STATEMENTS OF FINANCIAL ACCOUNTING STANDARDS

(continued on inside back cover)

Intermediate Accounting

INTERMEDIATE

EDITION 6

ACCOUNTING

LANNY G. CHASTEEN
Oklahoma State University

RICHARD E. FLAHERTY
Arizona State University

MELVIN C. O'CONNOR
Michigan State University

Case Contributor
H. FRED MITTELSTAEDT
University of Notre Dame

Irwin McGraw-Hill

Boston   Burr Ridge, IL   Dubuque, IA   Madison, WI   New York   San Francisco   St. Louis
Bangkok   Bogotá   Caracas   Lisbon   London   Madrid
Mexico City   Milan   New Delhi   Seoul   Singapore   Sydney   Taipei   Toronto

WB

McGraw-Hill

A Division of The McGraw-Hill Companies

Intermediate Accounting

domestic   2 3 4 5 6 7 8 9 0 VNH VNH 9 0 0 9 8
international   1 2 3 4 5 6 7 8 9 0 VNH HNV 9 0 0 9 8 7

ISBN 0-07-011901-5

Editorial Director: Michael Junior
Publisher: Jeff Shelstad
Associate editor: Becky Page
Developmental editor: Marc Chernoff
Marketing manager: Rhonda Seelinger
Project manager: Sharla Volkersz
Production supervisor: Tanya Nigh
Designer: Amanda Kavanagh
Cover designer: Amanda Kavanagh
Cover art: Vasily Kandinsky, *Jetzt Auf! (Now Upwards!)*, 1931. Watercolor, wash and ink on paper, 19 × 24 inches (48.1 × 61 cm). The Hilla Von Rebay Foundation, Guggenheim Museum, New York. Photograph by David Heald © The Solomon R. Guggenheim Foundation, New York. (FN 1970.46)
Photo researcher: Susan Friedman
Editorial assistant: Donna Hayes
Compositor: York Graphic Services, Inc.
Typeface: Stone Serif
Printer: Von Hoffman Press

Because this page cannot legibly accommodate all the acknowledgements, page 1284 constitutes an extension of the copyright page.

Library of Congress Cataloging-in-Publication Data
Chasteen, Lanny G., 1942–
    Intermediate accounting / Lanny G. Chasteen, Richard E. Flaherty,
Melvin C. O'Connor. —6th ed.
        p.   cm.
    Includes index.
    ISBN 0-07-011901-5
    1. Accounting.   I. Flaherty, Richard E., 1944–   . II. O'Connor,
Melvin C.   III. Title.
HF5635.C474   1997
657'.044—dc21   97-39530
                                                                                          CIP

http://www.mhhe.com

ABOUT THE AUTHORS

Lanny G. Chasteen, Ph.D., CPA, is the Arthur Andersen Alumni Centennial Professor and Head of the School of Accounting at Oklahoma State University. He holds a B.B.A. from the University of Texas at Austin, and an M.B.A. and Ph.D. from the University of Arkansas. Professor Chasteen has published articles on financial accounting theory and practice in *The Accounting Review, Abacus,* the *Journal of Accounting Education, Issues in Accounting Education,* and the *Journal of Accountancy.* He has received the Outstanding Teacher Award in the College of Business Administration at OSU and the Oklahoma Outstanding Accounting Educator Award from the Oklahoma Society of Certified Public Accountants. In addition to his 28 years on the OSU faculty, Professor Chasteen has taught at the University of Texas at Austin, the University of Arkansas, Texas Tech University, the University of Texas at Arlington, and the University of Tulsa. His public accounting experience was with Haskins and Sells (now Deloitte & Touche). Professor Chasteen is a member of the American Accounting Association (AAA), the Administrators of Accounting Program Group of the AAA, the American Institute of Certified Public Accountants, the Financial Executives Institute, the Oklahoma Society of Certified Public Accountants, Beta Alpha Psi, and Beta Gamma Sigma, and has served on committees of these organizations. Professor Chasteen is also active in accreditation activities of the American Assembly of Collegiate Schools of Business (AACSB).

Richard E. Flaherty, Ph.D., CPA, is professor of accounting at Arizona State University and served as the Executive Director of the Accounting Education Change Commission from 1993–1996. Formerly, he was Director of the School of Accountancy at Arizona State University. He received his B.S., M.S., and Ph.D. degrees from The University of Kansas. Professor Flaherty previously served on the faculties of Oklahoma State University and the University of Illinois. He also served as a research associate at the Financial Accounting Standards Board, has served as a consultant on financial reporting issues to a number of businesses, and has taught in numerous professional development programs. He has published articles on financial accounting theory and practice in several journals, including *The Accounting Review* and the *CPA Journal.* In addition, he is the author of Accounting Education Research Monograph No. 3, *The Core of the Curriculum for Accounting Majors,* published by the American Accounting Association.

Professor Flaherty is a member of the American Accounting Association (AAA), the American Institute of Certified Public Accountants (AICPA), the Financial Executives Institute (FEI), the Arizona Society of Certified Public Accountants, Beta Alpha Psi, and Beta Gamma Sigma. He has served on a number of AAA committees, and currently serves on the Accounting Education Advisory Committee and the Accounting Accreditation Committee. Also, he has served on the Board of Examiners of the AICPA and on numerous committees, subcommittees, and task forces of the Board. He has been on the Board of Directors of the Arizona Chapter of the FEI, the Board of Trustees of the Arizona Society's Foundation for Education and Research, and on the governing boards of the AAPG and the Federation of Schools of Accountancy. He has also been actively involved in the AACSB, having served as Chair of the Accounting Accreditation Committee and the Peer Review Improvement Task Force, and as a member of several peer review teams and other committees.

Melvin C. O'Connor, Ph.D., CPA, is the Deloitte & Touche Professor of Accounting and Director of the Program in Professional Accounting at Michigan State University. He earned his bachelor's, master's, and doctorate degrees at The University of Kansas. Professor O'Connor has been Chairperson of the Department of Accounting and Director of the Accounting Doctoral Program, has been twice recognized as the outstanding teacher in the Department of Accounting, and in 1994–1995 received the Withrow Award as the outstanding teacher in the College of Business. He has published in *The Accounting Review,* the *Journal of Accountancy, Management Accounting,* and the *Financial Analysts Journal.* Professor O'Connor is a co-author of two monographs published by the National Association of Accountants—*Replacement Costing: Complying with Disclosure Requirements* and *Replacement Cost Disclosures: A Study of Compliance with the SEC Requirement.* He is a member of the American Accounting Association, the American Institute of Certified Public Accountants, the Michigan Association of Certified Public Accountants, Phi Kappa Phi, Beta Gamma Sigma, and Beta Alpha Psi. Professor O'Connor has been a member of the AAA Council, has served on many AAA committees, including the Committee on Financial Accounting Standards, is a past president of the AAA Administrators of Accounting Programs Group, and has been a member of the Editorial Board of *Issues in Accounting Education.* He also served for several years as a member of the Accounting Accreditation and Visitation Committees of the American Assembly of Collegiate Schools of Business. Professor O'Connor was a charter member of the Accounting Education Change Commission and was the only accounting educator to serve on the Commission throughout its entire existence.

*To Our
Families*

CONTENTS

CHAPTER 2

Financial Accounting and Reporting: A Theoretical Structure

CHAPTER

3

CHAPTER 4

The Income Statement
167

The Balance Sheet (Statement of Financial Position)   207

C H A P T E R

5

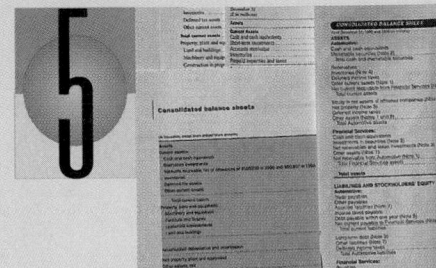

CHAPTER 6

The Statement of Cash Flows

Revenue Recognition and Income Determination   329

C H A P T E R 7

CHAPTER 8

Cash, Current Receivables and Payables, and Contingencies

Inventory Valuation: Determining Cost and Using Cost Flow Assumptions

CHAPTER

CHAPTER 10

Inventory Valuation: Departures From Historical Cost and Methods of Estimating Inventory Cost   531

Plant Assets and Intangibles: Acquisition and Subsequent Expenditures

Financial Instruments: Debt Securities   715

C H A P T E R

Leases   787

C H A P T E R

15

C H A P T E R

16

Pensions and Other Postretirement Benefits   843

Accounting for Income Taxes   907

C H A P T E R

17

CHAPTER 18

Stockholders' Equity — 953

Accounting Changes and Error Analysis   1021

CHAPTER 20

Earnings per Share

CHAPTER 21

Revisiting the Statement of Cash Flows; Additional Disclosure Topics

APPENDIX

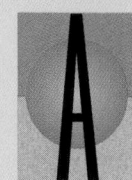

Concepts of Present and Future Value 1177

APPENDIX

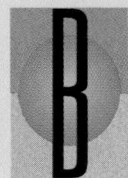

PREFACE

We were originally motivated to write this book because we recognized the need for an intermediate accounting book that would help students sharpen their ability to think, while simultaneously teaching the important financial accounting procedures. We are grateful for the positive response we have had to our approach in previous editions. We want to thank the many instructors and students who have taken the time to contact us and share their comments. We carefully considered their feedback while preparing this edition.

The sixth edition of Intermediate Accounting continues our vision for a more conceptual approach to intermediate accounting and offers many significant improvements. We hope that you will benefit from using this text in your course.

Strong Conceptual Orientation
. . . Along with a Balance of Procedures

Like other texts, our text provides a *conceptual framework* which is introduced in Chapters 1 and 2. Unique to our text, this framework is then consistently used throughout the text to explain and evaluate accounting procedures. Developing an understanding of the bigger picture benefits students not only in this course, but throughout their college experience and beyond. Along the way, students develop stronger communication, intellectual, and interpersonal skills. Students gain the ability to critically evaluate accounting practices and contribute to improvements when necessary. We feel that this conceptual orientation is consistent with the goals and recommendations of the Accounting Education Change Commission (AECC).

The organization of the book continues to include *early flexible coverage of rev-*

CONCEPTUAL

Financial statements are prepared in accordance with the time period assumption.

To provide relevant and timely information, corporations prepare financial statements periodically in accordance with the *periodicity* (or *time-period*) *assumption*. The accounting equation shown in Exhibit 3–1 may be interpreted within a time-period context. The first two equations in Exhibit 3–1 apply at the *end* of an accounting period. The third equation shows that the change in retained earnings *during* a period equals the beginning-of-period retained earnings plus net income for the period less dividends declared during the period. The last equation shows that net income *for the period* equals revenues less expenses plus gains less losses.

These margin notes appear frequently throughout the text to explain the underlying concepts behind various procedures.

The Accounting Entity Assumption

The essence of the accounting entity assumption is that accountants account for and report the financial information of a specific *accounting* entity. Thus the **accounting entity assumption** establishes boundaries or limits as to what information should be included in the financial statements of a given accounting entity. For example, you learned in introductory accounting that the economic activities of a single (sole) proprietorship are accounted for separately from the personal economic activities of the proprietor.

The accounting entity for which financial reports are prepared may or may not correspond to a legal entity. For example, under certain circumstances the accounting entity may be a corporation (a legal entity), a division or department within a corporation (within a legal entity), or a group of legal entities (for which consolidated

CONCEPTUAL

The accounting entity assumption limits the transactions and events that should be reported in an entity's financial statements.

enue recognition. We firmly believe that a thorough understanding of revenue recognition criteria as a means of compensating for uncertainty about future cash flows is essential to understanding specific accounting procedures. Therefore, revenue recognition is presented in Chapter 7, but can be covered at any time after Chapter 2. We were the first to offer this organization, but other books have since followed our lead.

The necessary procedural aspects of accounting have been kept intact. We continue to thoroughly present, explain, and illustrate common accounting procedures and reporting alternatives. They are evaluated routinely in terms of their usefulness in predicting and assessing cash flows to the company and to investors and creditors.

Student Friendly Focus

For the sixth edition, we have added new features that make this text extremely accessible and easy to understand.

- ■ **Learning objectives** now open each chapter to prepare students for the important material ahead of them. These objectives also appear as margin notes to alert students where an objective is discussed. The learning objectives are summarized at the end of the chapter to reinforce content and to serve as a study tool.

- ■ **Key terms** are highlighted in boldface text within the chapter and are listed at the end of each chapter with a page reference to the location in the chapter where the term is defined.

- ■ **Margin icons** direct students to interesting and important chapter material. These icons, appearing both within the text and end-of-chapter material, have the following functions:

 **Real World** Signify numerous excerpts from actual financial statements that are presented to relate the text coverage to the practice of accounting.

 **International** Highlight frequent discussions of how accounting practices vary by country and how they compare to the U.S. standards.

 **Economic Consequences** Indicate places in the text that discuss how the economic environment may be affected by financial accounting and reporting practices.

 **Ethics** High ethical standards are imperative for the future of the accounting profession; therefore, we raise ethical issues throughout the text, and include a number of cases dealing with ethical issues.

 **Group Assignment** Appear in the end-of-chapter material and feature assignments which are amenable to group activities.

 Research Problem Denote where students must study authoritative literature to support their answers.

 **Critical Thinking** Appear beside the end-of-chapter problems that require analysis, synthesis, and/or evaluation by students.

 **Financial Reporting** Show students problems that relate to actual financial statements.

 **Writing Assignment** Appear in the end-of-chapter material where students must demonstrate writing skills.

Stronger Problem Material

In an effort to strengthen student skills, we have greatly improved our *end-of-chapter assignments.* We have added more critical thinking exercises, more group assignments, and new financial reporting problems related to the **General Electric Annual Report** (located in Appendix B).

In addition, Professor Fred Mittelstaedt of the University of Notre Dame has prepared a number of exciting, integrative cases based on real accounting situations. Teaching notes for these cases appear in the Instructor's Manual.

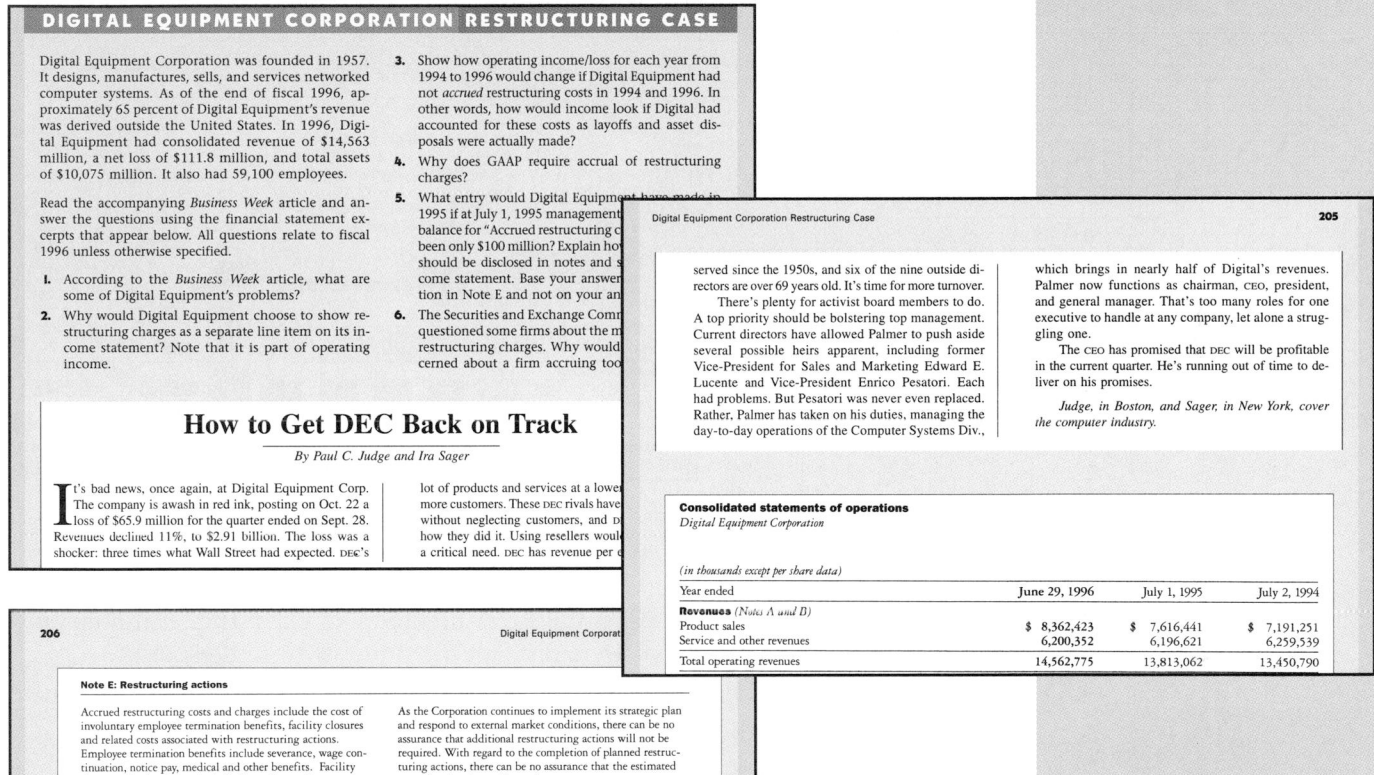

DIGITAL EQUIPMENT CORPORATION RESTRUCTURING CASE

Digital Equipment Corporation was founded in 1957. It designs, manufactures, sells, and services networked computer systems. As of the end of fiscal 1996, approximately 65 percent of Digital Equipment's revenue was derived outside the United States. In 1996, Digital Equipment had consolidated revenue of $14,563 million, a net loss of $111.8 million, and total assets of $10,075 million. It also had 59,100 employees.

Read the accompanying *Business Week* article and answer the questions using the financial statement excerpts that appear below. All questions relate to fiscal 1996 unless otherwise specified.

1. According to the *Business Week* article, what are some of Digital Equipment's problems?

2. Why would Digital Equipment choose to show restructuring charges as a separate line item on its income statement? Note that it is part of operating income.

3. Show how operating income/loss for each year from 1994 to 1996 would change if Digital Equipment had not *accrued* restructuring costs in 1994 and 1996. In other words, how would income look if Digital had accounted for these costs as layoffs and asset disposals were actually made?

4. Why does GAAP require accrual of restructuring charges?

5. What entry would Digital Equipment have made in 1995 if at July 1, 1995 management ... balance for "Accrued restructuring c... been only $100 million? Explain ho... should be disclosed in notes and s... come statement. Base your answe... tion in Note E and not on your an...

6. The Securities and Exchange Comm... questioned some firms about the m... restructuring charges. Why would... cerned about a firm accruing too...

How to Get DEC Back on Track

By Paul C. Judge and Ira Sager

It's bad news, once again, at Digital Equipment Corp. The company is awash in red ink, posting on Oct. 22 a loss of $65.9 million for the quarter ended on Sept. 28. Revenues declined 11%, to $2.91 billion. The loss was a shocker: three times what Wall Street had expected. DEC's

lot of products and services at a lower... more customers. These DEC rivals have... without neglecting customers, and D... how they did it. Using resellers woul... a critical need. DEC has revenue per...

Digital Equipment Corporation Restructuring Case   205

served since the 1950s, and six of the nine outside directors are over 69 years old. It's time for more turnover.

There's plenty for activist board members to do. A top priority should be bolstering top management. Current directors have allowed Palmer to push aside several possible heirs apparent, including former Vice-President for Sales and Marketing Edward E. Lucente and Vice-President Enrico Pesatori. Each had problems. But Pesatori was never even replaced. Rather, Palmer has taken on his duties, managing the day-to-day operations of the Computer Systems Div.,

which brings in nearly half of Digital's revenues. Palmer now functions as chairman, CEO, president, and general manager. That's too many roles for one executive to handle at any company, let alone a struggling one.

The CEO has promised that DEC will be profitable in the current quarter. He's running out of time to deliver on his promises.

Judge, in Boston, and Sager, in New York, cover the computer industry.

Consolidated statements of operations
Digital Equipment Corporation

(in thousands except per share data)

Year ended	June 29, 1996	July 1, 1995	July 2, 1994
Revenues (*Notes A and B*)			
Product sales	$ 8,362,423	$ 7,616,441	$ 7,191,251
Service and other revenues	6,200,352	6,196,621	6,259,539
Total operating revenues	14,562,775	13,813,062	13,450,790

---

206   Digital Equipment Corporat...

Note E: Restructuring actions

Accrued restructuring costs and charges include the cost of involuntary employee termination benefits, facility closures and related costs associated with restructuring actions. Employee termination benefits include severance, wage continuation, notice pay, medical and other benefits. Facility closure and related costs include disposal costs for property, plant and equipment, lease payments and related costs.

As the Corporation continues to implement its strategic plan and respond to external market conditions, there can be no assurance that additional restructuring actions will not be required. With regard to the completion of planned restructuring actions, there can be no assurance that the estimated cost of such actions will not change.

Technology

The most sophisticated intermediate accounting software available today, *Interactive Intermediate Accounting Lab,* by Ralph E. Smith and Rick Birney, was developed using the problem material from this text. This software package educates students on the mechanics of the accounting discipline, allowing more class time to be devoted to the conceptual learning of intermediate accounting. Both network and portable versions are available.

- As an employee for a virtual company, students enter an exciting virtual office complete with a fax machine, e-mail, and a desk calendar, which all play a functional role in the software.

- Students are motivated by salaries and promotions based on their performance working in this virtual company with their classmates.

■ The instructor can manipulate the "calendar" of assignments the students are required to complete, and can also monitor the performance of a complete class roster.

■ New Button Bar, Tutorial Lessons, and on-line reference make the program simple to learn and use.

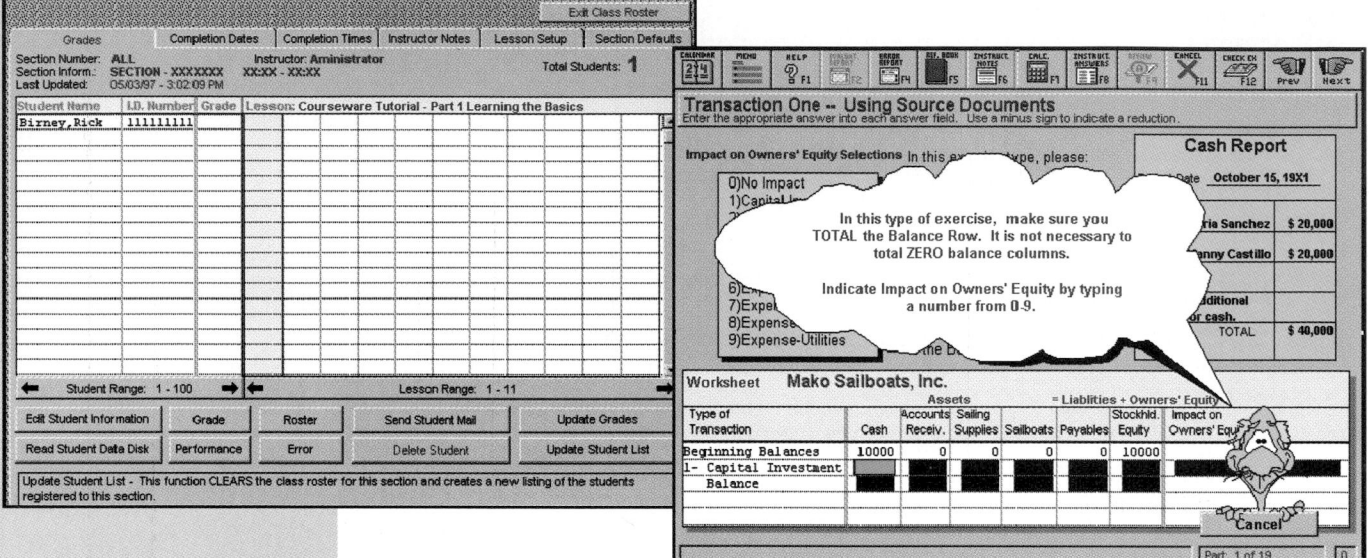

■ After completing the exercises, students come to class understanding the assigned material and prepared for advanced applications and collaborative exercises.

■ Since instructors receive performance results prior to class, they can prepare according to concepts that were difficult for students to understand.

■ If your students need a review of the accounting cycle, the *Interactive Financial Accounting Lab* is also available.

Currency

As always, we are committed to providing the most up-to-date information available. The latest FASB pronouncements have been fully integrated where appropriate. Through the help of our publisher, the author team will continue to provide updates as they relate to the intermediate course throughout the life of this edition. The following list details many of the changes we have made on a chapter-by-chapter basis.

CHAPTER-BY-CHAPTER CONTENT CHANGES IN THE SIXTH EDITION

■ **Chapter 1** contains revised and enhanced coverage of international accounting and reporting standards, as well as the environment and role of financial accounting and reporting.

■ **Chapter 2** now includes an additional section on the role of financial reporting in assessing management stewardship. An updated section on comprehensive income reflects the requirements of *FASB Statement No. 130*.

■ **Chapter 3** presents an expanded overview of the accounting process. A complete set of transactions is used throughout the accounting cycle rather than using fragmented illustrations.

■ **Chapter 4** now includes a brief discussion of the current operating performance approach and the all-inclusive approach to reporting income information. This coverage enables students to better understand the comprehensive income issue, which has also been updated in this chapter to incorporate the recently issued FASB *Statement No. 130*.

- Coverage of the statement of retained earnings, and prior period adjustments, has been moved to **Chapter 5** from **Chapter 4**. We have eliminated the coverage of currently-maturing obligations, callable obligations, and short-term obligations expected to be refinanced.

- **Chapter 6** modifications include a change of emphasis from the direct approach to the indirect approach for reporting cash flows from operating activities. We have also added material on cash flow analysis.

- We have subdivided **Chapter 8** into Part A (cash and current receivables) and Part B (current payables and contingencies). The end-of-chapter material has been subdivided accordingly. To reflect *FASB Statement No. 125*, we have also updated the material on using receivables to obtain immediate cash.

- The coverage of research and development costs in **Chapter 11** has been condensed.

- **Chapter 12** has been updated to reflect FASB activities related to liabilities for closure or removal of long-lived assets, and asset impairment.

- Based on the FASB *Exposure Draft,* **Chapters 13** and **14** include a discussion of derivatives and hedging activities. **Chapter 14** goes into some detail on accounting for derivatives and hedging activities and includes end-of-chapter material on the topic. Both chapters have been updated to reflect the comprehensive income reporting requirements of FASB *Statement No. 130.*

- **Chapter 16** has been completely revised to emphasize the conceptual aspects of "immediate recognition" of pension expense as contrasted to the "delayed recognition" approach which is permitted for some components of pension expense under *FASB Statement No. 87*. We have also incorporated a worksheet to account for the components of pension expense under the delayed recognition approach.

- In **Chapter 17**, we condensed the historical coverage leading to current requirements in accounting for income taxes. We made the comprehensive, multi-period example more concise by shortening it from five to four years.

- The coverage of stock options in **Chapter 18** has been updated to reflect *FASB Statement No. 123*. Coverage of stock subscriptions has been condensed. We have deleted coverage of donated treasury stock and scrip dividends.

- **Chapter 20**, covering earnings per share, has been completely rewritten based on *FASB Statement No. 128*. The chapter is shorter and more concise, but retains the conceptual aspects of previous editions.

- The section on segment reporting in **Chapter 21** has been revised to reflect the requirements of *FASB Statement No. 131*.

Important Retained Features

- **Treatment of complex issues** A building block approach is used to present accounting for leases (Chapter 15), pensions and other postretirement benefits (Chapter 16), income taxes (Chapter 17), and earnings per share (Chapter 20). A conceptual introduction to these topics is followed by explanations of progressively more complex procedural issues. The presentations are organized so that the material may be covered in varying degrees of detail.

- **Bonds and notes** Accounting for bonds and notes from the standpoint of the issuer and the investor are covered in one chapter. Because most of the concepts and procedures applicable to bonds and notes apply to both issuer and investor, it is both pedagogically sound and efficient to study them together.

- **Present and future value coverage** Concepts of present and future value are discussed in Appendix A and are used in several chapters. Time diagrams are used extensively to clarify the concepts of present and future value.

■ **Flexibility** There is a great deal of flexibility in both sequencing and depth of coverage of various topics. Some examples:
- The present value appendix can be covered at any point or not covered at all.
- The statement of cash flows is covered at two different levels of complexity in two different places. Some instructors may prefer only the introductory level coverage in Chapter 6, while others may include the in-depth coverage in Chapter 21.
- The building block approach allows the instructor to choose the depth of coverage for complex topics such as leases, pensions and other postretirement benefits, income taxes, and earnings per share.

SUPPLEMENTS FOR THE INSTRUCTOR

Instructor's Manual by Stephen J. Dempsey (University of Vermont). This manual increases the breadth of teaching materials available to professors. Each chapter begins with a restatement of the learning objectives. This section is followed by a detailed lecture outline. Lecture topics are provided, as are issues for reflection and discussion. An annotated bibliography suggests extra reading materials. A summary of chapter and problem material coverage and tables of assignment characteristics also are provided. Much of the material is accompanied by detailed illustrations that expand the extensive visual exhibits in the text. Teaching notes to accompany the integrative cases prepared by Fred Mittelstaedt (University of Notre Dame) are also included.

Solutions Manual by the authors. This volume provides fully worked solutions to questions, cases, exercises, and problems in the text. The solutions are thoroughly explained and each step is illustrated to enhance discussion of assignment and other materials.

Solutions Transparencies Solutions from the Solutions Manual for end-of-chapter exercises and problems are available on transparencies for use as a classroom aid in reviewing homework assignments. Fifty exhibits from the text and chapter outlines are also included in the transparency set.

Check Figures by the authors. This booklet provides key figures in the solutions to the end-of-chapter assignments. These figures allow students to check the accuracy of their work.

Ready Shows, Ready Slides by Paula Irwin (Muhlenberg College) are teaching enhancement packages. (See also "Ready Notes" under Supplements for Students).

> **Ready Shows** A package of multimedia lecture enhancement aids that uses PowerPoint software to illustrate chapter concepts.
> **Ready Slides** These selected four-color teaching transparencies are printed from the PowerPoint Ready Shows.

Instructor's Manual for* Understanding Corporate Annual Reports, *3/e by William R. Pasewark (University of Houston). The manual contains extensive instructional and grading suggestions, and a 50-question exam. (See description under Supplements for Students.)

Interactive Accounting Labs (Financial or Intermediate) by Ralph E. Smith and Rick Birney (both of Arizona State University) were designed to educate students on the mechanics of the accounting discipline, allowing class time to be devoted to other learning activities. This software is interactive, motivating, and provides immediate feedback. The Administration Module and Gradebook features allow you to manipulate the assignments your students are required to complete and easily track their performance. This software is available in either network or portable stand-alone versions.

Test Bank by Alan H. Falcon (Loyola Marymount University) and John A. Marts (The University of North Carolina—Wilmington). The Test Bank includes approximately 1,500 questions and problems. Each chapter offers multiple-choice questions, extended problems, and, in most chapters, essay questions. Also in this edition are guides to all questions indicating the topics tested by multiple-choice questions and the difficulty level of all questions.

Computest   A computerized version of the manual testbank for more efficient use is available in the Windows platform.

Teletest   By calling a toll free number, instructors can specify the content of exams and have a laser-printed copy of the exams mailed to them.

SUPPLEMENTS FOR STUDENTS

Study Guide by John Cumming and Clayton Hock (both of Miami University, Oxford, Ohio). Each chapter contains a list of objectives and a detailed chapter review. The Self-Study Learning section includes a review of key terms and concepts, true-false questions, multiple-choice questions, and extended problems—all with solutions. A final section discusses common errors.

Work Papers by Diane Adcox (University of North Florida). This supplement provides students with the forms necessary to work the problems and exercises at the end of each chapter in the text.

Ready Notes   This booklet of Ready Show screen printouts enables students to take notes during Ready Show or Ready Slide presentations. This supplement changes the nature of note-taking. Rather than spending time copying material that is already in the book, students can focus on the most important aspects of what the instructor is saying.

Understanding Corporate Annual Reports, 3/e by William R. Pasewark (University of Houston) offers students hands-on experience in the analysis and understanding of corporate annual reports. This Practice Set requires students to obtain an annual report and then use the information to answer the questions. Appendices provide instructions for obtaining an annual report from a corporation, making industry comparisons, and referencing generally accepted accounting principles. The latest edition has been updated to include recent FASB Statements and a discussion of internet sources for corporate financial data.

Interactive Accounting Labs (Financial or Intermediate) by Ralph E. Smith and Rick Birney are available in portable versions for the individual user. (See descriptions under Supplements for the Instructor.)

Seascapes Floral Expressions Practice Set by Marilyn E. Vito and Gulprit Chhatwal (both of the Richard Stockton College of New Jersey). Designed to address the growing demand for accountants skilled in small business accounting and administration, this practice set asks students to analyze data common to a small business environment, while providing a review of basic accounting concepts. Sales transactions are presented in a variety of formats to simulate the complexity of small businesses involved in several different service and product lines. The practice set also includes supplemental stand-alone problems that build on the text end-of-chapter material. Students may complete the practice set manually or with its accompanying spreadsheet templates, available in Lotus and Excel.

SPATS (Spreadsheet Applications Template Software)   This includes Excel templates for selected problems and exercises from the text. The templates gradually become more complex, requiring students to build a variety of formulas. "What if" questions are added to show the power of spreadsheets and a simple tutorial is included. Instructors may request either a free master template for students to use or copy, or shrink-wrapped versions are available for a nominal fee.

ACKNOWLEDGMENTS

Many individuals have contributed generously of their time in the development of the sixth edition. Their comments and suggestions on accounting teaching matters as well as on technical issues have been invaluable. They are: Margaret Conway, *Kingsborough Community College*, Ralph Smith, *Arizona State University*, Rose Marie Bakics, *Lafayette College*, John Crain, *Southeastern Louisiana University*, Linda Wade, *Tarleton State University*, Harvey Hendrickson, *Florida International University*, Paula Irwin, *Muhlenberg College*, Deborah Smiach, *University of Pittsburgh at Johnstown*.

We also want to thank the many instructors who provided valuable assistance in previous editions, including: Diana L. Adcox, *University of North Florida;* W. David Albrecht, *Bowling Green University;* John Alcorn, *Morehead State University;* Matthew J. Anderson, *Michigan State University;* Joseph H. Anthony, *Michigan State University;* Mary Barnum, *Grand Valley State University;* Deborah Beard, *Southeast Missouri State University;* Lila Bergman, *City University of New York/Hunter College;* Michele Blazek, *University of New Mexico;* Russell F. Briner, *The University of Texas at San Antonio;* Clifford D. Brown, *Bentley College;* Thomas Buchman, *University of Colorado at Boulder;* Joseph Bylinski, *University of North Carolina;* Barney R. Cargile, *University of Alabama;* Ronald E. Carlson, *St. Cloud State University;* Janice Carpenter, *Northern Arizona University;* Gyan Chandra, *Miami University;* Robert C. Chang, *University of Bridgeport;* Eugene G. Chewning, Jr., *University of South Carolina;* Joseph C. Colgan, *Fort Lewis College;* Doris M. Cook, *University of Arkansas;* James S. Cox, *Ohio University;* Joann Noe Cross, *University of Wisconsin/Oshkosh;* Stephen J. Dempsey, *The University of Vermont;* David M. Dennis, *University of South Florida;* Carleton Donchess, *Bridgewater State College;* C. Dwayne Dowell, *Texas Tech University;* Matthew Dowling, *San Francisco State University;* Joanne Duke, *San Francisco State University;* John A. Elfrink, *Southeast Missouri State University;* Alan H. Falcon, *Loyola Marymount University;* Martha A. Fasci, *The University of Texas at San Antonio;* David R. Finley, *Simon Fraser University;* Mary L. Fischer, *University of Texas/Tyler;* John D. Fitzsimmons, *Western Connecticut State University;* Thomas Frecka, *University of Notre Dame;* Martin Freedman, *State University of New York at Binghamton;* Monica D. Frizzell, *Western Connecticut State University;* Gouranga Ganguli, *University of Texas/Pan American;* David R. Ganz, *University of Missouri/St. Louis;* Bruce R. Gaumnitz, *St. Cloud State University;* Carol B. Gaumnitz, *University of Northern Kentucky;* William Geary, *College of William and Mary;* Joyce S. Goldstone, *Adelphi University;* Ellsworth Granger, Jr., *Mankato State University;* Julia Grant, *Case Western Reserve University;* James W. Greenspan, *Seton Hall University;* Robert Gruber, *University of Wisconsin–Whitewater;* Marcia Halvorsen, *University of Cincinnati;* John M. Hassell, *Indiana University at Indianapolis;* Carol Anne Hilton, *Ohio University;* George C. Holdren, *University of Nebraska;* Robert E. Holtfreter, *Central Washington University;* Carol Olson Houston, *San Diego State University;* Dennis Hudson, *University of Tulsa;* Herbert G. Hunt III, *University of Vermont;* H. Fenwick Huss, *Georgia State University;* Kenneth H. Johnson, *Georgia Southern University;* Allan L. Karnes, *Southern Illinois University;* Stuart B. Keller, *University of Kentucky;* Tim Kelley, *University of San Diego;* Robert Kirsch, *Southern Connecticut State University;* Thomas P. Klammer, *University of North Texas;* Harry E. Knight, *Southern Oregon State University;* James M. Kurtenbach, *Iowa State University;* Raef Lawson, *State University of New York–Albany;* Louis Lebensbaum, *Adelphi University;* Susan A. Lynn, *University of Baltimore;* Calvert C. McGregor, *Elon College;* Malcolm McKenzie McClure, *Illinois State University;* Reed McKnight, *Fort Lewis College;* Robert E. Malcom, *Pennsylvania State University;* John A. Marts, *University of North Carolina/Wilmington;* R. David Mautz, Jr., *University of North Carolina at Greensboro;* David Meeting, *Cleveland State University;* Paul B. W. Miller, *University of Colorado/Colorado Springs;* Thomas I. Miller, *Murray State University;* Ralph M. Newkirk, Jr., *Rutgers University;* Donald R. Nichols, *Texas Christian University;* Marcia S. Niles, *University of Idaho;* Priscilla O'Clock, *Xavier University;* Emeka Ofobike, *University of Akron;* Dorian Olson, *Moorhead State University;* William H. Parrott, *University of South*

Florida; Victor S. Pastena, *State University of New York/Buffalo;* Kathy Petroni, *Michigan State University;* David Plumlee, *The University of Kansas;* Susan Pourciau, *Florida State University;* Mahmood A. Qureshi, *California State University/Northridge;* Kris K. Raman, *University of North Texas;* Charles Ransom, *Oklahoma State University;* Charles Reichert, *University of Wisconsin;* Sara Ann Reiter, *State University of New York/Binghamton;* John Rich, *Emporia State University;* Frederick M. Richardson, *Virginia Polytechnic Institute and State University;* John T. Rigsby, *Mississippi State University;* Donald Rogoff, *California State University/Northridge;* Jeffrey Romine, *Truman State University;* Eugene R. Rozanski, *Illinois State University;* Victoria S. Rymer, *University of Maryland;* Clayton Sager, *University of Wisconsin;* William Schwartz, *Virginia Commonwealth University;* Mary Alice Seville, *Oregon State University;* D. Shores, *University of Washington;* Sheldon R. Smith, *Brigham Young University–Hawaii;* Matthew J. Stephens, Jr., *Wharton School, University of Pennsylvania;* Barbara R. Stewart, *Towson State University;* Donald Tang, *Portland State University;* Nancy O'Rourke Tang, *Portland State University;* Michael G. Tearney, *University of Kentucky;* Mary Tharp, *Kirkwood Community College;* Joel E. Thompson, *Northern Michigan University;* Michael Trebesh, *Alma College;* Terry Unruh, *Oral Roberts University;* Nancy A. Wagner, *Georgia Southern College;* Larry E. Watkins, *Northern Arizona University;* David N. Wiest, *University of Massachusetts–Boston;* Paul Wertheim, *East Carolina University;* Michael D. Wilson, *University of Wisconsin;* and David A. Ziebart, *University of Illinois.*

We also wish to thank John A. Marts (*University of North Carolina/Wilmington*) and Barbara Schnathorst (The Write Solution, Inc.) for reviewing the end-of-chapter assignment material. They carefully checked the questions, cases, exercises, and problems for consistency with text discussions and reworked our solutions, examining them for accuracy, completeness, and clarity.

We appreciate the cooperation of the American Institute of Certified Public Accountants and the Financial Accounting Standards Board for allowing us to draw on their pronouncements for much of the text discussion. We also acknowledge permission from the American Institute of Certified Public Accountants, The Canadian Institute of Chartered Accountants, the Certified General Accountants Association of Canada, and the Institute of Management Accountants to adapt materials from their professional examinations.

Finally, we are most appreciative of the outstanding assistance and guidance provided by the professionals of Irwin/McGraw-Hill: Sharla Volkersz, Project Manager, for her careful attention to presentation and detail; Marc Chernoff, Developmental Editor, for his efforts in attending to the preparation of ancillary materials; and Tanya Nigh, Production Supervisor. We particularly wish to recognize Jeff Shelstad, Publisher, and Becky Page, Associate Editor, for their overall leadership on the project.

Lanny G. Chasteen
Richard E. Flaherty
Melvin C. O'Connor

Financial Accounting and Reporting:
An Introduction

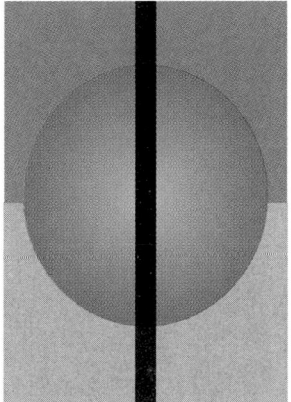

LEARNING OBJECTIVES

After studying this chapter, you should be able to:

1. Describe the nature of accounting, and differentiate between financial and managerial accounting.

2. Describe the role of the financial accountant.

3. Describe the concept of generally accepted accounting principles (GAAP), and describe the purposes those principles serve.

4. Discuss the importance of ethical behavior by accounting professionals.

5. Name the four financial statements required under GAAP.

6. Explain the role of the Securities and Exchange Commission in financial accounting and reporting.

7. Describe the organizational structure and standard-setting process of the Financial Accounting Standards Board, and identify the types of pronouncements it issues.

8. Describe the political nature of financial accounting and reporting standard setting.

9. Describe the state of international accounting standard setting, and describe the activities of some of the key groups in setting international standards.

10. Discuss the interrelationships among the corporation, suppliers of its inputs, regulatory authorities, and investors.

11. Explain the general role of financial accounting and reporting in the business environment.

12. Give examples of how the economic environment has influenced financial accounting and reporting.

13. Give examples of how financial accounting and reporting have impacted the economic environment.

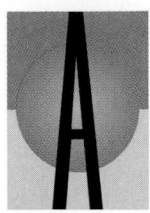

1 Describe the nature of accounting, and differentiate between financial and managerial accounting.

2 Describe the role of the financial accountant.

3 Describe the concept of generally accepted accounting principles (GAAP), and describe the purposes those principles serve.

ccounting is a service activity. Its function is to provide useful financial information about economic entities to managers, investors, creditors, and other interested parties. Accounting may be described as a measurement-communication activity, since the usefulness of accounting information depends on effective measurement of economic activities and effective communication of those measurements to users of accounting information.

Accounting information can be divided into two broad categories, according to the type of decision maker who uses it. **Management accounting information** is prepared primarily for decision makers inside an economic entity—that is, managers at various organizational levels. **Financial accounting information** is prepared primarily for decision makers outside an economic entity—investors, creditors, suppliers, and governmental agencies. Financial accounting information also is useful to top-level management inside an entity.

The term **financial accounting and reporting** encompasses the dual role of the financial accountant: (1) measuring and recording an entity's economic activities, and (2) communicating the recorded data to external users. Those who prepare accounting reports assume that users have a reasonable understanding of business and economic activities and are willing to study the reported data with reasonable diligence.

In this chapter we will review the nature and content of financial accounting and reporting, and the professional and regulatory institutions that oversee accounting practice. We will take a close look at the way financial accounting and reporting standards are set and the political influences on the standard-setting process. Next, we will consider the environment of financial accounting and reporting, concentrating particularly on the interrelationships and interests of corporations, suppliers of inputs, regulatory authorities, and investors. The chapter closes with some examples of how the economic environment and financial accounting and reporting impact each other.

THE NATURE AND CONTENT OF FINANCIAL ACCOUNTING AND REPORTING

In the words of the Accounting Principles Board, financial accounting and reporting provide "a continual history, quantified in money terms, of economic resources and obligations of a business enterprise, and economic activities that change those resources and obligations."[1] This description encompasses the published financial statements and supplementary information required under generally accepted accounting principles. In this section we will discuss the nature of financial accounting and reporting under those principles, explain why financial accounting and reporting standards are important, discuss why ethical behavior by accountants is essential, and review the four required financial statements and other aspects of external financial reporting.

Generally Accepted Accounting Principles (GAAP)

Generally accepted accounting principles (GAAP) consist of the financial accounting and reporting conventions, rules, and procedures that a business entity must use in preparing external financial statements subject to audit by an independent certified public accountant. Generally accepted accounting principles—standards, as they are sometimes called—usually are prescribed by authoritative

---

[1]"Basic Concepts and Accounting Principles Underlying Financial Statements of Business Enterprises," *Statement of the Accounting Principles Board No. 4* (New York: AICPA, October 1970), para. 41.

bodies, such as the Financial Accounting Standards Board, although some are simply practices accountants generally follow. They are based on both practical and theoretical considerations and often represent a consensus among accountants as to what is considered acceptable practice.

Generally accepted accounting principles serve three basic purposes. They help increase the confidence of financial statement users that the financial statements are representationally faithful. They provide companies and accountants who prepare financial statements with guidance on how to account for and report economic activities. And they provide independent auditors of financial statements with a basis for evaluating the fairness and completeness of those statements.

Generally accepted accounting principles (GAAP) are particularly important to independent auditors. An independent auditor's (certified public accountant's) unqualified opinion about a company's financial statements asserts that the financial statements fairly present the company's financial position, results of operations, and cash flows *in conformity with generally accepted accounting principles*. Because of the importance of GAAP to independent auditors, the Auditing Standards Board issued *Statement on Auditing Standards No. 69*, which identifies **sources of U.S. GAAP.**[2] The summary in *Statement No. 69* lists sources of GAAP for both nongovernmental and governmental entities and categorizes those sources in a hierarchy of relative authority. Sources of GAAP in the first category of the hierarchy have more authority than sources in the second category, and so on. (See Exhibit 1–1.)

Financial accounting and reporting standards (GAAP) require many estimates, assumptions, and professional judgments by both management and accountants. Calculations of depreciation expense and estimates of uncollectible accounts receivable are two examples. As a result, personal bias, misassessments of facts, errors in estimation, and ambiguity may enter into the measurement and communication of economic events. The potential for such factors to influence financial accounting information is not surprising when one considers the significance of accounting information in wage negotiations, management bonuses, bank lending decisions, and other resource allocations.

Needless to say, financial statements must have credibility to external users. Furthermore, the information in financial statements must be useful in decision making. Thus, the existence of standards or principles for financial accounting and reporting is very important both to the credibility and to the usefulness of financial data. Without standards to guide accounting and reporting practice, all accountants would, in effect, have to develop their own financial accounting theory, practices, and procedures. Under these circumstances, users of financial accounting information would find reported information of little help in making comparisons among competing uses for scarce resources. Moreover, without standards, users would have little assurance of the credibility of reported data. Historically, setting standards for financial accounting and reporting has proven to be in the public interest.

Ethical Behavior by Accounting Professionals

As has just been stated, financial accounting and reporting standards are essential to the credibility and usefulness of financial accounting information in general and of financial statements in particular. Even so, standards are not a substitute for ethical behavior by accounting professionals. Remember that the dual role of the financial accountant is to objectively measure and record the economic activities of an entity and to communicate the recorded data to interested parties outside the entity. Given the potential for personal bias, misassessments of facts, errors in estimation, and ambiguity to affect the measurement and communication of economic

---

[2]"The Meaning of Present Fairly in Conformity with Generally Accepted Accounting Principles in the Independent Auditor's Report," *Statement on Auditing Standards No. 69* (New York: AICPA Auditing Standards Board, January 1992). The Auditing Standards Board is the senior technical body of the American Institute of Certified Public Accountants (AICPA) designated to issue pronouncements on auditing matters.

	Nongovernmental Entities	**State and Local Governments**

EXHIBIT 1–1   **GAAP Hierarchy Summary**[a]

Established Accounting Principles

	Nongovernmental Entities	**State and Local Governments**
.10a	FASB Statements and Interpretations, APB Opinions, and AICPA Accounting Research Bulletins[b]	**.12a** GASB Statements and Interpretations, plus AICPA and FASB pronouncements if made applicable to state and local governments by a GASB Statement or Interpretation[c]
.10b	FASB Technical Bulletins, AICPA Industry Audit and Accounting Guides, and AICPA Statements of Position	**.12b** GASB Technical Bulletins, and the following pronouncements if specifically made applicable to state and local governments by the AICPA: AICPA Industry Audit and Accounting Guides and AICPA Statements of Position
.10c	Consensus positions of the FASB Emerging Issues Task Force and AICPA Practice Bulletins	**.12c** Consensus positions of the GASB Emerging Issues Task Force and AICPA Practice Bulletins if specifically made applicable to state and local governments by the AICPA
.10d	AICPA accounting interpretations, "Qs and As" published by the FASB staff, as well as industry practices widely recognized and prevalent	**.12d** "Qs and As" published by the GASB staff, as well as industry practices widely recognized and prevalent

Other Accounting Literature[c]

.11	Other accounting literature, including FASB Concepts Statements; APB Statements; AICPA Issues Papers; International Accounting Standards Committee Statements; GASB Statements, Interpretations, and Technical Bulletins; pronouncements of other professional associations or regulatory agencies; AICPA *Technical Practice Aids;* and accounting textbooks, handbooks, and articles	**.13** Other accounting literature, including GASB Concepts Statements; pronouncements in categories (*a*) through (*d*) of the hierarchy for nongovernmental entities when not specifically made applicable to state and local governments; APB Statements; FASB Concepts Statements; AICPA Issues Papers; International Accounting Standards Committee Statements; pronouncements of other professional associations or regulatory agencies; AICPA *Technical Practice Aids;* and accounting textbooks, handbooks, and articles

[a]*Statement on Auditing Standards No. 69* **(New York: AICPA Auditing Standards Board, January 1992). The reference numbers in each box of the hierarchy refer to the paragraphs of** *Statement No. 69* **that describe the categories of the GAAP hierarchy.**
[b]**FASB (Financial Accounting Standards Board); APB (Accounting Principles Board); AICPA (American Institute of Certified Public Accountants); and GASB (Governmental Accounting Standards Board).**
[c]**In the absence of established accounting principles, the auditor may consider other accounting literature, depending on its relevance in the circumstances.**

4

Discuss the importance of ethical behavior by accounting professionals.

events, business ethics and ethical behavior are particularly important to the accounting profession. Indeed, the higher the ethical standards followed by accountants who prepare or audit financial statements, the lower will be the number of accounting or reporting abuses that must be addressed by authoritative bodies like the FASB.

Each year business transactions become more complex, and new areas of business activity are explored. These conditions provide a multitude of ethical dilemmas that must be faced by the businessperson. Insider trading scandals in investment banking; restructuring of business for quick profit rather than for improved long-term operating performance; misleading or unfair marketing techniques; overcharging on government contracts; widespread failures of savings and loan institutions—all have plagued the business community in recent years. As businesspeople, accountants face the same ethical dilemmas that confront others in the business community. In addition, they face some ethical dilemmas that are associated more particularly with the activities of accountants and accounting (auditing) firms.

For instance, a certified public accountant (independent auditor) may have to resolve conflicts between GAAP and a client's preference for a non-GAAP accounting or reporting practice. Or, an independent auditor may not agree with a client's action regarding what should be disclosed in the financial statements. How will the accountant reconcile the responsibility to serve the public good with the obligation to keep the client happy? If the disagreement between the auditor and the client is substantial, the auditor may resign from the audit—as was the case when Coopers & Lybrand resigned from its Audre Recognition Systems audit because of "an impaired ability to rely on management's representations."[3] Independent auditors may face situations in which the confidentiality of their client relationship conflicts with their responsibility to disclose certain information for the benefit or protection of the public. They may also find themselves in a position in which what they know about one client would be extremely valuable to another client or could significantly affect their audit of another client. Both independent auditors and management (internal) accountants may have access to information about the company that is not publicly available and could therefore be used for their personal gain. Finally, a management accountant may have to choose between following GAAP or using a procedure that appears inconsistent with GAAP but puts a more favorable light on the company's operating results.

These examples are but a few of the many ethical dilemmas accountants may encounter during their professional careers. It is therefore important that accountants enter their profession with a strong sense of their own values and morals, as well as a good understanding of ethical professional behavior.

Ethical behavior typically is viewed as behavior consistent with the values of society. The basic issue is not whether a decision or action is legal or illegal, but whether the decision or action is defensible in a public forum. Thus, the FASB airs proposed new standards in an open forum prior to reaching its conclusions.

Ethical principles require accountants to consider the impact of their actions, as well as the effects of accounting standards and procedures and their application on the public good. To do otherwise would be to fail to fulfill the public service aspect of financial accounting and reporting. As you study financial accounting and reporting standards and procedures, you will begin to see that ethical considerations arise often. Accountants must be aware of potential ethical issues associated with financial accounting and reporting and must be prepared to respond to those issues.

Financial Statements

Financial statements are a central feature of financial reporting, and are the principal means of communicating the effects of business transactions and other economic events. A **financial statement** is a formal tabulation of account names and dollar amounts derived from the accounting records maintained by a business entity. Financial statements display either the financial position of the entity at a point in time or various kinds of changes in financial position of the entity over a period of time. Because individual financial statements are derived from the same underlying economic data—they merely report different aspects of the same

---

[3]*San Diego Daily Transcript,* August 4, 1995, Section A, p. 1.

transactions or other economic events—they *articulate* (interrelate) with one another. Since each presents a different type of information, however, no individual statement is likely to serve a single purpose or provide all the information necessary for a particular decision.

The financial statements required under GAAP are:

5 **Name the four financial statements required under GAAP.**

1. The *balance sheet* or *statement of financial position.*
2. The *income statement* or *statement of earnings.*
3. The *statement of owners' equity.*
4. The *statement of cash flows.*

Information provided in notes to these financial statements or shown parenthetically on the face of the statements (such as information about significant accounting policies, a pension plan description, or segment financial data) enhances or explains the information in the statements themselves. Supplementary information, such as disclosures of the effects of changing prices on the entity's financial statements, along with voluntary management discussion and analysis, adds support and additional explanation to the statements and notes. Many companies also voluntarily disclose certain financial information, such as expenditures for employee training and social welfare expenditures. This information, along with the financial statements, notes to the financial statements, and supplementary data, is useful for investment, credit, and similar decisions.

Exhibit 1–2 shows the total set of information that may be used in making investment, credit, and similar decisions. Reading from the left side of the exhibit, notice that the financial information subject to an independent auditor's opinion includes both the financial statements and the notes to the financial statements. As the exhibit shows, the FASB's area of interest is **general purpose external financial reporting**—reporting designed to serve the needs of external users of financial information as a whole, rather than the needs of particular groups. General purpose external financial reporting is directed toward a company's ability to generate positive net cash flows from operating activities—a common interest among external users. Information about cash flows is the basis for the financial reporting objectives and other concepts of financial accounting theory discussed in Chapter 2.

As the exhibit also indicates, financial reporting may go beyond the information provided by general purpose external financial statements. Financial reporting also may include the preparation of special reports for specific users. For example, a potential lender, such as a bank, often can demand additional financial information before making a lending decision.

Preparation and dissemination of the financial statements of a business entity are the responsibility of the management of that entity. Because of the importance of the financial statements, management often engages independent auditors (certified public accountants) to attest to the fairness of the statements. In the next section we will discuss the professional and regulatory institutions responsible for establishing financial accounting and reporting standards.

ⓟ ROFESSIONAL AND REGULATORY INSTITUTIONS OF FINANCIAL ACCOUNTING AND REPORTING

Until about 1930 accountants generally relied on their own judgment to determine the most useful practice in a given situation. Although accounting was a recognized profession, accounting practices varied widely and fell far short of the standards of GAAP today. In the aftermath of the 1929 stock market crash, criticism of

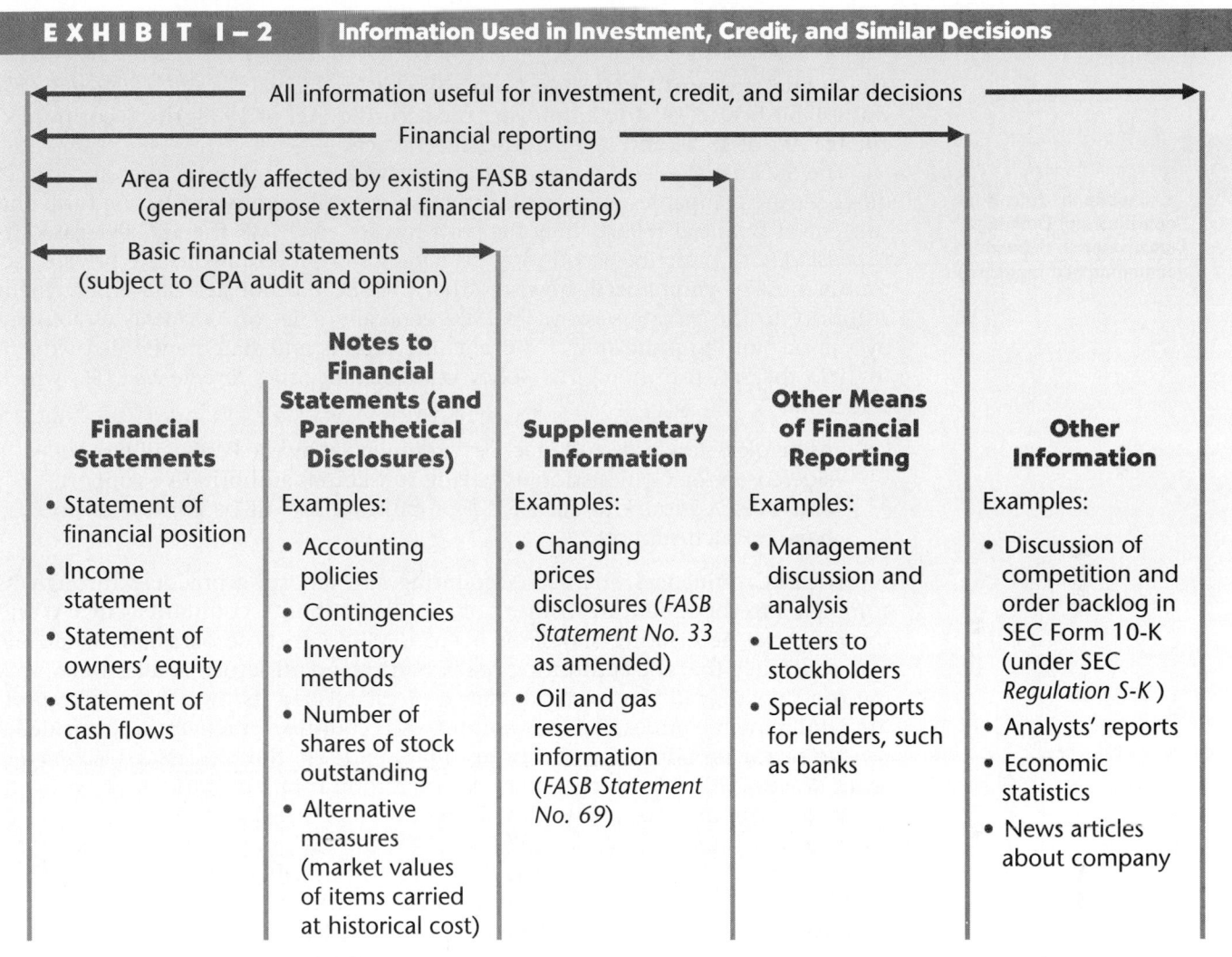

EXHIBIT 1-2   Information Used in Investment, Credit, and Similar Decisions

All information useful for investment, credit, and similar decisions

Financial reporting

Area directly affected by existing FASB standards (general purpose external financial reporting)

Basic financial statements (subject to CPA audit and opinion)

Financial Statements	Notes to Financial Statements (and Parenthetical Disclosures)	Supplementary Information	Other Means of Financial Reporting	Other Information
• Statement of financial position • Income statement • Statement of owners' equity • Statement of cash flows	Examples: • Accounting policies • Contingencies • Inventory methods • Number of shares of stock outstanding • Alternative measures (market values of items carried at historical cost)	Examples: • Changing prices disclosures (*FASB Statement No. 33* as amended) • Oil and gas reserves information (*FASB Statement No. 69*)	Examples: • Management discussion and analysis • Letters to stockholders • Special reports for lenders, such as banks	Examples: • Discussion of competition and order backlog in SEC Form 10-K (under SEC *Regulation S-K*) • Analysts' reports • Economic statistics • News articles about company

Source: "Recognition and Measurement in Financial Statements of Business Enterprises," *Statement of Financial Accounting Concepts No. 5* (Stamford, Conn.: FASB, 1984), p. 5.

financial accounting and reporting practices came from both inside and outside the accounting profession. In 1930, the American Institute of Accountants (AIA)[4] appointed two committees, one to work with the New York Stock Exchange on issues of common interest to stock exchanges, investors, and accountants, and one to address accounting issues and procedures. These appointments were in response to a change in accounting objectives. Whereas financial information previously had been intended strictly for management and creditors, it was now intended to meet the needs of investors and stockholders as well.

The stock market crash and the events that preceded and contributed to it also influenced federal legislation related to security exchanges. In an effort to restore investor confidence, to reestablish integrity in the capital markets, and to supplement intrastate regulation, Congress passed the Securities Act of 1933 and the Securities Exchange Act of 1934.

---

[4]The American Institute of Accountants was renamed the American Institute of Certified Public Accountants (AICPA) in 1957. The AICPA is the professional organization for CPAs. In that sense, it is similar to the American Bar Association (for lawyers) and the American Medical Association (for doctors).

Securities and Exchange Commission (SEC)

The **Securities and Exchange Commission** is a federal regulatory agency that was established in 1934 to administer the Securities Act of 1933, the Securities Exchange Act of 1934, and several other federal acts.

The SEC has the legal authority to prescribe accounting principles and procedures for the companies under its jurisdiction, as well as to prescribe the form and content of financial reports they file with the SEC. In 1938 the SEC delegated its *responsibility* to prescribe accounting principles and procedures to the private sector. (It must be emphasized, however, that the SEC did not delegate enforcement authority to the private sector.) The SEC generally relies on GAAP, as established by the accounting profession, for evaluating reports and statements filed with it. In 1973 the SEC reaffirmed this policy in *Accounting Series Release No. 150,* which states that

> principles, standards and practices promulgated by the FASB will be considered by the Commission as having substantial authoritative support, and those contrary to such FASB promulgations will be considered to have no such support.[5]

The SEC influences financial accounting and reporting practices through its comments to the American Institute of Certified Public Accountants (AICPA) and the Financial Accounting Standards Board (FASB). On those occasions when the SEC concluded that the accounting profession's standard-setting bodies were moving too slowly or in the wrong direction, it established its own financial reporting requirements, imposed a moratorium on accounting practices, or overruled a private sector pronouncement. For example, in 1974, the SEC issued *Accounting Series Release No. 163,* which imposed a moratorium on the capitalization of interest cost. This moratorium was lifted after the FASB issued *Statement No. 34,* "Capitalization of Interest Cost," in 1979. In 1978, the SEC, in effect, overruled a pronouncement of the FASB, when the SEC rejected the standards prescribed by *FASB Statement No. 19,* "Financial Accounting and Reporting for Oil and Gas Producing Companies." As a result, the FASB issued *Statement No. 25,* "Suspension of Certain Accounting Requirements for Oil and Gas Producing Companies," which suspended the effective dates of most of the requirements of *Statement No. 19.* In 1982, the FASB amended *Statements No. 19* and *25* with *Statement No. 69,* "Disclosures about Oil and Gas Producing Activities." Shortly thereafter, the SEC amended its disclosure requirements for oil and gas producers to require compliance with the provisions of *FASB Statement No. 69.* During the early 1990s, the SEC put substantial pressure on the FASB to require market value accounting for investment securities. Ultimately, the FASB issued *Statement No. 115,* which was responsive to the SEC pressure.

American Institute of Certified Public Accountants (AICPA)

Until 1973 the **American Institute of Certified Public Accountants (AICPA)** provided the private sector with leadership in developing financial accounting and reporting principles and practices. From 1938 through 1959 the AICPA acted primarily through its Committee on Accounting Procedure (CAP) and from 1959 through 1973 through the Accounting Principles Board (APB). When the Financial Accounting Standards Board (FASB) was established in 1973 as an independent standard-setting body, the AICPA continued to participate in

---

[5]"Statement of Policy on the Establishment and Improvement of Accounting Principles and Standards," *Accounting Series Release No. 150* (Washington, D.C.: SEC, December 20, 1973).

6 Explain the role of the Securities and Exchange Commission in financial accounting and reporting.

standard setting through its **Accounting Standards Executive Committee (AcSEC),** the senior technical committee to speak for the AICPA on matters of financial accounting and reporting. AcSEC frequently advises the FASB on agenda items and also provides guidance to AICPA members on issues not resolved by existing pronouncements.

Committee on Accounting Procedure (CAP)

In its two-decade history, the **Committee on Accounting Procedure (CAP),** a 21-member committee, issued 51 *Accounting Research Bulletins* **(ARBs)** on matters of financial accounting and reporting practice. Many are still in effect. The CAP devoted most of its time to resolving specific accounting and reporting problems. It gave little attention to developing either general accounting principles or a theoretical framework that could be used to resolve future accounting and reporting problems.

Accounting Principles Board (APB)

When the **Accounting Principles Board (APB)** replaced the CAP in 1959, its objectives were (1) to establish broad accounting principles, (2) to set up rules or guidelines for applying those principles to specific situations, and (3) to conduct research on which principles, rules, and guidelines would be based. An Accounting Research Division with a permanent research staff assisted the Board.

The APB operated from 1959 through June 1973 and had from 18 to 21 members, all of whom belonged to the AICPA. Members were selected primarily from the accounting profession but also from industry, the academic community, and government. During its existence, the APB issued 31 *Opinions* and 4 *Statements*. **APB Opinions** are authoritative pronouncements that set forth GAAP. **APB Statements** are primarily informative and basically serve to enhance interested parties' understanding of accounting matters.

Before 1964, enforcement of *APB Opinions* and effective *Accounting Research Bulletins* depended almost entirely on the prestige of the AICPA and the APB. A major factor in the APB's prestige was the SEC's delegation of authority to it. In 1964, the AICPA took the position that GAAP are those principles that have substantial authoritative support. Subsequently, the AICPA adopted a general requirement (Rule 203 of the Code of Professional Conduct of the AICPA) that no member of the AICPA may give an opinion that financial statements are presented in conformity with GAAP if those statements contain any material departures from generally accepted accounting principles, unless the member can demonstrate that, because of unusual circumstances, the financial statements would otherwise be misleading.

The APB was criticized for its inability to reduce the areas of difference and inconsistency in financial accounting and reporting. Much of the criticism focused on the APB's structure, specifically (1) its large size (18 to 21 members); (2) the part-time status of APB members (all were full-time employees of CPA firms, universities, or companies); (3) the lack of compensation for Board members; (4) their brief meeting times—only a few days each month; (5) the inability of the Accounting Research Division to provide timely research for *APB Opinions;* and (6) the excessive influence of CPA firms and, by implication, their clients on *APB Opinions.*

Because of the dissatisfaction with the system for developing accounting principles, the AICPA appointed two committees in 1971: the Study Group on Establishment of Accounting Principles and the Study Group on the Objectives of Financial Statements. The Study Group on Establishment of Accounting Principles recommended establishment of the Financial Accounting Standards Board to replace the APB. The Study Group on the Objectives of Financial Statements attempted to identify the objectives of financial accounting and reporting. Its report, published in 1973, was an important input to the FASB's work on a conceptual framework for financial accounting and reporting.

Financial Accounting Standards Board (FASB)

1 Describe the organizational structure and standard-setting process of the Financial Accounting Standards Board, and identify the types of pronouncements it issues.

The **Financial Accounting Standards Board (FASB)** began operations in July 1973. The mission of the FASB is to establish and improve standards of financial accounting and reporting. In addition, the FASB develops broad accounting concepts and provides guidance on the implementation of standards. The FASB is a privately funded, nongovernmental, independent entity responsible to the entire economic community, not just to the public accounting profession.

Organization

The FASB is a key part of the standard-setting structure shown in Exhibit 1–3. Notice that the FASB has seven members, one of whom is the Chair. FASB members

EXHIBIT 1–3	The Formal Structure for Setting Financial Accounting and Reporting Standards

Financial Accounting Foundation (FAF)

- Oversees the operations of the FASB and the GASB.
- Raises and manages the funds for FASB and GASB operations.
- Appoints the members of the FASB and the GASB and their respective Advisory Councils.

Financial Accounting Standards Board (FASB)

- Establishes financial accounting and reporting standards, develops broad accounting concepts, and provides guidance on implementation of standards.
- Issues several types of official pronouncements:

  1. *Statements of Financial Accounting Standards*
  2. *Interpretations*
  3. *Technical Bulletins*
  4. *Statements of Financial Accounting Concepts*

- Has seven members including the Chair.

Governmental Accounting Standards Board (GASB)

- Establishes financial accounting and reporting standards for state and local governments.
- Has five members.

Governmental Accounting Standards Advisory Council (GASAC)

- Advises the GASB on policy matters, agenda items, project priorities, technical issues, and task forces.

Emerging Issues Task Force (EITF)

- Identifies, investigates, and reviews emerging issues.
- When the EITF cannot reach consensus, advises the FASB on whether the issue merits FASB attention.

Financial Accounting Standards Advisory Council (FASAC)

- Advises the FASB on policy matters, agenda items, project priorities, technical issues, and task forces.

are well compensated and are assisted by a research and technical staff of approximately 40 professionals. FASB members are appointed by the **Financial Accounting Foundation (FAF),** which also appoints the Financial Accounting Standards Advisory Council, obtains and manages the FASB's funding, and exercises general oversight of the Board's operations.

The **Financial Accounting Standards Advisory Council (FASAC)** has about 30 members. Its role is to consult with the FASB on major policy questions, technical issues on the Board's agenda, project priorities, potential agenda items, and other matters as requested. Identification of potential agenda items is also one outcome of the activities of the FASB's **Emerging Issues Task Force (EITF),** formed in 1984. The EITF includes individuals from public accounting, large companies, and organizations such as the Financial Executives Institute—people who are in a position to identify emerging accounting and reporting issues before divergent practices in those areas become entrenched. The EITF discussions of issues and relevant accounting pronouncements help the FASB to better understand and resolve emerging issues. If the EITF is able to reach a consensus on an issue, the FASB usually will conclude that no Board action is needed. As a result, many items that might otherwise have been on the Board's agenda are resolved by the EITF. If consensus is not reached by the EITF, it may indicate that FASB action is warranted.

In 1984, the Financial Accounting Foundation also established a **Governmental Accounting Standards Board (GASB)** to set standards of financial accounting and reporting for state and local governmental units. The GASB is organized similarly to the FASB, with its own Advisory Council (the Governmental Accounting Standards Advisory Council) and technical staff. The GASB deals with public sector accounting rather than private sector accounting, which is the subject of this textbook.

Official Pronouncements

As shown in Exhibit 1–3, the FASB issues four types of official pronouncements:

Statements of Financial Accounting Standards. *Statements of Standards,* along with *APB Opinions* and *CAP Accounting Research Bulletins* that remain effective, are considered to be GAAP and are binding in accounting practice.

Interpretations of *CAP Accounting Research Bulletins, APB Opinions,* and *FASB Statements of Standards.* FASB *Interpretations* clarify, explain, or elaborate on existing *Statements of Standards* and predecessor documents and have the same authority as *Statements of Standards.*

Technical Bulletins. *Technical Bulletins* provide guidance in the application of *FASB Statements of Standards* or *Interpretations, APB Opinions,* and *CAP Accounting Research Bulletins.* They may address issues not directly covered by existing standards.

Statements of Financial Accounting Concepts. *Statements of Concepts* present the conceptual framework of financial accounting and reporting. *Statements of Concepts* do not establish GAAP.

Since June 1985 these four types of official pronouncements, as well as several other FASB documents, have been published under a single title, ***Financial Accounting Series.*** Documents included in the series are subtitled *Statement of Financial Accounting Standards, Technical Bulletin,* and so on, as appropriate.

Due Process Procedure

In an effort to be responsive to public opinion, the FASB completes a lengthy process of preparation and review before issuing either a *Statement of Financial Accounting Standards* or a *Statement of Financial Accounting Concepts.* This process helps to ensure that the Board deals fairly and equitably with various competing interests in developing its standards. The usual steps of this **due process procedure** are:

1. An accounting or reporting problem is identified and placed on the FASB's agenda. Topics are added to the Board's agenda after evaluating four factors: pervasiveness of the problem, alternative solutions, technical feasibility, and practical consequences.[6]

2. Research and analysis are conducted by the FASB's technical staff. For each major project, the Board appoints an advisory task force of experts from outside the FASB structure. The task force plays an important role by providing expertise, a diversity of viewpoints, and a means for communicating with those who might be affected by a proposed standard. The Board studies existing literature on the subject and commissions outside research projects when necessary.

3. A *Discussion Memorandum* or other discussion document presenting the issues and possible solutions is prepared and distributed to the public for comment.

4. A public hearing is held (usually after at least 60 days) to discuss the issues raised by the *Discussion Memorandum.* If a *Discussion Memorandum* is not issued, an *Exposure Draft* (see item 6) may provide the basis for an initial public hearing.

5. The public's oral and written comments in response to the public hearing are carefully analyzed by the FASB and its staff. After available input has

---

[6]L. Todd Johnson and Robert J. Swieringa, "Anatomy of an Agenda Decision: Statement No. 115," *Accounting Horizons,* June 1996, pp. 149–179.

been thoroughly studied, the Board begins formal discussions, meeting as necessary to resolve the issues. All meetings are open to the public.

6. A preliminary draft of a proposed *Statement,* called an *Exposure Draft,* is issued. At least five of the seven Board members must approve an *Exposure Draft* before its issuance.

7. All responses to the *Exposure Draft* received by a specified date, generally at least 60 days after its issuance, are analyzed by the staff and reviewed by Board members. When the analysis and review are complete, the Board begins discussion of a final *Statement.*

8. If substantial changes in the Board's position result from comments on the *Exposure Draft,* a revised *Exposure Draft* may be issued, and a second public hearing may be held.

9. After the Board concludes that all reasonable alternatives have been considered, a vote is taken on a final *Statement.* At least five of the seven Board members must support a *Statement* before it is issued.

Conceptual Framework Project

As shown by the list of accounting pronouncements inside the covers of this text, the FASB has been very productive. Like pronouncements of the CAP and APB, many of the FASB's *Statements of Financial Accounting Standards* and *Interpretations* are directed toward specific problems. However, the FASB also has made significant strides toward establishing a **conceptual framework.** Its conceptual framework project deals with both theoretical and conceptual issues, and is intended to provide an underlying structure for future *Statements of Standards.* It has been described as

> a constitution, a coherent system of interrelated objectives and fundamentals that can lead to consistent standards and that prescribes the nature, function, and limits of financial accounting and reporting. The fundamentals are the underlying concepts of accounting, concepts that guide the selection of events to be accounted for, the measurement of those events, and the means of summarizing and communicating them to interested parties.[7]

The *Statements of Financial Accounting Concepts* the FASB has issued provide a common language and starting point for discussion within the FASB and among its constituents. Much of the theoretical foundation underlying financial accounting and reporting, the subject of Chapter 2, is found in the conceptual framework.

THE POLITICS OF STANDARD SETTING IN FINANCIAL ACCOUNTING AND REPORTING

Dictionaries provide several definitions of *political* and *politics,* including competition among interest groups or individuals for power and leadership in government or other groups. Such competition is, in part, evidenced by attempts to influence the governing system so that particular views are reflected in the policies of the system, and/or a particular group's self-interest is benefited, perhaps to the detriment of others. This "political" type of environment is essentially the standard-setting environment of the FASB and the individuals who are its members. With the SEC looking over its shoulder, the Board is expected to serve a constituency composed of entities

8 Describe the political nature of financial accounting and reporting standard setting.

---

[7]"Conceptual Framework for Financial Accounting and Reporting: Elements of Financial Statements and Their Measurement," *Discussion Memorandum* (Stamford, Conn.: FASB, 1976), p. 2.

whose interests often are at variance and to reconcile the resulting divergent viewpoints in a manner that best serves the public interest.

SEC Influence

The FASB must bear in mind that its responsibility for establishing accounting and reporting standards is *delegated* to it by the SEC, which holds the legal authority to prescribe accounting and reporting standards. Furthermore, with regard to its constituency, the Board must maintain a delicate balance between dependence and independence. The FASB is dependent on *general* constituency support as the basis for its power to establish "generally accepted" standards. At the same time, the Board's credibility resides in its independence from any *particular* constituent. Finally, the Board must attempt to respond to both theoretical and practical considerations in developing accounting and reporting standards.

Recall that although the SEC delegated its responsibility for standard setting to the private sector (currently the FASB), it did not delegate its enforcement authority. As a result, the SEC's power in setting standards is substantial. In general, the SEC has supported standards established by the private sector. But, on rare occasions, it has established its own financial reporting requirements, imposed a moratorium on accounting practices, or refused to support a private sector action.

The first occasion on which the SEC failed to support the private sector occurred in 1962, when the APB issued *Opinion No. 2*[8] requiring the deferral method to account for the investment tax credit. (Although the Tax Reform Act of 1986 eliminated this tax credit retroactive to the beginning of 1986, it could reappear as an investment incentive in the future.) The effect of an investment tax credit is to reduce taxes payable by a company in the year in which the company puts qualifying assets into use. The accounting question raised by the investment tax credit was whether the tax credit benefit should be recognized in the company's income statement (1) as the asset was used in operations (the deferral method) or (2) entirely in the period of the asset's acquisition (the flow-through method). In *Opinion No. 2* the APB chose the deferral method.

Companies were not pleased that the APB chose the deferral method, because it spread income statement recognition of the tax credit benefit over several years. So much criticism was directed at the deferral method that the SEC declared that it would accept either the deferral or the flow-through method. In 1964 the APB issued *Opinion No. 4,*[9] which specified a preference for the deferral method but also permitted the flow-through method. Because of political pressure, two accounting alternatives became acceptable where previously only one had been permitted.

Pressure from Interested Parties

As discussed earlier, several steps normally precede the publication of an *FASB Statement* to ensure public input to the decision-making process and consideration of the views of all interested parties. Often referred to as "due process," the FASB's procedure involves lobbying, debate, negotiation, and compromise before yielding a "generally accepted" standard.

During the course of the due process procedure, the SEC, other agencies, and business groups (among others) may try to influence the FASB's action. For example, during deliberations on accounting for investments in debt securities, the FASB received substantial pressure from the SEC in favor of market value accounting, and pressure opposing market value accounting from banks, the Federal Reserve Board staff, and others. On numerous occasions efforts have been made

---

[8]"Accounting for the 'Investment Credit,'" *Opinions of the Accounting Principles Board No. 2* (New York: AICPA, 1962).
[9]"Accounting for the 'Investment Credit,'" *Opinions of the Accounting Principles Board No. 4* (New York: AICPA, 1964).

to sway Board decisions to protect specific self-interests, even to the point of arguing that a standard under consideration would "lead to the economic ruin of a particular industry or group of companies."[10] Assertions of this sort regarding economic consequences were made during the course of deliberations on accounting for oil and gas reserves, troubled debt restructuring, leases, research and development expenditures, pensions and other postretirement benefits, investments in debt securities, and employee stock options. Some of the arguments that were made in these cases are described later in this chapter.

Individual FASB members may need to make concessions on some aspects of a standard in order to achieve other points they consider more important. Such compromises sometimes are essential if the Board is to arrive at a favorable vote on a standard. The role of individuals on the FASB is *not* to represent the views of particular constituents of the Board, but to make independent and objective decisions that will increase the reliability, relevance, and usefulness of reported financial information.

In summary, standard setting by the FASB is a *political* as well as a technical process. Choices must be made among alternatives, and the alternatives selected are unlikely to satisfy everyone who will be affected by them. Pressure is exerted on those who set standards, and compromises often are necessary in order to make a proposed financial accounting or reporting practice generally acceptable. If the FASB and its standards are to remain credible, it is essential that the Board maintain its independence and objectivity in decision making.

Professional Influence

In addition to the SEC, the AICPA, and the FASB, a number of other organizations and regulatory agencies have influenced financial accounting and reporting. Among the more prominent professional groups are the American Accounting Association (AAA), the Institute of Management Accountants (IMA), and the Financial Executives Institute (FEI).

The AAA is an organization primarily for accounting educators, although many public accountants, industrial accountants, and governmental accountants also are members. Its broad objectives are to contribute to the development of accounting theory, to encourage and sponsor accounting research, and to improve the quality of accounting education. The academic members of the AAA conduct much of the research on accounting issues, and many of their research findings are published in the AAA's quarterly journal, *The Accounting Review*. The AAA also publishes *Accounting Horizons* and *Issues in Accounting Education*.

The IMA was organized in 1919 and is oriented toward managerial accounting issues. In 1968, however, the IMA broadened its research interests to include all information needed by business managers and investors. In addition to publishing its periodical, *Management Accounting*, the IMA has funded several major accounting research projects, and it tends to provide a broad perspective on standard setting.

The FEI was founded in 1931. Through its Financial Executives Research Foundation, the FEI has undertaken and published several studies related to financial accounting and reporting issues. The FEI has contributed to the development of financial accounting and reporting standards through the cooperation of its technical committee on corporate reporting with both the APB and the FASB. The FEI also publishes a monthly journal, *Financial Executive*. Recently (1996), the FEI "mounted a behind-the-scenes campaign to shrink the FASB" to five members and increase business's influence on its rule-setting process.[11]

---

[10]For example, see *Financial Accounting Series Status Report No. 186* (Stamford, Conn.: FASB, 1987), p. 3; or Robert J. Swieringa, "The First 100 Days in the Life of a New Board Member," *Accounting Horizons*, June 1987, pp. 1–7.
[11]Lee Burton, "Business Group Wants Smaller FASB, More Influence on Rule-Setting Process," *The Wall Street Journal*, February 28, 1996, p. C20.

IRS Influence

The Internal Revenue Service (IRS) also influences financial accounting and reporting through its administration of the income tax law. In many instances the accounting profession has been willing to accept tax accounting requirements as generally accepted accounting principles. Moreover, many companies prefer to avoid maintaining separate sets of records, one for accounting purposes and one for tax purposes. Therefore, companies often will select financial accounting procedures because those procedures are followed for tax purposes.

Congressional Influence

Congress has become an active and powerful force in the setting of accounting and reporting standards. In 1976 and 1977, the U.S. Senate and House of Representatives formed separate subcommittees that studied the accounting profession concurrently and reached similar conclusions. The subcommittees recommended that the setting of accounting and reporting standards should remain in the private sector. They made it clear, however, that the accounting profession, working in cooperation with the SEC, must act in a timely manner to implement certain recommended policy goals.

In response to the subcommittees' concerns, the FASB reorganized its operations to increase due process, openness, and consistency in its actions. Reorganization also occurred within the AICPA, which established a public board to oversee peer reviews of CPA firms that audit businesses registered with the SEC. In June 1985 the National Commission on Fraudulent Financial Reporting (known as the Treadway Commission) was established in response to increasing allegations of financial reporting fraud and growing numbers of SEC enforcement actions regarding fraud. A multiorganizational effort funded by the AICPA, the AAA, the FEI, the IMA, and the Institute of Internal Auditors, the Commission made several recommendations to the independent public accounting profession, the SEC and other regulatory agencies, and accounting educators. In general, the recommendations were intended to help reduce the incidence of fraudulent reporting, improve the audit process, enhance regulation of reporting, and increase awareness of the risks of fraudulent reporting.

In 1985 the House of Representatives Subcommittee on Oversight and Investigation, known as the Dingell Committee, initiated hearings on the SEC's effectiveness in overseeing the accounting profession's progress in improving the usefulness, integrity, and credibility of financial reporting by public companies. The Dingell Committee hearings covered quality control, independence, enforcement, and standard setting in the accounting profession. The Dingell hearings highlighted a growing concern about white-collar crime in financial reporting.

INTERNATIONAL ACCOUNTING AND REPORTING STANDARDS

9   **Describe the state of international accounting standard setting, and describe the activities of some of the key groups in setting international standards.**

Though the focus of this text is on financial accounting and reporting in the United States, the increasing number of multinational companies and the global nature of capital markets make some mention of the status of international accounting and reporting standards appropriate. In this section we begin by describing the diversity of international accounting practices and discussing the need for harmonization of conflicting accounting and reporting standards. We then describe the activities of some key groups in the international standard-setting forum.

International Accounting Differences

Substantial differences exist from one country to another in financial accounting and reporting practices. Those differences result from a variety of causes, including the legal environment, political forces, and cultural differences, as well as different economic models. Most countries fall into one of two general groups. In countries such as France, Germany, and Japan, businesses obtain their financial resources largely from borrowing. Accounting practices tend to be rather conservative, and are greatly influenced by tax rules, legal systems, and social norms (e.g., an emphasis on privacy). In countries such as the United States, the United Kingdom, Australia, and the Netherlands, businesses more often obtain financial resources from equity transactions. In these countries accounting practices tend to be less conservative and relatively independent of tax rules; some private sector body usually is responsible for standard setting.

The potential for substantial differences in reported business outcomes due to differences in accounting systems is startling. For example, in 1994 the German company Daimler Benz reported a profit of DM895 million under German accounting rules, and DM1,052 million under U.S. standards. An even more dramatic difference existed in 1993, when Daimler Benz reported a *profit* of DM615 million under German rules but a *loss* of DM1,839 million under U.S. accounting rules. Even in countries that are considered "in the same group" for purposes of financial reporting, notable differences in reported business outcomes can occur. Thus, Norsk Hydro reported a profit of NKR167 million in 1992 using Norwegian accounting rules, whereas U.S. accounting yielded a profit of NKR1,763 million. And News Corporation (an Australian company) reported a profit of A$502 million using Australian rules, compared to A$241 under U.S. accounting rules.[12] Differences in specific accounting practices between countries also illustrate the point. For example, United Kingdom accounting allows the cost of purchased goodwill to be charged directly to stockholders' equity, while in the United States the cost of goodwill must be capitalized and charged against earnings over a period of 40 years. It has been argued that U.S. companies cannot compete successfully with United Kingdom companies in acquiring other companies because of the high goodwill charge against earnings under U.S. accounting rules.[13]

Because of the increasing number of multinational companies and the globalization of capital markets, the need for greater uniformity in financial accounting and reporting practices around the world has greatly increased in recent years. Furthermore, given the diversity of reported outcomes that is possible under the accounting practices of different countries, the very credibility of financial accounting is at risk. For users to feel that they can rely on published financial statements when making resource allocation decisions, reported business outcomes must not vary dramatically merely because of international differences in financial accounting practices. Without more uniform accounting practices, the efficient allocation of scarce resources in an international marketplace may be substantially impaired. Three groups are particularly active in the effort to establish more uniform international financial accounting and reporting standards: the International Accounting Standards Committee, the International Organization of Securities Commissions, and the European Union.

International Accounting Standards Committee (IASC)

The **International Accounting Standards Committee (IASC)** was founded in 1973, with the American Institute of Certified Public Accountants as one of its

[12]J. A. Schweikart, S. J. Gray, and S. B. Salter, "An Interview with Sir Bryan Carsberg, Secretary-General of the International Accounting Standards Committee," *Accounting Horizons,* March 1996, pp. 110–117.

[13]J. C. Corry, "Accounting Aspects of Takeovers," *Management Accounting,* September 1990, pp. 47–51.

founding members. It has a membership of over 100 professional bodies from 86 countries. The IASC's objectives are:

1. To formulate and publish in the public interest accounting standards to be observed in the presentation of financial statements and to promote their worldwide acceptance and observance.

2. To work generally for the improvement and harmonization of regulations, accounting standards, and procedures relating to the presentation of financial statements.

The IASC's work is carried out by a board of representatives that includes representatives of 13 countries and the International Coordinating Committee of Financial Analysts' Associations. The United States is represented on the IASC board by a two-person delegation appointed, one each, by the AICPA and the Institute of Management Accountants. The IASC follows a due process procedure similar to that of the FASB. Before an IASC standard is issued, a steering committee is appointed to study the topic in detail and make recommendations to the board. An exposure draft is then prepared and distributed to member bodies as well as to governments, stock exchanges, regulatory authorities, and others involved with or interested in financial accounting and reporting. After the exposure period (usually six months), the draft is revised on the basis of comments received. It is issued as a standard if approved by three-quarters of the board. The IASC has issued 32 statements of International Accounting Standards in this way. It also has compiled a conceptual framework document that addresses the objectives of financial reporting, defines the qualities of useful financial reporting, and describes the elements of the financial statements.

The IASC's International Accounting Standards have been criticized for permitting too many alternative accounting treatments for some transactions and events. In the late 1980s, the IASC embarked on a major effort to eliminate many of the alternative treatments in existing standards. Since the IASC has no legal power to establish accounting standards, it must rely on the voluntary actions of member bodies and other groups to support and enforce its standards. Recently the IASC has been focusing on completing a core set of International Accounting Standards as an alternative to national standards.

International Organization of Securities Commissions (IOSCO)

The **International Organization of Securities Commissions (IOSCO),** of which the U.S. Securities and Exchange Commission is a member, consists of regulators representing the securities markets of nearly 70 countries. With cooperation from the IASC, IOSCO hopes to complete a core set of 16 standards on subjects such as intangibles, financial instruments, interim reporting, segments, and leasing by 1999—at which time it is expected to endorse the core set of standards. Under IOSCO's agreement with the IASC, IOSCO's Technical Committee will recommend to national securities commissions that financial statements issued by foreign companies based on the IASC's core International Accounting Standards be accepted for cross-border capital raising and listing purposes in all global markets. IOSCO's cooperation with the IASC and its endorsement of the IASC's efforts are indicative of the growing support for the establishment of generally accepted International Accounting Standards.

European Union (EU)

The **European Union (EU),** formed in 1957, consists of 15 member countries. The EU is engaged in a program to harmonize accounting and reporting within the

Union and to encourage capital formation and the free flow of capital among member countries. The EU's program has the full weight of law behind it. Each member country's laws must be adapted to the EU's *Directives*. The *Directives* (the *Fourth Directive* in particular) contain optional accounting practices; each country's legislature selects the options it prefers. For example, the United Kingdom and the Netherlands allow companies to use either historical cost or current cost, while Germany allows only historical cost.[14] The accounting provisions of the *Directives* are mandatory for any company—even for non-European companies—doing business within a member country.

The two most important *Directives* affecting financial accounting and reporting are the *Fourth* and *Seventh Directives*. The *Fourth Directive* governs the content and format of financial statements, including the disclosures they must contain. The *Seventh Directive* deals with consolidated financial statements. In general, however, the *Directives* are not an ideal way to set accounting standards because they are like statutes; and changing their requirements can be a lengthy political process. In the mid-1990s there was some discussion about forming a European accounting standards board. However, the EU is much more likely to increase its involvement with, and support of, the IASC as the primary group for harmonizing international financial accounting and reporting standards.

THE ENVIRONMENT AND ROLE OF FINANCIAL ACCOUNTING AND REPORTING

In this section we will discuss some important aspects of the environment in which business operates, and in which financial accounting and reporting exist. We will begin by discussing four groups that have significant interests in financial accounting and reporting issues. We will then describe how those groups are interrelated, and how financial accounting information enters into their relationships—that is, the general role of financial accounting and reporting in the business environment. Finally, we will provide some examples of how the economic environment influences financial accounting and reporting and, in turn, how financial accounting and reporting has impacted the economic environment.

The Economic Environment

The United States has a highly developed exchange economy. In recent years, many other countries have achieved similar, though often less sophisticated, economies, so that there now exists a highly developed global exchange economy. In an exchange economy, most companies do not consume the goods and services they produce. Instead, they exchange goods and services produced for money or claims to money (e.g., accounts receivable), with the objective of maximizing the economic welfare of their owners. Since money is the basis of exchange in this economy, those participating in the economy make decisions and take actions based on their present and expected money resources.

Financial accounting is an important source of information for those who make resource allocation decisions in the business world. In particular, four general groups (parties) have a significant interest in financial accounting and reporting issues: corporations (corporate management); nonstockholders (nonowners) who supply inputs to corporations (e.g., lenders, employees, and suppliers of materials and

---

[14]Stephen A. Zeff, unpublished comments, January 1995.

goods); various regulatory authorities; and existing and potential investors (stockholders) in corporations.

Corporations (Corporate Management)

Producing and marketing goods and services are long, costly, and complicated processes that require continuous access to large amounts of physical and money capital and are best managed by professionals. The corporate form of business enables companies to obtain large amounts of money capital by issuing stocks and bonds in organized securities markets. To conduct the day-to-day business activities of the company, the owners (stockholders) of corporations engage professional managers. These managers, who are directly accountable to the stockholders, are responsible for developing and implementing a strategy for profitable operation of the corporation. Their effectiveness in doing so is assessed by the owners, in large part, on the basis of information provided in the corporation's periodic financial statements, which are prepared by management.

The accounting and reporting process, procedures, and practices followed by corporate management in preparing the financial statements are significantly influenced by generally accepted accounting and reporting principles. Thus, GAAP plays an important role in helping stockholders to effectively monitor, evaluate, and reward (through compensation agreements) the stewardship of corporate management.

Suppliers of Inputs

Other than stockholders, those who supply the necessary inputs for operating a corporation are interested in financial information about the corporation for contracting and settling purposes. Lenders (e.g., bondholders) expect to receive interest on the amounts they lend and to have the principal returned on the due date of the loan. They examine the financial accounting information of a potential borrower when making decisions about whether to enter into a lending contract, and when assessing a borrower's ability to settle up at the end of a contract. During the lending period, lenders often require borrowers to maintain particular financial ratios or to meet certain other loan covenants based on financial accounting data.

Employees too use financial accounting information about their employers in negotiations related to their working hours, wages, and fringe benefits. Employees also may look at their employer's financial success as a measure of their own performance. Suppliers may rely on financial accounting data about a potential buyer to ascertain the extent to which they may be called upon to provide production inputs. They may find that such financial accounting data influences the extent to, and the terms under which, they are willing to extend credit to buyers.

Regulatory Authorities

Various regulatory authorities, especially units of the federal government, are a significant part of the environment of financial accounting and reporting. U.S., foreign, state, and local government units play a major role in resource allocation by levying and collecting taxes and by borrowing and spending money. In addition, the federal government regulates the activities of companies and individuals through legislation and agencies like the Federal Trade Commission and the Securities and Exchange Commission. Government agencies often use financial accounting information to monitor the activities of regulated companies and assist in policy making.

10 **Discuss the interrelationships among the corporation, suppliers of its inputs, regulatory authorities, and investors.**

Investors (and Securities Markets)

Investors in corporations usually expect to receive dividends from their investments. They also expect that the market value of their shares of stock will increase. Organized securities markets, such as the New York Stock Exchange, allow investors to easily buy and sell securities. Transactions in these markets are referred to as secondary market transactions because they occur after the securities have been issued by the corporation. No part of the exchange price in secondary market transactions goes to the corporation.

Even though secondary market transactions do not transfer resources to the corporation that issued the securities, they are important to the issuing corporation, because they help to set market prices for later security issues. While many factors, such as worldwide, national, or industry economic conditions, may affect the market prices of securities, security prices are significantly influenced by the cash flows corporations generate from earnings and other operating activities. Therefore, financial accounting information that helps investors and others to assess the amounts, timing, and degree of certainty of the corporation's future cash flows is particularly desirable. Because most investors are far removed from a corporation's day-to-day activities, they rely on published financial accounting data as a principal source of information when making decisions about buying, selling, or holding investments in the corporation.

Research has shown that securities markets are "efficient" with respect to published financial accounting information; that is, security prices react to published financial accounting information quickly and without bias. When securities markets are efficient, investors cannot expect to use published accounting information to earn abnormal or above-average returns on their investments. Rather, they can expect to earn a return that is consistent with the risk associated with their investment. In fact, publishing financial accounting information is believed to contribute to the efficiency of securities markets and to help prevent abnormal returns to individuals who trade on inside information.[15] Of course, published accounting information must be relevant and reliable if it is to help securities markets function efficiently and be useful to investors in efficiently allocating their resources.

Summary of Interrelationships

The interrelationships of the four groups just discussed and the way in which financial accounting and reporting influences those interrelationships are summarized in Exhibit 1–4.

As shown in Exhibit 1–4, corporations (corporate managers) are in effect constrained in their business activities by the decisions and actions of other parties, including suppliers of inputs, regulatory authorities, and investors. Thus, the degree of success of business operations depends greatly on resource allocations and other actions taken by suppliers, regulators, and investors. At the same time, the welfare and other interests of suppliers, regulators, and investors are affected by the results of business operations. The decisions and actions of those parties are substantially dependent on the information provided in financial statements about the activities and potential activities of the corporation and its managers.

Numerous conflicts of interest exist regarding the way in which business activities and events are accounted for and reported in the financial statements. For example, management might like to provide existing and potential investors and creditors with substantial detail about the corporation's activities; yet to do so could compromise proprietary information, ultimately damaging investors' and creditors'

---

[15]William H. Beaver, "What Should Be the FASB's Objective?," *Journal of Accountancy,* August 1973, pp. 49–56.

EXHIBIT 1–4   **Summary of Interrelationships**

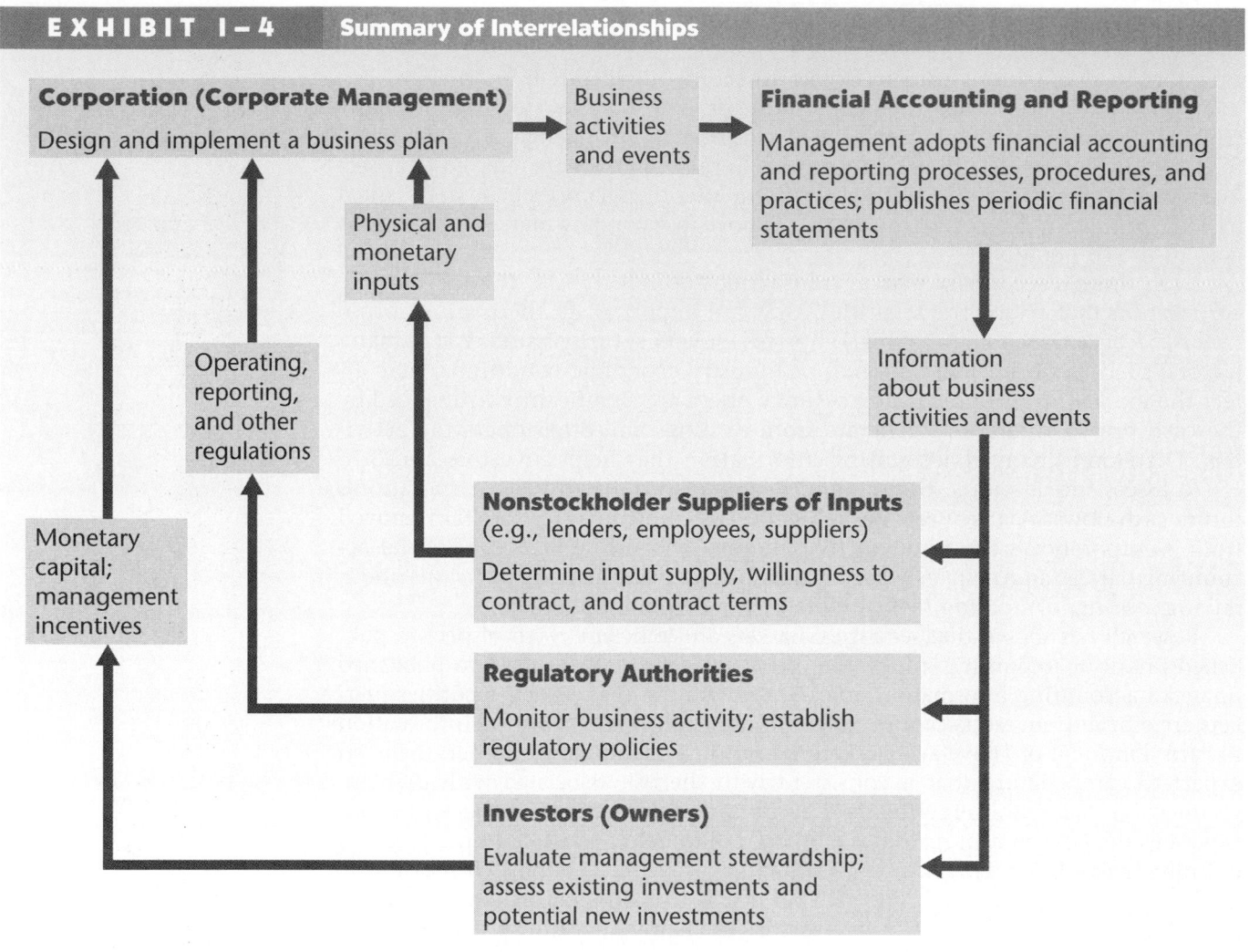

interests. Publication of information that pleases investors or creditors might also attract unwanted attention from regulatory authorities or employees (labor unions). And though disclosure of management's plans and expectations for the future might be very useful to investors and creditors, it could create competitive problems, diminishing management's ability to enact its plans and realize its expectations. Finally, the more information that is disclosed, the more likely management will be subjected to higher levels of scrutiny by those who are concerned about management's stewardship. Because management prepares all published financial information, the information most useful for assessing management's stewardship might be difficult to obtain.

The different—and often conflicting—interests served by published financial accounting information require that the general role of financial accounting and reporting be to provide information that is useful to a variety of parties (primarily external to the company) who make a variety of lending, supplying, regulating, investing, monitoring, and other resource allocation decisions. To contribute to the efficient allocation of scarce resources, financial accounting and reporting must provide evenhanded (neutral or unbiased) financial information—information that is not intended to influence a user's behavior in a particular direction. Useful information must be relevant, reliable, and comparable over time and across similar companies. Following generally accepted accounting and reporting principles increases the likelihood that reported information will be useful in the efficient allocation of scarce resources.

11 **Explain the general role of financial accounting and reporting in the business environment.**

Economic Influences on Financial Accounting and Reporting

The economic environment in which businesses operate, as well as the information needs of those who use financial accounting data, changes continuously. Changes in the economic environment often are major factors in determining which financial accounting and reporting issues are of the greatest concern to accountants and authoritative accounting standard-setting bodies such as the Financial Accounting Standards Board (FASB) and the Securities and Exchange Commission (SEC). We will look at several examples of changes or conditions in the economic environment that have influenced the amount of attention given to particular accounting and reporting issues.

12 Give examples of how the economic environment has influenced financial accounting and reporting.

Multinational Corporations

In the 1960s the growing number and size of multinational corporations increased the importance of the way in which the financial statements of foreign subsidiaries (which are prepared in terms of foreign currencies) are translated into U.S. dollars. As a result, since 1972 the FASB has issued several *Statements of Financial Accounting Standards* that address accounting and reporting issues associated with foreign currency transactions and translation.

Inflation

Another example of the influence of the economic environment on financial accounting and reporting is provided by the inflationary period of the 1970s and early 1980s, which was followed by a period of comparatively little inflation. In the 1970s considerable attention, research, and effort were directed at setting standards for reporting accounting data during periods of inflation. A result of much of this activity was the FASB's 1979 *Statement of Financial Accounting Standards No. 33,* "Financial Reporting and Changing Prices." This document *required* disclosure of both historical cost/constant dollar data and current cost data in order to conform to generally accepted accounting principles.

As inflation began to subside in the mid-1980s, and the cost of preparing changing prices data disclosures in financial statements became more apparent, enthusiasm for data on changing prices declined. In 1986 the FASB issued *Statement of Standards No. 89,* which superseded its 1979 *Statement* and made supplementary reporting of data on changing prices *voluntary.*

Postretirement Benefits

A third example of the influence of the economic environment on financial accounting and reporting is employer-sponsored plans that promise pension and other postretirement benefits (e.g., health care) to employees. Beginning in the 1950s, and increasingly in the 1960s and 1970s, postretirement benefits grew as a percentage of employees' overall compensation. Then, in 1974 Congress passed the Employee Retirement Income Security Act (ERISA), which significantly impacted virtually all private pension plans in the United States.

The substantial increase in the economic burden and importance of employer-sponsored postretirement benefit plans, as well as the existence of ERISA, prompted increased standard-setting activity by the FASB and its predecessor, the Accounting Principles Board (APB). In 1966 the APB issued *Opinion No. 8,* "Accounting for the Cost of Pension Plans," which was superseded in 1985 by two FASB *Statements of Standards* (*Nos. 87* and *88*), the more significant of which was titled "Employers'

Accounting for Pensions." In 1990 the FASB issued *Statement of Standards No. 106,* "Employers' Accounting for Postretirement Benefits Other than Pensions." The general result of these standards was to cause previously unreported or understated expenses and liabilities to appear in employers' financial statements.

International Accounting Standards

A final example of how the economic environment can influence financial accounting and reporting is in the area of international accounting standards. Discussions about the desirability and feasibility of such standards began in the 1960s. As discussed earlier, by 1973 the International Accounting Standards Committee (IASC) had been formed. However, the standards issued by the IASC between 1973 and 1996 have done little more than endorse the accounting and reporting standards of various developed countries, such as the United States, as acceptable alternatives. In general, for about 25 years after discussion of the issue began, there was not a great deal of enthusiasm for, and relatively little was accomplished toward, internationalizing accounting standards—in spite of the fact that the IASC existed during the last 15 or so of those 25 years.

Beginning in the mid-1980s, however, the demand for international accounting standards has increased dramatically because of the growing number of multinational companies and the globalization of financial markets. Participants in these global markets have a common interest in financial accounting and reporting. Therefore, the International Accounting Standards Committee and others are directing substantial effort toward establishing a core set of international accounting standards.

Economic Consequences of Accounting Standards

13 **Give examples of how financial accounting and reporting have impacted the economic environment.**

Just as financial accounting and reporting standards and practices are affected by aspects of and changes in the economic environment, so also the economic environment may be affected by financial accounting and reporting practices. Occurrences of this sort are sometimes referred to as *economic consequences* of accounting and reporting practices. Often businesses and others who oppose a proposed change in generally accepted accounting principles argue that the change will produce economic consequences that are not in the public interest. Indeed, many accountants, businesses, and users of accounting information believe that the potential economic consequences of accounting and reporting practices should be considered by authoritative accounting standard-setting bodies such as the FASB and the SEC. There are many examples of circumstances in which accounting or reporting practices have been viewed as having economic consequences. Several of these are described in the next few paragraphs. More detailed discussion of each of the following examples is provided in later chapters.

Oil and Gas Exploration

Potential adverse economic consequences were emphasized by opponents of the FASB's 1977 position on accounting and reporting practices for oil and gas exploration. At that time the FASB required that if the exploration did not result in a successful well (i.e., discovery of oil or gas), the costs of exploration should be included in the current year's expense. Small, exploratory oil and gas companies, which had been recording exploration costs as assets and expensing them over several years, argued that the FASB's accounting requirement would reduce their reported income, making them less attractive to investors and creditors and reducing their ability to raise capital. They argued further that the FASB's position would have an adverse impact on society, because it would reduce efforts to find new energy reserves. Ultimately the SEC rejected the FASB's 1977 requirement and allowed the costs of unsuccessful exploration to be recorded either as an expense or as an asset and then expensed over several years. (More detailed discussion of the oil and gas accounting controversy appears in Chapter 12.)

Debt Restructuring

By the mid-1970s, liquidity problems, high interest rates, and other adverse economic conditions had resulted in increasing numbers of troubled debt restructuring agreements between debtors and creditors. Under a restructuring agreement, the creditor makes concessions to the debtor, changing the terms of the debt agreement in the debtor's favor. Restructuring reduces the possibility that the debtor will default, increasing the creditor's chances of recovering the maximum amount of principal and interest.

In 1977 the FASB issued the *Statement of Standards* "Accounting by Debtors and Creditors for Troubled Debt Restructuring." Perhaps the most discussed accounting issue that arose during the FASB's deliberations related to whether the creditor should write down its receivable and report a loss when debt terms are modified to benefit the debtor. Creditors, potential creditors, and credit regulators argued that there would be certain adverse economic consequences of requiring creditors to write down receivables and report losses from debt restructuring: (1) creditors would avoid engaging in restructurings and (2) public confidence in financial institutions would be eroded. The FASB concluded that, except for certain rare cases, creditors would not be required to write down their receivables and show a loss due to restructuring.

In a 1993 *Statement of Standards,* "Accounting by Creditors for Impairment of a Loan," the FASB reversed its position. This *Statement* requires that, for troubled loans restructured after the effective date of the *Statement,* a creditor must report a loss when debt terms are modified to benefit the debtor. (Further discussion of accounting for troubled debt restructuring is presented in Chapter 14.)

Postretirement Benefits

Having dealt with accounting and reporting for employer-sponsored pension plans in its 1985 *Statements,* the FASB turned its attention to accounting and reporting for other postretirement benefits, such as health care. The Board found that most employers were waiting until expenditures for benefits were actually made before recording any expense. This "cash basis" type of accounting meant that no liability to pay future benefits appeared on employers' balance sheets, even though obligations to pay employees' postretirement benefits clearly existed—in many cases as part of a written compensation contract with employees. The FASB concluded that, as with pension plans, employers' commitments to pay other postretirement benefits represent a liability and a cost that should be recorded when the commitment is incurred, rather than ignored until benefits are paid.

Employers and employee groups argued that having to record liabilities and cost equal to the extremely large dollar amounts of employer commitments would cause employers to substantially reduce their promises of postretirement benefits to employees, and perhaps to drop health care and other benefits entirely. Indeed, in 1992, Unisys Corporation stated that it planned to stop paying retiree medical benefits in three years, and McDonnell-Douglas Corporation announced it would pay health benefits for salaried retirees only for the next four years.[16] (A more thorough discussion of accounting for postretirement benefits other than pensions is presented in Chapter 16.)

real world

---

[16]"Unisys Corp. Says It Will Stop Paying Medical Benefits in Three Years," *The Wall Street Journal,* November 4, 1992, p. C9.

Investments in Debt Securities

During the 1980s, hundreds of savings and loan institutions engaged in highly speculative—and ultimately disastrous—investment activities. The balance sheets of these institutions did not show the declining values of some of their investments, however, because at the time accounting standards allowed investments in debt securities to be reported at original cost. This practice masked how much the securities might have dropped in value. In fact, reporting investments in debt securities at original cost is viewed as one reason savings and loan investors learned too late about their institutions' multibillion-dollar losses. The savings and loan debacle, SEC pressure, and conceptual considerations resulted in the FASB's 1993 *Statement of Financial Accounting Standards No. 115,* "Accounting for Certain Investments in Debt and Equity Securities," which requires that certain investments in debt or equity securities be reported at fair value.[17]

Those who opposed the FASB's position, including bankers, savings and loan officials, and the Federal Reserve Board, described numerous undesirable economic consequences of the *Statement.* For example, bank representatives stated that the new requirement would cause them to shift bank holdings into variable-rate mortgage-backed securities, which could eventually make getting fixed-rate mortgages more difficult.[18] Bank representatives also indicated that they would hesitate to invest bank resources in unrated local municipal debt issues, thus raising the cost of borrowing for many school boards and other municipal issuers.[19] Finally, the Federal Reserve Board staff expressed its concern that the fair value requirement would erect barriers to the control of interest rate risk by financial institutions and give an inaccurate picture of banks' financial condition.[20] (More about what is commonly called "mark-to-market" accounting appears in Chapters 13 and 14.)

Executive Stock Options

In 1993, the FASB reached a tentative conclusion that the fair value of executive stock compensation, including stock options, should be treated as an expense and deducted from revenues in determining corporate income. This FASB position, like those discussed in previous paragraphs, stimulated a rash of opposition based on economic consequences. Many corporations indicated they would accelerate the granting of stock options so the options would be granted before the FASB standard took effect, thus avoiding the requirement that stock options granted must be reported as an expense. It was argued that the proposed requirement might actually threaten the use of stock options as a compensation tool.[21] Ultimately, the FASB decided not to require expense recognition for employee stock-based compensation.[22] Corporations praised the Board's turnabout, and predicted it would lead to further blossoming of stock option plans. (Accounting for stock options is discussed thoroughly in Chapter 18.)

National Competitiveness

With the growing importance of international business, the potentially adverse effect of an accounting or reporting practice on the competitiveness of U.S. companies has been mentioned as a possible economic consequence of some accounting

---

[17]The FASB views quoted market prices, if available, as the most reliable measure of fair value. When market prices are not available, a reasonable estimate of fair value can be made using pricing techniques such as discounted cash flow analysis.

[18]"Some Banks Alter Investment Strategies due to New Accounting Rule Proposal," *The Wall Street Journal,* December 18, 1992, p. A2.

[19]"SEC Renews Call for Pressure on Banks and S&Ls to Update Accounting Rules," *The Wall Street Journal,* January 8, 1992, p. A3.

[20]"Fed Warns against FASB's Proposed Accounting Rule," *The Wall Street Journal,* January 18, 1993, p. B3E.

[21]"Executives Say Accounting Idea Is Poorly Timed," *The Wall Street Journal,* December 4, 1992, p. B1.

[22]"Accounting for Stock-Based Compensation," *Statement of Financial Accounting Standards No. 123* (Norwalk, Conn.: FASB, 1995).

and reporting standards. For example, it has been argued that recording postretirement benefit costs, such as health care costs, on an accrual basis rather than a "pay-as-you-go" cash basis would hurt the competitiveness of U.S. companies. Those taking this position pointed out that non-U.S. companies do not have to meet U.S. accounting and reporting standards, and therefore are not burdened by increased expenses reported under the FASB's accrual requirement. And since most other countries have national health care coverage paid through taxation, most non-U.S. companies report health care costs on a cash basis rather than an accrual basis.

Changes in Accounting Methods

Even changing from one generally accepted accounting principle to another can have substantial economic consequences. For example, in 1994 Sony Corporation took a $2.7 billion write-off on Sony Pictures Entertainment as part of a change in accounting methods. This write-off caused Standard & Poor's to give notice that it might downgrade Sony's debt rating. Sony's American shares dropped in price by $3.25 to $55.25 and its share price in Tokyo plunged 8.1 percent.[23] And in 1995, when Chambers Development Company changed accounting methods, the resulting $362 million drop in profits for the year sent the company's high-flying stock into a nosedive, dropping nearly $20 in one day.[24]

[23]"Sony Takes a $2.7 Billion Hit on Studios," *Los Angeles Times,* November 18, 1994, Section A, p. 1.
[24]"Chambers Merger Hinges on Settlement of Suit," *Pittsburgh Post-Gazette,* May 20, 1995, Section C, p. 6.

SUMMARY OF LEARNING OBJECTIVES

1. Describe the nature of accounting, and differentiate between financial and managerial accounting.

Accounting is a service activity. Its function is to provide useful financial information about economic entities to interested parties, such as managers, investors, and creditors. Financial accounting provides information primarily for decision makers who are outside the economic entity, such as investors and creditors. Managerial accounting provides information for decision makers (various levels of managers) who are inside the economic entity.

2. Describe the role of the financial accountant.

The financial accountant has a dual role: (1) measuring and recording an entity's economic activities and (2) communicating the recorded data to external users.

3. Describe the concept of generally accepted accounting principles (GAAP), and describe the purposes those principles serve.

Generally accepted accounting principles (GAAP) consist of the financial accounting and reporting conventions, rules, and procedures that a business entity must use in preparing external financial statements subject to audit by an independent certified public accountant. GAAP serve three basic purposes. They help increase the confidence of financial statement users that the statements are representationally faithful. They provide companies and accountants who prepare financial statements with guidance on how to account for and report economic activities. And they provide independent auditors with a basis for evaluating the fairness and completeness of a company's financial statements.

4. Discuss the importance of ethical behavior by accounting professionals.

Given the service nature of financial accounting, the role of the financial accountant, and the potential for personal bias, misassessments of facts, errors in estimation, and ambiguity to affect the measurement and communication of economic events, ethical behavior by accounting professionals is particularly important. The higher the ethical standards followed by accountants who prepare or audit financial statements, the lower will be the number of accounting or reporting abuses that must be addressed by authoritative bodies like the FASB.

5. Name the four financial statements required under GAAP.

The financial statements required under GAAP are the balance sheet or statement of financial position, the income statement or statement of earnings, the statement of owners' equity, and the statement of cash flows.

6. Explain the role of the Securities and Exchange Commission in financial accounting and reporting.

The Securities and Exchange Commission has the legal authority to prescribe accounting principles and procedures for companies under its jurisdiction and to prescribe the form and content of financial reports filed with the SEC. The SEC has delegated the responsibility to prescribe accounting principles and procedures to the private sector (currently, the FASB), but it retains enforcement authority. The SEC also influences financial accounting and reporting practices through its own filing requirements.

7. Describe the organizational structure and standard-setting process of the Financial Accounting Standards Board, and identify the types of pronouncements it issues.

The FASB has seven members, one of whom is the Chair. It is supported by a research and technical staff. The Financial Accounting Foundation appoints the FASB members and the Financial Accounting Standards Advisory Council, obtains and manages the FASB's funding, and exercises general oversight of the FASB's operations. The Financial Accounting Standards Advisory Council consults with the FASB on major policy questions, technical issues of the Board's agenda, project priorities, potential agenda items, and other matters requested by the Board or its Chair. The Emerging Issues Task Force helps the Board by identifying potential agenda items and discusses issues and relevant accounting pronouncements. When consensus is reached by the EITF, the FASB usually concludes that no Board action is needed.

In general, the FASB's standard-setting process has the following steps: an accounting or reporting problem is identified and analyzed, and an external task force is appointed; a *Discussion Memorandum* or other discussion document is prepared; a public hearing is held; public input is carefully analyzed; an *Exposure Draft* is issued; responses to the *Exposure Draft* are reviewed and analyzed; a revised *Exposure Draft* may be issued; a vote is taken on a final *FASB Statement*.

The FASB issues four types of official pronouncements: *Statements of Financial Accounting Standards, Statements of Financial Accounting Concepts, Interpretations,* and *Technical Bulletins.*

8. Describe the political nature of financial accounting and reporting standard setting.

There are several aspects of the financial accounting and reporting standard-setting process that are "political" in nature. First, the SEC has veto power because it has the legal authority to prescribe accounting and reporting standards. The FASB is expected to serve a constituency composed of entities whose interests often are at variance and to reconcile the resulting divergent viewpoints in a manner that best serves the public interest. With regard to its constituency, the Board must maintain a balance between dependence and independence. General constituency support is needed for general acceptance of its standards, yet the Board must remain independent of any particular constituent. The FASB's due process procedure results in lobbying, debate, negotiation, and compromise prior to the issuance of a final standard. Within the FASB itself, it may be necessary for individual Board members to make concessions on some aspects of a standard in order to achieve other points they consider more important.

9. Describe the state of international accounting standard setting, and describe the activities of some of the key groups in setting international standards.

Substantial differences exist in financial accounting and reporting practices among countries. Because of the increasing number of multinational companies and the globalization of capital markets, the need for greater uniformity in financial accounting and reporting practices around the world has greatly increased in recent years. As a result of this situation, by the mid-1990s several groups were involved in a major effort to harmonize international accounting standards.

The International Accounting Standards Committee (IASC), the International Organization of Securities Commissions (IOSCO), and the European Union (EU) are key groups in setting international standards. The IASC, in cooperation with IOSCO, is in the process of developing a core set of 16 International Accounting Standards. If these standards are completed, it is expected that in 1999 IOSCO will recommend to national securities commissions that financial statements issued by foreign companies based on the core standards be accepted for cross-border capital raising and listing purposes in all global markets. The EU is expected to increase its involvement with the IASC effort to harmonize international financial accounting and reporting rather than forming a European accounting standards board.

10. **Discuss the interrelationships among the corporation, suppliers of its inputs, regulatory authorities, and investors.**

The corporation (corporate management) designs and implements a business plan. However, corporation activities and opportunities are constrained by the resources available to the corporation and various operating, reporting, and other regulations. Those who provide resources to the corporation and monitor the corporation's activities for regulatory or stewardship evaluation purposes depend to a great extent on the corporation's published financial statements for information about business activities and events related to the corporation. (The relevance, reliability, comparability, and, in general, usefulness of these financial statements are a result, in large part, of generally accepted accounting principles.) Based on what nonstockholder suppliers of corporate inputs, regulatory authorities, and investors learn from the financial statements and other sources, resource allocation, regulatory, management incentive, and other decisions are made—thereby affecting the corporation's business plan and its implementation.

11. **Explain the general role of financial accounting and reporting in the business environment.**

The different, and often conflicting, interests served by published financial accounting information require that the general role of financial accounting and reporting be to provide information that is useful to a variety of parties (primarily external to the company) who make a variety of lending, supplying, regulating, investing, monitoring, and other resource allocation decisions. To contribute to the efficient allocation of scarce resources, financial accounting and reporting must provide evenhanded financial information that is relevant, reliable, and comparable over time and across similar companies.

12. **Give examples of how the economic environment has influenced financial accounting and reporting.**

Changes in the economic environment often are major factors in determining which financial accounting and reporting issues are of the greatest concern to accountants and authoritative accounting standard-setting bodies such as the FASB and the SEC. Examples of the influence of the economic environment on accounting and reporting include the growing number of multinational corporations causing increased importance of issues related to foreign currency transactions and translation; the impact of the amount of inflation on the degree of interest in how to report accounting data in inflationary periods; the substantial increase in the importance of employer-sponsored postretirement benefit plans resulting in increased standard-setting activities related to such plans; and the globalization of financial markets and growing number of multinational companies resulting in an increased demand for harmonized international accounting standards.

13. **Give examples of how financial accounting and reporting have impacted the economic environment.**

The economic environment may be affected by financial accounting and reporting practices. Examples of circumstances in which particular accounting or reporting practices have had or have been viewed as having economic consequences include the adverse effect on oil and gas exploration of the FASB's initial position that, in cases of unsuccessful exploration, exploration costs should be expensed; employers reducing their promises of certain postretirement benefits to employees because of the FASB's position that employer commitments to pay other postretirement benefits represent a liability and cost that should be recorded when the commitment is incurred; and corporations indicating they would accelerate the granting of stock options so the options would be granted before the FASB required employee stock options be reported as an expense. (The FASB ultimately decided not to require stock options to be reported as an expense.)

Even changes in accounting methods used by a company can impact the economic environment of the company. For example, the stock prices of Sony Corporation (in 1994) and Chambers Development Company (in 1995) fell significantly because the companies changed accounting methods, thus greatly reducing reported profits.

KEY TERMS

Accounting Principles Board (APB) 9

APB Opinions 9

APB Statements 9

Accounting Research Bulletins (ARB) 9

Accounting Standards Executive Committee (AcSEC) 9

American Institute of Certified Public Accountants (AICPA) 8

Committee on Accounting Procedures (CAP) 9

conceptual framework 13

due process procedure 12

Emerging Issues Task Force (EITF) 11

ethical behavior 5

European Union (EU) 18

financial accounting and reporting 2

Financial Accounting Foundation (FAF) 11

financial accounting information 2

Financial Accounting Series 12

Financial Accounting Standards Advisory Council (FASAC) 11

Financial Accounting Standards Board (FASB) 10

financial statement 5

generally accepted accounting principles (GAAP) 2

general-purpose external financial reporting 6

Governmental Accounting Standards Board (GASB) 11

International Accounting Standards Committee (IASC) 17

International Organization of Securities Commissions (IOSCO) 18

Interpretations 11

management accounting information 2

Securities and Exchange Commission (SEC) 8

sources of U.S. GAAP 3

Statements of Financial Accounting Concepts 12

Statements of Financial Accounting Standards 11

Technical Bulletins 12

QUESTIONS

Q 1-1. What is the distinction between management accounting information and financial accounting information?

Q 1-2. What is the dual role of the financial accountant?

Q 1-3. What do *generally accepted accounting principles* consist of?

Q 1-4. How do generally accepted accounting principles help users, preparers, and auditors of financial statements, respectively?

Q 1-5. What is a common view of what constitutes ethical behavior?

Q 1-6. Which financial statements are required under GAAP?

Q 1-7. What is meant by the term *general purpose external financial reporting*?

Q 1-8. How do the following rank with respect to authoritativeness in establishing GAAP for nongovernmental entities: *FASB Statements of Concepts,* consensus positions of the FASB's Emerging Issues Task Force, *FASB Statements of Standards, AICPA Statements of Position,* and *APB Opinions*?

Q 1-9. Financial reporting is not the only source of information needed for decision making by people outside a company. Give some examples of information sources other than a company's financial reports.

Q 1-10. How does the SEC influence financial accounting and reporting?

Q 1-11. Distinguish between *APB Opinions* and *APB Statements*.

Q 1-12. What is AcSEC, and what is its role in financial accounting and reporting standard setting?

Q 1-13. What does Rule 203 of the Code of Professional Conduct of the AICPA state?

Q 1-14. What were some of the specific criticisms made about the APB?

Q 1-15. In what ways does the FASB structure respond to criticisms of the APB?

Q 1-16. What is the EITF's role in the process of establishing financial accounting and reporting standards?

Q I-I7. Describe the FASB organization.

Q I-I8. Identify and characterize the types of final official pronouncements issued by the FASB.

Q I-I9. How does an *FASB Statement of Financial Accounting Concepts* differ from a *Statement of Financial Accounting Standards*?

Q I-20. Why might it be appropriate to describe financial accounting and reporting standard setting as a political process?

Q I-2I. What are some of the ways in which standard setting is a political process?

Q I-22. What steps usually are followed by the FASB in issuing a *Statement of Financial Accounting Standards*?

Q I-23. Why do international accounting standards need to be more uniform?

Q I-24. What is the IASC, and what are its objectives?

Q I-25. What organizations are key participants in international standard setting?

Q I-26. What does it mean to say that the securities markets are efficient with respect to published financial accounting information?

Q I-27. What four general groups have significant interests in financial accounting and reporting issues?

Q I-28. What are the interrelationships between the corporation, suppliers of its inputs, regulatory authorities, and investors?

Q I-29. What are some of the conflicts of interest regarding how business activities and events are accounted for and reported?

Q I-30. What is the general role of financial accounting and reporting?

Q I-3I. Using an example or two, explain how the economic environment and financial accounting and reporting impact each other.

Q I-32. Describe two situations for which it was argued that a financial accounting and reporting requirement would have an adverse economic consequence. What was the nature of the anticipated economic consequence(s) in each situation?

Q I-33. Why are "standards" or "principles" of financial accounting and reporting important?

CASES

C I-I. **DISCUSSION OF FINANCIAL ACCOUNTING AND REPORTING** At Best University, where you are an accounting major, the last required accounting course for all accounting majors is a "capstone" course intended to provide students with a series of opportunities to tie together, compare, and contrast what they have learned in their previous accounting courses. One of the first assignments in the capstone course, in which you are enrolled, is for students to write three or four paragraphs discussing a key aspect of their area of emphasis, which for you is financial accounting and reporting.

REQUIRED In response to the first assignment, your task is to discuss what financial accounting and reporting is, the general role of financial accounting and reporting in the business environment, the role of the financial accountant, the interaction of financial accounting and reporting and the business environment, the users and uses of financial information, and the four financial statements required under generally accepted accounting principles.

C I-2. **THE ECONOMIC ENVIRONMENT OF FINANCIAL ACCOUNTING AND REPORTING** You are one of several individuals being considered as a potential member of the FASB. As part of the interview process, you are asked to characterize and briefly comment on the economic environment in which financial accounting and reporting exists.

REQUIRED Write a memorandum to the interviewers describing how financial accounting and reporting "fits" in the business environment, particularly with respect to corporations and users of external financial reports.

C I-3. **DEVELOPMENT OF FINANCIAL ACCOUNTING AND REPORTING STANDARDS** One of the assignments in a history class you are taking is to describe some aspect of fundamental development that has occurred in the 20th century in a profession of your choice. Since you also are taking an intermediate financial accounting course, you decide to discuss the development of financial accounting and reporting standards in the United States and, in recent years, internationally. You intend to focus on the period since the 1929 stock market crash.

REQUIRED Write a brief paper tracing the development of financial accounting and reporting standards, beginning immediately after the 1929 stock market crash and continuing through the international standard-setting efforts of the mid-1990s. As part of your presentation, indicate all relevant professional groups about which you are aware, and indicate the role of each in standards development.

C I-4. **ALTERNATIVE FINANCIAL ACCOUNTING REPORTS** An article, "Proposed Cut-Rate Financial Statements for Small Business Meet Opposition," (author, Lee Berton), that appeared in the August 18, 1995 edition of *The Wall Street Journal* included the following:

> The 328,000-member American Institute of Certified Public Accountants said it expects to propose a rule next month permitting CPAs to provide small closely held companies with a new, abbreviated form of financial data, reserved for internal use. Auditors would charge 20 percent to 50 percent less for such data than for audits and audit-like reports requiring a certified public accountant's signature, accountants estimate.
>
> Under the proposal, the auditor could issue financial data on plain paper, without the accounting firm's letterhead or the auditor's signature. The data would be less detailed than that in an audit, and it wouldn't need to follow generally accepted accounting principles, known as GAAP, or any other standards.

REQUIRED Prepare two memoranda, each mentioning as many specific issues as possible, presenting arguments, first, by proponents of the AICPA's proposed rule and, second, by opponents of the rule.

C I-5. **SEC INVOLVEMENT IN STANDARD SETTING** You recently attended a presentation by a member of the FASB. Several times during the presentation, the Board member referred to the Board's need to be sure that the SEC is aware of the Board's standard-setting activities and tentative positions on agenda items. The Board member also mentioned in passing that she had never had a job more difficult than being on the FASB, because never before had she worked for an organization with so much responsibility and so little authority.

REQUIRED Write a paragraph or two explaining why the FASB member may have made her statements about the need to keep the SEC informed and the lack of balance between the Board's responsibility and its authority.

C I-6. **USE OF FINANCIAL ACCOUNTING INFORMATION** Investors, creditors, suppliers of materials, employees, and regulatory authorities are among the more important users of published financial statements. Each of these groups has particular reasons for being interested in an entity's financial statements.

REQUIRED Write a memorandum discussing how financial accounting information may be useful to investors, creditors (including suppliers), employees, and regulatory authorities, giving attention to the specific issues about which each group may need to make decisions.

C I-7. **THE NATURE OF FINANCIAL STATEMENTS** Your daughter has been assigned the task of providing her seventh-grade class with an "expert" who will comment on some aspect of a profession the students might choose to enter for their careers. She has come to you for help. As a practicing accountant, you wonder if a career in the accounting profession might be of interest to your daughter's classmates, and you ask if she would like you to make a presentation on external financial statements and the accountant's role in preparing those statements. In particular, you intend to concentrate your remarks on the nature of external financial statements and the notes and supplementary information that often accompany the financial statements.

REQUIRED Prepare a brief written discussion of financial statements, notes, and supplementary information to take with you as a handout for your daughter's class.

C I-8. **GENERALLY ACCEPTED ACCOUNTING PRINCIPLES** Your uncle is looking over the annual report he recently received from one of the companies in which he has an investment in common stock. He notices that in the Independent Auditor's Report, following the presentation of financial statements and notes, the auditor states that the financial statements are presented fairly "in conformity with generally accepted accounting principles." He asks you what generally accepted accounting principles are, in what ways they are important (especially to independent auditors and external users of financial statements, like himself), and where they come from.

REQUIRED Prepare a two- or three-paragraph response to your uncle's questions.

C 1-9. **A STUDENT'S ETHICAL DILEMMA** Sandy Lowe is completing her junior year as an accounting major at State College. She recently interviewed for summer internship positions with both Lawson Corporation and Cole and Farr, a major public accounting company. Following the interviews, Sandy was particularly hopeful that Cole and Farr would offer her a summer position. She knows several people who work for Cole and Farr and has heard many good things about the company. In fact, Sandy's goal is to work for Cole and Farr when she graduates from college.

About 10 days after completing her interviews, Sandy received an offer from Lawson Corporation for a summer internship position. It was a good offer, but she had her heart set on a position with Cole and Farr. Unfortunately, Sandy did not hear from Cole and Farr before the deadline for responding to the Lawson offer. Sandy was not sure what to do, so, just before the Lawson deadline, she asked for advice from Laura Hall, a good friend who had graduated from State College the previous year.

Laura told Sandy that it was better to accept Lawson's offer than to reject it in hopes of receiving an offer from Cole and Farr. After all, Laura argued, it had been almost three weeks since Sandy had interviewed with Cole and Farr, and it was only a summer internship position anyway. Laura pointed out that Sandy could still interview next year for an entry-level position with Cole and Farr. In addition, Laura felt the experience Sandy would gain during a summer with Lawson would give her some insight into corporate accounting, and would benefit her during next year's interview process. Sandy decided to take Laura's advice, and she accepted the summer internship with Lawson Corporation.

One week after verbally accepting the Lawson internship, Sandy was contacted by Cole and Farr with an offer of a summer internship position. The director of personnel, Mary Jacobs, apologized for the delay in contacting Sandy, explaining that the recent firm merger had made it difficult to determine how many summer internships were available. Jacobs told Sandy that the staff members who had met her were very impressed and she was hopeful Sandy would accept Cole and Farr's offer.

Sandy did not know what to do. She was afraid that if she did not take the Cole and Farr internship it might hurt her chances of getting an entry-level position with the company following her graduation. On the other hand, although she had not signed a written agreement, she had already verbally accepted the Lawson offer.

REQUIRED Assume that you are in Sandy's position. What, if anything, might you have done differently during the process up to the point when Cole and Farr made its offer, and what would you do now?

C 1-10. **AN INDEPENDENT AUDITOR'S ETHICAL DILEMMA** You are a partner in the public accounting company of Griffey, Griffey & Company. One of your larger clients is a company that designs and produces small engines used in lawn mowers, lawn edgers, snowblowers, and similar types of equipment. Last year your client's research and development division had a major breakthrough in small engine design. During the current year your client continued its research and development efforts related to the new engine design, in the hope of creating an innovative new automobile engine. Even though automobile engines are not part of the normal design and production activities of your client, it had every intention of producing automobile engines if the small-engine breakthrough could be successfully adapted to automobile engines.

The research and development costs during this year for the automobile engine project have been extremely large, almost double all small-engine research and development costs for the same period. Your client's management has made it clear to you that they intend to capitalize the automobile engine research and development costs, and then write them off to expense over several years. Your client's position is that this approach will better match the research and development costs against revenues earned from the automobile engine project. Your client feels very strongly that to record the automobile research and development costs as an expense of the current year, which is the company's usual practice with its small-engine research and development costs, would be entirely unfair because to do so would turn a relatively profitable year into a year in which the company would report its largest loss ever. In your client's opinion, to report a substantial loss would be totally inconsistent with the fact that the design application to automobile engines could be the greatest positive event in company history. The client's management feels so strongly about their position that they have told you they will engage a different CPA firm as their auditor if you will not agree to the cost capitalization plan.

Your client's plan puts you in a difficult position because (1) it is one of your firm's more important clients, producing audit fees in excess of $250,000 each year, and (2) your understanding is that generally accepted accounting principles require that research and development costs be expensed in the year in which they are incurred.

REQUIRED What issues will you consider, and how will you deal with your dilemma?

C 1-11.   **AN INTERNAL AUDITOR'S ETHICAL DILEMMA**   You are 57 years old and have spent most of your professional life working for Martel Trucking, Inc., which provides truck transportation services to a variety of businesses, including produce farms, salad oil manufacturers, lumber companies, and chemical manufacturers. For the past 17 years you have been on Martel's internal audit staff, having been appointed as director of internal audit only two years ago. You plan to work for five more years, and then retire. You are particularly happy with your new position in the company because the company's retirement plan uses the last five years' compensation levels to determine the amount of annual retirement benefits. As director of internal audit, your compensation is substantially higher than previously.

During the current year's internal audit of the western region shipping terminal, your staff brings data to your attention strongly suggesting a most unsettling possibility. The turnaround time records indicate sufficiently short turnaround times that you are virtually certain that for the last six months many of Martel's tanker trucks, which took toxic chemicals to the East Coast, failed to receive the thorough cleaning required by company operating policies before making the return trip to the West Coast. This, in itself, is a matter of concern to you, and your concern is heightened by the fact that several of those tanker trucks hauled salad oil back to the West Coast.

Your investigation into who (if anyone) authorized skipping the appropriate cleaning process reveals that a senior vice president, who is responsible for the shipping volume of the western terminal, issued a memorandum a little more than six months earlier "encouraging" his drivers to minimize their turnaround times. This memorandum was part of an overall effort to boost the performance measures for the western terminal. It seems inconceivable to you that the vice president would be unaware that, following his memorandum, proper cleaning procedures were not being followed by many Martel trucks going east and, in some cases, improperly cleaned trucks were carrying salad oil on their return trips west.

You are uncertain whether anyone other than the vice president is aware of the truck cleaning/salad oil issue. You also are uncertain about both the legal implications and the health risks associated with improperly cleaning the tankers. You do know that you do not want your family to eat salad oil hauled in the improperly cleaned Martel trucks. After a few days, you contact the senior vice president with your concerns. The vice president tells you the matter has already been investigated and the tankers were adequately cleaned. In addition, the vice president makes it clear that you should stick to auditing issues and "mind your own business."

REQUIRED What issues does this situation raise for you personally and professionally? In light of your concerns, as well as the senior vice president's comments to you, will you go any further in pursuing the matter?

C 1-12.   **AN INTERNAL AUDITOR'S ETHICAL DILEMMA**   Dave Grimsley recently joined the internal audit staff of Allen Industries, a company that manufactures large machinery, including road graders, dump trucks, street sweepers, and bulldozers. In addition to producing machinery for several private sector customers, Allen Industries usually has several government contracts in process, sometimes earning as much as 50 percent of total revenues from government work. Dave is very excited about his new position because he spent almost two years after graduating from college looking for the "right" job. Dave still has several thousand dollars of college loans to repay, and he hopes to replace his 14-year-old car with a new sporty model, so he has every intention of staying with Allen for several years.

About eight months after joining Allen Industries, Dave becomes a member of a four-person team assigned to evaluate the effectiveness of an experimental cost containment program started two years earlier at Allen's Wilmington, Delaware, plant. The cost containment program was developed by the Wilmington plant manager in concert with the manager of Allen's internal audit division, who also is Dave's boss. The plant manager and the manager of internal audit have had considerable positive visibility in Allen Industries because of the apparent success of their cost containment program. Both individuals are likely to receive significant promotions if the program is found by the study team to have been successful.

Dave's specific assignment on the team is to determine the percentage amount by which costs have been reduced in producing dump trucks that are being sold to several large coal mining companies that are long-time Allen Industries customers. Dave is aware that Allen has been able to minimize increases in the selling prices of these dump trucks (much to the delight of its customers), supposedly in large part because of the new cost containment program.

After working on his assignment for a few weeks, Dave concludes that the total cost of producing dump trucks at the Wilmington plant is 22 percent less than was the case before the cost containment program was initiated. He is puzzled, however, by the fact that even though most of the cost reductions are in the areas of labor and materials, his on-site analysis of the production process revealed that essentially the same number of employee hours and the same amounts and types of materials are currently being used to produce the trucks as was reported by the on-site observer two and a half years earlier. In addition, supplier invoices show that unit material costs have risen slightly in the last two years, and nine months ago a new labor contract increased hourly pay by 7 percent.

Dave cannot understand how it is possible that the reported costs of labor and materials used in producing dump trucks for the coal mining companies have decreased. One day, as he is continuing his review of the plant's production records, Dave stumbles on the answer—a substantial portion of the labor costs and material costs incurred in producing the coal mining company dump trucks is being recorded as cost on a government contract for dump trucks. Moreover, the government contract specifies that Allen will be paid for the dump trucks on a "cost plus" basis. Whoever is responsible for shifting some of the costs of producing the coal mining company trucks to the government truck contract is accomplishing two things. First, the cost shifting makes it appear that the cost containment program at the Wilmington plant is working. Second, revenues from the government contract will increase because the government pays Allen for all production costs reported for the contract plus a 30 percent profit.

REQUIRED   What would you do if you were in Dave's position? Discuss the possible implications for affected parties of any action you may decide to take.

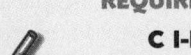

C 1-13.   **APPROACHES TO POLICY MAKING**   Suppose you have been called to testify before a U.S. Senate subcommittee studying the development of accounting standards. The specific question put to you by the subcommittee is: "What are the similarities and differences among the Committee on Accounting Procedures, the Accounting Principles Board, and the Financial Accounting Standards Board with respect to their organizational structures, their output of principles or standards, and their approaches to policy making?"

REQUIRED   Prepare a written response to the subcommittee's question.

C 1-14.   **THE FASB'S STRUCTURE AND PROCESS**   Assume that you are the Chair of the FASB and that you recently saw the following headlines in *The Wall Street Journal:* "Accounting Board Rulings Make Business See Red" and "FASB Rule on Retirees to Cause Furor." A few months earlier you read a *Business Week* article titled "First Thing We Do Is Kill All the Accountants." Moreover, you are aware of general rumblings in the business community that the FASB moves too slowly in establishing standards, that the FASB is ignoring its constituency's concerns, and that the FASB should give more attention to the potential economic consequences of its actions. All of this "feedback" causes you to attempt to cast a more favorable light on the FASB.

REQUIRED   As the basis of a potential journal article, prepare several paragraphs (1) describing the FASB's organizational structure, (2) describing the FASB's due process procedures, and (3) discussing how the FASB's structure, procedures, and independence contribute to the Board's ability to serve the public interest.

C 1-15.   **POLITICAL PRESSURES AND POLICY MAKING**   In the early 1970s, a noted academician and former member of the APB stated: "My hypothesis is that the setting of accounting standards is as much a product of political action as of flawless logic or empirical findings" (C. T. Horngren, "Statements in Quotes," *Journal of Accountancy,* October 1973, p. 61). Today this view is more widely held than ever before.

REQUIRED   Identify and comment on some of the groups and agencies that exist in the current environment of financial accounting and reporting, and that may influence accounting policy making.

C 1-16.   **POLITICAL ASPECTS OF STANDARD SETTING**   Private sector standard setting, especially as conducted by the Financial Accounting Standards Board and its predecessor, the Accounting Principles Board, provides several opportunities for political interaction. For example, members of the Board must interact with one another, the Board must interact with its constituents, and the Board must interact with the Securities and Exchange Commission and other government agencies.

REQUIRED   Write a few paragraphs discussing the political nature of the interactions among members of the FASB, between the FASB and its constituents, and between the FASB and the SEC. In your discussion be sure to comment on how these interactions are dealt with and, indeed, enhance the standard-setting process.

C I-I7.   INTERNATIONAL ACCOUNTING STANDARDS   There are many differences in financial accounting and reporting practices among countries. An example of differences in perspectives was provided in the article "Bean Counters, Unite" (*The Economist,* June 10, 1995, pp. 67–68).

> America, led by its Securities and Exchange Commission (SEC) and Financial Accounting Standards Board (FASB), believes that the guiding principle should be for companies to give a "true and fair" view to shareholders. Germany, in contrast, prefers that companies exercise "prudence" on behalf of stakeholders—which, in practice, thanks to Germany's weak equity culture, means on behalf of creditors and employees rather than shareholders. German accounts are largely driven by tax considerations.

Differences in accounting and reporting standards and practices, such as those described for the United States and Germany, can cause substantial tension between countries and between foreign companies and a country.

REQUIRED   Write a brief paper identifying possible causes of differences among countries in accounting and reporting practices, discussing what, if anything, might motivate countries to seek international accounting standards, and describing organizations and activities that may help to establish standardized international accounting practices.

C I-I8.   INTERRELATION OF ACCOUNTING AND ITS ECONOMIC ENVIRONMENT   Assume that as a member of the FASB you are aware there has been considerable negative reaction by corporations to a recently proposed *Statement of Financial Accounting Standards* on accounting for leases. The essence of most of the negative reaction is that "if the proposed *Standard* is implemented, it will change the types of lease agreements into which corporations will enter. In effect, the *Standard* will *cause* certain lease agreements to be made, even though such agreements are economically unsound."

In an effort to reduce the level of negativism surrounding the proposed lease accounting *Standard,* and to enlighten the business community, you have been selected by the FASB to attend a forthcoming national corporate seminar on the lease accounting issue. Your specific responsibility at the seminar, however, is not to discuss lease accounting but rather to present some brief comments, including examples, regarding the interrelation between financial accounting and reporting and the economic environment.

REQUIRED   Prepare a rough draft of the comments you plan to make at the seminar.

EXERCISES

E I-I.   SOURCES OF ACCOUNTING PRONOUNCEMENTS   Several organizations and documents that have influenced or might influence financial accounting and reporting practices in the United States are listed below.

ORGANIZATION	DOCUMENT
A. Accounting Principles Board	1. *Opinions*
B. Financial Accounting Standards Board	2. *Statements of Concepts*
C. Committee on Accounting Procedure	3. *Technical Bulletins*
	4. *Statements of Standards*
	5. *Accounting Research Bulletins*
	6. *Discussion Memoranda*

REQUIRED   Identify (by number) all documents related to each organization listed above.

E I-2. **IMPORTANT ACCOUNTING ORGANIZATIONS, GROUPS, AND TERMS** Several acronyms appearing in this chapter are listed below. What is the organization, group, or term represented by each, and (briefly) what is (or was) the task of each organization or group, or the meaning of each term?

FASB   AICPA   CPA   EITF   APB   CAP
GAAP   FAF   AcSEC   FASAC   AIA

E I-3. **IMPORTANT ACCOUNTING ORGANIZATIONS, GROUPS, AND TERMS** Several acronyms appearing in this chapter are listed below. What is the organization, group, or term represented by each, and (briefly) what is the task of each organization or group, or the meaning of each term?

SEC   AAA   IRS   EU   FEI
GASB   IMA   IASC   GASAC   IOSCO

E I-4. **OFFICIAL PRONOUNCEMENTS** Which description in the right-hand column below best matches each of the official pronouncements listed in the left-hand column?

OFFICIAL PRONOUNCEMENT	DESCRIPTION
1. *Statements of Financial Accounting Standards*	A. Explain or elaborate on existing *FASB Statements of Standards* and predecessor documents and have the same authority as *Statements of Standards.*
2. *Statements of Financial Accounting Concepts*	B. Provide guidance in the application of *FASB Statements of Standards, APB Opinions,* and *CAP Accounting Research Bulletins.*
3. *APB Opinions*	C. States that principles, standards, and practices established by the FASB will be viewed by the Securities and Exchange Commission as having substantial authoritative support.
4. *Accounting Research Bulletins*	D. Predecessor documents to the *FASB Statements of Standards.*
5. *Technical Bulletins*	E. Predecessor documents to *APB Opinions.*
6. *Accounting Series Release No. 150*	F. Present the conceptual framework of financial accounting and reporting.
7. *FASB Interpretations*	G. Currently produced documents that establish standards for financial accounting and reporting.

Financial Accounting and Reporting: A Theoretical Structure

LEARNING OBJECTIVES

After studying this chapter, you should be able to:

1. List and describe the four environmental assumptions that provide the foundation for financial accounting and reporting theory.

2. List and discuss the three objectives of financial reporting.

3. Identify and describe the qualitative characteristics of useful accounting information.

4. Discuss the benefits of versus the constraints on strict application of financial accounting and reporting standards.

5. Define the elements of the financial statements.

6. State the four criteria of the fundamental recognition principle.

7. Describe and give examples of the difference between accrual and cash-basis accounting.

8. Discuss the realization principle and its two criteria.

9. Discuss the matching principle and the three general guidelines for applying it.

10. Describe what the FASB believes are the four purposes of disclosure.

11. Describe (1) three alternative concepts of capital maintenance and (2) five alternative asset/liability valuation methods.

12. Explain and illustrate the interrelationship between capital maintenance and asset/liability valuation in the determination of income.

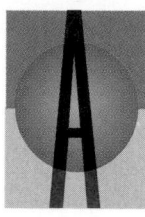s the business environment becomes more complex, companies engage in increasingly complex transactions. Accountants must be able to analyze these complex transactions and resolve the related accounting and reporting issues. Effective analysis of business transactions and related accounting and reporting issues requires an understanding of the underlying theoretical structure of financial accounting and reporting.

Accounting theory can be helpful in resolving accounting issues.[1] For example, assume a major television network has entered into a noncancelable agreement with the National Basketball Association (NBA) for the exclusive right to televise all NBA games during the next 20 years, and the network has agreed to pay the NBA $20 million annually, plus 1 percent of all revenues derived from the telecasts of NBA games.

This agreement raises several accounting issues for both the television network and the NBA:

1. Is the exclusive right to televise the games an *asset* to the television network? If so, how should this asset be measured and reported in the network's financial statements?

2. Has the network incurred a *liability* to the NBA as a result of this 20-year noncancelable agreement? If so, how should the obligation ($20 million annually, plus 1 percent of *future* revenues) be measured and reported?

3. Should the NBA report the cash inflows to be received as *revenue*? If so, at what point or points in time should this revenue be reported?

4. Should this agreement be disclosed in the financial statements of the network and the NBA? If so, what is the most *useful* method of disclosing this agreement?

Questions like these can be answered with the help of financial accounting theory. As shown in Exhibit 2–1, financial accounting and reporting theory includes the objectives of financial reporting, the qualitative characteristics of useful accounting information, the nature and definitions of the elements of financial statements (assets, liabilities, revenues, etc.), and the recognition and measurement principles for the elements of financial statements. All of these have the potential to be helpful in resolving the accounting issues facing the television network and the NBA. The objectives of financial reporting may help to determine what should be reported. The qualitative characteristics help to further determine the information that may be helpful to users of financial information. The nature and definitions of the elements of the financial statements should help in determining whether the network has an asset or a liability, and whether the NBA has revenue. The principles of accrual accounting, particularly the realization and matching principles, should help to determine what should be reported in the financial statements of the network and the NBA, and when it should be reported. Disclosure and financial statement presentation concepts may help in deciding the most useful method of reporting the transaction.

As pointed out in Chapter 1, financial accounting and reporting are affected by the economic environment. Correspondingly, financial accounting and reporting theory is affected by the environment of financial accounting and reporting. We will begin Chapter 2 with a discussion of the environmental assumptions underlying GAAP. Next, we will present the objectives of financial reporting, which focus on providing useful information to users of financial reports and are derived from environmental influences. Following the objectives, we will consider the characteristics of useful accounting information, which the FASB calls qualitative characteristics. Discussion of the qualitative characteristics is followed by definitions of the financial statement elements, which are the building blocks of the financial statements; they include assets, liabilities, equity, revenues, expenses, gains, losses,

---

[1]As we pointed out in Chapter 1, political considerations also play a role in the resolution of accounting issues. Thus, theory may *assist* rather than dictate resolution.

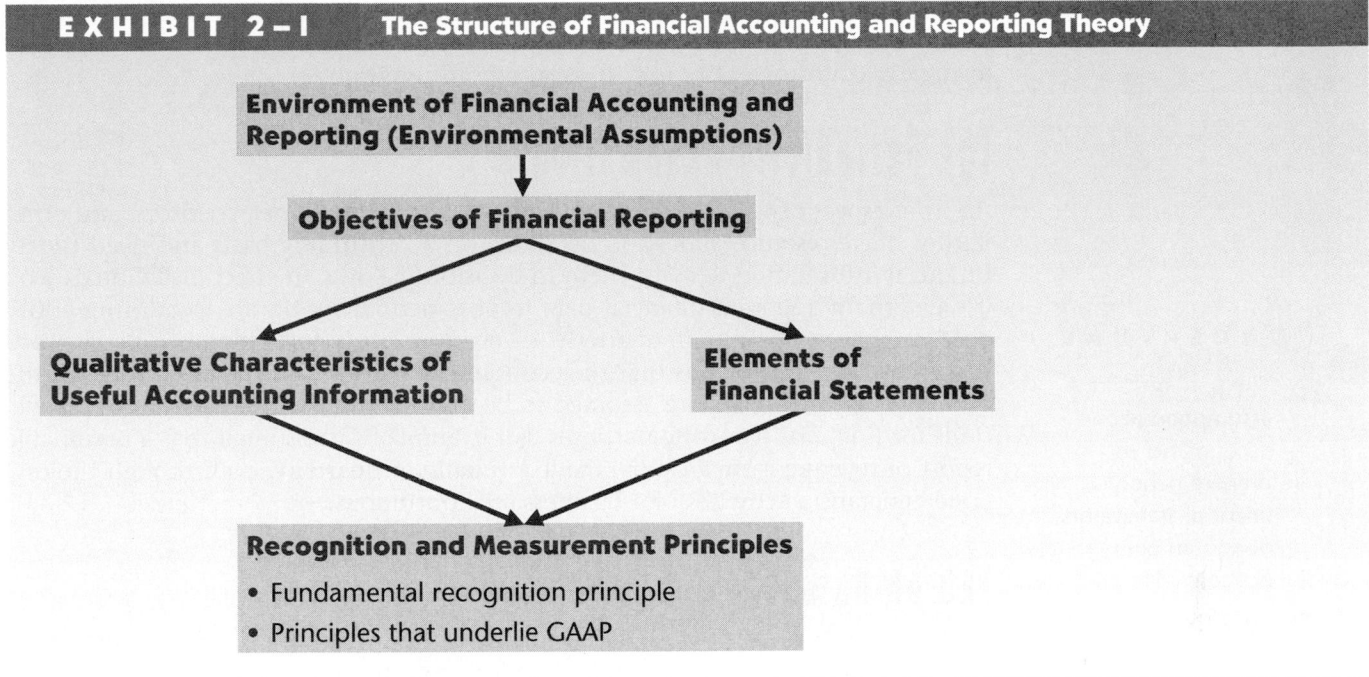

EXHIBIT 2–1   The Structure of Financial Accounting and Reporting Theory

Environment of Financial Accounting and Reporting (Environmental Assumptions)

Objectives of Financial Reporting

Qualitative Characteristics of Useful Accounting Information

Elements of Financial Statements

Recognition and Measurement Principles
- Fundamental recognition principle
- Principles that underlie GAAP

net income or loss, and other comprehensive income. After defining the elements, we examine the principles for recognition and measurement of the elements, discussing first the fundamental recognition principle, then the recognition and measurement principles that underlie GAAP. The format of the chapter follows the structure of financial accounting and reporting theory shown in Exhibit 2–1.

ENVIRONMENTAL ASSUMPTIONS

In Chapter 1 we described the economic environment in which financial accounting and reporting exist. In this section we look more closely at the environmental assumptions that provide the context for financial accounting and reporting theory. These assumptions are:

1. The *accounting entity assumption*.
2. The *periodicity assumption*.
3. The *going concern assumption*.
4. The *monetary assumption*.

The Accounting Entity Assumption

The essence of the accounting entity assumption is that accountants account for and report the financial information of a specific *accounting* entity. Thus the **accounting entity assumption** establishes boundaries or limits as to what information should be included in the financial statements of a given accounting entity. For example, you learned in introductory accounting that the economic activities of a single (sole) proprietorship are accounted for separately from the personal economic activities of the proprietor.

The accounting entity for which financial reports are prepared may or may not correspond to a legal entity. For example, under certain circumstances the accounting entity may be a corporation (a legal entity), a division or department within a corporation (within a legal entity), or a group of legal entities (for which consolidated

1 List and describe the four environmental assumptions that provide the foundation for financial accounting and reporting theory.

CONCEPTUAL

The accounting entity assumption limits the transactions and events that should be reported in an entity's financial statements.

financial statements are prepared). In the latter case, even though the parent company and subsidiary companies are separate legal entities, they are combined into a single accounting entity for financial reporting purposes.

The Periodicity Assumption

Another aspect of the economic environment is that investors, creditors, and other parties make resource allocation decisions on a continuing basis and need timely financial information to assist them in decision making. In effect, individuals who use externally reported financial data impose periodicity on an accounting entity because they need annual, quarterly, or even monthly information. The **periodicity assumption** means that the economic activities undertaken during the life of an accounting entity are assumed to be divisible into various artificial time periods for financial reporting purposes. For example, it is assumed that a reasonable report of revenue earned can be made annually or quarterly, even though the revenue generating activities of a business are continuous.

The Going Concern Assumption

Typically, business entities expect to continue in operation on a relatively permanent basis. Although some companies may encounter financial difficulties and may cease operation, such occurrences are not the normal expectation. The **going concern assumption** means that in the absence of evidence to the contrary, it is assumed a business will continue to operate indefinitely—at least long enough to carry out existing plans, commitments, and contracts. Often, it is the external auditor of a company who raises the going concern issue. For example, in 1995 the auditors of Samuel Goldwyn Co. included in their audit report a clause raising questions about the company's ability to continue as a going concern.[2]

Perhaps the going concern assumption can be best explained by analogy to the way people conduct their own lives. Most people have no reason to expect death in the near future, and conduct their affairs as if they have an indefinite, but not infinite, remaining life. Similarly, the accountant assumes the accounting entity has a future life of undetermined length, unless there is evidence of imminent failure.

When an accounting entity appears not to be a going concern, it may be appropriate to change the method of accounting and reporting for that entity. For example, it may be proper to report liquidation values in the financial statements, if there is reasonable doubt about a company's ability to continue as a going concern. Accounting for entities not considered to be going concerns usually is studied in an advanced accounting course.

The Monetary Assumption

In our society exchanges are conducted in terms of dollars. Therefore, accountants assume that the number of dollars or dollar equivalents (in noncash transactions) should be the measure of the results of an accounting entity's economic activities and that those results should be reported in dollars. The **monetary assumption** implies that the dollar has the same characteristic—stability over time—as all other generally accepted measuring units, such as the inch or the pound. Just as an inch in 1998 is the same length as an inch in 1968, so it is assumed that a dollar in 1998 should have the same purchasing power as a dollar in 1968. This is a major weakness of the monetary assumption. That is, in terms of general purchasing power, a 1998 dollar is not the same as a 1968 dollar. A 1998 dollar is in fact much smaller (has less purchasing power) than a 1968 dollar.

CONCEPTUAL

The periodicity assumption allows accountants to prepare periodic financial statements during an entity's economic life.

CONCEPTUAL

The going concern assumption causes accountants to presume an indefinite economic life, unless there is evidence to the contrary.

CONCEPTUAL

The monetary assumption allows accountants to measure economic events and transactions in terms of dollars with assumed stable purchasing power.

[2]"Goldwyn Says 'Very Bad Year' Could Spell Doom for Company," *Los Angeles Times,* June 16, 1995, Section D, p. 5.

When inflation or deflation occurs and the purchasing power of the dollar changes, many people question the use of the dollar as the measuring unit for financial reporting purposes. One suggested alternative is that the dollar should be adjusted for changes in its general purchasing power. *FASB Statement No. 89,* issued in 1986, encourages, but does not require, supplementary disclosures of the impact of inflation and changing prices on financial statement numbers.[3]

◎ OBJECTIVES OF FINANCIAL REPORTING

As we saw in Chapter 1, financial accounting and reporting practices are influenced by the economic environment. Similarly, the objectives of financial reporting are responsive to the economic environment, including the uses and users of financial accounting information that were identified in Chapter 1. In this section we present and discuss the role and objectives of financial reporting.

In Chapter 1 the general role of financial accounting and reporting was described as being to provide information that is useful to a variety of external users who make a variety of resource allocation decisions. Financial accounting and reporting must provide evenhanded (neutral or unbiased) information that helps to promote the efficient allocation of scarce resources in capital and other markets. The **objectives of financial reporting** are concerned with fulfilling this role and are directed at general purpose financial reporting by business companies.

The FASB's *Statement of Financial Accounting Concepts No. 1* sets forth three basic financial reporting objectives. We will examine each of them.

Providing Information for Financial Decision Making

The first objective of financial reporting is to provide information that is useful to present and potential investors and creditors, as well as other users, in making rational investment, credit, and similar decisions. The information should be comprehensible to those who have a reasonable understanding of business and economic activities and are willing to study the information with reasonable diligence.

This objective is quite broad in that investors, creditors, and others who may use financial information have varying degrees of understanding of financial information. The way, and extent to which, they rely on and use financial information may also vary greatly. Since financial information is a tool, it cannot be of much use to those who do not understand it, who are unable or unwilling to use it, or who misuse it. As a result, *the FASB's first objective specifies that financial reporting should provide information that can be used by all who have a reasonable understanding of business and economic activities, and who are willing to learn to properly use the information.*

> **2** List and discuss the three objectives of financial reporting.

Providing Information on Cash Flows

The second objective of financial reporting is to provide information that will help present and potential investors and creditors, and other users, to assess the amounts, timing, and uncertainty of prospective cash receipts from dividends or interest, as well as the proceeds from the sale, redemption, or maturity of securities or loans. Since investors' and creditors' cash flows are related to enterprise cash flows, financial reporting should also provide information to help investors, creditors, and others assess the amounts, timing, and uncertainty of prospective net cash inflows to an enterprise.

---

[3]"Financial Reporting and Changing Prices," *Statement of Financial Accounting Standards No. 89* (Stamford, Conn.: FASB, 1986).

This objective relates to investors' and creditors' interests in receiving cash flows from their investments in or loans to companies. It also relates investors' and creditors' cash flow prospects to the cash flow prospects of the company. That is, the company's ability to pay dividends and interest, as well as the market prices of its securities, is affected by its ability to generate favorable cash flows. Thus, in assessing their own cash flow prospects, investors, creditors, and others can benefit from information helpful in assessing the amounts, timing, and uncertainty of prospective net cash inflows to the company.

Providing Information on Economic Resources

The third objective of financial reporting is to provide information about the economic resources of an enterprise, which are sources, direct or indirect, of future cash inflows; about the claims to those resources (obligations to transfer resources to other entities and owners' equity), which are sources, direct or indirect, of future cash outflows; and about the effects of transactions, events, and circumstances that can cause changes in resources and claims to those resources.[4]

This objective emphasizes the need to provide information about the scarce economic resources needed to carry on economic activity, as well as claims to those resources, and changes in them that are brought about by earnings and other business activities. Such information helps investors, creditors, and others to identify the company's financial strengths and weaknesses and to assess its liquidity and solvency. Moreover, it provides direct indications of the cash flow potentials of some resources, and of the cash needed to satisfy many, if not most, obligations. However, many cash flows cannot be linked with specific resources and obligations, because they result from the combining of resources in the company's operating activities. For this reason, financial reporting should provide information about the company's financial performance during a period. According to the FASB, "the primary focus of financial reporting is information about an enterprise's performance provided by measures of earnings and its components."[5] Investors and creditors may use evaluations of the company's past earnings performance to develop expectations about future earnings performance, which in turn affects their expectations about cash flows from investing in or lending to the company.

In summary, the three objectives of financial reporting emphasize information that is useful for investment and credit decisions. The objectives of financial reporting provide a perspective that is helpful in resolving specific financial accounting and reporting issues. They are consistent with the role of providing financial information that is useful in making economic decisions and are not concerned with what those decisions should be.

Providing Information on Managerial Stewardship

Though the need for information that is useful in making investment, credit, and similar decisions is at the core of the objectives of financial reporting, financial reporting also plays another role. The need to monitor and evaluate management's stewardship of company resources is met by financial reporting, because valuation and managerial decision making are interrelated.

Those who monitor the stewardship of the company's management are concerned with management's efficiency, effectiveness, and integrity. Stockholders' evaluations of management's stewardship help them assess the potential for their investments in the company. Those who are not satisfied with management's stewardship may decide to sell their shares of the company's stock. Potential stockholders who are not satisfied with management's stewardship may decide not to invest in the company's

CONCEPTUAL

Both valuation and stewardship concerns are addressed by the objectives of financial reporting.

---

[4]"Objectives of Financial Reporting by Business Enterprises," *Statement of Financial Accounting Concepts No. 1* (Stamford, Conn.: FASB, 1978).
[5]Ibid., para. 43.

stock. Creditors are interested in the company's (management's) compliance with the terms of loan agreements. They may take legal action if the terms are not being met. At a minimum, they may decide not to extend additional credit to the company.

In both roles—that of providing information to investors and creditors and that of providing information on managerial stewardship—financial accounting compiles and reports information related to an entity's past performance. Users of that information can compare their expectations about an entity's performance with its reported performance. Their satisfaction, or lack of it, with the outcomes of those comparisons becomes the basis for their resource allocation decisions. The critical issue is to determine what characteristics make accounting information useful. In the next section we will discuss some of those characteristics.

QUALITATIVE CHARACTERISTICS OF USEFUL ACCOUNTING INFORMATION

The qualitative characteristics of useful accounting information help in choosing among accounting and reporting alternatives, such as alternative depreciation methods, alternative methods of valuing assets, and alternative methods of disclosure. The qualitative characteristics help to provide an answer to the question, What accounting information will be useful for decision making?

3 Identify and describe the qualitative characteristics of useful accounting information.

User-Specific Qualities

Exhibit 2–2 presents the FASB's hierarchy of qualitative characteristics of useful accounting information. The boxes representing decision makers and **decision usefulness** relate the qualitative characteristics to the financial reporting objectives, which stress providing information that will be useful for decision making. **Understandability** means that the user must be able to understand the information presented if the information is to be useful in decision making. Understandability, like decision usefulness, is a user-specific quality. Information may be useful to one user but not to another, depending on the decision being made and how well the particular user understands the information presented. Remember, the first financial reporting objective is that information should be comprehensible to those who have a reasonable understanding of business and economic activities and who are willing to study the information. Therefore, the understandability characteristic implies that financial reporting should not exclude useful information simply because it is difficult to understand. Special effort, such as additional education, may be needed to increase a user's understanding of financial information.

Primary Qualitative Characteristics

The primary qualities that make accounting information useful are *relevance* and *reliability*. They are called primary qualities because information *must* possess some measure of each of these two qualities to be useful. Relevance and reliability, and their components, are discussed below.

Relevance

Relevance means that the accounting information is capable of making a difference in a decision. To be relevant, information must either confirm or change the decision maker's expectations. If information confirms expectations, it increases the probability that the results will be as expected. For example, learning that the All-American tailback on your football team is injured probably will add to your already existing belief that your team will lose its next game. If information

CONCEPTUAL

Information is relevant if it is capable of making a difference in a decision.

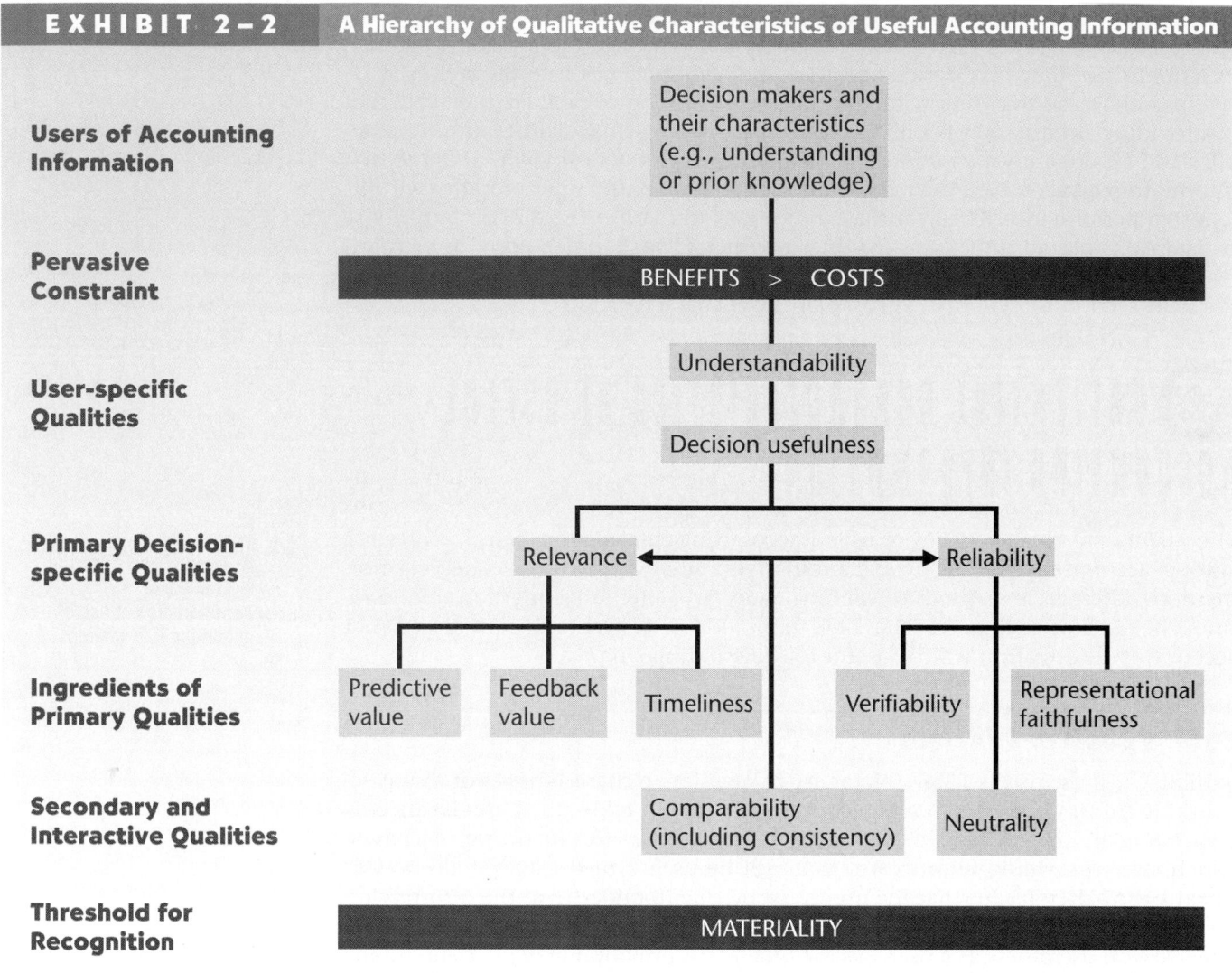

EXHIBIT 2–2 **A Hierarchy of Qualitative Characteristics of Useful Accounting Information**

Users of Accounting Information
— Decision makers and their characteristics (e.g., understanding or prior knowledge)

Pervasive Constraint
— BENEFITS > COSTS

User-specific Qualities
— Understandability
— Decision usefulness

Primary Decision-specific Qualities
— Relevance ⟷ Reliability

Ingredients of Primary Qualities
— Predictive value / Feedback value / Timeliness / Verifiability / Representational faithfulness

Secondary and Interactive Qualities
— Comparability (including consistency) / Neutrality

Threshold for Recognition
— MATERIALITY

Source: "Qualitative Characteristics of Accounting Information," *Statement of Financial Accounting Concepts No. 2* (Stamford, Conn.: FASB, 1980), p. 15.

changes expectations, it changes the perceived probabilities of previously identified possible outcomes. For example, you may have expected to go to the next football game until you learned that the game was sold out.

In summary, information makes a difference to a decision maker who does not already have that information. Relevance of information, however, does not mean that a decision already made must be changed, or that a course of action already taken must be altered. If someone decides to hold an investment rather than sell it, information that supports the hold decision is relevant, just as information that supports a sell decision would be relevant.

Predictive value, feedback value, and timeliness are the components of relevance. Information can affect a decision by improving the decision maker's ability to forecast the outcome of past or present events. If so, it has **predictive value.** For example, if the injury status of your football team's star players helps in predicting the likelihood that your team will lose its next game, then an injury status report has predictive value.

Information can also affect a decision by confirming or altering the decision maker's earlier expectation. As such it has **feedback value.** For example, if learning that the next football game is a sellout before you have a chance to buy a ticket causes you to change your plan to go to the game, then the ticket sales information has feedback value.

Often information has both feedback value and predictive value, since knowledge about the outcomes of actions already taken will generally improve the decision maker's ability to predict the outcomes of similar future actions. For example, a tabulation of past game results showing that your football team has lost 95 percent of all games when two or more of its star players were injured probably will help you to predict the outcome of the next game played under such circumstances. Predictive value and feedback value are consistent with the second financial reporting objective, providing information to help users predict and assess cash flows.

If accounting information is to be capable of affecting a decision, the information must be **timely,** or available at the time the decision is to be made. **Timeliness** alone cannot make information relevant, but information that is not timely is not relevant. For example, information that a football game is sold out is not timely, and therefore not relevant, unless you get it before you drive to the game.

In many situations it may be necessary to sacrifice some of the precision of accounting information to make the information timely. For example, although interim (e.g., quarterly) financial statements tend to be less complete and less precise than annual financial statements, they are more timely. Therefore, many users want quarterly financial statements. Notice the relationship of timeliness to the periodicity assumption and periodic reporting. The need for timely financial information is a major reason that a company's economic activities are divided into artificial time periods for financial reporting purposes.

Reliability

Reliability means that a user can depend on or have confidence in information. Accounting information is considered reliable when it actually represents what it is intended to represent (a quality called representational faithfulness); is reasonably free from error and bias (is neutral); and can be verified. **Representational faithfulness** means there is agreement between a financial measure or description and the underlying economic phenomenon being measured or described. The information must be free from bias and complete in the sense that nothing material is left out.

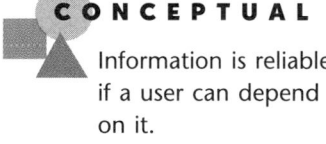

CONCEPTUAL

Information is reliable if a user can depend on it.

In financial accounting, economic resources and obligations and events that change those resources and obligations are presented in financial statements. Let us return to the hypothetical agreement between the television network and the NBA. The network acquired the exclusive right to televise NBA games over a 20-year period, and agreed to make payments to the NBA over this same period. Therefore, many people believe the network should report the right acquired as an asset and the related obligation as a liability on its balance sheet. This disclosure would make the television network's financial statements representationally faithful regarding the benefit obtained and obligation incurred by entering into the agreement with the NBA.

Verifiability increases the assurance that accounting measures represent what they are intended to represent. *Statement of Financial Accounting Concepts No. 2* states that "verifiable financial accounting information provides results that would be substantially duplicated by independent measurers using the same measurement methods."[6] That is, verification implies a consensus among accountants on the measurement of an economic event and on the way it is reported. For example, the amount of cash reported on a balance sheet is highly verifiable. The book value of a depreciable asset, however, may have low verifiability, because different accountants may use different methods to determine cost, salvage value,

---

[6]"Qualitative Characteristics of Accounting Information," *Statement of Financial Accounting Concepts No. 2* (Stamford, Conn.: FASB, 1980), para. 82.

and the estimated life of the asset. Objectivity is often used as a synonym for verifiability.

Relevance vs. Reliability

CONCEPTUAL

There may be a conflict between providing relevant information and providing reliable information.

Accounting information must be both relevant and reliable if it is to be useful for decision making. Relevance and reliability often conflict with each other, however. It is sometimes necessary to sacrifice some degree of one in order to increase the other. For example, there has been much controversy over the possibility of including management's forecasts in annual reports. Many people believe that forecasts provide users with information that is *relevant* to efforts to assess a company's future cash flows. Others, however, believe that the information contained in a forecast is too *unreliable* because of the subjectivity of such estimates. To give another example of the trade-off between relevance and reliability, information about the current values of a company's assets may be more *relevant* than the historical costs of those assets, but the historical cost information may be much more *reliable* than the current value information.

Although relevance and reliability may conflict, apparently the FASB has not emphasized one over the other in its standard-setting activities. A 1994 study reports that "the Board does not appear to sacrifice one quality for the other to any significant extent when promulgating standards."[7]

Secondary Qualitative Characteristics

As shown in Exhibit 2–2, the secondary characteristics of useful accounting information are *neutrality* and *comparability*. Though these are desirable qualities of accounting information, they are not as important as relevance and reliability.

Neutrality

Neutrality means that accounting information should be neutral, or unbiased, with respect to its impact on users' behaviors. Accounting information should not be biased in an effort to attain a predetermined result or to cause users to behave in a particular way. For example, financial reporting should not be aimed at accomplishing a particular economic goal, such as increasing (or decreasing) research and development efforts by companies. *Freedom from such bias (neutrality) is an important characteristic of reliable information.*

Notice the relationship of neutrality to the discussion of economic consequences in Chapter 1. Since accounting information may affect the economic environment, it is important that it be unbiased. Financial reporting should assist in efficient resource allocation, but should be neutral with respect to all other economic consequences. Even though financial accounting and reporting standards may have economic consequences, neutrality in standard setting is important to maintaining the credibility of standards and is thus in the public interest.

Comparability (Including Consistency)

The usefulness of accounting information in decision making is increased if that information is **comparable** with similar information about other accounting entities and with similar information about the same accounting entity over time. Interfirm comparability is achieved when companies use similar accounting procedures to account for similar economic circumstances. For this reason, audited financial statements must be prepared in conformity with GAAP. For example,

---

[7]L. R. Hudack and J. P. McAllister, "An Investigation of the FASB's Application of Its Decision Usefulness Criteria," *Accounting Horizons*, September 1994, pp. 1–18.

interfirm comparability would be increased if both Chrysler and Ford used the same inventory method, such as LIFO, in accounting for automobile inventories. Interperiod comparability, or **consistency,** requires consistent application of accounting procedures over time. For example, continuous use of LIFO by Ford would increase interperiod comparability.

Consistency does *not* mean that an entity can never make a change in its accounting practices, such as a change from FIFO to LIFO in accounting for inventories. If a change in accounting practice is made, however, it should be because of a change in economic circumstances. The entity must also be able to demonstrate that the new accounting practice is preferable to the old practice, given the change in economic circumstances. In addition, the nature of the accounting change and its effect on the financial statements should be disclosed.

Other Considerations and Constraints

Two other concepts, *information benefits versus information costs* and *materiality,* appear in Exhibit 2–2 and are discussed in this section. On occasion, application of these concepts may modify or constrain the choice of an accounting or reporting practice that might otherwise have been made based only on qualitative characteristics.

Information Benefits versus Information Costs

Since the preparation of accounting information is not without cost, those who set accounting standards must consider whether the information benefits derived from a particular accounting disclosure are greater than the costs of making that disclosure. To give one example, the FASB's 1979 *Statement of Standards* required disclosure of both historical cost/constant dollar data and current cost data for financial statements to be in conformity with GAAP. This standard resulted from the perceived need to report such information, given the high levels of inflation in the 1970s. While the cost of preparing changing price data was certainly not insignificant, it seemed to be outweighed by the potential benefits to financial statement users. However, as inflation declined in the mid-1980s, the potential benefits to users also declined. As a result, the benefits of having this information no longer justified the very high costs of preparing the data. This conclusion was a major reason why the FASB issued its 1986 *Statement of Standards,* which superseded the 1979 *Statement* and made supplementary reporting of changing prices data *voluntary.*

What makes accounting information different from commodities that are traded in the marketplace? Commodities traded in the marketplace are *private* goods. The associated benefits and costs of a private good can be determined with reasonable precision and traced to a particular buyer or seller. Accounting information, on the other hand, is a *public* good, the benefits of which cannot always be determined with reasonable precision or confined to those who "pay" for it. For example, the financial statements of a publicly held company are available to all, regardless of whether financial statement users buy the company's products or invest in its securities.

Furthermore, the costs of providing accounting information may be widely diffused. Is the cost of preparing financial statements absorbed by those who buy the company's products? Or is it borne by investors in the company as increased expense and reduced profit? Do employees "pay" for financial statements by receiving lower wages than they would if the company did not have to incur the cost of preparing financial statements? Because it is difficult to determine and compare the benefits and costs of a public good such as accounting information, application of the "benefit must exceed cost" rule to the problem of choosing among alternative accounting and reporting practices is at best very subjective. Nevertheless, the benefits and costs associated with accounting and reporting choices should

4 Discuss the benefits of versus the constraints on strict application of financial accounting and reporting standards.

CONCEPTUAL

The benefits of reporting particular information should exceed the costs of providing that information.

be evaluated to the extent possible. One of the FASB's guidelines is to prescribe an accounting or reporting requirement only when the expected benefits exceed the expected costs.

Materiality

CONCEPTUAL

GAAP must be strictly followed only when accounting for and reporting material items.

Information is considered to be material if it is likely to have a significant effect on a user's decision. **Materiality** implies that generally accepted accounting principles need to be strictly followed only when accounting for and reporting material items. Lack of materiality justifies expedient, cost-effective treatment of an item—for example, expensing rather than capitalizing the cost of an extremely low-cost, long-lived item, like a metal wastebasket, would be acceptable in many cases.

Materiality is an important consideration that has an impact on financial accounting and reporting practices, as illustrated by this statement from the end of *FASB Statements of Financial Accounting Standards:* "The provisions of this Statement need not be applied to immaterial items." Materiality considerations have been cited in court cases. In one case, a judge ruled that a material fact was one "which if it had been correctly stated or disclosed would have deterred or tended to deter the average prudent investor from purchasing the securities in question."[8]

Materiality is a somewhat elusive concept because it depends on (1) the relative dollar amount of an item, (2) the nature of an item (e.g., a legal payment versus an illegal payment), or (3) some combination of the relative dollar amount and nature of an item. For example, a decision by Exxon to record the purchase of a $10 metal wastebasket as an expense instead of as an asset (the wastebasket has future service potential) may be based on the immateriality of the $10 in comparison with the dollar amount of Exxon's total assets. A decision to disclose a small loan to an officer of a company in the external financial statements, on the other hand, is likely to be based on the nature of the transaction rather than on the dollar amount of the loan.

The materiality of an item must be considered in conjunction with other items. For example, neither the dollar amount nor the nature of a $500 shortage of 2×4 lumber in a lumberyard may make the shortage material. However, if similar small dollar amounts of inventory shortage occur in the hardware, roofing, fencing, and other departments of the lumberyard, then the 2×4 shortage may become material. Finally, the materiality threshold may vary from company to company. A $70,000 loss from a lawsuit would be material for many companies but might not be material for a company as large as Exxon. Because materiality judgments often involve factors peculiar to a particular situation, the FASB has not yet been able to develop a set of general guidelines on materiality.

International Qualitative Characteristics

The International Accounting Standards Committee has published a *Framework for the Preparation and Presentation of Financial Statements,* which discusses the qualitative characteristics of useful financial statements. The views of the IASC are broadly consistent with those of the FASB. However, according to the IASC, comparability is of equal importance to relevance or reliability—a statement that may reflect the fact that there is much less comparability among statements internationally than there is domestically.

Two other qualitative characteristics discussed in the IASC's *Framework* are "substance over form" and "prudence." Substance over form refers to accounting for transactions and economic events according to their substance and economic

---

[8]Escott et al. v. BarChris Construction Corporation et al., 283 Fed. Supp. (District Court S.D., New York, 1968), p. 681.

reality, not merely their legal form. While it is not made explicit in the FASB's discussion, substance over form nevertheless underlies U.S. GAAP. Prudence refers to exercising a certain amount of caution in dealing with the uncertainties of future events so that assets or income are not overstated and liabilities or expenses understated.

The qualitative characteristics enumerated by both the FASB and the IASC are based on the view that financial reporting is designed to provide useful information to investors and others interested in making resource allocation decisions. This perspective is particularly relevant for companies that raise capital internationally by listing their stock on overseas stock exchanges.

ELEMENTS OF THE FINANCIAL STATEMENTS

The elements of the financial statements are "the building blocks with which financial statements are constructed"[9]—the major categories of items that make up the statements. The basic elements—*assets, liabilities, equity, revenues, expenses, gains, losses,* and *net income* or *loss,* and *other comprehensive income*—represent an entity's economic resources; claims to or interests in those resources; and the financial effects of transactions or other economic events that cause changes in those economic resources or claims to them. The following section defines the basic elements of the financial statements.

CONCEPTUAL

Elements of the financial statements are the general categories of items (e.g., assets) reported in the financial statements.

Definitions and Interrelationships of the Elements

Definitions of the elements of financial statements are important, because they help in determining how a transaction or other economic event should be accounted for and reported in the financial statements. For example, assume that a manufacturing company suddenly discovers that the land it owns and on which its plant is located contains several thousand tons of valuable minerals. Should the minerals be recorded as an asset? Does this discovery create revenue? The definitions of asset and revenue should help to answer these questions.

To give another example, assume that a large corporation establishes a pension plan for its employees. In determining employees' retirement benefits, the corporation agrees to give its employees credit for services rendered before the plan was adopted. Is the obligation to pay those benefits whose amounts are based on prior service a liability at the date the pension plan is established? The definition of liability may be helpful in answering this question.

Assets

Assets are defined as probable future economic benefits obtained or controlled by a particular entity as a result of past transactions or events. Three essential characteristics are included in the definition of an asset. First, an asset has expected future economic benefit or future service potential in the form of positive cash flows.[10] For example, a delivery van owned by a florist is an asset if it is expected to contribute to the florist's future cash inflows. Second, an entity can obtain the future

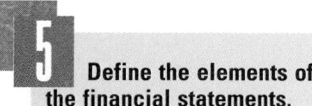

5 Define the elements of the financial statements.

CONCEPTUAL

An asset has future economic benefit obtained by a particular entity as a result of a past transaction or event.

---

[9]"Elements of Financial Statements," *Statement of Financial Accounting Concepts No. 6* (Stamford, Conn.: FASB, 1985), para. 5. (*Statement of Concepts No. 6* replaced *Statement of Concepts No. 3.*) Also see "The Elements of Financial Statements," *Framework for the Preparation and Presentation of Financial Statements* (London: International Accounting Standards Committee, July 1989), paras. 47–81.

[10]These positive cash flows may be direct or indirect. For example, an account receivable has a direct future cash flow benefit. On the other hand, the future cash inflow associated with a machine is indirect, if the machine is used to produce a product that is then sold for cash.

economic benefit from use of the asset and can control other entities' access to that benefit. For example, an interstate highway in front of a company's factory, while probably beneficial to the company, is not an asset of the company because other entities also have free use of the highway. On the other hand, an access road built by a company to its factory, and controlled by that company, is an asset. Third, the transaction that gives rise to the future economic benefit must already have occurred; that is, the asset's existence is not dependent on a future transaction or event. For example, a contract may call for a company to purchase specific goods to be delivered by a second company in the future. The company that signs the purchase contract to buy those goods should not record the goods as assets because the actual delivery of the goods has not taken place. This kind of event is an exchange of promises called an executory contract. Under current GAAP, the rights existing under an executory contract are not considered to possess the characteristics of an asset.

If we apply these three essential characteristics of an asset to the hypothetical agreement between the television network and the NBA that was described at the beginning of this chapter, the network's right to televise NBA games for the next 20 years appears to be an asset. First, the television rights should have future economic benefit to the network in the form of revenues from commercials shown during telecasts. Second, the agreement gives the network exclusive television rights and is noncancelable. Third, the existence of the television rights is the result of a signed agreement and does not require any future transaction or event to occur.

Liabilities

CONCEPTUAL

A liability is a present obligation to transfer assets or provide services in the future as a result of a past transaction or event.

Liabilities are defined as probable future sacrifices of economic benefits arising from present obligations of the accounting entity to transfer assets or provide services to other entities in the future, as a result of past transactions or events. Like assets, liabilities have three essential characteristics. First, a liability obligates a company to transfer cash or some other asset, or to provide services, at some future time. For example, a dividend payable in cash is a liability because the declaration of a cash dividend obligates the company to transfer cash (an asset) to stockholders on the payment date. A dividend distributable in stock of the declaring company, however, is not a liability because the obligation is to distribute the company's own stock, not cash or other assets, to stockholders. Second, the obligation to transfer assets or to provide services must be a present obligation of the accounting entity. For example, if Company A guarantees to pay a note issued by Company B in the event that Company B is unable to pay the debt at maturity, Company A does not incur a liability as a result of the guarantee. Company A's obligation as a guarantor is not a present obligation; it becomes a liability only if Company B defaults on the note. Third, the transaction or event that obligates the entity to transfer assets or provide services must already have taken place. Using the example that was given in the definition of assets, the agreement to purchase goods in the future does not give rise to a liability. A liability to pay for the goods arises only when the goods are received by the accounting entity at a future date.

Returning to the hypothetical television network agreement with the NBA, it appears that the network has, at a minimum, incurred a liability to pay the NBA $20 million annually. The obligation to pay $20 million annually requires the future payment of assets, specifically by the network, and is dependent only on the agreement that has already been signed. Whether the obligation to pay 1 percent of future telecast revenues should be recorded as a liability at the time of signing the agreement is doubtful because future payments by the network depend on a future event—namely, earning revenues. Even if future revenues are likely, the amount of revenue for each of the 20 years of the agreement is highly uncertain.

Equity

Equity, or net assets, is the residual interest in the assets of an entity after its total liabilities have been deducted from its total assets. Because equity is a residual interest, it cannot be measured independently of assets and liabilities. The relationship between assets, liabilities, and equity is the basis for the **accounting equation:**

Assets = Liabilities + Equity

or, rearranging the equation to emphasize equity:

Equity = Assets − Liabilities

Equity usually is described as **stockholders' equity** or **owners' equity.**

Investments in the company by owners and distributions to owners are called equity transactions or capital transactions. A company's sale (issuance) of its own common stock results in an investment by the owners. A cash dividend declared and paid by a company to holders of its common stock is a distribution to the owners. Both the issuance of stock and the payment of a cash dividend are equity transactions.

CONCEPTUAL

Equity equals total assets minus total liabilities.

Revenues

Revenues are periodic inflows of assets or settlements of liabilities, or both, as a result of the delivery or production of goods, the rendering of services, or other earnings activities that constitute an entity's major or *primary* operations. Revenues have two essential characteristics: (1) they arise from a company's primary earnings activities, and (2) they are recurring or continuing in nature. For example, a supermarket's sales of groceries each year result in revenues. An isolated sale of land by the supermarket does *not* result in revenue, but instead might yield a gain or loss. (Gains and losses will be defined and contrasted with revenues and expenses later.) Accounting theorists sometimes describe revenue as "entity accomplishments" or "the product of the enterprise."

Again considering the network-NBA agreement, the NBA should report the annual cash inflows from the network as revenue. Certainly, one component of the NBA's primary earnings activities is the sale of television rights to NBA games. Also, cash flows related to the sale of the television rights will be continuing for the foreseeable future.

CONCEPTUAL

Revenues are inflows of assets or settlements of liabilities as a result of an entity's primary operations.

Expenses

Expenses are the periodic use of assets or the incurring of liabilities, or both, as a result of the delivery or production of goods, the rendering of services, or other earnings activities that constitute an entity's major or *primary* operations. The essential characteristic of expenses is that they are incurred in the process of generating revenue. Referring to the network-NBA example, as years pass and the network uses up its right to televise NBA games, it should record an expense each year that is equal to the dollar amount of the right (the asset) that is used up. Expenses are sometimes described as "entity efforts" or "entity sacrifices" associated with the earning of revenue.

CONCEPTUAL

Expenses are the use of assets or incurrence of liabilities as a result of an entity's primary operations.

Gains and Losses

Gains are *increases* in equity or net assets that result from *peripheral* or incidental transactions by an entity. In other words, gains arise from transactions and economic events that do not result in either revenues or owner investments. **Losses** are *decreases* in equity or net assets arising from *peripheral* or incidental transactions by an entity. Losses arise from transactions and economic events that do not result in either expenses or distributions to owners.

CONCEPTUAL

Gains (losses) are increases (decreases) in equity as a result of an entity's peripheral transactions.

There are two important distinctions between revenues and gains and between expenses and losses. First, both revenues and expenses relate to the major or *primary* operating activities of a company, whereas both gains and losses relate to *peripheral* activities. Consequently, revenues and expenses provide different cash flow signals from those provided by gains and losses. Because revenues and expenses are ongoing and are associated with a company's primary operating activity, users of financial statements should assess and predict cash flows associated with revenues and expenses and make predictions of future revenues and expenses differently than they would cash flows associated with gains and losses, which are not ongoing and are peripheral to a company's activities.

Second, revenues and expenses refer to *gross* inflows and outflows, whereas gains and losses refer to *net* inflows and outflows. For example, sales revenue is a major revenue item for a merchandising company; it represents a gross inflow of resources resulting from its sales activity. To determine profit (a net amount) from sales, it is necessary to subtract cost of goods sold from sales revenue. In contrast, a gain on the sale of a company's plant, property, or equipment is the difference (a net amount) between the book value of the plant, property, or equipment sold and the cash or other resources received from the sale.

Net Income or Net Loss

CONCEPTUAL

Net income (loss) is the change in equity from revenues, expenses, gains, and losses.

Under GAAP, **net income** or **net loss** refers to the periodic change in equity (that is, the change in net assets) of an entity as a result of transactions and other economic events that result in revenues, expenses, gains, and losses. Thus, net income or net loss includes all changes in equity during a period, except for investments by and distributions to owners and certain other changes in net assets. Mathematically, net income or net loss is determined by revenues, expenses, gains, and losses as follows:

Net income or net loss = Revenues – Expenses + Gains – Losses

In this textbook, as in current practice, the term **earnings** sometimes will be used as a synonym for *net income,* or as a way of capturing the elements (i.e., revenues, expenses, gains, losses) that make up income. The items included in net income are displayed in four classifications: continuing operations, discontinued operations, extraordinary items, and cumulative effects of changes in accounting principles.

Comprehensive Income

The FASB first introduced the concept of **comprehensive income** in 1980 in *Statement of Financial Accounting Concepts No. 3.* In 1984, in *Statement of Financial Accounting Concepts No. 5,* the FASB took the position that earnings (net income) should to the extent possible be a measure of performance for the current period only and that items extraneous to the current period should be included, not in earnings, but in the broader concept of comprehensive income.[11] In 1985, the Board again addressed comprehensive income in *Statement of Financial Concepts No. 6,* defining it as "the change in equity (net assets) of a business enterprise during a period from transactions and other events and circumstances from nonowner sources. It includes all changes in equity during a period except those resulting from investments by owners and distributions to owners."[12] In short, by 1985 the Board saw comprehensive income as traditional earnings (net income) *plus* all other changes in equity for the period, except investments by owners and distributions to owners.

---

[11]"Recognition and Measurement in Financial Statements of Business Enterprises," *Statement of Financial Accounting Concepts No. 5* (Stamford, Conn.: FASB, 1984).
[12]*FASB Statement of Concepts No. 6,* para. 70.

Until 1997, the concept of comprehensive income remained just that—a concept. Meanwhile, on several occasions between 1980 and 1997, the Board issued *Statements* specifically requiring that certain changes in assets and liabilities—that is, changes in equity that had nothing to do with owner-related transactions—be reported as a separate component of equity in the balance sheet rather than in the income statement. In other words, items that would have been reported in a statement of comprehensive income, had one existed, were not included in the income statement, which reported only earnings as traditionally defined. FASB *Statements* that specifically require that certain changes in equity *not* be reported in the income statement, even though those changes were not the result of owner-related transactions, are *Statements No. 52,* "Foreign Currency Translation"; *No. 80,* "Accounting for Futures Contracts"; *No. 87,* "Employers' Accounting for Pensions"; and *No. 115,* "Accounting for Certain Investments in Debt and Equity Securities."

By the 1990s, users of financial statements were expressing increasing concern about the number of items that were bypassing the income statement and going directly to equity in the balance sheet. Users also indicated their dislike for the effort required to analyze those types of items. Among those expressing concerns and/or advocating adoption of a more inclusive concept of income were the Association for Investment Management and Research and the Accounting Policy Committee of the Robert Morris Associates. Internationally there was also some movement toward a broader concept of income, including the position taken by the United Kingdom Accounting Standards Board in its 1992 *Financial Reporting Standard 3,* "Reporting Financial Performance."

In June 1997, in response to these kinds of pressure and with the knowledge that other important items (such as some of the gains and losses resulting from valuing financial instruments at fair value) might end up bypassing the traditional income statement in forthcoming FASB *Statements,* the Board issued *Statement of Financial Accounting Standards No. 130,* "Reporting Comprehensive Income." This *Statement* became effective for fiscal years beginning after December 15, 1997, and applies to all enterprises that provide a full set of financial statements that report financial position, results of operations, and cash flows.[13] The Board's view was that information provided in a report of comprehensive income, if used with information provided in the other financial statements, would help users of the financial statements to assess a company's financial performance and the timing and amounts of its future cash flows.

Statement No. 130 "requires that all items that meet the definition of components of comprehensive income be reported in a financial statement for the period in which they are recognized. In doing so, this *Statement* amends *Statements 52, 80, 87,* and *115* to require that changes in the balances of items that under those *Statements* are reported directly in a separate component of equity in a statement of financial position be reported in a financial statement that is displayed as prominently as other financial statements."[14] The *Statement* also discusses how to report and display comprehensive income and its components, including net income.

Statement No. 130 defines comprehensive income as the total of all components of comprehensive income, including net income (earnings). In other words, it divides comprehensive income into net income and other comprehensive income. Those revenues, expenses, gains, and losses included in comprehensive income but excluded from net income are designated as **other comprehensive income.** Specific items included in other comprehensive income, given accounting standards existing in June 1997, would include foreign currency items, minimum pension liability adjustments, and unrealized gains and losses on certain investments in debt and equity securities. The *Statement* does not require that the terms *comprehensive income* or *other comprehensive income* be explicitly used in the financial statements.

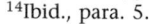

[13]"Reporting Comprehensive Income," *Statement of Financial Accounting Standards No. 130* (Norwalk, Conn.: FASB, June 1997) paras. 6 and 34.
[14]Ibid., para. 5.

Statement No. 130 encourages the use of either of two formats for reporting comprehensive income—a one-statement format and a two-statement format. In either format, net income must be reconciled with comprehensive income. If the one-statement format is used, net income will appear as a subtotal within a statement of income and comprehensive income, and comprehensive income will be the "bottom line." If the two-statement format is used, a statement of income will be followed by a statement of comprehensive income that must begin with the net income that is the bottom line of the statement of income. Components of other comprehensive income may be displayed either net of related tax effects or before related tax effects, with a single amount shown for the aggregate tax effect related to the total amount of other comprehensive income. The total of other comprehensive income for a period must be transferred to a component of equity that is displayed separately from retained earnings and additional paid-in capital in the statement of financial position, using a descriptive title such as *accumulated other comprehensive income.*

Throughout this textbook, the terms "net income," "income," "net earnings," and "earnings" are used with their traditional meaning, as suggested by the FASB. The term "comprehensive income" will be used only to refer to items characterized by the FASB as other comprehensive income.

Financial Statements Based on the Elements

When discussing the objectives of financial reporting, we pointed out that financial reporting should provide information about economic resources, claims to or interests in resources, and changes in resources and obligations from earnings and other activities that are helpful in assessing a company's cash flows. Economic resources, claims to or interests in resources, and changes in resources and obligations are represented by the elements of financial statements defined in the preceding section. Now we will briefly describe the contents of the four required financial statements introduced in Chapter 1.

The **balance sheet,** also called the **statement of financial position,** reports an entity's assets, liabilities, and equity at the end of each accounting period. The **income statement** reports revenues, expenses, gains, losses, and the resulting net income or loss. Thus it summarizes a company's earnings performance during an accounting period. The **statement of changes in owners' equity** summarizes transactions affecting owners' equity during an accounting period. Finally, the **statement of cash flows** summarizes cash inflows and outflows from operating activities, investing activities, and financing activities during the accounting period. Each of the financial statements is discussed in detail later in the textbook.

Effects of Economic Events on the Elements

An economic event is an occurrence or a happening that has an economic consequence to an entity, involving one or more of the elements of financial statements. Economic events may be external or internal to the entity. An external event occurs when an entity is affected by something in its environment, such as the activity of another entity, an increase in the cost of materials purchased, or a natural disaster. An internal event occurs within an entity, such as the use of raw materials in making a product that is to be sold.

External economic events may be classified as either transactions or events other than transactions. A transaction is the transfer of something of value between two or more entities. If an entity both receives and sacrifices something of value, the transaction is an exchange or a reciprocal transfer. A company's purchase of merchandise for cash or on account is an exchange transaction. On the other hand, if the transaction is such that an entity either receives something of value or sacrifices

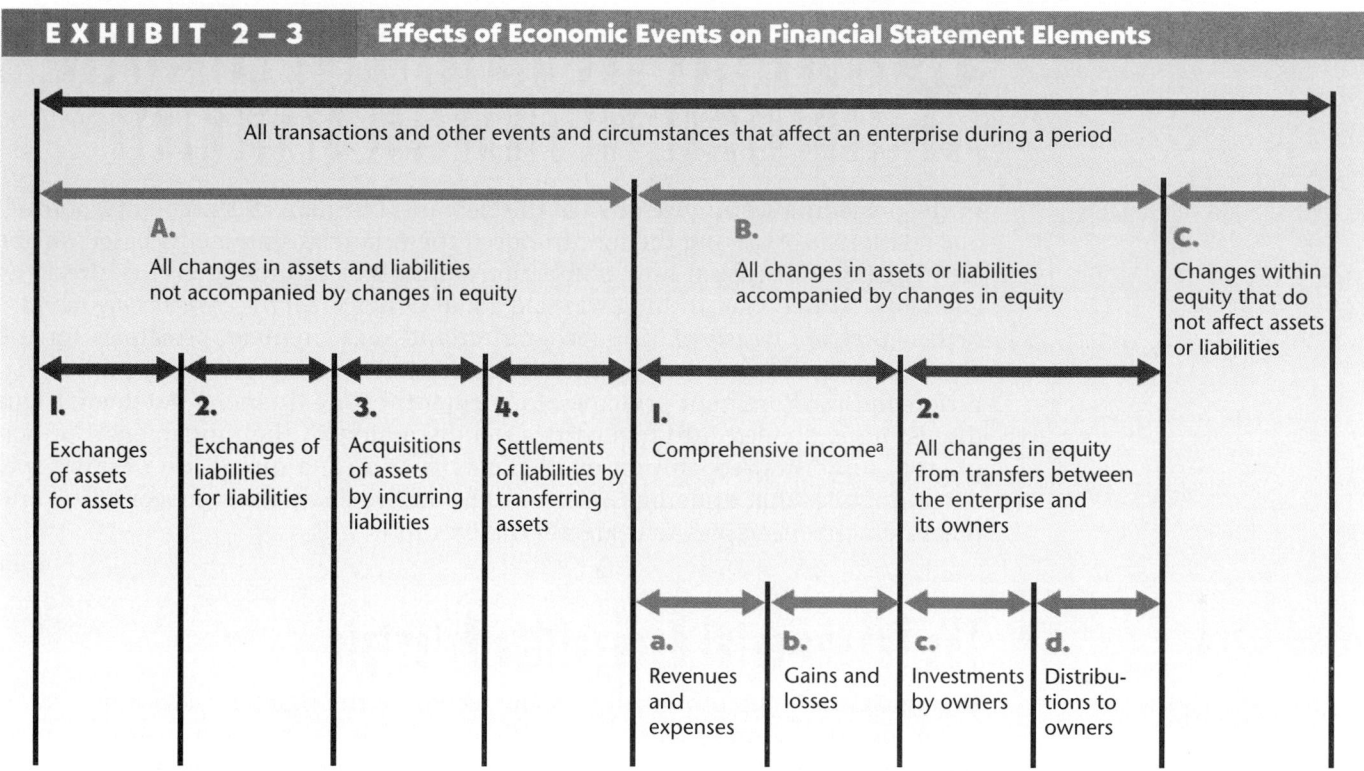

EXHIBIT 2-3   Effects of Economic Events on Financial Statement Elements

[a]Very similar to net income in current practice. One difference is that comprehensive income would include changes in market values of certain debt and equity securities, whereas such changes are not part of net income in current practice.

Source: "Elements of Financial Statements," *Statement of Financial Accounting Concepts No. 6* (Stamford, Conn.: FASB, 1985).

something of value, but not both, the transaction is called a nonreciprocal transfer. A city's donation of land to a company for operating purposes is a nonreciprocal transfer. External events other than transactions include price changes, changes in market interest rates, and natural disasters.

Economic events have various effects on the elements of a company's financial statements. These effects are shown in Exhibit 2–3. As the exhibit illustrates, all economic events that are recognized have a dual effect on the financial statement elements. That is, if a transaction or other economic event causes an increase or a decrease in one element, another element also increases or decreases. This duality is the basis for double-entry bookkeeping, discussed in Chapter 3. Some examples of the dual effect of economic events on the financial statement elements are presented below:

ECONOMIC EVENT	EXAMPLE
Exchange of assets for assets	**Acquisition of inventory by paying cash. Inventory is increased, cash is decreased. (A.1 in Exhibit 2–3)**
Acquisition of assets by incurring liabilities	**Acquisition of land by issuing a note. Land is increased, notes payable is increased. (A.3 in Exhibit 2–3)**
Change in assets accompanied by change in equity	**A consulting firm earns revenue by performing consulting services in exchange for cash. Cash is increased, equity is increased. (B.1.a in Exhibit 2–3)**
Change in assets accompanied by change in equity	**A company issues its own stock in exchange for cash. Cash is increased, equity is increased. (B.2.c in Exhibit 2–3)**

Under GAAP, not all economic events are captured and reported in the financial statements. Only those economic events that can be both identified with the accounting entity and quantified in dollars are recorded and reported.

RECOGNITION AND MEASUREMENT PRINCIPLES FOR ELEMENTS OF THE FINANCIAL STATEMENTS

In the preceding section we defined the elements of financial statements, pointed out relationships among them, introduced the financial statements based on the elements, and discussed how transactions and other economic events affect the elements. Notice that nothing was said about either *when the elements are recorded* or *how they are measured*. The recognition and measurement principles for the elements provide guidance on these issues. In this section we discuss the recognition and measurement principles for elements of the financial statements. Our discussion is divided into two parts: (1) a discussion of the fundamental principle that underlies recognition of all elements and (2) a discussion of more specific principles that underlie GAAP. In addition, we discuss some recognition and measurement principles that are alternatives to GAAP.

The Fundamental Recognition Principle

Recognition is the process of formally recording the financial effects of a transaction or other economic event and including that information in the financial statements as an asset, a liability, a revenue, an expense, or some other element. Recognition includes both the *initial* recognition (recording) of an item and recognition of subsequent *changes* in the recorded amount of that item. Under the fundamental recognition principle, an item resulting from a transaction or other economic event should be recognized (reported in the financial statements) if the following criteria are met:

6 State the four criteria of the fundamental recognition principle.

1. The item meets the *definition* of an element of financial statements.

2. The item has an attribute that *can be measured* reliably.

3. Information about the item is *relevant*—that is, capable of making a difference in user decisions.

4. Information about the item is *reliable*—that is, representationally faithful, verifiable, and neutral.[15]

These four criteria for recognition apply to *all* elements of the financial statements, and are subject to the cost-benefit constraint. The expected benefits from recognition of an item should exceed the expected costs of providing and using the information. In addition, lack of materiality justifies expedient, cost-effective treatment of an item. Notice how the four recognition criteria listed above, along with the cost-benefit constraint and the materiality threshold, build on and incorporate the qualitative characteristics and the definitions of elements discussed in preceding sections. (These relationships also are shown in Exhibit 2–1.)

Before discussing the more specific principles that underlie GAAP, we should elaborate on recognition criterion 2, because it may not be clear what is meant by the term "attribute." *Attribute* refers to a characteristic of an item. For example, attributes of an asset include its volume, its color, and its weight. Users of financial statements are interested in *financial* attributes, such as the historical cost or the current replacement cost of an item. Although criterion 2 permits any attribute to be reported, the selected attribute must be reliably measurable in dollars.

---

[15]"Recognition and Measurement in Financial Statements of Business Enterprises," para. 63.

Principles and Concepts for Determining Income Under GAAP

Now that we have discussed the fundamental recognition principle and its four criteria, we examine the specific principles and concepts underlying GAAP. These principles are discussed and illustrated in the following subsections.

Accrual Accounting versus Cash-Basis Accounting

Although a company's earnings and related operating activities are continuous, they are reported for specific intervals in order to provide useful information for decision making on a timely basis. Some activities may begin and end during the accounting period, while others may require two or more accounting periods for completion. An automobile dealer, for example, may spend cash for an inventory of automobiles, sell the automobiles, and collect cash from the buyers all in one accounting period. Or the dealer may spend cash for an inventory of cars in one accounting period, sell the cars in the second period, and collect cash from the buyers in the third period. In addition, though the dealer's showroom was purchased in one period, it will provide economic benefits over several accounting periods.

In measuring earnings, which provide signals about cash flows, should revenues and expenses be reported on the basis of cash inflows and outflows or on the basis of transactions that have present and future cash consequences? **Accrual accounting** focuses on transactions and other economic events that have cash consequences (affect cash flows), rather than strictly on cash receipts or cash disbursements. Under accrual accounting, transactions and other economic events are recorded when they occur, but revenues are reported (recognized) when they are earned and the amount and timing of their revenue can be reasonably estimated. Expenses are reported in accordance with the matching principle (discussed on page 65), and are deducted from revenue to determine net income. Under **cash-basis accounting,** in contrast, revenues are reported when cash is received and expenses are reported when cash is paid. The following examples illustrate both accrual accounting and cash-basis accounting. They will allow us to contrast the two methods from the standpoint of financial reporting objectives and the definitions of financial statement elements.

Suppose that a contractor begins business in period 1 and agrees to construct a $60,000 building for a local bank. During period 1, the contractor incurs costs *on credit* of $35,000 in constructing the building and delivers the completed building to the client. In period 2, the contractor collects the sales price of $60,000 from the client. In period 3, the contractor pays his creditors the $35,000 due.

On the basis of the above data, the contractor's net income for each period, first under cash-basis accounting and then under accrual accounting, is as follows:

7 Describe and give examples of the difference between accrual and cash-basis accounting.

	PERIOD			
	1	2	3	TOTAL
Cash-basis accounting:				
Cash receipts	$ –0–	$60,000	—	$60,000
Cash disbursements	–0–	—	$(35,000)	(35,000)
Net income	$ –0–	$60,000	$(35,000)	$25,000
Accrual accounting:				
Revenues	$60,000	—	—	$60,000
Expenses	(35,000)	—	—	(35,000)
Net income	$25,000	$ –0–	$ –0–	$25,000

CONCEPTUAL

The difference between accrual accounting and cash-basis accounting is the timing of net income.

Notice that for the three periods combined, both methods result in the same total net income. The difference between accrual accounting and cash-basis accounting is the *timing* of net income.[16]

Under *cash-basis accounting,* net income is zero in period 1, since the sale of the building and purchase of materials, labor, and other assets or services used in constructing the building were on credit. Net income in period 2 is $60,000 because the sales price was collected in cash. In period 3 there is a net loss of $35,000 because $35,000 cash was paid to the creditors.

Under *accrual accounting,* because the contractor constructs and delivers the building to the bank in period 1, and because the net cash consequences (net cash flows) of this earnings activity are known with a high degree of certainty at the end of period 1, net income of $25,000 is reported. The revenue has been earned, and a claim to cash (an account receivable) is held, which is measurable with a high degree of reliability. In periods 2 and 3, however, no earnings activities take place, so no income or loss is reported.

Let us modify the situation slightly. If the contracting company were a publicly held company with several buildings under construction, its profitability ultimately would affect the dividends paid to its stockholders and the market value of its outstanding shares. Thus, in making decisions to purchase or sell shares, owners and potential investors need timely information about present and future cash flows to the company to help in evaluating the company and in making assessments of future cash flows to them. *Accrual accounting provides this information by reporting the net cash flows associated with earnings activities as soon as those cash flows can be estimated with some acceptable level of confidence.* In the earlier example, these net cash effects were known and reported in period 1 on an accrual basis, but spread out over several periods on a cash basis. For example, at the end of period 1, cash-basis accounting indicates that the contractor had not engaged in any profitable construction activity during the period. At the end of the second period, the cash-basis income statement data indicated that net cash flows on the contract were or ultimately would be $60,000. The user would not know until the end of the third period that net income and net cash flow on the project were only $25,000.

In summary, accrual accounting is grounded in cash flows but reports transactions and other events with cash consequences at the time the transactions occur rather than at the time cash is received or paid. Accrual accounting is also superior to cash-basis accounting from the standpoint of the definitions of financial statement elements, as our next illustration shows.

Suppose that on January 1, 1998, Dave Brown formed a used car company by investing $20,000 cash. A summary of the company's transactions during January is as follows:

1. Purchased three cars for cash at $6,000 each.
2. Sold three cars for $9,000 each. Two sales were for cash. The third was on a deferred payment plan; $1,000 was collected on this sale during January.
3. Rented a building for an office and a showroom and paid three months' rent in advance—$3,000.
4. Purchased another car for $6,000 cash.
5. Salespeople earned a $300 commission on each car sold. At the end of January, commissions were paid on the two cars sold for cash, and the company owed a salesperson the commission on the third sale.
6. Office salaries incurred and paid totaled $800.

[16]For example, when the Wichita, Kansas, public school district switched from cash-basis to accrual accounting, it had to record 13 months of salaries expense instead of 12 months for the first year after the switch. "Accounting Changes Account for USD259's Budget 'Overrun,'" *Wichita Business Journal,* April 7, 1995, Section 1, p. 9.

EXHIBIT 2-4	Financial Statements Based on Cash-Basis and Accrual Accounting

Brown Used Cars
Income Statement
for the Month Ended January 31, 1998

	CASH BASIS	ACCRUAL
Revenues	$ 19,000[a]	$ 27,000[b]
Expenses:		
Cost of cars: Purchased (4 @ $6,000)	$ 24,000	
Sold (3 @ $6,000)		$ 18,000
Commissions	600	900
Salaries	800	800
Rent	3,000	1,000
Total expenses	$(28,400)	$(20,700)
Net income (loss)	$ (9,400)	$ 6,300

Balance Sheet
as of January 31, 1998

	CASH BASIS	ACCRUAL
Assets:		
Cash	$10,600[c]	$10,600[c]
Receivable from customer ($9,000 − $1,000)		8,000
Inventory		6,000
Prepaid rent		2,000
Total assets	$10,600	$26,600
Liabilities and equity:		
Commissions payable		$ 300
Dave Brown, equity	$10,600[d]	26,300[c]
Total liabilities and equity	$10,600	$26,600

[a]($9,000 × 2) + $1,000.
[b]$9,000 × 3.

[c]Original investment	$20,000
Cash sales (2 @ $9,000)	$18,000
Collection on deferred payment sale	1,000
Cars purchased (4 @ $6,000)	(24,000)
Rent payment	(3,000)
Sales commission paid	(600)
Office salaries paid	(800)
Current cash balance	$10,600

[d]Beginning investment less net loss: $20,000 − $9,400.
[e]Beginning investment plus net income: $20,000 + $6,300.

Cash-basis and accrual-basis financial statements for January based on this illustration appear side-by-side in Exhibit 2–4. Several aspects of this comparison show cash-basis accounting is inconsistent with the theory underlying the financial statement elements:

1. The cash-basis approach understates the amount of revenue and inflows of assets in January from the sale of the three cars. The $8,000 receivable on the third sale is a future cash inflow that is ignored in January if cash-basis accounting is used.

2. Under cash-basis accounting, the expense associated with the cost of cars sold in January is overstated because only three cars were actually sold. The fourth car is an asset in the form of inventory. This car has future cash inflow potential because it can be sold later.

3. The cash-basis approach ignores the portion of the commissions that have been earned by the sales staff. Since three cars were sold, salespeople have earned $900 in commissions even though only $600 has been paid. Also, the company is obligated to pay a salesperson a $300 commission on the noncash car sale. That obligation is a liability.

4. Rent expense for January is overstated under the cash-basis approach because the $3,000 payment for rent provides economic benefits over three months. The right to use the building for two more months is a prepaid rent asset.

In accrual accounting, cash flows that precede the related earnings activities are called prepayments (from cash outflows) or unearned (from cash inflows). For example, the prepaid rent of $2,000 shown in the balance sheet in Exhibit 2–4 is a prepayment. Earnings activities that precede the related cash flows are called accruals. The receivable of $8,000 shown in Exhibit 2–4 is an example of accrued revenue, and the commission payable of $300 is an example of accrued expense.

The Historical Cost Principle

CONCEPTUAL

Under pure historical cost, the reported amounts for assets and liabilities are derived from the exchange price or cost at the time the asset was acquired or the liability was incurred.

Under the **historical cost principle,** the exchange price established or cost incurred at the time a transaction occurs is the basis for initially recording assets and liabilities. This principle is used for initial recording because cost usually is the best estimate of an asset's or a liability's fair value.[17] When a cost is not incurred at the acquisition date, such as when a company acquires a machine by issuing shares of its stock, the historical exchange price is determined by reference to the fair value of what is received or given, whichever is more clearly determinable.

After the acquisition or exchange date, the continued use of historical cost, less depreciation if applicable, often results in reported data that are based on out-of-date prices. Asset prices may change because of inflation, changes in supply and demand, technology, and other factors. Thus, historical cost may become irrelevant for decision-making purposes. Under GAAP, the carrying value of an asset is occasionally written down to recoverable value if that value is below cost. But an asset is rarely written up and reported above historical cost. Many accountants believe that the merit of reporting verifiable, actual transaction costs in the financial statements exceeds the possible disadvantage of those data being out of date. In other words, many accountants would prefer to give up some relevance in order to increase the reliability of the reported data.

The Realization Principle or Concept

Discuss the realization principle and its two criteria.

CONCEPTUAL

Realization is an abstract concept that governs *when* revenue should be recognized (recorded).

The realization concept provides additional guidance beyond the four fundamental recognition criteria (page 58) for determining when *revenue* (or *gains*) should be recognized and reported in the income statement. Although the terms "realization" and "recognition" sometimes are used interchangeably, they have different meanings in accounting. Recognition is the *act of recording* revenue in the accounting records and reporting it in the income statement. Thus, recognition refers to an *action* taken or to be taken. **Realization** is an abstract *concept* that governs *when* revenue should be recognized. Realization appears in the accounting literature in several contexts. It sometimes is used to describe the conversion of noncash assets to

---

[17]Conceptually, the cost and fair value of an asset are equal at the acquisition date.

cash or claims to cash. It (and two derivative terms, "realized" and "unrealized") may be associated with the occurrence of a transaction. For example, increases in the value of an asset that occur before the asset is sold are said to be *unrealized* until the asset is sold. At the date of sale, these value increases are said to be *realized* by the sale. Realization also is used to describe the occurrence of an event that reduces uncertainty about future cash flows to a level acceptable to justify recognition.[18]

Under the realization principle or concept, revenue should be recognized and reported in the income statement when:

1. The amount and timing of revenue are reasonably determinable; that is, revenue has been realized or is realizable.

2. The earnings process is complete or virtually complete; that is, revenue has been earned.

These two criteria are more operational than the four fundamental recognition criteria on page 58, and provide further guidance related only to the recognition of revenues or gains. The first criterion of the realization concept means that the expected cash flows related to revenue must be objectively determinable before the revenue can be recorded. In its *Statement of Concepts No. 5, the FASB's discussion of the first criterion refers to revenue being "realized" (when goods or services are exchanged for cash or claims to cash) or being "realizable" (when related assets received or held are readily convertible to known amounts of cash or claims to cash).*[19] The second criterion can be interpreted as meaning that the event(s) critical to earning the revenue must have occurred before revenue can be recognized. *The FASB's discussion of the second criterion says the revenue must be "earned," meaning that the entity has substantially accomplished what it must do to be entitled to the benefits represented by the revenue.*[20] For  example, in its 1995 Annual Report Whitman Corporation states, "Revenue is recognized when title to a product is transferred to the customer or upon completion of a service."[21]

The Earnings Process   Certain aspects of the earnings process may be generalized across companies and types of business. We have identified these common aspects of the earnings process on the time line in Exhibit 2–5. This exhibit illustrates a company's earnings process on a conceptual basis, and is equally applicable to a manufacturing company, a merchandising company, or a service company. A manufacturing company acquires the components of production, manufactures the product, sells it, and then collects cash from the sale. The period between the sale and the collection of cash may be of zero duration, as in a cash sale, or quite long, as in a sale in exchange for a long-term receivable.

The earnings process of a merchandising company differs slightly. The merchandise company acquires inventory from a manufacturer and then holds it until the time of sale. From the point of sale on, the earnings process of a merchandising company is the same as that for a manufacturing company. In a service company, the production period is replaced by the period of providing services. The point of sale is the point at which performance of the service is complete.

Conceptually, the earnings process is continuous, as utility or value is constantly being added to the service or good. For example, value is added to goods as inputs such as raw materials and labor are transformed into finished products. In a given situation, the two criteria set forth by the realization principle (above)

---

[18]"Report of the Committee on Concepts and Standards—External Reporting," *Accounting Review 49* (1974), supplement. This third use of realization seems conceptually preferable. It is more robust and acknowledges the possibility that, of many events that might occur, one critical event may reduce uncertainty about an asset's future cash flows to an acceptable level. In addition, it allows many existing accounting practices to be consistent with the concept of realization, rather than being viewed as exceptions to the realization concept.

[19]*FASB Statement of Concepts No. 5*, para. 83a.

[20]Ibid., para. 83b.

[21]"Consolidated Financial Statements," Whitman Corporation, 1995, Note 1.

| EXHIBIT 2-5 | The Earnings Process |

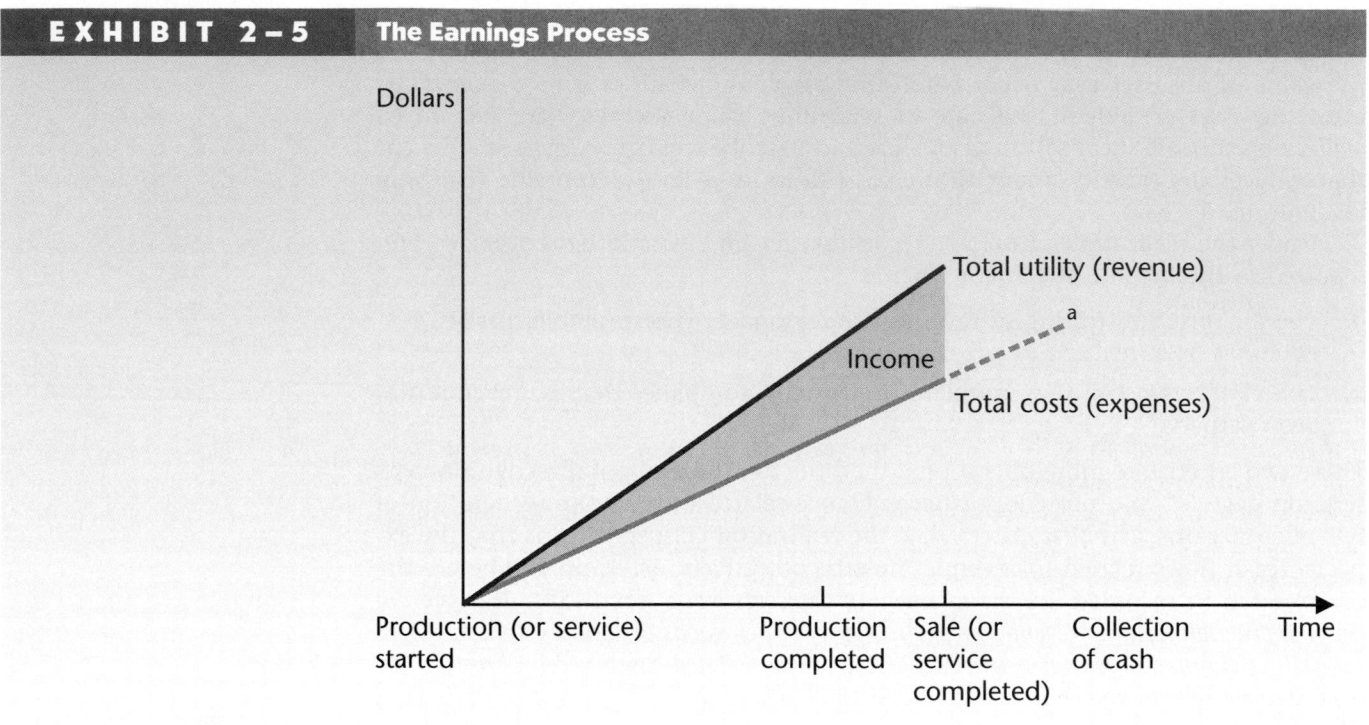

[a]Although the earnings process may be virtually complete at the date of sale, occasionally sale-related costs are incurred subsequent to the date of sale.

could be met, and revenue would be recognized, at any point during the earnings process. In the next few sections we will discuss revenue recognition at several different points during the earnings process.

Revenue Recognition at the Time of Sale   The sale is the most critical event in the earnings processes of most companies. Therefore, the normal (or most common) case is to recognize revenue at the time of sale. The sale event typically occurs when (1) ownership of goods is transferred to a buyer, (2) services are performed, or (3) asset services (e.g., apartment rentals) have been provided (e.g., the apartment has been occupied during the period).

Revenue Recognition During Production   Contractual arrangements between the producer or seller and the buyer sometimes specify and guarantee selling prices to an extent sufficient to meet the criteria of revenue recognition before sale and delivery. Revenue may be recognized during production if (1) the contract price is fixed or determinable, (2) total production cost can be reasonably estimated, and (3) the cost incurred during the current accounting period or the percentage of production completed to date is known or can be reasonably estimated. Revenue often is recognized during production under long-term construction contracts. In these circumstances—for example, when a bridge is being built under a fixed-price contract—production is the critical event in the earnings process.

   Note that if the three conditions for revenue recognition during production are met, it is possible to determine with a high degree of certainty the net cash flows that will result from the transaction. Thus, users can be provided with information that will help them to assess and predict cash flows. Revenue recognition during production is discussed thoroughly in Chapter 7.

Revenue Recognition at the Completion of Production   Revenue may be recognized before the sale in circumstances other than long-term construction contracts as long as the two revenue recognition criteria are met. Precious minerals, such as gold and silver, and some agricultural commodities, such as wheat and corn, are not produced under long-term contracts, but the two criteria for recognition of revenue are often met at the completion of production. The ready marketability of such goods results in a reasonably certain market price; that is, the amount and timing of revenue to be received are reasonably determinable. Furthermore, marketing or selling costs are zero or minimal, so the earnings process is virtually complete. When there is a ready market for a product at a known market price and the marketing costs are immaterial, the critical event in the earnings process is the completion of production, not the sale of the product. In these cases, it is appropriate to recognize revenue when production is completed. Recognition at the completion of production is discussed in Chapter 7.

Revenue Recognition When Cash Is Collected   When sales are made on account and reasonable estimates of uncollectible accounts cannot be made, revenue is recognized as cash is collected. Under circumstances such as these, even though a sale has occurred, there is too much uncertainty about the amount of cash to be received to justify recognition of revenue before the cash is collected. When sales are made under a deferred payment plan, revenue is sometimes recognized as cash is collected. Two methods of revenue recognition when sales are made on account are the *installment method* and the *cost-recovery method*. Both are illustrated in Chapter 7.

The Matching Principle

The **matching principle** means that revenues generated and expenses incurred in generating those revenues should be reported in the same income statement. Revenues for an accounting period are recognized in accordance with the realization principle. Then the expenses incurred in generating those revenues are determined in accordance with the matching principle. Thus, expenses are reported in the income statement for the accounting period in which the related revenues are recognized.

The matching principle emphasizes the cause-and-effect relationship between expense and revenue. This relationship, however, is sometimes difficult to identify. For example, an expense that is incurred may not generate any obvious revenue. Such a situation occurs when an interior decorator employed by a retail furniture store provides free advice to customers about wallpaper, paint, or room arrangements. While little or no revenue can be associated directly with the interior decorator's service, there is no doubt that the expense of employing the decorator is incurred by the furniture store in the expectation that providing this service will contribute to revenues.

Because of the difficulty of associating expenses with revenues, three general guidelines are used to apply the matching principle:

1. Associating cause and effect.
2. Systematic and rational allocation.
3. Immediate recognition.

Associating Cause and Effect   The most obvious matching of expenses and revenues occurs when the cost of goods sold is related to or associated with revenues generated from the sale of goods. In this instance there is a clear and direct relationship between the revenue recognized and the associated cost of goods sold. For example, the cost of an electronic TV game sold by a hardware store can be determined and matched with the revenue from its sale. Any sales commissions on the sale can also be matched against the associated revenue.

Systematic and Rational Allocation   Some costs are incurred to acquire assets that provide benefits to the entity over several accounting periods. A typical example is the cost of a depreciable plant asset. Even though there is no clear-cut relationship to specific revenues during each year in which the asset is used, the

9   **Discuss the matching principle and the three general guidelines for applying it.**

CONCEPTUAL

Expenses incurred in generating revenues should be reported in the same income statement as the revenues generated.

CONCEPTUAL

Three guidelines for applying the matching principle: (1) associating cause and effect, (2) systematic and rational allocation, and (3) immediate recognition.

asset contributes to revenues over its useful life. Therefore, a *systematic and rational allocation method* of matching the cost of using the asset with the revenues generated is employed. For example, if the asset is expected to provide equal benefits each month, an equal amount of cost should be expensed each month. Rocky Mountain Chocolate Factory reports in the Notes to its 1995 financial statements that when it opens a new retail store it capitalizes $12,000 of pre-opening costs and "amortizes such costs over the 12-month period following a store's opening."

Immediate Recognition   Finally, some costs may be incurred when there is no ascertainable future benefit, or when the future benefits are highly uncertain. These costs, such as advertising, supervisors' salaries, and the salary of the interior decorator mentioned earlier, are recorded as expenses in the period in which they are incurred.

The Concept of Capital Maintenance

Capital maintenance is a concept of investment recovery. It defines what amount must be recovered through revenues before an entity can have income. Under GAAP, the capital maintenance concept generally used in income determination is *originally invested dollars* or *nominal dollars.* Income results only if a company recovers more dollars from sales revenue than it originally invested in the asset sold. For example, under GAAP, if you bought shares of Intel common stock for $1,000 and later sold those shares for $1,500, your income would be $500, because you have recovered $500 more than you invested. This is the nominal dollar concept of capital maintenance.

However, persistent inflation in the United States in the 1970s caused many people to question the usefulness of the monetary assumption and the nominal dollar capital maintenance concept currently followed under GAAP. Later in this chapter, we will examine some alternative income determination models that may provide more useful information about earnings in periods of changing prices. We defer our discussion of these alternatives until after we have completed our discussion of the recognition and measurement principles of GAAP.

Modifications of the Basic Principles and Concepts

Under GAAP, the recognition and measurement principles underlying accrual accounting are used to record transactions that are then reported in the financial statements. In some circumstances, however, accountants depart from a strict application of the principles of accrual accounting. Two circumstances that may result in such departures are discussed below.

Conservatism

Many accounting and reporting practices require judgments and estimates, because future economic events are uncertain. **Conservatism** is a practice followed in an effort to ensure that the risk or uncertainty inherent in business situations is adequately considered. Conservatism does not mean there should be deliberate, consistent understatement of net assets and income; it is simply a method of dealing with uncertainty about future cash flows. Under conservatism, when two or more accounting alternatives appear to be equally capable of fulfilling financial reporting objectives, the alternative with the least favorable impact on net income and financial position is chosen. For example, conservatism would result in expensing the cost of an asset over a shorter, rather than a longer, period of time. Companies sometimes are known for using generally liberal or

CONCEPTUAL

Under GAAP, the nominal dollar concept of capital maintenance is normally used.

CONCEPTUAL

Conservatism results in the use of accounting practices with the least favorable impact on net income and financial position.

generally conservative accounting practices. For example, Livent, Inc., is characterized by its chief financial officer as having accounting that is "conservative, rather than liberal-within-GAAP."[22]

Special Industry Practices

Special industry accounting or reporting practices are used in some industries, such as utilities, railroads, oil and gas companies, and investment companies. If the special accounting practices are followed by all companies in an industry, comparability is improved.

DISCLOSURE AND METHODS OF FINANCIAL STATEMENT PRESENTATION

Having discussed GAAP's recognition and measurement principles, we now turn our attention to disclosure and methods of financial statement presentation. These concepts are very important in deciding how information should be displayed in the financial statements and notes to the financial statements in order to satisfy the financial reporting objectives discussed at the beginning of this chapter.

Disclosure

In Chapter 1 we pointed out that securities markets are efficient with respect to *publicly available* information, which includes information provided by financial statements and notes to those statements. Yet recognition of an asset or a liability, or the effects of a transaction, in the financial statements may not provide all the information financial statement users need. Therefore, disclosure of information in addition to that which appears in the financial statements is important. The concept of **disclosure** means that published financial statements and related notes should include any economic information about the accounting entity that is significant enough to affect the decisions of informed and prudent users of the financial statements. Disclosure increases the relevance and reliability of accounting information.

> **CONCEPTUAL**
>
> Any economic information that is significant enough to affect the decisions of informed, prudent users should be disclosed.

The FASB believes there are four purposes of disclosure.[23] First, *disclosures are meant to describe and provide additional relevant measures of items that are recognized on the face of the financial statements.* For some recognized items, such as cash, the account title and the dollar amount are normally sufficient. For other items, however, descriptive information and measures beyond those which appear on the face of the financial statements may be needed to fully inform decision makers. For example, an explanatory footnote disclosure about inventories for a manufacturing company might be needed to provide information regarding the particular inventory system and cost flow assumptions the company uses, as well as a breakdown of total inventory into the amounts for raw materials, work in process, and finished goods.

10   **Describe what the FASB believes are the four purposes of disclosure.**

Second, disclosures describe and provide useful measures of items that are not recognized in the financial statements. Some items do not qualify under GAAP for

[22]"Livent's Accounting May Puzzle the Experts," *The Financial Post* (Toronto), September 23, 1995, Section 1, p. 6.

[23]"Disclosure of Information about Financial Instruments with Off-Balance-Sheet Risk and Financial Instruments with Concentrations of Credit Risk," *Statement of Financial Accounting Standards No. 105* (Norwalk, Conn.: FASB, 1990), paras. 75–85.

recognition in the financial statements, yet information related to those items would be useful to decision makers. Disclosed information about such items might include a description of the company's organizational structure, a summary of the company's significant accounting policies, a discussion of events that occurred between the financial statement date and the date the financial statements were issued (called "subsequent events"), and a commentary on the company's business acquisitions and disposals during the accounting period. Disclosures of certain of these items might include both commentary and dollar amounts or other measures. For example, the dollar amounts of cost incurred and liabilities assumed in a business acquisition would be appropriate disclosures.

Third, disclosures provide information to help investors and creditors assess the risks and potentials of both recognized and unrecognized items. When an asset, a liability, or other element is recognized in the financial statements, the dollar amount reported is only a single-point estimate. Even though it has been determined in accordance with GAAP, a point estimate may not convey the degree of information needed by statement users. Additional information may be necessary to help users assess the inherent uncertainties and the potential effects on the entity of the possible outcomes. For example, CSS Industries, Inc., reported long-term obligations, net of current portion, of $17,865,000 in its 1995 consolidated balance sheet. To provide users with more information about this dollar amount, CSS prepared a substantial footnote (Note 6) identifying the several components of the long-term obligations and describing related interest rates, loan covenants, possible loan extensions, security required by the loans, and long-term obligation maturity dates.

Finally, disclosures provide important information in the interim while accounting issues are being studied in more depth. This type of disclosure is sometimes required by *FASB Statements of Standards*. For example, the Board added a project on accounting and reporting for financial instruments to its agenda in the mid-1980s. Initially, it decided that improved disclosure of information was called for and issued *Statement of Standards No. 105,* "Disclosure of Information about Financial Instruments with Off-Balance-Sheet Risk and Financial Instruments with Concentrations of Credit Risk" (1990) and *Statement of Standards No. 107,* "Disclosure about Fair Value of Financial Instruments" (1991). Later, in 1993, the Board progressed to addressing the accounting issues and published *Statement of Standards No. 115,* "Accounting for Certain Investments in Debt and Equity Securities."

Common methods of providing disclosures include adding notes and clarifying parenthetical comments on the face of the financial statements, and explanatory footnotes and supplementary information following the financial statements. You may want to refer to Exhibit 1–2 (page 7) for a summary of forms of disclosure and examples of items typically disclosed.

Disclosure is arguably even more important when reporting internationally, given the substantial differences in accounting practices that exist worldwide. Indeed, research shows that companies operating in global capital markets voluntarily disclose more information in their financial statements than they are required to—sometimes substantially more.[24] They do this because investors are demanding the extra information, and companies are obliged to provide it in order to secure capital.

There is growing concern about the extensiveness of disclosures in financial statements; some people believe there are too many required disclosures, a condition sometimes characterized as "disclosure overload." The FASB, along with the AICPA, SEC, and other regulatory and professional bodies, is a major source of disclosure requirements. In July 1995 the Board issued a Prospectus calling for research and comment on concerns about disclosures. Although the Board has

---

[24]G. K. Meek and S. J. Gray, "Globalization of Capital Markets and Foreign Listing Requirements: Voluntary Disclosures by Continental European Companies Listed on the London Stock Exchange," *Journal of International Business Studies,* Summer 1989, pp. 315–336.

concluded that disclosure effectiveness and disclosure overload are matters about which opinion is strong, it has not yet decided to make disclosure an agenda item. In the meantime, the FASB is specifically evaluating disclosure concerns as part of every one of its agenda items.

The way in which items are presented in the financial statements is associated with the disclosure issue. In fact, one of the causes of disclosure overload may be the lack of a standardized format for presenting information in the financial statements. In the next section we discuss some of the issues related to methods of presentation.

Methods of Presentation

Methods of financial statement presentation—especially of information about earnings—have generated much discussion and research. The following questions illustrate some considerations with regard to methods of presenting or otherwise disclosing data to help users assess and predict future cash flows, evaluate a company's earnings performance, and in general make intelligent investment decisions necessary for efficient allocation of scarce resources:

1. What guidelines are necessary to distinguish between normal, recurring earnings activities and those that are unusual and nonrecurring?

2. Is information about earnings activities by segments (e.g., product segments and geographical segments) useful? If so, how should segments be defined?

3. Should distinctions be made between costs that vary with volume and costs that remain fixed regardless of changes in volume?

4. Are distinctions between committed and discretionary expenditures helpful in assessing future cash flows?

5. How can financial statement information be presented to reveal a company's liquidity and ability to adapt financially to a changing environment?

6. What level of aggregation or disaggregation of income statement data is necessary to allow users to analyze and assess the components of income?

7. Is a single net income number desirable, or should multiple income measures be disclosed?

8. What type of reporting should be required for economic events that relate to operations in earlier periods?

Conceptually, these questions must be answered by reference to the financial reporting objectives. Chapters 4, 5, and 6 examine financial statements in some detail and provide discussions of the manner in which many of these presentation issues are resolved under GAAP.

LTERNATIVE SYSTEMS OF DETERMINING INCOME

We have now completed our discussion of asset and liability measurement and income determination under conventional standards (GAAP). There are a variety of income determination systems that are conceptual alternatives to GAAP. Any system that might be used to measure a company's income for a given accounting period consists of a combination of (1) a capital maintenance concept and (2) an asset/liability valuation method. For example, GAAP incorporates the nominal dollar capital maintenance concept and the historical cost asset/liability valuation method to determine income. To develop your understanding of income determination systems other than GAAP, in the next section we provide some alternative capital maintenance concepts and asset/liability valuation methods and then illustrate how they can be combined to yield alternative (to GAAP) income determination systems.

Alternative Capital Maintenance Concepts

11 Describe (1) three alternative concepts of capital maintenance and (2) five alternative asset/liability valuation methods.

As stated earlier in the chapter, the general meaning of capital maintenance is that investment must be recovered through revenues before a company can have income. A concept of capital maintenance is necessary to determine the portion of a company's cash inflows that is a return *of* capital (or investment recovery) and the portion that is a return *on* capital (or income). A discussion of three different concepts of capital maintenance follows.

Maintenance of Nominal Dollars

Under the **nominal dollar concept of capital maintenance,** income exists only if a company recovers more dollars from sales revenue than the number of dollars invested in the asset sold. For example, if a retail clothing company purchases a shirt at a cost of $20 and later sells it for $50, nominal dollar income on the sale is $30:

Revenue (cash inflow from sale)	**$50**
Investment to be recovered (return *of* capital)	**(20)**
Income (return *on* capital)	**$30**

As indicated earlier, the nominal dollar concept of capital maintenance is used in GAAP. The nominal dollar concept of capital maintenance is sometimes called financial capital maintenance, as is the case in *FASB Statement of Concepts No. 5.*

Maintenance of General Purchasing Power

Many accountants believe that in periods of inflation, maintenance of the number of dollars is not useful for measuring a company's income. They feel that because the dollar loses general purchasing power in a period of inflation, more useful financial statement data are provided by the **general purchasing power concept of capital maintenance.** Under this concept, income arises only if a company is able to recover more from revenues than the general purchasing power equivalent of its investment.

In the preceding example, if the general price level, such as the consumer price index, doubled from the time the company purchased the inventory until the inventory was sold, income from the sale would be only $10:

Revenue (cash inflow from sale)	**$50**
Investment of general purchasing power to be recovered (return *of* capital):	
$20 × 2	**(40)**
Income (return *on* capital)	**$10**

Because the general price level has doubled since the inventory was purchased, the company would have to sell the shirt for at least $40 to maintain the same level of general purchasing power as it invested in the shirt inventory. Thus, income under the general purchasing power concept of capital maintenance is only one-third ($10, as compared with $30) of that calculated when the nominal dollar capital maintenance concept was used.

The general purchasing power concept of capital maintenance is also called **constant dollar accounting.** The significant feature of this concept is that the measuring units are general price-level adjusted dollars or constant dollars, rather than nominal dollars.

Maintenance of Physical Capital

Another concept of capital maintenance that has received support in inflationary periods is the **physical capital maintenance concept.** Under this concept, income arises only if a company can recover more from sales revenue than the current replacement cost of the item sold. In the clothing store example, if the shirt that originally cost $20 was sold for $50 at a time when the current cost of replacement was $45, income would be $5:

Revenue (cash inflow from sales)	**$50**
Current cost of replacement (return *of* capital)	**(45)**
Income (return *on* capital)	**$ 5**

If the company plans to continue its operations by replacing the shirt and repeating the earnings activity, income will be only $5, because $45 of the $50 cash inflow is necessary to replace the shirt that was sold.

Alternative Asset/Liability Valuation Methods

The second necessary part of any income determination system is an asset and liability valuation method. Different asset and liability valuation methods focus on measuring different attributes of assets and liabilities. Five attributes that can be measured, or valuation methods that can be used, for assets are (1) historical cost, (2) current replacement cost, (3) current exit value, (4) expected exit value, and (5) present value of expected cash flows. The generic term "current value" sometimes is used to describe all of the last four valuation methods, even though each is a different form of current value.

Historical Cost

The historical cost method of valuing assets is used in the GAAP income determination system. The historical cost method initially values assets in terms of the cash or cash equivalent price at the time the asset is acquired. Many accountants prefer the historical cost method because it uses prices from the transaction through which the asset was acquired.

Current Replacement Cost

Current replacement cost is the amount of cash that would have to be paid if an asset, or equivalent asset service, were to be acquired currently. Although historical cost and current replacement cost are the same on the date an asset is acquired, these attributes can be quite different later on. Assume that one of your relatives bought a home in 1988 for $100,000. Because costs have increased in the home building industry, the current cost of replacing this home in 1998 is $160,000, even though the historical cost of the home is $100,000. Under current replacement cost, the home would be reported at $160,000.

Current Exit Value

Current exit value is the amount of cash that would be received currently if an asset were sold under conditions of orderly liquidation. Assume you own 100 shares of AT&T stock. The currently quoted price of an AT&T share on the New York Stock Exchange times the 100 shares that you own, less brokerage commission, is the current exit value of your investment (what you can sell it for) on the date of the quoted price. When assets are to be sold in the normal course of business, current exit value sometimes is called current market selling price.

Expected Exit Value

Expected exit value is the nondiscounted cash flow associated with the expected sale or conversion of an asset at some future time. Risk and the time value of money are ignored. For example, if you hold a $1,000 non-interest-bearing note receivable that is due one year from now, the expected exit value of the receivable (what you expect to receive on the maturity date) is $1,000.

Present Value of Expected Cash Flows

Present value of expected cash flows is similar to expected exit value, except that expected future cash flows are discounted at an appropriate interest rate to reflect risk and the time value of money. If we use the one-year, $1,000 note receivable case just presented, and assume the current market interest rate on notes of similar risk is 10 percent, the present value of the expected cash flows from the note is $909 ($1,000 ÷ 1.10). The present value of $909 means that because of the time value of money, the cash inflow to be received in one year is not worth $1,000 today.

Application of Alternative Methods to Liabilities

The five attributes or valuation methods may be applied to liabilities as follows:

Historical proceeds: the amount of cash or cash equivalent received at the exchange date.

Current proceeds: the amount that would be received if the same liability were incurred currently.

Current exit value: the amount of cash that would have to be paid currently to eliminate or settle the liability.

Expected exit value: the amount of cash expected to be paid in the future to eliminate or settle the liability in the due course of business.

Present value of expected cash flows: same as the expected exit value, except that the future cash flows are discounted at an appropriate rate of interest.

Historical Cost versus Alternative Methods

The conventional accounting system that underlies GAAP often is called the *historical cost system*. (A more appropriate name would be the *historical exchange price system*.) This name means that assets and liabilities generally are measured and recorded at historical cost (historical exchange price). In addition to historical cost, however, other attributes of assets and liabilities are measured and may be reported under GAAP in certain situations. For example, *current cost* is used in lower-of-cost-or-market procedures for inventories. *Current exit value* is used in accounting for certain investments in debt and equity securities, and *expected exit value* is used for short-term accounts receivable and accounts payable. *Present value of expected cash flows* is used for long-term receivables and payables. Moreover, some assets are acquired, and some liabilities incurred, without exchanges.

For example, an asset might be found or given to a firm. In these circumstances there is no exchange price, and some attribute other than historical cost must be measured.

In recent years, the FASB and the accounting profession have given a lot of attention to "fair value" as an alternative to the historical cost method of asset/liability valuation. During the deliberations leading to *Statement of Standards No. 107,* "Disclosures about Fair Value of Financial Instruments," and *Statement of Standards No. 115,* "Accounting for Certain Investments in Debt and Equity Securities," the FASB stated that quoted securities market prices (current exit values), if available, are the best evidence of the fair values of financial instruments. Otherwise, the FASB said, the best estimate of fair value may be based on the quoted market price of a financial instrument with similar characteristics or on valuation techniques such as the present value of estimated future cash flows. More about fair value accounting applied to investments in equity and debt securities is presented in Chapters 13 and 14.

Since several asset and liability valuation methods actually are used in the conventional system, it is misleading to refer to GAAP as a "historical cost system." We believe it is more appropriate to characterize the conventional system that underlies GAAP as a *modified historical cost system.*

CONCEPTUAL

GAAP actually is a modified historical cost system.

The Interrelationship of Capital Maintenance Concept and Asset/Liability Valuation in the Determination of Income

As stated earlier, both a concept of capital maintenance and an asset/liability valuation method are necessary to determine a company's income for an accounting period. From a balance sheet standpoint, asset and liability valuation methods (or measured attributes) are used to determine the total dollar amount of net assets at the end of an accounting period. A specified capital maintenance concept determines how much of this dollar total is necessary to maintain the beginning-of-period invested capital and how much is income:

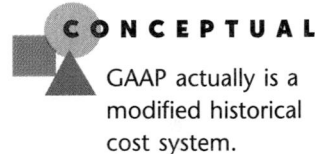

Explain and illustrate the interrelationship between capital maintenance and asset/liability valuation in the determination of income.

Total net assets − Invested capital = Net income
(end of period) (beginning of period) (for the period)

determined by   determined by the
the valuation   concept of capital
method used   maintenance

Exhibit 2–6 demonstrates how capital maintenance and asset/liability valuation interact in income determination. Under alternative 1 in Exhibit 2–6, income for 1998 is zero, because the land is valued at historical cost (historical exchange price) and capital is maintained in nominal dollars. This is the historical cost system, the primary income determination approach used under GAAP. Under alternative 2, the land is valued at its current exit value of $1,500. Because invested capital is to be maintained in nominal dollars, income of $500 results. This value change of $500, recognized as income under alternative 2, sometimes is called a holding gain. Under alternative 3, the land is valued at $1,500, but because the general price level has increased 20 percent during the year, invested capital in end-of-1998 constant dollars is $1,200, and income for 1998 is only $300 (considered a holding gain). Notice that under alternative 3, if the land's

EXHIBIT 2-6	Interaction of Capital Maintenance and Asset Valuation in Income Determination

Facts:

1. Company X organized at the beginning of 1998 with only one asset, land, acquired at a cost of $1,000. The company did not sell the land during 1998.

2. The current exit value of the land increased during 1998 by $500 and was $1,500 at the end of 1998.

3. The general price level increased 20 percent during 1998.

	Net Income for 1998 Under the Following Alternatives:		
Asset Valuation Method/ Capital Maintenance Concept	**1 Historical Cost/Nominal Dollars**	**2 Current Exit Value/Nominal Dollars**	**3 Current Exit Value/General Purchasing Power or Constant Dollars**
Total assets at the end of 1998	$1,000	$1,500	$1,500
Amount needed to maintain invested capital	(1,000)	(1,000)	(1,200)
Net income for 1998	$ –0–	$ 500	$ 300

current exit value had been $1,200 at the end of 1998, income would have been zero, because the $200 increase in the value of the land would have allowed the company to maintain a constant amount of general purchasing power during the year.

UMMARY OF LEARNING OBJECTIVES

1. List and describe the four environmental assumptions that provide the foundation for financial accounting and reporting theory.

The four environmental assumptions are (1) the accounting entity assumption, (2) the periodicity assumption, (3) the going concern assumption, and (4) the monetary assumption. The accounting entity assumption limits the transactions and events that should be reported in an entity's financial statements. The periodicity assumption allows accountants to prepare periodic financial statements during an entity's economic life. The going concern assumption allows accountants to presume an indefinite economic life for the accounting entity unless there is evidence to the contrary. The monetary assumption allows accountants to measure economic events and transactions in terms of dollars with assumed stable purchasing power.

2. List and discuss the three objectives of financial reporting.

The first broad objective of financial reporting focuses on information that is useful in investor and creditor decision making. It specifies that financial reporting should provide information that can be used by all who have a reasonable understanding of business and economic activities, and are willing to learn to use the information properly. The second objective relates to investors' and creditors' interest in receiving cash flows from investments in, or loans to, companies. It also relates investors' and creditors' cash flow prospects to the company's cash flow prospects. Thus, financial reporting should provide information that is useful in assessing potential cash flows to investors and creditors and to the company. The third objective emphasizes the need to provide information about the scarce economic resources needed to carry on economic activity, about claims to those economic resources, and about changes in economic resources and obligations brought about by a company's earnings and other business activities.

3. **Identify and describe the qualitative characteristics of useful accounting information.**

The qualitative characteristics of useful accounting information are:

Decision usefulness. Accounting information should be useful for decision making.

Understandability. The user must be able to understand the information, given reasonable attempts.

Relevance. Accounting information must be capable of making a difference in a decision by either confirming or changing the decision maker's expectations.

Predictive value. If information improves the decision maker's ability to forecast the outcome of past or present events, it has predictive value.

Feedback value. If information confirms or corrects the decision maker's earlier expectation, it has feedback value.

Timeliness. If information is to be capable of affecting a decision, it must be available at the time the decision is to be made.

Reliability. Information is reliable when it actually represents what it is intended to represent, is neutral, and can be verified.

Representational faithfulness. Information is representationally faithful when there is agreement between a financial measure and the economic phenomenon being measured.

Verifiability. Information about which there is a consensus among accountants on its measurement and how to report it is considered to be verifiable.

Neutrality. Information should be neutral, or unbiased, with respect to its impact on users' behaviors.

Comparability. Information should be comparable with similar information about other accounting entities and with similar information about the same accounting entity over time.

4. **Discuss the benefits of versus the constraints on strict application of financial accounting and reporting standards.**

The benefits of reporting particular accounting information should exceed the costs of providing that information. However, because accounting information is a public good, the benefits and costs of that information are difficult, if not impossible, to measure. Furthermore, the benefits cannot always be confined to those who incur the costs, and vice versa. Even so, one of the guidelines followed by the FASB is to prescribe an accounting or reporting requirement only when the expected benefits exceed the expected costs.

5. **Define the elements of the financial statements.**

Assets are defined as probable future economic benefits obtained or controlled by a particular entity as a result of past transactions or events. *Liabilities* are defined as probable future sacrifices of economic benefits arising from present obligations of the accounting entity to transfer assets or provide services to other entities in the future as a result of past transactions or events. *Equity* is the residual interest in the assets of an entity after its total liabilities have been deducted from its total assets. *Revenues* are periodic inflows of assets or settlements of liabilities, or both, as a result of the delivery or production of goods, the rendering of services, or other earnings activities that constitute an entity's primary operations. *Expenses* are the periodic use of assets or the incurring of liabilities, or both, as a result of the delivery or production of goods, the rendering of services, or other earnings activities that constitute an entity's primary operations. *Gains (losses)* are increases (decreases) in equity or net assets that result from peripheral transactions of an entity. *Net income (earnings)* or *net loss* equals revenues plus gains minus expenses and losses.

6. **State the four criteria of the fundamental recognition principle.**

The four criteria of the fundamental recognition principle are:

1. The item to be recognized meets the definition of an element of the financial statements.
2. The item has an attribute that can be measured reliably.
3. Information about the item is relevant.
4. Information about the item is reliable.

7. Describe and give examples of the difference between accrual and cash-basis accounting.

The difference between accrual accounting and cash-basis accounting is the timing of net income. Under accrual accounting, revenues are reported when they are earned and when the amount and timing of the revenue can be reasonably estimated. Expenses are reported in accordance with the matching principle. Under cash-basis accounting, revenues are reported when cash is received, and expenses are reported when cash is paid.

Assume a company begins operations on December 15 and pays its employees on the 15th of each month, making the first payment of wages on January 15. Under accrual accounting, the company would report half a month's wage expense at the end of December. Under cash-basis accounting, there would be no wage expense for December; all the wage expense for the first month of operation would be reported in January.

If a publishing company received $240 in advance from a subscriber for a 24-month subscription to an upscale monthly magazine, no revenue would be reported under accrual accounting until the delivery of the magazines. (For example, $10 of revenue might be recognized with the delivery of each monthly edition of the magazine.) Under cash-basis accounting, the company would report $240 of revenue when the subscription was received, even though nothing had been done to earn the revenue and no magazines had been delivered.

8. Discuss the realization principle and its two criteria.

The realization principle states that revenue should be recognized and reported in the income statement when (1) the amount and timing of revenue are reasonably determinable and (2) the earnings process is complete or virtually complete. The FASB interprets these criteria as meaning that (1) the revenue must be realized (goods or services exchanged for cash or claims to cash) or realizable (assets readily convertible to known amounts of cash or claims to cash) and (2) the revenue must have been earned.

9. Discuss the matching principle and the three general guidelines for applying it.

The matching principle means that expenses incurred in generating revenues should be reported in the same income statement as the revenues generated. The general guidelines for applying the matching principle are (1) associating cause and effect, (2) systematic and rational allocation, and (3) immediate recognition. Expenses should be matched against revenues when they are directly related to the generation of those revenues. In some cases, like depreciation, it is necessary to allocate or match a cost to (record an expense in) those periods in which that cost contributes to creating revenues. Some costs must be recorded as expenses in the period in which they are incurred (immediate recognition), because there is no ascertainable future benefit, or because the future benefits are highly uncertain.

10. Describe what the FASB believes are the four purposes of disclosure.

The four purposes of disclosures are:

1. To describe and provide additional relevant measures of items that are recognized on the face of the financial statements.
2. To describe and provide useful measures of items that are not recognized in the financial statements.
3. To provide information to help investors and creditors assess the risks and potentials of both recognized and unrecognized items.
4. To provide important information in the interim while accounting issues are being studied in more depth.

11. Describe (1) three alternative concepts of capital maintenance and (2) five alternative asset/liability valuation methods.

Three alternative concepts of capital maintenance are:

1. *Maintenance of nominal dollars.* Income exists when a company recovers a greater number of dollars from sales revenue than the number of dollars invested in the asset sold.
2. *Maintenance of general purchasing power.* Income exists only when a company is able to recover more from revenues than the general purchasing power equivalent of its investment.
3. *Maintenance of physical capital.* Income exists only when a company can recover more from sales revenue than the current replacement cost of the item sold.

Five alternative asset valuation methods are:

1. *Historical cost.* Assets are initially valued in terms of the cash or cash equivalent price at the time the asset is acquired. Subsequently, the asset's cost is depreciated, amortized, or depleted over the economic or useful life of the asset.
2. *Current replacement cost.* An asset is valued at the amount of cash that would have to be paid if the asset, or the equivalent asset service, were to be acquired currently.
3. *Current exit value.* An asset is valued at the amount of cash that would be received currently if the asset were sold under conditions of orderly liquidation.
4. *Expected exit value.* An asset is valued at the sum of the nondiscounted future cash flows associated with its expected sale or conversion.
5. *Present value of expected cash flows.* An asset is valued in terms of the discounted future cash flows associated with its expected sale or conversion.

12. Explain and illustrate the interrelationship between capital maintenance and asset/liability valuation in the determination of income.

Both a capital maintenance concept and an asset/liability valuation method are necessary to determine a company's income for an accounting period. An asset/liability valuation method is used to determine the total dollar amount of net assets at the end of an accounting period. A capital maintenance concept determines how much of that dollar total is necessary to maintain the beginning-of-period invested capital and how much is income. To illustrate, if the combination of historical cost (an asset/liability valuation method) and maintenance of nominal dollars (a capital maintenance concept) is used to determine income, a company would have income when the nominal dollar amount of its net assets at the end of the period, valued in terms of historical cost, exceeds the nominal dollar amount of its net assets at the beginning of that period, valued in terms of historical cost.

KEY TERMS

accounting entity assumption 41

accounting equation 53

accrual accounting 59

assets 51

balance sheet 56

capital maintenance 66

cash-basis accounting 59

comparable 48

comprehensive income 54

conservatism 66

consistency 49

constant dollar accounting 70

current exit value 71

current replacement cost 71

decision usefulness 45

disclosure 67

earnings 54

equity 53

expected exit value 72

expenses 53

feedback value 46

gains 53

general purchasing power concept of capital maintenance 70

going concern assumption 42

historical cost principle 62

income statement 56

information benefit vs. cost 49

liabilities 52

losses 53

matching principle 65

materiality 50

monetary assumption 42

net income (or loss) 54

neutrality 48

nominal dollar concept of capital maintenance 70

objectives of financial reporting 43

other comprehensive income 55

owners' equity 53

periodicity assumption 42

physical capital concept maintenance 71

QUESTIONS

Q 2-I.   Four environmental assumptions underlie financial accounting and reporting. What are they?

Q 2-2.   Discuss the accounting entity assumption.

Q 2-3.   Can a distinction be made between a legal entity and an accounting entity? Explain.

Q 2-4.   What is meant by the periodicity assumption?

Q 2-5.   What is the going concern assumption?

Q 2-6.   What is assumed under the monetary assumption?

Q 2-7.   What is the general role of financial accounting and reporting?

Q 2-8.   List and discuss the objectives of financial reporting.

Q 2-9.   Given the need for accounting information that is useful for decision making, what are the two primary qualities of useful accounting information?

Q 2-10. What does it mean for accounting information to be relevant? What are the components of relevant information?

Q 2-II. What is the nature of reliable accounting information?

Q 2-12. What does it mean to say that information has representational faithfulness?

Q 2-13. In the context of accounting, what does verifiability mean?

Q 2-14. Why does the fact that accounting information is a public good cause a problem in operationalizing the traditional cost-versus-benefit rule for choosing among alternatives?

Q 2-15. Why is materiality important in financial accounting and reporting? What does materiality mean in financial accounting and reporting practice?

Q 2-16. What is an asset? A liability?

Q 2-17. Distinguish between revenues and gains, and between expenses and losses.

Q 2-18. Explain what is meant by *comprehensive income,* and how it differs from net income (earnings).

Q 2-19. Economic events may be classified by the nature of the event and by the effect of the event on the financial statement elements. Discuss each classification.

Q 2-20. What are the five basic principles underlying the conventional financial accounting and reporting system?

Q 2-21. Distinguish between accrual accounting and cash-basis accounting.

Q 2-22. Explain the historical cost principle.

Q 2-23. How is the historical cost principle modified when assets are acquired at zero cost to an entity?

Q 2-24. Distinguish between revenue realization and revenue recognition.

Q 2-25. What is meant by the phrase *the earnings process,* and what are the components of the earnings process for (1) a merchandising company, (2) a manufacturing company, and (3) a service organization?

Q 2-26. What are the four criteria of the fundamental recognition principle?

Q 2-27. Why is the realization principle important?

Q 2-28. What are the two criteria of the realization principle?

Q 2-29. Under what circumstances might revenue be recognized at the completion of production?

Q 2-30. Under what circumstances should revenue recognition be deferred until cash has been collected?

Q 2-31. Explain the matching principle. Describe the general guidelines that are used in matching expenses and revenues.

Q 2-32. Discuss the following concepts of capital maintenance: (1) maintenance of nominal dollars, (2) maintenance of general purchasing power, and (3) maintenance of physical units.

Q 2-33. Explain the concept of conservatism within the context of financial accounting and reporting.

Q 2-34. To what does the phrase *attributes to be measured* refer?

Q 2-35. List and discuss five attributes of elements of financial statements that could be measured.

Q 2-36. Why might the conventional financial accounting and reporting system best be referred to as a *modified* historical cost system?

Q 2-37. According to the FASB, what are the four purposes of disclosure?

CASES

C 2-1. **ENVIRONMENTAL ASSUMPTIONS** The economic environment of financial accounting and reporting is relatively complex. As often is the case in complex situations, some simplifying assumptions about the business and economic environment are needed as a foundation for the theory and practice of financial accounting and reporting.

REQUIRED Describe the environmental assumptions that underlie the theory and practice of financial accounting and reporting, and discuss how each assumption affects financial accounting and reporting. For each assumption, give an accounting or reporting practice that seems to be based primarily, if not entirely, on that assumption.

C 2-2. **THE ACCOUNTING ENTITY ASSUMPTION** The concept of the accounting entity often is considered to be the most fundamental of the accounting concepts, one that pervades all of accounting.

REQUIRED **1. a)** What is an accounting entity?
  b) Explain why the accounting entity assumption is so fundamental that it pervades all of accounting.
2. For each of the following, indicate whether the accounting entity assumption is applicable; discuss and give illustrations.
  a) A unit created by or under law.
  b) A product-line segment of an enterprise.
  c) A combination of legal units and/or product-line segments.
  d) All of the activities of an owner or a group of owners.
  e) An industry.
  f) The economy of the United States.

C 2-3. **FINANCIAL REPORTING OBJECTIVES** Recently, a potential investor entered your brokerage office and inquired about investing in common stocks. He said he was interested in returns through dividends and market price appreciation of the stock, and he had concluded that financial statements of publicly held firms were of absolutely no use to him in evaluating investment alternatives. In fact, he was of the opinion that financial statements published in annual reports were of little or no value to society's allocation of scarce resources among competing investments.

REQUIRED Write a response to the potential investor outlining the following:
1. The general role of financial reporting.
2. How financial reporting objectives meet that role.
3. How published financial statement information may be useful in evaluating possible cash flows to individual investors.

(AICPA, adapted)

C 2-4. **FINANCIAL REPORTING OBJECTIVES** Assume you belong to a country club that is the "in" place for young professionals in your community. In addition to a number of CPAs, such as yourself, the club's membership includes doctors, dentists, lawyers, and members of several other professions. One day you and a few other club members, who are not accountants, are discussing the purposes served by your respective professions. A lawyer member of the group asserts that "accountants are only in it for the money" and that "everyone knows that financial statements are useless because financial reporting is intended to help management keep the stockholders in the dark about what's going on." Being offended by the lawyer's assertion and mildly amused by what seems to you to be a case of the "pot calling the kettle black," you are determined to convince the rest of the group that the lawyer is wrong.

REQUIRED For the benefit of the lawyer and the others who are discussing their professions' roles and purposes, write a short paper stating and explaining the objectives of financial reporting. Go into some detail regarding the intent of each objective, how the objectives are related to each other, and how they relate to the general role of financial reporting.

C 2-5. **FINANCIAL REPORTING IN THE '90s: A CALL FOR CHANGE** This case is adapted from a presentation by Lawrence Weinbach, Managing Partner and Chief Executive of Andersen Worldwide (Arthur Andersen/Andersen Consulting), given to the Institute of Management Accountants in September 1995:

> . . . we have reached a time when the very nature of the profession is changing, as the demands for, and expectations of, financial information have evolved . . . It is within this framework—the demands of a changing global marketplace—that I suggest we must face two significant issues: (1) *Our present financial reporting model is broken.* It is failing to keep pace with change, and not always providing the most useful information to the marketplace. The current model focuses only on hard assets. I believe that we must provide information about a company's soft assets, which are the "drivers" of a company's future cash flows and value in the marketplace. There are several categories of soft assets that should be considered in developing a new financial reporting paradigm—measuring knowledge capital, accounting for software and technology, reporting on intellectual property, and the value of human capital. (2) *Whether historical financial information is what the marketplace really wants and needs, or whether there should be greater emphasis on more forward-looking information.* Technology has created an information explosion. Our predecessors had to worry about whether they had enough information to make intelligent decisions. Our problem is just the opposite. We are drowning in information. When it comes to providing management and investor information, the traditional financial statement is not as important as it once was. A growing volume of information with a forward-looking perspective is available over multiple on-line, easy-access data bases.

REQUIRED For each of the above two issues, write a paragraph either agreeing or disagreeing with the suggestions made by Mr. Weinbach. Be sure your position is supported by the financial reporting objectives, qualitative characteristics, and other conceptual material covered in this chapter.

C 2-6. **INTERRELATIONSHIP OF VALUATION AND STEWARDSHIP** In its 1994 "Comprehensive Report," the AICPA's Special Committee on Financial Reporting (commonly called the Jenkins' Committee) made the following two statements:

> An investor's primary objective is to form opinions about the absolute and relative value of companies and their equity securities. (p. 18)

> A creditor's primary objective is to assess the ability of a company to meet its obligations related to current or future debt. (p. 18)

The statement about investor's objectives emphasizes valuation, while the statement about creditor's objectives relates more to stewardship.

REQUIRED Write a brief paper commenting on how financial reporting can address the informational needs of both those who are concerned about valuation and those who are concerned about stewardship. Explain, using examples, how valuation decision making and assessing stewardship are interrelated.

C 2-7. **QUALITATIVE CHARACTERISTICS** Assume you are a member of the FASB technical staff. You have been assigned to provide corporate accountants with guidance on how to choose among alternative financial accounting and reporting practices. You have decided to schedule several free regional seminars for this purpose, and to answer any questions the participants may have about particular accounting or reporting choices they face.

REQUIRED Write some opening comments for the seminars, discussing the qualitative characteristics of useful accounting information and indicating the importance of these characteristics to choices among alternative accounting and reporting practices.

C 2-8. **QUALITATIVE CHARACTERISTICS** You are engaged in the audit of Barstow, Inc., which opened its first branch office in 1998. During the audit Nancy Barstow, president, raises the question of the accounting treatment of the operating loss of the branch office for its first year.

Barstow proposes to capitalize the operating loss as a start-up cost to be amortized over a five-year period. She states that branch offices of other firms in the same field generally suffer a first-year operating loss that is invariably capitalized, and you are aware of this practice. She argues, therefore, that the loss should be capitalized so that the accounting will be "conservative." Further, she argues that the accounting must be "consistent" with established industry practice.

REQUIRED Discuss the president's use of the words *conservative* and *consistent* from the standpoint of accounting terminology. Discuss the accounting treatment you would recommend.

(AICPA, adapted)

C 2-9. **QUALITATIVE CHARACTERISTICS** The FASB has issued six *Statements of Financial Accounting Concepts*. These *Statements* describe objectives and fundamentals that are intended to be the basis for developing financial accounting and reporting standards. The objectives identify the goals and purposes of financial reporting. The fundamentals are the underlying concepts of financial accounting—concepts that guide the selection of transactions, events, and circumstances to be accounted for; their recognition and measurement; and the means of summarizing and communicating them to interested parties.

The purpose of *Statement of Financial Accounting Concepts No. 2*, "Qualitative Characteristics of Accounting Information," is to examine the characteristics that make accounting information useful. The characteristics or qualities of information discussed in *Statement of Concepts No. 2* are the ingredients that make information useful and are the qualities to be sought when accounting choices are made.

REQUIRED
1. Identify and discuss the benefits that can be expected to be derived from the FASB's conceptual framework study.
2. What is the most important quality for accounting information as identified in *Statement of Concepts No. 2*? Explain why it is the most important.
3. *Statement of Concepts No. 2* describes a number of key characteristics or qualities for accounting information. Briefly discuss the importance of any three of these qualities for financial reporting purposes.

(IMA, adapted)

C 2-10. **RELEVANCE AND RELIABILITY** D. Miller recently joined the financial reporting division of Hanson Industries. Miller's initial position in the company is in the current reporting practices section, which is responsible for making all of Hanson's external financial statements and reports conform to relevant Financial Accounting Standards Board pronouncements.

The head of the current reporting practices section, S. Davis, is considering the possibility of supplementing Hanson Industries' financial statements with a report of the current replacement costs of all the company's assets. Davis has just returned from a three-day current reporting issues conference at a local university, at which one of the speakers stated that "financial reporting issues usually boil down to assessing the relevance and reliability of the information to be reported." Davis cannot remember much of what the speaker said to clarify this statement and is uncertain about what the statement means. Davis assigns Miller to prepare a brief report about the nature of relevance and reliability in the context of accounting information. In addition, Davis wants Miller to comment on relevance and reliability as they relate to the issue of providing supplementary replacement cost data for Hanson's assets.

REQUIRED Write Miller's report.

C 2-11. **NEUTRALITY** Watson Company is a manufacturer of heavy equipment that employs almost 2,500 people. In addition to having a very good pension plan for its retirees, Watson provides health care benefits to employees and their spouses from the time of the employee's retirement until both the employee and the spouse are deceased. Watson's practice has been to record health care expense in the accounting period in which health care benefits are actually paid. No attempt has been made to estimate the amount of future health care benefits that may be paid to retired employees and their spouses, nor has any liability for future health care payments been shown on Watson's balance sheet.

Watson's chief financial officer reads in *The Wall Street Journal* that the Financial Accounting Standards Board has established a requirement that companies must report a liability for any commitments they have to their employees to pay postretirement benefits such as health care. His reaction to this report is that Watson cannot tolerate having a liability on its balance sheet of the magnitude that will result from the FASB's new requirement. Therefore, his view is that Watson probably will substantially reduce future health care benefits in order to minimize its reported liability.

The chief financial officer shares his opinion with his assistant who reacts by saying, "It's too bad the FASB took an action that probably will result in economic hardship for our employees. Why can't they stick to requiring accounting practices that don't have such adverse economic consequences?"

REQUIRED   Write a statement to Watson's chief financial officer and his assistant. Explain neutrality as a quality of useful accounting information, and comment on the relationship between FASB neutrality in standard setting and the economic consequences issue. As part of your statement, indicate how FASB neutrality relates to the issue of establishing accounting and reporting standards for postretirement benefits.

C 2-12.   **THE MATERIALITY CONCEPT**   Your friend has started a small manufacturing business. Recently, she had her initial meeting with a CPA about preliminary drafts of the first year's financial statements. During that meeting, the CPA mentioned "materiality" several times. Your friend has asked you to help her understand the materiality concept.

REQUIRED   Write a memorandum to your friend about the meaning of the materiality concept, indicating its essential characteristics. Comment on why materiality might be considered the most important concept in financial accounting and reporting.

C 2-13.   **FINANCIAL STATEMENT ELEMENTS**   Dave's Engine Repair is a relatively new business that repairs engines on a "carry-in" as well as a contract basis. The management of the company has never fully understood what constitutes each of the elements of financial statements. As a result, each year there are some transactions or events for which the management has difficulty determining the appropriate accounting treatment. For example, in the current year management is uncertain about how to account for the following transactions and events:

a)   The city required the company to put a sidewalk across company property parallel to the street.

b)   The company signed an agreement to buy engine parts for small engines from Jason Distributing for the next two years.

c)   Full payment was received in advance for a four-year motorcycle engine maintenance contract with a local motorcycle club.

d)   A three-year insurance policy covering the company building and equipment was purchased and paid in full.

e)   Several old engine-boring machines were sold in anticipation of replacing them with new models.

REQUIRED   Write a brief general description of what constitutes assets, liabilities, revenues, expenses, gains, and losses, respectively, and use your general descriptions to tell the management of Dave's Engine Repair how to account for each of the transactions and events listed above.

C 2-14.   **FINANCIAL STATEMENT ELEMENTS: ASSETS**   The general ledger of New Views, a corporation engaged in the development and production of television programs for commercial sponsorship, contains the following accounts before amortization at the end of the current year:

ACCOUNT	DEBIT BALANCE
Madison Heights	$58,000
Wilderness Adventure	46,000
Destiny	17,200
The Home Chef	11,000
Studio rearrangement	6,100

An examination of contracts and records reveals the following information:

a)   The first two accounts listed above represent the total cost of completed programs that were televised during the accounting period just ended. Under the terms of an existing contract, *Madison Heights* will be rerun during the next accounting period, at a fee equal to 50 percent of the fee for the first televising of the program. The contract for the first run produced $400,000 of revenue. The contract with the sponsor of *Wilderness Adventure* provides that he may, at his option, rerun the program during the next season at a fee of 75 percent of the fee for the first televising of the program.

b) The balance in the *Destiny* account is the cost of a new program that has just been completed and is being considered by several companies for commercial sponsorship.

c) The balance in the *The Home Chef* account represents the cost of a partially completed program for a projected series that has been abandoned.

d) The balance of the studio rearrangement account consists of payments made to a firm of engineers that prepared a report relative to the more efficient use of existing studio space and equipment.

REQUIRED

1. Which of the above accounts should be considered assets? Give reasons for your answers.

2. How would you report each of the accounts in the financial statements of New Views? Explain.

(AICPA, adapted)

C 2-15. **FINANCIAL STATEMENT ELEMENTS** Ryan Corporation purchased $170,000 of computer equipment for $120,000 cash and an obligation to deliver an unspecified number of shares of its $10 par common stock, with a market value of $15,000, on January 1 of each year for the next five years. Hence, $75,000 in market value of common shares will be required to discharge the $50,000 balance due on the equipment.

The corporation immediately acquired 3,000 shares of its own stock for $45,000, expecting the market value of the stock to increase substantially before the delivery dates. A total of 2,500 of these shares, costing $37,500, were subsequently issued in settlement of the equipment contract.

REQUIRED

1. Discuss the propriety of recording the cost of the equipment as:
a) $120,000 (the cash payment).
b) $170,000 (the cash equivalent price of the equipment).
c) $195,000 (the $120,000 cash payment plus the $75,000 market value of the stock that must be issued in order to settle the obligation in accordance with the terms of the agreement).
d) $157,500 (the $120,000 cash payment plus the $37,500 cost of the 2,500 shares issued for the equipment).

2. Discuss the arguments for treating the obligation as:
a) A liability.
b) Common stock subscribed (part of stockholders' equity).

3. Would any of your answers to part 2 be different if previously unissued shares had been used to settle the obligation?

4. Discuss the arguments for treating the corporation's repurchased shares as (*a*) an asset; (*b*) a reduction in stockholders' equity.

5. Has the corporation earned revenue or made a gain by holding its own shares while their market value increased?

C 2-16. **REVENUES, EXPENSES, ASSETS, AND NET LOSS** The following information relating to the movie *Forrest Gump* was taken from "Now You See It, Now You Don't," *Forbes,* June 5, 1995, pp. 42–43.

Released last July, Paramount Pictures' *Forrest Gump* has grossed over $657 million at box offices around the world. That's not counting videocassette and sound-track revenues. It's before licensing fees on such products as *Forrest Gump* wristwatches, Ping-Pong paddles, and cookbooks. Larry Gerbrandt, a senior analyst with Paul Kagan Associates, figures *Gump* could generate up to $350 million in cash flow for Paramount's parent, Viacom, Inc.

But, believe it or not, the film lost money. That's right. By Hollywood standards it "lost" money, $62 million through December 31, 1994. How do you show a loss on one of the most profitable Hollywood properties of all time? You get yourself a Hollywood accountant. Here's what they cooked up for the movie through December 31, according to a confidential net profit statement:

After splitting the box office take with the theater owners, about 50-50, Paramount received $191 million in gross *Gump* receipts. Right off the top

Paramount keeps for itself something called a "distribution fee" equal to 32 percent of gross. What exactly is this distribution fee? It's not really to cover the costs of getting the movie out and to the public. That's covered with a separate category called "distribution expense," which includes advertising, making prints, holding screenings, throwing a premiere party, transporting and storing film reels. Paramount claimed these expenses came to some $67 million. No, the "distribution fee" isn't for these things. It's just a rake-off by Paramount; almost pure profit. In this case, $61.6 million through the end of last year (1994). Paramount tacked on another charge: an advertising "overhead" fee equal to 10 percent of the distribution expenses. Again, this is not an expense at all, just another way of siphoning some profits. Another $6.7 million.

Okay, add up all the "distribution" charges and they come to $135 million. But so far we haven't allowed anything for the cost of making the damned thing. That was $112 million—"negative costs," the Hollywood bean counters call them. Does that sound like a lot of money to shoot a flick? Well, actor Tom Hanks and director Robert Zemeckis each got around $20 million of the $112 million (with more to come). Paramount got into the act, here, too. Included in "negative costs" is $14.5 million for studio overhead, a charge equal to 15 percent of the cost of making the film.

And, of course, it wanted to be paid for the money tied up in making the film. That added a separate $6 million in "interest on negative costs." . . . With this kind of bookkeeping, anyone can lose money. Sure enough, Paramount claimed *Gump* lost $62 million through year's end (1994).

REQUIRED   Write a short paper commenting on the accounting treatments given to the various items mentioned in the *Forbes* article. Your discussion should include GAAP definitions for revenues, expenses, assets, and net loss, and should provide analyses of the *Gump* accounting procedures in terms of the GAAP definitions. Where appropriate, indicate what you think should have been accounted for differently by the *Gump* accountants, and give reasons why.

C 2-17.   **EARNINGS VS. COMPREHENSIVE INCOME**   In "Is a Second Income Statement Needed?" (*Journal of Accountancy,* April 1996, pp. 69–72), D. R. Beresford, L. T. Johnson, and C. L. Reither mention that several important nonowner changes in equity are taken directly to equity in the balance sheet and are not included in the traditional income statement. They go on to say that the FASB is concerned about this situation and feels reporting comprehensive income, which would include items not included in traditional net income (earnings), would enhance the understandability of the financial statements.

REQUIRED   Write a memorandum discussing what is included in traditional net income, what is meant by comprehensive income, and how net income and comprehensive income differ. In addition, comment on how comprehensive income might be reported and on how the display of comprehensive income would relate to the display of net income.

C 2-18.   **ACCRUAL VS. CASH-BASIS ACCOUNTING**   Generally accepted accounting principles require the use of accrual accounting in the determination of income.

REQUIRED   1.   How does accrual accounting affect the determination of income? Include in your discussion what constitutes an accrual and give some examples of accruals.
2.   Contrast accrual accounting with cash-basis accounting.

C 2-19.   **CASH-BASIS VS. ACCRUAL ACCOUNTING**   Bob Lemon, owner of Lemon's Retail Hardware, states that he calculates income on a cash basis. At the end of each year he takes a physical inventory and calculates the cost of all merchandise on hand. To this amount he adds the ending balance of accounts receivable because he considers the related goods to be a part of inventory (not yet sold) on the cash basis. He deducts from this total the ending balance of accounts payable for merchandise (because he considers such goods not yet "bought"), to arrive at what he calls inventory (net).

The following information has been taken from Lemon's cash-basis income statements for the years indicated:

	2000	1999	1998
Cash received	$ 173,000	$ 164,000	$150,000
Cost of goods sold:			
Inventory (net), Jan. 1	$ 8,000	$ 11,000	$ 3,000
Total purchases	109,000	100,000	95,000
Goods available for sale	$ 117,000	$ 111,000	$ 98,000
Inventory (net), Dec. 31	(1,000)	(8,000)	(11,000)
Cost of goods sold	$(116,000)	$(103,000)	$ (87,000)
Gross margin	$ 57,000	$ 61,000	$ 63,000

Additional information is as follows for the years indicated:

	2000	1999	1998
Cash sales	$151,000	$147,000	$141,000
Credit sales	24,000	18,000	14,000
Accounts receivable, Dec. 31	8,000	6,000	5,000
Accounts payable for merchandise, Dec. 31	33,000	22,000	13,000

REQUIRED

1. Without reference to the specific situation described above, discuss cash-basis and accrual accounting and indicate their conceptual merits.
2. Is the gross margin for Lemon's Retail Hardware being calculated on a cash basis? Evaluate and explain the approach used with illustrative calculations of the cash-basis gross margin for 1999.
3. Explain why the gross margin for Lemon's Retail Hardware shows a decrease, while sales and cash receipts are increasing.

(AICPA, adapted)

C 2-20.   **ASSUMPTIONS AND PRINCIPLES**   The current financial reporting practices followed by business organizations reflect the growth and development of the U.S. and world economies, and the informational needs of today's sophisticated users of financial reports. Since the Middle Ages, when simple reports of stewardship were prepared, the scope of accounting information has been increasing, as has the responsibility for its content. From the beginning of the Industrial Revolution, when businesses became separate legal entities and the emphasis on financial position began to emerge, accounting information has evolved to meet the objectives of those supplying and relying on capital to fulfill the needs of society. Today the concept of income has taken on greater importance and the measurement of earnings is more closely scrutinized in both the public and private sectors. Thus, the evolution of financial reporting has witnessed a shift from an emphasis on financial position to an emphasis on income, cash flows, and the details of these items, which often are disclosed in the notes accompanying the financial statements.

REQUIRED

1. Identify some of the external users of general purpose financial statements and describe the contexts in which they use the statements.
2. Several basic assumptions are critical to the development of accounting. If a user does not understand the basic assumptions made by accountants, he or she cannot understand the information that is presented. Explain each of the following basic assumptions of accounting and indicate its effect on general purpose financial statements:
   a) Accounting entity assumption.
   b) Periodicity assumption.
   c) Going concern assumption.
   d) Monetary unit assumption.
3. Basic principles of accounting relate to how assets, liabilities, revenues, and expenses are to be identified, measured, and reported. Explain each of the following basic

principles of accounting and indicate its impact on the presentation of general purpose financial statements:

a) Historical cost principle.

b) Realization principle.

c) Matching principle.

(IMA, adapted)

C 2-21. **THE FUNDAMENTAL RECOGNITION PRINCIPLE** You and a friend decide to establish a small antiques business. Your friend has a great deal of experience with antiques, and her responsibilities in the new business are to be primarily acquiring, grading, and selling antiques. You have a business background, with expertise in finance and accounting. Your responsibilities will be obtaining capital and accounting for the firm's transactions.

One day, your friend asks how you know when an asset, a liability, a revenue, or an expense exists and should be recorded in the firm's accounts. You respond that you rely on the "fundamental recognition principle."

REQUIRED To help clarify your response to your friend, identify the four fundamental criteria that should be met before an item is recorded in the accounts. In addition, mention any other conditions or circumstances that may constrain the accounting procedures or practices applied to an item.

C 2-22. **REVENUE RECOGNITION** Revenue earned by a business entity is recognized for accounting purposes when the transaction is recorded. In some situations, revenue is recognized approximately as it is earned in the economic sense. In other situations, however, accountants have developed guidelines for recognizing revenue by other criteria, such as at the point of sale.

REQUIRED Write three paragraphs explaining (1) why revenue is often recognized as earned at time of sale, and justify the practice; (2) in what situations it would be appropriate to recognize revenue as the production activity takes place; and (3) at what times, other than those included in your first two paragraphs, it may be appropriate to recognize revenue.

(AICPA, adapted)

C 2-23. **REVENUE RECOGNITION** LeaseCo was organized in 1998 to bid on natural gas leases. LeaseCo resells the leases on which it bids to gas exploration companies. Because considerable time, effort, and cost are incurred in gathering information for purposes of submitting bids, LeaseCo sells the leases before it actually acquires them. It collects the sale price shortly after a sale is made. If LeaseCo is unable to obtain the lease, it refunds 95 percent of the sale price to the buyer and keeps the other 5 percent to cover the cost, time, and effort of gathering information associated with the bidding process.

LeaseCo's management is uncertain about when to recognize revenue in connection with its bidding operation, and has asked you to evaluate the following recognition alternatives and to make a recommendation as to when revenue should be recognized. The alternatives are:

a) When the lease is sold to the exploration company, subject to LeaseCo's obtaining the lease.

b) When the cash is collected from the exploration company.

c) When LeaseCo incurs the costs associated with the bidding process.

d) When the lease is obtained by LeaseCo.

REQUIRED Evaluate the above alternatives and select the appropriate point for revenue recognition. Give reasons for your recommendation.

C 2-24. **REVENUE RECOGNITION** After you present your report on your examination of Liston Publishing Company's financial statements to its board of directors, one of the new directors expresses surprise that the income statement assumes that an equal proportion of the revenue is earned with the publication of every issue of the company's magazine. He feels that the "crucial event" in the process of earning revenue in the magazine business is the cash sale of a subscription. He says that he does not understand why most of the revenue cannot be "realized" in the period of the sale.

REQUIRED **1.** List the various accepted methods for recognizing revenue in the accounts and explain when the methods are appropriate.

2. Discuss the propriety of timing the realization of revenue in Liston Publishing Company's account with:

a) The cash sale of a magazine subscription.

b) The publication of the magazine every month.

c) Both events, by realizing a portion of the revenue with cash sale of a magazine subscription and a portion of the revenue with the publication of the magazine every month.

(AICPA, adapted)

C 2-25. **REVENUE REALIZATION AND RECOGNITION** Parson Racing Tecnics is a small, diversified company that builds high-performance racing cars for retail sale, leases a limited number of high-performance racing cars to professional drivers on an annual basis, and provides maintenance service to several racing teams under long-term maintenance contracts. It takes Parson as long as three years to build a car for sale or lease.

When a car is built and sold on a custom basis, its selling price is received in several payments that occur throughout the production process. The contracts on leased cars call for one-half of the lease amount to be paid to Parson on the first day of the lease and one-half of the lease amount to be paid on the last day of the lease. All maintenance service contracts specify that Parson is to be paid a flat fee at the time of signing the contract and that parts as well as labor in excess of 100 hours per contract will be billed at the time the service is rendered.

The management of Parson is uncertain about when revenue should be recognized in each of its three lines of business and has come to you, a local accountant, for advice.

REQUIRED   Write a short response to Parson addressing the following:

1. The distinction between earning revenue, recognition of revenue, and realization of revenue.
2. The circumstances that justify recognition of revenue (*a*) during production, (*b*) at the completion of production, and (*c*) during cash collection.
3. The formulation of a definition of revenue realization that encompasses all the alternatives in such a way that they are not considered exceptions. Justify your definition with respect to each alternative.
4. Specific guidance for Parson as to when revenue should be recognized in each of its three lines of business.

C 2-26. **EXPENSE RECOGNITION** Quick Start sells and builds shell houses—frame structures that are completely finished on the outside, but are unfinished on the inside except for flooring, partition studding, and ceiling joists. Shell houses are sold chiefly to customers who are handy with tools and who have time to do the interior wiring, plumbing, wall completion and finishing, and other work necessary to make the shell houses livable dwellings.

Quick Start buys shell houses from a manufacturer in unassembled packages consisting of all lumber, roofing, doors, windows, and similar materials necessary to complete a shell house. Upon commencing operations in a new area, Quick Start buys or leases land as a site for its local warehouse, field office, and display houses. Sample display houses are erected at a total cost of from $30,000 to $40,000, including the cost of the unassembled packages. The chief cost element of the display houses is the unassembled packages, since construction is a short, low-cost operation. Old sample models are torn down or altered into new models every three to seven years. Sample display houses have little salvage value because dismantling and moving costs amount to nearly as much as the cost of an unassembled package.

REQUIRED   1. A choice must be made between (*a*) expensing the costs of sample display houses in the period in which the expenditure is made and (*b*) spreading the costs over more than one period. Discuss the advantages of each method.
2. For 1b, discuss amortizing the costs of sample display houses on the basis of time versus on the basis of the number of shell houses expected to be sold.

(AICPA, adapted)

C 2-27. **EXPENSE RECOGNITION** An accountant must be familiar with the concepts involved in determining earnings of a business entity. The amount of earnings reported for a business entity is dependent on the proper recognition, in general, of revenue and expense for a given time period. In some situations, costs are recognized as expenses at the time of product sale; in other situations, guidelines have been developed for recognizing costs as expenses or losses by other criteria.

REQUIRED   1. Explain the rationale for recognizing costs as expenses at the time of product sale.
2. What is the rationale for treating costs as expenses of a period rather than assigning the costs to an asset? Explain.
3. In what general circumstances would it be appropriate to treat a cost as an asset instead of as an expense? Explain.

4. Some expenses are assigned to specific accounting periods on the basis of systematic and rational allocation of asset cost. Explain the underlying rationale for recognizing expenses on the basis of systematic and rational allocation of asset cost.

5. Identify the necessary conditions in which it would be appropriate to treat a cost as a loss.

C 2-28. **EXPENSE RECOGNITION: AN ETHICAL DILEMMA** Deb Johnson had successfully operated a chain of health and fitness centers in Europe for many years. She opened her first center in the United States in 1998. The center was located in Los Angeles. Johnson planned to expand to several additional cities within five years.

David White was hired to help prepare Johnson's first set of financial statements for the year ended December 31, 1998. White discovered that Johnson had capitalized as a deferred charge $20,000 of advertising cost. Johnson's intention was to amortize the deferred charge over a five-year period. White questioned Johnson about the treatment of the advertising cost and was informed that the $20,000 was spent before opening the Los Angeles center. According to Johnson, it was customary to offer 30-day discount memberships before opening a center in order to attract a large number of initial members. The advertising cost had been incurred in selling the preopening promotional memberships. All advertising costs incurred after opening the center were expensed in 1998. Johnson indicated that she had followed the practice of capitalizing preopening promotional advertising costs for years in accounting for her European operations.

After listening to Johnson's explanation, White informed her that the preopening advertising cost should be expensed in 1998, because it was material in amount and could not be shown with reasonable certainty to yield a future benefit to the center. Johnson responded that, based on past experience, the members who joined during the preopening promotional period usually renewed their memberships for at least five years and, therefore, a five-year deferral period was appropriate. White persisted in expressing his viewpoint until Johnson interrupted him to say, "I have been following this practice for many years. It is especially important to show the highest possible earnings during 1998 because I hope to raise investment capital in 1999 for planned future expansion. If you cannot support me in this matter, then I will find an accountant who can support me."

White did not know what to do. He knew that his position with Johnson's Health and Fitness Center held great promise for the future growth and expansion of his accounting practice with emerging businesses. Still, White did not feel comfortable with Johnson's treatment of the preopening advertising costs.

REQUIRED Discuss the ethical and professional concerns that exist for White in deciding on a course of action. What would you do? Why?

C 2-29. **THE MATCHING PRINCIPLE** Mary Owens is planning to finance most of her college education with her earnings from being the owner and manager of a Nice'N Cold ice cream franchise in Willis, Florida. Nice'N Cold ice cream is sold nationwide through franchises like Mary's, which use neighborhood ice cream trucks. Mary recently obtained her five-year franchise by paying a $100,000 fee to the national office of Nice'N Cold. This fee entitles Mary to use the Nice'N Cold name and logo, to buy her ice cream wholesale from the national distribution center, and to take advantage of any nationwide advertising campaigns for Nice'N Cold.

In addition to the franchise fee, Mary determines that her business expenses will include: annual interest on the $130,000 she borrowed from her parents, the cost of the ice cream she sells, the cost of two delivery trucks, the cost of periodic advertisements in the local newspaper, the wages she will pay to the drivers of her two trucks, and her own salary of $15,000 per year. If all goes as Mary plans, she should be able to cover her expenses over the five years she owns the franchise, and at the end of the franchise period she will have saved $130,000 of her profits to pay back the loan from her parents.

Part of Mary's agreement with her parents is that she will provide them with an annual income statement for her franchise that has been prepared using generally accepted accounting principles. Mary has come to you, her friend and unpaid accountant, for guidance on how to report her various expenses each year.

REQUIRED Write a memorandum describing the matching principle to Mary, including the general guidelines used to apply the matching principle. Explain how each of Mary's expenses would be accounted for in accordance with the matching principle.

C 2-30. **THE NEED FOR REPORTING STANDARDS** In its 1994 report, the AICPA's Special Committee on Financial Reporting wrote the following:

> Some constituents, including many companies, while acknowledging the importance of high-quality business reporting, question the need for a study of business reporting and recommendations to improve it. They ask: Why not let the marketplace for capital determine the nature and quality of business reporting? The marketplace, they argue, already offers powerful incentives for high-quality reporting. It rewards higher quality reporting and punishes lower quality reporting by easing or restricting access to capital or raising or lowering the cost of capital. Additional reporting standards, they argue, would only distort a market mechanism that already works well and would add costs to reporting, with no benefit. They liken reporting standards to costly, inefficient, unnecessary bureaucratic regulations.

REQUIRED Write a few paragraphs discussing four or five reasons why reporting standards play an important role in helping the market mechanism work effectively for the benefit of companies, users, and the public. More specifically, discuss why reporting standards are needed.

C 2-31. **CAPITAL MAINTENANCE**

1. A and B each invested $4,000 in a nightclub operation. C invested $4,000 in common stock of X Corporation in the hope that the price of the stock would rise so that he could buy a piece of land that was for sale for $4,400. After two years, A, B, and C cashed in their investments for $6,000 each. In talking with them you find that A considers that he earned a profit over the two-year period, B considers that he broke even, and C considers that he lost money because the owner of the land now wants $7,400 for it. The general price level increased 50 percent over the two-year period.

REQUIRED Discuss the capital maintenance concepts apparently employed by A, B, and C.

2. Assume that you purchased a home for $50,000 in 1985 by paying $10,000 down and signing a 30-year mortgage at an interest rate of 8 percent. Today your house has an estimated selling price of $150,000, interest rates are now 10 percent, and the general level of prices has increased 50 percent since 1985.

REQUIRED Ignoring income taxes, what factors should you consider in determining whether your capital has been maintained during this time period, and whether you are better off as a result of making this home investment in 1985?

C 2-32. **EXIT VALUE** Your boss wants to learn more about several concepts of current value that were introduced during a recent seminar she attended. She has asked you to prepare brief written comments about the concept of exit value.

REQUIRED In your written comments, discuss the meaning of *exit value*, distinguish between current exit value and expected exit value, and explain how exit values may be useful in meeting financial reporting objectives.

EXERCISES

E 2-1. **QUALITATIVE CHARACTERISTICS** Identify by letter the qualitative characteristic or characteristics of useful accounting information that best relate to each numbered concept or phrase below. A characteristic may be used more than once.

a) Understandability	**f)** Feedback value	**k)** Neutrality
b) Decision usefulness	**g)** Materiality	**l)** Comparability
c) Relevance	**h)** Timeliness	**m)** Consistency
d) Reliability	**i)** Verifiability	**n)** Benefit exceeds cost
e) Predictive value	**j)** Representational faithfulness	

1. Accounting information may confirm the decision maker's earlier expectation.

2. A primary qualitative characteristic.

3. Expedient, cost-effective treatment of some items is justified by this concept.

4. Essential for interperiod comparisons.

5. Characteristic dealing with consensus of a group.

6. Agreement between a measure and the thing being measured.

7. Essential for interfirm comparisons.

8. Periodic reporting, especially interim reporting, relates to this characteristic.

9. Balancing relevant disclosures with resources required to generate such disclosures.
10. This characteristic implies that standards do not favor a particular user group.
11. Accounting information should be capable of making a difference in a decision.
12. To be useful, accounting information must be available to the decision maker when the decision is being made.

E 2-2. **DEFINITIONS OF CONCEPTUAL TERMS**   Identify by letter (a through r) the term that best corresponds to each definition or description (1 through 18). A term may be used more than once.

a) Asset	**g)** Loss	**m)** Cash-basis accounting
b) Liability	**h)** Realization	**n)** Matching
c) Equity	**i)** Recognition	**o)** Conservatism
d) Revenue	**j)** Net income	**p)** Current exit value
e) Expense	**k)** Other comprehensive income	**q)** Comprehensive income
f) Gain	**l)** Accrual accounting	**r)** Current replacement cost

1. A decrease in net assets arising from an incidental transaction of the entity.
2. Focuses on transactions and economic events that have cash consequences rather than strictly on transactions involving only cash inflows or outflows.
3. A future economic benefit controlled by an entity, as a result of a past transaction.
4. The accounting alternative with the least favorable impact on net income is used.
5. The net amount of all revenues, expenses, gains, and losses.
6. The act of recording a transaction or economic event.
7. Expenses incurred in generating revenues should be reported in the same income statement as those revenues.
8. A probable future sacrifice of economic benefits.
9. The amount of cash that would be received, if an asset were sold under conditions of orderly liquidation.
10. Revenues are recorded when cash is received.
11. An increase in equity from peripheral transactions.
12. All changes in equity during a period, other than investments by owners and distributions to owners.
13. Net assets.
14. An abstract concept that governs when revenue should be recognized.
15. The amount of cash required to purchase an asset currently.
16. An inflow of assets as a result of the delivery of goods.
17. Items included in comprehensive income, but excluded from net income.
18. The using of an asset or incurring of a liability.

E 2-3. **QUALITATIVE CHARACTERISTICS**   Listed below are statements that relate to the qualitative characteristics of useful accounting information and to modifications of the basic principles underlying GAAP.

a) Companies usually record as expenses all expenditures for supplies that do not exceed a specified amount.
b) All companies in the utility industry disclose interest expense but do not include the expense in the operating section of the income statement.
c) The SEC requires that the 10-K report include comparative statement data.
d) When a company adopts LIFO, a change cannot be made to FIFO unless economic circumstances change.
e) Although the cost of polluting the environment may be relevant information for inclusion in annual reports, few companies provide such disclosures.
f) Most accountants, if asked to determine the cost of K-Mart's inventory by using, say, FIFO, would probably reach similar conclusions.
g) Ace Trucking Company made an expenditure of $35,000 to remodel and improve its warehouse facilities. The company's manager could not decide whether to expense this amount. After discussing the matter with the company's accountant and external auditor, he expensed the amount.
h) Before the 1930s, many companies did not disclose the amount of sales revenue. Today all companies disclose such items.
i) The use of footnotes and supplementary disclosures in annual reports has increased dramatically in recent years.
j) Real estate investment trust companies report their real estate investments at market value, while other companies generally use either cost or lower of cost or market.

REQUIRED   What concept is described by or relates to each of the above statements?

E 2-4.   **THE MATERIALITY CONCEPT** M. Peters is responsible for the external financial reporting function of Reece, Inc., a merchandising company. In recent years, Reece's income has averaged about $3 million, with expenses and losses totaling approximately $33 million each year. During the current fiscal year, four situations arise for which the proper accounting and reporting depend on applying the materiality concept. The four situations are as follows:

a) Reece purchased 150 clerk/typist chairs for an average price of $130 per chair. Similar dollar amounts are spent on office equipment each year. It is expected that the chairs, like most office equipment, will have to be replaced in four years.

b) A senior officer of Reece received a $30,000 advance against his next year's salary to be used to purchase shares of Reece stock in an employee stock purchase program that is available only for the last three months of the current fiscal year.

c) Inventory shortages of $3,000 to $8,000 have been found in almost 40 percent of Reece's 38 merchandise departments. During the same period, four inventory overages occurred. Usually, inventory overages and shortages occur about equally often at the rate of three to six per fiscal year and average about $5,000 per department.

d) Reece lost a $45,000 lawsuit that was filed by an individual whose two-year-old daughter was seriously burned on the right arm when her supposedly nonflammable sleeper suit was ignited by a large spark that flew out of the family's fireplace on Christmas Day. As part of the lawsuit settlement, Reece also recalled nearly 10,000 similar sleeper suits that had been sold for $4.95 each during the two-week period just before Christmas.

REQUIRED   After giving full consideration to materiality, write a memorandum to Peters regarding the proper accounting and reporting treatment for each situation.

E 2-5.   **FINANCIAL STATEMENT ELEMENTS** Akins Corporation requests your advice on determining how the items below should be classified as financial statement elements:

a) Akins wishes to know if its own stock, which has not yet been issued, should be classified as an asset.

b) Several years ago Akins issued long-term bonds for financing purposes. The bond contract specifies that in two years Akins must issue 10 shares of its common stock for each $1,000 bond outstanding. Akins wonders if the obligation for the common shares should be reported as a liability.

c) During the current year Akins sold land that had been purchased for speculative purposes. The company is unsure whether to classify the sale as revenue or as a gain.

d) Akins recently made some improvements to a state-owned bridge that provides access to Akins's property. Akins wishes to show the fair value of these improvements as an intangible asset.

REQUIRED   On the basis of the definitions and relevant characteristics of the financial statement elements, write a brief response regarding the classification of each of the four items above.

E 2-6.   **REVENUES AND EXPENSES** In the chapter, revenues are defined as "inflows of assets or settlements of liabilities, or both . . ." and expenses are defined as "the using of assets or the incurring of liabilities, or both . . ."

REQUIRED   Present and explain two examples of each of the following:
1. Revenues occurring in conjunction with the inflow of assets.
2. Revenues occurring in conjunction with the settlement of liabilities.
3. Expenses occurring in conjunction with using assets.
4. Expenses occurring in conjunction with incurring liabilities.

E 2-7.   **CASH-BASIS VS. ACCRUAL ACCOUNTING** Bernard Wholesale began operations on January 1, 1998. The following data pertain to the operating activities of Bernard for the years 1998, 1999, and 2000:

	1998	1999	2000
Cash sales	$13,000	$ 9,000	$ 9,000
Credit sales	15,000	19,000	24,000
Expenses (cash)	9,000	11,000	5,000
Accrued expenses	12,000	14,000	20,000

Accounts receivable are collected and accounts payable are paid entirely within the immediately following year.

1. Calculate the income for each year under cash-basis accounting.
2. Calculate the income for each year under accrual accounting.

E 2-8. **CASH-BASIS VS. ACCRUAL ACCOUNTING** The following cash-basis income statements pertain to Nelson Company's operations:

	1998	1999
Cash receipts from customers	$142,000	$137,000
Cash disbursements to creditors, employees, etc.	(110,000)	(115,000)
Cash-basis income	$ 32,000	$ 22,000

Additional data are as follows:

	1998	1999
Accounts receivable:		
Beginning of year	$20,000	$58,000
End of year	58,000	30,000
Payables:		
Beginning of year	$18,000	$4,000
End of year	4,000	6,000

Calculate the accrual-basis income for 1998 and 1999.

E 2-9. **CASH-BASIS VS. ACCRUAL ACCOUNTING** Arnold, Inc., reported net income of $33,000 for the year just ended. Since Arnold uses cash-basis accounting, the following items were excluded from the determination of net income:

Cost of sales:	
Beginning inventory	$ 5,000
Purchases on account	5,000
Ending inventory	3,500
Bad debts expense	2,500
Write-down of damaged equipment	2,100
Depreciation expense	2,000
Interest accrued on bonds held	3,200
Sales on account	15,000

On the basis of the above data, and assuming that the $33,000 reported net income included (*a*) a $4,000 payment to a creditor for purchases made the previous year and (*b*) $3,100 in customer payments for goods that will be completed and delivered next year, calculate the accrual-basis net income for Arnold, Inc.

E 2-10. **CAPITAL MAINTENANCE CONCEPTS** Joe's Shoe Company purchased two pairs of shoes at the beginning of 1998 for $80 per pair. At the end of 1998, the shoes were sold for $120 per pair. During the year, the general level of prices increased by 40 percent; if Joe's Shoe plans to operate in 1999, however, the shoes must be replaced at a cost of $130 per pair.

Calculate the earnings for Joe's Shoe Company for 1998 under the following capital maintenance concepts:
1. Nominal dollars.
2. General purchasing power units at the end of 1998.
3. Physical capital.

E 2-11. **CAPITAL MAINTENANCE CONCEPTS** In this chapter, three capital maintenance concepts were discussed and illustrated. Assume that the president of a small business knows the following facts about inventory item A and about the general level of prices in the economy:
a) Five units of item A were bought at the beginning of the current year and were sold at the end of the current year.

b) Each unit was purchased for $95 and was sold for $121.

c) The general level of prices rose by 12 percent during the year.

d) Each unit of item A could be replaced for $105 at the end of the year.

REQUIRED In order that she may better understand the alternative concepts of capital maintenance, the president asks you to calculate income related to inventory of item A under each of the capital maintenance concepts discussed in the chapter. Be sure to identify clearly each concept as you use it.

E 2-12. BASIC ASSUMPTIONS, PRINCIPLES, AND CONCEPTS UNDERLYING CONVENTIONAL FINANCIAL REPORTING Several statements related to financial reporting appear below. List and describe the assumption, principle, or concept applicable to each statement.

a) Annual reports usually cover a one-year period.

b) Liquidation values usually are not reported in financial statements filed with the SEC and other agencies.

c) IBM Corporation reports revenue associated with computer sales at the point of sale.

d) Rockwell International depreciates equipment over its estimated useful life.

e) Allman Corporation bought the assets of a failing competitor at a price substantially below estimated fair value but recorded the assets acquired at the cash price paid.

f) Companies record goodwill only when goodwill is purchased in a merger transaction.

g) Dacey operates a grocery store. During the current year, he withdrew $2,000 in cash for personal use at the local dog track. The amount was not expensed on the books of the grocery store.

E 2-13. BASIC ASSUMPTIONS, PRINCIPLES, AND CONCEPTS UNDERLYING CONVENTIONAL FINANCIAL REPORTING Several statements related to financial reporting practice appear below. List and describe the assumption, principle, or concept applicable to each statement.

a) Wilshire, Inc., owns a controlling stock interest in several music publishing companies. Financial statements for Wilshire, Inc., include the dollar amounts of relevant financial data pertaining to these (legally separate) companies.

b) Costs incurred to improve the efficiency of the Talson Company are recorded as assets and subsequently expensed as revenue is earned and reported in Talson's income statement.

c) In addition to the basic financial statements, most companies include extensive footnotes and other supplementary data in their published financial statements.

d) *APB Opinion No. 22* requires that a statement of accounting policies (inventory pricing methods used, depreciation policies, revenue recognition policies, lease commitments, etc.) be included as an integral part of published financial statements.

e) The city of Barton, Texas, recently donated a tract of land to Yamasaki Motorcycle Corporation in connection with a manufacturing plant to be built in Barton. Yamasaki recorded the land at its fair value of $780,000.

f) For the past 13 years, Silas Corporation has used the installment method of revenue recognition because of an inability to estimate uncollectible accounts.

g) Brown Exploration Company depletes (depreciates) its mineral deposits on a cost-per-ton basis but depreciates its mine shafts on a straight-line basis.

E 2-14. BASIC ASSUMPTIONS, PRINCIPLES, AND CONCEPTS UNDERLYING CONVENTIONAL FINANCIAL ACCOUNTING AND REPORTING Several transactions and events that have affected Smith Woodworking Company during the current year are listed below.

a) Smith gave about $3,500 of oak lumber to one of its employees in lieu of wages for June and part of July. This transaction was recorded as follows:

Cost of goods sold 3,500
    Inventory 3,500

b) A delivery truck purchased for $10,000 was being depreciated using the straight-line method applied over a five-year useful life and assuming no salvage value. At the beginning of the fourth depreciation year for the truck, Smith's accountant learned that the current replacement cost of the truck was $6,000 and, therefore, made the following entry:

Accumulated depreciation 2,000
    Gain on truck appreciation 2,000

c) Several of Smith's employees are carpenters who were hired to work in the prefabricated kitchen cabinets shop. In recent weeks, when individual carpenters have not been needed in cabinet construction, they have been assigned to help build Smith's new warehouse. Smith's accountant concludes that since the carpenters were hired to build cabinets, are on salary and must be paid regardless of whether they are building cabinets or not, and are working on the warehouse project only about 15 percent of their time, it is appropriate to include all of their monthly wages in the cost of work-in-process inventory.

d) Smith employs an interior design specialist, who works with individuals in designing new or remodeled kitchens, bathrooms, etc. The services of the designer are made available without cost to potential woodworking customers because Smith's management believes that some people who would not otherwise use Smith's woodworking services will choose to remodel if given some design assistance. The interior design specialist's monthly salary of $3,000 is recorded as follows:

Salary expense 3,000
Cash. 3,000

e) Smith was able to purchase several table saws and drill presses for $42,300 at the bankruptcy sale of a former competitor company. The saws and drill presses were in "like new" condition and if purchased at normal prices would have cost $59,000. Smith made the following entry to record the purchase:

Table saws and drill presses 59,000
Cash 42,300
Income 16,700

REQUIRED State whether you agree or disagree with Smith's accounting treatment in each of the above situations. Support your conclusions by discussing the applicable assumption, principle, or concept.

E 2-15. **BASIC ASSUMPTIONS, PRINCIPLES, AND CONCEPTS UNDERLYING CONVENTIONAL FINANCIAL ACCOUNTING AND REPORTING** Several transactions and events involving Hudson Industries are listed below.

a) A three-year insurance policy on Hudson's administrative building was acquired for $15,000 and recorded as follows:

Insurance expense. 15,000
Cash 15,000

b) Inventory costing $63,000 was on hand at the end of the current year, at which time its replacement cost was $75,000. Hudson made the following entry to record this fact:

Inventory 12,000
Income 12,000

c) Hudson reports accumulated depreciation on its equipment as a liability, because it feels obligated to replace the equipment in order to stay in business.

d) Hudson purchased a few acres of land for plant expansion. The cash price of the land was $125,000, but Hudson acquired the land by paying $95,000 immediately, and agreeing that in one year it would issue 2,000 shares of Hudson's no-par common stock to the owner of the land. Under the agreement, Hudson was entitled to take possession of the land upon signing the purchase agreement. Hudson made the following entry to record the transaction:

Land for plant expansion 125,000
Liability to issue common stock 30,000
Cash 95,000

e) Hudson's treasurer borrowed $6,000 from the company. The loan was recorded by the company as follows:

Accounts receivable 6,000
Cash. 6,000

f) Hudson signs a contract to manufacture and deliver 30 small tractors at the rate of 10 per year for the next three years. The total price of the tractors is $150,000, one-half of which is paid to Hudson in advance. Hudson records receipt of the cash as follows:

Cash 75,000
Sales revenue. 75,000

REQUIRED State whether you agree or disagree with Hudson's accounting treatment in each of the above situations. Support your conclusions by discussing the applicable assumption, principle, or concept.

E 2-16. **REVIEW OF CONCEPTS** Identify the element definition, concept, principle, or assumption that appears to be violated in each independent situation outlined below, and write a brief explanation of your reasoning.

a) Included among the liabilities in the balance sheet for NewTone Corporation is this item: "Obligation for fees related to consulting services yet to be received, $35,000."

b) During 1998, Carson, Inc., paid a customer $300,000 in settlement of a lawsuit stemming from a golf-cart accident. The company recorded the event as follows:

  Intangibles 300,000
  Cash   300,000

c) In 1997, Ranger Watercraft received a contract for 300 jet ski machines. The contract was recorded as revenue in 1997, although work on the contract did not begin until mid-1998.

d) Anderson Antiques recently purchased an antique Volkswagen at an auction for $4,000. Anderson's owner felt that the car was worth at least $7,000 and directed her controller to record the purchase as follows:

  Merchandise inventory 7,000
  Cash.   4,000
  Gain on bargain purchase   3,000

e) When the corporation that owned the Half-Mile Island nuclear plant was assessed a stiff penalty by a governmental unit for a nuclear accident, the corporation recorded the penalty as a "deferred charge," arguing that future revenues would easily cover the penalty.

f) In 1998, Hale Railroad Company entered into a 100-year noncancelable agreement to lease railroad cars at an annual lease payment of $4 million. Hale excluded information about this transaction from its 1998 financial statements, since technically it was not considered a liability (the amount is material).

E 2-17. **REVIEW OF CONCEPTS** Identify the element definition, concept, principle, or assumption that appears to be violated in each independent situation below, and write a brief explanation of your reasoning.

a) Recently Benton Oil Company built a pipeline to carry petroleum products from the oil field to its refinery. The cost of the pipeline, which was $30 million, was expensed. Benton's net assets have averaged $50 million over the past 15 years.

b) Deep Discount sells microwave ovens on a deferred payment plan. The company recognizes revenue on a cash-collection (i.e., installment) basis even though no uncollectible accounts have occurred since the company began operating 20 years ago.

c) The Gulf Airport Authority (a governmental unit) constructed two new runways at the municipal airport it owns and operates. One common carrier, Mid-South Airlines, recognized the benefits that the construction would have on its ability to increase the number of flights into the airport, and it accordingly made the following entry on its books:

  Runway improvements (intangibles) 300,000
  Contributed capital.   300,000

d) Branson, Inc., adopted a depreciation policy by which the depreciation method (e.g., accelerated, straight-line, units of production, etc.) used each year would be selected in accordance with its ability to permit the firm to maintain (and thus report) a 20 percent rate of return on beginning owners' equity.

e) Newton Corporation recently reported a dividend distributable in its own shares as a liability.

f) In 1998, Slayer Company resold shares of its own stock that it had previously purchased in the open market for more than it had paid for previous purchases. The excess was reported as a gain on Slayer's 1998 income statement.

E 2-18. **REVIEW OF CONCEPTS** Identify the element definition, concept, principle, or assumption that appears to be violated in each independent situation below, and write a brief explanation of your reasoning.

a) Upon learning that the replacement cost of its forklift was $1,200 more than its book value, Walsh Company added $1,200 to the forklift's book value.

b) Hardy, Inc., sold a three-year fast-food franchise to Bob Wilson for $150,000, which was received at the time the contract was signed. Hardy reported a $150,000 franchise sale revenue when the cash was received.

c) The federal government filed and won an $85,000 lawsuit against French Chemicals for polluting a local lake. French Chemicals, with annual profits in excess of $5 million, did not separately report either the lawsuit or its settlement in its financial statements or accompanying footnotes.

d) Stacey Computers, a chain of retail computer hardware and software stores, spends a material amount each year on 45-day training programs for new salespeople. Stacey expects that each salesperson will have to be retrained or brought up to date every four years. Stacey debits expense for the entire cost of each year's training program.

e) In 1998, Dobson Landscape, Inc., signed a $180,000 contract with Link Company to landscape the corporate headquarters during the summer of 1999. It is understood that Link Company will make no payments to Dobson until the project is at least 50 percent complete. Dobson reports a $180,000 liability to landscape Link Company in its 1998 balance sheet.

f) The neighborhood surrounding Bill's Paint Shop has been an eyesore and a high-crime area for several years. During the current year, the city did a major renovation of the area and also widened and resurfaced all the streets in the blocks adjacent to Bill's business. Bill is convinced that the improvements that have been made will substantially improve his retail sales, and that it is appropriate to recognize the improvements by recording an intangible asset in his books.

E 2-19. **REVIEW OF CONCEPTS** Identify the element definition, concept, principle, or assumption that appears to be violated in each independent situation below, and write a brief explanation of your reasoning. If there is no violation and the accounting treatment is appropriate, explain why.

a) During the current accounting period, Harris, Inc., sold $4,500,000 of merchandise on account to several thousand different customers. Based on past experience, Harris expected about $45,000 of the receivables to be uncollectible. Therefore, Harris reduced its receivables balance and recorded a loss of $45,000 on its income statement for the period.

b) Grace Company decided to expand its sheet metal–forming business by adding two new $65,000 metal-forming presses, giving it a total of 12 presses. Each of the two new presses is expected to have a useful life of 10 years. Grace recorded its cash purchase of the metal-forming presses by recording a $130,000 expense.

c) Having net assets of $2,000,000, Reese Company considered itself to be a midsize company. During the current year, Reese replaced 60 of the electric pencil sharpeners in its drafting department with new commercial-grade units costing $100 each. On the average, the new sharpeners are expected to have four-year useful lives. Reese recorded its purchase by debiting office equipment expense for $6,000.

d) Carson Builders, a building contractor specializing in new home construction, needed a new storage facility for some of its equipment. Carson learned that it would cost $80,000 to have the storage facility custom-built for them. Since some of its employees were not being fully utilized at the moment, Carson decided to build its own storage facility; which it did for a cost of $50,000, including materials, employee wages, and interest incurred on money borrowed to finance the project. Carson put the new facility on the books for its $80,000 fair value, and recorded a $30,000 gain on the construction project.

e) Absolute Best Painting received $40,000 from Modern Construction as payment for doing the exterior paintwork on 10 custom-built homes that Modern expected to build over the next two years. Absolute Best recorded the receipt of the cash and recognized a $40,000 gain.

f) A two-acre lot in an area zoned commercial was purchased by Thomas Auto as the site for an auto body shop. Local township ordinances required that Thomas install a five-foot-wide sidewalk across the entire 500-foot frontage of its lot so that pedestrians could cross Thomas's property. The sidewalk, which would be maintained by the township, cost Thomas $25,000. Thomas included the sidewalk cost in the overall cost of developing the property, shown as an asset on Thomas's balance sheet.

E 2-20. **ENVIRONMENTAL ASSUMPTIONS, QUALITATIVE CHARACTERISTICS, AND RECOGNITION AND MEASUREMENT PRINCIPLES** Several widely used financial accounting and reporting practices are listed below.

a) The costs of assets are initially capitalized and then debited to expense over the periods benefited.

b) Revenues are recorded when earned and expenses are recorded when incurred.

c) The exchange price established in a transaction actually entered into by the accounting entity is the proper basis for initially recording assets.

d) Revenue is recorded in the accounting records and reported in the financial statements.

e) Revenue normally is reported in the income statement in the period of sale.

f) Inventories are valued on the basis of lower of cost or market.

g) The assets and liabilities of stockholders are not included with the assets and liabilities of the corporation whose stock they hold.

h) Income occurs when the number of dollars of revenue earned exceeds the number of dollars of expenses incurred. (Do not use the matching principle.)

REQUIRED   Identify the environmental assumption, qualitative characteristic, or recognition and measurement principle that best supports each of the above accounting and reporting practices.

E 2-21.   ENVIRONMENTAL ASSUMPTIONS, QUALITATIVE CHARACTERISTICS, RECOGNITION AND MEASUREMENT PRINCIPLES, AND OTHER CONCEPTS   Several widely used financial accounting and reporting practices are listed below.

a) All economic information that is significant enough to affect users' decisions is reported in financial statements.

b) Financial statements usually are prepared on a consolidated basis, with the financial data of the various activities of the subsidiary companies aggregated with those of the parent company.

c) Financial reports issued between the dates of annual financial statements, which are called interim reports, are available from many companies.

d) Financial statements are issued at regular intervals, such as annually.

e) When the useful economic life of a plant asset is determined, it is assumed that the business that owns the asset will continue operations indefinitely.

f) In order for a company's financial statements to be comparable from year to year, changes in accounting practices should be made only when economic circumstances change.

g) Current values are not generally reported, and one argument supporting continuation of this practice is that it is very costly to prepare current value disclosures.

h) Plant assets are depreciated over their useful lives.

REQUIRED   Identify the environmental assumption, qualitative characteristic, recognition and measurement principle, or other concept that best supports each of the above accounting and reporting practices.

PROBLEM

P 2-1.   FINANCIAL REPORTING PROBLEM (GENERAL ELECTRIC)   In a *Wall Street Journal* article, "How General Electric Damps Fluctuations in Its Annual Earning," (November 3, 1994, pp. A1, A6), the following statement appeared:

> One way GE stores profits for future use is, ironically, by following fairly conservative accounting practices.

REQUIRED   Examine the General Electric consolidated financial statements and notes to those statements in Appendix B. Find at least three examples of situations in which GE uses what appear to you to be "conservative" accounting and reporting practices. For each example, explain why you believe the practice is conservative.

FASB AND STOCK COMPENSATION CASE

Many public companies give stock options to their employees, especially top management. Stock options allow employees to buy company stock at some future date for a predetermined (exercise) price, usually the price of the stock at the time the stock options are issued (granted). These contracts can provide tax benefits and align employee incentives with stockholder interests; the options do not benefit the employees unless stock prices increase.

Under *APB Opinion No. 25* (issued in 1972), no compensation expense is recognized if the exercise price is greater than or equal to the stock price at the date of the grant. As a result, most firms did not expense anything for the options even though employees were able to acquire stock for much less than the current market value. For example, in 1992 Michael Eisner, chairman of Disney, used stock options to purchase Disney stock for $197 million below market value.

The FASB added the stock option issue to its agenda in 1984. After much research, discussion, and deliberation, the FASB issued an *Exposure Draft* in 1993. The *Exposure Draft* would have required firms to use an option pricing model to measure compensation expense at the date of grant. The accounting would have forced firms to increase compensation expense for the estimated value of the options as of the date of grant, thereby decreasing income. Firms which made the most extensive use of stock options would have seen the most drastic decreases to income.

The FASB was criticized by many businesses and some members of Congress. Bills in favor of and against the pronouncement were introduced in Congress. One concern was that although option pricing models had proved useful for pricing publicly traded options, they might not provide reliable values for employee stock options. In addition, some argued that the exchange did not meet the definition of an expense. Other concerns are discussed in the accompanying articles.

Ultimately, the FASB softened its position by allowing firms to continue to use *APB Opinion No. 25* for recognition purposes and to merely disclose the effect on income under the *Exposure Draft* accounting method. Chapter 18 discusses the accounting and disclosure for stock compensation in detail.

Read the accompanying *Business Week* articles, which describe some of the pressure received by the FASB and manager incentives for pressuring the FASB. Answer the questions using the background information and the articles.

1. Explain why it is important for the FASB to remain independent of the groups that it regulates.

2. Explain why the FASB pays attention to the desires of groups like the Financial Executives Institute.

3. Explain why business leaders would object to the FASB's *Exposure Draft* on stock options. You should go beyond what is given in the Koretz article and also include reasons based on accounting theory.

4. Explain why business leaders would object to the FASB's increasing disclosure for stock options, derivatives, and so on.

5. Explain why firm managers strongly opposed expense recognition but offered little opposition to disclosure of the pro forma expense.

6. Explain how your answer to question 5 is consistent or inconsistent with market efficiency.

How a Corporate Watchdog Nearly Lost Its Bite

By Robert Kuttner

A newly assertive Securities & Exchange Commission is trying to save the Financial Accounting Standards Board from a power play by large corporations and banks seeking more latitude for creative accounting. At stake is not only FASB's integrity and independence but also investor confidence that accountants and their clients aren't colluding to cook corporate books—in short, the efficiency of capital markets.

The story is also significant for what it reveals about the limits of self-regulation. FASB was created in 1973 as the officially recognized body in charge of accounting standards, responsible to a nonprofit Financial Accounting Foundation. The SEC is empowered by law to set corporate accounting standards. But since 1936, the Commission has delegated that job to private bodies affiliated with the accounting profession, mostly with happy results—until now.

For its first two decades, FASB enjoyed a well-deserved reputation as an independent body committed to the public interest. The main criticism was that it took too long writing new standards. In recent months, however, trustees of the foundation nominally in charge of FASB have campaigned to clip its wings. This campaign is advertised as an effort to streamline FASB, but the reality is that key business and banking leaders are opposed to the degree of disclosure FASB champions.

Wiggle Room. What could have business so annoyed? For one thing, FASB is working on a new standard requiring derivative securities to be counted at present market value—not their issue price. At present, accounting practices for derivatives and hedging exposures are a hodge-podge, allowing corporations and banks to hide potential losses. For another, beginning in 1993, FASB has sought clearer accounting of executive stock options. In the face of furious opposition, it backed down in October, 1995, and issued a disclosure standard with lots of wiggle room.

The board of the Financial Accounting Foundation, which governs FASB, is the corporate power elite in cameo. Its trustees include the chief financial officers of General Electric, Microsoft, Citicorp, and Morgan Stanley; as well as executives of major accounting firms. The sole "public-interest" representative is currently Kathryn D. Wriston, wife of Walter B. Wriston, the retired Citicorp chairman. Even worse, FASB depends on the same foundation board to raise much of its operating budget, which sets up an exquisite conflict of interest in which the industries affected by FASB rulings raise its money.

The most recent attack on FASB independence has been led by J. Michael Cook, the foundation's president and CEO of Deloitte & Touche, the Big Six accounting firm. Cook began the skirmish with a letter last February proposing to rein in FASB by reducing its agenda-setting powers. This followed a demand last November by the 14,000-member Financial Executives Institute, a lobbying group for increased business influence on the standards-setting process. The lobbying group accused FASB of "an implicit antibusiness bias."

Civilian Reps. In April, SEC Chairman Arthur Levitt, Jr., weighed in, declaring that what FASB needed was more independence from business pressure, not less. In a public speech to the Economic Club of Chicago and in follow-up discussions with Cook, Levitt asked FASB trustees to restructure their board to produce a majority of public-interest members, with SEC involvement in the selection process. As a last resort, the SEC could take away the existing trustees' jurisdiction over FASB or even reclaim control of the standard-setting process.

Levitt says he would prefer to keep FASB as an independent body, but that "quasi-public bodies like FASB should look, smell, and feel like the public that they are mandated to represent." Levitt wants a governing body of public figures and representatives of the investor community committed to FASB's operating independence. At this juncture, the SEC chairman and the trustees still have major differences on whether a representative of an industry affected by FASB decisions can be considered a "public" trustee of its governing body.

The attack on FASB's independence has been blunted, for now. But this episode shows the brazenness of leading segments of the corporate and banking community seeking latitude to mislead investors. It has been a long slide since the original trustees reliably defended FASB's independence. The affair also suggests that FASB, as a quasi-public body, should get its appropriations directly from the Treasury Dept. Finally, the attack on FASB is a reminder that self-regulation is only as good as the public regulation that stands behind it.

Keeping Options Under Wraps
Why execs fought FASB so fiercely

By Gene Koretz

The economic logic seems unassailable: Since the pay and fringes received by rank and file workers are a business cost that is recognized as an expense item on income statements, so too should the big chunk of top executives' compensation made up of stock options.

Now that option pricing models have made it relatively easy to place a value on options, however, corporations argue that expensing options would have harmful economic effects. By reducing reported earnings, they say, the practice would cause stock prices to fall and thus raise the cost of capital.

Such views were the gist of the 1,700 or so comment letters received in 1993 by the Financial Accounting Standards Board (FASB) when it finally dropped the other shoe and unveiled a proposal to make companies recognize the cost of employee options as an expense. As a result of the firestorm of resistance, the FASB backed off, and companies will now be required merely to disclose the estimated costs of options in a footnote.

In a new study, Patricia M. Dechow and Richard G. Sloan of the Wharton School and Amy P. Sweeney of the

Harvard Business School have assessed the validity of corporate objections to the FASB proposal. They find no evidence that companies dependent on external financing make especially intense use of stock options as compensation. More important, they find that the stock prices of companies making heavy use of options did not react negatively when the news of the FASB proposal broke.

The three accounting professors also looked at the companies registering written objections to the expensing proposal. On average, they found that the top five executives in each of the companies heard from received both much higher total compensation ($1.2 million vs. $880,000) and a higher fraction of their pay in the form of stock options (28% vs. 21%) than the top brass of a matched sample of companies that registered no complaints.

The study's bottom line: The concerns expressed about the impact of expensing options on stock prices and borrowing costs seem to have been a smoke screen to avoid publicizing bosses' high pay.

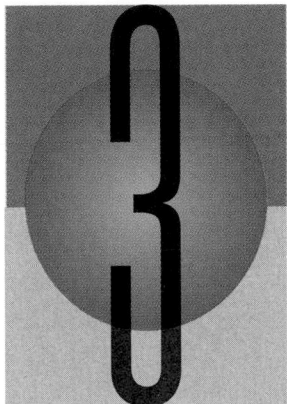
The Accounting Process: An Overview

LEARNING OBJECTIVES

After studying this chapter, you should be able to:

1. Explain the effects of transactions on the accounting equation.

2. State the basic rules for debits and credits to accounts.

3. Analyze transactions and determine their effects on financial statements.

4. Record transactions in the general journal.

5. Post transactions from the journal to the ledger.

6. Explain the purpose of and prepare a trial balance.

7. Identify and prepare the four basic types of adjusting entries.

8. Explain the purpose of and prepare the four basic financial statements.

9. Explain the purpose of and prepare closing entries.

10. Explain the purpose of reversing entries; identify adjusting entries that could be reversed, and prepare entries to reverse them.

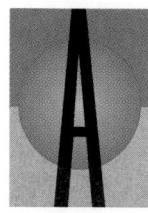

n accurate and effective accounting system is crucial to the operation of both for-profit and nonprofit organizations. As the following example illustrates, poor record keeping can spell trouble for an enterprise:

> A recently released independent audit of Tulsa Community Action Agency's 1994 financial records found problems so serious, auditors said the troubles could threaten the agency's ability to continue operating. The report found the agency had poor cash-handling procedures, checks were written without sufficient funds, and thousands were spent in questionable costs.
>
> "Because of the inadequacies in Tulsa Community Action Agency's accounting records, we were unable to form an opinion regarding the amounts recorded in the accompanying financial statements for cash, receivables, payables, beginning net assets, revenues earned and expenses incurred," the report said.[1]

Besides supporting the day-to-day operation of an entity, an accurate accounting system provides the information managers need to evaluate an entity's effectiveness over the long term. In for-profit enterprises, the information provided by financial accounting and reporting enables managers and external users to answer such questions as:

Did the company make a profit this year?

What was the profit trend over the past several years?

Should the company pay a dividend this year?

Is the company generating cash flows according to expectations?

Are sales keeping step with a growing market?

What is the company's rate of return on invested capital?

Whether for-profit or nonprofit, large or small, most entities share similar accounting systems. As you might expect, Wal-Mart has more complex accounting systems and financial reports than a small grocery store. A retailer with an international market, Wal-Mart carries more products, does a larger volume of business, and has greater management information needs and more interaction with governmental agencies than a local grocer. Despite such differences in the size and complexity of operations, however, the accounting systems and related procedures of both companies share these three common features:

1. The types of economic events the systems capture.

2. The accounting model used to express the financial effects of those events.

3. The accounting process or cycle used to record and process data.

Not all economic events are captured and reported in the financial statements. As was pointed out in Chapter 2, to be recognized an event must fit the definition of a financial statement element, it must have a relevant attribute that is measurable with sufficient reliability, and information about the event must be both relevant and reliable. For example, Wal-Mart would recognize a sale to a customer because the sale satisfies these criteria. Wal-Mart would not recognize a tax cut that may increase consumers' spendable income, ultimately producing increased sales, because the tax cut does not meet the definition of an asset, revenue, or any other financial statement element, nor is its effect on Wal-Mart's sales and income measurable with sufficient reliability.

In this chapter we will review the process through which companies capture, process, and summarize the economic events that affect them, and which are reported in the financial statements. (We will discuss the financial statements in more detail in Chapters 4, 5, and 6.) Our review begins with a discussion of the

---

[1]"Audit Scours TCAA Books, Finds Trouble," *Tulsa World,* April 18, 1996, p. A-9.

accounting equation, which expresses the financial effects of economic events. We will then turn to the ten (or eleven) steps in the accounting process or cycle. A discussion of the differences in accounting for proprietorships and partnerships follows. The chapter concludes with a comparison of cash-basis and accrual accounting.

THE ACCOUNTING EQUATION

In its simplest form, the equation used to express the financial effects of economic events is as follows:

Assets = Liabilities + Equity

Assets are probable future economic benefits, obtained or controlled by an accounting entity as a result of past transactions or events. **Liabilities** are probable future sacrifices of economic benefits arising from an entity's present obligations to transfer assets or provide services to other entities as a result of past transactions or events. **Equity** is the residual interest in an entity's assets that remains after deducting its liabilities from its assets. Sometimes equity is referred to as *net assets.* In a business enterprise equity is the ownership interest, called **owners' equity.**

Effects of Transactions on the Accounting Equation

We saw in Chapter 2 that each economic event affecting a business has a *dual effect* on the accounting equation. The five transactions that follow illustrate how this dual effect maintains the balance of the accounting equation:

I. An attorney invested $10,000 cash in a legal practice.

Assets = Liabilities + Owners' equity
+$10,000   +$10,000

2. The legal practice purchased supplies on account at a cost of $800.

Assets = Liabilities + Owners' equity
+$800   +$800

3. Legal services are performed for clients on account, $1,000.

Assets = Liabilities + Owners' equity
+$1,000   +$1,000

4. Supplies costing $300 are used.

Assets = Liabilities + Owners' equity
−$300   −$300

5. The legal practice pays $600 due on an account with a supplier.

Assets = Liabilities + Owners' equity
−$600   −$600

1 Explain the effects of transactions on the accounting equation.

CONCEPTUAL

Each economic event has a dual effect on the accounting equation.

The first transaction is a capital transaction that increases assets and owners' equity. The second transaction is an asset and liability transaction because both assets and liabilities are increased. The third and fourth transactions are revenue and expense transactions, respectively; each meets the definition of revenues or expenses discussed in Chapter 2. The fifth transaction is an asset and liability transaction because both assets and liabilities are affected.

For a corporation, the accounting equation may be expanded as shown in Exhibit 3–1. In corporate entities, owners' equity is called **stockholders' equity.** Stockholders' interests in the assets of a corporation arise from two sources—their

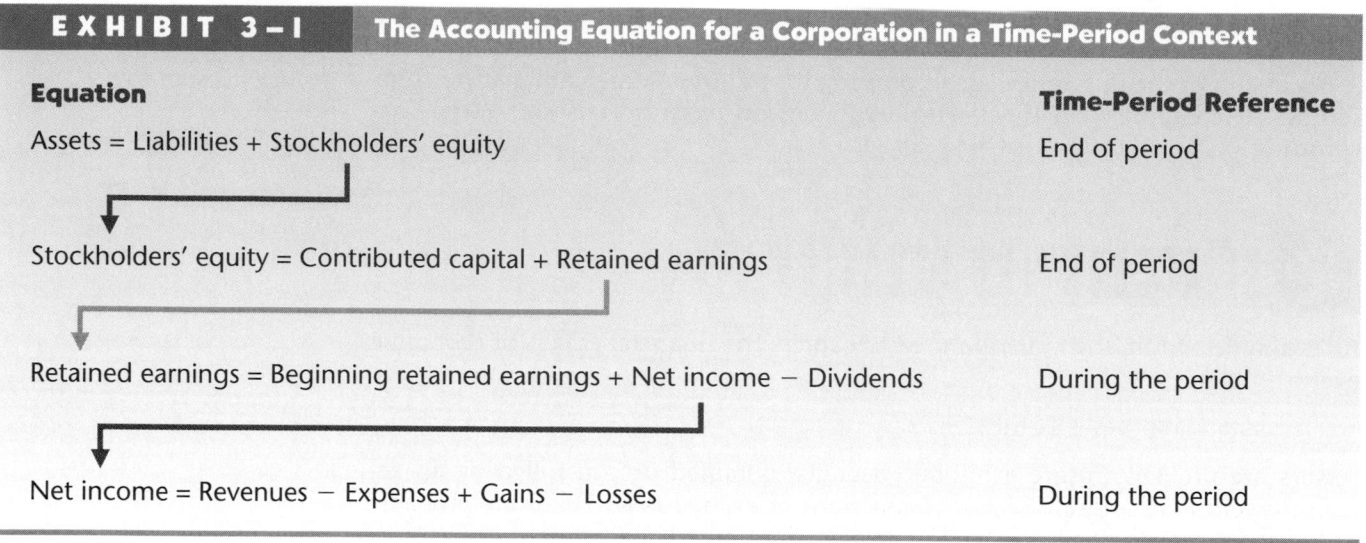

EXHIBIT 3–1   The Accounting Equation for a Corporation in a Time-Period Context

Equation	Time-Period Reference
Assets = Liabilities + Stockholders' equity	End of period
Stockholders' equity = Contributed capital + Retained earnings	End of period
Retained earnings = Beginning retained earnings + Net income − Dividends	During the period
Net income = Revenues − Expenses + Gains − Losses	During the period

CONCEPTUAL

Financial statements are prepared in accordance with the time period assumption.

investments in the corporation and the corporation's earnings or net income. The term **contributed capital** represents the stockholders' investments and **retained earnings** is the cumulative net income retained in the corporation rather than distributed as dividends to stockholders. **Dividends** are distributions to stockholders of assets resulting from profitable operations.

To provide relevant and timely information, corporations prepare financial statements periodically in accordance with the *periodicity* (or *time-period*) *assumption*. The accounting equation shown in Exhibit 3–1 may be interpreted within a time-period context. The first two equations in Exhibit 3–1 apply at the *end* of an accounting period. The third equation shows that the change in retained earnings *during* a period equals the beginning-of-period retained earnings plus net income for the period less dividends declared during the period. The last equation shows that net income *for the period* equals revenues less expenses plus gains less losses.

Accounts: Summaries of the Effects of Transactions

A company may have many assets and liabilities, and many revenues, expenses, gains, and losses. The effects of transactions that cause changes in the various financial statement elements are summarized in **accounts.** Accounts are used to accumulate the dollar effects of transactions and other economic events on each financial statement item. In "T-account" form, an account appears this way:

Account title   No.
Debit side   │   Credit side

The vertical portion of the T divides the account into two sides, the left side or **debit** side, and the right or **credit** side.[2] Entered on the left side, a dollar amount is said to be *debited* to an account; entered on the right side, it is said to be *credited* to the account. The account title is the name of the account (e.g., cash or inventory). The account number is simply a number assigned for record-keeping purposes and is helpful in processing data, especially in computerized accounting systems. To illustrate

---

[2]The words *debit* and *credit* are derived from the Latin words *debitum* (debt) and *creditum* (loan). The terms arose because early records were kept initially to show amounts due to and from individual merchants. In modern accounting, however, *debit* and *credit* simply mean the left side and right side, respectively, of an account.

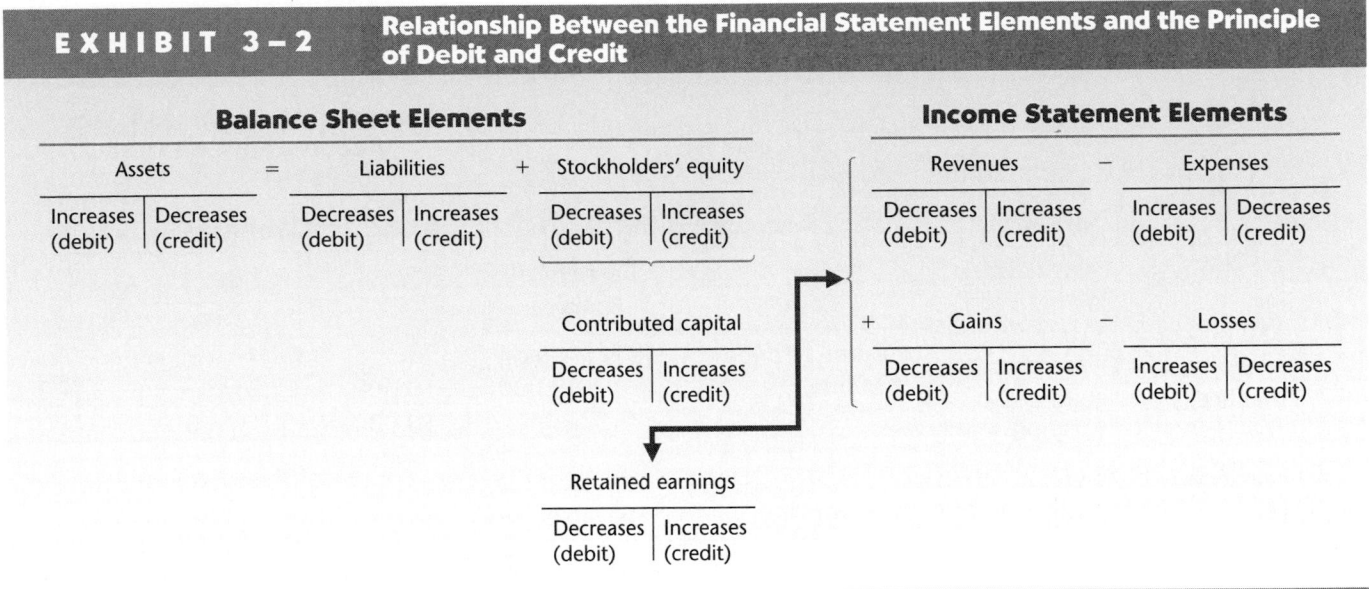

EXHIBIT 3–2 Relationship Between the Financial Statement Elements and the Principle of Debit and Credit

how accounts may be numbered, a corporation might use the following three-digit account numbers for the financial statement elements:

Asset accounts	**100–199**
Liability accounts	**200–299**
Stockholders' equity accounts	**300–399**
Revenue and gain accounts	**400–499**
Expense and loss accounts	**500–599**

Exhibit 3–2 shows the elements of the balance sheet and income statement in the form of T-accounts. Exhibit 3–3 summarizes the effects of debits and credits on those elements.

Assets, which appear on the left side of the accounting equation, are debited for increases. Liabilities and stockholders' equity, which appear on the right side of the accounting equation, are credited for increases. As Exhibits 3–2 and 3–3 show, revenues increase stockholders' equity and are credited for increases. Expenses decrease stockholders' equity and are debited for increases. At any point in time, the balance in an account is the difference between its debit and credit entries. *Asset, expense, and loss accounts normally have debit balances; liability, stockholders' equity, revenue, and gain accounts normally have credit balances.*

Exhibit 3–4 illustrates both the dual effect of transactions on the accounting equation and the rules for debits and credits, using the example of the legal practice presented earlier. Several points are important:

2 State the basic rules for debits and credits to accounts.

EXHIBIT 3–3 Summary of Debit/Credit and Increase/Decrease Relationships

Element	Debit	Credit
Assets	Increase	Decrease
Liabilities	Decrease	Increase
Equity	Decrease	Increase
Revenues	Decrease	Increase
Expenses	Increase	Decrease
Gains	Decrease	Increase
Losses	Increase	Decrease

EXHIBIT 3-4	The Effects of Transactions on the Accounting Equation and the Rules for Debits and Credits

Economic Event	Analysis of Event	Accounting Entry	Cumulative Balances in the Accounting Equation Assets = Liabilities + Owners' Equity
1. An attorney invests $10,000 in a legal practice.	Assets (cash) increased by $10,000. Owners' equity increased by $10,000.	**Cash** — Debit 10,000 / Credit — **Owners' Equity** — Debit / Credit 10,000	+10,000 / 10,000 = 0 + +10,000 / 10,000
2. The legal practice purchases supplies on account at a cost of $800.	Assets (supplies) increased by $800. Liabilities (accounts payable) increased by $800.	**Supplies** — Debit 800 / Credit — **Accounts Payable** — Debit / Credit 800	+800 / 10,800 = +800 / 800 + 10,000
3. Legal services are performed for clients on account, $1,000.	Assets (accounts receivable) increased by $1,000. Owners' equity (revenue) increased by $1,000.	**Accounts Receivable** — Debit 1,000 / Credit — **Revenues** — Debit / Credit 1,000	+1,000 / 11,800 = 800 + +1,000 / 11,000
4. Supplies costing $300 are used.	Assets (supplies) decreased by $300. Owners' equity decreased (expenses increased) by $300.	**Supplies Expense** — Debit 300 / Credit — **Supplies** — Debit 800[a] / Credit 300	−300 / 11,500 = 800 + −300 / 10,700
5. The practice pays $600 on account.	Assets (cash) decreased by $600. Liabilities (accounts payable) decreased by $600.	**Accounts Payable** — Debit 600 / Credit 800[a] — **Cash** — Debit 10,000[b] / Credit 600	−600 / 10,900 = −600 / 200 + 10,700

[a]From transaction #2.
[b]From transaction #1.

1. Each transaction is analyzed first in terms of its effect on the elements of the accounting equation. Notice that each transaction has a dual (balancing) effect on the equation.

2. The dollar amounts of the transactions are entered into the appropriate accounts as increases and decreases, in accordance with the rules for debits and credits.

3. For every debit made to an account, a corresponding credit is made to another account. Thus for every transaction the debits and credits are equal. Because at least two accounts are affected by each transaction, this practice is sometimes described as a *double-entry* system.

4. The effects of the transactions on the accounting equation are shown on the right-hand side of Exhibit 3–4. Notice that the equality of the equation, Assets = Liabilities + Owners' equity, is maintained after each transaction.

Before we begin our discussion of the accounting process, we should point out that balance sheet and income statement accounts are classified on the basis of their permanency. Accounts for balance sheet items are called real or permanent accounts because they provide an ongoing, cumulative record of assets, liabilities, and owners' equity. Income statement accounts are called nominal or temporary accounts because they are used to accumulate changes in assets and liabilities that arise from earnings activities during each accounting period. At the end of each accounting period nominal account balances are closed (reduced to zero) to ready them for recording of the next period's transactions.

THE ACCOUNTING PROCESS OR CYCLE

This section provides an overview of the accounting process and is the most important section of this chapter.

The **accounting process** or **cycle,** shown in Exhibit 3–5, consists of the procedures used to collect, process, and report the effects of economic events on an entity during an accounting period.

Advances in computer technology and accounting software have changed the way in which the accounting process is applied. Inexpensive software, called *general ledger packages,* can now be used to record transactions and accumulate their effects in accounts. The accounts reside on some storage medium, such as floppy disks or hard disks in a personal computer or on magnetic tape or a direct-access disk in a mainframe computer. Software packages usually include (1) the capability to construct financial statements based on recorded transactions, (2) inventory control routines, (3) accounts receivable and accounts payable routines, (4) payroll routines, and (5) the capability to print hard copies of system output. In short, these software packages provide a comprehensive accounting system.

The concepts presented here in a pen-and-paper approach apply equally well to most, if not all, computerized accounting processes. Any differences in application are due to the efficiency and speed in which data can be processed with the computer.

Step 1: Collecting Data About Economic Events

The first step in the accounting cycle is to collect data about those economic events that will enter a company's accounting system. Data about economic events are collected from source documents, which provide evidence that an economic event has occurred. Some examples of source documents that provide verification of the occurrence of economic events are listed in Exhibit 3–6.

| EXHIBIT 3–5 | The Accounting Cycle |

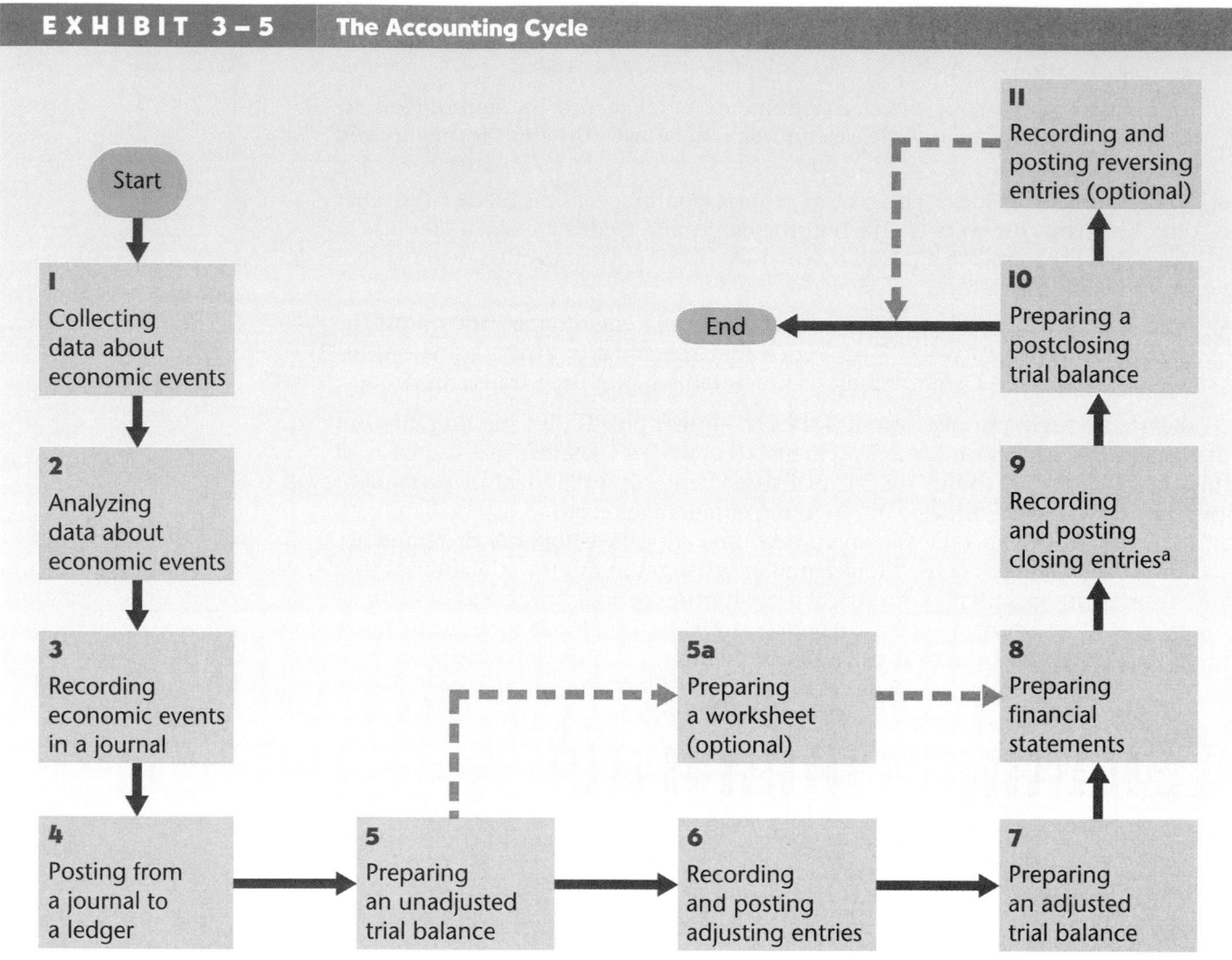

Note: Steps 1–4 occur during the accounting period. Steps 5–10 occur at the end of the accounting period. Step 11 (optional) occurs at the beginning of the following accounting period.

[a]At this time, adjusting entries also must be recorded and posted if a worksheet is used.

| EXHIBIT 3–6 | Some Source Documents for Selected Economic Events |

Economic Event	Source Document
Cash sales	Cash register tapes
Credit sales	Sales invoices
Purchases of merchandise, supplies, and other assets	Purchase orders, purchase invoices, freight bills
Purchases of labor services (e.g., salaries and wages)	Time tickets, clock cards
Depreciation of long-lived assets	Depreciation schedules
Interest on notes held as investments	Note contract
Interest on savings accounts; service charges on checking accounts	Monthly bank statements
Customer defaults on accounts	Letters from customer or from customer's attorney
Warranty claims on merchandise sold	Warranty claim forms

Step 2: Analyzing Data About Economic Events

Once economic data on business transactions have been collected through source documents, the next step is to analyze the data to determine the effects of each transaction on the company's financial statement elements. This step is very important because transaction analysis will determine how an event is to be entered into the accounting system in the recording step that follows. Recall that we analyzed the effects of the economic events in the examples in Exhibit 3–4 and that the entries in the T-accounts were based on that analysis.

A knowledge of accounting theory helps the accountant analyze transactions, determine the effect of each transaction on the financial statements, and record that effect. For example, the realization principle is used to determine when revenue should be recognized. The definition of an asset must be applied to determine whether a particular economic event gives rise to an asset. If an asset is recorded, expense recognition principles provide guidelines for determining how the cost of the asset should be expensed as the asset's service potential expires. Objectivity and verifiability govern whether or not particular economic events will be recorded. Consistency ensures that similar events will be recorded in a similar manner. These examples illustrate the importance of accounting theory in analyzing transactions.

3 Analyze transactions and determine their effects on financial statements.

CONCEPTUAL

Accounting theory assists in data analysis.

Step 3: Recording Economic Events in a Journal

The recording process is the first step in entering economic data that have been collected and analyzed into a company's accounting records. The device used to record transactions is called a book of original entry, or a **journal.** A journal provides a chronological record of transactions and other economic events that affect the company.

Journals may take many forms. A journal in which entries are made by hand may take the form shown in Exhibit 3–7. In a highly sophisticated computerized accounting system, the journal may consist of a document that authorizes a computer operator to enter data into the accounting system. In practice, an actual journal may not exist. Data for entry into the accounts may consist of business source documents, such as sales invoices.

In Exhibit 3–4 the effects (increases and decreases or debits and credits) of economic events were shown directly in T-accounts. This approach was used for illustration only. In practice, transactions are first entered into a journal and then transferred (posted) to the appropriate accounts. The advantage of recording transactions in a journal is that the procedure provides a chronological record of the economic events recognized during a period, with all the information about each transaction in one place. Notice that when the events were recorded directly into the T-accounts in Exhibit 3–4, no record of an entire transaction appeared in one place. The debit part of a transaction appeared in one account, the credit part in another. With a journal, if a question about the transaction were to arise, the journal could be used for purposes of verification.

In the next section, we will review the recording process for a general journal. Then we will take a brief look at special journals.

The General Journal

One method of recording transactions involves a single journal, called a **general journal.** Assume that the following transactions took place in May 1998, during its first month of operations, for The Garden Shop.

May 1 Corporate charter was received authorizing the issuance of 100,000 shares of $5 par common stock. Issued 16,250 shares at $8 per share.

May 1 Borrowed $30,000 from City Bank by issuing a $30,000 note due in two years. Interest at 10% is payable annually.

May 1 Purchased the assets of Real-Value Landscapers for $75,000 in cash. The assets consisted of inventory of $60,000, supplies of $4,000, and fixtures and equipment of $11,000.

May 2 Paid rent on a building for 12 months in advance, $7,200. Debited rent expense.

May 3 Purchased display equipment for $10,000 from Northern Supply Company. Paid $2,000 cash, the balance to be paid in 60 days.

May 4 Purchased merchandise on account from Quik Wholesale. Cost of the merchandise was $44,100. The Garden Shop uses the periodic inventory method.

May 4 Paid $1,800 cash for supplies, which were recorded as an asset.

May 5 Sold miscellaneous items totaling $25,000 to Ace Nursery on account.

May 9 Purchased merchandise costing $30,000 from Plants, Inc., on account. The transportation cost for the merchandise totaled $250 and was paid in cash.

May 11 Received $12,000 of the amount due from Ace Nursery.

May 12 Paid sales salaries totaling $3,000.

May 20 Cash sales of lawn supplies, $15,000.

May 20 Subleased the top floor of the building rented on May 2 for $300 per month. Credited rent revenue.

May 22 Received $5,000 from the sale of gift certificates. Credited unearned revenue—gift certificates.

May 24 Purchased temporary investments for cash at a cost of $3,600.

May 25 Returned defective merchandise costing $1,200 to Plants, Inc.

May 26 Sold miscellaneous lawn supplies totaling $24,000 to Rite-Way Construction. Rite-Way paid $6,000 cash and put the balance on account.

May 28 Paid the amount due to Quik Wholesale, $44,100.

May 29 Purchased merchandise on account from Handy Dandy Supply for $6,000.

May 30 Cash sales of lawn supplies, $18,000.

These transactions will be used as the underlying data for illustrating and discussing the remaining steps of the accounting cycle. We shall assume that The Garden Shop prepares monthly financial statements; therefore the accounting cycle in this example is one month.

The transactions just listed are recorded in general journal form in Exhibit 3–7. Notice the format of the general journal and its entries. The first column in the journal shows the date of the transaction. Listed next are the accounts debited and credited and a brief explanation of the transactions. The "folio" column is also called a "posting reference" column. In the next step of the accounting cycle, when the journal entries are posted (transferred) to the individual accounts, the account numbers of the accounts that are affected by the entries will be entered in this column to indicate that the amounts have been transferred to the appropriate accounts. The last two columns in the journal are for the dollar amounts of the debits and credits.

An analysis and a brief explanation of each entry in Exhibit 3–7 follow.

Record transactions in the general journal.

May 1	Cash 130,000	
	Common stock	81,250
	Contributed capital in excess of par	48,750

This transaction (a nonreciprocal transfer) increases an asset, cash, and stockholders' equity by $130,000. Cash is debited since increases in assets are recorded as debits. Stockholders' equity accounts are credited because increases in equity are recorded as credits. You learned in your introductory accounting course that when common stock is issued above par value, the difference between the issue price and par value is credited to contributed capital in excess of par, which is part of contributed capital.

| May 1 | Cash .... | 30,000 | |
| | Notes payable .... | | 30,000 |

The issuance of this note increases both an asset, cash, and a liability, notes payable. Cash is debited because asset increases are recorded as debits. Notes payable is credited because liability increases are recorded as credits.

May 1	Inventory.............................	60,000	
	Supplies	4,000	
	Fixtures and equipment..................	11,000	
	Cash...............................		75,000

This exchange transaction increases the assets, inventory, supplies, and fixtures and equipment, and decreases the asset, cash, by $75,000. The assets purchased are recorded as debits to the individual accounts, and cash is credited.

| May 2 | Rent expense .... | 7,200 | |
| | Cash............................... | | 7,200 |

The payment of $7,200 provides the company with the use of a building for 12 months. Even though this expenditure represents the acquisition of an asset, it is recorded *temporarily* in an expense account. (More will be said about this entry later.)

May 3	Fixtures and equipment..................	10,000	
	Cash...............................		2,000
	Accounts payable....................		8,000

This exchange transaction increases total assets and total liabilities by $8,000. Fixtures and equipment is debited (increased) by $10,000, cash is credited for $2,000, and accounts payable is credited for $8,000.

| May 4 | Purchases .... | 44,100 | |
| | Accounts payable.................... | | 44,100 |

This exchange transaction increases both the asset, inventory, and the liability, accounts payable by $44,100. The purchase of merchandise is recorded *temporarily,* however, in a purchases account. This procedure is a feature of the periodic inventory system used by The Garden Shop. Under the **periodic inventory system,** purchases of inventory are not recorded in the inventory account. Instead, the inventory account is adjusted at the end of the accounting period to show the cost of the merchandise still on hand at that time. Likewise, when sales are made (see the May 5 transaction), the cost of goods sold is not recorded. Instead, the cost of goods sold is determined and accounted for at the end of the accounting period on the basis of the following relationship:[3]

$$\begin{matrix} \text{Beginning} \\ \text{inventory} \end{matrix} + \begin{matrix} \text{Net cost of} \\ \text{purchases} \end{matrix} - \begin{matrix} \text{Ending} \\ \text{inventory} \end{matrix} = \begin{matrix} \text{Cost of} \\ \text{goods sold} \end{matrix}$$

| May 4 | Supplies .... | 1,800 | |
| | Cash............................... | | 1,800 |

[3]An alternative inventory system is a perpetual system. Under a **perpetual inventory system,** the cost of merchandise purchased for resale is debited to (recorded directly in) the inventory account. When merchandise is sold, in addition to the sales entry, the cost of goods sold is recorded at that time by debiting cost of goods sold and crediting inventory. Many computerized systems, especially those that capture sales information with UPC bar codes on the products, employ a perpetual inventory system. Periodic and perpetual inventory systems are examined in more detail in Chapter 9.

EXHIBIT 3-7	General Journal Entries

The Garden Shop
General Journal   *Page 1*

Date 1998	Account Title and Explanation	Folio	Debit	Credit
May 1	Cash		130,000	
	Common stock			81,250
	Contributed capital in excess of par			48,750
	To record sale of common stock.			
May 1	Cash		30,000	
	Notes payable			30,000
	To record issuance of note payable.			
May 1	Inventory		60,000	
	Supplies		4,000	
	Fixtures and equipment		11,000	
	Cash			75,000
	To record acquisition of assets of Real-Value Landscapers.			
May 2	Rent expense		7,200	
	Cash			7,200
	To record advance payment of rent.			
May 3	Fixtures and equipment		10,000	
	Cash			2,000
	Accounts payable			8,000
	To record purchase of equipment.			
May 4	Purchases		44,100	
	Accounts payable			44,100
	To record purchase of merchandise.			
May 4	Supplies		1,800	
	Cash			1,800
	To record purchase of supplies.			
May 5	Accounts receivable		25,000	
	Sales			25,000
	To record sales on account.			
May 9	Purchases		30,000	
	Transportation in		250	
	Accounts payable			30,000
	Cash			250
	To record purchases of merchandise and related freight costs.			

This purchase of supplies increases the asset, supplies, and decreases the asset, cash. Supplies is debited and cash is credited for the amount of the purchase.

		Debit	Credit
May 5	Accounts receivable	25,000	
	Sales		25,000

The sale of merchandise on account increases the asset, accounts receivable, and stockholders' equity. This increase in stockholders' equity is temporarily recorded in the revenue account, sales. At the end of the accounting period, in the closing step of the accounting cycle, the company's revenues less its expenses (i.e., net income or net loss) will be transferred to retained earnings (part of stockholders' equity).

The Garden Shop
General Journal

Date 1998	Account Title and Explanation	Folio	Debit	Credit
May 11	Cash		12,000	
	Accounts receivable			12,000
	To record collections from customers.			
May 12	Salaries expense		3,000	
	Cash			3,000
	To record salaries expense.			
May 20	Cash		15,000	
	Sales			15,000
	To record cash sales of merchandise.			
May 20	Cash		300	
	Rent revenue			300
	To record receipt of rent in advance for sublease.			
May 22	Cash		5,000	
	Unearned revenue—gift certificates			5,000
	To record receipt of cash for gift certificates.			
May 24	Investments		3,600	
	Cash			3,600
	To record purchase of investments.			
May 25	Accounts payable		1,200	
	Purchase returns			1,200
	To record return of defective merchandise.			
May 26	Cash		6,000	
	Accounts receivable		18,000	
	Sales			24,000
	To record cash sales and sales on account.			
May 28	Accounts payable		44,100	
	Cash			44,100
	To record payment of amount due.			
May 29	Purchases		6,000	
	Accounts payable			6,000
	To record purchases on account.			
May 30	Cash		18,000	
	Sales			18,000
	To record cash sales.			

May 9	Purchases	30,000		
	Transportation in	250		
	Accounts payable		30,000	
	Cash		250	

We analyzed a purchase of merchandise in the May 4 entry. The transportation cost for this purchase represents an additional cost of the merchandise and is recorded temporarily in a separate account. At the end of the period, transportation in will be added to purchases in the calculation of the cost of goods available for sale and the cost of goods sold.

May 11	Cash	12,000		
	Accounts receivable		12,000	

Collections from customers increase the asset, cash, and decrease the asset, accounts receivable. Cash is debited and accounts receivable is credited for $12,000.

May 12   Salaries expense   3,000
             Cash.   3,000

This entry recognizes the labor services received through May 12. Since these services already have helped to generate revenue through May 12, an expense results. Salaries expense is debited (which decreases stockholders' equity) and cash is credited.

May 20   Cash   15,000
             Sales   15,000

This transaction is similar to the sale transaction on May 5 except that it is a cash sale rather than a credit sale. The analysis is the same.

May 20   Cash   300
             Rent revenue   300

The Garden Shop received $300 in exchange for permitting a tenant to use a portion of its building for a month. Both assets and liabilities are increased by $300. Because the $300 will not be fully earned until June 20, it represents a liability at the time the cash is received. For *bookkeeping purposes,* however, a revenue account is *temporarily* credited. Rent revenue and a liability account, unearned rent, will be adjusted at the end of May for the portion of the rent earned as of May 31. (More will be said about this entry later.)

May 22   Cash   5,000
             Unearned revenue—gift certificates   5,000

The receipt of cash for sales of gift certificates increases assets and liabilities (unearned revenue) because the company has an obligation to deliver merchandise to customers who redeem the certificates. As the gift certificates are redeemed for merchandise, the obligation will be satisfied and revenue will be earned.

May 24   Investments   3,600
             Cash   3,600

In this transaction The Garden Shop exchanged the asset, cash, for the asset, investments. Investments is increased (debited) and cash is decreased (credited) for $3,600.

May 25   Accounts payable   1,200
             Purchase returns   1,200

The return of defective merchandise decreases liabilities and reduces merchandise available for sale. Because The Garden Shop uses a periodic inventory system, however, this decrease is recorded as purchase returns (a reduction in purchases). Purchase returns will be considered further when inventory adjustments are made at the end of the accounting period.

May 26   Cash   6,000
             Accounts receivable   18,000
             Sales   24,000

The above entry records the partial cash and partial credit sale. This transaction can be analyzed in the same manner as previous cash sales and credit sales transactions.

May 28   Accounts payable   44,100
             Cash.   44,100

This entry decreases liabilities by $44,100 and decreases assets by $44,100.

May 29   Purchases   6,000
             Accounts payable   6,000

This purchase transaction can be analyzed in the same manner as the credit purchase made on May 4.

May 30   Cash 18,000
               Sales   18,000

This transaction can be analyzed in the same way as previous cash sales.

Before moving to our discussion of how journal entries are posted to the accounts, we shall briefly look at how special journals are used to record transactions of a similar nature.

Special Journals

Many companies use special journals to record economic events of a similar nature. For example, if a department store has many sales of merchandise for cash, it may use a cash receipts journal to record these cash transactions. A cash disbursements journal may be used to record all transactions involving cash disbursements. The use of special journals may permit more efficient use of labor services because work may be more easily divided. For example, one employee may be assigned to record cash sales in the cash receipts journal, while another may be assigned to record cash payments in a cash disbursements journal.

The most commonly used special journals are:

SPECIAL JOURNAL	TRANSACTIONS RECORDED
Cash receipts	Cash receipts from all sources
Cash disbursements	Cash disbursements for all purposes
Sales	Sales on account
Purchases	Purchases of merchandise on account

When special journals are employed, the general journal is used to record those transactions that are not recorded in the special journals. Because special journals are normally covered in courses on accounting information systems, they are not discussed further in this chapter.

Step 4: Posting to Ledger Accounts

Once transactions have been recorded in the journal, the next step in the accounting cycle is to transfer the journalized information to the ledger. The process of transferring journalized information to ledger accounts is called **posting.** In a manual system, the ledger may consist of a notebook containing a sheet of paper for each account. In a computerized system, the ledger may consist of tracks on a tape, floppy disk, or hard drive.

The Posting Process

Posting of the journal entries shown in Exhibit 3–7 to the ledger accounts is presented in Exhibit 3–8. Some of the original journal entries are shown with the folio column completed; the numbers in the folio column indicate the accounts to which the data are posted. In the T-accounts, "GJ 1" indicates the page number in the general journal from which the data were posted. To review the posting process thoroughly, trace each journal entry's debit and credit to the appropriate account.

5 Post transactions from the journal to the ledger.

General and Subsidiary Ledgers

The composite of all the accounts shown in Exhibit 3–8 is known as a company's **general ledger.** Notice that the general ledger does not provide additional detail about items included in an account balance. For example, the balance in the accounts receivable account represents the sum of amounts due from various customers.

EXHIBIT 3 – 8   **Posting of Journal Entries to Ledger Accounts**

The Garden Shop
Selected Journal Entries

Date	Account Title and Explanation	Folio	Debit	Credit
May 1	Cash	100	130,000	
	Common stock	310		81,250
	Contributed capital in excess of par	320		48,750
1	Inventory	140	60,000	
	Supplies	120	4,000	
	Fixtures and equipment	150	11,000	
	Cash	100		75,000
2	Rent expense	560	7,200	
	Cash	100		7,200

Accounts after Posting of Journal Entries from Exhibit 3–7

		Cash					100				Supplies		120

	Cash	100			Supplies	120
May 1 GJ 1 130,000	May 1 GJ 1 175,000		May 1 GJ 1 4,000			
1 GJ 1 30,000	2 GJ 1 7,200		4 GJ 1 1,800			
11 GJ 1 12,000	3 GJ 1 2,000		31 Balance 5,800			
20 GJ 1 15,000	4 GJ 1 1,800					
20 GJ 1 300	9 GJ 1 250		Investments	130		
22 GJ 1 5,000	12 GJ 1 3,000		May 24 GJ 1 3,600			
26 GJ 1 6,000	24 GJ 1 3,600					
30 GJ 1 18,000	28 GJ 1 44,100		Inventory	140		
31 Balance 79,350			May 1 GJ 1 60,000			
Accounts receivable	110		Fixtures and equipment	150		
May 5 GJ 1 25,000	May 11 GJ 1 12,000		May 1 GJ 1 11,000			
26 GJ 1 18,000			3 GJ 1 10,000			
31 Balance 31,000			31 Balance 21,000			

Likewise, the balance in the accounts payable account represents amounts owed to several suppliers.

In order to provide detailed information about the composition of an account balance, some companies use subsidiary ledgers. For example, The Garden Shop might use a subsidiary ledger to show amounts owed to individual suppliers. The relationship between The Garden Shop's accounts payable balance and the amounts due to individual creditors is shown in Exhibit 3–9.

When subsidiary ledgers are used, the general ledger account is called a controlling account. In practice, companies often use subsidiary ledgers with controlling accounts for accounts such as accounts receivable, plant and equipment, accounts payable, and expenses. Subsidiary ledgers reduce the need for several general ledger accounts related to similar transactions.

Step 5: Preparing an Unadjusted Trial Balance

6 Explain the purpose of and prepare a trial balance.

Once transactions and other economic events have been recorded in the journal and posted to the appropriate ledger accounts, the next step in the accounting cycle is to prepare an unadjusted trial balance. The **unadjusted trial balance,** prepared at the end of the accounting period, is a listing of each account and its balance in the general ledger before any adjusting entries are made. Exhibit 3–10 presents the

Accounts payable				200
May 25 GJ 1	1,200	May 3 GJ 1	8,000	
28 GJ 1	44,100	4 GJ 1	44,100	
		9 GJ 1	30,000	
		29 GJ 1	6,000	
		31 Balance	42,800	

Notes payable		205
	May 1 GJ 1	30,000

Unearned revenue–gift certificates		210
	May 22 GJ 1	5,000

Common stock		310
	May 1 GJ 1	81,250

Contributed capital in excess of par		320
	May 1 GJ 1	48,750

Sales		400
	May 5 GJ 1	25,000
	20 GJ 1	15,000
	26 GJ 1	24,000
	30 GJ 1	18,000
	31 Balance	82,000

Rent revenue		420
	May 20 GJ 1	300

Purchases		510
May 4 GJ 1	44,100	
9 GJ 1	30,000	
29 GJ 1	6,000	
31 Balance	80,100	

Purchase returns		520
	May 25 GJ 1	1,200

Transportation in		540
May 9 GJ 1	250	

Salaries expense		550
May 12 GJ 1	3,000	

Rent expense		560
May 2 GJ 1	7,200	

unadjusted trial balance for The Garden Shop on May 31, 1998. The accounts are listed in the following order: assets, liabilities, stockholders' equity, revenues, and expenses.

The unadjusted trial balance is a useful step in the accounting process for the following reasons:

1. The unadjusted trial balance verifies the equality of the debits and credits posted to the ledger accounts before adjusting entries are made. Although it does not prove that all transactions have been recorded and posted correctly (e.g., if a purchase of supplies is debited to revenue, the transaction has been incorrectly recorded, but the debits and credits are still equal), it does reveal errors such as posting a debit as a credit, or posting a debit but failing to post the related credit.

2. The unadjusted trial balance facilitates the preparation of adjusting entries, because it provides a listing of each account's debit or credit balance.

After the unadjusted trial balance has been prepared, an *optional* step in the accounting cycle is to prepare a worksheet. The worksheet facilitates the recording of adjusting entries and the preparation of financial statements. Because worksheet preparation is an optional step that does not replace any of the remaining steps in the accounting cycle, it is presented in Appendix 3–1 at the end of this chapter.

EXHIBIT 3-9   **Accounts Payable in General Ledger and in Subsidiary Ledger**

	General Ledger		Accounts Payable Subsidiary Ledger		
Accounts payable		200	Northern Supply Company		204
Balance		42,800 ←		May 3	8,000
			Quik Wholesale		201
	May 28	44,100	May 4		44,100
			Plants, Inc.		202
	May 25	1,200	May 9		30,000
				Balance	28,800
			Handy Dandy Supply		203
				May 29	6,000

EXHIBIT 3-10   **Unadjusted Trial Balance**

The Garden Shop
Unadjusted Trial Balance
May 31, 1998

Account	DR	CR
Cash	$ 79,350	
Accounts receivable	31,000	
Supplies.	5,800	
Investments	3,600	
Inventory	60,000	
Fixtures and equipment	21,000	
Accounts payable		$ 42,800
Notes payable		30,000
Unearned revenue—gift certificates		5,000
Common stock.		81,250
Contributed capital in excess of par.		48,750
Sales		82,000
Rent revenue		300
Purchases	80,100	
Purchase returns		1,200
Transportation in.	250	
Salaries expense	3,000	
Rent expense	7,200	
	$291,300	$291,300

Step 6: Preparing Adjusting Entries

To this point, all of The Garden Shop's external transactions have been recorded in the accounts. However, additional internal transactions may have occurred but not been recorded. For example, unrecorded salary expenses may have accrued since the last payday. Or supplies may have been used but not recorded as expenses. Under accrual accounting and the related principles of matching and revenue and expense recognition, these events must be recorded to permit proper measurement of the company's net income for the month of May and to facilitate the preparation of financial statements at the end of the month. The recording of these additional transactions and internal events is accomplished through preparing **adjusting entries,** the next step in the accounting cycle.

At the end of May, The Garden Shop has gathered the following information:

I. Prepaid rent, end of May, $6,600.

2. Supplies used during May, $1,300.

3. Rent revenue from sublease earned during May, $100.

4. Sales from redemptions of gift certificates, $3,500.

5. Interest accrued on notes payable, $250.

6. Salaries accrued, end of May, $2,500.

7. Depreciation on fixtures and equipment, $350. (The Garden Shop uses straight-line depreciation on its assets, which have an estimated useful life of five years and no salvage value.)

8. Estimated uncollectible accounts receivable, $215.

9. Ending inventory, based on a physical count of merchandise on hand and priced at cost, $72,000.

Using these data, we will prepare adjusting entries for The Garden Shop for the month of May. We will classify the adjusting entries as follows:

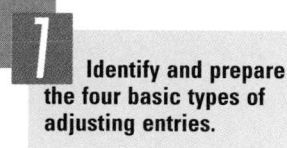

Identify and prepare the four basic types of adjusting entries.

I. Prepayments and unearned items (deferrals)—cash flows that *precede* earnings activities.

   a) Prepaid expenses.

   b) Unearned revenues.

2. Accruals—cash flows that *follow* earnings activities.

   a) Accrued expenses.

   b) Accrued revenues.

3. Estimated items.

   a) Depreciation expense.

   b) Uncollectible accounts expense.

4. Inventory adjustments.

Prepayments and Unearned Items (Deferrals)

Prepayments and **unearned items,** often called **deferrals,** are transactions in which assets are acquired in advance of their use, or in which obligations to deliver goods or services result from assets received. For prepayments and unearned items, *the cash flows precede the earnings activity.* For example, a company may acquire supplies for cash and later use the supplies in the earnings process. Because prepayments have been recorded in the accounts, an adjusting entry must allocate their amounts between asset and expense accounts or between liability and revenue accounts.

Why are prepayments and unearned items called deferrals? According to one dictionary, to defer means "to put off to a future time, to delay, or to keep something from occurring until a future time."[4] In the context of the accounting process, to "put off to a future time" means that deferrals are not recognized immediately in the income statement as expenses and revenues. Deferrals *are* recognized immediately in the balance sheet as assets and liabilities, but their income statement recognition is

CONCEPTUAL

For prepayments/unearned items, cash flows precede the earnings activity.

CONCEPTUAL

Deferrals are not recognized immediately in the income statement as expenses and revenues.

---

[4]*The Random House Dictionary of the English Language* (New York: Random House, 1987), p. 522. Some accounting theorists would call almost all assets carried at historical cost deferred expenses, in the sense that these items will eventually find their way into the income statement as expenses when they are sold, used, consumed, or as their service potential expires.

"delayed" or "put off" until they are used or consumed (in the case of assets such as supplies) or earned (in the case of liabilities such as unearned revenues).

In the next two sections we will discuss and illustrate adjusting entries for prepaid expenses and unearned revenue.

Prepaid Expenses   **Prepaid expenses** are the costs of assets acquired when a company makes an expenditure that gives rise to future economic benefits. For example, a company may acquire insurance protection by purchasing an insurance policy. Or it may acquire the future use of a factory building by making an advance rental payment. These two examples are usually categorized as prepaid insurance and prepaid rent. Other prepaid expenses include prepaid advertising and supplies. As the economic benefits are received, these prepayments are transferred to expense accounts.

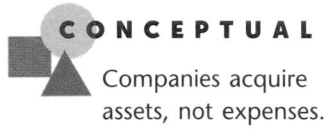

C O N C E P T U A L

Companies acquire assets, not expenses.

Companies acquire assets, not expenses. Even though prepaid expenses represent assets, some companies first *record* them by debiting an expense account instead of an asset account. This bookkeeping procedure may be followed for several reasons:

1. The company expects to receive the benefits of the asset during the current accounting period. Thus, this procedure avoids the necessity of making an end-of-period adjusting entry.

2. The company's practice is to record all prepayments as expenses, and make the appropriate adjustments at the end of the accounting period.

3. The dollar amount of the prepayment, which in theory should be recorded as an asset, may be immaterial.

Adjustments for prepaid expenses assign the cost of asset services used to an expense account, while leaving the cost of asset services applicable to future accounting periods in the asset account. The adjusting entry necessary for prepaid expenses depends on whether the initial expenditure was recorded as an asset or as an expense. This point will be illustrated for two types of prepaid expenses for The Garden Shop.

The Garden Shop's first prepaid expense requiring adjustment is prepaid rent. On May 3 the company paid $7,200 for 12 months' rent on a building; rent expense for May (one month) is $600. Since the company originally recorded the rent payment in the rent expense account, the following adjusting entry is required on May 31:

Prepaid rent 6,600
    Rent expense   6,600

After this adjusting entry has been posted to the appropriate ledger accounts, the prepaid rent (asset) account has a balance of $6,600, and the rent expense account has a balance of $600.

Prepaid rent				Rent expense			
May 31				May 3	7,200	May 31	
Adjusting	6,600					Adjusting	6,600
				Balance	600		

The second prepaid expense to be adjusted is supplies. The company made two purchases of supplies, at a total cost of $5,800, and recorded both transactions in the asset account, supplies. Supplies costing $1,300 were used during May; thus the following adjusting entry is necessary:

Supplies expense 1,300
    Supplies.   1,300

After posting, the supplies and supplies expense accounts appear as follows:

Supplies				Supplies expense			
May 1	4,000	May 31		May 31			
May 4	1,800	Adjusting	1,300	Adjusting	1,300		
Balance	4,500						

Note that the adjusting entry for prepaid rent required the debiting of an asset account (prepaid rent) and the crediting of an expense account (rent expense), while this adjusting entry requires the debiting of an expense account (supplies expense) and the crediting of an asset account (supplies). However, the purpose of both entries is the same—to assign the cost of assets or asset services used to an expense account while leaving the cost of assets on hand or the cost of services to be received in the future in an asset account. In formal terms, the portion of prepaid expenses applicable to future periods is known as unexpired costs; the portion of prepaid expenses expensed during the current period is called expired costs.

Unearned Revenue **Unearned revenues** represent obligations to provide goods or services arising from receipts of assets (usually cash). As the company provides the goods or services, the related revenues are earned. End-of-period adjustments record the amounts earned as revenues and the amounts unearned as liabilities. The two adjustments related to unearned revenue are made as follows.

On May 20, 1998, The Garden Shop subleased the upper floor of its building at a monthly rental of $300. However, only one-third of the rent has been earned between the sublease date, May 20, and the end of May. Because The Garden Shop credited rent revenue when it received the cash, an adjustment is necessary:

Rent revenue 200
    Unearned rent revenue 200

Once the adjustment has been posted to the ledger accounts, the rent revenue account will have a credit balance of $100, which is the amount of rent earned during May.[5] The unearned rent revenue account will have a balance of $200, which is the amount unearned at the end of May.

Rent revenue				Unearned rent revenue	
May 31		May 20	300		May 31	
Adjusting	200				Adjusting	200
		Balance	100			

Another adjustment must be made for sales and redemptions of gift certificates. On May 22, 1998, The Garden Shop sold gift certificates totaling $5,000. The $5,000 was credited to unearned revenue from gift certificates because The Garden Shop is obligated to deliver merchandise to those customers who redeem the certificates. By the end of May, gift certificates totaling $3,500 have been redeemed. Therefore, the following adjusting entry is required.[6]

Unearned revenue—gift certificates. 3,500
    Sales 3,500

After this adjustment is posted to the ledger accounts, unearned revenue—gift certificates will have a credit balance of $1,500, which is the sales value of the gift certificates still outstanding at the end of May.

---

[5]Since the company leased the building and is now subleasing a part of it, the rent received for subleasing could be viewed as a reduction in rent expense. If this approach were used, the following adjustment would be made:

Rent revenue 300
    Rent expense 100
    Unearned rent revenue 200

[6]Because a periodic inventory system is in use, the cost of the goods related to redemptions of gift certificates will be included in the cost of goods sold when the end-of-year inventory and purchases adjustments are made.

Sales			Unearned revenue—gift certificates			
	May 31		May 31		May 22	5,000
	Adjusting	3,500	Adjusting	3,500		
					Balance	1,500

In the prepaid expense adjustments illustrated on pages 119–121, The Garden Shop initially recorded some prepayments as expenses and others as assets. Likewise, in these unearned revenue adjustments, one cash receipt is offset by a credit to revenue and the other by a credit to a liability. These bookkeeping inconsistencies are *for illustration only* to show the various forms adjusting entries might take. In practice, a company would probably record all prepayments as either expenses or assets and all unearned items as either revenues or liabilities.

Accruals

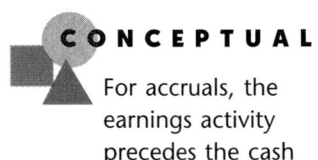

CONCEPTUAL

For accruals, the earnings activity precedes the cash flows.

Accruals arise from earnings activities that precede the related cash flows. They are transactions or internal events that have occurred but have not been recorded. Revenues that are earned before their collection are called accrued revenues, and expenses that are incurred before they are paid are called accrued expenses. Accruals necessitate adjustments that affect either (1) expense and liability accounts or (2) asset and revenue accounts. Revenue accruals always increase assets (receivables) and owners' equity (revenue). Expense accruals always decrease owners' equity (by increasing expenses) and increase liabilities (payables).

The Garden Shop's first adjusting entry is to record interest of $250 accrued on notes payable:

Interest expense 250
    Interest payable 250
($30,000 × .10 × 1/12)

If the company continues to prepare monthly statements, this adjusting entry will be made each month; and on May 1, 1999, the balance in the interest payable account will be $3,000 ($250 × 12). When the interest is paid on May 1, 1999, interest payable will be debited and cash will be credited for $3,000.

The second adjustment is for accrued salary expense. The Garden Shop has received employee services from the last payday (May 12) to the end of May but has neither recorded nor paid for those services. Therefore, the following adjusting entry is necessary:

Salaries expense 2,500
    Salaries payable 2,500

Assuming that salaries of $5,500 are paid in June at the end of the regular payment period, $3,000 constitutes payment for employee services received in June (salaries expense in June), and $2,500 constitutes payment of the liability, salaries payable, that exists at the end of May.

Distinction between Prepayments and Accruals

Note the distinction between prepayment and accruals. Accrual accounting and the matching principle require adjustments for these two groups of items for quite different reasons:

1. *Prepayments* have been recorded but necessitate end-of-period allocations between asset and expense accounts and between liability and revenue accounts.

2. *Accruals* have occurred but have not yet been recorded and necessitate end-of-period adjustments of either expense and liability accounts or asset and revenue accounts.

EXHIBIT 3-11	Adjustments for Prepayments and Accruals

Income Statement

Balance Sheet	Revenue	Expense

Assets	Accrued revenues[a]
	Asset Dr
	    Revenue Cr
		Prepaid expenses[b]
		Expense Dr
		    Asset Cr

Liabilities	Unearned revenue[b]
	Liability Dr
	    Revenue Cr
		Accrued expenses[a]
		Expense Dr
		    Liability Cr

[a]Earnings activity occurs before the related cash flow.
[b]Cash flow occurs before the related earnings activity.

Prepayments and accruals may also be distinguished on the basis of the relationship between earnings activities and related cash flow. For prepayments, the cash flow leads (occurs before) the related earnings activity; for accruals, the cash flow lags (follows) the related earnings activity. These "leads and lags" are summarized in Exhibit 3–11, which shows balance sheet elements in the rows and income statement elements in the columns. The intersection of each row and column represents an adjustment involving either a prepayment or an accrual. With respect to the prepayments (unearned items), it is assumed that a real account was debited (credited) when the cash outflow (inflow) occurred.

Estimated Items

Two of the three remaining adjustments required in The Garden Shop's accounts are for expenses that must be estimated at the end of the accounting period in order to match revenues and expenses in determining net income for the month. These two estimated expenses are depreciation expense and uncollectible accounts expense. Although estimates are an inherent part of the accounting process, required in making adjustments for prepayments and accruals as well, it is accepted practice to use the term **estimated items** to describe adjustments for depreciation and uncollectibles.

Depreciation Expense **Depreciation expense** is the estimated cost of services received (or potential services expired) during a period from the use of plant and equipment. Plant and equipment services generally cannot be purchased in small amounts, as can labor services or raw materials. When a company purchases an asset that provides economic benefits that extend over several accounting periods, the estimated cost of its services in the generation of revenue during a given accounting period must be deducted from the revenue recognized in that period in order to determine income. This procedure is based on the matching principle. Under GAAP, depreciation is considered a cost allocation process in which an asset's cost, less its salvage value, if any, is allocated over its estimated useful life in a systematic and rational manner.[7]

On the basis of the information given on page 119, the following adjusting entry would be made to record The Garden Shop's depreciation expense for the month of May:

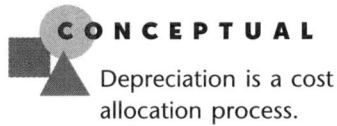

CONCEPTUAL
Depreciation is a cost allocation process.

Depreciation expense 350
    Accumulated depreciation—fixtures and equipment. 350

---

[7]The cost of plant and equipment may be viewed as a long-term prepayment.

The $350 is calculated as follows:

$$\frac{\text{Cost minus salvage value}}{\text{Useful life}} = \begin{array}{l}\text{Annual depreciation, assuming the} \\ \text{use of the straight-line method}\end{array}$$

$$\frac{\$21,000 - \$0}{5} = \$4,200 \text{ annual depreciation expense}$$

$$\frac{\$4,200}{12} = \$350 \text{ monthly depreciation expense}$$

Accumulated depreciation is shown on the balance sheet as a deduction from fixtures and equipment. This type of account is called a **contra asset** or asset valuation account. Conceptually, the fixtures and equipment account could be credited for depreciation instead of the accumulated depreciation account. However, that approach would not allow a financial statement user to determine the original cost of the fixtures and equipment. Thus, the use of a contra asset account provides additional information to financial statement users. (Accounting for depreciation of plant and equipment is discussed in more detail in Chapter 12.)

Uncollectible Accounts Expense   **Uncollectible accounts expense,** or bad debt expense, is an expense arising from uncollectible accounts receivable.[8] Under some circumstances, uncollectible accounts are not recorded as expenses until it is known for certain that they are uncollectible. However, these expenses are usually estimated and recorded each period in order to match revenue and expense on the income statement and report receivables on the balance sheet at the amount expected to be collected.

The Garden Shop estimates that the dollar amount of its uncollectible accounts will be $215. Thus the following entry would be made:

Uncollectible accounts expense 215
    Allowance for uncollectible accounts   215

CONCEPTUAL

The allowance for uncollectible accounts measures receivables not expected to be collected.

The allowance for uncollectible accounts is a measure of those receivables not expected to be collected. Because The Garden Shop does not know *which* accounts receivable will prove to be uncollectible, the allowance account, instead of accounts receivable, must be credited.

The allowance account is reported on the balance sheet as a deduction from accounts receivable. It is a contra asset or asset valuation account. Because receivables are reported net of the allowance, the net receivables balance represents the amount of cash that is expected to be collected in the near future. Thus it better satisfies the financial reporting objective of providing information about future cash inflows to the company. As individual customers' accounts become uncollectible, the allowance account is debited and accounts receivable credited for the amount of each customer's account written off.

CONCEPTUAL

Uncollectible accounts expense is similar to an accrual.

Adjusting entries for uncollectible accounts expense are similar to accruals. That is, the entry to record uncollectible accounts expense may be viewed as an adjustment of a previously recorded accrual of sales on account. (Accounting and reporting for accounts receivable and estimating uncollectible accounts are covered in greater detail in Chapter 8.)

Inventory Adjustments

Recall that The Garden Shop uses a periodic inventory system. Under this system, merchandise purchases and related items such as transportation costs on merchandise, returned merchandise, and cash discounts from early payments on purchases are not recorded in the inventory account. Instead, temporary (nominal) accounts

---

[8]Some accountants consider classification of uncollectible accounts as a reduction in sales rather than as an expense to be conceptually appealing.

arc used to record these transactions. The use of temporary accounts provides the management of The Garden Shop with information about the cost of current purchases, transportation cost incurred, and the dollar amount of purchase returns. Otherwise, this information would be buried in the inventory account.

Under a periodic inventory system, no entries are made to record the cost of merchandise sold on each sale date. To determine the cost of goods sold during May (which is deducted, along with other expenses, from sales to determine income), we must compare the cost of merchandise on hand at the end of May with the total cost of merchandise available for sale during May.

At the end of the accounting period, a physical inventory of merchandise on hand is taken, and the cost of the merchandise is determined. The inventory account must then be adjusted to show the cost of merchandise on hand at the end of the period. An adjustment must also be made to record the cost of goods sold during the period.

The cost of goods sold by The Garden Shop during May may be calculated on the basis of the account balances in Exhibit 3–8, as follows:

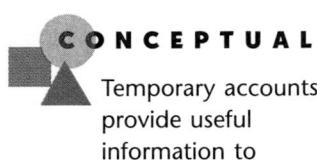

Beginning inventory		$ 60,000
Purchases	$ 80,100	
Transportation in	250	
Purchase returns	(1,200)	
Net cost of purchases		79,150
Cost of goods available for sale during May		$139,150
Ending inventory		(72,000)
Cost of goods sold		$ 67,150

As shown, the company had $60,000 of merchandise at the beginning of May and purchased merchandise costing $79,150 during the month. Therefore, merchandise costing $139,150 was available for sale during the month. Since merchandise costing $72,000 remains at the end of May, the cost of goods sold is $67,150.

Two hypothetical questions clarify this calculation:

1. If *no* inventory remained at the end of May, what would be the cost of goods sold?

2. If *no* sales were made during May, what would be the cost of goods sold and the cost of the ending inventory?

It should be clear that the answer to the first question is $139,150, and the answer to the second is $0 for the cost of goods sold and $139,150 for the cost of the ending inventory.[9] The following equation sets forth the relationship between inventories, purchases, and cost of goods sold:

Beginning inventory (BI)	+	Net cost of purchases (P)	−	Ending inventory (EI)	=	Cost of goods sold (CGS)

The adjusting entries to record the cost of goods sold for May are as follows:

Cost of goods sold 60,000
    Inventory (beginning) 60,000
To transfer the beginning inventory balance
to cost of goods sold.

Cost of goods sold 79,150
Purchase returns 1,200
    Purchases 80,100
    Transportation in 250
To transfer the net cost of purchases to cost of goods sold.

---

[9]These hypothetical questions ignore the possibility of shrinkage (i.e., theft, breakage, or spoilage) and errors in recording purchase transactions and in taking inventory. Technically, these factors should be considered. Here, however, they unnecessarily complicate and detract from the conceptual discussion.

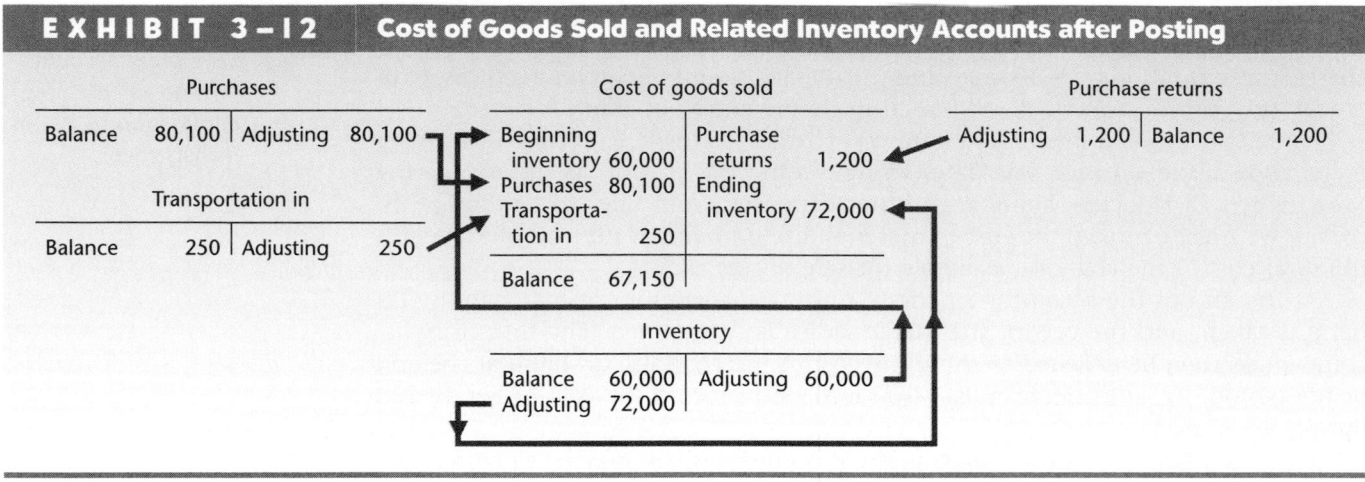

EXHIBIT 3–12 **Cost of Goods Sold and Related Inventory Accounts after Posting**

	Inventory (ending)	. . . .	72,000	
	Cost of goods sold	. . . .		72,000

To record the ending inventory in the accounts
as an asset.

These entries could be combined into one cost of goods sold adjusting entry. When these entries have been posted, the accounts affected will appear as shown in Exhibit 3–12.

Although we have referred to these entries as *adjusting entries* for inventory and cost of goods sold, they could also be described as **closing entries,** or even *adjusting/closing entries*. To illustrate, the first entry closes the beginning inventory balance to cost of goods sold; the second entry closes purchases and related accounts to cost of goods sold. One reason for using the term *closing entries* is that some companies close the beginning inventory and purchases and related accounts directly to income summary in the closing step of the accounting cycle. Under this approach, income summary would replace cost of goods sold in the entries just illustrated.

Adjusting Entries: A Summary

Once the adjustments have been recorded in the general journal, they are posted to the general ledger (see GJ2 posting references in Exhibit 3–18 on pages 132–133). The reason for and purpose of adjusting entries may be summarized as follows:

1. Under accrual accounting, adjusting entries are necessary to record economic events related to earnings activities that have occurred but have not been recorded at the end of the period.

2. Adjusting entries are necessary to match revenues earned and expenses incurred in order to determine net income for the period. In addition, assets and liabilities are properly measured after the adjusting entries are made.

3. Each adjusting entry affects a real (balance sheet) account and a nominal (income statement) account.

4. For prepayments and unearned items, the form of the adjusting entry depends on how the prepaid expense or unearned revenue item was recorded initially. However, the purpose of the adjustment is the same. For prepaid expenses, that portion of the cost of asset services that represents future economic benefits

appears on the balance sheet as an asset, and that portion of the cost of asset services that provided benefits during the current year appears on the income statement as an expense. For unearned revenues, the portion earned during the period is shown on the income statement as revenue, and the portion that will be earned in a subsequent period is reported on the balance sheet as a liability.

5. In short, adjusting entries are necessary to make the financial statements representationally faithful and thus more useful to investors, creditors, management, and others.

Step 7: Preparing the Adjusted Trial Balance

The **adjusted trial balance** for The Garden Shop appears in Exhibit 3–13. The adjusted trial balance is useful because it tests the accuracy of the account balances *after* the adjusting entries have been posted. In addition, it contains all the information necessary to complete the next step in the accounting cycle, preparation of the financial statements.

EXHIBIT 3–13	Adjusted Trial Balance

The Garden Shop
Adjusted Trial Balance
May 31, 1998

Account	DR	CR
Cash	$ 79,350	
Accounts receivable	31,000	
Allowance for uncollectible accounts		$ 215
Supplies	4,500	
Prepaid rent	6,600	
Investments	3,600	
Inventory	72,000	
Fixtures and equipment	21,000	
Accumulated depreciation—fixtures and equipment		350
Accounts payable		42,800
Notes payable		30,000
Salaries payable		2,500
Interest payable		250
Unearned revenue—gift certificates		1,500
Unearned rent		200
Common stock		81,250
Contributed capital in excess of par		48,750
Sales		85,500
Rent revenue		100
Cost of goods sold	67,150	
Depreciation expense	350	
Interest expense	250	
Salaries expense	5,500	
Rent expense	600	
Supplies expense	1,300	
Uncollectible accounts expense	215	
	$293,415	$293,415

Step 8: Preparing the Financial Statements

Now that we have recorded and posted The Garden Shop's transactions for the month of May, we are ready to prepare the financial statements, the end product of the accounting process. As stated in Chapter 1, the financial statements are a central component of financial reporting and a principal means of communicating the effects of transactions and other economic events to interested users. The Garden Shop's financial statements appear in Exhibits 3–14 through 3–17.

The Income Statement

The **income statement** presents a summary of a company's earnings activities for the period, including the revenues earned and the expenses incurred in earning them. Gains and losses from activities not related to a company's primary operating activities also appear on the statement. The income statement allows users to determine whether a company made a profit during the period, and may also help in assessing the company's future cash flows.

The Garden Shop's income statement for the month of May appears in Exhibit 3–14. Net income for May was $10,235. Net income is added to stockholders' equity on the May 31, 1998, balance sheet. (The format, classification, and other aspects of the income statement are discussed in more detail in Chapter 4.)

The Balance Sheet (Statement of Financial Position)

The **balance sheet,** also called the **statement of financial position,** reports a company's financial position at a point in time. The elements of the balance sheet—assets, liabilities, and equity—correspond to the elements of the accounting equation.

The Garden Shop's balance sheet at May 31, 1998, appears in Exhibit 3–15. Assets are listed on the balance sheet, generally according to liquidity. *Current assets* are those that are expected to be converted into cash or consumed within a relatively short period of time, generally one year or the company's operating cycle, whichever is longer. For example, accounts receivable are classified as current since

---

EXHIBIT 3–14 **Income Statement**

The Garden Shop
Income Statement for the Month of May 1998

Sales		$85,500
Cost of goods sold		(67,150)
Gross margin		$18,350
Selling and administrative expenses:		
Depreciation expense	$ 350	
Interest expense	250	
Salaries expense	5,500	
Rent expense	600	
Supplies expense	1,300	
Uncollectible accounts expense	215	
Total		(8,215)
		$10,135
Other revenues and expenses:		
Rent revenue		100
Net income		$10,235

EXHIBIT 3–15   Balance Sheet

The Garden Shop
Balance Sheet
May 31, 1998

Assets			Liabilities and Stockholders' Equity		
Current assets:			Current liabilities:		
Cash		$ 79,350	Accounts payable		$ 42,800
Accounts receivable	$31,000		Interest payable		250
Less: Allowance for			Salaries payable		2,500
uncollectible accounts	(215)	30,785	Unearned revenue from gift certificates		1,500
Investments		3,600	Unearned rent		200
Inventory		72,000	Total current liabilities		$ 47,250
Supplies		4,500			
Prepaid rent		6,600	Long-term liabilities:		
Total current assets		$196,835	Notes payable (due in 2000)		30,000
			Total liabilities		$ 77,250
Plant and equipment:					
Fixtures and equipment	$21,000		Stockholders' equity:		
Less: Accumulated			Common stock ($5 par, 100,000		
depreciation	(350)	20,650	shares authorized, 16,250		
			shares issued)		$ 81,250
Total assets		$217,485	Contributed capital in excess of par		48,750
			Retained earnings		10,235
			Total stockholders' equity		$140,235
			Total liabilities and		
			stockholders' equity		$217,485

they are expected to be collected shortly after the balance sheet date. Investments are classified as current because The Garden Shop does not plan to hold them over a long period. Assets whose benefits extend over longer periods include plant and equipment, intangibles, and long-term investments. They are sometimes called *noncurrent assets*.

Liabilities also are classified in a similar manner. *Current liabilities* are those that will require the use of current assets or will be discharged within a relatively short period, usually one year. In Exhibit 3–15, interest payable is classified as current since it will be paid within the next year. Notes payable, on the other hand, are classified as *long-term* or *noncurrent,* since they will not be paid until 2000. By providing information about the timing of future cash inflows and outflows, these classifications increase the usefulness of the financial statements.

Because net income increases stockholders' equity, the net income for May is included on the balance sheet as part of retained earnings in the stockholders' equity section. In the closing step of the accounting cycle, the balances in the income statement accounts will be transferred to the income summary account and finally to the retained earnings account. (The format, classification, and other related aspects of balance sheet reporting are discussed more thoroughly in Chapter 5.)

The Statement of Retained Earnings

The **statement of retained earnings** for The Garden Shop is shown in Exhibit 3–16. This statement is designed to reconcile the beginning and ending retained

EXHIBIT 3-16	Statement of Retained Earnings

The Garden Shop
Statement of Retained Earnings
for the Month of May 1998

Retained earnings, May 1, 1998	$ –0–
Net income for May	10,235
Retained earnings, May 31, 1998	$10,235

earnings balances. Net income for the period increases retained earnings; dividends for the period decrease retained earnings. The only item affecting The Garden Shop's retained earnings in May was the income.

If The Garden Shop declares and pays a cash dividend of $7,500 in June 1998, the entry to record the declaration and payment would be as follows:

Dividends declared	7,500	
Cash		7,500

At the end of June the dividends declared account would be closed to retained earnings.[10] This dividend would appear as a deduction on the statement of retained earnings for the month of June. (The statement of retained earnings is covered in more detail in Chapters 4 and 18.)

The Statement of Cash Flows

The **statement of cash flows** discloses the amount of cash generated and used by a company's operating, financing, and investing activities during an accounting period. The Garden Shop's statement of cash flows appears in Exhibit 3–17. The information presented in Exhibit 3–17 was taken from the company's cash ledger account, which appears in Exhibit 3–8 on page 116. Other approaches to preparing the statement of cash flows and additional disclosures about cash flows are discussed in Chapters 6 and 21.

Step 9: Recording and Posting Closing Entries

9 **Explain the purpose of and prepare closing entries.**

After the financial statements have been prepared, the income statement account balances in the ledger must be closed (reduced to zero) so that these accounts can be used to collect revenue and expense transactions in the following period. This procedure is called closing the accounts. To facilitate the closing process, one new nominal account, income summary, is opened, and the revenue and expense account balances are transferred to it. The income summary account balance is then transferred to owners' equity, or in the case of The Garden Shop, to retained earnings.

Three steps are used to close the income statement accounts and to transfer the resulting balance in the income summary account to retained earnings:[11]

1. All income statement accounts with *credit* balances are *debited,* and the income summary account is credited in an amount equal to the total debits.

---

[10]Many companies record dividends directly in the retained earnings account, as follows:

Retained earnings	xx	
Cash		xx

[11]These three steps could be combined and only one closing entry made. Additionally, the income statement accounts could be closed directly to retained earnings, instead of being closed to income summary.

EXHIBIT 3-17 Statement of Cash Flows

The Garden Shop
*Statement of Cash Flows
for the Month of May 1998*

Cash flows from operating activities:
Cash sales and collections on credit sales	$ 51,000	
Revenue collected in advance	5,000	
Purchases of merchandise	(104,350)	
Purchases of supplies	(5,800)	
Payment of salaries	(3,000)	
Payment of rent (net of $300 sublease)	(6,900)	
Net cash used by operating activities		$(64,050)
Cash flows from investing activities:		
Purchases of fixtures and equipment	$ (13,000)	
Purchases of investments	(3,600)	
Net cash used by investing activities		(16,600)
Cash flows from financing activities:		
Issued common stock	$130,000	
Issued notes payable	30,000	
Net cash provided by financing activities		160,000
Net increase in cash		$ 79,350

2. All income statement accounts with *debit* balances are *credited,* and the income summary account is debited in an amount equal to the total credits.

3. The balance in the income summary account is transferred to retained earnings. If earnings activities have resulted in net income, income summary is debited and retained earnings is credited. If instead a net loss results, retained earnings is debited and income summary is credited.

Closing entries for The Garden Shop are as follows:

Sales	85,500	
Rent revenue	100	
Income summary		85,600
To close revenues to income summary.		

Income summary	75,365	
Cost of goods sold		67,150
Depreciation expense		350
Salaries expense		5,500
Rent expense		600
Supplies expenses		1,300
Uncollectible accounts expense		215
Interest expense		250
To close expenses to income summary.		

Income summary	10,235	
Retained earnings		10,235
To close net income to retained earnings.		

Exhibit 3–18 shows the general ledger accounts for The Garden Shop after these closing entries have been posted. The adjusting entries that were recorded earlier have also been posted to these accounts. This exhibit assumes that all transactions *during* the period were recorded on page 1 of the company's general journal (GJ 1), all *adjusting* entries on page 2 (GJ 2), and all *closing* entries on page 3 (GJ 3).

EXHIBIT 3–18   **Accounts after Closing**

The Garden Shop
General Ledger Accounts after Posting of Closing Entries

		Cash					100
May	1	GJ 1	130,000	May	1	GJ 1	75,000
	1	GJ 1	30,000		2	GJ 1	7,200
	11	GJ 1	12,000		3	GJ 1	2,000
	20	GJ 1	15,000		4	GJ 1	1,800
	20	GJ 1	300		9	GJ 1	250
	22	GJ 1	5,000		12	GJ 1	3,000
	26	GJ 1	6,000		24	GJ 1	3,600
	30	GJ 1	18,000		28	GJ 1	44,100
			216,300				136,950
						Balance	79,350
			216,300				216,300
31	Balance		79,350				

		Accounts receivable					110
May	5	GJ 1	25,000	May 11		GJ 1	12,000
	26	GJ 1	18,000				
			43,000				12,000
						Balance	31,000
			43,000				43,000
31	Balance		31,000				

	Allowance for uncollectible accounts		111
		May 31 GJ 2	215

		Supplies					120
May	1	GJ 1	4,000	May 31		GJ 2	1,300
	4	GJ 1	1,800				
			5,800				1,300
						Balance	4,500
			5,800				5,800
31	Balance		4,500				

	Prepaid rent		121
May 31	GJ 2	6,600	

	Investments		130
May 24	GJ 1	3,600	

		Inventory					140
May	1	GJ 1	60,000	May 31	GJ 2	60,000
	31	GJ 2	72,000			
			132,000			60,000
				Balance		72,000
			132,000			132,000
31	Balance		72,000			

		Fixtures and equipment					150
May	1	GJ 1	11,000	
	3	GJ 1	10,000	
31	Balance	21,000	

	Accumulated depreciation— fixtures and equipment		151
		May 31 GJ 2	350

		Accounts payable					200
May 25	GJ 1	1,200	May	3	GJ 1	8,000
28	GJ 1	44,100		4	GJ 1	44,100
				9	GJ 1	30,000
				29	GJ 1	6,000
		45,300				88,100
31 Balance		42,800				
		88,100				88,100
			31 Balance			42,800

	Notes payable		205
		May 31 GJ 1	30,000

	Unearned revenue—gift certificates		210
May 31 GJ 2	3,500	May 22 GJ 1	5,000
Balance	1,500		
	5,000		5,000
		31 Balance	1,500

	Unearned rent		211
		May 31 GJ 2	200

Step 10: Preparing a Postclosing Trial Balance

Once the income statement accounts have been closed, a company prepares a **postclosing trial balance.** The postclosing trial balance lists the real accounts and their respective balances in the general ledger after the closing entries have been posted. The purpose of a postclosing trial balance is to test the equality of the debits and credits in the ledger after the closing entries have been posted. This trial balance shows

Salaries payable			212
	May 31	GJ 2	2,500

Interest payable			213
	May 31	GJ 2	250

Common stock			310
	May 1	GJ 1	81,250

Contributed capital in excess of par			320
	May 1	GJ 1	48,750

Retained earnings			321
	May 31	GJ 3	10,235

Sales							400
May 31	GJ 3	85,500	May 5	GJ 1	25,000
			20	GJ 1	15,000
			26	GJ 1	24,000
			30	GJ 1	18,000
			31	GJ 2	3,500
		85,500			85,500

Rent revenue							420
May 31	GJ 2	200	May 20	GJ 1	300
31	GJ 3	100			
		300			300

Cost of goods sold							500
May 31	GJ 2	60,000	May 31	GJ 2	72,000
	GJ 2	79,170		GJ 3	67,150
		139,150			139,150

Purchases							510
May 4	GJ 1	44,100	May 31	GJ 2	80,100
9	GJ 1	30,000			
29	GJ 1	6,000			
		80,100			80,100

Purchase returns							520
May 31	GJ 2	1,200	May 25	GJ 1	1,200

Transportation in							540
May 9	GJ 1	250	May 31	GJ 2	250

Depreciation expense							541
May 31	GJ 2	350	May 31	GJ 3	350

Salaries expense							550
May 12	GJ 1	3,000	May 31	GJ 3	5,500
31	GJ 2	2,500			
		5,500			5,500

Rent expense							560
May 2	GJ 1	7,200	May 31	GJ 2	6,600
			31	GJ 3	600
		7,200			7,200

Interest expense							565
May 31	GJ 2	250	May 31	GJ 3	250

Supplies expense							570
May 31	GJ 2	1,300	May 31	GJ 3	1,300

Uncollectible accounts expense							580
May 31	GJ 2	215	May 31	GJ 3	215

Income summary							590
May 31	GJ 3	75,365	May 31	GJ 3	85,600
31	GJ 3	10,235			
		85,600			85,600

the real accounts and their balances, which will be carried forward to the next accounting period. The postclosing trial balance for The Garden Shop, based on the account balances presented in Exhibit 3–18, appears in Exhibit 3–19.

At this point the accounting cycle has been completed. The nominal accounts have been closed, the real account balances have been determined, and the ledger accounts are ready to accumulate transaction data and other economic events for the next accounting period.

EXHIBIT 3–19	Postclosing Trial Balance

The Garden Shop
Postclosing Trial Balance
May 31, 1998

Account	DR	CR
Cash	$ 79,350	
Accounts receivable	31,000	
Allowance for uncollectible accounts		$ 215
Supplies	4,500	
Prepaid rent	6,600	
Investments	3,600	
Inventory	72,000	
Fixtures and equipment	21,000	
Accumulated depreciation—fixtures and equipment		350
Interest payable		250
Accounts payable		42,800
Notes payable		30,000
Unearned revenue—gift certificates		1,500
Unearned rent		200
Salaries payable		2,500
Common stock		81,250
Contributed capital in excess of par		48,750
Retained earnings		10,235
	$218,050	$218,050

Step 11 (Optional): Recording and Posting Reversing Entries

10 Explain the purpose of reversing entries; identify adjusting entries that could be reversed, and prepare entries to reverse them.

If desired, reversing entries may be made at the *beginning* of the following accounting period. A **reversing entry** is a reversal of an adjusting entry that was made at the end of the previous period. As we shall see, the purpose of a reversing entry is to simplify the recording of transactions in the next period. Keep in mind that *reversing entries are optional, not mandatory.*

In the next two sections, we will review the procedure for reversing two types of adjusting entries: (1) prepayments and unearned items and (2) accruals.

Prepayments and Unearned Items

Not all adjusting entries may be reversed. Reversing entries may be made only for prepayments and unearned items for which the original transactions involving them were recorded in nominal accounts. This procedure assumes that prepayments and unearned items will be recorded in nominal accounts during the following period, thus increasing bookkeeping consistency.

To illustrate, assume that on October 1, 1998, XYZ Company purchased a two-year insurance policy on its buildings, paid the two-year premium of $2,400 in advance, and recorded the transaction as follows:

Insurance expense	2,400	
Cash		2,400

If the company closes its books on December 31, 1998, the adjusting entry required at the end of the year is as follows:

Prepaid insurance	2,100	
Insurance expense		2,100

(21/24 × $2,400)
To adjust insurance expense to the correct expense
for 1998 and to record the unexpired insurance
as an asset.

Once the closing entries are made, the prepaid insurance account has a balance of $2,100, and the $300 balance in the insurance expense account ($2,400 − $2,100) has been closed to income summary. Because the company recorded the original transaction as an expense, and presumably will do so for future insurance coverage, the following reversing entry is appropriate on January 1, 1999:

Insurance expense	2,100	
Prepaid insurance		2,100

After this reversing entry has been posted at the beginning of 1999, the prepaid insurance account balance is zero, and the insurance expense account has a debit balance of $2,100. An adjusting entry, similar to the one just shown but in the amount of $900 ($2,100 − $1,200), would be required at the end of 1999. Reversal of this amount at the beginning of the year 2000 eliminates the necessity of an adjusting entry at the end of 2000, because coverage will expire on October 1, 2000.

Accruals

Reversing entries may be made for accrued revenue and expense adjustments in order to simplify the accounting procedures for these items in the following period, when the receivable is collected or the liability is paid. To illustrate, assume that a company pays its employees' salaries of $30,000 every other Friday (based on 10 working days). The company's fiscal year ends on December 31, which falls on a Wednesday. Assuming that three working days have elapsed since the last payday, the adjusting entry required to record the accrued salaries on December 31 is as follows:

Salaries expense	9,000	
Salaries payable		9,000

(3/10 × $30,000)

After all closing entries have been made on December 31, this adjusting entry will be reversed on January 1 of the following year:

Salaries payable	9,000	
Salaries expense		9,000

What is the effect of this reversing entry? The entry reduces the salaries payable account to zero and creates a credit balance of $9,000 in salaries expense. When the salaries of $30,000 are paid on the next payday, the following entry will be made:

Salaries expense	30,000	
Cash		30,000

After the $30,000 has been posted to the salaries expense account, the account will show a debit balance of $21,000, which is the correct amount of salaries expense to date.

These concepts may be further illustrated with T-accounts:

Accounts after adjustment:

Salaries expense			Salaries payable		
Assumed balance before adjustment				Adjusting	9,000
153,000					
Adjusting 9,000					

Accounts after closing:

Salaries expense			Salaries payable		
162,000	Closing	162,000		Adjusting	9,000

Accounts after reversing:

Salaries expense			Salaries payable		
162,000		162,000	Reversing 9,000		9,000
	Reversing	9,000			

Salaries expense account after the first pay period in the following accounting period:

Salaries expense		
162,000		162,000
30,000	Reversing	9,000
Balance 21,000		

Without reversing entries, when salaries are paid for the first time in the following year, it would be necessary to determine what portion of the $30,000 payment relates to current expense and what portion represents payment of the beginning-of-year liability. That determination is unnecessary when reversing entries are used because the amount is shown automatically in the accounts.

Reversing Entries: A Summary

Reversing entries are *not* mandatory but may help to simplify bookkeeping. If a company *chooses* to make reversing entries, the following rule is a useful reminder of which adjustments should and should not be reversed: If the adjusting entry increases the balance in an asset or liability account, reverse the adjusting entry; otherwise, do not reverse it. This rule is illustrated in Exhibit 3–20.

PROPRIETORSHIP AND PARTNERSHIP EQUITY ACCOUNTS

In the illustration of the accounting cycle just completed, the accounting entity was a corporation. As a result, owners' (stockholders') equity was subdivided into the following accounts: common stock, contributed capital in excess of par, and retained earnings. The first two accounts were used to record the issuance of stock. The corporation's net income for the accounting period was transferred to retained earnings at the end of the accounting period.

EXHIBIT 3-20	To Reverse or Not to Reverse		

Adjusting Entry		Reverse?	Reason
Prepaid rent . . . . *xx*		Yes	Adjusting entry increases an asset account balance.
Rent expense	*xx*		
Unearned revenue . . . . *xx*		No	Adjusting entry does not increase a liability account balance.
Revenue	*xx*		
Depreciation expense . . . . . . *xx*		No	Adjusting entry does not increase an asset account balance; accumulated depreciation is a contra asset account balance.
Accumulated depreciation .	*xx*		
Interest expense . . . . *xx*		Yes	Adjusting entry increases a liability account balance.
Interest payable	*xx*		

In a single proprietorship, one real account (e.g., owner's equity) replaces all the stockholders' equity accounts. In a partnership, an owner's equity account is established for each partner. If the owner or owners withdraw assets for personal use during an accounting period, a nominal or drawing account is established to record withdrawals. The drawing account is closed to the capital account at the end of the period.

To illustrate, assume that Bud Lacy begins a single proprietorship. Transactions and other events that affect owner's equity would be recorded as follows:

Initial investment by owner:

> Assets (detailed) . . . . *xx*
>   B. Lacy, capital . . . .   *xx*

Withdrawals by owner:

> B. Lacy, drawings . . . . *xx*
>   Assets (detailed) . . . .   *xx*

Closing of income summary account (assuming a profit):

> Income summary . . . . *xx*
>   B. Lacy, capital . . . .   *xx*

Closing of withdrawals to capital account:

> B. Lacy, capital . . . . *xx*
>   B. Lacy, drawings . . . .   *xx*

CASH-BASIS ACCOUNTING VERSUS ACCRUAL ACCOUNTING REVISITED

Chapter 2 included a comparison of cash-basis and accrual accounting. This chapter has provided a comprehensive review of accrual accounting within the context of the accounting cycle. In practice, accountants are often required to convert a cash-basis income statement to an accrual-basis statement so that the company's financial statements will conform to GAAP. Because this task requires a thorough understanding of the principles of accrual accounting, it is an appropriate way to end this chapter.

Exhibit 3–21 presents an analysis of cash flows versus income flows for The Garden Shop. The left-hand side of Exhibit 3–21 represents the cash flows from operating activities taken from The Garden Shop's statement of cash flows in Exhibit 3–17.

EXHIBIT 3-21   **Cash Flows versus Income Flows**

The Garden Shop
Analysis of Cash Flows vs. Income Flows

Cash Flows (from Exhibit 3–17)		Adjustments[a]		Income Flows (from Exhibit 3–14)	
Collections from customers					
($51,000 + $5,000)	$56,000	A	$31,000		
		B	(1,500)	$85,500	Sales
Payments for merchandise	(104,350)	C	72,000		
		D	(34,800)	(67,150)	Cost of goods sold
Payments for supplies	(5,800)	E	4,500	(1,300)	Supplies expense
Payments for salaries	(3,000)	F	(2,500)	(5,500)	Salaries expense
Payments for rent	(7,200)	G	6,600	(600)	Rent expense
Less: Sublease	300	H	(200)	100	Rent revenue
		I	(350)	(350)	Depreciation expense
		J	(215)	(215)	Uncollectible account expense
		K	(250)	(250)	Interest expense
Net cash used by operating activities	($64,050)			$10,235	Net income

[a]Key to adjustments:
  A: **Increase in accounts receivable**
  B: **Increase in unearned revenue—gift subscriptions**
  C: **Ending inventory**
  D: **Increase in accounts payable related to operating activities**
  E: **Increase in supplies**
  F: **Increase in salaries payable**
  G: **Increase in prepaid rent**
  H: **Increase in unearned rent**
  I: **Depreciation expense**
  J: **Uncollectible accounts expense**
  K: **Increase in interest payable**

The middle column contains the adjustments necessary to convert The Garden Shop's operating cash flows to an accrual-basis income statement. The income statement on the right-hand side is reproduced from Exhibit 3–14. An analysis of each adjustment follows. As we proceed through it, trace the amounts in the adjustments column to the appropriate financial statement.

A. This amount is the increase in the accounts receivable account ($31,000 ending – $0 beginning) during the month. It is added to customer collections because the amount represents sales on account that have not been collected by the end of the month.

B. This amount is the increase in the unearned revenue account ($1,500 ending – $0 beginning) during the month. It is deducted from customer collections because the amount it represents will not be recorded as sales until customers redeem the outstanding gift certificates.

C. This amount is The Garden Shop's inventory at the end of the month. It will not appear on the Shop's accrual-basis income statement until the goods it represents are sold. Normally, cash paid to suppliers is adjusted to cost of goods sold by deducting the increase (or adding the decrease) in inventory during the period, because beginning inventory sold during the period increases the cost of goods sold but has no effect on cash. In The Garden Shop's case, however, part of the cash payments to suppliers was for its initial inventory.

D. During the month, The Garden Shop's accounts payable account increased by $42,800: $34,800 for merchandise purchases (an operating activity) and $8,000 for purchases of fixtures and equipment (an investing and financing activity). Because the $34,800 amount represents additional purchases of merchandise on account during the month, it is added to payments to suppliers.

E. This amount is the increase in the supplies account during the month. The ending supplies will become expenses as they are used in the following period(s).

F. This amount is the increase in the salaries payable account during the month. It is added because it represents additional salaries expense accrued but not paid during the month.

G. This amount is the increase in the prepaid rent account during the month. It is deducted because it represents that portion of rent payments applicable to future periods.

H. This amount is the increase in the unearned rent account during the month; it can be interpreted in the same way as adjustment B.

I. Though the depreciation expense of $350 had no effect on cash flows, it must be included in the income statement as an expense under GAAP.

J. Though uncollectible accounts expense of $215 had no effect on cash flows, it must be included in the income statement as an expense under GAAP.

K. This amount is the increase in the interest payable account during the month. It is added because it represents an expense in excess of any cash outflows for interest.

After the adjustments are added or subtracted, as appropriate, from The Garden Shop's operating cash flows, the resulting accrual-basis revenues and expenses appear as they did on The Garden Shop's income statement in Exhibit 3–14.

As we shall see in Chapter 6, companies often prepare the statement of cash flows by converting the accrual-basis income statement to a cash basis (operating cash flows). An analysis similar to that in Exhibit 3–21, except working from right to left, is used. For example, to convert the accrual-basis sales to a cash basis, the increase in accounts receivable would be deducted from sales and the increase in unearned revenue would be added to sales. Similar analyses could be made for the other income statement items.

SUMMARY OF LEARNING OBJECTIVES

1. Explain the effects of transactions on the accounting equation.
Every transaction has a dual (balancing) effect on the accounting equation. For example, if a transaction causes an increase in assets, it will also cause an increase in liabilities or equity.

2. State the basic rules for debits and credits to accounts.
Debits are recorded on the left side of an account, credits on the right. Debits indicate asset increases, liability decreases, stockholders' equity decreases, and increases in expenses and losses. Credits indicate asset decreases, liability increases, stockholders' equity increases, and increases in revenues and gains.

3. Analyze transactions and determine their effects on financial statements.
Transaction analysis determines how the financial effects of each transaction will be entered (recorded) in the accounting system. Each transaction has a dual effect on the financial statements. For example, a sale to a customer on account increases an asset account, accounts receivable, and increases a revenue account (revenue being a component of equity).

4. Record transactions in the general journal.

Transactions are recorded in the general journal by listing the accounts affected by the transaction. Each account is debited or credited, as appropriate, for the dollar amount of the transaction.

5. Post transactions from the journal to the ledger.

Accounts, each with a cumulative record of debits and credits, are kept in a ledger. The posting process involves transferring the dollar amounts from each transaction recorded in the journal to the appropriate ledger account.

6. Explain the purpose of and prepare a trial balance.

A trial balance verifies the equality of the debits and credits posted to the ledger accounts. Although a trial balance does not verify that all transactions have been recorded and posted correctly, it does reveal errors such as posting a debit as a credit or posting a debit but failing to post the related credit. The trial balance also facilitates the preparation of adjusting entries, because it provides a listing of each account's debit or credit balance.

7. Identify and prepare the four basic types of adjusting entries.

Prepayments and unearned items (deferrals) are transactions in which assets are acquired in advance of their use, or in which obligations to deliver goods or services result from assets received. Adjusting entries for the transactions are designed to allocate assets used (or revenues earned) to expense accounts (or revenue accounts) from asset accounts (or liability accounts). Accruals represent transactions and internal events that have occurred but have not yet been recorded. Adjusting entries for accruals are designed to record expenses and liabilities (or assets and revenues) that have taken place but have not yet been recorded. Adjusting entries for estimated items include depreciation expense and uncollectible accounts expense. Adjusting entries for inventory are designed to transfer the dollar cost of purchases and related accounts to cost of goods sold and to adjust the inventory account (through cost of goods sold) to the proper dollar amount at the end of an accounting period. These procedures result in allocating the total cost of goods available for sale during the period to cost of goods sold and ending inventory.

8. Explain the purpose of and prepare the four basic financial statements.

The income statement reports the revenues, expenses, gains, and losses during the accounting period. The balance sheet reports the company's financial position at a point in time, the end of the accounting period, by listing the company's assets, liabilities, and owners' equity. The statement of retained earnings reports the changes in retained earnings during the period. The statement of cash flows reports the cash inflows and outflows from operating, investing, and financing activities.

9. Explain the purpose of and prepare closing entries.

Closing entries are designed to reduce the income statement account balances to zero so the accounts can be used to summarize revenue and expense transactions data for the following period.

10. Explain the purpose of reversing entries; identify entries that could be reversed, and prepare entries to reverse them.

The purpose of reversing entries is to simplify the recording of transactions in the following accounting period. If entries are reversed, a reversing entry should be made for any adjusting entry that has increased an asset or liability account balance.

KEY TERMS

accounting process (or cycle) 107

accounts 104

accruals 122

adjusted trial balance 127

adjusting entries 119

assets 103

balance sheet
   (statement of financial position) 128

closing entries 126

contra asset 124

APPENDIX 3-1

Use of a Worksheet

A worksheet may be used to facilitate the preparation of both adjusting entries and the financial statements. A worksheet permits the accountant to assemble all the ledger account balances and adjustment information on one schedule. In addition, it permits a company to prepare interim (e.g., monthly or quarterly) statements even though it may close its books only once a year. The worksheet is not a formal statement but merely a working paper. As Exhibit 3–5 on page 108 indicates, its preparation is optional.

A worksheet for The Garden Shop is presented in Exhibit 3–22. It was prepared as follows.

Preparing the Worksheet

1. The unadjusted trial balance (see Exhibit 3–10) is recorded in the first two columns of the worksheet.

2. The worksheet adjusting entries, prepared from and keyed to the adjustments information on page 119, are entered into the second pair of columns. If a new account is needed for an adjustment, it is added at the bottom of the worksheet (e.g., prepaid rent or supplies expense). Just as was illustrated on pages 125–126, entries (9), (10), and (11) are used to record the cost of goods sold.

3. The adjusted trial balance is constructed by extending the unadjusted trial balance and adjustments data into the third pair of columns. This third pair of columns is often omitted, and the unadjusted trial balance and adjustment data extended directly into the income statement and balance sheet columns. In that case, the worksheet consists of only eight columns. The nominal account balances are extended into the appropriate income statement columns (preserving the previous debit or credit balances), and the real account balances are extended into the balance sheet columns.

4. The worksheet illustration assumes that The Garden Shop's income tax rate is 40 percent. Net income before taxes is $10,235, which is the difference between

EXHIBIT 3–22 10-Column Worksheet

The Garden Shop
Worksheet for the Month of May 1998

Account	Unadjusted Trial Balance DR	Unadjusted Trial Balance CR	Adjustments DR	Adjustments CR	Adjusted Trial Balance DR	Adjusted Trial Balance CR	Income Statement DR	Income Statement CR	Balance Sheet DR	Balance Sheet CR
Cash	79,350				79,350				79,350	
Accounts receivable	31,000				31,000				31,000	
Supplies	5,800			(2) 1,300	4,500				4,500	
Investments	3,600				3,600				3,600	
Inventory	60,000		(11)72,000	(9)60,000	72,000				72,000	
Fixtures and equipment	21,000				21,000				21,000	
Accounts payable		42,800				42,800				42,800
Notes payable		30,000				30,000				30,000
Unearned revenue—gift certificates		5,000	(4) 3,500			1,500				1,500
Common stock		81,250				81,250				81,250
Contributed capital in excess of par		48,750				48,750				48,750
Sales		82,000		(4) 3,500		85,500		85,500		
Rent revenue		300	(3) 200			100		100		
Purchases	80,100			(10)80,100						
Purchase returns		1,200	(10) 1,200							
Transportation in	250			(10) 250						
Salaries expense	3,000		(6) 2,500		5,500		5,500			
Rent expense	7,200			(1) 6,600	600		600			
	291,300	291,300								
Cost of goods sold			(9)60,000 (10)79,150	(11)72,000	67,150		67,150			
Prepaid rent			(1) 6,600		6,600				6,600	
Supplies expense			(2) 1,300		1,300		1,300			
Unearned rent				(3) 200		200				200
Interest expense			(5) 250		250		250			
Interest payable				(5) 250		250				250
Salaries payable				(6) 2,500		2,500				2,500
Depreciation expense			(7) 350		350		350			
Accumulated depreciation				(7) 350		350				350
Uncollectible accounts expense			(8) 215		215		215			
Allowance for uncollectible accounts				(8) 215		215				215
			227,265	227,265	293,415	293,415	75,365	85,600		
Income tax expense			4,094				4,094[a]			
Income tax payable				4,094						4,094
Net income							6,141[b]			6,141
							85,600	85,600	218,050	218,050

[a] .40($85,600 − $75,365).
[b] $85,600 − $75,365 − $4,094.

the income statement credit and debit column totals ($85,600 − $75,365 = $10,235). Thus, one more adjusting entry is made in the adjustments columns to record the tax: income tax expense is debited and income tax payable credited for $4,094 (.40 × $10,235). Income tax expense is then extended to the income statement debit column, and income tax payable is extended to the balance sheet credit column as a liability. Finally, the net income of $6,141 is shown as a debit to balance the income statement columns, and as a credit to balance the balance sheet columns. (If the adjustment for taxes were not made, net income for May would have been $10,235, per the income statement in Exhibit 3–14; that amount would have been the balancing debit and credit in the income statement and balance sheet columns, respectively.)

Preparing Financial Statements from the Worksheet

The income statement and balance sheet for The Garden Shop may be prepared directly from the income statement and balance sheet columns of the worksheet. The adjusting entries (including the entry for taxes) can be transferred directly from the worksheet to the general journal and posted to the appropriate accounts. Closing entries also can be made on the basis of the income statement columns in the worksheet. Income summary would be debited for the total debits in the income statement column, and the individual accounts would be credited. Likewise, income summary would be credited for the total credits in the income statement column and the individual accounts would be debited.

Since The Garden Shop began operations in May, the worksheet shown in Exhibit 3–22 does not incorporate a retained earnings account at the beginning of May. Exhibit 3–23 illustrates a partial worksheet for The Garden Shop at the end of June 1998.

Several points should be noted about this worksheet.

1. This worksheet actually has 12 columns, but the first four columns have been omitted here to avoid repetition. This worksheet differs from the 10-column worksheet shown in Exhibit 3–22 only in the addition of a pair of columns for retained earnings.

2. Many of the accounts shown in the adjusted trial balance carry over from the May 31 postclosing trial balance (e.g., the prepaid rent account balance has been reduced by the $600 for the rent expense for June; accumulated depreciation has been increased by the $350 in depreciation expense for June).

3. The retained earnings account balance of $6,141 represents the beginning-of-June balance and is the same amount as shown on the worksheet in Exhibit 3–22.

4. The Garden Shop declared and paid dividends of $5,000 during June. Note that the beginning retained earnings, the net income of $10,800, and the dividends of $5,000 are entered into the retained earnings column. The balancing debit in this column represents the retained earnings balance at the end of June; it is extended to the balance sheet credit column.

The existence of beginning retained earnings does not necessitate the use of a 12-column worksheet. An 8- or 10-column worksheet can be prepared by extending beginning retained earnings (and dividends declared, if appropriate) from the adjusted trial balance directly to the balance sheet columns. For balance sheet reporting purposes, the ending retained earnings figure would be determined as follows:

$$\frac{\text{Beginning}}{\text{retained earnings}} + \frac{\text{Net}}{\text{income}} - \text{Dividends} = \frac{\text{Ending}}{\text{retained earnings}}$$

EXHIBIT 3–23 | **12-Column Worksheet (Partial)**

The Garden Shop
Partial Worksheet for the Month of June 1998

Account	Adjusted Trial Balance DR	Adjusted Trial Balance CR	Income Statement DR	Income Statement CR	Retained Earnings DR	Retained Earnings CR	Balance Sheet DR	Balance Sheet CR
Cash	52,041						52,041	
Accounts receivable	54,000						54,000	
Allowance for uncollectible accounts		500						500
Supplies	7,000						7,000	
Investments	3,600						3,600	
Prepaid rent	6,000						6,000	
Inventory	65,000						65,000	
Fixtures and equipment	21,000						21,000	
Accumulated depreciation		700						700
Accounts payable		54,000						54,000
Interest payable		500						500
Salaries payable		3,800						3,800
Common stock		81,250						81,250
Contributed capital in excess of par		48,750						48,750
Retained earnings		6,141				6,141		
Sales		104,000		104,000				
Rent revenue		200		200				
Cost of goods sold	76,500		76,500					
Salaries expense	6,300		6,300					
Rent expense	600		600					
Interest expense	250		250					
Depreciation expense	350		350					
Uncollectible accounts expense	400		400					
Supplies expense	1,800		1,800					
Dividends declared	5,000				5,000			
	299,841	299,841	86,200	104,200				
Income tax expense			7,200					
Income tax payable								7,200
Net income (to retained earnings)			10,800			10,800		
			104,200	104,200		16,941		
								11,941
Retained earnings (to balance sheet)					11,941		208,641	
					16,941	16,941	208,641	208,641

Q 3-1. What are the features common to accounting and reporting systems, regardless of the complexity of the entity?

Q 3-2. Give an example of each of the following types of economic events:
1. External event—exchange.
2. External event—nonreciprocal transfer.
3. Internal event.

Q 3-3. What is the distinguishing characteristic of an exchange?

Q 3-4. For each transaction below, indicate the effect on the accounting equation. Use + for increase, – for decrease, and N for no effect.

| | EFFECT ON: | | |
TRANSACTION	ASSETS	LIABILITIES	OWNERS' EQUITY
a) Purchased a machine with cash			
b) Borrowed cash by issuing a note			
c) Revenue earned during the period			
d) Owner investment in the business			
e) Owner withdrawal of cash from the business			
f) Paid the note in item *b*			
g) Sold a building at a gain			
h) Sold a building at a loss			
i) Purchased supplies on account			

Q 3-5. What are source documents? What is their role in the accounting cycle?

Q 3-6. Explain the process and purpose of journalizing transactions.

Q 3-7. Why is the posting step in the accounting cycle useful?

Q 3-8. The steps in the accounting cycle are listed below, but not necessarily in the proper order. Number them in the proper order.
Financial statement preparation
Collection of data about economic events
Analysis of effects of transactions and other events
Reversing entries
Unadjusted trial balance preparation
Adjusted trial balance preparation
Recording transactions during the period
Postclosing trial balance preparation
Posting transactions during the period
Recording and posting closing entries
Recording and posting adjusting entries

Q 3-9. How are subsidiary ledgers related to general ledger controlling accounts?

Q 3-10. Many companies use special journals to record transactions. What are some of the advantages of using special journals?

Q 3-11. Why might a company elect to make reversing entries? What guidelines may be used to determine when an adjusting entry should be reversed?

Q 3-12. What is the purpose of adjusting entries?

Q 3-13. An unadjusted trial balance is prepared at the end of the accounting period as a step in the accounting cycle. Why is this step important? Which of the following errors would be revealed by an unadjusted trial balance? Why?
1. A debit item was posted twice from the journal to the ledger.
2. Debit and credit items in equal amounts were not posted.

3. A purchase of merchandise was recorded as an expense.

4. A purchase of merchandise was recorded as a debit to sales.

5. An error was made in totaling the cash account, which resulted in an overstatement of the account.

*Q 3-14. Where would each of the following items appear on a 10-column worksheet?

1. Balance, before adjustment, of the salaries expense account.

2. Adjusting entry for depreciation expense.

3. Ending inventory.

4. Dividends declared and paid during the period.

5. Beginning inventory.

6. Sales discounts.

7. Beginning retained earnings.

Q 3-15. Classify each of the following as a real or nominal account:

1. Allowance for doubtful accounts.   **5.** Cost of goods sold.

2. Ending inventory.   **6.** Mr. X, withdrawals.

3. Purchase returns.   **7.** Mr. X, capital.

4. Interest receivable.   **8.** Prepaid insurance.

Q 3-16. What types of transactions would be recorded in the following special journals?

1. Purchases journal.

2. Cash receipts journal.

3. General journal.

4. Sales journal.

5. Cash disbursements journal.

Q 3-17. A company recorded the following transaction in general journal form:

Notes receivable 12,000

Cash 24,000

  Sales   36,000

To record sales of merchandise.

Assume that the company uses special journals. How would this transaction be recorded?

Q 3-18. A company's ledger accounts showed a debit of $2,600 posted to interest revenue at the beginning of 1998. What kind of account is this (e.g., revenue, expense, etc.) and how did it arise?

Q 3-19. Why are closing entries necessary? What accounts are affected by closing entries?

*Q 3-20. How is a worksheet used in the accounting cycle? What are the advantages of preparing a worksheet?

*Q 3-21. The bookkeeper for Work, Inc., made the following errors in extending items in the adjusted trial balance columns to the income statement and balance sheet columns of a worksheet. What effect would each error have on the affected columns? Also state why the error would or would not be automatically detected.

1. A revenue item was extended into the balance sheet credit column.

2. An asset item was extended into the income statement credit column.

3. An expense item was extended into the balance sheet debit column.

4. A revenue item was extended into the income statement debit column.

CASES

C 3-1.   **DOUBLE-ENTRY BOOKKEEPING**   For some time Mr. Jordan has operated a small convenience store. He has limited his accounts to single-entry records and has engaged outside accounting assistance only for preparation of his tax return. He has never needed to obtain credit and does not expect to do so. Mr. Jordan approaches you with the statement that he has heard of double-entry bookkeeping and would like to know how double-entry bookkeeping would record his store's transactions. He has maintained a record of the store's cash receipts and disbursements. The cash records for April of the current year appear as follows:

Balance, April 1		$ 6,500
Receipts:		
Cash sales	43,610	
Additional investment by Mr. Jordan	5,000	48,610
Disbursements:		
Purchases of merchandise	$11,900	
Withdrawals by Mr. Jordan	2,000	
Purchases of supplies	460	
Clerical salaries	14,600	
Other	750	(29,710)
Balance, April 30		25,400

REQUIRED Write a memo to Mr. Jordan explaining how the above cash transactions would be recorded in a double-entry system.

C 3-2. **ACCRUAL ACCOUNTING CONCEPTS** On January 1, 1998, Slim Sloan opened a western wear shop in a neighborhood shopping center. Recently, he came to you for advice in connection with a bank loan. The bank has requested financial statements for the six months ending June 30, 1998. Slim has kept limited records, and he asks you how the following items should be considered in the preparation of financial statements:

a) No records have been maintained for merchandise purchases, although the company's checkbook indicates that $50,000 has been paid to creditors since January 1. You also determine that there are purchase invoices outstanding at June 30 that total $12,000.

b) During the six-month period, the company has returned unsalable merchandise that was purchased for $4,000. Since the merchandise was paid for, the manufacturer issued the company a credit to be used against future purchases.

c) The company took a physical inventory on June 30. The merchandise on hand had a cost of $18,000. On June 30, immediately after the inventory, Slim's ex-wife took clothing with a cost of $2,400 and sales value of $3,200 as a draw against Slim's personal child-support check.

d) The western store borrowed $10,000 from a savings and loan company shortly after commencing operations. By June 30, $6,000 has been repaid, as has interest of $600. The company's records show revenue of $10,000 and expenses of $6,600 in connection with these events.

e) The owner of the shop next door told Slim that prepayments and accruals must be considered in preparing the financial statements on June 30. Slim is confused about these terms and considers them irrelevant, arguing that a banker once said, "All that really matters is cash flows."

f) Fixtures and display equipment costing $9,000 were acquired on a deferred payment plan. As of June 30, $3,200 of this amount has been repaid. Slim's uncle has advised him that this should be considered depreciation on the fixtures and equipment, since "things wash out eventually."

g) Slim has inquired about what financial statements should be prepared for the bank in addition to the statement of cash receipts and disbursements, which he thinks measures the western store's earnings for the first six months of operation.

h) Just before your arrival at the western store, Slim glanced at a trade association manual that described a system of record keeping in terms of the accounting cycle. He is confused about the meaning of the accounting cycle and the steps involved in it.

REQUIRED Write a brief response to each of the items above.

C 3-3. **ADJUSTMENTS; PREPAYMENTS VS. ACCRUALS** The ability to distinguish between prepayments (deferrals) and accruals is important to accounting graduates, both in terms of having a full understanding of cash flow and income "leads/lags" and in being able to communicate clearly and effectively with those outside the profession as discussions of this type arise. For example, a marketing employee could become quite confused if an accounting employee described sales commissions earned but not paid as a prepayment. Or a finance employee might wonder about an accounting employee describing "accrued depreciation."

In the context of adjusting entries, some accountants contrast prepayments (deferrals) and accruals as follows: One type of adjustment adds amounts to both the income statement and balance sheet; the other type moves amounts from one financial statement to another financial statement.

REQUIRED

1. Write a paragraph that distinguishes between prepayments (deferrals) and accruals as the terms are used in financial accounting. In your paragraph, relate these terms to "leads and lags" between cash flows and income.

2. Write a brief paragraph that clarifies the view expressed in the second paragraph above.

C 3-4. **PURPOSE OF ADJUSTING ENTRIES** Two students are taking the accounting principles course in different sections with different instructors. Both sections recently completed studying adjusting entries, and the two students are discussing what they have learned about the subject. They are somewhat confused about adjusting entries, because their instructors described the purpose of adjusting entries differently.

Instructor A told his class that the sole purpose of adjusting entries is to properly match revenues and expenses on the income statement. Instructor B told her class that the sole purpose of adjusting entries is to properly report assets and liabilities on the balance sheet.

REQUIRED   Write a brief paragraph to these two students that will help overcome their confusion.

EXERCISES   The exercise marked with an asterisk (*) refers to Appendix 3–1.

E 3-1. **RULES OF DEBIT AND CREDIT** Below is a list of accounts, with each account name preceded by a letter. Indicate the account debited and credited to record each transaction below by placing the letter corresponding to the correct account to the right of each transaction.

a) Cash   **f)** Rent expense
b) K. Kaminski, capital   **g)** Accounts payable
c) Accounts receivable   **h)** Agency revenue
d) Office equipment   **i)** Salaries expense
e) Supplies   **j)** Unearned revenue

	DEBIT	CREDIT
Example: K. Kaminski started an advertising agency by investing cash.	a	b
1. Purchased office equipment and office supplies on account.		
2. Rented a building and paid the monthly rent.		
3. Completed layout work on a magazine for a client and received cash.		
4. Returned a portion of the office equipment purchased in transaction 1.		
5. Placed a TV advertisement for a client on account.		
6. Paid the balance due on the equipment and supplies purchased in transaction 1.		
7. Paid the salary of her secretary.		
8. Withdrew supplies for her personal use.		
9. Received cash as an advance payment for art and layout work to be completed next year.		
10. Collected cash from client in transaction 5.		

E 3-2. **TRIAL BALANCE PREPARATION** The unadjusted trial balance below was prepared by your client and does not balance. Additional information relating to the trial balance also appears below.

Rebenar Racquet Club
Trial Balance
December 31, 1998

ACCOUNT	DEBIT	CREDIT
Cash	$ 3,300	
Receivables from club members	41,600	
Supplies	1,400	
Building	75,000	
Accumulated depreciation—building		$ 34,000
Land	61,000	
Accounts payable		38,200
Notes payable		10,000
M. Rebenar, capital		50,000
Club member advances		5,400
Club revenues		110,400
Salaries expense	46,500	
Advertising expense	12,000	
Tournament expense	19,000	
	$259,800	$248,000

a) M. Rebenar withdrew supplies totaling $800 for personal use. The withdrawal was not recorded.

b) Salaries expense for November was $5,000 and was recorded correctly in the journal. However, the debit was posted twice to the salaries expense account.

c) Advertising expenses of $6,000 were incorrectly debited to the land account.

d) Club revenues for the month of May 1998 totaled $3,400. When the transaction was posted from the journal to the ledger, the club revenue account was debited instead of credited for $3,400.

e) On December 5, 1998, the company received a bill for $2,500 for newspaper advertising for November. The transaction had not been recorded nor had the bill been paid at the end of 1998.

REQUIRED

1. Give appropriate entries required to correct the accounts. Also, explain how the remaining accounts would be corrected if a formal entry is not required.

2. Prepare a corrected trial balance.

E 3-3. **ADJUSTING ENTRIES** Prepare adjusting entries for the data below:

a) Revenue of $6,000 was recorded during the year when cash was received. By the end of the year, only $4,400 had been earned.

b) Salaries of $3,000 have accrued since the last payment period.

c) Interest revenue of $500 has been earned but is unrecorded at the end of the year.

d) Uncollectible accounts expense is determined by adjusting the allowance for doubtful accounts to 4 percent of the ending accounts receivable balance. At the end of the year, the balance in the accounts receivable account was $120,000, and the credit balance in the allowance account was $3,000.

e) Assets are depreciated by the straight-line method. Assets subject to depreciation had a cost of $64,000, estimated useful life of 10 years, and estimated salvage value of $4,000.

f) Included among the accounts on the unadjusted trial balance were supplies expense with a debit balance of $6,000 and supplies with a debit balance of $9,000. Supplies on hand at the end of the year totaled $3,000.

E 3-4.   **ADJUSTING AND REVERSING ENTRIES**   The following transactions and other data relate to operating activities of Flynn Company, which closes its books each December 31 and makes reversing entries:

a)   Flynn purchased $2,000 in office supplies on March 1. On December 31, $400 in office supplies were on hand.

b)   Flynn received $18,000 on November 1, which represented an advance payment for six months' rent on a building owned by Flynn.

c)   Flynn holds a $4,000 note, dated November 1. Interest accrued at December 31 totals $60.

d)   On December 31, Flynn had accrued salaries of $3,600. Salary payments of $9,000 are made during the first week of each month.

REQUIRED   1.   Prepare the adjusting entries for the above four items, assuming that the original debits or credits for prepayments and unearned items were recorded in real accounts.

2.   Repeat the requirement in part 1, this time assuming that the original debits or credits for prepaid and unearned items were recorded in nominal accounts.

3.   Prepare any reversing entries appropriate for part 1.

4.   Prepare any reversing entries appropriate for part 2.

E 3-5.   **ACCRUAL ACCOUNTING RELATIONSHIPS**   Eight independent items of information relating to transactions and adjusting entries appear below. For each item, make the required calculation.

1.   Accounts payable, beginning of period, $33,000; end of period, $40,000. Purchases for the period, $100,000. Calculate cash payments to creditors during the period.

2.   Unearned revenues, end of period, $2,000. Cash collections from customers during the period, $12,000. Revenues for the period, $30,000. Calculate unearned revenues, beginning of period.

3.   Plant and equipment, beginning of period, $100,000; end of period, $95,000. Equipment with an original cost of $25,000 and accumulated depreciation of $20,000 was sold during the period at a gain of $3,000. Calculate the amount of cash received from sale of the equipment.

4.   Refer to part 3. Calculate plant and equipment purchased during the period.

5.   Refer to part 3. Given accumulated depreciation on plant and equipment, beginning of period, $66,000, and depreciation expense for the period, $14,000, calculate accumulated depreciation at the end of the period.

6.   Prepaid rent, beginning of period, $10,000; end of period, $3,000. Cash payments for rent during the period, $22,000. Calculate rent expense for the period.

7.   Salaries payable, beginning of period, $12,000. Cash payments for salaries during the period, $58,000. Salaries expense for the period, $50,000. Calculate salaries payable at the end of the period.

8.   Inventory, end of period, $10,000. Merchandise purchases for the period, $80,000. Cost of goods sold for the period, $75,000. Calculate inventory at the beginning of the period.

E 3-6.   **ACCRUAL ACCOUNTING RELATIONSHIPS**   Information relating to the balances of various balance sheet and income statement accounts is given below. For each case, prepare the journal entry that would logically account for the changes in the account balances.

1.   Unearned rent, beginning of the year, $18,000. Cash of $250,000 was received during the year and credited to unearned rent. Rent revenue appearing on the year's income statement, $255,000.

2.   Prepaid rent, beginning of the year, $9,600; end of the year, $18,000. Rent expense appearing on the year's income statement, $76,600. Prepaid rent was debited for $85,000, when cash was paid during the year.

3.   Accumulated depreciation—machinery, beginning of the year, $100,000; end of the year, $140,000. During the year, machinery with a cost of $40,000 (60 percent depreciated) was sold.

4.   Interest payable, beginning of the year, $1,200. During the year, cash interest payments were $10,400. Interest expense reported on the year's income statement, $12,200.

5.   Allowance for uncollectible accounts, beginning of year, $30,000; end of year, $46,000. Uncollectible accounts written off during the year, $10,000.

6.   Salaries payable, beginning of year, $15,000. Salaries expense on current year's income statement, $120,000. Cash payments to employees during the year, $100,000.

E 3-7. **ADJUSTING ENTRIES** Five independent transactions appear below. Each company's accounting period ends on December 31, 1998.

a) In December 1998, Company A started and completed a project with a sales price of $60,000. The project has not been recorded on the books of the company, and the company will not receive payment from the client until mid-January of 1999. Costs incurred on the project were $22,000 and have been recorded in a prepaid expense account.

b) Company B always debits prepaid insurance when it purchases or renews an insurance policy. An expiring policy was renewed on July 31, 1998, and was debited to the asset account. The three-year renewal cost $61,200, which was $18,000 more than the policy had cost three years earlier.

c) At the end of 1997, Company C reported salaries payable of $25,000 on its balance sheet. Salary payments to employees during 1998 were $210,000, and this amount was debited to salaries expense. At the end of 1998, the balance in salaries payable is still $25,000, and salaries of $23,000 for services rendered in December 1998 remain unpaid.

d) On April 1, 1998, Company D rented a building for a two-year period and paid $30,000 rent in advance; this amount was debited to rent expense. During November and December, the company subleased one floor of the building for $2,000 per month. The sublease revenue was credited to rent revenue. The company wishes to show sublease revenue as a reduction in rent expense.

e) Company E began the 1998 fiscal year with a balance of $15,000 in the supplies account. During the year, supplies were purchased at a cost of $32,000, and this amount was debited to the supplies expense account. An inventory on December 31, 1998, showed supplies of $10,000 on hand.

REQUIRED Prepare the proper adjusting entry for each company.

E 3-8. **ADJUSTING ENTRIES; TRIAL BALANCE; CLOSING ENTRIES** The unadjusted trial balance and year-end adjustments information for Trennepohl Corporation for the year ending December 31, 1998, appear below:

ACCOUNT	DR	CR
Cash	$ 23,000	
Accounts receivable	14,500	
Allowance for uncollectible accounts		$ 1,800
Inventory (1/1/98)	57,500	
Prepaid insurance	3,200	
Plant and equipment	50,000	
Accumulated depreciation		13,000
Accounts payable		25,000
Unearned rent		28,000
Common stock		2,000
Contributed capital in excess of par		8,000
Retained earnings		12,400
Sales		100,000
Purchases	25,000	
Supplies expense	6,000	
Salaries expense	11,000	
	$190,200	$190,200

Adjusting entry information at December 31, 1998:
a) Uncollectible accounts expense, $900.
b) Ending inventory, $25,000.
c) Insurance expired, $1,700.
d) Supplies on hand, $1,500.
e) Rent earned, $23,000.
f) Depreciation expense, $3,000.
g) Salaries accrued, $2,000.

REQUIRED   **I.** Prepare the December 31, 1998, adjusting entries in general journal form.
           2. Prepare an adjusted trial balance at December 31, 1998.
           3. Prepare closing entries for the year ending December 31, 1998.

*E 3-9.   **ADJUSTING ENTRIES; USE OF A WORKSHEET**   The unadjusted trial balance for Trennepohl Corporation in the preceding exercise (E3-8) is reproduced below, along with
some additional accounts.

ACCOUNT	UNADJUSTED DR	UNADJUSTED CR	ADJUSTMENTS DR	ADJUSTMENTS CR	ADJUSTED DR	ADJUSTED CR
Cash	$ 23,000					
Accounts receivable	14,500					
Allowance for uncollectible accounts ..		$ 1,800				
Inventory (1/1/98)	57,500					
Prepaid insurance	3,200					
Supplies						
Plant and equipment	50,000					
Accumulated depreciation .		13,000				
Accounts payable		25,000				
Unearned rent		28,000				
Salaries payable						
Common stock		2,000				
Contributed capital in excess of par		8,000				
Retained earnings		12,400				
Sales		100,000				
Rent revenue						
Cost of goods sold						
Purchases..............	25,000					
Insurance expense.......						
Supplies expense........	6,000					
Depreciation expense						
Uncollectible accounts expense						
Salaries expense	11,000					
	$190,200	$190,200				

REQUIRED   Using the adjustments information in the preceding exercise, complete the above worksheet for Trennepohl Corporation.

E 3-10.   **ADJUSTING, CLOSING, AND REVERSING ENTRIES**   For the year ending June 30, 1998,
Alaina Corp. had recorded salaries expense of $34,000 by debiting salaries expense and
crediting cash. On June 30, 1998, salaries expense of $2,000 had accrued since the last
payday but had not been recorded.

REQUIRED   Using T-accounts:
           I. Record Alaina's salaries expense of $34,000, record the end-of-year adjusting entry,
           and close all appropriate accounts to income summary.
           2. Reverse the June 30, 1998, adjusting entry.
           3. What is the nature of the balance in salaries expense immediately after the revers-
           ing entry has been made?
           4. On July 10, 1998, the first payday in July, $3,000 was paid; salaries expense was deb-
           ited, and cash was credited. Record this transaction.
           5. How much of the $3,000 amount in part 4 represents salaries expense thus far for
           the month of July 1998?

E 3-11. **COST OF GOODS SOLD RELATIONSHIPS** For each of the situations below, determine the missing amounts.

	BEGINNING INVENTORY	PURCHASES	PURCHASE RETURNS	ENDING INVENTORY	COST OF GOODS SOLD
1.	$20,000	$36,000	$7,000	$14,000	?
2.	18,000	61,000	3,000	?	$42,000
3.	10,000	?	–0–	–0–	40,000
4.	?	40,000	5,000	4,000	41,000

E 3-12. **CLOSING ENTRIES** The following information was taken from Oessyou Ltd.'s adjusted trial balance:

Prepaid rent	$ 6,000
Sales..	200,000
Other expenses..	20,000
Dividends	16,000
Salaries payable...	18,000
Cost of goods sold	120,000
Allowance for doubtful accounts	10,000
Other revenue...	8,000
Stockholders' equity...	180,000

REQUIRED Prepare the appropriate closing entries.

E 3-13. **ACCRUALS; PREPAYMENTS; FINANCIAL STATEMENT RELATIONSHIPS** At the beginning of 1998, Scotty Moore's balance sheet was as follows:

ASSETS		LIABILITIES AND EQUITY	
Cash	$50,000	Unearned revenue	$ 5,000
Accounts receivable	11,000	Accounts payable	3,000
Prepaid expenses	15,000	S. Moore, capital	68,000
Total	$76,000	Total	$76,000

Scotty Moore's income statement and statement of cash flows for the year ending December 31, 1998, reported the following:

Income statement: Net income, $1,000 [Revenues ($36,000) less expenses ($35,000)]. *Statement of cash flows:* Cash collections from customers, $44,000 ($2,000 of this amount represented unearned revenue at the end of 1998); cash payments to suppliers, employees, and other parties, $18,000 ($3,000 of this amount represented prepaid expenses at the end of 1998).

REQUIRED Prepare Scotty Moore's balance sheet on December 31, 1998.

E 3-14. **CASH BASIS VERSUS ACCRUAL BASIS** Shedrick owns and operates a small convenience store. He is interested in comparing the gross profit from gasoline sales with the gross profit from sales of sodas, chips, candy, and so on. His wife prepared the following "cash gross profit," based on information taken from the store's checkbook:

	GASOLINE	OTHER
Receipts from sales	$180,000	$100,000
Payments to suppliers	(190,000)	(80,000)
Profit	$(10,000)	$ 20,000

Shedrick was able to obtain the following information from records kept in the store's safe:

	GASOLINE	OTHER
Inventory, beginning	$20,000	$ 5,000
Inventory, ending	30,000	2,000
Accounts payable, beginning	50,000	–0–
Accounts payable, ending	30,000	10,000

REQUIRED Prepare a statement that shows the accrual-basis gross profit for Shedrick's convenience store.

E 3-15. **RECORDING TRANSACTIONS; ADJUSTING ENTRIES** The following transactions and related information for Bowen Corporation occurred during 1998:

March 1   Rented a building to a customer for a one-year period. Rent of $3,600 was received, which was credited to a liability account.

March 15   Purchased 300 boxes of typing paper at a total cost of $2,400 to be used as office supplies. During 1998, 190 boxes were used. Bowen records supplies initially as an asset.

April 1   Borrowed $4,000 from a bank. The loan was for a two-year period. Interest at 8 percent is due on March 31 of each year.

June 30   Sales commissions totaling $18,000 for the first six months of 1998 were recorded but not paid.

July 3   Paid the sales commissions in the previous transaction.

REQUIRED **1.** Record the above transactions in journal form.

2. Prepare any adjusting entries required at the end of 1998, the end of Bowen Corporation's fiscal period.

E 3-16. **ACCRUAL ACCOUNTING APPLICATIONS** Several sets of facts appear below. For each set, calculate the required amount.

1. Supplies on hand at the beginning of the year, $9,000; supplies purchased during the year, $20,000; supplies used during the year, $12,000. Determine the supplies on hand at the end of the year.

2. Salaries payable at the end of the year, $7,000; salaries expense for the year, $34,000; salaries payable at the beginning of the year, $6,000. Determine the cash paid for salaries during the year.

3. Unearned rent (reported as a liability) at the beginning of the year, $1,100; unearned rent at the end of the year, $2,200; rent revenue for the year, $12,800. Determine the amount of cash received for rent during the year.

4. Purchases of inventory during the year, $86,000; cost of goods sold during the year, $100,000; inventory returned to suppliers during the year, $6,000; inventory on hand at the end of the year, $40,000. Determine inventory on hand at the beginning of the period.

5. Interest revenue for the year, $10,000; interest receivable at the beginning of the year, $2,000; cash received as interest during the year, $11,500. Determine interest receivable at the end of the year.

6. Accounts receivable collected in cash during the year, $50,000; accounts receivable at the end of the year, $12,000; sales on account during the year, $53,500. Determine accounts receivable at the beginning of the year.

E 3-17. **COST OF GOODS SOLD** The following data relate to Sutton Sporting Goods' inventory and cost of merchandise sold:

Beginning inventory	$ 7,000
Transportation in	500
Purchase	12,500
Purchase returns	1,000
Ending inventory	11,000

REQUIRED **1.** Calculate cost of goods sold for Sutton Sporting Goods.

2. Prepare adjusting entries to transfer the inventory, purchases, and related accounts to cost of goods sold.

E 3-18. **SPECIAL JOURNALS** A business uses the following special journals: cash receipts (CR), cash disbursements (CD), single-column sales (S), single-column purchases (P), and general journal (GJ). Indicate, by inserting CR, CD, S, P, or GJ in the space provided, in which journal each of the following transactions would be recorded.

1. ____ Purchase of office equipment for cash.
2. ____ Payment to a creditor for merchandise previously purchased on account.
3. ____ Return of a cash sale (cash was refunded).
4. ____ Purchase of merchandise on credit.
5. ____ Sale of merchandise on credit.
6. ____ Adjusting entries.
7. ____ Sale of office equipment on credit.
8. ____ Return on a credit purchase.
9. ____ Return of a credit sale.
10. ____ Purchase of office supplies on credit.
11. ____ Customer collections.
12. ____ Payment of monthly salaries.
13. ____ Cash sales.
14. ____ Closing entries.
15. ____ Purchase of land by issuance of common stock.

E 3-19. **TRANSACTION ANALYSIS** Your employer approaches you for help regarding the effects of the following transactions on the financial statements prepared for the years ending December 31, 1997 and 1998:

a) Sales made on credit, end of 1997, $1,000; end of 1998, $3,000.
b) A three-year insurance policy was purchased for $3,600 cash on June 30, 1997.
c) On October 1, 1997, the company purchased at par $10,000 of 8 percent corporate bonds. The bonds were dated October 1, 1997, and pay interest annually.
d) Depreciation expense was $1,600 for 1997 and $2,000 for 1998.
e) Accrued wages at the end of 1997 and 1998 amounted to $500 and $400, respectively.

REQUIRED Indicate the dollar amount of each effect in the table below. The first transaction serves as an example.

	NET INCOME		TOTAL ASSETS, 12/31		TOTAL LIABILITIES, 12/31		OPERATING CASH FLOWS	
	1997	1998	1997	1998	1997	1998	1997	1998
a)	+$1,000	+$3,000	+$1,000	+$3,000	–0–	–0–	–0–	+$1,000
b)								
c)								
d)								
e)								

E 3-20. **ACCRUAL ACCOUNTING CONCEPTS** During 1998, Sandmeyer's cash inflows from customers were $98,000, and cash outflows to suppliers, employees, and governments totaled $102,400. Assets, liabilities, and equity at the beginning and end of 1998 were as follows:

	BEGINNING OF 1998	END OF 1998
Sandmeyer, capital	$33,500	$38,800
Prepaid expenses	19,000	16,000
Payables	2,500	800
Receivables	4,000	11,000
Unearned revenues	7,000	3,000
Cash	20,000	15,600

REQUIRED   **1.** Calculate the following on an accrual basis:
   a) Revenues for the year.
   b) Expenses for the year.
   c) Net income for the year.
2. Verify that Sandmeyer Company's owners' equity at the beginning of 1998 plus net income for 1998 equals owners' equity at the end of 1998.

<hr>

PROBLEMS   Problems marked with an asterisk (*) refer to Appendix 3–1.

P 3-1. **JOURNAL ENTRIES, POSTING, TRIAL BALANCE** The following transactions occurred for Greer Music Company during its first year of operations:
   a) C. Greer invested $150,000 cash in the business.
   b) Purchased a building at a cost of $60,000. Paid $20,000 down with the balance due in 120 days.
   c) Purchased record display equipment for $25,000 cash.
   d) Purchases on account, $100,000. The periodic inventory system is used.
   e) Sales: on account, $60,000; for cash, $80,000.
   f) Paid clerical salaries totaling $20,000.
   g) Collected $45,000 from credit customers.
   h) Paid $25,000 on accounts payable.
   i) Borrowed $50,000 by issuing a short-term note.
   j) C. Greer withdraw $8,000 in cash for personal use.

REQUIRED   **1.** Record the above transactions in general journal form.
2. Set up T-accounts for the necessary accounts. Post the journal entries to the T-accounts.
3. Prepare an unadjusted trial balance.

P 3-2. **JOURNAL ENTRIES; ACCOUNTING CYCLE** At the beginning of the current year, Megan Dorr invested $200,000 cash in a VHS movie rental store. In addition to this transaction, the following transactions, in summary form and not in chronological order, occurred during the year:
   a) Rented a building under a five-year lease at an annual rental of $18,000. Under the terms of the rental agreement, Dorr paid the first two annual rentals in advance.
   b) Purchased supplies for cash, $8,000.
   c) Purchased 6,000 movie tapes for cash at a cost of $12 per tape. Dorr plans to rent the tapes for $2 per day. Customers are required to make a cash deposit of $.50 per tape, which will be refunded when the tapes are returned.
   d) Purchased fixtures and equipment on account at a cost of $30,000.
   e) Purchased 2,000 additional movie tapes for cash, $24,000.
   f) 30,000 tape rentals totaling $60,000 were made during the year; tape deposits totaled $15,000, and refunds of tape deposits totaled $13,200 (see also item *g* below).
   g) At the end of the year, 3,600 tapes were in the hands of customers on rentals. The rentals on these 3,600 tapes are included in the $60,000 revenues in item *f*.
   h) Paid $25,000 on the fixtures and equipment purchased in item *d*.
   i) Salaries paid during the year, $12,000.
   j) During the year, Dorr withdrew $2,500 in cash for personal use.
       Items *k* through *o* relate to adjusting entry information at the end of the year:
   k) Supplies on hand at the end of the year, $3,200.
   l) Depreciation expense for the year, $1,350.
   m) Salaries accrued but unpaid at the end of the year, $1,400.
   n) Rent expense for the year, $18,000.
   o) During the inventory count of VHS tapes at the end of the year, Dorr found 1,200 worn-out tapes that were not suitable for future rentals.

REQUIRED   **1.** Prepare journal entries for Dorr's initial investment and for transactions items *a* through *j*.
2. Set up T-accounts and post the journal entries in part 1 to the appropriate accounts.
3. Prepare adjusting entries for items *k* through *o* and post them to the appropriate accounts.

4. Prepare Megan Dorr's income statement for the year.
5. Prepare Megan Dorr's balance sheet at the end of the year.

P 3-3.   **REVIEW OF ACCOUNTING CYCLE**   The January 1, 1998, balance sheet for TJ's Golf-Around was as follows:

ASSETS			LIABILITIES AND STOCKHOLDERS' EQUITY	
Cash		$ 2,500	Accounts payable	$ 3,300
Accounts receivable	$12,000		Salaries payable	600
Less: Allowance for doubtful			Interest payable	250
accounts	(2,400)	9,600	Notes payable	20,000
Interest receivable		150	Capital stock	40,000
Supplies		4,000	Retained earnings	21,600
Inventories		29,500		
Investment in bonds		5,000		
Buildings and equipment ..	$50,000		Total	$85,750
Less: Accumulated depreciation	(15,000)	35,000		
Total		$85,750		

The following transactions and other economic events took place during the year ending December 31, 1998.
a) Paid the $250 interest accrued on the notes payable.
b) Purchased merchandise on account at a cost of $17,500 (assume a periodic inventory system).
c) Sales: on account $13,500; for cash, $8,000.
d) Paid salaries totaling $2,400, including salaries accrued on January 1.
e) Cash collections from customers, $11,600.
f) Purchased merchandise for cash at a cost of $13,000.
g) Wrote off a customer's account of $300 as uncollectible.
h) Sales: on account, $6,500; for cash, $10,000.
i) Made payment on accounts payable of $17,640.
j) One customer returned $150 of merchandise that was purchased on account.
k) Paid sales salaries totaling $3,600.
l) Purchased merchandise on account at a cost of $5,400.
m) Sales: on account, $12,000; for cash, $5,400.
n) Received cash interest on investments, $150.
o) Cash collections from customers, $8,000.
p) Declared a cash dividend of $5,000 to be paid in January 1999.

REQUIRED
1. Open T-accounts and enter the beginning balance sheet information in the various T-accounts.
2. Record the 1998 transactions in general journal form.
3. Post the journal entries in part 2 to the appropriate T-accounts.
4. Prepare the end-of-year adjusting entries in journal form. Information for adjustments:
   a) Uncollectible accounts expense, $319.
   b) Supplies used, $2,800.
   c) Depreciation expense, $5,000.
   d) Salaries accrued, end of year, $740.
   e) Interest accrued on notes payable, $250.
   f) For cost of goods sold, the cost of the ending inventory was $35,000.
5. Prepare TJ's Golf-Around income statement for the year ending December 31, 1998.
6. Prepare TJ's Golf-Around balance sheet at December 31, 1998.

P 3-4.   **CLOSING ENTRIES**   Refer to the data in Problem 3-3. Prepare the journal entries to close the nominal accounts.

P 3-5.   **ADJUSTING ENTRIES**   Adjustment data for Green LLP for the year ending December 31, 1998, are as follows:
a) Green holds a $50,000 note receivable dated April 1, 1998. The note is a one-year note with interest payable at 6 percent.

b) During 1998, Green purchased supplies at a cost of $20,000. The supplies were originally recorded as assets. On December 31, 1998, there were supplies on hand costing $3,000.

c) Green depreciates its assets on a straight-line basis and records one-half of a year's depreciation on acquisitions made during the year. The plant and equipment account appears as follows:

DATE OF ACQUISITION	ITEM	USEFUL LIFE	SALVAGE	COST
4/1/94	Building	30	$5,000	$50,000
12/10/97	Machinery	10	–0–	24,000
6/3/98	Equipment	4	3,000	33,000

d) Green rents the land on which its plant and equipment are located. At the beginning of 1998, Green made a rent payment covering 1998 and 1999. The amount paid was $40,000 and was debited to prepaid rent.

e) In 1998, Green received $78,000 in advance fees for consulting to be performed over the next two years. Green accounted for the receipt as unearned revenue and $40,000 had been earned at the end of 1998.

f) In 1994, Green issued 10-year, $100,000, 6 percent notes payable. Interest is payable each March 1 and September 1.

g) At the end of 1998, Green had accrued salaries payable of $42,000.

h) On December 1, 1997, Green purchased a three-year fire insurance policy at a cost of $10,800. The debit was made to the prepaid insurance account.

REQUIRED   Prepare adjusting entries for the above data.

P 3-6.   **ADJUSTING ENTRIES** The following information about year-end adjusting entries applies to Jenkins Video Games, Inc.

a) On March 1, 1998, Jenkins purchased a four-year liability insurance policy at a total cost of $9,600. Jenkins's accounting policy is to record prepaid insurance transactions as assets.

b) On November 30, 1998, Jenkins renewed the annual rent on the store by making a $18,000 rent payment, which was recorded as rent expense.

c) On November 1, 1998, Jenkins purchased 10 $1,000 bonds of the local city at a cost of $10,000. The stated annual interest rate on the bonds is 6 percent, payable quarterly on May 1, August 1, November 1, and February 1.

d) Jenkins's depreciable assets have a cost of $50,000 and are being depreciated on a straight-line basis with an estimated 20-year useful life and estimated salvage value of $2,000.

e) At the end of 1998, Jenkins's concession and video revenue account had a credit balance of $300,000. During 1998, Jenkins received $35,000 in advances for private video parties; $20,000 of the proceeds was credited to unearned revenue, and the remainder was credited to concession and video revenue. At the end of 1998, advances of $8,000 were still unearned, since these parties had not been held.

f) Salary transactions during 1998 appear as follows:

Salaries payable

Salary payments in January 1998	21,000	Beginning of 1998	15,000

Salaries expense

Salary payments February 1 through December 26	100,000	

Salaries of $10,000 are payable on December 31.

g) On the unadjusted trial balance, a "suspense" (miscellaneous) account with a debit balance of $32,000 was composed of the following:

Withdrawals by J. Jenkins, owner	$19,000
Miscellaneous postage expenses	10,000
Cost of having store cleaned	15,000
Sale of fully depreciated jukebox with an original cost of $50,000 (proceeds debited to cash)	(12,000)
	$32,000

h) At the beginning of 1998 the video supplies account had a debit balance of $6,000. Purchases of supplies during 1998 were debited to the supplies account and totaled $18,500. Supplies on hand at the end of 1998 totaled $12,000.

i) On December 28, 1998, Jenkins received a bill for $8,000 for night security services received during December. This transaction has not been recorded.

REQUIRED Prepare the necessary December 31, 1998, adjusting entries from the above information.

P 3-7. ADJUSTING ENTRIES The January 31, 1998, unadjusted trial balance for Larry's Plumbing Company was as follows:

	DEBIT	CREDIT
Cash	$ 8,000	
Accounts receivable	36,000	
Allowance for uncollectible accounts		$ 4,800
Supplies	6,500	
Prepaid insurance	8,000	
Inventory, 1/31/97	94,000	
Fixtures and equipment	50,000	
Accumulated depreciation		10,000
Accounts payable		33,000
Larry Hummer, capital		198,500
Sales		250,000
Purchases	156,800	
Rent expense	60,000	
Salaries expense	40,000	
Advertising expense	28,000	
Other expenses	9,000	
	$496,300	$496,300

Information for adjustments for the fiscal year ending January 31, 1998, is as follows:

a) Estimated uncollectible accounts expense, $1,500.

b) Supplies on hand at January 31, 1998, $2,000.

c) Insurance expense for the year ending January 31, 1998, $1,000.

d) Inventory on January 31, 1998, $80,000.

e) Fixtures and equipment are depreciated at the rate of 5 percent per year.

f) Prepaid rent applicable to the following period, $24,000.

g) Sales salaries accrued on January 31, 1998, $7,400.

h) On January 27, 1998, Larry paid $12,000 in connection with advertising to be conducted during February 1998.

REQUIRED Prepare adjusting entries for Larry's Plumbing Company.

*P 3-8. PREPARATION OF A WORKSHEET Refer to Problem 3-7.

REQUIRED Prepare a 10-column worksheet for Larry's Plumbing Company.

*P 3-9. FINANCIAL STATEMENTS FROM WORKSHEET DATA Refer to the worksheet that was prepared in Problem 3-8.

REQUIRED Prepare the income statement and balance sheet for Larry's Plumbing Company for the year ending January 31, 1998.

P 3-10. JOURNAL ENTRIES; TRANSACTION ANALYSIS Kim's Style Shop cuts and styles hair and sells a complete line of hair care products. The trial balance below contains Kim's Style

Shop's beginning account balances *and* the total debits and credits to each account during the year ending December 31, 1998.

ACCOUNT	DEBIT	CREDIT
Cash	$102,800	$ 27,200
Inventory of hair care products	24,000	8,000
Supplies	9,000	4,000
Prepaid rent	4,000	2,000
Equipment	20,000	4,000
Accumulated depreciation—equipment	2,500	3,000
Accounts payable	9,500	25,000
Notes payable	3,000	14,000
Kim Murray, capital	2,200	50,000
Styling revenue		50,000
Sales of hair care products		24,000
Cost of hair care products sold	28,000	16,000
Purchases of hair care products	20,000	20,000
Supplies expense	4,000	
Rent expense	2,000	
Depreciation expense	3,000	
Salaries expense	11,000	
Interest expense	1,500	
Loss on sale of equipment	700	
	$247,200	$247,200

Additional Information:
a) All styling revenue and sales of hair care products are for cash.
b) All purchases of hair care products were made on account.
c) Equipment costing $14,000 was purchased by issuing a note.
d) Equipment transactions and events were the purchase in item *c,* depreciation expense, and the sale of equipment at a loss.
e) Near the end of the year, Kim withdrew $2,200 in cash for personal use.
f) Kim uses the periodic inventory method for her hair care products.

REQUIRED   In summary form, prepare journal entries for Kim's transactions and adjusting entries for the year ending December 31, 1998.

P 3-11.   **JOURNAL ENTRIES; FINANCIAL STATEMENTS**   The December 31, 1997, balance sheet and the combined statement of income and retained earnings for the year ending December 31, 1998, and additional information for Charlotte's Candy Company (CCC) follow.

Charlotte's Candy Company
Balance Sheet
December 31, 1997

ASSETS

Cash		$140,000
Accounts receivable	$88,000	
Less: Allowance for uncollectable accounts	(19,000)	69,000
Notes receivable		42,000
Prepaid insurance		46,000
Candy inventory		146,000
Plant and equipment	$340,000	
Less: Accumulated depreciation	(100,000)	240,000
Land		75,000
		$758,000

LIABILITIES AND STOCKHOLDERS' EQUITY

Accounts payable	$164,000
Salaries payable	8,000
Income taxes payable	130,000
Notes payable	200,000
Common stock	50,000
Contributed capital in excess of par	125,000
Retained earnings	81,000
	$758,000

Charlotte's Candy Company
Statement of Income and Retained Earnings
for the Year Ended December 31, 1998

Revenues and gains:	
Sales of candy	$700,000
Interest revenue	8,400
Gain on sale of land	20,000
Expenses:	
Cost of goods sold	(375,000)
Depreciation expense	(68,000)
Insurance expense	(46,000)
Salaries expense	(190,000)
Uncollectible accounts expense	(10,000)
Interest expense	(20,000)
Income tax expense	(10,000)
Net income	$ 9,400
Retained earnings, December 31, 1997	81,000
Cash dividends	(8,000)
Retained earnings, December 31, 1998	$ 82,400

a) All candy sales are initially recorded on account.
b) The land that was sold had a cost of $40,000.
c) $6,000 of the interest revenue was an end-of-year accrual.
d) Payments on income taxes, $135,000.
e) Customers' accounts aggregating $17,500 were written off as uncollectible.
f) Collections on accounts receivable, $625,000.
g) Purchases of candy on account totaled $400,000.
h) The ending accounts payable balance was $225,000.
i) Accrued salaries payable, December 31, 1998, $20,000.
j) There was no interest payable at the end of 1998.

REQUIRED

1. Prepare, in summary form, journal entries to record CCC's transactions for 1998.
2. Prepare CCC's balance sheet on December 31, 1998.

P 3-12. **THE ACCOUNTING CYCLE** Usry Brothers' Clothiers was organized on September 1, 1998. Below are the summary transactions for the store's first two months of operations:

SEPTEMBER
a) Usry invested $120,000 cash and a building and land in the business. The building had a fair value of $60,000, and the fair value of the land was $20,000.
b) The business acquired the clothing inventory of Milton Company for $75,000. Milton was going out of business. Because Usry acquired the inventory of another company, the inventory account was debited.
c) Supplies were purchased for cash at a cost of $6,000.
d) Clothing purchases on account, $45,000. Usry uses the periodic inventory method.
e) Clothing sales for cash, $36,000; on account, $40,000.
f) Salary expenses paid in cash, $26,000.
g) Accounts receivable collections, $35,000.
h) Payments on accounts payable, $28,000.

i) Other expenses paid in cash, $5,600.

j) Owner withdrawals of cash, $3,500.

k) End-of-month adjustment data:

Depreciation	**$ 1,000**
Uncollectible accounts expense	**250**
Supplies used	**1,200**
Ending inventory	**90,000**
Accrued salaries	**1,200**

OCTOBER

a) Purchases of clothing on account, $65,000.

b) Supplies purchased for cash, $3,000.

c) Write-off of customer accounts, $100.

d) Clothing sales for cash, $50,000; on account, $72,000.

e) Salaries paid in cash, $31,000.

f) Accounts receivable collections, $48,000.

g) Payments on accounts payable, $70,000.

h) Usry invested additional cash of $35,000 in the business.

i) Other expenses paid in cash, $6,000.

j) End-of-month adjustment data:

Depreciation	**$ 1,000**
Uncollectible accounts expense	**600**
Supplies used	**6,000**
Ending inventory	**80,000**

REQUIRED

1. Record the September transactions in general journal form and post the transactions to the necessary T-accounts.

2. Prepare adjusting entries for September and post to the T-accounts.

3. Prepare closing entries for September and post to the T-accounts.

4. Record the October transactions in general journal form and post the transactions to the T-accounts. Usry does not make reversing entries.

5. Record the adjusting entries for October and post to the T-accounts.

6. Prepare the income statement for October and the balance sheet at the end of October.

P 3-13. **RECORDING TRANSACTIONS; FINANCIAL STATEMENTS** Big T is a T-shirt boutique owned by Joey Michelle. Although the store does not have complete records on a double-entry basis, you have been provided with the information below:

a) Big T's balance sheet on December 31, 1997, prepared by an outside CPA firm, was as follows:

ASSETS

Cash..		**$10,350**
Accounts receivable..	**$21,112**	
Less: Allowance for doubtful accounts	**(1,480)**	19,632
Inventory		38,486
Prepaid insurance..		316
Supplies..		158
Equipment	**$6,260**	
Less: Accumulated depreciation	**(2,220)**	4,040
Total assets		**$72,982**

LIABILITIES AND OWNER'S EQUITY

Accounts payable...	**$ 8,488**
Notes payable..	10,000
Other payables	816
Joey Michelle, capital......................................	53,678
Total liabilities and owner's equity	**$72,982**

b) The boutique's checkbook revealed the following for the period January 1– December 31, 1998:

Cash sales	$79,600
Collections on accounts receivable	86,166
Payments on accounts payable	(115,082)
Salaries expense	(21,976)
Rent, telephone, electricity expenses	(7,988)
Supplies purchased	(560)
Insurance purchased	(682)
Miscellaneous expenses, including interest	(3,616)
Payment on notes payable	(6,000)
Cash withdrawals by Joey Michelle	(12,280)
Decrease in cash	($2,418)

c) All T-shirts are purchased on account. Purchases during 1998 totaled $116,902.

d) During 1998, $1,600 in accounts receivable were written off as uncollectible. Uncollectible accounts expense for 1998 was $1,920. Accounts receivable at December 31, 1998, totaled $23,842.

e) The T-shirt inventory on December 31, 1998, was $35,614.

f) On December 31, 1998, prepaid insurance was $244, supplies on hand totaled $210, and other miscellaneous payables were $578.

g) Depreciation expense for 1998 was $626.

REQUIRED Prepare Big T's income statement for the year ending December 31, 1998, and Big T's balance sheet as of December 31, 1998. Before preparing these statements, you may find it helpful to prepare journal entries for Big T's 1998 transactions.

P 3-14. **ANALYSIS OF TRANSACTIONS; FINANCIAL STATEMENTS** Linehan Oil Jobbers has never had an audit until 1998. Based on the limited records kept by the company, you constructed the following December 31, 1997, postclosing trial balance and gathered the following information about 1998 transactions:

a) Postclosing trial balance on December 31, 1997:

	DEBIT	CREDIT
Cash	$ 36,000	
Accounts receivable	155,000	
Inventory	80,000	
Plant and equipment	120,000	
Accumulated depreciation		$ 36,000
Land (held for speculative purposes)	19,000	
J. Linehan, capital		374,000
	$410,000	$410,000

b) On December 31, 1998, Linehan owed creditors $36,000 for unpaid purchases and had accrued salaries of $1,600.

c) Plant and equipment are depreciated on a straight-line basis over 15 years with no estimated salvage value. Some equipment was sold on December 31, 1998.

d) In 1998, Linehan began selling on a cash-only basis. Any receivables not collected during 1998 were written off as uncollectible.

e) Linehan's cost of goods sold equals 70 percent of sales.

f) On December 31, 1998, Linehan exchanged the land held for speculative purposes for McPherson Brothers' common stock. A gain of $4,000 was recognized.

g) The income tax rate is 30 percent.

h) Deposits during 1998:

Cash sales	$250,000
Proceeds of $5,000 note issued on October 1 and bearing interest at 8%, payable annually	5,000
Customer collections	146,000
Proceeds on sale of fully depreciated equipment (original cost, $20,000)	5,000
Total deposits	$406,000

Checks written during 1998:

Purchases of merchandise	$120,000
Payments to creditors	60,000
Salaries	10,000
Advertising (to be run in 1999)	10,000
Owner withdrawals	10,000
Other expenses	5,500
Total checks written	$215,500

REQUIRED   Prepare an income statement for the year ended December 31, 1998, and a balance sheet at December 31, 1998, for Linehan Oil Jobbers.

*P 3-15.   **PREPARATION OF A 12-COLUMN WORKSHEET**   Unadjusted trial balance data and adjustment information for Rauh LLP for the year ended December 31, 1998, appear below.

Unadjusted trial balance data:

Cash	$ 4,000
Accounts receivable (net of allowance)	5,200
Supplies	2,900
Investments	3,000
Prepaid insurance	2,500
Inventory	10,000
Plant and equipment (net of accumulated depreciation)	15,000
Accounts payable	6,000
Notes payable	3,000
Common stock	20,000
Retained earnings	15,000
Dividends declared	2,000
Interest revenue	500
Sales	60,300
Sales returns	4,000
Purchases	44,000
Salaries expense	9,000
Insurance expense	3,000
Interest expense	200

Adjustment information:

Uncollectible accounts expense	$ 200
Depreciation expense	1,500
Supplies on hand	900
Insurance expense for the period	2,000
Accrued interest revenue	200
Ending inventory	23,000
Accrued salaries payable	800
Accrued interest payable	200
Unearned revenue (when cash was received, the offsetting credit was made to the sales account)	280
Accrued property taxes	150

Income tax expense equals 30% of income before taxes.

REQUIRED   Prepare a 12-column worksheet similar to the worksheet illustrated in Exhibit 3–23.

*P 3-16. **WORKSHEET PREPARATION** A partially completed worksheet appears below. However, certain data are missing.

	TRIAL BALANCE DR	CR	ADJUSTMENTS DR	CR	INCOME STATEMENT DR	CR	BALANCE SHEET DR	CR
Cash	45						45	
Receivables	70		25				95	
Prepaid insurance				5			10	
Plant and equipment	80						80	
Accumulated depreciation ..		20						
Accounts payable		40						40
Unearned revenue			20					5
Salaries payable		0						
Common stock		20						
Contributed capital in excess of par		20						
Retained earnings		45						
Revenues		100						
Salaries expense			15		40			
Depreciation expense	0				10			
Insurance expense								
Other expenses	35	—	—	—	35	—		
Total	=	=	=	=				
Net income (loss)					—	—	—	—
Total					=	=	=	=

REQUIRED Complete the worksheet by filling in the missing data.

P 3-17. **ACCOUNTING CYCLE; FINANCIAL STATEMENT RELATIONSHIPS** On December 31, 1998, the balance sheet for Jeremy's Men's Wear, Inc., was as follows:

ASSETS		LIABILITIES AND CAPITAL	
Cash	$184,000	Notes payable	$60,000
Inventory	120,000	Unearned revenue	10,000
Equipment	29,000	Contributed capital	200,000
Less: Accumulated depreciation .	(3,000)	Retained earnings	60,000
Total	$330,000	Total	$330,000

Prior to 1998, Jeremy had a "cash only" sales policy. Beginning on January 1, 1998, Jeremy also began selling on credit in order to increase sales revenues. The income statement and statement of cash flows for the year ending December 31, 1998, appear as follows:

Income Statement
for the Year Ending December 31, 1998

Sales revenue		$171,000
Expenses:		
Cost of goods sold	$134,300	
Depreciation expense	700	
Interest expense	500	
Salaries expense	11,000	
Rent expense	1,000	
Supplies expense	2,600	
Uncollectible accounts expense	430	
Total expenses		150,530
Net income		$ 20,470

Statement of Cash Flows
for the Year Ending December 31, 1998

Cash flows from operating activities:

Cash sales and collections from customers	$102,000	
Purchases of merchandise	(88,700)	
Purchases of supplies	(11,600)	
Payment of salaries	(6,000)	
Payment of rent	(13,800)	
Net cash used by operating activities		(18,100)

Cash flows from investing activities:

Purchase of investments		(7,200)

Cash flows from financing activities:

Dividends declared and paid		(6,000)
Decrease in cash		($31,300)
Cash balance, December 31, 1997		184,000
Cash balance, December 31, 1998		$152,700

Additional information:

a) All merchandise purchases initially are made on account.

b) Of the unearned revenue balance on December 31, 1997, $7,000 was earned during 1998 and was reported as sales revenues.

c) Merchandise inventory on December 31, 1998, was $144,000.

REQUIRED Prepare the balance sheet on December 31, 1998, for Jeremy's Men's Wear, Inc. You may wish to prepare summary journal entries for the year, although they are not required.

P 3-18. **FINANCIAL REPORTING PROBLEM; GENERAL ELECTRIC** Refer to the financial statements for General Electric Corporation that are presented in Appendix B at the end of the text.

REQUIRED

1. Identify GE's assets and liabilities that would probably be classified as prepayments and unearned items (deferrals).

2. Identify GE's assets and liabilities that would probably be classified as accruals.

3. Using the balance sheet and income statement, make a list of the adjusting entries that GE probably made at the end of its 1995 fiscal year.

P 3-19. **RESEARCH PROBLEM ON THE ACCOUNTING PROCESS** Visit a discount store, department store, grocery store, or another type of retail business in your area that uses an optical scanning machine to scan UPC bar codes in recording sales transactions. If you are not familiar with this technology, take some time to observe how the process works and perhaps purchase some merchandise and study your cash receipt. Also, try to interview a store manager about the type of information that is captured from the bar codes.

REQUIRED Write a short report that addresses the following questions and issues:

1. What do you perceive to be some of the advantages and disadvantages of using optical scanning devices to record sales transactions?

2. What type of information is captured by the scanning process?

3. How might the use of this technology modify the steps in the accounting cycle presented in Exhibit 3–5?

The Income Statement

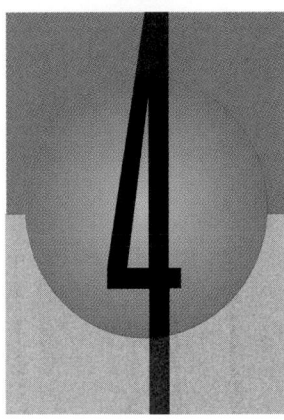

CHAPTER 4

Motor Company And Subsidiaries

CONSOLIDATED STATEMENT OF INCOME	1996	1995
For the Years Ended December 31, 1996, 1995 and 1994 (in millions, except amounts per share)		
AUTOMOTIVE		
Sales (Note 1)	$118,023	$110,496
Costs and expenses (Notes 1 and 15):		
Costs of sales	108,882	101,171
Selling, administrative and other expenses	6,625	6,044
Total costs and expenses	115,507	107,215
Operating income	2,516	3,281
Interest income	841	800
Interest expense	695	622
Net interest income/(expense)	146	178
Equity in net (loss)/income of affiliated companies (Note 1)	(6)	(154)
Net expense from transactions with Financial Services (Note 1)	(85)	(139)
Income before income taxes - Automotive	2,571	3,166
FINANCIAL SERVICES		
Revenues (Note 1)	28,968	26,641
Costs and expenses (Note 1):		
Interest expense	9,704	9,424
Depreciation	6,875	6,500
Operating and other expenses	6,217	5,499
Provision for credit and insurance losses	2,564	1,818
Asset write-downs and dispositions (Note 15)	121	-
Total costs and expenses	25,481	23,241
Net revenue from transactions with Automotive (Note 1)	85	139
Gain on sale of The Associates' common stock (Note 15)	650	-
Income before income taxes - Financial Services	4,222	3,539
TOTAL COMPANY		
Income before income taxes	6,793	6,705
Provision for income taxes (Note 6)	2,166	2,379
Income before minority interests	4,627	4,326
Minority interests in net income of subsidiaries	181	187
Net Income	$ 4,446	$ 4,139
Income attributable to Common and Class B Stock after preferred stock dividends (Note 1)	$ 4,381	$ 3,839
Average number of shares of Common and Class B Stock outstanding	1,179	1,071
AMOUNTS PER SHARE OF COMMON AND CLASS B STOCK (Note 1)		
Income	$ 3.72	$ 3.58
Income assuming full dilution	$ 3.64	$ 3.33

LEARNING OBJECTIVES

After studying this chapter, you should be able to:

1. Differentiate between the net assets approach and the transactions approach to the determination of net income.

2. Distinguish between the single-step and multiple-step formats of reporting income from continuing operations.

3. Distinguish between the current operating performance approach and the all-inclusive approach to reporting income.

4. Identify a discontinued segment or operation of a business entity and prepare the related income statement disclosures.

5. Identify an extraordinary item and prepare the related income statement disclosures.

6. Calculate the cumulative effect of a change in accounting principle on prior periods and prepare the related income statement disclosures.

7. Define other comprehensive income and comprehensive income and explain the reporting requirements for these items.

8. Explain the importance of earnings per share (EPS) and required EPS disclosures.

9. Explain the meaning and purpose of intraperiod tax allocation.

10. Discuss the issues confronting the FASB in its attempt to develop a format for the reporting of earnings activities.

11. Prepare an income statement.

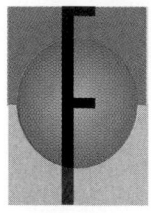

Financial statements are the end product of the accounting process. The income statement, which reports the net income or loss from operating activities, forms the basis of investment and other decisions. For example, net income per share, also called earnings per share, is used extensively in security investment decision making. Financial statement users also require information on income from operations and other sources, including gains and losses from discontinued operations and extraordinary items like the one reported in this excerpt from *The Wall Street Journal:*

Ben & Jerry's Homemade Inc., writing down an investment in a glitch-plagued automated packing plant, reported a fourth-quarter loss of $4.9 million, or 69 cents a share.

The write-down represents the first major action by the company's new chief executive, Robert Holland, named last month to head the offbeat seller of super-premium ice cream. The Waterbury, Vt., company earlier warned that it might report a sizable fourth-quarter loss due to problems with its new automated plant in St. Albans, Vt., but it wasn't expected to write down its investment. The write-down resulted in an after-tax charge of about $4.1 million.

Ben & Jerry's fourth-quarter loss compared with year-earlier earnings of $1.1 million, or 15 cents a share. Sales fell to $31.2 million from $31.7 million. . . .

In a press release, Mr. Holland said that without the write-down, the company would have reported 1994 earnings of $2.2 million. . . .

Mr. Holland said the company decided to write down its investment in the automated packing technology because of continuing start-up delays and concern that it wouldn't perform up to expectations. He added that the company will "move to simpler, proven processes" at the St. Albans plant.[1]

Investors rely heavily on reported income information to assess future income and cash flow prospects for the firm and for them as investors in the firm through dividends and stock price increases. Thus, components of reported income must be described fully and accurately to enable financial statement users to determine which items are expected to recur and which are transitory in nature. That is why Ben and Jerry's chief executive described in some detail the financial impact of writing down the investment in the automated packaging plant, an unusual event that was not expected to recur.

This chapter covers the two basic issues that underlie the reporting of income: (1) determination of income—the *measurement issue,* and (2) reporting of income—the *format issue.* It begins with a brief review of the theory underlying the measurement of accounting income. The major portion of the chapter is then devoted to an analysis of the way income information is reported, including the significant components of income and alternative reporting formats. Earnings per share is discussed briefly. The chapter concludes with a discussion of unresolved issues in income reporting and a comprehensive illustration of a multiple-step income statement.

Many of the illustrations in this and other chapters are taken from actual financial statements. You can gain a better perspective, however, by looking at a complete set of financial statements. The financial statements, notes, and auditor's report from the 1995 annual report of General Electric Company (GE) are reproduced in Appendix B at the end of the book. You may wish to scan the GE income statement and related notes at this point. You may also want to refer to these statements as we discuss various items in this chapter and throughout the book. Many subsequent chapters contain one or more end-of-chapter items that are related to the 1995 GE financial statements.

---

[1]*The Wall Street Journal,* March 6, 1995, p. B7E.

 NCOME MEASUREMENT

One of the objectives of financial accounting and reporting is to provide information on the effects of those transactions, events, and circumstances related to a company's earnings activities that change its resources and claims to those resources. This information appears in the income statement and related notes and supplementary information. It is generally referred to as *income.*

As we pointed out in Chapter 2, income measurement requires the measurement of a particular asset and liability attribute, together with a particular capital maintenance concept. Under current accounting requirements in the United States, historical cost is the primary attribute measured; thus, we refer to current requirements as the **modified historical cost accounting system.** The predominant capital maintenance concept underlying the determination of income in this system is the maintenance of original invested dollars (nominal dollars). That is, an entity earns income when it generates revenues in excess of the historical cost of the resources consumed in producing those revenues. The principles of realization and matching govern the timing of recognition of changes in the amounts of resources and obligations that result from earnings activities. In sum, income determination is an attempt to match effort with accomplishment: revenues are the accomplishment, and expenses are the effort expended in attaining revenues.

We may report income either from a net assets approach or from a transactions approach. These two approaches are described and evaluated in the remainder of this section.

CONCEPTUAL

Income measurement requires both a capital maintenance concept and the measurement of an attribute.

CONCEPTUAL

The realization and matching principles govern earnings recognition.

Net Assets Approach

Conceptually, **net income or net loss** for a period of time is the change in equity (assets minus liabilities, also known as **net assets**) that results from transactions and from economic events other than transactions with owners. The FASB refers to the change in net assets from nonowner sources as **comprehensive income.**[2] If we compare the net assets of an entity at two points in time, assuming no investments or withdrawals of assets by owners, an increase in net assets represents net income; a decrease in net assets represents a net loss. For example, a company's net assets were as follows at the beginning and end of 1998:

Net assets, January 1, 1998	**$100,000**
Net assets, December 31, 1998	**110,000**

Assuming no assets were invested or withdrawn by the owners during the period, the increase in net assets of $10,000 is the net income for the period.

What if we assume instead that the owners invested assets of $4,000 during 1998 and withdrew assets of $9,000 during 1998? Net income can be calculated as follows:

Net assets, December 31, 1998	**$110,000**
Add: Asset withdrawals by owners	**9,000**
Deduct: Asset investments by owners	**(4,000)**
Ending net assets excluding effect of capital transactions	**$115,000**
Deduct: Net assets, January 1, 1998	**(100,000)**
Net income	**$ 15,000**

Though transactions with owners affect net assets, they are not related to a company's earnings activities. Thus, owners' withdrawals must be added back and

[2]"Reporting Comprehensive Income," *Statement of Financial Accounting Standards No. 130* (Norwalk, Conn.: FASB, 1997), para. 8. Later in the chapter, we distinguish between net income and comprehensive income. For many companies, these two amounts may be the same. Thus, for simplicity the following presentation assumes they are the same.

owners' investments deducted to determine accounting income. Still, this approach to income determination does not explain why net income was $15,000. To provide that information, accountants have adopted a **transactions approach** to measuring and reporting income. This is the approach that underlies the income statement.

Transactions Approach

The transactions approach reports revenues and expenses related to the company's primary earnings activities plus gains and losses from peripheral activities. For example, net income of $15,000 would be measured by listing the revenues, expenses, gains, and losses for the period (amounts assumed):

Revenues	$180,000
Expenses	(160,000)
Gains	17,000
Losses	(22,000)
Net income	$ 15,000

Differentiate between the net assets approach and the transactions approach to the determination of net income.

Although conceptually it is feasible to determine net income using the net assets approach, the transactions approach is used in practice because it discloses the component transactions and events that caused net income or net loss. Disclosure of those components allows users to better evaluate a company's performance, and thus provides a better basis for decision making.

INCOME REPORTING

Although accountants use a transactions approach to measure income and construct the income statement, several reporting issues remain:

> Should the income statement distinguish between recurring and nonrecurring income items?
>
> How much detail should the income statement include?
>
> What information might be better presented in the notes to the income statement?
>
> Should some nonowner changes in equity be excluded from the income statement?

We will address these questions in this section as we discuss how income information must be reported under generally accepted accounting principles. At the end of the chapter we will briefly examine some unresolved reporting issues.

Under GAAP the income statement reports revenues, expenses, gains, and losses related to transactions and events that occurred during a specified period. *APB Opinion No. 30* provides the format requirements for reporting components of net income.[3] Exhibit 4–1 summarizes them. Note that the order of presentation in Exhibit 4–1 is inflexible: *The income components that follow income from continuing operations must be presented in the order shown.* In the remainder of this section we will discuss each of the income components, beginning with income from continuing operations. Also, we describe the requirements for reporting comprehensive income and its components.

---

[3]"Reporting the Results of Operations," *Opinions of the Accounting Principles Board No. 30* (New York: AICPA, 1973).

EXHIBIT 4-1	Required Reporting Format for the Components of Net Income

Income from continuing operations before taxes[a]	$xxx
Income tax expense.	(xx)
Income from continuing operations	$xxx
Discontinued operations (net of tax)	xx
Extraordinary gains and losses (net of tax)	xx
Cumulative effect of change in accounting principle (net of tax)	xx
Net income	$xxx

[a]Components of income from continuing operations include revenues, expenses, gains, and losses.

Income from Continuing Operations

Several alternative formats are used for reporting the individual revenues, expenses, gains, and losses that enter into the determination of **income from continuing operations.** Here we will discuss two distinct formats—the single-step format and the multiple-step format—which are representative of the variety of formats used in practice.

Single-Step Format

Under the **single-step format,** income from continuing operations consists of two categories: (1) revenues and gains and (2) expenses and losses. As Exhibit 4–2 illustrates, Motorola, Inc., uses this format to match total expenses with total revenues in determining the net income or loss from continuing operations. Note that income taxes are deducted separately, as the last item to arrive at "net earnings." The primary advantage of the single-step format is its simplicity.

Multiple-Step Format

The multiple-step format is illustrated by the Coca-Cola Company statement in Exhibit 4–3. An advantage of the **multiple-step format** is that it provides a number of subtotals not shown in a single-step income statement. For example, cost of goods sold is deducted from net operating revenues to obtain gross profit on sales. This subtotal allows comparison of period-to-period gross profit rates, which is useful in assessing performance and predicting future cash flows. Separate identification of operating income also is useful for predictive purposes because of the recurring nature of that item. Likewise, nonoperating revenues, expenses, gains, and losses are reported separately from operating items in this format. As Exhibit 4–3 shows, income tax expense is deducted separately at the end. Another illustration of a multiple-step income statement is provided in Exhibit 4–11 (pages 186–187).

2 Distinguish between the single-step and multiple-step formats of reporting income from continuing operations.

More important than the format a company uses is consistency in format from year to year because users of financial statements need comparative data. The format adopted should be the one management believes will be most informative to users.

Nonoperating Income

The vast majority of a firm's transactions relate to its current or primary operating activities. However, certain types of gains and losses and other economic events that affect income are unrelated or only remotely related to current

EXHIBIT 4-2	Single-Step Income Statement

Motorola, Inc., and Consolidated Subsidiaries
Statement of Consolidated Earnings
(in millions)

Year ended December 31	1995
Net sales	$27,037
Costs and expenses	
Manufacturing and other costs of sales	17,545
Selling, general and administrative expenses	4,642
Depreciation expense	1,919
Interest expense, net	149
Total costs and expenses	$24,255
Earnings before income taxes	$ 2,782
Income taxes provided on earnings	1,001
Net earnings	$ 1,781

EXHIBIT 4-3	Multiple-Step Income Statement

The Coca-Cola Company and Subsidiaries
Consolidated Statement of Income
(in millions)

Year Ended December 31	1995
Net operating revenues	$18,018
Cost of goods sold	6,940
Gross profit	$11,078
Selling, administrative and general expenses	6,986
Operating income	$ 4,092
Interest income	245
Interest expense	272
Equity income	169
Other income (deductions)-net	20
Gain on issuance of stock by Coca-Colá Amatil	74
Income before income taxes	$ 4,328
Income taxes	1,342
Net income	$ 2,986

operations. For example, a firm may dispose of a major product line, sell a company it owns, or experience an unusual loss as a result of litigation or catastrophe. Such events have significantly different cash flow implications than ongoing earnings activities. For some time controversy has existed over how firms should report the income effect of events and transactions not directly related to current operating activities. Two approaches to presenting such income information have evolved: the *current operating performance approach* and the *all-inclusive approach*.

Current Operating Performance Approach

An income statement prepared under the **current operating performance approach** includes only regularly recurring operating revenues and expenses. Unusual or nonrecurring items are reported directly in the statement of retained earnings. Supporters of this approach argue that an earnings figure should be useful for predicting future earnings and the inclusion of unusual, irregular, or nonrecurring gains and losses may cause users to draw misleading conclusions. They argue further that statement preparers are in a better position to distinguish between recurring and nonrecurring items than users. Finally, supporters of this approach maintain that even if nonrecurring items are clearly identified, users may focus solely on income ("the bottom line") and neglect to study its components.

3 Distinguish between the current operating performance approach and the all-inclusive approach to reporting income.

All-Inclusive Approach

In the **all-inclusive approach,** all revenues, expenses, gains, and losses are reported in the income statement. Thus, an entity's accumulated net income over its existence is the sum of its periodic net income. Advocates of this approach point out that manipulation of earnings is possible if firms are allowed to omit the effects of some transactions from the income statement. The absence of detailed criteria for determining which items should be included in the income statement creates an opportunity for selective inclusion and exclusion.

As Exhibit 4–1 indicates, the all-inclusive approach comes closest to describing current reporting practice under GAAP, especially with the issuance of *Statement No. 130* on comprehensive income. In the following sections we will discuss the reporting requirements for the remaining items identified in Exhibit 4–1: gain or loss from discontinued operations, extraordinary items, and the cumulative effect of a change in accounting principle.

Gain or Loss from Discontinued Operations

Discontinuing the operations of a segment of a business (e.g., by selling a major line of business) has an impact on a company's ability to generate future cash flows. Thus, to enable financial statement users to predict future cash flows, discontinued operations must be adequately disclosed. The three major issues associated with discontinued operations are (1) the identification of discontinued operations, (2) the measurement of the resulting gain or loss, and (3) the relevant reporting and disclosure requirements. Each of these issues is discussed in the remainder of this section.

CONCEPTUAL

Prediction of future cash flows requires measurement and disclosure of discontinued operations.

Identification of Discontinued Operations

The term **discontinued operations** is used to describe "the operations of a segment of a business . . . that has been sold, abandoned, spun off, or otherwise disposed of or, although still operating, is the subject of a formal plan for disposal."[4] Thus, discontinued operations may include both actual dispositions during the period and planned dispositions. However, only those discontinued business segments that constitute (1) separate major lines of business or (2) separate classes of customer qualify for treatment as discontinued operations. In addition, the discontinued operation's

4 Identify a discontinued segment or operation of a business entity and prepare the related income statement disclosures.

---

[4]Ibid., para. 8.

assets, operating results, and activities must be clearly distinguishable, both physically and operationally, from those of the rest of the company. For example, a sale by a diversified company of a major division that represents the company's only activities in the electronics industry would qualify as a discontinued operation.

On the other hand, disposals of assets in the normal course of an entity's business, such as the disposal of part of a line of business, the phasing out of a product line, or changes occasioned by technological improvements, do not constitute discontinued operations. Examples of transactions that would *not* be reported as discontinued operations include (1) the sale by a mining company of a major foreign subsidiary engaged in silver mining, which represents all the company's activities in that particular country; and (2) the sale by a diversified company of one of its two subsidiaries that manufacture furniture.

Measurement of Gain or Loss

To measure gain or loss from discontinued operations, we must first identify the measurement date and the disposal date. The **measurement date** is the date on which management commits itself to a formal plan to dispose of a segment. At a minimum, such a plan must include: identification of major assets to be disposed of, the expected method of disposal, the expected period required for disposal (usually not more than one year from the measurement date), an active program to find a buyer if disposal is by sale, the estimated results of operations from the measurement date to the disposal date, and the estimated proceeds upon disposal. The **disposal date** is the date the sale is closed if disposal is by sale or the date when operations cease if disposal is by abandonment.[5]

The reported gain or loss from discontinued operations consists of two parts: (1) the operating income or loss (net of taxes) from the beginning of the period to the measurement date, and (2) the operating income or loss (net of taxes) during the *phase-out period* (between the measurement date and the disposal date) combined with the gain or loss on disposal of the segment (net of taxes). If the measurement date and the disposal date fall in the same accounting period, all disposal gains and losses are realized during the period. When the disposal date occurs in a *subsequent* period, the measurement problem becomes more complex.

In the case of disposal during a subsequent period, the second part of the recognized gain or loss must be separated into two components: (1) the *realized* gain or loss between the measurement date and the end of the accounting period, and (2) the *estimated* gain or loss from the end of the accounting period to the disposal date. *Remember that each of these two components consists of operating income or loss plus gain or loss on disposal.* If there is an *estimated loss* from the end of the accounting period to the disposal date, it should be recognized as part of the phase-out gain or loss. If there is an *estimated gain,* it may be recognized only to the extent of realized losses between the measurement date and the end of the accounting period. This situation, in which *anticipated* gains may be recognized (but only to the extent of realized losses), is rare.

These measurement rules may seem rather detailed and complex, but they will make sense if you think about them for a moment. The operating gain or loss *before* the measurement date has already occurred and therefore presents no measurement difficulty. But the gain or loss in the phase-out period has not occurred as of the measurement date. To the extent that the phase-out period extends beyond the current period, estimates are required. A projected *loss* in a subsequent period is always recognized currently. However, a projected *gain* may be recognized currently only to the extent of a realized loss between the measurement date and the end of the current period. Since the projected gain and the realized loss are combined, a company can never show a projected net gain for the second part of

---

[5]Ibid., para. 14.

the gain or loss calculation. The second part of the gain or loss calculation will always yield either a loss or zero effect.

To illustrate the application of these measurement guidelines, assume the following amounts, all net of tax:

	CASE 1	CASE 2
Income from continuing operations	$560,000	$560,000
Operating income (loss) for discontinued operation during period prior to measurement date	(42,000)	42,000
Operating income (loss) for discontinued operation during period from measurement date to end of accounting period	(14,000)	14,000
Gain (loss) on disposal prior to end of accounting period	70,000	(49,000)
Estimated operating income (loss) during subsequent period	(21,000)	(14,000)
Estimated gain (loss) on disposal during subsequent period	(56,000)	77,000

Note that in both cases, the disposal of segment assets occurs over two accounting periods.

The solutions to Cases 1 and 2 are shown in time-line format in Exhibit 4–4. All the amounts in the exhibit are net-of-tax. In Case 1, the $42,000 operating loss prior to the measurement date is added to the $21,000 realized and estimated loss during the phase-out period. Thus, the loss from discontinued operations recognized in the year of the measurement date would be $63,000.

In Case 2, the gain from discontinued operations in the year of the measurement date would be reported at $42,000, which is the operating income from the discontinued segment prior to the measurement date. The realized loss of $35,000 between the measurement date and the end of the accounting period is offset by a portion of the $63,000 estimated gain between the end of the accounting period and the disposal date. As a result, $35,000 of the anticipated $63,000 gain for year 2 is accrued in year 1 to absorb the $35,000 loss after the measurement date, producing a net effect of zero. If the anticipated results are realized in year 2, the remaining $28,000 ($63,000 – $35,000) of the anticipated gain will be realized and reported as a gain from discontinued operations.

Reporting and Disclosure Requirements

Exhibit 4–5 illustrates the required format for reporting discontinued operations using the figures from Case 1. Note the two components of discontinued operations: (1) loss from operations (up to the measurement date) and (2) loss on disposal, including operating loss (from the measurement date to the disposal date). As Exhibit 4–1 indicates, this information must be presented after income from continuing operations and before extraordinary items. All components are to be shown on a net-of-tax basis.

The income taxes applicable to the components must be disclosed either in the income statement or in the notes that accompany the financial statements. Revenues from the discontinued operations must also be disclosed, in the related notes. For prior periods presented on a comparative basis, the net operating results of the discontinued segment should be reported separately in the income statements for the prior periods. Data on earnings per share must be presented for (1) income from continuing operations and (2) net income. Per share data are optional for discontinued operations and the gain or loss on disposal. As a result of these disclosures, income from continuing operations is kept "clean" for predictive purposes.

The following additional information must be disclosed in the notes to the financial statements for the year in which the measurement date occurs:

1. The identity of the discontinued segment.

2. The expected disposal date, if known.

3. The expected manner of disposal.

EXHIBIT 4–4 **Calculation of Gain/Loss from Discontinued Operations**

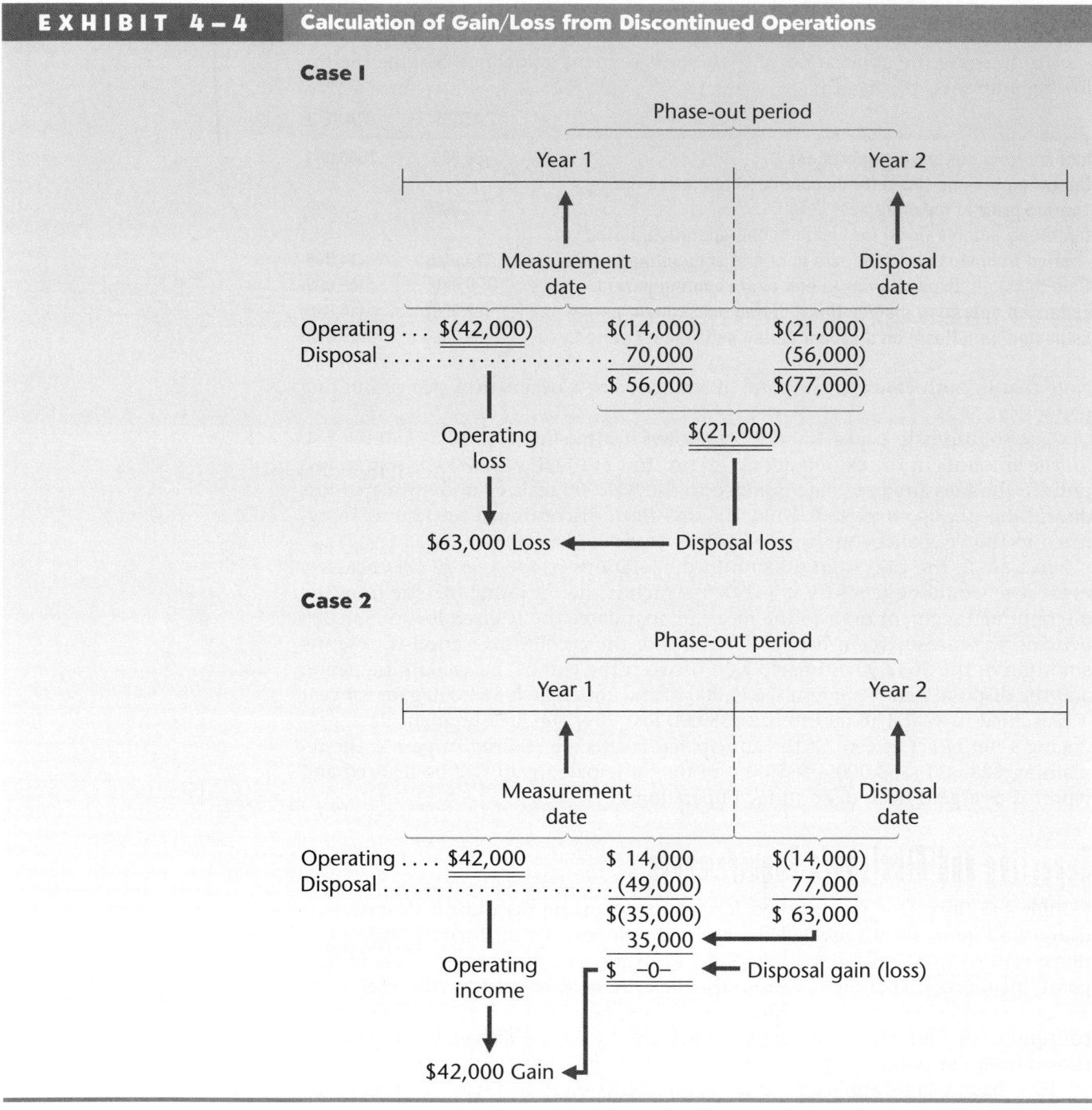

Case 1

Phase-out period

	Year 1		Year 2

Measurement date — Disposal date

Operating ...	$(42,000)	$(14,000)	$(21,000)
Disposal		70,000	(56,000)
		$ 56,000	$(77,000)

Operating loss → $63,000 Loss ← Disposal loss

$(21,000)

Case 2

Phase-out period

	Year 1		Year 2

Measurement date — Disposal date

Operating	$42,000	$ 14,000	$(14,000)
Disposal		(49,000)	77,000
		$(35,000)	$ 63,000
		35,000	

Operating income → $42,000 Gain ← $ –0– ← Disposal gain (loss)

4. A description of the remaining assets and liabilities of the discontinued segment at the balance sheet date.

5. The operating income or loss, and any proceeds from the disposal during the period from the measurement date to the balance sheet date.[6]

In sum, the objective is to disclose fully the impact of the disposal on the company through separate disclosure of the remaining net assets of the segment and through separate reporting of the impact of the disposal.

[6]Ibid., para. 18.

EXHIBIT 4-5	**Required Income Statement Format for Reporting Discontinued Operations (Based on Case I)**

Income from continuing operations.............		$560,000
Discontinued operations:		
Loss from operations of discontinued Division *X* (less applicable income tax savings)..........	$(42,000)	
Loss on disposal of Division *X*, including provision of $35,000 for operating losses during phase-out period (less applicable income tax savings).....	(21,000)	(63,000)
Net income..............................		$497,000

An actual example of reporting and disclosure of discontinued operations is provided in the General Electric income statement in Appendix B. Note 2 to the financial statements explains the source of the items in the income statement. GE sold its Kidder, Peabody securities business to Paine Webber in 1994 and its aerospace operations to Martin Marietta in 1993.

Another illustration of the disclosure requirements associated with discontinued operations is shown in Exhibit 4–6. In its comparative income statements, The Clorox Company reported earnings from discontinued operations of $32,064,000 in 1994 and a loss from discontinued operations of $867,000 in 1993. This note to the financial statements explained that those results arose from disposal of Clorox's bottled water and frozen foods businesses.

EXHIBIT 4-6	**Disclosure Requirements for Discontinued Operations**

The Clorox Company
From 1995 Annual Report

2. Discontinued Operations

The Company sold its bottled water and frozen foods businesses during 1994 for $159,293,000. The sale of these businesses resulted in a net gain of $31,430,000. In June 1993, the Company sold its Prince Castle business which did not result in a material gain or loss. Results of discontinued operations are classified separately in the Statements of Consolidated Earnings and include (in thousands):

	1994	1993
Net sales.....................	$18,700	$173,291
Earnings (losses) from operations before income taxes......................	$ 1,043	$ (1,437)
Income tax (expense) benefits.................	(409)	570
Net earnings (losses) from discontinued operations ..	$ 634	$ (867)
Gain on sale of businesses....................	$42,177	—
Income taxes............................	10,747	—
Net gain on sale of businesses................	$31,430	—
Earnings (losses) from discontinued operations	$32,064	$ (867)

5 Identify an extraordinary item and prepare the related income statement disclosures.

CONCEPTUAL

Disclosures for extraordinary items allow users to better assess future earnings power.

Extraordinary Items

Another category of items that must be reported separately from income from continuing operations is **extraordinary items.** According to *APB Opinion No. 30, both* the following criteria must be met for an item to be classified as extraordinary:

1. *Unusual nature.* The underlying event or transaction should possess a high degree of abnormality and be of a type clearly unrelated to, or only incidentally related to, the ordinary and typical activities of the entity, *taking into account the environment in which the entity operates.* [Emphasis added.]

2. *Infrequency of occurrence.* The underlying event or transaction should be of a type that would not reasonably be expected to recur in the foreseeable future, *taking into account the environment in which the entity operates.*[7] [Emphasis added.]

The purpose of these criteria for separate disclosure of extraordinary items is to allow financial statement users to better assess a company's future earning power.

Note that both criteria conclude with the phrase "taking into account the environment in which the entity operates." What is extraordinary for one entity may not be extraordinary for another because of environmental differences. For example, a casualty loss from flood damage to a company's plant along the Mississippi River in Louisiana may not constitute an extraordinary item, but a casualty loss from flood damage in the Arizona desert may. Likewise, classification of similar events as either extraordinary or ordinary may differ from one year to another as environmental conditions change. The environment includes factors such as the characteristics of the industry or industries in which a company operates, its geographical location, and the extent of government regulation.

To give another example, assume that a large, diversified company sells a block of shares from its securities portfolio which it has acquired for investment purposes. The company owns several securities for investment purposes; this is the first sale. Would the gain or loss qualify as extraordinary? It would not.

Unless the available evidence clearly indicates that an item is both unusual and infrequent, the presumption is that items are ordinary and usual. The following events typically do not qualify as extraordinary items because they are not unusual or because they may be expected to recur regularly:

1. Write-down or write-off of receivables, inventories, equipment leased to others, . . . or intangible assets.

2. Gains or losses from exchange or translation of foreign currencies, including those relating to major devaluations and revaluations.

3. Gains or losses on disposal of a segment of a business.

4. Other gains or losses from sale or abandonment of property, plant, or equipment used in the business.

5. Effects of a strike, including those against competitors and major suppliers.

6. Adjustment of accruals on long-term contracts.[8]

Occasionally one of these items may be part of an event or a transaction that gives rise to an extraordinary item. In those rare instances, the portion of the item that is "the direct result of a major casualty (such as an earthquake), an expropriation, or a prohibition under a newly enacted law or regulation that clearly meets both criteria" for an extraordinary item should be reported as an extraordinary gain or loss.

In reporting extraordinary items, companies must include descriptive captions and amounts for individual items where practicable, along with disclosure of the

---

[7]Ibid., para. 20.
[8]Ibid., para. 23.

nature of the items involved and the applicable income taxes. Earnings per share must be disclosed in the income statement for both income before extraordinary items and net income. (Since earnings per share for extraordinary items can be determined by subtraction, disclosure of that figure is not required.) Exhibit 4–7 illustrates the reporting requirements for extraordinary items. In 1995 Pacific Telesis reported an extraordinary charge of $3.36 billion—more than three times its operating income! The note indicates that the charge occurred because its subsidiary, Pacific Bell, changed from regulatory accounting rules to GAAP in the third quarter of that year.

Gains and losses from the extinguishment of debt must always be reported as extraordinary items if the effect is material.[9] The reporting of debt extinguishments as extraordinary items without concern for whether they meet the criteria for extraordinary items does not seem supportable from an accounting theory standpoint. The FASB may have wished to "flag" the huge gains resulting from debt retirement when the market values of companies' debts were driven down below book value because of high interest rates in the 1970s and early 1980s. One might question whether the circumstances that gave rise to this requirement justify its continued existence.

Unusual or Infrequent Items

Some items meet one, but not both, of the criteria for classification as extraordinary items. That is, they are either **unusual or infrequent,** but not both. Those items should be reported as components of income from continuing operations at their gross amounts (*not* net of taxes). They should either be listed separately in the income statement or disclosed in the notes to the financial statements. They should not be reported in any manner that implies that they are extraordinary items. For example, Coca-Cola explained in the notes to its 1995 financial statements that selling, administrative, and general expenses included a nonrecurring charge of $86 million "to increase efficiencies in the Company's operations in the United States and Europe."

Restructuring Charges

Recently, the income statements of many companies have included **restructuring charges.** For example, Bristol-Myers Squibb included a restructuring charge of $310 million in its 1995 income statement. As explained in Note 4 to the financial statements, this charge "relates to the consolidation of plants and facilities, and related employee terminations. The restructuring charge consists of employee-related costs of $190 million, $100 million of asset write-downs and $20 million of other related expenses."

Restructuring charges must be presented as a component of income from continuing operations and must be separately disclosed if they are material. Restructuring charges related to assets or activities for which the associated revenues and expenses have historically been included in operating income may not be included as "other expense" but should instead be included as a component of operating income. It is not appropriate to report the per share impact of restructuring charges.

A Note on International Reporting Practices

The U.S. GAAP requirements for classifying an item as extraordinary are generally the most restrictive in the world. For example, under British GAAP the sale of an investment in a subsidiary and the disposal of fixed assets may be classified as extraordinary if they are not expected to recur regularly or frequently. British GAAP

[9]"Reporting Gains and Losses from Extinguishment of Debt: An Amendment of *APB Opinion No. 30,*" *Statement of Financial Accounting Standards No. 4* (Stamford, Conn.: FASB, 1975), para. 8.

EXHIBIT 4 – 7   **Reporting Requirements for Extraordinary Items**

Pacific Telesis Group and Subsidiaries
Consolidated Statements of Income
For the Year Ended December 31, 1995
(Dollars in millions, except per share amounts)

Income from continuing operations before income taxes (details omitted)	$ 1,611
Income taxes	563
Income before extraordinary item	$ 1,048
Extraordinary item, net of tax (Note C)	(3,360)
Net income (loss)	$(2,312)
Earnings (loss) per share:	
Income from continuing operations	$ 2.46
Income before extraordinary item	$ 2.46
Extraordinary item	(7.89)
Net income (loss)	$ (5.43)
Dividends per share	$ 2.18
Average shares outstanding (thousands)	425,996

The accompanying Notes are an integral part of the Consolidated Financial Statements.

C. Discontinuance of Regulatory Accounting - SFAS 71

Effective third quarter 1995, the Corporation's Pacific Bell subsidiary discontinued its application of SFAS 71 in accordance with the provisions of SFAS 101, "Accounting for the Discontinuance of Application of FASB Statement No. 71." As a result, the Corporation recorded a non-cash, extraordinary charge of $3.4 billion, or $7.89 per share, during 1995 which is net of a deferred income tax benefit of $2.4 billion. The charge includes a write-down of net telephone plant and the elimination of net regulatory assets as summarized in the following table.

(Dollars in millions)	Pre-Tax	After-Tax
Increase in telephone plant and equipment accumulated depreciation.	$4,819	$2,842
Elimination of net regulatory assets.	962	518
Total	$5,781	$3,360

Pacific Bell historically accounted for the economic effects of regulation in accordance with the provisions of SFAS 71. Under SFAS 71, Pacific Bell depreciated telephone plant using lives prescribed by regulators and, as a result of actions of regulators, deferred recognizing certain costs, or recognized certain liabilities (referred to as "regulatory assets" and "regulatory liabilities").

Effective third quarter 1995, management determined that, for external financial reporting purposes, it is no longer appropriate for Pacific Bell to use the special SFAS 71 accounting rules for entities subject to traditional regulation. Management's decision to change to the general accounting rules used by competitive enterprises was based upon an assessment of the emerging competitive environment in California. Pacific Bell's prices for its products and services are being driven increasingly by market forces instead of regulation.

also requires that discontinued operations be disclosed as an extraordinary item, rather than separately as discontinued operations. In the reports of non-U.S. companies unusual items are sometimes included in income from continuing operations and other times disclosed separately. Thus, users of financial statements of non-U.S. companies must pay close attention to unusual and extraordinary items, since there is little comparability in international reporting practices.

Cumulative Effect of a Change in Accounting Principle

In our discussion of the qualities of useful information (Chapter 2), we pointed out the importance of consistency in the use of accounting principles over time. Occasionally, however, a company may adopt a different accounting principle from the one used in previous periods, either voluntarily or to conform to a new professional pronouncement. For example, a company may change from FIFO to average cost in accounting for inventories, or from the straight-line method to an accelerated method for depreciation of plant assets.

The cumulative effect of most **changes in accounting principle** must be disclosed in the income statement in the period in which the company makes the change.[10] The cumulative effect is the difference between (1) the present carrying value of the affected asset or liability, calculated under the previously used principle, and (2) the carrying value under the newly adopted principle. The cumulative effect must be reported in the income statement net of applicable taxes. Accounting for the asset or liability in the current period is based on the new principle. This method of reporting the change in accounting principle is referred to as the *current period approach.*

In addition to reporting the cumulative effect in the income statement, net income and earnings per share for all prior periods presented on a comparative basis must be disclosed as if the new method had been in effect during those periods. This pro forma information is *supplementary* to the actual reported net income and earnings per share numbers in prior periods.

To illustrate, assume that at the beginning of 1996, Miller Corporation purchased equipment costing $30,000. The equipment was being depreciated by the sum-of-the-years'-digits method, on the basis of an estimated five-year life and zero salvage value. In 1998, Miller changed to straight-line depreciation, with no change in the estimated life or salvage value. Miller will continue to use the sum-of-the-years'-digits method for tax purposes; the applicable tax rate is 40 percent. The cumulative effect of this change is calculated as follows:

CONCEPTUAL

Consistency is a necessary quality of useful accounting information.

6 Calculate the cumulative effect of a change in accounting principle on prior periods and prepare the related income statement disclosures.

	DEPRECIATION UNDER		
	SUM-OF-THE-YEARS'-DIGITS	**STRAIGHT-LINE**	**DIFFERENCE**
1996	5/15 × $30,000 = $10,000	$6,000	$4,000
1997	4/15 × $30,000 = 8,000	6,000	2,000
	Cumulative effect, before taxes		$6,000

Exhibit 4–8 shows how the change in accounting principle is disclosed in Miller's income statement for 1998. A footnote would describe the change, set forth the reason for it, and point out that depreciation expense for 1998 is based on the straight-line method.

Our purpose has been to provide an overview of the reporting requirements for changes in accounting principle. Accounting and disclosure requirements for accounting changes are covered in depth in Chapter 19. You may wish to refer to the GE annual report in Appendix B, where Note 20 explains a change in accounting principle that occurred in 1993.

---

[10]"Accounting Changes," *Opinions of the Accounting Principles Board No. 20* (New York: AICPA, 1971). *Opinion No. 20* requires that the cumulative effect of some changes in accounting principle be disclosed by restating prior period financial statements instead of reporting the cumulative effect in the current period income statements. Additionally, many FASB transition rules require statement of prior period financial statements. These types of changes and disclosure requirements are discussed in Chapter 19.

| EXHIBIT 4-8 | Reporting a Change in Accounting Principle |

Income before extraordinary item and change
in accounting principle (assumed) $22,200
Extraordinary gain on early extinguishment of debt,
net of applicable taxes of $2,000 (assumed) 3,000
Cumulative effect of change in accounting principle,
net of applicable taxes of $2,400[a] 3,600
Net income $28,800

[a]$6,000 × .40.

Reporting Comprehensive Income

> **1** Define other comprehensive income and explain the reporting requirements for those items.

The FASB stated in *Concepts Statement No. 5* that a full set of financial statements for a period should show (among other things) comprehensive income (total nonowner changes in equity) for the period. Recall that *Concepts Statements* do not establish GAAP. Prior to the issuance of *Statement No. 130*, there was no requirement for reporting comprehensive income, nor was there a recommended format for displaying comprehensive income. Thus, *Statement No. 130* represents the Board's first step in implementing the concept of comprehensive income.

If all revenues, expenses, gains, and losses were included in net income, net income and comprehensive income would be the same. However, the perceived need for reporting comprehensive income and its components arose because a number of gain and loss items were being reported directly in stockholders' equity rather than as a part of net income. For example, unrealized gains and losses on certain investments in debt and equity securities are reported directly in stockholders' equity. The purpose of reporting comprehensive income is to summarize *all* nonowner changes in equity for a period. In connection with other disclosures, this information should assist financial statement users in assessing the timing and amount of an entity's future cash flows.

Comprehensive income includes net income and all revenues, expenses, gains, and losses that are *included* in comprehensive income but *excluded* from net income. *Statement No. 130* requires that companies must divide comprehensive income into *net income* and *other comprehensive income*. They must continue to report net income. Companies with no other comprehensive income items in any of the periods presented need not report comprehensive income.

Items included in other comprehensive income must be classified according to their nature. Currently, these items would include no more than three categories: foreign currency items, minimum pension liability adjustments, and unrealized gains and losses on certain debt and equity securities. To avoid double counting in comprehensive income items that are included in the current year's net income that have been included in other comprehensive income in current or prior periods, *reclassification adjustments* may be necessary. For example, the portion of *realized* gains on the sale of investment securities (included in net income) that was included as *unrealized* gains in other comprehensive income of prior periods must be deducted through other comprehensive income to avoid double counting.

There is no specific format required for reporting comprehensive income and its components. However, net income must be displayed as a component of comprehensive income, and comprehensive income and its components must be displayed in a financial statement that has the same prominence as other required financial statements. The Board provides several alternative acceptable formats in an appendix to *Statement No. 130,* but *encourages* companies to display the components of other comprehensive income and total comprehensive income either

EXHIBIT 4-9	Reporting Comprehensive Income—Two-Statement Approach

X Company
Statement of Comprehensive Income
For the year ended December 31, 1998
(numbers assumed)

Net income		$80,000
Other comprehensive income, net of tax:		
Foreign currency translation adjustments		$10,000
Unrealized gains on securities:		
Unrealized holding gains arising during period	$7,000	
Less: reclassification adjustment for gains		
included in net income	(1,000)	6,000
Other comprehensive income		$16,000
Comprehensive income		$96,000

(1) below net income in a statement that reports results of operations (*one-statement approach*), or (2) in a separate statement of comprehensive income that starts with net income (*two-statement approach*). An illustration of the second alternative above for the hypothetical X Company is provided in Exhibit 4–9. Note that X Company would continue to present its income statement as in the past. The "bottom line" on the income statement is the beginning point for the statement of comprehensive income. In Chapter 5 we illustrate another acceptable format for presenting comprehensive income and its components in the statement of changes in equity.

The total of other comprehensive income for a period is transferred to a separate component of equity—accumulated other comprehensive income (just as net income is transferred to retained earnings). The accumulated balances for each classification of accumulated other comprehensive income (for example, unrealized gains/losses on certain debt and equity securities) must be disclosed either in the balance sheet, in a statement of changes in equity, or in notes to the financial statements.

Earnings per Share

Perhaps the most often quoted figure related to a company's performance is **earnings per share** (EPS). In the simplest setting, earnings per share is calculated by dividing net income by the number of common stock shares outstanding. Users find earnings on a per share basis easier to comprehend than total earnings, and price/earnings (P/E) ratios are quoted frequently in the financial press.

EPS information, which usually appears on the face of the income statement, must be disclosed by publicly held companies for each year for which an income statement is presented. If discontinued operations, extraordinary items, and changes in accounting principles all exist within a particular reporting period, companies must report EPS for income from continuing operations, income before extraordinary items, the cumulative effect of a change in accounting principle, and net income. Since income statement users may calculate the per share amounts for discontinued operations and extraordinary items by subtraction, disclosure of the EPS effect of discontinued operations and extraordinary items is optional. However, most entities do disclose the per share effect of those items. A per-share amount is not required for comprehensive income.

Many complexities may arise in calculating and reporting EPS. Under some circumstances, companies must make a dual presentation of EPS in the income state-

8 Explain the importance of earnings per share (EPS) and required EPS disclosures.

EXHIBIT 4–10   **Dual Presentation of Earnings per Share**

Glick Company
Schedule of Basic and Diluted EPS
For the Year Ended December 31, 1998

Earnings per share of common stock (basic):
Income from continuing operations before extraordinary items $3.63
Income from discontinued operations 0.47
Extraordinary items 0.92
Net income $5.02

Earnings per share of common stock (diluted):
Income from continuing operations before extraordinary items $3.54
Income from discontinued operations 0.43
Extraordinary items 0.85
Net income $4.82

ment. The two presentations are called basic EPS and diluted EPS, respectively. Exhibit 4–10 illustrates a dual presentation of EPS by Glick Company. Detailed guidelines for calculating EPS are presented in Chapter 20.

We have now discussed the major issues associated with income reporting, from continuing operations through earnings per share disclosures. In the next section, we briefly describe the process of associating income tax expense with various income components.

ASSOCIATING INCOME TAX EXPENSE WITH INCOME COMPONENTS

> **9**
> **Explain the meaning and purpose of intraperiod tax allocation.**

> **CONCEPTUAL**
>
> Disaggregation of income tax expense contributes to the objectives of financial reporting.

In reporting income tax expense (or the income tax benefit associated with a tax-deductible loss), companies must disaggregate total income tax expense (or benefit) and associate it with the major income components that caused the expense (or benefit). Referring back to Exhibit 4–1 (page 171), we see that an income tax effect, where applicable, should be related to each of the income components in the exhibit. For example, if a company incurred a tax-deductible extraordinary loss of $100,000 as a result of a catastrophe, and the applicable tax rate was 40 percent, the loss would be reported as $60,000 [$100,000 – (.40 × $100,000)]. (Since the loss is tax-deductible, income taxes otherwise payable are reduced by $40,000 and the $40,000 tax benefit is reported as a reduction in the amount of the loss.)

The association of income tax expense with income components, which is referred to as the **disaggregation of income tax expense,** or **intraperiod tax allocation,** contributes to the objectives of financial reporting by presenting income statement information that permits users to evaluate, assess, and predict net cash flows to the company. To illustrate, assume that Valenzuela Corporation's revenues and expenses for 1998 were $160,000 and $60,000, respectively. In addition, the corporation had an extraordinary gain of $40,000. The income tax rate was 40 percent, except for the extraordinary gain, which was taxed at a 25 percent rate. Assume these same revenues, expenses, and extraordinary gain also appeared on the corporation's tax return. The total income tax liability would have been $50,000 [.40($160,000 – $60,000) + .25($40,000)]. Therefore net income for 1998 was $90,000:

$160,000 – $60,000 + $40,000 – $50,000 = $90,000
Revenues – Expenses +   Gain   – Taxes = Net income

EXHIBIT 4–11	Income Statement with and without Disaggregation of Income Tax Expense (Intraperiod Tax Allocation)

Valenzuela Corporation
Income Statement for 1998

	Without Disaggregation	With Disaggregation
Revenues	$160,000	$160,000
Expenses	(60,000)	(60,000)
Income from operations before income taxes	$100,000	$100,000
Income tax expense	(50,000)	(40,000)
Income before extraordinary gain	$ 50,000	$ 60,000
Extraordinary gain	40,000	
Extraordinary gain (net of $10,000 taxes)		30,000
Net income	$ 90,000	$ 90,000

Two versions of the corporation's income statement, one with and one without disaggregation of income tax expense, are shown in Exhibit 4–11. Which one better depicts the net cash flow effects of Valenzuela Corporation's primary and peripheral operating activities? The income statement prepared *with* disaggregation of income tax expense is the better presentation, because had the gain *not* occurred, net income would have been $60,000 instead of $50,000. Which of the two presentations provides the better basis for users to predict *future* net income and cash flows? Again, the income statement prepared *with* disaggregation of income tax expense provides a better basis. Since the extraordinary gain is by definition unusual and nonrecurring, the figure of $60,000 for income before the extraordinary gain is probably a better predictor of future income than the figure $50,000. If 1999 operations were identical to those of 1998 except for the extraordinary item, net income would be $60,000.

In sum, disaggregation of income tax expense allows the user to assess the after-tax impact of the events and transactions that affect net income. Income tax expense (or benefit) must be reported separately for (1) income from continuing operations, (2) discontinued operations, (3) extraordinary items, (4) cumulative effect adjustments, and (5) prior period adjustments. Items affecting income from continuing operations are reported at their gross amount, and then one amount for income taxes is related to income from continuing operations. Each of the items included in the income statement after income from continuing operations should be reported net of any related income tax expense or income tax benefit. The amount of income tax expense or benefit associated with each component of other comprehensive income must be disclosed either on the face of the statement where the components are displayed or in the notes to the financial statements.

This concludes our coverage of the current requirements for income reporting. To provide a conceptual summation of the income statement, a few unresolved income reporting issues are described in the following section.

U NRESOLVED INCOME REPORTING ISSUES

Historically, the development of rules for reporting income and its components has not been related to a set of basic concepts because there has been no general agreement on concepts. Instead, the accounting profession has developed reporting rules piecemeal. Not surprisingly, the rules have often been criticized for their inadequacies and inconsistencies.

10 Discuss the issues confronting the FASB in its attempt to develop a format for the reporting of earnings activities.

EXHIBIT 4-12 Detailed Multiple-Step Income Statement

WRL Company, Inc.
Income Statement
For the Year Ended December 31, 1998

Sales		$300,000	
Less: Sales discounts, returns, and allowances		(5,000)	$295,000
Cost of goods sold:			
Beginning inventory		$ 30,000	
Purchases	$200,000		
Less: Discounts, returns, and allowances	(25,000)	175,000	
Freight in		5,000	
Cost of goods available for sale		$210,000	
Less: Ending inventory		(20,000)	190,000
Gross profit on sales			$105,000
Less: Operating expenses			
Selling expenses:			
Sales salaries	$ 11,000		
Advertising and promotion	19,000		
Freight out	7,000		
Travel and entertainment	5,000		
Depreciation	18,000		
Bad debt expense	5,000	$ (65,000)	
General and administrative expenses:			
Administrative salaries	$ 20,000		
Property taxes	1,000		
Utilities	6,000		
Depreciation	4,000		
Insurance expense	900		
Research and development	1,600	(33,500)	(98,500)
Operating income			$ 6,500
Other revenues and gains:			
Interest revenue	$ 600		
Dividend revenue	1,400		
Gain on sale of fixed assets	7,700	$ 9,700	

Users complain that existing income statements do not provide enough information about past income activities to enable them to assess future income and cash flows. They complain specifically about inadequate disclosure of the effects of unusual events or transactions, as well as economic changes that affect the relationship between recurring revenues and expenses (such as a large price change in an important resource). Furthermore, some professional pronouncements, such as the requirement that research and development costs be recorded as expenses as they are incurred, may increase the variability of income without disclosing the reasons for the increased variability. Even with disclosure, interpretation is often difficult. Small wonder users tend to focus on the final net income number rather than on the components of income.

Some income components are reasonably stable over time. Disclosure of the stable components of income assists users in predicting future amounts for these items. Reporting of historical data on the *volume* of goods and services sold, selling *prices,* and the *range* of goods and services provided further helps users to project future cash flows. Historical reporting of the fixed and variable components of expenses and of changes in the prices of major resources also helps.

Other expenses and losses:			
Interest on long-term debt	$ 700		
Loss on disposal of part of a division	8,000	(8,700)	1,000
Income from continuing operations before income taxes			$ 7,500
Income tax expense			(2,100)
Income from continuing operations			$ 5,400
Discontinued operations:			
Income from operations of discontinued segment X			
(less related tax of $4,000)		$ 8,000	
Loss on disposal of segment X, including provision			
of $10,000 for operating losses during phase-out period			
(less related tax savings of $5,000)		(12,000)	(4,000)
Income before extraordinary item and cumulative effect			
of a change in an accounting principle			$ 1,400
Extraordinary item:			
Gain on debt extinguishment (net of $1,600 tax)			4,400
Cumulative effect on prior years of retroactive application			
of new depreciation method (net of $7,000 tax)			6,000
Net income			$ 11,800
Earnings per common share:[a]			
Income from continuing operations			$ .54
Income from discontinued segment X			.80
Loss on disposal of segment X			(1.20)
Income before extraordinary item and cumulative effect			$ .14
Extraordinary item			.44
Cumulative effect of change in an accounting principle			.60
Net income			$1.18

[a]Assuming 10,000 shares outstanding.

Other income components may be highly volatile. Information about those components should be reported so that users may separate their effects from the effects of more stable components. Examples of relatively volatile income components are gains and losses from discontinued operations, extraordinary items, and the cumulative effects of accounting changes.

Despite efforts over the last few years to make income statements more informative, many income statement users are still dissatisfied with current practice. As we said in Chapter 1, financial information is disclosed (1) in the main body of the statements, (2) in notes accompanying the statements, and (3) as supplementary information. Thus, information about income and its components could appear in any of those places. Additional questions concern the amount of detail to be reported and the manner in which it should be presented. Accountants currently lack definitive guidance for those decisions.

Partially in response to these criticisms, as was mentioned earlier in this chapter, the FASB devoted several paragraphs of *Statement of Financial Accounting Concepts No. 5* to a discussion of the statement of earnings and comprehensive income. That discussion emphasizes the need for information about the various components of earnings and comprehensive income that differ in risk, stability, and predictability.

As described earlier in this chapter, the FASB issued *Statement No. 130,* "Reporting Comprehensive Income," in 1997. *Statement No. 130* requires that comprehensive income and its components be reported, either in a one-statement or two-statement format or in the statement of changes in equity. Still unanswered, however, are the issues of when components of comprehensive income should be recognized in financial statements and how they should be measured, and the characteristics of items that should be included in net income and in other comprehensive income.

SUMMARY OF INCOME REPORTING

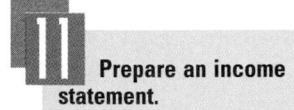

Prepare an income statement.

Exhibit 4–12 summarizes the format requirements discussed in this chapter. This exhibit shows how items included in income from continuing operations are displayed in a detailed, multiple-step income statement. Although this amount of detail would seldom be found in financial statements prepared for external users, the exhibit does show where the various revenues, expenses, and gains and losses are typically included.

SUMMARY OF LEARNING OBJECTIVES

I. Differentiate between the net assets approach and the transactions approach to the determination of net income.

Conceptually, net income is the periodic change in net assets, excluding transactions with owners such as dividends or the issue of capital stock. This manner of calculating net income may be referred to as the net assets approach. The transactions approach, on the other hand, summarizes the periodic inflows (revenues) and outflows (expenses) that cause net assets to change. The transactions approach underlies income reporting under GAAP.

2. Distinguish between the single-step and multiple-step formats of reporting income from continuing operations.

Under the single-step approach, income from continuing operations consists of two categories: (1) revenues and gains, and (2) expenses and losses. The multiple-step approach matches various revenues, expenses, gains, and losses to produce various subtotals, such as operating income.

3. Distinguish between the current operating performance approach and the all-inclusive approach to reporting income.

The current operating performance approach includes only regular, recurring operating revenues and expenses in income. Unusual or nonrecurring items are reported directly in retained earnings. Under the all-inclusive approach, all revenues, expenses, gains, and losses are included in income. The all-inclusive approach comes closer to describing current income reporting practice under GAAP.

4. Identify a discontinued segment or operation of a business entity and prepare the related income statement disclosures.

A discontinued operation is a segment of a business that has been sold, abandoned, spun off, or otherwise disposed of; or a business that, although it is still operating, is the subject of a formal plan for disposal. The gain or loss, after income from continuing operations, is reported in two parts: (1) net operating income or loss from the beginning of the period to the measurement date, and (2) operating income or loss plus disposal gain or loss during the phase-out period. Required disclosures include the identity of the discontinued segment, the expected disposal date, the expected manner of disposal, a description of the remaining assets and liabilities of the discontinued segment, the operating income or loss, and any disposal proceeds during the period from the measurement date to the balance sheet date.

5. **Identify an extraordinary item and prepare the related income statement disclosures.**
An extraordinary item is a material income item that is unusual and infrequent in occurrence, taking into account the environment in which an entity operates. Gains and losses from the extinguishment of debt must always be reported as extraordinary items. The net-of-tax effect of the event or transaction must be reported in the income statement after any gain or loss from discontinued operations and before the cumulative effect of an accounting change. The nature of the item and its income tax effect must be disclosed.

6. **Calculate the cumulative effect of a change in accounting principle on prior periods and prepare the related income statement disclosures.**
The cumulative effect of a change in accounting principle on prior periods is the difference between (1) the carrying value of the affected asset or liability and (2) what the carrying value would have been if the newly adopted principle had been in effect in prior periods. This effect is reported net of tax effect after extraordinary items in the income statement. Net income and earnings per share for prior periods reported currently must be disclosed as if the new method had been in effect in those periods, as a supplement to the actual reported net income in prior periods. The nature of and the reason for the change must be described in the notes to the financial statements. Current period statements should reflect the use of the new principle.

7. **Define other comprehensive income and explain the reporting requirements for these items.**
Other comprehensive income is the portion of comprehensive income not included in net income. Comprehensive income is the change in net assets for a period from nonowner sources. Net income must be displayed as a component of comprehensive income, and comprehensive income and its components must be displayed in a financial statement that has the same prominence as other required financial statements. Several alternative reporting formats are acceptable, including the one-statement approach, the two-statement approach, and presentation of comprehensive income and its components in the statement of changes in equity.

8. **Explain the importance of earnings per share (EPS) and required EPS disclosures.**
Earnings per share is commonly used by investors and other financial statement users to assess the productivity of an investment on a per share basis. The price-earnings (P/E) ratio, another commonly used ratio, is based on EPS (EPS is the denominator). Public companies must disclose EPS for each year for which an income statement is presented. EPS must be disclosed separately for income from continuing operations, income before extraordinary items, the cumulative effect of a change in accounting principle, and net income. Under some circumstances, companies must make a dual presentation of EPS.

9. **Explain the meaning and purpose of intraperiod tax allocation.**
Intraperiod tax allocation refers to the required association of income tax expense (benefit) with income components; it is also referred to as disaggregation of income tax expense. A single tax effect is reported for continuing operations. The tax effects of a gain or loss from discontinued operations, extraordinary items, and the cumulative effect of changes in accounting principle must also be reported with those items on a net-of-tax basis. The purpose of intraperiod tax allocation is to enable financial statement users to better assess the cash flow impact of operating and nonoperating income components.

10. **Discuss the issues confronting the FASB in its attempt to develop a format for the reporting of earnings activities.**
Issues confronting the FASB include the lack of an accepted set of basic concepts, and user complaints about the "backward-looking" nature of financial accounting information and about inadequate disclosures regarding income components. The FASB's project on comprehensive income is an attempt to resolve some of these issues.

11. **Prepare an income statement.**
The preparation of an income statement must follow the format shown in Exhibit 4–1. Income from continuing operations may be presented in a single-step or multiple-step format. Exhibit 4–11 provides a comprehensive illustration of a detailed multiple-step income statement. Other examples include the GE income statements in Appendix B at the end of the book and Exhibits 4–2 (Motorola), 4–3 (Coca-Cola), and 4–7 (Pacific Telesis).

KEY TERMS

all-inclusive approach 173

change in accounting principle 182

comprehensive income 169

current operating performance approach 173

disaggregation of income tax expense 184

discontinued operations 173

disposal date 174

earnings per share 183

extraordinary item 178

income from continuing operations 171

intraperiod tax allocation 184

measurement date 174

modified historical cost accounting system 169

multiple-step format 171

net assets 169

net income (loss) 169

restructuring charges 179

single-step format 171

transactions approach 170

unusual or infrequent items 179

QUESTIONS

Q 4-1. Why is it necessary to measure a particular attribute and to adopt a particular capital maintenance concept in order to determine accounting income?

Q 4-2. What is the revenue realization principle, and what is its role in income determination?

Q 4-3. What is the periodicity assumption, and what is its relationship to income determination?

Q 4-4. What are the advantages to a transactions approach to reporting of accounting income as opposed to a net assets approach?

Q 4-5. What is the matching principle, and what is its role in income determination?

Q 4-6. What are (1) the single-step format and (2) the multiple-step format for presenting earnings information? Describe the advantages and disadvantages of each format.

Q 4-7. Describe and explain the rationale for the current operating performance and all-inclusive approaches to reporting income information.

Q 4-8. What are discontinued operations, and how are they required to be reported?

Q 4-9. What is meant by *measurement date* and *disposal date* with respect to discontinued operations? What is the *phase-out period*?

Q 4-10. What are the two criteria that must be met in order for an item to qualify as extraordinary? What item must always be reported as an extraordinary item?

Q 4-11. How should extraordinary items be reported in the financial statements?

Q 4-12. How should material items that meet one, but not both, of the criteria for extraordinary items be reported in the financial statements?

Q 4-13. What are restructuring charges, and how should they be reported?

Q 4-14. Define a change in accounting principle, give an example of such a change, and describe the *general rule* of accounting for and disclosing changes in accounting principles.

Q 4-15. What is meant by *disaggregation of income tax expense*? How does disaggregation relate to the assessment of past and future cash flows?

Q 4-16. Where should earnings per share data be disclosed in the financial statements? For which reported figures are earnings per share data required?

Q 4-17. In what ways have current reporting practices been criticized as inadequate with respect to stable and volatile components of earnings?

CASES

C 4-1. **INCOME STATEMENT CLASSIFICATION** Kent Company is engaged primarily in commercial and agricultural land sales but also makes some retail land sales and condominium sales. Kent recently acquired a retail land sales project with the agreement that it could return the property with no liability to Kent if it did not desire to pursue the project. Kent invested considerable money in the project before deciding, because of a declining economy, to return the project to the original owner before any sales were made.

REQUIRED Describe the appropriate income statement presentation of the amount invested in the retail land sales project in the period in which the project was abandoned and returned to the original owner. Cite authoritative literature to support your answer.

(AICPA, adapted)

C 4-2. **EXTRAORDINARY ITEMS** David Company, a textile manufacturer, entered into firm purchase commitments for cotton at a very favorable price. David currently has a very long position of purchase commitments at a low fixed price. Some of these contracts may be sold at a tremendous profit, as the cost of raw cotton has increased tremendously in recent months. The profit that might be realized from the sale of these contracts is extremely material in relation to normal operating income. The company has not sold such commitment contracts in the past, nor does it anticipate selling such contracts in the future.

REQUIRED Should the sale of cotton futures commitment contracts be considered an extraordinary item? Explain your answer.

(AICPA, adapted)

C 4-3. **INCOME STATEMENT CLASSIFICATION** You are a staff accountant for a deep-sea fishing boat rental company in Florida. In an effort to reduce audit fees, your company has agreed to prepare the financial statements prior to the auditor fieldwork. The controller has delegated the job to you and has asked you to pay particular attention to the proper presentation of the following material items:
a) Loss on the sale of the portion of a subsidiary that leased life preservers to the boat renters. The subsidiary continues to lease fishing equipment to the boat renters.
b) Gain on the sale of the company's subsidiary that distributes the inspected and cleaned fish (caught during the fishing excursions) to supermarkets in the region.
c) The total loss of one-third of the company's boats during a tidal wave. This happens approximately every six years, and the company is not insured.
d) Costs incurred as a result of the relocation of the rental operations from the Miami area to the Tampa area.

The controller believes that items *a* and *b* should be presented as discontinued operations and that items *c* and *d* should be presented as extraordinary items. He is unaware of *SEC Staff Accounting Bulletin No. 67.*

REQUIRED For each item, prepare a short summary indicating the appropriate financial presentation and justification for such treatment. Be sure to address the controller's opinions.

C 4-4. **INCOME STATEMENT CLASSIFICATION** You are a staff accountant in a public accounting firm. One day, while you are in the office library during a summer lull in activity, one of the audit partners stops by to chat. In the course of conversation, she discovers that you feel a little uncomfortable with your ability to classify nonoperating items on the income statement. To give you some drill with these items, she comes back later with a list of items that she has come across in recent audit engagements. The items were as follows (assume all are material):
a) A meat-packing company sold its 25 percent interest in a professional baseball team. All other activities of the company are in the meat-packing business.
b) A clothing manufacturer sold all of the assets related to the manufacture of men's wool suits in order to concentrate on the production of synthetic suits.
c) A company reported a gain from the sale of an office building.
d) A company sold a block of common stock of a publicly traded company. The stock was the only security investment the company had ever owned.
e) A company that operates a chain of warehouses sold excess land surrounding one of its warehouses. In the past five years the company has twice sold such land.

f) A communications company sold all of its radio stations. The company's remaining activities are in television and publishing. The radio stations' assets and operating results are clearly distinguishable.

g) A retail company changed its method of inventory costing from first in, first out to average cost.

REQUIRED   Indicate the appropriate income statement classification of each of the items. Briefly explain each item's classification.

C 4-5. **INCOME STATEMENT PRESENTATION**   The following events and transactions are to be considered independently. Assume that each item is material.

a) The U.S. government exercises its right of eminent domain on some land owned by a rancher. This land is then designated as a wilderness area. The transaction results in a gain to the rancher.

b) As a result of a court decision, Griffin Brothers must write off the cost of its trademark on a board game that has been quite profitable.

c) A company discovers that it has been misapplying the guidelines for accounting for leases. The company begins to apply the guidelines correctly in the current year.

d) As a result of a bank failure, a company loses part of its cash balance in excess of the $100,000 FDIC guarantee.

e) A company suffers a loss on the value of its investment in Johnson Corporation after it is disclosed that Johnson issued false and misleading financial statements that materially overstated income.

f) A major customer declares bankruptcy, causing a write-off of that customer's receivable.

g) A company incurs a loss on the abandonment of some equipment formerly used in the business. This is the only time in the company's history that it has had such an abandonment.

REQUIRED   Determine the effect of each of the above items on the income statement in the period in which the event occurred. Include in your answer the appropriate classification of the income statement effect.

C 4-6. **INCOME STATEMENT PRESENTATION** Behn Company's income statements for the years ended December 31, 1998, and December 31, 1997, were as follows:

Behn Company
Income Statement
(*in thousands, except per share amounts*)

	YEAR ENDED DECEMBER 31	
	1998	1997
Net sales	$ 900,000	$ 750,000
Costs and expenses:		
Cost of goods sold	$ 720,000	$ 600,000
Selling, general, and administrative expenses	112,000	90,000
Other, net	11,000	9,000
Total costs and expenses	$(843,000)	$(699,000)
Income from continuing operations before income taxes	$ 57,000	$ 51,000
Income taxes	(23,000)	(24,000)
Income from continuing operations	$ 34,000	$ 27,000
Loss on disposal of Bear Division, including provision of $1,500,000 for operating losses during phase-out period, less applicable income tax savings of $8,000,000	(8,000)	
Cumulative effect on prior years of change in depreciation method, less applicable income taxes of $1,500,000		3,000
Net income	$ 26,000	$ 30,000
Earnings per share of common stock:		
Income before cumulative effect of change in depreciation method	$2.60	$2.70
Cumulative effect on prior years of change in depreciation method, less applicable income taxes		.30
Net income	$2.60	$3.00

Additional facts are as follows:
a) On January 1, 1997, Behn Company changed its depreciation method for previously recorded plant machinery from the double-declining balance method to the straight-line method. The effect of applying the straight-line method for the year of and year after the change is included in Behn Company's income statements for the two years in cost of goods sold.
b) The loss from operations of the discontinued Bear Division from January 1, 1998, to September 30, 1998 (the portion of the year prior to the measurement date), and from January 1, 1997, to December 31, 1997, is included in Behn Company's income statements for the two years in "Other, net."
c) Behn Company has a simple capital structure with only common stock outstanding. There are no stock options or convertible securities outstanding.

REQUIRED Determine from the additional facts above whether the presentation of those facts in Behn Company's income statements is appropriate. If the presentation is appropriate, explain the theoretical rationale for the presentation. If the presentation is not appropriate, specify the appropriate presentation and explain its theoretical rationale.

(AICPA, adapted)

EXERCISES

E 4-I. **NET ASSETS APPROACH TO INCOME DETERMINATION** The records of Bradley Company disclosed the following information:

Total assets, 1/1/98	$411,500
Total liabilities, 1/1/98	286,000
Total assets, 12/31/98	480,750
Total liabilities, 12/31/98	303,700
Cash dividends declared and paid during 1998	16,050
Additional investments of cash by stockholders in exchange for common stock	42,000
Fair value of land donated to Bradley during 1998 (also amount at which recorded)	4,350

REQUIRED
1. Calculate net income for Bradley Company for 1998.
2. What weakness do you see in presenting earnings information as calculated in part 1?

E 4-2. **TRANSACTIONS APPROACH TO INCOME DETERMINATION** The following account balances were taken from the ledger of Nealy's Warehouse at the end of the year:

Sales revenue	$1,700,000
Purchases	992,600
Beginning inventory	160,000
Ending inventory	137,600
Selling expenses	212,800
Lease revenues	96,000
Interest expense	38,400
Income tax expense	115,980
Investment revenue	19,600
Purchase discounts	17,800
Freight in	33,200
Administrative expenses	183,400
Dividends declared	72,600
Sales discounts	47,800

REQUIRED
1. Calculate net income for the current year.
2. What advantage does the transactions approach have over the net assets approach to presenting earnings information?

E 4-3. **TRANSACTIONS APPROACH TO INCOME DETERMINATION** The following account balances were taken from the ledger of Trivedi Corporation at the end of the year:

Income tax expense	$ 35,000
Sales revenue	470,100
Investment revenue	14,900
Purchases	249,000
Purchase discounts	4,600
Beginning inventory	36,000
Freight in	8,000
Ending inventory	34,400
Administrative expenses	46,000
Selling expenses	53,600
Dividends declared	19,000
Lease revenues	25,000
Sales discounts	12,100
Interest expense	9,500

REQUIRED
1. Calculate net income for the year.
2. What advantage does the transactions approach have over the net assets approach?

E 4-4. **SINGLE-STEP INCOME STATEMENT** The following items relate to the current year's operations of Drieke Equipment Company:

Inventory, beginning of year	$ 51,844,875
Depreciation	5,774,150
Sales	220,215,750
Purchases	149,051,700
Inventory, end of year	47,575,125
Sales returns and allowances	3,083,775
Freight in	24,755,400
Income taxes	8,859,750
Purchase discounts, returns, and allowances	20,425,875
Miscellaneous revenue	11,773,000
Selling, general, and administrative expenses	34,533,975
Interest expense	3,714,150
Other expenses	502,575

There were 4.5 million shares of common stock outstanding during the period.

REQUIRED Prepare a single-step income statement, including EPS.

E 4-5. **SINGLE-STEP INCOME STATEMENT** Vaughn Railroad Corporation has the following revenue and expense items at the end of the current year (in thousands of dollars):

State and local taxes	$ 108,194
Sales	1,599,444
Crude oil and other raw materials used	937,454
Depreciation, depletion, and amortization	259,432
Transportation revenues	2,349,088
Other operating costs	353,322
Salaries, wages, and employee benefits	1,228,702
Interest expense	121,344
Materials and supplies used	547,118
Other revenue	81,396
Federal income taxes	119,012

Also, 40 million shares of common stock were outstanding during the period.

REQUIRED Prepare a single-step income statement, including EPS.

E 4-6. **SINGLE-STEP AND MULTIPLE-STEP INCOME STATEMENTS** The following income statement items were taken from the accounts of King Computer Corporation (in thousands of dollars):

Sales	$2,845,700
Interest expense	39,300
Research and development costs	187,200
Gain on sale of fixed assets	16,700
Cost of sales	2,239,300
Computer rental and service revenue	762,100
Income taxes	150,700
Gain from extinguishment of debt, net of taxes	19,900
Selling, general, and administrative expenses	794,000
Interest revenue	17,500

There were 40 million shares of common stock outstanding during the year.

REQUIRED
1. Prepare a single-step income statement, including EPS.
2. Prepare a multiple-step income statement, including EPS.
3. Which format do you prefer? Why?

E 4-7.   **SINGLE-STEP AND MULTIPLE-STEP INCOME STATEMENTS** Diamondback Company had the following items to be reported in the current period financial statements (in thousands of dollars):

Interest expense	$ 59,542
Cost of sales	5,445,908
Income taxes	135,000
Depreciation, depletion, and amortization	160,292
Sales	6,902,448
Excise taxes on petroleum products	471,114
Interest revenue	202,086
Selling, administrative, and general expenses	548,032
Gain from extinguishment of debt (net-of-tax effect)	25,810
Exploration costs of nonproductive wells (expensed as incurred)	42,658

In addition, 50 million shares of common stock were outstanding during the period.

REQUIRED   **1.**   Prepare a single-step income statement, including EPS.
2.   Prepare a multiple-step income statement, including EPS.
3.   Which format do you prefer? Why?

E 4-8.   **DISCONTINUED OPERATIONS; INCOME STATEMENT PREPARATION** Accountants for Kraft Grocers, Inc., obtained the following information from the accounting records of the company for 1998 (in thousands of dollars):

Selling, general, and administrative expenses	$ 52,555
Sales	655,486
Depreciation and amortization	7,952
Cost of sales	579,265
Interest expense	13,631
Provision for uncollectible note	1,135
Other revenue	4,162
Income taxes	739

The "provision for uncollectible note" relates to a mortgage note receivable from Bungling Bakery, a company that has filed for the protection of the court under Chapter XI of the federal bankruptcy act. During the year, Kraft Grocers disposed of its apparel segment. The operating loss from segment operations during the year prior to the measurement date was $3,020,000, net of taxes of $990,000. After the measurement date, the combined operating loss and loss on disposal of the segment was an additional $3,290,000, net of tax benefits of $2,212,000.

REQUIRED   Prepare a multiple-step income statement for Kraft Grocers, Inc., for 1998.

E 4-9.   **DISCONTINUED OPERATIONS; INCOME STATEMENT PRESENTATION** As chief accountant for Burke Fish Company, you have received the following information regarding 1998 activities:

Advertising expense	$ 595,000
Gain on disposition of fixed assets	601,800
Gross sales	105,271,800
General, selling, and administrative expenses	6,778,200
Sales discounts	3,333,600
Cost of sales	84,065,400
Gain from extinguishment of debt, net of taxes	786,000
Miscellaneous expenses	112,200
Interest revenue	454,000
Interest expense	2,841,600
Income taxes	2,744,400

During the year, the company decided to discontinue its pet food division, which produces pet food from residuals of the company's seafood processing operations. The operating income from the discontinued division during the year prior to the measurement date was $21,000, net of taxes of $6,000. The company is continuing to operate the division until a buyer is found. It is anticipated that a buyer will be found within the first few months of the next year and that a loss of $762,000 (net of tax benefit of $560,400) will result from the disposal.

In addition, several unusual operations were being phased out during the year, including tropical shrimp product lines, frozen retail products, a fleet of scallop fishing vessels, and a crabmeat processing operation. The loss during the year from these operations, which do not qualify as discontinued operations according to *APB Opinion No. 30*, was $2,410,400. The number of common shares outstanding during the year was 700,000.

REQUIRED Prepare a multiple-step income statement for Burke Fish Company for the year ended December 31, 1998.

E 4-10. **DISCONTINUED OPERATIONS** On July 1, 1998, the board of directors of Morgan, Inc., approved a formal plan to sell its furniture division. The sale qualifies for reporting as a discontinued operation. It is expected that the actual sale will occur in 1999. During 1998, the furniture division had a loss from operations, before any tax effect, of $3.6 million, which was incurred evenly throughout the year. Morgan's effective tax rate for 1998 is 30 percent.

REQUIRED Calculate the amount that Morgan should report as loss from operations of the discontinued furniture division for the year ended December 31, 1998.

E 4-11. **DISCONTINUED OPERATIONS** On April 30, 1998, Baginski Corporation, whose fiscal year-end is September 30, adopted a plan to discontinue the operations of Stith Division on November 30, 1998. Stith contributed a major portion of Baginski's sales volume. Baginski estimated that Stith would sustain a loss of $460,000 from May 1, 1998, through September 30, 1998, and would sustain an additional loss of $220,000 from October 1, 1998, to November 30, 1998. Baginski estimated that it would realize a gain of $500,000 on the sale of Stith's assets. On September 30, 1998, Baginski determined that Stith had actually lost $1,120,000 for the fiscal year, of which $420,000 represented the loss from May 1 to September 30, 1998.

REQUIRED Ignoring income tax effects, how much should Baginski report in its income statement for the year ending September 30, 1998, as gain or loss on disposal of Stith?

(AICPA, adapted)

E 4-12. **INCOME STATEMENT PREPARATION** LaFrentz Corporation calculated after-tax income of $800,000 from continuing operations for 1998. The following information was not considered in arriving at the $800,000:

a) During 1998, LaFrentz sold its headquarters building for an after-tax gain of $1 million.

b) In 1998, LaFrentz sold its Dix Division, a major segment of its business. LaFrentz realized a gain of $650,000 after taxes on the disposal of the assets of Dix. Operating losses of Dix in 1998 prior to the decision to dispose of the division were $710,000 (net of tax benefits).

c) In 1998, LaFrentz adopted the double-declining-balance method of depreciation. Previously, the straight-line method had been used. The change decreased 1998 income by $20,000 (before taxes). The cumulative effect on prior periods' income was a $180,000 decrease (before taxes).

REQUIRED Prepare the 1998 income statement for LaFrentz Corporation, beginning with income from continuing operations. Assume an income tax rate of 40 percent on all items for all years. There were 500,000 shares of common stock outstanding throughout 1998.

E 4-13. **INCOME STATEMENT PRESENTATION OF ACCOUNTING CHANGES AND DISCONTINUED OPERATIONS** Lorek, Inc., reported income from continuing operations after taxes for 1998 of $4,840,000. In addition, the following information relates to 1998:

a) The company disposed of its heat treating equipment division during the year at a loss (net of $68,000 tax benefit) of $131,000. The loss from operations of this division during the year prior to the measurement date (net of tax benefit of $152,000) was $170,000.

b) The company changed its accounting policy for commission revenues at the beginning of 1998 in order to better match marketing expenses and commission revenues within the same accounting period. The company adopted the policy of recognizing commission revenues when all of its marketing services are completed and the order is accepted by the supplier; previously, commissions were recognized at the time the supplier shipped the product. The effect of this change, which was included in income from continuing operations, was to increase income from continuing operations after taxes by $11,000 for 1998. The cumulative effect of the change on previous years' income (net of income tax of $100,000) was an increase of $230,000.

c) There were 1 million shares of common stock outstanding during the period.

REQUIRED Prepare the income statement for Lorek, Inc., for 1998, beginning with income from continuing operations.

E 4-14. **CHANGE IN ACCOUNTING PRINCIPLE; INCOME STATEMENT PRESENTATION** Dusenbury, Inc., a soft drink company, has the following items to be reflected in its 1998 financial statements:

Net sales	$542,016
Administrative, marketing, and general expenses	167,938
Federal and state income taxes	37,690
Uninsured casualty loss, net of tax benefit of $2,200 (extraordinary)	2,928
Cost of sales (average cost)	282,186
Other revenue	3,890

In addition, you determine that Dusenbury changed its method of inventory costing from FIFO to average cost as of the beginning of 1998. The effect of this change was to decrease current earnings (net of applicable taxes of $1,788) by $1,972. The cumulative effect on prior years was a decrease in net income (net of taxes of $5,698) of $12,356.

REQUIRED Prepare a multiple-step statement of income for Dusenbury, Inc., for the year ended December 31, 1998.

E 4-15. **ACCOUNTING CHANGES; DEPRECIABLE ASSETS** During 1998, the management of Schaefer Corporation decided to change from sum-of-the-years'-digits to straight-line depreciation for equipment that was acquired at the beginning of 1995 at a cost of $440,000. The equipment has a useful life of 10 years from the date of purchase and no salvage value. Accumulated depreciation through 1997 was $216,000. If Schaefer had used the straight-line method, it would have been $132,000. Assume the applicable income tax rate is 40 percent. Net income for the years ending December 31, before consideration of the cumulative effect of the change, was as follows:

1995	$230,000
1996	238,000
1997	246,000
1998	266,000 (depreciation expense for this year is based on the new method)

REQUIRED Show how the change would be disclosed on the December 31, 1998, income statement, and on income statements for 1995–1997, which are presented for comparative purposes.

P 4-1.   SINGLE-STEP INCOME STATEMENT   You are charged with the responsibility of preparing the income statement for Frecka Oil Company for the year ended March 31, 1998. Pertinent information for accomplishing this task is set forth below (in thousands of dollars):

	DR	CR
Provision for income taxes	$1,840	
Production expenses	1,696	
Well supervisory fees		$1,748
Drilling program marketing expenses	556	
Commissions and drilling arrangements revenue		3,784
Interest expense	1,204	
Gain from extinguishment of debt, net of taxes		1,068
General and administrative expenses	5,868	
Oil and gas sales		10,240
Management fees		1,288
Provision for losses on advances	364	
Depreciation, depletion, and amortization	1,932	
Cumulative effect on prior years of change in method of allocating administrative overhead (net of tax effect)		418

On average, there were 2 million shares of stock outstanding during the year.

REQUIRED   **1.**   Prepare a single-step income statement for the year ended March 31, 1998, including EPS.

2.   What disclosures are necessary with respect to the change in method of overhead allocation?

P 4-2.   SINGLE-STEP INCOME STATEMENT   Naus Van Lines, Inc., presents its results of operations and retained earnings reconciliation in a combined statement. Selected information from the accounts of Naus Van Lines, Inc., for 1998 is as follows (in thousands of dollars):

Communications and utilities expense	$ 445
Rent expense	327
Operating revenues	25,309
Salaries, wages, and fringe benefits	2,883
Depreciation and amortization	215
Leasing revenues	123
Interest expense	271
Loss on disposal of equipment	23
Supplies expense	286
Purchased transportation costs (current expense)	12,500
Administrative and general expenses	1,589
Miscellaneous revenue	131
Insurance expense	969
Agent commission fees	3,663
Taxes and licenses	890

There were 2 million shares of stock outstanding during the year.

REQUIRED   Prepare a single-step statement of income for 1998, including EPS.

P 4-3. **SINGLE-STEP INCOME STATEMENT** Kiel Hotels, Inc., is in the process of preparing financial statements for 1998. Relevant data are as follows (in thousands of dollars):

	DR	CR
Food and beverage revenues.....................................		$101,895
Medical revenues...		39,883
Room and related services expense............................	$65,859	
Construction expense...	4,798	
License sales and royalties...................................		11,545
General and administrative expense............................	42,373	
Room and related services revenue		171,462
Medical expenses	31,497	
Construction revenue...		6,064
Interest and dividend revenue.................................		8,540
Depreciation...	16,752	
Provision for income taxes	15,367	
Other revenue...		5,877
Other operating expenses	49,192	
Gain on extinguishment of debt (net of taxes of $5,673)............		9,859
Extraordinary loss from expropriation of Jamaican resort facilities (net of tax benefit of $496)	1,396	
Loss from discontinuance of furniture manufacturing division (net of tax benefit of $518)...............	636	

There were 30 million shares of common stock outstanding during the year.

REQUIRED

1. Prepare a single-step income statement, including EPS, for the year ended December 31, 1998.

2. Describe the disclosures required for any items presented after income from continuing operations.

P 4-4. **MULTIPLE-STEP INCOME STATEMENT; DISCONTINUED OPERATIONS** Accounts of Houser Drug Corporation showed the following balances at the end of 1998 (in thousands of dollars):

Inventory, 1/1/98	$ 29,534
Purchase discounts, returns, and allowances	10,560
Sales..	196,394
Inventory, 12/31/98	21,038
Purchases..	143,300
Sales discounts, returns, and allowances	14,960
Freight in	4,642
Interest expense	2,790
Other revenue..	538
Selling, general, and administrative expenses	27,972
Provision for loss on closed facilities	336
Income taxes	1,878

a) The provision for loss on closed facilities was established to cover the estimated loss on the disposal of certain facilities associated with the company's wholesale drug operations, which have been or are in the process of being closed. This item does not qualify for treatment as a discontinued operation.

b) In December 1998, the board of directors determined that the company's wholesale surgical supply operations were to be discontinued. In connection with this planned disposition, realized and estimated losses from disposal of assets are expected to total $222,864 (net of tax benefit of $148,464). The loss from operations of the discontinued segment (net of tax benefit of $1,356,490) was $3,897,980 in 1998.

c) There were 2 million shares of common stock outstanding during the year.

REQUIRED Prepare a multiple-step income statement for 1998, including EPS.

P 4-5. **DISCONTINUED OPERATIONS** Condensed income statements for Aspen Corporation, a diversified company, were as follows for the two years ended December 31, 1998 and 1997 (in thousands of dollars):

	1998	1997
Net sales	$10,000	$9,600
Cost of sales	(6,200)	(6,000)
Gross profit	$ 3,800	$3,600
Operating expenses	(2,200)	(2,400)
Operating income	$ 1,600	$1,200
Gain on sale of division	900	—
	$ 2,500	$1,200
Provision for income taxes	(625)	(300)
Net income	$ 1,875	$ 900

On January 1, 1998, Aspen entered into an agreement to sell for $3,200,000 the assets and product line of one of its separate operating divisions. The sale was consummated on December 31, 1998, and resulted in a gain of $900,000. This division's contribution to Aspen's reported income before income taxes for each year was as follows:

1998 .... $640,000 loss
1997 .... $500,000 loss

REQUIRED Assuming an income tax rate of 25 percent, prepare revised comparative income statements for 1998 and 1997, beginning with income from continuing operations, and properly reporting the effect of the discontinued operation.

(AICPA, adapted)

P 4-6. **DISCONTINUED OPERATIONS** Assume the following notation (all figures net of tax effect) related to a segment disposal:

o = operating income (loss) from beginning of period to measurement date
r_1 = realized operating income (loss) from measurement date to end of fiscal year
r_2 = realized gain (loss) on disposal of segment assets to end of fiscal year
e_1 = estimated operating income (loss) from end of fiscal year to disposal date
e_2 = estimated gain (loss) on disposal of segment assets from end of fiscal year to disposal date

Now assume the following amounts (in thousands of dollars):

	CASE 1	CASE 2	CASE 3	CASE 4
o	$60	$(60)	$60	$60
r_1	20	30	20	20
r_2	50	(50)	(70)	50
e_1	10	10	10	20
e_2	(110)	(90)	90	90

REQUIRED For each case, calculate the amount that should be reported as discontinued operations in the income statement.

P 4-7. **ACCOUNTING CHANGES; INVENTORIES, RECEIVABLES** Near the end of 1998, before the books were closed, management of Solomon Corporation decided to make the following accounting changes:

a) Management decided to change from average cost to FIFO in accounting for inventories. Assume FIFO has been used in determining income for 1998. The resulting effect on net income was as follows:

YEAR	INCREASE IN INCOME
Before 1997	$234,000
1997	38,000
1998	26,000

b) The company uses the allowance method of accounting for uncollectible accounts and determines annual uncollectible accounts expense by aging accounts receivable. Aging of the receivables at the end of 1998 indicated that the allowance account should be reduced by $4,800.

c) Net income for 1997 was $275,000.

d) Net income for 1998 before the effect of (*b*) was $290,000.

e) Ignore all income tax effects.

REQUIRED

1. Prepare all necessary journal entries related to the above accounting changes at the end of 1998.

2. Calculate net income for 1998 and for 1997 for comparative purposes.

P 4-8. **REPORTING EARNINGS INFORMATION**   Mori Corporation has tentatively calculated income from continuing operations before taxes as $4,200,000 for 1998. The following items have *not* been considered in arriving at income from continuing operations:

a) The company sold investments from its portfolio during the year for $623,000. The cost of the securities disposed of was $767,000.

b) During the year, a patent with an original cost of $221,000 and book value of $84,000 was written off as worthless because a competitor marketed a slightly modified but significantly improved product at a similar price.

c) As the result of a strike by union employees which lasted 45 days, the company incurred excess labor costs of $318,000 associated with the employment of short-term nonunion laborers and additional security forces during the strike.

d) In July 1998, Mori purchased and retired a portion of its long-term debt in the open market at a price of $1,281,000. The carrying value of the debt at the date of purchase was $1,549,000 (applicable tax rate, 25 percent).

e) In December 1998, the company decided to change its method of inventory costing effective as of January 1, 1998, for a major portion of its inventories from average cost to FIFO. This change decreased cost of goods sold for 1998 by $148,000, which is already reflected in tentative income. Prior years' income would have been $861,000 more (net of taxes of $427,000) if the company had been using FIFO during those years.

Except as specified in item *d*, the applicable tax rate was 40 percent. There were 3 million shares of stock outstanding during the year.

REQUIRED

1. Describe the required disclosures for items *a–e*, assuming that each item is material.

2. Prepare an income statement for 1998, including EPS, beginning with income from continuing operations before taxes.

P 4-9. **REPORTING EARNINGS INFORMATION**   Finley Media Corporation calculated income from continuing operations before taxes as $44,850,000 for 1998. The accountant who prepared the tentative income statement, however, had some doubts about the appropriate treatment of certain items that appeared to be nonroutine and did not consider the following items:

a) Finley had invested $5,000,000 over a three-year period in the production of a television show. At the time the expenditures were made, there was little doubt about the ability to recover these costs through the sale of commercial time. Thus, Finley deferred these costs, to be matched against future revenues. During 1998, however, the National Television Viewing Board issued a regulation that effectively prohibited the televising of the show to the general public. Finley determined that revenues of approximately $800,000 could be generated through the sale of rights to the show to various pay television operations. Accordingly, the deferral was reduced to $800,000.

b) During the year, fixed assets with a book value of $1,321,000 were sold for $989,000.

c) A major production facility in Los Angeles was totally destroyed by an earthquake. The book value of the property, which was insured for $2 million, was $3.4 million. The loss does not qualify as an extraordinary item.

d) The applicable tax rate was 40 percent.

e) There were 10 million shares of stock outstanding during the year.

REQUIRED

Prepare an income statement for 1998, beginning with income from operations before taxes and including EPS.

P 4-10. **REPORTING EARNINGS INFORMATION** Marie Corporation is accumulating financial data needed to prepare the financial statements for the year ended December 31, 1998. The 1998 estimated income before taxes, without considering the five items described below, is $600,000. The information regarding the following activities has been taken from the company's records:

a) A lawsuit against the company arising from a 1996 claim was settled during 1998 for $70,000. The loss has not been accrued and is due for payment in March 1999.

b) The company sold one of several buildings in its Finishing Division at a gain of $40,000.

c) Marie experienced a $200,000 loss of timber in 1998 due to a flood resulting from the eruption of a volcano that had been inactive for over 50 years. The loss was not covered by insurance.

d) The company changed its method for depreciating its buildings in 1998 from an accelerated method to straight line. Total depreciation on the buildings through the end of 1997 would have been $260,000 lower if the straight-line method had been used. The change was made for both book and tax purposes.

e) Office equipment purchased in January 1997 for $45,000 was incorrectly debited to office supplies expense. The straight-line method is used to depreciate office equipment for book and tax purposes. The office equipment was estimated to have a three-year life with no expected scrap value. This error has not been corrected.

Assume that Marie Corporation is subject to a 30 percent income tax rate on all items.

REQUIRED

I. Calculate the 1998 income from operations before income taxes for Marie Corporation, identifying adjustments, if any, that need to be made to the estimated income of $600,000.

2. Prepare a partial income statement for Marie Corporation for the year ended December 31, 1998, beginning with the amount for adjusted income from operations before income taxes as calculated in requirement 1.

*P 4-11. **FINANCIAL REPORTING PROBLEM** This problem is based on the 1995 annual report of GE, reproduced in Appendix B at the end of the text. Assume the questions refer to the consolidated results, rather than the GE or GECS components, unless stated otherwise.

REQUIRED Answer the following questions, and indicate the specific part of the report where you found the answer.

I. When are sales of goods and services recorded?

2. What inventory method is used to determine cost of goods sold?

3. What is the largest component of "other income"?

4. In what years did GE report discontinued operations? Describe the events that gave rise to the reporting of discontinued operations.

5. Describe the nature of the cumulative effect adjustment in the 1993 income statement. What was the per share impact of the accounting change?

6. Were restructuring charges included in the determination of earnings in any of the three years? Explain.

7. How did the operating margin of the GE portion of consolidated earnings change over the three years? What were the primary reasons for the change?

8. What was the largest revenue source for the GE portion of consolidated results? For the GECS portion?

9. How did international revenues for 1995 compare with 1994?

DIGITAL EQUIPMENT CORPORATION RESTRUCTURING CASE

Digital Equipment Corporation was founded in 1957. It designs, manufactures, sells, and services networked computer systems. As of the end of fiscal 1996, approximately 65 percent of Digital Equipment's revenue was derived outside the United States. In 1996, Digital Equipment had consolidated revenue of $14,563 million, a net loss of $111.8 million, and total assets of $10,075 million. It also had 59,100 employees.

Read the accompanying *Business Week* article and answer the questions using the financial statement excerpts that appear below. All questions relate to fiscal 1996 unless otherwise specified.

1. According to the *Business Week* article, what are some of Digital Equipment's problems?

2. Why would Digital Equipment choose to show restructuring charges as a separate line item on its income statement? Note that it is part of operating income.

3. Show how operating income/loss for each year from 1994 to 1996 would change if Digital Equipment had not *accrued* restructuring costs in 1994 and 1996. In other words, how would income look if Digital had accounted for these costs as layoffs and asset disposals were actually made?

4. Why does GAAP require accrual of restructuring charges?

5. What entry would Digital Equipment have made in 1995 if at July 1, 1995 management believed that the balance for "Accrued restructuring costs" should have been only $100 million? Explain how this adjustment should be disclosed in notes and shown on the income statement. Base your answer on the information in Note E and not on your answer to part 3.

6. The Securities and Exchange Commission (SEC) has questioned some firms about the magnitude of their restructuring charges. Why would the SEC be concerned about a firm accruing too much expense?

How to Get DEC Back on Track

By Paul C. Judge and Ira Sager

It's bad news, once again, at Digital Equipment Corp. The company is awash in red ink, posting on Oct. 22 a loss of $65.9 million for the quarter ended on Sept. 28. Revenues declined 11%, to $2.91 billion. The loss was a shocker: three times what Wall Street had expected. DEC's stock ended the day at 29, down 5⅜, and nearly 50-points below this year's high of 75⅝, on Feb. 8. For all the restructurings, layoffs, executive exits, and product initiatives, DEC still is flailing about, unable to formulate a cohesive strategy and deliver results.

Clearly, there are no easy fixes for what ails Digital. But customers, employees, and investors are getting whiplash from the constant changes of plan. Two years ago, CEO Robert B. Palmer cut back the direct sales force in the name of cost-cutting. After customers complained of being ignored, Palmer this summer reversed course, more than doubling the number of customers Digital will call on directly, from fewer than 1,000 to more than 2,500. The disruption was severe: Palmer blamed most of Digital's quarterly earnings drop on the strategy overhaul.

DEC should set a course and stick to it. Here are some suggestions:

- Go back to Palmer's plan for a pared-down sales force, and hand off the sales responsibility to more third-party resellers. As IBM, Hewlett-Packard, and others have figured out, these outside sales companies can deliver a lot of products and services at a lower cost per sale to more customers. These DEC rivals have made the switch without neglecting customers, and DEC should study how they did it. Using resellers would help cut costs, a critical need. DEC has revenue per employee of just $246,000, compared with an average of $372,000 for IBM, Hewlett-Packard, and Sun Microsystems.

- Get out of personal computers. It's a $2 billion business that lost $200 million in the fiscal year that ended on June 30. Focus instead on selling Intel-based PC servers, where margins are higher.

  Digital doesn't have to make or sell every computer product. Customers want technology that will make them more productive or solve a particular business problem. High-end services are more remunerative than making hardware, anyway. So are good software technologies. Digital's profitable Internet-security products, which meet a critical need for companies setting up Intranets, should become the core of the company's Intranet offering.

- Recruit new management and freshen up the board. DEC badly needs new blood throughout the company. Calling for help from outsiders is all too often a knee-jerk response to strategic blunders, but Digital has been in decline for years. And its board has been little more than a passive witness. Meanwhile, two directors have served since the 1950s, and six of the nine outside directors are over 69 years old. It's time for more turnover.

There's plenty for activist board members to do. A top priority should be bolstering top management. Current directors have allowed Palmer to push aside several possible heirs apparent, including former Vice-President for Sales and Marketing Edward E. Lucente and Vice-President Enrico Pesatori. Each had problems. But Pesatori was never even replaced. Rather, Palmer has taken on his duties, managing the day-to-day operations of the Computer Systems Div., which brings in nearly half of Digital's revenues. Palmer now functions as chairman, CEO, president, and general manager. That's too many roles for one executive to handle at any company, let alone a struggling one.

The CEO has promised that DEC will be profitable in the current quarter. He's running out of time to deliver on his promises.

Judge, in Boston, and Sager, in New York, cover the computer industry.

Consolidated statements of operations
Digital Equipment Corporation

(in thousands except per share data)

Year ended	June 29, 1996	July 1, 1995	July 2, 1994
Revenues *(Notes A and B)*			
Product sales	$ 8,362,423	$ 7,616,441	$ 7,191,251
Service and other revenues	6,200,352	6,196,621	6,259,539
Total operating revenues	14,562,775	13,813,062	13,450,790
Costs and expenses *(Notes A, D, G, H and K)*			
Cost of product sales	5,541,792	5,397,723	4,968,025
Service expense and cost of other revenues	4,214,412	3,993,970	3,943,612
Research and engineering expenses	1,062,253	1,040,028	1,301,347
Selling, general and administrative expenses *(Note J)*	3,295,865	3,272,913	4,027,869
Restructuring charges *(Note E)*	492,000	–	1,206,000
Operating income/(loss)	(43,547)	108,428	(1,996,063)
Interest income	76,438	57,497	49,422
Interest expense *(Notes F and I)*	100,418	90,268	73,353
Income/(loss) before income taxes and cumulative effect of changes in accounting principles	(67,527)	75,657	(2,019,994)
Provision for income taxes *(Note C)*	44,285	18,342	85,043
Income/(loss) before cumulative effect of changes in accounting principles	(111,812)	57,315	(2,105,037)
(Benefit)/charge due to cumulative effect of changes in accounting principles, net of tax *(Notes C, G and J)*	–	(64,503)	51,026
Net income/(loss)	(111,812)	121,818	(2,156,063)
Dividends on preferred stock *(Note L)*	35,500	35,500	10,650
Net income/(loss) applicable to common stock	$ (147,312)	$ 86,318	$ (2,166,713)
Per common share *(Note A)*			
Income/(loss) applicable before cumulative effect of changes in accounting principles	$ (.97)	$ .15	$ (15.43)
Benefit/(charge) due to cumulative effect of changes in accounting principles	–	.44	(.37)
Net income/(loss) applicable per common share *(Note A)*	$ (.97)	$ .59	$ (15.80)
Weighted average common shares outstanding *(Note A)*	152,052	146,331	137,090

The accompanying notes are an integral part of these financial statements.

Note E: Restructuring actions

Accrued restructuring costs and charges include the cost of involuntary employee termination benefits, facility closures and related costs associated with restructuring actions. Employee termination benefits include severance, wage continuation, notice pay, medical and other benefits. Facility closure and related costs include disposal costs for property, plant and equipment, lease payments and related costs. Restructuring costs were accrued and charged to expense in accordance with approved management plans.

As a result of initiatives to increase sales productivity, further consolidate manufacturing plants and distribution sites, improve service delivery and further reduce overhead in support areas, the Corporation accrued a restructuring charge of $492,000,000 in the fourth quarter of fiscal 1996.

The cost of employee separations associated with the fiscal 1996 charge includes termination benefits for approximately 7,000 employees in fiscal 1997 as well as employee termination benefits incurred in the fourth quarter of fiscal 1996. The majority of the employee separations will come from administrative and overhead functions, located in Europe and the United States. Most other organizations and functions also will be affected by the planned reduction in employees. The fiscal 1996 charge also includes costs associated with the closure of an additional 3.5 million square feet of office and manufacturing space, principally in the United States and Europe.

As the Corporation continues to implement its strategic plan and respond to external market conditions, there can be no assurance that additional restructuring actions will not be required. With regard to the completion of planned restructuring actions, there can be no assurance that the estimated cost of such actions will not change.

During fiscal 1996, restructuring actions resulted in approximately 2,400 employee separations, a portion of which were covered under the fiscal 1994 restructuring plan. The number of involuntary separations was less than originally planned due principally to a higher level of voluntary separations and employees transferred in connection with divesting activities. However, associated cost savings were offset by higher than planned separation costs for certain non-U.S. employees.

The Corporation's experience in property dispositions has been consistent with the restructuring plan provided for in fiscal 1994. In the past two fiscal years, the Corporation has sold 6.2 million square feet of space and reduced space under lease by 4.7 million square feet.

Accrued restructuring costs (in thousands)

Year ended	June 29, 1996	July 1, 1995	July 2, 1994
Balance, beginning of year	$ 492,046	$1,351,075	$ 738,989
Charges to operations:			
Employee separations	363,000	–	679,000
Facility closures and related costs	129,000	–	527,000
Total charges to operations	492,000	–	1,206,000
Costs incurred:			
Employee separations	153,025	507,816	372,450
Facility closures and related costs	177,593	323,029	212,300
Other	34,012	28,184	9,164
Total costs incurred	364,630	859,029	593,914
Balance, end of year	$ 619,416	$ 492,046	$ 1,351,075
Cash expenditures:			
Employee separations	$ 175,839	$ 562,629	$ 532,000
Facility closures and related costs, net of proceeds	61,000	(38,850)	67,550
Net cash expenditures	$ 236,839	$ 523,779	$ 599,550
Number of employee terminations due to restructuring actions	2,400	7,400	12,000

The Balance Sheet
(Statement of
Financial Position)

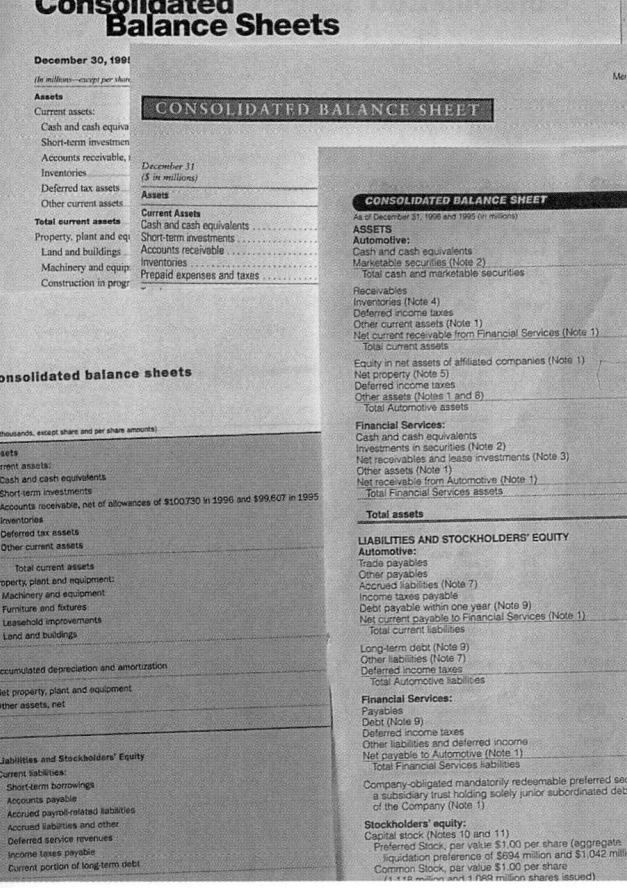

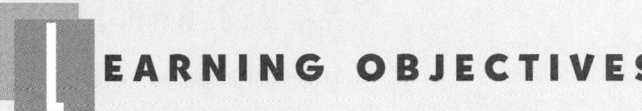

LEARNING OBJECTIVES

After studying this chapter, you should be able to:

1. Describe the uses and limitations of the balance sheet.

2. Distinguish between the two common formats for the balance sheet—the account form and the report form.

3. Define and identify the valuation methods for current assets and prepare the current assets section of the balance sheet.

4. Define and identify the valuation methods for current liabilities and prepare the current liabilities section of the balance sheet.

5. Define and identify the valuation methods for noncurrent assets and prepare the noncurrent assets section of the balance sheet.

6. Define and identify the valuation methods for long-term liabilities and prepare the long-term liabilities section of the balance sheet.

7. Define a contingency and describe the three possible treatments of a loss contingency.

8. Prepare a statement of retained earnings.

9. Define and describe the appropriate accounting and reporting for prior period adjustments.

10. Describe the statement of stockholders' equity (statement of changes in equity).

11. Describe the options for the placement and display of balance sheet information and discuss the purpose of the notes and supplementary information.

12. Define subsequent events and describe the accounting and reporting guidelines for them.

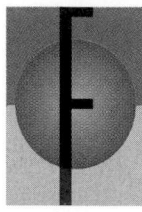

or many years investors and other financial statement users concentrated their analysis on the income statement, focusing specifically on net income and earnings per share. However, in recent years users have become increasingly concerned about liquidity and financial flexibility—two characteristics that can be evaluated properly only by studying the balance sheet (also called the statement of financial position) and the statement of cash flows. Indeed, many investors have discovered the hard way that reasonable expectations regarding future cash flows require a study of *all* the basic financial statements.

This chapter describes and illustrates the purpose, format, and content of the balance sheet; it provides the background you need to understand later chapters. As various components of the balance sheet are discussed, you may wish to refer to the GE balance sheet in Appendix B. The chapter begins with a discussion of the uses and limitations of the balance sheet, followed by an analysis of classification and valuation of items in the balance sheet. A brief discussion of the statement of stockholders' equity follows. The chapter closes with discussions of the notes and supplementary information and the reporting of subsequent events. (Notes and supplementary disclosures may relate to the income statement or statement of cash flows as well as to the balance sheet.) Appendix 5–1 illustrates some basic techniques of financial statement analysis.

USES AND LIMITATIONS OF THE BALANCE SHEET

As transactions and events occur during a period, the effects are recorded in the appropriate accounts according to generally accepted accounting principles, always maintaining the equality in the accounting equation Assets = Liabilities + Owners' equity. On a specific date a summary of assets, liabilities, and owners' equity accounts and their related account balances, called the **balance sheet,** is prepared. One may think of the balance sheet as a statement of the economic resources (assets) available to an entity and of the claims to, or interests in, those resources (liabilities and owners' equity) at the statement date.

Another way to think of the information contained in the balance sheet is to view it as a still photograph of a dynamic process. In preparing a balance sheet, we are momentarily halting the inflows and outflows associated with earnings and other activities in order to assess the entity's resources and claims to those resources. This set of resources and obligations represents the results of all past activities, and thus the base with which the entity enters the next period.

Assessment of Liquidity and Financial Flexibility

The balance sheet is a primary source of information about a company's liquidity and financial flexibility. **Liquidity** depends on the amount of time expected to lapse until an asset is converted into cash or a liability is paid. For example, analysis of a company's current assets, which represent short-term sources of cash, in relation to its current liabilities, which represent short-term obligations to pay cash, permits an assessment of a company's ability to meet its financial obligations as they mature as well as its ability to pay dividends over the short term. **Financial flexibility** is a company's ability to alter its future cash flows by responding to unexpected needs and opportunities. Thus, financial flexibility is a measure of a company's adaptability. The balance sheet, by reporting available resources and the amounts and timing of claims on those resources, provides information useful for assessing a company's financial flexibility. For example, a company's ratio of long-term debt to owners' equity may be so high as to indicate that the company has no additional long-term borrowing capacity. To raise additional capital, the company may be forced to issue additional capital stock, which could

CONCEPTUAL

A balance sheet presents an entity's economic resources and claims to or interests in those resources.

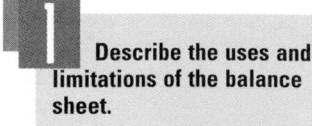

Describe the uses and limitations of the balance sheet.

dilute its earnings per share. Such information is relevant to present and prospective investors.

Assessment of Profitability

In addition to providing information on liquidity and financial flexibility, the balance sheet is useful in assessing a company's profitability. By relating net income to assets or owners' equity, investors can determine the company's return on invested resources. Also, a comparison of certain balance sheet items with related income statement items provides users with a measure of the efficiency with which resources are being employed. For example, cost of goods sold, an income statement item, divided by inventory, a balance sheet item, provides a measure of the company's ability to generate sales by maintaining a given amount of inventory.

Limitations of the Balance Sheet

There are limitations to what the balance sheet can convey, however. Under generally accepted accounting principles, current market values are not disclosed for many balance sheet items because the underlying accounting process is based on the (modified) historical cost principle. Furthermore, some resources that are used to generate future cash flows are not recorded in the accounts because the accounting process is based on transactions. For example, the value of a superior management group is not recorded in the accounts even though future cash flows are enhanced by a superior management team. Finally, the balance sheet does not portray the fair value of the total entity. Because some resources are not recorded, and because many resources that are recorded are not reported at current market value, the amount of recorded assets minus liabilities is not likely to represent the entity's fair value. Information reported in the balance sheet is useful to those interested in assessing the entity's fair value, however. In the next section we will take a closer look at how balance sheet items are classified and valued.

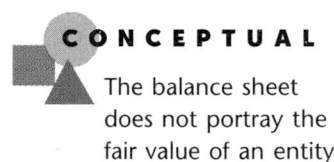

CONCEPTUAL

The balance sheet does not portray the fair value of an entity.

CLASSIFICATION AND VALUATION IN THE BALANCE SHEET

In the balance sheet, assets, liabilities, and owners' equity accounts are grouped together in certain classes to assist users. In general, the classifications should indicate the amounts and liquidity of available resources, management's intent with respect to the use of those resources, and the amounts and timing of obligations that require liquid resources for settlement. Assets that differ in their *expected function* should be reported separately. For example, inventories generate cash flows through sales, whereas property, plant, and equipment generate cash flows through internal use in operations. Therefore, these two categories of asset should be reported separately. Assets and liabilities with different implications for financial flexibility should also be reported separately. For example, because operating assets such as property, plant, and equipment afford a company less financial flexibility than assets held for investment, such as investments in the capital stock of other companies, those two categories of asset should be reported separately.

The sequence of items shown in Exhibit 5–1 is currently the most commonly used balance sheet sequence. (See also the balance sheet of GE in Appendix B.) The classification scheme shown in the exhibit is based primarily on liquidity. Within the assets category, current assets are more liquid than noncurrent assets. Within the liabilities category, current liabilities are expected to be paid sooner than long-term liabilities. The items under owners' equity in Exhibit 5–1 are those

EXHIBIT 5–1	**Typical Balance Sheet Classifications**

Assets	**Liabilities and Owners' Equity**
Current assets	Current liabilities
Noncurrent assets	Long-term liabilities
Investments and funds	Contingencies
Property, plant, and equipment	Stockholders' (Owners') equity
Intangible assets	Contributed capital
Other assets	Retained earnings
	Accumulated other
	Comprehensive Income

that appear in the reports of corporations. In the report of a proprietorship or partnership, the owners' equity section would consist only of the capital accounts of the owners.

Two Common Formats

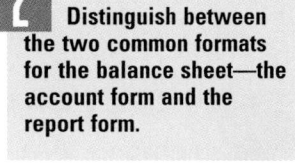

Distinguish between the two common formats for the balance sheet—the account form and the report form.

There are two common formats for the balance sheet: the *account form* and the *report form.* A balance sheet presented under the **account form** lists assets on the left side of the balance sheet and liabilities and owners' equity on the right side, as in Exhibit 5–1. In the **report form,** assets are listed first, with liabilities and owners' equity beneath them. GE's balance sheet (in Appendix B) is presented in report form.

Other balance sheet formats may be observed in other countries. For example, many European companies list their assets in reverse order of liquidity. Noncurrent assets are shown before current assets; within the current asset category, inventory is shown before receivables, which is shown before cash. Also common are report-form balance sheets in which current liabilities are subtracted from total assets and the difference added to noncurrent liabilities. The structure of such a balance sheet, in terms of the accounting equation, is Assets – Liabilities = Stockholders' equity, rather than Assets = Liabilities + Stockholders' equity. Overall, these differences in format should create few difficulties for users of financial statements, since they involve merely a rearrangement of the balance sheet amounts.

A somewhat more serious problem can arise as a result of differences in terminology. Even between the United States and Great Britain, two nations that share the same language, numerous differences exist in accounting terminology. Consider, for example, the following comparison:

UNITED STATES	UNITED KINGDOM
Corporation	**Company**
Consolidated	**Group**
Financial statements	**Accounts**
Accounts receivable	**Debtors**
Inventory	**Stocks**
Accounts payable	**Creditors**
Common stock	**Ordinary shares**
Additional paid-in capital	**Share premium**
Retained earnings	**Reserves**
Leverage	**Gearing**
Income statement	**Profit and loss account**
Sales revenue	**Turnover**
Operating income	**Trading profit**

The remainder of this section describes the content of each balance sheet classification, and summarizes the basic valuation guidelines for balance sheet items. Detailed studies of individual balance sheet items appear in subsequent chapters.

Current Assets

In the balance sheet, assets may be divided into two broad categories: current assets and noncurrent assets. **Current assets** are cash and other assets that can reasonably be expected to be converted to cash or consumed during one year or the normal operating cycle of the business, whichever is longer.[1] The operating cycle is the time between the acquisition of inventory and the conversion of that inventory back into cash. For example, the operating cycle of a whiskey distillery may extend 10 years, whereas the operating cycle of a grocery store may be no more than several days. For the distiller, the distinction between current and noncurrent assets is based on the 10-year period. For the grocery store, the distinction is based on a one-year period because the store's operating cycle is less than one year. Any asset whose use is restricted for purposes other than current operations must be excluded from current assets. For example, cash set aside in a special fund to repay long-term debt would not be classified as a current asset.

The current asset presentation in Exhibit 5–2 is reproduced from a recent annual report of The Clorox Company. Note that the current assets are ordered according to their liquidity.

Cash and Cash Equivalents

Cash is the most common current asset. It is listed first under current assets because it is the most liquid. All cash balances on hand and on deposit that are readily available for current operating purposes should be included in the cash category under current assets. **Cash equivalents** are short-term marketable securities, generally with original maturities of 90 days or less, that are readily convertible to known amounts of cash. These securities usually are combined with cash for reporting purposes.

Short-Term Investments

The next most liquid group of assets, and thus the next category presented under current assets, consists of short-term investments. At the time of acquisition, debt

> **3** Define and identify the valuation methods for current assets and prepare the current assets section of the balance sheet.

EXHIBIT 5–2	Presentation of Current Assets

The Clorox Company
From 1995 Annual Report
(in thousands)

Current Assets	
Cash and short-term investments	$137,330
Accounts receivable, less allowance	311,868
Inventories	121,095
Deferred income taxes	11,495
Prepaid expenses	18,543
Total current assets	$600,331

[1]Committee on Accounting Procedures, "Restatement and Revision of Accounting Research Bulletins," *Accounting Research Bulletin No. 43* (New York: AICPA, 1953), chap. 3, sec. A.

and equity securities must be classified as trading, available for sale, or held to maturity.[2] **Trading securities,** which are securities that have been bought and held principally for the purpose of resale in the near term, are always included in short-term investments. **Available-for-sale securities** that are expected to be sold in the next year or operating cycle, whichever is longer, are also considered short-term investments. Securities that are being **held to maturity** and will mature within the year or operating cycle, whichever is longer, should similarly be reported as short-term investments. Trading securities and available-for-sale securities are reported at fair value. Held-to-maturity securities, which are debt instruments, are reported at amortized cost. (The reporting requirements for investments in debt and equity securities are described in more detail in Chapters 13 and 14.)

Short-Term Receivables

Short-term receivables are claims to cash that are expected to be exercised within one year or the operating cycle, whichever is longer. They often constitute a significant portion of current assets. Note in Exhibit 5–2 that Clorox's receivables comprise more than half of its current assets. In our credit-based society, a firm's receivables and its credit and collection policies have a strong influence on its profitability.

There are two types of short-term receivables. Trade receivables result from sales of goods or services on account. That is, a company sells goods or services in exchange for a promise from the customer to pay according to specified terms. For example, a routine credit sale of inventory to a customer creates a trade receivable. Nontrade receivables arise when a company lends money on a short-term basis. For example, a company may lend cash to a company officer on a short-term basis. Usually, nontrade receivables are supported by a formal contractual agreement specifying the terms of repayment and are called notes receivable.

Short-term receivables are reported at net realizable value, which is the amount of cash expected to be collected. Net realizable value is the difference between the gross amount of receivables and anticipated uncollectible accounts, discounts, and returns and allowances.

Inventories

In manufacturing and in wholesale and retail merchandising, a large percentage of a company's resources is tied up in inventory. **Inventories** are those assets that merchandising companies acquire for resale or that manufacturers produce for sale to customers in the ordinary course of business. In terms of the operating cycle, inventories are one step further removed from cash than receivables. Consequently, inventories follow receivables in the current assets section of the balance sheet.

Inventories generally are accounted for in accordance with the historical cost principle. However, when the revenue-producing ability of inventory falls below its cost, the inventory is revalued at the lower market value. That is, a lower-of-cost-or-market valuation approach is applied to inventories. Occasionally, inventories are valued at net realizable value. This approach is used only when selling prices are known, the sale is not a critical event in the earnings process, and selling costs are minimal.

CONCEPTUAL

A manufacturing company has three types of inventory.

A manufacturing concern has three major types of inventory: (1) raw materials, which are goods and materials that will ultimately become part of the finished product but have not yet entered the production process; (2) work in process, which consists of partially completed goods; and (3) finished goods, which are goods ready for sale to customers. Some companies also report miscellaneous supplies as a category of inventory. Miscellaneous supplies are those items that are consumed in

---

[2]"Accounting for Certain Investments in Debt and Equity Securities," *Statement of Financial Accounting Standards No. 115* (Norwalk, Conn.: FASB, 1993), para. 6.

the production process but are not primary materials. The balance sheet (or notes) for a manufacturing concern should include the three major inventory categories. A merchandising concern has no raw materials or work-in-process inventories since there is no production process.

Prepaid Expenses

Prepaid expenses that are included under current assets are expenditures made in exchange for benefits, usually in the form of services, not yet received but expected to be received within one year or the operating cycle, whichever is longer. For example, payment in advance for a one-year insurance policy should be classified as a prepaid expense at the time of the expenditure because the payment precedes the receipt of benefits. Companies often include premium prepayments for two, three, or more years in current assets even though part of the advance payment applies to periods beyond the current operating cycle or one year. Such a presentation is acceptable only if the amounts included are not material. Other common prepaid expenses include prepaid rent, office supplies, and taxes. Prepaid expenses are reported at cost.

Current Liabilities

Current liabilities are obligations that are expected to be eliminated either through the use of existing current assets or by the creation of other current liabilities. To be classified as a current liability, (1) the obligation must mature within one year or the operating cycle, whichever is longer, and (2) management must *intend* to use existing current assets or to create other current liabilities to satisfy the obligation. For example, accounts payable resulting from short-term credit purchases from a supplier should be classified as a current liability because of the expectation that existing current assets will be used to eliminate the obligation. Likewise, if a company borrows cash in exchange for a 90-day note, expecting to eliminate the note by replacing it with another short-term note, the original note should be classified as a current liability because it is expected to be eliminated by the creation of another current liability. This category also includes liabilities whose liquidation is expected to occur within a relatively short period of time, usually 12 months, such as serial maturities of long-term obligations.

4 **Define and identify the valuation methods for current liabilities and prepare the current liabilities section of the balance sheet.**

Financial statement users pay particular attention to the relationship between current assets and current liabilities. The difference between current assets and current liabilities, called **working capital,** is an approximation of the pool of resources available to management to conduct daily operations. Likewise, current assets divided by current liabilities, called the current ratio, provides a rough indication of the short-term debt-paying ability of a company. For example, if a company has a 2-to-1 current ratio, that means that the book value of current assets is twice as large as the book value of current liabilities. In most circumstances, a company with a 2-to-1 current ratio will have little difficulty paying its debts as they become due. More specifically, a comparison of cash, temporary investments, and receivables to current liabilities provides information about a company's solvency and short-term dividend-paying potential.

In general, the valuation of current liabilities is straightforward because most current liabilities are monetary obligations. That is, they are obligations to pay a fixed amount of cash in the near future. Current liabilities are reported at the number of dollars expected to be required to eliminate the obligations. Exhibit 5–3 illustrates the presentation of current liabilities by McDonald's.

Notes Payable

Notes payable are short-term promises to pay cash that are supported by written promissory notes. Notes payable may be classified as trade payables or nontrade

EXHIBIT 5-3	Presentation of Current Liabilities

McDonald's Corporation
From 1995 Annual Report
(in millions)

Current Liabilities	
Notes payable	$ 413.0
Accounts payable	564.3
Income taxes	55.4
Other taxes	127.1
Accrued interest	117.4
Other accrued liabilities	352.5
Current maturities of long-term debt	165.2
Total current liabilities	$1,794.9

payables, as described earlier in our discussion of short-term receivables (page 212). Such notes usually are reported at their face amount.

Accounts Payable

Accounts payable are the counterpart of accounts receivable. Accounts payable arise when a company purchases goods, supplies, or services on credit. They are recorded at the amount expected to be paid to eliminate the obligation.

Accrued Expenses (Accrued Liabilities)

During an accounting period, companies incur certain expenses that have not been paid by the end of the accounting period, called **accrued expenses** or **accrued liabilities.** For example, interest on notes payable accrues as time passes. When interest payment dates do not coincide with the end of an accounting period, a liability exists at the end of the year for interest that has accrued but has not yet been paid. Likewise, obligations for wages and salaries that have been earned by employees but not paid as of the end of the period are accrued expenses (accrued liabilities). Other examples include property taxes, payroll taxes, and income taxes. Income taxes often are reported separately, since they typically constitute a significant liability.

Noncurrent Assets

5 Define and identify the valuation methods for noncurrent assets and prepare the noncurrent assets section of the balance sheet.

Assets are classified as **noncurrent** if they are not expected to be converted into cash or consumed during one year or the operating cycle, whichever is longer. Noncurrent assets include investments and special-purpose funds; property, plant, and equipment; and intangible assets.

Investments and Special-Purpose Funds

Most large companies own a variety of nonoperating assets. That is, a company purchases assets that are not used to produce the goods or services that comprise its ongoing operations. For example, a company may invest in the securities of other companies, with the intention of holding them for a long period. Or a company may make long-term loans to other companies or persons, such as corporate officers. Special-purpose funds may be set up to accumulate the resources to accomplish certain long-term objectives, such as a plant expansion or the elimination of long-term debt. Or a manufacturing concern may purchase land for speculative purposes.

EXHIBIT 5–4 **Presentation of Investments**

The Coca-Cola Company
From 1995 Annual Report
(*in millions*)

Investments and Other Assets
  Equity method investments
    Coca-Cola Enterprises Inc. . . . . $ 556
    Coca-Cola Amatil Limited   682
    Other, principally bottling companies   1,157
  Cost method investments, principally bottling companies   319
  Finance subsidiary receivables and investments   351
  Marketable securities and other assets   1,246
                                                                                 $4,311

These assets and others like them are classified as **investments** and funds. Although they appear to be quite diverse, they are all noncurrent nonoperating assets. All are expected to generate future cash flows to the company. Investments in other companies are expected to produce dividends and stock price appreciation. Long-term loans create a claim for cash. Cash set aside in special-purpose funds is invested in securities to earn a return. And investment in land creates an expectation of future cash flows when the property is sold.

Investments and funds are reported after current assets on the balance sheet. Although historical cost is the primary basis for valuation of investments and funds, significant exceptions exist. As discussed earlier, available-for-sale securities must be reported at fair value. (Departures from historical cost are discussed later in the book, as the appropriate topics are covered.) The specific methods used to assign values to assets included in investments and special-purpose funds must be disclosed. A knowledge of these methods is necessary to understand the cash flow implications of various assets. (See Exhibit 5–4 for the investments section of Coca-Cola's 1995 balance sheet.)

Property, Plant, and Equipment

The next major category on the balance sheet is **property, plant, and equipment** (also called fixed assets or plant assets). Most business entities have a substantial investment in physical property that provides benefits over several accounting periods as it is used in operations. The major assets included in this category are land, buildings, machinery and equipment, furniture and fixtures, leasehold improvements, and land improvements. Inclusion of an asset within the property, plant, and equipment section implies that a company is using the asset to generate revenues from operations. If any such assets are not actively used in operations, they should be excluded from the property, plant, and equipment category and reported as other assets.

At acquisition, property, plant, and equipment is recorded at cost. Because the benefit period for most types of property, plant, and equipment is limited, the cost is allocated to an expense account over the periods in which the company uses the assets. The amount allocated each period is called depreciation. The objective of this process is to match the costs invested in plant and equipment with the benefits derived in the form of revenues. Depreciable assets are reported in the balance sheet at cost less accumulated depreciation up to the balance sheet date. Because land has an unlimited life, it is not depreciated. Exhibit 5–5 demonstrates the reporting of property, plant, and equipment by Gannett Co., Inc.

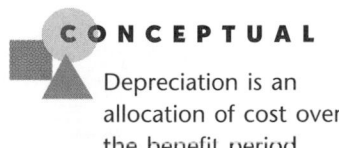

CONCEPTUAL

Depreciation is an allocation of cost over the benefit period.

EXHIBIT 5–5   **Presentation of Property, Plant, and Equipment**

Gannett Co., Inc.
From 1995 Annual Report
(in thousands)

Property, plant, and equipment

Land	$ 138,601
Buildings and improvements	739,510
Cable and security systems and outdoor advertising structures	665,471
Machinery, equipment and fixtures	1,894,893
Construction in progress	121,191
Total	$3,559,666
Less accumulated depreciation	(1,488,979)
Net property, plant and equipment	$2,070,687

Intangible Assets

Like property, plant, and equipment, **intangible assets** produce benefits over several periods. The major distinction between property, plant, and equipment and intangible assets is that intangibles lack physical substance. They are valuable because of the rights and privileges they convey to their owners. Examples of intangible assets are patents, copyrights, trademarks, franchises, and goodwill.

Intangible assets are recorded initially at cost. After acquisition, their cost is allocated to an expense account and matched against the related revenues. Intangible assets are reported at cost less accumulated amortization, which is the term used to describe the amount of cost allocated to expense each period. The cost of an intangible asset must be amortized over the asset's expected useful life or 40 years, whichever is less.[3] Exhibit 5–6 shows the presentation of intangibles in the 1995 balance sheet of The Clorox Company.

EXHIBIT 5–6   **Presentation of Intangibles**

The Clorox Company
From 1995 Annual Report
(in thousands)

From Balance Sheet:

Brands, Trademarks, Patents and Other Intangibles—Net	$592,792

From Notes:

6. Brands, Trademarks, Patents and Other Intangibles—Net

The major classes are (in thousands):

	1995	1994
Brands and trademarks	$583,902	$484,574
Patents and other intangibles	129,076	129,076
Accumulated amortization	(120,186)	(93,608)
Net	$592,792	$520,042

---

[3]"Intangible Assets," *Opinions of the Accounting Principles Board No. 17* (New York: AICPA, August 1970).

Other Assets

The balance sheet category other assets includes assets that do not fit logically into some other category. For example, many companies include costs associated with beginning the business, such as attorneys fees and the costs of printing and engraving stock certificates, in this category. The book value of idle plant often is included in this category. Items that are immaterial to the balance sheet as a whole may be reported here. Because of the vagueness of the term *other assets,* any significant items within this category should be clearly described in the footnotes to the financial statements.

Long-Term Liabilities

Long-term liabilities are obligations that will be settled beyond the operating cycle or one year, whichever is longer. The most common long-term liabilities are long-term notes, bonds, deferred taxes, pension and other postretirement obligations, and lease obligations. For balance sheet users to understand fully the impact of these commitments on a company's future operations, the terms of repayment, including principal, interest payments, conversion features, and restrictions on dividend payments and borrowing, must be disclosed. Generally, these obligations are reported at the present value of the future cash payments. Exhibit 5–7 shows the footnote disclosure that supports the balance sheet amount of $5.503 billion for long-term debt and capital lease obligations in the 1995 balance sheet of Texaco Inc.

One of the more controversial issues in accounting is *off-balance-sheet financing,* a term that refers to forms of financing not reported in the balance sheet, such as certain long-term lease commitments and other obligations. These issues are discussed more fully in connection with related topics throughout the text.

> **6** Define and identify the valuation methods for long-term liabilities and prepare the long-term liabilities section of the balance sheet.

real world

Contingencies

At the balance sheet date, certain conditions or circumstances exist that may affect whether a firm should report a gain or loss, depending on the occurrence or nonoccurrence of a future event. These conditions are called *contingencies*. A **loss contingency** represents a possible reduction in an entity's future net cash flows. For example, if a firm sells its product on credit, a portion of the receivables generated may not be collected. The possible loss due to uncollectible receivables is a loss contingency.

There are three possible treatments of a loss contingency: (1) accrual and disclosure of an estimated loss, (2) disclosure without accrual of the potential loss, and (3) neither disclosure nor accrual. The first treatment is required only if a loss contingency is probable and the amount can be reasonably estimated. If both the foregoing criteria are not met but a loss contingency is at least reasonably possible, only disclosure is required. For all other loss contingencies, neither accrual nor disclosure is required.

To illustrate the accrual of a loss contingency, assume that Boatsman Corporation has recently learned that the government of the country Crooch will take over all Boatsman's operating assets in that country without reimbursing Boatsman. The company has no insurance on these assets. The book value of the assets is $42 million. Because it is probable that a loss has been incurred and the amount is reasonably determinable, Boatsman must accrue the loss as follows:

> **7** Define a contingency and describe the three possible treatments of a loss contingency.

Loss from expropriation of assets	42,000,000	
Assets (individual asset accounts credited)		42,000,000

EXHIBIT 5 – 7	Disclosures for Long-Term Debt

Texaco Inc.
From 1995 Annual Report
(*in millions*)

From Notes:
Long-term debt and capital lease obligations
As of December 31   1995

Long-Term Debt

6-7/8% Guaranteed notes, due 1999	$ 200
6-7/8% Guaranteed debentures, due 2023	195
7-1/2% Guaranteed debentures, due 2043	198
7-3/4% Guaranteed debentures, due 2033	199
7-7/8% Guaranteed notes, due 1995	—
8% Guaranteed debentures, due 2032	147
8-1/4% Guaranteed debentures, due 2006	150
8-3/8% Guaranteed debentures, due 2022	198
8-1/2% Guaranteed notes, due 2003	199
8-5/8% Guaranteed debentures, due 2010	150
8-5/8% Guaranteed debentures, due 2031	199
8-5/8% Guaranteed debentures, due 2032	199
8.65% Guaranteed notes, due 1998	200
8-7/8% Guaranteed debentures, due 2021	150
9% Guaranteed notes, due 1996	400
9% Guaranteed notes, due 1997	200

Long-Term Debt (*continued*)

9% Guaranteed notes, due 1999	200
9-3/4% Guaranteed debentures, due 2020	250
Medium-term notes, maturing from 1996 to 2043 (7.9%)	573
Revolving Credit Facility, due 1998–2002—variable rate (6.1%)	330
Pollution Control Revenue Bonds, due 2012—variable rate (3.7%)	166
Other long-term debt:	
Texaco Inc.—Guarantee of ESOP Series B and F loans—fixed and variable rates (5.4%)	213
U.S. dollars (6.7%)	295
Other currencies (7.3%)	38
Total	$5,049
Capital Lease Obligations (see Note 9)	118
	$5,167
Less current portion of long-term debt and capital lease obligations	711
	$4,456
Short-term obligations intended to be refinanced	1,047
Total long-term debt and capital lease obligations	$5,503

The percentages reflected for variable-rate debt are the interest rates at December 31, 1995. The percentages reflected for the categories "Medium-term notes" and "Other long-term debt" are the weighted average interest rates at year-end 1995. Where applicable, principal amounts reflected in the preceding schedule include unamortized premium or discount.

At December 31, 1995, Texaco was also party to a revolving credit facility with commitments of $2 billion with a syndicate of major U.S. and international banks, available as support of the issuance of the company's commercial paper, as well as for working capital and for other general corporate purposes. Texaco had no amounts outstanding under this facility at year-end 1995. Texaco pays a facility fee on the $2 billion facility. The banks reserve the right to terminate the credit facility upon the occurrence of certain specific events, including change in control. In

addition, a partially owned subsidiary of Texaco maintains a revolving credit facility for $330 million, which was fully utilized as of December 31, 1995.

At December 31, 1995, Texaco's long-term debt included $1,047 million of short-term obligations scheduled to mature during 1996, which the company has both the intent and the ability to refinance on a long-term basis, through the use of its $2 billion revolving credit facility.

Contractual annual maturities of long-term debt, including sinking fund payments and other redemption requirements, for the five years subsequent to December 31, 1995 are as follows (in millions): 1996–$684; 1997–$344; 1998–$315; 1999–$534; and 2000–$179. The preceding maturities are before consideration of short-term obligations intended to be refinanced and also exclude capital lease obligations.

A **gain contingency** represents a possible increase in an entity's future net cash flows, such as a claim against others for patent infringement. Gain contingencies usually should not be accrued. They typically are reported in the financial statements only when they are realized. Accounting for loss contingencies and gain contingencies is discussed in detail in Chapter 8.

Owners' Equity (Stockholders' Equity)

Rearranging the accounting equation, we know that Assets – Liabilities = **Owners' equity.** In a sole proprietorship, owner's equity is a single account. In a partnership, there are multiple owners, and a separate amount is reported in owners' equity for each partner. Reporting the owners' equity of a corporation, called stockholders' equity, is considerably more complex. Legal constraints, accounting guidelines, and the separation of corporate ownership and management interact to produce substantial information requirements for the equity interests in a corporation.

Stockholders' equity typically consists of three categories: (1) contributed capital, (2) retained earnings, and (3) accumulated other comprehensive income. An illustration of the stockholders' equity section of a corporate balance sheet (Motorola's) is presented in Exhibit 5–8. See also GE's presentation in Appendix B. Because the reporting requirement for accumulated other comprehensive income is new, these statements do not include this category. However, GE's unrealized gains (losses) on investment securities would be included in this category.

CONCEPTUAL

Stockholders' equity consists of contributions by owners (contributed capital) and reinvested earnings (retained earnings).

Contributed Capital

When a corporation issues stock for cash, its assets increase by the amount of cash contributed. The amount of the increase in assets is credited to **contributed capital,** indicating that the additional assets came from the owners.

Contributed capital may be divided into the par or stated value and other contributed capital. Legal capital, which is defined by state law, usually is the par or stated value of the shares issued and outstanding. Par value or stated value is an arbitrary amount per share, specified in the corporate charter and printed on the stock certificate. When stock is issued at an amount in excess of par or stated value, the amount received in excess of par or stated value is called other contributed capital. If a company has more than one class of stock issued and outstanding, such as preferred stock and common stock, a further subdivision within contributed capital informs users what portion of contributed capital came from each class of stock.

EXHIBIT 5–8   *Presentation of Stockholders' Equity*

Motorola, Inc.
From 1995 Annual Report
(in millions)

Stockholders' equity
  Common stock, $3 par value
  Authorized shares: 1995 and 1994, 1,400
  Issued and outstanding shares: 1995, 591.4; 1994, 588.0 $ 1,774
  Preferred stock, $100 par value issuable in series
  Authorized shares: 0.5 (none issued) . . . .   —
  Additional paid-in capital   1,813
  Retained earnings   7,461
    Total stockholders' equity $11,048

A variety of terms is used to describe the components of contributed capital. Balance sheet users must become familiar with terms such as *capital surplus, additional contributed capital,* and *additional paid-in capital,* all of which refer to amounts received for stock in excess of par or stated value.

Retained Earnings

8 Prepare a statement of retained earnings.

Retained earnings is the account used to record net income (or net loss) and dividend distributions. Net income increases retained earnings; net losses and dividends decrease retained earnings. The balance of the retained earnings account, which is reported under stockholders' equity in the balance sheet, is the amount by which total net income exceeds total dividends since the company began operations.

Generally, companies include a reconciliation of the balance of the retained earnings account from the beginning to the end of the year in their annual reports. This reconciliation is called a **statement of retained earnings.** To illustrate, Bristol-Myers Squibb included the following schedule in its 1995 annual report (in millions of dollars):

Retained Earnings, January 1	**$7,600**
Net earnings	**1,812**
	$9,412
Less dividends	**1,495**
Retained Earnings, December 31	**$7,917**

9 Define and describe the appropriate accounting and reporting for prior period adjustments.

Besides net income or loss and dividends, prior period adjustments affect retained earnings. A **prior period adjustment** is the income effect of an error correction related to prior period financial statements. The income effect is reported as an addition to, or deduction from, the beginning balance of retained earnings in the year in which the error is discovered and corrected.

Errors may occur as a result of mathematical mistakes, misapplication of accounting principles, or misuse of facts. Companies must exclude the effects of error corrections related to prior periods from the determination of current period net income because the errors have no relationship to current period results. Prior period statements reported currently for comparative purposes must be restated to report the amounts that would have been reported had the error not occurred.[4]

S TATEMENT OF STOCKHOLDERS' EQUITY

10 Describe the statement of stockholders' equity (statement of changes in equity).

In addition to the balance sheet disclosures of stockholders' equity categories and account balances, many companies include in their annual report a **statement of stockholders' equity** (or **statement of changes in equity**). This statement reconciles changes in the balances of the major components of stockholders' equity from the beginning to the end of the year. Thus, it is broader than the statement of retained earnings, which merely reconciles changes in retained earnings. Corporations are required to disclose the number of shares of each class of stock authorized, issued, outstanding, and held in the treasury. They also must disclose the characteristics of each class of stock, such as par or stated value, dividend rate, liquidation preference, call price, and conversion terms.

An illustration of a hypothetical statement of changes in equity for Company Z is presented in Exhibit 5–9. Note that the retained earnings reconciliation is a component of Company Z's statement of changes in equity. Also, the presentation of comprehensive income and its components is included in Exhibit 5–9. As we discussed in Chapter 4, this reporting format is acceptable under *Statement No. 130.*

---

[4]"Prior Period Adjustments," *Statement of Financial Accounting Standards No. 16* (Stamford, Conn.: FASB, 1977). In addition to error corrections, tax loss carryforwards may allow companies to reduce taxes otherwise payable in future periods. Under some circumstances, realization of the tax benefits of these carryforwards must be reported as a prior period adjustment. Ibid., para. 11.

EXHIBIT 5-9	Hypothetical Illustration of Statement of Changes in Equity—Comprehensive Income Disclosures

Company Z
Statement of Changes in Equity
For the year ended December 31, 1998

	Total	Comprehensive Income	Retained Earnings	Accumulated Other Comprehensive Income	Common Stock	Paid-In Capital
Beginning balance	$281,750		$44,250	$12,500	$75,000	$150,000
Comprehensive income						
Net income	31,625	$31,625	31,625			
Other comprehensive income, net of tax						
Unrealized gains on securities, net of reclassification adjustment (see disclosure)	5,750	$ 5,750				
Foreign currency translation adjustments	4,000	4,000				
Minimum pension liability adjustment	(1,250)	(1,250)				
Other comprehensive income		$ 8,500		8,500		
Comprehensive income		$40,125				
Common stock issued	75,000				25,000	50,000
Dividends declared on common stock	(5,000)		(5,000)			
Ending balance	$391,875		$70,875	$21,000	$100,000	$200,000

 # NOTES AND SUPPLEMENTARY INFORMATION

In reporting financial information to assist users in decision making, a company faces two decisions: a placement decision and a display decision. The **placement decision** governs whether information should be reported in the main body of the financial statements, in the notes to the financial statements, or as supplementary information. Financial reporting encompasses all three of these possibilities. The **display decision** governs the amount of detail to be reported and the manner of presentation. Note that the display and placement decisions are pertinent to all financial statements, not just to the balance sheet.

Two general criteria are useful in deciding where information should be reported. First, to be reported in the main body of financial statements, an item must be a material financial statement element and must meet other recognition criteria described in Chapter 2. For items that meet these recognition criteria, disclosure by other means is not an acceptable substitute. The notes should amplify or explain the items presented in the main body of financial statements. For example, the notes might include a schedule of lease payments to explain a lease liability in the balance sheet. Supplementary information, on the other hand, could provide a different perspective from that adopted in the financial statements. For example, supplementary information might include the current market values of assets or information about the effects of inflation on operating activities. Management's discussion of the financial reports might also be included as supplementary information.

Second, because different users may require different levels of detail, the notes should present detail that cannot reasonably be included in the main body of the financial statements. Supplementary information can provide even more detailed

11 **Describe the options for the placement and display of balance sheet information and discuss the purpose of the notes and supplementary information.**

data that are useful only for specialized analyses. When this guideline is followed, users can minimize the cost of using the information. Also, if supplementary information need not be audited, preparers can lower their audit cost by including data in that category. Users, on the other hand, should be aware that unaudited supplementary information may not be as reliable as audited information.

Three types of disclosures deserve particular mention here. Details of long-term commitments and property, plant, and equipment should be included in the notes, along with an explanation of the company's accounting policies. These disclosures are discussed in the following sections.

Long-Term Commitments

Many companies finance their expansion by incurring long-term commitments, such as notes, bonds, or leases. For the statement user to understand fully the impact of such commitments (some of which may not meet the fundamental recognition criteria) on a company's future cash flows, supporting schedules are often necessary. Exhibit 5–10 illustrates the types of disclosure typically made with respect to long-term commitments. Because due dates and amounts of the obligations are reported,

---

EXHIBIT 5–10	**Disclosures of Long-Term Commitments**

Teleflex Incorporated
From 1995 Annual Report
(in thousands)

From notes:

Borrowings and Leases	1995	1994
Senior Notes at an average rate of 7.2% due in installments through 2008	$ 98,000	$101,000
Mortgage notes secured by certain assets with a net book value of $12,084	10,294	11,161
Deutsche Mark denominated notes at an average rate of 6.4% due in installments through 2000	73,710	50,085
Other debt and capital lease obligations, at interest rates ranging from 3% to 9%	27,571	39,691
	$209,575	$201,937
Current portion of borrowings	(12,731)	(11,438)
	$196,844	$190,499

The various senior note agreements provide for the maintenance of minimum working capital amounts and ratios and limit the purchase of the company's stock and payment of cash dividends. Under the most restrictive of these provisions, $50,000 of retained earnings was available for dividends at December 31, 1995.

The weighted average interest rate on the $61,487 of demand loans due to banks was 6.3% at December 31, 1995. In addition, the company has approximately $100,000 available under several interest rate alternatives in unused lines of credit.

Interest expense in 1995, 1994, and 1993 did not differ materially from interest paid, nor did the carrying value of year end long-term borrowings differ materially from fair value.

The aggregate amounts of debt, including capital leases, maturing in each of the four years after 1996 are as follows: 1997–$25,639; 1998–$50,940; 1999–$23,436; 2000–$33,609.

The company has entered into certain operating leases which require minimum annual payments as follows: 1996–$11,813; 1997–$10,778; 1998–$9,814; 1999–$8,378; 2000–$8,511. The total rental expense for all operating leases was $11,855, $9,418 and $8,460 in 1995, 1994, and 1993, respectively.

users can determine the amount and timing of the related future cash flows for long-term obligations by analyzing the notes.

Property, Plant, and Equipment

Because the balance sheet condenses financial information, the balance sheet presentation of property, plant, and equipment is a summary of information about many separate assets. Property, plant, and equipment may include several categories, such as land, buildings, machinery and equipment, leasehold improvements, and perhaps construction in progress. So users may assess a company's ability to generate cash by using plant and equipment and the possibility of future cash outflows for investment in additional plant and equipment, entities must disclose, either in the balance sheet or in the notes, the major categories of its assets and accumulated depreciation. The disclosure of accumulated depreciation, along with the depreciation methods used, permits users to estimate the timing of future cash outflows to replace existing plant and equipment. Exhibit 5–11 illustrates the disclosures related to property, plant, and equipment for Ford Motor Company.

Accounting Policies

Accounting policies are the specific accounting principles and the methods of applying them that have been adopted by a company's management for preparation of the financial statements. Despite efforts to reduce the number of acceptable alternatives, many alternatives exist; therefore management must exercise judgment in the selection and application of accounting policies. Companies that issue financial statements prepared in accordance with U.S. GAAP must include as an integral part of the statements a summary of significant accounting policies.[5] The disclosure of accounting policies also is required by the generally accepted accounting principles in most other nations. Indeed, disclosure is perhaps more important in an international context because of the substantial accounting differences that exist worldwide. If financial statement users know and understand the accounting principles used and the methods of applying them, the comparability of financial data is improved. As discussed in Chapter 2, in order for information to be useful, it must be *comparable* and it must be *understandable*.

CONCEPTUAL

To be useful, information must be comparable and understandable.

The summary of significant accounting policies should include, where applicable, information such as the basis of consolidation, depreciation methods, inventory pricing, amortization of intangibles, and foreign currency translation practices. The footnote describing policies should not duplicate details provided elsewhere in the financial statements. *Opinion No. 22,* while recognizing the need for flexibility with respect to format, expresses a preference for placement of the summary of significant accounting policies before the notes or as the initial note to the financial statements. An example of a summary of significant accounting policies is included in GE's annual report in Appendix B.

S UBSEQUENT EVENTS

Because of the time required to complete the year-end closing, perform the audit, and prepare the annual report, companies usually issue financial statements several weeks after the end of the accounting period. Certain events other than

12 Define subsequent events and describe the accounting and reporting guidelines for them.

---

[5]"Disclosure of Accounting Policies," *Opinions of the Accounting Principles Board No. 22* (New York: AICPA, 1972).

EXHIBIT 5–11	Disclosures of Property, Plant, and Equipment

Ford Motor Company
From 1995 Annual Report

Note 5. Net Property, Depreciation and Amortization — Automotive

Net property at December 31 was as follows (in millions):

	1995	1994
Land	$ 381	$ 359
Buildings and land improvements	7,539	6,939
Machinery, equipment, and other	38,954	33,551
Construction in progress	1,609	1,685
Total land, plant, and equipment	$ 48,483	$ 42,534
Accumulated depreciation	(25,313)	(22,738)
Net land, plant, and equipment	$ 23,170	$ 19,796
Unamortized special tools	8,103	7,252
Net property	$ 31,273	$ 27,048

Property, equipment and special tools are stated at cost, less accumulated depreciation and amortization. Property and equipment placed in service before January 1, 1993 are depreciated using an accelerated method that results in accumulated depreciation of approximately two-thirds of asset cost during the first half of the estimated useful life of the asset. Property and equipment placed in service after December 31, 1992 are depreciated using the straight-line method of depreciation over the estimated useful life of the asset. On average, buildings and land improvements are depreciated based on a 30-year life; machinery and equipment are depreciated based on a 14-year life. Special tools are amortized using an accelerated method over periods of time representing the estimated productive life of those tools.

Depreciation and amortization expenses were as follows (in millions):

	1995	1994	1993
Depreciation	$2,454	$2,297	$2,392
Amortization	2,765	2,129	2,012
Total	$5,219	$4,426	$4,404

When property and equipment are retired, the general policy is to charge the cost of those assets, reduced by net salvage proceeds, to accumulated depreciation. Maintenance, repairs, and rearrangement costs are expensed as incurred and were $2,529 million in 1995, $2,377 million in 1994, and $1,934 million in 1993. Expenditures that increase the value or productive capacity of assets are capitalized. Preproduction costs related to new facilities are expensed as incurred.

CONCEPTUAL

Timeliness is an important characteristic of accounting information.

normal operating activities may occur between the statement date (the end of the accounting period) and the date of issuance of the financial statements. Because *timeliness* is an important characteristic of accounting information, it is essential that management inform investors and other users of significant events that occur during this interim period. The information could alter cash flow projections for the company, and thus for individuals who rely on the company for cash flows. Such events, referred to as poststatement events, or **subsequent events,** are of two types: (1) events that provide further evidence of conditions that existed at the statement date and (2) events that provide evidence of conditions that did not exist at the balance sheet date.[6]

Because events in the first category relate to conditions existing at the statement date, they require adjustment of the amounts reported in the financial statements. All available information should be used to make the amounts reported in the financial statements as accurate as possible. For example, an accrued liability related to litigation may require adjustment if the company settles the litigation after the statement date but before the financial statements are issued for an amount significantly different from the accrued amount. Because the event that gave rise to the liability occurred prior to the statement date, all available evidence, including evidence arising after the statement date but before the issue date, should be reflected in the financial statement amounts.

Events in the second category do not require adjustment of amounts in the financial statements. Footnotes, schedules, and pro forma statements (supplementary statements reflecting the impact of the new information) are common methods of disclosure for these events. For example, if a company engages in major new debt or equity financing during the poststatement period, disclosure is necessary to enable users to make meaningful cash flow projections. Other common events in this category include casualty losses (e.g., due to fires or floods), litigation settlements related to events occurring after the balance sheet date, and the sale of part of the company or the purchase of another company.

EXHIBIT 5–12   **Disclosure of Subsequent Events**

Storage USA, Inc.
From 1995 Annual Report

Note 12. Subsequent Events

Formation of Strategic Alliance

On March 1, 1996, the Company entered into a Stock Purchase Agreement with Security Capital U.S. Realty (US Realty), an affiliate of Security Capital Group. Under the Stock Purchase Agreement, subject to the terms and conditions thereof, US Realty will invest a total of $220,000 in the Company, initially place two of its nominees on the Company's Board of Directors, one of whom the Company has been informed will be William D. Sanders, Chairman of the Board and Chief Executive Officer of Security Capital Group, and make available to the Company certain strategic advice, research and related information and expertise (the "Strategic Alliance"). As part of the transaction, on March 19, 1996, the Company issued to US Realty 1,948,882 shares of Common Stock, approximately 10.0% of the outstanding Common Stock, at a price of $31.30 per share, plus a purchase price adjustment for accrued dividends. At the same time, the Company executed a Strategic Alliance Agreement and a Registration Rights Agreement with US Realty.

After the Strategic Alliance has been approved by the shareholders of the Company, and prior to December 31, 1996, the Company will issue to US Realty an additional 5,079,872 shares of the Company's common stock at the same price for an aggregate of $159,000. After acquiring the additional shares (and assuming no other change in the number of outstanding shares), US Realty will own approximately 28.6% of the outstanding Common Stock. The proceeds of both fundings will be contributed to the Operating Partnership in exchange for additional Operating Partnership Units and used to support the acquisition and development of self-storage facilities.

The Company has agreed to submit to the shareholders a proposal to amend the ownership limitations of the Company's Charter to permit US Realty to acquire up to 37.5% of the Company's capital stock. The Strategic Alliance, the amendment and certain related transactions are expected to be submitted to shareholders for approval at the Company's 1996 annual meeting.

---

[6]The accounting and reporting requirements described in the remainder of this section under U.S. GAAP are consistent with *International Accounting Standard 10,* "Contingencies and Events Occurring after the Balance Sheet Date," October 1978.

Note that the effect of events in both categories just discussed can be isolated and quantified in the financial statements. Other subsequent events that may affect the company require neither statement adjustment nor disclosure in the statements or notes. Examples include changes in management, new or pending legislation that might alter the entity's expectations, and changes in product emphasis. While such events clearly are important in assessing future cash flows, the effect of such items on the financial statements is not readily quantifiable.

Finally, *Statement of Concepts No. 5* indicates that recognition involves reporting an item in the financial statements in both words and numbers. When such reporting is not feasible, management's letter to stockholders is the appropriate location for a disclosure.

Exhibit 5–12 illustrates the disclosure of a subsequent event. Note that these events are relevant to the assessment of the company's future cash flows.

SUMMARY OF LEARNING OBJECTIVES

I. Describe the uses and limitations of the balance sheet.

The balance sheet provides a summary of an entity's assets, liabilities, and owners' equity at a specific date. It provides information about a company's liquidity and financial flexibility. Along with the income statement, it is useful in assessing profitability and efficiency in the utilization of resources. However, because many items are not reported at current value and some items of value are not reported at all, the balance sheet does not portray the fair value of the entity.

2. Distinguish between the two common formats for the balance sheet—the account form and the report form.

The account form reports assets on the left side of the balance sheet and liabilities and owners' equity on the right side. The report form lists assets first, followed by liabilities and equity items.

3. Define and identify the valuation methods for current assets and prepare the current assets section of the balance sheet.

Current assets are cash and other assets that can reasonably be expected to be converted to cash or consumed during one year or the normal operating cycle, whichever is longer. Cash is valued at its face amount, short-term investments are valued at fair value, currently maturing held-to-maturity securities are valued at amortized cost, accounts and notes receivable are valued at net realizable value, inventories are usually valued at lower of cost or market, and prepaid expenses are valued at cost.

4. Define and identify the valuation methods for current liabilities and prepare the current liabilities section of the balance sheet.

Current liabilities are obligations that are expected to be eliminated either through the use of existing current assets or by the creation of other current liabilities. Notes payable are valued at their face amount. Accounts payable are valued at the amount expected to be paid to eliminate the obligation, as are accrued expenses (liabilities).

5. Define and identify the valuation methods for noncurrent assets and prepare the noncurrent assets section of the balance sheet.

Noncurrent assets are assets that are not expected to be converted into cash or consumed during one year or the operating cycle, whichever is longer. Long-term investments that are available for sale are valued at fair value, while those that are expected to be held to maturity are valued at amortized cost. Property, plant, and equipment is valued at depreciated cost, except for land, which is not depreciated. Intangible assets are valued at amortized cost.

6. Define and identify the valuation methods for long-term liabilities and prepare the long-term liabilities section of the balance sheet.

Long-term liabilities are obligations that are expected to be settled beyond the operating cycle or one year, whichever is longer. Common examples include long-term notes, bonds, deferred taxes, pension and other postretirement obligations, and lease obligations. In general, these obligations are valued at the present value of the future obligation.

7. Define a contingency and describe the three possible treatments of a loss contingency.

A contingency is a condition or circumstance existing at the balance sheet date that creates the possibility of a future gain or loss, depending on the occurrence or nonoccurrence of a future event. The three possible treatments for a loss contingency are accrual and disclosure, disclosure only, and neither accrual nor disclosure. If accrual is appropriate, the contingency is valued at the amount expected to be required to eliminate it.

8. Prepare a statement of retained earnings.

The statement of retained earnings is a reconciliation of the beginning and ending retained earnings for a period of time. The most common reconciling items are net income (loss) and dividends.

9. Define and describe the appropriate accounting and reporting for prior period adjustments.

A prior period adjustment is the income effect of an error correction related to prior period financial statements. The effect of such an adjustment should be reported as an addition to or deduction from the beginning balance of retained earnings in the year in which the error is discovered.

10. Describe the statement of stockholders' equity (statement of changes in equity).

The statement of stockholders' equity is a reconciliation of the beginning and ending balance of all stockholders' equity accounts for a period of time. A company may choose to display comprehensive income and its components in this statement.

11. Describe the options for the placement and display of balance sheet information and discuss the purpose of the notes and supplementary information.

The placement decision governs whether information should be reported in the body of financial statements, in the notes, or as supplementary information. The display decision governs the amount of detail reported and the manner of presentation. The purpose of notes is to amplify or explain items included in the body of the financial statements. Supplementary information may provide a different perspective from that adopted in the financial statements, or more detail than the notes provide, and includes management's discussion of the financial statements.

12. Define subsequent events and describe the accounting and reporting guidelines for them.

Subsequent (poststatement) events are events that occur after the end of an accounting period but before the financial statements for that period are issued. If the events provide further evidence of conditions that existed at the statement date, the financial statements should reflect the new information. If the events provide evidence of conditions that did not exist at the end of the period, the financial statements should not be adjusted, but disclosure may be appropriate.

KEY TERMS

account form 210

accounting policies 223

accounts payable 214

accrued expenses (accrued liabilities) 214

available-for-sale securities 212

balance sheet 208

cash equivalents 211

contributed capital 219

current assets 211

current liabilities 213

display decision 221

financial flexibility 208

gain contingency 219

held-to-maturity securities 212

APPENDIX 5–1

Analysis of Financial Statements

Evaluation of investment or lending alternatives involves, among other things, the analysis of financial information about individual companies. Chapters 4 and 5 have described the preparation, content, and typical classifications in the income statement and balance sheet. In Appendix 5–1, we describe some of the techniques of financial statement analysis. As you proceed through the remainder of this textbook, you should keep in mind how the information reported in financial statements is used. Such knowledge is helpful in making decisions regarding disclosure, classification, and aggregation.

The relationship between security prices and information like that contained in financial statements is called market efficiency. As discussed in Chapter 1, the securities market is efficient with respect to some specified information system, such as a company's financial statements, if and only if the company's security prices act *as if* everyone observes the information system.[7] There is considerable evidence that security prices *do* react in such a fashion—that is, in a manner consistent with the hypothesis that the securities market is efficient with respect to published financial statement data.

The securities market's efficiency with respect to financial statement information means that security prices *fully reflect* financial statement information. This suggests that little if anything is to be gained by analyzing financial statements in an attempt to discover over- or undervalued securities. Rather than engaging in such an activity, an investor generally would be better off to decide on an acceptable level of risk and invest in a well-diversified securities portfolio that yields returns commensurate with that risk level. Thus, individual securities should be evaluated with respect to their effect on the entire portfolio's risk and return distributions. Investors who cannot afford to buy well-diversified personal portfolios should invest in something else with the desired risk/return level, such as a mutual fund.

Since considerable evidence supports the existence of an efficient securities market, it is reasonable to ask, "Why bother to explain financial statement analysis techniques?" There are several reasons why financial accountants should have some understanding of financial statement analysis.

---

[7]William A. Beaver, *Financial Reporting: An Accounting Revolution* (Englewood Cliffs, N.J.: Prentice-Hall, 1981), p. 147.

First, financial statement analysis may be viewed as bringing new information into the marketplace.[8] If so, financial statement analysis is not necessarily inconsistent with the efficient market hypothesis. That is, analysis may be a significant part of the process that causes security prices to fully reflect all available information.

Second, many decision makers are not aware of, or do not believe in, securities market efficiency and do not behave in a manner that is consistent with market efficiency. Therefore, regardless of the market's efficiency, many decision makers analyze financial statements. A knowledge of financial statement analysis techniques may also help accountants to prepare more useful financial statements.

Third, the securities of many companies are not traded in organized markets. When these securities are made available to the public, it is necessary to determine the appropriate offering price. This determination usually is made by underwriters and is based partially on analysis of financial statement data.

Fourth, lending institutions often require prospective borrowers to submit financial statements for analysis before they extend loans. In addition, many loan covenants require that the borrower maintain certain financial relationships, or ratios. The lender monitors these ratios.

Finally, the relative risk of a given security may change over time. Changes in risk may be related to changes in a company's capital structure, product mix, industry, or other relevant variable. Careful assessment of such factors, as disclosed in financial statements and other sources of financial information, may enable an investor to forecast expected returns more accurately.

The Financial Analysis Process

Evaluation of investment or lending alternatives typically consists of a three-step process: (1) analysis of general economic conditions, (2) analysis of the industry, and (3) analysis of individual companies in the industry. The remainder of this appendix is concerned with techniques often used in Step 3—analysis of individual companies.

Much of the information that is considered in evaluating a company's financial strength and future prospects is derived from interim and annual financial statements, schedules and commentary that supplement those statements, notes to the statements, and the external auditors' report. Many of these sources of information are illustrated by the annual report of GE, reprinted in Appendix B. Specific sections of that annual report are referred to throughout the following discussion.

Financial analysis of a company should include, at a minimum, consideration of the following sources of information. First, the *auditors' report* (see GE's auditor's report in Appendix B). The auditors' report informs the reader that the financial statements have been audited in accordance with generally accepted auditing standards. In addition, it indicates whether the financial statements fairly present the company's financial position, changes in its financial position, and cash flows in conformity with generally accepted accounting principles. In general, the auditors' report provides the user of the financial statements with some guidance as to the amount of confidence the user may place in the information reported in the statements and the related footnotes. The auditors' report also alerts financial statement users about accounting practices followed by the company and about special conditions within the company or its operating environment. Interim financial statements usually are not audited. If they are not audited, they must be so labeled.

Second, analysts should also consider the *notes to the financial statements* (see GE's  notes in Appendix B). The notes to the financial statements explain the accounting policies of the company, and often provide explanations of how those policies were applied. We discussed the typical content of notes to the financial statements in Chapter 5. Companies often make supplementary disclosures that elaborate on specific

---

[8] Paul M. Healy and Krishna G. Palepu, "The Effect of Firms' Financial Disclosure Strategies on Stock Prices," *Accounting Horizons*, March 1993, p. 7.

amounts reported in the financial statements. Sometimes the notes are used to explain specific actions by management and the reasons for those actions. The notes to the financial statements must be read carefully if the statements are to be understood fully.

Finally, analysts should consider the *financial statements* themselves (see GE's financial statements in Appendix B). The basic financial statements are, of course, the balance sheet, the income statement, the statement of cash flows, and the statement of shareholders' equity.

Financial Analysis Techniques

Analysis of financial statements often involves some transformation of the reported data. It is difficult to assess how well a company is doing merely by examining the dollar amounts reported for individual items. Techniques such as percentage analysis and ratio analysis allow analysts to identify, highlight, and summarize significant relationships in a company's financial data. These techniques are most effective when they are applied to data for several accounting periods—which usually is possible, because most companies report two or three years of comparative financial statement data at each report date. In fact, companies often provide a five- or even ten-year summary of selected financial data as a supplement to the annual financial statements. Exhibit 5–13 shows a five-year summary of data for the hypothetical Commex Company.

The following sections explain the general procedures used in percentage analysis and ratio analysis.

Percentage Analysis

Percentage analysis is a technique in which particular accounts or line items in the financial statements, such as cost of goods sold or net earnings, are evaluated *over time,* as a percentage of their value in a designated base period, or *within a particular period,* as a percentage of some designated account (line item), such as net sales. Percentage analysis is useful for highlighting trends in individual line items. The two most common versions of percentage analysis are horizontal and vertical analysis.

Horizontal Analysis

Horizontal analysis expresses financial data from two or more accounting periods in terms of a single designated base period; it compares data in each succeeding period with the amount for the preceding period. These two types of horizontal analysis are illustrated in Exhibits 5–14 and 5–15 using the summary data for Commex Company presented in Exhibit 5–13.

An examination of Exhibits 5–14 and 5–15 raises at least three questions about the operations of Commex Company that might cause an analyst to conduct further research:

1. Why did the overall level of operations, as measured by net sales, drop off in 1998 after several years of growth?
2. Why did net income deteriorate significantly?
3. Why did interest expense increase so much in 1997 and 1998?

Some additional information related to these questions is provided by the notes that accompany Commex's five-year summary data in Exhibit 15–13. These notes mention charges to income for plant closings in 1996 and 1998, and a credit to income in 1996 for a gain on the sale of securities.

EXHIBIT 5-13 Five-Year Summary Data

Commex Company
Five-Year Summary of Selected Consolidated Financial Data
(in thousands, except per share data)

	1998	1997	1996	1995	1994
Operations:					
Net sales	$1,159,863	$1,208,061	$1,107,128	$978,692	$871,505
Cost of products sold	952,176	966,568	882,362	760,312	663,840
Interest expense	21,891	16,038	9,526	8,151	8,400
Income taxes	6,300	35,300	42,300	43,900	46,600
Net earnings	28,831[a]	58,078	65,800[b]	58,944	58,864
Dividends on Series A preferred stock	4,817	4,817	4,818	4,830	4,992
Earnings attributable to common stock	24,014	53,261	60,982	54,114	53,872
Per share data:					
Basic:					
Average shares outstanding	11,088	11,093	11,084	11,084	10,958
Per share amount	2.17	4.80	5.50	4.88	4.92
Diluted:					
Average shares outstanding	12,609	12,615	12,605	12,608	12,542
Per share amount	2.17	4.60	5.22	4.67	4.69
Cash dividends per share:					
Preferred	4.75	4.75	4.75	4.75	4.75
Common	1.70	2.30	2.30	2.20	2.00
Financial position:					
Cash, short-term investments, and marketable securities	$ 38,951	$ 39,064	$ 49,410	$ 26,331	$ 64,126
Receivables (net)	162,521	138,459	129,221	117,632	92,931
Inventories	267,663	270,592	242,558	233,380	196,770
Plants and properties (cost)	834,743	805,408	689,113	637,041	599,660
Plants and properties (net)	361,949	347,581	260,194	231,308	224,973
Total assets[c]	903,841	846,010	726,588	653,632	627,556
Current assets[c]	494,961	457,525	427,931	384,070	363,419
Current liabilities[c]	181,308	163,453	148,279	121,021	129,882
Working capital[c]	313,653	294,072	279,652	263,049	233,537
Long-term debt	190,521	165,033	90,916	83,834	81,816
Stockholders' equity[c]	509,992	504,716	476,807	441,238	410,072
Book value per common share[c]	36.84	36.38	33.88	30.68	28.10
Other data:					
Expenditures for plants and properties (includes properties of businesses acquired)	$ 58,840	$128,398	$ 64,032	$ 39,618	$ 24,233
Depreciation	42,551	37,172	33,262	31,298	32,352
Employee compensation and benefits	453,502	463,037	430,046	384,020	340,740
Return on average stockholders' equity[c]	5.7%	11.8%	14.3%	13.8%	14.9%
Shares outstanding at December 31:					
Preferred	1,014	1,014	1,014	1,014	1,017
Common	11,090	11,085	11,080	11,077	10,973
Number of employees at December 31	17,817	19,916	20,997	20,578	19,417

[a]Includes charge for provision for plant-closing costs ($11,000 pretax, $5,850 net, equal to $.53 per share).
[b]Includes charge for provision for plant-closing costs ($12,000 pretax, $5,952 net, equal to $.53 per share) and credit for gain on sale of securities ($16,885 pretax, $11,820 net, equal to $1.07 per share).
[c]Amounts for years prior to 1998 restated for a change in accounting principle.

EXHIBIT 5–14	Horizontal Analysis Using 1994 as a Base

Commex Company
Horizontal Analysis of 1994–1998 Summary Data
(*as percentage of 1994 amount*)

	1994		1995		1996		1997		1998	
	Thousands of Dollars	% of 1994	Thousands of Dollars	% of 1994	Thousands of Dollars	% of 1994	Thousands of Dollars	% of 1994	Thousands of Dollars	% of 1994
Net sales	$871,505	100%	$978,692	112%	$1,107,128	127%	$1,208,061	139%	$1,159,863	133%
Cost of products sold	663,840	100	760,312	115	882,362	133	966,568	146	952,176	143
Interest expense	8,400	100	8,151	97	9,526	113	16,038	191	21,891	261
Income taxes.	46,600	100	43,900	94	42,300	91	35,300	76	6,300	14
Net income.	58,864	100	58,944	100	65,800	112	58,078	99	28,831	49

EXHIBIT 5–15	Horizontal Analysis on a Year-to-Year Basis

Commex Company
Horizontal Analysis of 1994–1998 Summary Data
(*as percentage of preceding year's amount*)

	1994		1995		1996		1997		1998	
	Thousands of Dollars	% of 1994	Thousands of Dollars	% of 1994	Thousands of Dollars	% of 1995	Thousands of Dollars	% of 1996	Thousands of Dollars	% of 1997
Net sales	$871,505	100%	$978,692	112%	$1,107,128	113%	$1,208,061	109%	$1,159,863	96%
Cost of products sold	663,840	100	760,312	115	882,362	116	966,568	110	952,176	99
Interest expense	8,400	100	8,151	97	9,526	117	16,038	168	21,891	136
Income taxes	46,600	100	43,900	94	42,300	96	35,300	83	6,300	18
Net income	58,864	100	58,944	100	65,800	112	58,078	88	28,831	50

When we use percentage analysis, we must remember that percentages are relative to the designated base. If the base amount is small, even a comparatively small change in dollar amount will yield a substantial percentage change. For example, in Exhibit 5–14 the 1998 interest expense is 261 percent of the 1994 interest expense, partially because the 1994 interest expense was a comparatively small dollar amount. Also, when the period-to-period type of horizontal analysis is used, as in Exhibit 5–15, the changes in percentage for a particular item result partially from the period-to-period change in the base. Finally, percentage changes from period to period in a particular item are meaningful when the base period remains the same, as in Exhibit 5–14. Such changes are not as meaningful when the base changes from period to period, as in Exhibit 5–15.

Vertical Analysis

In *vertical analysis,* all the data in a particular financial statement are presented as a percentage of a single designated line item in that statement. For example, we might report income statement items as a percentage of net sales, balance sheet items as a percentage of total assets, and items in the statement of cash flows as a percentage of the change in cash. Vertical analysis is illustrated in Exhibit 5–16, based on the Commex Company data in Exhibit 5–13.

The vertical analysis in Exhibit 5–16 adds further concerns about the questions raised earlier by the analyses in Exhibits 5–14 and 5–15. For example, we can

EXHIBIT 5–16	Vertical Analysis as a Percentage of Net Sales

Commex Company
Vertical Analysis of 1994–1998 Summary Data
(as percentage of net sales)

	1994		1995		1996		1997		1998	
	Thousands of Dollars	% of Net Sales	Thousands of Dollars	% of Net Sales	Thousands of Dollars	% of Net Sales	Thousands of Dollars	% of Net Sales	Thousands of Dollars	% of Net Sales
Net sales	$871,505	100%	$978,692	100%	$1,107,128	100%	$1,208,061	100%	$1,159,863	100%
Cost of products sold	663,840	76	760,312	78	882,362	80	966,568	80	952,176	82
Interest expense	8,400	1	8,151	1	9,526	1	16,038	1	21,891	2
Income taxes..............	46,600	5	43,900	4	42,300	4	35,300	3	6,300	1
Net income	58,864	7	58,944	6	65,800	6	58,078	5	28,831	2

see from Exhibit 5–16 that net income as a percentage of net sales fell to only 2 percent in 1998. That decline is partly explained by increases in both the cost of products sold and interest expense as a percentage of net sales. We can also observe that the relative amount of income tax fell, but that is not surprising given the apparent drop in taxable income.

If more than one year's data are used in vertical analysis, as in Exhibit 5–16, care must be exercised in comparing percentages from period to period. For example, although interest expense in Exhibit 5–16 was 1 percent of net sales in 1997, and 2 percent of net sales in 1998, it would be incorrect to say that interest expense was twice as much in 1998 as in 1997. The purpose of vertical analysis is to highlight relationships between components of the financial statements, not to assess trends in individual components over time.

Ratio Analysis

Probably the most widely used financial analysis technique is *ratio analysis,* the analysis of relationships between two or more line items on the financial statements. For example, one commonly used financial ratio is the *current ratio,* or the relationship between current assets and current liabilities.

Generally, financial ratios are calculated for the purpose of evaluating four aspects of a company's operations: (1) liquidity, (2) activity in or turnover of assets, (3) leverage, and (4) profitability. *Liquidity ratios* help users assess a company's ability to meet currently maturing or short-term obligations. *Activity* or *turnover ratios* are useful for evaluating the effectiveness with which a company uses its assets. *Leverage ratios* provide information about a company's ability to meet both current and long-term obligations. *Profitability ratios* are helpful for evaluating management's success in generating returns for those who provide capital to the company. Each of these financial ratio types is discussed in the following sections. Ratio calculations are illustrated by using the Commex Company data in Exhibits 5–17, 5–18, and 5–19.

Liquidity Ratios

Liquidity ratios are used to evaluate a company's short-term financial strength. The most common liquidity ratios are the current ratio, the quick ratio, and the defensive interval ratio.

EXHIBIT 5–17   Consolidated Balance Sheets

Commex Company
Consolidated Balance Sheets
As of December 31, 1998 and 1997
(*in thousands*)

	December 31	
	1998	**1997**
Assets:		
Currents assets:		
Cash and short-term investments, at cost (approximate market).	$ 38,951	$ 39,064
Receivables, less allowances of $8,511,000 and $7,672,000, respectively. . . .	162,521	138,459
Inventories	267,663	270,592
Federal income tax refund receivable	14,700	
Deferred tax asset and other current assets	11,126	9,410
Total current assets	$494,961	$457,525
Investments and other assets:		
Investments in and advances to affiliates	$ 17,037	$ 13,760
Other assets	7,562	4,812
	$ 24,599	$ 18,572
Plants and properties:		
Land	$ 13,500	$ 13,316
Land improvements	22,998	19,941
Buildings.	215,208	206,343
Machinery and equipment	567,901	494,824
Construction in progress	15,136	70,984
	$834,743	$805,408
Less: Accumulated depreciation	(472,794)	(457,827)
	$361,949	$347,581
Excess of cost of investments in subsidiaries over net assets acquired	$ 22,332	$ 22,332
Total assets	$903,841	$846,010

Current Ratio

The *current ratio,* also called the *working capital ratio,* is an indicator of a company's ability to meet its short-term obligations with current assets. It is calculated by dividing current assets by current liabilities. For example, Commex Company's 1998 current liabilities equal $181,308. Can Commex meet these current obligations when they are due? Since in theory noncash current assets are expected to be converted into cash in the near term, the ratio of current assets to current liabilities should provide an indication of the company's ability to satisfy short-term creditors.

Commex's 1998 current ratio is calculated as follows:

$$\text{Current ratio} = \frac{\text{Current assets}}{\text{Current liabilities}} = \frac{\$494,961}{\$181,308} = 2.73$$

This ratio indicates that Commex's short-term creditors can feel reasonably secure about receiving payment from Commex when it is due. Analysts view a low current ratio with concern because short-term cash flow problems could force a company into bankruptcy. On the other hand, a current ratio that is too high may indicate bad management of liquid resources. Excessive current assets might be better used to pay dividends or retire long-term debt, or invested as capital. The current ratio should be evaluated in light of the company's circumstances, including management plans as well as industry and general economic conditions.

	December 31	
	1998	**1997**
Liabilities and stockholders' equity:		
Current liabilities:		
Notes payable to banks	$ 25,540	$ 18,428
Accounts payable........................	41,079	40,248
Employees' compensation and amounts withheld therefrom	41,731	37,683
Taxes, other than federal and foreign income taxes	16,700	18,134
Accrued product warranty expense	19,250	16,250
Other accrued liabilities	26,561	22,846
United States and foreign income taxes	9,536	8,900
Current maturities of long-term debt	911	964
Total current liabilities	$181,308	$163,453
Deferred tax liability	13,468	6,663
Unfunded pension costs of closed plants	8,552	6,145
Long-term debt (9% promissory notes)	190,521	165,033
Total liabilities	$393,849	$341,294
Stockholders' equity:		
Serial preferred stock, authorized 4,000,000 shares:		
$4.75 cumulative convertible, Series A, upon liquidation entitled		
to $100 per share, $101,414,500 in the aggregate		
at December 31, 1998; outstanding, 1,014,145 shares, stated value	$ 39,074	$ 39,074
Common stock (par value $5.00 a share):		
Authorized, 20,000,000 shares		
Outstanding, 11,089,956 and 11,084,938 shares, respectively		
(after deducting 80,772 and 85,790 shares, respectively, in treasury)	55,450	55,425
Contributed capital in excess of par	10,499	10,415
Retained earnings........................	404,969	399,802
Total stockholders' equity........................	$509,992	$504,716
Total liabilities and stockholders' equity........................	$903,841	$846,010

The current ratio can be manipulated by techniques such as irregular dividend payments. Such activity is known as *window dressing*. In analyzing financial statements, keep in perspective information that is derived from any single financial ratio.

Quick Ratio and Defensive Interval Ratio

One problem with the current ratio is that current assets have varying degrees of liquidity. To allow for differences in liquidity, analysts often calculate other liquidity ratios. Two of those ratios are the quick, or acid-test, ratio and the defensive interval ratio.

The *quick ratio* is calculated by dividing the most liquid assets—generally, the total of cash, short-term marketable securities, and net short-term receivables—by total current liabilities. Excluding inventories, prepaid items, and other comparatively nonliquid assets from the numerator of the quick ratio provides a better indication of a company's liquidity than the current ratio. When calculating and evaluating the quick ratio, however, one should consider the particular circumstances of the company being studied. Some companies, such as a jewelry store, may have very liquid inventories, while other normally liquid current assets, such as short-term receivables, may be comparatively nonliquid.

EXHIBIT 5-18   **Statements of Consolidated Net Income**

Commex Company
Statements of Consolidated Net Income
for the Years Ended December 31, 1996–1998
(in thousands, except per share data)

	1998	1997	1996
Revenues and gains:			
Net sales	$ 1,159,863	$ 1,208,061	$ 1,107,128
Royalties and interest	7,562	7,127	5,259
Gain on sale of securities			16,885
Other revenues	4,019	2,569	5,791
Total revenues	$ 1,171,444	$ 1,217,757	$ 1,135,063
Costs and expenses:			
Cost of products sold	$ 952,176	$ 966,568	$ 882,362
General and administrative, selling, advertising, and other expenses	128,176	120,880	104,651
Engineering, research and development	23,070	20,893	18,424
Interest expense	21,891	16,038	9,526
Provision for plant closing costs	11,000		12,000
Total costs and expenses	$(1,136,313)	$(1,124,379)	$(1,026,963)
Income before income taxes	$ 35,131	$ 93,378	$ 108,100
Income taxes	(6,300)	(35,300)	(42,300)
Net income	$ 28,831	$ 58,078	$ 65,800
Dividends on preferred stock	(4,817)	(4,817)	(4,818)
Income attributable to common stock	$ 24,014	$ 53,261	$ 60,982
Net income per share of common stock:			
Basic	$2.17	$4.80	$5.50
Diluted	2.17	4.60	5.22

Commex Company's 1998 quick ratio is calculated as follows:

$$\text{Quick ratio} = \frac{\text{Cash} + \text{Short-term marketable securities}^a + \text{Net short-term receivables}}{\text{Current liabilities}}$$

$$= \frac{\$38,951 + \$162,521}{\$181,308} = 1.11$$

[a]Commex has no short-term marketable securities.

Although Commex's quick ratio is substantially lower than its current ratio, it is greater than 1.0, which means that Commex can probably meet all its current obligations using only its most liquid current assets.

The *defensive interval ratio* is equal to *defensive assets* (cash, short-term marketable securities, and net short-term receivables) divided by average daily expenditures for operations. The defensive interval ratio addresses a company's survivability in the absence of external cash flows. This ratio measures the length of time that a company could carry on its daily operations with only its liquid assets. The defensive interval ratio is useful because it considers the size and timing of average daily cash flows.

In theory, the average daily expenditures for operations (the denominator of the defensive interval ratio) should be based on a company's cash budget for the coming period. In practice, however, the cash budget is not available to external analysts. Therefore, analysts must estimate average daily expenditures for operations by summing the cost of goods sold, selling and administrative expenses, and all other

EXHIBIT 5–19 **Statements of Consolidated Stockholders' Equity**

Commex Company
Statements of Consolidated Stockholders' Equity
For the Years Ended December 31, 1996–1998
(in thousands)

	Preferred Stock	Common Stock	Additional Paid-in Capital	Retained Earnings
Balance at January 1, 1996..............	$39,074	$55,384	$10,246	$338,904
Cumulative effect of change in accounting principle.................				(2,370)
Balance at January 1, 1996, as restated	$39,074	$55,384	$10,246	$336,534
Issuance of 3,220 common shares under employee stock option plans		16	53	
Net income for the year..................				65,800
Cash dividends paid:				
Common stock ($2.30 a share)				(25,482)
Preferred stock ($4.75 a share)...........				(4,818)
Balance at December 31, 1996.............	$39,074	$55,400	$10,299	$372,034)
Issuance of 4,856 common shares under employee stock option plans		25	116	
Net income for the year..................				58,078
Cash dividends paid:				
Common stock ($2.30 a share)				(25,493)
Preferred stock ($4.75 a share)				(4,817)
Balance at December 31, 1997.............	$39,074	$55,425	$10,415	$399,802
Issuance of 5,018 common shares under employee stock option plan		25	84	
Net income for the year				28,831
Cash dividends paid:				
Common stock ($1.70 a share)				(18,847)
Preferred stock ($4.75 a share)				(4,817)
Balance at December 31, 1998.............	$39,074	$55,450	$10,499	$404,969

ordinary daily cash expenditures and dividing the total by 365 days. If total expense is used in the denominator, noncash expenses (such as tax expense for which payment is deferred and depreciation) must be subtracted from total expenses.

Commex's 1998 defensive interval is:

$$\frac{\text{Defensive}}{\text{interval}} = \frac{\text{Defensive assets}}{\text{Average daily expenditures for operations}}$$

$$= \frac{\text{Cash} + \text{Short-term marketable securities} + \text{Net short-term receivables}}{\left(\begin{array}{c}\text{Cost of} \\ \text{goods sold}\end{array} + \begin{array}{c}\text{Selling and administrative} \\ \text{expenses}\end{array} + \begin{array}{c}\text{Other ordinary} \\ \text{expenses}\end{array} - \text{Depreciation}\right) \div 365 \text{ days}}$$

$$= \frac{\$38,951 + \$162,521}{(\$952,176 + \$128,176 + \$23,070 + \$21,891 - \$42,551) \div 365 \text{ days}}$$

$$= \frac{\$201,472}{\$1,082,762 \div 365 \text{ days}} = \frac{\$201,472}{\$2,966 \text{ per day}}$$

$$= 67.9 \text{ days}$$

Based on this defensive interval, it appears Commex could carry on normal operations for more than two months using only its most liquid assets to finance its operating expenses.

Activity or Turnover Ratios

Turnover ratios are used to measure the relative efficiency with which a company uses its assets. Both current and long-term aspects of asset management can be analyzed in this way. The three most important turnover ratios are inventory turnover, accounts receivable turnover, and total assets turnover.

Inventory Turnover

Inventory turnover is cost of goods sold divided by average inventory for the period. Cost of goods sold is used as the numerator instead of sales because sales includes profit, and inventory (the denominator) is a cost figure. *Average* inventory is used as the denominator because this ratio is a measure of inventory activity *during* the period.

Commex's inventory turnover for 1998 is calculated as follows:

$$\text{Inventory turnover} = \frac{\text{Cost of goods sold}}{\text{Average inventory}}$$

$$= \frac{\text{Cost of goods sold}}{(\text{Beginning inventory} + \text{Ending inventory}) \div 2}$$

$$= \frac{\$952,176}{(\$270,592 + \$267,663) \div 2}$$

$$= 3.54 \text{ times per year, or every 103 days}$$

The amount of time inventory takes to turn over is a good indicator of a company's cash inflow prospects. Low values for the inventory turnover ratio may indicate sluggish sales or too much inventory on hand, which increases inventory carrying costs. High inventory turnover ratios may indicate problems with stockouts; such problems would necessitate an increase in inventory levels.

Accounts Receivable Turnover

In theory, the *accounts receivable turnover ratio* is net credit sales divided by average net accounts receivable outstanding during the period. In practice, however, the numerator used is often net total sales, since most companies do not report their credit sales. If the relationship between credit sales and cash sales is fairly stable, use of net total sales will not adversely affect the information provided by the ratio.

Commex Company's 1998 accounts receivable turnover is calculated as follows:

$$\text{Accounts receivable turnover} = \frac{\text{Net sales}}{\text{Average accounts receivable}}$$

$$= \frac{\text{Net sales}}{\left(\text{Beginning net accounts receivable} + \text{Ending net accounts receivable}\right) \div 2}$$

$$= \frac{\$1,159,863}{(\$138,459 + \$162,521) \div 2}$$

$$= 7.71 \text{ times per year, or every 47 days}$$

This ratio indicates that Commex's average dollar balance of accounts receivable is outstanding for a little more than 47 days before it is converted to cash. If we combine the accounts receivable turnover period with Commex's inventory turnover period (103 days), we see that each credit sale ties up cash for about 150 days (including the inventory holding period). If credit sales are a substantial part of total sales, 150 days is a good estimate of the length of Commex's operating cycle. If most sales are for cash, then the inventory turnover period of 103 days is a better estimate. An excessively long accounts receivable turnover period would suggest a need to investigate, and perhaps to modify the company's policy for granting credit or its accounts receivable collection practices.

Total Assets Turnover

The *total assets turnover ratio* is net sales divided by the average total assets for the period. This ratio emphasizes how productive total assets have been during a period.

Commex's 1998 total assets turnover is calculated as follows:

$$\text{Total assets turnover} = \frac{\text{Net sales}}{\text{Average total assets}}$$

$$= \frac{\text{Net sales}}{(\text{Beginning total assets} + \text{Ending total assets}) \div 2}$$

$$= \frac{\$1,159,863}{(\$846,010 + \$903,841) \div 2}$$

$$= 1.33 \text{ times per year, or every 274 days}$$

An excessively low total assets turnover suggests the existence of high opportunity costs for asset use, or at least inefficient use of assets. In such cases, reduction of the asset base may be called for. In extreme cases, liquidation of the company may be preferable to the inefficient use of company assets. As we suggested earlier, however, no ratio should be analyzed in isolation, without examining other measures of financial strength.

Leverage Ratios

Leverage ratios indicate to investors and long-term creditors the riskiness of a company as an investment or lending alternative. These ratios provide information to investors about the relative emphasis on debt in a company's capital structure. As debt increases and debt-servicing requirements grow, uncertainty about the return on an investment in the company's common stock increases. Leverage ratios also are useful for evaluating a company's ability to service both current and long-term debt, whether on a continuing basis or on a liquidation basis.

The two major leverage ratios are total liabilities to total assets and times interest earned.

Total Liabilities to Total Assets

The *total liabilities to total assets ratio* provides information about a company's ability to absorb asset reductions arising from losses without jeopardizing the interests of creditors. A high value for this ratio indicates increased risk to creditors because of the possibility that the company will become insolvent before all creditors' claims are met. Because of the interest charges that accompany debt, investors prefer that the total liabilities to total assets ratio not be too high. Loan covenants often require that companies not exceed specified levels of this ratio. Desired levels usually vary with the stability of a company's income. Generally, the more stable a company's historical income, the greater the likelihood that investors and creditors will tolerate increased debt.

Commex's 1998 total liabilities to total assets ratio is calculated as follows:

$$\text{Total liabilities to total assets} = \frac{\text{Total liabilities}}{\text{Total assets}}$$

$$= \frac{\$393,849}{\$903,841} = .44$$

Since less than half of Commex's financing comes from debt, further limited growth in its debt may be possible. Given the increase in this ratio from .40 in 1997 to .44 in 1998, however, stockholders may oppose further debt financing, especially if restrictions on cash dividends are part of Commex's existing debt arrangements.

Times Interest Earned

The *times interest earned ratio* is ordinary income before interest expense and taxes divided by interest expense. Ordinary income before interest and taxes is used as the numerator because that is the amount that is available for interest payments. This ratio is useful for assessing a company's ability to make annual interest payments using only its ongoing income.

Commex would calculate its 1998 times interest earned ratio as follows:

$$\text{Times interest earned} = \frac{\text{Income before taxes} + \text{Interest expense} + \text{Provision for plant closings}}{\text{Interest expense}}$$

$$= \frac{\$35{,}131 + \$21{,}891 + \$11{,}000}{\$21{,}891}$$

$$= 3.1 \text{ times}$$

Note that in calculating the ratio, we added the $11,000 special provision for plant closings to income before taxes and interest expense, in order to obtain normal operating income. Both investors and creditors prefer a high value for times interest earned because it indicates a margin of safety for their investments or loans. That is, normal operating income available to pay interest will be well in excess of annual interest expense.

Sometimes the times interest earned ratio is modified to include all fixed expenses (e.g., interest payments, lease payments, and pension payments) in the denominator. Fixed expenses usually do not include preferred dividends because declaration of dividends is a management prerogative. When the times interest earned ratio is modified in this way, it is called a *fixed expenses* (or *fixed charges*) *coverage ratio*. The fixed expenses (fixed charges) coverage ratio provides a more severe test of the company's ability to meet its obligations from ongoing income.

Profitability Ratios

Management's ultimate goal should be to maximize the return to stockholders. Net income probably is the best single measure under management's control of how well that goal has been achieved. Thus, investors are quite interested in net income and consider profitability ratios to be among the most important of financial ratios.

We will consider the different profitability ratios: profit margin on sales; net operating margin; return on total assets; return on stockholders' equity; trading on the equity; earnings per share; price-earnings ratio; dividend yield; book value per share; and the DuPont method of combining ratios to assess return on investment.

Profit Margin on Sales

The *profit margin on sales* is net income divided by net sales. This ratio indicates the return a company receives for each dollar of sales. The most obvious weakness of this ratio is that many items included in net income, such as financing costs, are not directly related to the company's sales activity.

Commex's profit margin on sales in 1998 is calculated as follows:

$$\text{Profit margin on sales} = \frac{\text{Net income}}{\text{Net sales}}$$

$$= \frac{\$28{,}831}{\$1{,}159{,}863} = .025$$

Commex's profit margin on sales is fairly low. But this ratio does not provide the best evidence of profitability in 1998. Better evidence is provided by the net operating margin and the return on total assets.

Net Operating Margin

The *net operating margin* is operating income divided by net sales. In this ratio nonoperating items, such as interest revenue and interest expense, royalties, and gains or losses on disposals of assets, are excluded from operating income. Since operating income is the numerator, this ratio is a better measure of the effectiveness with which a company produces and sells its products than profit margin on sales.

Commex's 1998 net operating margin is calculated as follows:

$$\text{Net operating margin} = \frac{\text{Operating income}}{\text{Net sales}}$$

$$= \frac{\text{Net sales} - \left(\frac{\text{Cost of}}{\text{goods sold}} + \frac{\text{Operating}}{\text{expenses}}\right)}{\text{Net sales}}$$

$$= \frac{\$1,159,863 - (\$952,176 + \$128,176 + \$23,070)}{\$1,159,863}$$

$$= \frac{\$56,441}{\$1,159,863} = .049$$

Commex's net operating margin is almost twice as large as its profit margin on sales, indicating that Commex has large nonoperating charges. Remember that we first saw this phenomenon in connection with interest expense in percentage analyses—see, for example, Exhibits 5–14 and 5–15.

Return on Total Assets

The *return on total assets* equals net income divided by average total assets. This ratio is a better measure of profitability than either profit margin on sales or net operating margin because it indicates management's effectiveness at using company assets to generate net income.

Commex's 1998 return on total assets is calculated as follows:

$$\text{Return on total assets} = \frac{\text{Net income}}{\text{Average total assets}}$$

$$= \frac{\text{Net income}}{(\text{Beginning total assets} + \text{Ending total assets}) \div 2}$$

$$= \frac{\$28,831}{(\$846,010 + \$903,841) \div 2}$$

$$= \frac{\$28,831}{\$874,925} = .03$$

Here the denominator is *average* total assets because the return on total assets is earned during the entire period.

Some analysts contend that the numerator of this ratio should be net income before interest expense (net of tax savings resulting from interest expense), because interest expense is a cost of obtaining additional assets, and therefore should not be considered as a deduction in determining return on assets. If we follow this reasoning, Commex's 1998 return on total assets is calculated as follows:

$$\text{Return on total assets} = \frac{\text{Net income} + \text{Interest expense}(1 - \text{Tax rate})}{\text{Average total assets}}$$

$$= \frac{\$28,831 + (\$21,891)\left(1 - \frac{\$6,300}{\$35,131}\right)}{(\$846,010 + \$903,841) \div 2}$$

$$= \frac{\$28,831 + (\$21,891)(.82)}{\$874,925}$$

$$= \frac{\$46,782}{\$874,925} = .05$$

Return on Stockholders' Equity

Return on stockholders' equity is net income minus preferred dividends, divided by average common stockholders' equity. Since dividends on common stock are paid after preferred dividends have been paid, only net income minus preferred dividends is available for distribution to common stockholders.

Commex Company's 1998 return on stockholders' equity is calculated as follows:

$$\frac{\text{Return on}}{\text{stockholders' equity}} = \frac{\text{Net income} - \text{Preferred dividends}}{\text{Average common stockholders' equity}}$$

$$= \frac{\text{Net income} - \text{Preferred dividends}}{\left(\begin{array}{c}\text{Beginning common} \\ \text{stockholders' equity}\end{array} + \begin{array}{c}\text{Ending common} \\ \text{stockholders' equity}\end{array}\right) \div 2}$$

$$= \frac{\$28,831 - \$4,817}{(\$465,642 + \$470,918) \div 2}$$

$$= \frac{\$24,014}{\$468,280} = .05$$

Return on stockholders' equity summarizes management's success at maximizing the return to common stock investors. When Commex's return on stockholders' equity is compared with its profit margin on sales, net operating margin, and return on total assets, it appears the interests of common stockholders have been reasonably well served. That is, the return on stockholders' equity is greater than or equal to all those measures of company profitability. As we shall see shortly, however, Commex's return on stockholders' equity may still be less than satisfactory.

Trading on the Equity

The terms *trading on the equity* and *financial leverage* describe the practice of borrowing money at fixed interest rates, or issuing preferred stock with fixed dividend rates, with the expectation of investing the money received in assets that will yield a return that exceeds the interest and preferred dividends paid. Because the claims of creditors and preferred stockholders come before the claims of common stockholders, common stockholders benefit from trading on the equity only when the yield on assets exceeds the fixed returns due to creditors and preferred stockholders. In that case, the margin of excess return will accrue to the benefit of the common stockholders, and trading on the equity is *favorable* to them. But when the cost of nonequity capital is greater than the return on assets, trading on the equity is *unfavorable* to common stockholders.

How can we quantify the concept of leverage? One way of writing the accounting equation is:

$$\text{Total assets} = \text{Creditors' equity} + \begin{array}{c}\text{Preferred} \\ \text{stockholders' equity}\end{array} + \begin{array}{c}\text{Common} \\ \text{stockholders' equity}\end{array}$$

We know from earlier calculations that Commex Company's 1998 return on total assets was 3 percent. Therefore, based on the accounting equation, *aggregate return on creditors', preferred stockholders', and common stockholders' equities*, which together equal total assets, also was 3 percent. Since the return on common stockholders' equity was 5 percent, we can conclude that the combined returns to creditors and preferred stockholders must have been less than 3 percent because the return on *all* equity was 3 percent. On this basis, trading on the equity was favorable to Commex's common stockholders.

On the other hand, in examining Commex's balance sheet (see Exhibit 5–17), we see that a substantial portion of Commex's creditors' equity is short-term and essentially interest-free. The 9 percent long-term debt and the preferred stock (4.75 percent cumulative) both have returns exceeding 3 percent, and the long-term debt return exceeds the 5 percent return on Commex's common stockholders' equity. Viewed from this perspective, Commex's return on common stockholders' equity might not be satisfactory to some investors.

Earnings per Share

Investors often are interested in measures of profitability on a per share basis. While there are several such measures, perhaps the most widely used figure is earnings per share. When a company has no potentially dilutive securities outstanding, the *earnings per share ratio* is calculated by dividing net income minus senior claims on earnings, such as dividends on preferred stock, by the weighted average number of common stock shares outstanding during the period. When potentially dilutive securities, such as stock options, stock warrants, and convertible securities, are outstanding, analysts may need to calculate two earnings per share figures: (1) basic earnings per share and (2) diluted earnings per share.[9] Commex Company has potentially dilutive securities outstanding—for example, the $4.75 cumulative convertible preferred stock—so it reports both basic earnings per share and diluted earnings per share for 1998 (see Exhibit 5–18).

Care must be exercised in relying on the earnings per share figure. Earnings per share may be increased simply by reducing the number of shares outstanding. In addition, as with all per share figures, too much emphasis may be placed on performance with respect to a single share of stock, and not enough on total company operations and profitability.

Price-Earnings Ratio

The *price-earnings ratio* (P/E) is the market price of a share of stock divided by earnings per share. Assuming *The Wall Street Journal* reported a December 31, 1998, closing price for Commex common stock of 22 7/8 ($22.875), Commex's price-earnings ratio would be calculated as follows:

$$\text{Price-earnings ratio} = \frac{\text{Market price per share}}{\text{Earnings per share}}$$

$$= \frac{\$22.875}{\$2.17} = 10.54$$

The trend of the price-earnings ratio is indicative of the long-term growth potential of a company. A rising price-earnings ratio reflects a favorable investor view of growth potential; a declining price-earnings ratio indicates doubt about a company's growth potential.

Dividend Yield

The *dividend yield* is the ratio of the dividend per common share to the market price per common share.

Commex's 1998 dividend yield is calculated as follows:

$$\text{Dividend yield} = \frac{\text{Dividend per common share}}{\text{Market price per common share}}$$

$$= \frac{\$1.70}{\$22.875} = .07$$

---

[9]Chapter 20 contains a thorough discussion of earnings per share.

The dividend yield can be added to the percentage change in stock price for the period to derive a reasonable measure of a common stockholder's total return for the period.

The *dividend payout ratio* is closely related to the dividend yield. The dividend payout ratio is the total cash dividends paid divided by net income available to common stockholders.

Commex's dividend payout ratio for common stock in 1998 is calculated as follows:

$$\text{Dividend payout ratio} = \frac{\text{Cash dividends}}{\text{Net income} - \text{Preferred dividends}}$$

$$= \frac{\$18,847}{\$24,014} = .78$$

Book Value per Share

Book value per share equals common stockholders' equity divided by the number of common shares outstanding at the end of the period. Common stockholders' equity is total stockholders' equity minus any preferred stockholder claims, such as a redemption or liquidation value, dividends in arrears on cumulative preferred stock, or preferred stock participation rights.

Commex's 1998 book value per share is calculated as follows:

$$\frac{\text{Book value}}{\text{per share}} = \frac{\text{Common stockholders' equity}}{\text{Number of common shares outstanding}}$$

$$= \frac{\text{Total stockholders' equity} - \text{Preferred stockholder claims}}{\text{Number of common shares}}$$

$$= \frac{\$509,992,000 - \$101,414,500^a}{11,089,956 \text{ shares}}$$

$$= \frac{\$408,577,500}{11,089,956 \text{ shares}} = \$36.84 \text{ per share}$$

[a]As of 12/31/98, Commex's preferred shares had an aggregate liquidation value of $101,414,500 (see Exhibit 5–17).

Although book value per share is quoted often for common stock, and can be found regularly in supplementary schedules to annual financial statements (see, for example, Commex's five-year summary data in Exhibit 5–13), normally it is not a good measure of the economic or market value of a share of common stock. Because modified historical cost accounting practices typically do not yield market-based values for net assets, only under unusual circumstances will book value per share be a reasonable approximation of the economic value of a share of stock. Only when a company has just started operations or is being accounted for on a liquidation basis is book value likely to be close to economic or market value.

The DuPont Method

Financial ratios can be combined in a series to assess return on investment. The use of ratios in a system of interrelationships is known as the *DuPont method,* after E. I. DuPont de Nemours & Company, one of the first companies to use this approach to financial control and management. The system can yield several forms of equations, one of which is:

$$\frac{\text{Return on}}{\text{investment}} = \frac{\text{Net sales}}{\text{Total assets}} \times \frac{\text{Total assets}}{\text{Stockholders' equity}} \times \frac{\text{Net income} - \text{Preferred dividends}}{\text{Net sales}}$$

The benefit of the DuPont method is that it can be used to consider several responses to a single question simultaneously. For example, the question "How can return on investment be increased?" might be answered in several ways—increasing asset turnover through increased sales; increasing net income through cost-cutting policies; or a combination of changes.

Exhibit 5–20 summarizes the financial ratios that have been discussed. Financial ratios as a group often are evaluated using time series analysis or cross-section analysis, discussed in the next two sections.

Time Series Analysis

Time series analysis is the study of increases and decreases in variables over time. A knowledge of trends or other relationships among variables should permit increased precision in the estimation of future levels of these variables, provided that past relationships continue into the future. Time series analysis can be applied to many of the ratios discussed in this appendix, as well as to net earnings and cash flow measures. Time series analysis often is combined with cross-section analysis in the development of investment strategies.

Cross-Section Analysis

Analysts often compare the operating results or financial condition of one company with those of other companies in the same industry, or of companies in different industries during the same period. This type of analysis is known as *cross-section analysis,* or *comparative analysis.* Although cross-section analysis is widely used, the technique has several potential problems. For example, the operating results of some companies may be interdependent, especially when they are in the same industry. Also, similar companies may use different accounting techniques, which makes comparisons difficult. In addition, economies of scale or other economic factors may affect different companies differently.

Another problem with cross-section analysis arises when industry average ratios are used for comparative purposes. This practice implies that the industry level of performance is desirable. Although that may be true, entire industries sometimes do poorly, as was the case in the mid-1980s in the oil and gas industry. Such comparisons do provide a benchmark for assessing how well a particular company's management has performed in relation to others in the industry. And because many enterprises operate in several industries, deciding which industry is the appropriate one for comparisons may be difficult or impossible. For example, the hypothetical Commex Company had operations in several industries.

A company should be compared with other companies that have the same general characteristics, such as products, markets, and size. Care also should be taken to ensure that companies that are compared are as similar as possible in terms of their accounting techniques, capital structure, and other variables. While matching companies perfectly for comparative purposes is virtually impossible, reasonably valid conclusions can be drawn from a comparison of companies that are reasonably well matched. One must remember that many industry ratios are not weighted for the size of member companies; a large multinational company may be weighted equally with a regional company. Very likely the requirements for success of a multinational company differ substantially from those for the success of a regional company. Analysts must consider issues such as these in order to maximize the value of cross-section analysis when industry average ratios are used for comparison.

| EXHIBIT 5–20 | Summary of Financial Ratios |

Evaluating Financial Strength

Ratio	Formula for Calculation
Liquidity ratios:	
Current ratio	$\dfrac{\text{Current assets}}{\text{Current liabilities}}$
Quick ratio..................................	$\dfrac{\text{Cash} + \text{Short-term marketable securities} + \text{Net short-term receivables}}{\text{Current liabilities}}$
Defensive interval	$\dfrac{\text{Cash} + \text{Short-term marketable securities} + \text{Net short-term receivables}}{\text{Average daily expenditures for operations}}$
Activity or turnover ratios:	
Inventory turnover	$\dfrac{\text{Cost of goods sold}}{\text{Average inventory}}$
Accounts receivable turnover	$\dfrac{\text{Net sales}}{\text{Average net accounts receivable}}$
Total assets turnover	$\dfrac{\text{Net sales}}{\text{Average total assets}}$
Leverage ratios:	
Total liabilities to total assets	$\dfrac{\text{Total liabilities}}{\text{Total assets}}$
Times interest earned	$\dfrac{\text{Income before taxes} + \text{Interest expense}}{\text{Interest expense}}$

Limitations of Ratio Analysis

Ratio analysis is a popular technique for analyzing financial statements because ratios are simple to calculate, convenient to use, and widely published. In addition, ratios provide some types of financial information much more effectively than does study of the line item amounts reported in the financial statements. However, users of financial statements must be aware of the limitations of ratio analysis so that financial ratios are not inappropriately emphasized while other types of financial information are overlooked or underutilized.

As was indicated earlier, one factor that limits the usefulness of ratio analysis is that not all companies use the same accounting principles and practices. A variety of accounting practices are used in several areas, such as:

1. Inventory accounting (LIFO, FIFO, average cost, etc.).
2. Depreciation method (double-declining balance, straight-line, etc.).
3. Capitalizing versus expensing of various expenditures.
4. Bases for accounting for investments in stocks (cost, equity, fair value).

Differences among companies in accounting for these and other items make care in the use of intercompany ratio comparisons essential. Accounting data should be adjusted for differences in accounting practices among companies whenever possible.

Because ratios can be calculated precisely, greater precision may be attached to financial ratios than exists in the data used in their calculation. Ratios can be no

Evaluating Profitability

Ratio	Formula for Calculation
Profitability ratios:	
Profit margin on sales	$\dfrac{\text{Net income}}{\text{Net sales}}$
Net operating margin	$\dfrac{\text{Operating income}}{\text{Net sales}}$
Return on total assets	$\dfrac{\text{Net income}}{\text{Average total assets}}$
Return on total assets (income before interest expense)	$\dfrac{\text{Net income + Interest expense(1 - Tax rate)}}{\text{Average total assets}}$
Return on stockholders' equity	$\dfrac{\text{Net income - Preferred dividends}}{\text{Average common stockholders' equity}}$
Earnings per share	$\dfrac{\text{Net income - Senior claims on earnings}}{\text{Weighted average number of common shares}}$
Price-earnings ratio	$\dfrac{\text{Market price per share of stock}}{\text{Earnings per share}}$
Dividend yield	$\dfrac{\text{Cash dividend per common share}}{\text{Market price per share of stock}}$
Dividend payout ratio	$\dfrac{\text{Cash dividends}}{\text{Net income - Preferred dividends}}$
Book value per share	$\dfrac{\text{Common stockholders' equity}}{\text{Number of common shares outstanding}}$

more precise than the accounting data used in their calculation. Because accounting data often are based on judgments, estimations, and allocations, ratios based on accounting data will be affected by those same factors. Ratios are also sensitive to management policies, and are affected by the particular accounting practices used by a company.

Furthermore, the accounting data used in ratios generally are not based on current values. In the modified historical cost system, judgments, estimations, and allocations cause the amounts for many items, particularly assets, to differ significantly from current values in many cases.

Note also that some financial ratios provide information about different aspects of a company and its operations *at a point in time.* Since companies operate continuously and in a changing environment, those ratios have the same deficiencies in describing a company as snapshots do in describing a running event at a track meet.

Recall that individual financial ratios should not be used in isolation. A broader perspective on a company is needed than is provided by a single ratio in isolation. Because many financial ratios are correlated with other ratios, a change in one may affect several others.

Finally, ratio analysis is only one of several types of financial statement analysis, and a company's annual financial statements are only one of several sources of information about that company. Proper evaluation of a company's economic status and its potential for future success must include attention to all available sources of information.

Q 5-1. What is the relationship between the fundamental accounting equation, the balance sheet, and cash flows of an entity?

Q 5-2. What are liquidity and financial flexibility, and how does the balance sheet provide information useful for the assessment of liquidity and financial flexibility?

Q 5-3. Does a balance sheet show the fair value of an entity? Explain.

Q 5-4. Why is a reasonably standard classification system, consistently applied, important in financial statements?

Q 5-5. What classifications typically are presented in a balance sheet? Describe them briefly.

Q 5-6. What are current assets, current liabilities, and working capital, and what are their roles in an economic entity?

Q 5-7. Current assets are valued variously at their face amount, cost, net realizable value, and lower of cost or market. Why?

Q 5-8. What is the typical order of presentation of current assets for statement presentation purposes? Why?

Q 5-9. How do inventories in a manufacturing concern differ from inventories for a wholesale or retail concern?

Q 5-10. What is the justification for classifying prepaid expenses as current assets?

Q 5-11. What is the theoretically correct valuation of a monetary obligation? Why are current liabilities typically not recorded at their theoretically correct valuation?

Q 5-12. What are accrued liabilities? Give three examples.

Q 5-13. What are four major categories within the property, plant, and equipment classification?

Q 5-14. How do tangible assets differ from intangible assets?

Q 5-15. Why is the classification *other assets* necessary?

Q 5-16. Does the valuation approach for long-term liabilities differ from that for current liabilities? Explain.

Q 5-17. Define *contingency,* identifying the three essential elements of the definition.

Q 5-18. What three ways are available to account for and report loss contingencies?

Q 5-19. Identify the two conditions that must be satisfied before it is proper to accrue an estimated loss from a loss contingency.

Q 5-20. What are the two basic categories of owners' equity in a corporation? Describe each category and explain the reason for the distinction.

Q 5-21. What is the purpose of a statement of retained earnings?

Q 5-22. What is a prior period adjustment? How should prior period adjustments be reported in financial statements?

Q 5-23. What is the purpose of a statement of stockholders' equity (statement of changes in equity)?

Q 5-24. Why do footnotes and supplementary schedules always accompany financial statements?

Q 5-25. What are accounting policies? Why is it important that they be disclosed?

Q 5-26. What are three balance sheet items for which the accounting policies would probably be disclosed in the summary of significant accounting policies?

Q 5-27. What is a subsequent (poststatement) event? Under what conditions would a subsequent event require accrual as of the statement date?

*****Q 5-28.** Distinguish between horizontal and vertical percentage analyses.

*****Q 5-29.** What is the primary objective of vertical analysis?

*****Q 5-30.** Most financial ratios can be classified as one of four types of ratios. What are the four general types of financial ratios, and what sort of information is provided by each general type of ratio?

*****Q 5-31.** Name, and write the formulas for, financial ratios that can be used to evaluate the short-term liquidity of a company.

*Q 5-32. What information is provided by turnover ratios? Name three commonly used turnover ratios.

*Q 5-33. Explain how the accounts receivable turnover ratio and the inventory turnover ratio can be used to estimate a company's operating cycle.

*Q 5-34. What information is provided by leverage ratios?

*Q 5-35. Explain why creditors and investors usually prefer that the total liabilities to total assets ratio not be too high.

*Q 5-36. Write the formulas for at least four profitability ratios. Explain what an analyst might learn from each of the ratios you have listed.

*Q 5-37. What is meant by the term *trading on the equity*?

*Q 5-38. Explain the DuPont method.

*Q 5-39. Describe some of the problems that may be associated with cross-section analysis.

*Q 5-40. Discuss the limitations of ratio analysis.

CASES   Cases marked with an asterisk (*) refer to Appendix 5–1.

C 5-1. **ENTITY VALUATION VERSUS ASSET VALUATION**   The following statement has been taken with some modification from the accounting literature:

> If the value of an entity were to be determined by calculating the sum of the present values of the marginal (or incremental) expected net receipts of individual tangible and intangible assets, the resulting valuation would tend to be less than if the value were determined by calculating the present value of total expected net receipts for the entire entity (that is, the resulting valuation of parts would yield a sum that was less than that for the whole). This would be true even if the same pattern of interest or discount rates were used for both valuations.

REQUIRED Evaluate the above statement, indicating and explaining your agreement or disagreement with each point made.

(AICPA, adapted)

C 5-2.   **FINANCIAL STATEMENT PRESENTATION** The following year-end financial statements were prepared by the Morley Corporation's bookkeeper. The Morley Corporation operates a chain of retail stores.

Morley Corporation
Balance Sheet
As of June 30, 1998

Assets:			
Current assets:			
Cash			$ 100,000
Notes receivable			90,000
Accounts receivable, less reserve for doubtful accounts			75,000
Inventories			395,500
Investment securities			100,000
Total current assets			$ 760,500
Property, plant, and equipment:			
Land (at cost) (Note 1)		$175,000	
Buildings, at cost less accumulated depreciation of $350,000		500,000	
Equipment, at cost less accumulated depreciation of $180,000		400,000	1,075,000
Intangibles			450,000
Other assets:			
Prepaid expenses			6,405
Total assets			$2,291,905
Liabilities and owners' equity:			
Current liabilities:			
Accounts payable			$ 100,500
Estimated income taxes payable			160,000
Total current liabilities			$ 260,500
Long-term liabilities:			
9% serial bonds, $50,000 due annually on December 31			
Maturity value		$850,000	
Less unamortized discount		(35,000)	815,000
Total liabilities			$1,075,500
Owners' equity:			
Common stock, stated value $10 (authorized and issued, 75,000 shares)		$750,000	
Retained earnings:			
Appropriated (Note 2)	$110,000		
Free	356,405	466,405	1,216,405
Total liabilities and owners' equity			$2,291,905

Morley Corporation
Income Statement
For the Year Ended June 30, 1998

Sales			$2,500,000
Interest revenue			6,000
Total revenue			$2,506,000
Cost of goods sold			(1,780,000)
Gross margin			$ 726,000
Operating expenses:			
Selling expenses:			
Salaries..................................	$95,000		
Advertising	85,000		
Sales returns and allowances	50,000	$230,000	
General and administrative expenses:			
Salaries..................................	$84,000		
Property taxes	38,000		
Depreciation and amortization	86,000		
Rent....................................	75,000		
Interest on serial bonds	48,000	331,000	(561,000)
Income before income taxes			$ 165,000
Income taxes			(160,000)
Net income			$ 5,000

FOOTNOTES TO FINANCIAL STATEMENTS

1. Includes a future store site acquired during the year at a cost of $75,000.
2. Retained earnings in the amount of $110,000 have been set aside to finance expansion.

REQUIRED   Identify and discuss the defects in the financial statements above with respect to terminology, disclosures, and classification. Your discussion should explain why you consider them to be defects.

(AICPA, adapted)

C 5-3.   **CURRENT ASSET AND CURRENT LIABILITY CLASSIFICATION** Below are the account titles of a number of debit and credit accounts as they might appear on the balance sheet of Tammy Corporation as of October 31, 1998.

DEBITS

Cash in bank	Goodwill
Land	Inventory of finished goods
Patents	Inventory of work in process
Cash and U.S. government bonds	Inventory of operating parts and supplies
set aside for property additions	Inventory of raw materials
Investment in subsidiary	Interest accrued on U.S. government
Accounts receivable	securities
U.S. government contracts	Notes receivable
Regular	Petty cash fund
Installments, due in 1998	U.S. government securities
Installments, due in 1999–2000	Treasury stock

CREDITS

Accrued payroll	9 1/2% first mortgage bonds due in 2005
Notes payable	Preferred stock dividend, payable
Accrued interest on bonds	November 1, 1998
Accumulated depreciation	Allowance for doubtful accounts
Accounts payable	Provision for federal income taxes
Capital in excess of par	Customers' advances (on contracts to be
Accrued interest on notes payable	completed in 1999)
8% first mortgage bonds to be redeemed	Officers' 1998 bonus accrued
in 1998 out of current assets	
Capital stock, preferred	

REQUIRED   Select the current asset and current liability items from among these debits and credits. If there appear to be certain borderline cases that you are unable to classify without further information, give your reasons for making questionable classifications, if any.

(AICPA, adapted)

C 5-4.   **LOSS CONTINGENCIES**   The following three independent sets of facts relate to the possible accrual of a loss contingency or its possible disclosure by other means.

Situation 1:   A company has adopted a policy of recording self-insurance for any possible losses resulting from injury to others by its vehicles. The premium for an insurance policy for the same risk from an independent insurance company would have an annual cost of $2,000. During the period covered by the financial statements, there were no accidents involving the company's vehicles which resulted in injury to others.

Situation 2:   A company offers a one-year warranty for the product that it manufactures. A history of warranty claims has been compiled and the probable amount of claims related to sales for a given period can be determined.

Situation 3:   After the date of a set of financial statements but before they have been issued, a company enters into a contract that will probably result in a significant loss to it. The amount of the loss can be reasonably estimated.

REQUIRED   For each of the three independent sets of facts above, describe the accrual or type of disclosure necessary (if any) and the reason why such disclosure is appropriate.

(AICPA, adapted)

C 5-5.   **ETHICS; LOSS CONTINGENCIES**   Searfoss Oil Company is one of the largest independent oil and gas producing companies in the United States. Even though Searfoss has a clean record with respect to oil spill occurrences, insurance coverage for such an event is prohibitive because of recent industrywide spills and increased insurance claims. Therefore, Searfoss established a policy several years ago to self-insure against possible losses resulting from its involvement in oil spills. Searfoss charged earnings on a systematic basis as if it were expensing an insurance premium. It established a corresponding contingent liability against which actual losses would be charged. The contingent liability account had a $2 million balance at December 31, 1998.

Gleason and Company recently contracted with Searfoss Oil to conduct an audit of the financial statements for the year ended December 31, 1998. Gleason was awarded the contract after a competitive bidding process was instituted by Searfoss to replace its prior auditors. Gleason noted during the course of its audit that Searfoss's accounting for self-insurance was not proper. The auditors suggested that any losses resulting from oil spills should be recorded in the period incurred, because it is only at this point that an asset has been impaired or a liability incurred and a reasonable estimate of loss can be made.

Searfoss's chief financial officer, Sara Kenny, disagreed with the auditors' opinion. Kenny stated that the accrual approach to self-insurance was generally accepted and widely used in the industry. This approach simply spread out the potential expense over current and future periods. According to Kenny, Searfoss follows a similar approach in accounting for other contingencies such as potential bad debts.

In an attempt to reach a compromise on the issue, the auditors suggested that retained earnings could be appropriated over time to match anticipated future losses.

This suggestion did not appease Kenny, who informed the auditors that Searfoss would not compromise on the issue. The auditors were asked to reconsider their position in light of the fact that the accrual approach to self-insurance had been used for many years.

REQUIRED   What ethical and professional concerns exist for Gleason and Company in deciding whether to go along with Searfoss Oil's accounting for self-insurance? Assume that you were asked to advise Gleason and Company on a proper course of action. What would your recommendation be?

C 5-6.   **SUBSEQUENT EVENTS**   The following events and transactions related to Solomon Company occurred after the balance sheet date of December 31, 1998, and before the financial statements were issued in 1999. None of the items is reflected in the financial statements as of December 31, 1998.

a) In order to secure a bank loan of $50,000, Solomon pledged as collateral certain fixed assets with a net book value of $100,000. Solomon applied for the loan on December 20, 1998, and the bank approved the loan on January 10, 1999.

b) On November 31, 1998, Solomon initiated a lawsuit seeking $400,000 in damages from a firm that Solomon claims infringed on one of its patents. Solomon's attorneys have stated that the chances of winning and of getting the $400,000 are "excellent."

c) On March 3, 1999, the IRS assessed Solomon an additional $200,000 for the 1996 tax year. However, both the tax attorneys for Solomon and the tax accountants have indicated that it is likely that the IRS will agree to a $150,000 settlement.

d) On March 1, 1999, Solomon issued bonds at an interest rate 2 percentage points above the prime rate.

e) A warehouse containing a substantial portion of Solomon's inventory was destroyed by fire on February 7, 1999.

f) A supplier to whom Solomon owes $10,000 declared bankruptcy on February 2, 1999.

REQUIRED   Prepare a memorandum describing the appropriate accounting and reporting for each of the above items in the financial statements and related notes as of December 31, 1998. Treat each item independently.

C 5-7.   **SUBSEQUENT EVENTS**   There are three types of reporting available for subsequent (post-statement) events:

1. Adjust amounts in financial statements.
2. Disclose but not adjust.
3. Neither disclose nor adjust.

The following subsequent events must fit into one of the three categories listed above:

a) Issuance of a significant amount of common stock.
b) Retirement of the company treasurer.
c) Material loss on the sale of marketable securities.
d) Settlement of litigation against the company when the event giving rise to the claim took place prior to the balance sheet date.
e) Employee strike.
f) Material loss on a receivable due to a customer's bankruptcy.
g) Introduction of a new product line.
h) Loss of a warehouse and contents due to fire.
i) Settlement of a federal income tax obligation at considerably more than anticipated at year-end.
j) Sale of a significant portion of the company's assets.

REQUIRED   Describe the appropriate treatment of each item.

C 5-8.   **DISCLOSURES**   The preliminary draft of the statement of financial position at the end of the current fiscal year for Falcon Industries follows. The statement will be incorporated into the annual report to stockholders and will present the dollar amounts at the end of both the current and prior years on a side-by-side comparative basis. The accounts in the statement are properly classified, and the dollar amounts have been determined in accordance with generally accepted accounting principles. The company does not intend to provide any more detailed information in the body of the statement.

Falcon Industries
Statement of Financial Position
November 30, 1998
(in millions)

Assets:
  Current assets:

Cash	$ 9.0
Short-term investments	4.5
Accounts receivable—trade (net)	75.3
Inventories	152.0
Prepayments and other	3.2
Total current assets	$244.0
Investments in equity securities (available for sale)	36.8
Plant, property, and equipment (net)	524.7
Total assets	$805.5

Liabilities and stockholders' equity:
  Current liabilities:

Current maturities on long-term debt	$ 24.3
Notes payable	53.0
Accounts payable	93.2
Accrued taxes	28.2
Accrued interest	7.3
Other	2.9
Total current liabilities	$208.9
Long-term debt	318.1
Total liabilities	$527.0

Stockholders' equity:

Preferred stock	$ 20.0
Common stock	51.3
Paid-in capital on common stock	43.6
Retained earnings—appropriated	27.2
Retained earnings—unappropriated	136.4
Total stockholders' equity	$278.5
Total liabilities and stockholders' equity	$805.5

REQUIRED   Identify the accounts that most likely would require further disclosure in the notes to the financial statements, and describe what information would have to be disclosed in those notes by Falcon Industries before the statement can be included as part of the annual report for presentation to its stockholders.

(IMA, adapted)

*C 5-9.   **INFORMATION PROVIDED BY FINANCIAL RATIOS** Information provided by several financial ratios is given below.
  a) Primary test of solvency.
  b) A more severe test of immediate solvency.
  c) Measures efficiency of collection of accounts receivable.
  d) Indicates liquidity of inventory.
  e) Measures use of total assets.
  f) Indicates ability to protect creditor interests.
  g) Indicates net productivity of each sales dollar.
  h) Measures success at maximizing common stockholders' return.
  i) Indicates the long-term growth potential of the company.

j) Useful for determining the company's ability to make annual interest payments.

REQUIRED
1. Name the financial ratio that provides each of the above pieces of information and give the formula for calculating that ratio.
2. For each ratio named in part 1, indicate what a high or low value of the ratio may mean.

*C 5-10. **SOLVENCY RATIOS** As the CPA responsible for an "opinion" audit engagement, you are requested by the client to organize the work to provide him at the earliest possible date with some key ratios based on the final figures appearing on the comparative financial statements. This information is to be used to convince creditors that the client business is solvent and to support the use of going concern valuation procedures in the financial statements. The client wishes to save time by concentrating on only these key data.

The data requested and the calculations taken from the financial statements follow:

	LAST YEAR	THIS YEAR
Current ratio	2.0:1	2.5:1
Quick (acid-test) ratio	1.2:1	.7:1
Property, plant, and equipment to owners' equity	2.3:1	2.6:1
Sales to owners' equity	2.8:1	2.5:1
Net income	Down 10%[a]	Up 30%[a]
Earnings per common share	$2.40	$3.12
Book value per common share	Up 8%[a]	Up 5%[a]

[a]As compared with the previous year.

REQUIRED
1. The client asks that you prepare comments stating how each of these items supports the solvency and going concern potential of his business. He wishes to use these comments to support his presentation of data to his creditors. Prepare the comments as requested, giving the implications and the limitations of each item separately and then the collective inference one may draw from them about the client's solvency and going concern potential.
2. Having done as the client requested in part 1, prepare a listing of additional ratio analysis data for this client which you think his creditors are going to ask for to supplement the data provided in part 1. Explain why you think the additional data will help these creditors to evaluate this client's solvency.
3. What warnings should you offer these creditors about the limitations of ratio analysis for the purpose stated here?

(AICPA, adapted)

E 5-1.   BALANCE SHEET CLASSIFICATION   The following classification scheme typically is used in the preparation of a balance sheet:

a) Current assets.
b) Investments and funds.
c) Property, plant, and equipment.
d) Intangible assets.
e) Other assets.
f) Current liabilities.
g) Long-term liabilities.
h) Contributed capital.
i) Retained earnings.

Using the letters above and the format below, indicate the category in which an entity typically would place each of the following items. Indicate a contra account by inserting a dash before the letter.

____ Income taxes payable
____ Goodwill
____ Bonds payable (due in eight years)
____ Petty cash
____ Trade accounts receivable
____ Investment in subsidiary
____ Accrued wages
____ Patents
____ Raw materials inventory
____ Mortgage payable
____ Preferred stock

____ Accounts payable
____ Organization costs
____ Premium on common stock
____ Buildings
____ Bond sinking fund
____ Cash
____ Deferred rearrangement costs
____ Accumulated depreciation
____ Discount on bonds payable
____ Land (held for speculative purposes)
____ Prepaid expenses

E 5-2.   BALANCE SHEET CLASSIFICATION   The following classification scheme typically is used in the preparation of a balance sheet:

a) Current assets.
b) Investments and funds.
c) Property, plant, and equipment.
d) Intangible assets.
e) Other assets.
f) Current liabilities.
g) Long-term liabilities.
h) Contributed capital.
i) Retained earnings.

Using the letters above and the format below, indicate the balance sheet category in which an entity typically would place each of the following items. Indicate a contra account by inserting a dash before the letter.

____ Long-term receivables
____ Accumulated amortization
____ Current maturities of long-term debt
____ Notes payable (short-term)
____ Accrued payroll taxes
____ Leasehold improvements
____ Retained earnings appropriated for plant expansion
____ Machinery
____ Donated capital
____ Deferred tax liability (long-term)

____ Allowance for uncollectible accounts
____ Premium on bonds payable
____ Supplies inventory
____ Additional paid-in capital
____ Work-in-process inventory
____ Notes receivable (short-term)
____ Copyrights
____ Unearned revenue (long-term)
____ Inventory
____ Short-term investments

E 5-3.   BALANCE SHEET CLASSIFICATION   Answer each of the following multiple-choice questions related to balance sheet items and justify your answer.

1. An example of an item that is not an element of working capital is:
   a) Goods in process.
   b) Short-term investments.
   c) Accrued interest on notes receivable.
   d) Treasury stock.
2. The test of marketability must be met before an entity can classify securities owned as:
   a) Bonds payable.
   b) Treasury stock.
   c) Long-term investments.
   d) Current assets.

3. An example of an item that is not a liability is:
   a) The portion of long-term debt due within one year.
   b) Advances from customers on contracts.
   c) Accrued estimated warranty costs.
   d) Dividends payable in the corporation's own stock.

E 5-4. **BALANCE SHEET CLASSIFICATION** Forsyth Corporation has the following items that must be included in the balance sheet:
   a) Advances from customers.
   b) Temporary investment in U.S. Treasury bills.
   c) Accrued payroll.
   d) Land held for possible future expansion.
   e) Fund for plant expansion.
   f) Allowance for doubtful accounts.
   g) Accumulated depreciation.
   h) Goodwill.
   i) Supplies inventory.
   j) Prepaid expenses.

REQUIRED Indicate the appropriate balance sheet classification of each of the items.

E 5-5. **BALANCE SHEET CLASSIFICATION** Guidry Corporation has the following items that must be included in its balance sheet:
   a) Guidry Corporation common stock outstanding, par value.
   b) Dividends payable.
   c) Bonds payable, maturing three years from the balance sheet date.
   d) Machinery used in operations.
   e) Patent.
   f) Idle plant for which there is no intent of future use.
   g) Investment in subsidiary.
   h) Raw materials inventory.
   i) Short-term investment in marketable securities.
   j) Leasehold improvements.

REQUIRED Indicate the appropriate balance sheet classification for each of the items.

E 5-6. **BALANCE SHEET PREPARATION** Following is a list of items taken from the December 31, 1998, balance sheet of Nix Company (amounts omitted):

Work-in-process inventory	Prepaid expenses
Buildings	Accrued expenses
Cash	Income taxes payable
Notes payable to banks (short-term)	Preferred stock
Raw materials	Contributed capital in excess of par
Allowance for depreciation—buildings	Machinery and equipment
Deferred tax liability (noncurrent)	Finished products inventory
Current portion of long-term debt	Trade accounts receivable
Land	Bonds payable
Short-term investments	Allowance for depreciation—machinery and
Deferred charges	equipment
Retained earnings	Goodwill
Accounts payable	Common stock

REQUIRED Using the above information, prepare a balance sheet in account form.

E 5-7. **BALANCE SHEET PREPARATION** Olsen Photo, Inc., had the following balance sheet items at December 31, 1998 (amounts omitted):

Inventories	Notes payable (noncurrent)
Accumulated depreciation	Picture island kiosks (film drop centers)
Deferred expenses	Goodwill
Machinery and equipment	Deferred revenues (current)
Accounts payable	Notes receivable (current)
Allowance for bad debts	Notes payable (short-term)
Land	Common stock
Current maturities of notes payable	Notes receivable (noncurrent)
Preferred stock	Accrued liabilities
Automobiles and trucks	Amounts payable under noncompetition
Accrued income taxes	agreements (noncurrent)
Prepaid expenses	Additional paid-in capital
Accounts receivable	Furniture and fixtures
Life insurance loans payable (long-term)	Retained earnings
Leasehold improvements	Cash
Refundable federal income taxes	Buildings

REQUIRED Using the above information, prepare a balance sheet in account form.

E 5-8. **EFFECT OF TRANSACTIONS ON BALANCE SHEET** Using the following format, indicate the effect on assets, liabilities, and stockholders' equity of the items set forth below. For no change, indicate 0; for increase, +; for decrease, –.

	ASSETS	LIABILITIES	STOCKHOLDERS' EQUITY
a) Declaration of a cash dividend.			
b) Payment of cash dividend in *a*.			
c) Retirement of bond liability by issuance of stock.			
d) Issuance of shares for land to be held as an investment.			
e) Issuance of shares for cash.			

E 5-9. **BALANCE SHEET FORMAT** The following balance sheet, which has some weaknesses in terminology and classification, has been submitted to you for review:

Ramanan Company
Balance Sheet
As of 12/31/98
(*in thousands*)

Assets:
  Fixed assets—tangible:

Land	$300	
Buildings and equipment	120	
Less: Reserve for depreciation	(40)	$380
Factory supplies		30

  Current assets:

Inventory	$ 97	
Accounts receivable	52	
Cash	43	192

  Fixed assets—intangibles:

Patents	$ 37	
Goodwill	26	63

  Deferred charges:

Discount on bonds payable	$ 5	
Returnable containers	21	26
Total assets		$691

Liabilities:
  Current liabilities:

Accounts payable	$ 80	
Allowance for doubtful accounts	6	
Wages payable	100	$186

  Long-term liabilities:

Bonds payable	$200	
Reserve for contingencies	50	250

  Equity:

Capital stock, $5 par value, 10,000 shares issued and outstanding	$ 50	
Capital surplus	34	
Earned surplus	196	
Dividends paid	(25)	255
Total liabilities		$691

REQUIRED Prepare a corrected balance sheet in report form.

E 5-10. **ACCOUNTING FOR A LOSS CONTINGENCY** Neyhart Corporation, a manufacturer of automobile tires, is preparing annual financial statements as of December 31, 1998. Because of a recently identified flaw in one of its specialty tires, the government has clearly indicated that Neyhart will be required to recall all of the specialty tires sold in the last six months. Neyhart's management estimates that this recall will cost $2.5 million.

REQUIRED **1.** What accounting recognition, if any, should be given to this situation?
2. Assume the situation justifies accrual of a loss contingency. Prepare the appropriate accrual entry.

E 5-11. **FOOTNOTE DISCLOSURES; PROPERTY, PLANT, AND EQUIPMENT** Robinson Corporation's presentation of property, plant, and equipment in its December 31, 1998, balance sheet was as follows:

Property, plant, and equipment, at cost:

Land	$ 18,200,000
Buildings	43,600,000
Machinery and equipment.......................................	26,700,000
Leasehold improvements	14,100,000
	$102,600,000
Less accumulated depreciation and amortization	(38,400,000)
Net property, plant, and equipment	$ 64,200,000

In addition, the following information is available regarding Robinson's property, plant, and equipment assets:

> Robinson capitalizes property, plant, and equipment expenditures expected to benefit future periods, including major renewals and betterments. Ordinary repairs and maintenance expenditures are charged to expense as incurred. Equipment and machinery have been acquired regularly over the years of the company's existence. In general, the buildings are well maintained and are expected to be serviceable for many years. The assets are recorded at cost and then depreciated or amortized, after considering estimated salvage value, over their estimated useful lives, primarily using the straight-line method. Buildings are depreciated over 20 to 40 years, and machinery and equipment is depreciated over 5 to 15 years. Leasehold improvements are amortized over the shorter of the lease term or the life of the improvement. Most of the leasehold improvements are amortized over the lease term.

REQUIRED Prepare the note related to property, plant, and equipment for Robinson Corporation.

E 5-12. **SUBSEQUENT EVENTS** Assume the following events occurred after the end of a company's fiscal year and before the annual report was released:
a) Settlement of a major lawsuit against the company related to events that occurred three years ago.
b) Loss of a significant portion of the plant due to earthquake damage.
c) Issuance of common stock.
d) Expropriation of significant operations in a foreign country, with proceeds significantly less than anticipated at year-end.
e) Resignation of the president and chief executive officer.

REQUIRED Indicate how each item should be accounted for and reported in the company's financial statements for the fiscal year preceding the occurrence of the event.

E 5-13. **SUBSEQUENT EVENTS** Assume the following events occurred after the end of a company's fiscal year and before the annual report was released:
a) A significant, unanticipated increase in the rate of inflation, which will adversely affect the profitability of the company.
b) Introduction of a major new product line.
c) Bankruptcy and loss of a major customer.
d) Out-of-court settlement of litigation arising from an event that occurred immediately after the end of the fiscal year.
e) Acquisition of a significant block of outstanding shares of the company's own common stock.

REQUIRED Indicate how each item should be accounted for and reported in the company's financial statements for the fiscal year preceding the occurrence of the event.

*E 5-14. **HORIZONTAL AND VERTICAL ANALYSIS** Barton, Inc., manufactures and sells portable radios. Condensed comparative income statements for 1997 and 1998 are as follows:

Barton, Inc.
Comparative Income Statements

	1998	1997
Sales	$486,100	$305,200
Sales returns	(20,400)	(6,100)
Beginning inventories	131,250	110,100
Cost of manufactured radios	291,600	143,700
Ending inventories	(160,400)	(131,250)
Cost of goods sold	262,450	122,550
Selling expenses	110,000	91,500
Administrative expenses	48,600	45,750
Income before tax	44,650	39,300

REQUIRED

1. Prepare a horizontal percentage analysis using 1997 as the base year. Round each figure to the nearest percentage point.
2. Prepare a vertical percentage analysis for both 1997 and 1998, using sales as the basis for comparison. Round each figure to the nearest percentage point.
3. Barton is concerned with its 1998 profit. On the basis of your analysis in parts 1 and 2, identify those financial statement items that appear to be problem areas for Barton. Give reasons for your choices.

(CGAA, adapted)

*E 5-15. **LIQUIDITY RATIOS** Information from Michelman Company's income statement and balance sheet is as follows:

Loss on sale of building	$ 10,000,000
Cost of goods sold	565,500,000
Selling and administrative expense	121,000,000
Depreciation expense	250,000,000

Current assets:
Cash	$ 2,100,000
Short-term investments	7,500,000
Accounts receivable (net)	40,400,000
Inventories	66,300,000
Prepaid expenses	1,200,000
Total current assets	$117,500,000

Current liabilities:
Notes payable	$ 1,500,000
Accounts payable	19,500,000
Accrued expenses	12,500,000
Income taxes payable	500,000
Payments due within one year on long-term debt	3,500,000
Total current liabilities	$ 37,500,000

REQUIRED Calculate the current ratio, quick ratio, and defensive interval for Michelman Company.

*E 5-16. **TURNOVER RATIOS** Selected information from the accounting records of the Warren Company is as follows:

Net accounts receivable, 12/31/97	$ 900,000
Net accounts receivable, 12/31/98	$1,100,000
Accounts receivable turnover	5:1
Inventories, 12/31/97	$1,100,000
Inventories, 12/31/98	$1,300,000
Inventory turnover	4:1

REQUIRED   **I.** Calculate Warren's gross margin for 1998.

            2. Assuming a business year consisting of 300 days, what was the number of days' sales in average receivables for 1998 and the number of days' sales in average inventories for 1998?

            (AICPA, adapted)

*E 5-17. **CALCULATING PROFITABILITY RATIOS**   As of December 31, 1997, Weber Company had 100,000 shares of $10 par value common stock issued and outstanding. There was no change in the number of shares outstanding during 1998. Total stockholders' equity as of December 31, 1998, was $2.8 million. The net income for the year ended December 31, 1998, was $900,000. During 1998, Weber Company paid $3 per share in dividends on its common stock. The quoted market price of Weber's common stock on a national stock exchange was $20 on December 31, 1997, and $28 on December 31, 1998.

REQUIRED   Calculate the price-earnings ratio, dividend yield, dividend payout, and estimated common stockholders' return for 1998.

            (AICPA, adapted)

*E 5-18. **CALCULATING BOOK VALUE PER SHARE OF COMMON STOCK**   Swayze Corporation's stockholders' equity as of June 30, 1998, consisted of the following:

Preferred stock, 10%, $50 par value: liquidating value,
  $55 per share; 20,000 shares issued and outstanding **$1,000,000**
Common stock, $10 par value: 500,000 shares authorized;
  300,000 shares issued and outstanding **3,000,000**
Retained earnings **400,000**

REQUIRED   What is Swayze Corporation's book value per share of common stock at June 30, 1998?

            (AICPA, adapted)

*E 5-19. **COMPONENTS OF FINANCIAL RATIOS**   The following information has been taken from the financial statements of Hassell Company:

Current assets **$200,000**
Current liabilities **$100,000**
Common stock **$100,000**
Retained earnings **$100,000**
Long-term debt to stockholders' equity . . . .   **.5:1**
Inventory turnover . . . . **9 times per year**
Gross margin . . . .   **.10**
Acid-test ratio **1:1**
Average collection period . . . .   **18 days**
Sales **$1,000,000**

REQUIRED   Assuming a 360-day year and that all sales are on credit, determine the amounts of the following items:

            I. Cash.
            2. Average accounts receivable.
            3. Average inventory.
            4. Long-term debt.

            (CGAA, adapted)

Problems marked with an asterisk (*) refer to Appendixes B and/or 5–1.

P 5-I. **BALANCE SHEET PREPARATION** Schroeder Company had the following account balances at December 31, 1998 (in thousands of dollars):

	DEBIT	CREDIT
Inventories	$ 7,576	
Furniture and office equipment	317	
Investments (noncurrent)	5,408	
Notes payable (long-term)		$ 300
Additional paid-in capital		792
Prepaid expenses	729	
Short-term investments	3,877	
Accumulated depreciation—buildings		3,014
Unearned revenues (long-term)		1,384
Bonds payable		679
Land improvements	719	
Accumulated depreciation—furniture and office equipment		161
Leasehold improvements (net of amortization)	22	
Accumulated depreciation—machinery and equipment		9,832
Special tools	992	
Preferred stock		283
Unearned revenues (current)		94
Common stock		480
Accounts payable		4,612
Machinery and equipment	14,434	
Cash	177	
Retained earnings		?
Accounts receivable	1,624	
Accumulated depreciation—land improvements		431
Land	268	
Income taxes payable		944
Notes receivable	4,007	
Buildings	9,975	
Accrued liabilities		6,113
Allowance for bad debts		7

REQUIRED Prepare a balance sheet in account form.

P 5-2.   **BALANCE SHEET AND INCOME STATEMENT PREPARATION**   The accounts of DeBerg Industries, Inc., at December 31, 1998, disclose the following information (credits in parentheses; all amounts in thousands of dollars):

Goodwill	$ 59,558
Contributed capital in excess of par	(100,967)
Lease obligations (long-term)	(39,036)
Selling, general, and administrative expenses	174,126
Accounts receivable	182,879
Investment property	19,110
Allowance for doubtful notes	(7,007)
Cash	50,351
Retained earnings	(127,822)
Trucks, tractors, trailers	95,749
Accounts payable	(135,383)
Net sales	(1,643,364)
Income taxes payable	(18,393)
Interest expense	34,172
Allowance for doubtful accounts	(6,363)
Inventories	169,198
Accrued liabilities	(88,084)
Cost of goods sold	1,283,978
Notes payable (current)	(11,241)
Terminals and improvements	39,490
Bonds payable (long-term)	(203,258)
Income tax expense	26,523
Buildings and improvements	88,034
Prepaid expenses	8,294
Notes receivable (noncurrent)	31,536
Deferred tax liability (noncurrent)	(11,761)
Land (used in operations)	21,499
Other assets	18,029
Other expense (net of other revenue)	5,323
Machinery and equipment	110,955
Preferred stock	(1,980)
Accumulated depreciation (combined)	(129,759)
Common stock	(13,628)

REQUIRED   **1.** Prepare a single-step income statement.
           2. Prepare a balance sheet in account form.

P 5-3. **PREPARATION OF CORRECTED BALANCE SHEET** The following balance sheet has been submitted to you for consideration:

Stolle Corporation
Balance Sheet
For the Year Ended December 31, 1998
(in millions)

Debits:

Inventories	$ 706
Long-term investments	732
Cash and short-term investments	110
Deferred charges and other assets	330
Property, plant, and equipment	5,737
Accounts receivable	641
Prepaid expenses	16
Total	$8,272

Credits:

Retained earnings	$2,165
Pension and other liabilities	277
Accumulated depreciation and amortization	1,937
Accounts payable	500
Accrued and other liabilities	173
Common stock	1,520
Allowance for doubtful accounts	20
Notes payable, short-term	110
Long-term debt	1,570
Total	$8,272

REQUIRED Prepare a balance sheet in report form.

P 5-4.   **PREPARATION OF CORRECTED BALANCE SHEET**   Forest Products, Inc., drafted the following balance sheet:

Forest Products, Inc.
Balance Sheet
For the Year Ended December 31, 1998
(*in thousands*)

Assets:

Refundable income taxes	$ 4,110
Timber and timberlands	17,397
Prepaid expenses	9,113
Cash	14,247
Inventories	86,723
Investments (long-term)	6,530
Receivables	48,394
Machinery and equipment	220,413
Assets held for disposal	2,955
Short-term investments	482
Land	6,956
Long-term receivables	20,101
Buildings	49,670
	$487,091

Equities:

Accounts payable	$ 25,612
Bonds payable	174,542
Allowance for doubtful accounts	1,127
Preferred stock	1,149
Common stock	5,533
Accumulated depreciation	76,868
Notes payable (short-term)	41,000
Contributed capital in excess of par	78,550
Retained earnings	63,257
Accrued payables	19,453
	$487,091

In addition, in reviewing the information underlying the balance sheet, you discover the following:

a) The refundable income taxes relate to income taxes paid in prior years by the company. Although the item is still being contested by the IRS, the company believes there is a reasonable possibility that the amount will be refunded. Therefore, at the end of 1998, it accrued the receivable with a corresponding credit to retained earnings, since the item related to prior years' operations.

b) Of the amount reported as bonds payable, $12,874,000 is due within the next year.

REQUIRED   Prepare a corrected balance sheet in account form.

P 5-5. **PREPARATION OF BALANCE SHEET** Houser Company had the following condensed balance sheet at December 31, 1998.

Houser Company
Statement of Financial Position
As of December 31, 1998
(in thousands)

Current assets	$2,844,292
Property, plant, and equipment, net	1,355,198
Other assets	440,015
	$4,639,505
Current liabilities	$2,477,166
Long-term debt	41,340
Contingencies	—
Stockholders' equity	2,120,999
	$4,639,505

The following information regarding balance sheet items also is available (dollar amounts in thousands):

a) Current assets: cash and short-term investments, $108,056; accounts receivable (net of allowance for doubtful accounts of $14,720), $709,024; contracts in process, $1,133,424; inventories, $726,264; prepaid expenses, $167,524.

b) Property, plant, and equipment: land, $48,644; buildings and leasehold improvements, $711,100; machinery and equipment, $2,108,114; equipment leased to others, $49,183; accumulated depreciation and amortization on all property, plant, and equipment items, $1,561,843.

c) Current liabilities: notes payable and current portion of long-term debt, $911,443; advance payments (less contracts in process of $101,740), $411,754; accounts payable, $439,534; accrued salaries and wages, $203,285; federal and foreign income taxes, $125,636; other accrued expenses, $385,514.

d) Contingencies: Houser is the defendant in numerous court proceedings which are generally incident to the normal course of business. In the opinion of management, the results of such litigation are either indeterminable or will not have a materially adverse effect on the company.

e) Long-term debt consists solely of bonds payable; with unamortized discount of $3,660.

f) Stockholders' equity: preferred stock, no par, authorized, 3 million shares, outstanding, none; common stock, $1 par, authorized, 200 million shares, outstanding, 66,373,000 shares (after deducting treasury shares of 22,361,000), $66,373; additional paid-in capital, $182,808; retained earnings, $1,871,818.

REQUIRED Prepare a corrected balance sheet.

P 5-6. **CONTINGENCIES** Consider the following independent situations:

a) Donnelly Company is being sued for negligence in permitting the local residents to be exposed to highly toxic chemicals from its plant and thereby causing numerous illnesses among them. Donnelly's lawyer states that, as of December 31, 1998, it is probable that Donnelly will lose the suit and be found liable for a judgment, but the amount of the expected judgment is not determinable.

b) George Corporation, a manufacturer of household paints, is preparing annual financial statements. Because of a recently proven health hazard in one of its paints, the government has clearly indicated its intent to order George to recall all cans of this paint sold in the last six months. George's management estimates that this recall will cost $3,000,000.

c) Before the year's financial statements (1998) are issued, a company learns that by the end of its fiscal year it probably will have incurred a liability for obligations related to product warranties. The company can reasonably estimate the amount of the loss involved.

d) Chewning Company sells football helmets. In 1998 Chewning discovered a defect in the helmets, which has produced lawsuits that are reasonably estimated to result in losses of $4 million. On the basis of its own experience and the experience of other enterprises in the business, Chewning considers it probable that additional lawsuits will result in material losses, but the amount of additional losses cannot be reasonably estimated.

e) In January 1995, Munter Corporation purchased a patent for a new consumer product for $200,000. At the time of purchase, the patent was valid for 15 years. Owing to the competitive nature of the product, however, Munter estimated that the patent would have a useful life of only 10 years. During 1998, Munter permanently removed the product from the market because of a potential health hazard present in the product. Munter records amortization in each year, and did so in 1998.

REQUIRED   Indicate the appropriate accounting and disclosure requirements for each of the above situations. All requirements relate to 1998 financial statements.

P 5-7.   **CONTINGENCIES**   Jack's Pizza Company, which sells boxed pizza mixes through grocery stores, encountered the following situations during fiscal 1998:

a) On April 30, Jack's filed a lawsuit against Little Italy Pizza Company for infringing on one of Jack's pizza dough patents. Jack's management believes that the infringement may ultimately cost Jack's as much as $2 million in lost sales. The company's legal counsel, however, expects that proving an infringement may be very difficult.

b) During the third week of October, an unhappy employee put small amounts of sand in a number of batches of dry pizza dough mix. Most of the ruined mix was located before it was boxed and shipped, but a few boxes of bad mix did manage to reach customers. While no customer claims have been filed as of the end of the fiscal year, management thinks that it is very likely that one or more lawsuits will be filed and that an unfavorable outcome is almost certain. However, the nature of the problem is such that a reasonable estimate of any loss that may arise is not yet possible.

c) Jerry Johnson, a former Jack's employee, has filed a suit against Jack's for injuries alleged to have occurred on Jack's property after the period of time during which he worked for Jack's. The suit seeks to recover $1 million in damages. Jack's is insured for this sort of claim up to $200,000, although the coverage is being contested by the insurance company. Johnson's claim is still pending in the county court and legal counsel has advised Jack's that a favorable outcome is likely.

d) A small overseas division of Jack's with a book value of $300,000 and a current market value of $450,000 was taken over by the new government of the country in which it is located shortly after a bloodless coup in August. At the present time it appears unlikely that any of the company's investment in the division will be recovered.

REQUIRED   Indicate the appropriate 1998 accounting treatment (including journal entries, if any) for each of the above situations. Justify your choices of treatments.

P 5-8.   **BALANCE SHEET AND INCOME STATEMENT PREPARATION**   The Jim and Joyce Company, a partnership, was organized on January 1, 1998, with each partner investing $25,000 in cash. The partners failed to provide an adequate system of records, and when asked to present financial statements as of December 31, 1998, they were unable to do so. You were called in to prepare the required statements. Your investigation of available data and your discussions with the partners revealed the following:

a) Total cash receipts (including partners' investments) from January 1 to December 31, 1998, were $109,840. Included in receipts was a bank loan of $2,000, on which $120 of interest had accrued on December 31, 1998.

b) An analysis of cash disbursements showed the following:

Payment for land ($5,000) and building ($30,000)	$35,000
Payment for furniture and fixtures	8,000
Payment of salaries and wages	6,100
Payment of other expenses	825
Payment of accounts payable	51,165

c) On December 31, you ascertained the following account balances:

Accounts payable	$2,160
Accounts receivable	5,680
Inventory	8,920
Prepaid expenses	180
Accrued payables other than interest	210

d) You also learned that goods costing $500 were purchased during the year and paid for by the company but were found to be for the personal use of Joyce, who had not reimbursed the company.

e) You determined that recognition of the following was required: depreciation of building at a rate of 10 percent; depreciation of furniture and fixtures at a rate of 20 percent; estimated uncollectible accounts receivable, $350.

REQUIRED
I. Prepare a balance sheet in account form as of December 31, 1998.
2. Prepare an income statement for the year ended December 31, 1998.

(CGAA, adapted)

P 5-9. **BALANCE SHEET PREPARATION AND ANALYSIS** Albrecht Company began business as a corporation on December 3, 1996. The accounting for the business since its inception has been done by Ken Rowe. Rowe's primary responsibilities are in the marketing area, and his previous experience in accounting was limited. Kevin Stocks, a qualified accountant, was hired to perform the company's accounting functions in December 1998. The first task he was assigned was to review the accounting for the company's first two years and to make any corrections that might be necessary to ensure that the company's 1997–1998 financial statements were proper. The preclosing trial balance as of November 30, 1998, includes year-end adjustments that were prepared by Rowe.

Albrecht Company
Preclosing Trial Balance
November 30, 1998

	DEBIT	CREDIT
Cash	$ 2,150	
Accounts receivable	10,350	
Note receivable	3,000	
Inventory	10,500	
Land	8,000	
Furniture and fixtures	20,000	
Unexpired insurance	600	
Accounts payable		$ 5,950
Notes payable		5,000
Common stock, $10 par		25,000
Additional paid-in capital		2,700
Retained earnings		8,950
Sales		103,800
Purchases	78,750	
Purchase returns		450
Selling expenses	11,000	
Administrative expenses	7,500	
Total	$151,850	$151,850

Stocks' review of the accounting records and other records uncovered the following additional information:

a) Checks totaling $2,350 had been written to vendors and recorded in the November 1998 cash disbursements journal but were still in the vault on December 7.

b) All receivables from 1996–1997 credit sales had been either collected or written off. The estimate for bad debts arising from 1997–1998 sales was $1,000, and the following entry was made to recognize this fact:

Selling expense	1,000	
Accounts receivable		1,000

c) The note receivable for $3,000 is from a customer. This three-month note is dated November 1, 1998, and has an annual interest rate of 18%.

d) The physical inventory on November 30, 1998, includes $9,900 of product on hand and $2,100 of inventory that Apex Company is holding and attempting to sell for Albrecht.

e) The furniture and fixtures were acquired on December 3, 1996. These fixed assets are being depreciated on a straight-line basis over a 10-year life with no salvage value. The following adjusting entry was made by Rowe in November 1998 to recognize depreciation:

Selling expense	2,000	
Administrative expense	500	
Furniture and fixtures		2,500

The same adjusting entry was made for the 1996–1997 fiscal year.

f) The company has one prepaid insurance policy. The policy covers a one-year period and was purchased for $1,200 on June 1, 1998.

g) The notes payable were issued on November 1, 1998, with an annual interest rate of 12 percent. The principal and interest are payable on August 1, 1999.

h) The tax return for the 1997–1998 fiscal year appears to be prepared properly and shows no tax liability.

REQUIRED   Prepare a statement of financial position for the Albrecht Company as of November 30, 1998.

(IMA, adapted)

*P 5-10.   **FINANCIAL REPORTING PROBLEM**   The following questions relate to the financial statements and related information of GE presented in Appendix B. Your answers should relate to 1995 only, unless otherwise indicated.

REQUIRED

I. Investment securities are a highly significant portion of GE's assets and increased substantially from 1994 to 1995. What is included in this category and what caused the increase in 1995?

2. What is GE's largest asset? Describe the nature of this item.

3. Describe GE's depreciation and amortization policy.

4. How does GE value its inventories for financial reporting purposes? What is the largest inventory component?

5. What was the total accumulated depreciation, depletion, and amortization?

6. What is the largest component of intangible assets? All other assets?

7. Short-term borrowings exceeded $64 billion at the end of 1995. What are the two largest components of this liability category?

8. What was the amount of accrued taxes payable? Where are these shown in the balance sheet?

9. How much was GE's total line of credit at the end of 1995?

I0. Describe GE's stock repurchase plan and explain how these transactions are reflected in the balance sheet.

II. GE's two primary businesses are manufacturing (GE) and financial services (GECS). What is the largest source of revenue within each of these businesses?

I2. What type of stock does GE have authorized? Issued?

*P 5-11. **FINANCIAL STATEMENT CONTENT AND ANALYSIS** Tabor Company is listed on the New York Stock Exchange. The market price of its common stock was quoted at \$20 per share on both December 31, 1998, and December 31, 1997. Tabor's balance sheets as of December 31, 1998, and December 31, 1997, and statements of income and retained earnings for the years then ended are presented below.

Balance Sheets
(in thousands)

	12/31/98	12/31/97
Assets:		
Current assets:		
Cash	\$ 3,800	\$ 3,600
Short-term investments	13,000	11,000
Accounts receivable, net of allowance		
for doubtful accounts	105,000	95,000
Inventories at lower of cost or market	134,000	154,000
Prepaid expenses	2,500	2,400
Total current assets	\$258,300	\$266,000
Property, plant, and equipment, net		
of accumulated depreciation	311,000	308,000
Other assets	29,000	34,000
Total assets	\$598,300	\$608,000
Liabilities and stockholders' equity:		
Current liabilities		
Notes payable	\$ 5,000	\$ 15,000
Accounts payable and accrued expenses	62,500	74,500
Income taxes payable	1,000	1,000
Payments due within one year on long-term debt	6,500	7,500
Total current liabilities	\$ 75,000	\$ 98,000
Long-term debt	177,300	180,000
Deferred tax liability	74,000	67,000
Other liabilities	9,000	8,000
Total liabilities	\$335,300	\$353,000
Common stock, par value \$1 per share:		
authorized, 20,000,000 shares; issued and outstanding,		
10,000,000 shares	\$ 10,000	\$ 10,000
Contributed capital in excess of par	111,000	111,000
Retained earnings	142,000	134,000
Total stockholders' equity	\$263,000	\$255,000
Total liabilities and stockholders' equity	\$598,300	\$608,000

Statements of Income and Retained Earnings
(in thousands)

	YEAR ENDED	
	12/31/98	12/31/97
Net sales	$600,000	$500,000
Costs and expenses:		
Cost of goods sold $480,000		$400,000
Selling, general, and		
administrative expenses 66,000		60,000
Other expenses, net 17,000		6,000
Total costs and expenses	(563,000)	(466,000)
Income before income taxes	$ 37,000	$ 34,000
Income taxes	(16,800)	(15,800)
Net income	$ 20,200	$ 18,200
Retained earnings at beginning of period,		
as previously reported $141,000		$132,000
Adjustment required for correction of error . . (7,000)		(6,000)
Retained earnings at beginning of period,		
as restated	134,000	126,000
Dividends on common stock	(12,200)	(10,200)
Retained earnings at end of period	$142,000	$134,000

Additional facts are as follows:

a) Selling, general, and administrative expenses for 1998 included a usual but infrequently occurring loss of $10 million.

b) Other expenses, net, for 1998 included an extraordinary item (loss) of $10 million. If the extraordinary item (loss) had not occurred, income taxes for 1998 would have been $21.8 million instead of $16.8 million.

c) Adjustment required for correction of error was a result of a change from an accounting principle that is not generally accepted to one that is generally accepted.

d) Tabor Company has a simple capital structure and has disclosed earnings per common share for net income in the notes to the financial statements.

REQUIRED   **1.** Determine from the additional facts above whether the presentation of those facts in Tabor Company's statements of income and retained earnings is appropriate. If the presentation is appropriate, discuss the theoretical rationale for the presentation. If the presentation is not appropriate, describe the appropriate presentation and discuss its theoretical rationale. Do not discuss disclosure requirements for the notes to the financial statements.

2. Describe the general significance of the following financial analysis tools:
   a) Quick (acid-test) ratio.
   b) Inventory turnover.
   c) Return on stockholders' equity.

3. On the basis of the Tabor Company balance sheets, statements of income and retained earnings, and additional information, describe how to determine each of the above financial analysis tools (for the year 1998 only).

(AICPA, adapted)

*P 5-12.   **CALCULATING FINANCIAL RATIOS**

REQUIRED   Using the information given for Tabor Company in Problem 5-11, calculate the following (for 1998 only). Show supporting calculations.

1. Current (working capital) ratio.

2. Profit margin on sales.

3. Number of days' sales in average receivables, assuming a business year of 300 days and all sales on account.

4. Inventory turnover.
5. Book value per share of common stock.
6. Earnings per share on common stock.
7. Price-earnings ratio on common stock.
8. Dividend payout ratio on common stock.

(AICPA, adapted)

*P 5-13.   **CALCULATING FINANCIAL RATIOS**   The accounting staff of Yeary Enterprises has completed the preparation of financial statements for the 1998 calendar year. The statement of income for 1998 and comparative statements of financial position for 1997 and 1998 are presented below and on the next page:

Yeary Enterprises
Statement of Income
Year Ended December 31, 1998
(*in thousands*)

Revenues:	
Net sales	$ 800,000
Other	60,000
Total revenue	$ 860,000
Expenses:	
Cost of goods sold	$(540,000)
Research and development	(25,000)
Selling and administrative	(155,000)
Interest	(20,000)
Total expenses	$(740,000)
Income before income taxes	$ 120,000
Income taxes	(48,000)
Net income	$ 72,000

Yeary Enterprises
Statements of Financial Position
December 31, 1998 and 1997
(*in thousands*)

	1998	1997
Assets:		
Current assets:		
Cash and short-term investments	$ 26,000	$ 21,000
Receivables, less allowance for doubtful accounts		
($1,100 in 1998 and $1,400 in 1997).....................	48,000	50,000
Inventories, at lower of FIFO cost or market	65,000	62,000
Prepaid items and other current assets	5,000	3,000
Total current assets..................................	$144,000	$136,000
Other assets:		
Investments, at cost	$106,000	$106,000
Deposits	10,000	8,000
Total other assets	$116,000	$114,000
Property, plant, and equipment:		
Land	$ 12,000	$ 12,000
Buildings and equipment, less accumulated		
depreciation ($126,000 in 1998 and $122,000 in 1997)	268,000	248,000
Total property, plant, and equipment	$280,000	$260,000
Total assets	$540,000	$510,000
Liabilities and stockholders' equity:		
Current liabilities:		
Short-term loans	$ 22,000	$ 24,000
Accounts payable	72,000	71,000
Salaries, wages, and other	26,000	27,000
Total current liabilities	$120,000	$122,000
Long-term debt	160,000	171,000
Total liabilities	$280,000	$293,000
Stockholders' equity:		
Common stock, at par	$ 44,000	$ 42,000
Paid-in capital in excess of par	64,000	61,000
Total paid-in capital	$108,000	$103,000
Retained earnings	152,000	114,000
Total stockholders' equity	$260,000	$217,000
Total liabilities and stockholders' equity	$540,000	$510,000

The accounting staff calculates selected financial ratios, using average balance sheet amounts to calculate ratios involving income statement accounts and using ending balance sheet amounts to calculate ratios involving only balance sheet accounts.

REQUIRED

1. Briefly explain how each of the following types of financial ratios is useful: liquidity ratio, activity or turnover ratio, leverage ratio, and profitability ratio.
2. Calculate the following ratios for 1998 for Yeary Enterprises:
   a) Times interest earned.
   b) Return on total assets.
   c) Return on common stockholders' equity.
   d) Total liabilities to total assets.
   e) Accounts receivable turnover.
   f) Current ratio.
   g) Quick ratio.

The Statement of Cash Flows

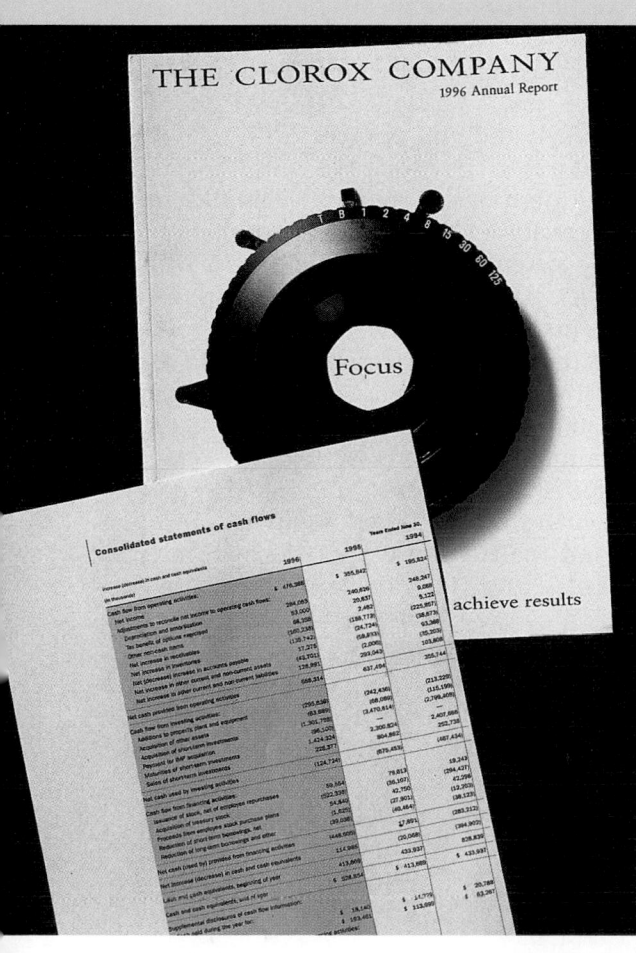

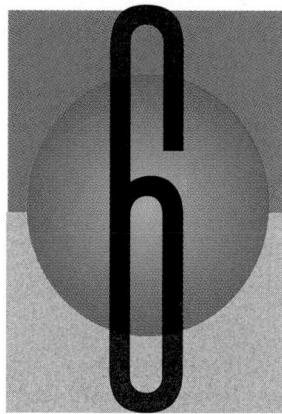

LEARNING OBJECTIVES

After studying this chapter, you should be able to:

1. State the purpose of the statement of cash flows and describe its format.

2. Discuss various types of questions that might be answered and types of information that might be obtained by examining a statement of cash flows.

3. Explain why net income for a period and net cash flow from operations for the same period may differ in amount.

4. Use the indirect approach to determine cash flows from operating activities.

5. Use the direct approach to determine cash flows from operating activities.

6. Determine cash flows from investing activities.

7. Determine cash flows from financing activities.

8. Prepare a statement of cash flows.

9. Discuss the relative merits of the indirect and direct approaches for determining cash flows from operating activities.

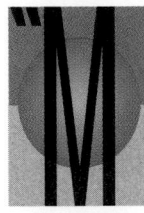

erger mania" began in the 1960s, accelerated in the 1980s, and has continued into the 1990s. Over this period, many companies have acquired substantial amounts of economic resources through merger activities that were financed with cash, as well as with long-term borrowing and capital stock issues. Information about such merger activities is of interest to investors. How did DuPont finance its acquisition of Conoco? And how did General Motors finance the acquisitions of Electronic Data Systems and Hughes Aircraft? How did Boeing finance its purchase of McDonnell Douglas—a deal described as "akin to shrinking America's Big Three automakers to just two, leaving Boeing and Europe's Airbus"?[1]

Leveraged buyouts (LBOs) provided the means by which many companies were bought and sold during this period. Because these arrangements involve the use of large debt issues to finance acquisitions, cash requirements for interest payments can be significant. Information about these large cash flows is therefore of interest to lenders as well as investors.

Investors also need answers to questions about the billions of dollars U.S. automobile companies have spent to compete with foreign automobile makers. How much did Ford Motor Company spend to retool and modify its operating assets to meet the shift in consumer demand toward faster, sportier cars? How can other companies report large profits yet face severe shortages of cash? Answers to questions like these generally cannot be found by examining only a company's income statement or its statement of financial position (balance sheet). Another important financial statement—the statement of cash flows—may be more useful to investors and other financial statement users seeking answers to questions about cash flows for investing and financing.

In this chapter we will discuss the background and purpose of the statement of cash flows and the reasons for its usefulness to investors. We will show how to prepare the statement of cash flows. The illustrations are relatively simple and use only those accounts and transactions normally encountered in introductory accounting. Students who did not study the statement of cash flows in their introductory courses should still be able to understand the statement of cash flows and follow the process of its preparation. Students who *did* study the statement of cash flows in introductory accounting will find that this chapter provides a good review of the basics of statement preparation. All students should find that this chapter provides a "capstone" review of many traditional introductory accounting topics, including how the results of accrual accounting relate to cash flows.

The chapter begins with a description of the evolution in "funds" reporting that led to the development of the statement of cash flows. A discussion of the purposes and format of the statement and the two basic approaches to preparing it is followed by a brief section on the uses for the statement. The major portion of the chapter covers the preparation of the statement of cash flows. Two approaches to preparing the section on cash flows from operating activities are presented, with an emphasis on the indirect approach. The chapter closes with a comparison of the indirect and direct approaches and an illustration of cash flow analysis based on General Electric's statement of cash flows (in Appendix B of the book).

VOLUTION OF THE STATEMENT OF CASH FLOWS

"Funds flow" reporting, including the reporting of cash flows, has been of interest to accounting theorists, practitioners, and financial statement users for decades. During the 1960s and 1970s, authoritative bodies issued documents either recommending or requiring the inclusion of a funds flow statement in companies'

---

[1]"Boeing Shakes Up Aerospace World with Latest Buy," *Lansing State Journal,* December 16, 1996, p. 1A.

financial reports. This statement became known as the "statement of changes in financial position."[2]

Various concepts of "funds" were used in the statement of changes in financial position. Historically, the term *funds* usually meant cash or working capital (current assets minus current liabilities). But other concepts, such as cash plus temporary investments (cash equivalents) and net current monetary assets, also were permitted.[3] Relatively few companies used the cash or the cash and cash equivalents concept of funds. The APB permitted the use of ambiguous terms, such as *funds,* rather than more descriptive terms, such as *cash* or *cash and cash equivalents.* Variations in the focus of the statement (cash, cash and cash equivalents, or working capital), differences in reporting formats, and the reporting of net changes in the amounts of assets and liabilities rather than the flows of funds (e.g., cash) created a lack of comparability among statements. Furthermore, many people believed that the concept of working capital was not as useful as the cash (or cash and cash equivalents) concept in assessing, predicting, and evaluating cash flows, and therefore conflicted with financial reporting objectives.

In *Statement of Concepts No. 5,* the FASB took the position that a full set of financial statements for a period should show *cash flows* for that period. And in 1987, acknowledging the importance of cash flow information, the FASB issued *Statement of Accounting Standards No. 95,* "Statement of Cash Flows."[4] This *Statement,* as amended by *Statements No. 102* and *104,* requires that a company present a statement of cash flows with any set of financial statements that purports to report both the company's financial position and the results of its operations.[5]

From an international standpoint, providing either a funds or a cash flow statement is now commonplace among the world's multinational corporations. In 1992, the International Accounting Standards Committee issued *International Accounting Standard 7* (revised), titled "Cash Flow Statements." However, a funds or cash flow statement is not required in all countries. For example, Germany and the Netherlands are notable European Community countries without a requirement. However, even when not required, the presentation of some type of statement by multinational corporations, often on a voluntary basis, is now the rule rather than the exception.

VERVIEW OF THE STATEMENT OF CASH FLOWS

Exhibit 6–1 shows the relationships among the income statement, balance sheet, statement of retained earnings, and statement of cash flows. The balance sheet is a static statement, analogous to a snapshot of a business at a point in time. The income statement, statement of retained earnings or stockholders' equity, and statement of cash flows are statements of *flows* during a period of time. These statements are more comparable to movies than to snapshots. Of these, the statement of cash flows is much broader than the income statement. Whereas the income statement reports the *profitability* of a company's operating activities, the statement of cash flows reports the *cash flows* from operating and other activities.

---

[2]"Reporting Changes in Financial Position," *Opinions of the Accounting Principles Board No. 19* (New York: AICPA, 1971).

[3]The use of the term *funds* in this chapter should not be confused with accounting for various funds (e.g., assets restricted for certain purposes), which is discussed in Chapter 13.

[4]"Statement of Cash Flows," *Statement of Financial Accounting Standards No. 95* (Stamford, Conn.: FASB, 1987).

[5]"Statement of Cash Flows—Exemption of Certain Enterprises and Classification of Cash Flows from Certain Securities Acquired for Resale," *Statement of Financial Accounting Standards No. 102* (Norwalk, Conn.: FASB, 1989), and "Statement of Cash Flows—Net Reporting of Certain Cash Receipts and Cash Payments and Classification of Cash Flows from Hedging Transactions," *Statement of Financial Accounting Standards No. 104* (Norwalk, Conn.: FASB, 1989).

| EXHIBIT 6-1 | Relationship of the Statement of Cash Flows to Other Financial Statements |

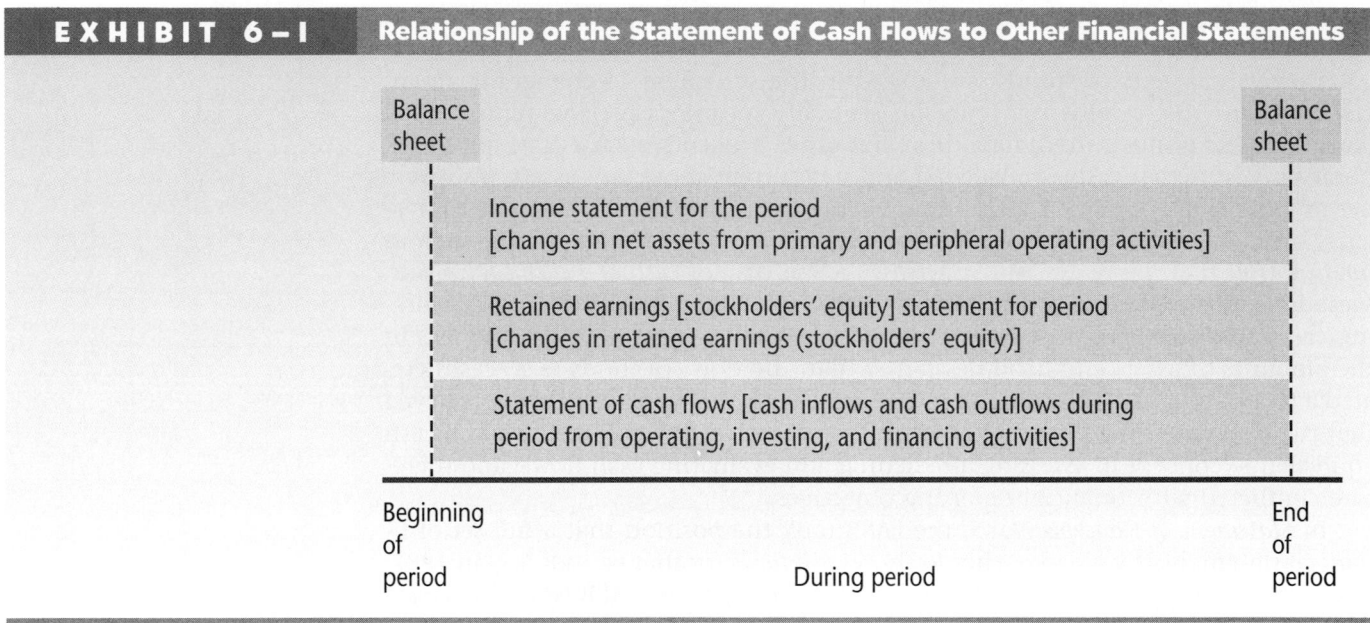

Purpose of the Statement

1

State the purpose of the statement of cash flows and describe its format.

The primary purpose of the **statement of cash flows** is to provide information regarding a company's cash inflows and outflows during an accounting period. The statement of cash flows provides information that, together with information in the other financial statements, should help users to (1) assess a company's ability to generate positive future net cash flows; (2) assess a company's ability to meet its obligations and its need for external financing and to pay dividends; (3) understand the difference between a company's net income and its net cash flow; and (4) determine the effects on a company's financial position of its investing and financing transactions during the period.[6]

The statement of cash flows must provide information about a company's operating, investing, and financing activities. In an effort to respond to the common practice of investing idle cash in highly liquid assets, *Statement No. 95* requires that companies treat cash and cash equivalents as a single pool for reporting purposes. The *Statement* defines **cash equivalents** as short-term, highly liquid investments that are readily convertible to known amounts of cash.[7] Treasury bills, commercial paper, and money market funds are examples of cash equivalents. The cash and cash equivalents grouping is preferable to a "pure" cash analysis for at least two reasons:

1. Users' assessments of cash flows probably are unaffected by whether cash is on hand, on deposit, or invested in highly liquid short-term assets.

2. Reporting numerous purchases and sales ("rollovers") of highly liquid investments could result in the presentation of information about a company's investing activities that is not representationally faithful.

Format of the Statement

The statement of cash flows is based on an **activity format,** which means that cash inflows and outflows are classified in terms of operating, investing, and financing activities. **Operating activities** relate to a company's primary revenue-

---
[6]*Statement No. 95,* paras. 4–5.
[7]*Statement No. 95,* para. 8. Generally, only investments with original maturities of three months or less qualify as cash equivalents.

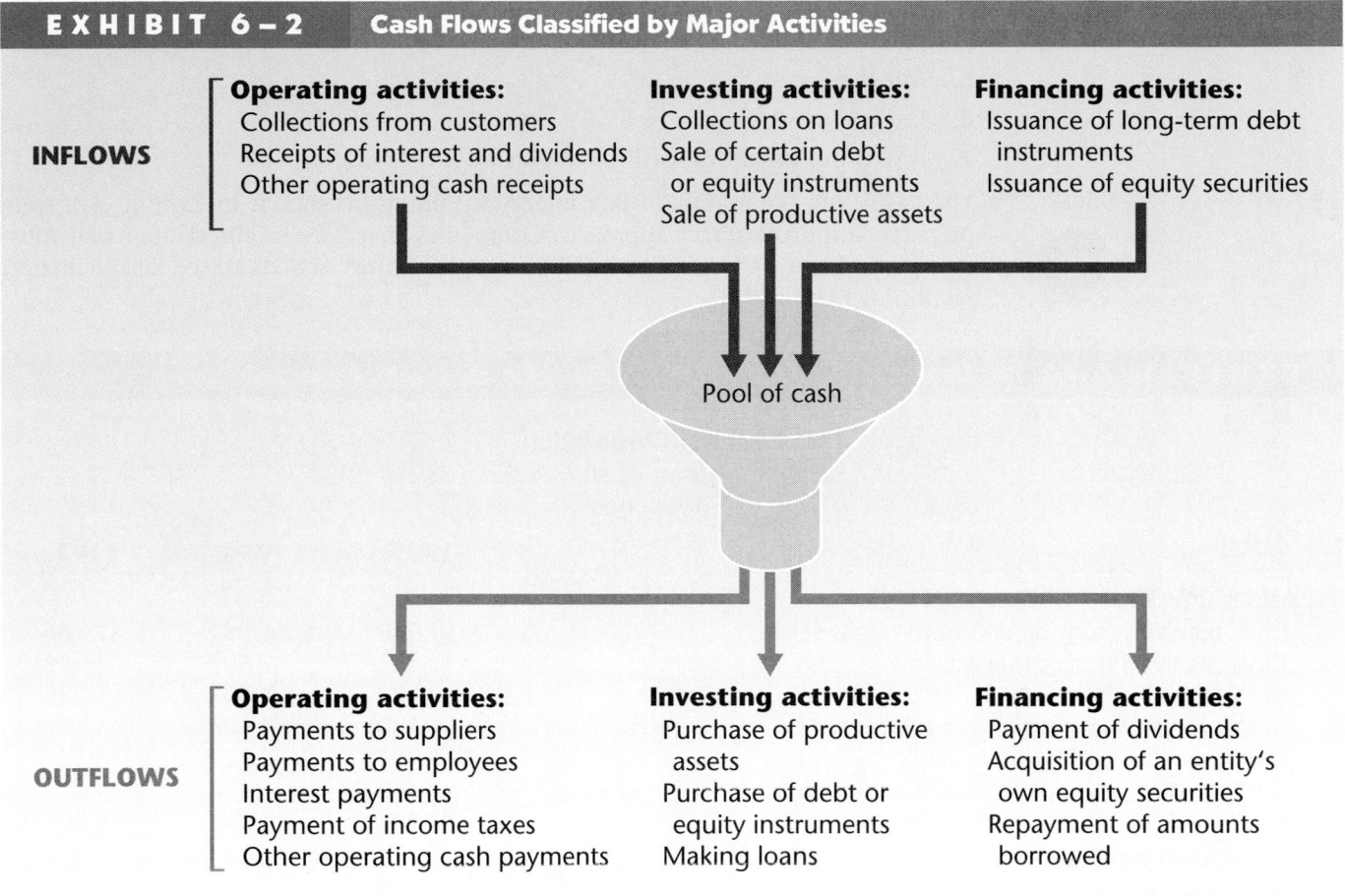

EXHIBIT 6-2   **Cash Flows Classified by Major Activities**

INFLOWS

Operating activities:
Collections from customers
Receipts of interest and dividends
Other operating cash receipts

Investing activities:
Collections on loans
Sale of certain debt
 or equity instruments
Sale of productive assets

Financing activities:
Issuance of long-term debt
 instruments
Issuance of equity securities

Pool of cash

OUTFLOWS

Operating activities:
Payments to suppliers
Payments to employees
Interest payments
Payment of income taxes
Other operating cash payments

Investing activities:
Purchase of productive
 assets
Purchase of debt or
 equity instruments
Making loans

Financing activities:
Payment of dividends
Acquisition of an entity's
 own equity securities
Repayment of amounts
 borrowed

generating activities. Cash flows from operating activities are generally the cash effects of transactions and economic events included in the determination of income. **Investing activities** include lending money and collecting on those loans, buying and selling productive assets that are expected to generate revenues over long periods, and buying and selling securities not classified as cash equivalents. **Financing activities** include borrowing money from creditors and repaying the amounts borrowed and obtaining resources from owners and providing them both a return *on* their investment (through dividends) and a return *of* their investment.

Exhibit 6–2 summarizes the types of transactions that appear on the statement of cash flows. Investing and financing transactions that do not affect cash, such as the issuance of common stock to acquire land, must be reported (including dollar amounts) either in a *supplementary schedule* or in a *narrative footnote* to the statement of cash flows.

Two Approaches to Reporting Operating Activities

Two approaches may be used to report cash flows from operating activities—the direct approach and the indirect approach. *Statement No. 95* encourages use of the direct approach but permits the indirect approach as an alternative.

Under the **direct approach,** the following major sources of operating cash inflows and outflows must be reported:

1. Cash collected from customers and cash collected from lessees, licensees, and similar parties.

2. Interest and dividends received.

3. Any other operating cash receipts.

4. Cash paid to employees and other suppliers of goods or services, including suppliers of insurance, advertising, and similar services.

5. Interest paid.

6. Income taxes paid.

7. Any other operating cash payments.

The cash flow statements of Box Energy Corporation, shown in Exhibit 6–3, were prepared using the direct approach. Companies that use the direct approach must also present the indirect approach in a supplementary schedule (see Reconciliation section of Exhibit 6–3).

EXHIBIT 6–3	**Consolidated Statements of Cash Flows, Direct Approach**

Box Energy Corporation
Statements of Cash Flow
(*in thousands*)

	1995	1994	1993
CASH FLOW FROM OPERATIONS			
Cash received from oil and natural gas sales	$ 50,958	$ 56,769	$ 32,166
Cash received from other sources	1,851	1,607	905
Cash received from interest income	2,127	1,601	1,228
Cash paid to suppliers and employees	(14,280)	(14,427)	(14,129)
Cash paid for net profits expense	(11,906)	(12,920)	(4,464)
Cash paid for income taxes	(80)	(238)	—
Cash paid for interest and financing expense	(4,623)	(4,748)	(4,700)
Net cash flow from operations	$ 24,047	$ 27,644	$ 11,006
CASH FLOW FROM INVESTMENTS			
Payments for capital expenditures	$(21,274)	$(16,648)	$(18,901)
Proceeds from sale of property	1,375	2,879	39
Sales of marketable securities	—	—	104,039
Investments in marketable securities	—	—	(95,259)
Net cash flow from investments	$(19,899)	$(13,769)	$(10,082)
CASH FLOW FROM FINANCING			
Proceeds from notes payable	—	—	$ 3
Principal payments on notes payable	—	$ (1,970)	(517)
Net cash flow from financing	—	$ (1,970)	$ (514)
Net increase in cash and cash equivalents	$ 4,148	$ 11,905	$ 410
Cash and cash equivalents at beginning of period	$ 17,496	$ 5,591	$ 5,181
Cash and cash equivalents at end of period	$ 21,644	$ 17,496	$ 5,591
RECONCILIATION OF NET INCOME TO NET CASH FLOW FROM OPERATIONS			
Net income	$ 5,392	$ 9,157	$ 2,161
Depreciation, depletion, and amortization	14,967	11,075	10,141
Amortization of deferred charges	254	261	228
Amortization of premium on marketable securities	15	15	—
Dry hole and impairment costs	2,223	1,619	604
Loss (gain) on sale of assets	(1,080)	739	(808)
Deferred income tax expense (benefit)	1,995	4,820	(43)
(Increase) in accounts receivable	(3,492)	(21)	(1,993)
(Increase) in prepaid expenses and other current assets	(127)	(292)	(44)
Increase (decrease) in accounts payable	3,306	(708)	(10)
Increase in net profits expense payable	594	979	770
Net cash flow from operations	$ 24,047	$ 27,644	$ 11,006

Under the **indirect approach,** cash flows from operating activities are reported by adjusting net income for revenues, expenses, gains, and losses that appear on the income statement but do not have an effect on cash. Net income is also adjusted for operating cash inflows and outflows that do not appear on the income statement.[8] Companies that use the indirect approach must disclose in footnotes the amounts of interest and income taxes paid. The cash flow statements of U.S. Air Group, Inc., shown in Exhibit 6–4 (see page 282), were prepared using the indirect approach.

Although the FASB prefers the direct approach, in practice the indirect approach is far more widely used. We will illustrate how to determine operating cash flows using both approaches. Later in the chapter we will compare the two approaches in terms of the qualitative characteristics of financial reporting. Regardless of which approach is used, the statement of cash flows is useful for a variety of purposes, as we shall see in the next section.

USEFULNESS OF THE STATEMENT OF CASH FLOWS

Because of its *activity format,* the statement of cash flows provides information about the following activities and company characteristics:

2 Discuss various types of questions that might be answered and types of information that might be obtained by examining a statement of cash flows.

I. *Cash provided by or used by operating activities.* While income as reported in the income statement is of primary importance in evaluating a company's performance, many revenues and expenses shown on the income statement result from accruals and cost allocations that do not affect cash. For example, depreciation expense does not cause an outflow of cash. The statement of cash flows provides useful information about the cash generated from a company's primary operating activities, information that may help to answer the following types of questions:

a) Why would a company that operates at a profit be continually short of cash?

b) How can a company operate at a loss and still generate huge inflows of cash from operations?

2. *Cash provided by or used by investing activities.* The statement of cash flows can provide information needed to answer questions about investing activities such as:

a) Is the company making capital expenditures to modernize, expand, or replace worn-out or obsolete plant and equipment?

b) Has the company acquired any long-term investments or other income-producing assets?

c) Did the company obtain cash from the disposal of long-lived assets? If so, how much?

3. *Cash provided by or used by financing activities.* The statement of cash flows can provide answers to the following types of questions about a company's financing activities:

a) Did the company obtain financing during the period through the issuance of debt or equity securities? If so, how much cash did it obtain?

b) Did the company use cash to retire any long-term debt or equity securities during the period?

Answers to these questions are not provided by the income statement and may not be easily obtained by an analysis of successive balance sheets.

---

[8]When preparing its *Proposed Statement of Financial Accounting Standards,* "Reporting Comprehensive Income" (Norwalk, Conn.: FASB, 1996), the FASB considered whether the operating activities section of an indirect-approach statement of cash flows, or the supplementary schedule provided with the operating activities section of a direct-approach statement of cash flows, should begin with comprehensive income instead of net income as specified by *Statement No. 95.* The Board decided not to amend *Statement No. 95.*

EXHIBIT 6-4   **Consolidated Statements of Cash Flows, Indirect Approach**

USAir Group, Inc.
Consolidated Statements of Cash Flows
(in thousands)

Years Ended December 31,	1995	1994	1993
Cash and cash equivalents beginning of year.	$ 429,538	$ 368,347	$ 296,038
Cash flows from operating activities			
Net income (loss)	119,287	(684,923)	(393,116)
Adjustments to reconcile net income (loss)			
to cash provided by (used for) operating activities			
Depreciation and amortization	352,447	408,587	352,467
Loss (gain) on disposition of property.	(17,043)	(24,099)	10,328
Amortization of deferred gains and credits	(27,817)	(27,396)	(27,309)
Other.	6,294	(11,605)	24,635
Changes in certain assets and liabilities			
Decrease (increase) in receivables	2,417	41,101	(180,152)
Decrease (increase) in materials, supplies,			
prepaid expenses and intangible pension assets	(74,980)	74,663	24,234
Increase (decrease) in traffic balances payable			
and unused tickets	38,955	(61,932)	35,517
Increase (decrease) in accounts payable			
and accrued expenses	120,422	235,105	84,787
Increase (decrease) in postretirement benefits			
other than pensions, non-current	56,667	51,613	65,967
Net cash provided by (used for)			
operating activities.	$ 576,649	$ 1,114	$ (2,642)
Cash flows from investing activities			
Aircraft acquisitions and purchase deposits, net	$ (61,689)	$ (46,022)	$(202,085)
Additions to other property	(84,980)	(134,086)	(159,031)
Proceeds from disposition of property	222,325	75,075	178,387
Change in short-term investments	2,430	(21,994)	—
Change in restricted cash and investments	71,980	2,578	(14,221)
Other	(1,134)	1,110	(4,378)
Net cash provided by (used for)			
investing activities	$ 148,932	$(123,339)	$(201,328)
Cash flows from financing activities			
Issuance of debt.	$ 1,162	$ 308,856	$ 597,834
Reduction of debt.	(283,160)	(87,073)	(889,872)
Issuance of common stock.	8,733	52	230,891
Issuance of preferred stock.	—	—	400,719
Sale of treasury stock	—	11,244	8,273
Dividends paid	—	(49,663)	(71,566)
Net cash provided by (used for)			
financing activities	$(273,265)	$ 183,416	$ 276,279
Net increase (decrease) in cash and cash equivalents	$ 452,316	$ 61,191	$ 72,309
Cash and cash equivalents end of year	$ 881,854	$ 429,538	$ 368,347
Noncash investing and financing activities			
Issuance of debt for aircraft acquisitions, net	$ 169,725	$ 224,614	$ 343,188
Issuance of debt for additions to other property	$ —	$ —	$ 669
Reduction of debt—aircraft purchase deposits	$ 70,837	$ —	$ —
Reduction of debt—aircraft related	$ —	$ —	$ 47,685
Supplemental information			
Cash paid during the year for interest,			
net of amounts capitalized	$ 299,871	$ 251,943	$ 236,122
Net cash received (paid) during the year			
for income taxes	$ (6,637)	$ 317	$ (967)

4. *The "quality" of earnings.* One view of the **quality of earnings** is based on how closely income is correlated with cash flows—the higher the correlation, the higher the quality of earnings. A comparison of net income with cash generated from operating activities may provide useful information for assessing the quality of earnings.

5. *Solvency, liquidity, and financial flexibility.* **Solvency** is the ability to pay debts as they mature. **Liquidity** is the ability to generate adequate amounts of cash for specific purposes; the concept also refers to assets' and liabilities' "nearness to cash." **Financial flexibility** refers to the ability to adapt during a period of financial adversity—to obtain financing, to liquidate nonoperating assets for cash, and to modify operations to increase short-run cash inflows. The statement of cash flows helps users to evaluate solvency, liquidity, and financial flexibility.

The statement of cash flows provides vital information not provided by the other financial statements. One measure of a company's profitability, for instance, is net income. *Over the life of the company,* total reported net income or net loss (assuming a nominal dollar concept of capital maintenance) will equal net cash inflow or outflow. Since income determination is based on *accrual accounting,* however, the equality of income and cash flows rarely holds for shorter time periods, such as annual accounting periods. A company may operate for several years because its annual cash inflows exceed its annual cash outflows, yet be unprofitable in the long run. Or a profitable company may experience severe short-run cash flow problems.

The statement of cash flows complements the income statement by disclosing the amount of cash generated by the company's operating activities. It complements the balance sheet by disclosing cash flow transactions that cause changes in assets, liabilities, and stockholders' equity. For example, the amount of cash used to purchase long-lived assets during an accounting period is reported on the statement of cash flows.

Many users believe that the statement of cash flows presented with an income statement better satisfies many of the qualitative characteristics of accounting information discussed in Chapter 2 than the income statement alone. For example, in addition to its *relevance,* which underlies the five points listed on page 281 and above, the statement of cash flows may be more *reliable* than the income statement. The information presented in the statement of cash flows avoids many of the arbitrary allocations and estimates (e.g., depreciation expense) necessary to determine income. Furthermore, the statement of cash flows may enhance *comparability* among companies. Because GAAP permits the use of many alternative accounting procedures to determine income, intercompany comparisons based on income alone often are difficult. Finally, a statement of cash flows is readily *understandable.*

The usefulness of the statement of cash flows does not lessen the importance of the income statement and balance sheet as sources of information to users. When investors make decisions, they must assess many factors. The income statement and balance sheet provide information about some, but not all, of those factors; the statement of cash flows provides information about others. A significant body of empirical research suggests that cash flow information is indeed useful.

CONCEPTUAL

The statement of cash flows enhances relevance, reliability, and comparability, and is readily understandable.

REPARATION OF THE STATEMENT OF CASH FLOWS

The statement of cash flows is organized according to the activity format shown in Exhibit 6–5. As discussed earlier, the activity format is divided into three sections— cash flows from operating activities, cash flows from investing activities, and cash flows from financing activities. This activity format should be used for any cash flow statement, regardless of whether the direct approach or the indirect approach is used to determine cash flows from operating activities. Notice that a schedule of investing

EXHIBIT 6-5	**Activity Format for the Statement of Cash Flows**

Company Name
Statement of Cash Flows
Period Covered

Cash flows from operating activities:

         .
         .
         .

    Net cash provided (or used) by operating activities . . . . $xx

Cash flows from investing activities:

         .
         .
         .

    Net cash provided (or used) by investing activities xx

Cash flows from financing activities:

         .
         .
         .

    Net cash provided (or used) by financing activities xx

Net increase (or decrease) in cash . . . . $xx

Cash at beginning of period xx

Cash at end of period . . . . $xx

Investing and financing activities not affecting cash:
(List of individual transactions including cash and noncash portions) . . . . . $xx

---

and financing activities not affecting cash appears at the bottom of the statement of cash flows. As mentioned earlier, a narrative footnote is an alternative means of presenting *noncash* investing and financing activities.

When preparing a company's statement of cash flows for an accounting period, the company's income statement for that period, its balance sheets for that period and for the immediately preceding period, and summary information about transactions in which the company was involved during the period are used. For purposes of preparing the 1998 cash flow statement for KDM, Inc., we will use KDM's 1997 and 1998 balance sheets (shown in Exhibit 6–6) and KDM's 1998 income statement and additional information (shown in Exhibit 6–7). Preparation of the statement involves the following steps:

I. *Determine the net increase or decrease in cash and cash equivalents for the period.* Referring to Exhibit 6–6, we see that KDM, Inc., has no cash equivalents and that its cash balance increased by $250,000 during 1998. This amount can be used as a "check" for our statement of cash flows. When the 1998 statement of cash flows is completed, the net cash inflow must equal KDM's $250,000 cash increase.

2. *Analyze any available income statement data, changes in noncash balance sheet accounts, and available additional information* to determine the transactions that caused inflows and outflows of cash during the period.

3. *Using an activity format, prepare the statement of cash flows on the basis of the two previous steps.*

Cash Flows from Operating Activities

The first section of the statement of cash flows summarizes the cash flows associated with a company's operating activities. As you probably suspect, the major recurring *inflow* of cash from operating activities, for most companies, is from sales of products or services—or stated another way, cash inflows from customer collections. Operating cash *outflows* include payments to suppliers of merchandise, payments to employees for wages and salaries, payments to creditors for interest, and payments to government agencies for taxes.

3 Explain why net income for a period and net cash flow from operations for the same period may differ in amount.

EXHIBIT 6–6 Balance Sheets

KDM, Inc.
Balance Sheets
As of December 31, 1998 and 1997
(*in thousands*)

	12/31/98	12/31/97
Assets:		
Current assets:		
Cash	$ 2,750	$ 2,500
Accounts receivable	6,000	4,750
Inventory	12,500	13,000
Prepaid rent	1,000	750
Total current assets	$22,250	$21,000
Long-term investments	$ –0–	$ 2,500
Property, plant, and equipment:		
Equipment	$15,500	$10,000
Buildings	31,250	23,750
Less: Accumulated depreciation on plant		
and equipment	(10,050)	(10,000)
Total property, plant, and equipment	$36,700	$23,750
Total assets	$58,950	$47,250
Liabilities:		
Current liabilities:		
Salaries payable	$ 500	$ 750
Accounts payable	2,000	3,000
Short-term notes payable	3,250	2,250
Total current liabilities	$ 5,750	$ 6,000
Long-term notes payable	8,750	7,500
Total liabilities	$14,500	$13,500
Stockholders' equity:		
Contributed capital:		
Capital stock, $10 par value	$20,000	$16,000
Contributed capital in excess of par	17,500	14,000
Total contributed capital	$37,500	$30,000
Retained earnings	6,950	3,750
Total stockholders' equity	$44,450	$33,750
Total liabilities and stockholders' equity	$58,950	$47,250

We have seen that because the income statement is based on accrual accounting, the revenues, expenses, gains, and losses reported in the income statement do not necessarily represent cash inflows and outflows. For example, depreciation expense is an item that appears on the income statement under accrual accounting, but is a noncash expense and therefore would not be part of net cash flows. As another example, interest revenue accrued on notes receivable would appear on the income statement under accrual accounting. However, this revenue accrual would not represent a cash inflow. In general, two distinct classes of items cause differences between "income flows" and cash flows and must be kept in mind when using an income statement to determine cash flows from operating activities:

I. *Items that appear on the income statement that do not represent cash inflows or outflows,* such as depreciation, depletion, or amortization expense, or items whose

CONCEPTUAL

The components of the income statement are based on accrual accounting and do not necessarily represent cash inflows and outflows.

EXHIBIT 6–7 Income Statement and Additional Information

KDM, Inc.
Income Statement
For the Year Ended December 31, 1998
(in thousands)

Sales		$ 30,000
Less: Cost of goods sold		(10,500)
Gross profit.		$ 19,500
Operating expenses:		
Salaries expense	$ 7,500	
Rent expense	900	
Depreciation expense	2,300	(10,700)
Operating income		$ 8,800
Other income (deductions):		
Interest expense.	$(2,000)	
Loss on sales of equipment	(500)	
Gain on sale of investments	500	(2,000)
Net income before income taxes		$ 6,800
Less: Income taxes		(350)
Net income.		$ 6,450

Additional information for 1998:
(a) Purchased equipment costing $3,750,000; paid one-third in cash and issued a five-year interest-bearing note for the balance.
(b) Purchased equipment costing $6,250,000 by issuing 350,000 shares of common stock.
(c) Made a $7,500,000 addition to a building; paid cash.
(d) Paid a $1,250,000 long-term note by issuing 50,000 shares of common stock.
(e) Sold investments for $3,000,000 cash.
(f) Paid cash dividends.
(g) Depreciation expense was $2,300,000.
(h) Sold for $1,750,000 equipment that originally cost $4,500,000 and that was one-half depreciated.
(i) Proceeds from the short-term note were used to purchase inventory.

cash effects do not relate to operating activities, such as gains or losses on sales of depreciable assets.

2. *Operating cash inflows and outflows that do not appear on the income statement,* but appear instead on the balance sheet as prepayments, deferrals, unearned items, or reductions of accruals. These cash flows must be reported on the statement of cash flows.

To give an example of the second type of item, a company may collect in the current period cash arising from credit sales made in a previous period. Or it may pay cash this period for rent that relates to the current period plus one or more future periods. To give another example, a company may make current period cash payments to employees for settlement of salary expenses accrued in the previous accounting period. Because most current asset and current liability accounts arise from, and are affected by, transactions related to a company's operating activities, an analysis of changes in current assets and current liabilities is necessary in order to adjust the amounts in an accrual-basis income statement to obtain net cash flows from operating activities.

As stated earlier, there are two approaches for determining and reporting net cash flows from operating activities: the *indirect approach* and the *direct approach.* Under the indirect approach, net income is adjusted as necessary to convert it to a cash basis. This process includes adjustments for revenues, expenses, gains, and losses that appear on the income statement but do not affect cash, and adjustments for operating cash inflows and outflows that do not appear on the income statement. The latter adjustments are based on analysis of the current asset and liability accounts. The general process of the indirect approach is shown in Exhibit 6–8. Under the direct approach, each operating item in the income statement is adjusted to a cash flow basis by adjusting for changes during the period in related balance sheet accounts. The result is that the calculation of net cash flows from operating activities includes cash inflows from customers, from interest revenue, and from dividends, followed by cash outflows for payments for purchases of goods, for operating expenses, for interest expense, and for taxes. The general process of the direct approach is shown in Exhibit 6–10.

Both the indirect approach and the direct approach are acceptable under GAAP, and both produce the same result. In practice, however, the more widely used, by far, is the indirect approach; for this reason the indirect approach may have been emphasized in your introductory accounting course. On the other hand, as stated earlier, the FASB prefers the direct approach, with the indirect approach presented as a supplementary schedule to the cash flow statement. In the next two sections we will illustrate both the indirect approach and the direct approach of determining cash flows from operating activities. Later in the chapter, after preparing a cash flow statement, we will suggest some reasons why we believe the direct approach is preferable and conceptually superior to the indirect approach.

Indirect Approach

KDM's 1998 income statement reports net income of $6,450,000. Our task using the indirect approach is to adjust from this accrual accounting net income amount to a net cash flow from operating activities amount. Before specifically addressing the facts for KDM, it will be useful to identify the more common types of items for which accrual-based net income must be adjusted to determine cash flows from operating activities using the indirect approach.

4 Use the indirect approach to determine cash flows from operating activities.

Exhibit 6–8 summarizes the overall adjustment process under the indirect approach. In general, items that are added back to net income in Exhibit 6–8 are items that are peripheral to operating activities and/or items that are associated with reductions in net income but that do not require cash outflows. Items that

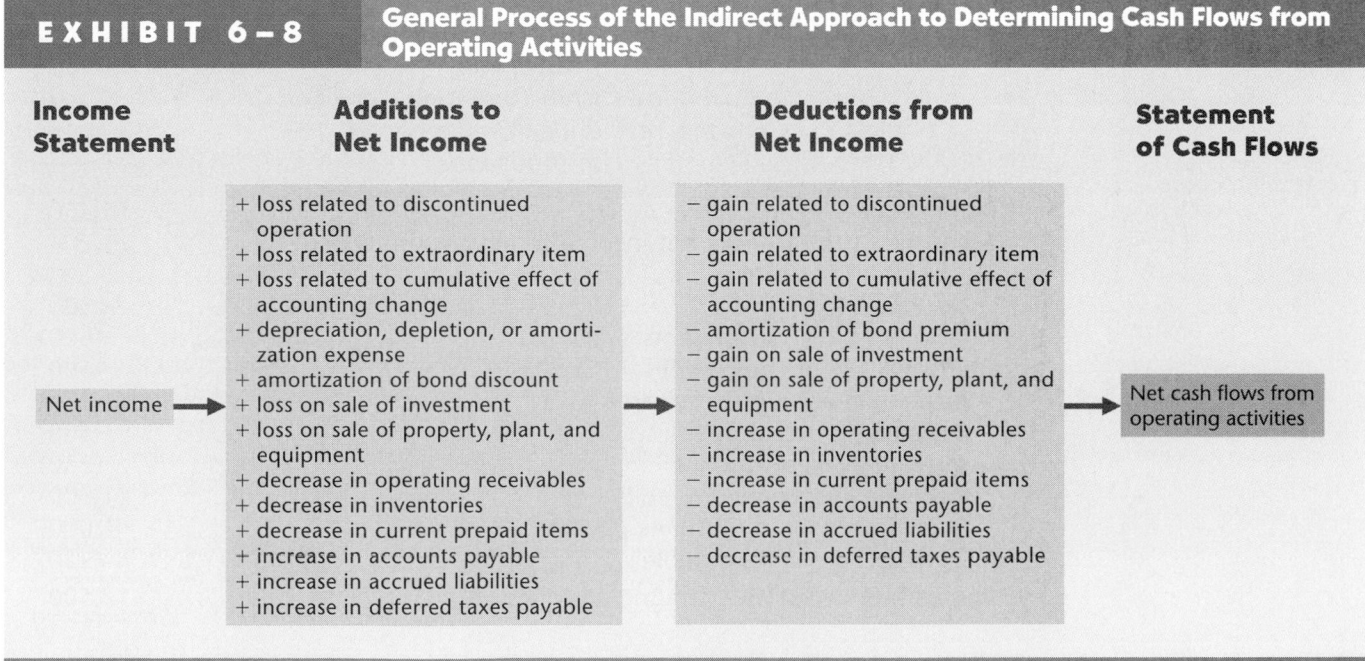

EXHIBIT 6–8 General Process of the Indirect Approach to Determining Cash Flows from Operating Activities

Income Statement	Additions to Net Income	Deductions from Net Income	Statement of Cash Flows
Net income	+ loss related to discontinued operation + loss related to extraordinary item + loss related to cumulative effect of accounting change + depreciation, depletion, or amortization expense + amortization of bond discount + loss on sale of investment + loss on sale of property, plant, and equipment + decrease in operating receivables + decrease in inventories + decrease in current prepaid items + increase in accounts payable + increase in accrued liabilities + increase in deferred taxes payable	− gain related to discontinued operation − gain related to extraordinary item − gain related to cumulative effect of accounting change − amortization of bond premium − gain on sale of investment − gain on sale of property, plant, and equipment − increase in operating receivables − increase in inventories − increase in current prepaid items − decrease in accounts payable − decrease in accrued liabilities − decrease in deferred taxes payable	Net cash flows from operating activities

are deducted from net income are items that are peripheral to operating activities, items that are associated with increases in net income that did not result in corresponding cash inflows, or items that required cash outflows but did not reduce net income. In the following sections we will discuss how these general guidelines apply to the particular items shown as additions to, or deductions from, net income in Exhibit 6–8. At the same time, we will indicate where appropriate how the indirect approach applies to KDM's case.

Additions to Net Income

Any losses related to discontinued operations, extraordinary items, or cumulative effects of accounting changes that have been included in net income must be added back to net income because they are not part of ordinary operating activities. (Any cash flows related to such items will be reported in other parts of the statement of cash flows.) KDM has no nonoperating transactions, but you can see how such items are treated for cash flow purposes by examining General Electric's statement of cash flows (in Appendix B of the text), which shows adjustments to net income for both discontinued operations and the cumulative effect of an accounting change.

Depreciation, depletion, and amortization expense are added back to net income because they are expenses for which there are no cash outflows. (Such expenses are sometimes referred to as noncash expenses.) In KDM's case, 1998 depreciation expense was $2,300,000, which is added to net income to determine operating cash flows (see Exhibit 6–9). Likewise, amortization of a bond discount by the bond issuer increases interest expense for the period, but does not require a cash outflow. It is therefore added back to net income. (KDM had no bond discount amortization.)

Losses on sales of investments or on sales of property, plant, and equipment are added back to net income for two reasons. First, these losses result from transactions that are peripheral to normal operating activities (they are related to investing activities). Second, such losses do not necessarily cause cash outflows. KDM had a $500,000 loss on the sale of equipment, which is added to net income (see Exhibit 6–9).

E X H I B I T   6 – 9   **Cash Flows from Operating Activities, Indirect Approach**

KDM, Inc.
Cash Flows from Operating Activities
For the Year Ended December 31, 1998
(in thousands)

Net income	$6,450
Adjustments to reconcile net income to net cash provided by operating activities:	
Depreciation expense	2,300
Gain on sale of investments	(500)
Loss on sale of equipment	500
Increase in accounts receivable	(1,250)
Decrease in inventory	500
Increase in prepaid rent	(250)
Decrease in accounts payable	(1,000)
Increase in short-term notes payable	1,000
Decrease in salaries payable	(250)
Net cash provided by operating activities	$7,500

A decrease in operating receivables, such as accounts receivable, is added to net income because a cash inflow has occurred without a corresponding increase in net income. (KDM's *increase* in accounts receivable is discussed in the section on deductions from net income.) A decrease in inventories is added to net income because to the extent that inventory was used as part of the cost of goods sold for the period, some of the cost of goods sold did *not* require cash outflows. Without adjustment, therefore, cash flows from operating activities are understated. In 1998 KDM had a $500,000 decrease in inventory, which is added to net income (see Exhibit 6–9).

A decrease in a current prepaid item, such as prepaid rent, means that some expense (e.g., rent expense) recorded for the period did not require a cash outflow in the current period. To calculate cash flows, therefore, this decrease must be added to net income. KDM had an *increase* in prepaid rent of $250,000, which we will discuss in the section on deductions from net income.

An increase in accounts payable results from purchasing goods (inventory) on credit (not for cash), and to that extent the cost of goods sold (which is derived from the cost of goods available for sale) for the period is overstated on a cash basis. Therefore, an increase in accounts payable must be added to net income to determine cash flows. KDM had a *decrease* in accounts payable, which we will discuss among the deductions from net income. KDM did, however, have a $1,000,000 increase in short-term notes payable, which was related to the purchase of goods (inventory). This increase must be added to net income because no cash outflow occurred, even though inventory was acquired.

An increase in accrued liabilities (e.g., salaries payable) or in deferred taxes payable means that an expense was reported during the period for which there was no related cash outflow. To determine cash flow from operating activities, the increase in liabilities must be added to net income. In 1998 KDM actually *decreased* salaries payable—an item we will discuss in the next section under deductions from net income.

Deductions from Net Income

Gains related to discontinued operations, extraordinary items, or cumulative effects of accounting changes must be deducted from net income. Because such events are not ordinary operating activities, any cash flows associated with them will be accounted for in other sections of the statement of cash flows. (KDM had no nonoperating transactions in 1998.)

Amortization of a bond premium decreases interest expense for the bond issuer, causing the bond issuer's net income for the period to be larger than it would otherwise have been. Since no cash inflow is related to the larger income amount, amortization of the bond premium must be deducted from the reported net income to determine cash flows from operating activities. (KDM had no bond premium amortization.)

Gains on the sale of investments or of property, plant, and equipment do not result from ordinary operating activities. Furthermore, they do not necessarily produce an equivalent cash inflow. For these reasons such gains must be deducted from net income to determine cash flows from operating activities. (KDM had a $500,000 gain on the sale of investments in 1998. Exhibit 6–9 shows this gain deducted from net income to arrive at net cash provided by operating activities.)

An increase in operating receivables occurs when revenue is recognized without a corresponding cash inflow, thus increasing net income. Such increases, like KDM's $1,250,000 increase in accounts receivable in 1998, must be deducted from net income to yield cash flows from operating activities.

An increase in inventories occurs when more inventory is acquired during a period than is used up as part of cost of goods sold. Because the cash outflow to increase the inventories is not associated with cost of goods sold for the period, it must be deducted from net income (in effect, added to cost of goods sold) to arrive at cash outflows for operating activities. (KDM's inventory *decreased* rather than increased in 1998.)

An increase in a current prepaid item means that some cash was spent to acquire an asset, but the cash outflow was not included when expenses were deducted in calculating net income. To adjust net income to a cash basis, the increase in a current prepaid item must be deducted from reported net income. (In 1998 KDM had a $250,000 increase in prepaid rent, which is deducted from KDM's net income in Exhibit 6–9 to determine cash flows from operations.)

A decrease in accounts payable occurs when cash has been used to pay accounts due. Payment of accounts payable does not increase cost of goods sold. Therefore, to the extent that accounts payable has decreased, cost of goods sold for the period does not fully reflect all cash outflows for goods. To adjust net income to a cash basis, a decrease in accounts payable must be deducted from net income, as is done in Exhibit 6–9. (KDM had a $1,000,000 decrease in accounts payable for 1998.)

Like a decrease in accounts payable, a decrease in accrued liabilities or in deferred taxes payable is associated with a cash outflow that is not reflected in the income statement. Accordingly, such decreases must be deducted from net income. (In Exhibit 6–9, KDM's $250,000 decrease in salaries payable is deducted from net income to arrive at net cash provided by operating activities.)

Summary of the Indirect Approach

We have completed our explanation of how to determine net cash flows from operating activities under the indirect approach. Along the way, we illustrated the specific adjustments to KDM's net income that were necessary to determine net cash provided by operating activities in 1998 was $7,500,000 (see Exhibit 6–9). We will now turn our attention to the direct approach for determining cash flows from operating activities, again using KDM's data.

Direct Approach

5 **Use the direct approach to determine cash flows from operating activities.**

The process under the direct approach to preparing the operating activities section of the statement of cash flows is summarized in Exhibit 6–10. The process begins with a systematic assessment of each income statement item. Those items having nothing to do with operating activities (e.g., a gain on the sale of investments), as well as all noncash expenses (e.g., depreciation expense), are excluded. Those items that are part of normal operating activities (e.g., sales, cost of goods sold, various expenses) are adjusted to a cash basis using the changes in related balance sheet accounts during the period. For example, to adjust sales to a cash basis, an increase

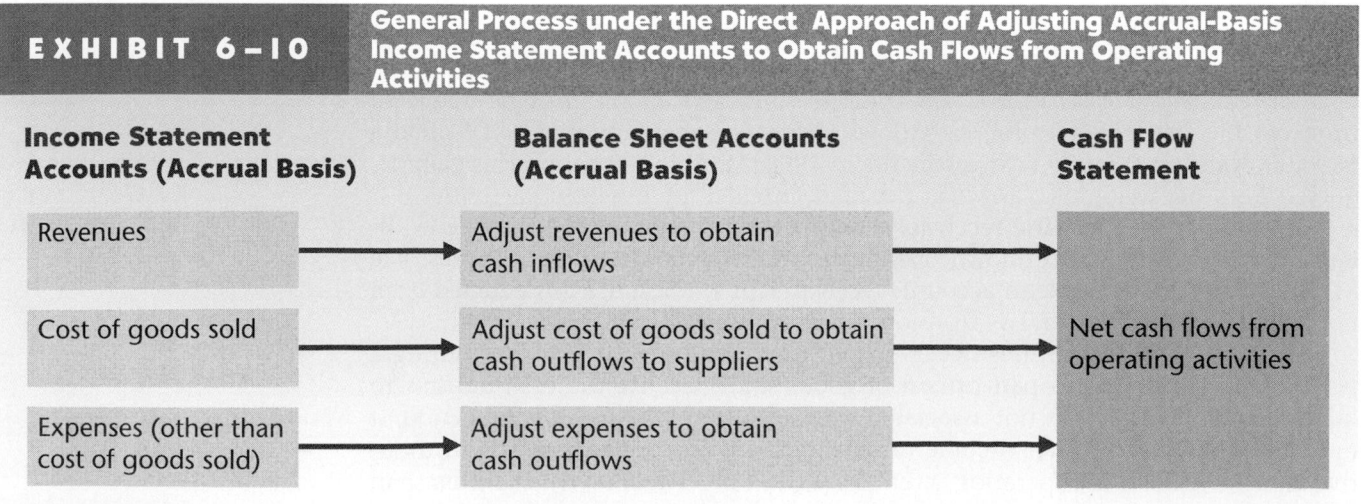

EXHIBIT 6–10	**General Process under the Direct Approach of Adjusting Accrual-Basis Income Statement Accounts to Obtain Cash Flows from Operating Activities**

Income Statement Accounts (Accrual Basis)	Balance Sheet Accounts (Accrual Basis)	Cash Flow Statement
Revenues	Adjust revenues to obtain cash inflows	
Cost of goods sold	Adjust cost of goods sold to obtain cash outflows to suppliers	Net cash flows from operating activities
Expenses (other than cost of goods sold)	Adjust expenses to obtain cash outflows	

EXHIBIT 6–11	Cash Flows from Operating Activities, Direct Approach

KDM, Inc.
Cash Flows from Operating Activities
For the Year Ended December 31, 1998
(in thousands)

Cash flows from operating activities:
Collections from customers	$28,750
Payments to merchandise suppliers	(10,000)
Payments to employees for salaries	(7,750)
Payments for rent	(1,150)
Payments to creditors for interest	(2,000)
Payments for taxes	(350)
Net cash provided by operating activities	$ 7,500

(decrease) in the accounts receivable balance is deducted from (added to) the reported income from sales.

Once each income statement item has been considered and dealt with appropriately, the next step is to assess the operating cash flow implications of changes in any current asset and current liability accounts not considered in the assessment of the income statement items. This information is obtained from the comparative balance sheets. We will use data from KDM's 1998 income statement and additional information (Exhibit 6–7) and its 1997 and 1998 balance sheets (Exhibit 6–6) to illustrate the direct approach to determining cash flow from operating activities. Exhibit 6–11 shows this part of KDM's cash flow statement for 1998.

Cash Collections from Customers

We can see from the income statement in Exhibit 6–7 that KDM, Inc., had sales revenue of $30,000,000 in 1998. However, we are interested in the amount of cash collected from customers. Therefore, we must adjust sales revenue by the change in accounts receivable during 1998. For example, an increase in accounts receivable would be deducted from sales revenue, because the increase would reflect sales for which cash had not yet been collected. The process of adjusting from accrual-basis sales revenue to cash collections from customers is shown in Exhibit 6–12. Using this process, we calculate cash collections from customers as follows:

Sales revenue (Exhibit 6–7)	$30,000,000
Less: Increase in accounts receivable (Exhibit 6–6)	(1,250,000)
Cash collections from customers	$28,750,000

Cash Collections from Other Operating Activities

A company may have sources of cash inflow other than sales revenue that must be considered when determining cash collections related to operating activities. For example, even though interest revenue and cash dividends received are associated with investing activities, *Statement No. 95* requires that any cash received from these items must be included in cash flows from operating activities. (Correspondingly, interest expense, which we will discuss later, is treated as a cash outflow from operating activities.) Exhibit 6–13 summarizes the process of adjusting accrual-basis revenues (except sales revenue) to cash inflows from operating activities. We can see from Exhibit 6–7 that KDM had no other sources of operating cash inflow besides sales.

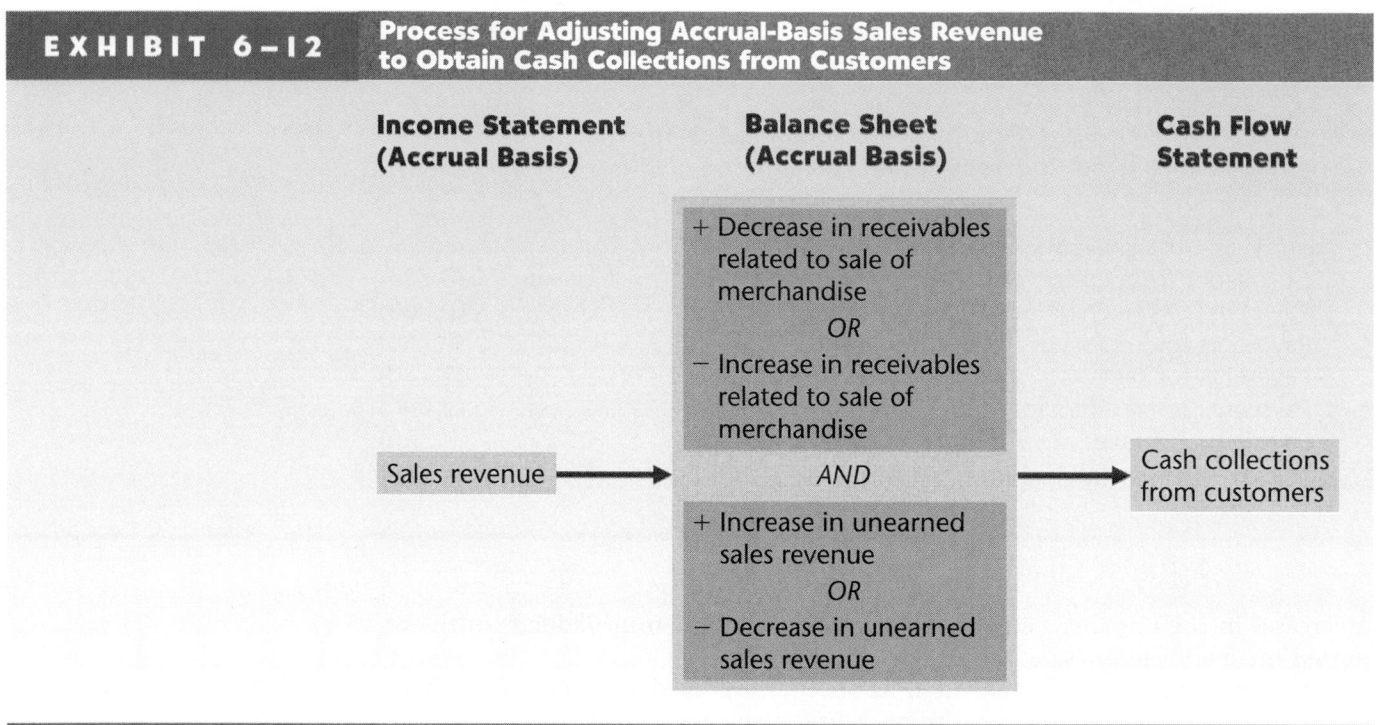

EXHIBIT 6–12 — Process for Adjusting Accrual-Basis Sales Revenue to Obtain Cash Collections from Customers

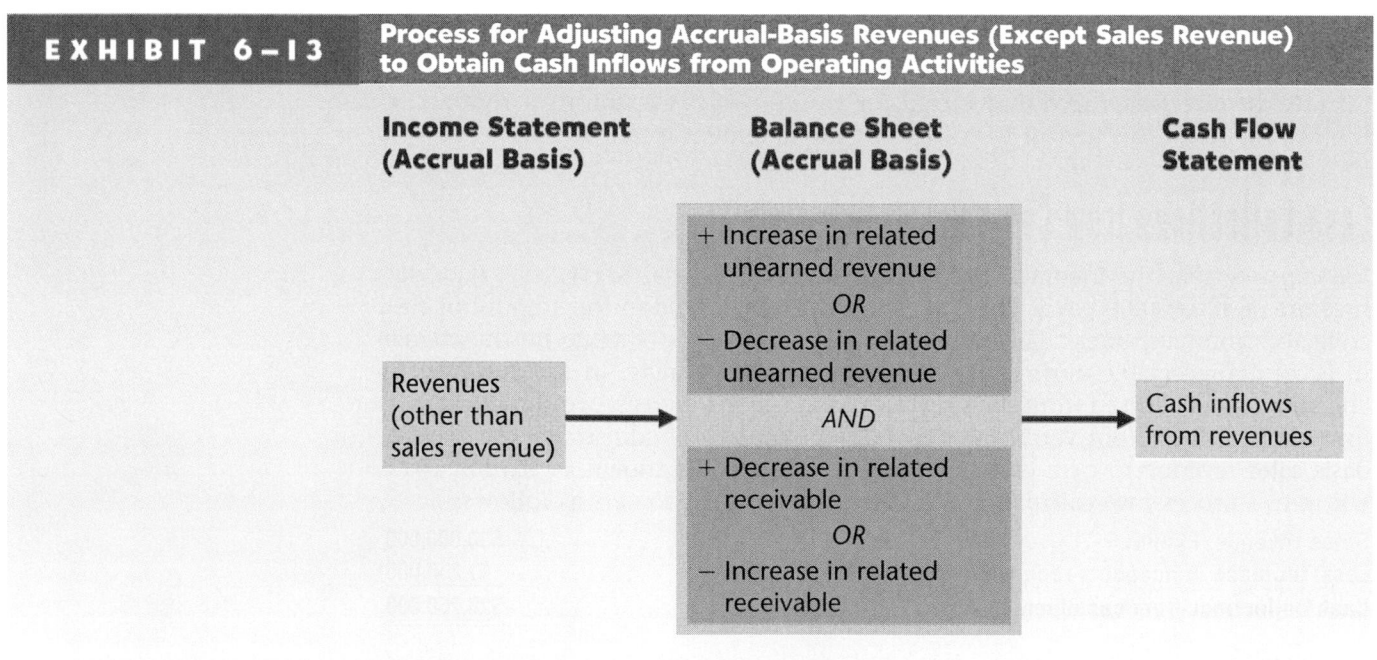

EXHIBIT 6–13 — Process for Adjusting Accrual-Basis Revenues (Except Sales Revenue) to Obtain Cash Inflows from Operating Activities

Cash Paid to Merchandise Suppliers

To determine the amount of cash paid to merchandise suppliers, cost of goods sold must be adjusted for changes in two balance sheet accounts: inventory and accounts payable to suppliers (see Exhibit 6–14). An increase in inventory means that more goods were purchased during the period than were sold. Therefore, an increase in inventory must be added to cost of goods sold to determine purchases from suppliers. A decrease in inventory means that more goods were sold during the period than were purchased. Therefore, a decrease in inventory must be subtracted from cost of goods sold to determine purchases from suppliers.

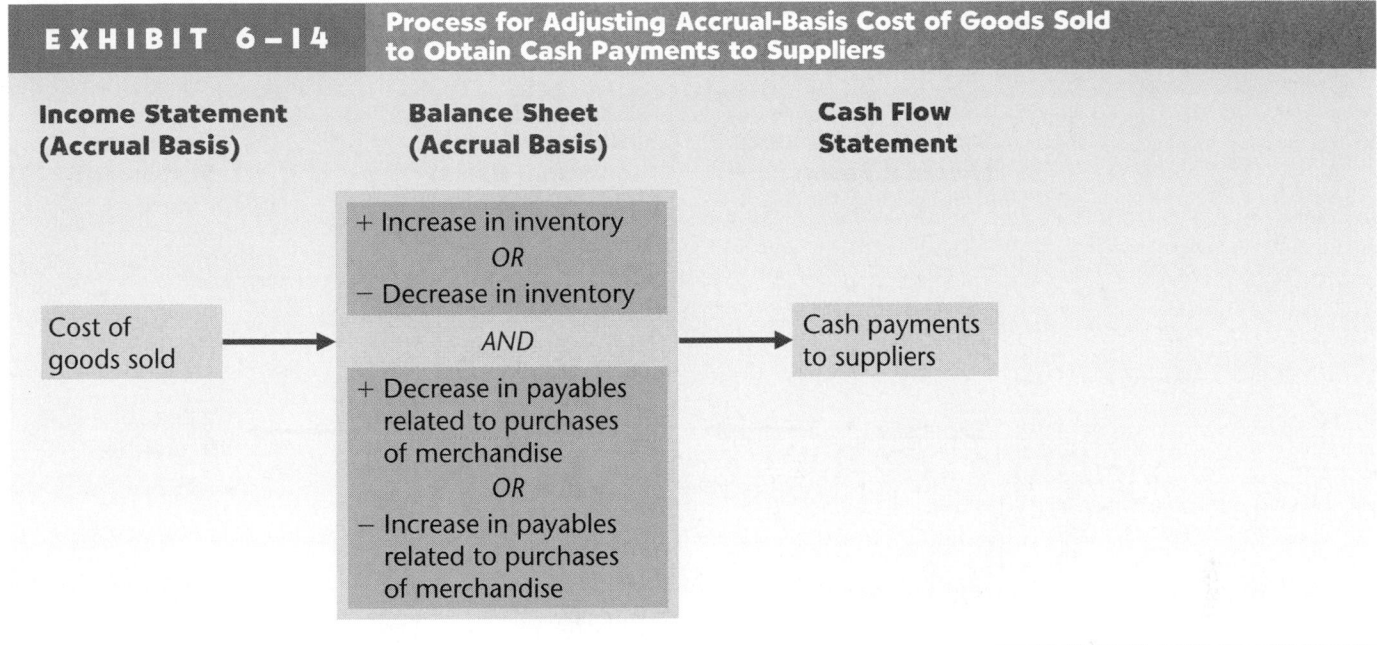

EXHIBIT 6–14 **Process for Adjusting Accrual-Basis Cost of Goods Sold to Obtain Cash Payments to Suppliers**

Income Statement (Accrual Basis)	Balance Sheet (Accrual Basis)	Cash Flow Statement
Cost of goods sold	+ Increase in inventory *OR* – Decrease in inventory *AND* + Decrease in payables related to purchases of merchandise *OR* – Increase in payables related to purchases of merchandise	Cash payments to suppliers

An increase in accounts payable to suppliers arises because goods were purchased during the period for which cash was not paid during the same period. As a result, an increase in payables to suppliers must be subtracted from cost of goods sold to determine cash payments. A decrease in payables to suppliers means that cash was paid during the period over and above cash payments for current period purchases. Therefore, a decrease in payables to suppliers must be added to cost of goods sold to determine cash payments for the period.

KDM's cash payments to suppliers would be determined as follows:

Cost of goods sold (Exhibit 6–7).	$10,500,000
Less: Decrease in inventory (Exhibit 6–6)	(500,000)
Add: Decrease in accounts payable (Exhibit 6–6).	1,000,000
Less: Increase in short-term notes payable [Exhibit 6–6 and item (i) in Exhibit 6–7].	(1,000,000)
Cash payments to merchandise suppliers.	$10,000,000

We turn now to cash *outflows* from operating activities.

Cash Payments for Operating Expenses

KDM reported three operating expenses in 1998 (Exhibit 6–7): salaries expense ($7,500,000), rent expense ($900,000), and depreciation expense ($2,300,000). The process we will use to adjust these accrual-basis expenses (not including depreciation expense, which is a noncash expense) to cash outflows for expenses is shown in Exhibit 6–15.

Cash Payments to Employees for Salaries

Salaries expense must be adjusted for any increase or decrease in prepaid salaries (an unlikely account) as well as for any increase or decrease in salaries payable. An increase in prepaid salaries would result from paying salaries in advance of when the expense was incurred. This amount must be added to salaries expense to determine cash outflows for salaries. A decrease in prepaid salaries would result from

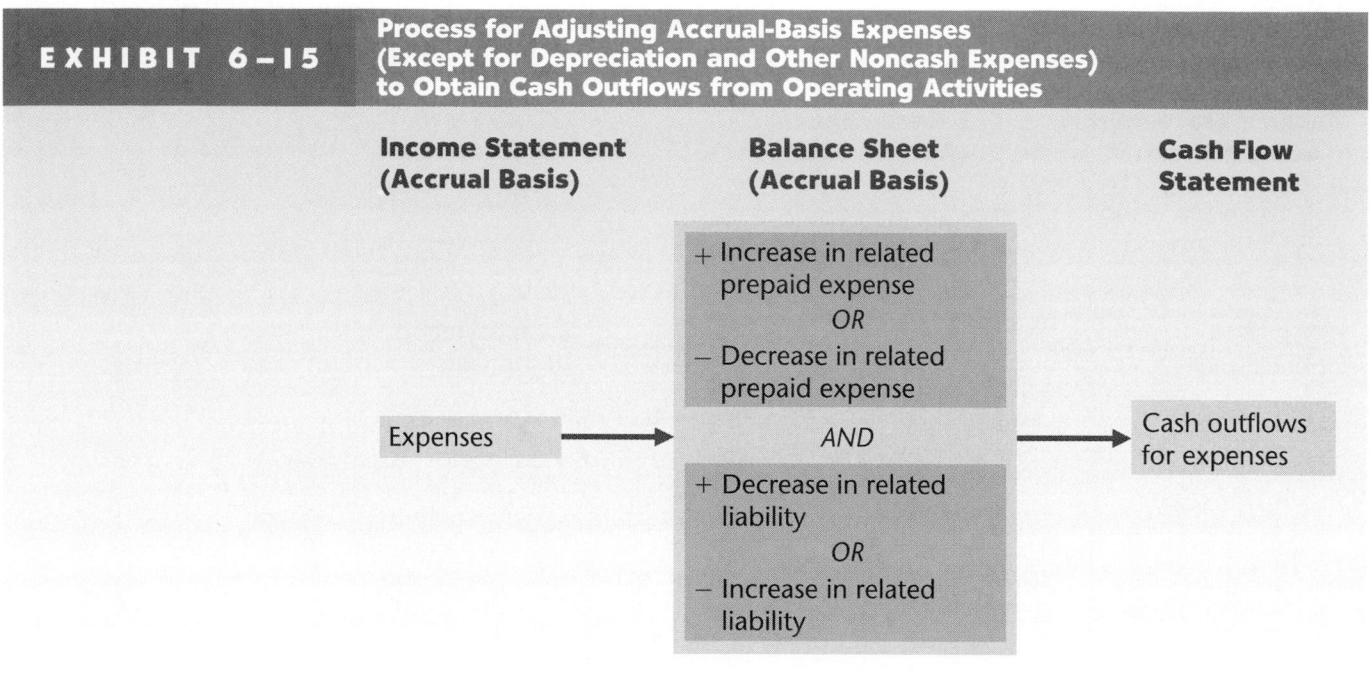

EXHIBIT 6-15

Process for Adjusting Accrual-Basis Expenses (Except for Depreciation and Other Noncash Expenses) to Obtain Cash Outflows from Operating Activities

Income Statement (Accrual Basis)	Balance Sheet (Accrual Basis)	Cash Flow Statement
Expenses	+ Increase in related prepaid expense OR − Decrease in related prepaid expense AND + Decrease in related liability OR − Increase in related liability	Cash outflows for expenses

incurring salaries expense for which cash payments were made in previous periods. This amount must be subtracted from salaries expense in order to calculate the current period's cash payments to employees for salaries.

An increase in salaries payable means that salaries expense has been incurred but not paid in the current period. This amount must be subtracted from salaries expense to calculate cash outflows for salaries. A decrease in salaries payable results from having paid salaries that were accrued as expenses in a previous period. This amount must be added to salaries expense to determine cash payments for salaries in this period. In the case of KDM, cash payments to employees would be determined as follows:

Salaries expense (Exhibit 6–7).	$7,500,000
Add: Decrease in salaries payable (Exhibit 6–6).	250,000
Cash payments to employees for salaries	$7,750,000

Cash Payments for Rent

Rent expense, like salaries expense, must be adjusted for changes in prepaid rent expense and rent payable to calculate cash payments for rent. The appropriate adjustments are shown in Exhibit 6–15. The analysis is the same as that for adjustments to salaries expense. KDM's cash payments for rent would be calculated as follows:

Rent expense (Exhibit 6–7).	$ 900,000
Add: Increase in prepaid rent (Exhibit 6–6).	250,000
Cash payments for rent.	$1,150,000

Depreciation Expense and Other Noncash Income Statement Items

Three items on KDM's income statement—depreciation expense, loss on sale of equipment, and gain on sale of investments—are not part of net cash flows from operating activities. When depreciation expense is recorded, no cash flow occurs. Therefore, this expense is a noncash expense.

KDM's $500,000 loss on the sale of equipment and its $500,000 gain on the sale of investments (see Exhibit 6–7) are not reported as cash flows from operating activities for *two* reasons. First, the dollar amount of a gain or loss is not a measure of the related cash flow. The equipment was sold for $1,750,000 [Exhibit 6–7, item (h)], and the investment was sold for $3,000,000 [Exhibit 6–7, item (e)]. Second, such gains and losses do not relate to operating activities; rather, they arise from a company's peripheral activities—in KDM's case, from its investment activities. Accordingly, cash flows arising from the sale of equipment and investments will be reported in the section of the statement of cash flows that is concerned with cash flows from investing activities (see pages 297–298).

Cash Payments to Creditors for Interest

As mentioned earlier (page 291), *Statement No. 95* requires that cash payments for interest be included in the calculation of cash flows from operating activities, even though interest expense arises because of a company's financing activities. Since KDM has no interest payable accounts (Exhibit 6–6), we know that the $2,000,000 of reported interest expense resulted in $2,000,000 of cash payments to creditors for interest. If KDM's balance sheet did show prepaid interest or interest payable accounts, interest expense would be adjusted to determine cash paid for interest in the same way salary expense and rent expense are adjusted (see pages 293–294).

Cash Payments for Taxes

Taxes are another operating expenditure that affects net cash flow. The process for adjusting reported expenses to cash outflows for expenses (shown in Exhibit 6–15) can be used for adjusting tax expense. Because KDM had no prepaid or accrued balance sheet accounts related to taxes, we know the reported income taxes of $350,000 was equal to the amount of cash paid for taxes.

We have now completed our analysis of KDM's cash flows from operating activities. Thus, we have the data necessary to prepare the cash flows from operating activities section of KDM's statement of cash flows. The section appears in Exhibit 6–11 and is the first section of the complete statement of cash flows shown in Exhibit 6–16.

Reconciliation of Income Flows and Cash Flows

Statement No. 95 requires that if a company uses the direct approach to report cash flows from operating activities, it must provide a supplementary schedule that reconciles net income with net cash provided or used by operating activities. Because we used the direct approach to prepare the operating activities section of KDM's cash flow statement shown in Exhibit 6–16, we must also prepare the required supplementary schedule. *This reconciliation schedule is exactly the same as the operating activities section of a cash flow statement prepared using the indirect approach.* Therefore, in KDM's statement of cash flows (Exhibit 6–16), the reconciliation of net income to net cash provided by operating activities that appears at the bottom of the statement looks exactly like Exhibit 6–9 minus the statement heading. (If KDM were to use the indirect approach to prepare the cash flows from operating activities section of its statement of cash flows, the reconciliation in Exhibit 6–9 would replace the first section of Exhibit 6–16, and a supplementary schedule would not be required.)

Investing and Financing Activities

As discussed earlier (page 279) and shown in Exhibit 6–5, the two other major activities that result in cash inflows and outflows are investing activities and financing activities. *Investing activities* include purchases and sales of productive assets that are expected to generate revenues over long periods of time, purchases and sales

EXHIBIT 6–16	**Statement of Cash Flows, Direct Approach**

KDM, Inc.
Statement of Cash Flows
For the Year Ending December 31, 1998
(in thousands)

Cash flows from operating activities:		
Collections from customers.	$28,750	
Payments to merchandise suppliers	(10,000)	
Payments to employees for salaries	(7,750)	
Payments for rent	(1,150)	
Payments to creditors for interest	(2,000)	
Payments for taxes	(350)	
Net cash provided by operating activities		$ 7,500
Cash flows from investing activities:		
Sale of investments	$ 3,000	
Purchase of equipment	(1,250)	
Sale of equipment	1,750	
Addition to building	(7,500)	
Net cash used by investing activities		(4,000)
Cash flows from financing activities:		
Payment of dividends	$ (3,250)	
Net cash used by financing activities		(3,250)
Net increase in cash		$ 250
Cash at beginning of year		2,500
Cash at end of year		$ 2,750
Investing and financing activities not affecting cash:		
Purchased $3,750 of equipment for $1,250 cash		
and by issuing a long-term note		$ 2,500
Extinguished a $1,250 long-term note		
by issuing common stock		1,250
Purchased $6,250 of equipment		
by issuing common stock		6,250
		$10,000
Reconciliation of net income to net cash		
provided by operating activities:		
Net income		$ 6,450
Adjustments to reconcile net income to net cash		
provided by operating activities:		
Depreciation expense		2,300
Gain on sale of investments		(500)
Loss on sale of equipment		500
Increase in accounts receivable		(1,250)
Decrease in inventory		500
Increase in prepaid rent		(250)
Decrease in accounts payable		(1,000)
Increase in short-term notes payable		1,000
Decrease in salaries payable		(250)
Net cash provided by operating activities		$ 7,500

of securities that are not classified as cash equivalents, and lending money and collecting interest on the loans. *Financing activities* include borrowing money from creditors and repaying the amounts borrowed, as well as obtaining resources from owners and providing them with both a return *on* their investment (through dividends) and a return *of* their investment.

KDM's investing and financing activities are analyzed in the next section. You should refer to Exhibit 6–16 in order to see how each transaction is reported on the statement of cash flows. Remember, the investing activities and financing activities sections of the statement of cash flows are unaffected by how the operating activities section is prepared.

Cash Flows from Investing Activities

The second section of the statement of cash flows presents cash flows from investing activities. To identify items relevant to this section, we must focus particularly on noncurrent asset accounts and transactions that affect those accounts. In addition, we must consider transactions that affect certain short-term investments, as well as gains and losses that are reported on the income statement. A review of KDM's comparative balance sheets, income statement, and additional information (Exhibits 6–6 and 6–7) reveals that KDM has three long-term assets (investments, equipment, and buildings), no short-term investments, a loss on the sale of equipment, and a gain on the sale of investments. From the additional information provided in Exhibit 6–7, we learn that there were four transactions in 1998 that affected cash flows from investing activities: a $3,000,000 sale of long-term investments, a $3,750,000 purchase of equipment ($1,250,000 of which was for cash), a $1,750,000 sale of equipment, and a $7,500,000 addition to the building. In the following sections we will analyze each of the accounts and transactions related to KDM's investing activities to determine their effects on net cash flow from investing activities.

6 Determine cash flows from investing activities.

Long-Term Investments

During 1998 long-term investments decreased by $2,500,000. Our objective is to determine why this decrease occurred and in the process to ascertain the effect on cash flows. Item (e) of the additional information in Exhibit 6–7 states that investments were sold for $3,000,000. This selling price explains the $500,000 gain on the sale of investments. Having no information to the contrary, we can conclude that the sale was for cash. This investing transaction should appear on the statement of cash flows as follows:

Sale of investments **$3,000,000**

Equipment

During 1998 KDM's equipment balance increased by $5,500,000. We must therefore analyze the increases and decreases in equipment to assess their impact on cash flows. Item (a) of the additional information in Exhibit 6–7 reports a purchase of equipment for $3,750,000, of which $1,250,000 represented an outflow of cash. (According to *Statement No. 95,* the $2,500,000 remainder of the purchase, which did not affect cash, must be reported either in a supplementary schedule to the statement of cash flows or in a related narrative. This disclosure must clearly indicate the cash and noncash portions of the transaction, as shown in Exhibit 6–16 for the $2,500,000 noncash portion of the equipment purchase.) The $1,250,000 cash used to purchase the equipment should be reported in the statement of cash flows as follows:

Purchase of equipment. **$1,250,000**

We observe from item (b) in the additional information that another $6,250,000 of equipment was purchased by issuing common stock. This transaction did not affect cash flows. Like the $2,500,000 noncash portion of the equipment purchase just discussed, it must be reported in a supplementary schedule or narrative.

Item (h) of the additional information tells us that equipment with a recorded cost of $4,500,000 was sold for $1,750,000. Since this equipment was only one-half depreciated, we can determine that there was a loss of $500,000 on the sale, which we see reported in the income statement. Having no other information, we can conclude that $1,750,000 in cash was received from the sale. It should be reported in the statement of cash flows as follows:

Sale of equipment. **$1,750,000**

We are aware of no other transactions involving equipment. Based on what we know about equipment, summarized in the T-account below, we have explained the $5,500,000 increase in equipment. (As you can see, a T-account analysis sometimes is helpful when preparing a cash flow statement.)

Equipment

Beginning balance	10,000,000	Sale	4,500,000
Purchased for stock	6,250,000		
Purchased for cash/note	3,750,000		
Ending balance	15,500,000		

Buildings

The buildings account increased by $7,500,000 during 1998. That amount is exactly equal to the cash paid for the addition to buildings mentioned in item (c) of the additional information in Exhibit 6–7. This addition to buildings affected cash flows and must therefore be reported in the statement of cash flows as follows:

Addition to buildings **$7,500,000**

Accumulated Depreciation on Property, Plant, and Equipment

The accumulated depreciation account balance has increased $50,000 by the end of 1998. A T-account analysis will be helpful as we attempt to explain the end-of-1998 balance in this account. The beginning balance was $10,000,000. The sale of equipment that had $2,250,000 of accumulated depreciation would have reduced the accumulated depreciation balance. We also know that depreciation expense of $2,300,000 (Exhibit 6–7) was recorded in 1998. We can summarize these facts as follows:

Accumulated depreciation

Sale of equipment	2,250,000	Beginning balance	10,000,000
		Depreciation expense	2,300,000
		Ending balance	10,050,000

Since the effects on cash flows of all transactions involving accumulated depreciation have been considered elsewhere, our analysis of this account does not call for an entry to the statement of cash flows.

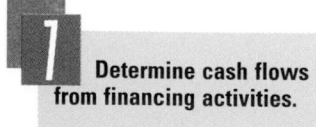
Determine cash flows from financing activities.

Cash Flows from Financing Activities

The third section of a statement of cash flows reports cash flows from financing activities. This section of the statement of cash flows focuses on the long-term liability and stockholders' equity accounts. We will analyze these accounts in the same manner as we did the investment activity accounts. KDM has long-term notes payable, common stock, contributed capital in excess of par, and retained earnings accounts that we must consider. The additional information available to us is that a $2,500,000, five-year (long-term) note was issued as part of an equipment purchase, 350,000 shares of $10 par common stock were issued to purchase $6,250,000 of equipment, a $1,250,000 long-term note was paid by issuing 50,000 shares of common stock, and dividends were paid.

Long-Term Notes Payable

During 1998, KDM's long-term notes payable increased by $1,250,000. We know that long-term notes payable increased by $2,500,000 as part of an equipment purchase and decreased by $1,250,000 as the result of settling (or extinguishing) a note by issuing common stock. These two transactions explain the $1,250,000 net increase in long-term notes payable. However, neither the issuance of long-term notes nor the settlement of a long-term note by issuing common stock affected cash. Therefore, *Statement No. 95* requires that these transactions be reported in a schedule of investing and financing activities that did not affect cash as follows:

Purchased equipment by issuing note. **$2,500,000**
Extinguished a long-term note by issuing common stock **$1,250,000**

This schedule is supplementary to the statement of cash flows (a narrative footnote could be used instead).

Contributed Capital Accounts

The $4,000,000 increase in common stock and the $3,500,000 increase in contributed capital in excess of par are explained by the issuance of a total of 400,000 shares of common stock involved in the purchase of equipment and the extinguishment of a long-term note. The extinguishment of the long-term note was dealt with in the previous section. The $6,250,000 purchase of equipment by issuing common stock did not affect cash flows, and therefore should be included in the supplementary schedule of investing and financing activities that did not affect cash flows as follows:

Purchased equipment by issuing common stock **$6,250,000**

Retained Earnings

KDM's retained earnings at the end of 1998 were $3,200,000 greater than at the end of 1997 (Exhibit 6–6). We know that 1998 net income would increase retained earnings by $6,450,000. Since we are aware of no transactions other than the payment of dividends that would have reduced retained earnings, producing a $3,200,000 net increase, we can conclude that dividends paid in 1998 were $3,250,000. This amount is reported as a cash outflow from financing activities as follows:

Payment of dividends **$3,250,000**

Had dividends been declared but not paid, the resulting decrease in retained earnings would be associated with a $3,250,000 liability for dividends payable (probably current) on KDM's 1998 balance sheet. In that case, no cash outflow would be listed under financing activities. However, the declared but unpaid dividends would be included among the financing activities that did not affect cash.

Summary of Statement Preparation and Reporting Objectives

We have followed the three-step procedure for preparing the statement of cash flows described on page 284. First, we determined that KDM had a $250,000 increase in its cash balance during 1998. (Later, this fact was used to confirm the result of KDM's statement of cash flows.) Then we analyzed the available income statement data, changes in the noncash balance sheet accounts, and other information to identify transactions that caused cash inflows and outflows during the period. Finally, we prepared KDM's statement of cash flows using the direct approach as shown in Exhibit 6–16. Study Exhibit 6–16 carefully, noting each of the components of the three activity sections, as well as the list of investing and financing activities that did not affect cash. In particular, observe that the statement of cash flows yields the same $250,000 increase in cash shown by KDM's comparative balance sheets for 1997 and 1998 (Exhibit 6–6). In short, the statement of cash flows explains why KDM's cash balance increased by $250,000 during 1998.

For comparative purposes, refer to the consolidated statements of cash flows for USAir Group, Inc., that are presented in Exhibit 6–4. USAir prepares its statement of cash flows using the indirect approach for determining cash flows from operating activities. The next section compares the direct and indirect approaches.

COMPARISON OF THE DIRECT AND INDIRECT APPROACHES

The KDM, Inc., data were used to illustrate both the indirect and the direct approaches to determining net cash provided (or used) by operating activities. As stated earlier, *Statement No. 95* encourages use of the direct approach but permits the indirect approach as an alternative, apparently because of its popularity. Because many companies feel their accounting systems cannot capture the data required by the direct approach, the indirect approach is also considered to be less costly.

The KDM illustration should make it clear that the direct and indirect approaches are merely alternative methods of arriving at the same result. Whereas the indirect approach arrives at net cash provided or used by operating activities by adjusting net income, the direct approach converts the accrual-basis income statement (and other accruals and deferrals) directly to a cash basis.

The major conceptual argument in support of the indirect approach is that because the calculation begins with net income, users are better able to link operating cash flows to net income. As a result, users can better assess a company's earnings "quality"—that is, how closely income flows are correlated with cash flows. Arguments against the indirect approach are that (1) the major sources of gross cash inflows and outflows from operating activities are not reported and (2) users of financial statements may become confused by the adjustments to net income that are necessary to arrive at net cash provided or used by operating activities. For example, depreciation often has been viewed—quite incorrectly—as a source of "funds," or cash, because it is added back to net income under the indirect approach.

Proponents of the direct approach argue that it is much more straightforward than the indirect approach and therefore much less confusing. It shows clearly that cash inflows are from customers and other sources, and that cash outflows are for merchandise, salaries, interest, taxes, and other operating items.[9] Furthermore,

---

[9]A similar point has been made by Loyd C. Heath. See Loyd C. Heath, "Let's Scrap the Funds Statement," *Journal of Accountancy*, October 1978, pp. 94–103.

the direct approach provides more information than the indirect approach because of the requirement that the direct analysis be accompanied by the indirect reconciliation.

Conceptually, we agree with the FASB's preference for the direct approach. The direct approach is more *understandable,* more *relevant,* and more *representationally faithful* than the indirect approach, even though it may be more costly to apply. Furthermore, a statement of cash flows that is prepared using the direct approach to report operating cash inflows and outflows should be the more logical and simpler statement from the viewpoint of financial statement users, because those cash flows are not affected by *recognition, measurement,* or *estimation* issues. Finally, much of the apparent "mystery" that has surrounded funds (cash) flow reporting over the past several decades can be attributed to the widespread use of the indirect approach.

CASH FLOW ANALYSIS

The statements of cash flows for General Electric Company (GE) and consolidated affiliates for 1993 through 1995 appear in the first three columns on pages 1232–1233 of Appendix B of the textbook. The next three columns show the 1993–1995 statements of cash flows for GE alone. We will use the separate GE statements of cash flows to illustrate how a statement of cash flows might be analyzed.

A statement of cash flows provides information about both the sources of cash inflows and the uses of cash resources during an accounting period. In GE's case, there was an overall decrease in cash and cash equivalents of $499 million during 1995. The source of almost all of GE's cash inflows was operating activity. The major uses of cash resources were additions to property, plant, and equipment; payment of nonoperating debt; purchase of treasury stock; and payment of dividends. Note that the pattern of sources and uses of cash in 1995 was very similar to the pattern in 1993 and 1994, except for the purchase of treasury shares, which was primarily a 1995 event. We can conclude that over the 1993–1995 period, GE generated most of its cash inflows from operating activities, and used most of its cash to pay dividends; invest in new property, plant, and equipment; reduce its debt; and acquire, and place in treasury, shares of its common stock.

The amount of cash inflows generated by GE's operating activities, plus the company's ability to continue to generate cash inflows from operations, is particularly important because business success depends on successful operating activities. Since operating activities were the main source of GE's cash inflows for several years, it is reasonable to expect that GE will continue to generate substantial cash inflows from operations in the future. Furthermore, GE's acquisitions of property, plant, and equipment indicate that management expects increased demand for the company's goods and services, which suggests even greater cash inflows from operations in the future.

The fact that GE is using substantial amounts of cash to purchase treasury stock is also a positive sign. By decreasing the number of shares of common stock outstanding, GE will reduce a major use of cash (namely, the payment of dividends), making more cash available for other uses. Even if GE's profitability remains stable, dividends per share can be increased for those shares that remain outstanding.

There is a good correlation between GE's cash inflows from operating activities and its earnings—both increased each year in the 1993–1995 period—which indicates a high quality of earnings. GE's ability to generate substantial operating cash inflows allows it to pay its debts as they mature; that is, GE's solvency is good. In fact, as mentioned earlier, one of the main uses of GE's cash resources during the 1993–1995 period was the reduction of debt (a financing activity). Finally, because of its ability to

CONCEPTUAL

The direct approach is more understandable, more relevant, and more representationally faithful than the indirect approach.

CONCEPTUAL

The cash flows reported under the direct approach are not affected by the recognition, measurement, or estimation issues that impact the income statement.

generate substantial cash inflows from operating activities, GE has the liquid resources, or financial flexibility, to adapt to changing business conditions.

⑤UMMARY OF THE USES AND OBJECTIVES OF FINANCIAL STATEMENTS

We have now explained and illustrated all the basic concepts and procedures related to preparing the statement of cash flows. As stated earlier, information reported in the statement of cash flows, when used with other financial statement information, helps users to assess a company's future cash flow potential. It also helps users in assessing a company's ability to pay its debts, to pay dividends, and to meet its need for external financing. Finally, the statement of cash flows helps users to understand differences between a company's income flows and cash flows, and to assess both the cash and noncash aspects of the company's investing and financing activities.

In this chapter and Chapters 4 and 5, we have described the objectives and content of the basic financial statements. Individually and as a set, these financial statements are designed to meet the objectives of financial reporting. These statements are interrelated; they complement one another. No single statement is likely to be adequate in meeting the need for accounting information required for a particular decision. For example, the income statement provides profitability information, but rate-of-return calculations also require information found in the balance sheet. The statement of cash flows provides useful cash flow information but must generally be used with the income statement and balance sheet to obtain meaningful projections of future cash flows. In summary, the financial statements are intended to meet the needs of investors, creditors, and other users who have a common interest in the amount, timing, and uncertainty of a company's cash flows. The fact that the financial statements are general-purpose statements means that they do not satisfy all users equally well, nor are they all-purpose statements.

⑤UMMARY OF LEARNING OBJECTIVES

1. **State the purpose of the statement of cash flows and describe its format.**
   The primary purpose of the statement of cash flows is to provide information regarding a company's cash inflows and outflows during the accounting period. The statement is organized according to an activity format, which means that cash inflows and outflows are classified in terms of operating, investing, and financing activities. Noncash investing and financing activities must be reported in a separate schedule below the statement of cash flows or in a narrative footnote.

2. **Discuss various types of questions that might be answered and types of information that might be obtained by examining a statement of cash flows.**
   Questions that might be answered by examining the statement of cash flows include: (1) If a company operates at a profit, how can it be continually short of cash? (2) How can a company operate at a loss and still generate huge inflows of cash from operations? (3) Is the company making capital expenditures to modernize, expand, or replace worn-out or obsolete plant and equipment? (4) Did the company acquire any long-term investments or other income-producing assets during the period? (5) Did the company obtain cash from the disposal of long-lived assets during the period? If so, how much? (6) Did the company obtain financing during the period through the issuance of debt or equity securities? If so, how much? (7) Did the com-

pany use cash to retire any long-term debt or equity securities during the period? In addition to helping to answer these questions, a statement of cash flows may provide information about the quality of a company's earnings and its solvency, liquidity, and financial flexibility.

3. **Explain why net income for a period and net cash flow from operations for the same period may differ in amount.**
The income statement is based on accrual accounting. Therefore, the revenues, expenses, gains, and losses reported in the income statement do not necessarily represent cash inflows and outflows. In general, two distinct classes of items cause differences between income flows and cash flows: (1) items on the income statement that do not represent inflows and outflows of cash, or for which actual cash flows differ from the amounts on the income statement; and (2) items reflecting cash flows that appear not on the income statement, but on the balance sheet as prepayments, deferrals, unearned items, or reductions of accruals.

4. **Use the indirect approach to determine cash flows from operating activities.**
Under the indirect approach, cash flows from operating activities are determined by adjusting net income to a cash basis. Adjustments are made for revenues, expenses, gains, and losses that appear on the income statement but do not affect cash. Net income is also adjusted for operating cash inflows and outflows that do not appear on the income statement. The latter adjustments are based on analysis of the current asset and liability accounts.

5. **Use the direct approach to determine cash flows from operating activities.**
Under the direct approach, each operating item in the income statement is adjusted to a cash flow basis by adjusting for changes during the period in related balance sheet accounts. The calculation of net cash flows from operating activities begins with cash collections from customers, interest revenue, and dividends, followed by deductions for cash payments for purchases of goods, operating expenses, interest expense, and taxes. Companies that use the direct approach must also present the indirect approach in a supplementary schedule.

6. **Determine cash flows from investing activities.**
The second section of a statement of cash flows presents cash flows from investing activities. Cash flows related to the noncurrent asset accounts and transactions affecting those accounts must be analyzed. Cash flows related to transactions that affect certain short-term investments and investment income (including gains and losses) reported on the income statement must also be identified.

7. **Determine cash flows from financing activities.**
The third section of a statement of cash flows reports cash flows from financing activities. The long-term liability and stockholders' equity accounts must be analyzed and the cash flow effects of activities involving those accounts assessed.

8. **Prepare a statement of cash flows.**
Preparation of a statement of cash flows is a three-step procedure. First, the amount of change in the cash account for the period is calculated. Next, the available income statement data, changes in noncash balance sheet accounts, and other information are analyzed to determine cash inflows and outflows during the period. Finally, the statement of cash flows is prepared using an activity format, with separate sections for cash flows from operating activities, investing activities, and financing activities. Significant noncash investing and financing activities should be disclosed in a supplementary schedule or supporting footnote.

9. **Discuss the relative merits of the indirect and direct approaches for determining cash flows from operating activities.**
The major conceptual argument in favor of the indirect approach is that it links operating cash flows with a company's net income more clearly because the calculation begins with net income. Thus, users can better assess earnings quality. The indirect approach is used more widely than the direct approach, probably because it is the traditional format, and as such does not require significant changes in recordkeeping.
   Arguments against the indirect approach are that (1) it does not report the major sources of gross cash inflows and outflows from operating activities and (2) users of financial statements may become confused by the adjustments to net income

(e.g., some users view depreciation as a source of cash because it is added to net income under the direct approach).

The direct approach is more straightforward than the indirect approach and is much less confusing. It clearly shows that cash inflows are from customers and other sources, and that cash outflows are for merchandise, salaries, interest, taxes, and other operating items. Furthermore, the direct approach provides more information than the indirect approach because of the requirement that it be accompanied by an indirect reconciliation. In summary, the direct approach is more understandable, more relevant, and more representationally faithful than the indirect approach, and the cash flows it reports are not affected by recognition, measurement, or estimation issues.

KEY TERMS

activity format 278	investing activities 279
cash equivalents 278	liquidity 283
direct approach 279	operating activities 278
financial flexibility 283	quality of earnings 283
financing activities 279	solvency 283
indirect approach 281	statement of cash flows 278

QUESTIONS

Q 6-1. What is the purpose of the statement of cash flows?

Q 6-2. How does the statement of cash flows relate to *Statement of Financial Accounting Concepts No. 5?*

Q 6-3. List the various concepts of funds discussed at the beginning of the chapter.

Q 6-4. Distinguish among a company's operating activities, investing activities, and financing activities.

Q 6-5. List three examples of investing activities and three examples of financing activities.

Q 6-6. How can the statement of cash flows provide information related to the quality of earnings?

Q 6-7. List three types of transactions that have no effect on cash but that must be disclosed either in a narrative or in a supplementary schedule to the statement of cash flows.

Q 6-8. Give two examples of a cash equivalent.

Q 6-9. Two approaches that can be used to determine the amount of cash flows from operating activities are the direct approach and the indirect approach. What are the differences between the two approaches?

Q 6-10. When cash collections from customers are calculated under the direct approach, why must sales revenue be adjusted for a change in accounts receivable during the period?

Q 6-11. How would interest revenue accrued on a cash equivalent be reported on the statement of cash flows?

Q 6-12. A company acquired a tract of land with a fair value of $300,000 by paying $125,000 cash and issuing a 10-year note for the balance. Explain how this transaction would be reported on the statement of cash flows.

Q 6-13. Explain how a company could report a net loss for the year and still have cash flows generated from operations.

Q 6-14. A partial statement of cash flows for Harsons Company appears below. What changes would you suggest for this statement?

Cash flows from operating activities:

Net income..	$360,352
Depreciation charged to income.......................	196,159
Net book value of property, plant, and equipment retired	18,730
Other noncash items	(44,881)
Net cash provided by operating activities	$530,360

Q 6-15. Indicate how the transactions below would appear on a statement of cash flows prepared using the direct approach. Use the following key for your answers:
  a) Income statement adjustment for determining operating cash flows.
  b) Investing activity.
  c) Financing activity.
  d) Supplementary schedule (noncash investing and/or financing activity).
  e) None of the above.
    I. ____ Declaration (but not payment) of a cash dividend.
    2. ____ Gain on disposal of equipment.
    3. ____ Interest accrued on short-term notes receivable.
    4. ____ Interest accrued on long-term notes receivable.
    5. ____ Issuance of long-term notes for cash.
    6. ____ Issuance of short-term notes for cash.
    7. ____ Depreciation expense.
    8. ____ Proceeds from sale of land.
    9. ____ Dividends received from investments.
    10. ____ Loss on sale of equipment.
    II. ____ Issue of common stock at a price in excess of par.

CASES

C 6-I. **STATEMENT OF CASH FLOWS: OBJECTIVES AND ISSUES** For several years Brown Corporation has prepared a statement of cash flows in accordance with GAAP. Because Brown invests idle cash in short-term government obligations, the company's statement of cash flows combines cash and cash equivalents in a single pool. Brown uses the direct approach in reporting cash flows from operating activities.

REQUIRED **I.** Why are cash and cash equivalents thought to be superior to cash in preparing the statement of cash flows?
  2. Brown's controller has asked you to explain briefly how the following transactions should be disclosed, if at all, in the company's statement of cash flows:
    a) During the year, Brown issued common stock in an acquisition of land.
    b) Brown reported a net loss of $100,000 for the year, based on cash revenues of $300,000 and total expenses of $400,000. However, 75 percent of Brown's total expenses were noncash expenses. These noncash expenses included depreciation and other allocations of amounts from balance sheet asset accounts.
    c) Brown owns some of the common stock of Nathan Corporation. During the current year. Brown purchased additional shares of Nathan for $100,000 and received cash dividends of $12,000 from Nathan.
    d) Near the end of the year, Brown sold land at its fair value of $40,000 and recorded a gain of $8,000.

C 6-2.   **WEAKNESSES IN PREPARATION OF STATEMENT OF CASH FLOWS**   The following statement was prepared by the accountant for the Ramon Corporation:

Ramon Corporation
Statement of Sources and Applications of Cash
For the Year Ended September 30, 1998

Sources of cash:

Net income	$ 35,000
Depreciation and amortization	59,000
Interest	22,000
Increase in long-term debt	178,000
Changes in current receivables and inventories, less current liabilities (excluding current maturities of long-term debt)	3,000
	$297,000

Uses of cash:

Cash dividends	$ 33,000
Expenditures for property, plant, and equipment	202,000
Investments and other uses	9,000
Change in cash	53,000
	$297,000

The following additional information is available for Ramon Corporation for the year ended September 30, 1998:

a)

Increase in long-term debt	$600,000
Retirement of debt	(422,000)
Net increase	$178,000

b)   During the year, Ramon's interest expense was $22,000 less than its cash payments to creditors.

c)

Expenditures for property, plant, and equipment	$212,000
Proceeds from retirements of property, plant, and equipment	(10,000)
Net expenditures	$202,000

d)   On July 1, 1998, when its market price was $5 per share, 16,000 shares of Ramon Corporation common stock were issued in exchange for a plot of land with a fair value of $80,000.

REQUIRED   **1.**   Identify the weaknesses in the form and format of Ramon Corporation's statement of sources and applications of cash, without reference to the additional information.

2.   For each of the four items of additional information, indicate the proper disclosure on the statement of cash flows.

(AICPA, adapted)

C 6-3.   **NET CASH FLOWS FROM OPERATING ACTIVITIES**   A friend of yours recently formed a new business and, after three years of operations, wishes to expand the business. She has approached a local financial institution about the possibility of a substantial loan and has been told by the potential lender that she will need to submit a complete set of financial statements (including a statement of cash flows) for the business. Your friend is aware that there are two approaches for preparing the statement of cash flows, and she has come to you for an explanation of the two alternative approaches and, relatedly, is interested in how several items would appear on the statement of cash flows under each of the approaches for preparing the statement.

REQUIRED   **1.**   Write two or three paragraphs discussing the two approaches that can be used to prepare the cash flows from operating activities section of the statement of cash flows. As part of your discussion, comment on the arguments supporting each of the approaches.

2. How would each of the items below affect cash flows from operating activities prepared under (1) the direct approach and (2) the indirect approach?

   a) Decrease in accounts receivable.

   b) Increase in interest receivable.

   c) Loss on sale of equipment.

   d) Decrease in merchandise inventory.

   e) Depreciation expense.

   f) Decrease in accounts payable to suppliers.

C 6-4. **RECONCILING INCOME FLOWS AND CASH FLOWS** ADC Corporation is a computer service company. The company's business consists of computer consulting and installing computer systems that have been purchased by clients from computer manufacturers. The company has reported large amounts of net income for many years. However, ADC management consistently has been forced to borrow large amounts from creditors in order to finance the company's operations. Additional information about the operating activities of ADC is as follows:

a) ADC owns 100 percent of the common stock of Hill Company. Because of cash pressures, Hill has never paid a cash dividend but has reported substantial amounts of net income for several years. Because it controls Hill, ADC has been reporting Hill's income each year as a debit to investment in Hill and as a credit to investment revenue.

b) ADC allows its customers very lenient credit terms. In fact, over the past several years, the company's accounts receivable balances have been increasing at a rate in excess of 15 percent per year. The company's uncollectible accounts expense has remained fairly constant during this period.

c) For several years, ADC has paid cash for an option to bid on a large government computer contract. To date, the company has not been awarded a contract but has submitted a bid each year. ADC has recorded the cost of each option as an asset to be matched against contract revenue should a contract be awarded at some future date.

d) Because of the nature of their operations, very few of ADC's suppliers sell on credit. In fact, many suppliers require that cash accompany a purchase order. Over the past several years, the supplies inventory of ADC has been increasing at a fairly substantial rate.

REQUIRED For each item above, write a brief paragraph discussing how the item could cause significant differences between the income flows of ADC and the company's cash flows from operating activities.

EXERCISES

E 6-1. **CALCULATING CASH FLOWS** Baker Corporation's comparative balance sheets and income statement are presented here:

Baker Corporation
Comparative Balance Sheets

	12/31/97	12/31/98
Assets:		
Cash	$ 19,000	$ 50,000
Accounts receivable	24,000	15,000
Inventory	31,000	59,000
Plant and equipment	40,000	77,000
Accumulated depreciation	(12,000)	(29,000)
Land	28,000	4,000
Total	$130,000	$176,000
Liabilities and stockholders' equity:		
Accounts payable	$ 16,000	$ 20,000
Notes payable (short-term)	7,000	–0–
Bonds payable	–0–	20,000
Common stock (no-par)	90,000	102,000
Retained earnings	17,000	34,000
Total	$130,000	$176,000

Income Statement
For the Year Ended December 31, 1998

Revenues	$190,000
Cost of goods sold	(125,000)
Depreciation	(17,000)
Other expenses	(20,000)
Loss on sale of land	(6,000)
Net income	$ 22,000

The notes were issued in 1997 for the acquisition of plant and equipment.

REQUIRED Calculate the following for Baker for 1998:
1. Cash flows from operating activities under the:
   a) Direct approach.
   b) Indirect approach.
2. Proceeds received on the sale of land.
3. Amount of cash received from issuing the bonds.
4. Dividends paid during the year.
5. Proceeds received on the issuance of common stock.
6. Cash used to purchase plant and equipment.

E 6-2. **PREPARING A STATEMENT OF CASH FLOWS** Using the information for Baker Corporation in E6-1, prepare Baker's statement of cash flows using the indirect approach for determining cash flows from operating activities.

E 6-3.   **CASH PROVIDED (USED) BY OPERATIONS** An income statement for the first year of operations for Darcy Company appears below:

Sales	$300,000
Dividend revenue	30,000
Interest revenue	18,500
Cost of goods sold	(160,000)
Salary expense	(20,000)
Depreciation expense	(54,000)
Income tax expense	(84,000)
Net income	$ 30,500

Additional information:
a) Salaries payable, end of year, $6,500.
b) Accounts payable, end of year, $10,000.
c) Inventories, end of year, $20,000.
d) Accounts receivable, end of year, $25,000.
e) Customers' accounts with credit balances (included in item *d*), end of year, $2,000.

REQUIRED   Calculate the cash provided (used) by operating activities for Darcy Company. Use the direct approach.

E 6-4.   **CASH PROVIDED BY OPERATIONS** Using the information for Darcy Company in E6-3, prepare the cash provided (used) by operating activities section of Darcy's statement of cash flows under the indirect approach.

E 6-5.   **CASH PAYMENTS TO SUPPLIERS** Dillon Company reported cost of goods sold of $237,800 on its 1998 income statement. Other information for Dillon is as follows:

	BEGINNING OF 1998	END OF 1998
Inventory	$32,600	$35,800
Accounts payable	17,500	16,230

REQUIRED   Prepare a schedule showing the amount of cash paid to suppliers in 1998.

E 6-6.   **CASH PAYMENTS TO SUPPLIERS** Ernest reported cost of goods sold of $70,000 for the current year. Other information about the company's operating activities is as follows:

	BEGINNING OF YEAR	END OF YEAR
Inventories	$4,600	$6,000
Accounts payable	3,000	–0–

Of the $4,600 in beginning inventory, $500 was written off as obsolete during the year.

REQUIRED   Prepare a schedule showing the amount of cash paid to Ernest's suppliers during the current year.

E 6-7.   **REPORTING NONCASH TRANSACTIONS** During the current year, Nair Realty Corporation acquired rental real estate, a long-term investment, with a fair value of $300,000. Resources sacrificed in the transaction were as follows:

Issuance of long-term notes	$ 95,000
Issuance of common stock	80,000
Cash	125,000
Total	$300,000

REQUIRED   Show how the above transaction would be reported in the corporation's statement of cash flows.

E 6-8. **CASH FLOWS FROM OPERATING ACTIVITIES** Nilson, Inc., has the following balance sheets for the beginning and end of the current year:

	BEGINNING BALANCE	ENDING BALANCE
Cash..	$ –0–	$17,000
Accounts receivable..	8,500	12,500
Inventories	8,000	5,000
Plant and equipment		
(net of accumulated depreciation)	2,000	–0–
Salaries payable.......................................	(4,000)	–0–
Income taxes payable	(1,000)	(4,500)
Owners' equity	$13,500	$30,000

Nilson's income statement for the current year is:

Sales		$70,000
Cost of goods sold		(16,000)
Gross margin...		$54,000
Expenses:		
Salaries...	$(19,000)	
Interest	(5,000)	
Depreciation	(2,000)	(26,000)
Income before taxes...................................		$28,000
Income tax expense		(11,000)
Net income		$17,000

REQUIRED Using the direct approach, prepare a schedule calculating Nilson's net cash flows from operating activities. Were there any nonoperating cash flows this year? If so, for what purpose and for what amount?

E 6-9. **CASH FLOWS FROM OPERATING ACTIVITIES** Using the information for Nilson Company in E 6-8, prepare the cash provided (used) by the operating activities section of Nilson's statement of cash flows under the indirect approach. Were there any nonoperating cash flows this year? If so, for what purpose and for what amount?

E 6-10. **CASH COLLECTIONS FROM CUSTOMERS** The information below was taken from the accounting records of Willard Company:

	BEGINNING BALANCE	ENDING BALANCE
Accounts receivable....................................	$70,000	$12,500
Allowance for doubtful accounts........................	8,000	11,500

Credit sales for the year were $90,000. Uncollectible accounts expense for the year was $11,000, and $7,500 in customers' accounts were written off as uncollectible during the year.

REQUIRED Prepare a schedule showing the amount of cash collected from customers during the year.

E 6-11. **CASH FLOWS FROM INVESTING ACTIVITIES** The following information relates to the plant and equipment accounts of Hasting Corporation:

	BEGINNING BALANCE	ENDING BALANCE
Land...	$ 65,000	$ 77,000
Building and equipment	200,000	250,000
Accumulated depreciation	50,000	39,000

Land with a carrying value of $38,000 was sold at a loss of $6,000. Equipment with an original cost of $20,000 and accumulated depreciation of $17,000 was written off as obsolete. During the year, a building with an original cost of $60,000 and accumulated depreciation of $30,000 was sold at a $20,000 gain. Depreciation expense for the period was $36,000.

REQUIRED   Prepare a schedule showing Hasting's cash flows from investing activities for the year.

E 6-12.   **CASH FLOWS FROM FINANCING ACTIVITIES**   The following data apply to Derrick Company:

	BEGINNING BALANCE	ENDING BALANCE
Dividends payable	$ 10,000	$ 17,000
Retained earnings	150,000	200,000

Net income for the year was $80,000.

REQUIRED   Prepare a schedule showing the amount of cash dividends paid by Derrick Company during the year.

E 6-13.   **CASH FLOWS; EXTRAORDINARY ITEMS**   Gill Corporation began the current year with the following balance sheet:

Land	$200,000	Capital stock	$200,000

During the year, Gill leased the land to a lessee for $8,000 per month. At the end of the year, federal authorities condemned the land because of carcinogenic materials discovered by the lessee. Gill received $130,000 from authorities as a condemnation award. The company's income statement for the year and its balance sheet at the end of the year appeared as follows:

Income Statement for the Year

Rental revenues	$96,000
Operating expenses	(6,000)
Income before taxes and extraordinary item	$90,000
Income tax expense	(36,000)
Income before extraordinary item	$54,000
Extraordinary item:	
Loss on condemnation of land (net of $28,000 tax benefit)	(42,000)
Net income	$12,000

Balance Sheet, End of Year

Cash	$212,000	Capital stock	$200,000
		Retained earnings	12,000
	$212,000		$212,000

REQUIRED   Prepare the statement of cash flows for Gill for the current year. Gill uses the direct approach. You need not prepare a reconciliation schedule.

E 6-14.   **RELATIONSHIP BETWEEN BALANCE SHEET AND STATEMENT OF CASH FLOWS**   Selected financial statements for Lindal Corporation appear below:

Balance Sheet
December 31, 1997

Assets:		Equities:	
Cash	$35,000	Capital stock (no par)	$30,000
Buildings and equipment	48,000	Retained earnings	38,000
Accumulated depreciation—			
buildings and equipment	(15,000)		
	$68,000		$68,000

Statement of Cash Flows
For the Year Ended December 31, 1998

Cash flows from operating activities:		
Collected from customers	$50,000	
Paid for salaries	(11,000)	
Paid for other expenses	(8,000)	
Net cash provided by operating activities		$31,000
Cash flows from investing activities:		
Sale of buildings	$ 8,000	
Purchase of land	(18,000)	
Purchase of buildings and equipment	(30,000)	
Net cash used by investing activities		(40,000)
Cash flows from financing activities:		
Issue of capital stock	$20,000	
Payment of dividends	(16,000)	
Net cash flows from financing activities		4,000
Net decrease in cash		$ (5,000)

Other information:
a)   Depreciation expense for 1998, $11,000.
b)   Accumulated depreciation on the building sold, $6,000; gain on sale, $4,000.
c)   Net income for 1998, $24,000.

REQUIRED   On the basis of the above data, prepare the balance sheet for Lindal Corporation as of December 31, 1998.

E 6-15.   **ANALYSIS OF CHANGES IN ACCOUNT BALANCES IN PREPARATION OF STATEMENT OF CASH FLOWS**   In preparing the statement of cash flows for Sherrill Corporation, you find the following data related to the equipment and bonds payable accounts:
a)   Account balances and information related to equipment during the year:

	BALANCE, BEGINNING OF YEAR	BALANCE, END OF YEAR
Equipment	$66,000	$210,000
Accumulated depreciation	30,000	38,000

Equipment with an original cost of $32,000 and a book value of $19,000 was sold at a gain of $6,000.
b)   Account balances and information relating to bonds payable during the year:

	BALANCE, BEGINNING OF YEAR	BALANCE, END OF YEAR
Bonds payable (maturity values, $80,000 and $60,000, respectively)	$92,000	$ 70,000

Bonds with a par (face) value of $20,000 were issued for $22,000 in exchange for land. Bonds with a book value of $44,000 were retired. The amount paid was $50,000, and the loss of $6,000 was extraordinary.

REQUIRED Based on the information given in items *a* and *b* above, prepare schedules showing Sherrill's:
1. Cash flows from investing activities.
2. Cash flows from financing activities.

E 6-16. **ANALYSIS OF CHANGES IN ACCOUNT BALANCES** Account balances related to equipment and accumulated depreciation on equipment at the beginning and end of a company's fiscal year are as follows:

	BALANCE, BEGINNING OF YEAR	BALANCE, END OF YEAR
Equipment	$96,000	$200,000
Accumulated depreciation	30,000	38,000

Equipment with a book value of $10,000 and an original cost of $22,000 was sold at a gain of $9,000. All equipment purchases were for cash.

REQUIRED Calculate:
1. The amount of cash provided by the sale of equipment.
2. The amount of cash used to purchase equipment.
3. The current year's depreciation expense.

E 6-17. **CONVERSION OF STATEMENT OF CASH FLOWS TO ACCRUAL-BASIS INCOME STATEMENT** The statement of cash flows for the fiscal year ended November 30, 1998, and other data for Patton Corporation are shown below:

Cash flows from operating activities:
Cash collections from customers	$330,000	
Dividends received	20,000	
Cash outflows for:		
Merchandise	(100,000)	
Salaries	(50,000)	
Taxes	(25,000)	
Other operating expenses	(20,000)	
Net cash provided by operating activities		$155,000
Cash flows from investing activities:		
Sales of investments	$ 30,000	
Purchased machinery	(100,000)	
Net cash used by investing activities...................		(70,000)
Cash flows from financing activities:		
Issue of capital stock		75,000
Net increase in cash		$160,000

Additional data:
a) Patton's dividends receivable account increased by $2,000 during the year.
b) The machinery account, net of accumulated depreciation, increased by $70,000 during the year. The only other transaction, exclusive of depreciation, was the write-off on May 1, 1998, of obsolete machinery that had a book value of $5,000.
c) Accounts receivable increased by $60,000 during 1998. The allowance account increased by $5,000. There were no write-offs of uncollectible accounts.
d) Salaries payable at the beginning of the year were $6,000; at the end of the year, $9,000.
e) Inventories decreased $24,000 during 1998.
f) Taxes payable decreased $6,000 during the year.
g) The investments that were sold had a book value of $20,000.

REQUIRED On the basis of the above data, prepare Patton Corporation's income statement for the year ended November 30, 1998.

E 6-18. **CONVERSION OF CASH-BASIS INCOME STATEMENT AMOUNTS TO AN ACCRUAL BASIS**
Green Company keeps its books on the cash basis. The 1998 cash-basis income statement, along with additional information, follows:

Green Company
Income Statement (Cash Basis)
For the Year Ended December 31, 1998

Cash receipts		$195,000
Cash payments:		
Wages	$(60,000)	
Taxes	(40,000)	
Insurance	(20,000)	(120,000)
Net income		$ 75,000

Additional information:

a)

	BALANCES	
	JANUARY 1, 1998	**DECEMBER 31, 1998**
Accounts receivable	$30,000	$20,000
Allowance for doubtful accounts	1,500	1,200
Prepaid insurance	2,000	1,000
Prepaid interest	3,000	1,000
Accumulated depreciation	30,000	45,000
Wages payable	5,000	10,000
Taxes payable	10,000	15,000

b) Accounts receivable written off during 1998 amounted to $4,000.
c) A piece of equipment was sold during 1998 for $7,000 cash. It originally cost $10,000 and had a book value at the time of sale of $3,000.

REQUIRED Calculate the following amounts that Green Company should show on its 1998 income statement, prepared on an accrual basis:
1. Sales revenue.
2. Depreciation expense.
3. Uncollectible accounts expense.
4. Wage expense.
5. Taxes expense.
6. Insurance expense.
7. Interest expense.
8. Net income.

E 6-19. **RECONCILING INCOME FLOWS AND CASH FLOWS** A schedule that reconciles net loss and cash flows from operating activities for Taylor Corporation appears below:

	INCOME STATEMENT	ADJUSTMENT	CASH FLOWS
Sales	$140,000	(1)	$180,000
Rent revenue	8,000	(2)	12,000
Cost of goods sold	(100,000)	(3)	
		(4)	(90,000)
Salaries expense	(30,000)	(5)	(36,000)
Depreciation expense	(20,000)	(6)	–0–
Insurance expense	(5,000)	(7)	(6,000)
Income tax expense	(10,000)	(8)	(4,000)
Net income	$ (7,000)		
Net cash provided by operating activities			$ 56,000

Additional information:
a) During the year, accounts payable decreased by $15,000.
b) There was no change in interest payable during the year.

REQUIRED   For each number in parentheses in the adjustment column above, indicate the most probable transaction or event that led to the adjustment.

PROBLEMS

P 6-1.   **STATEMENT OF CASH FLOWS**   Jackson Corporation's income statement for the year ended December 31, 1998, and comparative balance sheets at December 31, 1997 and 1998 appear below:

Jackson Corporation
Comparative Balance Sheets

	12/31/97	12/31/98
Assets:		
Cash	$ 80	$ 240
Accounts receivable	100	150
Inventory	190	130
Long-term investments	220	180
Plant and equipment	400	440
Accumulated depreciation	(200)	(220)
Land	–0–	580
Total	$790	$1,500
Liabilities and stockholders' equity:		
Accounts payable	$210	$ 90
Wages payable	80	60
Notes payable (long-term)	100	270
Common stock (no par)	100	600
Retained earnings	300	480
Total	$790	$1,500

Income Statement
For the Year Ended December 31, 1998

Sales revenue	$1,340
Cost of goods sold	(760)
Depreciation	(100)
Other expenses	(300)
Loss on sale of equipment	(20)
Gain on sale of long-term investments	100
Net income	$ 260

Additional data for 1998:
a) Plant and equipment costing $160 (50 percent depreciated) was sold at the end of 1998 for $60 cash.
b) Purchased land costing $200; paid $50; gave long-term note for the balance.
c) Paid $80 on long-term notes.
d) Issued common stock for $200 cash.
e) Purchased plant and equipment for $200; paid one-half cash; gave a long-term note for the balance.
f) Issued 300 shares of common stock for land with a fair value of $380 and paid the balance in cash. The shares were actively traded at $1 per share.
g) Sold long-term investments for $140.
h) Dividends are declared and paid in the same year.

REQUIRED   **I.** Calculate the cash flows from operating activities using:
  a) The direct approach.
  b) The indirect approach.
  2. Prepare the statement of cash flows using the direct approach. You need not prepare a reconciliation schedule.

P 6-2. **STATEMENT OF CASH FLOWS** The following comparative balance sheets and income statement are available for Bolton, Inc.:

Bolton, Inc.
Comparative Balance Sheets

	12/31/97	12/31/98
Assets:		
Cash	$ 2,375	$ 7,400
Accounts receivable	3,000	1,875
Inventory	3,875	7,375
Plant and equipment	5,000	9,625
Accumulated depreciation	(1,500)	(3,625)
Land	3,500	500
Total	$16,250	$23,150
Liabilities and stockholders' equity:		
Accounts payable	$ 2,000	$ 2,400
Notes payable (short-term)	875	–0–
Bonds payable	–0–	2,500
Common stock (no par)	11,250	12,750
Retained earnings	2,125	5,500
Total	$16,250	$23,150

Income Statement
For the Year Ended December 31, 1998

Sales revenue	$25,000
Cost of goods sold	(15,625)
Depreciation	(2,125)
Other expenses[a]	(2,500)
Loss on sale of land	(750)
Net income	$ 4,000

[a]Other expenses were paid in cash.

REQUIRED   Prepare Bolton's statement of cash flows using the direct approach.

P 6-3. **STATEMENT OF CASH FLOWS** The records of Victory Flower Shop showed the following information related to the balance sheet accounts and the income statement:

Income Statement for 1998

Revenues and gains	$15,000
Cost of goods sold	(7,000)
Salaries expense	(3,000)
Interest expense	(600)
Other expenses and losses	(1,400)
Net income	$ 3,000

Balance Sheet at End of Year

	12/31/97	12/31/98
Debits:		
Cash	$ 1,000	$ 1,100
Accounts receivable	1,900	2,400
Inventory	5,200	5,000
Prepaid expenses	800	800
Long-term investments	1,000	–0–
Buildings	9,000	12,000
Machinery	4,000	6,200
	$22,900	$27,500
Credits:		
Accounts payable	$ 1,200	$ 800
Notes payable—short-term (operating)	900	1,300
Accrued wages	300	200
Accumulated depreciation	4,000	3,900
Notes payable—long-term	3,000	3,500
Common stock	12,000	15,000
Retained earnings	1,500	2,800
	$22,900	$27,500

Additional date for 1998:

a) Proceeds from the short-term note were used to purchase inventory.

b) Sold for $700 old machinery that originally cost $1,800 and that was one-half depreciated.

c) Depreciation expense recorded on buildings and machinery, $800.

d) Sold investment for $1,200 cash.

e) Paid a $500 long-term note by issuing common stock.

f) Made addition to building costing $3,000; paid cash.

g) Purchased machinery costing $2,500 by issuing common stock.

h) Purchased machinery costing $1,500; paid one-third in cash and issued a five-year, interest-bearing note for the balance.

i) Dividends are declared and paid in the same year.

REQUIRED   Prepare Victory's statement of cash flows using the indirect approach.

P 6-4. **STATEMENT OF CASH FLOWS** Dart Swimming Club is applying for a bank loan and furnishes you with the following trial balances:

	12/31/97, POSTCLOSING		12/31/98, PRECLOSING	
	DR	CR	DR	CR
Cash	$ 73,000		$ 40,000	
Accounts receivable	71,000		108,000	
Inventories	26,000		20,000	
Plant and equipment	180,000		250,000	
Accumulated depreciation		$ 22,000		$ 70,000
Land	40,000		20,000	
Accounts payable		80,000		40,000
Commissions payable		8,000		9,000
Salaries payable		5,000		3,000
Other current liabilities		7,000		28,000
Long-term notes payable		50,000		40,000
I. Dart, capital		118,000		108,000
D. Monroe, capital		100,000		90,000
Membership and pool revenues				90,000
Sales of swimsuits, towels, etc.				78,000
Cost of goods sold			20,000	
Depreciation expense			48,000	
Salaries and other expenses			36,000	
Loss on sale of land			14,000	
	$390,000	$390,000	$556,000	$556,000

Additional information:
a) There were no sales of plant and equipment.
b) There were no purchases of land.
c) The partners share income equally. Their cash withdrawals during 1998 were as follows: Dart, $10,000; Monroe, $10,000.

REQUIRED Prepare the following for Dart Swimming Club's statement of cash flows for 1998:
1. Cash flows from operating activities under the direct approach.
2. Cash flows from investing activities.
3. Cash flows from financing activities.

P 6-5. **STATEMENT OF CASH FLOWS** The following financial data were furnished to you by Greer Company:

Greer Company
Comparative Trial Balances
At Beginning and End of Fiscal Year
Ended January 31, 1998

	FEBRUARY 1, 1997	INCREASE	DECREASE	JANUARY 31, 1998
Debits:				
Cash	$ 5,000	$14,400		$ 19,400
Accounts receivable	9,500	4,000		13,500
Inventories	30,000		$ 900	29,100
Prepaid insurance	1,200		450	750
Long-term investments	12,000		2,000	10,000
Plant and equipment	28,500	12,500		41,000
Cost of goods sold				53,900
Other expenses				32,200
Loss on sale of equipment				100
Total	$86,200			$199,950

	FEBRUARY 1, 1997	INCREASE	DECREASE	JANUARY 31, 1998
Credits:				
Accumulated depreciation	$ 5,000	1,900		$ 6,900
Accounts payable...........	8,000		500	7,500
Note payable—current	–0–	5,000		5,000
Accrued expenses payable	2,500	2,800		5,300
Unearned revenue	1,000		750	250
Note payable—long-term	30,000		6,000	24,000
Common stock	20,000	10,000		30,000
Contributed capital in excess of par	500	11,100		11,600
Retained earnings	19,200		800	18,400
Sales.....................				85,000
Gain on sale of investments....				6,000
Total	$86,200			$199,950

The following additional information was available:
a) All purchases and sales were on account.
b) Equipment with an original cost of $1,500 was sold for $700.
c) Other expenses included the following:

Insurance expired	$ 450
Depreciation expense	2,600
Interest expense...	1,800

d) All dividends declared were paid in cash.
e) New equipment was purchased; cash and a six-month note payable in the amount of $5,000 were issued.
f) The long-term note payable requires the payment of $6,000 per year plus interest until paid.

REQUIRED
1. Prepare a schedule showing the cash flows from operating activities for the year under the:
   a) Direct approach.
   b) Indirect approach.
2. Prepare a statement of cash flows for Greer Company. Use your answer to part 1 for the cash flows from operating activities. You need not prepare a supplementary reconciliation schedule.

P 6-6.   **STATEMENT OF CASH FLOWS**   Knott Company is an established firm specializing in the manufacture of plastic bottles. The company is well known nationally for the novelty and quality of its product line.

The company's accounting department is in the process of preparing the financial statements for the fiscal year just completed on December 31, 1998. The income statement for 1998 and comparative statements of financial position for 1997 and 1998 appear below.

Knott Company
Income Statement
For the Year Ended December 31, 1998
(in thousands)

Revenues:		
Sales...		$6,000
Interest and dividends		28
Total revenues		$6,028
Expenses and losses:		
Cost of goods sold	$4,740	
Selling expenses	620	
Administrative expenses	515	
Interest expense..	83	
Loss on sale of investment	25	(5,983)
Net income..		$ 45

Knott Company
Statements of Financial Position
December 31, 1997 and 1998
(in thousands)

	1997	1998
Assets:		
Cash	$ 420	$ 11
Marketable securities	80	40
Accounts receivable (net of allowance		
for uncollectible accounts)	960	1,152
Inventories	1,580	1,802
Investment in Cooper Products Co...........................	320	135
Property, plant, and equipment		
(net of accumulated depreciation)	1,320	1,370
Total assets	$4,680	$4,510
Liabilities and equities:		
Short-term notes payable (nontrade)..........................	$ 350	$ 430
Accounts payable	600	545
Cash dividends payable.......................................	–0–	30
Accrued and other liabilities	120	130
Current portion of long-term debt	200	200
Long-term debt..	1,000	800
Common stock, $4 par	1,120	1,164
Paid-in capital in excess of par	280	291
Retained earnings	1,010	920
Total liabilities and equities	$4,680	$4,510

The following additional data regarding Knott's operations have been assembled by the accounting department:

a)   The allowance for uncollectible accounts had a balance of $70,000 on December 31, 1997, and a balance of $85,000 on December 31, 1998. A total of $40,000 in accounts receivable was written off as uncollectible during 1998. A provision for uncollectible accounts of $55,000 in 1998 was included in selling expenses.

b) The company liquidated some of its investments during 1998 in order to raise cash. Marketable securities were sold at their recorded cost of $40,000. In addition, Knott sold part of its investment in Cooper Products Company for cash.

c) Equipment costing $215,000 was purchased during 1998, and used equipment was sold at its book value of $25,000. Depreciation on plant and equipment included in the operating expenses amounted to $140,000 for 1998.

d) Long-term debt is being retired at the rate of $200,000 per year.

e) The company issued 11,000 shares of its common stock for cash during 1998.

f) Knott declared cash dividends of $135,000 during 1998.

REQUIRED
Using the direct approach, prepare a complete statement of cash flows for Knott for the year ending December 31, 1998. Include marketable securities as cash equivalents.

P 6-7. **STATEMENT OF CASH FLOWS** The net changes in the balance sheet accounts of Grand Hotel for the year ended December 31, 1998, are shown below.

	DEBIT	CREDIT
Investments		$ 25,000
Land	$ 3,200	
Buildings	35,000	
Machinery	6,000	
Office equipment		1,500
Accumulated depreciation:		
Buildings		2,000
Machinery		900
Office equipment	600	
Dividends payable		21,000
Long-term debt		40,000
Common stock		12,400
Contributed capital in excess of par—common		6,200
Retained earnings		7,000
Cash	71,200	
	$116,000	$116,000

Additional information:

a) Cash dividends of $21,000 were declared on December 15, 1998, payable January 15, 1999.

b) The investments were sold at a gain of $2,500.

c) A building that cost $45,000 and had a depreciated basis of $40,500 was sold for $50,000.

d) The following entry was made to record an exchange of an old machine for a new one:

```
Machinery ....................................... 13,000
Accumulated depreciation—machinery................... 5,000
    Machinery......................................         7,000
    Cash...........................................         11,000
```

e) A fully depreciated office machine that cost $1,500 was written off.

f) The company issued 1,240 shares of its common stock (par value $10) on June 15, 1998, for $15 a share. There were 13,240 shares outstanding on December 31, 1998.

g) Cash was received from issuing long-term debt.

h) Other than any gains and losses, the only items appearing on the hotel's income statement of 1998 were room revenues of $36,000, interest revenue from investments of $5,000, depreciation expense, interest expense of $4,400, and miscellaneous cash expenses of $7,300.

REQUIRED
Using the indirect approach, prepare Grand Hotel's statement of cash flows for the year ended December 31, 1998.

P 6-8.   STATEMENT OF CASH FLOWS   To facilitate the preparation of its statement of cash flows, the management of High Corporation has provided you with a comparative analysis of changes in account balances between December 31, 1997, and December 31, 1998, as follows:

	12/31/98	12/31/97	INCREASE (DECREASE)
Accounts with debit balances:			
Cash	$ 54,800	$ 86,000	$ (31,200)
Accounts receivable	239,000	256,000	(17,000)
Inventories	485,000	538,000	(53,000)
Prepaid expenses	114,800	117,000	(2,200)
Securities held for plant expansion purposes	150,000	–0–	150,000
Machinery and equipment	927,000	647,000	280,000
	$1,970,600	$1,644,000	$326,600
Accounts with credit balances:			
Accumulated depreciation of machinery and equipment	$ 474,000	$ 421,000	$ 53,000
Accounts payable	232,800	105,000	127,800
Cash dividends payable	40,000	–0–	40,000
Long-term debt	300,000	350,000	(50,000)
Common stock	500,000	500,000	–0–
Retained earnings	423,800	268,000	155,800
Total	$1,970,600	$1,644,000	$326,600

High's income statement for the year ended December 31, 1998, was as follows:

Sales		$736,000
Cost of goods sold		(382,800)
Gross margin		$353,200
Other expenses and losses:		
Depreciation	$98,000	
Salaries expense	26,200	
Interest expense	18,000	
Insurance expense	2,200	
Loss on sale of machinery	13,000	(157,400)
Net income		$195,800

During 1998 the following transactions occurred:
a) New machinery was purchased for $386,000. In addition, obsolete machinery having a book value of $61,000 was sold for cash. No other entries were recorded in machinery and equipment or related accounts other than for depreciation.
b) High extinguished long-term debt that matured during 1998.
c) On December 10, 1998, the board of directors declared a cash dividend payable to holders of common stock on January 10, 1999.

REQUIRED   Using the direct approach, prepare a statement of cash flows for High Corporation for the year ended December 31, 1998.

P 6-9. **STATEMENT OF CASH FLOWS; RECONCILING INCOME FLOWS AND CASH FLOWS** Allen Corporation's income statement for the year ended December 31, 1998, and comparative balance sheets at December 31, 1997 and 1998 appear below.

Allen Corporation
Income Statement
For the Year Ended December 31, 1998

Revenues (sales, interest, dividends)........................		$2,432,363
Expenses and losses:		
Materials and supplies used	$896,752	
Salaries expense	906,387	
Depreciation expense....................................	114,079	
Loss on sale of investments	6,016	
Miscellaneous expenses, including interest................	21,006	
Income tax expense	284,442	(2,228,682)
Net income		$ 203,681

Allen Corporation
Comparative Statements of Financial Position
As of December 31, 1998 and 1997

	1998	1997	INCREASE (DECREASE)
Assets:			
Cash	$ 214,421	$ 225,351	$ (10,930)
Marketable securities	180,767	251,388	(70,621)
Receivables	281,612	195,991	85,621
Inventories, at cost	322,438	359,175	(36,737)
Prepaid expenses	15,009	17,894	(2,885)
Plant and equipment, net	1,356,132	1,200,816	155,316
Total assets	$2,370,379	$2,250,615	$ 119,764
Liabilities and equity:			
Accounts payable	$ 404,203	$ 553,647	$(149,444)
Salaries payable	12,602	11,495	1,107
Dividends payable	23,726	25,591	(1,865)
Other payables.......................	13,372	15,238	(1,866)
Long-term debt.......................	50,000	–0–	50,000
Common stock, par value, $100	1,532,600	1,357,500	175,100
Contributed capital in excess of par.......	61,524	42,043	19,481
Retained earnings	272,352	245,101	27,251
Total liabilities and equity............	$2,370,379	$2,250,615	$ 119,764

Additional information:
a) During the year, marketable securities (not considered cash equivalents) were purchased at a cost of $24,692.
b) The only entries in retained earnings were for net income and dividend declarations.
c) There were no sales or retirements of plant and equipment during the year.

REQUIRED
1. Prepare a schedule summarizing Allen's cash flows from operating activities. The schedule should be constructed to convert Allen's accrual-basis income statement for the year ending December 31, 1998, to a cash basis on an item-by-item basis.
2. Prepare a schedule summarizing Allen's cash flows from investing activities for the year ending December 31, 1998.
3. Prepare a schedule summarizing Allen's cash flows from financing activities for the year ending December 31, 1998.

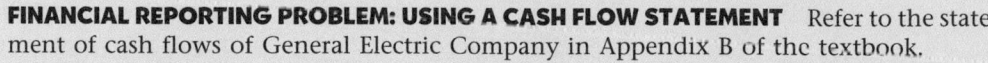

P 6-10.

REQUIRED

FINANCIAL REPORTING PROBLEM: USING A CASH FLOW STATEMENT   Refer to the statement of cash flows of General Electric Company in Appendix B of the textbook.

Answer the following questions. Your answers should relate to the consolidated statement for 1995 only, unless otherwise indicated.

1. Does General Electric use the direct approach or the indirect approach in reporting cash flows from operating activities?
2. Why did General Electric add back depreciation, depletion, and amortization to net income in determining net cash provided by operating activities?
3. What were General Electric's major cash inflow and outflow from investing activities?
4. What were General Electric's major cash inflow and outflow from financing activities?
5. Did General Electric have any noncash investing and financing activities?
6. Is General Electric's statement of cash flows based on an activity format? Explain.
7. If the answer to part 6 is "yes," what activity generated the greatest cash inflow? What activity generated the greatest cash outflow?
8. Was there a net cash increase or decrease for the year?

P 6-11.

FINANCIAL REPORTING PROBLEM: ANALYZING A STATEMENT OF CASH FLOWS   Using the statements of cash flows for USAir Group, Inc., shown in Exhibit 6–4 (page 282), analyze the 1995 cash flows. The illustrative analysis of a statement of cash flows on pages 301–302 may be useful as a guide.

GENERAL ELECTRIC COMPANY   CASH FLOW CASE

General Electric Company, incorporated in 1892, is one of the largest and most diversified companies in the world. It produces aircraft engines, appliances, industrial products and systems, engineered materials, power generation equipment, and medical equipment and systems. In addition, it has large subsidiaries in broadcasting (NBC) and finance (General Electric Capital Services). As of the end of 1995, 25 percent of GE's revenue was generated outside the United States. In 1995, GE had consolidated revenue of $70 billion, net income of $6.6 billion, and total assets of $228 billion. It also had 220,000 employees at the end of 1995.

Answer the following questions using the financial statement excerpts that appear below. All questions relate to 1995 unless stated otherwise.

1. Explain the main items that cause differences between net income and cash from operating activities.

2. Cash from operating activities is significantly higher than net earnings for all years presented. Will cash from operating activities always be higher than net earnings or will the relation reverse at some point? Explain.

3. The balance sheet shows an increase in current receivables of $1,208 million ($8,735 – $7,527 million), but the statement of cash flows shows an increase in GE current receivables of $632 million. Explain why the two statements report different increases in receivables.

4. Does GE's statement of cash flows raise any concerns about income quality? Explain.

5. Show how the 1995 cash from operating activities section would change if the direct approach were used. Estimate amounts for the broad categories of cash sales, cash cost of goods and services sold, other cash expenses, interest paid, and income taxes paid.

6. Explain some possible reasons why the FASB encourages the direct approach for the operating activities segment.

Statement of Earnings

For the years ended December 31 (In millions)	General Electric Company and consolidated affiliates		
	1995	1994	1993
Revenues			
Sales of goods	**$33,157**	$30,740	$29,509
Sales of services	**9,733**	8,803	8,268
Other income (note 3)	**752**	793	735
Earnings of GECS from continuing operations	**—**	—	—
GECS revenues from operations (note 4)	**26,386**	19,773	17,189
Total revenues	**70,028**	60,109	55,701
Costs and expenses (note 5)			
Cost of goods sold	**24,288**	22,748	22,606
Cost of services sold	**6,682**	6,214	6,308
Interest and other financial charges	**7,286**	4,949	4,054
Insurance losses and policyholder and annuity benefits	**5,285**	3,507	3,172
Provision for losses on financing receivables (note 8)	**1,117**	873	987
Other costs and expenses	**15,429**	12,987	12,287
Minority interest in net earnings of consolidated affiliates	**204**	170	151
Total costs and expenses	**60,291**	51,448	49,565
Earnings from continuing operations before income taxes and accounting change	**9,737**	8,661	6,136
Provision for income taxes (note 9)	**(3,164)**	(2,746)	(1,952)
Earnings from continuing operations before accounting change	**6,573**	5,915	4,184
Earnings (loss) from discontinued operations (note 2)	**—**	(1,189)	993
Earnings before accounting change	**6,573**	4,726	5,177
Cumulative effect of accounting change (note 20)	**—**	—	(862)
Net earnings	**$ 6,573**	$ 4,726	$ 4,315
Net earnings per share (in dollars)			
Continuing operations before accounting change	**$ 3.90**	$ 3.46	$ 2.45
Discontinued operations before accounting change	**—**	(0.69)	0.58
Earnings before accounting change	**3.90**	2.77	3.03
Cumulative effect of accounting change	**—**	—	(0.51)
Net earnings per share	**$ 3.90**	$ 2.77	$ 2.52
Dividends declared per share (in dollars)	**$ 1.69**	$ 1.49	$ 1.305

The notes to consolidated financial statements on pages 45-64 are an integral part of this statement.

Statement of Financial Position

At December 31 (In millions)	General Electric Company and consolidated affiliates 1995	1994
Assets		
Cash and equivalents	$ 2,823	$ 2,591
Investment securities (note 10)	41,067	30,965
Current receivables (note 11)	8,735	7,527
Inventories (note 12)	4,395	3,880
GECS financing receivables (investment in time sales, loans and financing leases) — net (notes 8 and 13)	93,272	76,357
Other GECS receivables	12,417	5,763
Property, plant and equipment (including equipment leased to others) — net (note 14)	25,679	23,465
Investment in GECS	—	—
Intangible assets (note 15)	13,342	11,373
All other assets (note 16)	26,305	23,950
Total assets	**$228,035**	**$185,871**
Liabilities and equity		
Short-term borrowings (note 18)	$ 64,463	$ 57,781
Accounts payable, principally trade accounts	9,061	6,766
Progress collections and price adjustments accrued	1,812	2,065
Dividends payable	767	699
All other GE current costs and expenses accrued (note 17)	5,898	5,543
Long-term borrowings (note 18)	51,027	36,979
Insurance liabilities, reserves and annuity benefits (note 19)	39,699	29,438
All other liabilities (note 20)	15,363	13,161
Deferred income taxes (note 22)	7,380	5,205
Total liabilities	195,470	157,637
Minority interest in equity of consolidated affiliates (note 23)	2,956	1,847
Common stock (1,857,013,000 shares issued)	594	594
Unrealized gains (losses) on investment securities	1,000	(810)
Other capital	1,663	1,122
Retained earnings	34,528	30,793
Less common stock held in treasury	(8,176)	(5,312)
Total share owners' equity (notes 24 and 25)	29,609	26,387
Total liabilities and equity	**$228,035**	**$185,871**

The notes to consolidated financial statements on pages 45-64 are an integral part of this statement. Year-end 1994 assets and liabilities of Kidder, Peabody Group Inc., the discontinued securities broker-dealer of GECS, have been reclassified to "All other liabilities."

Statement of Cash Flows

For the years ended December 31 (In millions)	General Electric Company and consolidated affiliates		
	1995	1994	1993
Cash flows from operating activities			
Net earnings	$ 6,573	$ 4,726	$ 4,315
Adjustments for discontinued operations	—	1,189	(993)
Adjustments to reconcile net earnings to cash provided from operating activities			
Cumulative effect of accounting change	—	—	862
Depreciation, depletion and amortization	3,594	3,207	3,223
Earnings retained by GECS — continuing operations	—	—	—
Deferred income taxes	1,047	1,228	548
Decrease (increase) in GE current receivables	(632)	668	(571)
Decrease (increase) in GE inventories	55	(56)	750
Increase (decrease) in accounts payable	244	697	639
Increase in insurance liabilities, reserves and annuity benefits	2,490	1,624	1,479
Provision for losses on financing receivables	1,117	873	987
All other operating activities	458	(2,399)	782
Cash from operating activities	14,946	11,757	12,021
Cash flows from investing activities			
Additions to property, plant and equipment	(6,447)	(7,492)	(4,727)
Dispositions of property, plant and equipment	1,542	2,506	1,139
Net increase in GECS financing receivables	(11,309)	(9,525)	(4,164)
Payments for principal businesses purchased	(5,641)	(2,606)	(2,090)
All other investing activities	(3,362)	372	(6,518)
Cash used for investing activities	(25,217)	(16,745)	(16,360)
Cash flows from financing activities			
Net change in borrowings (maturities of 90 days or less)	(3,487)	(2,784)	2,406
Newly issued debt (maturities longer than 90 days)	37,604	23,239	15,468
Repayments and other reductions (maturities longer than 90 days)	(18,580)	(13,098)	(11,851)
Net purchase of GE shares for treasury	(2,523)	(353)	(364)
Dividends paid to share owners	(2,770)	(2,462)	(2,153)
All other financing activities	259	181	(69)
Cash from (used for) financing activities	10,503	4,723	3,437
Cash from (used for) discontinued operations	—	(200)	962
Increase (decrease) in cash and equivalents during year	232	(465)	60
Cash and equivalents at beginning of year	2,591	3,056	2,996
Cash and equivalents at end of year	$ 2,823	$ 2,591	$ 3,056
Supplemental disclosure of cash flows information			
Cash paid during the year for interest	$ (6,645)	$ (4,524)	$ (3,754)
Cash recovered (paid) during the year for income taxes	(1,483)	(1,777)	(1,644)

The notes to consolidated financial statements on pages 45-64 are an integral part of this statement. Data for 1994 and 1993 have been reclassified to combine cash flows of discontinued operations.

Revenue Recognition and Income Determination

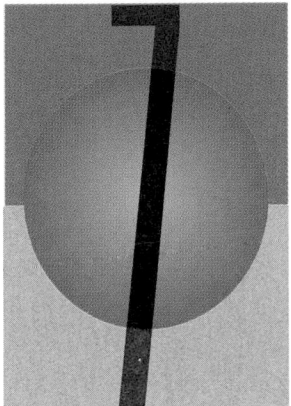

LEARNING OBJECTIVES

After studying this chapter, you should be able to:

1. Distinguish among revenue, revenue measurement, and revenue recognition.

2. Describe the earnings process.

3. Explain the concept of realization.

4. List and apply the two basic revenue recognition criteria.

5. Account for revenue recognition at the point of sale, including credit sales, after-sale costs, and return privileges.

6. Explain how revenue recognition applies to service transactions.

7. Distinguish between the percentage-of-completion and completed-contract methods of accounting for long-term construction contracts and apply each.

8. Explain how revenues and expenses are recognized for services that extend over several periods.

9. Identify situations in which revenue should be recognized when production is complete and account for revenue in those situations.

10. Differentiate between the installment and the cost-recovery methods of accounting and prepare journal entries under each method.

11. Describe some of the accounting issues related to revenue recognition in franchises, real estate, and other specialized industries.

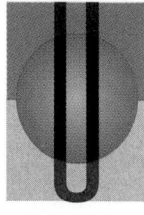

nder accrual accounting, accountants measure the net cash flow effects of earnings activities by recording and reporting transactions that have cash consequences as they occur, rather than waiting until the cash is received or paid. Revenue is recognized based on the realization concept, and expenses are matched against revenues to determine income. As we saw in Chapter 2, accrual accounting generally provides better signals about future cash flows than does cash-basis accounting. Thus, it better satisfies the objectives of financial reporting.

Revenue and income recognition is and has always been one of the most controversial issues in accounting. Many companies have experienced financial difficulties (and often bankruptcy and lawsuits) from "premature" recognition of revenue and income. In the 1980s many retail land sales companies experienced losses and cash flow problems that arose from premature recognition of revenue from credit sales transactions. Purchasers made only token down payments and were given many years to pay for the land. Additionally, the sellers had not fulfilled their obligations to the purchasers—revenue had not been earned—on the revenue recognition date. As illustrated by the following news articles, revenue recognition problems have also arisen in other industries, such as energy and drug and clinical testing:

But one Enron tactic—its aggressive accounting—is a bit too fast for some. In 1991 Enron became perhaps the only major gas or oil company to adopt its method of booking all estimated profit on multiyear gas contracts at the time they are signed. In other words, if Enron expects net income of $400,000 annually for five years on the fixed-price sale of gas to a local utility or manufacturer, it books $2 million in the first year. Such accounting boosts short-term earnings while increasing the potential for exposure to losses. Although the SEC has approved Enron's accounting, critics say the practice invites abrupt writedowns because it won't allow the company to spread out its losses over time if customers cancel or if accidents, such as weather, cut off supplies. Just in case, Enron has set aside $100 million in reserves.[1]

Cincinnati's highest-flying young company, Future Healthcare Inc., crashed on Wall Street after the company reported it had found accounting discrepancies and may have overstated its earnings for years. The company conducts clinical studies for drug and medical companies. At issue were the length of time the company took to collect receivables and the point at which it counted a contract as earned revenue. Future Healthcare said the discrepancies involved its accounts receivable and earned "unbilled" revenue.[2]

Revenue recognition issues like these apply to service transactions as well as to the manufacture and sale of goods. In **service transactions,** revenue results from providing a service rather than the production and sale of a product, like natural gas. Our society is rapidly becoming a service economy; service employment outnumbers industrial employment four to one.[3] Some examples of service businesses are:

Accounting	Business and home security
Advertising and public relations	Computer services
Architecture	Continuing education
Automobile repair	Entertainment
Brokerage services	Franchises

---

[1]"Piping Up: Natural-Gas Industry Is Reinventing Itself by Going International," *The Wall Street Journal,* April 19, 1994, pp. A-1 and A-12.
[2]"Future Healthcare Stock Crashes, President Quits," *Cincinnati Inquirer,* March 14, 1995, p. A-1.
[3]*The Atlantic Monthly,* January 1990, p. 45.

Health care	Medical services
Job placement	Outdoor recreation
Legal services	Physical fitness training
Management consulting	Travel services

Because of the importance of income information to investors and other financial statement users, we will examine revenue recognition and income determination concepts in detail in this chapter. The chapter begins with an overview based on our discussion of revenue and income in Chapters 2 and 4. Next, we discuss the rationale for and illustrate the recording and reporting of revenue and income at various points in a company's earnings cycle. This discussion will cover revenue recognition for both sales of products and sales of services. Finally, we present some special applications of revenue recognition concepts. Appendix 7–1 covers accounting for consignment transactions.

N OVERVIEW OF REVENUE CONCEPTS

It is important to distinguish among (1) the nature or definition of revenue, (2) the measurement of revenue, and (3) the recognition of revenue. Revenues were *defined* in Chapter 2 as increases in net assets arising from the delivery or production of goods, the rendering of services, or other activities that constitute a company's primary operations. Revenues are *measured* at the fair value or cash equivalent price of assets received. **Revenue recognition** is a *timing* issue—when should revenue be recognized (recorded) and reported in the income statement? The answer to this question has to do with the process by which revenue is earned and the concept of realization—the subjects of the next two sections.

The Revenue Earning Process

Exhibit 7–1, reproduced from Chapter 2, illustrates a company's **earnings process.** Revenue is *earned* throughout the process as value—in the form of time, place, and form utility—is added through productive inputs. For example, a company may acquire raw materials and add *form* utility by transforming those materials and labor inputs into a final product. Or a transportation company may add *place* utility to products by bringing them closer to final consumers.

Earnings activities may overlap—that is, some goods may be sold while other goods are being produced. In addition, the economic resources used to generate revenue and income may benefit either one product in one accounting period (e.g., cost of merchandise sold) or many products over several accounting periods (e.g., long-lived depreciable assets). While the economic events pictured in Exhibit 7–1 may not represent the sequence of earnings activities in all companies, the exhibit does illustrate the general *nature* of the earnings process.

Revenue Recognition and the Realization Concept

Even though revenue may be earned continuously, recognizing it on a continuous basis is impractical, and associating portions of it with each revenue-generating activity is not feasible. Therefore, accountants select a point or points in the earnings process at which to recognize revenue. There are many points at which revenue

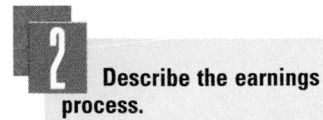

EXHIBIT 7–1	The Earnings Process

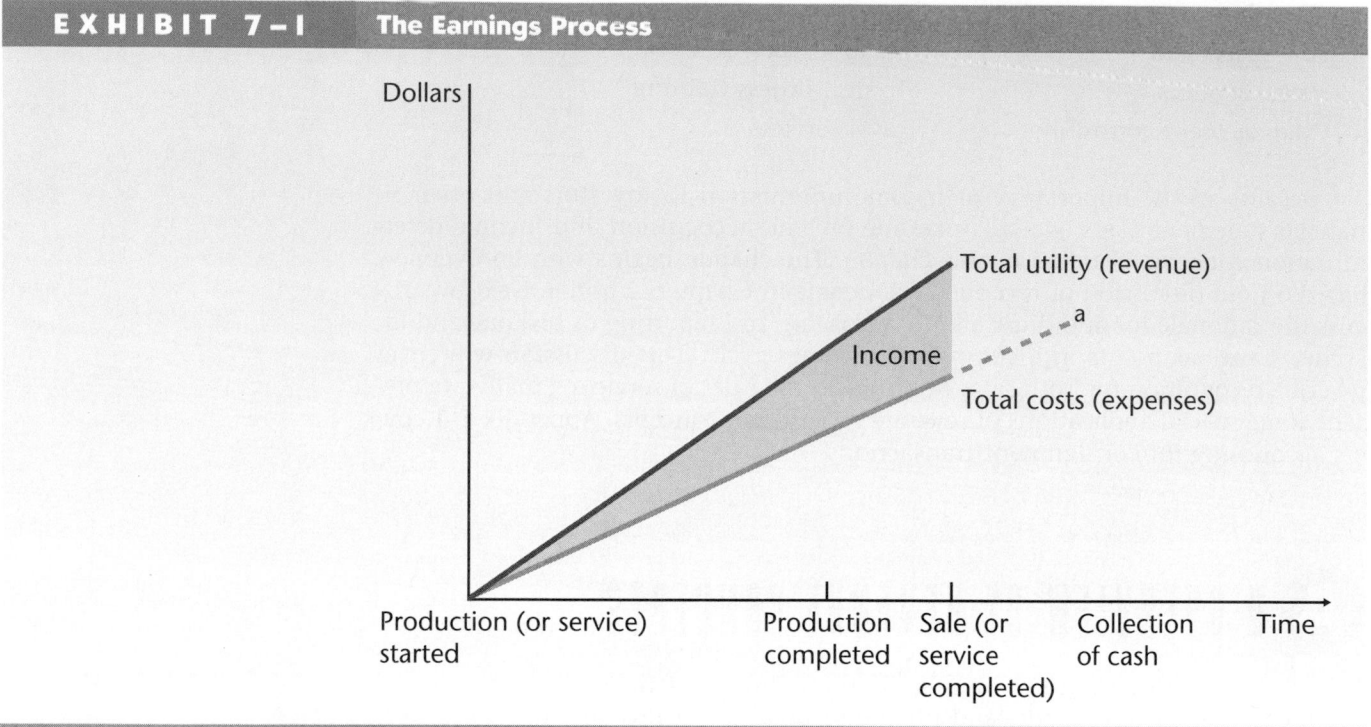

^a**Occasionally, sale-related costs are incurred after the sale date. Ideally, these costs should be estimated and accrued as expenses at the sale date or at the end of the accounting period in which the sale occurs.**

could be recognized. Depending on the circumstances, revenue could be recognized during production, at the completion of production, while the completed product is awaiting sale, at the point of sale, or, for credit sales, when cash is collected. As we saw in Chapter 2, accountants use the realization concept as a guideline for determining when revenue should be recognized. Conceptually, **realization** refers to the occurrence of an event or events that reduce to an acceptable level the uncertainty about the net cash flow effect of an earnings activity. The occurrence of that event or events triggers the recognition of revenue (and associated expenses).

In practice, the realization concept is applied through two revenue recognition criteria or guidelines. As stated in Chapter 2 on page 63, revenues should be recognized and reported in the income statement when:

1. The amount and timing of revenue are reasonably determinable; that is, revenue has been realized or is realizable.

2. Revenue has been earned; that is, the earnings process is complete or virtually complete.

Notice that these criteria are consistent with the fundamental recognition principle for all financial statement elements presented in Chapter 2 on page 58. The first criterion means that expected cash inflows must be objectively determinable before revenue can be recorded. The second criterion means that until the earnings process is complete or virtually complete, the company has not fulfilled all its economic obligations related to the transaction. Thus, expenses or *expected cash outflows* associated with the transaction are too uncertain. In summary, revenues are recorded on the basis of the realization principle. Expenses incurred in the earnings process are matched against revenues on the basis of one or more of the expense recognition guidelines presented in Chapter 2 (see pages 65–66).

Some accounting theorists have proposed a **critical event** theory of revenue recognition. Under this theory, revenue should be recognized when the most critical (crucial) event in the earnings process has been completed. As examples, in most industries, the sale is the critical event in the earnings process. In some industries, however, production of the goods may be the most critical event in the

---

3 **Explain the concept of realization.**

4 **List and apply the two basic revenue recognition criteria.**

earnings process. In most cases, application of the critical event theory would yield results similar to those obtained by applying the two revenue recognition criteria just presented.

The two revenue recognition criteria illustrate the need to balance *relevance* and *reliability* in order to meet the financial reporting objective of providing information that assists users in predicting, evaluating, and assessing cash flows. The *earlier* revenue is recognized in the earnings process, the more *relevant* the information is likely to be. However, in many cases, early recognition of revenue may not be as *reliable*. Thus, *timely* information about revenue, income, and cash flows increases the relevance of the reported information. On the other hand, the information also must be reliable—*verifiable* and *representationally faithful*—in order to be useful. Notice how the revenue recognition criteria incorporate both qualitative characteristics.

In the following sections we will discuss revenue recognition at various points in the earnings process. As you read and study this material, which covers revenue from sales of products as well as from services, remember that the specific practices discussed and illustrated are applications of these conceptual considerations.

CONCEPTUAL

Revenue recognition criteria meet the qualitative characteristics of accounting information.

REVENUE RECOGNITION AT THE POINT OF SALE

Most merchandising and manufacturing companies recognize revenue at the point of sale because for them the two recognition criteria are met at that point.[4] The amount of revenue that is recognized is established by the exchange price at the time of the sale. If the sale is for cash or on short-term account, there usually is no uncertainty about the amount or timing of the cash flows. In addition, the point of sale represents the completion of the earnings process because the merchandise has been transferred to the buyer. Thus, the seller usually has fulfilled all obligations to the buyer at that point.

Revenue recognition at the point of sale is often complicated, however, by the following factors:

1. Sales made on credit, trade and cash discounts, uncollectible accounts, and interest on receivables that are collectible over extended periods.

2. Costs related to the sale that are incurred after the sale date.

3. Return privileges on merchandise that has been sold.

In the following sections we will address each of these considerations. Because not all of these considerations apply to service transactions, revenue recognition for services will be discussed separately.

5 Account for revenue recognition at the point of sale, including credit sales, after-sale costs, and return privileges.

Sales Made on Credit

Accounting for receivables that arise from credit sales is discussed in detail in Chapter 8; only an overview is presented here. Since revenue is measured at the fair value or cash equivalent price of the assets received in exchange, revenue from credit sales should be recorded net of any trade and sales discounts. Unless cash inflows are expected to be received within a short period of time, revenue should be measured at the present value of the cash flows to be received.

---

[4]In practice, liquidity or nearness to cash often plays a role in revenue and income recognition. Revenues and income usually are recognized when an exchange results in an increase in liquidity. Interestingly, the change in liquidity (more liquidity or less liquidity) resulting from an exchange may be the primary distinction between a purchase and a sale. When an asset received in an exchange transaction is less liquid than the asset sacrificed, the transaction is classified as a purchase. When the asset received is more liquid than the asset sacrificed, the transaction is classified as a sale.

Because the amount of cash expected from the sale should be reported on the income statement, an allowance must be made for any sales estimated to be uncollectible. This allowance procedure also results in the reporting of accounts receivable on the balance sheet at the amount of cash expected to be collected. Unless the waiting period is short, this amount should be discounted. The procedures for estimating uncollectible accounts was introduced in our discussion of the accounting cycle in Chapter 3. It is discussed at greater length in Chapter 8.

Costs Incurred after the Point of Sale

Although the earnings process may be virtually complete at the date of sale, occasionally sale-related costs are incurred after the sale date. For example, a hardware store that sells television sets may offer a two-year warranty on the sets. According to the concepts underlying accrual accounting, the cost of servicing the warranty should be estimated and accrued as an expense at the date of sale or at the end of the accounting period in which the sale is made so that expenses will be properly matched against the revenue recognized.

To illustrate, assume that Murphy Corporation sells 200 television sets. On the basis of past experience, the company estimates that warranty costs will average about $12 per set. The following entry would be made to record the warranty expense for expenditures expected to be made after the sale date:

Warranty expense. 2,400
    Estimated warranty obligations.   2,400

Actual warranty costs incurred during the warranty period would be recorded as a debit to a liability account, estimated warranty obligations, and as a credit to the appropriate asset accounts. Accounting for warranty obligations is covered in more detail in Chapter 8.

Return Privileges

In some industries, such as newspaper and book publishing, perishable foods, and record and tape sales, customers are allowed to return goods under certain circumstances. Goods may be returned for a refund, for a credit to be applied to other purchases or amounts owed, or in exchange for other merchandise. In determining the amount of revenue to be recognized at the point of sale, therefore, the seller must consider the fact that some goods may be returned. If possible returns are not considered, the amount of revenue reported may overstate the expected cash inflow.

If returns are infrequent, are small in amount, and occur over a fairly short period following the sale, sales returns should be debited and accounts receivable or cash credited as goods are returned. Mismatching of sales and returns is probably immaterial in these circumstances, even though the sale may be recorded in a different accounting period than the related sales return.

When the return privilege covers a longer period and a significant amount of returns is expected and can be estimated, an allowance for sales returns account should be established. If the return privilege applies to a cash sale or if the customer has otherwise paid for the goods, a liability for returns should be established.

To illustrate, assume that McDonald Corporation sells merchandise on credit and allows customers to return merchandise for several weeks after the sale. Experience indicates that sales returns average approximately 15 percent of sales. During 1998, sales were $200,000, cash collections $110,000, and actual returns $18,000. Merchandise is sold at a gross margin of 40 percent, and the company uses a perpetual inventory system.

The following summary entries illustrate how McDonald would use the allowance method to record sales returns:

Accounts receivable	200,000	
Sales		200,000
To record sales on account during 1998.		

Cost of goods sold	120,000	
Inventory		120,000
(.60 × $200,000)		
To record cost of goods sold.		

Cash	110,000	
Accounts receivable		110,000
To record cash collections during 1998.		

Sales returns	18,000	
Accounts receivable		18,000
To record actual returns during 1998.		

Inventory	10,800	
Cost of goods sold		10,800
(.60 × $18,000)		
To record cost of merchandise returned.		

At the end of 1998, the following adjusting entries would be required:

Sales returns	12,000	
Allowance for sales returns		12,000
To record returns associated with 1998 sales but expected to take place in 1999 [(.15 × $200,000) − $18,000].		

Inventory	7,200	
Cost of goods sold		7,200
(.60 × $12,000)		
To record cost of merchandise expected to be returned in the next accounting period.		

These transactions would be reported on McDonald's 1998 income statement and balance sheet in the following manner:

INCOME STATEMENT		**BALANCE SHEET**	
Sales	$200,000	Accounts receivable	$72,000
Less: Sales returns	(30,000)	Less: Allowance	
Net sales	$170,000	for sales returns	(12,000)
Cost of goods sold	(102,000)	Accounts receivable (net)	$60,000
Gross margin	$ 68,000		

In some circumstances, the risk associated with return privileges may be so great that a sale should *not* be recorded initially. Circumstances that increase the level of uncertainty about future cash flows related to return privileges include (1) lack of a fixed or determinable sales price, (2) lack of an obligation by the purchaser to pay the seller if the merchandise cannot be resold by the seller or is stolen or damaged, (3) an obligation on the part of the seller to assist the purchaser in product resale, and (4) an inability to reasonably estimate future returns. Under such circumstances, any collections received should be recorded as deposits or as unearned revenue.[5]

---

[5]"Revenue Recognition When Right of Return Exists," *Statement of Financial Accounting Standards No. 48* (Stamford, Conn.: FASB, 1981).

In practice, companies sometimes do record sales under uncertain circumstances. For example, *The Wall Street Journal* published an interesting article about IBM's liberal treatment of sales with return privileges:

IBM's former chief outside auditor, Price Waterhouse's Donald Chandler, wrote IBM a blistering 20-point memo in November 1988 suggesting that the company was reporting revenue that it might never get. For example, Mr. Chandler wrote, IBM's computer shipments to dealers "are recorded as sales at time of shipment" even though the dealers have the right to return the computers. He worried that some revenue from such shipments would "be difficult to defend at

very best." In some cases, he found, IBM was recording revenue when it shipped products merely to its own warehouses. "This seems clearly inappropriate," he wrote. IBM defends its continuing practice of booking revenue as soon as it ships a product and says it makes allowances for returns. "The earnings process is substantially complete upon shipment," IBM contends, adding, "Price Waterhouse was, and continues to be, in full agreement."[6]

Service Transactions

6 Explain how revenue recognition applies to service transactions.

Service companies also engage in "sales" transactions. Such transactions may require the performance of a single short-term service or of several services extending over several accounting periods. When the service to be performed is a single act, no particular accounting problems arise. Revenues and related expenses should be recognized when the service (the earnings process) has been completed.[7] Revenue recognition for services that consist of several acts extending over a period of time is discussed later in this chapter.

REVENUE RECOGNITION DURING PRODUCTION

Some companies engage in earnings activities that extend over several accounting periods. For example, bridges, airplanes, office buildings, and oil refineries all require several years to complete. A timber company may plant pine seedlings that require decades of growth before the timber can be cut, processed, and sold as lumber. Service transactions may also extend over several years.

To provide timely information about earnings and future cash flows to investors and other users, should some revenue and income from these types of production be recognized each year? If the net cash flows from these earnings activities can be estimated with a high degree of certainty, the answer is yes. Revenue recognition for these types of transactions is covered in the following sections.

Long-Term Construction Contracts

7 Distinguish between the percentage-of-completion and completed-contract methods of accounting for long-term construction contracts and apply each.

Under generally accepted accounting principles, there are two methods of accounting for revenues, expenses, and income earned under long-term construction contracts (such as those for buildings, bridges, airplanes, and ships):

1. The percentage-of-completion method.

2. The completed-contract method.

---

[6]"As IBM's Woes Grew, Its Accounting Tactics Got Less Conservative," *The Wall Street Journal*, April 7, 1993, pp. A-1 and A-6.

[7]This procedure, as applied to service companies, has been described as the *specific performance method.* See "Accounting for Certain Service Transactions," *FASB Invitation to Comment* (Stamford, Conn.: FASB, 1978). Other terms used in this chapter to describe revenue recognition procedures for service transactions are based on this document. Although the *Invitation to Comment* does not represent GAAP, it does provide a basis for discussing revenue recognition issues for service transactions.

Under the **percentage-of-completion method,** revenue, expenses, and income are recognized during production. The amount of revenue and income recognized generally is in proportion to the amount of progress made toward completing the construction contract (based on costs incurred). Under the **completed-contract method,** revenue, expenses, and income are not recognized until the construction project (the earnings process) is completed. These two methods are presented together in this section for comparative purposes.

The Percentage-of-Completion Method

When contractual arrangements and production processes extend over several accounting periods, the producer-seller should recognize revenue and income *during* production under the following circumstances:

1. The total price of the contract—the price the buyer agrees to pay—is known.

2. The total cost of the construction project is reasonably estimable by the producer-seller.

3. The cost incurred by the producer-seller during the current accounting period, or the percentage of production completed, is known or is reasonably estimable. Stated another way, the producer-seller can reliably measure the extent of completion of production during each accounting period.

CONCEPTUAL

Some circumstances requiring the percentage-of-completion method.

The presence of these circumstances means that the net cash flow effects of the construction activity are reasonably determinable through time. That is, because the contract price is known, the amount of revenue can be estimated with reasonable certainty. The percentage of the project completed during a period is assumed to represent the portion of revenue and income earned during that period.

Applying the Percentage-of-Completion Method At the end of each accounting period, estimated total construction costs are subtracted from the total contract price to determine the estimated total income on the project. In some instances total estimated income may change from period to period because estimated total construction costs may change as construction progresses. Once estimated total income on the project has been determined, the portion of the total income that should be recognized to date (the period between the start of the project and the end of the current accounting period) is calculated. This calculation is based on some measure of the percentage of completion of the total project.

Assume, for example, that at the end of year 2 of a long-term contract to construct a bridge at a contract price of $5 million, the total cost of construction is estimated to be $4.5 million. Therefore, at the end of year 2 total income on the project is estimated to be $500,000. If the bridge is estimated to be 80 percent complete at the end of year 2, then 80 percent of $500,000, or $400,000, is the amount of income that should be recognized for the period between the start of the project and the end of year 2.

Once the amount of income that should be recognized on the project through the end of the current accounting period has been determined, any income that has already been recognized on the project (in prior accounting periods) must be deducted. The result of this calculation is the amount of income that should be recognized in the current accounting period. If $240,000 of income has already been recognized on the construction of the bridge (in year 1), then $160,000 (the $400,000 total income to date less the $240,000 income recognized in year 1) should be recognized as income in year 2.

Measuring the Percentage of Completion The percentage of completion of a project may be based on the relationship between costs incurred up to the current date and total estimated construction costs. That is, any new information about estimated costs necessary to complete the project may be included in the latest cost estimates. Alternatively, the percentage of completion may be based on some physical measure of completion. For example, units of input—such as the number of hours of labor used to date compared with estimated total labor hours needed—might be an appropriate measure of completion. Or units of output, such as the number of miles of road completed compared to total contract miles, might be appropriate.

The components of construction costs—direct materials costs, direct labor costs, and overhead costs—are similar to those of manufacturing costs. With respect to direct materials, an interesting accounting question arises. Should the cost of direct materials *purchased* be included in the calculation of the percentage of completion? This question is important for two reasons: (1) Construction companies typically acquire a large portion of their construction materials early in construction to avoid price increases and take advantage of quantity discounts, and (2) if the cost of those material purchases is included in the percentage of completion, larger amounts of income will be recognized in the early years of the contract.

As a practical example, several years ago Frigitemp, a diversified corporation that manufactured custom-made refrigeration equipment for ships and hotels, built food service systems, and decorated hotels and casinos, declared bankruptcy. The company used the percentage-of-completion method to account for many of its construction contracts. One factor that caused problems for the company was the resulting "front-end loading" of its income from such contracts. Frigitemp included materials *purchased* in its percentage-of-completion calculations, which increased both the percentage of completion and the reported income for that period. In one instance, the company issued promissory notes to a supplier, who in turn invoiced the company for $4.2 million in deck planking—most of which was still in the form of trees growing on the West Coast!

Clearly, the costs of *purchased* materials should not be included in the percentage-of-completion calculation. Instead, material costs should be included in the percentage of completion only as they are used.

Accounting and Reporting under the Percentage-of-Completion Method   In accounting for long-term construction contracts, an inventory account, construction in progress, is debited for the costs incurred in completing the project. This account is also debited for income that is recognized on the project. Thus, under the percentage-of-completion method, the construction-in-progress inventory account is composed of costs incurred to date plus income recognized to date. If the project continues to be profitable, the balance in the construction-in-progress account at the end of each accounting period will equal the contract price times the percentage of completion—that is, the amount of revenue recognized to date. When the project is completed, the balance in the construction-in-progress inventory account will equal the contract price.

Because of the extended construction period required to fulfill a long-term contract and the need to finance continuing construction costs, a construction contract typically specifies that the contractor may bill the purchaser periodically for part of the contract price. These billings are recorded by debiting accounts receivable and crediting an account called billings on construction contract. Because revenue and income are recognized on a percentage-of-completion basis, billings have no effect on the amount of revenue and income to be recognized.

The billings on construction contract account may be interpreted as a dollar measure of the contractor's obligation to perform. In this same vein, the construction-in-progress account may be interpreted as a dollar measure of the contractor's performance to date. Consequently, the billings on the construction contract account and the construction-in-progress account are reported as offsets on the contractor-seller's balance sheet. If the sum of construction in progress and income to date exceeds the billings on construction to date, the net debit amount is reported on the balance sheet as an asset because it represents an amount to be recovered from future billings. If the reverse relationship exists, the net credit amount is reported on the balance sheet as a liability representing unfulfilled obligations to customers. A detailed illustration of accounting for and reporting of long-term

CONCEPTUAL

Revenue and income recognition are not affected by contract billings.

construction projects follows the discussion of the completed-contract method (see pages 332–345.

The Completed-Contract Method

When reasonably dependable estimates of the extent of completion cannot be made, the completed-contract method should be used for long-term construction contracts. Conceptually, the completed-contract method is similar to revenue recognition at the completion of production (and also at the date of sale, since the product is delivered to the purchaser at completion).

As the name implies, under the completed-contract method no income is recognized until the project is completed. During the course of construction, costs incurred on the project are debited to construction in progress. Billings to the customer are recorded by debiting accounts receivable and crediting billings on construction contract. In this respect, and in terms of reporting these accounts on the balance sheet, the completed-contract method is like the percentage-of-completion method. From a balance sheet standpoint, the essential difference between the two methods is that since no income is recognized under the completed-contract method until construction is completed, the construction-in-progress inventory account includes only construction costs incurred. At the completion date, the construction-in-progress account balance will be less than the contract price by the amount of the income from the project.

The percentage-of-completion method and the completed-contract method are not alternatives available for use under the same set of circumstances. When the contract price or revenue is known and future construction costs can be reasonably estimated, the percentage-of-completion method must be used because it provides better signals about net cash flows and therefore more relevant and useful data. If these two conditions are not met however, the completed-contract method must be used to avoid reporting data that may not be reliable.

Accounting for and Reporting Long-Term Construction Contracts: The Two Methods Compared

Assume that at the beginning of 1998, Sunny Corporation entered into a contract to construct a revolutionary solar generating plant for the city of Texarkana. The contract price was $1 million. Information related to construction activity from the beginning of 1998 through the end of 2000, when construction was completed, is as follows:

	1998	1999	2000
Construction costs incurred to date...............	$200,000	$500,000	$875,000
Estimated cost to complete construction...........	600,000	350,000	–0–
Estimated total construction costs................	$800,000	$850,000	$875,000
Billings on contract	180,000	490,000	330,000
Cash payments by purchaser	170,000	240,000	590,000

Observe that the estimated *total* cost of construction (construction costs incurred to date plus estimated costs to complete) changes from year to year. Such changes are common under long-term contracts because the future is never predictable with certainty. Estimates of total construction costs become more certain, however, as time passes.

Exhibit 7–2 shows how the amount of income that would be recognized each year is calculated under the percentage-of-completion method. Exhibit 7–3 presents the journal entries that would be made under both the percentage-of-completion and completed-contract methods. Note the following points about the journal entries in

CONCEPTUAL

The percentage-of-completion method and the completed-contract method are not alternatives available for use under similar circumstances.

EXHIBIT 7-2	Gross Profit (Income) to Be Recognized under the Percentage-of-Completion Method			

	1998	1999	2000
Construction costs incurred to date	$200,000	$500,000	$875,000
Estimated cost to complete construction.	600,000	350,000	–0–
Estimated total cost of construction	$800,000	$850,000	$875,000
Estimated percentage of completion to date (construction costs incurred to date ÷ estimated total cost of construction)	25%	59%ᵃ	100%
Estimated total income ($1,000,000 contract price less estimated total cost of construction).	$200,000	$150,000	$125,000
Income to be recognized to date (estimated percentage of completion × estimated total income)	$ 50,000	$ 88,500	$125,000
Income to be recognized in current year (income to be recognized to date less income recognized in previous years) . . .	$ 50,000	$ 38,500ᵇ	$ 36,500ᶜ

ᵃRounded.
ᵇ$88,500 – $50,000.
ᶜ$125,000 – $88,500.

Exhibit 7–3. First, in all years other than the year in which the project is completed and accepted by the purchaser, the percentage-of-completion method and the completed-contract method require the same journal entries, with one exception: the annual revenue and expense recognition entry made under the percentage-of-completion method. Second, when income is recognized under the percentage-of-completion method, it increases the balance in the inventory account, construction in progress. Third, under the percentage-of-completion method, the construction in progress account includes both costs incurred and income recognized to date. By the time the project is completed, the construction-in-progress account and the billings on construction contract account both equal the contract price. Finally, because no income is recognized during the course of construction under the completed-contract method, in the year the project is completed the difference between the construction-in-progress account and billings on construction contract account equals total income ($1,000,000 revenue – $875,000 expense) to be recognized on the project.

As indicated earlier, if construction in progress exceeds billings on a construction contract, the difference is reported on the balance sheet as a *current asset*. If the amount in the billings on construction contract account exceeds the amount in the construction-in-progress account, the difference is reported as a *current liability*. The difference is reported as a current item because the contractor's operating cycle includes the length of the construction period.

Exhibit 7–4, which is based on data for the Sunny Corporation illustration and the journal entries in Exhibit 7–3, illustrates financial statement reporting and disclosures for companies with long-term construction contracts.

Recognition of Losses on Long-Term Construction Contracts

To this point we have assumed that construction contracts are profitable, in terms of both the income recognized each period and total income on the contract. In this section we shall consider accounting for and reporting of losses on long-term construction contracts.

CONCEPTUAL

Losses on long-term construction contracts are recognized as soon as the losses are probable.

When cost estimates indicate that a loss is *probable,* the loss should be recognized immediately, under both the percentage-of-completion and the completed-contract methods. There are two types of losses: (1) when the percentage-of-completion method is used, the periodic calculation of income to be recognized may indicate that though the overall contract is expected to be profitable, a loss must be reported for the current period, or (2) under either method, a loss may be sustained on the contract as a whole.

Periodic Losses under a Profitable Contract   Periodic losses are caused by upward revisions of estimated construction costs. They will occur when the income recognized in previous accounting periods exceeds the income that should have been recognized to date. To illustrate this type of loss, assume that Feldman Construction has reached the end of the third year of a four-year, $800,000 construction contract. Cumulative construction costs and income data for years 1, 2, and 3, the current year, are as follows:

	YEAR 1	YEAR 2	YEAR 3
Construction costs incurred to date	$210,000	$432,000	$600,000
Estimated cost to complete construction	490,000	288,000	150,000
Estimated total cost of construction	$700,000	$720,000	$750,000
Estimated percentage of completion	30%	60%	80%
Estimated total income	$100,000	$80,000	$50,000
Income recognized to date	30,000	48,000	40,000
Income recognized in current year	30,000	18,000	(8,000)

Notice that $48,000 of construction income has been recognized through the end of year 2—$8,000 *more* than the $40,000 income that should be recognized by the end of year 3. Thus, an $8,000 loss must be recognized for year 3. Since construction costs incurred during year 3 were $168,000 ($600,000 − $432,000), the following entry would be made at the end of year 3:

Construction expenses.........................	168,000	
Construction revenue........................		160,000
Construction in progress		8,000

Given the conditions under which the percentage-of-completion method is used, this type of loss should occur only infrequently. It will not arise under the completed-contract method because no income is recognized under that method until the construction project is completed.

Continuing with the Feldman Construction example, if actual construction costs in year 4 are $150,000, total income on the contract will be $50,000. Thus, $10,000 in income will be recognized in year 4 ($50,000 − $40,000).

Losses under an Unprofitable Contract   The second type of loss arises when total construction costs are expected to exceed the contract price. This type of loss can arise under either the completed-contract method or the percentage-of-completion method. Like a periodic loss, a loss on the contract as a whole arises because of unexpected increases in construction costs.

To illustrate this type of loss, refer to the Feldman Construction example above. Assume the same facts for years 1 and 2 and for the construction costs incurred in year 3 ($168,000). Assume also that the estimated completion costs for year 4 are $220,000. Under these assumptions, the cost data at the end of year 3 would be as follows:

	END OF YEAR 3
Construction costs incurred to date....................................	$600,000
Estimated cost to complete construction.................................	220,000
Estimated total cost of construction.....................................	$820,000

Under these circumstances, the construction contract is expected to result in an overall loss of $20,000 ($820,000 − $800,000). Because Feldman has already recognized

| EXHIBIT 7-3 | **Journal Entries for Long-Term Construction Contracts, Percentage-of-Completion and Completed-Contract Methods** |

	Percentage-of-Completion Method		Completed-Contract Method	
1998				
To record construction costs:				
Construction in progress............................	200,000		200,000	
Materials, wages payable, cash, etc.		200,000		200,000
To record billings:				
Accounts receivable	180,000		180,000	
Billings on construction contract		180,000		180,000
To record cash collections:				
Cash	170,000		170,000	
Accounts receivable		170,000		170,000
To record income recognized:[a]				
Construction in progress............................	50,000		No entry	
Construction expenses	200,000			
Construction revenue		250,000		
1999				
To record construction costs:				
Construction in progress............................	300,000		300,000	
Materials, wages payable, cash, etc.		300,000		300,000
To record billings:				
Accounts receivable	490,000		490,000	
Billings on construction contract		490,000		490,000
To record cash collections:				
Cash	240,000		240,000	
Accounts receivable		240,000		240,000

$48,000 in income through the end of year 2, the following entry for construction revenue and expense would be required at the end of year 3:

> Construction expenses......................... 168,000
>   Construction revenue ($168,000 – $68,000).......   100,000
>   Construction in progress ($48,000 + $20,000)   68,000

If Feldman Construction had been using the completed-contract method, the following entry would have been required at the end of year 3:

> Loss on construction contract 20,000
>   Construction in progress ($820,000 – $800,000)....   20,000

The loss account is used because under the completed-contract method, revenues and expenses are not recognized until the contract is completed.

    Notice that under both methods, the construction-in-progress account balance at the end of year 3 is $580,000. (Percentage-of-completion method—$600,000 costs incurred plus $48,000 income minus $68,000 adjusting entry; completed-contract method—$600,000 costs incurred minus $20,000 adjusting entry.) Thus, the loss and its unfavorable net cash flow effect are reported on a timely basis in the year in

	Percentage-of-Completion Method		Completed-Contract Method	
To record income recognized:[a]				
Construction in progress.	38,500		No entry	
Construction expenses	300,000			
Construction revenue		338,500		

2000

	Percentage-of-Completion Method		Completed-Contract Method	
To record construction costs:				
Construction in progress	375,000		375,000	
Materials, wages payable, cash, etc.		375,000		375,000
To record billings:				
Accounts receivable	330,000		330,000	
Billings on construction contract		330,000		330,000
To record cash collections:				
Cash	590,000		590,000	
Accounts receivable		590,000		590,000
To record income recognized and to close construction contract accounts:				
Percentage-of-completion method:[a]				
Construction in progress	36,500			
Construction expenses	375,000			
Construction revenue		411,500		
Billings on construction contract	1,000,000			
Construction in progress		1,000,000		
Completed-contract method:				
Construction expenses			875,000	
Construction in progress			125,000	
Construction revenue				1,000,000
Billings on construction contract			1,000,000	
Construction in progress				1,000,000

[a]Since construction income is based on the percentage of completion, construction revenue equals the costs incurred in the current period plus the amount of income recognized in the current period. Construction expenses, then, equal the costs incurred in generating the revenue.

Equivalent entries to show the amount of *income* recognized each year under the percentage-of-completion method would be:

	1998		1999		2000	
Construction in progress	50,000		38,500		36,500	
Income on long-term construction contract.		50,000		38,500		36,500

which they first become known. In addition, the construction-in-progress account is reported at the amount expected to be *recoverable* on the contract: $580,000 = the $800,000 contract price less the $220,000 expected completion cost.

Assuming that actual costs in year 4 are $220,000, the balance in the construction-in-progress account at the end of year 4 will be $800,000. A percentage-of-completion income statement for year 4 would show revenues and expenses of $220,000 each; a completed-contract income statement would show revenues and expenses of $800,000 each.

The recognition of losses on long-term construction contracts when those losses first become known is an example of how conservatism deals with uncertainty

EXHIBIT 7-4	Financial Statement Reporting and Footnote Disclosures for a Long-Term Construction Contract

Percentage-of-Completion Method

	1998	1999	2000
Partial Income Statement			
Revenue from long-term construction contracts	$250,000	$338,500	$411,500
Costs of construction revenue	(200,000)	(300,000)	(375,000)
Income (gross profit) on long-term construction contracts.	$ 50,000	$ 38,500	$ 36,500

Partial Balance Sheet

CURRENT ASSETS:				
Accounts receivable		$ 10,000	$260,000	
Inventories:				
Construction in progress	$250,000			
Less: Billings	(180,000)	70,000		
CURRENT LIABILITIES:				
Billings on construction contract			$670,000	
Less: Construction in progress			(588,500)	81,500

Note I. Significant Accounting Policies (in Part)

Long-term construction contracts: The company recognizes profit on long-term construction contracts by using the percentage-of-completion method of accounting. The percentage of completion is based on the ratio of cost incurred to date as compared to estimated total construction cost. When costs incurred plus profits recognized to date exceed amounts billed, a current asset equal to the difference and classified as inventory is reported on the balance sheet. In 1998, this amount equaled $70,000. When amounts billed exceed costs incurred plus profits recognized to date, a current liability equal to the difference is reported on the balance sheet. In 1999, this amount was $81,500. Construction costs include direct materials, direct labor, and overhead costs associated with the project.

CONCEPTUAL

Accounting for losses on long-term construction contracts illustrates the concept of recoverable value.

about future cash flows. It also illustrates the application of the concept of *recoverable value,* discussed in connection with balance sheet valuation and reporting in Chapter 5.

As a practical example of revenue recognition on long-term contracts, the following disclosure appeared in the 1995 annual report of MFS Communications Company:

The Company recognizes revenue on telecommunications services in the month the related service is provided. Network systems integration revenue is recognized on the percentage-of-completion method of accounting. Under the percentage-of-completion method, an estimated percentage for each contract, as determined by the Company's engineering estimate based on the amount of work performed, is applied to total estimated profit. Provisions for losses are recognized on uncompleted contracts when they become known. Claims for additional revenue are recognized in the period when settled. Revisions in cost and profit estimates, which are always reasonably possible to occur in the near term under the percentage-of-completion method, are reflected in the accounting period in which the facts which require the revision become known.

Completed-Contract Method

	1998	1999	2000
Partial Income Statement			
Completed-contract method:			
Revenue from long-term			
construction contracts.	—	—	$1,000,000
Costs of construction revenue	—	—	(875,000)
Income (gross profit) on long-term			
construction contracts.	—	—	$ 125,000
Partial Balance Sheet			
CURRENT ASSETS:			
Accounts receivable.	$10,000	$260,000	
Inventories:			
Construction in progress. $200,000			
Less: Billings . . . . (180,000)	20,000		
CURRENT LIABILITIES:			
Billings on construction contract		$670,000	
Less: Construction in progress.		(500,000)	170,000

Note I. Significant Accounting Policies (in Part)

Long-term construction contracts: The company uses the completed-contract method of accounting for long-term construction contracts. Under this method, no profit is recognized until the construction project is either complete or substantially complete. During the period of construction, construction costs are accumulated in a construction-in-progress account and customer billings are accumulated in a billings on construction contract account. Construction costs include direct materials, direct labor, and overhead costs associated with the project. Any excess of costs incurred to date over billings is reported among inventories as a current asset. In 1998, this amount was $20,000. Any excess of billings over costs incurred to date is reported as a current liability. In 1999, this amount was $170,000.

Service Transactions

Many service transactions require the performance of *several* acts extending over a long period of time. When service performance consists of a number of similar acts, a percentage-of-completion method called the **proportional-performance method** is often used. If the number of acts to be performed is fixed, revenue is recognized proportionally as each act is performed. If the number of acts to be performed is not fixed, revenue must be recognized proportionately on the basis of the number of acts performed as a percentage of the estimated total number of acts.

Professional examination review courses, such as CPA and law review courses, provide a good illustration for applying the proportional-performance method. Companies that offer these courses often charge a one-time fixed fee. This fee permits participants to take the courses either a fixed number of times or an *unlimited* number of times. Because companies incur operating costs each time the courses are offered, recognizing the entire fixed fee as revenue at the time the cash is received would produce misleading operating income and cash flow signals. Consequently, these companies must estimate the number of times a candidate will take the course and recognize revenue accordingly. Obviously, professional judgment is required in making these estimates.

8 Explain how revenues and expenses are recognized for services that extend over several periods.

Another illustration of a service company that performs several acts over an extended period is a health and physical fitness club. These clubs, which offer members activities such as racquetball, tennis, sauna, and weightlifting privileges, often charge a membership fee up front, in addition to monthly fees. A few clubs have offered *lifetime* membership fees, payable at the joining date, with no monthly fees. To properly match revenues with expenses, these membership fees must be allocated over future usage periods. Recently, several of these health clubs have experienced financial difficulties because of declining membership, an inability to estimate the costs of servicing members over time, and improper revenue recognition methods. Several years ago, for example, International Fitness Centers, a large chain of clubs, filed for bankruptcy.[8] The bankruptcy was attributed to mounting legal and financial problems, as well as to questionable bookkeeping practices related to revenue recognition.[9]

Finally, an example of a unique type of service transaction is provided by Thousand Trails, Inc., an outdoor recreation company. Several years ago, Thousand Trails began developing campgrounds for use by campers who were willing to pay a one-time membership fee of several thousand dollars. The fee gave members access to well-maintained campgrounds in various parts of the country; Thousand Trails called them "the poor man's country club." Some people raised questions about the company's revenue recognition methods. Thousand Trails recorded the entire membership fee as revenue shortly after a member's contract was signed, despite the fact that members paid only about 10 percent down, with the balance payable over a period of up to seven years. The company had little recourse against contract defaults other than suspension of membership privileges.

Another questionable aspect of income recognition was the method the company used to match expenses with revenues. Thousand Trails prorated its actual and projected expenses to revenue on the basis of the number of members who eventually would use the facilities. For example, if a campground could support 5,000 members, 1/5,000th of current and projected expenses was matched against revenue from each new member. One year the company prorated expenses on the basis of 240,000 estimated members although there were only 70,000 actual members. As a result of the company's methods of revenue recognition, reported earnings were $16.2 million, or $1.51 per share, through the first nine months of that year. For that same period, however, cash flows were negative (estimated to be a negative $40 million for that year).[10]

Service transactions often require a company to perform several acts, with the *final act* considered the "critical event" in the earnings process. Under these circumstances, a revenue recognition method called the **completed-performance method** is applied in a manner similar to the completed-contract method discussed earlier. That is, revenue is not recognized and costs are deferred until the final act has been completed. Upon completion of the critical event, revenue is recognized, and costs, which were previously deferred, are matched against revenue to determine income. For example, a computer service company that contracts with a school system to install, test, and debug a sophisticated computer network probably would not recognize revenue until the system was operational.

Products Requiring Aging

Many products require lengthy periods of preparation before they are finally in salable form. For example, tree seedlings require care—fertilizing, watering, thinning, treating with insecticides—for a number of years before they are sold. Fine whiskeys are aged for several years before they are marketed and sold. Thus, these products

---

[8]"Fitness Centers File for Bankruptcy," *Daily Oklahoman,* March 4, 1987, p. 10.
[9]*Daily Oklahoman,* March 5, 1987, p. 11.
[10]"A Look at Thousand Trails Raises Questions about Viability of Its Plan," *The Wall Street Journal,* November 11, 1984, pp. 35, 63.

become more valuable over time. Should the *accretion* in their value be recognized as income on a periodic basis?

Generally, the answer is no. Even though some products do increase in value through time, future economic conditions, such as consumer demand, technological change, selling prices, and production costs, are so uncertain that the net cash flow effects of the accretion in value cannot be reasonably estimated. As a result, income usually is not recognized on an accretion basis. An exception may arise when a contract to age a specific product for a customer is agreed upon before the aging process begins. If future costs can be estimated and the seller is relieved of any obligation in the event the purchaser is dissatisfied with the product, the percentage-of-completion method would appear to be appropriate.

REVENUE RECOGNITION AT COMPLETION OF PRODUCTION

> **9** Identify situations in which revenue should be recognized when production is complete and account for revenue in those situations.

As Exhibit 7–1 indicates, revenue may be recognized when production is completed. The circumstances that justify revenue recognition at this point are:

1. The product is sold in a market with a reasonably assured selling price.

2. The costs of selling and distributing the product are insignificant and can be reasonably estimated.

3. Production, rather than sale, is considered to be the most critical event in the earnings process. For a farm implement manufacturer, the most crucial event in earning revenue probably is *selling* wheat combines and other farm implements, not producing them. But for a wheat farmer, the most crucial event probably is *harvesting* the mature wheat. Thus, the wheat farmer might recognize revenue at harvest—the completion of production. In the following section we discuss this method and compare it to the point-of-sale method.

Comparison to Recognition at the Point of Sale

Revenue often is recognized at the completion of production of food products and some precious metals. To illustrate this method, assume that Kinney Farms began operating at the beginning of 1998. During 1998, the company planted and harvested 10,000 bushels of corn. Eight thousand of those bushels were sold in 1998, and the remaining bushels were sold in 1999. Additional data are as follows:

Selling price of corn, per bushel	**$3.00**
Variable production cost (paid in cash), per bushel	**$1.00**
Depreciation on production equipment	**$6,000**
Selling cost, per bushel (incurred and paid at time of sale)	**$.20**

Cash collected on sales:	1998	$18,000
	1999	10,000
	2000	2,000
		$30,000

Financial position of Kinney Farms at the beginning of 1998:
  Equipment, $60,000   Contributed capital, $60,000

Exhibit 7–5 presents the financial statements for Kinney Farms for 1998 and 1999. Columns 1 and 2 show the statements as they appear when revenue is recognized at the completion of production. For comparative purposes, columns 3 and 4 show the financial statements when revenue is recognized at the point of sale. As Exhibit 7–5 indicates, both methods show the same amount for total net

| EXHIBIT 7–5 | Revenue Recognition at the Completion of Production versus at the Point of Sale | | | |

	At Completion of Production		At Point of Sale	
	1998	1999	1998	1999
Income Statement				
Revenues	$ 30,000	—	$ 24,000	$ 6,000
Expenses:				
Cost of goods produced/sold:				
Variable production costs	$(10,000)	—	$ (8,000)	$ (2,000)
Depreciation	(6,000)	—	(4,800)[a]	(1,200)
Total cost of goods produced/sold	$(16,000)	—	$(12,800)	$ (3,200)
Selling expenses	(2,000)	—	(1,600)	(400)
Net income.	$ 12,000	—	$ 9,600	$ 2,400
Balance Sheet				
Cash	$ 6,400	$16,000	$ 6,400	$16,000
Accounts receivable	6,000[b]	2,000[c]	6,000[b]	2,000[c]
Inventory of corn.	5,600[d]	—	3,200[e]	—
Equipment (net of accumulated depreciation)	54,000	54,000	54,000	54,000
	$ 72,000	$72,000	$ 69,600	$72,000
Contributed capital	$ 60,000	$60,000	$ 60,000	$60,000
Retained earnings	12,000	12,000	9,600	12,000
	$ 72,000	$72,000	$ 69,600	$72,000

[a].80 × $6,000.

[b]
Sales in 1998	$24,000
Collections in 1998	(18,000)
	$ 6,000

[c]
Beginning balance	$ 6,000
Sales in 1999	6,000
Collections in 1999	(10,000)
	$ 2,000

[d]$6,000 (sales price) − $400 (future selling costs).

[e].20 × $16,000 production costs.

income once all the corn has been sold. The difference between the two methods lies only in the *timing* of the recognition of net income.

When revenue and income are recognized at the completion of production, inventory is reported at *net realizable value* or *expected exit value*. Notice that at the end of 1998, the carrying value of the corn inventory is $5,600. This amount represents the future selling price of $6,000 (2,000 × $3) less future selling costs of $400 (2,000 × $.20). In other words, $5,600 represents the *future net cash flows* associated with sale of the corn.

When the sales price is assured and future selling costs can be estimated, revenue and income recognition at the completion of production provide earlier signals about future net cash flows than the point-of-sale method does. In Exhibit 7–5, notice that the net income of $12,000 is reported in 1998 under the completed-production method, but only partially in 1998 ($9,600) and partially in 1999 ($2,400) under the point-of-sale method.

Accounting and Reporting at the Completion of Production

How would Kinney Farms incorporate revenue recognition at the completion of production into its accounts? Although many procedures are possible, one approach would be to record the corn at its selling price as production is completed and the corn is placed in inventory. The following summary entries illustrate this approach:

Inventory	16,000	
Cash		10,000
Accumulated depreciation		6,000

[(10,000 × $1) + $6,000]
To record cost of corn harvested in 1998.

Inventory ($30,000 – $16,000)	14,000	
Cost of goods produced (expenses)	16,000	
Revenue (10,000 × $3)		30,000

To record revenue, costs to be matched against revenue,
and inventory at selling price for 1998.

Sales would be recorded by debiting accounts receivable and crediting inventory, and collections would be recorded in the usual manner:

Accounts receivable	24,000	
Inventory.		24,000

(8,000 × $3)
To record sales made in 1998.

Cash	18,000	
Accounts receivable		18,000

To record collections in 1998.

During 1998, selling expenses would be recorded as the sales are made. In addition, an adjusting entry would be necessary at the end of 1998 to accrue selling expenses to be paid when the remaining inventory is sold in 1999:

Selling expenses	1,600	
Cash.		1,600

(8,000 × $.20)
To record selling expenses on 1998 sales.

Selling expenses	400	
Inventory		400

(2,000 × $.20)
To accrue selling expenses on unsold inventory.

Notice that the selling expense accrual reduces the carrying value of inventory to its net realizable value of $5,600 ($6,000 – $400).

When Kinney Farms sells the remaining inventory in 1999, the following entry would be made:

Accounts receivable (2,000 × $3)	6,000	
Inventory		5,600
Cash (2,000 × $.20)		400

Accounts receivable is debited for the dollar amount of sales, inventory is credited for its net realizable (carrying) value, and cash is credited for the costs incurred in selling the remaining bushels. Since revenue and income were recognized when production was completed in 1998, revenue and expense accounts are not affected in 1999. The entry to record 1999 cash collections from customers is the same under both the point-of-sale method and the completed-production method.

Notice that by recognizing income at the completion of production, Kinney Farms becomes something of a grain speculator during the holding period from production to sale. If grain prices fluctuate during this holding period, holding gains and losses on the inventory, similar to those discussed on page 13 in Chapter 2, result and perhaps the inventory should be "marked-to-market." However, if the holding gains and losses are frequent and material, one might argue that Kinney Farms should not be using this revenue recognition method because the net cash flow uncertainty is too great to warrant revenue and income recognition before the sale occurs.

Reserve Recognition Accounting

Several years ago, a variation of the completion-of-production method, called **reserve recognition accounting** (RRA), was proposed for oil and gas exploration companies. Many people felt that the *discovery* of proven oil and gas reserves was the critical event in the earnings process. They asserted further that more relevant and timely financial information would result from basing income on the discovery of energy resources rather than on their sale. Under RRA, income is measured at the present value of the estimated future sales of the discovered reserves less the exploration costs incurred in finding the reserves and the present value of the cost of extracting them.[11] Opponents of RRA felt that although it would provide relevant information, its usefulness was impaired by its lack of reliability. For theoretical, practical, and political reasons, RRA became a very controversial concept. Because of its controversial nature, oil and gas companies were never required to use the method to recognize revenue and income. However, under generally accepted accounting principles, oil and gas companies are required to make certain supplementary *disclosures,* similar to RRA, in their financial statements.[12]

REVENUE RECOGNITION DURING CASH COLLECTION

So far in this chapter, we have seen that when the revenue recognition criteria are met before or at the point of sale, revenue should be recognized and reported in the income statement. Also, under the matching concept, expenses incurred in earning revenue should be recognized and deducted from revenue to obtain net income. If sales are made on account, the allowance (accrual) method of accounting for uncollectible accounts should be used to estimate the dollar amount of receivables expected to be uncollectible.

Under certain circumstances, uncertainty about the ultimate cash collection of a credit sale may be so great that revenue should not be recognized until cash is collected. For example, a company may have no basis for estimating the dollar amount of uncollectibles. Or the net cash flow effect of its earnings activity may be so uncertain that revenue and income should be recognized only when cash is collected. Two methods of recognizing revenue during cash collection are the *installment method* and the *cost-recovery method*. In the following sections we will examine both methods, including the circumstances under which each should be used.

CONCEPTUAL

Recognition of revenue during cash collection is appropriate when uncollectibles cannot be estimated.

10 Differentiate between the installment and the cost-recovery methods of accounting and prepare journal entries under each method.

---

[11]Other components of RRA income include (1) interest on the carrying value of reserves and (2) revisions of previously reported income due to changes in estimated selling prices, costs, and quantities of proven reserves.
[12]"Disclosures about Oil and Gas Producing Activities," *Statement of Financial Accounting Standards No. 69* (Stamford, Conn.: FASB, 1982).

The Installment Method

The **installment method,** as the name implies, is sometimes used to account for certain installment sales. The sale of an item such as a television set, a refrigerator, or an automobile on an installment or deferred payment plan does not in itself justify the use of the installment method, however. If the criteria for revenue recognition are met on the date an installment sale occurs, revenue and related expenses, including uncollectible accounts expense, should be recognized at that point. As a practical example, Dillard's Department Stores has annual installment sales in the millions of dollars, yet it recognizes revenue and income at the point of sale. When the collection period on a credit sale extends over a long period and there is no reasonable basis for estimating uncollectible accounts, the installment method of accounting is appropriate. Under this method, gross profit (sales less cost of goods sold) arising from a sale is deferred and recognized only as cash collections take place. In the next section, we will illustrate how the method is used. The following sections will address considerations such as variations in gross profit rates, interest on receivables, and credit defaults.

Income Recognition under the Installment Method

Assume that Jay Electronics sells computers for $5,000 each on a deferred payment plan—$1,000 down, the balance payable in four equal quarterly installments of $1,000. Jay manufactures the computers at a cost of $3,000 each. On October 1, 1998, Jay sells one computer under these terms. Jay's accounting period ends on December 31. (Jay also charges interest on the outstanding unpaid installment balance. Although the interest payments are due each quarter in addition to the quarterly installment payments, to simplify the illustration we shall ignore the interest at this point.)

To apply the installment method, we must calculate the gross profit percentage on the sale. The gross profit percentage on Jay's 1998 sales is 40 percent:

$$\frac{\text{Gross profit}}{\text{percentage}} = \frac{\text{Sales} - \text{Cost of goods sold}}{\text{Sales}} = \frac{\$5,000 - \$3,000}{\$5,000} = \frac{\$2,000}{\$5,000} = 40\%$$

This calculation means that as cash collections are made, 40 cents (40 percent) of each dollar collected is assumed to represent profit, and 60 cents (60 percent) of each dollar to represent a recovery of cost. Thus, Jay would recognize gross profit each year as follows:

	1998	1999	TOTAL
Cash collections	$2,000	$3,000	$5,000
Gross profit percentage	40%	40%	40%
Gross profit recognized	$800	$1,200	$2,000

Journal Entries for the Installment Method Jay Electronics would make the following entries in 1998:

10/1/98:

1. Cash 1,000
   Accounts receivable 4,000
       Sales   5,000
   To record sales.

2. Cost of goods sold 3,000
       Inventory   3,000
   To record the cost of sales. (The perpetual inventory method is assumed.)

12/31/98:

3. Cash 1,000
    Accounts receivable   1,000
To record collection of the first quarterly
installment payments.

4. Sales 5,000
    Cost of goods sold. 3,000
    Deferred gross profit   2,000
To close the sales and cost of goods sold accounts
and defer the gross profit.

5. Deferred gross profit 800
    Realized gross profit   800
($2,000 × .40)
To recognize gross profit based on cash collections.

The first two entries are to record the sale and related cost of goods sold. Entry 3 is to record the first installment payment received from the customer. Entries 4 and 5 are year-end adjustments necessary under the installment method. Because profit is to be recognized on the basis of cash collections, the entire gross profit applicable to the sale made in 1998 is initially deferred. This deferral is accomplished in the fourth entry. Entry 5 records the amount of gross profit recognized in 1998.

Financial Statement Presentation   Financial statement data regarding these transactions would appear as follows:

INCOME STATEMENT FOR 1998

Sales (based on cash collections)	**$2,000**
Cost of sales (.60 × $2,000)	**(1,200)**
Realized gross profit	**$ 800**
Expenses	**(xx)**
Net income	**$ xx**

BALANCE SHEET, END OF 1998

Accounts receivable	**$3,000**
Loss: Deferred gross profit (.40 × $3,000)	**(1,200)**
Accounts receivable (net)	**$1,800**

The income statement reports the $800 realized gross profit and the usual expenses that are deducted to arrive at net income. Sales of $5,000 for 1998, along with the related cost of goods sold and deferred gross profit, could be disclosed in a footnote. This disclosure provides information about the company's sales activities, and the related gross profit that has not been recognized because of uncertainty about the collection of accounts receivable. The materiality of the sales transaction would determine the amount of detail that is reported in the income statement.

    On the balance sheet the deferred gross profit is reported as a contra asset to accounts receivable. The net receivable balance of $1,800 may be interpreted as the unrecovered cost of the computers sold:

CONCEPTUAL

Accounts receivable, net of deferred gross profit, represents the unrecovered cost of the assets sold.

Cost of computers sold	**$3,000**
Less: Cash collections ($2,000) × cost percentage (.60)	**(1,200)**
Unrecovered cost, end of 1998	**$1,800**

At this point it should be clear why a *gross profit percentage,* rather than a net profit percentage, is used to recognize profit under the installment method. Since the accounts receivable balance, net of the deferred gross profit, represents the un-recovered cost of the assets sold, only those costs that normally would be considered inventoriable costs are included in the calculation of deferred gross profit.

Variations in the Gross Profit Percentage

Changes in costs, selling prices, and the mix of merchandise sold may cause the gross profit percentage to vary from year to year. Therefore, it is necessary to segregate accounts receivable by the year in which sales were made. This segregation is necessary in order to determine the amount of gross profit to be recognized on cash collections in a given year. Alternatively, a company might maintain only one controlling account and use a subsidiary receivables ledger to distinguish among the sales of the various years. If desired, separate deferred gross profit accounts also could be maintained for each year's receivables.

Interest on Receivables

Interest usually is charged on receivables when they are collectible over a period of time. Interest may be charged on the unpaid balance and collected in cash each period, in addition to the cash installment payments. Or interest may be implicit in the installment payments.

To illustrate, refer to the Jay Electronics example on page 351. Assume, however, that $5,000 is the cash selling price. The deferred payment plan price is $1,000 down, with the balance payable in four equal quarterly installments of $1,076.11. Thus, the installment payments include interest at 3 percent per quarter.

The present value of these installment payments may be treated as an ordinary annuity, as discussed in Appendix A at the back of the text. Together with the down payment, it equals $5,000:

Down payment. **$1,000**
Present value of installments:
$1,076.11 × $P_{\overline{4}|3\%}$ = $1,076.11 × 3.7171 . . . . __4,000__
Total (cash equivalent exchange price) . . . . __$5,000__

Interest revenue associated with this credit sale would be recognized using the *effective interest method.* The following schedule could be used to calculate the amount of interest and gross profit recognized over the payment period:

EVENT	(1) INTEREST REVENUE (CR)[a]	(2) CASH (DR)[b]	(3) ACCOUNTS RECEIVABLE (CR)[c]	(4) ACCOUNTS RECEIVABLE BALANCE[d]	(5) REALIZED GROSS PROFIT[e]
				$5,000.00	
Down payment	—	$1,000.00	$1,000.00	4,000.00	$ 400.00
1st payment	$ 120.00	1,076.11	956.11	3,043.89	382.44
2nd payment	91.32	1,076.11	984.79	2,059.10	393.92
3rd payment	61.77	1,076.11	1,014.34	1,044.76	405.74
4th payment	__31.34__	1,076.11	1,044.76[f]	–0–	__417.90__
	$ 304.43				$2,000.00

[a].03 × previous balance in column (4).
[b]Given.
[c]Col. (2) − col. (1).
[d]Previous balance − col. (3).
[e].40 × col. (3).
[f]Rounded.

Credit Defaults

When a customer defaults on a credit sale contract, normally the seller repossesses the merchandise. Usually the installment payments are large enough so that if the buyer defaults, the fair value of the merchandise repossessed is at least equal to the seller's unrecovered cost (the unpaid receivable balance, net of any deferred gross profit). In accounting for defaults under the installment method, the unpaid receivable balance and related deferred gross profit are removed from the accounts. The difference between the net receivable balance (the unpaid balance less the applicable deferred gross profit) and the fair value of the repossessed merchandise is the gain or loss on repossession.

To illustrate, refer to the original Jay Electronics example on page 351. Assume that Jay's customer defaults shortly after making the second (March 31, 1999) installment payment. Assuming that the repossessed computer has a fair value of $900, the following entries would be made to record the default:

Deferred gross profit	400	
Realized gross profit		400
(.4 × $1,000)		

To record realized gross profit on second installment payment of $1,000 on March 31, 1999.

Inventory of repossessed merchandise	900	
Deferred gross profit (.4 × $2,000)	800	
Loss on repossession	300	
Accounts receivable ($5,000 − $3,000)		2,000

To record the default.

The fair value of the repossessed merchandise represents its selling price in its present condition. If the merchandise must be reworked or reconditioned before being resold, it should be recorded at its expected selling price after reconditioning less estimated reconditioning costs.

The Cost-Recovery Method

Under the **cost-recovery method,** no income is recognized on credit sales until the cost of the merchandise sold has been *fully* recovered through cash collections. After the cost of the merchandise sold has been recovered, all remaining cash collections are reported as income in the period in which they are collected.

Journal entries under the cost-recovery method are identical to the entries under the installment method, except for the *amount* of realized gross profit recognized each year. In the Jay Electronics example presented on page 351, the amounts recognized each year under the cost-recovery method would be as follows:

	1998	1999
Collections	$2,000	$3,000
Cost recovered	(2,000)	(1,000)
Profit recognized	$ 0	$2,000

The cost-recovery method is also used when there is significant uncertainty about the profitability of a specific venture or contract. For example, aircraft manufacturers, such as Boeing, sometimes use the cost-recovery method when they are uncertain whether revenues will be sufficient to produce a profit on the construction or modification of airplanes.

Some service companies also use the cost-recovery method. Many service transactions result in an initial inflow of receivables instead of cash. When there is no basis for estimating the collectibility of receivables, the cost-recovery method should be used. (Since service transactions do not involve cost of goods sold, the cost-recovery method appears to be more appropriate than the installment method.)

Evaluation of Cash-Collection Methods

In practice, the installment and cost-recovery methods are used primarily in real estate transactions. The installment method is more popular than the cost-recovery method, in part because it is the method commonly used for income tax purposes. However, we prefer the cost-recovery method on theoretical grounds. Postponing revenue (gross profit) recognition until cash collection occurs is justifiable only when reasonable estimates of uncollectible accounts cannot be made. Yet the installment method assumption—for each dollar collected, one portion is cost recovery and another portion is profit—is valid only if the seller expects to collect the entire receivable arising from the sale. This expectation runs counter to the circumstances under which the installment method is normally used. For this reason we prefer the cost-recovery method whenever significant uncertainty exists about future cash inflows from receivables.

SUMMARY OF REVENUE AND INCOME RECOGNITION CONCEPTS

We have pointed out that under accrual accounting, the net cash flow effects of earnings activities are reported when they can be measured at an acceptable level of certainty. Professional judgment is often necessary to make this determination. The two revenue recognition criteria, together with the matching principle, provide guidance for recognizing revenues and expenses. While these criteria generally are met at the point of sale, they sometimes are met before a sale occurs or even after a sale occurs.

The *amount* of revenue and income that is *ultimately* recognized is the same under all revenue recognition methods. The differences among the various methods relate to *timing—when* revenue and income are recognized. Timing differences are not trivial, however, given the financial reporting objectives of providing useful and timely information to help users predict and assess cash flows.

Exhibit 7–6 summarizes the effects on periodic income of some of the revenue and income recognition approaches discussed in this chapter. The data in Exhibit 7–6 are based on the Kinney Farms example on pages 347–351 and in Exhibit 7–5.

In accordance with the concept of full disclosure, companies that sell goods or services usually include a description of their revenue recognition procedures in the Summary of Significant Accounting Policies section of the annual report. Refer, for example, to General Electric's annual report in Appendix B at the end of this text. Footnote 1 under accounting policies contains the following disclosure: "*Sales of goods and services.* A sale is recorded when title passes to the customer or when services are performed in accordance with contracts." To give another example, the following disclosure appeared in Southwest Airlines' annual report:

> *REVENUE RECOGNITION* Passenger revenue is recognized when the transportation is provided. Tickets sold but not yet used are included in "Air traffic liability," which includes estimates that are evaluated and adjusted periodically. Any adjustments resulting therefrom are included in results of operations for the periods in which the evaluations are completed.

To this point in the chapter, we have discussed and illustrated how revenue and income can be recognized at various points in a company's earnings process.

CONCEPTUAL

Revenue recognition methods differ in the *timing* of revenue and income recognition.

EXHIBIT 7–6	Summary of the Income Effects of Several Revenue Recognition Methods (Based on Exhibit 7–5)

Revenue Recognition Method	Income Reported	
At completion of production:	1998	$12,000
	1999	—
	2000	—
	Total	$12,000
At point of sale:	1998	$9,600
	1999	2,400
	2000	—
	Total	$12,000
During cash collection: Installment method: Profit rate is 40% $\left(\dfrac{\$12,000}{\$30,000} = .4\right)^{a}$	1998	$18,000 cash collected × .4 = $ 7,200
	1999	10,000 cash collected × .4 = 4,000
	2000	2,000 cash collected × .4 = 800
	Total	$12,000
Cost-recovery method:	1998	$18,000 −$14,400[b] = $3,600
	1999	10,000 − 3,600[c] = 6,400
	2000	2,000 − 0 = 2,000
	Total	$12,000

[a]For instructional purposes only, we have included the selling expenses in the calculation of the profit rate.
[b]$12,800 (cost of goods sold) +$1,600 (selling costs).
[c]$3,200 (cost of goods sold) + $400 (selling costs).

In the next section we will discuss some specialized applications of revenue recognition concepts to franchises, real estate sales, and barter transactions.

Ⓢ PECIALIZED APPLICATIONS OF REVENUE RECOGNITION CONCEPTS

11 **Describe some of the accounting issues related to revenue recognition in franchises, real estate, and other specialized industries.**

Authoritative accounting bodies have issued detailed procedural standards for revenue and income recognition in some companies and certain industries because of special economic circumstances and practices. An overview of some of these applications follows, beginning with franchises.

Franchises

Sales of franchises occur in restaurant, fast-food, motel, auto rental, and similar businesses. Exhibit 7–7 lists the ten fastest-growing franchises in the United States in 1996. In a typical franchise arrangement, the buyer, or franchisee, obtains the right to sell the franchisor's products and to use the franchisor's name for a specified period in a specified location. In addition, the franchisor often promises to assist the franchisee in selecting a business site, constructing facilities, training employees, establishing and

EXHIBIT 7-7	Ten Fastest-Growing Franchises in the United States

Company	Type of Franchise
Subway	Sandwiches
7-Eleven	Convenience store
Burger King	Hamburgers
McDonald's	Hamburgers
Dunkin' Donuts	Donuts
Yogen Fruz/Bresler's	Frozen yogurt/ice cream
Baskin-Robbins	Ice cream and yogurt
Jani-King	Commercial cleaning
Coverall Cleaning Concepts	Commercial cleaning
CleanNet	Commercial cleaning

Source: *Entrepreneur,* April 1996, pp. 150–152.

maintaining a recordkeeping system, planning sales promotion and advertising, and other business activities. In return, the franchisor earns revenue from (1) an *initial franchise fee* related to the sale of the franchise and the services performed and (2) *continuing periodic fees* for services provided on a continuing basis. The periodic fee usually is based on a percentage of the franchisee's sales. Separate accounting issues apply to these two types of fees, as we shall see in the following two sections.

The Initial Franchise Fee

There is no difficulty in accounting for the *continuing periodic fees* received by a franchisor; these fees are accounted for as revenue in the periods in which they are received. Accounting for the *initial franchise fee,* however, raises a difficult revenue recognition issue. For many years it was common practice for franchisors to "front-end" income. That is, they reported the entire franchise fee as revenue in the period in which the franchise contract was signed—regardless of the fact that the fee was to be collected in installments over an extended period and that many services remained to be performed. In terms of the revenue recognition criteria presented earlier, this practice is inappropriate if collectibility of future installments of the fee cannot be estimated or if the franchisor must perform a significant number of the promised services in the future. *FASB Statement No. 45* requires that the initial franchise fee be recognized as revenue only after the franchisor has substantially performed the services promised in the franchise arrangement, and the collectibility of the initial franchise fee is reasonably assured.[13]

Assume, for instance, that Burger Boy sells restaurant franchises for $20,000. This fee is payable 10 percent down with the balance due in four annual installments plus interest on the unpaid balance. In return for the $20,000 initial franchise fee, Burger Boy will assist the franchisee in selecting a location, obtaining financing, and installing an accounting system and will provide expert advice over a specified period on such matters as employee motivation, advertising, planning, and financing. In addition to the initial franchise fee, Burger Boy will receive 1 percent of each restaurant's monthly sales in return for permitting franchisees to purchase meal ingredients below market prices.

There are several methods of accounting for the initial franchise fee, depending on the circumstances. *If no services have been provided by the franchisor at the time*

---

[13]"Accounting for Franchise Fee Revenue," *Statement of Financial Accounting Standards No. 45* (Stamford, Conn.: FASB, 1981).

the initial payment is received, but collectibility of the receivable is assured, the following entry would be appropriate:

Cash.	2,000	
Receivable from franchisee.	18,000	
Unearned franchise fee.		20,000

Despite the receipt of $2,000 in cash, the franchise fee is recorded as unearned because no services have been provided. As the franchisor provides services to the franchisee, the following entry would be made by the franchisor to record the franchise fee earned. (The *amounts* to be debited and credited would depend on the amount of the services provided relative to the total estimated services to be provided.)

Unearned franchise fee	*xx*	
Franchise fee revenue.		*xx*

If substantially all services have been provided by the franchisor, and collectibility of the receivable is reasonably assured, the following entry would be appropriate:

Cash.	2,000	
Receivable from franchisee.	18,000	
Franchise fee revenue.		20,000

If substantially all services have been provided but there is no basis for estimating uncollectibles (i.e., uncertainty exists about the ultimate cash inflows), the following entry would be appropriate:

Cash.	2,000	
Receivable from franchisee.	18,000	
Deferred franchise fee.		18,000
Franchise fee revenue.		2,000

Note that in this case a deferred franchise fee is credited; in the first case (no services provided), an unearned franchise fee was credited. This distinction may appear subtle, but it is very important. In the first case the franchise fee had not yet been earned. In this case the fee has been earned—that is, all the services have been provided—but there is some uncertainty about collecting the receivable. Thus, the deferred franchise fee account is similar to the deferred gross profit account used under the installment method of accounting. Either the installment method or cost-recovery method could be used to recognize franchise fee revenue as cash collections occur. Other approaches are possible, depending on the circumstances. Professional judgment is necessary in applying the revenue recognition guidelines in a given situation.

Some franchise agreements stipulate that any payments made to the franchisor will be refunded if for any reason the franchisee fails to open. Since this stipulation may create uncertainty about net cash inflows to the franchisor, it should be considered in determining the amount of revenue to be recognized before the franchisee's opening date.

Continuing Periodic Fees

Each month Burger Boy would make the following entry to record the receipt of continuing service fees:

Cash (or accounts receivable)	*xx*	
Service revenue		*xx*

To determine periodic income from these service activities, expenses incurred by the franchisor in providing continuing services would be deducted from service revenue.

The following disclosure of revenue recognition for initial franchise fees and continuing periodic fees appeared in the annual report of Rocky Mountain Chocolate Factory, Inc., a manufacturer of chocolate candy and franchisor of stores that sell Rocky Mountain Chocolates:

Franchise and Royalty Fees

Franchise fee revenue is recognized upon completion of all significant initial services provided to the franchisee and upon satisfaction of all material conditions of the franchise agreement. In addition to the initial franchise fee, the Company receives a royalty fee of five percent (5%) and a marketing and promotion fee of one percent (1%) of the store's gross sales.

Real Estate and Retail Land Sales

Real estate sales often involve relatively small down payments—perhaps 20 percent or less—and an extended period, often 25 years or more, for payment of the balance due. Because of the lengthy payment period, uncertainty about the collectibility of payments on a real estate sale may be greater than it is for many other sales transactions. Also, the seller may be required by contract to perform significant services after the sale, such as managing or maintaining the property. Thus, many real estate transactions may not meet the revenue recognition criteria at the time of the sale.

If a substantial number of services are to be performed by the seller, estimating the costs yet to be incurred may be difficult. In addition, uncertainty about the collectibility of payments due may make estimating the amount of cash to be received difficult. Hence, recognition of all or part of the revenue may have to be postponed until the revenue recognition criteria are met. Until the services are performed, collections should be recorded as a deposit (unearned revenue). Even after the seller has performed the required services, if estimates of uncollectibles cannot be made, the installment sales method or the cost-recovery method may be the only appropriate methods for recognizing revenue.

Sales of undeveloped land are similar to real estate sales except that the volume of sales usually is much greater; the down payment usually is a smaller percentage of the sales price; and the seller usually agrees to develop the land by subdividing it, obtaining regulatory approvals, selling the lots, and making improvements such as grading, landscaping, and paving. Furthermore, the sales contract generally is unenforceable (the seller's only recourse is repossession of the property), and the purchaser may have refund privileges for a specified period.

Under rules established by the FASB, revenue should be recognized on retail land sales only when the following conditions are met: (1) the refund period has expired, (2) the cumulative payments equal or exceed 10 percent of the sales price, (3) the receivables are collectible and are not subordinate to new loans on the property, and (4) the seller either is not obligated to make improvements on the lots sold or has made progress on any promised improvements.[14] Cash received before these conditions are met should be recorded as a deposit (unearned revenue).

Barter Transactions

Many economic circumstances have encouraged companies to engage in barter transactions. For example, an automobile dealer may contract with a cleaning company to sell a truck in exchange for cleaning services over an extended period.

---

[14]"Accounting for Sales of Real Estate," *Statement of Financial Accounting Standards No. 66* (Stamford, Conn.: FASB, 1982).

To give another example, broadcasters often barter unused airtime for goods and services. Some companies derive a major portion of their revenues from barter transactions that result in inflows of nonfinancial assets or services instead of cash. Since revenue transactions normally result in cash inflows, some interesting questions arise. Should revenue be recognized on these barter transactions? If so, how is it to be measured? From another perspective, if revenue recognition is deferred until an expected cash inflow materializes, what effect does this delay, which may extend over several periods, have on the timeliness of earnings reporting?

No revenue recognition guidelines currently exist specifically for barter transactions, although *APB Opinion No. 29,* on nonmonetary exchanges, addresses some transactions that are similar to barter transactions. The nature of a barter transaction appears to differ little from that of a sales transaction. Therefore, perhaps revenue should be recognized and measured at the exchange price (called a trading unit in barter transactions) established in the transaction. Accounting for barter transactions presents some real challenges to accountants and raises some interesting theoretical questions. To the extent that these types of transactions continue to grow, we may see FASB involvement.

Other Industry Standards

We have presented and discussed some practical applications of revenue recognition concepts. This presentation was designed to illustrate issues and to show how revenue recognition concepts are applied in different circumstances. The FASB also has issued detailed revenue recognition standards for the following industries:

Insurance industry. Some insurance contracts cover a short period and others a longer period. Standards encompass the recognition of revenue under different types of contracts.[15]

Record and music industry. Owners of record masters or copyrights may earn substantial revenue by entering into license agreements. Standards cover how licensors of record masters and music copyrights are to recognize revenue.[16]

Cable television industry. Standards cover how cable companies are to recognize "hook-up" revenues.[17]

Motion picture industry. Film exhibition rights generally are sold or licensed to theaters for a flat fee or a percentage of box office receipts. License agreements to broadcast a film on television also fall in this category. Many years ago, for example, CBS obtained a license to televise the classic *Gone With the Wind* several times over a period of years. Standards cover how the licensor is to recognize the revenue associated with these agreements.[18]

In summary, special industry characteristics have prompted the FASB to issue rather detailed standards. Consistent with the financial reporting objectives discussed in Chapter 2, the objective of these standards is to allow companies to recognize revenue and income when *uncertainty about the net cash flow effects of the transaction or transactions has been reduced to an acceptable level.* These standards also represent applications of the two revenue recognition criteria discussed and illustrated throughout this chapter.

---

[15]"Accounting and Reporting by Insurance Companies," *Statement of Financial Accounting Standards No. 60* (Stamford, Conn.: FASB, 1982).

[16]"Financial Reporting in the Record and Music Industry," *Statement of Financial Accounting Standards No. 50* (Stamford, Conn.: FASB, 1981).

[17]"Financial Reporting by Cable Television Companies," *Statement of Financial Accounting Standards No. 51* (Stamford, Conn.: FASB, 1981).

[18]"Financial Reporting by Producers and Distributors of Motion Picture Films," *Statement of Financial Accounting Standards No. 53* (Stamford, Conn.: FASB, 1981).

SUMMARY OF LEARNING OBJECTIVES

1. **Distinguish among revenue, revenue measurement, and revenue recognition.**
   Revenues are increases in net assets that arise from delivery or production of goods, the rendering of services, or other activities that constitute a company's primary operations. Revenues are measured at the fair value or cash equivalent price of the assets received in exchange. Revenue recognition is a timing issue—when revenue should be recognized and reported in the income statement.

2. **Describe the earnings process.**
   The earnings process is continuous. Revenue is earned throughout this process as value—in the form of place, form, and/or time utility—is added to the cost of productive inputs.

3. **Explain the concept of realization.**
   Conceptually, realization refers to the occurrence of an event or events that reduce the uncertainty about the net cash flow effects of an earnings activity to an acceptable level. In practice, the realization concept is applied through two revenue recognition criteria or guidelines used to determine when revenue should be recognized.

4. **List and apply the two basic revenue recognition criteria.**
   Revenue should be recognized when the following two criteria are met: (1) the amount and timing of revenue are reasonably determinable and (2) the earnings process is complete or virtually complete.

5. **Account for revenue recognition at the point of sale, including credit sales, after-sale costs, and return privileges.**
   Revenue normally is recognized at the point of sale, at which time expenses are matched against revenue to determine income. To account for credit sales, an estimate of uncollectible expenses must be made. To properly match revenue with expenses, costs to be incurred after the point of sale must also be estimated. Adequate allowances must be made for returns when goods are sold with return privileges.

6. **Explain how revenue recognition applies to service transactions.**
   When a service is performed in a single act, revenues and related expenses are recognized when the act is completed. When a service includes several acts performed over an extended period, it is accounted for as if it were a long-term contract.

7. **Distinguish between the percentage-of-completion and the completed-contract methods of accounting for long-term construction contracts and apply each.**
   The percentage-of-completion method should be used when the contract price is known, the total cost of the contract is reasonably estimable, and the percentage of completion can be estimated each period. If these circumstances are not met, the completed-contract method should be used. Under the percentage-of-completion method, profit is recognized in proportion to the amount of progress made on the contract. Under the completed-contract method, profit is not recognized until the contract has been completed. Under both methods, losses are recognized as they occur.

8. **Explain how revenues and expenses are recognized for services that extend over several periods.**
   Revenue recognition for services that extend over several periods is similar to accounting for long-term contracts. The two methods used are (1) the proportional-performance method, which is similar to the percentage-of-completion method for long-term contracts, and (2) the completed-performance method, which is similar to the completed-contract method for long-term contracts.

9. **Identify situations in which revenue should be recognized when production is complete and account for revenue in those situations.**
   Revenue can be recognized at the completion of production under the following conditions: The product is sold in a market with a reasonably assured selling price; the costs of selling and distributing the product are not significant and can be reasonably estimated; and production (rather than sale) is considered to be the critical event in the earnings process. Accounting for revenue and associated expenses at the completion of production requires that inventory be debited for the increase

from cost to net realizable value (sales price less selling costs), that cost of goods sold and estimated disposal costs be increased (debited), and that revenue be increased (credited) for the sales price.

10. Differentiate between the installment method and the cost-recovery methods of accounting and prepare journal entries under each method.

Both the installment and cost-recovery methods of accounting are appropriate when there is significant uncertainty about the collection of a credit sale. Both methods recognize revenue on the basis of cash collections. Under the installment method, each dollar collected is considered to be part cost recovery and part gross profit. Under the cost-recovery method, gross profit is not recognized until cash collections equal to the cost of the goods sold have been received.

11. Describe some of the accounting issues related to revenue recognition in franchising, real estate, and other specialized industries.

In franchising, the initial franchise fee and in real estate, revenue from land sales are recognized as revenue when they are earned and collectibility can be estimated. For barter sales, the primary issue is determining the exchange price. In all special industries, the guiding concept is that revenue should be recognized when uncertainty about the net cash flow effect of the transaction or event has been reduced to an acceptable level.

KEY TERMS

completed-contract method 337

completed-performance method 346

cost-recovery method 354

critical event 332

earnings process 331

installment method 351

percentage-of-completion method 337

proportional-performance method 345

realization 332

reserve recognition accounting 350

revenue recognition 331

service transactions 330

APPENDIX 7–1

Consignment Sales

Many manufacturers and distributors arrange for their products to be sold by retailers or dealers on a consignment basis. Under such an arrangement, the seller, or consignor, retains title to the merchandise. The dealer, or consignee, acts as a selling agent, accepts the merchandise, and agrees to sell it. The dealer earns a commission on any products sold and periodically remits the cash from sales, less the commission earned, to the seller/consignor—usually a manufacturer or distributor. For example, grocery stores often do not wish to make a substantial investment in cosmetics and drugs. Instead, they sell them on consignment, earning a commission on sales.

Assume, for example, that Movie Town sells VHS movies on a consignment basis. The company ships 800 tapes to Marvin Foods for sale at $60 each, paying $1,600 in transportation costs. The tapes cost Movie Town $20 each. Marvin Foods is allowed a commission of 20 percent on each tape sold. During the year Marvin sells 300 tapes and spends $2,400 for 800 plastic storage boxes—an amount Movie Town has agreed to reimburse. At the end of the year, Marvin

---

EXHIBIT 7–8   Accounting for Consignments

I. Consignor ships 800 tapes costing $20 each to consignee:

Consignor (Movie Town)		**Consignee (Marvin Foods)**
Inventory on consignment 16,000		No entry
Inventory.	16,000	

2. Consignor pays $1,600 in transportation costs ($2 per tape):

Consignor		**Consignee**
Inventory on consignment 1,600		No entry
Cash	1,600	

3. Consignee spends $2,400 for tape storage boxes ($2,400/800 tapes = $3 per tape):

Consignor	**Consignee**	
No entry	Payable to consignor. 2,400	
	Cash	2,400

4. Consignee sells 300 tapes at $60 each and earns a 20% commission on tapes sold:

Consignor	**Consignee**	
No entry	Cash 18,000	
	Commission revenue	3,600
	Payable to consignor	14,400

5. Consignee notifies consignor of tapes sold and remits sales proceeds, less commissions earned and reimbursable costs:

Consignor		**Consignee**	
Cash. 12,000		Payable to consignor. 12,000	
Inventory on consignment 2,400		Cash	12,000
Commission expense 3,600		($14,400 – $2,400)	
Consignment sales	18,000		
Cost of consignment sales. 7,500			
Inventory on consignment	7,500		
(300 × $25ᵃ)			

6. Reconstruction of the inventory on consignment account:

Inventory on consignment			
Initial shipment	16,000	Cost of sales	7,500
Transportation costs	1,600	Balance	12,500
Storage boxes	2,400		
	20,000		20,000
Balance (500 tapes at $25 each)	$12,500		

ᵃ$20 + $2 transportation costs + $3 cost of storage boxes.

remits the sales proceeds, net of commissions and reimbursable costs, to Movie Town.

Journal entries for this consignment appear in Exhibit 7–8. Several points about these journal entries are pertinent:

1. The shipment of merchandise on consignment is not a sale because the two revenue recognition criteria have not been satisfied. Inventory has simply been transferred to another location. Instead, an inventory account, inventory on consignment, is established so that the consignor knows the cost of goods on consignment.

2. The transportation costs represent an additional cost of the inventory on consignment and are recorded accordingly.

3. As the consignee records the merchandise sold, the commissions earned and the liability to the consignor are also recorded.

4. The consignee notifies the consignor of the merchandise sold through the use of an *account sales* document. This document, which summarizes the consignment activities and the net proceeds from sales, is forwarded to the consignor. The consignor records the sales, cost of goods sold, commissions expense, and cost of the storage boxes.

5. The balance in the inventory account represents the cost of the merchandise remaining on consignment.

QUESTIONS

The question marked with an asterisk (*) refers to Appendix 7–1.

Q 7-1. How is accrual accounting related to the measurement of cash flows?

Q 7-2. Distinguish among *earning* revenue, revenue *recognition,* and *realization*.

Q 7-3. Realization has nothing to do with the income concept but does determine the timing of income recognition. Explain.

Q 7-4. What two criteria must be met to recognize revenue?

Q 7-5. Methods of revenue recognition are also methods of recognizing income. Briefly explain.

Q 7-6. What factors must be considered when revenue is recognized at the point of sale?

Q 7-7. Under what circumstances is it proper to recognize revenue as productive activity takes place?

Q 7-8. Distinguish between the percentage-of-completion method and the completed-contract method of accounting for long-term construction contracts in terms of the following:
  1. Income recognition.
  2. Valuation of construction in progress.
  3. Recognition of losses on construction contracts.

Q 7-9. Discuss two methods that may be used to estimate the percentage of completion of long-term construction contracts.

Q 7-10. What is meant by accretion?

Q 7-11. Why is value accretion generally not recognized under GAAP?

Q 7-12. Discuss the critical event concept in revenue recognition.

Q 7-13. Under what circumstances is it preferable to recognize revenue at the completion of production?

Q 7-14. Explain how inventories are reported at net realizable value when income is recognized at the completion of production.

Q 7-15. Discuss some acceptable methods of accounting for initial franchise fee revenue.

Q 7-16. Why is revenue usually not recognized when a sale is made in connection with retail land sales?

Q 7-17. How are the revenue recognition concepts explained in relation to the objectives of financial reporting?

Q 7-18. In accounting for long-term construction contracts (those taking longer than one year to complete), the two methods commonly followed are the percentage-of-completion method and the completed-contract method. Discuss how earnings on long-term construction contracts are recognized and calculated under these two methods.

Q 7-19. Refer to Question 7-18. Under what circumstances is it preferable to use one method rather than the other?

*Q 7-20. Briefly explain the nature of a consignment arrangement.

CASES

C 7-1. **REVENUE RECOGNITION** (The following case is adapted from an article in *Fortune* magazine, December 4, 1989, pp. 89–101.) "Trade loading" is a crazy, uneconomic, insidious practice through which manufacturers—trying to show sales, profits, and market share they don't actually have—induce their wholesale customers, known as the trade, to buy more products than they can promptly sell. RJR Nabisco engaged in this practice aggressively enough over the past few years to overstate operating profits in its tobacco division by an estimated $250 million.

Trade loading is a kind of economic treadmill. In the first step, manufacturers induce wholesalers to buy more cases of a product than they really need. The inducements—price discounts, for example—are called the "push," and wholesalers love them. Next comes the "pull"—promotions at the retail level, also financed by the manufacturer, to help the wholesaler unload those mountains of boxes stacked in warehouses. Pushes and pulls are costly enough for manufacturers, but suppose they are trying to work this magic in a business like tobacco that has certain troublesome characteristics. First, cigarette unit sales are declining in the United States; that makes the pull all the more difficult. Second, cigarette manufacturers must pay federal excise taxes of 16 cents a pack on the goods they ship to the wholesalers—which means they automatically incur a sizable, up-front cost when they pad volume. Third, this industry has a full-return policy for cigarettes the manufacturer regards as too stale to sell, typically those more than six months old.

Alas, this whole process is addictive to an extreme. If manufacturers load up the trade in the fourth quarter of year *A* and thereby inflate sales, profits, and unit shipments, they will, in the interests of continuing to look good, be powerfully tempted to repeat the exercise in the fourth quarter of year *B*. In an industry showing unit growth, they might settle for simply matching the first year's load. If the industry is declining, or if manufacturers are losing ground to competitors—as RJR has been doing to Philip Morris—they are apt to be seduced into increasing the load year after year. By this strategy, they disguise the extent to which they are losing both their customer base and their market share.

Hearing about trade loading, an excise-tax expert in the U.S. Treasury sized up the facts and cut through the smoke with the statement "It's like getting in with a loan shark!"

REQUIRED Based on the principles of revenue recognition, discuss these trade loading practices.

C 7-2. **REVENUE RECOGNITION FOR SERVICES; BUSINESS ETHICS** A few years ago PTL, the Jim and Tammy Bakker religious organization, initiated a plan to construct an elaborate hotel complex at Heritage Village, Heritage USA, South Carolina, for use by financial supporters of PTL. Under the plan, PTL received cash for Heritage Grand Lifetime Partnerships (memberships) that provided the "partners" with lifetime use of the hotel. In order to stay at the hotel, a partner would make a reservation, much like making any other hotel reservation. Assuming available space, the reservation was confirmed, and the partner could stay at Heritage Village without charge. There was no limit on the number of times a partner could use the hotel facilities, assuming space was available.

This arrangement provided PTL with almost $70 million in cash with which to build the hotel. In fact, the number of partnerships sold greatly exceeded hotel capacity. (For purposes of this case, assume that the entire $70 million was received prior to the time the hotel began operating.) The excess demand created by the success of the partnership sales forced PTL to begin constructing a second unit, Heritage Towers, in order to meet its obligations to partners. PTL also began selling Towers Lifetime Partnerships for the second unit.

For various reasons, PTL began having financial difficulty and was declared bankrupt in 1989. Jim Bakker and other PTL officers ultimately ended up in prison. One issue relating to the PTL fiasco was how the company should recognize revenue and income on the sales of the Grand Lifetime Partnerships. Possible alternatives range from recognizing the $70 million as revenue "up front," accruing all of the expenses expected to be incurred and matching these expenses with the $70 million in revenue, to spreading the $70 million over future periods based on expected total hotel occupancy and matching expenses incurred each period with the revenue recognized. Another issue was whether the "overselling" of the hotel capacity was ethical (or perhaps constituted fraud).

REQUIRED

1. Discuss how PTL should recognize revenue and income on sales of the Heritage Grand Lifetime Partnerships. If you believe that the $70 million should be recognized in future periods, consider whether the amounts recognized should be the same each year or whether an "accelerated" method of revenue recognition, for example, sum of the years' digits, should be used.

2. Discuss any ethical issues that may arise from "overselling" of the hotel.

C 7-3. FRANCHISES Cajun Catfish sells franchises to independent operators throughout the southeastern United States. The contract with the franchise includes the following provisions:

The franchisee is charged an initial fee of $25,000. Of this amount, $5,000 is payable when the agreement is signed and a $4,000 non-interest-bearing note is payable at the end of each of the five subsequent years. The credit ratings of all franchises would entitle them to borrow at the current interest rate of 10 percent.

All of the initial franchise fee collected by Cajun Catfish is to be refunded and the remaining obligation canceled if for any reason the franchisee fails to open his or her store.

In return for the initial franchise fee, Cajun Catfish agrees (1) to assist the franchisee in selecting the location for the business, (2) to negotiate the lease for the land, (3) to obtain financing and assist with building design, (4) to supervise construction, (5) to establish accounting and tax records, and (6) to provide expert advice over a five-year period on such matters as employee and management training, quality control, and promotion.

In addition to the initial franchise fee, the franchisee is required to pay to Cajun Catfish a monthly fee of 2 percent of sales for menu planning, recipe innovations, and the privilege of purchasing ingredients from Cajun Catfish at or below prevailing prices.

Management of Cajun Catfish estimates that the value of the services rendered to the franchisee at the time the contract is signed amounts to at least $5,000. All franchisees to date have opened their stores at the scheduled time, and none has defaulted on any of the notes receivable.

REQUIRED

1. Discuss the alternatives that Cajun Catfish might use to account for the initial franchise fee, evaluate each by applying generally accepted accounting principles to this situation, and prepare illustrative entries for each alternative.

2. Given the nature of its agreement with its franchisees, when should Cajun Catfish recognize revenue? Discuss the question of revenue recognition for both the initial franchise fee and the additional monthly fee of 2 percent of sales and give illustrative entries for both types of revenue.

(AICPA, adapted)

C 7-4. REVENUE RECOGNITION ISSUES Two criteria that must be met before revenue (and income) can be recognized are that (1) the amount of revenue and its timing are reasonably determinable, and (2) the earnings process must be complete. At the beginning of this chapter, we pointed out that many companies have experienced financial difficulties from "premature" recognition of revenue and income.

These financial difficulties often have appeared at opposite ends of the revenue recognition spectrum. To paraphrase some media writers:

a) Premature recognition was associated with "revenue that was not there," or

b) Premature recognition was associated with "revenue that was there but was not revenue."

REQUIRED

Write a short paper that explains the intended meanings of statements *a* and *b* above and that relates these meanings to the two criteria for revenue recognition. Provide an example to support your discussion.

C 7-5. REVENUE RECOGNITION BASED ON SALES ORDERS Kramer Corporation manufactures playground swing sets. The company has a very aggressive marketing organization throughout the country and a very sophisticated standard cost system in its manufacturing division.

Recently, Cindy Copp, head of the sales division, suggested to you, the controller of Kramer, that the company should consider recognizing revenue (and resulting income) on the basis of *sales orders received* instead of in the traditional manner, on the basis of delivery. (There is a time lag between receipt of an order and delivery of the swing sets to customers.)

REQUIRED

I. Briefly discuss the arguments for and against Copp's proposal.

2. Assume that the company implemented Copp's proposal. The swing sets sell for $400 per unit, and the standard cost per unit is $280. Prepare entries to record the following events (the company's fiscal year ends December 31):

December 30 Received order for 1,000 swing sets. Sales commissions, 8% of sales price.

January 10 Completed production of 1,000 swing sets at a cost of $282 per unit.

January 20 Shipped sets to customers (customers pay transportation costs).

February 1 Received cash from customers.

C 7-6. **REVENUE RECOGNITION FOR SERVICES** You are the senior person in charge of the audit of Andersen Affiliates for the year ended December 31, 1998. At the beginning of 1998, Andersen acquired Office Assistance Marketing (OAM), which develops and markets a "comprehensive office management" package. The package consists of computer software and "trailing" services—education and training, videotapes, minor systems modifications, office efficiency evaluations, and consulting services. The contract sets an upper limit on the number of staff hours that OAM must provide for training and other trailing services.

The package is sold at a price that varies, depending on the customer's potential cost savings and the nature of the business. Sales are made on a contract basis and do not include any guarantees, other than what is specified in the contract. Each contract requires from 12 to 20 months to fulfill. Although OAM performs several distinct acts in connection with the package, customers cannot purchase part of a package. Under the contract terms, the entire package must be purchased. Revenues and costs of a typical package are as follows:

Revenue based on contract price	**$840,000**
Costs associated with revenue:	
Software	(44,000)
Videotapes	(15,000)
Training	(200,000)
Other	(12,000)
Income (profit contribution)	**$569,000**

During the course of the audit, you have discovered that OAM has recognized all the income on the sales of its comprehensive office management package at the time of shipment of the computer software. Andersen's management gave the following justifications for this practice:

a) The *primary* item being sold is technology, which is represented by the software. The value of the software makes up most of the contract price.

b) Several years ago, OAM sold the package in parts. Although the computer software was sold at a substantial profit, the trailing services sold at or near cost (gross profit was about 6 percent of sales).

c) Except in a few instances, OAM has adequately serviced, trained, and educated several Chicago Board of Trade companies on the use of this technology. (In two instances, costs associated with trailing services exceeded the company's estimates by 65 percent. These two instances occurred in 1992, shortly after OAM was organized.)

d) Because the cost of the trailing services varies but usually is immaterial to the price of the contract, customer acceptance of the software is the critical event for revenue recognition.

Your superior has questioned OAM's method of revenue recognition. She has suggested that perhaps revenue should be recognized over the contract period or that some portion of revenue should be deferred and matched against the trailing services as they are performed. She also has pointed out that if the costs of the trailing services were to increase significantly in the future, perhaps these services should be considered the critical event for revenue recognition.

REQUIRED Is OAM's method of revenue recognition acceptable? Discuss.

C 7-7.   **REVENUE RECOGNITION ALTERNATIVES**   At the beginning of 1997, Charlotte Company began a business to manufacture and sell an imitation of Water Wiggle. Near the end of 1997, a sales order was received that called for delivery of 100,000 of these items on October 1, 1998. Production was started late in 1997 but was not completed until mid-1998.

REQUIRED   For each independent situation below, discuss whether revenue (and income) should be recognized at the point in time indicated. Your answers should be brief but comprehensive.

1. Recognize revenue when the sales order is received. Charlotte is able to predict manufacturing costs perfectly. The purchaser pays in full on the date of the sales order, and the purchase price is not refundable.

2. Same as part 1, except that Charlotte will not receive the cash from the sale until December 31, 1998. The purchaser has a history of defaulting on purchase agreements.

3. Recognize revenue on October 1, 1998. Charlotte agrees to allow the purchaser to pay in monthly installments beginning on November 1, 1998. While some possibility of noncollection is present, Charlotte can make reasonable estimates of such amounts.

4. Recognize revenue on October 1, 1998. The purchaser will pay cash on that date but has the right to return any unsold water tubes for refund (or credit against future purchases) on or before December 1, 1998. Charlotte can make reasonable estimates of returns.

5. Recognize revenue when production is complete. Substantial delivery costs may be incurred upon delivery. These costs cannot be estimated before actual delivery.

C 7-8.   **RECOGNITION OF INTEREST REVENUE**   Bass Savings and Loan (BSL) is an aggressive financial institution located in the Midwest. It is located in a heavy manufacturing area and specializes in making short-term loans (generally, less than three years to maturity) to manufacturers to assist them in financing their production activities. BSL's policy is to make non-interest-bearing loans only and to discount the maturity value in determining the amount of cash loaned to each manufacturer. For example, if BSL wished to earn 10 percent interest on a non-interest-bearing note of $10,000 to be repaid at the end of two years, the company would discount the $10,000 at 10 percent for two years and give the borrower cash of $8,264 ($10,000/1.10 = $9,091; $9,091/1.10 = $8,264).

You are conducting the audit for the year ended December 31, 1998. During the course of your audit, you discover that BSL has been recognizing interest revenue in full at the date the loan is made. Using the example above, BSL would make the following entry at the date of the loan:

Notes receivable	10,000	
Cash		8,264
Interest revenue		1,736

When the customer repaid the loan, BSL would debit cash and credit notes receivable for $10,000. Since many of the loans made in 1998 mature in 1999 and later years, the amount of interest revenue reported on the 1998 income statement under this procedure is material.

When you question BSL's controller about this practice, he responds that the company applies the revenue recognition criteria under GAAP. You question this response, and he replies, "The amount of interest earned is known at the date that the loan is made. Making the loan is the critical event in the company's earning cycle. Our company has no other obligation to the borrowers at the time the loan is made, and all borrowers are excellent credit risks. In fact, all we have to do is sit back and wait for the money to come in. Surely, 'waiting' is not part of our earnings process! We believe in reporting income and expected cash flows 'sooner than later.' Isn't that the essence of the financial reporting objectives?"

REQUIRED   Do you approve of BSL's revenue recognition procedure? Explain.

C 7-9.   **REVENUE RECOGNITION FOR SERVICES**   Haskins, Whinney, & Mitchell (HWM) is a public accounting firm that specializes in providing consulting services to colleges and universities. HWM prepared and submitted a proposal for $540,000 to perform an administrative cost/operations analysis consulting project for Orion State University (OSU). The project consisted of three stages: (1) studying and making recommendations for changes in OSU's organizational structure, (2) analyzing and recommending improvements in OSU's operations and processes, and (3) analyzing and recommending improvements in OSU's systems and controls. The estimated cost of the project was $400,000.

After evaluating several proposals, OSU awarded the contract to HWM. Information about project activities and cash receipts (per the contract agreement) is as follows:

ACTIVITY	COSTS INCURRED
During HWM's first fiscal period:	
Proposal preparation and presentation	**Estimated, $40,000; actual, $50,000**
During HWM's second fiscal period:	
Received contract and $180,000 from OSU	
Organization restructure completed	**Estimated, $80,000; actual, $75,000**
During HWM's third fiscal period:	
Received $180,000 from OSU	
Operations analysis completed	**Estimated, $165,000; actual, $180,000**
During HWM's fourth fiscal period:	
Systems and controls study completed	**Estimated, $115,000; actual, $110,000**
Received $180,000 from OSU	

REQUIRED

1. Discuss the propriety of HWM's use of the following methods of revenue recognition for the consulting project:
   a) Specific-performance method.
   b) Proportional-performance method.
   c) Completed-performance method.
   d) Collection method.
2. Assume that HWM decides to use the proportional-performance method. Prepare summary journal entries to record each fiscal period's transactions.

C 7-10. **REVENUE RECOGNITION FOR SERVICES** Diana Jacobs recently opened a health club, The Svelte Place. Membership fees are payable to the health club under one of two methods: (1) monthly membership fees of $50 or (2) a onetime, nonrefundable membership fee of $1,500, payable in cash at the joining date. Both membership fee arrangements give club members unlimited use of the club facilities, which include weight lifting, aerobics classes, racquetball, squash, locker room storage, showers, and saunas.

The health club was organized as a partnership, and Diana Jacobs is the primary investor. The club's substantive investment in its physical facilities was financed by partner contributions and a bank loan. These facility costs include the building, sports equipment, and the locker room. Recurring monthly costs include instructor and staff salaries, electricity, water, supplies, and minor maintenance.

Diana Jacobs and her partners are discussing how membership fee revenue should be recognized each month, given the company's rather capital-intensive cost structure. The partners are in agreement that monthly membership fees should be recognized as revenue when collections occur. There is some disagreement, however, about how to recognize revenue associated with the lifetime membership fees. Some of the partners prefer recognizing revenue at the time the lifetime membership fees are received by The Svelte Place. These partners base their arguments primarily on the certainty of the cash inflows and the fact that lifetime membership fees are not refundable.

REQUIRED Discuss how The Svelte Place should recognize revenue from the lifetime membership fees. As part of your discussion, summarize the financial statement effects of each alternative that you present.

C 7-11. **REVENUE RECOGNITION WITH GUARANTEES** Tucker AutoMart is a high-volume automobile dealer, selling thousands of cars each year. Tucker finances purchases of its cars at a local bank and arranges financing for sales to its customers at the same bank. The dealer's operating and financing procedures are described in the following paragraph.

Tucker borrows cash by issuing a demand note (payable on demand) to its bank. The cash is then used to purchase cars from the manufacturer. When a sale is made, the customer signs an interest-bearing note payable to the bank. The bank substitutes the customer's note for Tucker's demand note and remits the difference to Tucker. The difference represents Tucker's gross profit on the sale of the car. Tucker guarantees payment of the customer's note to the bank by serving as a cosigner. In the event that a customer defaults on payment of the note, Tucker must pay the bank the balance due and repossess the car from the customer.

REQUIRED
1. Discuss how and when Tucker should recognize revenue on sales of its cars.
2. Assume that it is proper for Tucker to recognize revenue at the sale date. If Tucker buys a car for $18,000 and sells it for $22,000, what entries would be required by Tucker, the bank, and the customer under the above arrangement?

C 7-12. **REVENUE RECOGNITION BASED ON DISCOVERY** In the year 2025, medical researchers and geologists discovered a unique mineral effective in preventing a form of illness that was common during this decade. As a result, an entire industry developed to explore, extract, and produce this mineral for sale to the general public. In many ways, this industry resembled the oil and gas industry.

During 2025, Haberdashery Exploration Corporation (HEC) spent $3 million on exploration costs for this new mineral. Near the end of the year, the company discovered an undeterminable number of pounds of the mineral. However, geologists estimated the "reserve" to contain, at a minimum, approximately 2 million pounds of the mineral, which, at the current market price of $20 per pound, had a value of $40 million. The process of extracting and readying the mineral for sale to the general public is somewhat lengthy but relatively inexpensive (currently approximately $3 per pound). Management estimated that the extracting process would extend over several years.

HEC's management is preparing financial statements for the year ending December 31, 2025, and is concerned about reporting the discovery deposit (reserves) at its $3 million cost, given that the undiscounted net realizable value (sales price less production costs) could be well over $34 million [2,000,000 × ($20 – $3)]. Management argues that *discovery* of the mineral deposit is the critical event in the earnings process, especially given the immense market for the product in health care. Furthermore, management believes that reporting income based on discovery and valuing the deposit at net realizable value on HEC's balance sheet would provide much more relevant information about future cash flows to financial statement users than would reporting the deposit at its historical cost of $3 million. Management also believes that, unlike profits on most business ventures, the spread between cost and value is simply too great to ignore in the primary financial statements.

REQUIRED
1. Discuss strengths and weaknesses of the revenue and income recognition method proposed by HEC management.
2. Disregarding your discussion in part 1, assume that the revenue recognition method proposed by HEC management was approved by an authoritative accounting body. Also assume the following additional estimated information on December 31, 2025, about HEC's operations for the following four years:

END OF YEAR	POUNDS EXTRACTED	SELLING PRICE PER POUND	EXTRACTING COST PER POUND
2026	800,000	$20	$ 3
2027	600,000	22	5
2028	400,000	25	8
2029	200,000	30	10

Because the mineral will be extracted and sold over a four-year period, a discount rate of 10 percent per year is applicable in calculating the present value of the net cash flows. (The use of the tables in Appendix A or a calculator with present value functions will be necessary for present value calculations.)

Based on the above data:

a) Calculate the amount of income HEC would report on its income statement for the year ending December 31, 2025, and the amount at which the mineral deposit would be reported on its December 31, 2025, balance sheet.

b) Prepare summary journal entries for HEC's transactions for the year ending December 31, 2026, under the assumption that the actual number of pounds extracted was 750,000 and that extracting costs per pound were $4. All other estimates (pounds extracted, selling prices, and extracting costs) for the three future years remain unchanged.

Exercises marked with an asterisk (*) refer to Appendix 7–1.

E 7-1. PERCENTAGE-OF-COMPLETION METHOD The Fingland Construction Corporation uses the percentage-of-completion method of accounting. In 1998, Fingland began work on a contract for construction of a hotel at a contract price of $8 million. Other details follow:

Costs incurred during the year $2,400,000
Estimated costs to complete as of 12/31/98 4,000,000
Billings during the year 2,100,000
Collections during the year 900,000

REQUIRED Calculate the income that should be recognized in 1998.

E 7-2. PERCENTAGE-OF-COMPLETION METHOD In 1998, Baird Dynamics began construction work under a three-year contract. The contract price was $400,000. Baird uses the percentage-of-completion method for financial accounting purposes. The income to be recognized each year is based on the proportion of cost incurred to total estimated costs for completing the contract. Trial balance information related to this contract at December 31, 1998, was as follows:

	DR	CR
Accounts receivable...	7,500	
Construction in progress..	25,000	
Billings on construction contract.................................		23,500
Construction revenue		25,000
Construction expenses	20,000	

REQUIRED
1. What was the initial estimated total income before tax on this contract?
2. How much cash was collected on this contract in 1998?

E 7-3. INCOME RECOGNITION ON LONG-TERM CONTRACTS Kurtz Construction Company began operating on January 1, 1998, and during the year the company contracted with the city of Enid to build a superdome. Kurtz Construction estimated that it would take four years to complete the facility at a total cost of $19.2 million. The total contract price was $24 million. During 1998, the company incurred $5.8 million in construction costs related to the dome construction, including $800,000 in materials purchased but not used in 1998. The estimated cost to complete the contract was $15 million as of December 31, 1998. The city of Enid was billed $6 million of the contract price and had paid $4 million by December 31, 1998.

REQUIRED Prepare schedules to calculate the amount of income to be recognized by Kurtz for the year ended December 31, 1998, using each of the following methods:
1. Completed-contract method.
2. Percentage-of-completion method.

E 7-4. JOURNAL ENTRIES FOR LONG-TERM CONTRACTS Refer to the data in Exercise 7-3.
REQUIRED
1. Prepare all necessary journal entries for 1998 for Kurtz Construction Company, assuming that the percentage-of-completion method is appropriate.
2. Prepare all necessary journal entries for 1998 for Kurtz Construction Company, assuming that the completed-contract method is appropriate.

E 7-5. INCOME RECOGNITION ON LONG-TERM CONTRACTS Dobson Construction Corporation contracted to construct a building for $400,000. Construction began in 1998 and was completed in 1999. End-of-year data related to the contract are summarized below:

	12/31/98	12/31/99
Costs incurred...	$250,000	$70,000
Estimated costs to complete	62,500	–0–

Dobson used the percentage-of-completion method as the basis for income recognition.

REQUIRED
1. What income should Dobson report on the contract for 1998 and 1999, respectively?
2. Prepare all necessary journal entries for 1998 and 1999.
3. If Dobson used the completed-contract method to account for the above contract, how much income would be reported for 1998 and 1999, respectively?

E 7-6. **REVENUE RECOGNITION WITH RIGHT OF RETURN**   Sallee Corporation distributes movies on VHS videocassettes to grocery stores, discount houses, and other cassette dealers. Dealers have the right to return unsold cassettes to Sallee for a full refund within two months of the date of purchase. During the current year, Sallee sold 60,000 cassettes. All sales were for cash. Each cassette costs Sallee $8 and sells for $12. Sallee uses a perpetual inventory system.

REQUIRED   Prepare journal entries to record Sallee's sales, cost of goods sold, and any other necessary entries for the current year under each of the following independent assumptions:

1. Returns have varied over the past several years but generally are insignificant. During the current year, 450 cassettes were returned.
2. Returns have been very stable over the past several years and have averaged 3,000 per year. As of the end of the current year, actual returns were 2,700.
3. Returns have been significant, have varied greatly over the past several years, and are not estimable. Cassette sales for the last two months of the current year were 8,000, and actual returns as of the end of the current year were 13,000.

E 7-7. **LONG-TERM CONSTRUCTION CONTRACTS**   William LLP is engaged in a long-term construction contract. At the end of 1997, the company's construction-in-progress account had a balance of $800,000, which included $100,000 of construction income. At the end of 1997, William estimated that the contract was 40 percent complete. During 1998, William incurred construction costs of $160,000.

REQUIRED   1. Calculate the contract price and the estimated total income expected on the construction contract at the end of 1997.
2. Calculate the amount of construction income or loss for 1998, assuming that estimated completion costs at the end of 1998 were:
   a) $560,000.
   b) $740,000.
   c) $940,000.

E 7-8. **CASH-COLLECTION METHODS**   Abraham appropriately uses the installment sales method of accounting. The following information is taken from Abraham's accounting records for 1998 and 1999.

	1998	1999
Sales	$250,000	$290,000
Cost of goods sold	200,000	246,500
Cash collected on 1998 sales	190,000	60,000
Cash collected on 1999 sales	–0–	180,000

REQUIRED   1. Calculate the income recognized in 1998 and 1999, respectively.
2. What is the aggregate balance of the deferred gross profit account at the end of 1999?
3. Assume now that Abraham uses the cost-recovery method. Calculate the amount of income recognized in 1998 and 1999.

E 7-9. **REVENUE RECOGNITION METHODS**   McDonald Company, a farm corporation, produced the following in its first year of operations:

	SELLING PRICE PER BUSHEL
9,000 bushels of soybeans	$2.40
6,000 bushels of corn	1.40

During the year it sold three-fourths of the grain produced and collected four-fifths of the selling price on the bushels sold; the balance is to be collected in equal amounts during each of the two following years.

Additional data for the first year are:

Depreciation on productive plant and equipment	$3,000
Other production costs (cash)	8,100
Selling and delivery costs (incurred and paid at time of sale), per bushel	.10

REQUIRED   1. If revenue were recognized when production is complete (i.e., inventory is carried at net selling price), what would be McDonald's income for year 1?

2. If revenue were recognized on the sales basis, McDonald's income for year 1 would be what amount?

3. If revenue were recognized on the installment basis, McDonald's income for year 1 would be what amount?

E 7-10. **THE INSTALLMENT METHOD AND COST-RECOVERY METHOD** Middlemist Corporation sells pianos on a deferred payment plan. Summary information appears below:

	1998	1999	2000
Sales	$100,000	$120,000	$250,000
Cost of goods sold	(70,000)	(90,000)	(180,000)
Gross profit	$ 30,000	$ 30,000	$ 70,000
Customer collections on:			
1998 sales	$ 40,000	$ 55,000	$ 5,000
1999 sales		60,000	20,000
2000 sales			200,000

REQUIRED

1. Calculate the amount of gross profit that would be recognized each year under the installment method.

2. Calculate the amount of gross profit that would be recognized each year under the cost-recovery method.

E 7-11. **THE INSTALLMENT METHOD OF ACCOUNTING** The following information relates to activities of Clayton Trucking Sales, which sells trucks on a deferred payment plan and uses the installment method of accounting:

	1998	1999
Sales	$800,000	$900,000
Cost of goods sold	640,000	630,000
Operating expenses	60,000	80,000
Cash collections:		
On 1998 sales	650,000	150,000
On 1999 sales	—	750,000

REQUIRED

1. Prepare all required journal entries for Clayton for 1998 and 1999.

2. Show how the above information would appear on Clayton's balance sheet at the end of 1998 and 1999.

3. In early 2000 a customer defaults on a 1999 installment sale. The truck, with a fair value of $6,000, is repossessed. The unpaid balance on the installment is $9,000. Prepare the entry to record the repossession.

E 7-12. **SALE OF INSTALLMENT PAYMENTS** At the beginning of 1997, Jeremiah Bootery began manufacturing and selling cowboy boots to shoe stores throughout the southwestern part of the United States. In order to stimulate boot sales, Jeremiah sold the boots on a deferred payment plan. Because of the poor credit ratings of many of these shoe stores, Jeremiah used the installment method of accounting. Information relating to Jeremiah's sales, cost of sales, and collections during 1997 and 1998 is as follows:

	1997	1998
Sales	$300,000	$400,000
Cost of sales	225,000	240,000
Collections on		
1997 sales	180,000	70,000
1998 sales	—	230,000

At the beginning of 1999, Jeremiah decided to begin selling on a cash-only basis. As a result, Jeremiah sold all of its uncollected receivables to a bank for 60 percent of the face amounts.

REQUIRED

Calculate Jeremiah's gain or loss on the sale of its receivables.

E 7-13.   **REVENUE RECOGNITION METHODS**   Zuhair Corporation manufactures and sells a special device for finding natural gas. In 1998, Zuhair manufactured 400 devices at a cost of $100 each. Each device has a selling price of $180.

During 1998, the company sold 250 devices and collected $30,000 from customers on such sales. During 1999, the company sold 150 devices, and total cash collections were $40,000. The remainder of the receivables was collected in 2000.

REQUIRED   Calculate the amount of income (revenue less expense) to be recognized for 1998, 1999, and 2000 under the following revenue recognition alternatives:

   I.   Revenue is recognized when production is completed.
   2.   Revenue is recognized when a sale is made.
   3.   Revenue is recognized under the installment method.
   4.   Revenue is recognized under the cost-recovery method.

E 7-14.   **REVENUE RECOGNITION WITH RIGHT OF RETURN**   Bennett distributes paperback books. The books are sold to retail stores with the stipulation that up to 35 percent of the books can be returned within three months. Actual returns have averaged 30 percent in each of the last eight years.

Bennett shipped 10 million books to retail stores during the current fiscal year ending May 31, 1998. All books have a unit sales price of $2.00 and a unit cost of $1.50. Actual returns on 1997–1998 shipments have been 29 percent to date.

As of May 31, 1997, a total of 1.8 million books shipped during the 1996–1997 fiscal year still had a right of return. Collections on these shipments during the 1997–1998 fiscal year totaled $2,844,000, and 450,000 books were returned for credit. Bennett uses the perpetual inventory system.

REQUIRED   **I.**   Determine the net sales revenue to be recognized for the year ending May 31, 1998, from shipments made during this fiscal year.

   2.   Prepare journal entries to record the following transactions related to Bennett's operations (Bennett uses the allowance method for returns):

     a)   Shipments made during the current year and associated costs.
     b)   Actual returns from current year shipments.
     c)   Remaining estimated returns from current year shipments.
     d)   Collections on shipments made during the previous year.
     e)   Actual returns from the shipments made during the previous year.

                                                           (IMA, adapted)

E 7-15.   **LONG-TERM CONSTRUCTION CONTRACTS**   Atlanta Construction Corporation entered into a construction contract with Walker Associates on July 1, 1998, to construct a television tower. At that time, Atlanta estimated that it would take between two and three years to complete the project. The total contract price for construction of the tower was $4 million. Atlanta accounts for this contract under the percentage-of-completion method. The tower was completed on December 31, 2000. Accumulated contract costs incurred, estimated costs to complete the contract, and accumulated billings to Walker under the contract were as follows:

	12/31/98	12/31/99	12/31/00
Contract costs incurred to date	$ 350,000	$2,640,000	$4,300,000
Estimated costs to complete the contract	3,150,000	1,760,000	—
Billings to Walker to date..................	600,000	2,800,000	4,000,000

REQUIRED   **I.**   Determine the profit or loss to be recognized as a result of this contract for the years ended December 31, 1998, 1999, and 2000.

   2.   Calculate the balance in the construction-in-progress account on December 31, 1998, 1999, and 2000. Comment briefly on these balances.

E 7-16. **LONG-TERM CONSTRUCTION CONTRACTS** Thompson Industries contracted to construct a building for $2 million. Construction began in 1998 and was completed in 1999. Information relating to the contract is summarized below:

	1998	1999
Costs incurred during the year	$1,160,000	$ 540,000
Estimated additional costs to complete	580,000	–0–
Billings during the year	920,000	1,080,000
Cash collections during the year	800,000	1,000,000

REQUIRED Using the information above, complete the financial statement information below for Thompson Industries.

	METHOD	
	COMPLETED CONTRACT	PERCENTAGE OF COMPLETION
Balance sheet, end of year:		
Accounts receivable:		
1998	_____	_____
1999	_____	_____
Construction in progress, net of billings:		
1998	_____	_____
1999	_____	_____
Income statement, for the year:		
Construction revenue:		
1998	_____	_____
1999	_____	_____
Construction expenses:		
1998	_____	_____
1999	_____	_____

E 7-17. **FRANCHISES** Arterbery Center Courts sells franchises. The initial franchise fee is $60,000, payable 25 percent down with the balance in five equal annual installments plus interest at 12 percent on the unpaid balance. In return for the initial fee, the corporation agrees to assist in designing and constructing a clubhouse, to help the franchisee obtain financing, to help train a club pro, and to provide management advice to the franchisee over a five-year period.

REQUIRED Prepare the franchisor's entry to record the initial franchise fee, the first annual installment, and interest revenue under the following independent assumptions:

1. At the time the franchise is signed, none of the services promised have been provided; however, at least 90 percent of the services have been provided on the date of the first installment. Collectibility of the franchise fee is assured.
2. Same as part 1, except that collectibility of the remaining installments cannot be estimated.
3. At the time the franchise is signed, the value of the services rendered is estimated to be at least $5,000. The remaining services are performed equally over the five-year period, and collectibility of the franchise fee is assured.
4. At the time the franchise is signed, all the services promised have been provided, and collection of the franchise fee is assured.
5. Same as part 4, except that collectibility of the remaining installments cannot be estimated.

E 7-18. **FRANCHISES; INITIAL FRANCHISE FEE** GrabHold Here has an international reputation as a bodybuilding franchise. A Grabhold Here franchise sells for $100,000, payable as follows: $50,000 down and four $12,500 payments at the end of each of the following four years. GrabHold Here normally would charge franchisees 8 percent interest on a deferred payment plan.

REQUIRED   Prepare GrabHold Here's journal entries to record the initial franchise fee under the four assumptions given below. Below each journal entry for each assumption, also indicate how you applied the revenue recognition criteria in preparing the appropriate journal entry.

Assumptions:

1. GrabHold Here has provided all necessary services and collectibility of the deferred payments is reasonably assured.
2. GrabHold Here has provided all necessary services but there is a substantial amount of uncertainty about collectibility of the deferred payments.
3. GrabHold Here has provided no services and collectibility of the deferred payments is reasonably assured.
4. GrabHold Here has provided services estimated to equal the down payment. Collectibility of the deferred payments is reasonably assured.

E 7-19.   **RETAIL SALES OF UNDEVELOPED LAND**   On January 1, 1998, Nancy's Homes was organized to purchase raw land for development into residential housing lots. The following transactions occurred during 1998:

January 15   Acquired 10 acres of land at a cost of $175,000. The company plans to subdivide the land into 10 building sites.

January 31   Obtained sales contracts for all 10 sites at a sales price of $25,000 per site, payable $5,000 down with the balance in 10 quarterly installments. Purchasers can void their sales contracts and receive refunds of all previous payments up until the due date of the third installment.

March 10   Subcontracted grading and paving of the development area and advanced the subcontractor $18,000.

May 1   Received first installment from all purchasers.

August 1   Received second installment from all purchasers.

August 30   The paving and grading work was completed, and the subcontractor was paid the remaining $22,000 due.

October 19   Two purchasers decided to cancel the sales contract and were given refunds of amounts previously paid.

November 1   Received third installment from the remaining purchasers.

November 30   Landscaping and other expenditures on the 10 lots, $20,000. These activities completed Nancy's obligations to the purchasers.

Until all services have been performed by Nancy's Homes, customer payments are to be recorded as unearned revenue. In addition, no receivables should be recorded until the refund privilege has expired. Costs should be deferred and not recognized as expenses until the related revenue is recognized. Once the services have been performed, the sales method is appropriate.

REQUIRED   Prepare entries to record the 1998 transactions for Nancy's Homes.

*E 7-20.   **CONSIGNMENTS**   Valdez sells special blends of coffee and tea on a consignment basis. During 1998, the following transactions, given in summary form, occurred:

a) Shipped merchandise costing $36,000 to various dealers on a consignment basis.
b) Transportation costs incurred on consignment shipments totaled $6,400.
c) Account sales documents submitted by consignees indicated that 80 percent of the consignment merchandise had been sold for $45,000. Commissions amounted to $4,500, and the balance of $40,500 was received from various consignees.
d) Valdez recorded the consignment sales and related expenses upon receipt of the account sales.

REQUIRED   Prepare all necessary entries to record the above transactions.

*E 7-21.   **CONSIGNMENTS**   Jerrie Company sells bicycles on a consignment basis. During the current year the following transactions occurred:

a) Shipped 100 bikes on a consignment basis. The cost of each bike was $300, and each was to be sold for $800. Consignees are to receive a commission of $90 for each bike sold.
b) Freight on the consignment shipment was $1,800 and was paid by Jerrie Company.
c) The account sales remitted to Jerrie at the end of the year showed that consignees sold 60 bikes during the year. Also, advertising incurred and paid by consignees (reimbursable by Jerrie Company) was $500. Finally, cash remitted by consignees at the end of the year was $10,000.

REQUIRED   Prepare all journal entries for the above transactions for Jerrie Company.

PROBLEMS	The problem marked with an asterisk (*) refers to Appendix 7–1.

P 7-I.   **REVENUE RECOGNITION METHODS**   On January 1, 1998, Kittleman Corporation's balance sheet consisted of $600,000 in cash and $600,000 in equity. On this date, the company began production of an electronic device for improving the sound quality of cassette tapes. During 1998, Kittleman produced 50,000 devices at a cost of $8 each. These devices had a selling price of $12 each and were to be sold on credit to various dealers in Kittleman's geographic area. The selling cost per device (for example, sales commissions), incurred at the time of sale, was $.40. During 1998, 1999, and 2000, the 50,000 units produced were sold and cash was collected as follows:

	1998	1999	2000
Units sold......................................	20,000	30,000	–0–
Cash collections	$120,000	$420,000	$60,000

REQUIRED   **I.** Calculate the amount of Kittleman's net income each year, assuming that revenue and income are recognized:
   a) At the completion of production.
   b) At the point of sale.
   c) As cash is collected (installment method).
   2. Prepare Kittleman's journal entries for 1998 under each of the methods in part 1.

P 7-2.   **REVENUE AND INCOME RECOGNITION ALTERNATIVES**   At the beginning of 1998, Elizabeth Limited was organized as a partnership to explore for, mine, and sell diamonds to diamond dealers. The partners contributed $180,000 in cash, which was used to purchase exploration and mining equipment. During 1998, Elizabeth discovered and mined 300 diamonds of similar size and quality. The diamonds had an estimated selling price of $300 each. Elizabeth sold 240 of these diamonds to dealers for $72,000 cash during 1998. Additional data about Elizabeth's operations for 1998 are as follows:

Variable mining and production cost per diamond...........................	$ 80
Depreciation on exploration and mining equipment	36,000
Shipping and insurance cost per diamond (paid in cash at time of shipment)	30

REQUIRED   **I.** Prepare Elizabeth Limited's income statement for 1998, assuming that revenue and income are recognized at:
   a) The completion of production.
   b) The date of sale.
   2. Calculate the inventory valuation of diamonds at the end of 1998, assuming that revenue and income are recognized at:
   a) The completion of production.
   b) The date of sale.
   3. Assume that it is appropriate for Elizabeth Limited to recognize revenue and income at the completion of production. Prepare all necessary journal entries for 1998 under this method.

P 7-3.   **REVENUE RECOGNITION; RETURNS**   Record Exchange sells compact discs (CDs) and recognizes revenue at the point of sale. At the beginning of 1998, it had the following balance sheet:

Cash	$ 40,000	Contributed capital	$100,000
Disc inventory (4,000 units)	40,000	Retained earnings	40,000
Plant and equipment	60,000		
Total	$140,000		$140,000

During 1998, the following transactions occurred:
a) Sales of CDs at $30 each on account:
1st quarter, 300 units
2nd quarter, 1,000 units
3rd quarter, 600 units
4th quarter, 400 units

b) The company allows unlimited sales returns for one quarter *following* the sale and estimates that 10 percent of all CDs sold on account will be returned. Actual returns were as follows:

1st-quarter sales, 28 units
2nd-quarter sales, 120 units
3rd-quarter sales, 42 units
4th-quarter sales, 10 units

c) A one-year warranty on the CDs is offered. Warranty costs generally average about $6 per CD. Actual warranty costs incurred during 1998 totaled $9,000.

d) Cash collections during 1998 totaled $48,000, and customer accounts totaling $3,500 were written off as uncollectible during the year.

e) The company estimates that 6 percent of the accounts receivable balance, net of estimated returns, at the end of 1998 will prove uncollectible.

f) Depreciation expense for 1998 was $3,000, and operating expenses of $8,000 were paid in cash.

g) Recorded cost of goods sold.

REQUIRED
1. Prepare journal entries to record the above transactions and end-of-year adjustments.
2. Prepare Record Exchange's income statement for the year ended December 31, 1998.
3. Prepare Record Exchange's balance sheet at December 31, 1998.

P 7-4. **PERCENTAGE-OF-COMPLETION METHOD** In 1998 Bossey Builders agreed to construct an apartment house for $720,000. Information relating to costs, billings, and collections for this contract is as follows:

	1998	1999	2000
Costs incurred to date...........................	$180,000	$351,000	$740,000
Estimated costs yet to be incurred................	420,000	429,000	–0–
Customer billings to date	75,000	270,000	720,000
Customer collections to date	60,000	225,000	700,000

Bossey uses the percentage-of-completion method of accounting for long-term construction contracts.

REQUIRED
1. Calculate the amount of income (loss) to be recognized each year.
2. Prepare all necessary journal entries each year.
3. Prepare partial balance sheets at the end of each year.

P 7-5. **REVENUE RECOGNITION; DISCOUNTS AND CANCELLATIONS** Buddys Bend State Park (BBSP) was formed during 1997 to begin operating 120 campground spaces for rent to the general public on January 1, 1998. The camp spaces rent for $250 per week. The campground is open for 15 weeks from Memorial Day through Labor Day, and BBSP has a December 31 fiscal year. The company spends the offseason making repairs, maintenance, and improving its camping spaces. Because of demand, camp spaces are rented in advance (from January 1 through September 1) and require a 20 percent down payment. A 6 percent discount is provided if full payment accompanies the current-season reservation. BBSP allows a 10 percent discount for "following season" reservations made and paid for between Labor Day and December 31. Reservations that are cancelled are subject to a $25 fee.

The following is a summary of BBSP's campground activities for the fiscal year ending December 31, 1998:

a) Balance sheet, January 1, 1998:

ASSETS		LIABILITIES AND EQUITY	
Cash	$ 60,000	Notes payable..............	$350,000
Land	80,000	Partners' capital............	175,000
Campground equipment......	300,000		
Supplies	85,000		
Total	$525,000	Total	$525,000

b) Reservations received:

Current season (1998) reservations, weeks 1,800
  (1,200 of these 1,800 qualified for a 6 percent discount;
  50 of these 1,800 were down payments only and were cancelled)
Following season (1999) reservations, weeks 800
  (all qualified for 10 percent discount)

c) Reservations cancelled:

Current season (1998) reservations, weeks 250
  (none of these had received 6 percent discount;
  50 of these were down payments only; see [b] above)
Following season (1999) reservations, weeks 75
  (all qualified for 10 percent discount)

d) Expenses for 1998:

Depreciation on campground equipment . . . . $ 45,000
Supplies used 15,000
Salaries (including 12/31/98 accrual of $20,000) 250,000
Interest expense 18,000
Other cash expenses 90,000

REQUIRED
1. Prepare BBSP's journal entries for its 1998 transactions.
2. Prepare BBSP's income statement for the year ending December 31, 1998.
3. Prepare BBSP's balance sheet at December 31, 1998.

P 7-6. **INCOME DETERMINATION FOR VARIOUS METHODS OF REVENUE RECOGNITION** The following information relates to a three-year period for Fonda Corporation, a manufacturer and distributor of short-range satellite receivers made to sell for $400 each.

1998   Produced 1,000 dishes and incurred costs of $280 per dish. Sold 400 dishes on account; collected $120,000 in cash from customers.

1999   Sold 500 dishes on account; collected cash from customers as follows: on 1998 sales, $40,000; on 1999 sales, $160,000.

2000   Sold the remaining 100 dishes for cash; collected the remaining cash due on previous years' sales.

REQUIRED Calculate the amount of income to be recognized each year under each of the following methods of revenue recognition:
1. Revenue recognized when production is complete.
2. Revenue recognized at point of sale.
3. Revenue recognized using the installment method.
4. Revenue recognized using the cost-recovery method.

P 7-7. **REVENUE RECOGNITION FOR SERVICES** On January 1, 1998, Buddy Baskin organized Buddy's Fitness Center, which had the following balance sheet:

ASSETS		LIABILITIES AND EQUITY	
Cash	$ 40,000	10% notes payable	$200,000
Plant and equipment	560,000	Baskin, capital	400,000
	$600,000		$600,000

The fitness center charges a one-time cash membership fee of $200. This fee allows members unlimited lifetime use of the facilities. The following information shows memberships sold and expenses incurred during 1998 and 1999:

	1998	1999
Memberships sold	1,000	800
Depreciation expense	$28,000	$28,000
Interest expense	20,000	18,000
Other expenses	16,000	10,000

Industry statistics indicate that members tend to use such facilities for approximately four years after they join. Accordingly, the company decided to recognize membership revenue using a sum-of-the-years'-digits method over a four-year period. Except for depreciation, all expenses were paid in cash. The note payable is repaid in $20,000 installments at the end of each year. In 1998, Baskin withdrew $35,000 in cash for personal use.

REQUIRED

1. Prepare the fitness center's income statements for the years ending December 31, 1998 and 1999.

2. Prepare the fitness center's balance sheet on December 31, 1998.

3. Prepare all journal entries for the fitness center for the year ending December 31, 1998.

P 7-8. **LONG-TERM CONSTRUCTION CONTRACTS** The controller's department of Pilloff Construction Company is comparing the impact of the completed-contract method and the percentage-of-completion method of accounting for long-term contracts on the company's financial statements. You have been engaged to assist Pilloff's controller in the preparation of a presentation to be given at the board meeting. The controller provides you with the following information:

a) Pilloff commenced doing business on January 1, 1998.

b) Construction activities for the year ended December 31, 1998, were as follows:

PROJECT	TOTAL CONTRACT PRICE	BILLINGS THROUGH 12/31/98	CASH COLLECTIONS THROUGH 12/31/98	CONTRACT COSTS INCURRED THROUGH 12/31/98	ADDITIONAL COSTS TO COMPLETE CONTRACTS
A	$ 520,000	$ 350,000	$ 310,000	$ 424,000	$106,000
B	670,000	210,000	210,000	126,000	504,000
C	475,000	475,000	395,000	315,000	–0–
D	200,000	70,000	50,000	112,750	92,250
E	460,000	400,000	400,000	370,000	30,000
	$2,325,000	$1,505,000	$1,365,000	$1,347,750	$732,250

c) Each contract is with a different customer.

d) Any work remaining to be done on the contracts is expected to be completed in 1999.

REQUIRED

1. Prepare a schedule by project, computing the amount of income (or loss) before selling, general, and administrative expenses for the year ended December 31, 1998, which would be reported under:

a) The completed-contract method.

b) The percentage-of-completion method.

2. The balance sheet that follows compares balances resulting from the use of the two methods of accounting for long-term contracts. For each numbered space on the statement, supply the correct balance (indicating DR or CR as appropriate). Disregard income taxes.

Pilloff Construction Company
Balance Sheet
December 31, 1998

	COMPLETED-CONTRACT METHOD	PERCENTAGE-OF-COMPLETION METHOD
Assets:		
Cash...	$xx	$xx
Accounts (contracts) receivable	1	2
Cost of uncompleted contracts in excess of billings........................	3	—
Costs and estimated earnings in excess of billings on uncompleted contracts	—	4
Property, plant, and equipment, net	xx	xx
Other assets	xx	xx
	$xx	$xx
Liabilities and stockholders' equity:		
Accounts payable and accrued liabilities..........	$xx	$xx
Billings on uncompleted contracts in excess of cost............................	5	—
Billings in excess of costs and estimated earnings on uncompleted contracts..............	—	6
Notes payable.................................	xx	xx
Pilloff, capital	xx	xx
	$xx	$xx

(AICPA, adapted)

P 7-9. **REVENUE RECOGNITION ALTERNATIVES** At the beginning of 1998, Ross Shelby began a business manufacturing and selling a super turbocharger designed to increase the performance of four-cylinder automobiles. Financial data related to production costs, sales price, and sales commissions are given below (the devices are sold through auto parts houses, and a commission is allowed on all units sold):

Production costs..	$25 per device
Selling price	$80 per device
Sales commission......................................	20% of sales per device

To encourage sales, Shelby agreed that the parts houses could sell the devices on credit and that they could remit all cash collections annually after deducting the 20 percent commission on all units sold during the year. Production, sales, and cash remittance data for 1998, 1999, and 2000 are as follows:

	1998	1999	2000
Units produced and delivered to parts houses	30,000	44,000	–0–
Units sold.............................	18,000	50,000	6,000
Cash remittances:			
Collections.............................	$1,000,000	$3,600,000	$1,320,000
Sales commissions	(288,000)	(800,000)	(96,000)
Net remittances......................	$ 712,000	$2,800,000	$1,224,000

REQUIRED

I. Calculate the income to be recognized each year under the following alternatives:
- **a)** Production basis.
- **b)** Sales basis.
- **c)** Installment basis. Do not include sales commissions in calculating the gross profit ratio.

Use the following format for alternatives *a* and *b:*

Revenues	**$xx**
Production costs matched against revenue	**(xx)**
Sales commissions	**(xx)**
Income	**$xx**

2. Verify that each of the above alternatives gives identical results for the three years combined.

P 7-I0. **THE INSTALLMENT METHOD** Todd Wholesale Company sells tires on a deferred payment plan. Because of an inability to estimate bad debts, Todd uses the installment method of accounting.

The balances of accounts receivable at the beginning and end of 1998 were:

	1/1/98	12/31/98
Accounts receivable, 1996....................................	$ 24,020	$ –0–
Accounts receivable, 1997....................................	344,460	67,440
Accounts receivable, 1998....................................		410,090

As collections are made, the company debits cash and credits accounts receivable. During 1998, upon default in payment by customers, the company repossessed merchandise having an estimated wholesale value of $1,200. The sales were made in 1997 for $10,000, and $7,800 had been collected before default. Todd recorded the default and repossession by debiting inventory of repossessed merchandise and crediting accounts receivable, 1997, for the uncollected receivable balance.

Todd's sales and cost of goods sold for the applicable three years are as follows:

	1996	1997	1998
Sales	$380,000	$432,000	$602,000
Cost of goods sold...........................	247,000	285,120	379,260

REQUIRED

Prepare journal entries to record at December 31, 1998, (1) the recognition of profits and (2) any other adjustments arising from the above data. Give complete explanations in support of your entries.

(AICPA, adapted)

P 7-II. **SERVICE REVENUE** At the beginning of 1998, Stay-and-Pass (SAP) began a CPA review course for prospective CPA examination candidates. SAP's tuition fee was $800, which covered a review of all parts of the Uniform CPA Examination. The tuition fee was payable in cash at the first review session and permitted the candidate to take one or more parts of SAP's review course as many times as necessary to pass the exam. The review course is offered twice each year.

SAP's statement of financial position at the beginning of 1998 consisted of cash, $100,000; notes payable, $60,000; and partners' capital, $40,000.

The following information applies to SAP's review course and other activities for 1998 and 1999:

	1998	1999
Number of first-time candidates	1,500	2,800
Number of retake candidates	45	165
Direct cost per candidate	$ 175	$ 195
Instructional costs...	200,000	450,000
Overhead costs (including facilities, administrative, interest, and miscellaneous costs)	140,000	180,000
Payments on note..	20,000	30,000
Partners' cash withdrawals.................................	80,000	115,000

In addition to the above information, a 1997 study by AASBA (American Association of State Boards of Accountancy) showed that, on the average, 8 percent of first-time candidates are unsuccessful and take the course a second time. After the first retake, the percentage of unsuccessful candidates who repeat the review course is almost zero.

SAP's fiscal year ends each year on December 31.

REQUIRED
1. Prepare summary general journal entries for SAP's operating activities for 1998 and 1999. Assume that all expenses are paid in cash.
2. Prepare income statements for SAP for 1998 and 1999.
3. Prepare balance sheets for SAP at the end of 1998 and 1999.

P 7-12.   REVENUE RECOGNITION; MISCELLANEOUS   Gerhardt Inc. has several diversified divisions, each of which maintains its own accounting system and method of revenue recognition. Three of these divisions are described below.

Paul Engineering: Paul is a civil engineering firm that specializes in building tunnels under rivers and lakes. On January 1, 1998, Paul received a $40,000,000, four-year contract to build an interstate highway tunnel under the Arkansas River; the estimated cost of the project was $35,200,000. Paul uses the percentage-of-completion method of revenue recognition, and data regarding the status of this contract at the end of the last two fiscal years are as follows:

	MAY 31, 1998	MAY 31, 1999
Estimated total costs	$35,200,000	$34,000,000
Actual costs incurred to date	4,224,000	11,900,000
Total progress billings to date	3,800,000	10,680,000
Total cash collections to date	2,950,000	10,100,000

Sarasota Tree Services: Sarasota provides tree trimming and spraying to both residential and commercial customers. Although commercial customers provide the majority of Sarasota's revenue, the company views the residential sector as an expanding market and recently introduced a discount program for two-year and three-year contracts. Residential service includes seven monthly trims and sprays from April 1 to October 31. Between January 1 and April 1 of 1998, Sarasota signed the following new residential contracts:

	CONTRACT AMOUNT	NUMBER
One-year-contract	$280	400
Two-year contract	490	80
Three-year contract	630	50

Grandpa's Joys: Grandpa's Joys manufactures baby car seats that are sold by infant stores and discount chains throughout the world. Because of rapid changes in government regulations regarding car safety, Grandpa's Joys allows retailers to return up to 25 percent of the merchandise purchased. Although returns on individual styles fluctuate, the returns have averaged 20 percent in each of the past five years. Grandpa's gross car seat sales totaled $12,500,000 during the year ended May 31, 1998. At year end, $5,800,000 of these sales were still subject to return privileges over the next several months. The remaining $6,700,000 of fiscal 1998 sales had actual returns of 18 percent. Grandpa's Joys meets all applicable criteria with respect to revenue from sales where the right of return exists, and records revenue accordingly.

REQUIRED
1. Calculate the revenue that should be recognized by Paul Engineering for the highway tunnel project for the fiscal years ended May 31, 1998, and May 31, 1999.
2. Calculate the revenue to be recognized in the fiscal year ended May 31, 1998, for the new residential contracts by Sarasota Tree Services.
3. Calculate the revenue to be recognized in the fiscal year ended May 31, 1998, for the sales for Grandpa's Joys.

(CMA adapted)

P 7-13.   **REVENUE RECOGNITION FOR FRANCHISES**   Sho and Go is a nationwide seller of the Sho and Go franchise. Two types of franchises are offered for sale, and the terms of each are as follows:

FRANCHISE	TYPE	FRANCHISE FEE	DETAILS
S	Use of name only.	$ 50,000	The franchisee may use the Sho and Go name for an unlimited period of time; no services are required by the franchisor.
G	Use of name and access to franchisor services.	100,000	Same as S except that for an additional $50,000, the franchisor also agrees to provide financial and managerial advice to franchisee over a five-year period.

Both types of franchises require a 50 percent down payment, with the balance payable in four equal annual installments. Interest is also received on the outstanding balance but can be ignored in this problem.

Information related to franchise sales and operating costs for the franchisor for 1998 and 1999 is summarized below.

		1998	1999
a)	Number of type *S* franchises sold (collectibility of the installments could not be estimated for four franchises sold in 1998 and six franchises sold in 1999; for the remaining franchises, it is estimated that 1% will not be collected).	20	24
b)	Number of type *G* franchises sold (for these franchises, it is estimated that 1% will not be collected).	8	12
c)	For type *G* franchises, it is estimated that the financial and managerial services are provided equally over the five-year period.		
d)	As of 12/31/99, all installments have been received on schedule.		
e)	For simplicity, assume that all franchises are sold on the first day of each year.		
f)	Cash operating expenses (exclusive of any uncollectible accounts provisions).	$236,000	$270,000

REQUIRED

1. Prepare income statements for 1998 and 1999 for Sho and Go.

2. Assume that Sho and Go's balance sheet at the beginning of 1998 consisted of cash of $100,000 and owners' equity of $100,000. Prepare balance sheets at the end of 1998 and 1999.

P 7-14. **COMPREHENSIVE REVIEW** Hardage Corporation sells tractors and also uses some of them in landscape construction. Its trial balance at the end of 1998 is as follows:

	DEBIT	CREDIT
Cash	$ 80,000	
Accounts receivable (net of uncollectible accounts)	150,000	
Construction in progress	470,000	
Inventory of tractors	250,000	
Plant and equipment	185,000	
Accumulated depreciation		$ 66,000
Accounts payable		100,000
Billings on contracts		560,000
Deferred gross profit		20,000
Common stock		180,000
Retained earnings		170,000
Sales of tractors		330,000
Cost of tractors sold	231,000	
Operating expenses	60,000	
	$1,426,000	$1,426,000

Additional information about 1998 operations is as follows:

a) The gross profit rate on tractors has remained constant for many years.

b) Hardage has two long-term landscape projects in progress on which the percentage-of-completion method is used. Financial data about these projects are as follows:

	PROJECT #300	PROJECT #400
Project started	January 1, 1997	January 1, 1998
Contract price	$800,000	$200,000
Costs incurred:		
During 1997	100,000	—
During 1998	200,000	110,000
Estimated completion costs:		
At the end of 1997	400,000	—
At the end of 1998	300,000	100,000
Billings on contract:		
1997	150,000	—
1998	300,000	110,000
Cash collections:		
Through the end of 1998	150,000	10,000

No adjusting entries, including construction income or loss adjustments, have been made for 1998.

c) During 1998, a tractor that was previously used for landscaping was sold for $12,000, and the proceeds were credited to the plant and equipment account. The tractor's original cost was $50,000, and it was 40 percent depreciated.

d) Hardage uses the accrual (sales) method of accounting for sales of tractors and has not recorded uncollectible accounts expense for 1998, which should be 4 percent of sales. During 1997, two sales were made to Customers *A* and *B*, and because collectibility could not be estimated on these two isolated sales, the installment method was used. Customer *A* has an account balance of $30,000 at the end of 1998. In August of 1998, Customer *B* defaulted on the remaining $12,000 owed. Since the repossessed tractor was worthless, the company wrote off Customer *B*'s account to operating expenses.

REQUIRED
1. Prepare any necessary adjusting and correcting entries at the end of 1998.
2. Prepare the income statement for 1998 for Hardage Corporation.
3. Prepare the balance sheet at the end of 1998 for Hardage Corporation.

P 7-15.   **REVENUE RECOGNITION FOR BARTER TRANSACTIONS**   Cocoa Trading Corporation was organized on January 1, 1998, to act as a bartering agent for companies and individuals who wish to trade assets under a bartering arrangement. The corporation's initial pool of assets, contributed by two partners who share profits and losses equally, consisted of $70,000 in cash, a warehouse with a fair value of $80,000, and goods to be bartered with a fair value of $150,000.

The bartering arrangements are as follows:

a)   A membership fee of $100 is required of each customer. This fee is payable "up front" and is not refundable. However, $50 of this amount may be applied in barter transactions in which the customers' goods sacrificed are valued at less than the goods received (see item *b* below). No portion of the fee may be applied toward agent commissions (see item *c* below). Industry experience indicates that a member uses the services of a bartering agent for approximately four years.

b)   Customers bring to the warehouse any goods that they wish to barter. The corporation determines the fair value of the goods by consulting a nationally distributed "barter black book." Customers either pay cash or are paid cash for the difference between the fair values of the bartered goods.

c)   The corporation charges a service fee equal to 10 percent of the established value of each barter transaction. This fee is payable in cash at the time the barter transaction takes place.

The following information pertains to Cocoa Trading Corporation's operating activities for 1998:

Membership fees	**$800,000**
Portion of membership fees applied to bartering	280,000
Fair value of goods accepted from customers	900,000
Fair value of goods delivered to customers	950,000
Concessions revenue (soft drinks, candy, etc.)	28,000
Operating expenses:	
Depreciation expense	16,000
Cost of concessions	8,000
Salaries	48,000
Miscellaneous (includes telephone, electricity, supplies, and advertising)	16,000

REQUIRED

1.   Calculate Cocoa Trading Corporation's service fees for 1998.

2.   Prepare journal entries for Cocoa Trading Corporation's operations for 1998.

3.   Prepare the income statement for 1998 and the statement of financial position for Cocoa Trading Corporation at the end of 1998.

P 7-16.   **INSTALLMENT METHOD OF ACCOUNTING**   The following trial balance consists of the beginning account balances *and* the total debits and credits to the accounts of Ross McAlister, which sells sailboats on a deferred payment plan and uses the installment method of accounting:

ACCOUNT	DEBIT	CREDIT
Cash	$ 333,000	$ 142,000
Accounts receivable	310,000	285,000
Inventory (new sailboats)	320,000	196,000
Inventory (repossessed sailboats)	900	
Accounts payable	120,000	220,000
Deferred gross profit	80,600	104,000
Common stock		100,000
Retained earnings		50,000
Sales	300,000	300,000
Interest earned on accounts receivable		10,000
Cost of goods sold	196,000	196,000
Expenses	22,000	
Loss on repossession	500	
Realized gross profit		80,000
	$1,683,000	$1,683,000

Additional information:

a) Interest collected during the year was $8,000.

b) During the year, a customer defaulted on an account, and the merchandise was repossessed. The amount debited to deferred gross profit was $600, which represented a 30 percent gross profit on the uncollected amount.

c) McAlister uses a perpetual inventory system. The beginning inventory was $120,000.

d) Because of varying gross profit rates, you need not verify realized gross profit.

REQUIRED

1. Prepare, in summary form, all journal entries made by Ross McAlister during the year.

2. Construct Ross McAlister's balance sheet at the beginning of the year.

*P 7-17. **CONSIGNMENTS; ADJUSTING AND CORRECTING ENTRIES** During your audit of Franklin Corporation for the year ended December 31, 1998, the following information comes to your attention:

a) Franklin sells big-screen television sets on a consignment basis. The television sets are sold by consignees for $1,800 each. Consignees are allowed a 30 percent commission on each sale and are reimbursed for all expenses paid in connection with the television sets.

b) The television sets cost Franklin $1,000 each.

c) Franklin shipped 140 televisions to consignees during 1998. Franklin paid crating and packing costs of $1,680. Freight charges paid by consignees totaled $5,320.

d) Television sets unsold by consignees as of the end of 1998, 60.

e) During 1998, the following entries were made by Franklin Corporation relative to the above information:

Accounts receivable	252,000	
Sales		252,000

To record television sets shipped to consignees.

Miscellaneous expenses	1,680	
Cash		1,680

To record crating and shipping expenses.

Cash	45,480	
Accounts receivable		45,480

To record cash received from consignees, based
on the following account sales report:

Television sets sold	$144,000
Less: Freight	(5,320)
Commissions (.30 × $144,000)	(43,200)
Balance due (to follow)	(50,000)
Cash remitted	$ 45,480

REQUIRED Prepare the necessary adjusting or correcting entries for Franklin Corporation.

P 7-18. **RESEARCH PROBLEM—FREQUENT-FLYER MILES** (The following material was taken from an article entitled "Are Air-Miles Programs in a Tailspin?") The much-anticipated move of the airlines to devalue their frequent-flyer miles is now a fact of life. Faced with the ever-rising number of unredeemed frequent-flyer miles and the colossal liability locked away in the escalating mileage accounts of 30 million enrolled frequent flyers, the airlines decided it was time to put the squeeze on their best customers. This, of course, confirms what the skeptics have been saying all along—frequent-flyer programs must eventually sink of their own weight. The brilliant marketing ploy of the '80s is destined to become a costly burden in the '90s. Right? Wrong. To understand the latest twists in the marketing strategy followed by the airlines, you first must confront the four misleading myths about these programs:

Myth No. 1.   There is no cost to the airline when an unsold seat is awarded.

Myth No. 2.   The airlines regret the day American Airlines launched the first frequent-flyer program in 1981. The growing liability of 1.4 trillion frequent-flyer miles threatens the very survival of the industry.

Myth No. 3.   Today's loyalty reward programs are the latest version of the S & H Green Stamps craze of the '50s and '60s. They'll fade away as stamps did, once people tire of the game.

Myth No. 4.   The key to success in any customer-reward program is to give away as little as possible while creating the impression that the customer is getting a great deal.

REQUIRED   Go to your school or local library and research the accounting and economics of frequent-flyer programs. Once you have performed your research, write a short paper that addresses the above myths.

Cash, Current Receivables and Payables, and Contingencies

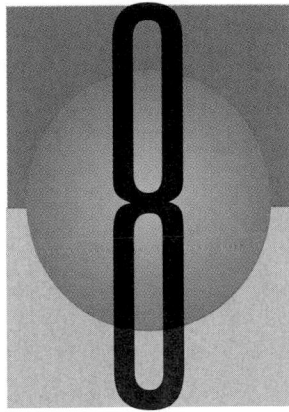

LEARNING OBJECTIVES

PART A • Cash and Current Receivables

After studying this part of the chapter, you should be able to:

1. Identify items considered to be cash.
2. List the three accounting considerations related to accounts receivable.
3. State the issues related to determining the amounts due on accounts receivable.
4. Identify and discuss the available alternatives for accounting for uncollectible accounts receivable.
5. Identify various transactions in which receivables are used to obtain immediate cash and describe the general objective in accounting for such transactions.
6. List the three conditions that must be met for a transfer of receivables to be considered a sale of assets.
7. Describe the appropriate accounting for a transfer of receivables that is not considered a sale.

PART B • Current Payables and Contingencies

After studying this part of the chapter, you should be able to:

8. Define current liabilities and describe the amount at which they normally are recorded.
9. State the accounting and evidence issues related to short-term obligations expected to be refinanced.
10. Identify the three general categories of current liabilities and discuss the nature of the liabilities in each category.
11. Specify the circumstances under which the currently due portion of a long-term obligation would not be classified as a current liability.
12. List the conditions under which an accrual should be made for compensated employee absences.
13. Define a contingency.
14. Describe the appropriate accounting and reporting for loss contingencies, including litigation contingencies.

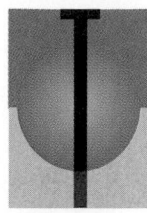

he collapse of Drexel Burnham Lambert Group, Wall Street's largest bankruptcy, in February 1990 was attributed to Drexel's lack of liquidity:

> Coming due the following Monday was $30 million of commercial paper for the firm's commodities subsidiary. Says a Drexel managing director: "The bank called up on Friday and said, 'Sorry, fellas, it's too risky for us. We're outta here.' We were caught with our pants down." . . .
>
> The commercial paper was an obligation of the holding company, Drexel Burnham Lambert Group, whose assets consisted of an illiquid junk bond portfolio. The firm's liquid capital was housed in its broker-dealer subsidiary, where there was in excess of $1 billion.[1]

Drexel had been using its broker-dealer subsidiary's cash to meet the holding company's obligations, a practice the SEC finally prohibited. The Commission had ruled that the parent company must borrow against its own assets to raise capital because the broker-dealer subsidiary needed to retain its liquid capital to protect its own customers. Drexel found itself in the unfortunate position of having to meet its obligations with illiquid assets.

Liquidity is important to investors, creditors, and others who want to assess a company's potential future cash flows and its ability to adapt to changes in its operating environment. In accounting for cash and other short-term monetary assets and liabilities, the accountant is concerned with providing disclosures that will help financial statement users assess the company's liquidity.

Chapters 4, 5, and 6 covered the financial statements and the concepts and principles that underlie their preparation. Most of the remaining chapters in this book examine more closely the specific asset, liability, and stockholders' equity components of the balance sheet along with income and cash flow effects of these items. Some chapters, such as those dealing with debt securities (Chapter 14) and leases (Chapter 15), cover both the asset and the liability sides of an issue to minimize redundancy and provide more efficient explanations. For the same reasons, this chapter covers both current monetary assets and current monetary liabilities, together with a few other current liabilities. The authors recognize that in some courses, current assets and liabilities will not be covered together. To facilitate coverage of the two topics at different points, this chapter is divided into two parts: Part A on cash and current receivables and Part B on current liabilities and contingencies.

Part A • Cash and Current Receivables

According to the FASB, the primary objective of financial accounting and reporting is to provide existing and potential investors, creditors, and others with information about an enterprise that is useful for decision making. Accordingly, the FASB has specified that financial reporting should provide information about the amounts, timing, and degree of certainty of a company's prospective cash inflows and outflows. The ease with which a company's assets can be converted into cash, and how quickly its obligations must be settled using cash, determine a company's **liquidity.** The more liquid a company's assets, the more likely the company will meet its obligations as they come due. The sooner its obligations must be settled, the more important for the company to have liquid assets available to meet those obligations.

Assets are classified as monetary or nonmonetary depending on the nature of cash claims. **Monetary assets** include money (cash) and claims to receive a sum of money, the amount of which is fixed or determinable without reference to the future prices of specific goods and services. The current monetary assets discussed in this part of the chapter are cash, accounts receivable, and notes receivable.

---

[1]"Did Drexel Get What It Deserved?" *Fortune*, March 12, 1990, p. 81.

 **ASH**

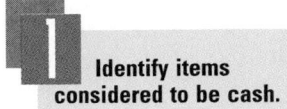

Cash, the most liquid of all assets, is a medium of exchange used to purchase goods and services and to discharge obligations. Cash is so widely accepted as a medium of exchange that there are almost no restrictions on its use in business transactions. Cash includes U.S. currency and coins, personal checks, money orders, demand deposits, cashiers' checks, bank drafts, petty cash, change funds, and most savings deposits. (Banks seldom enforce the requirement that depositors give prior notice before withdrawing funds from savings accounts.) Foreign currencies are included in cash if they are freely convertible into U.S. currency. Sums of money held as an asset but restricted to specific uses should not be included in cash, because they are not available as a general medium of exchange. Restricted deposits, postdated checks, IOUs, stamps, money-market accounts, and certificates of deposit are not included in cash because they are not readily exchangeable and are not freely available for purchasing goods and services or for paying obligations. These items, which are *not* available as a general medium of exchange, should be classified as shown in Exhibit 8–1.

Management of Petty Cash

Many companies establish a fixed-amount petty cash fund for small expenditures that do not justify a formal authorization and disbursement procedure. The size of the petty cash fund is a function of many factors, such as the expected total amount of small expenditures over a period, say, a month. Under an *imprest system,* an individual is placed in charge of the petty cash fund and made responsible for making payments for expenditures that are supported by proper vouchers. (The word *imprest* means to be held responsible.) Periodically, a check to replenish the fund, made payable to petty cash, is written on the company's regular checking account. At this time the expenditures made from petty cash and the related replenishment are recorded in the accounts.

Assume, for example, that on June 1 The Cycle Shop established a $300 petty cash fund for small expenditures. On June 16 the petty cash trustee submitted vouchers for several petty cash expenditures made through June 16 and requested replenishment of the fund. On June 16 the petty cash fund would contain the following vouchers and cash balance:

Postage expenditures	$ 75
Freight paid on purchases	110
Supplies purchased and used	30
Cash on hand	85
Total	$300

EXHIBIT 8–1	Balance Sheet Classification of Restricted Cash Items	
Item	**Classification**	**Reason for Classification**
Deposits with a trustee (e.g., construction funds advanced)	Noncurrent assets	Cannot be used to discharge current obligations because they are earmarked for a specific purpose.
Postdated checks	Receivables	Generally, banks do not accept such checks for deposit.
IOUs	Receivables	Generally, banks do not accept IOUs for deposit.
Postage stamps	Supplies	Not an accepted medium of exchange.
Certificates of deposit	Investments	Not available for immediate withdrawal without a substantial penalty.
Money-market accounts	Investments	Only a limited number of transactions permitted.

The entries to record the establishment of this fund, the expenditures, and its replenishment would be:

June 1	Petty cash	300	
	Cash		300
	To record the establishment of the petty cash fund.		
June 16	Supplies expense ($75 + $30)	105	
	Transportation in	110	
	Cash		215
	To record expenditures and replenishment of the fund.		

Occasionally, errors made in payments or unaccounted-for expenditures will result in the amount of petty cash on hand differing from the amount that should be on hand. To resolve such discrepancies, cash short-and-over should be debited or credited, and the offsetting debit or credit made to cash. The cash short-and-over account should be closed to miscellaneous expenses at the end of the accounting period.

Petty cash on hand is considered a monetary asset because it is part of the company's cash balance. The size of a petty cash fund may be increased or decreased. An increase in the size of the fund is recorded by debiting petty cash and crediting cash. A decrease is recorded by debiting cash and crediting petty cash. The petty cash fund should always be replenished at the end of an accounting period, so that expenses will be properly recorded and cash correctly stated.

Reconciliation of Cash Balances

Banks send depositors monthly statements of the activities in their checking accounts. Each month, depositors should reconcile these statements with the cash balances shown in their own accounting records, as a part of the overall control over cash. The purpose of the **bank reconciliation** is to ensure that entries in the company's cash account agree with the bank's independent records of the company's cash receipt and disbursement activities.

The ending cash balance shown on the monthly bank statement seldom will agree with the ending cash balance in the company's records, for one or more of the following reasons:

1. The bank may show deposits to its customer's account that have not been recorded as cash receipts in the customer's books. An example of this type of transaction is a note receivable collected by the bank for the benefit of the customer. The customer may have no knowledge of the collection until the bank statement is received.

2. The bank may have decreased the customer's account balance for transactions not known to the customer until the bank statement is received. For example, a bank normally increases a customer's cash balance immediately for checks deposited. However, if the maker of a check does not have adequate funds deposited to cover the check, the bank will then decrease the customer's cash balance. Normally, these so-called NSF (not sufficient funds) checks are returned to the customer depositor. Other items that reduce depositor balances include service charges, charges for safe deposit boxes, and charges for printing checks.

3. A customer may have recorded cash receipts that have not yet been recorded by the bank as deposits. For example, if near the end of the month the customer makes a deposit, it may not appear in the bank statement as a deposit until the following month.

4. A customer may have recorded cash disbursements that have not been paid by the bank as of the bank statement date. For example, a customer may have written checks in payment for goods and services, but those checks may not have been presented to and paid by the bank at the time the statement is prepared and mailed to the customer. These checks, called *outstanding* checks, will appear on the monthly bank statement in the month when they are paid by the bank. (Outstanding *certified* checks are excepted from this category, since the bank immediately reduces the customer's account balance when a certified check is prepared.)

5. Finally, errors on the part of the bank or the customer can cause the bank balance to disagree with the customer's accounting records.

Notice that items 1 and 2 have been recorded by the bank but not by the company, and therefore will cause the *company's* ending cash balance to differ from the correct cash balance. On the other hand, items 3 and 4 have been recorded by the company but not by the bank; they will cause the reported cash balance on the *bank statement* to differ from the correct cash balance. Finally, item 5 will affect the reported balance of the company or the bank, depending on which party made the error. Obviously, any bank error should be called to the bank's attention promptly.

To illustrate, assume that Lacey Corporation's accounting records show a cash balance of $8,672.89 on January 31, 1998. The January bank statement reported an ending balance in Lacey Corporation's bank account of $1,768.22. After examining the monthly transactions on the bank statement and comparing the statement with the cash account, Lacey discovered the following:

I. Four checks were written during January but were not included on the bank statement, or returned with it.

CHECK NUMBER	AMOUNT
394	$ 400.00
407	1,870.00
412	500.00
413	870.00
	$3,640.00

2. A deposit of $400 was made on January 29 but did not appear on the bank statement.

3. On January 28, Lacey Corporation redeemed a two-month certificate of deposit at the bank's suburban branch. The face amount was $10,000, and interest totaled $600. The cash proceeds were deposited at the branch bank. Because the information did not reach the main bank for processing until February 2, this deposit did not appear on the January bank statement.

4. Bank service charges for January, $2.30, were not recorded by Lacey.

5. One of Lacey's customer's checks was returned with the bank statement. The $26.37 check was marked "NSF."

6. The bank collected a note for Lacey on January 21 totaling $214, of which $14 was interest revenue.

7. On January 26, Lacey Corporation made a $630 deposit, which represented receivable collections. Lacey's bookkeeper made a transposition error in recording the deposit in the cash account and recorded the deposit as $360.

Exhibit 8–2 shows how the bank statement ending balance of $1,768.22 may be reconciled with Lacey's ending cash balance of $8,672.89. Note that items 2 and 3 are added to the bank balance, while item 1 is deducted from the bank balance. Items 6 and 7 are added to the book balance, and items 4 and 5 are deducted.

The bank reconciliation shown in Exhibit 8–2 is useful for at least two reasons. First, the reconciliation yields the correct cash balance of $9,128.22 for financial

EXHIBIT 8-2	Bank Reconciliation

Lacey Corporation
January 31, 1998

Balance per bank statement................		$ 1,768.22
Add: Deposit in transit	$ 400.00	
Proceeds from matured CD	10,600.00	11,000.00
		$12,768.22
Deduct: Outstanding checks		(3,640.00)
Corrected cash balance..................		$ 9,128.22
Balance per books		$ 8,672.89
Add: Understatement of deposit from		
transposition error..................	$ 270.00	
Proceeds of note collected by bank	214.00	484.00
		$ 9,156.89
Deduct: Service charge..................	$ 2.30	
NSF check......................	26.37	(28.67)
Corrected cash balance		$ 9,128.22

statement purposes.[2] Second, items that increase and decrease the balance per books to arrive at the correct cash balance provide the necessary information to adjust Lacey Corporation's cash account in the general ledger. The entries required to adjust and correct Lacey Corporation's books at January 31, 1998, are as follows:

Cash	484.00	
Accounts receivable		270.00
Notes receivable		200.00
Interest revenue		14.00
Accounts receivable	26.37	
Miscellaneous expense	2.30	
Cash		28.67

Notice that the adjusting entries shown above consist of reconciling items in the lower section of the bank reconciliation shown in Exhibit 8–2.

Another form of reconciliation often used in practice, especially in auditing, is a cash receipts and disbursements reconciliation (sometimes called a **comprehensive reconciliation** or **proof of cash**). The comprehensive reconciliation provides not only a reconciliation of the ending accounting balance with the ending book balance, but a reconciliation of beginning cash balances and all cash receipts and disbursements during the period.

Cash Disclosures

Disclosures related to cash in the balance sheet should help financial statement users to assess a company's liquidity. Two important cash disclosures are overdrafts and compensating balances.

Overdrafts

Occasionally, a company may write checks that cause an **overdraft** in its bank account at a balance sheet date. If the company has other unrestricted checking ac-

---

[2]A variation of the format shown in Exhibit 8–2 begins with the bank balance, adds and deducts the reconciling items as appropriate, and reconciles to the book balance. This approach, however, does not clearly indicate the correct ending cash balance.

count balances at the same bank that are greater than the amount of the overdraft, the overdraft may be offset in the balance sheet against these positive cash balances. Otherwise, an overdraft should be classified as a current liability, similar to a temporary loan.

Compensating Balances

Banks often require borrowers to maintain compensating balances. A **compensating balance** is a cash amount that must remain on deposit during the period of the loan. For example, a company may borrow $50,000 from a bank and be required to maintain a 10 percent compensating balance of $5,000 on deposit at the bank during the loan period. Since a compensating balance requirement reduces a company's liquidity by restricting its use of a portion of its reported cash balance at a statement date, disclosure of such compensating balance requirements is necessary to enable users to assess future cash flows and liquidity. *SEC Financial Reporting Release No. 1* requires that companies disclose information related to compensating balance arrangements made in connection with short-term debt and lines of credit.

This concludes our discussion of cash. We next turn to receivables.

THE CLASSIFICATION AND VALUATION OF RECEIVABLES

Receivables arise when a company sells goods or services on credit, obtaining the right to receive cash in the future; or when it lends money to another company, receiving a note in exchange. Receivables are considered monetary assets because they represent claims to receive fixed amounts of cash. In theory, receivables should be valued at the present value of future cash flows to be received. In practice, however, most short-term receivables are valued at net realizable value (the face amount of the receivable) instead of present value, because the discount or interest factor is not material.

CONCEPTUAL

Receivables are monetary assets because they represent claims to receive fixed amounts of cash.

The two most common types of receivables are accounts receivable and notes receivable. Other receivables arise from loans to employees and officers, advances made to affiliated companies (such as a branch office or a subsidiary), tax refund claims from governmental units, long-term leasing agreements, and accruals such as interest.

In recent years the use of bank credit cards (for example, Visa and MasterCard) for consumer purchases has increased dramatically. When a retailer's customers purchase goods with bank credit cards, the retailer deposits the credit card slips in its bank checking account. Periodically, the bank deducts from the retailer's account a credit card or service fee for processing the slips. The customers make credit card payments directly to the bank that acts as a clearing agent; therefore, from the retailer's standpoint, credit card sales do *not* produce receivables.

ACCOUNTS RECEIVABLE

Accounts receivable, sometimes called **trade receivables,** arise from the sale of goods or services on account. In our economic system, many exchanges at the manufacturing, wholesale, and retail levels take place on credit. Companies expect that by selling on credit, they will achieve greater sales and profits than they would if their sales were made on a cash-only basis. Even though a company runs the risk of not being able to collect some receivables, it expects that any uncollectible receivables, along with the costs of credit sales, will be more than offset by an increase in sales and, in turn, profitability.

A sale made on account is an informal contract between the buyer and seller. The terms of sale vary depending on the business or industry. The accounting considerations associated with sales of goods and services on account are as follows:

2 List the three accounting considerations related to accounts receivable.

1. Determining the amount of the receivable due from the customer.
2. Determining when the receivable should be recognized as an asset.
3. Determining what recognition should be given to the possibility that the amount owed may not be collected.

These considerations, which were introduced briefly in Chapter 7, are important in applying the *historical cost principle* to receivables. Our discussion in Chapter 7 focused primarily on the revenue side of the transaction and the resulting income statement effect. Our discussion here will focus primarily on the accounts receivable side of the transaction and the resulting balance sheet effect.

3 State the issues related to determining the amounts due on accounts receivable.

Determining Amounts Due on Accounts Receivable

Because revenue arises from the sale of goods or services, the determination of the amount due from sales transactions made on account is precisely the same problem as determining the amount of revenue to be recognized from the transaction. Conceptually, the amount due is equal to the *current cash equivalent exchange price* arising from the transaction between buyer and seller. Although the exchange price may sometimes be blurred in practice because of trade and cash discounts, customer returns, and the length of the collection period, the amount to be recognized is clear conceptually: *It is the exchange price established in the transaction.* This amount is the initial recorded amount for accounts receivable; it is also the amount of revenue recorded in the transaction.

CONCEPTUAL

The amount recorded for an account receivable is the exchange price established in the transaction.

Trade Discounts

Some manufacturing companies publish suggested retail prices or list prices for their products, then grant **trade discounts** to various groups of buyers, such as distributors, wholesalers, and retailers. By using list prices and trade discounts, manufacturers can price their products differently for different groups without publishing a separate price list for each group. Trade discounts also enable manufacturers to adjust their selling prices simply by adjusting the trade discount, rather than by publishing a new price list when costs change.

Trade discounts are never recorded. For example, if a manufacturer sold goods with a list price of $700 at a trade discount of 40 percent, the selling price, and the amount to be recorded as a receivable, would be $420 [$700 × (1 − .40)], the amount which represents the exchange price of the asset.

Sales Discounts

Many companies grant their customers **cash** or **sales discounts** to encourage prompt payment for purchases made on account. For example, a company may offer the following terms: "2%/10, net 30." Thus, if a customer who purchases supplies on account at a sales price of $1,000 pays within 10 days of the invoice date, that customer may deduct 2 percent of $1,000, or $20, from the sales price, and remit only $980. If the same customer pays *after* 10 days, however, the entire $1,000 must be paid.[3] Although many customers do not take advantage of cash discounts,

---

[3]Another common type of sales discount is "2%/10 EOM," where EOM means "end of the month." The customer is allowed a 2 percent discount if payment is received within 10 days following the end of the month. For example, if a purchase is made anytime in March, the discount is allowed if payment is made before April 10.

EXHIBIT 8–3	Accounting for Sales Discounts

Situation	Entry		
At the time of sale, the receivable and sale are recorded net of the cash discount	Accounts receivable . . .	980	
	Sales		980[a]
and			
if the customer pays within the discount period and remits $980	Cash	980	
	Accounts receivable . .		980
or			
if the customer does not pay within the discount period and thus remits $1,000	Cash	1,000	
	Accounts receivable . .		980
	Interest revenue		20

[a]**Although conceptually less desirable, sales and accounts receivable could be recorded at the gross amount of $1,000. If payment is received within the discount period, sales discounts (a contra sales account) would be debited for $20.**

rational customers should do so, even if they must borrow the money needed to pay within the 10-day period. The loss of the 2 percent discount in exchange for an additional 20 days to make payment is roughly equivalent to a 36 percent annual interest rate (.02 times 18, the number of 20-day periods in a year).

Because companies offer cash discounts on such favorable terms, the discounted amount ($980) provides the best measure of the cash inflow to be realized from the sale. Therefore, the sale should be recorded net of the sales discount, at $980, the amount that represents the "cash equivalent price" at the exchange date. Exhibit 8–3 illustrates the accounting for sales discounts.

One more point should be made regarding accounting for sales discounts. If the seller's fiscal period ends after the discount period has elapsed but before the customer has made full remittance, an adjusting entry debiting accounts receivable and crediting interest revenue for $20 is necessary to adjust the receivable to the full amount to be received and to record the interest revenue.

Sales Returns

In Chapter 7 (pages 334–336) we discussed accounting for sales returns in connection with measuring the amount of revenue to be reported on the income statement. When goods are sold on account, consideration of sales returns is necessary in order to report at the balance sheet date the amount of receivables that is expected to result in a cash inflow.

The following accounting procedures for sales returns were presented in Chapter 7:

1. If sales returns are infrequent and small in dollar amount, they may be recorded as they occur. Though mismatching may occur, it should not be material.

2. If companies experience a significant dollar amount of sales returns, and can make reasonable estimates of expected returns, the allowance method should be used.

3. Under certain circumstances, the seller's risk from customer return privileges may be so great that a sale should not be recorded until the return period has expired.

Interest

Most accounts receivable do not bear interest if the customer pays the amount owed within the period specified by the terms of sale. However, if payment is not

made within this time period, the purchaser must pay interest or a finance charge on the unpaid balance. For example, Sears, Inc., offers a revolving credit plan in which customers must pay a finance charge of 1.5 percent per month on the average unpaid balance, unless credit purchases are paid for within approximately 20 days from the date a statement is received.[4]

Determining When Accounts Receivable Should Be Recorded

CONCEPTUAL

Recognition of accounts receivable as assets parallels revenue recognition.

In the previous section we discussed how to determine the amount due on accounts receivable. We pointed out that this problem is precisely the same as that of determining the amount of revenue that arises from a company's earnings activities. Similarly, the issue of *when* a receivable should be recorded as an asset is directly related to *when* revenue should be recognized from an exchange transaction.

In Chapters 2 and 7 we discussed the realization concept, which governs the recognition of revenue. Under this concept, revenue should be recognized when (1) the amount and timing of the revenue can be reasonably estimated (revenue has been realized or is realizable) and (2) the earnings process is complete or virtually complete (revenue has been earned). Until these criteria have been met, there is too much uncertainty about a transaction's ultimate net cash flow effect to justify recognition of revenue. Though in many cases these criteria are met at the point of sale, occasionally they may be met, and revenue recognized, at other points. Where receivables are concerned, revenue sometimes is recognized on the basis of cash collections from customers. The two methods of revenue recognition on a cash-collection basis—the installment method and the cost-recovery method—and the circumstances that justify their use were discussed in Chapter 7.

Estimating Uncollectible Accounts Receivable: The Allowance Method

4 **Identify and discuss the available alternatives for accounting for uncollectible accounts receivable.**

Companies that sell on account generally expect that most, but perhaps not all, of their credit sales will be collected in cash. They assume, moreover, that the increased sales and profits that result from selling on account will more than offset any uncollectible receivables or increased costs associated with credit sales, such as the cost of mailing periodic billings.

CONCEPTUAL

In accordance with the matching principle and the objective of providing useful information, estimated uncollectible accounts receivable expense should be recorded in the period of the sale.

In accordance with the matching principle and the financial reporting objective of providing information that helps users to predict, assess, and evaluate future cash flows, estimates of **uncollectible accounts expense** (sometimes called **bad debt expense**) should be made and recorded in the period in which sales take place if (1) it is highly probable that some accounts will prove uncollectible and (2) the dollar amount of uncollectible accounts reasonably can be estimated.[5] The method most often used to account for uncollectible accounts is called the allowance method.[6] (Because the allowance method applies the matching principle under accrual accounting, it sometimes is called the accrual method.)

In the **allowance method** of accounting for uncollectible accounts, an estimate of uncollectible accounts is made each period and reported in the income

---

[4]There are many methods of calculating the finance charge. This finance charge is similar in concept to interest charged by credit card companies such as Visa and MasterCard.

[5]"Accounting for Contingencies," *Statement of Financial Accounting Standards No. 5* (Stamford, Conn.: FASB, 1975).

[6]Sometimes the allowance method is not used. Instead, uncollectible accounts receivable are written off with a corresponding debit to uncollectible accounts expense at the time the accounts are determined to be uncollectible. This treatment is called the direct write-off method.

statement as an expense.[7] On the balance sheet, estimated uncollectible receivables are represented by an accounts receivable valuation or contra account called an allowance for uncollectible accounts. (Alternatively, accounts receivable may be reported "net" of the allowance for uncollectible accounts.) An allowance account is used because, at the time the estimate of uncollectible accounts is made, it is not known *which* customers' accounts will prove uncollectible. Three generally accepted procedures may be used in applying the allowance method: aging of accounts receivable, percentage of ending accounts receivable, and percentage of credit sales.

Aging of Accounts Receivable

The **aging of accounts receivable** procedure stresses the reporting of receivables at net realizable value. The procedure is based on the assumption that the longer a receivable is outstanding, the less likely it is to be collected. In this procedure, the individual account balances are classified according to the number of days outstanding. Once the aging schedule has been completed, a separate estimate of the percentage of uncollectible receivables is applied to each age classification group. The longer receivables have been outstanding, the higher the percentage that is expected to be uncollectible.

The aging procedure is illustrated in Exhibit 8–4 for Larson Corporation. Most computerized accounting packages include a software routine that ages accounts receivable. Conceptually, the routine operates in a manner similar to that illustrated in the exhibit. On the basis of the aging procedure illustrated in Exhibit 8–4, the required ending credit balance in Larson's allowance account would be $1,523. If the ending balance in the allowance account had a *debit* balance of $200,[8] the adjusting entry to record the uncollectible accounts expense for 1998 would be:

Uncollectible accounts expense. 1,723
    Allowance for uncollectible accounts   1,723
[$1,523 (from Exhibit 8–4) + $200]

Percentage of Ending Accounts Receivable

The **percentage of ending accounts receivable** procedure is similar to, but less precise than, the aging procedure. In this procedure, the dollar amount of accounts receivable that is not expected to be collected is determined by applying an *overall* percentage to the end-of-the-period balance of accounts receivable. The allowance account is then adjusted to this amount using an entry like the one just shown in connection with the aging procedure.

Percentage of Credit Sales

In the **percentage of credit sales** procedure, the estimate of uncollectible accounts expense is based on a historically determined percentage of each period's *credit* sales. Assume, for instance, that Liston Corporation's experience indicates that ultimate uncollectible accounts average about 2 percent of its credit sales. If credit sales in 1998 were $110,000, the uncollectible accounts expense for 1998 would be $2,200 ($110,000 × .02). The end-of-year adjusting entry would be as follows:

Uncollectible accounts expense 2,200
    Allowance for uncollectible accounts   2,200

---

[7]Some accountants prefer to report uncollectible accounts expense as a deduction from sales, since it represents that portion of reported sales not expected to be collected. In practice, however, the tendency is to consider uncollectibles expense as an administrative expense, since granting of credit and collection are management responsibilities.

[8]A debit balance, before adjustment, is possible because the entry to record uncollectible accounts expense is made at the *end* of the period, while actual write-offs of accounts are made periodically *during* the period. In other words, the expense of $1,723 in the example above includes $200 of receivables *known* to be uncollectible plus $1,523 of receivables *estimated* to be uncollectible.

EXHIBIT 8-4	Accounts Receivable Aging Schedule

Larson Corporation

Customer	Balance 12/31/98	Age of Account (Days)			
		Less than 30	30–60	61–90	Over 90
Willis Corporation	$ 3,000	$3,000			
Janson Company	4,000	1,900	$2,100		
Hillard, Inc.	2,000			$1,600	$400
Nason, Ltd.	4,000		2,000	2,000	
Lind, Inc.	1,000	1,000			
Ross, Ltd.	700			700	
Total	$14,700	$5,900	$4,100	$4,300	$400

Age (Days)	Amount	Percent Estimated Uncollectible	Required Ending Balance in Allowance Account
Less than 30	$ 5,900	3%	$ 177
30–60	4,100	6	246
61–90	4,300	20	860
Over 90	400	60	240
Total	$14,700		$1,523

CONCEPTUAL

The percentage of credit sales procedure emphasizes good matching on the income statement, whereas the percentage of receivables procedures emphasizes good matching on the balance sheet.

This uncollectible accounts expense of $2,200 would be reported on the income statement. The allowance account balance would be reported as a deduction from accounts receivable. Note that this procedure emphasizes associating (matching) uncollectible accounts expense with sales revenue. The ending balance in the allowance account is the balance before the adjusting entry plus the amount of the adjustment to the allowance.

The first two procedures are concerned with good matching on the balance sheet because they emphasize valuation of the receivables at net realizable value. The percentage of credit sales procedure is concerned with good matching on the income statement because of its emphasis on determining uncollectible accounts expense.

A Summary of the Allowance Method

The two procedures that adjust the allowance account to a desired ending balance are sometimes called *balance sheet approaches* because both emphasize valuation of the receivables at net realizable value on the balance sheet. The percentage of credit sales procedure sometimes is called an *income statement approach* because it emphasizes matching uncollectible accounts expense against current revenues. Regardless of the procedure followed, if experience indicates that the percentages used in making accruals are too low or too high, the percentages should be adjusted accordingly. These adjustments represent changes in estimates; their impact on income should be disclosed in the financial statements in the period of the change.[9]

Writing Off a Customer's Account

Under all three procedures for applying the allowance method, an actual write-off of a customer's account has no effect on the net carrying value (book value) of accounts

[9]"Accounting Changes," *Opinions of the Accounting Principles Board No. 20* (New York: AICPA, 1971).

receivable. Refer back to Exhibit 8–4. Note that accounts receivable and the related allowance would appear on the balance sheet as follows:

Accounts receivable	**$14,700**
Less: Allowance for uncollectible accounts	**(1,523)**
Accounts receivable (net)	**$13,177**

Now assume that in early January 1999, it was determined that Ross, Ltd., could not pay the $700 owed. The following entry would be made to record the write-off of Ross's account:

Allowance for uncollectible accounts	700	
Accounts receivable		700

After the write-off, the net carrying value of total receivables would still be $13,177:

Accounts receivable ($14,700 – $700)	**$14,000**
Less: Allowance for uncollectible accounts ($1,523 – $700)	**(823)**
Accounts receivable (net)	**$13,177**

In practice, write-offs of uncollectible accounts receivable can be significant. Several years ago, for example, Montgomery Ward wrote off uncollectible accounts totaling $118.4 million, or 3.05 percent of its credit sales.

Occasionally, a customer whose account has been written off will pay all or a portion of the amount previously owed. When this occurs, the customer's account should first be restored by debiting accounts receivable and crediting the allowance account for the amount to be received. Then, cash should be debited and accounts receivable credited for the amount received.

Summary of Accounts Receivable

We have seen how accounts receivable should be measured initially; when they should be recognized; and how sales discounts, sales returns, and uncollectible accounts should be accounted for and reported. These procedures, when viewed together, determine how accounts receivable are reported on the balance sheet. The overall conceptual picture appears in Exhibit 8–5. Next, we will discuss accounting issues related to short-term *notes* receivable.

SHORT-TERM (CURRENT) NOTES RECEIVABLE

Notes receivable are monetary in nature, and like other monetary items, they represent rights to receive a specified amount of cash in the future. Short-term notes receivable covering a period of one year or less are discussed in this section. Long-term notes receivable, which rely more heavily on present value concepts, are discussed in Chapter 14.

Though notes receivable may arise from credit extended in a sales transaction, most notes originate from lending transactions. In contrast to an account receivable, which arises from an informal agreement between a buyer and seller, a note receivable is a written contractual agreement in which the maker—the party who issues the note and who must pay it at maturity—agrees to pay a specified sum of money to the payee under the terms of the note.

Short-term notes receivable may be either interest-bearing or non-interest-bearing. **Interest-bearing notes** usually have an interest rate that corresponds to the market rate of interest for notes of similar risk. **Non-interest-bearing notes** have no stated interest rate. The *principal* or *face value* of a note is the amount printed on the note. The amount to be received when the note is due is called the *maturity*

EXHIBIT 8-5	Valuation and Reporting of Accounts Receivable: A Summary

When recognized: ⟶ Governed by the realization principle

How measured:

   Initially: ⟶ Current cash equivalent exchange price (or present value if discount is material)

Events reducing initial measurement:

   Returns: ⟶ Allowance established (allowance for returns)

   Uncollectibles: ⟶ Allowance established (allowance for uncollectible accounts)

Balance sheet reporting: ⟶ Net realizable value (amount expected to be collected)

value. For an interest-bearing note, the maturity value equals the principal amount plus interest during the term of the note. For a non-interest-bearing note, the maturity value is the principal amount.

Calculating Interest on Short-Term Notes

Appendix A to this text illustrates interest calculations. For simple interest, which is most applicable for short-term notes of one year or less, interest is calculated as follows:

$$I = \text{Principal} \times \text{Interest rate per year} \times \text{Time (portion of a year)}$$

An interest rate specified by the note, unless otherwise stated, is assumed to be an annual rate. For example, if Craig Robison has a note receivable with a face value of $1,000 due in nine months at an interest rate of 8 percent, the interest for nine months is calculated as follows:

$$I = \$1,000 \ (.08)(9/12)$$
$$= \$60$$

Thus, the amount the note will pay when it matures (its maturity value) is $1,060.

When lenders accept non-interest-bearing notes, they usually lend an amount that is less than the note's maturity value. For example, assume that First National Bank, which has a 10 percent discount rate, accepts a customer's one-year, $2,000, non-interest-bearing note. The bank will deduct 10 percent interest from the note's maturity value and give the customer $1,800 [$2,000 − .10 ($2,000)].[10]

Accounting for Short-Term Notes and Interest

To illustrate accounting for short-term notes and interest, refer back to the Craig Robison example. Since Mr. Robison is the payee of the note, he would record the note receivable and the cash loaned as follows:

Note receivable	1,000	
Cash		1,000

When the note is due, Mr. Robison would record the interest revenue and receipt of the note's maturity value as follows:

Cash.	1,060	
Note receivable		1,000
Interest revenue ($1,000 × .08 × 9/12).		60

---

[10]Notice that, because the bank deducts the 10 percent interest (the discount) in advance, the effective rate of interest on the note is 11.11 percent ($200 ÷ $1,800).

If Mr. Robison's accounting period ended before the note was due, an end-of-period adjusting entry would be necessary to accrue a portion of the $60 interest revenue for the period the note had been outstanding. The maker of the note would make a similar accounting entry to record accrued interest expense and interest payable.

In the First National Bank example, the bank would make the following entry on the date of the loan:

Notes receivable	1,800	
Cash		1,800

When the note is paid by the maker, First National would make the following entry:

Cash.	2,000	
Interest revenue		200
Notes receivable		1,800

Adjusting entries to accrue the interest revenue would require a debit to notes receivable and a credit to interest revenue.

TRANSFERS OF RECEIVABLES

Receivables, whether accounts receivable or notes receivable, are financial assets because they convey a right to receive cash from another party (a customer or lender). As such, receivables may be sold, put into trust, or used as collateral for a loan. Companies often use accounts and notes receivable to obtain immediate cash, rather than waiting to collect the amount due under the terms of the receivable. Some years ago, for example, J. C. Penney sold several million dollars of its credit card receivables to Citicorp. Citicorp received as income from Penney a service charge plus interest on the purchased receivables.

A good illustration of the circumstances in which a company might use receivables to obtain cash quickly follows:

> Last year Jennifer Barclay, founder of Blue Fish, a Frenchtown, N.J. apparel business, was looking for credit to keep up with her company's growth. Though profitable at revenues of $5 million, Blue Fish was struggling to pay its suppliers on time. "Our customers weren't paying us fast enough," Barclay says. Fortunately, she found a solution that didn't require her to sell a single stitch of equity. What Blue Fish *does* sell is its accounts receivable—to a "factor."[11]

A certified factoring specialist explains further:

> A typical business that extends credit will have 10 percent to 20 percent of its annual sales tied up in accounts receivable at any given time. Just think for a moment about how much money is tied up in 60 days worth of receivables. You can't pay the electric bill or this week's payroll with a customer's invoice. But you can sell that invoice for the cash to meet those obligations.[12]

Several methods may be used to generate cash from receivables, ranging from using receivables as collateral for a loan to selling receivables outright.

Methods of Transfer

All uses of receivables to obtain immediate cash fall within the general category of **transfers of financial assets.** Pledging, assigning, factoring, securitizing receivables,

5 Identify various transactions in which receivables are used to obtain immediate cash and describe the general objective in accounting for such transactions.

---

[11]"How to Pick a Factor," *Inc.,* February 1994, p. 89.
[12]"Alternative Financing," *Black Enterprise,* September 1994, p. 28.

and discounting of notes receivable are all transfers of financial assets made to raise immediate cash. Under a **pledging** arrangement, for example, receivables are used as security or collateral for a loan. In case of default, the lender has a legal right to the receivables in satisfaction of the debt.

Receivables also serve as collateral in an **assignment** of receivables. The assignor (the borrower) agrees that the proceeds from the collection of the assigned receivables will be used to pay back the loan. Legally, the assignment gives the assignee (the lender) the right to collect the receivables. Customers' payments may be made to the assignor, or they may be made directly to the assignee. To provide some additional security or "cushion" for the loan agreement, the assignee usually lends less than the face amount of the receivables. In addition, the assignee usually deducts a finance fee or service charge, as well as interest on the unpaid balance.

CONCEPTUAL

Most factoring arrangements are outright sales of receivables.

Factoring of receivables, as in the Blue Fish example, is common in many industries, such as clothing and textiles. Most factoring arrangements are outright sales of receivables. Cash receipts are accelerated by transferring (factoring) the receivables to financial institutions known as *factors*. Collection risks shift to the factor, usually without recourse to the transferor in the event of a loss. The factoring company earns income by paying the transferor less than the expected realizable value of the receivables. The difference between the amount received by the transferor and the expected realizable value of the receivables is composed of a factoring fee (which may be relatively high if the factor bears the collection risks) and interest over the waiting period before the receivables are collected. Customers of the transferor usually are notified of the factoring arrangement and make payments directly to the factor.

Financial assets such as mortgage loans, automobile loans, trade receivables, credit card receivables, and other revolving charge accounts are commonly transferred in **securitizations.** In a typical securitization, the transferor transfers a portfolio of financial assets to a special-purpose entity, often a trust. **Beneficial interests** in the special-purpose entity (rights to receive all or some of the cash inflows of the special-purpose entity) are sold to investors, and the proceeds from the sale are used to pay the transferor for the receivables. In "pass-through" and "pay-through" securitizations, receivables are transferred to the special-purpose entity, and no further transfers are made. All cash collections are paid to the holders of beneficial interests in the special-purpose entity. In "revolving" securitizations, receivables are transferred both at the beginning of the securitization and periodically thereafter for a specified period (commonly three to eight years). During this specified period, the special-purpose entity uses most of the cash collections to purchase additional receivables from the transferor on prearranged terms. An example of a securitization is described in the notes to the 1994 financial statements of Dixie Yarns, Inc.:

> On October 15, 1993, the Company entered into a seven-year agreement to sell an undivided interest in a revolving pool of its trade accounts receivable. At December 31, 1994 and December 25, 1993, a $45,000,000 interest had been sold under this agreement and is reflected as a reduction of accounts receivable in the accompanying consolidated balance sheets. Fees of this program were fixed at 6.08 percent per annum on the amount of the interest sold plus administrative fees typical in such transactions. These costs, which were approximately $2,983,000 for 1994 and $574,000 for 1993, are included in other (income) expense—net.

Occasionally, a company may transfer short-term notes receivable to a third party, usually a bank, to obtain cash. This type of transfer of financial assets is called **discounting notes receivable.** If the transfer is **without recourse,** the transferor has no further obligation should the maker of the note fail to pay the bank on the note's maturity date. Most notes transferred are discounted **with recourse,** which means the transferor is contingently liable and must pay the amount due in the event the maker of the note defaults on payment at maturity. The interest the bank earns from holding the note to maturity equals the discount, or the difference between the proceeds paid to the transferor of the note and the amount due on the note at maturity.

Next, we will discuss the accounting standards for transfers of financial assets. Numerical examples of some of the types of transfers of receivables just described will illustrate the various accounting treatments.

Accounting Standards for Transfers

A desire on the part of many companies to engage in "off-balance-sheet financing" has created a gray area between sales and borrowing transactions. That is, is a transfer of receivables in exchange for cash a *sale* transaction, or is it a *borrowing* transaction? The distinction is important because in a sale transaction, the receivables are removed from the seller's books and a gain or loss on the sale recorded by the seller. In a borrowing transaction, a liability is recorded on the transferor's books, and the receivables serve merely as collateral for the loan.

Accounting for transfers of financial assets in which the transferor retains no continuing involvement with the transferee or the transferred assets is straightforward—the transferred assets have been sold. But the appropriate accounting for transfers in which there is a continuing involvement by the transferor—such as when there is an opportunity for recourse by the transferee, an agreement to reacquire by the transferor, or a pledge of collateral—depends on the extent of the transferor's control over the transferred assets. *The general objective in accounting for transfers of financial assets by the involved entities is that each entity should "recognize only assets it controls and liabilities it has incurred" and "derecognize" (remove from its balance sheet) assets over which it has surrendered control and liabilities it has extinguished.* The FASB describes this type of accounting as a "financial-components approach that focuses on control."

■▲ CONCEPTUAL

Transfers of financial assets in which the transferor has no continuing involvement are sales of those assets.

Sales of Receivables

As we have seen, a transfer of financial assets (e.g., receivables) in which the transferor surrenders control over those financial assets should be accounted for as a sale. The transferor is considered to have surrendered control over the transferred assets, and a sale of the assets to have occurred, only if *all* the following conditions are met:

1. The transferred assets have been isolated from the transferor (put beyond the reach of the transferor under all circumstances, even bankruptcy).

2. Transferees have the right to pledge or exchange either the transferred assets or beneficial interests in the transferred assets. (A beneficial interest is the right to receive all or portions of the cash flows from the transferred assets received by a trust or other entity.)

3. The transferor does not maintain effective control over the transferred assets through an agreement to repurchase or redeem them before their maturity.[13]

6 List the three conditions that must be met for a transfer of receivables to be considered a sale of assets.

If a transfer of receivables meets all three of these conditions for treatment as a sale, the transferor (seller) should:

1. Remove (derecognize) the receivables from its balance sheet accounts.

2. Recognize all assets obtained and liabilities incurred in connection with the sale.

3. Measure all assets received and liabilities incurred from the sale at fair value (or at some alternative amount, if estimating fair value is not practicable).

---

[13]"Accounting for Transfers and Servicing of Financial Assets and Extinguishment of Liabilities," *Statement of Financial Accounting Standards No. 125* (Norwalk, Conn.: FASB, 1996), para. 9.

4. Recognize a gain or loss on the sale equal to the difference between the proceeds of the sale and the book value of the receivables sold.[14]

To illustrate the accounting for a transfer of receivables that is considered a sale, consider a normal factoring arrangement. Assume that Drake Corporation transfers without recourse to Factors, Inc., accounts receivable with a book value of $94,000 (face amount of $100,000 less an allowance for uncollectible accounts of $6,000). Because the transfer is without recourse, Factors, Inc., charges a comparatively high factoring fee equal to 12 percent of the receivables' face value, plus interest of $2,000 to compensate for the waiting period before the receivables are collected. After the transfer, Drake has no access to the receivables, Factors, Inc., is free to pledge or exchange the receivables, and Drake has no effective control over the transferred receivables. Drake's entry to record this *sale* of receivables would be:

Cash [$100,000 − (.12 × $100,000) − $2,000]	86,000	
Allowance for uncollectible accounts	6,000	
Loss on sale of receivables ($94,000 − $86,000)	8,000	
Accounts receivable		100,000

Even if the receivables were transferred to Factors, Inc., *with* recourse, as long as the three conditions for treatment as a sale are met, Drake would record the transfer as a sale of receivables. For example, assume all the same facts just presented, except that Drake has accepted a recourse obligation (agreed to reimburse the factor) for uncollectible receivables up to a fair value of $2,000. Drake's liability related to the recourse obligation must be recorded as part of the sale entry (and would reduce the proceeds of the sale, thereby increasing the loss) as shown below:

Cash	86,000	
Allowance for uncollectible accounts	6,000	
Loss on sale of receivables	10,000	
Recourse obligation		2,000
Accounts receivable		100,000

As mentioned earlier, the typical securitization arrangement (such as in the example of Dixie Yarns, Inc.) would meet the three necessary conditions for treatment as a sale of receivables. The same is also true in most cases in which notes receivable are discounted, whether with or without recourse. Entries to record the sale of receivables transferred in qualifying securitizations or through discounting of notes receivable would be similar to those for factored receivables.

Nonsale Transfers (Borrowings)

1 **Describe the appropriate accounting for a transfer of receivables that is not considered a sale.**

If a transfer of receivables in exchange for cash or other consideration (except for a beneficial interest in the transferred assets) *does not meet* all three conditions for treatment as a sale, the transferor and transferee must account for the transfer as a **secured borrowing,** with the transferred receivables serving as a pledge of collateral.[15] Appropriate accounting for collateral by the debtor and the lender (the secured party) in a secured borrowing depends on (1) whether the lender has control over the collateral and (2) the lender's and debtor's rights and obligations arising from the collateral arrangement.

If either (1) the lender *is not free* to sell or repledge the collateral or (2) the debtor *has the right and ability* to redeem the collateral on short notice, the debtor should continue to carry the collateral receivables among its other receivables, and the lender should not record the pledged assets (the collateral receivables) on its books.[16] To illustrate, assume that on March 1, Wilson, Inc., assigns $75,000 in

---

[14]Ibid., para. 11.
[15]Ibid., para. 12.
[16]Ibid., para. 15b.

accounts receivable to First Finance as collateral for a loan. First Finance lends Wilson cash equal to 80 percent of the face amount of the assigned receivables, charges a finance fee equal to 4 percent of the face amount of the loan, charges 1 percent interest per month on the unpaid loan balance, and is not free to sell or repledge the assigned receivables. Wilson's customers continue to make their payments to Wilson. The following entries show how Wilson would account for the March 1 loan transaction, and for subsequent collection and payment transactions.

March 1	Cash ($75,000 × .8 × .96).	57,600	
	Finance fee expense (.04 × $60,000)	2,400	
	Payable to First Finance		60,000

The above entry is to record the loan. The fact that $75,000 of accounts receivable are assigned should be clearly indicated in a footnote, since the proceeds from their collection are restricted specifically for repayment of the loan from First Finance.

March 31	Collected receivables totaling $40,000. Paid this amount to First Finance as interest and a reduction in the payable.		
	Cash	40,000	
	Accounts receivable.		40,000
	Interest expense (.01 × $60,000)	600	
	Payable to First Finance	39,400	
	Cash		40,000
April 30	Collected receivables totaling $30,000. Paid the interest and balance due to First Finance.		
	Cash	30,000	
	Accounts receivable.		30,000
	Interest expense [.01 × ($60,000 – $39,400)]. .	206	
	Payable to First Finance	20,600	
	Cash		20,806

If, instead, Wilson's customers had remitted directly to First Finance, and Wilson had received periodic reports from First Finance, Wilson would make the following entries at the end of March and April:

March 31	Interest expense	600	
	Payable to First Finance	39,400	
	Accounts receivable.		40,000
April 30	Cash	9,194	
	Interest expense	206	
	Payable to First Finance	20,600	
	Accounts receivable.		30,000

In Wilson's balance sheet, the amount payable to First Finance is offset against (deducted from) accounts receivable because a portion of the receivables is restricted specifically for retirement of the loan.

To give another example of accounting for a secured borrowing, assume that Harlen, Inc., enters a two-month agreement under which it borrows $94,000 from New Bank and transfers accounts receivable with a face of $100,000 and a related $6,000 allowance for uncollectible accounts to New Bank. The agreement calls for Harlen's customers to send their payments directly to New Bank. Harlen agrees to pay New Bank for any portion of the loan New Bank is unable to recover from collection of the receivables during the two-month agreement. New Bank is not permitted to sell or repledge the receivables. Although New Bank loans Harlen $94,000, New Bank actually gives Harlen only $87,300. This amount is calculated by subtracting an assumed finance fee equal to 5 percent of the loan amount and interest of $2,000 (to compensate for the period until the receivables are collected) from the amount of the loan [$87,300 = $94,000 – ($94,000 × .05) – $2,000].

Harlen still has effective control over the receivables because of the recourse agreement. Therefore, this transaction must be accounted for as a secured borrowing, in which the debtor (Harlen) should continue to carry the receivables on its books. To record the receipt of cash from New Bank, Harlen would make the following entry:

Cash.	87,300	
Fees and interest expense ($4,700 + $2,000)	6,700	
Payable to New Bank		94,000

As customers' payments are received, New Bank would notify Harlen, which would debit the payable to New Bank and credit accounts receivable for the amount collected. Notification by New Bank that an account is uncollectible would result in a write-off of an uncollectible account on Harlen's books. For example, if at the end of the first month, New Bank notifies Harlen that $50,000 of receivables have been collected and $3,500 of receivables due are uncollectible, Harlen would make the following entry:

Payable to New Bank.	50,000	
Allowance for uncollectible accounts	3,500	
Accounts receivable		53,500

Assume that as of the end of the second month of this agreement, New Bank has collected a total of $94,000 and has determined that a total of $6,000 of the accounts are uncollectible. Given these facts, at the end of month two Harlen would make the following entry:

Payable to New Bank.	44,000	
Allowance for uncollectible accounts	2,500	
Accounts receivable		46,500

Alternatively, if New Bank has collected a total of only $93,000 by the end of the second month, with the remaining $3,500 of receivables judged to be uncollectible, Harlen would make the following entry at the end of the two-month agreement:

Payable to New Bank.	44,000	
Allowance for uncollectible accounts	3,500	
Accounts receivable		46,500
Cash		1,000

In a secured borrowing situation in which the secured party (the lender) *is free* to sell or repledge the collateral and the debtor does not have the right and ability to redeem the collateral on short notice, the debtor is *required* to reclassify receivables that are collateral assets and report them separately from other receivables not so encumbered in its balance sheet.[17] The secured party should recognize the collateral as its asset, record it at fair value, and also recognize its obligation to return the receivables to the debtor.

Assume, for example, that Neas Corporation has a $20,000, 9 percent, 60-day note receivable that it received from a customer in settlement of an account. After holding the note for 24 days, Neas Corporation discounts the note with recourse at Local Bank, which has a 10 percent discount rate. Under the recourse terms, if the maker of the note fails to pay the maturity value to Local Bank in full on the maturity date, Neas Corporation must pay the maturity value to Local Bank. Local Bank is free to sell or pledge the note, but Neas does not have the right to redeem the note on short notice.

---

[17]Ibid., para. 15a.

Local Bank calculates the discount on the note and the proceeds to be received by Neas in the following way:

Face amount of the note...	**$20,000**
Interest to maturity ($20,000 × .09 × 60/360).............................	**300**
Maturity value...	**$20,300**
Less: discount ($20,300 ×.10 × 36/360)...............................	**(203)**
Proceeds to Neas..	**$20,097**

The discount of $203 is the interest Local Bank will earn from holding the note for the remaining 36 days until maturity.

Neas would record the discounting transaction as follows:

Cash..	20,097	
Payable to Local Bank.........................		20,000
Interest revenue..............................		97

In addition, Neas should reclassify the discounted note:

Discounted notes receivable......................	20,000	
Notes receivable.............................		20,000

When the maker of the note pays Local Bank, Neas will be relieved of the liability and should make the following entry:

Payable to Local Bank..........................	20,000	
Discounted notes receivable		20,000

If the maker of the note fails to pay Local Bank on the maturity date, Neas must pay the maturity value of $20,300 and should make the following entry:

Receivable from customer	20,300	
Payable to Local Bank	20,000	
Discounted notes receivable		20,000
Cash		20,300

If Neas is unable to collect the receivable from the customer, the note should be written off as uncollectible.

Default on a Secured Borrowing

If the debtor defaults under the terms of a secured contract and is no longer entitled to redeem collateral assets, the debtor should remove them from its balance sheet accounts. (To the extent that the lender has not already done so, it should recognize the collateral as an asset at fair value.) For example, assume that Wallace, Inc., pledged $5,000 book value of accounts receivable ($5,500 face, with an allowance of $500) as collateral for a $5,000 loan from East Bank. At the due date, Wallace failed to repay the loan. Under the loan terms, East Bank would take possession of and legal title to the accounts receivable. Wallace would record its default as follows:

Payable to East Bank...........................	5,000	
Allowance for uncollectible accounts	500	
Accounts receivable		5,500

Our discussion of cash and current receivables is complete. Part B addresses accounting for current payables and contingencies. It begins with a discussion of the general nature of liabilities and their valuation. Part B then focuses specifically on accounting for current payables and closes with a discussion of accounting for and reporting of contingencies.

Part B • Current Payables and Contingencies

C O N C E P T U A L

Monetary liabilities are obligations to pay fixed or determinable sums of money.

Monetary liabilities are obligations to pay a sum of money, the amount of which is fixed or determinable without reference to the future prices of specific goods and services. The current monetary liabilities discussed in this part of the chapter include trade accounts payable, notes payable, collections made for third parties, various accrued liabilities, income taxes payable, and bonuses payable. In order to cover all current liabilities in this part, we also discuss accounting for customer prepayments and deposits. The obligations (usually short-term) resulting from prepayments and deposits are classified as nonmonetary items, because meeting those obligations requires the delivery of goods or services rather than cash payments. Part B concludes with a thorough discussion of accounting for contingencies.

THE CLASSIFICATION AND VALUATION OF LIABILITIES

In Chapter 2, **liabilities** were defined as probable future sacrifices of economic benefits arising from present obligations of a particular entity to transfer assets or provide services to other entities in the future as a result of past transactions or events.[18] According to this definition, a liability has three basic characteristics:

1. There is a present duty or responsibility to one or more other entities that is expected to be settled by the transfer of assets or the provision of services in the future.

2. This duty or responsibility obligates a particular entity.

3. The transaction or event that caused the entity to be obligated has already occurred.

Classification

Define current liabilities and describe the amount at which they normally are recorded.

In the balance sheet, liabilities usually are divided into two classifications: (1) current, or short-term, liabilities and (2) noncurrent, or long-term, liabilities. The distinction between current and noncurrent liabilities is based on the period that will pass before the obligation will be settled. A **current liability** (current payable) requires the transfer of resources or the incurrence of another liability within the *longer* of one fiscal year or one operating cycle. This definition means that a current liability is an obligation that is expected to be settled by the use of resources classified as current assets, or by the creation of another current liability. All liabilities that are not classified as current are considered noncurrent.

C O N C E P T U A L

The entity's operating cycle determines which liabilities are current.

Whether an obligation is a current or noncurrent liability depends on the operating cycle of the accounting entity. It is possible for a particular type of obligation to be a current liability for one entity and a noncurrent liability for another. For example, a note payable due in three years would be a noncurrent liability for most companies, but would be classified as a current liability for a distiller of seven-year whiskey because of the distiller's more-than-seven-year operating cycle.

While an obligation that must be settled within the longer of one year or one operating cycle normally is classified as a current liability, there are exceptions to

---

[18]"Elements of Financial Statements," *Statement of Financial Accounting Concepts No. 6* (Stamford, Conn.: FASB, 1985), para. 35.

this rule. If the debtor intends to refinance a short-term obligation on a long-term basis, and can demonstrate the ability to refinance the obligation, the obligation should be classified as a noncurrent liability. The debtor can satisfactorily demonstrate the ability to refinance the obligation by either (1) refinancing on a long-term basis during the period between the balance sheet date and the date the financial statements are issued or (2) entering into an agreement, before the financial statements are issued, that clearly permits refinancing on a long-term basis.[19]

If refinancing occurs, the amount of short-term obligation that should be included in noncurrent liabilities should not exceed the proceeds from the new long-term obligation incurred, or the capital stock issued, to retire the short-term obligation. For example, assume that Davis Company had $8 million of short-term notes payable as of December 31, the end of its fiscal year. Also assume that before issuing its balance sheet, Davis issued $5 million of 10-year bonds, with the intention of using the proceeds of the bond issue to liquidate the short-term notes payable at maturity. Since the bond issue was for $5 million, only $5 million of the short-term notes should be reclassified from current liabilities to noncurrent liabilities on the December 31 balance sheet. The remaining $3 million of the short-term notes payable would continue to be reported as a current liability.

If the ability to refinance is demonstrated by entering into a long-term financing agreement before the balance sheet is issued, the amount of short-term obligation excluded from current liabilities on the balance sheet should not exceed the amount available for refinancing under the financing agreement. If the funds obtainable under the financing agreement fluctuate in proportion to some factor, such as the value of collateral, the amount of short-term obligation excluded from current liabilities should be limited to the *minimum* amount expected to be available for refinancing. For example, assume that the financing agreement limits the amount that can be borrowed to no more than the replacement cost of inventory, which is pledged as collateral and is expected to have a replacement cost ranging from $3 million to $4.5 million during the period beginning with the maturity date of the refinanced short-term obligation. Since the minimum amount expected to be available for refinancing is $3 million, only $3 million of short-term obligations should be reclassified from current liabilities to noncurrent liabilities on the balance sheet.

For a financing agreement to be acceptable evidence of the ability to refinance, the agreement must meet *all* the following conditions:

1. The agreement must not expire within the longer of one operating cycle or one year from the date of the balance sheet, and it must not be cancelable, except for violation of a provision with which compliance is objectively determinable.

2. There must be no violation or evidence of violation of any provision in the agreement before the balance sheet is issued.

3. The lender or investor is expected to be financially capable of honoring the agreement.

Valuation

Theoretically, every liability should be valued at the present value of the services or assets that must be given up in the future to settle the obligation.[20] However, many current liabilities are due within very short periods, so their present value is not materially different from the future payment amount. Therefore, most current liabilities are customarily recorded at their future payment amounts (or face

> **9**
> State the accounting and evidence issues related to short-term obligations expected to be refinanced.

> **CONCEPTUAL**
> Although all liabilities should be recorded at present value, for practical reasons most current liabilities are recorded at their future payment amounts.

---

[19]"Classification of Short-Term Obligations Expected to Be Refinanced," *Statement of Financial Accounting Standards No. 6* (Stamford, Conn.: FASB, 1975).
[20]The appropriate interest rate to be used in calculating the present value would incorporate both a risk factor and a factor that reflects expectations about the future purchasing power of the dollar.

amounts) rather than at their present values. This concession to practical considerations, such as expediency and materiality, results in minor overstatements of current liabilities before their due dates.

Although all current (short-term) liabilities must have the three characteristics of liabilities presented earlier (page 410), other characteristics may vary. The existence and amounts of some current liabilities are determined by contracts or by the transactions in which they arise. The amounts of other current liabilities must be estimated. While either the existence or the amount, or both, of some current liabilities depend on operating results, still other current liabilities, called *contingent liabilities,* are uncertain as to their existence, amount, or both. They are contingent instead on the outcome of some future event, such as a court settlement. Because of the differences among types of current liabilities, our discussion of current liabilities is divided into (1) determinable current liabilities, (2) current liabilities dependent on operating results, and (3) contingencies.

Current liabilities normally are presented as the first group of items in the liabilities section of the balance sheet. This presentation follows the traditional practice of ordering items in the balance sheet according to their liquidity. Current liabilities should not be offset against current assets that may be used to liquidate them. The General Electric balance sheet in Appendix B of the text provides an example of how current liabilities are reported. Another example is shown in Exhibit 8–6.

10 Identify the three general categories of current liabilities and discuss the nature of the liabilities in each category.

DETERMINABLE CURRENT LIABILITIES

Determinable current liabilities are known with certainty to exist as of the balance sheet date, and the amount ultimately to be paid is known with certainty or can be reasonably estimated. In most cases the existence, amounts to be paid, and due dates of determinable current liabilities are prescribed by written or implied contracts. Therefore, the primary accounting problem related to most determinable current liabilities is simply to be certain that they are recorded and are properly classified in the balance sheet.

Determinable current liabilities include trade accounts payable, current notes payable, current maturities of long-term obligations, callable obligations, cash dividends payable, collections for third parties, accrued liabilities (e.g., accrued wages payable), and prepayments or deposits from customers.

Trade Accounts Payable

Trade accounts payable, usually called **accounts payable,** arise when an entity purchases goods, supplies, or services in the normal course of business but does not pay for them immediately. Because the time lag between the time of purchase and the time of payment generally is short (often less than 60 days), accounts payable normally are recorded at their face amount rather than at their present value. Accounts payable can be recorded net of purchase discounts (sometimes called cash discounts). Alternatively, an allowance for purchase discounts can be deducted from gross accounts payable in the balance sheet to obtain a proper valuation of accounts payable. A typical purchase entry for a company that has a perpetual inventory system and that records accounts payable net of purchase discounts follows. A gross purchase price of $1,000 and payment terms of 2%/10, net 30 are assumed. Thus, the net purchase price is $980:

Inventory 980
    Accounts payable 980

The amount and due date of an account payable normally are stated in the invoice from the seller. Usually, accounts payable and purchases are recorded when title passes to the buyer. It is important that purchases and the corresponding account

EXHIBIT 8–6	Reporting of Current Liabilities

Caterpiller, Inc.
Partial Consolidated Statement of Financial Position
December 31, 1995
(dollars in millions)

	1995	1994
Liabilities		
Current liabilities:		
Short-term borrowings	$ 1,174	$ 740
Accounts payable and accrued expenses	2,579	2,624
Accrued wages, salaries, and employee benefits	875	1,047
Dividends payable	68	50
Deferred and current income taxes payable	91	144
Long-term debt due within one year (*note 6B*)	1,262	893
Total current liabilities	$ 6,049	$ 5,498
Long-term debt due after one year (*note 6B*)	3,964	4,270
Liability for postemployment benefits	3,393	3,548
Deferred income taxes.	36	23
Total liabilities	$13,442	$13,339

Note 6B

B. Long-term Debt: Long-term debt, including that due within one year and classified as current, totaled $5,226 million at December 31, 1995: $2,205 million related to *Machinery and Engines*, and $3,021 million related to *Financial Products*. This includes $294 million of commercial paper outstanding at December 31, 1995, which was classified as long-term debt due after one year in conjunction with *Financial Products'* revolving credit agreement. The aggregate amounts of maturities and sinking fund requirements of long-term debt during each of the years 1996 through 2000 are:

(*millions of dollars*)	1996	1997	1998	1999	2000
Machinery and Engines	$ 156	$ 129	$ 41	$ 61	$ 169
Financial Products . . .	1,106	711	486	238	82
	$1,262	$ 840	$ 527	$ 299	$ 251

payable not be misstated. Such errors affect both the buyer's income statement (via purchases) and balance sheet (via accounts payable).

Short-Term (Current) Notes Payable

Current notes payable are written promissory notes. The maker of the note promises to pay the face amount of the note at the due date, which also is called the maturity date. The note may or may not specify an interest rate—called the stated, nominal, or contract interest rate—to be applied to the face value of the note. If an interest rate is stated, it may or may not be the same as the prevailing interest rate in the money market for notes of similar risk. However, the stated rate normally is the same as the market rate.

In theory, notes payable should be recorded at the present value of the cash outflows (payments of principal and interest) associated with the note. If they are not recorded at present value, the liability reported in the balance sheet will be over-stated, and interest expense reported in the income statement will be understated. If notes payable are secured by collateral, that fact, as well as the dollar amount of specific assets pledged as collateral, should be disclosed in the financial statements.

Trade Notes Payable

Trade notes payable are current obligations to suppliers for which there are written promissory notes. Trade notes payable typically arise when the terms of payment include a longer payment period than is normal for trade accounts payable. The due date, the amount of the obligation, and the interest rate, if any, usually are stated in the promissory note. The generally accepted practice is to report a trade note payable at its face amount, because the dollar amount and the relatively short duration of such a note make the difference between its face amount and its present value immaterial.

Other Short-Term Notes

Short-term notes payable typically are issued in exchange for cash or for special purposes, such as the purchase of equipment on short-term credit. Short-term notes payable usually include all current notes payable other than trade notes payable.

Sometimes cash is borrowed from a bank or other lending institution in return for a non-interest-bearing note. These short-term notes payable often are referred to as discounted notes. Instead of specifying an interest rate in a contract, the bank discounts the note and gives only the proceeds to the borrower. As described in the discussion of current receivables in part A (page 409), the bank applies its discount rate to the face amount of the note to calculate the amount of the discount, which is then subtracted from the face amount of the note to determine the proceeds. A borrower's entry to record a discounted note transaction involving a one-year, $1,000 note and a 10 percent annual bank discount rate would be as follows:

Cash ($1,000 – $100) 900
Discount on notes payable ($1,000 × .10) 100
    Notes payable.   1,000

For financial reporting purposes, the discount on notes payable is deducted from the notes payable account on the balance sheet so that the liability is reported at its present value.[21]

Current Maturities of Long-Term Obligations

An obligation previously classified as long-term but now due within the longer of one year or the company's operating cycle generally should be reclassified as a current liability. There are three exceptions to this rule: (1) when the currently due portion of the long-term obligation will be retired by the use of assets classified as noncurrent; (2) when the currently due portion of the long-term obligation will be refinanced on a long-term basis (e.g., by use of the proceeds from a long-term debt contract); and (3) when the currently due portion of the long-term obligation will be retired by issuance of capital stock. In these three cases the currently due portion of the long-term obligation should not be reclassified as a current liability. Only the portion of long-term obligations requiring the use of a current asset or

11   **Specify the circumstances under which the currently due portion of a long-term obligation would not be classified as a current liability.**

---

[21]An alternative borrower's entry for a one-year, $1,000 note and a 10 percent per year bank discount rate would be:

Cash ($1,000 – $100) 900
    Notes payable   900

In this case, there is no discount account, yet the liability is still reported at present value.

the incurrence of a current liability should be reclassified as a current liability. Exhibit 8–6 shows long-term debt due within one year among Caterpiller's current liabilities. Notice the discussion of the current portion of debt in Note 6B.

Obligations That Are Callable by the Creditor

An obligation is **callable** by the creditor at a given date if the creditor has the right on that date to demand, or to give notice of its intention to demand, repayment of the obligation owed by the debtor.[22] Companies must report as current liabilities those obligations that, by their terms, are or will be due on demand within the longer of one year or one operating cycle from the balance sheet date. Long-term obligations that are callable by the creditor because the debtor has violated a provision of the debt agreement must be classified as current liabilities. In addition, long-term obligations that will be callable within the longer of one year or one operating cycle, if the debtor's violation of a debt provision is not corrected within a specified grace period, also must be classified as current liabilities, unless it is probable that the violation will be corrected within the grace period. The only exception to these requirements occurs when the creditor has waived or subsequently lost the right to demand repayment for more than the longer of one year or one operating cycle.

Dividends Payable

Most dividends payable are determinable current liabilities. The term **dividend** is generally understood to mean a cash dividend. However, three other types of dividends also are recognized: property dividends (dividends in the form of assets other than cash), liability or scrip dividends (promissory notes to pay cash dividends at some future date), and stock dividends (dividends of shares of the company's own stock). Except for stock dividends, all these types of dividends ultimately will require the distribution of the company's assets. Therefore, declarations of dividends other than stock dividends create liabilities on the date of declaration. A stock dividend requires distribution of shares of the declaring company's own stock, which is not an asset of the company. Hence, stock dividends distributable are not liabilities.

Because **cash dividends payable, property dividends payable,** and **liability** or **scrip dividends payable** all are liabilities that will be met in a relatively short period of time, they normally appear among the current liabilities. Of course, if payment of the dividend is not expected to occur within one year or one operating cycle, whichever is longer, the dividend payable should be classified as a noncurrent liability.

Collections for Third Parties

Another determinable liability arises when an entity collects or withholds assets, usually cash, from one party for the purpose of remitting them to a third party. During the period between the time of withholding or collecting the assets and the time of remitting them to the third party, the entity that is withholding or collecting the assets has an obligation that should be reported as a liability.

Assets are collected for third parties on many occasions. Perhaps the most common examples are (1) the collection of sales taxes from customers at the time of sale and (2) the withholding of payroll-related taxes, insurance premiums, union dues, and other amounts from employees' paychecks. In these examples, as in all collections for third parties, the withholding entity acts as an agent of the third party—a

---

[22]"Classification of Obligations That Are Callable by the Creditor," *Statement of Financial Accounting Standards No. 78* (Stamford, Conn.: FASB, 1983).

government unit, an insurance company, or a labor union—and is obligated to remit the collected or withheld amounts to that third party.

When a sales tax is included in the total amount collected by the seller, the seller should make an entry including a liability, as shown in the following example. A $100 sales price and a 4 percent sales tax are assumed.

Cash.	104	
Sales revenue		100
Sales taxes payable		4

The Federal Insurance Contributions Act (FICA) requires that the employer withhold and remit to the federal government 7.65 percent of the first $65,400 of an employee's wages and 1.45 percent of wages in excess of $65,400. (These percentages and wage levels were effective for 1997.) This tax commonly is referred to as the *social security tax*. In addition, federal tax law, some state tax laws, and some local tax laws require employers to withhold income taxes from employees' paychecks and to remit those taxes to the appropriate governmental taxing unit. Until the withheld payroll tax is conveyed to the proper taxing unit, the employer has a current liability. A hypothetical entry to record liabilities related to payroll taxes withheld from total salaries of $70,000 (assuming that no single employee received more than $65,400 in wages) would be:

Salaries expense 70,000		
Federal, state, and local income taxes payable		
(amount assumed)	11,000	
Employee FICA taxes payable (7.65% × 70,000)	5,355	
Cash or salaries payable	53,645	

Accrued Liabilities

As you learned in principles of accounting and have seen in earlier chapters of this text, there are many types of **accrued liabilities,** all of which arise when expenses have been incurred but not yet paid as of the end of the accounting period. For example, assume a company has a December 31 fiscal year-end, and pays employee wages and rent on a building on the 15th day of each month. That company must make December 31 adjusting entries to accrue one-half month's wages expense and wages payable and one-half month's rent expense and rent payable. Although accrued liabilities are recorded in separate accounts such as wages payable and rent payable, most accrued liabilities—except for taxes payable—are combined for reporting purposes under the current liability heading "accrued liabilities" in the balance sheet.

In this chapter we discuss a few accrued liabilities that are fairly common, yet are seldom, if at all, covered in beginning accounting courses. The next three sections cover payroll taxes payable, compensated employee absences, and property taxes payable. Income taxes payable and employee bonuses payable are discussed later, in the section on current liabilities dependent on operating results.

Payroll Taxes Payable

Under the Federal Insurance Contributions Act (FICA), employers must make a contribution matching the employee's share of FICA tax. The employer's share of FICA tax (7.65 percent of employee wages to $65,400 and 1.45 percent of wages in excess of $65,400 in 1997) accrues as wages and salaries are earned by employees, and must be remitted monthly to the federal government along with the employee's withheld share. Any unremitted portion of the employer's share, as well as any unremitted employee's share withheld, should be recorded as payroll taxes payable.

The Federal Unemployment Tax Act (FUTA) imposes a tax on all employers who either (1) employ one or more individuals for some portion of a day in each of 20 weeks in the current or preceding calendar year or (2) pay $1,500 or more wages in a calendar quarter of the current or preceding calendar year. The FUTA tax for 1997 was 6.2 percent on the first $7,000 of wages paid to each employee. The employer receives a credit against the FUTA tax rate equal to the *standard* state unemployment tax rate in the state of employment. This credit is limited to 5.4 percent of taxable wages. The result of the state tax credit is that the effective FUTA tax rate normally does not exceed .8 percent (6.2 percent less the 5.4 percent credit).

Hypothetical entries for *employer* payroll tax expense and payroll taxes payable on wages of $5,000, given the FICA tax (7.65 percent), the FUTA tax (.8 percent after state unemployment tax credit), and a state unemployment tax of 5.4 percent, are:

Payroll taxes expense	692.50	
Employer FICA taxes payable (7.65% × $5,000)		382.50
FUTA taxes payable (.8% × $5,000)		40.00
State unemployment taxes payable (5.4% × $5,000). . .		270.00

When the taxes are remitted to the proper taxing units, the respective current liability accounts are debited, and cash is credited to account for settlement of the obligations.

Compensated Employee Absences

Compensated employee absences are future absences from work, such as for vacations, illnesses, and holidays, for which the employee is expected to be paid. An employer must accrue a liability for employees' rights to receive compensation for future absences when *all* the following conditions are met:[23]

12 List the conditions under which an accrual should be made for compensated employee absences.

1. The employer's obligation to pay compensation for future absences is attributable to services already rendered by the employee.

2. The employee's right to compensation for future absences is not contingent on the employee's future service (that is, the right is vested), or the right can be accumulated over time.

3. Payment of the compensation by the employer is probable.

4. The amount of compensation that will be paid for future absences can be reasonably estimated.

If conditions 1, 2, and 3 are met, but an accrual cannot be made because condition 4 is not met, that fact should be disclosed.

A modification of the general rule for accounting for compensated future absences exists for sick pay. If employees are allowed to use accumulated sick pay to take compensated time off from work, even though they are not ill, or if employees are routinely allowed to receive compensated "terminal leave" for non-vested accumulated sick pay prior to retirement, a liability must be accrued. If employees receive sick pay *only* if they are absent from work because of future illness, accrual of a liability is not required, because an obligation does not exist unless illness occurs.

The expense and accrued liability arising from an employee's right to be compensated for future absences should be recorded in the year in which the right is earned by the employee. For example, assume that at the beginning of fiscal year 1998 Foster Manufacturing Company hired 15 new employees at salaries of $500 per week. Foster's policy is to give two weeks of paid vacation for each year of work

---

[23]"Accounting for Compensated Absences," *Statement of Financial Accounting Standards No. 43* (Stamford, Conn.: FASB, 1980).

and to grant vacation time only after one full year of employment. The entry to record the wages expense and accrued vacation wages payable at the end of Foster's 1998 fiscal year would be:

Wages expense	15,000	
Vacation wages payable		15,000
(15 × $500 × 2 weeks)		

The vacation wages payable liability normally would appear among the current liabilities on Foster's 1998 balance sheet. The liability would be noncurrent to the extent that it is probable that employees will not take paid vacations during the longer of one year or one operating cycle.

Assume that Foster's new employees take their paid vacations in fiscal year 1999, at which time their rate of pay is $550 per week. Payment of their vacation wages would be recorded as follows:

Vacation wages payable	15,000	
Wages expense	1,500	
Cash (15 × $550 × 2 weeks)		16,500

Note that additional wages expense of $1,500 must be recorded in 1999 because of the $50 increase in the weekly rate of pay.

Property Taxes Payable

Property taxes based on the assessed value of real and personal property are the primary source of revenue for most local governments. There are two basic questions in accounting for property taxes:

1. When should the liability for property taxes be recorded on the taxpayer's books?

2. When should property tax expense be recognized in the taxpayer's income statement?

In practice, two different procedures are used to account for property taxes. Both recognize property tax expense over the fiscal year of the governmental taxing unit. They differ with respect to when the liability for property taxes is recorded. Under one procedure, the property taxes payable account is credited on the lien date[24] for the *entire year's* property tax obligation, because the taxes become a legal claim against the property on the lien date. Under the other procedure, property taxes payable are accrued *monthly* on the taxpayer's books during the fiscal year of the governmental taxing unit.

Recognition of the entire property tax liability on the lien date, which typically precedes the payment date, results in the recording of a debit to deferred property tax expense and a credit to property taxes payable. The debit to deferred property tax expense is conceptually troublesome, because it implies that unpaid property taxes are an asset, which of course they are not. Accruing property taxes payable monthly as each month's property tax expense is recognized avoids this recording of a nonexistent asset. Monthly accrual of property taxes payable is illustrated in the following example.

Assume that James Company's fiscal year ends on December 31. In February James receives its property tax bill for $12,000, which is based on a January 1 assessment. The government's fiscal year begins on April 1, which is the lien date for the property taxes. Taxes must be paid in equal installments on June 1 and August 1.

---

[24]The *lien date* is established by the government taxing unit and is the date on which property taxes become a lien or legal claim against the taxed property.

If property taxes are accrued monthly, the following entry would be made at the end of both April and May, the first two months of the property tax year:

Property tax expense	1,000	
Property taxes payable		1,000

When the first $6,000 payment is made on June 1, the following entry would be made:

Property taxes payable	2,000	
Deferred property tax expense	4,000	
Cash		6,000

An asset account, deferred property tax expense, would be debited for the excess of the cash payment over the amount of property taxes payable accrued by June 1. On June 30 and July 31, property tax expense for June and July would be recorded with this entry:

Property tax expense	1,000	
Deferred property tax expense		1,000

Prepayments and Deposits from Customers

A payment received from a customer before goods or services are delivered to the customer creates an obligation either to provide the goods or services or to return the **prepayment.** Prepayments from customers normally result in *nonmonetary* liabilities, because goods or services are used to settle the obligation.

An example of a prepayment would be the advance receipt of the $24 price of a one-year subscription to a monthly magazine. On receiving the cash, the seller of the magazine would record unearned revenue, a liability account representing an obligation to deliver the magazines:

Cash	24	
Unearned revenue		24

On delivery of each magazine the customer has paid for, the seller would reduce its obligation and record the revenue earned:

Unearned revenue	2	
Revenue from magazine sales		2

Deposits are payments made by customers to guarantee the performance of a contract, the delivery of services, or to guarantee against damage to or loss of property in the customer's possession. Examples include deposits made with utility companies, security deposits on apartment rentals, and deposits on returnable bottles and cans. Like prepayments, deposits normally result in a *nonmonetary* liability for the recipient of the deposit. An obligation arising from prepayments or deposits is classified as current or noncurrent depending on whether it is expected to be met within the longer of one year or one operating cycle.

CURRENT LIABILITIES DEPENDENT ON OPERATING RESULTS

The amounts of some obligations depend on the company's operating results, which cannot be known with certainty until the end of the accounting period. Perhaps the most common of the current liabilities that are dependent on operating results are income taxes payable and bonuses payable.

Income Taxes Payable

Income taxes payable are common current liabilities of corporations. They are not found on the balance sheets of sole proprietorships or partnerships because individual proprietors and partners are taxed personally for their share of the business entity's profits.

Most corporations must pay income taxes in advance of the due date in the form of an estimated tax. Payments of estimated taxes should be debited to prepaid income tax, an asset account. At the end of the accounting year an adjusting entry should be made to recognize income tax expense and reduce the prepaid income tax account. If the total tax obligation for the year exceeds the total estimated tax payments, income tax expense must be debited and income taxes payable credited for the additional obligation. If the total tax obligation for the year is less than the total estimated tax payments, a tax refund receivable account should be debited for the difference between income tax expense and prepaid income tax.

Bonuses Payable

Bonuses payable is another current liability that often is dependent on a company's operating results. Key employees often receive compensation bonuses in addition to their basic wage or salary. If bonuses are based on revenues earned or output produced, calculating the bonus due is not difficult. All that is necessary to calculate the bonus at any time is to determine the revenue or output to date that is subject to the bonus and multiply by the bonus factor. (For example, the bonus factor might be $.10 per unit produced.)

Bonus arrangements that are based on a company's income make the determination of the amount of bonus due more difficult. From the point of view of the company, bonuses paid to employees are additions to wages or salaries, and are accounted for as an expense when income for the period is calculated. Moreover, in most cases employee bonuses are considered deductible expenses for tax purposes. As such, bonuses affect taxes, which in turn affect income. Thus, there is a circular relationship between bonus and income—the bonus is dependent on the amount of income and the amount of income is dependent on the bonus expense. Various bonus plans, plus an illustrative bonus calculation, are presented in Appendix 8–1.

 ONTINGENCIES

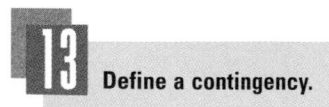

Define a contingency.

According to *Statement of Financial Accounting Standards No. 5,* a **contingency** is defined as:

> an existing condition, situation, or set of circumstances involving uncertainty as to possible gain (hereinafter a "gain contingency") or loss (hereinafter a "loss contingency") to an enterprise that will ultimately be resolved when one or more future events occur or fail to occur. Resolution of the uncertainty may confirm the acquisition of an asset or the reduction of a liability or the loss or impairment of an asset or the incurrence of a liability.[25]

Contingencies are classified as either *loss contingencies* or *gain contingencies.* Our primary concern in Part B is loss contingencies, because they are the source of contingent liabilities. However, near the end of Part B we shall briefly consider accounting for gain contingencies.

---

[25]*FASB Statement of Financial Accounting Standards No. 5,* para. 1.

Loss Contingencies

A **loss contingency** arises when an uncertain existing condition, situation, or set of circumstances will be resolved by the occurrence or nonoccurrence of a future event that may result in the impairment of an asset or the incurrence of a liability. Among the examples of loss contingencies provided by *FASB Statement No. 5* are collectibility of receivables; obligations related to product warranties and product defects; risk of loss or damage of property by fire, explosion, or other hazards; pending or threatened litigation; actual or possible claims or assessments; guarantees of the indebtedness of others; and agreements to repurchase receivables that have been sold.

14 Describe the appropriate accounting and reporting for loss contingencies, including litigation contingencies.

When a loss contingency exists, the likelihood that a future event or events will confirm the impairment of an asset or the incurrence of a liability can range from very likely to very unlikely. Within this range, the FASB has identified three levels of likelihood:

1. *Probable.* The future event or events are likely to occur.

2. *Reasonably possible.* The chance that the future event or events will occur is more than remote but less than probable.

3. *Remote.* The chance that the future event or events will occur is slight.

Under U.S. GAAP, the accounting treatment for a particular loss contingency depends in part on whether the related future event has a probable, reasonably possible, or remote chance of confirming the impairment of an asset or the incurrence of a liability.

There are three basic ways to account for and report loss contingencies:

1. *Accrual* of an estimated loss from the contingency, which should be reported in the body of the financial statements.

2. *Disclosure, but not accrual,* of the loss contingency.

3. *Neither accrual nor disclosure* of the loss contingency.

In the following sections we will examine each of these treatments.

Loss Contingencies That Should Be Accrued

An estimated loss from a loss contingency should be accrued if *both* the following conditions are met:

1. Information available before issuance of the financial statements indicates that it is *probable* that an asset has been impaired or a liability has been incurred by the date of the financial statements. It is implicit in this condition that it must be *probable* that one or more future events will occur confirming the fact of the loss.

2. The amount of loss can be reasonably estimated.

In addition to requiring accrual of a loss contingency that meets *both* of the conditions for accrual, satisfactory disclosure would include a footnote in the financial statements describing the circumstances surrounding the loss contingency. For example, in 1995 Mercer International, Inc. reported a $7 million litigation settlement expense, accompanied by the following partial footnote:

Note 12 (partial)

During 1994, the Company and its senior management were named as defendants in class action lawsuits filed in U.S. federal court. The lawsuits alleged violations of federal and state securities laws in connection with a drop in market price of the Company's common stock. The lawsuit was settled between the parties in September 1995 with final approval by the court to occur in April 1996. The Company paid $6,450,000 in cash under the terms of the settlement, which was accrued as a 1995 expense plus legal and other fees of $550,000.

In some situations, condition 1 is met, but in response to condition 2 only a *range* of loss can be reasonably estimated. For example, an unfavorable verdict on a lawsuit against the firm might be probable, but the amount of the loss can only be estimated to be in the range of $3 million to $6 million. In these situations, if some amount within the range appears to be a better estimate of the loss than any other amount within the range, that amount should be accrued through a charge to income. If no single amount within the range appears to be a better estimate of loss than any other, the minimum amount in the range should be accrued.[26]

A good example of a footnote supporting the accrual of the most likely amount within a range of possible losses is provided by Note 17 from the 1994 financial statements of Air Products and Chemicals, Inc.:

Note 17 (partial)

The company has accrued for certain environmental investigatory and noncapital remediation costs consistent with the policy set forth in Note 1. The potential exposure for such costs is estimated to range from $24 million to a reasonably possible upper exposure of $55 million. The balance sheet at 30 September 1994 includes an accrual of $29.6 million. The company does not expect that any sums it may have to pay in connection with these environmental matters would have a materially adverse effect on its consolidated financial position, nor is there any material additional exposure expected in any one year in excess of the amounts the company currently has accrued.

If there is a reasonable possibility of loss in excess of the amount accrued, the potential additional loss should be disclosed. When the minimum loss in a range of possible losses is accrued (because there is no better estimate within the range), the difference between the maximum and minimum possible losses should be disclosed as an upper limit on potential additional loss.

The next few paragraphs discuss various loss contingencies that generally should be accrued. Accruable loss contingencies other than those discussed here should be accounted for by procedures similar to those discussed.

Guarantee and Product Warranties   Most products and many services are accompanied by a guarantee or warranty that the product or service will be as advertised, and that it is free of defects. Guarantees and warranties typically are effective for some limited period, such as 90 days or one year, during which the seller or manufacturer will repair or replace the product without charge or refund some, all, or even more than the original purchase price—for example, "double your money back." Costs of warranties can be substantial, as indicated in the following excerpt from *The Wall Street Journal:*

Chrysler Corp.'s costs for providing warranty-covered repairs have shot up 48 percent per vehicle over the past two years, Chrysler planning documents indicate. As a result, the No. 3 auto maker's repair bills may exceed industry standards, analysts say.

According to documents obtained by *The Wall Street Journal,* Chrysler this year expects to spend $2.38 billion, or $959 for each vehicle it sells in 1995, on warranty repairs. That is up from $1.91 billion, or $763 a vehicle, last year and $1.45 billion, or $647 a vehicle, in 1993, the documents indicate.[27]

---

[26]"Reasonable Estimation of the Amount of a Loss: An Interpretation of *FASB Statement No. 5,*" *Interpretation No. 14* (Stamford, Conn.: FASB, 1976).
[27]"Chrysler Documents Show Sharp Rise in Costs for Warranty-Covered Repairs," *The Wall Street Journal,* October 23, 1995, pp. A3 and A5.

Guarantees or warranties create loss contingencies because there is an existing circumstance—the guarantee—that will be resolved by future events—either nonfailure of the product or failure of the product combined with a customer claim. These future events may result in the impairment of an asset or the incurrence of a liability by the seller or manufacturer.

Estimating the amount of the seller's potential warranty expense and the related liability for any *particular item* sold normally is not possible. However, on the basis of past experience, the seller can usually estimate the potential warranty expense associated with *total* sales during some period, such as a month. For example, suppose Kinney Manufacturing Company sold 10 drill presses during July for $3,000 cash each. Past experience indicates that warranty expense is equal to about 2 percent of sales revenue. In this case, entries to record the aggregate sales and estimated warranty expense and liability for July would be:

Cash	30,000	
Sales revenue		30,000
(10 × $3,000)		
Estimated warranty expense	600	
Estimated liability under warranties		600
(2% × $30,000)		

If actual costs of $400 are incurred when warranty work is done, those costs are recorded as follows:

Estimated liability under warranties.	400	
Wages payable, parts inventory, cash, etc..		400

When warranty expense is not a material item, or developing a reasonable estimate of warranty expense and the related liability during the period of sale is not possible, the cash basis of accounting for warranty expense may be used. That is, warranty expense is debited, with an offsetting credit to cash, materials, wages payable, and so forth, at the time the warranty obligations are met.

Premiums and Coupons   Sellers or manufacturers frequently give customers premiums such as cash or merchandise in exchange for coupons, labels, or wrappers accompanying purchased merchandise. Examples include cash refunds in exchange for jar labels, toys given in exchange for cereal boxtops, and household utensils given in exchange for coupons included in boxes of detergent. Since premium offers are made in an effort to increase sales of the product, the matching principle requires that the expense of premium offers be included among the expenses of the period in which the related product sales occur. When recognizing the premium expense, the accountant should also record an obligation to provide the premium to those customers who turn in their coupons before the expiration date. This obligation will be met when the premiums are distributed to the customers.

To illustrate, assume that Super Cereal Company has offered an official-size football in exchange for 10 Super Cereal boxtops plus $10. A total of 100,000 boxes of Super Cereal were sold at $3.00 each during the accounting period. Estimates are that 40 percent of the boxtops will eventually be turned in for footballs. Super Cereal must first obtain an inventory of footballs to be given out as premiums. If the company has acquired 5,000 footballs at $12.50 each, the entry to record the acquisition would be:

Inventory of premiums.	62,500	
Cash		62,500
(5,000 × $12.50)		

The entry to record sales of the 100,000 boxes of Super Cereal at $3.00 per box would be:

Cash.	300,000	
Sales revenue		300,000
(100,000 × $3.00)		

In conjunction with the current period's sales, estimated premium expense would be debited for the $2.50 per football cost (in excess of the $10 charge to the customer) for the 4,000 footballs given out or expected to be given out in exchange for boxtops (100,000 boxtops divided by 10 boxtops per football multiplied by a 40 percent return rate on the boxtops equals 4,000 footballs). Redemption of 30,000 boxtops and receipt of $30,000 in exchange for 3,000 footballs given out during the accounting period would be recorded as:

Cash.	30,000	
Premium expense (3,000 × $2.50).	7,500	
Inventory of premiums (3,000 × $12.50)		37,500

At the end of the accounting period, the adjusting entry to record the estimated premium expense and the associated obligation for premiums still outstanding that are related to the current period's sales would be:

Premium expense	2,500	
Estimated premium obligation		2,500
(1,000 × $2.50)		

Litigation, Claims, and Assessments   Accrual of loss contingencies for threatened litigation (a lawsuit not yet filed), pending litigation (a lawsuit filed but not settled), claims, or assessments is appropriate only if:

1. The cause for action occurs by the date of the financial statements.

2. Information available *before* the issuance of the financial statements indicates that it is *probable* that an asset has been impaired or a liability has been incurred as of the date of the financial statements.

3. It is possible to make a reasonable estimate of the amount of loss that may arise from the loss contingency.

Among the factors that should be considered in determining the probability that an asset has been impaired or a liability incurred are the nature of the litigation, claim, or assessment; the progress of the case; the opinions or views of management, legal counsel, and other advisers; the experiences of the entity in previous similar cases; the experiences of other entities; and any decision by management as to how the entity will respond to the lawsuit, claim, or assessment. Though legal counsel for the entity may not be able to express an opinion that the outcome will be favorable, the lack of a favorable opinion should not necessarily be interpreted to mean that an unfavorable outcome is probable.

Making a reasonable estimate of the amount of loss that may result from pending litigation is seldom possible. Even if the evidence available prior to the issuance of the financial statements suggests an unfavorable outcome for the defendant, publishing a specific estimate of a loss in the financial statements cannot reasonably be expected. To do so could weaken the company's position in the litigation. Therefore, footnote disclosure of contingencies associated with litigation is the norm. An example typical of such disclosure is provided by Note 9 of the 1994 financial statements of Icot Corporation:

Note 9. Litigation

In November 1993, an action was brought against the Company for damages related to the use of the Company's products. The plaintiff filed a suit claiming repetitive stress injuries resulting from the use of the Company's product in the course of employment with American Airlines from the period May 1981 through July 1991. The plaintiff alleges damages in the amount of $1 million and punitive damages of $10 million. The Company believes that the claim is without merit and has tendered defense of this action to its insurance carriers. In the opinion of management, the outcome of this litigation will not have a material adverse effect on the

Company's financial position or its results of operations. The Company is not involved in any other substantial litigation.

Loss Contingencies That Should Be Disclosed but Not Accrued

A loss contingency that fails to meet either or both of the two conditions for accrual mentioned earlier (page 421) should not be accrued. Instead, it should be disclosed in a footnote or by other means if there is at least a *reasonable possibility* that a loss may have been incurred. *Remote* loss contingencies that have the characteristics of guarantees should also be disclosed. Such remote loss contingencies include direct or indirect guarantees of the indebtedness of others,[28] obligations of commercial banks under "standby letters of credit," and guarantees to repurchase receivables.

Acceptable forms of disclosure include parenthetical notes in the financial statements, showing items "short" in the financial statements, appropriations of retained earnings, and footnotes to the financial statements. By far the most common form of disclosure for loss contingencies is footnotes. Disclosure of a loss contingency should indicate the nature of the contingency, and should either (1) give an estimate of the possible loss or range of loss or (2) state that such an estimate cannot be made. For a remote loss contingency with the characteristics of a guarantee, the amount of the guarantee should be disclosed. If estimable, amounts that are expected to be recovered from outside parties should also be disclosed.

Disclosure is not required for a loss contingency related to an unasserted claim or assessment when there is no evidence that a potential claimant is aware that a claim or assessment is possible. If a claim is *probable,* however, *and* there is a *reasonable possibility* that the outcome will be unfavorable, a loss contingency should be disclosed. For example, an accident resulting from faulty brakes on a new automobile will probably generate a claim that has a reasonable possibility of an unfavorable outcome for the manufacturer or its insurer. In this case, the automobile manufacturer should disclose the loss contingency even though no claim has yet been asserted.

Occasionally, information becomes available before the financial statements are issued indicating that an asset was impaired or a liability incurred *after* the date of the financial statements or that there is at least a reasonable possibility that an asset was impaired or a liability incurred after that date. In such circumstances, the first condition for accrual of a loss contingency is not met because there was no asset impairment or liability incurrence *by* the date of the financial statements. However, *disclosure* of losses or loss contingencies of this type may be necessary to keep the financial statements from being perceived as misleading.

Loss Contingencies That Are Neither Accrued nor Disclosed

General or unspecified business risks—for example, strikes, wars, and recessions—do not meet the conditions for accrual of loss contingencies. Therefore no accrual or disclosure of loss or possible loss from such risks should be made. Disclosure is not required for *remote* loss contingencies that are not guaranteed or for which a reasonable estimate of possible loss cannot be made.

Accounting practices in other countries are less restrictive than U.S. GAAP in the accrual of loss contingencies. Many European companies accrue for general risks with no specific contingency. This approach allows a company to smooth income from one period to the next by adjusting the amount of general risk "reserves," as they are often called.

---

[28]In a *direct* guarantee of the indebtedness of others, if the debtor fails to make payment to the creditor when the debt is due, the guarantor must pay the creditor. In an *indirect* guarantee, instead of paying the creditor, the guarantor must transfer funds to the debtor.

Having discussed proper accounting and reporting for loss contingencies, we shall briefly consider accounting for gain contingencies.

Gain Contingencies

A **gain contingency** arises when an uncertain existing condition, situation, or set of circumstances will be resolved with the occurrence or nonoccurrence of a future event that may increase assets or decrease liabilities. Claims against others for patent infringement, upward price revision, and claims for reimbursement under condemnation proceedings are examples of gain contingencies.

Both the realization principle and conservatism influence accounting for gain contingencies. Gain contingencies are not recorded and reported in the body of the financial statements. Instead, a material gain contingency should be given adequate disclosure in the notes to the financial statements, but only when it is highly likely the gain will be realized. Notice the caution regarding a gain contingency in the following footnote to the 1994 financial statements of BMC Industries:

13. Subsequent Event

In January 1995, a U.S. District Court jury in Miami, Florida, awarded the Company a verdict totaling $5.1 million against Barth Industries (Barth) of Cleveland, Ohio, and its parent, Nesco Holdings, Inc. (Nesco). The verdict relates to an agreement under which Barth and Nesco were to help automate the plastic lens production plant in Ft. Lauderdale. The Company has not recorded any income relating to this verdict as a final judgement has not yet been rendered and Barth and Nesco are expected to appeal.

SUMMARY OF LEARNING OBJECTIVES

PART A • Cash and Current Receivables

I. Identify items considered to be cash.
Cash includes U.S. currency and coins, personal checks, money orders, demand deposits, cashiers' checks, bank drafts, petty cash, change funds, and most savings deposits. Foreign currencies are included in cash if they are freely convertible into U.S. currency.

2. List the three accounting considerations related to accounts receivable.
The three considerations are (1) determining the amount of the receivable due from the customer, (2) determining when the receivable should be recognized as an asset, and (3) determining what recognition should be given to the possibility that the amount owed may not be collected.

3. State the issues related to determining the amounts due on accounts receivable.
Conceptually, the amount due is equal to the current cash equivalent exchange price that results from the transaction between buyer and seller. In determining the exchange price, any trade discount should be deducted from the list price. Receivables should be recorded net of any sales discount.

4. Identify and discuss the available alternatives for accounting for uncollectible accounts receivable.
When it is highly probable that some accounts receivable will not be collected and the seller can make a reasonable estimate of the uncollectible amount, the allowance method should be used. Under this method, an estimate of uncollectible accounts is made each period and reported in the income statement as an expense. On the

balance sheet, estimated uncollectible receivables are represented by an accounts receivable valuation or contra account called allowance for uncollectible accounts. Three generally accepted procedures may be used in applying the allowance method: aging of accounts receivable, percentage of ending accounts receivable, and percentage of credit sales. Under the aging procedure, receivables are classified according to the number of days they have been outstanding, and a separate estimate of the percentage of uncollectible receivables is applied to each age classification group. The longer receivables have been outstanding, the higher the percentage expected to be uncollectible. Once the total dollar amount of uncollectible receivables has been estimated, the allowance for uncollectible accounts is adjusted *to* the estimated uncollectible amount. In the percentage of ending accounts receivable procedure, as in the aging procedure, the amount of estimated uncollectible receivables is determined, and the allowance for uncollectible accounts is adjusted *to* that amount. Because receivables are not classified by age, however, this procedure is less precise than the aging procedure. Both the aging procedure and the percentage of ending accounts receivable procedure emphasize good matching on the balance sheet. The percentage of credit sales procedure estimates uncollectible accounts expense based on the amount of credit sales for the period. The calculated amount of uncollectible accounts expense is recorded, with a corresponding increase in the allowance for uncollectible accounts. This procedure emphasizes good matching on the income statement.

5. **Identify various transactions in which receivables are used to obtain immediate cash and describe the general objective in accounting for such transactions.**
Transactions in which receivables are used to obtain immediate cash include pledging receivables, assigning receivables, factoring receivables, securitizations of receivables, and discounting of notes receivable. In a transfer of receivables in which the transferor retains no continuing involvement with the transferred receivables, the transferred receivables should be accounted for as sold. Accounting for transfers in which there is continuing involvement by the transferor depends on the extent of the transferor's control over the transferred assets. The general objective in accounting for transfers of receivables is that each of the involved entities should recognize only those assets it controls and those liabilities it has incurred and should derecognize those assets over which it has surrendered control and those liabilities it has extinguished.

6. **List the three conditions that must be met for a transfer of receivables to be considered a sale of assets.**
The three conditions are (1) the transferred assets have been isolated from the transferor under all circumstances, (2) the transferees have the right to pledge or exchange either the transferred assets or beneficial interests in those assets, and (3) the transferor does not maintain effective control over the transferred assets through an agreement to repurchase or redeem them before their maturity.

7. **Describe the appropriate accounting for a transfer of receivables that is not considered a sale.**
A transfer of receivables that does not meet all three of the conditions necessary for it to be accounted for as a sale must be accounted for as a secured borrowing. Appropriate accounting for a secured borrowing depends on (1) whether the lender has control over the collateral and (2) the lender's and debtor's rights and obligations resulting from the collateral arrangement. If either (1) the lender is not free to sell or repledge the collateral or (2) the debtor has the right and ability to redeem the collateral on short notice, the debtor should continue to carry the collateral receivables among its receivables, and the lender should not record the collateral receivables on its books. In a secured borrowing situation in which the secured party (the lender) *is free* to sell or repledge the collateral and the debtor does not have the right and ability to redeem the collateral on short notice, the debtor is *required* to reclassify those receivables that are collateral assets and to report them in its balance sheet separately from other receivables not so encumbered. The secured party should recognize the collateral as its asset, initially recorded at fair value, and also recognize its obligation to return the receivables to the debtor.

PART B • Current Payables and Contingencies

8. **Define current liabilities and describe the amount at which they normally are recorded.**

   A current liability requires the transfer of resources or the incurrence of another liability within the longer of one fiscal year or one operating cycle. Most current liabilities are recorded at their future payment amounts.

9. **State the accounting and evidence issues related to short-term obligations expected to be refinanced.**

   If the debtor intends to refinance a short-term obligation on a long-term basis and can demonstrate the ability to refinance the obligation, the obligation should be classified as a noncurrent liability. The ability to refinance can be shown by either (1) refinancing on a long-term basis during the period between the balance sheet date and the date the financial statements are issued or (2) entering into an agreement before the financial statements are issued that clearly permits refinancing on a long-term basis.

10. **Identify the three general categories of current liabilities and discuss the nature of the liabilities in each category.**

    The three general categories of current liabilities are (1) determinable current liabilities, (2) current liabilities that are dependent on operating results, and (3) contingencies. Determinable current liabilities are known with certainty to exist as of the balance sheet date, and the amount ultimately to be paid is known with certainty or can be reasonably estimated. The amounts of current liabilities that are dependent on operating results cannot be known with certainty until the end of the accounting period. Contingencies resulting in liabilities are loss contingencies. A loss contingency arises when an uncertain existing condition, situation, or set of circumstances will be resolved by the occurrence or nonoccurrence of a future event that may result in the impairment of an asset or the incurrence of a liability.

11. **Specify the circumstances under which the currently due portion of a long-term obligation would not be classified as a current liability.**

    The currently due portion of a long-term obligation would not be classified as a current liability if it (1) will be retired by the use of assets classified as noncurrent, (2) will be refinanced on a long-term basis, or (3) will be retired by issuance of capital stock.

12. **List the conditions under which an accrual should be made for compensated employee absences.**

    An accrual should be made when all of the following conditions are met: (1) the employer's obligation to pay compensation for future absences is attributable to services already rendered by the employee, (2) the employee's right to compensation for future absences is not contingent on the employee's future service, or can be accumulated over time, (3) payment of the compensation by the employer is probable, and (4) the amount of compensation that will be paid for future absences is reasonably estimable.

13. **Define a contingency.**

    A contingency is an existing condition, situation, or set of circumstances involving uncertainty about a possible gain or loss that will ultimately be resolved when one or more future events occur or fail to occur. Resolution of the uncertainty may confirm the acquisition of an asset or the reduction of a liability, or the loss or impairment of an asset or the incurrence of a liability.

14. **Describe the appropriate accounting and reporting for loss contingencies, including litigation contingencies.**

    A loss contingency should be accrued if (1) it is probable that an asset has been impaired or a liability has been incurred by the date of the financial statements and (2) the amount of the loss can be reasonably estimated. In addition, for a litigation contingency to be accrued, the cause for action must have occurred by the date of the financial statements. A loss contingency should be disclosed but not accrued if it fails to meet either or both of the two conditions for accrual, assuming there is at least a reasonable possibility that a loss may have been incurred. If there is not at least a reasonable possibility that a loss has been incurred, a loss contingency should be neither accrued nor disclosed.

KEY TERMS

PART A

accounts receivable 395

aging of accounts receivable 399

allowance method 398

assignment 404

bad debt expense 398

bank reconciliation 392

beneficial interests 404

cash 391

cash discounts 396

compensating balance 395

comprehensive reconciliation 394

discounting notes receivable 404

factoring 404

interest-bearing notes 401

liquidity 390

monetary assets 390

non-interest-bearing notes 401

notes receivable 401

overdraft 394

percentage of credit sales 399

percentage of ending accounts receivable 399

pledging 404

proof of cash 394

receivables 395

sales discounts 396

secured borrowing 406

securitizations 404

trade discounts 396

trade receivables 395

transfers of financial assets 403

uncollectible accounts expense 398

with recourse 404

without recourse 404

PART B

accounts payable 412

accrued liabilities 416

callable 415

cash dividends payable 415

contingency 420

current liability 410

current notes payable 413

deposits 419

determinable current liabilities 412

dividend 415

gain contingency 426

liabilities 410

liability (scrip) dividends payable 415

loss contingency 421

monetary liabilities 410

prepayment 419

property dividends payable 415

short-term notes payable 414

trade accounts payable 412

trade notes payable 414

Bonus Plans and Calculations

A bonus plan based on the company's income may be formulated in a variety of ways. For example, bonuses may be based on:

1. Income before bonus expense and before income taxes ($B = bI$).

2. Income after bonus expense but before income taxes [$B = b(I − B)$].

3. Income after income taxes but before bonus expense [$B = b(I − T)$].

4. Income after bonus expense and after income taxes [$B = b(I − B − T)$].

> where b = the bonus rate
> I = income before bonuses and income taxes
> B = the bonus in dollars
> T = income taxes

Given the tax rate (t) and the fact that a bonus is a tax-deductible expense, income taxes (T) can be determined as follows:

$T = t(I − B)$.

The procedure for solving income-based bonus problems involves the following steps:

Step 1. Construct an equation that mathematically describes the bonus plan.

Step 2. Construct an equation for calculating income taxes (if the amount of income taxes must be known for the bonus calculation).

Step 3. Substitute known data in the equation(s).

Step 4. Solve for any unknown variables.

For example, assume that the third bonus plan (income after income taxes but before bonus expense) is in place. Income before bonuses and taxes is $100,000; the bonus rate is 2 percent, and the tax rate is 30 percent. The bonus would be calculated as follows:

$$B = b(I − T), \text{ where } T = t(I − B)$$
$$B = b[I − t(I − B)]$$
$$B = .02[\$100,000 − .30(\$100,000 − B)]$$
$$B = .02(\$100,000 − \$30,000 + .30B)$$
$$B = \$2,000 − \$600 + .006B$$
$$.994B = \$1,400$$
$$B = \$1,408.45$$

An adjusting entry would be made to record this bonus expense and the related obligation:

Bonus expense.	1,408.45	
Bonus payable		1,408.45

The bonus expense account should appear on the income statement, probably in combination with other salary and wage expenses. The bonus payable liability should be included among the current liabilities on the balance sheet until the bonus is paid.

PART A • Cash and Current Receivables

Q 8-1. Define monetary assets.

Q 8-2. Define monetary liabilities.

Q 8-3. What is cash, and what items normally are included in the cash account?

Q 8-4. What is a petty cash fund, and what purposes are served by the use of such a fund?

Q 8-5. How should a bank overdraft at the end of the fiscal year be classified on the balance sheet?

Q 8-6. In what numbered space in the following bank reconciliation format should each of the items listed below appear? If an item should not appear, so indicate by marking it 5.

Balance, per bank statement . . . . **$xx**	**Balance, per books** . . . . **$xx**
Add: . . . . (1)	**Add:** . . . . (3)
Deduct: . . . . _(2)_	**Deduct:** . . . . _(4)_
Corrected bank balance . . . . **$xx**	**Corrected book balance** . . . . **$xx**

a) ____ Note collected by bank on behalf of company.
b) ____ Service charge for month.
c) ____ NSF check returned to company by bank.
d) ____ Outstanding checks.
e) ____ An outstanding certified check.
f) ____ Deposits in transit.
g) ____ A deposit the company failed to record.

Q 8-7. Given the following information, calculate the balance per books (before adjustment):

Balance, per bank statement **$3,000.00**
Service charge for month **4.00**
Outstanding checks, end of month **129.00**
Deposit in transit **400.00**

Deposit of $120 recorded by the company as a deposit of $12.

Q 8-8. Identify three considerations that arise in accounting for accounts receivable.

Q 8-9. Distinguish between trade discounts and cash discounts offered by sellers of merchandise and discuss the purpose of each type of discount.

Q 8-10. Why should estimated uncollectible accounts expense be recorded in the same period in which credit sales occur?

Q 8-11. What is the primary distinction between the percentage-of-credit-sales procedure and the percentage-of-receivables procedure of accounting for uncollectible accounts receivable?

Q 8-12. Why is the percentage-of-credit-sales procedure sometimes called an income statement approach to accounting for uncollectible accounts receivable?

Q 8-13. Company *A* follows the practice of *factoring* receivables, Company *B* uses receivables as *pledges*, while Company *C assigns* receivables periodically. How do these practices differ?

Q 8-14. Describe a typical securitization.

Q 8-15. What is the distinction between a "pass-through" securitization and a "revolving" securitization?

Q 8-16. The following items appear as receivables for Joelle Corporation:

	DR	CR
Accounts receivable..	$45,000	
Allowance for doubtful accounts...............................		$4,400
Receivable from officer	1,200	
Notes receivable...	16,000	
Unearned interest..		2,700
Receivables with credit balances—customers....................		400
Allowance for loan losses		1,600
Notes receivable discounted		1,000
Interest on notes receivable..................................	600	
Purchase advances..	1,500	

How should each item be presented on a classified balance sheet?

Q 8-17. Big Apple, Inc., assigned $35,000 of accounts receivable as a basis for a loan. The assignee advanced $32,000 to Big Apple. What accounts of Big Apple would be affected by the transaction? How would the accounts be presented on a balance sheet?

Q 8-18. What is the nature of the account *discounted notes receivable*?

Q 8-19. What is the general objective in accounting for transfers of financial assets?

Q 8-20. What are the three conditions that must be met for a transfer of financial assets to be accounted for as a sale of assets?

PART B • Current Payables and Contingencies

Q 8-21. What three characteristics are common to all liabilities?

Q 8-22. What is the theoretically correct valuation of a liability?

Q 8-23. Distinguish between current liabilities and noncurrent liabilities.

Q 8-24. Why might a liability that is current for one entity be properly classified as noncurrent for another entity?

Q 8-25. Under what circumstances might currently maturing long-term debt properly be excluded from current liabilities?

Q 8-26. Under what conditions would a long-term obligation that is callable be classified as a current liability?

Q 8-27. What two conditions must be satisfied before a short-term obligation that is expected to be refinanced can be classified as a noncurrent liability?

Q 8-28. Explain how a company can satisfactorily demonstrate the ability to refinance a short-term obligation on a long-term basis.

Q 8-29. Why are stock dividends declared not recognized as liabilities?

Q 8-30. How do accrued liabilities arise?

Q 8-31. Under what conditions must an employer accrue a liability for employees' rights to receive compensation for absences from work?

Q 8-32. When should the expense and accrued liability arising from an employee's right to be compensated for absences be recorded?

Q 8-33. What are the two different procedures for accounting for property taxes?

*Q 8-34. Why is bonus calculation on the basis of income after *all* expenses a "circular" problem?

Q 8-35. Define a contingency.

Q 8-36. When does a loss contingency arise?

Q 8-37. Identify and describe the three levels of likelihood of the occurrence of a future event related to accounting for loss contingencies.

Q 8-38. What are the three basic ways to account for and report a loss contingency?

Q 8-39. What two conditions must be met to accrue a loss contingency?

Q 8-40. Under what conditions is accrual of a loss contingency for threatened litigation appropriate?

Q 8-41. In the case of loss contingencies that should be disclosed but not accrued, what information should be disclosed?

Q 8-42. What loss contingencies are neither accrued nor disclosed?

Q 8-43. What are the two fundamental provisions related to accounting for and reporting gain contingencies?

CASES

PART A • Cash and Current Receivables

C 8-1. **ESTIMATING UNCOLLECTIBLE ACCOUNTS** During the audit of accounts receivable, your client asks why the current year's income statement reports bad debt expense when some accounts may not become uncollectible until *next* year. He says that he has read that financial statements should be based on verifiable, objective evidence. It seems to him to be much more objective to wait until individual accounts receivable are actually determined to be uncollectible before recording them as expenses.

REQUIRED Write a memorandum to your client explaining the theoretical justification of the allowance method of accounting for bad debts. Include a description of the percentage-of-sales method and the aging method of estimating bad debts, and explain how well each method accomplishes the objectives of the allowance method of accounting for bad debts.

(AICPA, adapted)

C 8-2. **ALLOWANCES: RECEIVABLE VALUATION** The president and the controller of Riley Corporation were discussing the merits of the use of allowances in connection with accounts receivable. The controller suggested that the following allowances be used in connection with the company's receivables: an allowance for bad debts and an allowance for sales returns.

The president strongly opposed the controller's suggestion on the basis that (1) too much subjectivity is introduced into the statements, (2) the resulting data are hypothetical, and (3) the resulting financial statements are not useful or reliable.

REQUIRED Discuss the objectives underlying the use of allowances in connection with accounts receivable and describe the circumstances under which the allowances suggested by the controller would be appropriate?

C 8-3. **CASH GENERATION FROM RECEIVABLES** Dannon Corporation is a nationwide distributor of custom carpeting for recreational vehicles. At the beginning of the current year, its accounts and notes receivable appeared as follows:

Accounts receivable $7,000,000
Notes receivable 850,000

During the current year, the company continually has found itself without the cash necessary to conduct its day-to-day operations. Dannon has considered borrowing $6 million from a local bank, but the company president is concerned about the effect of such a loan on the company's balance sheet. During a recent lunch at the local country club, a friend of the president's suggested that Dannon use its accounts and notes receivable as a way to generate the cash needed for operations. The president was intrigued by this suggestion and has asked you to analyze the effects of the following alternatives on the company's income statement, the statement of cash flows, and the statement of financial position:

a) Pledge the accounts receivable as security for a $6 million loan.

b) Transfer (sell) the receivables, without recourse, to a factor. Factors normally pay only about 80 percent of face value for receivables on a nonrecourse basis.

c) Same as part *b,* except that the transfer will be with recourse. Dannon cannot estimate its obligation to the factor and will receive cash approximating 95 percent of the receivables' face value on a recourse basis.

d) Discount the notes receivable at the local bank. The notes have a maturity value of $880,000, and the bank's discount will be approximately $40,000.

e) Assign both the notes and the accounts receivable to a bank in another state. This bank will advance 85 percent of the face value of the receivables, less a service charge and periodic interest on the uncollected receivables. The president's friend favors this alternative and points out that it is the most attractive way to obtain needed funds without "loading up the debt section of the company's balance sheet."

REQUIRED   Draft a response to each alternative. In your responses, indicate what the effects would be on each financial statement mentioned. You may indicate the effects in general terms.

C 8-4.   ACCOUNTING FOR AND REPORTING TRANSACTIONS INVOLVING RECEIVABLES   Carlton, Inc., normally sells its products on account in exchange for 30-day accounts receivable. Occasionally, Carlton will agree to a longer term financing arrangement with a customer in which a three- to six-month note receivable is held by Carlton. Carlton uses the allowance method to account for uncollectible accounts.

During the current year, Carlton had the following transactions involving its receivables:

a)   Carlton factored, without recourse, some of its accounts receivable with Finance, Inc. After the transfer, Carlton had no access to and no effective control over the factored receivables. Finance, Inc., had the right to pledge or exchange the factored receivables.

b)   Carlton assigned some of its accounts receivables to Finance, Inc., as collateral for a loan. Finance, Inc., is not free to sell or repledge the collateral.

c)   Carlton discounted one of its six-month notes receivable at a local bank, with recourse. The bank is free to sell or repledge the note.

d)   Some of Carlton's accounts receivable were written off as uncollectible and some accounts receivable that had previously been written off were collected.

REQUIRED   Explain how Carlton should account for and report each of the above transactions.

C 8-5.   ACCOUNTING FOR CURRENT RECEIVABLES AND PAYABLES: ETHICAL ISSUES   The management of Foster, Inc., has adopted some policies related to accounting for current receivables and payables that caught the attention of the company's internal auditor. For the first time in its five-year history, the company changed its estimate of uncollectible accounts receivables as a percentage of credit sales. Estimated uncollectible receivables had been 5 percent of credit sales for the first four years, yet in the current year the estimated uncollectible percentage had been lowered to 4 percent of credit sales. The internal auditor saw no evidence that there had been any change in the history of uncollectible accounts to justify lowering the estimate.

Foster's management has reclassified some of its notes payable that are due in less than one year to long-term notes payable. Management has expressed its intent to refinance the notes on a long-term basis and apparently has entered an agreement to accomplish the refinancing. However, the auditor is concerned when it is determined that the long-term refinancing agreement is with one of Foster's major suppliers and the supplier is known to be willing to do almost anything to keep Foster's business.

The internal auditor's concern about the actions taken regarding current receivables and payables is heightened by the fact that he knows management wishes to show a strong income picture for the current year and to have minimal current liabilities in order to maximize the company's chances of obtaining a substantial loan to be used for plant expansion.

REQUIRED   **1.**   Does the internal auditor have reason to be concerned with the actions taken by management in the current year? Explain why.

2.   Do management's actions cause an ethical dilemma for the internal auditor? What arguments should be made or actions taken by the internal auditor?

PART B • Current Payables and Contingencies

C 8-6.   CURRENT AND NONCURRENT LIABILITIES   The following items are listed as liabilities on the balance sheet of Thomas Company on December 31, 1998:

Accounts payable.	$ 170,000
Notes payable.	280,000
Bonds payable	2,500,000

The accounts payable represent payments to be made to suppliers that are due in January 1999. The notes payable mature on various dates during 1999. The bonds payable mature on July 1, 1999.

REQUIRED   **1.**   What is the general rule for determining whether a liability is classified as current or noncurrent?

2. Under what conditions may any of Thomas Company's liabilities be classified as noncurrent? Explain your answer.

(IMA, adapted)

C 8-7. **CURRENT AND NONCURRENT LIABILITIES** A close friend of yours, Debra Jacobs, has a retail business that sells kitchen appliances, including refrigerators, ovens, dishwashers, and a variety of countertop appliances. Jacobs is aware that you have recently graduated from college as an accounting major and comes to you late in 1998 with some questions about how several accounts in her company's records should be classified on the December 31, 1998, balance sheet. She indicates that she is particularly interested in keeping the current liability total at a minimum because to do so will improve the company's current ratio (current assets ÷ current liabilities), which is preferred by one of the banks that the company hopes to borrow more money from within the next eight or nine months.

The particular balance sheet items that Jacobs is asking you about are:

a) A $150,000 note payable, of which $75,000 is due on April 1, 1999, and $75,000 is due on April 1, 2001.

b) A $130,000 note payable, due March 1, 1999.

c) Stock dividends of $20,000 that have been declared and are distributable on January 20, 1999.

d) Customer deposits of $42,500 toward the purchase prices of appliances that are scheduled for delivery during the period December 15, 1998, through March 15, 1999.

REQUIRED Prepare a memorandum to Jacobs describing what constitutes a current liability in general and outlining the circumstances, if any, under which items *a* through *d* would *not* be classified as current liabilities.

C 8-8. **CLASSIFICATION OF OBLIGATIONS** On January 1, 1992, Farber Company borrowed $150,000 and signed two long-term notes payable. One note payable was for $100,000 and specified that the creditor is to be paid back in four annual installments of $25,000, $25,000, $30,000, and $20,000, beginning December 31, 1997. The second note was for $50,000, is payable in 10 years, and is callable any time after six years, if Farber fails to make any of the annual interest payments specified in the note contract. Because of poor sales in most of its product lines and low 1998 income, Farber was unable to make the 1998 interest payment on the $50,000 note.

You are on the staff of Farber's financial reporting office and have been assigned to prepare the 1998 financial statements. As part of this assignment, you are evaluating the two notes payable in an effort to determine how much, if any, of each note payable should be reported as current and noncurrent liabilities in the December 31, 1998, balance sheet.

REQUIRED **1.** Determine the amount, if any, of the $100,000 note that should be reported as a current liability on the 1998 balance sheet. As an aid to your superior, prepare a brief written statement describing what conditions would have to exist in order for the current maturities of long-term obligations *not* to be classified as current liabilities.

2. How much of the $50,000 note payable should be reported as a current liability for 1998? Under what conditions would long-term obligations that are callable by the creditor or that will be callable within the longer of one year or one operating cycle *not* be classified as current liabilities?

C 8-9. **CLASSIFICATION OF OBLIGATIONS** On June 14, 1998, Jackson Manufacturing borrowed $1.2 million on a six-month note payable. Jackson's fiscal year ends on July 31, and it normally issues its financial statements on September 15. On August 30, 1998, Jackson arranges a 10-year financing agreement with Wilshire Finance Corporation, with the intention of using funds obtained under the 10-year agreement to refinance the six-month note payable. The financing agreement with Wilshire allows Jackson to borrow up to $1.5 million, but no more than 90 percent of the replacement cost of Jackson's inventory at the time of the borrowing. During the year following the maturity date of the six-month note, the replacement cost of Jackson's inventory is expected to range from $1.3 to $1.6 million.

REQUIRED **1.** Prepare a memorandum to the chief financial officer of Jackson Manufacturing describing (*a*) the conditions under which the six-month note payable should be classified as a long-term liability in the 1998 balance sheet and (*b*) the amount, if any, of the six-month note payable that should be reported as a long-term liability as of July 31, 1998.

2. If any part of the six-month note payable should not be reported as a long-term liability as of July 31, 1998, explain why not.

C 8-10. **REFUNDS OF DEPOSITS; ETHICAL AND PROFESSIONAL ISSUES** Regency Chemicals, Inc., ships its chemical products in large metal containers. Regency collects a $1,000 deposit on each container and refunds this money when the container is returned in acceptable condition. On the average, 50 containers are returned each week and refund checks totaling $50,000 are issued by the accounting supervisor, Pete Smith. Returned containers are received and inspected by Smith, who draws up the necessary papers to support reimbursement and issues checks in the appropriate amount.

During the course of a routine internal audit, one of the staff auditors, Larry Benson, determined that Pete Smith had issued 70 checks to Hillery Manufacturing Company during the last six months of 1998. Since Benson had not previously heard of Hillery Manufacturing, he investigated and discovered that Hillery Manufacturing had no record of receiving chemical shipments from Regency or returning containers to Regency. Further, Benson discovered that Pete Smith's brother, Harold, was the president and chief executive officer of Hillery Manufacturing.

Larry Benson and Pete Smith were good friends. Benson could not believe that Smith would do anything wrong. However, he knew that he had to question Smith about the refund checks to Hillery Manufacturing. Upon questioning, Smith admitted that he had falsified information to support refund checks to Hillery Manufacturing for returned containers. He had issued the checks and mailed them to his brother, who had cashed them on Pete's behalf. When asked why he had done it, Smith broke down and told Benson that he had been experiencing severe personal financial problems during the past year. He was close to declaring bankruptcy. He had been turned down by several banks for loans, and even Hillery Manufacturing had refused to loan him money.

Pete Smith admitted that he had made a mistake. He was sorry for what he had done, but he had felt pushed into a corner with nowhere to turn. In order to make amends, Smith asked Benson to talk with Bob Jennings, the controller of Regency Chemicals, and explain the situation to Jennings. Smith suggested that he be allowed to repay the $70,000 through salary deductions over a period of time.

REQUIRED What ethical and professional issues should be of concern to Larry Benson in deciding a course of action? What would you do?

C 8-11. **LOSS CONTINGENCIES; LIABILITY ON COUPONS** Butler Company is a manufacturer of toys. During the year, the following situations arose:

Situation 1: A safety hazard related to one of Butler's toy products was discovered. It is considered probable that liabilities have been incurred. A reasonable estimate of the amount of loss can be made on the basis of past experience.

Situation 2: One of Butler's small warehouses is located on the bank of a river and can no longer be insured against flood losses. No flood losses have occurred since the date when the insurance became unavailable.

Situation 3: This year, Butler began to promote a new toy by including a coupon, redeemable for a movie ticket, in each toy's carton. The movie ticket, which costs Butler $2, is purchased in advance and then mailed to the customer when the coupon is received by Butler. Butler estimated, on the basis of past experience, that 55 percent of the coupons would be redeemed. Forty percent of the coupons were actually redeemed this year, and the remaining 15 percent of the coupons are expected to be redeemed next year.

REQUIRED
1. How should Butler report the safety hazard? Why?
2. How should Butler report the uninsurable flood risk? Why?
3. How should Butler account for the toy promotion campaign this year?

(AICPA, adapted)

PART A • Cash and Current Receivables

E 8-1. **PETTY CASH FUND** On May 1, 1998, Laverne Company installed a petty cash fund of $600. On May 20, 1998, the fund custodian presented reimbursement vouchers for the following expenditures:

Supplies purchased and used	$158
Postage	94
Withdrawal of money by Laverne for personal use	200
Freight paid on purchases	90

The fund was replenished on May 20, 1998. On May 27, 1998, the petty cash fund was decreased by $100.

REQUIRED Prepare entries to record:
1. Establishment of the fund.
2. Replenishment of the fund.
3. Decrease in the balance of the fund.

E 8-2. **BANK RECONCILIATION** The following data apply to the cash records of Pearson Company:

Ending cash balance, per books	$5,135
Ending cash balance, per bank statement	5,300
Outstanding checks	1,212
Service charge for month	20
Proceeds from bank collection of note (including interest of $8)	108
Deposits in transit	1,000

In error, Pearson Company recorded a deposit of $135 for cash sales twice.

REQUIRED
1. Prepare a bank reconciliation for the month.
2. Prepare the journal entry to adjust Pearson's accounts.

E 8-3. **DETERMINING A CASH SHORTAGE THROUGH A BANK RECONCILIATION** As auditor for Hock Corporation, you are attempting to determine an apparent cash shortage that Hock believes resulted from an employee's theft. You have assembled the following information for the month of March:

Cash balance per books, 3/1	$11,596.37
Cash receipts for March, per books	25,247.50
Cash disbursements for March, per books	34,270.91
Cash balance, per bank statement, 3/31	1,534.14
Deposit in transit, 3/31	800.00
Outstanding checks, 3/31	270.38
Service charge for month	9.20

You have reason to believe that a cash payment on account to a creditor in the amount of $500 was not recorded by Hock.

REQUIRED Verify the amount of the suspected cash shortage.

E 8-4. **BANK RECONCILIATION** The following data are available for the *Arkansas Gazette:*
a) The newspaper's bank statement shows a balance of $68,334.87 at September 30, 1998.
b) The bank balance per the *Gazette's* records is $56,232.06.
c) Deposits in transit, September 30, $5,025.50.
d) Checks outstanding as of September 30, $9,540.84.
e) On September 29, the bank collected a note for the *Gazette* for $7,889.00, including interest of $889. The bank charged a collection fee of $25.20.
f) In recording a check from an advertiser in the amount of $480.00, the *Gazette's* bookkeeper recorded the amount of $48.00.
g) Bank service charges for the month, $15.93.

h) Included in the bank statement was a check from a customer in the amount of $558.00 which was marked NSF by the bank.

i) Included in the bank statement was a debit memo for $134.40 that the bank had erroneously charged to the *Gazette*.

REQUIRED

1. Prepare a bank reconciliation for the *Arkansas Gazette* on September 30, 1998.

2. Prepare the necessary journal entries for the newspaper on September 30, 1998.

E 8-5.   **ESTIMATING UNCOLLECTIBLE ACCOUNTS EXPENSE**   Harris Corporation had the following accounts receivable and allowance for uncollectible accounts balances at the end of 1998 before any expense adjustment:

Accounts receivable . . . . **$60,000 Dr**
Allowance for uncollectible accounts . . . .   **4,000 Cr**

Sales in 1998 totaled $400,000 (8 percent of sales were for cash), and write-offs of customer accounts totaled $2,500.

REQUIRED

1. Calculate the balance in the allowance account at the beginning of 1998.

2. Prepare the adjusting entry to record uncollectible accounts expense under the following independent assumptions:

    a) 1.5 percent of credit sales will prove uncollectible.

    b) 10 percent of ending accounts receivable are uncollectible.

    c) Aging of the receivables indicates that $6,800 is probably uncollectible.

E 8-6.   **UNCOLLECTIBLE ACCOUNTS EXPENSE; CUSTOMER COLLECTIONS**   The following year-end information relates to Fuller Corporation's credit sales for 1998, 1999, and 2000:

YEAR	ACCOUNTS RECEIVABLE	ALLOWANCE FOR UNCOLLECTIBLE ACCOUNTS	ACCOUNTS WRITTEN OFF
1998	$39,000	$1,600	$800
1999	42,000	1,800	900
2000	47,000	1,500	600

REQUIRED

1. Calculate the uncollectible accounts expense for 1999 and 2000.

2. Assume that in 1999 and 2000 sales (all credit) total $280,000 each year. Calculate the customer collections for these years.

E 8-7.   **JOURNAL ENTRIES FOR SALES AND UNCOLLECTIBLE ACCOUNTS**   At the beginning of December 1998, Ham Enterprises had a debit balance in accounts receivable of $380,000 and a credit balance of $32,000 in allowance for doubtful accounts. During December, the following transactions occurred:

a) Sales on account, $660,000.

b) Sales returns and allowances, $9,800.

c) Cash collections on accounts receivable from customers, $644,500.

d) Write-off of a customer's account, $9,000.

On December 31, 1998, Ham decided that the allowance account balance should be adjusted to $48,700 to reflect the net realizable value of the receivables.

REQUIRED

1. Prepare journal entries for items *a* through *d* and for the adjusting entry to the allowance account.

2. Calculate the balance in accounts receivable and the allowance account at December 31, 1998.

3. In July 1999, the customer in item *d* paid to Ham the amount previously written off. Prepare Ham's journal entry to record this receipt.

E 8-8.   **DETERMINING SALES FROM RECEIVABLES DATA**   For the month of December 1998, the records of Brain Corporation show the following information:

Cash received on accounts receivable **$140,000**
Cash sales **120,000**
Accounts receivable, 1/1/98 . . . . **325,000**
Accounts receivable, 12/31/98 . . . . **300,000**
Accounts receivable written off during the year **3,000**
Allowance for uncollectible accounts, 1/1/98 . . . .   **10,000**
Allowance for uncollectible accounts, 12/31/98 . . . .   **15,000**

REQUIRED	**I.**	Calculate total sales for the year ending December 31, 1998.
	2.	Calculate uncollectible accounts expense for the year ending December 31, 1998.

E 8-9. **ACCOUNTING FOR SALES DISCOUNTS** Watson sells merchandise on a credit basis under the following terms: 3%/10, net 30. The corporation records sales net of sales discounts. The following data apply to credit sales made during 1998, Watson's first year of operation:

Credit sales at gross amount..	$135,000
Gross accounts receivable collected within the discount period...............	80,000
Gross accounts receivable collected after the discount period had expired......	10,000
Accounts receivable (gross) written off as uncollectible	5,000
Portion of accounts receivable at the end of the year estimated	
to be uncollectible	2%

Assume that the sales discount period had expired for accounts receivable written off during the period and on hand at the end of the period.

REQUIRED Prepare journal entries, including adjusting entries, for the above transactions and events.

E 8-10. **ACCOUNTS RECEIVABLE; UNCOLLECTIBLE ACCOUNTS** Silvan's first year of operations began on January 1, 1998. On December 31, 1998, the company's accounts receivable balance of $155,600 include the following:

Customers' accounts not past due and considered collectible	$137,900
Customers' accounts past due and estimated to be uncollectible..............	7,400
Customers' accounts known to be uncollectible	5,700
Amounts due from the state government for tax rebates for recycling efforts	6,600
Customers' accounts with credit balances...............................	(2,000)
Total	$155,600

REQUIRED	**I.**	Prepare the journal entry to correctly state accounts receivable and to reclassify items that do not belong in the accounts receivable account.
	2.	Prepare the journal entry to record uncollectible accounts expense for the year ending December 31, 1998.

E 8-11. **UNCOLLECTIBLE ACCOUNTS EXPENSE** At the beginning of the current year, Wilburn Corporation's allowance for doubtful accounts had a credit balance of $3,500. During the current year, Wilburn had credit sales of $600,000 and wrote off uncollectible customers' accounts totaling $12,000. An aging of the ending accounts receivable balance of $325,000 indicated that accounts totaling $9,000 probably were uncollectible.

REQUIRED Calculate Wilburn Corporation's uncollectible accounts expense for the year.

E 8-12. **ACCOUNTING FOR SALES DISCOUNTS** Artman Appliance Wholesale sells washers to appliance stores with credit terms of a 2 percent discount on payments within 10 days of the purchase. The washers have a sales price of $1,200 each. During March and April the following transactions occurred:

March 3	Sold three washers on account to Steve's Discount.
March 12	Received payment in full from Steve's Discount.
March 17	Sold four washers on account to Green Joy Stores.
March 26	Green Joy returned one washer because of paint defects.
April 15	Received payment in full from Green Joy Stores.

Artman records sales net of sales discounts.

REQUIRED Prepare entries for Artman Appliance to record the transactions for March and April.

E 8-13. **DISCOUNTING NOTES RECEIVABLE** The following short-term notes are held by a company:
a) A two-month, 9 percent note receivable for $12,000 dated November 1, 1998.
b) A six-month, 10 percent note receivable for $20,000 dated October 1, 1998.
c) A one-month, 12 percent note receivable for $50,000 dated December 1, 1998.
d) A one-year, 10 percent note receivable for $16,000 dated September 1, 1998.

REQUIRED Prepare the appropriate entry for each of the above cases, assuming that the notes were discounted at a bank on December 1, 1998, under conditions justifying treatment as a sale. No interest accruals were made before discounting and the discount rate was 12 percent. Use monthly intervals, not days, and calculate to the nearest whole dollar.

E 8-14. **TRANSFERS OF RECEIVABLES** On March 1, Bay Corporation transferred receivables with a face value of $240,000 to Clark Factors.

REQUIRED Prepare Bay's March 1 entry to record the transfer of receivables under the following two independent assumptions:

1. The transfer was without recourse under conditions justifying treatment as a sale. Clark Factors charged a $15,000 factoring fee plus interest of $2,000 during the three-month period. On March 1, Bay estimated and recorded uncollectible accounts of $9,000 and cash discounts of $7,200.

2. Same facts as in part 1, except that the transfer was with recourse, Clark charged an $11,000 factor fee, and Bay accepted a recourse obligation with a fair value of $1,000.

E 8-15. **ASSIGNMENT OF ACCOUNTS RECEIVABLE** On March 1, Post Corporation assigned accounts receivable of $80,000 and received $64,000 less a 2 percent finance fee. On April 1, $36,000 was collected on receivables and forwarded to the finance company; $300 of that amount represented interest. Also during April, $10,000 of the assigned accounts was written off as uncollectible under the allowance method. On May 1, $40,000 was collected, and the loan was paid in full plus $170 in interest. The transfer is a secured borrowing in which the lender is not free to sell or repledge the receivables.

REQUIRED Prepare the appropriate entries.

E 8-16. **RECEIVABLES FACTORED WITH RECOURSE** On January 1, 1998, Wilder Corporation transferred all its accounts receivable to Manx Factors. Manx Factors has the right to pledge the receivables and Wilder has no effective control over the receivables. The transfer was with recourse, and Manx charged Wilder a factoring fee equal to 2 percent of the receivables' face value of $160,000. Manx also levied an interest charge equal to 1 percent of the receivables' face value. Under the recourse provisions, Wilder accepted a $3,000 recourse obligation. Wilder Corporation's fiscal year ends on December 31.

REQUIRED 1. Prepare Wilder's entry to record the transfer of receivables and explain briefly the reasons for your entry.

2. Now assume that Wilder and Manx also agreed that in two months Wilder would purchase all receivables outstanding at that time. Prepare Wilder's entry to record the transfer of receivables and briefly explain the reasons for your entry.

E 8-17. **SALE OF RECEIVABLES**

A. Hiller, Inc., factors $200,000 of accounts receivable without recourse to Acme Financial. The allowance for uncollectible accounts related to the receivables is $10,000. Acme Financial charges a factoring fee of 10 percent of the face value of the receivables, plus $3,000 interest. The transfer meets all of the conditions necessary to justify treatment as a sale of the receivables by Hiller.

REQUIRED Prepare Hiller's journal entry to record the above transfer of financial assets.

B. Assume the same facts as in part A, except that Hiller agreed to reimburse Acme Financial for uncollectible receivables up to a fair value of $5,000 in exchange for Acme reducing its factoring fee to 8 percent of the receivables' face value.

REQUIRED Prepare Hiller's journal entry to record the transfer of financial assets described in part B.

E 8-18. **ACCOUNTING FOR A SECURED BORROWING** On July 31, 1998, Janson Company assigned $90,000 in accounts receivable to Miller Finance, Inc., as collateral for a loan. Miller Finance loaned Janson cash equal to 75 percent of the face amount of the assigned receivables, charged Janson a finance fee equal to 5 percent of the amount of the loan, and charged interest of 1 percent per month on the outstanding balance of the loan. Under the terms of the agreement, Miller Finance is not free to sell or repledge the assigned receivables.

Janson's customers make their payments to Janson, and $50,000 of the assigned receivables were collected as of the end of August 1998.

REQUIRED 1. Prepare Janson's journal entries (a) to record the July 31 loan and (b) to record the first month's collections of receivables and related payments to Miller Finance.

2. How should the assigned accounts receivable be reported by Janson?

E 8-19. **DEBTOR DEFAULT ON A SECURED BORROWING** Harris Company borrowed $12,000 for six months at 10 percent annual interest from New Castle Bank. As collateral for the loan, Harris pledged accounts receivable with a face value of $14,000 and a related allowance for uncollectible accounts of $1,000. Under the loan terms, New Castle would take possession of and legal title to the accounts receivable in proportion to the extent, if any, that Harris failed to pay either principal or interest on the due date of the loan. On the due date, Harris failed to pay either the principal or the interest amounts due.

REQUIRED Prepare the journal entry for Harris to record the default on the loan agreement.

PART B • Current Payables and Contingencies

E 8-20. **RECORDING TRANSACTIONS INVOLVING LIABILITIES** Selected transactions of Strong Corporation for the current fiscal year ending December 31 are listed below.

a) On December 27, Strong purchased $7,000 of inventory, with payment terms of 3%/10, net 30. Strong has a perpetual inventory system and records purchases net of available purchase discounts.

b) Strong receives $3,458 on December 21 from a bank in return for a non-interest-bearing note due in one year. The bank has a 9 percent discount rate.

c) Employee salaries accrued, but not paid, as of December 31 were $13,850.

REQUIRED Prepare the journal entries to record the above transactions.

E 8-21. **RECORDING TRANSACTIONS INVOLVING LIABILITIES** Selected transactions of Riley Manufacturing for the fiscal year ended December 31, 1998, are listed below.

a) On November 1, Riley borrowed cash from the local bank in exchange for a six-month $110,000 note discounted at 8 percent.

b) December sales were $520,000, including a 4 percent sales tax that is to be remitted to the state before March 15, 1999. Sales and sales taxes are recorded in separate accounts.

c) On December 1, Riley received a $55,000 deposit from a customer to be applied against a parts delivery scheduled to be made on January 20, 1999.

d) On December 15, monthly wages and salaries of $275,000 were paid.

REQUIRED 1. Prepare the appropriate journal entries to record the above transactions.

2. Prepare any 1998 year-end adjusting entries related to interest. Assume straight-line amortization of discounts.

E 8-22. **ACCOUNTING FOR SHORT-TERM NOTES PAYABLE** Assume that Joyce Smith wishes to obtain $630, after bank charges, from her local bank for the purpose of buying a television set. The note signed by Smith is a one-year, non-interest-bearing note, which the bank intends to discount at 10 percent.

REQUIRED 1. What is the face value of the note?

2. Prepare the entry on Smith's books to record her transaction with the bank.

3. What is the effective interest rate incurred by Smith on this transaction?

E 8-23. **ACCOUNTING FOR SHORT-TERM OBLIGATIONS EXPECTED TO BE REFINANCED** Grace Company has a September 30 fiscal year-end, and on September 30, 1998. Grace has $2.4 million of short-term notes payable outstanding. On October 15, 1998, Grace issued 115,000 shares of its $5 par value common stock at $20 per share to generate funds to be used to retire short-term notes payable due on November 7, 1998. After paying brokerage fees and other costs of issuing the common stock, Grace received proceeds from the stock sale of $2.2 million, which was used on October 28 to liquidate short-term notes payable. Grace's 1998 financial statements were published on November 15.

REQUIRED Show how the short-term notes payable that were liquidated on October 28 should be reported on the September 30, 1998, financial statements, including footnote disclosures.

E 8-24. **CURRENT MATURITIES OF LONG-TERM OBLIGATIONS** Wallace Industries has $1 million of long-term debt originally incurred two years ago that is due at the rate of $250,000 annually, beginning six months from now.

REQUIRED 1. What is the general rule for determining how much, if any, of Wallace's $1 million debt would be classified as a current liability on a balance sheet that is prepared one month from now?

2. Under what conditions would the general rule given in your response to part 1 *not* be followed?

E 8-25. **DIVIDENDS PAYABLE** Types of dividends payable include cash dividends payable, stock dividends distributable, property dividends payable, and scrip dividends payable.

REQUIRED 1. Which of these types of dividends payable require recognition of a liability at the date of declaration?

2. If declaration of any of the above dividends does not result in a liability, why not? Be specific about the type of dividend.

E 8-26. **SALES TAXES COLLECTED** The current fiscal year's sales for Farr, Inc., totaled $3 million, including a 3.2 percent sales tax. The sales taxes are to be remitted to the proper taxing authority within six months of the end of the fiscal year.

REQUIRED   Prepare the appropriate journal entries (a) to record Farr's total sales revenue and sales tax obligation for the current year and (b) to record remittance of the sales taxes collected for each of the following independent cases.

1. Farr separates sales revenues and sales taxes when recording sales transactions.
2. Farr does not separate sales revenues and sales taxes when recording sales transactions.

(AICPA, adapted)

E 8-27. **AMOUNTS WITHHELD FROM PAYROLL** In 1998, Easton Company paid total wages and salaries of $350,000, all of which was subject to a 7.65 percent FICA tax rate. Federal, state, and local income taxes withheld from wages and salaries amounted to $90,000, and union dues withheld were $12,200.

REQUIRED   Make the appropriate entry to record wages and salaries expense, the various amounts withheld from employees' wages and salaries, and payment of employees' wages and salaries.

E 8-28. **ACCOUNTING FOR COMPENSATED EMPLOYEE ABSENCES** Peter Corporation began operations on January 1, 1998, at which time it hired 30 new employees at a wage of $20 per hour for a 40-hour workweek. Peter's vacation policy allows 90 hours of paid vacation to be vested for each full year of employment. No paid vacation can be taken until after one year of employment. All of Peter's new employees took paid vacations during 1999, with 2,200 total vacation hours taken. All vacation hours were taken when the wage rate was $21 per hour.

REQUIRED   Prepare the necessary entries for 1998 and 1999 to record the accrual and payment of vacation wages.

E 8-29. **ACCOUNTING FOR EMPLOYER PAYROLL TAX EXPENSE** Total wages and salaries paid by Sam's TV Repair were $173,000 in 1998. Sam has 15 employees, each of whom earns more than $10,000 but less than $16,000 per year. Because of his outstanding record of providing stable employment, Sam is subject to a state unemployment tax rate of only 2.7 percent, although the standard rate in his state is 5.4 percent on the first $7,000 earned by any employee. In 1998, the FUTA tax rate, before credit for state unemployment taxes paid, is 6.2 percent on the first $7,000 paid to each employee and the FICA tax rate is 7.65 percent of the first $60,600 earned by each employee.

REQUIRED   Prepare the appropriate journal entry to record the employer's payroll tax expense for 1998.

E 8-30. **ACCOUNTING FOR PROPERTY TAXES** Owasco Township assesses property in January, sends out property tax bills in February, and expects payment of property taxes in two equal installments on June 30 and December 31. Owasco Township's fiscal year begins on March 1, which also is the lien date for property taxes. Fisher Company received a $6,000 property tax bill on February 17.

REQUIRED   1. What two basic questions must be answered in accounting for property taxes?
2. Assuming that property taxes payable are accrued at the end of each month, what entries would be made by Fisher Company on February 17, March 31, June 30, and December 31?

E 8-31. **PREPAYMENTS FROM CUSTOMERS** Action Publishing Company sells subscriptions to a *Basketball Card Price Guide* that is delivered to customers at the end of every other month, beginning with the end of January. Subscriptions are $12 for one year and are received as follows for the first three months of the current year: January (700 subscriptions), February (675 subscriptions), and March (770 subscriptions).

REQUIRED   1. Prepare the necessary entries for January through March to record subscriptions from, and deliveries to, new customers.
2. Under normal circumstances, unearned subscriptions revenue would be classified as what kind of account? Why?

*E 8-32. **CALCULATING AND RECORDING BONUS EXPENSE** Janice Blake, president of Blake Office Supplies, receives an annual bonus of 15 percent of income after tax expense. Her bonus is deductible for tax purposes and for purposes of bonus calculation. The current year's income before taxes and bonus is $780,000 and the tax rate is 34 percent.

REQUIRED   1. Calculate the tax expense and Blake's bonus for the current year. (Round your answer to the nearest dollar.)
2. Prepare the appropriate journal entries to record the bonus and income taxes.

*E 8-33. **CALCULATING BONUS AND TAX EXPENSES** The chief administrative officer of White Cosmetics, Inc., Mary White, receives a bonus of 12 percent of income each year. Assume effective tax rates for 1998 and 1999 of 32 percent and 34 percent, respectively. Income in 1998 before bonus and taxes is $230,000, and the bonus is deductible for tax purposes; but only taxes are deductible for the purpose of calculating the bonus. Income in 1999 before bonus and tax expenses is $300,000, and the 1999 bonus is based on income after bonus expense but before income taxes.

REQUIRED
1. Calculate White's bonus and the corporation's tax expense for 1998.
2. Calculate White's bonus and the corporation's tax expense for 1999.

E 8-34. **ACCOUNTING FOR PREPAYMENTS AND INCOME TAXES** All the revenue of Tapeland, Inc., comes from selling videotapes on a subscription basis. Its customers buy one-, two-, or three-year subscriptions to a videotape service that allows them to select and order five videotapes per year from a library of more than 3,000 movie tapes. Cash receipts from customers are credited to unearned tape subscription revenue, which had a balance of $3.5 million before December 31, 1998, year-end adjusting entries. Outstanding subscriptions at December 31, 1998, will expire as follows: $700,000 during 1999; $850,000 during 2000; and $975,000 during 2001.

REQUIRED
1. Prepare the appropriate December 31, 1998, adjusting entry to record tape subscription revenue.
2. Assuming expenses of $310,000, taxable income equal to pretax accounting income, and a 34 percent tax rate, prepare the entry to record Videotape's income tax payable for 1998.

E 8-35. **REPORTING LIABILITIES** Indicate how each of the following items should be reported in the financial statements:
1. Discount on note payable.
2. A declared, but unpaid, cash dividend.
3. Prepayments by customers.
4. Employee taxes that have been withheld but not yet remitted.
5. Employee bonuses payable.

E 8-36. **LITIGATION LOSS CONTINGENCY** A truck owned and operated by Marsh Company was involved in an accident with an auto driven by Harder on November 15, 1998. Marsh received notice on January 10, 1999, of a lawsuit for $2 million damages for a personal injury suffered by Harder. The company counsel believes it is probable that the company will have to pay Harder $450,000 but that the award could be as much as $500,000. Marsh's accounting year ends on December 31, and the 1998 financial statements were issued on March 15, 1999.

REQUIRED
1. What amount of loss, if any, must be accrued by a charge to income in 1998?
2. What disclosures, if any, should accompany any contingent loss reported in the 1998 income statement?

(AICPA, adapted)

E 8-37. **LITIGATION LOSS CONTINGENCIES** In May 1998, Walton Company became involved in litigation. As a result, it is probable that Walton will have to pay $2.1 million. In July 1998, a competitor commenced a suit against Walton alleging violation of antitrust laws and seeking damages of $4.2 million. Walton denies the allegations, and the likelihood that Walton will have to pay any damages is remote. In September 1998, Ness County brought action against Walton for $1.5 million for polluting Perch Lake. It is possible that the county's suit will be successful, but the amount of damages Walton will have to pay is not reasonably determinable.

REQUIRED
1. What amount, if any, should be accrued in 1998?
2. Draft the disclosures, if any, that should appear in Walton Company's 1998 financial statements as the result of the litigation in 1998.

(AICPA, adapted)

E 8-38. **CALCULATING AND ACCOUNTING FOR A WARRANTY LIABILITY** In 1998, Ash Company began selling a new line of products with a two-year warranty against defects. Industry experience with similar products indicates that estimated warranty costs are 2 percent of sales during the first year of the warranty and 5 percent of sales during the second year of the warranty. Sales and actual warranty expenditures for 1998 and 1999 are:

YEAR	SALES	ACTUAL WARRANTY EXPENDITURES
1998	$220,000	$ 4,000
1999	500,000	15,000

REQUIRED

1. Give entries for 1998 and 1999 to (*a*) record the sales (on account), (*b*) record estimated warranty expense, and (*c*) record actual warranty expenditures.
2. Calculate the balance of the estimated warranty liability account at the end of 1999.

E 8-39. **CALCULATING ESTIMATED LIABILITY ON PRODUCT PREMIUMS** Cola Corporation has inaugurated a new sales promotional program. For every 10 bottle caps from one-liter bottles that are returned to Cola, customers will receive a beach ball that costs Cola $.50 per unit. Cola estimates that 30 percent of the bottle caps in the hands of customers will be redeemed. During the year, 3 million one-liter bottles of Cola are sold at a total retail price of $4.5 million. Cola has purchased 100,000 beach balls and distributed 60,000 of them to customers. At the end of the year, Cola recognizes a liability equal to the estimated cost of beach balls that may be distributed in the future.

REQUIRED Calculate the estimated liability for beach balls still to be distributed.

E 8-40. **ACCOUNTING FOR ESTIMATED LIABILITY ON PRODUCT PREMIUMS** Ringer Company includes one coupon in each box of dog food it sells. In return for 10 coupons, customers receive a doggy toy that the company purchases in large quantities for $1.50 each. Ringer's experience indicates that 70 percent of the coupons will be redeemed. During 1998, 7,000 toys were purchased, 90,000 boxes of dog food were sold, and 50,000 coupons were redeemed. During 1999, an additional 4,000 toys were purchased, 80,000 boxes of dog food were sold, and 60,000 coupons were redeemed.

REQUIRED Prepare the appropriate 1998 and 1999 journal entries to record the following events:
1. The purchase of toys.
2. Premium expense.
3. Coupon redemption.

(CGAA, adapted)

E 8-41. **CALCULATING AND ACCOUNTING FOR LIABILITY ON COUPONS** Brown Dog Food Company distributes to consumers coupons that may be presented (on or before a stated expiration date) to grocers for discounts on purchases of Brown Dog Food. The grocers are reimbursed when they send the coupons to Brown. Brown has found that in the past an average of 45 percent of the coupons have been redeemed. During 1998, Brown issued two separate series of coupons, as follows:

ISSUE DATE	EXPIRATION DATE	TOTAL VALUE ISSUED	AMOUNT DISBURSED ON REDEMPTION AS OF 12/31/98
1/1/98	6/30/99	$50,000	$16,000
7/1/98	12/31/99	60,000	18,000

REQUIRED

1. Calculate the amount of the liability for unredeemed coupons as of December 31, 1998.
2. Prepare the appropriate December 31 adjusting entry, given your answer to part 1 and assuming no liability account existed before December 31.

The problems marked with an asterisk (*) refer to Appendix 8–1.

PART A • Cash and Current Receivables

P 8-1. **RECONCILING A BANK STATEMENT** The following information pertains to the cash account and bank account of Tillman Corporation for the month of December:

a) Bank checking account balance, December 31, $271.90.
b) Cash balance per books, December 31, $94.50.
c) A customer's check for $100 was returned with the November bank statement. The check was redeposited in December but was returned with the December bank statement marked NSF. Tillman decided to forgo the possibility of trying to collect on the check.
d) Deposits in transit on December 31:

#1247 $49.70
#1248   20.00

e) The bank charged Tillman's account in December for $21 for a check written by Alfred Company.
f) Outstanding checks at December 31:

#64 $ 76.25
#73   128.00
#75   53.50
#79   94.85
#82   560.00

(Check #64 was also outstanding at the end of November.)
g) Bank charges for the month of December:

Service charge, $2.70
Charge for note collections (see part *h*), $9

h) Notes collected by bank but not recorded in Tillman's records:

Principal $360.00
Interest 7.20

i) Deposit #1230 in the amount of $258 from collection of an account receivable was recorded by Tillman in the cash account as $658.
j) Check #70 in the amount of $500 was written to establish a petty cash fund. Tillman failed to record the check.

REQUIRED 1. Construct a bank reconciliation for the month of December.
2. Prepare the entries necessary to adjust and correct the accounts of Tillman Corporation.

P 8-2.   **RECONCILING A BANK STATEMENT**   The cash account and bank statement for Ireland Company for the month of July are as follows:

CASH

July 1 Bal.	4,829	Check #216	July 3	140
3	480	217	5	316
5	629	218	5	219
9	780	219	9	160
9	79	221	14	80
12	810	222	14	68
14	635	223	15	104
23	90	224	16	394
28	14	225	19	175
31	220	226	20	175
31	165	227	21	314
	8,731	228	24	48
		229	29	96
		230	30	112
				2,401

IRELAND ACCOUNT #NB990

CHECKS				DEPOSITS	DATE	BALANCE
					July 1	6,077
48		1,040		165	2	5,154
	325			480	3	5,309
140				692	5	5,861
219	316	160		79	9	5,245
1,260				780	10	4,765
	79DM			1,445	14	6,131
80	68	394	104		18	5,485
				110NC	20	5,595
175	314			90	23	5,196
48					25	5,148
				14	29	5,162
96	4SC			165	31	5,227

DM: debit memorandum (NSF check)   SC: service charge   NC: note collection

Additional information:
a) The bank statement is correct in all respects.
b) Ireland failed to record check #220, which was written on July 9 to acquire equipment.
c) The interest on the note collected by the bank was $10.
d) Check #225, written to a supplier, was destroyed in the check-writing machine, and check #226 was issued as a replacement.

REQUIRED   **I.** Prepare a bank reconciliation statement for the months of June and July.
2. Prepare the entries at July 31 to adjust the accounts of Ireland Company.

P 8-3. **RECONCILING A BANK STATEMENT** You are engaged in the audit of Justin Corporation and have gathered the following information about the company's cash account balance at December 31, 1998.

a) The cash account (in summary form) is as follows:

Cash

Balance, 12/1/98	7,906	Disbursements during	
Receipts for December	35,627	December	38,927

b) The bank statement for December contained the following:

11/30 balance...	$ 6,750
Total deposits and other credits.......................	35,962
Checks and other debits...............................	39,029
(Including a service charge of $7, an NSF check of $48, and a safety deposit charge of $20)	

c) Deposit in transit, December 31, $1,333.

d) On December 10 the company failed to record a deposit made to the bank totaling $420.

e) The only check outstanding at December 31 was check #1046, which also was outstanding at November 30.

f) The November 30 bank reconciliation was as follows:

Balance per bank...		$6,750
Add:		
Deposit in transit......................................		1,500
Service charge for November............................		20
Error made by Justin in recording check written for $180; check was recorded at $18......................................		162
Deduct:		
Outstanding checks:		
#1043	$100	
#1044	70	
#1046	65	
#1048	39..	(274)
Note collected by bank (including interest).........................		(252)
Balance per books...		$7,906

REQUIRED
1. Calculate the cash balance at November 30.
2. Prepare a bank reconciliation statement for December that arrives at the correct cash balance per books and per bank.

P 8-4.   **PETTY CASH**   Green Cartage Company had the following transactions in March and April:

March 1   Established a petty cash fund in the amount of $700.

March 19   The custodian of the fund requested replenishment of the fund and submitted the following vouchers:

Postage stamps and envelopes	$ 22
Warehouse supplies	100
Cash withdrawal by owner	75
Miscellaneous garage repairs	80
Cash in fund	523

April 3   Decreased the amount of the fund by $100.

April 20   The custodian requested replenishment of the fund and submitted the following vouchers:

Garage repairs	$170
Warehouse supplies	43
Miscellaneous expenditures	39
Cash in fund	400

REQUIRED

1. Prepare the entries to record the above petty cash transactions.
2. How would the petty cash fund appear on a March 31 balance sheet?

P 8-5.   **SALES DISCOUNTS; ESTIMATING UNCOLLECTIBLE RECEIVABLES**   Oliver Company records credit sales net of cash (sales) discounts. Its balance sheet presentation for accounts receivable at the end of 1997 was as follows:

Accounts receivable	$200,000[a]
Allowance for uncollectible accounts	15,000

[a]The cash discount period has expired for the receivables, and the appropriate adjusting entry was made at the end of 1997.

During 1998, the following transactions occurred:

Cash sales	$350,000
Credit sales, net of cash discounts	439,000
Returns on credit sales, net of cash discounts	4,000
Cash collections from customers:	
Within the cash discount period	186,200
After the discount period had expired (includes interest of $20,000)	400,000
Accounts written off as uncollectible	10,000
Interest accrued on accounts receivable not paid within the discount period	2,200

REQUIRED

1. Prepare the entries to record the 1998 transactions.
2. Prepare the adjusting entry to record uncollectible accounts expense for 1998, assuming that the expense is based on adjustment of the allowance account to equal 15 percent of the ending accounts receivable balance.

P 8-6.   **ACCOUNTS RECEIVABLE AND ALLOWANCE TRANSACTIONS AND RELATIONSHIPS**   The following information is available for the Bossier Company (in thousands of dollars):

	1998	1999	2000
Charge sales	$ 900	$1,100	$1,000
Cash sales	600	800	700
Total	$1,500	$1,900	$1,700
Accounts receivable (end of year)	$ 170	$ 230	$ 220
Allowance for doubtful accounts (end of year)	47	30	56
Accounts written off as uncollectible (during year)	2	50	4

REQUIRED

Assuming there was no change in the method used to estimate doubtful accounts during 1998, 1999, and 2000, what was the balance in the allowance for doubtful accounts at the beginning of 1998?

(AICPA, adapted)

P 8-7. **UNCOLLECTIBLE ACCOUNTS EXPENSE; AGING** Blue Corporation uses the allowance method of accounting for bad debts and has used a historical rate of 2.5 percent of credit sales to estimate this expense. The aging schedule of Blue's accounts receivable at the end of the current year appears as follows:

DAYS OUTSTANDING	AMOUNT	PROBABILITY OF COLLECTION
0–30 days	$700,000	.98
31–60 days	200,000	.90
61–90 days	80,000	.60
Over 90 days	50,000	.30

Total credit sales for the current year were $3,200,000. The allowance account had a credit balance of $29,400 at the beginning of the current year, and accounts totaling $18,000 were written off during the current year.

REQUIRED

1. Calculate the expense for the current year if Blue continues to use the percentage-of-sales method to estimate its bad debt expense.

2. Calculate the expense for the current year if bad debt expense is based on an aging of the accounts receivable.

3. Refer to part 2. Calculate the balance in the allowance account at the end of the current year.

P 8-8. **DISCOUNTING NOTES RECEIVABLE** Quick Company had the following notes receivable and related accounts at December 31, 1997:

Notes receivable (net of $4,800 discount) **$68,000**
Less: Discounted notes receivable.. **(20,000)**
    Total **$48,000**

The notes receivable account consists of two notes. The note not discounted is a non-interest-bearing note due at the end of 1998 and accepted at a 10 percent effective rate of interest, which yielded a present value of $48,000.

During 1998, the following note transactions occurred:

March 1   Quick was notified that the maker of the note discounted by Quick paid the note at maturity.

July 1   Sold land by accepting a one-year, 6 percent note with a face value of $10,000. The market rate of interest for notes of similar risk was 6 percent, and the cost of the land sold was $7,000.

Dec. 1   Discounted the note accepted in July. The note was discounted by Slippery Books Savings and Loan at a discount rate of 8 percent. The transaction was a secured borrowing and Slippery Books was free to pledge the note.

REQUIRED Prepare journal entries to record the above transactions.

P 8-9. **SALES RETURNS** Newt Cassette Distributors sells tapes and records to record shops and discount stores. These retailers have the privilege of returning to Newt any unsold merchandise for full credit or for other merchandise in exchange. Because of obsolescence, returned goods are normally resold overseas for 35 percent of the original selling price. Newt uses a perpetual inventory system and records returned merchandise at net realizable value less a normal profit.

The following transactions occurred during the year:

a) Sold, on account, 10,000 record albums of "Sonny's Back" for $48,000. The cost per album was $2.

b) Customers returned 2,000 albums for credit.

c) The returned albums were sold (no return privilege) for cash to an overseas discount shop for $1.75 per album.

REQUIRED

1. Prepare the entries to record the above transactions, assuming that Newt does not use an allowance for sales returns account.

2. Prepare the entries to record the above transactions, assuming that Newt uses an allowance for sales returns account and that it is estimated that 30 percent of the albums originally sold will be returned.

P 8-10.   **MISCELLANEOUS RECEIVABLE TRANSACTIONS**   Hot Tubbs has a fiscal year that ends on December 31. The company sells health equipment and had the following transactions during 1998:

April 1   Hot Tubbs sold a special-order sauna on credit for $5,000 and received in return an 8 percent note receivable. Both interest and principal are due on April 1, 1999. The interest rate on the note equaled the market rate for a note of this type.

June 30   Hot Tubbs sold a special-order bathtub on credit for $4,320 and received in return a non-interest-bearing note receivable due on June 30, 1999. The market rate of interest for notes of this type is 8 percent per year.

Nov. 1   Hot Tubbs has substantial accounts receivable arising from credit sales of its regular merchandise. On this date, the company transferred receivables with a face value of $40,000 to a factor on a nonrecourse basis. The terms of the transfer met the conditions of a sale of the receivables. The factor paid Hot Tubbs $35,000 for the receivables. Hot Tubbs had recorded allowances for sales returns and doubtful accounts of $2,500.

Dec. 1   Hot Tubbs discounted a customer's $18,000, 9 percent note, which had been accepted in settlement of an account receivable on October 1. The note had a maturity date of April 1, 1999. The bank discounted the note at 10 percent. The discounting is a secured borrowing; the lender is not free to pledge the note.

REQUIRED

1. Prepare the necessary journal entries for Hot Tubbs on April 1, June 30, November 1, and December 1.

2. Prepare a schedule showing how the above transactions and any required adjusting entries will affect Hot Tubbs's income statement for the year ending December 31, 1998.

3. Show how the above transactions, including the effects of any adjusting entries, will appear on Hot Tubbs's balance sheet at December 31, 1998.

P 8-11.   **ASSIGNMENT OF ACCOUNTS RECEIVABLE**   Robinson Company finances some of its current operations by assigning accounts receivable to a finance company. On July 1, 1998, it assigned accounts receivable amounting to $180,000, and the finance company lent 80 percent of the accounts assigned less a commission charge of 1/2 of 1 percent of the total accounts assigned. Robinson's customers were instructed to make payments directly to the finance company.

On July 31, Robinson Company received a statement that the finance company had collected $90,000 of these accounts and had made an additional charge of 1/2 of 1 percent of the total accounts outstanding as of July 31. This charge was to be deducted at the time of the first remittance due Robinson Company from the finance company. On August 31, the Robinson Company received a second statement from the finance company, together with a check for the amount due. The statement indicated that the finance company had collected an additional $60,000 and had made a further charge of 1/2 of 1 percent of the balance outstanding as of August 31.

REQUIRED

1. Prepare the entry to record the assignment of the accounts.

2. Prepare Robinson's entry to record the data from the first report from the finance company (July 31).

3. Prepare Robinson's entry to record the data in the report of August 31.

4. Explain how the items should be reported on the financial statements of Robinson Company at July 31 and August 31.

P 8-12.   **AGING RECEIVABLES**   Dell Company sells office equipment and supplies to many organizations in the city and surrounding area on contract terms of 2/10, n/30. In the past, over 75 percent of the credit customers have taken advantage of the discount by paying within 10 days of the invoice date.

The number of customers taking the full 30 days to pay has increased within the last year. Current indications are that less than 60 percent of the customers are now taking the discount. Bad debts as a percentage of gross credit sales have risen from the 1.5 percent provided in past years to about 4 percent in the current year.

The controller has responded to a request for more information on the deterioration in collections of accounts receivable with the report reproduced on page 451.

The fact that some credit accounts will prove uncollectible is normal. Annual bad debt write-offs have been 1.5 percent of gross credit sales over the past five years. During the last fiscal year, this percentage increased to slightly less than 4 percent. The current accounts receivable balance is $1.2 million. The condition of this balance in terms of age and probability of noncollection is as follows:

Dell Company
Finance Committee Report
Accounts Receivable Collections
May 31, 1998

AGE CATEGORY	AMOUNT IN CATEGORY	PROBABILITY OF NONCOLLECTION
Not yet due	$ 816,000	1.0%
Less than 30 days past due	180,000	3.5
30–60 days past due	96,000	5.0
61–120 days past due	60,000	9.0
121–180 days past due	30,000	25.0
Over 180 days past due	18,000	80.0
	$1,200,000	

The allowance for doubtful accounts had a credit balance of $8,000 on June 1, 1997. Dell has provided for a monthly bad debts expense accrual during the current fiscal year based on the assumption that 4 percent of gross credit sales will be uncollectible. Total gross credit sales for the 1997–1998 fiscal year amounted to $3 million. Write-offs of bad accounts during the year totaled $112,000.

REQUIRED

1. Prepare an accounts receivable aging schedule for Dell Company using the age categories identified in the controller's report to the Finance Committee, showing the estimated amount that is uncollectible for each category and in total.
2. Calculate the amount of the year-end adjustment necessary to bring the allowance for doubtful accounts to the balance indicated by the aging analysis. Then prepare the necessary journal entry to adjust the accounting records.

(IMA, adapted)

P 8-13. **REVIEW OF ACCOUNTS RECEIVABLE AND UNCOLLECTIBLE ACCOUNTS** Rust Corporation makes all sales on credit. The company records sales net of sales discount and gives its customers a 3 percent sales discount for prompt payment. You are performing an audit for Rust Corporation and are provided the following summary of transactions affecting accounts receivable for the current year:

	DR	CR
ACCOUNTS RECEIVABLE		
Beginning balance	$120,000	
Credit sales	72,000	
Sales returns		$ 6,000
Collections		40,000
	$192,000	$46,000
Ending balance per books	$146,000	
ALLOWANCE FOR UNCOLLECTIBLE ACCOUNTS		
Beginning balance		$10,000
Note accepted in settlement of accounts		1,200
Write-offs of customers' accounts	$ 3,600	
	$ 3,600	$11,200
Ending balance per books		$ 7,600

During the audit, the following items are brought to your attention:

a) Credit sales amounted to $110,000 but were recorded in accounts receivable at cost.
b) A customer gave a note in full settlement of her account. The entry was recorded by debiting notes receivable and crediting allowance for uncollectible accounts.
c) At the end of the year, there were accounts receivable totaling $32,010 for which

the sales discount period had expired. Rust Corporation did not recognize this event in its accounts.

1. Prepare all necessary entries to correct any errors made by Rust Corporation relative to the above information.

2. Prepare the adjusting entry to record uncollectible accounts expense for the year under the assumption that the expense is determined by adjusting allowance for uncollectible accounts to equal 6 percent of ending accounts receivable.

P 8-14. **ACCOUNTS RECEIVABLE; MISCELLANEOUS**   Tinker Textile Corporation had the following transactions, listed in summary form, for 1998 and 1999, its first two years of operations. For simplicity, assume that the transactions are in chronological order.

1998

a) Sales on account, $300,000. Tinker allows return privileges and uses the allowance method at the end of each year to estimate returns expected in the following year. Actual returns during 1998 were $28,000.

b) Collections from customers, $175,000.

c) Accepted a $10,000 note in settlement of an account receivable. Interest on the note, payable at maturity, was $800.

d) Customer accounts written off as uncollectible, $4,000. Tinker will use the allowance method of accounting for bad debts.

e) Discounted the note in part *c* at a local savings and loan. Interest earned prior to the discount date, $300; proceeds received, $10,100. The transfer qualifies as a sale of the note and related interest revenue.

f) Estimated returns in 1999 on sales in part *a*, $5,000.

g) Aging indicated that $3,500 of the ending balance of accounts receivable probably was uncollectible.

(*Note:* Tinker's cost of goods sold for 1998 was adjusted appropriately for the cost of goods expected to be returned in 1999.)

1999

h) The savings and loan notified Tinker that the customer's note and interest had been paid.

i) Transferred, with recourse, the balance of accounts receivable to State Factoring Company. Under the recourse provisions, Tinker had an obligation to absorb all returns and uncollectibles. The balances in Tinker's allowance accounts for returns and uncollectible accounts were reasonable estimates of this obligation. In addition to a factoring fee of $2,000, State Factoring withheld $8,500 for customer returns and uncollectible accounts. Tinker also agreed to repurchase, on demand, up to $22,000 in receivables from State Factoring.

j) State Factoring reported that receivables totaling $53,200 had been collected and that $3,000 in receivables were uncollectible. Additionally, customer returns to Tinker totaled $4,800.

k) State Factoring mailed a check for $700 to Tinker in final settlement and requested that Tinker repurchase the remaining outstanding receivables of $22,000.

l) Tinker mailed a check for $22,000 in exchange for the outstanding receivables.

1. Prepare all necessary journal entries for the above transactions.

2. Prepare a schedule summarizing the effects of Tinker's transfer of receivables arrangement with State Factoring.

3. Prepare a schedule showing Tinker's receivables and related allowances immediately after transaction *l*. Assume that the return period has not expired.

P 8-15. **UNCOLLECTIBLE ACCOUNTS, ASSIGNMENTS, FACTORING, VALUATION OF NOTES**
A. At January 1, 1998, the credit balance in the allowance for doubtful accounts of the Master Company was $400,000. For 1998 the provision for doubtful accounts is based on an aging of accounts receivable. Net sales for 1998 were $50 million. The 1998 ending allowance for doubtful accounts, based on the latest available facts, is required to be $350,000. During 1998 uncollectible receivables amounting to $410,000 were written off against the allowance for doubtful accounts.

Prepare a schedule showing the balance in Master's doubtful accounts allowance at December 31, 1998.

B. The Guide Company requires additional cash for its business. Guide has decided to use its accounts receivable to raise the additional cash as follows:

a) On July 1, 1998, Guide assigned $200,000 of accounts receivable to the Cell Finance Company. Guide received an advance from Cell of 85 percent of the assigned accounts receivable less a commission on the advance of 3 percent. Before December 31, 1998, Guide collected $150,000 on the assigned accounts receivable and remitted $160,000 to Cell, $10,000 of which represented interest on the advance from Cell.

b) On December 1, 1998, Guide sold $300,000 of net accounts receivable to the Factoring Company for $260,000. The receivables were sold outright on a nonrecourse basis.

c) On December 31, 1998, Guide received an advance of $100,000 from the Domestic Bank by pledging $120,000 of its accounts receivable. Guide's first payment to Domestic is due on January 30, 1999.

REQUIRED Prepare a schedule showing the income statement effect for the year ended December 31, 1998, as a result of the above facts.

C. Allen Corporation transfers receivables with a face value of $80,000 to Ford Factors. The transfer is with recourse, and Allen has recorded allowances for sales discounts and uncollectible accounts totaling $3,000, which are reasonable estimates of these amounts. Ford Factors pays Allen $76,500 for the receivables. Allen accepts a recourse obligation for uncollectible receivables up to a fair value of $2,500.

REQUIRED Prepare Allen Corporation's entry to record the transfer.

P 8-16. **COMPREHENSIVE REVIEW OF CASH AND RECEIVABLES** You are conducting an audit of Dave & Don Partnership for the year ending December 31, 1998. Below are several transactions engaged in by the company from January 1996, when it began operations, through 1998.

a) D&D uses the allowance method of accounting for uncollectible accounts and calculates uncollectible accounts expense as a percentage of sales. Recoveries of previously written-off amounts are credited to miscellaneous revenues. Past recoveries are as follows:

1996	**$1,800**
1997	8,800
1998	9,200

b) On January 2, 1997, D&D made an installment sale for $25,000. The installment contract called for 25 monthly payments of $1,000 plus 1 percent interest on the unpaid balance beginning January 31, 1997. The item sold had cost D&D $14,000. Since collectibility of the installment could not be estimated, D&D used the installment method of accounting for the transaction. After making the payment on June 30, 1998, the customer defaulted on the contract and D&D repossessed the item sold, which had an estimated fair value of $2,000. D&D recorded the default and repossession as follows:

Repossessed merchandise	2,000	
Installment receivables		2,000

c) On July 1, 1998, D&D sold a tract of land that cost $45,000 by accepting a one-year, non-interest-bearing note receivable for $55,000. At the date of sale, the market rate of interest for similar notes was 10 percent. D&D recorded the sale and related interest as follows:

7/1/98	Notes receivable	55,000	
	Land		45,000
	Gain on sale		10,000
12/31/98	No entry because D&D's bookkeeper decided that any interest revenue would be recorded when the note was collected.		

d) On November 1, 1998, D&D discounted a 90-day, $12,000, 6 percent customer's note dated September 1, 1998. The bank discounted the note and gave D&D proceeds of $12,080. The bank is free to sell or pledge the note and D&D does not have the right to redeem the note on short notice. D&D recorded the transaction as follows:

Cash	12,080	
Notes receivable		12,080

REQUIRED Prepare adjusting or correcting entries, as necessary, for each of the above transactions. All errors that affect years prior to 1998 should be corrected through the partners' capital accounts. Dave and Don share profits and losses equally.

P 8-17. COMPREHENSIVE REVIEW OF CASH AND RECEIVABLES Several 1998 transactions of Wilson Company are listed below:

a) On December 1, 1998, Wilson Co. assigned $60,000 in accounts receivable to a finance company with recourse, receiving 85 percent of the accounts assigned less a service charge of 2 percent of the advance. Customers were directed to remit directly to the finance company. The assignment was recorded as follows:

Cash ($51,000 – $1,020).	49,980	
Interest expense.	10,020	
Accounts receivable.		60,000

At the end of December, Wilson was notified by the finance company that $40,000 of receivables assigned had been collected and that $750 of such collections should be considered interest. No entry had been made for the collections and interest.

b) Wilson's bank reconciliation for the month of December 1998 was as follows:

Balance per bank.	**$16,000**
Deposit in transit	**2,000**
Service charge.	**20**
Error by Wilson bookkeeper on check #166	**300**
Outstanding checks	**(3,000)**
Balance per books.	**$15,320**

Wilson made the following adjusting entry for the above:

Cash.	3,000	
Accounts payable		3,000

c) Wilson has a petty cash fund of $1,500. When the cash fund was replenished in September for expenditures of $1,150, the following entry was made:

Petty cash	1,150	
Cash		1,150

d) On December 31, 1998, Wilson transferred receivables with a face value of $40,000 to Bank of Brewster County under conditions justifying treatment as a sale of the receivables. The transfer was with recourse, and Wilson agreed to accept responsibility for any of the receivables that were uncollectible. Wilson also agreed to take back a maximum of $5,000 fair value of these receivables at the bank's request. The bank charged a factoring fee of $1,000, held back $1,500 as a standard bank procedure to cover uncollectibles, and remitted $37,500 in cash to Wilson. Wilson recorded the transfer as follows:

Cash	37,500	
Due from Bank of Brewster County	1,500	
Loss on sale of receivables	1,000	
Accounts receivable.		40,000

REQUIRED Prepare adjusting or correcting entries, as necessary, for each of the above transactions.

P 8-18. FINANCIAL REPORTING PROBLEM: CURRENT RECEIVABLES The 1995 Annual Report of General Electric Company is presented in Appendix B of the textbook. The consolidated financial statements of both General Electric (GE) and General Electric Capital Services, Inc. (GECS), and separate financial statement data for GE and GECS are presented.

REQUIRED Use the financial statement data for GE alone, plus information provided in Management's Discussion of Financial Resources and Liquidity and the footnotes to the financial statements, to answer the following questions:

I. What dollar amount of current receivables did GE have in 1995 and 1994, respectively?

2. What was GE's ratio of current receivables to total assets in 1995? In 1994?

3. What amount of GE's current receivables was due specifically from customers in 1995? In 1994?

4. What was GE's customer receivables turnover in 1995? In 1994?

5. What is one source of current receivables other than amounts owed by customers?

6. In terms of dollar amounts, what four areas of GE's business activity accounted for the most current receivables?

7. What economic entity is GE's largest customer?

PART B • Current Payables and Contingencies

P 8-19. **RECORDING TRANSACTIONS INVOLVING LIABILITIES** Selected transactions of Hondo Company for the current fiscal year ending December 31 are listed below.

a) On December 3, Hondo received a $3,000 prepayment from a customer for goods that Hondo is to deliver on January 10 of the next year.

b) During December, deposits from customers on returnable containers amounted to $415.

c) During December, cash sales of products totaled $19,734, which included a 4 percent sales tax that must be remitted to the state by February 1 of the next year.

d) Salaries expense for December was $13,400, which included federal, state, and local income taxes payable of $4,800 and employee FICA taxes withheld at the rate of 7.65 percent.

e) Hondo follows the practice of recording its current property tax liability on the lien date and then recognizing an equal amount of property tax expense each month over the fiscal year of the taxing unit. Property taxes of $14,400 became a lien on March 1, the beginning of the taxing unit's current fiscal year, and were paid in equal amounts on June 30 and December 31.

REQUIRED Prepare the necessary journal entries to record the above events and transactions on Hondo's books. For part *d*, prepare only the withholding entry. For part *e*, prepare all necessary entries for events that occurred during the current fiscal year.

P 8-20. **RECORDING TRANSACTIONS INVOLVING LIABILITIES** Selected transactions of Urton, Inc., for the fiscal year ended December 31, 1998, are listed below.

a) Salaries, which are paid on the fifteenth of each month, were $135,700 for the period December 16–31, 1998.

b) Urton purchased $275,300 of inventory between December 23 and December 31. Eighty-five percent of the purchases were on account. All purchases on account have terms of 3%/12, net 30. Urton has a perpetual inventory system and records accounts payable net of purchase discounts. No accounts were paid by December 31.

c) On November 15, Urton borrowed cash from a local savings and loan in exchange for a 90-day, $200,000 note discounted at 8.70 percent.

d) December sales were $391,440, including a 5 percent sales tax that must be paid to the state during the first quarter of 1999. Sales and sales taxes are recorded in separate accounts.

e) On December 11, a $50,000 forklift truck was purchased for use in the warehouse. The equipment was paid for with $15,000 cash and by signing a $35,000, one-year, 10 percent note.

f) During 1998, estimated federal income taxes of $78,750 were paid each quarter. On December 31, it was determined that actual federal income tax expense (for both accounting and tax return purposes) for 1998 was $347,500.

REQUIRED 1. Prepare the necessary journal entries to record the above transactions.

2. Prepare any 1998 year-end adjusting entries related to interest expense on notes payable. (Assume that 50 percent of the discount on the note payable in part *c* is amortized on December 31, 1998.)

P 8-21. **RECORDING TRANSACTIONS INVOLVING LIABILITIES** Selected transactions for Barstow Corporation, which has a December 31 fiscal year-end, are listed below.

a) On August 31, Barstow retired $80,000 of its $300,000, 12 percent, long-term note payable to New Town Bank. The long-term note had been signed six months earlier. The $80,000 portion of the note, plus related accrued interest, was retired by using $27,800 of Barstow's own cash and signing a six-month, $60,000 note discounted at 10 percent by New Town Bank.

b) Prepayments by customers on orders that will be delivered within six months of the end of Barstow's current fiscal year were $125,000.

c) Total sales of goods in the current year totaled $1,005,795, which includes a 3 percent sales tax that must be remitted to the state within two months of Barstow's fiscal year-end. Cash sales were one-third of total sales. Sales and sales taxes payable are recorded in separate accounts.

d) Barstow's practice is to accrue its property taxes monthly. Barstow received a $16,500 property tax bill on September 10, based on an August 1 assessment. The fiscal year of the governmental taxing unit begins on September 1, which also is the lien date for property taxes. Property taxes must be paid in equal installments on November 1 and April 1.

e) On December 12, Barstow purchased $213,600 of inventory from Wallace Whole-sale, with payment terms of 2%/10, net 30. Barstow has a perpetual inventory system and records accounts payable net of available purchase discounts. The invoice was paid on December 20.

REQUIRED

1. Prepare the necessary journal entries to record the above transactions, including all property tax entries for September through December.

2. Prepare the year-end adjusting entry related to interest on the $60,000 note in item *a*. (Assume that two-thirds of the discount on the note is amortized.)

P 8-22. **ACCOUNTING FOR SHORT-TERM OBLIGATIONS TO BE REFINANCED** The fiscal year of Hewit Implement Company ends on June 30, and Hewit normally issues its financial statements about August 15. As of the end of the current fiscal year, Hewit has $300,000 in one-year notes payable that are due within the next six to eight months, but Hewit intends to refinance them by replacing them with a five-year series of guaranteed renewable short-term obligations. On July 20 Hewit signs just the sort of refinancing agreement that it has been looking for, except that the new agreement provides a maximum of only $280,000 worth of refinancing, and the total amount available is limited to 75 percent of the fair value of the collateral provided by Hewit. Because of restrictive aspects of other financing agreements to which Hewit is a party, it is determined that collateral available for the new agreement is $370,000.

REQUIRED

1. Identify and discuss the circumstances under which a short-term obligation should be reported in the financial statements as other than a current liability.

2. What are the important factors to be considered in determining Hewit's proper accounting for and disclosure of the $300,000 of one-year notes in the current year's financial statements?

3. Demonstrate, by balance sheet classification and appropriate footnote disclosure, how Hewit should report this situation in its current financial statements.

P 8-23. **CALCULATING AND ACCOUNTING FOR PAYROLL OBLIGATIONS** Wages for the period January 1 through June 30 and wages for June for the four employees of Heston Manufacturing are listed below:

EMPLOYEE	WAGES THROUGH 6/30	WAGES FOR JUNE
J. Alden	$45,300	$8,000
P. Watson	32,000	5,500
M. Fields	21,500	4,000
S. Golden	17,000	3,000

Assume a FICA tax rate of 7.65 percent for both the employee and the employer applicable to the first $65,400 of an employee's wages. Further assume a FUTA tax rate of 6.2 percent (before credit for contributions to state unemployment) and a state unemployment tax rate of 5.4 percent, only two-thirds of which is applicable to Heston because of the company's stable employment record. Both unemployment tax rates are applicable to the first $7,000 of wages paid to each employee. The federal income tax rate for Alden and Watson is 30 percent, while Fields and Golden are subject to a 25 percent federal tax rate.

REQUIRED

1. Calculate the federal income tax withheld, the employer and employee FICA taxes, and the state and federal unemployment taxes related to each employee's wages for June.

2. Prepare the necessary entry to record wages expense, various payroll liabilities, and payment of June wages to the four employees.

3. Prepare the necessary entry to record Heston's payroll tax expense for June.

P 8-24. **ACCOUNTING FOR COMPENSATED EMPLOYEE ABSENCES** Swanson Company's policy is to allow one hour of paid sick leave to accrue for each two weeks of employment. During its first year of operation, Swanson's employees accumulated 650 hours of sick leave, 240 hours of sick leave were taken, and hourly wage rates were $16. Swanson's employees are allowed to use accumulated sick leave to take compensated time off from work even though they are not ill.

REQUIRED

1. What conditions must exist in order for an employer to accrue a liability for employees' rights to receive compensation for future absences from work?

2. Under what sick pay benefits policy might an employer not accrue a liability for sick pay benefits?

3. Assuming that accrual of a sick leave pay liability is appropriate, prepare any entry(ies) that may be necessary for Swanson in its first year of operations.

P 8-25. **ACCOUNTING FOR PROPERTY TAXES** Gibson Distributing Company, a calendar-year company, receives a property tax bill for $18,000 on February 20. The bill is for one year and is based on an early January assessment of the value of Gibson's business property. Gibson employs two accountants, T. Davis and S. Cline, who normally have similar views about accounting issues. Accounting for property taxes, however, is one subject about which the two simply cannot agree. Davis believes that property taxes for the year should be recorded as a liability on the lien date, April 30, while Cline thinks that the property tax liability should be accrued on a monthly basis over the taxing authority's fiscal year, which begins on April 30. In any case, the taxes are due in two equal installments on July 1 of the current year and January 1 of the following year.

REQUIRED
1. Present the best argument you can in support of Davis's view.
2. Give two reasons why Davis's approach may be inferior to Cline's approach.
3. Assume that Cline's opinion is adopted as Gibson's property tax accounting policy. Make the necessary entries (if any) on February 20, April 30, July 1, and December 31 (the end of Gibson's fiscal year).

*P 8-26. **PAYROLL WITHHOLDING LIABILITIES, BONUS PAYABLE, AND INCOME TAX PAYABLE** Hartman, Inc., has 12 employees, all of whom are on salary. Based on the employees' contracts, total salary expense for 1998 is $637,450, on which $191,325 was withheld for employee income taxes. On January 1, Hartman estimates that its total accounting and taxable income for 1998 will be $680,000. Income at this level will subject Hartman to a 34 percent income tax rate. Hartman's record of stable employment entitles the company to a favorable state unemployment tax rate of 3.8 percent, even though the standard for the state is 5.4 percent on the first $7,000 earned by each employee. All of Hartman's employees' salaries are above $7,000. In 1998, the FUTA rate, before credit for state unemployment taxes paid, is 6.2 percent on the first $7,000 paid to each employee, and the FICA rate is 7.65 percent of the first $65,400 earned by each employee and 1.45 percent of each employee's earnings in excess of $65,400. Each of Hartman's employees earns less than $65,400 in 1998. Thus, none of Hartman's total salaries is subject to the 1.45 percent for wages in excess of $65,400.

In addition to her basic salary, the president of Hartman is entitled to a bonus equal to 5 percent of corporate income after all expenses, including both her bonus and the corporation's tax expense. The president's annual salary is sufficiently high that her bonus is not subject to the state unemployment tax, FUTA, or FICA.

REQUIRED
1. a) Prepare an entry to record salary expense, payroll withholdings, and payment of salaries for all of 1998.
   b) Prepare an entry to record Hartman's payroll tax expense for 1998.
2. Prepare the quarterly entry for Hartman to record estimated income taxes paid. Show supporting calculations.
3. a) Calculate the president's bonus for 1998.
   b) Prepare the journal entry to record payment of the president's bonus.
4. Prepare the year-end entry to record actual tax expense for 1998. Show supporting calculations. (Assume that actual taxable income for 1998 is $680,000.)

*P 8-27. **CALCULATING BONUSES PAYABLE** Aston Tool Company has four district sales managers. Each district manager receives a basic salary plus an annual bonus based on income for his or her district. Because the four managers have different levels of experience and have been with the company for different lengths of time, each is compensated under a different bonus arrangement. The four bonus arrangements are described below.

D. Jacobs (District 1): 3 percent bonus based on district income before either bonus expense or income taxes are deducted.

B. Barster (District 2): 4 percent bonus based on district income after deduction of income taxes, but the bonus is not treated as an expense in determining income subject to the bonus.

S. Swenson (District 3): 3 percent bonus based on district income after deduction of both bonus expense and income tax expense.

M. Markel (District 4): 2 percent bonus based on district income after deduction of bonus expense but before deduction of income taxes.

The income figures for the four districts, before deduction of either bonus expense or income taxes, are as follows for the current year:

DISTRICT	INCOME
1	$72,400
2	68,300
3	75,600
4	69,000

Aston Tool Company is subject to a 34 percent income tax rate, and bonus expense is deductible for purposes of calculating income taxes payable.

REQUIRED   Calculate the amount of income taxes payable for each district and the bonus due to each district sales manager for the current year. Round to the nearest dollar.

P 8-28.   **CONTINGENCIES; PRODUCT WARRANTIES**   Eller Company manufactures and sells remote computer terminals. In the current year Eller sold 280 terminals for $3,000 each. The terminals have a two-year warranty on labor and a one-year warranty on parts. Eller estimates that warranty expenses will average about $20 per year for labor and 5 percent of selling price for parts for each terminal sold. During the current year there were 35 warranty claims requiring a total of $5,000 for labor and $24,000 for parts.

REQUIRED   **I.** Assuming the estimates of warranty expenses are reasonable and that warranty expenses are a material income statement item, prepare the necessary entries to record (*a*) aggregate sales, (*b*) warranty expense, (*c*) warranty work on claims, and (*d*) year-end adjustments (if any).
     2. For the current year, what accounts and dollar amounts would be reported in the income statement? In the balance sheet?

P 8-29.   **CONTINGENCIES; LITIGATION**   Brake failures on a special run of automobiles manufactured and sold by U.S. Auto Company between November 1 and December 15, 1998, resulted in 69 personal injury lawsuits for damages totaling $23 million. Of this amount, $12.8 million related to suits filed before the end of the company's fiscal year, December 31, and the remainder arose from suits filed during January 1999. U.S. Auto's lawyers expect that essentially all of the 69 suits will result in unfavorable outcomes, but that total damages will probably not exceed $8 million. Management expects that about 25 similar additional suits will be filed before the 1998 financial statements are issued on February 20, 1999.

REQUIRED   **I.** What conditions must be met before it is acceptable accounting practice to accrue a loss contingency for litigation, claims, or assessments?
     2. Give some factors that must be considered in determining the probability of asset impairment or liability incurrence in litigation loss contingency situations.
     3. Prepare any journal entries or 1998 financial statement disclosures called for by the facts given above.

P 8-30.   **ACCOUNTING FOR PRODUCT WARRANTIES**   Fuller is an 18-month-old firm that sells office equipment and supplies. A major part of Fuller's business is sales of a well-known brand of electronic word processor. The marketing arrangement for this particular brand of word processor requires that the seller, rather than the manufacturer, take total responsibility for any warranty that may be offered in conjunction with the sale of a word processor. While Fuller has essentially no experience with either the cost or the number of repairs associated with the word processor it is selling, the word processor does have a long history of industrywide performance that is available for Fuller's consideration. With each word processor sold, Fuller provides a one-year warranty covering all parts and labor. In addition, purchasers of new word processors have the option of buying an additional two-year service contract at the time of purchase. About 80 percent of the customers purchase this contract. The additional two-year service contract costs $50 and provides the owner with free labor on word processor maintenance and repair for two years beyond the initial one-year warranty. Necessary parts must be paid for by the customer. On the basis of industry experience, Fuller estimates that labor costs under the two-year service contracts will average about $40 per contract, and labor and parts under the warranty given with each word processor sold will average about $20 and $15, respectively, per unit sold.

REQUIRED

I. Which of the two methods of accounting for product warranties do you think is more appropriate in Fuller's case? Why?

2. Prepare pro forma entries (use account titles, but enter no dollar amounts) for each of the two accounting methods (*a*) at the time a word processor is sold, (*b*) at the time a service contract is sold, (*c*) at the time warranty work is performed, and (*d*) at the time service contract work is performed.

3. Explain the effect(s) each of the two accounting methods would have on the income statement and balance sheet during the term of a warranty or a service contract.

P 8-31.   **ACCOUNTING FOR COUPON OFFERS**   In a massive promotional campaign the Classical Compact Disc Club sent coupons to 2 million families in the United States on November 1, 1998. In order to benefit from the coupon, the recipient had to return it along with an order for a $49.95 five-disc set within six months of November 1. Each customer who did so would receive, in addition to the five-disc set, a free classical compact disc with a retail value of $9.95. Any customer who was not satisfied with the five-disc set could return it within 30 days for a full refund and keep the free disc without obligation. Classical expected about 34 percent of the families who received coupons to respond to the offer. Of those who responded to the offer, Classical estimated that about 10 percent would return the five-disc set within 30 days of receipt. In preparation for the campaign, Classical purchased 680,000 of the discs to be given as premiums at a price of $3.95 per disc on October 25. As of December 31 (end of the fiscal year), 416,000 coupons had been received by Classical and 21,000 customers had subsequently returned the five-disc set for a refund.

REQUIRED   Prepare all journal entries for 1998 suggested by the above facts.

P 8-32.   **ACCOUNTING FOR PREMIUM OFFERS**   The Best Detergent Company hopes to stimulate sales by inserting a coupon in each box of Best that can be sent to the Best Company, along with $1.25, to obtain a set of three towels retailing for $6.95. Fifty cents of the $1.25 charge is to cover shipping charges. Best Detergent sells for $1.89 a box, and the three-towel sets cost Best $1.50 each. Shipping the towels to customers is expected to cost the Best Company an average of $.38 per set. Data related to the towel promotion in 1998 and 1999 are:

	1998	1999
Towel sets purchased by Best	94,000	97,480
Boxes of Best Detergent sold	179,300	169,340
Coupons redeemed by customers	76,670	82,390
Percent of coupons expected to be redeemed	50%	48%

REQUIRED

I. Prepare any journal entries necessary for 1998 and 1999 to account for the Best Detergent towel promotion.

2. Indicate the account titles, the dollar amounts, and the financial statement classification of accounts arising from the towel promotion that would be reported at the end of fiscal 1998 and 1999, respectively.

P 8-33.   **ACCOUNTING FOR WARRANTIES AND PREMIUMS**   Foster Music Emporium carries a wide variety of musical instruments, sound reproduction equipment, recorded music, and sheet music. Foster uses two sales promotion techniques—warranties and premiums—to attract customers.

Musical instruments and sound equipment are sold with a one-year warranty for replacement of parts and labor. The estimated warranty cost, based on experience, is 1.5 percent of sales.

The premium is offered on recorded music and on sheet music. Customers receive a coupon for each dollar spent on recorded music or sheet music. Customers may exchange 200 coupons and $20 for a cassette player. Foster pays $32 for each cassette player and estimates that 55 percent of the coupons given to customers will be redeemed.

Foster's total sales for 1998 were $7.2 million—$5.4 million from musical instruments and sound reproduction equipment and $1.8 million from recorded music and sheet music. Replacement parts and labor for warranty work totaled $85,000 during 1998. A total of 6,200 cassette players used in the premium program were purchased during the year. There were 1.2 million coupons redeemed in 1998.

Foster uses the accrual method to account for the warranty and premium costs for financial reporting purposes. The balances in the accounts related to warranties and premiums on January 1, 1998, were as shown below.

Inventory of premium cassette players..................................... **$32,000**
Estimated premium claims outstanding **41,000**
Estimated liability from warranties.. **63,000**

REQUIRED   Foster Music Emporium is preparing its financial statements for the year ended December 31, 1998. Determine the amounts that will be shown on the 1998 financial statements for the following:

  1. Warranty expense.
  2. Estimated liability from warranties.
  3. Premium expense.
  4. Inventory of premium cassette players.
  5. Estimated premium claims outstanding.

(IMA, adapted)

P 8-34.   **FINANCIAL REPORTING PROBLEM: CURRENT LIABILITIES**   Use the 1995 Annual Report of General Electric Company in Appendix B to answer the following questions. Your answers should be based on financial statement data, management discussion, and related footnotes for GE *alone*. Do not use the consolidated data for GE and GECS.

  1. What dollar amount of short-term borrowings did GE have in 1995? In 1994?
  2. What dollar amount of accounts payable did GE have in 1995? In 1994?
  3. What was GE's ratio of accounts payable to total liabilities in 1995? In 1994?
  4. What does GE identify as the components of its short-term borrowings?
  5. What average rate of interest on payables to banks did GE incur in 1995? In 1994?

PHILIP MORRIS COMPANIES INC. CONTINGENCY CASE

Philip Morris operates in the tobacco (Marlboro, Virginia Slims), food (Kraft, Oscar-Mayer), beer (Miller Brewing, Red Dog), and financial services industries. Approximately 52 percent of its revenue in 1996 came from sales outside the United States. In 1996, Philip Morris had total revenues of $69.21 billion, net income of $6.30 billion, and total assets of $54.9 billion. Philip Morris also had 154,000 employees at the end of 1996.

Read the article from *Business Week* and answer the following questions, using the financial statement excerpts that are included here.

1. On the balance sheet Philip Morris indicates zero liabilities for contingencies and refers the reader to Note 13, which is over **7 pages long. Don't read the entire note.** Read the first sentence of several paragraphs and all of the last paragraph. Explain how this accounting/reporting is consistent and in-consistent with accounting theory (see Chapter 2). Consider the *Business Week* article in your answer and do not rely on *SFAS No. 5*.

2. The *Business Week* article suggests that the market is pricing Philip Morris stock as if it has a tobacco liability of $60 billion. What entry would Philip Morris make if it were forced to accrue this amount?

3. What would happen to Philip Morris's ability to pay cash dividends if it booked this liability?

4. The market to book ratio is defined as the market price of a share of common stock divided by the book value of a share of common stock (common shareholders' equity on the balance sheet divided by the number of common shares outstanding). This ratio is one tool used by investors to evaluate the market price of a firm's stock. Explain how Philip Morris's current accounting for its potential tobacco liability affects its market to book ratio.

Big Tobacco May Be Ready to Deal
Plaintiffs' lawyers see signs that makers want to bargain

By Mike France, with Lori Bongiorno and David Greising

The tobacco industry spends a lot of time these days reminding the public that it has no interest in settling any of the hundreds of lawsuits filed against it. When a proposed congressional pact surfaced in late August, the companies quickly denied any participation in the alleged settlement talks. And they insisted they had no plans to bargain with opponents in the future. Cigarette makers continue to go out of their way to hammer the point home. After a Florida judge handed manufacturers a minor victory on Sept. 16 by dismissing most counts in that state's suit against them, R. J. Reynolds Tobacco Co. zapped out the following statement: "This ruling should clarify for doubters why the tobacco industry has taken the firm position that it will not settle litigation that has no merit in law or fact."

But there are signs that tobacco companies are becoming increasingly interested in striking a deal that would put their legal woes behind them. Several leading plaintiffs' attorneys say that since mid-August they have received phone calls from lawyers, lobbyists, and politicians claiming to represent the industry and trying to lay the groundwork for a possible settlement. Washington-based John Coale of Coale & Van Susteren says he had a 20-minute conversation with an industry lobbyist in mid-September who wanted to know whether he would be willing to go along with a deal brokered by Congress.

Phone Calls. Such a deal, which both sides consider the only plausible method of settling the tobacco litigation, would likely require the manufacturers to shell out billions for injured smokers and teenage-prevention programs. In exchange, Big Tobacco would receive immunity from legal liability, in effect ridding itself in one fell swoop of its many lawsuits.

Plaintiffs' attorneys Elizabeth Cabraser of San Francisco's Lieff, Cabraser, Heimann & Bernstein, and Patrick J. Coughlin, partner at Milberg Weiss Bershad Hynes & Lerach in San Diego, said that they, or partners at their firms, have received similar calls. The lawyers declined to identify the callers, saying only that none of them worked directly for cigarette manufacturers. "There are a lot of folks surfacing right now, putting out feelers, trying to test the waters for a potential settlement," says anti-tobacco attorney Russ Herman of Herman, Herman, Katz & Cotlar in New Orleans. He says he has also been approached by industry representatives.

The standard pitch, says Herman, goes like this: "I have on occasion represented X, Y, and Z [a tobacco company]. I'm very interested in settling this issue, and I know they would be. If I can be of assistance in bringing you folks together or floating proposals, I'm more than willing to do that." Such feelers, adds attorney Coale, are the first part of "a real courtship" between the two sides, "where you are going to have this type of thing, and then you'll have negotiation through intermediators, and then you'll have direct negotiations."

The cigarette manufacturers deny that they are putting out any settlement feelers, and say that several plaintiffs' lawyers lied about the industry's participation in the proposed August congressional deal. Noting that the anti-tobacco bar has invested millions in suing the industry and is at best years away from recouping any money, they argue that the plaintiffs' attorneys are simply trying to force a settlement by drumming up support for a deal with politicians, the public, and the media. "The company is talking to absolutely no one about [a litigation settlement]," says Philip Morris Cos. spokesman Michael York. "We remain absolutely confident of our position both legally and factually, and I can't think of a case where I don't think we'll prevail."

Depressed Stock. But there's no doubt that the companies have plenty of incentive to settle. They're spending tens of millions annually defending themselves, and analysts say that their share prices are depressed by at least 50% because of the threat of litigation and increased regulatory oversight. Says industry analyst Jeffrey A. Altman, a vice-president at major tobacco shareholder Mutual Series Fund Inc. in Short Hills, N.J.: "In my opinion, the companies have to think about a settlement very seriously."

Evidence is mounting that that's just what the companies are doing. In early September, Gary D. Black, a tobacco analyst at investment banking and money management firm Sanford C. Bernstein & Co., which holds a large chunk of Philip Morris, wrote that "for the first time since we started covering this group, we detect a clear willingness by the industry to bargain." Because the share prices of tobacco companies are heavily discounted, a settlement would be appealing even if the companies had to spend billions to achieve it. The market value of Philip Morris alone is discounted by $60 billion because of litigation risk, estimates Black. And it would not be hard for the industry to fund a settlement simply by upping prices: a 25¢-per-pack increase, Black calculates, would yield at least $6 billion a year—even taking into account a drop in consumption.

Other large institutional investors are starting to hear conciliatory words from the tobacco companies themselves. Lon West, a securities analyst at San Antonio-based USAA Investment Management Co., a large shareholder in several of the companies, recalls that in private meetings with attorneys from RJR and Philip Morris on Sept. 16 and 17, they told him they would be interested in a global settlement in order "to limit the downside risk, get out from under the cloud of litigation, and carry on with business," says West. While those same lawyers denied the existence of any current negotiations, they did discuss legislative precedents for a global settlement, citing the 1969 Federal Coal Mine Health & Safety Act and the 1986 National Childhood Vaccine Injury Act as proof that a congressional grant of immunity to an industry is plausible, according to West.

The tobacco companies also have made attempts to reach out to the state attorneys general who are suing to recover Medicaid expenses. North Carolina Attorney General Michael F. Easley says the tobacco companies have asked to use his office "as a vehicle through which they can communicate with the other AGs—especially those with whom they have pending litigation—because it's just hard to communicate once the suit is filed." He adds that the companies have not asked him to air any settlement proposals.

Teen Smoking. Nonetheless, Easley says that Philip Morris and RJR representatives did meet face-to-face with North Carolina state officials this summer to craft a statute aimed at curbing teen smoking. Among other measures, the proposal called for the manufacturers to give up to $100 million annually to eligible states to prevent youth smoking—double the amount that Philip Morris and U.S. Tobacco offered in a comparable federal proposal floated in May. Easley says the industry originally hoped to use his plan to fend off states considering Medicaid suits. When the tobacco companies sued the Food & Drug Administration to stave off new teen-smoking rules, they dropped their support for the state proposal.

The one thing everybody can agree on is that hammering out a deal would be a Herculean feat. Before forking over billions to its adversaries, the industry would insist on a global settlement that would insulate it from any further litigation. That alone would take an act of Congress, which could easily choke on the divisive politics of tobacco. Moreover, a deal would require the approval of plaintiffs' lawyers, the FDA, state attorneys general, and health activists. But compared with all-out war for the next few years, Big Tobacco just may decide that negotiating is a risk that is worth taking.

Consolidated Balance Sheets (in millions of dollars, except per share data)

at December 31,	1996	1995
Assets		
Consumer products		
Cash and cash equivalents	$ 240	$ 1,138
Receivables, net	4,466	4,508
Inventories:		
Leaf tobacco	4,143	3,332
Other raw materials	1,854	1,721
Finished product	3,005	2,809
	9,002	7,862
Other current assets	1,482	1,371
Total current assets	15,190	14,879
Property, plant and equipment, at cost:		
Land and land improvements	664	726
Buildings and building equipment	5,168	4,976
Machinery and equipment	12,481	11,542
Construction in progress	1,659	1,357
	19,972	18,601
Less accumulated depreciation	8,221	7,485
	11,751	11,116
Goodwill and other intangible assets		
(less accumulated amortization of $4,391 and $3,873)	18,998	19,319
Other assets	3,015	2,866
Total consumer products assets	48,954	48,180
Financial services and real estate		
Finance assets, net	5,345	4,991
Real estate held for development and sale	314	339
Other assets	258	301
Total financial services and real estate assets	5,917	5,631
Total Assets	$54,871	$53,811

See notes to consolidated financial statements.

	1996	1995
Liabilities		
Consumer products		
Short-term borrowings	$ 260	$ 122
Current portion of long-term debt	1,846	1,926
Accounts payable	3,409	3,364
Accrued liabilities:		
Marketing	2,106	2,114
Taxes, except income taxes	1,331	1,075
Employment costs	942	995
Other	2,726	2,706
Income taxes	1,269	1,137
Dividends payable	978	834
Total current liabilities	14,867	14,273
Long-term debt	11,827	12,324
Deferred income taxes	731	356
Accrued postretirement health care costs	2,372	2,273
Other liabilities	5,773	5,643
Total consumer products liabilities	35,570	34,869
Financial services and real estate		
Short-term borrowings	173	671
Long-term debt	1,134	783
Deferred income taxes	3,636	3,382
Other liabilities	140	121
Total financial services and real estate liabilities	5,083	4,957
Total liabilities	40,653	39,826
Contingencies (Note 13)		
Stockholders' Equity		
Common stock, par value $1.00 per share (935,320,439 shares issued)	935	935
Earnings reinvested in the business	22,478	19,779
Currency translation adjustments	192	467
	23,605	21,181
Less cost of repurchased stock (124,871,681 and 104,150,433 shares)	9,387	7,196
Total stockholders' equity	14,218	13,985
Total Liabilities and Stockholders' Equity	$54,871	$53,811

Consolidated Statements of Earnings (in millions of dollars, except per share data)

for the years ended December 31,	1996	1995	1994
Operating revenues	$69,204	$66,071	$65,125
Cost of sales	26,560	26,685	28,351
Excise taxes on products	14,651	12,932	11,349
Gross profit	27,993	26,454	25,425
Marketing, administration and research costs	15,630	15,337	15,372
Amortization of goodwill	594	591	604
Operating income	11,769	10,526	9,449
Interest and other debt expense, net	1,086	1,179	1,233
Earnings before income taxes and cumulative effect of accounting changes	10,683	9,347	8,216
Provision for income taxes	4,380	3,869	3,491
Earnings before cumulative effect of accounting changes	6,303	5,478	4,725
Cumulative effect of changes in method of accounting		(28)	
Net earnings	$ 6,303	$ 5,450	$ 4,725
Per share data:			
Earnings before cumulative effect of accounting changes	$ 7.68	$ 6.51	$ 5.45
Cumulative effect of changes in method of accounting		(.03)	
Net earnings	$ 7.68	$ 6.48	$ 5.45

Consolidated Statements of Stockholders' Equity
(in millions of dollars, except per share data)

	Common Stock	Earnings Reinvested in the Business	Currency Translation Adjustments	Cost of Repurchased Stock	Total Stockholders' Equity
Balances, January 1, 1994	$935	$15,718	$(711)	$(4,315)	$11,627
Net earnings		4,725			4,725
Exercise of stock options and issuance of other stock awards		(217)		324	107
Cash dividends declared ($3.03 per share)		(2,623)			(2,623)
Currency translation adjustments			664		664
Stock repurchased				(1,600)	(1,600)
Net unrealized depreciation on securities		(114)			(114)
Balances, December 31, 1994	935	17,489	(47)	(5,591)	12,786
Net earnings		5,450			5,450
Exercise of stock options and issuance of other stock awards		(77)		470	393
Cash dividends declared ($3.65 per share)		(3,065)			(3,065)
Redemption of stock rights		(9)			(9)
Currency translation adjustments			514		514
Stock repurchased				(2,075)	(2,075)
Net unrealized depreciation on securities		(9)			(9)
Balances, December 31, 1995	935	19,779	467	(7,196)	13,985
Net earnings		6,303			6,303
Exercise of stock options and issuance of other stock awards		(28)		609	581
Cash dividends declared ($4.40 per share)		(3,606)			(3,606)
Currency translation adjustments			(275)		(275)
Stock repurchased				(2,800)	(2,800)
Net unrealized appreciation on securities		30			30
Balances, December 31, 1996	$935	$22,478	$ 192	$(9,387)	$14,218

See notes to consolidated financial statements.

Note 13. Contingencies:

Legal proceedings covering a wide range of matters are pending in various U.S. and foreign jurisdictions against the Company and its subsidiaries, including Philip Morris Incorporated ("PM Inc."), the Company's wholly-owned domestic tobacco subsidiary. Various types of claims are raised in these proceedings, including but not limited to products liability, antitrust, securities law, tax and patent infringement matters.

Pending claims related to tobacco products generally fall within three categories: (i) smoking and health cases alleging personal injury brought on behalf of individual smokers, (ii) smoking and health cases alleging personal injury and purporting to be brought on behalf of a class of plaintiffs, and (iii) health care cost recovery actions brought primarily by states and local governments seeking reimbursement for Medicaid and other health care expenditures allegedly caused by cigarette smoking.

In the individual and class action smoking and health cases pending against PM Inc. and, in some cases, the Company and/or certain of its other subsidiaries, plaintiffs allege personal injury resulting from cigarette smoking, "addiction" to cigarette smoking or exposure to environmental tobacco smoke ("ETS") and seek compensatory and, in some cases, punitive damages in amounts ranging into the billions of dollars. During the past two years, there has been a substantial increase in the number of such smoking and health cases in the United States, with a majority of the new cases having been filed in Florida on behalf of individual plaintiffs. As of December 31, 1996, there were 185 smoking and health cases filed and served on behalf of individual plaintiffs in the United States against PM Inc. and, in some cases, the Company, compared to 115 such cases as of December 31, 1995, and 84 such cases as of December 31, 1994. One hundred twenty-two of the cases filed and served as of December 31, 1996, were filed on behalf of individual plaintiffs in the state of Florida. Ten of the individual cases involve allegations of various personal injuries allegedly related to exposure to ETS.

In addition to the foregoing individual smoking and health cases, there are 17 purported smoking and health class actions pending in the United States against PM Inc. and, in some cases, the Company, including one that involves allegations of various personal injuries related to exposure to ETS. Twelve of these actions purport to constitute state-wide class actions and were filed after the Fifth Circuit Court of Appeals, in the *Castano* case discussed below, reversed a federal district court's certification of a purported nation-wide class action on behalf of persons who were allegedly addicted to tobacco products. One purported smoking and health class action is pending in Canada and another in Brazil against affiliates of the Company. In California, individuals and local governments and other organizations purportedly acting as "private attorneys general" have filed suits seeking, among other things, injunctive relief, restitution and disgorgement of profits for alleged violations of California's consumer protection statutes. As discussed below, 26 health care cost recovery actions are currently pending.

In August 1996, a jury awarded a former smoker and his spouse $750,000 in a smoking and health case against another United States cigarette manufacturer (*Carter v. American Tobacco Co., et al.*). Neither PM Inc. nor the Company was a party to that litigation. Defendant in that action has appealed the verdict. Later that month, a jury returned a verdict for defendants in a smoking and health case in Indiana against United States cigarette manufacturers, including PM Inc. (*Rogers v. R.J. Reynolds Tobacco Company,.et al.*). Plaintiff has appealed the verdict.

Several smoking and health cases and health care cost recovery actions are scheduled for trial in 1997, although trial dates are subject to change. One individual smoking and health case in which PM Inc. is a defendant is scheduled for trial during the first quarter of 1997 and a number of other individual cases against the industry are scheduled for trial later in the year. A purported class action on behalf of flight attendants alleging injury caused by exposure to ETS aboard aircraft is set for trial in June 1997 in Florida state court. A purported class action on behalf of Florida residents who allege injury from alleged nicotine addiction is set for trial in September 1997. A similar action on behalf of Pennsylvania residents is set for trial in October 1997. Health care cost recovery actions are currently scheduled for trial in Mississippi in June 1997, in Florida in August 1997 and in Texas in September 1997.

A description of smoking and health class actions, health care cost recovery litigation and certain other actions pending against the Company and/or its subsidiaries and affiliates follows.

Smoking and Health Litigation

Plaintiffs' allegations of liability in smoking and health cases are based on various theories of recovery, including negligence, gross negligence, strict liability, fraud, misrepresentation, design defect, failure to warn, breach of express and implied warranties, conspiracy, concert of action, and violations of deceptive trade practice laws and consumer protection statutes. Defenses raised by defendants in these cases include lack of proximate cause, assumption of the risk, comparative fault and/or contributory negligence, statutes of limitations or repose, and preemption by the Federal Cigarette Labeling and Advertising Act, as amended (the "Labeling Act"). In June 1992, the United States Supreme Court held that the Labeling Act, as enacted in 1965, does not preempt common law damage claims but that the Labeling Act, as amended in 1969, preempts claims arising after July 1969 against cigarette manufacturers "based on failure to warn and the neutralization of federally mandated warnings to the extent that those claims rely on omissions or inclusions in advertising or promotions." The Court also held that the 1969 Labeling Act does not preempt claims based on express warranty, fraudulent misrepresentation or conspiracy. The Court also held that claims for fraudulent concealment were preempted except "insofar as those claims relied on a duty to

disclose...facts through channels of communication other than advertising or promotion." (The Court did not consider whether such common law damage claims were valid under state law.) The Court's decision was announced by a plurality opinion. The effect of the decision on pending and future cases will be the subject of further proceedings in the lower federal and state courts. Additional similar litigation could be encouraged if legislation to eliminate the federal preemption defense, proposed in Congress in recent years, were enacted. It is not possible to predict whether any such legislation will be enacted.

A smoking and health class action against United States cigarette manufacturers has been pending in Florida state court since October 1991 in which a class has been certified consisting of "all non-smoking flight attendants who are or have been employed by airlines based in the United States" and who are allegedly suffering from exposure to ETS aboard aircraft. *Broin, et al. v. Philip Morris Incorporated, et al., Circuit of the Eleventh Judicial Circuit in and for Dade County Florida, Case No. 91-49738-CA-20.* Various challenges to the class certification have been denied on appeal, and the case is currently set for trial in June 1997.

Another smoking and health class action against United States cigarette manufacturers has been pending in Florida state court since May 1994 in which a class has been certified consisting of all Florida citizens and residents and their survivors who have suffered injury "caused by their addiction to cigarettes that contain nicotine." *Engle, et al. v. R.J. Reynolds Tobacco Company, et al., Circuit Court of the Eleventh Judicial Circuit in and for Dade County, Florida, Case No. 94-08273-CA-20.* Various challenges to the class certification have been denied on appeal, and the case is currently set for trial in September 1997.

In March 1994, a smoking and health class action was filed in Alabama state court against three United States cigarette manufacturers, and was subsequently removed to federal court. *Lacey, et al. v. Lorillard Tobacco Company, Inc. et al., United States District Court, Northern District of Alabama, Jasper Division, Civil Action No. 94-4-B-0901-J.* Plaintiffs, claiming to represent all smokers who have smoked or are smoking cigarettes sold by defendants in the State of Alabama, seek compensatory and punitive damages not to exceed $48,500 per each class member as well as injunctive relief arising from defendants' alleged failure to disclose additives used in their cigarettes. In August 1996, the judge orally granted defendants' motion for summary judgment on the grounds that the suit is preempted by the Labeling Act.

In March 1994, a smoking and health class action was filed in federal district court in Louisiana against United States cigarette manufacturers and others, including the Company, seeking certification of a purported class consisting of all United States residents who allege that they are addicted, or are the legal survivors of persons who were addicted, to tobacco products. *Castano, et al. v. The American Tobacco Company Inc., et al., United States District Court, Eastern District of Louisiana, Case No. 94-1044.* Plaintiffs alleged that the cigarette manufacturers concealed and/or misrepresented information regarding the addictive nature of nicotine and manipulated the levels of nicotine in their tobacco products to make such products addictive. In February 1995, the trial court certified the class and in

May 1996, the Fifth Circuit Court of Appeals reversed the trial court's class certification and remanded the case with instructions that the class allegations be dismissed. Summary judgment motions against the two remaining named plaintiffs in this case are pending.

Following the announcement of the Fifth Circuit's class decertification decision in *Castano,* lawyers for the plaintiffs announced that they would file "state-wide" smoking and health class actions in state courts. Subsequently, smoking and health class actions based on claims similar to those in *Castano* (a "nicotine-dependence class action") and, in some cases, claims of physical injury as well (a "physical injury class action") were filed in a number of states, as described below.

Immediately prior to the Fifth Circuit's decision in the *Castano* case, a purported nicotine-dependence class action was filed in Indiana state court against United States cigarette manufacturers and others. In June 1996, defendants removed the case to federal court. *Norton, et al. v. RJR Nabisco Holdings Corporation, et al., United States District Court for the Southern District of Indiana, Case No. IP96-0798-C-M/S.* Plaintiffs' motion to remand the case to state court is pending.

In May 1996, a purported physical injury class action was filed in Maryland state court against United States cigarette manufacturers and others, including the Company. The case was removed by defendants to federal court and was subsequently remanded to state court. *Richardson, et al. v. Philip Morris Incorporated, et al., Circuit Court for Baltimore City, No. 96145050.*

In May 1996, a purported nicotine-dependence class action was filed in Louisiana state court against four United States cigarette manufacturers and others, including the Company. *Scott, et al. v. The American Tobacco Company, Inc., et al., Civil District Court for the Parish of Orleans, State of Louisiana, Docket No. 96-8461.* A hearing on plaintiffs' motion for class certification has been scheduled for February 1997.

In June 1996, a purported nicotine-dependence class action was filed in New York state court against PM Inc., the Company, the Tobacco Institute and the Council for Tobacco Research—U.S.A., Inc. *Frosina, et al. v. Philip Morris Inc., et al., Supreme Court of the State of New York, County of New York, Case No. 96110950.* In December 1996, defendants filed motions to dismiss the complaint and to deny class certification.

In June 1996, a purported physical injury class action was filed in the Superior Court of the District of Columbia against United States cigarette manufacturers and others, including the Company. *Reed v. Philip Morris Incorporated, et al., Superior Court of the District of Columbia, Case No. CA-05070-96.* A hearing on whether plaintiffs can pursue a class action has been scheduled for June 1997.

In August 1996, a purported nicotine-dependence class action was filed in Pennsylvania state court against United States cigarette manufacturers and others, including the Company, and was subsequently removed to federal court. *Arch, et al. v. American Tobacco Company Inc., et al., United States District Court for the Eastern District of Pennsylvania, Case No. 96-5903-CN.* A hearing on class certification is set for March 1997, and the trial is scheduled for October 1997.

In August 1996, a purported nicotine-dependence class action was filed in Alabama state court, on behalf of Alabama and North Carolina residents, against four United States cigarette manufacturers and others, including the Company. In September 1996, the case was removed by defendants to federal court. *Lyons, et al. v. The American Tobacco Co., Inc., et al., United States District Court for the Southern District of Alabama, Southern Division, Civil Action No. 96-0881-BH-S.* Plaintiffs' motion to remand the case to state court is pending.

In August 1996, a purported nicotine-dependence class action was filed in Ohio state court against United States cigarette manufacturers and others, including the Company, and was subsequently removed to federal court. *Chamberlain, et al. v. The American Tobacco Co., et al., United States District Court, Northern District of Ohio, Case No. 1:96CV2005.* Plaintiffs' motion to remand the case to state court is pending.

In August 1996, a purported physical injury class action was filed in Florida state court against United States cigarette manufacturers, and others. *Walters, et al. v. Brown & Williamson Tobacco Corp., et al., Circuit Court, Fourth Judicial District, Duval County, Florida.*

In September 1996, a purported nicotine-dependence class action was filed in Minnesota state court against four United States cigarette manufacturers and others, including the Company. The case was removed by defendants to federal court in September 1996. *Masepohl, et al. v. The American Tobacco Co., Inc., et al., United States District Court, District of Minnesota, Third Division, Case No. CV3-96-888.* Plaintiffs' motion to remand the case to state court is pending.

In October 1996, a purported nicotine-dependence class action was filed in New Mexico state court against four United States cigarette manufacturers and others, including the Company. *Connor, et al. v. The American Tobacco Co., et al., Second Judicial District Court, County of Bernalillo, State of New Mexico, Case No. CV-96-9422.*

In October 1996, a purported nicotine-dependence class action was filed in federal court in Puerto Rico against four United States cigarette manufacturers and others. *Ruiz, et al. v. The American Tobacco Co., et al., United States District Court for the District of Puerto Rico, Civil Action No. 96-2300.*

In November 1996, a purported nicotine-dependence class action was filed in federal court in Arkansas against United States cigarette manufacturers and others, including the Company. *McGinty, et al. v. The American Tobacco Co., et al., United States District Court for the Eastern District of Arkansas, Western Division, Case No. LRC 96-881.*

In February 1995, Rothmans, Benson & Hedges, Inc. (in which the Company, through subsidiaries, owns a 40% interest) was served with a statement of claim commencing a purported class action in the Ontario Court of Justice, Toronto, Canada, against Imperial Tobacco Limited, RJR-MacDonald Inc., and Rothmans, Benson & Hedges, Inc. *LeTourneau v. Rothmans et al., Ontario Court of Justice, Toronto, Canada, Court File No. 95-CU-82186* (now captioned *Caputo v. Imperial Tobacco Limited, et al.*). The lawsuit seeks damages in the amount of $1,000,000 (Canadian) per class member and punitive and exemplary damages and an order requiring the funding of rehabilitation centers. Plaintiffs seek certification of a class of persons consisting of all current and former cigarette smokers in Ontario, their families and the estates of deceased smokers. Defendants' request for a more particular statement of claim prior to delivering their statement of defense was partially granted and partially denied in April 1996. Defendants have appealed that order.

In July 1995, a purported class action on behalf of all Brazilian smokers and former smokers was filed in state court in Sao Paulo, Brazil, naming Philip Morris Marketing, S.A., a wholly-owned subsidiary of the Company, as a co-defendant. *The Smoker Health Defense Association, et al. v. Souza Cruz, S.A. and Philip Morris Marketing, S.A., 19th Lower Civil Court of the Central Courts of the Judiciary District of Sao Paulo, Brazil.* Plaintiffs allege that defendants failed to warn that smoking is "addictive" and engaged in misleading advertising. Plaintiffs have obtained an order, which was upheld on appeal, reversing the burden of proof and placing the burden on defendants. Defendants are seeking further appellate review of this order.

Pro se prisoners have filed two purported class actions against United States cigarette manufacturers and others seeking, in one case, class certification on behalf of prisoners in two Mississippi prisons based on alleged exposure to ETS *(Lyle, et al. v. Brown & Williamson Tobacco Corporation, et al., United States District Court for the Northern District of Mississippi, Civil Action No. 3:96-CV-268WS)* and, in the other, on behalf of all allegedly nicotine-dependent persons in the United States *(Harris, et al. v. Philip Morris Incorporated, et al., United States District Court for the Eastern District of Pennsylvania, Civil Action No. 3:96-CV 652).* In October 1996, the court issued an order dismissing the *Lyle* action. In November 1996, the court in *Harris* entered an order denying class certification.

Health Care Cost Recovery Litigation

In certain of the pending proceedings, state and local government entities and others seek reimbursement for Medicaid and/or other health care expenditures allegedly caused by tobacco products. The claims asserted in these health care cost recovery actions vary. All plaintiffs assert the equitable claim that the tobacco industry was "unjustly enriched" by plaintiffs' payment of health care costs allegedly attributable to smoking and seek reimbursement of those costs. Other claims made by some but not all plaintiffs include the equitable claim of indemnity, common law claims of negligence, strict liability, breach of express and implied warranty, violation of a voluntary undertaking or special duty, fraud, negligent misrepresentation, conspiracy, public nuisance, claims under state and federal statutes governing consumer fraud, antitrust, deceptive trade practices and false advertising, and claims under the Federal Racketeer Influenced and Corrupt Organization Act ("RICO") or state RICO statutes.

Each plaintiff seeks reimbursement of Medicaid and/or other health care costs. Other relief sought by some but not all plaintiffs includes punitive damages, treble damages for alleged antitrust law violations, injunctions prohibiting alleged marketing and sales to minors, disclosure of research, disgorgement of profits, funding of anti-smoking programs, disclosure of nicotine yields and payment of attorney and expert witness fees.

Defenses raised by defendants include failure to state a valid claim, lack of benefit, adequate remedy at law, "unclean hands" (namely, that plaintiffs cannot recover because they participated in, and benefited from, the sale of cigarettes), lack of antitrust injury, federal preemption, lack of proximate cause and statute of limitations. In addition, defendants argue that they should be entitled to "set-off" any alleged damages to the extent a state benefits economically from the sale of cigarettes through the receipt of excise taxes or otherwise. Defendants also argue that all of these cases are improper because plaintiffs must proceed under principles of subrogation and assignment. Under traditional theories of recovery, a payor of medical costs (such as an insurer or a state) can seek recovery of health care costs from a third party solely by "standing in the shoes" of the injured party. Defendants argue that plaintiffs should be required to bring an action on behalf of each individual health care recipient and should be subject to all defenses available against the injured party. In certain of these cases, defendants have also challenged the ability of the plaintiffs to use contingency fee counsel to prosecute these actions. Further, certain cigarette companies, including PM Inc., have filed related declaratory judgment actions in several states seeking to block the health care cost recovery actions in those states and/or to prevent the state from hiring contingency fee counsel.

The following is a summary of certain developments in each of the health care cost recovery suits pending against PM Inc. and, in some cases, the Company and the related declaratory judgment actions filed by cigarette manufacturers.

Florida—In May 1994, the State of Florida enacted a statute which purports, among other things, to abolish affirmative defenses in Medicaid recovery actions. In June 1994, PM Inc. and others filed suit in Florida state court challenging the constitutionality of the statute. *Associated Industries of Florida, Inc., et al. v. State of Florida Agency for Health Care Administration, et al., Circuit Court of the Second Judicial Circuit in and for Leon County, Florida, Case No. 94-3128.* In June 1996, the Florida Supreme Court ruled that the provisions of the statute that permitted the state to pursue its action without identifying individual Medicaid recipients violated defendants' due process rights under the Florida constitution and that defendants may rebut the state's claims of causation and damages on a recipient-by-recipient basis. The court held constitutional on its face the statutory provision abolishing affirmative defenses normally available to a third party, including assumption of the risk, but stated that this provision might be unconstitutional as applied in the state's case. The court also held that the state's independent cause of action created by the statute could apply only to Medicaid costs paid after the amendment became effective in July 1994, that defendants could be held individually liable under a market share theory, that the state could use statistical evidence to present its case, and that the agency charged with enforcing the statute was constitutionally established. In September 1996, plaintiffs' petition for rehearing on the Florida Supreme Court's rulings on abrogation of affirmative defenses and application of the statute to conduct occurring before July 1994 was denied. In December 1996, PM Inc. and another party filed a petition for a writ of certiorari to the United States Supreme Court on the grounds that the statute violates due process because it creates a unique cause of action on behalf of the state which abrogates certain common law and equitable principles, including affirmative defenses.

In February 1995, the State of Florida filed a health care cost recovery action under the statute in Florida state court. *The State of Florida, et al. v. The American Tobacco Company, et al., Circuit Court of the Fifteenth Judicial Circuit in and for Palm Beach County, Florida, Case No. CL 95 1466 AO.* In September 1996, the trial court dismissed all of the state's claims except for its negligence and strict liability counts arising from Medicaid payments made after July 1, 1994, and its count for injunctive relief. The court also ordered the state to disclose the identity of the Medicaid recipients. In October 1996, the state filed a coded listing (without names) for all Medicaid recipients with alleged smoking-related illnesses. The trial court accepted the coded listing and, in January 1997, the Florida Supreme Court determined not to hear and denied defendants' challenge to the sufficiency of the state's purported identification of Medicaid recipients. In November 1996, plaintiffs amended their complaint to add claims for violations of Florida's RICO and consumer protection statutes. In December 1996, the court granted defendants' motion to dismiss various claims brought under state statutes and denied the motion to dismiss claims based on Florida's RICO statute and on a state false advertising statute. In January 1997, defendants waived their rights to a pretrial determination of whether plaintiffs can amend their complaint to include a punitive damages claim. Defendants have reserved their rights to challenge the punitive damages claim on factual or legal bases. Plaintiffs' motion to strike defendants' affirmative defenses was heard on January 24, 1997. The trial in this case is scheduled to begin in August 1997.

Mississippi—In May 1994, the Attorney General of Mississippi filed a health care cost recovery action in Mississippi state court. *Moore v. The American Tobacco Company, et al., Chancery Court of Jackson County, Mississippi, Case No. 94-1429.* In February 1995, the court granted plaintiff's motion to strike certain of defendants' challenges to the sufficiency of the complaint and denied defendants' motion for judgment on the pleadings. In July 1995, plaintiff filed a motion seeking to preclude defendants from asserting their "set off" defenses. That motion is pending. The Governor of Mississippi and defendants have filed petitions with the Mississippi Supreme Court challenging the authority of the Attorney General to pursue this action. The Mississippi Supreme Court heard arguments on both petitions in September 1996, but has not issued a decision on either petition. The trial is scheduled to begin in June 1997.

Minnesota—In August 1994, the Attorney General of Minnesota and Blue Cross and Blue Shield of Minnesota filed a health care cost recovery action in Minnesota state court. *Minnesota, et al. v. Philip Morris Incorporated, et al., Minnesota District Court, Second Judicial District, County of Ramsey, Case No. C1-94-8565.* In July 1996, the Minnesota Supreme Court ruled that Blue Cross did not have standing to pursue its tort claims against defendants, but that it could proceed against defendants for claims brought under antitrust and consumer protection statutes. The Supreme Court also held that Blue Cross could pursue directly its equitable claims, but only for injunctive (not monetary) relief. The case is scheduled to go to trial in January 1998.

West Virginia—In September 1994, the Attorney General of West Virginia filed a health care cost recovery action in West Virginia state court. *McGraw v. The American Tobacco Company, et al., Circuit Court of Kanawha County, West Virginia, Case No. 94-1707.* In October 1995, the court dismissed eight of ten counts of the complaint and granted defendants' motion to prohibit prosecution of this case pursuant to a contingent fee agreement with private counsel. In June 1996, the Attorney General added the Public Employees' Insurance Agency as a plaintiff. In November 1996, plaintiffs added the West Virginia Department of Health and Human Resources as a plaintiff, and three law firms as defendants, and asserted additional counts under theories of indemnity, negligent misrepresentation, negligence, and strict product liability. In December 1996, the court heard oral argument on defendants' motion to dismiss plaintiff's common law and equitable claims. A hearing on defendants' motion to dismiss plaintiff's statutory claims is scheduled for February 1997.

Texas—In March 1996, the Texas Attorney General filed a health care cost recovery action in federal court in Texas. *The State of Texas v. The American Tobacco Company, et al., United States District Court, Eastern District of Texas, Civil No. 5-96CV91.* Trial in this action is set for September 1997 and defendants have filed a number of motions to dismiss it. Defendants and others had previously filed an action in Texas state court in November 1995, seeking a declaration that the Texas Attorney General cannot pursue a health care cost recovery action. *Philip Morris Incorporated, et al. v. Dan Morales, Attorney General of the State of Texas, et al., District Court of Travis County, Texas, No. 94-14807.* The state court has stayed the action for declaratory relief pending the outcome of the Attorney General's suit.

Massachusetts—In December 1995, the Massachusetts Attorney General filed a health care cost recovery action in Massachusetts state court. *Commonwealth of Massachusetts v. Philip Morris Inc., et al., Superior Court, Middlesex County, Civil Action No. 95-7378.* Defendants have moved to dismiss the complaint. Defendants had previously filed an action in Massachusetts federal court in November 1995, seeking to enjoin the Attorney General from prosecuting a health care cost recovery action. *Philip Morris Incorporated, et al. v. Scott Harshbarger, United States District Court, District of Massachusetts, Case No. 95-12574-GAO.* In November 1996, the federal district court denied the Attorney General's motion to dismiss the complaint and stayed the injunction action.

Maryland—In May 1996, the State of Maryland filed a health care cost recovery action in Maryland state court. *State of Maryland v. Philip Morris Incorporated, et al., Circuit Court for Baltimore County, Maryland, Case No. 96-122017/CL211017.* Defendants' motion to dismiss the state's complaint is scheduled to be heard on January 28, 1997. The trial is scheduled for January 1999. Defendants and others had previously filed a separate action in Maryland state court seeking to enjoin the Maryland Attorney General from prosecuting a health care cost recovery action pursuant to a contingent fee arrangement with special counsel. *Philip Morris Incorporated, et al. v. Parris N. Glendening, Governor of the State of Maryland, et al., Circuit Court for Talbot County, Maryland, Case No. CG 2829.* In August 1996, the court granted defendants' motion for summary judgment and dismissed the injunction action. Plaintiffs have appealed.

Louisiana—In March 1996, the Attorney General of Louisiana filed a health care cost recovery action in Louisiana state court. *Ieyoub, et al. v. The American Tobacco Company, et al., 14th Judicial District Court, Parish of Calcasieu, Louisiana, Case No. 96-1209.* In January 1997, the court denied defendants' motion to dismiss which argued that the Attorney General lacked the authority to bring this action.

San Francisco—In June 1996, the City and County of San Francisco filed a health care cost recovery action in California federal court and has since been joined by ten other California counties. *City and County of San Francisco, et al. v. Philip Morris, Inc. et al., United States District Court, Northern District of California, Civil No. C 96-2090.* In January 1997, the court denied defendants' motion to disqualify plaintiffs' contingency-fee counsel and took under advisement defendants' motion to dismiss. In September 1996, plaintiffs in the federal court action, joined by several medical associations, filed an action in California state court seeking, among other things, injunctive relief and disgorgement of profits for alleged violations of California's consumer protection statutes. *People of the State of California, et al. v. Philip Morris, Inc. et al., San Francisco Superior Court, County of San Francisco, Case No. 980864.* In January 1997, the court granted in part defendants' motion to dismiss by requiring plaintiffs to replead certain causes of action and denied the motion on other grounds.

Washington—In June 1996, the Attorney General of the State of Washington filed a health care cost recovery action in Washington state court. *State of Washington v. American Tobacco Co., Inc., et al., Superior Court of Washington, King County, No. 96-2-15056-8.* In November 1996, the court dismissed claims based on special duty, unjust enrichment and restitution to the state, but did not dismiss claims brought under Washington's antitrust laws. The State of Washington recently moved to amend its complaint with the stated intention of correcting deficiencies found by the court to exist in the special duty and unjust enrichment claims and to add a claim for restitution under Washington's consumer protection statute. Trial is scheduled for September 1998.

Connecticut—In July 1996, the State of Connecticut filed a health care cost recovery action in Connecticut state court. *State of Connecticut v. Philip Morris Inc., et al., Superior Court, Judicial District of Litchfield, Case No. CV-96-01534405.* Defendants had previously filed an action in federal district court in June 1996, seeking to enjoin the Connecticut Attorney General from bringing the health care cost recovery action. *Philip Morris Inc., et al. v. Richard Blumenthal, United States District Court, District of Connecticut, Case No. 396CV01221 (PCD).* This injunction action was dismissed in December 1996 and, in January 1997, plaintiffs appealed the dismissal.

Utah—In September 1996, the Utah Attorney General filed a health care cost recovery action in federal court in Utah. *State of Utah v. R.J. Reynolds Tobacco Company, et al., United States District Court, District of Utah, Case No. 2:96CV 0829W.* Defendants had previously filed an action in Utah state court in July 1996, challenging the right of the Attorney General to bring such an action and to prosecute the case pursuant to a contingent fee arrangement with special counsel. *Philip Morris Incorporated, et al. v. Janet C. Graham, Attorney General of the State of Utah, et al., Third Judicial District Court of Salt Lake County, Utah, No. 960904948CV.* The parties have agreed that the state court action will be stayed while the federal action is proceeding, except for the challenge to the Attorney General's contingent fee arrangement with special counsel. In December 1996, a motion for partial summary judgment challenging the contingent fee arrangement was argued before the state court.

Los Angeles County—In August 1996, the County of Los Angeles filed a health care cost recovery action in California state court. *County of Los Angeles v. R.J. Reynolds Tobacco Company, et al., Superior Court of California, San Diego County.*

Alabama—In August 1996, a health care cost recovery action was filed in Alabama state court as a putative class action on behalf of taxpayers of the State of Alabama. Following local rules, the state court entered an order conditionally certifying the class. This action was subsequently removed by defendants to federal court. *Crozier, et al. v. The American Tobacco Company, et al., United States District Court for the Middle District of Alabama, Case No. 96-A-1403-N.* Plaintiffs' motion to remand to state court is pending.

Kansas—In August 1996, the Attorney General of Kansas filed a health care cost recovery action in Kansas state court. *State of Kansas, ex rel. Carla J. Stovall, Attorney General v. R.J. Reynolds Tobacco Co., et al., District Court of Shawnee County, Kansas, Case No. 96-CV-919.* Defendants' motion to dismiss this case is scheduled to be heard in April 1997.

Michigan—In August 1996, the Attorney General of Michigan filed a health care cost recovery action in Michigan state court. *Frank J. Kelley, Attorney General, ex rel. State of Michigan v. Philip Morris Incorporated, et al., Circuit Court for the 30th Judicial Circuit, Ingham County, Michigan, Case No. 96-84281-CZ.* In October 1996, defendants moved to dismiss certain counts of the complaint and to strike claims for compensatory and punitive damages.

Oklahoma—In August 1996, the Attorney General of Oklahoma filed a health care cost recovery action in Oklahoma state court. *State of Oklahoma, et al. v. R.J. Reynolds Tobacco Co., et al., District Court for Cleveland County, Oklahoma, Case No. CJ-96-1499-L.*

Arizona—In August 1996, the Attorney General of Arizona filed a health care cost recovery action in Arizona state court. *State of Arizona, et al. v. American Tobacco Co., Inc., et al., Superior Court, Maricopa County, Arizona, No. CV 96-14769.* The Governor of Arizona has instructed the Attorney General to dismiss the case. Subsequently, the Attorney General filed an amended complaint that abandons claims for Medicaid payments, but seeks recovery of other health care costs as well as other damages and forms of relief. Motions to dismiss the complaint are pending. The trial is scheduled for October 1998.

Hawaii—In August 1996, PM Inc. and three other cigarette manufacturers filed suit against the Hawaii Attorney General in federal district court in Hawaii seeking declaratory and injunctive relief invalidating a threatened health care cost recovery action by Hawaii. A hearing on defendant's motion to dismiss is scheduled for March 1997. The action is scheduled to go to trial in December 1997. *Philip Morris Inc., et al. v. Margery Bronster, U.S. District Court, Hawaii, Civ. No. 96-00722 HG.*

Ohio—In September 1996, two Ohio local officials filed a health care cost recovery action in Ohio state court, purportedly on behalf of the State of Ohio and all Ohio taxpayers.

Defendants removed the case to federal court in Ohio and have filed a motion to dismiss challenging the standing of plaintiffs to bring this action. *State ex rel. Coyne, Jr., et al. v. The American Tobacco Co., et al., United States District Court, Northern District of Ohio, Case No. 96-2247.* Plaintiffs motion to remand this action to state court is pending.

New Jersey—In September 1996, the New Jersey Attorney General filed a health care cost recovery action in New Jersey state court. *The State of New Jersey v. R.J. Reynolds Tobacco Company, et al., Chancery Court, Middlesex County, Case No. C-254-96.* In August 1996, defendants filed a separate suit challenging the right of the Attorney General to bring such an action and to prosecute the case pursuant to a contingent fee arrangement with special counsel. *Philip Morris Incorporated, et al. v. Peter Verniero, Attorney General of the State of New Jersey, et al., Superior Court of New Jersey, Chancery Division, Mercer County, Case No. MER-C-000114-96.* Defendants' motion to dismiss the complaint and plaintiffs' motion for summary judgment are pending.

New York City—In October 1996, the City of New York and the New York City Health and Hospitals Corporation filed a health care cost recovery action in New York state court. *City of New York, et al. v. The Tobacco Institute, et al., Supreme Court of the State of New York, County of New York, Case No. 406225/96.*

Illinois—In November 1996, the Attorney General of Illinois filed a health care cost recovery action in Illinois state court. *People of the State of Illinois v. Philip Morris, Inc., et al., Circuit Court of Cook County, Illinois, Case No. 96 L 13146.*

Iowa—In November 1996, the State of Iowa filed a health care cost recovery action in Iowa state court. *State of Iowa, ex rel. Thomas J. Miller, in his capacity as Attorney General of the State of Iowa v. R.J. Reynolds Tobacco Co., et al., District Court for Polk County, Iowa, Case No. CL71048.*

Alaska—In January 1997, PM Inc. and three other cigarette manufacturers filed suit against the Alaska Attorney General in federal district court seeking declaratory and injunctive relief to prohibit a threatened health care cost recovery action by Alaska on grounds that it would violate federal law. *Philip Morris Inc., et al. v. Bruce Botelho, U.S. District Court, Alaska, No. A 97-003 Civil (JWS).*

Erie County—In January 1997, the County of Erie filed a health care cost recovery action in New York state court. *County of Erie v. The Tobacco Institute, Inc., et al., Supreme Court of the State of New York, County of Erie, Case No. I1997/359.*

New York—On January 27, 1997, it was reported in the press that the State of New York filed a health care cost recovery action.

Other state and local government entities have announced that they are considering filing similar health care cost recovery actions.

In September 1996, a purported class action was filed in Tennessee state court against four United States cigarette manufacturers and others on behalf of all individuals and entities in the United States who have paid premiums to a Blue Cross or Blue Shield organization for medical insurance. The complaint alleges that defendants' actions have resulted in increased medical insurance premiums for all class members and seeks recovery under various consumer protection statutes as well as under theories of breach of special duty and unjust enrichment. This case was removed by defendants to federal court. *Perry, et al. v. Philip Morris Incorporated, et al., United States District Court for the Eastern District of Tennessee, Winchester Division, Civil Action No. 4:96-CV-106.* Plaintiffs' motion to remand the case to state court is pending.

Other Tobacco Related Class Actions

In May 1995, PM Inc. announced a recall of certain of its products and in June and July four purported class actions relating to the recall were filed. Three of these cases have been dismissed. In October 1995, plaintiffs in the remaining action, *Tijerina, et al. v. Philip Morris, Inc., et al., United States District Court, Northern District of Texas, Amarillo Division, Case No. 2-95-CV-120,* filed an amended complaint alleging that PM Inc. has, for many years, knowingly manufactured filtered products that are defective because they contain "defective filters." Plaintiffs purport to bring this action on behalf of all persons who "are Texas residents and who have smoked Philip Morris filtered cigarettes manufactured with Hoechst Celanese filter materials" and who have suffered adverse health effects. Plaintiffs allege that the filters in these products contain hazardous chemicals and that cellulose acetate fibers break away from the filters and are inhaled and ingested by the consumer when the filtered products are used. Plaintiffs further allege that they relied on PM Inc.'s false and fraudulent misrepresentations, made through advertising, regarding the safety of the use of the filters. Motions to dismiss certain of plaintiffs' claims and motions for summary judgment are pending. In October 1996, the court denied plaintiffs' motion for class certification.

In June 1995, an action was filed in federal court in Maryland against PM Inc. seeking certification of a purported class consisting of "all persons and estates injured as a result of the defendant's alleged failure to manufacture a fire safe cigarette since 1987." *Sacks, et al. v. Philip Morris Inc., United States District Court, District of Maryland, Case No. WMN-95-1840.* Plaintiffs alleged in their complaint that PM Inc. intentionally withheld and suppressed material information relating to technology to produce a cigarette less likely to cause fires and failed to design and sell its cigarettes using the alleged technology. Compensatory and punitive damages were sought. In September 1996, an order was entered denying plaintiffs' motion for leave to file an amended complaint and granting defendant's motion to dismiss. Plaintiffs have appealed the order.

Certain Other Actions

In April 1994, the Company, PM Inc. and certain officers and directors were named as defendants in a complaint filed as a purported class action in federal court in New York. *Lawrence, et al. v. Philip Morris Companies Inc., et al., United States District Court, Eastern District of New York, Case No. 94 Civ. 1494 (JG).* Plaintiffs allege that defendants violated the federal securities laws by maintaining artificially high levels of profitability through an inventory management practice pursuant to which defendants allegedly shipped more inventory to customers than was necessary to satisfy market demand. In August 1995, the court granted plaintiffs' motion for class certification, certifying this action as a class action on behalf of all persons (other than persons associated with defendants) who purchased common stock of the Company during the period July 10, 1991 through

April 1, 1993, inclusive, and who held such stock at the close of business on April 1, 1993. In September 1996, the United States Court of Appeals for the Second Circuit denied the Company's Petition for Writ of Mandamus which had requested that the Court of Appeals direct the trial court to withdraw its order granting class certification. In January 1997, the court granted a motion by an alleged class member to intervene in the action and to be named an additional class representative.

In April 1994, the Company, PM Inc. and certain officers and directors were named as defendants in several purported class actions that were consolidated in the United States District Court in the Southern District of New York. *Kurzweil, et al. v. Philip Morris Companies Inc., et al., United States District Court for the Southern District of New York, Case Nos. 94 Civ. 2373 (MBM) and 94 Civ. 2546 (MBM)* and *State Board of Administration of Florida, et al. v. Philip Morris Companies Inc., et al., United States District Court for the Southern District of New York, Case No. 94 Civ. 6399 (MBM).* In those cases, plaintiffs asserted that defendants violated federal securities laws by, among other things, making allegedly false and misleading statements regarding the allegedly "addictive" qualities of cigarettes. In each case, plaintiffs claimed to have been misled by defendants' knowing and intentional failure to disclose material information. In September 1995, the court granted defendants' motion to dismiss the two complaints in their entirety. The court granted plaintiff in the *State Board* action leave to replead one of its claims. In April 1996, the court entered an order stipulating the dismissal of the *State Board* claims. In August 1996, the court entered judgment dismissing the claims in *Kurzweil*. In September 1996, the *Kurzweil* plaintiffs filed an appeal from the judgment in the United States Court of Appeals for the Second Circuit; plaintiffs withdrew the appeal without prejudice in December 1996. In September 1996, the *Kurzweil* plaintiffs filed a motion in the district court to vacate the judgment and for leave to amend their complaint; this motion remains pending.

In March 1995, an antitrust action was filed in California state court against four United States cereal manufacturers, including the Post Division of Kraft Foods, Inc. ("Kraft"), by plaintiffs purporting to represent all California residents who purchased defendants' cereal products during the four years preceding the date upon which the complaint was filed. *McIver, et al. v. General Mills, Inc., et al., Superior Court of the State of California, County of Santa Barbara, Case No. 206663.* Plaintiffs seek treble damages and the return of profits resulting from defendants' alleged conspiracy to fix and raise prices of cereal products sold to California consumers. In April 1995, a second purported class action similar to the earlier action was filed in the same court. In August 1995, the two cases were consolidated. In September 1995, the court granted defendants' motions for summary judgment. In December 1995, plaintiffs filed an appeal of that decision with the California Court of Appeals and, in January 1997, the Court of Appeals affirmed the trial court's dismissal of this action.

In April 1996, an antitrust action was filed in federal court in Wisconsin against Kraft as a purported class action. *Stuart, et al. v. Kraft Foods, Inc., et al., United States District Court, Eastern District of Wisconsin, Case No. 96-C-391.* An amended complaint filed in July 1996, named two other leading dairy products manufacturers and the National Cheese Exchange as defendants.

Plaintiff purports to represent all persons and entities in the United States (excluding governmental entities and political subdivisions) that sold milk and/or bulk cheese directly to Kraft or any of its alleged co-conspirators at any time since January 1, 1988. Plaintiff alleges that defendants engaged in a conspiracy to fix and depress the prices of bulk cheese and milk through their trading activity on the National Cheese Exchange and failed to deal in good faith with their bulk cheese and milk suppliers by paying them prices based on the National Cheese Exchange. Plaintiff seeks injunctive and equitable relief and treble damages. In December 1996, plaintiffs' motion for class certification was denied and defendants' motion to dismiss plaintiffs' action was denied without prejudice.

In September 1996, a second antitrust action was filed in federal court in Wisconsin against Kraft as a purported class action. *Sheeks, et al. v. Kraft Foods, Inc., et al., United States District Court, Eastern District of Wisconsin, Case No. 96-C-1100.* Plaintiffs are dairy farmers and assert virtually identical claims to those in the *Stuart* case discussed above. In December 1996, the court denied plaintiffs' motion to consolidate this action with the *Stuart* case.

During 1996, tax assessments alleging the underpayment of Italian value added taxes for the years 1988 to 1994 and income taxes for the year 1987 were asserted against certain affiliates of the Company. The aggregate amount of taxes claimed to be assessed to date, together with interest and penalties, is $798.4 million. The Company anticipates that further substantial value added and income tax assessments may be claimed. The Company and its affiliates believe they have complied with applicable Italian tax laws and intend to vigorously contest the assessments. A hearing concerning value added taxes is scheduled in the Italian tax court for February 4, 1997.

The Company and each of its subsidiaries named as a defendant believe, and each has been so advised by counsel handling the respective cases, that it has a number of valid defenses to all litigation pending against it. All such cases are, and will continue to be, vigorously defended. It is not possible to predict the outcome of this litigation. Litigation is subject to many uncertainties, and it is possible that some of these actions could be decided unfavorably. An unfavorable outcome of a pending smoking and health case, such as the *Carter* case discussed above, could encourage the commencement of additional similar litigation. There have also been a number of adverse legislative, regulatory, political and other developments concerning cigarette smoking and the tobacco industry. These developments generally receive widespread media attention. The Company is not able to evaluate the effect of these developing matters on pending litigation and the possible commencement of additional litigation.

Management is unable to make a meaningful estimate of the amount or range of loss that could result from an unfavorable outcome of all pending litigation. It is possible that the Company's results of operations or cash flows in a particular quarterly or annual period or its financial position could be materially affected by an ultimate unfavorable outcome of certain pending litigation. Management believes, however, that the ultimate outcome of all pending litigation should not have a material adverse effect on the Company's financial position.

Inventory Valuation: Determining Cost and Using Cost Flow Assumptions

LEARNING OBJECTIVES

After studying this chapter, you should be able to:

1. List and describe the major inventory classifications that a company's inventory might comprise.

2. Describe and distinguish between the periodic and perpetual inventory systems.

3. Identify the types of items that should be included in inventory.

4. Determine the effects of inventory errors on financial statement accounts.

5. Determine the costs that should be included in inventory cost.

6. Explain the procedure for each of the following cost flow assumptions: average cost, FIFO, and unit LIFO.

7. Discuss the characteristics, advantages, and disadvantages of the FIFO, LIFO, and average cost assumptions.

8. Explain the dollar-value LIFO procedure.

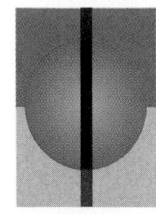

Inventory is the term used in the United States to describe assets that are intended for sale in the ordinary course of business, are in the process of being produced for sale, or are to be used currently in producing goods for sale. (In many other countries, the term *stock* is used for inventory.) What constitutes inventory for a particular company depends on that company's normal operating activities. For example, a securities dealer would treat trading securities as inventory, but a manufacturer of drill presses would classify them as an investment. A manufacturer of road graders would classify a road grader as inventory, but a road construction company would treat it as property, plant, and equipment.

Proper identification and valuation of inventory items are important because inventory can have a material effect on both the balance sheet and the income statement. Inventory may be one of the most significant assets, in dollar amount, reported on the balance sheet of manufacturing and merchandising companies. For example, these data from Whitman Corporation's 1995 balance sheet reveal that total inventories were more than 35 percent of total current assets (amounts are in millions of dollars).

Inventories:

Raw materials and supplies	**$ 84.5**
Work in process	**48.1**
Finished goods	**134.5**
Total inventories	**$267.1**
Other current assets	**62.2**
Total current assets	**$761.1**

Furthermore, the cost of inventory sold, normally called the cost of goods sold, is a major expense for many companies. In 1995, General Electric's cost of goods sold was more than 40 percent of total expenses (see Appendix B of the textbook). Inventory on hand at the end of an accounting period is reported as a current asset on the balance sheet because it is expected to be sold or used to produce goods for sale within one year or one operating cycle, whichever is longer.

The basic issues related to accounting for and reporting inventory are:

1. Classifying inventories by type.

2. Selecting an inventory accounting system.

3. Identifying items to be included in inventory.

4. Determining the expenditures and cost allocations to be included in inventory cost.

5. When necessary, making assumptions about inventory cost flow.

6. When necessary, choosing among alternatives to the cost basis of valuing inventory.

7. Estimating inventory costs when a physical count of inventory items is not practicable or possible.

Issues 1 through 5 are discussed in order in this chapter. Alternatives to the cost basis of valuing inventory and methods of estimating inventory costs (issues 6 and 7) are discussed in Chapter 10.

 **MAJOR INVENTORY CLASSIFICATIONS**

The inventory classifications reported on the balance sheet and the costs included in those inventory classifications depend on a company's normal operating activities. A merchandising company ordinarily purchases goods for resale to customers, at wholesale or retail. As consumers, most of us are more familiar with retail merchandisers than with wholesalers. Sears, Montgomery Ward, a Ford dealership, and the local grocery store are all retailers, because most if not all of their sales are to individual consumers. All merchandising companies, whether wholesalers or retailers, have only one general class of inventory—**merchandise inventory,** or simply inventory. The merchandise inventory account, however, often consists of several specific categories of goods intended for sale. For example, the merchandise inventory of an automobile dealership might consist of several car models. Merchandise inventory costs normally include the purchase price of the inventory plus any other costs incurred to get the inventory items on location and ready for sale to customers.

Rather than purchasing completed goods for resale, a manufacturing company produces the goods it sells. As a result, manufacturing companies normally have three types of inventory, each of which is associated with a stage of the production process: raw materials, work in process, and finished goods.

Raw materials inventory consists of goods and materials that will ultimately become part of the manufactured product but have not yet entered the production process. For example, the raw materials inventory of an automobile manufacturer might include sheet metal, nuts, bolts, and paint. The cost of raw materials inventory generally includes the purchase price of the materials plus shipping and similar costs necessary to get the materials into place for use in the production process.

Work-in-process inventory consists of units in the production process that require additional work before becoming finished goods. The costs normally included in work-in-process inventory are the costs of the raw materials incorporated into the product and the cost of labor applied directly to its completion, plus manufacturing overhead costs incurred before the date when the amount of work-in-process inventory is determined. Manufacturing overhead costs include the cost of supplies used in the production process, such as machine oil; the cost of labor necessary to support the production process; insurance and utilities expense; and depreciation on property, plant, and equipment employed in the production process.

Finished goods inventory consists of units that have been completed and are available for sale at the end of the accounting period. The cost of finished goods includes the costs of raw materials and labor that can be traced directly to the completed product, as well as manufacturing overhead costs incurred during the production process.

Exhibits 9–1 and 9–2 present the inventory accounts and the costs flowing into and out of those accounts for a merchandising company and a manufacturing company, respectively. Additional inventory accounts are sometimes found on the balance sheet—for example, an inventory of supplies to be used in the production process.

INVENTORY ACCOUNTING SYSTEMS

In accounting for inventory we need to determine both the amount of inventory on hand at the end of the accounting period, which is reported as a current asset on the balance sheet, and the cost of inventory sold during the accounting period, which is reported as a deduction from sales on the income statement. The amount of inventory on hand and the cost of inventory sold can be determined using either the periodic or the perpetual inventory system.

The Periodic Inventory System

2 Describe and distinguish between the periodic and perpetual inventory systems.

As the name implies, when the **periodic inventory system** is used, the amount of inventory on hand is determined only periodically. All inventory acquired

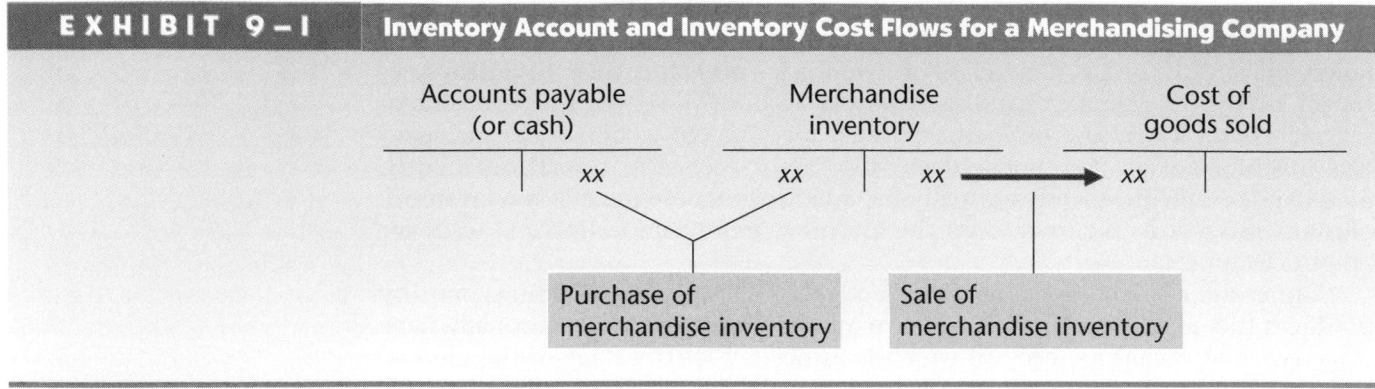

EXHIBIT 9-1   **Inventory Account and Inventory Cost Flows for a Merchandising Company**

Accounts payable (or cash) | Merchandise inventory | Cost of goods sold

Purchase of merchandise inventory

Sale of merchandise inventory

EXHIBIT 9-2   **Inventory Account and Inventory Cost Flows for a Manufacturing Company**

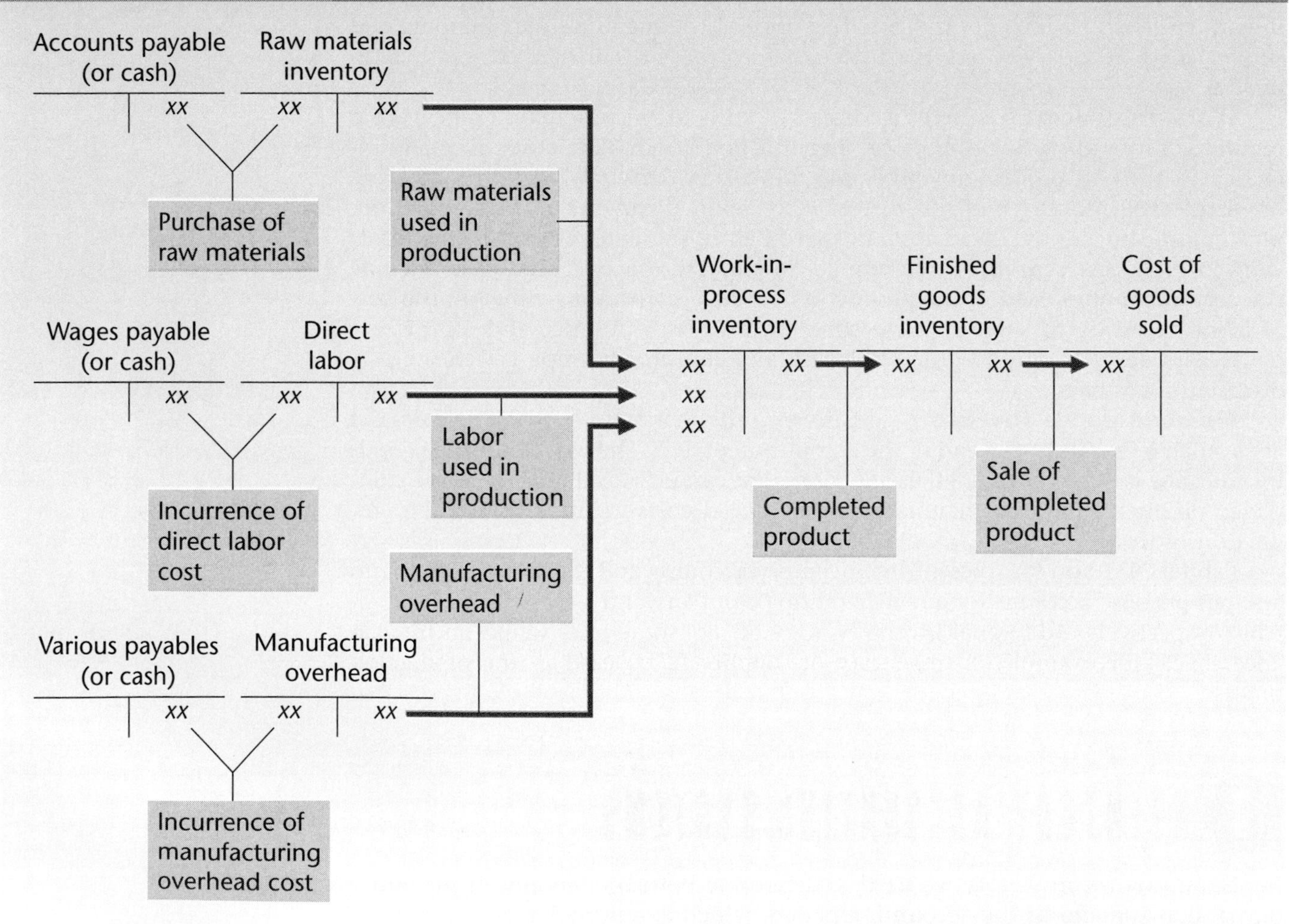

Accounts payable (or cash) — Raw materials inventory

Purchase of raw materials

Raw materials used in production

Wages payable (or cash) — Direct labor

Incurrence of direct labor cost

Labor used in production

Work-in-process inventory — Finished goods inventory — Cost of goods sold

Completed product

Sale of completed product

Manufacturing overhead

Various payables (or cash) — Manufacturing overhead

Incurrence of manufacturing overhead cost

during an accounting period is recorded by debiting the purchases account. The dollar amount in the purchases account at the end of the accounting period is added to the cost of the inventory on hand at the beginning of the period to determine the total cost of goods available for sale. The amount of inventory at the end of the accounting period is determined by counting inventory units. The cost of this ending inventory is then deducted from the cost of goods available for sale to determine the cost of goods sold. In summary, when the periodic inventory system is used, a physical count of inventory is required; and cost of goods sold is a *residual* amount dependent on the amount of ending inventory·

Beginning inventory	$10,000
Plus: Net inventory purchases during the period	80,000
Cost of goods available for sale	$90,000
Less: Ending inventory	(15,000)
Cost of goods sold	$75,000

Under the periodic inventory system, the balance in the inventory account is adjusted only when a physical count is made. Once the inventory on hand has been determined by physical count at the end of an accounting period, the inventory account is credited for the beginning inventory balance, and the purchases account is closed with a credit. The inventory account is then debited for the dollar amount of ending inventory (based on the physical count), and cost of goods sold is debited for the dollar amount of inventory that was available for sale but not included in the ending inventory balance. The usual entries made under the periodic inventory system are illustrated in the left-hand column of Exhibit 9–3.

The Perpetual Inventory System

When the **perpetual inventory system** is used, a continuous record is kept of changes in inventory. Inventory, rather than purchases, is debited when inventory is acquired. Sales of inventory are recorded by debiting the cost of goods sold account and crediting the inventory account for the cost of merchandise sold. Thus, the perpetual inventory system provides a *continuous record* of the balances in both the inventory account and the cost of goods sold account. If the company has a computerized bookkeeping system, additions to and withdrawals from inventory can be recorded almost instantaneously. Moreover, the advent of computerized bookkeeping systems has made the perpetual inventory system cost-effective for an increasing number of companies. The use of optical scanners when recording sales at the cash register can be incorporated into such a system.

Even though a physical inventory count is not required to determine the inventory on hand, all inventory items should be counted at least once each year in order to verify the perpetual inventory balance. Since the purpose of this physical count is to verify the perpetual inventory records, the count need not be made at a single point in time and need not occur at or near the end of the accounting period. Counts of various inventory items can be staggered throughout the fiscal year, reducing the inconvenience and cost often associated with a shutdown of operations for a complete inventory count.

Because of accounting or counting errors or because of inventory losses, theft, or waste, the physical inventory count may yield an inventory balance that differs from the balance in the perpetual inventory records. Should such a difference occur, the balance of the inventory account should be adjusted to agree with the physical count. When the adjustment is made, an inventory shortage account is debited, or an inventory overage account credited, as appropriate. Illustrative entries for the perpetual inventory system are shown in the right-hand column of Exhibit 9–3.

The Periodic and Perpetual Inventory Systems Compared

The essential distinction between the periodic and the perpetual inventory systems is that under the periodic system the cost of inventory sold is determined by subtracting the cost of the ending inventory from the cost of inventory available for sale during the period. Under the perpetual system, in contrast, the cost of inventory sold is subtracted from the cost of inventory available for sale to obtain the cost of the ending inventory. We have seen too that the periodic system *requires* a physical inventory count before ending inventory and cost of goods sold can be recorded, whereas the perpetual system does not. The periodic inventory system is best suited to companies with large quantities of low-cost inventory items, such as a hardware store. The perpetual system is better suited to high-cost inventory items, for which continuous monitoring of inventory is important—as in the case of an automobile dealership.

The periodic inventory system has several disadvantages compared with the perpetual inventory system. One is the periodic system's dependence on a complete physical inventory count at the end of each accounting period. Physical inventory counts can be time-consuming, inconvenient, and costly, and they may interfere with the company's normal operation. A second disadvantage of the periodic system is that cost of goods sold is calculated by deducting ending inventory from goods available for sale. The underlying assumption is that inventory that is not on hand at the end of the accounting period must have been sold. This assumption ignores the possibility that various inventory shortages, such as breakage, theft, loss, and waste, may have occurred during the period. Finally, when the periodic system is used, reporting a reasonably accurate interim inventory figure is difficult unless some sort of supplementary perpetual inventory records are available, or an interim count is made of physical inventory.

To illustrate the differences between the periodic and perpetual inventory systems, consider the following data for the Thompson Stereo Shop and the related comparative entries presented in Exhibit 9–3.

Beginning inventory (25 units @ $400)	**$10,000**
Purchases (80 units @ $400)	**32,000**
Ending inventory (30 units @ $400)	**12,000**
Sales (74 units @ $500 selling price)	**37,000**
Inventory shortage (1 unit @ $400)	**400**

EXHIBIT 9–3   Journal Entries under the Periodic and Perpetual Inventory Systems

Periodic Inventory System			Perpetual Inventory System		
To record purchase of speaker systems for sale:					
Purchases	32,000		Inventory	32,000	
Accounts payable		32,000	Accounts payable		32,000
(80 × $400)			(80 × $400)		
Entries made as sales occur:					
(No entry for inventory withdrawal or to record cost of goods sold)			Cost of goods sold	29,600	
			Inventory		29,600
			(74 × $400)		
Accounts receivable	37,000		Accounts receivable	37,000	
Sales revenue		37,000	Sales revenue		37,000
(74 × $500)			(74 × $500)		
Year-end adjusting and closing entries:					
Cost of goods sold (residual)	30,000		Inventory shortage	400	
Ending inventory (30 × $400)	12,000		Inventory		400
Beginning inventory			(1 × $400)		
(25 × $400)		10,000			
Purchases (80 × $400)		32,000			
Income summary	30,000		Income summary	30,000	
Cost of goods sold		30,000	Inventory shortage		400
			Cost of goods sold		29,600

Observe that both inventory systems produce a $30,000 debit to the income summary for the year. Under the periodic system, however, the $400 inventory shortage is not separately identifiable because of the assumption that all speaker systems that are not included in the physical inventory count must have been sold.

ITEMS INCLUDED IN INVENTORY

Generally, identifying items that should be included in inventory is not difficult, because the company has the items in its possession and holds legal title to them. In some situations, however, the identification of items that should be included in inventory is more difficult. For example, a company may hold goods that it does not own, or own goods that it does not hold—such as when goods are in transit from a supplier, but title already has passed to the company that is purchasing the goods. When determining which items should be included in the current period's inventory is difficult, several factors should be considered, including legal title, physical possession, contractual terms, special industry practices, and the intentions of the parties involved. When inventory identification problems must be resolved, there is no substitute for sound professional judgment by the accountant.

3 Identify the types of items that should be included in inventory.

Goods in Transit

Acquisitions of inventory should be recorded by the buyer when legal title passes to the buyer. Often, however, determining exactly when title passes is not easy. Because the financial statements normally are not materially affected by such transactions, companies usually record inventory acquisitions as the goods are received. When a company follows this practice, the purchases account (under the periodic system) or the inventory account (under the perpetual system) as well as related accounts payable must be adjusted for any goods in transit for which title has passed to the buyer as of the end of the accounting period.

When determining whether goods in transit should be included in inventory, accountants must review the terms of the shipping agreement. If goods are shipped "**f.o.b. [free on board] shipping point,**" legal title and the responsibilities of ownership, such as insurance and shipping costs, pass to the buyer when the seller delivers the goods to the shipping agent. In this case, goods in transit should be included in the buyer's inventory. If goods are shipped "**f.o.b. destination,**" the goods belong to the seller until they are delivered to their destination by the shipping agent. In this case, title and the responsibilities of ownership remain with the seller until the goods reach the specified destination. The goods in transit should therefore be included in the seller's inventory, and their transportation cost included in the seller's expense.

When there is some question as to whether title has passed to the buyer, the accountant must consider the intent of the sales agreement, special industry practices, the buyer's normal accounting policy, and similar factors. For example, it is common practice to treat goods manufactured for a special order as being sold as soon as they are physically separated from the manufacturer's regular inventory. Special-order goods are not assets (inventory) of the manufacturer, because the economic benefit embodied in such goods can accrue only to the customer who placed the order.

Consigned Goods

A **consignment** is a transaction in which one party, the consignor, ships goods to a second party, the consignee, who attempts to sell the goods for the consignor. Legal title to the goods remains with the consignor. The consignee is responsible for exercising due care and protecting the goods from loss or damage, but incurs no liability to the consignor. When goods are sold by the consignee, the sales price less a selling commission is remitted to the consignor. Goods that are not sold are returned to the consignor.

Consigned goods must be considered when determining inventory because even though they are in the possession of the consignee, the merchandise is part of the consignor's inventory. Consigned goods should be included in inventory at their cost to the consignor plus the costs of handling and shipping the goods to the consignee. An artist's agreement to sell paintings through an art gallery is typical of consignment arrangements. The details of accounting for consignments are discussed and illustrated in the appendix to Chapter 7.

Sales on Approval

Sales on approval are similar to consignment sales, except that the party who owns the goods ships them directly to potential buyers "on approval," rather than attempting to sell them through a consignee. For example, companies that sell postage stamps to stamp collectors often send stamps to collectors who might be interested in buying them. The collectors return to the seller the stamps they do not purchase along with payment for the stamps they decide to keep. Goods sent on approval to a potential buyer should remain as inventory on the seller's books until payment is received for items kept by the buyer.

Product Financing Arrangements

A **product financing arrangement** is a transaction in which a company "sells" (transfers) inventory items at the same time agreeing to repurchase them, or substantially identical items, from the buyer at a specified price over a specified period. For example, Axle Corporation "sells" (transfers) inventory to Gilson Company, and as part of the transaction, agrees to repurchase the goods at a specified price within the next three months. Transactions such as these are often called **parking transactions** because for a short period the "seller" (Axle) in effect "parks" its inventory among the "buyer's" (Gilson's) assets. (For the seller, "parking" is an example of off-balance-sheet financing, a topic that was introduced in Chapter 5.)

The FASB has concluded that in most cases parking transactions should not be recorded as sales, because the earnings process is not complete or virtually complete.[1] In particular, when the specified repurchase price can be adjusted as necessary to cover fluctuations in carrying and financing costs, the original seller (Axle) actually bears the risks of ownership even though the legal title may have passed to the buyer (Gilson). In such cases, *FASB Statement No. 49* requires that the items "sold" must continue to be reported as part of the seller's inventory (i.e., no sale can be recorded). The cash received by the seller should be recorded along with an obligation to repurchase the items from the buyer—an obligation that is reported as a liability on the seller's balance sheet.

Conditional Sales

The extended payment period of an installment sale, or uncertainty about possible returns, often increases the seller's risk of not collecting the entire amount due. As a result, goods are often sold on a conditional basis. The seller may retain legal title until all payments have been received, or sales may not be recorded until returns can be reasonably estimated. For example, book publishers often allow bookstores to return unsold books for a refund.

---

[1]"Accounting for Product Financing Arrangements," *Statement of Financial Accounting Standards No. 49* (Stamford, Conn.: FASB, 1981).

In such a case, should all or only part of the books shipped by the publisher to the bookstore be recorded as sold and removed from the publisher's inventory? The answer depends on the degree of certainty about the number of unsold books that may be returned. If a reasonable estimate of book returns can be made, then all the books shipped should be considered as sold and removed from inventory, and an account for estimated sales returns and allowances established. If such an estimate cannot be made, the publisher should not remove shipped books from the inventory account until they are sold by the bookstore.[2]

INVENTORY ERRORS AND THEIR EFFECTS ON THE FINANCIAL STATEMENTS

Errors can occur in identifying or counting items that should be included in inventory, as well as in recording inventory acquisitions or sales. The great variety of goods often found in inventory makes overlooking or mispricing items easy, and makes physical counts of inventory items tedious. The extended periods required to ship goods from a seller to a buyer may mean that several items will be in transit from suppliers or to customers at the end of each accounting period. When vast numbers of transactions involve inventory, individual purchase or sale transactions may be erroneously omitted from the accounting records.

Errors in accounting for inventory can affect one or more of the following: beginning inventory, purchases, ending inventory, cost of goods sold, income, and retained earnings. In analyzing the effects of inventory accounting errors, the following guidelines should be remembered:

I. If multiple inventory errors occur in a particular accounting period, the effects of each error should be separately evaluated.

2. Use the following interrelationships to reduce the complexity of the process of analyzing inventory errors.

For a periodic inventory system:

$$
\underset{\text{BI}}{\text{Beginning}\atop\text{inventory}} + \underset{\text{P}}{\text{Purchases}} - \underset{\text{EI}}{\text{Ending}\atop\text{inventory}} = \underset{\text{CGS}}{\text{Cost of}\atop\text{goods sold}}
$$

For a perpetual inventory system:

$$
\underset{\text{BI}}{\text{Beginning}\atop\text{inventory}} + \underset{\text{P}}{\text{Purchases}} - \underset{\text{CGS}}{\text{Cost of}\atop\text{goods sold}} = \underset{\text{EI}}{\text{Ending}\atop\text{inventory}}
$$

Gross margin is calculated as:

$$
\underset{\text{SR}}{\text{Sales}\atop\text{revenue}} - \underset{\text{CGS}}{\text{Cost of}\atop\text{goods sold}} = \underset{\text{GM}}{\text{Gross}\atop\text{margin}}
$$

Exhibits 9–4 and 9–5 present analyses of two inventory errors to demonstrate the effects of errors and the procedures for their analysis. Both exhibits show how inventory and purchase errors can have multiple effects on the financial statements, and of course, on financial data and analyses based on the financial statements. In addition, the exhibits demonstrate that some inventory errors are

4 Determine the effects of inventory errors on financial statement accounts.

CONCEPTUAL

Inventory accounting errors can affect both the balance sheet and the income statement.

---

[2]"Revenue Recognition When Right of Return Exists," *Statement of Financial Accounting Standards No. 48* (Stamford, Conn.: FASB, 1981).

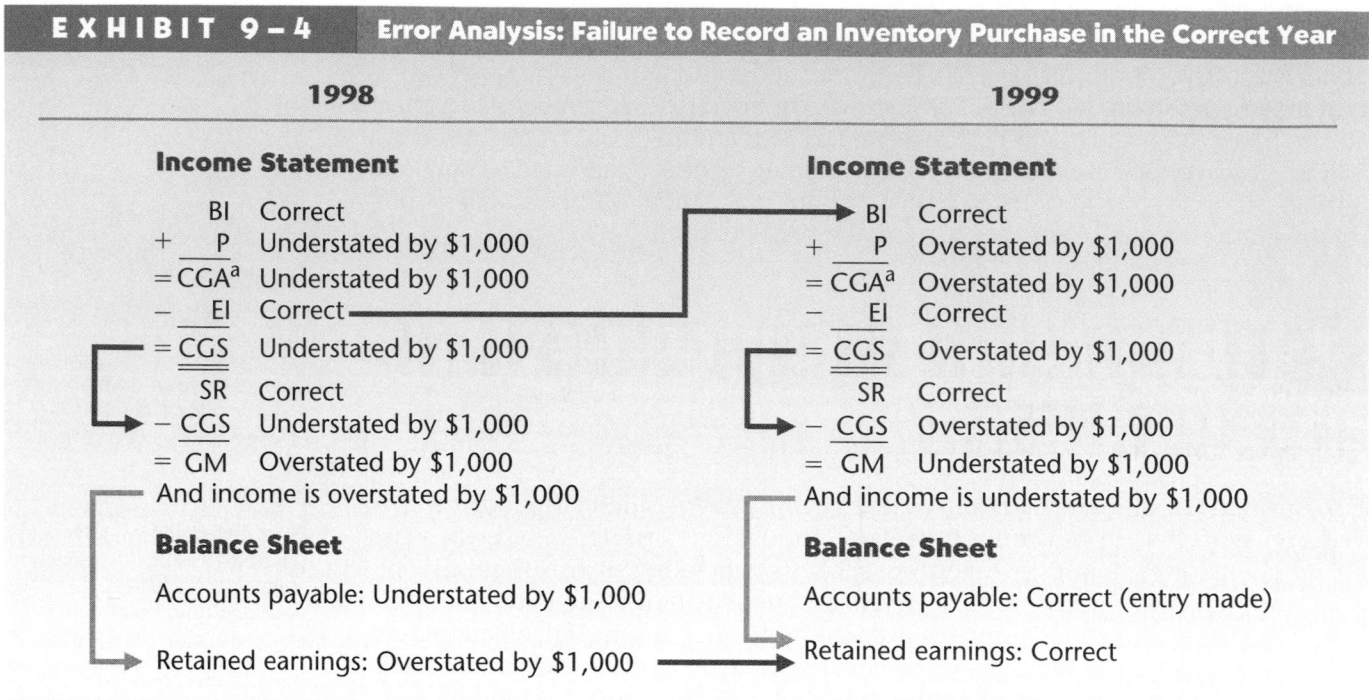

EXHIBIT 9-4   **Error Analysis: Failure to Record an Inventory Purchase in the Correct Year**

1998	1999
Income Statement	**Income Statement**
BI Correct	BI Correct
+ P Understated by $1,000	+ P Overstated by $1,000
= CGA[a] Understated by $1,000	= CGA[a] Overstated by $1,000
– EI Correct	– EI Correct
= CGS Understated by $1,000	= CGS Overstated by $1,000
SR Correct	SR Correct
– CGS Understated by $1,000	– CGS Overstated by $1,000
= GM Overstated by $1,000	= GM Understated by $1,000
And income is overstated by $1,000	And income is understated by $1,000
Balance Sheet	**Balance Sheet**
Accounts payable: Understated by $1,000	Accounts payable: Correct (entry made)
Retained earnings: Overstated by $1,000	Retained earnings: Correct

[a]CGA: Cost of goods available.

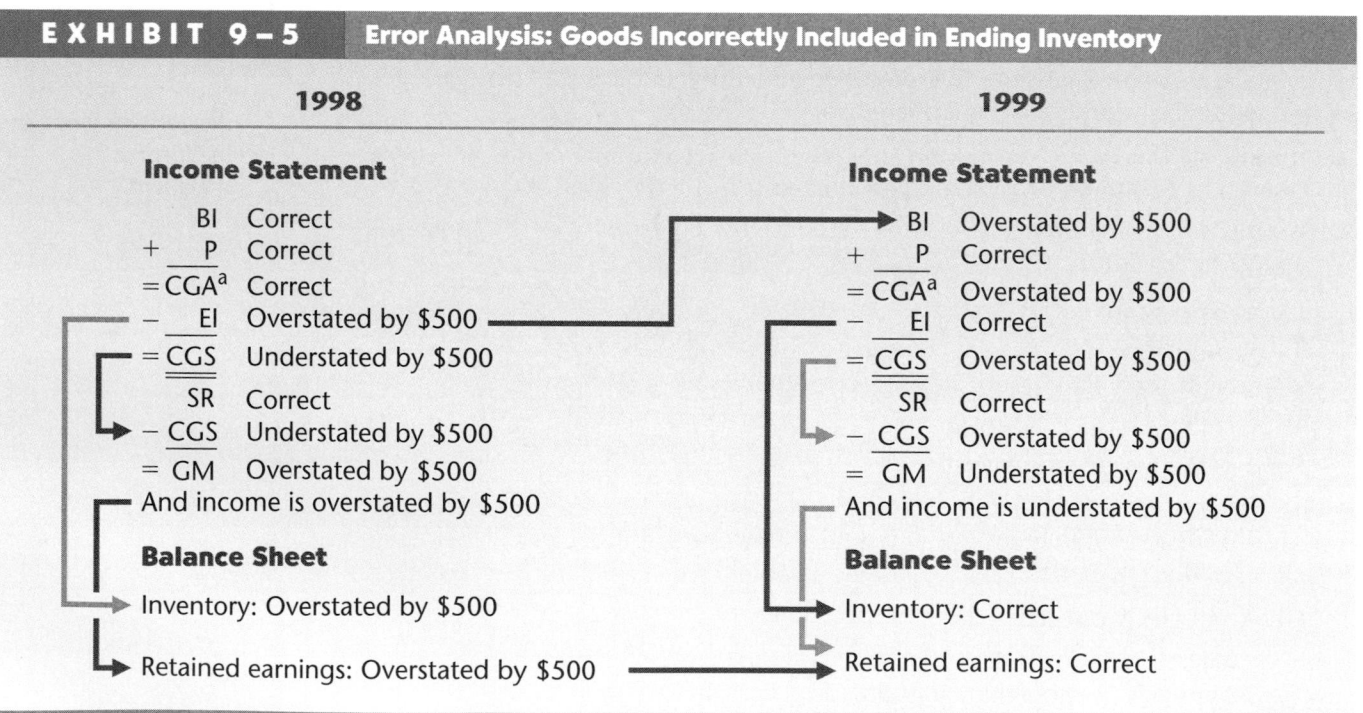

EXHIBIT 9-5   **Error Analysis: Goods Incorrectly Included in Ending Inventory**

1998	1999
Income Statement	**Income Statement**
BI Correct	BI Overstated by $500
+ P Correct	+ P Correct
= CGA[a] Correct	= CGA[a] Overstated by $500
– EI Overstated by $500	– EI Correct
= CGS Understated by $500	= CGS Overstated by $500
SR Correct	SR Correct
– CGS Understated by $500	– CGS Overstated by $500
= GM Overstated by $500	= GM Understated by $500
And income is overstated by $500	And income is understated by $500
Balance Sheet	**Balance Sheet**
Inventory: Overstated by $500	Inventory: Correct
Retained earnings: Overstated by $500	Retained earnings: Correct

[a]CGA: Cost of goods available.

self-correcting or counterbalancing over two accounting periods. That is, an overstatement or understatement in one period is offset by an error in the opposite direction in the following period. Since the ending inventory of one period is the beginning inventory of the next period, errors in ending inventory are carried into the next period.

In tracing the effects of the error in Exhibit 9–4, for instance, we can see that erroneous recording of a 1998 purchase in 1999 caused 1998 purchases, goods available for sale, and cost of goods sold to be understated, and income and retained earnings to be overstated. On the other hand, 1999 purchases, goods available for sale, and cost of goods sold were overstated, and 1999 income understated. Since 1998 income was overstated and 1999 income understated by the same amount, however, retained earnings is correct at the end of 1999. A similar analysis can be made of the data in Exhibit 9–5. Try doing so as a means of developing your error analysis skills.

ⒺXPENDITURES AND COST ALLOCATIONS INCLUDED IN INVENTORY COST

An important aspect of accounting for inventory is to properly determine the expenditures to be included in inventory cost. Inventory, like other assets, generally is accounted for in accordance with the historical cost principle (discussed in Chapter 2). **Inventory cost** (for a merchandising company) or **product cost** (for a manufacturing company) is the sum of all expenditures required to get inventory items into condition and location for sale. Inventory cost includes the original purchase price plus expenditures for freight in, handling, storage related to goods purchased, applicable insurance and taxes, and materials and labor used to manufacture inventory.

5 Determine the costs that should be included in inventory cost.

CONCEPTUAL

Inventory cost includes all expenditures needed to get inventory into condition and location for sale.

In theory, it also would be appropriate to allocate to inventory a portion of some other expenditures, such as expenses of the purchasing department and costs of handling and storing goods before they are sold. Because of the difficulty of allocating such expenditures, however—and because they often are not material in amount compared with other expenditures included in inventory cost—such expenditures are seldom included in practice. Instead, they are accounted for separately as period expenses, or **period costs.**[3] Also, expenditures not related directly to the acquisition or production of inventory normally are accounted for as period expenses. For example, selling costs are accounted for as period costs and are expensed when incurred.

Likewise, interest costs incurred to finance the purchase of inventory are treated as period costs, even though they seem more directly related to inventories than most other period costs. In fact, some accountants argue that inventory financing expenditures are a direct cost of getting inventory into condition and location for sale and should therefore be included as part of the cost of inventory. But others argue that interest expenditures related to inventories are no different from other financing costs, and should therefore be accounted for as a period cost, like other financing costs. The FASB has taken the position that interest costs for inventories that are routinely and continuously manufactured in large quantities—for example, automobiles—should not be included in inventory cost because the value of the information provided by such treatment is outweighed by the cost of providing it. On the other hand, material amounts of interest incurred in the construction of assets for the company's own use or as discrete projects for sale or lease—for example, ships—should be capitalized (recorded as part of the cost of the asset), provided such assets require considerable time to be readied for use. The FASB assumes that the value of the information provided by assigning these interest costs to inventory will exceed the cost of making the assignment.[4] (Accounting for interest costs incurred during construction is discussed in more detail in Chapter 11.)

Merchandise Inventory Costs and Cost Adjustments

As indicated earlier and illustrated in Exhibit 9–3, when merchandise is purchased, a debit is made to either inventory (in a perpetual inventory system)

---

[3]Interestingly, under the Tax Reform Act of 1986, expenditures such as these must be included in inventory cost for purposes of determining *taxable income* by companies with more than $10 million in sales.
[4]"Capitalization of Interest Cost," *Statement of Financial Accounting Standards No. 34* (Stamford, Conn.: FASB, 1979).

or purchases (in a periodic inventory system). Ideally, the dollar amount debited should be the invoice price of the goods purchased, less any available purchase discount. (Alternatively, inventory acquisitions may be recorded at the invoice price, and purchase discounts taken recorded in a separate account.) Additional costs may be incurred for shipping and handling of the goods; and reductions in acquisition cost may result from returns of purchased goods and other allowances, or adjustments of the invoice price. Although additions to and reductions of the invoice price can be accounted for by adjusting the purchases or inventory account directly, normal accounting practice is to use a number of separate accounts for these adjustments. Use of separate accounts for freight in, purchase returns, purchase allowances, and similar adjustments provides a breakdown of information that helps management to analyze the elements of inventory acquisition cost.

Lump-Sum Purchases

Sometimes a company purchases two or more different kinds of inventory for a single lump sum. In these instances, the company must allocate the single purchase amount among the various items purchased. The procedure that should be used to allocate a lump-sum or "basket" purchase price is the **relative sales value method.**

Assume that Donna's Dress Shop purchased 10 identical blouses and 15 identical dresses from Wholesale Fashions for a total amount of $1,500. As a "package deal," the invoice provided no breakdown of the costs of the blouse and dress groups separately. Further assume that Donna's intends to sell the blouses for $75 each, and the dresses for $150 each. Using the relative sales value method, the $1,500 lump-sum cost would be allocated between the blouse and dress groups as follows:

$$\text{Blouses:} \quad \frac{10 \text{ blouses} \times \$75}{(10 \text{ blouses} \times \$75) + (15 \text{ dresses} \times \$150)} \times \$1,500 = \$375$$

$$\text{Dresses:} \quad \frac{15 \text{ dresses} \times \$150}{(10 \text{ blouses} \times \$75) + (15 \text{ dresses} \times \$150)} \times \$1,500 = \$1,125$$

Note that the selling prices of the blouses and dresses are used as a percentage of the combined selling prices to calculate the portion of the lump-sum purchase price that should be allocated to blouses and the portion to be allocated to dresses.

Purchase Discounts

Sellers offer **purchase discounts** to buyers as an incentive to make prompt payment on purchases. For example, typical sale terms are "2%/10, net 30," which means that a 2 percent discount from the invoice price is offered for payment within 10 days, and the full invoice price is due within 30 days.

As with sales discounts (see Exhibit 8–3), the preferable method of accounting for purchase discounts is the net method because both purchases and accounts payable are recorded at their cash equivalent amounts at the time of purchase. Under the **net method,** purchases and accounts payable are recorded *net* of the purchase discount, and purchase discounts not taken are recorded as purchase discounts lost. Illustrative entries for the net method are shown in Exhibit 9–6.

There are several reasons to use the net method rather than record inventory acquisitions at the invoice price. First, on the purchase date, purchases and accounts payable are recorded at the cash equivalent exchange price, or the invoice price *net* of the purchase discount. Therefore, the cost of the purchased

EXHIBIT 9-6	Net Method of Accounting for Purchase Discounts (Terms: 2%/10, Net 30)

To record purchase on 12/15:

Purchases (inventory)	980[a]	
Accounts payable		980

To record payment within discount period (by 12/25):

Accounts payable	980	
Cash		980

To record payment after discount period but before end of fiscal year (12/16–12/31):

Accounts payable	980	
Purchase discounts lost	20	
Cash		1,000

Adjusting entry at end of fiscal year (12/31) when invoice is unpaid but discount period has expired:

Purchase discounts lost	20	
Accounts payable		20

[a]**Although conceptually less desirable, purchases (inventory) and accounts payable could be recorded at the gross amount of $1,000. If payment is made within the discount period, purchase discounts (a contra purchases account) would be credited for $20.**

goods and the related liability are correctly stated as of the purchase date, and the purchase discount is recorded at the time the purchase is recorded. Second, purchase discounts lost are recorded separately from purchases, which is appropriate because the expense arose from failure to make a timely payment rather than from the purchase transaction itself. Third, accounts payable are adjusted at the end of the year for purchase discounts lost. This adjustment results in proper reporting of the liability. Finally, if purchase discounts lost is reported in the income statement as a financing expense or general operating expense, rather than hidden in the cost of merchandise purchased, users of the financial statements are made aware of the period expense that arose from failure to pay accounts payable on time.

Some users may consider failure to make payments within the discount period an important matter because the *effective* interest rate paid by the buyer, assuming that payment on a 2%/10, net 30 purchase is not made until the thirtieth day, is approximately 36 percent:

$$2\% \times \frac{360 \text{ days}}{30 \text{ days} - 10 \text{ days}} = 36\%$$

Indeed, it is almost always better financing policy to borrow money elsewhere and take advantage of a purchase discount than to defer payment and lose a purchase discount.

Freight In

In accordance with the historical cost principle, transportation costs, called **transportation in** or **freight in,** as well as handling costs and other incidental costs a company incurs in getting inventory into location and in condition for sale, should be included in inventory cost. If it is impractical to identify such costs with specific purchases of goods, however, or if the amounts of such costs are material in comparison with other inventoriable costs, they may be recorded in separate accounts, such as freight in. A typical entry to record $100 of freight in would be:

Freight in	100	
Accounts payable		100

In practice, freight in increases the cost of goods sold under a periodic inventory system, because it is added to purchases when goods available for sale is calculated. Under a perpetual inventory system, freight in should be debited to merchandise inventory at the time of purchase. If freight in is recorded in a separate account, it normally is added to cost of goods sold at the end of the accounting period. Although adjustment of the cost of goods sold for freight in during the accounting period is a common practice, it is theoretically unsound, because only the freight costs associated with goods sold should be included in cost of goods sold. The remainder of the freight costs should be assigned to the goods still in inventory at the end of the accounting period.

Purchase Returns and Allowances

When the buyer returns goods to the seller, the buyer is given a **purchase return** credit against existing accounts payable or future purchases. As soon as the amount of the credit is known, it should be recorded on the buyer's books. Assuming that the buyer has accounts payable to the seller, a $30 purchase return would be recorded as follows:

Accounts payable	30	
Purchase returns (Inventory, in a perpetual system)		30

The purchase returns account is a contra account to the purchases account. It is closed along with the purchases account in the year-end adjusting and closing entries made under a periodic inventory system.

Sellers occasionally ship damaged or otherwise unsatisfactory goods. Rather than return the goods, the buyer usually elects to accept an appropriate adjustment of the purchase price, called a **purchase allowance.** Under a periodic inventory system, a purchase allowance is credited to a purchase allowances account, which is a contra account to the purchases account, and is closed in the year-end adjusting and closing entries. Under a perpetual inventory system, purchase allowances are credited directly to inventory. A $50 purchase allowance would be recorded as follows:

Accounts payable	50	
Purchase allowance (Inventory, in a perpetual system)		50

Manufactured Inventory Costs

As Exhibit 9–2 indicates, manufacturing companies typically divide their inventories into three major categories: raw materials inventory, work-in-process inventory, and finished goods inventory. Work in process and finished goods include three types of costs: raw materials cost, direct labor cost, and allocated manufacturing overhead cost. The cost of the raw materials inventory purchased by a manufacturing company is calculated exactly as is the cost of purchased merchandise inventory, including adjustments for freight in, purchase discounts, and purchase returns and allowances. Direct labor cost is the cost of labor employed directly in the production process. For example, production supervisors' salaries and the wages of assembly-line workers are included in direct labor. Manufacturing overhead cost includes all manufacturing costs other than the costs of raw materials and direct labor. For example, manufacturing overhead cost would include the salary of the vice-president for manufacturing, indirect materials cost, indirect labor cost, and properly allocated portions of general overhead expenses, such as depreciation, taxes, insurance, and utilities.

COST FLOWS AND COST FLOW ASSUMPTIONS

A company usually begins an accounting period with some units of inventory on hand, and purchases or manufactures additional units during the period. Units on hand plus units acquired constitute the units available for sale. Assuming no waste, theft, or other loss, goods available for sale either are sold during the accounting period or remain in inventory at the end of the period.

Since purchases occur at different times during the period, identical units of inventory may be acquired at different costs. Thus, the dollar amounts reported for inventory and cost of goods sold at the end of the accounting period depend on the answer to the question, "Which of the costs of beginning inventory and purchases should be included in cost of goods sold, and which in the cost of ending inventory?"

Generally accepted accounting principles allow several different procedures for assigning costs to ending inventory and cost of goods sold. Those procedures may not only produce different dollar amounts for ending inventory and cost of goods sold; some of them will yield one inventory value when used in conjunction with a perpetual inventory system, and another inventory value when used with a periodic inventory system. In the next several pages, the most common cost flows, cost flow assumptions, and corresponding inventory accounting procedures are discussed. The data in Exhibit 9–7 will be used to illustrate each procedure.

Specific Identification

One procedure used to determine the cost of goods sold and the cost of ending inventory is known as **specific identification.** In this procedure, the flow of costs through goods available for sale to either cost of goods sold or cost of ending inventory is exactly the same as the physical flow of units. That is, specific identification traces *actual cost flows*. Each unit of inventory obtained, held, and sold, as well as its cost, must be specifically identified. For example, each of the 100 units sold by Sloan Company on May 10 must be specifically identified as being either a $10 unit from beginning inventory or a $12 unit from the March 7 purchase. Since the cost of a unit in the beginning inventory differs from the cost of a unit purchased on March 7, the cost of goods sold on May 10 will depend on which units were actually sold.

EXHIBIT 9–7	Inventory Units and Costs for Sloan Company		
	Number of Units	**Cost per Unit**	**Total Cost**
Inventory, 1/1	500	$10.00	$ 5,000
Purchase, 3/7	200	12.00	2,400
Purchase, 7/12	100	13.25	1,325
Purchase, 10/24	300	14.00	4,200
Goods available for sale.	1,100		$12,925
Sale, 2/5 250			
Sale, 5/10. 100			
Sale, 11/7. 150			
Goods sold	(500)		
Inventory, 12/31	600		

Because the specific identification procedure is based on the actual flow of goods through inventory, it is easiest to use when inventory consists of a relatively small number of easily distinguishable items. Specific identification is most likely to provide useful information about relatively costly inventory items—high-priced jewelry, for example, or automobiles. It becomes less practical, and less likely to produce information that justifies the extra bookkeeping effort required, as the number of inventory units increases and the cost per unit declines. This relationship is especially true if units of inventory are not easily distinguishable from one another. To give an extreme example, consider the high cost and low benefit of using specific identification to account for an inventory of sixteen-penny nails, which are sold by the handful at a relatively small unit acquisition cost that fluctuates substantially.

Some accountants argue that besides being impractical, specific identification allows management to manipulate the cost of ending inventory, cost of goods sold, and net income. That is, by selecting particular goods to be sold, management can exercise some control over the cost of goods sold and the cost of inventory remaining on hand. For example, if on May 10 Sloan Company selected 100 of the $10 units in beginning inventory to be sold (Exhibit 9–7), cost of goods sold would be $1,000. But if Sloan chose to sell 100 of the $12 units purchased on March 7, cost of goods sold would be $1,200. Whether this opportunity for management to influence cost of goods sold and inventory cost by selecting particular units for sale is manipulation or simply the result of reporting actual physical inventory flows, which management is certainly entitled to control, is debatable.

Because of the impracticality of specific identification in most accounting applications, this procedure is not widely used. Instead, most companies use one or more of several generally accepted inventory **cost flow assumptions.** The three most often used inventory cost flow assumptions are first in, first out (FIFO), last in, last out (LIFO), and average cost. The AICPA reports that in a 1995 survey of 600 companies, 42 percent of the companies used the FIFO assumption, 35 percent used LIFO, and 19 percent used average cost. Four percent used some other inventory cost flow assumption.[5]

These inventory cost flow assumptions and related accounting procedures are not departures from historical cost. Instead, they are simplifying assumptions about the flow of cost through goods available for sale into cost of goods sold and cost of ending inventory. As cost flow *assumptions,* they have no necessary relationship to the actual physical flow of goods through the enterprise. In this sense, cost flow assumptions are fundamentally different from the specific identification procedure, which is based on actual, not assumed, cost flows.

As long as each unit of inventory is acquired at the same cost, the dollar amounts of cost of goods sold and ending inventory are unaffected by which units of goods available for sale are sold and which remain in ending inventory. But as in the Sloan Company example, when units of inventory are acquired at different costs, the dollar amounts of cost of goods sold and ending inventory can vary significantly, depending on which units are assumed to be sold and which are assumed to remain in ending inventory. Cost flow assumptions relate to just which costs are associated with goods sold and goods held in ending inventory, respectively. Thus, when units of inventory have different acquisition costs, the selection of a cost flow assumption can be very important. The impact on cost of goods sold and earnings, as reported in the income statement, and on the valuation of ending inventory, as reported in the balance sheet, can be substantial. To illustrate, consider the following description of the comparative effects of LIFO and FIFO on the earnings of The Neiman Marcus Group, Inc.:

> Inventories at October 28, 1995, were $477.1 million, compared to $429.8 million a year earlier. The Company reported that the effect of the LIFO method of accounting for inventories compared to the FIFO

CONCEPTUAL

Inventory cost flow assumptions are not necessarily related to the actual physical flow of inventory items.

[5]*Accounting Trends & Techniques,* Forty-ninth Ed., American Institute of Certified Public Accountants, 1995, p. 177.

method was to decrease pre-tax earnings by $2.0 million in the first quarter of fiscal 1996 and $3.1 million in the first quarter of 1995.[6]

The following sections describe the average cost, FIFO, and LIFO cost flow assumptions.

Average Cost

Under the **average cost procedure,** the costs of goods are divided equally, or averaged, among the units in inventory. The average cost procedure can be used in either a periodic or a perpetual inventory system. When used in the periodic inventory system, it is known as the weighted average method; when used in the perpetual system, it is called the moving average method.

Weighted Average Method

The **weighted average method** is the average cost procedure used in the periodic inventory system. Sloan Company's weighted average cost of goods sold for the year and its cost of ending inventory (Exhibit 9–7) would be determined as follows:

$$\text{Average cost of goods available for sale during the period} = \frac{\text{Total } \textit{cost} \text{ of goods available for sale during the period}}{\text{Total } \textit{units} \text{ of goods available for sale during the period}}$$

$$= \frac{\$12,925}{1,100 \text{ units}} = \$11.75$$

Cost of goods sold = 500 units @ $11.75 = $5,875

Ending inventory = 600 units @ $11.75 = $7,050

Moving Average Method

The **moving average method** is the average cost procedure used in the perpetual inventory system. The perpetual system requires the use of a continuous, or moving, average cost of goods available for sale, so that the average cost can be used to determine cost of goods sold at the time of any sale. As a result, the moving average method requires the recalculation of the average unit cost after each purchase. The new average cost is then used to record the cost of goods sold for any sale made before the next purchase. The only exception to this rule occurs when the purchase price per unit is the same as the average cost per unit before the purchase in question. When applied to the Sloan Company data, the moving average method yields the results shown in Exhibit 9–8.

Notice in Exhibit 9–8 that the average cost per unit of units on hand at the time of each sale is assigned to units sold as well as to units retained in inventory. For example, when 250 units are sold on February 5, they are assigned the $10 average cost per unit that exists at that time. The 250 units that remain in inventory also are assigned a $10 per unit cost. When 200 additional units are purchased on March 7 at a cost of $12 per unit, a new average unit cost must be calculated for the 450 units then on hand. Given 250 units with a cost of $10 each, and 200 units with a cost of $12 each, the average cost per unit for the 450 units is $10.89, shown in the right-hand column of Exhibit 9–8. This average cost per unit is then assigned to the 100 units sold on May 10, as well as to the 350 units remaining in inventory after that sale. The pattern of calculations just described is followed throughout the remainder of Exhibit 9–8.

---

[6]"The Neiman Marcus Group Reports Strong Earnings Gains," *Business Wire,* November 16, 1995.

EXHIBIT 9–8	Cost of Goods Sold and Ending Inventory Using the Moving Average Method

Sloan Company

	Number of Units	Cost per Unit	Total Cost	Moving Average Cost
Beginning inventory, 1/1......................	500		$5,000	$10.00
Sale, 2/5 (CGS)................................	(250)	$10.00	(2,500)	
Inventory balance...........................	250	10.00	$2,500	
Purchase, 3/7	200	12.00	2,400	
Inventory balance...........................	450		$4,900	10.89[a]
Sale, 5/10 (CGS)	(100)	10.89	(1,089)	
Inventory balance...........................	350	10.89	$3,811[a]	
Purchase, 7/12	100	13.25	1,325	
Inventory balance...........................	450		$5,136	11.41[a]
Purchase, 10/24	300	14.00	4,200	
Inventory balance	750		$9,336	12.45[a]
Sale, 11/7 (CGS)	(150)	12.45	(1,867)[a]	
Inventory balance..........................	600	12.45	$7,469[a]	
Ending inventory	600		$7,469	
Cost of goods sold	250		$2,500	
	100		1,089	
	150		1,867	
	500		$5,456	

[a]Reflects minor rounding.

First In, First Out (FIFO)

The **first in, first out** inventory cost flow assumption, abbreviated **FIFO,** treats the earliest inventory costs of the period as the cost of goods sold and the latest inventory costs as the cost of ending inventory. In other words, regardless of the actual physical flow of goods, cost of goods sold and ending inventory are calculated as if the goods entering inventory first are sold first, and the goods entering inventory last are sold last, or remain in ending inventory. During periods of *rising* inventory acquisition costs, FIFO yields a lower cost of goods sold and a higher ending inventory cost than the average cost approach.

Exhibit 9–9 shows the calculations of Sloan Company's cost of goods sold and ending inventory using the FIFO assumption under both the periodic and perpetual inventory systems. When FIFO is applied in the periodic system, ending inventory is valued using the cost of the last goods purchased during the period. The ending inventory cost is then subtracted from the cost of goods available for sale to determine the cost of goods sold, or $5,000 in Exhibit 9–9. In contrast, when FIFO is applied in the perpetual system, cost of goods sold is determined at the time of each sale, based on the cost of the earliest purchased goods on hand at the time of the sale. The total cost of goods sold for the period is then subtracted from the cost of goods available to obtain the ending inventory cost of $7,925.

Notice that in both the periodic and perpetual systems, FIFO yields the same cost of goods sold and ending inventory cost. This result occurs because the same goods and costs are first in, and therefore first out, whether the cost of goods sold

CONCEPTUAL

FIFO yields the same results in the periodic system as in the perpetual system.

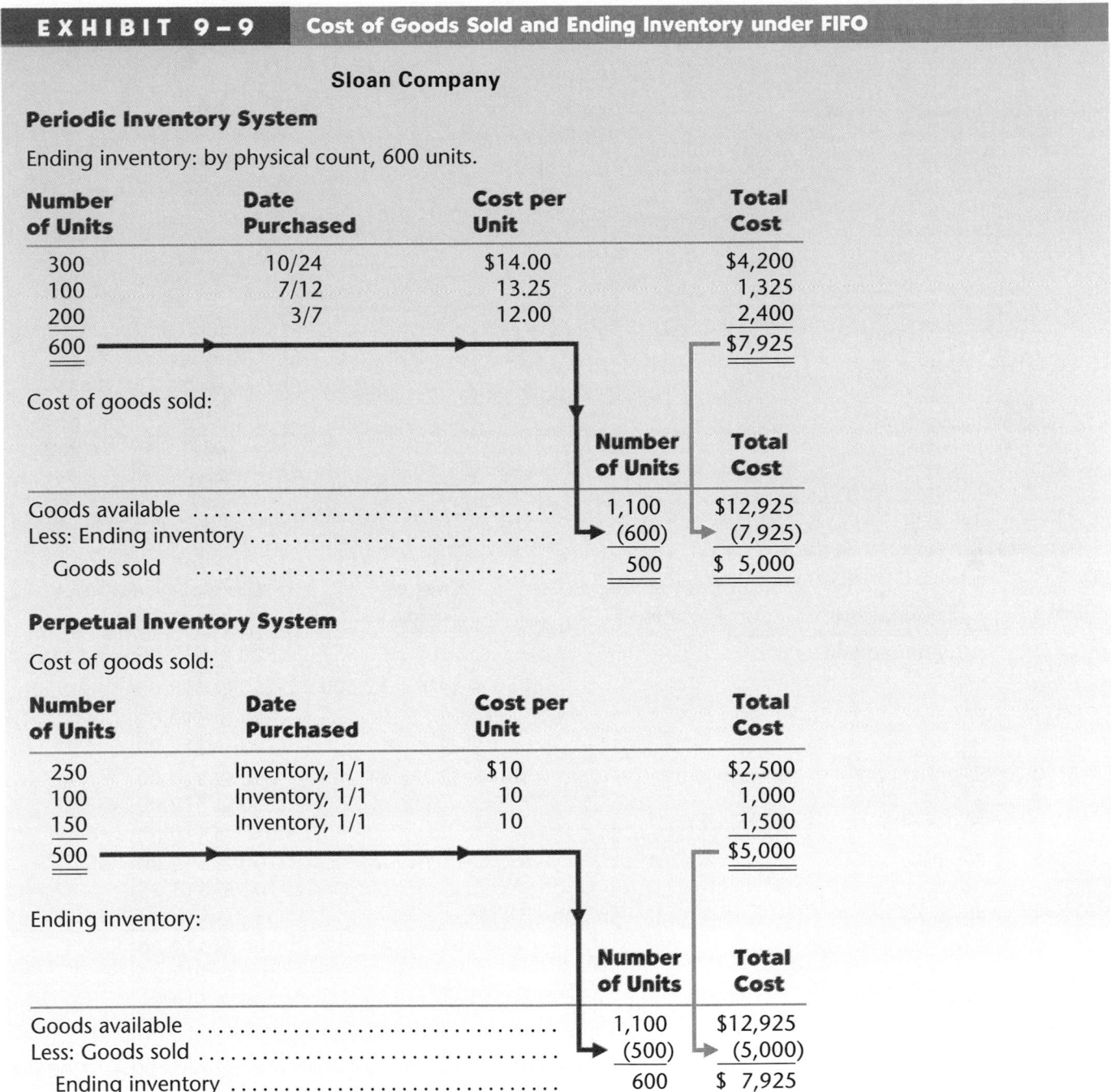

EXHIBIT 9–9 Cost of Goods Sold and Ending Inventory under FIFO

Sloan Company

Periodic Inventory System

Ending inventory: by physical count, 600 units.

Number of Units	Date Purchased	Cost per Unit	Total Cost
300	10/24	$14.00	$4,200
100	7/12	13.25	1,325
200	3/7	12.00	2,400
600			$7,925

Cost of goods sold:

	Number of Units	Total Cost
Goods available	1,100	$12,925
Less: Ending inventory	(600)	(7,925)
Goods sold	500	$ 5,000

Perpetual Inventory System

Cost of goods sold:

Number of Units	Date Purchased	Cost per Unit	Total Cost
250	Inventory, 1/1	$10	$2,500
100	Inventory, 1/1	10	1,000
150	Inventory, 1/1	10	1,500
500			$5,000

Ending inventory:

	Number of Units	Total Cost
Goods available	1,100	$12,925
Less: Goods sold	(500)	(5,000)
Ending inventory	600	$ 7,925

is determined throughout the accounting period as goods are sold, as in the perpetual system, or as a residual amount at the end of the accounting period, as in the periodic system.

Last in, First Out (LIFO)

Under the **last in, first out** cost flow assumption, abbreviated **LIFO,** the cost of the most recent purchases is assigned to the cost of goods that are sold first, and the cost of the earliest inventory acquisitions is assigned to the cost of goods that are sold last or remain in the inventory account. Regardless of the actual physical flow of goods, the cost of goods sold and the inventory balance are calculated as if the goods that entered inventory last were sold first, and the goods that entered

EXHIBIT 9–10   Cost of Goods Sold and Ending Inventory Under LIFO

Sloan Company

Periodic Inventory System

Ending inventory: by physical count, 600 units.

Number of Units	Date Purchased	Cost per Unit	Total Cost
500	Inventory, 1/1	$10	$5,000
100	3/7	12	1,200
600			$6,200

Cost of goods sold:	Number of Units	Total Cost
Goods available	1,100	$12,925
Less: Ending inventory...	(600)	(6,200)
Goods sold..	500	$ 6,725

Perpetual Inventory System

Date	Transaction	Cost of Goods Purchased	Cost of Goods Sold	Cumulative Balance of Inventory
1/1	Beginning inventory			500 @ $10.00 = $5,000
2/5	Sale		250 @ $10 = $2,500	250 @ $10.00 = 2,500
3/7	Purchase	200 @ $12 = $2,400		250 @ $10.00 ⎤ 200 @ $12.00 ⎦ = 4,900
5/10	Sale		100 @ $12 = $1,200	250 @ $10.00 ⎤ 100 @ $12.00 ⎦ = 3,700
7/12	Purchase	100 @ $13.25 = $1,325		250 @ $10.00 ⎤ 100 @ $12.00 ⎬ = 5,025 100 @ $13.25 ⎦
10/24	Purchase	300 @ $14 = $4,200		250 @ $10.00 ⎤ 100 @ $12.00 ⎪ 100 @ $13.25 ⎬ = 9,225 300 @ $14.00 ⎦
11/7	Sale		150 @ $14 = $2,100	250 @ $10.00 ⎤ 100 @ $12.00 ⎪ 100 @ $13.25 ⎬ = 7,125 150 @ $14.00 ⎦

Total cost of goods sold $5,800   Ending inventory $7,125

inventory first were sold last or remained in inventory. During periods of *rising* acquisition costs, LIFO yields higher cost of goods sold, lower income, and lower ending inventory cost than the average cost approach. Most U.S. corporations use LIFO. This is not the case elsewhere in the world. Since LIFO has the effect of reducing income, its use in the United States contributes to the view that U.S. accounting is more conservative than that of other countries.

Given the use of LIFO in the periodic and perpetual inventory systems, Sloan Company's ending inventory and cost of goods sold are calculated as shown in Exhibit 9–10. As you can see from the top part of Exhibit 9–10, under the periodic inventory system LIFO requires relatively simple calculations. The costs associated with units remaining in inventory at the end of the period are assumed to be the costs of the earliest units purchased. The cost of ending inventory is subtracted from the cost of goods available for sale to determine the cost of goods sold.

LIFO in the perpetual system is illustrated in the bottom part of Exhibit 9–10. The calculations for the period are relatively complex, because the cost of goods sold calculated at the time of each sale must be based on the cost of the goods most recently purchased prior to the sale. The total cost of goods sold for the period can be subtracted from the cost of goods available for sale to determine the ending inventory cost.

As Exhibit 9–10 shows, under LIFO, inventory is composed of *layers*. In periods in which more units are purchased than sold, the increase in inventory will result in the addition of one or more new layers of inventory. In periods in which more units are sold than purchased, layers of inventory that were added in previous accounting periods will be eliminated, beginning with the most recent layer added. *Once a specific layer is eliminated, it is never replaced.*

Exhibit 9–10 demonstrates that in contrast to the FIFO cost flow assumption, during periods of changing inventory costs LIFO does not yield the same results for ending inventory and cost of goods sold when used with the perpetual system as it does when used with the periodic system. It yields different results because LIFO in the periodic system assumes sale of the most recent purchases over the entire accounting period, while LIFO in a perpetual system assumes sale of the most recent purchases as of the time of each sale.

COMPARATIVE EVALUATION OF COST FLOW ASSUMPTIONS

CONCEPTUAL

When inventory acquisition costs change, LIFO does not yield the same results in the periodic system as in the perpetual system.

Exhibit 9–11 shows the comparative effects of the average cost, FIFO, and LIFO cost flow assumptions on Sloan Company's cost of goods sold and ending inventory, under both the periodic and perpetual inventory systems. The results of using specific identification, which is based on actual cost flows, are not presented, because the amounts for cost of goods sold and ending inventory are strictly dependent on the particular inventory items that actually are sold.

As Exhibit 9–11 shows, whether the periodic or the perpetual inventory system is used, during periods of *rising* acquisition costs (as is the case for Sloan Company), FIFO yields a lower cost of goods sold, and LIFO yields a higher cost of goods sold, than does the average cost approach. Conversely, ending inventory is higher under FIFO and lower under LIFO. During periods of *falling* acquisition costs, the results would be the reverse of those reported in Exhibit 9–11. The average cost procedure would continue to yield cost of goods sold and inventory

| EXHIBIT 9–11 | Comparative Financial Statement Effects of Cost Flow Assumptions |

Sloan Company

Account	Periodic Inventory System			Perpetual Inventory System		
	Weighted Average	FIFO	LIFO	Moving Average	FIFO	LIFO
Cost of goods sold.	$5,875	$5,000	$6,725	$5,456	$5,000	$5,800
Ending inventory.	7,050	7,925	6,200	7,469	7,925	7,125

amounts between those of FIFO and LIFO. In the following sections we will look more closely at the comparative advantages and disadvantages of these cost flow assumptions.

FIFO

Discuss the characteristics, advantages, and disadvantages of the FIFO, LIFO, and average cost assumptions.

Companies normally attempt to sell the oldest goods in inventory first. In fact, perishable goods and goods subject to obsolescence must be handled in a first in, first out manner. Although generally accepted accounting principles do not require inventory *cost flows* to conform to the *physical flow* of goods, cost flow assumptions that do parallel the physical flow of goods are conceptually appealing. In fact, one of the advantages claimed for the FIFO cost flow assumption is that it conforms to the actual physical flow of many inventory items. Hence, for many types of inventory, FIFO yields the same cost of goods sold and ending inventory figures as does the specific identification procedure.

Other advantages of FIFO are that it is simple to employ and comparatively inexpensive when used with either the periodic or the perpetual inventory system. FIFO is also systematic and objective, and less subject to manipulation by management than other inventory cost flow assumptions, particularly LIFO. Under the FIFO assumption, the cost assigned to ending inventory is based on the most recent inventory acquisition costs. Therefore, FIFO approximates the current replacement cost of inventory on the balance sheet, particularly when inventory turnover is rapid, and most of the costs assigned to ending inventory are very recent.

Perhaps the primary disadvantage of FIFO is that because it assigns the most recent costs to ending inventory, relatively noncurrent or out-of-date costs are assigned to goods that have been sold. This problem becomes more severe when inventory acquisition costs rise rapidly during the accounting period, and the quantity of inventory either remains stable or increases. Under these conditions, FIFO results in poor matching on the income statement. Old and comparatively low inventory acquisition costs are included in the cost of goods sold and matched against current, comparatively high sales revenue. This matching of old, comparatively low inventory acquisition costs against current revenue can yield an income number that is inflated by **inventory holding profits (gains)**—the difference between the old, low inventory costs and the current replacement cost of inventory.

For example, if a unit of inventory that was purchased at the beginning of the accounting period for $10 costs $15 to replace at the end of the accounting period, the potential inventory holding profit is $5. If the old cost of $10 is then matched against sales revenue, profit will be $5 higher than if the current replacement cost of $15 were matched against sales revenue. Furthermore, when management increases the selling prices for its goods in order to cover increased inventory acquisition costs, the inventory holding profit that results from using FIFO can cause misleading income and cash flow signals. FIFO ignores the cost of replacing inventory at higher prices (in a period of rising inventory prices), producing an income number that includes a "paper profit" (the inventory holding profit) that is not really available for distribution to owners, because it is needed to replace inventory.

LIFO

One of LIFO's most important advantages is that it matches the most recently incurred inventory cost against sales revenue. This matching is especially critical during accounting periods when inventory acquisition costs are rising and inventory turnover is slow. Although the cost of goods sold under LIFO probably will not equal the replacement cost of inventory sold, it may *approximate* replacement cost and thus minimize the inventory holding profit. When LIFO is used during periods of rising inventory prices, reported income is more likely to approximate the amount that really is available for distribution to owners.

Because LIFO yields a comparatively low net income during periods when inventory acquisition costs are rising and inventory quantities are not decreasing, it can be used to defer income taxes through reductions in current taxable income. From management's perspective, this is perhaps the major advantage of LIFO. In fact, the income tax advantage of LIFO during inflationary periods is considered to be the primary reason for the growth in its use. An example of the tax-motivated reasoning that often causes a company to use the LIFO procedure is provided by a recent newspaper article:

Because prices in most industries have held steady until recently, many businesses have been using the FIFO (first in, first out) method of inventory valuation. This means simply that the cost assigned to the goods sold would reflect the oldest purchase price of that inventory.

While this method is probably the most practical during economically stable times, it isn't necessarily the best option from a tax standpoint when prices are following a predictable upward path. This is especially true today in the paper industry, where prices are rising faster than businesses can pass them on to the consumer.

If your business fits the aforementioned profile, you may want to consider switching to the LIFO (last in, first out) method, where the cost assigned to the goods sold would reflect the most recent purchase price of that inventory. The switch to LIFO from FIFO will allow your company to report a lower profit on goods sold, which ultimately will reduce the amount of taxable income you must report.[7]

The Internal Revenue Service adopted "LIFO conformity" regulations, requiring companies that use LIFO for tax purposes to use it in their external financial statements as well. Although it is almost always advantageous to defer taxes by reducing taxable income, the use of LIFO to obtain such a deferral also results in lower reported income in external financial statements than would be the case under some other cost flow assumption. The IRS does allow companies that use LIFO to disclose the income or loss that would have resulted if an assumption other than LIFO had been used. These disclosures can be made in notes to the financial statements, in the president's letter, or in other supplementary sections of the annual report. A company that uses LIFO also is allowed to disclose the FIFO value of inventory, adjusted to LIFO, in the balance sheet, but only LIFO may be used for reporting in the income statement.[8]

While the FIFO and average cost assumptions are used commonly around the world, the United States is the only major country in which LIFO is used on a widespread basis. There are two primary reasons for this difference in usage. First, some countries (e.g., France and Great Britain) do not allow the use of LIFO. Second, even where LIFO is allowed for accounting purposes, it is not allowed for tax purposes. (This point adds credibility to the view that the primary motivation for using LIFO is its tax-saving potential during periods of rising acquisition costs.) At the international level, it should be mentioned that the International Accounting Standards Committee has proposed the elimination of LIFO for international financial reporting.[9]

Because LIFO yields lower reported income during periods of rising inventory acquisition costs, its use may be disadvantageous when management would like to avoid reporting a low income to external users of financial data. Furthermore, some

[7]"Price Rises Make Look at Valuing Inventory Timely," *Crains Cleveland Business,* March 13, 1995, p. S–3.
[8]*U.S. Treasury Regulation* 1.472-2(e), 1981.
[9]International Accounting Standards Committee, *Statement of Intent—Comparability of Financial Statements* (London: IASC, July 1990).

management compensation plans are tied to reported income. And although LIFO may approximate the current replacement cost for goods that have been sold, it does not yield a true current-cost income. During periods of rising inventory acquisition costs, LIFO may also yield very low balance sheet amounts for ending inventory, because the oldest acquisition costs remain in the inventory account.[10] To the extent that inventory is reported at a lower amount, financial analysis that is based on current or total assets may be impaired.

Because inventory costs tend to be outdated under LIFO, liquidation (using up) of early inventory layers during periods of rising costs can result in the matching of very old and low inventory costs against sales revenue in the income statement. Hence, liquidation of early layers of LIFO inventory during periods of rising prices can lead to an unusually *large* reported income. During periods of rising inventory costs and positive tax rates, LIFO provides a cash flow incentive (resulting from reduced taxes) to avoid inventory liquidations.[11] But when inventory costs continue to rise, and companies continue to avoid liquidation of early LIFO inventory layers, the difference between balance sheet inventory amounts and current inventory replacement costs continues to grow. Under these conditions, reported inventory amounts can be quite misleading to financial statement users.

When an inventory decline that causes liquidation of early LIFO layers is *temporary,* some LIFO users avoid potential distortion of income by debiting the cost of goods sold for the current inventory replacement cost—even though some of the goods actually sold were carried at older, lower costs. This procedure, which is an application of next in, first out (NIFO) inventory accounting, is a temporary departure from the historical cost principle. An account such as "excess of replacement cost over LIFO cost of basic inventory temporarily liquidated" is credited for the excess of the current replacement cost over the LIFO carrying cost for inventory that has been temporarily liquidated. When the inventory is replenished, the temporary "excess of replacement cost" account is removed from the books, and the goods acquired are placed in inventory at the old LIFO costs.

While it exists, the temporary account is reported among the current liabilities on the balance sheet to disclose the expected reduction in reported working capital when the inventory is replaced. In *Statement of Concepts No. 6,* the FASB stated explicitly that such a temporary account is in fact *not* a liability, as defined in the conceptual framework, because the company is not obligated to sacrifice assets in the future. (Of course, *Statements of Concepts* do not establish GAAP.) Use of the current replacement cost for cost of goods sold when early LIFO layers have been temporarily liquidated avoids the reporting of an artificially high net income, and helps to improve the comparability of past, present, and future income statements.

The increases in net income and related increases in income taxes that can result from the liquidation of early LIFO inventory layers during periods of rising acquisition costs may cause management to make economically unsound inventory purchasing decisions at the end of the accounting period. If unit sales have exceeded unit purchases for the period, management may be faced with the necessity of including some very old and very low inventory costs in cost of goods sold. To avoid dipping into old inventory layers, management may elect to purchase additional inventory. If the additional purchase causes unusually high inventory costs or a shortage of liquid assets, it may be economically unsound, even though it may contribute to a tax saving. Some accountants view management's opportunity to affect the amount of net income by strategic inventory acquisitions as a manipulation of net income.

A final disadvantage of the LIFO cost flow assumption is that it seldom conforms to the normal physical flow of inventory units. (Some inventories do conform to a LIFO flow. Piled coal inventory is one; new coal is added to the outside of the pile

---

[10]Perhaps the greatest limitation of LIFO is the distortive effects that it may have on a company's balance sheet. See J. M. Reeve and K. G. Stanga, "Balance Sheet Impact of Using LIFO: An Empirical Study," *Accounting Horizons,* September 1987, p. 9.

[11]Reeve and Stanga, *Accounting Horizons,* September 1987, p. 10.

and inventory withdrawals are from the outside of the pile.) This disparity is not critical, however, because generally accepted accounting principles do not require that cost flows correspond to physical flows. GAAP requires only that a cost flow assumption be systematic; that it be based on cost; and that it appropriately match expenses and revenues. LIFO meets these requirements.

Average Cost

The average cost procedure of determining the cost of goods sold and the value of inventory steers a middle course between FIFO and LIFO. Whether inventory acquisition costs are rising or falling, the average cost approach tends to produce a cost of goods sold and ending inventory amounts that fall between the results produced by FIFO and LIFO. In its effect on the balance sheet, however, the average cost assumption is much more like FIFO than LIFO. In fact, when inventory turnover is rapid, the inventory cost figures produced by the average cost method are almost as close to current replacement cost as those produced by FIFO.

The main advantage of the average cost procedure is its practicality. It is a fairly simple procedure, objective, and easy to apply. Another advantage is that average cost does not lend itself so readily to manipulation as do the specific identification and LIFO approaches.

ALTERNATIVES TO THE UNIT LIFO APPROACH

The LIFO approach described to this point in the chapter can be called **unit LIFO.** (Another name is "specific goods LIFO.") That is, we have been discussing the use of LIFO on individual types of inventory units. Unfortunately, problems may arise when unit LIFO is used. First, unit LIFO requires a complete record of the quantity and cost of each type of inventory unit purchased during an accounting period, as well as the number of units and the specific unit costs making up the beginning balance for each type of inventory unit for the period. When a company has numerous inventory transactions involving varied acquisition costs for several types of inventory units, compiling such detailed inventory records can be a significant recordkeeping task.

Second, if it becomes necessary to liquidate early layers of LIFO inventory containing low and out-of-date inventory acquisition costs, LIFO's primary advantage becomes a major disadvantage. That is, matching the low, early inventory costs against current sales revenue may result in a large reported income and a large tax obligation. The possibility of liquidating early LIFO layers increases when LIFO is used on a unit basis. For example, while a lumber company's overall inventory might increase during a period, and even groups of inventory items, such as finish-grade hardwoods, might increase, there could be a liquidation of early LIFO layers of one or more particular types of inventory units, such as board feet of finish-grade walnut. In such cases, liquidation of individual types of inventory units can negate much of the tax advantage of using LIFO.

A Pooled Approach to LIFO

Because of the problems that may occur when LIFO is used on an individual unit basis, inventory units often are combined into groups or pools before the LIFO assumption is applied. This is a **pooled approach** to LIFO. Each inventory pool consists of units that are similar in nature, such as the lumber company's pool of board feet of finish-grade hardwoods. In general, when units are pooled for LIFO purposes, the pools are defined based on the natural similarities among units.

When inventory units are pooled, all units in the beginning inventory pool are considered to have been purchased at the same time and at the same price. Thus, the average cost of the units in the pool is used to value the beginning inventory.

Similarly, the average cost of all units purchased for the pool during an accounting period is the unit cost assigned to any incremental units added to the pool during that period. Units that are added to the pool during a period form a single inventory layer. If the pool were to decrease in size during the next accounting period, the cost assigned to this inventory layer would be the first layer of inventory cost to be eliminated. On the other hand, if the next period's ending inventory is not lower in quantity than the inventory pool at the beginning of the period, the unit costs already in the pool would remain in inventory.

To illustrate the pooled approach to applying LIFO, we shall use the example of the finish-grade hardwood group for the lumber company. Assume that at the beginning of its first year of operations the lumber company had the following units in its finish-grade hardwood pool:

HARDWOOD	QUANTITY (BOARD FEET)	COST (PER FOOT)	TOTAL COST
Walnut	3,000	$1.50	$ 4,500
Oak	7,500	1.10	8,250
Maple	4,200	1.25	5,250
	14,700		$18,000

Given this inventory pool, the average cost per board foot of hardwood in beginning inventory is approximately $1.2245 ($18,000 ÷ 14,700 ft.).

Now assume that the following transactions involving units in the finish-grade hardwood pool occurred during the first year of operations:

HARDWOOD	PURCHASES QUANTITY (BOARD FEET)	PURCHASES COST (PER FOOT)	PURCHASES TOTAL	SALES QUANTITY (BOARD FEET)	ENDING QUANTITY (BOARD FEET)
Walnut	1,500	$1.60	$2,400	1,700	2,800
Oak....................	2,500	1.15	2,875	2,200	7,800
Maple..................	2,000	1.20	2,400	1,900	4,300
	6,000		$7,675		14,900

Note that the average cost per board foot of hardwood purchased during year 1 was approximately $1.2792 ($7,675 ÷ 6,000 ft.). A new layer of 200 board feet (14,900 ending board feet less 14,700 beginning board feet) was added to inventory.

In the pooled approach to LIFO, the average cost per board foot purchased during year 1 ($1.2792) will be used to value the 200-board-foot layer added in year 1. The ending inventory for year 1 would be determined as follows:

	QUANTITY (BOARD FEET)	COST (PER FOOT)	TOTAL COST
Beginning inventory..................	14,700	$1.2245	$18,000
Layer added in year 1.................	200	1.2792	256
Ending inventory....................	14,900		$18,256

The pooled approach to LIFO reduces the recordkeeping related to the LIFO approach. Compared with unit LIFO, it also reduces the chance that early LIFO layers will be liquidated, since a reduction in the quantity of one type of unit in the pool, such as board feet of finish-grade walnut, may be offset by an increase in the quantity of another type of unit in the pool, such as board feet of finish-grade maple. This pooled approach is not without its problems, however. Technological changes, style changes, changes in the inventory mix, and other changes in inventory may occur, sometimes quite often. Such changes probably will require the company to redefine its inventory pools, which can be a time-consuming and costly process. In addition, even in the pooled approach to LIFO, the possibility remains that one or more inventory pools may suffer total or partial liquidation, reducing the overall advantage of using LIFO.

Dollar-Value LIFO

Dollar-value LIFO is an inventory valuation procedure that provides the benefits of LIFO, but avoids or reduces the problems that arise under unit LIFO or the pooled approach to LIFO. Dollar-value LIFO can be applied to inventory pools consisting of a greater variety of goods than is possible under traditional LIFO, resulting in fewer inventory pools. In fact, in some cases the entire inventory can be included in one dollar-value LIFO pool.[12] It has been asserted that if managers are following a strategy of deferring income taxes by the use of dollar-value LIFO, the objective should be to minimize the number of pools.[13] Others have disagreed with this assertion, calling it overly simplistic.[14] Because fewer and larger inventory pools exist under dollar-value LIFO, both the possibility of liquidating early LIFO layers and the chance that liquidation of inventory pools will diminish the overall advantage of using LIFO are reduced. It has been reported that as many as 95 percent of LIFO companies use either dollar-value LIFO or dollar-value retail LIFO (discussed in Chapter 10).[15]

In dollar-value LIFO calculations, period-end acquisition costs and inventory cost indexes are used to determine reported ending inventory values for the inventory pools. Dollar-value LIFO inventory pools consist of *layers of costs* that are related to past and present accounting periods. The dollar-value LIFO procedure may seem more complicated than unit LIFO, but it does not require detailed records of individual inventory units and unit costs to be maintained. Thus, it completely avoids one of the problems associated with the traditional unit LIFO approach.

The dollar-value LIFO procedure begins with the valuation of ending inventory at period-end acquisition cost. Next, any change in inventory acquisition cost during the period is removed from the dollar amount of ending inventory using an inventory cost index. Then, to determine whether there was a *physical* increase or decrease in inventory over the period, the cost-adjusted ending inventory is compared with the beginning inventory for the period. If the physical inventory has increased (that is, if a layer has been added to inventory), the new layer is valued in terms of the current-period acquisition cost. If the physical inventory has decreased (that is, if previously added layers have been taken from inventory), the cost of beginning inventory for the period is reduced accordingly.

CONCEPTUAL

Dollar-value LIFO either avoids or reduces the problems of unit LIFO or the pooled approach to LIFO.

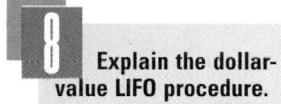

8 Explain the dollar-value LIFO procedure.

Illustration of the Dollar-Value LIFO Method

To illustrate, assume that a company's beginning inventory for the year had a cost of $1,000, and that the cost index at that time was 1.00. Assume also that the company's ending inventory for the year has an end-of-year acquisition cost of $1,200. But has the company's *physical* inventory actually increased during the year? The answer depends on the amount of increase or decrease in inventory acquisition cost during the year. The increase of $200 in the dollar amount of ending inventory over the dollar amount of beginning inventory may be due to a higher unit acquisition cost, to more units of inventory, or both. In this case, if the acquisition cost has increased 20 percent during the year (the cost index has risen to 1.20), then the physical level of inventory must be unchanged, because the entire $200 increase in the dollar amount

---

[12]It has been reported that most companies have only a few inventory pools, with retailers having a median of six pools and nonretailers having a median of three pools. See J. M. Reeve and K. G. Stanga, "The LIFO Pooling Decision: Some Empirical Results from Accounting Practice," *Accounting Horizons,* June 1987, p. 27.

[13]Reeve and Stanga, *Accounting Horizons,* June 1987, p. 27.

[14]W. R. Cron and R. B. Hayes, "The Dollar Value LIFO Pooling Decision: The Conventional Wisdom Is Too General," *Accounting Horizons,* December 1989, p. 57.

[15]Reeve and Stanga, *Accounting Horizons,* June 1987, p. 27.

of inventory is the result of the 20 percent increase in acquisition cost. Accordingly, ending inventory should be reported at $1,000 because after adjustment for the cost change, the amount of inventory is the same as it was at the beginning of the year.

On the other hand, if there has been no increase in acquisition cost during the year (if the cost index remains at 1.00), the entire $200 increase must be due to additional inventory units on hand at the end of the year. Since those additional units were acquired during the current year, the ending inventory will consist of beginning inventory plus the new layer added during the current year:

Cost of beginning inventory	**$1,000**
Cost of current layer added	**200**
Dollar-value LIFO ending inventory	**$1,200**

Suppose the acquisition cost has increased by only 10 percent during the current year (the cost index has risen to 1.10). In this case, the ending inventory under dollar-value LIFO will be $1,100 because only a $100 new layer is added in the current year. The dollar-value LIFO ending inventory would be calculated as follows:

Ending inventory at year-end acquisition cost	**$1,200**
Ending inventory in terms of beginning-of-year cost ($1,200 ÷ 1.10)	**$1,091**
Less: Beginning inventory in terms of beginning-of-year cost ($1,000 ÷ 1.00)	**(1,000)**
Cost of layer added in terms of beginning-of-year cost	**$ 91**
Cost of layer added restated using end-of-year cost ($91 × 1.10)	**$ 100**
Cost of beginning inventory	**$1,000**
Plus: Cost of layer added	**100**
Dollar-value LIFO ending inventory	**$1,100**

Next, we will discuss the application of the dollar-value LIFO approach in more complex situations.

Procedure for the Dollar-Value LIFO Method

The first year in which the dollar-value LIFO procedure is used is called the **base year.** The inventory at the beginning of the base year, called the **base inventory,** is equal to the number of units times the unit cost at the beginning of the base year. The unit costs of the base inventory are referred to as the **base year costs.** The cost index at the beginning of the base year is assumed to be 1.00.

We have seen that inventory cost indexes are necessary in making dollar-value LIFO calculations. Therefore, an early step in the dollar-value LIFO procedure each year is to calculate or otherwise obtain inventory cost indexes. Such cost indexes can be obtained by calculation, either using the *double-extension method* or the *link-chain method,* or by consulting a published index such as the Consumer Price Index or the Producer Price Index.

An inventory cost index relates the end-of-current-period acquisition cost of a unit to the beginning-of-base-year acquisition cost of the same type of unit. For example, if the cost of inventory at the beginning of the base year (year 1) is $10.00 per unit, and the cost of the same type of inventory at the end of the base year (year 1) is $12.50 per unit, then the inventory cost index for the end of Year 1 is $12.50 ÷ $10.00 = 1.25. Similarly, if the unit cost of the same type of inventory is $15.00 at the end of year 2, the inventory cost index for the end of year 2 is $15.00 ÷ $10.00 = 1.50. (Notice that the cost index always relates current acquisition cost to the *base year* cost.)

Cost indexes are then used to restate each year's total ending inventory in terms of beginning-of-base-year cost. If total year 1 ending inventory has a year-end acquisition cost of $14,000, that same inventory can be restated in terms of beginning-of-base-year acquisition cost as follows: $14,000 ÷ 1.25 = $11,200. As you will see in the following discussion, the current year's total ending inventory, restated in terms of beginning-of-base-year cost, is a key component of the dollar-value LIFO procedure.

Under the dollar-value LIFO procedure, the addition of a new LIFO layer as a result of an *increase* in inventory during the year, or the loss of one or more previously added layers as a result of a *decrease* in inventory, is determined by comparing year-end inventory priced in terms of base year acquisition cost with beginning-of-the-year inventory priced in terms of base year acquisition cost. Since both beginning and ending inventories for the current year are priced in terms of base year cost, any difference between the two inventories must be the result of a change in the *quantity* of inventory units held.

Use of the dollar-value LIFO method requires the following information: (1) the base year and base inventory cost; (2) an inventory cost index for each year (compared to the beginning of the base year), beginning with the end of the base year; and (3) year-end unit quantities and unit costs for each year, beginning with the end of the base year.

Summary of Dollar-Value Calculations

Assume that the base year is Year 1 and that we have the following information for Mason Corporation:

DATE	INVENTORY AT CURRENT YEAR-END COST	INVENTORY COST INDEX
1/1/Year 1	$10,000[a]	1.00
12/31/Year 1	14,000	1.25
12/31/Year 2	16,000	1.50
12/31/Year 3	15,000	1.30
12/31/Year 4	17,000	1.65
12/31/Year 5	20,000	1.70

[a]Base inventory.

Calculations of the amounts of ending inventory that Mason Corporation would report in its financial statements for years 1 through 5 under dollar-value LIFO are summarized in Exhibit 9–12. Study the calculations and procedure carefully. In doing so, you will see that the calculations follow the sequence presented in the description of the dollar-value LIFO procedure on page 501. The essential steps of the dollar-value LIFO procedure are as follows:

1. Determine the total ending inventory for the current year in terms of current year-end costs. Typically, the actual costs of the most recent purchases are used for current year-end costs (see col. 1, Exhibit 9–12).

2. Calculate the inventory cost index for the current year or use a price index from an external source. (Inventory cost indexes used in Exhibit 9–12 are given above in the data for Mason.)

3. Restate the current year's ending inventory in terms of base year costs (see col. 2, Exhibit 9–12).

4. Identify the layers included in inventory, stated in terms of base year costs (see col. 3, Exhibit 9–12).

5. Restate the inventory layers using the cost index (or indexes) associated with the inventory layer(s) in question (see col. 4, Exhibit 9–12).

6. Add the restated inventory layers to determine the current year's dollar-value LIFO ending inventory to be reported in the financial statements (see col. 5, Exhibit 9–12).

To assist you further in understanding the addition and reduction of layers in dollar-value LIFO, Exhibit 9–13 displays graphically the layers developed in Exhibit 9–12.

EXHIBIT 9–12   Calculation of Ending Inventory for Year I Through Year 5 Under Dollar-Value LIFO

Mason Corporation

Date of Calculating Dollar-Value LIFO Ending Inventory	(1) Inventory Stated in Terms of Current Year-End Cost	(2) Inventory Stated in Terms of Base Year Costs[a]	(3) Inventory Layers Stated in Terms of Base Year Costs (Date)	(4) Inventory Layers Restated Using the Proper Inventory Cost Indexes	(5) Dollar-Value LIFO Inventory
1/1/Year 1 (base point)	$10,000 (base inventory)	$\dfrac{\$10,000}{1.00} = \$10,000 \longrightarrow$	$\$10,000$ (base)	$\$10,000 \times 1.00 = \$10,000$	$\longrightarrow \$10,000$
12/31/Year 1	14,000	$\dfrac{\$14,000}{1.25} = \$11,200 \longrightarrow$	$\$10,000$ (base) 1,200 (Year 1)	$\$10,000 \times 1.00 = \$10,000$ $1,200 \times 1.25 = 1,500$	$\longrightarrow 11,500$
12/31/Year 2	16,000	$\dfrac{\$16,000}{1.50} = \$10,667 \longrightarrow$	$\$10,000$ (base) 667 (Year 1)[b]	$\$10,000 \times 1.00 = \$10,000$ $667 \times 1.25 = 834$	$\longrightarrow 10,834$
12/31/Year 3	15,000	$\dfrac{\$15,000}{1.30} = \$11,538 \longrightarrow$	$\$10,000$ (base) 667 (Year 1) 871 (Year 3)	$\$10,000 \times 1.00 = \$10,000$ $667 \times 1.25 = 834$ $871 \times 1.30 = 1,132$	$\longrightarrow 11,966$
12/31/Year 4	17,000	$\dfrac{\$17,000}{1.65} = \$10,303 \longrightarrow$	$\$10,000$ (base) 303 (Year 1)[c]	$\$10,000 \times 1.00 = \$10,000$ $303 \times 1.25 = 379$	$\longrightarrow 10,379$
12/31/Year 5	20,000	$\dfrac{\$20,000}{1.70} = \$11,765 \longrightarrow$	$\$10,000$ (base) 303 (Year 1) 1,462 (Year 5)	$\$10,000 \times 1.00 = \$10,000$ $303 \times 1.25 = 379$ $1,462 \times 1.70 = 2,485$	$\longrightarrow 12,864$

[a]Rounded to the nearest dollar.
[b]$11,200 – $10,667 = $553 decrease.
$1,200 (Year 1 layer) – $553 decrease = $667 (from Year 1 layer).
[c]$11,538 – $10,303 = $1,235 decrease.
$871 (Year 3 layer) + $667 (Year 1 layer) – $1,235 decrease = $303 (from Year 1 layer).
Notice that when a decrease occurs, previous layers are "used up" in accordance with the LIFO cost flow assumption.

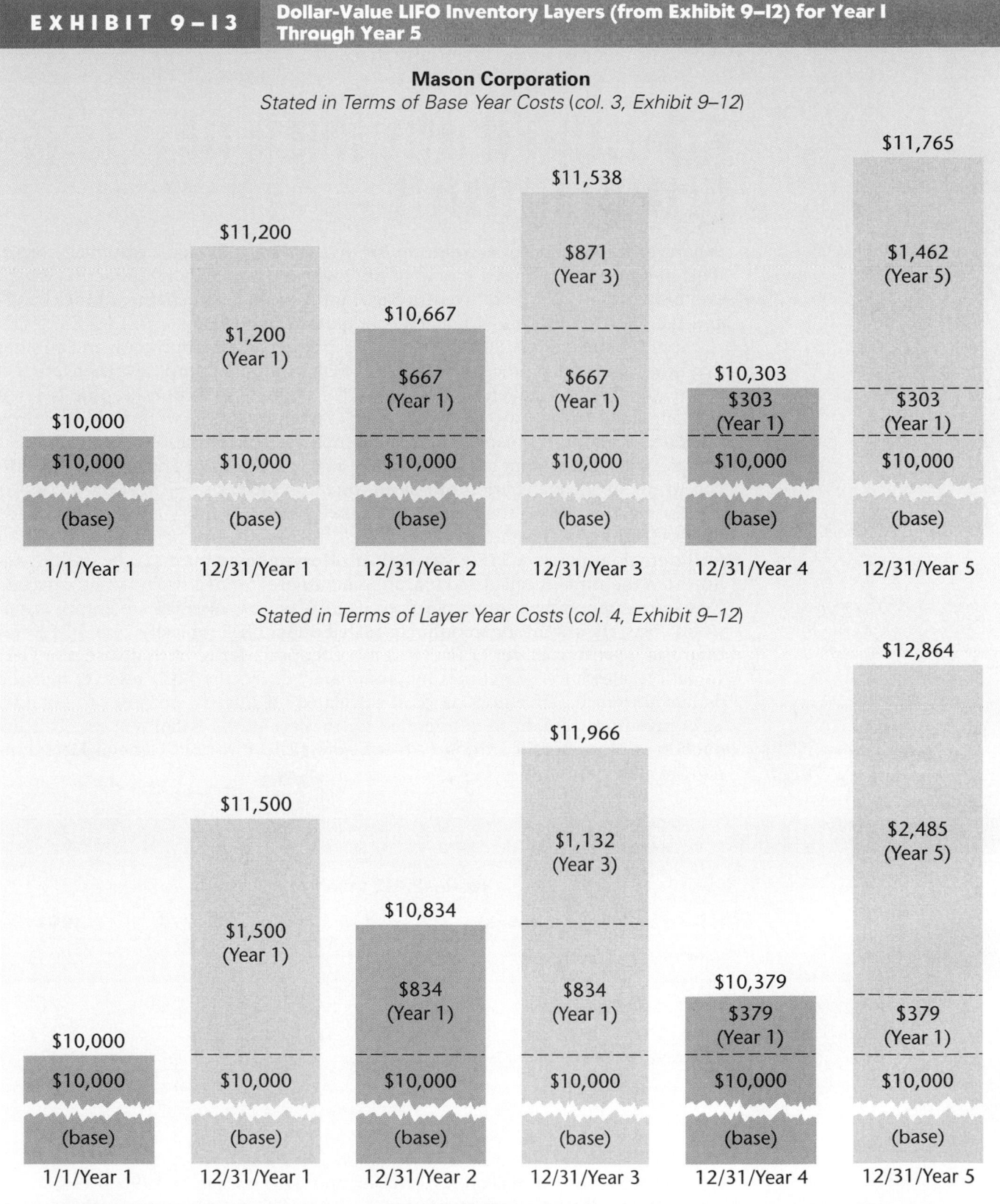

EXHIBIT 9–13 Dollar-Value LIFO Inventory Layers (from Exhibit 9–12) for Year 1 Through Year 5

Mason Corporation
Stated in Terms of Base Year Costs (col. 3, Exhibit 9–12)

Stated in Terms of Layer Year Costs (col. 4, Exhibit 9–12)

Having completed our discussion of dollar-value LIFO and the other historical cost-based inventory cost flow assumptions, we next consider how inventories should be reported in the financial statements.

ⓇEPORTING OF INVENTORIES IN THE FINANCIAL STATEMENTS

Whatever the method of accounting for inventories, it should be applied consistently, and the method used should be disclosed in the financial statements. Whenever a significant change in inventory accounting is made, the nature of the change and the effect on income, if material, should be disclosed.

Some companies use LIFO for external reporting and tax purposes, and another inventory accounting procedure, such as FIFO, for internal purposes. There are several reasons why a company might do so. For example, (1) recordkeeping is easier with methods other than LIFO because LIFO often does not conform to the physical flow of goods; (2) management and employee compensation plans related to company income seldom are based on the LIFO assumption; and (3) LIFO is difficult to use in the preparation of interim financial reports.

Normally, there will be a difference between the inventory amount calculated under LIFO and the inventory amount resulting from the inventory procedure used for internal purposes. A **LIFO valuation allowance** account can be used to adjust from the amount calculated for internal purposes to the LIFO inventory needed for external reporting and tax purposes. During periods of rising inventory acquisition costs, the inventory amount calculated under LIFO typically would be lower than the inventory amount calculated by other procedures. In that case, the LIFO valuation allowance, sometimes inappropriately called the LIFO reserve, must be deducted from the inventory amount calculated for internal purposes to obtain a LIFO inventory amount to be reported on the face of the balance sheet. This deduction is illustrated in Exhibit 9–14 in Note 12 to the 1995 General Electric financial statements.

real world

EXHIBIT 9-14	Illustration of a LIFO Valuation Allowance

Note 12. GE Inventories

December 31 (in millions)	1995	1994
Raw materials and work in process	$ 3,205	$ 2,933
Finished goods	2,277	2,165
Unbilled shipments	258	214
	5,740	5,312
Less revaluation to LIFO	(1,345)	(1,432)
	$ 4,395	$ 3,880

LIFO revaluations decreased $87 million in 1995, compared with decreases of $197 million in 1994 and $179 million in 1993. Included in these changes were decreases of $88 million, $72 million and $101 million in 1995, 1994, and 1993, respectively, that resulted from lower LIFO inventory levels. There was no cost change in 1995 and net cost decreases in 1994 and 1993. As of December 31, 1995, GE is obligated to acquire raw materials at market prices through the year 2000 under various take-or-pay or similar arrangements. Annual minimum commitments under these arrangements are insignificant.

SUMMARY OF LEARNING OBJECTIVES

I. List and describe the major inventory classifications that a company's inventory might comprise.

Typical inventory classifications are merchandise inventory, raw materials inventory, work-in-process inventory, and finished goods inventory. A merchandising company has only one class of inventory—merchandise inventory. A manufacturing company normally has three types of inventory—raw materials, work in process, and finished goods. Raw materials inventory consists of goods and materials that ultimately will become part of a manufactured product but have not yet entered the manufacturing process. Work in process consists of units that are in the production process but require additional work before becoming finished goods. Finished goods are units of inventory that have been completed and are available for sale.

2. Describe and distinguish between the periodic and perpetual inventory systems.

In a periodic inventory system, the amount of inventory on hand is determined only when a periodic physical inventory count is made. All inventory acquired is recorded as a purchase. At the end of the accounting period, purchases are added to beginning inventory to arrive at the amount of goods available for sale. Ending inventory, determined through a physical count, is subtracted from goods available for sale to determine the cost of goods sold. All goods not in the ending inventory are assumed to have been sold. Since cost of goods sold is a residual amount, the periodic inventory system is not a good system for inventory control. The periodic system is best suited to companies with large quantities of low-cost inventory items.

In the perpetual inventory system, a continuous record is kept of changes in inventory. Inventory, rather than purchases, is recorded when goods are acquired. When goods are sold, the inventory account is reduced and cost of goods sold is increased. Hence, there is a continuous record of both inventory and cost of goods sold. A physical inventory count is not required to determine the inventory on hand under the perpetual system. Even so, a physical count of inventory should be made at least once each year in order to verify the perpetual inventory balance. If a difference is found between the perpetual system's inventory balance and the physical count, the inventory account is adjusted to agree with the physical count, and an inventory overage or shortage is recorded. The perpetual system is good for inventory control and is best suited to companies with high-cost inventory items for which continuous monitoring of inventory is important.

3. Identify the types of items that should be included in inventory.

Generally, items available for sale in the ordinary course of business, which a company has in its possession and holds legal title to, should be included in inventory. Goods in transit shipped f.o.b. shipping point *to* the company or shipped f.o.b. destination *from* the company are part of the company's inventory. Goods in transit shipped f.o.b. destination *to* the company or shipped f.o.b. shipping point *from* the company are not part of the company's inventory. Consigned goods should be included in the consignor's inventory. Goods sent on approval to a potential buyer should remain as inventory on the seller's books until payment is received for items kept by the buyer. Goods "sold" under a product financing arrangement are not really sold and should continue to be included in the inventory of the "seller." Goods sold on a conditional basis, such as when the right to return exists, should be treated as sold if a reasonable estimate of returns can be made. If such an estimate cannot be made, the shipped goods should remain in the seller's inventory until the possibility of return no longer exists. Goods manufactured for a special order may be accounted for as sold by the manufacturer if they are physically separated from the manufacturer's regular inventory, even though they have not yet been shipped to the buyer.

4. Determine the effects of inventory errors on financial statement accounts.

Errors in accounting for inventory can affect one or more of the following: beginning inventory, purchases, ending inventory, cost of goods sold, income, and retained earnings. If multiple errors occur in a particular period, the effects of each error should be separately evaluated. When analyzing errors, it is important to remember that in a periodic inventory system:

Beginning inventory + Purchases − Ending inventory = Cost of goods sold

And, for a perpetual system:

Beginning inventory + Purchases − Cost of goods sold = Ending inventory

Gross margin is calculated as:

Sales revenue − Cost of goods sold = Gross margin

5. Determine the costs that should be included in inventory cost.

Inventory cost includes all expenditures needed to get inventory into condition and on location for sale. Inventory cost includes the original purchase price (preferably net of any purchase discount) less purchase returns and allowances and plus expenditures for freight in, handling, storage related to goods purchased, applicable insurance and taxes, and materials and labor used in manufacturing. Normally, interest expenditures related to inventories should be treated as period costs rather than as inventory costs. However, material amounts of interest incurred in the construction of discrete projects for sale or lease should be included in the cost of the project.

6. Explain the procedure for each of the following cost flow assumptions: average cost, FIFO, and unit LIFO.

In the average cost procedure, the costs of goods are divided equally, or averaged, among the inventory units. When used in the periodic inventory system, the average cost procedure is known as the weighted average method. Total cost of goods available for sale during the period is divided by total units available for sale during the period. When used in the perpetual system, the average cost procedure is called the moving average method. Average unit cost is recalculated after each purchase, unless the purchase price per unit is the same as the average cost per unit before the purchase in question.

The FIFO assumption treats the earliest inventory costs of the period as the cost of goods sold and the latest inventory costs as the cost of ending inventory. FIFO yields the same results in the periodic system as in the perpetual system.

In the LIFO method, the costs of the most recent purchases are assigned to the cost of goods sold first, and the costs of the earliest inventory acquisitions are assigned to the cost of goods sold last, or they remain in the inventory account. In a periodic system, the costs assigned to ending inventory for the period are assumed to be the costs of the earliest units purchased. The cost of ending inventory is subtracted from the cost of goods available for sale to determine the cost of goods sold. In a perpetual system, the cost of goods sold is calculated at the time of each sale and is based on the cost of the goods most recently purchased. Ending inventory can be determined by subtracting the total cost of goods sold during the period from the cost of goods available for sale. If inventory acquisition costs have changed, LIFO will not yield the same results in the periodic system as it does in the perpetual system.

7. Discuss the characteristics, advantages, and disadvantages of the FIFO, LIFO, and average cost assumptions.

FIFO conforms to the actual physical flow of many inventory items. It is also comparatively simple to employ. FIFO approximates the current replacement cost of inventory on the balance sheet, especially when inventory turnover is rapid, because it assigns the most recent acquisition costs to ending inventory. A major disadvantage of FIFO is that it assigns relatively noncurrent inventory acquisition costs to the cost of goods sold. During periods of rapidly rising acquisition costs, FIFO results in the matching of a cost of goods sold based on earlier, lower acquisition costs with current revenue on the income statement.

In contrast to FIFO, LIFO matches the most recently incurred inventory costs against sales revenue. LIFO approximates replacement cost, and thus minimizes inventory holding profit. When inventory acquisition costs are rising and inventory quantities are not decreasing, LIFO can be used to defer income taxes through reductions in current taxable income. Under these circumstances, however, LIFO can result in the reporting of inventory on the balance sheet at comparatively low, early acquisition costs, which may be misleading to financial statement users. If early layers of LIFO are liquidated, an unusually large reported income may be reported simply because inventory replacement did not occur prior to the end of the accounting period. LIFO seldom conforms to the normal physical flow of inventory units.

Whether inventory acquisition costs are rising or falling, the average cost approach tends to produce amounts for cost of goods sold and ending inventory that fall between the amounts produced by FIFO and LIFO. The main advantage of the average cost method is its practicality. It is a fairly simple, objective procedure that is easy to apply.

8. Explain the dollar-value LIFO procedure.

The dollar-value LIFO procedure begins with the valuation of ending inventory for the period at period-end acquisition cost. Next, any change in inventory acquisition cost during the period is removed from the dollar amount of ending inventory using an inventory cost index. To determine whether there was a physical increase or decrease in inventory for the period, the cost-adjusted ending inventory is compared with the beginning inventory for the period. If the physical inventory has increased (if a new layer has been added to inventory), the new layer is valued in terms of the current-period acquisition cost. If the physical inventory has decreased (if previously added layers have been taken from inventory), the cost of the beginning inventory for the period is reduced accordingly.

KEY TERMS

average cost procedure 491
base inventory 502
base year 502
base year costs 502
consignment 481
cost flow assumptions 490
dollar-value LIFO 501
finished goods inventory 477
first in, first out (FIFO) 492
f.o.b. destination 481
f.o.b. shipping point 481
freight in 487
inventory 476
inventory cost 485
inventory holding profits (gains) 496
last in, first out (LIFO) 493
LIFO valuation allowance 506
merchandise inventory 477
moving average method 491

net method 486
parking transaction 482
period costs 485
periodic inventory system 477
perpetual inventory system 479
pooled approach 499
product cost 485
product financing arrangement 482
purchase allowance 488
purchase discounts 486
purchase return 488
raw materials inventory 477
relative sales value method 486
sales on approval 482
specific identification 489
transportation in 487
unit LIFO 499
weighted average method 491
work-in-process inventory 477

QUESTIONS

Q 9-1. What are the major inventory classifications that might be reported in the balance sheet of a manufacturing company? Of a merchandising company?

Q 9-2. How does the periodic inventory system differ from the perpetual inventory system?

Q 9-3. What is meant when cost of goods sold is referred to as a *residual* amount under the periodic inventory system?

Q 9-4. What disadvantages does the periodic inventory system have?

Q 9-5. What should be done if the inventory amount determined by physical count differs from the inventory balance calculated in a perpetual inventory system?

Q 9-6. What are some of the factors that should be considered when you determine whether or not a particular item should be included in inventory?

Q 9-7. Distinguish between the terms *f.o.b. shipping point* and *f.o.b. destination.*

Q 9-8. Describe a consignment arrangement, particularly as it relates to inventory accounting.

Q 9-9. What is a product financing arrangement? How does a product financing arrangement affect the inventory of the company that "sells" the goods?

Q 9-10. Describe the net method of accounting for purchase discounts.

Q 9-11. Distinguish between purchase returns and purchase allowances, and describe how each would be accounted for (*a*) in a periodic inventory system and (*b*) in a perpetual inventory system.

Q 9-12. The cost of manufactured inventory consists of what three types of costs?

Q 9-13. Discuss the specific identification method of inventory accounting and comment on the practical and conceptual strengths and weaknesses of the method.

Q 9-14. Comment on the argument that the specific identification method of accounting for inventory allows management to manipulate the cost of ending inventory, cost of goods sold, and net income.

Q 9-15. Why are FIFO and LIFO called cost flow assumptions?

Q 9-16. Compare and contrast the weighted average method and the moving average method of accounting for inventory.

Q 9-17. How would the reported amounts of ending inventory and cost of goods sold vary under the average cost approach, FIFO, and LIFO during periods of *rising* inventory acquisition costs? During periods of *falling* inventory acquisition costs?

Q 9-18. Discuss the advantages and disadvantages of FIFO.

Q 9-19. Discuss the advantages and disadvantages of LIFO.

Q 9-20. What is an inventory holding profit? Under what conditions do inventory holding profits occur, and how can the use of LIFO help to minimize inventory holding profit?

Q 9-21. How does the pooled approach to LIFO differ from traditional unit LIFO?

Q 9-22. How is dollar-value LIFO preferable to traditional LIFO with regard to recordkeeping and the problem of liquidating layers of specific inventories within total inventory?

Q 9-23. If you saw a credit balance account called *excess of replacement cost over LIFO cost of basic inventory temporarily liquidated* among the current liabilities of a company, what transaction or event would you think might have occurred?

Q 9-24. If you saw a credit balance account with the title *allowance to reduce inventory to LIFO basis* in the current assets section of the balance sheet, what do you think that account would represent and under what circumstances would it be used?

CASES

C 9-1. **MANUFACTURING COMPANY INVENTORIES** Dave Miller has come to you, a local accountant, for advice in setting up inventory accounts for his new paint manufacturing company. Miller is particularly interested in obtaining some guidance regarding how to distinguish one type of inventory from another.

Among the items that Miller believes might be appropriately classified as inventory are supplies used to service the two assembly lines and supplies used in the general and accounting offices. A fairly substantial number of parts for machines used in the manufacturing process also must be maintained to avoid lengthy shutdowns for machine repairs. Other items that Miller is considering for inclusion in inventory are barrels of linseed oil, alkyd resin, and mineral spirits, all of which are used in paint manufacture. In addition, the company always has on hand substantial supplies of paint pigments and driers.

The manufacture of paint almost always results in partly completed paint as well as completed, but not yet canned, paint on hand. There also tend to be several hundred cans of paint in the factory that have not had labels attached and several hundred labeled cans of paint that have been boxed but not yet shipped to customers. Occasionally, Miller will have some custom color paint prepared in response to a special order by a customer that is completed and boxed but not yet shipped.

REQUIRED   Prepare a written report for Dave Miller discussing the types of inventory that normally exist in a manufacturing company. As part of your report, indicate whether each of the various items that Miller believes might qualify as inventory actually should be included in inventory and, if so, mention what type of manufacturing inventory the item is.

C 9-2.   PERIODIC AND PERPETUAL INVENTORY SYSTEMS   Heather Jackson is considering starting a small business and recently attended a seminar on setting up an accounting system. The seminar was sponsored by the small business division of the state government. After leaving the seminar, Jackson realized that she did not understand some of the points that had been made about inventory accounting and she has come to you, a CPA, for assistance in understanding what she believes she was told.

In particular, Jackson does not understand several statements she wrote in her seminar notes. First, her notes indicate that "purchases are not recorded when using a perpetual inventory system." Jackson does not see how any inventory system can be reliable if goods are not recorded when they are purchased. Second, her notes state that "inventory shortages normally are recorded only when a perpetual inventory system is used." Jackson views this as a positive feature of the perpetual inventory system because she would prefer not to have any inventory shortages and would like to know when they exist. Finally, the statement "a physical inventory count is not required to determine ending inventory when a perpetual inventory system is used" appears in her notes. Jackson believes that this is another positive feature of the perpetual inventory system because another small business owner told her that taking a complete physical inventory at the end of each business year is extremely time-consuming and interferes with normal business activities.

REQUIRED   Write a brief comment on each of the statements Jackson recorded in her notes. Be sure to clarify what was probably meant by each statement. As an additional aid to Jackson, give general comparative descriptions of the periodic and perpetual inventory systems.

C 9-3.   ITEMS AND EXPENDITURES INCLUDED IN INVENTORY   As controller of Hilton Appliance Company, you have decided to hire an assistant to help with the increasing workload. Because inventory is one of the company's most significant assets and much of your work involves inventory accounting, you plan to select your new assistant on the basis of his or her knowledge of inventory accounting. For purposes of testing applicants, you have listed the following issues for discussion: (a) goods in transit, (b) consignments, (c) inventory financing expenditures, and (d) purchase discounts.

REQUIRED   Prepare what you consider to be a good written response to the following: "Explain how each of these issues affects inventory accounting and describe the acceptable accounting treatment of each."

C 9-4.   INVENTORIABLE COSTS   Nash Company is a retailer and wholesaler of national brandname household lighting fixtures. Nash purchases its inventories from various suppliers, and its management is uncertain about (a) what criteria should be used to determine inventoriable costs and (b) whether administrative costs are inventoriable.

REQUIRED   Draft a brief response to each of the issues raised by Nash's management.

C 9-5.   PURCHASE DISCOUNTS; FIFO VS. LIFO   Jones Corporation is a household appliance dealer that purchases its inventory from suppliers throughout the United States. Jones uses the FIFO cost flow assumption. As part of an overall inventory accounting review, Jones is considering alternative methods of accounting for the purchase discounts it receives when suppliers are paid promptly. Among the alternatives it is considering are (a) recording purchase discounts as interest revenue when payments are made, (b) reducing cost of goods sold for the period in which payments are made, and (c) directly reducing the purchase cost at the time of acquiring the goods.

A second matter under review is the possibility of switching from the FIFO cost flow assumption to the LIFO cost flow assumption. Jones is considering this switch because inventory costs have been continuously rising in recent years and Jones would like to take advantage of this condition to increase its net cash inflow.

REQUIRED   **1.**   Prepare a memorandum to Jones discussing, from a theoretical standpoint, each of the alternative methods of accounting for purchase discounts that is being considered by Jones, indicating whether the method should be used.

2.   In your memorandum, comment on both the balance sheet effect and the income effect of using the LIFO cost flow assumption instead of the FIFO assumption over a substantial period of time during which inventory costs are increasing. Indicate why these effects take place. Explain how Jones can increase its net cash flow by using LIFO.

(AICPA, adapted)

C 9-6. **ADVANTAGES AND DISADVANTAGES OF LIFO** J. White owns a company in which inventories are a major component of total assets. Indeed, for the past few years reported inventory amounts have increased dramatically for the company, which currently uses the FIFO inventory method. White is considering switching from FIFO to LIFO because she has read in the financial press that in recent years many other firms in her company's industry have chosen to use LIFO. White has heard several reasons why LIFO seems to be so popular, including (a) LIFO can help to avoid inventory holding profits, (b) LIFO can help to offset the impact of rising inventory prices on financial statements, and (c) LIFO can help to improve net cash flows during periods of inflation.

REQUIRED Prepare a written discussion of the advantages and disadvantages related to the use of LIFO. Within your discussion, describe inventory holding profits and comment on each of the reasons White has heard for the popularity of LIFO. Explain whether what she has heard is true and, if so, why.

(AICPA, adapted)

C 9-7. **LIFO VS. FIFO; LIQUIDATION OF LIFO LAYERS** Because you are the senior accountant for your company, the president of the company has asked you to prepare a brief paper comparing the LIFO and FIFO cost flow assumptions. The president is considering a switch from the FIFO assumption currently used to the LIFO assumption and is particularly interested in (a) the comparative effects of the two cost flow assumptions on reported income during periods of rising inventory costs and (b) how the company might minimize the potential income distortion caused by liquidating early LIFO layers during periods of rising inventory costs.

REQUIRED In response to the president's request, compare the LIFO and FIFO cost flow assumptions, paying particular attention to their effects on reported income and to the financial statement effects of switching from FIFO to LIFO. In addition, outline an accounting procedure that might be used to avoid distortion of reported income should early LIFO layers be liquidated during periods of rising inventory costs.

(AICPA, adapted)

C 9-8. **LIFO AND DOLLAR-VALUE LIFO** One of your clients, Vision Optical, has called you for advice regarding the possibility of switching from the FIFO inventory method to the LIFO inventory method. The purchase prices of Vision's inventory have risen constantly for three or four years. In two of those years, price increases were dramatic and Vision found that its taxable income and cash outflow for taxes in those years were unusually large. In fact, concern about having sufficient funds available to pay taxes is beginning to interfere with Vision's plans for expanding its business into several new locations.

Based on conversations with several other local businesses, Vision's management has tentatively concluded that use of the LIFO inventory method would substantially reduce some of their current inventory-related problems. On the other hand, the management has heard that LIFO requires detailed records of individual units and unit costs and that severe tax problems can be encountered if it ever becomes necessary to liquidate specific inventory items.

REQUIRED Prepare a written discussion of how LIFO may be helpful to Vision Optical, given the recent trends in their inventory prices. Comment on the recordkeeping and liquidation problems raised by Vision's management and, if possible, suggest an approach that Vision might follow to minimize those problems.

C 9-9. **THE DOLLAR-VALUE LIFO PROCEDURE** For several years Drake Company has used the unit LIFO inventory method. The senior financial officer of the company has never liked unit LIFO because of the extensive recordkeeping involved. However, she does like the favorable effects that LIFO has on both taxable income and cash outflows during inflationary periods. After much discussion, Drake's management concludes that serious consideration should be given to using the dollar-value LIFO method.

Before switching to dollar-value LIFO, however, the senior financial officer wants to see a step-by-step presentation of how the dollar-value LIFO approach works so that she can be sure recordkeeping will be minimized. At your request, she tells you that at the ends of the last two years it would have cost $330,000 and $380,000, respectively, to replace all the inventory. She also indicates that the company's inventory purchase prices increased about 15 percent between the first year and the second year.

REQUIRED Using the inventory data given to you by the senior financial officer, describe and illustrate the dollar-value LIFO procedure.

EXERCISES

E 9-1. **MERCHANDISE TO BE INCLUDED IN INVENTORY** As part of preparing the June 30, 1998, financial statements for your company, you must decide whether each of the following year-end transactions involving inventory requires any further adjustment:

a) Merchandise inventory costing $250 was ordered on June 25, 1998. This merchandise was shipped to your company f.o.b. destination and arrived on July 2, 1998. At the moment, this merchandise is included in your 1998 ending inventory.

b) On June 30, 1998, your company held $325 of merchandise on consignment from Joyce Barnes. This merchandise has been included in your 1998 ending inventory.

c) Your company ordered $410 of merchandise from a supplier on June 26, 1998. This merchandise was shipped f.o.b. shipping point on June 28 but had not arrived at your company by June 30. As a result, this merchandise has not been included in your 1998 ending inventory.

d) On June 27, 1998, one of your customers ordered a shipment of 25 units, which was to be sent f.o.b. destination for arrival at the customer's warehouse on July 5, 1998. These goods have been included in your 1998 ending inventory even though they were shipped to the customer on June 29, 1998.

REQUIRED For each of the above cases, state whether the transaction has been handled properly and indicate the reasons for your conclusion.

E 9-2. **CALCULATING THE DOLLAR AMOUNT IN INVENTORY** The inventory account of Little Paint Company at December 31, 1998, had a balance of $71,300, including the following items:

	INVENTORY AMOUNT
Merchandise out on consignment at sales price (cost = $3,800)	$6,000
Goods purchased, in transit (shipped f.o.b. shipping point)	5,000
Goods held on consignment by Little Paint	4,000
Goods out on approval (sales price $2,500, cost $2,000)	2,500

REQUIRED Calculate the correct inventory account balance at December 31, 1998.

(AICPA, adapted)

E 9-3. **CALCULATING COST OF GOODS AVAILABLE** The following information is available for Carson, Inc., for 1998:

Freight in	$ 20,000
Purchase returns	70,000
Selling expenses	200,000
Ending inventory	80,000

The cost of goods sold is equal to 600 percent of selling expenses.

REQUIRED Calculate the cost of goods available for sale.

(AICPA, adapted)

E 9-4. **DETERMINING COST OF GOODS SOLD** Hickok Company supplies you with the following information:

Freight in	$ 2,000
Freight out (selling expense)	2,000
Gross sales	100,000
Merchandise inventory, 1/1/98	10,000
Merchandise inventory, 12/31/98	14,000
Purchases	70,000
Office supplies used	7,000
Purchase discounts	4,000
Purchase returns and allowances	5,000
Sales returns and allowances	10,000
Supplies inventory, 12/31/98	5,000

REQUIRED   Calculate the cost of goods sold for Hickok Company. Make entries to (1) record cost of goods sold and (2) close cost of goods sold.

(CGAA, adapted)

E 9-5.   **ADJUSTING THE COST OF MERCHANDISE INVENTORY**   Brandon Equipment Company made a large "group" purchase of lawn mowers from Honda International in order to obtain a special price. The invoice price for the entire group of mowers was $160,000. The purchased mowers consisted of 180 self-propelled Model A machines (normally sold by Brandon for $600 each), 120 self-propelled Model B machines (normally sold by Brandon for $550), and 105 push-type Model C machines (normally sold by Brandon for $400). Since the lawn mowers were bought as a group purchase. Honda International agreed to accept up to 40 mowers as purchase returns at unit purchase price amounts determined by Brandon using the relative sales value method of allocating the total cost to individual models.

The purchase terms were 2%/10, net 30, and Brandon paid for all but 10 percent of the purchase within the purchase discount period. The remaining 10 percent of the invoice price was not paid within the discount period because 22 of the self-propelled Model A machines were damaged on receipt by Brandon and were returned to Honda International along with the balance due to Honda on the invoice. Brandon uses a periodic system for its lawn mower inventory.

REQUIRED   **1.** Using the relative sales value method, determine the cost per unit (to the nearest whole penny) of each of the models of lawn mowers purchased by Brandon.

   2. Record (*a*) the purchase using the net method of recording purchase discounts and (*b*) payment for 90 percent of the purchase within the discount period.

   3. Record (*a*) the purchase returns and (*b*) payment of the balance due to Honda. The balance due was paid after the purchase discount period.

E 9-6.   **DETERMINING COSTS TO BE INCLUDED IN INVENTORY**   At its fiscal year-end, August 31, 1998, Nelson Jewelers took a physical inventory count and determined its cost to be $383,500. Accounts payable and sales for 1998 were recorded as $29,000 and $865,000, respectively. Additional information related to 1998 transactions is as follows:

a) Several pieces of jewelry were in transit from Nelson Jewelers to Hillside Jewelers on August 31, 1998. These items, costing $17,200, were shipped f.o.b. destination on August 28 and were not included in Nelson's ending inventory. At the time of shipment a $22,000 sale had been recorded.

b) Jewelry on consignment from Wallace Gems has a cost of $7,900 and was included in Nelson's 1998 ending inventory and in accounts payable.

c) Nelson Jewelers had consigned $12,350 worth of jewelry to Hillside Jewelers on August 20, 1998. These jewelry items had a retail value of $15,575 and were not included in Nelson's 1998 ending inventory.

d) $26,430 of watches were purchased from Wholesale Jewelers, Inc., and paid for in late August 1998. The watches were sold by Nelson Jewelers for $29,400 and were shipped f.o.b. shipping point on August 31, 1998. The watches were included in Nelson's year-end 1998 physical inventory count. The sale was not recorded until the watches were received at the buyer's office on September 5, 1998.

e) On August 31, 1998, goods costing $15,700 were in transit to Nelson Jewelers. These goods had been shipped f.o.b. shipping point. A purchase had not been recorded and the goods were not included in Nelson's 1998 ending inventory.

REQUIRED   Prepare a schedule of adjustments to the unadjusted balances of inventory, accounts payable, and sales using the format shown below. For any case where the additional information does not require a change to the unadjusted balance, indicate by inserting –0–.

	INVENTORY	ACCOUNTS PAYABLE	SALES
Unadjusted balances.............	$383,500	$29,000	$865,000
Adjustments:			
a			
b			
c			
d			
e			
Adjusted balances...........			

E 9-7. **ACCOUNTING FOR PURCHASE DISCOUNTS** Mock Company, which uses a periodic inventory system, bought $50,000 of inventory on September 10, 1998, at terms of 2%/10, net 30. $34,000 of the inventory was paid for on September 19, 1998, and the remaining $16,000 was paid for on October 5, 1998.

REQUIRED Make the journal entries to record (1) the purchase, (2) the September 19 payment, and (3) the October 5 payment under the net method of accounting for purchase discounts.

E 9-8. **EFFECTS OF INVENTORY ERRORS** A company that uses a periodic inventory system neglected to record a $2,500 purchase of merchandise on account at the end of the year. This merchandise also was omitted from the year-end physical count.

REQUIRED Give the dollar amount and direction of effect (overstate, understate, no effect) of these errors on (1) assets, (2) liabilities, (3) stockholders' equity, and (4) net income for the year.

(AICPA, adapted)

E 9-9. **EFFECTS OF INVENTORY ERRORS** The December 31, 1997, year-end physical inventory of Grayson Company was adjusted to include $2,100 worth of goods ordered by Grayson from Peters, Inc., on December 28. Peters shipped the goods f.o.b. destination, and the goods arrived at Grayson's on January 2, 1998, at which time the purchase was recorded.

Grayson's December 31, 1998, physical inventory appropriately included $3,600 of merchandise that was not recorded as a purchase on account until January 1999.

REQUIRED What effect, in dollar amount and direction of effect (overstate, understate, no effect), will these errors have on (1) assets, (2) liabilities, (3) retained earnings, and (4) net income for 1998?

E 9-10. **EFFECTS OF INVENTORY ERRORS** In examining the books of Riston Company, you discover the following errors:
  a) Incorrect exclusion from the ending inventory of goods costing $3,500 for which the purchase was not recorded.
  b) Inclusion in the ending inventory of goods costing $7,000, although the purchase was not recorded. The goods in question were being held on consignment from Sonya Company.
  c) Incorrect exclusion of $3,000 from the inventory count at the end of the period. The goods were in transit (f.o.b. shipping point); the invoice was received and the purchase was recorded.
  d) Items on the receiving dock that were being held for return to the vendor because of damage were incorrectly included in inventory and a purchase of $6,000 was recorded.
  The records (uncorrected) showed the following amounts:
  e) Purchases, $141,000.
  f) Income before tax, $25,000.
  g) Accounts payable, $30,000.
  h) Inventory at the end of the period, $40,000.

REQUIRED Determine the corrected amounts for items *e* through *h* (show calculations).

(CGAA, adapted)

E 9-11. **CORRECTION OF INVENTORY ERRORS** During the course of your examination of the financial statements of Tallon Company, a new client, for the year ended December 31, 1998, you discover the following:
  a) Inventory at January 1, 1998, was overstated by $2,500.
  b) Inventory at December 31, 1998, was understated by $5,000.
  c) During 1998 Tallon Company received a $1,500 cash advance from a customer for merchandise to be manufactured and shipped during 1999. The $1,500 was credited to sales revenue.
  d) Net income reported on the 1998 income statement (before reflecting any adjustments for the above items) was $20,000.

REQUIRED **1.** Calculate the correct net income for 1998.
  2. Assuming that the 1998 books have not been closed, make the appropriate adjusting entry or entries to correct any errors that you discover in examining your new client's financial statements.

E 9-12.   **WEIGHTED AVERAGE METHOD AND MOVING AVERAGE METHOD** The following information was available from the inventory records of Frank Company for January 1998:

	UNITS	UNIT COST	TOTAL COST
Balance at 1/1/98	2,000	$10.00	$20,000
Purchases:			
1/6/98	1,600	10.30	16,480
1/26/98	3,400	10.72	36,448
Sales:			
1/7/98	(1,800)		
1/31/98	(3,200)		
Balance at 1/31/98	2,000		

REQUIRED   **I.** Assuming that Frank maintains perpetual inventory records, what should be the inventory at January 31, 1998, using the moving average method, rounded to the nearest dollar?

2. Assuming that Frank does *not* maintain perpetual inventory records, what should be the inventory at January 31, 1998, according to the weighted average inventory method, rounded to the nearest dollar?

(AICPA, adapted)

E 9-13.   **CALCULATING INVENTORY UNDER ALTERNATIVE COST FLOW ASSUMPTIONS** Crystal Company was formed on January 1, 1998. The following information is available from Crystal's 1998 inventory records:

	UNITS	UNIT COST
Initial inventory, 1/1/98	800	$10.00
Purchases:		
1/5/98	1,500	9.50
1/25/98	1,200	10.50
2/16/98	600	11.00
3/26/98	800	11.50

A physical inventory on March 31, 1998, shows 1,600 units on hand.

REQUIRED   Prepare schedules to calculate the ending inventory at March 31, 1998, under each of the following inventory methods:
I. FIFO.
2. LIFO.
3. Weighted average.

(AICPA, adapted)

E 9-14.   **PERIODIC INVENTORY SYSTEM AND LIFO COST FLOW** Barton, Inc., started its second year of operations with 80 units of inventory costing $26 each. During the second year the summary transactions listed below affected Barton's inventory. Barton uses the LIFO cost flow assumption in accounting for its inventory. All purchases and sales were for cash.

    1/24 Purchased 10 units costing $25 each.
    3/10 Sold 20 units for $30 each.
    7/21 Purchased 30 units costing $30 each.
    9/15 Sold 20 units for $32 each.
  11/27 Purchased 25 units costing $30 each.
  12/3 Sold 27 units for $38 each.

REQUIRED   Make summary journal entries, including adjusting and closing entries, for Barton, Inc., under the periodic inventory system.

E 9-15.   **PERPETUAL INVENTORY SYSTEM AND LIFO COST FLOW** Use the accounting information and the transactions data given in E9-14.

REQUIRED   Make summary journal entries, including adjusting and closing entries, for Barton, Inc., under the perpetual inventory system.

E 9-16. **FIFO, LIFO; PERPETUAL VS. PERIODIC INVENTORY RECORDS** The records of Gaylord Corporation show the following for the inventory account for 1998:

	UNITS	UNIT COST	UNIT SELLING PRICE	TOTAL
Beginning inventory, 1/1	250	$10.50		$2,625.00
Purchase, 3/7	200	11.00		2,200.00
Purchase, 7/15	275	11.75		3,231.25
Sale, 5/20	(120)		$14.00	(1,680.00)
Sale, 6/30	(55)		15.00	(825.00)
Sale, 9/17	(245)		16.00	(3,920.00)
Ending inventory, 12/31	305			

REQUIRED

1. Assuming that Gaylord maintains perpetual inventory records, what is the cost of the ending inventory according to (*a*) FIFO and (*b*) LIFO?

2. Assuming that Gaylord does *not* maintain perpetual inventory records, what is the cost of the ending inventory according to (*a*) FIFO and (*b*) LIFO?

E 9-17. **USE OF ALTERNATIVE COST FLOW ASSUMPTIONS** Tilton Faucets Ltd. sells only one product. During the year just ended, Tilton sold 153,000 units, generating total sales of $2.6 million. Inventory at the beginning of the year was 30,000 units at a cost of $230,000. During the year purchases were as follows:

February 1..	40,000 units @ $15.50
April 1...	57,000 units @ $16.00
June 1..	42,000 units @ $16.60
September 1...	29,000 units @ $16.80
Total	168,000 units

REQUIRED

1. Calculate the year-end inventory using:
  a) FIFO.
  b) LIFO.
  c) Weighted average cost.

2. Construct a partial income statement (down to gross profit on sales), with separate columns side by side, for each of the above inventory cost flow assumptions.

(CGAA, adapted)

E 9-18. **USE OF ALTERNATIVE COST FLOW ASSUMPTIONS** Nixon Product Company had the following inventory transactions during the month of December 1998:
  12/1 Inventory of 20 units at $4.60 each.
  12/8 Purchased 80 units at $5.00 each.
  12/15 Purchased 40 units at $5.30 each.
  12/22 Purchased 60 units at $5.60 each.
  12/29 Purchased 40 units at $5.50 each.
By December 31, 1998, 175 units of inventory had been sold by Nixon.

REQUIRED Calculate the cost of the ending inventory under (*a*) FIFO, (*b*) LIFO, and (*c*) average cost.

E 9-19.   **USE OF ALTERNATIVE COST FLOW ASSUMPTIONS**   Heller Company has one inventory item for which the 1998 beginning inventory was 175 units purchased for $58.00 per unit. Heller uses a periodic inventory system and has the following additional inventory data for 1998:

MONTH		UNITS	UNIT COST
January...............................	Purchased	180	$59.50
	Sold	75	
February..............................	Purchased	100	60.00
	Sold	225	
March................................	Purchased	900	60.50
April.................................	Purchased	200	61.50
May..................................	Sold	400	
June.................................	Sold	175	
November.............................	Purchased	175	62.50
	Sold	125	
December.............................	Purchased	125	63.00
	Sold	400	

REQUIRED   1. Calculate the cost of 1998 ending inventory under (*a*) FIFO, (*b*) LIFO, and (*c*) average cost.

2. Which of the inventory methods listed in part 1 will produce the highest net income for Heller? Why?

E 9-20.   **DOLLAR-VALUE LIFO**   Rendel Company carries only one type of inventory item. On January 1, 1998, Rendel adopted the dollar-value LIFO inventory method. At the time, the inventory was valued at $300,000 under dollar-value LIFO. Inventory data for subsequent years are as follows:

YEAR	ENDING INVENTORY AT YEAR-END PRICES	PRICE INDEX (JAN. 1998 = 1.00)
1998	$330,000	1.06
1999	345,000	1.12
2000	370,000	1.08

REQUIRED   Calculate the inventory value at the end of 1998, 1999, and 2000 using the dollar-value LIFO method.

E9-21.   **DOLLAR-VALUE LIFO**   Snow Company adopted dollar-value LIFO on January 1, 1998, at which time it had $200,000 worth of inventory. On December 31, 1998, the current cost of inventory on hand was $230,000 and the cost index was 1.07, as compared to the January 1, 1998, cost index of 1.00.

REQUIRED   1. Calculate Snow Company's December 31, 1998, ending inventory by the dollar-value LIFO procedure.

2. Assuming that at December 31, 1999, Snow Company had ending inventory with a current cost of $260,000 and the cost index was 1.11, calculate the company's December 31, 1999, ending inventory by dollar-value LIFO.

3. What principal advantages does dollar-value LIFO have over traditional LIFO?

E 9-22.   **DOLLAR-VALUE LIFO**   Justin Corporation manufactures one product. On December 31, 1997, Justin adopted the dollar-value LIFO inventory method. The inventory on that date was evaluated by the dollar-value LIFO method at $200,000.

Inventory data are as follows:

YEAR	ENDING INVENTORY AT YEAR-END PRICES	PRICE INDEX (1997 = 1.00)
1998...............................	$231,000	1.04
1999...............................	285,000	1.14
2000...............................	306,000	1.20

REQUIRED   Calculate the inventory at December 31, 1998, 1999, and 2000 using the dollar-value LIFO method.

(AICPA, adapted)

E 9-23.   **LIFO VALUATION ALLOWANCE**   Crandel Company maintains its inventory records for internal purposes on a FIFO basis, but it reports inventory on a LIFO basis for external reporting and tax purposes. At the end of 1998 the following inventory information is available:

	ENDING INVENTORY	
	1997	1998
FIFO	$180,000	$210,000
LIFO	160,000	180,000

REQUIRED   Assuming the proper adjustment from FIFO to LIFO was made in 1997:
1. Using the cost of goods sold account and an allowance to reduce inventory to a LIFO basis, make the necessary 1998 entry to adjust inventory from a FIFO basis to a LIFO basis.
2. Describe how the adjustment would be reported in the external financial statements for 1998.

PROBLEMS

P 9-1.   **PERIODIC VS. PERPETUAL INVENTORY**   Watson Company started Year 3 with 100 units of inventory costing $10 per unit. During Year 3 the summary transactions listed below affected Watson's inventory. Watson uses the FIFO cost flow assumption in accounting for its inventory.

4/30	Purchases (170 × $10)	$1,700
9/20	Purchases (150 × $11)	1,650
5/10	Sales (220 sold for $15 each)	3,300
11/15	Sales (100 sold for $17 each)	1,700
	Ending inventory (physical count)	90 units

REQUIRED   1. Make summary journal entries, including adjusting and closing entries, for Watson Company under (a) the periodic inventory system and (b) the perpetual inventory system.
2. Compare the advantages and disadvantages of the periodic and perpetual inventory systems.

P 9-2.   **PERIODIC VS. PERPETUAL INVENTORY**   Faxon, Inc., began the current year with 80 units of inventory costing $25 each. During the current year, Faxon had the transactions listed below that affected its inventory. Faxon uses the LIFO cost flow assumption. All purchases and sales were for cash.

2/7	Purchased 10 units costing $24 each.
4/17	Sold 20 units for $30 each.
6/9	Purchased 30 units costing $28 each.
8/24	Sold 20 units for $32 each.
10/19	Purchased 25 units costing $30 each.
11/25	Sold 27 units for $38 each.

REQUIRED   1. Prepare summary journal entries, including adjusting and closing entries, for Faxon, Inc., under the periodic inventory system.
2. Prepare summary journal entries, including adjusting and closing entries, for Faxon, Inc., under the perpetual inventory system.

P 9-3.   **MERCHANDISE TO BE INCLUDED IN INVENTORY**   As you prepare the December 31, 1998, financial statements for Ellis Electronics, you must decide whether each of several year-end transactions involving inventory requires any further adjustment of the inventory balance. The transactions under consideration are listed below.
a) Merchandise worth $750 was ordered by Ellis Electronics on December 28, 1998, and was shipped to Ellis f.o.b. shipping point on December 30, arriving January 3, 1999. This merchandise was not included in Ellis's 1998 ending inventory.

b) Ellis ordered $500 of goods on December 24, 1998. Those goods, shipped to Ellis f.o.b. destination, arrived on January 2, 1999. They were not included in Ellis's 1998 ending inventory.

c) On December 29, 1998, Ellis received $1,500 of merchandise on consignment from Barney, Inc. The merchandise was on hand at December 31 and was included in Ellis's physical inventory count.

d) Ellis's December 31 physical inventory count included $400 worth of merchandise set aside for shipment to Paxon's Radio Shop. Paxon had ordered the goods on December 23 and had enclosed a 30 percent down payment with the order.

e) Goods worth $600 were in Ellis's warehouse at December 31, 1998, but were not included in ending inventory. These goods had been ordered by Lester Company on December 22 and Ellis had billed Lester $600, although the goods were not shipped until January 1, 1999, because of an error on the shipping dock.

f) Ellis's December 31, 1998, inventory included $1,200 of goods Ellis had shipped on consignment to Gray Electronics on December 20, 1998. It had cost Ellis $120 to ship the goods to Gray.

REQUIRED   Examine each transaction carefully and determine whether it was handled properly in Ellis's December 31, 1998, inventory determination. In each case state what you think is the proper inventory treatment and give your reasons.

P 9-4.   **MERCHANDISE TO BE INCLUDED IN INVENTORY**   Haslett Stamp and Coin is a large retail and wholesale dealer in rare collectible postage stamps and coins that has a March 31 fiscal year-end. During the preparation of Haslett's 1998 financial statements, you become aware of the following late March 1998 transactions that may require additional adjustments to the ending inventory balance that was determined by physical count:

a) On March 25, Haslett sold a large lot of U.S. commemorative stamps to a dealer in Chicago. The stamps were sold for $18,600 on an installment basis. The Chicago dealer sent Haslett $6,200 on March 25 and is to pay Haslett $6,200 on both April 25 and May 25, 1998, after which Haslett will ship the entire lot to the Chicago dealer. While waiting for the remaining installments, Haslett has separated the stamps from its regular inventory and did not include the stamps in its 1998 year-end inventory count. Haslett has dealt with the Chicago dealer several times before and is virtually certain that there will be no difficulty in collecting the installment payments.

b) Haslett entered into an agreement on March 27, 1998, with Dawson Quality Coin Shop. Under this agreement, Haslett agreed to sell Dawson 50 uncirculated $10 U.S. gold coins on March 27 and to buy at least 50 of the same type of coins from Dawson during the first six months of Haslett's 1999 fiscal year. The price that Haslett agreed to pay Dawson is specified as being the going market price on the date Haslett makes each coin transaction. The 50 coins were shipped to Dawson f.o.b. shipping point on March 28, 1998, and were not included in Haslett's 1998 ending inventory.

c) Haslett ordered $30,300 worth of foreign postage stamps from a dealer in Great Britain on March 26, 1998. These stamps were shipped to Haslett f.o.b. shipping point on March 27 and arrived on April 2. The stamps were not included in Haslett's 1998 ending inventory.

d) Coins worth $10,000 were shipped on consignment to a West Coast coin dealer on March 29, with arrival expected in three days. Since the coins were in transit on March 31, Haslett did not include them in its 1998 ending inventory.

e) Coins worth $20,500 were ordered and paid for by Haslett on March 29, 1998. These coins were shipped to Haslett f.o.b. destination and arrived on April 3. Since the coins had been paid for, Haslett included them in its 1998 ending inventory.

f) As of March 31, 1998, Haslett had $73,250 in stamps and coins sent to various customers on approval. Even though these stamps and coins were not in Haslett's possession on March 31, they were included in its 1998 ending inventory.

g) On March 28, 1998, Haslett shipped $17,100 worth of stamps to a Miami dealer on terms of f.o.b. destination. These stamps arrived in Miami on April 1 and were included in Haslett's ending inventory for 1998.

REQUIRED   State whether each of the preceding transactions was handled properly in determining Haslett Stamp and Coin's 1998 ending inventory. If the transaction was not handled properly, state what you think is the correct treatment.

P 9-5. **DETERMINING COSTS TO BE INCLUDED IN INVENTORY** Master Corporation is a wholesale distributor of automotive replacement parts. At the end of 1998, Master took a physical count of its inventory and determined its cost to be $1,200,000 at December 31. Accounts payable at that date were as follows:

VENDOR	TERMS	AMOUNT
Best Company	2%/10, net 30	$250,000
Swanson Company	Net 30	210,000
Jones Company	Net 30	300,000
Falen Company	Net 30	225,000
Post Company	Net 30	—
Wyler Company	Net 30	—
		$985,000

Sales in 1998 were $9.3 million.

Additional information is as follows:

a) Parts held on consignment from Swanson to Master, the consignee, amounting to $155,000, were included in the physical count of goods in Master's warehouse on December 31, 1998, and in accounts payable at December 31, 1998.

b) $22,000 of parts that were purchased from Post and paid for in December 1998 were sold in the last week of 1998 and appropriately recorded as sales of $28,000. The parts were included in the physical count of goods in Master's warehouse on December 31, 1998, because they were on the loading dock waiting to be picked up by the customers.

c) Parts in transit to customers on December 31, 1998, shipped f.o.b. shipping point on December 28, amounted to $34,000. The parts were not included in Master's December 31, 1998, inventory. The customers received the parts on January 6, 1999. Sales of $39,000 to the customers for the parts were recorded by Master on January 2, 1999.

d) On December 31, 1998, retailers were holding goods on consignment from Master, the consignor, with a value of $200,000 at cost ($250,000 at retail). These goods were not included in Master's ending inventory.

e) Goods were in transit from Wyler to Master on December 31, 1998. The cost of the goods was $25,000, and they were shipped f.o.b. shipping point on December 29, 1998.

f) A quarterly freight bill in the amount of $2,000, specifically related to merchandise purchased in December 1998, was received on January 3, 1999. All of that merchandise was still in the inventory at December 31, 1998. The freight bill was not included in either inventory or accounts payable at December 31, 1998.

g) All the purchases from Best occurred during the last seven days of the year. These items have been recorded in accounts payable and accounted for in the physical inventory at cost before discount. Master's policy is to pay invoices in time to take advantage of all cash discounts, adjust inventory accordingly, and record accounts payable net of cash discounts.

REQUIRED Prepare a schedule of adjustments to the initial amounts using the format shown below. Show the effect, if any, of each of the transactions separately. If any transaction would have no effect on the amount shown, indicate by inserting –0–.

	INVENTORY	ACCOUNTS PAYABLE	SALES
Initial amounts	$1,200,000	$ 985,000	$9,300,000
Adjustments—increase (decrease)			
a			
b			
c			
d			
e			
f			
g			
Total adjustments			
Adjusted amounts	$	$	$

(AICPA, adapted)

P 9-6.   DETERMINING COSTS TO BE INCLUDED IN INVENTORY Jasper Corporation, a manufacturer of small tools, provided the following information from its accounting records for the year ended December 31, 1998:

Inventory at December 31, 1998 (based on physical count
of goods in Jasper's plant at cost on December 31, 1998) $1,800,000
Accounts payable at December 31, 1998 1,100,000
Net sales (sales less sales returns) 8,300,000

Additional information is as follows:

a) Included in the physical count were tools billed to a customer f.o.b. shipping point on December 31, 1998. These tools had a cost of $28,000 and were recorded as sales at $33,000. The shipment was on Jasper's loading dock waiting to be picked up by the common carrier.

b) Goods were in transit from a vendor to Jasper on December 31, 1998. The invoice cost was $39,000, and the goods were shipped f.o.b. shipping point on December 29, 1998.

c) Work-in-process inventory costing $20,000 was sent to an outside processor for plating on December 30, 1998, and was not included in physical inventory.

d) Tools returned by customers and held pending inspection in the returned goods area on December 31, 1998, were not included in the physical count. On January 8, 1999, the tools, costing $25,000, were inspected and returned to inventory. Credit memos totaling $41,000 were issued to the customers on the same date.

e) Tools shipped to a customer f.o.b. destination on December 26, 1998, were in transit at December 31, 1998, and had a cost of $25,000. Upon notification of receipt by the customer on January 2, 1999, Jasper issued a sales invoice for $42,000.

f) Goods received from a vendor at 5:00 P.M. on December 31, 1998, were recorded on a receiving report dated January 2, 1999. The goods, with an invoice cost of $30,000, were not included in the physical count, but the invoice was included in accounts payable at December 31, 1998.

g) Goods received from a vendor on December 26, 1998, were included in the physical count. However, the related $55,000 vendor invoice was not included in accounts payable at December 31, 1998, because the accounts payable copy of the receiving report was lost.

h) On January 3, 1999, a monthly freight bill in the amount of $4,000 was received. The bill specifically related to merchandise purchased in December 1998, one-half of which was still in the inventory at December 31, 1998. The freight charges were not included either in inventory or in accounts payable at December 31, 1998.

REQUIRED   Using the following format, prepare a schedule of adjustments as of December 31, 1998, to the initial amounts per Jasper's accounting records. Show separately the effect, if any, of each of the eight transactions on the December 31, 1998, amounts. If the transactions would have no effect on the initial amount shown, indicate by inserting –0–.

	INVENTORY	ACCOUNTS PAYABLE	NET SALES
Initial amounts..........................	$1,800,000	$1,100,000	$8,300,000
Adjustments—increase (decrease)			
a.................................			
b.................................			
c.................................			
d.................................			
e.................................			
f.................................			
g.................................			
h.................................			
Total adjustments			
Adjusted amounts	$	$	$

(AICPA, adapted)

P 9-7. **DETERMINING COSTS TO BE INCLUDED IN INVENTORY** The 1998 beginning inventory for Instill Company was $18,700. During 1998, the following inventory-related transactions took place:

a) Instill incurred $3,100 of interest expense related to the manufacture of its primary product. Instill elected to include this interest expense in the cost of its inventory.

b) Instill purchased $10,000 (invoice price) of merchandise inventory at terms of 2%/15, net 30, on July 10, 1998. Instill uses the net method of accounting for purchase discounts. The inventory was recorded at $10,000 on July 10 and payment was made by Instill on July 22. Freight in costs from the inventory acquisition were $200. Instill elected to exclude these costs from the inventory account.

c) Instill purchased $1,700 worth of merchandise inventory for cash from Ellison, Inc., on August 17, 1998. The inventory was recorded at the time of purchase. Upon receipt of the goods, Instill discovered that $600 worth of the merchandise was the wrong model and returned the goods to Ellison for credit. Instill did not record the return.

d) On December 28, 1998, Instill shipped $12,300 worth of merchandise to Miller Company. The shipping terms were f.o.b. destination, and the goods arrived on Miller's receiving dock on January 4, 1999. The goods were not included in Instill's 1998 ending inventory.

e) Instill's 1998 ending inventory included $4,000 of goods held on consignment from Jackson, Inc., the consignor.

f) Before paying the amount due, Instill received a $350 allowance from Marsh Company for part of a $3,000 order received from Marsh on November 20, 1998, and recorded on that date. No record of the allowance was made.

g) On December 27, 1998, Instill ordered $6,000 worth of goods from Ellison, Inc. Those goods were shipped f.o.b. destination by Ellison on December 29, 1998, and were received by Instill on January 2, 1999. Instill included the goods in its 1998 ending inventory.

REQUIRED **1.** Comment on Instill's accounting treatment of each transaction, indicating which treatments were correct and which were not. If you consider an entry incorrect, indicate what entry should have been made. Give your reasons.

2. Calculate Instill's correct ending inventory balance.

P 9-8. **ACCOUNTING FOR PURCHASE DISCOUNTS** Harris Company uses a periodic inventory system. Its fiscal year ends June 30. The company's purchase transactions for June of the current year are as follows:

June 4 Purchased $9,000 worth of merchandise inventory on account; terms 2%/10, net 20.

June 10 Returned 4% of the June 4 purchase and received a credit on account.

June 15 Purchased $5,000 worth of merchandise on account; terms 2%/10, net 30.

June 20 Paid 90% of the amount due on the June 4 purchase.

June 23 Paid all of the amount due on the June 15 purchase.

Harris uses the *net method* of accounting for purchase discounts.

REQUIRED **1.** Make a journal entry to record each of the above transactions. Date each entry.

2. Make any year-end adjusting entry or entries that may be required.

3. Describe how the accounts used in your entries would be reported in the financial statements.

4. Outline the conceptual strengths of the net method of accounting for purchase discounts.

P 9-9. **EFFECTS OF INVENTORY ERRORS** You are the auditor for Handy, Inc., for the year ended December 31, 1998. In your examination of Handy's accounts you discover the following:

a) $1,000 of goods purchased by Handy have been shipped f.o.b. shipping point. The goods have not been received, but the invoice has been received. The purchase has been recorded but does not appear in the inventories account.

b) Items costing $2,600 are being held in the receiving department for return as unacceptable. The purchase has been recorded and is included in the inventories account.

c) Goods costing $700 are included in the inventories account but the purchase has not been recorded. The goods were shipped f.o.b. destination and were received December 30, 1998.

d) Goods costing $5,000 have been received on consignment but have not been recorded as purchases and do not appear in the inventories account.

REQUIRED

1. What effect, in dollar amount and in direction (overstate, understate, no effect), will each of these errors have on (*a*) assets, (*b*) liabilities, and (*c*) retained earnings?

2. Handy reported net income of $38,000 without considering items *a* through *d* above. Starting with the reported net income of $38,000, calculate the correct net income as of December 31, 1998.

(CGAA, adapted)

P 9-10. **EFFECTS OF INVENTORY ERRORS** During your audit of Ellen Company's ending inventory at December 31, 1998, you find the following inventory accounting errors:

a) Merchandise purchased on account by Ellen on December 30, 1998, and shipped f.o.b. shipping point was excluded from ending inventory and the purchase was not recorded.

b) On December 29, 1998, Ellen shipped goods costing $5,000 to Jacobs, f.o.b. destination. Jacobs received the goods on January 3, 1999. The goods were not included in Ellen's 1998 ending inventory.

c) Goods in Ellen's warehouse on consignment from Hill, Inc., were included in Ellen's ending inventory.

d) On December 28, 1998, Ellen received $3,500 worth of inventory, which was included in the 1998 ending inventory. However, the invoice on the shipment was not received by Ellen until January 3, 1999, at which time the purchase was recorded. The purchase should have been recorded in 1998.

e) Some of Ellen's merchandise, on consignment with Allison, Inc., was excluded from Ellen's ending inventory.

REQUIRED

Assume that Ellen uses the periodic inventory system. Indicate the effect (overstate, understate, no effect) each of the above errors would have on:

1. 12/31/98 ending inventory.
2. 12/31/99 ending inventory.
3. 12/31/98 cost of goods sold.
4. 12/31/99 cost of goods sold.
5. 12/31/98 accounts payable.
6. 12/31/99 accounts payable.

P 9-11. **USE OF ALTERNATIVE COST FLOW ASSUMPTIONS** The inventory records of Fuller Company showed the following inventory transactions for January:

	UNITS	UNIT COST
Beginning inventory	110	$5.25
Purchases:		
1/5	100	5.50
1/9	50	5.75
1/17	120	6.00
1/25	90	6.20
Sales:		
1/10	120	
1/15	30	
1/21	110	
1/24	60	
1/27	90	

REQUIRED

1. Assuming that Fuller Company uses a periodic inventory system, calculate the cost of goods sold and cost of ending inventory under (*a*) FIFO, (*b*) LIFO, and (*c*) average cost.

2. Assuming that Fuller Company uses a perpetual inventory system, calculate the cost of goods sold and cost of ending inventory under (*a*) FIFO, (*b*) LIFO, and (*c*) average cost.

P 9-12. **USE OF ALTERNATIVE COST FLOW ASSUMPTIONS** The following data relate to Lyon Company Ltd. for the month of March 1998. There was no beginning inventory.

MERCHANDISE PURCHASED			MERCHANDISE SOLD	
	UNITS	COST PER UNIT		UNITS
3/4.............	1,900	$4.90	3/5	1,100
3/11.............	1,600	5.20	3/12	1,000
3/23.............	3,200	4.60	3/17	1,000
3/29.............	1,000	4.75	3/27	800
	7,700		3/30	1,150
				5,050

REQUIRED

1. Calculate the number of units and the cost of the ending inventory using the following methods:

   a) First in, first out, periodic basis.

   b) Last in, first out, periodic basis.

   c) Weighted average method, periodic basis.

2. Assuming a perpetual inventory system is being used, prepare journal entries to record purchases and sales under methods *a* and *b* above. Selling price is $10 per unit.

(CGAA, adapted)

P 9-13. **CALCULATING GROSS PROFIT UNDER ALTERNATIVE COST FLOW ASSUMPTIONS** Hudson Merchandising Company started operations on June 1, 1998. Purchases and sales data for the first three months of operations are provided below. Assume that Hudson had no inventory when it began operations, and that the company uses a periodic inventory system.

	PURCHASES	SALES
June 4	200 units @ $2.50	
June 9		150 units @ $4.00
June 17	250 units @ $2.80	
June 22		220 units @ $4.20
July 8		40 units @ $4.25
July 19	150 units @ $2.90	
July 22	150 units @ $3.00	
July 25		240 units @ $4.50
August 10		50 units @ $4.60
August 12	120 units @ $3.10	
August 25		150 units @ $4.75

REQUIRED

1. Calculate the company's gross profit for each of the first three months of operation under:

   a) First in, first out.

   b) Last in, first out.

   c) Weighted average.

2. Comment on the impact of each of the above three inventory cost flow assumptions on gross profit during a period of rising prices such as was faced by Hudson Merchandising during its first few months of operation.

P 9-14. **CALCULATING INVENTORY UNDER ALTERNATIVE COST FLOW ASSUMPTIONS** The controller of Lister Corporation, a retail company, prepared three different schedules of gross margin for the first quarter ended September 30, 1998. These schedules appear below.

	SALES ($10 PER UNIT)	COST OF GOODS SOLD	GROSS MARGIN
Schedule *A*	$270,000	$114,550	$155,450
Schedule *B*	270,000	112,690	157,310
Schedule *C*	270,000	111,250	158,750

The calculation of cost of goods sold in each schedule is based on the following data:

	UNITS	COST PER UNIT	TOTAL COST
Beginning inventory, 7/1	6,000	$4.00	$24,000
Purchase, 7/25	8,000	4.15	33,200
Purchase, 8/15	5,000	4.13	20,650
Purchase, 9/5	7,000	4.35	30,450
Purchase, 9/25	12,000	4.25	51,000

The president of the corporation cannot understand how three different gross margins can be calculated from the same set of data. As controller, you have explained to him that the three schedules are based on three different assumptions concerning the flow of inventory costs: first in, first out; last in, first out; and weighted average. Schedules A, B, and C were not necessarily prepared in this sequence of cost flow assumptions.

REQUIRED   Prepare three separate schedules calculating cost of goods sold and supporting schedules showing the composition of the ending inventory under each of the three cost flow assumptions.

(AICPA, adapted)

P 9-15.   CALCULATING INVENTORY UNDER ALTERNATIVE COST FLOW ASSUMPTIONS   Yale Department Store maintains separate inventory records for each type of merchandise it sells. The inventory records for product type A show the following for the month of September:

	UNITS	UNIT COST	UNIT SELLING PRICE
Beginning inventory, 9/1	200	$3.00	
Purchase, 9/8	150	3.20	
Sale, 9/13	130		$5.00
Purchase, 9/19	50	3.50	
Sale, 9/22	80		5.25
Purchase, 9/26	100	3.55	
Purchase, 9/29	50	3.60	
Sale, 9/30	80		5.50

REQUIRED   **I.**   Assume that Yale uses a periodic inventory system and calculate the cost of ending inventory and the cost of goods sold for September under (a) FIFO, (b) average cost, and (c) LIFO.

2.   Assume that Yale uses a perpetual inventory system and calculate the cost of ending inventory and the cost of goods sold for September under (a) FIFO, (b) average cost, and (c) LIFO.

3.   September was a month of increasing inventory acquisition cost for Yale. Will FIFO or LIFO yield the lower net income under these circumstances? Explain why.

P 9-16.   CALCULATING MANUFACTURING INVENTORY COST   You are engaged in an audit of Perry Manufacturing Company for the year ended December 31, 1998. To reduce the workload at the end of the year, the company took its annual physical inventory under your observation on November 30, 1998. The company's inventory account, which includes raw material and work in process, is on a perpetual basis, and the first in, first out method of pricing is used. There is no finished goods inventory. The company's physical inventory revealed that the book inventory of $60,000 was understated by $2,900. To avoid distorting the interim financial statements, the company decided not to adjust the book inventory until the end of the year except for obsolete inventory items.

Your audit revealed the following information regarding the November 30 inventory:

a)   Pricing tests showed that the physical inventory was overpriced by $1,800.

b)   Footing and extension errors resulted in a $180 understatement of the physical inventory.

c)   Direct labor included in the physical inventory amounted to $10,000. Overhead was included at the rate of 200 percent of direct labor. You determined that the amount of direct labor was correct and the overhead rate was proper.

d) The physical inventory included obsolete materials recorded at $250. During December these obsolete materials were removed from the inventory account by a charge to cost of sales.

Your audit also disclosed the following information about the December 31 inventory:

e) Total debits to certain accounts during December are listed below:

Purchases.	**$24,500**
Direct labor.	**13,000**
Manufacturing expense.	**25,200**
Cost of goods sold.	**68,600**

f) The cost of goods sold of $68,600 included direct labor of $13,800.

g) Normal scrap loss on established product lines is negligible. A special order started and completed during December, however, had excessive scrap loss of $700, which was charged to manufacturing expense.

REQUIRED

1. Calculate the correct amount of the physical inventory at November 30, 1998.

2. Without prejudice to your solution to part 1, assume that the correct amount of the physical inventory at November 30, 1998, was $58,000. Calculate the amount of the inventory at December 31, 1998.

(AICPA, adapted)

P 9-17. **DETERMINING COST OF GOODS SOLD** Wallace Wholesale Company has been growing rapidly, but during this period of rapid growth the accounting records have not been properly maintained. You were recently employed to correct the accounting records and to assist in the preparation of the financial statements for the fiscal year ended February 28, 1998. One of the accounts you have been analyzing is titled "Merchandise." That account, in summary form, follows. Letters following each entry correspond to the lettered explanations and additional information below, which you have accumulated during your analysis.

Merchandise

Balance, 3/1/97	*a*	Merchandise sold		*e*
Purchases	*b*	Consigned merchandise		*f*
Freight in	*c*			
Insurance	*d*			
Freight out on				
consigned merchandise	*g*			
Freight out on				
merchandise sold	*h*			

a) You have satisfied yourself that the March 1, 1997, inventory balance represents the approximate cost of the few units in inventory at the beginning of the year. Wallace uses the FIFO method of accounting for inventories.

b) The merchandise purchased was recorded in the account at the vendors' catalog list price, which is the price that appears on the face of each vendor's invoice. All purchased merchandise is subject to trade (chain) discounts. These discounts have been accounted for as revenue when the merchandise was paid for.

All merchandise purchased was also subject to cash terms of 2%/15, net 30. During the fiscal year Wallace recorded $3,500 in cash discounts as revenue when the merchandise was paid for. Some cash discounts were lost because payment was made after the discount period ended. All purchases of merchandise were paid for in the fiscal year during which they were recorded as purchased.

c) All merchandise is purchased f.o.b. vendors' business locations. The freight in amount is the cost of transporting the merchandise from the vendors' business locations to Wallace.

d) The insurance charge is for an all-perils policy to cover merchandise in transit to Wallace from vendors.

e) The credit to this account for merchandise sold represents the vendors' catalog list price of merchandise sold plus the cost of the beginning inventory; the debit side of the entry was made to the cost of goods sold account.

f) Consigned merchandise represents goods that were shipped to Seitz Company during January 1998, priced at the vendors' catalog list price. The offsetting debit was made to accounts receivable when the merchandise was shipped to Seitz. Wallace does not account for consigned goods and consignment profits separately; it commingles all consignment inventories, costs, expenses, and revenues with those from nonconsigned goods.

On March 5, 1998, Wallace received a payment from Seitz for one-third of the consigned merchandise, the quantity that was sold through February 28, 1998; the payment was recorded as a reduction in accounts receivable. Seitz sold the merchandise at the agreed price, deducted its 16 percent sales commission and 4 percent advertising allowance, and remitted the difference. The remaining two-thirds of the consigned merchandise was unsold and held by Seitz on February 28, 1998.

g) The freight out on consigned goods is the cost of trucking the consigned goods to Seitz from Wallace.

h) Freight out on merchandise sold is the amount paid trucking companies to deliver merchandise sold to Wallace's customers.

REQUIRED   Consider each of the eight lettered items independently and explain specifically how and why each item should have (if correctly accounted for) affected:

1. The amount of cost of goods sold to be included in Wallace's income statement.

2. The amount of any other account to be included in Wallace's February 28, 1998, financial statements.

Organize your answer in the following format:

ITEM	HOW AND WHY THE AMOUNT OF COST OF GOODS SOLD SHOULD HAVE BEEN AFFECTED	HOW AND WHY THE AMOUNT OF ANY OTHER ACCOUNT SHOULD HAVE BEEN AFFECTED

(AICPA, adapted)

P 9-18.   **LIFO VS. FIFO; DOLLAR-VALUE LIFO**   Eller Company is considering a change from the first in, first out (FIFO) method of inventory valuation to the dollar-value last in, first out (LIFO) method for the fiscal year ended May 31, 1998. Eller manufactures two staplers—compact and standard—that would be combined into a single inventory pool if dollar-value LIFO is adopted.

Selected financial data for Eller's two products are presented in the schedule shown below. Pretax income for the 1997–1998 fiscal year would be $420,000 under the FIFO method of inventory valuation. Eller is subject to an income tax rate of 40 percent.

	COMPACT STAPLER			STANDARD STAPLER			
	UNITS	COST PER UNIT	TOTAL COST	UNITS	COST PER UNIT	TOTAL COST	TOTAL INVENTORY
Ending inventory at May 31, 1997 (FIFO)	64,000	$5.00	$ 320,000	36,000	$8.00	$ 288,000	$608,000
1997–1998 fiscal year:							
Production[a]	500,000	5.52	2,760,000	600,000	9.00	5,400,000	
Sales	525,000			583,000			
Ending inventory at May 31, 1998 (FIFO)	40,000	5.52	220,800	52,000	9.00	468,000	688,800

[a]The unit production costs are annual averages.

REQUIRED **I.** Discuss the advantages and disadvantages of a switch from the FIFO method of inventory valuation to the LIFO method.

2. Explain the following terms that are commonly used with the LIFO method of inventory valuation:

a) LIFO pool.

b) Dollar-value method.

c) LIFO increment.

d) LIFO valuation allowance.

3. a) Calculate the ending inventory as of May 31, 1998, for Eller Company using the dollar-value LIFO method of inventory valuation and a single inventory pool.

b) Calculate the effect the change to the dollar-value LIFO inventory method would have on pretax income and on income taxes.

(IMA, adapted)

P 9-19. **DOLLAR-VALUE LIFO** On December 31, 1997, Peters Company adopted the dollar-value LIFO inventory method. The company's inventory records provide the following information:

DATE	YEAR-END-COST	RELEVANT COST INDEX
12/31/97	$300,000	1.00
12/31/98	363,000	1.10
12/31/99	426,000	1.20
12/31/2000	434,000	1.25

REQUIRED What inventory amounts would be reported in the financial statements at December 31, 1997, 1998, 1999, and 2000, using the dollar-value LIFO method?

(AICPA, adapted)

P 9-20. **DOLLAR-VALUE LIFO** Savoy Company began using dollar-value LIFO on January 1, 1998. The following information is available from the company's records and other sources:

DATE	CURRENT COST OF ENDING INVENTORY	PRICE LEVEL IN ACQUISITION MARKET
1/1/98	$12,000	120
12/31/98	15,000	140
12/31/99	17,550	150
12/31/2000	18,744	170

REQUIRED Calculate the ending inventory for Savoy Company for 1998, 1999, and 2000, using the dollar-value LIFO method.

Hint: The cost index for each year, with 1.00 for January 1, 1998, can be obtained by dividing the price level for each year by the price level at January 1, 1998.

P 9-21. **DOLLAR-VALUE LIFO** Nash, Inc., adopted the dollar-value LIFO inventory method on July 31, 1997. Nash's inventory records provide the following information:

DATE	YEAR-END CURRENT COST	RELEVANT COST INDEX
7/31/97	$248,000	1.00
7/31/98	246,000	.95
7/31/99	285,000	1.03
7/31/2000	290,000	1.08
7/31/01	305,000	1.10

REQUIRED Calculate the ending inventory for Nash, Inc., for 1998, 1999, 2000, and 2001, using the dollar-value LIFO method.

P 9-22.

FINANCIAL REPORTING PROBLEM   Use the information available in General Electric's 1995 Annual Report (Appendix B of the textbook).

1. What is GE's consolidated inventories amount for 1995?
2. What amount of change in GE's consolidated inventories occurred from 1994 to 1995?
3. What is GE's inventory turnover for 1995?
4. What inventory valuation procedures are used by GE?
5. What are the general categories included in GE's total inventories?
6. GE's 1995 consolidated inventories are what percentage of total assets?

Inventory Valuation: Departures from Historical Cost and Methods of Estimating Inventory Cost

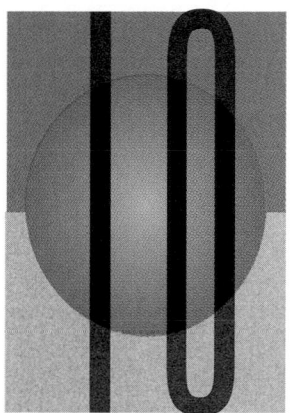

LEARNING OBJECTIVES

After studying this chapter, you should be able to:

1. Explain the rationale for the ceiling and floor constraints on the use of replacement cost as "market" when valuing inventory at the lower of cost or market.

2. Apply the lower-of-cost-or-market procedure to the valuation of inventory.

3. Estimate ending inventory using the gross profit method.

4. Describe the proper treatment of the various complicating factors in the retail inventory method.

5. Use the retail inventory method to estimate ending inventory on an average cost basis, a lower-of-cost-or-market basis, and a LIFO basis.

6. Estimate ending inventory using the dollar-value retail LIFO method.

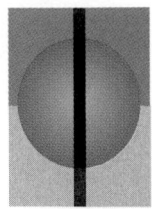

n Chapter 9 we discussed the use of historical cost and cost flow assumptions to value inventory and to determine cost of goods sold. However, departures from the cost basis of inventory valuation may sometimes be appropriate. For example, in their 1995 annual reports, Sherwin Williams, Armstrong, and Amdahl Corporation all report that their inventories are valued at lower of cost or market. Under what conditions should inventory be valued at lower of cost or market? Should changes in inventory value after the acquisition date be recognized before the point of sale? Should inventory valuation be based on the selling price when production rather than sale of the inventory is the critical event? How should inventory be valued when a physical count is not possible, such as when inventory has been destroyed by a flood? Questions like these have led to the development of inventory valuation methods other than historical cost, including techniques for estimating the value of inventory without a physical count. In this chapter we will examine methods of inventory valuation other than historical cost, including methods of estimating inventory costs.

VALUATION OF INVENTORY AT LOWER OF COST OR MARKET

U.S. generally accepted accounting principles require a departure from the historical cost basis of valuing inventory if the value (revenue-producing ability) of inventory falls below its original cost. When physical deterioration, obsolescence, a change in price level, or any other event causes the value of inventory to fall below its cost, a loss should be recognized, and the inventory should be reduced in value on the balance sheet. In these circumstances, inventory is valued at the lower of cost or market (LCM) rather than at historical cost. The reduced utility of the inventory is reported as a loss in the current period. If the amount of damaged, obsolete, or otherwise devalued goods is material, such goods should be segregated from regular inventories on the balance sheet. In its 1995 edition of *Accounting Trends & Techniques* the AICPA reported that "approximately 90 percent of the survey companies use lower of cost or market, an acceptable basis for pricing inventories when circumstances require a departure from cost, to price all or a portion of their inventories."[1] Lower of cost or market is used throughout the world. It is recommended by *International Accounting Standard 2* and is required by the *Fourth Directive* of the European Community.

What is meant by *cost* and *market* when inventory is valued at LCM? **Cost** is the inventory value calculated using one of the historical-cost-based methods discussed in Chapter 9—specific identification, average cost, FIFO, or LIFO. **Market** generally is the replacement cost of the inventory. For a merchandising company, replacement cost is the market price at which the inventory is purchased. For a manufacturing company, replacement cost is the cost to produce inventory, called the reproduction cost.

GAAP limits the "market" that is used to value inventory at LCM to an amount that does not exceed **net realizable value,** which is the estimated selling price in the ordinary course of business minus reasonably predictable costs of completion and disposal. For example, the net realizable value of an inventory item that normally sells for $100 and that costs $5 to deliver to the customer is $95. In effect, net realizable value is a *ceiling* on the amount used as "market." GAAP also requires that "market" *should not be less than* net realizable value reduced by an amount that approximates a normal profit margin on inventory sales. A **normal profit margin** is the amount by which the net realizable value *normally* exceeds

---

[1]*Accounting Trends & Techniques,* 1995, Forty-ninth Edition (New York: AICPA), p. 176.

the cost of inventory. For example, if an inventory item normally sells for $100, with a net realizable value of $95, and normally costs $70, then the normal profit margin is $25. In effect, net realizable value minus a normal profit margin is a *floor* on the amount used as "market."

Rationale for Ceiling and Floor Constraints on "Market"

In the normal course of business, the selling price of inventory will increase as its replacement cost increases. Conversely, the selling price of inventory will decline as the replacement cost declines. This relationship between selling price and replacement cost underlies the use of the LCM procedure for valuing inventory. Accountants accept a decline in replacement cost as evidence of a decline in the sale utility of inventory. However, replacement cost and selling price do not always move together. When they do not, replacement cost should not be used in valuing inventory because it could produce misleading cash flow signals.

The purpose of the ceiling and floor constraints on the use of replacement cost as "market" is to avoid the use of replacement cost when the *normal* gross profit relationship between replacement cost and selling price does not exist. Net realizable value serves as a ceiling, or an upper constraint, on the use of replacement cost as "market," because the utility of inventory is no greater than the cash inflow that can be realized through the sale of that inventory. Bear in mind that inventory is useful only because it can be sold. Therefore, a company would replace inventory at a cost that exceeds net realizable value only under unusual circumstances and only for a limited time. Since replacement cost in excess of net realizable value is not a normal condition, net realizable value serves as an appropriate ceiling on replacement cost as a measure of utility. For example, if the net realizable value of an item of inventory is $60, only under unusual circumstances would a company pay more than $60 to replace that inventory. Therefore, $60 is an appropriate upper limit on "market" as a value for inventory.

We have seen that when the normal relationship between selling price and replacement cost of inventory exists, replacement cost will be below net realizable value by the amount of a normal profit margin. For example, if the normal profit margin is $20 for an item that has a net realizable value of $100, then the normal replacement cost of that item is $80. Any replacement cost that is below net realizable value by more than the normal profit margin would not be a "normal" replacement cost, and therefore is not an appropriate measure of "market" in valuing inventory. Thus, the use of net realizable value minus a normal profit margin is a floor, or lower constraint, on the use of replacement cost as "market" in valuing inventory.

Application of Lower of Cost or Market

Exhibit 10–1 explains how the LCM procedure is applied to inventory. Notice that cost, as calculated by one of the historical-cost-based methods, is compared with "market," which is replacement cost constrained by the ceiling (net realizable value) and the floor (net realizable value minus a normal profit margin). Exhibit 10–2 presents examples of how to determine "market" for use in valuing inventory at LCM. Exhibit 10–2 assumes that net realizable value is $60 and net realizable value minus a normal profit margin is $40.

To illustrate the use of the LCM procedure, consider Johnson Corporation, a manufacturing company. The cost of Johnson's inventory is calculated using the FIFO method. The replacement cost of its inventory is the current production cost; the cost to complete each inventory item at the time inventory is valued includes the costs of minor mechanical adjustments and touch-up painting. The

CONCEPTUAL

Replacement cost should not be used in LCM when misleading cash flow signals might result.

1 Explain the rationale for the ceiling and floor constraints on the use of replacement cost as "market" when valuing inventory at the lower of cost or market.

2 Apply the lower-of-cost-or-market procedure to the valuation of inventory.

EXHIBIT 10–1	The Lower-of-Cost-or-Market Procedure Applied to Inventory

Step 1 Determine the cost of the inventory using one of the historical-cost-based inventory valuation methods (specific identification, average cost, FIFO, or LIFO).

Step 2
(a) Obtain the current replacement cost of the inventory.
(b) Calculate the net realizable value (the ceiling) of the inventory.
(c) Calculate the net realizable value minus a normal profit margin (the floor) of the inventory.

Step 3 Determine the "market" value of the inventory.

General rule: "Market" value = replacement cost (RC).

Exceptions:
(a) If RC > net realizable value (NRV), "market" value = NRV.
(b) If RC < net realizable value (NRV) minus a normal profit margin (NPM), "market" value = (NRV − NPM).

Step 4 Compare cost (from Step 1) with "market" (from Step 3) and use the lower amount as the value of the inventory.

EXHIBIT 10–2	Determining "Market" in Three Hypothetical Cases

Case	Assumed Replacement Cost	Ceiling Limit	Floor Limit	Amount to Be Used as "Market" in Lower of Cost or Market
A	$62	$60	$40	The ceiling ($60) should be used as "market" because replacement cost exceeds the ceiling.
B	55	60	40	Replacement cost should be used as "market" because replacement cost is between the ceiling and floor.
C	38	60	40	The floor ($40) should be used as "market" because replacement cost is below the floor.

normal profit margin used in pricing Johnson's inventory is derived from the relationship between net realizable value and replacement cost for the most recent two-year period. Detailed data about the five items in Johnson's inventory are as follows:

INVENTORY ITEM	COST	CURRENT REPLACEMENT COST	ESTIMATED SELLING PRICE	COST TO COMPLETE	NORMAL PROFIT MARGIN
1	$100	$110	$130	$–0–	$30
2	95	90	125	5	20
3	110	105	128	3	25
4	115	120	120	6	4
5	80	70	100	10	15

The LCM procedure can be applied to individual inventory items, such as a particular model of clock radio, to *groups* of similar inventory items, or to *total* inventory. Suppose the LCM procedure is *applied separately to each item* in Johnson's inventory. Exhibit 10–3 shows how to determine the total inventory value. But suppose that items 1, 2, and 3 are clock radios, and items 4 and 5 are portable TVs. Exhibit 10–4 shows the results of grouping these items. Notice that as the pool of inventory to which LCM is applied is broadened from individual items to groups, and finally to total inventory, the dollar amount that is reported for inventory increases from $489 to $494 to $500. As individual items are combined into groups, amounts for which market is below cost will tend to be offset by amounts for which

---

EXHIBIT 10–3   **The LCM Procedure Applied to Individual Inventory Items**

Johnson Corporation

Inventory Item	Analysis	Inventory Value at Lower of Cost or Market
1	Cost is $100. Market is the $110 replacement cost, because it is less than the ceiling ($130 – $0) and greater than the floor ($130 – $0 – $30).	$100 (cost)
2	Cost is $95. Market is $100, which is net realizable value minus the normal profit margin (floor = $125 – $5 – $20), because replacement cost is below the floor.	95 (cost)
3	Cost is $110. Market is the $105 replacement cost because it is less than the ceiling ($128 – $3) and greater than the floor ($128 – $3 – $25).	105 (market)
4	Cost is $115. Market is the $114 net realizable value (ceiling = $120 – 6), because replacement cost is above the ceiling.	114 (market)
5	Cost is $80. Market is $75, which is net realizable value minus the normal profit margin (floor = $100 – $10 – $15), because replacement cost is below the floor.	75 (market)
Total		$489

EXHIBIT 10–4   **The LCM Procedure Applied to Individual Items, Groups of Items, and Total Inventory**

Johnson Corporation

Inventory Item	Cost	Market	Lower of Cost or Market Applied to: Individual Items	Groups of Items	Total Inventory
1	$100	$110	$100		
2	95	100	95		
3	110	105	105		
	$305	$315		$305	
4	$115	$114	114		
5	80	75	75		
	$195	$189		189	
Total	$500	$504	$489	$494	$500

market is above cost, reducing the LCM effect and increasing the dollar amount of inventory.

In practice, the LCM procedure is commonly applied to individual items. As a general rule, LCM must be used on an item-by-item basis for income tax purposes. However the procedure is applied, it should be applied consistently over time.

The Conservative Effect of Lower of Cost or Market

CONCEPTUAL

When inventory is valued at market, the new inventory value becomes the cost used in the next period's LCM test.

The LCM procedure provides an excellent example of the influence of conservatism on GAAP. In this procedure, if market is below cost, the value of inventory is reduced to market, and the new, lower inventory value is considered the cost in future comparisons of cost and market. Furthermore, any recovery in the value of inventory previously reduced to market is ignored. These practices bias the LCM procedure toward the reporting of lower inventory values on the balance sheet. The LCM procedure also has a conservative effect on the income statement of the period in which inventory value is reduced to market, because the reduction in value requires a loss to be reported. When the inventory is sold in a subsequent period, however, income will be higher, because the reduced inventory values are then included in cost of goods sold.

Recording the Reduction of Inventory to "Market"

Special accounting and reporting issues arise when the LCM procedure is used and the "market" value of inventory falls below cost. When this occurs, the inventory value that is included in current assets must be reduced to "market," and the loss of inventory value must be included in the income statement for the period. There are several ways to record and report this reduction of inventory value and the corresponding inventory holding loss.

On the balance sheet, reduction of inventory value from cost to a lower market value can be recorded by (1) directly reducing the inventory account by the amount that market is below cost or (2) indirectly reducing reported inventory through the use of a contra inventory allowance account that is equal to the amount by which market is below cost. In the balance sheet, this inventory allowance account would be subtracted from inventory valued at cost to obtain inventory valued at market. When a contra account is used, it is necessary at the beginning of each new accounting period to adjust the allowance account balance to zero and to make a corresponding reduction in the beginning inventory balance so that beginning inventory will not be overstated.

When market value falls below cost, the income statement effect of the loss of inventory value can be recorded by (1) directly increasing (debiting) cost of goods sold for the period or (2) debiting a separate inventory holding loss account. The weakness of directly increasing cost of goods sold—and the strength of using a separate inventory holding loss account—is that the loss of inventory value was not caused by the sale of inventory items, but by the *holding* of inventory during a period when its value declined. Hence, including the amount by which market value has fallen below cost in reported cost of goods sold for the period is conceptually unsound. Furthermore, when a holding loss is included in cost of goods sold, cost of goods sold is overstated and financial statement users cannot determine the amount of the holding loss. On the other hand, when a separate inventory holding loss is reported in the income statement as a component of operating income, the amount of loss is easily determined.

Conceptually, *the best entry for recording the reduction of inventory from cost to an LCM value is to (1) directly reduce the inventory account with a credit and (2) debit an inventory holding loss account by the amount that the LCM value falls below cost.* For example, based on the individual-item analysis in Exhibit 10–4, in which LCM is

$489 and cost is $500, the journal entry to reduce inventory from cost to LCM would be:

Inventory holding loss	11	
Inventory		11

A typical footnote related to inventories for a company that uses LCM appears in the 1995 annual report of Armstrong:

INVENTORIES

Inventories were $30.9 million higher at the end of 1995. The higher inventory levels were primarily due to increasing inventory levels for insulation products in order to ensure customer service while starting up new production facilities at Mebane, North Carolina, and the softening of sales in the floor industry segment. The translation of foreign currency inventories to U.S. dollars at higher exchange rates increased inventories by $3.1 million.

Approximately 51% in 1995 and 49% in 1994 of the company's total inventory was valued on a LIFO (last-in, first-out) basis. Such inventory values were lower than would have been reported on a total FIFO (first-in, first-out) basis, by $62.4 million at the end of 1995 and $55.5 million at year-end 1994.

INVENTORIES (MILLIONS)	1995	1994
Finished goods	$119.9	$103.1
Goods in process	24.0	22.9
Raw materials and supplies	51.6	38.6
Total	$195.5	$164.6

Inventories are valued at the lower of cost or market. Approximately 90 percent of 1995's domestic inventories are valued using the LIFO method. Other inventories are generally determined on a FIFO method.

Valuation of Firm Purchase Commitments at LCM

A business sometimes will enter into a contract to purchase inventory items at a fixed price by a specified date, to ensure a supply of the goods or protect against future price increases. Some purchase contracts can be revised or canceled under particular conditions; others cannot be changed, and are noncancelable. Non-cancelable purchase commitments, as well as other purchase commitments under which performance is probable because of large disincentives for nonperformance, are called **firm purchase commitments.**

GAAP requires that goods contracted for under a firm purchase commitment be accounted for by LCM, just as if they were already in inventory.[2] A buyer who enters into and executes a firm purchase commitment within a single fiscal year need make no entry until the contract is executed. For example, suppose that on April 30 Anderson Company, whose fiscal year ends on December 31, signs a firm purchase commitment to buy goods from Gillard Company for $20,000 by September 15 of the same year. If the open market price of the goods at the purchase date (i.e., September 15) is equal to or greater than the $20,000 contract price, Anderson simply records the purchase at the contract price:

Inventory (or purchases)	20,000	
Accounts payable (or cash)		20,000

---

[2]"Restatement and Revision of Accounting Research Bulletins Nos. 1–42," *Accounting Research Bulletin No. 43* (New York: AICPA, 1953), chap. 4, statements 5 and 10.

However, if the open market price on the date the contract is executed (September 15) is below the contract price—for example, $18,000—Anderson must record the purchase at the lower market price, and show a loss on the purchase:

Inventory (or purchases)	18,000	
Loss on purchase commitment	2,000	
Accounts payable (or cash)		20,000

If the purchase contract period extends beyond the end of the buyer's fiscal year, accounting for a firm purchase commitment is somewhat more complicated. First, if the contract is for a material dollar amount, the terms and the amount of the contract should be disclosed, usually in a footnote, in the buyer's financial statements. Moreover, if the fiscal year-end market price is below the contract price, and the price decline appears to be a reasonable estimate of a probable loss at the time the purchase actually will occur, then a loss on the purchase commitment should be recorded in the period of the price decline. For example, if a $20,000 purchase commitment made by Anderson extends into February of the next fiscal year and the market price of the contracted goods is $17,000 at the end of Anderson's fiscal year, Anderson would make the following adjusting entry at the end of the year:

Estimated loss on purchase commitment	3,000	
Estimated liability on purchase commitment		3,000

The liability account in this entry would be included in Anderson's current liabilities if the purchase commitment is to be executed within the longer of the next fiscal year or the next operating cycle. In the period in which the purchase is made, the liability account would be debited to the extent of its credit balance. The estimated loss on purchase commitment account would be closed to Anderson's income summary, and would appear in Anderson's income statement as a component of operating income.

When Anderson executes the purchase commitment in February, several possibilities exist with respect to the relationship between the open market price and the contract price of the goods:

I. The market price remains exactly $3,000 below the contract price.

2. The market price is more than $3,000 below the contract price.

3. The market price is less than $3,000 below the contract price.

4. The market price is equal to or above the contract price.

If the market price remains exactly $3,000 below the contract price, Anderson would make the following entry at the time of purchase to record the purchase at the lower market price:

Inventory (or purchases)	17,000	
Estimated liability on purchase commitment	3,000	
Accounts payable (or cash)		20,000

If the market price at the time of purchase is more than $3,000 below the contract price, Anderson would need to recognize an additional loss in the period of the purchase to record the purchase at the lower market price. For example, assume that the open market price is $5,000 below the contract price when the contract is executed. The following entry would be made:

Inventory (or purchases)	15,000	
Estimated liability on purchase commitment	3,000	
Loss on purchase commitment	2,000	
Accounts payable (or cash)		20,000

If, however, the open market price has recovered, and is now less than $3,000 below the contract price, equal to the contract price, or above the contract price,

Anderson should ignore the market price recovery and record the purchase at the $17,000 market price that existed when the loss was recognized at year-end. In this case, Anderson would make the same purchase entry as if the market price had remained $3,000 below the contract price, namely:

Inventory (or purchases)........................	17,000	
Estimated liability on purchase commitment..........	3,000	
Accounts payable (or cash)		20,000

In short, recovery of the market price of the goods is ignored when accounting for a firm purchase commitment, just as it is when the LCM rule is applied to inventories on hand. This procedure for handling improvement in the market price–contract price relationship when a firm purchase commitment exists has the same theoretical deficiency as does the application of LCM to inventory on hand. That is, the increased utility of the contract owing to the market price improvement is not reported in the period of the increase, but instead is reported indirectly in the gross margin related to future sales at the time the undervalued inventory passes through cost of goods sold.

A business that is the buyer in a firm purchase commitment may hedge against the possibility of market price movements for goods under contract. Hedging can be accomplished through a futures contract in which the buyer in a firm purchase commitment simultaneously agrees to a future sale of the same quantity of similar, perhaps identical, goods at a fixed price. When the market price of the goods changes, a company that holds a sell position in a futures contract and a buy position in a corresponding purchase commitment will be better off under one contract by approximately the same amount by which it is worse off under the other contract. For example, if the market price of the goods drops, the buyer may suffer from having signed the purchase commitment, but will also benefit from the fixed selling price in the futures contract. (If the goods specified in the two contracts are not identical, some difference in the value of the two contracts may develop, but it should be small.)

The widespread use of hedging arrangements resulted in the issuance of *FASB Statement No. 80*. The general principle set forth in *Statement No. 80* is that a change in the market value of a futures contract should be recognized in income in the period in which the change occurs. However, when a futures contract exists as a hedge against a firm purchase commitment, changes in the market value of the futures contract should be recognized in income when the effects of related changes in the market prices of the hedged items are recognized.

OTHER ALTERNATIVES TO HISTORICAL COST INVENTORY VALUATION

There are circumstances when measures of inventory value other than historical cost may be used. In the following sections, three alternatives to historical cost—replacement cost, net realizable value, and standard costs—are discussed.

Replacement Cost

Some accountants believe that the current value of inventory, as measured by replacement cost, is more useful than historical cost as a measure of inventory utility. Those accountants would report the replacement cost of inventory in the balance sheet whether it is above or below historical cost. In those situations in which the net realizable value of inventory is more clearly determinable than the replacement cost, however, they would report inventory at net realizable value.

A major argument for valuing inventory at replacement cost is that if replacement cost measures the utility of inventory when it is below historical cost (the LCM argument), then it is also a valid measure of utility when it is above historical cost. This argument is very persuasive—unless the LCM use of replacement cost is justified on the basis of conservatism, rather than as an effort to report information about future cash flows.

If replacement cost were used as the primary basis of inventory valuation, a gain or loss on holding inventory would be reported in each accounting period in which replacement cost was above or below that of the previous period. Valuation of inventory at replacement cost would result in the reporting of inventory gains and losses in the income statement before the period in which the inventory was sold. Under current GAAP, revenue is reported at the time inventory is sold, except for the holding losses that arise under LCM. If inventory were valued at replacement cost, both changes in replacement cost *and* the sale of inventory would justify the recognition of revenue.

Currently, U.S. GAAP limits the use of replacement cost in the financial statements to inventory items that have suffered a reduction in value below historical cost (i.e., the LCM procedure). The use of replacement costs that are higher than historical cost to report inventory values in the financial statements is not a generally accepted accounting principle. However, replacement costs may be reported as supplementary data to the financial statements, whether they are below or above historical costs.[3]

Internationally, the Dutch are noted proponents of replacement cost accounting. While most Dutch companies use historical cost accounting, several large ones use replacement cost for valuing tangible assets, including inventories. Dutch companies do not report inventory holding gains as income. Instead, they credit holding gains directly to stockholders' equity when the inventory is sold.

Net Realizable Value

Net realizable value is another alternative to historical cost inventory values. As we saw earlier, net realizable value serves as the upper limit, or ceiling, on market in the LCM procedure. Therefore, net realizable value is used to value inventory under LCM whenever replacement cost is below historical cost but above net realizable value.

Under GAAP, inventory may also be valued at net realizable value when two special conditions exist: (1) Inventory has a known and reasonably certain selling price and (2) any costs of completing and selling the inventory are known or are not material. In Chapter 2 we stated that revenue should be recognized when the amount and timing of revenue to be received and the costs to be incurred are reasonably determinable, and when the earnings process is virtually complete. Therefore, when the inventory selling price is known and reasonably certain, and the costs of completing and selling the inventory are known or are not material, revenue may be recognized before the point of sale, and inventory may be reported at net realizable value.

The most common types of inventory that meet the conditions for revenue recognition before sale—and therefore for valuation at net realizable value—are (1) inventories of precious metals and minerals, some agricultural goods, and some other readily marketable items and (2) inventories associated with long-term construction contracts accounted for by the percentage-of-completion method. For these types of inventory, the essential conditions are that (1) the selling price is reasonably certain because of ready marketability at an established price (as in the case of wheat) or because of contractual agreement (as in a long-term construction contract) and (2) the costs of completion and disposal are reasonably predictable

---

[3]"Financial Reporting and Changing Prices," *Statement of Financial Accounting Standards No. 89* (Stamford, Conn.: FASB, 1986).

(as in some long-term construction contracts) or are not material (as they are once a bushel of wheat has been harvested). These conditions were discussed and illustrated in Chapter 7.

Standard Costs

A third alternative to historical cost valuation is standard costs. Many manufacturing companies use a standard cost system in which the unit costs for material, labor, and manufacturing overhead are predetermined. Standard costs usually are based on the cost of material, labor, and overhead per unit of product when a plant is operating at normal capacity. Standard costs provide management with an ideal or a goal against which to compare actual costs. By recording and analyzing variances from standard costs, management can obtain information that is helpful in controlling and managing inventory costs.

Standard costs can be used under GAAP for external reporting purposes, provided that they are adjusted at reasonable intervals to reflect current conditions, so that at the balance sheet date they reasonably approximate costs determined under one of the cost bases discussed in Chapter 9—namely, specific identification, average cost, FIFO, and LIFO.

METHODS OF ESTIMATING INVENTORY COSTS

In the preceding sections and in Chapter 9 we discussed the valuation of inventory when a physical count of inventory is taken. Sometimes the dollar amount of ending inventory must be *estimated,* however, because making a physical count is either impractical or impossible. For example, the determination of an inventory figure for interim financial statements normally does not justify the cost and inconvenience of a physical count. Or a corporate executive might want an estimate of ending inventory to use in verifying an inventory figure developed through normal inventory procedures. Occasionally, the dollar amount of ending inventory must be estimated because inventory and the inventory records have been lost, stolen, or destroyed by fire or some other catastrophe. The remainder of this chapter is devoted to two methods of estimating the dollar amount of inventory—the gross profit method and the retail inventory method.

The Gross Profit Method

The **gross profit method** of estimating inventory costs, sometimes called the **gross margin method,** uses the gross profit percentage to convert goods sold during the period from a selling price to a cost basis. The resulting cost of goods sold amount is then subtracted from the cost of goods available for sale to yield an estimate of the cost of goods remaining in inventory.

The gross profit method must be based on a reasonable estimate of the relationship between gross profit and selling price. This estimate may be obtained by analyzing the historical relationship between the gross profit and the selling price of the inventory in question. Once an estimate of gross profit as a percentage of sales has been obtained, the dollar amount of estimated gross profit may be calculated as follows:

$$\text{Estimated gross profit percentage} \times \text{Selling price in dollars} = \text{Estimated gross profit in dollars}$$

The estimated dollar amount of gross profit can then be subtracted from the dollar amount of sales to yield an estimate of the dollar amount of cost of goods sold. Finally, under the assumption that all goods available for sale are either sold or in

3 Estimate ending inventory using the gross profit method.

inventory, the estimated cost of goods sold can be subtracted from the cost of goods available for sale to yield an estimate of the cost of inventory. The cost of goods available for sale, of course, can be determined from beginning inventory and the purchase records for the accounting period.

To illustrate, assume that the following current-year data are available for Murry Company:

Beginning inventory (at historical cost). **$12,000**
Net purchases. **68,000**
Net sales (retail prices) **90,000**
Estimated gross profit as a percentage of net sales
  (derived from past accounting records). **30%**

Under the gross profit method, Murry's ending inventory for the current year would be estimated as follows:

Step 1: Estimated gross profit = 30% × $90,000 = $27,000.

Step 2: Estimated cost of goods sold = $90,000 − $27,000 = $63,000.

Step 3: Goods available for sale = $12,000 + $68,000 = $80,000.

Step 4: Estimated ending inventory = Goods available for sale − Estimated cost of goods sold.

  Estimated ending inventory = $80,000 − $63,000 = $17,000.

As you can see, the gross profit method employs simple calculations. It does, however, require an estimate of gross profit as a percentage of sales. Since companies typically maintain records of their gross profit as a percentage of sales, the required data usually are readily available. Occasionally, however, companies calculate gross profit as a *percentage of cost,* in which case gross profit must be restated as a percentage of sales before the gross profit method can be used.

Assume that gross profit has been calculated as a percentage of cost rather than a percentage of sales. If gross profit is 25 percent of cost, that means in effect that the selling price equals cost plus 25 percent of cost. If we recall the relationship in column A below, and choose arbitrary numerical values for each element of the relationship, as in column B, we can ascertain the relationship between gross profit and sales.

COLUMN A	COLUMN B[a]
Sales	5
− Cost of goods sold	−4
= Gross profit	1

[a]Values are chosen arbitrarily; that is, any values can be used such that gross profit is 25 percent of cost of goods sold.

Because we knew that gross profit is 25 percent, or one-fourth, of cost, we chose the values 1 and 4 in column B for gross profit and cost of goods sold, respectively. So the column A relationship would hold, we assigned the value to sales in column B. We can now inspect the numbers in column B and conclude that gross profit is one-fifth, or 20 percent, of sales. This sort of analysis can be used to derive gross profit as a percentage of sales whenever it is available only as a percentage of cost.[4]

The primary weakness of the gross profit method is that the gross profit percentage is based on *past* relationships between gross profit and selling price or gross profit and cost. If past relationships between selling price and cost differ from present relationships, then the gross profit method will not provide good estimates.

CONCEPTUAL

The primary weakness of the gross profit method is that it is based on *past* relationships.

---

[4]Alternatively, the following formula could be used to arrive at gross profit as a percentage of sales, given gross profit as a percentage of cost:

$$\text{Gross profit as percentage of sales} = \frac{\text{Gross profit as percentage of cost}}{1.00 + \text{Gross profit as percentage of cost}}$$

Because the gross profit method is so dependent on the gross profit percentage, the percentage must be adjusted when the relationship between gross profit and sales changes. In addition, the gross profit method must be applied separately to different types of inventory that bear different relationships between cost and selling price. Finally, the gross profit percentage depends on the cost flow assumption that was used and the inventory conditions that existed during the period over which the percentage was calculated. Data for periods in which inventory cost flow assumptions differed from those of the current period, or for periods in which special circumstances existed, such as the liquidation of a LIFO layer or the use of market values, should *not* be used in calculating the current gross profit percentage.

In most cases, the gross profit method is a comparatively inaccurate method of estimating inventory cost because the gross profit percentage used in the method typically is an *average* figure for several prior years. The gross profit method therefore should be relied on to estimate ending inventory only as a last resort. For example, it may provide a reasonable estimate of inventory when an inventory has been destroyed or when the retail inventory method—the subject of the next section—cannot be used.

The Retail Inventory Method

Like the gross profit method, the **retail inventory method** is used to estimate the dollar amount of ending inventory. Compared with the gross profit method, however, the retail inventory method is capable of providing more accurate estimates. The retail method is acceptable for external reporting purposes if it yields results that reasonably approximate results that would be obtained using one of the cost flow methods described in Chapter 9.

While the gross profit method relies on *past* relationships between cost and selling price, the retail inventory method uses the *current* relationship between cost and selling price. As a result, the retail inventory method is used in circumstances that invite the use of the gross profit method. It is also widely used by retail stores on a daily basis, with at least annual confirmation of the inventory amount by a physical count valued at retail. The method is particularly appealing to retailers with high-volume, low-unit-cost inventories, such as hardware and clothing stores.

In its simplest form, the retail inventory method requires the following data: (1) beginning inventory, expressed in both cost and retail selling prices, (2) the current period's purchases, expressed in both cost and retail prices, and (3) the retail sales for the period. Current purchases are first added to beginning inventory to calculate total goods available for sale, at both cost and retail selling prices. Cost and retail prices are then compared, and a cost-to-retail percentage is calculated by dividing cost by selling price. Next, sales for the period, expressed in retail selling prices, are subtracted from goods available for sale, also expressed in retail selling prices, to obtain ending inventory expressed in retail selling prices. Finally, ending inventory is multiplied by the cost-to-retail percentage to obtain an estimate of the cost of ending inventory.

Assume the following data for year 2 for Edison Corporation:

	COST	RETAIL
Beginning inventory	$ 6,000	$ 8,000
Purchases	40,000	45,000
Sales		47,000

Using the retail inventory method, ending inventory for year 2 is estimated as shown in Exhibit 10–5.

The retail inventory method is most effective when there is a consistent relationship between the cost and retail selling price of inventory items. Therefore, the

CONCEPTUAL

The gross profit method relies on *past* cost to selling price relationships. The retail inventory method uses the *current* cost to retail relationship.

EXHIBIT 10 – 5   **Estimation of Ending Inventory, Retail Inventory Method**

Edison Corporation

	Cost	Retail
Beginning inventory	$ 6,000	$ 8,000
Purchases	40,000	45,000
Goods available for sale	$46,000	$53,000

Cost-to-retail percentage: $\dfrac{\$46,000}{\$53,000} = 86.8\%$

Less: Sales		(47,000)
Estimated ending inventory at retail		$ 6,000
Estimated ending inventory at cost ($6,000 × 86.8%) . . .	$ 5,208	

retail inventory method is particularly appropriate in cases in which a consistent markup over acquisition cost is used to establish retail prices. To increase the effectiveness of the retail inventory method, a separate cost-to-retail percentage should be calculated for each group or type of goods for which there is a relatively uniform markup over cost. For example, if a store that uses the retail inventory method sells both tobacco products and toiletry items, and the markup on tobacco products is different from the markup on toiletry items, one cost-to-retail percentage should be calculated for tobacco products and another for toiletry items.

The retail inventory method of estimating inventory has several advantages. It can be used to estimate ending inventory when a physical count is not practical or not possible. It can be used when inventory has been lost, stolen, or destroyed, and thus it is used often to generate inventory data for insurance purposes. The retail inventory method also quickly provides comparatively accurate figures on inventory and cost of goods sold for use in interim financial statements. When used daily, the method simplifies bookkeeping and expedites confirmation of physical inventory counts. Because the store maintains records of inventory, purchases, and sales expressed in terms of retail selling prices, when a physical count is made, units are simply recorded at retail. There is no need to refer to records of cost.

Retail Inventory Method Terminology

So far in our discussion of the retail method we have assumed that inventory is purchased and assigned a retail selling price that remains constant until the inventory is sold. In reality, the selling prices of goods often change, rising with increases in cost or demand and falling with decreases in demand and sometimes with decreases in cost. Special terminology is used to describe such changes in retail selling price. If the retail inventory method is to be applied correctly, this terminology must be understood.

When a retail merchant acquires inventory, the sum of all the expenditures required to get it into condition and location for sale is known as its **original cost.** Each inventory item is then assigned an initial or **original selling price.** The difference between the original selling price and the original cost of goods is called the **original markup.** If the selling price of an item is raised above the original selling price, the increase is called an additional markup, or simply a markup. (In this book, we refer to an increase in selling price above the original selling price as a **markup.**) If the selling price of an item is reduced to an amount below the original selling price, the difference between the original selling price and the new, lower selling price is called a **markdown.** Over the course of a season a selling price might be raised and lowered many times. If a selling price that was previously raised above the original selling price is subsequently lowered, the amount by which it is lowered is called a **markup cancellation** until the price has been reduced to the level of the original selling price. Any further lowering of the selling price results in a markdown. If a selling price that was previously reduced below the original selling price (i.e., a markdown) is subsequently increased, the amount by which it is increased is called a **markdown cancellation** until the price has been increased to the level of the original selling price. Any further increases of the selling price result in markups. Markups less markup cancellations are called **net markups;** markdowns less markdown cancellations are called **net markdowns.** Exhibit 10–6 illustrates retail inventory method terminology.

Complicating Factors in the Retail Inventory Method

Markups, markup cancellations, markdowns, and markdown cancellations add to the complexity of the retail inventory method. Several other factors, such as freight in and purchase returns and allowances, also complicate the calculations. Note that the format used to calculate Edison's retail inventory cost in Exhibit 10–5 includes two columns—the *cost column* and the *retail column*. We will refer to those columns in describing the proper treatment of several factors that complicate the retail inventory method.

Freight in is part of the cost of inventory purchases and should therefore appear only in the cost column of retail inventory calculations, as an addition to purchases. The retail column is not adjusted for freight in because normal management practice is to establish an initial retail price that will cover incidental costs such as freight in. Likewise, *purchase allowances* should be deducted from purchases in the cost column, but not from the retail column. Factors that normally lead to purchase allowances, such as damage, are taken into consideration when the initial retail price is established. However, *purchase returns* should be deducted from purchases in *both* the cost column and the retail column because returned goods reduce both the total cost and the total selling price of purchased goods. If purchases are recorded at gross amounts, *purchase discounts taken* should be deducted from purchases in the cost column.

4 Describe the proper treatment of the various complicating factors in the retail inventory method.

EXHIBIT 10–6   **Terminology Applied to Price Changes in the Retail Inventory Method**

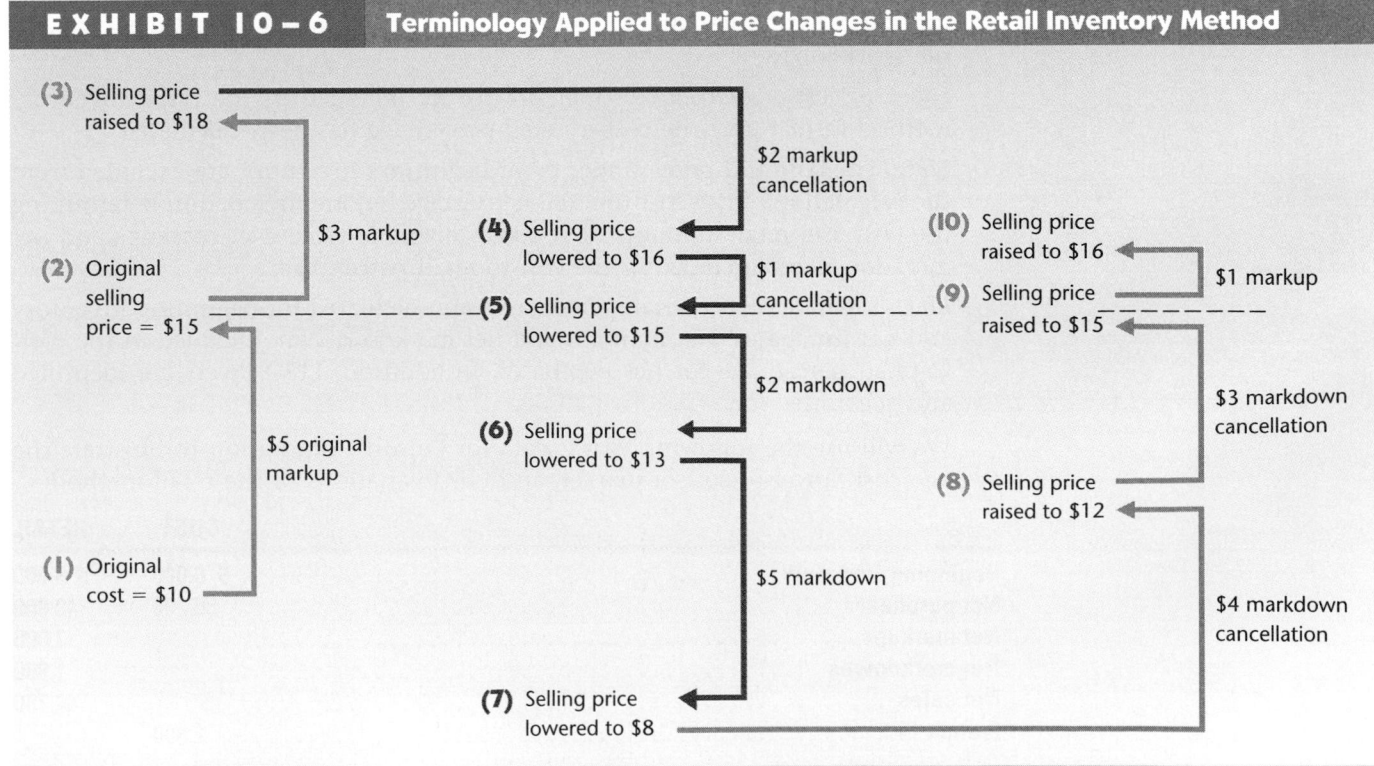

To illustrate the adjustment of purchases, assume that Edison Corporation's purchase allowances totaled $1,000. Purchase returns had a cost of $900 and a retail price of $1,200. Purchases were recorded gross, with purchase discounts of $2,900. Given these amounts, the adjusted (net) cost and retail purchases would be: $40,000 − $1,000 − $900 − $2,900 = $35,200 cost; $45,000 − $1,200 = $43,800 retail.

Sales returns and *sales allowances* should be deducted from sales in the retail column if sales are recorded on a gross basis. When sales to employees are recorded net of (after subtracting) employee discounts, *employee discounts* should be added to sales in the retail column. This treatment is necessary to obtain a total sales figure for the current period. To illustrate the adjustment of sales, assume that Edison Corporation records sales on a gross basis. Sales returns and allowances are $2,800, and employee discounts total $500. Edison's adjusted (net) sales amount would be $44,700 ($47,000 − $2,800 + $500).

Normal spoilage, such as normal breakage during handling or deterioration in the quality of items such as fresh vegetables, should be deducted from goods available in the retail column *after* the cost-to-retail percentage has been calculated. This treatment is appropriate because though spoiled goods are not available to be sold, the cost of *normal* spoilage is relevant to the establishment of the normal cost-to-retail percentage. *Abnormal spoilage* should be deducted from both the cost and retail columns *before* the normal cost-to-retail percentage is calculated because the goods are not available for sale and the cost of such goods is not relevant to the normal cost-to-retail percentage.

Variations of the Retail Inventory Method

So far we have discussed the retail inventory method in its most fundamental form. In practice, it can become considerably more complex. Several variations of the retail inventory method exist, including the average cost, lower of cost or market, FIFO, and LIFO versions. Basically, each variation differs from the others with respect to the components that are included in the calculation of the cost-to-retail percentage, as follows:

Average cost: The cost-to-retail percentage includes the cost and retail amounts for both beginning inventory and net purchases, adjusted for net markups and net markdowns.

Lower of cost or market: Net markdowns are included in the retail inventory method format *after* the cost-to-retail percentage has been calculated.

FIFO: The cost and retail amounts for beginning inventory are excluded from the calculation of the cost-to-retail percentage but are included in determining the cost and retail amounts of goods available for sale. Net markups and net markdowns are included in the cost-to-retail percentage.

LIFO: Separate cost-to-retail percentages are calculated for beginning inventory and net purchases. Net markups and net markdowns are included in the cost-to-retail percentage for net purchases. In addition, LIFO layers are identified and accounted for.

We will use the following year 2 data for Edison Corporation to illustrate the average cost, lower-of-cost-or-market, and LIFO variations of the retail method:

	COST	RETAIL
Beginning inventory	$ 6,000	$ 8,000
Net purchases	35,200	43,800
Net markups		3,000
Net markdowns		1,800
Net sales		44,700
Freight in	2,000	

Note that purchases and sales are *net* amounts, after adjustment for purchase returns, purchase allowances, purchase discounts, sales returns and allowances, and employee sales discounts. These amounts were obtained earlier, in the section on complicating factors (see pages 545–546).

Average Cost Ending Inventory Recall that when ending inventory is estimated under the average cost variation of the retail inventory method, the cost-to-retail percentage includes the cost and retail amounts for both beginning inventory and net purchases, adjusted for net markups and net markdowns. The average cost variation is the most straightforward use of the retail method, and is therefore a good starting point for developing an understanding of the retail method. An average cost basis for estimating Edison's year 2 ending inventory is illustrated in Exhibit 10–7.

Careful examination of the format of Exhibit 10–7 reveals why this particular variation of the retail inventory method provides an estimate of ending inventory at average cost. Beginning inventory and net purchases are combined, and net markups and net markdowns are applied to *all* goods available for sale. As a result, the cost-to-retail percentage is an average percentage, weighted by the dollar value of goods in beginning inventory and net purchases adjusted for overall retail price changes. This "average" cost-to-retail percentage is applied to the retail ending inventory to yield ending inventory at average cost.

Lower-of-Cost-or-Market Ending Inventory When net markdowns are not included in the retail inventory method until *after* the cost-to-retail percentage has been calculated, the method yields an estimate of ending inventory on a lower-of-cost-or-market basis. Use of a lower-of-cost-or-market basis to estimate Edison's year 2 ending inventory is shown in Exhibit 10–8. Notice that the estimated ending inventory in this exhibit, $6,540, is less than the estimated ending inventory that was calculated on an average cost basis, $6,765 (see Exhibit 10–7). This relationship will hold whenever net markdowns exist. By excluding net markdowns from the cost-to-retail percentage, the lower-of-cost-or-market variation yields a lower cost-to-retail percentage. If there are no net markdowns, the lower-of-cost-or-market variation will yield the same results as the average cost variation.

The lower-of-cost-or-market variation is used widely, and is commonly known as the **conventional retail inventory method.** In most cases it only *approximates* the lower-of-cost-or-market valuation of inventory. However, since it yields a lower ending inventory figure than the average cost method only when net

5 Use the retail inventory method to estimate ending inventory on an average cost basis, a lower-of-cost-or-market basis, and a LIFO basis.

EXHIBIT 10–7	**The Retail Inventory Method, Average Cost Basis**

Edison Corporation

	Cost	Retail
Beginning inventory	$ 6,000	$ 8,000
Net purchases	35,200	43,800
Freight in	2,000	
Net markups		3,000
Net markdowns		(1,800)
Goods available for sale	$43,200	$53,000

Cost-to-retail percentage: $\dfrac{\$43,200}{\$53,000} = 81.5\%$

Net sales		(44,700)
Estimated ending inventory at retail		$ 8,300
Estimated ending inventory at average cost ($8,300 × 81.5%)	$ 6,765	

EXHIBIT 10–8	The Retail Inventory Method, Lower-of-Cost-or-Market Basis ("Conventional Retail Method")	

Edison Corporation

	Cost	Retail
Beginning inventory	$ 6,000	$ 8,000
Net purchases	35,200	43,800
Freight in	2,000	
Net markups		3,000
	$43,200	$54,800

Cost-to-retail percentage: $\dfrac{\$43,200}{\$54,800} = 78.8\%$

	Cost	Retail
Net markdowns		(1,800)
Goods available for sale	$43,200	$53,000
Net sales		(44,700)
Estimated ending inventory at retail		$ 8,300
Estimated ending inventory at lower of cost or market ($8,300 × 78.8%)	$ 6,540	

markdowns exist, net markdowns obviously are responsible for a lower inventory figure in this method. As was noted earlier, reductions in retail selling price (i.e., markdowns) are evidence of a loss of utility. Therefore, a net markdown of a selling price implies that the utility of the merchandise has fallen below its acquisition cost. Thus, the merchandise should be reported at a figure below cost. As can be seen by comparing the estimate of ending inventory in Exhibit 10–8 with the estimate in Exhibit 10–7, the lower-of-cost-or-market variation does report inventory at less than cost when net markdowns exist.

LIFO Cost Ending Inventory   To estimate the cost of ending inventory under the LIFO cost flow assumption, separate cost-to-retail percentages must be calculated for beginning inventory and net purchases. Net markups and net markdowns are included in the cost-to-retail percentage for net purchases. In addition, LIFO layers must be identified and accounted for. Exhibit 10–9 shows how to generate an estimate of Edison Corporation's year 2 ending inventory on a LIFO cost basis.

Notice that the ending inventory in Exhibit 10–9 consists of two layers, the beginning inventory ($6,000 cost, $8,000 retail) and the new layer ($248 cost, $300 retail) from the current year's purchases. If the retail amount of ending inventory had been less than the retail amount of beginning inventory, only the 75 percent cost-to-retail percentage would have been used to calculate the cost of ending inventory. It would not have been necessary to calculate a cost-to-retail percentage for the current year's net purchases because none of those purchases would be included in ending inventory. As the number of years of LIFO use increases, beginning inventory for each year will consist of more layers from prior years' additions to inventory. The normal LIFO cost flow assumption would apply to the liquidation of any layers included in beginning inventory each year.

The Dollar-Value Retail LIFO Method

In illustrating the retail LIFO method (Exhibit 10–9), we assumed the *same* retail price level for (1) beginning inventory, (2) net purchases for the period, and (3) ending inventory. That is, in Exhibit 10–9 we assumed that the selling prices associated with (1) the $8,000 retail beginning inventory, (2) the $43,800 net purchases (adjusted for net markups and net markdowns), and (3) the $8,300 retail

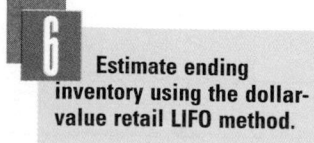

6 Estimate ending inventory using the dollar-value retail LIFO method.

EXHIBIT 10-9	The Retail Inventory Method, LIFO Cost Flow Basis		

Edison Corporation

		Cost	Retail
Beginning inventory		$ 6,000	$ 8,000
Cost-to-retail percentage, beginning inventory:			
$\frac{\$6,000}{\$8,000} = 75\%$			
Net purchases		$35,200	$43,800
Freight in		2,000	
Net markups			3,000
Net markdowns			(1,800)
		37,200	45,000
Cost-to-retail percentage, excluding beginning inventory:			
$\frac{\$37,200}{\$45,000} = 82.7\%$			
Goods available for sale		$43,200	$53,000
Net sales			(44,700)
Estimated ending inventory at retail			$ 8,300
Estimated ending inventory at LIFO cost:			
Beginning inventory layer ($8,000 × 75%)		$ 6,000	
Current layer ($300 × 82.7%)		248	
		$ 6,248	

ending inventory were the same. Thus, we could conclude that the $300 increase in retail inventory represented the selling prices of *additional* merchandise that Edison Corporation had on hand at the end of year 2, rather than only an increase in selling price.

Suppose that, instead, the retail selling price had changed during year 2. For example, assume that as a result of inflation, the retail price level for Edison's goods rose 3 percent during year 2. In that case, the dollar amount of ending inventory, as measured by retail prices could be 3 percent more than the dollar amount of beginning inventory simply because of the change in the retail price level—with no *real* increase in the physical amount of inventory. If that were the case, the cost of the ending inventory under LIFO would be the same as the cost of the beginning inventory. In the case of Edison Corporation, the assumption of a 3 percent increase in the retail price level during year 2 would mean that the $8,300 retail ending inventory amount shown in Exhibit 10–9 would have to be deflated by the 3 percent increase in the retail price level before it could be compared with beginning inventory at retail.

Deflation of the year-end dollar amounts of inventory to reflect changes in price levels was discussed in Chapter 9 (see pages 501–506). There the dollar-value LIFO method was discussed as a technique for adjusting the dollar amount of inventory *cost* for changes in the inventory cost index (or cost price level). Thus, calculated changes in total inventory *cost* from period to period would be the result of increases or decreases in the physical level of inventory, rather than merely the result of changes in cost. When the *retail* price level changes during an accounting period, a dollar-value LIFO adjustment to *retail* prices should be used in conjunction with the retail LIFO method. This combination of the retail LIFO method and

CONCEPTUAL

Dollar-value retail LIFO makes adjustments for changes in *retail* price indexes rather than for changes in cost indexes.

the dollar-value LIFO adjustment for unstable retail prices is known as the **dollar-value retail LIFO method.**

The effect of a changing retail price level and of the appropriate dollar-value adjustments on retail LIFO calculations can be seen if we add two assumptions to the Edison Corporation data in Exhibit 10–9. First, assume that the beginning inventory for year 2 is the base inventory for dollar-value LIFO purposes. Second, assume that during year 2 the retail price level increased by 3 percent, causing the retail price index to rise from 1.00 to 1.03. Given these additional assumptions, the dollar-value retail LIFO method as applied to the Edison Corporation data for year 2 is shown in Exhibit 10–10.

Dollar-value retail LIFO is a combination of the retail LIFO method discussed in this chapter (Exhibit 10–9) and the dollar-value LIFO procedure that was discussed in Chapter 9 (Exhibit 9–12). Notice that the top part of Exhibit 10–10 is the same as Exhibit 10–9. The difference between Exhibit 10–10 (dollar-value retail LIFO) and Exhibit 10–9 (retail LIFO) is that in dollar-value retail LIFO, the ending inventory at current retail prices ($8,300) must first be adjusted to base retail prices ($8,058) and then to layered retail prices ($8,060) before it is adjusted to a cost basis. Adjustment to cost is accomplished by multiplying each inventory layer by the appropriate cost-to-retail percentage (column 4, Exhibit 10–10).

In review, the principal steps of the dollar-value retail LIFO method are:

I. Calculate the cost-to-retail percentages for beginning inventory and net purchases by means of the LIFO cost variation of the retail inventory method. In addition, calculate the ending inventory, stated in terms of current retail prices,

---

EXHIBIT 10–10   **The Dollar-Value Retail LIFO Method**

Edison Corporation

	Cost		Retail
Beginning inventory (cost-to-retail percentage = 75%)		$ 6,000	$ 8,000
Net purchases	$35,200		$43,800
Freight in	2,000		
Net markups			3,000
Net markdowns			(1,800)
		37,200	45,000

Cost-to-retail percentage, excluding beginning inventory:

$$\frac{\$37,200}{\$45,000} = 82.7\%$$

	Cost		Retail
Goods available for sale		$43,200	$53,000
Net sales			(44,700)
Ending inventory stated in terms of current retail prices (retail price index = 1.03)			$ 8,300

(1) Ending Inventory Stated in Terms of Base Retail Prices	(2) Inventory Layers Stated in Terms of Base Retail Prices	(3) Inventory Layers Restated Using Proper Retail Price Indexes	(4) Inventory Layers Stated in Terms of Cost	(5) Dollar-Value Retail LIFO Ending Inventory
$\dfrac{\$8,300}{1.03} = \$8,058$ →	$\left\{\begin{array}{l}\$8,000 \text{ (base)}\\ 58 \text{ (year 2)}\end{array}\right.$	$\begin{array}{l}\$8,000 \times 1.00 = \$8,000\\ 58 \times 1.03 = 60\end{array}$	$\left.\begin{array}{l}\$8,000 \times .75 = \$6,000\\ 60 \times .827 = 50\end{array}\right\}$ →	$\underline{\underline{\$6,050}}$

in accordance with the retail inventory method (Exhibit 10–9 or the top part of Exhibit 10 10).

2. Adjust the ending inventory, stated in terms of current retail prices, to base year retail prices by means of the current year's retail price index (column 1, bottom part of Exhibit 10–10).

3. Break down the current ending inventory, stated in terms of base year retail prices, into layers of retail prices (column 2, bottom part of Exhibit 10–10).

4. Restate the retail price layers of inventory using the retail price indexes related to the year of each layer (column 3, bottom part of Exhibit 10–10).

5. State the layers of ending inventory in terms of cost by using the cost-to-retail percentages related to each layer (column 3, bottom part of Exhibit 10–10).

6. Total the cost layers to obtain the dollar-value retail LIFO ending inventory (column 5, bottom part of Exhibit 10–10).

As you can see, if the basic concepts of both the retail LIFO variation and dollar-value LIFO are understood, dollar-value retail LIFO is not difficult to grasp. It is simply a combination of retail LIFO (the top part of Exhibit 10–10) and dollar-value LIFO (the bottom part of Exhibit 10–10). However, in dollar-value LIFO (Chapter 9), adjustments were made using *cost* indexes, whereas in dollar-value retail LIFO, the price index used is for *retail* selling prices. A retail price index must be used because the retail method initially determines ending inventory in terms of current retail prices.

As an additional aid to understanding the dollar-value retail LIFO method, the necessary data for Edison Corporation for year 3 are added to the data for year 2 in Exhibit 10–11 and are used in Exhibit 10–12 to demonstrate use of the dollar-value retail LIFO method over a two-year period. In studying Exhibit 10–12, note the following:

1. The base inventory, as well as each year's purchases (adjusted for freight, net markups, and net markdowns), has its own cost-to-retail percentage.

2. Ending inventory, expressed in current retail prices for each year, is adjusted to base retail prices by means of the retail price index for that particular year.

3. The relevant cost associated with each inventory layer is determined by means of the cost-to-retail percentage related to that layer.

| **EXHIBIT 10–11** | **Cost and Retail Data for Dollar-Value Retail LIFO Method, Years 2 and 3** |

Edison Corporation

	Year 2		Year 3	
	Cost	Retail	Cost	Retail
Beginning inventory[a]	$ 6,000	$ 8,000		
Net purchases	35,200	43,800	$37,500	$45,000
Freight in	2,000		3,000	
Net markups		3,000		4,000
Net markdowns		1,800		2,000
Net sales		44,700		45,060
Retail price indexes:				
1/1, year 2				1.00
12/31, year 2				1.03
12/31, year 3				1.12

[a]It is assumed that dollar-value retail LIFO was adopted at the beginning of year 2, so that the year 2 beginning inventory is the base inventory and the retail selling price index at January 1, year 2, is the base year index.

EXHIBIT 10–12 The Dollar-Value Retail LIFO Method: Two-Year Example

Edison Corporation
Year 3

	Cost		Retail
Beginning inventory (ending inventory, year 2: Exhibit 10-10).	$ 6,050		$ 8,300
Net purchases $37,500		$45,000	
Freight in 3,000			
Net markups		4,000	
Net markdowns		(2,000)	
	40,500		47,000

Cost-to-retail percentage, excluding beginning inventory:

$$\frac{\$40,500}{\$47,000} = 86.2\%$$

	Cost		Retail
Goods available for sale	$46,550		$55,300
Net sales			(45,060)
Ending inventory stated in terms of current retail prices (retail price index = 1.12)			$10,240

(1) Ending Inventory Stated in Terms of Base Retail Prices	(2) Inventory Layers Stated in Terms of Base Retail Prices	(3) Inventory Layers Restated Using Proper Retail Price Indexes	(4) Inventory Layers Stated in Terms of Cost	(5) Dollar-Value Retail LIFO Ending Inventory
$\dfrac{\$10,240}{1.12} = \$9,143 \longrightarrow$	$8,000 (base) 58 (year 2) 1,085 (year 3)	$8,000 \times 1.00 = \$8,000$ $58 \times 1.03 = 60$ $1,085 \times 1.12 = 1,215$	$8,000 \times .75 = \$6,000$ $60 \times .827 = 50$ $1,215 \times .862 = 1,047$ $\longrightarrow$	$7,097

4. The cost and retail ending inventories for year 2 are the cost and retail beginning inventories for year 3.

5. The ending inventory at cost that is calculated for each year ($6,050 in Exhibit 10–10 and $7,097 in Exhibit 10–12) is the ending inventory amount that would be reported in the financial statements for that year under dollar-value retail LIFO.

SUMMARY OF LEARNING OBJECTIVES

1. Explain the rationale for the ceiling and floor constraints on the use of replacement cost as "market" when valuing inventory at the lower of cost or market.
The purpose of the ceiling and floor constraints on the use of replacement cost as "market" is to avoid using a replacement cost that is "not normal"—that is, a replacement cost that is above net realizable value or below net realizable value minus a normal profit margin. A company would not normally replace inventory at a cost that exceeds net realizable value because to do so would make no economic sense. Nor would inventory normally be replaced at an amount that is below net realizable value minus a normal profit margin. By definition, a replacement cost below the floor amount would not be a normal replacement cost because it would yield an abnormally large profit margin.

2. Apply the lower-of-cost-or-market procedure to the valuation of inventory.
Cost, as calculated by one of the historical-cost-based methods, is compared with "market," which is replacement cost constrained by the ceiling (net realizable value)

and the floor (net realizable value minus a normal profit margin). The lower of cost or market can be applied to individual items, groups of items, or total inventory. If it is determined that market is lower than cost, the amount by which market is lower than cost should be recorded by a credit to the inventory account and a debit to an inventory holding loss account.

3. Estimate ending inventory using the gross profit method.

The gross profit method of estimating inventory is based on the use of an historically based gross profit percentage (the relationship between gross profit and selling price) for the inventory. This gross profit percentage is used to convert goods sold during the period from a selling price to a cost basis. The resulting cost of goods sold amount is then subtracted from the cost of goods available for sale to yield an estimate of the cost of goods remaining in inventory.

4. Describe the proper treatment of the various complicating factors in the retail inventory method.

Freight in is added to purchases only in the cost column. Purchase allowances should be deducted from purchases only in the cost column. Purchase returns should be deducted from purchases in both the cost column and the retail column. Purchases should be recorded net of purchase discounts or, if they are recorded at gross amounts, purchase discounts taken should be deducted from purchases in the cost column. Sales returns and sales allowances should be deducted from sales in the retail column if sales are recorded on a gross basis. When sales are recorded net of employee discounts, employee discounts should be added to sales in the retail column. Normal spoilage should be deducted from goods available for sale in the retail column after the cost-to-retail percentage has been calculated. Abnormal spoilage should be deducted in both the cost and retail columns before the normal cost-to-retail percentage is calculated.

5. Use the retail inventory method to estimate ending inventory on an average cost basis, a lower-of-cost-or-market basis, and a LIFO basis.

For an estimate of average cost, the cost-to-retail percentage includes the cost and retail amounts for both beginning inventory and net purchases, adjusted for both net markups and net markdowns. For an estimate of lower of cost or market, the net markdowns are included in the retail inventory method format after the cost-to-retail percentage has been calculated. For an estimate of LIFO cost, separate cost-to-retail percentages are calculated for beginning inventory and net purchases. Both net markups and net markdowns are included in the cost-to-retail percentage for net purchases. In addition, LIFO layers are identified and accounted for.

6. Estimate ending inventory using the dollar-value retail LIFO method.

The cost-to-retail percentages for beginning inventory and net purchases, respectively, are calculated by means of the LIFO cost variation of the retail inventory method. Ending inventory, stated in terms of current retail prices, is calculated in accordance with the retail inventory method. The ending inventory is then adjusted to base year retail prices by means of the current year's retail price index. The current ending inventory, stated in terms of base year retail prices, is then broken down into layers of retail prices. Next, these retail price layers are restated using the retail price indexes related to the year of each layer. Finally, the layers of ending inventory are stated in terms of cost by using the cost-to-retail percentages related to each layer. The total of the cost layers is the dollar-value retail LIFO ending inventory.

KEY TERMS

QUESTIONS

Q 10-1.   Define *replacement cost* and *net realizable value* as they pertain to inventory.

Q 10-2.   Define *cost* and *market* as these terms are used in lower-of-cost-or-market inventory accounting.

Q 10-3.   Why is net realizable value an appropriate upper constraint, or ceiling, on market in lower-of-cost-or-market valuation of inventory?

Q 10-4.   Why is net realizable value less a normal profit margin an appropriate lower constraint, or floor, on market in lower-of-cost-or-market valuation of inventory?

Q 10-5.   Lower of cost or market can be applied to individual inventory items, to groups of inventory items, or to total inventory. Which level of application would you expect to yield the highest inventory value? Why?

Q 10-6.   Why is the lower-of-cost-or-market procedure an excellent example of the influence of conservatism on GAAP?

Q 10-7.   What is a firm purchase commitment? Why might a business enter into a firm purchase commitment?

Q 10-8.   Under GAAP, what is the general accounting treatment for goods contracted for in a firm purchase commitment?

Q 10-9.   What does it mean to hedge against the possibility of market price movements of goods included in a firm purchase commitment? How can the buyer in a firm purchase commitment hedge against the purchase commitment?

Q 10-10.   According to *FASB Statement No. 80,* when should a change in market value of a futures contract be recognized if that contract is a hedge against a firm purchase commitment?

Q 10-11.   Give some examples of situations in which it might be necessary to estimate the dollar amount of ending inventory.

Q 10-12.   What is the key variable that must be estimated in order to use the gross profit method of estimating inventory cost? What are the basic steps of the gross profit method?

Q 10-13.   When the gross profit method of estimating inventory cost is used, available information sometimes includes gross profit as a percentage of cost. In this case, it is necessary to restate gross profit as a percentage of sales. How would you make this restatement?

Q 10-14.   What are the comparative advantages and disadvantages of the gross profit method and the retail inventory method of estimating ending inventory?

Q 10-15.   What data are required in order to use the retail inventory method in its simplest form?

Q 10-16.   Provide examples of what is meant by the following retail inventory method terminology: original markup, markup, markdown, markup cancellation, markdown cancellation, net markup, net markdown.

Q 10-17.   Explain how and why purchase returns and purchase allowances should be incorporated into retail inventory calculations.

Q 10-18.   Explain how and why normal and abnormal spoilage should be incorporated into retail inventory calculations.

Q 10-19.   Distinguish among the calculation procedures of the average cost, lower-of-cost-or-market, and LIFO variations of the retail inventory method.

Q 10-20.   Describe the calculation procedure for the conventional retail method.

Q 10-21.   What inventory estimation method would be used if a company chose to use the retail inventory method on a LIFO basis to estimate inventory during a period of changing retail price levels?

Q 10-22.   What are the principal steps of the dollar-value retail LIFO method?

CASES

C 10-1. **LOWER OF COST OR MARKET** One of your clients has a small-appliance retail sales and repair business. There have been continuous innovations in small-appliance technology in recent years, and this has caused obsolescence to occur in several of your client's product lines. In addition, the competitive nature of small-appliance wholesale and retail markets has caused numerous price-level changes in the wholesale market. These conditions have caused the value of much of your client's inventory to fall to near, or below, cost. In your opinion, the client may need to depart from the use of cost-based inventory valuation.

REQUIRED
1. Explain to your client some of the conditions under which historical cost may no longer be appropriate for inventory valuation. Relate these conditions to your client's circumstances.
2. Describe, in general terms, the lower-of-cost-or-market method of inventory valuation, including the levels of inventory groupings to which it can be applied.
3. Mention some of the arguments that can be made against the lower-of-cost-or-market method of valuing inventory.

C 10-2. **LOWER OF COST OR MARKET** The CPA firm that conducts your company's annual independent audit has determined that the circumstances surrounding your company's inventory require application of the lower-of-cost-or-market inventory valuation procedure. This fact, along with a brief description of what is meant by *cost* and *market* in the lower-of-cost-or-market procedure, has been communicated to your company's management group by the partner in charge of the independent audit team. During the discussion of the lower-of-cost-or-market procedure, the terms *ceiling* and *floor* were mentioned as being relevant in determining market for use in lower of cost or market. However, no details about the ceiling or floor, or about the logic for their existence, were provided. As a result, you have been assigned to write a brief report that defines both the ceiling and the floor and explains the underlying logic of the ceiling and the floor.

REQUIRED Write the required report and support the text of your report with a simple numerical illustration of how the ceiling and floor act as constraints on market in lower of cost or market.

C 10-3. **LOWER OF COST OR MARKET: ETHICAL ISSUES** Dale Davis is the sole owner and manager of an automobile repair shop, Dale's Auto Repair. Net income rose steadily during the first three years of operation. In the current year, 1998, however, net income through June 30 declined by 20 percent in comparison with the comparable period in 1997. Condensed income statements appear below.

Dale's Auto Repair
Income Statements

	FOR THE YEAR ENDED DECEMBER 31, 1997	1998 MARCH 31	1998 JUNE 30
Revenue.......................	$535,400	$126,400	$124,800
Cost of sales	(364,100)	(87,384)	(90,212)
Gross margin	$171,300	$ 39,016	$ 34,588
Operating expenses	(91,100)	(21,408)	(20,606)
Operating profit...............	$80,200	$ 17,608	$ 13,982
Other income...................	4,800	1,156	1,108
Profit before tax	$ 85,000	$ 18,764	$ 15,090
Income tax.....................	(28,900)	(6,380)	(5,131)
Net income	$ 56,100	$ 12,384	$ 9,959

Declining revenue from repair services and sales of automobile parts created a need for additional financing in order to acquire new equipment and to restock inventory. Davis applied for a $100,000 bank loan. The bank requested audited financial statements for the year ended December 31, 1997, and financial statements that were reviewed for the first two quarters of 1998. Additionally, audited annual financial statements were required for each year that the loan was outstanding.

Sue Smith is the chief accountant of Dale's Auto Repair. In reviewing the June 30, 1998, inventory records, she became aware of items in the repair parts inventory that were related to discontinued models. She estimated that at least $6,000 of the repair parts inventory was obsolete and should be written off the books. Smith informed Davis of her finding. Davis resisted the suggestion that the repair parts inventory should be written down, stating that such a reduction in the second quarter's net income would negatively affect the ability of the business to secure needed bank financing.

During the ensuing discussion between Davis and Smith, a disagreement arose over whether it was necessary to write down inventory as of June 30, 1998. Smith maintained that there was little or no market value for the repair parts in question and, therefore, it was appropriate to reduce the value of the June 30 repair parts inventory. Davis countered by stating that the $6,000 amount was not material since it represented less than 10 percent of the total ending inventory at June 30. Additionally, he felt that any write-down should occur at year-end, after bank financing had been secured. It was Davis' opinion that the auditors would not question the absence of a write-down, since the June 30 quarterly statements would only be reviewed, not audited.

Smith responded to Davis by insisting that the auditors would inquire about the physical condition and valuation of inventories included in the quarterly statements. Under these circumstances, she felt that the best approach would be to reduce the repair parts inventory now because she felt an obligation to inform the auditors of the status of the obsolete inventory.

Davis became agitated with Smith and stated that any further reduction in net income might negate the bank loan. Without such financing the business would be unable to compete. There was not enough available cash in bank accounts to purchase needed equipment and to restock inventory. The potential existed for a significant loss of business. If this occurred, employees might have to be laid off.

Sue Smith was not sure what to do. She felt quite strongly about her position. However, she did not want to take any action that would jeopardize the ability of the business to continue its operations.

REQUIRED   What are the ethical and professional considerations for Sue Smith in choosing a course of action? What would you do? Discuss the possible implications of your actions.

C 10-4.   **FIRM PURCHASE COMMITMENTS**   Cheryl Miller, the vice-president of marketing for your company, is seriously considering a new policy of entering into firm purchase commitments for inventory items as a way of coping with a seemingly endless series of inventory market price increases over the past three years. While recent market prices have only increased, vice-president Miller is concerned with the "downside risk" of market price decreases. She has come to you to learn about the accounting implications of market price decreases when a firm purchase commitment exists. She also is interested in learning whether it is possible to protect the company against losses that might arise from having a firm purchase commitment.

REQUIRED   **1.**   Discuss the application of the LCM procedure to goods contracted for under firm purchase commitments. Include in your discussion commitments that are both made and executed within one of the buyer's fiscal years and commitments that extend beyond the end of the buyer's fiscal year. Also discuss the impact of additional market price changes between the end of the fiscal year in which the buyer makes the commitment and the time the commitment is met in a subsequent fiscal year. It might be useful to include illustrative journal entries in your discussion.

2.   Describe how it might be possible to reduce the adverse accounting impact of market price decreases when a firm purchase commitment exists.

C 10-5.   **METHODS OF ESTIMATING INVENTORY**   Sam's Card and Gift Shop recently suffered major damage to the building in which it was housed and almost total loss of its inventory as the result of a fire. The owner, Sam Falcon, has come to you for help in preparing some statements of loss for submission to the insurance company and slightly different financial reports to show the local banker in an attempt to obtain financing to be used in reestablishing the business. Inspection of the property and review of a backup set of accounting records reveal that the only way to get a total value for inventory on hand at the time of the fire will be to estimate the inventory value.

REQUIRED   Write a report that describes how Sam may be able to estimate the value of lost inventory. Include a discussion of the relative advantages or disadvantages of the inventory estimation methods available to Sam.

C 10-6. **RETAIL INVENTORY METHOD** The Newsom Paint Company, your client, manufactures paint. The company's president, Bill Newsom, has decided to open a retail store to sell Newsom Paint as well as wallpaper and other supplies that he would purchase from other companies. Bill is thinking about using the retail method to value his store's inventory and has asked you to write a report describing the retail method. He wants the report to describe: (1) the retail method, (2) the conditions that may distort the results under the retail method, (3) the advantages of using the retail method as compared with cost methods of inventory pricing, and (4) the accounting theory underlying the treatment of net markdowns and net markups under the retail method.

REQUIRED   Write the necessary report.

(AICPA, adapted)

C 10-7. **RETAIL INVENTORY METHOD** When the retail inventory method is used, markups, markdowns, markup cancellations, and markdown cancellations all must be considered. In addition, several other factors can complicate retail inventory calculations, including freight in, purchase returns, purchase allowances, sales returns, sales allowances, purchase discounts taken, employee discounts, normal spoilage, and abnormal spoilage.

REQUIRED   Explain the proper treatments of each of the complicating factors mentioned above when the retail inventory method is used.

C 10-8. **DOLLAR-VALUE RETAIL LIFO METHOD** One of your client companies has used the retail inventory method for several years. After reviewing the company's inventory accounting records and considering the retail price movements of its inventory items, you have determined that there have been substantial changes in the retail prices of the inventory from year to year.

REQUIRED   Write a brief paper discussing the dollar-value retail LIFO method, which your client probably should use for inventory valuation. Include comments on the motivation for using dollar-value retail LIFO and outline the principal steps of the method.

EXERCISES

E 10-1. **LOWER OF COST OR MARKET** Falls Corporation has two products in its ending inventory, each accounted for at lower of cost or market. A profit margin of 30 percent of selling price is considered normal for each product. Specific data with respect to each product follow:

	PRODUCT 1	PRODUCT 2
Historical cost.	$17	$ 47
Replacement cost	14	48
Estimated cost to dispose.	6	26
Estimated selling price	30	100

REQUIRED   If Falls values its ending inventory by the lower-of-cost-or-market method, what unit values should be used for products 1 and 2, respectively?

(AICPA, adapted)

E 10-2. **LOWER OF COST OR MARKET** Maine Company uses the lower-of-cost-or-market method of valuing its inventory. Data for four of its inventory items are:

ITEM	COST	CURRENT REPLACEMENT COST	EXPECTED SELLING PRICE	EXPECTED COST TO COMPLETE AND DISPOSE	NORMAL PROFIT MARGIN (PERCENT OF SELLING PRICE)
1	$24	$23.00	$30	$3.00	12%
2	30	28.00	35	2.00	20
3	18	17.50	23	6.00	5
4	39	41.00	48	6.00	8

REQUIRED   Calculate unit inventory values for items 1 through 4. As part of your answer, clearly indicate the ceiling and floor used in determining market for each inventory item.

E 10-3. **LOWER OF COST OR MARKET**   The following inventory data are available for Olsen Corporation:

INVENTORY ITEM	COST	CURRENT REPLACEMENT COST	CURRENT SELLING PRICE	COST OF COMPLETION AND DISPOSAL	NORMAL PROFIT MARGIN
A	$1.10	$1.04	$1.00	$–0–	$.05
B	1.50	1.55	1.80	.20	.10
C	2.30	2.50	3.00	.55	.20
D	1.80	1.90	2.00	.25	.10
E	2.40	1.80	2.60	.20	.50

REQUIRED   Using the lower-of-cost-or-market method, calculate the dollar amount of inventory:
1. On an individual-item basis.
2. On a group basis, assuming that group 1 consists of items A and B, and group 2 consists of items C, D, and E.
3. On the basis of total inventory.

E 10-4. **LOWER OF COST OR MARKET**   Tavner Company has six inventory items, data for which are as follows:

ITEM	COST	CURRENT REPLACEMENT COST	EXPECTED SELLING PRICE	EXPECTED COST TO COMPLETE AND DISPOSE	NORMAL PROFIT MARGIN (PERCENT OF COST)
1	$72.00	$75.00	$80.00	$7.00	5%
2	84.00	85.00	90.00	5.00	5
3	61.00	59.00	70.00	3.00	8
4	69.00	70.00	74.50	2.50	4
5	81.00	80.00	87.00	3.00	10
6	76.00	74.00	81.00	.75	7

REQUIRED   Using the lower-of-cost-or-market method, calculate the dollar amount of inventory:
1. On an individual-item basis.
2. On a group basis, assuming that group 1 consists of items 2, 5, and 6, and group 2 consists of items 1, 3, and 4.
3. On the basis of total inventory.

E 10-5. **LOSS ON FIRM PURCHASE COMMITMENT**   On November 15, 1998, Harmon Company signed a noncancelable contract to purchase 12,000 units of inventory at $5 per unit in six months. On December 31, 1998, the end of Harmon's fiscal year, the same units of inventory could be bought in the open market at $4.90 per unit. By the end of the first quarter of 1999, the open market price per unit of inventory had risen to $5.25.

REQUIRED   Assuming that on December 31, 1998, the open market price appeared to be a reasonable estimate of the open market price that would exist at the time the contract was fulfilled, how should the facts related to this firm purchase commitment be accounted for:
1. At December 31, 1998?
2. At the end of the first quarter of 1999?

E 10-6. **FIRM PURCHASE COMMITMENT**   On June 10, 1998, Crane Corporation entered into a noncancelable purchase contract specifying the purchase of 10,000 units of inventory for $4.40 per unit. Crane has a December 31 fiscal year-end. In addition, the following price information is available:

DATE	MARKET PRICE OF GOODS
August 31, 1998	$4.00
September 27, 1998	4.20
November 30, 1998	4.40
December 31, 1998	4.35
January 31, 1999	5.00
February 20, 1999	4.28

REQUIRED   **1.** Assuming that the contract is executed with a cash purchase on September 27, 1998, what entries (if any) would Crane make on August 31 and September 27, 1998?

2. If the contract is executed on September 27 and the market price at that time is $4.75 rather than $4.20, what entry would Crane make to record the purchase?

3. If the contract is executed on February 20, 1999, with a cash payment, what entries (if any) would Crane make on November 30, 1998; on December 31, 1998; on January 31, 1999; and on February 20, 1999?

4. If the contract is executed on February 20, 1999, but the market price at that time is $4.50 instead of the $4.28 specified above, what entry would Crane make to record the cash purchase?

E 10-7.   **GROSS PROFIT METHOD**   The following information is available for Riley Company for the three months ended March 31, 1998:

Merchandise inventory, 1/1/98	**$ 800,000**
Purchases	**3,400,000**
Freight in	**150,000**
Sales	**4,400,000**

The gross profit margin was 25 percent of sales.

REQUIRED   What is the estimated cost of merchandise inventory at March 31, 1998?

(AICPA, adapted)

E 10-8.   **GROSS PROFIT METHOD**   On January 1, 1998, the merchandise inventory of Krupa Company was $350,000. During 1998, Krupa purchased merchandise costing $1.8 million and recorded sales of $2 million. The gross profit, based on cost, was 20 percent.

REQUIRED   What is the estimated cost of merchandise inventory of Krupa at December 31, 1998?

(AICPA, adapted)

E 10-9.   **GROSS PROFIT METHOD**   On June 13, 1998, a fire destroyed the entire uninsured merchandise inventory of Harris Merchandising Company. The following data are available:

Inventory, 1/1/98	**$ 50,000**
Purchases, 1/1/98–6/13/98 (including $20,000 of goods	
in transit on 6/13/98, shipped f.o.b. destination)	**160,000**
Sales, 1/1/98–6/13/98	**200,000**
Markup percentage on cost	**25%**

REQUIRED   Calculate the approximate inventory loss as a result of the fire.

(AICPA, adapted)

E 10-10.   **GROSS PROFIT METHOD**   On April 10, 1998, a flood destroyed the entire merchandise inventory on hand of Peters Wholesale Company. The following information is available:

Sales, 1/1/98–4/10/98	**$420,000**
Inventory, 1/1/98	**90,000**
Freight in	**30,000**
Merchandise purchases, 1/1/98–4/10/98 (including $40,000 of goods	
in transit on 4/10, shipped f.o.b. shipping point)	**340,000**
Purchase returns	**20,000**

REQUIRED   **1.** Assuming that the markup percentage on cost is 15 percent, what is the estimated inventory on April 10, 1998, immediately before the flood?

2. Assuming that the gross profit is 30 percent of sales, what is the estimated inventory on April 10, 1998, immediately before the flood?

E 10-11.   **AVERAGE COST; RETAIL INVENTORY METHOD**   Value Department Store uses the retail inventory method. Information related to the calculation of the inventory at December 31, 1998, is as follows:

	COST	RETAIL
Inventory, 1/1/98	$ 20,000	$ 38,000
Sales		280,000
Purchases	135,000	300,000
Freight in	3,800	
Net markups		25,000
Net markdowns		10,000

REQUIRED   What should be the estimated ending inventory in terms of average cost at December 31, 1998, under the retail inventory method?

(AICPA, adapted)

E 10-12.   **AVERAGE COST; RETAIL INVENTORY METHOD**   The retail inventory method is used by Bryan Company. Inventory, purchases, and sales data for 1998 are:

	COST	RETAIL
Beginning inventory	$ 12,000	$ 20,000
Purchases	115,000	220,000
Freight in	4,300	
Net markups		17,500
Net markdowns		13,300
Net sales		197,800

REQUIRED   Estimate the average cost of Bryan's year-end inventory using the retail inventory method.

E 10-13.   **LOWER OF COST OR MARKET; RETAIL INVENTORY METHOD**   Green Department Store uses the retail inventory method to approximate the lower-of-cost-or-market value of inventory. The following information is available for the month of August 1998:

	COST	RETAIL
Goods available for sale	$190,000	$225,000[a]
Net markups		40,000
Net markdowns		10,000
Sales		170,000

[a]Before net markups and net markdowns.

REQUIRED   Using the retail inventory method, calculate the approximate value of inventory, in terms of lower of cost or market, at August 31, 1998.

(AICPA, adapted)

E 10-14.   **LOWER OF COST OR MARKET; RETAIL INVENTORY METHOD**   Haskin Company uses the retail inventory method to approximate the lower-of-cost-or-market value of inventory. The following information is available for 1998:

	COST	RETAIL
Beginning inventory	$ 90,000	$140,000
Purchases	280,000	410,000
Freight in	15,000	
Normal spoilage		9,000
Net markups		14,000
Net markdowns		7,000
Sales		380,000

REQUIRED   What amount would Haskin Company report for its 1998 ending inventory under the lower-of-cost-or-market version of the retail method?

E 10-15. **LIFO RETAIL INVENTORY METHOD** Killen Company plans to use the retail inventory method to estimate its 1998 ending inventory on a LIFO basis. The following data are available related to inventory, purchases, and sales:

	COST	RETAIL
Beginning inventory	$ 8,300	$12,950
Purchases	70,000	89,200
Purchase returns	5,600	7,780
Purchase allowances	500	
Net markups		8,100
Net markdowns		4,270
Freight in	5,800	
Normal spoilage		1,600
Abnormal spoilage	730	1,200
Sales (recorded on a gross basis)		85,360
Sales returns and allowances		3,770

REQUIRED Calculate Killen Company's 1998 ending inventory using the retail inventory method and the LIFO cost flow assumption.

E 10-16. **RETAIL INVENTORY METHOD** Quick Sales Company uses the retail inventory method to value its merchandise inventory. The following information is available:

	COST	RETAIL
Beginning inventory	$ 40,000	$ 70,000
Purchases	280,000	410,000
Freight in	3,000	
Markups (net)		3,000
Markdowns (net)		5,000
Employee discounts		2,000
Sales		380,000

REQUIRED
1. Calculate the ending inventory at retail.
2. If the ending inventory is to be valued at the lower of cost or market, what is the cost-to-retail ratio?
3. If the ending inventory is valued on a LIFO basis, what is the cost-to-retail ratio for the current year's purchases?

E 10-17. **RETAIL INVENTORY METHOD** The following data concerning the retail inventory method are taken from the financial records of Rorick Corporation:

	COST	RETAIL
Beginning inventory	$17,800	$ 30,000
Purchases	87,000	155,000
Freight in	1,400	
Net markups		2,000
Net markdowns		1,740
Sales		156,760

REQUIRED
1. What should be the ending inventory at retail?
2. If the ending inventory is to be valued at approximately the lower of cost or market, what dollar amounts of cost and retail would be used for goods available for sale in calculating the cost-to-retail percentage?
3. If the ending inventory for the current period at cost amounts to $15,000, how does the gross profit for the current year, as a percentage of sales, compare with the gross profit percentage of the preceding year?
4. If the LIFO cost flow assumption were used, the retail inventory method would provide an estimate of ending inventory of how much?

E 10-18. **DOLLAR-VALUE RETAIL LIFO METHOD** One year ago Stricter Corporation adopted the dollar-value retail LIFO method of inventory valuation. Current year inventory and price index data are:

	COST	RETAIL
Beginning inventory (cost to retail = 80%)	$400,000	$?
Net purchases	220,000	240,000
Net markups...		13,000
Net markdowns		14,000
Net sales		230,000

Price index at beginning of year: 1.13
Price index at end of year: 1.15

REQUIRED Calculate Stricter Corporation's ending inventory using dollar-value retail LIFO.

E 10-19. **DOLLAR-VALUE RETAIL LIFO METHOD** The following information is available for Marvin Corporation, which uses the dollar-value retail LIFO method in valuing its inventory:

	COST	RETAIL
Beginning inventory (a single layer)..........................	$ 68,000	$ 91,000
Net purchases	110,000	140,000
Freight in	6,000	
Net markups...		8,000
Net markdowns		4,000
Net sales		142,000
Normal spoilage..		2,000

Price index at beginning of year: 1.10
Price index at end of year: 1.20

REQUIRED Calculate Marvin Corporation's ending inventory using dollar-value retail LIFO.

E 10-20. **DOLLAR-VALUE RETAIL LIFO METHOD** Lopez Company adopted the dollar-value retail LIFO inventory method on January 1, 1998. The following information is available for Lopez Company:

	RETAIL PRICE INDEX	LIFO INVENTORY COST	RETAIL	COST-TO-RETAIL PERCENTAGE
Inventory, 1/1/98	1.00	$16,000	$20,000	80%
Inventory, 12/31/98...............	1.12	?	29,000	87
Inventory, 12/31/99...............	1.23	?	34,000	83

REQUIRED Using the dollar-value retail LIFO method, calculate the ending inventories on December 31, 1998, and December 31, 1999.

E 10-21. **DOLLAR-VALUE RETAIL LIFO METHOD** Arden Corporation adopted the dollar-value retail LIFO method of inventory valuation at the beginning of 1997, at which time the retail price index was 1.00. As of the beginning of 1998, the retail price index had risen to 1.05. In addition, the following information is available for Arden Corporation.

	LIFO INVENTORY COST	RETAIL	COST-TO-RETAIL PERCENTAGE	RETAIL PRICE INDEX
Inventory, 1/1/98	$15,750	$21,000	?	
Inventory, 12/31/98	?	27,000	90%	1.09
Net purchases, 1999...............	28,000	33,000		
Net markups, 1999		400		
Net sales, 1999		31,000		
Inventory, 12/31/99	?	?		1.12

REQUIRED Using the dollar-value retail LIFO method, calculate the inventory costs on December 31, 1998, and December 31, 1999.

PROBLEMS

P 10-1. **LOWER OF COST OR MARKET** Berris Distributing Company has a perpetual inventory system and uses the lower-of-cost-or-market method of valuing its inventories. The following information is available from the inventory records as of December 31, 1998:

INVENTORY ITEM	NUMBER OF UNITS	UNIT COST	CURRENT REPLACEMENT COST PER UNIT	ESTIMATED SELLING PRICE	UNIT COST TO COMPLETE	NORMAL UNIT PROFIT
A	300	$2.50	$2.60	$3.00	$.25	$1.00
B	500	2.50	2.90	2.75	.15	.50
C	150	5.40	5.30	5.90	.20	1.20
D	450	3.50	3.25	4.50	.40	.65
E	280	2.65	2.55	4.00	.30	.80
F	375	4.30	4.20	4.60	.50	1.25

REQUIRED
1. Calculate the ending inventory on December 31, 1998, using lower of cost or market applied on an individual-item basis.
2. If you find that market is below cost in part 1, make at least two alternative journal entries that could be used to record this fact.
3. Calculate the ending inventory on December 31, 1998, on a group basis, treating inventory items A, B, and C as group 1 and items D, E, and F as group 2.
4. Why might lower of cost or market yield a higher inventory value when applied to groups than when applied to individual items?

P 10-2. **LOWER OF COST OR MARKET** Detter Company manufactures and sells four products. Its inventories are priced at cost or market, whichever is lower. A normal profit margin rate of 30 percent of selling price is maintained on each of the four products.

The following information was compiled as of December 31, 1998:

PRODUCT	ORIGINAL COST	COST TO REPLACE	ESTIMATED COST TO DISPOSE	EXPECTED SELLING PRICE
A	$40.00	$42.00	$15.00	$ 80.00
B	47.50	45.00	20.50	95.00
C	17.50	16.00	5.00	28.00
D	45.00	48.00	26.00	100.00

REQUIRED
1. Why are expected selling prices important in the application of the LCM method?
2. Prepare a schedule containing unit values (including floor and ceiling) for determining the lower-of-cost-or-market value of each of the four products. The last column of the schedule should contain the unit value of each product for the purpose of inventory valuation resulting from the application of the lower-of-cost-or-market method.
3. What effects, if any, do the expected selling prices have on the valuation of products A, B, C, and D by the lower-of-cost-or-market method?

(AICPA, adapted)

P 10-3. **GROSS PROFIT METHOD** On November 21, 1998, a fire at Fox Company's warehouse caused severe damage to its entire inventory. Fox estimates that all usable damaged goods can be sold for $10,000. The following information is available from Fox's accounting records for inventory:

Inventory cost, 11/1/98 .... $ 80,000
Purchases, 11/1/98–11/21/98 145,000
Net sales, 11/1/98–11/21/98 210,000

In recent periods Fox had a gross profit margin of 30 percent of net sales.

REQUIRED
1. Prepare a schedule to calculate the estimated loss on the inventory in the fire, using the gross profit method. Show supporting calculations in good form.
2. Discuss the weaknesses of the gross profit method.

(AICPA, adapted)

P 10-4.   **ESTIMATING INVENTORY BY THE GROSS PROFIT METHOD**   Meridian Mall housed the premises of the Complete Hardware Company. On the morning of November 1, 1998, fire gutted the hardware store and some of the other tenants. Complete Hardware had been a popular store and had consistently earned a gross profit equal to about two-thirds of cost.

Appropriate data covering the period from January 1, 1998, until the date of the fire are as follows:

Sales	$1,220,000
Purchases	750,000
Purchase returns	18,000
Sales returns	16,000
Delivery expense	30,000
Freight in	12,000
Administrative expenses	8,000
Inventory, 1/1/98	200,000
Advertising expense	20,250
Sales clerks' salaries	85,500
Sales discounts	5,000

REQUIRED   Prepare a schedule and calculate Complete Hardware's estimated inventory on November 1, 1998.

(CGAA, adapted)

P 10-5.   **ESTIMATING INVENTORY BY THE GROSS PROFIT METHOD**   On June 30, 1998, a flash flood damaged the warehouse and factory of Allen Corporation, completely destroying the work-in-process inventory. There was no damage to either the raw materials or finished goods inventories. A physical inventory count taken after the flood revealed the following valuations:

Raw materials	$ 60,000
Work in process	–0–
Finished goods	117,000

The inventory on January 1, 1998, consisted of the following:

Raw materials	$ 35,000
Work in process	95,000
Finished goods	150,000
	$280,000

A review of Allen's records disclosed that the gross profit margin historically approximated 30 percent of sales. The sales for the first six months of 1998 were $340,000. Raw material purchases were $115,000. Direct labor costs for this period were $85,000, and manufacturing overhead historically has been applied at 45 percent of direct labor.

REQUIRED   Calculate the value of the work-in-process inventory lost at June 30, 1998. Show supporting calculations.

(AICPA, adapted)

P 10-6.   **GROSS PROFIT RATIO AND GROSS PROFIT METHOD**   Ranvel Corporation is an importer and wholesaler. Its merchandise is purchased from a number of suppliers and is warehoused by Ranvel until it is sold to consumers.

In conducting her audit for the year ended June 30, 1998, the company's CPA determined that the system of internal control was good. Accordingly, she observed the physical inventory at an interim date, May 31, 1998, instead of at the end of the year.

The following information was obtained from the general ledger:

Inventory, 7/1/97	$ 90,000
Physical inventory, 5/31/98	95,000
Sales for eleven months ended 5/31/98	850,000
Sales for year ended 6/30/98	960,000
Purchases for eleven months ended 5/31/98 (before audit adjustments)	675,000
Purchases for year ended 6/30/98 (before audit adjustments)	800,000

The CPA's audit disclosed the following information:

Shipments received in May and included in the physical inventory but recorded as June purchases	$ 7,500
Shipments received in unsalable condition and excluded from physical inventory; credit memos not received and charge-backs to vendors not recorded	
Total at 5/31/98	1,000
Total at 6/30/98 (including the May unrecorded charge-backs)	1,500
Deposit made with vendor and charged to purchases in April 1998; product shipped in July 1998	3,000
Deposit made with vendor and charged to purchases in May 1998; product shipped f.o.b. shipping point 5/29/98 and included in 5/31/98 physical inventory as goods in transit	5,500
Through carelessness of receiving department, June shipment damaged by rain; sold later in June at cost	10,000

REQUIRED When interim physical inventory counts are made, a frequently used auditing procedure is to test the reasonableness of the year-end inventory by the application of gross profit ratios.

Prepare in good form the following schedules:

1. Calculation of the gross profit ratio for the eleven months ended May 31, 1998.

2. Calculation by the gross profit method of cost of goods sold during June 1998.

3. Calculation by the gross profit method of June 30, 1998, inventory.

(AICPA, adapted)

P 10-7. **LOWER OF COST OR MARKET; RETAIL INVENTORY METHOD** Ken's Clothing Store values its inventory under the retail inventory method at the lower of cost or market. The following data are available for the month of November 1998:

	COST	SELLING PRICE
Inventory, 11/1/98	$ 50,000	$ 75,000
Markdowns		30,000
Markups		29,000
Markdown cancellations		13,000
Markup cancellations		11,000
Purchases	175,000	223,600
Sales		244,000
Purchase returns	3,000	3,600
Sales returns and allowances		10,000

REQUIRED On the basis of the data presented above, prepare a schedule to calculate the estimated inventory at November 30, 1998, at lower of cost or market under the retail inventory method.

(AICPA, adapted)

P 10-8. **LOWER OF COST OR MARKET AND LIFO; RETAIL INVENTORY METHOD** Great Variety Store uses the retail inventory method. Information related to the calculation of the inventory at December 31, 1998, follows:

	COST	RETAIL
Inventory, 1/1/98	$ 30,600	$ 45,000
Purchases	150,000	190,000
Freight in	15,000	
Sales		187,000
Net markups		38,000
Net markdowns		13,000

REQUIRED

I. Assuming that there was no change in the price index during the year, calculate the inventory at December 31, 1998, using the lower-of-cost-or-market retail inventory method.

2. Assuming that there was no change in the price index during the year, calculate the inventory at December 31, 1998, using the LIFO retail inventory method.

(AICPA, adapted)

P 10-9. **THE CONVENTIONAL RETAIL METHOD** Martin Department Store, Inc., uses the conventional retail inventory method to estimate ending inventory for its monthly financial statements. The following data pertain to a single department for the month of October 1998.

Inventory, 10/1/98:	
At cost	$ 22,000
At retail	40,000
Purchases (exclusive of freight and returns):	
At cost	99,300
At retail	146,495
Freight in	4,900
Purchase returns:	
At cost	2,100
At retail	2,800
Additional markups	2,500
Markup cancellations	265
Markdowns (net)	900
Normal spoilage and breakage	4,500
Sales	140,100

REQUIRED

I. Prepare a schedule to calculate estimated lower-of-cost-or-market inventory for October 31, 1998.

2. Martin estimates the cost of the ending inventory of another department as $31,000. An accurate physical count reveals only $25,000 of inventory at lower of cost or market. List the factors that may have caused the difference between the estimated inventory and the physical count.

(AICPA, adapted)

P 10-10. **LOWER OF COST OR MARKET; RETAIL INVENTORY METHOD** Dotson Department Store uses the retail inventory method. Information related to the calculation of its inventory at December 31, 1998, is as follows:

	COST	RETAIL
Inventory at 1/1/98	$ 50,000	$ 80,000
Sales		595,000
Purchases	260,000	600,000
Freight in	7,600	
Markups		60,000
Markup cancellations		10,000
Markdowns		25,000
Markdown cancellations		5,000

Estimated normal spoilage: 3% of sales

REQUIRED

I. Prepare a schedule to calculate the estimated ending inventory at the lower of cost or market at December 31, 1998, using the retail inventory method. Show supporting calculations.

2. What are some of the advantages of the retail inventory method?

(AICPA, adapted)

P 10-11. **VARIATIONS OF THE RETAIL INVENTORY METHOD** The following data are available for Tiller Company for 1998:

Sales	$99,000
Sales returns	5,000
Markups	9,000
Markup cancellations	2,500
Markdowns	6,000
Markdown cancellations	1,500
Freight in	8,000
Purchases at cost	75,000
Purchases at retail	98,000
Purchase returns at cost	3,000
Purchase returns at retail	4,000
Beginning inventory at cost	6,000
Beginning inventory at retail	11,000
Employee discounts	3,000
Normal spoilage	1,000

REQUIRED Using the retail inventory method, estimate ending inventory in terms of:
1. Average cost.
2. Lower of cost or market.
3. LIFO.

P 10-12. **VARIATIONS OF THE RETAIL INVENTORY METHOD** The following data are available for Biltner Company for 1998:

Sales	$214,000
Sales returns	17,000
Markups	16,000
Markup cancellations	6,500
Markdowns	9,000
Markdown cancellations	2,100
Freight in	10,500
Purchases at cost	170,000
Purchases at retail	210,000
Purchase returns at cost	4,200
Purchase returns at retail	5,800
Beginning inventory at cost	23,000
Beginning inventory at retail	30,000
Employee discounts	4,300
Abnormal spoilage at cost	1,200
Abnormal spoilage at retail	1,500
Normal spoilage	2,000

REQUIRED Using the retail inventory method, estimate ending inventory in terms of:
1. Average cost.
2. Lower of cost or market.
3. LIFO.

P 10-13. **LIFO RETAIL METHOD; DOLLAR-VALUE RETAIL LIFO METHOD** Under your guidance, on January 1, 1998, the Allsports Sporting Goods Store implemented the retail method of accounting for its merchandise inventory.

When you undertook the preparation of the store's financial statements at June 30, 1998, the following data were available:

	COST	SELLING PRICE
Inventory, 1/1/98..	$32,000	$ 39,000
Markdowns		10,500
Markups...		19,500
Markdown cancellations		6,500
Markup cancellations..		5,000
Purchases	91,500	111,800
Sales		120,500
Purchase returns...	1,500	1,800
Sales returns and allowances		7,000

REQUIRED

1. Prepare a schedule to calculate Allsports Sporting Goods Store's June 30, 1998, inventory under the retail method of accounting for inventories. The inventory is to be valued at cost under the LIFO method.

2. Without prejudice to your solution to part 1, assume that you calculated the June 30, 1998, inventory to be $45,000 at retail and the ratio of cost to retail to be 80 percent. The retail price level has increased from 100 at January 1 to 104 at June 30. Prepare a schedule to calculate the June 30, 1998, inventory at the June 30 price level under the dollar-value retail LIFO method.

(AICPA, adapted)

P 10-14. **LIFO RETAIL METHOD; DOLLAR-VALUE RETAIL LIFO METHOD** Marshall Music uses the retail method of accounting for its inventory and assumes a LIFO cost flow. The following data are available for Marshall Music for fiscal year 1998:

	COST	RETAIL
Beginning inventory (all same layer)...........................	$ 9,345	$ 14,770
Purchases	93,575	132,890
Purchase returns...	3,650	5,880
Purchase allowances...	1,125	
Net markups		11,330
Net markdowns..		6,500
Freight in...	9,200	
Normal spoilage		2,700
Sales (see note)		128,000
Sales returns and allowances		4,200
Employee discounts		2,680

Note: Sales to nonemployee customers are recorded on a gross basis, and sales to employees are recorded net of employee discounts.

REQUIRED

1. Prepare a schedule to calculate Marshall Music's ending inventory for 1998 using the retail inventory method and the LIFO cost flow assumption.

2. Assume that in part 1 you calculated the 1998 year-end inventory to be $18,000 at current retail, and the cost-to-retail percentage for 1998 purchases was determined to be 73 percent. In addition, assume that, compared to the base retail price level, the beginning-of-1998 retail price level was 1.03, and the end-of-1998 retail price level was 1.04. Prepare a schedule to calculate the 1998 ending inventory under the dollar-value retail LIFO method.

P 10-15. **DOLLAR-VALUE RETAIL LIFO METHOD** New Electronics began using the dollar-value retail LIFO method on January 1, 1998. Information related to inventory, purchases, sales, and retail price levels for 1998 and 1999 is as follows:

	1998 COST	1998 RETAIL	1999 COST	1999 RETAIL
Beginning inventory	$10,000	$12,000	$?	$?
Gross purchases	52,000	60,000	48,000	54,200
Freight in	5,000		4,000	
Purchase allowances	2,500		2,015	
Purchase returns	1,000	1,800	500	1,000
Purchase discounts	3,400		2,400	
Net markups		5,200		4,000
Net markdowns		3,100		2,800
Abnormal spoilage	200	300	100	300
Normal spoilage		600		500
Gross sales		53,500		53,100
Employee discounts		2,300		2,000
Sales returns		1,200		1,100
Sales allowances		1,800		1,700

Retail selling price indexes:
   1/1/98 .... 1.00
   12/31/98 .... 1.04
   12/31/99 .... 1.06

REQUIRED Prepare a schedule to calculate the costs of 1998 and 1999 ending inventories under the dollar-value retail LIFO method.

P 10-16. **CONVENTIONAL RETAIL; LIFO RETAIL; DOLLAR-VALUE RETAIL LIFO** Draper Department Store converted from the conventional retail method to the LIFO retail method on January 1, 1998, and is now considering converting to the dollar-value retail LIFO inventory method. During your examination of the financial statements for the year ended December 31, 1999, management requested that you furnish a summary showing certain calculations of inventory costs for the past three years.

Available information follows:
a) The inventory at January 1, 1997, had a retail value of $50,000 and a cost of $30,000 based on the conventional retail method.
b) Transactions during 1997 were as follows:

	COST	RETAIL
Gross purchases	$282,000	$490,000
Purchase returns	6,500	10,000
Purchase discounts	3,000	
Gross sales		492,000
Sales returns		5,000
Employee discounts		3,000
Freight in	26,500	
Net markups		28,000
Net markdowns		10,000

c) The retail value of the December 31, 1998, inventory was $66,100, the cost ratio for 1998 under the LIFO retail method was 62 percent, and the regional price index was 103 percent of the January 1, 1998, price level.
d) The retail value of the December 31, 1999, inventory was $58,300, the cost ratio for 1999 under the LIFO retail method was 61 percent, and the regional price index was 105 percent of the January 1, 1998, price level.

REQUIRED

1. Prepare a schedule showing the calculation of the cost of inventory on hand at December 31, 1997, based on the conventional retail method.

2. Prepare a schedule showing the calculation of the cost of inventory on hand at the store on December 31, 1997, based on the LIFO retail method.

3. Without prejudice to your solution to part 2, assume that you calculated the December 31, 1997, inventory (retail value $60,000) under the LIFO retail method at a cost of $48,000. Prepare a schedule showing the calculations of the costs of the store's 1998 and 1999 year-end inventories under the dollar-value retail LIFO method. Assume that January 1, 1998, is the beginning of the base year.

(AICPA, adapted)

P 10-17. **CONVENTIONAL RETAIL; LIFO RETAIL; DOLLAR-VALUE RETAIL LIFO** Keller Company has the following data available for 1997, 1998, and 1999:

For 1997:

	COST	RETAIL
Beginning inventory (January 1)	$ 9,780	$ 13,250
Gross purchases	136,890	165,770
Purchase allowances	2,600	
Purchase returns	3,500	4,990
Freight in	11,350	
Net markups		8,440
Net markdowns		3,820
Normal spoilage		1,700
Gross sales		154,640
Sales returns		2,760
Employee discounts		6,500

Additional data:

	RETAIL PRICE INDEX	RETAIL INVENTORY	COST-TO-RETAIL PERCENTAGE
January 1, 1998	1.00		
December 31, 1998	1.03	$19,700	75.0 (for 1998)
December 31, 1999	1.05	18,950	71.0 (for 1999)

REQUIRED

1. Prepare a schedule calculating the cost of December 31, 1997, inventory using the lower-of-cost-or-market variation of the retail inventory method.

2. Prepare a schedule calculating the cost of December 31, 1997, inventory using the LIFO variation of the retail inventory method.

3. Instead of your solution to part 2, assume that the December 31, 1997, inventory had a retail value of $18,000 and a cost under the LIFO retail inventory method of $15,120. Prepare a schedule calculating the costs of the 1998 and 1999 ending inventories under the dollar-value retail LIFO method.

P 10-18.   **DOLLAR-VALUE RETAIL LIFO METHOD**   Petroni Corporation has just completed its second year of operations. When it began operations, it adopted the dollar-value retail LIFO method of inventory valuation. Inventory, purchases, sales, and retail price data for the two years Petroni has been in existence are provided as follows:

	YEAR 1		YEAR 2	
	COST	RETAIL	COST	RETAIL
Beginning inventory	$ 9,000	$12,000	$?	$?
Gross purchases	30,000	37,000	28,500	35,600
Purchase returns	800	1,000	620	1,050
Purchase discounts	1,400			
Net markdowns		2,100		2,130
Net markups				380
Gross sales		33,500		37,300
Sales returns		1,300		1,600
Sales allowances		1,100		1,500

Retail selling price indexes:
  1/1/Year 1 . . . . 1.00
  12/31/Year 1 . . . . 1.03
  12/31/Year 2 . . . . 1.06

REQUIRED   Prepare a schedule to calculate the costs of Year 1 and Year 2 ending inventories under the dollar-value retail LIFO method.

Plant Assets and Intangibles: Acquisition and Subsequent Expenditures

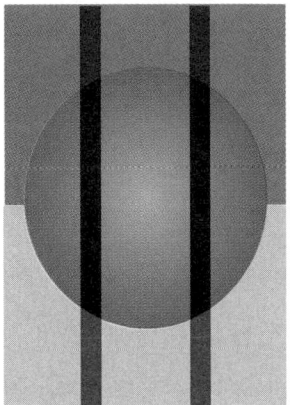

EARNING OBJECTIVES

After studying this chapter, you should be able to:

1. Describe the characteristics of plant assets and intangibles.

2. State the general guideline for valuing plant assets and intangibles at acquisition and explain how it is applied to common transactions involving plant assets and intangibles.

3. Account for interest during construction.

4. Describe the characteristics by which intangibles may be classified.

5. Summarize the accounting requirements for intangibles.

6. Account for research and development (R&D) costs and computer software costs.

7. Explain the concept of goodwill and account for goodwill.

8. Account for assets acquired in nonmonetary exchanges.

9. State the conceptual guideline for accounting for expenditures after acquisition and apply it to common categories of expenditures after acquisition.

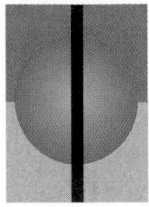

n Chapters 11 and 12 we continue our coverage of accounting and reporting for assets by examining plant assets and intangibles. In this chapter we present the financial accounting and reporting issues related to the acquisition of plant assets and intangibles and expenditures made after acquisition. In Chapter 12 we describe accounting for and reporting of the use and disposition of plant assets and intangibles.

For many entities, one of the largest categories of resources (assets) is property, plant, and equipment, also known as plant assets. For example, Intel Corporation's plant assets constituted 43 percent of its total assets in 1995. For other companies, intangible assets represent a large investment. Also, in 1995, 52 percent of the total assets of Gannett Co., Inc., a diversified news and information company, were classified as goodwill.

In spite of some obvious differences between plant assets and intangibles, the accounting and reporting issues for these two types of assets are virtually identical. What are the common characteristics of these resources? What are their typical components? How do accountants determine whether expenditures related to plant assets and intangibles should be recorded in an asset account or an expense account? For those expenditures that are recorded in an asset account, how should the costs be matched with revenues over the benefit period? How should the disposition of plant assets and intangibles be accounted for? The purpose of Chapters 11 and 12 is to address these questions.

We begin by describing the characteristics of plant assets and intangibles. We then describe the general process of valuation at acquisition for various types of plant assets and intangibles. Next, noncash acquisitions of plant assets and intangibles are covered. The chapter concludes with a discussion of the appropriate accounting treatment for expenditures after acquisition, and the reporting and disclosure requirements for plant assets and intangibles.

CHARACTERISTICS OF PLANT ASSETS AND INTANGIBLES

Describe the characteristics of plant assets and intangibles.

CONCEPTUAL

Plant assets and intangibles are acquired for use in operations and provide benefits over several accounting periods.

Virtually all business firms acquire some assets for use over an extended period. If these assets have a physical existence, they are referred to by one of three terms: property, plant, and equipment; fixed assets; or **plant assets.** In this chapter we generally use the latter term. If the assets do not have a physical existence—for example, patents—they are referred to as **intangible assets.**

In general, plant assets and intangibles may be distinguished from other assets by two major characteristics. First, *they are acquired to be used in operations.* That is, the value of plant assets and intangible assets results from the services they provide, not from their potential resale. A company acquires plant assets and intangibles for use in its operations; it considers selling or otherwise disposing of them only after they have generated revenue for the company for several periods. Second, *plant assets and intangibles provide benefits over several accounting periods.* According to the matching principle, the cost of a resource that provides service potential only during the period in which it is acquired should be expensed entirely in that period. Because plant assets and intangibles provide benefits over several accounting periods, they are classified in the balance sheet as noncurrent assets.

Typical plant assets include buildings, improvements, machinery, furniture, tools, certain leased property, and leasehold improvements. Typical intangible assets include patents, copyrights, trademarks, franchises, and goodwill. The service potential—that is, cash-generating ability—of most plant assets and intangibles decreases as they are used in producing revenues. Therefore, according to the matching principle, companies must allocate the cost of the service potential embodied in these assets to expense over the periods in which their service potential is consumed. We will discuss the process of allocating their *initial* cost in Chapter 12.

When a company acquires service potential in the form of plant assets and intangibles, it must record the new assets in the accounts. In the next section we will describe the guidelines for valuing plant assets and intangibles at acquisition.

VALUATION OF PLANT ASSETS AND INTANGIBLES AT ACQUISITION

The general guideline for valuation at acquisition is the same for all assets, including plant assets and intangibles. *Assets acquired should be recorded at the best estimate of their fair value at the date of acquisition.* While this guideline is easily understood from a conceptual standpoint, its application in practice sometimes becomes quite complex. In this section we will discuss the application of the valuation guideline, first to plant assets and then to intangibles.

Plant Assets

Like other assets, plant assets are recorded in the accounts when an exchange transaction occurs, such as when a building is purchased. Plant assets may also be acquired without an exchange transaction, such as when a company constructs its own plant or receives donations. In both these cases long-term service potential is obtained, so an asset must be recorded.

When a company acquires a plant asset, cost on the acquisition date usually is the best estimate of the asset's fair value. Thus, plant assets usually are recorded initially at the cost incurred in a transaction actually entered into by the company. This method of valuation is an application of the historical cost (historical exchange price) principle. When a cost is not incurred at acquisition—such as when a company issues shares of its own stock to acquire a plant asset—both the asset and the stock should be recorded at the fair value of what is received or given, whichever is more reasonably determinable. Keep in mind, however, that the reason for recording an asset at cost is that at the date an asset is acquired, cost is the best estimate of its fair value.

Few accountants disagree with the use of this valuation method *at acquisition.* However, there is much disagreement about the appropriate valuation of plant assets *after* they are acquired. The greater the time that has passed since the acquisition date, the more likely it is that an asset's fair value will differ from its acquisition cost. Under U.S. GAAP, however, plant assets are reported at depreciated historical cost subsequent to their acquisition.

Internationally, valuation methods differ from country to country. Like the United States, Canada, Germany, and Japan adhere strictly to historical cost in valuing plant assets. Other countries, such as the Netherlands and most English-speaking countries other than the United States and Canada, allow periodic revaluation to current value. In these circumstances, companies typically disclose the historical cost as well as the current values.

Application of the historical cost principle to plant assets means that all necessary sacrifices made to obtain the asset's service potential and place it into position for its intended use should be recorded in the asset account. This principle was discussed in Chapter 2. It is also the same guideline we used to record inventory acquisitions in Chapter 9. We will now consider how this principle is applied to each of the major types of plant assets.

2 State the general guideline for valuing plant assets and intangibles at acquisition and explain how it is applied to common transactions involving plant assets and intangibles.

CONCEPTUAL

Assets should be recorded at the best estimate of fair value at the date of acquisition.

CONCEPTUAL

Cost usually is the best estimate of fair value at acquisition.

CONCEPTUAL

Cost includes all necessary sacrifices made to obtain an asset's service potential and place it into position for its intended use.

Land and Land Improvements

The cost of obtaining land and readying it for its intended use may include, in addition to the purchase price, closing costs (e.g., attorneys' fees), survey costs, earth-moving costs, and unpaid taxes or mortgages assumed by the purchaser. The purchaser may incur some or all of these costs before the land is put into use. The fact that the buyer is willing to incur the purchase price and other costs implies that the land's service potential is at least equal to the cost incurred. Thus, the buyer should record all costs incurred in an asset account.

The cost of land improvements that produce permanent benefits, such as landscaping, sewer installation, and special tax assessments for paving and streetlights, may be included in the land account. Because these improvements provide benefits indefinitely, and are often replaced and maintained by an outside agency, depreciation is an inappropriate way to account for them. On the other hand, the cost of improvements that provide benefits over limited periods, such as fences, parking lots, and other items that are not maintained by an outside agency, should be recorded separately in a land improvements account. The company then depreciates them over the expected benefit period.

Companies often acquire land with the objective of constructing a factory, an office building, or a warehouse. In such circumstances, the company should record all costs incurred up to the point where construction begins as part of the cost of the land, because the company is merely readying the land for its intended use. If the company must remove old structures, the cost of removing them, net of any salvage value, is considered a cost of the land. At first glance it may not seem to matter whether such costs are treated as part of the land cost or part of the building cost. However, considering that buildings are depreciated, but land is not, proper treatment of these costs is clearly important.

To be properly classified as a plant asset, an asset must be used for operating purposes. If a company acquires land primarily for speculative purposes, even though management may ultimately construct a plant on it, the land should be classified as an investment rather than a plant asset.

Machinery and Equipment

The cost of machinery and equipment usually is determined by the amount paid for an item. However, companies often buy machinery and equipment at a price that is subject to a discount for prompt payment. Theoretically, the invoice price *net* of the cash discount is the asset's cash-equivalent exchange price. If the buyer does not pay promptly, and thus forgoes the discount, the additional cost incurred represented by the discount not taken is *not* a cost of the asset. Instead, it should be considered a financing charge incurred for the use of the seller's cash over the discount period. In practice, however, many companies include discounts not taken as part of the asset cost if they are not material amounts.

In addition to the net invoice cost, the cost of machinery and equipment (and furniture and fixtures) includes freight charges; in-transit insurance costs; taxes applicable to the acquisition; the cost of special foundations or bases; and assembly, installation, and testing costs. All these costs are necessary to acquire the asset and get it in position for its intended use.

Buildings

A company may acquire buildings by purchasing them, by constructing them, or by contracting with an outside party to construct them. Regardless of the way a building is acquired, the general valuation guideline remains the same. The company should record in the building account all costs necessary to obtain the building and get it into position for its intended use.

When a company acquires a building from an outside party, through either contracted construction or purchase of an existing building, an objective market transaction occurs. This market transaction establishes a value for the building. Additional costs incidental to the purchase, such as attorneys' fees and building permits, should be recorded in the building account along with the acquisition price.

Self-Constructed Assets

When a company constructs its own plant, the asset should be recorded at cost. Cost, however, often is difficult to determine, since there is no exchange transaction to provide an objective figure. Instead of a purchase price, the company incurs material, labor, overhead, and incidental costs. Direct material, direct labor, and direct overhead costs pose no problems in valuation because they clearly are incremental costs associated with the construction of the asset. However, two items create valuation difficulties for self-constructed assets: (1) indirect manufacturing costs and (2) interest during construction. We will discuss these two items in the remainder of this section.

Indirect Manufacturing Costs **Indirect manufacturing costs** include items such as electricity, taxes on manufacturing facilities, factory supervisory costs, manufacturing supplies, factory janitorial services, and depreciation on manufacturing facilities. By definition, *indirect* manufacturing costs cannot be attributed *directly* to a self-constructed asset. Instead, if a company wishes to assign these costs to a self-constructed asset, the costs must be allocated, just as a manufacturing company allocates indirect costs (factory overhead costs) to inventories. To a large extent, indirect manufacturing costs will be incurred whether or not the company is constructing a plant asset, so they are not incremental costs of self-construction. If they were, the company could trace them directly to the self-constructed asset.

CONCEPTUAL

Indirect manufacturing costs cannot be attributed directly to self-constructed assets.

Three methods have been proposed for dealing with this issue:

1. Assign none of the indirect manufacturing overhead to self-constructed assets **(direct costing approach).**

2. Assign indirect manufacturing overhead to self-constructed assets on the same basis the company uses to assign indirect costs to normal inventory production **(full costing approach).**

3. Include in the cost of the self-constructed asset the profit the company would have earned in normal business operations, but instead sacrificed to build the asset **(opportunity cost approach).** This method is appropriate only if a company is operating at full capacity.

Of these three methods, the *full costing approach* is the most commonly used. It is consistent with the way in which the historical cost principle is applied to inventories. The *direct costing approach* may be useful for management purposes but is not acceptable for external reporting under current generally accepted accounting principles. The *opportunity cost approach* has considerable theoretical appeal. However, its subjective "what if" nature (i.e., determining the profit a company would have earned if it had dedicated its operating capacity to inventory production instead of to self-construction) renders it rather impractical, so it is rarely used.

Interest During Construction To place this issue in perspective, recall that interest costs are typically treated as period costs; that is, they are expensed when they are incurred. The rationale for this treatment is that the funds for which interest costs are incurred are being used currently to generate revenues. Therefore, proper matching requires that the costs of using the funds (interest) be expensed as they are incurred. When a company incurs interest costs in the process of constructing assets that are not yet generating revenues, however, a question arises as to whether these costs should be treated as period costs.

The historical cost principle requires that a company capitalize all necessary costs incurred in obtaining an asset and getting it into position for its intended use. Proper matching is then achieved by allocating the capitalized costs as depreciation expense over the periods in which the company generates revenues by using the asset. Accordingly, **interest** costs **during construction** should be capitalized for all assets that require a period of time to ready them for their intended use—that is, all assets that have an *acquisition period*.[1] If the effect of interest capitalization is not material, interest capitalization is not required.

The basic requirements for interest capitalization may be divided into three categories: (1) the qualifying assets, (2) the amount to be capitalized, and (3) the capitalization period. We will discuss the requirements in that order, beginning with qualifying assets.

Qualifying assets. A company should capitalize interest for assets that it constructs (or that are constructed for the company by others) *for its own use* (e.g., an office building or a nuclear power plant), as well as for assets it constructs as discrete projects *for sale or lease* (e.g., a ship or a shopping center). Interest costs *cannot* be capitalized for routinely manufactured inventories, assets in use or ready for use, and assets not ready for use in the earning process and not being prepared for use (e.g., vacant land held for future expansion).

When land qualifies for interest capitalization, the capitalized interest is considered a cost of the asset that results from the construction activities. For example, if a building results from the construction activities, the interest cost is considered a cost of the building. If developed land, such as lots that have been readied for sale, results from the construction activities, the interest cost is considered a cost of the developed land.

Amount to be capitalized. In determining the amount of interest to be capitalized, *the basic conceptual objective is to capitalize interest that could have been avoided had the qualifying assets not been constructed.* This objective can be implemented by considering actual expenditures, actual borrowings, and actual interest cost incurred for qualifying assets during the period. The amount of interest to be capitalized is determined by multiplying actual expenditures for the qualifying asset during the period times the number of months outstanding times the appropriate interest rate. This process can be demonstrated by a simple example.

Assume that three companies, *A, B,* and *C,* are undertaking self-construction that qualifies for interest capitalization. All three companies spend $1,000,000 on qualifying expenditures related to self-construction during the period. However, Company *A* incurs the entire expenditure at the beginning of the period; Company *B* incurs the expenditure halfway through the period; and Company *C* incurs the entire expenditure on the last day of the period. Assume that the appropriate interest rate is 10 percent. The amount of interest each company would capitalize is calculated as follows:

Company *A*: $1,000,000 × 12/12 × .10 = $100,000
Company *B*: $1,000,000 × 6/12 × .10 = $50,000
Company *C*: $1,000,000 × 0/12 × .10 = $0

If a company borrows specifically to finance construction of a qualifying asset, the interest rate on the specific borrowing may be applied to expenditures on the project up to the amount of the specific borrowing. Expenditures in excess of specific borrowings would then be multiplied by the company's weighted average rate on other outstanding borrowings during the period.[2] Capitalized interest cannot

---

[1]"Capitalization of Interest Costs," *Statement of Financial Accounting Standards No. 34* (Stamford, Conn.: FASB, 1979).

[2]Interest rates used generally are the actual rates on borrowings outstanding during the period. However, if some borrowings originated in periods when interest rates were substantially different from the current rates, those interest rates may be excluded from the weighted average calculation, because the objective is to approximate *avoidable* interest costs, which implies *current* borrowing costs. Judgment is required to determine which of the historical rates should be used to approximate avoidable interest costs.

exceed actual interest costs incurred during the period. Companies must disclose both total interest costs incurred during the period and the amount capitalized.

Capitalization period. The capitalization period begins when three conditions have been met: (1) expenditures for the asset have been made, (2) activities necessary to prepare the asset for its intended use (e.g., planning, obtaining permits, and physical construction) are in progress, and (3) interest cost is being incurred. As long as all three conditions are met, interest capitalization continues. The capitalization period ends when the asset is substantially complete and ready for its intended use.

To illustrate the application of these requirements, assume that Murphy Corporation began construction activity on a new office building on January 2, 1998. On that date, Murphy obtained a $3,000,000 construction loan with an 11 percent annual interest rate. Expenditures on the construction project during 1998 and 1999 were as follows:

January 2, 1998	**$ 800,000**
July 1, 1998	**1,000,000**
October 1, 1998	**600,000**
March 1, 1999	**900,000**
June 1, 1999	**1,800,000**

The project was completed on June 30, 1999.

Murphy's only other outstanding interest-bearing debt during the construction period consisted of two long-term notes in the principal amounts of $4,000,000 and $8,000,000, bearing interest at the rates of 12 percent and 15 percent, respectively. These notes were outstanding throughout the construction period. The weighted average interest rate on these notes is 14 percent, calculated as follows:

$$\begin{array}{ll} \$\ 4,000,000 \times .12 = \$\ 480,000 \\ \underline{8,000,000} \times .15 = \underline{\ 1,200,000} \\ \$12,000,000 \qquad\quad \$1,680,000 \end{array}$$

$$\frac{\$1,680,000}{\$12,000,000} = .14$$

The amount of interest Murphy can capitalize for 1998 is $159,500, calculated as follows:

$$\begin{array}{llll} 1/2/98 & \$\ 800,000 \times 12/12 \times .11 = \$\ 88,000 \\ 7/1/98 & 1,000,000 \times\ 6/12 \times .11 = & 55,000 \\ 10/1/98 & \underline{\ 600,000} \times\ 3/12 \times .11 = & \underline{\ 16,500} \\ & \$2,400,000 & \$159,500 \end{array}$$

Note that the company's actual expenditures, $2,400,000, are less than $3,000,000, the amount Murphy borrowed for the construction. Therefore, the weighted average rate on its other borrowings is not used. The company would make the following aggregate journal entry for its expenditures in 1998:

Building	2,559,500	
Cash		2,559,500

($800,000 + $1,000,000 + $600,000 + $159,500)

With the March 1, 1999, expenditure of $900,000, Murphy's total expenditures exceed its $3,000,000 loan. For all expenditures over $3,000,000, interest is capitalized at 14 percent, the weighted average rate on Murphy's other borrowings. Capitalized interest in 1999 would be $199,367.50, calculated as follows:

$$\begin{array}{lll} 1/1/99 & \$2,559,500 \times 6/12 \times .11 = \$140,772.50 \\ 3/1/99 & 440,500 \times 4/12 \times .11 = & 16,151.67 \\ & 459,500 \times 4/12 \times .14 = & 21,443.33 \\ 6/1/99 & 1,800,000 \times 1/12 \times .14 = & \underline{\ 21,000.00} \\ & & \$199,367.50 \end{array}$$

For the six months ending June 30, 1999 the balance in Murphy's building account will increase by $2,899,367.50:

Building 2,899,367.50
    Cash 2,899,367.50
($900,000 + $1,800,000 + $199,367.50)

The noncapitalizable portion of the interest incurred in 1999 would be recorded as interest expense.[3]

Note that if a company's expenditures exceed the sum of its specific and other borrowings, interest can be capitalized only on that portion of the expenditures supported by specific and other borrowings. For example, if Murphy had made expenditures in excess of $15 million, the total of its specific and other borrowings, no interest would be capitalized on its excess expenditures.

Before we turn our attention to intangible assets, we will briefly discuss a special category of long-term assets, natural resources.

Natural Resources

As a company consumes the services embodied in its plant and equipment and other depreciable assets, the physical characteristics of those assets often remain virtually unchanged. On the other hand, **natural resources,** also called **wasting assets,** are consumed physically in the production process. Examples of wasting assets include timberland, oil and gas deposits, and mineral deposits. As in the case of depreciable assets, a major problem in accounting for natural resources is to determine their cost and match it with the revenues generated from their sale. The amount of natural resource cost expensed each period is called **depletion**— an appropriate designation because companies physically *deplete* a natural resource in the production process.

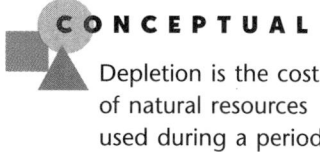

C O N C E P T U A L

Depletion is the cost of natural resources used during a period.

Costs associated with natural resources may be divided into four categories: (1) acquisition costs, (2) exploration costs, (3) development costs, and (4) production costs. *Acquisition costs* include all costs incurred to acquire the property on which a resource is located; the right to search for the natural resource; or the right to a previously discovered resource. *Exploration costs* are costs incurred in the process of searching for natural resources, such as drilling and excavation costs. *Development costs* relate either to tangible assets, such as the cost of constructing or purchasing special-purpose equipment, or to intangible assets, such as the cost of drilling wells or digging shafts and tunnels. *Production costs* include the cost of labor used to extract the resource.

In general, all costs necessary to place a wasting asset in position for its intended use should be capitalized (recorded as a cost of the asset), including acquisition costs. The accounting treatment of exploration costs, which is controversial, is discussed in detail in Chapter 12. Tangible assets related to exploration, development, or production must be depreciated or amortized, as appropriate. Other capitalized costs related to wasting assets must be matched against revenues as the resources are used up—a process which is discussed in Chapter 12.

Accounting policies related to natural resources should be disclosed in the notes to the financial statements. Texaco included the following disclosure in a note to its 1995 annual report:

Exploratory costs, excluding the costs of exploratory wells, are charged to expense as incurred. Costs of drilling exploratory wells, including stratigraphic test wells, are capitalized pending determination whether the wells have found proved reserves which justify commercial development. If such reserves are not found, the drilling costs are charged to

---

[3]Note that if interest expense had been recorded during the year, interest expense, instead of cash, would be credited at the end of the year for the amount of capitalized interest.

exploratory expenses. Intangible drilling costs applicable to productive wells and to development dry holes, as well as tangible equipment costs related to the development of oil and gas reserves, are capitalized.

Intangible Assets

Accounting for intangibles is complicated by the nature of these assets. The accounting issues have been summarized as follows:

> Accounting for an intangible asset involves the same kinds of problems as accounting for other long-lived assets, namely, determining an initial carrying amount, accounting for that amount after acquisition under normal business conditions (amortization), and accounting for that amount if the value declines substantially and permanently. Solving the problems is complicated by the characteristics of an intangible asset: its lack of physical qualities makes evidence of its existence elusive, its value is often difficult to estimate, and its useful life may be indeterminable.[4]

Intangible assets may be classified, based on their characteristics, as follows:

1. *Identifiability.* Many intangibles, such as patents, copyrights, trademarks, and franchises, are *separately identifiable.* Goodwill, however, is a combination of several factors that cannot be separately identified and evaluated. Thus, goodwill is often referred to as an *unidentifiable intangible asset.*

2. *Manner of acquisition.* Companies may either develop intangible assets internally or acquire them from external sources. A patent, for example, may be developed or purchased. If intangibles are acquired externally, they may be acquired singly, in groups, or as part of a business combination.

3. *Expected period of benefit.* Some intangible assets, such as organization costs, may provide benefits indefinitely. The benefit periods of others may be limited by economic factors or by legal or contractual restrictions. Patents, for example, have a legal life of 17 years.

4. *Separability* (exchangeability). Some intangibles, such as patents and franchises, may be sold separately. Others, such as goodwill and organization costs, relate solely to the enterprise as a whole and cannot be sold separately.[5]

4 Describe the characteristics by which intangibles may be classified.

The accounting profession considered each of these characteristics in establishing the accounting requirements for intangibles.

Exhibit 11–1 summarizes the accounting requirements for intangibles. The costs of intangibles acquired from others, whether specifically identifiable or unidentifiable (i.e., goodwill), must be recorded as assets and matched against revenues (amortized) over the periods benefited. The maximum amortization period for the cost of an intangible asset is 40 years. Entities must use the straight-line method of amortization unless they can demonstrate that some other systematic method is more appropriate. The method used should be disclosed in the financial statements. For example, Coca-Cola included the following description of its accounting policy for goodwill and other intangible assets in its 1995 annual report:

> Goodwill and other intangible assets are stated on the basis of cost and are amortized, principally on a straight-line basis, over the estimated future periods to be benefited (not exceeding 40 years). Goodwill and other intangible assets are periodically reviewed for impairment based on an assessment of future operations to ensure that they are appropriately valued.

The last sentence relates to possible impairment beyond the amortized book value, a subject we will discuss in Chapter 12.

---

[4]"Intangible Assets," *Opinions of the Accounting Principles Board No. 17* (New York: AICPA, 1970), para. 2.
[5]Ibid., para. 10.

EXHIBIT 11-1	Summary of Accounting Requirements for Intangibles	
	Method of Acquisition	
Type of Intangible	**Purchased**	**Internally Developed**
Specifically Identifiable	Capitalize and amortize over shorter of 40 years or useful life	Expense as incurred *or* Capitalize and amortize over shorter of 40 years or useful life
Unidentifiable (Goodwill)	Capitalize and amortize over shorter of 40 years or useful life	Expense as incurred

5 **Summarize the accounting requirements for intangibles.**

CONCEPTUAL

Recorded assets must have a relevant attribute that is measurable with sufficient reliability.

The costs of developing intangibles internally are accounted for in one of two ways, depending on whether the intangible is or is not specifically identifiable. Intangibles that are not specifically identifiable must be expensed as they are incurred. There is no specific authoritative guidance for how companies should record costs incurred to *develop* specifically identifiable intangibles, such as patents, trademarks, and copyrights. Consequently, companies may either (1) record the costs as assets and amortize them over the periods benefited or (2) expense them as they are incurred.

In spite of the lack of definitive guidance for internally developed intangible assets that can be specifically identified, the conceptual framework assists us in determining the appropriate accounting treatment. To be reported as an asset in the balance sheet, an item must meet the definition of an asset. However, that criterion provides only a "first cut" for items to be reported as assets. Items that meet the definition of an asset must also have a relevant attribute that is measurable with sufficient reliability. Keeping these criteria in mind, a company should be able to establish a conceptually acceptable and consistent approach to accounting for the costs incurred in developing specifically identifiable intangibles.

Now that we have described the general guidelines for accounting for intangibles, we will look at how those guidelines are applied to specific intangibles. Intangibles that can be specifically identified can be accounted for individually using the guidelines in Exhibit 11–1. The following sections describe common types of specifically identifiable intangibles and the appropriate accounting for each type. The very last section, on goodwill, describes accounting for unidentifiable intangibles.

Patents

A **patent,** granted by the U.S. Patent Office, is the exclusive right to use, manufacture, and sell a product or process. Patents are granted for a period of 17 years. Ownership of a patent does not guarantee that an asset exists, however. If a patent is not expected to increase a company's future cash flow, then it is not an asset. A company may defer and amortize the cost of a patent only if that patent provides the company with measurable future benefits.

Research and development costs incurred to develop products or processes that become patented must be expensed as they are incurred.[6] Since the actual costs of obtaining a patent from the government are minimal (government processing fees and attorneys' fees), for all practical purposes the only patents that

---

[6]Guidelines for research and development costs are provided by "Accounting for Research and Development Costs," *Statement of Financial Accounting Standards No. 2* (Stamford, Conn.: FASB, 1974). These guidelines are discussed later in this chapter.

companies capitalize are existing patents purchased from another party. The amount capitalized should include the direct costs of acquiring the patent plus other costs incurred in securing it, such as attorneys' fees.

Copyrights

A **copyright** is a grant by the federal government providing the owner the exclusive right to reproduce and sell an artistic or literary work. The government grants copyrights to business firms for 75 years.[7] The owner of a copyright may assign or sell it to other parties.

Trademarks and Trade Names

Trademarks and **trade names** are words, symbols, or other devices that identify particular products. The right of exclusive use of a trademark resides with the original user as long as the original user employs the trademark continuously. Companies may register trademarks with the U.S. Patent Office for a period of 20 years. Registrations are renewable for additional 20-year periods as long as the trademark is used continuously. From a practical standpoint, the period over which the exclusive use of the trademark provides benefits in the form of increased cash flows may be only a few years. Conversely, the trademark's benefit may extend indefinitely, as in the case of "Coke," Coca-Cola's widely recognized product.

Franchises

As discussed in Chapter 7, a **franchise** is an agreement in which one party (the franchisor) grants another party (the franchisee) the exclusive right to market a product or service within a designated area. For example, governmental units often grant franchise rights to utility companies. Likewise, individuals and companies often operate under franchise arrangements with organizations such as fast-food operations (e.g., Subway and Burger King), motels (e.g., Holiday Inn), and professional sports teams (e.g., the Kansas City Royals).

If the franchisee pays an initial franchise fee, the fee should be recorded as an intangible asset. The franchisee should amortize the franchise fee over the life of the franchise if the fee is for a specified number of years, or over 40 years if the franchise term exceeds 40 years. If the franchise is indefinite in duration or perpetual, the franchisee should amortize the initial franchise fee over the estimated benefit period, not to exceed 40 years. The periodic payments required under a franchise arrangement, such as fees based on periodic operating income, should be expensed when they are incurred in accordance with the matching principle.

Lease Prepayments and Leasehold Improvements

A lease is a contractual agreement in which one party (the lessor) grants another party (the lessee) the right to use specified property for a specific period in exchange for periodic cash payments.[8] In many instances the lessee must make a lump-sum payment, also called a **lease prepayment,** to the lessor at the time of signing the lease agreement. The lessee should capitalize this prepayment and amortize it to lease expense over the lease period. Because lease prepayments usually relate to tangible property, companies sometimes include them under plant assets in the balance sheet.

---

[7]In an interesting, related development, the U.S. Copyright Office has provided 10-year copyright protection to registrants who manufacture microchips. The penalty for infringement is $250,000 for each "mask work" (circuit pattern) that is reproduced without the copyright owner's permission.

[8]We describe the detailed accounting and reporting requirements for leases in Chapter 15.

Leasehold improvements made to leased property by the lessee, such as buildings, usually revert to the lessor at the termination of the lease. Thus, although the lessee pays for the improvements, the lessee does not own them. Rather, the lessee has the right to use the improvements over the lease term. The cost of leasehold improvements usually is reported under plant assets in the lessee's balance sheet. However, some companies include such costs under intangible assets. Since the lease term establishes a maximum benefit period, the lessee should amortize the cost of the improvements to lease expense over the lease term or the life of the improvement, whichever is shorter. For example, McDonald's Corporation included leasehold improvements under property and equipment in its 1995 annual report, with the following disclosure in its summary of significant accounting policies: ". . . leasehold improvements—lesser of useful lives of assets or lease terms including option periods. . . ."

Organization Costs

Companies incur a variety of costs in the process of organizing. Legal fees, accounting fees, state fees and taxes, and promotional costs are common examples of **organization costs.** A company usually incurs these costs either before it begins operating or during the early stages of operation.

A company would not incur organization costs if it did not anticipate that future revenues would be sufficient to recover the costs and provide a fair rate of return. Furthermore, if the company expects to continue in existence indefinitely, conceptually its organization costs should be capitalized and reported as an intangible asset. The rationale is that those costs were incurred to benefit the company over its entire life. However, since intangible assets must be amortized over not more than 40 years, this conceptually attractive alternative is not feasible. Most companies amortize organization costs over a short arbitrary period on a straight-line basis. For income tax purposes, organization costs must be amortized over five years or more.

Other Assets

Many companies have a balance sheet classification called **other assets** or **deferred charges.** Items in this category might include long-term prepayments (such as license fees, rent, insurance, and taxes), plant rearrangement or relocation costs, the book value of idle plant assets, and sometimes organization costs. The category seems to be a catchall for items that do not fit conveniently into some other asset category and are not material enough individually to constitute a separate category. Companies must amortize each item in the other assets or deferred charges category over its estimated benefit period, not to exceed 40 years.

Research and Development Costs

Expenditures aimed at developing new products or processes, or at modifying existing products or processes, are called **research and development costs,** or simply **R&D.** R&D often is a highly significant portion of the cost of doing business. For example, in 1995, GE reported R&D expense of nearly $2 billion (see Appendix B).

The inability to reasonably estimate the amount and timing of the benefits from R&D expenditures makes the capitalization and amortization of R&D expenditures impractical. Therefore, in general, companies must expense research and development costs as they are incurred. The FASB defines *research* and *development* in *Statement No. 2* as follows:

> *Research* is planned search or critical investigation aimed at discovery of new knowledge with the hope that such knowledge will be useful in de-

6   **Account for research and development (R&D) costs and computer software costs.**

veloping a new product or service (hereinafter "product") or a new process or technique (hereinafter "process") or in bringing about a significant improvement to an existing product or process.

Development is the translation of research findings or other knowledge into a plan or design for a new product or process or for a significant improvement to an existing product or process whether intended for sale or use.[9]

Several examples of activities that typically would constitute R&D activity, as well as activities that typically would *not* constitute R&D activity, are presented in Exhibit 11–2. In general, the FASB's intent appears to be to include in R&D those activities related to *preproduction* efforts and to exclude from R&D those activities related to *existing and ongoing production.*

The FASB has specified five cost elements that should be associated with R&D activities:[10] (1) materials, equipment, and facilities; (2) personnel; (3) purchased intangibles; (4) contract services; and (5) indirect costs. The costs of materials, equipment, or facilities that have been acquired or constructed for a specific R&D project and have no alternative future use (and thus no separate economic value) must be expensed as incurred. The costs of materials, equipment, or facilities that have an alternative future use (in other research and development projects or otherwise) should be capitalized as tangible assets. To the extent that such materials subsequently are consumed in R&D activities, they must be expensed as R&D costs. Likewise, depreciation on other equipment and facilities used in research and development activities constitutes research and development cost.

The costs of personnel engaged in R&D activities must be expensed as R&D costs as they are incurred. The costs of intangibles that have been purchased from others for use in a specific R&D project, and that have no alternative future use, must be expensed as they are incurred. If the intangibles have an alternative future use (in R&D activities or otherwise), the costs should be capitalized as intangible assets and amortized. The amortization of those intangibles used in R&D activities constitutes R&D expense.

The costs of services performed by others in connection with a company's R&D activities must be expensed as they are incurred, as R&D costs. A *reasonable* allocation of indirect costs should be included in R&D costs and expensed as the costs are incurred. General and administrative costs, however, should *not* be included as R&D costs unless they are clearly related to R&D activity.

FASB Statement No. 2 does *not* cover costs incurred in performing R&D activities under *contractual arrangement.* For example, if Company A agrees to pay Company B $100,000 to conduct research, *Statement No. 2* does not govern Company B's treatment of costs incurred under the contract. If, however, the activities of Company B constitute R&D as defined by *Statement No. 2,* Company A must expense the $100,000 as the cost is incurred. Likewise, accounting for indirect costs that are reimbursable under the terms of a contract are not covered by the *Statement.* For example, a company that incurs costs for R&D activity conducted under a government contract may capitalize and amortize the costs. As a result, companies that perform R&D both under contract and on their own account (for themselves) may capitalize costs associated with the contract R&D, but must expense the costs incurred in connection with R&D done for themselves.

Finally, the amount of R&D costs charged to expense must be disclosed for each period for which an income statement is presented since the amount of R&D expenditures may be useful for assessing an entity's future cash flows. The method of expensing R&D costs as they are incurred is a practical solution to a complex problem. This approach does not deny that there may be future benefits associated with R&D expenditures. It is merely a practical, conservative way of dealing with

CONCEPTUAL

The amount of R&D expenditures is useful in assessing future cash flows.

---

[9]*FASB Statement No. 2,* para. 8.
[10]Ibid., para. 11.

EXHIBIT 11-2	R&D Activities versus Non–R&D Activities

R&D Activities[a]

1. Laboratory research aimed at discovery of new knowledge.
2. Searching for applications of new research findings or other knowledge.
3. Conceptual formulation and design of possible product or process alternatives.
4. Testing in search for or evaluation of product or process alternatives.
5. Modification of the formulation or design of a product or process.
6. Design, construction, and testing of preproduction prototypes and models.
7. Design of tools, jigs, molds, and dies involving new technology.
8. Design, construction, and operation of a pilot plant that is not of a scale economically feasible to the enterprise for commercial production.
9. Engineering activity required to advance the design of a product to the point where it meets specific functional and economic requirements and is ready for manufacture.

Non–R&D Activities[b]

1. Engineering follow-through in an early phase of commercial production.
2. Quality control during commercial production.
3. Troubleshooting in connection with breakdowns during commercial production.
4. Routine, ongoing efforts to refine, enrich, or otherwise improve upon the qualities of an existing product.
5. Adaptation of an existing capability to a particular requirement or customer's need as part of a continuing commercial activity.
6. Seasonal or other periodic design changes to existing products.
7. Routine design of tools, jigs, molds, and dies.
8. Activity, including design and construction engineering, related to the construction, relocation, rearrangement, or start-up of facilities or equipment other than pilot plants and facilities or equipment whose sole use is for a particular research and development project.
9. Legal work in connection with patent applications or litigation, and the sale or licensing of patents.

[a]FASB *Statement* No. 2, para. 9.
[b]Ibid., para. 10.

the uncertainty and measurement difficulties inherent in research and development programs.

Computer Software Costs

Costs incurred to purchase or develop computer software to be sold, leased, or otherwise marketed must be expensed as incurred as research and development costs *until the technological feasibility of the product or process is established.*[11] Technological feasibility is deemed to be established when a company has completed all planning, designing, coding, and testing activities necessary to determine that a product can be produced to design specifications. To establish technological feasibility, a detailed program design must be completed. In the absence of such a design, a working model of the product must be completed and confirmed by testing.

Once technological feasibility has been established, costs incurred to produce product masters must be capitalized as **computer software costs.** Product masters include a completed version of the software product, ready for copying; the associated documentation; and training materials. As soon as the product is available for release to customers, capitalization of these costs must cease. Capitalized costs must be amortized on a product-by-product basis.

Costs of duplicating the software, documentation, and training materials from the product masters, and of physically packaging the product for distribution, are

---

[11]"Accounting for the Costs of Computer Software to Be Sold, Leased, or Otherwise Marketed," *Statement of Financial Accounting Standards No. 86* (Stamford, Conn.: FASB, 1985).

capitalized as inventory, as they are for other products. These costs should be recorded as cost of sales when sales revenue from the product is recognized. Maintenance and customer support costs must be expensed when the related revenue is recognized, or when the costs are incurred, if earlier.

Several unresolved issues remain in the area of accounting for computer software. For example, GAAP does not cover accounting for the costs of computer software to be used internally. Also, there are no specific guidelines for revenue recognition from the sale of computer software. As the emphasis in our economy continues to shift from tangible, physical outputs to intangible, creative outputs, more guidance is likely to be needed to account for these important issues.

Goodwill

Goodwill is perhaps the most misunderstood asset in financial accounting and reporting. A primary reason for this misunderstanding is that most discussions of goodwill fail to distinguish clearly between the *definition* and the *measurement* of goodwill. **Goodwill** consists of the favorable characteristics of a business enterprise that are intangible and cannot be separately identified and valued. Examples of favorable characteristics that often make up goodwill include the following:

Explain the concept of goodwill and account for goodwill.

CONCEPTUAL

Goodwill consists of intangible favorable characteristics of a business that cannot be separately identified and valued.

1. Superior management team.
2. Outstanding sales management or organization.
3. Weakness in the management of a competitor.
4. Effective advertising.
5. Secret manufacturing process.
6. Good labor relations.
7. Outstanding credit rating.
8. Top-flight training program for employees.
9. High standing in the community.
10. Unfavorable developments in operations of a competitor.
11. Favorable association with another company.
12. Strategic location.
13. Discovery of talents or resources.
14. Favorable tax conditions.
15. Favorable government regulation.[12]

Unlike inventory, property, and even specifically identifiable intangibles such as patents and copyrights, the components of goodwill cannot be bought or sold separately because they cannot exist apart from the company to which they belong. By increasing a company's earning power, these components increase the company's value; they are, then, assets. Goodwill is recorded as an asset, however, only when part of a company's acquisition cost is identified with goodwill. A company may generate goodwill in its normal business operations, such as when it develops resources or gains a favorable image in the community. But to value this goodwill without a market transaction is so difficult, and the results so subjective, that the company generating the goodwill cannot record it as an asset. *Only by acquiring another entity may a company record goodwill as an asset.*

In an actual situation involving the acquisition of a company, both the buyer and the seller probably would use several methods to estimate the value of goodwill in the acquired entity. These estimates, along with many other considerations, such as the bargaining power and persuasiveness of the two parties, would then

CONCEPTUAL

Goodwill cannot be bought or sold separately from the company.

---

[12]George R. Catlett and Norman O. Olson, "Accounting for Goodwill," *Accounting Research Study No. 10* (New York: AICPA, 1968), pp. 17–18.

serve as inputs in the process of negotiating the final transaction price. The amount recorded as goodwill for accounting purposes depends on (1) the total purchase price of the company and (2) the fair value of the company's identifiable net assets. The excess of the total acquisition price over the fair value of the identifiable net assets is recorded as goodwill.[13]

For example, assume that Company *A* acquires Company *B* for $1,000,000 cash. The book value of Company *B*'s net assets is $600,000, composed of assets with a book value of $1,100,000 less liabilities with a book value of $500,000. However, the *fair value* of Company *B*'s assets is $1,300,000, and the fair value of its liabilities $500,000—the same as their book value. Therefore, Company *A* would record goodwill of $200,000 as part of the acquisition:

Cash purchase price		**$1,000,000**
Fair value of net assets:		
Assets	**$1,300,000**	
Liabilities	**(500,000)**	**(800,000)**
Goodwill		**$ 200,000**

Note that the *book value* of *B*'s net assets has no relevance when calculating the amount of goodwill to be recorded.

CONCEPTUAL

Goodwill appears on the balance sheet only when an entity has purchased it in connection with the acquisition of another entity.

Companies must expense the internal costs of developing, maintaining, or restoring goodwill as they are incurred. Thus, goodwill appears on the balance sheet only when an entity has purchased it in connection with the acquisition of another entity. For tax purposes, the cost of goodwill is not a deductible expense, unless the goodwill was acquired in a cash transaction after August 10, 1993 (in which case the amortization period is 15 years).

In sum, goodwill is recorded as an asset only when it is "bought and paid for" in connection with the acquisition of a company. This approach does not deny the existence of goodwill in the absence of a market transaction. Instead, it recognizes the lack of verifiability in the valuation of goodwill in circumstances other than a market transaction.

The practice of recording purchased goodwill on the balance sheet and amortizing it over not more than 40 years is peculiarly American. In many countries, goodwill is written off against retained earnings in the year of purchase. In others it is recorded as an asset but never amortized. In still others it is recorded as an asset and amortized over a period much shorter than 40 years—in many cases as few as 5 years.

NONCASH ACQUISITION OF PLANT ASSETS AND INTANGIBLES

So far in this chapter, we have assumed that plant assets and intangibles have been acquired for cash or promises to pay cash. In this section, we discuss events and transactions in which plant assets and intangibles are acquired without paying cash.

---

[13]It is possible to have a situation in which the fair value of the identifiable net assets *exceeds* the purchase price of a company. This difference is called *negative goodwill* or *badwill.* When negative goodwill arises, the acquiring company must apply it to reduce the values otherwise assignable to noncurrent (long-term) assets, except long-term investments in marketable securities, in proportion to their fair values. If through this process the company reduces its noncurrent assets to zero value and an excess of fair value over cost remains, the company should establish a deferred credit, excess of assigned value of identifiable assets over cost, and amortize it over the periods benefited, not exceeding 40 years.

The rationale for the accounting requirements for negative goodwill is that companies should not record assets at more than cost. Also, the measured consideration given up usually provides a more reliable estimate of fair value of noncurrent assets acquired, except for securities, than does direct valuation of the assets. See "Business Combinations," *Opinions of the Accounting Principles Board No. 16* (New York: AICPA, 1970), para. 91.

We begin by describing the accounting when stock is issued to acquire assets. Next, we describe the accounting for donated assets. Lump-sum purchases are then described, and we conclude the section with a discussion of accounting for exchanges of nonmonetary assets.

Issuance of Stock

Plant assets and intangibles (and other assets) acquired by issuing stock should be recorded at their fair values or the fair value of the stock given up, whichever is more readily determinable. If the stock is traded actively on an organized stock exchange, the market value of the stock probably provides the better estimate of the fair value of the acquired assets. If the market value of the stock is not readily determinable, then the accountant must attempt to determine the fair value of the acquired assets directly, either by analyzing current market activity for those assets or by appraisal. As a last resort, if the market value of neither the stock nor the acquired assets is readily determinable, the board of directors of the acquiring company must establish a value for both the acquired assets and the stock. In such a case, the board of directors normally would seek expert advice.

Donations

A company may receive donated property either from its owners or from outsiders—such as when a local government donates land to attract industry. Donated property from outsiders often is subject to contingencies, such as a requirement that the recipient maintain a certain level of employment for a number of years before title passes. Unless there is substantial doubt that the contingencies will be met, the donated assets should be recorded in the accounts at the time of donation. The financial statements should disclose any contingencies.

The conventional system of accounting relies on exchange transactions. Usually, something is given up and something is received, and the exchange determines what the acquired asset is worth. Determining the value of an asset received through donation may be difficult, however. This type of transaction is called a **nonreciprocal transfer**—that is, an asset is received without a corresponding sacrifice, either at the time of receipt or in the future.

The historical cost principle cannot be used to determine the amount at which to record donated assets. The only costs incurred by the recipient (e.g., legal fees) are likely to be insignificant in relation to the fair value of the donated assets. As a result, the historical cost to the recipient is not a reasonable estimate of fair value. Therefore, donated assets should be recorded at their fair value at the date of donation, as determined by quoted market prices for the asset, if available. If quoted market prices are not available, then quoted market prices for similar assets, appraisals, or valuation techniques such as the present value of estimated cash flows should be used.[14] This method is not a violation of the historical cost principle, but rather a recognition that historical cost is used to value assets at acquisition only when such an approach produces a reasonable estimate of the fair value of the acquired assets. When historical cost does not accomplish that objective, it should be abandoned in favor of an approach that produces more realistic results.

In general, the fair value of an asset received by donation is also recorded as revenue or as a gain in the period it is received.[15] For example, assume Schultz Corporation donated a building with a fair value of $10 million to Somewhere State

CONCEPTUAL

Historical cost is not useful in recording donated assets.

[14]"Accounting for Contributions Received and Contributions Made," *Statement of Financial Accounting Standards No. 116* (Norwalk, Conn.: FASB, June 1993), para. 19.
[15]Ibid., para. 8. However, contributed services that do not require specialized skills and contributed works of art and similar items that are held for public exhibition rather than for financial gain need not be recognized as assets and revenues. Ibid., paras. 9 and 11.

University, to be used to house the Schultz College of Business. Somewhere State would record the fair value of the building both as an asset and as revenue:

Building 10,000,000
 Revenue from receipt of donated building   10,000,000

However, the fair value of assets received by business enterprises from governmental units usually are not recognized as revenues.[16] Instead, it is typically recorded as donated capital, an owners' equity account. As an example, assume the city of Prescott gave five acres of land with a fair value of $300,000 to Fox Company, to be used as the site of a manufacturing facility. Fox would record the receipt of the land as follows:

Land.   300,000
 Donated capital   300,000

Lump-Sum Purchases

It is not unusual for a company to buy two or more different assets for a single "package" price. Such a transaction is referred to as a "lump-sum" or "basket" purchase. Normally, the total cost of the package is presumed to be the best evidence of the combined fair values of all the assets in the package. Somehow an appropriate share of the total cost must be allocated to each asset.

The standard practice is to allocate the acquisition cost among the assets on the basis of their relative fair values. The buyer may have to rely on appraisals, tax assessments, insurance data, and the like to arrive at a fair value for each asset. The seller's book values, which may or may not be known to the buyer, are seldom realistic indicators of fair value. If the fair value of only one of the assets is determinable, that fair value is recorded, and the other assets are valued at the difference between the cash paid and the known fair value. (See Chapter 9 for a discussion of this allocation process related to inventory acquisitions.)

Nonmonetary Exchanges

We have already noted that companies may acquire plant assets, intangibles, or other nonmonetary assets, such as inventories, in exchange for nonmonetary assets. Such transactions are called **nonmonetary exchanges.** We will first consider the general guideline for accounting for nonmonetary exchanges. Then we will provide several illustrations.

General Guideline

Account for assets acquired in nonmonetary exchanges.

CONCEPTUAL

Fair values generally govern the recording process for nonmonetary exchanges.

In *all* exchanges, including nonmonetary exchanges, the general guideline is that acquired assets are recorded at their own fair values or at the fair value of the sacrificed asset, whichever is clearer. That is, *fair values govern the recording process.* Assets are recorded at the best estimate of their worth to the company that acquires them at the time it acquires them—the point at which the earning process begins for those assets. Gains and losses are recognized on surrendered assets, since the earning process ends when they are given up.

The accounting guidelines for nonmonetary exchanges basically implement and reiterate this guideline. Under two circumstances, however, the general guideline does *not* apply:

I. The fair value of neither the surrendered asset nor the acquired asset is determinable.

---
[16]*Statement No. 116* does not apply to transfers of assets from governmental units to business enterprises. Ibid., para. 4.

2. An exchange involving *similar* assets results in a gain.

We will discuss the first of these two exceptions at the end of the next section. We will describe the second exception in our discussion of exchanges of similar assets.

Exchanges of Dissimilar Assets

Many nonmonetary exchanges involve assets with dissimilar functions. For example, a tract of land may be exchanged for a patent. Such transactions are referred to as nonmonetary exchanges of **dissimilar assets.** Accounting for these exchanges follows the general guideline. Gains or losses are recognized in full at the time of the exchange.

Assume that Bain surrenders a tract of land (book value, $60,000; estimated fair value, $150,000) to Pitt in exchange for a patent whose fair value is not readily determinable. Bain would record the exchange as follows:

Patent.	150,000	
Land		60,000
Gain on exchange		90,000

The earning process for the land has culminated, and the patent's earning process has just begun. Now let us modify the example slightly. If the fair value of the patent is determinable—say, $140,000—and that value is more clearly evident than the fair value of the land, Bain would record the patent at its fair value, and the gain would be $80,000—the difference between the fair value of the patent ($140,000) and the book value of the land ($60,000):

Patent.	140,000	
Land		60,000
Gain on exchange		80,000

Note that when the fair value of only the land was determinable, Bain recognized a gain on the disposal of the land and recorded the patent at its estimated fair value, basing the estimate on the fair value of the land. If the fair value of the land were less than its book value, Bain would recognize a loss. For example, if the fair value of the land (and patent) were $50,000, Bain would make the following entry:

Patent.	50,000	
Loss on exchange	10,000	
Land		60,000

A small amount of cash, called *boot,* may be included in a nonmonetary exchange. Boot is included whenever the fair values of the exchanged assets differ. Boot *surrendered* along with a nonmonetary asset may be thought of as increasing the fair value surrendered in a nonmonetary exchange of dissimilar assets. On the other hand, boot *received* decreases the *net* fair value surrendered.

As stated earlier, the general guideline does not apply when the fair value of neither the surrendered asset nor the acquired asset is objectively determinable. In such instances, the acquired asset is recorded at the book value of the surrendered asset; no gain or loss is recognized. This situation, caused by an inability to measure the exchange objectively, is the only case involving *dissimilar* assets in which accountants depart from the fair value approach.

Exchanges of Similar Assets

A departure from the fair value approach also occurs in *some* nonmonetary exchanges involving similar assets. **Similar assets** are defined as assets that are of the same general type or that perform the same function. Specific examples of similar asset exchanges are:

1. An exchange of inventory for inventory in the same line of business, to facilitate sales to outside customers.

2. An exchange of a productive asset normally not held for sale for a similar productive asset. (A productive asset is one that is held for or used in the production of goods or services.)[17]

Consider how these exchanges differ from the exchange of dissimilar assets described earlier. In an exchange of dissimilar assets, a company gives up one asset for a distinctly different type of asset. Therefore, recognition of a gain or loss on disposal and recording of the acquired asset at fair value make sense, since the earning process has culminated for the old asset. In an exchange of similar assets, however, the company is *trading* one nonmonetary asset for another that performs the same function. Thus, the earning process has not ended for the surrendered asset, or begun for the acquired asset; it is simply continuing. Though a new asset has replaced the old, the process goes on.

When the exchange is seen from this perspective, it seems logical to transfer the book value of the old asset to the new asset. This is the reasoning that underlies the general rule for accounting for exchanges of similar assets. *In exchanges of similar assets, gains are not recognized unless boot is received (and then only partially); losses, however, are recognized fully.* When a company *receives* boot in an exchange of similar assets, the old asset is considered to be *partially sold* (and thus the earning process is complete, and a gain can be recognized on that portion) and *partially exchanged* (and thus the earning process is continued rather than ended for that portion). In the sections that follow, we will consider exchange first at a loss and then at a gain.

Exchange at a Loss   Assume that Deberg Company exchanges some old machinery (cost, $100,000; accumulated depreciation, $40,000) for similar new machinery. Assume further that the fair value of the old machinery is not reasonably determinable, and the fair value of the new machinery is $64,000. Deberg also pays boot (cash) of $10,000. Deberg thus gives up assets with a total book value of $70,000 (the $60,000 book value of the old machinery, net of depreciation, and the $10,000 cash) and receives in return an asset with a fair value of $64,000. The difference of $6,000 ($70,000 – $64,000) is a loss. The old machinery apparently is worth only $54,000 ($6,000 less than its book value), as evidenced by the terms of the exchange.

Recalling that losses are recognized fully, whether the assets exchanged are dissimilar or similar, Deberg records the transaction as follows:

Machinery (new).	64,000	
Accumulated depreciation	40,000	
Loss [($60,000 + $10,000) – $64,000]	6,000	
Machinery (old).		100,000
Cash		10,000

A loss is recorded on disposal of the old machinery and the new machinery is recorded at its fair value. If the fair value of the old machinery had been more clearly evident than the fair value of the new machinery, the old machinery's fair value would have been used to determine the amount of the loss. The old machinery's fair value, along with the boot given, would have been recorded as the cost of the new machinery.

Exchange at a Gain, Boot Given   Now let us assume that Baginski Corporation surrenders a tract of land (book value, $20,000; fair value, $24,000) and $8,000 in

CONCEPTUAL

In an exchange of similar assets, the earnings process does not culminate, but instead continues.

CONCEPTUAL

Losses are recognized fully for both similar and dissimilar exchanges.

[17]"Accounting for Nonmonetary Transactions," *Opinions of the Accounting Principles Board No. 29* (New York: AICPA, 1973), para. 21.

cash to Schaefer Corporation, in exchange for similar land where fair value is not readily determinable. Because the fair value of the sacrificed land exceeds its book value ($24,000 – $20,000), a gain to Baginski of $4,000 is implicit in the transaction. However, since Baginski receives no cash, the exchange is considered to be a continuation of the earning process for the land and no gain is recognized. Baginski merely transfers the book value of the old land, along with the boot given, to the new land:

Land (new)	28,000	
Land (old)		20,000
Cash		8,000

A further implication of this transaction is that the new land is worth $32,000, the sum of the fair values of the assets surrendered to obtain it ($24,000 land + $8,000 cash). The gain of $4,000, however, is suppressed at this point. If the new land is later disposed of in a dissimilar exchange, or in a similar exchange involving a loss, the $4,000 will appear as an increase in the gain or a decrease in the loss resulting from the exchange.

Consider again for a moment an exchange of similar assets in which no cash is involved. In such an exchange neither company has purchased or sold anything; each has merely traded an asset. Therefore, neither company is more or less liquid than it was before the exchange. Also, a company that gives up boot has moved to a position of less liquidity. Because realization has not occurred, no gain can be recognized in either of these instances.

Exchange at a Gain, Boot Received   Now consider a case in which a company *receives* both cash and a nonmonetary asset in an exchange of similar assets. The company has given up a strictly nonmonetary asset, partly for cash and partly for a similar nonmonetary asset. We may think of this transaction as consisting of two parts:

I. A portion of the old asset has been converted to cash (or sold). The company may recognize a gain on *this part* of the transaction since it is a *sale*—that is, the conversion of a nonmonetary asset to cash, which terminates the earning process.[18]

2. The other portion of the old asset has simply been replaced by a similar asset. The company may not recognize a gain on this portion because the earning process has not been completed.

To demonstrate the accounting procedures involved, consider the exchange described earlier, between Baginski and Schaefer, from Schaefer's point of view. Schaefer receives $8,000 cash and land with a fair value of $24,000 in exchange for similar land. The only additional information we need is the book value of the land that Schaefer surrenders. Let us assume that the fair value of the land surrendered by Schaefer is not reasonably determinable but that its book value is $18,000. The total gain is $14,000, calculated as follows:

Fair value received:

Cash	$ 8,000	
Similar asset	24,000	$32,000
Book value surrendered		(18,000)
Total gain		$14,000

Since similar assets have been exchanged, only one-fourth of the book value (.25 × $18,000 = $4,500) is presumed to have been sold. Thus, Schaefer may recognize a gain only on the portion of the book value that was converted to cash

CONCEPTUAL

When boot is given no gain is recognized because realization has not occurred.

---

[18]More generally, we could view any dissimilar asset received (not just cash) as the culmination of the earning process for the portion of the old asset converted to a dissimilar asset and as a basis for gain recognition.

(sold), which is determined by the ratio of cash received to the total fair value received ($8,000 ÷ $32,000 = .25). Since the cash received for this portion of the book value was $8,000, Schaefer should recognize a gain of only $3,500 ($8,000 – $4,500). Schaefer cannot recognize the remainder of the gain ($14,000 total gain – $3,500 recognized gain = $10,500 unrecognized gain), because that applies to the portion of the transaction that is considered to be an exchange of similar assets. Thus Schaefer must record the acquired land at $13,500 ($24,000 fair value – $10,500 unrecognized gain). Stated another way, Schaefer must record the new asset at the book value of the old asset ($18,000) minus the portion of that book value that was converted to cash ($4,500), or $13,500. Schaefer would record the exchange as follows:

Land (new). . . . . 13,500[a]
Cash 8,000
　Land (old). . . . . 　18,000
　Gain . . . . 　3,500[b]

[a]Recorded amount for asset acquired = book value of asset given up – portion of book value converted to cash
　　= $18,000 – $4,500
　　= $13,500

[b]Recognized gain = total gain × ratio of cash received to total fair value received
　　= ($24,000 + $8,000 – $18,000) × $\dfrac{\$8,000}{\$32,000}$
　　= $14,000 × .25 = $3,500

　　or

　Recognized gain = cash received – book value of portion of land converted to cash (sold)
　　= $8,000 – \left(\dfrac{\$8,000}{\$32,000} \times \$18,000 \right)$
　　= $8,000 – $4,500 = $3,500

Summary of Nonmonetary Exchanges

In summary, losses are recognized fully, whether assets are similar or dissimilar. A loss occurs when the surrendered asset has a book value greater than either its own fair value or the fair value of the asset received. Gains are recognized fully in exchanges of dissimilar assets. However, they are not recognized in exchanges of similar assets unless a company receives boot, and even then only a portion of the gain is recognized. Exhibit 11–3 summarizes the accounting requirements for exchanges of nonmonetary assets.

To this point, we have been concerned with the appropriate accounting for plant assets and intangibles when they are acquired. Once an asset has been placed in service, additional costs may be incurred. In the following section we explain how to account for costs incurred after acquisition.

9 State the conceptual guideline for accounting for expenditures after acquisition and apply it to common categories of expenditures after acquisition.

CONCEPTUAL

Capital expenditures benefit future periods; revenue expenditures benefit only the current period.

EXPENDITURES AFTER ACQUISITION

Many costs are incurred for plant assets and intangibles after they are placed in service. Some of those costs represent normal repair and maintenance; others represent significant enhancements, such as the addition of a new floor to an existing building.

The general guideline for accounting for expenditures made after acquisition is that if the expenditures provide additional service potential beyond the current period, they should be recorded as assets (capitalized); if they do not provide additional service potential, they should be expensed as incurred. Expenditures that provide future benefits are referred to as **capital expenditures.** Expenditures that do not result in a significant increase in future service potential are referred to as **revenue expenditures** because they are matched against current period revenues to determine net income.

EXHIBIT 11–3 **Summary of Accounting for Exchanges of Nonmonetary Assets**

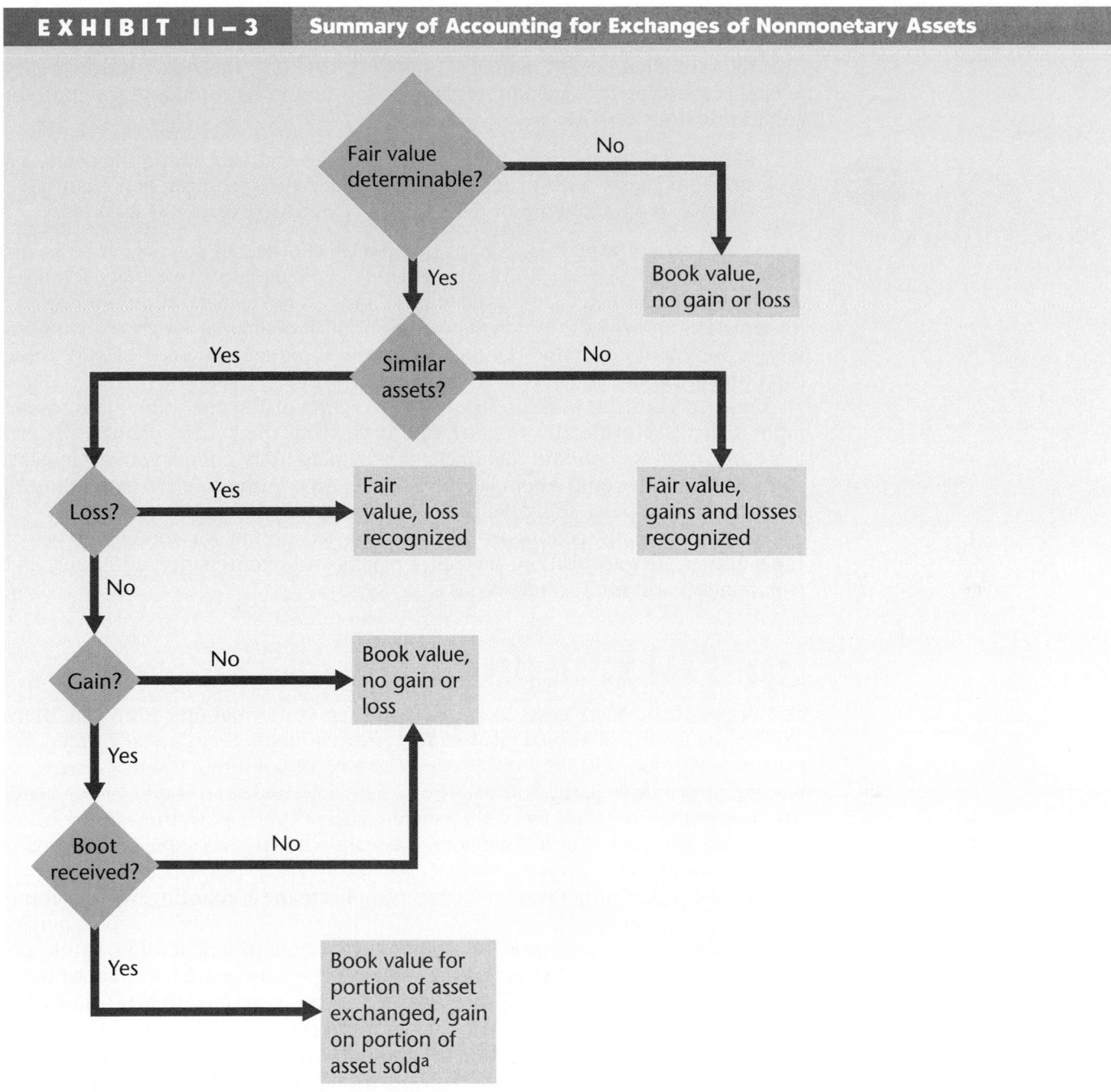

[a]Acquired asset recorded at book value of asset given up minus portion of book value sold, or fair value minus suppressed (unrecognized) gain. Recognized gain is cash received minus book value of portion of asset

A company may obtain future benefits from an asset by making current expenditures that:

1. Extend the useful life of the asset beyond original expectations.
2. Increase the quantity of services provided by the asset beyond original expectations.
3. Increase the quality of services provided by the asset beyond original expectations.

If an expenditure causes one or more of these results, then according to the historical cost principle and the matching principle, the expenditure should be recorded in an asset account. Through depreciation, depletion, or amortization charges, the company should then match the cost against the revenues generated over the estimated benefit period. In 1995 Gannett Co., Inc., disclosed its policy toward accounting for expenditures after acquisition in its summary of significant accounting policies as follows:

> Major renewals and improvements and interest incurred during the construction period of major additions are capitalized. Expenditures for maintenance, repairs and minor renewals are charged to expense as incurred.

As a matter of expediency, many companies expense all costs incurred below a certain amount (e.g., $100) on the grounds of materiality. This practice makes distinguishing between capital expenditures and revenue expenditures unnecessary for costs falling below the materiality threshold. Professional judgment is necessary, however, to determine the materiality threshold and properly classify those costs that are material.

Often it is difficult to determine whether a particular expenditure increases the future benefits provided by an asset, and if so, what the benefit period is. Given this difficulty, it is important that financial statement users, company management, and auditors understand a company's policy on accounting for such expenditures, and that the company apply the policy consistently.

In the following sections we will describe accounting for common types of expenditures after acquisition, including repairs and maintenance, additions, and replacements and improvements.

Repairs and Maintenance

Companies incur many costs to keep plant assets in normal operating condition. These costs are called **repair and maintenance costs.** Costs are associated, for example, with lubrication of machinery, cleaning of buildings and machinery, replacement of minor parts, and painting. These activities do not add to the benefits provided by the plant asset; they merely enable the asset to provide the benefits originally expected of it. Therefore, costs of such activities should be expensed as they are incurred.

In practice, two situations sometimes complicate the accounting for repairs and maintenance expenditures. First, these expenditures may be seasonal. For example, a manufacturing company may overhaul machinery routinely at a low point during the year's production activity. If the company prepares quarterly financial statements, it should accrue the expense evenly over the year, crediting allowance for repairs, a contra asset account. As expenditures occur, they should be debited to allowance for repairs. For interim reporting purposes, the allowance would be reported as a deduction from the asset(s) to which it relates. Any remaining balance at the end of the year must be eliminated by a debit to allowance for repairs and a credit to the repairs and maintenance expense account.

For example, assume that Pratt Company incurs annual repair and maintenance expenditures of $100,000 at the end of the second quarter each year. Pratt would accrue one-fourth of the annual amount at the end of each quarter, as follows:

Repairs and maintenance expense.	25,000	
Allowance for repairs.		25,000

When Pratt spends $100,000 at the end of the second quarter, it would make the following entry:

Allowance for repairs	100,000	
Cash, payables, etc..		100,000

A second complication arises when a company incurs routine repair and maintenance costs only once every few years, as when oil tankers are dry-docked for cleaning and repainting. Such activities are usually predictable, and the amounts often can be estimated with reasonable accuracy well in advance. Some people argue that these costs should be accrued as an expense in the years preceding the repair and maintenance activity. However, it is difficult to justify recognition of an expense for an activity that has not yet begun. Furthermore, the credit portion of the entry certainly cannot be classified as a liability, because the company does not have an obligation as the result of a past transaction. Consequently, these costs should *not* be accrued in advance of their incurrence. Usually, the appropriate treatment is to record the costs as an expense in the period in which they are incurred. However, some major repairs enhance the future service potential of the related asset. In that case, capitalization of the cost as a part of the asset cost would be appropriate.

Additions

Additions, as the term implies, are enlargements, expansions, or extensions of existing plant assets—for example, the addition of a wing to an existing building, or the addition of air-conditioning to a fleet of cars. Since an addition provides future benefits to the company, it is a capital expenditure. Therefore, the company should capitalize the cost of an addition and match it to revenues in future periods. The cost of any work required on the existing asset because of the addition, such as the cost of removing walls or strengthening foundations, also should be capitalized as a part of the cost of the addition. If the addition is an integral part of the older asset, the company should depreciate the addition over the remaining life of the older asset or its own useful life, whichever is shorter. If the addition has an existence separate from the older asset, it should be depreciated over its own useful life.

CONCEPTUAL

Additions enhance future service potential, and thus addition costs should be capitalized.

Replacements and Improvements

Companies often dispose of and replace major components of existing plant assets. If the new component has virtually the same operating capabilities as its predecessor, it is referred to as a **replacement.** For example, the substitution of a new air conditioning system for an old one with essentially the same characteristics is a replacement. If the new component substantially improves the operating capabilities of the asset, it is referred to as an **improvement** or a **betterment.** For example, the substitution of a new and significantly more powerful air conditioning system for an old one is an improvement or betterment.

Both replacements and improvements provide additional future benefits to the company; thus, they are capital expenditures. In practice, it often is difficult to distinguish repairs from replacements and improvements. Three methods are used to record replacements and improvements:

1. The substitution method.

2. Capitalization of the new cost.

3. Reduction of accumulated depreciation.

Each of these three methods is acceptable under certain circumstances. All three produce an increase in the book value of the related asset. In the remainder of this section, we will describe each method.

Substitution Method

The **substitution method** recognizes that a company is disposing of an old component of an asset and acquiring a new one. If the cost and accumulated depreciation associated with the old component can be identified, its cost can be eliminated from the accounts and a gain or loss recorded on the disposal. Then the cost of the new component can be debited to the asset account.

Suppose that at the beginning of 1998 Tahoe Company replaced the air conditioning unit in its manufacturing facility with a new unit. Although the cost of the old air conditioning unit ($45,000) was included in the buildings account, Tahoe depreciated the unit separately from the building. Through 1997, Tahoe had recorded accumulated depreciation of $40,000 on the old unit. The new unit had a cost of $70,000, which Tahoe paid in cash.

Under the substitution method, Tahoe would make the following entries at the beginning of 1998:

Accumulated depreciation, buildings	40,000	
Loss on disposal	5,000	
Buildings		45,000
Buildings	70,000	
Cash		70,000

This method cannot be used if a company does not have a record of the cost and accumulated depreciation for the old component. In that case, a company must use one of the following two methods.

Capitalization of the New Cost

Under the capitalization method, the cost of the new asset is debited to the asset account. The only difference between this approach and the substitution approach is that under this method, the company does not remove the book value of the old asset from the accounts. Capitalization may be appropriate when it can be assumed that the company has reduced the book value of the old component to an insignificant amount through depreciation charges. Even though this approach may be unrealistic, companies often use it when the book value of the old component is not determinable.

Reduction of Accumulated Depreciation

It may be argued that if a replacement or an improvement extends the useful life of an asset, the result is equivalent to a partial recovery or recapture of previously recorded depreciation. Therefore, rather than adding the cost of a replacement or improvement to the asset account, a company may debit accumulated depreciation for the cost.

This method and the capitalization method both produce the same book value. However, cost and accumulated depreciation differ under the two approaches. A debit to accumulated depreciation for the cost of a replacement is acceptable only when the expenditure extends the useful life of the asset. Even then, there is some question about the logic of the method, since it is unlikely that the cost of the new component will equal the depreciation previously recorded on the old component.

Rearrangement and Relocation

Companies sometimes rearrange machinery and equipment to increase operating efficiency. Similarly, plants or portions of plants often are relocated, with the objective of obtaining additional future benefits. If *rearrangement or relocation costs* are material and the benefits clearly extend beyond the current period, the company should capitalize the costs as deferred rearrangement (relocation) costs (usually included in other assets on the balance sheet) and amortize them over the estimated benefit period. If it is not possible to determine with reasonable certainty whether significant future benefits will occur, then the company should expense the costs as they are incurred.

Litigation Costs of Intangibles

Companies often incur litigation costs related to intangibles such as patents, copyrights, and trademarks. The outcome of the litigation determines the appropriate accounting treatment of the litigation costs. For example, if a company successfully defends a patent, the litigation costs should be recorded in the patent account. However, if a company is unsuccessful in defending against patent infringement, the litigation costs should be expensed as incurred. In addition, the company should assess the recoverable value of the patent, to determine whether a partial or total write-down of the patent book value is required, since presumably the reason for the litigation was to attempt to protect the value of the patent.

In 1988 Apple Computer, Inc., filed suit against Microsoft and Hewlett-Packard (HP) for infringing the Macintosh user interface with their Windows and NewWave programs, respectively. The suit, which was unsuccessful, was finally settled in 1995. Apple described the litigation as follows in its 1995 annual report:

Litigation

Apple v. Microsoft Corporation and Hewlett-Packard Company

In March 1988, the Company filed suit in the U.S. District Court for the Northern District of California (the "Court") against Microsoft Corporation ("Microsoft") and Hewlett-Packard Company ("HP") alleging that their Microsoft Windows and HP NewWave computer programs infringe the Company's audiovisual copyrights protecting the Macintosh user interface. On August 24, 1993, the district court entered final judgment for Microsoft and HP, dismissing the Company's action.

On September 21, 1993, the Court denied defendants' motions for an award of full defense costs and attorneys' fees under 17 U.S.C. Section 505, but allowed defendants to renew their motions should the Supreme Court alter the standard for the award of attorneys' fees in copyright cases in the case of *Fogerty v. Fantasy, Inc.,* 114 S. Ct. 1023 (1994).

On September 20, 1993, the Company appealed the case to the U.S. Court of Appeals for the Ninth Circuit. On September 24, 1994, the Court of Appeals issued its decision affirming the district court judgment on the merits but remanding the case on the issue of attorneys' fees in light of the *Fogerty* decision. The Company filed a petition for a *writ of certiorari* in the Supreme Court of the United States on December 19, 1994.

The Company's petition for a *writ of certiorari* was denied by the Supreme Court of the United States on February 21, 1995. Accordingly, the decision of the appellate court affirming the dismissal of the Company's copyright infringement case against Microsoft and HP is now final. The requests of Microsoft and HP for attorneys' fees have been resolved by settlement agreements. Accordingly, the matter has been entirely resolved.

® EPORTING AND DISCLOSURE REQUIREMENTS

As you now know, transactions involving plant assets and intangibles often produce significant cash flows. The statement of cash flows must reflect those cash inflows and outflows. Additions to and dispositions of plant assets are reported separately under investing activities. Note, for example, that GE's statement of cash flows for 1995 (Appendix B) reported over $6 billion of additions to property, plant, and equipment and about $1.5 billion of dispositions of plant assets (in the investing activities section). To the extent that acquisitions are financed, the financing activities section of the statement of cash flows should disclose the new debt.

Companies must also disclose the major components of, and accounting policies for, plant assets and intangibles. Disclosure of accounting policies is usually

made in the accounting policies note to the financial statements. For example, GE discloses its depreciation and amortization policies in Note 1 (Appendix B). Note 14 to GE's statements breaks down the major components of property, plant, and equipment and discloses committed cash flows over the next five years. Note 15 provides similar information for intangible assets.

SUMMARY OF LEARNING OBJECTIVES

1. Describe the characteristics of plant assets and intangibles.

Plant assets and intangibles (1) are acquired to be used in operations and (2) provide benefits over several accounting periods.

2. State the general guideline for valuing plant assets and intangibles at acquisition and explain how it is applied to common transactions involving plant assets and intangibles.

The general guideline is that assets acquired should be recorded at the best estimate of their fair value at the date of acquisition. Cost is usually the best estimate of fair value, including all costs necessary to get the asset into position for its intended use. For self-constructed assets, cost usually includes a share of the indirect manufacturing costs. When a cost is not incurred, such as when stock is issued in exchange for an asset, fair value must be estimated by some other means.

3. Account for interest during construction.

Interest cost must be capitalized for all assets that have an acquisition period. The amount of interest to be capitalized is the amount that could have been avoided had construction not occurred. Interest on specific borrowings must be capitalized first, followed by interest on other outstanding borrowings during the period (using a weighted average rate).

4. Describe the characteristics by which intangibles may be classified.

Intangibles may be classified according to their (1) identifiability (either separately identifiable or unidentifiable), (2) manner of acquisition (either internally developed or purchased), (3) expected benefit period (either limited life or indefinite life), and (4) separability (either capable of being sold separately or related solely to the business as a whole and thus not capable of being sold separately, as in the case of goodwill).

5. Summarize the accounting requirements for intangibles.

Exhibit 11–1 summarizes the accounting requirements for intangibles. The cost of all purchased intangibles must be capitalized and amortized over their useful lives, not to exceed 40 years. The cost of specifically identifiable intangibles that are developed internally may either be expensed as incurred or capitalized and amortized over the shorter of their useful lives or 40 years. The cost of developing goodwill internally must be expensed as incurred.

6. Account for research and development (R&D) costs and computer software costs.

In general, R&D costs are expensed as they are incurred. However, materials, equipment, and facilities and purchased intangibles that have alternative future uses are capitalized and expensed over their useful lives. Costs incurred to purchase or develop computer software to be sold, leased, or otherwise marketed must be expensed as R&D costs until the technological feasibility of the product or process has been established. After that point, production and packaging costs must be capitalized as inventory and expensed as cost of sales when the related sales revenue is recognized. GAAP does not provide specific guidance on accounting for the costs of computer software developed for internal use or on revenue recognition from the sale of computer software.

7. Explain the concept of goodwill and account for goodwill.

Goodwill consists of the favorable characteristics of a business enterprise that cannot be separately identified and valued. Purchased goodwill (the excess of the purchase price of an entity over the fair value of its identifiable net assets) must be capitalized and amortized over its estimated useful life, not to exceed 40 years. Internal costs of developing goodwill must be expensed as incurred.

8. **Account for assets acquired in nonmonetary exchanges.**

   The accounting requirements for nonmonetary exchanges are summarized in Exhibit 11–3. If the asset's fair value is determinable, it is generally recorded at fair value, and a gain or loss is recognized. However, if similar assets are involved in the exchange, gains may be recognized only if boot is received. In that case the recognized gain is the total gain times the boot received divided by the total fair value received. If the asset's fair value is not determinable, the book value of the old asset should be assigned to the new asset.

9. **State the conceptual guideline for accounting for expenditures after acquisition and apply it to common categories of expenditures after acquisition.**

   In general, expenditures that provide future benefits (capital expenditures) should be capitalized; expenditures that do not result in significant future benefits (revenue expenditures) should be expensed as incurred. Repair and maintenance expenditures generally are expensed as incurred. Additions, replacements, and improvements generally are capitalized and depreciated over the estimated remaining life of the related asset.

KEY TERMS

additions 597	natural resources (wasting assets) 580
capital expenditure 594	nonmonetary exchange 590
computer software costs 586	nonreciprocal transfer 589
copyright 583	opportunity cost approach 577
deferred charges 584	organization costs 584
depletion 580	other assets 584
direct costing approach 577	patent 582
dissimilar assets 591	plant assets 574
franchise 583	rearrangement and relocation costs 598
full costing approach 577	repair and maintenance costs 596
goodwill 587	replacements 597
improvement (betterment) 597	research and development costs (R&D) 584
indirect manufacturing costs 577	revenue expenditure 594
intangible assets 574	similar assets 591
interest during construction 578	substitution method 597
lease prepayment 583	trademark (trade name) 583
leasehold improvement 584	

QUESTIONS

Q 11-1. What two characteristics distinguish plant assets and intangibles from other assets?

Q 11-2. What is the general guideline governing the amount that an entity should assign to an asset at the time it is acquired?

Q 11-3. What types of costs do entities typically incur in connection with the acquisition of land?

Q 11-4. What is the appropriate accounting and reporting treatment for land improvements that (*a*) produce relatively permanent benefits and (*b*) have a limited life?

Q 11-5. What are the two major accounting problems associated with self-constructed assets that are not associated with assets acquired from an external source?

Q 11-6. Describe the three possible approaches to accounting for indirect manufacturing costs when a company constructs assets for its own use. Which method is the most common in practice? Why?

Q 11-7. Describe briefly the requirements for accounting for interest during construction. In your description, include (*a*) an identification of qualifying assets, (*b*) a discussion of the amount to be capitalized, and (*c*) a definition of the capitalization period.

Q 11-8. What distinguishes natural resource assets from depreciable assets?

Q 11-9. What four types of costs do companies incur in connection with wasting assets (natural resources)? Briefly describe each category.

Q 11-10. Identify and describe four criteria by which we may classify intangibles.

Q 11-11. What is the appropriate accounting treatment for each of the following categories of expenditures related to intangibles?
 1. Specifically identifiable, purchased.
 2. Unidentifiable, purchased.
 3. Specifically identifiable, internally developed.
 4. Unidentifiable, internally developed.

Q 11-12. Describe the following intangibles:
 1. Patents.
 2. Copyrights.
 3. Trademarks and trade names.
 4. Franchises.

Q 11-13. What is a lease prepayment? How should a company account for lease prepayments and report them in financial statements?

Q 11-14. Over what period should a company amortize the cost of leasehold improvements? Why?

Q 11-15. Give some examples of organization costs. What is the appropriate accounting treatment for such costs? Why?

Q 11-16. How should costs incurred internally for research and development be recorded in the accounts? Describe briefly the justification for this requirement.

Q 11-17. What are the five elements of cost that a company should identify with research and development activities? Under certain circumstances, a company may capitalize two of these cost elements rather than expensing them as incurred as a part of R&D expense. What are the circumstances and which two cost elements are involved?

Q 11-18. What is the significance of the requirement that companies must disclose the amount of research and development expenditures charged to expense?

Q 11-19. Under what circumstances should costs of developing or purchasing computer software be charged to expense as research and development costs?

Q 11-20. When should costs of developing computer software be capitalized?

Q 11-21. Give several examples of characteristics that might make up goodwill. Why can we not record these items separately rather than combining them into a category called goodwill?

Q 11-22. Why is goodwill capitalized only when it is acquired in connection with the acquisition of another company?

Q 11-23. When a company acquires assets by issuing its own capital stock, at what amount should the assets and the capital stock be recorded?

Q 11-24. What is a nonreciprocal transfer? At what amount should a company record assets acquired by donation at acquisition? Subsequent to acquisition?

Q 11-25. How is the cost of assets acquired in a lump-sum purchase allocated to the separate assets?

Q 11-26. What is the general guideline governing the valuation at acquisition of assets acquired in a nonmonetary exchange? In what two circumstances does this general guideline not apply?

Q 11-27. Give two examples of exchanges of similar assets. Describe the appropriate accounting for exchanges of similar assets in a loss situation. Describe the appropriate accounting for exchanges of similar assets in a gain situation where (*a*) boot is given and (*b*) boot is received.

Q 11-28. Explain why companies recognize gains fully in exchanges of dissimilar assets and why they do not recognize, or only partially recognize, gains resulting from exchanges of similar assets.

Q 11-29. What is the basic accounting guideline governing costs related to assets after they have been acquired? Distinguish between capital expenditures and revenue expenditures.

Q 11-30. Describe the appropriate accounting treatment for (*a*) repair and maintenance costs, (*b*) additions, (*c*) replacements and improvements, (*d*) rearrangement and relocation costs, and (*e*) litigation costs related to intangible assets.

Q 11-31. Describe how plant asset transactions affect the statement of cash flows.

CASES

C 11-1. ACQUISITION COST OF LAND In February 1998, Peck Company acquired a tract of land as a site for a new plant facility. In addition to the purchase price, Peck incurred legal fees; title, recording, and escrow fees; and a broker's commission on the transaction. Also, the seller had not paid taxes on the property for the last year. Peck agreed to assume the tax obligation as part of the transaction.

Prior to beginning construction on the new plant, an old building on the land was torn down and the materials removed. The property was then surveyed and graded in preparation for the new construction.

REQUIRED

1. What is the general guideline regarding the appropriate costs to be capitalized in connection with the acquisition of land?
2. Describe the costs that Peck should capitalize as part of the cost of the land acquired as a new plant site.

C 11-2. ACQUISITION COST OF MACHINERY Owen Corporation acquired a machine with an invoice price of $10,000. Various other costs related to the acquisition and installation of the machine, including transportation, electrical wiring, and a special base, amounted to $2,000. The machine has an estimated life of 10 years, with no residual value at the end of that period.

Pat Owen, the president and owner of the business, suggests to you, the company controller, that the incidental costs of $2,000 be charged to expense immediately, for the following reasons: (*a*) If the machine is sold, the company cannot recover these costs in the sales price; (*b*) the inclusion of the $2,000 in the machinery account on the books will not necessarily result in a closer approximation of the market price of this asset over the years, because of the possibility of changing price levels; and (*c*) charging the $2,000 to expense immediately will reduce federal income taxes.

REQUIRED

Prepare a memo to Ms. Owen discussing each of the points raised.

(AICPA, adapted)

C 11-3. ACQUISITION COST OF PLANT ASSETS Following are three independent situations involving application of the guidelines for valuing plant assets.

1. Miller Corporation acquired a site for the construction of a building 10 years ago. At that time a building on the site had an estimated expected life of 40 years. Currently, the building is being demolished because of obsolescence, and a completely new structure is being built. Should the undepreciated cost of the old building be carried forward as part of the cost of the new building, or should it be expensed in the current period?
2. Several years ago, Dawes Corporation entered into an agreement with a customer, Nash Corporation, whereby Nash would take the entire output of one of Dawes' plants. As part of the consideration, Dawes gave Nash an option to purchase the land and plant at a future date at a price that is adjusted annually for capital additions and depreciation. As the option date approaches, Dawes would now like to negotiate with Nash for the cancellation of the option. This would require Dawes to make some payment to Nash. If this transaction occurs, how should the matter be accounted for and shown in the financial statements?
3. Dole Corporation entered into a contract to purchase certain plant assets. As part of the transaction, Dole received a commission from the real estate broker, who was paid by the seller. Would the commission be considered as income to Dole or as a reduction of the cost of the property acquired?

C 11-4. **SELF-CONSTRUCTED ASSETS** Steve Manufacturing, Inc., began operations in 1993 to produce probos, a new type of instrument it hoped to sell to doctors, dentists, and hospitals. The demand for probos far exceeded initial expectations, and Steve was unable to produce enough of them to fill its orders.

For a time Steve manufactured its product using equipment that it had built at the start of its operations. To meet the demand, it needed more efficient equipment. Steve decided to design and build new equipment, because the equipment available on the market was unsuitable for the production of probos.

In 1998, Steve devoted a section of the plant to development of the new equipment and hired a special staff. Within six months, at a cost of $400,000, a machine was developed that increased production and reduced labor costs substantially. Elated by the success of the new machine, Steve built three more machines of the same type at a cost of $250,000 each.

REQUIRED

1. In addition to satisfying a need that outsiders cannot meet within the desired time, why might a company construct assets for its own use?
2. In general, what costs should a company capitalize for a self-constructed asset?
3. Discuss the propriety of including in the capitalized cost of self-constructed assets:
   a) The increase in overhead caused by the self-construction.
   b) A proportionate share of overhead on the same basis as that applied to goods manufactured for sale.
4. Discuss the proper accounting treatment of the $150,000 ($400,000 – $250,000), the amount by which the cost of Steve's first machine exceeded the cost of the subsequent machines.

(AICPA, adapted)

C 11-5. **PATENTS** In examining the books of Clark Company, you, a staff auditor, find on the December 31, 1998, balance sheet the item "Patents, $350,000."

Referring to the ledger accounts, you note the following regarding one patent acquired in 1995:

1995 legal costs incurred in successfully defending the validity of the patent **$26,000**
1997 legal costs in successfully prosecuting an infringement suit **38,000**
1997 legal costs (additional expenses) in the infringement suit **10,400**
1997 cost of improvements (unpatented) on the patented device **24,300**

There are no credits in the account, and no allowance for amortization has been set up on the books for any of the patents. Three other patents were issued in 1992, 1994, and 1995. All were developed by the staff of your client. The patented articles are currently very marketable, but it is estimated that they will be in demand for only the next few years.

REQUIRED Prepare a memo to the senior accountant on the audit engagement evaluating the items included in the patent account from an accounting standpoint.

(AICPA, adapted)

C 11-6. **START-UP COSTS** After securing lease commitments from several major stores, Verde Valley Shopping Center, Inc., was organized and built a shopping center in a growing suburb.

The shopping center would have opened on schedule on January 1, 1998, if it had not been struck by a severe tornado in December 1997; instead, it opened for business on October 1, 1998. All additional construction costs that were incurred as a result of the tornado were covered by insurance.

In July 1997, in anticipation of the scheduled January opening, a permanent staff had been hired to promote the shopping center, obtain tenants for the uncommitted space, and manage the property.

A summary of some of the costs incurred in 1997 and the first nine months of 1998 follows.

	1997	1/1/98–9/30/98
Interest on mortgage bonds	$75,000	$60,000
Cost of obtaining tenants	48,000	22,000
Promotional advertising	34,000	38,000

The promotional advertising campaign was designed to familiarize shoppers with the center. Had it been known in time that the center would not open until October

1998, the 1997 expenditures for promotional advertising would not have been made. The advertising had to be repeated in 1998.

All the tenants who had leased space in the shopping center at the time of the tornado accepted the October occupancy date on condition that the monthly rental charges for the first nine months of 1998 be canceled.

REQUIRED Explain how each of the costs for 1997 and the first nine months of 1998 should be treated in the accounts of the shopping center corporation. Give the reasons for each treatment.

(AICPA, adapted)

C 11-7. RESEARCH AND DEVELOPMENT COSTS Lehman Company is in the process of developing a revolutionary new product. A new division of Lehman was formed to develop, manufacture, and market this new product. As of December 31, 1998, the new product has not been manufactured for resale. However, a prototype unit has been built and is in operation.

Throughout 1998 the new division incurred certain costs. These costs include design and engineering studies, prototype manufacturing costs, administrative expenses (including salaries of administrative personnel), and market research costs. In addition, approximately $900,000 in equipment (estimated useful life, 10 years) was purchased for use in developing and manufacturing the new product. Approximately $200,000 of this equipment was built specifically for the design development of the new product. The remaining $700,000 of equipment was used to manufacture the preproduction prototype and will be used to manufacture the new product once it is in commercial production.

REQUIRED **1.** What is the definition of *research* and of *development* according to *FASB Statement No. 2*?
2. How should the various costs of Lehman described above be recorded in the financial statements for the year ended December 31, 1998?

(AICPA, adapted)

C 11-8. COMPUTER SOFTWARE COSTS RB Software Company has recently completed the development and testing of an integrated software package called EvReThing. The software has a common command structure that allows a user to perform database, spreadsheet, presentation, and word processing functions. While operating within any one of these programs, the user may integrate data from the other programs.

Because of its past success with stand-alone database, spreadsheet, presentation, and word processing software, RB has no doubts about the commercial profitability of EvReThing. Thus, management believes that the costs of designing, developing, coding, and testing the software package should be capitalized and amortized on a straight-line basis over three years, which is the length of time EvReThing is expected to produce revenues.

REQUIRED **1.** Is RB's proposed accounting for the development costs acceptable? Explain.
2. Explain how the costs incurred to produce product masters, after technological feasibility has been established, should be accounted for.
3. Explain how the costs of duplicating the software, documentation, and training materials should be accounted for.

C 11-9. GOODWILL Winn Corporation, a retail fuel oil distributor, has increased its annual sales volume to a level three times that of the dealer it purchased in 1996 in order to begin operations.

Winn's board of directors recently received an offer to negotiate the sale of Winn Corporation to a large competitor. The majority of the board wants to increase the stated value of goodwill on the balance sheet to reflect the larger sales volume developed through intensive promotion and the current market price of oil. A few of the board members, however, would prefer to eliminate goodwill from the balance sheet altogether in order to prevent "possible misinterpretations." Goodwill was recorded properly in 1996.

REQUIRED **1.** Discuss the meaning of the term *goodwill*.
2. Why does the book value of Winn's goodwill differ from its market value?
3. Discuss the propriety of:
    a) Increasing the stated value of goodwill before the negotiations.
    b) Eliminating goodwill from the balance sheet before negotiations.

(AICPA, adapted).

C 11-10. CAPITAL EXPENDITURES VS. REVENUE EXPENDITURES Dawn Hill was hired recently as president of Jackson Corporation, a large manufacturing concern. When reviewing the proposed annual report with the controller, John Torrance, Hill wondered aloud, "How do we determine which expenditures related to plant assets go into the balance sheet and which ones go directly to the income statement?" It seemed to her intuitively that certain expenditures do not enhance the value of the asset and that others probably do enhance the value of the asset. Torrance explained to Hill the distinction between capital expenditures and revenue expenditures. Torrance noted further that Jackson expenses all expenditures related to plant assets of less than $1,000 as incurred.

REQUIRED
1. Explain why the concepts of capital expenditure and revenue expenditure exist and why it is important to classify expenditures properly in these two categories.
2. How can Jackson justify expensing all costs incurred related to plant assets of less than $1,000, even though some of these may be capital expenditures?

C 11-11.   **REPAIR AND MAINTENANCE EXPENDITURES**   The controller for Jensen, Inc., has asked a staff member to review the repair and maintenance expense account to determine if all the charges are appropriate. The staff member has reviewed this account and has identified the following 10 transactions from 1998 for further scrutiny. All of these amounts are considered material.

DATE	AMOUNT	DESCRIPTION
a) Jan. 3	$10,000	Service contract on office equipment.
b) March 7	10,000	Initial design fee for proposed extension of office building.
c) April 12	18,500	New condenser for central air conditioning unit located on the roof of office building.
d) April 20	7,000	Purchase of two executive chairs and desks.
e) May 12	40,850	Purchase of storm and screen windows and installation of same on all office windows.
f) May 18	38,450	Sealing of roof leaks over entire production plant.
g) June 19	28,740	Replacement of large door to production area.
h) July 3	11,740	Installation of automatic door opening system on the above door to speed opening.
i) Sept. 14	38,500	Purchase of overhead crane for the assembly department to speed up production.
j) Oct. 18	11,000	Replacement of broken gear on machine in the machining department.

REQUIRED   For each of the above transactions identified by the controller's staff member, indicate whether the amount is properly charged to the repair and maintenance expense account, and if not, indicate the appropriate account to which the amount should be charged. Explain your reasoning in each case.

C 11-12.   **SUBSEQUENT EXPENDITURES: ETHICS**   Consolidated Delivery operates a trucking service that delivers merchandise for businesses operating in the northwest region of the United States. Typically, the businesses do not have their own delivery services for customers so they contract with Consolidated.

Consolidated has been experiencing cash flow problems during the past few years, due in part to its acquisition of a new fleet of trucks in order to modernize and eventually expand its operations into California. To effectuate the expansion, Consolidated planned to borrow about $1 million during the first quarter of 1999. In an effort to conserve funds and maximize net cash inflows during 1998, top management of Consolidated placed restrictions on capital expenditures until after the loan was secured. Restrictions were placed on discretionary and nonessential expenditures. The burden of proof was placed on the operations and accounting managers, Charlie Smith and Jim Benjamin, respectively, to jointly approve any capital expenditures during 1998.

Charlie Smith and Jim Benjamin routinely met to discuss proposed capital expenditures. At a recent meeting Smith solicited Benjamin's support for the expenditure of $60,000 to overhaul the engines of approximately 40 trucks that are several years old. Recent engine problems had affected the efficiency of the trucks, and repair bills were mounting up. Smith stated that it is in Consolidated's best interest to overhaul the engines now rather than wait for additional breakdowns to occur, especially in light of the proposed expansion of operations in 1999.

Jim Benjamin was sensitive to Smith's request. However, he was reluctant to approve the expenditure because of the restrictions that are in place. Benjamin was not convinced that the expenditure is essential at this time. He suggested that repairs continue to be made until the restrictions are removed.

Charlie Smith persisted in his request. He told Benjamin that the $60,000 should be expensed since the expenditure merely kept the trucks in good operating condition. According to Smith, there would be no increase in the useful life of the trucks and the expenditure did not add to or improve the trucks in any significant way. Smith concluded his argument by stating that any loss of customers and revenue resulting from delivery problems caused by truck breakdowns could jeopardize Consolidated's ability to secure needed bank financing.

Jim Benjamin carefully thought about his options. He does not agree with Smith's assessment that the overhaul expenditure should be expensed. However, he does recognize that it is not a clear-cut situation. He knows that the expenditure cannot be made without his approval. Benjamin feels an obligation to support Smith, who is a longtime friend and business associate.

REQUIRED What ethical and professional issues should be of concern to Jim Benjamin in deciding upon a course of action? What would you do?

EXERCISES

E 11-1. **CLASSIFICATION OF PLANT ASSET EXPENDITURES** Magill Company incurred the following costs in connection with plant assets:
   a) Cash paid for land.
   b) Attorneys' fees connected with land purchase.
   c) Improvements to land—limited life.
   d) Survey costs for new building.
   e) Architect's fee.
   f) Net invoice cost of machinery.
   g) Insurance on machinery in transit.
   h) Unpaid taxes on land assumed by Magill.
   i) Cost of assembling and installing machinery.
   j) Removal costs of old building on land.
   k) Landscaping costs—indefinite life.
   l) Excavation costs for new building.
   m) Freight costs on machinery.
   n) Material, labor, and overhead on new building.
   o) Foundation for machinery (not usable elsewhere).
   p) Interest costs incurred on debt associated with construction of building.
   q) Cost of testing new machinery.
   r) Mortgage assumed on land.

REQUIRED Indicate whether each of the items listed should be included in land (L), buildings (B), machinery and equipment (M), or other (O). Where your response is "other," indicate the appropriate treatment of the item in the accounts.

E 11-2. **BALANCE SHEET CLASSIFICATION OF ASSETS** The following types of assets may be held by a company at various times:
   a) Land held for future plant site.
   b) Leasehold improvements.
   c) Fully depreciated assets still in use.
   d) Land held for investment purposes.
   e) Idle machinery awaiting disposal.

REQUIRED What is the appropriate balance sheet classification of each of the items listed?

E 11-3. **ACQUISITION COST OF LAND** On November 1, 1998, Berryman Company purchased for $700,000 a tract of land as a factory site. A building on the property was razed, and salvaged materials resulting from demolition were sold. Additional costs incurred and salvage proceeds realized during November were as follows:

Demolition of old building	$80,000
Legal fees for purchase contract and recording ownership	8,000
Title guarantee insurance	7,000
Proceeds from sale of salvaged materials	23,000

REQUIRED   Prepare a schedule showing the amount that Berryman should report for land in its balance sheet at November 30, 1998.

(AICPA, adapted)

E 11-4.   **INTEREST CAPITALIZATION**   Johnson Company is constructing a production facility for an estimated cost of $10 million. Construction began on January 1, 1998, and is expected to take about two years. Also on January 1, 1998, to finance the construction, Johnson borrowed $10 million at a 9 percent annual interest rate. During 1998, Johnson incurred construction expenditures of $2 million on April 1 and $1 million on July 1.

REQUIRED   **1.**   Calculate the amount of interest that Johnson should capitalize for 1998.
2.   Prepare the journal entries to reflect the aggregate construction costs for 1998 and to reflect interest costs incurred. Assume cash was paid for all expenditures.

E 11-5.   **INTEREST CAPITALIZATION**   On January 2, 1998, Glezen Corporation began construction on a new plant facility for its own use. The expected cost of the facility was $8 million. Glezen did not undertake any specific borrowing to finance the self-construction. However, throughout 1998, Glezen did have outstanding debt with an aggregate principal amount of $7,000,000 and an average interest rate of 11 percent.
Cash expenditures on the project during 1998 were as follows:

March 1	$ 600,000
June 30	800,000
September 30	600,000
December 31	700,000
	$2,700,000

REQUIRED   **1.**   Calculate the amount of interest incurred during 1998.
2.   How much interest should be capitalized for 1998?
3.   Prepare the journal entry to record the aggregate expenditures for the self-construction and for interest costs incurred during 1998.

E 11-6.   **INTEREST CAPITALIZATION**   On January 2, 1998, Briner Corporation began construction on a new office building for its own use. At the beginning of 1998, Briner borrowed $4,000,000 at 12 percent, payable annually on December 31, specifically to help finance the construction. Briner had no other outstanding debt during 1998.
Cash expenditures on the project during 1998 were as follows:

March 1	$ 900,000
June 30	800,000
September 30	600,000
October 30	600,000
	$2,900,000

REQUIRED   **1.**   Calculate the amount of interest incurred during 1998.
2.   How much interest should be capitalized for 1998?
3.   Prepare the journal entry to record the aggregate expenditures for the self-construction and for interest costs incurred during 1998.

E 11-7.   **INTEREST CAPITALIZATION**   On January 2, 1998, Manning Corporation began construction on a new office building for its own use. On July 1, 1998, Manning borrowed $1,000,000 at 12 percent, with interest payable semiannually on June 30 and December 31, specifically to help finance the construction. In addition to the construction loan, Manning had the following outstanding debt throughout 1998:
$2,000,000, 14% bonds, annual interest payable 12/31.
$1,000,000, 11% note, annual interest payable 12/31.
Cash expenditures on the project during 1998 were as follows:

March 1	$ 900,000
June 30	800,000
September 30	600,000
October 31	700,000
	$3,000,000

REQUIRED
  1. Calculate the amount of interest incurred during 1998.
  2. How much interest should be capitalized for 1998?
  3. Prepare the journal entry to record the aggregate expenditures for the self-construction and for interest costs incurred during 1998.

E 11-8. **INTEREST CAPITALIZATION** On January 2, 1998, Esiason Corporation began construction on a new office building for its own use. On July 1, 1998, Esiason borrowed $2,000,000 at 12 percent, with interest payable semiannually on June 30 and December 31, specifically to help finance the construction. In addition to the construction loan, Esiason had a $1,000,000, 11 percent note, with annual interest payable 12/31, outstanding throughout 1998.

Cash expenditures on the project during 1998 were as follows:

March 1	$1,800,000
June 30	800,000
September 30	900,000
November 30	1,200,000
	$4,700,000

REQUIRED
  1. Calculate the amount of interest incurred during 1998.
  2. How much interest should be capitalized for 1998?
  3. Prepare the journal entry to record the aggregate expenditures for the self-construction and for interest costs incurred during 1998.

E 11-9. **INTEREST CAPITALIZATION** During 1998, Wu Corporation constructed and manufactured certain assets and incurred the following interest costs in connection with these activities:

	INTEREST COSTS INCURRED
Warehouse constructed for Wu's own use	$90,000
Special-order machine for sale to customer, produced according to customer specifications	18,000
Inventories routinely manufactured, produced on a repetitive basis	14,000

All of these assets required an extended period of time for completion.

REQUIRED Calculate the amount of interest cost that should be capitalized for 1998.

(AICPA, adapted)

E 11-10. **CLASSIFICATION OF INTANGIBLES** The following account balances were taken from the general ledger of Sterling Corporation at the end of 1998:

Patents	$ 16,400
Trademark	8,000
Organization costs	32,000
Discount on bonds payable	4,200
Franchise	28,600
Research and development costs	132,000
Excess of cost over fair value of net assets of acquired business	80,000
Trade accounts receivable (net)	61,000

REQUIRED Prepare the intangible assets section of the balance sheet for Sterling Corporation as of December 31, 1998.

E 11-11. **ORGANIZATION COSTS** Pei Company was organized in 1997 and began operations on January 1, 1998. Pei is engaged in conducting market research studies on behalf of manufacturers. Before the start of operations, the following costs were incurred:

Attorneys' fees in connection with organization of Pei	$16,000
Improvements to leased offices prior to occupancy	28,000
Meetings of incorporators, state filing fees, and other organization expenses	40,000
	$84,000

Pei has elected to record amortization of organization costs over the maximum period allowable under generally accepted accounting principles.

REQUIRED
I. Prepare the journal entry to record amortization of organization costs for 1998.
2. If any of the above items should be excluded from organization costs, explain how they should be accounted for.

(AICPA, adapted)

E 11-12. **RESEARCH AND DEVELOPMENT COSTS** In 1998 Bennett Corporation developed a new product to be marketed in 1999. In connection with the development of this product, the following costs were incurred in 1998:

Research and development department costs	$ 600,000
Materials and supplies consumed	300,000
Compensation paid to research consultants	220,000
	$1,120,000

It is anticipated that these costs will be recovered in 2001.

REQUIRED
What is the amount of research and development costs that should be expensed in 1998?

(AICPA, adapted)

E 11-13. **RESEARCH AND DEVELOPMENT COSTS** Tabor Company incurred research and development costs in 1998 as follows:

Materials used in research and development projects	$ 700,000
Equipment acquired that will have alternate uses in future research and development projects	3,000,000
Depreciation for 1998 on above equipment	500,000
Personnel costs of persons involved in research and development projects	1,300,000
Consulting fees paid to outsiders for research and development projects	400,000
Indirect costs reasonably allocable to research and development projects	400,000

REQUIRED
Calculate the amount of research and development expense that Tabor Company should record in 1998.

(AICPA, adapted)

E 11-14. **RESEARCH AND DEVELOPMENT COSTS** Carpenter Corporation incurred the following costs in connection with the indicated activities during 1998:

Searching for applications of new research findings	$140,000
Consulting fees paid to outsiders in connection with research and development activities	30,000
Quality control during commercial production	16,000
Design changes to existing products	80,000
Laboratory research aimed at discovering new knowledge	100,000
Adaptation of existing capability to meet a customer's need	13,000
Engineering activity required to advance the design of a product to the manufacturing stage	30,000
Design of tools involving new technology	25,000

REQUIRED
Calculate the amount that Carpenter should include in research and development cost for 1998.

E 11-15. **COMPUTER SOFTWARE COSTS** SoftSmith Corporation is a computer software development and marketing company. During 1998, SoftSmith incurred the following costs related to the development and marketing of AccSys, an accounting software package:

Testing to determine consistency with product design	$ 30,000
Coding	180,000
Program planning and design	120,000
Production of product masters	22,000
Duplication of product masters	6,000
Packaging	17,000
Advertising	18,000

All coding, testing, and program planning and design costs were incurred prior to the establishment of technological feasibility. Assume all costs were paid in cash.

REQUIRED Prepare the journal entries required to record the costs incurred by SoftSmith.

E 11-16. **COMPUTER SOFTWARE COSTS** Blazek, Inc., a computer software company, incurred the following costs in the process of developing and producing a new software program:

Program planning and design	$110,000
Production of product masters	35,000
Coding	160,000
Testing to determine consistency with product design	30,000
Duplication of product masters and packaging	28,000

The costs of planning and design, coding, and testing all were incurred before the technological feasibility of the product was determined.

REQUIRED Prepare journal entries to record the costs incurred by Blazek.

E 11-17. **GOODWILL** On July 31, 1998, Landry Company purchased for $10 million cash all the outstanding common stock of Irvin Company when Irvin's balance sheet showed net assets of $6.2 million. The fair values of Irvin's assets and liabilities differed from their book values, as follows:

	BOOK VALUE	FAIR VALUE
Property, plant, and equipment (net)	$10,000,000	$11,000,000
Other assets	1,000,000	800,000
Long-term debt	6,000,000	5,800,000

REQUIRED Calculate the amount paid for goodwill.

(AICPA, adapted)

E 11-18. **GOODWILL** Roark Company is contemplating the purchase of all the outstanding common stock of Shaver Corporation. Shaver's recorded assets and liabilities are as follows:

Cash	$ 40,000
Receivables (net)	180,000
Inventory	320,000
Property, plant, and equipment (net)	500,000
Liabilities	(220,000)

Roark estimated that the fair value (net realizable value) of Shaver's receivables was $160,000, the fair value of inventory was $400,000, and the fair value of property, plant, and equipment was $475,000. The fair value of Shaver's liabilities did not differ significantly from book value.

REQUIRED
1. If Roark paid $1,400,000 for all of Shaver's common stock, what amount would Roark record for goodwill?
2. What should be the minimum amount that Shaver would be willing to accept for its net assets? Why?

E 11-19. **EXCHANGE OF STOCK FOR LAND** On December 1, 1998, Autry Corporation exchanged 10,000 shares of its $5 par value common stock for a parcel of land to be held for a future plant site. On the exchange date a common share of Autry Corporation had a fair value of $60. Autry received $30,000 for selling scrap when an existing building on the property was removed from the site.

REQUIRED Prepare the journal entry to record the transaction.

E 11-20. **LUMP-SUM ACQUISITION** On December 1, 1988, Murphy Corporation purchased for $300,000 a tract of land on which a warehouse and office building were located. The following data were available concerning the property:

	CURRENT APPRAISED VALUE	SELLER'S BOOK VALUE
Land	$130,000	$ 70,000
Warehouse	26,000	40,000
Office building	114,000	90,000
	$270,000	$200,000

REQUIRED   Prepare the journal entry to record the property acquisition.

(AICPA, adapted)

E 11-21.   **EXCHANGE OF DISSIMILAR NONMONETARY ASSETS**   Jayhawk Corporation exchanged a building for a patent. The building had cost Jayhawk $160,000; the book value at the time of the exchange was $70,000. The patent could have been purchased for $20,000 cash; the fair value of the building was not readily determinable.

REQUIRED   Prepare the journal entry to record the exchange.

E 11-22.   **EXCHANGE OF SIMILAR NONMONETARY ASSETS**   Platt Baseball Company had a player contract with Stewart that was recorded in its accounting records at $2,500,000. Beaton Baseball Company had a player contract with Norman that was recorded in its accounting records at $1,800,000. Platt traded Stewart to Beaton for Norman by an exchange of contracts. The estimated fair value of each contract was $3,000,000.

REQUIRED   Prepare the journal entries to record the exchange for both Platt and Beaton.

(AICPA, adapted)

E 11-23.   **EXCHANGE OF SIMILAR NONMONETARY ASSETS**   On January 2, 1998, Brown Delivery Company traded in an old delivery truck for a newer model. Data relative to the old and new trucks follow:

OLD TRUCK:

Original cost	**$8,000**
Accumulated depreciation as of 1/2/98	**5,000**
Average published retail value	**2,700**

NEW TRUCK:

List price	**$10,000**
Cash price without trade-in	**9,200**
Cash paid with trade-in	**7,800**

REQUIRED   Prepare the appropriate journal entry to record the exchange on Brown's books.

E 11-24.   **ACCOUNTING FOR COSTS INCURRED FOR PLANT ASSETS AND INTANGIBLES**   During 1998, Gardner Company made the following expenditures:

Jan. 2   Acquired land and building for $300,000 cash. The appraised values of the land and building were $110,000 and $220,000, respectively.

Feb. 15   Acquired machinery for $30,000 cash. Paid freight charges of $1,000 and an insurance premium of $300 to cover goods in transit.

April 10   Completed remodeling of building acquired on January 2 at a cost of $48,000, paid in cash.

June 13   Incurred legal fees of $30,000 in connection with a successful defense of a patent infringement suit.

July 20   Performed periodic maintenance on machinery at a cost of $3,800.

Aug. 3   Completed new foundation for machinery acquired on February 15 at a cost of $3,000. The original foundation, which was included in the cost of the machinery, was inadequate. Scrap from the old foundation was sold for $400.

Nov. 12   The machinery and equipment in the plant were rearranged to enhance the efficiency of the production process at a cost of $8,300.

REQUIRED   Prepare journal entries to record the above transactions.

E 11-25.   **ACCOUNTING FOR COSTS INCURRED FOR PLANT ASSETS AND INTANGIBLES**   Cook Corporation incurred the following costs (all paid in cash) related to plant assets and intangibles during 1998:

a) $23,000 for painting of a major plant facility. The plant was last painted in 1993.

b) $51,000 for cleaning and repainting of oil tanker. This activity occurs about every three years.

c) $700,000 for addition to building.

d) $4,400 for replacement of a motor in a machine. The cost of the old motor was not available, as it was purchased as a part of the original machine.

e) $112,000 in connection with relocating certain plant and equipment items. While Cook expects that the new arrangement should continue for several years, there is a reasonable possibility that the new arrangement will not produce the desired results and that the items will be returned to their original locations and setups.

f) Incurred legal fees of $36,000 in connection with the unsuccessful defense of a patent. The patent had been acquired at a cost of $700,000 several years ago and had a book value of $300,000 when the litigation outcome was determined. As a result of the litigation outcome, the patent was determined to be worthless.

REQUIRED Prepare journal entries to record the above transactions.

PROBLEMS

P 11-1. ACQUISITION OF PLANT ASSETS On January 2, 1998, Lin Corporation acquired from Chang Corporation a truck, equipment, and some land with an old building on it. Lin did not want the old building and, according to plan, demolished it during the first week of January to make way for a new building on the site. The net demolition costs were $3,000.

A local garage appraised the truck at $5,500. The *Gold Book of Used Trucks,* a survey of 200 similar trucks in the area in December, estimated the average price of such trucks in similar condition at $6,000.

On the date of acquisition, a local equipment dealer offered to buy the equipment from Lin for $8,000. The equipment cost Chang $9,000 in 1995, and in his opinion it was worth $8,000.

To acquire these assets, Lin put $6,000 down and signed a $24,000 interest-bearing note with Chang on which it agreed to pay $4,000 interest over the next two years. The company also promised to pay the 1997 property tax arrearages of $600. Legal fees associated with the purchase were $1,800.

REQUIRED Prepare the journal entry or entries required to record the January 1998 plant asset acquisitions by Lin Corporation.

(CGAA, adapted)

P 11-2. ACQUISITION OF PLANT ASSETS Taylor, Inc., needs to acquire additional machine capacity to meet the growing demand for its product. The Machine Supply Company offers to provide the machines to Taylor under any of the options listed below. Each option gives Taylor exactly the same machines and gives Machine Supply approximately the same net present value cash equivalent at 8 percent.

a) Cash purchase, $100,000.
b) Installment purchase, 15 equal payments of $11,700.
c) 10-year lease with right to purchase for $1,000; annual lease payments of $14,800.
d) 15-year rental contract at $11,300 per year.

The expected economic life of these machines to Taylor is 15 years. Salvage value is estimated to be $10,000 at the end of that time. All cash flows are at the end of the year.

REQUIRED For each option, prepare the journal entry (if any) required by Taylor to record the transaction.

(IMA, adapted)

P 11-3. SELF-CONSTRUCTED ASSETS Mueller Machine Company manufactures small and large milling machines. Selling prices of these machines range from $35,000 to $200,000. During the five-month period from August 1, 1998, through December 31, 1998, the company manufactured a milling machine for its own use. This machine was built as part of the regular production activities. The project required a large amount of planning and supervisory personnel's time, as well as that of some of the company's officers, because it was a more sophisticated type of machine than their regular production models.

Throughout the five-month period, all costs directly associated with the construction of the machine were charged to a special asset construction account. An analysis of the debits to this account as of December 31, 1998, follows.

Mueller Machine Company
Asset Construction Account

ITEM DESCRIPTION			COST
Raw materials:			
Iron castings:			
Main housing, 3 sections		$37,480	
Movable heads, 2 @ $3,900		7,800	
Machine bed		4,760	
Table, 2 sections @ $6,000		12,000	$ 62,040
Other raw materials:			
Electrical components and wiring		$32,000	
Worm screws and housing		8,600	
Cutter housings		2,700	
Conveyor system		8,400	
Other parts		2,500	54,200
Direct labor costs:			
Layout	90 hrs. @ $5.00	$ 450	
Electricians	380 hrs. @ 9.00	3,420	
Machining	1,100 hrs. @ 8.00	8,800	
Heat treatment	100 hrs. @ 7.50	750	
Assembly	450 hrs. @ 7.00	3,150	
Testing	180 hrs. @ 8.00	1,440	18,010
Other direct charges:			
Repairs and maintenance during testing period		$ 1,340	
Interest expense from 8/1/98 to 12/31/98 on funds borrowed for construction purposes		4,260	
Additional labor to assist during machine testing period, 180 hrs. @ $5		900	6,500
Balance, 12/31/98			$140,750

Factory overhead is allocated to normal production as a percentage of direct labor dollars, as follows:

	FACTORY OVERHEAD RATES (PERCENTAGE OF DIRECT LABOR DOLLARS)		
DEPARTMENT	**VARIABLE**	**FIXED**	**TOTAL**
Layout and electricians	50%	20%	70%
Machining,[a] heat treatment, and assembly	50	50	100

[a]All testing is conducted by employees in the machining department.

Mueller uses a flat rate of 40 percent of direct labor dollars to allocate general and administrative overhead.

During the machine-testing period, a cutter head malfunctioned and did extensive damage to the machine table and one cutter housing. This damage was the result of an error in the assembly operation. Although no additional raw materials were needed to make the machine operational after the accident, the following labor for rework was required:

	DIRECT LABOR HOURS
Electric	80
Machining	250
Assembly	100
Testing (conducted by machining department)	20

Mueller included all of these labor charges in the asset construction account. In addition, the repairs and maintenance charges of $1,340 included in the account were incurred as a result of the malfunction.

REQUIRED Calculate the amount that Mueller should capitalize for the milling machine as of December 31, 1998, when the machine was declared operational.

(IMA, adapted)

P 11-4. **INTEREST CAPITALIZATION** At the beginning of 1997, Davey Jones Corporation signed a construction contract to have a deluxe swimming pool, spa, and club built at its apartment complex. Construction was to begin in late 1997 and was to be completed by the end of 1998. In anticipation of construction expenditures, on October 1, 1997, Davey Jones borrowed $1 million by issuing a two-year, 12 percent note with a maturity value of $1,000,000. Interest is payable annually on September 30.

Because of bad weather, construction did not begin until April 1, 1998; it was completed on December 31, 1998. Construction expenditures during 1998 (all in cash) were as follows:

April 1	$400,000
May 1	100,000
June 1	500,000
October 1	200,000
December 31	100,000

Davey Jones's only other outstanding debt was a 10 percent, 10-year bond issue sold three years ago at its par value of $4 million. Davey Jones's fiscal year ends on December 31.

REQUIRED **1.** Calculate Davey Jones's actual interest cost for 1997 and 1998.
2. Calculate the amount of interest that Davey Jones should capitalize for 1997 and 1998.
3. Prepare the journal entry to record the aggregate expenditures for the construction and for interest costs incurred during 1998.

P 11-5. **INTEREST CAPITALIZATION** Refer to Problem 11-4 and assume the same facts except that the expenditures in 1998 were as follows:

April 1	$500,000
June 1	800,000
August 1	600,000
October 1	300,000
December 1	300,000

REQUIRED Calculate the amount of interest that Davey Jones should capitalize for 1998.

P 11-6. **INTEREST DURING CONSTRUCTION** At the beginning of 1998, Gilbert Interiors, Inc., undertook construction of a building that it planned to use for office space, warehousing, and retail/wholesale sales. On January 2, 1998, Gilbert borrowed $100,000 specifically to help finance the construction. The stated rate and market rate were both 11 percent, and interest was payable annually on December 31. In addition, Gilbert had outstanding debt throughout the construction period as follows:

$100,000, 9% note, interest payable annually on 6/30.
$400,000, 10% note, interest payable annually on 9/30.

During 1998, Gilbert incurred the following expenditures related to the construction:

3/1	$42,000
5/31	36,000
7/31	24,000
9/30	72,000
12/31	18,000

During 1999, the following costs were incurred prior to completion on March 31:

1/31	$24,000
3/31	36,000

REQUIRED
1. Calculate Gilbert's actual interest cost for 1998 and 1999.
2. Calculate the amount of interest cost that Gilbert should capitalize for 1998 and 1999.
3. Prepare the journal entries to record construction costs and interest costs for 1998 and 1999.
4. Describe the rationale for capitalizing interest incurred during self-construction.

P 11-7.　ACCOUNTING FOR INTANGIBLES　Sedona Corporation commenced operations at the beginning of 1998. During 1998, the following selected transactions and events took place:

a) During January, Sedona incurred organization costs of $44,000.
b) On January 31, Sedona acquired a patent for $42,000. The remaining legal life at the time of acquisition was seven years. Sedona estimated, however, that the useful economic life was four years.
c) Throughout the year, the firm incurred costs of $28,000 to publicize its products.
d) Sedona acquired a franchise on July 1. The company paid an initial franchise fee on July 1 of $70,000. The franchise term is five years.
e) Sedona incurred research and development costs of $48,000. Of this amount, $16,000 relates to equipment acquired on October 1, which Sedona can use for other research and development activities. The estimated useful life of the equipment is 10 years, and Sedona anticipates that there will be no salvage value. Sedona depreciates similar equipment on a straight-line basis.

REQUIRED
1. Prepare journal entries in 1998 related to the above expenditures. Assume that Sedona amortizes organization costs over five years.
2. Prepare the intangible assets section of the balance sheet for December 31, 1998.

P 11-8.　ACCOUNTING FOR INTANGIBLES　Selected transactions for Pylipow Company at the beginning of 1998 were as follows:

a) Pylipow acquired a patent for $28,000 cash. The remaining legal life was 15 years; the estimated remaining economic life was 7 years.
b) The company incurred promotional costs of $18,000 related to existing products. Pylipow anticipates that these expenditures will generate additional revenues for approximately 3 years.
c) Pylipow paid $9,000 in legal fees for successful defense of a patient infringement suit. The related patent had a book value of $3,000, a remaining useful life of 3 years, and a remaining legal life of 12 years at the beginning of 1998.
d) The company paid $8,000 in legal fees connected with unsuccessful defense of a patent infringement suit. The related patent, which Pylipow subsequently determined was worthless, had a book value of $20,000 at the beginning of 1998 and a remaining legal life of 4 years.
e) Pylipow acquired a trademark from another company for $60,000.
f) Pylipow paid $4,000 cash for media ads to promote the new trademark.

REQUIRED
Prepare journal entries to record the above transactions in the accounts of Pylipow, including year-end adjusting entries where appropriate. Unless the information provided indicates otherwise, amortize intangibles over their legal life.

P 11-9.　RESEARCH AND DEVELOPMENT COSTS　During 1996, XYZ Company purchased a building site for its proposed research and development laboratory at a cost of $250,000. Construction of the building was started in 1996. The building was completed on December 31, 1997, at a cost of $900,000, and was placed in service on January 2, 1998. The estimated useful life of the building for depreciation purposes was 20 years; the straight-line method of depreciation was to be employed, and there was no estimated net salvage value.

Management estimates that about 50 percent of the projects of the research and development group will result in long-term benefits (i.e., at least 10 years) to the corporation. The remaining projects either benefit the current period or are abandoned before completion. A summary of the number of projects and the direct costs incurred in conjunction with the research and development activities for 1998 appears below.

At the recommendation of the research and development group, XYZ Company acquired a patent for manufacturing rights at a cost of $200,000. The patent was acquired on April 1, 1997, and has an economic life of 10 years.

	NUMBER OF PROJECTS	SALARIES AND EMPLOYEE BENEFITS	OTHER EXPENSES (EXCLUDING BUILDING DEPRECIATION CHARGES)
Completed projects with long-term benefits...............	15	$ 85,000	$35,000
Abandoned projects or projects that benefit current period	10	60,000	30,000
Projects in process— results indeterminate	_5_	_25,000_	_20,000_
Total.........................	30	$170,000	$85,000

REQUIRED

How should the above items related to research and development activities be reported:

1. On the company's income statement for 1998?

2. On the company's balance sheet as of December 31, 1998?

P 11-10. **GOODWILL** At the beginning of 1998, Conrad Corporation entered into an agreement to acquire Ford Company by acquiring all of the outstanding common stock of Ford. The agreement specifies that the purchase price will be equal to the sum of the fair values of the identifiable net assets of Ford at December 31, 1997, and an amount for goodwill equal to five times the average annual earnings for the last four years from normal operations in excess of 10 percent of the fair values of identifiable net assets at December 31, 1997.

Ford's balance sheet at December 31, 1997, was as follows:

Current assets..	$ 300,000
Investments..	80,000
Fixed assets (net)..	820,000
Total	$1,200,000
Liabilities	$ 400,000
Stockholders' equity..	800,000
Total	$1,200,000

The fair value of Ford's inventory exceeded its book value by $80,000 and the fair value of fixed assets exceeded book value by $140,000. Fair value and book value are the same for all other assets and liabilities.

Ford's average annual earnings for the last four years was $120,000. This average included a $20,000 extraordinary gain in 1996 from expropriation of property.

REQUIRED

1. Determine the purchase price to be paid for Ford Company according to the agreement.

2. Prepare the journal entry by Conrad to record the acquisition of Ford.

3. Explain the rationale for recording goodwill only when it is "purchased."

P 11-11. **NONMONETARY EXCHANGE** Hoyt Company owns a warehouse with a fair value of $1,300,000, a recorded cost of $1,800,000, and accumulated depreciation of $900,000. Cottell Corporation owns an office building with a fair value of $1,224,000, a recorded cost of $2,160,000, and accumulated depreciation of $1,288,000. Hoyt and Cottell exchange assets. Cottell also gives Hoyt cash of $76,000 in the exchange. The exchange is considered an exchange of dissimilar assets.

REQUIRED

Record the exchange on the books of:

1. Hoyt.

2. Cottell.

P 11-12. **NONMONETARY EXCHANGE** Assume the same data as given in Problem 11-11, except that the exchange is considered an exchange of similar assets.

REQUIRED

1. Record the exchange on the books of:

a) Hoyt.

b) Cottell.

2. Explain the rationale for the accounting treatment in part 1 by Hoyt and Cottell.

P 11-13.   **NONMONETARY EXCHANGE**   Two independent companies, Ruland and Rahman, are in the home building business. Each owns a tract of land that it is holding for development, but each company would prefer to build on the other's land. Accordingly, they agree to exchange their land.

An appraiser is hired, and from his report and the companies' records, the following information is obtained:

	RAHMAN COMPANY'S LAND	RULAND COMPANY'S LAND
Cost and book value................................	$ 800,000	$500,000
Fair value based on appraisal	1,000,000	900,000

The exchange of land is made and, in view of the difference in appraised fair values, Ruland pays $100,000 cash to Rahman.

REQUIRED   Prepare the necessary journal entries to record the exchange for both Rahman and Ruland.

P 11-14.   **COMPREHENSIVE**   On December 31, 1997, certain accounts included in the property, plant, and equipment section of Diamond Company's balance sheet had the following balances:

Land...	$1,200,000
Buildings..	900,000
Leasehold improvements	400,000
Machinery and equipment	600,000

During 1998 the following transactions occurred:

a)   Land site number 621 was acquired for $1 million. In addition, Diamond paid a $60,000 commission to a real estate agent. Costs of $35,000 were incurred to clear the land. During the course of clearing the land, timber and gravel were recovered and sold for $5,000.

b)   A second tract of land (site number 622) with a building was acquired for $300,000. The closing statement indicated that the land's value was $200,000 and the building's value was $100,000. Shortly after acquisition, the building was demolished at a cost of $30,000. A new building was constructed for $150,000 plus the following costs:

Excavation fees	$11,000
Architectural design fees	8,000
Building permit fee	1,000
Imputed interest on funds used during construction	6,000

The building was completed and occupied on September 30, 1998.

c)   A third tract of land (site number 623) was acquired for $600,000 and was put on the market for resale.

d)   Extensive work was done to a building occupied by Diamond under a lease agreement that expires on December 31, 2004. The total cost of the work was $125,000, which consisted of the following:

WORK DONE	COST	ESTIMATED USEFUL LIFE (YEARS)
Ceilings painted	$ 10,000	1
Electrical work.............................	35,000	10
Extension to current work area constructed......	80,000	30
Total	$125,000	

The lessor paid one-half of the costs incurred in connection with the extension to the current working area.

e)   During December 1998, costs of $65,000 were incurred to improve leased office space. The related lease will terminate on December 31, 2000, and is not expected to be renewed.

f) A group of new machines was purchased under a royalty agreement that provides for payment of royalties based on units of production for the machines. The invoice price of the machines was $75,000, freight costs were $2,000, unloading charges were $1,500, and royalty payments for 1998 were $13,000.

REQUIRED Prepare a detailed analysis of the changes in each of the following balance sheet accounts for 1998:
1. Land.
2. Buildings.
3. Leasehold improvements.
4. Machinery and equipment.

Disregard the related accumulated depreciation accounts.

(AICPA, adapted)

P 11-15. **COMPREHENSIVE** Selected transactions for Johnson Company during 1998 were as follows (assume cash transactions unless otherwise indicated).

a) The company acquired a tract of land. The purchase price was $1,200,000, real estate brokerage fees of $50,000 were incurred, and other miscellaneous costs related to the purchase totaled $30,000. Existing structures on the land were demolished, and the land was cleared at a cost of $40,000. Scrap was sold for $12,000.

b) At the beginning of the year, Johnson acquired an office building at a cost of $3,000,000. The terms were 10 percent down, with a mortgage note payable for the balance. Additional costs related to the purchase included brokerage fees of $100,000 and remodeling costs of $800,000. Later in the year, Johnson removed asbestos from the building at a cost of $250,000.

c) Johnson began construction on a warehouse/headquarters facility at the beginning of the year. Total expenditures incurred on the facility were $1,400,000, average accumulated expenditures were $500,000, no specific borrowing occurred, the average interest rate on other borrowings was 10 percent, and total interest cost incurred during 1998 was $120,000.

d) Relocation and rearrangement costs of $400,000 were incurred. The company incurred the costs to meet the requirements of a government contract that will be completed in five years.

e) The company replaced turbine engines in plant machinery at a cost of $600,000. The cost of the old engines was not determinable.

f) Johnson closes its manufacturing facilities for two weeks once every three years to undertake a thorough repair and maintenance of its plant facilities. This was done in 1998 at a cost of $180,000.

g) A research and development facility was acquired at a cost of $620,000. This building would be useful for the foreseeable future and was not related to any single R&D project.

REQUIRED Prepare journal entries for Johnson to record the transactions. Prepare one journal entry for each lettered item. Do not record year-end adjusting entries.

P 11-16. **FINANCIAL REPORTING PROBLEM** The following questions relate to the financial statements of GE in Appendix B. Unless stated otherwise, assume the questions relate to 1995 only and to the consolidated results only. Please indicate the source of each answer (e.g., income statement, balance sheet, footnote X, etc.). Note: Items 5 and 6 are related to the appendix to Chapter 5.

REQUIRED
1. Describe the composition of GE's property, plant, and equipment.
2. Describe the composition of GE's intangible assets.
3. How much cash did GE spend on new plant assets during 1995?
4. How much cash was generated from the disposal of plant assets during 1995?
5. What is GE's total assets turnover ratio for 1995? Evaluate this ratio.
6. What is GE's return on total assets? Evaluate this ratio.

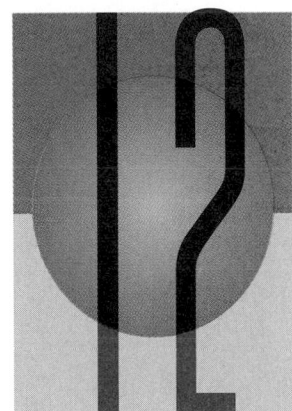
Plant Assets and Intangibles: Depreciation, Depletion, Amortization, and Disposition

LEARNING OBJECTIVES

After studying this chapter, you should be able to:

1. Describe the purpose and process of depreciation, depletion, and amortization.

2. Calculate depreciation expense using the straight-line method, the production or use method, the sum-of-the-years'-digits method, the declining balance method, and the group and composite methods; describe the circumstances under which each is preferred.

3. Calculate depletion expense.

4. Distinguish between and apply the successful efforts method and the full-cost method of accounting for exploration costs.

5. Describe and apply the accounting requirements for amortization of intangible assets.

6. Discuss the issue of impairment of value of long-lived assets and apply the accounting guidelines to impairment situations.

7. Account for the disposition of plant assets, natural resources, and intangible assets.

8. Describe and prepare the appropriate disclosures for plant assets, natural resources, and intangible assets.

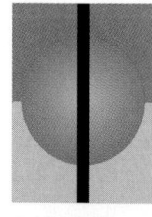

n Chapter 11 we discussed how to account for and report plant assets and intangible assets both at acquisition and when subsequent expenditures occur. In this chapter we extend our coverage by discussing the processes of depreciation, depletion, and amortization. We describe common depreciation methods and typical approaches to partial-year depreciation. We then describe circumstances in which impairment of value may cause write-downs to occur above and beyond normal depreciation or amortization expense. Finally, the chapter concludes with an explanation and illustration of the required disclosures for plant assets and intangible assets.

THE NATURE OF DEPRECIATION, DEPLETION, AND AMORTIZATION IN ACCOUNTING

Describe the purpose and process of depreciation, depletion, and amortization.

CONCEPTUAL

Depreciation is a process of cost allocation and an application of the matching principle.

To those who are not familiar with accounting, depreciation often implies a decline in the "value" or "worth" of an asset. For example, you may hear someone lament that a car is *depreciating* at the rate of $2,000 per year. What he probably means is that the resale value of the car is declining by $2,000 annually. He is using the term *depreciation* to refer to the amount by which the market value of the car is declining each period.

One could argue that this common perception of depreciation as a decline in value, if applied to accounting for depreciable assets, would provide relevant information. However, because of the emphasis in accounting on reliable information and cost-benefit considerations, **depreciation** *is more accurately thought of as a process of cost allocation rather than a means of valuation.* Depreciation is also an application of the matching principle, in which the cost of plant assets used up during a period is matched with the revenues generated by their use.

Likewise, **depletion** is the process of cost allocation for wasting assets (natural resources) and **amortization** the process of cost allocation for intangible assets. Because the processes are identical for all three types of assets—plant assets, natural resources, and intangibles—for simplicity we will focus our discussion in the remainder of this section on plant assets and depreciation.

Cost Allocation versus Valuation

When an asset is acquired, it usually is recorded at cost, because cost (i.e., the sacrifice made to obtain the asset) usually is the best estimate of its fair value. The cost of a plant asset may be thought of as a long-term prepayment, because a company incurs the cost in one period and realizes the service potential over future periods as it uses the asset in the earning process.

For a plant asset, the matching principle is applied by allocating a part of the acquisition cost to a nominal account, called depreciation expense, during each accounting period in which the asset is used to generate revenues. In other words, the amount initially invested in the asset (its acquisition cost) is allocated to the accounting periods in which the company uses the asset.

Generally, the only market values that are relevant in accounting for a plant asset are (1) the market value at the time the asset is acquired and (2) the estimated market value at the time the asset is disposed of—its salvage value.[1] The difference between these two values becomes **depreciation expense,** or the part of the acquisition cost that the company does not expect to recover at the time it disposes

---

[1]However, as we discuss in more detail later in this chapter, in recent years many companies have reduced the book value of plant assets to recoverable value to recognize impairment (loss of economic value).

of the asset. Thus, depreciation may be thought of as a valuation process only when viewed over the entire life of the asset. On a periodic basis, depreciation is merely a method of allocating cost.

Consider a plant asset acquired for $40,000 cash. It has an estimated useful life of 10 years, and an estimated salvage value of $5,000 at the end of the 10 years. The process for this asset is shown graphically in Exhibit 12–1. The objective of recording depreciation is to decrease the book value (the acquisition cost minus accumulated depreciation) from $40,000 (point A) to $5,000 (point B) over the 10-year period. Curves I and II indicate only two of the many depreciation patterns that could be used to depreciate the asset. Curve I shows the straight-line method, and curve II an accelerated method. In either case, the asset's market value is expected to decline by $35,000 over the 10 years. This $35,000 expense may be thought of as the cost of the asset's service potential that is used up over its 10-year life.

Depreciation and Cash Flows

Some users of financial statements incorrectly perceive depreciation to be a source of cash. Although the *acquisition* of an asset does represent a *use* of cash, the *subsequent depreciation is neither a source nor a use of cash.* Depreciation is merely a current allocation of a previously incurred cost.

Because depreciation is a deductible expense for income tax purposes, however, the pattern of depreciation expense that is used for income tax purposes does affect cash flows through its impact on taxes. For example, using an accelerated depreciation method for income tax purposes results in greater tax savings in the earlier years of an asset's useful life than in later years. Using straight-line depreciation for income tax purposes produces the same tax savings each year (assuming tax rates remain constant).

In summary, depreciation is a process of cost allocation. That part of the asset's cost that is not expected to be recovered on disposal is deducted from revenues during the years in which the company uses the asset to generate revenues.

CONCEPTUAL

Depreciation is an allocation of a previously incurred cost and is neither a source nor a use of cash.

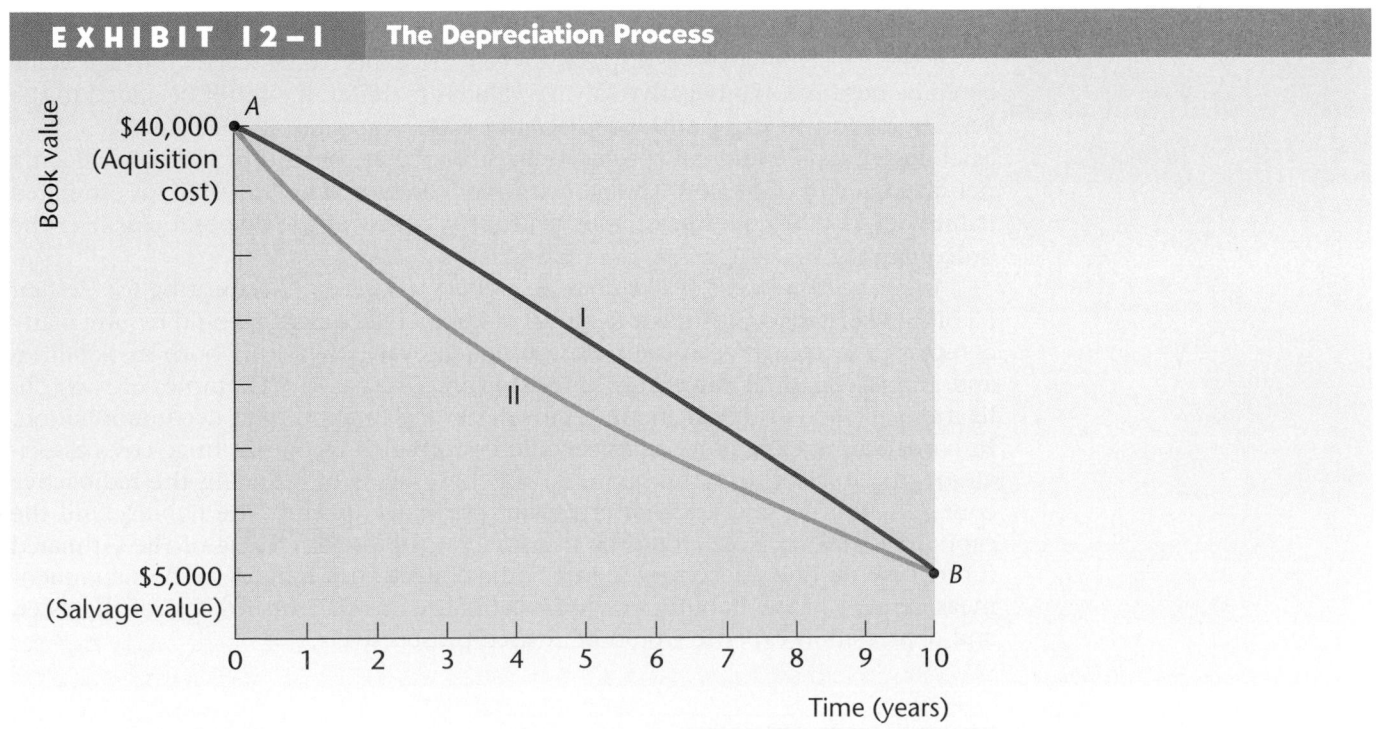

| EXHIBIT 12–1 | The Depreciation Process |

Book value

The only cash flow implications related to depreciation are the income tax savings provided because depreciation is deductible for income tax purposes.

In the next section, we describe the factors that enter into the determination of depreciation expense for financial reporting.

Relevant Factors in Calculating Depreciation

Estimates are an inherent part of the accounting system. One of the best examples of the lack of certainty in accounting, and the resultant need for the exercise of well-informed professional judgment, is the depreciation of plant assets (and for similar reasons, the depletion and amortization of other assets).

Three factors enter into the determination of depreciation expense for plant assets: (1) the depreciation base, (2) the asset's useful life, and (3) the pattern of cost allocation (*i.e.,* the depreciation method).

Depreciation Base

The term **depreciation base** refers to the difference between the acquisition cost, which is the amount at which an asset is initially recorded, and the estimated salvage (residual) value. Put another way, the depreciation base is the amount that ultimately is recorded as the total depreciation expense—that is, the total cost of using the asset—over the accounting periods in which a company uses an asset.

Salvage or residual value is the amount a company expects to receive for an asset upon its disposal. As one might expect, estimating a plant asset's salvage value is a very subjective matter given the uncertainty about the future. If a company expects to incur disposal costs, those estimated costs must be deducted from the estimated proceeds from disposal; the difference is the net salvage value. Because of uncertainty and immateriality, accountants often assume that salvage value is zero—an assumption that is quite valid for assets a company expects to use until they are virtually worthless. Many companies, however, prefer to replace certain plant assets (e.g., a fleet of trucks) long before their utility has expired. In such cases the salvage value usually is relatively large and must therefore be considered in determining the depreciation base.

If the expected costs of disposal exceed the expected proceeds, salvage value could be negative. If a negative salvage value is material, it should be added to the acquisition cost to arrive at the depreciation base. For example, assume that a plant asset costs $10,000 and is expected to be scrapped at the end of its useful life at a net disposal cost of $1,000. The depreciation base would be $11,000. An estimated liability of $1,000 would be established for the excess of the disposal cost over the proceeds.

A *Proposed Statement of Financial Accounting Standards,* "Accounting for Certain Liabilities Related to Closure or Removal of Long-Lived Assets," would require many companies to recognize certain closure or removal obligations both as liabilities and as an increase in the cost of a related long-lived asset.[2] Examples of such obligations include dismantlement, removal, site reclamation, and decontamination. In particular, nuclear power plants could be forced to recognize huge costs associated with "nuclear decommissioning," or the process of reducing the radioactive contamination to safe levels after a plant ceases to operate. The liability and the capitalized cost increase would be measured at the present value of the estimated future cash outflows necessary to satisfy the obligation. Changes in the subsequent measurement of the liability would be capitalized as part of the cost of the asset, and depreciation expense would be revised prospectively.

---

[2]"Accounting for Certain Liabilities Related to Closure or Removal of Long-Lived Assets," *Exposure Draft of Proposed Statement of Financial Accounting Standards* (Norwalk, Conn.: FASB, February 7, 1996).

After a company determines the depreciation base, it must estimate the time period over which an asset will generate revenues. This period is referred to as the asset's *useful life*. The factors that must be considered in estimating an asset's useful life are the subject of the next section.

Useful Life

The **useful life** of a plant asset is the period during which a company expects to use the asset in the earning process. Clearly, the *useful* life of a plant asset cannot exceed the asset's *physical* life. Several different entities may use an asset during its physical life, however.

During the latter years of an asset's physical life, the cost of maintaining it in efficient operating condition is usually very high. That is, an asset's useful life is often shorter than its physical life. Thus, both physical and economic factors must be considered in estimating the useful life of a plant asset. From a practical standpoint, income tax considerations can also play a role in determining an asset's useful life, as can a company's previous experience with similar plant assets.

Physical factors that affect an asset's useful life are the normal wear and tear that result from usage and the passage of time. With the exception of land, the service potential of a plant asset expires as a company uses the asset in the earning process. The estimated useful and physical lives of identical plant assets may differ from one company to the next because repair and maintenance policies (which are designed to delay the inevitable trip to the junkyard) vary among companies.

More often than not, economic factors are the limiting factors in the determination of an asset's useful life, especially in a highly industrialized, technology-rich economy. Economic factors include *obsolescence, inadequacy*, and *changing economic conditions*. Obsolescence is the process by which an existing plant asset becomes outmoded as improved, more efficient substitutes become available. Consider, for example, the continuing development of computers, in which each new generation renders the previous generation obsolete. To remain competitive, companies may have to continually replace their assets with the most up-to-date resources available, even though the assets they replace may not be near the end of their physical lives.

Assets may become inadequate as a result of a company's growth. A company may reach the point at which its existing assets simply cannot perform the work required. Therefore, the company must replace its existing assets with more efficient assets. Finally, changing economic conditions can reduce an asset's service potential. Such economic changes include inflation, energy crises, and changes in consumer tastes. For example, much of the equipment used in the manufacture of large cars, such as the body molds, is no longer useful, even though the equipment's physical life may still be substantial.

The 1986 Tax Reform Act, as amended, requires companies to use a modified accelerated cost recovery system (MACRS) to write off the cost of plant assets for tax purposes.[3] The original purpose of the MACRS provision was to encourage capital investment by allowing rapid recovery of capital expenditures through tax deductions. The MACRS established classes of depreciable assets, each with a prescribed life much shorter than an asset's useful life. Thus, for tax purposes, companies that invest in these assets may depreciate the cost over a prescribed life that may be much shorter than the actual useful life.

The concept of depreciation under the MACRS provision differs greatly from the traditional financial accounting approach of matching costs with the revenues generated over a plant asset's useful life. Based on the historical influence of taxation on financial accounting, it is certainly possible that the MACRS guidelines may spill over into the traditional financial accounting approach to depreciation.

CONCEPTUAL

Both physical and economic factors affect an asset's useful life.

---

[3]Actually, companies still could elect the straight-line depreciation method over a life at least as long as the MACRS life.

Pattern of Cost Allocation

The third factor that affects determination of periodic depreciation expense is the **pattern of cost allocation,** more commonly referred to as the depreciation method. GAAP requires only that the depreciation method used be systematic and rational. Given this rather permissive guideline, a number of depreciation methods are used in practice, as described in the next section.

DEPRECIATION METHODS

CONCEPTUAL

Depreciation should depict the decline in usefulness of an asset.

2 Calculate depreciation expense using the straight-line method, the production or use method, the sum-of-the-years'-digits method, the declining balance method, and the group and composite methods; describe the circumstances under which each is preferred.

Depreciation methods are used to allocate costs that have actually been incurred. Conceptually, the best depreciation method for an asset is the one that best represents the decline in the asset's usefulness. To determine which method accomplishes this objective, we must be able to estimate the net cash flows that arise from the use of the asset each year of its useful life, because an asset's usefulness is determined by its ability to generate cash flows. However, the cash flows generated from the use of a plant asset are indirect, and thus difficult to assess. Often, the choice of depreciation method is made on more practical grounds. In practice, the most common cost allocation methods are:

1. the straight-line method.
2. the production or use method.
3. two accelerated depreciation methods:
   a) the sum-of-the-years'-digits method
   b) the declining balance method
4. group and composite methods.

Each of these methods produces a different cost allocation pattern. The methods and some of the issues relating to their use are discussed in the sections that follow.

Straight-Line Method

For financial reporting purposes, the **straight-line method** of depreciation is the most common depreciation method. Under this method, the amount of depreciation is a linear function of time. That is, depreciation expense is the same amount every accounting period. The amount of activity during a period has no bearing on the amount of depreciation expense recorded for that period. In this method, the depreciation expense allocated to each year is determined by dividing the depreciation base by the estimated useful life of the asset in years.

To illustrate, assume that on the first day of the year, Ricci Company acquires a plant asset for $120,000 cash. Its estimated useful life is five years, and its estimated salvage value is $20,000. Under the straight-line method, depreciation expense would be $20,000 per year, calculated as follows:

$$\text{Depreciation expense} = \frac{\text{Acquisition cost} - \text{Estimated salvage value}}{\text{Estimated useful life}}$$

$$= \frac{\$120,000 - \$20,000}{5 \text{ years}}$$

$$= \$20,000$$

Note that the annual depreciation expense may also be expressed as a rate, in this case, $\frac{1}{5} = 20$ percent.

When approximately the same amount of an asset's service potential is used up each period, straight-line depreciation provides a reasonable estimate of the decline in service potential. The expiration of an equal amount of service potential each period, however, implies that the *net* cash flows generated by the asset (the difference between the revenues generated and the costs of maintaining the asset) are approximately equal each period—an unrealistic assumption in most cases.

The straight-line method is popular because of its simplicity. It often produces results that are reasonable approximations of the depreciation expense that would be calculated under more conceptually appealing but more complex depreciation methods.

Whereas the straight-line method results in a constant amount of depreciation *per time period,* the production or use method, described in the next section, produces a constant amount of depreciation *per unit of activity.*

Production or Use Method

The **production** or **use method** of depreciation may be thought of as an *activity* method, because the depreciation expense that is allocated to a period under this method is based on some measure of the asset's activity during the period. The activity measure that is used in this method should be related to the actual decline in the asset's service potential. Examples of commonly used activity measures include miles driven (for trucks and cars), number of hours used (for machinery), and number of units produced (for machinery). Depreciation expense for a particular accounting period is calculated as the depreciation per unit of activity times the number of units of activity during that period. Depreciation per unit of activity is calculated as follows:

$$\text{Depreciation per unit of activity} = \frac{\text{Acquisition cost} - \text{Estimated salvage value}}{\text{Total estimated number of units of activity during useful life}}$$

To illustrate, refer back to the example on page 626. Assume that the number of hours Ricci Company's new plant asset is used is a reasonable measure of its activity. If Ricci estimates the asset may be used for 20,000 hours over its useful life, the depreciation cost per hour would be $5 [($120,000 – $20,000) ÷ 20,000 hours]. Assume further that during each of the next five years Ricci uses the plant asset as indicated in Column 2 of the following schedule. Column 3 shows the depreciation expense per year for this asset.

YEAR	(1) DEPRECIATION EXPENSE PER HOUR	(2) NUMBER OF HOURS USED	(3) DEPRECIATION EXPENSE PER YEAR (COL. 1 × COL. 2)
1	$5	3,000	$ 15,000
2	5	6,000	30,000
3	5	4,000	20,000
4	5	5,000	25,000
5	5	2,000	10,000
		20,000	$100,000

The use method is a logical approach to determining depreciation expense when (1) actual usage varies substantially over time, (2) the company can reliably estimate the total units of activity over the asset's useful life, and (3) the decline in service potential is closely related to the extent of the asset's use. In such circumstances, matching is best achieved by the use method. However, this method is generally a bit more difficult to apply than the straight-line method, because it is often easier to estimate an asset's useful life in years than to estimate its useful life in total units of activity. The use method also requires that a company keep a record of the actual use of an asset during each period.

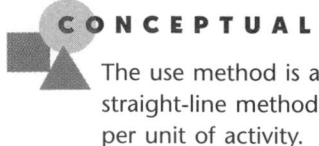

The use method allocates a fixed depreciation charge per unit used or produced. Hence, it may be thought of as a straight-line method per unit of activity. That is, the book value declines in a straight line, but as a function of activity rather than of time.

Some depreciation methods are designed to produce decreasing depreciation amounts each period. Because they result in higher depreciation charges in the early years of an asset's life, they are called accelerated depreciation methods.

Accelerated Methods

Accelerated depreciation methods provide higher depreciation expense in the early years of an asset's useful life and lower depreciation expense in the later years. That is, they speed up, or "accelerate," the recognition of depreciation expense. Accelerated depreciation methods provide an excellent example of the impact of income tax regulations on financial reporting practices. Before the IRS accepted accelerated methods for tax purposes in 1954, virtually all companies used straight-line depreciation for financial reporting. After the IRS accepted accelerated methods, many companies began to use them for financial reporting purposes as well as for tax reporting, to avoid the necessity of keeping two separate sets of records.

Using accelerated depreciation methods for tax purposes allows companies to defer some of their tax payments. An increase in depreciation expense in the early years of an asset's life reduces the company's taxable income in those years. Of course, the taxes saved in the early years must be paid later, when depreciation expense is lower. But the *present value* of the total tax obligation is reduced.[4] Hence, tax savings resulting from accelerated depreciation decrease the cost of owning plant assets, encouraging capital investment.

Although the decision to use accelerated depreciation methods often is based on the tax savings they provide, there is also some theoretical basis for their use. The amount of service potential obtained from a plant asset may well decline each year. When plant assets are new, they are very efficient and require little maintenance. As they age, their efficiency declines, and maintenance costs rise. Because the net cash flows from assets decline over the years, a depreciation expense pattern that recognizes higher depreciation expense in the early years, when an asset is generating larger cash flows, and lower depreciation expense in the later years, when an asset is contributing smaller cash flows, is theoretically sound.

Recall that a depreciation method must be systematic and rational. In the remainder of this section, we describe two common accelerated depreciation methods that fit this description.

Sum-of-the-Years'-Digits

One commonly used accelerated method is the **sum-of-the-years'-digits.** In this method, the amount of depreciation expense for a period is determined by multiplying the depreciation base by a fraction. The *numerator* of the fraction is the number of years of useful life remaining at the beginning of the year for which depreciation is being calculated. The *denominator* of the fraction is the sum of the numbers representing each year of useful life—the sum of the years' digits.

For example, if the estimated useful life of an asset is five years, the sum of the years' digits is $1 + 2 + 3 + 4 + 5 = 15$. The denominator also may be calculated using the relationship $n(n + 1)/2$, where n is the number of years of useful life. The numerator would be 5 for the first year, 4 for the second year, and

---

[4]Furthermore, if a company is expanding its fixed asset base in a growth situation, the high depreciation on the new assets may offset the lower depreciation on the old assets, so that the taxes are postponed indefinitely.

so on. Thus, by multiplying successively smaller fractions by the fixed depreciation base, a decreasing amount of depreciation expense is allocated to each successive year. Exhibit 12–2 illustrates the calculation using data for the Ricci Company.

Declining Balance

Under the **declining balance method,** a depreciation fraction, or rate, is determined and then multiplied by the asset's declining book value to determine the depreciation expense each year. One widely used declining balance method is the **double-declining-balance method,** historically the maximum rate acceptable to the IRS for tax purposes. Under the double-declining-balance method, the rate applied to the book value is twice the straight-line rate. Note that the rate is multiplied by the *book value,* not the depreciation base. Thus, the salvage value is not deducted when calculating depreciation expense under the double-declining-balance method. However, toward the end of an asset's useful life, the salvage value must be considered. Otherwise, the asset might be depreciated below its salvage value.

To illustrate, consider again Ricci Company's data. Since the straight-line depreciation rate is 20 percent ($20,000 ÷ $100,000), the double-declining-balance rate would be 40 percent (2 × 20 percent). Exhibit 12–3 illustrates the calculation of the depreciation expense to be recorded each year. Applying the 40 percent rate to the $25,920 book value at the beginning of year 4, Ricci would allocate depreciation expense of $10,368 to year 4, producing a book value of $25,920 – $10,368 = $15,552—less than the estimated salvage value of $20,000. One solution to this problem would be to depreciate the asset down to its salvage value in year 4 ($25,920 – $20,000 = $5,920). To do so, however, would eliminate depreciation expense in year 5, even though the asset still possesses some service potential in that year. The solution commonly found in practice, and illustrated in Exhibit 12–3, is to switch to the straight-line method in the year in which the double-declining-balance method would depreciate the asset below its salvage value.

So far in our discussion, we have been describing the depreciation of individual plant assets. When a company owns a large number of relatively low-cost plant assets or groups of similar or dissimilar plant assets, the methods we have just described are costly to apply. In this case, the group or composite method may be used.

EXHIBIT 12–2	Sum-of-the-Years'-Digits Method of Depreciation			
	Ricci Company			
Year	Depreciation Base (Acquisition Cost – Salvage Value)	Remaining Life (Years)	Fraction	Annual Depreciation Expense
1	$100,000	5	5/15	$ 33,333
2	100,000	4	4/15	26,667
3	100,000	3	3/15	20,000
4	100,000	2	2/15	13,333
5	100,000	1	1/15	6,667
15 (sum of the years' digits)				$100,000

| EXHIBIT 12 – 3 | Double-Declining Balance Method of Depreciation |

Ricci Company

Year	Book Value, Beginning of Year	Double-Declining Depreciation Rate	Annual Depreciation Expense
1	$120,000	.40	$48,000
2	72,000	.40	28,800
3	43,200	.40	17,280
4	25,920	—	2,960[a]
5	22,960	—	2,960[a]
6	20,000		

[a]($25,920 – $20,000) ÷ 2.

Group and Composite Methods

Many companies group assets to simplify the depreciation process. An average depreciation rate can then be applied to depreciate the entire group. If the assets in a group are *similar,* as they are in a fleet of delivery trucks, the method is called **group depreciation.** If they are *dissimilar*—for instance, all the machinery and equipment in a particular factory—the method is called **composite depreciation.** From an accounting standpoint, the two methods are identical. The primary purpose in using either of them is to minimize the work required to depreciate plant assets.

Assume that a company acquires three dissimilar assets, *A, B,* and *C,* within the same year. The company decides to depreciate the assets using composite depreciation. Relevant data are as follows:

ASSET	ACQUISITION COST	SALVAGE VALUE	DEPRECIATION BASE	USEFUL LIFE	STRAIGHT-LINE DEPRECIATION PER YEAR
A	$17,000	$2,000	$15,000	6	$2,500
B	11,000	1,000	10,000	5	2,000
C	10,000	1,000	9,000	3	3,000
	$38,000	$4,000	$34,000		$7,500

The **average depreciaton rate** for this group is determined by dividing the straight-line depreciation per year ($7,500) by the acquisition cost ($38,000): $7,500 ÷ $38,000 = 19.74 percent.[5] The **average composite life** of the group is determined by dividing the depreciation base by the straight-line depreciation per year, or $34,000 ÷ $7,500 = 4.53 years. If no changes occur in the composition of the assets in this group, applying the 19.74 percent average depreciation rate to the total acquisition cost of $38,000 for 4.53 years will reduce the book value of the group to the salvage value of $4,000 (subject to a rounding error).

In practice, however, each year the company is likely to add some new assets to the group and retire others. As those changes occur, the amount of depreciation expense will change. Depreciation expense for the period is therefore calculated by multiplying the average depreciation rate by the acquisition cost of assets *in use during the period.* For example, if Asset *C* is retired as expected at the end of year 3,

---

[5]Other methods of calculating the average depreciation rate occasionally are found in practice, such as basing the rate on the longest-lived asset in the group (here, 1/6, or 16 2/3 percent), or on the average useful life of the assets that make up the group (here, 1/[(6 + 5 + 3)/3], or 21.4 percent).

depreciation expense for year 4 will be [.1974 × ($38,000 − $10,000)] = $5,527. (Recall that while Asset C was in use with the others during years 1, 2, and 3, depreciation expense each year was [.1974 × $38,000] = $7,500.)

Because depreciation records are not kept on a unit basis under the group or composite method, it is assumed that assets are disposed of at their book value. Therefore, when a company retires assets from the group, it recognizes no gain or loss. Even so, most companies probably do retire some assets early, and use others beyond their originally expected useful lives. To record a disposal under this method, the asset account is credited for the acquisition cost of the retired asset; cash (or other assets) is debited for the amount received upon disposal; and accumulated depreciation is debited for the difference. As a result, any gain or loss that might otherwise be recognized is "buried" in the accumulated depreciation account. For example, if Asset C were disposed of for $500 at the end of year 3, the following entry would be made:

CONCEPTUAL

When assets are disposed of under the group or composite method, no gain or loss is recognized.

Accumulated depreciation	9,500	
Cash	500	
Asset C		10,000

The average depreciation rate is calculated when a group is first established. Normally, this rate is used throughout the life of the group. Estimating the useful life and salvage value of assets added to the group generally is not necessary, since they are depreciated by applying the average depreciation rate to their acquisition cost. If, however, additions to the group have useful lives that differ significantly from the average composite life of the assets in the initial group, it may be necessary to calculate a new average depreciation rate for the group.

Often, plant assets are acquired and disposed of at times other than the beginning or end of an accounting period. Companies must adopt some logical and consistent means of allocating depreciation expense to these periods of acquisition and disposition. The process of calculating partial-year depreciation is described in the next section.

Partial-Year Depreciation

Return to the Ricci Company example (page 626). Assume that Ricci acquired its $120,000 plant asset on April 1 and that the company's accounting period coincides with the calendar year. Since the asset provided service potential for only 9 months in the year of its acquisition, Ricci should charge only three-fourths of a year's depreciation to the first accounting period. If Ricci uses the asset for five years, as it expects to, each of the next four years will absorb depreciation charges for 12 months. The fifth year, the year of its retirement, Ricci will record 3 months of depreciation expense. Exhibit 12–4 shows how Ricci's plant asset would be depreciated using three basic methods (1) if it were acquired on January 1 and (2) if it were acquired on April 1.

Companies use various methods to simplify this process. One common approach is to take one-half year's depreciation in the year of acquisition and one-half year's depreciation in the year of disposal. Another approach is to record no depreciation in the year of acquisition and a full year's depreciation in the year of disposal. Still another is to record a full year's depreciation on assets acquired during the first half of the year and no depreciation on assets acquired during the last half of the year. In large companies that frequently acquire and dispose of plant assets, the results from using one of the simpler approaches tend to approximate the results obtained by depreciating to the nearest whole month. In this book, unless a problem states otherwise; you should assume that depreciation is to be calculated to the nearest whole month.

So far in this chapter, our discussion has focused on depreciation of plant assets. In the next section, we discuss the cost allocation process for natural resources.

EXHIBIT 12–4	Partial-Year Depreciation: Three Basic Methods	

Ricci Company
(Cost = $120,000; Salvage Value = $20,000; Useful Life = 5 Years)

Year	Straight-Line Method[a]	Sum-of-the-Years'-Digits Method[b]	Double-Declining Balance Method[c]
January 1 acquisition:			
1	$20,000	$33,333	$48,000
2	20,000	26,667	28,800
3	20,000	20,000	17,280
4	20,000	13,333	2,960
5	20,000	6,667	2,960
April 1 acquisition:			
1 (4/1–12/31)	3/4 × $20,000 = $15,000	3/4 × $33,333 = $25,000	3/4 × $48,000 = $36,000
2	$20,000	(1/4 × $33,333) + (3/4 × $26,667) = $28,333	.4 × ($120,000 − $36,000) = $33,600 *or* (1/4 × $48,000) + (3/4 × $28,800) = $33,600
3	$20,000	(1/4 × $26,667) + (3/4 × $20,000) = $21,667	.4 × ($120,000 − $36,000 − $33,600) = $20,160
4	$20,000	(1/4 × $20,000) + (3/4 × $13,333) = $15,000	12/27 × ($30,240 − $20,000) = $4,551[d]
5	$20,000	(1/4 × $13,333) + (3/4 × $6,667) = $8,333	12/27 × ($30,240 − $20,000) = $4,551[d]
6 (1/1–3/31)	1/4 × $20,000 = $5,000	1/4 × $6,667 = $1,667	3/27 × ($30,240 − $20,000) = $1,138[d]

[a]($120,000 − $20,000) ÷ 5.
[b]See Exhibit 12–2.
[c]See Exhibit 12–3.
[d]**Because continued application of the double-declining-balance method in year 4 would reduce the book value below the $20,000 estimated salvage value, the company depreciates the book value at the beginning of year 4 in excess of salvage value, $30,240 − $20,000 = $10,240, on a straight-line basis over the remaining 27 months.**

 # DEPLETION OF NATURAL RESOURCES

As we saw in Chapter 11, a major task in accounting for natural resources is to determine their cost and to match that cost with the revenues generated by their sale. Recall that the amount of natural resource cost expensed each period is called depletion. Capitalized costs should be amortized (recorded as depletion expense) over the periods in which a company realizes the benefits. The depletion base is the amount of capitalized cost not expected to be recovered through residual value. Any expected residual value thus reduces the depletion base. If the expected net residual value is negative, it increases the depletion base. For example, additional costs may be required to restore the property after the company has depleted the resource.[6]

---

[6]As we discussed earlier in this chapter, a Proposed Statement of Financial Accounting Standards would require the accrual of a liability and capitalization of costs for certain obligations incurred in the acquisition or development of long-lived assets. Examples of such costs include costs related to the removal of offshore oil and gas production facilities and closure, reclamation, and removal of mining facilities.

Companies also must depreciate the cost of tangible assets used in the exploration, development, or production of natural resources. If a tangible asset—a drilling rig, for instance—can be moved from site to site, the company should depreciate it over its useful life. If a tangible asset is not movable—for example, most buildings cannot be moved at reasonable cost—the company should amortize its cost over the shorter of its expected useful life or the expected life of the natural resource.

Calculation of Depletion

3 Calculate depletion expense.

For most capitalized natural resource costs, the most logical method of calculating depletion is the **units-of-production (activity) method.** First, depletion expense per unit is calculated, as follows:

$$\text{Depletion expense per unit} = \frac{\text{Depletion base}}{\text{Estimated recoverable units}}$$

The depletion expense per unit is then multiplied by the number of units produced and sold during the period to determine depletion expense for the period.

Assume, for example, that Foster Corporation, a major copper producer, incurred costs of $2 million in connection with property acquisition, exploration, and development of an open-pit copper mine. Foster expects that the property can be sold for $500,000 after it has depleted the copper and spent $300,000 to restore the property. The total estimated recoverable units in the property are 1 million tons of copper ore. Depletion expense per unit would therefore be calculated as:

$$
\begin{aligned}
\text{Depletion expense per unit} &= \frac{\text{Depletion base}}{\text{Estimated recoverable units}} \\
&= \frac{\$2,000,000 - (\$500,000 - \$300,000)}{1,000,000 \text{ tons}} \\
&= \frac{\$1,800,000}{1,000,000 \text{ tons}} \\
&= \$1.80 \text{ per ton}
\end{aligned}
$$

If Foster were to recover and sell 200,000 tons of copper ore during the first year of production, depletion expense would be 200,000 × $1.80 = $360,000. The entry to record depletion expense would be as follows:

```
Depletion expense. . . . . . . . . . . . . . . . . . . . . . . . . . . . 360,000
     Mining property. . . . . . . . . . . . . . . . . . . . . . . . . .        360,000
```

Note that the credit is made directly to an asset account, mining property, rather than to an accumulated depletion account. While this approach is used most often, it is acceptable to credit a contra asset account, *accumulated depletion.*

Depletion expense is considered part of the product cost. When the product is sold, the depletion expense associated with the product becomes a part of the cost of goods sold. If a company does not sell all of its production for a period, the depletion on the unsold portion is considered an inventory cost. The unamortized portion of the capitalized costs of natural resources are included under property, plant, and equipment in the balance sheet.

CONCEPTUAL

Depletion expense is part of the product cost.

Changes in Estimates

There usually is substantial uncertainty regarding the number of recoverable units of a natural resource. Frequently, then, a company must revise its estimates, after which it calculates a new depletion rate per unit. Rather than revising prior period depletion charges to reflect the new estimate, the company should spread the remaining book value over the new estimate of recoverable units. For example, assume the Foster Corporation recovered and sold 100,000 tons in its second year (refer back to page 633). However, Foster now estimates *total* recoverable units at only 800,000 units. Therefore, the depletion rate in the second year will be $2.40 per ton [($1,800,000 − $360,000) ÷ (800,000 tons − 200,000 tons)]. Depletion expense in the second year will be $240,000.

An income tax provision regarding the calculation of depletion expense for tax purposes often creates a difference between the depletion reported for tax purposes and the depletion reported for financial reporting purposes. We will discuss this issue in the next section.

Percentage (Statutory) Depletion

For many years the Internal Revenue Code has permitted taxpayers to deduct the greater of cost depletion (as described to this point in this chapter) or **percentage depletion** for oil, gas, and most minerals. Percentage depletion, also known as **statutory depletion,** is calculated by multiplying a rate specified by the Internal Revenue Service by the *gross income* from the property for the period. Because percentage depletion is based on revenues rather than on costs, the total amount of depletion taken for tax purposes over the life of the property may exceed the amount invested in the property.

From time to time the IRS has changed the percentage depletion rates, which vary depending on the type of natural resource. Because the depletion reported for tax purposes can exceed the cost depletion reported in the financial statements, the use of percentage depletion creates a difference between taxable income and income reported for financial accounting purposes.[7]

So far in our discussion of accounting for natural resources, little has been said about exploration costs. One of the most complex theoretical issues in accounting relates to the appropriate accounting for the exploration costs of oil and gas companies. This issue, and the alternative accounting methods developed to deal with it, are discussed in the following section.

The Oil and Gas Controversy

CONCEPTUAL

Oil and gas exploration costs are comparable to R&D in other types of companies.

4 Distinguish between and apply the successful efforts method and the full-cost method of accounting for exploration costs.

Oil and gas companies engage in exploration with the expectation that it will produce benefits in excess of costs. That is, they expect an acceptable return on their investment in the exploration. However, at the time these costs are incurred, it usually is not possible to determine which exploratory efforts will be successful and which will not. This is precisely the same issue that companies face with respect to research and development. As we saw in Chapter 11, the FASB resolved the R&D controversy by requiring companies to expense R&D costs other than for contract R&D as they are incurred.

Historically, oil and gas companies have used one of two methods to account for exploration costs. Many capitalize exploratory costs associated with successful exploration, and expense costs associated with unsuccessful exploration. This approach, called the **successful efforts method,** is prevalent among the larger oil companies. Other companies, primarily the smaller, exploration-oriented oil companies, capitalize all exploration costs. This latter approach is called the **full-cost method.**

To illustrate these alternative methods, assume that Global Company incurs costs of $2 million for each of 10 oil wells during 1998. Nine of the 10 wells prove

---

[7]We discuss the financial accounting implications of this and similar differences in Chapter 17.

to be dry. The journal entries to record the cost incurred under the two approaches would be as follows:

FULL-COST		SUCCESSFUL EFFORTS	
Oil reserves . 20,000,000		Oil reserves. . 2,000,000	
Cash.	20,000,000	Exploration	
		expense . . . 18,000,000	
		Cash	20,000,000

Under the full-cost method, Global would expense $20 million in subsequent periods as the successful well is depleted. Under the successful efforts method, only $2 million would remain to be expensed in the future as the successful well is depleted.

In 1977, as part of its efforts to narrow acceptable alternatives in accounting for exploratory efforts, the FASB issued *Statement No. 19,* which would have required all oil and gas companies to employ the successful efforts method.[8] However, extensive pressure brought to bear by the industry, legislators, the Department of Energy, the Justice Department, and the SEC forced the FASB to retreat from its proposed requirement in 1979.[9] As a result, both the successful efforts and full-cost methods are currently accepted. This controversy provides another illustration of the rather tenuous relationship between the SEC and the FASB. The SEC has the *authority* to establish financial accounting standards, but it has delegated the *responsibility* for establishing such standards to the FASB. Yet when the FASB attempted to implement its charge of narrowing the number of accounting alternatives, and the SEC did not like its choice, the FASB was unable to carry out its responsibilities.

The FASB's pronouncement on research and development costs (*Statement No. 2*), its attempted pronouncement on the exploration costs of oil and gas companies (*Statement No. 19*), and its pronouncement on computer software (*Statement No. 86*) reflect a preference for expensing costs in the face of uncertainty. Furthermore, *Statement No. 7,* issued in 1975, prohibits development-stage companies (companies that have not yet commenced their principal operations) from capitalizing costs that other entities cannot capitalize.[10] The primary consideration in all these instances appears to be the uncertainty regarding cost recoverability at the time the expenditures occur. Because of this uncertainty, the FASB requires that such costs must be recorded as expenses as they are incurred. Taken together, these *Statements* indicate that the FASB is emphasizing conservatism and reliability of information, as well as the definitions of the elements (of financial statements discussed in Chapter 2), in the reporting of items on the balance sheet.

In the next section, we turn to the matching of the costs of intangible assets with their future revenues, a process referred to as amortization. Keep in mind that amortization is conceptually the same as depreciation and depletion.

CONCEPTUAL

The FASB emphasizes conservatism and reliability of information.

AMORTIZATION OF INTANGIBLE ASSETS

In Chapter 11 we saw that the costs of intangible assets acquired from others must be capitalized and amortized (recorded in an expense account) over not more than 40 years. This rule is arbitrary and theoretically unappealing. Certain intangible assets, such as a perpetual franchise and some copyrights, may provide benefits for more than 40 years. The 40-year limit on the amortization period appears to be a

5 Describe and apply the accounting requirements for amortization of intangible assets.

[8]"Financial Accounting and Reporting by Oil and Gas Producing Companies," *Statement of Financial Accounting Standards No. 19* (Stamford, Conn.: FASB, 1977).

[9]"Suspension of Certain Accounting Requirements for Oil and Gas Producing Companies," *Statement of Financial Accounting Standards No. 25* (Stamford, Conn.: FASB, 1979).

[10]"Accounting and Reporting by Development Stage Enterprises," *Statement of Financial Accounting Standards No. 7* (Stamford, Conn.: FASB, 1975).

compromise between the view that companies should not amortize certain intangibles without evidence of a decline in value, and the view that all intangibles have a limited life and thus should be systematically amortized over the periods benefited. Limiting the number of years in the amortization period forces companies to amortize all intangibles, and thus reflects the latter view. The selection of a period of 40 years (rather than some smaller number) enables companies to minimize the impact of amortization on net income—a move to appease proponents of the former view.

Companies must use the straight-line method of amortization unless they can demonstrate that some other systematic method is more appropriate. This requirement implies that equal amounts of service potential are being used up each period and that companies should therefore allocate equal amounts of the cost of an intangible asset to expense each period. Theoretically, there appears to be no more basis for this assumption with respect to intangible assets than there is with respect to plant assets or natural resources. When amortization expense is recorded, the credit entry may be made either directly to the asset account or to an accumulated amortization account.

CONCEPTUAL

Accounting for intangibles often sacrifices relevance for reliability.

As with many other accounting issues, the shortcomings evident in the accounting standards for intangibles exist primarily because of measurement difficulties. As was indicated in Chapter 2, relevance is often sacrificed in order to increase reliability. If the value and benefit period of internally generated intangibles were more readily determinable, accounting data could be made more relevant without a loss of reliability. This increased emphasis on relevance would minimize the theoretical flaws in accounting standards. Perhaps the FASB's conceptual framework project will provide the impetus for improved accounting for intangibles.

In the remainder of this section, we will briefly discuss the application of the general guideline for amortization to specific intangible assets. We begin with specifically identifiable intangible assets such as patents and follow with goodwill.

Specifically Identifiable Intangible Assets

If the estimated benefit period for a *patent* acquired from another party extends beyond the year of acquisition and the patent has not been acquired in connection with a specific R&D project, patent costs should be capitalized and amortized over the shorter of the patent's remaining legal life (17 years for a newly issued patent) or its useful life. The useful economic life of a patent is often considerably less than 17 years because of such factors as competing products or processes and changing consumer demand. Companies should periodically review the amortization period for their patents. If these reviews produce revised estimates, the unamortized patent cost should be allocated over the estimated remaining useful lives of the patents.

Copyrights are granted to business firms for 75 years. Because of the difficulty in estimating the useful life of a copyright, companies generally amortize their copyright costs over some short and arbitrary period. The amortization period may not exceed 40 years. In accordance with the historical cost principle, increases in the value of copyrights above unamortized cost are not recorded.

The right of exclusive use of a *trademark* resides with the original user as long as that user employs the trademark continuously. Trademarks are registered with the U.S. Patent Office for a period of 20 years and are renewable for additional 20-year periods as long as they are used continuously. From a practical standpoint, the period over which the exclusive use of a trademark provides benefits to a company in the form of increased cash flows may be only a few years. Conversely, a trademark's benefits may extend indefinitely into the future, as in the case of Coca-Cola's "Coke." The maximum amortization period is 40 years.

Franchise fees must be amortized over the life of the franchise if the fee is for a specified number of years, or over 40 years if the franchise term exceeds 40 years. If a franchise is perpetual or indefinite in duration, the franchisee should amortize the initial franchise fee over the estimated benefit period, but not longer than 40 years.

Lease prepayments, which are lump-sum payments made at the beginning of a lease term, must be amortized to lease expense over the lease term. *Leasehold improvements* represent the rights to use lease improvements over the lease term. Therefore, the cost of the improvements must be amortized to lease expense over the life of the improvements or the lease term, whichever is shorter.

Conceptually, *organization costs* provide benefits to a company over its entire life. However, the maximum amortization period is 40 years. Most companies amortize these costs over a much shorter period, usually 5 years, to coincide with the income tax reporting requirement that such costs must be amortized over 5 years or more.

As described in Chapter 11, research and development costs for materials, equipment, and facilities, as well as the cost of purchased intangibles that have alternative future uses, are capitalized. The guidelines for depreciation and amortization of these costs are the same as for other plant assets and intangible assets. To the extent that these assets are used in R&D, their depreciation and amortization are classified as R&D expense in the income statement.

Capitalized computer software costs must be amortized on a product-by-product basis. The periodic amortization amount is *the greater of* (1) the ratio of current gross revenues from the product to total current and anticipated gross revenues from the product or (2) the amount determined by applying the straight-line method over the product's remaining estimated economic life. For example, assume that HiTec Company appropriately capitalized computer software costs of $120,000 in connection with the production of ABC, a word processing program that is expected to produce revenues for three years. Revenues for the first year were $800,000; total expected revenues for the three years combined are $2,000,000. The amortization for the first year would be $48,000 [($800,000 ÷ $2,000,000) × $120,000], because that amount is greater than the straight-line amortization of $40,000 ($120,000 ÷ 3 years).

Goodwill

Goodwill appears on the balance sheet only when an entity has purchased it in connection with the acquisition of another entity. The cost of acquired goodwill, like that of other intangible assets, must be amortized over not more than 40 years. The straight-line method of amortization must be used, unless it can be demonstrated that another systematic method is more appropriate.

We have now discussed the acquisition and subsequent expenditures for plant assets and intangibles (Chapter 11) and their depreciation, depletion, or amortization. Generally, long-lived assets are recorded at cost, and that cost reduced periodically by depreciation, depletion, or amortization. However, events or changes in circumstances may indicate that the carrying amount of a long-lived asset is not recoverable—that is, that its value has been impaired or has suffered **impairment.** To round out our discussion of plant assets and intangibles, we turn now to the issue of impairment of value.

IMPAIRMENT OF VALUE OF LONG-LIVED ASSETS

In its 1995 annual report, Brown Group, Inc., owner of the Famous Footwear retail group and other wholesale and retail footwear operations, explained it had written down its retail store assets by $2.1 million because "an evaluation of the fair value of the assets associated with the corporation's retail store operations resulted in the determination that certain store assets were impaired." The write-down was included in the "other expense" section of Brown's income statement.

How did Brown decide when and in what amount to record this impairment? In this section we will describe the nature of the issues involved in accounting for impairments of value, and describe the recently issued accounting guidelines for recording impairment of long-lived assets (plant assets and intangibles).

real world

Discuss the issue of impairment of value of long-lived assets and apply the accounting guidelines to impairment situations.

CONCEPTUAL

A decline in value of a long-lived asset represents relevant information that should be reported on a timely basis.

Until recent years, the recognition of losses on long-lived assets that a company plans to continue to use or operate has been rare. Because accounting standards have not specifically addressed when an impairment of value should be recognized, or how it should be measured and reported, actual practice has been diverse. From a conceptual viewpoint, write-downs to reflect significant declines in the value of long-lived assets should be recognized as soon as they are objectively determinable, because they and the lower book values they produce provide *relevant* and *reliable* information regarding future cash flows. As soon as an impairment of value is reasonably certain to exist and the decline in its value can be reasonably determined, it should be reported.

The measurement of a decline in value is often subject to considerable uncertainty. The need for guidelines is clear, both for companies faced with making the decision about whether and when to record a write-down, and in what amount, and for auditors charged with determining whether the decline in value has been dealt with properly. In the absence of such guidelines, different accountants will deal with similar circumstances in different ways; auditors will have no basis for assessing the propriety of their accounting; and users will not be able to reasonably interpret the resulting financial statements.

In 1995 the FASB issued much-needed guidance in *Statement of Financial Accounting Standards No. 121*.[11] The *Statement* requires that long-lived assets and certain identifiable intangibles held for further use must be reviewed for impairment "whenever events or changes in circumstances indicate that the carrying amount of an asset may not be recoverable."[12] Examples of events or changes in circumstances that suggest the carrying amount of an asset should be reassessed are:

1. A significant decrease in market value.

2. A significant change in the extent or manner in which an asset is used or a significant physical change in an asset.

3. A significant adverse change in legal factors or in the business climate or an adverse action or assessment by a regulator.

4. An accumulation of acquisition or construction costs significantly in excess of the amount originally expected.

5. A current-period operating or cash flow loss combined with a history of operating or cash flow losses or with a projection or forecast of continuing losses associated with an asset that is used to produce revenue.[13]

Reassessment of a carrying amount requires a comparison between the estimated net future cash flows from the asset (undiscounted, and without interest charges) and the asset's carrying amount. If the projected net future cash flows are less than the carrying amount, an impairment loss equal to the excess of the carrying amount over the asset's *fair value* must be recognized. For assets expected to be disposed of, impairment would be recognized if the fair value minus disposal costs is less than the carrying amount.[14] Quoted market prices in active markets are considered the best measure of fair value. If such prices are not available, management should use the best information available. The fair value then becomes the asset's new cost basis.

To apply the future cash flow test, assets must be grouped at the lowest level for which identifiable, independent cash flows exist. If goodwill is identified with assets subject to an impairment loss, it must be eliminated before the carrying amount of the related long-lived assets or identifiable intangibles is reduced.

Impairment losses are reported as a component of income from continuing operations before taxes. Recall that Brown Group reported the impairment of its store

---

[11]"Accounting for the Impairment of Long-Lived Assets and for Long-Lived Assets to Be Disposed of," *Statement of Financial Accounting Standards No. 121* (Norwalk, Conn.: FASB, 1995).
[12]Ibid., para. 4.
[13]Ibid., para. 5.
[14]However, assets covered by APB *Opinion No. 30* would continue to be reported at the lower of cost or net realizable value.

assets under other expenses. The following disclosures are required in the financial statements for the period of the write-down:

1. A description of the impaired assets and the facts and circumstances leading to their impairment.

2. The amount of the impairment loss and how the asset's fair value was determined.

3. The part of the income statement in which the impairment loss has been aggregated if that loss has not been presented separately on the face of the statement.

4. If applicable, the business segment affected.[15]

When a company first applies the provisions of *Statement No. 121,* restatement of prior years' financial statements is not permitted. Impairment losses must be reported in the period in which the criteria are first met and applied. For assets being held for disposal at the date of adoption of the *Statement,* initial application of its provisions should be reported as the cumulative effect of a change in accounting principle.

Statement No. 121 should eliminate much of the uncertainty and flexibility that have existed in accounting for the impairment of long-lived assets. *Comparability* should be enhanced as a result of the new guidance. To round out our coverage of plant assets, natural resources, and intangibles, we turn next to accounting for the disposition of those assets.

DISPOSITION OF PLANT ASSETS, NATURAL RESOURCES, AND INTANGIBLE ASSETS

Companies may dispose of plant assets, natural resources, and intangible assets (and other assets as well) *voluntarily* through sale, abandonment, exchange, or donation. They also may dispose of assets *involuntarily,* through acts of nature (e.g., fire, flood, and earthquake) or as a result of condemnation by a governmental body.

Regardless of the method of disposal, the objectives in accounting for the disposition are to (1) eliminate the book value of the asset, (2) record the consideration received (if any), and (3) record any resulting gain or loss. If the consideration received exceeds the asset's book value, a gain arises. If the asset's book value is greater than the consideration received, a loss results. Depreciation, depletion, or amortization expense must be recorded up to the date of disposal to bring the book value up to date so that the gain or loss may be calculated properly. Gains and losses from the disposal of assets enter into the determination of income from continuing operations unless the disposition meets the criteria for treatment as an extraordinary item or a discontinued operation.

The appropriate accounting disposition of assets depends on the method of disposal. In the following sections we will consider accounting procedures for the sale, abandonment, donation, and involuntary conversion of assets.

7 Account for the disposition of plant assets, natural resources, and intangible assets.

Sale

Companies often sell assets before their service potential has been exhausted. Since assets are not carried at their fair value after acquisition, but rather at depreciated historical cost, it is likely that their book value will differ from the amount of consideration received from their sale. Thus, a gain or loss is likely to arise when an asset is sold.

---

[15]Ibid., para. 14.

For example, if a company sold for $80,000 cash a building with a historical cost of $200,000 and accumulated depreciation of $140,000, the sale would be recorded as follows:

Cash	80,000	
Accumulated depreciation	140,000	
Building		200,000
Gain on sale of building		20,000

A gain of $20,000 results because the cash received ($80,000) exceeds the book value of the building ($200,000 cost – $140,000 accumulated depreciation) by $20,000.

Abandonment

A company may simply stop using an asset that no longer has service potential. If such an asset has been fully depreciated (depleted, amortized), no gain or loss arises. If the asset has a positive book value, however, the company must recognize a loss equal to the book value. Any residual value received for the asset decreases the loss, and any disposal costs incurred increase the loss.

Assume, for example, that at the end of 1998, Pitt Corporation disposes of office equipment with a historical cost of $8,000, on which accumulated depreciation of $7,000 has been recorded. A local salvage yard operator pays Pitt $200 for the equipment. Pitt must record the disposal as follows:

Cash	200	
Accumulated depreciation	7,000	
Loss on disposal	800	
Office equipment		8,000

The loss of $800 results from the disposal of equipment with a book value of $1,000 ($8,000 – $7,000) in exchange for $200 cash.

Donation

A company may dispose of an asset by donating it to an individual or another organization. The donated asset's fair value is unlikely to be the same as its book value. From an economic standpoint, the cost of the donation to the company that is donating it is the asset's fair value. The donor should recognize this fair value as donation expense.[16] A gain or loss on the donation equal to the difference between the asset's book value and fair value should be recognized.

. . . . Assume that Nice Corporation donates five acres of land to a city in which Nice has production facilities. The city will construct a community center on the land. The land originally cost Nice Corporation $25,000; it has a fair value of $40,000 at the time of the donation. Nice would make the following entry to record the donation:

Donation expense	40,000	
Land		25,000
Gain on donated land		15,000

Involuntary Conversion

Not infrequently, assets are partially or totally destroyed by fire, flood, and other catastrophes. Governmental bodies may also, through their right of eminent domain, force companies to give up assets in exchange for a consideration that may be more or less than the asset's book value. Both these sets of circumstances may be referred to as **involuntary conversions** of assets.

---

[16]"Accounting for Contributions Received and Contributions Made," *Statement of Financial Accounting Standards No. 116* (Norwalk, Conn.: FASB, June 1993), para. 18.

When a company disposes of an asset involuntarily, it must record any asset received in the process (usually cash) at its fair value; eliminate the book value of the asset; and recognize a gain or loss, just as in voluntary disposals. If the gain or loss meets the criteria for treatment as an extraordinary item, the company would show it as an extraordinary item on the income statement. Otherwise, it would be included in income from continuing operations.

Companies sometimes immediately reinvest the proceeds from involuntary conversion in similar assets. Some people argue that in this case the company is in the same economic situation as it was before the conversion. Because the investment amounts to an exchange of similar nonmonetary assets, no gain or loss should be recognized. However, the FASB requires that even when reinvestment of the proceeds from involuntary conversion occurs or is contemplated, companies must fully recognize gains and losses.[17]

FINANCIAL STATEMENT DISCLOSURES

Chapters 11 and 12 have covered the acquisition, use, and disposal of plant assets and intangibles. In the final section of this chapter, we will describe and illustrate the general reporting requirements for plant assets, natural resources, and intangible assets, respectively.

8 Describe and prepare the appropriate disclosures for plant assets, natural resources, and intangible assets.

Plant Assets

Plant assets, measured in dollars invested, represent the most significant resources of many companies. The financial statements must include disclosures about plant assets that will enable users to determine how efficiently management has used those assets, and what their future cash flow potential is. Specifically, companies must disclose the following information in the financial statements or notes:[18]

CONCEPTUAL

Disclosures should enable users to assess efficiency of usage and cash flow potential.

1. Depreciation expense for the period.

2. Balances of major classes of depreciable assets, by nature or function, on the balance sheet date.

3. Accumulated depreciation, either by major classes of depreciable assets or in total, on the balance sheet date.

4. A general description of the method or methods used to calculate depreciation with respect to major classes of depreciable assets.

For an illustration of disclosures for plant assets, see the financial statements and notes of GE in Appendix B. Specifically note the policies disclosures in Note 1 and the supporting schedule of property detail in Note 14. Note that GE uses the indirect method of reporting cash flows from operating activities in the statement of cash flows. Thus, depreciation and amortization are added to net earnings to obtain cash flow from operating activities.

real world

Natural Resources

In general, the disclosure requirements for natural resources are similar to those for plant assets. However, for oil and gas producing companies, the disclosure requirements are much more extensive.

In *Statement No. 69,* the FASB required that companies engaged in oil and gas producing activities must disclose the method of accounting for costs incurred in those activities. That is, oil and gas producers must disclose whether

---

[17]"Accounting for Involuntary Conversions of Nonmonetary Assets to Monetary Assets," *FASB Interpretation No. 30* (Stamford, Conn.: FASB, 1979).
[18]"Omnibus Opinion—1967," *Opinions of the Accounting Principles Board No. 12* (New York: AICPA, 1967), para. 5.

they use successful efforts or full costing, and the manner of disposal of any capitalized costs related to those activities.[19] In addition, oil and gas companies must include supplementary, unaudited information about the following items in their annual reports:

1. Proved oil and gas reserves.

2. Capitalized costs related to oil and gas producing activities.

3. Costs incurred for property acquisition, exploration, and development activities.

4. Results of operations for oil and gas producing activities.

5. A standardized measure of discounted future net cash flows relating to proved oil and gas reserves.[20]

Intangible Assets

Financial statements should disclose the method and period of amortization of intangible assets. This disclosure normally is included in the accounting policies note to the financial statements. As discussed earlier, companies must periodically evaluate the carrying value and future benefits of assets. If a significant reduction in unamortized cost results from such an evaluation, the reason for it should be disclosed. In Appendix B, GE's policy disclosure for intangible assets can be seen in Note 1, and supporting detail for the balance sheet amount can be seen in Note 15.

---

[19]"Disclosures about Oil and Gas Producing Activities," *Statement of Financial Accounting Standards No. 69* (Stamford, Conn.: FASB, 1982), para. 6.
[20]Ibid., para. 7.

SUMMARY OF LEARNING OBJECTIVES

1. Describe the purpose and process of depreciation, depletion, and amortization.
Depreciation, depletion, and amortization are processes of allocating the costs of long-lived assets over their useful lives. They are applications of the matching principle, in which cost is matched against the revenues generated from the use of assets.

2. Calculate depreciation expense using the straight-line method, the production or use method, the sum-of-the-years'-digits method, the declining balance method, and the group and composite methods; describe the circumstances under which each is preferred.
Under the straight-line method, depreciation expense is calculated by dividing the depreciation base by the years of useful life. Under the production or use method, depreciation expense is calculated by multiplying the depreciation per unit by the number of units of activity during the period. Under sum-of-the-years'-digits depreciation, the depreciation base is multiplied by a fraction, in which the numerator is the number of years of useful life remaining as of the beginning of the period and the denominator is the sum of the years of useful life. Under the declining balance method, a depreciation rate (usually twice the straight-line rate) is multiplied by the book value of the asset to obtain depreciation expense. Under the group and composite methods, an average depreciation rate is applied to the cost of a group of assets to obtain depreciation expense.

The straight-line method is preferred for its simplicity, when the decline in an asset's usefulness is relatively constant over time, or when the results it yields are approximately the same as a conceptually preferable method. The production or use method is preferred when the decline in an asset's usefulness can be related to a measure of activity that varies significantly from period to period. Accelerated methods such as the sum-of-the-years'-digits and declining balance are preferred for practical reasons—to simplify accounting; for tax reasons—when they produce tax savings; and for conceptual reasons—when assets have greater utility in their early years than in their later years. The group and composite methods are used to simplify recordkeeping when a company has many assets to depreciate.

3. **Calculate depletion expense.**

   Depletion expense is calculated by multiplying the depletion per unit by the number of units sold during a period.

4. **Distinguish between and apply the successful efforts method and the full-cost method of accounting for exploration costs.**

   Under the successful efforts method, only exploration costs associated with successful exploration are capitalized; all other exploration costs are expensed as incurred. Under the full-cost method, all exploration costs are capitalized and expensed over the periods in which revenues are generated from the successful efforts.

5. **Describe and apply the accounting requirements for amortization of intangible assets.**

   The costs of intangible assets must be amortized over the shorter of their useful lives or 40 years. The straight-line method must be used unless it can be demonstrated that another method is more appropriate.

6. **Discuss the issue of impairment of value of long-lived assets and apply the accounting guidelines to impairment situations.**

   Long-lived assets and certain identifiable intangibles must be assessed for impairment whenever events or changes in circumstances indicate that the carrying amount may not be recoverable. The assessment involves a comparison of the undiscounted net future cash flows from the asset and the carrying amount. If the future cash flows are less than the carrying amount, an impairment loss equal to the excess of the carrying amount over the fair value of the asset must be recognized as a part of income from continuing operations.

7. **Account for the disposition of plant assets, natural resources, and intangible assets.**

   When assets are disposed of, their book value must be eliminated from the accounts; any consideration received must be recorded; and a gain or loss equal to the difference between the two must be recognized. The expense of donated assets is recorded at fair value, and a gain or loss equal to the difference between book value and fair value is recognized.

8. **Describe and prepare the appropriate disclosures for plant assets, natural resources, and intangible assets.**

   Accounting policies for long-lived assets must be disclosed, typically in the policies note to the financial statements. Depreciation expense for the period, cost and accumulated depreciation of major classes of assets, and a general description of the depreciation methods used must also be disclosed. For intangible assets, the method and period of amortization of major intangibles must be disclosed.

KEY TERMS

QUESTIONS

Q 12-1. Distinguish between the concept of depreciation in accounting and the use of the term in everyday language.

Q 12-2. What role do market prices play in the process of depreciation in accounting?

Q 12-3. Describe the relationship between depreciation expense and cash flows. Does depreciation provide funds for replacement of assets? Explain.

Q 12-4. Name and describe the three relevant factors in calculating depreciation expense.

Q 12-5. If, at the time a company acquires a plant asset, the expected disposal costs exceed the expected proceeds from disposal, what effect does this have on the depreciation base?

Q 12-6. Distinguish between estimated useful life and physical life in accounting for assets. Discuss the factors that enter into the estimate of useful life.

Q 12-7. In general, what would be the effect on a company's financial statements of using the modified accelerated cost recovery system required for income tax purposes for determining the depreciation period for financial reporting? Explain.

Q 12-8. Under what circumstances might it be appropriate to use a depreciation method in which the periodic depreciation charge is a function of (*a*) the passage of time or (*b*) use or productive activity?

Q 12-9. What is the practical reason for the popularity of accelerated depreciation methods? What conceptual support exists for accelerated depreciation methods?

Q 12-10. Explain the numerator and denominator in the fraction used to calculate depreciation expense under the sum-of-the-years'-digits method.

Q 12-11. Why would a company prefer group or composite depreciation rather than depreciation on a unit basis? Distinguish between group depreciation and composite depreciation.

Q 12-12. Explain the process for recording retirement or disposal of assets being depreciated by a group or composite depreciation method. What is the rationale for this treatment?

Q 12-13. Explain why there is often a conflict between the depreciation method deemed most desirable for financial reporting and the method deemed most desirable for income tax purposes.

Q 12-14. How do companies usually allocate the capitalized cost of natural resources to expense? Why?

Q 12-15. What accounting issues exist with regard to tangible assets constructed or purchased in connection with wasting assets? What are the accounting requirements for such assets?

Q 12-16. What is percentage (statutory) depletion?

Q 12-17. Describe the similarity between (*a*) research and development expenditures and (*b*) exploration costs of oil and gas companies.

Q 12-18. Distinguish between the successful efforts method and the full-cost method of accounting for exploration costs.

Q 12-19. What are the current accounting guidelines for accounting for exploration costs by oil and gas companies?

Q 12-20. Explain why a company may record a write-down in the book value of a noncurrent asset, other than through depreciation, depletion, or amortization, even though the company may not be planning to dispose of the asset.

Q 12-21. List three methods of voluntarily disposing of noncurrent assets. Describe the appropriate accounting treatment for each method of disposal.

Q 12-22. How should an entity record involuntary conversions of assets? How should a loss from an involuntary conversion be reported in the financial statements?

Q 12-23. Identify the information that must be disclosed in the financial statements or notes with respect to plant assets, natural resources, and intangible assets.

CASES

C 12-1. **DEPRECIATION CONCEPTS** Syracuse Manufacturing Company was organized January 1, 1998. During 1998 it used the straight-line method of depreciating its plant assets in its reports to management.

In November, you are having a conference with Syracuse's officers to discuss the depreciation method to be used for income tax and stockholder reporting. The president of Syracuse has suggested the use of a new method, which she feels is more suitable than the straight-line method for the company's needs during the period of rapid expansion of production and capacity that she foresees. Following is an example in which the proposed method is applied to a fixed asset with an original cost of $32,000, an estimated useful life of five years, and a scrap value of approximately $2,000.

YEAR	YEARS OF LIFE USED	FRACTION	DEPRECIATION EXPENSE	ACCUMULATED DEPRECIATION AT END OF YEAR	BOOK VALUE AT END OF YEAR
1	1	1/15	$ 2,000	$ 2,000	$30,000
2	2	2/15	4,000	6,000	26,000
3	3	3/15	6,000	12,000	20,000
4	4	4/15	8,000	20,000	12,000
5	5	5/15	10,000	30,000	2,000

The president favors the new method because she has heard that it will (*a*) increase the funds recovered during the years near the end of the assets' useful lives, when maintenance and replacement disbursements will be high, and (*b*) result in increased write-offs in later years and thereby reduce taxes.

REQUIRED Write a memo to the president which includes answers to the following questions:
1. What is the purpose and nature of accounting for depreciation?
2. Is the president's proposal within the scope of generally accepted accounting principles? In making your decision, discuss the circumstances, if any, under which the method would be reasonable and those, if any, under which it would not be reasonable.
3. The president wants your advice on the following:
   a) Do depreciation charges recover or create funds? Explain.
   b) Assume that the Internal Revenue Service will accept the proposed depreciation method in this particular case. If the proposed method were used for stockholder and tax reporting purposes, how would it affect the availability of funds generated by operations?

(AICPA, adapted)

C 12-2. **SELECTION OF DEPRECIATION METHOD** Pinetop Corporation sells and erects shell houses—frame structures that are completely finished on the outside but are unfinished on the inside except for flooring, partition studding, and ceiling joists. Shell houses are sold chiefly to customers who are handy with tools and who have time to do the interior wiring, plumbing, wall completion and finishing, and other work necessary to make the houses livable.

Pinetop buys shell houses from a manufacturer in unassembled packages consisting of all lumber, roofing, doors, windows, and similar materials necessary to complete a shell house. Upon commencing operations in a new area, Pinetop buys or leases land as a site for its local warehouse, field office, and display houses. Sample display houses are erected at a total cost of from $3,000 to $7,000, including the cost of the unassembled packages. The chief element of cost of the display houses is the unassembled packages, since erection is a short, low-cost operation. Old sample models are torn down or altered into new models every three to seven years. Sample display houses have little salvage value because dismantling and moving costs amount to nearly as much as the cost of an unassembled package.

REQUIRED Would it be preferable to depreciate the cost of display houses on the basis of (*a*) the passage of time or (*b*) the number of shell houses sold? Explain.

(AICPA, adapted)

C 12-3.   **SELECTION OF A DEPRECIATION METHOD**   White Corporation recently acquired an apartment building. As chief accountant for White, you have the responsibility of determining the appropriate depreciation method for the appliances (stoves, refrigerators, etc.) that are provided in the apartments.

REQUIRED   Describe the depreciation method that you believe is the most practical for depreciating appliances in the apartment buildings. In addition to describing the method, explain why you believe this method is the most practical and identify any theoretical shortcomings of the method.

C 12-4.   **ACCOUNTING FOR EXPLORATION COSTS**   Soon after hiring you as the controller of a small oil exploration and production company, the executive vice-president for finance calls you into his office to discuss an issue that has been bothering him for some time. He is concerned about a recent proposal by the FASB that would allow oil and gas companies to capitalize only those exploration costs associated with successful exploration efforts. The executive vice-president is adamantly opposed to the proposed requirement, preferring to capitalize all exploration costs, as is the company's current practice.

    After an extended discussion of the issues involved, the executive vice-president decides that the best course of action is to send a letter to the FASB in response to the proposed requirement. As a basis for drafting the letter, he requests that you prepare a memorandum summarizing all arguments supporting the company's current practice.

REQUIRED
1.   Why is the executive vice-president so concerned about the method of accounting for exploration costs? Why might a small, exploration-oriented company be more concerned about this proposal than a large, integrated oil company?
2.   Draft a memorandum to the executive vice-president that summarizes the arguments in favor of capitalization and subsequent amortization of all exploration costs.

C 12-5.   **PATENTS**   You are part of the audit team reviewing the books of Tobin Company. The December 31, 1998, balance sheet contains the item "Patents" in the amount of $324,000. Upon reviewing the supporting ledger account and documentation, you note the following debits to the account related to a patent acquired from another company at the beginning of 1993, at which time the patent had a remaining legal life of 10 years:

a)   In 1994, Tobin incurred legal costs of $23,000 in successfully defending the validity of the patent.
b)   In 1995, Tobin incurred legal costs of $28,000 in successfully prosecuting an infringement suit.
c)   During 1996, Tobin incurred additional legal costs of $9,000 related to the infringement suit.
d)   During 1997, Tobin incurred costs of $31,000 for improvements on patented items.

    In addition, you determine that a patent on the books at December 31, 1998, at a cost of $74,000 had no material value to Tobin. Several other patents that had been developed by Tobin during the last five years relate to products that currently are generating revenues, but the life cycle of the products is expected to be fairly short. There were no credits to the patent account.

REQUIRED   Discuss the appropriate accounting treatment of the items in the patent account. Include in your discussion the considerations underlying the amortization of and appropriate amortization period for patents.

C 12-6.   **PATENTS**   On June 30, 1998, your client, Creative Corporation, was granted two patents covering plastic cartons that it has been producing and marketing profitably for the past three years. One patent covers the manufacturing process and the other covers the related products.

    Creative executives tell you that these patents represent the most significant breakthrough in the industry in the past 30 years. The products have been marketed under the registered trademarks Safetainer, Duratainer, and Sealrite. Licenses under the patents have already been granted by your client to other manufacturers in the United States and abroad and are producing substantial royalties.

    On July 1, Creative commenced patent infringement actions against several companies whose names you recognize as those of substantial and prominent competitors. Creative's management believes that these suits will result in a permanent injunction against the manufacture and sale of the infringing products and collection of damages for loss of profits caused by the alleged infringement.

REQUIRED
I. Assuming no practical problems of implementation and ignoring generally accepted accounting principles, what is the preferable basis of valuation for patents? Explain.
2. What would be the preferable theoretical basis of amortization? Explain.
3. What basis of valuation for Creative's patents would be generally accepted in accounting? Give supporting reasons for this basis.

(AICPA, adapted)

C 12-7. **START-UP COSTS** You are the chief financial officer for Factory Outlets, Inc. (FOI), a developer of shopping centers for factory outlet merchandise of major retailers. One of its current projects, Fiesta Factory Outlets, was scheduled to open in January 1999, but a disastrous flood occurred at the end of 1998. As a result, the center did not open until July 1, 1999.

Prior to the flood, FOI had secured lease commitments from a number of retailers and had incurred substantial costs related to construction (including interest on borrowed funds), promotion of the center among shoppers, leasing activities, and property management. In addition, as a result of the flood, during the first half of 1999 FOI incurred additional interest costs on the funds borrowed to finance the construction (additional construction costs were covered by insurance), as well as additional advertising costs because the flood rendered the 1998 promotional activities ineffective. All but two of the tenants who had committed before the flood accepted the six-month-late July opening.

The president of FOI is concerned about the financial reporting impact of the costs related to the flood and the delayed opening. She suggests rather strongly to you that she would prefer to see as few of these costs as possible hit the income statement now, because it will take some time for Fiesta Factory Outlets to become established and substantial unanticipated costs were incurred as a result of the flood.

REQUIRED
Describe how each of the costs incurred prior to 1999 and for the first six months of 1999 related to Fiesta Factory Outlets should be accounted for by FOI. For the benefit of the president, a nonaccountant, explain the rationale for the accounting treatments that you recommend.

C 12-8. **RESEARCH AND DEVELOPMENT COSTS** Cobra Company is a large manufacturing concern that routinely engages in research and development activities in connection with new products. During 1998, a significant amount of Cobra's research and development activities were devoted to a new product that has extraordinary market potential.

By the end of 1998, the product had not yet been manufactured, but a working prototype had been built and tested. In addition, costs related to conceptual formulation and design were incurred during the year. Also, during 1998 Cobra acquired additional patents and some machinery, and the company incurred certain administrative and marketing research costs in connection with the development activities. The usefulness of the patents and some of the machinery is related solely to the development of the new product. The remainder of the machinery will be used during commercial manufacture of the product.

REQUIRED
Describe the appropriate accounting for the various costs incurred by Cobra during 1998. Explain the rationale for the accounting treatments that you recommend.

C 12-9. **SOFTWARE DEVELOPMENT COSTS** During an examination of the financial statements of Tracie Company, your assistant calls attention to significant costs incurred in the development of software programs for major segments of the sales and inventory scheduling systems.

The software program development costs will benefit future periods to the extent that the systems change slowly and the program instructions are compatible with new equipment acquired at three- to six-year intervals. The service value of the software programs is affected almost entirely by changes in the technology of systems and hardware and does not decline with the number of times the program is used. Because many system changes are minor, program instructions can frequently be modified with only minor losses in program efficiency. The frequency of such changes tends to increase with the passage of time.

REQUIRED
I. Discuss the propriety of classifying the unamortized software program development costs as:
a) A prepaid expense.
b) An intangible asset.
c) A tangible fixed asset.

2. Discuss the propriety of amortizing the software program development costs by means of:

a) The straight-line method.

b) A decreasing charge method (e.g., the sum-of-the-years'-digits method).

c) A variable charge method (e.g., the units-of-production method).

(AICPA, adapted)

C 12-10. **IMPAIRMENT OF VALUE OF PLANT ASSETS** Kingman Corporation has just completed construction of a plant facility designed for use in manufacturing a consumer product. However, during the latter stages of construction, the release onto the market of a substitute product at a lower cost caused the market potential of Kingman's product to decline considerably. It now appears that Kingman will be able to recover only about 60 percent of the cost of the plant unless the market for the product recovers, which appears highly unlikely at this time.

REQUIRED **1.** Explain why a company may record impairment of value of a plant asset. Include in your explanation a discussion of when the impairment should be recorded and how the amount of the impairment should be determined.

2. Should Kingman write down the book value of the plant? Explain.

EXERCISES

E 12-1. **CALCULATION OF DEPRECIATION EXPENSE** Snyder Company acquired machinery on January 2, 1998, for $220,000 in cash. The estimated useful life is 10 years, and estimated salvage value is $20,000. Snyder estimates that the machine will produce 10,000 units of product and that 25,000 direct labor hours will be utilized over the useful life of the machine. During 1998, Snyder manufactured 900 units of product and used 1,600 direct labor hours.

REQUIRED Calculate depreciation expense for 1998 under each of the following methods:

1. Straight-line method.

2. Production method (units of output).

3. Use method (units of input—direct labor hours).

4. Sum-of-the-years'-digits method.

5. Double-declining-balance method.

E 12-2. **CALCULATION OF DEPRECIATION EXPENSE** On April 1, 1998, Bader Company acquired machinery for $104,000 cash. The estimated useful life is six years, and estimated salvage value is $8,000. Bader estimates that the machine can produce 20,000 units of product. During 1998 and 1999, 2,400 and 3,500 units were produced, respectively. Bader's reporting year ends on December 31.

REQUIRED Calculate depreciation expense for 1998 and 1999 under each of the following methods (assuming Bader calculates depreciation expense to the nearest month in the year of acquisition):

1. Straight-line method.

2. Production method (units of output).

3. Sum-of-the-years'-digits method.

4. Double-declining-balance method.

E 12-3. **CALCULATION OF DEPRECIATION EXPENSE** NHE, Inc., a manufacturer of imaging equipment for the medical profession, acquired a custom machine on January 2, 1998, to use in the production process. The machine cost $120,000, and freight and other miscellaneous costs associated with the purchase amounted to $6,000. It is expected that the machine will be useful to NHE for five years before it is obsolete, and at the end of that time the expected salvage value is $10,000.

REQUIRED Calculate the amount of depreciation expense for 1998 and 1999 under each of the following methods:

1. Straight-line method.

2. Sum-of-the-years'-digits method.

3. Double-declining-balance method.

E 12-4. **CALCULATION OF DEPRECIATION EXPENSE** At the beginning of 1997, Cassell Company acquired machinery at a cost of $87,000. It was expected that the machine would have an estimated life of six years, during which time it could produce 36,000 units of product and be used for 18,000 hours. Expected salvage value is $6,000.

REQUIRED   Calculate depreciation expense for the second year of operation, 1998, under each of the following methods:

1. Straight-line method.
2. Sum-of-the-years'-digits method.
3. Double-declining-balance method.
4. Production method, assuming 8,000 units are produced in 1998.
5. Use method, assuming the machine was operated 3,800 hours in 1998.

E 12-5.   **SUM-OF-THE-YEARS'-DIGITS DEPRECIATION**   On January 2, 1997, Horry Company acquired equipment to use in its manufacturing operations. The equipment has an estimated useful life of 10 years and an estimated salvage value of $15,000. The depreciation applicable to this equipment was $40,000 for 1999, calculated under the sum-of-the-years'-digits method.

REQUIRED   Determine the acquisition cost of the equipment.

E 12-6.   **DEFERRED PAYMENTS; DOUBLE-DECLINING-BALANCE METHOD**   On January 2, 1998, Vaughn Company purchased a machine having an estimated life of 10 years with no salvage value. The terms of the purchase included a $4,000 cash down payment plus three equal annual payments of $10,000 each, which included interest on the unpaid balance at 10 percent per annum. The first payment was due January 2, 1999.

REQUIRED   1. Prepare the January 2, 1998, entry to record the purchase of the machine.
2. Prepare the entry to record depreciation for 1998, assuming Vaughn uses the double-declining-balance method of depreciation.
3. Prepare the entry to record the final $10,000 payment, assuming the effective interest method is used to record interest expense.

(CGAA, adapted)

E 12-7.   **GROUP DEPRECIATION**   Pearce Delivery Company began operations in 1998. At the beginning of the year, the company acquired three delivery trucks. An accountant friend told the owners that they could save considerable bookkeeping by treating the trucks as a group for depreciation purposes. Relevant data on the trucks are as follows:

TRUCK	ACQUISITION COST	SALVAGE VALUE	USEFUL LIFE
A	$14,000	$2,000	5
B	11,000	1,500	4
C	13,000	1,000	6

REQUIRED   1. Calculate depreciation expense for 1998 by the group method of depreciation.
2. If Truck C is sold at the beginning of 2001 for $4,000, what journal entry will be required?

E 12-8.   **COMPOSITE DEPRECIATION**   Desert Airways opened a new maintenance facility in Phoenix at the beginning of 1998. Desert decided to minimize the clerical work associated with depreciation by using the composite depreciation method for the four major machinery and equipment assets. Relevant information for the four assets is as follows:

ASSET	ACQUISITION COST	SALVAGE VALUE	USEFUL LIFE
1	$64,000	$ 4,000	6
2	90,000	10,000	10
3	42,000	6,000	9
4	30,000	–0–	5

REQUIRED   1. Calculate depreciation expense for 1998.
2. If Asset 3 is sold at the beginning of 2000 for $28,000, what journal entry would be required?

E 12-9.   **CHANGE IN ESTIMATED LIFE**   Bryant Company acquired a machine in 1988 for $60,000. Bryant has been depreciating the machine over an estimated useful life of 20 years, assuming no salvage value, by the straight-line method of depreciation. At the beginning of 1998, Bryant overhauled the machine at a cost of $12,000. As a result of the overhaul, Bryant estimated that the useful life of the machine would extend five years beyond the original estimate.

REQUIRED   1. Prepare the journal entry to record the overhaul.
2. Calculate depreciation expense for 1998.

E 12-10. **DEPRECIATION BASE; ADDITIONS; DEPRECIATION EXPENSE** Perry Manufacturing Company, a calendar-year company, purchased a machine for $90,000 on January 1, 1997. At the date of purchase, Perry incurred the following additional items:

Loss on sale of old machinery	$2,000
Freight in	1,000
Installation cost	3,000
Testing costs prior to regular operation	800

The estimated salvage value of the machine was $5,000, and Perry estimated that the machine would have a useful life of 20 years. Depreciation was calculated by the straight-line method. In January 1999, accessories costing $3,400 were added to the machine in order to reduce its operating costs. These accessories neither prolonged the machine's life nor provided any additional salvage value.

REQUIRED   Calculate depreciation expense for 1999.

E 12-11. **EXTRAORDINARY REPAIRS; IMPROVEMENTS; DEPRECIATION EXPENSE** On January 2, 1995, Patten Limited purchased a new machine at a cost of $75,000. Installation costs for the machine were $2,000. The machine has a salvage value of $7,000 and an expected useful life of 10 years. The company uses straight-line depreciation.

On January 2, 1997, an extraordinary repair was made to the machine in the amount of $8,000. The repair extended the machine's life to 16 years but left the salvage value unchanged.

On January 2, 1999, an improvement was made to the machine in the amount of $4,800, which increased the machine's productivity and increased the residual value to $9,400 but did not affect the remaining useful life.

REQUIRED   Determine depreciation expense for the years ended December 31, 1995, 1997, and 1999.

(CGAA, adapted)

E 12-12. **CHANGE IN ESTIMATED LIFE AND SALVAGE VALUE** In reviewing its depreciation schedules at the end of 1998, Penley Company decides that, due to changing market conditions, both the estimated life and salvage value of a major piece of equipment have changed significantly from prior estimates. The equipment was acquired at the beginning of 1994, had an original cost of $62,000, and has been depreciated over an estimated 10-year life with an estimated $6,000 salvage value using the straight-line method. Penley now estimates that the equipment will be useful only through 2001 and that the salvage value will be $1,000.

REQUIRED   Calculate depreciation expense for 1998.

E 12-13. **DEPLETION** Pacter Company acquired a tract of land containing an extractable natural resource. Pacter is required by its purchase contract to restore the land to a condition suitable for recreational use after it has extracted the natural resource. Geological surveys estimate that the recoverable reserves will be 2 million tons and that the land will have a value of $3 million after restoration. Relevant cost information follows:

Land	$14,000,000
Estimated restoration costs	1,200,000

Pacter maintains no inventories of extracted material.

REQUIRED   What should be the depletion expense per ton of extracted material?

(AICPA, adapted)

E 12-14. **DEPLETION** During 1998, Snyder Corporation acquired a mine for $3,600,000, of which $600,000 was allocable to land value after the mineral has been removed. Geological surveys have indicated that 4 million units of the mineral could be extracted. During 1998, 1.2 million units were extracted and 1 million units were sold.

REQUIRED   What is the amount of depletion for 1998?

(AICPA, adapted)

E 12-15. **DEPLETION** In January 1998, Mother Lode Corporation purchased for $9 million a mine with removable ore estimated at 2 million tons. The property has an estimated value of $1,200,000 after the ore has been extracted. The company incurred $800,000 of development costs preparing the mine for production. During 1998, 400,000 tons were removed and 350,000 tons were sold.

REQUIRED   What is the amount of depletion that Mother Lode should record for 1998?

(AICPA, adapted)

E 12-16.   **DEPLETION; TANGIBLE ASSETS ACQUIRED FOR PRODUCTION OF NATURAL RESOURCE**
On July 1, 1998, Houser Mining, a calendar-year corporation, purchased the rights to a mine. Of the total purchase price, $6.4 million was appropriately allocable to the mineral. Estimated reserves were 1,350,000 tons. Production began immediately. Houser found it could extract and sell 10,000 tons of ore per month. The selling price was $25 per ton.

To aid production, Houser also purchased some new equipment on July 1, 1998. The equipment cost $85,000 and had an estimated useful life of 12 years. After all the ore was removed from this mine, the equipment would be of no use to Houser and would be sold for an estimated $4,000.

REQUIRED   **1.**   What was Houser's depletion expense on this mine for 1998?
2.   What was Houser's depreciation expense on the new equipment for 1998?

(AICPA, adapted)

E 12-17.   **ACCOUNTING FOR EXPLORATION COSTS**   Resources, Inc., incurred exploration costs as follows on oil-drilling efforts during 1998:

Well A	$ 60,000
Well B	80,000
Well C	30,000
Well D	50,000
Well E	40,000
	$260,000

As a result of these efforts, Wells A, B, and C were abandoned, Well D was determined to be commercially successful, and Resources plans to continue drilling on Well E during 1999 to determine its feasibility.

REQUIRED   Prepare a summary journal entry to account for the above costs at the end of 1998, assuming that Resources uses (a) the full-cost method of accounting for exploration costs and (b) the successful efforts method of accounting for exploration costs.

E 12-18.   **PATENTS**   At the beginning of 1998, Erin Company purchased a patent on a product for $800,000. The remaining legal life of the patent was 14 years. The estimated economic life of the patent, however, was 10 years. In January 1999, Erin incurred legal fees of $60,000 in connection with a successful defense of a patent infringement suit. At the beginning of 2001, Erin withdrew the product from the market because of a potential health hazard.

REQUIRED   Prepare journal entries related to the patent for 1998, 1999, 2000, and 2001.

E 12-19.   **AMORTIZATION OF COMPUTER SOFTWARE COSTS**   Software House has appropriately capitalized computer software costs associated with internally developed products that were determined to be technologically feasible. One of these products, Xscape, has a carrying amount of $120,000 at the end of 1998. Straight-line amortization would be $40,000. Estimated current and future revenues from the product are $240,000 for 1998, $160,000 for 1999, and $80,000 for 2000.

REQUIRED   Calculate the amount of amortization expense for 1998.

E 12-20.   **DISPOSAL OF PLANT ASSETS**   Altman Company has a machine that is no longer useful. The machine cost $60,000, and as of December 31, 1998, accumulated depreciation of $45,000 had been recorded. The machine's market value on that date was $13,000.

REQUIRED   Prepare the journal entry to record the disposal of the machine on January 2, 1999, under each of the following *independent* assumptions:
1.   Altman sells the machine for $13,000 cash.
2.   Altman abandons the machine, incurring $600 of removal costs.
3.   Altman donates the machine to a newly formed small business in the community.

PROBLEMS

P 12-1. **ACQUISITION, SUBSEQUENT EXPENDITURES, AND DEPRECIATION OF PLANT ASSETS**
The following information relates to the purchase and upkeep of machinery of Heath Company during the years 1998 and 1999:

1998:

April 1   Purchased Machine *A* for $8,000 cash; paid $500 for installation and $300 for freight. Machine *A* is expected to have a useful life of 8 years from this date and no scrap value.

July 1   Purchased Machine *B* for $12,000, including delivery and installation. No scrap value is anticipated, and the machine is expected to have a useful life of 10 years.

Dec. 31   Recorded depreciation on a straight-line basis.

1999:

March 31   Paid repair bills of $294, of which $100 applied to Machine *A* and $194 to Machine *B*.

July 1   Traded in Machine *A* plus $3,000 cash for Machine *C*. The new machine has a life expectancy of 10 years and no salvage value.

Oct. 1   Sold Machine *B* for $8,000 cash.

Dec. 31   Recorded depreciation on a straight-line basis.

REQUIRED   Prepare journal entries to record each of the above items.

P 12-2. **ACQUISITION, SUBSEQUENT EXPENDITURES, AND DEPRECIATION OF PLANT ASSETS**
On the first business day of 1994, KCR Truckers purchased for cash a new truck from its local dealer. The truck was a heavy-duty type, and records indicated it should have a 10-year life span and no salvage value. The vehicle cost $36,000. The straight-line depreciation method is used.

During the first week of January 1998, the truck was repaired and rebuilt at a total cost of $6,400: $4,800 for additions and $1,600 for ordinary repairs. The additions increased the efficiency of the vehicle but no change was contemplated in life expectancy or salvage value.

On April 1, 1999, the truck was completely wrecked. Alpha Insurance Company settled the claim for $17,000.

REQUIRED   Prepare journal entries for:
1. The purchase of the vehicle.
2. Depreciation during the first year.
3. The 1998 transaction involving the rebuilding.
4. The 1998 depreciation.
5. The 1999 entries.

(CGAA, adapted)

P 12-3. **CALCULATION OF DEPRECIATION EXPENSE; PARTIAL-YEAR DEPRECIATION** Petras Health Services, a provider of diagnostics to health care organizations, was founded by Greg Petras at the beginning of 1998. Operations began on July 1, 1998.

Just prior to commencing operations, Petras acquired a machine at a cost of $120,000 that performs multiple diagnostics on clients. Freight and installation costs were $4,000. Because of rapid technological changes, Petras estimated that the machine would be useful for only four years and that salvage value would be negligible. It was also estimated that the machine could be used for about 5,000 hours.

REQUIRED   Calculate depreciation expense for 1998 and 1999 under each of the following depreciation methods:
1. Straight-line method.
2. Sum-of-the-years'-digits method.
3. Double-declining-balance method.
4. Use method, assuming the machine is used 500 hours in 1998 and 1,600 hours in 1999.

P 12-4. **EFFECT OF DEPRECIATION METHODS ON INCOME** On January 1, 1996, Rankin Company, a small machine tool manufacturer, acquired for $1 million a piece of new industrial equipment. The new equipment had a useful life of 10 years, and Rankin estimated that the salvage value would be $200,000. Rankin estimated that the new equipment could produce 10,000 machine tools in its first year. Production would then decline by 1,000 units per year over the remaining useful life of the equipment.

The following depreciation methods may be used:

Double-declining-balance.

Straight-line.

Sum-of-the-years'-digits.

Production (units of output).

REQUIRED

1. Which depreciation method would result in the maximization of profits for financial statement reporting for the three-year period ending December 31, 1998? Prepare a schedule showing the amount of accumulated depreciation as of December 31, 1998, under the method selected. Show supporting calculations. Ignore present value, income tax, and deferred income tax considerations in your answer.

2. Which depreciation method would result in the minimization of profits for financial reporting for the three-year period ending December 31, 1998? Prepare a schedule showing the amount of accumulated depreciation as of December 31, 1998, under the method selected. Show supporting calculations. Ignore present value considerations.

(AICPA, adapted)

P 12-5. **ANALYSIS OF PLANT ASSET ACCOUNTS** Selected accounts included in the property, plant, and equipment section of Gardner Corporation's balance sheet on December 31, 1997, had the following balances:

Land	**$300,000**
Land improvements	**90,000**
Buildings	**900,000**
Machinery and equipment	**550,000**

During 1998, the following transactions occurred:

a) A plant facility consisting of land and building was acquired from Nostrand Company in exchange for 10,000 shares of Gardner's common stock. On the acquisition date, Gardner's stock had a closing market price of $45 per share on a national stock exchange. Current appraised values for the land and building, respectively, are $160,000 and $320,000.

b) Items of machinery and equipment were purchased at a total cost of $300,000. Additional costs were incurred as follows:

Freight and unloading	**$ 5,000**
Sales and use taxes	**12,000**
Installation	**25,000**

c) Expenditures totaling $75,000 were made for new parking lots, streets, and sidewalks at the corporation's various plant locations. These expenditures had an estimated useful life of 15 years.

d) A machine costing $50,000 on January 1, 1990, was scrapped on June 30, 1998. Double-declining-balance depreciation has been recorded on the basis of a 10-year life.

e) A machine was sold for $20,000 on July 1, 1998. Original cost of the machine was $36,000 on January 1, 1995, and it was depreciated on a straight-line basis over an estimated useful life of 7 years, with a salvage value of $1,000.

REQUIRED Prepare a detailed analysis of the changes in each of the following balance sheet accounts for 1998:

1. Land.

2. Land improvements.

3. Buildings.

4. Machinery and equipment

Disregard the related accumulated depreciation accounts.

P 12-6.   **ANALYSIS OF PLANT ASSET ACCOUNTS**   Colby Corporation, a manufacturer of steel products, began operations on October 1, 1998. Colby's accounting department has started the fixed asset and depreciation schedule presented below. You have been asked to assist in completing this schedule. In addition to ascertaining that the data already on the schedule are correct, you have obtained the following information from the company's records and personnel:

a)   Depreciation is calculated from the first of the month of acquisition to the first of the month of disposition.

b)   Land A and Building A were acquired from Beeson Corporation. Colby paid $812,500 for the land and building together. At the time of acquisition, the land had an appraised value of $72,000 and the building had an appraised value of $828,000.

c)   Land B was acquired on October 2, 1998, in exchange for 3,000 newly issued shares of Colby's common stock. At the date of acquisition, the stock had a par value of $5 per share and a market price of $40 per share. During October 1998, Colby paid $14,000 to demolish an existing building on this land so it could construct a new building.

d)   Construction of Building B on the newly acquired land began on October 1, 1999. By September 30, 2000, Colby had paid $210,000 of the estimated total construction costs of $300,000. Estimated completion and occupancy are scheduled for July 2001.

e)   Certain equipment was donated to the corporation by a local university. An independent appraisal of the equipment when it was donated placed the fair value at $24,000 and the salvage value at $2,000.

f)   Machinery A's total cost of $110,000 includes installation expense of $550 and normal repairs and maintenance of $11,000. Salvage value is estimated to be $5,500. Machinery A was sold on February 1, 2000.

g)   On October 1, 1999, Machinery B was acquired with a down payment of $4,000, the remaining payments to be made in 10 annual installments of $4,000 each beginning October 1, 2000. The prevailing interest rate was 8 percent.

Fixed Asset and Depreciation Schedule

ASSETS	ACQUI-SITION DATE	COST	SALVAGE	DEPRE-CIATION METHOD	ESTIMATED LIFE (YEARS)	DEPRECIATION EXPENSE, YEAR ENDED 9/30	
						1999	2000
Land A	10/1/98	(1)	N/A	N/A	N/A	N/A	N/A
Building A	10/1/98	(2)	$47,500	Straight-line	(3)	$14,000	(4)
Land B	10/2/98	(5)	N/A	N/A	N/A	N/A	N/A
Building B	Under construction	$210,000 to date	—	Straight-line	30	—	(6)
Donated equipment	10/2/98	(7)	2,000	150% declining-balance	10	(8)	(9)
Machinery A	10/2/98	(10)	5,500	Sum-of-years'-digits	10	(11)	(12)
Machinery B	10/1/99	(13)	—	Straight-line	15	—	(14)

N/A = Not applicable.

REQUIRED   For each numbered item in the schedule, calculate the correct amount. Show supporting calculations.

(AICPA, adapted)

P 12-7. **MISCELLANEOUS PLANT ASSET TRANSACTIONS** At the beginning of 1991, Advanced Semi, Inc. (ASI), a semiconductor manufacturer, purchased machinery to be used in its manufacturing operations. ASI paid $360,000 cash for the machinery and began using it immediately upon acquisition. Initially, it was anticipated that the machinery would be useful to ASI for about 15 years and that salvage value would be minimal. ASI uses the straight-line method of depreciation.

Selected events during the next few years were as follows:

a) At the beginning of 1994, ASI paid $30,000 for an upgrade to the machinery, which supposedly would increase output by 20 percent but would not alter the expected useful life or salvage value.

b) In January 1998, the machinery was overhauled at a cost of $24,000. This overhaul extended the estimated useful life by five years.

c) On September 1, 1999, the machinery was totally destroyed as the result of a plant fire. ASI received insurance proceeds of $160,000.

REQUIRED Prepare journal entries to record:
1. The original purchase of the machinery.
2. 1994 depreciation.
3. 1998 depreciation.
4. The fire loss and settlement.
Show supporting calculations.

P 12-8. **DEPRECIATION; EXCHANGE OF PLANT ASSETS** Riley Corporation purchased Machine A at a cost of $22,000 on January 2, 1992. From 1992 through 1995, the machine was depreciated on a straight-line basis, under the assumption that it would have a 10-year useful life and a $2,000 salvage value. After more experience and before recording 1996 depreciation, Riley revised its estimate of the machine's useful life downward from 10 years to 8 years and revised the estimated salvage value downward to $1,000.

On April 2, 1998, the company traded in Machine A for Machine B, a newer model, receiving a $5,000 trade-in allowance. Machine B cost $16,300, less the trade-in allowance, and the balance of $11,300 was paid in cash. Machine B was depreciated on a straight-line basis under the assumption that it would have a 7-year useful life and a $1,300 salvage value.

REQUIRED Prepare journal entries to record:
1. The purchase of Machine A.
2. 1992 depreciation.
3. 1996 depreciation.
4. The exchange of the machines.
5. 1998 depreciation.

P 12-9. **DEPRECIATION; CHANGES IN ESTIMATED LIFE AND SALVAGE VALUE** Coleman Company, which uses the straight-line method of depreciation, purchased three machines on the first day of business in January 1993. Details of the purchase are as follows:

	MACHINE X	MACHINE Y	MACHINE Z
Cost	$20,000	$15,000	$15,000
Estimated life	5 years	6 years	8 years
Estimated scrap value	None	$2,400	$600

During the first week of business in January 1998, Machine X was sold for $2,400. This prompted management to reexamine not only the estimated useful life but also the expected scrap value of machines Y and Z. They decided that Machine Y had a remaining life of two years as of January 1, 1998, and that the scrap evaluation of $2,400 was about right. Machine Z, however, had a remaining life of five years and there probably would be no salvage value.

REQUIRED Prepare journal entries to reflect all of the events and information related to the three machines during 1998, including depreciation expense.

(CGAA, adapted)

P 12-10. **DEPLETION** Simon Copper Company purchased a tract of mining property in 1997 for $6.4 million. Simon constructed buildings on the property during 1997 at a cost of $400,000. Simon estimated that the buildings would have a physical life of 20 years, but Simon does not intend to use the buildings after it has depleted the copper ore from the property. Simon acquired machinery for $360,000 to be used in its mining operation and estimated that two-thirds of the machinery (in terms of book value) will be used up by the mining of the tract in question.

Mining operations commenced at the beginning of 1998. At that time, Simon estimated that it would extract 1,800,000 tons of low-grade ore from the property. Simon incurred production costs of $220,000 during 1998 to extract 140,000 tons of ore.

In 1999, Simon extracted 200,000 tons of ore and incurred production costs of $260,000. At the end of 1999, the company estimated that 1,200,000 tons of ore remained that could be extracted economically.

REQUIRED Assuming that Simon Copper maintains no inventories and that restoration costs negate any residual value, calculate depletion expense for 1998 and 1999 by the units-of-production method.

P 12-11. **DEPLETION** Lowder Resources, Inc., is engaged in the exploration and production of natural resources. Lowder acquires properties, extracts and markets the resources, and then disposes of the depleted properties after meeting restoration obligations. In 1998, Lowder purchased a tract of land in Utah for $3.6 million. In addition, Lowder constructed facilities on the property, which could be used only in the mining operation, at a cost of $200,000 with no anticipated salvage value.

Lowder estimated that 900,000 tons of the natural resource could be extracted economically from the property. Also, it anticipated that restoration costs of $80,000 would be incurred after production was completed and that the property could then be sold for $400,000.

In 1998, Lowder extracted 40,000 tons, of which 10,000 tons were unsold at the end of the year, and incurred production costs of $180,000. During 1999, a refiner entered into an agreement to purchase all that Lowder could produce. Lowder extracted 60,000 tons in 1999 and, at the end of the year, estimated that 600,000 recoverable tons remained. Production costs of $280,000 were incurred in 1999.

REQUIRED **1.** Calculate the depletion rate per ton in 1998 and 1999.
2. Prepare the journal entries at the end of 1998 and 1999 to record production activities.

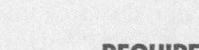

P 12-12. **ACCOUNTING FOR INTANGIBLES** Selected information related to Henry Corporation for 1998 is as follows:
a) Patent *A,* acquired at the beginning of 1995 for $24,000, was being amortized over a 10-year period. At the end of 1998, the remaining legal life of the patent was 12 years, but Henry estimated that the patent would have only an 8-year useful life to the company (from the date of acquisition).
b) During 1998, Henry incurred legal fees of $5,000 in connection with the unsuccessful defense of Patent *B.* Patent *B* had been acquired at the beginning of 1993 for $40,000 and was being amortized over an 8-year period. As a result of the unsuccessful litigation, Patent *B* was determined to be worthless.
c) Henry incurred research and development costs of $60,000 during 1998. Of this amount, $36,000 was for personnel costs and $24,000 was for a July 1 equipment purchase. The equipment will be used for a number of research and development projects over a 5-year period. Henry anticipates no salvage value and depreciates similar equipment using the straight-line method.
d) Henry acquired a franchise on April 1, 1998, by paying an initial franchise fee of $120,000 cash. The franchise term is 10 years.
e) Henry incurred advertising fees of $40,000 related to products in the marketplace. Henry's research indicates that advertising can generate revenues for approximately 3 years.

REQUIRED Prepare the 1998 journal entries to record the above information, including any necessary year-end adjustments.

P 12-13. **INTANGIBLES—STATEMENT PRESENTATION** Kraft Company has provided information on intangible assets as follows:
a) A patent was purchased from Johnson Company for $1.5 million on January 1, 1997. Kraft estimated the remaining useful life of the patent to be 10 years. The patent

was carried in Johnson's accounting records at net book value of $1.25 million when Johnson sold it to Kraft.

b) During 1998, a franchise was purchased from Greenberg Company for $600,000. In addition, 5 percent of revenue from the franchise must be paid to Greenberg. Revenue from the franchise for 1998 was $2 million. Kraft estimates the useful life of the franchise to be 10 years and takes a full year's amortization in the year of purchase.

c) Kraft incurred research and development costs in 1998 as follows:

Materials and equipment	**$220,000**
Personnel	**140,000**
Indirect costs	**60,000**
	$420,000

Kraft estimates that these costs will be recovered by December 31, 2000.

d) At the end of 1998, Kraft estimated, on the basis of recent events in the field, that the remaining life of the patent purchased on January 1, 1997, was only 4 years.

REQUIRED **1.** Prepare a schedule showing the intangibles section of Kraft's balance sheet on December 31, 1998. Show supporting calculations.

2. Prepare a schedule showing the income statement effect for the year ended December 31, 1998, as a result of the above facts. Show supporting calculations.

(AICPA, adapted)

P 12-14. **INTANGIBLES—CLASSIFICATION** Fane Corporation began operations in 1998. As the senior accountant assigned to the audit of Fane Corporation for 1998, you discover a ledger account, "intangibles," consisting of the following items:

Jan. 2	**Organization costs**	**$14,000**
Feb. 1	**Advertising costs**	**6,300**
March 30	**Registered a patent to be used in R&D activities**	
	($15,000 of the cost constitutes research and development costs	
	related to development of patent)	**17,400**
July 1	**Operating loss, first six months**	**8,000**
Oct. 1	**Acquired copyright, estimated remaining economic life of 5 years**	**12,000**
Oct. 15	**Labor costs associated with R&D activities**	**8,000**
Dec. 1	**Acquired two patents to be used for R&D activities: patent no. 1**	
	(cost of $6,000), to be used solely for current R&D project,	
	has remaining legal life of 4 years; patent no. 2 (cost of $21,000),	
	to be used for several R&D projects over 3-year period,	
	has remaining legal life of 14 years	**27,000**

REQUIRED Prepare correcting entries to eliminate the intangibles account, including year-end adjusting entries. You should amortize organization costs over the minimum period allowable for tax purposes.

P 12-15. **GOODWILL** On September 1, 1998, Kelley Company purchased 200,000 shares representing 45 percent of the outstanding stock of Moore Company for cash. Goodwill of $500,000 was appropriately recognized by Kelley at the date of the purchase.

On December 1, 1996, Kelley purchased 300,000 shares representing 30 percent of the outstanding stock of Powell Company for $2.5 million cash. The stockholders' equity section of Powell's balance sheet at the date of the acquisition was as follows:

Common stock, par value $2 a share	**$2,000,000**
Contributed capital in excess of par	**1,000,000**
Retained earnings	**3,000,000**
	$6,000,000

At the date of acquisition, the fair value of Powell's property, plant, and equipment (net) was $3.8 million, whereas the book value was $3.5 million. The fair values of all of Powell's other assets and liabilities were equal to their book values.

Kelley amortizes goodwill over the maximum period allowed and takes a full year's amortization in the year of purchase.

REQUIRED   Prepare a schedule calculating the amount of goodwill and accumulated amortization on December 31, 1999, and the goodwill amortization for the year ended December 31, 1999. Show supporting calculations.

(AICPA, adapted)

P 12-16.   **INTANGIBLES—COMPREHENSIVE**   Eskew Corporation was founded in 1985 and experienced only moderate growth until the last 3 years, when it became a leader in the field of robotics. Eskew has experienced a 30 percent growth rate in revenues during the last 3 years and is planning several expenditures that would enable it to meet increased demand and continue its excellent growth rate.

Dan Johnson, of Eskew's accounting department, is having some difficulty determining the appropriate accounting for several transactions that occurred during the first quarter of 1998. These transactions are described below. All amounts are considered to be material.

a)   Eskew paid $600,000 for land on which to build a new research facility. The cost to raze and remove an old building on the site of the newly proposed research facility was $50,000. Usable fixtures from the old building were sold for $10,000. Eskew paid $4,000 to the architect who designed the new building, $30,000 for excavation of the basement, and $550,000 to a contractor for construction of the building. The new building is expected to be appropriate for the needs of the company for about 20 years.

b)   Eskew gave a 1-year, non-interest-bearing note for $165,000 to Roberts Industries in exchange for a conveyor to be installed in the new facility and a temperate monitoring system (TMS). The imputed interest rate on the note is 10 percent per year. The conveyor had an estimated value of $60,000 at the date of the exchange, is expected to last for 30 years, and will be needed as long as the research facility is used by the company. The TMS had an estimated value of $100,000 at the date of the exchange and is expected to last 5 years.

c)   Eskew incurred the following costs in developing and securing a trademark:

Design costs	**$6,000**
Registration fees	**300**
Attorneys' fees	**700**

Eskew's marketing manager believes the trademark will be of value to the company for 50 years.

d)   Eskew incurred $8,000 in legal fees to defend its rights in a patent. The patent was purchased at the beginning of 1996 for $15,000 and is being amortized over 12 years.

e)   Eskew spent $60,000 searching for practical applications of new research findings that are believed to be of use to the company for the next 20 years.

REQUIRED   As controller for Eskew Corporation, you are to review the five items described, summarize the amounts to be capitalized and expensed in 1998, and determine the number of years over which capitalized amounts are to be written off.

(IMA, adapted)

P 12-17.   **FINANCIAL REPORTING RESEARCH PROBLEM: IMPAIRMENT OF VALUE OF LONG-LIVED ASSETS**   Texaco, Inc., adopted *Statement of Financial Accounting Standards No. 121* in 1995. As a result, Texaco reported significant write-downs of oil and gas properties in its 1995 annual report.

REQUIRED   **1.**   Obtain Texaco's 1995 annual report (hard copy, EDGAR, or other means). Locate information in the report about the adoption of *SFAS 121* and the effect of that adoption on the financial statements for 1995. Summarize where that information is found.

   2.   Assume that, as an example of the impact of changing accounting standards, you have been asked to explain the adoption of *SFAS 121* and its impact on Texaco at a luncheon speech to a group of businesspeople who are not accountants and who are not in the oil and gas industry. Write your explanation, including an analysis of the broader significance of *SFAS 121*.

P 12-18.   **DISPOSAL OF PLANT ASSETS AND INTANGIBLES**   Selected transactions and events related to Wilk Company's plant assets and intangible assets were as follows during 1998:

a) A machine was disposed of on June 30 for $21,000 cash. The machine had cost $30,000 on January 2, 1994, and had an estimated salvage value of zero. Accumulated depreciation on December 31, 1997, calculated using the straight-line method, was $12,000.

b) On September 30, Wilk sold a patent to TechCo for $21,000 cash. The patent had been acquired at the beginning of 1993, had cost $40,000, and was being amortized over 10 years.

c) On April 1, Wilk acquired special-purpose machinery from Bowmar Company by exchanging a trademark and a patent. The fair value of the machinery on April 1 was $30,000. The trademark, acquired on January 2, 1992, had a cost of $32,000 and was being amortized over 10 years. The patent, acquired on July 1, 1993, had a cost of $28,000 and was being amortized over 7 years.

d) As a result of acquiring another company several years ago, Wilk had goodwill of $180,000 on its books at the beginning of 1998. The company has been amortizing the goodwill in the amount of $15,000 per year. However, in assessing the future profitability of the acquired net assets, Wilk determines that the conditions that led to the payment for goodwill no longer exist, and that the goodwill no longer has value.

e) At the end of 1998, Wilk decides that it no longer has any need for a vacant piece of land that it had acquired several years ago to allow for the possibility of expanding its plant facilities. Thus, the company donates the land, which had a cost of $300,000, to the city, with the understanding that the land will be developed into a city park. The fair value of the land at the end of 1998 was $420,000.

REQUIRED   Prepare journal entries to record each of the events and transactions, including any necessary year-end adjusting entries.

P 12-19.   **FINANCIAL REPORTING PROBLEM**   This problem relates to the annual report of GE in Appendix B. Using that report, answer the following questions about plant assets and intangibles. Indicate the source of each answer. The questions relate only to consolidated results and only to 1995 unless specified otherwise.

REQUIRED   **1.** What depreciation method does GE use for manufacturing plant and equipment?
2. How is goodwill amortized? Other intangible assets?
3. What proportion of total assets is composed of property, plant, and equipment and intangible assets?
4. What are the major components of property, plant, and equipment? Intangible assets?
5. What was the total depreciation, depletion, and amortization for 1995?
6. How much cash was generated from the disposition of property, plant, and equipment?
7. How much cash was used for property, plant, and equipment additions?

SONY CORPORATION IMPAIRMENT CASE

Sony Corporation was founded in 1946 and is headquartered in Tokyo, Japan. Sony develops, produces, and distributes audio and video equipment, musical entertainment, and motion pictures. Its American Depositary Receipts (ADRs) are listed on the New York Stock Exchange. The accounting presented in annual reports distributed in the United States conforms with U.S. GAAP. As of the end of fiscal 1995, approximately 37 percent of Sony's revenue came from Japan, and approximately 29 percent came from the United States. In 1995, Sony had consolidated revenue of $44.8 billion, a net loss of $3.3 billion, and total assets of $47.5 billion. It also had 138,000 employees.

Read the *Business Week* article and answer the questions using the accompanying financial statement excerpts. The impairment loss was booked prior to the issuance of *Statement No. 121,* but much of the disclosure is consistent with what one would see under *Statement No. 121.* All questions relate to fiscal 1995 unless stated otherwise. Note that many amounts are given in yen and dollars. Answer questions using dollars.

1. What conditions necessitated Sony's review of its carrying value of Columbia Pictures?

2. How did Sony determine the amount of goodwill impairment?

3. What entry did Sony make to record the impairment?

4. How does the entry affect future return on equity or return on asset calculations?

5. Based on the write-down, what amount should Sony have paid for Columbia Pictures?

A Real-Life Hollywood Horror Story
Book Review: Hit & Run: How Jon Peters and Peter Guber Took Sony for a Ride in Hollywood (By Nancy Griffin and Kim Masters)

By Ronald Grover

It was 1989, and Frank Price had just finished a job interview he would not soon forget. Price, a Hollywood insider who had run the studio operations of both Columbia Pictures Entertainment Inc. and Universal Studios, had been job hunting in New York. Sony Corp. was about to plunk down $3.4 billion to buy Columbia from Coca-Cola Co. and was looking for someone to head it. But to get the post, Price needed the approval of Walter Yetnikoff, the volatile head of Sony's CBS Records unit. At a lunch at Yetnikoff's New York office, the mood was hostile and dismissive. The meeting—and Price's bid for the job—ended abruptly when a barber arrived and Yetnikoff donned a kimono to have his hair cut.

Why Sony deferred to Yetnikoff, an executive whose Hollywood track record consisted of a few movie soundtracks and who had just returned from treatment for substance abuse at the Hazelden clinic, is still unclear. What is known is that Yetnikoff immediately called a candidate he preferred, Peter Guber, producer of such hits as *Rain Man*—and of $100 million in losses at a film company he had run for PolyGram.

The story of how Sony blundered into Hollywood reads like a train wreck ready to happen. With Yetnikoff's blessing, Sony hired the ponytailed Guber and his partner Jon Peters, a seventh-grade dropout and onetime hairdresser to the stars. As co-chairmen, they proceeded to take Sony for the ride of its life, wildly bidding up the cost of movies and building the most lavish studio in a town that thrives on lavishness. In addition to annual salaries of $2.7 million, each man got his own corporate jet. Peters sometimes used his to fly flowers to an actress working in London. Inevitably, they ran up losses the likes of which Hollywood may never see again.

In *Hit & Run,* Nancy Griffin and Kim Masters skillfully chronicle the lunacy of the deals, personalities, and excesses that made up Sony's Hollywood nightmare. Both are accomplished Hollywood reporters—Griffin formerly at *Premiere* and Masters for *Time.* As they tell the story, Sony's misadventures serve as a cautionary tale for any investor seeking Tinseltown riches. And despite the notorious history of Sony and archrival Matsushita Electric Industrial Co., overseas investors can't seem to resist this glamorous but treacherous business. The current buzz: Korean executives may be behind bids for MGM, now being peddled by banker Crédit Lyonnais. If so, they had better put on their reading glasses.

Lesson No. 1: Find someone who knows the business. To negotiate the deal with Coke, Sony relied on Mickey Schulhof, a PhD in physics who had risen to head the consumer-electronics company's U.S. operations. But Schulhof was hardly a dealmaker, and pitting him against veteran entertainment investment banker Herbert Allen

Jr.—representing Coke—was "like putting my Labrador retriever Thunder against a Chihuahua," Yetnikoff said later. And the $5 billion in cash and debt assumption that Sony paid for Columbia showed the mismatch. Only five years later, Sony would take a $2.7 billion write-down to erase the overpayment.

Still, Sony might have weathered the purchase by putting the studio in better hands. Superagent Michael Ovitz, who had brokered the deal by putting Coke and Schulhof together, wanted the job. But Sony resisted his demands: total control, a chunk of stock, and freedom to buy more companies. Ovitz then took himself out of the running—and walked away with an $11 million fee.

That left Guber and Peters. Guber, dressed in flannel shirt and jeans, flew to New York and seduced Schulhof with his trademark charisma and a hyperkinetic flow of ideas. In the end, Sony agreed not only to hire the two men but also to pay an astounding $200 million for their film-production company. Only later did Sony find that it would also have to pay an estimated $500 million worth of concessions to free the duo from an existing contract with Warner Brothers.

By then, money was no object. Guber and Peters were left alone to spend whatever they wanted to restore Columbia's shopworn Culver City studio and to revive a near-moribund company. Costs spiraled out of control for Steven Spielberg's *Hook,* for the Michael Douglas-produced *Radio Flyer,* and for *Hudson Hawk,* produced by and starring Bruce Willis. None made money; *Hudson Hawk* alone lost $42 million for Sony. Emblematic of the prevailing mood was Willis' response to the soaring costs—as reported in *Hit & Run:* "I don't give a s---."

In the end, it seems, no one did. Not Yetnikoff, who was forced out by Sony when his sway evaporated with such key talent as Bruce Springsteen and Michael Jackson. Not Peters, who was shoved out by Guber. And certainly not Guber, who even as he was being forced to resign from the studio he had mismanaged, finagled a package valued at $200 million to make films for the company. Schulhof was ousted from his Sony USA post a few months later.

The writing in *Hit & Run* isn't flashy, but Griffin and Masters have produced a readable if slightly dated account of one of Hollywood's real-life horror stories. This is no *Indecent Exposure,* David McClintick's brilliant account of the David Begelman check-kiting scandal at Columbia in the '70s. But that was crime, greed, and venality. The Sony story is primarily one of stupidity.

CONSOLIDATED BALANCE SHEETS
Sony Corporation and Consolidated Subsidiaries
March 31

	Yen in millions		Dollars in thousands (Note 2)
	1994	1995	1995
ASSETS			
Current assets:			
Cash and cash equivalents (Notes 5 and 10)	¥ 484,231	¥ 475,555	$ 5,343,315
Time deposits (Note 10)	45,095	16,173	181,719
Marketable securities (Note 8)	35,756	66,617	748,506
Notes and accounts receivable, trade (Notes 7 and 10)	592,774	675,111	7,585,516
Allowance for doubtful accounts and sales returns	(45,485)	(48,185)	(541,404)
Inventories (Note 6)	671,992	723,383	8,127,899
Deferred income taxes (Note 12)	70,968	77,883	875,089
Prepaid expenses and other current assets	168,397	160,161	1,799,562
Total current assets	2,023,728	2,146,698	24,120,202
Noncurrent inventories—film (Note 6)	168,133	141,651	1,591,584
Investments and advances:			
Affiliated companies	23,189	39,313	441,719
Securities investments and other (Note 8)	275,288	445,539	5,006,056
	298,477	484,852	5,447,775
Property, plant and equipment (Notes 9 and 15):			
Land	155,897	153,347	1,723,000
Buildings	617,752	638,282	7,171,708
Machinery and equipment	1,449,980	1,481,053	16,641,045
Construction in progress	55,681	65,312	733,843
	2,279,310	2,337,994	26,269,596
Less—Accumulated depreciation	1,229,888	1,308,693	14,704,416
	1,049,422	1,029,301	11,565,180
Other assets:			
Intangibles (Note 4)	100,994	82,555	927,584
Goodwill (Notes 3 and 4)	424,482	121,383	1,363,854
Other (Note 12)	204,649	217,480	2,443,596
	730,125	421,418	4,735,034
	¥4,269,885	¥4,223,920	$47,459,775

The accompanying notes are an integral part of these statements.

CONSOLIDAIED STATEMENTS OF INCOME AND RETAINED EARNINGS
Sony Corporation and Consolidated Subsidiaries
Year ended March 31

	Yen in millions			Dollars in thousands (Note 2)
	1993	1994	1995	1995
Sales and operating revenue:				
Net sales (Note 7)	¥3,879,427	¥3,609,873	**¥3,826,693**	**$42,996,550**
Operating revenue	113,491	123,848	**156,745**	**1,761,180**
	3,992,918	3,733,721	**3,983,438**	**44,757,730**
Costs and expenses:				
Cost of sales (Note 14)	2,928,912	2,755,840	**2,916,475**	**32,769,382**
Selling, general and administrative	937,546	878,213	**972,417**	**10,926,034**
Goodwill write-off (Note 3)	—	—	**265,167**	**2,979,404**
	3,866,458	3,634,053	**4,154,059**	**46,674,820**
Operating income (loss)	126,460	99,668	**(170,621)**	**(1,917,090)**
Other income:				
Interest and dividends	46,086	38,395	**33,965**	**381,629**
Foreign exchange gain, net	22,432	35,435	**22,789**	**256,056**
Other	43,660	46,318	**32,396**	**364,000**
	112,178	120,148	**89,150**	**1,001,685**
Other expenses:				
Interest	91,361	69,217	**69,283**	**778,461**
Other	54,716	48,437	**70,194**	**788,696**
	146,077	117,654	**139,477**	**1,567,157**
Income (loss) before income taxes	92,561	102,162	**(220,948)**	**(2,482,562)**
Income taxes (Note 12):				
Current	83,322	59,869	**84,108**	**945,034**
Deferred	(33,528)	18,743	**(18,935)**	**(212,753)**
	49,794	78,612	**65,173**	**732,281**
Income (loss) before minority interest	42,767	23,550	**(286,121)**	**(3,214,843)**
Minority interest in consolidated subsidiaries	6,507	8,252	**7,235**	**81,292**
Net income (loss)	36,260	15,298	**(293,356)**	**(3,296,135)**
Retained earnings:				
Balance, beginning of year	861,227	887,788	**883,776**	**9,930,067**
Common stock issue costs, net of tax	(17)	(11)	**(8)**	**(90)**
Cash dividends	(18,656)	(18,673)	**(18,692)**	**(210,022)**
Transfer to legal reserve	(2,043)	(2,221)	**(4,238)**	**(47,618)**
Reversal of special allowances, net of taxes	11,017	1,595	**1,902**	**21,371**
Balance, end of year	¥ 887,788	¥ 883,776	**¥ 569,384**	**$ 6,397,573**

	Yen			Dollars (Note 2)
Per common share:				
Net income (loss)	¥92.2	¥42.1	**¥(696.9)**	**$(7.83)**
Cash dividends	50.0	50.0	**50.0**	**0.56**

The accompanying notes are an integral part of these statements.

2. U.S. dollar amounts

U.S. dollar amounts are included solely for convenience. These translations should not be construed as representations that the yen amounts actually represent, or have been or could be converted into U.S. dollars. As the amounts shown in U.S. dollars are for convenience only, the rate of ¥89=U.S.$1, the approximate current rate at March 31, 1995, has been used for the purpose of presentation of the U.S. dollar amounts in the accompanying consolidated financial statements.

3. Investments in acquired businesses including goodwill

During the second quarter of the fiscal year ended March 31, 1995, the company changed its method of accounting for assessing the carrying value of its investments in acquired businesses including goodwill. Previously, the company assessed the carrying value of its investments in acquired businesses including goodwill on the basis of projections of undiscounted future operating cash flows plus an amount for an anticipated residual value. Operating cash flows for this purpose are all cash flows expected to be generated by business, net of taxes and after capital investment, but exclusive of financing activity (interest and principal).

Under the new method adopted in the second quarter, the company applies a discount factor to those projected cash flows. The company believes that the new method provides a better measurement of the recoverability of its investments because the discounted cash flows method recognizes the effect of the substantial cost of capital employed to carry the investments.

The effect of this accounting change was to reduce the goodwill of the Entertainment segment associated with the Pictures Group by ¥265,167 million ($2,979,404 thousand). This new accounting methodology was also applied to unrelated acquisitions and it was determined that the book value of these investments was recoverable from future operating cash flows of those businesses over the forecast period. Accordingly, no additional write-offs were necessary.

Since its acquisition in November 1989, there had been slower than expected growth of the businesses of the Pictures Group, higher than expected levels of operating costs and expenses and higher than anticipated capital investment requirements. The deterioration experienced in the year ended March 31, 1994 gave rise to a thorough internal review. Similar results experienced in the first half of the fiscal year, together with the resignation of the Pictures Group top management, caused the company to conclude that additional funding would be needed to attain acceptable levels of profitability. In light of the level of investments and likelihood of additional funding requirements, the company determined in the second quarter of the fiscal year that a discounted cash flows method provided a preferable measurement of the recoverability of its investments in acquired businesses because this method recognizes the effect of the cost of capital. The discounted future results of the Pictures Group, based on the company's forecasts, were not sufficient to justify the carrying value as of the end of the second quarter.

In formulating the financial forecasts, the company considered historical performance and the medium-term plans as well as the longer-term economic outlook. These forecasts took into consideration market conditions during the second quarter of the fiscal year as well as foreseeable opportunities for future growth in existing lines of business. Although the company believed it could fund the Pictures Group over the entire forecast period, it had not determined whether additional investments would be made in areas other than the existing lines of business.

The operating cash flows were based upon the short-term plans in effect in the second quarter of the fiscal year that called for a substantial improvement in earnings through recovered market share and cost reductions. For the longer term, it was assumed that the low levels of inflation during the second quarter would continue and that the industry would grow at a slightly better rate than the economy as a whole. At the end of the forecast period a residual was included based on an appropriate multiple of the final year's results.

The company believes that the forecast results, based on the historical financial trends and market conditions during the second quarter, were the best estimate of the company's future performance.

In arriving at the discounted net present value, the company used a discount rate of 9% reflecting its weighted average cost of funds, including a factor for equity allocated to the Pictures Group commensurate with the risk associated with that business as indicated by reference to comparable industry statistics.

Over the entire forecast period, after giving effect to significant additional investment required to complete the investment program contemplated during the second quarter of the fiscal year, the company forecast total operating cash flows of ¥4,166,374 million ($46,813,191 thousand). Based on such forecasts, the cumulative results of the Pictures Group's operating cash flows on a discounted net present value basis of ¥309,005 million ($3,471,966 thousand) as of September 30, 1994 were insufficient to recover a significant portion of the investment. The amount of the resultant shortfall reduced the goodwill balance arising from the Pictures Group to ¥85,197 million ($957,270 thousand) as of September 30, 1994.

The changes in the company's goodwill during the fiscal year ended March 31, 1995 are summarized as follows:

	Yen in millions	Dollars in thousands
Balance at March 31, 1994	¥424,482	$4,769,460
Amortization of goodwill	(8,037)	(90,303)
Goodwill write-off	(265,167)	(2,979,404)
Translation adjustment and other	(29,895)	(335,899)
Balance at March 31, 1995	¥121,383	$1,363,854

PHILIP MORRIS COMPANIES INC. INTANGIBLES CASE

Philip Morris operates in the tobacco (Marlboro, Virginia Slims), food (Kraft, Oscar-Mayer), beer (Miller Brewing, Red Dog), and financial services industries. The Marlboro brand name alone has been estimated to be worth $39 billion.[1] Approximately 52 percent of its revenue in 1996 came from sales outside the United States. In 1996, Philip Morris had total revenues of $69.2 billion, net income of $6.30 billion, and total assets of $54.9 billion. Philip Morris also had 154,000 employees at the end of 1996.

Use the above information and the accompanying financial statements to answer the following questions.

1. Philip Morris owns numerous brand names. Explain how these names are valued on the balance sheet.

2. Explain how advertising expenditures are probably handled for accounting purposes.

[1]K. Badenhausen, "Brands: The Management Factor," *Financial World,* August 1, 1995, pp. 50–69.

3. Explain why U.S. GAAP handles brand names and advertising in the manner described in questions 1 and 2.

4. Explain how the answers to questions 1 and 2 affect Philip Morris's market to book ratio. The market to book ratio is computed as the market value of outstanding common stock divided by common shareholders' equity. Another approach that yields the same answer is dividing market price per share by book value per share (common shareholders' equity divided by the number of common shares outstanding).

5. At the end of 1996, the market value of Philip Morris common stock was $113 per share. Compute the market value to book value ratio as of December 31, 1996. Label calculations.

6. Explain why the ratio in your answer to question 5 exceeds 1.0.

Consolidated Balance Sheets (in millions of dollars, except per share data)

at December 31,	1996	1995
Assets		
Consumer products		
Cash and cash equivalents	$ 240	$ 1,138
Receivables, net	4,466	4,508
Inventories:		
Leaf tobacco	4,143	3,332
Other raw materials	1,854	1,721
Finished product	3,005	2,809
	9,002	7,862
Other current assets	1,482	1,371
Total current assets	15,190	14,879
Property, plant and equipment, at cost:		
Land and land improvements	664	726
Buildings and building equipment	5,168	4,976
Machinery and equipment	12,481	11,542
Construction in progress	1,659	1,357
	19,972	18,601
Less accumulated depreciation	8,221	7,485
	11,751	11,116
Goodwill and other intangible assets		
(less accumulated amortization of $4,391 and $3,873)	18,998	19,319
Other assets	3,015	2,866
Total consumer products assets	48,954	48,180
Financial services and real estate		
Finance assets, net	5,345	4,991
Real estate held for development and sale	314	339
Other assets	258	301
Total financial services and real estate assets	5,917	5,631
Total Assets	$54,871	$53,811

	1996	1995
Liabilities		
Consumer products		
Short-term borrowings	$ 260	$ 122
Current portion of long-term debt	1,846	1,926
Accounts payable	3,409	3,364
Accrued liabilities:		
Marketing	2,106	2,114
Taxes, except income taxes	1,331	1,075
Employment costs	942	995
Other	2,726	2,706
Income taxes	1,269	1,137
Dividends payable	978	834
Total current liabilities	14,867	14,273
Long-term debt	11,827	12,324
Deferred income taxes	731	356
Accrued postretirement health care costs	2,372	2,273
Other liabilities	5,773	5,643
Total consumer products liabilities	35,570	34,869
Financial services and real estate		
Short-term borrowings	173	671
Long-term debt	1,134	783
Deferred income taxes	3,636	3,382
Other liabilities	140	121
Total financial services and real estate liabilities	5,083	4,957
Total liabilities	40,653	39,826
Contingencies (Note 13)		
Stockholders' Equity		
Common stock, par value $1.00 per share (935,320,439 shares issued)	935	935
Earnings reinvested in the business	22,478	19,779
Currency translation adjustments	192	467
	23,605	21,181
Less cost of repurchased stock (124,871,681 and 104,150,433 shares)	9,387	7,196
Total stockholders' equity	14,218	13,985
Total Liabilities and Stockholders' Equity	$54,871	$53,811

Financial Instruments:
Equity Securities

LEARNING OBJECTIVES

After studying this chapter, you should be able to:

1. Identify and define the six types of fundamental financial instruments.

2. Account for common stock investments at acquisition, including those acquired for cash, for noncash consideration, and in a lump-sum acquisition.

3. Account for and report common stock investments using the fair value method and describe the circumstances under which the fair value method should be used.

4. Account for common stock investments using the cost method and describe the circumstances under which the cost method should be used.

5. Account for and report common stock investments using the equity method, and describe the circumstances under which the equity method should be used.

6. Define and account for investments in preemptive stock rights.

7. Account for purchased stock warrants.

8. Define and account for special-purpose funds.

9. Define and account for the cash surrender value of life insurance.

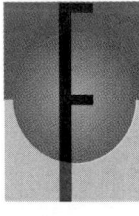

or many years, the U.S. economic environment was characterized by stable interest rates, relatively little global trading, and close regulation of financial institutions. Traditional equity instruments, such as common and preferred stock, and debt instruments, such as notes and bonds, met the investment needs of most companies, and accounting for them was fairly straightforward. But in the 1980s, deregulation of financial institutions, along with changes in federal monetary policy that allowed the market to dictate interest rates, increased the complexity of the U.S. economic environment. Greater volatility in interest rates, foreign exchange, and other markets also increased the market, credit, and liquidity risks companies must bear. What is more, attempts to manage these risks, combined with advances in computer and information technology, have produced an ever-increasing array of new and complex financial instruments, including LYONS, OPPOSSMs, ZEBRAs, bunny bonds, and the much-publicized junk bonds.[1]

At the same time, many companies have issued securities with characteristics that blur the distinction between debt and equity. Some examples include bonds that are convertible into common stock, and preferred stock with a mandatory redemption feature. Many investors would include *junk bonds* in this category because of the high risk of investing in them and because in many cases the likelihood of repayment of the principal is small. Should these types of securities be accounted for as debt or equity securities?

These novel financial instruments have created accounting and reporting complexities not just for preparers but for users and standard setters. In some cases, their issuance to finance mergers and leveraged buyouts, complicated by the market and credit risk associated with them, has compounded rather than solved companies' financial problems. This account from *The Wall Street Journal* will illustrate:

> RJR Nabisco, Inc. and its main shareholder, Kohlberg Kravis Roberts & Co., have begun a $5.3 billion refinancing effort that will drastically reshape the tobacco and food company's balance sheet. The plan aims to retire more than $4 million of RJR's poorest-performing below-investment-grade "junk" bonds . . . and pay off $1 billion of increasing-rate notes later this year.
>
> Since January, bond-market investors and KKR partners have worried about RJR's obligations on more than $6 billion of low-rated junk bonds. . . . These (bunny) bonds have proved unpopular with many investors, in part because they pay interest in the form of more bonds, rather than in cash.[2]

As the result of pressure from regulators and others about the recognition and measurement of investments in such securities, particularly by financial institutions, the FASB has spent the last several years studying the problems and potential solutions. The most controversial outcome of the FASB's efforts was a recent pronouncement that requires "mark-to-market" (fair value) accounting for certain debt and equity securities that have a readily determinable fair value.[3] This revolutionary change in accounting was opposed strongly by financial institutions, for reasons discussed later in the chapter. A spokesman for the 630-member American Council of Life Insurance, for instance, complained that the rule would "cause wide swings in the amount of surplus [equity] reported by insurers" and "force insurers to shorten bond maturities to reduce volatility from interest-rate change."[4]

---

[1]In 1988, Coopers & Lybrand issued a booklet, *Guide to Financial Instruments,* which sets forth purposes, risk considerations, accounting considerations, and tax considerations for more than *130* financial instruments. That the given list is a small sample is demonstrated by the fact that the booklet is 119 pages in length.
[2]"RJR and Its Main Shareholder, KKR, Begin $5.3 Billion Refinancing Effort," *The Wall Street Journal,* June 20, 1990, pp. A-2 and A-5.
[3]"Accounting for Certain Investments in Debt and Equity Securities," *Statement of Financial Accounting Standards No. 115* (Norwalk, Conn.: FASB, 1993). Equity method investments and investments in consolidated subsidiaries are not included within the scope of *Statement No. 115.*
[4]"FASB Votes to Make Banks and Insurers Value Certain Bonds at Current Prices," *The Wall Street Journal,* April 14, 1993, p. A-3.

A major part of Chapters 13 and 14 is devoted to explaining the FASB's objectives in this new pronouncement and to illustrating the associated accounting and reporting requirements. In this chapter we will discuss accounting for traditional equity financial instruments—that is, investments in equity securities such as common stocks. We will also describe the accounting for stock rights and stock warrants. In Chapter 14 we will discuss accounting for bonds and notes. Before we begin our coverage of equity securities, however, a short overview of financial instruments is in order.

N OVERVIEW OF FINANCIAL INSTRUMENTS

Defined formally, a **financial instrument** is cash, evidence of an ownership interest in an entity, or a contract that both:

1. Imposes on one entity a contractual obligation (1) to deliver cash or another financial instrument to a second entity or (2) to exchange financial instruments on potentially unfavorable terms with the second entity, and

2. Conveys to that second entity a contractual right (1) to receive cash or another financial instrument from the first entity or (2) to exchange other financial instruments on potentially favorable terms with the first entity.[5]

Familiar examples include common stocks and bonds. Based on this definition, six types of fundamental financial instruments can be identified. Each type is introduced and discussed briefly in the following section.

Fundamental Financial Instruments

The six types of financial instruments that are referred to as fundamental are the building blocks of other, more complicated instruments. Some financial instruments represent combinations of some of the six fundamental types and are called **compound financial instruments.** A bond issued with detachable warrants to purchase common stock is an example of such a compound instrument.

1 Identify and define the six types of fundamental financial instruments.

CONCEPTUAL

Compound financial instruments are combinations of fundamental types.

Unconditional Receivables/Payables

An **unconditional receivable (payable)** is a right (obligation) to receive (pay) cash or another financial asset on demand or on or before a specified date. Examples of this type of fundamental financial instrument include accounts receivable/payable, notes receivable/payable, and bond investments/bonds payable. Accounting for accounts receivable was covered in Chapter 8. Accounting for notes and bonds is the major topic of Chapter 14.

Conditional Receivables/Payables

A **conditional receivable (payable)** differs from an unconditional receivable (payable) in that the right (obligation) to receive (pay) cash or another financial asset depends on the occurrence of an event that is beyond the control of either party. An example of a conditional receivable (payable) is a term life insurance policy. The policyholder's right to receive cash and the insurance company's obligation to pay cash are conditional on the death of the insured.

---

[5]"Disclosure of Information about Financial Instruments with Off-Balance-Sheet Risk and Financial Instruments with Concentrations of Risk," *Statement of Financial Accounting Standards No. 105* (Norwalk, Conn.: FASB, 1991).

Forward Contracts

A **forward contract** represents an unconditional right (obligation) to exchange financial instruments. One example is a forward exchange contract, an agreement between two parties to purchase/sell a specific quantity of foreign currency at a specific price with delivery and payment made at a future date. Accounting for foreign exchange contracts is beyond the scope of this text.

Options

An **option** is a right (obligation) to exchange other financial instruments on potentially favorable (unfavorable) terms, conditional on the occurrence of an event within the control of one party. In most cases, the option holder's right to exercise is the conditional event. Options to purchase common stock are covered on page 688.

Guarantees or Other Conditional Exchanges

A **guarantee** or other conditional exchange is similar to an option, except that the right (obligation) to exchange the financial instrument is conditional on the occurrence of an event that is beyond the control of both parties. A loan guarantee is an example.

Equity Instruments

An **equity instrument** represents an ownership interest in an entity. Common and preferred stocks, discussed in this chapter, are examples of equity instruments, or equity securities.

To conclude our overview of financial instruments, we will briefly discuss derivative financial instruments in the next section.

Derivative Financial Instruments

Some financial instruments, called **derivatives,** derive their value from the value of another security. A stock option, for example, derives its value from the value of the underlying common shares. These financial instruments are called derivatives. The four basic types of derivatives are forward contracts, future contracts, options, and swaps. Forward contracts and options were discussed above.

Derivatives are designed to achieve a certain economic result when the price of an underlying security, index, interest rate, commodity, or other financial instrument changes. Companies generally use them in risk management. One common use is in **hedging** activities, or actions taken to avoid or reduce an identified exposure to risk. For example, a company that sells merchandise overseas and receives payment in a foreign currency is exposed to fluctuations in exchange rates. The company can hedge that exposure through a forward contract in the foreign currency that allows the company to "lock in" the dollar selling price of its merchandise. A company can also hedge its exposure to interest rate fluctuations using derivatives, namely, options (caps and floors) and interest swaps.

As was pointed out in Chapter 2 (page 72), the measurement model used under GAAP is a "mixed attribute" measurement model. As a result—and because of many of the unique characteristics of derivative financial instruments—accounting for derivatives is in a formative stage. However, the FASB has issued several *Statements* on disclosure of derivative financial instruments and is studying how derivatives should be recognized, measured, and reported in the financial statements. We will revisit this topic at the end of Chapter 14, after we have completed coverage of investments in debt securities.

Recognition and Measurement of Financial Instruments

Recognition and measurement concepts were introduced in Chapter 2. These concepts underlie the issues in accounting for financial instruments that are discussed in this chapter and Chapter 14. More specifically, we will discuss:

1. When should a financial instrument be recognized by an investor (debtor) as an asset (liability) in the balance sheet?

2. How should a financial instrument be accounted for (initially measured) if recognized?

3. How should a financial instrument be accounted for during the time it is outstanding (if a liability) or held (if an investment)?

4. Under what circumstances should a financial instrument be accounted for at fair value ("marked to market"), and how should unrealized holding gains and losses be reported?

5. When should a financial instrument be removed from the balance sheet, and should a gain or loss be recognized at that time?

These concepts will be applied primarily to our discussion of bonds and notes—unconditional receivables/payables—in Chapter 14. However, in a few cases they also will be applied to other fundamental and compound financial instruments. We turn now to accounting for investments in equity securities.

VALUATION OF COMMON STOCK AT ACQUISITION

Securities that represent an ownership interest in an enterprise (e.g., common stock, preferred stock, and other capital stock), or the right to acquire an ownership interest (e.g., warrants, rights, and call options) or dispose of an ownership interest (e.g., put options) at fixed or determinable prices, are called equity securities.[6] Companies acquire equity securities for a number of reasons. For example, an entity may acquire a significant portion of the common stock of another company to gain control of or significant influence over the company's operating and financial policies. In many instances, companies acquire equity securities with the expectation that their price will increase, producing gains when the securities are sold.

Equity securities may be acquired for cash or noncash considerations. In the sections that follow, we will concentrate on the valuation of common stocks, touching briefly on other types of securities in connection with lump-sum purchases. Later in the chapter we will look more closely at other equity securities, such as stock rights and warrants.

Acquisition for Cash

Investors buy many common stocks through organized stock exchanges, such as the New York Stock Exchange or the American Stock Exchange, or "over the counter" through dealers who make a market in certain securities. Common stocks may also be acquired directly from the issuing company or from a current owner of the stocks. Regardless of how an investor acquires these securities, the historical cost or historical exchange price principle governs their valuation at acquisition. In other words, the stock is recorded at the best estimate of its fair value at the date of acquisition. When a company pays cash for an investment in common stock, the amount of cash sacrificed is recorded as the stock's value. Any broker's fees, taxes, or other miscellaneous costs incurred in connection with the acquisition also must be included as part of the cost of the investment.

> **2** **Account for common stock investments at acquisition, including those acquired for cash, for noncash consideration, and in a lump-sum acquisition.**

> **CONCEPTUAL**
> Historical cost or the historical exchange price principle governs valuation at acquisition.

---

[6]*FASB Statement No. 115*, para. 137.

Acquisition for Noncash Consideration

In stock acquisitions involving only the payment of cash, the number of dollars given up usually represents the best measure of the securities' fair value. When only nonmonetary items are involved in an exchange, however, fair value must be determined by assessing the values of both the securities acquired and the resources given up. When a company purchases stock in exchange for noncash resources, it should record the investment either at the fair value of the securities received or the fair value of the resources sacrificed, whichever is more readily determinable.[7] Thus, *cost,* as measured by the fair value of the resources sacrificed, is used to value acquired resources only when that approach produces the best estimate of the fair value of the acquired resources.[8]

Assume, for example, that Sterling Corporation acquires 200 shares of Rice Corporation's common stock in exchange for certain machinery no longer needed in Sterling's operations. The machinery, which originally cost $15,000, has a book value of $8,000 at the time of the exchange and an estimated fair value of $10,000. The fair value of the Rice shares is not determinable because the company is "closely held" (i.e., Rice has relatively few stockholders, who make a limited number of stock transactions). No recent exchanges of the stock have been made.

In this case, the more readily determinable fair value is that of the machinery—$10,000. Therefore, Sterling assigns a fair value of $10,000 to the stock, and records the exchange as follows:

Investment in stock of Rice Corp.	10,000	
Accumulated depreciation—machinery	7,000	
Machinery		15,000
Gain on exchange		2,000

The gain of $2,000 is the difference between the machinery's book value ($8,000) and its fair value ($10,000). As far as Sterling's operations are concerned, this transaction marks the culmination of the earning process for its machinery. Consequently, Sterling will recognize the gain on the exchange at this time. Likewise, Rice's stock begins its earning process for Sterling at this time, so Sterling records the stock at the best estimate of its fair value.[9]

Lump-Sum Purchase

CONCEPTUAL

Cost allocation is based on relative fair values.

Sometimes a company acquires two or more types of securities in a single transaction. For example, a company that is issuing new common shares may include preferred stock as a "sweetener" to enhance the marketability of the common shares. When such a *lump-sum* or *basket purchase* is made, the company must allocate the cost among the acquired assets on the basis of the relative fair values of the assets.[10]

Assume, for example, that Rubin Company pays $25,000 for 500 shares of newly issued $10 par common stock of Fox Company, plus one share of Fox's $5 par preferred stock for every 5 shares of common Rubin purchases. The common stock is traded at $40 per share on the date of the sale; the preferred stock is traded at $60

---

[7]"Accounting for Nonmonetary Transactions," *Opinions of the Accounting Principles Board No. 29* (New York: AICPA, 1973), para. 18.
[8]For a related discussion of the historical exchange price principle, see p. 62.
[9]Exchanges of nonmonetary assets are described in detail in Chapter 11.
[10]We described this process with respect to lump-sum purchases of plant assets in Chapter 11.

per share. The $25,000 purchase price is therefore allocated between the common and preferred shares as follows:

Common ($40 × 500 shares) **$20,000**
Preferred ($60 × 100 shares) **6,000**
   Total fair value **$26,000**

Purchase price allocated to common shares:	Purchase price allocated to preferred shares:
$\dfrac{\$20,000}{\$26,000} \times \$25,000 = \$19,231$	$\dfrac{\$6,000}{\$26,000} \times \$25,000 = \$5,769$

The journal entry to record this transaction would be:

Investment in Fox Co. common	19,231	
Investment in Fox Co. preferred	5,769	
Cash		25,000

If Rubin knew the market value of only one of these securities at the time of the transaction, it would assign that market value to the appropriate security and then allocate the remainder of the $25,000 purchase price to the remaining security. In cases in which neither security is actively traded, the total purchase price could be recorded in one account pending the availability of subsequent market data or appraisals.

In summary, the objective in valuing common stock at acquisition is to record it at the best estimate of its fair value. Although different circumstances require different means of estimating fair value at acquisition, the basic principle is the same regardless of circumstance or the type of equity security involved. Accounting and reporting for common stocks *subsequent to acquisition,* the subject of the next section, become more complex.

ⓥ ALUATION OF COMMON STOCK FOLLOWING ACQUISITION

Exhibit 13–1 summarizes the required accounting methods for both debt and equity security investments. As the exhibit indicates, investments in equity securities may be accounted for using the fair value, cost, or equity method, depending on the circumstances. The fair value method is required for investments in securities that have a readily determinable fair value. The cost method is required for those investments that do not have a readily determinable fair value. For investments in equity securities that convey significant influence to the investor, the equity method is required. In the following sections, we will discuss and illustrate each of these methods.

Fair Value Method

Statement No. 115 requires **mark-to-market (fair value)** accounting for certain investments in equity securities that have a readily determinable fair value. An equity security can be said to have a readily determinable fair value if sales prices or bid-and-asked quotations are currently available for it, either on a securities exchange that is registered with the SEC or in an over-the-counter market.[11] *Statement No. 115* does not cover equity securities that do not have a readily determinable fair value or that are accounted for by the equity method. Companies must

> **3** Account for and report common stock investments using the fair value method and describe the circumstances under which the fair value method should be used.

---

[11]*FASB Statement No. 115,* para. 3.

EXHIBIT 13-1	Summary of Accounting Methods for Investments in Debt and Equity Securities

Investment Characteristics	Accounting Method
Trading securities (debt and equity)	Fair value (unrealized holding gains and losses are included in earnings)
Available-for-sale securities (debt and equity)	Fair value if determinable (unrealized holding gains and losses are reported as other comprehensive income); otherwise, cost or amortized cost
Held-to-maturity securities (debt)	Amortized cost (effective interest method)
Significant influence investments in equity securities (common stock)	Equity method
Control investments in equity securities (common stock)	Consolidated financial statements

classify equity securities covered by *SFAS No. 115* at acquisition as *trading securities* or *available-for-sale securities*.[12] **Trading securities** are bought and held principally for the purpose of resale in the near term. That is, they are actively and frequently bought and sold with the objective of generating profits from short-term price increases. **Available-for-sale securities** are security investments that are not bought for trading purposes. At each reporting date, the appropriateness of these classifications should be reassessed.

Investments in both trading securities and available-for-sale securities must be "marked-to-market"—that is, reported in the statement of financial position at their fair value. **Unrealized holding gains and losses**—that is, value changes in investments still owned at the reporting date—must be reported as follows:

1. For trading securities, they are included in earnings on the income statement.

2. For available-for-sale securities, they are reported as other comprehensive income and included in accumulated other comprehensive income in stockholders' equity.

Dividend revenue from investments in equity securities that are reported at fair value is included in earnings. Likewise, *realized* gains and losses from the sale of equity securities that are reported at fair value are also included in earnings.

CONCEPTUAL

Fair value provides a market assessment of prospective cash inflows.

Why is fair value now the required valuation method for equity securities of readily determinable value? Many accountants believe that fair value assists financial statement users in evaluating a firm's investment strategies. Fair value also provides a market assessment of prospective cash inflows. Furthermore, in recent years, research has indicated the potential usefulness of market value information on investment securities as an indicator of the solvency of financial institutions. In a liquidity crisis, fair value indicates the amount that is available to cover an enterprise's obligations.

Why are unrealized gains and losses for trading securities reported differently from unrealized gains and losses on available-for-sale securities? Consider again the objectives of the two types of investment. Trading securities are purchased with the intent of speculating on short-term price changes. Thus, they may be viewed as operating assets, for which changes in fair value should be included in earnings in the period in which the changes occur. According to the realization criteria (see Chapters 2 and 6), those fair value changes are treated as unrealized because of the uncertainty regarding the ultimate cash flow effects.

---

[12]Ibid., para. 6.

In the *Exposure Draft* that preceded the issuance of *Statement No. 115,* the FASB proposed that unrealized holding gains and losses on available-for-sale securities should also be included in earnings. However, many respondents to the *Exposure Draft* emphasized that doing so would cause undue volatility in reported earnings, which would not be representative of the way enterprises, particularly financial institutions, manage their business. Though the investment strategy of these enterprises involves both assets and liabilities, their liabilities are not reported at fair value. Thus, reporting the unrealized holding gains and losses on equity investments in available-for-sale securities outside of earnings (as other comprehensive income) alleviates the potential for earnings volatility that is unrepresentative of an entity's economic circumstances. Furthermore, unlike trading securities, available-for-sale securities relate more to investment than to operating activities. As a result of these arguments, the FASB was persuaded to require that unrealized holding gains and losses on available-for-sale securities be excluded from earnings and reported instead as other comprehensive income and included directly in stockholders' equity.

In the following sections we will apply the requirements of *Statement No. 115* to the two types of equity securities.

Application to Trading Securities

To illustrate the accounting for trading securities, assume that during 1998, Stockton Company acquired 500 shares of common stock of Wood Company for $25 per share, or a total of $12,500. The journal entry to record this acquisition would be as follows:

Investment in Wood common	12,500	
Cash		12,500

Assume that Stockton receives dividends of $625 ($1.25 per share) in November. Stockton would make the following journal entry:

Cash	625	
Dividend revenue		625

Now assume that Stockton still owns the Wood shares at December 31, 1998, and that the quoted market price at that time is $30 per share. Stockton would make the following adjusting entry on December 31:

Investment in Wood common	2,500	
Unrealized holding gain		2,500
[($30 − $25) × 500 shares]		

Because the investment in Wood is a trading security, the unrealized holding gain of $2,500 would be included in Stockton's earnings for 1998. The unrealized holding gain account is a nominal account, and would thus be closed at the end of 1998.

Now assume that Stockton receives dividends of $625 during 1999. The company still owns the shares at the end of 1999, at which time the quoted market price is $27 per share. The journal entries required to record these events would be as follows:

Cash	625	
Dividend revenue		625
To record dividends received.		
Unrealized holding loss	1,500	
Investment in Wood common		1,500
To record change in fair value [($30 − $27) × 500 shares].		

The unrealized holding loss of $1,500 would be reported in the income statement and closed at the end of the period.

Finally, assume that Stockton sells the Wood shares on February 15, 2000, for $18,000 ($36 per share). The following journal entry would be required:

Cash	18,000	
Investment in Wood common		13,500
Realized gain on sale of securities		4,500

Note that the carrying amount for the investment account is $13,500, the fair value on December 31, 1999 ($27 per share × 500 shares). The realized gain is the difference between the cash received of $18,000 and the carrying amount at the last reporting date, December 31, 1999 ($13,500).

Application to Available-for-Sale Securities

To demonstrate the difference between the accounting and reporting for trading securities and available-for-sale securities, assume the same data for Stockton's investment in Wood, except that the investment is classified at acquisition as an available-for-sale security. The journal entry to record the acquisition would be the same as for a trading security:

Investment in Wood common	12,500	
Cash		12,500

Likewise, the journal entry to record dividends received during 1998 and to mark the shares to market at year end would be the same, except for a minor adjustment to the account title for the unrealized holding gain:

Cash	625	
Dividend revenue		625

To record dividends received.

Investment in Wood common	2,500	
Unrealized holding gain/loss		2,500

To record change in fair value [($30 – $25) × 500 shares].

The account title *unrealized holding gain/loss* simplifies subsequent accounting, as we will soon see. A debit balance signifies a loss; a credit balance, a gain. Because we are assuming this investment in Wood is an available-for-sale security, the unrealized holding gain is excluded from earnings and reported instead as other comprehensive income, which is part of accumulated other comprehensive income in stockholders' equity. The account is not closed out at the end of the period but remains on the books until the security is sold.

In 1999, Stockton again received dividends of $625. They are accounted for just as they were in the trading securities example:

Cash	625	
Dividend revenue		625

At the end of 1999, the investment must be marked to market:

Unrealized holding gain/loss	1,500	
Investment in Wood common		1,500

Note that at the end of 1999, the balance of the unrealized holding gain/loss account is a credit of $1,000 (the $2,500 credit at the end of 1998 minus the $1,500 debit at the end of 1999). This credit balance of $1,000 represents the net fair value change in the Wood common shares since acquisition.

To record the sale of the Wood shares on February 15, 2000, for $18,000, Stockton would make the following journal entry:

Cash	18,000	
Unrealized holding gain/loss	1,000	
Investment in Wood common		13,500
Realized gain on sale of securities		5,500

CONCEPTUAL

For available-for-sale securities, the balance in the unrealized gain/loss account is the net fair value change since acquisition.

Notice that in this case the realized gain is $5,500, as opposed to $4,500 in the trading securities example (page 678). The reason for the difference is that the realized gain for the trading securities was the difference between the sales proceeds and the end-of-1999 fair value, whereas the realized gain for the available-for-sale securities is the difference between the sales proceeds and the acquisition cost. Remember that unrealized holding gains/losses have been excluded from earnings and reported instead directly in stockholders' equity. Therefore, when the securities are disposed of, the *accumulated* unrealized holding gain/loss must be closed out. In essence, the net carrying amount of the Wood shares at the time of sale is $12,500 (the $13,500 book value of the asset minus the $1,000 unrealized holding loss). Thus, the realized gain of $5,500 is the difference between the sales proceeds ($18,000) and the net carrying amount (acquisition cost) of $12,500.

In summary, for available-for-sale securities, unrealized holding gains/losses are excluded from earnings. Instead, they are carried forward to future periods as part of accumulated other comprehensive income in stockholders' equity. Thus, the end-of-period adjustment is the change in fair value during the period. It is also the *difference* between the desired balance in the unrealized holding gain/loss account and the existing balance. Upon disposal of the securities, the realized gain/loss calculation is affected by the net unrealized holding gains/losses that have been "deferred" and recognized in accumulated other comprehensive income. The realized gain/loss is the difference between the sales proceeds and the acquisition cost.

Reclassification of Investments

Recall that equity investments must be classified at acquisition as either trading securities or available-for-sale securities. At each reporting date, the appropriateness of the original classification must be reevaluated, and if necessary, the classification must be changed. Any resulting transfers of securities between categories must be accounted for at fair value.[13]

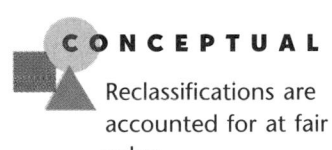

CONCEPTUAL

Reclassifications are accounted for at fair value.

Because of the nature of trading securities, transfers into or out of the trading securities category should be rare. Should such transfers occur, however, unrealized holding gains and losses at the date of reclassification must be accounted for as follows:

1. For securities transferred *from* the trading category, unrealized gains or losses will already have been recognized in earnings. Thus, no adjustment is required.

2. For securities transferred from the available-for-sale category *to* the trading category, any unrealized holding gains or losses must be recognized in earnings immediately. That is, the balance of the unrealized holding gain or loss, shown as part of accumulated other comprehensive income in stockholders' equity, must be recognized in earnings for the period in which the reclassification occurs.

The two sections that follow illustrate the application of these guidelines.

From Trading to Available-for-Sale Return to the Stockton example on page 677. Assume that by the end of 1999, Stockton had ceased to actively manage the investment in Wood common stock, so the investment was appropriately reclassified as available for sale. Recall that at the end of 1998 Stockton had recognized an unrealized holding gain of $2,500. The change in classification does not require any adjustment to that gain recognition. Likewise, the adjustment made at the end of 1999 is the same as before, except that the account title changes to unrealized holding gain/loss, consistent with the treatment of an available-for-sale security:

> Unrealized holding gain/loss 1,500
>   Investment in Wood common 1,500

Because this investment is now classified as an available-for-sale security, the unrealized holding gain/loss is excluded from earnings and reported instead as other

---

[13]Ibid., para. 15.

comprehensive income. In summary, no adjustment is required. The investment is merely accounted for as an available-for-sale security from 1999 forward.

From Available-for-Sale to Trading   Now refer back to the example on page 678, in which Stockton first classified its investment as an available-for-sale security. If at the end of 1999, Stockton determines that the investment is more appropriately classified as a trading security, the following two entries (or one combined entry) would be required:

Unrealized holding gain/loss	2,500	
Realized gain on reclassification of equity securities		2,500
To record reclassification of Wood investment		
from available-for-sale security to trading security.		
Unrealized holding loss	1,500	
Investment in Wood common		1,500
To record decline in fair value for 1999.		

The first entry reclassifies the "deferred" gain at the end of 1998, which was recorded as other comprehensive income to a realized gain (included in that income) in 1999, the year in which the reclassification occurred. The second entry is an application of the accounting requirements for trading securities to the investment at the end of 1999. It recognizes the 1999 change in fair value as earnings and adjusts the book value of the investment to end-of-1999 fair value.

Financial Statement Presentation and Disclosures

C O N C E P T U A L

Investments in trading securities are current assets.

real world

On a classified balance sheet, investments in equity securities must be categorized as either current or noncurrent assets. As you might expect given the nature of trading securities, all investments in trading securities must be reported as current assets. Investments in available-for-sale securities should be reported as either current or noncurrent, as appropriate. If an investment in available-for-sale securities is expected to be converted into cash within the next year or operating cycle, whichever is longer, it should be reported as a current asset. Otherwise, it should be reported as a noncurrent asset.[14]

For example, Dell Computer Corporation reported short-term (current) investments of over $484 million in its balance sheet at January 29, 1995. In the notes to the financial statements, Dell explained that these investments "are classified as available-for-sale and accordingly are reported at fair value, with unrealized gains and losses reported net of taxes in a separate component of stockholders' equity." In stockholders' equity, Dell reported an unrealized loss on short-term investments of $2,628,000.

In the statement of cash flows, cash flows from the purchase and sale of trading securities should be included in *operating* activities. Cash flows from the purchase and sale of available-for-sale securities should be included in *investing* activities. For these securities, companies must disclose the aggregate fair value, gross unrealized holding gains, and gross unrealized holding losses by major security type. Disclosure must be made for each period for which a statement of financial position is presented.[15]

For each period for which an income statement is presented, companies must disclose the following:

I. Proceeds from sales of available-for-sale securities and gross realized gains and losses on those sales.

2. The cost basis used to calculate realized gain or loss (i.e., specific identification, average cost, or other method).

---

[14]Ibid., para. 17.
[15]Ibid., para. 19. In addition, financial institutions must include in their disclosures specified major security types.

3. Gross gains and losses on transfers of securities from the available-for-sale to the trading category included in earnings.

4. The change in net unrealized holding gain or loss on available-for-sale securities (reported as other comprehensive income for the period).

5. The change in net unrealized holding gain or loss on trading securities (included in earnings for the period).[16]

Unresolved Issues

With *Statement No. 115,* the FASB took a significant step toward more general use of fair value accounting. However, the Board recognizes that problems remain, and that *Statement No. 115* is most likely an interim solution pending the outcome of its financial instruments project. At least two problems that the FASB set out to solve remain unresolved. First, "gains trading"—the practice of selling appreciated securities in order to recognize gains in earnings, and holding securities with unrealized holding losses in order to avoid the recognition of losses—can still occur. Reporting unrealized losses on available-for-sale securities as other comprehensive income allows the practice to continue. Second, accounting for investment securities based on management's intent impairs comparability, because the treatment of unrealized holding gains and losses for trading securities differs from that for available-for-sale securities. Thus, identical securities can be accounted for differently in different companies, based on management's intent to hold or trade them.

CONCEPTUAL

Accounting based on management intent impairs comparability.

Cost Method

So far in our discussion we have assumed that equity securities have a readily determinable fair value. As a result, fair value governed our balance sheet valuation of an investment, and we reported unrealized holding gains and losses either in earnings (trading securities) or as a separate component of stockholders' equity (available-for-sale securities). By their very nature, trading securities will virtually always have a readily determinable fair value. That is, a company is extremely unlikely to invest in an equity security for the purpose of generating profits from short-term price increases if an active market does not exist for that security. However, some available-for-sale securities may not have a readily determinable fair value. In that case, the cost method must be used to account for the investment.

4 Account for common stock investments using the cost method and describe the circumstances under which the cost method should be used.

Under the **cost method,** an equity security investment is carried at its acquisition cost, including brokerage fees and other incidental costs. For example, if Plummer Company acquires 1,000 shares of common stock in Poole Corporation at $35 per share, Plummer would record the transaction as follows:

CONCEPTUAL

The cost method is used only if fair value is not readily determinable.

Investment in Poole Corp. common	35,000	
Cash		35,000

Now assume that the Poole shares are not actively traded. Under the cost method, dividends received from Poole are recognized as revenue, just as they are under the fair value method. For example, if Poole paid dividends of $2,000 to Plummer, Plummer would record the dividends as follows:

Cash	2,000	
Dividend revenue		2,000

To give another example, assume that on January 3, 1998, Redmond Company purchases 1,000 shares (2%) of the common stock of Martin Corporation, a closely

[16]Ibid., para. 21.

held company, at $50 per share. Martin Corporation's net income and dividend distributions for 1998 and 1999 are as follows:

YEAR	NET INCOME	DIVIDENDS
1998	$150,000	$100,000
1999	50,000	50,000
	$200,000	$150,000

In 1998 and 1999, Redmond's journal entries for this investment would be:

```
1/3/98   Investment in Martin Corp. common . . . . . . . 50,000
            Cash . . . . . . . . . . . . . . . . . . . . . . . . . . . . .        50,000
         To record investment in 1,000 shares at $50.

12/31/98 Cash . . . . . . . . . . . . . . . . . . . . . . . . . . . . . . 2,000
            Dividend revenue . . . . . . . . . . . . . . . . . . . .        2,000
         To record share of dividends received
         during 1998 (2% × $100,000).

12/31/99 Cash . . . . . . . . . . . . . . . . . . . . . . . . . . . . . . 1,000
            Dividend revenue . . . . . . . . . . . . . . . . . . . .        1,000
         To record share of dividends received
         during 1999 (2% × $50,000).
```

Note that Redmond continues to carry the investment at its cost of $50,000. The company reports the dividends received from the investment in its income statement.

Under the cost method, the investment account must be reduced if the investor receives dividends *in excess of* the investor's percentage share of earnings. Note that Redmond's share of Martin Corporation's earnings exceeds the dividends it received, both in 1998 and *in total* for 1998 and 1999:

YEAR	SHARE OF NET INCOME (2%)	DIVIDENDS RECEIVED (2%)
1998	$3,000	$2,000
1998 and 1999	4,000	3,000

The cumulative dividends Redmond received in 1998 and 1999 represent a distribution that is less than Redmond's share of Martin's cumulative earnings.

Now assume instead that Martin had a net loss of $50,000 in 1999:

YEAR	MARTIN NET INCOME (LOSS)	MARTIN DIVIDENDS
1998	$150,000	$100,000
1999	(50,000)	50,000
	$100,000	$150,000

Redmond's journal entries to record the dividends received in 1998 and 1999 would be as follows:

```
12/31/98 Cash . . . . . . . . . . . . . . . . . . . . . . . . . . . . . . 2,000
            Dividend revenue . . . . . . . . . . . . . . . . . . . .        2,000

12/31/99 Cash . . . . . . . . . . . . . . . . . . . . . . . . . . . . . . 1,000
            Investment in Martin Corp. common . . . . . . .        1,000
```

In this case, Martin's cumulative earnings for 1998 and 1999 are $100,000 ($150,000 − $50,000). Redmond's share of those earnings would be $2,000 (2% × $100,000). Therefore, any dividends received in excess of $2,000 represent a return *of* Redmond's investment rather than a return *on* the investment. Because

Redmond received dividends of $2,000 in 1998, the $1,000 it received in 1999 must be considered a *liquidating dividend,* and thus a reduction in the investment rather than dividend revenue.

In summary, to the extent that Martin distributes assets that represent income earned before 1998 (when Redmond acquired its interest in Martin), that distribution is a return of a portion of Redmond's original investment. A portion of Redmond's investment is converted to cash and distributed to Redmond. The investor determines whether a particular dividend payment is a liquidating dividend or an ordinary dividend by comparing its *cumulative* share of earnings since acquisition of the investment with its *cumulative* dividends since acquisition of the investment.

Equity Method

Up to this point, our discussion has focused on common stock investments that do not permit the investor to exert significant influence or control over the investee company. We now shift our attention to common stock investments that are made with the intent of influencing the management and financial policies of the investee company.

The **equity method** of valuation must be used to account for long-term investments in common stock which allow the investor to exercise **significant influence.** Evidence of significant influence may be indicated by (1) representation on the board of directors, (2) participation in policy making, (3) material intercompany transactions, (4) the exchange of management personnel, (5) technological dependency, and (6) the extent of ownership relative to the concentration of other shareholdings.[17] *An investment of 20 percent or more of the outstanding common stock of an investee carries with it the presumption of an ability to exercise significant influence.* However, if there is predominant evidence to the contrary, the investment should be reported at fair value if determinable, or at cost if fair value is not determinable. Evidence of an inability to exercise significant influence could include the following situations:

1. The investee, through litigation or regulatory authorities, challenges the investor's ability to exercise significant influence.

2. The investor and investee enter into an agreement in which the investor surrenders significant rights as a stockholder. (A "standstill agreement," in which the investor agrees to limit its percentage of ownership in an investee, is an example of such an agreement.)

3. Majority ownership of the investee is concentrated in a small group of stockholders who control the investee without regard to the investor's views.

4. In order to apply the equity method, the investor attempts but fails to obtain financial information beyond that normally available to stockholders.

5. The investor attempts but fails to obtain representation on the investee's board of directors.[18]

This list is illustrative rather than all-inclusive; the existence of any one of these circumstances does not necessarily overcome the presumption of significant influence. The presence of one or more of these or similar circumstances, however, does require an evaluation of the facts to determine whether or not significant influence exists.

It is important to emphasize that *the percentage of ownership does not determine whether the equity method is appropriate. Rather, the determinant is whether or not the investor is able to exercise significant influence over the investee's financing and operating*

CONCEPTUAL

A liquidating dividend occurs when cumulative dividends since acquisition exceed cumulative earnings since acquisition.

5 Account for and report common stock investments using the equity method and describe the circumstances under which the equity method should be used.

CONCEPTUAL

The equity method is appropriate for common stock investments in which the investor significantly influences the investee company.

---

[17]"The Equity Method of Accounting for Investments in Common Stock," *Opinions of the Accounting Principles Board No. 18* (New York: AICPA, 1971), para. 17.
[18]"Criteria for Applying the Equity Method of Accounting for Investments in Common Stock," *Interpretation No. 35* (Stamford, Conn.: FASB, 1981), para. 4.

policies. The 20 percent guideline is merely a starting point in the determination of whether significant influence exists. All the facts and circumstances surrounding an investment, not simply the percentage of ownership, must be evaluated to determine whether significant influence exists, and thus which accounting method is appropriate for the investment.

Under the equity method, as income is earned by the investee, a proportionate share of that income is presumed to accrue to the investor. Therefore, when the investee's net assets increase as a result of earnings, the investor increases its investment account to record its share of the increase in the investee's net assets:

Investment. . . . . *xx*
      Investment revenue (or equity in income of investee) . . . .   *xx*

When the investee declares dividends, the dividends reduce the investee's net assets. Accordingly, the investor reduces its investment account by its share of the decrease in net assets:

Cash (or dividends receivable). . . . . *xx*
      Investment . . . .   *xx*

CONCEPTUAL

Investee net asset changes are presumed to flow through to the investor.

Thus, increases in the investee's net assets (via earnings) and decreases in net assets (via losses and dividends) are presumed to "flow through" to the investor as they occur. Since the investor presumably can influence the investee's dividend policy, the investor could "realize" (convert to cash) the recorded increase in the investment account by influencing the investee to pay dividends. Conversely, dividends received represent a realization of earnings previously recorded in the investment account. Thus, *the equity method may be thought of as an extension of accrual accounting to common stock investments.*

Application of the Equity Method

The following steps are involved in the application of the equity method:

1. Record the initial investment at its acquisition cost.

2. Record the investor's share of the investee's net income as an increase in the investment account and as investment revenue. Record the investor's share of the investee's net loss as a decrease in the investment account and an investment loss.

3. Record the investor's dividends received as a decrease in the investment account.

4. The acquisition cost may differ from the book value of the investor's interest in the investee's net assets at the date of acquisition. If so, the investor must adjust the recorded earnings by amortizing the excess of cost over book value (or book value over cost) that arises from the following circumstances:
   a) An excess of *cost over book value,* because:
      i. The investee's assets were *undervalued* in terms of the price the investor paid.
      ii. The investor paid a premium because of *unrecorded goodwill.*
   b) An excess of *book value over cost,* because the investee's assets were *overvalued* in terms of the price the investor paid.

CONCEPTUAL

The investor's investment account moves in tandem with changes in the net assets of the investee.

To the extent that such overvaluations or undervaluations would affect the investee's net income *if the investee recorded them,* the investor must adjust the investment account and investment revenue. For example, undervalued depreciable assets understate depreciation expense, and thus overstate the investee's net income. Thus, the investor must reduce the amount of earnings recorded as investment revenue to reflect the fair value of the depreciable assets (as evidenced by the price paid for the investee's stock). If the overvalued or undervalued assets are not depreciable or amortizable, no adjustment to investment revenue and the investment account is required. As a result of following steps 2 through 4, the investor's investment account moves in tandem with changes in the investee's net assets.

5. The investor's share of the investee's extraordinary items, and of the cumulative effect of a change in accounting principle, if material to the investor, should be reported in a similar fashion in the investor's income statement.

To illustrate, assume that at the beginning of 1998, Takeover Company acquires 40 percent (10,000 shares) of the outstanding common stock of Easymark Corporation, at a cost of $400,000. In doing so Takeover gains significant influence over Easymark's operating and financing policies. The book value of Easymark's net assets at the beginning of 1998 is $900,000. The entry to record the acquisition would be:

Investment in Easymark	400,000	
Cash		400,000

Easymark earns net income of $120,000 in 1998. Takeover would record its share as follows:

Investment in Easymark	48,000	
Investment revenue.		48,000
(.40 × $120,000)		

Dividends declared and paid by Easymark during 1998 amount to $60,000. Takeover would record its share as follows:

Cash	24,000	
Investment in Easymark		24,000
(.40 × $60,000)		

Note that Takeover paid $40,000 [$400,000 − .4($900,000)] more than book value for its 40 percent interest in Easymark Corporation. Of that amount, assume that $10,000 is attributable to undervalued depreciable plant assets with a remaining life of 4 years. The remainder ($30,000) is attributable to unrecorded goodwill. Takeover decides that 30 years is a reasonable period over which to amortize the unrecorded goodwill. Since Takeover's investment account moves in tandem with changes in Easymark's net assets, Takeover must eliminate the excess of cost over book value that is recorded in its investment account as Easymark's undervalued assets are consumed in operations. Easymark does not adjust the carrying value of its assets to reflect their implied fair values. However, Takeover must adjust its investment account and investment revenue to reflect Easymark's net income, which is calculated on the basis of the implied fair values established in Takeover's acquisition of Easymark's stock. Thus, Takeover makes the following adjusting entry:

Investment revenue	3,500	
Investment in Easymark		3,500
To record amortization of unrecorded goodwill of $1,000		
($30,000 ÷ 30 years) and depreciation on undervalued		
plant assets of $2,500 ($10,000 ÷ 4 years).		

At the end of 1998, Takeover's investment in Easymark Corporation has a balance of $420,500:

Acquisition cost	**$400,000**
Net income, 1998.	**48,000**
Dividends, 1998	**(24,000)**
Amortization of unrecorded goodwill	**(1,000)**
Depreciation of undervalued plant assets	**(2,500)**
Balance, 12/31/98	**$420,500**

If Takeover were to sell 4,000 of its 10,000 shares for $200,000 at the beginning of 1999, the following journal entry would be required:

Cash	200,000	
Investment in Easymark		168,200[a]
Gain on sale of investment		31,800

[a]$420,000 × $\frac{4,000 \text{ shares}}{10,000 \text{ shares}}$ = $168,200.

In the remainder of this section we will extend our discussion of the equity method by describing the required financial statement disclosures, investigating further the concept of significant influence, and looking briefly at the concept of consolidated financial statements. Appendix 13–1 describes the appropriate accounting and reporting for changes to and from the equity method.

Required Disclosures

The significance of an investment to the investor is one factor that determines the extent of disclosure required of an investor. Generally, the following disclosures are appropriate for equity method investments:

1. The name of each investee and the percentage of ownership of the investee's common stock.

2. The investor's accounting policies with respect to investments in common stock.

3. Any difference between the carrying value of an investment and the underlying equity in the investee's net assets, and the accounting treatment of the difference.

4. The market value of each common stock investment for which a quoted market price is available (except for investments in the common stock of subsidiaries).

5. When equity method investments are material to the investor, summarized information on the investee's assets, liabilities, and results of operations, either individually or in groups.[19]

When the investor has investments in common stock of more than one company, these disclosures may be combined. Investors must also disclose the reasons for using the equity method for investments of less than 20 percent and for not using the equity method for minority investments of 20 percent or more.

The Concept of Significant Influence

We have seen that judgment is required to determine whether or not significant influence exists. This point has been highlighted by some investors who have claimed significant influence even though the circumstances indicated otherwise.  For example, a few years ago Curtiss-Wright Corporation changed to the equity method of accounting for its 14.3 percent investment in Kennecott Copper Corporation, which is about six times larger than Curtiss-Wright. In the preceding year, Curtiss-Wright had failed in an attempt to change Kennecott's board of directors, but later gained representation on the board following court actions. Curtiss-Wright also entered into an agreement with Kennecott that limited Curtiss-Wright's ownership to not more than 21 percent. Curtiss-Wright claimed—and its auditors concurred—that the presence of 3 Curtiss-Wright directors on Kennecott's 18-member board was adequate evidence of an ability to exercise significant influence, and thus justified the use of the equity method. The change from the cost method to the equity method increased Curtiss-Wright's earnings from $13.8 million ($1.64 per share) to $21.3 million ($2.55 per share).[20]

Such situations led to the issuance of *Interpretation No. 35* by the FASB in May 1981. The purpose of the *Interpretation* was to clarify the criteria for use of the equity method. The *Interpretation* reemphasized the need to evaluate all the facts and circumstances surrounding an investment, rather than relying solely on the percentage of ownership.

 Immediately after *Interpretation No. 35* was issued, the SEC filed suit against McLouth Steel Corporation, accusing McLouth of incorrectly using the equity method to account for its 19.87 percent interest in Jewell Coal & Coke Company

---

[19]*APB Opinion No. 18*, para. 20.
[20]*The Wall Street Journal*, January 21, 1980, p. 14.

from 1974 until 1978. According to the SEC, McLouth had tried and failed to obtain representation on Jewell's board of directors. Jewell had also ignored McLouth's wishes on several corporate issues. The SEC argued that McLouth did not have the ability to influence Jewell. Without admitting or denying the charges, McLouth agreed to a court order barring future violations of both the antifraud section and the periodic reporting section of federal securities laws.[21]

The SEC's action against McLouth, coupled with *Interpretation No. 35,* emphasizes that *all* the facts and circumstances surrounding a minority ownership of common shares must be evaluated to justify the use of the equity method. Thus the 20 percent ownership guideline now appears to be less important than it once was. Companies, and their auditors, must now look a little more closely even at investments in excess of 20 percent to determine whether the use of the equity method is justified.

Consolidated Financial Statements

Some investments convey *control,* rather than merely significant influence, to the investor. Generally, investments of more than 50 percent of the outstanding voting common stock of an investee provide such control. In these situations, which are referred to as *parent-subsidiary relationships,* the combined entities are generally viewed as one economic entity. The financial statements of the combined entities are referred to as **consolidated financial statements.** GE's financial statements, presented in Appendix B, provide an example of consolidated financial statements.

When consolidated financial statements are prepared, the investment account is eliminated for reporting purposes and replaced with the subsidiary company's assets and liabilities. The rationale for this approach is that users should view the combined entities as one economic entity. Combining the individual financial statement elements is thought to be more meaningful than showing a "one-line consolidation"—that is, an investment account. In rare circumstances, a majority-owned subsidiary may not be controlled by the parent. In such instances, the parent company normally would use the cost method to account for the investment.

CONCEPTUAL

Consolidated financial statements permit users to view combined entities as a single economic entity.

The process of preparing consolidated financial statements is beyond the scope of this discussion. Likewise, a full understanding of the circumstances in which consolidation is appropriate is beyond our purposes at this point. Advanced accounting textbooks describe those circumstances and the consolidation process in detail.

International Practice

Two *International Accounting Standards* deal with accounting for investments: *Standard No. 25,* "Accounting for Investments," and *Standard No. 28,* "Accounting for Investments in Associates." Both these *Standards* are consistent with U.S. GAAP. However, in 1989, the International Accounting Standards Committee (IASC) proposed revisions to *Standard No. 25,* recommending that investments that are classified as current assets be reported at market value, while investments that are classified as noncurrent assets be reported at cost. Those recommendations are incompatible with U.S. GAAP. However, the IASC has deferred consideration of the proposed revisions to *Standard No. 25* pending further investigation.

Standard No. 28 recommends use of the equity method for investments in "associates," the term most commonly used in international practice for entities over which an investor exerts significant influence. As with U.S. GAAP, *Standard No. 28* uses 20 percent as the cutoff point for the presumption of an ability to exert significant influence. The *Seventh Directive* of the European Community (EC) also requires use of the equity method and a 20 percent cutoff point. Prior to the *Seventh*

---

[21]*The Wall Street Journal,* June 18, 1981, p. 10. See also "A Bit More Equity," *Forbes,* August 17, 1981, p. 79.

Directive, the equity method was either not allowed or not practiced in a number of EC countries. By harmonizing accounting practices among member countries, the EC is improving comparability. In many other parts of the world, the equity method is still not used, though it is gradually becoming an internationally accepted practice.

ALUATION OF OTHER EQUITY SECURITIES

So far in this chapter, we have focused primarily on the appropriate accounting for common stock investments. In addition to common stock, investors may hold investments in other equity securities, such as preferred stock and stock rights. To complete our coverage of investments in equity securities, we will discuss these investments.

Preferred Stock

Statement No. 115 defines nonredeemable preferred stock as an equity security. Companies must report at fair value these investments in nonredeemable preferred stock that have a readily determinable fair value, and must classify them appropriately as trading securities or available-for-sale securities. If an investment in nonredeemable preferred stock does not have a readily determinable fair value, or if the preferred stock is redeemable either at the option of the investor or by the issuer, under mandatory redemption terms, the cost method is appropriate. Preferred stock that is held as a trading security should be reported as a current asset. Available-for-sale investments in preferred stock should be classified as current or noncurrent, depending on management's intent with respect to their disposal.

Stock Rights

Owners of common stock or preferred stock often receive a *preemptive right* to purchase additional shares from a pending new issue, proportionate to their present holdings. The right to acquire stock in exchange for cash and a *warrant* (a certificate evidencing such a right) may also be *purchased,* either separately or in conjunction with another security. These **stock rights,** which are a form of stock option, indicate the price at which stock can be acquired (the exercise price), the number of shares that may be acquired for each right, and the expiration date. Because the source of their value is their relationship to a particular equity security, these stock rights are equity securities. They are classified as either current or noncurrent, depending on the investor's intent.

Preemptive Rights

6 Define and account for investments in preemptive stock rights.

Preemptive rights may be granted to existing stockholders to allow them to maintain their ownership proportion. When preemptive rights are part of a stock contract, a company must issue stock rights to existing stockholders whenever it attempts to sell additional shares. Such rights provide existing stockholders with an opportunity to purchase additional shares at a specified price. One right is issued for each share held; the number of rights that are required to purchase an additional share depends on the terms of the offering. For example, the warrant evidencing the preemptive rights may require five rights, plus a specified amount of cash, to acquire each additional share. Thus, each stockholder would be entitled to one additional share for each five shares held.

Acquisition of Preemptive Rights When an investor receives preemptive stock rights, the *total* book value of the investment remains unchanged. The investee has given up nothing, and the investor has invested nothing beyond the original investment. Between the announcement of the pending rights and the date the rights are actually issued, the stock to which the rights relate is bought and sold in the marketplace **rights on,** meaning that the value of the rights is embedded in the stock price. After the issuance date, the rights trade separately from the stock, and the stock is said to trade **ex-rights.** Though the total book value of the investment remains unchanged by the issuance of rights, the investment is no longer represented solely by the original shares held. Instead, it is represented by these shares *and* the rights. As a result, the company must allocate the book value of its investment between the shares held and the rights received, using the relative fair market value method.

To illustrate, assume that Sizer Company owns 1,000 shares of common stock in Bush Corporation, which it acquired for $20,000. Sizer subsequently receives one right for each share held. The company may purchase additional common shares in exchange for two rights and $15 cash per share. The market price of the common stock is $22 per share immediately after the rights are issued (ex-rights). The market price of the rights at issuance is $3.50.

Sizer would allocate its $20,000 investment between the original shares and the new rights as follows:

Market value of stock (ex-rights):
$22 × 1,000 shares	$22,000

Market value of rights:
$3.50 × 1,000 rights	3,500
Total market value of investment	$25,500

Portion of cost allocated to stock:

$$\frac{\$22,000}{\$25,500} \times \$20,000 = \$17,255$$

$17,255 ÷ 1,000 shares = $17.255 per share

Portion of cost allocated to rights:

$$\frac{\$3,500}{\$25,500} \times \$20,000 = \$2,745$$

$2,745 ÷ 1,000 rights = $2.745 per right

Note that the investment account still has a carrying value of $20,000 ($17,255 + $2,745). However, $2,745 of that $20,000 has been allocated to the rights. If desired, the following entry could be made:

Investment in Bush Corp. rights	2,745	
Investment in Bush Corp. common		2,745

At this point, the *book value* of the investment in common shares is $17.26 per share. Each right has a book value of $2.745.

Like investments in common stock, accounting and reporting for investments in stock rights is governed by *Statement No. 115.* Thus, stock rights must be classified as either trading or available-for-sale securities at acquisition. They must be reported subsequent to acquisition at fair value (or at cost if fair value is not reasonably determinable).

Disposal of Preemptive Rights Preemptive rights may be disposed of in one of three ways:

1. The rights may be exercised.
2. The rights may be sold by selling the warrants that evidence them to other investors.
3. The rights may be allowed to expire.

To illustrate these various possibilities, we will return to the previous example of Sizer Company. Assume that Sizer appropriately classifies its rights as trading securities, and that their fair value at the end of the first reporting period is $3.10 per right. In this case, the book value of the stock rights should be adjusted to $3.10 at the end of the period:

Investment in Bush Corp. rights	355	
Unrealized holding gain		355

[($3.10 – $2.745) × 1,000 rights]

The unrealized holding gain should be reported in Sizer's income statement.

Assume that during the second period, Sizer exercises all 1,000 of the rights to acquire additional shares of Bush. This transaction would be recorded as follows:

Investment in Bush Corp. stock	10,600	
Investment in Bush Corp. rights		3,100
Cash ($15 × 500)		7,500

The book value per share of the common stock Sizer acquires by exercising its rights is $21.20. This figure includes $15 cash and two stock rights with a book value of $3.10 each ($3.10 × 2 = $6.20).

If, instead, Sizer sold all the rights for $3,000 ($3 each), it would make the following entry:

Cash	3,000	
Loss on sale of rights	100	
Investment in Bush Corp. rights		3,100

Because the rights have a carrying value of $3.10 each, and Sizer sells them for $3 each, the company sustains a loss of $100 [($3.10 – $3.00) × 1,000].

Finally, assume Sizer allows the rights to expire. The company should do so only if the rights have no value—for instance, if shares could be purchased in the open market for less than the price specified by the rights. If the rights were to expire, Sizer would make the following journal entry:

Loss on expiration of stock rights	3,100	
Investment in Bush Corp. rights		3,100

Purchased Stock Warrants

Investors who buy warrants, whether from an issuing corporation or from another investor, may either sell them to other investors or exercise them to obtain a specified number of shares at the specified price per share. Warrants generally expire at a particular date, although companies sometimes issue warrants without an expiration date (these are referred to as "perpetual" warrants). The issuing company may sell warrants either separately or as part of a bond or preferred stock offering, as a "sweetener." In the latter case, the investor may detach the warrants and either sell or exercise them.

Account for purchased stock warrants.

Investors record stock warrants at their acquisition cost and report them subsequently at fair value (assuming that fair value is readily determinable). If the issuing company sells the warrants in conjunction with another security, the investor must allocate the total cost of the securities between the warrants and the other security according to their relative fair market values. When the investor exercises the warrants, the book value of the warrants plus the cash paid when they are exercised becomes the cost basis for the new shares.

To illustrate, assume that Boyd Corporation acquires 500 warrants for $2,500 cash, or $5 per warrant. Each warrant is exchangeable, along with $20 cash, for one share of Gartin Products common. Boyd would make the following journal entries to record the acquisition of the warrants and their subsequent exercise, assuming a carrying value (fair value) of $6 per warrant at the time of exercise:

Investment in Gartin Products warrants	2,500	
Cash		2,500
To record acquisition of warrants.		

Investment in Gartin Products common	13,000	
Cash ($20 × 500 warrants)		10,000
Investment in Gartin Products warrants		
($6 × 500 warrants)		3,000
To record exercise of warrants.		

If the investor sells stock warrants rather than exercising them, the difference between the selling price and the carrying value is recorded as a gain or loss. If the warrants are allowed to expire, their carrying value is eliminated and recorded as a loss on their expiration. Expiration should be a rare occurrence, because the exercise period generally is quite long.

Stock Splits and Stock Dividends

In addition to acquiring securities through purchases and the exercise of warrants, companies also may obtain shares as the result of investee stock splits and stock dividends. When a company issues a stock split or a stock dividend, current stockholders receive additional shares on a pro rata basis—that is, in proportion to their current holdings. A **stock split** usually is accompanied by a proportionate reduction in the par value or stated value per share. A **stock dividend** involves the distribution of additional shares, without a proportionate reduction in par value or stated value. For example, if a company has 100,000 shares of $10 par value common stock outstanding, a 2-for-1 stock split would result in the issuance of 100,000 more shares and an accompanying reduction of par value to $5 per share. A 100 percent stock dividend, in contrast, would result in the issuance of 100,000 more shares *without* a reduction in par value.

While the legal distinction between a stock split and a stock dividend affects the issuer's accounting, the investor's accounting is not affected. The *total* carrying value (book value) of the investment is unaffected by the receipt of additional shares, via either a stock split or a stock dividend. The situation is comparable to the receipt of stock rights from an investee. The investor simply reduces the *per share* book value in proportion to the increase in the number of shares received. The same amount is now represented by—and must be spread over—more shares.

Suppose that Soza Corporation owns 1,000 shares of common stock in Stephens Company, acquired at a cost of $15,000 ($15 per share) and accounted for by the fair value method. If Soza receives one additional share for each 10 shares held (a 10 percent stock dividend) at a time when the book value is $17 per share, the book value per share will be reduced to $15.45 ($17,000 ÷ 1,100 shares). Soza makes no entry upon receipt of the additional shares, except to note the change in the book value per share for future use. If 100 shares were subsequently sold for $2,000 ($20 per share) prior to any change in book value, Soza would record the sale as follows:

Cash	2,000	
Investment in Stephens common		1,545
Gain on sale of investments		455
To record sale of 100 shares with a cost basis of $15.45		
per share for $20 per share.		

In many cases, investors do not receive a whole number of shares in stock splits and stock dividends. For example, if a 10 percent stock dividend were declared, an investor who owned 95 shares would be entitled to 9.5 additional shares. In such

CONCEPTUAL

The total carrying value of an investment is not changed by the receipt of shares via a stock split or stock dividend.

instances, the issuing company either (1) pays cash equal to the market value of the fractional share, which the investor records as a credit to the investment account (because the receipt of cash constitutes a reduction in the cost of the remaining shares); or (2) issues **fractional share warrants,** which may be bought and sold in the marketplace.

Two other common equity securities are special-purpose funds and the cash surrender value of life insurance. Both constitute long-term investments.

⑤ PECIAL-PURPOSE FUNDS

The notion of a special-purpose fund was introduced in Chapter 8, in connection with petty cash. Companies use the petty cash fund to make small expenditures for specified purposes without going through the formal, time-consuming procedures required for other expenditures. Many establish other short-term funds for purposes such as the payment of dividends, payroll, and interest. All these funds constitute short-term segregations of cash for specified operating purposes. All are classified as current assets.

In addition, many companies establish **special-purpose funds** for the long-term, systematic accumulation of resources to meet future objectives. These funds may be required by contractual commitments, or they may be voluntary. Some common types of special-purpose funds required by contract are:

8 **Define and account for special-purpose funds.**

1. Bond sinking fund to retire long-term debt.

2. Stock redemption fund to retire capital stock, usually preferred stock.

3. Pension fund to meet pension obligations.

Funds required by contractual agreement usually are administered by an outside trustee. The trustee invests and accounts for the fund's assets and reports the fund's income and expenses periodically to the company that established it.

Funds may also be established voluntarily by companies to accumulate resources for purposes such as plant expansion and environmental improvements. While an outside trustee may administer this type of fund, often the company that establishes the fund administers it.

Transactions involving a long-term fund include cash contributions to the fund; investment of the fund's cash in securities; receipt of income on securities; incurrence of expenses; the sale of investments; the use of the fund's assets to fulfill the purpose for which the fund was created; and the transfer of any unused assets into unrestricted asset accounts.

A separate account must be maintained for each type of transaction. For example, a bond sinking fund typically would require the following accounts:

Sinking fund cash

Sinking fund investments

Sinking fund revenue

Sinking fund expense

Gain on sale of sinking fund investments

Loss on sale of sinking fund investments

To illustrate the accounting for a bond sinking fund, assume that the terms of a bond agreement require Beaton Company to establish a bond sinking fund and to contribute $10,000 at the end of each year for 10 years. The maturity value of the bonds, due in 10 years, is $200,000. Assuming a 16 percent rate of return, Beaton must pay $9,380 ($200,000 ÷ 21.3215) into the fund each year in order to accumulate $200,000 by the end of the tenth year (see Table C in Appendix A). Thus, if Beaton contributes $10,000 annually, the fund's investments could earn slightly less than 16 percent and still accumulate to $200,000 by the end of the tenth year. Selected transactions over the life of the fund, and accompanying journal entries, would be as follows:

Contribution of $10,000 to the fund at end of the first year:

Sinking fund cash	10,000	
Cash		10,000

Purchase of securities for $9,500:

Sinking fund investments	9,500	
Sinking fund cash		9,500

Receipt of $1,700 in dividends and interest revenue:

Sinking fund cash	1,700	
Sinking fund revenue		1,700

Incurrence of expenses (e.g., trustee's fee for managing the fund) of $400:

Sinking fund expense	400	
Sinking fund cash		400

Sale of securities (several years later) with a cost basis of $36,000 for $44,000:

Sinking fund cash	44,000	
Sinking fund investments		36,000
Gain on sale of sinking fund investments		8,000

Payoff of the bonds at the end of the tenth year, when the fund balance is $204,000:

Bonds payable	200,000	
Sinking fund cash		200,000

Return of the remaining balance of $4,000 to Beaton Company:

Cash	4,000	
Sinking fund cash		4,000

The last entry eliminates the sinking fund. Beaton would report the nominal (temporary) accounts used in accounting for its sinking fund (revenue, expense, gain, and loss) in its income statement and close them to retained earnings at the end of each year. The sum of sinking fund cash and the sinking fund investments would be reported in the investment section of the balance sheet as a trusteed sinking fund.

CASH SURRENDER VALUE OF LIFE INSURANCE

Many business entities purchase life insurance policies for key executives, naming the company as beneficiary. In addition to a payment to the beneficiary in the event of death, these whole-life insurance policies provide a **cash surrender value,** which the policy owner receives if the policy is canceled or expires. Thus, the cash surrender value, which increases each period as the company pays the premiums, is an asset of the company that owns the policy. Since the normal intent is to continue the policies indefinitely, the cash surrender value constitutes a long-term investment, and is classified under investments and funds in the balance sheet.

In essence, the owner of such a whole-life policy is paying premiums (1) to provide protection against losses and disruptions from the untimely death of key executives and (2) to generate a cash surrender value.[22] Accounting for whole-life policies recognizes both these aspects of the investment: (1) The current period's protection against loss is recognized as insurance expense, and (2) the investment in cash surrender value is recorded as an asset. Any dividends received on the policies reduce the insurance expense.

9 Define and account for the cash surrender value of life insurance.

---

[22]Whole-life policies also provide the owner with borrowing capacity, because the owner may borrow against the cash surrender value.

Assume that Pioneer Paint Company, a small paint manufacturer, acquires a whole-life insurance policy on its president with a face amount of $70,000. The annual premiums are $2,000, payable at the beginning of each year. There is no cash surrender value until the beginning of year 2, at which time $600 of the $2,000 premium represents an increase in cash surrender value. Pioneer would make the following entries, starting with the beginning of year 1:

Prepaid insurance	2,000	
Cash		2,000

At the end of year 1:

Insurance expense	2,000	
Prepaid insurance		2,000

At the beginning of year 2:

Prepaid insurance	1,400	
Cash surrender value of life insurance	600	
Cash		2,000

At the end of year 2:

Insurance expense	1,400	
Prepaid insurance		1,400

If the president of Pioneer Paint were to die at the beginning of year 6, and the cash surrender value of the policy at that time is $3,300 (assumed), Pioneer would record the event as follows:

Cash	70,000	
Cash surrender value of life insurance		3,300
Gain on life insurance		66,700

Insurance premiums on whole-life policies for which the company is the beneficiary are not tax-deductible, nor are the proceeds taxable as part of the company's income.

UMMARY OF LEARNING OBJECTIVES

1. Identify and define the six types of fundamental financial instruments.

The six types of fundamental financial instruments are (1) unconditional receivables/payables, or the right (obligation) to receive (pay) cash or another financial asset on demand or on or before a specified date; (2) conditional receivables/payables, or the right (obligation) to receive (pay) cash or another financial asset, dependent on the occurrence of an event that is beyond the control of either party; (3) forward contracts, which are unconditional rights (obligations) to exchange financial instruments; (4) options, which are rights (obligations) to exchange other financial instruments on potentially favorable (unfavorable) terms, conditional on the occurrence of an event that is within the control of one party to the contract; (5) guarantees or other conditional exchanges, which are similar to options, except the right (obligation) to exchange financial instruments is conditional on the occurrence of an event that is beyond the control of both parties; and (6) equity instruments, or ownership interests in an entity.

2. Account for common stock investments at acquisition, including those acquired for cash, for noncash consideration, and in a lump-sum acquisition.

Acquisitions for cash are recorded at cost. Acquisitions for noncash consideration are recorded at the fair value of the securities received or the consideration given, whichever is more clearly evident. The cost of securities acquired in a lump-sum purchase is allocated among the securities on the basis of their relative fair values.

3. **Account for and report common stock investments using the fair value method and describe the circumstances under which the fair value method should be used.** In the fair value method, stocks must be classified as either trading or available-for-sale securities at acquisition. The carrying value of both categories must be adjusted to fair value at the end of each period. Unrealized gains and losses on trading securities are included in income. Unrealized gains and losses on available-for-sale securities are reported as a separate component of stockholders' equity. The fair value method should be used to account for common stocks that have a readily determinable fair value, except those that are appropriately accounted for using the equity method.

4. **Account for common stock investments using the cost method and describe the circumstances under which the cost method should be used.** In the cost method, equity securities are carried at cost, and dividends received are usually recorded as dividend revenue. Liquidating dividends are recorded as a reduction in the investment account. The cost method is required for common stock whose fair value is not readily determinable.

5. **Account for and report common stock investments using the equity method and describe the circumstances under which the equity method should be used.** In the equity method, the investment account is increased (decreased) by the investor's share of the investee's earnings (loss). Dividends received are recorded as a reduction in the investment account. In other words, changes in the investee's net assets flow through the investor's investment account.

6. **Define and account for investments in preemptive stock rights.** Preemptive stock rights are rights granted to existing stockholders that allow them to maintain their share of ownership when additional shares are issued, if they desire. When such rights are received, the total cost of existing shares must be reallocated to include the rights. The rights are subsequently marked-to-market using the fair value method.

7. **Account for purchased stock warrants.** Purchased stock warrants are recorded at cost, and are subsequently marked to market at the end of the accounting period. If they are acquired in combination with another security, the cost of the purchase must be allocated between the two types of security using the relative fair value method.

8. **Define and account for special-purpose funds.** Special-purpose funds are accumulations of resources for the purpose of achieving specific future objectives. Each fund is accounted for as a separate entity, including cash contributions to the fund, investments in earning assets, receipt of income, incurrence of expenses, the sale of investments, the use of fund assets to achieve the fund's objectives, and the transfer of unused assets back to unrestricted asset accounts.

9. **Define and account for the cash surrender value of life insurance.** The cash surrender value of life insurance is the amount the policy owner will receive if the policy is canceled or allowed to expire. Cash surrender value is an asset to the owner of the policy; it reduces insurance expense.

KEY TERMS

available-for-sale securities 676	equity instrument 672
cash surrender value 693	equity method 683
compound financial instrument 671	ex-rights 689
conditional receivable/payable 671	fair value (mark-to-market) method 675
consolidated financial statements 687	financial instrument 671
cost method 681	forward contract 672
derivatives 672	fractional share warrants 692

PPENDIX 13–1

Additional Issues Related to the Equity Method

The material presented in the body of this chapter covered the basic issues associated with the equity method of accounting for long-term investments in common stock. This appendix deals with accounting for changes to and from the equity method.

Changes to the Equity Method

Circumstances may not permit an investor in common stock to exercise significant influence over the investee. In such cases, the investment does not qualify for the equity method. If the investor subsequently gains significant influence (e.g., by increasing the proportion of ownership), the investment must be accounted for using the equity method. This change in accounting principle from the fair value or cost method to the equity method requires the investor to adjust (1) the investment account, (2) prior period income statements presented currently, and (3) retained earnings.[23] The objective is to make prior period financial statements appear as they would have had the equity method been applied during those periods, thus making them comparable to current and future statements based on the equity method.

Assume, for example, that at the beginning of 1998, Mann Corporation acquires 10 percent of the outstanding common shares of Percha Corporation, a closely held company, for $240,000. Mann's 10 percent interest does not permit significant influence over Percha. Mann therefore uses the fair value method to account for the investment, and classifies the securities as available for sale. The book value of Percha's net assets at the acquisition date is $2 million. Net income and dividend payments for the next three years are as follows:

YEAR	NET INCOME	DIVIDENDS
1998	$300,000	$100,000
1999	400,000	150,000
2000	500,000	200,000

At the beginning of 2000, when the book value of Percha's net assets is $2.6 million, Mann acquires an additional 30 percent of the outstanding common shares for $850,000. Acquisition of the additional shares enables Mann to exercise significant influence over Percha's operations. The difference between the acquisition price and the book value of both its initial 10 percent acquisition and the subse-

---

[23]This retroactive treatment of the effect of the change in accounting principle is an exception to the *general* requirement that the cumulative effect of changes in accounting principles should be reflected in the income statement in the period of change. For further discussion of changes in accounting principles, see Chapter 19.

quent 30 percent acquisition is attributed to unrecorded goodwill, which should be amortized over not more than 40 years from the acquisition date.

Given the significant influence Mann has acquired over Percha, Mann must change to the equity method at the beginning of 2000. The following journal entries are required to account for Mann's investment in Percha Corporation, beginning with its first acquisition in 1995:

```
Investment in Percha Corp. . . . . . . . . . . . . . . . . . . . 240,000
    Cash . . . . . . . . . . . . . . . . . . . . . . . . . . . .              240,000
To record investment.
```

At the end of 1998:

```
Cash . . . . . . . . . . . . . . . . . . . . . . . . . . . . . .  10,000
    Dividend revenue . . . . . . . . . . . . . . . . . . . . . .              10,000
To record dividends received (.10 × $100,000).
```

At the end of 1999:

```
Cash . . . . . . . . . . . . . . . . . . . . . . . . . . . . . .  15,000
    Dividend revenue . . . . . . . . . . . . . . . . . . . . . .              15,000
To record dividends received (.10 × $150,000).
```

At the beginning of 2000:

```
Investment in Percha Corp. . . . . . . . . . . . . . . . . . . 850,000
    Cash . . . . . . . . . . . . . . . . . . . . . . . . . . . .              850,000
To record additional investment.

Investment in Percha Corp. . . . . . . . . . . . . . . . . . .  43,000
    Retained earnings . . . . . . . . . . . . . . . . . . . . . .              43,000
To adjust investment account and retained earnings
to reflect equity method applied retroactively,
calculated as follows:
```

	1998	1999	TOTAL
Mann's interest (10%) in Percha's earnings	$30,000	$40,000	$70,000
Amortization of unrecorded goodwill			
{[$240,000 − .10($2,000,000)] ÷ 40 years}	(1,000)	(1,000)	(2,000)
Equity method revenue	$29,000	$39,000	$68,000
Dividends (already recorded as revenue			
under the cost method)	(10,000)	(15,000)	(25,000)
Increase in investment and retained earnings			
to reflect the equity method	$19,000	$24,000	$43,000

At the end of 2000:

```
Investment in Percha Corp. . . . . . . . . . . . . . . . . . . 200,000
    Investment revenue. . . . . . . . . . . . . . . . . . . . . .              200,000
To record share of Percha's earnings: (.40 × $500,000).

Investment revenue . . . . . . . . . . . . . . . . . . . . . .   2,750
    Investment in Percha Corp. . . . . . . . . . . . . . . . . . .              2,750
To adjust share of earnings for amortization
of unrecorded goodwill:
    1998 acquisition:
        [$240,000 − .10($2,000,000)] ÷ 40 years = $1,000
    2000 acquisition:
        [$850,000 − .30($2,600,000)] ÷ 40 years =  1,750
                                                   $2,750

Cash . . . . . . . . . . . . . . . . . . . . . . . . . . . . . .  80,000
    Investment in Percha Corp. . . . . . . . . . . . . . . . . . .              80,000
To record dividends received (.4 × $200,000).
```

Note that Mann changes to the equity method at the beginning of 2000 by crediting retained earnings and debiting investment in Percha Corporation for $43,000. This adjustment reflects the fact that retained earnings and the investment account would have been $43,000 greater if Mann had been using the equity method in 1998 and 1999. The adjustment has no effect on reported earnings in 2000, the period of change. The financial statements for 1998 and 1999, if presented at the end of 2000 or later for comparative purposes, must be restated to reflect the retroactive application of the equity method.

Changes from the Equity Method

When circumstances cause the investor to lose significant influence over the investee, either because of a reduction in the number of shares held or for other reasons, the investor must change from the equity method of valuation to either the fair value method or the cost method. When such a change is made, the carrying value of the investment at the time of the change becomes the cost basis for subsequent accounting. No retroactive calculation is made to determine what the balance in the investment account would have been had a different method been used in prior periods. The effect of using the equity method in prior periods remains in the investment account and in retained earnings.

A change from the equity method also means that at the time of change, the investor discontinues the amortization of undervalued or overvalued assets. Since the investor does not record its share of the investee's earnings under either the fair value method or the cost method, there is no need to adjust those earnings for overvalued or undervalued assets.

QUESTIONS

The question marked with an asterisk (*) refers to Appendix 13–1.

Q 13-1. Define a financial instrument.

Q 13-2. List six types of fundamental financial instruments.

Q 13-3. Discuss the meaning of the term *equity securities*.

Q 13-4. Define the term *derivative financial instrument*.

Q 13-5. What is the general principle governing the valuation of common stock at the date of acquisition if (*a*) cash is given up and (*b*) noncash consideration is given up?

Q 13-6. If two or more types of securities are acquired as a unit, how is the transaction recorded?

Q 13-7. Distinguish between trading securities and available-for-sale securities.

Q 13-8. What is the appropriate valuation method for trading and available-for-sale securities that have a readily determinable fair value?

Q 13-9. How should unrealized holding gains and losses be reported for (*a*) trading securities and (*b*) available-for-sale securities?

Q 13-10. How is dividend revenue reported for security investments reported at fair value?

Q 13-11. How is the realized gain or loss determined in accounting for the sale of trading securities? Of available-for-sale securities? Why is there a difference?

Q 13-12. How should unrealized holding gains or losses be accounted for when an available-for-sale security investment is reclassified as a trading security?

Q 13-13. When the cost method is used to account for investments in equity securities, what circumstances require a write-down of the investment account after acquisition?

Q 13-14. Why are dividends received accounted for as a reduction in the investment account for equity method investments and as revenue under the fair value and cost methods?

Q 13-15. Explain why the investor's share of investee earnings must be adjusted for amortization of the excess of cost over book value, or for the excess of book value over cost, for investments accounted for by the equity method.

Q 13-16. Give four examples that may provide evidence of significant influence by an investor in common stock. How does this evidence relate to the presumption that investments of less than 20 percent do not convey significant influence to the investor?

Q 13-17. Give four examples of evidence of an investor's inability to exercise significant influence over an investee. How does this evidence relate to the presumption that investments of 20 percent or more convey to the investor the ability to exercise significant influence over the investee?

Q 13-18. How should investments that constitute more than 50 percent of the outstanding voting common stock of the investee usually be reported in the financial statements?

Q 13-19. What is the appropriate accounting method for preferred stock investments that have a readily determinable fair value and are nonredeemable?

Q 13-20. Distinguish between stock rights and stock warrants and describe the investor's accounting for the receipt of stock rights and stock warrants.

Q 13-21. Distinguish between a stock split and a stock dividend. What must the investor do from an accounting standpoint upon the receipt of shares resulting from a stock split or a stock dividend? Explain.

Q 13-22. Describe the nature of special-purpose funds. Give three examples of long-term special-purpose funds.

Q 13-23. Explain the relationship between the cash surrender value of a life insurance policy and the periodic premiums on the policy. Where is the cash surrender value reported in the balance sheet of the company that owns the policy?

***Q 13-24.** Describe the procedure required to change (*a*) *to* the equity method and (*b*) *from* the equity method of accounting for investments in common stock.

CASES	The case marked with an asterisk (*) refers to Appendix 13–1.

C 13-1. **REPORTING UNREALIZED HOLDING GAINS AND LOSSES** As the chief financial officer of a large, publicly held company, you have primary responsibility for seeing that the company complies with generally accepted accounting principles. In preparation for your next annual shareholders' meeting, you are going over with your controller some potential areas of questioning from stockholders on financial reporting issues. One of the subjects brought to your attention by the controller is the reporting of unrealized holding gains and losses on equity securities. The controller believes that some stockholders may not understand or agree with the difference in reporting for unrealized holding gains and losses on trading securities as compared to available-for-sale securities.

REQUIRED Write an analysis of the differing treatment of unrealized holding gains and losses for trading securities and available-for-sale securities. This analysis should both explain and justify the differing treatment and should serve as a basis for your response to any questions on this issue at the annual shareholders' meeting.

C 13-2. **TRANSFERS BETWEEN EQUITY SECURITY INVESTMENT CLASSIFICATIONS** The president of the company that you serve as controller is looking for a way to maximize reported annual earnings. It is her understanding that one means of accomplishing this task is through the classification of investments in equity securities. She is aware that managerial intent determines the appropriate classification of equity security investments and that unrealized holding gains and losses related to trading securities flow through the income statement, whereas unrealized holding gains and losses on available-for-sale securities are taken directly to stockholders' equity. It is her belief that if equity securities are classified in a certain manner at the end of each year, the income effect of the securities portfolio can be maximized. The president comes to you for advice.

REQUIRED Is the president correct in her analysis? Write a memo to the president supporting your position.

C 13-3. **VALUATION OF EQUITY SECURITY INVESTMENTS SUBSEQUENT TO ACQUISITION** Harvey Company, a manufacturing company, has invested in equity securities of many corporations. The company buys and sells the securities in small blocks strictly for dividend revenue and appreciation. Although Harvey's total investment in equity securities is large, the amount invested in each security is small in terms of both the total amount of its investments and the market for the security. All securities are traded regularly on one or more organized exchanges.

Harvey's board of directors is attempting to determine whether to report its investment in these securities at cost or at fair value.

REQUIRED   Write a summary of the *conceptual* merits (GAAP notwithstanding) of Harvey Company's reporting of its investment in equity securities:

1. At cost.
2. At fair value.

(AICPA, adapted)

C 13-4.   CLASSIFICATION OF SECURITY INVESTMENTS; EQUITY METHOD   Dean Systems, Inc., a chemical processing company, has been operating profitably for many years. On March 1, 1998, Dean purchased 50,000 shares of McClure Company common stock for $2 million. The 50,000 shares represented 25 percent of McClure's outstanding stock. The fiscal years of both Dean and McClure end August 31.

For the fiscal year ended August 31, 1998, McClure reported net income of $800,000 earned evenly throughout the year. During November 1997 and February, May, and August 1998, McClure paid its regular quarterly cash dividend of $100,000.

REQUIRED   1. What criteria should Dean consider in determining how to account for its investment in McClure in its August 31, 1998, balance sheet? Confine your discussion to the decision criteria for determining the balance sheet classification of the investment.
2. Assume that the investment in McClure is determined to be an equity method investment. The cost of Dean's investment equaled its equity in the recorded values of McClure's net assets; recorded values were not materially different from fair values (individually or collectively). For the fiscal year ended August 31, 1998, how did the net income reported and dividends paid by McClure affect Dean's accounts? Indicate each account affected, whether it increased or decreased, and explain the reason for the change in the account balance (cash, investment in McClure, etc.).

(AICPA, adapted)

C 13-5.   LONG-TERM INVESTMENTS   Hare Company acquired 15 percent of the outstanding voting common stock of Nasif Company. Hare also made a loan to Nasif that is convertible into voting common stock of Nasif and is secured by voting common stock of Kadet Company, which is a wholly owned subsidiary of Nasif. For as long as the loan is outstanding, Hare will have several seats on Nasif's board of directors. Hare also has options to purchase a substantial number of shares of Kadet.

REQUIRED   What method of accounting should Hare Company use to account for its investment in Nasif? Explain.

(AICPA, adapted)

C 13-6.   ACCOUNTING FOR CASH SURRENDER VALUE   At the beginning of 1998, Burton Corporation purchased a $200,000 life insurance policy on the life of the corporation's president. Information relating to this whole-life policy for the first 10 years is as follows:

YEAR	ANNUAL PREMIUM	INCREASE IN CASH SURRENDER VALUE	TOTAL CASH SURRENDER VALUE
1	$6,000	$ –0–	$ –0–
2	6,000	2,000	2,000
3	6,000	3,000	5,000
4	6,000	4,000	9,000
5	6,000	5,500	14,500
6	6,000	6,000	20,500
7	6,000	7,000	27,500
8	6,000	7,500	35,000
9	6,000	8,000	43,000
10	6,000	10,000	53,000

Two employees in Burton's accounting department are discussing the proper method of accounting for the policy, especially in view of the substantial increase in cash surrender value. Mr. Budge believes that, because the net cost to Burton by the end of the tenth year is only $7,000 ($60,000 – $53,000), this $7,000 should be allocated equally over the 10-year period. For example, the entries to record the insurance expense for years 1 and 2 and for years 9 and 10 would be as follows:

YEAR 1		
Insurance expense	700	
Deferred charge	5,300	
Cash		6,000

YEAR 2		
Insurance expense	700	
Cash surrender value	2,000	
Deferred charge	3,300	
Cash		6,000

YEAR 9		
Insurance expense	700	
Cash surrender value	8,000	
Deferred charge		2,700
Cash		6,000

YEAR 10		
Insurance expense	700	
Cash surrender value	10,000	
Deferred charge		4,700
Cash		6,000

Mr. Budge further maintains that this approach would "even out" the cash value increases and would better match insurance expense against the revenues generated (indirectly) by the company's president.

Ms. Jenne believes that the periodic insurance expense should be the difference between the annual premium paid and the periodic increase in cash surrender value. Although Mr. Budge's idea is attractive to her, something about the idea bothers her.

REQUIRED Write an explanation as to why Jenne's approach is superior to Budge's. Be specific in regard to the aspects of Budge's proposal that are not in accord with the concepts discussed in Chapter 2 of the text.

C 13-7. **CASH SURRENDER VALUE** Oliver Company has secured a short-term loan from an insurance company against the cash surrender value of its life insurance policies. According to generally accepted accounting principles, the cash surrender value is excluded from current assets.

REQUIRED Discuss whether it is appropriate for Oliver to classify a readily liquid asset (cash surrender value) as noncurrent, while simultaneously showing the related borrowings as a current liability. Include in your discussion any alternative reporting practice(s) that you consider acceptable.

*C 13-8. **CHANGE TO EQUITY METHOD** For the past five years, Benson has maintained an investment in Falk amounting to a 10 percent interest in Falk's voting common stock. The Falk stock is not actively traded. The purchase price was $700,000, and the underlying net equity in Falk at the date of purchase was $620,000. On January 2 of the current year, Benson purchased an additional 14 percent of Falk's voting common stock for $1.2 million. Now, for the first time, Benson is able to exercise significant influence over Falk's operations. The underlying net equity of the additional investment at January 2 was $1 million. Falk has been profitable and has paid dividends annually since Benson's initial acquisition.

REQUIRED Write a discussion of how this increase in ownership affects Benson's accounting for and reporting on the investment in Falk. Include in your discussion any adjustments that might be made to the amount shown before the increase in investment to bring the amount into conformity with generally accepted accounting principles. Also, discuss how the investment would be reported in current and subsequent periods.

(AICPA, adapted)

EXERCISES The exercise marked with an asterisk (*) refers to Appendix 13–1.

E 13-1. **ACQUISITION OF SECURITIES** Beck Company acquired the following securities during 1998 in exchange for the consideration indicated:

a) 500 shares of X Company common at $60 per share. Beck paid cash for the shares. Brokerage fees of $300 were incurred.

b) 1,000 shares of Y Company preferred were acquired in exchange for land. The land had a carrying value of $40,000 and an appraised value of $45,000; the preferred stock had a market price per share (on the New York Stock Exchange) of $50 on the date the shares were acquired. Brokerage fees of $1,000 were incurred.

REQUIRED Prepare the journal entries required by Beck Company to record the securities acquisitions.

E 13-2. **LUMP-SUM PURCHASE OF SECURITIES** Martin Corporation invested in 4,000 shares of Linton Corporation's $5 par value common. To increase the marketability of the common shares, Linton issued one share of its $10 par preferred with each 10 shares of common. Martin paid $70,000 for the securities. The market prices per share of the securities on the date of the transaction were $16 for the common and $25 for the preferred.

REQUIRED 1. Prepare the journal entry to record the acquisition of the securities by Martin. Show calculations.
2. How would the journal entry in part 1 differ if there were no readily determinable market price for the preferred shares?

E 13-3. **FAIR VALUE METHOD** Bain Corporation acquired 4,000 shares of Taylor Corporation common at $30 per share on January 2, 1998. The purchase, which did not permit Bain to exercise significant influence over Taylor, was classified as an available-for-sale security and reported as a long-term investment. On December 31, 1998, the market price per share was $21.

REQUIRED 1. Prepare journal entries required by Bain Corporation in 1998 to account for its investment in Taylor.
2. Where would the temporary (nominal) accounts in your answer to part 1 appear in Bain's financial statements? Explain.

E 13-4. **FAIR VALUE METHOD** On August 1, 1998, Mickelson Company acquired 2,000 shares of the common stock of Mayfair Corporation at $10 per share, plus brokerage fees of $300. The Mayfair shares were actively traded on the New York Stock Exchange, and approximately 5 million shares were outstanding in 1998. Mickelson purchased the shares as trading securities, expecting to be able to sell them within a few months at a substantial profit.

On October 10, 1998, Mickelson acquired 8,000 common shares of Norman Company at $18 per share, plus brokerage fees of $2,000. The Norman shares also were actively traded on the New York Stock Exchange, and approximately 4 million shares were outstanding. Because these securities furnished an attractive dividend yield, Mickelson intended to hold the Norman Company shares for the foreseeable future.

Market prices of the Mayfair and Norman shares at December 31, 1998, the end of Mickelson's accounting period, were as follows:

Mayfair **$13**
Norman **16**

At the end of 1998, Mickelson's intent with respect to the Mayfair and Norman shares was the same as at acquisition.

REQUIRED 1. Prepare the journal entries required by Mickelson to record (*a*) the acquisition of the securities and (*b*) any year-end adjustments at December 31, 1998.
2. For each unrealized holding gain/loss recorded in part 1, where would this amount be reported in the financial statements of Mickelson?
3. Where would the investments in Mayfair and Norman be reported in Mickelson's statement of financial position at December 31, 1998?

E 13-5. **FAIR VALUE METHOD; SUBSEQUENT PERIODS** Refer to the data in Exercise 13-4. Assume that both the Mayfair and Norman shares are still held by Mickelson at the end of 1999, at which time the share prices are as follows:

Mayfair **$17**
Norman **25**

Mickelson's intent with respect to the two investments remains the same at the end of 1999. That is, Mickelson still expects to sell the Mayfair shares within the near term and intends to hold the Norman shares for the foreseeable future.

REQUIRED Prepare the journal entries to record any year-end adjustments required by Mickelson at December 31, 1999.

E 13-6. **FAIR VALUE METHOD; SALE** Clark Corporation acquired 5,000 shares of Brenner Company common stock during 1998 at $15 per share, plus a brokerage commission of $1,000. The Brenner shares were actively traded in the over-the-counter market, and Clark planned to hold the shares for the foreseeable future. The investment did not allow Clark to exercise significant influence over the operating and financing policies of Brenner.

Market prices of the Brenner common shares at the end of 1998 and 1999 were as follows:

December 31, 1998 .... **$23 per share**
December 31, 1999 .... **21 per share**

On April 10, 2000, Clark sold all of the Brenner shares for $26 per share and paid a brokerage commission on the sale of $800.

Until immediately prior to the sale, Clark had continued to view the investment as one that would be held for the foreseeable future. However, a rapid run-up in the market price of the Brenner shares, combined with the need for cash to take advantage of another investment opportunity, led Clark to sell the Brenner shares.

REQUIRED

1. At acquisition, should the investment in Brenner common stock be classified by Clark as a trading security or as an available-for-sale security?
2. Prepare the journal entry to record the acquisition of the Brenner stock by Clark.
3. Prepare the journal entries required at the end of 1998 and 1999 by Clark for its investment in Brenner common stock.
4. How should the investment in Brenner common stock be reported in Clark's statement of financial position at December 31, 1998? At December 31, 1999?
5. Prepare the entry required by Clark on April 10, 2000, to record the sale of the Brenner common stock.

E 13-7. **FAIR VALUE METHOD; RECLASSIFICATION** Siegel Company purchased two equity security investments during 1998. On April 20, 1998, Siegel acquired 5,000 shares of Brown Corporation nonredeemable preferred at $30 per share plus brokerage fees of $350. On July 10, 1998, Siegel acquired 3,000 shares of Bauer, Inc., common for $24 per share plus brokerage fees of $250. At acquisition, Siegel's intent for both of these securities was to hold them for the foreseeable future rather than to dispose of them in the short term. Neither of these security investments conveyed significant influence, and both securities were actively traded on a regional stock exchange.

The market prices of the Brown and Bauer shares at the end of 1998 and 1999 were as follows:

	BROWN	BAUER
12/31/98	$33	$18
12/31/99	38	22

At the end of 1999, Siegel decided that it would probably dispose of the Bauer shares within the first few months of 2000, and reclassified the investment as a trading security.

REQUIRED

1. Prepare the appropriate journal entries to record the acquisition of the Brown and Bauer equity securities by Siegel.
2. Prepare the end of period adjusting entries for Siegel at the end of 1998 and 1999.
3. For each unrealized holding gain/loss recorded in part 2, where would this amount be reported in the financial statements of Siegel?
4. Where would the investments in Brown and Bauer be reported in Siegel's statement of financial position at December 31, 1999?

E 13-8. **COST METHOD** Tucker Corporation acquired 1,000 shares of common stock of Boyle Company on January 2, 1998, for $30,000 plus brokerage costs of $1,000. Boyle, which had 2 million common shares outstanding throughout 1998 and 1999, had net income and dividend payments as follows for 1998 and 1999:

	NET INCOME	DIVIDENDS
1998	$4,000,000	$1,000,000
1999	5,000,000	2,000,000

Because Boyle's stock was not actively traded, a fair value was not readily determinable.

REQUIRED Prepare all entries required by Tucker in 1998 and 1999 in connection with the investment in Boyle.

E 13-9. **COST METHOD** At the beginning of 1998, Bailey Corporation acquired 500 (6 percent) of the outstanding common shares of Li Company for $20,000. Incidental costs incurred in connection with the acquisition amounted to $600. In 1998, Li's net income was

$40,000 and dividend payments totaled $20,000. In 1999, Li's net income was $30,000 and dividend payments totaled $40,000. The Li Company common stock was not actively traded, and therefore, fair value was not readily determinable. Bailey has no ability to influence Li's operations.

REQUIRED

1. Prepare all entries required by Bailey Corporation in 1998 and 1999 in connection with the investment.
2. How would the entries in part 1 differ if Li's net income in 1999 had been $10,000 instead of $30,000? Explain.

E 13-10. **COST METHOD AND EQUITY METHOD**   Fazzi Company made the following investments in the common stock of Melnick Company, a closely held concern (fair value not readily determinable):

| 1/2/98 | 4,000 shares at $20 per share |
| 1/2/99 | 4,000 shares at $28 per share |

Melnick has 40,000 shares outstanding and reported net income in 1998 and 1999 of $60,000 and $100,000, respectively. Dividends of $50,000 were paid each year.

REQUIRED

1. Prepare entries for Fazzi for 1998 and 1999, assuming that the investment does not allow Fazzi to influence the operating and financial policies of Melnick.
2. Prepare entries for Fazzi for 1998 and 1999, assuming that, as a result of the investment, Fazzi exercises significant influence over the operating and financial policies of Melnick in those years.

E 13-11. **COST METHOD AND EQUITY METHOD**   On January 2, 1998, Brown Company purchased 15,000 shares of the common stock of Brewer Corporation, a closely held company, for $225,000. During 1998 and 1999, Brewer had 100,000 common shares outstanding. Brewer reported net income of $200,000 and $150,000 in 1998 and 1999, respectively. Dividends paid by Brewer were $80,000 in 1998 and in 1999.

REQUIRED

1. Assuming that the investment does *not* allow Brown to exert significant influence over the operating and financial policies of Brewer, prepare journal entries for Brown related to the investment in Brewer for 1998 and 1999.
2. Assuming that the investment *does* allow Brown to exert significant influence over the operating and financial policies of Brewer, prepare journal entries for Brown related to the investment in Brewer for 1998 and 1999.

E 13-12. **EQUITY METHOD**   On January 3, 1998, Scotney Corporation paid $700,000 for 20,000 shares of Ball Corporation common. The investment represents a 25 percent interest in the net assets of Ball and gave Scotney the ability to exercise significant influence over Ball's operations. Scotney received dividends of $1.25 per share in 1998, and Ball reported net income of $300,000 for the year ended December 31, 1998.

REQUIRED

1. Assuming that the book value of Ball's net assets was $2.8 million on January 3, 1998, prepare the journal entries required by Scotney for 1998.
2. Assume instead that the book value of Ball's net assets was $2.4 million and that the excess of cost over book value was attributable to unrecorded goodwill, to be amortized over 40 years. How would the entries in part 1 differ?

E 13-13. **EQUITY METHOD**   At the beginning of 1998, Atkins Company bought 30,000 shares of Valenzuela Corporation common for $600,000 cash. Valenzuela had 150,000 common shares outstanding during 1998 and 1999. The book value of Valenzuela's net assets at the time of purchase was $2.6 million. The excess of cost over book value was attributable to unrecorded goodwill, to be amortized over 10 years. Atkins's purchase provided it with the ability to significantly influence the operating and financial policies of Valenzuela.

Valenzuela reported net income of $340,000 and paid dividends of $100,000 in 1998. In 1999, Valenzuela reported net income of $380,000 and paid dividends of $120,000.

REQUIRED   Prepare journal entries for 1998 and 1999 for Atkins related to the investment in Valenzuela.

E 13-14. **STOCK RIGHTS**   Chaney Corporation purchased 10,000 shares of Solomon Company for $660,000 in 1996. Since then the securities have been accounted for by the cost method because fair value was not readily determinable. At the beginning of 1998, Solomon issued one preemptive right per share to existing stockholders in connection with a new issue of securities. The purchase of each additional common share required five rights and $50. Immediately after the rights were issued, active trading in the securities began. The stock was selling for $70 per share, and the market price of each right was $5.

REQUIRED

1. Prepare the journal entry that could be made (optional) by Chaney on receipt of the rights.

2. Prepare the journal entry to record the disposal of the rights during 1998 under each of the following alternatives (assuming the entry in part 1 was made):

a) All the rights are exercised.

b) All the rights are sold for $50,000.

c) All the rights are allowed to expire.

E 13-15. **STOCK WARRANTS** On September 1, 1998, Clayton Company acquired 4,000 shares of Fern Corporation's preferred stock for $216,000. Each share had one warrant attached. Warrant holders could acquire one share of Fern common in exchange for two warrants and $19. The market price of the preferred stock (without warrant) was $50 per share, and the market price of the stock warrants was $10 per warrant on September 1, 1998.

REQUIRED

1. Prepare the journal entry required to record the acquisition of the preferred shares and warrants on September 1, 1998.

2. Prepare the entry required by Clayton under each of the following two independent assumptions:

a) Clayton sold the warrants on November 1, 1998, for $40,000.

b) All the warrants were exercised on November 1, 1998.

E 13-16. **STOCK WARRANTS** Gill Company issued common stock with detachable warrants on July 1, 1998. Each share of common had one warrant attached. An additional share of Gill common stock could be acquired in exchange for five warrants and $10. Immediately after issuance, the common stock traded at $40 per share (without warrants) and the warrants traded at $6 each.

Teague Corporation acquired 10,000 of the Gill shares on July 1, 1998, for $420,000.

REQUIRED

1. Prepare the journal entry by Teague to record the acquisition of the common stock and warrants on July 1, 1998.

2. Assume that Teague exercised all the warrants on December 10, 1998. Prepare the journal entry to record the exercise.

3. Assume, instead, that Teague sold half the warrants on October 1, 1998, for $8.50 each and exercised the other half on November 15, 1998. Prepare the journal entries to record these transactions.

E 13-17. **SPECIAL-PURPOSE FUNDS** Ortiz Corporation established a trusteed fund to accumulate resources over a five-year period to be used for environmental improvements. The following selected transactions involving the fund took place:

a) Transferred $240,000 cash to the trustee.

b) Common stock of Hopkins Corporation was acquired for $80,000 by the trustee.

c) Dividends of $6,000 were received on the Hopkins common.

d) Trustee's fee of $8,000 was charged against the fund.

e) At the end of the fifth year, after all fund investments were converted to cash, $600,000 was spent on environmental improvements.

f) Remaining cash in the fund ($12,000) was returned to unrestricted cash.

REQUIRED Prepare the journal entries required by Ortiz Corporation to reflect the above transactions.

E 13-18. **CASH SURRENDER VALUE OF LIFE INSURANCE** Chapman Company owns and pays premiums on insurance policies on several of its key executives. Chapman Company is designated as the beneficiary of all the policies. At the end of 1998, Chapman paid premiums of $5,000 and the cash surrender value of policies owned increased by $1,200. At the beginning of 1999, an executive covered by a $100,000 face value policy with a cash surrender value of $24,000 died and Chapman received the face amount.

REQUIRED

1. Prepare the entry required by Chapman at the end of 1998 to record the premium payments and the increase in cash surrender value.

2. Prepare the entry required by Chapman at the beginning of 1999 to record the collection of the face amount of the $100,000 policy.

*E 13-19. **CHANGE FROM THE EQUITY METHOD** Lattan Company acquired 40 percent (40,000 shares) of the outstanding common stock of Klein Corporation for $510,000 at the beginning of 1996, enabling Lattan to exercise significant influence over Klein. The book value of Klein's net assets at the date of acquisition was $1 million. The difference between the cost and the book value of Lattan's 40 percent interest in Klein was attributable to undervalued depreciable assets that were being depreciated on a straight-line basis with a remaining life of 10 years. The investment in Klein account appeared as follows at the beginning of 1998:

Investment in Klein

1/2/96		510,000	12/27/96	Dividends		33,000
12/31/96	Income	60,000	12/31/96	Amortization		
12/31/97	Income	70,000		of under-		
				valued assets		11,000
			12/27/97	Dividends		37,000
			12/31/97	Amortization		
				of under-		
				valued assets		11,000

At the beginning of 1998, Lattan sold 30,000 of the Klein shares for $330,000, thus losing its ability to influence Klein's operating and financial policies. In 1998 Klein had net income of $75,000 and paid dividends of $50,000. The market price of the Klein stock was $10 per share at the end of 1998. Lattan appropriately classified the remaining investment in Klein as available-for-sale.

REQUIRED   Prepare the journal entries required by Lattan in 1998 related to its investment in Klein.

PROBLEMS

Problems marked with an asterisk (*) refer to Appendix 13–1.

P 13-1.   **ACQUISITION OF SECURITY INVESTMENTS**   During 1998, Kirk Corporation acquired the following securities:

a) 6,000 shares of Wahlen Corporation's common stock at $32 per share, plus brokerage fees of $2,000.

b) 1,000 shares of Weekly Company's preferred at $26 per share. Included with each preferred share was a warrant that permitted the holder to acquire common shares of Weekly at a specified price. Immediately after the transaction, the preferred shares had a market price of $24 per share (without the warrant), and the market price of the warrants was $4 per warrant.

c) 3,000 shares of Galligan Corporation preferred and 300 shares of Galligan's common stock in exchange for land with a book value of $120,000 and an appraised value of $165,000. The market prices of the preferred and common shares at the date of the transaction were $56 and $23 per share, respectively. Both securities were actively traded on an organized exchange.

d) 200 of Bowen Corporation's 10 percent, $1,000 face value bonds maturing in 2008 at 102 (102 percent of face value).

REQUIRED   Prepare the journal entries required by Kirk to record the purchases.

P 13-2.   **FAIR VALUE METHOD**   Lafrenz Company has invested in a number of equity securities of other companies over the years, sometimes to speculate on short-term price changes, sometimes with the intent of establishing a long-term relationship but with the willingness to dispose of such securities should circumstances warrant, and other times to exert significant influence over the financing and operating policies of the investee company. At the end of 1998, Lafrenz owned equity securities in only five companies, all of which were acquired during 1998. The carrying amount and market value of each investment at December 31, 1998, before any year-end adjustments, and dividends received, were as follows:

	CARRYING AMOUNT	MARKET VALUE	DIVIDENDS
Company *A*	$10,000	$13,000	$ 600
Company *B*	6,000	5,000	0
Company *C*	24,000	18,000	1,000
Company *D*	35,000	43,000	0
Company *E*	88,000	61,000	2,600

All of these securities were actively traded. Investments in Companies *A, B,* and *C* were classified as trading securities, and investments in Companies *D* and *E* were classified as available-for-sale securities.

REQUIRED

1. Prepare journal entries for Lafrenz Company (*a*) to record dividends received and (*b*) at December 31, 1998, related to the five equity security investments.

2. How would the (*a*) dividends received and (*b*) unrealized holding gains/losses be reported in Lafrenz's financial statements?

3. How would the investments be reported in Lafrenz's statement of financial position at December 31, 1998?

P 13-3. **FAIR VALUE METHOD; RECLASSIFICATION AND SALE** Refer to the data in P13-2. Assume that in 1999 Lafrenz sold the equity securities of Companies *A, B, C,* and *D* for $15,000, $8,000, $23,000, and $42,000, respectively. No dividends were received on these shares during 1999. Also, Lafrenz determined at the end of 1999 that the Company *E* shares should be reclassified as trading securities. At December 31, 1999, the market value of the equity security investment in Company *E* was $70,000. Dividends of $2,600 were received on the Company *E* shares in 1999.

REQUIRED

1. Prepare journal entries to record the sale of the investments in equity securities of Companies *A, B, C,* and *D.*

2. Prepare journal entries for Lafrenz Company (*a*) to record dividends received in 1999, and (*b*) at December 31, 1999, related to Company *E.*

3. How would the effect of the reclassification of the investment in Company *E* be reported in the financial statements of Lafrenz?

P 13-4. **TRADING SECURITIES** Cain Corporation owned the following equity securities at the end of 1998:

	CARRYING AMOUNT (BEFORE YEAR-END ADJUSTMENT)	MARKET VALUE
A Corporation	$12,000	$15,000
B Corporation	8,000	6,000
C Corporation	24,000	28,000
D Corporation	16,000	11,000
E Corporation	7,000	4,000

All these securities are classified as trading securities at the end of 1998, as they have been since they were acquired.

During 1999, Cain engaged in the following transactions involving trading securities:

a) Sold one-half of its shares in *C* Corporation for $14,000.

b) Acquired additional shares of *A* Corporation for $11,000.

c) Acquired shares of *F* Corporation for $18,000.

d) Disposed of its shares of *E* Corporation for $6,500.

At the end of 1999, market data were as follows:

	MARKET VALUE
A Corporation	$26,000
B Corporation	8,000
C Corporation	12,000
D Corporation	15,000
F Corporation	20,000

REQUIRED

1. Prepare any required year-end adjusting entries at December 31, 1998.

2. Prepare entries to record the four securities transactions during 1999.

3. Prepare any end-of-period adjusting entries required at December 31, 1999.

P 13-5. **FAIR VALUE METHOD** Munter Company, which began operations in 1998, had the following equity securities appropriately classified as trading securities at the end of 1998 and 1999:

	DECEMBER 31, 1998	
	COST	MARKET VALUE
Altman Corp.	$10,000	$ 9,000
Murphy Corp.	30,000	26,000
Chandra Co.	20,000	23,000

	DECEMBER 31, 1999 MARKET VALUE
Altman Corp.	$10,000
Murphy Corp.	14,000
Chandra Co.	27,000
Decker Corp. (cost $14,000)	12,000

During 1999, Munter sold half of its shares of Murphy for $16,000.

REQUIRED

I. Prepare the adjusting entries required at the end of 1998 related to the trading securities.

2. Prepare the entry required to record the sale of Murphy Corporation shares in 1999.

3. Prepare the adjusting entries required at the end of 1999 related to the trading securities.

P 13-6. **FAIR VALUE METHOD AND EQUITY METHOD** On January 2, 1997, Lyon Company purchased 25 percent (40,000 shares) of the outstanding common stock of Hock Corporation for $2.4 million. Hock experienced the following net income (loss) and dividends from 1997 through 2001:

YEAR	NET INCOME (LOSS)	DIVIDENDS
1997	$1,600,000	$ 800,000
1998	(1,200,000)	400,000
1999	2,400,000	1,200,000
2000	1,200,000	800,000
2001	(1,600,000)	400,000

At acquisition, Lyon intended to hold the investment for the foreseeable future because of the attractive dividend payout and because of its interest in maintaining a strong business relationship with Hock. The market price of the Hock shares, for which there was an active market, was as follows at December 31 of each year:

YEAR	PRICE
1997	$68
1998	56
1999	72
2000	75
2001	65

Lyon's intent with respect to its investment in Hock did not change over these years.

REQUIRED

I. Prepare the journal entry to record the investment in Hock on January 2, 1997.

2. Assume that the investment does *not* convey significant influence to Lyon. Prepare entries by Lyon related to the investment from 1997 through 2001.

3. Assume, instead, that the investment *does* convey significant influence over the operating and financial policies of Hock. Prepare entries by Lyon related to the investment from 1997 through 2001.

4. Explain the difference in the treatment of dividends received under parts 2 and 3.

5. Discuss the meaning of the balance of the investment in Hock account at the end of 2001 under parts 2 and 3.

P 13-7. **COST METHOD AND EQUITY METHOD** At the beginning of 1997, Phillips Corporation acquired 30 percent of the outstanding voting common stock of Chang Company for $7 million. The Chang common is closely held, and thus fair value is not readily determinable. The book value of Chang's net assets at the acquisition date was $18 million. Any amount paid in excess of book value is attributable to goodwill, to be amortized over 40 years. Chang's net income (loss) and dividends from 1997 through 2000 were as follows:

YEAR	NET INCOME (LOSS)	DIVIDENDS
1997	$2,400,000	$1,200,000
1998	1,100,000	800,000
1999	(1,000,000)	400,000
2000	500,000	600,000

REQUIRED
I. Prepare entries by Phillips to account for its investment in Chang from 1997 through 2000 under the cost method.
2. Prepare entries by Phillips to account for its investment in Chang from 1997 through 2000 under the equity method.
3. Summarize the balance sheet amount and the income statement amount reported for the investment for each of the four years (1997–2000) under (a) the cost method and (b) the equity method.

P 13-8. **EQUITY METHOD** Kaufman Corporation has been manufacturing industrial products for over 30 years. Kaufman decided to diversify into the home products industry and purchased 60 percent of the outstanding common stock of McKnight Company for $9 million in cash on December 1, 1997, the first day of the 1997–1998 fiscal year for both Kaufman and McKnight.

Information pertaining to McKnight Company as of December 1, 1997, is presented below:
a) The book value of McKnight's total stockholders' equity was $10 million.
b) McKnight's inventory, valued at lower of cost (determined by the FIFO method) or market, was undervalued by $500,000.
c) Included in McKnight's plant and equipment were some depreciable assets that had a market value of $1.3 million in excess of book value. These undervalued assets had a remaining life of 10 years.

McKnight reported net income of $1,200,000 for the 1997–1998 fiscal year. Dividends in the amount of $300,000 were declared and paid by McKnight in the 1997–1998 fiscal year. None of the items in McKnight's inventory on December 1, 1997, were in the inventory on November 30, 1998.

Kaufman uses the equity method to account for its investment in McKnight, recognizes only its portion of the undervalued assets for any amortization, and amortizes any goodwill over the maximum period allowed under generally accepted accounting principles.

REQUIRED
I. Prepare a schedule to calculate the balance of investment in McKnight common that would appear on the balance sheet of Kaufman Corporation at November 30, 1998.
2. Prepare a schedule to calculate the amount of equity in subsidiary earnings that would appear on the income statement of Kaufman Corporation for the year ended November 30, 1998. Ignore income taxes.

(IMA, adapted)

P 13-9. **EQUITY SECURITIES** On December 31, 1997, Brady Corporation properly reported as current assets the following trading securities:

Tang Corp., 1,000 shares, $2.40 convertible preferred	**$40,000**
Hull, Inc., 6,000 shares, common	**60,000**
Crane Co., 2,000 shares, common	**48,000**

On January 2, 1998, Brady paid $1.7 million to purchase 100,000 shares of Skousen Corporation common stock, representing 30 percent of Skousen's outstanding common stock and an underlying equity of $1.4 million in Skousen's net assets at January 2. Brady amortizes goodwill over a 40-year period. As a result of Brady's 30 percent ownership of Skousen, Brady has the ability to exercise significant influence over Skousen's financial and operating policies. Skousen's net income for the year ended December 31, 1998, was $1,200,000.

During 1998, Brady disposed of the following securities:
January 18—Sold 2,500 shares of Hull for $13 per share.
June 1—Sold 500 shares of Crane for $21 per share.

The following 1998 dividend information pertains to the stock held by Brady:
April 5 and October 5—Tang paid dividends of $1.20 per share on its $2.40 preferred stock to stockholders of record on March 9 and September 9, respectively.
June 30—Hull paid a $1 per share dividend on its common stock.
March 1, June 1, September 1, and December 1—Skousen paid quarterly dividends of $0.50 per share on each of these dates.

At December 31, 1998, Brady's management intended to hold the Skousen stock as a long-term investment, with the remaining investments being held as trading securities. Market prices per share of the equity securities were as follows at December 31, 1998:

Tang Corp. preferred	$56
Hull, Inc. common	12
Crane Co. common	22
Skousen Corp. common	16

All the foregoing stocks are listed on national stock exchanges.

REQUIRED

1. Prepare entries to record the transactions during 1998.
2. Prepare the required adjusting entries at December 31, 1998, related to the trading securities.
3. Prepare a schedule to show the carrying amount of the Skousen investment at December 31, 1998.

P 13-10. EQUITY METHOD, UNDERVALUED ASSETS On January 2, 1998, Wild Company purchased for cash 60 percent of the 20,000 outstanding common shares of Sepe Corporation at $16 per share. The following additional data were available for Sepe Corporation on January 2, 1998:

	BOOK VALUE	FAIR VALUE
Assets not subject to depreciation	$160,000	$170,000
Assets subject to depreciation (10-year remaining life)	120,000	134,000
Total	$280,000	$304,000
Liabilities	$ 20,000	
Contributed capital	200,000	
Retained earnings	60,000	
Total	$280,000	

In 1998, Sepe Corporation reported net income of $60,000 (including a $10,000 extraordinary gain) and paid cash dividends of $20,000.

REQUIRED   Prepare journal entries on the books of Wild Company for 1998 related to its investment in Sepe Corporation. Show calculations.

(CGAA, adapted)

P 13-11. EQUITY METHOD On September 1, 1997, Mark Company purchased 200,000 shares representing 45 percent of the outstanding stock of White Company for cash. As a result of the purchase, Mark has the ability to exercise significant influence over White's operating and financial policies. Goodwill of $900,000 was appropriately recognized by Mark at the date of the purchase.

On December 1, 1998, Mark purchased 300,000 shares representing 30 percent of the outstanding stock of Jabara Company for $2.7 million cash. The stockholders' equity section of Jabara's balance sheet at the date of the acquisition was as follows:

Common stock, par value $2	$2,000,000
Contributed capital in excess of par	1,000,000
Retained earnings	4,000,000
Total	$7,000,000

Furthermore, at the date of acquisition, the fair value of Jabara's net property, plant, and equipment was $3.8 million, whereas the book value was $3.5 million. The fair value and book value of all of Jabara's other assets and liabilities were equal. As a result of the transaction, Mark has the ability to exercise significant influence over Jabara's operating and financial policies.

Mark amortizes goodwill over the maximum period allowed and takes a full year's amortization in the year of purchase.

REQUIRED Prepare a schedule calculating the amount of goodwill and accumulated amortization on December 31, 1998, and the goodwill amortization for the year ended December 31, 1998. Show supporting calculations.

(AICPA, adapted)

P 13-12. **COMPREHENSIVE** During the course of your examination of the financial statements of Hiltner Corporation for the year ended December 31, 1998, you find a new account, *investments*. Your examination reveals that during 1998 Hiltner began a program of investments, and all investment-related transactions were entered in this account. Your analysis of this account for 1998 follows:

Analysis of Investments
for the Year Ended December 31, 1998

DATE		DEBIT	CREDIT
Bradley Company Common Stock:			
3/15	Purchased 1,000 shares @ $25 per share	25,000	
6/28	Received 50 shares of Bymore Sales Co. common stock (quoted market price of $8 per share) as a dividend on Bradley Co. common stock (memorandum entry in general ledger).		
9/30	Sold 50 shares of Bymore Sales Co. common stock @ $14 per share.		700
10/31	Awarded 500 shares of Bradley Co. common stock (quoted market price of $44 per share) to selected members of Hiltner's management as an incentive award and accounted for as employee compensation.		12,500
12/31	Market price, $52 per share.		
Mori, Inc., Common and Preferred Stock:			
3/15	Purchased 600 units of common and preferred stock @ $36 per unit. Each unit consists of one share of preferred and two shares of common stock. Quoted market prices of common and preferred were $10 and $20 per share, respectively.	21,600	
4/30	Sold 300 shares of common stock @ $13 per share		3,900
6/28	Received 900 common stock rights. Each right (which had a quoted market price of $3 per right) entitles the holder to purchase one share of common stock for $12 (memorandum entry in general ledger). The common stock market price (ex-rights) was $15 per share.		
9/30	Exercised 450 common stock rights to acquire 450 shares of common stock @ $12 per share.	5,400	
9/30	Sold remaining 450 common stock rights @ $4 per right.		1,800
12/31	Market price, $16 per share for common, $21 per share for preferred.		

(continued on page 712)

Grace Service, Inc., Common Stock:

3/15	Purchased 10,000 shares @ $17 per share.	170,000
10/31	Received dividend of $.75 per share.	7,500
12/31	Market price, $20 per share.	

Pinto Instruments, Inc., Common Stock:

3/15	Purchased 4,000 shares @ $28 per share.	112,000
4/30	Purchased 2,000 shares @ $30 per share.	60,000
6/28	Received dividend of $.40 per share.	2,400
12/31	Market price, $34 per share.	

Additional information:

a) Grace Service, Inc., has only one class of stock authorized, and 30,000 shares of its common stock were outstanding throughout 1998. Hiltner's cost of its investment in Grace was *not* materially different from its equity in the recorded values of Grace's net assets; recorded values were *not* materially different from fair values. Grace's net income from the date of acquisition of Hiltner's investment to December 31, 1998, was $390,000. As a result of this investment, Hiltner exerts significant influence over the financing and operating policies of Grace.

b) Pinto Instruments, Inc., has only one class of stock authorized, and there were 40,000 shares of its common stock outstanding throughout 1998. Hiltner's cost of its investment in Pinto was *not* materially different from its equity in the recorded values of Pinto's net assets; recorded values were *not* materially different from fair values. Pinto's net income from the date of acquisition of Hiltner's investment to December 31, 1998, was $120,000. Hiltner does not exert significant influence over the financing and operating policies of Pinto.

c) All other investments of Hiltner are widely held, Hiltner's percentage of ownership in each is nominal (5 percent or less), and they are classified as trading securities.

REQUIRED   Prepare necessary adjusting journal entries at December 31, 1998, classified by each of the securities analyzed, to adjust the investments account properly. Show supporting calculations. Ignore income taxes.

(AICPA, adapted)

P 13-13.   **COMPREHENSIVE**   Ushman Company owned trading securities on December 31, 1997, which were appropriately reported as current assets at fair value as follows:

Caldwell Corp., 500 shares of $200 par value 6% preferred stock	$240,000
Hart Corp., 1,000 shares of $3 no-par convertible preferred stock	230,000
Gorman Co., 10,000 shares of common stock	250,000
Gentry, Inc., 3,000 shares of common stock	92,000
Brown Co., 4,000 shares of common stock	25,000

Ushman appropriately recorded $42,000 cash surrender value of life insurance carried on the life of Ushman's president on December 31, 1997.

During 1998, the following transactions occurred:

a) The market value of Caldwell Corporation stock was $250,000 on December 31, 1998.

b) Hart Corporation issues cash dividends once a year to stockholders of record on May 31. The cash was received on June 10, 1998. On June 15, 1998, Ushman converted 500 shares of Hart $3 no-par convertible preferred stock into 1,000 shares of Hart common stock, which had a market value of $114,000 at the date of the conversion and $116,000 on December 31, 1998. The market value of the remaining $3 no-par convertible preferred stock was $117,000 on December 31, 1998.

c) Gorman Company issued a 10 percent stock dividend in 1998. The market value of the common stock on December 31, 1998, was $24 per share.

d) Gentry, Inc., effected a 2-for-1 stock split in 1998. The market value of the stock on December 31, 1998, was $91,000.

e) Brown Company declared cash dividends of $.30 per share to stockholders of record on March 31 and June 30, 1998. The cash was received on April 15 and July 15. On July 4, 1998, Ushman sold all its shares of Brown for $7 per share.

f) In January 1998, premiums of $2,500 for the six months ended June 30, 1998, were paid on the president's $100,000 life insurance policy. During this six-month period, the cash surrender value of the policy increased $1,300. The president of Ushman died on July 1, 1998, and Ushman received the proceeds from the insurance policy shortly thereafter.

g) On October 1, 1998, Ushman purchased 100,000 shares representing 40 percent of the outstanding stock of Levy Company for $1.6 million cash; on that date, the underlying equity in net assets of 40 percent of Levy was $1.2 million. Ushman amortizes goodwill over a 40-year period and takes a full year's amortization in the year of the purchase. As a result of this transaction, Ushman has the ability to exercise significant influence over Levy's operating and financial policies. Levy's net income for the three months ended December 31, 1998, was $60,000 and for the year ended December 31, 1998, $170,000. On December 1, 1998, Ushman made a long-term loan of $400,000 to Levy. The market value of the stock was $1,605,000 on December 31, 1998. On January 20, 1999, cash dividends of $.20 per share were paid to stockholders of record on December 31, 1998.

REQUIRED

1. Prepare a schedule of Ushman's trading securities as of December 31, 1998. Show supporting calculations.

2. Prepare a schedule of Ushman's long-term investments as of December 31, 1998. Show supporting calculations.

(AICPA, adapted)

*P 13-14.   **CHANGE TO EQUITY METHOD**   On January 1, 1998, Wood, Inc., paid $700,000 for 10,000 shares of Park Company's voting common stock, which represented a 10 percent interest in Park. At that date Park's net assets totaled $6 million. The fair values of all of Park's identifiable assets and liabilities were equal to their book values. Wood does not have the ability to exercise significant influence over Park's operating and financial policies. Wood received dividends of $.90 per share from Park on October 1, 1998. Park reported net income of $450,000 for the year ended December 31, 1998. The market price of Park's common, which was actively traded, was $80 per share at December 31, 1998.

On July 1, 1999, Wood paid $2.5 million for 30,000 additional shares of Park Company's voting common stock, which represents a 30 percent investment in Park. The fair values of all of Park's identifiable assets net of liabilities were equal to their book values of $6.5 million. As a result of this transaction, Wood has the ability to exercise significant influence over Park's operating and financial policies. Wood received dividends of $1.10 per share from Park on April 1, 1999, and $1.35 per share on October 1, 1999. Park reported net income of $500,000 for the year ended December 31, 1999, and $300,000 for the six months ended December 31, 1999. Wood amortizes goodwill over 40 years.

REQUIRED

1. Prepare a schedule showing the income or loss that Wood should report from its investment in Park in its income statement for the year ended December 31, 1998, assuming that Wood classifies the security as an available-for-sale security. Ignore income taxes.

2. During March 2000, Wood issues comparative financial statements for 1998 and 1999. Prepare schedules showing the income or loss for the years ended December 31, 1998 and 1999, which Wood should report from its investment in Park. Ignore income taxes.

(AICPA, adapted)

*P 13-15.   **CHANGE TO EQUITY METHOD**   On January 2, 1998, Chewning Corporation acquired 15 percent of the outstanding common stock of Spiller Company for $120,000. The book value of Spiller's net assets on that date totaled $700,000. The Spiller Company common was not actively traded. The 15 percent interest did not give Chewning the ability to exercise significant influence over Spiller's operating and financial policies. On January 3, 1999, Chewning acquired another 10 percent of Spiller's outstanding shares for $80,000. The book value of Spiller's net assets at this date totaled $750,000. As a result of this latter transaction, Chewning was able to exercise significant influence over Spiller's operating and financial policies. The difference between Chewning's cost and its share of the book value of Spiller at both acquisition dates is attributed to depreciable assets with a remaining estimated life of five years at the date of acquisition.

Spiller's income and dividends for 1998 and 1999 were:

	NET INCOME	DIVIDENDS PAID
1998	$100,000	$ 60,000
1999	200,000	150,000

REQUIRED

1. Prepare the journal entries required by Chewning during 1998 to account for its investment in Spiller.

2. Prepare the journal entries required by Chewning during 1999 to account for its investment in Spiller. Show supporting calculations.

Financial Instruments: Debt Securities

LEARNING OBJECTIVES

After studying this chapter, you should be able to:

1. Describe the major characteristics of debt securities.

2. Calculate the issue price (market price) of an unconditional receivable/payable debt security.

3. Prepare journal entries to record the issuance/purchase of a bond or note (1) on the contract date and (2) between interest dates.

4. Explain the relationship that exists between (1) a bond or note's stated rate of interest and the market rate of interest and (2) the security's issue price and its face (maturity) value.

5. Calculate interest expense/interest revenue under the effective interest method and prepare the related journal entries for the issuer/investor.

6. Discuss the primary features and advantages of the effective interest method.

7. Explain the basic accounting concepts for bonds and notes.

8. Describe the three classifications of debt securities held as investments under *Statement No. 115.*

9. Apply the fair value accounting requirements of *Statement No. 115* to debt securities held as investments.

10. Describe the two methods of extinguishing debt prior to maturity and prepare journal entries to record early extinguishment of debt.

11. Describe the general accounting requirements of *Statement No. 114* with respect to accounting for loan impairments.

12. Discuss the accounting issues related to convertible debt and debt issued with detachable warrants and prepare journal entries for those compound financial instruments.

13. Explain how derivatives are used in hedging activities to manage risk.

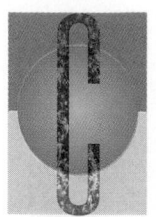

hapter 13 provided an introduction to financial instruments. In Chapter 13 we defined financial instruments and discussed the six major types of financial instruments. The discussion also touched briefly on the major recognition and measurement concepts that apply to financial instruments. The major part of Chapter 13 covered accounting for equity instruments—investments in common stock and preferred stock, stock options, and other equity financial instruments.

In this chapter we continue our discussion of financial instruments by focusing on accounting for debt instruments, such as bonds and notes. These types of financial instruments represent a significant source of debt financing for many corporations. For example, General Electric's long-term borrowings exceeded $51 billion at the end of 1995 (see Appendix B, footnote 18). Financial instruments, such as bonds and notes, also provide significant investment opportunities, and their prices and rates of return (yields) are monitored very closely by the investment community:

How low can yields go? That is the burning question among bond investors, in light of the explosive rally in fixed-income markets since last November. With bond prices soaring on the evidence that the economy has slowed sharply, the yield on the benchmark 30-year Treasury has plummeted from 8.25% late last year to 6.5% on June 6. Bond yields are plunging abroad, too. And with the recent spate of bearish economic news, forecasters are betting that the rally won't end any time soon. While the European markets offer value, fund managers and economists believe the story in the U.S. is the most compelling: "Invest in America," says Madis Senner, manager of Van Eck Global Income Fund. "Buy bonds."[1]

We begin this chapter by describing the major characteristics of bonds and notes and how their prices are determined in the market. Following this discussion, we cover the basic methods of accounting for bonds and notes issued at par or at a discount or premium. We then discuss some related issues, including debt issued for noncash assets, debt issue costs, and interest accruals when debt is issued between interest dates. The use of fair value in accounting for debt investment securities is presented next, followed by a brief discussion of debt extinguishment and loan impairments. We then discuss how to account for compound financial instruments, such as convertible debt and debt issued with detachable stock warrants. The chapter concludes with a discussion of some of the more complex financial instruments, such as derivatives, and how to account for them. This part of the chapter also includes a brief overview of the FASB's financial instruments project.

BONDS AND NOTES: THEIR NATURE AND CHARACTERISTICS

Describe the major characteristics of debt securities.

CONCEPTUAL

An issuer of bonds usually incurs two cash flow obligations—one for interest and one for the maturity value.

A **bond** or a **note** is a borrowing agreement between the issuer of the debt security and the purchaser or investor. The terms of a bond agreement are specified in writing in the bond indenture or contract. Bonds are offered for sale through a *prospectus*, a brochure that sets forth details of the bond issue. The terms of a note, which is a less formal agreement, are usually specified directly on the note.

A company that issues bonds or notes generally incurs two obligations: (1) an obligation to pay investors a specified amount of cash, called the maturity value (also called the par value or face value), on a specified maturity date; and (2) an obligation to pay investors cash interest on specified dates to compensate them for the use of their funds. Bonds are often traded in organized security markets

---

[1]"This Rally Still Has a Full Head of Steam," *Business Week,* June 19, 1995, p. 100.

established to facilitate transfers of ownership. Notes are negotiable instruments and are transferable by endorsement.

Bonds or notes that become due or mature on the same date as all other debt in the same issue are called **term bonds or notes,** while bonds or notes that mature in installments are called **serial bonds or notes.** For example, a company may issue 100 $1,000 term bonds with a maturity value of $100,000, all of which mature 10 years from the date of issue. It may also issue 100 $1,000 serial notes that mature at the rate of $10,000 per year over a 10-year period.

Bonds and notes are usually issued with a fixed or stated contract rate of interest. This stated rate is also called the nominal rate, or if interest coupons are attached, as is sometimes the case with a bond, the coupon rate. Interest may be payable monthly, quarterly, semiannually, or annually. Historically, bonds and notes have been issued at fixed stated interest rates. More recently, however, these financial instruments have been issued with interest rates that vary according to market conditions. Variable rate debt securities are discussed later in the chapter.

In recent years, many companies, such as General Motors Acceptance Corporation (GMAC), J. C. Penney, BankAmerica Corporation, and Macy's, have issued non-interest-bearing bonds and notes, which are called **deep discount or zero-coupon bonds (notes).** As your knowledge of present value would lead you to suspect, these non-interest-bearing instruments sell for much less than their face values. The GMAC bonds, for example, were issued at approximately 25 percent of par; that is, for each $1,000 in face value, the buyer paid only $250. Since the company must pay investors the face value at maturity, the discount represents interest over the life of the bonds. This selling price for the GMAC bonds represented a 14.25 percent annual yield to maturity (annual rate of return). Because the investor's interest revenue is taxable even though no cash is received until maturity, zero-coupon bonds and notes have been most attractive to tax-exempt entities.

Other characteristics of debt securities, such as bonds and notes, are listed in Exhibit 14–1. Before discussing how an issuing company or an investor accounts for bonds and notes, we need to address how market prices are determined.

DETERMINING ISSUE PRICES FOR BONDS AND NOTES

Appendix A at the end of this text presents a comprehensive review of present value concepts. In particular, pages 1199–1201 show how present value concepts apply to bond prices. Because of the importance of this topic, we shall summarize these concepts at this point. For further help, you may wish to study Appendix A in more detail.

Market Pricing of Debt on Contract Date

The market price of a bond or note is determined by supply and demand among buyers and sellers in the financial market. In theory, the market price is equal to the present value of the future cash flows for interest and principal. The interest (discount) rate used to determine this present value is the *market rate of interest* at the issue date for similar instruments with similar risk.

To illustrate, assume that on January 2, 1998, Oklahoma Gas Company issues for cash a financial instrument with a five-year term and a face value of $100,000. The instrument has a stated interest rate of 10 percent, payable annually each December 31, and is dated January 2, 1998 (interest begins to accrue on that date). The instrument matures and the principal amount of $100,000 is payable on December 31, 2002.

CONCEPTUAL

A bond's selling price equals the present value of the future cash flows for interest and principal.

	EXHIBIT 14–1	**Characteristics of Various Types of Long-Term Debt**

	Characteristic	**Explanation**
Interest:	Interest-bearing debt	Cash interest paid periodically.
	Non-interest (zero-coupon) debt	No cash interest paid; interest part of debt maturity value.
Maturity:	Term debt	Entire debt issue matures on a single date.
	Serial debt	Debt issue matures in a series of installments.
Security:	Debenture debt	No security for debt; debt issued on basis of company's general financial strength.
	Secured debt	Assets pledged as debt collateral.
	Senior debt	Debt holders have priority claim in the event of issuer default.
	Subordinated (or junior) debt	Priority claim of debt holders follows another class of creditors.
	Guaranty debt	Debt repayment guaranteed by another party.
Ownership registration:	Registered debt	Records maintained of ownership for purposes of paying principal and interest.
	Bearer debt	Interest and principal paid to whoever demonstrates ownership.
	Coupon debt	Interest paid to coupon holders; similar to bearer debt.
Risk:	Credit risk	Risk that issuer will default on interest and principal obligations.
	Market risk	Risk of market (fair) value changes due to changes in interest rates.
Other:	Sinking fund requirement	Issuer required to set aside (earmark) periodic amounts of cash to service debt.
	Callable debt	Issuer has option (right) to retire debt at a specified price prior to maturity.
	Convertible debt	Purchaser has option (right) to exchange debt for common shares.
	Revenue debt	Debt serviced from specific revenue source; usually issued by cities, counties, turnpike authorities, schools, and other governmental units.

This instrument is an example of a fundamental financial instrument—an unconditional payable (from Oklahoma Gas Company's standpoint) and an unconditional receivable (from the investors' standpoint). It could be either a bond or a note. As we shall see, the same accounting concepts and procedures apply to both. For purposes of illustration, we will assume that it is a bond.

The issue price of these bonds (the amount of cash received by Oklahoma Gas Company) depends on the market rate of interest on January 2, 1998. Because some time may have elapsed since the company decided to sell the bonds and had them printed and readied for sale, the market rate of interest may have changed. Thus, it may be different from the bonds' stated rate of 10 percent. (If the instrument had been a note, the stated rate might also differ from the market rate. However, the difference would probably arise from a decision by the note's maker, rather than from time lapse.) Exhibit 14–2 presents the calculation of the issue price of the Oklahoma Gas Company bonds under three different market rates of interest on January 1, 1998. The time diagram in the exhibit shows the cash flows associated with the issue. The issue price is calculated by discounting the face value (a single amount) and the interest payments (an ordinary annuity) at the *market rate of interest*.

If the rate that investors can earn on investments of similar risk is 10 percent, the bonds will sell at par (face value) and *yield* 10 percent. On the other

2   **Calculate the issue price (market price) of an unconditional receivable/payable debt security.**

EXHIBIT 14-2	Determining the Issue Price of a Five-Year, 10 Percent Bond Under Three Different Market Rates of Interest

$100,000 Principal

PV = ? $10,000 $10,000 $10,000 $10,000 $10,000 Interest

|—————|—————|—————|—————|—————→

1/2/98 12/31/98 12/31/99 12/31/00 12/31/01 12/31/02

	Market Rate on 1/2/98		
	10%	8%	12%
Present value of principal:			
$100,000($p_{\overline{5}|10\%}$)			
$100,000(.6209)[a]	$62,090		
$100,000($p_{\overline{5}|8\%}$)			
$100,000(.6806)[a]		$68,060	
$100,000($p_{\overline{5}|12\%}$)			
$100,000(.5674)[a]			$56,740
Present value of interest:			
$10,000($P_{\overline{5}|10\%}$)			
$10,000(3.7908)[b]	37,908		
$10,000($P_{\overline{5}|8\%}$)			
$10,000(3.9927)[b]		39,927	
$10,000($P_{\overline{5}|12\%}$)			
$10,000(3.6048)[b]			36,048
Issue price	$100,000[c]	$107,987	$92,788

[a]From Table B in Appendix A at the end of this text.
[b]From Table D in Appendix A at the end of this text.
[c]$2 rounding error.

hand, if the market rate of interest is 8 percent, investors will bid up the price of the bonds to $107,987 because the stated rate of 10 percent is more favorable than the current market rate. Thus, the *effective yield* will correspond to the market rate of 8 percent, and the bonds will sell at a *premium* of $7,987, or 107.987 percent of par. Finally, if the market rate of interest is 12 percent, the bond price will be only $92,788 because the stated rate is *less* than the market rate. The effective rate will be 12 percent, and the bonds will sell at a *discount* of $7,212, or 92.788 percent of par. On any subsequent interest date, a bond's market price can be calculated by discounting the remaining cash flows for interest and principal at the prevailing market rate of interest on that date.

The Oklahoma Gas Company bonds paid interest in addition to principal (face value). But these pricing concepts would apply equally well if a bond or note was non-interest-bearing (a zero-coupon bond or note). To illustrate, assume the same facts for Oklahoma Gas Company, except that the bonds are non-interest-bearing. Under these circumstances, the issue price of the bonds under the three different market interest rates is shown in the "present value of principal" portion of Exhibit 14-2. For example, if the market rate of interest was 10 percent on January 2, 1998, the bonds would sell for $62,090, a discount of $37,908 or 62.09 percent of par. As we stated with reference to the GMAC example, because the issuer (Oklahoma Gas Company) must pay investors $100,000 at maturity, the discount of $37,908 represents interest over the term of the bonds.

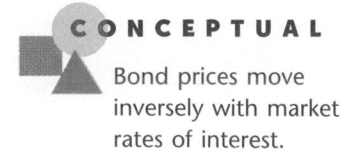

CONCEPTUAL

Bond prices move inversely with market rates of interest.

Exhibit 14–2 also shows that there is an inverse relationship between interest rates and prices of debt securities, such as bonds. When interest rates go up, bond prices go down and vice versa. This relationship holds both for interest-bearing and non-interest-bearing debt. To illustrate, the following information is reproduced from Exhibit 14–2 for the $100,000, 10 percent stated-rate bonds of Oklahoma Gas Company:

MARKET INTEREST RATE	PRICE OF BOND
8 percent	$107,987
10 percent	100,000
12 percent	92,788

If these same bonds were non-interest-bearing (zero-coupon bonds), the following interest rate/bond price relationships would result:

MARKET INTEREST RATE	PRICE OF BOND (PRINCIPAL ONLY PORTION OF EXHIBIT 14–2)
8 percent	$68,060
10 percent	62,090
12 percent	56,740

The inverse relationship between interest rates and bond prices is also presented in the illustration at the beginning of this chapter.

These same pricing concepts apply to debt that matures in installments, such as serial bonds and installment notes. Debt that has a series of maturities can be perceived as a "package" of term debt. To illustrate, assume that a company issues $100,000 in serial debt. The debt issue has a stated rate of interest of 6 percent and matures at the rate of $25,000 per year, beginning at the end of the first year. The issue price would be determined by discounting the interest and principal cash flows, shown in the following time diagram, at the market rate of interest on the issue date:

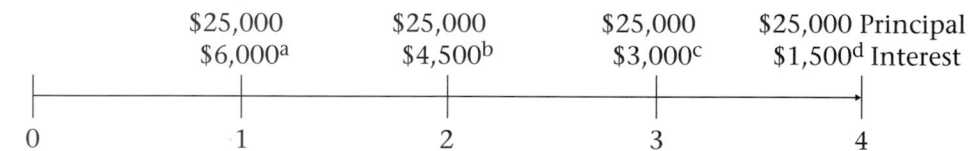

	$25,000	$25,000	$25,000	$25,000 Principal
	$6,000[a]	$4,500[b]	$3,000[c]	$1,500[d] Interest
0	1	2	3	4

[a].06 × $100,000.
[b].06 × $75,000.
[c].06 × $50,000.
[d].06 × $25,000.

Under the "yield-curve" theory as well as in practice, debt securities markets may use different discount rates to value different series, under the theory that the longer the life of a series, the higher the yield demanded by the market to compensate for increased risk. Under these circumstances, each series could be treated as term debt, and the pricing concepts illustrated for Oklahoma Gas Company's bonds applied to each.

real world

To illustrate, in 1996 the Oklahoma Development Finance Authority issued $10,000,000 in tax-exempt serial and term bonds in connection with the construction of a new engineering building on the Oklahoma State University campus. The following maturity schedule, extracted from information about the bond issue, shows how the market demanded a higher yield as the length of each series increased:

$10,000,000
The Oklahoma Development Finance Authority
Public Facilities Financing Program Revenue Bonds
(Oklahoma State University Project)
Series 1996

MATURITY SCHEDULE
$6,425,000 SERIAL BONDS

MATURITY	AMOUNT	RATE	YIELD	MATURITY	AMOUNT	RATE	YIELD
1997	$265,000	10.00%	3.95%	2005	$440,000	5.05%	5.10%
1998	295,000	9.50	4.20	2006	465,000	5.20	5.20
1999	320,000	8.00	4.45	2007	490,000	5.30	5.30
2000	345,000	5.70	4.60	2008	515,000	5.35	5.40
2001	365,000	4.70	4.70	2009	545,000	5.45	5.50
2002	385,000	4.75	4.80	2010	570,000	5.55	5.60
2003	400,000	4.85	4.90	2011	605,000	5.60	5.65
2004	420,000	4.95	5.00				

$3,575,000.00   5.625% Term Bonds Due July 1, 2016 @ 5.795%
(Plus Accrued Interest)

The series that matures in 2004, for example, was sold to yield 5 percent; that is, the market discounted the cash flows for interest and the $420,000 maturity amount at 5 percent. On the other hand, the series that matures in 2008 was sold to yield 5.4 percent; the market discounted the cash flows for interest and the $515,000 maturity amount at 5.4 percent.

Pricing Between Interest Dates

Bonds are not always issued on the date stated in the indenture or on an interest date. Frequently they are issued between interest dates because of time delays in the printing of the bonds, or the issuer's desire to wait until market interest rates are more favorable, or even because of a lack of demand. Furthermore, purchases and sales of outstanding bonds and notes *rarely* occur on an interest date.

When bonds or notes are issued between interest dates, the market price is equal to the present value of the debt, including any accrued interest, on the date of sale. Assume, for example, that the Oklahoma Gas Company bonds, dated January 2, 1998, are actually sold on May 1, 1998, when the market interest rate is 8 percent. The issue price would be calculated as follows:

Issue price at 1/2/98 (Exhibit 14–2). $107,987
Growth in bond value for first four months of 1998 at market rate of 8%
  ($107,987 × .08 × 4/12)   2,879
Issue price on 5/1/98 (including accrued interest) $110,866

Notice that because the market rate is 8 percent, four months' interest at 8 percent must be added to the January 2, 1998, issue price of $107,987. Thus, the issue price on May 1, 1998, is $110,866.

Exhibit 14–3 shows the pattern of values or issue prices of the Oklahoma Gas Company bonds throughout their term at an 8 percent yield. The initial issue price is $107,987. Each year the bonds' value grows at 8 percent. At the end of the first year, for example, *immediately before the first interest cash flow of $10,000*, the bonds have a value of $116,626 ($107,987 × 1.08). The first interest payment of $10,000 causes the bond value to decrease to $106,626. In Exhibit 14–3, the growth each year is shown by the solid, upward-sloping lines; the annual cash interest flows are

EXHIBIT 14–3	Value of a Five-Year, 10 Percent, Principal $100,000 Bond at a Yield of 8 Percent

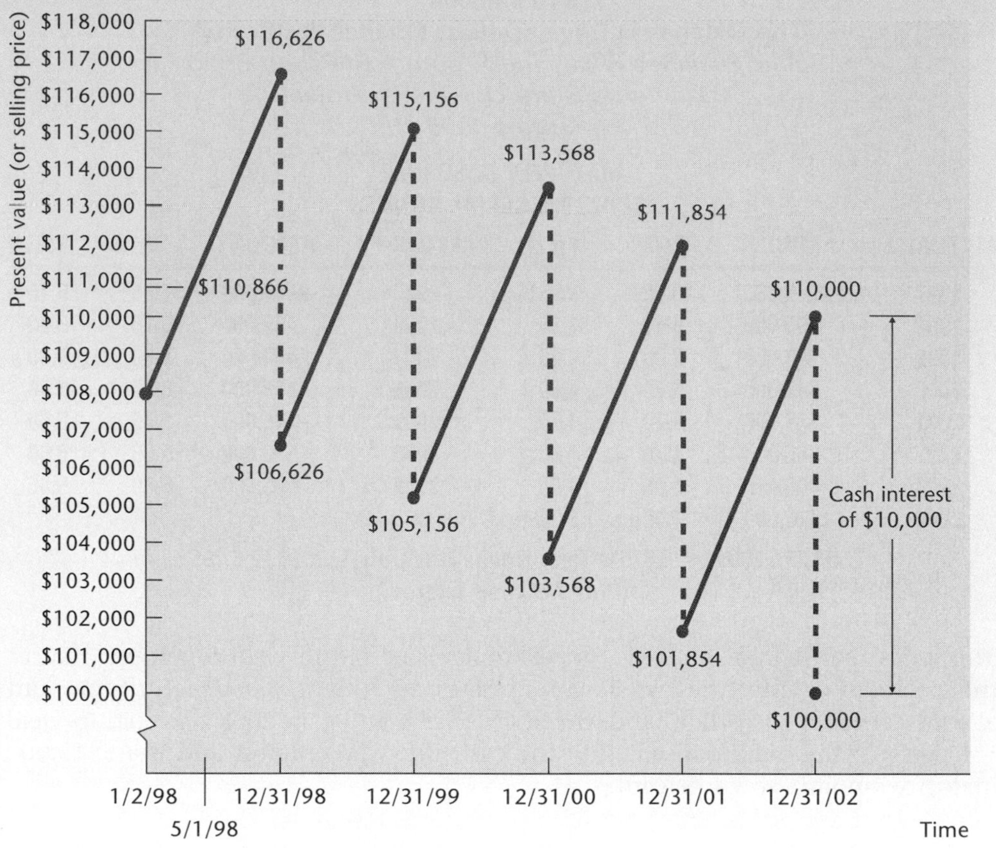

Present value (or selling price)

$118,000
$117,000
$116,000 ··· $116,626
$115,000 ··· $115,156
$114,000
$113,000 ··· $113,568
$112,000
$111,000 ─ $110,866 ··· $111,854
$110,000 ··· $110,000
$109,000
$108,000
$107,000
$106,000 ··· $106,626
$105,000 ··· $105,156
$104,000
$103,000 ··· $103,568
$102,000
$101,000 ··· $101,854
$100,000 ··· $100,000

Cash interest of $10,000

1/2/98   12/31/98   12/31/99   12/31/00   12/31/01   12/31/02
5/1/98   Time

shown by the vertical dashed lines. At the end of the fifth year (the maturity date), the bonds have a value of $100,000, which is the face value. The May 1, 1998, issue price of $110,866 also is shown in Exhibit 14–3. The issue price at an 8 percent yield at any other date can be determined by reference to the solid, upward-sloping lines. The concepts in Exhibit 14–3 also apply to notes.

In practice, bond prices are quoted net of the accrued interest at the *stated rate*. For example, the Oklahoma Gas Company bonds would be quoted on May 1, 1998, at $107,533, plus accrued interest of $3,333 from January 2, 1998:

Issue price on 5/1/98 (including interest)	**$110,866**
Less accrued interest from 1/2/98 at 10% stated rate	
($100,000 × .10 × 4/12)	(3,333)
Issue price, net of accrued interest	**$107,533**

A CCOUNTING FOR BONDS AND NOTES: BASIC METHODS

We are now ready to discuss the procedures used to account for bonds and notes. The procedures will be discussed from both the issuer's and the investor's standpoints. An unconditional receivable/payable is recognized when an exchange takes place. Initial recognition (recording) is based on the cash or cash equivalent exchange price on the exchange date. After the exchange date, unconditional receivables/payables, which are monetary assets/liabilities, are measured and recorded at their present value. As we shall see, this present value approach is equivalent to accounting for them using the effective interest method discussed in Appendix A at the end of this text.

In the following section, we will examine the accounting procedures for bonds or notes sold on an interest date. These procedures will include bonds issued at par and bonds issued at a discount or premium. Later, we will cover a more complicated procedure when bonds are issued between interest dates.

Bonds Issued at Par

Assume that on January 2, 1998, Oklahoma Gas Company issues its bonds at par to yield 10 percent. The following entries are necessary for the issuer (Oklahoma Gas Company) and the investor:

> **3** Prepare journal entries to record the issuance/purchase of a bond or note (1) on the contract date and (2) between interest dates.

ISSUER			**INVESTOR**		
Cash	100,000		Investment in		
Bonds payable . .		100,000	Oklahoma Gas		
			Company bonds . .	100,000	
			Cash		100,000

We stated earlier that the accounting concepts and procedures for an unconditional payable/receivable, such as the Oklahoma Gas Company bonds, apply equally to bonds and notes. This same accounting procedure would apply to a note. If Oklahoma Gas Company prepared a balance sheet immediately after the above transaction, it would report the bonds payable as a long-term liability.

After the issue date, assuming that both the issuer's and the investor's accounting period ends on December 31, the entry to record bond interest each year would be as follows:

ISSUER			**INVESTOR**		
Interest expense	10,000		Cash	10,000	
Cash		10,000	Interest revenue . . .		10,000
($100,000 × .10)					

At maturity, the issuer and investor would make the following entries:

ISSUER			**INVESTOR**		
Bonds payable	100,000		Cash	100,000	
Cash		100,000	Investment in		
			Oklahoma Gas		
			Company bonds .		100,000

Bonds Issued at a Discount or Premium

When bonds are issued at a **discount** or **premium,** both the issuer and the investor may record the discount or premium in a separate account. For the sake of simplicity—and because we believe that your understanding will be enhanced by using as few accounts as possible—we will record Oklahoma's bonds in one account, net of the discount or including the premium. This approach will also allow you to better relate the accounting for bonds and notes to the "saw-toothed" pattern of bond (and note) values shown in Exhibit 14–3.

To record the bonds described in Exhibit 14–2, first at a 12 percent market rate (at a discount) and then at an 8 percent market rate (at a premium), the issuer and investor would make the following entries:

	ISSUER			INVESTOR		

Bonds issued/purchased at a discount:

ISSUER		INVESTOR		
Cash 92,788		Investment in		
Bonds payable . .	92,788	Oklahoma Gas		
		Company bonds .	92,788	
		Cash		92,788

Bonds issued/purchased at a premium:

ISSUER		INVESTOR		
Cash 107,987		Investment in		
Bonds payable . .	107,987	Oklahoma Gas		
		Company bonds .	107,987	
		Cash		107,987

Nature of Discount and Premium

4 Explain the relationship that exists between (1) a bond or note's stated rate of interest and the market rate of interest and (2) the security's issue price and its face (maturity) value.

CONCEPTUAL

A bond discount increases interest expense (revenue) over the life of the bond. A bond premium reduces interest expense (revenue) over the life of the bond.

At the issue date, the issuer receives the par value plus the premium or less the discount. Over the term of the bonds, the issuer must pay interest at the stated rate and pay the face (par) value at maturity. Thus, when the bonds mature, the issuer pays more or less than it received at the time it issued the bonds. The difference between what it received on the date of issue and what it must pay at maturity is the discount or premium.

Earlier, we pointed out that bonds sell at a discount or premium because of differences between the current market interest rate and the interest rate stated on the bonds. If the market rate at the date of issue exceeds the stated rate, the bonds will be issued at a discount; if the market rate is less than the stated rate, the bonds will be issued at a premium. In Exhibit 14–2, for example, note that the 10 percent bonds were issued at a discount when the market rate was 12 percent and at a premium when the market rate was 8 percent. For bonds issued at a discount, the amount of the discount represents additional interest (over and above any cash interest) over the term of the bonds. For bonds issued at a premium, the amount of the premium represents a reduction in interest over the term of the bonds. These concepts and relationships are summarized in Exhibit 14–4.

Let us apply these concepts to the Oklahoma Gas Company example. Assume that the bonds are issued on January 2, 1998, and remain outstanding throughout their term. Oklahoma Gas Company's *total* interest expense and the investor's

EXHIBIT 14–4	Relationship Between the Issue of Debt at a Discount or Premium and Interest Over the Debt Term	
Transaction	**Issuer**	**Investor**
Debt issued at par; market rate = stated rate	Interest expense over term of debt equals cash interest paid	Interest revenue over term of debt equals cash interest received
Debt issued at a discount; market rate > stated rate	Interest expense over term of debt equals cash interest paid plus discount	Interest revenue over term of debt equals cash interest received plus discount
Debt issued at a premium; market rate < stated rate	Interest expense over term of debt equals cash interest paid less premium	Interest revenue over term of debt equals cash interest received less premium

total interest revenue under three different market interest rates—10 percent, 12 percent, and 8 percent—would be as follows:

IF ISSUED AT PAR TO YIELD 10%		IF ISSUED AT A DISCOUNT TO YIELD 12%		IF ISSUED AT A PREMIUM TO YIELD 8%	
Cash interest ($10,000[a] × 5) ..	$50,000	Cash interest ..	$50,000	Cash interest ..	$50,000
		Plus discount ..	7,212	Less premium ..	(7,987)
Total	$50,000	Total.........	$57,212	Total	$42,013

[a].10 × $100,000.

How should interest expense/interest revenue be recognized over the bond term? Should the amount of interest recognized each year be determined by applying the effective yield (interest) rate, or should equal amounts of interest be recognized each year? These choices describe the two methods of accounting for interest and for amortizing[2] discount/premium on bonds and notes—the straight-line method and the effective interest method. We will discuss each, beginning with the straight-line method. (These methods do not apply when bonds are issued/purchased at par value, because the stated rate on the bonds equals the market rate.)

Straight-Line Method

Under the **straight-line method,** interest expense or revenue is recognized as a *constant amount* each year, and any discount or premium is spread equally over the term of the bond or note. For bonds sold at a premium, annual interest expense equals the cash interest less the annual premium amortization. For bonds sold at a discount, annual interest expense equals the cash interest plus the annual discount amortization.

Assume, for example, that the Oklahoma Gas Company bonds in Exhibit 14–2 were sold at a discount of $7,212—that is, for $92,788. Since the bonds mature in five years, the annual discount amortization would be $1,442.40 ($7,212 ÷ 5). Thus, the annual interest expense would be $11,442.40 ($10,000 stated interest plus $1,442.40). Similar reasoning applies to the investor.

Assuming instead that the Oklahoma Gas Company bonds sold for $107,987, the annual premium amortization would be $1,597.40 ($7,987 ÷ 5). Oklahoma Gas Company's annual interest expense and the investor's annual interest revenue would be $8,402.60 ($10,000 – $1,597.40).

Effective Interest Method

The **effective interest method** is introduced and discussed in Appendix A on present value. Under this method, the issuer's periodic interest expense (the investor's periodic interest revenue) is determined by multiplying the instrument's book value at the beginning of each period by the effective interest rate (also called the yield rate) at the time the bonds were issued. (Because the effective rate was established in an exchange transaction when the bonds were issued, this rate may also be described as a *historical rate*.) The increase or decrease in the book value of

---

[2]According to *Statement of Financial Accounting Concepts No. 6,* terms such as *unamortized* or *deferred discount and premium* and *to amortize discount and premium* are carryovers from earlier days when debt discount was considered to be an amortizable asset. ["Elements of Financial Statements," *Statement of Financial Accounting Concepts No. 6* (Stamford, Conn.: FASB, 1985), para. 239.] We agree with this *Concept Statement* that these terms do not describe accurately (1) bond or note investments or payables or (2) the interest method of accounting for them. Thus, although the terms *discount and premium amortization* and *unamortized discount and premium* appear in this text and are part of acceptable present accounting practice, we have tried to downplay their usage by focusing instead on the interest expense/revenue and cash flows associated with these types of debt securities.

the bonds (discount or premium amortization) for each interest period is the difference between the interest calculated at the stated rate and the interest calculated at the effective rate. The schedules in Exhibits 14–5 and 14–6 illustrate the interest calculations and the related change in book value under the effective interest method. The schedule in each exhibit is based on the data in Exhibit 14–2. Exhibit 14–5 assumes that the bonds were issued at a discount for $92,788 to yield 12 percent; Exhibit 14–6 assumes that the bonds were issued at a premium for $107,987 to yield 8 percent.

EXHIBIT 14–5	Schedule of Interest and Book Value, Effective Interest Method—Discount Case			
Year Ending	(1) Interest Expense/Revenue[a]	(2) Cash[b]	(3) Increase in Book Value[c] (Discount Amortization)	(4) Book Value of Bonds[d]
				$ 92,788.00
12/31/98	$11,134.56	$10,000.00	$1,134.56	93,922.56
12/31/99	11,270.71	10,000.00	1,270.71	95,193.27
12/31/00	11,423.22	10,000.00	1,423.22	96,616.49
12/31/01	11,594.00	10,000.00	1,594.00	98,210.49
12/31/02	11,789.51[e]	10,000.00	1,789.51	100,000.00
	$57,212.00	$50,000.00	$7,212.00	

[a].12 × book value at beginning of year.
[b].10 × $100,000.
[c]Col. 1 minus col. 2.
[d]Previous book value balance plus col. 3. Also, previous book value plus col. 1 minus col. 2.
[e]Rounding error of $4.25.

EXHIBIT 14–6	Schedule of Interest and Book Value, Effective Interest Method—Premium Case			
Year Ending	(1) Interest Expense/Revenue[a]	(2) Cash[b]	(3) Decrease in Book Value[c] (Premium Amortization)	(4) Book Value of Bonds[d]
				$107,987.00
12/31/98	$ 8,638.96	$10,000.00	$1,361.04	106,625.96
12/31/99	8,530.08	10,000.00	1,469.92	105,156.04
12/31/00	8,412.48	10,000.00	1,587.52	103,568.52
12/31/01	8,285.48	10,000.00	1,714.52	101,854.00
12/31/02	8,146.00[e]	10,000.00	1,854.00	100,000.00
	$42,013.00	$50,000.00	$7,987.00	

[a].08 × book value at beginning of year.
[b].10 × $100,000.
[c]Col. 2 minus col. 1.
[d]Previous book value balance minus col. 3. Also, previous book value plus col. 1 minus col. 2.
[e]Rounding error of $2.32.

Note that under the effective interest method, each period the issuer's liability and the investor's investment (1) grow (increase) at the effective rate because of interest and (2) decline (decrease) because of the cash flows. This pattern, called the "saw-toothed curve," is introduced in the discussion of the effective interest method in Appendix A. In fact, Exhibit 14–3 shows this pattern. If the periodic interest exceeds the periodic cash flows, the asset/liability will increase over time. This concept applies in Exhibit 14–5, where the bonds were issued at a discount and gradually grow to maturity value. On the other hand, if the periodic interest is less than the periodic cash flow, the asset/liability will decrease over time. This concept applies in Exhibit 14–6, where the bonds were issued at a premium and gradually decrease to face value.

CONCEPTUAL

The effective interest method patterns a "saw-toothed curve."

Journal Entries   The information presented in Exhibits 14–5 and 14–6 can be used to prepare journal entries for both the issuer and the investor. For example, assuming that the Oklahoma Gas Company bonds were sold at a discount, the following entries would be required to record Oklahoma Gas Company's interest expense and the investor's interest revenue for the first year:

ISSUER			INVESTOR		
Interest expense.	11,134.56		Cash		10,000.00
Bonds			Investment in		
payable		1,134.56	Oklahoma Gas		
Cash		10,000.00	Company		
			bonds	1,134.56	
			Interest		
			revenue		11,134.56

Balance Sheet Reporting and Valuation   Exhibits 14–5 and 14–6 present the book (carrying) value of the bonds net of the discount or including the premium. The journal entries just presented are consistent with this approach. Should the issuer or investor wish to disclose the bonds' face value less discount (or plus premium), that information can be obtained easily from the exhibits. In Exhibit 14–5 the unamortized discount on December 31, 1999, is $4,806.73 ($100,000 face value – $95,193.27 book value); in Exhibit 14–6 the unamortized premium on December 31, 2000, is $3,568.52 ($103,568.52 book value – $100,000 face value).

Perhaps more important, at least from a conceptual standpoint, is the balance sheet valuation (measurement) of unconditional receivables and payables such as bonds and notes. There is an important relationship between the present value method of valuing monetary assets and the effective interest method of accounting for bonds and notes. In terms of balance sheet valuation, the effective interest method gives precisely the same results as would discounting the remaining cash flows at the historical (effective) rate of interest.

CONCEPTUAL

Under the effective interest method, monetary assets and monetary liabilities are valued at present value, and the discount rate is the historical (effective) rate.

To illustrate, refer to the book (carrying) values of the bonds in Exhibit 14–6. Except for slight rounding errors, these carrying values are exactly the same as the ones we would obtain if we discounted the remaining cash flows at the effective rate of 8 percent. The time diagrams and calculations shown in Exhibit 14–7 illustrate this relationship. Again, except for rounding errors, the present value amounts in Exhibit 14–7 are the same as the bond values in Exhibit 14–3. In fact, investors would use a present value approach to determine the issue prices in Exhibit 14–3.

Quarterly and Semiannual Interest Payments   Interest on bonds or notes often is paid quarterly or semiannually. To apply the effective interest method in these cases, we must use *interest periods* rather than years in determining selling prices and accounting for the debt. For example, for a five-year, 12 percent note paying 3 percent interest each quarter, we would determine the selling price by discounting the quarterly cash interest and maturity value for 20 periods at the effective rate per period. If the quarterly market rate at the date of sale were 2 percent, we would discount the cash flows at 2 percent per quarter for 20 quarters.

EXHIBIT 14-7	Valuation of Debt at Present Value

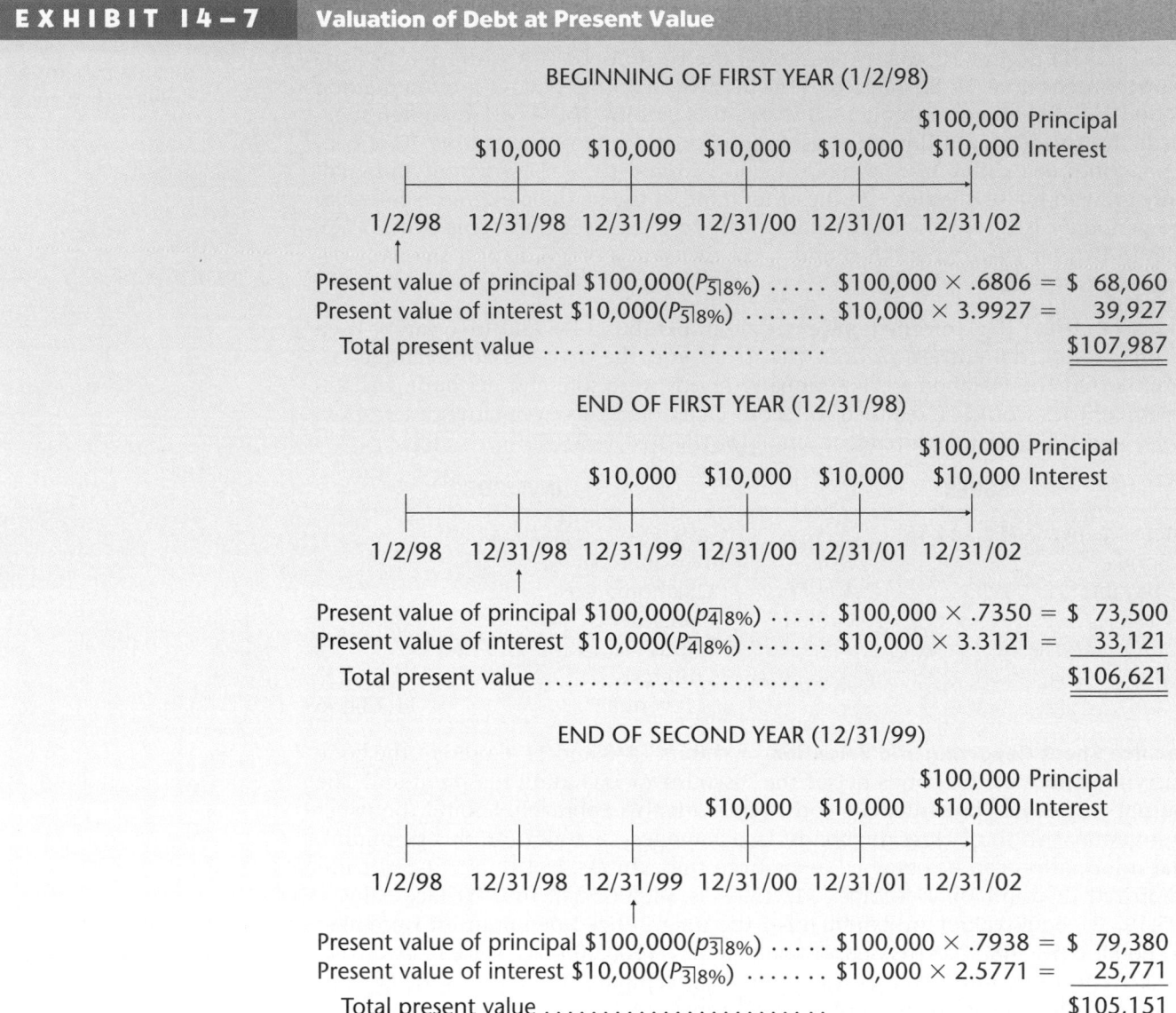

BEGINNING OF FIRST YEAR (1/2/98)

Present value of principal $100,000($P_{\overline{5}|8\%}$) . . . . . $100,000 \times .6806 = \$ 68,060$
Present value of interest $10,000($P_{\overline{5}|8\%}$) . . . . $10,000 \times 3.9927 = 39,927$
Total present value $107,987

END OF FIRST YEAR (12/31/98)

Present value of principal $100,000($p_{\overline{4}|8\%}$) . . . . . $100,000 \times .7350 = \$ 73,500$
Present value of interest $10,000($P_{\overline{4}|8\%}$) . . . . $10,000 \times 3.3121 = 33,121$
Total present value $106,621

END OF SECOND YEAR (12/31/99)

Present value of principal $100,000($p_{\overline{3}|8\%}$) . . . . . $100,000 \times .7938 = \$ 79,380$
Present value of interest $10,000($P_{\overline{3}|8\%}$) . . . . $10,000 \times 2.5771 = 25,771$
Total present value $105,151

Furthermore, the interest expense/revenue schedule would be constructed on a quarterly basis covering 20 periods. The effective interest rate of 2 percent per quarter would then be used to calculate the issuer's quarterly interest expense and the investor's quarterly interest revenue.

Application to Zero-Coupon Bonds   Effective interest method concepts also apply to zero-coupon bonds or notes. Assume that Oklahoma Gas Company issued non-interest-bearing notes that were sold to yield 10 percent. Earlier, we used Exhibit 14–2 to determine that the issue price would be $62,090. Exhibit 14–8 presents the interest expense/revenue schedule for these bonds. At the end of each year, the issuer's interest expense would be debited, and notes payable would be credited for the amounts in column (1). Investors would debit notes receivable and credit interest revenue for the same amounts.

Evaluation of Effective Interest and Straight-Line Methods

The effective interest method employs a constant *rate* of interest each period, which is applied to the book value of the bonds at the beginning of each period

END OF THIRD YEAR (12/31/00)

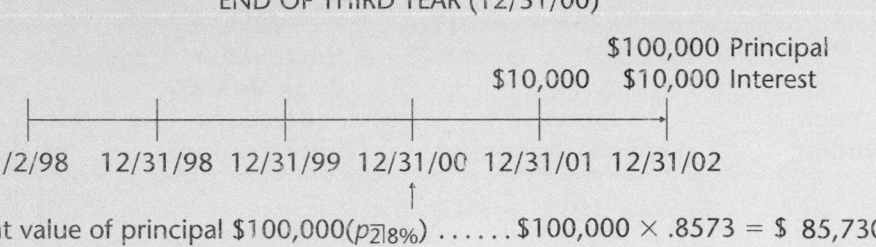

$100,000 Principal
$10,000 $10,000 Interest

| | | | | | |
1/2/98   12/31/98 12/31/99 12/31/00 12/31/01 12/31/02

Present value of principal $100,000($p_{\overline{2}|8\%}$) ...... $100,000 × .8573 = $ 85,730
Present value of interest $10,000($P_{\overline{2}|8\%}$) .... $10,000 × 1.7833 = 17,833
    Total present value $103,563

END OF FOURTH YEAR (12/31/01)

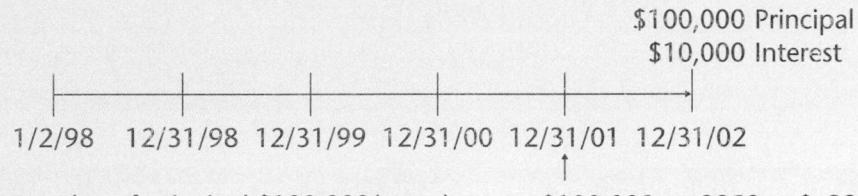

$100,000 Principal
$10,000 Interest

| | | | | | |
1/2/98   12/31/98 12/31/99 12/31/00 12/31/01 12/31/02

Present value of principal $100,000($p_{\overline{1}|8\%}$) ...... $100,000 × .9259 = $ 92,590
Present value of interest $10,000($P_{\overline{1}|8\%}$ .... $10,000 × .9259 = 9,259
    Total present value $101,849

END OF FIFTH YEAR (12/31/02)

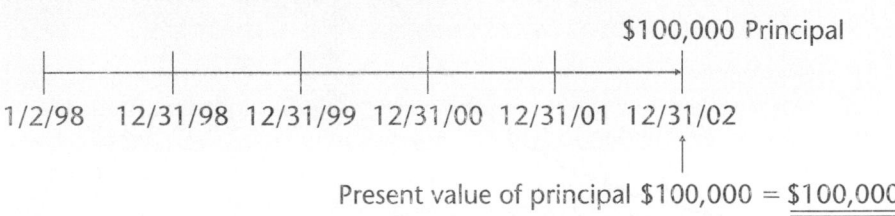

$100,000 Principal

| | | | | | |
1/2/98   12/31/98 12/31/99 12/31/00 12/31/01 12/31/02

Present value of principal $100,000 = $100,000

to determine interest expense/revenue. The amount of interest expense/revenue changes each period as the book value of the bonds changes. As the book value of bonds issued at a discount increases to face value, the periodic interest also increases. As the book value of bonds issued at a premium decreases to face value, the periodic interest also decreases. The straight-line method, in contrast, assigns a constant *amount* of interest to each period.

Though the straight-line method and the effective interest method result in the same amount of *total* interest over the life of the bonds, the interest patterns under the effective interest method conform more closely to economic reality. That is, *interest expense/revenue should be a function of the amount of the liability or investment.* Exhibit 14–9 compares the interest patterns under the two methods.

Historically, the straight-line method has been used widely in practice, probably because of its simplicity. *Under GAAP, however, the effective interest method must be used if the results are materially different from those of the straight-line method.*[3]

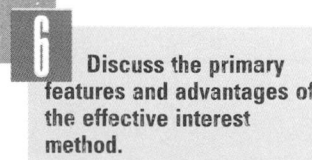

Discuss the primary features and advantages of the effective interest method.

CONCEPTUAL

The effective interest method conforms to economic reality—the amount of interest should be a function of the amount of the liability or the investment.

---

[3]"Interest on Receivables and Payables," *Opinions of the Accounting Principles Board No. 21* (New York: AICPA, 1971).

EXHIBIT 14–8	Schedule of Interest and Book Value, Effective Interest Method—Zero-Coupon Note		

Year Ending	(1) Interest Expense/Revenue[a]	(2) Increase in Book Value[b] (Discount Amortization)	(3) Book Value of Note[c]
			$ 62,090.00
12/31/98	$6,209.00	$6,209.00	68,299.00
12/31/99	6,829.90	6,829.90	75,128.90
12/31/00	7,512.89	7,512.89	82,641.79
12/31/01	8,264.18	8,264.18	90,905.97
12/31/02	9,090.60	9,090.60	100,000.00[d]

[a].10 × book value at beginning of year.
[b]Same as col. 1.
[c]Previous book value balance plus col. 3.
[d]Rounding error of $3.43.

EXHIBIT 14–9	Interest Patterns Under the Straight-Line and Effective Interest Methods of Accounting for Bond Discounts and Premiums

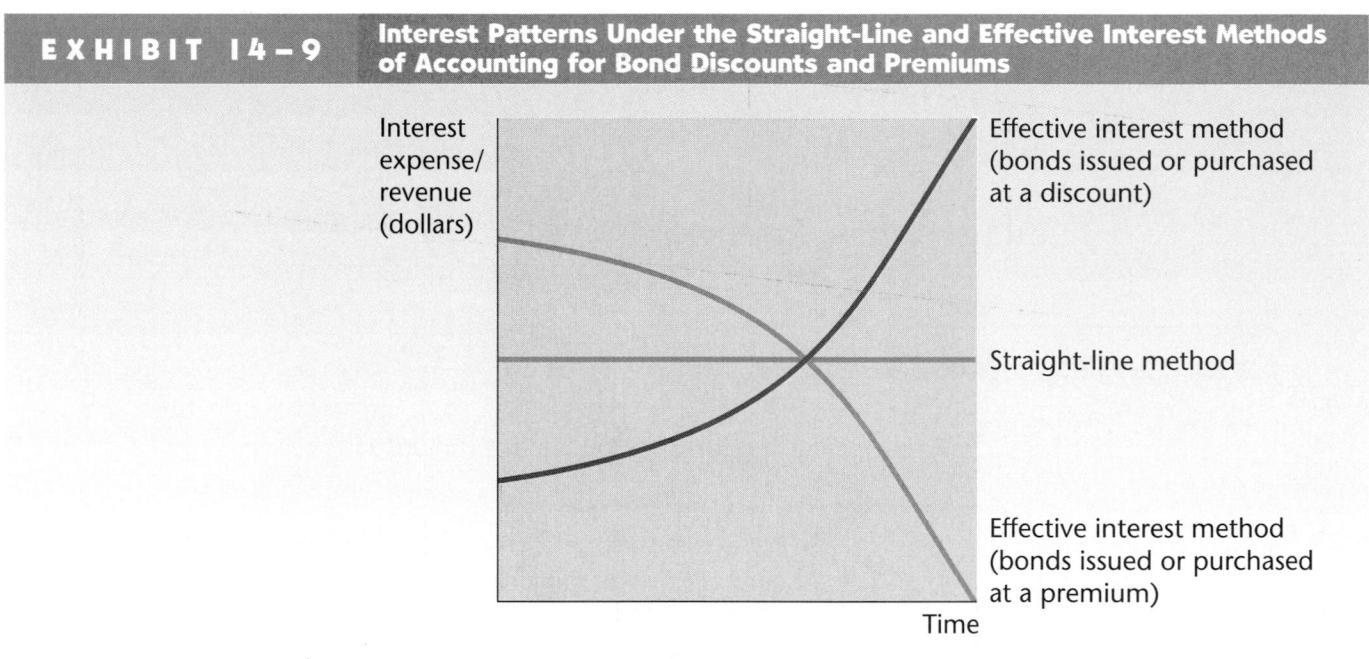

Because materiality varies among companies, the method used by the bond issuer may differ from the method used by the investor. Because of the conceptual superiority of the effective interest method and because computer spreadsheet technology has simplified its application in practice, the effective interest method will be used throughout the remainder of this chapter, as well as in the end-of-chapter assignment material.

To this point we have discussed the basic concepts in accounting for unconditional payables/receivables, such as bonds and notes. We have also seen how these financial instruments and their related interest appear on the financial statements. In the following section we will discuss some additional considerations in accounting for bonds and notes.

ACCOUNTING FOR BONDS AND NOTES: ADDITIONAL CONSIDERATIONS

The previous section covered the basic concepts in accounting for bonds and notes. In this section we discuss some additional considerations related to accounting for bonds and notes. These considerations include accounting for serial debt, debt exchanged for noncash assets, debt and other obligations exchanged for cash, interest accruals when a debt security's interest period does not coincide with a company's accounting period, and accounting for debt issued between interest dates. Although the accounting procedures for these additional considerations are a bit more involved, the basic concepts covered in the previous section continue to apply.

Serial Debt Issued at a Premium or Discount

Accounting for serial debt is very similar to accounting for term debt. The only difference is that in addition to cash flows for interest, there are also cash flows for maturing amounts of principal. Exhibit 14–10 presents an interest and book value schedule for an issuer of serial debt. Notice that an additional column has been inserted in this exhibit to show the principal amounts that mature each period. In addition to the required journal entries each year for interest expense, the following additional entry would be made at the end of 1999 and 2000 to record the maturing debt:

Bonds (or notes) payable 20,000
    Cash   20,000

E X H I B I T 1 4 – 1 0   Schedule of Interest and Book Value—Serial Debt

Facts:
1. Serial debt ($40,000 face value) issued on January 1, 1998, for $38,364.
2. Stated interest rate, 10 percent.
3. Effective interest rate, 12 percent.
4. Debt matures at the rate of $20,000 per year, beginning December 31, 1999.

Year Ending	(1) Interest Expense[a]	(2) Cash[b]	(3) Increase in Book Value[c] (Discount Amortization)	(4) Decrease in Book Value (Face Value of Debt Maturing)[d]	(5) Book Value of Debt[e]
					$38,364
12/31/98	$ 4,604	$ 4,000	$ 604	$ —	38,968
12/31/99	4,676	4,000	676	20,000	19,644
12/31/00	2,356[f]	2,000	356	20,000	–0–
	$11,636	$10,000	$1,636	$40,000	

[a].12 × book value of debt at beginning of year.
[b].10 × par value of debt outstanding.
[c]Col. 1 minus col. 2.
[d]Given.
[e]Previous book value balance plus col. 3 minus col. 4.
[f]Rounded by $1.

Debts Exchanged for Noncash Assets

Most debt transactions are for cash; an issuer of debt receives cash or an investor pays cash in exchange for a bond or note investment. Occasionally, however, a company will accept noncash consideration, such as a note, in exchange for merchandise or other assets or for services performed. Also, a company may acquire a noncash asset, such as a building or land, by issuing debt. Although the present value of the debt and the fair value of the noncash consideration exchanged are assumed to be equal, circumstances may be such that one of these values is uncertain or unknown. *APB Opinion No. 21* requires that in those circumstances, the present value of the note or the fair value of the noncash consideration, whichever is more reliable, should be used to value the exchange.

Assume, for example, that at the beginning of year 1, Carl, Inc., sold a tract of land that originally cost $9,000. In return, Carl accepted a $15,000 serial note payable as follows: end of year 1, $5,000; end of year 2, $5,000; end of year 3, $5,000. The note also paid interest at the rate of 2 percent each year. Because five appraisers had given five very different estimates of the land's value, its fair value was not objectively determinable. The market rate of interest at the beginning of year 1 for notes of similar risk was 10 percent.

The present value of the note and imputed fair value of the land would be determined as follows:[4]

Present value of principal (present value of a
$5,000 ordinary annuity for three years at 10%):
$\quad$ $5,000($P_{\overline{3}|10\%}$) .... $5,000 × 2.4869 = $12,435
Present value of interest:
$\quad$ $300($p_{\overline{1}|10\%}$) .... $300 × .9091 = $\quad$ 273
$\quad$ $200($p_{\overline{2}|10\%}$) .... 200 × .8264 = $\quad$ 165
$\quad$ $100($p_{\overline{3}|10\%}$) .... 100 × .7513 = $\quad\underline{\quad 75}$
$\quad$ **Total present value** .... $\underline{\underline{\$12,948}}$

The entry to record the sale would be:

Notes receivable 12,948		
$\quad$ Land		9,000
$\quad$ Gain on sale of land ($12,948 – $9,000).		3,948

At the end of each year, interest revenue would be calculated under the effective interest method. For example, for year 1 the entry to record the interest and maturing note would be as follows:

Cash	300	
Notes receivable ($1,295 – $300)	995	
$\quad$ Interest revenue (.10 × $12,948)		1,295
Cash	5,000	
$\quad$ Notes receivable.		5,000

-----

[4]A time diagram would appear as follows:

^{a}$15,000 × .02.
^{b}$10,000 × .02.
^{c}$5,000 × .02.

If the fair value of the land were known with a high degree of certainty, it could be used to establish the exchange price. In that case the interest rate implicit in the exchange would be calculated for purposes of recording interest revenue.[5]

Debt and Other Obligations Exchanged for Cash

Occasionally a company may lend money and receive, along with a note, the *right to buy assets,* such as merchandise, from the borrower at a discount from regular selling prices. The lender may be willing to accept a non-interest-bearing note or a note with an unreasonably low rate of interest and to sacrifice cash equal to the face amount of the note in return for the right to buy at a discount. The borrower, in turn, may be willing to grant the discount in exchange for a lower-than-market rate of interest. Thus, the cash exchanged represents not just a borrowing but a prepayment on assets to be purchased.

Before *Opinion No. 21* was issued, many companies ignored the right (obligation) that had been acquired (incurred) in such cases and recorded the note at its face value. *Opinion No. 21* requires that the right acquired (obligation incurred) be recorded as an asset (liability) at an amount equal to the discount on the note. That amount is determined by discounting the cash flows associated with the note at the then-current rate of interest.

Assume, for example, that at the beginning of year 1 Gibco Automart accepts a two-year, $6,000 non-interest-bearing note from Carter Supply Company, plus the right to purchase 200 cases of oil from Carter at a discount price in exchange for $6,000. Notice that the right to buy at a discount has all of the characteristics of an asset that we discussed in Chapter 2. Similarly, the obligation to sell merchandise at a discount has all of the characteristics of a liability. If the current market rate of interest is 10 percent, Gibco and Carter should record the transaction as follows:

GIBCO AUTOMART		**CARTER SUPPLY COMPANY**	
Notes receivable 4,958		Cash 6,000	
Prepaid purchases 1,042		Notes payable	4,958
Cash	6,000	Unearned revenue . . .	1,042

The present value of the note is calculated by multiplying $6,000 times the present value of $1 for two years at 10% (from Appendix A, Table B).

$$\$6,000 \times .8264 = \$4,958$$

The recorded amount for prepaid purchases and unearned revenue is calculated by subtracting the note's present value from its face value:

$$\$6,000 - \$4,958 = \$1,042$$

To recognize interest over the two-year period, Gibco Automart and Carter Supply Company would use the effective interest method:

GIBCO AUTOMART		**CARTER SUPPLY COMPANY**	
END OF YEAR 1			
Notes receivable 496		Interest expense 496	
Interest revenue	496	Notes payable	496
(.10 × $4,958)			
END OF YEAR 2			
Notes receivable 545		Interest expense 545	
Interest revenue	545	Notes payable	545
[.10 × ($4,958 + $496)]			

---

[5]In this example, it would be necessary to use a trial-and-error method to find the effective interest rate, because the cash flows are not uniform.

At the end of the second year, when the note is exchanged for cash at maturity, its carrying value would be $6,000 ($4,958 + $496 + $545).

Gibco's asset, prepaid purchases, would be allocated to purchases or inventory in proportion to the number of cases of oil purchased each year, as compared with the total purchases to be made. Carter Supply's liability, unearned revenue, would be allocated to sales in a similar manner. For example, if Gibco purchased 60 cases of oil from Carter Supply during the first year, the following entries would be appropriate:

GIBCO AUTOMART		CARTER SUPPLY COMPANY	
Purchases (inventory) 313		Unearned revenue 313	
Prepaid purchases	313	Sales.	313
[(60/200) × $1,042]			

In accordance with the historical cost (exchange price) principle, the addition to Gibco's purchases/sales in year 1 is considered part of the cost of those purchases because Gibco has sacrificed a portion of the right to purchase at a discount. The same line of reasoning applies to Carter Supply. In accordance with the realization principle, Carter has fulfilled a portion of its obligation to Gibco, so part of the unearned revenue has now been earned.

Debt Issue Costs

A company incurs many types of expenditures when it issues bonds, such as the cost of printing the bonds, the cost of preparing the prospectus, attorneys' fees, and sales commissions if the bonds are sold through a broker. Issue costs for notes are usually minimal. Under GAAP, the issue costs are recorded as an asset, **deferred debt issue costs,** and are expensed over the period from the issue date to the maturity date. The rationale for this practice is that the company should expense the costs over the period in which the debt proceeds contribute to the earning process.

On the other hand, some accountants argue that debt issue costs should be treated as a reduction in the proceeds from the issue price. This method either increases the debt discount or decreases the debt premium. Therefore, the issue costs effectively increase interest expense over the term of the debt. Debt issue costs have been cited by the FASB in *Statement of Financial Accounting Concepts No. 6* as an expenditure that does *not* meet the definition of an asset.[6] Thus, the second method is preferable conceptually and is supported by *Statement of Financial Accounting Concepts No. 6.*

Accruals When Interest and Accounting Periods Do Not Coincide

A company's accounting period seldom coincides with the interest period stated in the bond indenture or on the note. In the Oklahoma Gas Company example, we made the simplifying assumption that they did coincide, which permitted us to focus on conceptual issues. Such a coincidence rarely occurs in practice, however. If the two periods do not coincide, adjusting entries must be made for accruing interest on the bond or note.

Assume that on March 1, 1998, a company issues a five-year note with a face value of $100,000. The note is dated March 1, 1998, and has a stated interest rate of 12 percent, payable 6 percent semiannually on September 1 and March 1. The

---

[6]"Elements of Financial Statements," *Statement of Financial Accounting Concepts No. 6* (Stamford, Conn.: FASB, 1985), para. 237. In Chapter 1 we pointed out that *Concepts Statements* do not constitute or modify generally accepted accounting principles.

EXHIBIT 14–11 Partial Schedule of Interest, Book Value, and Adjusting Entries

Six Months Ended	(1) Interest Expense[a]	(2) Cash[b]	(3) Increase in Book Value[c] (Discount Amortization)	(4) Book Value of Notes[d]
				$86,581.00
9/1/98	$6,926.48	$6,000.00	$ 926.48	87,507.48
3/1/99	7,000.60	6,000.00	1,000.60	88,508.08
9/1/99	7,080.65	6,000.00	1,080.65	89,588.72
3/1/01	7,167.10	6,000.00	1,167.10	90,755.82

9/1/98	Interest expense..	6,926.48	
	Notes payable		926.48
	Cash		6,000.00
12/31/98	Interest expense (4/6 × $7,000.60)	4,667.07	
	Notes payable (4/6 × $1,000.60).........................		667.07
	Interest payable (4/6 × $6,000)		4,000.00
3/1/99	Interest payable	4,000.00	
	Interest expense (2/6 × $7,000.60)	2,333.53	
	Notes payable (2/6 × $1,000.60).....................		333.53
	Cash		6,000.00
9/1/99	Interest expense.......................................	7,080.65	
	Notes payable		1,080.65
	Cash		6,000.00
12/31/99	Interest expense (4/6 × $7,167.10)	4,778.07	
	Notes payable (4/6 × $1,167.10).......................		778.07
	Interest payable (4/6 × $6,000)		4,000.00
3/1/00	Interest payable	4,000.00	
	Interest expense (2/6 × $7,167.10)	2,389.03	
	Notes payable (2/6 × $1,167.10).......................		389.03
	Cash		6,000.00

[a].08 × book value at beginning of period.
[b].06 × $100,000.
[c]Col. 1 minus col. 2.
[d]Previous book value balance plus col. 3.

note is issued for $86,581 to yield an effective rate of 8 percent semiannually.[7] The issuing company's accounting period ends on December 31. Exhibit 14–11 shows a partial schedule of interest and book value and adjusting entries through March 1, 2000. Notice that the schedule is based on the debt's *interest periods,* not on the issuer's accounting periods. When interest periods do not coincide with a company's accounting periods, the amounts in the schedule must be apportioned to the proper accounting periods. For example, the entries on December 31 and March 1 for the first two years are based on the data for the six months ended March 1, 1999, and March 1, 2000, and on the fact that the company closes its books on December 31.

---

[7]The issue price is calculated as follows:

$$\text{Present value of principal} = \$100,000(p_{\overline{10}|8\%}) = \$100,000(.4632) = \$46,320$$
$$\text{Present value of interest} = \$6,000(P_{\overline{10}|8\%}) = \$6,000(6.7101) = \underline{40,261}$$
$$\underline{\underline{\$86,581}}$$

Debt Issued or Purchased Between Interest Dates

Notes are usually written and issued at the same time; that is, a note is prepared, dated, and issued simultaneously. However, an entity may not always issue bonds on the date specified in the bond indenture. And because bonds and notes are often traded on organized security markets, investors rarely purchase them on an interest payment date. When debt is issued between interest dates, the accounting issues are twofold: (1) accounting for accrued interest at the issue date and (2) accounting for interest expense/revenue for the first (partial) interest period. If the debt is issued at par (face value), these two issues are uncomplicated. If the debt is issued at a premium or discount, they are somewhat more complex. The following sections address both cases.

Debt Issued at Par (Face Value)

We pointed out earlier (page 721) that when debt is issued between interest dates, the exchange price includes the growth in (interest on) the debt from the previous interest date to the issue date. For example, assume that a $100,000, five-year bond pays interest at a stated rate of 12 percent annually. It is dated January 1, 1998, but is issued on April 1, 1998, at face value plus accrued interest from January 1, 1998. (Note that because the bond is issued at face value, the market rate of interest is also 12 percent.) The issuer's fiscal period ends on December 31. Under these assumptions, the issue price is $103,000:

Issue price at 1/1/98	**$100,000**
Add growth in bond value for first three months of 1998 at _market_ rate of 12% ($100,000 × .12 × 3/12)	**3,000**
Issue price on 4/1/98 (including interest)	**$103,000**
Less accrued interest from 1/1/98 to 4/1/98 at _stated_ rate of 12% ($100,000 × .12 × 3/12)	**(3,000)**
Issue price, net of accrued interest	**$100,000**

The entry to record the issue is as follows:

Cash	103,000	
Bonds payable		100,000
Interest payable		3,000

When the first interest payment is made on December 31, 1998, the following entry is made:

Interest payable	3,000	
Interest expense	9,000	
Cash		12,000

Interest expense of $9,000 for the year ending December 31, 1998, represents interest from April 1, 1995, through December 31, 1998 ($100,000 × .12 × 9/12 = $9,000), which is consistent with the length of time the bonds were outstanding during 1998.

Debt Issued at a Premium or Discount

Although slightly more complicated, the same concepts and procedures apply to debt issued at a premium or discount between interest dates. To illustrate, assume that a company with a December 31 fiscal year issues two-year, 8 percent term bonds with a maturity value of $200,000. The bonds are dated January 1, 1998, and pay $8,000 interest semiannually (.04 × $200,000 = $8,000) on July 1 and December 31. They are issued on March 1, 1998, for $196,123, which includes accrued interest from January 1, 1998, to March 1, 1998, to yield 5 percent semi-annually:

Issue price at 1/1/98:

Present value of principal ($200,000 × $p_{\overline{4}	5\%}$ = $200,000 × .8227)	$164,540
Present value of interest ($8,000 × $P_{\overline{4}	5\%}$ = $8,000 × 3.5460)	28,368
Issue price at 1/1/98	$192,908
Add growth in bond value for first two months of 1998 at *market* rate	
of 5% semiannually ($192,908 × .05 × 2/6)	3,215
Issue price on 3/1/98 (including interest)	$196,123
Less accrued interest from 1/1/98 to 3/1/98 at *stated* (semiannual) rate	
of 4% ($200,000 × .04 × 2/6)	(2,667)
Issue price, net of accrued interest	$193,456

The entry to record the issue on March 1, 1998, is as follows:

Cash ($193,456 + $2,667)	196,123	
Bonds payable		193,456
Interest payable		2,667

Note that when debt is issued at a premium or discount between interest dates, *interest expense for the first (partial) period must be calculated under the assumption that the debt security was issued on the security's contract date—the date on which interest begins to accrue.* (If the security is not a new issue, the assumption is that it was purchased after the previous interest date.) This assumption is necessary to achieve consistency between the applicable effective rate and the compounding period that underlies the effective rate.

This concept is applied in the construction of the schedule of interest and book value shown in Exhibit 14–12. The schedule, which is based on the example on page 736 and above, is constructed as of January 1, 1998 (when the book value of the bonds was $192,908), even though the bonds were not issued until March 1, 1998. Thus, interest expense and the increase in book value for the four months from March 1, 1998, to July 1, 1998, would be calculated by multiplying the line entries for the first interest period, ending July 1, 1998, by the fraction of time the bonds were outstanding. Interest expense for the four months ending July 1, 1998, would be $6,430 (4/6 × $9,645). Because the compounding period is semiannual,

EXHIBIT 14–12	Schedule of Interest and Book Value for Debt Issued Between Interest Dates			
Six Months Ending	**(1) Interest Expense[a]**	**(2) Cash[b]**	**(3) Increase in Book Value[c] (Discount Amortization)**	**(4) Book Value of Bonds[d]**
				$192,908
7/1/98	$ 9,645	$ 8,000	$1,645	194,553
12/31/98	9,728	8,000	1,728	196,281
7/1/99	9,814	8,000	1,814	198,095
12/31/99	9,905	8,000	1,905	200,000
	$39,092	$32,000	$7,092	

[a].05 × book value of bonds at beginning of period.
[b]$200,000 × .04.
[c]Col. 1 minus col. 2.
[d]Previous book value balance plus col. 3.

interest expense of $6,430 may also be calculated as $192,908 × .05 × 4/6 = $6,430. The fraction used is 4/6 because the bonds were outstanding for four months of the six-month interest period.

Journal entries to record interest expense for the first two interest periods would be as follows:

7/1/98	Interest expense (4/6 × $9,645)	6,430	
	Interest payable	2,667	
	Bonds payable (4/6 × $1,645).		1,097
	Cash.		8,000
12/31/98	Interest expense	9,728	
	Bonds payable.		1,728
	Cash		8,000

ⓈUMMARY OF ACCOUNTING CONCEPTS FOR BONDS AND NOTES

7 Explain the basic accounting concepts for bonds and notes.

CONCEPTUAL

Present value concepts underlie debt recognition and measurement.

To this point, we have discussed the basic recognition and measurement principles for one type of fundamental financial instrument—unconditional receivables/payables. Our discussion focused on bonds and notes as examples of unconditional receivables/payables. We covered recognition and measurement (1) at the time these instruments are issued/purchased and (2) during the period over which they are outstanding.

The concept of *present value* underlies recognition and measurement both at the issue/acquisition date and subsequent to that date. At the issue/acquisition date, bonds and notes are valued at the present value of their future cash flows, using a discount rate equal to the market interest rate for instruments of similar risk. This interest rate is called the *effective rate* or *historical rate,* because it is an interest rate established at the exchange (issue/acquisition) date.

After the issue/acquisition date, the effective interest method is used to account for bonds and notes. Under the effective interest method, the bond/note investment or liability increases each period because of interest (at the effective rate) and decreases each period by any cash flows. Use of the effective interest method is equivalent to valuing these instruments at the present value of their future cash flows, where the interest (discount) rate used is the historical (effective) rate.

Up to this point we have not addressed the use of *current market rates of interest* in valuing and accounting for bonds and notes after their issuance or acquisition. However, we have seen that market prices (fair values) of debt securities move *inversely* with market interest rates. *Decreases in market interest rates (relative to the historical rate) cause the market prices (fair values) of debt securities to exceed their carrying values. Conversely, increases in market interest rates (relative to the historical rate) cause the market prices (fair values) of debt securities to fall below their carrying values.*

CONCEPTUAL

Valuing debt securities at fair value increases relevance and is reliable.

Many people believe that valuing debt securities at market prices (fair value)—especially those securities held for sale or potential sale—provides information that is useful in predicting, assessing, and evaluating the cash flows related to those securities. They point out that in addition to providing *relevant* information, fair value information is *reliable* because debt securities are usually traded on organized security exchanges. In summary, they believe that for certain debt securities, fair values provide more useful information than "historical values." Reporting debt security investments at fair value is the subject matter of *Statement No. 115,* "Accounting for Certain Investments in Debt and Equity Securities." It is discussed in the following section.

Accounting for and Reporting Certain Debt Securities Held as Investments

As we saw in the previous chapter, *Statement No. 115* requires that certain debt and equity securities held as investments be reported at fair value and that unrealized gains and losses from holding those securities be reported in firms' financial statements. We applied these "mark-to-market" procedures to equity securities in Chapter 13. The following discussion applies them to debt securities held as investments.

Statement No. 115 Definition of a Debt Security

Statement No. 115 defines a debt security as "any security representing a creditor relationship with an enterprise."[8] Examples of debt securities include corporate bonds, convertible debt, U.S. Treasury securities, municipal securities, commercial paper, redeemable preferred stock, and all secured debt instruments. Trade accounts receivable arising from credit sales and loans and notes receivable arising from consumer, commercial, and real estate lending activities by financial institutions are *not* considered debt securities under this definition unless they have been securitized. The primary reason for excluding instruments such as consumer loans and individual notes from the *Statement No. 115* definition has to do with cost/benefit considerations. Given that consumer loans and individual notes receivable normally are not traded in organized exchange markets, the FASB was concerned about the effort and cost required to make reasonable estimates of fair value for those types of instruments. In the next section we will discuss the classification of debt securities held as investments under *Statement No. 115*.

Classification of Debt Securities

Statement No. 115 requires that for purposes of applying fair value, debt securities be classified as follows:

1. Held-to-maturity securities.

2. Trading securities.

3. Available-for-sale securities.

> **8** Describe the three classifications of debt securities held as investments under *Statement No. 115*.

It may help to view these three categories on a continuum, with held-to-maturity securities at one end and trading securities at the opposite end. Available-for-sale securities would fall somewhere in between. Keeping this continuum in mind will be useful as we discuss the reporting procedures for securities in each class.

Held-to-Maturity Debt Securities

A debt security should be classified as **held to maturity** only if the investor has the positive intent and ability to hold it until it matures. Although a significant change in circumstances could cause a change in the investor's intent,[9]

---

[8]*Statement No. 115,* para. 137, also defines a *security* as a share, participation, or other interest in property or in an enterprise of the issuer or an obligation of the issuer that meets three characteristics: (1) either is represented by an instrument issued in bearer or registered form or, if not represented by an instrument, is registered in books maintained to record transfers by or on behalf of the issuer; (2) is of a type commonly dealt in on securities exchanges or markets or, when represented by an instrument, is commonly recognized in any area in which it is issued or dealt in as a medium for investment; and (3) either is one of a class or series or by its terms is divisible into a class or series of shares, participations, interests, or obligations.
[9]Paragraph 8 of *Statement No. 115* discusses several circumstances that could cause a change of intent but that would not be inconsistent with the original held-to-maturity classification. These circumstances include a deterioration in the issuing company's creditworthiness, a tax law change that eliminates or reduces the tax-exempt status of interest on the debt security, and a change in statutory or regulatory requirements that might force or cause an investor to dispose of a held-to-maturity debt security. These regulatory requirements apply primarily to financial institutions.

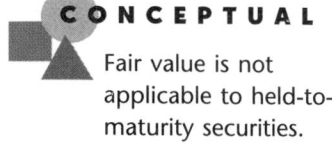

a debt security should not be classified as held to maturity if the investor intends to hold the security for an indefinite period or sell it in response to changes in market interest rates, liquidity needs, availability of and yield on alternative investments, funding sources and terms, and foreign currency risk.

Fair value reporting is not applicable to held-to-maturity securities. Securities in this class are accounted for using the effective interest method and are reported on the balance sheet at the carrying amount from using the effective interest method. (The effective-interest-method carrying amount is called "amortized cost" in *Statement No. 115.*) The logic of this requirement is that if management intends to hold investment securities to maturity, fair (market) values are not relevant for predicting, assessing, and evaluating the associated cash flows.

Trading and Available-for-Sale Securities

Debt securities *not* held to maturity fall into one of two classes—**trading securities** and **available-for-sale securities.** As stated in Chapter 13, trading securities are securities that are held for resale in the near term. The objective of buying and holding trading securities is to sell them and generate profits due to short-term differences between cost and sales price. Trading securities are usually held by companies that buy and sell securities on a regular basis as part of their primary operating activities. For example, financial institutions normally hold trading securities, which they buy and sell regularly. Profits result from differences between buying and selling prices.

In terms of length of time held and intent, available-for-sale securities fall somewhere in between held-to-maturity securities and trading securities. The available-for-sale classification is almost a *default* classification. That is, *Statement No. 115* requires that debt securities that are not classified as either trading securities or held-to-maturity securities be classified as available-for-sale securities.

Reporting of Fair Value and Changes in Fair Value

Statement No. 115 requires that trading securities and available-for-sale securities be reported at fair value on the balance sheet and that changes in fair value (unrealized gains and losses) be reported:

1. On the income statement if the security is classified as a trading security.

2. As a component of other comprehensive income if the security is classified as available for sale.

These "mark-to-market" procedures have no effect on the calculation of periodic interest revenue using the effective interest method. That is, although a debt security is reported at fair value (marked to market) at the end of each period for financial reporting purposes, the periodic calculation of interest revenue is based on the carrying value that results from the effective interest method.

In order to account for and report a debt security at fair value, one must first calculate the unrealized gain or loss from holding it over the accounting period. The next section explains this procedure.

Calculation of Unrealized Holding Gain or Loss

To illustrate the mark-to-market procedure, assume that on January 1, 1999, Troccoli Company purchased zero-coupon debt securities issued by Finley-Mart Corporation at a cost of $34,150. The securities had a maturity value of $50,000 and a maturity date of December 31, 2002. They were purchased to yield 10 percent. A schedule of interest and book value and the calculation of unrealized holding gains and losses for these securities appear in Exhibit 14–13. Column 7 shows Troccoli's unrealized holding gain/(loss) at the end of each year—the difference between the securities'

| EXHIBIT 14–13 | Schedule of Interest and Book Value and Calculation of Unrealized Holding Gains and Losses |

End of Year	(1) Interest Revenue[a]	(2) Increase in Book Value (Discount Amortization)[b]	(3) Effective Interest Method Carrying Value[c]	(4) Fair Value[d]	(5) Change in Fair Value[e]	(6) Adjusting Entry for Gain (Loss)[f]	(7) Unrealized Holding Gain (Loss) End of Year[g]
			$34,150	$34,150			
1999	$3,415	$3,415	37,565	39,000	$4,850	$1,435	$1,435
2000	3,757	3,757	41,322	40,000	1,000	(2,757)	(1,322)
2001	4,132	4,132	45,454	46,000	6,000	1,868	546
2002	4,545	4,545	50,000	50,000	4,000	(545)	0

[a].10 × previous balance in col. 1.
[b]Same as col. 1.
[c]Previous balance in col. 3 plus col. 2.
[d]Given.
[e]Col. 4 minus previous balance in col. 4.
[f]Col. 5 minus col. 2.
[g]Col. 4 minus col. 3.

fair value and their book (carrying) value at the end of the year. Column (6) shows the amount of unrealized holding gain/(loss) that must be recognized in the form of an adjusting entry at the end of each year. As is shown in the legend at the bottom of the schedule (Step f), the amount *recognized* each period is the change in fair value during the period (column 5) minus the increase in book value discount amortization (column 2). For a debt security purchased at a *premium,* the amount recognized each period would be the change in fair value during the period *plus the decrease* in book value (premium amortization). In summary, *for debt securities purchased at a discount, the increase in book value (discount amortization) each year either (1) reduces any unrealized holding gain resulting from an increase in fair value or (2) increases any unrealized holding loss resulting from a decrease in fair value. For debt securities purchased at a premium, the decrease in book value (premium amortization) each year either (1) increases any unrealized holding gain resulting from an increase in fair value or (2) decreases any unrealized holding loss resulting from a decrease in fair value.* More will be said about Exhibit 14–13 later, when we present the appropriate journal entries.

Accounting for and Reporting Trading Securities at Fair Value

Assume that Troccoli considers the Finley-Mart securities it has purchased to be trading securities. (This assumption may appear somewhat unrealistic, in that trading securities would probably not be held for a long period. Nevertheless, it allows us to compare accounting for trading securities with accounting for available-for-sale securities.)

At the end of 1999, Troccoli would record interest revenue and the unrealized holding gain as follows:

```
Investment in debt securities . . . . . . . . . . . . . . . . . . . . . . . 3,415
    Interest revenue . . . . . . . . . . . . . . . . . . . . . . . . . . . . .        3,415
To record interest revenue (from Exhibit 14–13).

Investment in debt securities . . . . . . . . . . . . . . . . . . . . . . . 1,435
    Unrealized holding gain (to income) . . . . . . . . . . . . . . .        1,435
To record unrealized holding gain (from Exhibit 14–13).
```

The amount of unrealized holding gain that is recognized is $1,435—the increase in fair value of $4,850 ($39,000 − $34,150) less the increase in book value (discount amortization) of $3,415 for 1999 ($4,850 − $3,415 = $1,435). Because these securities are classified as trading securities, both the interest revenue and the unrealized holding gain would appear on Troccoli's income statement for the year ending December 31, 1999.

At the end of 2000, Troccoli would make the following entries:

Investment in debt securities 3,757
  Interest revenue   3,757
To record interest revenue (from Exhibit 14–13).

Unrealized holding loss (to income) 2,757
  Investment in debt securities.   2,757
To record unrealized holding loss (from Exhibit 14–13).

Notice that at the end of 2000, the securities' carrying value exceeds their fair value by $1,322 (column 7). Their fair value increased $1,000 during the year ($40,000 − $39,000), but that amount must be reduced by the $3,757 increase in book value discount amortization (column 2). Thus, an unrealized holding loss of $2,757 ($1,000 − $3,757) must be recognized in the adjusting entry (column 6).

At the end of 2001, Troccoli would make the following entries:

Investment in debt securities 4,132
  Interest revenue   4,132
To record interest revenue (from Exhibit 14–13).

Investment in debt securities 1,868
  Unrealized holding gain (to income)   1,868
To record unrealized holding gain (from Exhibit 14–13).

At the end of 2001, the securities' fair value exceeds their carrying value by $546. The change in their fair value during the year was $6,000 ($46,000 − $40,000), an amount that must be reduced by the $4,132 increase in book value (discount amortization) for 2001. Thus, recognition of an unrealized holding gain of $1,868 is required.

As stated earlier, because Troccoli classifies these securities as trading securities, the unrealized gain or loss recognized each year would be reported as part of net income. On the other hand, had Troccoli classified these securities as available-for-sale securities, the unrealized gain or loss would be reported as a component of Troccoli's other comprehensive income, as we shall see in the following section.

Accounting for and Reporting Available-for-Sale Securities at Fair Value

For the available-for-sale security category, the unrealized holding gain/loss is reported as a component of other comprehensive income rather than included in income and closed to retained earnings at the end of each period. One procedural point should be noted: the use of a single account—unrealized holding gain/loss—instead of separate gain and loss accounts greatly simplifies the bookkeeping process. At each reporting date, a debit balance signifies an unrealized holding loss; a credit balance signifies an unrealized holding gain.

At the end of 1999, for example, Troccoli's unrealized holding gain (credit balance), reported on the balance sheet as a component of accumulated other comprehensive income, would be $1,435. At the end of 2000, the unrealized holding loss, reported in the same way (accumulated other comprehensive income), would be $1,322 [the $1,435 credit balance before adjustment + the $2,757 loss (debit) for 2000]. At the end of 2001, the reported unrealized holding gain would be $546 [the $1,322 debit balance before adjustment + the $1,868 gain (credit) for 2001].

Sales of Debt Securities

How are sales of debt securities accounted for? Assume that Troccoli sold its debt securities at the beginning of 2002 for $46,000. *Assuming the securities were classified as trading securities,* the following entry would be made to record the sale:

Cash.	46,000	
Investment in debt securities		46,000

Notice that no gain or loss would result from the sale, because the fair value of the securities at the date of sale (and the end of 2001) is $46,000. The unrealized gains and losses *have already been included* in Troccoli's income each year prior to the date of sale.

Assuming the securities were classified as available-for-sale securities, the following entry would be made:

Cash.	46,000	
Unrealized holding gain/loss		
(from accumulated other comprehensive income)	546	
Investment in debt securities		46,000
Realized gain on sale of securities (to income)		546

The $546 debit would be reported in other comprehensive income as a reclassification adjustment for the realized gain included in net income.

Assets often are sold *during* a period. As with depreciable assets sold during a period, an adjusting entry is necessary to adjust the beginning-of-period carrying value to the sale-date carrying value so that the gain or loss on sale may be calculated. Extending this concept to Troccoli's case, it would be necessary to accrue interest up to the sale date using the effective rate before recording the gain or loss on the sale. To illustrate, assume that Troccoli sold the Finley-Mart securities at the end of the first quarter of 2002 for $47,000. *Assuming the securities were classified as trading securities,* the adjusting entry for interest and the entry to record the sale would be as follows:

Investment in debt securities	1,136	
Interest revenue		1,136
(1/4 × $4,545)		
To record accrued interest revenue (from Exhibit 14–13).		

Cash.	47,000	
Realized loss on sale of debt securities	136	
Investment in debt securities ($46,000 + $1,136)		47,136
To record the sale.		

The realized loss of $136 results because the interest revenue (discount amortization) for the first quarter, $1,136, exceeded the increase in fair value ($1,000) for the same period.

Assuming the securities were classified as available-for-sale securities, the adjusting entry would be as follows:

Investment in debt securities	1,136	
Interest revenue		1,136
(1/4 × $4,545)		
To record interest revenue (from Exhibit 14–13).		

Cash.	47,000	
Unrealized holding gain/loss		
(from accumulated other comprehensive income)	546	
Investment in debt securities ($46,000 + $1,136)		47,136
Realized gain on sale of securities (to income)		410
To record the sale.		

The realized gain of $410 equals the net unrealized holding gain of $546 minus the $136 difference between the $1,000 increase in fair value and the interest revenue (discount amortization) of $1,136.

As an example of how unrealized and realized gains and losses are calculated on debt securities in practice, the following footnote appeared in MFS Communications Company's 1995 annual report:

> The Company has classified all marketable securities other than cash equivalents as available-for-sale. The amortized costs of the securities used in computing unrealized and realized gains and losses are determined by specific identification. Fair values are estimated based on quoted market prices.

In the preceding illustrations, interest revenue was accounted for using the effective interest method, which meant that the discount (in this case) was amortized during the holding period. In practice, *many companies ignore discount and premium amortization in accounting for interest on trading securities.*[10] The logic of this practice is based on three factors: (1) materiality considerations; (2) the fact that amortization of any premium or discount is not relevant in assessing, evaluating, and predicting cash flows for securities held for only a short time; and (3) the fact that any increase (decrease) in interest revenue due to discount (premium) amortization will be offset by a lower (higher) unrealized holding gain or a higher (lower) unrealized holding loss. Thus, net income will not be affected.

In all end-of-chapter materials, you should use the effective interest method and amortize any premium or discount.

Impairments of Available-for-Sale and Held-to-Maturity Securities

As with equity securities discussed in the previous chapter, the fair value of an available-for-sale or held-to-maturity debt security may decline, and the decline may be judged to be permanent ("nontemporary"). *If the decline in fair value is judged to be nontemporary, the security should be written down to fair value and the amount of the write-down accounted for as a realized loss and reported in the income statement.* The fair value then becomes the new carrying value. For securities classified as available for sale, any *subsequent temporary* increases and decreases in fair value should be accounted for as unrealized holding gains and losses and reported as a component of other comprehensive income, as in the Troccoli example (pages 740–743).

Transfers Between Debt Categories

As with equity securities, companies occasionally transfer debt securities between investment categories—that is, reclassify them. When a debt security is transferred between categories, *Statement No. 115 requires that the transfer be accounted for at fair value.* The following paragraphs summarize the accounting procedures for any unrealized gain or loss on the transferred security.

If a debt security is transferred *from* the trading category to either the held-to-maturity or available-for-sale category, any unrealized gain or loss at the date of transfer will have already been recognized in earnings. If the security is transferred *to* the trading category, the unrealized holding gain or loss is recognized in earnings at the date of transfer. In cases in which the transfer is from the held-to-maturity

---

[10]Discussions with several practitioners and with representatives of the FASB indicated that many companies ignore premium and discount amortization on trading securities that are held for less than three months. For securities held for more than three months, any premium/discount is usually amortized.

category, the unrealized gain or loss would be the difference between the held-to-maturity carrying value and the fair value at the date of transfer. With respect to securities transferred either to or from the trading category, note that any unrealized holding gain or loss is not carried forward. At the transfer date, a new effective interest (yield) rate must be determined based on fair value in order to apply the effective interest method in future periods.

If a debt security is transferred *to* the available-for-sale category from the held-to-maturity category, the unrealized gain or loss at the date of transfer would be reported as a component of other comprehensive income. As stated in the previous paragraph, the unrealized gain or loss would be the difference between the held-to-maturity carrying value and the fair value at the date of transfer. Because any unrealized holding gain or loss is carried forward, the historical effective rate is used to apply the effective interest method in future periods.

If a debt security is transferred *to* the held-to-maturity category from the available-for-sale category, *Statement No. 115,* as modified by *Statement No. 130,* states that "the unrealized holding gain or loss at the date of transfer shall continue to be reported as a separate component of other comprehensive income but shall be amortized over the remaining life of the security as an adjustment of yield in a manner consistent with the amortization of any premium or discount."[11] Given that the security's fair value minus (plus) any unrealized holding gain (loss) at the date of transfer must equal the security's effective-interest-method carrying value, the net result of this requirement is that interest revenue in subsequent periods will equal the amount of interest revenue that would have been reported had the security been in the held-to-maturity category all along.[12]

To illustrate, refer to the Troccoli example in Exhibit 14–13. Assume that at the end of 1999, Troccoli transfers the Finley-Mart security from the available-for-sale category to the held-to-maturity category. The following entry would be made at the date of transfer:

Investment in debt securities (held to maturity)	39,000	
Investment in debt securities (available for sale).		37,565
Unrealized holding gain (other comprehensive		
income)		1,435

To amortize the unrealized holding gain, we must determine the effective yield based on the fair value at the transfer date. The difference between the interest calculated at the original (historical) rate and interest calculated at the new effective rate will be the amount of the amortization. Interest revenue for 2000 calculated at the historical rate would be $3,757 [.10 × ($39,000 − $1,435)]. The effective interest (yield) rate that corresponds to a present value of $39,000 accumulating to a future value of $50,000 by the December 31, 2002, maturity date is 8.634 percent. Thus, the unrealized holding gain amortization for 2000 would be calculated as follows:

Interest revenue at 10 percent on $37,565	**$3,757**
Interest revenue at 8.634 percent on $39,000 (.08634 × $39,000)	**(3,367)**
Amortization of unrealized holding gain	**$ 390**

This amortization of the unrealized holding gain would be recorded with interest revenue for 2000 as follows:

Investment in debt securities	3,367	
Unrealized holding gain (calculated above)	390	
Interest revenue (.10 × $37,565)		3,757

Similar analyses would be made for subsequent years.

---

[11]*Statement No. 115,* para. 15D, as modified by *Statement No. 130.*
[12]A much simpler implementation requirement would have been to require that transfers to the held-to-maturity category from the available-for-sale category be transferred at the effective-interest-method carrying value [fair value minus (plus) any unrealized holding gain (loss)]. Presumably, however, such a requirement would have violated the "fair value spirit" of *Statement No. 115.*

EXHIBIT 14-14   **Accounting for Transfers of Debt Securities Held as Investments**

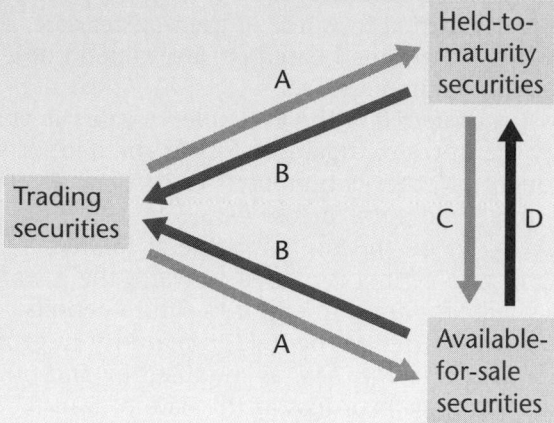

Transfers are accounted for at fair value and:

A. Unrealized holding gains/losses already have been recognized in income. The effective interest method using a new yield rate, based on fair value, is used in accounting for interest in future periods.

B. Unrealized holding gain/loss at the date of transfer is recognized in income. The effective interest method using a new yield rate, based on fair value, is used in accounting for interest in future periods.

C. Unrealized holding gain/loss at the date of transfer is reported as a component of other comprehensive income. The effective interest method using the historical yield rate is used in accounting for interest in future periods.

D. Unrealized holding gain/loss at the date of transfer is reported as a component of other comprehensive income. The gain/loss amount is amortized over remaining maturity as an adjustment of yield (interest) and as a reclassification adjustment in other comprehensive income. Since fair value minus unrealized holding gain (plus unrealized holding loss) equals the effective-interest-method carrying value, the net result is that the debt security is accounted for under the effective interest method using the historical (effective) interest rate (at amortized cost).

A summary of the requirements for transfers between debt categories appears in Exhibit 14–14.

Financial Statement Presentation and Investment Disclosures

Statement No. 115 requires that trading securities be classified as current assets if a company presents classified balance sheets. Held-to-maturity securities and available-for-sale securities should be classified as current or noncurrent on the balance sheet following the concepts presented in Chapter 5.

On the statement of cash flows, cash flows from sales, purchases, and maturities of available-for-sale and held-to-maturity securities should be classified as cash flows from investing activities. Cash flows from sales, purchases, and maturities of trading securities should be classified as cash flows from operating activities.

Statement No. 115 also requires an extensive set of disclosures related to investments in debt securities. These disclosures, similar to those presented in

Chapter 13 are aimed at providing information that is useful in analyzing a company's investment strategies and risk exposure. For an illustration of these disclosures, you may wish to refer to footnote 10 in GE's annual report in Appendix B at the end of the text.

Fair Value Accounting: Summary and Analysis

Many people believe that *Statement No. 115* represents an improvement in financial reporting in terms of addressing the inconsistency in accounting for debt securities and of requiring relevant fair values. Fair value reporting is also thought to be more "evenhanded" than the lower-of-cost-or-market method used prior to *Statement No. 115.* However, two issues were not resolved by *Statement No. 115:* accounting based on intent and the opportunity for "gains trading." Gains trading can occur when managers selectively sell held-to-maturity and available-for-sale securities. In doing so, they cause realized gains to be reported in income and unrealized losses to be excluded from income. Accounting based on intent is subjective and does not promote comparability across firms. Although the *Statement No. 115* disclosures are designed to reveal gains trading, many people believe that the only way to resolve the issues of gains trading and accounting based on intent is to require the use of fair values for *all* debt and equity securities within the scope of *Statement No. 115,* and to include *all* unrealized gains and losses (changes in fair value) in income.

The *Statement No. 115 mark-to-market procedures just discussed and illustrated above for investments in debt securities do not apply to the issuing firm's liabilities.*[13] Many preparers and users, especially those constituents of financial institutions, believe that mark-to-market accounting procedures should be extended to these liabilities. They have argued that banks and other financial institutions, whose assets and liabilities are interest rate sensitive and are managed as a group, should not be required to recognize losses on debt securities held as assets without also being permitted to recognize gains on debt liabilities. While the FASB was sensitive to these arguments, it was unable to identify any approach to valuing liabilities that was workable yet not too complex or permissive.

As a general rule, the valuation of liabilities at fair value is a substantive accounting issue for many reasons. First, many people believe there is a fundamental difference between the relevance of fair values for assets versus fair values for liabilities. They argue that an asset's fair value can be realized by simply selling it in the market. On the other hand, extinguishing a liability at fair value requires that the debtor have the cash or liquidity to do so. Second, the market prices of a company's outstanding debt or equity securities are determined to a large extent by the company's profitability. Following this line of reasoning, the fair (market) values of a company's outstanding debt securities, while correlated negatively with market interest rates, may be correlated positively with the company's profitability. To recognize unrealized holding gains and losses on outstanding debt securities in a company's income creates a "Catch-22." That is, the normal relationship between income and market prices is that a company's ability to generate profits and cash impacts the prices of its stock and bonds outstanding. If the fair value of a company's debt outstanding is allowed to impact its profits, the relationship goes the other way.

Though *Statement No. 115* does not deal with fair values for debt securities outstanding, very often the carrying value of outstanding debt differs from its current fair (market) value. This difference creates an opportunity for the issuing company to extinguish debt at an amount that is different from its carrying value. Extinguishment of debt is the subject of the following section.

CONCEPTUAL

Statement No. 115 mark-to-market procedures do not apply to liabilities.

---

[13]As we shall see, however, in our discussion of derivatives and hedging activities at a later point in this chapter, fair values are applicable to liabilities that have been hedged by a derivative contract.

EXTINGUISHMENT OF DEBT

Although long-term unconditional receivables/payables, such as bonds and notes, often remain outstanding until maturity, economic conditions sometimes cause companies to extinguish (retire) them before maturity. There are two common methods of extinguishing debt, as described below.[14]

Methods of Extinguishing Debt

10 Describe the two methods of extinguishing debt prior to maturity and prepare journal entries to record early extinguishment of debt.

1. The debtor may pay the creditor, thus discharging any present and future obligations. A debtor may accomplish this type of extinguishment in one of several ways. The company may choose to retire its debt by purchasing it on the open market at the current market price. Or, if the debt is callable, the company may extinguish it by exercising the call privilege at the call price. Finally, the company may substitute a new debt issue for the original one through a process called **refunding.** In refunding, the proceeds of the new issue are used to extinguish the original issue.

2. The debtor may be legally released from responsibility for the debt, either judicially or by the creditor. For example, a parent company may agree to become the primary obligor for a subsidiary's debt. From the subsidiary company's viewpoint, the debt has been extinguished. This process sometimes is called **defeasance,** meaning release from legal liability.

In addition to these common methods, a debt may be extinguished through an arrangement in which a creditor makes a concession to a debtor in financial stress. Accounting for concessions made because of a debtor's financial difficulties is discussed in Appendix 14–1. A conversion of debt to common stock is not considered an extinguishment, because the conversion option rests with the investor.[15]

Several factors may motivate a company to extinguish outstanding debt. First, as pointed out earlier, when market interest rates are high, a debt issue will often trade in the market at a "deep discount." If the debt's current market price is below its current book value, the issuer may be able to retire the debt at a substantial gain. Second, a company with callable debt outstanding may wish to lower its debt-equity ratio in order to increase its borrowing capacity. It can do so by exercising its call option. Finally, current market interest rates and other economic conditions may be such that a company finds it advantageous to refund its debt at a lower rate of interest.

Accounting for and Reporting Extinguishment of Debt

When debt is extinguished prior to its maturity, current GAAP requires that *the gain or loss on extinguishment,* if material, *be reported as an extraordinary item, net of related taxes.*[16] The gain or loss is the difference between the book value of the debt, including any unamortized debt issue costs, and the amount of cash (or other consideration) given.

Assume that on January 1, 1986, Gilmer Corporation issued 6 percent, 20-year $100,000 bonds for $80,360—an 8 percent effective yield. Interest is payable annually. On April 1, 1998, when the current market rate of interest for bonds of similar risk is 12 percent, Gilmer retires 60 percent of the bonds outstanding for

---

[14]"Accounting for Transfers and Servicing of Financial Assets and Extinguishments of Liabilities," *Statement of Financial Accounting Standards No. 125* (Norwalk, Conn.: FASB, 1996).
[15]"Early Extinguishment of Debt," *Opinions of the Accounting Principles Board No. 26* (New York: AICPA, 1972).
[16]"Reporting Gains from Extinguishment of Debt," *Statement of Financial Accounting Standards No. 4* (Stamford, Conn.: FASB, 1975), para. 8.

$43,380, an amount that includes accrued interest of $900 from January 1 through March 31. Gilmer uses the effective interest method; the company's fiscal year ends on December 31.

Before recording the retirement, Gilmer must first accrue the interest expense on the retired bonds for the first three months of 1998:

Interest expense [.6($88,510 $\times$ .08 $\times$ 3/12)]	1,062	
Bonds payable		162
Interest payable ($60,000 $\times$ .06 $\times$ 3/12)		900

On January 1, 1998, eight years from maturity, the book value of Gilmer's bonds is $88,510:

Present value of principal:
  $100,000 ($p_{\overline{8}|8\%}$) = $100,000 (.5403) $54,030
Present value of interest:
  $6,000 ($P_{\overline{8}|8\%}$) = $6,000 (5.7466) . . . . <u>34,480</u>
Total . . . . <u>**$88,510**</u>

The gain on retirement is $10,788 and would be calculated, based on the above figures, as follows:

Book value of bonds retired:
  Book value of 100% of bonds on 1/1/98 . . . . **$88,510**

  Book value of 60% of bonds on 1/1/98 ($88,510 $\times$ .6) **$53,106**

  Add discount amortization in journal entry above for Jan.–Mar. 1998 . . . . <u>**162**</u>

  Book value of 60% of bonds on 4/1/98 . . . . **$53,268**
Cash paid *excluding* accrued interest of $900 ($43,380 – $900) . . . . **(42,480)**
Gain on retirement. . . . . <u>**$10,788**</u>

The April 1 entry to record the retirement would be as follows:

Interest payable.	900	
Bonds payable.	53,268	
Cash ($42,480 + $900)		43,380
Extraordinary gain on retirement of bonds		10,788

For the remaining bonds outstanding, Gilmer would continue to use 40 percent of the amounts in the interest and book value schedule.

When serial debt is extinguished before maturity, the calculations are identical conceptually to the calculations for term debt. The book value of the debt retired is determined by discounting the remaining cash flows on the series at the effective (historical) rate of interest established when the debt was issued. The gain or loss on extinguishment is the difference between the book value of the series and the amount paid.

Debt Extinguishment: A Summary

The history behind the "extraordinary item" classification of gain or loss on debt extinguishments is interesting, in view of the fact that many extinguishments do not appear to be unusual and nonrecurring, especially within the environment in which they arose. In the 1970s, inflationary pressures and extremely high interest rates depressed debt security prices, motivating many companies to extinguish their debt at huge gains. Many companies were reporting large gains that distorted their income statements. *FASB Statement No. 4*, issued in 1975, required that gains and losses on early extinguishment be classified as extraordinary items in order to "flag" those numbers, so financial statement users would not get a misleading impression of companies' future cash-generating abilities.

The following excerpts from an article in *The Wall Street Journal* describe the rush to extinguish debt at a gain:

Corporate buy-backs of junk bonds hit a record $2.5 billion during the first quarter and are expected to set new highs for the year. Dozens of companies that sold junk bonds to investors now are rushing to buy them back at a steep discount. . . .

In recent months, traders have spotted Burlington Industries Inc., Mark IV Industries Inc., Coltec Industries Inc., Levi Strauss & Co., and many others actively buying back their bonds. . . .

But don't expect to hear much about the trend. Traders said the buy-backs are often kept secret, at least long enough for the companies to buy the bonds while prices are still cheap. . . .

Burlington said the [extinguishment] transaction resulted in a $14 million net extraordinary gain to first-quarter earnings.[17]

ACCOUNTING FOR LOAN IMPAIRMENTS

Describe the general accounting requirements of *Statement No. 114* with respect to accounting for loan impairments.

CONCEPTUAL

The impairment provisions of *Statement 114* and *Statement 115* are similar.

Our discussion of accounts receivable in Chapter 8 explained how to account for uncollectibles using the accrual (allowance) method. That discussion covered short-term receivables. Generally, present value considerations are ignored in accounting for short-term receivables, because the collection period is so short that there is no material difference between face value and present value. Thus, our objective in using the allowance method in Chapter 8 was to report receivables at net realizable value—the amount of cash expected to be collected from customers.

Statement No. 114, "Accounting by Creditors for Impairment of a Loan," addresses a creditor's measurement and reporting of impaired loans.[18] *The impairment provisions of Statement No. 114 are similar to the impairment (nontemporary decline in fair value) provisions of Statement No. 115. Statement No. 115* covers impairments of available-for-sale and held-to-maturity securities; *Statement No. 114* applies to long-term loans such as accounts receivable (with terms exceeding one year) and notes receivable. Thus, these provisions address an issue similar to that of uncollectible accounts.

Prior to the issuance of *Statement No. 114,* proper accounting for **loan impairments**—i.e., the inability of a creditor to collect all amounts due (principal *and* interest) according to the contractual terms of a loan agreement—had gone unresolved for many years. Perhaps the most significant issue with respect to accounting for loan impairments related to interest and present value. To illustrate, assume that on January 1, 1998, XYZ Finance Company loans money to a customer by accepting a five-year non-interest-bearing note with a maturity value of $12,000. On that date, the market rate of interest for notes of similar risk is 6 percent. The amount of cash loaned and the note receivable would therefore be recorded at its present value of $8,968:

$$\text{Present value} = \$12,000 \ (p_{\overline{5}|6\%})$$
$$= \$12,000 \ (.7473)$$
$$= \underline{\underline{\$8,968}}$$

Now assume that one year later, when the note's carrying value is $9,506 [$8,968 (1.06)], XYZ Finance Company determines that only $10,000 may be collected at maturity. Is the loan impaired at 12/31/99? Some people would argue

---

[17]"Junk Buy-Backs Take Off; Issuers Spring at Discounts," *The Wall Street Journal,* June 1, 1990, pp. C-1, C-13.
[18]"Accounting by Creditors for Impairment of a Loan," *Statement of Financial Accounting Standards No. 114* (Norwalk, Conn.: FASB, 1993).

no, saying XYZ still expects to recover more than its $9,506 recorded investment. Others would argue yes, saying that the *present value* of the expected future cash flow of $10,000 is less than $9,506. For those that argue yes, another related issue arises. Because an impaired loan may be more risky than a nonimpaired loan, should the discount rate be the historical (effective) rate of 6 percent or should it be a higher rate?

 Statement No. 114 resolved some of these issues. The *Statement* requires the creditor to determine whether and in what amount the loan is impaired based on the present value of the expected future cash flows. The discount rate used to calculate its present value is the loan's historical (effective) interest rate. As a practical expedient, *Statement No. 114* permits the measure of impairment to be based on the loan's observable fair value or on the fair value of any collateral involved with the loan.

 Returning to the XYZ Finance Company example and applying the provisions of *Statement No. 114,* the amount of impairment would be calculated as follows:

Note receivable 12/31/99	$9,506
Present value of expected future cash flows:	
$10,000(p\ \overline{{}_{4|6\%}}) = \$10,000\ (.7921)$	(7,921)
Amount of impairment	$1,585

The impairment would be recorded by debiting uncollectible accounts expense and crediting notes receivable (or allowance for uncollectible accounts) for $1,585. The effective interest method, using the 6 percent rate, would be used to account for the note receivable in subsequent periods. Should any subsequent changes occur in the amount or timing of expected future cash flows, the amount of impairment would be recalculated.

COMPOUND FINANCIAL INSTRUMENTS WITH DEBT AND EQUITY CHARACTERISTICS

The 1980s were a decade of mergers, as were the 1960s. Also like the 1960s, the 1980s were characterized by the issuance of compound financial instruments with both debt and equity characteristics. Many companies issued these "hybrid" securities to finance the acquisition of either the net assets or the common stock of other companies.

 Two hybrid securities that became popular during this period, and have remained popular in the 1990s, are (1) convertible debt and (2) debt issued with detachable stock warrants, which may be used to purchase shares of the issuing company's common stock. Conversion features and detachable warrants are called "sweeteners" because they allow securities to command a higher price than those issued without such features.

 Convertible debt and debt with detachable stock warrants are good examples of compound financial instruments. Both combine (1) an unconditional receivable/payable (the right to receive or obligation to pay cash) and (2) an option. As we stated at the beginning of Chapter 13, an option gives the holder (obligation of the writer) the right to exchange the security for other financial instruments on potentially favorable terms.

 In the following sections we will discuss accounting for convertible debt and debt issued with detachable stock warrants. Our discussion focuses primarily on current generally accepted accounting principles for these securities at the issue date and at the conversion/exercise date. However, because the current economic environment is quite different from the environment that existed at the time GAAP was established for these financial instruments, this discussion is followed by a

12 **Discuss the accounting issues related to convertible debt and debt issued with detachable warrants and prepare journal entries for those compound financial instruments.**

summary of some of the conceptual issues related to financial instruments with both debt and equity characteristics.

Convertible Debt

Convertible debt—a convertible bond or convertible note—gives the investor the option of converting the security into a specified number of shares of common stock within a specified time period. Companies issue convertible debt as a means of raising equity capital, assuming conversion takes place, and also as a means of issuing debt at a lower effective interest cost. Convertible debt may also be attractive to investors, because if the market price of the company's common shares increases, the holder of convertible debt can convert it into common stock. If the common shares do not increase in price and conversion does not become attractive, the investor can continue to hold the debt and receive interest.

Two accounting issues related to convertible debt are (1) valuation at the date of issue and (2) accounting for the conversion.

Date-of-Issue Valuation

If market participants perceive a conversion feature to have value, convertible debt can be issued at a higher price than similar debt issued without a conversion feature. In these cases, the market places value on the conversion option. To illustrate, assume that Meek Corporation issues $100,000 in 12 percent convertible bonds at par at a time when 12 percent bonds of similar risk, but without a conversion privilege, are selling at only 82 percent of par. The market value of the conversion option appears to be $18,000 ($100,000 − $82,000).

There are two views regarding accounting for convertible debt at the time of issuance. Under the first, convertible debt is considered to consist of a liability component and a debt component. Thus, the total proceeds received on the sale of convertible debt are allocated between debt and stockholders' equity. There are several methods of making this allocation. Under one method, called the with-and-without method, the amount assigned to the debt is based on the selling price of similar bonds *without* the conversion privilege. The amount assigned to the option (contributed capital) is the difference between the total proceeds received and the amount assigned to the debt.[19] Under this view, Meek would make the following entry to allocate the proceeds between the liability and equity:

Cash 100,000		
Bonds payable	82,000	
Contributed capital from conversion option	18,000	

Proponents of this view argue that each component of convertible debt should be recognized in the accounts. The bond investor has paid for the option to become a common stockholder along with the right to receive cash flows. Since the conversion privilege has economic value, the proceeds related to the conversion privilege should be accounted for as contributed capital. Similar reasoning applies to the issuer.

Under the second view, convertible debt is considered to be *entirely* a liability instrument or *entirely* an equity instrument, depending on which characteristic (liability or equity) governs at the issue date. Because convertible debt has the characteristics of an unconditional receivable/payable until converted, one could argue that it should be accounted for entirely as a liability. Following this argument, none of the proceeds would be assigned to the conversion option or accounted for as contributed capital.

---

[19]Other methods include the relative value method if both compound instrument components can be measured directly, basic option pricing models, and convertible debt pricing models.

Considering convertible debt as a liability, Meek would record the bond issue as follows:

```
Cash. . . . . . . . . . . . . . . . . . . . . . . . . . . . . . . . . . 100,000
    Bonds payable . . . . . . . . . . . . . . . . . . . . . . . . . .      100,000
```

Notice that periodic interest expense will be less under this view, because the initial book value of the bond will be decreased by either a discount or a reduced premium.

A supporting argument for treating convertible debt this way is that the conversion option is *inseparable* from the debt. That is, exercising the conversion option means surrendering the bond. Proponents of this argument also feel that practical measurement problems prohibit the objective allocation of the proceeds between debt and equity. Subjective allocation would reduce the reliability of the financial statements.

The APB opted for the second view in *Opinion No. 14,* which requires that convertible debt be accounted for as a liability at issuance. This approach represents GAAP at the present time. *Opinion No. 14* places greater weight on the inseparability of the debt and conversion option than on practical measurement problems. It concludes that no portion of the proceeds from the issuance of convertible debt should be assigned to the conversion option.

When convertible debt is issued at a premium or discount, a question arises regarding the time period over which the premium or discount should be amortized, since conversion may occur before the debt matures. Because there is no way to predict with certainty when conversion will occur, the premium or discount should be amortized as if the bonds will remain outstanding until maturity.

CONCEPTUAL

Convertible bonds are accounted for in the same manner as nonconvertible bonds.

Conversion of Debt into Common Shares

Convertible debt generally is convertible into common shares on or immediately after an interest date. When convertible debt is converted into common shares, the debt must be removed from the accounts and the shares issued must be recorded.

To illustrate conversion, assume that Joseph Corporation has convertible notes outstanding with a book value of $300,000. Each $1,000 note is convertible into 10 shares of Joseph's $50 par common stock. Thus, the conversion price per note is $100 ($1,000 ÷ 10 shares). The notes are converted into common shares at a time when the common shares are selling at $125 per share.

In practice, the most common method of accounting for conversions is the **book value method.** Under this method, no gain or loss is recognized when the notes are converted, because the conversion occurs under terms of a preexisting contract that has already been recognized in the financial statements. Instead, the conversion is recorded at the book value of the converted notes.[20] Joseph would record the conversion as follows:

```
Notes payable . . . . . . . . . . . . . . . . . . . . . . . . . . . 300,000
    Common stock. . . . . . . . . . . . . . . . . . . . . . . . . .      150,000ᵃ
    Contributed capital in excess of par. . . . . . . . . . .       150,000ᵇ
```

ᵃ$\frac{\$300,000}{\$1,000}$ = 300 notes × 10 common shares per note = 3,000 shares;
3,000 shares × $50 par value per share = $150,000.
ᵇ$300,000 – $150,000 = $150,000.

Assuming an investor also carried the notes at $300,000, the investor would record the conversion as follows:

```
Investment in Joseph stock . . . . . . . . . . . . . . . . . . . 300,000
    Investment in Joseph notes. . . . . . . . . . . . . . . . .      300,000
```

[20]A less used method is the **market value method.** Under this method, a gain or loss is recognized equal to the difference between the book value of the bonds and their market value at the time of conversion. The market value of the common shares issued may be used for measurement if it is more easily determinable. Many people believe that the market value method would have stronger conceptual appeal if the proceeds at issuance were allocated to *both* liability and equity components.

Induced Conversions of Debt

To encourage or induce prompt conversion, many companies with outstanding convertible debt offer creditors additional consideration, such as cash, warrants, or a more favorable conversion ratio of debt to common stock. Companies may be motivated to induce conversion for various reasons, including the desire to reduce interest expense or to improve their debt-equity ratio. The additional consideration usually is offered only for a specified time. *Statement No. 84* requires that when a company induces conversion, it must recognize the additional consideration as an expense. This expense is measured by the fair value of the additional securities or other consideration issued to induce conversion. Unlike a gain or loss on extinguishment, in which an existing contract between the debtor and debt holder is voided, the conversion contract remains in effect. The inducement is viewed as the sacrifice made to effect conversion.

To illustrate accounting for an induced conversion, refer to the Joseph Corporation example. Assume that to induce conversion, Joseph Corporation offers a more favorable conversion ratio of 12 common shares instead of 10 for each $1,000 note converted within a specified period. Thus, the conversion price is $83.33 ($1,000 ÷ 12 shares). During the inducement period, 66 notes, or 22 percent of the total issue, are converted. The entry to record the induced conversion would be as follows:

Notes payable (66 × $1,000).	66,000	
Conversion expense [66 × (12 − 10) × $125]	16,500	
Common stock (66 × 12 × $50)		39,600
Contributed capital in excess of par		42,900

The $16,500 conversion expense represents the fair value of the additional shares issued in conversion. Any notes converted after the inducement period would be accounted for under the original conversion terms, 10 common shares for each $1,000 note.

Debt Issued with Detachable Warrants

Some companies sweeten their debt issues by offering debt with detachable—that is, physically separable—stock purchase warrants. This type of financial instrument is similar to convertible debt, except that the option to purchase common stock is physically separable from the debt rather than *imbedded* in it. A **warrant** is simply a certificate that gives its holder the right (option) to purchase stock at a specified price during a specified period. A warrant may have economic value, because the market price of the shares may increase in relation to the option price. *Opinion No. 14* requires that the proceeds received from bonds issued with detachable warrants be allocated between the debt and the warrants.[21] This allocation may be based on the relative market values of the warrants and bonds of similar risk issued without warrants. If only one of these market values is known, the known market value is subtracted from the total proceeds to determine the amount assigned to the other security.

To illustrate, assume that Short Corporation has issued 10 percent, $150,000 par value bonds with 1,500 detachable stock warrants (10 detachable warrants for each $1,000 bond). Each warrant could be used to purchase one share of Short's $2 par common stock for $25 per share. The bond issue sold for $160,000. Shortly after issuance the warrants sold in the market for $3 each.

---

[21]This approach is similar to the allocation of cost in a "basket purchase" of plant and equipment.

Short would record the bond issuance as follows:

Cash	160,000	
Bonds payable ($160,000 − $4,500)		155,500
Contributed capital—stock warrants outstanding (1,500 × $3)		4,500

If 1,200 of the warrants were later exercised at a time when the stock was selling at $30 per share, Short would make the following entry:

Cash (1,200 × $25)	30,000	
Contributed capital—stock warrants outstanding (1,200 × $3)	3,600	
Common stock (1,200 × $2)		2,400
Contributed capital in excess of par		31,200

Notice that neither the issuer nor the investor recognizes the $30 market price per share because of the $25 fixed price in the warrant contract.

Compound Financial Instruments: A Summary

As we have seen in the two previous sections, financial accounting standards for convertible debt are not the same as the standards for debt issued with detachable stock warrants, although in substance these two types of securities are similar. Convertible debt is accounted for as debt; debt with detachable stock warrants is accounted for as part debt and part equity.

In today's economic environment—in contrast to the environment in which *Opinion No. 14* was issued—it is fairly common for market agents, such as financial institutions, to combine and/or unbundle financial rights and obligations. For example, financial institutions often sell "stripped" bonds or notes—securities that have had their cash flows for interest and principal unbundled and sold separately. Because such combining and unbundling activities do occur, many people believe formal accounting recognition should be given to both the debt and equity components of compound financial instruments. Some people maintain that accounting information would be more useful if convertible bonds and bonds with detachable stock warrants were accounted for in a similar way.

As a part of its financial instruments project, the FASB is studying the issue of (1) whether an instrument with both liability and equity characteristics should be accounted for *entirely* as debt or *entirely* as equity or (2) whether separate liability and equity components should be recognized. For the "all debt versus all equity" alternative, the FASB is studying how to determine which characteristic (debt or equity) governs at the issue date. For the "part liability and part equity" alternative, the FASB is studying methods of allocating the proceeds at issuance between the two components.[22]

DERIVATIVES AND OTHER COMPLEX FINANCIAL INSTRUMENTS

The list of financial instruments presented at the beginning of Chapter 13 showed how the changing nature of financial markets and other environmental circumstances, such as information technology, have produced an explosion of

---

[22]"Distinguishing between Liability and Equity Instruments and Accounting for Instruments with Characteristics of Both," *Discussion Memorandum* (Norwalk, Conn.: FASB, 1990).

novel and complex financial instruments. Perhaps the most important of these are derivatives.

Explain how derivatives are used in hedging activities to manage risk.

CONCEPTUAL

Derivatives are often used to hedge a risk exposure.

Derivatives and Hedging Activities

As we stated in Chapter 13, the most common types of **derivatives** include forward contracts, futures contracts, options, and swaps. Although derivative financial instruments are often used in speculative activities, most companies use them in hedging activities. **Hedging** means taking an action, such as entering into a derivatives contract, in order to mitigate exposure to risk. Consider the following example of how derivatives can be used to manage risk exposure. Company A's asset—a term bond—might be exposed to fair (market) value risk; that is, its fair value would decline if interest rates rise. Company B's asset—a variable interest rate note—might be exposed to cash flow risk; that is, a decline in market interest rates would reduce its cash flows. In summary, Company A is exposed to fair value risk (sometimes called market value risk) but not cash flow risk; Company B is exposed to cash flow risk but not fair value risk.

Company A could hedge its exposure to a decline in the fair value of its bond investment by *selling* (taking a short position in) a bond futures contract whose value change is correlated with the fair value of its term bond. If interest rates rise, bond prices fall. But the unrealized holding loss on the bond investment will be offset by a realized gain on the futures contract, which has a fixed selling price that exceeds the bond's current fair value. Exchange-traded futures contracts are marked to market and settled in cash on a daily basis. Company A would receive cash equal to the difference between the two prices. (If interest rates decrease, the opposite would happen, and the company would have to pay cash.)

Company B could hedge its exposure to a decline in future cash flows by *purchasing* (taking a long position in) a note futures contract. If interest rates fall, the reduced cash flows on the variable-interest-rate note would be offset by a gain on the futures contract. The gain results because Company B would receive cash equal to the difference between the (higher) current price of the note and the (lower) contracted purchase price. (If interest rates fall, the opposite would happen, and the company would have to pay cash.)

In addition to derivatives, two other interesting complex financial instruments are price-indexed debt and commodity bonds and notes. The following section summarizes some of the issues related to these instruments.

Price-Indexed Debt and Commodity Bonds and Notes

Price-indexed debt requires the issuer to pay at maturity an amount that is tied to a price index—either a general price index like the Consumer Price Index or an index related to a specific good. The periodic interest, if any, may or may not be indexed. For example, the Mexican development bank (NAFINSA) has issued several "petro-bonds." The maturity value of these bonds is indexed to the price of oil. The accounting issue is whether the potentially higher maturity value should be recognized over the term of the bond, and if so, in what manner.

A **commodity bond** (or **note**) is payable at maturity in terms of a specified commodity or its cash equivalent. This type of debt security is usually linked to a commodity produced by the company that issues the debt. For example, several years ago Texas International Company, an Oklahoma City-based oil and gas producer, issued $50 million in 9 percent commodity notes. The notes were redeemable at maturity for 29 times the free-market price of one barrel of oil or $1,000, whichever was greater. The company had the option of calling the notes if oil reached $69.86 per barrel, a price that would place each $1,000 note's value at approximately $2,000.

Several possibilities exist in accounting for commodity bonds, depending on how the transaction is viewed. First, if the issuer does not own the commodity in which the debt is payable, accounting for the transaction may be viewed as similar to accounting for price-indexed debt. Second, if the issuer does own the commodity, the obligation and the commodity used to satisfy it could be recorded at their fair values on the debt issue date. Subsequently, the asset and the liability may or may not be adjusted to their fair values at the end of each year. Third, if the transaction is viewed as a below-market-interest-rate borrowing, accounting may follow the guidelines of *Opinion No. 21*, which deals with debt and other obligations exchanged for cash. We discussed this approach on pages 733–734. Finally, the transaction may be viewed as a sale of the commodity with future delivery. Under this view, the debt proceeds would be recorded as unearned revenue. When the commodity is delivered to satisfy the debt obligation, the revenue is recognized as earned.

The FASB's Financial Instruments Project
Summary of Documents Issued to Date

In 1986, the FASB added a project on financial instruments and off-balance-sheet financing to its agenda. Called a "mini-conceptual framework," this project has as its objective the development of broad standards for resolving financial accounting and reporting issues involving financial instruments.

As of this writing, the FASB has issued four *Statements* related to the financial instruments project. In 1990, the FASB issued *Statement No. 105*, "Disclosure of Information about Financial Instruments with Off-Balance-Sheet Risk and Financial Instruments with Concentrations of Risk." *Statement No. 105* was intended as an interim step in the financial instruments project, pending completion of the recognition and measurement stage of the project. **Off-balance-sheet risk** refers to the risk of accounting loss in an amount that exceeds the amount reported for financial instruments as assets and liabilities in the balance sheet. The disclosures required by *Statement No. 105* are designed to provide information about off-balance-sheet risk and concentrations of credit risk arising from financial instruments.

Statement No. 107, "Disclosures about Fair Value of Financial Instruments," was issued in 1991. *Statement No. 107* sets forth certain fair value *disclosure* requirements for some financial instruments, including instruments reported as assets *and* liabilities, as well as certain financial instruments not currently reported as assets and liabilities under GAAP. Because *Statement No. 107* is concerned with disclosure, it has had no impact on the recognition, measurement, or classification of financial instruments in financial statements. As discussed and illustrated earlier in this chapter and in Chapter 13, *Statement No. 115* is somewhat narrower than *Statement No. 107*. It does impact the recognition, measurement, and classification of some financial instruments (certain debt and equity securities held as investments).

In 1994, the FASB issued *Statement No. 119*, "Disclosure about Derivative Financial Instruments and Fair Value of Financial Instruments." The objective of this *Statement* was to improve disclosures about derivative financial instruments—futures, forward, swap, or option contracts, or other financial instruments with similar characteristics. The *Statement* also amended certain disclosure requirements of *Statements No. 105 and 107*. Examples of these financial instrument disclosures for GE appear in its financial statements (footnotes 18 and 29) in Appendix B at the end of this text.

Except for *Statement No. 115,* all of the FASB *Statements* about financial instruments and derivatives to date have dealt with *disclosure* of fair values rather than *recognition* of fair values. This result has stemmed partly from considerations of feasibility and political and economic consequences, and from the fact that the current accounting model under GAAP does not embrace fair values for all assets and liabilities—including financial instruments. Thus, the FASB has been concerned about issues of consistency across standards and comparability across firms, in addition to issues of relevance and reliability.

In July 1996, the FASB issued an *Exposure Draft* of a *Proposed Statement of Financial Accounting Standards,* "Accounting for Derivatives and Similar Financial Instruments and for Hedging Activities."[23] A brief summary of this *Proposed Statement* is presented in the following section. An example will clarify some of the *Proposed Statement* requirements.

Accounting for Derivatives and Similar Financial Instruments and for Hedging Activities

The scope of the *Proposed Statement* on accounting for derivatives and hedging is much broader and the issues are more complex than the material covered in this chapter and in Chapter 13. Thus, the following summary omits many accounting and technical issues that are beyond the scope of this text.

First, a derivative financial instrument provides the holder (or writer) with the right (or obligation) to participate in some or all of the price changes of an underlying financial instrument or other items, such as commodities and other assets or specific items to which a rate, price index, or other market indicator is applied. The instrument does not require that the holder (writer) own or deliver the underlying financial instrument or other item. A contract that *requires* ownership or delivery of the underlying financial instrument or other item is a derivative financial instrument if it meets either of the following conditions: (1) the underlying financial instrument or other item is another derivative; (2) the parties involved can close the contract with only a net cash settlement through some market mechanism, such as an organized exchange; (3) the contract is customarily settled with only a net cash payment based on changes in the price of the underlying item.

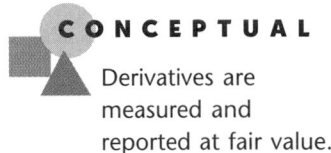

CONCEPTUAL

Derivatives are measured and reported at fair value.

Second, all derivatives must be recognized in the balance sheet as assets (or liabilities) depending on the contractural rights (or obligations) involved and measured at fair value. Companies must use the guidelines in *Statement No. 107* for determining fair value.

Third, changes in the fair value of a derivative (gains and losses) are accounted for in the following manner:

1. If the derivative is designated as a fair value hedge, the gain or loss is recognized in net income (together with an offsetting gain or loss on the asset or liability being hedged, as discussed below).

2. If the derivative is designated as a cash flow hedge, the gain or loss is reported not as part of net income but as a component of other comprehensive income. The gain or loss is recognized in net income on the projected date of the forecasted transaction.

3. If the derivative is not designated as a hedge (if it is speculative in nature), the gain or loss is recognized in net income.

CONCEPTUAL

Items hedged by derivatives are measured and reported at fair value.

Fourth, the item being hedged is also measured at fair value. Changes in the fair value of the hedged item (gains and losses) are recognized in net income only to the extent of any offsetting changes in the fair value of the derivative hedging instrument. When the change in fair value of the hedged item exceeds the offsetting change in the fair value of the derivative hedging instrument, any portion of a change in the fair value of the hedged item that is not recognized in net income in one period is available for income recognition in a subsequent period.

---

[23]"Accounting for Derivatives and Similar Financial Instruments and for Hedging Activities," *Proposed Statement of Financial Accounting Standards* (Norwalk, Conn.: FASB, 1996).

Fifth, the effective interest rate of a hedged interest-bearing asset or liability must be recalculated (both at the termination of the hedge and for periodic reporting in the balance sheet and income statement) based on the adjusted carrying amount of the hedged item and its expected future cash flows.

Finally, a set of lengthy disclosure requirements is designed to provide information to external users about the company's risk management objectives and its strategies for issuing or holding derivatives. Required disclosures include the types of risk being hedged and the types of derivative used to hedge them "to help investors and creditors understand what an entity is trying to accomplish with its derivatives."[24] These disclosure requirements are similar to those in *Statements No. 107 and 119,* both of which would be superseded by the *Proposed Statement.*

As we shall see in the following example, the third and fourth requirements can be described, at least conceptually, in two ways. In one—mark-to-market accounting applied to the derivative and to the item being hedged—the gain or loss on the derivative is offset by the gain or loss on the hedged item on the income statement. In the other—mark-to-market accounting applied to the derivative and to the item being hedged—to the extent that the derivative is offset by a loss or gain on the hedged item since the inception of the hedge, the gain or loss on the derivative is deferred as an adjustment to the carrying value of the hedged item.

To illustrate these requirements, assume that at the beginning of year 1, Linsmeyer has a $100,000 note outstanding. The note pays 8 percent interest each December 31 and matures at the end of year 3. Although the market interest rate at the beginning of year 1 is 8 percent, Linsmeyer is concerned that interest rates might fall, causing the fair value of its note payable to increase. As part of its risk-management strategy, Linsmeyer therefore decides to hedge its fair (market) value risk by entering into a three-year interest rate swap.

Under the swap's terms, Linsmeyer will receive fixed interest at an 8 percent rate and will pay interest at a variable rate. The interest rate swap, based on a **notational amount** of $100,000 (an amount noted or designated for periodic settlement purposes), will produce a cash settlement to be paid or received by Linsmeyer each December 31. The settlement is to be the net of the 8 percent fixed rate receipt and a variable interest payment based on the market interest rate at the *beginning* of each year.

Over the three-year period, market rates of interest are as follows: beginning of year 1, 8 percent; end of year 1, 6 percent; end of year 2, 5 percent; end of year 3, 5 percent.

Exhibit 14–15 shows the calculation of fair value and changes in fair values for the derivative hedging instrument (the interest rate swap) and the hedged instrument (the fixed-rate note payable). Notice how the derivative serves to mitigate the risk associated with changes in the fair value of the liability.

Based on Exhibit 14–15, the following journal entries would be made over the three-year period:

End of year 1

Interest expense	8,000	
Cash		8,000
To record interest for year 1.		
Derivative—interest rate swap	3,667	
Holding gain—interest rate swap		3,667
To record gain on derivative.		
Holding loss—note	3,667	
Notes payable		3,667
To record loss on note.		

---

[24]*Statement No. 119,* para. 58; *Proposed Statement,* para. 176.

EXHIBIT 14-15	Calculation of Fair Values and Changes in Fair Value of a Derivative (Interest Rate Swap) Used to Hedge an Exposure to Fair Value Risk

	BOY1	EOY1	EOY2	EOY3
Balance sheet fair values:				
Asset: Derivative		$ 3,667[a]	$ 2,857[c]	$–0–
Liability:				
Notes payable	$100,000	$103,667[b]	$102,857[d]	$100,000[e]
Changes in fair values [gain (loss)]:				
Derivative		$3,667[f]	$1,190[f]	$143[f]
Notes payable		$(3,667)[g]	$(970)[g]	$–0–[g]

[a]Present value of $2,000 annuity (expected net payments) for two periods discounted at 6 percent.
[b]Present value of two $8,000 cash flows discounted at 6 percent plus present value of $100,000 principal discounted at 6 percent.
[c]Present value of $3,000 (expected net payment) for one period discounted at 5 percent.
[d]Present value of one $8,000 cash flow discounted at 5 percent plus present value of $100,000 principal discounted at 5 percent.
[e]Before payment of principal.
[f]Ending fair value minus beginning fair value plus net cash receipt.
[g]Ending fair value minus beginning fair value plus periodic amortization.

End of year 2

Interest expense (.06 × $103,667)	6,220	
Notes payable ($8,000 − $6,220)	1,780	
Cash		8,000

To record interest for year 2.
Note: The effective interest method is used. The effective rate is 6 percent and is applied to the beginning fair value of the note payable.

Cash	2,000	
Derivative—interest rate swap		
($8,000 fixed − $6,000 variable)		2,000

To record net cash receipt.

Derivative—interest rate swap.	1,190	
Holding gain—interest rate swap		1,190

To record gain on derivative.

Holding loss—note	970	
Notes payable		970

To record loss on note.

End of year 3

Interest expense (.05 × $102,857)	5,143	
Notes payable ($8,000 − $5,143)	2,857	
Cash		8,000

To record interest for year 3.
Note: The effective interest method is used. The effective rate is 5 percent and is applied to the beginning fair value of the note payable.

Cash	3,000	
Derivative—interest rate swap		
($8,000 fixed − $5,000 variable)		3,000

To record net cash receipt.

Derivative—interest rate swap	143	
Holding gain—interest rate swap		143

To record gain on derivative.

Based on the information in Exhibit 14–15 and these journal entries, Linsmeyer's income statement over the three-year period would report the following:

	END OF YEAR 1	END OF YEAR 2	END OF YEAR 3
Interest expense	$(8,000)	$(6,220)	$(5,143)
Holding gain on derivative	3,667	1,190	143
Holding loss on notes payable	(3,667)	(970)	–0–
Net	$ 8,000	$ 6,000	$ 5,000

Because interest rates decreased over the three-year period, the net expense on Linsmeyer's income statement each year is consistent with the company's risk-management strategy. It reflects the fact that the derivative allowed Linsmeyer to pay interest at a variable rate and to hedge any increase in the fair value of its liability. Finally, the total net cash settlement of $5,000 ($2,000 at the end of year 2 and $3,000 at the end of year 3) is recognized in the income statement as holding gains on the derivative ($3,667 + $1,190 + $143 = $5,000). The *Proposed Statement* does not prescribe how gains and losses on derivatives should be classified on the income statement. Therefore, other ways of classifying the three items in Linsmeyer's income statement are possible.

UMMARY OF LEARNING OBJECTIVES

1. **Describe the major characteristics of debt securities.**
   The major characteristics of debt securities include: whether they mature at one time (term debt) or in installments (serial debt); whether they are interest-bearing or non-interest-bearing; whether there is security for the debt issued; whether the debt is registered; whether there is a sinking fund requirement; whether the debt is callable; whether the debt is convertible into equity; and whether the debt is serviced from specific revenue sources.

2. **Calculate the issue price (market price) of an unconditional receivable/payable debt security.**
   The issue price of an unconditional receivable/payable, such as a bond or note, equals the present value of the cash flow(s) for principal (maturity value) plus the present value of any interest cash flows. The discount rate used to calculate these present values is the market rate of interest at the issue date. When debt is issued between interest dates, the present values must be calculated at the immediately preceding interest date, then accumulated to the issue date at the current market rate of interest.

3. **Prepare journal entries to record the issuance/purchase of a bond or note (1) on the contract date and (2) between interest dates.**
   When a bond or note is issued, cash is debited for the amount of cash received; interest payable is credited for any accrued interest based on the stated rate; and bonds (or notes) payable is credited for the difference. An investor would make a parallel entry for a bond or note investment.

4. **Explain the relationship that exists between (1) a bond or note's stated rate of interest and the market rate of interest and (2) the security's issue price and its face (maturity) value.**
   If the market rate of interest is *greater* than the stated rate of interest on a bond or note, the issue price will be *less* than the face value (par value or principal amount), and the bond or note will be issued at a discount. For example, a zero-coupon bond is always issued at a discount. If the market rate of interest is *less* than the stated rate of interest on a bond or note, the issue price will be *greater* than the face value (par value or principal amount), and the bond or note will be issued at a premium.

5. **Calculate interest expense/interest revenue under the effective interest method and prepare the related journal entries for the issuer/investor.**

   When the interest period and the fiscal period coincide, interest expense is debited for an amount equal to the beginning book value of the debt times the effective interest rate. Cash is credited for any cash interest, and the debt is debited (or credited) for the difference. (Any difference represents amortization of the premium or discount.) When the interest period and the fiscal period do *not* coincide, interest expense must be based on an apportionment of the current interest period's interest expense for the number of months between the beginning of the interest period and the end of the fiscal period. An investor would make similar entries for an investment in a bond or note.

6. **Discuss the primary features and advantages of the effective interest method.**

   The effective interest method uses a constant rate of interest (the effective or historical rate) to calculate interest expense/revenue for each period. This method conforms to economic reality, in the sense that the amount of interest recognized each period is a function of the amount of the liability/investment. More important, the effective interest method values a liability/investment at the present value of the remaining cash flows for interest and principal.

7. **Explain the basic accounting concepts for bonds and notes.**

   The concept of present value provides the conceptual underpinnings for the recognition and measurement of bonds and notes, both at issue or acquisition date and after. At the issue/acquisition date, bonds and notes are valued at the present value of their future cash flows, where the discount rate is the market rate at issue or acquisition. This interest rate is called the effective (historical) rate. After issue or acquisition, the effective interest method is used to account for bonds and notes. The use of the effective interest method results in the valuing and reporting of bonds and notes at the present value of their future cash flows, where the interest rate is the historical (effective) rate.

8. **Describe the three classifications of debt securities held as investments under *Statement No. 115*.**

   At acquisition, debt securities are classified as belonging to one of the following three categories: trading, available-for-sale, or held-to-maturity. Trading securities are purchased and held with the intent of selling them in the near term at a profit. Held-to-maturity securities are purchased with intent of being held to earn interest to maturity. Securities not classified as either trading or held-to-maturity are classified as available-for-sale securities.

9. **Apply the fair value accounting requirements of *Statement No. 115* to debt securities held as investments.**

   Fair value accounting applies to trading and available-for-sale securities but not to held-to-maturity securities. At the end of each period, investments in debt securities classified as trading and available-for-sale securities are reported at their fair value ("marked to market"). For trading securities, changes in fair value (unrealized holding gains and losses) are reported in the income statement. For available-for-sale securities, changes in fair value (unrealized holding gains and losses) are reported as a component of other comprehensive income. When such debt securities are purchased at a discount or premium, the unrealized holding gain (loss) for the period equals the change in fair value adjusted for the change in book value (discount or premium amortization).

10. **Describe the two methods of extinguishing debt prior to maturity and prepare journal entries to record early extinguishment of debt.**

    A debtor may extinguish debt prior to maturity by paying the creditor through an open market purchase of the debt, calling the debt if callable, or by refunding or by being legally released from an obligation by the creditor. When debt is extinguished prior to maturity, the difference between the amount paid to extinguish the debt and the carrying (book) value of the debt must be accounted for as an extraordinary gain or loss.

II. Describe the general accounting requirements of *Statement No. II4* with respect to accounting for loan impairments.

When a creditor is unable to collect all the principal and interest due, the collectible amounts (the future cash flows expected to be collected) must be discounted at the loan's historical (effective) rate. If the resulting present value is less than the carrying amount, the impairment is recorded by debiting uncollectible accounts expense and crediting the asset (or allowance).

I2. Discuss the accounting issues related to convertible debt and debt issued with detachable warrants and prepare journal entries for those compound financial instruments.

Debt is often issued with an option—either a conversion feature or detachable warrants. The two primary accounting issues are (1) allocating the issue proceeds between the debt and the option and (2) accounting for conversions (the exercise of the warrants). When convertible debt is issued, the entire proceeds are recorded as debt because of the inseparability of the option and the debt. When debt is issued with detachable warrants, the proceeds are allocated between the debt and the warrants. When convertible debt is converted to common stock, the book value method is used. When warrants are exercised, the sum of the carrying value of the warrants and the cash received is credited to contributed capital.

I3. Explain how derivatives are used in hedging activities to manage risk.

Although derivatives may be used for speculative purposes, most companies use them in hedging activities. Hedging means to take an action, such as entering into a derivatives contract in order to reduce or mitigate an exposure to risk. For example, a company might have variable interest rate debt outstanding. To avoid paying larger amounts of interest should interest rates rise, the company could hedge its exposure by entering into an interest rate swap. Should interest rates rise, the larger interest payments would be offset by gains on the interest rate swap.

KEY TERMS

available-for-sale securities 740

bond 716

book value method 753

commodity bond (note) 756

convertible debt 752

deep discount or zero-coupon bonds (notes) 717

defeasance 748

deferred debt issue costs 734

derivatives 756

discount 723

effective interest method 725

hedging 756

held to maturity 739

loan impairments 750

market value method 753

notational amount 759

note 716

off-balance-sheet risk 757

premium 723

price-indexed debt 756

refunding 748

serial bonds or notes 717

straight-line method 725

term bonds or notes 717

trading securities 740

warrant 754

Troubled Debt Restructuring

In recent years, liquidity problems, high interest rates, and other unfavorable economic circumstances have forced many debtors in the United States to arrange *debt-restructuring* agreements with creditors. For example, both Cleveland and Orange County, California, have effected debt-restructuring arrangements because of an inability to meet their obligations (interest or principal) as they became due. Many businesses, such as Southland Corporation and Donald Trump's company, Trump Organization, have also restructured their debt. Rather than force troubled debtors into bankruptcy proceedings, creditors, especially banks, often make concessions through restructuring agreements that may allow creditors maximum recovery of their investment.

A *troubled debt restructuring* occurs when a creditor makes a concession that is *favorable* to a debtor. The restructuring may take either one or both of the following forms:

1. The debtor may transfer assets or equity securities in *settlement* of a debt obligation.

2. The terms of the debt agreement may be *modified*.[25]

Both forms are discussed in the following sections.

Transfer of Assets or Equity Securities in Settlement of Debt

When a debtor sacrifices assets or issues equity securities in settlement of an outstanding debt, the debtor recognizes an *extraordinary gain* on restructure equal to the difference between the book value of the debt and the fair value of the assets sacrificed or securities issued. The extraordinary classification may help users to assess cash flows when a troubled debtor who has experienced continuing losses from operations suddenly shows a gain due to restructuring of an outstanding debt. (Since the creditor makes a concession to the debtor, *the restructuring will never result in a loss to the debtor.*) Furthermore, when assets are transferred to the creditor, the debtor also recognizes a gain or loss equal to the difference between the book value of the assets transferred and their fair value. This gain or loss is classified according to the criteria for extraordinary items in *APB Opinion No. 30.* The creditor either recognizes a loss or reduces the allowance for doubtful accounts, whichever is applicable, for the difference between the book value of the receivable and the fair value of the assets or securities received. Since a concession has been made, *the creditor will never record a gain.*

To illustrate, assume that Creditor Corporation holds a $150,000 note receivable that is currently due with interest payable of $7,500. Debtor Corporation is unable to pay the amounts due. Therefore, Creditor agrees to accept land with a fair value of $135,000 in full settlement. The carrying value of the land on Debtor's books is $100,000.

---

[25]"Accounting by Debtors and Creditors for Troubled Debt Restructurings," *Statement of Financial Accounting Standards No. 15* (Stamford, Conn.: FASB, 1977).

The following entries would be made by both debtor and creditor to record the debt restructuring:

CREDITOR			DEBTOR		
Land 135,000			Notes payable. 150,000		
Loss on			Interest payable . . .	7,500	
restructuring[a]	22,500		Land		100,000
Notes receivable .		150,000	Extraordinary gain		
Interest			on debt		
receivable		7,500	restructuring		
			($157,500 –		
			$135,000)		22,500
			Gain on transfer		
			of land		
			($135,000 –		
			$100,000)		35,000

[a]Or allowance for doubtful accounts.

If instead of sacrificing land, the debtor issued stock with a par value of $90,000 and a fair value of $135,000, the creditor would debit investments instead of land in the entry just shown. The debtor would make the following entry:

Notes payable	150,000	
Interest payable	7,500	
Common stock.		90,000
Contributed capital in excess of par		
($135,000 – $90,000)		45,000
Extraordinary gain on debt restructuring		22,500

Modification of Debt Terms

As an alternative to restructuring by the transfer of assets or equity securities, the debtor may receive a concession in the form of a modification of the terms of the debt agreement. Modification of terms may take one or more of the following forms:

1. Forgiveness of the interest currently due or forgiveness of part of the principal amount owed.

2. Deferral of the principal or interest due to a later date.

3. Reduction of the rate of interest on the original debt.

The following example will illustrate. Assume that on January 1, 1995, Debtor Company issued a four-year, 10 percent note for $100,000, with interest payable annually. Debtor made the interest payments for 1995 and 1996 but began to have severe financial difficulties in 1997. At the end of 1997, Debtor was unable to pay the $10,000 interest due. Furthermore, it was unlikely that Debtor would be able to meet the principal obligations under the original debt contract. Creditor Company therefore agreed to forgive the $10,000 interest payable at the end of 1997; to reduce the original principal to $95,770; to extend the due date of the new principal to the end of 2000; and to lower the rate of interest to 5.743 percent beginning in 1998.

In this example, the accounting issue centers around what recognition should be given to the restructuring arrangements in the accounts and in the financial statements. Some accountants argue that an exchange has occurred—that new debt has been issued to replace debt currently outstanding. They reason that a gain or loss should be recognized in the same manner for early extinguishment of debt through debt refunding. Other accountants argue that an exchange of resources or obligations has not occurred and that the original debt is still outstanding albeit with modified terms. Since the ability of a debtor in financial stress to meet future cash flow obligations may be highly uncertain, the FASB opted for this second more conservative approach represented by the latter argument.

In the following sections we will examine accounting for restructured debt with modified terms, first by the debtor and then by the creditor.

Accounting by the Debtor

CONCEPTUAL

Debt restructuring is treated prospectively.

Under *FASB Statement No. 15,* restructuring effects are treated *prospectively.* That is, the debtor recognizes no gain unless the *total cash flows,* as restructured, are *less* than the *book value* of the debt *before* restructuring. If the restructured cash flows *exceed* the current book value of the debt, a new effective interest rate on the debt is imputed by finding the interest rate that equates the present value of the restructured cash flows with the book value of the debt before restructuring. Thus, the book value of the debt is considered to be the present value of the restructured cash flows, and an effective interest rate on the debt is imputed for purposes of recording interest expense in future periods. Both situations are illustrated in the next two sections.

Cash Flows in Excess of Book Value   In the example on page 765, Debtor Company's restructured cash flows exceeded the book value of the original debt:

Restructured cash flows:		
Principal (due at end of 2003)	**$95,770**	
Interest ($95,770 × .05743 for		
six years = $5,500 × 6)	**33,000**	**$128,770**
Current book value:		
Principal (due at end of 1998)	**$100,000**	
Interest due at end of 1997	**10,000**	**(110,000)**
Excess of restructured cash flows		
over book value of debt		**$ 18,770**

Since the restructured cash flows exceed the book value of the debt, no gain is recognized.

A time diagram showing the current book value of the debt, the restructured cash flows, and the new effective interest rate calculations appears in Exhibit 14–16. As the calculations in the exhibit indicate, the effective interest rate, determined by a trial-and-error process, is 3 percent. This rate, when applied to the restructured cash flows, equates their present value with the debt's original book value.

A reclassification entry for Debtor at the date of restructure might be as follows:

Notes payable	100,000	
Interest payable	10,000	
Notes payable		110,000

Next, annual interest expense is calculated using the effective interest method. The difference between the cash interest paid and the interest expense represents a reduction in the carrying value of the debt. Entries for interest expense for 1998 and 1999 would be as follows:

Interest expense (.03 × $110,000)	3,300	
Notes payable ($5,500 − $3,300)	2,200	
Cash		5,500
To record interest for 1998		
Interest expense [.03 × ($110,000 − $2,200)]	3,234	
Notes payable ($5,500 − $3,234)	2,266	
Cash		5,500
To record interest for 1999.		

EXHIBIT 14–16   Imputation of an Effective Interest Rate for Restructured Debt

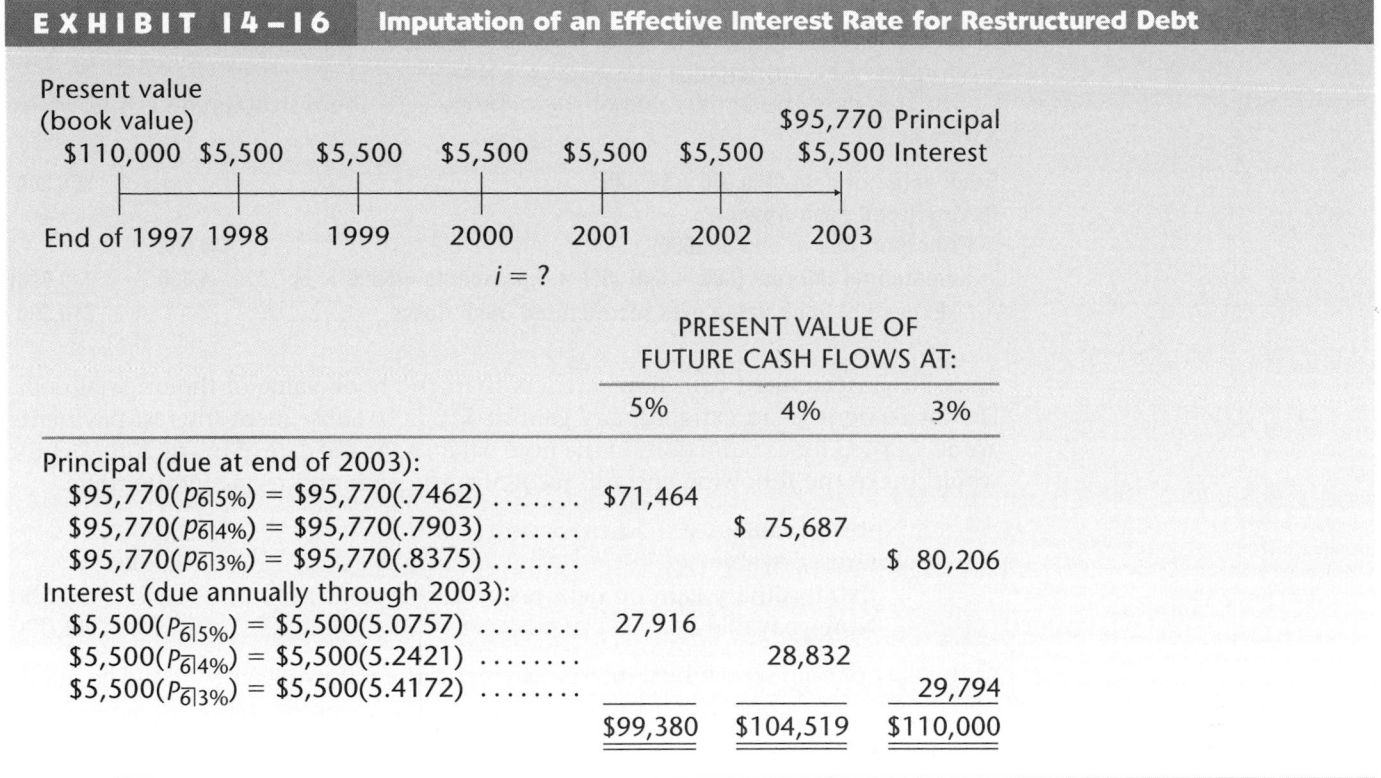

	PRESENT VALUE OF FUTURE CASH FLOWS AT:		
	5%	4%	3%
Principal (due at end of 2003):			
$95,770(p\overline{6}|_{5\%})$ = $95,770(.7462)	$71,464		
$95,770(p\overline{6}|_{4\%})$ = $95,770(.7903)		$ 75,687	
$95,770(p\overline{6}|_{3\%})$ = $95,770(.8375)			$ 80,206
Interest (due annually through 2003):			
$5,500(P\overline{6}|_{5\%})$ = $5,500(5.0757)	27,916		
$5,500(P\overline{6}|_{4\%})$ = $5,500(5.2421)		28,832	
$5,500(P\overline{6}|_{3\%})$ = $5,500(5.4172)			29,794
	$99,380	$104,519	$110,000

Since the interest expense is less than the cash interest paid, the difference represents a reduction in the notes payable balance. By the end of the sixth year, the note will be reduced to $95,770, the amount due at that time.

In this example, we used a trial-and-error approach because the rate of interest was applied both to a single amount and an annuity. If the restructured cash flows are either a single future amount or an annuity, the effective rate can be determined using the present value concepts discussed in Appendix A at the back of this text. For example, if Creditor agreed to accept a lump-sum amount of $139,183 at the end of 2003 in full settlement of the debt, we could determine the effective rate using the formula for the present value of a single amount:

$$p = a(p\overline{6}|_{i\%})$$
$$\$110,000 = \$139,183(p\overline{6}|_{i\%})$$
$$p\overline{6}|_{i\%} = \frac{\$110,000}{\$139,183}$$
$$p\overline{6}|_{i\%} = .7903$$

As Table B in Appendix A at the back of this text indicates, the rate of interest that corresponds to the present value factor of .7903 for six periods is 4 percent. In this situation, periodic interest expense would be calculated by multiplying each beginning-of-year liability by 4 percent. Thus, the liability would increase by 4 percent each year and would total $139,183 at the end of 2003.

Cash Flows Less Than Book Value   If the restructured cash flows are *less* than the book value of the debt, an extraordinary gain on restructuring is recognized at the date of restructuring. The gain is the difference between the book value of the debt and the restructured cash flows. Subsequent cash payments are accounted for as reductions in the book value of the debt, and *no periodic interest expense is recorded.*

To illustrate, assume that on June 30, 1998, Debtor owes Creditor $50,000 on a note. Interest of $4,500 has also accrued. Because of Debtor's financial difficulties, Creditor agrees to forgive the interest currently due; to reduce the note principal to

$40,000; to extend the due date of the note until December 31, 2000; and to reduce the interest rate on the note from 9 percent annually to 2 percent semiannually on the new principal.

In this case the book value of the debt exceeds the restructured cash flows by $10,500:

Book value of debt ($50,000 + $4,500)		**$54,500**
Restructured cash flows:		
Principal (due at end of 2000)	**$40,000**	
Semiannual interest [(.02 × $40,000) × 5 payments = $800 × 5] . . .	**4,000**	**(44,000)**
Excess of book value over restructured cash flows		**$10,500**

Since the restructured cash flows are less than the book value of the original debt, Debtor recognizes an extraordinary gain of $10,500. Subsequent interest payments are accounted for as reductions in the note balance. At the date of restructure, Debtor would make the following entry to recognize the gain and reclassify the note:

Notes payable	50,000	
Interest payable	4,500	
Extraordinary gain on debt restructuring		10,500
Notes payable		44,000

At the date of each semiannual interest payment, the following entry would be made:

Notes payable	800	
Cash		800

EXHIBIT 14–17	**Accounting for Troubled Debt Restructuring, *FASB Statement No. 15* (as Modified for the Creditor by *FASB Statement No. 114*)**

---

^aIf the creditor maintains an allowance for doubtful accounts, all or part of the loss might be debited to this account.

At the note's maturity date, the following entry would be made:

Notes payable.	40,000	
Cash		40,000

Accounting by the Creditor

Prior to the issuance of *Statement No. 114,* the accounting procedures for the creditor of restructured debt with modified terms generally paralleled those of the debtor. *Statement No. 114,* dealing with loan impairments, was discussed and illustrated on pages 750–751. When the terms of the debt are modified, the provisions of *Statement No. 114* supersede *Statement No. 15's* provisions for the creditor. *Statement No. 114* requires that the creditor account for any modifications of debt terms under a troubled debt restructuring in the same manner as a loan impairment.

A summary of the accounting procedures for debt-restructuring agreements appears in Exhibit 14–17.

QUESTIONS Questions marked with an asterisk (*) refer to Appendix 14–1.

Q 14-1. Identify and discuss at least two similarities and two differences between bonds and notes.

Q 14-2. Listed below are various types of debt instruments. Briefly describe each.
I. Coupon bonds.
2. Serial notes.
3. Mortgage bonds (in which assets are pledged).
4. Revenue bonds.
5. Zero-coupon notes.
6. Registered bonds.
7. Sinking fund bonds.
8. Debenture bonds.
9. Convertible notes.
10. Bonds with detachable warrants.

Q 14-3. Explain how prices of debt securities are determined in the marketplace.

Q 14-4. Under what conditions will a bond sell:
I. At par (face) value?   **2.** At a premium?   **3.** At a discount?

Q 14-5. A $1,000 bond was quoted in the market for "97 1/2 plus accrued interest." Explain the phrase in quotation marks.

Q 14-6. What effects do risk and inflation have on market prices of debt?

Q 14-7. Explain two methods of accounting for debt premium and discount.

Q 14-8. What is the relationship between interest expense and cash interest payments for debt issued at:
I. A discount?   **2.** A premium?

Q 14-9. Discuss the accounting and reporting procedures for debt issue costs.

Q 14-10. Long-term debt sometimes is issued as a means of obtaining cash. Describe the valuation principles for long-term debt under the following circumstances:
I. Debt is issued in exchange for cash.
2. Debt is issued in exchange for fixed assets.
3. Debt and other obligations are exchanged for cash.

Q 14-11. When debt is issued, under what circumstances will the amount of cash received be equal to the face (principal) amount of the debt?

Q 14-12. Under what circumstances will the present value of debt be less than its face value?

Q 14-13. Distinguish among the following categories of debt security investments: held-to-maturity securities, available-for-sale securities, and trading securities.

Q 14-14. Why is fair value reporting not applicable to held-to-maturity securities?

Q 14-15. For trading securities and available-for-sale securities, explain briefly how unrealized holding gains and losses from applying fair value are accounted for and reported in the financial statements.

Q 14-16. Briefly explain how impairments of held-to-maturity securities and available-for-sale securities are accounted for under *Statement No. 115.*

Q 14-17. When debt securities are transferred between categories, how are the transfers measured and what disposition is made of any unrealized gain or loss at the date of transfer?

Q 14-18. How are purchases, sales, and maturities of debt securities held as investments reported on the statement of cash flows?

Q 14-19. Identify and describe three methods of extinguishing (retiring) outstanding debt before maturity.

Q 14-20. How are gains and losses on early extinguishment of debt calculated and reported?

Q 14-21. When debt is retired before maturity, what disposition is made of unamortized debt issue costs?

Q 14-22. Issuing debt under an arrangement whereby lenders receive an option to buy common stock during all or a portion of the time the debt is outstanding is a frequent corporate financing practice. In some situations the result is achieved through the issuance of convertible bonds. In other situations, debt is issued with detachable warrants to buy stock. Describe the differences that exist under present GAAP in accounting for original proceeds of the issuance of convertible bonds and of debt instruments with separate warrants to purchase common stock. Also, discuss the underlying rationale for the differences in accounting.

(AICPA, adapted)

Q 14-23. Describe accounting for the conversion of debt into common stock.

Q 14-24. Discuss how to account for "sweeteners" offered to holders of convertible debt to induce them to exercise a conversion privilege.

Q 14-25. Identify the accounting procedures necessary to record the exercise of warrants issued in connection with debt.

Q 14-26. On December 31, 1998, Opela Corporation had serial debt outstanding totaling $4 million. The carrying (book) value of this debt on December 31, 1998, was $4,240,000. Ten percent of the maturity value is payable on January 4, 1999. How should this debt be presented on Opela Corporation's balance sheet as of December 31, 1998.

Q 14-27. Define a derivative financial instrument and give some examples of derivative financial instruments.

Q 14-28. Explain how derivatives are used to manage risk.

*Q 14-29. What is meant by troubled debt restructuring?

*Q 14-30. Describe two methods set forth in *FASB Statement No. 15* that are used to restructure debt.

CASES	The case marked with an asterisk (∗) refers to Appendix 14–1.

C 14-1. **VALUATION OF DEBT** On January 1, 1998, Haworth Corporation issued for $79,000, three-year, 10 percent notes with a face value of $100,000 that pay interest annually on December 31. The following are three presentations of the long-term liability section of the balance sheet that might be used for these notes at the issue date:

a)
Notes payable (maturing 12/31/2000)	$100,000
Discount on notes payable	(21,000)
Total note liability	$ 79,000

b)
Notes payable—principal (face value $100,000, maturing 12/31/2000)	$ 58,000a
Notes payable—interest (annual payment $10,000)	21,000b
Total note liability	$ 79,000

c)
Notes payable—principal (maturing 12/31/2000)	$100,000
Notes payable—interest ($10,000 per year for 3 years)	30,000
Total note liability	$130,000

aThe present value of $100,000 due at the end of three years at the yield rate of 20 percent per year.
bThe present value of $10,000 per year for three years at the yield rate of 20 percent per year.

REQUIRED

1. Discuss the conceptual merits of each of the date-of-issue balance sheet presentations shown above.
2. Explain why investors would pay only $79,000 for notes that have a face value of $100,000.

3. Assuming that an interest (discount) rate is needed to calculate the carrying value of the obligations arising from a note issue at any date during its term, discuss the conceptual merits of using:

   a) The stated or nominal rate.

   b) The market or effective rate at date of issue.

4. If the obligations arising from these notes are to be carried at their present value calculated by means of the *current* market rate of interest, how would the note valuation at dates subsequent to the date of issue be affected by an increase or a decrease in the market rate of interest?

(AICPA, adapted)

C 14-2. **CONVERTIBLE DEBT—INITIAL VALUATION AND CONVERSION** Janine Corporation recently issued several $1,000, 5 percent notes at a discount. Each $1,000 note is callable at $1,050 by Janine at any date on 30 days' notice five years after the issue date. The notes are convertible into $10 par value common stock of the company at the conversion price of $12.50 per share for each $1,000 note (each $1,000 note is convertible into 80 shares of common: $1,000 ÷ $12.50 = 80).

REQUIRED

1. Explain how the notes' conversion feature has value to (*a*) the issuer and (*b*) the investor.

2. Janine's management has suggested that when the issuance of the notes is recorded, a portion of the proceeds should be assigned to the conversion feature.

   a) What are the arguments for according *separate* accounting recognition to the notes' conversion feature?

   b) What are the arguments supporting accounting for the convertible notes as a *single* element?

3. Assume that no value was assigned to the conversion feature when the notes were issued. Assume further that five years after issuance, notes with a face value of $100,000 and book value of $96,000 are tendered for conversion on an interest payment date when the market price of the common stock is $14 per share, and that the company records the conversion as follows:

Notes payable. 96,000		
Common stock	80,000	
Contributed capital in excess of par	16,000	

   Discuss the propriety of the above accounting treatment.

4. Now assume instead that 12 years after issuance, Janine's management wants to sweeten the conversion rate in order to induce conversion. Therefore, management lowers the conversion price from $12.50 per share for each $1,000 note to $10 per share. Management argues that since the inducement did not affect cash or other assets, an expense need not be recognized in connection with conversions during the inducement period. Draft a brief response to Janine's management.

C 14-3. **PREMIUMS PAID ON BOND INVESTMENTS** The following article appeared in *The News Press*, Stillwater, Oklahoma, January 23, 1995, p. 1:

> State Treasurer Robert Butkin said today that earnings from Oklahoma's investment portfolio will be nearly $5 million less than his predecessor had predicted. Butkin said former Treasurer Claudette Henry used improper accounting practices to arrive at her projection of more than $70 million. The figure is closer to $66 million, Butkin said at his news conference.
>
> The discrepancy comes from coupon bonds for which premiums were paid to gain higher interest rates. Butkin gave an example: A bond worth $100,000 yields that amount when it matures five or six years down the road. But it may have been purchased for $125,000 to get higher interest rates. The result, he said, is a "juiced up" estimate of earnings.
>
> "Under the old practice, as soon as the bond matured, you would take that huge loss," Butkin said. He promised to use a new system to account for higher premiums. Butkin said most banks don't pay premiums higher than three or four percent, and his new chief investment officer will be looking into "whether it ever makes sense to pay a 25 percent premium."
>
> Butkin said Mrs. Henry paid premiums of $18.2 million for coupon bonds that will mature from now [1995] to the year 2001. His office did not yet know the average amount her office paid for the premiums. He said Mrs. Henry purchased $25 million worth of bonds at a 25 percent premium. It will take his office about 20 months to catch up, he said. The State Board of

Equalization uses the estimate from the Treasurer's office when it establishes the amount available to the Legislature for appropriation. Butkin submitted his revised figures to the board today.

REQUIRED

1. What is meant by paying a premium "to gain higher interest rates"?

2. The article mentions an old practice and a new practice for accounting for the premiums paid. What accounting procedure is suggested by:
   a) the old practice?
   b) the new practice?

3. Assume that the $100,000 bond in the article example matures in six years and that the market (effective) rate of interest at the purchase date is 6 percent. Determine what the coupon rate would have been in order for the State Treasurer's office to pay $125,000 (a 25 percent premium) for the bond investment.

4. Discuss how the State Treasurer's office may have "juiced up" earnings.

C 14-4. **MARK-TO-MARKET ACCOUNTING** Crooch Cotton Corporation is a financial institution that factors receivables for several cotton producers along the Mississippi River. In addition to its factoring activities, Crooch also is actively engaged in buying and selling corporate debt and equity securities on the New York Stock Exchange, the American Stock Exchange, and several over-the-counter and international markets. Crooch's security transactions are designed to complement the seasonal nature of its cotton-factoring activities.

You are conducting an audit of Crooch Cotton Corporation for the year ending December 31, 1998. In the course of your examination, you find that on January 1, 1997, Crooch purchased a non-interest-bearing corporate bond at a cost of $683,000. The bond matures on December 31, 2000, and was purchased to yield 10 percent. The following information is a summary description of the manner in which Crooch applied mark-to-market accounting procedures for this bond during 1997 and 1998:

a) During 1997, Crooch recognized interest revenue using the 10 percent rate. At the end of 1997, the market rate of interest for bonds of similar risk was 8 percent, and Crooch recognized an unrealized holding gain.

b) During 1998, Crooch applied the 8 percent rate to the end-of-1997 fair value amount in recording interest revenue. At the end of 1998, the market rate of interest for bonds of similar risk was 12 percent, and Crooch recognized an unrealized holding loss.

c) Crooch plans to apply the 12 percent rate to the end-of-1998 fair value in recording interest revenue for 1999.

REQUIRED

1. Discuss how Crooch Cotton Corporation should classify the corporate bond for purposes of applying the mark-to-market procedures under *Statement No. 115*.

2. What were the fair values of the bond at the end of 1997 and 1998?

3. Discuss the propriety of the mark-to-market procedures being used by Crooch Cotton Corporation.

4. Following the mark-to-market procedures set forth in *Statement No. 115*, calculate the correct amounts of interest revenue and unrealized holding gain or loss that Crooch should have reported for 1997 and 1998.

C 14-5. **MARK-TO-MARKET ACCOUNTING** You are a partner with a national CPA firm and have three clients who are preparing to apply the accounting and reporting requirements of *Statement No. 115*, "Accounting for Certain Investments in Debt and Equity Securities." Each client has brought to your attention an accounting issue related to applying the provisions of *Statement No. 115*. These three issues are summarized below.

a) Client *A*, a manufacturing company, holds a long-term bond that is classified as held to maturity. The issuer of the bond is experiencing financial difficulty, and it is highly likely that noteholders, including Client *A*, will allow the issuer to reduce the stated interest rate on the note significantly. The effect of this restructuring will be to reduce the fair value of the bond below the carrying value on Client *A*'s books. Client *A* believes that "mark to market" does not apply since the bond is being held to maturity and would like to simply record the reduced amount of interest revenue in future periods.

b) Client *B*, a bank, holds a bond investment classified as a trading security. Like other financial institutions, Client *B* has been reporting changes in the fair values of its trading securities as unrealized gains and losses on its income statement. Client *B* is considering reclassifying the bond investment as held to maturity. Because of the change in classification, Client *B* wishes to restate the investment from fair value to the amount that would have resulted had the investment been accounted for using the effective interest method since acquisition. Client *B* considers the change from mark-to-market accounting to the effective interest method as a change in accounting principle and would like to report the cumulative effect of the change in the current year's income statement.

c) Client *C*, a retail institution, holds a bond investment classified as available for sale. The market price of this investment has been on an upswing in recent months. Since Client *C* does not intend to hold the investment to maturity, Client *C* believes that the available-for-sale category implies that fair values and changes in fair values provide meaningful signals about present and future cash flows. Therefore, Client *C* believes that these changes in fair value should be reported in its income statement.

REQUIRED   Write a brief response to each of your clients.

C 14-6.   **INNOVATIVE FINANCIAL INSTRUMENTS** Brando Computer Company wishes to raise $100,000 in cash for expansion and is exploring ways to finance this expansion. Because Brando's operating cash flows have been close to a break-even level, the company is considering issuing a new financial instrument, called a "PIK (pay-in-kind) note." A PIK note pays no cash interest during the period over which it is outstanding. In substance, investors reinvest the interest income in notes with the same terms and conditions as the "host" note. Thus, the issuer's liability and the investor's asset increase (compound) over time. On the notes' maturity date, the issuer extinguishes the liability balance by paying cash to investors.

On January 1, 1998, Brando issues a five-year, $100,000 PIK note with a stated interest rate of 10 percent. Brando's controller is uncertain about how the market will determine the value of the PIK note at the issue date, given that there are no interest cash flows.

REQUIRED   **I.** Assuming that the market rate of interest at the issue date for notes of similar risk is 10 percent, explain why the note's issue price would be $100,000. Your explanation should be supported by a time diagram and any necessary calculations.

2. Assuming that the market rate of interest at the issue date for notes of similar risk is 12 percent, explain why the note would be issued at a discount.

3. Explain how Brando Computer Corporation should account for the PIK note, assuming that the effective interest rate at the issue date is:

   a)   10 percent.   **b)**   12 percent.

You may wish to support your explanations with calculations.

4. Discuss any similarities between an interest-bearing PIK note and a zero-coupon (non-interest-bearing) note.

C 14-7.   **ZERO-COUPON DEBT; DEBT EXTINGUISHMENT** Studebaker Motor Works, a truck manufacturer, is experiencing declining earnings due to an influx of foreign models into its sales territories. The president's young grandson, a student of financial engineering, has been trying to find creative ways to improve Studebaker's financial statements. You are the controller, and he recently entered your office with the following financing and accounting idea:

> The foreign government of Moontrek plans to issue some 20-year zero-coupon notes with a 12 percent yield. As a result of three revolutions in five years, this government has borrowed to the hilt and is forced to pay high prices for money. Each $1,000 note can be purchased for only $103.70. Where do we get our money to buy these notes? Our brokers say we can issue our own 20-year zero-coupon notes for $311.80 for each $1,000 in maturity value. Now here's the deal. Since the maturity value of each Moontrek note equals the maturity value of each note we issue, we designate the Moontrek investment as a "note sinking fund" dedicated to retiring our own debt. Since our own debt is now effectively retired—the maturity values are covered—we treat both transactions as one debt extinguishment and make the following entries (for each $1,000 in maturity value):

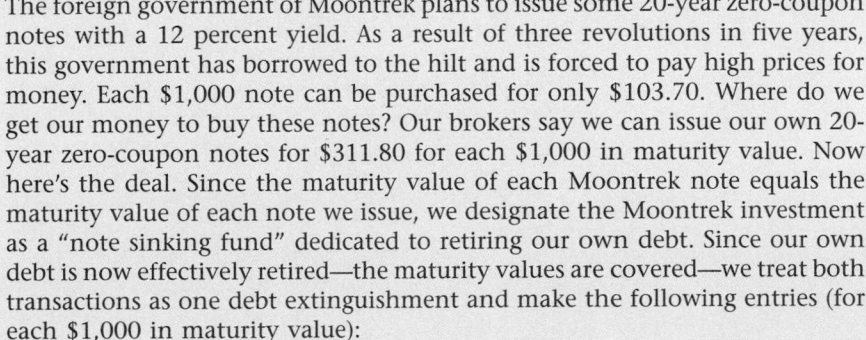

Cash	311.80	
Notes payable.		311.80
To record issue of notes.		
Investment in Moontrek notes	103.70	
Cash		103.70
To record purchase of notes.		
Notes payable	311.80	
Investment in Moontrek notes		103.70
Gain on note extinguishment		208.10
To record extinguishment.		

The more debt we issue, the more money we get to buy Moontrek notes, the larger the reported gain, and the more cash we put in the bank. Creative financing and creative accounting. What a nice pair.

REQUIRED Write a response to the president's grandson's proposal. In your response, address any issues that the proposed transactions would have on the company's risk and point out accounting deficiencies of the proposal.

C 14-8. **EMERGING DEBT INSTRUMENTS** Plastics Incorporated is a manufacturer and distributor of plastic bags. The company is considering an expansion program that will require it to raise $10 million for financing purposes. Plastics has decided to issue some form of debt instead of common stock. Since the current market rate of interest is 12 percent, the company is considering one of the following types of emerging debt instruments:

a) $10 million, zero-coupon bonds that will mature in 20 years.

b) A $10 million, floating rate bond issue that will mature in 15 years. Plastics predicts that future interest rates will fall drastically and desires not to be locked in at 12 percent.

c) A $10 million bond issue whose maturity value is linked to the Consumer Price Index. Plastics believes that investors would buy this issue at a yield of only 5 percent if the maturity value is linked to an inflation index.

d) A $10 million, non-interest-bearing commodity bond payable in 100 million plastic bags. The commodity bond will mature in six years, and at that time plastics promises to pay the par value or the cash equivalent price of the plastic bags, whichever is higher.

REQUIRED

1. What proceeds are likely to be received if Plastics selects debt instrument *a*?

2. If Plastics finances with debt instrument *b*, explain how the company might account for the bond issue.

3. Assume that Plastics finances with debt instrument *c*. If the CPI has *fallen* 50 percent from the issue date to the maturity date, how might Plastics account for this maturity date discount? (*Note:* The final decrease in the CPI is *not known* until the maturity date.)

4. Assume that Plastics finances with debt instrument *d* and that 100 million plastic bags are immediately transferred to an outside trustee, Merchant's Bank. Discuss some alternative approaches for accounting for these commodity bonds.

*C 14-9. **TROUBLED DEBT RESTRUCTURING; RECOVERABLE VALUE** Computers-R-Yours-and-Ours (CORYOS) began operations in 1993 as a retail computer store. Its hottest selling computer was a hand-held model—Small Fry—that was sold throughout the country for $3,600. The computers were manufactured overseas for CORYOS at a cost of $2,400.

In early 1997, severe competition and a new generation of credit-card-sized computers caused the company's profits and cash flows to decline. Several retail outlets were closed, and CORYOS was forced to borrow $400,000 from a savings and loan company in order to finance operations. Profits and cash flow continued to decline, and CORYOS was unable to pay the interest on the loan. By the end of 1998, $32,000 in interest had accrued.

On December 31, 1998, CORYOS reached an agreement with the savings and loan whereby the savings and loan would accept 144 Small Frys in full settlement of the $432,000 loan. CORYOS recorded the loan settlement as follows:

Notes payable	432,000	
Intangible asset	86,400	
Sales (144 × $3,600)		518,400
To record Small Fry sales.		
Cost of goods sold	345,600	
Inventory		345,600
(144 × $2,400)		
To record cost of sales.		

CORYOS believed that the intangible asset represented goodwill as the transaction maintained good relations with the savings and loan.

You are currently performing the audit of CORYOS for the year ending December 31, 1998. You have determined that CORYOS had 600 Small Frys in its stores and warehouses immediately prior to the transaction with the savings and loan. You also determine that Small Fry's manufacturer has been quoting a price of $1,700 to computer dealers in the United States.

REQUIRED Write a short paper discussing whether CORYOS has followed proper accounting procedures for its computer transactions. In the course of your discussion, determine if any adjusting entries are necessary. If so, prepare any necessary adjusting entries.

E 14-1. **BOND PRICING** Calculate the selling prices and prepare entries to record the issue for each of the following bond issues.

ISSUE	MATURITY VALUE	STATED INTEREST RATE	INTEREST PAYABLE	LIFE OF ISSUE (YEARS)	MARKET RATE AT ISSUE DATE
1	$200,000	8%	Annually	10	8% per year
2	200,000	10%	Quarterly	5	3% per quarter
3	150,000	10%	Semiannually	4	6% semiannually
4	200,000	0%	Annually	20	12% per year

E 14-2. **BOND PREMIUM** On November 1, 1998, a corporation issued bonds having a maturity value of $100,000 on November 1, 2003. A schedule of interest and book value for the issue appears below:

DATE	(1) INTEREST PAYMENT (CASH)	(2) INTEREST EXPENSE	(3) DECREASE IN BOOK VALUE (1 − 2)	(4) CARRYING VALUE (PREVIOUS 4 − 3)
11/1/98				$102,194.99
11/1/99	$5,000	$4,598.77	$401.23	101,793.76
11/1/00	5,000	4,580.72	419.28	101,374.48
11/1/01	5,000	4,561.85	438.15	100,936.33
11/1/02	5,000	4,542.13	457.87	100,478.46
11/1/03	5,000	4,521.54	478.46	100,000.00

REQUIRED
1. Interest is calculated by the _____ method.
2. The annual rates of interest are _____ percent nominal and _____ percent effective.
3. The issuing corporation's fiscal year ends on December 31. Prepare entries for its books as follows:
   a) On November 1, 2001.
   b) On December 31, 2001.

E 14-3. **EFFECTIVE INTEREST METHOD** On March 1, 1998, Dahliwal issued five-year, zero-coupon secured notes with a face value of $300,000. The notes were issued to yield 6 percent. Dahliwal's fiscal year ends on December 31, and the company uses the effective interest method.

REQUIRED
1. Calculate the issue price of the notes.
2. Prepare a schedule of interest and book value for Dahliwal's notes.
3. Prepare Dahliwal's adjusting entry for interest expense on December 31, 1998.

E 14-4. **EFFECTIVE INTEREST METHOD; MARK-TO-MARKET** Refer to the information about the Dahliwal notes in Exercise 14-3. Assume that on June 1, 1999, Gladys Trust Company purchased 30 percent of Dahliwal's notes from another investor.

REQUIRED
1. Calculate the purchase price on June 1, 1999, assuming that on June 1, 1999, the market rate of interest for notes of similar risk was:
   a) 6 percent.
   b) 10 percent.
2. Assuming that the market rate of interest for notes of similar risk was 10 percent, prepare Gladys Trust's entry to record:
   a) The purchase of Dahliwal's notes.
   b) Interest revenue for the year ending December 31, 1999.
3. Assume that Gladys Trust classifies the Dahliwal notes as trading securities. Prepare the mark-to-market adjusting entry on December 31, 1999, assuming that the fair value of the notes on this date was $65,000.

E 14-5.   **EFFECTIVE INTEREST METHOD**   On January 1, 1998, Arktex issued $120,000 of five-year, 12 percent term bonds for $129,096 to yield 10 percent. Interest is paid annually on December 31, and Arktex's accounting period ends on December 31. Arktex uses the effective interest method.

REQUIRED   **1.**   Prepare a schedule of interest and book value for Arktex.
2.   Prepare the entry to record interest expense on December 31, 2000.

E 14-6.   **BONDS ISSUED BETWEEN INTEREST DATES**   On April 1, 1998, Tyson sold a six-year, $200,000 bond issue to Weaver for $222,868, which included accrued interest. The issue price represented an effective rate of 8 percent. The bonds were dated January 1, 1998, and the stated interest rate was 10 percent, payable annually on December 31. The fiscal year for both companies ends December 31, and both use the effective interest method.

REQUIRED   **1.**   Verify the issue price on April 1, 1998.
2.   Prepare all required entries on the books of Tyson (issuer) and Weaver (investor) from April 1, 1998, through December 31, 1999.

E 14-7.   **MARK-TO-MARKET PROCEDURES**   Refer to the information in Exercise 14-6 and assume that Weaver classifies the Tyson bonds as available-for-sale.

REQUIRED   **1.**   Calculate the unrealized holding gain or loss on December 31, 1998, and December 31, 1999, assuming that the investment's fair value on these dates was $217,000 and $214,000, respectively.
2.   Briefly discuss how the unrealized gain or loss at the end of each year would be reported on Weaver's financial statements.

E 14-8.   **BOND INVESTMENTS—ACCRUALS**   On November 1, 1998, Grace acquired a long-term bond investment for $47,543. The 10 percent bonds have a par value of $50,000, mature on November 1, 2001, and pay interest (5 percent) semiannually on April 30 and October 31. Grace's accounting period ends on December 31. The purchase price represented a 6 percent yield (semiannually). On November 1, 1999, Grace sold a portion of the bonds held as a long-term investment. The par value of the bonds sold was $15,000, and the proceeds from the sale were $17,200. Grace classifies the bond investment as held to maturity.

REQUIRED   Prepare the required entries on Grace's books on the following dates (you may wish to prepare a schedule of interest and book value):
1.   November 1, 1998.
2.   December 31, 1998.
3.   April 30, 1999.
4.   October 31, 1999.
5.   November 1, 1999.

E 14-9.   **MARK-TO-MARKET PROCEDURES**   Refer to Exercise 14-8 and assume that Grace's bond investment was classified as available-for-sale. On December 31, 1998 and 1999, the fair values were as follows:

DATE	FAIR VALUE
December 31, 1998	$49,000
December 31, 1999	34,000

REQUIRED   **1.**   Calculate the unrealized holding gain recognized for 1998 and 1999.
2.   Explain how Grace should report the unrealized holding gain at the end of each year on its financial statements.

E 14-10.   **ACCRUALS FOR BOND ISSUES**   On June 1, 1998, Stickler issued six-year, $300,000 par bonds for $250,653. The bonds pay 8 percent interest each May 31 and were sold to yield 12 percent. Stickler's fiscal year ends on December 31.

REQUIRED   Prepare journal entries for the following dates. (*Hint:* You also may wish to prepare a schedule of interest and book value.)
1.   June 1, 1998 (the date of the issue).
2.   December 31, 1998 (to record interest expense for 1998).
3.   May 31, 1999 (to record interest expense and the interest payment).
4.   December 31, 1999 (to accrue interest to the end of 1999).

E 14-11. **BONDS PURCHASED AT A DISCOUNT** On January 1, 1998, Mary Melody purchased for $278,686 a $400,000 par value, five-year bond paying 2 percent interest on December 31 of each year. The purchase price represented a 10 percent effective annual yield. Mary Melody classifies the bond investment as held-to-maturity.

REQUIRED   **1.** Verify that the annual yield on the bond is 10 percent.
             2. Prepare the entries for interest revenue on December 31, 1998 and 1999.

E 14-12. **MARK-TO-MARKET; TRANSFERS BETWEEN INVESTMENT CATEGORIES** Refer to the information in Exercise 14-11. Assume that on January 1, 2000, circumstances were such that Mary Melody reclassified the bond investment into the trading security category. The fair value of the bond on January 1, 2000, based on a 12 percent market rate of interest at that date, was $303,934. Mary Melody held the bond as a trading security during 2000. On April 1, 2001, the company sold the bond for $340,000, including accrued interest.

REQUIRED   Prepare journal entries for the following dates:
             1. January 1, 2000 (to record the transfer).
             2. December 31, 2000 (to record interest).
             3. December 31, 2000 (to record the bond's fair value of $335,000).
             4. April 1, 2001 (to record the sale of the bond).

E 14-13. **VALUATION OF NOTES** Three independent note transactions appear below:
   a) Mr. *X* gave Mr. *Y* $7,118 cash. In exchange, Mr. *Y* gave Mr. *X* a three-year, non-interest-bearing note with a face value of $10,000.
   b) Ms. *A* gave Ms. *B* a parcel of land. In exchange, Ms. *B* gave Ms. *A* a three-year, $8,000, 6 percent note with interest payable annually. Although the land's fair value was not objectively determinable, Ms. *A* had paid $3,000 for the land several years ago. The market rate of interest for notes of similar risk was 10 percent.
   c) Mr. *P* gave Ms. *Q* a truck with a fair value of $8,264. In exchange, Ms. *Q* gave Mr. *P* a two-year, $10,000, non-interest-bearing note. According to Mr. *P*'s accounting records, the truck had a book value of $7,000.

REQUIRED   For each of the three transactions above:
             1. Prepare the entry for both parties to record the transaction.
             2. Prepare a schedule of interest and book value suitable for both parties.

E 14-14. **SERIAL BONDS** Gardere Corporation issued $360,000 in serial bonds at the beginning of 1998. The stated rate on the bond issue was 12 percent, payable annually. The bonds mature at the rate of $120,000 each year, beginning on December 31, 1999. Assume that each series was sold to yield 16 percent.

REQUIRED   **1.** Calculate the issue price of each series and of the total bond issue.
             2. Prepare a schedule of interest and book value.

E 14-15. **DEBT ISSUED FOR NONCASH ASSETS** At the beginning of 1998, Sawyer issued a five-year, non-interest-bearing note with a maturity value of $20,000 in exchange for land with a fair value of $13,612. Using the straight-line method inappropriately, Sawyer recognized interest expense each year of $1,278 ($20,000 − $13,612 = $6,388; $6,388 ÷ 5 = $1,278).

REQUIRED   **1.** Prepare the entry to record the exchange of the note for land.
             2. Calculate the overstatement or understatement of interest expense for 1998 and 1999.

E 14-16. **NOTES AND PRIVILEGES EXCHANGED FOR CASH** On January 1, 1998, Neas Distributing borrowed $10,000 from Gas-N-Go Service Centers by issuing a two-year, $10,000 note with interest at 4 percent payable annually. As part of the borrowing agreement and because Neas would normally have to pay 12 percent to borrow money, Neas gave Gas-N-Go the right to purchase 400 automobile tires at a discount during the two-year period.

REQUIRED   **1.** Prepare entries for Neas Distributing and Gas-N-Go Service Centers on January 1, 1998.
             2. Calculate Neas Distributing's interest expense and Gas-N-Go's interest revenue for 1998 and 1999.
             3. Assume that Gas-N-Go paid Neas $8,400 for purchases of 280 automobile tires during 1998. Prepare both parties' entries to record these purchases/sales.

E 14-17. **DEBT EXCHANGED FOR NONCASH ASSETS** At the beginning of the current year, Lybrand acquired a tract of land with a fair value of $122,016 by issuing a four-year, non-interest-bearing note with a maturity amount of $192,000.

REQUIRED   **1.** What is the effective (implicit) rate of interest on the note?
             2. Prepare the entry at the beginning of the current year to record the acquisition.
             3. Prepare the entries to record interest expense for the first and second years.

E 14-18.   **NON-INTEREST-BEARING NOTES**   Davidson sold a machine at the beginning of the current year by accepting a non-interest-bearing note with a face value of $150,000. The note is payable in four annual installments of $37,500 beginning at the end of the current year. The current rate of interest for notes of similar risk is 10 percent. Davidson's machine had a book value of $100,000.

REQUIRED

1. What is the imputed fair value of the machine?
2. Prepare the entry to record the acquisition at the beginning of the current year.
3. Prepare the entries to record interest revenue and the note receivable at the end of each of the next four years. (*Hint:* You also may wish to prepare a schedule of interest and book value.)

E 14-19.   **NOTES AND OTHER OBLIGATIONS EXCHANGED FOR CASH**   Jetblack Supply Corporation borrowed $50,000 from a customer by issuing a three-year, 2 percent note for $50,000 (interest payable annually). Jetblack also agreed to sell 800 cases of hair coloring to its customer at a discount in exchange for such a favorable rate of interest. The current rate of interest on notes of similar risk is 12 percent.

REQUIRED

1. Calculate the present value of the note and the fair value of the obligation to sell at a discount.
2. Prepare the entries to record the note issue and annual interest expense for the three-year period.
3. Assume that Jetblack's customer purchased 200 cases of hair coloring during the first year at the reduced price of $20 per case. Prepare the entry to record the sale and recognition of other revenue on the basis of your answers to parts 1 and 2.

E 14-20.   **EARLY EXTINGUISHMENT OF DEBT**   Jesse Garon Corporation issued 12-year, $100,000, 6 percent bonds at par. Bond issue costs totaled $3,000. After the bonds had been outstanding for four years and when they were selling at a 10 percent yield, Garon issued $80,000 in 10 percent bonds at par and used the proceeds to retire the old issue. Issue costs for the new issue were $2,000. Garon uses the straight-line method of accounting for bond issue costs and the effective interest method of accounting for interest.

REQUIRED   Prepare the entry to record the new issue and the extinguishment.

E 14-21.   **DEBT EXTINGUISHMENT**   On January 1, 1998, Gladstone issued five-year, 9 percent bonds with a face value of $150,000 for $133,779, which represented an effective interest rate of 12 percent. Interest is payable annually. On January 1, 2000, Gladstone extinguished the entire issue on the open market when the bonds were priced to yield 16 percent. Gladstone uses the effective interest method.

REQUIRED

1. Record Gladstone's interest expense for 1998 and 1999.
2. Record the extinguishment on January 1, 2000.

E 14-22.   **ZERO-COUPON DEBT—ISSUER**   At the beginning of the current year, the City of Broken Arrow issued $9 million of 10-year, par value, zero-coupon secured notes for $2,898,000. The effective interest method is used by Broken Arrow in accounting for interest expense.

REQUIRED

1. What is the effective interest rate?
2. Prepare Broken Arrow's entry to record the note issue.
3. Prepare Broken Arrow's entries to record interest expense for the first two years that the notes are outstanding.
4. Prepare Broken Arrow's entry to record extinguishment at maturity.

E 14-23.   **ZERO-COUPON DEBT—INVESTOR; MARK-TO-MARKET**   Refer to Exercise 14-22. At the beginning of the third year, Dowell purchased 40 percent of the Broken Arrow notes on the open market at a price to yield 10 percent. Dowell also uses the effective interest method. Dowell classifies the notes as available-for-sale.

REQUIRED

1. Calculate Dowell's purchase price.
2. Prepare Dowell's entries to record interest revenue for years 3 and 4.
3. Prepare Dowell's entries to record the unrealized holding gain/loss on the notes, assuming that the fair value at the end of years 3 and 4 was $1,600,000 and $2,100,000, respectively.

E 14-24. **IMPAIRMENT OF A LOAN** On January 1, 1998, a financial institution loaned a customer $100,000 by accepting a five-year 6 percent note in the amount of $100,000. Interest was payable annually on December 31. Three years later, on January 1, 2001, the financial institution determined that the loan had become impaired and that it was probable that the customer could pay none of the contractual interest payments and only 90 percent of the principal payment.

REQUIRED Prepare the journal entry to record the loan impairment.

E 14-25. **IMPAIRMENT OF A LOAN** At the beginning of year 1, a bank loaned a customer $15,000 by accepting a seven-year non-interest-bearing note. The note required seven annual installment payments of $2,881, beginning at the end of year 1. The note's effective interest rate was 8 percent.

At the beginning of year 3, the bank determined that the loan had been impaired and estimated that the customer would be able to pay only $2,000 annually on the remaining installment payments.

REQUIRED
1. Prepare the journal entry at the beginning of year 3 to record the loan impairment.
2. Prepare the journal entry at the end of year 3 to record interest and the customer's payment, assuming that the customer made a $2,000 payment.
3. Now assume that at the end of year 4, the customer made the contractual payment of $2,881 and that the bank determined that the loan was no longer impaired. Prepare the journal entry to record interest, the customer's payment, and any adjustment related to the nonimpairment.

E 14-26. **CONVERTIBLE DEBT** Orange Corporation issued $120,000 of 10-year, 10 percent convertible bonds for $136,105 (an 8 percent effective yield). Each $1,000 bond was convertible to eight shares of Orange common stock (par $100) on any interest date beginning two years from date of issue. Black Company acquired 40 percent of this issue.

REQUIRED
1. Prepare the entries to record the issuance by Orange and the acquisition by Black.
2. Calculate Orange's interest expense for years 1 and 2.
3. At the end of the sixth year, Black converted the bonds to Orange common stock. Give the entries for Orange and Black to record the conversion under the book value method.

E 14-27. **BONDS AND DETACHABLE WARRANTS** On December 1, 1998, Mott Corporation issued 100 $1,000, 5 percent bonds at 103. Attached to each bond was a detachable stock purchase warrant entitling the holder to purchase 10 shares of Mott's $5 par common stock for $80 per share. On December 1, 1998, the market value of each stock purchase warrant was $100. Several years later, investors exercised the warrants and purchased Mott's shares.

REQUIRED Prepare Mott's entries to record the bond issue and the exercise of the warrants.

E 14-28. **DETACHABLE WARRANTS** On April 7, 1998, Northern Corporation issued 20-year, $2 million, 8 percent bonds at 103 of par. Each $1,000 bond had a detachable warrant that permitted the purchase of one share of the corporation's $25 par value common stock for $30. Immediately after the sale of the bonds, the warrants were selling for $10 each. Western acquired the entire bond issue.

REQUIRED Prepare the entry to record the bond transaction for both Northern and Western.

E 14-29. **CONVERTIBLE NOTES; INDUCEMENTS** On January 1, 1995, Brown Company issued 100 $1,000, 12 percent convertible notes at par. The maturity date of the notes was December 31, 2004, and each note was convertible into 25 shares of Brown's $2 par common stock. On January 1, 1998, Brown induced conversion by making each note convertible into 30 shares of its common stock if conversions took place within 90 days of January 1, 1998.

During the inducement period, 80 percent of the notes were converted when the market price of Brown's common stock was $40. The remaining notes were converted to Brown's common stock during 1999 when the market price of the stock was $48.

Brown uses the book value method for bond conversion.

REQUIRED
1. Prepare Brown's journal entry to record the conversions during the inducement period.
2. Prepare Brown's journal entry to record the conversions during 1999.

E 14-30.   **BONDS WITH DETACHABLE WARRANTS**   Mustang Company sold five-year, $100,000, 8 percent bonds with detachable stock warrants to Kravis Investments for $114,000. Each $1,000 bond included detachable warrants for 25 shares of Mustang common stock ($10 par value). The option price was $30. Shortly after the sale, the warrants were selling for $3 each. At a later date, when Mustang's shares were selling at $44 per share, Kravis exercised 1,500 warrants and acquired 1,500 of Mustang's shares.

REQUIRED   **1.**   Prepare the entries for Mustang and Kravis at the date of issue.
          2.   Prepare the entries for Mustang and Kravis to record the exercise of the warrants.

*E 14-31.   **TROUBLED DEBT RESTRUCTURING**   Debtor owes $100,000 principal plus $15,000 of accrued interest to Creditor. The debt is a 10-year, 15 percent note due today, October 31, 1998. Creditor makes a concession because Debtor is in financial stress.

REQUIRED   Prepare Debtor's entries to record the following restructurings. Consider each one independently.
          1.   Creditor agrees to accept some of Debtor's real estate in full settlement of the debt. The property cost Debtor $75,000 and has a market value of $90,000.
          2.   Creditor agrees to forgive the $15,000 accrued interest, extend the maturity date to October 31, 2000, and reduce the interest rate to 6 percent.
          3.   Creditor agrees to forgive the $15,000 accrued interest and to accept 4,000 shares of Debtor's $10 par common stock in full settlement of the debt. Each share of Debtor's common stock has a market value of $22.
          4.   Creditor agrees to extend the maturity date to October 29, 2000, with no additional interest being charged.

*E 14-32.   **DEBT RESTRUCTURING—TRANSFERS OF ASSETS/EQUITY SECURITIES**
          a)   Marvin Corporation has bonds payable outstanding that are now due in the amount of $80,000. Accrued interest on the bonds totals $8,000. Since Marvin is having financial difficulties, Jobe Corporation, the holder of Marvin's bonds, agrees to accept inventory in full settlement of the debt. Marvin carries the inventory at historical cost of $55,000, although the fair value is $72,000.
          b)   Assume that instead of accepting inventory, Jobe Corporation agrees to accept 1,000 shares of Marvin's common stock (par value $5 per share, market value $75 per share).

REQUIRED   Prepare the entries to record both of the above restructuring agreements in the books of both the debtor (Marvin) and creditor (Jobe).

PROBLEMS   The problem marked with an asterisk (*) refer to Appendix 14–1.

P 14-1.   **DEBT ISSUED AT A PREMIUM—ISSUER**   On January 1, 1998, Connor Corporation issued $800,000 in 10-year, par value, 6 percent bonds. The bonds were dated January 1, 1998, pay interest annually each December 31, and were sold for $861,762 (a 5 percent effective rate). Connor uses the effective interest method. The company's fiscal year ends on December 31.

REQUIRED   **1.**   Prepare a schedule of interest and book value for Connor's bond issue.
          2.   Prepare journal entries to record the bond issue and to record interest expense for 1998.
          3.   Prepare the journal entry to record the bond issue, assuming that the bonds were issued on March 1, 1998, to yield 5 percent.
          4.   Refer to part 3. Calculate interest expense for 1998.

P 14-2.   **DEBT ISSUED AT A PREMIUM—INVESTOR**   Refer to the Connor Corporation information in Problem 14-1. On April 1, 2001, Pierce-Fenner Investment Partners purchased, as a long-term, held-to-maturity investment, 20 percent ($160,000 par value) of the Connor Corporation bonds on the open market. The purchase price was $146,208, which included accrued interest from January 1, 2001. The purchase price reflected an 8 percent yield to Pierce-Fenner. Pierce-Fenner's fiscal year ends on June 30.

REQUIRED   **1.**   Prepare Pierce-Fenner's journal entry to record the purchase on April 1, 2001.
          2.   Prepare Pierce-Fenner's schedule of interest and book value over the remaining bond term.
          3.   Prepare Pierce-Fenner's adjusting entry to record interest revenue for the year ending June 30, 2001.
          4.   Prepare Pierce-Fenner's journal entry to record the receipt of cash interest on December 31, 2001.
          5.   Calculate Pierce-Fenner's interest revenue for the year ending June 30, 2002.

P 14-3. **ZERO-COUPON BONDS—ISSUER** On January 1, 1998, Zachary Manufacturing Company issued four-year, zero-coupon bonds. The bonds had a maturity value of $300,000 and were dated January 1, 1998. The issue price was $220,500, which reflected an effective yield of 8 percent annually.

REQUIRED
1. Prepare journal entries for Zachary on the following dates (Zachary's fiscal year ends on December 31):
   a) January 1, 1998.
   b) December 31, 1998.
   c) December 31, 1999.
2. Prepare Zachary's entry to retire the bonds on the maturity date.

P 14-4. **ZERO-COUPON BONDS—INVESTOR; MARK-TO-MARKET** Refer to the information in Problem 14-3. Assume that Taylor Investments acquired the entire Zachary bond issue on the issue date and classifies the bond investment as available-for-sale.

REQUIRED
1. Prepare journal entries for Taylor Investments on the following dates (Taylor's fiscal period ends on December 31):
   a) January 1, 1998.
   b) December 31, 1998. The fair value of the Zachary bonds was $240,000.
   c) December 31, 1999. The fair value of the Zachary bonds was $267,000.
2. On January 1, 2000, Taylor Investments sold 80 percent of the Zachary bonds to another investor for $213,600. Prepare Taylor's entry to record the sale.
3. On April 1, 2000, Taylor Investments sold the remaining 20 percent of the Zachary bonds to another investor for $54,000. Prepare Taylor's entry to record the sale.

P 14-5. **NOTES EXCHANGED FOR NONCASH ITEMS** The following three transactions are independent. Assume a December 31 fiscal year end for each transaction.
   a) On January 1, Broyles, Inc., sold a truck, which had a book value of $8,000, and accepted cash of $5,000 and a three-year, non-interest-bearing note for $15,000. The note will be paid off at the rate of $5,000 per year, beginning December 31. On January 1, the market rate of interest for notes of similar risk was 10 percent.
   b) On April 1, Jadlow issued a three-year, 8 percent note for $80,000 in exchange for a customized travel bus. Interest is payable each March 31. The note's stated interest rate equaled the market rate for notes of similar risk.
   c) On January 1, Trivitt Glass Company acquired equipment with a suggested list price of $80,000 by issuing a five-year, 5 percent note for $80,000. Interest is payable annually each December 31. On January 1, the market rate of interest for notes of similar risk was 8 percent.

REQUIRED
Prepare entries to record the above transactions and to record interest for the first year.

P 14-6. **EFFECTIVE INTEREST METHOD—ISSUER AND INVESTOR** On January 1, 1998, Chance Motors issued $200,000 of term bonds, dated January 1, 1998. The bonds mature on December 31, 2000, carry a stated rate of 12 percent, payable annually at the end of each year, and were sold for $209,948 to yield 10 percent. Wayne Investment Company acquired the entire issue and plans to hold the issue until maturity. Both parties have fiscal years ending on December 31.

REQUIRED
1. Prepare a schedule of interest and book value suitable for both parties.
2. Prepare all entries for 1998 and 1999 for Chance Motors and Wayne Investment Company.
3. Assume instead that Wayne Investment Company classified the Chance Motors bonds as available-for-sale securities at the acquisition date. Prepare Wayne Investment Company's mark-to-market adjusting entries on December 31, 1998, and December 31, 1999, assuming the following fair values on the indicated dates:

DATE	FAIR VALUE
December 31, 1998	$210,000
December 31, 1999	203,000

P 14-7.   **BOND INVESTMENTS; MARK-TO-MARKET**   On December 31, 1998, Fun and Sun Brothers, Inc. (FASBI), reported the following on its balance sheet:

Assets (at fair value):

8% Al-Shaieb Corporation bonds (par value, $100,000;
     effective-interest-method carrying value, $95,022;
     interest payable annually on 12/31; maturity date, 12/31/01;
     purchased to yield 10%) **$98,000**

10% Zuhair secured notes (face value, $50,000;
     effective-interest-method carrying value, $48,778; interest payable
     annually on 12/31; maturity date, 12/31/01; purchased to yield 11%) 47,000

Accumulated other comprehensive income (part of stockholders' equity):

Unrealized holding gain (loss) on Al-Shaieb bonds........................ 2,978

FASBI classifies the Al-Shaieb bonds as available-for-sale and the Zuhair notes as trading securities. FASBI's fiscal year-end is December 31.

The following transactions occurred through December 31, 2001:

Dec. 31, 1999   Recorded interest revenue on the Al-Shaieb bonds and the Zuhair notes.

Dec. 31, 1999   Made adjusting entries to mark investment securities to market: fair value of Al-Shaieb bonds, $98,500; fair value of Zuhair notes, $48,000.

July 1, 2000   Sold the Zuhair notes for $51,000, including accrued interest from January 1, 1997.

Dec. 31, 2000   Recorded interest revenue on the Al-Shaieb bonds.

Dec. 31, 2000   Made adjusting entry to mark Al-Shaieb bonds to market: fair value, $98,176.

Dec. 31, 2000   Sold 40 percent of the Al-Shaieb bonds for $39,271.

Dec. 31, 2001   Recorded interest revenue on the Al-Shaieb bonds.

Dec. 31, 2001   Received maturity value of Al-Shaieb bonds.

REQUIRED   Prepare entries for FASBI to record the above transactions and events.

P 14-8.   **IMPROPER VALUATION OF NOTES RECEIVABLE**   On January 1, 1998, Hardage sold a tract of land that had an original cost of $20,000 by accepting four 8 percent notes for $10,000 each. The notes are due as follows:

12/31/98... **$10,000**
12/31/99... **10,000**
12/31/2000... **20,000**

While the fair value of the land could not be determined objectively by appraisers, the current rate of interest on January 1, 1998, was 12 percent. Hardage recorded the sale on January 1, 1998, and the cash interest and note collected on December 31, 1998, as follows:

Jan. 1   Notes receivable 40,000
         Land..   20,000
         Gain on sale of land   20,000

Dec. 31   Cash 3,200
         Interest revenue   3,200
         (.08 × $40,000)
         Cash 10,000
         Notes receivable   10,000

REQUIRED   **I.** Prepare the entries at December 31, 1998, to correct the errors made by Hardage with respect to the gain and the interest revenue.

        2. Prepare the entries to record interest revenue and note collections at the end of 1999 and 2000.

P 14-9.   **VALUATION OF NOTES; INTEREST**   Jason Realty Renovating Company invests in apartment and office buildings. The properties are renovated and remodeled and then resold to apartment leasing syndicates. The sales price of a property varies but usually averages about $200,000 per property. Jason requires a small down payment and accepts a note, payable in 10 annual installments, for the balance of the sales price. The notes bear interest at 2 percent, although the syndicates normally would have to borrow at a much higher rate.

During your audit of Jason, you discover that the company has been recording its notes receivable at face value and crediting sales revenue for the notes' face value. Interest revenue on the notes then is calculated on the basis of the 2 percent stated interest rate.

REQUIRED

1. Discuss the impact on the financial statements of the company's methods of accounting for notes receivable and interest revenue. In the course of your discussion, indicate the proper method of accounting.
2. Assume that the prevailing market rate of interest applicable to the notes accepted by Jason is 10 percent. On the basis of an average sales price per property of $200,000 and an average down payment of $10,000, calculate the amount of misstatement of the following items in the company's financial statements (for simplicity, assume that the sale is made at the beginning of the year and that each installment payment is received at the end of the year):
   a) Sales revenue in the year of sale.
   b) Interest revenue for the first and second years that the note is outstanding.
   c) Notes receivable at the end of the first and second years.

P 14-10. **EFFECTIVE INTEREST METHOD, ACCRUALS, EARLY EXTINGUISHMENT OF DEBT** On March 1, 1998, Day Housing Corporation issues $250,000 in 10 percent term bonds. The bonds are dated March 1, 1998, pay 5 percent interest semiannually on March 1 and September 1, mature on March 1, 2001, and are issued to yield 6 percent semiannually. On September 1, 2000, after paying the semiannual interest, Day extinguishes 40 percent of the bonds through an open-market purchase at $92,000. Day's fiscal year ends on December 31, and the company uses the effective interest method.

REQUIRED

1. Calculate the total cash received on the bond sale on May 1, 1998.
2. Prepare the entries on the following dates:
   a) March 1, 1998 (date of sale).
   b) September 1, 1998 (to record interest expense and the first interest payment).
   c) December 31, 1998 (to record accrued interest expense and interest payable).
   d) March 1, 1999 (to record interest expense and the second interest payment).
   e) September 1, 2000 (to record the bond retirement).

P 14-11. **EARLY EXTINGUISHMENT OF DEBT** In each of the two independent cases below, the effective interest method is appropriate.
   a) Immediately after a semiannual interest payment, Nelson extinguished outstanding debt with a par value of $200,000 for $195,000. The 10-year, 6 percent (3 percent semiannually) bonds had been outstanding for 5 1/2 years and were originally issued for $215,595 (a 2 1/2 percent semiannual yield).
   b) On April 1, 1991, Conn issued bonds for $255,000 (including accrued interest). The bonds had a par value of $250,000, were dated January 1, 1991, pay 8 percent interest annually, and mature on December 31, 2005. Expenditures associated with the bond issue total $22,125. The bonds are callable at 103 percent after January 1, 1992. On January 1, 1998, Conn exercises the call privilege and retires the bonds.

REQUIRED Prepare the entry to record the debt extinguishment in each case.

P 14-12. **DEBT EXTINGUISHMENT** At the beginning of 1995, Crowe Corporation issued, for $107,360, 10-year, 7 percent term bonds with a maturity value of $100,000. Interest is payable annually. Interest expense for 1995, 1996, and 1997 was accounted for under the effective interest method (6 percent effective yield). At the beginning of 1998, these bonds were selling in the market to yield 10 percent, and Crowe decided to extinguish this debt.

REQUIRED Prepare the entry to record Crowe's debt extinguishment under each of the following independent methods of extinguishment:
1. Crowe purchases the 7 percent bonds on the open market and retires them.
2. Crowe issues, at a discount, seven-year, zero-coupon bonds with a maturity value of $175,000. Investors required a 12 percent effective yield to maturity. The proceeds and additional cash are used to extinguish Crowe's 7 percent term bonds.

P 14-13. **SERIAL DEBT** At the end of year 2, Bauman, Inc., issued 9 percent serial bonds with a maturity value of $150,000. Interest is payable annually, and the bonds were issued to yield 12 percent. They mature as follows:

DATE	PAR VALUE
End of year 4	$20,000
End of year 5	20,000
End of year 6	30,000
End of year 7	30,000
End of year 8	50,000

REQUIRED

1. Calculate the proceeds of the bond issue.
2. Prepare an interest expense schedule using the effective interest method.
3. Referring to the schedule made for part 2, prepare the entry to record interest expense and maturing bonds at the end of year 6.

*P 14-14. **DEBT RESTRUCTURING—MODIFICATION OF TERMS** The three independent cases below represent situations in which a creditor has made a concession to a debtor in financial difficulty.

a) Book value of debt at beginning of current year: $58,000. Terms of restructuring agreement: Principal is reduced to $40,000 and due at the end of three years. The interest rate is changed to 8 percent, payable annually at the end of each year.

b) Book value of debt at beginning of current year: principal, $100,000; accrued interest, $6,950. Terms of restructuring: All payments are deferred until the end of the fourth year, at which time $130,000 will be due and payable.

c) Book value of debt:

Bonds payable (including premium of $2,710)...........................$102,710
Interest payable 2,000

Terms of restructuring: Accrued interest payable is forgiven; bond principal is deferred to the end of the fifth year; the interest rate on the bonds is changed to 3 percent, payable annually.

REQUIRED Complete the following requirements for each case:

1. Determine if an entry by the debtor is required at the date of restructure.
2. If no entry is required, calculate the effective interest rate applicable to the restructure agreement.
3. Prepare any necessary entries at the date of restructure and at the end of the first year on the books of the debtor.

P 14-15. **DERIVATIVES** On January 1, 1998, Hedger LLP acquires, as an available-for-sale security, a bond for $50,000. The bond pays 5 percent interest each December 31 and the $50,000 maturity value is due on December 31, 2000. Hedger is concerned that interest rates might rise and decrease the fair value of the bond investment. On January 1, 1998, Hedger enters into a three-year interest rate swap. Under the swap terms, Hedger will pay fixed interest at a 5 percent rate and will receive interest at a variable rate. The notational amount of the swap is $50,000; a cash settlement will be paid or received by Hedger each December 31. The cash settlement at the end of each year is the net of the 5 percent fixed rate payment and a variable interest receipt based on the market rate of interest at the *beginning* of each year. Over the three-year period, market rates of interest are as follows: 1/1/98, 5 percent; 12/31/98, 8 percent; 12/31/99, 6 percent; 12/31/00, 6 percent.

REQUIRED

1. Prepare a schedule showing the fair values of the note receivable and the derivative instrument (interest rate swap) on December 31, 1998, 1999, and 2000.
2. Prepare a schedule showing the changes in fair value of the note receivable and the derivative instrument (interest rate swap) for the years ending December 31, 1998, 1999, and 2000.
3. Show how these transactions would appear on Hedger's income statement for the years ending December 31, 1998, 1999, and 2000.
4. Comment briefly on the success of Hedger's risk-management strategy.

P 14-16. **COMPREHENSIVE REVIEW PROBLEM** You are conducting the audit for Supergum Corporation for the year ending December 31, 1998, and the transactions below have come to your attention:

a) On January 1, 1997, Supergum accepted a three-year, non-interest-bearing note with a maturity value of $50,000 in exchange for land. The land had cost Supergum $30,000, and the market rate of interest for notes of similar risk was 10 percent. Supergum recorded the transaction as follows:

Notes receivable	50,000	
Land		30,000
Gain on sale of land		20,000

Supergum has recorded no interest on the note to date, arguing that this omission is offset by the gain on sale. Supergum plans to hold the note until maturity.

b) On July 1, 1998, Supergum borrowed $20,000 in cash from a bank by issuing a two-year, non-interest-bearing note. In exchange for such a favorable interest rate, Supergum agreed to repair as needed, and without charge, the bank's air-conditioning system for two years. No repairs have been necessary to date. The market rate of interest on July 1, 1998, was 10 percent.

c) On January 1, 1995, Supergum acquired IROC bonds with a par value of $100,000 for $117,115 (an 8 percent yield). The bonds pay interest at 10 percent each December 31 and mature 15 years from January 1, 1995. Although Supergum classified the bonds as held-to-maturity, a decline in IROC's credit rating led Supergum to sell the bonds on April 1, 1998, for $110,000 including accrued interest of $2,500 ($100,000 × .10 × 1/4). The sale was recorded as follows (no decrease in book value was recorded by Supergum during the time it held the bonds, although the effective interest method is proper):

Cash	110,000	
Realized loss on sale of bonds	7,115	
Investment in IROC bonds		117,115

d) At the end of 1998, Supergum Company issued $6 million of zero-coupon bonds with detachable warrants for 400,000 shares of its $10 par value common stock at $18 per share. The bonds mature over 10 years, starting one year from date of issuance, with annual maturities of $600,000. At the time, Supergum had 3.2 million shares of common stock outstanding and the market price was $23 per share. The company received $6,680,000 for the bonds and the warrants. The bonds would have been issued at an 8 percent interest rate had they been issued without the warrants. Supergum recorded the transaction as a debit to cash and a credit to notes payable in the amount of $6,680,000.

e) On July 1, 1998, Supergum purchased convertible bonds for $40,000 (par value) plus accrued interest of $2,400. The bonds have a 12 percent stated rate of interest and a scheduled maturity date of December 31, 2001. Supergum reasoned that the bonds would have sold for $37,000 without the conversion privilege and recorded the purchase and interest during 1998 as follows:

July 1 Investment in bonds ($37,000 + $2,400)	39,400	
Conversion privilege	3,000	
Cash		42,400
Dec. 31 Cash	4,800	
Interest revenue		4,800

f) On January 1, 1997, Supergum purchased, as a trading security, a zero-coupon note for $55,840. The note matures 10 years from January 1, 1997, and the purchase price represented an effective yield of 6 percent. Supergum did not mark the note to its fair value of $60,000 at the end of 1997. At the end of 1998, when the note's fair value was $65,000, Supergum transferred the note to the available-for-sale category and made the following entry to record the transfer:

Note investment (available for sale)	65,000	
Note investment (trading)		62,741
Unrealized holding gain (to other comprehensive income)		2,259

The $62,741 credit to note investment (trading) represented the effective-interest-method carrying value at the transfer date, and Supergum shows the unrealized holding gain as a component of accumulated other comprehensive income on its 12/31/98 balance sheet.

g) Supergum has a $100,000 variable-rate note payable outstanding, which paid 8 percent interest (the market rate on January 1, 1997) for the year ending December 31,

1997. The note matures on December 31, 2002. In anticipation of continued rising interest rates over the note term, on January 1, 1998 Supergum entered into a five-year pay-fixed, receive-variable interest rate swap. The notational amount of the swap was $100,000, and cash settlement to be paid or received by Supergum is the net of 8 percent fixed payment and a variable interest receipt based on the market rate of interest at the beginning of each year. On December 31, 1998, the market rate of interest was 6 percent.

REQUIRED   For each transaction, prepare any necessary adjusting or correcting entry.

P 14-17.   **FINANCIAL REPORTING PROBLEM; GENERAL ELECTRIC**   The financial statements and notes for General Electric Corporation appear in Appendix B at the end of the text. Two items on GE's December 31, 1995, balance sheet that relate to the material covered in this chapter are:

Assets: **Investment securities** .... **$41,067 million**
Liabilities: **Long-term borrowings** .... **$51,027 million**

Additional disclosures related to these balance sheet amounts appear in footnotes 1 (summary of significant accounting policies), 10 (investment securities), and 18 (borrowings).

REQUIRED   Study these two items and the related footnote disclosures and write a brief report that answers the following questions (all questions refer to the 1995 financial statements):

1. Specify how GE classifies its investment securities and list the types of securities included.

2. For the investment securities, prepare a schedule comparing estimated fair value with amortized cost (effective-interest-method carrying value). Your schedule should include an analysis of unrealized gains and unrealized losses.

3. What were the amounts of gross *realized* gains and gross *realized* losses on sales of investment securities during 1995?

4. Are GE's investment securities a significant portion of total assets? Support your answer with any necessary calculations.

5. List the types of debt securities included under long-term borrowings.

6. Are GE's long-term borrowings a significant portion of its liabilities and equity? Support your answer with any necessary calculations.

7. Discuss how GE uses interest rate and currency swaps to manage risk and interest costs.

Leases

LEARNING OBJECTIVES

After studying this chapter, you should be able to:

1. Distinguish between a lease that is a rental of property and a lease that is an acquisition of property by financing.

2. Describe how to account for a lease that represents a transfer of ownership from the lessor to the lessee.

3. Classify leases that transfer ownership and those that do not transfer ownership from the lessor to the lessee.

4. Identify the *Statement No. 13* criteria used by (1) the lessee and (2) the lessor to classify a lease.

5. Distinguish between and account for guaranteed residual values and unguaranteed residual values.

6. Describe a bargain purchase option and explain how to account for it.

7. Distinguish between the interest rate implicit in a lease and the lessee's incremental borrowing rate and apply the proper rate for the lessee.

8. Describe a sale-leaseback transaction and prepare journal entries for such a transaction.

9. Prepare lessee journal entries for a capital lease and an operating lease.

10. Prepare lessor journal entries for a direct-financing lease, a sales-type lease, and an operating lease.

11. Describe the purpose of lease disclosures.

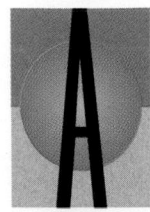

lease is an arrangement in which one party, called the **lessor,** transfers property and the rights to use it to another party, called the **lessee,** in return for cash payments that extend over a given period. Leasing arrangements extend into many areas of our society and cover many types of property. The grocer's building where you shop probably is leased rather than owned by the grocer. The mainframe computer at your college or university probably is leased from a computer manufacturer or financial institution. Other commonly leased properties include warehouses, railroad cars, trucks, automobiles, space satellites, land, and airplanes. Several years ago, for example, American Airlines leased 40 new jets from Airbus and Boeing in an innovative arrangement called "rent-a-plane." More recently, International Lease Finance Corporation, a company that specializes in leasing jets to airlines, placed orders worth $6 billion for new airliners from Airbus and Boeing.[1] Even clothing is leased:

Top Shelf, a Minnesota company, deals in made-to-measure garments for men and women. Last year it got into suit leasing. The company leases custom-made suits to executives with a signed agreement and a down payment of 40 percent of the lease cost. The minimum two-year lease costs $5,000, for which Top Shelf provides 12 to 15 suits costing around $420 apiece. The balance is paid off in monthly payments made over two years. At the end of the two-year lease period, the suits are returned to Top Shelf.

A "direct buy option" also is offered. If interest rates or other factors make leasing unrealistic for a company, the suits can be purchased.

Suit leasing began about four years ago in England, where some companies were embarrassed by the tacky appearance of their executives. Because of Britain's lower wage rates and high taxes, some executives couldn't afford expensive clothes.

In the United States the Internal Revenue Service is thought to be watching for potential abuses. Leased suits are intended for business, but who's going to make sure they're not worn at nonbusiness parties?[2]

At the consumer level, there has been a significant increase in the number of automobile dealers engaged in leasing. These dealers offer to lease cars to their customers under a long-term lease arrangement as an alternative to a purchase plan. The leasing alternative usually is made available to a dealer by the automobile manufacturer, such as General Motors, or by a financing subsidiary of the manufacturer, such as GMAC. By the year 2000, manufacturers expect that 50 percent of all new cars will be financed under a leasing program, whether for single cars or entire fleets.[3] In the automobile industry, leasing became popular about five years ago, when new car prices rose so high the industry was forced to promote leasing to survive. In the past, those on limited budgets could buy a car with monthly payments spread over two to five years. But as loan periods lengthened with the rising cost of new cars, owners had to wait almost five years to build up equity in a car before trading it in on a new one. Car manufacturers found the way to get people back into the showrooms was leasing.[4]

Why has there been such an unprecedented growth in leasing in recent years? Proponents of leasing claim it has advantages. First, the lessee obtains greater financing without having to make the substantial down payment required under a credit purchase. Second, leasing may offer larger tax deductions than a purchase does. Third, leasing may reduce the risk of property obsolescence. Finally, under some circumstances, a lessee may not be required to report a lease obligation as a liability on the balance sheet. This method of "off-balance-sheet financing" may increase the lessee's apparent borrowing capacity.

---

[1]"International Lease to Buy Airbus and Boeing Planes," *The Wall Street Journal,* March 5, 1996, p. A-3.
[2]"Suit Leasing Firm Can Help You Fit the Company Image," *Tulsa World,* March 22, 1981, p. F-9.
[3]"Behind the Wheel," *Entrepreneur,* January 1996, p. 162.
[4]"Clearing the Fog Surrounding Car Leasing," *Tulsa World,* August 25, 1995, p. W-9.

Not surprisingly, accounting for leases, especially by the lessee, has been controversial for decades. Many lessees have "window-dressed" their financial statements through leasing arrangements; that is, they have acquired the use of assets through a lease without showing either the assets or the related liabilities on the balance sheet. Lessees have also opposed disclosing long-term lease obligations on their balance sheets. The motives for window dressing include a desire to increase the apparent return on investment, to obtain a more favorable debt-equity ratio, and to increase borrowing capacity.

In the following section, we will consider two basic concepts underlying accounting for leases: the question of whether a lease transfers ownership of property and the classification of leases based on the answer to that question. We will then apply these concepts using *Statement No. 13* criteria for classifying leases. The next section describes and covers accounting for other features of leases, including residual values, purchase options, and sale-leaseback transactions. The chapter concludes with a section on lease disclosures.

CONCEPTUAL CONSIDERATIONS

The basic conceptual issue in accounting for leases is whether a lease is (1) a *rental of property* or (2) an *acquisition of property by financing*. This distinction is important because accounting for rentals of property is quite different from accounting for the acquisition and financing of property. In fact, this conceptual distinction underlies classification of all leases, as we shall see later in this section. First, we will discuss how to determine whether a lease constitutes a rental or an acquisition of property.

Acquisition or Rental? The Question of Ownership Transfer

To determine whether a lease is a rental or an acquisition of property, one must ask the following question: *Has the lessor transferred substantially all ownership rights, risks, and rewards associated with the property to the lessee?* If so, the lessor has either financed property for the lessee or sold property to the lessee and financed the purchase. The lessee has acquired an asset—property—and in doing so has incurred a liability—the lease obligation. If these conditions have *not* been met, the lessor is merely renting the property to the lessee.

Exhibit 15–1 provides a perspective on this issue. The line in the exhibit should be thought of as a continuum. The far left end represents a lease agreement that *does* transfer ownership rights, risks, and rewards from the lessor to the lessee. The far right end represents a lease agreement that *does not* transfer ownership rights, risks, and rewards from the lessor to the lessee. Keep these end points in mind as we discuss the following example.

At the beginning of 1998, Lessor Bank, Inc., entered into a noncancelable lease agreement with Lessee Telecommunications Company in which the bank purchased and transferred computer equipment to Lessee Telecommunications. The equipment had a fair value of $2,486, a useful life of three years, and no residual value at the end of the third year. The term of the lease covered three years—1998, 1999, and 2000. Lessee Telecommunications was an excellent credit risk and agreed to assume all ownership risks associated with the equipment, such as maintenance, taxes, and insurance. Lessor Bank recently had purchased the equipment for $2,486.

> **1** Distinguish between a lease that is a rental of property and a lease that is an acquisition of property by financing.

EXHIBIT 15-1	An "Acquisition/Rental" Continuum for a Lease (Conceptual)

Lessor Transfers
Ownership Rights, Risks,
and Rewards to Lessee

Lessor Retains
Ownership Rights,
Risks, and Rewards

$$\xleftarrow{\hspace{6cm}}\xrightarrow{}$$

Lessee: Purchase by
    financing

Lessee: Rental

Lessor: Sale and/or
    financing

Lessor: Rental

Because the bank desired a 10 percent rate of return on its investment, it established the annual lease payments as follows:

$$\text{Investment to be recovered} = \text{Lease payments} \times P\overline{_{3|}}_{10\%}$$
$$\$2,486 = \text{Lease payments} \times 2.4869^{a}$$
$$\text{Lease payments} = \frac{\$2,486}{2.4869}$$
$$= \$1,000 \text{ (rounded)}$$

ᵃFrom Table D of Appendix A.

The bank charged Lessee Telecommunications $1,000 per year, payable at the end of each year.[5] Had Lessee Telecommunications borrowed the money to purchase the equipment, it would have had to pay a 10 percent interest rate.

We can analyze this lease agreement with reference to the theory concepts presented in Chapter 2. There we defined assets as probable future economic benefits obtained or controlled by a particular entity as a result of past transactions or events. Liabilities were defined as probable future sacrifices of economic benefits arising from present obligations of a particular entity to transfer assets or provide services to other entities in the future as a result of past transactions or events.

CONCEPTUAL

Definitions of financial statement elements are applied to a lease.

Applying these definitions, clearly Lessee Telecommunications has both acquired an asset and has incurred a liability. As an asset, the computer equipment is expected to provide future economic benefits to Lessee Telecommunications by contributing to its revenue-generating activities and thus to its net cash inflows. Lessee Telecommunications will obtain those economic benefits by using the computer equipment. Furthermore, it can control others' access to those benefits because it possesses the equipment. Also, an exchange transaction has occurred; Lessee Telecommunications has acquired the right to use the equipment as it wishes.

CONCEPTUAL

If the lease terms transfer ownership risk and benefits to the lessee, the lessee has purchased the equipment by financing.

Lessee has also incurred a liability. It has a noncancelable obligation to pay $1,000 at the end of each year for the next three years. The obligation, which will be discharged in the future, was created by an exchange transaction that has already occurred. In exchange for the use of the asset throughout its useful life, Lessee Telecommunications has agreed to assume responsibility for its maintenance, insurance, and taxes, and is essentially paying Lessor Bank its fair value plus 10 percent interest.

In summary, Lessor Bank has transferred all ownership rights, risks, and rewards to Lessee Telecommunications. The concept of **substance over form** implies that Lessee has purchased the computer equipment from Lessor. Lessor is merely financing the purchase for Lessee.

---

[5]At this point the lease payments are assumed to be made at the *end* of each period. In practice, lease payments usually are made at the *beginning* of each period. Later in this chapter we will use beginning-of-period payments. End-of-year payments are used here for instructional purposes.

Accounting for a Lease That Transfers Ownership

Based on our analysis above, on January 1, 1998, Lessor would make the following entries to record the lease as a financing transaction:

LESSOR

Lease receivable	2,486	
Equipment		2,486

To record the receivable from financing.

Describe how to account for a lease that represents a transfer of ownership from the lessor to the lessee.

CONCEPTUAL

Lease receivables are recorded at present value.

As with other long-term monetary assets, the receivable is recorded at the present value of the future cash flows (in this case, the lease payments). Recording the lease receivable at present value is sometimes called the **net method** of recording a lease.[6]

Note that the *lease receivable equals the fair value of the equipment* transferred to Lessee. The interest (discount) rate of 10 percent, which when applied to the annual lease payments of $1,000 equates the present value of the lease payments with the equipment's fair value of $2,486, is called the **interest rate implicit in the lease.** Notice that this 10 percent interest rate is also the rate of return desired by Lessor.

Turning to the lessee, Lessee would make the following entry on January 1, 1998:

LESSEE

Leased property	2,486	
Lease liability		2,486

To record the asset acquired and the liability incurred.

Lessee records an asset, leased property, at its fair value of $2,486, and a lease liability at $2,486, the present value of the three $1,000 annual lease payments. As with the lessor's lease receivable, Lessee records the liability using the net method.[7]

We have determined that the lease agreement between Lessor Bank and Lessee Telecommunications is, in substance, an acquisition of property by financing. The accounting procedures over the term of the lease are relatively uncomplicated. Lessor Bank would account for the lease as if it were a long-term loan. During 1998, 1999, and 2000, Lessor's only entries would be to record (1) receipt of the annual lease payments and (2) interest revenue. Lessee Telecommunications would account for the lease in a manner similar to that of the purchase of plant and equipment by incurring debt. Lessee would make parallel entries for (1) the lease payments and (2) interest expense. In addition, Lessee would depreciate the leased property over the three-year period on the basis of the services it expects to receive from the use of the asset.

A schedule of interest and book value for the lessor's receivable and lessee's payable appears in Exhibit 15–2. This schedule is suitable for *both* parties in this example, because both the lessor's rate of return and the lessee's cost of borrowing are 10 percent. (Later, we will discuss situations in which the lessor's schedule of

---

[6]Under the gross method, the entry would be:

Lease receivable	3,000	
Equipment		2,486
Unearned interest revenue		514

Unearned interest revenue is a contra account to the lease receivable account. Notice that the net receivable (lease receivable minus unearned interest revenue) is $2,486.

[7]Lessee's entry under the gross method would be:

Leased property	2,486	
Discount on lease liability	514	
Lease liability		3,000

The discount is a contra account to the lease liability account and is interpreted in the same manner as a discount on a debt security. Notice that the net liability (lease liability minus discount on lease liability) is $2,486.

EXHIBIT 15–2	Schedule of Interest and Book Value

Year	(1) Interest Revenue/ Expense[a]	(2) Annual Lease Payment	(3) Reduction in Receivable/ Payable[b]	(4) Lease Receivable/ Payable Balance (End of Year)[c]
			(1/1/98)	$2,486
1998	$249	$1,000	$ 751	1,735
1999	174	1,000	826	909
2000	91	1,000	909	–0–
	$514	$3,000	$2,486	

[a]10% of beginning-of-period receivable/payable balance.
[b]Col. 2 minus col. 1.
[c]Beginning balance of receivable/payable minus col. 3.

CONCEPTUAL

The effective interest method is used to account for the lessor's receivable and the lessee's payable.

interest and book value differs from the lessee's schedule.) Notice that interest is calculated using the *effective interest method.* Lessor and Lessee make the following entries, based on the information in Exhibit 15–2, at the end of 1998 to record the lease payments and interest:

LESSOR

Lease receivable	249	
Interest revenue		249
To recognize interest earned in 1998.		

Cash	1,000	
Lease receivable		1,000
To record receipt of lease payment at the end of 1998.		

LESSEE

Interest expense	249	
Lease liability		249
To record interest expense for 1998.		

Lease liability	1,000	
Cash		1,000
To record the lease payment at the end of 1998.		

One more point should be made about Exhibit 15–2 and the journal entries just presented. Note that, as with other monetary assets and liabilities accounted for at present value, the lessor's receivable (lessee's payable) *increases* during the year (column 3) because of interest revenue (interest expense) and *decreases* at the end of the year (column 4) because of the cash flows (lease payments). This pattern, typical of the effective interest method, should not be new to you. It was a fundamental concept in the previous chapter on financial instruments. Exhibit A–9 in Appendix A to this text presents the pattern as a "saw-toothed curve."

CONCEPTUAL

The pattern of the lease receivable/payable follows a "saw-toothed" curve.

In our example, Lessee has acquired all the ownership rights associated with the equipment and has essentially purchased it on an installment basis. Therefore, Lessee makes the following entry at the end of each year to record depreciation, assuming the straight-line method is appropriate:

Depreciation expense—leased property	829	
Accumulated depreciation		829
($2,486 ÷ 3)		

Financial Statement Presentation of Leases That Transfer Ownership

The following data about the lease would appear on Lessor Bank's and Lessee Telecommunications's income statements for the year ended December 31, 1998:

LESSOR'S INCOME STATEMENT
Interest revenue (from Exhibit 15–2) **$249**

LESSEE'S INCOME STATEMENT
Interest expense (from Exhibit 15–2) **$249**
Depreciation expense—leased property **829**

Lessor's and Lessee's December 31, 1998, balance sheets would show the following information:

LESSOR'S BALANCE SHEET
Assets:
   Lease receivable (from Exhibit 15–2) **$1,735**

LESSEE'S BALANCE SHEET
Assets:
   Leased property **$2,486**
   Less: Accumulated depreciation . . . . **(829)**
                                                                                                    $1,657

Liabilities:
   Lease liability (from Exhibit 15–2) **$1,735**

As with other long-term monetary assets and liabilities, Lessor's lease receivable and Lessee's lease liability are valued and reported at present value—in this case, the present value of the minimum lease payments. In their financial statements for the year ending December 31, 1998, Lessor and Lessee could disclose in footnotes the gross amount of lease payments remaining, less interest if that information were thought useful. The gross lease payments remaining ($2,000), less the interest portion of those payments ($265), provide additional information about the composition of the Lessor's lease receivable balance (Lessee's lease liability balance) of $1,735 on December 31, 1998.

If Lessor and Lessee prepare *classified* balance sheets at the end of 1998, they should allocate the lease receivable (lease liability) balances between the current and noncurrent classifications. This allocation may be made from the data presented in Exhibit 15–2. The portion of the receivable and payable that will be reduced in 1999 is $826. Therefore, $826 is the current portion, and $909 is the noncurrent portion:

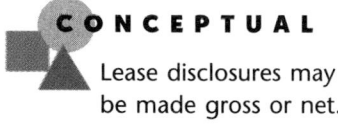
CONCEPTUAL
Lease disclosures may be made gross or net.

Lessor's receivable and Lessee's payable balance
   at the end of 1998: $ 826 classified as current
                                                                    909 classified as noncurrent
                                                              $1,735 total

Notice in Exhibit 15–2 that although Lessor will receive $1,000 in cash at the end of 1998, $174 of that amount is interest that will accrue in 1999 and thus is *not*

EXHIBIT 15-3	**Classification of Leases by Lessor and Lessee**	
	Lessee	**Lessor**
Ownership rights, risks, and rewards transferred from lessor to lessee	Capital lease	**1.** Direct-financing **2.** Sales-type **3.** Leveraged
Ownership rights, risks, and rewards not transferred from lessor to lessee	Operating lease	Operating lease

part of the lease receivable at the end of 1998. Similar reasoning also applies to the lease liability on Lessee's balance sheet.[8]

This extended example has allowed us to focus on conceptual issues and procedures involved in accounting for a lease that transfers substantially all ownership rights, risks, and rewards from the lessor to the lessee. In the following section we shall discuss how those types of leases, as well as others that do *not* transfer ownership rights, risks, and rewards, are classified in practice.

Classification of Leases

3

Classify leases that transfer ownership and those that do not transfer ownership from the lessor to the lessee.

Exhibit 15–3 shows how lessors and lessees classify leases in practice. A lessee classifies a lease as either a capital lease or an operating lease. A capital lease is, in substance, a purchase of property on an installment basis. (The use of the term *capital* has probably arisen from accountants' use of the term *capitalize* to mean "record as an asset.") A lessor would classify a lease of this type as either a direct financing lease, a leveraged lease, or a sales-type lease. An operating lease is similar to a property rental. These lease classifications are discussed in more detail in the following sections.

Capital Leases–Lessee

A **capital lease** is a lease that transfers ownership rights, risks, and rewards from the lessor to the lessee. *Lessee Telecommunications' lease with Lessor Bank was a capital lease to Lessee Telecommunications.* From the lessee's standpoint, accounting for a capital lease is similar to accounting for any other exchange transaction in which it acquires an asset and incurs a liability.

Direct-Financing Leases–Lessor

If ownership rights, risks, and rewards are transferred from the lessor to the lessee and if the terms of the lease are such that the lessor essentially *finances* the property acquisition for the lessee, the lease is called a **direct-financing lease.** Under a direct-financing lease, no income accrues to the lessor at the inception of the lease because the present value of the lease payments equals the lessor's investment

---

[8]Under GAAP, unanimity is lacking on the current/noncurrent balance sheet classification of lease receivables and lease obligations. As alternatives to the approach shown above, many accountants would classify as the current portion either (1) the next year's lease payment or (2) the *present value* of next year's lease payment and the remainder of the receivable or obligation as the noncurrent portion. In terms of our example, these additional alternatives would lead to the following classifications:

ALTERNATIVE	CURRENT POSITION	+	NONCURRENT PORTION	=	TOTAL
1	$1,000		$735		$1,735
2	$1,000/1.10 = $909		826		1,735

in the property. *Lessor Bank had a direct-financing lease with Lessee Telecommunications.* Notice that Lessor Bank's only source of income from the transaction is interest over the lease term. Most direct-financing leases involve financial institutions, which profit by lending money at interest. Such institutions do not sell property but merely finance property acquisitions.

Sales-Type Leases—Lessor

If ownership rights, risks, and rewards are transferred from the lessor to the lessee and if the lease terms are such that the lessor has income (gross profit) on the transfer (sale) of property to the lessee *in addition* to providing financing to the lessee, the lease is a **sales-type lease.** Thus, the lessor has two sources of earnings under a sales-type lease:

1. A profit (loss) at the lease inception date.

2. Interest revenue over the lease term.

Most sales-type leases involve companies that are in the business of both selling and leasing property, such as equipment manufacturers or dealers. Under this type of lease, the lessor not only sells property to the lessee but also finances the sale for the lessee.

Return to the lease between Lessor Bank and Lessee Telecommunications. Assume that Lessor is an equipment manufacturer rather than a bank. Lessor normally sells such equipment for $2,486. Assume further that Lessor paid $1,800 to manufacture the equipment. Lessor would make the following entries to record this sales-type lease.

Lease receivable	2,486	
Sales		2,486
Cost of goods sold	1,800	
Inventory		1,800

The gross profit $686 ($2,486 − $1,800) would appear on Lessor's income statement for 1998. Lessor's other entries for 1998 (and subsequent years) would be the same as those entries shown on page 792. The other items on Lessor's financial statements would also appear the same. Finally, Lessee's entry would be the same as that shown on page 792.

Leveraged Leases—Lessor

A **leveraged lease** is a special type of direct-financing lease and has been attractive to lessors because of the tax advantages it offers. Under a leveraged lease, the lessor finances a large portion of the property purchased and leased to the lessee with nonrecourse debt issued to a third party. For tax purposes, the lessor "owns" the property. Although the lease payments represent taxable income, the lessor receives tax savings from depreciation and interest deductions on the debt. The pattern of net cash flows over the lease term is such that the lessor enjoys a high rate of return on the investment in the leased property. Because of their technical complexity, leveraged leases are not discussed further in this chapter.

Operating Leases—Lessee and Lessor

If a lease does not transfer ownership rights, risks, and rewards from the lessor to the lessee, it is an **operating lease** for both the lessor and lessee. An operating lease is similar to a rental. Assume Lessee has an operating lease with a computer equipment distributor, the terms of which are shown in Exhibit 15–4. Under these terms, which are quite different from those of our earlier example, the lessor has not transferred any rights, risks, and rewards of ownership to Lessee.

EXHIBIT 15-4	Terms of Operating Lease Between Lessee Telecommunications and a Computer Distributor

Item in Lease Agreement	Lease Terms
Cancelability	Cancelable at lessee's option
Lease term	3 years
Useful life of leased property	15 years
Residual value of leased property, end of lease term	$6,500
Fair value (and cost) of leased property	$8,000
Annual lease payments	$800
Responsibility for maintenance, taxes, insurance, etc.	Lessor

CONCEPTUAL

An operating lease is similar to a rental agreement.

Let us see why. First, Lessee can cancel the lease at any time. Second, the future economic benefits accruing to Lessee are relatively small, since the three-year term of the lease is short relative to the life of the property. Third, the annual lease payments of $800 are small relative to the equipment's fair value of $8,000 even if they are *not* discounted. Thus, Lessee is not purchasing the equipment at fair value but is merely renting it. Finally, because the lessor agrees to maintain the equipment and pay the insurance and property taxes, the lessor retains the risks of ownership. In summary, the lessor retains the rights to most of the service potential associated with the equipment.

This operating lease agreement is similar to a typical rental agreement on an apartment, with which you may be familiar. The landlord or landlady assumes responsibility for maintenance, taxes, and insurance on the apartment. The tenant can cancel the lease at any time but will probably forfeit a deposit and/or a month's advance rent. In any event, under no circumstances would the tenant be considered to have "bought" the apartment and received financing from the building's owner.

Accounting for an operating lease is much less complicated than accounting for a capital lease. The lessor records the annual lease payments as rent revenue. The equipment remains on the lessor's books and is depreciated over its useful life. The lessee records the annual lease payments as rent expense. The two parties would make the following entries each year based on the information in Exhibit 15-4:

LESSOR

Equipment under operating lease	8,000	
Inventory (or equipment)		8,000
Cash	800	
Rental revenue		800
Depreciation expense	xx^a	
Accumulated depreciation		xx^a

LESSEE

Rent expense	800	
Cash		800

[a]The amount of depreciation recorded each year would depend on the depreciation method used by the lessor.

Capital Leases Accounted for as Operating Leases

At the beginning of the chapter, we pointed out that many lessees have resisted reporting leased property and the corresponding lease obligation in their financial statements. Referring to our earlier example, what would be the financial statement effects of recording Lessee Telecommunication's capital lease as an operating lease?

EXHIBIT 15-5	Effects on Lessee's Income of Recording a Capital Lease as an Operating Lease[a]						
	Recorded as a Capital Lease				**Recorded as an Operating Lease**		
1998	Interest expense	$249		1998	Rent expense		$1,000
	Depreciation expense	829	$1,078				
1999	Interest expense	$174		1999	Rent expense		1,000
	Depreciation expense	829	1,003				
2000	Interest expense	$ 91		2000	Rent expense		1,000
	Depreciation expense	828	919				
	Total expenses		$3,000		Total expenses		$3,000

[a]Based on data given on pages 789–790.

The effects on Lessee's income statements are shown in Exhibit 15–5. Notice that Lessee reports total expenses of $3,000 under both methods over the three-year period. However, the *timing* of the income effect differs. (The income effects are similar for a lessor.)

Incorrectly recording a capital lease as an operating lease also has significant balance sheet effects. Under a capital lease, the lessee reports the leased property as an asset and the lease obligation as a liability. Under an operating lease, the lessee's balance sheet shows neither an asset nor a liability. Significant balance sheet differences also apply to the lessor. In terms of financial reporting objectives, these financial statement differences send quite different cash flow signals to investors and other users of financial statements. For example, a lessee's reporting of leased property as an asset informs users that this asset will contribute to future revenue-generating (and cash-generating) activities. Reporting a lease liability on the balance sheet provides information about a lessee's expected future cash outflows.

CONCEPTUAL

Proper lease accounting improves cash flow signals to users of financial statements.

Difficulties in Classifying Leases

In practice, classifying a lease as a capital lease or an operating lease is often difficult for several reasons. First, the terms of a lease agreement may fall somewhere between the two ends of the continuum presented in Exhibit 15–1, and illustrated in the examples. Determining the intentions of the lessor and lessee may be difficult. Was the intent to rent or purchase? Second, as we have mentioned, many lessees have attempted to avoid recording capital leases in order to improve their financial position, and many lease agreements have been structured *specifically* to avoid capitalization.

To provide perspective on the difficulties in classifying leases, Exhibit 15–6 presents the acquisition/rental continuum as it exists in practice. Exhibit 15–6 is similar to the conceptual acquisition/rental continuum in Exhibit 15–1 but shows that in practice many leases fall between the two extremes of a purchase/sale and a rental. The shaded area in Exhibit 15–6 represents a "gray area" in which the question of whether a lease transfers ownership rights, risks, and rewards from lessor to lessee cannot be clearly answered. Leases in this gray area are not easily classified as capital or operating by lessees, or as direct financing/sales-type or operating leases by lessors. Authoritative guidelines or standards are needed to apply the conceptual distinction between an acquisition and a rental to these leases. In the next section we will look at how this conceptual distinction is applied using the lease classification criteria set forth in *Statement No. 13*.

EXHIBIT 15-6   **The Acquisition/Rental Continuum for a Lease in Practice**

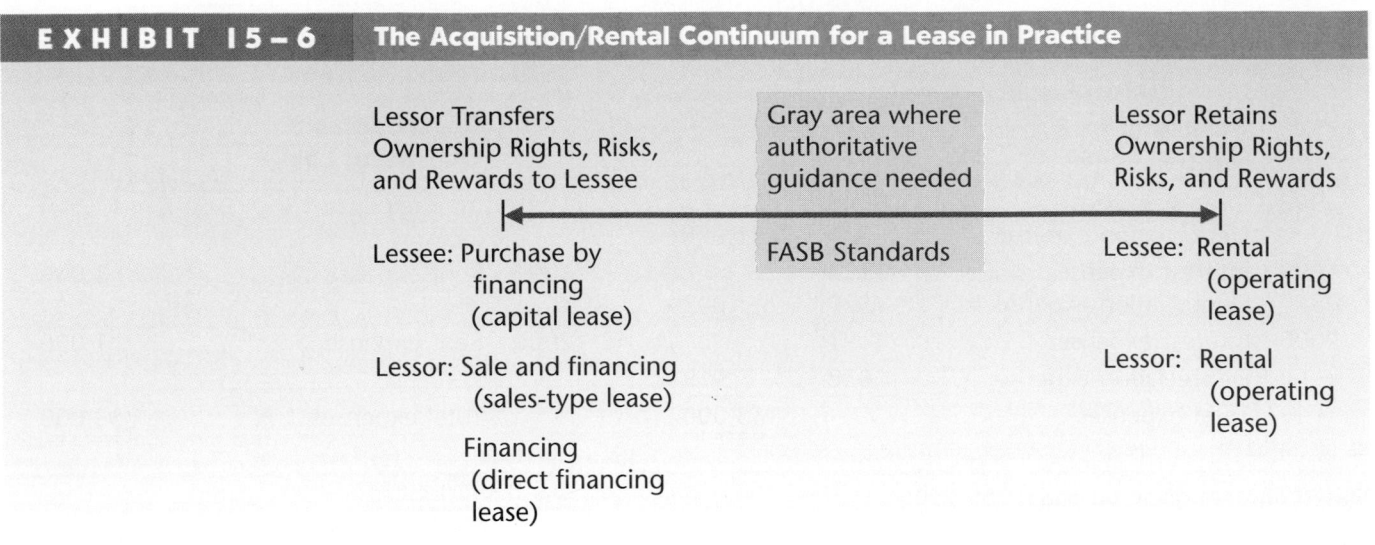

APPLICATION OF THE CONCEPTUAL CONSIDERATIONS

Although leases have been used for many years as a means of obtaining the right to use property, lease arrangements have expanded rapidly and have become increasingly complex since the 1960s. Lease contracts now include such complexities as clauses prohibiting cancellation; provisions for insurance, repair, and maintenance; sublease agreements; contingent rental agreements; renewal options; bargain purchase options; sale-and-lease-back provisions; and guarantees of the leased property's residual values. Also, third parties are often part of a lease agreement. They may provide financing, guarantee a property's residual value, or agree to purchase an interest in a property's residual value. Complexities such as these have made it increasingly difficult for accountants to classify leases and account for them.

To increase financial statement comparability, to thwart accounting abuses, and to reduce user confusion, the accounting profession has made several attempts to develop criteria for distinguishing between capital leases and operating leases. The accounting profession's first attempt to improve lease accounting was *Accounting Research Bulletin No. 38*, "Disclosure of Long-Term Leases in Financial Statements of Lessees," issued in 1949. *Bulletin No. 38* recommended that leases that were equivalent to installment purchases be accounted for as capital leases. However, it did not establish the criteria to determine equivalence.

In 1962, the Accounting Research Division of the AICPA issued *Accounting Research Study No. 4*, "Reporting of Leases in Financial Statements." *Study No. 4* recommended that *all* long-term, noncancelable leases be accounted for as capital leases. Between 1964 and 1973, the Accounting Principles Board attempted to narrow the accounting alternatives for leases by issuing four *Opinions*, two affecting the lessor and two affecting the lessee. In 1974 the FASB placed the lease issue on its agenda and issued a *Discussion Memorandum* on the subject. Two years later the FASB issued *Statement No. 13*. Amended by and clarified through many additional *Statements, Interpretations,* and *Technical Bulletins,* this *Statement* is now considered the authoritative document on leases.[9]

---

[9]"Accounting for Leases," *Statement of Financial Accounting Standards No. 13* (Stamford, Conn.: FASB, 1976). In January 1990, the FASB issued an amended version that integrated *Statement No. 13* with subsequent amendments and interpretations. As a result, except for pronouncements issued after January 1990, financial accounting standards for leases are set forth in one document.

Statement No. 13 Lease Classification Criteria

Statement No. 13 established criteria for classifying leases from both the lessee's and the lessor's points of view. Four basic criteria apply to both the lessor and lessee. Also, two additional criteria apply to the lessor.

Criteria for the Lessee

If, at the date of the lease agreement, a lease meets *any one* of the following criteria, the lessee classifies and accounts for it as a capital lease.

1. The lease transfers ownership of the property to the lessee by the end of the lease term.

2. The lease contains a bargain purchase option.

3. The lease term is equal to 75 percent or more of the leased property's estimated economic life.

4. The present value of the minimum lease payments at the beginning of the lease term equals or exceeds 90 percent of the excess of the leased property's fair value at the date of the agreement.[10]

> **4** Identify the *Statement No. 13* criteria used by (1) the lessee and (2) the lessor to classify a lease.

If *none* of these criteria is met, the lessee classifies and accounts for the lease as an operating lease.

Let us explain these criteria more fully. The **lease term** generally includes the fixed, noncancelable term of the lease. A **bargain purchase option** gives the lessee the option to purchase the property at a price that is substantially below the expected fair value at the date the option may be exercised, that is, a price that seems so favorable at the date of the lease agreement that the option is reasonably certain to be exercised. If the beginning of the lease term falls within the last 25 percent of the estimated economic life of the property, the third and fourth criteria above are not applicable.[11] The fourth criterion sometimes is called a **fair value recovery criterion.** Excluded from the minimum lease payments are *executory costs.* Executory costs include insurance, maintenance, and taxes on the leased property. These costs are period costs, rather than part of the acquisition cost of the property.

In our presentation of the conceptual issues in the previous section, the implicit rate in the lease and the lessee's borrowing rate were the same. In practice, these interest rates may be different. In addition, the lessee may not be able to determine the implicit rate in the lease. Therefore, *FASB Statement No. 13 requires the lessee to use its incremental borrowing rate to calculate the present value of the minimum lease payments unless (1) it is practicable for the lessee to learn the implicit rate in the lease and (2) the implicit rate is less than the lessee's incremental borrowing rate.*[12] As we saw in the Lessee Telecommunications example, the **incremental borrowing rate** is the rate the lessee would have to pay to borrow the funds necessary to purchase the property.

The fair value of the leased property is the price at which the leased property could be sold in an arm's-length exchange transaction. In a sales-type lease, the fair value of the leased property equals the dealer's normal selling price. In a direct-financing lease, the fair value normally would equal the cost of the leased property to the lessor.

---

[10]Ibid., para. 7a–d. The leased property's fair value is reduced by any investment credit retained and expected to be realized by the lessor. However, the Tax Reform Act of 1986 repealed the investment credit.
[11]Excluding the third and fourth criteria in this circumstance thus prevents, for example, a lease of property with a 20-year life under, say, four separate and succeeding five-year leases from being classified as an operating lease at the beginning of each of the first three leases but as a capital lease at the beginning of the last lease.
[12]*FASB Statement No. 13,* para. 7d.

Criteria for the Lessor

If *all* of the following criteria are met, the lessor classifies and accounts for the lease as a direct-financing lease or sales-type lease:

1. The lease meets *any one* of the four criteria on page 799.
2. Collectibility of the lease payments is reasonably predictable.
3. There is no significant uncertainty related to the amount of unreimbursable costs yet to be incurred by the lessor under the lease.

If these criteria are met, the lessor classifies the lease as a sales-type lease if a profit arises on the transfer of property in addition to the interest revenue earned over the lease term. If these criteria are met and the lessor's only source of earnings is interest over the lease term, the lessor classifies the lease as a direct-financing lease. If *any* of the criteria are *not* met, the lessor classifies and accounts for the lease as an operating lease.

Application of the *Statement No. 13* Criteria

We have discussed the conceptual considerations in a lease and have presented the lease classification criteria in *FASB Statement No. 13*. Now let us apply these criteria to the conceptual issue of whether the lessor transfers ownership risks and rewards to the lessee.

Criterion 1: Passage of Title

If title to the property passes to the lessee at the end of the lease term, then *all* ownership benefits accrue to the lessee. Furthermore, the property's residual value, if any, will accrue to the lessee.

Criterion 2: Bargain Purchase Option

If the lease contains a bargain purchase option, it is assumed that the lessee will exercise the option and obtain title to the leased property. Thus, the discussion in the previous paragraph applies here.[13]

Criterion 3: Relationship Between Lease Term and Life of Property

If the lease term equals the economic life of the property, the lessee will obtain all the benefits associated with the property (assuming a nominal residual value) throughout its economic life. These benefits will accrue to the lessee even though the property may revert to the lessor at the end of the lease term. (Notice that a company could easily avoid classifying a lease as a capital lease if the criteria stated that the lease term had to equal *100 percent* of the economic life of the property. Under those circumstances, a lease contract could be drafted so that the lease term was slightly less than the life of the property, thereby circumventing this criterion.)

The FASB concluded that the lessee obtains essentially all ownership risks and rewards if the lease term is a substantial portion of the life of the leased property. The FASB quantified "substantial" as 75 percent of the leased property's estimated

---

[13]If a bargain purchase option is the vehicle that transfers ownership risks and rewards to the lessee, the lease payments determined by the lessor should ensure a specified rate of return on the lessor's investment. Thus, higher lease payments should be required if a bargain purchase option, as opposed to an ordinary purchase option, is included.

economic life. In summary, the third criterion means that if the lease term covers at least 75 percent of the property's useful life, the parties are presumed to have entered into a capital lease agreement.

Criterion 4: Fair Value Recovery

If the present value of the lease payments equals 100 percent of the property's fair value, obviously the lessor either has financed a purchase for the lessee (i.e., a direct-financing lease) or has sold the property to the lessee and financed its purchase (i.e., a sales-type lease). In either case, the lessee is paying the fair value (cash equivalent exchange price) for the leased property plus interest over the lease term. However, a requirement that the present value of the lease payments must equal *100 percent* of the property's fair value would not allow for any residual value that might accrue to the lessor at the end of the lease term. If residual value accrues to the lessor at the end of the lease term, then the lessor can reduce the lease payments and still obtain the desired rate of return. To illustrate, assume that on January 1, 1998, Lessee enters into a 10-year lease with Lessor for equipment with a fair value of $10,000. Title to the equipment is retained by the lessor at the end of the lease term. The equipment has a useful life of 10 years and an estimated residual value of $3,000. Because the $3,000 residual value will accrue to Lessor, the lessor need not recover the entire $10,000 in lease payments. (Later we will show how lease payments are determined when residual values are present.)

In addition, a 100 percent requirement could be abused by a lessee because a lease contract could be drafted specifically to avoid this criterion. Because of residual value considerations and potential abuses with a 100 percent requirement, the FASB requires that the present value of the lease payments be compared to 90 percent of the fair value of the leased property. Conceptually, the essence of this criterion is that the lessee pays *fair value* for the leased property (plus interest over the lease term), and receives substantially all ownership benefits associated with the property.

Additional Lessor Criteria

The two additional lessor criteria are applications of the realization principle discussed in Chapter 2. Collectibility of the lease payments is a criterion for revenue recognition at the point of sale and thus applies to sales-type leases. Collectibility of lease payments also applies to direct-financing leases; a lender would not finance a purchase for a lessee unless reasonable estimates of uncollectible amounts could be made.

The second criterion—no significant uncertainties exist in regard to nonreimbursable costs to be incurred by the lessor—is another way of saying the lessor's earnings process must be complete before income can be recognized. In summary, the two additional criteria also ensure that the lessor is transferring the risks and rewards of ownership.

Lessee Depreciation of Leased Property under a Capital Lease

The lease criteria affect the period over which the lessee depreciates property under a capital lease. If the lease meets either the first or second criterion listed on page 799, the lessee depreciates the property over its useful life (because the lessee will have the use of the property over its entire useful life). If neither of the first two criteria is met but either criterion 3 or 4 is met, the lessee depreciates the property over the term of the lease. Exhibit 15-7 provides a summary of these depreciation requirements.

CONCEPTUAL

The additional lessor criteria are applications of the revenue recognition principle.

EXHIBIT 15–7	Depreciation Period for Assets Acquired under a Capital Lease		
		Lessee Depreciates Leased Property Over:	
Statement No. 13 Criterion Met		**Property's Useful Life**	**The Lease Term**
Criterion 1: Title passes to lessee by end of lease term		*x*	
Criterion 2: Lease contains a bargain purchase option		*x*	
If neither criterion 1 nor 2 is met:			
Criterion 3: Term of lease at least 75% of property's useful life.			*x*
Criterion 4: Present value of lease payments at least 90% of property's fair value.			*x*

Summary of the Application of *Statement No. 13* Criteria

To this point, we have learned how lessors and lessees apply the lease criteria set forth in *Statement No. 13* to classify leases in practice. Exhibit 15–8 offers a quick review. The exhibit applies the *Statement No. 13* criteria to Lessee Telecommunications' lease with a bank (a capital lease) and its lease with a computer distributor (an operating lease). Exhibit 15–8 should also strengthen your understanding of the major objective of *Statement No. 13:* to establish criteria for deciding whether a lease transfers ownership rights, risks, and rewards from the lessor to the lessee.

CONCEPTUAL

One objective of *Statement No. 13* was to increase comparability between purchased assets and leased assets.

A secondary objective of *FASB Statement No. 13* was to increase comparability between companies that *buy* their long-lived assets and companies that *lease* their long-lived assets. Since lessees often attempt to avoid capitalization of a lease, still another objective was to eliminate lease abuses and to close loopholes in previous accounting pronouncements that allowed lessees to engage in off-balance-sheet financing. At the end of this chapter, we will discuss the apparent success of *Statement No. 13* and also discuss some of its alleged weaknesses. First, however, we shall look briefly at international accounting standards for leases, then we shall examine some additional accounting issues for leases.

International Accounting Standards for Leases

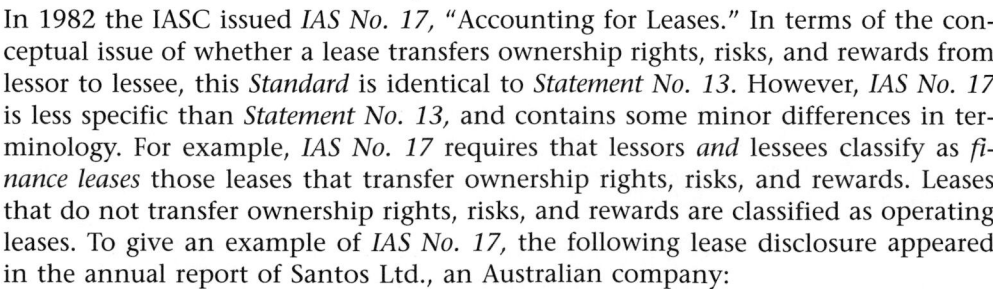

In 1982 the IASC issued *IAS No. 17,* "Accounting for Leases." In terms of the conceptual issue of whether a lease transfers ownership rights, risks, and rewards from lessor to lessee, this *Standard* is identical to *Statement No. 13.* However, *IAS No. 17* is less specific than *Statement No. 13,* and contains some minor differences in terminology. For example, *IAS No. 17* requires that lessors *and* lessees classify as *finance leases* those leases that transfer ownership rights, risks, and rewards. Leases that do not transfer ownership rights, risks, and rewards are classified as operating leases. To give an example of *IAS No. 17,* the following lease disclosure appeared in the annual report of Santos Ltd., an Australian company:

I. Statement of Accounting Policies

Leases

Finance leases, which effectively transfer to the lessee substantially all of the risks and benefits incidental to ownership of the leased item, are capitalised at the present value of the minimum lease payments, disclosed

EXHIBIT 15-8   Lease Classification: A Summary Analysis

Lease Between Lessee Telecommunications and Lessor Bank (pp. 789–794):

	Criterion met for:	
Criterion:	Lessee?	Lessor?
1. Passage of title?	No	No
2. Bargain purchase option?	No	No
3. Term of lease ≥ 75 percent of life of property?	Yes	Yes
4. Present value of lease payments ≥ 90 percent of property's fair value?	Yes	Yes
Additional lessor criteria:		
a) Collectibility of lease payments?		Yes
b) Uncertainty about unreimbursable costs to be incurred during lease term?		No
Classification of lease based on above analysis:	Capital lease	Direct-financing lease

Lease Between Lessee Telecommunications and Computer Distributor (Exhibit 15–4, p. 796):

	Criterion met for:	
Criterion:	Lessee?	Lessor?
1. Passage of title?	No	No
2. Bargain purchase option?	No	No
3. Term of lease ≥ 75 percent of life of property?	No	No
4. Present value of lease payments ≥ 90 percent of property's fair value?	No	No
Additional lessor criteria:		
a) Collectibility of lease payments?		Not applicable
b) Uncertainty about unreimbursable costs to be incurred during lease term?		Not applicable
Classification of lease based on above analysis:	Operating lease	Operating lease

as capitalised leases and amortised over the period the lessee is expected to benefit from the use of the leased assets. A corresponding liability is also established and each lease payment is allocated between the principal component and the interest expense Operating lease payments, where the lessors effectively retain substantially all the risks and benefits of ownership of the leased items, are charged against operating profit in equal instalments over the lease term.

DDITIONAL LEASING ISSUES

To this point, we have covered the basic concepts of how leases are classified and accounted for by a lessor and lessee. In this section, we build on these basic concepts by discussing the following topics:

1. A closer examination of what is included in minimum lease payments.

2. Accounting for residual values and bargain purchase options.

3. A closer examination of the discount rate used by the lessee to calculate the present value of minimum lease payments.

4. Accounting for initial direct costs incurred by the lessor at the lease inception date.

5. The nature of and accounting for sale-and-leaseback transactions.

Minimum Lease Payments

The **minimum lease payments** consist of all payments that the lessee is reasonably expected to make under the terms of the lease agreement. An accountant needs to know what must be included in the minimum lease payments, since they apply to the fourth lease criterion and are a part of the recorded amount for capital, sales-type, and direct-financing leases.

If a lease agreement contains a bargain purchase option, the minimum lease payments include (1) the periodic lease payments up to the date on which the bargain purchase option becomes exercisable and (2) the amount of the bargain purchase option. If a lease agreement does *not* contain a bargain purchase option, the minimum lease payments include (1) the periodic lease payments over the lease term, (2) the amount of any guaranteed residual value at the end of the lease term, and (3) any payment required by the lessee for failing to renew or extend the lease at the end of the lease term. In any given lease, a bargain purchase option and a residual value guarantee are mutually exclusive. That is, one or the other could be part of the terms of the lease, but not both.

Residual Value at the End of the Lease Term

5 **Distinguish between and account for guaranteed residual values and unguaranteed residual values.**

As we learned in Chapter 12, property usually has residual value at the end of its useful life. Thus, when the lease term equals the expected useful life of the leased property, the property may have some residual value at the end of the lease term. When the lease term is *less* than the estimated economic life of the leased property, the property's residual value at the end of the lease term may be substantial. In practice, a lessee may guarantee all, part, or none of the property's residual value.

Residual values at the end of the lease term are an integral part of automobile leases in the United States and abroad. Leases with unguaranteed residual values are called "closed-end leases"; leases with guaranteed residual values are called "open-end leases." We will examine both types, beginning with those that guarantee residual value.

Guaranteed Residual Value

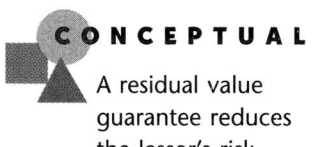

CONCEPTUAL

A residual value guarantee reduces the lessor's risk.

A lease agreement may include a **guaranteed residual value** (GRV), in which the lessee assures that the lessor will recover at least a guaranteed amount at the end of the lease term. Lessors often insert a GRV clause in lease contracts in order to minimize their risk associated with the property's value. In essence, the guarantee transfers the risk of a decrease in value to the lessee or in some cases to a third-party guarantor. A residual value guarantee also may encourage the lessee to make prudent use of the leased property.

If the actual residual value is below the amount guaranteed, the lessee must pay the difference to the lessor. For example, assume that a lessee guarantees a residual value of $3,000. The amount paid to the lessor at the end of the lease term, assuming four different residual values, would be as follows:

GUARANTEED RESIDUAL VALUE	ACTUAL RESIDUAL VALUE	AMOUNT PAID BY LESSEE TO LESSOR
$3,000	$ 500	$2,500
3,000	2,700	300
3,000	3,000	–0–
3,000	3,800	–0–

If the actual residual value exceeds $3,000, the difference between the actual residual value and $3,000 is a gain to the lessor. Some lease agreements provide that the lessor and lessee share the gain.

Establishing the Lease Payments   As we stated above, a residual value guarantee is part of the minimum lease payments. The lessor considers a GRV when establishing the lease payments. The lessee considers a GRV when applying the fourth lease criterion and when accounting for the lease if it is a capital lease. To illustrate, assume that on January 1, 1998, Lessor Corporation, a financial institution, leased equipment with a six-year useful life to Lessee Corporation. The following data pertain to this lease:

1. Cost to Lessor and fair value of equipment, $20,000.

2. Term of lease, four years.

3. At the end of the lease term, Lessee guarantees 100 percent of the residual value, estimated to be $3,000.

4. Implicit rate of interest in the lease payments and Lessee's incremental borrowing rate, 12 percent.

5. Annual lease payments to be made at the beginning of each year (an annuity due) were determined by Lessor as follows:[14]

Cost and fair value of equipment....................................	**$20,000**
Present value of guaranteed residual value:	
$3,000 × $p_{\overline{4}|12\%}$	
$3,000 × .6355...	(1,906)
Amount to be recovered through lease payments.......................	**$18,094**
Annual lease payments:	
$18,094 ÷ $P_{D_{\overline{4}|12\%}}$	
$18,094 ÷ 3.4018..	**$ 5,319**

6. Lessee uses straight-line depreciation on the leased asset.

The present value of the minimum lease payments is $20,000 ($5,319 × 3.4018 = $18,094; $3,000 × .6355 = $1,906; $18,094 + $1,906 = $20,000). Since the fourth criterion is met for the lessee (the present value exceeds 90 percent of the fair value of the equipment), the lease is a capital lease for the lessee. The fourth criterion is also met for the lessor, and assuming that the two additional lessor criteria (page 800) are met, the lease is a direct-financing lease for the lessor.

Exhibit 15–9 shows a schedule of interest and book value suitable for use by both Lessor and Lessee. Notice that the schedule is slightly different from the one in Exhibit 15–2 because the lease payments (cash flows) occur at the beginning instead of the end of each year. In Exhibit 15–2, the receivable/payable increased during the year because of interest and then decreased at the end of the year because of the cash lease payments. In that exhibit, the lease payments were an ordinary annuity. In Exhibit 15–9, the receivable/payable *decreases* at the beginning of the year because of the cash lease payments and then *increases* during the year because of interest. In Exhibit 15–9, the lease payments are an annuity due. (Refer to Exhibit A-5 in Appendix A to this text for a pictorial representation of this pattern.) Note in Exhibit 15–9 that the lessor's net receivable balance and the lessee's lease liability balance at the end of 2001 (column 5) equal the amount of the residual value guarantee.

---

[14]A time diagram for the cash flows associated with the lease would appear as follows:

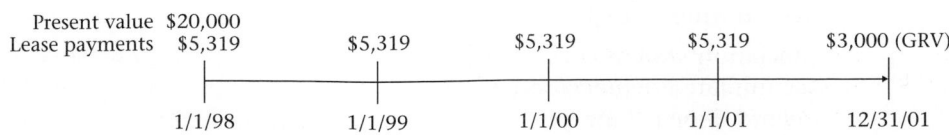

EXHIBIT 15–9	Schedule of Interest and Book Value with Guaranteed Residual Value

Year	(1) Annual Lease Payments (Beginning of Year)a	(2) Net Receivable/ Payable Outstanding During Yearb	(3) Interest Revenue/ Expensec	(4) Reduction in Receivable/ Payabled	(5) Net Receivable/ Payable Balance (End of Year)e
(1/1/98)					$20,000
1998	$ 5,319	$14,681	$1,762	$ 3,557	16,443
1999	5,319	11,124	1,335	3,984	12,459
2000	5,319	7,140	857	4,462	7,997
2001	5,319	2,678	322f	4,997	3,000
	$21,276		$4,276	$17,000	

aPreviously calculated.
bPrevious balance in col. 5 minus col. 1.
c.12 × col. 2.
dCol. 1 minus col. 3.
ePrevious balance minus col. 4 (or col. 2 + col. 3).
fRounded by $1.

Accounting for the Lease Payments On January 1, 1999, Lessor and Lessee would make the following entries to record the capital lease:

LESSOR

Lease receivable 20,000
    Equipment   20,000
To record the direct financing lease.

Cash 5,319
    Lease receivable   5,319
To record the first lease payment.

LESSEE

Leased property 20,000
    Lease liability   20,000
To record the capital lease.

Lease liability 5,319
    Cash   5,319
To record the first lease payment.

Notice that the lessor's beginning receivable balance and the lessee's beginning liability balance, both $20,000, are the sum of (1) the present value of the lease payments ($18,094) and (2) the present value of the guaranteed residual value ($1,906).

On December 31, 1998, lessor and lessee would make the following entries:

LESSOR

Lease receivable 1,762
    Interest revenue   1,762
To record interest earned.

LESSEE

Interest expense 1,762
    Lease liability   1,762
To record interest expense.

Depreciation expense 4,250
    Accumulated depreciation   4,250
To record depreciation on the leased equipment for 1998
[($20,000 – $3,000) ÷ 4].

Similar entries, based on the numbers from Exhibit 15–9, would be made in 1999, 2000, and 2001. At the end of 2001, entries would be made to record the return of the equipment to the lessor and the final settlement based on the residual value guarantee. First, assume that the *actual* residual value was $3,000:

LESSOR

Equipment	3,000	
Lease receivable		3,000

LESSEE

Accumulated depreciation	17,000	
Lease liability	3,000	
Leased property		20,000

If instead the *actual* residual value were $2,000, the following entries would be made:

LESSOR

Cash ($3,000 – $2,000)	1,000	
Equipment	2,000	
Lease receivable		3,000

LESSEE

Loss on residual value guarantee	1,000	
Accumulated depreciation	17,000	
Lease liability	3,000	
Leased property		20,000
Cash		1,000

If the actual residual value *exceeded* $3,000, a gain would accrue to the lessor (and perhaps to the lessee, depending on the agreement). Until the lessor sold the asset, however, the equipment would be reported at the amount of the guarantee, since the earnings process would not be complete. In practice, the leased equipment need not be physically transferred to the lessor. The lessee may sell the equipment and remit the proceeds to the lessor, including any amount required under the guarantee.

An interesting example of a residual value guarantee was IBM's use of Merrill Lynch as a *third-party guarantor* of residual value in the 1980s. According to an article in *The Wall Street Journal,* IBM wanted to account for its computer leases as sales-type rather than operating leases to improve its profits. By paying Merrill Lynch a fee to guarantee the residual value of the computers it leased to other companies, IBM was able to meet the fourth lease criterion (fair value recovery) and thus was able to account for its leases as sales-type leases:

> In the hotly competitive market, IBM was offering terms that didn't add up to the 90% mark. Merrill's solution: It sold IBM "7D insurance" guaranteeing a certain value of the computer at the end of the lease—enough to push IBM over 90%. "Helping IBM keep the accounting proper for these leases was a simple matter, and we were able to provide this service for them," says Frederick Butler, a former Merrill director of lease financing. "Without this guarantee, these leases would be just under the [90%] line and would have to be taken as operating leases." IBM says its deal with Merrill lasted until 1990. Today, IBM uses an offshore 7D insurer it won't identify.[15]

Unguaranteed Residual Value

Establishing the Lease Payments   The portion of a leased property's residual value that is *not* guaranteed by a lessee or another party is called the **unguaranteed**

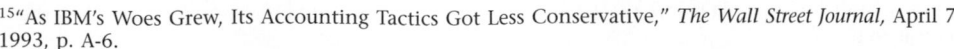

[15]"As IBM's Woes Grew, Its Accounting Tactics Got Less Conservative," *The Wall Street Journal,* April 7, 1993, p. A-6.

residual value (URV). When some or all of the residual value is not guaranteed, the lessor still determines the lease payments so as to recover the fair value of the property plus interest. However, because of a lessor's higher risk and uncertainty associated with an unguaranteed residual value, the lessor would require a higher rate of return than if the entire residual value were guaranteed.

To illustrate, refer to the example on pages 805–807, but assume that the estimated residual value of $3,000 was *not* guaranteed by Lessee. For purposes of comparison, assume also that in both cases Lessor's required rate of return was 12 percent. Lessor would determine the annual lease payments as follows:

Cost and fair value of equipment	$20,000
Present value of unguaranteed residual value ($3,000 × .6355)	(1,906)
Amount to be recovered (present value)	$18,094

Annual lease payments:
$18,094 ÷ $P_{D\overline{4}|12\%}$
$18,094 ÷ 3.4018 .... $ 5,319

Because none of the residual value is guaranteed by the lessee, only the periodic lease payments would be included when Lessee calculates the present value of the minimum lease payment:

$$\begin{aligned} \text{Present value} &= \text{Lease payments} \times P_{D\overline{4}|12\%} \\ &= \$5,319 \times 3.4018 \\ &= \$18,094 \end{aligned}$$

Since the present value of the minimum lease payments exceeds 90 percent of the equipment's fair value [$18,094 ≥ .90($20,000)], the lease still qualifies as a capital lease to Lessee and a direct-financing lease to Lessor.

Accounting for the Lease Payments Lessor's entries to record the lease receivable and subsequent entries to record interest would be the same as the entries on page 806. If the actual residual value at the end of the lease term were to differ from the $3,000 estimate, Lessor would record a loss or a gain when the asset is sold.[16]

Because Lessee did not guarantee any residual value, Lessee would record the capital lease as follows:

Leased property	18,094	
Lease liability		18,094
Lease liability	5,319	
Cash		5,319

These entries are similar to Lessee's entries on page 806. The difference of $1,906 in the amount recorded for the asset and liability is the present value of the residual value, which was guaranteed in the entry on page 806 but is *not* guaranteed in this example. Exhibit 15–10 presents Lessee's schedule of interest and book value with no residual value guarantee. Subsequent entries for interest expense and lease payments would be based on the amounts in the exhibit. Note that since Lessee makes no residual value guarantee, the liability is fully discharged at the beginning of 2001.

When unguaranteed residual value exists *in a sales-type lease,* the lessor's entry to record the lease is modified slightly. Let us modify our first example by assuming that the equipment had a cost to the lessor of $15,000, not $20,000. Lessor would make the following entries on January 1, 1998:

Lease receivable	20,000	
Cost of goods sold ($15,000 – $1,906)	13,094	
Sales ($5,319 × 3.4018)		18,094
Inventory		15,000
To record the sales-type lease.		

---

[16]A loss might be recognized before the actual sale, whereas a gain would not be recognized until the asset was sold.

EXHIBIT 15–10	Schedule of Interest and Book Value—No Residual Value Guarantee

Year	(1) Annual Lease Payments (Beginning of Year)[a]	(2) Liability Outstanding During Year[b]	(3) Interest Expense[c]	(4) Reduction in Liability[d]	(5) Liability Balance (End of Year)[e]
(1/1/98)					$18,094
1998	$ 5,319	$12,775	$1,533	$ 3,786	14,308
1999	5,319	8,989	1,079	4,240	10,068
2000	5,319	4,749	570	4,749	5,319
2001	5,319	–0–	–0–	5,319	–0–
	$21,276		$3,182	$18,094[f]	

[a]Previously calculated.
[b]Previous balance in col. 5 minus col. 1.
[c].12 × col. 2.
[d]Col. 1 minus col. 3.
[e]Previous balance minus col. 4 (or col. 2 + col. 3).

```
Cash. . . . . . . . . . . . . . . . . . . . . . . . . . . . . . . . . . . . . 5,319
     Lease receivable  . . . . . . . . . . . . . . . . . . . . . . . . . . . . .        5,319
     To record receipt of the first lease payment.
```

The lease receivable account is debited for $20,000, which is the present value of the minimum lease payments ($18,094) plus the present value of the unguaranteed residual value ($1,906). Under *Statement No. 13,* the amount recorded for sales is the present value of the minimum lease payments. Had the residual value been guaranteed, the present value of the minimum lease payments (which includes GRV) and corresponding sales would have been $20,000. Because the residual value is not guaranteed, however, the present value of the minimum lease payments (and sales) is only $18,094 ($20,000 – $1,906). This accounting procedure has no effect on Lessor's gross profit of $5,000 ($20,000 – $15,000), since $18,094 less $13,094 also equals $5,000.

The following rationale applies in accounting for unguaranteed residual value under a sales-type lease. When the residual value is guaranteed, the lessor's sacrifice is measured by the entire cost of the property transferred to the lessee; in return the lessor is *assured* of the normal (entire) sales price (lease payments plus guaranteed residual value). When the residual value is *not* guaranteed, the lessor's sacrifice is the original cost of the property less the present value of its unguaranteed residual value. The lessor does not recover the normal (entire) sales price *from the lessee* when the estimated residual value is *not* guaranteed.

Unguaranteed residual values pose a potential problem in the classification of leases, especially from the lessee's standpoint. If unguaranteed residual value is quite large relative to the fair value of leased property, many leases will not qualify as capital leases under the fourth criterion, fair value recovery. For example, in the illustration just discussed, the present value of the lease payments was $18,094, only slightly more than 90 percent of the equipment's fair value. In practice, lessees can circumvent this criterion by paying an unrelated third party to guarantee the residual value. (In fact, a whole new industry has arisen in which an unrelated company guarantees, for a fee similar to an insurance premium, the residual value to the lessor.) Since the lessor considers residual value (both GRV and URV) in determining the lease payments but the lessee considers only guaranteed residual value, the lease may fail the 90 percent test when the lessee calculates present values. (*Both* the lessor and lessee may fail the 90 percent test when the unguaranteed residual value is large.)

Given that unguaranteed residual value affects a lessor's determination of lease payments, failure to make realistic estimates of this residual value can affect a lessor's profits. For example, many computer-leasing companies purchase computers from computer manufacturers and then lease them to users. The leasing companies attempt to compete with the computer manufacturers by setting lower lease payments based on overly optimistic estimates of unguaranteed residual values. Many computer-leasing companies have experienced huge losses, financial difficulties, and even bankruptcy because of overly optimistic estimates of residual value.

Bargain Purchase Options

6 **Describe a bargain purchase option and explain how to account for it.**

Bargain purchase options were discussed briefly on page 799. The lessor's treatment of a bargain purchase option is similar to the treatment of a residual value guarantee. To illustrate, assume that on January 1, 1998, Lessor acquired equipment at a cost of $90,000 and leased it to Lessee under a 10-year noncancelable lease agreement. The terms of the lease were as follows:

I. The lease was 10 years, and the useful life of the equipment was 20 years. The lease contract included a bargain purchase option of $20,000 at the end of the fourth year.

2. Lessor's required rate of return was 10 percent.

3. The lessor established annual lease payments due at the beginning of each year of $21,893:

Cost and fair value of property on 1/1/98	$90,000
Less present value of bargain purchase option:	
$20,000 \times p\,\overline{_{4}}\,|_{10\%} = \$20,000 \times .6830$	(13,660)
Amount to be recovered through annual lease payments	$76,340
Annual lease payments:	
$\$76,340 \div (P_{D\,\overline{_{4}}|_{12\%}})$	
$\$76,340 \div 3.4869$	$21,893

4. Collectibility of the lease payments was assured, and Lessor would not incur any additional costs associated with the lease.

As we stated on page 804, Lessee's minimum lease payments cover the period up to the date of the bargain purchase option (four years) plus the $20,000 option. Because of the bargain purchase option, the lease is classified as a capital lease to Lessee. Because of the bargain purchase option and because the two additional lessor criteria are met, Lessor classifies the lease as a direct-financing lease.

A schedule of interest and book value for this lease appears in Exhibit 15–11. As the exhibit shows, at the end of 2001 the balance of Lessor's receivable and Lessee's payable (column 5) equals the amount of the bargain purchase option. Because the lease contains a bargain purchase option, Lessee would depreciate the equipment over its useful life.

A bargain purchase option should be distinguished from an ordinary purchase option. Under a bargain purchase option, the lessee is given the option to purchase the leased property at a price substantially below fair value. An ordinary purchase option allows the lessee to acquire the asset by paying approximately fair value at the exercise date.

Implicit Rate versus the Lessee's Incremental Borrowing Rate

7 **Distinguish between the interest rate implicit in a lease and the lessee's incremental borrowing rate and apply the proper rate for the lessee.**

As stated earlier, *Statement No. 13* requires the lessee to use its incremental borrowing rate in calculating the present value of the minimum lease payments unless (1) the lessee can determine the rate implicit in the lease and (2) the implicit rate

EXHIBIT 15-11		Schedule of Interest and Book Value with a Bargain Purchase Option			
Year	(1) Annual Lease Payments[a]	(2) Receivable/ Payable Outstanding During Year[b]	(3) Interest Revenue/ Expense[c]	(4) Reduction in Receivable/ Payable[d]	(5) Receivable/ Payable Balance (End of Year)[e]
					$90,000
1998	$21,893	$68,107	$ 6,811	$15,082	74,918
1999	21,893	53,025	5,303	16,590	58,328
2000	21,893	36,435	3,644	18,249	40,079
2001	21,893	18,186	1,819	20,079[f]	20,000
	$87,572		$17,577	$70,000	

[a]Previously calculated.
[b]Previous balance in col. 5 minus col. 1.
[c].10 × col. 2.
[d]Col. 1 minus col. 3.
[e]Previous balance minus col. 4.
[f]Rounding error of $5.

is less than the lessee's incremental borrowing rate. In establishing this requirement, the FASB apparently had two concerns, both related to the lessee's calculation of present value and the leased property's fair value:

1. The *higher* the interest rate used to discount the minimum lease payments, the *lower* the present value. Thus, if the lessee's "claimed" borrowing rate were *higher* than the implicit rate, the lessee could avoid the all-important 90 percent of fair value criterion.

2. Under GAAP, assets are not recorded in excess of their fair value. If the lessee's borrowing rate was actually *lower* than the implicit rate, in the absence of a substantial unguaranteed residual value, the present value of the lease payments (calculated using the incremental borrowing rate) would probably exceed the fair value of the property.

To avoid these problems, *Statement No. 13* requires the lessee to use the *lower* of (1) the incremental borrowing rate, subject to the fair value limitation, or (2) the rate implicit in the lease in discounting the minimum lease payments. This approach means that the lessee will always record a capital lease at the lower of (1) the leased asset's fair value or (2) the present value of the minimum lease payments. In practice, the number of instances in which the incremental borrowing rate should apply probably is small, for the following reasons:

1. Most lessors disclose the implicit interest rate in the lease agreement.

2. The lessee usually knows virtually as much about the fair value of the property as the lessor, since the lessee presumably has already made the decision to lease rather than to borrow and buy the asset.

3. Leased property may be subject to a high rate of obsolescence, which may make expected residual values nominal. Furthermore, when the lease term is fairly long, the present value of unguaranteed residual values, obsolescence notwithstanding, is likely to be small. As a result, the lessor's determination of the required lease payments will be based for the most part on the fair value of the property at the date of the agreement. In that case, a *lower* incremental borrowing rate would probably cause the present value of the lease payments to exceed the property's fair value.[17]

---

[17]A strong case against the use of the incremental borrowing rate was made by John Coughlan in "Regulation, Rents, and Residuals," *Journal of Accountancy*, February 1980, pp. 58–66.

Lessor's Initial Direct Costs of Leasing

Lessors usually incur various costs in negotiating and completing lease transactions. Those costs that can be *directly* related to the lease are called **initial direct costs.** They include commissions, credit investigations, legal fees, and costs associated with preparation of the lease contract. Should these costs, incurred by a lessor at the date of the lease agreement, be expensed or recorded as an asset? We can answer by recalling the distinction between assets and expenses. *Assets* represent probable future economic benefits resulting in direct or indirect future cash inflows. *Expenses* are sacrifices that contribute to the revenue-generating or earning process in the current accounting period.

For operating leases, the lessor's initial direct costs should be recorded as assets and amortized over the lease term. The amortization pattern should be similar to the pattern of rent revenue recognition, which typically is straight-line. This procedure is consistent with the fact that the lessor incurred these costs in order to earn rental revenue over the lease term. Therefore, these direct costs, along with depreciation of the leased asset and other expenses, should be matched against the revenue generated.

For sales-type leases, the lessor's initial direct costs should be expensed and deducted, along with the cost of the property sold, from the revenue from the sale. This treatment is consistent with the accounting for direct costs incurred in connection with an outright sale of property. While an argument could be made for deferring a portion of the costs related to the financing portion of the lease because the lessor also earns interest revenue over the lease term, *Statement No. 13* does not permit that treatment.

For direct-financing leases, the lessor's initial direct costs should be recorded as an asset and matched against interest revenue over the lease term. In this instance, the lessor has incurred the costs in order to finance the property acquisition for the lessee. Although there are several ways to achieve this matching objective, perhaps the simplest technique is to include initial direct costs as part of the lessor's investment in the lease receivable. When the effective interest method is used to account for interest revenue and the lease receivable, initial direct costs will then be implicitly matched against interest revenue.[18]

Sale-Leaseback Transactions

A **sale-leaseback** transaction occurs when a company "sells" property and immediately leases it back from the purchaser. This type of transaction has become popular as another means for the seller-lessee to obtain cash through off-balance-sheet financing yet still retain substantially all ownership rights associated with the property. Many corporations, including Ramada Inns, Inc. (now Aztar), Entergy Corp., and Dr Pepper, have recently engaged in sale-leaseback transactions.

To illustrate a sale-leaseback, assume that the Wilton Transit Authority (WTA) owns a railroad car with a book value of $600,000. The car has a useful life of 10 years and no salvage value. At the beginning of 1998, to obtain cash, WTA sells the car to Financial Services for $800,000 (its fair value), then immediately leases it back under a 10-year noncancelable lease agreement. Financial Services desires a 12 percent rate of return and determines the lease payments as follows:

$$\$800,000 \div P\overline{_{10|}}_{12\%} = \$800,000 \div 5.6502 = \$141,588$$

WTA must make annual lease payments of $141,588, payable at the end of each year. How should WTA account for this transaction? In the next section we will

---

[18]When direct costs are involved in a direct-financing lease, the *interest rate implicit in the lease,* which equates the present value of the lease payments with the fair value of the leased property, will be higher than the interest rate used by the lessor to calculate the required lease payments.

analyze this sale-leaseback arrangement. In the section that follows, we will account for it.

Analysis of Sale-Leasebacks

At first glance, it appears that WTA could record the sale as follows:

Cash.	800,000	
Equipment.		600,000
Gain on sale of equipment		200,000

The above entry does not capture the *substance* of the transaction, however. Compare WTA's financial position before the sale-leaseback with its financial position after the sale-leaseback. Before the transaction occurred, WTA had equipment with a book value and fair value of $600,000 and $800,000, respectively. After the sale-leaseback, WTA has all rights to the services of the same equipment, cash of $800,000, and a noncancelable obligation to pay $141,588 each year for 10 years, which has a present value of $800,000. One could argue that, in substance, WTA has simply borrowed $800,000 and has an obligation to pay it back over a 10-year period, at 12 percent interest.

This reasoning underlies accounting for sale-leaseback transactions. First, when the sale-leaseback occurs, the "profit" or "gain" is deferred, both because the earnings process is incomplete and because of the interdependency between the sales price and the lease terms. That is, because the property is sold to the same party from whom it is simultaneously leased back, the terms of the sale and the terms of the lease are usually negotiated as a package. Second, the seller-lessee and the purchaser-lessor apply the *Statement No. 13* criteria in classifying and accounting for the lease. WTA's lease agreement satisfies both the third and the fourth capital lease criteria: The term of the lease exceeds 75 percent of the useful life of the property, and the present value of the lease payments exceeds 90 percent of the fair value of the property. Therefore, the lease is a capital lease to WTA as seller-lessee. Finally, the seller-lessee amortizes the deferred gain over the life of the leased property or the lease term, whichever is more appropriate.

CONCEPTUAL

A sale-leaseback is a financing transaction.

Accounting for Sale-Leasebacks

WTA would make the following entries on January 1, 1998:

Cash.	800,000	
Equipment.		600,000
Deferred gain on sale-leaseback		200,000
To record the sale and deferred gain.		
Leased property.	800,000	
Lease liability.		800,000
To record the capital lease.		

On December 31, 1998, WTA would make the following entries:

Interest expense	96,000	
Lease liability.		96,000
(.12 × $800,000)		
To record interest expense for the year.		
Lease liability	141,588	
Cash		141,588
To record the first lease payment.		
Depreciation expense.	80,000	
Accumulated depreciation.		80,000
To record depreciation expense on the leased equipment,		
assuming straight-line depreciation.		

Deferred gain on sale-leaseback 20,000

    Depreciation expense 20,000

($200,000 ÷ 10)

To reduce depreciation expense by the amount
of the deferred gain recognized in 1998.

The effects of these transactions would appear on WTA's 1998 income statement as follows:

Interest expense **$96,000**

Depreciation expense ($80,000 − $20,000) **60,000**

These transactions would appear on WTA's balance sheet as of December 31, 1998, as follows:

ASSETS		LIABILITIES	
Leased property	**$800,000**	**Lease liability**	**$754,412**
Less: Accumulated		**($800,000 + $96,000 − $141,588)**	
depreciation	**(80,000)**		
Deferred gain	**(180,000)**		
	$540,000		

On the income statement, the deferred gain is amortized as a reduction in depreciation expense. On the balance sheet, the unamortized deferred gain is offset against the leased property. The effect of this procedure is to reduce the depreciation expense and the book value of the leased property to the cost basis originally used by WTA. If a sale-leaseback of nondepreciable property qualifies as a capital lease, amortization of the deferred gain is recorded as miscellaneous revenue. If a sale-leaseback transaction does not meet the criteria for a capital lease and is instead classified as an operating lease, the seller-lessee amortizes the deferred gain as a reduction in rent expense related to the annual lease payments. For example, if WTA's lease had been an operating lease, WTA would have made the following entry on January 1, 1998:

Cash 800,000

    Equipment 600,000

    Deferred gain on sale-leaseback 200,000

To record the sale and deferred gain.

WTA would have made these entries on December 31, 1998:

Rent expense 141,588

    Cash 141,588

To record the lease payment.

Deferred gain on sale-leaseback 20,000

    Rent expense 20,000

To amortize the deferred gain for 1998.

Thus, WTA recognizes the gain as it uses the equipment over the lease term.

An anomalous situation arises in presenting the deferred gain on the financial statements when the seller-lessee classifies the lease as an operating lease. The presence of a deferred gain suggests that a financing transaction rather than a sale has occurred. Yet neither the equipment nor the obligation appears on the seller-lessee's balance sheet. Thus, the deferred gain cannot be treated as a contra asset to the leased equipment. In practice, a deferred gain is often reported as a deferred credit on the seller-lessee's balance sheet.

Sale-Partial Leasebacks

In the previous example, the seller-lessee sold and leased back the entire property over its remaining useful life. Thus, it retained *all* the ownership rights to use the property. In many sale-leaseback transactions, however, property is sold and only

a portion of it leased back. Several years ago, for example, First National Bank of Boston sold its 37-story headquarters building and leased back some of the space to maintain its headquarters.[19] A company may also sell property and lease it back for only a *portion* of its useful life. Transactions of this kind are called **sale-partial leaseback** transactions.

With two exceptions, any gain on a sale-partial leaseback should be deferred and amortized as previously illustrated. According to *Statement No. 28,* the two exceptions to this rule are:

1. When only a *minor portion* of the property is leased back, the sale and leaseback should be considered separate transactions and should be accounted for separately. "Minor" means that the present value of the lease payments equals or is less than 10 percent of the fair value of the leased property. Any gain should be recognized in the income statement for the period that includes the lease inception date, because the sale represents the completion of an earnings process rather than a financing transaction.

2. When the portion of the property that is leased back represents *more than a minor part but not substantially all of it,* the gain should be deferred and amortized in the manner previously illustrated. However, if the gain is greater than (*a*) the recorded amount of the leased property (if a capital lease) or (*b*) the present value of the lease payments (if an operating lease), that portion of the gain in excess of *a* or *b* should be recognized in the income statement. The remainder should be deferred and amortized.[20]

ACCOUNTING FOR LEASES: A SUMMARY

The beginning of this chapter presented the major conceptual issue in accounting for leases, whether a lease transfers the rights, risks, and rewards of ownership from the lessor to the lessee. A discussion of how the *Statement No. 13* criteria apply this conceptual issue to the classification of leases followed. The next section covered additional leasing issues, such as minimum lease payments, residual values, bargain purchase options, lessee's use of the implicit rate versus an incremental borrowing rate, initial direct costs, and sale-leaseback transactions. Before going on to the *disclosure* of information by the lessor and lessee, perhaps we should summarize our discussion and illustrations to this point.

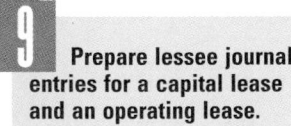

Exhibit 15–12 summarizes how a lessor and a lessee account for different types of leases. The journal entries for the lessee cover capital leases and operating leases. The journal entries for the lessor cover direct-financing leases, sales-type leases, and operating leases. This exhibit serves as an overview of the major topics in this chapter; study it carefully. You will find it useful as a reference for many of the end-of-chapter materials.

LEASE DISCLOSURES

In accordance with the full disclosure principle, *FASB Statement No. 13* requires various types of disclosures by lessors and lessees. These disclosures are designed to help users assess both risk and future cash flows. They also increase comparability among companies, thus enhancing the usefulness of financial reporting.

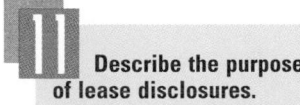

---

[19]"Bank of Boston to Sell, Lease Back Its Headquarters," *The Wall Street Journal,* November 15, 1984, p. 10.
[20]"Accounting for Sales with Leasebacks," *Statement of Financial Accounting Standards No. 28* (Stamford, Conn.: FASB, 1979). The 10 percent test for the first exception can be related to the 90 percent of fair value recovery criterion for a capital lease. Stated another way, when the present value of the lease payments exceeds 90 percent of the fair value of the leased property, the lessee is presumed to have acquired substantially all of the ownership rights associated with the property.

EXHIBIT 15–12   Summary Journal Entries for Lessee and Lessor

Journal Entries for Lessee

Capital lease:

Leased property	xx	
Lease liability		xx

The amount recorded is the present value of the minimum lease payments, which, if applicable, includes either a bargain purchase option or a residual value guarantee. The discount rate used is the lower of the implicit rate in the lease or the lessee's incremental borrowing rate; the amount recorded cannot exceed the fair value of the leased property. Over the term of the lease, the leased property is depreciated over the lease term or the life of the leased asset, whichever is applicable. The lease liability is accounted for using the effective interest method.

Operating lease:

Rent expense	xx	
Cash		xx

Rent expense equals the periodic lease payments.

Journal Entries for Lessor

Direct-financing lease:

Lease receivable	xx	
Property		xx

The lease receivable amount is the present value of the minimum lease payments plus the present value of any unguaranteed residual value. The property amount is its fair value. Over the term of the lease, the lease receivable is accounted for using the effective interest method.

Sales-type lease:

Lease receivable	xx	
Cost of goods sold	xx	
Sales		xx
Inventory		xx

The lease receivable amount is the present value of the minimum lease payments plus the present value of any unguaranteed residual value. The cost of goods sold amount is the property's cost less the present value of any unguaranteed residual value. The sales amount is the present value of the minimum lease payments. The inventory amount is its cost. Over the term of the lease, the lease receivable is accounted for using the effective interest method.

Operating lease:

Cash	xx	
Rent revenue		xx
Property under operating lease	xx	
Inventory (or property)		xx

Rent revenue equals the periodic lease payments. The property is reclassified and depreciated over the lease term to its residual value at the end of the lease term.

Lessee Disclosures

FASB Statement No. 13 requires *lessees* to disclose certain information related to leasing activities. For capital leases, lessees must disclose information regarding capital leases and lease liabilities. For capital leases and noncancelable operating leases, lessees must disclose future lease payments to be made. Lessees should also provide a general description of leasing arrangements. Lease disclosures for Southwest Airlines are shown in Exhibit 15–13.

EXHIBIT 15–13   Southwest Airlines Lease Disclosures

Leases*

Total rental expense for operating leases charged to operations in 1995, 1994, and 1993 was $247,033,000, $198,987,000, and $167,303,000, respectively. The majority of the Company's terminal operations space, as well as 100 aircraft, were under operating leases at December 31, 1995. The amounts applicable to capital leases included in property and equipment were (in thousands):

	1995	1994
Flight equipment	$223,844	$233,324
Less accumulated amortization	101,641	88,656
	$122,203	$144,668

Future minimum lease payments under capital leases and noncancelable operating leases, with initial or remaining terms in excess of one year, at December 31, 1995, were (in thousands):

	Capital Leases	Operating Leases
1996	$ 27,796	$ 223,279
1997	25,858	207,875
1998	32,026	187,662
1999	20,245	173,846
2000	16,871	165,692
After 2000	172,751	1,935,372
Total minimum lease payments	$295,547	$2,893,726
Less amount representing interest	(117,851)	
Present value of minimum lease payments	$177,696	
Less current portion	(13,505)	
Long-term portion	$164,191	

The aircraft leases can generally be renewed at rates, based on fair market value at the end of the lease term, for one to five years. Most aircraft leases have purchase options at or near the end of the lease term at fair market value, but generally not to exceed a stated percentage of the lessor's defined cost of the aircraft.

---

*From Southwest Airlines 1995 annual report.

Lessor Disclosures

For sales-type and direct-financing leases, the *lessor* is required to disclose the components of and information about the net investment in lease receivables, together with related income statement information. For noncancelable operating leases, the lessor must disclose information about equipment leased to lessees and future lease payments to be received from lessees. The lessor must also describe the nature of these leasing arrangements. In summary, the required lessor disclosures are very similar to those required of lessees. Footnote 13 in Appendix B illustrates lessor disclosures by General Electric.

Gross versus Net Disclosures

For instructional purposes, throughout this chapter (and, indeed, this text) we have been recording monetary assets and liabilities, such as lease receivables and lease liabilities, at their present values. In practice, companies are often required to supplement these present values with disclosures of the gross (undiscounted) cash flows and applicable interest. These requirements apply especially to leases. For example, we discussed this disclosure possibility with Lessee Telecommunications and Lessor Bank at the beginning of this chapter.

We have now completed our discussion of leases and how they must be accounted for and disclosed under *Statement No. 13*. We conclude this chapter by summarizing some of the continuing controversies about leases.

CONTINUING CONTROVERSIES SURROUNDING LEASES

While *Statement No. 13* has resolved many leasing issues, others remain unresolved. Many lessees continue to structure lease agreements to avoid meeting the four capital lease criteria.

Classification Inconsistency Between Lessor and Lessee

Given the criteria set forth in *Statement No. 13,* sales-type or direct-financing leases to the lessor are usually capital leases to the lessee. The reverse, however, is not necessarily true. A lease agreement may satisfy one or more of the first four criteria and thus be a capital lease to the lessee, but may not satisfy both of the additional criteria for the lessor. As a result, a lease may be classified as a capital lease by the lessee and an operating lease by the lessor. In that case, the leased property appears on *both* the lessor's and the lessee's balance sheets.

On the other hand, the case of the "disappearing asset" occurs if the lessor classifies and records a lease as a sales-type or direct-financing lease, but the lessee classifies and records it as an operating lease. In this instance, the leased property appears on *neither* the lessor's *nor* the lessee's balance sheet. This situation could arise with unguaranteed residual value, when the lessee cannot ascertain the rate implicit in the lease and uses an incremental borrowing rate higher than the implicit rate.

Leases and Economic Consequences

One of the most controversial aspects of *Statement No. 13* has been its alleged economic consequences, especially to lessees. Many opponents of *Statement No. 13* assert that the *Statement* has increased the number of leasing arrangements that must be accounted for as capital leases, increased the cost of financing for lessees, and adversely affected lessees' security prices. An *FASB Research Report* issued several years ago did not substantiate these assertions. The comprehensive research study examined preparer, user, and auditor attitudes toward and perceptions of information required by *Statement No. 13*. Although the study concluded that *Statement No. 13* did not adversely affect lessee companies' security prices, the *Statement* apparently did have some effect on economic behavior. For example:

1. Many respondents indicated that new lease contracts were drafted and many existing contracts renegotiated to avoid capitalization.

2. There appeared to be an increase in assets purchased instead of leased.

3. In analyzing the financial statements of two identical companies, one of which capitalized its leases while the other did not, many bankers and analysts considered the company that did not capitalize its leases to be more profitable and better able to pay its debts.[21]

Thus, although *Statement No. 13* appears to have affected the behavior and perceptions of some participants in the *FASB Research Report,* the economic consequences generally have not been unfavorable.

A "Property-Rights" Approach to Leases

Under present financial accounting and reporting standards, the conceptual distinction between a capital lease and an operating lease is whether the lease transfers substantially all ownership risks and rewards from the lessor to the lessee. Many people believe that this "all or nothing" approach is not in the best interests of society, given continuing abuses in practice. Those who hold this view believe that lease accounting should adopt a **property-rights approach,** in which a lessee would record property rights acquired under a noncancelable lease as an asset and the obligation incurred as a liability, *even if the lease agreement does not transfer substantially all ownership risks and rewards*. The asset and liability would be measured at the present value of any required lease payments. Proponents of the property-rights approach maintain that it would preserve the conceptual aspects of leases when substantially all ownership risks and rewards *are* transferred from lessor to lessee. In addition, this approach would reduce the amount of resources expended to circumvent *Statement No. 13* criteria. Thus, accounting abuses would be reduced, and society would be better served.

Interestingly, *Accounting Research Study No. 4,* issued in 1962, also stated that noncancelable leases should be considered transfers of rights to use property. This study made accounting recommendations similar to those of the property-rights approach. Also, in 1996 a special report issued jointly by the FASB, IASC, and other organizations recommended a similar approach.[22] Whether the FASB will formally adopt the property-rights approach remains to be seen. In any event, because many leasing issues remain unresolved, further changes in standards for lease accounting and disclosure are likely.

CONCEPTUAL

Many people advocate a "property-rights" approach to lease accounting and reporting.

Leases: An International Perspective

Change is likely worldwide as well as in the United States. Though the United States was the first nation in the world to require the capitalization of leases that are in substance installment purchases, many other nations—for example, Great Britain,

[21]"The Economic Effect on Leases of *SFAS No. 13*: Accounting for Leases," *FASB Research Report* (Stamford, Conn.: FASB, 1981).
[22]"Accounting for Leases: A New Approach," *Financial Accounting Series Special Report* (Norwalk, CT: FASB, 1996).

where substance over form is an overriding consideration in accounting—have since adopted similar requirements. While U.S. GAAP is consistent with *International Accounting Standard No. 17,* "Accounting for Leases," U.S. requirements are the most detailed and prescriptive of any in the world. The standards in other nations, as well as *Standard No. 17,* establish the broad objectives of accounting for leases and leave accountants to use their judgment in accomplishing them. In some nations, like Germany, accounting standards emphasize legal form. In those countries, leases are seldom capitalized; instead, all lease payments are expensed. Because the *Fourth* and *Seventh Directives* of the European Community have no specific requirements regarding leases, this issue is one where there is likely to be a diversity of practice in Europe—and internationally, for that matter—for some time to come.

SUMMARY OF LEARNING OBJECTIVES

I. **Distinguish between a lease that is a rental of property and a lease that is an acquisition of property by financing.**
Leases that transfer the risks, rewards, and benefits associated with ownership of an asset are considered to be acquisitions of property by financing. Leases that do *not* transfer these risks, rewards, and benefits from the lessor to the lessee are essentially rentals.

2. **Describe how to account for a lease that represents a transfer of ownership from the lessor to the lessee.**
The lessor accounts for a lease that transfers ownership from the lessor to the lessee as a sale/financing transaction. The lessee accounts for this type of lease as a purchase/financing transaction. Both the lessor and lessee use the effective interest method to account for the lease receivable/lease liability over the lease term. In addition, the lessee depreciates the leased property over the period benefited by the lease agreement.

3. **Classify leases that transfer ownership and those that do not transfer ownership from the lessor to the lessee.**
Lessees classify leases that transfer the rights, risks, and rewards of ownership from the lessor to the lessee as capital leases. Lessors classify these types of leases as direct-financing, sales-type, or leveraged leases. Leases that do *not* transfer the rights, risks, and rewards of ownership from lessor to lessee are classified as operating leases by both the lessor and lessee.

4. **Identify the *Statement No. 13* criteria used by (a) the lessee and (b) the lessor to classify a lease.**
  a. If a lease meets any one of the following four criteria, the lessee must classify and account for it as a capital lease; otherwise, the lessee must classify and account for it as an operating lease: (1) the lease transfers ownership of the property to the lessee by the end of the lease term; (2) the lease contains a bargain purchase option; (3) the lease term is equal to 75 percent or more of the estimated economic life of the leased property; (4) the present value of the minimum lease payments equals or exceeds 90 percent of the fair value of the leased property.
  b. If a lease meets all of the following criteria, the lessor must classify and account for it as a direct-financing lease or a sales-type lease: (1) the lease meets *any one* of the four criteria listed above; (2) collectibility of the lease payments is reasonably predictable; and (3) there is no significant uncertainty related to the amount of unreimbursable expenses to be incurred by the lessor under the lease; otherwise, the lessor must classify and account for it as an operating lease.

5. **Distinguish between and account for guaranteed residual values and unguaranteed residual values.**
The value of leased property at the end of the lease term is called its residual value. That portion of the residual value that the lessee guarantees or assures the lessor will

recover is called the guaranteed residual value. That portion of the residual value that is not guaranteed by the lessee is called the unguaranteed residual value. Both the lessor and lessee account for guaranteed residual value as a component of the minimum lease payment—that is, as part of the lessor's lease receivable and the lessee's lease liability. The unguaranteed residual value is accounted for as part of the lessor's lease receivable.

6. **Describe a bargain purchase option and explain how to account for it.**
   A bargain purchase option gives the lessee the option to purchase the property at a price substantially below the expected fair value at the date the option may be exercised. Accounting for a bargain purchase option is similar to accounting for guaranteed residual values.

7. **Distinguish between the interest rate implicit in a lease and the lessee's incremental borrowing rate and apply the proper rate for the lessee.**
   The interest rate implicit in the lease is the rate of interest (discount) that equates the present value of the minimum lease payments plus the present value of any unguaranteed residual value with the property's fair value. The lessee's incremental borrowing rate is the rate of interest the lessee would have to pay if it purchased the leased asset with debt. In calculating the present value of the minimum lease payments, the lessee uses the lower of the two rates, subject to the fair value limitation.

8. **Describe a sale-leaseback transaction and prepare journal entries for such a transaction.**
   A sale-leaseback transaction is a financing transaction. Any gain on the sale must be deferred. On the income statement, the deferred gain is amortized as a reduction in depreciation expense or rent expense, depending on whether the seller-lessee classifies the leaseback as a capital lease or an operating lease. On the balance sheet, the deferred gain is reported as a deduction from the leased property or as a deferred credit, depending on whether the seller-lessee classifies the leaseback as a capital lease or an operating lease. When only a minor portion of the property is sold and leased back, the sale and leaseback are accounted for as separate transactions.

9. **Prepare lessee journal entries for a capital lease and an operating lease.**
   The journal entry for a capital lease is as follows:
   ```
   Leased property. . . . . . . . . . . . . . . . . . . . . . . . . . . . . . . . . . . . . . . . . . . . . . . . . x
        Lease liability. . . . . . . . . . . . . . . . . . . . . . . . . . . . . . . . . . . . . . . . . . . . . . . . . x
   ```
   The amount recorded is the present value of the minimum lease payments, which if applicable includes either a bargain purchase option or a residual value guarantee. The discount rate used is the lower of the rate implicit in the lease or the lessee's incremental borrowing rate. The amount recorded cannot exceed the fair value of the leased property. The leased property is depreciated over the term of the lease or the life of the leased asset, whichever is applicable. The lease liability is accounted for using the effective interest method.
   The journal entry for an operating lease is as follows:
   ```
   Rent expense . . . . . . . . . . . . . . . . . . . . . . . . . . . . . . . . . . . . . . . . . . . . . . . . . . x
        Cash. . . . . . . . . . . . . . . . . . . . . . . . . . . . . . . . . . . . . . . . . . . . . . . . . . . . . . . . x
   ```
   The amount recorded is the periodic lease payment.

10. **Prepare lessor journal entries for a direct-financing lease, a sales-type lease, and an operating lease.**
    The journal entry for a direct-financing lease is as follows:
    ```
    Lease receivable . . . . . . . . . . . . . . . . . . . . . . . . . . . . . . . . . . . . . . . . . . . . . . . x
         Property . . . . . . . . . . . . . . . . . . . . . . . . . . . . . . . . . . . . . . . . . . . . . . . . . . . x
    ```
    The lease receivable amount is the present value of the minimum lease payments plus the present value of any unguaranteed residual value. The property amount is the property's fair value. Over the term of the lease, the lease receivable is accounted for using the effective interest method.
    The journal entry for a sales-type lease is as follows:
    ```
    Lease receivable . . . . . . . . . . . . . . . . . . . . . . . . . . . . . . . . . . . . . . . . . . . . . . . x
    Cost of goods sold . . . . . . . . . . . . . . . . . . . . . . . . . . . . . . . . . . . . . . . . . . . . . x
         Sales. . . . . . . . . . . . . . . . . . . . . . . . . . . . . . . . . . . . . . . . . . . . . . . . . . . . . . x
         Inventory . . . . . . . . . . . . . . . . . . . . . . . . . . . . . . . . . . . . . . . . . . . . . . . . . . x
    ```
    The lease receivable amount is the present value of the minimum lease payments plus the present value of any unguaranteed residual value. The cost of goods sold

amount is the property's cost less the present value of any unguaranteed residual value. The sales amount is the present value of the minimum lease payments. The inventory amount is the cost of inventory. Over the term of the lease, the lease receivable is accounted for using the effective interest method.

The journal entries for an operating lease are as follows:

```
Cash ....................................................... x
    Rent revenue ..........................................        x
Property under operating lease ...........................        x
    Inventory (or property) ...............................            x
```

The amount recorded for rent revenue is the periodic lease payment. The property is reclassified from inventory and is depreciated over the lease term to its residual value at the end of the term.

11. Describe the purpose of lease disclosures.

The lease disclosures required under *Statement No. 13* are designed to help users assess risk and future cash flows. The disclosures also increase the comparability among financial statements of different companies, thus increasing the usefulness of financial reporting.

KEY TERMS

bargain purchase option 799

capital lease 794

direct-financing lease 794

fair value recovery criterion 799

guaranteed residual value 804

incremental borrowing rate 799

initial direct cost 812

interest rate implicit in the lease 791

lease 788

lease term 799

lessee 788

lessor 788

leveraged lease 795

minimum lease payments 804

net method 791

operating lease 795

property-rights approach 819

sale-leaseback 812

sale-partial leaseback 815

sales-type lease 795

substance over form 790

unguaranteed residual value 807

QUESTIONS

Q 15-1.   Describe a *lease*.

Q 15-2.   The president of Ransom Corporation stated that his company would prefer to lease rather than purchase property in almost all instances. Explain why the president might have a preference for leasing.

Q 15-3.   For a lessor, distinguish among the following types of leases:
   1.   Sales-type lease.
   2.   Direct-financing lease.
   3.   Operating lease.
   4.   Leveraged lease.

Q 15-4.   For a lessee, distinguish between the following types of leases:
   1.   Capital lease.
   2.   Operating lease.

Q 15-5. Conceptually, under what circumstances would a lease be equivalent to a purchase or sale of property?

Q 15-6. *Statement No. 13* sets forth certain criteria for classifying and accounting for leases.
1. List the criteria for the lessee.
2. List the criteria for the lessor.

Q 15-7. Generally, what items are included in the lessee's minimum lease payments?

Q 15-8. Explain how a lessor would calculate the annual lease payments for purposes of a lease agreement.

Q 15-9. From the lessor's standpoint, briefly discuss the accounting procedures for:
1. A sales-type lease.
2. A direct-financing lease.
3. An operating lease.

Q 15-10. From the lessee's standpoint, briefly discuss the accounting procedures for:
1. A capital lease.
2. An operating lease.

Q 15-11. What is a bargain purchase option, and how does it affect the lessee's minimum lease payments to the lessor?

Q 15-12. What are residual values within a leasing context?

Q 15-13. Under what circumstances would no residual value accrue to a lessor?

Q 15-14. Distinguish between unguaranteed and guaranteed residual values.

Q 15-15. How would a lessor consider residual value (either guaranteed or unguaranteed) in determining the annual lease payments to be paid by the lessee?

Q 15-16. Define the following terms:
1. Interest rate implicit in the lease.
2. Incremental borrowing rate.

Q 15-17. How are the interest rates in Question 15-16 used by the lessee in accounting for capital leases?

Q 15-18. Although *Statement No. 13* requires the lessee, under certain circumstances, to use the incremental borrowing rate in discounting minimum lease payments, this rate may not be used in many instances. Explain.

Q 15-19. Define and give some examples of initial direct costs of leasing.

Q 15-20. Describe the lessor's accounting for initial direct costs for the following types of leases:
1. Sales-type leases.
2. Direct-financing leases.
3. Operating leases.

Q 15-21. Discuss the nature of a sale-leaseback transaction.

Q 15-22. Explain how the following parties account for a sale-leaseback:
1. The seller-lessee.
2. The purchaser-lessor.

Q 15-23. Certain lease criteria and other data that pertain to a lessor follow. For each independent situation, determine whether the lessor should classify the lease as a sales-type lease, a direct-financing lease, or an operating lease.

SITUATION	TITLE TRANSFERRED AT END OF LEASE TERM?	BARGAIN PURCHASE OPTION?	COLLECTIBILITY PREDICTABLE?	UNCERTAINTY REGARDING OTHER COSTS TO BE INCURRED?	DEALER PROFIT?
1	Yes	Yes	Yes	Yes	No
2	No	No	No	Yes	No
3	Yes	No	Yes	No	No
4	No	Yes	Yes	No	Yes
5	Yes	Yes	No	No	No
6	Yes	Yes	Yes	No	Yes
7	Yes	Yes	No	Yes	Yes
8	No	Yes	No	No	No

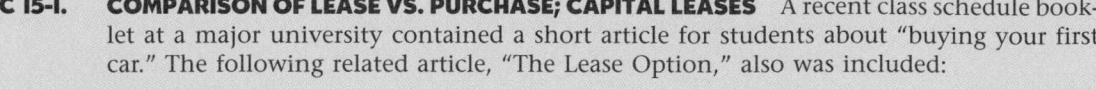

CASES

C 15-1. **COMPARISON OF LEASE VS. PURCHASE; CAPITAL LEASES** A recent class schedule book-let at a major university contained a short article for students about "buying your first car." The following related article, "The Lease Option," also was included:

THE LEASE OPTION

Buying a car, as outlined above, is a relatively simple procedure. You choose the model you want, arrange a bank loan, come up with the down payment, sign on the dotted line, and the car is yours . . . and the bank's.

Then there is leasing. Leasing is a more complicated concept than buying, but it has an advantage, particularly if you are a graduating senior. When you lease a car the down payment and monthly payments required will usually be smaller than when you buy.

One important difference between the two is that when you buy a car you own it, but when a lease agreement expires, you do not own the car because you have not paid for all of it.

Basically, lease payments are determined by subtracting the amount of money the car is worth at the end of the lease from the estimated value of the car when new. That is why leasing is less expensive than buying. Lease payments can also include taxes, maintenance costs, replacement tires and insurance.

There are two major types of lease arrangements: a closed-end lease and an open-end lease. Under a closed-end lease, the lessee simply returns the car to the lessor at the end of the lease.

When an open-end lease expires, the customer is liable for any difference between the estimated value of the car when the lease began and the selling price of the car when the lease expires.

Of course, there are variations, subparagraphs and fine print on these basics that are best carefully examined by you on a situation-by-situation basis.

The chart on the right, based on data supplied by Chrysler Financial Corporation, compares the costs of a theoretical purchase against leasing the same car.

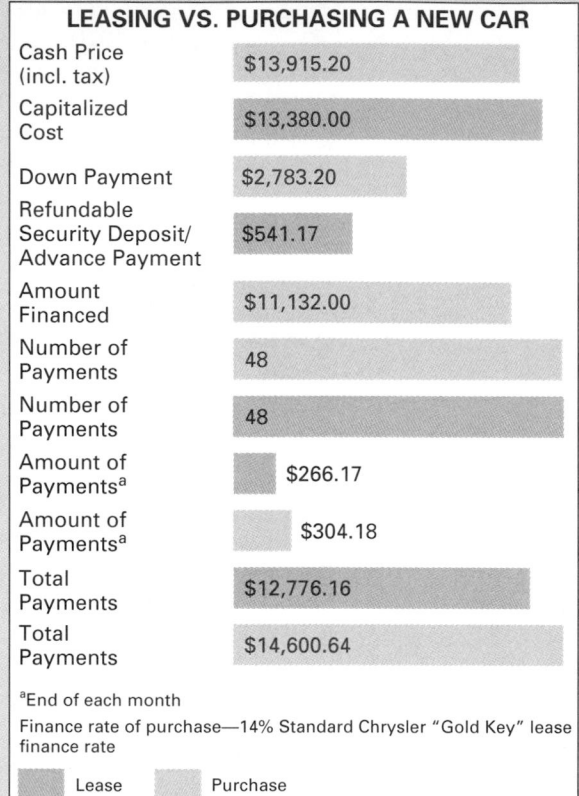

LEASING VS. PURCHASING A NEW CAR	
Cash Price (incl. tax)	$13,915.20
Capitalized Cost	$13,380.00
Down Payment	$2,783.20
Refundable Security Deposit/ Advance Payment	$541.17
Amount Financed	$11,132.00
Number of Payments	48
Number of Payments	48
Amount of Payments[a]	$266.17
Amount of Payments[a]	$304.18
Total Payments	$12,776.16
Total Payments	$14,600.64

[a]End of each month

Finance rate of purchase—14% Standard Chrysler "Gold Key" lease finance rate

▓ Lease   ░ Purchase

REQUIRED

1. Write a short critique of the above article. For this requirement, ignore the lease-versus-purchase numerical comparison.

2. Using the lease-versus-purchase numerical comparison data, derive the monthly lease and purchase payments of $266.17 and $304.18, respectively. The finance rate of purchase, reported to be 14 percent, has been rounded downward, but you must determine the exact monthly *purchase* finance rate. The residual value of the automobile at the end of the lease term is $5,000; you must determine the monthly *lease* finance rate. Assume that "capitalized cost" equals the automobile's cash price less the refundable security deposit/advance payment. (Because the present value tables in Appendix A have a limited number of interest rates, you will find it useful to perform this requirement on either a programmable calculator or spreadsheet software such as Excel.)

3. Based on the article information and your analysis in part 2, discuss whether the lease should be classified as a capital lease or an operating lease.

C 15-2. **LEASE CRITERIA, CLASSIFICATION, AND ACCOUNTING** Arthur Corporation entered into a lease arrangement with Whinney Leasing Corporation for a certain machine. Whinney's primary business is leasing. It is neither a manufacturer nor a dealer. Arthur will lease the machine for a period of three years, which is 50 percent of the machine's economic life. Arthur does not guarantee any residual value for the machine and will not purchase it at the end of the lease term.

Arthur's incremental borrowing rate is 10 percent, and the rate implicit in the lease is 8 1/2 percent. Arthur has no way of knowing the implicit rate used by Whinney. At either rate, the present value of the minimum lease payments is more than 90 percent of the fair value of the machine at the date of the lease agreement.

Arthur has agreed to pay all executory costs directly, and no allowance for these costs is included in the lease payments. Whinney is reasonably certain that Arthur will pay all lease payments, and because Arthur has agreed to pay all executory costs, there are no important uncertainties regarding costs to be incurred by Whinney.

REQUIRED

1. With respect to Arthur (the lessee):
   a) What type of lease has been entered into? Explain the reason for your answer.
   b) How should Arthur calculate the appropriate amount to be recorded for the lease or asset acquired?
   c) What accounts will be created or affected by this transaction, and how will the lease or asset and other costs related to the transaction be matched with revenue?
   d) What disclosures must Arthur make regarding this lease or asset?

2. With respect to Whinney (the lessor):
   a) What type of leasing arrangement has been entered into? Explain the reason for your answer.
   b) How should Whinney record this lease, and how are the appropriate amounts determined?
   c) How should Whinney determine the appropriate amount of income to be recognized from each lease payment?
   d) What disclosures must Whinney make regarding this lease?

(AICPA, adapted)

C 15-3. **PURCHASE OF RESIDUAL VALUE** Farmers and Ranchers Mutual Group, an insurance company, is leasing a Boeing 767 jet to Southeast Airlines. The 10-year lease is a capital lease to Southeast Airlines and a direct-financing lease to Farmers and Ranchers. There is no bargain purchase option, no transfer of title at the end of the lease term, and no guarantee of the residual value, which is estimated to be $10 million at the end of the lease term.

Shortly after the inception of the lease, Donald Liquidators purchases, at a cost of $4 million, the right to the residual value of the jet at the end of the lease term. Donald believes that the jet will be worth at least $10 million at that time. Donald proposes to you, the auditor, that it be permitted to account for the acquisition of residual value interest in one of two ways:

a) Recognize a profit of $6 million at the date of acquisition. Donald argues that the only thing it must do over the remaining lease term is wait. Thus, its earnings process is complete at the date of acquisition (entering into the agreement and paying the $4 million are the *critical events* in its earnings process).

b) Record the residual value acquisition at its present value of $4 million. Subsequent to acquisition, the residual value would be increased each period by an amount "equal to the interest factor." This approach would be identical to valuing the company's residual value interest at present value, both at the date of acquisition and subsequent to acquisition. Donald argues that this approach is consistent with, if not identical to, the method that lessors use to account for unguaranteed residual value in a sales-type or direct-financing lease.

REQUIRED Discuss how Donald should account for its purchase of an interest in the residual value of the Boeing 767.

C 15-4. **LESSOR INTEREST IN RESIDUAL VALUE** Mittelstaedt is a financial institution that specializes in leasing telecommunications equipment. Mittelstaedt purchases this equipment from various vendors and leases the equipment under both operating and direct-financing leases.

You are conducting an audit of Mittelstaedt and have noted two types of leasing transactions that have a material effect on the company's income statement. These leases will be referred to as *Type X* and *Type Y,* and a description of each type is given below.

Type X lease: Mittelstaedt purchases equipment with a six-year life for $100,000 and immediately leases it to a lessee under a four-year lease. The implicit rate in the lease is 10 percent, and the expected residual value, which is unguaranteed, is $15,000. The annual lease payments are $28,315, payable at the end of each year. Mittelstaedt appropriately accounts for this lease as a direct-financing lease.

Type Y lease: Mittelstaedt purchases the same equipment as described in the *Type X* lease and enters into the same leasing agreement as in *Type X*. However, to improve cash flow, Mittelstaedt immediately assigns the lease payments (but not the residual value) to another financial institution. In essence, Mittelstaedt sells the rights to the lease payments to the other financial institution. The financial institution determines the cash to be given to Mittelstaedt by discounting the lease payments using an 8 percent discount rate. The lease payments discounted at 8 percent equal proceeds of $93,782, and the present value of the lease payments discounted at 10 percent is $89,756. At the time of assignment, Mittelstaedt recognizes a gain equal to $4,026 ($93,782 − $89,756). Using the effective interest method, Mittelstaedt also recognizes interest revenue on the present value of the unguaranteed residual value from the date of the lease to the end of the lease. (This same procedure is used, at least implicitly, for *Type X* leases.)

As an auditor, you are concerned that the ultimate profit on these transactions depends on the amount of residual value actually realized at the end of the lease term. You feel that this residual value is more likely to be $5,000 instead of $15,000.

REQUIRED

1. Prepare a schedule of interest and book value for the *Type X* lease, assuming that the residual value at the end of the fourth year will be $15,000. Comment on the total amount of income over the four-year period.

2. Prepare a schedule of interest and book value for the *Type Y* lease, assuming that the residual value at the end of the fourth year will be $15,000. Comment on the total amount of income (gain plus interest) over the four-year period.

3. Now assume that the actual residual value at the end of the fourth year is $5,000 and that this amount is not known until the end of the fourth year. Calculate the total amount of income to be recognized for the *Type X* and *Type Y* leases over the four-year period.

4. Comment on why you are concerned about Mittelstaedt's accounting procedures for these leases.

5. What accounting procedures would you recommend to address your concerns in part 4?

C 15-5. **LEASE PAYMENTS FOR AN AUTOMOBILE LEASE** (This case is adapted from the following article, "New Data Help Car Lessees Shop Smarter," *The Wall Street Journal,* July 11, 1995, p. B-1.) Auto dealers are starting to disclose a number that could increase consumers' bargaining power when they lease new cars—if consumers can figure out how to use it. The number is a lease's "capitalized cost," a figure that roughly matches a vehicle's purchase price in a traditional transaction. In the past, the number rarely appeared in leasing contracts. But now most of the automobile industry is moving to disclose the figure as pressure builds for leasing reform. Consumer advocates fear that most leasing customers won't use the new information effectively because auto dealers will be reluctant to explain it, and consumers won't know enough to ask.

Joanne Gordon said she understood very little about the lease she signed when she drove away with a new Chevrolet Cavalier. She simply paid $10,000 to cover her leasing costs up-front—a $6,000 credit for the car she traded in and $4,000 in cash. In return, she got the right to drive the Cavalier for three years and as many as 45,000 miles. "I didn't think costs had anything to do with me because I wasn't actually buying anything," said Ms. Gordon.

"Had she known the Cavalier's capitalized cost, Ms. Gordon might have discovered she was letting the dealer keep too much profit," said Remar Sutton, president of the Consumer Affairs Task Force for Automobile Issues, an Atlanta-based group that offers a "reality checklist" for reviewing lease deals.

John Scura was an exception. Before driving away with his Jeep Wrangler, he assessed not only the contract's capitalized cost, but also its "money factor"—the interest-like rate that leasing companies use to calculate lease charges. He reduced his monthly payments by $100. His advice: Never shop for a lease by comparing payments alone; also consider factors like capitalized cost, residual value, and leasing charges.

REQUIRED Write a paragraph that explains how knowledge of an automobile's capitalized cost (and other factors) can help a lessee evaluate the "cost" of an automobile lease.

C 15-6. **LEASE CLASSIFICATION; AUTOMOBILE LEASE** Several years ago, a Lincoln-Mercury dealer had the following advertising headline in a local newspaper: "Lease a cat with nine lives." The dealer was offering to lease a new Mercury Cougar GS for $265 per month. The car was fully equipped with a V-6 electronic fuel-injected engine, air-conditioning, electronic AM/FM four-speaker stereo, LCD digital speedometer, and other options. The information below is reproduced from the advertisement:

THE TERMS

a) Lessee may have the option to purchase the car at lease end, at a price to be negotiated with the dealer at lease inception; however, lessee has no obligation to purchase the car at lease end.

b) Lessee is responsible for excess wear and tear.

c) Refundable security deposit, cash down payment, and first lease payment due at lease inception.

THE ARITHMETIC

Monthly lease payment	$265
Number of months	48
Refundable security deposit	$275
Cash down payment	$1,500
Total amount due at inception	$1,775
Total amount of payments	$12,720
Total mileage allowed	60,000
Mileage penalty over 60,000	$.06 per mile

REQUIRED 1. Assume that you are the lessee. Based on the above terms, discuss whether the lease is a capital lease or an operating lease.

2. Again assume that you are the lessee. The actual "window sticker" price of the Cougar was $14,065, which included a manufacturer's discount of $600. Assuming that your incremental borrowing rate was 1 percent per month and applying the *Statement No. 13* criteria, how should you classify the lease? You may want to consider the nature of a "window sticker" price in arriving at your answer. (*Note:* The factor for the present value of an annuity due for 48 rents at 1 percent is 38.3537.)

C 15-7. **LEASES; UNCERTAINTY ABOUT LEASE PAYMENT COLLECTIBILITY** You are a senior accounting professor at a small state university and teach leases in your intermediate accounting class. Recently, while discussing the lessor criteria for sales-type leases, one of your students raised the following issue: "In Chapters 2 and 7 of this text, revenue recognition concepts were discussed. We learned that revenue is normally recognized at the point of sale. However, when the seller is unable to make reasonable estimates of uncollectible accounts, the installment method may be used. Given this concept, instead of accounting for a lease as an operating lease, why shouldn't lessors use the installment method for a sales-type lease when the only criterion lacking is that collectibility of the lease payments is not reasonably predictable?"

REQUIRED Draft a response to the issue raised by your student.

C 15-8. **CAPITAL LEASE VS. OPERATING LEASE—LESSEE** A Cadillac dealer ran the following advertisement in the local newspaper:

Lease from the Best
SMART LEASE

Sedan de Ville

Lease this new Cadillac for only $499.77* per month (plus use tax.)

■ New, more powerful 4.5 liter V8

■ True, six-passenger comfort

■ 4-year, 50,000-mile Gold Key Bumper to Bumper Warranty

■ Distinctive design & luxury appointments

*48-month closed end lease. Option to purchase at end of lease is $9,709, with no customer liability or obligation. Up-front money includes (1) first month payment of $534.75, (2) security deposit of $550, and (3) tag and tax of $1,350. Total of payments is $25,668. 15,000 miles per year limit.

Additional information:

a) The monthly payment of $534.75 includes the lease payment of $499.77 plus a 7 percent use tax of $34.98.

b) The effective monthly rate of interest implicit in the lease is .8 percent.

c) "Closed end" means that the lessee does not guarantee residual value.

d) The Sedan de Ville's "window sticker" price is $28,000. Most dealers offer discounts from the window sticker prices.

REQUIRED   Assume that you have agreed to lease the Sedan de Ville described above. Discuss all factors that should be considered in determining whether you have entered into a capital lease or an operating lease. Include calculations where necessary.

C 15-9.   **SOUTHWEST AIRLINES LEASE DISCLOSURES**   Refer to the lease disclosures presented on page 817 for Southwest Airlines.

REQUIRED   Answer each of the following questions about Southwest Airlines's lease disclosures (your answers should be written and should have supporting calculations, as appropriate):

1. What is the probable reason that most of Southwest's terminal operations space is accounted for as an operating lease?

2. Except for 100 aircraft, Southwest's flight equipment is accounted for as leased property under capital leases. How does the use of this equipment affect Southwest's income statement?

3. What is Southwest's lease liability reported on its current year's balance sheet?

4. In the disclosure of the future minimum lease payments under capital leases, Southwest reports lease payments to be made in 1996 of $27,796,000, and the current portion of the present value of minimum lease payments is reported to be $13,505,000. What method does Southwest use to distinguish between the current portion and the long-term portion of its lease obligation?

5. Refer to part 4. Assume that the lease payments are made at the beginning of each year. Prepare journal entries to record Southwest's lease payments and interest for 1996. Also calculate the apparent interest rate—that is, the implicit interest rate—used by Southwest to account for its lease obligation.

6. How is the disclosure of the future minimum lease payments under noncancelable operating leases useful to Southwest's current and potential investors and creditors?

7. Do any of Southwest's aircraft leases contain bargain purchase options?

EXERCISES

E 15-1.   **LESSOR'S DETERMINATION OF ANNUAL LEASE PAYMENTS**   Below are four independent cases that deal with the lessor's use of present value and other concepts in determining annual lease payments to be received at the end of each year.

	CASE 1	CASE 2	CASE 3	CASE 4
Cost of equipment to lessor	$27,000	$50,000	$150,000	$64,000
Fair value of equipment	$27,000	$70,000	$150,000	$80,000
Residual value:				
Guaranteed	—	$10,000	—	$4,800
Unguaranteed	—	—	$40,000	$3,200
Life of lease	20 years	10 years	10 years	15 years
Initial direct costs	$500	—	$2,000	—
Rate of return required by lessor.	12%	12%	10%	12%

REQUIRED   Calculate the lease payments for each case above.

E 15-2.   **SALES-TYPE AND CAPITAL LEASES**   Alaina Corporation manufactures and sells computerized telephone systems. Alaina's normal selling price for the system, which costs $43,000 to manufacture, is $65,000. Because of competition and obsolescence, the estimated useful life of a system is four years.

On January 1, 1998, Alaina Corporation leased a telephone system to Nebo Consulting. The term of the lease was four years, and the annual lease payments, due at the end of each year, were $21,400. The implicit interest rate in the lease (and Nebo's incremental borrowing rate) was 12 percent. At the end of the lease term, the system was to be returned to the lessor.

The terms of the lease meet the criteria for a sales-type lease to Alaina and for a capital lease to Nebo. Both companies have a December 31 fiscal year-end.

REQUIRED
1. Construct a schedule of interest and book value suitable for Alaina and Nebo.
2. In parallel columns, prepare all entries for the lessor and lessee for the first two years of the lease. Nebo uses sum-of-the-years'-digits depreciation on its other telephone equipment.
3. Prepare all necessary balance sheet data for both parties on December 31, 1999.

E 15-3. **OPERATING LEASES** Refer to the data in Exercise 15-2. Assume that the lease qualifies as an operating lease to both parties (even though the facts indicate otherwise). Alaina uses straight-line depreciation on all depreciable assets.

REQUIRED In parallel columns, prepare all entries for the lessor and lessee for the first two years of the lease.

E 15-4. **BARGAIN PURCHASE OPTION** At the beginning of the current year, a bank (lessor) and a construction company (lessee) entered into a lease agreement. The construction company leased equipment with a fair value of $100,000 from the bank, which had recently purchased the equipment for lease purposes at a cost of $100,000. Under the terms of the lease, the annual lease payments were $28,100, payable at the end of each year. Although the lease was for a 20-year period, the lessee was given a bargain purchase option, exercisable at the end of the fourth year, for $16,000. The implicit rate in the lease (and the lessee's incremental borrowing rate) was 10 percent.

REQUIRED Prepare a schedule of interest and book value that both parties could use in accounting for the annual lease payments.

E 15-5. **IMPLICIT RATE IN LEASE** Gloria's Computer Market has a large mainframe computer for sale or lease. The cash selling price is $92,442. Under the lease terms, the lessee must sign a noncancelable lease and make 15 annual payments of $10,000 each, beginning on the first day of the lease term. Title passes to the lessee at the end of the lease term.

REQUIRED Calculate the implicit rate in the above lease.

E 15-6. **CAPITAL LEASES AND SALES-TYPE LEASES; RESIDUAL VALUE** The following information pertains to a lease agreement between a lessor and lessee for plant and equipment with a fair value of approximately $60,000:
a) Term of lease—4 years; life of leased property—5 years
b) Annual lease payments (end of each year)—$17,200
c) Implicit rate in lease (and lessee's incremental borrowing rate)—10 percent.
d) Estimated residual value at the end of the lease term—$8,017. *The lessee guaranteed 75 percent of the residual value.*
e) Cost of plant and equipment to lessor—$42,000.
f) At the end of the lease term, the equipment is returned to the lessor.
Based on the above information, the lease is a capital lease to the lessee and a sales-type lease to the lessor.

REQUIRED
1. Prepare the journal entries for the lessor and the lessee at the lease inception date.
2. Prepare all other journal entries for the lessor and lessee during the first year. The lessee uses straight-line depreciation on the leased property.
3. Prepare the lessor's journal entry to record receipt of the equipment at the end of the lease term. Assume that the residual value is $8,017 at the end of the lease term.

E 15-7. **RESIDUAL VALUE GUARANTEE** A lessor and lessee enter into a lease agreement whereby an 18-wheeler with a fair value of $100,000 will be leased for a period of four years at an annual rental of $25,740, payable at the beginning of each year. The lessee guarantees that at the end of the lease term, the truck's residual value will be at least $15,000. The lessee is aware of the truck's fair value and that a discount rate of 10 percent is used by the lessor to calculate the annual lease payments, although the lessee's incremental borrowing rate is 8 percent. This lease is a direct-financing lease to the lessor and a capital lease to the lessee, and the lessee plans to depreciate the truck by the sum-of-the-years'-digits method. The truck is returned to the lessor at the end of the lease term.

1. Explain why the lessee cannot use the incremental borrowing rate as a basis for recording the capital lease.

2. Prepare entries to record the lease on the books of the lessor and lessee at the date of the lease agreement.

3. Prepare a schedule of interest and book value for the lessor and lessee.

4. Prepare all necessary entries on the books of the lessor and lessee at the end of the lease term, assuming that the actual residual value of the truck at that time is:

    a) $20,000.

    b) $10,000.

    c) $18,000 (the lease term provides that all gains shall accrue to the lessor).

E 15-8. **UNGUARANTEED RESIDUAL VALUE** Refer to Exercise 15-7. Assume that the facts in that exercise apply here, except for the following changes: (a) the $15,000 estimated residual value at the end of the lease term is not guaranteed by the lessee; (b) the beginning-of-period annual lease payments, established by the lessor, were $26,169 based on a higher implicit interest rate (11 percent) to compensate for the increased risk of unguaranteed residual value; and (c) the lessee cannot determine the 11 percent implicit interest rate in the lease.

1. Prepare entries to record the lease on the books of the lessor and lessee at the date of the lease agreement.

2. Prepare schedules of interest and book value for the lessor and lessee. *Note:* Separate schedules will be necessary because different interest rates are used by the parties.

3. Assume that the actual residual value at the end of the lease term is $12,800. Prepare any entries in the lessor's journal needed to record this event.

E 15-9. **SALES-TYPE LEASES; RESIDUAL VALUE** The following information relates to a sales-type lease for Sugarland Corporation, a dealer-lessor:

Term of lease	**10 years**
Cost of leased property	**$240,000**
Normal selling price of leased property	**$270,000**
Residual value, end of lease term	**$30,000**
Lease payments required at end of each year	
on basis of a 12% implicit interest rate	**$46,077**

1. Prepare the lessor's entry to record the sales-type lease under the assumption that the residual value is guaranteed.

2. Prepare the lessor's entry to record the sales-type lease under the assumption that the residual value is not guaranteed. Although the lessor's required rate of return probably would be higher, assume that the 12 percent interest rate still applies.

E 15-10. **INITIAL DIRECT COSTS** The following information pertains to a lease agreement between a lessor and a lessee:

Fair value of equipment	**$7,460**
Term of lease	**3 years**
Initial direct costs incurred by lessor (attorneys' fees,	
filing fees, and contract fees)	**$480**
Discount rate used by lessor in calculating	
annual end-of-year lease payments	**10%**

1. Assume that the lease is a sales-type lease and that the lessor calculated the lease payments in order to recover the normal sales price of the equipment as follows:

$$\frac{\text{Sales price}}{P_{\overline{3}|10\%}} = \frac{\$7,460}{2.4869} = \$3,000 \text{ (rounded)}$$

The leased property had a cost of $5,000 to the lessor. Prepare the lessor's entries to record the lease and the receipt of the first year's lease payment.

2. Assume that the lease is a direct-financing lease and that the lessor calculated the lease payments in order to recover cost ($7,460) plus the initial direct costs over the lease term as follows:

$$\frac{\$7,460 + \$480}{2.4869} = \$3,193$$

Prepare the lessor's entries to record the lease and receipt of the first year's lease payment.

3. Assume that the lease is an operating lease with annual payments of $2,400. Prepare the lessor's entries to record the initial direct costs, the receipt of the first year's rental, and amortization of the initial direct costs for the first year.

E 15-11. LEASE CLASSIFICATION AND ACCOUNTING—LESSEE On July 1, 1998, Red River Airlines (RRA) leased a small plane from Spider Aircraft Corporation. The lease covered a 10-year period and required annual lease payments of $58,000, beginning on July 1, 1998. On July 1, 1998, the plane had a fair value of $400,000 and an estimated life of 16 years. RRA could not determine the implicit rate in the lease but had an incremental borrowing rate of 10 percent. RRA's fiscal year ends on December 31, and the company depreciates its other equipment on a straight-line basis.

REQUIRED
1. Determine whether RRA should classify the lease agreement with Spider as a capital lease or as an operating lease.
2. Prepare the appropriate journal entry for RRA on July 1, 1998.
3. Prepare the appropriate journal entries for RRA on the following dates:
   a) December 31, 1998.
   b) July 1, 1999.
   c) December 31, 1999.

E 15-12. IMPLICIT RATE AND UNGUARANTEED RESIDUAL VALUE Refer to the data in Exercise 15-11. Notice that Red River Airlines did not guarantee any residual value at the end of the lease term.

REQUIRED Calculate the estimated residual value, assuming that the implicit rate in the lease was:
1. 10 percent.
2. 12 percent.

E 15-13. LEASE CLASSIFICATION AND ACCOUNTING—LESSOR Dubois Company manufactures concert electric pianos at a cost of $28,500 and sells them for $35,000. On January 1, 1998, Dubois leased a piano with an estimated useful life of 10 years to a country music band. The lease term covered an 8-year period. The annual lease payments were $4,785, payable at the end of each year, in addition to a $7,500 payment to Dubois on the date of the lease agreement. At the end of the lease term, the band could purchase the piano for $1. Collectibility of the lease payments was reasonably assured, and Dubois expected to incur no other costs during the 8-year lease period, except for expenses of $2,000 in negotiating and closing the lease with the band. The implicit rate in the lease was 8 percent. Dubois's fiscal year ends on December 31.

REQUIRED
1. How should Dubois classify the lease with the country music band? Explain.
2. Prepare Dubois's journal entry or entries on January 1, 1998.
3. Prepare all necessary journal entries for Dubois Company on December 31, 1998, and December 31, 1999.

E 15-14. SALE-LEASEBACK On January 1, 1998, Germain sold a travel bus to Nashville Finance Company for $32,000, then immediately leased it back under a 15-year, noncancelable lease at an annual rental of $4,195, payable at the beginning of each year. Nashville used an implicit rate of 12 percent (known by Germain) to determine the annual lease payments. The bus had a carrying value of $24,000 on Germain's books. Both parties' fiscal year ends on December 31.

REQUIRED
1. Assume the lease qualifies as a capital lease to the lessee and a direct-financing lease to the lessor. Prepare all necessary entries for 1998 for Germain (seller-lessee) and Nashville Finance Company (purchaser-lessor). Germain will depreciate the bus on a straight-line basis over the lease term.
2. Assume that the lease is an operating lease for both parties (though the facts indicate otherwise). Prepare all necessary entries for 1998 for Germain and Nashville Finance Company. Nashville will depreciate the bus on a straight-line basis over its estimated useful life of 20 years.

E 15-15. SALE AND LEASEBACK On January 1, 1998, Krull Corporation sold a machine to Georgie Company and simultaneously leased it back for two years. Pertinent data are as follows:

Estimated remaining useful life on 1/1/98	**8 years**
Sales price	**$100,000**
Krull's carrying value on 1/1/98	**$50,000**
Monthly rental under leaseback, payable end of month	**$1,500**
Interest rate implicit in lease (per month)	**1%**

REQUIRED   **1.** Prepare Krull's entry to record the sale and leaseback on January 1, 1998.
                2. Calculate Krull's monthly rental expense under the sale and leaseback.

E 15-16.   **LESSEE CLASSIFICATION AND ACCOUNTING**   On January 1, 1998, Bolivar signed a five-year, noncancelable lease on a nuclear barge. The barge had a fair value of $665,000 and an estimated useful life of six years. The lease specified that Bolivar would make five annual payments of $170,000, beginning on December 31, 1998.

        Title to the barge does not transfer to Bolivar at the end of the lease term, and the lease agreement does not contain a bargain purchase option. Bolivar depreciates similar assets on a straight-line basis. Bolivar's incremental borrowing rate is 10 percent (Bolivar cannot determine the implicit rate in the lease). Bolivar's fiscal year ends on December 31.

REQUIRED   **1.** Determine how Bolivar must classify and account for the nuclear barge lease.
                2. Prepare all necessary journal entries for Bolivar for 1998.

E 15-17.   **LESSOR CLASSIFICATION AND ACCOUNTING**   Refer to the information provided in Exercise 15-16. Assume that on January 1, 1999, Bolivar terminated the lease by transferring the lease and barge to Rauh Corporation. Under the terms of the sublease, Rauh agreed to assume all obligations previously held by Bolivar.

REQUIRED   What journal entry, if any, should Bolivar make on January 1, 1999, to account for its lease with Rauh?

E 15-18.   **SALE-LEASEBACK TRANSACTION**   Miami Nice, Inc., owns and operates a luxury charter boat service. Because customer demand for its services has increased in recent years, Miami decided to have a larger charter boat constructed. Construction began in 1997 and was expected to be completed January 1, 2000.

        At the beginning of 1998, Miami began seeking a buyer for its smaller boat. On November 1, 1998, the smaller boat was sold for $87,500. At the date of sale, the boat had an estimated remaining life of 50 months (salvage value is negligible) and was carried on Miami's books at $40,000, net of accumulated depreciation.

        Because the larger boat was not scheduled to be completed until January 1, 2000, the terms of sale provided that Miami could rent the smaller boat for a 14-month period, beginning November 1, 1998, and ending December 31, 1999. The monthly rentals were $2,500, payable at the end of each month, and represented a "market price" rental based on the boat's fair value of $87,500 and its useful life of 50 months.

REQUIRED   **1.** Determine the interest rate implicit in the monthly rental payments of $2,500.
                2. Explain why Miami must classify the 14-month lease of the smaller boat as an operating lease.
                3. Prepare Miami's entry to record the sale and leaseback on November 1, 1998.
                4. Calculate Miami's rent expense for the two-month period ending December 31, 1998.

E 15-19.   **INCOME EFFECTS OF CAPITAL VS. OPERATING LEASES**   On January 1, 1998, Fulkerson Corporation entered into an 8-year lease agreement to lease a fleet of horse trailers. The annual lease payments were $12,269, payable at the beginning of each year. Fulkerson should have accounted for the lease as a capital lease in the amount of $72,000, because title to the trailers passed to Fulkerson at the end of the lease term. Fulkerson, however, mistakenly accounted for it as an operating lease. The trailers had an estimated life of 10 years with no residual value and should have been depreciated by the straight-line method.

REQUIRED   Calculate the effect of Fulkerson's error for the years 1998 and 1999.

E 15-20.   **DETERMINING ANNUAL LEASE PAYMENTS**   Duckworth Investments has been requested by Rocky Transit Corporation to purchase and lease a fleet of small planes to Rocky. The cost of the fleet is $5.4 million. The lease term will be 10 years with annual lease payments due at the beginning of each year. Rocky Transit will guarantee a residual value for the fleet of $150,000 at the end of the lease term, although Duckworth estimates that the residual value will be at least $400,000. Duckworth will incur direct costs of $48,000 in negotiating and closing the lease agreement. Duckworth desires a 10 percent rate of return on the investment. Rocky's incremental borrowing rate is 12 percent; the rate implicit in the lease is unknown to Rocky.

REQUIRED   **1.** Calculate the annual lease payments that Duckworth Investments would have in the lease agreement.
                2. Assume that the lease is classified as a direct-financing capital lease for Duckworth and as a capital lease for Rocky Transit. Prepare the entries for both parties to record the lease and to record any adjusting entries at the end of the first year. Rocky uses straight-line depreciation on its other planes.

PROBLEMS

P 15-1. **LEASE CLASSIFICATION AND ACCOUNTING—LESSOR** Hometime Builders manufactures camp trailers for $20,000 each and sells them for $30,000 each. The trailers have a useful life of 20 years with no salvage value after that time.

On January 1, 1998, Hometime entered into a 12-year noncancelable lease agreement with Redstone Park for a fleet of five trailers. The annual lease payments, payable at the end of each year, were $22,972. The residual value of the trailers was estimated to be $30,000 at the end of the lease term. None of this residual value was guaranteed by Redstone Park. The interest rate implicit in the lease was 12 percent.

Collectibility of the lease payments by Hometime is reasonably predictable, and Hometime will not incur any additional unreimbursable costs during the term of the lease.

REQUIRED
1. Determine how Hometime should classify the lease.
2. Prepare the journal entry or entries for Hometime on January 1, 1998.
3. Prepare all journal entries for Hometime for the first two years of the lease. Hometime has a fiscal year ending on December 31.
4. Prepare Hometime's entry at the end of the lease term, assuming that the camp trailers have a fair value of only $22,000 at that time.

P 15-2. **LEASE CLASSIFICATION AND ACCOUNTING—LESSEE** Refer to the lease agreement in Problem 15-1. Redstone Park's incremental borrowing rate also is 12 percent.

REQUIRED
1. Determine how Redstone Park should classify the lease.
2. Prepare the journal entry or entries for Redstone Park on January 1, 1998.
3. Prepare all journal entries for Redstone Park for the first two years of the lease. Redstone Park uses straight-line depreciation.
4. If Redstone Park's incremental borrowing rate had been 16 percent and if Redstone had been unable to ascertain the implicit rate in the lease, would the lease still be classified as a capital lease by Redstone? Explain and show calculations.

P 15-3. **FINANCIAL STATEMENT EFFECTS OF LEASES** At the beginning of year 1, Jeremy Lessor and Jamie Lessee entered into a four-year lease agreement and made the following entries to record the lease:

JEREMY LESSOR			JAMIE LESSEE		
Lease receivable	120,000		Leased property	114,523	
Cost of sales	74,523		Lease liability		114,523
Sales		114,523			
Inventory		80,000			

Subsequent to recording the lease, Jeremy and Jamie misplaced the lease agreement. During your audit for year 1, you pieced together the following information about the lease:
a) The annual lease payments were $34,400, payable at the end of each year.
b) The implicit rate in the lease (and Jamie's incremental borrowing rate) was 10 percent.
c) Jamie guaranteed 50 percent of the property's residual value at the end of the lease term; the estimated useful life of the property was 5 years.
d) The lease did not transfer title to the lessee and did not contain a bargain purchase option.
e) Straight-line depreciation is appropriate.
f) Jamie was a good credit risk and agreed to assume responsibility for maintenance and all other expenses associated with the property during the lease term.

REQUIRED
1. Verify that both parties classified the lease correctly.
2. Calculate the leased property's residual value at the end of the lease term.
3. Verify the numbers recorded by Jeremy Lessor and Jamie Lessee at the date of the lease agreement.
4. Indicate the financial effects that the above lease would have on Jeremy Lessor's and Jamie Lessee's income statement and statement of cash flows for year 1 and their balance sheets at the end of year 1.

P 15-4. **CAPITAL LEASES** Ramesh Consulting Corporation was incorporated in 1997 and has a fiscal year ending December 31. On October 1, 1998, Ramesh leased a computerized management information system from the manufacturer. The lease calls for a monthly rental of $5,000 for the 50 months of the lease term. The estimated useful life of the system is five years.

Each scheduled monthly rental payment includes $400 for full-service maintenance on the system, to be performed by the manufacturer. All rentals are payable on the first day of the month, beginning October 1, 1998. At the end of the lease term, Ramesh can purchase the system from the manufacturer at its then-current fair value.

This lease is to be accounted for as a capital lease by Ramesh, and it will be depreciated by the straight-line method. Borrowed funds for this type of transaction would cost Ramesh 1 percent per month. Ramesh does not know the implicit rate in the lease.

REQUIRED
1. Why is the lease a capital lease to Ramesh?
2. Prepare journal entries for Ramesh on October 1, 1998.
3. Calculate the amounts at which the capital lease and the lease liability would appear on Ramesh's balance sheet on December 31, 1998.

P 15-5.   BARGAIN PURCHASE OPTIONS   Downs Corporation sells and leases cruise ships. The ships normally sell for $6 million and cost Downs $4 million each. At the beginning of 1998, Downs leased one of these ships to Arthur Company with the following terms:

Lease term	**10 years**
Bargain purchase option (end of 2002)	**$500,000**
Estimated life of ship	**12 years**
Lease payments (payable at beginning of each year)	**$1,517,021**
Interest rate implicit in lease (known to Arthur)	**16%**
Estimated residual value:	
End of lease term	**$300,000**
End of useful life of ship	**$100,000**

Downs expects to collect the lease payments in full from Arthur and does not expect to incur any future costs related to the lease. The fiscal years of both parties coincide with the calendar year.

REQUIRED
1. Show how Downs calculated the annual lease payments.
2. Determine how each party should classify the lease.
3. Give the necessary entries on the books of Downs and Arthur on January 1, 1998.
4. Prepare a schedule of interest and book value that would be suitable for both parties.
5. On the basis of the schedule in part 4, prepare all entries for Downs and Arthur relative to any lease receivable/payable accruals and payments on December 31, 1998, and January 1, 1999.
6. Arthur Company uses straight-line depreciation on other cruise ships that it owns. Calculate the annual depreciation expense on the leased cruise ship.
7. Assume that Arthur Company exercised the bargain purchase option at the end of 2002. Prepare the entries to record the exercise on the books of Downs and Arthur.

P 15-6.   CLASSIFICATION AND ACCOUNTING FOR LEASES   Jay Guaranty and Trust purchases new jets from manufacturers and used jets from airlines and leases them to other airlines and charter companies. On June 29, 1998, Jay purchased a used wide-body jet at its fair value of $5 million from Nordic Airlines. The jet had a remaining useful life of 18 years with minimal salvage value at the end of its useful life.

On July 1, 1998, Jay leased the wide-body jet to Thompson Airways. The term of the lease was 12 years, and Thompson was to obtain title to the jet at the end of the lease term. Annual lease payments were $750,000 and were due on July 1 of each year, beginning July 1, 1998. The annual lease payments included $29,300 for insurance and taxes on the aircraft.

The implicit rate in the lease was 12 percent, although Thompson's incremental borrowing rate was 10 percent. Jay was not able to make a reasonable prediction of the collectibility of the lease payments, because Thompson recently had experienced some difficulty in meeting its obligations with creditors. Both companies' fiscal years end on December 31.

REQUIRED
1. Verify how Jay Guaranty and Trust determined the lease payments on the jet.
2. Determine how this lease should be classified and accounted for by the lessor and the lessee.
3. Prepare all necessary entries for Jay and Thompson on July 1, 1998.

4. Prepare all adjusting entries for both companies on December 31, 1998. Straight-line depreciation is appropriate for the aircraft.

P 15-7. **LEASE CLASSIFICATION AND ACCOUNTING; DISCLOSURE** On January 1, 1998, Cash signed a three-year noncancelable contract to lease construction equipment from Leasequip. Cash agreed to pay Leasequip $52,862 at the beginning of each year, and Cash made the first payment on January 1, 1998. The contract did not transfer title to Cash, but it did allow Cash a bargain purchase option of $25,000 on December 31, 2000. Cash agreed to maintain the equipment and to pay insurance, taxes, and all other costs associated with the use of the equipment. Because of Cash's credit history, collectibility of the lease payments was reasonably certain.

On January 1, 1998, the equipment was carried on Leasequip's books at $120,000, although the equipment's fair value was approximately $160,000. The equipment has an estimated useful life of five years and an estimated salvage value of $10,000 at the end of that time.

Leasequip will account for the lease as a sales-type lease. Cash will account for the lease as a capital lease. Cash will use straight-line depreciation on the equipment. The implicit rate used by Leasequip and Cash's incremental borrowing rate are 12 percent. Leasequip and Cash both have fiscal years ending on December 31.

REQUIRED

1. Explain why Leasequip and Cash classified the lease as a sales-type lease and capital lease, respectively.

2. Prepare all necessary journal entries for Leasequip and Cash on January 1, 1998, and on December 31, 1998.

3. Cash also will be required to disclose the following capital lease items in the financial statement footnotes for the year ending December 31, 1998:

   a) The total remaining minimum lease payments.

   b) Amounts representing interest.

   c) Net lease obligation.

   Calculate these amounts for Cash.

P 15-8. **ACCOUNTING FOR LEASES—LESSEE** Ardmore Corporation, a company with nationwide interests in commercial real estate, has leased a helicopter for business use. The noncancelable lease agreement is for 10 years and covers a Bell XR-1 that has a fair value of $900,000. Ardmore must make annual payments of $127,912 at the beginning of each year; the first payment is due on January 1, 1998. These payments include $5,000 per year for taxes and insurance, which are paid by the lessor. Ardmore agrees to pay costs for all maintenance, which has been scheduled by the lessor. At the end of the 10-year lease term, Ardmore can purchase the helicopter for $20,000. The helicopter has an estimated useful life of 15 years. Its fair value at the end of the lease term is estimated to be $75,000. Its fair value at the end of 15 years is estimated to be $30,000.

The implicit rate in the lease is not stated expressly in the lease agreement, but Ardmore has determined, based on the helicopter's fair value, that this rate is 8 percent. Ardmore's line of credit would allow the company to borrow approximately $900,000 under a 10-year loan agreement at an annual interest rate of 12 percent. On January 1, 1998, the present value of the net rental payments and the purchase option of $20,000 is approximately $784,000 on the basis of a 12 percent rate. Ardmore has determined that this lease agreement constitutes a capital lease. Ardmore will use straight-line depreciation on the helicopter.

REQUIRED

1. Discuss why Ardmore must classify this lease as a capital lease.

2. Prepare the necessary journal entries for Ardmore on January 1, 1998, and on December 31, 1998, the end of its fiscal year.

3. Prepare all necessary journal entries for Ardmore on January 1, 1999, and December 31, 1999.

4. Show how the capital lease and related obligation would appear on Ardmore's balance sheet for the year ending December 31, 1999. Ardmore does not prepare classified balance sheets.

5. Assume that Ardmore exercises the purchase option at the end of the lease term. Prepare all required journal entries on this date.

P 15-9. **CAPITAL LEASES** At the beginning of 1998, MoPac entered into a 20-year, noncancelable, long-term lease agreement for a warehouse that had been constructed on MoPac's land. The warehouse has a useful life of 40 years, and MoPac can acquire title to the facility at the end of the lease term by paying the lessor $1. The annual lease payments over the lease term, payable at the beginning of each year, are as follows:

First 10 years	**$600,000 per year**
Second 10 years	**$400,000 per year**

MoPac also must make annual payments to the lessor of $8,000 for property taxes and $18,000 for insurance. The implicit rate in the lease (known by MoPac) is 6 percent; MoPac's incremental borrowing rate is 8 percent. On January 1, 1998, MoPac made the first payment of $626,000 to the lessor.

REQUIRED

1. Discuss how MoPac should classify the lease.
2. Prepare all necessary entries for MoPac on January 1, 1998.
3. Calculate the following items affecting MoPac's financial statements:
   a) Depreciation expense, if any, for 1998. Assume that straight-line depreciation is appropriate and that the salvage value of the warehouse is zero.
   b) Interest expense, if any, for 1998 and 1999.

P 15-10. **LEASE CLASSIFICATION AND UNGUARANTEED RESIDUAL VALUE** On July 1, 1998, Wetzel Corporation, a manufacturer and distributor of compact disk recorders (CDRs), entered into a lease with Mac Tape Rentals, Inc. Mac agreed to lease 40 CDRs for a period of six years beginning July 1, 1998. Other lease terms are as follows:

Annual lease payments beginning 7/1/98	**$2,269**
Manufacturing cost of each CDR	**$170**
Normal selling price of each CDR	**$300**
Estimated economic life for CDRs	**9 years**
Estimated residual value of each CDR at end of lease term (not guaranteed by Mac)	**$50**
Implicit rate in lease (not known by Mac)	**10%**

Mac can borrow money at 12 percent and agrees to assume full responsibility for all repairs and maintenance of the machines. At the end of the lease term, Mac will return the CDRs to Wetzel. Since Mac is a good credit risk, Wetzel is certain to collect the lease payments and will not incur any additional costs after the date of the lease agreement.

REQUIRED

1. Determine how Wetzel, the lessor, and Mac, the lessee, should classify the lease.
2. Prepare all required entries for the lessor and the lessee on July 1, 1998.
3. Prepare all required entries for the lessor and the lessee on December 31, 1998 (both companies' fiscal year-end), and July 1, 1999.
4. Assume that when the CDRs are returned to Wetzel at the end of the lease term, the residual value of each CDR is only $35. Prepare the entry for Wetzel to record the receipt of the machines.

P 15-11. **UNGUARANTEED RESIDUAL VALUE; IMPLICIT RATE IN LEASE** Super Shuttle, Inc. (SSI), enters into a lease agreement with Kevin Industrial Complex (KIC) whereby KIC agrees to lease 35 shuttle flights from SSI. The cost and fair value of the shuttle is $48 million. The term of the lease is 10 years. KIC must utilize its 35 flights during this 10-year period and has exclusive use during this period. The estimated life of the shuttle is 100 flights, after which its residual value will be zero. At the end of the 10-year lease term, the estimated residual value is $25 million, which is not guaranteed by KIC. SSI sets the lease payments, payable at the beginning of each year, to earn a 12 percent rate of return. KIC's incremental borrowing rate is 8 percent, and KIC may purchase the shuttle at the end of the lease term for its fair value at that time. KIC agrees to pay all costs associated with operating the shuttle and does not know the implicit rate in the lease.

REQUIRED

1. Calculate the annual lease payments required by SSI.
2. What type of a lease is the above to SSI? To KIC? Explain and show calculations.
3. Prepare all necessary entries for SSI and for KIC (*a*) at the inception of the lease and (*b*) for the first year of the lease. KIC made five shuttle flights during the first year. Both parties base depreciation on usage.

P 15-12. **GUARANTEED RESIDUAL VALUE** On July 1, 1998, Fast Freight Forwarders leased a fleet of trucks from Aron Corporation. Aron had recently manufactured the trucks at a cost of $3 million. The fleet's normal selling price was $3.5 million. Terms of the lease agreement were as follows:

Length of lease	4 years
Semiannual lease payments, beginning 7/1/98	$474,532
Estimated life of trucks	6 years
Estimated residual value of trucks at end of lease term (guaranteed by Fast Freight Forwarders)	$600,000
Implicit (semiannual) rate in lease (known to Fast Freight Forwarders)	6%

The lessee agreed to assume full responsibility for periodic maintenance and service on the fleet. The full amount of the lease payments was expected to be collectible, and no other costs were expected to be incurred by the lessor. Both the lessor and the lessee have fiscal years that end on December 31.

REQUIRED

1. Determine how Aron Corporation (the lessor) and Fast Freight Forwarders (the lessee) should classify the lease.
2. Prepare all necessary journal entries for the lessor and the lessee on July 1, 1998.
3. Prepare all necessary journal entries for the lessor and the lessee on December 31, 1998, January 1, 1999, and July 1, 1999. Straight-line depreciation is appropriate.
4. At the end of the lease term, the actual residual value of the truck fleet was determined to be $680,000. On behalf of Aron Corporation, Fast Freight Forwarders sold the trucks at this price and remitted the appropriate amount to Aron Corporation. Prepare journal entries for the lessor and the lessee to record this transaction. Under the terms of the lease, any residual value in excess of the amount guaranteed by Fast Freight Forwarders accrues to Aron Corporation.

P 15-13. **CAPITAL LEASES—LESSEE** Trennepohl Transmission entered into an agreement with UFOS, Inc., to lease a video transmission satellite for sports programming. Terms of the lease agreement were as follows:

Date of lease agreement	January 1, 1998
Term of lease	15 years
Semiannual lease payments (end of each 6 months)	$40,000
Life of satellite	18 years
Semiannual interest rate implicit in lease	6%

Due to the nature and distant location of the satellite, its residual value at the end of the lease term is minimal. Trennepohl's incremental borrowing rate also is 6 percent (per each six months).

REQUIRED

1. Explain how Trennepohl Transmission should classify the lease.
2. Calculate the present value of the minimum lease payments, and prepare a schedule of interest and book value for the first two years of the lease.
3. Prepare entries related to the lease agreement for Trennepohl on January 1, 1998, June 30, 1998, and December 31, 1998. Straight-line depreciation is appropriate.
4. Prepare Trennepohl's income statement and balance sheet disclosures related to the lease for the year ended December 31, 1998. Trennepohl does not prepare a classified balance sheet.

P 15-14. **CAPITAL LEASES—LESSOR** Consider the data in Problem 15-13 from the standpoint of UFOS, Inc., the lessor. The space satellite was manufactured by the lessor at a cost of $400,000, and initial direct costs associated with the lease were $45,000. UFOS is assured of collecting the lease payments and will not incur any other costs after the lease inception date.

REQUIRED

1. Explain how UFOS, Inc., should classify the lease.
2. What is your estimate of the fair value of the space satellite on January 1, 1998? Explain.
3. Prepare all necessary journal entries related to the lease agreement for UFOS on January 1, 1998, June 30, 1998, and December 31, 1998.

P 15-15. **SALE-LEASEBACK** On February 1, 1998, Buy-N-Bye, a national chain, sold vending equipment to a financial institution for $12 million (the fair value) and leased back the equipment under a 10-year, noncancelable lease. Annual lease payments, beginning on January 31, 1999, were $1.5 million.

The lessor calculated the lease payments based on an implicit interest rate of 10 percent (known by Buy-N-Bye). The equipment had an estimated economic life of 16 years from February 1, 1998, and was carried on the books of Buy-N-Bye at $2 million, net of accumulated depreciation, on the date of sale.

REQUIRED

1. Explain why the sale-leaseback transaction qualifies as an operating lease to Buy-N-Bye.
2. Prepare the entry to record the sale of the equipment on February 1, 1998.
3. Prepare the entry to record the leaseback on February 1, 1998.
4. Calculate the annual rent expense for Buy-N-Bye.

P 15-16. SALE-LEASEBACK Joe Road Builders sold a heavy-duty backhoe with a carrying value of $280,000 to Dane Finance Company for $500,000, then immediately leased it back under the following lease terms:

Term of lease	**8 years, beginning 1/1/98**
Annual lease payments (beginning of each year)	**$89,867**
Interest rate implicit in lease payments (known by Joe)	**12%**

The lease qualified as a capital lease for Joe and a direct-financing lease for Dane Finance. The backhoe has a useful life of eight years and no salvage value.

REQUIRED

1. Prepare the entries for Joe Road Builders and Dane Finance on January 1, 1998, to record the sale-leaseback.
2. Prepare all entries, including any adjusting entries, for both parties on December 31, 1998; January 1, 1999; and December 31, 1999. Joe uses the straight-line method of depreciation.

P 15-17. LEASE CLASSIFICATION; UNEQUAL LEASE PAYMENTS On January 1, 1998, Jacinto Savings and Loan purchased a "floating casino" riverboat at a cost of $816,600 and immediately leased it to Dennis Vegas Charter Company. The lease agreement contained the following terms:

Term of lease	**6 years**
Annual year-end lease payments:	
End of 1998, 1999, and 2000	**$200,000**
End of 2001, 2002, and 2003	**$120,000**
Bargain purchase option, end of 2003	**$18,000**
Interest rate implicit in lease payments (known by lessee)	**6%**

Dennis Vegas Charter Company was a financially strong company; therefore, Jacinto Savings was assured of collecting the lease payments. In order to stimulate business growth and gaming in the area, Jacinto Savings agreed to assume all maintenance and upkeep of the boat during the term of the lease. The boat had an estimated salvage value of $40,000 at the end of its expected useful life of 40 years, and straight-line depreciation was appropriate.

REQUIRED

1. How should Dennis Vegas Charter Company and Jacinto Savings and Loan classify the lease?
2. Prepare journal entries for the lessee (Dennis Vegas) on the following dates:
   a) January 1, 1998.
   b) December 31, 1998.
   c) December 31, 1999.
   d) December 31, 2003 (to record exercise of the bargain purchase option).
3. Prepare journal entries for the lessor (Jacinto Savings and Loan) on the following dates:
   a) January 1, 1998.
   b) December 31, 1998.
   c) December 31, 1999.
   d) December 31, 2003 (to record exercise of the bargain purchase option).

P 15-18. RESEARCH PROBLEM ON LEASES Most airline companies lease a large portion of their operating aircraft. For example, we presented the lease disclosures for Southwest Airlines on page 817.

REQUIRED

Obtain annual reports for two airlines (not including Southwest Airlines) of your choice. Write a brief response to each of the following questions:

1. What differences exist between the two airline companies in terms of leasing versus purchasing their operating aircraft?

2. With respect to leasing, which type of lease—capital or operating—tends to be used more by each company?

3. What differences exist between the two airline companies in terms of the term (length) of their leases?

4. Do any of the companies have bargain purchase options associated with their leases?

5. Assume that a new *FASB Statement* required all companies to follow a "property-rights" approach in accounting for their leases. What general effects would such a new *Statement* have on the airline companies' balance sheets?

P 15-19.

REQUIRED

FINANCING REPORTING PROBLEM; GENERAL ELECTRIC Refer to the financial statements for General Electric Corporation presented in Appendix B at the end of the text.

Write a short report that addresses the following questions about GE's leases for the year ending December 31, 1995:

1. What types of leases are included on GE's balance sheet?

2. What percentage of GE's total assets is made up of GE's net investment in financing leases?

3. What is the amount of unguaranteed residual value of assets covered by direct-financing leases?

4. What is meant by the term "deferred income" in connection with GE's direct financing leases?

5. Prepare a list of the types of assets leased to others under operating leases.

6. At December 31, 1995, what is the amount of future rentals for equipment on operating leases?

WOOLWORTH LEASE CASE

Woolworth Corporation began in 1879 as a general merchandise store. Although Woolworth still has general merchandise stores, most of its revenue now comes from its Footlocker and Kinney Shoes subsidiaries. Approximately 37 percent of its sales in 1995 were generated outside the United States. In 1995, Woolworth had revenue of $8.22 billion, balance sheet liabilities of $2.28 billion, and balance sheet assets of $3.51 billion. Woolworth had approximately 94,000 employees at the end of 1995.

Use the accompanying financial statement footnote excerpts to answer questions related to Woolworth's capital and operating leases.

1. What accounts and amount(s) related to leases are on the balance sheet?

2. What journal entry will be made in 1996 to record the effects of capital leases existing at the end of 1995? Do not make an entry to record depreciation expense.

3. What journal entry will be made in 1996 to record the effects of operating leases existing at the end of 1995?

4. Firms are not required to disclose "Present value of operating lease commitments"; the schedule usually ends with "Total operating lease commitments." Why would Woolworth voluntarily disclose the present value?

5. Show how Woolworth's debt to asset ratio would change if its operating leases were treated as capital leases.

6. Assume that the interest rate is 8.5 percent and that the operating lease "thereafter" amount of $790 million is spread evenly over three years. Verify the "Present value of operating lease commitments" amount of $2,136 million. You will need to use a spreadsheet package or a financial calculator to compute present value factors for the 8.5 percent rate.

12 LONG-TERM DEBT AND CAPITAL LEASE OBLIGATIONS

During 1995, the Company issued in the United States $200 million of 7 percent notes with a 5-year maturity, $50 million of 6.98 percent notes with a 6-year maturity, and $40 million of 7 percent notes with a 7-year maturity. In connection with a European investment, a $41 million (DM 59 million) 6.45 percent note maturing in 1998 was issued.

Following is a summary of long-term debt and capital lease obligations:

(in millions)	1995	1994
8.5% debentures payable 2022	$ 200	$ 200
7.0% debentures payable 2000	200	—
6.93% to 7.43% medium-term notes payable through 2002	125	45
3.75% to 10.5% mortgage obligations on real estate payable through 2013	28	30
Other	48	15
Total long-term debt	601	290
Capital lease obligations	43	45
	644	335
Less current portion	25	26
	$ 619	$ 309

Maturities of long-term debt and minimum rent payments under capital leases in future periods are:

(in millions)	Long-term debt	Capital leases	Total
1996	$ 19	$ 11	$ 30
1997	13	10	23
1998	58	13	71
1999	2	6	8
2000	202	4	206
Thereafter	307	18	325
	601	62	663
Less: Imputed interest	—	16	16
Executory expenses	—	3	3
Current portion	19	6	25
	$ 582	$ 37	$ 619

13 LEASES

The Company is obligated under capital and operating leases for a major portion of its store properties. Some of the store leases contain purchase options or renewal options with varying terms and conditions. Management expects that in the normal course of business, expiring leases will generally be renewed or replaced by leases on other premises. Operating lease periods generally range from 5 to 10 years with options to renew, with terms ranging from 5 to 10 years. Certain leases provide for additional rent payments based on a percentage of store sales. Rent expense consists of the following:

(in millions)	1995	1994	1993
Minimum rent	$ 671	$ 634	$ 630
Contingent rent based on sales:			
Operating leases	45	47	57
Capital leases	—	3	3
Sublease income	(23)	(19)	(20)
Total rent expense	$ 693	$ 665	$ 670

Future minimum lease payments under noncancelable operating leases are:

(in millions)	
1996	$ 512
1997	474
1998	435
1999	376
2000	304
Thereafter	790
Total operating lease commitments	$ 2,891
Present value of operating lease commitments	$ 2,136

14 OTHER LIABILITIES

(in millions)	1995	1994
Pension benefits	$ 302	$ 260
Other post-retirement benefits	212	210
Repositioning/restructuring	115	146
Other	100	80
	$ 729	$ 696

Pensions and Other Postretirement Benefits

LEARNING OBJECTIVES

After studying this chapter, you should be able to:

1. Distinguish between a defined contribution plan and a defined benefit plan and describe other characteristics of postretirement benefit plans.

2. Identify the potential components of pension expense.

3. Calculate and account for the service component of pension expense.

4. Calculate and account for the interest component of pension expense and explain how the service and interest components are related to the projected benefit obligation.

5. Explain how the expected rate of return component of pension expense and periodic funding affect pension plan assets.

6. Define prior service cost and explain how it is accounted for under an immediate recognition approach.

7. Describe how pension gains and losses arise and explain how they are accounted for under an immediate recognition approach.

8. Explain how prior service cost is accounted for under the delayed recognition approach permitted by *Statement No. 87.*

9. Prepare a schedule to reconcile the funded status of a pension plan with the net pension asset (liability) reported in the employer's balance sheet.

10. Explain how pension gains and losses are accounted for under the delayed recognition (corridor) approach.

11. Calculate the minimum liability and explain the minimum liability requirement.

12. Prepare a worksheet for the various components of pension expense.

13. Identify the components of other postretirement benefit expense.

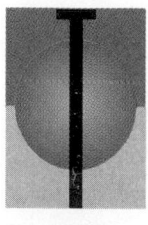

oday, millions of workers are covered by employer-sponsored plans that provide pension benefits and other postretirement benefits, such as health care. These plans are growing at such a rate—in terms of both the absolute and relative dollar worth of their assets, obligations, and expenses—that accounting and reporting on such plans has become very significant. In various sectors of the economy many pension plans are significantly underfunded, creating concerns for retirees and other interested parties. The following illustration was adapted from a newspaper question-and-answer column called "Action Line":[1]

> **Question:** The Oklahoma Teacher Retirement System (OTRS) is something that state legislative leaders will tackle this year. The system has $2.87 billion in assets but is burdened with future benefit liabilities of $7.48 billion. How did we get $4.61 billion in the hole? How long have we been there?
>
> **Answer:** According to the executive secretary of OTRS, the system was created in 1943 and liabilities have always exceeded assets. This is not unusual for a public pension plan. The simple answer to the unfunded liability issue is that the state has not properly funded promised benefits. Recent legislation requires greater contributions by both active employees and employers. A 16-member task force has been created to study the retirement system and long-term solutions. Teachers pay a certain percentage of their monthly salary into the retirement fund, and the state also contributes a certain percentage of members' pay (these percentages have varied over time). Money deposited by members and employers is invested in stocks and bonds.

CONCEPTUAL

Many conceptual aspects of financial accounting and reporting apply to postretirement benefits.

Accounting for postretirement benefits involves many of the conceptual aspects of financial accounting and reporting. Both *matching* and *expense recognition,* for example, provide guidance for when the employer should record the cost of postretirement benefits as an expense. *Present value* concepts are used to determine how a future retirement payment should be valued in exchange for services rendered currently. And professional disagreement about the nature and essential characteristics of a liability underlies controversies over whether pension obligations should be *recognized* in the balance sheet or merely *disclosed* in footnotes, and if recognized, the amount of the liability that should be reported by the employer.

CONCEPTUAL

Accounting for pension expense may be based on an "immediate recognition approach" or a "delayed recognition approach."

In this chapter, we will discuss accounting and reporting for pension and other postretirement benefit plans. First, we will discuss the major characteristics of postretirement benefit plans, showing how a typical plan operates. Next, using a pension plan as an illustration, we will explain how pension benefits are calculated and how the components of pension expense are determined and accounted for under a conceptual or "immediate recognition" approach. (**Immediate recognition** means that the components of pension expense are recognized in the financial statements as they occur.) Then, we will discuss the "delayed recognition" approach permitted by *Statement No. 87,* which modifies accounting for certain pension expense components. (**Delayed recognition** means that expense recognition of some components of pension cost is not recognized immediately, but rather their recognition is delayed to future periods.) We will also illustrate how a worksheet can be used to simplify accounting for pension expense. Following this discussion, we will consider other postretirement benefits, such as a health care plan. Finally, we will summarize the major disclosure requirements of *Statement No. 87,* for pensions, and *Statement No. 106,* for other postretirement benefits.

---

[1]"Teacher Pension System Poorly Funded," *Tulsa World,* Action Line, March 12, 1996, p. A-2.

POSTRETIREMENT BENEFIT PLANS

Postretirement benefit plans include pension benefits as well as other benefits, such as health care. A **pension plan** is an arrangement under which a governmental unit or private company provides income to retired workers. *Public* pension plans are established by law and are sponsored by a governmental unit, such as the federal government. The largest and best-known public pension plan was created by the Social Security Act of 1935, generally known as "social security." *Private,* or *employer-sponsored,* pension plans exist largely at the discretion of the employers who sponsor them and are established by agreement between employers and employees. This chapter concentrates on private pension plans.

Private pension plans began to appear in the United States in the late 1800s, but they became significant sources of financial support for retirees only after about 1950. Under early private pension plans, the payment of retirement benefits to employees was regarded by both the employer and employee as a discretionary gratuity for long and faithful service. But by the late 1940s, organized labor had begun to demand pensions in lieu of wage increases. In 1949 a federal court ruled that pensions, like wages, are a bargainable issue.[2]

In 1974 Congress passed the Employee Retirement Income Security Act (ERISA) to strengthen and encourage the growth of private pension plans. ERISA established standards for employee participation in a plan, vesting of pension benefits, and funding of the employer's obligation. The act applies to virtually all private pension plans in the United States. ERISA also created a new agency, the Pension Benefit Guaranty Corporation (PBGC). The PBGC is responsible for ensuring payment of minimum benefits by defined benefit pension plans (plans which promise *specified* benefits) and for administering defined benefit plans that have been terminated.

Postretirement benefit plans other than pension plans may promise a variety of benefits to retirees and their spouses, dependents, and beneficiaries. The most common of these plans promises payments for health care. A **health care plan** may reimburse retirees for payments made for health care services, pay those who render the services, or provide health care services directly to retirees. Promised postretirement benefits may also include life insurance, tuition assistance, legal and tax services, day care, and housing subsidies.

Characteristics of Postretirement Benefit Plans

There are essentially two types of private postretirement benefit plans: defined contribution plans and defined benefit plans. In a **defined contribution plan,** the employer promises to make specified contributions to the retirement fund but does not specify the benefits that will be paid to retired employees. An example of a defined contribution pension plan is TIAA-CREF, a program in which the faculty and staff of many U.S. colleges and universities participate. In this program, the university contributes a specified amount (say, 10 percent of an employee's annual salary) on behalf of each faculty or staff member. The amount a particular employee will receive during retirement depends on (1) the total funds contributed to TIAA-CREF on his or her behalf at the time of retirement, (2) the employee's retirement age, and (3) the employee's salary level. From an accounting standpoint, benefits are limited to contributions to the fund plus earnings on the fund's assets; therefore, the employer's periodic expense is the amount contributed by the employer during the period.

In a **defined benefit plan,** the employer promises to make benefit payments in specified amounts but does not specify the amount of the contribution that will

> **1** Distinguish between a defined contribution plan and a defined benefit plan and describe other characteristics of postretirement benefit plans.

---

[2]*Inland Steel Company v. National Labor Relations Board,* 170 F. 2d 247, 251 (1949).

be made to the retirement fund. In the case of pension plans, employers must meet ERISA's minimum contribution requirements, and the employer's contributions plus the fund's investment earnings must be sufficient to meet the specified benefit payments when they are due. The Oklahoma Teacher Retirement System, discussed at the beginning of this chapter, is an example of a defined benefit plan. In the case of postretirement plans such as those that provide health care benefits, employers may define the plan's benefits in monetary terms. For example, a health care plan may provide $100,000 of life insurance, or hospitalization coverage of up to $300 per day, or 90 percent of the cost of specific surgical procedures. *Throughout the remainder of this chapter, the discussion either assumes or states explicitly that the retirement plan in question, for example, a pension or health care plan, is a defined benefit plan.* Other characteristics of private postretirement benefit plans are listed in Exhibit 16–1.

A Typical Defined Benefit Plan

A typical defined benefit pension plan includes the following parties: (1) the company (employer) who sponsors the plan; (2) an independent funding agent who receives the cash contributions to the fund, manages its assets, and pays its benefits; and (3) the employees covered by the plan. Exhibit 16–2 shows the interrelationships and roles of these three parties. With some modification, Exhibit 16–2 also applies to other postretirement benefit plans, such as health care plans. Because most health care plans in the United States are not funded plans, the

EXHIBIT 16–1	**Characteristics of Private Postretirement Benefit Plans**

■ Employer obligation

Defined contribution plan:	Employer has obligation to make periodic contributions to retirement plan but employee retirement benefits are not specified.
Defined benefit plan:	Employer has obligation to make retirement benefits to employee retirees but employer contributions are not specified.

■ Contributing parties

Contributory plan:	Both employer and employee contribute to plan.
Noncontributory plan:	Only employer contributes to plan.

■ Vesting arrangements

Fully vested:	Employee's right to receive earned (or accumulated) benefits is not contingent on continued employment.
Partially vested:	Employee loses any non-vested claims to benefits if employment ceases.

■ Funding arrangements

Funded retirement plan:	Employer contributions are made to an independent funding agent (trustee) who administers the retirement plan by investing contributions in income-earning assets and making retirement payments to employee retirees. Most pension plans are funded plans.
Unfunded retirement plan:	Retirement fund remains under control of the sponsoring employer. Most health care plans have been unfunded plans.

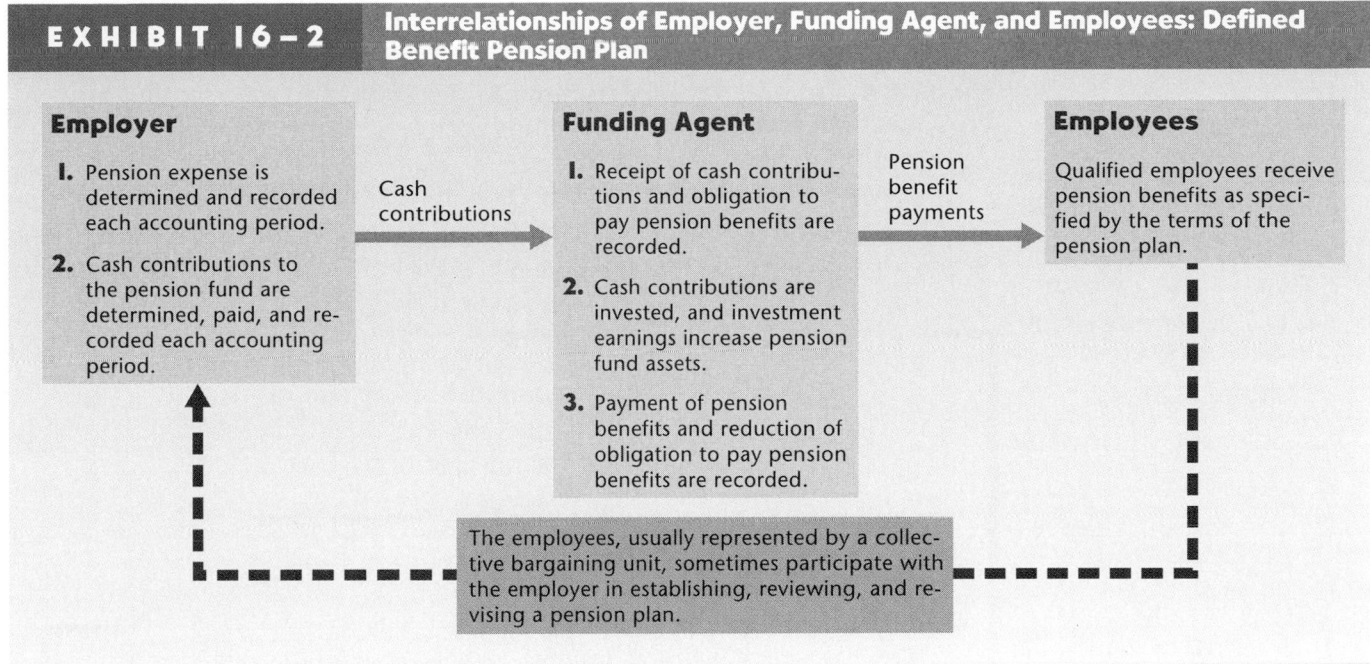

EXHIBIT 16–2 · **Interrelationships of Employer, Funding Agent, and Employees: Defined Benefit Pension Plan**

Employer

1. Pension expense is determined and recorded each accounting period.

2. Cash contributions to the pension fund are determined, paid, and recorded each accounting period.

Cash contributions →

Funding Agent

1. Receipt of cash contributions and obligation to pay pension benefits are recorded.

2. Cash contributions are invested, and investment earnings increase pension fund assets.

3. Payment of pension benefits and reduction of obligation to pay pension benefits are recorded.

Pension benefit payments →

Employees

Qualified employees receive pension benefits as specified by the terms of the pension plan.

The employees, usually represented by a collective bargaining unit, sometimes participate with the employer in establishing, reviewing, and revising a pension plan.

funding agent portion of the exhibit would not apply in most cases. Health care benefit payments usually are made directly by the employer.

Determination of the cost of providing pension benefits and the methods of funding the employer's obligation are based on the use of present value and probability techniques. Applying these techniques requires assumptions about interest rates, mortality rates, employee turnover, future salary levels, and inflationary trends. Health care plans also require assumptions about claim patterns, cost trends, and Medicare reimbursement rates. These statistics, called actuarial present values, are calculated for the employer and funding agent by actuaries—professionals trained in the use of statistics in making estimates. Because the resulting amounts are only estimates, they usually require revision as circumstances change over time.

Exhibit 16–3 shows the flow of information about a pension plan from the funding agent and actuary to the employer sponsor. As we shall see later, the employer uses this information to record pension expense and other events related to the plan. Although some of the terminology is different, the information flows and concepts in Exhibit 16–3 also apply to other postretirement benefit plans.

In the next two sections we will examine professional pronouncements on postretirement plans and the objectives in accounting for these plans.

Accounting Pronouncements on Postretirement Benefit Plans

From 1966 to 1986, *APB Opinion No. 8,* "Accounting for the Cost of Pension Plans," served as the primary source of GAAP related to employers' pension plans. In 1974, in response to the passage of ERISA and criticisms concerning deficiencies in *Opinion No. 8,* the FASB added two pension projects to its agenda: (1) accounting and reporting by employee benefit plans and (2) employers' accounting for pensions. Critics of *Opinion No. 8* had asserted that, because several measurement methods and assumptions were acceptable under *Opinion No. 8,* pension costs were not comparably measured from company to company and often not even from period to period within the same company.

EXHIBIT 16-3	Information Flows from Funding Agent and Actuary to Employer

Funding Agent and Actuary Determine the Following Information and Provide the Information to the Employer:

Information about the Employer's Pension Obligation:

	Projected benefit obligation (beginning of period)
+	Service cost for the period
+	Interest on the projected benefit obligation
+/−	Amendments to pension plan
+/−	Changes in projected benefit obligation from changes in estimates and assumptions (called pension gains/losses)
−	Payments to retired employees
=	Projected benefit obligation (end of period)

Information about the Assets of the Pension Fund:

	Plan assets at fair value (beginning of period)
+	Contributions to plan during the period
+	Earnings (return) on plan assets
	Note: Consists of long-run *expected* return on plan assets during the period plus/(minus) gains/(losses)
−	Payments to retired employees
=	Plan assets at fair value (end of period)

Employer/Sponser Uses the Information Supplied by the Funding Agent and Actuary to Record Pension Expense for the Period

The first of the FASB's two projects led to the issuance of *Statement No. 35,* "Accounting and Reporting by Defined Benefit Plans," in 1980. *Statement No. 35* addressed, for the first time, financial reporting by the pension plan itself. (The important aspects of *Statement No. 35* are presented in Appendix 16–1.) The central portion of the second pension project initiated in 1974 ultimately led to the issuance of *Statement No. 87,* "Employers' Accounting for Pensions," and *Statement No. 88,* "Employers' Accounting for Settlements and Curtailments of Defined Benefit Pension Plans and for Termination Benefits."[3]

In its effort to obtain more useful financial reporting, the FASB made three basic changes in *Statement No. 87:*

1. The *Statement* requires a standardized method for measuring pension expense. This requirement is intended to improve comparability and understandability. The compensation cost of an employee's pension is recognized over the employee's service period, and compensation cost is related to the terms of the pension plan.

2. The *Statement* requires immediate recognition of a liability (defined in the *Statement* as the minimum liability) under certain circumstances (to be discussed later).

3. The *Statement* requires expanded disclosures, intended to provide more complete and current information on employer-sponsored pension plans.

Statement No. 88 is closely related to *Statement No. 87.* (*Statement No. 88* is discussed in Appendix 16–1.)

---

[3]"Employers' Accounting for Pensions," *Statement of Financial Accounting Standards No. 87,* and "Employers' Accounting for Settlements and Curtailments of Defined Benefit Pension Plans and for Termination Benefits," *Statement of Financial Accounting Standards No. 88* (Stamford, Conn.: FASB, 1985).

In December 1990, the FASB issued *Statement No. 106,* "Employers' Accounting for Postretirement Benefits Other Than Pensions."[4] This *Statement* resulted from the Board's concern about the lack of information in financial statements regarding the cost of and obligation for postretirement benefits other than pensions. The Board had good reason to be concerned about the shortfall because of the magnitude of commitments by U.S. companies to provide such benefits. For example, at approximately the time *Statement No. 106* was issued, it was reported that "about 1/3 of all workers in the U.S. participate in company health plans that provide for the continuation of health coverage into retirement. The aggregate unfunded obligation has been estimated at between $100 and $500 billion."[5]

Furthermore, evidence showed that for employers with relatively low ratios of active employees to retirees, application of the *Statement No. 106* rules would increase employer expense related to other postretirement benefits from 2 to 7 times the expense reported under previous accounting practices and from 8 to 43 times the expense reported earlier for employers with relatively high ratios of active employees to retirees.[6] As an example, when IBM adopted the new accounting standard for other postretirement benefits, it reported a first-quarter deduction from income of $2.3 billion (about $4 per share), which produced IBM's first-ever quarterly loss.[7] Ford and General Motors also reported losses when they adopted *Statement No. 106.* Even the FASB felt the sting of the new accounting standard, noting in its 1990 annual report that it could cause the FASB's reported income to drop by at least $672,000.[8]

The accounting concepts underlying *Statement No. 106* are the same as for *Statement No. 87,* namely: (1) an employer's promise to provide retirees with postretirement benefits represents a form of deferred compensation to employees, in exchange for employees' current services; and (2) the cost of promised future benefits should be recognized systematically over the service periods for which employees are given credit toward postretirement benefits. These accrual accounting concepts contrast sharply with the predominant practice before the issuance of *Statement No. 106,* the "pay-as-you-go" or cash-basis method of recording the cost of postretirement benefits. Pay-as-you-go (cash-basis) accounting delays the recognition and measurement of the financial effects of postretirement benefits until those benefits are paid to or on behalf of retirees. As a result, costs incurred currently are not recognized until future periods.

Objectives in Accounting for Defined Benefit Plans

Because of the importance of postretirement benefits and the sheer magnitude of retirement funds, concerns about the economic consequences of accounting standards, as well as political compromises, have influenced the standards established for accounting for postretirement benefits. Acknowledging these issues, the FASB stressed several objectives in the work that produced *Statements No. 87, 88,* and *106:*

CONCEPTUAL

Accounting objectives for postretirement benefits incorporate qualitative characteristics and include improved financial reporting and disclosure.

I. To provide a more *representationally faithful* measure of pension expense and other postretirement benefit expenses, in the sense that they reflect the terms of the retirement plan and better approximate the cost of an employee's benefits over the employee's service period.

---

[4]"Employers' Accounting for Postretirement Benefits Other Than Pensions," *Statement of Accounting Standards No. 106* (Norwalk, Conn.: FASB, 1990).
[5]"New FASB Rules on Accounting for Other Postretirement Benefits," *Deloitte & Touche Review,* December 31, 1990.
[6]"Retiree Health Benefits: What Drives the Numbers?," *Executive Briefing, Coopers & Lybrand,* March 1991.
[7]"IBM to Record Large Charge for New Rule," *The Wall Street Journal,* March 29, 1991, p. A-3.
[8]"Accounting Board Feeling the Sting of Its Own Rule," *The Wall Street Journal,* April 26, 1991, p. B-5D.

2. To provide a more *understandable,* more *comparable,* and therefore more *useful* measure of expense.

3. To provide *disclosures* that help financial statement users understand the full extent and effect of an employer's commitment to provide postretirement benefits and to make related financial arrangements.

4. To improve *reporting* of the employer's resources and claims against those resources (financial position).

These objectives are reflected in the calculations, accounting procedures, and disclosures that are described and discussed in the remaining sections of this chapter. Before we discuss how pension benefits are determined and accounted for, however, we will examine two opposing or contrasting views of pension fund assets and obligations.

Pension Fund Assets and Obligations—Two Contrasting Views

CONCEPTUAL

There are two contrasting views of the nature of pension plan assets and obligations.

Two views or perspectives exist regarding the nature of pension obligations and pension fund assets: the separation perspective and the integration perspective.[9] These contrasting views provide a conceptual background that will help you to better understand several accounting issues connected with pensions.

The Separation Perspective

From the **separation perspective,** the employer-sponsor of a pension plan has no pension obligation as long as the amount of pension expense, determined by an acceptable actuarial method (such as *Statement No. 87* requirements), is funded. However, any difference between periodic expense and periodic funding represents a pension asset or a pension liability, as appropriate. Under the separation view, pension plan assets belong to the pension trust (or plan trustee), not to the employer-sponsor; therefore, any obligation to pay projected benefits is an obligation of the pension trust. One consequence of this view is that *many events that affect pension plan assets and the obligation to pay pension benefits either are not recorded or their recognition by the employer-sponsor is delayed.* (The notion of delayed recognition was introduced on page 844.) In summary, this perspective views the pension plan assets and the obligation to pay pension benefits as *separate* from the employer-sponsor. In terms of Exhibit 16–3, the information provided to the employer assists the employer in recording the debit to pension expense, the credit to cash (the amount funded), and the debit or credit to a pension asset or liability, as appropriate.

The Integration Perspective

Under a second view, called the **integration perspective,** pension plan assets are viewed as belonging to the employer-sponsor, along with the obligation to pay projected pension benefits. Under this view, the employer-sponsor reports both the pension plan assets and the obligation to pay benefits on its balance sheet. Because the pension plan assets are restricted to paying pension benefits/obligations, the

---

[9]M. J. Anderson and K. C. Chen, "Excess Asset Reversions and Shareholder Wealth," *Journal of Finance,* Volume 41, March 1986, pp. 225–241. See also C. DeBerg, H. F. Mittelstaedt, and P. Regier, "Employers' Accounting for Pensions: A Theoretical Approach to Financial Accounting Standards No. 87," *Journal of Accounting Education,* Fall 1987, pp. 227–242.

pension plan asset and pension liability accounts are offset and reported as a *net* asset or *net* liability. In summary, this perspective views the plan assets and any pension obligation as an *integral* part of the employer-sponsor's balance sheet. As a result, all events that affect pension plan assets and the obligation to pay pension benefits are recognized immediately as they occur. (The notion of immediate recognition was introduced on page 844.) In terms of Exhibit 16–3, the employer would record all of the information provided directly in the appropriate accounts.

As we shall see later when we discuss accounting for pension expense, both perspectives are evident in the accounting and reporting requirements of *Statement No. 87*. As a result of political considerations, economic consequences, and the need for compromise, *Statement No. 87* generally adopts a separation perspective for financial statement *recognition* and reporting but an integration perspective in required footnote *disclosures*.

DETERMINING PENSION AND OTHER POSTRETIREMENT BENEFITS

The concepts and accounting issues underlying pensions and other postretirement benefits, such as a health care plan, are similar. Because pension benefits are somewhat more common than postretirement health care benefits, we will use a pension example as an illustration. Later we will extend these same accounting concepts and procedures to other postretirement benefits, such as a health care plan.

Pension Benefits Under a Defined Benefit Plan

To illustrate the calculation of various pension amounts, we shall use the data on National Corporation's defined benefit pension plan and one of its employees, Dave Smith, given in Exhibit 16–4. The data there and in subsequent illustrations apply to a single employee in order to minimize the complexity of the explanation. In reality, an employer's pension calculations apply to large groups of employees and are somewhat more complex than the calculations shown.

The relationship between National Corporation's defined benefit pension plan and Dave Smith's employment and retirement can be diagrammed as follows:

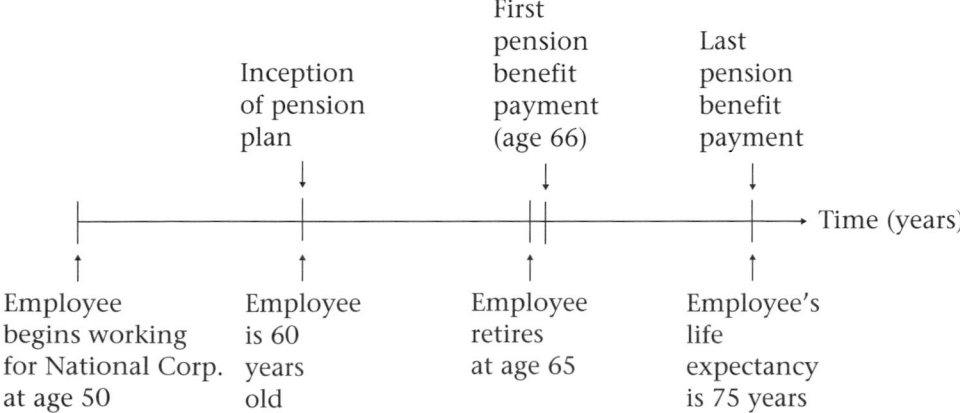

As we shall see, the way in which Dave Smith's benefits for services rendered to date are valued depends on the purpose of the calculation—whether to calculate Smith's pension benefits based on his salary levels to date or on his projected future salaries.

EXHIBIT 16–4	**Data for National Corporation's Pension Plan and Employee Dave Smith**

Description of Pension Plan

1. A defined benefit, noncontributory pension plan.
2. Pension benefits are paid at the *end* of each retirement year.
3. No credit toward pension benefits is given for employee service prior to the date the pension plan was adopted.
4. Assumed discount rate is 8%.
5. The pension plan pays annual pension benefits equal to 1.5% for each year of service that qualifies for pension credit, multiplied by the simple average of the employee's three highest annual salaries before retirement. Hence,

$$\begin{array}{c} \text{Pension benefit} \\ \text{received each year} \\ \text{of retirement} \end{array} = .015 \times n \times \begin{array}{c} \text{Average of three} \\ \text{highest annual} \\ \text{salaries} \end{array}$$

where *n* equals the number of years of service that qualify for pension credit.

Data About Employee (Dave Smith)

1. Will retire at age 65.
2. Has an expected retirement period of 10 years before death.
3. Is 60 years old at the time the pension plan is adopted.
4. Was employed by National Corporation for 10 years before the date the pension plan was adopted (the inception date).
5. Average of three highest annual salaries before retirement is expected to be $65,000.

Funding Arrangements

1. National will contribute $5,358 in cash to the pension fund at the end of each year. The funding agent will invest these contributions in a wide variety of income-earning assets—common stock, corporate bonds, treasury securities, etc.
2. The expected return on plan assets (stocks, bonds, securities, etc.) is 10 percent. The actual return on plan assets is also 10 percent.
3. The annual contributions were determined so that, assuming that the actual rate of return on plan assets also is 10 percent, the fair value of the plan assets at Dave Smith's retirement date will equal the pension obligation at his retirement date. (We will say more about how the annual contribution of $5,358 was calculated at a later point in the chapter.)

Accumulated Benefits versus Projected Benefits

Depending on its purpose, the calculation of pension benefits may be based on either *compensation levels to date* or *future compensation levels*. The benefit formula for Dave Smith is based on the average of his three highest annual salaries. At any time before Smith's retirement, calculation of his pension benefits based on services rendered to date and on this average of his three highest *expected* salaries yields his *projected pension benefits*. Calculation of Smith's pension benefits based on services rendered to date and on the average of his three highest salaries *to date* (rather than his three highest salaries at any time up to retirement) yields his *accumulated pension benefits*.

Which is more useful in determining pension cost for accounting purposes: accumulated pension benefits or projected pension benefits? This question is difficult to answer because of the trade-off between relevance and reliability. At any

CONCEPTUAL

Methods of calculating pension benefits involve trade-offs between relevance and reliability.

given time, the calculation of accumulated benefits is *more reliable* than the calculation of projected benefits because accumulated benefits are based on actual salaries to date. However, a projected benefit calculation may be considered *more relevant,* because it encompasses estimates of future salaries, which affect *future cash flows.* A pension benefit calculation based on future salary levels may also be *more representationally faithful* because under the *going concern assumption,* it is presumed that benefits paid will be based on salaries up to the retirement date. *Statement No. 87 requires that if the pension plan benefit formula incorporates future salary levels, the cost of pension benefits must be based on future salary levels.* Thus, Smith's pension benefits will be based on future salary levels, because National's benefit formula incorporates Smith's salary levels up to his retirement.

Calculating Projected Benefits

Returning to our example and to the data in Exhibit 16–4, the pension plan specifies that no credit will be given for service before the date the pension plan was begun (its inception date). Therefore, five years of Smith's service will qualify for pension credit. According to the benefit formula given in Exhibit 16–4, Smith's first year of service will earn him an estimated annual pension benefit of $975 (.015 × 1 × $65,000), which he will receive throughout his retirement (estimated to be ten years), beginning one year after his retirement date.

Likewise, Smith's second year of service also will earn him an estimated annual pension benefit of $975. Thus, at the end of the second year, his *projected* annual pension benefits total $1,950 ($975 × 2 years). By way of comparison, if Smith's *actual* average salary to date, as of the end of the second year, were $40,000, he would have an *accumulated* annual pension benefit at the end of the second year of only $1,200 (.015 × 2 × $40,000). Based on projected benefits, by the time of his retirement Smith's five years of qualifying service will entitle him to estimated annual pension payments of $4,875 ($975 × 5 years) beginning at age 66 and extending over his expected retirement period of 10 years.

Once these pension retirement benefits have been calculated, their cost to the employer must be determined and accounted for. Accounting for pension expense is covered in the following section.

ACCOUNTING FOR PENSION EXPENSE

Accrual accounting and the time period assumption require that the cost of Smith's retirement benefits be allocated to each of the five years during which Smith provides qualifying services to National Corporation. Actuaries have developed two general approaches for allocating or attributing the cost of pension benefits to accounting periods—a "cost" approach and a "benefit" approach. *Statement No. 87 requires the use of a benefit approach to allocate the cost of pension benefits to the relevant accounting periods.* In the following sections, we shall see how a benefit approach is used to determine periodic pension expense. First, however, let us summarize the six components of pension expense.

The Six Components of Pension Expense

Pension expense for an accounting period can include as many as six components:

1. Service cost.
2. Interest cost.
3. Expected earnings (return) on plan assets.
4. Amortization of prior service cost, including amendments to the plan.

2 Identify the potential components of pension expense.

5. Amortization of pension gains or losses.

6. Amortization of any net asset (gain) or obligation (loss) resulting from the initial adoption of *Statement No. 87*. Because this initial-adoption gain or loss represents a change in accounting principle, the resulting *Statement No. 87* accounting requirements are often called "transition requirements."

The first five of these components are discussed and illustrated in the following sections. The sixth component is rapidly becoming outdated due to the fact that *Statement No. 87* was issued almost 13 years ago. Therefore, it is discussed only briefly on page 879.

Pension Expense Component 1: Service Cost

3 **Calculate and account for the service component of pension expense.**

Smith provides labor services to National each year and in exchange receives wages and a pension benefit. The cost of the pension benefits Smith earns during a particular year of qualifying service is called the **service cost** for that year. The *service cost is equal to the present value of the benefits attributed by National Corporation's pension formula to Smith's services during the current year.* It is calculated using expected future salary levels and an assumed **discount rate,** which should reflect the interest rate at which the employer's obligation to pay benefits could be settled. In selecting a discount rate, a company should consider the interest rates implicit in the current prices of annuity contracts that could be used to settle the pension obligation. (We will say more about annuity contracts and settling the employer's obligation shortly.)

Given the 8 percent discount rate specified in Exhibit 16–4 and an expected annual pension benefit of \$975 in return for Smith's work during year 1, the service cost for year 1 is \$4,808, calculated as follows:

Present value *at Smith's retirement date* of a 10-year, \$975 per retirement year pension benefit arising from service during year 1
$= \$975 \times P\overline{_{10}|}_{8\%}$
$= \$975 \times 6.7101$ (Appendix A, Table D,
$= \underline{\$6,542}$ at the back of the text)

Present value *at the end of Smith's first service year* of future pension benefits of \$6,542
$= \$6,542 \times p\overline{_{4}|}_{8\%}$
$= \$6,542 \times .7350$ (Appendix A, Table B,
                    at the back of the text)
$= \underline{\$4,808}$ = Service cost for year 1

First \$975 benefit payment   Tenth \$975 benefit payment

```
        0  1  2  3  4  5  ↓                              ↓
        ├──┼──┼──┼──┼──┼──┼──┼──┼──┼──┼──┼──┼──┼──┼──→ Time (years)
        ↑              ↑  1  2  3  4  5  6  7  8  9  10
```

\$4,808 present value of future pension benefits at the end of year 1 of service

\$6,542 present value of future pension benefits at the retirement date

Based on this calculation, the entry to record the service cost component of pension expense for year 1 and National's obligation at the end of year 1 would be as follows:

Pension expense 4,808
    Pension liability   4,808

This pension obligation is called the **projected benefit obligation (PBO)**, because it is based on future salary levels. *The projected benefit obligation as of a particular date is the present value of all pension benefits attributed by the plan's benefit formula to employee service rendered prior to that date, based on salary levels up to retirement.* In Smith's case, the $4,808 projected benefit obligation can be interpreted as the amount National would have to pay if it wished to settle its pension obligation to Smith at the end of year 1. For example, National might settle the obligation by purchasing an **annuity contract** on Smith's behalf. Under an annuity contract, an insurance company agrees to pay pension benefits during a retirement period in return for a fixed premium. In effect, an annuity contract shifts the risk associated with having to pay the pension benefits from the employer to the insurance company.

The service cost component for each succeeding year is calculated as demonstrated above, except that each year it is discounted for one less year. Therefore each succeeding year's service cost is 8 percent larger than it was for the preceding year. These relationships are shown in Exhibit 16–5. In a manner identical to the service cost entry on page 854, each year's pension expense would be debited and pension liability would be credited using the service cost numbers in Exhibit 16–5.

CONCEPTUAL

The projected benefit obligation is based on services rendered to date and projected future salaries.

Pension Expense Component 2: Interest on the Projected Benefit Obligation

To calculate pension expense for year 2 of Smith's service and following years, another component, **interest on the projected benefit obligation,** which exists at the beginning of each year, must be added to the service cost for that year. Conceptually, the interest component of pension expense is identical to interest expense that accrues due to the passage of time on any other monetary liability, such as a note payable.

Exhibit 16–6 shows how the interest component of pension expense is calculated. The schedule includes the two components of pension expense—service cost and interest cost—that increase the projected benefit obligation over time. Since interest is calculated on the beginning-of-year projected benefit obligation balance, there is no interest cost for year 1; the projected benefit at the beginning of year

4 Calculate and account for the interest component of pension expense and explain how the service and interest components are related to the projected benefit obligation.

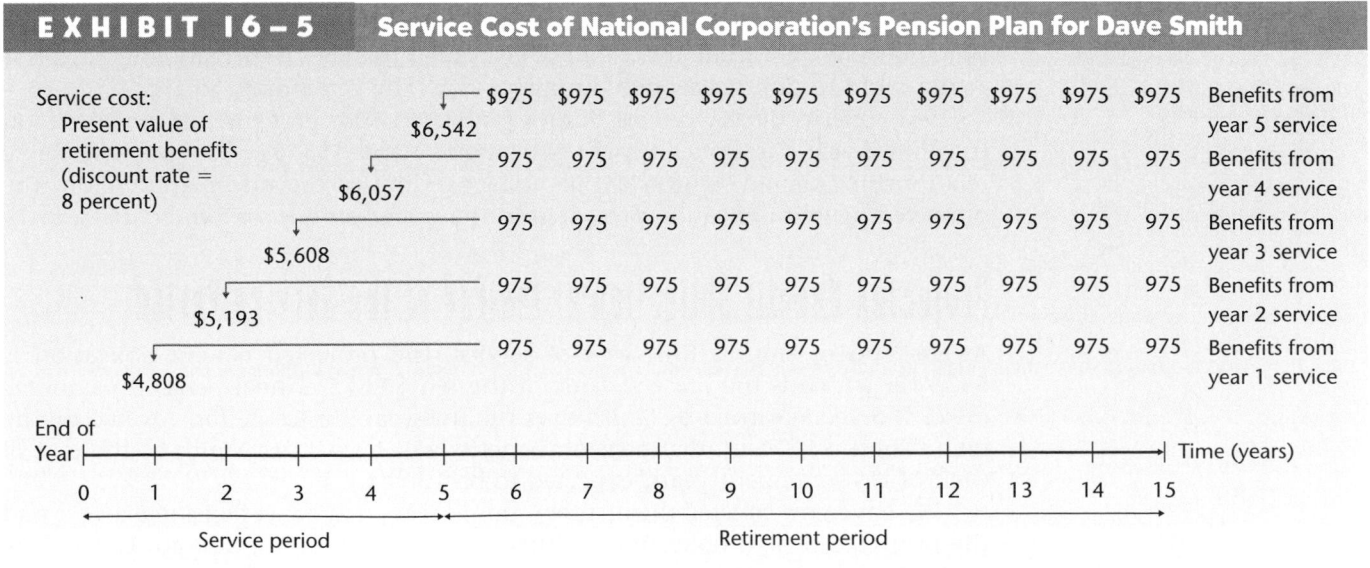

EXHIBIT 16–5 **Service Cost of National Corporation's Pension Plan for Dave Smith**

Service cost: Present value of retirement benefits (discount rate = 8 percent)		$6,542	$975	$975	$975	$975	$975	$975	$975	$975	$975	$975	Benefits from year 5 service
		$6,057		975	975	975	975	975	975	975	975	975	975	Benefits from year 4 service
	$5,608				975	975	975	975	975	975	975	975	975	Benefits from year 3 service
	$5,193					975	975	975	975	975	975	975	975	Benefits from year 2 service
$4,808						975	975	975	975	975	975	975	975	Benefits from year 1 service

End of Year: 0 1 2 3 4 5 6 7 8 9 10 11 12 13 14 15 Time (years)

Service period — Retirement period

EXHIBIT 16–6	Service Cost, Interest Cost, and Projected Benefit Obligation of National Corporation's Pension Plan for Dave Smith			

End of Year	Age	(I) Service Cost[a]	(2) Interest Cost[b]	(3) Projected Benefit Obligation[c]
1	61	$4,808	$ –0–	$ 4,808
2	62	5,193	385	10,386
3	63	5,608	831	16,825
4	64	6,057	1,346	24,228
5	65	6,542	1,938	32,712

[a]From Exhibit 16–5.
[b]Preceding balance in col. 3 × .08.
[c]Preceding balance in col. 3 + col. 1 + col. 2.

1 was zero. The entry to record the interest component of pension expense for year 2 would be:

Pension expense	385	
Pension liability		385

National's pension liability balance at the end of each year, which equals the projected benefit obligation at the end of each year, can be interpreted within the context of the discount rate used to calculate the present values of the retirement benefits. As was stated on page 855, National's pension liability balance at the end of each year can be interpreted as the amount that National would have to pay if it wished to settle its pension obligation by purchasing an annuity contract on Smith's behalf.

Relationship Between Service Cost, Interest Cost, and the Projected Benefit Obligation

In Exhibit 16–6, notice how the service cost component of pension expense is related to the measurement of the projected benefit obligation at the end of each year. Each year's service cost is that portion of the projected benefit obligation attributable to employee services rendered during the year. For example, the projected benefit obligation at the end of year 2 is $10,386. Of this amount, $5,193 is attributable to Smith's service during year 2. The remaining $5,193 ($10,386 – $5,193) consists of service cost during year 1 ($4,808) plus interest for year 2 on the end-of-year-1 projected benefit obligation balance ($385 = .08 × $4,808). These relationships should reinforce your understanding of the information about the projected benefit obligation presented in the upper portion of Exhibit 16–3.

Projected Benefit Obligation at the End of the Service Period

At the end of Smith's fifth year of service, the projected benefit obligation is $32,712, which is the present value of the ten $4,875 annual pension payments ($975 × 5 years) earned by Smith over the five-year service period covered by the plan. These $4,875 annual pension benefits will be paid to Smith at the end of each of his retirement years, expected to be 10 years.

We have now covered the first two components that affect pension expense and the projected benefit obligation. At this point, you should be able to see why the approach used by *Statement No. 87* to determine pension expense is called a "benefit" approach: In Dave Smith's case, each year the amount of expected pension benefits attributed to his service for that year is calculated. The service cost component is calculated as the present value of those expected benefits. A benefit formula like the one used for Dave Smith, which defines benefits in terms of years of service, is referred to as a **benefit/years-of-service approach.**

Pension Expense Component 3: Funding and Expected Return on Plan Assets

The data in Exhibit 16–4 assume that National established a pension fund and made annual contributions of $5,358 to the fund on Dave Smith's behalf. The amount funded (contributed to the pension fund) each period is based on methods used by actuaries and depends on many considerations, including the employer's working capital requirements, minimum funding requirements specified by ERISA, and tax deductibility. Thus, *funding of a pension plan is primarily a financial decision, while determining annual pension expense is an accounting issue.* As indicated under funding arrangements in Exhibit 16–4, the employer's contributions to the fund are invested by the funding agent or trustee in a variety of assets, including common stocks, bonds, real estate investment, and perhaps the employer's own securities.

Over time, earnings on pension fund assets increase the amount of assets in the fund. Because of the long-run nature of a pension plan, actuaries use an *expected* rate of return in making actuarial calculations. In determining the expected rate of return, consideration is given to the returns being earned by the assets in the fund and the rates of return expected to be available for reinvestment over the long term. *The rate of return on plan assets may differ from the discount rate discussed earlier, because the two rates are based on different considerations.* The discount rate is a *borrowing rate,* which reflects the rate of interest at which the employer's obligation to pay pension benefits could be settled. The **rate of return on plan assets** is a *lending* or *earnings* rate, which reflects the long-term return the employer expects to earn on its investments. For simplicity and pedagogical reasons, at this point we have assumed that the expected rate of return and the actual rate of return are the same for National's pension fund.

Earnings on plan assets increase the net assets of the fund, thus reducing the contributions the employer must make to the fund. To illustrate, had National waited until Smith's retirement date to fund its pension obligation, it would have had to contribute $32,712 (see Exhibit 16-6, page 856). However, by making five annual contributions of $5,358 (5 × $5,358 = $26,790) and investing them in assets that earn a 10 percent return, National amasses plan assets (contributions plus earnings) of $32,712 at Smith's retirement date.[10] In other words, the earnings on the plan assets *reduce* National's pension expense over Smith's service period. These concepts are illustrated in Exhibit 16–7.

The schedule in Exhibit 16–7 shows how the plan assets increase during each year of Smith's service. From left to right, it shows the return on plan assets each year (assuming a 10 percent rate of return), the contributions made to the fund, and the balance of the plan assets at the end of each year. National would use the numbers

> 5 **Explain how the expected rate of return component of pension expense and periodic funding affect pension plan assets.**

---

[10]The annual funding payments can be viewed as the five equal payments making up the ordinary annuity that has a future value of $32,712 at Smith's retirement date, given a 10 percent rate of return on plan assets:

$$\$32,712 = R(A_{\overline{5}|10\%})$$
$$\$32,712 = R(6.1051)$$
$$R = \$32,712 \div 6.1051$$
$$= \$5,358 = \text{Annual cash funding}$$

Because funding is a financial decision that is calculated using an accepted actuarial method, the funding amounts will be provided in the text from this point forward and also will be provided in the end-of-chapter material.

EXHIBIT 16–7	Funding, Return on Plan Assets, and Plan Assets of National Corporation's Pension Plan for Dave Smith			
End of Year	Age	(I) Return on Plan Assets[a]	(2) Funding[b]	(3) Plan Assets[c]
				$ –0–
1	61	$ –0–	$ 5,358	5,358
2	62	536	5,358	11,252
3	63	1,125	5,358	17,735
4	64	1,773	5,358	24,866
5	65	2,487	5,358	32,712
			$26,790	

[a]Preceding balance in col. 3 × .10.
[b]From Exhibit 16–4.
[c]Preceding balance in col. 3 + col. 1 + col. 2.

in Exhibit 16–7 to make journal entries each year for this component of pension expense. For example, National would make the following journal entries for year 2:

```
Pension asset. . . . . . . . . . . . . . . . . . . . . . . . . . . . . . . .    536
    Pension expense. . . . . . . . . . . . . . . . . . . . . . . . . . .            536
To record return on plan assets for year 2.

Pension asset. . . . . . . . . . . . . . . . . . . . . . . . . . . . . . . 5,358
    Cash . . . . . . . . . . . . . . . . . . . . . . . . . . . . . . . . . .          5,358
To record contributions at the end of year 2.
```

Summary of the First Three Components of Pension Expense

So far we have covered three components of pension expense: service cost, interest cost, and return on plan assets. In terms of our pension example in Exhibit 16–4, we have completed the accounting for National's pension plan during Smith's service period. Perhaps we should summarize our discussion to this point by bringing all three components together and relating National's accounting for its defined benefit pension plan to the information flow in Exhibit 16–3.

Exhibit 16–8 summarizes National's pension accounting over Smith's service period. The pension expense components and balance sheet information were taken from two preceding exhibits—Exhibit 16–6 for the service cost, interest cost, and projected benefit obligation (columns 1, 2, and 6) and Exhibit 16–7 for the funding, return on plan assets, and balance of plan assets (columns 5, 3, and 7). Note the following points:

■ The National Corporation example is a *model*. As with all models, *this model is oversimplified from the standpoint of reality but provides an overview of the components of pension expense and the balance sheet information related to a defined benefit pension plan.*

■ The total pension expense (column 4) and cash contributions (funding, column 5) of $26,790 reinforce the concept that in the long run, pension expense equals cash contributions to the pension fund. (In reality, however, this equality would hold only when all employees retire, receive their retirement benefits and die, and the company goes out of existence.)

■ For simplicity, we did not extend this example through Smith's retirement period. In the real world, Smith would receive retirement benefits until his death,

EXHIBIT 16–8 National Corporation's Pension Expense and Other Pension Information Over Dave Smith's Service Period

End of Year	Age	Calculation of Pension Expense					Balance Sheet Information		
		(1) Service Cost +	(2) Interest Cost −	(3) Return on Plan Assets =	(4) Pension Expense	(5) Funding	(6) Pension Liability (Also Equals Projected Benefit Obligation) +	(7) Pension Asset (Also Equals Pension Plan Assets) =	(8) Net Asset/ (Liability) (Also Equals Funded Status)
1	61	$4,808	$ –0–	$ –0–	$ 4,808	$ (5,358)	$ –0–	$ –0–	$ –0–
2	62	5,193	385	(536)	5,042	(5,358)	(4,808)	5,358	550
3	63	5,608	831	(1,125)	5,314	(5,358)	(10,386)	11,252	866
4	64	6,057	1,346	(1,773)	5,630	(5,358)	(16,825)	17,735	910
5	65	6,542	1,938	(2,487)	5,993	(5,358)	(24,228)	24,866	638
					$26,790ᵃ	$(26,790)	(32,712)	32,712	0

ᵃRounded by $3.

whenever it occurs. Based on assumed mortality tables, we estimated Smith's retirement period to be 10 years. However, if Smith were to live for 20 or 25 years after retirement, he would receive benefits for each of those years. To avoid extending this example beyond Smith's service period, we assumed that National settled its pension obligation *at the end of Smith's service period* by using plan assets to purchase an annuity on Smith's behalf. In reality, companies normally do not take this action. During an employee's retirement years, the employer continues to account for at least two pension expense components—interest on the projected benefit obligation and return on plan assets. These two components increase both the projected benefit obligation and the plan assets. As Exhibit 16–3 shows, the retirement benefits paid to retirees decrease both the projected benefit obligation and plan assets.

■ Applying the integration perspective discussed on pages 850–851, we have offset National's pension asset and pension liability accounts (column 8 of Exhibit 16–8). Since the pension asset account balance exceeded the pension liability account balance at the end of years 1–4, National would report a net pension asset at the end of years 1–4.

■ At any point in time, the difference between the projected benefit obligation (column 6) and the fair value of plan assets (column 7 of Exhibit 16–8) is called the **funded status** of the pension plan (column 8). The funded status of a pension plan provides information about whether a pension plan is overfunded or underfunded, which is useful to a wide variety of decision makers, including investors, creditors, employees, unions, and bond-rating agencies. Since National Corporation has *recognized* all pension events, the funded status of the plan equals National's net pension asset/(liability) at the end of each year.

When a company begins a defined benefit pension plan, it usually gives retirement benefit credits to employees who worked for the company *before* the pension plan was adopted. The cost associated with these credits for prior service is called prior service cost. Accounting for prior service cost is discussed in the following section.

Pension Expense Component 4: Retroactive Benefits (Prior Service Cost)

As we stated above, many pension plans give credit for service rendered prior to the plan inception date. An employer may decide to give credit for prior years' service in expectation of higher employee productivity and efficiency, perhaps due to higher morale. Prior service credit may also be given in recognition of long years of loyal service. The cost of retroactive pension benefits arising from prior service credit, whether that credit is given at the plan inception date or later as a result of a plan amendment, is called **prior service cost.** The relationship between prior service cost and the annual service cost component can be diagrammed as follows:

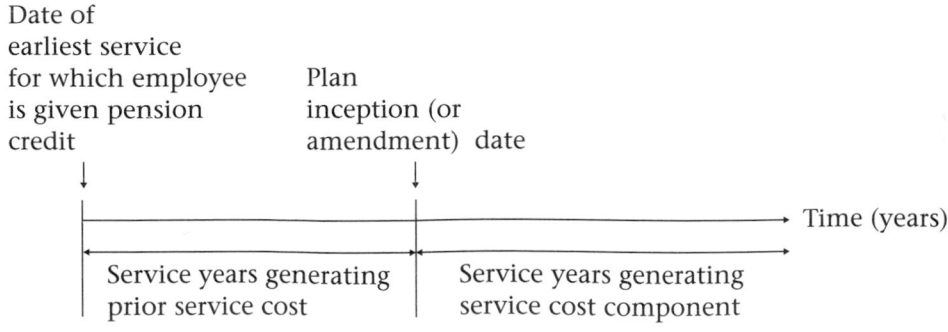

Calculation of Prior Service Cost

To illustrate the calculation of prior service cost, let us modify Dave Smith's case to give him credit for his 10 years of service before the plan's inception date. Thus, at the beginning of year 1 (the plan inception date), Smith's service prior to the plan's inception has earned him expected annual retirement benefits of $9,750:

Expected annual retirement benefits based
on credit for 10 years' prior service $= .015 \times 10 \times \$65,000$
$$= \underline{\$9,750}$$

Assuming an 8 percent discount rate, these annual retirement benefits have a present value of $65,423 as of Smith's retirement date (the end of year 5):

Present value at Smith's retirement
date of a $9,750 ordinary
annuity for 10 retirement $= \$9,750 \times P_{\overline{10}|8\%}$
years discounted at 8 percent $= \$9,750 \times 6.7101$ (Appendix A, Table D,
at the back of the text)

$$= \underline{\$65,423}$$

At the plan inception date, the present value of these benefits is:

Present value of $65,423 as of $= \$65,423 \times p_{\overline{5}|8\%}$
the plan inception date $= \$65,423 \times .6806$ (Appendix A, Table B,
at the back of the text)

$$= \underline{\$44,527} = \text{Prior service cost}$$

In terms of the time diagram, the pension obligation and retirement payments are as follows:

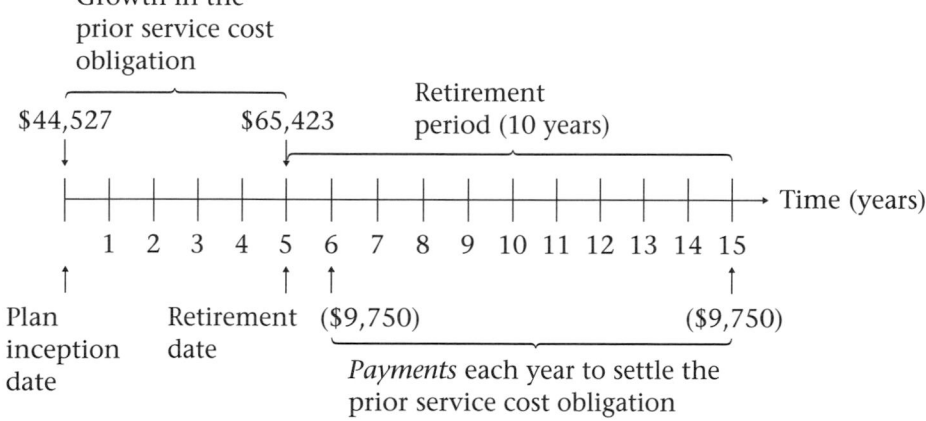

In summary, the prior service cost for Dave Smith is $44,527, which is the present value of Smith's expected future pension benefits resulting from his service prior to the pension plan inception date. Note that the procedure used to calculate prior service cost is similar to the procedure followed in calculating the annual service cost component. The prior service cost of $44,527 is also National's projected benefit obligation at the plan inception date.

Theoretical Considerations

The prior service cost raises some significant accounting questions and issues:

Is the obligation that arises from credit for prior service a liability?

If the obligation is a liability, what if anything has the company received in exchange for the obligation?

CONCEPTUAL

Accounting for prior service cost raises a number of significant accounting questions and issues.

Should the granting of credit for prior service and the related calculation of the projected benefit obligation be *recognized* (reported) immediately in National's financial statements or is footnote *disclosure* adequate?

Each of these questions will be addressed in the paragraphs below.

The Liability Issue   In Chapter 2, we saw that for an economic event to be reported, the following conditions must be satisfied:

1. The item must meet the definition of a financial statement element—in this case, a liability.

2. The item must have a relevant attribute that is measurable with sufficient reliability.

3. Information about the item must be relevant and reliable.

4. Providing information about the item must not be too costly in relation to the benefits to be derived.

The granting of prior service credit (resulting in prior service cost and an increase in the projected benefit obligation) meets this definition of a liability. National has a present obligation (estimated to be $44,527) to transfer economic resources to Dave Smith in the future as a result of a past transaction (Smith's 10 years of service before the plan's inception date). The prior service cost liability is measurable with as much *reliability* as the annual service cost, and would certainly appear *relevant* to financial statement users who need to assess National's future cash outflows. Thus, National has incurred a liability by granting prior service pension credit.

Some argue that the obligation arising from prior service credit should be measured using accumulated pension benefits rather than projected pension benefits. However, doing so would produce inconsistent accounting because measurement of annual service cost is based on projected pension benefits.[11]

The Issue of What Has Been Received in Exchange   What about the debit that is necessary to offset the credit from recording a liability for prior service cost? Has National acquired an asset worth $44,527? Or does the $44,527 represent an additional expense of the current period? Or, should the debit amount be deducted from stockholder's equity? The debit item does not meet the definition of an expense because the prior service credit was given in expectation of benefits in present *and* future years. Also, because any benefit the employer may receive will occur in the future, there appears to be no conceptually sound argument for a deduction from stockholders' equity.

As stated earlier, most companies grant retroactive pension benefits with the expectation that they will realize future economic benefits. Accordingly, National has acquired an asset—at least in theory—though there may be some uncertainty about the amount of economic benefit National will realize. Indeed, National probably would not incur the obligation for prior services if it did not believe the benefits would exceed the cost.

The Recognition Issue   Given that National has acquired an asset and has incurred a liability as a result of giving prior service credit, the following entry would record the prior service cost under the *immediate recognition* approach introduced on page 844:

Intangible asset 44,527
Pension liability   44,527

---

[11]At a more fundamental level, of course, one could question whether the determination of any current obligation should be contingent upon future events (such as future salary levels), as is the case under the projected benefits approach. However, this concept would apply to use of the projected benefits approach in general, not just to its use in measuring prior service cost.

Statement No. 87, however, adopts a delayed recognition approach for this component of pension expense and does not require that either an asset or a liability be recorded in recognition of prior service cost. For pedagogical reasons, we will not discuss the delayed recognition approach until a later point in the chapter. We turn now to the fourth component of pension expense—amortization of prior service cost.

Amortization of Prior Service Cost

Amortization for National Corporation Just as it accounts for other types of intangible assets, National should allocate prior service cost over the period during which it expects to receive the resulting economic benefits. The amortization pattern should parallel the manner in which the company expects to receive those benefits. Since Dave Smith is expected to work five more years at the date prior service credit is granted, five years is the amortization period. Assuming that National expects to receive economic benefits equally each year during Smith's remaining five years of work, straight-line amortization over the five-year service period would be appropriate. Thus, National would make the following journal entry each year to record this component of pension expense:

Pension expense $8,905
   Intangible asset   8,905
($44,527 ÷ 5)
To record amortization of prior service cost.

Exhibit 16–9 shows National Corporation's pension expense, including amortization of prior service cost, over Smith's service period. Note that Exhibit 16–9 is very similar to Exhibit 16–8. It also assumes that National's annual contribution to the pension fund was $16,074, which together with plan earnings at 10 percent, fully funds the projected benefit obligation at the end of Smith's service period.

There are three differences between Exhibits 16–9 and 16–8. First, amortization of prior service cost has been added as a component of pension expense. Second, the balance sheet part of the exhibit includes the intangible asset and shows how it decreases by the amount of prior service cost amortized each year. Third, until the end of year 5, National reports a net pension liability at the end of each year. This liability also equals the funded status of the plan, which is unfunded until the end of year 5.

Amortization for a Group of Employees In the National Corporation example, Dave Smith was National's only employee. Therefore, amortization of prior service cost over Smith's service period was not difficult. In practice, however, a company may have hundreds or thousands of employees who will either complete their service or leave the company at varying times.

To illustrate the amortization of prior service cost for a group of employees, assume that Coopers Company has eight employees to whom it has granted credit for prior service—an action that gives rise to a prior service cost of $66,000. The employees, *A* through *H*, are expected to retire from the company as follows:

A and *B* will retire after two years.

C, D, and *E* will retire after four years.

F will retire after five years.

G and *H* will retire after six years.

The relationship between the number of employees currently working and the expected total employee years (see the amortization fractions on page 865) can be used to amortize prior service cost for this group of employees. The method,

EXHIBIT 16-9 National Corporation's Pension Expense and Other Pension Information, Including Prior Service Cost, Over Dave Smith's Service Period

Calculation of Pension Expense

End of Year	Age	(1) Service Cost +	(2) Interest Cost −	(3) Return on Plan Assets +	(4) Amortization of Prior Service Cost =	(5) Pension Expense	(6) Funding
1	61	$4,808	$3,562	$ –0–	$ 8,905	$17,275	$(16,074)
2	62	5,193	4,232	(1,607)	8,905	16,722	(16,074)
3	63	5,608	4,986	(3,376)	8,905	16,123	(16,074)
4	64	6,057	5,833	(5,320)	8,905	15,475	(16,074)
5	65	6,542	6,784	(7,460)	8,907	14,774	(16,074)
					$44,527	$80,370	$(80,370)

Balance Sheet Information

(7) Intangible Asset (Prior Service Cost)	(8) Pension Liability (Also Equals Projected Benefit Obligation) +	(9) Pension Asset (Also Equals Pension Plan Assets) =	(10) Net Asset/ (Liability) (Also Equals Funded Status)
$44,527	$(44,527)	$ –0–	$(44,527)
35,622	(52,897)	16,074	(36,823)
26,717	(62,322)	33,755	(28,567)
17,812	(72,916)	53,205	(19,711)
8,907	(84,806)	74,599	(10,207)
–0–	(98,132)	98,132	–0–

All column totals have been rounded, as necessary.

called *service years outstanding,* produces a declining pattern of amortization over time, as employees' remaining service years decline through attrition, retirement, or termination:

YEAR	NUMBER OF EMPLOYEES	AMORTIZATION FRACTION		PRIOR SERVICE COST	ANNUAL PRIOR SERVICE COST AMORTIZATION
1	8	8/33	×	$66,000	$16,000
2	8	8/33	×	66,000	16,000
3	6	6/33	×	66,000	12,000
4	6	6/33	×	66,000	12,000
5	3	3/33	×	66,000	6,000
6	2	2/33	×	66,000	4,000
	33ᵃ				$66,000ᵇ

ᵃTotal employee years.
ᵇTotal prior service cost.

Statement No. 87 permits the use of other allocation methods as long as they are systematic, rational, and applied consistently over time, and as long as they amortize prior service cost at least as fast as the service-years-outstanding method. For example, *Statement No. 87* permits straight-line amortization of prior service cost over the average remaining service period of a group of employees. In the Coopers Company example, a total of 33 service years remain for the eight employees. Thus, the average remaining service period is 4.125 (33 total employees years ÷ 8 employees). Annual amortization of prior service cost for years 1 through 4 would therefore be $66,000 ÷ 4.125 = $16,000. Amortization in the fifth year of the straight-line method would be .125 × $16,000 = $2,000.

Plan Amendments

Companies often make amendments to defined benefit pension plans as economic conditions change. For example, a company might modify its plan benefit formula as a result of higher cost of living indexes. Since the projected benefit obligation represents the present value of promised retirement benefits earned to date, an amendment affects the balance of the projected benefit obligation. To illustrate, refer to Exhibit 16–9 on page 864 and assume that at the beginning of year 3, National amended Smith's benefit formula, increasing the annual benefits by one-third (that is, increasing it from 1.5 percent to 2.0 percent per year of qualifying service):

Original benefit formula = .015 × n × $65,000
Amended benefit formula = .02 × n × $65,000

This plan amendment would also increase the projected benefit obligation at the beginning of year 3 by one-third:

Amended projected benefit obligation = $62,322 × 4/3 = $83,096[12]

National would record this increase of $20,774 ($83,096 – $62,322) in its pension obligation as follows:

Intangible asset 20,774
Pension liability 20,774

---

[12]Alternatively, we could calculate the present value of annual retirement benefits, as amended, at the beginning of year 3.

The amount of prior service cost amortized during years 3 through 5 would be $15,830 [$8,905 + ($20,774 ÷ 3)]. In addition, National would have to increase the annual funding amount in order to fully fund the projected benefit obligation by the end of year 5.

We have now discussed and illustrated four components of pension expense. The fifth component arises when actuarial estimates and assumptions change as a result of environmental influences. A discussion of this component follows.

Pension Expense Component 5: Gains and Losses

1 **Describe how pension gains and losses arise and explain how they are accounted for under an immediate recognition approach.**

CONCEPTUAL

Changes in actuarial assumptions and estimates create pension gains and losses.

Actuarial valuations made in connection with a pension plan require many assumptions about future events, such as discount rates, rates of return on plan assets, mortality rates, employee service periods, and future compensation levels. Obviously such predictions are subject to error. When actual outcomes differ from estimates or predictions and from changes in assumptions about the economic environment in which a company operates, **pension gains and losses** result. *Gains* increase plan assets, decrease the projected benefit obligation, or both. *Losses* decrease plan assets, increase the projected benefit obligation, or both. For example, if the interest rate used to discount an employee's projected pension benefits is reduced to reflect the current and projected economic environment, a loss will result because the lower discount rate *increases* the projected benefit obligation.

To illustrate, assume that a pension plan's beginning assets total $100,000, and that the *expected* rate of return on plan assets for the current year is 10 percent, or $10,000. If the *actual* return for the current year is 8 percent, or $8,000, a pension loss of $2,000 results:

Actual return = Expected return −   Loss
   $8,000   = $10,000   − $2,000

This equation can be rearranged to emphasize how the loss (in this example) or gain is calculated:

Gain (Loss) = Actual return − Expected return
   $(2,000)   = $8,000   − $10,000

How should pension gains and losses be accounted for in calculating pension expense for a period? Under the immediate recognition approach, gains and losses are recognized *immediately* and included as a component of pension expense in the period in which they arise. In terms of the example just given, this approach would lead to the following entries:

Pension asset 10,000
   Pension expense.   10,000
To record the expected return on plan assets.

Pension expense 2,000
   Pension asset   2,000
To record the loss component of pension expense.

Similar entries would be made for a gain or loss that affected the projected benefit obligation.

Under the delayed recognition approach, pension gains and losses are not recognized immediately in the period in which they occur. Supporters of this view argue that immediate recognition creates unacceptable *volatility* in pension expense from period to period. They note that given the long-run nature of a pension plan, a gain or loss in one period may be offset partially or fully in subsequent periods. Perhaps more important, *because there may be considerable uncertainty about the ultimate cash flow effects of some gains and losses, for example, unrealized holding gains*

CONCEPTUAL

Immediate recognition of pension gains and losses can create volatility in pension expense from period to period.

on securities in the fund, immediate recognition may not provide reliable signals about future cash flows.

Under the delayed recognition approach, gains and losses are not recognized in pension expense as they occur; rather, they are recognized gradually in future periods as a component of pension expense. Because we believe that immediate recognition of gains and losses is easier for you to understand, we will not discuss the delayed recognition approach for pension gains and losses at this point. We will discuss it later, when we discuss the delayed recognition approach permitted under *Statement No. 87*.

Summary and Overview of the Five Primary Components of Pension Expense

We have now discussed the five primary components of pension expense introduced on pages, 853–854. These components, along with illustrative journal entries, are summarized in Exhibit 16–10. *Exhibit 16–10 is an important exhibit. Study it carefully. It includes a summary illustration of everything discussed so far in this chapter.*

In the National Corporation example and in Exhibit 16–10, we used a separate journal entry to record each component of pension expense. This approach showed clearly how each pension event affected National's balance sheet assets and liabilities. In practice, companies do not make separate entries for each component of pension expense. Rather, they record pension expense by making one or two compound journal entries upon receipt of the information outlined in Exhibit 16–3. To illustrate, refer to the year 1 data summarized in Exhibit 16–9. Instead of making a separate entry for each pension event and expense component, the company could combine them as follows:

Intangible asset	44,527	
Net pension asset/(liability)		44,527
To record prior service cost at the beginning of year 1.		
Pension expense	17,275	
Net pension asset/(liability)	7,704	
Cash		16,074
Intangible asset		8,905
To record pension expense for year 1.		

Notice that these combined journal entries produce the exact same income statement and balance sheet information shown in Exhibit 16–9. For example, the net pension asset/(liability) account has a credit balance of $36,823 ($44,527 – $7,704), which corresponds to the net asset/(liability) balance in column 10 of Exhibit 16–9 and which also equals the funded status of the plan.

We have now completed our discussion of the five primary components of pension expense. Using the National Corporation as an example, we recognized all transactions and events related to National's defined benefit pension plan. As we have stated, this approach is sometimes described as *immediate recognition*. For political reasons, concerns about potential economic consequences, and the need for compromise among various interest groups, *Statement No. 87* does not require immediate recognition for all components of pension expense. Instead, the *Statement* permits delayed recognition for three of the pension expense components. In the following section, we will discuss this approach. Because this approach is somewhat different from what you are probably used to, we will also illustrate how a pension worksheet can be used to accumulate pension expense and other information in a logical manner.

EXHIBIT 16–10	Accounting for Pension Expense Under Immediate Recognition: A Summary of Pension Transactions and Events

Component	Concept/Event	Accounting
(1) Service Component	Present value of retirement benefits earned in current period.	Pension expense . . . . xx 　　Pension liability . . . . 　　　xx
(2) Interest Component	Interest on the projected benefit obligation.	Pension expense . . . . xx 　　Pension liability . . . . 　　　xx
	Contributions made by employer to pension fund.	Pension asset . . . . xx 　　Cash. . . . . 　　　xx
(3) Return on Plan Asset Component	Expected return on plan assets.	Pension asset . . . . xx 　　Pension expense . . . . 　　　xx
	Prior service cost (PSC) from retro-active benefits and plan amendments.	Intangible asset (PSC) . . . . . xx 　　Pension liability . . . . 　　　xx
(4) Amortization of Prior Service Cost	PSC is allocated over periods benefited by employee service.	Pension expense . . . . xx 　　Intangible asset (PSC). . . . 　　　xx
(5) Pension Gains/Losses	Changes in assumptions and estimates that affect the projected benefit obligation.	Gains: Pension liability. . . . . xx 　　Pension expense . . . . 　　　xx Losses: Pension expense . . . . xx 　　Pension liability . . . . 　　　xx
	Differences between the expected return on plan assets and the actual return on plan assets.	Gains: Pension asset . . . . xx 　　Pension expense . . . . 　　　xx Losses: Pension expense . . . . xx 　　Pension asset . . . . 　　　xx
	Funded status of pension plan—difference between the projected benefit obligation and the fair value of plan assets at a point in time.	
	Balance sheet reporting of pension asset and pension liability: These two accounts are offset against each other and reported as a net pension asset/(liability). Net asset/(liability) equals the funded status of the plan.	

STATEMENT NO. 87 AND DELAYED RECOGNITION OF SOME PENSION EXPENSE COMPONENTS

During the FASB's deliberations on pension accounting, controversy arose over whether a company should be required to recognize a pension obligation for prior service cost when a defined benefit plan is started or an existing plan is amended. Opponents of immediate recognition of the obligation for prior service cost pointed out that it could have an adverse impact on a company's balance sheet and financial ratios. They also argued that immediate recognition of a substantive pension liability could violate certain contracts, creating sufficient liabilities on the employer's books to throw the company into technical default on certain debt limitation agreements. Finally, they pointed out that delayed recognition of certain events that change the projected benefit obligation and plan assets due to changes in assumptions and actuarial experience adjustments—for example, pension gains and losses—had long been an integral part of past pension accounting.

Statement No. 87 permits companies to use a delayed recognition approach for three components of pension expense: prior service cost, pension gains and losses, and the mandatory change in accounting principle arising from the initial adoption of (transition to) *Statement No. 87*. In the following sections we will discuss the delayed recognition approach for prior service cost and pension gains and losses. Transition requirements are discussed near the end of the chapter.

> **CONCEPTUAL**
>
> Delayed recognition applies to three components of pension expense.

Prior Service Cost

In the National Corporation example and the pension summary exhibit (Exhibit 16–10), we made the following entry to record the pension obligation that results from the granting of retroactive benefits.

Intangible assets	44,527	
Pension liability		44,527

Statement No. 87 does not require companies to make this entry to record prior service cost. However, it does require companies to include amortization of prior service cost as a component of pension expense, in the same way as was illustrated earlier for National Corporation (see page 864). The accounting effect of this modification is that prior service cost is accounted for as an *accrual* instead of as a *deferral*. The two methods compare as follows:

> **8** **Explain how prior service cost is accounted for under the delayed recognition approach permitted by *Statement No. 87*.**

> **CONCEPTUAL**
>
> Under *Statement No. 87*, prior service cost is accounted for as an accrual instead of as a deferral.

IMMEDIATE RECOGNITION		DELAYED RECOGNITION (*STATEMENT NO. 87*)	
(Accounted for as a deferral)		(Accounted for as an accrual)	
To record prior service cost at the beginning of year 1:			
Intangible asset 44,527			
Pension liability...	44,527	No entry	
To record amortization of prior service cost, years 1–5:			
Pension expense 8,905		Pension expense 8,905	
Intangible asset ...	8,905	Pension liability.....	8,905

Notice that eventually both approaches include the entire prior service cost of $44,527 in pension expense and record the pension liability of $44,527. Under the immediate recognition approach, the intangible asset and pension liability are recorded on the date retroactive benefits are granted, and the intangible asset is gradually reduced (amortized) to zero as a component of pension expense. Under the delayed recognition approach, the intangible asset is not recorded; however, prior service cost is recorded as a component of pension expense, and the pension liability is gradually increased (accrued) to $44,527.

Even though *Statement No. 87* does not require immediate recognition of a pension liability associated with prior service cost, *it does require the employer to disclose, in the notes to the financial statements, a reconciliation of the funded status of its pension plan with the net pension asset (liability) reported in its balance sheet.* This required reconciliation is the subject of the next section.

Reconciliation of Funded Status with the Balance Sheet Net Asset (Liability)

9 Prepare a schedule to reconcile the funded status of a pension plan with the net pension asset (liability) reported in the employer's balance sheet.

Exhibit 16–11 shows a reconciliation schedule for National Corporation for years 1 and 3. The amounts shown are based on the amounts in Exhibit 16–9, except for National's net pension asset (liability). Under the delayed recognition approach, National would not record the intangible asset or the pension liability of $44,527 at the beginning of year 1. As a result, National's net pension liability is smaller *by the amount of prior service cost not yet expensed (or amortized, to use Statement No. 87 terminology.)* The bottom portion of Exhibit 16–11 shows National's sheet data under the immediate recognition approach; the amounts were taken directly from Exhibit 16–9 [the intangible asset column (column 7) and the net pension asset (liability) column (column 10)].

Note that the *Statement No. 87* reconciliation schedule discloses, in "off-balance-sheet" form, exactly the same information that would appear in the primary financial statements under the immediate recognition approach. That is, the unrecognized prior service cost has the same balance each period as the intangible asset would have under the immediate recognition approach; the funded status corresponds to the net pension asset (liability) reported under the immediate recognition approach. During the FASB's deliberations, those who opposed immediate balance sheet recognition of the prior service cost liability apparently did not object to disclosure of the same information in footnotes to the financial statements.[13]

CONCEPTUAL

The *Statement No. 87* reconciliation schedule discloses information that would be recognized under the immediate recognition approach.

Gains and Losses (Corridor Approach)

10 Explain how pension gains and losses are accounted for under the delayed recognition (corridor) approach.

We pointed out earlier that immediate recognition of pension gains and losses could create unacceptable volatility in pension expense from period to period. Furthermore, past actuarial methods had not recognized such gains and losses as they occurred but had included them gradually over time in the calculation of pension expense. The FASB was sensitive to these considerations. As a result, *Statement No. 87* does not *require* that pension gains and losses be recognized as a component of pension expense in the period in which they occur. Instead, the *Statement* permits a delayed recognition approach that establishes a *minimum* amount of gain or loss subject to inclusion in pension expense. This approach is called the **corridor approach.**

Under the corridor approach, *no portion of a gain or loss is included (recognized) as a component of pension expense in the period in which it occurs.* In subsequent periods, however, the beginning-of-period unrecognized net gain or loss is compared with 10 percent of the greater of (1) the projected benefit obligation or (2) the fair value of plan assets. The amount of gain or loss subject to amortization is the net gain or loss *in excess* of 10 percent of the greater of (1) or (2). The excess net gain or loss (the amount "outside the corridor") is amortized over the average remaining service period of applicable employees. Each period, the corridor must be recalculated along with the average remaining service period of applicable employees. In summary, the corridor approach allows companies to dampen the effect of large gains and losses on pension expense by establishing a minimum amount subject to amortization.

Delayed Recognition: A Summary Example

To illustrate both the amortization of prior service cost and the corridor approach, assume that Presley Corporation has had a defined benefit pension plan for its

---

[13]More about *Statement No. 87* requirements as a reconciliation of the conflicting views on the pension obligation can be found in DeBerg, Mittelstaedt, and Regier, "Employers' Accounting for Pensions: A Theoretical Approach to Financial Accounting Standard No. 87," *Journal of Accounting Education,* Vol. 5, pp. 227–242.

EXHIBIT 16–11	Reconciliation Schedule Under Delayed Recognition (*Statement No. 87*) Compared to Immediate Recognition (Data from Exhibit 16–9)

National Corporation
Reconciliation Schedule

	END OF YEAR 1	END OF YEAR 3
Projected benefit obligation	$(52,897)	$(72,916)
Plan assets	16,074	53,205
Funded status	$(36,823)	$(19,711)
Unrecognized prior service cost:		
$44,527 − $8,905	35,622	
$44,527 − 3($8,905)		17,812
Net pension asset/(liability)	$ (1,201)	$ (1,899)

Immediate Recognition Approach
Balance Sheet Data

	END OF YEAR 1	END OF YEAR 3
Intangible asset (Dr)	$35,622	$17,812
Net pension asset/(liability) (Cr)	36,823	19,711

employees for many years. Presley uses the delayed recognition approach for prior service cost and pension gains and losses. At the beginning of 1998, the schedule to reconcile the funded status of Presley's pension plan with the company's balance sheet net pension asset/(liability) was as follows:

Projected benefit obligation	**$(60,000)**
Plan assets at fair value	**20,000**
Funded status	**$(40,000)**
Unrecognized prior service cost	**11,000**
Net pension asset/(liability)	**$(29,000)**

The following items resulted from Presley's pension plan during 1998:

1. Service component, $4,000.
2. Interest on the projected benefit obligation (6 percent rate), $3,600.
3. Expected return on plan assets, $2,000 (10 percent expected rate of return).
4. Average remaining service period of active employees, 5 years.
5. Amortization of prior service cost $2,200 ($11,000 ÷ 5).
6. Contributions made to the pension fund at the end of 1998, $15,000.
7. Actual return on plan assets during 1998, $9,000; pension gain of $7,000 (actual return of $9,000 less expected return of $2,000).
8. Retirement benefits paid to retirees, $5,000.

Under the delayed recognition approach, no portion of the $7,000 gain on plan assets would be included in pension expense in 1998. The journal entry to record pension expense for 1998 would be:

Pension expense ($4,000 + $3,600 − $2,000 + $2,200)	7,800	
Net pension asset/(liability)	7,200	
Cash		15,000

EXHIBIT 16–12	**Delayed Recognition Disclosures Under *Statement No. 87***

Kerr-McGee Corporation

17. Retirement Plans

Most of the company's employees are covered under noncontributory retirement plans of the company and certain of its subsidiaries. The benefits of these plans are based primarily on years of service and employees' remuneration near retirement. The company's policy is to fund the minimum amounts as permitted by the Employee Retirement Income Security Act of 1974 (ERISA).

The funded status of plans with assets in excess of accumulated benefits at December 31, 1995 and 1994, is as follows:

(In millions of dollars)	1995	1994
Plan assets at fair value	$ 492	$ 402
Actuarial present value of accumulated benefit obligations–		
Vested	$(323)	$(263)
Nonvested	(10)	(14)
Total	$(333)	$(277)
Plan assets in excess of accumulated benefit obligations	$ 159	$ 125
Plan assets at fair value	$ 492	$ 402
Projected benefit obligations–		
Actuarial present value of accumulated benefit obligations	$(333)	$(277)
Projected salary increases	(48)	(45)
Total	$(381)	$(322)
Plan assets in excess of projected benefit obligations	$ 111	$ 80
Unrecognized net asset at January 1, 1987	(22)	(26)
Unrecognized prior service costs	12	17
Unrecognized net gain	(73)	(51)
Pension prepayment at end of year	$ 28	$ 20

The schedule to reconcile the funded status of Presley's pension plan with the net pension asset/(liability) reported on the balance sheet at the end of 1998 would be as follows:

Projected benefit obligation ($60,000 + $4,000 + $3,600 − $5,000)	$ 62,600
Plan assets at fair value ($20,000 + $2,000 + $15,000 + $7,000 − $5,000)	39,000
Funded status	$(23,600)
Unrecognized prior service cost ($11,000 − $2,200)	8,800
Unrecognized gain	(7,000)
Net pension asset/(liability) ($29,000 − $7,200)	$(21,800)

In calculating pension expense for 1999, the amount of gain subject to amortization would be computed as follows:

Unrecognized gain at 1/1/99	$7,000
10 percent of the greater of the beginning projected benefit obligation ($62,600) or plan assets ($39,000): $62,600 × .10	(6,260)
Gain subject to amortization (amount outside of "corridor") ($7,000 − $6,260)	$ 740
Amount of gain included as a reduction of pension expense for 1999: ($740 ÷ 4 service years remaining)	$ 185

The unrecognized portion of the $555 gain ($740 − 185) would be netted against any pension gains or losses occurring during 1999. The resulting unrecognized

The net periodic pension credit, excluding charges of $1 million and $2 million in 1995 and 1994, respectively, related to the restructuring programs (see Note 10), for each of the three years ended December 31, 1995, 1994, and 1993, is summarized as follows:

(In millions of dollars)	1995	1994	1993
Service cost–benefits earned during the period	$ 8	$10	$ 9
Interest cost on projected benefit obligations	27	24	23
Return on plan assets	(115)	(6)	(69)
Net amortization and deferral	71	(35)	33
Net pension credit	$ (9)	$(7)	$(4)

The amount of benefits that can be covered by the funded plans is limited by ERISA and the Internal Revenue Code. Therefore, the company has unfunded supplemental plans designed to maintain benefits for all employees at the plan formula level and to provide senior executives with benefits equal to a specified percentage of their final average compensation. The projected benefit obligation for these unfunded plans totaled $15 million and $13 million at December 31, 1995 and 1994, respectively. To reflect the amount by which the accumulated benefit obligation exceeded the accrued pension expense for these plans, an additional liability totaling $4 million and $6 million at December 31, 1995 and 1994, respectively, is recorded in the Consolidated Balance Sheet with an offsetting intangible asset (see Note 5). Although not considered plan assets, a grantor trust was established from which payments for certain of these supplemental plans are made. The trust had a balance of $6 million and $4 million at December 31, 1995 and 1994, respectively. Net periodic pension expense for these plans was $4 million for each of the years 1995 and 1994 and $3 million for 1993.

The following assumptions were used in estimating the actuarial present value of the projected benefit obligation and net periodic pension costs:

	1995	1994	1993
Future compensation increases	5.00%	5.00%	5.00%
Discount rate	7.25	8.50	7.50
Long-term rate of return on plan assets	9.00	9.00	9.00

Source: Kerr-McGee 1995 Annual Report

net gain or loss would appear on Presley's reconciliation schedule at the end of 1999.

Footnote Disclosures of Pension Expense

In addition to the schedule that reconciles the funded status of a pension plan with the employer's balance sheet amounts, *Statement No. 87* also requires that the components of pension expense be disclosed in the notes to the financial statements. This disclosure must include the *actual return on plan assets.* Exhibit 16–12 illustrates Kerr-McGee's pension disclosures. Notice that the footnote includes both the reconciliation schedule and the schedule of pension expense components.

The reconciliation schedule in Exhibit 16–12 shows how Kerr-McGee arrives at the projected benefit obligation. The company starts with the **accumulated benefit obligation,** which is calculated in the same manner as the projected benefit obligation, except that it is based on *current* salary levels instead of *projected* salary levels. As a result of applying the delayed recognition approach, Kerr-McGee discloses three reconciling items: an unrecognized net asset (gain) resulting from the initial adoption of *Statement No. 87,* unrecognized prior service costs, and an unrecognized net gain.

In the schedule of Kerr-McGee's pension expense components (the right portion of Exhibit 16–12), the first two components—service cost and interest cost—are straightforward. The third component, the $115 million return on plan assets for 1995, is the *actual return,* as required by *Statement No. 87.* Since Kerr-McGee uses the expected return to calculate pension expense, the difference between the expected return and the

C O N C E P T U A L

The accumulated benefit obligation is similar to the projected benefit obligation except that it is based on actual salaries to date.

actual return is added back as part of the fourth component, net amortization and deferral. The fourth component also includes prior service cost amortization and amortization of the net asset (gain) arising when Kerr-McGee first adopted *Statement No. 87.*

To strengthen your understanding of these disclosures, let us apply the above concepts to the Presley Corporation example on pages 870–873. The following disclosure of the pension expense components would appear in the footnotes to Presley's financial statements for 1998:

Service cost	**$ 4,000**
Interest on the projected benefit obligation	**3,600**
Return on plan assets (actual)	**(9,000)**
Net amortization and deferral	**9,200**
Pension expense for 1998	**$ 7,800**

The net amortization and deferral of $9,200 includes the amortization of prior service cost of $2,200 and the $7,000 gain (the difference between the actual return of $9,000 and the expected return of $2,000).

Another disclosure requirement of *Statement No. 87* is the minimum liability requirement. This requirement is discussed and illustrated in the next section.

Recognition of a Minimum Liability

11 **Calculate the minimum liability and explain the minimum liability requirement.**

Under the delayed recognition approach permitted by *Statement No. 87,* a company is not required to recognize the projected benefit obligation as a pension liability. However, the *Statement* does require recognition of a **minimum liability,** at each balance sheet date, at least equal to the employer's *unfunded accumulated benefit obligation (accumulated benefit obligation minus the fair value of plan assets).* To illustrate this requirement, return to the reconciliation schedule in Exhibit 16–11. Assume that Smith's salary for year 1 was $39,000, which is only 60 percent of the $65,000 expected three-year average annual salary used to calculate his projected benefits. As a result, National's accumulated benefit obligation at the end of year 1 would be $31,738 (.60 × $52,897 from Exhibit 16–11). The minimum liability that must be reported under *Statement No. 87* is $15,664, calculated as follows:

Accumulated benefit obligation	**$(31,738)**
Plan assets at fair value	**16,074**
Unfunded accumulated benefit obligation	**$(15,664)**

This $15,664 minimum liability would be combined with the existing net pension asset (liability) balance, which appears on the company's balance sheet. Since National already has recorded a net pension liability of $1,201 at the end of year 1, an additional liability of $14,463 ($15,664 – $1,201) must be recognized in National's end-of-year-1 balance sheet. *Statement No. 87* requires that when recording this credit, the offsetting debit must be made to an intangible asset:

Intangible asset	14,463	
Net pension asset/(liability)		14,463

As you probably suspect, *the minimum liability requirements would not apply under the immediate recognition approach.* As the bottom of Exhibit 16–11 shows, National's net pension liability under the immediate recognition approach would be $36,823, which *exceeds* the minimum liability.

Four other points about the minimum liability adjustment are important:

CONCEPTUAL

Recognition of a minimum liability affects only the balance sheet; pension expense is not affected.

1. The adjustment affects only balance sheet accounts; the pension expense calculations and procedures are not affected. Thus, it is a balance sheet "tack on" procedure.

2. Since the calculation and adjustment, if any, are made at the end of each period based on pension data at that date, the amount and form of the journal entry are dependent on the balance already in the net pension asset (liability) account.

3. Each year's minimum liability journal entry records the amount necessary to *adjust to* the required minimum liability amount.

4. In some instances, the calculated minimum liability may *exceed* unrecognized prior service cost. Any amount greater than unrecognized prior service cost should be debited to an account titled "minimum pension liability adjustment" and reported as a component of other comprehensive income.

In summary, recognition of a minimum liability appears to be a compromise between the immediate recognition approach presented earlier in this chapter and the delayed recognition approach, under which a liability for prior service cost is not reported. It is also an interesting, although somewhat inconsistent, compromise on the issue of whether an employer's pension obligation should be based on projected benefits or accumulated benefits.

Now that we have discussed and illustrated the delayed recognition approach, the following section illustrates how a pension worksheet can be used to assemble and accumulate pension information in a logical and organized manner.

USING A PENSION EXPENSE WORKSHEET

12 Prepare a worksheet for the various components of pension expense.

Exhibits 16–8 and 16–9, based on the immediate recognition approach, were designed to provide an overview of National Corporation's pension expense over the service period of its only employee, Dave Smith. Although similar exhibits could have been used to illustrate the delayed recognition approach permitted by *Statement No. 87*, they would have become quite cumbersome as columns were added for unrecognized items such as prior service cost and gains and losses. In this section of the chapter, we will use the reconciliation schedule in Exhibit 16–11 to construct a worksheet for determining the components of pension expense. This worksheet will also provide an overview of pension expense under the delayed recognition approach. It should also be useful to you in studying the end-of-chapter materials.

Exhibit 16–13 shows a pension worksheet based on the data for Presley Corporation on pages 870–873. A few general comments about the worksheet are in order. First, the reconciliation schedule at the beginning of 1998 (reproduced from page 871) appears in the first column, in the upper left portion of the worksheet. Second, in columns 1 and 4, amounts in parentheses represent credits; amounts not in parentheses represent debits. For example, unrecognized prior service cost of $11,000 would be an asset (debit); the funded status of the plan (underfunded by $40,000) would be a net liability (credit). Third, *the items in bold type represent accounts that would appear on the employer's income statement or balance sheet, for example, pension expense and net pension asset/(liability).*

The worksheet is completed by entering the appropriate pension information for 1998 in columns 2 and 3 as follows:

1. The service cost of $4,000 is entered as a debit to (increase in) pension expense and a credit to (increase in) the projected benefit obligation.

2. Interest on the projected benefit obligation of $3,600 is entered as a debit to (increase in) pension expense and a credit to (increase in) the projected benefit obligation.

3. The expected return on plan assets of $2,000 is entered as a debit to (increase in) plan assets and a credit to (decrease in) pension expense.

4. Amortization of prior service cost of $2,200 is entered as a debit to (increase in) pension expense and a credit to (decrease in) unrecognized prior service cost.

5. The cash funding of $15,000 is entered as a debit to (increase in) plan assets and a credit to (decrease in) cash.

6. The pension gain of $7,000 is entered as a debit to (increase in) plan assets and a credit to (increase in) unrecognized gain.

| EXHIBIT 16-13 | A Pension Worksheet for Presley Corporation | | | |

	(1) Beginning of 1998	(2) Debit	(3) Credit	(4) End of 1998
Projected benefit obligation	(60,000)	(7) 5,000	(1) 4,000	
			(2) 3,600	(62,600)
Plan assets.	20,000	(3) 2,000		
		(6) 7,000		
		(5) 15,000	(7) 5,000	39,000
Funded status	(40,000)			(23,600)
Unrecognized prior service cost	11,000		(4) 2,200	8,800
Unrecognized gain			(6) 7,000	(7,000)
Net pension asset (liability)	**(29,000)**	**7,200**		**(21,800)**
Cash			(5) **15,000**	
Pension expense:				
Service cost		(1) 4,000		
Interest on projected benefit obligation		(2) 3,600		
Return on plan assets			(3) 2,000	
Amortization of prior service cost		(4) 2,200		
		38,800	38,800	
Formal journal entry:				
Pension expense		**7,800**		
Net pension asset/(liability)		**7,200**		
Cash			**15,000**	

7. Payments to retirees of $5,000 are entered as a debit to (decrease in) the projected benefit obligation and as a credit to (decrease in) plan assets.

Once the worksheet entries have been made, the formal journal entry can be made at the bottom of the worksheet. The debit of $7,800 to pension expense is the net of the debit and credit entries in the pension expense portion of the worksheet. The credit of $15,000 to cash is copied from the cash account in the middle of the worksheet. The debit to net pension asset/(liability) of $7,200 is the difference between the debit to pension expense and the credit to cash and is *posted* to the debit column in the upper portion of the worksheet. *Since this amount is posted after the debit and credit columns have been totaled, it is not part of the $38,800 column totals.* The reconciliation schedule at the end of 1998 in the upper right portion of the worksheet can now be completed by adding and subtracting, as appropriate, the debit and credit entries to or from the beginning-of-1998 balances.

In summary, the worksheet approach allows the accountant to assemble all the information necessary to record pension expense at the end of each period and to organize that information in a useful, logical, and understandable manner. It also facilitates the preparation of the reconciliation schedule required by *Statement No. 87.* Some of the end-of-chapter materials require that you use a worksheet.

◎THER POSTRETIREMENT BENEFITS

To this point we have focused on a defined benefit pension plan in presenting the concepts and fundamentals of accounting and reporting for postretirement benefit plans. Indeed, the concepts and fundamentals of accounting for pension plans parallel those of accounting for other postretirement benefit plans, such as health care plans. Because some of the pension terminology in *Statement No. 87* differs from that in *Statement No. 106* for other postretirement benefit plans, the purpose of this section is to note the similarities and differences in terminology and to describe some minor differences in concepts and procedures. We will first cover how the benefits of a postretirement plan, such as a health plan, are calculated. Then, in the following section, we will take a brief look at the components of other postretirement benefit costs.

Calculating Other Postretirement Benefits and Obligations

Two terms used in *Statement No. 106* relate to the calculation of other postretirement benefits. Those terms are the expected postretirement benefit obligation (EPBO) and the accumulated postretirement benefit obligation (APBO). An employer's **expected postretirement benefit obligation** to an employee as of the measurement date is the present value of the postretirement benefits expected to be paid the employee, the employee's beneficiaries, or any covered dependents. In other words, the EPBO is the present value of the estimated *total* expenditures needed to provide the promised future benefits as of the measurement date (the point in time that the EPBO is calculated)—usually the end of each fiscal year.

For example, assume that National Corporation's plan for Dave Smith (pages 852–857) is a health care plan instead of a pension plan and that actuarial calculations have yielded expected health care benefits of $4,875 per year during Smith's expected retirement period. The expected postretirement benefit obligation at the end of Smith's service period (end of year 5) would be $32,712, as calculated on page 856. The EPBO at the beginning of year 1 and the end of years 1 through 4 would be calculated as follows:

$$\text{Beginning of year 1:} \quad \$32,712 \div (1.08)^5 = \$22,263$$
$$\text{End of year 1:} \quad \$32,712 \div (1.08)^4 = \$24,044$$
$$\text{End of year 2:} \quad \$32,712 \div (1.08)^3 = \$25,968$$
$$\text{End of year 3:} \quad \$32,712 \div (1.08)^2 = \$28,043$$
$$\text{End of year 4:} \quad \$32,712 \div (1.08)^1 = \$30,289$$

The **accumulated postretirement benefit obligation** is used to describe the portion of the EPBO incurred as the result of employee service up to the measurement date. The APBO can be thought of as the portion of the EPBO that has been "earned" as a result of employee services provided up to the measurement date. *The APBO is conceptually identical to the projected benefit obligation under a pension plan.* Just as the service component for pensions was related to the projected benefit obligation, the service component of other postretirement benefits is related to the accumulated postretirement benefit obligation. Using the EPBO calculations above, these relationships are as follows:

END OF YEAR	EXPECTED POSTRETIREMENT BENEFIT OBLIGATION	ACCUMULATED POSTRETIREMENT BENEFIT OBLIGATION (PORTION OF EPBO EARNED)	SERVICE COST 1/5 × EPBO (FOR YEAR)
1	$24,044	1/5 × $24,044 = $ 4,808	1/5 × $24,044 = $4,808
2	25,968	2/5 × $25,968 = 10,386	1/5 × $25,968 = 5,193
3	28,043	3/5 × $28,043 = 16,824	1/5 × $28,043 = 5,608
4	30,289	4/5 × $30,289 = 24,228	1/5 × $30,289 = 6,057
5	32,712	5/5 × $32,712 = 32,712	1/5 × $32,712 = 6,542

The service cost numbers, shown in the last column, would be accounted for in the same manner as service cost for a pension plan (see page 856).

Recall that the period over which the service component of pension expense is accrued (attributed) ends on the employee's retirement date, because each year of service up to retirement increases the employee's pension benefits. This same concept applies to other postretirement benefits, unless the employee becomes fully eligible to receive all postretirement benefits prior to the expected retirement date. (In those cases, the attribution period ends on the date of full eligibility.[14])

Components of Other Postretirement Benefit Expense

13 Identify the components of other postretirement benefit expense.

The potential components of other postretirement benefit expense parallel those we have discussed for pension expense:

1. Service cost—the portion of the expected postretirement benefit obligation attributed to employee service during the period.
2. Interest on the accumulated projected benefit obligation. This interest (discount) rate is a settlement rate and has the same interpretation as the interest (discount) rate used in accounting for the projected benefit obligation for pensions.
3. Expected return on other postretirement benefit plan assets. (In practice this component may not exist, as very few plans have been funded.)
4. Amortization of prior service cost.
5. Amortization of gains (losses) arising from changes in assumptions and estimates.

Statement No. 106 does not require a minimum liability disclosure for other postretirement benefits. The reasons for not requiring this disclosure appear to be twofold. First, unlike the accumulated benefit obligation for pensions, the accumulated postretirement benefit obligation for other postretirement benefits does not vest, at least in a legal sense. Whereas the minimum liability provisions in *Statement No. 87* approximate the statutory liability a company would face if its pension plan were terminated, there are currently no similar statutory requirements for postretirement health care or welfare benefits. Second, because most pension plans were adequately funded when *Statement No. 87* was issued, the minimum liability provision served to identify those exceptional situations in which a pension plan was underfunded. Because most other postretirement benefits plans are unfunded, recognition of a minimum liability for such plans would be commonplace rather than exceptions.

T RANSITION AND OTHER DISCLOSURE REQUIREMENTS OF *STATEMENT NOS. 87* AND *106*

Statement No. 87 (for pensions) and *Statement No. 106* (for other postretirement benefits) represented mandatory changes in accounting principles. The initial application of their accounting and reporting requirements was addressed in transition requirements included in the two statements. The effective dates of the transition requirements are now quite old (fiscal years following December 15, 1986, for pensions and December 15, 1992, for other postretirement benefits), so the effects of

---

[14]According to paragraph 226 of *Statement No. 106,* most pension plans provide an incremental benefit for each year of service. Thus, the full eligibility date and the expected retirement date are the same for these types of plans. Paragraph 226 also states that "recent surveys suggest a trend among employers to amend their postretirement benefit plans to define the amount of benefits employees will receive based on the length of their service, similar to most pension plans. If that trend continues, the full eligibility date for many or most postretirement benefit plans also may be the employee's retirement date."

many of the requirements are disappearing from corporate annual reports. For this reason, transition requirements will be discussed only briefly. The disclosure requirements of the two statements follow.

Transition Requirements

As stated earlier, the initial adoption of *Statement Nos. 87* and *106* was a mandatory change in accounting principle. The cumulative effect of the change in accounting principle was calculated by comparing the funded status of the plan (projected benefit obligation less the fair value of plan assets for pensions; accumulated postretirement benefit obligation less the fair value of plan assets for other postretirement benefits) with the employer's balance sheet amount on the date of the change. *Statement No. 106* allowed companies to include the cumulative effect of the change in accounting principle in their income statement, and most companies followed that approach. (Refer to the IBM, Ford, General Motors, and FASB examples on page 849.) *Statement No. 87*, on the other hand, required companies to follow a delayed recognition approach by treating the cumulative effect as an unrecognized transition asset (gain) or an unrecognized transition obligation (loss) as appropriate. This cumulative effect (or transition amount) was recognized (amortized) gradually as a component of pension expense, similar to the procedure for prior service cost amortization. The amortization period permitted was the employees' average remaining service period (or fifteen years if the average remaining service period was less than fifteen years). *Given that at this writing, almost thirteen years had passed since the effective date of Statement No. 87, this component of pension expense soon will disappear.*

To illustrate, refer to Exhibit 16–12 for Kerr-McGee. Notice that unrecognized transition asset is being amortized by $4 million per year as a reduction in pension expense. Based on this amount of amortization each year, this component of pension expense will disappear in approximately five years.

Disclosure Requirements

Throughout this chapter we have referred to partial disclosures required by *Statements No. 87* and *106*. This section provides a summary of other disclosures required by the two *Statements*.

Statement No. 87 requires an employer sponsoring a defined benefit pension plan to disclose the following:

1. A description of the plan, including employee groups covered, type of benefit formula, funding policy, types of assets held and significant nonbenefit liabilities, if any, and the nature and effect of significant matters affecting the comparability of information for all periods.

2. The net periodic pension cost for the period, including separate figures for the service cost component, the interest cost component, the actual return on assets for the period, and the net total of other components.

3. A schedule reconciling the funded status of the plan with amounts reported in the employer's statement of financial position.

Statement No. 106 requires extensive disclosures, similar in many respects to the disclosures required for pensions. Required disclosures include:

1. A detailed description of the substantive plan, employee groups covered, funding policy, and types of assets held.

2. The components of net periodic postretirement benefit cost, including amortized amounts, for each year presented.

3. A schedule reconciling the funded status of the plan with amounts reported in the employer's balance sheet.

4. The assumed health care cost trend (rate) and the date it is expected to be achieved.

5. The effect of a 1 percent increase in the assumed health care cost trend (rate of change) for each future year on (1) the aggregate of the service and interest cost components of net periodic postretirement health care cost and (2) the APBO for health care benefits.

6. The weighted average of the assumed discount rate(s) and the weighted average rate(s) of compensation increase (for pay-related plans) used in making the actuarial calculations.

7. The amounts and types of securities included in plan assets.

8. The amount of gain or loss recognized during the period for a settlement or curtailment and a description of the nature of the event(s).

As you can see, the disclosure requirements of both *Statements* are quite extensive. Examples of these disclosures are presented in Exhibit 16–12 for Kerr-McGee Corporation and Appendix B (footnotes 6 and 7) at the end of the text for General Electric Corporation.

The FASB recently issued an *Exposure Draft* of a *Proposed Statement of Financial Accounting Standards,* "Employers' Disclosures about Pensions and Other Postretirement Benefits." This *Proposed Statement* would be effective for fiscal years beginning after December 31, 1997. The *Proposed Statement* would eliminate much of the descriptive disclosures required by *Statement Nos. 87, 88,* and *106,* e.g., disclosure item 1 on the previous page for pensions and for other postretirement benefits. The *Proposed Statement* would also require additional statistical data about pensions and other postretirement benefits. For example, the information flows in Exhibit 16–3 (page 848), which summarize changes during the period in the projected benefit obligation and the fair value of plan assets, would be a required disclosure both for pensions and other postretirement benefits.[15]

Accounting for Pensions and Other Postretirement Benefits: An Assessment

A substantial number of accounting concepts and issues are involved in accounting for postretirement benefits. Moreover, the behavioral implications and economic consequences of a given set of financial accounting standards for these benefits make the subject very controversial. Although the accounting framework provided by *Statements No. 87* and *106* appears to be an improvement over older accounting standards, several issues remain unresolved—especially in light of the FASB's conceptual framework project. The FASB has acknowledged that accounting for postretirement benefits is still in a transitional stage. Further changes in these standards are expected.

The United States has taken the lead internationally in standardizing accounting for postretirement benefits. U.S. GAAP provide the most detailed and comprehensive rules covering the subject. The influence of U.S. GAAP is apparent in the International Accounting Standards Committee's *IAS No. 19,* "Retirement Benefit Costs."[16] *IAS No. 19* recommends that the cost of retirement benefits be determined actuarially, based on services rendered to date and on an assumption about projected salaries. Furthermore, the effects of past service costs, experience adjustments, and changes in actuarial assumptions should be recognized systematically over the

---

[15]"Employers' Disclosures about Pensions and Other Postretirement Benefits," *Proposed Statement of Financial Accounting Standards* (Stamford, Conn: FASB, June 1997).
[16]International Accounting Standards Committee, "Retirement Benefit Costs," *IAS No. 19* (London: IASC, 1993).

expected remaining working lives of participating employees. Specifically prohibited are pay-as-you-go accounting, in which the cost is recognized as benefits are paid to retired employees, or as payments are made to the pension fund; and terminal funding accounting, in which the cost is recognized at the time an employee retires. *IAS No. 19* is similar in most respects to *Statement No. 87*.

Despite the recommendations of *IAS No. 19,* these methods—especially pay-as-you-go accounting—are common around the world. Tax laws also have an influence in that, in some countries, companies recognize cost to the extent that it is deductible for tax purposes. Most countries have either loose accounting standards for postretirement benefits or none at all—a fact that gives many companies an opportunity to manipulate reported income by varying the amount of benefit cost expensed. Moreover, few countries require disclosure of related costs and obligations. This situation is unlikely to change in the foreseeable future, despite the efforts of the International Accounting Standards Committee and the influence of U.S. GAAP.

SUMMARY OF LEARNING OBJECTIVES

1. **Distinguish between a defined contribution plan and a defined benefit plan and describe other characteristics of postretirement benefit plans.**

   In a defined contribution plan, the employer promises to make specified contributions to the retirement fund, but the benefits to be received by the employee are not specified. In a defined benefit plan, the employer promises to make specified payments to employees during their retirement, but the contributions to be made are not specified. Other characteristics of postretirement benefit plans include public versus private plans, contributory versus noncontributory plans, vested versus partially vested plans, funded versus unfunded plans, and pay-related versus non-pay-related plans.

2. **Identify the potential components of pension expense.**

   These components are service cost, interest cost, return on plan assets, amortization of prior service cost, amortization of pension gains (losses), and amortization of net asset (gain) or obligation (loss) from transition to the provisions of *Statement No. 87*.

3. **Calculate and account for the service component of pension expense.**

   The service component of pension expense is the present value of the retirement benefits attributed by a pension plan formula for services rendered during a particular period. The service component increases the projected benefit obligation and is that portion of the obligation related to benefits earned as a result of services rendered for the current year.

4. **Calculate and account for the interest component of pension expense and explain how the service and interest components are related to the projected benefit obligation.**

   The interest component of pension expense increases the projected benefit obligation and represents interest on the beginning obligation due to the passage of time. The projected benefit obligation (PBO) as of a particular date is the present value of all pension benefits attributed by the plan's benefit formula to employee service rendered prior to that date based on salary levels up to retirement.

5. **Explain how the expected rate of return component of pension expense and periodic funding affect pension plan assets.**

   Funding increases plan assets. Cash paid to the plan is invested in income-earning assets. The expected return (earnings) on assets in the fund increases the amount of assets in the pension fund and reduces pension expense.

6. **Define prior service cost and explain how it is accounted for under an immediate recognition approach.**

Prior service cost refers to the cost associated with retirement benefits granted to employees for services rendered prior to the time a pension plan is adopted. Under an immediate recognition approach, prior service cost would be recorded as an intangible asset and a liability (equal to the projected benefit obligation). The intangible asset would be amortized over the employees' remaining service periods as a component of pension expense.

7. **Describe how pension gains and losses arise and explain how they are accounted for under an immediate recognition approach.**

   Gains and losses arise from changes in either the projected benefit obligation or plan assets resulting from experience different from that assumed and from changes in assumptions. Under immediate recognition, these gains and losses would be included as a component of pension expense in the periods in which they occur.

8. **Explain how prior service cost is accounted for under the delayed recognition approach permitted by *Statement No. 87*.**

   Under the delayed recognition approach, an intangible asset and a liability (equal to the prior service cost) are not recognized (recorded) in the accounts. However, unrecognized prior service cost is amortized over the employees' remaining service periods as a component of pension expense.

9. **Prepare a schedule to reconcile the funded status of a pension plan with the net pension asset (liability) reported in the employer's balance sheet.**

   The difference between the projected benefit obligation for pensions and the fair value of plan assets is called the funded status of the plan. The funded status of the plan may be reconciled with the net pension asset (liability) amount reported in the employer's balance sheet by adding or deducting, as appropriate, items not required to be recognized under the delayed recognition approach permitted by *Statement No. 87*.

10. **Explain how pension gains and losses are accounted for under the delayed recognition (corridor) approach.**

    Under the delayed recognition approach permitted by *Statement No. 87,* the amount of gain or loss subject to amortization as a component of pension expense must exceed a minimum amount based on the corridor approach. Under the corridor approach, no portion of the gain or loss arising in a particular year is included in pension expense. In subsequent years, the amount of net gain or loss that is subject to amortization for that year is that portion "outside of the corridor," that is, that portion that exceeds 10 percent of the greater of the plan assets or projected benefit obligation. The portion that is subject to amortization in any year is amortized over the employees' remaining service period.

11. **Calculate the minimum liability and explain the minimum liability requirement.**

    The accumulated benefit obligation is similar to the projected benefit obligation, but the benefits attributed by the plan's benefit formula are based on salaries earned to date (accumulated benefits). *Statement No. 87* requires that any unfunded accumulated benefit obligation be recognized as a liability in the employer's balance sheet. The minimum liability requirement is a balance sheet disclosure requirement and has no effect on pension expense. Under an immediate recognition approach, the minimum liability requirement would not apply.

12. **Prepare a worksheet for the various components of pension expense.**

    The worksheet approach provides a "big picture" of pension expense under the delayed recognition approach. It also is helpful in showing how the various components of pension expense affect plan assets, the projected benefit obligation, any unrecognized items, and the net pension asset (liability) reported in the employer's balance sheet.

13. **Identify the components of other postretirement benefit expense.**

    These components are identical, conceptually, to the components of pension expense: service cost, interest cost, return on plan assets (if any), amortization of prior service cost, and amortization of gains (losses).

KEY TERMS

accumulated benefit obligation 873

accumulated postretirement benefit
obligation 877

annuity contract 855

benefit/years-of-service approach 857

corridor approach 870

defined benefit plan 845

defined contribution plan 845

delayed recognition 844

discount rate 854

expected postretirement benefit obligation 877

funded status 860

health care plan 845

immediate recognition 844

integration perspective 850

interest on the projected benefit obligation 855

minimum liability 874

pension gains and losses 866

pension plan 845

prior service cost 860

projected benefit obligation (PBO) 855

rate of return on plan assets 857

separation perspective 850

service cost 854

PPENDIX 16-1

Other Topics Related to Pension and Other Postretirement Benefits

This chapter has covered accounting for defined benefit pension plans. These concepts and procedures were also extended to other postretirement benefits, such as a health care plan. Two topics that are related to the chapter material are discussed in this appendix—settlements and curtailments of postretirement benefit plans and financial reporting requirements of the pension plan as a separate entity.

Settlements and Curtailments of Postretirement Benefit Plans

As a result of overfunded pension plans, many employers have terminated asset-rich pension plans and used the surplus assets in corporate projects unrelated to employee pension benefits. These asset reversions, with replacement of the plan by an annuity contract to cover pension benefits, have raised the question of whether any gain or loss should be recognized by the employer at the time the pension assets revert to the company. Employers may make lump-sum cash payments to plan participants in exchange for their right to receive specified pension or other postretirement benefits, or employers may purchase long-term nonparticipating insurance contracts to cover the accumulated postretirement benefit plan. Employers often terminate employees' services earlier than expected or terminate or suspend a plan so that employees do not earn additional benefits for future service.

Accounting for such events is addressed in *FASB Statement No. 88* for pensions and in *Statement No. 106* for other postretirement benefits. These events generally

EXHIBIT 16–14	Accounting for Settlements and Curtailments: Summary of Gain/Loss Recognition

1. Combine any transition net asset with any unrecognized net loss or gain.
2. Combine any transition net obligation with any unrecognized prior service cost.

Settlement

3. Maximum gain or loss from settlement is the amount in item 1 above.
4. a) For pensions, if the entire projected benefit obligation is settled, the maximum gain or loss (item 3) is recognized in the income statement.
   b) For other postretirement benefits, if the entire accumulated postretirement benefit obligation is settled and the maximum amount subject to recognition (item 3) is a gain, the settlement gain is used to reduce any unrecognized transition obligation and any excess gain is reported in income. If the maximum amount subject to recognition (item 3) is a loss, then the entire loss is recognized in the income statement.
5. a) For pensions, if only part of the projected benefit obligation is settled, a pro rata portion, equal to the percentage reduction in the projected benefit obligation, is recognized in the income statement.
   b) For other postretirement benefits, if only part of the accumulated postretirement benefit obligation is settled, a pro rata portion (equal to the percentage reduction in the accumulated postretirement benefit obligation) of the excess of the maximum settlement gain over any unrecognized transition obligation is recognized, or a pro rata portion of the maximum settlement loss is recognized.

Curtailment

6. The portion of item 2 above associated with reduced future services is recognized as a curtailment loss.
7. The decrease (or increase) in the projected benefit obligation (for pensions) or the accumulated postretirement benefit obligation (for other postretirement benefits) from curtailment is a gain or loss.
8. If the amount in item 1 is a net loss, the portion of gain in item 7 in excess of the net loss is a curtailment gain; if the amount in item 1 is a net gain, the entire gain in item 7 is a curtailment gain.
9. If the amount in item 1 is a net gain, the portion of loss in item 7 in excess of the net gain is a curtailment loss; if the amount in item 1 is a net loss, the entire loss in item 7 is a curtailment loss.
10. If the sum of item 6 and item 8 (or item 9) is a loss, it is recognized when curtailment is probable and the effects can be estimated. If the sum of item 6 and item 8 (or item 9) is a gain, it is recognized when the related employees terminate or when the plan is suspended or terminated, and is measured at that date.

are classified as either settlements or curtailments, and both *Statements* reach essentially the same conclusions about accounting for settlements and curtailments and set forth the requirements for recognizing gains and losses.

A *settlement* is an irrevocable action transaction that relieves the employer (or plan) of primary responsibility for a pension or other postretirement benefit obligation, eliminating significant risks related to the obligation and the assets used to affect the settlement. A *curtailment* is an event that significantly reduces the expected years of future service of active plan participants or eliminates the accrual of defined benefits for some or all future services of active plan participants. Settlements and curtailments may occur separately or together. They require gain or loss recognition of previously unrecognized amounts and adjustments to liabilities or assets appearing in the employer's balance sheet. Exhibit 16–14 summarizes accounting for pension and other postretirement benefit settlements and curtailments.

Accounting and Reporting by the Pension Plan

Consistent with the separation view, a pension plan is a separate entity from the employer who sponsors the plan and has its own accounting records and its own financial statements. As a result of the passage of ERISA, many defined benefit pension plans are required to prepare their financial statements in conformity with GAAP. *Statement of Financial Accounting Standards No. 35,* "Accounting and Reporting by Defined Benefit Pension Plans," applies to both private pension plans and plans of state and local governmental units. Though it does not require the preparation, distribution, or attestation of any of the plan's financial statements, external financial statements must meet its requirements. The disclosure requirements prescribed in *Statement No. 35* by the FASB are intended to provide information that is useful in assessing a plan's present and future ability to pay pension benefits when due.

QUESTIONS	Questions marked with an asterisk (*) refer to Appendix 16–1.

Q 16-1. What is a retirement plan? Distinguish between public and private retirement plans.

Q 16-2. What parties typically are involved in a private retirement plan arrangement, and what role does each party play in the arrangement?

Q 16-3. Distinguish between contributory and noncontributory retirement plans.

Q 16-4. What does it mean to say that contributions to a pension fund are fully vested?

Q 16-5. Private retirement plans are of essentially two types: defined contribution plans and defined benefit plans. Describe each of these two types of retirement plans.

*Q 16-6. Discuss and contrast accounting for pensions by the employer (sponsor) and accounting by the pension plan.

Q 16-7. What objectives were stressed by the FASB in its work leading to *Statements No. 87, 88, and 106*?

Q 16-8. Distinguish between projected pension benefits and accumulated pension benefits.

Q 16-9. Why may the calculation of accumulated pension benefits be more reliable than the calculation of projected pension benefits?

Q 16-10. Why may the calculation of projected pension benefits be more relevant and more representationally faithful than the calculation of accumulated pension benefits?

Q 16-11. What general approach to allocating the cost of pension benefits to accounting periods is required by *Statement No. 87*?

Q 16-12. What is meant by the concept of *service cost* when accounting for pensions and other postretirement benefits?

Q 16-13. What is included in the projected pension benefit obligation as of any particular date?

Q 16-14. List the potential components of pension expense.

Q 16-15. Distinguish between a final-pay pension benefit plan and a flat-benefit plan.

Q 16-16. How do earnings on plan assets affect each of the following: net assets of the pension fund, required contributions to the fund, and employer's pension expense?

Q 16-17. Define *prior service cost* as it relates to accounting for pensions.

Q 16-18. Why may prior service cost be considered to be a liability?

Q 16-19. How can gains and losses arise in the accounting for an ongoing pension plan?

Q 19-20. Under GAAP, how are we to account for actuarial gains and losses in measuring pension expense?

Q 16-21. When is the corridor approach used in accounting for pensions?

Q 16-22. What is the minimum liability that must be recognized at each balance sheet date under *Statement No. 87*?

Q 16-23. Outline the disclosures required for a defined benefit pension plan under *Statement No. 87*.

Q 16-24. When accounting for other postretirement benefit plans, how do the expected postretirement benefit obligation, service cost, and the accumulated postretirement benefit obligation relate to one another?

Q 16-25. How might the accumulated postretirement benefit obligation be described, as compared to the expected postretirement benefit obligation?

Q 16-26. Give a few examples of the types of retirement benefits, other than pension benefits, that may be included in a postretirement benefit plan.

Q 16-27. Describe how "pay-as-you-go" accounting differs from accounting for postretirement benefit expense on an accrual basis.

Q 16-28. Define or describe the expected postretirement benefit obligation and the accumulated postretirement benefit obligation in the context of other postretirement benefit plans.

*Q 16-29. In the context of pension plans, what is an asset reversion?

*Q 16-30. With respect to pension and other postretirement benefit plans, what is a settlement? A curtailment?

CASES

C 16-1. **PENSION COST COMPONENTS; DISCLOSURE** You are the controller for Barker Corporation, which established a noncontributory defined benefit pension plan for its employees at the beginning of year 1. At that time, the funded status of its pension plan was a deficiency of $300,000, because only $900,000 of the projected benefit obligation of $1.2 million arising from prior service cost was funded at the beginning of year 1. Barker used a "benefit/years-of-service" approach to measure the projected benefit obligation and will use this approach, in conjunction with a discount rate of 10 percent, to measure the service cost component of periodic pension cost. The expected return on plan assets is 7 percent. Finally, Barker decided to use the straight-line method to amortize the unrecognized prior service cost over the remaining 20-year period of service of employees expected to receive benefits under the plan.

Pension expense for year 1 was $317,000, and the company contributed $280,000 to the pension fund in year 1. No benefits were paid by the pension fund during year 1. At the end of fiscal year 1, the accumulated benefit obligation equaled 80 percent of the projected benefit obligation.

You have prepared the following footnote information for the year 1 annual report (amounts shown are in thousands of dollars):

COMPONENTS OF PENSION EXPENSE		RECONCILIATION OF PLAN FUNDED STATUS WITH AMOUNT SHOWN ON ENDING BALANCE SHEET	
Service cost	$200	Projected benefit obligation	$(1,520)
Interest cost	120	Plan assets at fair value	1,017
		Funded status	$ (503)
Actual loss on plan assets	163	Items not yet recognized in earnings:	
Net amortization and deferral	(166)	Unrecognized prior	
Total	$317	service cost	1,140
		Unrecognized net loss	226
		Net pension asset	$ 863

The president of Barker Corporation is very confused about the pension information for the annual report and has prepared the following questions for you to answer:

a) Why is interest included as a part of pension expense instead of being reported as interest expense?

b) What caused the unrecognized net loss, and what justification is there for deferring it rather than recognizing it in the year 1 income statement?

c) What is the rationale for amortizing the unrecognized prior service cost over the remaining service period of employees expected to receive benefits under the pension plan?

d) What makes up the "net amortization and deferral" portion of pension expense?

e) *Statement No. 87* requires the recording of a minimum liability under certain circumstances. Will Barker be required to record one? If so, what journal entry will be necessary?

The president also says that she does not quite understand why the reconciliation schedule is necessary. She recently has read *Statement of Concepts No. 5* and believes that if the information in the reconciliation schedule is useful, disclosure should not be a substitute for recognition in the financial statements.

REQUIRED

1. Write a brief response to each of the five questions raised by Barker Corporation's president. Support your responses with calculations where necessary.

2. Write a response to the president's concern about the reconciliation schedule both from a theoretical standpoint and from the standpoint of the standard-setting environment.

3. Refer to part 2. Indicate what journal entry would be required if immediate recognition were given to items in the reconciliation schedule presented above.

C 16-2.

PENSION DISCLOSURES; NEGATIVE PRIOR SERVICE COST; IMMEDIATE RECOGNITION
The following pension disclosure appeared in the notes to financial statements in the annual report of Owens Corning, a global corporation engaged in the manufacture and sale of glass composites and building materials systems:

7. Pension Plans: In August of 1995 the Company amended the pension plan for U.S. salaried employees to change from a final average pay formula to a cash balance formula. The change resulted in a reduction in the projected benefit obligation of $20 million. The change is expected to reduce pension expense in the future through the amortization of the reduction in the projected benefit obligation. The funded status at October 31, 1995 (in millions of dollars) is as follows:

	OVERFUNDED	UNDERFUNDED
Vested benefit obligation..............	$359	$312
Accumulated benefit obligation	395	355
Plan assets at fair value	$500	$316
Projected benefit obligation	447	365
Plan assets in excess of (less than) projected benefit obligation	$ 53	$(49)
Unrecognized loss	15	59
Unrecognized prior service cost	(30)	(31)
Projected benefit obligation	(35)	(11)
Net pension asset/(liability)	$ 3	$(32)

Note: Although not directly pertinent to this case, a "cash balance" pension plan is a defined-benefit pension plan that defines retirement benefits by reference to the amount of an employee's *hypothetical* account balance. This balance is credited with hypothetical contributions and hypothetical earnings determined under a formula. The allocations are designed to mimic the allocations of contributions and earnings that would occur under a defined contribution plan.

REQUIRED

1. Discuss the rationale for amortizing the decrease in the projected benefit obligation (prior service cost) over future periods as a reduction in pension expense.

2. Assume that Owens Corning followed an immediate recognition approach in accounting for the various components of pension expense. Discuss some alternatives that the company might use to account for a plan amendment that decreases the projected benefit obligation (prior service cost). Note that Owens Corning reports *negative* amounts of prior service cost in the above schedule.

C 16-3. **PRIOR SERVICE COST** Mitchell Corporation's board of directors recently approved a noncontributory defined benefit pension plan for the corporation's 3,000 employees. Mitchell has been in existence for over 30 years, and the board of directors decided to grant retroactive benefits to the employees. The benefit formula provides a fixed-dollar pension retirement benefit for each year of service. In addition, employees are given credit for prior service up to a maximum of 20 years prior to the plan inception date.

Mitchell's president majored in accounting in college and is curious about the nature of the retroactive pension benefits, which he also calls *prior service cost*. He has asked you, the controller, the following questions:

a) From a theoretical standpoint, does the obligation arising from the granting of retroactive benefits represent a liability to Mitchell?

b) If so, has Mitchell also incurred an expense or a loss, acquired an asset, or suffered a reduction in stockholders' equity?

c) Under the accounting requirements of *Statement No. 87,* what are the financial statement effects of prior service cost during the first year of the plan's existence?

REQUIRED Prepare a brief answer to each of the president's questions.

C 16-4. **GAINS AND LOSSES** O'Brian Company has had a defined benefit pension plan for its employees for several years. In making its cost calculations for 1998, O'Brian estimated that its plan assets would earn about 15 percent. In fact, a weak stock market during 1998 resulted in the plan assets actually earning only 4 percent for the year. Since the actual fair value of plan assets at the end of 1998 was less than the expected fair value, a loss occurred. The existence of this loss raised several questions at the year-end board of directors meeting, including the following:

a) Why do gains and losses sometimes arise in connection with the existence of a pension plan?

b) What are the two primary points of view on how gains and losses should be included in the calculation of pension expense?

c) What are the *Statement No. 87* requirements for accounting for gains and losses, and are those requirements responsive to the views described in part *b*?

REQUIRED Prepare brief responses to each of the questions raised in the board meeting.

C 16-5. **MINIMUM LIABILITY; PENSIONS** Your friend recently attended an accounting conference that featured a roundtable discussion of important accounting concepts. One participant discussed "financial statement articulation." He said that articulation means that "two classes of financial statement elements include statement of financial position elements and income statement elements. They are related in such a way that elements of the former class are changed by elements of the latter class and, at any time, are their cumulative result." He also stated that "articulation causes financial statements to be fundamentally related. Thus, information appearing on the balance sheet is related to information appearing on the income statement, and vice versa."

Upon returning home, your friend began to study *Statement No. 87,* "Employers' Accounting for Pensions." She noticed that the *Statement* requires that future compensation levels be used to calculate the service cost component of periodic pension expense and to determine the projected benefit obligation for disclosure purposes. (The projected benefit obligation also is used to calculate the interest component of pension expense.) However, she also noticed that the *Statement* requires that a minimum liability, equal to the unfunded accumulated benefit obligation, be recorded and presented in an employer's statement of financial position. Since the projected benefit obligation and some components of pension expense are based on *future* compensation levels, whereas the accumulated benefit obligation and the minimum liability are based on *current* compensation levels, she was puzzled about whether these requirements are consistent with the accounting concepts (especially articulation) presented at the conference.

REQUIRED Draft a brief response to your friend's concerns, explaining the apparent inconsistency. Perhaps you can provide other (nonpension) examples of GAAP where there is a lack of articulation between the financial statements.

C 16-6.

PENSIONS AND OTHER POSTRETIREMENT BENEFITS; A COMPARISON OF CONCEPTS
You recently graduated from a small private college and accepted a position in the accounting and finance department of WebScape, a large computer software company whose common shares are traded on the American Stock Exchange. A few years ago, the company established two postretirement benefit plans for its employees: a defined benefit pension plan and a defined benefit health care plan.

For the past several days, you have been assisting the controller in preparing the income statement expenses and related footnote disclosures related to the company's two postretirement benefit plans. The task has been fairly mechanical in that the company's computer system provides the output, based on the accounting requirements of *Statements No. 87* and *106* and data provided by an actuarial consulting firm.

This morning you and the controller were reviewing the expense numbers and related disclosures. In the course of your review, the controller questions whether the accounting requirements for these two retirement benefit plans are similar in concept. Specifically, the following questions were raised by the controller:

a) What is the similarity between the projected benefit obligation for pensions and the accumulated benefit obligation for other postretirement benefits?

b) From an actuarial standpoint, would the calculation of pension benefits entail more assumptions than the calculation of health care benefits?

c) What is the relationship between the expected postretirement benefit obligation and the accumulated postretirement benefit obligation associated with the health care plan?

d) What is the likely explanation for the fact that the reconciliation schedule for the pension plan contains a transition asset (gain or positive cumulative effect) while the reconciliation schedule for the health care plan contains neither a transition asset nor a transition obligation?

REQUIRED Draft a brief response to each of the questions raised by the company's controller.

EXERCISES Exercises marked with an asterisk (*) refer to Appendix 16–1

E 16-1.

CALCULATING ANNUAL PENSION EXPENSE Ellison Company sponsors a contributory pension plan. In 1998, a total of $180,000 was withheld from employees' paychecks and deposited in the pension fund. In addition, Ellison deposited $400,000 of its own money in the fund in 1998. Actuarial calculations as of the end of 1998 indicated that total pension cost for 1998 was $530,000, including $140,000 of prior service cost amortization. As a result of this information, Ellison contributed an additional $60,000 of its own money to the pension fund in early 1999.

REQUIRED **1.** Distinguish between contributory and noncontributory pension plans.
2. Calculate the amount of pension expense that Ellison should report for 1998.

(AICPA, adapted)

E 16-2.

CALCULATING AND RECORDING PENSION EXPENSE AND FUND CONTRIBUTIONS
Quick Company adopted a pension plan at the beginning of 1998 on a funded, noncontributory basis. Quick uses the delayed recognition approach and amortizes prior service cost over 17 years (the remaining service period of employees granted retroactive benefits). Pension information for 1998 and 1999 is as follows:

	1998	1999
17-year amortization of prior service cost....................	$110,000	$110,000
Interest on projected benefit obligation	149,600	181,568
Funding amount (end of year).................................	528,685	558,685
Return on plan assets.......................................	–0–	42,295
Pension asset/(liability) balance as of 12/31	19,085	48,497

Both the discount rate and the rate of return on plan assets are 8 percent.

REQUIRED **1.** If the service component of pension cost in 1998 was $250,000, what was Quick Company's pension expense for 1998?
2. If the service component of pension cost in 1999 was $280,000, what entry would Quick make in 1999 to record pension expense and funding?

E 16-3.   **FUNDED STATUS OF PENSION PLAN**   Refer to Exercise 16-2.

REQUIRED   Prepare a schedule that reconciles the funded status of the plan with the pension amounts reported on Quick's balance sheet on December 31, 1999.

E 16-4.   **PENSION EXPENSE; RECONCILIATION SCHEDULE**   Percy Company adopted a pension plan for its employees at the beginning of 1998. An actuary provided the following information:

a)   The service cost component for 1998 is $11,000.

b)   Prior service cost at the beginning of 1998 is $70,000.

Management contributed $70,000 to the pension fund at the beginning of 1998. Prior service cost will be amortized over the remaining service period (10 years) for employees given retroactive benefits. The discount rate is 9 percent, and the return on plan assets is 8 percent.

REQUIRED   **1.**   Calculate pension expense for 1998.

2.   Prepare a schedule that reconciles the funded status of Percy's pension plan with the amounts reported in the company's balance sheet at the end of 1998.

E 16-5.   **PENSION EXPENSE; RECONCILIATION SCHEDULE**   Sundy, Inc., adopted a defined benefit pension plan at the beginning of 1998. The following information is available regarding the plan:

a)   Service cost for 1998 is $14,000.

b)   Prior service cost at the beginning of 1998 is $75,000.

Sundy contributed $37,500 to the pension fund at the end of 1998. Prior service cost is to be amortized over the 15-year service period of the employees given retroactive benefits. The discount rate is 8 percent, and the rate of return on pension plan assets is 10 percent.

REQUIRED   **1.**   Calculate pension expense for 1998.

2.   Prepare a schedule reconciling the funded status of Sundy's pension plan with the amounts reported in the company's balance sheet at the end of 1998.

E 16-6.   **PENSION COST COMPONENTS; PENSION WORKSHEET**   Carter Corporation adopted a defined benefit pension plan for its employees. At the plan inception date the projected benefit obligation, arising from credit for prior service and based on an 8 percent discount rate, was $40,000. The annual service cost components for the first two years were $22,000 (year 1) and $27,000 (year 2).

Carter contributed $35,200 to the pension fund at the end of year 1 and $38,696 at the end of year 2. The expected return on plan assets was 10 percent. Prior service cost is to be amortized over five years, which is the remaining service period for employees granted retroactive benefits.

REQUIRED   **1.**   Prepare journal entries to record pension expense for years 1 and 2.

2.   Reconcile the funded status of Carter's pension plan at the end of year 2 with the amounts reported on the corporation's balance sheet at that date.

3.   Prepare a pension worksheet for Carter Corporation for year 2.

E 16-7.   **SERVICE COST AND ACCUMULATED POSTRETIREMENT BENEFIT OBLIGATION**   Darcy Company has a postretirement health care plan for its employees and accounts for the benefit costs according to *Statement No. 106.* Full eligibility for plan benefits is obtained after the employee reaches age 60, provided that the employee has worked for Darcy at least 12 continuous years ending with the full eligibility date. B. Gray was hired by Darcy when she was 40 years old. As of the end of 1998, Gray is 56; she expects to retire when she reaches 62. The expected postretirement benefit obligation for Gray is $60,000 as of the end of 1998 and is expected to be $66,000 at the end of 1999.

REQUIRED   **1.**   Calculate the service cost and accumulated postretirement benefit obligation related to Gray for 1998 and 1999.

2.   If the 2000 accumulated postretirement benefit obligation for Gray is $63,000, what is the 2000 expected postretirement benefit obligation and service cost?

E 16-8.   **SERVICE COST AND ACCUMULATED POSTRETIREMENT BENEFIT OBLIGATION**   The employees of Krupa, Inc., are fully eligible for health care coverage during their retirement years as of the date they retire, provided that they are at least 58 when they retire and have worked for Krupa for at least 15 years. By the end of 1998, employee R. Phel has worked for Krupa for 14 years since the day he was hired. He plans to retire in 8 years, at which time he will be 62. Based on the best information available to Krupa, the expected postretirement benefit obligation for Phel is $58,740 at the end of 1998 and is expected to be $64,020 for 1999 and $69,300 for 2000.

REQUIRED Calculate the 1998, 1999, and 2000 service costs and accumulated postretirement benefit obligations related to R. Phel.

E 16-9. **PENSION EXPENSE; RECONCILIATION SCHEDULE** Several years ago, Mexico Moe's initiated a noncontributory defined benefit pension plan for its employees. On December 31, 1997, the reconciliation of the firm's pension plan funded status with its balance sheet information was as follows:

Projected benefit obligation	**$(100,000)**
Plan assets at fair value	**80,000**
Funded status	**$ (20,000)**
Unrecognized prior service cost	**16,000**
Net pension asset/(liability)	**$ (4,000)**

Information about Mexico Moe's pension plan for the year ending December 31, 1998, is as follows:
a) Service cost component for the year, $15,000.
b) Rate of return on plan assets: expected, 6 percent; actual, 9 percent.
c) Discount rate for projected benefit obligation, 7 percent.
d) Prior service cost is being amortized over a remaining period (from January 1, 1998) of four years.
e) Amount paid to pension plan trustee (amount funded), $22,000. Funding occurred on December 31, 1998.

REQUIRED 1. Calculate Mexico Moe's pension expense for the year ending December 31, 1998.
2. Prepare the journal entry to record pension expense and funding for the year ending December 31, 1998.
3. Prepare a schedule to reconcile the funded status of Mexico Moe's pension plan with the firm's balance sheet information at December 31, 1998.

E 16-10. **USE OF A PENSION WORKSHEET** Refer to E16-9 above. Prepare a pension worksheet for the year ending December 31, 1998.

E 16-11. **PENSION GAINS AND LOSSES** The following table shows the projected benefit obligation (PBO) and fair value of plan assets for Rankin, Inc., for the years 1995–2000:

YEAR ENDING 12/31	PROJECTED PBO	PROJECTED PLAN ASSETS	ACTUAL PBO	ACTUAL PLAN ASSETS	REASONS FOR DIFFERENCE
1995	$100,000	$ 60,000	$100,000	$ 60,000	—
1996	130,000	76,000	130,000	96,000	Actual return > expected return
1997	173,000	123,600	173,000	110,000	Actual return < expected return
1998	225,300	146,960	180,000	180,000	Increased discount rate; actual return > expected return
1999	210,000	220,000	210,000	200,000	Actual return < expected return
2000	245,000	233,000	260,000	233,000	Decreased discount rate

REQUIRED 1. Using the data given for Rankin, Inc., calculate the pension gain or loss for each year.
2. Determine the amount of pension gain or loss amortization for each year, assuming that, at the end of 1995, the average remaining service period for employees expected to receive retirement benefits was 10 years. Rankin uses the corridor approach.
3. Calculate the unrecognized net gain or loss at the end of 2000.

E 16-12. **PENSION GAINS AND LOSSES** Clark Company had a $24,000 net pension gain at the end of 1997, when the projected benefit obligation (PBO) for its pension plan was $140,000 and the fair value of plan assets was $100,000. The following additional data are available for the PBO and fair value of plan assets at the end of 1998 and 1999:

	PROJECTED		ACTUAL	
	PBO	**PLAN ASSETS**	**PBO**	**PLAN ASSETS**
1998	$152,000	$125,000	$152,000	$128,500
1999	164,000	140,000	176,000	140,000

REQUIRED

I. Determine the amount of pension gain or loss amortization for 1998 and 1999. Assume that the average remaining service period of active employees expected to participate in the plan is 10 years in 1998 and 12 years in 1999.

2. What amount of unrecognized net pension gain or loss exists at the end of 1998 and the end of 1999?

E 16-13. **RECORDING PENSION EXPENSE** Simpson, Inc., a calendar-year corporation, adopted a noncontributory pension plan at the beginning of 1998. Simpson used a benefit approach actuarial method and determined the service cost component for 1998 and 1999 to be $35,000 and $36,000, respectively. These amounts were funded at the end of each of those years.

The granting of retroactive benefits gave rise to a projected benefit obligation at the beginning of 1998. Simpson funded this amount, plus accrued interest, in full on December 31, 1998, by contributing $110,000 to the pension fund. Prior service cost is being amortized over a 10-year period, based on the provisions of *Statement No. 87*. The assumed discount rate is 10 percent, as is the expected rate of return on plan assets. A delayed recognition approach is used by Simpson.

REQUIRED Prepare journal entries to record the funding of prior service cost on December 31, 1998, and the pension expense for the years 1998 and 1999. Assume actual experience equaled expectations.

E 16-14. **MINIMUM LIABILITY** Betty Thomas is the only employee covered by her employer's pension plan. Calculation of Betty's expected pension benefits is based on the assumption that the average of her five highest salaries before retirement will be $65,000. At the end of the current year, the average of Betty's five highest salaries to date is $52,000, her projected benefit obligation is $112,001, and pension plan assets related to her pension have a fair value of $34,688. The only account shown by Betty's employer on its current year-end balance sheet related to Betty's pension is a $33,413 net pension liability.

REQUIRED

I. Calculate the minimum liability that the employer must record in the current year with respect to Betty's pension.

2. Prepare any journal entry that is necessary at the end of the current year to recognize the employer's minimum liability.

3. Would the entry made to recognize the employer's minimum liability change if the unrecognized prior service cost at the end of the current year was $20,000?

E 16-15. **PENSION GAINS AND LOSSES** During 1998, Jacobs Company had a $33,000 net pension gain as the result of an unexpected plan asset appreciation. At the end of 1998, the projected benefit obligation (PBO) was $270,000, the fair value of the plan assets was $245,000, and the unrecognized prior service cost was $100,000. Jacob Company amortizes the prior service cost at the rate of $10,000 per year. The average remaining service period of active employees expected to participate in the plan is 9 years in 1998 and 12 years in 1999. The following additional data are available for the end of 1999:

PROJECTED		ACTUAL	
PBO	**PLAN ASSETS**	**PBO**	**PLAN ASSETS**
$300,000	$278,000	$300,000	$280,000

REQUIRED

I. Make any required year-end 1998 entry(ies) related to the net pension gain.

2. Calculate the amount of net pension gain, if any, to be amortized in 1999.

3. Prepare a year-end 1999 schedule that reconciles the net pension asset/(liability) account balance with the funded status of the pension plan.

E 16-16. **CALCULATING PENSION EXPENSE** Early in 1998, Joske Company adopted a noncontributory defined benefit pension plan. Using a 6 percent discount rate, an actuary calculated a $100,000 prior service cost at the plan inception date. The service cost components of net pension cost for the years ended December 31, 1998, 1999, and 2000 were $16,000, $18,000, and $24,000, respectively. The rate of return on plan assets is 8 percent. At the beginning of 2000, the pension plan was amended, resulting in an increase of $36,000 in the projected benefit obligation.

Joske contributed $20,000 to the pension fund at the end of each year. At the plan inception date, the average remaining years of service for employees expected to receive benefits under the plan was 20 years.

REQUIRED   Determine Joske Company's annual pension expense for 1998, 1999, and 2000.

E 16-17.   **PENSIONS: RECONCILIATION SCHEDULE**   Refer to Exercise 16-16.

REQUIRED   Prepare a schedule to reconcile the funded status of Joske's pension plan with the amounts reported on the company's balance sheet at December 31, 2000.

E 16-18.   **CALCULATING PENSION VARIABLES**   The following information relates to the status of a pension plan. For simplicity, assume that only a single employee, Joyce Boatsman, is covered by the plan.

a)   Benefit formula: Annual year-end payment of 2.5 percent of highest year's salary for each year of service (up to a maximum of 100 percent).
b)   Retirement date: December 31, 2000.
c)   Expected date of death: December 31, 2002.
d)   Projected benefit obligation as of January 1, 1998: $19,396.
e)   Fair value of plan assets as of January 1, 1998: $10,000.
f)   Unamortized prior service cost as of January 1, 1998: $9,396.
g)   Interest rate used to calculate benefit obligations: 10 percent.
h)   Employee's years of service as of January 1, 1998: 17.
i)   Salary during 1998: $26,250.
j)   Expected salary during 2000: $35,000.
k)   Earnings on plan assets during 1998: $1,200.
l)   Cash contribution to plan on December 31, 1998: $4,000.

REQUIRED   **1.**   Calculate the projected benefit obligation as of December 31, 1998.
2.   Calculate the accumulated benefit obligation as of December 31, 1998.
3.   Determine the fair value of the plan assets as of December 31, 1998 (after the $4,000 contribution on December 31, 1998).
4.   Calculate pension expense for 1998.
5.   Calculate the minimum liability to be reported on the balance sheet as of December 31, 1998.

E 16-19.   **PENSION EXPENSE COMPONENTS; RECONCILIATION SCHEDULE**   The following information pertains to the defined benefit pension plan of Smyrna Corporation:

Expected rate of return on plan assets	**10%**
Discount rate.	**8%**
Average service life (from 1/1/98).	**12 years**

	1/1/98	12/31/98
Projected benefit obligation	$660,000	$807,000
Fair value of plan assets.	720,000	820,000
Unrecognized prior service cost.	180,000	
Unrecognized pension gain.	108,000	
Net pension asset/(liability)	132,000	

Service cost for the year ending December 31, 1998, was $94,200. No benefits were paid and no contributions were made to the pension plan during 1998.

REQUIRED   **1.**   Calculate Smyrna Corporation's pension expense for the year ending December 31, 1998.
2.   Prepare a schedule to reconcile the funded status of Smyrna's pension plan with its balance sheet amount—net pension asset/(liability)—on December 31, 1998.

E 16-20.   **USE OF A PENSION WORKSHEET**   Refer to the Smyrna Corporation pension information in E16-19.

REQUIRED   Prepare a worksheet to calculate Smyrna's pension expense and to summarize other events related to Smyrna's pension plan for the year ending December 31, 1998.

E 16-21.   **GAIN AND LOSS ON POSTRETIREMENT BENEFIT PLAN**   On the last day of the fifth year following adoption of *Statement No. 106*, Gomer, Inc., determined that it had suffered a plan loss of $30,000 because of changes it had made in some actuarial assumptions. At the beginning of year 6, Gomer had an accumulated postretirement benefit obligation of $238,500, including the plan loss of $30,000, and plan assets with a fair value of $227,800. The average remaining service period of plan participants at the beginning of year 6 was 10 years, and the participant group remained unchanged during years 6 and 7. Near the end of year 6, Gomer had a $3,420 gain on its plan because of better-than-expected returns on its plan assets.

Gomer's service cost was $15,300 for year 6 and $14,900 for year 7. Year 6 and year 7 cash payments by Gomer were $14,000 and $16,200, respectively. In both years cash payments were exactly equal to benefit payments. In years 6 and 7, both the discount rate and the rate of return on plan assets were 8 percent.

REQUIRED   Calculate the amount, if any, of Gomer's loss or gain on its postretirement benefit plan that should be recognized in its year 5, year 6, and year 7 financial statements, assuming that Gomer uses the corridor approach.

*E 16-22.   **CALCULATING NET GAIN OR LOSS FROM CURTAILMENT OF A PENSION PLAN**   Listed below are four cases involving curtailment of a pension plan:

		CASE		
ITEM	**1**	**2**	**3**	**4**
Projected benefit obligation				
decrease (increase) from transition	$ 90,000	$ 80,000	$(65,000)	$ 90,000
Unrecognized net asset at transition				
plus unrecognized gain (loss).	60,000	(55,000)	(20,000)	(95,000)
Loss from reduced prior service cost				
(including net obligation at transition).	(25,000)	(35,000)	(20,000)	(29,000)

REQUIRED   For each case, calculate the net gain or loss from curtailment.

*E 16-23.   **PENSION SETTLEMENT, CURTAILMENT, TERMINATION**   Easton, Inc., sponsors a noncontributory defined benefit plan for its employees. The following pension disclosure appeared in the notes to Easton's financial statements for the year ending December 31, 1998:

Accumulated benefit obligation:		
Vested	$(90,000)	
Nonvested	(60,000)	$(150,000)
Effects of future compensation levels		(30,000)
Projected benefit obligation		$(180,000)
Plan assets at fair value		120,000
Unrecognized net asset at transition		(20,000)
Unrecognized prior service cost		50,000
Unrecognized net loss		38,000
Net pension asset/(liability)		$ 8,000

Consider each of the following situations separately.

A)   Assume that on January 1, 1999, Easton, Inc., settled the vested portion of the accumulated benefit obligation by using plan assets to purchase annuity contracts for employees covered by the plan.

REQUIRED   Prepare the journal entry to record the settlement.

B)   Assume that on January 1, 1999, Easton, Inc., terminated several of its employees. The termination resulted in the following:

   a)   Nonvested accumulated benefits were reduced by $20,000.

   b)   Projected benefits from future compensation levels were reduced by $12,000.

   c)   Unrecognized prior service cost associated with the terminated employees was $15,000.

REQUIRED   Prepare the journal entry to record the plan curtailment.

   C)   Assume that on January 1, 1999, Easton, Inc., terminated its pension plan. Nonvested accumulated benefits became vested upon termination. Pension plan assets and Easton's cash were used to pay a lump-sum settlement to employees covered by the plan. The plan then ceased to exist and was not replaced with another plan.

REQUIRED   Prepare the journal entry to record termination of the pension plan.

PROBLEMS	The problem marked with an asterisk (*) refers to Appendix 16–1.

Problems 16-1 through 16-4 are intended to increase your familiarity with and understanding of several important pension concepts. The employee data used in Problems 16-1 through 16-4 (see below) are single-employee data for the sake of simplicity. Problems 16-1 through 16-4 can be worked as a group or as independent problems.

Pension Plan Data and Employee Data
For Problems 16-1 through 16-4

PENSION PLAN DATA
a)   Defined benefit, noncontributory pension plan.
b)   Retirement benefits paid at year-end, with the first payment one year after retirement.
c)   Assumed discount rate is 8 percent.
d)   Pension plan formula is:

Annual retirement benefit $= .014 \times n \times$ Highest salary level

where n equals the number of years of service that qualify for pension credit, subject to a maximum of 30 years.

DATA FOR A PARTICULAR EMPLOYEE
e)   Retirement age of 62.
f)   Expected retirement period of 18 years.
g)   Employee is 40 years old when the plan is adopted.
h)   Employee began working for the company at age 38.
i)   Various salary levels for the employee:

AGE	SALARY LEVEL
38	$12,000
40	15,000
44	18,500
45	20,000
62	64,000

P 16-1.   **PENSION COST COMPONENTS; SERVICE COST AND INTEREST**   Assume the pension plan and employee data given above and assume that no credit is given for service before adoption of the plan.

REQUIRED
1.   Draw a diagram similar to the one on page 851 to show the relationship between the pension plan and the employment and retirement life of the employee.
2.   Calculate the estimated annual retirement benefit at the time of retirement.
3.   Calculate the projected benefit obligation at the time of retirement.
4.   Calculate the service cost and interest cost components of pension cost for years 1 and 2.
5.   Calculate pension expense for years 1 and 2, assuming $1,200 contributions to the pension fund at the end of each year. The expected and actual rate of return on plan assets was 10 percent.

P 16-2.   **PENSION COST COMPONENTS; PRIOR SERVICE COST**   Using the pension plan and employee data given before Problem 16-1, assume that pension credit is given for up to five years of service before adoption of the pension plan.

REQUIRED
1.   Explain how prior service cost is related to the service cost component of pension expense.
2.   Calculate the expected annual retirement benefit arising from prior service credit.
3.   Calculate the projected benefit obligation at the plan inception date.
4.   Calculate the amount of prior service cost amortization that would be included in pension expense each year.

P 16-3. **PENSION PLAN AMENDMENTS** Assume (1) the pension plan and employee data that are given before Problem 16-1, (2) pension credit is given for up to five years of service before adoption of the plan, and (3) five years after adoption, the plan benefit formula was amended to:

Annual retirement benefit = .021 × n × Highest salary level

REQUIRED   1. Discuss the impact of the plan amendment on (*a*) the annual expected retirement benefit and (*b*) the projected benefit obligation at the amendment date.

2. Calculate the projected benefit obligation at the amendment date based on the amended plan formula.

3. Calculate the amount of prior service cost amortization that would be included in pension expense each year following the amendment date.

P 16-4. **PENSIONS; ACCUMULATED BENEFIT OBLIGATION AND MINIMUM LIABILITY** Both *Statement No. 87* (employers' accounting for pensions) and *Statement No. 35* (accounting and reporting by the pension plan) require information about accumulated plan benefits. Therefore, an understanding of accumulated plan benefits, sometimes called the accumulated benefit obligation, and of the relationship between the accumulated benefit obligation and the projected benefit obligation is very important.

Assume (1) the pension plan and employee data given prior to Problem 16-1, (2) credit is given for a maximum of five years of service before the plan's adoption, and (3) a benefit information (actuarial valuation) date four years after adoption of the plan.

REQUIRED   1. Distinguish between the accumulated benefit obligation and the projected benefit obligation.

2. Calculate the accumulated plan benefit per year of retirement, as of the benefit information date.

3. Calculate the accumulated benefit obligation, as of the benefit information date.

4. *Statement No. 87* requires the recording, at the balance sheet date, of a minimum liability at least equal to the unfunded accumulated benefit obligation. Calculate the minimum liability, as of the benefit information date, assuming that the fair value of plan assets was $2,500 at that date.

5. Refer to part 4. Prepare the journal entry, if any, to record the minimum liability, assuming that at the benefit information date the employer's balance sheet showed a net pension asset of $650.

P 16-5. **PENSION COST COMPONENTS** Swenson Company adopted a noncontributory defined benefit pension plan on December 31, 1997, for three of its employees: John Davis, Sharon Estes, and Sue Manor. The plan benefit formula specified annual retirement benefit payments equal to 1 percent of each employee's highest salary received before retirement, multiplied by the number of years of service qualifying for pension credit. Under the new plan, Swenson Company gave each employee retroactive pension credit for all years of service prior to December 31, 1997. As of December 31, 1997, the highest salary each employee received was Davis, $42,000; Estes, $47,000; and Manor, $39,000. The highest salary expected to be paid to each before retirement is Davis, $57,000; Estes, $63,000; and Manor, $51,000.

John Davis and Sharon Estes began working for Swenson Company on January 1, 1989, and Sue Manor joined Swenson one year later. All three employees are expected to retire at the end of 2000. Each is expected to receive retirement payments until 2010, with the first retirement payment occurring on December 31, 2001.

Other data related to the pension plan are:

a) Expected return on plan assets is 8 percent.

b) Assumed discount rate is 6 percent.

c) Funding of the plan each year will equal net pension cost, less amortization of prior service cost.

d) Prior service cost will be funded in full on December 31, 2000.

e) The pension fund is administered by an outside trustee, and at the retirement date an annuity contract will be purchased to settle all pension obligations to Davis, Estes, and Manor.

f) Swenson will use the delayed recognition approach permitted by *Statement No. 87*.

REQUIRED   1. Calculate prior service cost as of December 31, 1997.

2. Calculate pension expense for 1998 and 1999.

3. Prepare all necessary journal entries for Swenson Company for 1998 and 1999.

4. Reconcile the funded status of Swenson's pension plan with its balance sheet amount on December 31, 1999.

P 16-6. **PENSION COST COMPONENTS; NON-PAY-RELATED PLAN** On December 31, 1997, Browner Corporation initiated a noncontributory defined benefit pension plan for all six employees in its word processing department. (Employees in other departments already were covered by a pension plan.) The plan benefit formula provides that each year of service earns each employee an annual retirement benefit of $3,000. The benefits are payable at the end of each retirement year. All six employees are expected to retire on December 31, 2002, and each is expected to live for four years following retirement.

Browner also provided retroactive benefits for employee services rendered prior to December 31, 1997. Total years of service for which retroactive benefits were granted equaled 20 years. Arrangements were made for an outside trustee to administer all aspects of the plan on Browner's behalf.

The following additional data are pertinent:
a) Expected return on plan assets is 10 percent.
b) Discount rate applicable to the projected benefit obligation is 8 percent.
c) Browner will contribute $73,979 to the pension fund each year, which, together with earnings at 10 percent, will fully fund the projected benefit obligation by December 31, 2002. Browner will make five annual contributions, beginning on December 31, 1997. Browner will purchase an annuity contract on December 31, 2002, to settle its pension obligation.
d) Browner uses the delayed recognition approach permitted by *Statement No. 87.* Assume that actual results equal the original estimates and assumptions, and that Browner's fiscal year ends on December 31.

REQUIRED
1. Draw a time diagram similar to the one on page 851 to show the relationship between the pension plan and the employment and retirement life of Browner's employees. (Be sure to show the total amount of benefits expected to be paid each year over the employees' retirement period.)
2. Calculate prior service cost on December 31, 1997.
3. Calculate pension expense for 1998, 1999, and 2000.
4. Prepare all necessary entries for 1998, 1999, and 2000.
5. Prepare a schedule that reconciles the funded status of Browner's pension plan with Browner's pension-related balance sheet amounts at the end of 2000.

P 16-7. **PENSION COST COMPONENTS; PLAN AMENDMENTS** Refer to Problem 16-6. Assume that on January 1, 2001, Browner amended the plan by increasing the annual retirement benefits to $3,450 for each year of service. Browner made no changes in the contributions to the pension fund. All other problem data remain the same.

REQUIRED
1. Calculate pension expense for 2001.
2. Prepare (*a*) all necessary journal entries for 2001 and (*b*) a schedule reconciling funded status with Browner's balance sheet amounts at December 31, 2001.

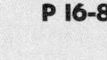

P 16-8. **PENSION COST COMPONENTS; PLAN ASSET GAIN** Refer to Problem 16-6. Assume that on December 31, 2000, the fair value of the pension plan assets was $390,000. During 2001 and 2002, however, the plan assets continued to earn a 10 percent rate of return. All other problem data remain the same.

REQUIRED
1. Calculate the gain or loss on plan assets for the year ending December 31, 2000.
2. Calculate Browner's pension expense for 2000 and 2001.
3. Prepare schedules to reconcile the funded status of Browner's pension plan with Browner's pension-related balance sheet amounts at December 31, 2000 and 2001.

P 16-9. **PENSION COST COMPONENTS; JOURNAL ENTRIES** When Richmond Corporation adopted its defined benefit pension plan, the projected benefit obligation arising from the grant of retroactive benefits to employees was $180,000, based on a benefit approach and an 8 percent discount rate. The service cost component of pension cost was $30,000 for year 1 and $35,000 for year 2. The following amounts were contributed to the pension fund at the end of each year: year 1, $40,000; year 2, $40,000. The rate of return on plan assets is 8 percent. The average remaining period of service for employees expected to receive benefits under the plan was 15 years. Richmond uses the delayed recognition approach permitted by *Statement No. 87.*

REQUIRED
1. Prepare the necessary journal entries in Richmond Corporation's books for years 1 and 2.
2. Indicate the accounts and amounts related to the pension plan that would appear on Richmond's balance sheet and income statement for year 1.

3. Prepare a schedule to reconcile the funded status of Richmond's pension plan with the amounts reported on the corporation's balance sheet at the end of year 2.

P 16-10. **PENSIONS; GAINS AND LOSSES; MINIMUM LIABILITY**   Koning Corporation, a calendar-year company, adopted a noncontributory defined benefit pension plan on January 1, 1998. The pension plan granted retroactive benefits for prior service. On the basis of the plan benefit formula, Koning's actuarial consultants used a "benefit/years-of-service" method and a 10 percent discount rate, and determined that the projected benefit obligation at the plan inception date was $300,000. This amount is to be amortized over a 16-year period, which, at the inception date, was the average remaining service period for employees expected to receive benefits under the plan. The employee group remained unchanged through 1999. Koning uses a delayed recognition approach in accounting for pensions.

Management decided to fund the service cost component of pension cost at the end of each year. Prior service cost would be funded by a $100,000 contribution to the pension fund's trustee at the beginning of 1998, followed by $23,491 payments at the end of each year for 20 years for the $200,000 balance. The rate of return on plan assets is expected to be 10 percent. The actuarial consultants and Koning's accountants provided the following information related to the pension plan for the years ending December 31, 1998 and 1999:

	1998	1999
Pension service cost component	$85,000	$90,000
Amortization of prior service cost	18,750	18,750
Funding of prior service cost	23,491	23,491

No changes in assumptions were necessary during the first two years. Actual results equaled the original estimates, except that during 1998 there was a $50,000 loss, which resulted from write-downs of plan assets to market value.

REQUIRED   **I.** Calculate pension expense for 1998 and 1999.
2. Prepare all necessary journal entries for Koning Corporation for both years.
3. Show how Koning's footnote disclosure of pension expense would appear for 1998.
4. **a)** Calculate the balance in the net pension asset/(liability) account after the 1999 journal entry in part 2.

b) Assume that on December 31, 1999, employees' accumulated plan benefits equaled 60 percent of the projected benefit obligation. Prepare any necessary entry for Koning Corporation to record the minimum liability at that date.
5. Prepare a schedule that reconciles the funded status of Koning's pension plan with amounts appearing on the corporation's balance sheet at December 31, 1999.

P 16-11. **PENSION COST; MINIMUM LIABILITY**   Darton, Inc., initiated a noncontributory defined benefit pension plan on January 1, 1998. The plan granted credit for prior service, resulting in a projected benefit obligation and a prior service of $375,000 on the plan inception date, at which time the average remaining service period for active plan participants was 15 years. The employee group remained unchanged for several years following the inception date.

Darton decided to fund service cost at the end of each year. Prior service cost was to be funded by a $75,000 deposit on the inception date and equal year-end payments of $35,049, beginning on December 31, 1998. The discount rate used for actuarial calculations is 10 percent, and the rate of return on plan assets is expected to be 8 percent. Other information related to the plan for 1998 and 1999 follows:

	1998	1999
Service cost	$106,250	$112,500
Amortization of prior service cost	25,000	25,000

No changes in assumptions were required during 1998 and 1999. The actual benefit obligation and plan assets were the same as the expected benefit obligation and plan assets for both years.

REQUIRED   **I.** Calculate the 1998 and 1999 pension expense for Darton.
2. Prepare all necessary journal entries for 1998 and 1999.

3. **a)** Calculate the balance in the net pension asset/(liability) account after the 1999 journal entry in part 2.

   b) Assume that the 1999 accumulated benefit obligation is 65 percent of the projected benefit obligation. Prepare any necessary journal entry to adjust to the minimum liability for Darton as of the end of 1999.

4. Prepare a schedule to reconcile pension plan amounts with amounts appearing on Darton's 1999 balance sheet.

P 16-12. **PENSION WORKSHEET; ANALYSIS OF RECONCILIATION SCHEDULES** Assume that you are given the following fiscal year-end reconciliation schedules of Searfoss Corporation for years 1998 and 1999:

	1999	1998
Actuarial present value of benefit obligations:		
Vested benefit obligation	$(620)	$(568)
Accumulated benefit obligation	$(803)	$(702)
Projected benefit obligation	$(959)	$(820)
Plan assets at fair value	767	650
Excess of projected benefit obligation over plan assets	$(192)	$(170)
Unrecognized prior service cost	144	156
Unrecognized net loss (gain)	33	(5)
Net pension asset/(liability)	$ (15)	$ (19)

The discount rate used to calculate the projected benefit obligation is 9 percent for both years. The expected long-run rate of return for both years is 10 percent. The service cost for 1999 is $25, and the actual return on plan assets for 1999 is $98.

REQUIRED

1. Prepare a pension worksheet for Searfoss Corporation's pension transactions and events for 1999 that will also explain all changes in the reconciliation schedules above.

2. Calculate the minimum liability for Searfoss at the end of each year.

P 16-13. **PENSION COST COMPONENTS; PENSION WORKSHEET** A schedule that reconciles the funded status of Darlene's pension plan with the amount reported on the company's balance sheet at the beginning and end of the current year appears below:

	BEGINNING	END
Projected benefit obligation	$(400,000)	$(478,000)
Plan assets at fair value	285,000	387,800
Funded status	$(115,000)	$ (90,200)
Unrecognized prior service cost	60,000	54,000
Unrecognized net gain	(50,000)	(49,000)
Net pension asset/(liability)	$(105,000)	$ (85,200)

Darlene recorded pension expense for the current year as follows:

Pension expense	60,200	
Net pension asset/(liability)	19,800	
Cash		80,000

No retirement payments were made during the year. Actual results for the current year equaled expectations, and there were no changes in assumptions. The service cost component of pension expense was $50,000.

REQUIRED Prepare a pension worksheet for Darlene.

*P 16-14. **SETTLEMENT OF A PENSION OBLIGATION** Refer to Problem 16-13. Assume that the plan benefit formula was based on future compensation levels. At the end of the current year, Darlene settled a $358,500 portion of the fully vested accumulated benefit obligation by using plan assets to purchase annuity contracts on its employees' behalf.

REQUIRED Prepare the entry to record the settlement.

P 16-15. **EPBO; APBO; POSTRETIREMENT BENEFIT COST** On January 1, 1998, Lonigan was organized and adopted a postretirement health plan for its employees. All of Lonigan's employees are 55 years of age and, under the terms of the plan, are eligible for full retirement benefits upon reaching age 60. Based on actuarial assumptions, the expected postretirement benefit obligation on January 1, 1998, was $500,000. The discount rate was 10 percent. Lonigan did not fund any of its postretirement benefit obligation until the end of 2002, at which time it funded the entire required amount.

REQUIRED
1. Prepare a schedule showing the expected postretirement benefit obligation, the service cost, and the accumulated postretirement benefit obligation for the years 1998–2002.
2. Prepare a schedule showing the calculation of Lonigan's postretirement benefit expense for 1998 through 2002.

P 16-16.   PENSIONS: COMPREHENSIVE On January 1, 1996, Sailer Company had a net pension asset of $600,000, and the funded status of the plan at that date was as follows:

Projected benefit obligation	$(1,400,000)
Plan assets at fair value	1,800,000
Funded status..	$ 400,000

Except for unrecognized prior service costs, there were no other unrecognized pension plan elements on January 1, 1996.

Financial data relating to the pension plan for the years 1996–1999 are as follows:

	1996	1997	1998	1999
Service cost component	$ 82,000	$ 86,400	$111,974	$121,870
Fund contributions (beginning of each year)............	80,000	90,000	159,000	100,000
Retirement payments by fund (end of each year).................	155,000	180,000	240,000	265,000
Plan asset loss	–0–	225,000	–0–	–0–
Liability gain (decrease in projected benefit obligation)	–0–	–0–	90,000	–0–

The expected return on plan assets was 10 percent, and the discount rate applicable to the projected benefit obligation was 8 percent. These estimates and assumptions were realized, except for the gain and loss above. On December 31, 1998, an amendment to the plan increased the projected benefit obligation by 20 percent. As of January 1, 1996, the average remaining service period for employees expected to receive plan benefits was 20 years. There were no changes in the employee group during the 1996–1999 period.

REQUIRED
1. Reconcile the funded status of Sailer's pension plan with the company's pension-related balance sheet amount on January 1, 1996.
2. Calculate the projected benefit obligation and the plan assets on December 31 for each of the four years above.
3. Prepare all necessary journal entries for Sailer Company for each year.
4. Prepare the footnote disclosure for fiscal years 1997 and 1998, showing the components of pension expense reported on Sailer's income statement.
5. Prepare the footnote disclosure that reconciles the funded status of Sailer's pension plan with amounts reported on the company's December 31, 1999, balance sheet.
6. Assume that the accumulated benefit obligation at December 31, 1999, is $1.5 million. Will Sailer be required to record a minimum liability? Explain.

P 16-17.   PENSIONS; IMMEDIATE RECOGNITION VERSUS DELAYED RECOGNITION At the beginning of 1998, Stet LLP adopted a defined benefit pension plan for its employees. Stet gave retroactive credit for prior service, resulting in $400,000 of prior service cost at the beginning of 1998.

Shortly after adopting the pension plan, Stet's controller resigned. Willie Chakraborty, a recent graduate of Arkoma State University, was appointed as the temporary controller and was placed in charge of accounting for Stet's pension plan. When Chakraborty attended college, his accounting instructors believed that students should be taught concepts, not simply existing practice. In the words of one of his professors, "Concepts never change; practices become obsolete overnight." As a result, Chakraborty was taught that pension accounting should follow a theoretical, immediate recognition approach (consistent with the integration view of the nature of pension assets and liabilities).

During 1998, Chakraborty made the following pension entries upon receipt of information from the plan trustee and actuarial company about Stet's pension plan:

Intangible asset	400,000	
Projected benefit obligation		400,000
To record prior service cost.		
Pension expense	50,000	
Projected benefit obligation		50,000
To record service cost and interest.		
Plan assets	120,000	
Cash		120,000
To record funding.		
Plan assets	18,000	
Pension expense		18,000
To record the actual return on plan assets (the expected return was $22,000).		
Pension expense	20,000	
Intangible asset		20,000
To record amortization of prior service cost.		
Pension expense	15,000	
Projected benefit obligation		15,000
To record a change in actuarial assumptions.		
Projected benefit obligation	35,000	
Intangible asset		35,000
To record a plan amendment at the end of 1998.		
Projected benefit obligation	430,000	
Plan assets		138,000
Net pension asset (liability)		292,000
To offset the PBO against plan assets for balance sheet reporting.		

The recording of these pension transactions under the immediate recognition approach had the following effects on Stet's financial statements for the year ending December 31, 1998:

INCOME STATEMENT FOR THE YEAR:	DR	CR
Pension expense	$ 67,000	
Balance sheet, end of year:		
Cash		$120,000
Intangible asset	345,000	
Net pension asset (liability)		292,000
Totals	$412,000	$412,000

When these financial statement effects were presented to Stet's CFO, she was horrified. She feared that pension expense for the year might not be representative of future years' pension expense because of the gains and losses that were included. She was especially upset at the balance sheet results. She stated, "The intangible asset gives us no help. Stock market analysts ignore these kinds of 'soft assets.' The pension obligation of $292,000 is even worse. It will kill our debt/equity ratio. Let's see if a delayed recognition approach permitted by *Statement No. 87* will make us look better."

REQUIRED
1. Reconstruct the income statement and balance sheet effects shown above, assuming that Stet uses a delayed recognition approach to account for its pension activities.
2. Prepare the journal entry or entries necessary to adjust Stet's accounts to a delayed recognition approach permitted by *Statement No. 87*.
3. Based on your solutions in parts 1 and 2 above, prepare a schedule to reconcile the funded status of Stet's pension plan with the amount that should be reported on its balance sheet under a delayed recognition approach.

4. Do you believe that analysts would evaluate Stet differently under a delayed recognition approach versus an immediate recognition approach in accounting for its pension activities? Give reasons for your answer.

P 16-18. **FINANCIAL REPORTING PROBLEM: RECONCILIATION SCHEDULE; PENSION DISCLOSURES** Alusuisse-Lonza Holding Ltd. is a multinational corporation headquartered in Zurich, Switzerland. The company manufactures and sells a wide range of chemicals, aluminum, and packaging materials. The following information about retirement benefits appeared in the accounting principles and footnotes sections of Alusuisse-Lonza's annual report for the year ending December 31, 1995:

Retirement benefits

Most of the subsidiaries operate their own pension schemes, mainly legally independent from the Group. Generally, they are funded by employees' and employer's contributions.

The Group adopted the revised IAS 19 for pension plans as of 1 January 1995 and performed actuarial valuations as of this date. The cumulative effect of the change in accounting principle is disclosed in the notes as a transitional amount and will be recognised as an asset or liability respectively, over a period not exceeding the expected remaining working lives of the participating employees.

31. Pension benefits

The Group sponsors pension plans according to the national regulations of the countries in which it operates. All significant plans provide defined benefits on retirement. The benefits are primarily based on years of service and the employee's compensation for certain periods during the last years of employment.

As of 1 January 1995 the Group has adopted the revised IAS 19 Retirement Benefit Costs. As of this date, actuarial valuations were performed for all significant defined benefit plans using the "projected unit credit" method. The cumulative effect of this change in accounting policy resulted in a net excess of plan assets over projected benefit obligations. This transitional amount of Sfr. 10 million has not been recorded as an asset in the Group's accounts but will be recognized over a period not exceeding the expected remaining working lives of the participating employees. The long-term provisions for retirement benefits relating to the Group's German subsidiaries have been included in this calculation.

A policy has been established whereby actuarial valuations will be performed on a three-year basis and roll forwards will be conducted as at 31 December each year during the intervening period.

The assumptions used in the actuarial valuations are according to the underlying national economic conditions of the respective countries as follows:

Discount rate 5.0%	to	9.5%
Expected long-term rates of return on plan assets 5.0%	to	9.0%
Rates of increase in compensation levels 3.0%	to	5.5%

Except for the Group's German subsidiaries, pension costs are funded on an ongoing basis within national regulatory limitations. The projected benefit obligation for the German subsidiaries is included in the table below. The funded status of the major defined benefit plans, shown separately for plans whose assets exceed and are less than the projected benefit obligation, is as follows:

IN MILLION SFR.	12/31/95 PLANS WITH ASSETS IN EXCESS OF PBO	12/31/95 PLANS WITH PBO IN EXCESS OF ASSETS
Projected benefits obligation (PBO) ...	(1567)	(1225)
Plan assets at fair value	1688	918
Plan assets in excess of (less than) projected benefit obligation	121	(307)
Long-term provisions for retirement benefits.............	—	196
Unrecognized transitional amount	121	(111)

Net periodic pension cost for the Group's significant defined benefit plans consists of the following:

	1995 IN MILLION SFR.
Service costs	48
Interest costs	162
Actual return on plan assets...........................	(152)
Net amortization and deferral	6
Total	64

REQUIRED

1. What kind of pension plan does Alusuisse-Lonza have for its employees?
2. How would you describe the manner in which employee retirement benefits are determined—for example, pay-related versus non-pay-related?
3. How does the discount rate used to calculate the projected benefit obligation compare with the expected long-term rate of return on plan assets?
4. Briefly discuss the funded status of Alusuisse-Lonza's pension plans.
5. In the schedule to reconcile the funded status of Alusuisse-Lonza's pension plans with the amount(s) reported on the company's balance sheet, explain how the unrecognized amounts will affect pension expense in future periods.
6. Compare the components of pension expense disclosed by Alusuisse-Lonza with the components of pension expense discussed in this chapter.
7. What events probably make up the "net amortization and deferral" portion of pension expense?
8. In general, comment on the similarity between *Statement No. 87* issued by the FASB and *IAS No. 19* issued by the International Accounting Standards Committee.

P 16-19. **FINANCIAL REPORTING RESEARCH PROBLEM** As pension benefits are a form of deferred compensation, one would normally expect companies to report pension expense from applying the accounting and reporting requirements of *Statement No. 87*. However, a large number of companies, including General Electric, whose annual report appears in Appendix B at the end of the text, have reported pension income (negative pension expense) over the past several years.

REQUIRED

1. Obtain access to a financial information database, such as *Lexis (NAARS)* or *Disclosure,* or to other data sources, such as *Accounting Trends and Techniques.* Study the pension disclosures of a sample of several companies whose financial statements and notes appear in these databases. (Include General Electric's pension disclosures, which appear in Appendix B at the end of the text, in your group of companies.)
2. Write a short report that summarizes the percentage of companies that report pension expense compared to the percentage of companies that report pension income. For the companies that report pension income, include in your report a brief analysis of which of the pension cost components resulted in the reporting of pension income instead of pension expense.

PHILLIPS PETROLEUM RETIREE BENEFIT CASE

Phillips Petroleum Company was founded in 1917 in Bartlesville, Oklahoma. Its businesses include petroleum exploration, production, refining, and marketing; natural gas gathering, processing, and marketing; and chemical production and distribution. Approximately 17 percent of its revenue in 1995 was generated outside the United States. In 1995, Phillips Petroleum had total revenues of $13,521 million, net income of $469 million, and total assets of $11,978 million. Phillips Petroleum also had 17,400 employees at the end of 1995.

Answer the following questions using the information in the accompanying financial statement excerpts. All questions refer to 1995 and the U.S. plans unless otherwise indicated and dollar amounts are in millions of dollars.

1. Explain why the funded status of the plan is different from the balance sheet amount.

2. The components of pension cost show a deferred gain of $57. Explain why this amount is added to pension cost.

3. Reconstruct the journal entry that was made to record pension cost and the contributions during 1995. Ignore the information below the reconciliation that relates to plan contributions. *Hint:* The change in "Prepaid (accrued) pension cost" is a debit of $6.

4. The change in the "Projected benefit obligation" can be analyzed as follows:

Beginning balance	$503
Service cost	26
Interest cost	48
Actuarial loss	205
Benefits paid to retirees	(22)
Ending balance	$760

By looking at information in the footnote, explain one cause of the $205 actuarial loss.

5. Using information from your answers above and the pension footnote, prepare analyses similar to the one for the "Projected benefit obligation" in part 4 for "Plan assets at fair value" and "Unrecognized net (gains) losses."

6. Refer to the "Other Postretirement Plans" note. Why is there zero return in the computation of retiree health plan expense?

7. Compare the reconciliations for pension plans and retiree health plans. Explain why the "Unrecognized prior service cost" reconciling items have different signs in the two reconciliations.

8. Explain how investors can use information in the pension and other postretirement plan notes to help them evaluate Phillips Petroleum's financial position or earnings potential.

Note 12 — Employee Benefit Plans
Defined Benefit Plans

The company has defined benefit retirement plans covering substantially all employees. The plans are generally non-contributory, with benefit formulas based on employee earnings and credited service.

Net pension cost was:

	Millions of Dollars					
	U.S. Plans			Foreign Plans		
	1995	1994	1993	**1995**	1994	1993
Service cost	**$ 26**	30	32	**14**	14	12
Interest cost	48	43	42	**18**	15	16
Return on assets						
Actual	**(86)**	2	4	**(36)**	(2)	(41)
Deferred gains (losses)	**57**	(30)	(36)	**14**	(14)	24
Amortization of						
Net asset	**(7)**	(7)	(7)	**—**	—	—
Net losses (gains)	**8**	12	8	**(1)**	1	—
Prior service cost	**3**	2	2	**1**	—	1
Net pension cost	**$ 49**	52	45	**10**	14	12

In determining net pension cost, Phillips has elected to amortize net gains and losses on a straight-line basis over 10 years. A table showing the funded status of the plans and a reconciliation with accrued pension cost and deferred gain on reversion at December 31 follows:

	Millions of Dollars			
	U.S. Plans		Foreign Plans	
	1995	1994	**1995**	1994
Plan assets at fair value	**$ 380**	261	**300**	246
Actuarial present value of benefit obligations				
Vested benefits	**439**	306	**193**	161
Non-vested benefits	**31**	18	**—**	—
Accumulated benefit obligation	**470**	324	**193**	161
Effect of projected future salary increases	**290**	179	**77**	69
Projected benefit obligation	**760**	503	**270**	230
Excess asset (obligation)	**(380)**	(242)	**30**	16
Unrecognized net asset	**(34)**	(41)	**(1)**	(1)
Unrecognized net (gains) losses	**191**	51	**(16)**	(9)
Unrecognized prior service cost	**35**	38	**9**	9
Prepaid (accrued) pension cost and deferred gain on reversion	**$ (188)**	(194)	**22**	15

Assumptions — Weighted Average at December 31

Rate of compensation increase	**4.25%**	4.25	**4.00**	4.20
Discount rate	**7.25**	8.75	**7.50**	7.70
Long-term rate of return on assets	**10.75**	11.25	**8.20**	8.50

The plan assets reflected in the above table include a participating annuity contract, commingled funds, real estate, stocks, bonds and insurance contracts. A foreign plan also holds employee home mortgage loans.

The accumulated benefit obligation reflected above includes $50 million and $36 million at December 31, 1995 and 1994, respectively, for supplemental retirement plans that are not qualified under the Employee Retirement Income Security Act of 1974 (ERISA). These non-qualified plans are funded by an irrevocable grantor trust, not out of the plan assets reflected in the above schedule. The plan assets shown above do not reflect contributions in 1996 and 1995 for plan years 1995 and 1994, respectively. After adding plan asset contributions of $42 million for the 1995 plan year and $30 million for the 1994 plan year, which are paid in the following year, and eliminating the non-qualified plan obligations that are not payable from plan assets, the plan assets exceed accumulated plan liabilities for both years.

For U.S. plans that are qualified under ERISA, which includes the company's primary retirement plan for employees, the company's funding policy is to contribute at least the minimum required by ERISA. The contribution requirements are determined by an independent actuary using actuarial assumptions and asset valuation techniques allowed by ERISA and generally accepted in the actuarial profession as appropriate for funding purposes. These ERISA funding calculations differ in some important respects from the assumptions and techniques required by financial accounting rules used to prepare the information in the above table. However, the company's qualified U.S. retirement plans have assets that exceed the value of the liabilities accumulated to date when valued under either set of requirements. For the foreign plans, the value of plan assets is also generally larger than the accumulated benefit obligation. Contributions to foreign plans are dependent upon local laws and tax regulations and, in most cases, are shared by co-venturers.

Other Postretirement Plans

Company plans provide certain health care and life insurance benefits for substantially all retired U.S. employees. The health care plan is contributory, while the life insurance plan is non-contributory. Retirees covered by the health care plan essentially pay their own way, except those persons who retired prior to March 1986 and early retirees not yet eligible for Medicare. The company's policy is to fund the health care plan in amounts sufficient to cover current claims. The life insurance plan is funded based on actuarial determinations.

Net postretirement benefit cost was:

| | Millions of Dollars | | | | | |
| | Health | | | Life | | |
	1995	1994	1993	**1995**	1994	1993
Service cost	**$ 2**	2	2	**1**	1	1
Interest cost	**6**	8	9	**4**	4	4
Return on assets						
Actual	—	—	—	**(2)**	(2)	(2)
Deferred losses	—	—	—	**—**	(1)	(1)
Amortization of						
Net losses	**1**	—	2	**1**	—	1
Prior service cost	**(4)**	—	—	**(1)**	—	—
Net postretirement benefit cost	**$ 5**	10	13	**3**	2	3

In determining net postretirement benefit cost, the company has elected to amortize net gains and losses on a straight-line basis over 10 years.

The following table shows the funded status of the plans and a reconciliation with accrued postretirement benefit cost at December 31.

| | Millions of Dollars | | | |
| | Health | | Life | |
	1995	1994	**1995**	1994
Accumulated postretirement benefit obligation (APBO)				
Retirees	**$ 68**	53	**52**	35
Fully eligible active participants	**9**	11	**4**	3
Other active participants	**11**	10	**4**	2
	88	74	**60**	40
Plan assets at fair value, held under a reserve deposit contract	**—**	—	**34**	35
APBO in excess of plan assets	**(88)**	(74)	**(26)**	(5)
Unrecognized net (gains) losses	**9**	(2)	**15**	(2)
Unrecognized prior service cost	**(17)**	(21)	**(4)**	(4)
Accrued postretirement benefit cost	**$(96)**	(97)	**(15)**	(11)
Financial Assumptions				
Discount rate	**7.00%**	8.75	**7.00**	8.75
Long-term rate of return on assets (non-taxable)	**—**	—	**7.00**	7.00
Rate of compensation increase	**—**	—	**4.25**	4.25

At December 31, 1995, the health care cost trend rate is assumed to decrease gradually from 8 percent in 1996 to 5 percent in 2003 and 2004. No increases in medical costs are assumed for years beginning in 2005 because of a provision in the health plan which freezes the company's contribution at 2004 levels. The same health care cost trend rate was used at December 31, 1994. Increasing the assumed health care cost trend rate by one percentage point in each year would increase the APBO by $4 million at both December 31, 1995 and 1994, and the aggregate of the service and interest cost components by $1 million for both 1995 and 1994.

For both defined benefit plans and other postretirement plans, certain financial assumptions are utilized in determining the company's projected benefit obligation. These assumptions are examined periodically by the company, and any required changes are incorporated in the subsequent determination of projected benefit obligations.

Accounting for Income Taxes

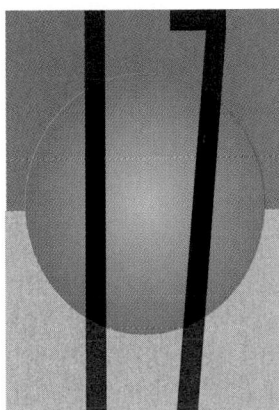

L EARNING OBJECTIVES

After studying this chapter, you should be able to:

1. Identify temporary differences between the tax basis and the book basis of an asset or liability.

2. Distinguish between partial and comprehensive recognition of deferred tax consequences.

3. Distinguish between the asset/liability method and the deferred method of accounting for income taxes.

4. State the current requirements for accounting for income taxes.

5. Explain the effect of changes in enacted marginal tax rates on deferred tax amounts.

6. Describe and account for net operating loss carrybacks and carryforwards.

7. Identify financial accounting events that do not have tax consequences.

8. Explain how to determine the appropriate valuation allowance for deferred tax assets.

9. Describe the financial statement presentation and disclosure requirements for deferred taxes.

10. Explain the role of tax planning strategies in accounting for income taxes.

11. Discuss the role of the alternative minimum tax in accounting for income taxes.

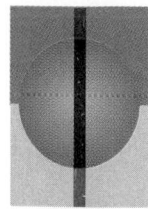

n its 1996 annual report, under current assets, The Clorox Company reported deferred income taxes in the amount of $10,987,000. In 1995, under long-term liabilities, Texaco Inc., reported deferred income taxes of $634 million. What are deferred income taxes? Do they meet the definitions of assets and liabilities? How are they measured? And what disclosures are necessary to explain them to financial statement users? This chapter answers these and other questions related to accounting for income taxes.

Most business entities that are organized as corporations must pay income taxes based on their taxable income. The basis for determining taxable income and for calculating the corporate income tax obligation for a period is the Internal Revenue Code and related Internal Revenue Service (IRS) pronouncements. In levying taxes, the government's primary objective is to obtain cash for its operations in a fair and equitable manner. Congress also designs tax law to encourage some types of economic and social activity and discourage other types of activity. The recognition, measurement, and reporting of events for financial accounting purposes, on the other hand, are based on generally accepted accounting principles (GAAP). The role of GAAP is to provide users of financial statements with the information they need for decision making, as well as to promote the efficient allocation of scarce resources.

CONCEPTUAL

The objectives of income tax law differ from the objectives of financial reporting.

Given the difference between the objectives of tax law and the role of GAAP in determining a company's income for financial reporting purposes, we should not be surprised that a corporation's *taxable income,* shown on its tax return, may differ considerably from its *pretax financial income,* shown in its income statement. Likewise, the tax bases of assets and liabilities may differ considerably from the amounts reported in the financial statements. For example, under some circumstances companies may use the installment (cash collection) method in accounting for sales made on credit for tax purposes, and the accrual method in accounting for those sales for financial reporting purposes. To give another example, warranty expenses often are accrued for financial reporting purposes but deducted on a cash basis in calculating taxable income. Furthermore, some revenues that are reported for financial reporting purposes, such as interest revenue on municipal bonds, are not taxable. And some expenses that are reported for financial purposes, such as fines and penalties for legal violations, are not deductible for tax purposes.

Several accounting complexities arise as a result of differences such as these. These complexities must be dealt with not only in the United States but in most of the English-speaking world and the Netherlands as well. In a number of other countries (e.g., Japan and most of continental Europe) there is no distinction between tax accounting and financial accounting.

The purpose of this chapter is to address the accounting complexities that arise because of the distinction between financial accounting and tax accounting. In the next section we will analyze the major conceptual issues to provide a foundation for the discussion of current accounting and reporting requirements that follows. A third section illustrates the application of current accounting and reporting requirements. The chapter concludes with a look at additional issues associated with accounting for income taxes: tax planning and the alternative minimum tax.

MAJOR CONCEPTUAL ISSUES IN ACCOUNTING FOR INCOME TAXES

For the most part, the tax consequences of events that are recognized in the current year's financial statements also are included in the determination of currently payable income taxes. However, significant differences do exist between the recognition and measurement of some financial statement items for financial accounting purposes and the treatment of those items for tax purposes. As a result, differences can arise between pretax financial income and taxable income. Differences can also arise between the tax bases (dollar amounts determined by following tax laws) of assets and liabilities and their reported amounts in the financial statements. These differences, called *temporary differences*, are central to accounting for income taxes.

Temporary Differences

A **temporary difference** is a difference between the tax basis of an asset or a liability and its reported balance sheet amount that is expected to result in taxable or deductible amounts in future years, without regard to other future events.[1] Most temporary differences are **timing differences,** which arise because of differences between the years in which some transactions affect taxable income and the years in which they affect pretax financial income. Timing differences create a temporary difference between the tax basis of an asset or a liability and its reported amount in the balance sheet; and therefore all timing differences are temporary differences.

For example, a credit sale may be recognized as revenue in the period of sale for financial reporting purposes but reported on the basis of cash collections for tax purposes. As a result, a receivable is recognized for financial reporting purposes but not for tax purposes. Other events, such as a reduction in the tax basis of depreciable assets because of tax credits, also may cause a difference between the tax bases of assets or liabilities and their reported amounts in the financial statements. Exhibit 17–1 provides some additional examples of temporary differences.

To illustrate the effect of a temporary difference, assume that in 1998, for financial accounting (book) purposes, Warren Company recognized revenue of $10,000 related to the performance of services in 1998. For tax purposes, Warren recognized the income on the basis of cash collections. Its cash collections were $4,000, and the tax rate for 1998 was 25 percent. Therefore, its tax liability was $1,000 (.25 tax rate × $4,000 taxable income). Based on these assumptions, relevant financial statement and tax return data at the end of 1998 were as follows:

FINANCIAL STATEMENTS		INCOME TAX RETURN	
Income statement:		Income (cash collections)	$4,000
Revenue	$10,000	Taxable income	$4,000
Pretax financial income	$10,000	Income tax payable (.25 × $4,000)..	$1,000
Balance sheet:			
Accounts receivable			
($10,000 − $4,000)	$ 6,000		

To simplify the example we will assume that Warren's only source of financial accounting income and taxable income in 1998, 1999, and 2000 is the $10,000 from the performance of services it rendered in 1998. As a result, at the end of 1998, the book basis of Warren's receivable is $6,000, and the tax basis is $0. Thus, the temporary difference at the end of 1998 is $6,000.

The fundamental question at the end of 1998 is whether the expected tax consequences of the existing temporary difference should be recognized in Warren's financial statements. That is, at the end of 1998, Warren Company has recognized a $6,000 asset (the uncollected receivable) in the balance sheet, and $6,000 of revenue in the income statement, which will not be recognized for tax purposes until a later period. Does the potential tax obligation related to the temporary difference at the end of 1998 constitute an expense for 1998 and a liability at the end of 1998? If so, an additional component of income tax expense should be reported at the end of 1998—the deferred tax consequences. If not, income tax expense consists only of the amount of income taxes

[1]"Accounting for Income Taxes," *Statement of Financial Accounting Standards No. 109* (Stamford, Conn.: FASB, 1992), paras. 11–13.

1
Identify temporary differences between the tax basis and the book basis of an asset or liability.

CONCEPTUAL

Most temporary differences are timing differences.

EXHIBIT 17–1	**Examples of Temporary Differences**

Timing Differences

1. Revenues or gains that are taxable in periods after they are recognized in pretax financial income (for example, a receivable from a credit sale).
2. Expenses or losses that are deductible for tax purposes in periods after they are recognized in pretax financial income (for example, a product warranty accrual).
3. Revenues or gains that are taxable in periods before they are recognized in pretax financial income (for example, cash received in advance for rent).
4. Expenses or losses that are deductible for tax purposes in periods before they are recognized in pretax financial income (for example, greater depreciation for tax purposes than for financial reporting purposes in the early periods of an asset's life).

Other Temporary Differences

5. A reduction in the tax basis of depreciable assets because of tax credits.
6. An investment tax credit accounted for by the deferral method.
7. An increase in the tax basis of assets because of indexing for inflation.

Source: Adapted from "Accounting for Income Taxes," *Statement of Financial Accounting Standards No. 109* (Stamford, Conn.: FASB, 1992), paras. 11–12.

currently payable. Conceptually, the two basic alternatives in accounting for this temporary difference are (1) *to ignore the temporary difference, recognizing income tax expense equal to income taxes payable ($1,000)* or (2) *to recognize the tax consequences of the temporary difference by including its tax effect as income tax expense on the income statement and as a liability (called a deferred tax liability) in the balance sheet.*[2]

The accounting theory concepts introduced in Chapter 2 support the second alternative. A basic objective of financial reporting is to provide information about economic resources and claims to those resources that will result in future cash inflows and outflows. *Accrual accounting* focuses on the present and future cash consequences of events and transactions, rather than strictly on present cash receipts and disbursements. Recall that under accrual accounting, *assets* represent probable future economic benefits obtained or controlled by an entity as a result of past transactions or events. *Liabilities* represent probable future sacrifices of economic benefits arising from present obligations of an entity to transfer assets or provide services as a result of past transactions or events.

CONCEPTUAL

Accrual accounting focuses on present and future cash consequences of events and transactions.

Underlying the valuation of assets and liabilities for financial reporting purposes is the notion that the *reported amounts will be recovered and settled, respectively.* Assets should not be reported at *more than* the amount expected to be *recovered* from their sale or use. Likewise, liabilities should not be reported at *less than* the amount required to *settle* the obligation. Stated another way, the reported amount for an asset is an estimate of the minimum amount expected to be recovered. The reported amount for a liability is an estimate of the maximum amount expected to be required for settlement. Note that the concept of *recoverable value* is also applied in the lower-of-cost-or-market valuation of inventories (Chapter 10); in the evaluation of long-lived assets to determine whether an impairment of value should be recognized (Chapter 12); and in the fair value limitation on the amount at which capitalized leases may be recorded (Chapter 15).

CONCEPTUAL

The recoverable value concept underlies asset and liability valuation.

Let us apply the recoverable value concept to the Warren Company example. If the entire $10,000 of revenue is recognized in the financial statements both as an asset and in pretax financial income, the implication is that the receivable will

---

[2]Prior to the issuance of *FASB Statement No. 96* in 1987, the process of recognizing the deferred tax consequences of temporary differences was referred to as *interperiod tax allocation.* That term, however, was not used by the FASB in *Statement No. 96*, nor is it used in *Statement No. 109.*

be collected, and that tax consequences (taxable income) will result when the receivable is collected. Therefore, the tax consequences related to the recognized asset and the recognized financial income should be recognized at the end of 1998.

Many accountants believe that the fundamental objectives of financial reporting, the accrual accounting model, and the definitions of assets and liabilities all support the view that both current and deferred tax consequences must be recognized for events that have been reported in the financial statements. Several different approaches to the recognition of deferred tax consequences have been proposed. Those approaches may be categorized as (1) partial versus comprehensive recognition and (2) the asset/liability versus the deferred method.

Partial versus Comprehensive Recognition

Although some theorists support the idea of recognizing the deferred tax consequences of temporary differences, two basic views exist about the *extent* to which deferred tax consequences should be recognized. One of those views supports partial recognition, while the other supports comprehensive recognition.

2 **Distinguish between partial and comprehensive recognition of deferred tax consequences.**

Partial Recognition

Proponents of **partial recognition** believe that the recognition of deferred tax consequences is not appropriate for recurring temporary differences that result in an *indefinite postponement or prepayment of taxes*. For example, an entity may use a modified accelerated cost recovery system (MACRS) depreciation schedule for tax purposes, and the straight-line method for financial accounting purposes. Partial recognition is used in a number of countries (e.g., Great Britain and the Netherlands).

Proponents of partial recognition view the tax effects of recurring temporary differences as *remote contingencies* that are not likely to affect cash flows in the foreseeable future. Because new temporary differences continually arise to offset the reversal of existing temporary differences (for example, a company keeps buying and depreciating new, higher-priced equipment), no cash flow consequences result from recurring temporary differences. Thus, the recognition of deferred tax consequences for such differences would misstate the cash flow consequences.

Those who favor partial recognition, then, argue that recognition of deferred tax consequences is appropriate only when temporary differences are not recurring and are expected to reverse in a relatively short time. The Warren Company illustration at the beginning of this chapter is one example. To give another example, suppose a company owns only one depreciable asset, which it depreciates using MACRS for tax purposes and the straight-line method for financial accounting purposes. Advocates of partial recognition would consider recognition of the deferred tax consequences of this temporary difference to be appropriate because no new temporary difference is expected to offset the reversal of the old temporary difference; therefore, the tax consequences probably will affect cash flows in the near future. Some people think that recognition of deferred tax consequences provides better cash flow signals in such cases than would be provided in the absence of such recognition.

Comprehensive Recognition

Under the **comprehensive recognition** approach, the deferred tax consequences of *all* existing temporary differences must be recognized in the financial statements. In this view, the fact that new temporary differences may arise in the future to offset taxable or deductible amounts related to existing temporary differences is irrelevant. Proponents of comprehensive recognition argue that accounting for the tax consequences of existing temporary differences should not depend on assumptions about future offsetting temporary differences for events that have not yet been recognized in the financial statements. *Existing temporary differences* are expected to have tax consequences in the future, whether they are recurring or nonrecurring, and their tax consequences are measurable.

Asset/Liability versus Deferred Method

There are two methods of recognizing deferred tax consequences: (1) the asset/liability method and (2) the deferred method. A significant difference between the two methods is the manner in which the tax consequences of temporary differences are viewed in the balance sheet. Both methods are described in this section.

Asset/Liability Method

Under the **asset/liability method,** the tax consequences of all events that have been recognized in the financial statements must be recognized as either (1) taxes payable or refundable (receivable) currently or (2) deferred tax liabilities or assets. Because deferred taxes are determined by future tax rates, the tax consequences of an event that produces a deferred tax asset or liability are measured using *enacted tax rates* applicable to future years. Thus, changes in tax rates will cause changes in the deferred tax asset or liability. From a conceptual standpoint, because a deferred tax asset or liability is a future claim or obligation for cash flows, a *long-term* deferred tax asset or liability, like other long-term monetary assets and liabilities, should be discounted and recorded at its present value. The appropriate interest rate for discounting the deferred tax liability or asset would be the rate that might be incurred on a payable/receivable of similar risk, duration, and repayment schedule. Because of its emphasis on recognition and measurement of the deferred tax asset or liability, the asset/liability method may be thought of as a *balance sheet approach.*

To illustrate the accounting procedures under the asset/liability method, refer to the Warren Company illustration on page 909. Recall that a temporary difference of $6,000 arose in 1998; recording this receivable as an asset assumes that the reported amount of $6,000 will be recovered (collected) in future periods. For financial accounting purposes, this amount was recognized as an asset in the balance sheet at the end of 1998. For tax return purposes, however, assume that $4,000 is expected to be recognized in 1999, and $2,000 to be recognized in 2000. Assume also that a tax rate of 35 percent was enacted in 1998 for 1999 and 2000.

Assuming a 10 percent discount rate, Warren Company would make the following two journal entries at the end of 1998 to record the taxes payable currently and the deferred tax liability, respectively:

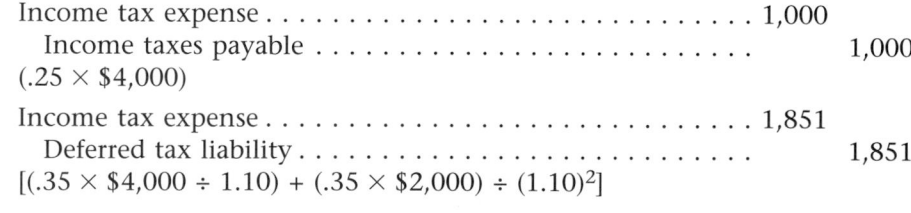

Income tax expense 1,000
   Income taxes payable   1,000
(.25 × $4,000)

Income tax expense 1,851
   Deferred tax liability   1,851
[(.35 × $4,000 ÷ 1.10) + (.35 × $2,000) ÷ (1.10)²]

Alternatively, a compound journal entry could be made to record this information:

Income tax expense 2,851
   Income taxes payable   1,000
   Deferred tax liability   1,851

As a result of recognizing the $6,000 as a receivable in the balance sheet for 1998 and as revenue in the income statement for 1998, Warren Company must recognize a liability for future taxes of $1,851, or the present value of the future taxes payable. *Note that income tax expense is the sum of the income taxes currently payable and the present value of the amount of tax payable in future years as the result of items currently recognized in the financial statements.*

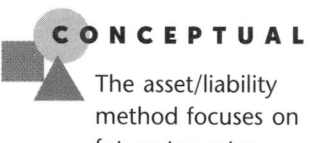

3 Distinguish between the asset/liability method and the deferred method of accounting for income taxes.

C O N C E P T U A L

The asset/liability method focuses on future tax rates.

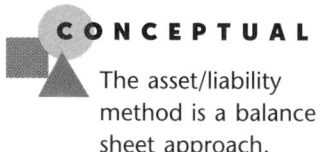

C O N C E P T U A L

The asset/liability method is a balance sheet approach.

Deferred Method

Under the **deferred method,** the primary objective is to match income tax expense with the related revenues and expenses included in pretax financial income. Income tax expense is the amount that would be payable currently if all revenues and expenses reported in pretax financial income also were included in taxable income. In determining the amount of deferred taxes, the emphasis is on the current period tax savings or the prepayment resulting from temporary differences. Future tax rates and changes in tax rates have no relevance under the deferred method, because the deferred amount and reversals are based on the tax rate existing in the period(s) when the temporary difference(s) arose.

Under the deferred method, the resulting debit or credit balance in the deferred tax account is not viewed as an asset or a liability, but rather as the cumulative effect of the periodic application of the deferred method in past periods. Proper valuation of the deferred amount in the balance sheet in terms of its cash flow consequences is not a primary consideration. Because of the emphasis on the income statement result and on matching the current period tax savings, or prepayment, resulting from temporary differences with reported revenues and expenses, the deferred method may be thought of as an *income statement approach.*

In the Warren Company illustration (page 909), the following journal entry would be made at the end of 1998:

Income tax expense (.25 × $10,000) 2,500		
Income taxes payable (.25 × $4,000)	1,000	
Deferred taxes ($2,500 – $1,000)	1,500	

Income taxes payable is determined as before. (The method of *accounting* for income taxes has no effect on income taxes payable.) The debit to income tax expense of $2,500 is determined by multiplying the 1998 tax rate (25 percent) times 1998 pretax financial income ($10,000). Deferred taxes is credited for $1,500, which is the difference between the debit to income tax expense ($2,500) and the credit to income taxes payable ($1,000).

Under the deferred method, income tax expense may not accurately measure the cash flow consequences of items recognized currently in the financial statements. Likewise, because the deferred tax credit is only a residual of the calculation of income tax expense over a number of years, the credit probably will not accurately measure the future taxes payable as a result of items recognized currently in the financial statements. The relevant tax rates for measuring the future tax consequences are the *future* tax rates, not the *current* period rate that is used under the deferred method.

Net-of-Tax Reporting of Deferred Taxes

Some have argued that a **net-of-tax display** of deferred tax consequences is appropriate under either the asset/liability method or the deferred method. The tax effects of temporary differences would be reported in the balance sheet as reductions of the amounts of the related assets and liabilities and in the income statement as a reduction of the related revenues and expenses. Those who support this method argue that taxability and tax deductibility are relevant factors in the valuation of assets and liabilities.

There are several difficulties with a net-of-tax display. First, some temporary differences cannot be associated with individual assets or liabilities. Second, if the tax effects of temporary differences were displayed with individual assets and liabilities, interpreting a company's overall tax situation would be difficult without significant additional information. Third, the meaning of the resulting balance sheet measure—for example, building cost less depreciation less deferred tax liability—would be questionable. Finally, a net-of-tax method of reporting is

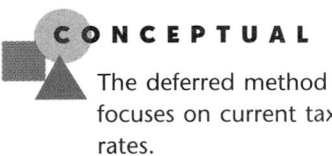

CONCEPTUAL

The deferred method focuses on current tax rates.

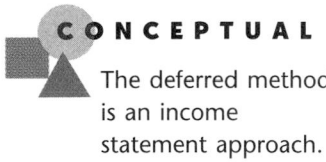

CONCEPTUAL

The deferred method is an income statement approach.

inconsistent with the view that the tax consequences of events that are recognized currently in the financial statements represent separate assets or liabilities—a fundamental concept underlying the asset/liability method.

Summary

In summary, the asset/liability method appears to be more in accord with the conceptual framework than the deferred method. The deferred method ignores future tax rates and creates a residual debit (credit) on the balance sheet that is not an asset (liability). Thus, the objective of providing measurements of assets and liabilities that are useful in assessing future cash flows is best met under the asset/liability method.

The following section explains and illustrates the current requirements for accounting for income taxes. As you will see, the asset/liability method forms the foundation for these requirements.

CURRENT REQUIREMENTS IN ACCOUNTING FOR INCOME TAXES

The purpose of this section is to describe and illustrate the basic requirements of accounting for income taxes. We will first detail the current requirements, then illustrate the calculation of a deferred tax liability. Next, we will discuss the effect of changes in enacted marginal tax rates. The following sections illustrate the accounting for both a deferred tax asset and a deferred tax liability. An explanation of a special case of deferred tax asset—net operating losses—follows. The section closes with a brief discussion of financial accounting events that do not have tax consequences.

Until fairly recently, the accounting and reporting requirements for income taxes were set forth in *APB Opinion No. 11*,[3] which required the comprehensive recognition of deferred tax consequences using the deferred method. However, in 1992, the FASB's *Statement No. 109* superseded previous pronouncements; it now represents GAAP in accounting for income taxes. Though comprehensive recognition is still required, the asset/liability method has replaced the deferred method.[4] Therefore, the deferred tax asset or liability related to temporary differences represents the *future* income tax effects of existing differences between the tax bases and the accounting bases of assets and liabilities. We assume here that the assets will be recovered and the liabilities will be settled at their reported amounts.

Deferred tax liabilities and assets are not discounted under Statement No. 109. Some FASB members argued that the issue of discounting future amounts was too complex, because of issues such as the selection of the appropriate discount rate(s) and the determination of the timing of the taxability or deductibility of temporary differences. Other Board members believed that discounting should be addressed in a broader study extending beyond accounting for income taxes. As a result, the issue of discounting was removed from the scope of the project on accounting for income taxes. Practical considerations appear to have outweighed the very strong conceptual arguments that support discounting of deferred tax assets and liabilities.

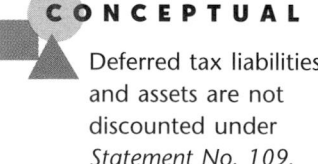

State the current requirements for accounting for income taxes.

CONCEPTUAL

Deferred tax liabilities and assets are not discounted under *Statement No. 109*.

---

[3]"Accounting for Income Taxes," *Opinions of the Accounting Principles Board No. 11* (New York: AICPA, 1967).
[4]Interestingly, the United States was essentially alone in the world in requiring the deferred method. Thus, the adoption of the asset/liability method made U.S. practice more comparable to that of other countries.

In summary, *Statement No. 109* requires comprehensive recognition of deferred tax consequences using the asset/liability method. The objective is to measure the expected tax consequences of an event in the same year in which the event is recognized in the financial statements, with an emphasis on accruing an asset or a liability for the future tax consequences of existing temporary differences. Therefore, companies must look ahead when measuring the tax consequences of existing temporary differences. Measurement of future tax consequences must be based on the *enacted* marginal tax rates applicable to future years. The **enacted marginal tax rate** is the enacted rate that is expected to apply to the last dollars of taxable income in future periods in which deferred tax liabilities or assets are expected to be settled or recovered. Anticipated tax rate changes that have *not* been enacted cannot be used to calculate the deferred tax consequences.

CONCEPTUAL

Statement No. 109 requires comprehensive recognition of deferred taxes using the asset/liability method.

Deferred Tax Liability

Let us apply *Statement No. 109* requirements to the Warren Company example (page 909). Recall that at the end of 1998, Warren Company had a $6,000 receivable on its balance sheet that was expected to have future tax consequences. The $6,000 amount was the difference between the $10,000 asset (and revenue) recognized in 1998 for financial accounting purposes and the $4,000 cash collection recognized for tax purposes. This temporary difference of $6,000 will become a taxable amount in 1999 ($4,000) and 2000 ($2,000).

This simple example illustrates several important points regarding the application of the asset/liability method under *Statement No. 109*. The procedure for calculating the deferred tax balance in this example is as follows:

1. Identify existing temporary differences between the book and tax bases of assets and liabilities. In Warren's case, it is $6,000 at the end of 1998.

2. Determine the expected *reversals* of existing temporary differences. Temporary differences *reverse* in periods in which the difference between the book basis and the tax basis decreases. In Warren's case, the existing temporary difference of $6,000 is expected to reverse as follows: $4,000 in 1999 and $2,000 in 2000.

3. Calculate the expected total tax effect of the reversals using *enacted* marginal tax rates for the years of reversal. In Warren's case:

$6,000 × .35 = $2,100

The journal entry required to record the income taxes currently payable and the deferred tax consequences at the end of 1998 would be as follows:

Income tax expense ($1,000 + $2,100) 3,100		
Income taxes payable	1,000	
Deferred tax liability	2,100	

The expected future tax consequence of the 1998 temporary difference is $2,100 (.35 × $6,000). Income tax expense for 1998 is the sum of the credit to income taxes payable and the credit to deferred tax liability. That is, income tax expense is the amount of tax currently payable plus the amount expected to be paid in the future as a result of existing temporary differences.

Now let us extend this example into the next two years, assuming no other revenue or expense items in those years. At the end of 1999 and 2000, a liability for income taxes payable will be reported based on cash collections in each year. At the end of 1999, the remaining temporary difference (which is scheduled to reverse in 2000) will be $2,000. Therefore, the required balance in the deferred tax liability account at the end of 1999 is $700 (.35 × $2,000). To obtain this balance, the deferred tax liability account must be reduced by (debited for) $1,400 ($2,100

**CONCEPTUAL**

Under the asset/liability method, income tax expense is a "plug" figure.

existing balance – $700 desired balance). Therefore, the following entry is required at the end of 1999:

> Deferred tax liability 1,400
>   Income taxes payable   1,400
> (.35 × $4,000)

Note that there is no income tax expense for 1999 because the debit to the deferred tax liability is equal to the credit to income taxes payable (and because we assumed there were no revenues or expenses in 1999).

At the end of 2000, no temporary difference remains. Therefore, the remaining balance of $700 must be eliminated from the deferred tax liability account:

> Deferred tax liability   700
>   Income taxes payable   700
> (.35 × $2,000)

Again, there is no income tax expense, because the debit to the deferred tax liability is equal to the credit to income taxes payable.[5]

Changes in Enacted Marginal Tax Rates

5   **Explain the effect of changes in enacted marginal tax rates on deferred tax amounts.**

Under *Statement No. 109,* subsequently enacted changes in the marginal tax rate require an adjustment to the deferred tax asset or liability. For instance, if at the end of 1999, a newly enacted law changed the marginal tax rate for the year 2000 to 40 percent, the deferred tax liability would have to be adjusted. Warren Company's journal entry at the end of 1999 would therefore be as follows:

> Deferred tax liability [$2,100 – (.40 × $2,000) 1,300
> Income tax expense ($1,400 – $1,300)   100
>   Income taxes payable (.35 × $4,000)   1,400

CONCEPTUAL

The effect of tax rate changes alters the measurement of the deferred tax liability/asset and income tax expense.

Note that income taxes payable in 1999 is unaffected by the marginal tax rate change. It is still calculated as the tax rate for 1999 (35 percent) times taxable income for 1999 ($4,000). However, the deferred tax liability must be debited for $1,300 to adjust it from the existing beginning-of-year balance of $2,100 to the new desired balance of $800 (.40 × $2,000). That is, the tax consequence of the temporary difference of $2,000 at the end of 1999 has changed from $700 to $800. The total tax consequence is now expected to be $3,200 rather than $3,100, the amount estimated at the end of 1998. The effect of this *change in estimate* (a $100 *increase* in the expected tax consequences) is reported as additional income tax expense at the end of 1999. *The effect of the tax rate change must be included in income from continuing operations,* even though the taxable or deductible temporary differences from prior years may have been related to items not reported in continuing operations, such as extraordinary items.

In the preceding example, the tax consequences of the temporary difference at the end of 1998 resulted in *taxable* amounts in 1999 and 2000. In other situations, temporary differences may lead to *deductible* amounts in future years. In the following section we will learn how to account for a combined deferred tax asset and liability.

Deferred Tax Asset and Liability

Let us continue the assumption of a $6,000 temporary difference arising from (a) accruing a receivable for financial accounting purposes and (b) recognizing income

---

[5]Because we assumed that there were no other items of revenue or expense in 1999 and 2000, income taxes payable in each of those years relates solely to the taxable amounts arising from the temporary difference at the end of 1998, and income tax expense is zero.

on the basis of cash collections for tax purposes. Assume also that a warranty expense of $5,500, accrued in 1998 for book purposes, will not be deducted for tax purposes until 1999. As a result, at the end of 1998, the balance sheet includes two items that have future tax consequences: an asset (accounts receivable) and a liability (estimated warranty obligation). The receivable is expected to be recovered in 1999 and 2000, while the accrued liability for warranty costs is expected to be settled in 1999.

In this case, the end-of-1998 adjustments for income taxes may be made in three separate entries. First, the liability for taxes currently payable must be accrued:

Income tax expense	1,000	
Income taxes payable		1,000
(.25 × $4,000)		

Second, the deferred tax liability must be recognized:

Income tax expense	2,100	
Deferred tax liability		2,100
(.35 × $6,000)		

Finally, the deferred tax asset must be recognized:

Deferred tax asset	1,925	
Income tax expense		1,925
(.35 × $5,500)		

Income taxes payable is credited for $1,000, which is the 1998 tax rate (25 percent) times taxable income for 1998 ($4,000). An offsetting debit is made to income tax expense. The credit to deferred tax liability of $2,100 (second entry) is the expected future tax consequence of the $6,000 temporary difference that is expected to reverse in 1999 and 2000. Income tax expense is debited for the $2,100 expected future consequence. The debit of $1,925 to deferred tax asset is the expected future tax consequence of the $5,500 deductible temporary difference at the end of 1998.

As an alternative to three simple journal entries, the aggregate effect of the three entries could be recorded in one compound journal entry, as follows:

Deferred tax asset	1,925	
Income tax expense ($1,000 + $2,100 – $1,925)	1,175	
Deferred tax liability		2,100
Income taxes payable		1,000

In some cases, a special type of deductible amount is created by net operating losses, the subject of the following section.

Net Operating Losses

If deductions exceed revenues when *taxable income* is calculated, a **net operating loss** (NOL) exists. Federal tax law provides that companies may use net operating losses to offset taxable income in other years, thereby reducing taxes payable in those years. Specifically, a company must elect one of two options, as Exhibit 17–2 demonstrates. Under the **loss carryback** election, shown above the time line in Exhibit 17–2, the company carries the loss back to the third year preceding the loss year, to offset that year's taxable income and claim a refund for all or part of the taxes paid that year. If the taxable income for year –3 is inadequate to absorb the entire net operating loss, the company may apply the remainder against the taxable income from years –2, –1, +1, +2, . . . , +15, respectively, until the loss has been absorbed. Under the **loss carryforward** election, shown below the time line in Exhibit 17–2, the company carries the net operating loss forward to offset taxable income, and reduce the taxes payable, in the 15 carryforward years.

6 Describe and account for net operating loss carrybacks and carryforwards.

| EXHIBIT 17–2 | Net Operating Loss Carryback and Carryforward Options |

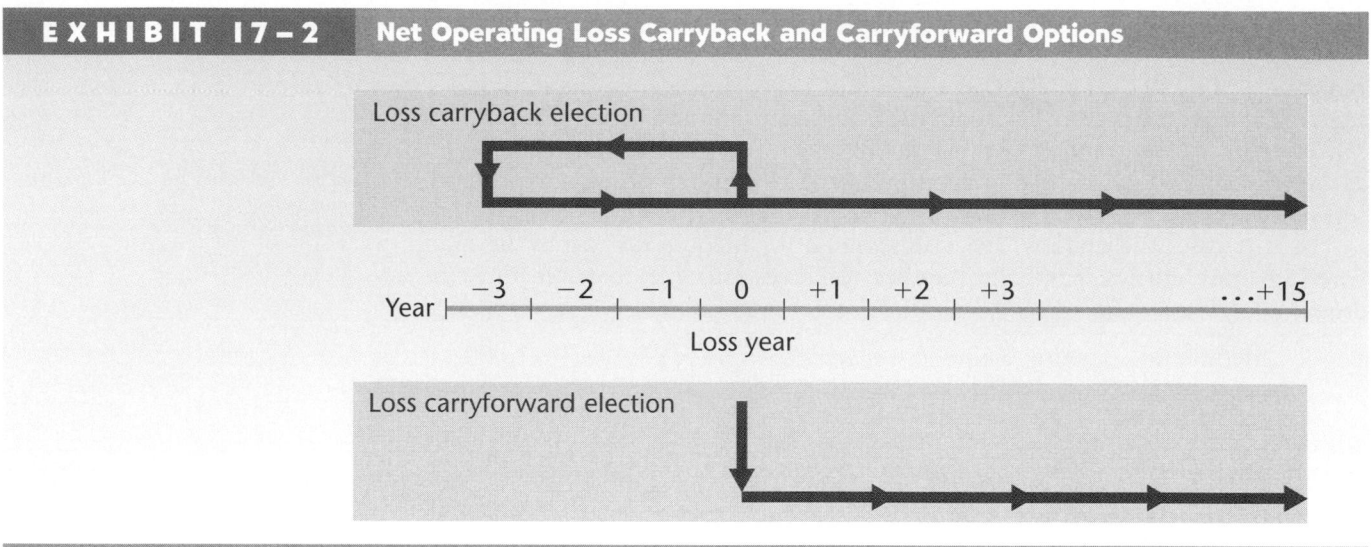

CONCEPTUAL

Loss carrybacks result in immediate cash inflows.

Under normal circumstances, a company with a net operating loss will elect the loss carryback option because the company will realize an immediate claim for a refund of taxes already paid. In most cases, an immediate claim is preferable to having to depend on future taxable income to realize the benefit of a net operating loss. However, if a company expects to have taxable income in the 15 carryforward years *and* expects tax rates to increase significantly in the future, it may benefit from electing the loss carryforward option. The carryforward option might also be preferable if special tax credits resulted in nominal tax payments in the carryback years. Finally, the time value of money might also be a factor in the decision to carry back versus carry forward. A claim for refund of taxes already paid results in an immediate cash inflow, which is worth more than the cash flow benefit from reducing taxes payable in future years, especially at high interest rates.

The objective of the net operating loss provision of the tax law is to equate the tax burden borne by companies that experience loss years in the midst of profitable years with the burden borne by companies with more stable earning patterns. Assume, for example, that Houser Company's taxable income, tax rate, and tax liability for the years 1996 through 1998 are as follows:

YEAR	TAXABLE INCOME	TAX RATE	TAX LIABILITY
1996	$100,000	40%	$40,000
1997	100,000	40	40,000
1998	100,000	40	40,000

Assume further that there is no difference between Houser's pretax financial income and taxable income for these three years. In 1999, however, Houser incurs a net operating loss of $300,000. The company calculates its tax refund claim by applying the $300,000 net operating loss against the taxable income of 1996, 1997, and 1998, and claims a refund for the taxes paid in those years. The $300,000 net loss exactly offsets the total taxable income for the three years preceding. Therefore, the tax refund claim is for all the income taxes paid during the preceding three years, or $120,000. The *net* tax payment over the four years is zero, which is reasonable because the *aggregate* taxable income over the same four years was also zero.

Loss Carryback

In the above example, Houser's tax rate was the same each period, and the amount of Houser's net operating loss was exactly equal to total taxable income for the three years preceding. Now let us look at a more realistic example. Assume the following figures for Plummer Corporation:

YEAR	TAXABLE INCOME	TAX RATE	TAX LIABILITY
1996	$100,000	40%	$ 40,000
1997	130,000	40	52,000
1998	160,000	45	72,000
	$390,000		$164,000

Also assume Plummer had a $300,000 net operating loss in 1999. Calculation of the tax refund claim at the end of 1999 would be as follows:

YEAR	TAXABLE INCOME ABSORBED BY LOSS CARRYBACK	TAX RATE	TAX REFUND
1996	$100,000	40%	$ 40,000
1997	130,000	40	52,000
1998	70,000	45	31,500
	$300,000		$123,500

Plummer first carries the loss back to 1996, leaving $200,000 to be carried back to 1997 and 1998. As a result, all 1996 and 1997 income taxes are refunded, as well as the taxes paid on $70,000 of taxable income in 1998. Note that the 50 percent tax rate in 1999, the year of the loss, has no bearing on the calculation of the tax refund. The loss carryback does not absorb the remaining $90,000 ($160,000 − $70,000) of taxable income in 1998. Therefore, related taxes of $40,500 ($90,000 × .45) are not refundable.

Plummer Corporation would make the following journal entry at the end of 1999 to record the effect of the loss carryback:

Income tax refund receivable 123,500
    Refund of taxes due to loss carryback   123,500

Loss Carryforward

If taxable income in the three years preceding a net operating loss is less than the amount of the loss, or if a company elects the loss carryforward option, the company may use the net loss to reduce taxes payable in the years following the loss year, up to a maximum of 15 years. Since *carrybacks* result in legal claims for amounts previously paid, there is no question regarding the realization of the claim. To realize the tax benefit of a loss carryforward, however, a company must have future taxable income. Otherwise, there will be no future taxes to be reduced by the carryforward. Despite the uncertainty regarding realization of the tax benefit, however, the *tax benefit* of a loss carryforward is recognized as a deferred tax asset. As described later in this chapter (pages 928–929), a valuation allowance may be required if uncertainty regarding realization is sufficiently high.

Assume that Booth Corporation experiences the following income (loss) for the years indicated:

CONCEPTUAL

Realization of tax benefits from loss carryforwards depends on future taxable income.

YEAR	TAXABLE INCOME (LOSS)	TAX RATE	CURRENT TAX[a]
1996	$ 50,000	40%	$20,000
1997	70,000	40	28,000
1998	40,000	40	16,000
1999	(200,000)	45	–0–
2000	20,000	35	7,000
2001	40,000	35	14,000

[a]Excludes carryback or carryforward effect, if any.

Because the taxable income in the three years preceding the loss is only $160,000, $40,000 of the $200,000 net loss results in a loss carryforward.

At the end of 1999, Booth records the following journal entry, assuming there are no temporary differences:

Deferred tax asset (.35 × $40,000).	14,000	
Income tax refund receivable		
($20,000 + $28,000 + $16,000)	64,000	
Refund of taxes due to loss carryback		64,000
Reduction of loss from loss carryforward		14,000

At the end of 2000, Booth can apply $20,000 of the remaining net loss against its $20,000 taxable income for that year, thus eliminating the tax on that income:

Income tax expense.	7,000	
Deferred tax asset		7,000

At the end of 2001, Booth can use the remaining loss carryforward of $20,000 to reduce its taxes by another $7,000 (.35 × $20,000). Booth will make the following entry:

Income tax expense ($7000 + $7000)	14,000	
Income taxes payable [.35 × ($40,000 – $20,000)]		7,000
Deferred tax asset (.35 × $20,000)		7,000

Companies must disclose the amount and expiration dates of unused loss carryforwards in the notes to the financial statements.

Some financial accounting events do not have tax consequences. We will look briefly at such events before turning to a comprehensive example of the accounting for income taxes.

Events That Do Not Have Tax Consequences

1

Identify financial accounting events that do not have tax consequences.

Some events that are reported for financial accounting purposes do not have tax consequences.[6] For example, the interest earned on municipal bonds generally is not taxable. Exhibit 17–3 summarizes the more common financial accounting events that do not have tax consequences.

Items that are reported for financial accounting purposes but do not have tax consequences should not affect income tax calculations. Since tax-exempt (nontaxable) revenues have no tax consequences, accruing income tax expense for those items would make no sense. Likewise, if financial accounting expenses are not tax-deductible, allowing them to affect income tax expense would be inappropriate.

EXHIBIT 17–3	**Examples of Financial Accounting Events That Do Not Have Tax Consequences**

I. Interest received on state and local government obligations.

2. Interest expense on debt incurred to acquire tax-exempt securities.

3. Life insurance proceeds received by a company as beneficiary of a policy on officers or employees.

4. Premiums paid for life insurance on officers or employees when the company is the beneficiary.

5. Fines and expenses incurred for violating the law.

---

[6]In the past, these items have been called *permanent differences* between financial accounting recognition and tax recognition.

The effect of events that do not have tax consequences on accounting for income taxes is not controversial. Such events do not enter into the calculation of income tax expense or income taxes payable. However, as explained later in this chapter, disclosure of those events may be necessary in order to reconcile the reported income tax expense with the amount of income tax expense that would be expected based on pretax financial income.

APPLICATION OF INCOME TAX ACCOUNTING REQUIREMENTS

This section brings together several issues discussed earlier. We will begin with the CFO Company example, which includes deferred tax assets and liabilities and a net operating loss. In addition, we will describe the process of evaluating the need for a valuation allowance for deferred tax assets and describe the financial statement presentation and disclosure requirements for income taxes.

Comprehensive Example

The basic facts for CFO Company are presented in Exhibit 17–4. Items 1 through 4 are temporary differences. (Assume there were no temporary differences prior to 1998.) Item 5, tax-exempt interest, is a revenue item that is included in pretax financial income but is not taxable. Therefore, item 5 does not create a temporary difference. Except as stated in Exhibit 17–4, revenues and expenses are the same for both financial accounting purposes and tax purposes.

End of 1998

Exhibit 17–5 provides an analysis of the items affecting the income tax accrual at the end of 1998. At this time, two items on CFO's balance sheet have future tax consequences that are related to existing temporary differences:

1. The fixed asset has a carrying amount of $75,000 ($100,000 cost – $25,000 depreciation for 1998) for financial accounting (book) purposes, and a tax basis of $55,000 ($100,000 cost – $45,000 depreciation for 1998). The discrepancy between the two results in a taxable temporary difference of $20,000 ($75,000 book basis – $55,000 tax basis) at the end of 1998. According to the data in Exhibit 17–4, the temporary difference will increase in 1999 and 2000 and decrease in 2001.

2. The $15,000 extraordinary loss was accrued as a liability at the end of 1998, but is deductible for tax purposes in 1999 and 2000. Therefore, the deductible temporary difference will reverse in 1999 and 2000.

The *net* temporary difference at the end of 1998 is $5,000 ($20,000 – $15,000).

The calculations underlying the end-of-1998 journal entry for income taxes are presented at the bottom of Exhibit 17–5. The entry to record income taxes at the end of 1998 would be as follows:

Deferred tax asset	4,500	
Income tax expense	1,750	
Income taxes payable		250
Deferred tax liability		6,000

To grasp more fully the notions of *future taxable amounts* and *future deductible amounts,* think of the last two columns in Exhibit 17–5 as "future mini-tax returns."

EXHIBIT 17–4	Basic Data for CFO Company

Facts

1. At the beginning of 1998, CFO was organized and acquired a fixed asset for $100,000 by issuing common stock. For financial accounting purposes, the fixed asset will be depreciated on the straight-line basis over four years, with no expected salvage value. For tax purposes, it will be depreciated over three years in amounts of $45,000, $35,000, and $20,000.

2. At the beginning of 1999, CFO received $60,000 cash representing rent for three years in advance. The rent revenue will be earned in equal amounts in 1999, 2000, and 2001.

3. Warranty expense is estimated and accrued for financial accounting purposes and amounted to $16,000 in each of 1999 and 2000. For tax purposes, the warranty costs are expected to be deducted in 2001.

4. An extraordinary loss of $15,000 (pretax) was accrued in 1998 for financial accounting purposes. For tax purposes, $10,000 and $5,000 will be deductible in 1999 and 2000, respectively.

5. CFO's pretax financial income each year included $2,000 of tax-exempt interest revenue. Note that, as a result, pretax financial income exceeds taxable income by $8,000 ($2,000 × 4 years) over the four-year period.

	Year				
	1998	**1999**	**2000**	**2001**	**Total**
Financial Accounting Recognition					
Revenues	$ 50,000	$ 50,000	$ 50,000	$ 20,000	$170,000
Interest (tax-exempt)	2,000	2,000	2,000	2,000	8,000
Rent revenue		20,000	20,000	20,000	60,000
Depreciation	(25,000)	(25,000)	(25,000)	(25,000)	(100,000)
Warranty expense		(16,000)	(16,000)		(32,000)
Extraordinary loss	(15,000)				(15,000)
Other expenses	(4,000)	(4,000)	(4,000)	(8,000)	(20,000)
Pretax financial income	$ 8,000	$ 27,000	$ 27,000	$ 9,000	$ 71,000
Tax Recognition					
Revenue	$ 50,000	$ 50,000	$ 50,000	$ 20,000	$170,000
Rent revenue		60,000			60,000
Depreciation	(45,000)	(35,000)	(20,000)		(100,000)
Warranty costs				(32,000)	(32,000)
Loss		(10,000)	(5,000)		(15,000)
Other expenses	(4,000)	(4,000)	(4,000)	(8,000)	(20,000)
Taxable income	$ 1,000	$ 61,000	$ 21,000	$(20,000)	$ 63,000
Enacted Marginal Tax Rate	**25%**	**30%**	**30%**	**30%**	

That is, the $20,000 temporary difference at the end of 1998 that is related to plant and equipment will cause future taxable income of $20,000. How do we know this? Remember that underlying the valuation of assets and liabilities is the assumption that assets will be recovered and liabilities will be settled, respectively. In this case, we are assuming that the $75,000 book value of plant and equipment at the end of 1998 will be recovered in future periods. When it is recovered, it will be reported on future tax returns as revenue. However, because only $55,000 of depreciation remains for tax purposes, the difference of $20,000 ($75,000 – $55,000) becomes taxable. Likewise, the $15,000 future deductible amount is the amount that will be deducted on future tax returns to settle the estimated loss liability reported at the end of 1998.

EXHIBIT 17–5	CFO Company: End of 1998			

	End of Current Year 1998	Future Taxable Amounts	Future Deductible Amounts
Temporary Differences			
Assets:			
Plant and equipment ($75,000 book basis − $55,000 tax basis)	$20,000	$20,000	
Liabilities:			
Estimated loss liability	(15,000)		$15,000
Net temporary difference	$ 5,000		
Taxable income (Exhibit 17–4)	$ 1,000		
TOTAL		$20,000	$15,000
Enacted marginal tax rate......................................		30%	30%
Deferred tax liability..		$ 6,000	
Deferred tax asset			$ 4,500
Journal Entry Information [Dr (Cr)]			
Income taxes payable (.25 × $1,000)		$ (250)	
Deferred tax liability:			
Ending	$ (6,000)		
Beginning	–0–		
Adjustment ··		(6,000)	
Deferred tax asset:			
Ending	$ 4,500		
Beginning	–0–		
Adjustment		4,500	
Income tax expense...		$ 1,750	

End of 1999

Exhibit 17–6 summarizes the information needed at the end of 1999 to record income taxes. At the end of the year, the balance sheet contains four items with future tax consequences that are related to existing temporary differences:

1. The fixed asset has a book value of $50,000 ($100,000 cost – $25,000 1998 depreciation – $25,000 1999 depreciation) and a tax basis of $20,000 ($100,000 cost – $45,000 1998 depreciation – $35,000 1999 depreciation). A temporary difference of $30,000 ($50,000 book basis – $20,000 tax basis) results.

2. Because in 1999 a tax deduction of $10,000 was allowed for the extraordinary loss, the remaining tax-deductible liability balance is $5,000.

3. Of the $60,000 rent received in 1999 and taxable in 1999, $40,000 was unearned at the end of 1999. It appears on the balance sheet as the liability unearned rent.

4. Because warranty expense of $16,000 was accrued at the end of 1999, a liability, estimated warranty obligation, appears on the balance sheet at the end of

EXHIBIT 17–6   **CFO Company: End of 1999**

	1998	End of Current Year 1999	Future Taxable Amounts	Future Deductible Amounts
Temporary Differences				
Assets:				
Plant and equipment ($50,000 book basis – $20,000 tax basis)		$ 30,000	$ 30,000	
Liabilities:				
Unearned rent		(40,000)		$40,000
Estimated loss liability		(5,000)		5,000
Warranty obligation		(16,000)		16,000
Net temporary difference		$(31,000)		
Taxable income (Exhibit 17–4)	$ 1,000	$ 61,000		
TOTAL			$ 30,000	$61,000
Enacted marginal tax rate			30%	30%
Deferred tax liability			$ 9,000	
Deferred tax asset				$18,300

Journal Entry Information [Dr (Cr)]

Income taxes payable (.30 × $61,000)		$(18,300)
Deferred tax liability:		
Ending	$ (9,000)	
Beginning (Exhibit 17–5)	(6,000)	
Adjustment		(3,000)
Deferred tax asset:		
Ending	$ 18,300	
Beginning (Exhibit 17–5)	4,500	
Adjustment		13,800
Income tax expense		$ 7,500

1999. The future deductible tax consequence of this temporary difference is expected to occur in 2001.

Based on the analysis at the bottom of Exhibit 17–6, the journal entry to record the various tax effects at the end of 1999 would be as follows:

Deferred tax asset	13,800	
Income tax expense	7,500	
Deferred tax liability		3,000
Income taxes payable		18,300

Note that the debit to deferred tax asset and the credit to deferred tax liability are the *differences* between the *desired* balances indicated in Exhibit 17–6 and the *existing* balances prior to adjustment. The debit to income tax expense of $7,500 is the net result of the credits to income taxes currently payable ($18,300) and deferred ($3,000) and the debit to deferred tax asset ($13,800).

Again, the last two columns of Exhibit 17–6 may be thought of as "future mini-tax returns." We have already discussed the rationale for the plant and equipment and estimated loss liability items. In addition, we now have a future deductible amount of $40,000 related to the liability unearned rent. Recall the assumption that liabilities will be settled. As the rent is earned, the following (summary) journal entry should be made:

Unearned rent.	40,000	
Rent revenue		40,000

This journal entry has no tax consequences, because the entire $60,000 of rent received in advance was reported in the 1999 tax return. However, implicit in the liability valuation approach is the notion that in the future, CFO will incur tax-deductible expenses of at least $40,000 to earn the unearned rent. The "hidden entry" to record these expenses is as follows:

Expenses.	40,000	
Cash (or other assets)		40,000

This $40,000 will be deductible in future tax returns.

The analysis of the $16,000 future deductible amount related to the warranty obligation is exactly the same as that for the estimated loss liability at the end of 1998 (page 922). That is, CFO expects to incur future tax-deductible expenses of $16,000 to settle the warranty obligation.

End of 2000

Exhibit 17–7 summarizes the information required to account for income taxes at the end of the year 2000. The balance sheet contains three items that have future tax consequences related to existing temporary differences:

1. The fixed asset has a book value of $25,000 [$100,000 – 3($25,000)] and a tax basis of zero ($100,000 – $45,000 – $35,000 – $20,000), resulting in a temporary difference at the end of 2000 of $25,000 ($25,000 – $0).

2. Of the $60,000 in rent received in 1999 and taxable in 1999, $20,000 was unearned at the end of 2000 and appears in the balance sheet as the liability unearned rent.

3. Because warranty expense of $32,000 is accrued as of the end of 2000 ($16,000 in 1999 and $16,000 in 2000), a liability, estimated warranty obligation, appears on the balance sheet at the end of the year.

These three temporary differences between the book basis and tax basis of assets and liabilities are summarized at the top of Exhibit 17–7. The expected future tax consequences of each of these items are also indicated in the exhibit.

The required journal entry to record income taxes at the end of 2000, as indicated at the bottom of Exhibit 17–7, would be as follows:

Income tax expense.	7,500	
Deferred tax liability	1,500	
Deferred tax asset.		2,700
Income taxes payable		6,300

The credit of $6,300 to income taxes payable is determined by multiplying the year 2000 tax rate (30 percent) times the taxable income for 2000 ($21,000). The debit to income tax expense of $7,500 is the sum of the two credits ($2,700 + $6,300) minus the debit of $1,500 to deferred tax liability.

End of 2001

The analysis presented in Exhibit 17–8 serves as the basis for the end-of-period accounting for income taxes in the year 2001. Because CFO has a taxable loss of

EXHIBIT 17–7   CFO Company: End of 2000

	1998	1999	End of Current Year 2000	Future Taxable Amounts	Future Deductible Amounts
Temporary Differences					
Assets:					
Plant and equipment ($25,000 book basis − $0 tax basis)			$ 25,000	$25,000	
Liabilities:					
Unearned rent..........................			(20,000)		$20,000
Warranty obligation			(32,000)		32,000
Net temporary difference			$(27,000)		
Taxable income (Exhibit 17–4)	$ 1,000	$61,000	$ 21,000		
TOTAL				$25,000	$52,000
Enacted marginal tax rate				30%	30%
Deferred tax liability......................				$ 7,500	
Deferred tax asset					$15,600

Journal Entry Information [Dr (Cr)]

Income taxes payable (.30 × $21,000)	$ (6,300)
Deferred tax liability:	
Ending	$ (7,500)
Beginning (Exhibit 17–6)	(9,000)
Adjustment	1,500
Deferred tax asset:	
Ending	$ 15,600
Beginning (Exhibit 17–6)	18,300
Adjustment	(2,700)
Income tax expense........................	$ 7,500

$20,000 for 2001, the company may choose either (1) the loss carryback option, to receive a refund of taxes paid in previous years, or (2) the loss carryforward option, to reduce its taxable income in the future. *Assuming that the loss carryback option is chosen,* the following entry would be made at the end of 2001 to record the receivable for the tax refund:

Income tax refund receivable	5,950	
Income tax expense		5,950

The calculations are:

YEAR	TAXABLE INCOME	TAXES PAID	REFUND
1998	$ 1,000	$ 250 (.25 × $1,000)	$ 250
1999	19,000	5,700 (.3 × $19,000)	5,700
	$20,000	$5,950	$5,950

EXHIBIT 17–8   CFO Company: End of 2001

	1998	1999	2000	End of Current Year 2001	Future Taxable Amounts	Future Deductible Amounts
Temporary Differences						
Taxable income (loss) (Exhibit 17–4)	$1,000	$61,000	$21,000	$(20,000)		
Loss carryback	(1,000)	(19,000)		20,000		
TOTAL	(1,000)	(19,000)			–0–	–0–
Enacted tax rate	25%	30%				
Deferred tax liability					–0–	
Deferred tax asset						–0–
Income tax refund receivable	$ 250	$ 5,700				

Journal Entry Information [Dr (Cr)]

Income tax refund receivable ($250 + $5,700)		$ 5,950
Deferred tax liability:		
Ending	$ –0–	
Beginning (Exhibit 17–7)	(7,500)	
Adjustment		7,500
Deferred tax asset:		
Ending	$ –0–	
Beginning (Exhibit 17–7)	15,600	
Adjustment		(15,600)
Income tax expense		$ 2,150

At the end of 2001, CFO has no remaining temporary differences. Because the beginning deferred tax liability and deferred tax asset balances were $7,500 and $15,600, respectively, the following entry would be made to record deferred taxes at the end of 2001:

Deferred tax liability	7,500	
Income tax expense	8,100	
Deferred tax asset		15,600

Alternatively, these two entries could be combined, as follows (and as indicated at the bottom of Exhibit 17–8):

Income tax refund receivable	5,950	
Deferred tax liability	7,500	
Income tax expense ($8,100 – $5,950)	2,150	
Deferred tax asset		15,600

Summary of CFO Company Example

The CFO Company example contains all the elements of the examples presented earlier. In addition, it demonstrates that items which enter into pretax financial income but do not have tax consequences, such as tax-exempt interest revenue, are not considered in accounting for income taxes.

We have also demonstrated that the adjustment to the deferred tax asset or deferred tax liability at the end of a period is the amount necessary to arrive at the end-of-period balance, given the beginning-of-period balance. The amounts generated in our schedules were the required balances at the end of the year, so that any existing balance had to be considered when preparing the year-end entry for income taxes.

In addition to the procedures we have described and illustrated, under some circumstances companies must recognize a valuation allowance for a deferred tax asset. In the next section we will describe the process of determining whether a valuation allowance is needed, and if it is, how the amount of the allowance is determined.

Valuation Allowance for Deferred Tax Assets

8 Explain how to determine the appropriate valuation allowance for deferred tax assets.

CONCEPTUAL

If tax benefits associated with deferred tax assets are not expected to be realized, deferred tax assets must be reduced by a valuation allowance.

As described earlier in this chapter, deferred tax assets are recognized for future deductible temporary differences and loss carryforwards. However, to realize the tax benefit from these items, taxable income must be earned within the appropriate time frame. Because of the uncertainty regarding the realization of such benefits, a valuation allowance may be called for. That is, if the tax benefits associated with some or all of deferred tax assets are not expected to be realized, the measurement of those assets must be reduced by a **valuation allowance.**

At the end of each period, all available evidence must be evaluated to determine whether a valuation allowance is needed. Sources of taxable income that would permit realization of the tax benefit may include the following:[7]

1. Future reversals of existing temporary differences that are taxable.
2. Future taxable income, exclusive of reversing temporary differences and carryforwards.
3. Taxable income in prior carryback year(s), if carryback is permitted under the tax law.
4. Tax planning strategies.

Tax planning strategies are prudent and feasible actions that a company ordinarily might not take, except to prevent a loss carryforward from expiring unused, and that would allow the company to realize deferred tax assets.[8] (Tax planning strategies are discussed in more detail later in this chapter.) Evidence concerning any one of these four sources may be sufficient to support a conclusion that no valuation allowance is needed. However, consideration of all the available evidence is required to determine the amount of any valuation allowance.

Examples of *negative* evidence regarding the realization of a tax benefit include:[9]

1. Cumulative losses in recent years.
2. A history of operating loss or tax credit carryforwards expiring unused.
3. Losses expected in the near future by a company that is presently profitable.
4. Unsettled circumstances that, if unfavorably resolved, would adversely affect future profit levels on a continuing basis.
5. A carryback, carryforward period that is so brief, it might limit the realization of tax benefits.

Examples of *positive* evidence that might indicate that a valuation allowance is not needed, even in the face of negative evidence, include:[10]

---

[7]*FASB Statement No. 109,* para. 21.
[8]Ibid., para. 22.
[9]Ibid., para. 23.
[10]Ibid., para. 24.

1. Existing contracts or sales backlog that will produce more than enough taxable income to realize the deferred tax asset.

2. An excess of appreciated asset value over the tax basis of the entity's net assets in an amount sufficient to realize the deferred tax asset.

3. A strong earnings history, exclusive of the loss that created the future deductible amount, coupled with evidence that the loss is an aberration rather than a continuing condition.

Based on an evaluation of all the available evidence, if the likelihood of *not* realizing some or all of the future benefits of a deferred tax asset is more than 50 percent, a valuation allowance must be established. The allowance should reduce the deferred tax assets to the amount that is more likely than not to be realized. If, on the other hand, the deferred tax asset is expected to be realized—meaning that the likelihood of realization is at least slightly more than 50 percent—no valuation allowance is required. The balance of the valuation allowance must be reviewed each year to determine whether changes in circumstances require a change in judgment regarding the realizability of the deferred tax assets. The effect of any adjustment should be allocated to income tax expense from continuing operations in the period in which it occurs.

To illustrate the application of these guidelines, return to the example of a deferred tax asset and liability that begins on page 916. In that example, we calculated a deferred tax asset of $1,925 (35 percent tax rate × $5,500 future deductible amount) at the end of 1998. Assume that all available evidence indicates it is more likely than not that only $3,000 of the $5,500 future deductible amount will produce tax benefits. Thus, a valuation allowance of $875 [.35 × ($5,500 − $3,000)] must be established at the end of 1998. A journal entry like the following would be required:

Income tax expense	875	
Allowance for reduction of deferred tax asset		875

This entry increases income tax expense by $875 to recognize the lack of realizability of a portion of the deferred tax asset. The carrying value of the deferred tax asset is reduced by $875 by reporting the balance of the allowance account as a deduction from the deferred tax asset.

In subsequent years, the allowance balance would be adjusted up or down, with a corresponding adjustment to income tax expense, to recognize any increase or decrease in the realizability of deferred tax assets. The amount of the adjustment would be the amount needed to change the allowance balance from the end-of-previous-period amount to the desired amount.

The discussion so far has emphasized the basic concepts and procedures associated with accounting for income taxes. Other important issues include the appropriate financial statement presentation and disclosure requirements, which are summarized in the following section.

Financial Statement Presentation and Disclosure

Exhibit 17–9 presents CFO Company's financial statements for the years 1998 through 2001. These exhibits demonstrate application of the *Statement No. 109* display requirements. We have assumed that all revenues and expenses (other than those that are the cause of temporary differences) are received or paid in cash, and that accrued income taxes payable and income tax refund receivable are always paid or received at the beginning of the following year. You should refer to Exhibit 17–9 as you proceed through the next two sections.

> **9** Describe the financial statement presentation and disclosure requirements for deferred taxes.

Statement of Financial Position

When an entity prepares a classified statement of financial position, income taxes payable is reported as a current liability. For example, CFO Company reports in-

EXHIBIT 17-9   Comparative Financial Statements for CFO Company

	1998	1999	2000	2001
Income Statement				
Revenue	$ 50,000	$ 50,000	$ 50,000	$ 20,000
Interest revenue	2,000	2,000	2,000	2,000
Rent revenue		20,000	20,000	20,000
Depreciation expense	(25,000)	(25,000)	(25,000)	(25,000)
Warranty expense		(16,000)	(16,000)	
Other expense	(4,000)	(4,000)	(4,000)	(8,000)
Income from continuing operations before taxes	$ 23,000	$ 27,000	$ 27,000	$ 9,000
Income tax expense	(5,250)	(7,500)	(7,500)	(2,150)
Extraordinary loss (net of tax benefit of $3,500)	(11,500)			
Net income	$ 6,250	$ 19,500	$ 19,500	$ 6,850
Balance Sheet				
Assets:				
Current assets:				
Cash	$ 48,000	$145,750	$170,450	$146,150
Income tax refund receivable				5,950
Deferred tax asset	3,000	12,300	15,600	
Noncurrent assets:				
Plant and equipment (net)	75,000	50,000	25,000	–0–
Total assets	$126,000	$208,050	$211,050	$152,100
Liabilities and stockholders' equity:				
Current liabilities:				
Income taxes payable	$ 250	$ 18,300	$ 6,300	
Estimated liability for loss	10,000	5,000		
Estimated warranty obligation		16,000	32,000	
Unearned rent		20,000	20,000	
Noncurrent liabilities:				
Estimated liability for loss	5,000			
Unearned rent		20,000		
Deferred tax liability	4,500	3,000	7,500	
Stockholders' equity:				
Contributed capital	100,000	100,000	100,000	100,000
Retained earnings	6,250	25,750	45,250	52,100
Total liabilities and stockholders' equity	$126,000	$208,050	$211,050	$152,100

come taxes payable as a current liability in every year except 2001, where an income tax refund receivable is reported as a current asset.

Deferred tax assets and deferred tax liabilities must be separated into current and noncurrent amounts. *The classification as current or noncurrent is based on the classification of the related assets or liabilities.* For example, the tax effect of temporary differences related to depreciation would be classified as noncurrent because the related depreciable assets are noncurrent. Deferred tax assets and liabilities that are *not* related to an asset or a liability must be classified based on the expected reversal date of the temporary differences.

After all deferred tax assets and deferred tax liabilities have been properly classified as current or noncurrent, all those classified as current are netted to produce either a *net current* deferred tax asset (debit) or a *net current* deferred tax liability (credit). Likewise, deferred tax assets and liabilities classified as noncurrent are netted to produce either a *net noncurrent* deferred tax asset (debit) or a *net noncurrent* deferred tax liability (credit). This netting, or aggregation, procedure is appropriate only to the extent that the deferred tax assets and liabilities relate to the same tax jurisdiction; deferred tax assets and liabilities from different tax jurisdictions may not be offset.

Assuming that the deferred tax consequences of CFO Company's 1998 extraordinary loss are not related to an asset or a liability, the classification as current or noncurrent is based on the expected timing of the reversal. Thus, at the end of 1998, CFO reports a current deferred tax asset of $3,000, which is determined by multiplying the enacted marginal tax rate for 1999 (30 percent) times the deductible amount expected to be recognized in 1999 ($10,000 of the extraordinary loss). To determine the noncurrent deferred amount, the expected tax benefit of the $5,000 deductible amount to be realized in 2000 (.3 × $5,000 = $1,500) is offset against the expected tax consequences of the temporary difference from depreciation (.3 × $20,000 = $6,000), resulting in a net noncurrent deferred tax liability of $4,500 ($6,000 − $1,500). All tax consequences of the depreciation temporary difference are classified as noncurrent because the related asset is classified as noncurrent. In summary, $3,000 of the $4,500 deferred tax asset is current and $1,500 is noncurrent. The noncurrent portion is offset against the noncurrent deferred tax liability of $6,000 to produce a net noncurrent deferred tax liability of $4,500.

We see from Exhibit 17–6 (page 924) that at the end of 1999 there is a deferred tax liability of $9,000 and a deferred tax asset of $18,300. The entire deferred tax liability of $9,000 is noncurrent. We must offset against the $9,000 a portion of the deferred tax asset representing the expected tax consequences of the $20,000 unearned rent that will not be earned until 2001 (.3 × $20,000 = $6,000). This offset produces a net noncurrent deferred tax liability of $3,000 ($9,000 − $6,000). The remainder of the deferred tax asset ($18,300 − $6,000 = $12,300) is classified as current. This amount relates to the $20,000 unearned rent, the $5,000 extraordinary loss, and the $16,000 warranty obligation, all expected to be recognized in 2000. Multiplying the enacted marginal tax rate (30 percent) times the sum of these three items ($20,000 + $5,000 + $16,000 = $41,000) produces the current deferred tax asset of $12,300. The deferred tax amounts for the years 2000 and 2001, shown in Exhibit 17–9, may be explained in similar fashion.

In addition to these classification requirements, *Statement No. 109* specifies the following disclosures related to the components of the net deferred tax liability or asset:[11]

1. The total of all deferred tax liabilities.

2. The total of all deferred tax assets.

3. The total valuation allowance recognized for deferred tax assets.

Companies must also disclose the net change in the valuation allowance during the year and the dollar amounts of temporary differences, carryforwards, or carrybacks responsible for significant portions of deferred tax assets and liabilities.

Income Statement and Statement of Stockholders' Equity

Total income tax expense (or benefit) must be associated with the appropriate components of net income, in addition to being related, as appropriate, to prior period adjustments, capital transactions, and items recognized in other comprehensive income that are reported directly in stockholders' equity. The process of associating total income tax expense with components of net income and with

---

[11]Ibid., para. 43.

EXHIBIT 17-10 **The Coca-Cola Company and Subsidiaries**
(Excerpted from Notes to 1995 Financial Statements)

Income tax expense (benefit) consists of the following (in millions):

Year Ended December 31,	United States	State & Local	International	Total
1995				
Current	$204	$41	$940	$1,185
Deferred	80	10	67	157
1994				
Current	$299	$38	$779	$1,116
Deferred	24	5	29	58
1993				
Current	$356	$34	$669	$1,059
Deferred[1]	(64)	5	(3)	(62)

[1]An additional deferred tax benefit of $8 million in 1993 has been included in the *Statement No. 112* transition effect charge.

The Company made income tax payments of approximately $1,000 million, $785 million and $650 million in 1995, 1994, and 1993, respectively.

A reconciliation of the statutory U.S. federal rate and effective rates is as follows:

Year Ended December 31,	1995	1994	1993
Statutory U.S. federal rate.	**35.0%**	35.0%	35.0%
State income taxes—net of federal benefit	**1.0**	1.0	1.0
Earnings in jurisdictions taxed at rates different from the statutory U.S. federal rate . .	**(3.9)**	(4.3)	(5.1)
Equity income.	**(1.7)**	(1.1)	(1.7)
Other—net	**.6**	.9	2.1
	31.0%	31.5%	31.3%

The Company's effective tax rate reflects the favorable U.S. tax treatment from manufacturing facilities in Puerto Rico that operate under a negotiated exemption grant that expires December 31, 2009. Changes to U.S. tax law enacted in 1993 limit the utilization of the favorable tax treatment from operations in Puerto Rico. The Company's effective tax rate also reflects the tax benefit derived from having significant operations outside the United States that are taxed at rates lower than the U.S. statutory rate of 35 percent. As a result of changes in U.S. tax law, the Company was required to record charges for additional taxes and tax-related expenses that reduced net income by approximately $51 million in 1993.

CONCEPTUAL

Income from continuing operations is the focal point of intraperiod tax allocation.

prior period adjustments, capital transactions, and elements of other comprehensive income included directly in stockholders' equity is called **intraperiod tax allocation.** Components of net income with which income taxes must be associated are (1) continuing operations, (2) discontinued operations, (3) extraordinary items, and (4) accounting changes.

Income from continuing operations is the focal point of the process of associating income tax expense with income components. In general, the amount of income tax expense (or benefit) associated with continuing operations is the tax consequence of items entering into pretax income or loss from continuing operations for the year. If there is only one item other than continuing operations, the

Appropriate U.S. and international taxes have been provided for earnings of subsidiary companies that are expected to be remitted to the parent company. Exclusive of amounts that would result in little or no tax if remitted, the cumulative amount of unremitted earnings from international subsidiaries that are expected to be indefinitely reinvested is approximately $577 million on December 31, 1995. The taxes that would be paid upon remittance of these indefinitely reinvested earnings are approximately $202 million based on current tax laws.

The tax effects of temporary differences and carryforwards that give rise to significant portions of deferred tax assets and liabilities consist of the following (in millions):

December 31,	1995	1994
Deferred tax assets:		
Benefit plans	$ 369	$324
Liabilities and reserves	178	169
Net operating loss carryforwards	97	108
Other	151	128
Gross deferred tax assets	$ 795	$729
Valuation allowance	(42)	(46)
	$ 753	$683
Deferred tax liabilities:		
Property, plant and equipment	$ 414	$362
Equity investments	170	188
Intangible assets	89	34
Other	205	72
	$ 878	$656
Net deferred tax asset (liability)[1]	$(125)	$ 27

[1]Deferred tax assets of $69 million and $207 million have been included in the consolidated balance sheet caption "marketable securities and other assets" at December 31, 1995 and 1994, respectively.

On December 31, 1995, the Company had $265 million of operating loss carryforwards available to reduce future taxable income of certain international subsidiaries. Loss carryforwards of $107 million must be utilized within the next 5 years, and $158 million can be utilized over an indefinite period. A valuation allowance has been provided for a portion of the deferred tax assets related to these loss carryforwards.

income tax expense or benefit remaining after the allocation to continuing operations is allocated to that item.[12]

To illustrate the disaggregation and display of income tax expense, consider the CFO Company example once more. At the end of 1998, CFO recorded income tax

---

[12]If two or more categories other than continuing operations exist, the allocation process may become more complex. Generally, in those circumstances, the incremental effect of all net loss categories is determined and the appropriate tax effect is allocated. Then the amount remaining to be allocated to net gain categories is the difference between the total tax expense or benefit and the amount allocated to net loss categories. See ibid., paras. 35–38.

expense of $1,750. The total income tax expense of $1,750 was associated with the two components of net income: (1) income from continuing operations ($5,250) and (2) the extraordinary loss item ($3,500 benefit).

Pretax income from continuing operations *having tax consequences* for 1998 was $21,000, calculated as follows (see Exhibit 17–4 for the amounts):

Pretax financial income	**$ 8,000**
Add: Extraordinary loss	**15,000**
Deduct: Tax-exempt interest	**(2,000)**
Pretax income from continuing operations having tax consequences	**$21,000**

Therefore, income tax expense associated with income from continuing operations is $5,250 (.25 × $21,000). The income tax *benefit* associated with the extraordinary loss is $3,500—the difference between the total income tax expense of $1,750 and the amount associated with income from continuing operations ($5,250).

In the notes to the financial statements, income tax expense attributed to income from continuing operations, using the approach just described, must be reconciled to the amount of income tax expense that would result from applying the statutory tax rates to pretax income from continuing operations. In the example just given, the amount of income tax expense that would result from applying the statutory rate to pretax income from continuing operations for 1998 would be $5,750 (.25 × $23,000). Therefore, $5,250 must be reconciled to $5,750 (although in this case the difference is probably not material). The amount and nature of significant reconciling items, such as the tax-exempt interest in the example, must be disclosed.

An example of the actual disclosure of income tax information is shown in Exhibit 17-10 which is excerpted from the notes to the 1995 financial statements of The Coca-Cola Company (Coke). Note that Coke first discloses the current and deferred portion of income tax expense, according to different tax jurisdictions. Total taxes paid each year are also disclosed. The reconciliation of the effective rate of 31 percent (1995) with the statutory rate of 35 percent indicates that the difference is caused largely by lower tax rates than the U.S. federal rate in some jurisdictions, especially Puerto Rico.

The Coca-Cola Company explains that taxes have not been provided on certain earnings of international subsidiaries, in which earnings are expected to be reinvested indefinitely. Reinvestment of earning in these situations allows the company to avoid paying U.S. taxes on the earnings; therefore, accrual of taxes would be inappropriate. Coke also discloses the major sources of deferred tax assets and liabilities and indicates the amount of operating loss carryforwards available, along with the valuation allowance established for such carryforwards.

ADDITIONAL ISSUES IN ACCOUNTING FOR INCOME TAXES

Two additional issues can affect the accounting for income taxes. In this section, we will first discuss the income tax effects of tax planning strategies. We will then describe the impact of the alternative minimum tax on deferred tax calculations.

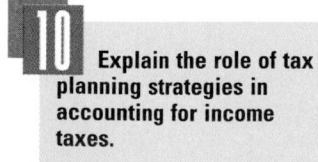

Explain the role of tax planning strategies in accounting for income taxes.

Tax Planning Strategies

Tax planning strategies refer to management actions that (1) are prudent and feasible; (2) might not be taken ordinarily, except to prevent an operating loss or tax credit carryforward from expiring unused; and (3) would result in the realization of deferred tax assets.[13] Tax planning strategies *must* be considered in determining the amount of valuation allowance required. However, if sufficient positive evidence exists to suggest that a valuation allowance is *not* needed, tax planning strategies need not be considered.

Examples of tax planning strategies that may be used include the following:

1. The sale-leaseback of plant assets.

2. A shift of estimated future taxable income from one year to another.

3. An election to waive the carryback option for a net operating loss deduction.

4. A shift in the estimated pattern and timing of future reversals of temporary differences.

Management must exercise due diligence to arrive at the lowest possible deferred tax liability or maximum deferred tax asset. Whatever tax planning strategy accomplishes this objective must be incorporated into the calculations.

Alternative Minimum Tax

Under current U.S. tax law, corporations must determine their potential federal income tax liability using both the regular tax system and an **alternative minimum tax (AMT)** system. The corporation's actual tax liability is the larger of the two liabilities. The calculation of taxable and deductible amounts for future years must consequently be carried out using both systems, and the deferred tax consequences for future years based on the results of both calculations. Furthermore, the same assumptions or tax strategies must be used under both systems. For example, if it is assumed that a liability will be settled in three years under the regular tax system, the same assumption must be made under the alternative minimum tax system.

> **11** Discuss the role of the alternative minimum tax in accounting for income taxes.

The alternative minimum tax not only complicates the calculation of the deferred tax consequences of existing temporary differences; it has other, more important implications. Specifically, the current Internal Revenue Code requires that in calculating income taxes payable under the alternative minimum tax system, a portion of the difference between pretax financial income and the tentative alternative minimum tax taxable income must be treated as a tax preference item. That is, the amount of taxes payable under the alternative minimum tax system is based partially on pretax financial income—an approach that represents a major policy change by the IRS and that could significantly influence the accounting principles companies use and the estimates they make for financial reporting purposes. Actual calculations under the alternative minimum tax system are more appropriately covered in corporate tax textbooks; they are beyond the scope of this discussion.

---

[13]Ibid., para. 22.

SUMMARY OF LEARNING OBJECTIVES

1. Identify temporary differences between the tax basis and the book basis of an asset or liability.

A temporary difference between the book basis and tax basis of an asset or a liability is a difference that is expected to result in taxable or deductible amounts on future tax returns, without regard to other future events.

2. Distinguish between partial and comprehensive recognition of deferred tax consequences.

Partial recognition means that only nonrecurring temporary differences that are expected to reverse in a relatively short time are recognized as having deferred tax consequences. Comprehensive recognition means that the future tax consequences of all temporary differences between book bases and tax bases are recognized in the financial statements.

3. Distinguish between the asset/liability method and the deferred method of accounting for income taxes.

Under the asset/liability method, which may be viewed as a balance sheet approach, the tax consequences of events that have been recognized in the financial statements must be recognized as either (1) taxes payable or refundable currently or (2) deferred tax assets or liabilities. Deferred amounts are measured using the enacted tax rates applicable to future years. Income tax expense is a "plug" figure, obtained after determining the appropriate adjustments to deferred tax assets and liabilities and the amount of income taxes payable currently. Under the deferred method, which may be viewed as an income statement approach, income tax expense is calculated directly, as the amount that would be payable currently if all revenues and expenses that were reported in pretax financial income were also reported in the current tax return. The deferred amount is then the difference between income tax expense and income taxes payable.

4. State the current requirements for accounting for income taxes.

Under *Statement No. 109*, the asset/liability method, applied on a comprehensive basis, is employed to account for the future tax consequences of temporary differences. The expected future tax consequences of temporary differences between the book bases and tax bases are not discounted. If uncertainty regarding the realization of deferred tax assets is sufficiently high, a valuation allowance is required.

5. Explain the effect of changes in enacted marginal tax rates on deferred tax amounts.

When enacted marginal tax rates change, the deferred tax asset or liability must be adjusted to reflect the new tax rate. The effect of this change in estimate is reported as an adjustment to income tax expense.

6. Describe and account for net operating loss carrybacks and carryforwards.

When a company's deductions exceed its revenues on the corporate tax return, a net operating loss (NOL) occurs. This loss may be used to claim a refund for taxes paid in the three years preceding the loss (starting with the third year back), an approach that is referred to as a loss carryback, or it may be used to reduce taxes that would otherwise be payable for up to fifteen years in the future (beginning with the first year after the loss), an approach referred to as a loss carryforward. A loss carryback creates a claim for a refund of income taxes already paid. A loss carryforward creates a future deductible amount and is thus recorded as a deferred tax asset. If uncertainty regarding the realization of the benefits of the carryforward is sufficiently high, a valuation allowance is required.

7. Identify financial accounting events that do not have tax consequences.

Examples of financial accounting events that do not have tax consequences include interest received on state and local government obligations, interest expense on debt incurred to acquire tax-exempt securities, life insurance proceeds received by a company as the beneficiary of a policy on officers or employees, premiums paid for life insurance on officers or employees when the company is the beneficiary, and fines and expenses incurred for violating the law.

8. Explain how to determine the appropriate valuation allowance for deferred tax assets.

At the end of each period, all available evidence must be evaluated to determine whether or not a valuation allowance is needed. If the likelihood is greater than 50 percent that some or all of the deferred tax assets will not be realized, a valuation allowance is required to reduce the deferred tax assets to the amount that is expected to be realized. The end-of-period adjustment is the amount needed to adjust the valuation allowance from its existing balance to the desired balance.

9. Describe the financial statement presentation and disclosure requirements for deferred taxes.

Deferred tax assets and liabilities must be classified as current or noncurrent, based on the classification of the related assets or liabilities. If there is no related asset or liability, the classification is based on the expected period of reversal of the temporary differences. For each tax jurisdiction, current deferred tax assets and liabilities are netted to produce a net current deferred tax asset or liability; likewise, noncurrent deferred tax assets and liabilities are netted to produce a net noncurrent deferred tax asset or liability. Companies must disclose (1) the total of all deferred tax liabilities, (2) the total of all deferred tax assets, and (3) the total valuation allowance recognized for deferred tax assets. They must also disclose the net change in the valuation allowance for the year and the amounts of significant components of deferred tax assets and liabilities. Intraperiod tax allocation is required in order to report income tax expense. Income from continuing operations is the focal point of the allocation. Income tax expense attributed to income from continuing operations must also be reconciled with the amount that would be expected using statutory tax rates.

10. Explain the role of tax planning strategies in accounting for income taxes.
Tax planning strategies may be used to prevent an operating loss or tax credit carryforward from expiring unused or to otherwise allow for the realization of deferred tax assets. These strategies must be considered in determining the amount of the valuation allowance required for deferred tax assets.

11. Discuss the role of the alternative minimum tax in accounting for income taxes.
Companies must calculate their potential federal income tax liability under both the regular tax system and the alternative minimum tax system. The actual tax liability is the larger of the two amounts. Thus, for financial reporting purposes, calculation of the tax consequences of future taxable and deductible amounts must be carried out using both systems.

KEY TERMS

alternative minimum tax (AMT) 935   net-of-tax display 913
asset/liability method 912   net operating loss 917
comprehensive recognition 911   partial recognition 911
deferred method 913   tax planning strategies 935
enacted marginal tax rate 915   temporary difference 909
intraperiod tax allocation 932   timing difference 909
loss carryback 917   valuation allowance 928
loss carryforward 917

QUESTIONS

Q 17-1. Without identifying specific items that are treated differently for tax purposes than for financial accounting purposes, provide a brief explanation of why taxable income and pretax financial income may differ.

Q 17-2. What is a *temporary difference*? Give four examples of temporary differences.

Q 17-3. What is the basic accounting issue resulting from temporary differences?

Q 17-4. Explain how the concept of accrual accounting and the definitions of assets and liabilities relate to the recognition and measurement of deferred tax consequences.

Q 17-5. Define *partial recognition* and *comprehensive recognition*. Describe the arguments for and against each of these approaches to recognition of the expected future tax consequences of temporary differences.

Q 17-6.   Identify and briefly describe the two methods of recognition of expected future tax consequences. What is the nature of deferred income taxes under each of these methods?

Q 17-7.   Describe the approach to recognition of deferred tax consequences that is required by GAAP.

Q 17-8.   Explain the meaning of the amounts reported in the balance sheet for deferred tax assets and deferred tax liabilities.

Q 17-9.   From a theoretical viewpoint, noncurrent deferred tax assets and liabilities should be discounted, as should other noncurrent monetary assets and liabilities. Why is discounting prohibited by *Statement No. 109*?

Q 17-10.   What tax rates must be used when determining the tax consequences of future taxable and deductible amounts? Why?

Q 17-11.   Explain how changes in marginal tax rates that were not enacted when the tax consequences of temporary differences were recorded affect deferred tax assets and liabilities and income tax expense.

Q 17-12.   Define *net operating loss*. Describe the two alternatives available to a company for obtaining a tax benefit from a net operating loss. Which alternative would you expect to be chosen more frequently? Why?

Q 17-13.   Explain the fundamental distinction between the tax benefit of a loss carryback and the tax benefit of a loss carryforward.

Q 17-14.   Describe the accounting and reporting requirements for tax benefits associated with (1) loss carrybacks and (2) loss carryforwards.

Q 17-15.   What are financial accounting events that do not have tax consequences? Give four examples.

Q 17-16.   Under what circumstances is a valuation allowance required for deferred tax assets?

Q 17-17.   How are the valuation allowance and adjustments to the valuation allowance reported in financial statements?

Q 17-18.   Explain how deferred tax assets and liabilities are separated into current and noncurrent amounts in a classified statement of financial position.

Q 17-19.   Explain briefly how total income tax expense is associated with income from continuing operations and other items.

Q 17-20.   What are *tax planning strategies,* and what is their significance in accounting for income taxes?

Q 17-21.   What is the significance of the *alternative minimum tax* to the process of recognizing the deferred tax consequences of temporary differences?

CASES

C 17-1.   **THEORETICAL ANALYSIS OF RECOGNITION OF EXPECTED FUTURE TAX CONSE-QUENCES**   Jennifer Bradley, the president of Bradley Corp., knows that business entities must recognize the expected future tax consequences of existing temporary differences. She is also aware that, even though generally accepted accounting principles require comprehensive recognition using the asset/liability method, other approaches are conceptually possible. However, she is not familiar with these other approaches, and believes that a better understanding of them might help her understanding of the asset/liability method.

REQUIRED   Write a memorandum to Ms. Bradley (1) explaining the theoretical justification for recognizing the expected future tax consequences of existing temporary differences, (2) describing and discussing the pros and cons of both partial recognition and comprehensive recognition, and (3) describing the asset/liability method and the deferred method of recognizing the expected future tax consequences of temporary differences. Explain the rationale underlying each method.

C 17-2.   **DEFERRED TAX ASSETS AND LIABILITIES**   For the current year, Baldwin Company includes in its income statement the following items:

   a)   Gross profit on credit sales.
   b)   Gross profit on long-term construction contracts.
   c)   Estimated costs of product warranty contracts.
   d)   Premiums on officers' life insurance with Baldwin Company as beneficiary.

REQUIRED   **I.**   Under what conditions should deferred tax assets or liabilities be reported in the financial statements?

2. For each of the items above, specify when a deferred tax asset or liability must be recognized, and indicate the rationale for such recognition.

C 17-3. **BALANCE SHEET CLASSIFICATION OF DEFERRED TAXES** Arens Company's president has heard that deferred tax assets and liabilities can be classified in a variety of ways in the statement of financial position. He does not have an accounting background, and he finds the classification guidelines rather confusing.

REQUIRED In a memo, describe for the president the conditions under which deferred tax assets and liabilities would be classified as current and noncurrent in the statement of financial position. Explain the justification for such classification.

C 17-4. **THEORETICAL BASIS FOR AND FINANCIAL REPORTING OF DEFERRED TAX ASSETS AND LIABILITIES** Wilk Company appropriately uses the asset/liability method to recognize the expected future tax consequences of temporary differences. For machinery purchased this year, Wilk uses a modified accelerated cost recovery system (MACRS) for tax purposes and the straight-line method for accounting purposes. The tax deduction is the larger amount this year. Also, Wilk received rent in advance this year. The rental receipts are included in this year's taxable income. For financial accounting purposes, however, the rent receipts are reported as unearned revenue, a current liability.

REQUIRED As the chief financial officer, write a brief report to the Board of Directors covering the following issues:
1. The theoretical justification for recognition of deferred tax assets and liabilities.
2. The appropriate accounting for the expected future tax consequences of the depreciation of machinery and the rent, including the rationale for the accounting.
3. Classification of the expected future tax consequences of the temporary differences related to the machinery and the rent on the balance sheet and income statement, including the rationale for such classification.

C 17-5. **EVENTS THAT DO NOT HAVE TAX CONSEQUENCES VS. TEMPORARY DIFFERENCES** The following differences enter into the reconciliation of financial accounting income and taxable income of Mona Corporation for the current year:
a) Tax depreciation exceeds book depreciation by $15,000.
b) Estimated warranty costs of $8,000 applicable to the current year's sales have not been paid.
c) Unearned rent revenue of $20,000 was deferred on the books but appropriately included in taxable income.
d) Life insurance premiums on officers' lives totaling $3,000 were recorded as an expense for book purposes but are not allowed as a deduction for tax purposes.

REQUIRED Consider each reconciling item independently. Explain whether each item would enter into the calculation of deferred tax assets and liabilities. For any item that is included in the calculation, explain the effect of the item on the current year's income tax expense. (Deferred tax calculations are not required.)

(AICPA, adapted)

EXERCISES

E 17-1. **EVENTS THAT DO NOT HAVE TAX CONSEQUENCES VS. TEMPORARY DIFFERENCES** The following items are treated differently for tax purposes and for financial accounting purposes:
a) Life insurance proceeds received by the company as beneficiary of a policy on an officer.
b) Interest revenue on municipal bonds.
c) Pension cost expensed for financial accounting purposes exceeds the amount deducted for tax purposes (the amount funded during the period).
d) Interest expense incurred to acquire municipal bonds.
e) Interest during construction capitalized as part of asset cost for financial accounting purposes but deducted as incurred for tax purposes.
f) Fines paid as a result of law violations.

g) Insurance premiums paid on policies on officers' lives for which the company is the beneficiary.

h) Warranty expenses accrued for financial accounting purposes but deducted as incurred for tax purposes.

i) Rent revenue recognized when received for tax purposes but deferred and recognized as revenue when earned for financial accounting purposes.

j) Goodwill amortization.

k) Modified accelerated cost recovery system (MACRS) depreciation used for tax purposes, but straight-line depreciation used for financial accounting purposes.

REQUIRED   Indicate whether each of the above items is an event that (1) does not have tax consequences or (2) results in a temporary difference.

E 17-2.   **DEFERRED TAX LIABILITY**   For financial accounting purposes, Hock Company accrued a gain of $80,000 on a casual sale of real estate in 1998, its first year of operations. For tax purposes, the gain was recognized on the basis of cash collections as follows:

YEAR	DEFERRED GAIN RECOGNIZED FOR TAX PURPOSES
1998	$20,000
1999	20,000
2000	20,000
2001	20,000

The enacted marginal tax rate was 30 percent in 1998 and 35 percent for subsequent years. Assume that Hock had no other items affecting pretax financial income or taxable income during 1998.

REQUIRED   Prepare the journal entry to record income taxes for Hock for 1998.

E 17-3.   **DEFERRED TAX ASSET**   In 1998, its first year of operations, Julie Company accrued, for financial accounting purposes, warranty expense of $50,000 related to 1998 sales. For tax purposes, the warranty costs are deducted in the period in which they are incurred. Tax deductions for warranty costs related to 1998 sales were $14,000 in 1998, $20,000 in 1999, and $16,000 in 2000. The tax rate was 35 percent in 1998 and 30 percent in 1999 and 2000. Taxable income in 1998 was $200,000.

REQUIRED   Prepare the journal entry to record income taxes for Julie Company at the end of 1998. Show supporting calculations.

E 17-4.   **DEFERRED TAX ASSET/LIABILITY**   At the beginning of 1998, its first year of operations, Regier Company purchased a machine for $10,000. The depreciation schedules for book (financial accounting) purposes and for tax purposes were as follows:

YEAR	BOOK PURPOSES	TAX PURPOSES
1998	$2,500	$4,000
1999	2,500	3,000
2000	2,500	2,000
2001	2,500	1,000

Assume an income tax rate of 34 percent for 1998 and 40 percent for all other years. Pretax financial income was $6,000 in 1998. The only temporary difference at the end of 1998 related to the depreciation difference.

REQUIRED   Prepare the journal entry to record income taxes at the end of 1998. Show supporting calculations.

E 17-5.   **DEFERRED TAX ASSET/LIABILITY; NET OPERATING LOSS**   Refer to the facts in Exercise 17-4, but assume that pretax financial income was $500.

REQUIRED   Prepare the journal entry to record income taxes at the end of 1998. Show supporting calculations.

E 17-6.   **DEFERRED TAX LIABILITY**   King's Auto Care began operations in January 1998. King invested $9,000 to purchase repair tools. For tax purposes, King will take $5,000, $2,500, and $1,500 in depreciation for 1998, 1999, and 2000, respectively. For financial statement purposes, King will depreciate the tools over three years using the straight-line method, with no salvage value. Pretax financial income in 1998 is $10,000. The enacted marginal tax rate for 1998 is 30 percent, and the enacted marginal tax rate for 1999 and 2000 is 40 percent. Assume that King's taxable income in 1999 and 2000 was $7,000 and $8,000, respectively, and that there are no other temporary differences.

REQUIRED   Prepare the journal entries to record income taxes in 1998, 1999, and 2000. Show supporting calculations.

E 17-7.   **DEFERRED TAX LIABILITY WITH CHANGE IN ENACTED MARGINAL TAX RATE**   Refer to the facts in Exercise 17-6, but assume that there is a tax law change in 1999 that reduces the tax rate to 34 percent for 1999 and 2000.

REQUIRED   Prepare the journal entries to record income taxes in 1998, 1999, and 2000. Show supporting calculations.

E 17-8.   **DEFERRED TAX ASSET ADJUSTMENT**   For financial accounting purposes, Maddox Corporation recognizes royalty income in the period earned. For tax purposes, royalties are taxed when they are collected. On December 31, 1997, Maddox reported a deferred tax asset of $160,000 related to the temporary difference at that time. Unearned royalties in Maddox's December 31, 1998, balance sheet amounted to $440,000. The income tax rate is 40 percent for 1998 and 30 percent for periods subsequent to 1998.

REQUIRED   Based on the above information, what should be the adjustment to the deferred tax asset account at December 31, 1998?

E 17-9.   **DEFERRED TAX LIABILITY ADJUSTMENT**   Grisham Company uses a modified accelerated cost recovery system method to depreciate its machinery for tax purposes and the straight-line method for financial accounting purposes. As a result, at the end of 1997, Grisham reported a deferred tax liability of $210,000. At the end of 1998, the book basis of the depreciable machinery exceeded the tax basis by $900,000. The income tax rate was 35 percent in 1998 and 30 percent in all subsequent years.

REQUIRED   Based on the above information, what should be the adjustment to the deferred tax liability account at the end of 1998?

E 17-10.   **DEFERRED TAX LIABILITY; EVENTS WITHOUT TAX CONSEQUENCES**   Dave's Cookies began selling cookie franchises in 1998. The franchisees agree to pay Dave $20,000 for each franchise over a four-year period. For financial accounting purposes, the franchise fee is recognized in the year in which the franchise is sold. In 1998, $240,000 of franchise fee revenue was recognized for financial accounting purposes, and $60,000 was recognized for tax purposes. In 1999, 2000, and 2001, the temporary difference of $180,000 will be recognized for tax purposes. There were no other temporary differences. Pretax financial income in 1998 was $430,000, which included interest from municipal bonds of $20,000. The enacted marginal tax rate was 40 percent for 1998 and 30 percent for all subsequent years.

REQUIRED   Prepare the journal entry to record income taxes in 1998. Show supporting calculations.

E 17-11.   **DEFERRED TAX LIABILITY; NOL CARRYFORWARD**   Refer to the facts in Exercise 17-10, but assume that pretax financial income in 1998 was $130,000, and that Dave elects the loss carryforward option.

REQUIRED   Prepare the journal entry to record income taxes in 1998. Show supporting calculations.

E 17-12.   **DEFERRED TAX ASSET/LIABILITY**   Hoyt Auto offers a three-year service warranty on all new cars sold. In 1998, its first year of operations, Hoyt has pretax financial income of $160,000, which includes an accrued expense of $50,000 for expected warranty costs. During 1998, Hoyt had cash expenditures of $13,000 associated with warranty work. Expenditures are expected to be $12,000, $21,600, and $3,400 in 1999, 2000, and 2001, respectively. For tax purposes, Hoyt recognizes income from some sales on the installment method. As a result, $24,000 of 1998 pretax financial income was deferred to future years for tax purposes. The enacted marginal tax rate was 42 percent in 1998 and 35 percent in all subsequent years.

REQUIRED   Prepare the journal entry to record income taxes for 1998. Show supporting calculations.

E 17-13.   **DEFERRED TAX ASSET/LIABILITY; NET OPERATING LOSS**   Refer to the facts in Exercise 17-12, but assume instead that Hoyt Auto experiences a $30,000 tax net operating loss in 1998 and elects to carry the loss forward.

REQUIRED   Prepare the journal entry to record income taxes for 1998. Show supporting calculations.

E 17-14.   **DEFERRED TAX LIABILITY; NET OPERATING LOSS**   In 1998, Hans and Franz Gym Equipment begins to manufacture weight machines, which are sold on the installment basis. For financial accounting purposes, revenue is recognized when equipment is sold. For tax purposes, income is recognized when installment payments are received. In 1998, the company recognized revenue of $250,000 for financial accounting purposes; for tax purposes, $70,000 was recognized. In 1999, 2000, and 2001, the temporary difference of $180,000 is expected to be recognized for tax purposes. The enacted marginal tax rate is 45 percent in 1998 and 35 percent in subsequent years. Pretax financial income in 1998 was $50,000.

REQUIRED   Prepare the journal entry to record income taxes in 1998. Show supporting calculations.

E 17-15.   **DEFERRED TAX ASSET ADJUSTMENT; CHANGE IN TAX RATE**   Mandel Corporation recognizes royalty income in the period earned for financial accounting purposes. For tax purposes, royalties are recognized in the period in which they are collected. As of December 31, 1998, unearned royalties of $400,000 are included in Mandel's balance sheet. Unearned royalties in Mandel's December 31, 1999, balance sheet amounted to $300,000. Taxable income in 1998 and 1999 was greater than the unearned revenue balance at the end of the year. No other temporary differences existed at the end of 1998 and 1999. The enacted marginal tax rate at the end of 1998 was 40 percent. During 1999, a new marginal tax rate of 30 percent was enacted for 1999 and subsequent years.

REQUIRED   What should be the change in the deferred tax asset account at the end of 1999? Show calculations.

E 17-16.   **NET OPERATING LOSS WITH DEFERRED TAX ADJUSTMENT**   Scrappy Dog Food Company had taxable income of $22,000 in 1998 and $15,000 in 1999. In 2000, Scrappy had a pretax financial accounting loss of $47,000 and had temporary differences relating to depreciation and franchise revenue. The book basis of fixed assets was $20,000 higher than the tax basis at the end of 1999, and $35,000 higher at the end of 2000. Franchise fees of $17,000 were received in 2000 but will not be included in pretax financial income until 2002. The enacted marginal tax rate was 40 percent in 1998, 38 percent in 1999, and 30 percent for all subsequent years. The deferred tax liability at the end of 1999 was $8,000. Scrappy elects the carryback option for net operating losses.

REQUIRED   Prepare the journal entry to record income taxes for 2000. Show supporting calculations.

E 17-17.   **VALUATION ALLOWANCE ADJUSTMENT**   After making the entries to record income taxes for 1998, Behn Corporation had a deferred tax asset balance of $22,000. Based on the available evidence, it is more likely than not that $10,000 of future deductible amounts will not produce future tax benefits. The enacted marginal tax rate in all subsequent periods is 40 percent. The balance in the valuation allowance before adjustment is $2,500.

REQUIRED   Prepare the journal entry required by Behn Corporation to adjust the valuation allowance at the end of 1998. Show supporting calculations.

E 17-18.   **VALUATION ALLOWANCE ADJUSTMENT**   Kraft Company had several temporary differences with expected future tax consequences at the end of 1998. After making the entries to record 1998 income taxes, Kraft had deferred tax assets of $32,000 and deferred tax liabilities of $56,000. After reviewing all available evidence, Kraft determined that it was more likely than not that $8,000 of future deductible amounts related to existing temporary differences would not produce tax benefits.

The valuation allowance had a balance of $5,000 prior to adjustment. The enacted marginal tax rate for all subsequent periods is 35 percent.

REQUIRED   Prepare the journal entry required by Kraft Company to adjust the valuation allowance at the end of 1998. Show supporting calculations.

E 17-19.   **BALANCE SHEET CLASSIFICATION OF DEFERRED TAXES**   At December 31, 1998, Green Company had a deferred tax liability of $48,000 related to the difference between the book basis and tax basis of a depreciable fixed asset because of differing depreciation methods for financial accounting purposes and tax purposes. The difference between the book basis and the tax basis was expected to be reduced by $12,000 in 1999. Also, Green accrued warranty costs for financial accounting purposes but deducted them as incurred for tax purposes, resulting in a deferred tax asset of $34,000 at the end of 1998. It is expected that in 1999, Green will incur warranty costs of $40,000 related to sales made prior to 1999. Income tax rates enacted as of the end of 1998 were 35 percent for 1998 and 45 percent for all subsequent years.

REQUIRED   How should deferred taxes be reported in Green's balance sheet at December 31, 1998?

E 17-20.   **BALANCE SHEET CLASSIFICATION OF DEFERRED TAXES**   Bedford Corporation had temporary differences related to three items at the end of 1998:
a)   Bedford discontinued a major segment of its business in 1998. As a result, Bedford accrued a liability of $1,400,000 for financial accounting purposes, which

represented the expected loss on disposal. For tax purposes, $300,000 of the loss was deducted in 1998, and it was expected that the other $1,100,000 would be deducted in 1999.

b) Bedford reported revenues from franchise fees as earned revenues for financial accounting purposes and on the basis of cash collections for tax purposes. As a result, unearned franchise fees of $300,000 were reported on the balance sheet at the end of 1998. It was expected that the balance of the unearned franchise fees account would decrease by $40,000 by the end of 1999.

c) Depreciable fixed assets were depreciated using a modified accelerated cost recovery system method for tax purposes and the straight-line method for financial accounting purposes. As a result, the book basis exceeded the tax basis by $800,000 at the end of 1998. It was expected that the book basis would exceed the tax basis by $650,000 at the end of 1999.

The enacted marginal tax rate was 34 percent for 1998 and 40 percent for subsequent years.

REQUIRED How should deferred taxes be reported in Bedford's balance sheet at the end of 1998?

E 17-21. **INCOME STATEMENT DISPLAY OF INCOME TAX EXPENSE** Trevino Company had net income of $4,200,000 in 1998. The following items entered into the determination of net income (all numbers are before taxes):

Income from continuing operations	$6,200,000
Loss from discontinued operations	(1,000,000)
Extraordinary gain—debt extinguishment	1,800,000
Total	$7,000,000

Assume that a tax rate of 40 percent applies to all income components.

REQUIRED Prepare the income statement for Trevino Company for 1998, beginning with income from continuing operations before taxes.

E 17-22. **INCOME STATEMENT DISPLAY OF INCOME TAX EXPENSE** Refer to the facts given in Exercise 17-21, but assume that income from continuing operations includes tax-exempt municipal bond income of $300,000 and that net income is $4,320,000.

REQUIRED **1.** Prepare the income statement for Trevino Company for 1998, beginning with income from continuing operations before taxes.

2. Prepare a note to the financial statements at the end of 1998 explaining why the income tax expense related to continuing operations differs from the amount that would be expected based on the statutory rate of 40 percent.

PROBLEMS

P 17-1. **DEFERRED TAX ADJUSTMENT** Berry Corporation, which commenced operations in 1998, follows the same accounting methods for financial accounting and tax purposes with the exception of accounting for warranty costs and franchise fee revenue. Warranty costs are recognized on the accrual basis for financial accounting purposes and when paid for tax purposes. Franchise fees are recognized when cash is received for tax purposes and when earned for financial accounting purposes. Warranty costs of $20,000 were accrued in 1998, but only $3,000 of warranty costs was incurred. Franchise fees of $170,000 were collected, but only $40,000 was recognized for financial accounting purposes. The enacted marginal tax rate was 40 percent for 1998 and 30 percent for subsequent years. Pretax financial income for 1998 is $500,000.

REQUIRED Prepare the journal entry to record income taxes in 1998. Show supporting calculations.

P 17-2. **DEFERRED TAX LIABILITY** Colby Company commenced operations in 1997. Colby uses the same accounting methods for both financial accounting and tax purposes, except for depreciation, which it determines by the sum-of-the-years'-digits method for tax purposes and by the straight-line method for book purposes. Colby's depreciable assets were acquired at the beginning of 1997 at a cost of $220,000 with an estimated salvage value of $20,000 and a useful life of four years. Pretax financial income for 1997 was $220,000. At the end of 1997, enacted marginal tax rates were 40 percent for 1997 and 30 percent for subsequent years.

REQUIRED   **1.** Prepare the journal entry to record income taxes at the end of 1997. Show supporting calculations.

2. Assume that the only temporary difference existing at the end of the years 1998–2000 relates to depreciation. Also assume that pretax financial income is $260,000 in 1998, $180,000 in 1999, and $200,000 in 2000. Prepare journal entries to record income taxes at the end of each of these three years. Show supporting calculations.

P 17-3.   **DEFERRED TAX LIABILITY**   Gardner Company, which began operations in 1997, accounts for certain credit sales on the accrual basis for accounting purposes and on the basis of cash collections for tax purposes. Data regarding temporary differences and expected future tax consequences for these credit sales for the years 1997 through 2000 follow:

YEAR	ENACTED MARGINAL TAX RATE AT END OF 1997	FUTURE TAXABLE AMOUNTS	EXPECTED FUTURE TAX CONSEQUENCES			
			1998	1999	2000	AFTER 2000
1997	40%	$ 80,000	$30,000	$40,000	$ 10,000	
1998	30	120,000		48,000	60,000	$ 12,000
1999	30	200,000			60,000	140,000
2000	30	160,000				160,000
After 2000	30					
			$30,000	$88,000	$130,000	$312,000

Pretax financial income is $300,000 in all years. There are no other temporary differences, and there are no events that do not have tax consequences.

REQUIRED   Prepare the journal entries to record income taxes at the end of 1997, 1998, 1999, and 2000. Show supporting calculations.

P 17-4.   **DEFERRED TAX ADJUSTMENT**   Shadow Cat Food, Inc., which began operations in 1998, follows the same accounting methods for financial accounting and tax purposes with the exception of accounting for depreciation expense and royalty income. Modified accelerated cost recovery system depreciation is taken for tax purposes, and the straight-line method is used for financial accounting purposes. Royalty income is recognized when received for tax purposes and later, when earned, for financial accounting purposes. Information concerning the temporary differences is given below (in the schedule of future tax consequences, taxable amounts are shown without parentheses and deductible amounts are shown in parentheses):

	DIFFERENCE BETWEEN TAX RETURN AND BOOKS IN CURRENT YEAR	CUMULATIVE DIFFERENCE BETWEEN TAX AND BOOK BASES	EXPECTED EFFECT ON TAX RETURNS OF FUTURE YEARS			
			1999	2000	2001	AFTER 2001
DEPRECIATION						
1998	$(30,000)	$ 30,000	$ 5,000	$ 10,000	$ 8,000	$ 7,000
1999	(15,000)	45,000		13,000	15,000	17,000
2000	(37,000)	82,000			21,000	61,000
ROYALTY INCOME						
1998	60,000	(60,000)	(40,000)	(20,000)		
1999	60,000	(120,000)		(100,000)	(20,000)	
2000	(70,000)	(50,000)			(46,000)	(4,000)

At the end of 1998, the enacted marginal tax rate is 40 percent for 1998 and 30 percent for 1999 and 2000. Pretax financial income for 1998, 1999, and 2000 is $340,000, $360,000, and $300,000, respectively.

REQUIRED   Prepare the journal entries to record income taxes in 1998, 1999, and 2000. Show supporting calculations.

P 17-5. **DEFERRED TAX ADJUSTMENT WITH A NET OPERATING LOSS** Refer to the data in Problem 17-4, but assume that Shadow had a pretax financial loss of $360,000 in 1999 and that Shadow elects the carryback option.

REQUIRED Prepare the journal entries to record income taxes in 1998, 1999, and 2000.

P 17-6. **BALANCE SHEET CLASSIFICATION; VALUATION ALLOWANCE** Dana Company had only two temporary differences between the book basis and tax basis of assets and liabilities at the end of 1998:

a) The book basis exceeded the tax basis for depreciable assets by $50,000 because of excess depreciation taken for tax purposes. An additional difference between book basis and tax basis of $40,000 will occur at the end of 1999, followed by decreases in the difference of $30,000 in each of the next three years.

b) Dana accrued a loss of $35,000 related to litigation, which is expected to be paid and deducted for tax purposes in 1999.

The enacted tax rates at the end of 1998 are 40 percent for 1998 and 35 percent for all subsequent years.

REQUIRED Determine the appropriate balance sheet presentation of resulting deferred tax assets and liabilities under each of the following two independent assumptions:

1. No valuation allowance is required, and no balance existed at the end of 1998.

2. A valuation allowance of $5,000 is required. The existing balance in the allowance is $1,500. Show supporting calculations.

P 17-7. **COMPREHENSIVE REVIEW** On December 31, 1998, Lacava Corporation's accounting records included a deferred tax asset account and a deferred tax liability account. During 1998 Lacava collected $30,000 of rent revenue. The rent was to be earned in equal amounts in 1999 and 2000. Lacava also acquired machinery in 1998 at a cost of $150,000 with no expected salvage value. In 1998, Lacava deducted $22,500 more depreciation for tax purposes than was recognized for financial accounting purposes. The machine is being depreciated on a straight-line basis over 5 years for tax purposes and on a straight-line basis over 20 years for financial accounting purposes. Lacava had no other temporary differences at December 31, 1998, and no transactions occurred in 2000 and 2001 that resulted in temporary differences.

The following transactions occurred during 1999 and gave rise to temporary differences between Lacava's pretax financial income and taxable income:

a) On January 1, Lacava sold land with a book value of $40,000 by accepting cash of $20,000 and an interest-bearing note for $80,000. The interest rate on the note equaled the prevailing market rate, and the note is due in five equal installments on December 31 of each year. For financial accounting purposes, the $60,000 gain is recognized at the date of sale. For tax purposes, the gain will be recognized on the basis of cash collections.

b) During 1999, Lacava accrued losses of $55,000 in connection with the planned disposal of a segment of its business. These losses are deductible for tax purposes on the disposal date, estimated to be in 2001.

c) Lacava established a construction division to build highways. Lacava's construction division uses the completed-contract method for tax purposes and the percentage-of-completion method for financial accounting purposes. At the end of 1999, Lacava estimated that the $38,000 in construction income recognized under the percentage-of-completion method would be recognized on its tax return as follows: 2000, $10,000; 2001, $20,000; 2002, $8,000.

The income tax rate was 30 percent for years prior to 1999. At the beginning of 1999, legislation was enacted that changed the marginal tax rate to 25 percent for 1999 and subsequent years.

REQUIRED Calculate the required balance in the deferred tax asset and deferred tax liability accounts at the end of 1999, 2000, and 2001. For each year, assume that loss carrybacks should be carried back to the year for which deferred tax asset and liability balances are being calculated.

P 17-8. **DEFERRED TAXES; OPERATING LOSSES** At the beginning of 1998, its first year of operation, Coleman Industries purchased a tract of land for $800,000 for development. The land was cleared and subdivided into 100 lots to sell for $20,000 per lot, resulting in a gross profit of $12,000 per lot [$20,000 − ($800,000 ÷ 100 lots)]. Sales of the lots were as follows: 1998, 30 lots; 1999, 30 lots; 2000, 40 lots. The lots were sold on credit, and purchasers paid one-third of the purchase price in cash each year. For financial accounting purposes, Coleman recognizes revenue on an accrual basis. For tax purposes, Coleman uses the installment method.

To clear the land, construction machinery was purchased at the beginning of 1998 at a cost of $240,000. Because low-income housing was to be constructed on the lots under a government contract, Coleman was permitted to deduct the entire cost of the machinery on its 1998 tax return. For financial accounting purposes, Coleman depreciated the construction equipment over a three-year period under the straight-line method with no estimated salvage value.

Other expenses associated with the clearing of the land and the sale of lots were $30,000 per year. These expenses were paid in cash each year.

Applicable enacted marginal income tax rates, known by Coleman at the beginning of 1998, were as follows: 1998, 25 percent; subsequent years, 30 percent.

REQUIRED

1. Prepare schedules showing Coleman's pretax financial income and taxable income over the three years 1998–2000.

2. Prepare journal entries to record Coleman's income taxes for 1998, 1999, and 2000.

3. Refer to part 2. Assume that Coleman has no transactions beyond 2000 other than collections on the installment sales. Indicate how the deferred tax asset or deferred tax liability, as applicable, will be reduced to zero when all collections have been received.

P 17-9. **DEFERRED TAX ASSET; EVENTS WITHOUT TAX CONSEQUENCES** Clayton Enterprises began marketing binoculars in 1998. Since the president, J. Clayton, is rather accident prone, the company maintains a $1 million life insurance policy on him, with the company named as the beneficiary. The annual premium for the insurance policy is $7,500. Each pair of binoculars comes with a two-year parts and service warranty. Warranty expense for financial reporting purposes was $37,000 in 1998. Cash expenditures for warranty work were $3,000 in 1998. Also in 1998, Clayton contributed $23,000 to a defined benefit pension trust but expensed only $15,000 for financial reporting purposes. The enacted marginal tax rates at the end of 1998 were 30 percent for 1998 and 40 percent for subsequent years. Clayton had pretax financial income of $70,000 in 1998.

REQUIRED Prepare the journal entry to record income taxes for 1998.

P 17-10. **DEFERRED TAX ASSET; EVENTS WITHOUT TAX CONSEQUENCES; VALUATION ALLOWANCE** Refer to the data in Problem 17-9, except assume that Clayton had a pretax financial loss of $30,000 in 1998. Also, assume that, based on all available evidence, Clayton determines that it is more likely than not that $6,000 of the future deductible amounts will not result in future tax benefits.

REQUIRED Prepare the journal entries to record income taxes for 1998. Show supporting calculations.

P 17-11. **DEFERRED TAX ADJUSTMENT** In 1999, its second year of operations, Rollo Company has several temporary differences. The impact of these temporary differences on future taxable income is given below:

Future taxable amounts. $290
Future deductible amounts 600

In 1998, when the tax rate was 40 percent, Rollo had taxable income of $300. At the end of 1998, there was a $220 balance in the deferred tax liability account and a $120 balance in the deferred tax assets account. The income tax rate in 1999 is 35 percent, and Rollo has $2,000 of taxable income. The enacted marginal tax rate for years subsequent to 1999 is 40 percent.

REQUIRED Prepare the journal entry to record income taxes for 1999. Show supporting calculations.

P 17-12. **COMPREHENSIVE REVIEW** In January 2000, you begin examining the financial statements of KCR Corporation, a new audit client, for the year ended December 31, 1999. KCR began operations in 1997. Your examination discloses the following information:

a) Federal tax liabilities reported on tax returns were:

1997	$48,500
1998	67,020
1999	61,966

b) On January 2, 1997, packaging equipment was purchased at a cost of $225,000. The equipment has an estimated useful life of five years and a salvage value of $15,000. The sum-of-the-years'-digits method was used for tax purposes and the straight-line method was used for financial accounting purposes.

c) On January 2, 1997, a patent acquired at a cost of $34,000 was granted to KCR. The corporation is amortizing the patent over a period of 17 years for financial accounting purposes and over 4 years for tax purposes.

d) On January 8, 1998, KCR collected $60,000 in advance rental of a building for a three-year period. The $60,000 was reported as taxable income in 1998, but $40,000 was reported as unearned revenue in 1998 for financial accounting purposes.

e) On February 12, 1999, the corporation sold land with a book and tax basis of $150,000 for $200,000. The gain, reported in full in 1999 on the financial statements, is being reported in equal installments on the income tax returns over a period of 10 years and is taxable as ordinary income.

f) Enacted tax rates at the end of 1997 were 30 percent for 1997 and 40 percent for all subsequent years.

REQUIRED

1. Calculate pretax financial income for 1997, 1998, and 1999.

2. Prepare the journal entries to record income taxes at the end of 1997, 1998, and 1999.

REYNOLDS METALS COMPANY TAX ACCOUNTING CASE

Reynolds Metals Company was founded in 1919 as the U.S. Foil Company. It produces, manufactures, and distributes aluminum and plastic products. For example, Reynolds Metals produces aluminum cans for many beverage firms and manufactures and distributes Reynolds Wrap aluminum foil and Reynolds Plastic Wrap. Approximately 23 percent of its revenue in 1995 came from sales outside the United States. In 1995, Reynolds Metals had total revenues of $7,213 million, net income of $389 million, and total assets of $7,740 million. Reynolds Metals also had 30,000 employees at the end of 1995.

Answer the following questions using the information in the accompanying financial statement excerpts.

1. What is the amount of "Deferred Income Tax Assets or Liabilities" recorded on the balance sheet? Where do the amounts appear and are they long term or short term?

2. What item has the largest effect on deferred tax assets or liabilities?

3. Explain the valuation allowance related to deferred tax assets.

4. What are the amounts of current and deferred portions of income tax expense?

5. What is total income tax expense on income before income taxes?

6. Look at the reconciliation of statutory rate to effective rate. How was the effective rate of 29 percent calculated? Do not merely sum the numbers in the reconciliation; the rate can be calculated independently of the schedule.

7. What amount of income taxes was paid during 1995?

8. Why might the answer to 7 differ from the amount of the current portion of income tax expense from 4?

CONSOLIDATED STATEMENT OF INCOME AND RETAINED EARNINGS

(In millions, except per share amounts)

Years ended December 31	1995	1994	1993
REVENUES			
Net sales	$7,213	$5,879	$5,269
Equity, interest and other income	39	46	25
Gains on sales of assets	—	88	—
	7,252	6,013	5,294
COSTS AND EXPENSES			
Cost of products sold	5,772	4,996	4,657
Selling, administrative and general expenses	449	376	358
Provision for depreciation and amortization	311	295	287
Interest — principally on long-term obligations	172	156	159
Operational restructuring and asset revaluation costs	—	—	348
	6,704	5,823	5,809
EARNINGS			
Income (loss) before income taxes	548	190	(515)
Taxes on income (credit)	159	68	(193)
NET INCOME (LOSS)	389	122	(322)
Preferred stock dividends	36	34	—
NET INCOME (LOSS) AVAILABLE TO COMMON STOCKHOLDERS	353	88	(322)
RETAINED EARNINGS			
Balance at beginning of year	980	954	1,348
Cash dividends on common stock	77	62	72
Retained earnings at end of year	$1,256	$ 980	$ 954
EARNINGS PER SHARE			
Average shares outstanding	73	62	60
Net income (loss)	$5.35	$1.42	$(5.38)
CASH DIVIDENDS PER COMMON SHARE	$1.20	$1.00	$ 1.20

CONSOLIDATED BALANCE SHEET

(In millions)

December 31	1995	1994
ASSETS		
Current assets		
Cash	$ 17	$ 26
Short-term investments (cash equivalents 1995 — $22, 1994 — $282)	22	408
Receivables		
Customers, less allowances of $20 (1994 — $19)	889	851
Other	154	111
Total receivables	1,043	962
Inventories	891	873
Prepaid expenses	41	53
Total current assets	2,014	2,322
Unincorporated joint ventures and associated companies	1,286	856
Property, plant and equipment — net	3,223	3,108
Deferred taxes	376	426
Other assets	841	749
Total assets	$7,740	$7,461
LIABILITIES AND STOCKHOLDERS' EQUITY		
Current liabilities		
Trade payables	$ 527	$ 658
Accrued compensation and related amounts	252	263
Payables to unincorporated joint ventures and associated companies	102	84
Short-term borrowings	111	120
Long-term debt	101	18
Other liabilities	274	281
Total current liabilities	1,367	1,424
Long-term debt	1,853	1,848
Postretirement benefits	1,213	1,145
Environmental	178	236
Deferred taxes	236	183
Other liabilities	276	353
Stockholders' equity		
Preferred stock	505	505
Common stock	941	870
Retained earnings	1,256	980
Cumulative currency translation adjustments	(22)	(43)
Pension liability adjustment	(63)	(40)
Total stockholders' equity	2,617	2,272
Contingent liabilities and commitments (Notes I and J)		
Total liabilities and stockholders' equity	$7,740	$7,461

Note H – Taxes On Income

At December 31, 1995, the Company had various U.S. and German income tax carryforward benefits of $37 million that expire primarily between 1998 and 2010 and $132 million that can be carried forward indefinitely. The Company has deferred tax assets primarily relating to certain state operating loss carryforwards, and foreign entities of approximately $45 million against which a full valuation reserve has been recorded. The Company is continuing to evaluate alternatives that may result in the ultimate realization of a portion of these assets.

Deferred income taxes reflect the net tax effects of temporary differences between the carrying amounts of assets and liabilities for financial reporting purposes and the amounts used for income tax purposes. At December 31, 1995, the Company had $902 million (1994 — $976 million) of deferred tax assets and $759 million (1994 — $717 million) of deferred tax liabilities that have been netted with respect to tax jurisdictions for presentation purposes. The significant components of these amounts as shown on the balance sheet were as follows:

	1995		1994	
	Asset	**Liability**	Asset	Liability
Retiree health benefits	**$415**	**—**	$414	—
Tax carryforward benefits	**213**	**$ (1)**	207	$ (61)
Environmental and restructuring costs	**121**	**(2)**	142	(3)
Other	**44**	**39**	69	17
Tax over book depreciation	**(369)**	**200**	(341)	230
Valuation reserve relating to tax carryforward benefits	**(45)**	**—**	(49)	—
Total deferred tax assets and liabilities	**379**	**236**	442	183
Amount included as current in balance sheet	**3**	**—**	16	—
Noncurrent deferred tax assets and liabilities	**$376**	**$236**	$426	$183

The significant components of the provision for income taxes were as follows:

	1995	1994	1993
Current:			
Federal	**$ 10**	$ 30	$ (55)
Foreign	**10**	15	14
State	**3**	1	4
Total current	**23**	46	(37)
Deferred:			
Federal	**66**	(13)	(99)
Foreign	**62**	32	(33)
State	**—**	(8)	(29)
Total deferred	**128**	11	(161)
Equity income	**8**	11	5
Total	**$159**	$ 68	$(193)

The deferred tax provision included state and foreign operating loss carryforward benefits of $9 million.

The Company has not provided taxes on the undistributed earnings ($992 million) of foreign subsidiaries. It is the intent of the Company to use such earnings to finance foreign expansion, reduce foreign debt, or support foreign operating requirements.

The Company's effective income tax rate varied from the U.S. statutory rate as follows:

	1995	1994	1993
U.S. rate	**35%**	35%	(35)%
Income taxed at other than the U.S. rate	**(5)**	2	3
Percentage depletion	**(1)**	(3)	(1)
State income taxes and other	**—**	2	(4)
Effective rate	**29%**	36%	(37)%

In 1995, income taxed at other than the U.S. rate includes a non-recurring foreign tax benefit of 3%.

Net income taxes paid (refunded) were $56 million, ($17 million) and $6 million in 1995, 1994 and 1993, respectively.

Stockholders' Equity

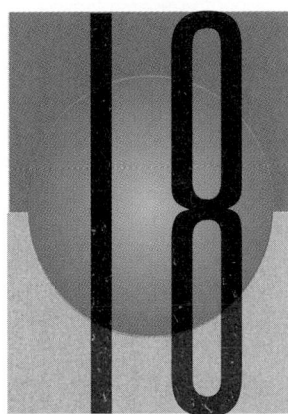

LEARNING OBJECTIVES

After studying this chapter, you should be able to:

1. Describe the four characteristics of the corporate form of organization that affect accounting for stockholders' equity.

2. Identify the two basic preferences possessed by preferred stockholders over common stockholders and describe other possible preferences and their impact on accounting for preferred stock.

3. Account for the issuance of stock for cash, for noncash consideration, on a subscription basis, and for a lump-sum consideration.

4. Account for the conversion of preferred stock to common stock.

5. Define and account for stock rights issued to existing stockholders.

6. Account for stock-based compensation under *APB Opinion No. 25* and evaluate the accounting guidelines set forth in that opinion.

7. Explain the accounting for stock-based compensation under *Statement No. 123.*

8. Account for the acquisition and retirement of capital stock and for treasury stock under the cost method and the par value method.

9. Account for cash dividends, property dividends, liquidating dividends, and stock dividends.

10. Explain how appropriations of retained earnings may be used and why.

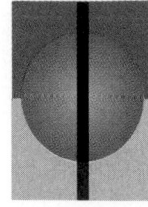

n previous chapters we discussed generally accepted principles underlying accounting and reporting for various assets and liabilities. Those principles are applicable to the three legal forms of business organization: the sole proprietorship, the partnership, and the corporation. However, accounting and reporting for the owners' equity of corporations—often called *stockholders' equity* or *shareholders' equity*—differs significantly from accounting and reporting for the owners' equity of partnerships and sole proprietorships, primarily because of legal requirements and complex terminology associated with corporations.

Stockholders' equity consists of (1) contributed capital, (2) retained earnings, and (3) accumulated other comprehensive income. In this chapter we will focus on accounting and reporting for transactions and events affecting the first two categories. Accumulated other comprehensive income was discussed in Chapters 2, 4, and 5. The chapter begins with a discussion of the corporate form of organization. We then describe accounting and reporting for contributed capital and retained earnings. The chapter concludes with a brief description of the statement of stockholders' equity. In Appendix 18–1 we discuss the accounting requirements for quasi-reorganizations.

THE CORPORATE FORM OF ORGANIZATION

In the United States, there are many more sole proprietorships and partnerships than corporations. The corporation, however, is the dominant form of business organization in the U.S. economy, whether measured by total revenue, total assets, number of employees, or any other characteristic. Its dominance is due to certain unique features of the corporate form, such as the limited liability owners enjoy, and its efficient system of capital accumulation.

Corporations may be classified as follows:

I. Private: privately owned corporations.
   A. Stock: private corporations that issue stock as evidence of ownership interest, and that seek profits and increased wealth for the owners.
      1. Open: stock corporations whose stock is widely held and available for purchase by the general public.
         a) Listed: open stock corporations whose stock is traded on an organized stock exchange, such as the New York Stock Exchange.
         b) Unlisted: open stock corporations whose stock is traded over the counter through securities dealers.
      2. Closed: stock corporations whose stock is held by a few individuals and is not available for purchase by the general public.
   B. Nonstock: private corporations that do not seek profits or issue stock, such as churches and charities.

II. Public: corporations owned by governmental units.

This chapter is concerned primarily with private corporations that issue stock. In the next section, we will discuss the impact of state laws on such corporations.

State Laws Governing Corporations

Each state has its own laws that govern the incorporation of businesses. Individuals who want to incorporate a business must apply to the appropriate governmental unit of the state in which they want to incorporate. Upon approval of their application by the state, a corporate charter, also called the articles of incorporation, is granted. The charter is an agreement between the state and the corporation in which the state grants the corporation the right to operate and to raise capital according to the terms of the charter. The state also recognizes the corporation as a legal entity separate from its owners. Thus, the corporation can enter into contracts, can sue and be sued, and can buy and sell property.

CONCEPTUAL

A corporation is recognized as a legal entity separate from its owners.

To accountants, the fact that laws govern both the incorporation process and the subsequent business activity of corporations is quite important. Corporate management must abide by state law regarding accounting terminology, permissible transactions, the distribution of profits, and the treatment of proceeds from stock issuances.

Learning the various state laws that govern corporations is not necessary to an understanding of the accounting for stockholders' equity. One must recognize only that because state laws are diverse, exceptions exist to any generalization we might make regarding stockholders' equity. Accountants learn about the exceptions as required in their practice of accounting.

In addition to state laws, four characteristics of corporations affect accounting for stockholders' equity:

1. The system of capital accumulation.
2. Limited liability.
3. Preferred stock.
4. Corporate dividend policy.

The impact of each of these characteristics is analyzed in the following sections.

> **1** **Describe the four characteristics of the corporate form of organization that affect accounting for stockholders' equity.**

The System of Capital Accumulation

Corporations obtain assets (and generate cash) primarily by borrowing, by issuing capital stock, and by operating at a profit. Of these three sources, only the issuance of capital stock is unique to corporations. The characteristics of stock, stockholders' rights, and the two major classes of stock are discussed in this section.

Characteristics of Stock

The issuance of ownership units in the form of capital stock enables corporations to accumulate large amounts of assets. Individual investments may range from one share of stock and only a few dollars to many shares and millions of dollars. An individual investor's proportion of ownership is equal to the proportion of total outstanding shares that investor owns. For example, if an investor owns 300,000 out of 1,000,000 outstanding shares, that investor has a 30 percent (300,000 ÷ 1,000,000) ownership interest in the corporation.

Investors may buy and sell outstanding shares of capital stock in listed or over-the-counter markets. The transfer of shares among investors affects neither the corporation's assets nor the continuity of its corporate operations. In a sole proprietorship or partnership, an ownership change generally terminates the entity's legal existence. The fact that the corporation continues despite frequent changes in ownership allows corporate management to plan and control operations to achieve long-run objectives.

CONCEPTUAL

Ownership changes do not affect the continuity of corporations.

Since investors buy and sell shares of capital stock frequently, corporations must periodically update their list of stockholders, called a *stockholders' ledger.* The stockholders' ledger provides a reference for allocating dividend payments and stock rights and for communicating with stockholders on other issues. Major corporations often employ a *registrar* to provide a current list of stockholders. In addition, many companies employ a *transfer agent* when they issue new shares.

Stockholders' Rights

Ownership of shares in a corporation conveys certain rights and privileges to the owner. A stock contract specifies the rights of each class of stock issued by a corporation. In the absence of specific provisions to the contrary, each class generally conveys the following rights:

1. The right to share in profits, as declared and distributed as dividends, in proportion to the number of shares held.

2. The right to vote for directors and on management policy issues.

3. The right to maintain a proportionate ownership by sharing proportionately in new issues of the same class of stock. This right is referred to as the **preemptive right.**

4. The right to share proportionately in corporate assets in the event of liquidation.

If the stock contract is silent with respect to these four rights, common law presumes that the rights exist. Thus, if the corporation wants to deny one or more of these rights, the stock contract must state specifically that the right does not exist. For example, because of difficulties associated with raising additional capital in the presence of a preemptive right, many stock contracts specifically exclude the preemptive right of stockholders.

Classes of Stock

A class of stock is a group of shares having the same rights and restrictions. When two or more classes of stock exist in a corporation, the stockholders of one class of stock control the management of the corporation, reap the rewards of its success, and bear the risk of its failure. The stock owned by this class of stockholders is called **common stock.** Common stock usually has the four rights listed above, with the possible exception of the preemptive right.

By excluding selected rights and conveying additional privileges, a corporation may create one or more special classes of stock called **preferred stock.** An extreme example of special classes is the General Motors Corporation's six classes of outstanding stock. The objective of creating two or more classes of stock, each with different risks and privileges, is to appeal to a broader spectrum of investors. For example, corporations often eliminate the voting privilege from a particular class of stock in exchange for a preference over common stockholders in dividend or asset distributions. In this arrangement, the corporation pays dividends to preferred stockholders at a specified rate (e.g., $6 per share); any remaining dividends are then distributed to common stockholders. In the event of liquidation, the corporation must pay preferred stockholders their stated liquidation value per share before common stockholders receive anything. In exchange for a dividend preference or a preferred claim on assets upon liquidation, preferred stockholders give up their rights to participate in management's policy decisions and to share in profits beyond the specified return.

Investors and creditors need information about the rights and privileges of various classes of stock. Dividend and liquidation preferences are relevant to users in assessing a stock's future cash flows. Thus, accounting reports must include such information.

In summary, the issuance of capital stock enables corporations to generate large amounts of capital and to continue operating indefinitely even though ownership of its stock may change. From the stockholders' viewpoint, a major advantage to stock ownership is its limited liability feature, discussed in the next section.

Limited Liability

The corporate form of organization limits the liability of stockholders by absolving them of responsibility for the corporation's debt. The corporation itself, as a separate legal entity, incurs the debt and bears the responsibility for its repayment. Thus, the personal assets of investors are not available for the satisfaction of corporate liabilities. Generally, the maximum loss that an individual stockholder can incur is the amount that has been invested in the stock. Investors in a stock may lose their entire investment, because the amount invested becomes part of corporate assets and therefore subject to the claims of creditors. But investors may not lose more than the amount they have invested.

The limited liability feature is a distinct advantage of the corporate form of business. In partnerships and sole proprietorships, creditors have a legal claim not only

2 Identify the two basic preferences possessed by preferred stockholders over common stockholders and describe other possible preferences and their impact on accounting for preferred stock.

CONCEPTUAL

Dividend preferences and liquidation preferences are relevant in assessing future cash flows.

CONCEPTUAL

Investors in corporate stock generally may not lose more than the amount invested.

to business assets, but also to the personal assets of the owners. The obligations of the partnership or proprietorship likewise are obligations of the owners; therefore, creditors may claim both business and personal assets to satisfy business debts.

Exception to the Limited Liability Rule

There is one exception to the generalization that a stockholder's loss is limited to the amount invested. That exception has to do with the issuance of stock at a discount. In many states, corporations issue **par value** stock, either by choice or because state laws require that the corporation designate a par value. The par value is an arbitrary dollar amount assigned to each share. There is no necessary relationship between the price at which a corporation issues stock, and the price at which the stock trades in the marketplace, and the par value of the stock. If a corporation issues par value stock at a price in excess of par, the stock is said to be issued at a **premium.** If a corporation issues stock at a price below par value, the stock is said to be issued at a **discount.**

Technically, shares of stock are not fully paid until the corporation receives at least the par value. Thus, stockholders who acquire stock at a price below par value bear a *contingent liability.* This contingent liability becomes an actual liability only if a corporation's liabilities exceed its assets. That is, a corporation may incur losses of such magnitude that the resulting decrease in corporate assets exceeds the total of its contributed capital and retained earnings. If claims exceed the assets available to meet them, creditors may force those stockholders who bought their stock at a discount to pay them the amount of the discount. Note that the contingent liability is to the creditors, not to the corporation. Unless a contractual arrangement transfers that liability to subsequent stockholders, it remains a liability of the original purchaser.

In summary, the limited liability feature means that investors who purchase shares from a corporation at a price equal to or exceeding par value cannot lose more than their investment. Investors who acquire shares at a discount may lose their original investment plus an amount equal to the discount.

Impairment of Contributed Capital

Corporations have a responsibility to maintain assets equal to the dollar amount of contributed capital as long as the business is in existence. At their dissolution, corporations must maintain assets equal to the capital contributed by stockholders until all other claims have been settled. Creditors' claims to corporate assets take priority over the claims of stockholders. That is, corporations may not distribute assets to stockholders *voluntarily* if prior claims (i.e., claims by creditors and preferred stockholders) exist, and if the dollar amount of the corporation's contributed capital would be impaired by such a distribution.[1]

To demonstrate the significance to creditors of this requirement, assume that Kesterson Corporation has assets valued at $120,000, liabilities of $20,000, contributed capital from the issuance of capital stock of $60,000, and retained earnings of $40,000, as shown in Exhibit 18–1. Kesterson may voluntarily distribute to stockholders (through dividends, for example) not more than $40,000 of assets. The state's requirement that Kesterson retain assets equivalent to the sum of liabilities and contributed capital ($20,000 + 60,000 = $80,000) is an attempt to protect creditors against shrinkage in asset value. Thus, contributed capital may be thought of as a buffer against loss for the protection of creditors.

CONCEPTUAL

Contributed capital is a buffer against losses for the protection of creditors.

---

[1]Technically, the dollar amount of net assets that a corporation must maintain is called *legal capital.* The definition of legal capital is not the same in all states. At a minimum, the par value of shares issued is included in legal capital, and in some states premiums paid in when a corporation issues shares also are included. Corporations cannot distribute assets to shareholders if the distribution would impair legal capital, however defined.

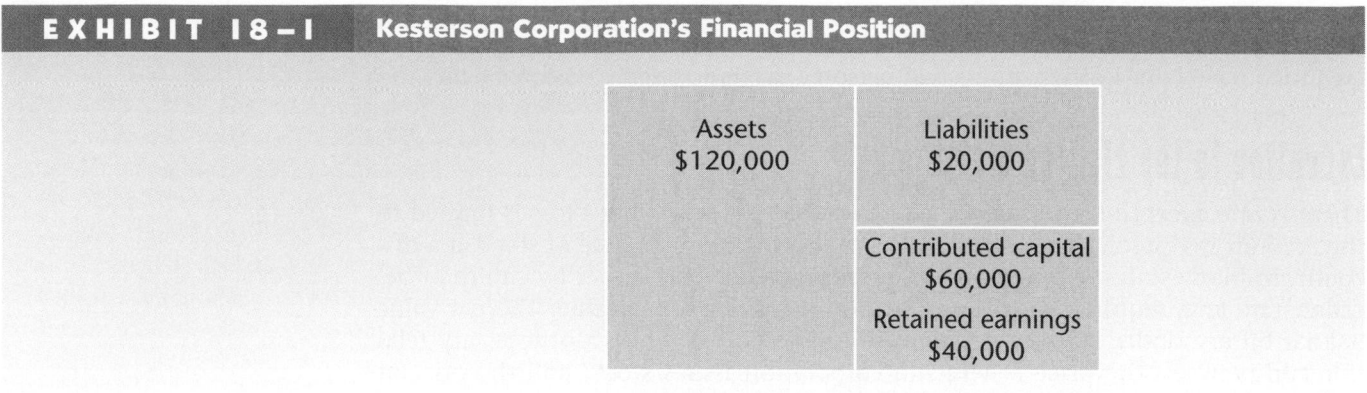

EXHIBIT 18-1   **Kesterson Corporation's Financial Position**

Assets $120,000	Liabilities $20,000
	Contributed capital $60,000
	Retained earnings $40,000

Because of the legal restrictions on the distribution of corporate assets, the board of directors of a corporation must formally approve dividend distributions to stockholders, and must maintain records of dividend declarations and distributions. If a corporation cannot pay creditors because illegal distributions have been made, the board may be held legally liable to the creditors.

Preferred stockholders also hold a prior claim on a corporation's assets. The characteristics of preferred stock are discussed in the next section.

Preferred Stock

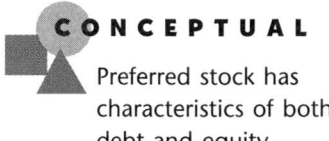

CONCEPTUAL

Preferred stock has characteristics of both debt and equity.

In terms of its characteristics, preferred stock occupies a position between long-term debt and common stock. It is similar to long-term debt, in that corporations usually pay preferred dividends at a specified rate per share, just as they make interest payments on long-term debt at a specified rate. However, the corporation often does not have an obligation to repay the preferred stockholders' investment at a specified date. In the absence of such an obligation, preferred stock tends to be a relatively permanent source of assets, like common stock. Consequently, preferred stock generally is classified as a part of stockholders' equity.

In addition to the normal preferences with respect to dividends and assets upon liquidation, preferred stock may possess one or more of the following features: (1) a cumulative feature, (2) a participation feature, (3) a call feature, and (4) a conversion feature. The stock contract specifies whether these features apply to a particular issue of preferred stock. Each is described in the following sections.

Cumulative Feature

Preferred stock is **cumulative** if the dividends not paid to the preferred shareholders in any year must be paid before holders of common shares may receive their dividends. In this arrangement, failure to declare dividends at the specified rate on cumulative preferred stock creates *passed dividends,* also called **dividends in arrears.** Thereafter, holders of common shares cannot receive a dividend until the corporation has paid both current dividends and dividends in arrears to preferred stockholders.

CONCEPTUAL

Dividends in arrears do not constitute a liability until formally declared.

Dividends in arrears do not constitute a liability to the corporation until the board of directors formally declares the dividend. However, corporations must disclose the amount of dividends in arrears in the footnotes to the financial statements because they represent a probable future outflow of cash and a potential constraint on dividends to common stockholders. If preferred stock is *noncumulative,* dividends in arrears cannot exist because the corporation is not obligated to pay passed dividends. Most preferred stock issues are cumulative because the feature appeals to many investors.

Participation Feature

Preferred stock is said to be **participating** if holders of both preferred and common stock share in dividends over and above the preferred dividend rate. For example, if a corporation had 9 percent, $100 par value, participating preferred stock, any dividends paid would go first to meet the preferred requirement, at $9 per share (.09 × $100). The corporation would then allocate additional dividends to the common stockholders, up to 9 percent of the par value of the common stock. If additional dividends were paid and the preferred stock was fully participating, the corporation would allocate the remainder to both preferred and common shares in proportion to the total par value of each class compared to the total par value of both classes.

Preferred stock also may be partially participating, meaning that the stock contract limits the payment of dividends over and above the preferred rate to a maximum amount per share. For example, a stock contract might specify a maximum 12 percent, or $12 per share, dividend on 9 percent participating preferred stock.

Although the participation feature was once common, today it is rare. Thus, in practice, dividends for a particular class of preferred stock tend to remain constant over time. If total dividends paid were to increase as a result of higher corporate earnings, the increased dividends would accrue to the common stockholders. (The effect of the cumulative and participating features on dividend distributions is illustrated later in this chapter; see pages 986–987.)

Call Feature

Many preferred stock issues are **callable,** meaning that the corporation may call, or redeem, the stock at a specified price. The company must pay any dividends in arrears when it redeems a preferred stock. For example, McDonald's recently issued $500 million of cumulative preferred stock that is callable at the liquidation preference amount plus accrued and unpaid dividends.

A call feature is advantageous to a corporation because it affords some flexibility in the timing of the retirement of preferred stock. A company is likely to exercise a call privilege when market interest rates have declined below the dividend rate on an outstanding preferred issue. At such times, the corporation can replace the outstanding issue with debt or stock issued at a lower interest or dividend rate. Because a call feature generally is not attractive to investors, a call price tends to put a ceiling on the market price of the preferred stock. To increase the attractiveness of the stock, companies may have to pay a **call premium**—an excess amount over and above the original issuance price.

Some preferred stock issues have **mandatory redemption** (retirement) terms, which require redemption at specified times—usually within 5 to 10 years—and in specified amounts. In recent years, many corporations have resorted to this type of financing to improve their debt-to-equity ratios. Because the issuing corporation commits itself to reacquire the shares at a definite date, preferred stock with mandatory redemption terms is much more like debt than equity. Recognizing the similarity between redeemable preferred stock and debt, the SEC has required corporations, in the financial statements they file with the SEC, to exclude from stockholders' equity amounts received from the issuance of redeemable preferred stock.[2] Corporations must describe the redemption feature and present a redemption schedule for the next five years.

GAAP does not require corporations to exclude redeemable preferred stock from stockholders' equity in annual reports made to stockholders. Because a redemption feature affects future cash flows, however, the issuing corporation must disclose the redemption terms in the notes to the financial statements. Exhibit 18–2 illustrates the disclosure of preferred stock issues in a recent annual report.

---

[2]"Presentation in Financial Statements of Redeemable Preferred Stocks," *Accounting Series Release No. 268* (Washington, D.C.: SEC, July 1979). The excluded amount should be reported immediately before stockholders' equity.

EXHIBIT 18-2   **Footnote Disclosure of Preferred Stock**

McDonald's Corporation
1995 Annual Report

Preferred Stock

In December 1992, the Company issued $500.0 million of Series E 7.72% Cumulative Preferred Stock; 10,000 preferred shares are equivalent to 20.0 million depositary shares having a liquidation preference of $25.00 per depositary share. Each preferred share is entitled to one vote under certain circumstances and is redeemable at the option of the Company beginning on December 3, 1997, at its liquidation preference plus accrued and unpaid dividends. On June 30, 1995, the Company completed an exchange of approximately 5.2 million depositary shares, representing 2,600 shares of Series E 7.72% Cumulative Preferred Stock, for subordinated debt securities. In the third quarter of 1995, the Company repurchased approximately .5 million depositary shares equivalent to 250 shares of Series E 7.72% Cumulative Preferred Stock.

In September 1989 and April 1991, the Company sold $200.0 million of Series B and $100.0 million of Series C ESOP Convertible Preferred Stock to the LESOP. The LESOP financed the purchase by issuing notes which are guaranteed by the Company and are included in long-term debt, with an offsetting reduction in shareholders' equity. Each preferred share had a liquidation preference of $14.375 and $16.5625, respectively, and was convertible to a minimum of .7692 and .8 common share (conversion rate), respectively. Upon termination of employment, employees were guaranteed a minimum value payable in common shares equal to the greater of the conversion rate; the fair market value of their preferred shares; or the liquidation preference plus accrued dividends, not to exceed one common share. Each preferred share was entitled to one vote and was redeemable at the option of the Company. In 1992, 8.2 million Series B shares were converted into 6.4 million common shares. During 1995, the remaining 5.2 million Series B shares and 5.8 million Series C shares were converted into 8.7 million common shares.

Conversion Feature

If a preferred stock is **convertible,** holders may exchange their preferred shares for common shares according to a specified ratio. A conversion privilege may be advantageous to both the corporation and the investor. The investor receives the dividend preferences of a holder of preferred stock, as well as the opportunity to convert the investment to common shares if conversion becomes attractive. When a conversion feature is available, preferred stock prices tend to rise with common stock prices. When common stock prices decline, the fixed-return aspect of preferred shares tends to keep their price relatively stable.

A company usually issues convertible preferred stock as an indirect, delayed means of issuing additional common stock. The attractiveness of the conversion privilege enables the issuing corporation to pay a lower dividend rate on the preferred stock than it would otherwise have to pay.

Corporate Dividend Policy

Corporations generally maintain a stable dividend pattern over time. Periodic dividends usually are considerably less than periodic net income, for one or more of the following reasons:

1. A corporation may desire to reinvest assets arising from profitable operations in internal expansion or growth.

2. A corporation's creditors may require the corporation to retain assets arising from earnings activities in order to provide additional protection to creditors.

3. A corporation may wish to smooth dividends over time, retaining assets arising from earnings in profitable years so that they can be distributed in less profitable years. Empirical evidence indicates that corporations are reluctant to lower their dividends in less profitable years.[3] For example, Coca-Cola's dividends have increased steadily for many years; the company has paid a dividend every year since 1893. Some companies even *borrow* money to pay dividends when their cash balances are temporarily low.

4. State law may require that retained earnings equal to the cost of treasury stock purchases be restricted from use as dividends. Such a requirement prevents any distribution of assets that would impair a corporation's legal capital.

One financial statistic that captures dividend policy is the **dividend payout ratio,** or annual dividends divided by annual net income. Historically, this ratio has varied among different industries as well as within industries.

While dividends are distributions of assets from a corporation to its stockholders, and therefore are not expenses, dividends paid to preferred stockholders may be viewed as an expense *from the standpoint of common stockholders*. This view underlies the calculation of *earnings per share,* which is discussed in detail in Chapter 20. In practice, many companies, especially those in the utility industry, deduct preferred dividends from net income in the income statement to arrive at net income available to common stockholders. The partial income statement of Dell Computer Corporation in Exhibit 18–3 illustrates this practice.

Unless legal restrictions prevent it, a company may distribute as dividends assets equal to the credit balance in retained earnings. In some cases, if a deficit (debit balance) exists in retained earnings, a corporation must eliminate the deficit by profitable operations or by quasi-reorganization (discussed in Appendix 18–1) before dividends can be declared. A corporation's financial position and financial strategies also influence its ability and inclination to pay dividends. Any dividend other than a stock dividend ultimately decreases a corporation's assets. Therefore, the amount and composition of cash and other assets, the amount of liabilities that require settlement in cash, and the need for future cash and future asset acquisitions may all affect dividend distributions.

To illustrate, return to the example of Kesterson Corporation introduced on page 957. Assume that Kesterson's balance sheet is as follows:

Cash	$ 30,000	Current liabilities		$ 20,000
Plant assets	90,000	Capital stock		30,000
		Other contributed capital		20,000
		Retained earnings		50,000
Total	$120,000	Total		$120,000

CONCEPTUAL

Dividends are not expenses but are distributions of assets. Preferred dividends may be viewed, however, as an expense from the standpoint of common stockholders.

We can draw some generalizations about dividends from this balance sheet.

First, assuming that there are no legal restrictions, Kesterson could distribute dividends equal to the retained earnings balance of $50,000. A dividend of that amount would represent a return on capital to the stockholders, since past profitable operations have increased net assets by $50,000. Because dividends are distributions of assets, however, Kesterson would have to either sell some plant assets or borrow money, since the amount of cash on hand is only $30,000. The maximum *cash* dividend that could be paid, given Kesterson's current financial position, is $30,000.

Second, assuming that Kesterson's legal capital is $30,000—the par value of the shares issued—Kesterson could pay dividends up to $70,000, the sum of the balances in the retained earnings and other contributed capital accounts. Again, since

[3]Thomas Copeland and J. Fred Weston, *Financial Theory and Corporate Policy* (Reading, Mass.: Addison-Wesley, 1980), chap. 14.

EXHIBIT 18-3 **Preferred Dividends Treated as Expenses**

Dell Computer Corporation
(*in thousands*)

	Fiscal Year		
	1995	**1994**	**1993**
Net income (loss)...............	$149,177	$(35,833)	$101,642
Preferred stock dividends	(8,750)	(3,743)	—
Net income (loss) applicable to common stockholders.........	$140,427	$(39,576)	$101,642

the cash balance is only $30,000, Kesterson would have to sell some plant assets or borrow to make such a cash distribution. If $70,000 were actually distributed, $50,000 would be considered a *distribution of earnings* (a return on capital), and the other $20,000 a *return of a portion of the stockholders' original investment* (a return of capital). Because this $20,000 distribution of assets would be a *liquidating dividend,* the stockholders would need to be so informed.[4] (Liquidating dividends will be discussed in more detail later in this chapter.) In summary, the maximum legal distribution of assets that could be paid to stockholders is:

$$\text{Maximum distribution (including liquidating dividends)} = \text{Stockholders' equity} - \text{Legal capital}$$

This concludes our discussion of the corporate form of organization. We turn now to accounting for the issuance of stock.

 EW STOCK ISSUES

As we have just seen, the issuance of capital stock constitutes a primary asset source for corporations. Every year corporations obtain billions of dollars through the issuance of capital stock. The processes by which they issue stock, and the associated accounting procedures, are discussed in this section.

Before issuing capital stock, a corporation must receive authorization to do so from the state in which it is incorporated. Once the company has received authorization, it offers the stock for sale. Interested investors then enter into a contract with the corporation to acquire the shares. When the investors pay the corporation for the shares, the corporation issues the stock. Investors may pay for the shares in several ways, including both cash and noncash considerations.

3 Account for the issuance of stock for cash, for noncash consideration, on a subscription basis, and for a lump-sum consideration.

Issuance for Cash

Corporations may issue several types of stock in return for cash, including par value stock, no-par stock with a stated value, and no-par stock with no stated value (also called true no-par stock). Each of these types of stock is described in the following sections, along with the process of accounting for the issue.

---

[4]An individual stockholder who receives a portion of the $70,000 distribution may or may not consider the receipt to be partially liquidating. Liquidating dividends were discussed from the standpoint of the investor in Chapter 13.

Par Value Stock

When a corporation issues par value stock, it usually establishes par value at an amount well below the issuance price, to avoid issuance at a discount. In fact, most states now prohibit the issuance of capital stock at a discount. The issuing corporation records any premium (the excess of the proceeds over the par value) in an account called *contributed capital in excess of par value.*

To illustrate, if Seymour Corporation issues 10,000 shares of $10 par value common stock for cash at $60 per share, the journal entry to record the issuance would be as follows:

Cash	600,000	
Common stock		100,000
Contributed capital in excess of par—common		500,000

Other names for the amount in excess of par include *additional paid-in capital—common, paid-in capital in excess of par—common,* and *premium on common stock.*

Stated Value Stock

In many states, corporations may issue capital stock without par value. Some of these states require that the issuing corporation assign such shares a **stated value** per share. The stated value serves the same purpose as par value—it distinguishes between legal (stated) capital and amounts paid in above legal capital. Thus, corporations account for no-par stock with a stated value in the same way that they account for par value stock.

True No-Par Stock

When a corporation issues no-par capital stock with no stated value, called **true no-par stock,** it credits the entire amount received for the stock to the capital stock account. No premiums or discounts are associated with true no-par capital stock. For example, if a corporation issues 10,000 shares of true no-par common stock for $60 per share, it makes the following journal entry:

Cash	600,000	
Common stock		600,000

The valuation of capital stock issued for cash is straightforward, because the number of dollars received provides the basis for recording the transaction. That is, the corporation records the number of dollars of cash received at the date of acquisition, and then assigns that amount to the shares issued. However, when a corporation issues stock in exchange for noncash consideration, such as property or services, accounting for the transaction becomes more complex. Accounting for these noncash transactions is described in the next section.

Issuance for Noncash Consideration

When a corporation issues stock for services or for assets other than cash, the general rule is that both the assets or services received and the stock issued should be recorded at the fair value of the consideration received or the stock issued, whichever is more readily determinable. In virtually all cases, the fair value of either the consideration received or the stock issued will clearly be more easily determinable than the other. If the two parties to the transaction are independent, the two fair values should be roughly the same.

If it is not possible to determine the fair value of either the noncash consideration received or the capital stock issued, the board of directors must assign a value

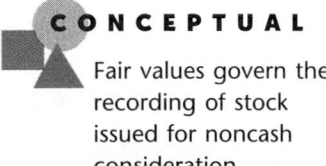

CONCEPTUAL

Fair values govern the recording of stock issued for noncash consideration.

to the transaction. In such circumstances the board often uses independent appraisals. Note that such an assignment of value is acceptable *only* if the fair value of neither the noncash consideration nor the capital stock is readily determinable.

To illustrate, assume that Arbaugh Corporation acquires a piece of equipment in exchange for 500 shares of its $1 par common stock. Given the following three assumptions, Arbaugh would record the transaction as follows:

I. The fair value of the equipment is $12,000; the fair value of the common stock is not readily determinable.

Equipment (fair value)	12,000	
Common stock ($1 × 500 shares)		500
Contributed capital in excess of par—common		11,500

2. The fair value of the equipment is not readily determinable; the fair value (market price) of the common stock is $22 per share.

Equipment ($22 × 500 shares)	11,000	
Common stock		500
Contributed capital in excess of par—common		10,500

3. Neither the fair value of the equipment nor the fair value of the stock is readily determinable. The board of directors assumes responsibility for assigning a value to the transaction. The board obtains three independent appraisals of the equipment's value and accepts the average appraisal value of $10,500 as a reasonable estimate.

Equipment	10,500	
Common stock		500
Contributed capital in excess of par—common		10,000

CONCEPTUAL

Watered stock is associated with overvalued assets. Secret reserves are associated with undervalued assets.

Some companies have misused this accounting guideline to overstate or understate their assets, and consequently their stockholders' equity. A company that receives noncash consideration and overvalues the assets received, producing a corresponding overvaluation of its capital stock, is said to have **watered stock.** A company that undervalues assets received and the capital stock it issues is said to possess **secret reserves.** In both cases, the company should eliminate any overstatement or understatement by restating its assets and capital stock to the best estimate of fair value.

In summary, when a corporation issues stock in exchange for noncash consideration, it should use the best evidence available to record the transaction. Occasionally, the corporation may have to rely on the board of directors to assign a value, pending receipt of better evidence.

So far in this section we have described transactions in which stock is issued for cash or noncash consideration. In the next section, we explain the accounting and reporting requirements for stock subscriptions.

Stock Subscriptions

CONCEPTUAL

Issuance of capital stock on a subscription basis is equivalent to issuing stock on credit.

Corporations sometimes issue capital stock by **subscription.** In this arrangement the purchasers of the stock, called *subscribers,* make a down payment in cash and pay the remainder of the purchase price later, according to the terms of the subscription agreement. The corporation does not actually issue the shares until it receives full payment for them. Newly formed companies, companies issuing capital stock to the public for the first time, and companies issuing stock to employees often offer stock by subscription.

Conceptually, issuance of capital stock on a subscription basis is equivalent to the issuance of stock on credit. The issuing company receives a down payment in cash and a promise to be paid cash, a receivable, in the amount of the deferred purchase price. The receivable, called *subscriptions receivable,* is the amount the company must collect before it issues the stock.

Suppose that Zall Corporation receives subscriptions for 5,000 shares of $5 par common stock at $40 per share. The subscription terms require a down payment of 20 percent, with the remainder of the purchase price to be paid in two equal installments, the first at the end of three months and the second six months from the subscription date. The entry to record the subscriptions would be as follows:

Cash	40,000	
Subscriptions receivable	160,000	
Common stock subscribed		25,000
Contributed capital in excess of par—common		175,000

Note that Zall credits common stock subscribed for the par value of the subscribed shares ($5 × 5,000 shares = $25,000), and contributed capital in excess of par—common for the excess of the purchase price over par value ($35 × 5,000 shares = $175,000).

At the end of three months, Zall would record collection of the first installment of the receivable as follows:

Cash	80,000	
Subscriptions receivable		80,000

At the end of six months, Zall would record collection of the remaining balance and issuance of the shares:

Cash	80,000	
Subscriptions receivable		80,000
Common stock subscribed	25,000	
Common stock		25,000

Note that the only new accounts associated with stock subscriptions are common stock subscribed (or preferred stock subscribed) and subscriptions receivable. *Common stock subscribed* is included in the balance sheet in the contributed capital section of stockholders' equity, along with common stock. Likewise, preferred stock subscribed is included with preferred stock in stockholders' equity.

There is some disagreement regarding the appropriate balance sheet presentation of subscriptions receivable. In most cases, companies include subscriptions receivable in the current assets section of the balance sheet, and report them separately from trade receivables. Some accountants, however, believe that in certain circumstances, showing subscriptions receivable as a deduction from the contributed capital account is more appropriate. Although both methods are used, presentation of subscriptions receivable as a current asset is preferable theoretically and is more common in practice.

So far, we have been discussing the issuance of a single class of security. Sometimes two or more types of stock are issued as a unit. Accounting for these transactions, which are known as lump-sum stock issuances, is described in the following section.

CONCEPTUAL

Generally, subscriptions receivable should be reported as current assets.

Lump-Sum Issuance

To increase the attractiveness of its stock and to generate additional capital, a corporation sometimes issues two or more types of stock as a single unit—for example, one share of common stock with one share of preferred stock. In this case the issuing company must allocate the amount received between the two classes of securities on the basis of their relative fair values at the time of issuance. If the company knows the fair value of only one of the securities issued, it must assign the known fair value to it and then allocate the remainder to the security whose fair value is not determinable.

To illustrate, assume that Malott Corporation offers a package consisting of one share of $10 par common stock and one share of $100 par preferred stock. Malott issues 1,000 of the units for $150 each. At the time of issuance, the market price of the common stock is $50 per share; the market price of the preferred stock is $130 per share. Malott allocates the $150,000 it receives for the issue ($150 × 1,000 units) to the common and preferred stock as follows:

Fair value of common ($50 × 1,000 shares) .... **$ 50,000**
Fair value of preferred ($130 × 1,000 shares) **130,000**
    Total fair value **$180,000**

Allocation to common:

$$\frac{\$50,000}{\$180,000} \times \$150,000 = \$41,667$$

Allocation to preferred:

$$\frac{\$130,000}{\$180,000} \times \$150,000 = \underline{108,333}$$

$$\text{Total allocated} \qquad \underline{\$150,000}$$

The required journal entry would be:

Cash	150,000	
Common stock ($10 × 1,000)		10,000
Contributed capital in excess of par—common		31,667
Preferred stock ($100 × 1,000)		100,000
Contributed capital in excess of par—preferred		8,333

If instead the market price of the preferred stock were not determinable, and the market price of the common stock were known to be $50 per share, Malott would allocate the $150,000 proceeds as follows:

Cash received **$150,000**
Allocated to common stock ($50 × 1,000 shares) .... **(50,000)**
Allocated to preferred stock **$100,000**

Note that the approach to valuing a lump-sum issuance is comparable to the problem of valuing two or more assets received in a lump-sum exchange (see page 590). In both cases, the allocation is based on fair values.

When stock is issued, various issuance costs are incurred. The next section describes the appropriate accounting for these costs.

Issue Costs

Corporations often incur legal, accounting, administrative, and promotional costs when they issue capital stock. For example, a company might announce a proposed offering of capital stock in *The Wall Street Journal*. The cost of the newspaper advertisement is a cost of the stock issue.

CONCEPTUAL

Stock issue costs relate to capital transactions, not earnings activities.

Because **stock issue costs** do not relate to operations, they should not affect reported earnings. Corporations incur these costs in association with capital transactions rather than earnings activities. Therefore, stock issue costs should be recorded as a reduction of the contributed capital associated with the shares. The net amount of capital generated is the issue price of the securities minus the stock issue costs.

Another type of transaction involving stock is the conversion of preferred stock into common stock. In the following section we look briefly at the accounting requirements.

Conversion of Preferred to Common

Companies sometimes issue common stock through conversion of preferred stock. When preferred stock is converted into common stock, the book value method is used to record the conversion. Because the conversion of preferred to common is a capital transaction, no gains or losses may be recognized. Instead, the amount recorded for the converted preferred is reclassified and transferred to the common stock issued in its place.

As an example, assume that McRae Company has $50 par value convertible preferred outstanding, issued at an average price of $70 per share. The conversion ratio is two shares of preferred to one share of common. If 20,000 shares of preferred are converted to common stock with a par value of $5 per share, the following entry would be made to record the conversion:

Preferred stock ($50 × 20,000)	1,000,000	
Contributed capital in excess of par—preferred		
($20 × 20,000)	400,000	
Common stock ($5 × 10,000)		50,000
Contributed capital in excess of par—common		
($135 × 10,000)		1,350,000

So far in this chapter we have discussed accounting for transactions in which corporations issue new capital stock. As we saw in Chapter 13 (pages 688–691), many corporations issue *stock rights* as a preliminary step to issuing additional shares. In the next section we will discuss the accounting requirements for stock rights, including the controversial topic of stock-based compensation.

4 Account for the conversion of preferred stock to common stock.

Stock Rights

A **stock right** entitles the holder to acquire shares of the issuing corporation's stock according to specified terms. The most common reasons for issuing stock rights are:

1. To enhance the marketability of another type of security, such as bonds. This situation was discussed in Chapter 14 (see pages 754–755).

2. To satisfy the preemptive right of existing stockholders in connection with the issuance of additional shares of stock.

3. To give executives and employees an opportunity to acquire shares of stock in connection with company stock plans.

The accounting procedures for stock rights depend on the circumstances under which the company issues the rights. We will describe accounting for stock rights in the second and third situations in the next two sections.

Rights Issued to Existing Stockholders

If existing stockholders have a *preemptive right,* the corporation must give them an opportunity to keep their proportion of ownership whenever it issues additional shares. The corporation issues stock rights to stockholders as evidence of this privilege. The certificate that verifies this right is called a **stock warrant.**

Stock rights permit stockholders to purchase more shares at a price that is generally below the current market price. Normally, the longer the period before the rights expire, the less the difference between the exercise price and the market price when the rights are issued. In fact, in some cases the exercise price may exceed the market price at the time the company issues the rights, as the following news story indicates:

> American Express Co. will issue to holders about 930,000 five-year warrants to purchase a common share at $55 each.

5 Define and account for stock rights issued to existing stockholders.

The warrants will be distributed to stock of record Feb. 11 at the rate of one warrant for each 100 shares held. These warrants would expire Feb. 28, 1987, but American Express said it reserves the right to move up the expiration date if the common rises to at least $95 a share for 10 consecutive days. Cash will be given in lieu of fractional warrants.

American Express common closed on the New York Stock Exchange composite tape yesterday at $39.625, down $2. The company currently has about 93 million shares outstanding.[5]

When a company issues warrants as evidence of preemptive rights, it does not need to make a formal accounting entry. The company should, however, make a **memorandum entry** in the general journal specifying the number of rights issued and describing the agreement. The corporation must be certain that enough unissued shares are available to permit exercise of the rights.

Stockholders can exercise the stock rights, sell them, or let them expire. Of these three options, the issuing company must account for only the exercise of the rights. For example, if a stockholder exercises preemptive rights to acquire 100 shares of $10 par common at $25 per share, the company must make the following journal entry:

Cash ($25 × 100 shares)	2,500	
Common stock		1,000
Contributed capital in excess of par—common		1,500

Stock-Based Compensation

For many years, corporations have employed stock option plans to compensate their employees and key executives, to raise capital, and to spread ownership of the business among their employees. Stock options and other forms of stock-based compensation have become increasingly common over the last twenty years. For example, in 1992, Walt Disney's CEO, Michael Eisner, realized $197 million in stock option gains; Thomas Frist of Hospital Corporation of America realized about $126 million.[6] Not a single penny of these gains was reported as a company expense.

Under current GAAP, companies may measure the cost of stock-based compensation under either of two official pronouncements: *APB Opinion No. 25*[7] or *Statement of Financial Accounting Standards No. 123*.[8] Because *Opinion No. 25* does not require recognition of compensation from many stock-based compensation agreements, while *Statement No. 123* does, most companies apply, and are expected to continue to apply, *Opinion No. 25*. Therefore, our coverage of accounting and reporting for stock-based compensation agreements will focus mainly on *Opinion No. 25*. Companies that follow the accounting requirements of *Opinion No. 25* must also provide pro forma disclosures of net income and earnings per share, as required by *Statement No. 123*. Therefore we conclude our coverage of stock-based compensation with a brief description of these required disclosures and the fair-value based method of accounting under *Statement No. 123*.

Accounting and Reporting under *APB Opinion No. 25* Under *Opinion No. 25,* stock option plans are classified as either *noncompensatory* or *compensatory.* In essence, a **noncompensatory plan** is one which is designed primarily to encourage stock ownership among employees rather than to provide compensation. These plans typically include substantially all employees and offer stock at an option price that is at least 85 percent of the market price. The company does not recognize com-

6 **Account for stock-based compensation under *APB Opinion No. 25* and evaluate the accounting guidelines set forth in that *Opinion*.**

---

[5]*The Wall Street Journal,* January 27, 1982, p. 37.
[6]"'Hands Off My Stock Pile,'" *Business Week,* April 12, 1993, p. 29.
[7]"Accounting for Stock Issued to Employees," *Opinions of the Accounting Principles Board No. 25* (New York: AICPA, 1972).
[8]"Accounting for Stock-Based Compensation," *Statement of Financial Accounting Standards No. 123* (Norwalk, Conn.: FASB, 1995).

pensation expense for noncompensatory stock option agreements, and the employee generally does not have to recognize income for tax purposes on stock purchases made under such plans.

A **compensatory plan** is one which does not meet the characteristics of a noncompensatory plan, as defined by *Opinion No. 25*. Typically, compensatory plans are designed to provide additional compensation to a select group of employees or executives. Thus, the option terms are more lenient (longer) than those of noncompensatory plans, allowing covered employees greater opportunity to reap benefits from the arrangement. The company's compensation expense is measured by the difference between the option price and the market price at the measurement date, which is often the date of grant. Under what might be called **fixed stock option plans,** companies usually avoid recognition of compensation expense by setting the option price equal to the market price at the date of grant. As a result, even though the plans are designed to provide compensation, typically no compensation expense is reported.

Other compensatory stock option plans, referred to as **performance options,** allow covered employees to receive cash, stock, or a combination of cash and stock based on the difference between a specified amount per share and the market price at some future date. For these plans, the amount and form of compensation are not determinable until the date of exercise. However, because the services for which the options are granted usually precede the date of exercise, compensation expense must be estimated for periods between the date of grant and the date of exercise.

To illustrate, assume that at the beginning of 1997, Erwin Corporation grants **stock appreciation rights (SARs)** to certain key executives. Under the terms of the SAR plan, the executives may receive either cash, Erwin Corporation $5 par common stock, or a combination of cash and common stock. The amount received is to be determined by the difference between the quoted market price of the stock and a price of $20 per SAR. Erwin grants a total of 20,000 SARs, exercisable between January 1, 2000, and December 31, 2004. The market price per share of Erwin Corporation common at the end of 1997, 1998, and 1999 was $35, $38, and $29, respectively.

Under this plan, the service period appears to be 1997 through 1999, since the executives cannot exercise the SARs until 2000. The calculation of compensation expense for the years 1997 through 1999 is shown below.

| | | | | | | | COMPENSATION | | |
| | ENDING | | | | | | | EXPENSE | |
YEAR	MARKET PRICE	OPTION PRICE	PER SHARE	AGGREGATE	ACCRUED PERCENTAGE	ACCRUED TO DATE	1997	1998	1999
1997	$35	$20	$15	$300,000	33 1/3	$100,000	$100,000		
1998	38	20	18	360,000	66 2/3	240,000		$140,000	
1999	29	20	9	180,000	100	180,000			$(60,000)

If Erwin is likely to pay the obligation in cash, journal entries at the end of each year would be as follows:

```
12/31/97  Compensation expense . . . . . . . . . . . . . . .  100,000
              Liability under stock plan . . . . . . . . . . . .          100,000

12/31/98  Compensation expense . . . . . . . . . . . . . . .  140,000
              Liability under stock plan . . . . . . . . . . . .          140,000

12/31/99  Liability under stock plan  . . . . . . . . . . . .   60,000
              Compensation expense . . . . . . . . . . . . . .           60,000
```

If Erwin were likely to meet the obligation through the issuance of stock instead of by paying cash, Erwin would credit an additional contributed capital account, *contributed capital—stock appreciation rights,* instead of crediting the liability. Note that compensation expense is *credited* in 1999, because estimated total compensation

CONCEPTUAL

Compensatory plans are designed to provide compensation.

expense at the end of 1999 is $180,000—whereas a total of $240,000 was recorded in the two previous years.

If the executives exercise all the SARs in 2000, when the quoted market price is $36 per share, total compensation expense will be $320,000 [($36 – $20) × 20,000 shares]. Because Erwin has recognized compensation expense of $180,000 in prior periods, an additional $140,000 arises at the measurement date in 2000, which in this case is also the date of exercise:

Liability under stock plan	180,000	
Compensation expense	140,000	
Cash		320,000

Application of the *Opinion No. 25* requirements leads to an anomaly in which compensation expense is recognized for most performance stock options, but not for most fixed stock options. This anomaly provides an incentive for companies to issue fixed stock options, because they generally prefer not to recognize compensation expense (and reduce reported earnings) in connection with their stock-based compensation plans. Many analysts and other financial statement users are troubled by the inconsistent treatment of performance and fixed stock options, even more so because performance options often are less valuable than fixed options. Michael Eisner's and Thomas Frist's stock options, which could hardly be considered valueless, were fixed stock options, yet no expense was reported for those options in the financial statements of the issuing companies.

As we indicated earlier, companies that continue to follow *Opinion No. 25* must also present pro forma disclosures of net income and earnings per share, as if they had followed *Statement No. 123*. We will briefly describe this method in the next section.

Accounting for Stock-Based Compensation under *Statement No. 123* Under *Statement No. 123,* compensation cost is measured at the fair value of stock-based compensation paid to employees. Equity instruments issued to employees, and the related services received as consideration, are measured and recognized based on the fair value of the equity instruments issued.[9] The amount attributed to employee services must be recognized as an expense over the periods in which the related employee services are rendered. When an award is made for past services, the expense should be recognized when the award is granted.[10]

The fair value of a financial instrument is defined as "the amount at which the instrument could be exchanged in a current transaction between willing parties, other than in a forced or liquidation sale."[11] For awards calling for settlement through the issuance of equity instruments (e.g., common stock), the fair value must be measured at the grant date, based on the stock price at that date and the best estimate of the outcome of service-related and performance-related conditions. The fair value of a stock option granted by a public entity (an entity whose equity securities are traded in an organized market) must be estimated using a pricing model. For stock-based compensation awards that call for settlement in cash, the employer incurs a liability instead of recognizing additional equity. The amount of the liability must be measured each period based on the current stock price, with changes in the amount of the liability recognized as compensation expense in the period in which the changes occur.

The fair value of equity instruments awarded to employees as compensation must be recognized as additional equity at the grant date. To the extent that the amount recognized is attributable to future services, it must also be recognized as an asset, *prepaid compensation,* and amortized over the employees' related service period. If the service period is not defined as an earlier or shorter period, it is pre-

1

Explain the accounting for stock-based compensation under *Statement No. 123*.

CONCEPTUAL

The fair value of equity instruments awarded to employees as compensation must be recognized as additional equity at the grant date.

---

[9]"Accounting for Stock-based Compensation," *Statement of Financial Accounting Standards No. 123,* (Norwalk, Conn.: FASB, 1995), para. 16.
[10]Ibid., para. 30.
[11]Ibid., para. 9.

sumed to be the vesting period. Stock option awards are **vested** when the employee's right to receive or retain stock or cash under the plan is not contingent on the performance of future services. Many stock option plans vest on the date the options become exercisable.

In conclusion, the FASB has advocated—unsuccessfully—a fair-value-based method of accounting for stock compensation plans. Though *Opinion No. 25* will undoubtedly continue to prevail in practice, the FASB has been able to require disclosure of the impact on net income of fair value recognition of stock compensation. As the Board pointed out, however, disclosure is not an acceptable substitute for recognition in the financial statements. The Board has also declared that the fair value method is preferable to the APB method for purposes of justifying a change in accounting principle.

The next section briefly describes the appropriate accounting and reporting for donated capital. The section following that addresses the accounting and reporting issues that arise when a company reacquires its own capital stock.

D ONATED CAPITAL

The issuance of stock is the primary source of a corporation's contributed capital. A less common source of capital is donations from stockholders or other parties. For example, a city may donate land to a corporation to induce it to locate a new plant or office there.

As indicated in the discussion of donated assets in Chapter 11 (pages 589–590), the corporation that receives the asset records it at its fair value, with a corresponding credit to *donated capital*. Because this event affects capital rather than earnings, no gain or loss arises. The donated capital account usually appears in the balance sheet in the additional contributed capital section of stockholders' equity. Alternatively, some companies report donated capital as a separate category between contributed capital from investments by stockholders and retained earnings.

A CQUIRED CAPITAL STOCK

As the following quotation indicates, buybacks of corporations' own capital stock have become increasingly common in recent years.

8 Account for the acquisition and retirement of capital stock and for treasury stock under the cost method and the par value method.

> Back in the 1980s, it was a defensive move. Many companies bought back big chunks of their stock—often with borrowed money—as a way to keep the shares away from unfriendly takeover types. But the demise of the dealmeisters in the early 1990s made buybacks less urgent. The recession forced Corporate America to focus on shrinking debt, not equity.
>
> But now, an increasing number of top-drawer companies are back in the buyback game with nary a raider in sight. This time, the reasons are mainly offensive, such as boosting stock prices and earnings per share. And the new tax bill should help fuel the buyback boom.[12]

Among the companies that have begun or approved large stock repurchase programs are Bristol-Myers Squibb, H. J. Heinz, Nike, PepsiCo, Quaker Oats, Reebok International, and Wachovia.[13] Quaker Oats repurchased 20 million common shares over a five-year period and was authorized to repurchase another 5 million shares. Quaker's treasurer said, "We spend on new products, we make acquisitions, and we raise the dividend, and we still can't soak up all the cash."[14] Because interest rates

[12]"The Great Buyback Boom of '93," *Business Week,* August 23, 1993, pp. 76–77.
[13]Ibid., p. 76.
[14]Ibid.

have declined, saving huge sums in interest expense, many corporations are generating more cash than they can spend. Mattel Inc., the giant toymaker, recently announced plans to buy 10 million of its own common shares over a four-year period.[15] The stated reason was that plant capacity was adequate to handle current sales growth, and excess cash was building up at the rate of $200 million per year.

When a corporation acquires shares of its own common stock, it may either retire them or hold them for subsequent reissue. If the company does not formally retire or cancel the shares, the acquired stock is called **treasury stock.** Laws governing the acquisition of a company's own shares vary from country to country. In Great Britain such shares must be canceled; thus, accounting for treasury stock is not an issue in that country.

The next section covers accounting for the retirement of capital stock. The section that follows covers the accounting procedures for treasury stock.

Retirement of Capital Stock

When a corporation acquires and retires its own capital stock, its net assets and stockholders' equity are both reduced. Since the selling price of shares varies over time, companies usually calculate an average paid-in price per share as a basis for determining the reduction in contributed capital. If the amount paid to retire the shares exceeds the average paid-in price per share, the difference must be debited to retained earnings. If the amount paid to retire the shares is less than the average paid-in price per share, the difference is credited to contributed capital from retirement of stock.

To illustrate, assume that Jackson Corporation has the following stockholders' equity account balances on December 31, 1998:

Common stock (1,000 shares, $10 par)	**$ 10,000**
Contributed capital in excess of par—common	**140,000**
Retained earnings	**500,000**

The average paid-in price per share is $150 ($150,000 ÷ 1,000). Assuming that the following three independent transactions occurred at the beginning of 1999, the required journal entries would be as follows:

1. Jackson acquires and retires 100 shares at $150 per share.

Common stock	1,000	
Contributed capital in excess of par—common	14,000	
Cash		15,000

2. Jackson acquires and retires 100 shares at $170 per share.

Common stock	1,000	
Contributed capital in excess of par—common	14,000	
Retained earnings ($20 × 100 shares)	2,000	
Cash		17,000

3. Jackson acquires and retires 100 shares at $135 per share.

Common stock	1,000	
Contributed capital in excess of par—common	14,000	
Cash		13,500
Contributed capital from retirement of stock ($15 × 100 shares)		1,500

CONCEPTUAL

A company cannot *increase* retained earnings through transactions in its own stock.

Note that a company may *decrease* retained earnings when it retires shares, but it cannot *increase* retained earnings through transactions in its own stock. The

---

[15]"Many Concerns Use Excess Cash to Repurchase Their Shares," *The Wall Street Journal,* July 2, 1993, p. C-1.

reduction in retained earnings may be viewed as an additional dividend paid to the stockholders whose shares are being retired.

Treasury Stock

As we saw earlier, a corporation may acquire its own stock for several purposes:

1. To meet its needs in connection with stock option plans.

2. To eliminate the ownership interests of a particular stockholder.

3. To increase earnings per share, by decreasing the number of shares outstanding.

4. To meet its needs in connection with convertible bonds or convertible preferred stock.

5. To increase the market price per share.

6. To make shares available for a pending merger.

7. To make shares available for the issuance of a stock dividend.

8. To reduce the size of the entity's operations.

Regardless of the reason for acquiring treasury shares, the accounting effect is the same as when stock is retired: *Net assets and stockholders' equity are reduced.* When a corporation issues capital stock, net assets and stockholders' equity increase; when a corporation acquires its own shares, the opposite effect occurs. Under U.S. GAAP, treasury stock constitutes a reduction of stockholders' equity rather than an asset. The fact that a company can reissue the treasury shares to generate additional resources is irrelevant, because the same can be said about authorized but unissued shares, which are also not assets. Note, however, that the *Fourth Directive* of the European Community requires that treasury stock be shown as an asset.

A company's retained earnings balance usually restricts the amount that can be paid for treasury stock, so that such acquisitions do not affect legal capital. Dividend distributions too usually are restricted by the cost of treasury shares held, so that subsequent dividends will not reduce contributed capital. Since a company cannot own a portion of itself, treasury shares do not confer voting rights, receive dividends, or confer liquidation rights.

Two methods of accounting for treasury stock are acceptable in practice: the cost method and the par value method. These methods are discussed in the next two sections.

CONCEPTUAL

Treasury stock is not an asset; it is a reduction in stockholders' equity.

The Cost Method

Under the **cost method,** the purchase of treasury stock is viewed as a *temporary* reduction in stockholders' equity. Thus, the purchase and subsequent reissue of treasury stock may be looked on as two parts of one transaction. The purchase temporarily reduces stockholders' equity; the reissue increases it. The cost method is therefore a "single-transaction" approach.

To record the acquisition of treasury shares under the cost method, the treasury stock account is debited for the *cost* of the acquired shares. Upon reissue, treasury stock is credited for the cost basis of the reissued shares. If acquisitions of treasury shares take place at different prices, a cost flow assumption, such as average cost, FIFO, or specific identification, must be adopted to record the reissuance of shares. *Under the cost method, the amount originally received for shares has no effect on the entries made to record the acquisition and reissuance of treasury shares.*

If a company reissues treasury shares for more than the cost of the shares, it should credit an additional contributed capital account, called *contributed capital from treasury stock transactions,* for the amount received in excess of cost. If a company reissues treasury shares for less than the cost, the difference between the proceeds and the cost reduces any additional contributed capital credit balance arising

CONCEPTUAL

Under the cost method, treasury stock is viewed as a temporary item awaiting ultimate disposition.

from earlier reissuances or retirements of treasury stock of the same class. If a difference remains after this additional contributed capital balance has been reduced to zero, retained earnings should be debited for the remainder. Note that *retained earnings may be decreased, but not increased, as a result of treasury stock transactions.* Accountants view any debit to retained earnings that is made as a result of treasury stock transactions as an additional dividend paid to retiring stockholders.

To illustrate, assume that Keane Corporation receives authorization to issue one million shares of $10 par common stock. To date, Keane has issued 300,000 shares at various prices. The balances of the contributed capital accounts are as follows:

Common stock **$3,000,000**
Contributed capital in excess of par—common **9,000,000**

Thus, the average price paid per share is $12,000,000 ÷ 300,000 shares = $40.

Now assume that the following transactions occur in the sequence indicated. Journal entries accompany each transaction.

I. Keane acquires 10,000 shares of common at a price of $53 per share.

Treasury stock	530,000	
Cash		530,000

2. Keane reissues 2,000 treasury shares at $56 per share.

Cash	112,000	
Treasury stock (2,000 × $53)		106,000
Contributed capital from treasury stock		
transactions—common (2,000 × $3)		6,000

3. Keane reissues 3,000 treasury shares at $48 per share.

Cash	144,000	
Contributed capital from treasury stock		
transactions—common	6,000	
Retained earnings	9,000	
Treasury stock (3,000 × $53)		159,000

4. Keane formally retires the remaining 5,000 treasury shares.

Common stock	50,000	
Contributed capital in excess of par—common	150,000	
Retained earnings	65,000	
Treasury stock (5,000 × $53)		265,000

Note that in transaction 3, the cost of the reissued treasury shares is $159,000, but the proceeds upon reissue are only $144,000. Of the $15,000 difference, Keane debits $6,000 to the additional contributed capital created in transaction 2, and the remaining $9,000 to retained earnings. Upon retirement of the remaining shares in transaction 4, the excess of the cost of the treasury shares ($265,000) over the amount originally paid in ($40 average price per share × 5,000 shares = $200,000) is $65,000. Keane debits the difference to retained earnings. If the cost of the treasury shares were less than the amount originally received for them, the company would credit the difference to an additional contributed capital account, called *contributed capital from retirement of common stock.*

The Par Value Method

The **par value method** is a "two-transaction" approach. Under this method, the acquisition of a company's own shares is viewed as equivalent to a retirement of the shares. Treasury stock is debited for the par or stated value of the acquired shares; the appropriate additional contributed capital account is debited for the amount originally received in excess of par or stated value; and cash is credited. If the cash paid to acquire the shares exceeds the amount originally received, retained earnings is debited for the difference. As mentioned in the example of stock retirement on page 972, the difference is viewed as a dividend to retiring stockholders. If the cash paid to acquire the shares is less than the amount originally received, the difference is credited to *contributed capital from treasury stock transactions.* This difference is viewed as a contribution from retiring stockholders.

Upon reissue of the treasury shares, cash is debited for the proceeds; treasury stock is credited for the par value of the reissued shares; and contributed capital in excess of par—common is credited for the excess of the proceeds over par value. The only difference between this entry and the entry to record the sale of previously unissued shares is that in the latter case, common stock rather than treasury stock is credited for the par value of the shares issued.

To illustrate the par value method, look again at the example of Keane Corporation. Keane has 300,000 shares of $10 par common stock outstanding. The following account balances imply an average price paid per share of $40:

Common stock **$3,000,000**
Contributed capital in excess of par—common 9,000,000

We will now account for the four transactions described earlier using the par value method.

1. Keane acquires 10,000 shares of common stock at $53 per share.

   Treasury stock 100,000
   Contributed capital in excess of par—common 300,000
   Retained earnings ($13 × 10,000 shares) 130,000
       Cash   530,000

2. Keane reissues 2,000 shares at $56 per share.

   Cash 112,000
       Treasury stock (2,000 × $10)   20,000
       Contributed capital in excess of par—common   92,000

3. Keane reissues 3,000 shares at $48 per share.

   Cash 144,000
       Treasury stock (3,000 × $10)   30,000
       Contributed capital in excess of par—common   114,000

4. Keane formally retires the remaining 5,000 treasury shares.

   Common stock 50,000
       Treasury stock (5,000 × $10)   50,000

The cost method is used more often than the par value method because it is simpler and requires less recordkeeping. The corporation does not have to keep track of original premiums and discounts arising from the original issue of reacquired shares. However, the par value method is conceptually preferable because when a company acquires shares, it eliminates the amounts originally received and replaces them upon reissue with the proceeds from reissue.

Balance Sheet Presentation

There are two acceptable methods of reporting treasury stock in the balance sheet; they correspond to the two methods of accounting for treasury stock. If a company uses the *cost method,* it reports the treasury stock account balance as a lump-sum reduction of total stockholders' equity. Under this method, the acquisition of treasury stock does not affect the individual contributed capital accounts. The unallocated reduction in stockholders' equity is consistent with the view that treasury stock is only a temporary account.

If a company uses the *par value method,* it deducts the treasury stock account balance from the par value of the issued shares of stock of the same class. Recall that when a company uses the par value method to account for treasury shares, it debits the additional contributed capital account for the excess over par received when the shares were originally issued. The treasury stock account balance is thus deducted from the capital stock account. This deduction, combined with the reduction of additional contributed capital, results in a reduction of contributed capital by the amount originally received for the shares. This reporting method is consistent with the view that the acquisition of treasury shares is equivalent to a retirement of the shares.

Exhibits 18–4 and 18–5 are based on Keane Corporation's transactions, with the following modifications: (1) Retained earnings before the treasury stock transactions was $18 million; and (2) transaction 4 has not yet occurred, so Keane Corporation has 5,000 treasury shares at the end of the period. Exhibit 18–4 illustrates the reporting that is consistent with the cost method of accounting for treasury stock. Exhibit 18–5 illustrates the reporting consistent with the par value method. Note that total stockholders' equity is the same under the two methods. In Exhibit 18–4 the cost of treasury stock is deducted as an unallocated amount; in Exhibit 18–5 the reduction from treasury stock acquisitions is allocated among the appropriate equity accounts.

As you might expect, given the popularity of the cost method, the reporting method demonstrated in Exhibit 18–4 is by far the most common. In most states,

CONCEPTUAL

Total stockholders' equity is the same under the cost method and the par value method.

EXHIBIT 18–4	Reporting of Treasury Stock Consistent with the Cost Method

Keane Corporation

Stockholders' equity:	
Common stock—$10 par value, authorized 1,000,000 shares, issued 300,000 shares	$ 3,000,000
Contributed capital in excess of par	9,000,000
	$12,000,000
Retained earnings ($265,000 restricted for cost of treasury stock held)	17,991,000
	$29,991,000
Less: Cost of 5,000 treasury shares	(265,000)
Total stockholders' equity	$29,726,000

EXHIBIT 18–5	Reporting of Treasury Stock Consistent with the Par Value Method

Keane Corporation

Stockholders' equity:	
Common stock—$10 par value, authorized 1,000,000 shares, issued 300,000 (of which 5,000 shares are held in the treasury)	$ 2,950,000
Contributed capital in excess of par	8,906,000
	$11,856,000
Retained earnings ($265,000 restricted for cost of treasury stock held)	17,870,000
Total stockholders' equity	$29,726,000

corporations must also restrict cash dividends to the balance of retained earnings less the cost of treasury shares held. Companies must disclose this restriction either parenthetically, as illustrated, or in a footnote to the financial statements.

Remember that corporations cannot "create earnings" through transactions in their own capital stock. In general, such transactions increase and decrease contributed capital. Though a company may occasionally *reduce* retained earnings through treasury stock transactions, it cannot increase retained earnings through such transactions.

The remainder of this chapter describes the accounting and reporting issues related to retained earnings. We first provide a general overview of retained earnings. We then consider the effect of dividends on retained earnings and, finally, appropriations of retained earnings.

R ETAINED EARNINGS

In Chapter 2, stockholders' equity was defined as the residual interest in the assets of a corporation that remains after its liabilities have been deducted. At the beginning of this chapter, we pointed out that stockholders' equity may be further subdivided into contributed capital and retained earnings (and possibly accumulated other comprehensive income). This subdivision provides useful financial information by indicating the portion of a company's net assets that has arisen from stockholder investments and other capital transactions and the portion that has arisen from profitable operating activities—called retained earnings. If a corporation operates at a profit, its net assets increase. If it operates at a loss, its net assets decrease. The increase or decrease is recorded in the retained earnings account. Thus, **retained earnings** is the balance sheet account that is debited or credited for changes in net assets that result from earnings activities.

The dollar amount of retained earnings makes up a significant portion of the stockholders' equity of most companies. Retained earnings may also represent a significant source of financing for many companies. Companies may "expand internally" by retaining assets that have arisen from profitable operations and using those assets to finance growth.

Trends in Terminology

While retained earnings is probably the term used most often for earnings that have been retained in the business, in practice terminology varies somewhat. Synonymous terms include *earnings retained in the business, accumulated earnings, earnings employed in the business,* and *retained income.* The accounting profession has discouraged the use of the term *earned surplus* to describe retained earnings and the term *capital surplus* to describe contributed capital in excess of par. Use of the term *surplus* can produce two possible misconceptions: (1) If a company has a "surplus," it has something it does not need; and (2) assets resulting from profitable operations are in distributable form.

Transactions That Affect Retained Earnings

Several types of transactions and other economic events affect retained earnings; see Exhibit 18–6. Under the all-inclusive form of the income statement discussed in Chapter 4, extraordinary, unusual, or infrequently occurring items are reported in the income statement rather than recorded directly in the retained earnings account.

EXHIBIT 18–6	Transactions and Other Economic Events That Affect Retained Earnings

Economic Event	Effect on Retained Earnings
Net income (loss)	Increase (decrease)
Prior period adjustments, e.g., error corrections	Increase or decrease
Some changes in accounting principle (discussed in Chapters 4 and 19)	Increase or decrease
Dividends (discussed later in this chapter)	Decrease
Some treasury stock transactions (discussed earlier in this chapter)	Decrease
Quasi-reorganizations (discussed in Appendix 18–1)	Increase

Dividends

9 Account for cash dividends, property dividends, liquidating dividends, and stock dividends.

CONCEPTUAL

Dividends are nonreciprocal transfers.

Other than stock dividends, **dividends** are *nonreciprocal transfers* between a company and its stockholders. As such, they represent a distribution of assets to stockholders. An earlier section in this chapter (pages 960–962) described corporate dividend policy in general and discussed the corporation's ability to pay dividends. This section explains the various types of dividends, including cash, property, liquidating, and stock dividends.

Cash Dividends

A cash dividend is a distribution of cash to stockholders. The *net effect* of a cash dividend is to reduce both retained earnings and cash:[16]

Retained earnings. xx
   Cash xx

Three dates are important with respect to cash and property dividends: the declaration date, the date of record, and the payment date. To illustrate, assume that on December 10, 1998, CD Corporation has 10,000 shares of common stock outstanding. On this date the board of directors declares a $1.50 per share cash dividend payable on January 10, 1999, to stockholders of record on December 30, 1998. In this example, the *declaration date* is December 10, the date on which the corporation's board of directors formally announces that a dividend is to be paid. Since dividends do not accrue with the passage of time, the declaration date is the date on which the corporation incurs an obligation (a liability) to pay the dividend. On December 10, 1998, therefore, the following entry would be made to record the dividend declaration:

Retained earnings 15,000
   Dividends payable 15,000
   (10,000 × $1.50)

If a balance sheet were to be prepared on December 31, 1998, dividends payable would be reported as a current liability.

The *date of record* is the date chosen by the corporation's board of directors on which to establish to whom the dividend will be paid. Generally, the date of record

[16]In Chapter 3 a temporary account, dividends declared, was debited for dividend declarations. This account was then closed to retained earnings at the end of the accounting period. For simplicity, this account is not used in this chapter.

is several days after the declaration date. No accounting entry is required at the date of record, since this date simply serves as the point at which stock ownership is established.

Stockholders who have purchased shares in the market before the ex-dividend date (which on the New York Stock Exchange is four trading days before the date of record) will receive the dividend whether or not they own the shares on the declaration or payment date. From the declaration date to the ex-dividend date, the common shares sell in the market "dividends on," meaning that the market price of the shares includes the forthcoming dividend. Thus, investors who purchase shares before the ex-dividend date will receive the dividend. After the ex-dividend date, the shares sell "ex-dividend," meaning that the price of the shares does not include the anticipated dividend. A stockholder who purchases shares after the ex-dividend date will not receive the dividend.

Finally, the payment date is the date when the dividend is paid, and the liability discharged. CD Corporation would make the following entry on January 10, 1999:

Dividends payable	15,000	
Cash		15,000

Property Dividends

A **property dividend** is a distribution of assets other than cash to stockholders. For example, Company *X* may declare a property dividend of some shares of Company *Z*'s stock, which it holds as an asset. Some years ago, Ranchers Exploration and Development Corporation, a New Mexico mining company, announced plans to pay its quarterly dividend in a specified quantity of gold per share. The company made the decision in recognition of "shareholders' concerns about inflation and the resultant loss of purchasing power or intrinsic value represented by paper currency and stock certificates."[17]

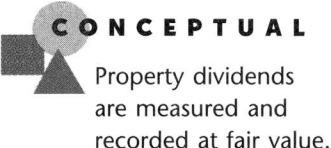

A property dividend may include any asset or group of assets. Most property dividends, however, consist of shares of other companies that are held as investments by the dividend-issuer. The shares are used as property dividends because they are easily divisible and their fair value readily determinable. In accordance with the historical exchange price principle discussed in Chapter 2 (page 000), assets that are distributed to stockholders as a property dividend should be adjusted to fair value at the declaration date, and a gain or loss should be recognized on the distribution.[18]

CONCEPTUAL

Property dividends are measured and recorded at fair value.

Assume, for instance, that Spinet Corporation holds 5,800 shares of TV Industries' common stock, which it acquired at $10 per share. Spinet declares a property dividend of 500 shares of TV Industries' stock at a time when the shares are carried on the books at $30 per share and are selling at $38 per share. The following entries would be necessary to record the declaration of the property dividend:

Investment in TV common	4,000	
Gain on disposition of investments		4,000
To record gain on 500 shares to be distributed		
[500 × ($38 − $30)].		
Retained earnings	19,000	
Property dividend payable		19,000
To record property dividend (500 × $38).		

At the payment date, the following entry would be made:

Property dividend payable	19,000	
Investment in TV common		19,000
To record payment of dividend.		

---

[17]*Arizona Republic,* May 19, 1981.
[18]"Accounting for Nonmonetary Transactions," *Opinions of the Accounting Principles Board No. 29* (New York: AICPA, 1973).

Some years ago, Eastern Airlines proposed an unusual type of "property" dividend. The company offered to allow stockholders to apply for travel vouchers good for 25 cents of travel for each common share owned. (Eastern had not paid a cash dividend on its common stock for many years.) One might question whether the travel vouchers represented property dividends or merely sales discounts. The rationale for treating the vouchers as a property dividend was that Eastern had obligated itself to deliver asset services—the services of its planes—in a nonreciprocal transfer between the company and its stockholders.[19]

Liquidating Dividends

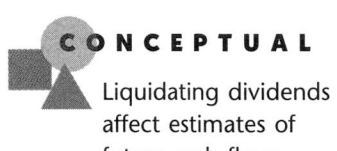

CONCEPTUAL

Liquidating dividends affect estimates of future cash flows.

From the company's perspective, a distribution of assets to stockholders in an amount greater than the dollar balance in retained earnings is a **liquidating dividend.** Stockholders should be informed if any portion of a dividend is liquidating, because such a distribution results in both a return *on* capital (the portion that represents the earnings distribution) and a return *of* capital (the portion that represents a return of contributed capital). Other things being equal, a return of capital to shareholders may result in decreased future cash flows to the company and its shareholders, because it reduces the asset base used to generate cash flows. Liquidating dividends usually are paid by companies that are ceasing operations or reducing their level of operations. If companies with wasting assets have no plans to acquire other wasting assets, they often pay dividends in an amount equal to *earnings before depletion.* In such cases the liquidating portion of the dividend is equal to the amount of depletion.

Liquidating dividends should be recorded by debiting retained earnings for the portion of the dividend that represents an earnings distribution. Other contributed capital should be debited for the liquidating portion of the dividend, and the asset that is distributed (usually cash) should be credited.

Stock Dividends

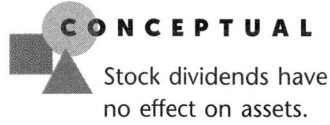

CONCEPTUAL

Stock dividends have no effect on assets.

A **stock dividend** is a distribution of additional shares of a corporation's own stock to its stockholders on a pro rata basis—that is, in proportion to the percentage of shares held. In this context, the word *dividend* is somewhat misleading because the dividends discussed thus far in this chapter have been distributions of cash, property, or other assets. A company's own stock, however, is not an asset to that company. Nevertheless, since the term is commonly used in practice, we will use it here.

Historically, corporations have distributed stock dividends for one or more of the following reasons:

1. A stock dividend increases the number of shares outstanding without changing the corporation's assets; therefore, it may cause the market price of the shares to fall, making the stock accessible to a greater number of investors.

2. Some corporations may wish to retain assets that have arisen from profitable operations and to distribute something else to stockholders in lieu of cash or other assets. A stockholder may be willing to accept stock instead of cash or other assets, since the shares may then be sold for cash (with a resulting decrease in the stockholder's interest). Thus, stock may be issued to satisfy stockholders' demands for dividends.

3. Management may desire to reduce the retained earnings available for future dividends. As we shall see, the recording of a stock dividend reduces retained earnings and increases contributed capital.

Accounting for a stock dividend depends on whether the dividend is considered large or small.[20] *Small stock dividends,* which are defined as less than approximately 20 to 25 percent of the shares outstanding, are recorded at the market price of the

---

[19]Also, the IRS indicated that the travel vouchers applied for would be considered as taxable income to the stockholders.

[20]"Restatement and Revision of Accounting Research Bulletins," *Accounting Research Bulletin No. 43* (New York: AICPA, 1953), chap. 7, sec. B, paras. 10–11.

shares distributed. *Large stock dividends,* which are defined as greater than 20 to 25 percent of the shares outstanding, are recorded, *at a minimum,* at the legal requirement, usually par value (stock dividends increase legal capital). Alternatively, large stock dividends may be measured at the average contributed amount per share.

The rationale for these practices is that because the market price of shares may not be affected by small stock dividends, those dividends may produce extra value to stockholders. Therefore, accounting for small stock dividends should be based on the market price of shares distributed, and retained earnings should be debited for the extra value. Theoretically, large stock dividends do not produce extra value, because the market price should decline proportionately. (In practice, market factors often cause a less-than-proportionate decline.) Therefore, retained earnings should be debited only to the extent of legal requirements.

To illustrate the accounting for stock dividends, assume that Lacy Industries has the following stockholders' equity balances:

Common stock ($10 par, 10,000 shares issued and outstanding)	$100,000
Contributed capital in excess of par	80,000
Retained earnings	160,000
Total	$340,000

If Lacy declares and distributes a 10 percent stock dividend when the market price of its shares is $32 per share, the following entry should be made:

Retained earnings (.10 × 10,000 × $32)	32,000	
Common stock (.10 × 10,000 × $10)		10,000
Contributed capital in excess of par ($32,000 – $10,000)		22,000

If Lacy declares and distributes a 50 percent stock dividend, the following entry would be required, assuming that par value is the basis of measurement:

Retained earnings	50,000	
Common stock		50,000
(.50 × 10,000 × $10)		

Alternatively, if the 50 percent stock dividend is recorded at the average contributed capital per share of $18 [($100,000 + $80,000) ÷ 10,000], the entry to record the dividend would be as follows:

Retained earnings (5,000 × $18)	90,000	
Common stock (5,000 × $10)		50,000
Contributed capital in excess of par (5,000 × $8)		40,000

Note that this measurement approach maintains the average contributed capital per share.

The effects of these stock dividends on total stockholders' equity may be summarized as follows:

		AFTER STOCK DIVIDEND		
	BEFORE STOCK DIVIDEND	SMALL STOCK DIVIDEND RECORDED AT MARKET PRICE	LARGE STOCK DIVIDEND RECORDED AT PAR VALUE	LARGE STOCK DIVIDEND RECORDED AT AVERAGE CONTRIBUTED CAPITAL PER SHARE
Common stock	$100,000	$110,000	$150,000	$150,000
Contributed capital in excess of par	80,000	102,000	80,000	120,000
Retained earnings	160,000	128,000	110,000	70,000
Total	$340,000	$340,000	$340,000	$340,000

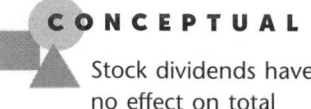

Note that in all three cases, the stock dividend has no effect on the *total* stock-holders' equity of $340,000. Accounting for the stock dividend merely results in a reclassification *within* stockholders' equity.

Up to this point we have assumed that stock dividends are declared and issued on the same date. If the issue date were to follow the declaration date, the following entries would be required to account for Lacy's small stock dividend.

On the declaration date:

Retained earnings	32,000	
Stock dividends distributable		10,000
Contributed capital in excess of par		22,000

On the issue date:

Stock dividends distributable	10,000	
Common stock		10,000

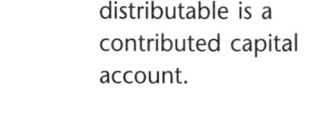

Stock dividends distributable is not a liability, since there is no obligation to transfer assets to stockholders. If a balance sheet is prepared between the declaration date and the issue date, stock dividends distributable are classified as part of contributed capital and are shown immediately below common stock issued and outstanding.

Stock Splits

Besides stock dividends, another way of increasing outstanding shares is through **stock splits.** Many corporations that have operated profitably, and whose stock has appreciated in value over a period, *split* their stock in order to make the market price more attractive to investors. For example, in 1993, Intel Corporation announced plans to split its stock 2 for 1. The price of Intel's stock had more than doubled in the year preceding the announcement. This split was Intel's ninth stock split since its initial public offering in 1971.

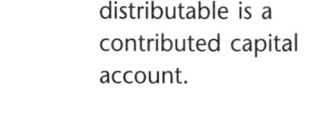

Conceptually, there is no difference between a stock dividend and a stock split; both result in an increased number of shares outstanding, with no effect on a corporation's net assets. Legally, however, there is a difference. As explained on page 980, a stock dividend increases the number of shares outstanding without changing par or stated value *per share.* As a result, the common stock account and legal capital both increase. A stock split also increases the number of shares outstanding, but it is accompanied by a proportional decrease in the par or stated value per share. The total dollar amount of the capital stock account does not change.[21]

No formal accounting entry is necessary to record a stock split. The corporation simply makes a memorandum entry to note the new shares outstanding and the lowered par value. As an alternative to a memorandum entry, the following formal entry could be made (assume a 3-for-1 stock split on 10,000 shares of $6 par common stock outstanding).

Common stock (10,000 shares, $6 par)	60,000	
Common stock (30,000 shares, $2 par)		60,000

Exhibit 18–7 compares the effects on stockholders' equity of a large stock dividend and a stock split. Since the usual objective of a large stock dividend is to lower the market price of a company's shares—and since the market impact is identical to that of a stock split—the Committee on Accounting Procedure suggested that a large stock dividend should be described as a "split-up effected in the form

---

[21]Corporations occasionally effect a *reverse* stock split by decreasing the number of shares outstanding. This strategy increases the market price of the (fewer) shares outstanding. For example, some years ago, Unicorp American effected a 15-for-1 reverse stock split designed to increase the market price of its stock, which sold for $.75 per share before the split.

EXHIBIT 18-7	Comparison of the Effects of a Large Stock Dividend and a Stock Split on Stockholders' Equity

Stockholders' Equity Before Stock Dividend or Stock Split

Common stock (par $10, 10,000 shares issued)	$100,000
Contributed capital in excess of par	100,000
Retained earnings	350,000
	$550,000

	Stockholders' Equity After	
	2-for-1 Stock Split	100% Stock Dividend
Common stock (par $5, 20,000 shares) . . .	$100,000	
(par $10, 20,000 shares) . .		$200,000[a]
Contributed capital in excess of par	100,000	100,000
Retained earnings	350,000	250,000[b]
	$550,000	$550,000

[a]100,000 + $100,000 (par value of shares issued in stock dividend).
[b]$350,000 − $100,000 (reduction from stock dividend, assuming that the dividend is measured at par).

of a dividend."[22] For instance, when Murphy Oil Corporation declared a 200 per-cent stock dividend, the event was described in the financial statements as follows:

> The shareholders approved an increase in the Company's authorized Common Stock to 40,000,000 shares and the Board of Directors declared a 200% stock dividend to effect a three-for-one stock split. Net income and dividends per share, average shares outstanding, shares subject to options and the related option prices have been adjusted to reflect the stock distribution.

Evaluation of Accounting for Stock Dividends

Although reporting stockholders' equity by source is a primary objective of financial reporting, accounting for stock dividends is inconsistent with that objective. Furthermore, the argument that accounting for small stock dividends should be based on the market price of shares distributed because such dividends produce extra value to stockholders has no apparent empirical support.[23] From the standpoint of the issuing company, stock dividends merely increase the number of shares outstanding and reduce the market price of the shares accordingly. Any *increases* in market price must be due to investors' expectations about future cash dividends, not to the stock dividends per se. Except for legal requirements, a logical accounting approach for all stock dividends would be to decrease proportionately the par value of the increased shares outstanding, which is the procedure used for stock splits. This approach appears to meet the qualitative characteristics of consistency and representational faithfulness discussed in Chapter 2.

Interestingly, the United States is one of the few countries, if not the only one, in which small stock dividends must be measured at market price. On the basis of

---

[22]*Accounting Research Bulletin No. 43,* para. 11.
[23]Sherman Chottiner and Allan Young, "A Test of the AICPA Differentiation between Stock Dividends and Stock Splits," *Journal of Accounting Research,* Autumn 1971, pp. 367–374; Eugene Fama, Lawrence Fisher, Michael Jensen, and Richard Roll, "The Adjustment of Stock Prices to New Information," *International Economic Review,* February 1969, pp. 1–21; Taylor Foster and Don Vickrey, "The Information Content of Stock Dividend Announcements," *Accounting Review,* April 1978, pp. 360–370.

an examination of historical events in the late 1930s and early 1940s, Stephen Zeff concluded that "evidently the New York Stock Exchange and a majority of the Committee on Accounting Procedure (of the AICPA) regarded periodic stock dividends as objectionable, and the CAP acted to make it more difficult for corporations to sustain a series of stock dividends out of their accumulated earnings."[24] Since market prices typically are much greater than par values, the requirement that a stock dividend be recorded at market price produces a much greater debit to (decrease in) retained earnings. This line of reasoning may partially explain the CAP's position on small stock dividends, and shows how accounting standards can affect the economic environment—in this case, by influencing corporate policy on stock dividends.

The Effect of Dividend Preferences on Dividend Distributions

Earlier in this chapter we discussed several characteristics of preferred and common stock. We pointed out that one characteristic of preferred stock is its preference with respect to dividends. If a company has both preferred stock and common stock issued and outstanding, preferred stockholders' claims to dividends must be satisfied before dividends are paid to common stockholders. If the preferred stock is *cumulative, dividends in arrears* must also be paid before distributions can be made to common stockholders. In addition, preferred stock that is *participating* allows preferred stockholders to share proportionately with common stockholders in dividends over and above the stated dividend rate on preferred shares. Participation may be either *full,* such that preferred stockholders are paid dividends at the same rate as common stockholders, or *partial* up to a maximum rate. For example, under partial participation, if a preferred share has a 10 percent stated dividend rate and is participating up to an additional 5 percent, the maximum total dividend rate is 15 percent.

To illustrate the effect of dividend preferences on dividend distributions, assume that Comanche Industries has the following capital stock outstanding:

Common ($10 par, 30,000 shares issued and outstanding) **$300,000**
8% preferred ($100 par, 2,000 shares issued and outstanding). **200,000**

Comanche plans to distribute cash dividends of $80,000 during the current year. Exhibit 18–8 (pages 986–987) shows the cash distribution to each class of stock under six different independent assumptions.

Appropriations (Restrictions) of Retained Earnings

Corporations often restrict the payment of dividends to amounts considerably less than the credit balance in retained earnings. Restrictions may arise because of one or more of the following circumstances:

10 Explain how appropriations of retained earnings may be used and why.

1. *Legal restrictions.* A corporation that purchases its own stock may be required to restrict retained earnings by an amount equal to the cost of the treasury stock. (This type of restriction was discussed on page 977.)

2. *A desire to retain assets for expansion.* A corporation may wish to retain assets that have arisen from profitable operations for purposes of internal expansion.

---

[24]Stephen Zeff, "The Rise of Economic Consequences," *Journal of Accountancy,* December 1978, pp. 57–58.

3. *Contractual restrictions.* A bond indenture, for example, may require a corporation to maintain not less than a specified amount of working capital, thus restricting the amount of liquid assets available for dividends. An indenture also may require that assets equal to a portion of retained earnings be restricted from availability for dividends over the life of a bond issue.

4. *Possibility of future losses.* Corporations often restrict dividends because of expected or possible losses arising from contingencies such as declines in inventory prices, lawsuits, or the risk of uninsured losses from casualties.[25]

These restrictions, if incorporated in the accounts, are referred to as **retained earnings appropriations.** Such appropriations communicate to stockholders that there are restrictions on dividends. Formal accounting entries are optional. When a corporation's board of directors approves a retained earnings restriction, the following entry may be made:

Retained earnings..	xx	
Retained earnings appropriated for (given purpose)..........		xx

When the appropriation is no longer necessary, the entry is reversed. Losses that may subsequently materialize should not be debited to the appropriation account. Those losses are a component of net income, and must therefore be reported on the income statement.

Whether or not formal entries are made, a restriction on retained earnings may be communicated by a disaggregation of retained earnings or a parenthetical or footnote disclosure. In the authors' opinion, disclosure of retained earnings restrictions by note is preferable to balance sheet disclosure, since it is less confusing than a formal appropriation. In many cases a formal appropriation may also require some commentary in the notes to the financial statements. Finally, because companies generally do not intend to pay dividends equal to the unappropriated retained earnings balance, subdividing the retained earnings balance appears to add little in the way of useful information.

In some countries, companies must provide "legal reserves." Each year a certain amount of income is appropriated until the reserve equals the legally prescribed percentage of stockholders' equity. Dividends may not be paid if doing so would impair the legal reserves. Thus, the main purpose of legal reserves is to protect creditors from overpayment of dividends. France, Japan, and Germany require companies to maintain legal reserves.

THE STATEMENT OF STOCKHOLDERS' EQUITY

The disclosure principle requires that financial reports include a statement showing the changes in retained earnings during the accounting period. When such a statement also includes changes in contributed capital, it is usually referred to as a statement of stockholders' (or shareholders') equity. This statement was described and illustrated in Chapter 5 (pages 220–221). Also, a statement of shareholders' equity for General Electric appears in Appendix B. Notice that the statement discloses all significant transactions affecting the shareholders' equity accounts during the last three accounting periods. This statement complements the other required financial statements by disclosing additional information and thus increasing their usefulness.

---

[25]The practice of not insuring against possible losses sometimes is described, quite incorrectly, as "self-insurance."

EXHIBIT 18-8	Distribution of Dividends to Common and Preferred Stockholders Under Six Independent Assumptions

Comanche Industries

Assumption 1: The preferred stock is noncumulative and nonparticipating.

	Preferred	Common	Total
8% of $200,000 (par value of preferred) to preferred stockholders . . .	$16,000		$16,000
Remainder ($80,000 − $16,000) to common stockholders		$64,000	64,000
Total	$16,000	$64,000	$80,000

Assumption 2: The preferred stock is cumulative and nonparticipating; dividends are in arrears for the three preceding years.

	Preferred	Common	Total
Dividends in arrears, $16,000 (8% of $200,000) for 3 years	$48,000		$48,000
Current year's dividend	16,000		16,000
Remainder ($80,000 − $64,000) to common stockholders		$16,000	16,000
Total	$64,000	$16,000	$80,000

Assumption 3: The preferred stock is noncumulative and fully participating.

	Preferred	Common	Total
Current year's dividend (8% of $200,000)	$16,000		$16,000
Ratable dividend to common (8% of $300,000)		$24,000	24,000
Amount available for participation: $80,000 − $40,000 = $40,000			
Participation rate: $\dfrac{\$40,000^a}{(\$200,000 + \$300,000)^b} = 8\%$			
Participating dividend:			
To preferred, 8% of $200,000	16,000		16,000
To common, 8% of $300,000		24,000	24,000
Total	$32,000	$48,000	$80,000

[a]Amount available for participation.
[b]Par value of preferred plus par value of common.

Assumption 4: The preferred stock is cumulative and fully participating; dividends are in arrears for the preceding year.

	Preferred	Common	Total
Dividends in arrears	$16,000		$16,000
Current year's dividend, including ratable dividend to common . . .	16,000	$24,000	40,000
Amount available for participation: $80,000 − $56,000 = $24,000			
Participation rate: $\dfrac{\$24,000}{\$500,000} = 4.8\%$			
Participating dividend:			
To preferred, 4.8% of $200,000	9,600		9,600
To common, 4.8% of $300,000		14,400	14,400
Total	$41,600	$38,400	$80,000

Assumption 5: The preferred stock is cumulative and participating up to an additional 3%;
dividends are in arrears for the two preceding years.

	Preferred	Common	Total
Dividends in arrears: $16,000 × 2 years	$32,000		$32,000
Current year's dividend, including ratable dividend to common . . .	16,000	$24,000	40,000
Amount available for participation: $80,000 − $72,000 = $8,000			
Participation rate: $\frac{\$8,000}{\$500,000}$ = 1.6%			
Participating dividend:[a]			
To preferred, 1.6% of $200,000	3,200		3,200
To common, 1.6% of $300,000		4,800	4,800
Total	$51,200	$28,800	$80,000

[a]Since the amount available for participation is less than 3%, the participating dividend in the current year is only 1.6%.

Assumption 6: The preferred stock is cumulative and participating up to an additional 3%;
no dividends are in arrears.

	Preferred	Common	Total
Current year's dividend, including ratable dividend to common . . .	$16,000	$24,000	$40,000
Amount available for participation: $80,000 − $40,000 = $40,000			
Participation rate:[a] $\frac{\$40,000}{\$500,000}$ = 8%			
Participating dividend:			
To preferred, 3% of $200,000	6,000		6,000
Remainder ($40,000 − $6,000) to common		34,000	34,000
Total	$22,000	$58,000	$80,000

[a]The participation rate should be calculated in order to determine if it exceeds 3%. If so, it is ignored in the participating dividend calculation, since preferred stock is limited to an additional 3%. Notice that the *actual* additional participation rate is as follows:

Preferred, 3%

Common, $\frac{\$34,000}{\$300,000}$ = 11.33%

SUMMARY OF LEARNING OBJECTIVES

I. Describe the four characteristics of the corporate form of organization that affect accounting for stockholders' equity.

The four characteristics that affect accounting for stockholders' equity are the system of capital accumulation, limited liability, stock preferences, and corporate dividend policy. The issuance of ownership units in the form of stock is a method of raising capital that is unique to corporations and creates some accounting and reporting complexities. *Limited liability* means that investors generally cannot lose more than the amount they invested and that the assets and liabilities of the corporation are separate and distinct from those of the owners. Stock preferences require significant disclosures in order for the financial statements to be understandable to users. Likewise, corporate dividend policy is governed by state corporation laws; financial accounting information assists users in evaluating that policy.

2. Identify the two basic preferences possessed by preferred stockholders over common stockholders and describe other possible preferences and their impact on accounting for preferred stock.

The two basic preferences possessed by preferred stockholders are preference with respect to dividend distributions and preference with respect to the distribution of assets upon liquidation. Other possible preferences include cumulative, participation, callable, and convertible features. If preferred stock is cumulative, dividends not paid on those shares in prior years must be paid before any dividend can be paid to common shareholders. Participating preferred shareholders share in any dividend distributions made after the preferred and common shareholders have received dividends equal to the preferred rate. If preferred stock is callable, the corporation may call, or redeem, the stock at a specified price. At the option of the stockholder, convertible preferred stock may be converted into shares of common stock at a specified ratio.

3. Account for the issuance of stock for cash, for noncash consideration, on a subscription basis, and for a lump-sum consideration.

In general, stock issued in any of these transactions should be recorded at the fair value of the stock or the consideration received, whichever is more readily determinable. The amounts recorded for the stock must be allocated, as appropriate, between par or stated value and contributed capital in excess of par or stated value. If a stock is sold on a subscription basis, common stock subscribed is shown as part of contributed capital; subscriptions receivable is usually reported as a current asset. When two or more classes of stock are issued for a lump-sum consideration, the amount received should be allocated based on the relative fair value of the stock issued.

4. Account for the conversion of preferred stock to common stock.

Upon conversion, amounts assigned to preferred stock should be eliminated from the preferred stock accounts and transferred to the common stock accounts using the book value method.

5. Define and account for stock rights issued to existing stockholders.

Stock rights entitle the holder to acquire shares of stock of the issuing corporation according to specified terms. When stock rights are issued to existing stockholders on a pro rata basis, no accounting is required, except perhaps for a memorandum entry. Upon exercise, the corporation must record the cash received in both the cash account and the appropriate common stock accounts.

6. Account for stock-based compensation under *APB Opinion No. 25* and evaluate the accounting guidelines set forth in that opinion.

For noncompensatory plans, no compensation expense is recognized. Compensatory plans may be divided into fixed stock option plans and performance options. Compensation expense generally is *not* recognized for fixed stock option plans. For performance options, however, compensation expense must be estimated and recognized for all periods from the date of grant to the date of exercise. Pro forma disclosure of net income and earnings per share is also required for performance options, based on fair value. These guidelines lead to an understatement of compensation expense in general, and an inconsistent treatment of fixed and performance option plans.

7. **Explain the accounting for stock-based compensation under *Statement No. 123*.**
Under *Statement No. 123*, compensation cost is measured at the fair value of stock-based compensation paid to employees. An option pricing model is used to determine fair value. Compensation expense is recognized over the periods in which the related services are rendered. Awards for past services are recognized as expense when they are granted. Awards calling for cash settlements are recognized as liabilities instead of as additional equity.

8. **Account for the acquisition and retirement of capital stock and for treasury stock under the cost method and the par value method.**
The retirement of capital stock is recorded by reducing assets and stockholders' equity by the amount paid for the retirement. Under the cost method, the acquisition of stock is recorded by reducing stockholders' equity by the cost of the shares acquired. When shares are subsequently reissued, the difference between the acquisition price and the reissue price is absorbed by either retained earnings (if the acquisition price is more than the reissue price) or additional paid-in capital (if the acquisition price is less than the reissue price). Under the par value method, the acquisition of shares is recorded by reducing the appropriate capital accounts for the average amount paid in per share. If the amount paid exceeds the average paid in per share, retained earnings is debited for the difference. If the amount paid is less than the average paid in per share, contributed capital from treasury stock transactions is credited for the difference. Upon reissuance, the reissued shares are accounted for as if they were newly issued shares.

9. **Account for cash dividends, property dividends, liquidating dividends, and stock dividends.**
Cash and property dividends both reduce retained earnings by the fair value of the assets distributed as dividends. A gain or loss may be recognized for property dividends. Liquidating dividends are recorded as a reduction of contributed capital. Stock dividends do not reduce net assets, but are recorded instead as a reduction of retained earnings and an increase in contributed capital, at either the fair value (for a small stock dividend) or the par value (for a large stock dividend) of the shares issued.

10. **Explain how appropriations of retained earnings may be used and why.**
Appropriations of retained earnings may be made to inform financial statement users of legal restrictions, company plans for the use of corporate assets, contractual restrictions, or the possibility of future losses. Appropriations are recorded by debiting retained earnings and crediting the appropriations account. Appropriations do not affect total retained earnings.

KEY TERMS

APPENDIX 18-1

Quasi-Reorganizations

A corporation that experiences continued losses may accumulate a debit balance—a *deficit*—in retained earnings. A deficit may also arise if assets—currently overstated because a change in economic conditions has diminished their value—are adjusted to their fair values. In many states a deficit in retained earnings may prevent the corporation from paying dividends until the retained earnings account is replenished with future net income. If potential investors are aware of the corporation's inability to pay dividends, the corporation may have difficulty obtaining capital, even though the operating activities may be capable of generating future cash flows and the business may have what appears to be a promising future. This inability to obtain capital may cause future losses and eventual insolvency or bankruptcy.

Under these circumstances, many states allow a company to eliminate its retained earnings deficit, revalue its assets, and proceed as a going concern without a legal reorganization. Such an arrangement, called a **quasi-reorganization,** may be preferable to a legal reorganization because of the time and money the latter requires. A quasi-reorganization, then, allows a company to make a fresh start from an accounting standpoint, as if it were beginning its operations at the date of the quasi-reorganization by acquiring assets and recording them at fair value. Quasi-reorganizations first became popular in the 1930s, as the result of the write-up of assets to artificially high appraisal values.

Before a quasi-reorganization takes place, stockholders must approve it. Furthermore, assets must be revalued based on reliable estimates of their fair value. The following procedures take place in a quasi-reorganization:

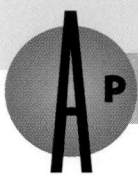

CONCEPTUAL

The accounting characteristics of a quasi-reorganization are a write-down of assets and the elimination of a retained earnings deficit.

1. Assets are revalued to their current fair values. While some individual assets may be written up to fair value, assets are generally written down in the aggregate.[26] This revaluation process increases the deficit in retained earnings.

2. The retained earnings deficit is eliminated (the balance is reduced to zero) by reducing the balances in the contributed capital accounts and increasing (crediting) retained earnings. In some instances, contributed capital may be decreased through stockholder donations of capital stock or by a reduction in the par value of shares outstanding.

3. In subsequent financial statements, retained earnings is "dated" for a reasonable number of years to show that a quasi-reorganization has occurred.

---

[26]We believe that a net *write-up* of assets is inconsistent with the economic conditions that originally led to the use of quasi-reorganizations. A sustained series of operating losses implies that an operating asset's (or group of operating asset's) present (fair) value is less than book value. An exception might occur when a *nonoperating* asset, such as land, is written up in an amount that exceeds the write-down of the *operating* assets in the aggregate.

To illustrate, assume that Indy Corporation has incurred operating losses for many years. With the approval of stockholders, the board decides to opt for a quasi-reorganization. Indy's balance sheet as of December 31, 1998, is as follows:

ASSETS		LIABILITIES AND STOCKHOLDERS' EQUITY	
Current assets	$ 70,000	Current liabilities	$ 30,000
Plant and equipment, net	100,000	Common stock (par $5,	
Other assets	30,000	40,000 shares outstanding)	200,000
		Contributed capital in excess	
		of par	20,000
		Retained earnings	(50,000)
Total	$200,000	Total	$200,000

The quasi-reorganization is carried out as follows:

1. Inventories, included in current assets, are written down by $10,000 to their net realizable value.
2. Plant and equipment are written down by $20,000 to their fair value.
3. Other assets are decreased by $10,000 to their fair value.
4. Stockholders agree to donate 5,000 shares of stock to Indy Corporation.
5. The par value of the remaining shares outstanding is reduced to $3 per share.

Indy would record the quasi-reorganization as follows:

Retained earnings	40,000	
Inventories (current assets)		10,000
Plant and equipment		20,000
Other assets		10,000
To revalue assets to fair value.		
Common stock	25,000	
Contributed capital in excess of par		25,000
To record donations (5,000 × $5).		
Common stock	70,000	
Contributed capital in excess of par		70,000
To record the reduction of par value from $5 per share to $3 per share on the remaining shares outstanding (35,000 × $2).		
Contributed capital in excess of par	90,000	
Retained earnings		90,000
To eliminate the deficit in retained earnings. The sum of the initial deficit of $50,000 in retained earnings plus the $40,000 debit to that account.		

Indy's balance sheet after the quasi-reorganization follows. The dating of retained earnings is shown parenthetically in the stockholders' equity section of the balance sheet.

ASSETS		LIABILITIES AND STOCKHOLDERS' EQUITY	
Current assets	$ 60,000	Current liabilities	$ 30,000
Plant and equipment	80,000	Common stock ($3 par,	
Other assets	20,000	35,000 shares outstanding)	105,000
		Contributed capital in excess	
		of par	25,000
		Retained earnings (quasi-	
		reorganization effected 12/31/98).	–0–
Total	$160,000	Total	$160,000

QUESTIONS   Questions marked with an asterisk (*) refer to Appendix 18–1.

Q 18-1.   Identify and describe the two primary components of stockholders' equity.

Q 18-2.   Describe the following types of corporations:
1. Private.   5. Open.
2. Public.   6. Closed.
3. Nonstock.   7. Listed.
4. Stock.   8. Unlisted.

Q 18-3.   How do state corporation laws affect accounting and reporting for stockholders' equity?

Q 18-4.   How does the system of capital accumulation for corporations differ from the system for partnerships and sole proprietorships?

Q 18-5.   What are the usual rights of corporate stockholders?

Q 18-6.   What is the difference between preferred stock and common stock?

Q 18-7.   What is the limited liability feature, and why is it advantageous to corporations?

Q 18-8.   Under what conditions might an investor in corporate stock be liable for more than the amount invested?

Q 18-9.   Why are corporations required to retain assets equivalent to contributed capital?

Q 18-10.   Describe the following features of preferred stock:
1. Cumulative.   3. Call.
2. Participation.   4. Conversion.

Q 18-11.   What are dividends in arrears? Do they constitute a liability? Explain.

Q 18-12.   Why does the SEC require corporations to exclude redeemable preferred stock from stockholders' equity?

Q 18-13.   What considerations influence a corporate board of directors' decisions regarding dividends?

Q 18-14.   Comment on the following statement: "A corporation pays dividends out of retained earnings."

Q 18-15.   What is the difference in accounting for the issuance of par value stock, stated value stock, and true no-par stock?

Q 18-16.   At what amount should a corporation record stock issued for noncash assets or services?

Q 18-17.   What is watered stock? What are secret reserves?

Q 18-18.   How should subscriptions receivable be reported in the financial statements? How should common stock subscribed be reported in the financial statements?

Q 18-19.   When two or more types of stock are issued as a unit, how does a corporation determine the amount to be assigned to each type of stock?

Q 18-20.   What is the acceptable method of accounting for stock issue costs? Why?

Q 18-21.   Describe the accounting for the conversion of preferred stock into common stock.

Q 18-22.   Identify three circumstances in which corporations commonly issue stock rights.

Q 18-23.   Distinguish between a *fixed* stock option plan and a *performance* stock option plan.

Q 18-24.   How should stock-based compensation cost be determined under *APB Opinion No. 25*?

Q 18-25.   Over what time period should stock-based compensation expense be recognized?

Q 18-26.   What are tandem plans? Why do these plans create accounting difficulties?

Q 18-27.   How should a company record donations of assets from stockholders or other parties?

Q 18-28.   Explain why retained earnings may decrease, but not increase, when a company retires its own capital stock.

Q 18-29.   What are some reasons that corporations acquire their own shares? What is the effect on a corporation of acquiring its own shares?

Q 18-30.   Describe the cost method and the par value method of accounting for treasury stock.

Q 18-31.   What is the difference between the cost method and the par value method in terms of their effect on (*a*) total stockholders' equity and (*b*) the components of stockholders' equity?

Q 18-32.   List the types of transactions that affect retained earnings.

Q 18-33.   Define the following dates related to cash dividends:
1. Declaration date.
2. Date of record.
3. Payment date.

Q 18-34. Describe a property dividend and the proper accounting for such dividends.

Q 18-35. Why is the distinction between large and small stock dividends important from an accounting standpoint?

Q 18-36. Compare a stock split and a large stock dividend in the following areas:
1. Par value of shares after issuance.
2. Shares outstanding after issuance.
3. Balance in the common stock account after issuance.
4. Effect on legal capital.
5. Market price of shares after issuance.
6. Effect on retained earnings.

Q 18-37. Discuss the purpose of an appropriation of retained earnings and give some examples of circumstances that may give rise to appropriations.

Q 18-38. Why is it important that liquidating dividends be identified as such in financial statements?

Q 18-39. What transactions and events could appear on a statement of changes in stockholders' equity?

Q 18-40. Indicate where the following items would appear in a corporation's financial statements:
1. Cash dividends declared.
2. Property dividends payable.
3. Warrants outstanding as a result of a stock dividend.
4. An appropriation of retained earnings for a purchase of treasury stock.
5. Stock dividends distributable.
6. A 4-for-1 stock split.

Q 18-41. Answer the following questions related to stock splits and stock dividends:
1. What is meant by a stock split effected in the form of a dividend?
2. From an accounting viewpoint, how does a stock split effected in the form of a dividend differ from an ordinary stock dividend?
3. How should a stock dividend that has been declared but not yet issued be classified in a statement of financial position? Why?

(AICPA, adapted)

*Q 18-42. Why do corporations sometimes initiate quasi-reorganizations?

*Q 18-43. Describe the procedures involved in accounting for a quasi-reorganization.

CASES

The case marked with an asterisk (*) refers to Appendix 18–1.

C 18-1. **ISSUANCE OF STOCK FOR NONCASH CONSIDERATION**   You have been engaged to examine the financial statements of Bay Corporation for the year ending December 31, 1998. Bay was organized in January 1998 by Moses and Price, original owners of options to acquire, for $400,000, oil leases on 5,000 acres of land. They contemplated that, first, the oil leases would be acquired by the corporation and, subsequently, 180,000 shares of the corporation's common stock would be issued to the public at $6 per share. In February 1998, they exchanged their options, $150,000 cash, and $50,000 of other assets for 75,000 shares of Bay's common stock. Bay's board of directors appraised the leases at $600,000, on the basis of leases recently issued for other acreage in the same area. The options were therefore recorded at $200,000 ($600,000 – $400,000 option price).

The options were exercised by Bay in March 1998, prior to the issuance of common stock to the public in April 1998. Leases on approximately 1,000 acres of land were abandoned as worthless during the year.

REQUIRED
1. Why is the valuation of assets acquired by a corporation in exchange for its own common stock sometimes difficult?
2. What reasoning might Bay Corporation use to support its valuation of the leases at $600,000, the amount of the appraisal by the board of directors?
3. Assuming the board's appraisal was sincere, what steps might Bay have taken to strengthen its position to use the $600,000 value and to provide additional information if questions are raised about possible overvaluation of the leases?
4. Discuss the propriety of charging one-fifth of the recorded value of the leases against income in 1998 because leases on 1,000 acres of land were abandoned during the year.

(AICPA, adapted)

C 18-2. **STOCK-BASED COMPENSATION** The following note accompanied the financial statements in McDonald's Corporation's 1995 annual report:

Stock options

At December 31, 1995, the Company had three stock-based compensation plans which were accounted for under *APB Opinion No. 25.* Accordingly, no compensation cost has been recognized in the consolidated financial statements for these plans because options to purchase common stock are granted at prices not less than the fair market value of the stock on date of grant.

Substantially all of the options under these plans become exercisable in four equal biennial installments, commencing one year from date of grant, and expire ten years from date of grant. At December 31, 1995, 105.1 and 37.0 million shares of common stock were reserved for issuance and for future grants, respectively, under these plans.

	NUMBER OF OPTIONS (IN MILLIONS)			WEIGHTED AVERAGE EXERCISE PRICE		
	1995	1994	1993	1995	1994	1993
Options outstanding at January 1	62.3	55.1	50.3	$21.02	$18.16	$15.54
Options granted	13.7	13.6	12.0	33.24	29.90	26.25
Options exercised	(6.0)	(4.1)	(5.3)	15.76	12.14	11.01
Options forfeited	(1.9)	(2.3)	(1.9)	24.55	18.72	17.28
Options outstanding at December 31	68.1	62.3	55.1	$23.86	$21.02	$18.16
Options exercisable at December 31	24.4	21.4	17.6			

Options granted during each year were 1.96%, 1.94%, and 1.69% of average common shares outstanding for 1995, 1994, and 1993, respectively. Stock options were granted to approximately 8,500, 7,700, and 6,800 employees in 1995, 1994, and 1993, respectively. Shares are issued from treasury stock to employees upon exercise of stock options.

The potential dilution of common shares outstanding upon exercise of stock options shown in the following table represents the number of common shares issuable upon exercise less the number of common shares that could be repurchased with proceeds from the exercise, based upon the respective December 31 prices of the Company's common stock. As such, this potential dilution was 2.9%, 1.6%, and 1.8% of shares outstanding at year-end 1995, 1994, and 1993, respectively.

(SHARES IN MILLIONS)	1995	1994	1993
Common shares outstanding at year end	699.8	693.7	707.3
Potential dilution of common shares outstanding from option exercises	20.4	11.4	12.6
Average option exercise price	$15.76	$12.14	$11.01
Average cost of treasury stock issued for option exercises	$ 7.16	$ 7.05	$ 6.65

As shown above, the average option exercise price has consistently exceeded the average cost of treasury stock issued for option exercises because of the Company's practice of prefunding the program through share repurchase. As a result, stock option exercises have generated additional capital, as cash received from employees has exceeded the Company's average acquisition cost of treasury stock.

DECEMBER 31, 1995

| | OPTIONS OUTSTANDING | | | OPTIONS EXERCISABLE | |
RANGE OF EXERCISE PRICES	NUMBER OF OPTIONS (IN MILLIONS)	WEIGHTED AVERAGE REMAINING CONTRACTUAL LIFE (YEARS)	WEIGHTED AVERAGE EXERCISE PRICE	NUMBER OF OPTIONS (IN MILLIONS)	WEIGHTED AVERAGE EXERCISE PRICE
$ 9 to 12	5.5	2.0	$11.05	5.5	$11.05
14 to 18	17.0	5.0	15.42	9.2	15.30
21 to 30	32.1	7.4	26.58	9.6	25.71
33 to 42	13.5	9.3	33.27	.1	33.19
$ 9 to 42	68.1	6.7	$23.86	24.4	$18.50

REQUIRED

1. Explain why McDonald's might have the stock option plans described in the note.

2. Explain, line by line, the meaning of each item in the first tabulation of stock option information in the note.

3. Is there a cost to McDonald's associated with these plans? If so, should the cost be recognized in McDonald's financial statements? Explain.

C 18-3. **ACCOUNTING FOR TREASURY STOCK** A corporation may acquire shares of its own capital stock for numerous reasons. When a company purchases treasury stock, it has two options as to how to account for the shares: (1) the cost method and (2) the par value method. In its 1990 annual report, for instance, Ford Motor Company made the following comments in its notes to the financial statements:

> There were 3.4 million shares of Common Stock of the company, with a cost of $52 million, included in Automotive other assets in the company's consolidated balance sheet at December 31, 1990. At December 31, 1989, there were 12.9 million shares of Common Stock of the company with a cost of $198 million included in Automotive other assets. Such shares were acquired for corporate purposes.

REQUIRED

1. Compare and contrast the cost method with the par value method for each of the following:

a) Acquisition of shares at a price less than par value.

b) Acquisition of shares at a price greater than par value.

c) Reissue of treasury shares at a price less than acquisition price but more than par value.

d) Reissue of treasury shares at a price greater than both acquisition price and par value.

e) Effect on net income.

2. a) Is Ford most likely using the cost method or the par value method to account for its treasury stock? Explain.

b) How can Ford justify reporting the treasury stock as an asset? (Note: Ford received a "clean opinion" from its external auditors in 1989 and 1990.)

(AICPA, adapted)

C 18-4. **DIVIDEND-PAYING ABILITY: ALTERNATIVE DIVIDEND PROPOSALS** The board of directors of Gratz Autos has met to discuss dividends for 1998 and has asked you to evaluate various proposals. Gratz Autos' December 31, 1998, balance sheet appears below:

ASSETS		LIABILITIES AND EQUITY	
Cash	$ 100,000	Current liabilities	$ 140,000
Trading securities	210,000	Long-term notes payable	60,000
Long-term investments, at market	595,000	Common stock ($10 par, 40,000 shares outstanding)	400,000
Plant and equipment, net	85,000	Contributed capital in excess of par	90,000
Other assets	40,000	Reserve for plant expansion	20,000
		Retained earnings (unappropriated)	320,000
Total	$1,030,000	Total	$1,030,000

The following alternative dividend proposals have been made by board members:
a) Mr. Nash proposes that a cash dividend be paid equal to the unappropriated balance in retained earnings.
b) Mr. Studebaker proposes that the reserves be used to pay dividends.
c) Mr. Fury proposes that all of the retained earnings be distributed.
d) Mr. De Soto proposes that dividends be paid equal to the cash balance of $100,000.
e) Mr. Edsel proposes that the trading securities be distributed as a dividend.
f) Mr. Morris proposes that trading securities and long-term investments be sold and that dividends be paid equal to total stockholders' equity less the par value of shares outstanding.
g) Mr. Saturn proposes that a 10 percent stock dividend be distributed and that the dividend be measured at par value.
h) Mr. Hudson proposes that 40,000 additional shares be distributed to the shareholders on a pro rata basis and that the dividend be measured at par value.

REQUIRED
1. Draft a response to each of the board members' proposals.
2. Draft a response outlining a recommendation for the payment of a cash dividend.

C 18-5. **STOCK DIVIDENDS** Beal Corporation, a client, is considering the authorization of a 5 percent stock dividend. The financial vice-president of Beal wishes to understand the accounting implications of such an authorization before the next meeting of the board of directors.

REQUIRED
1. The first topic he wishes to understand is the nature of the stock dividend to the recipient. Draft a memorandum to the financial vice-president describing:
a) The case *for* considering the stock dividend as income to the recipient.
b) The case *against* considering the stock dividend as income to the recipient.
2. The other topic is the propriety of issuing the stock dividend to all "stockholders of record" or to "stockholders of record exclusive of shares held in the name of the Corporation as treasury stock." Draft a memorandum describing:
a) The case *for* issuing stock dividends on treasury shares.
b) The case *against* issuing stock dividends on treasury shares.

(AICPA, adapted)

C 18-6. **STOCK SPLITS; LIABILITIES** Garrick Corporation entered into a reverse stock split whereby one $30 par common share was issued for every three $10 par common shares outstanding. This transaction produced a large number of fractional shares, which Garrick offered to acquire for cash. Under the terms of the transaction, fractional shares not presented to Garrick for acquisition by December 31, 1999, are to be stripped of voting rights and all rights to dividends. However, Garrick maintains the obligation to acquire such shares for cash. A material number of fractional shares were not presented for acquisition by the December 31, 1999, deadline.

REQUIRED
Discuss how Garrick should report the credit balance that represents the original issue price associated with the fractional shares outstanding at December 31, 1999.

C 18-7. **RETAINED EARNINGS RESTRICTIONS: APPROPRIATIONS VS. FOOTNOTE DISCLOSURES**

The stockholders' equity section of Flinn Corporation's balance sheet as of December 31, 1998, appears below:

Preferred stock (no par, 5,000 shares outstanding)	$ 40,000
Common stock ($5 par, 10,000 shares outstanding)	50,000
Contributed capital in excess of par—common	25,000
Retained earnings:	
Appropriated for plant expansion.....................................	5,000
Appropriated for inventory losses	2,500
Appropriated for treasury stock	3,000
Appropriated for bonded indebtedness	5,000
Unappropriated	10,000
Treasury stock (par value method)	(3,000)
Total	$137,500

Additional information:

a) The plant expansion appropriation represents an estimate of the cost of enlarging the plant. The expansion will begin next year.

b) The inventory appropriation represents a write-down of inventory to net realizable value, recorded as follows:

      Loss on inventory 2,500

         Retained earnings appropriated for inventory losses 2,500

c) State law requires that retained earnings be restricted equal to the cost of treasury stock purchases. Cost of purchases to date totals $5,000.

d) Flinn issued bonds several years ago. The bond indenture requires that retained earnings restrictions be in effect until the bonds mature. The bonds were extinguished before maturity during the 1998 fiscal year.

Flinn's management has asked you to reconstruct the stockholders' equity section of the balance sheet as of December 31, 1998, under the assumption that formal appropriations are to be eliminated and that restrictions of retained earnings are to be disclosed in notes to the financial statements.

REQUIRED Prepare the stockholders' equity section of Flinn's balance sheet and draft the notes to its financial statements to disclose the appropriate restrictions of retained earnings.

C 18-8. **STOCK DIVIDENDS** The board of directors of Warren, Inc., declared an "ordinary stock dividend" equal to 5 percent of the corporation's outstanding common stock, to be issued to common stockholders of record as of April 15, 1999. The corporation's treasury stock was to be used for this purpose to the extent available. The market value of the common stock just before the declaration was $64 per share, and it remained at substantially that figure for more than a month after the dividend shares were issued.

Warren's equity accounts at the dates of declaration and record included the following balances:

Preferred stock, $5 cumulative (no par): authorized, 25,000 shares;	
in treasury, 130 shares; outstanding, 10,402 shares.......................	$1,053,200
Common stock (par $50): authorized, 50,000 shares; in treasury, 880 shares;	
outstanding, 27,780 shares	1,433,000
Additional contributed capital—amounts contributed in excess of par value	
of common shares..	251,464
Retained earnings...	963,425
Treasury stock, $5 cumulative preferred (at cost).........................	14,922
Treasury stock, common (at cost)	40,920

At the time of declaration, the board directed that retained earnings in the amount of the aggregate par value of the dividend shares be transferred to the appropriate permanent capital accounts.

REQUIRED

1. Prepare an entry to record the net effect of the board's actions.

2. Evaluate the Warren board's action in regard to the retained earnings transfer in light of generally accepted accounting principles.

3. Assuming that the entry in part 1 had not been made and that the board had followed GAAP, prepare an entry that will give effect to the issuance of the stock dividend in accordance with the recommendations.

4. Assume the same facts as set forth above, except that the dividend declaration equaled 40 percent (instead of 5 percent) of the outstanding common shares and resulted in a substantial reduction in the market value of the common shares of Warren, Inc.

a) Describe the generally accepted method of accounting in these circumstances.

b) Does the board's transfer of retained earnings on a par value basis conflict with or conform to the generally accepted method? Explain.

(AICPA, adapted)

*C 18-9. **QUASI-REORGANIZATIONS** The Beyer Company, a medium-sized manufacturer, has been experiencing losses for the five years that it has been doing business. Although the operations for the year just ended resulted in a loss, several important changes resulted in a profitable fourth quarter, and the future operations of the company are expected to be profitable.

The treasurer suggests that there be a quasi-reorganization to (1) eliminate the accumulated deficit of $423,620, (2) write up the $493,100 cost of operating land and buildings to their fair value, and (3) set up an asset of $203,337 representing the estimated future tax benefit of the losses accumulated to date.

REQUIRED

1. What are the characteristics of a quasi-reorganization? That is, of what does it consist?

2. List the conditions under which a quasi-reorganization generally would be justified.

3. Evaluate the propriety of the treasurer's proposals to:

a) Eliminate the deficit of $423,620.

b) Write up the cost of the operating land and buildings to their fair value.

c) Set up an asset of $203,337 representing the future tax benefit of the losses accumulated to date.

(AICPA, adapted)

EXERCISES

The exercise marked with an asterisk (*) refers to Appendix 18–1.

E 18-1. **CAPITAL STOCK TRANSACTIONS** Wood Corporation has been in operation for several years. At the beginning of 1998, Wood had the following stock issues authorized:

Common stock, $5 par, 1,000,000 shares authorized, 200,000 shares issued and outstanding.

Preferred stock, 7 percent noncumulative, nonparticipating, $100 par, 500,000 shares authorized, 5,000 shares issued and outstanding.

During 1998, the following transactions occurred:

a) Wood issued 50,000 shares of common at $21 per share.

b) Wood issued 2,000 shares of preferred at $130 per share.

c) Subscriptions for 10,000 shares of common were taken at a purchase price of $22 per share. At December 31, 1998, $40,000 of the subscription amount remained unpaid. None of the shares was fully paid.

REQUIRED Prepare journal entries to record the transactions listed above. For item *c*, record both the original subscription and the collections.

E 18-2. **STOCK ISSUANCE FOR NONCASH CONSIDERATION** Utterback Corporation entered into the following transactions during 1998:

a) Issued 7,000 shares of its previously unissued $5 par common stock in exchange for a parcel of land to be used as a future plant site. Utterback's stock is actively traded on the American Stock Exchange and, on the date of this transaction, traded at an average price of $43 per share. The land was valued at $325,000 by an independent appraiser.

b) Issued 2,000 shares of its previously unissued $50 par preferred stock in exchange for the customer list of a competitor that was going out of business. The customer list was valued by a consultant from a valuation company at $430,000. The preferred stock was not actively traded. However, the president of Utterback estimated that the stock was worth about $250 per share.

REQUIRED Prepare the journal entries to record the above transactions.

E 18-3. **STOCK SUBSCRIPTIONS** On October 10, 1998, 200,000 shares of Erin Corporation's $5 par value common stock were sold at a subscription price of $40 per share. A down payment of $10 per share was received, with the remainder of the subscription price payable in three equal installments on November 10, 1998, December 10, 1998, and January 10, 1999.

REQUIRED Prepare journal entries on the books of Erin Corporation to record:
1. The subscription and collection of the down payment.
2. Collection of the three installments from all subscribers.
3. Issuance of the subscribed shares.

E 18-4. **LUMP-SUM ISSUES OF STOCK** Rayburn Corporation issued 200,000 shares of its $5 par common stock for $2,000,000. One share of Rayburn's $5 par preferred stock was issued with every 10 shares of common stock.

REQUIRED Record the issuance of the common and preferred stock under each of the following independent assumptions:
1. The market price per share for the common stock was $6; the market price per share for the preferred stock was $50.
2. The market price per share for the common stock was $6.50; the market price per share for the preferred stock was not readily determinable because it was not actively traded.

E 18-5. **CONVERTIBLE PREFERRED STOCK** At the beginning of 1998, Griffin Corporation issued 20,000 shares of $10 par convertible preferred stock at $40 per share. The stock is convertible into $5 par common shares on a share-for-share basis. During 1998, 2,000 of the preferred shares were converted into common. The market price of the preferred at the time of conversion was $47 per share; the market price of the common was $49 per share.

REQUIRED 1. Prepare the entry to record the issuance of the preferred stock at the beginning of 1998.
2. Prepare the entry to record the conversion of preferred into common.

E 18-6. **STOCK WARRANTS** On July 1, 1998, Denen Company issued, for $600,000, a total of 5,000 shares of $100 par value, 7 percent noncumulative preferred stock along with one detachable warrant for each share issued. Each warrant contains a right to purchase one share of Denen's $10 par value common stock for $15. The market price of the rights on July 1, 1998, was $3 per right. On October 31, 1998, when the market price of the common stock was $19 per share and the market value of the rights was $4 per right, 3,000 rights were exercised.

REQUIRED Prepare journal entries for Denen Company to record:
1. The issuance of the preferred stock and rights.
2. The exercise of the rights.

(AICPA, adapted)

E 18-7. **STOCK APPRECIATION RIGHTS** At the beginning of 1997, Kristin Corporation granted stock appreciation rights (SARs) to three of its key executives. Under the terms of the SAR plan, each executive was entitled to receive, at their option, cash, shares of Kristin's $1 par value common stock, or a combination of both cash and stock. The amount to be received was to be determined by the difference between the quoted market price of Kristin's common stock at the date of exercise and a predetermined price of $10 per SAR.

Kristin granted a total of 30,000 SARs, which were exercisable after January 1, 2000, and the executives were required to be in the employ of the company at the date of exercise. The per share market price of Kristin's common stock at the end of 1997, 1998, and 1999 was $19, $28, and $26, respectively. All of the SARs were exercised on January 2, 2000, and the appropriate amount of cash was paid.

REQUIRED Prepare all journal entries required in connection with the SAR plan for 1997 through 2000, assuming Kristin applies *APB Opinion No. 25*.

E 18-8. **RETIREMENT OF CAPITAL STOCK** Johnson Company's common stock has a $2.50 par value. Outstanding shares had been issued at prices ranging from $7 to $20 per share, with an average paid-in capital per share of $15. In 1998, Johnson acquired and immediately retired 40,000 of these common shares.

REQUIRED Prepare the journal entry to record the acquisition and retirement of the 40,000 shares, assuming:
1. The shares were acquired for $12 per share.
2. The shares were acquired for $18 per share.

E 18-9.   **TREASURY STOCK** The stockholders' equity accounts of O'Dell Company appeared as follows as of January 1, 1998:

Common stock, par value $10; authorized, 200,000 shares; issued and outstanding, 140,000 shares	$ 1,400,000
Contributed capital in excess of par value	700,000
Retained earnings	12,000,000
Total	$14,100,000

During 1998, O'Dell entered into the following transactions:
a) Acquired 10,000 shares of its stock for $180,000.
b) Reissued 4,000 treasury shares at $16 per share.
c) Retired the remaining treasury shares.

REQUIRED   Prepare the journal entries to record the treasury stock transactions using:
1. The cost method.
2. The par value method.

E 18-10.   **TREASURY STOCK** At the end of 1997, Middleton Corporation had the following balances in its stockholders' equity accounts:

Common stock, par value $5; authorized, 500,000 shares; issued and outstanding, 300,000 shares	$ 1,500,000
Contributed capital in excess of par value	4,500,000
Retained earnings	17,400,000
Total	$23,400,000

The following transactions occurred during 1998:
a) 10,000 shares were acquired for $340,000.
b) 12,000 shares were acquired for $240,000.
c) 15,000 shares of treasury stock were reissued at $28 per share.

REQUIRED   Prepare journal entries to record the treasury stock transactions using:
1. The cost method, assuming a FIFO cost flow.
2. The par value method.

E 18-11.   **TRANSACTIONS AFFECTING RETAINED EARNINGS** For each of the transactions below, indicate the effect on retained earnings, using + for increase, – for decrease, or 0 for no effect. Consider each transaction separately.
1. ____ Receipt of land as a donation.
2. ____ An extraordinary loss from a flood.
3. ____ Declaration and payment of a property dividend.
4. ____ Purchase of goodwill in the acquisition of another company.
5. ____ A quasi-reorganization.
6. ____ Correction of an error involving an asset acquired two years ago. The asset had a 10-year useful life but was expensed when it was purchased.
7. ____ An appropriation for contingencies.
8. ____ A net loss for the year.
9. ____ Distribution of a previously declared stock dividend.
10. ____ A sale of treasury stock in excess of cost.
11. ____ A 2-for-1 stock split.
12. ____ Reversal of a previously recorded appropriation.
13. ____ Declaration of a cash dividend.
14. ____ Net income for the year.

E 18-12. **CASH DIVIDENDS** Elliott Corporation's stockholders' equity accounts at the end of 1998 are:

8% preferred stock ($10 par, 50,000 shares issued)	$ 500,000
Common stock ($2 par, 90,000 shares issued).............................	180,000
Contributed capital in excess of par:	
Preferred	125,000
Common	180,000
Retained earnings ($64,000 restricted for cost of treasury stock)	500,000
Treasury stock (8,000 shares of common, at cost)	(64,000)
Total	$1,421,000

The following transactions occurred during 1999:

- 1/15   Declared the annual preferred stock dividend, payable on 2/10, to stockholders of record on 2/1.
- 1/20   Sold 1,000 shares of treasury stock for $10,000.
- 2/10   Paid the preferred dividend.
- 3/1   Declared a $1 per share cash dividend on outstanding common shares, payable on 4/15 to stockholders of record on 3/25.
- 4/15   Paid the common stock dividend.
- 12/31   Closed the net income of $226,000 for 1999 to retained earnings.

REQUIRED
1. Record the above transactions.
2. Prepare Elliott Corporation's stockholders' equity section of the balance sheet at the end of 1999.

E 18-13. **PROPERTY DIVIDENDS** Chan Corporation owned 1 million shares of equity securities of Boa Corporation. On December 31, 1998, when Chan's investment in common stock of Boa Corporation had a carrying value of $8 per share, Chan distributed these shares to its stockholders as a dividend. Boa has 2 million shares issued and outstanding, which are traded on a national stock exchange. The quoted market price for a Boa share was $10 on the declaration date.

REQUIRED Prepare the entry or entries to record the property dividend.

(AICPA, adapted)

E 18-14. **STOCK DIVIDENDS** The stockholders' equity of Cruzan Company on July 31, 1998, is as follows:

Common stock, par value $20: authorized, 400,000 shares;	
issued and outstanding, 150,000 shares	$ 3,000,000
Contributed capital in excess of par	140,000
Retained earnings	12,000,000
Total	$15,140,000

On August 1, 1998, the board of directors of Cruzan declared a 4 percent stock dividend on common stock, to be distributed on September 15. The market price of Cruzan's common stock was $38 on August 1, 1998, and $40 on September 15, 1998.

REQUIRED Prepare the entries to record the declaration on August 1, 1998, and the distribution on September 15, 1998.

E 18-15. **DIVIDENDS** Using the format shown below, indicate the effect on assets, liabilities, and stockholders' equity of the items set forth below. For no change write 0, for an increase +, and for a decrease –.

	ASSETS	LIABILITIES	STOCKHOLDERS' EQUITY
I. Declaration of a stock dividend.	_____	_____	_____
2. Declaration of a cash dividend.	_____	_____	_____
3. Distribution of stock dividend in item 1.	_____	_____	_____
4. Payment of cash dividend in item 2.	_____	_____	_____
5. Issuance of new shares in place of old shares associated with a stock split.	_____	_____	_____

(CGAA, adapted)

E 18-16. **STOCK DIVIDENDS; STOCK SPLITS** Berry Corporation had the following stockholders' equity balances at December 31, 1998:

Common stock ($2 par, 60,000 shares issued and outstanding)	$ 120,000
Contributed capital in excess of par	720,000
Retained earnings	3,400,000
Total	$4,240,000

At a time when the common stock is trading at $38 per share, Berry is considering the following four independent transactions and events:
a) Declaration and issuance of a 4 percent stock dividend.
b) Declaration and issuance of a 40 percent stock dividend, to be measured at the average paid in per share.
c) Declaration and issuance of a 100 percent stock dividend.
d) Declaration and issuance of a 2-for-1 stock split.

REQUIRED **I.** Prepare all entries to record the transactions being considered by Berry.
2. Prepare the stockholders' equity section resulting from each transaction.

E 18-17. **DIVIDEND PREFERENCES ON PREFERRED STOCK** Andrews Corporation has the following capital stock outstanding:

Common ($5 par, 100,000 shares outstanding)	$500,000
10% preferred ($50 par, 2,000 shares outstanding)	100,000

Andrews has decided to declare and issue a cash dividend of $100,000 during the current year.

REQUIRED Determine how the $100,000 dividend would be distributed among the common and preferred stockholders under the following five independent situations:
I. The preferred stock is cumulative and nonparticipating; dividends are in arrears for the three preceding years.
2. The preferred stock is noncumulative and fully participating.
3. The preferred stock is noncumulative and participating up to an additional 5 percent.
4. The preferred stock is cumulative and participating up to an additional 3 percent. Dividends are in arrears for the preceding two years.
5. The preferred stock is cumulative and fully participating. Dividends are in arrears for the preceding year.

E 18-18. **DIVIDEND PREFERENCES ON PREFERRED STOCK** During the current year Blum Company paid the following cash dividends to common and preferred stockholders:

Common	$33,000
Preferred	27,000

Par value of the outstanding preferred stock is $100,000, and par value of the outstanding common stock is $300,000. The dividend distribution includes an additional 3 percent participating dividend, as the preferred stock is fully participating. The preferred stock is cumulative, and dividends were in arrears for the two preceding years.

REQUIRED Calculate the stated dividend rate on the preferred shares.

E 18-19.   **STOCKHOLDERS' EQUITY TRANSACTIONS**   The following transactions occurred during the current year for Scott Industries:

a)   Declared and issued as a property dividend 1,200 shares of David Company held as a long-term (available-for-sale) investment. Information about the investment in David appears below:

Shares held: 3,600
Cost: $21,600 ($6 per share)
Market price at dividend date: $9 per share
Carrying amount at dividend date: $30,600 ($8.50 per share)

b)   Established a retained earnings appropriation of $30,000 for possible future losses on a contract to purchase minerals.

c)   Purchased at a cost of $11,000 its own no-par common shares to be held as treasury stock. Scott uses the par value method, and the issue price associated with the shares purchased was $9,000. State law requires that retained earnings equal to the cost of treasury shares held be appropriated.

d)   Established a retained earnings appropriation of $60,000 for future building expansion.

e)   Incurred a $16,000 loss on the mineral contract.

f)   Sold the treasury shares for $11,500.

g)   Scott has a bond sinking fund (and a retained earnings appropriation) established to retire long-term bonds payable. During the year, Scott transferred $15,000 in cash to the sinking fund.

h)   At the end of the year, Scott eliminated all previous retained earnings appropriations except for the sinking fund and established an appropriation for possible litigation totaling $120,000.

REQUIRED   Prepare the journal entries to record the above transactions.

E 18-20.   **TRANSACTIONS AFFECTING STOCKHOLDERS' EQUITY**   Using the format shown below, indicate the effect in terms of assets, liabilities, and stockholders' equity of the items set forth below. For no change write 0, for an increase +, and for a decrease −.

	ASSETS	LIABILITIES	STOCKHOLDERS' EQUITY		
			CAPITAL STOCK	OTHER CONTRIBUTED CAPITAL	RETAINED EARNINGS
1. Net income for period.	_____	_____	_____	_____	_____
2. Cash dividends declared.	_____	_____	_____	_____	_____
3. Payment of dividend in item 2.	_____	_____	_____	_____	_____
4. Declaration and distribution of small stock dividend.	_____	_____	_____	_____	_____
5. Declaration of large stock dividend.	_____	_____	_____	_____	_____
6. Distribution of stock dividend in item 5.	_____	_____	_____	_____	_____
7. 2-for-1 stock split.	_____	_____	_____	_____	_____
8. Prior period adjustment—correction of asset understatement.	_____	_____	_____	_____	_____
9. Prior period adjustment—correction of liability overstatement.	_____	_____	_____	_____	_____
10. Retained earnings appropriation.	_____	_____	_____	_____	_____
11. Reversal of appropriation in item 10.	_____	_____	_____	_____	_____
12. Declaration and payment of a property dividend.	_____	_____	_____	_____	_____
13. Liability canceled as a donation.	_____	_____	_____	_____	_____
14. Purchase of treasury stock at less than original issue price—par value method used.	_____	_____	_____	_____	_____
15. Resale of treasury stock in item 16 at more than par value.	_____	_____	_____	_____	_____
16. A change in accounting principle that increases liabilities.	_____	_____	_____	_____	_____
17. Acquisition of another company's common stock through an issuance of previously unissued preferred stock.	_____	_____	_____	_____	_____
18. Net loss for period.	_____	_____	_____	_____	_____

E 18-21. **STOCKHOLDERS' EQUITY TRANSACTIONS** For each of the following numbered items, select the corresponding lettered effect or effects on the corporation's statements. If there is no appropriate response among the effects listed, leave the item blank. If more than one effect is applicable to a particular item, list *all* applicable letters.

ITEM

1. ____ Declaration of a cash dividend due in one month on noncumulative preferred stock.
2. ____ Declaration and distribution of an ordinary stock dividend.
3. ____ Receipt of a cash dividend, not previously recorded, on stock of another corporation.
4. ____ Passing of a dividend on cumulative preferred stock.
5. ____ Receipt of preferred shares as a dividend on stock held as a trading security.
6. ____ Payment of dividend in item 1.
7. ____ Issue of new common shares in a 5-for-1 stock split.

EFFECT

a) Reduces working capital.
b) Increases working capital.
c) Reduces the dollar amount of total capital stock.
d) Increases the dollar amount of total capital stock.
e) Reduces total retained earnings.
f) Increases total retained earnings.
g) Reduces equity per share of common stock.
h) Reduces equity of each common stockholder.

(AICPA, adapted)

E 18-22. **RETAINED EARNINGS TRANSACTIONS** The retained earnings account for Nash Company had a credit balance of $900,000 at the end of 1998. Selected transactions affecting stockholders' equity during 1999 were as follows:

a) Net income for 1999, $124,000.
b) Cash dividends declared, $56,000.
c) Purchased treasury stock (par value, $6,000) at a cost of $10,000. Nash uses the par value method, and the stock was originally sold at par.
d) Stock dividends were declared and measured at $10,000.
e) Sold treasury stock in item *c* for $8,900.
f) Nash Company made a retained earnings appropriation of $8,000 for possible investment losses.
g) Declared and distributed a 3-for-1 stock split on 10,000 shares of $5 par common stock.
h) Corrected an error made in 1994. The correcting entry was as follows:

Plant and equipment 20,000
    Accumulated depreciation 6,000
    Prior period adjustment............................ 14,000

REQUIRED Calculate Nash's retained earnings balance as of December 31, 1999.

E 18-23. **APPROPRIATIONS; STOCK DIVIDENDS** On January 15, 1998, the directors of Fox Company voted to appropriate $80,000 of retained earnings and to retain assets equal to the appropriation for use in expanding the corporation's plant. This was the fifth such appropriation of $80,000. On January 16, the company had the following stockholders' equity accounts:

Common stock, $5 par value: 400,000 shares authorized, 300,000 shares issued . .	$1,500,000
Contributed capital in excess of par	50,000
Retained earnings appropriated for plant expansion	400,000
Unappropriated retained earnings......................................	2,200,000
Total stockholders' equity	$4,150,000

On February 15, Fox contracted for the construction of the plant addition for which appropriations had been made. On October 15, when the addition was completed, Fox paid Acme Builders, the contractor, $420,000, the amount of the contract.

On November 15, the directors returned the balance of the retained earnings appropriated for plant expansion account to unappropriated retained earnings. At the same time a stock dividend was declared and measured at the amount previously carried in the appropriation account. At that time the stock was trading at $12.50 per share. The dividend was distributed December 15.

REQUIRED

I. Prepare the journal entries on:
a) January 15, 1998.
b) October 15, 1998.
c) November 15, 1998.
d) December 15, 1998.

2. Prepare the stockholders' equity section of the balance sheet as of December 15, 1998.

(CGAA, adapted)

*E 18-24.   **QUASI-REORGANIZATION**   For the last several years Manning Lumber Company has suffered losses. The company's controller believes that a quasi-reorganization will allow the company to get on its feet, secure additional credit, operate profitably, and pay dividends in the near future.

The balance sheet prepared before the reorganization showed the following:

ASSETS		LIABILITIES AND STOCKHOLDERS' EQUITY	
Cash	$ 5,000	Current liabilities	$144,000
Receivables, net	38,000	Long-term liabilities	300,000
Inventories	126,000	Common stock (par $100)	250,000
Plant and equipment, net	300,000	Preferred stock (par $50)	50,000
Prepaid expenses	5,000	Other contributed capital	60,000
Goodwill	70,000	Retained earnings (deficit)	(225,000)
Deferred charges	35,000		
Total	$579,000	Total	$579,000

Stockholders and creditors have approved the following quasi-reorganization arrangement:
a) Receivables are to be reduced to $10,000.
b) Inventories are undervalued and are to be revalued to $160,000.
c) Plant and equipment is to be written down to $200,000 because of obsolescence.
d) Goodwill and all deferred charges are to be written off.
e) Short-term creditors have agreed to reduce all amounts owed to them by $40,000.
f) Long-term creditors have agreed to reduce amounts owed to them by $100,000.
g) The other contributed capital is to be closed (eliminated).
h) The par value of preferred is to be changed to $10 with no change in the number of shares outstanding.
i) Common stockholders have agreed to relinquish their shares and accept new no-par shares. The common stock account will be reduced in an amount necessary to reduce the retained earnings deficit to zero.

REQUIRED

I. Prepare separate entries for items *a* through *i* to record the quasi-reorganization agreement.
2. Prepare the balance sheet immediately after the quasi-reorganization.

PROBLEMS   The problem marked with an asterisk (*) refers to Appendix 18–1.

P 18-I.   **ACCOUNTING FOR STOCK ISSUANCE**   Fuhrman Corporation engaged in the following stock transactions during the year:
a) Issued 30,000 shares of $1 par value common stock for cash at $30 per share.
b) Issued 4,000 shares of $1 par common stock in exchange for a land site. The common stock, which was actively traded on a national stock exchange, had a market price per share of $26 at the time of the exchange. The appraised value of the land, based on the average appraisal from three independent appraisers, was $100,000. The appraisals ranged from $75,000 to $140,000.

c) Received subscriptions for 30,000 shares of $5 par preferred stock. The subscription price was $100; 20 percent was paid in cash as a down payment and the remainder was due in four equal installments in 30, 60, 90, and 120 days.

d) Collected the deferred portion of the subscription price as scheduled and issued the preferred stock.

e) Issued as a combination 32,000 shares of $1 par common stock and 4,000 shares of $5 par preferred stock for $1,250,000. The market prices per share of the common and preferred stock at the date of issuance were $30 and $120, respectively.

REQUIRED   Prepare journal entries to record the stock transactions.

P 18-2.   STOCK ISSUANCE AND CONTRIBUTED CAPITAL PRESENTATION   Dole Company began the 1998 calendar year with the following balances in its contributed capital accounts:

Preferred stock, $100 par value; authorized, 1 million shares;
  issued and outstanding, 200,000 shares $20,000,000
Common stock, $5 par value; authorized, 5 million shares;
  issued and outstanding, 1,500,000 shares   7,500,000
Contributed capital in excess of par—preferred   2,000,000
Contributed capital in excess of par—common 10,500,000

During 1998, the following stock transactions occurred:

a) Issued 100,000 shares of common at $18 per share. Incurred stock issue costs of $120,000.

b) Issued 20,000 shares of preferred for $2,400,000. As a "sweetener," Dole included one share of common stock with each five shares of preferred. The market prices of the common and preferred at the time of issuance were $15 and $120 per share, respectively. Stock issue costs were $140,000.

c) Received subscriptions for 200,000 shares of common at $18 per share. Subscribers paid one-third of the subscription price as a down payment, with the remainder due in two equal installments in 30 and 60 days. (The installments are due in 1999.)

REQUIRED   **1.** Prepare journal entries to record the stock transactions.

2. Prepare the contributed capital section of Dole Company's balance sheet at December 31, 1998.

P 18-3.   PRESENTATION OF STOCKHOLDERS' EQUITY   You have been provided with the following accounts and balances from the general ledger of the Lanin Company as of December 31, 1998:

Capital from land site donation $180,000
Cash dividend payable—common   20,000
Common stock dividend distributable   30,000
Retained earnings 850,000
Preferred stock 100,000
Subscriptions receivable—common stock   12,000
Common stock 200,000
Contributed capital in excess of par—preferred   16,000
Common stock subscribed   50,000
Loan payable to stockholders 300,000
Treasury stock—common   20,000

Additional information is as follows:

a) Common stock is $10 par value; authorization, 400,000 shares.

b) There are 2,000 common shares held as treasury stock.

c) Preferred stock is $100 par value, 6 percent cumulative and nonparticipating. The authorization is 4,000 shares.

REQUIRED   Prepare the stockholders' equity section of the balance sheet for Lanin Company as of December 31, 1998.

P 18-4.   VARIOUS STOCK TRANSACTIONS   During May 1997, Bailey, Inc., was organized with 3,000,000 authorized shares of $10 par value common stock, and 300,000 shares of its common stock were issued for $3,800,000. Net income for the year ended December 31, 1997, was $110,000.

On July 3, 1998, Bailey issued 500,000 shares of its common stock for $6,250,000. Bailey's net income for the year ended December 31, 1998, was $380,000.

During 1999, Bailey had the following transactions:

a) In February, Bailey acquired 30,000 shares of its common stock for $9 per share. Bailey uses the cost method to account for treasury stock.

b) In June, Bailey reissued 15,000 shares of its treasury stock for $12 per share.

c) In September, each stockholder was issued (for each share held) one stock right to purchase two additional shares of common stock for $13 per share. The rights expire on December 31, 1999.

d) In October, 250,000 stock rights were exercised when the market price of the common stock was $14 per share.

e) In November, 400,000 stock rights were exercised when the market price of the common stock was $15 per share.

f) On December 15, Bailey declared its first cash dividend to stockholders of $.20 per share, payable on January 10, 2000, to stockholders of record on December 31, 1999.

g) On December 21, in accordance with the applicable state law, Bailey formally retired 10,000 shares of its treasury stock. The market price of the common stock was $16 per share on this date.

h) Net income for 1999 was $750,000.

REQUIRED   Prepare a schedule of all transactions affecting the capital stock (shares and dollar amounts), additional paid-in capital, retained earnings, treasury stock (shares and dollar amounts), and the amounts that would be included in Bailey's balance sheet at December 31, 1997, 1998, and 1999, as a result of the above facts. Show supporting calculations.

(AICPA, adapted)

P 18-5.   **STOCK APPRECIATION RIGHTS**   Henry Company granted stock appreciation rights (SARs) to certain key executives at the beginning of 1998. The plan provides that the executives may receive either cash, Henry's $5 par value common stock, or a combination of cash and stock, with the amount to be received determined by the difference between the quoted market price at the date of exercise and a predetermined price of $20 per SAR.

Henry granted a total of 50,000 SARs in 1998, exercisable after January 1, 2001, and before January 1, 2010, by executives still employed by the company at the date of exercise. Henry assumed that the executives would choose to receive common stock. The per share market price of Henry's common stock was as follows:

DATE	QUOTED MARKET PRICE
12/31/98	$34
12/31/99	39
12/31/00	49
12/31/01	46
12/31/02	48

On December 31, 2001, 40,000 of the SARs were exercised and the appropriate amount of common stock was issued. The remaining 10,000 SARs were still outstanding at the end of 2002. Assume Henry applies *APB Opinion No. 25*.

REQUIRED   Prepare all journal entries required in connection with the SAR plan from 1998 through 2002.

P 18-6.   **TREASURY STOCK, COST METHOD**   Presented below is the stockholders' equity section of Raabe Corporation at December 31, 1997:

Common stock, par value $20; authorized, 50,000 shares;
  issued and outstanding, 30,000 shares .... $ 600,000
Contributed capital in excess of par value   150,000
Retained earnings 2,600,000
  Total $3,350,000

During 1998, the following transactions occurred relating to stockholders' equity:

a) 1,000 shares were acquired at $28 per share.

b) 900 shares were acquired at $30 per share.

c) 1,500 shares of treasury stock were reissued at $30 per share.

d) 200 shares of treasury stock were reissued at $26 per share.

Raabe accounts for treasury stock using the cost method, assuming a FIFO cost flow. For the year ended December 31, 1998, Raabe reported net income of $110,000.

REQUIRED
1. Prepare journal entries for the treasury stock transactions.
2. Prepare the stockholders' equity section of Raabe's balance sheet at December 31, 1998.

(AICPA, adapted)

P 18-7. **TREASURY STOCK, PAR VALUE METHOD** Refer to P18-6. Now assume that Raabe Corporation uses the par value method to account for treasury stock transactions.

REQUIRED
1. Prepare journal entries for the treasury stock transactions.
2. Prepare the stockholders' equity section of Raabe's balance sheet at December 31, 1998.

P 18-8. **TREASURY STOCK** Lopez Company had the following stockholders' equity account balances at the beginning of 1998:

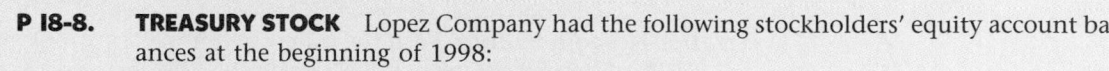

Common stock, $1 par, 2 million shares authorized	$ 500,000
Contributed capital in excess of par—common	3,500,000
Retained earnings	9,400,000
Total	$13,400,000

Treasury stock transactions for Lopez were as follows for 1998:
a) Acquired 22,000 of its own shares at $10 per share.
b) Acquired 8,000 of its own shares at $7 per share.
c) Reissued 18,000 treasury shares for $12 per share.
d) Reissued 6,000 treasury shares for $10 per share.
e) Retired 3,000 treasury shares.
Net income for 1998 was $300,000.

REQUIRED
1. Prepare journal entries to record the treasury stock transactions, assuming that Lopez Company uses the cost method and a FIFO cost flow.
2. Prepare the stockholders' equity section of Lopez's balance sheet at the end of 1998, assuming use of the cost method.
3. Prepare journal entries to record the treasury stock transactions, assuming that Lopez Company uses the par value method.
4. Prepare the stockholders' equity section of the balance sheet at the end of 1998, assuming use of the par value method.

P 18-9. **STOCKHOLDERS' EQUITY TRANSACTIONS; BALANCE SHEET REPORTING** At the end of 1998, Kent Corporation's stockholders' equity was as follows:

Common stock ($5 par, 100,000 shares authorized)		$125,000
Treasury stock (par value method)		(25,000)
Other contributed capital:		
Contributed capital in excess of par	$25,000	
Donated capital (receipt of land)	30,000	55,000
Retained earnings appropriated for self-insurance		25,000
Unappropriated retained earnings		1,400,000
Total		$1,580,000

During 1999, the following transactions and events occurred:
a) Net income, $70,000; cash dividends, $10,000.
b) Sold 3,000 treasury shares at $7 per share.
c) Reversed retained earnings appropriation.
d) Subsequent to sale of treasury stock in item *b,* declared and distributed a 30 percent stock dividend when the market price of the common was $10 per share.
e) Issued convertible bonds with a par value of $50,000 for $60,000. It was estimated that had the bonds not been convertible, they would have been issued for $46,000.
f) Sold previously donated land for a gain of $10,000; the gain was included in net income.

REQUIRED
Prepare the stockholders' equity section of the balance sheet for Kent Corporation as of December 31, 1999.

P 18-10.   **DIVIDENDS**   Weatherup Company presented the following stockholders' equity section of its balance sheet to the stockholders on December 31, 1998:

Capital stock:

Preferred: 6% cumulative, nonparticipating, par value $100; authorized, 10,000 shares; issued, 4,000 shares............	$ 400,000	
Common: par value, $10; authorized, 400,000 shares; issued, 200,000 shares......................................	2,000,000	$2,400,000
Contributed capital in excess of par.......................		300,000
Retained earnings		5,900,000
Total		$8,600,000

During the 1999 fiscal year, the following transactions took place:

2/20   Declared the regular 3% semiannual dividend on the preferred stock and a $.50 per share dividend on the common stock to holders of record 3/5/99, payable 4/1/99.

4/1   Dividends were paid.

4/5   Accepted subscriptions for 40,000 shares of common stock at $35 per share. The subscriptions were accompanied by a 25% down payment on the shares.

5/30   Issued stock subscribed on 4/5/99 on the basis of receipt of the balance due.

7/2   Issued $1 million, 8%, first mortgage bonds to Regional Trust at face value. The bonds have a 10-year maturity. Interest is payable semiannually on 12/31 and 6/30.

8/20   Declared the regular 3% semiannual dividend on the preferred and a dividend of $.50 per share on the common to stockholders of record 8/31/99, payable 10/1/99.

10/1   Paid dividends declared.

12/1   Declared a 10% stock dividend to the common stockholders of record on 12/20/99, to be issued on 1/15/2000. The common stock was actively traded on 12/1 at $40 per share.

12/31   Paid bond interest.

12/31   Closed to retained earnings net income of $370,000.

REQUIRED   **1.**   Prepare the journal entries to record the above transactions.

2.   Prepare the stockholders' equity section of the balance sheet as of December 31, 1999.

(CGAA, adapted)

P 18-11.   **DIVIDENDS AND STOCK SPLITS**   The stockholders' equity accounts for Junker, Inc., are as follows:

12% preferred stock: $50 par, 2,500 shares issued	$ 125,000
Common stock: $20 par, 10,000 shares issued...........................	200,000
Contributed capital in excess of par:	
Preferred..	50,000
Common	200,000
Donated capital from receipt of securities	100,000
Unrealized holding gain on investment in securities	120,000
Retained earnings	1,325,000
Total	$2,120,000

The following dividend declaration and distribution alternatives are being considered:

a)   Declaration of the 12 percent preferred cash dividend and a $4 per share cash dividend on common.

b)   Distribution of a 10 percent preferred stock dividend when the preferred shares are selling for $80 per share.

c)   Distribution of a 40 percent common stock dividend when the common shares are selling for $60 per share.

d)   Distribution of a 100 percent common and 100 percent preferred stock dividend. Both stock dividends are to be recorded at par.

e) Same as item *d,* except that the stock dividends are to be recorded at the average contributed capital per share.

f) Declaration of a 4-for-1 stock split on common.

g) Declaration of a 2-for-1 reverse stock split on preferred.

h) Declaration and distribution of a dividend from donated capital. Investment securities with a fair value at donation of $100,000, a carrying value of $220,000, and a fair value of $250,000 are distributed to common stockholders.

i) Distribution of a special stock dividend to common stockholders. Each common stockholder receives one share of preferred for each share of common held. The market prices of the shares are as follows:

Common **$60**

Preferred 80

REQUIRED Prepare the journal entries and the resulting stockholders' equity section of the balance sheet under each alternative.

P 18-12. **DIVIDENDS** Gifford, Inc., began operations in January 1994 and had the following reported net income or loss for each of its five years of operations:

1994	$ 150,000 loss
1995	130,000 loss
1996	120,000 loss
1997	250,000 income
1998	1,000,000 income

On December 31, 1998, Gifford's capital accounts were as follows:

Common stock, par value $10 per share: authorized, 100,000 shares;
issued and outstanding, 50,000 shares . . . . $ 500,000

4% nonparticipating, noncumulative preferred stock, par value
$100 per share: authorized, issued, and outstanding, 1,000 shares 100,000

7% fully participating, cumulative preferred stock, par value $100
per share: authorized, issued, and outstanding, 10,000 shares 1,000,000

Gifford has never paid a cash dividend or a stock dividend. There has been no change in the capital accounts since Gifford began operations. The appropriate state law permits dividends only from retained earnings.

REQUIRED Prepare a schedule showing the maximum amount available for cash dividends on December 31, 1998, and how it would be distributable to the holders of the common shares and each class of preferred shares.

(AICPA, adapted)

P 18-13. **APPROPRIATIONS; STOCKHOLDERS' EQUITY** Below are some of the accounts appearing in the trial balance of King Corporation, as of December 31, 1998:

	DR	CR
Common stock (no par, issued at $8 per share)		80,000
Preferred stock ($10 par)		30,000
Treasury stock (common, 1,000 shares at cost)	13,000	
Contributed capital in excess of par		10,000
Stock dividends distributable (common)		16,000
Unrealized holding loss on available-for-sale securities	28,000	
Reserve for treasury stock		13,000
Reserve for bond sinking fund		26,000
Donated capital		21,000
Prior period adjustment—error correction	16,700	
Prior period adjustment—inventory write-down	6,000	
Loss on fire at warehouse	20,000	
Reserve for contingencies		60,000
Retained earnings, 1/1/98		95,000
Dividends declared	16,000	

Net income for 1998 was $24,000.

REQUIRED

1. Prepare a statement of changes in unappropriated retained earnings for 1998.
2. Prepare the stockholders' equity section of the balance sheet as of December 31, 1998. Use appropriate account titles in this statement.

P 18-14. **STATEMENT OF STOCKHOLDERS' EQUITY** Stockholders' equity as of December 31, 1998, for Mayer Corporation was as follows:

8% preferred stock, $100 par value: 10,000 shares issued	$1,000,000
Common stock, $5 par value: 100,000 shares issued	500,000
Contributed capital in excess of par, common	1,000,000
Treasury stock, 10,000 shares of common at par value	(50,000)
Retained earnings:	
Appropriated for cost of treasury stock	60,000
Unappropriated	2,750,000
Total	$5,260,000

The following events, listed in chronological order, affected stockholders' equity during 1999:
a) Dividends declared: preferred, 8% of par; common, $2 per share.
b) Sold 5,000 treasury shares for $12 per share.
c) Declared and issued a 10 percent stock dividend on common shares outstanding. The market price of the shares on the declaration date was $20 per share.
d) The preferred stock was split 4 for 1.
e) Land with a fair value of $80,000 was donated to Mayer Corporation.
f) The directors appropriated $100,000 of retained earnings for a possible loss as a result of a lawsuit filed against Mayer Corporation.
g) 5,000 preferred shares were donated to Mayer Corporation by preferred stockholders.
h) Corrected an error that occurred two years earlier. At that time Mayer decided to record internally generated goodwill of $44,000. The credit was made to miscellaneous income. No amortization had been recorded.
i) Net income for 1999, $300,000.

REQUIRED Prepare a statement of changes in stockholders' equity using the following headings and format:

	PREFERRED STOCK	COMMON STOCK	CONTRIBUTED CAPITAL IN EXCESS OF PAR (COMMON AND PREFERRED)	OTHER CONTRIBUTED CAPITAL (OMIT DETAILS)	TREASURY STOCK	RETAINED EARNINGS		TOTAL
						APPRO-PRIATED	UNAPPRO-PRIATED	
End of 1998	$1,000,000	$500,000	$1,000,000	—	($50,000)	$60,000	$2,750,000	$5,260,000
1999 trans-actions								
End of 1999								

P 18-15. **PREFERRED DIVIDEND PREFERENCES** Sinclair Company has a capitalization of 2,000 shares of 6 percent, $100 par value preferred stock and 5,000 shares of $100 par value common stock. On December 31, 1998, there were no dividends in arrears. During the five following years, the company's dividend declarations were as follows:

1999	$77,000
2000	42,000
2001	6,000
2002	12,000
2003	54,000

REQUIRED Under the following independent assumptions, show the amount of dividends for each of the two classes of stock, using the format that follows the assumptions:
1. The preferred is cumulative and fully participating.
2. The preferred is noncumulative and fully participating.
3. The preferred is cumulative and nonparticipating.
4. The preferred is noncumulative and nonparticipating.

YEAR	STOCK	CUMULATIVE AND FULLY PARTICIPATING	NONCUMULATIVE AND FULLY PARTICIPATING	CUMULATIVE AND NON-PARTICIPATING	NONCUMULATIVE AND NON-PARTICIPATING
1999	Preferred				
	Common				
2000	Preferred				
	Common				
2001	Preferred				
	Common				
2002	Preferred				
	Common				
2003	Preferred				
	Common				

P 18-16.   **STOCKHOLDERS' EQUITY RELATIONSHIPS**   On December 31, 1999, Pinder Corporation's stockholders' equity appeared as follows:

Common stock ($10 par value)	$26,400,000
Contributed capital in excess of par	25,610,000
Retained earnings appropriated for plant expansion	600,000
Retained earnings, unappropriated	18,380,000
Less: Treasury stock (at cost)	(260,000)
Total	$70,730,000

During the year ended December 31, 1999, Pinder had the following transactions and events (in chronological order):

a) Convertible debt holders converted $10 million par value of bonds to Pinder's common stock. Each $1,000 bond was convertible into 40 shares of Pinder common stock. The bonds originally were issued at par, and Pinder uses the book value method of recording bond conversions.

b) Pinder declared and distributed a 10 percent stock dividend when the market price of its common stock was $25 per share.

c) Pinder acquired 20,000 shares of its common stock for $26 per share; shortly after the acquisition, the company issued 10,000 of these shares for $27 per share.

d) The company made a retained earnings appropriation of $600,000, the first in the company's history.

e) Cash dividends of $1 per share were declared and paid on the common shares.

f) Pinder's net income for 1999 was $3,000,000.

REQUIRED   Prepare the stockholders' equity section of Pinder's balance sheet on December 31, 1998.

P 18-17.   **STOCKHOLDERS' EQUITY REVIEW**   Beck Company was formed on July 1, 1996. It was authorized to issue 200,000 shares of $5 par value common stock and 50,000 shares of 6 percent, $10 par cumulative and nonparticipating preferred stock. Beck's fiscal year ends June 30.

The following information relates to Beck's stockholders' equity accounts:

COMMON STOCK

Before the 1998–1999 fiscal year, Beck had 105,000 shares of outstanding common stock issued as follows:

a) 95,000 shares were issued for cash on July 1, 1996, at $20 per share.

b) On July 24, 1996, 5,000 shares were exchanged for a plot of land that cost the seller $70,000 in 1990 and had an estimated fair value of $102,000 on July 24, 1996.

c) 5,000 shares were issued on March 1, 1998; the shares had been subscribed for $32 per share on October 31, 1997.

d) During the 1998–1999 fiscal year, the following common stock transactions took place:

     10/1/98   Subscriptions were received for 10,000 shares at $40 per share. Cash of $80,000 was received in full payment for 2,000 shares, and stock certificates were issued. The remaining subscriptions for 8,000 shares were to be paid in full by 9/30/99, at which time the certificates were to be issued.

     11/30/98   Beck purchased 2,000 shares of its own stock on the open market at $38 per share. Beck uses the cost method for treasury stock.

     12/15/98   Beck declared a 2 percent stock dividend for stockholders of record on 1/15/99, to be issued on 1/31/99. Beck was having a liquidity problem and could not afford a cash dividend at the time. Beck's common stock was selling at $43 per share on 12/15/98. (Stock dividends are not distributed on subscribed shares until the subscriptions are fully paid.)

     6/20/99   Beck issued 500 shares of the common stock that it had purchased on 11/30/98 for $21,000.

PREFERRED STOCK

e) Beck issued 30,000 shares of preferred stock at $20 per share on July 1, 1997.

CASH DIVIDENDS

f) Beck has followed a schedule of declaring cash dividends in December and June, with payment being made to stockholders of record in the following month. Cash dividends have been declared through June 30, 1999, as follows:

DECLARATION DATE	COMMON STOCK, PER SHARE	PREFERRED STOCK, PER SHARE
12/15/97	$.10	$.30
6/15/98	.10	.30
12/15/98	—	.30

No cash dividends were declared in June 1999 because of Beck's liquidity problems.

RETAINED EARNINGS

g) As of June 30, 1998, Beck's retained earnings account had a balance of $570,000. For the fiscal year ended June 30, 1999, Beck reported net income of $20,000.

h) In March 1998, Beck received a term loan from Union National Bank. The bank requires Beck to establish a sinking fund and restrict retained earnings in an amount equal to the sinking fund deposit. The annual sinking fund payment of $40,000 is due on April 30 each year; the first payment was made on schedule on April 30, 1999.

REQUIRED Prepare the stockholders' equity section of the statement of financial position, including appropriate notes, for Beck as of June 30, 1999.

(IMA, adapted)

P 18-18. **STOCKHOLDERS' EQUITY; COMPREHENSIVE** At the beginning of the current year, Martin Corporation had the following stockholders' equity balances:

Common stock ($10 par value) $2,500,000
Contributed capital in excess of par 1,500,000
Retained earnings 6,000,000

During the current year, Martin engaged in the following transactions, listed in chronological order:

a) Purchased 4,000 shares of its common stock for $18 per share. The company uses the cost method of accounting for treasury shares.

b) Issued 25,000 shares of $20 par convertible preferred stock, convertible 1 for 1 with its common, for $48 per share.

c) Issued 50,000 shares of previously unissued $10 par common stock for $20 per share.

d) Declared a cash dividend of $2 per share on the common shares outstanding.

e) Sold 3,000 shares of treasury stock for $22 per share.

f) Declared a cash dividend of $1 per share on the preferred shares.

g) Converted 10,000 preferred shares into common shares at stockholders' request.

h) Declared and distributed a 1 percent stock dividend on common when the market price of its common stock was $28 per share.

i) Corrected an error made several years ago. At that time, a purchase of land for $200,000 was incorrectly expensed.

j) Recorded net income of $800,000 for the year.

REQUIRED
1. Indicate the dollar effect of each transaction listed above on total stockholders' equity.
2. Prepare a statement of retained earnings for the current year.
3. Prepare the stockholders' equity section of Martin's balance sheet at the end of the current year.

P 18-19. **FINANCIAL REPORTING PROBLEM** This problem relates to the annual report of GE in Appendix B. Using that report, answer the following questions about stockholders' equity. Indicate the source of each answer. The questions relate only to consolidated results and only to 1995 unless stated otherwise.

REQUIRED
1. What type(s) of capital stock does GE have authorized? Outstanding?
2. How many shares of stock are issued? Outstanding?
3. How many shareowner accounts does GE have?

4. Describe GE's stock repurchase program. Why do you suppose GE initiated and expanded this program?

5. How much cash did GE pay in dividends during 1995?

6. GE adopted the disclosure-only option under *Statement No. 123* for the year ended December 31, 1995. What was the impact on 1995 net earnings?

*P 18-20. **QUASI-REORGANIZATION** Horton Corporation has $105,000 of dividends in arrears on its preferred stock as of March 31, 1998. While retained earnings are adequate to meet the accumulated dividends, the company's management does not wish to weaken its working capital position. It also realizes that a portion of the fixed assets are no longer used or useful in the company's operation. Therefore, the following reorganization is proposed and approved by stockholders, effective April 1, 1998:

a) The preferred stock is to be exchanged for $300,000 of 5 percent debenture bonds. Dividends in arrears are to be settled by the issuance of $120,000 of $10 par value, 5 percent, noncumulative preferred stock.

b) Common stock is to be assigned a value of $50 per share.

c) Goodwill is to be written off.

d) Property, plant, and equipment is to be written down, on the basis of appraisal and estimates of useful value, by a total of $110,000, consisting of $80,000 increase in accumulated depreciation and $30,000 decrease in certain assets.

e) Current assets are to be written down by $8,000 to reduce certain items to expected realizable values.

The condensed balance sheet as of March 31, 1998, is as shown below:

Assets:

Cash		$ 24,690
Other current assets		252,890
Property, plant, and equipment	$1,458,731	
Accumulated depreciation	(512,481)	946,250
Goodwill.		60,000
Total		$1,283,830

Liabilities and stockholders' equity:

Current liabilities.	$ 116,860
7% cumulative preferred stock ($100 par)ᵃ	300,000
Common stock (9,000 shares, no-par)	648,430
Contributed capital in excess of par—preferred	22,470
Retained earnings	196,070
Total	$1,283,830

ᵃ$105,000 dividends in arrears.

REQUIRED

1. Prepare the journal entries to give effect to the reorganization as of April 1, 1998. Give explanations with each entry and comment as to any possible options in recording the reorganization.

2. Prepare a balance sheet as of April 30, 1998, assuming that net income for April is $14,000 after provision for taxes and that operations result in $8,970 increase in cash, $10,660 increase in other current assets, $2,010 increase in current liabilities, and $3,620 increase in accumulated depreciation.

(AICPA, adapted)

BRISTOL-MYERS SQUIBB COMPANY STOCK COMPENSATION CASE

Bristol-Myers Squibb Company, incorporated in Delaware in 1933, traces its roots to a New York business started in 1887. It develops, manufactures, and distributes pharmaceuticals (Amoxicillin, Bufferin), beauty aids (Clairol, Keri), nutritional supplements (Enfamil, Theragram), and medical devices. Approximately 44 percent of its revenue in 1995 came from sales outside the United States. In 1995, Bristol-Myers Squibb had consolidated revenue of $13.8 billion, net income of $1.8 billion, and total assets of $13.9 billion. Bristol-Myers Squibb also had 49,000 employees at the end of 1995. Bristol-Myers Squibb is one of the few companies that adopted *Statement No. 123* in 1995; it was not required to be adopted until 1996.

Answer the following questions using the information in the accompanying financial statement excerpts. All questions relate to 1995 unless otherwise specified.

1. Note 13 states that no compensation expense has been recognized under *APB Opinion No. 25* for stock options. Using your knowledge of *APB Opinion No. 25* and other information in Note 13, explain why there is zero compensation expense. Note that Bristol-Myers Squibb has two types of option plans— one for executives and one for all employees.

2. Note 13 states that if the methodology of *Statement No. 123* had been used, net income would have been lowered by approximately $35 million. Show

how this amount was computed using the $12.94 fair value for each option granted and other information contained in the note. Assume that all options granted in 1995 were granted on May 1 and that there are no tax benefits.

3. As stated above, net income is $1.8 billion. Calculate the percentage effect on net income from using the *Statement No. 123* methodology.

4. What is the transfer of wealth to employees from shareholders in 1995 for the stock options *exercised*? The market price of Bristol-Myers Squibb stock at the end of 1995 was $86 per share.

5. Calculate the total excess of market price over exercise price for the options exercisable at the end of 1995. How should this amount be interpreted from an economic standpoint?

6. What is the percentage of the amount in part 5 to the total value of Bristol-Myers Squibb common stock outstanding?

7. Do you think that the percentages in parts 3 and 5 have anything to do with Bristol-Myers Squibb's adopting *Statement No. 123* prior to the mandatory adoption date?

8. How does the information in Note 13 assist shareholders or analysts?

CONSOLIDATED BALANCE SHEET

	DECEMBER 31,		
Dollars in Millions	1995	1994	1993
ASSETS			
Current Assets:			
Cash and cash equivalents	$ 1,645	$ 1,642	$ 2,421
Time deposits and marketable securities	533	781	308
Receivables, net of allowances	2,356	2,043	1,859
Inventories	1,451	1,397	1,322
Prepaid expenses	1,033	847	660
Total Current Assets	7,018	6,710	6,570
Property, Plant and Equipment	3,760	3,666	3,374
Insurance Recoverable	959	968	1,000
Excess of cost over net tangible assets received in business acquisitions	1,219	939	191
Other Assets	973	627	966
	$13,929	$12,910	$12,101
LIABILITIES			
Current Liabilities:			
Short-term borrowings	$ 575	$ 725	$ 177
Accounts payable	848	693	649
Accrued expenses	1,939	1,481	1,450
U.S. and foreign income taxes payable	744	740	689
Product liability	700	635	100
Total Current Liabilities	4,806	4,274	3,065
Product Liability	1,645	1,201	1,370
Other Liabilities	1,021	1,087	1,138
Long-Term Debt	635	644	588
Total Liabilities	8,107	7,206	6,161
STOCKHOLDERS' EQUITY			
Preferred stock, $2 convertible series: Authorized 10 million shares; issued and outstanding 19,023 in 1995, 21,857 in 1994 and 25,798 in 1993, liquidation value of $50 per share	—	—	—
Common stock, par value of $.10 per share: Authorized 1.5 billion shares; issued 540,185,639 in 1995, 540,173,669 in 1994 and 532,688,458 in 1993	54	54	53
Capital in excess of par value of stock	375	397	353
Cumulative translation adjustments	(327)	(301)	(332)
Retained earnings	7,917	7,600	7,243
	8,019	7,750	7,317
Less cost of treasury stock— 34,953,311 common shares in 1995, 32,887,848 in 1994 and 20,782,281 in 1993	2,197	2,046	1,377
Total Stockholders' Equity	5,822	5,704	5,940
	$13,929	$12,910	$12,101

The accompanying notes are an integral part of these financial statements.

NOTE 13 STOCKHOLDERS' EQUITY

Changes in capital shares and capital in excess of par value of stock were:

| | SHARES OF COMMON STOCK | | CAPITAL IN EXCESS OF PAR VALUE OF STOCK (dollars in millions) |
	ISSUED	TREASURY	
Balance, December 31, 1992	532,673,413	14,689,052	$435
Issued pursuant to stock plans, options, rights and warrants	3,530	(1,183,365)	(23)
Conversions of preferred stock	11,515	—	—
Purchases	—	7,276,594	—
Other	—	—	(59)
Balance, December 31, 1993	532,688,458	20,782,281	353
Issued pursuant to stock plans, options, rights and warrants	15,747	(518,733)	(15)
Conversions of preferred stock	16,646	—	—
Purchases	—	12,624,300	—
Other	7,452,818	—	59
Balance, December 31, 1994	540,173,669	32,887,848	397
Issued pursuant to stock plans, options and rights	—	(1,602,537)	(22)
Conversions of preferred stock	11,970	—	—
Purchases	—	3,668,000	—
Balance, December 31, 1995	540,185,639	34,953,311	$375

Each share of the company's preferred stock is convertible into 4.24 shares of common stock and is callable at the company's option. The reductions in the number of issued shares of preferred stock in 1995, 1994 and 1993 were due to conversions into shares of common stock.

Dividends per common share were $2.96 in 1995, $2.92 in 1994 and $2.88 in 1993.

Stock Compensation Plans

Under the company's stock option plans, officers, directors and key employees may be granted options to purchase the company's common stock at no less than 100% of the market price on the date the option is granted. Options generally become exercisable in installments of 25% per year on each of the first through the fourth anniversaries of the grant date and have a maximum term of ten years. Additionally, the plans provide for the granting of stock appreciation rights whereby the grantee may surrender exercisable options and receive common stock and/or cash measured by the excess of the market price of the common stock over the option exercise price. The plans also provide for the granting of performance-based stock options to certain key executives.

On May 4, 1993, the stockholders approved amendments to the 1983 Stock Option Plan extending its term for 10 years, authorizing additional shares in the amount of 0.9% of the outstanding shares per year for each of the additional 10 years, incorporating the company's existing long-term performance award plan and providing for the payment of long-term performance awards in shares of common stock.

Under the TeamShare Stock Option Plan, all full-time employees, excluding key executives, meeting certain years of service requirements are granted options to purchase the company's common stock at the market price on the date the options are granted. The company has authorized 15,000,000 shares for issuance under the plan. A total of 7,673,600 options were granted in 1995 under the plan with 200 options granted to each eligible employee. Individual grants generally become exercisable on or after the third anniversary of the grant date.

The company's restricted stock award plan provides for the granting of up to 3,000,000 shares of common stock to key employees, subject to restrictions as to continuous employment except in the case of death or normal retirement. Restrictions generally expire over a five-year period from date of grant. Compensation expense is recognized over the restricted period. At December 31, 1995, a total of 653,335 shares were outstanding under the plan.

The company applies Accounting Principles Board Opinion No. 25, Accounting for Stock Issued to Employees, and related interpretations in accounting for its plans. Accordingly, no compensation expense has been recognized for its stock-based compensation plans other than for restricted stock and performance-based awards. Had compensation cost for the company's other stock option plans been determined based upon the fair value at the grant date for awards under these plans consistent with the methodology prescribed under Statement of Financial Accounting Standards No. 123, Accounting for Stock-Based Compensation, the company's net income and earnings per share would have been reduced by approximately $35 million, or $.07 per share. The fair value of the options granted during 1995 is estimated as $12.94 on the date of grant using the Black-Scholes option-pricing model with the following assumptions: dividend yield 4.2%, volatility of 18.2%, risk-free interest rate of 6.9%, assumed forfeiture rate of 3%, and an expected life of 7 years.

Stock option and long-term performance award transactions were:

	SHARES OF COMMON STOCK		WEIGHTED AVERAGE OF EXERCISE PRICE OF SHARES UNDER PLAN
	AVAILABLE FOR OPTION/AWARD	UNDER PLAN	
Balance,			
December 31, 1992	4,259,730	14,955,760	$61.57
Authorized	4,661,859	—	—
Granted	(5,464,022)	5,464,022	56.58
Exercised	—	(1,264,638)	32.65
Lapsed	787,946	(790,981)	70.52
Balance,			
December 31, 1993	4,245,513	18,364,163	60.80
Authorized	4,607,156	—	—
Granted	(5,296,982)	5,296,982	51.93
Exercised	—	(686,507)	32.97
Lapsed	1,012,237	(1,027,651)	62.48
Balance,			
December 31, 1994	4,567,924	21,946,987	56.99
Authorized	19,565,572	—	—
Granted	(13,449,952)	13,449,952	61.79
Exercised	—	(2,012,827)	40.96
Lapsed	1,129,560	(1,129,574)	61.92
Balance,			
December 31, 1995	11,813,104	32,254,538	$59.76

The following table summarizes information concerning currently outstanding and exercisable options:

RANGE OF EXERCISE PRICES	OPTIONS OUTSTANDING			OPTIONS EXERCISABLE	
	NUMBER OUTSTANDING	WEIGHTED AVERAGE REMAINING CONTRACTUAL LIFE	WEIGHTED AVERAGE EXERCISE PRICE	NUMBER EXERCISABLE	WEIGHTED AVERAGE EXERCISE PRICE
$20-$40	782,226	1.09	$28.34	782,226	$28.34
$40-$50	1,103,858	2.33	43.44	1,103,858	43.44
$50-$60	11,811,741	1.57	53.64	7,370,348	53.82
$60-$70	12,928,294	9.01	62.11	80,325	64.37
$70-$90	5,628,419	9.39	77.23	4,897,199	77.31
	32,254,538			14,233,956	

At December 31, 1995, 51,379,361 shares of common stock were reserved for issuance pursuant to stock plans, options and conversions of preferred stock.

Attached to each outstanding share of the company's common stock is one Right. The Rights will be exercisable if a person or group acquires beneficial interest of 15% or more of the company's outstanding common stock, or commences a tender or exchange offer for 15% or more of the company's outstanding common stock. Each Right will entitle stockholders to buy one one-thousandth of a share of a new series of participating preferred stock of the company at an exercise price of $200. The Rights will expire on December 18, 1997. In the event of certain merger, sale of assets or self-dealing transactions, each Right will then entitle its holder to acquire shares having a value of twice the Right's exercise price. The company may redeem the Rights at $.01 per Right at any time until the 15th day following public announcement that a 15% position has been acquired.

Accounting Changes and Error Analysis

CHAPTER

LEARNING OBJECTIVES

After studying this chapter, you should be able to:

1. Distinguish among a change in accounting principle, a change in accounting estimate, and a change in the reporting entity.

2. Calculate the cumulative effect of a change in accounting principle and prepare the journal entry to record the change under the current period approach.

3. Calculate the cumulative effect of a change in accounting principle and prepare the journal entry to record the change under the retroactive approach.

4. Explain how to report the effects of a change in accounting principle under the current period approach.

5. Explain how to report the effects of a change in accounting principle under the retroactive approach.

6. Prepare the journal entry to record a change in accounting estimate and describe the disclosure requirements for the change.

7. Prepare correcting entries for errors and explain how error corrections are reported.

8. Distinguish among a classification error that does not affect income, a counterbalancing error, and a noncounterbalancing error.

9. Analyze the effects of counterbalancing errors on the financial statements and prepare any necessary correcting entries.

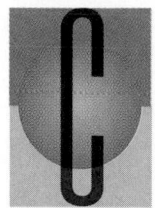

hanging economic circumstances often cause a company to change its methods of accounting. For example, rising prices may motivate a firm to switch from FIFO to LIFO inventory accounting. External conditions may also bring about revisions in estimates, as when a firm revises its estimate of the useful life of a depreciable asset. Whatever their cause, **accounting changes** are made to meet the financial reporting objective of providing information that is useful for decision making.

CONCEPTUAL

Accounting changes affect comparability and consistency.

Although accounting changes may increase the usefulness of information in one way, two qualitative characteristics of information—comparability and consistency—may suffer. Comparability helps users to make comparisons across firms; if firms use different accounting methods, comparability is impaired. Consistency helps users to evaluate a particular firm over time. If the firm changes its accounting methods, consistency may be sacrificed. An accounting change may also materially affect a company's reported earnings, even though it may not affect its cash flows. To illustrate, consider the following newspaper account of an accounting change made by McDonnell Douglas:

> Effective Oct. 1, 1995, McDonnell Douglas changed its accounting for the MD-11 trijet program from the program basis of accounting to the specific unit basis of accounting. The change had no impact on cash flow. Under the program basis, MD-11 costs for delivered aircraft were charged to cost of sales based upon the estimated average unit cost for the entire program. Actual costs in excess of the program average were deferred to be recovered by production and future delivery of lower-than-average cost units. Under the specific unit basis of accounting, MD-11 costs are charged to cost of sales based upon the unit cost of the delivered aircraft.[1]

One of the most significant accounting changes in history was the change in the method of accounting for employee health benefits required by *Statement No. 106.* (Accounting for postretirement benefits other than pensions was discussed in Chapter 16.) Although this accounting change had no effect on firms' cash flows, it had a significant effect on their reported earnings and statement of financial position—a negative one:

> Ford Motor Co. said on Wednesday it lost an unprecedented $7.4 billion in 1992 as accounting changes and one-time charges muddied an otherwise improving financial picture. The $7.4 billion loss amounted to $15.61 per common share, but included a one-time accounting charge of $7.5 billion to reflect a bookkeeping change for retiree health benefits.
>
> It was the biggest annual loss ever for a U.S. corporation, eclipsing the $4.97 billion that IBM lost in 1992. Ford's distinction will last for only a day, however. General Motors Corp. is expected to report on Thursday a 1992 loss exceeding $23 billion, including $22.2 billion in retiree health care accounting adjustments.
>
> The impact of the health care accounting change on Ford's latest results was reduced by the automaker's adoption of another accounting change that resulted in a one-time gain of $657 million. Shareholders' equity, or Ford's net worth, fell to $14.75 billion from $22.69 billion at the end of 1991 because of the accounting changes.[2]

CONCEPTUAL

Accounting changes that do not affect the value of a firm remain controversial, despite the efficiency of securities markets.

Although a significant body of empirical research indicates that the securities market is not fooled by accounting changes that do not affect a firm's value, accounting for these types of changes remains controversial. Accounting information is also used in many types of resource allocation decisions other than those made in securities markets. As examples, accounting information is used in lending decisions and in profit-sharing arrangements. Thus, the impact of an accounting change on a company's financial statements can be important.

---

[1]*PR Newswire,* January 18, 1996.
[2]*Tulsa World,* February 11, 1993, p. B-7.

Another problem arises when accounting errors are discovered. How should errors be corrected and disclosed? The objective of error correction and disclosure is to make the financial statements as useful as possible. *Meaningful disclosure of the effects of both accounting changes and error corrections increases the usefulness of financial statements by allowing users to distinguish between changes in resources and obligations and changes in the method of accounting for them.*

In this chapter we will discuss the various types of accounting changes and how to account for and disclose them in the financial statements. We will also examine accounting errors, their effect on the financial statements, and their correction.

ACCOUNTING CHANGES

To illustrate the potential diversity in the financial reporting of accounting changes if there were no standards for accounting changes, consider the following hypothetical situation:[3] At the beginning of 1994, four competing commuter airlines—Transtate, Southeast, Northern, and Alpha—acquired identical planes at a cost of $12 million to each airline. The companies operate in very similar business and economic environments. They estimated that the planes would have a useful life of six years, with no salvage value. All four estimated that the planes' services would be received equally each year, so all four decided to use straight-line depreciation.

In early 1998, after four years' service, the planes still had a remaining useful life of six years. That is, the total useful life of the planes now appeared to be ten years rather than six. Consequently, all four airlines decided to change the total estimated life of the planes from six years to ten years. At the date of the accounting change, the book value of each airline's planes was $4 million:

Airplanes (original cost)	**$12,000,000**
Accumulated depreciation ($12,000,000 ÷ 6 = $2,000,000;	
$2,000,000 × 4 years = $8,000,000)	**(8,000,000)**
Book value	**$ 4,000,000**

Transtate's controller reasoned that since the total useful life of the planes was now estimated to be ten years, depreciation to date should be reduced to show the (now) smaller depreciation for the four years already passed. Since four years of the ten years had elapsed, the planes should be depreciated by 40 percent. Transtate therefore made the following entries to record the accounting change and the 1998 depreciation:

Accumulated depreciation	3,200,000	
Miscellaneous income from accounting change. .		3,200,000

To record the change in estimate: 40 percent × original cost of $12,000,000 = $4,800,000 (new accumulated depreciation balance); $8,000,000 (accumulated depreciation before the change) – $4,800,000 = $3,200,000 (adjustment required).

Depreciation expense	1,200,000	
Accumulated depreciation		1,200,000

To record 1998 depreciation based on the revised 10-year life: $12,000,000 × .10 = $1,200,000.

---

[3]For simplicity, taxes are ignored. In addition, as we shall see later, not all of the alternatives considered here are acceptable under generally accepted accounting principles. This example does, however, illustrate the issues involved in accounting changes.

Southeast's controller reasoned in a similar manner. He argued, however, that the credit should be to retained earnings, since the adjustment applied to prior years rather than the current year. Southeast therefore recorded the change and 1998 depreciation as follows:

Accumulated depreciation.	3,200,000	
Retained earnings		3,200,000
Depreciation expense	1,200,000	
Accumulated depreciation		1,200,000

Southeast's controller also decided that the comparative income statements for the years 1994–1997 should be restated by reducing depreciation expense for each prior period by $800,000 ($3,200,000 ÷ 4). He thought this approach would help users to analyze trends and would also be more consistent, because prior years' depreciation expense would be the same as the current and future years' depreciation expense. (From a bookkeeping standpoint, the reduction in depreciation expense each year would increase net income each year by $800,000. Over four years, the increase in net income would equal the $3.2 million increase in retained earnings.)

Northern's controller reasoned in the same way as Southeast's and made the same entries for the accounting change and for 1998 depreciation. However, he decided not to restate the prior periods' statements. The controller argued that what was past was water over the dam. Northern simply reported the $3.2 million increase in retained earnings in the retained earnings statement for 1998.

Alpha's controller took a different approach. She felt that, because the original estimate was based on the best information available at the time the planes were purchased, no adjustment should be made to the accumulated depreciation account. Instead, the net book value of $4 million should be allocated over the (new) remaining life of six years. The controller also concluded that since estimates are inherent in accounting, adjustments to income or retained earnings arising from revisions of estimates might cause users to question the reliability of the financial statements. Alpha therefore made the following entry to record 1998 depreciation:

Depreciation expense.	666,667	
Accumulated depreciation		666,667
($4,000,000 ÷ 6 years)		

Alpha did disclose the change in estimated useful life and its impact on depreciation and net income for 1998 in the footnotes to its 1998 financial statement.

Information from the four airlines' comparative financial statements for 1994–1998 is shown in Exhibit 19–1. Obviously, the four companies' financial statements are not comparable. For example, Transtate's 1998 net income is $3.2 million more than Southeast's and Northern's. Alpha's 1998 net income is $533,333 more than Southeast's and Northern's. Though all four airlines have identical planes with identical useful lives, the asset carrying values on their balance sheets vary considerably. In addition, some of the companies' statements are not consistent over time. For example, Transtate, Northern, and Alpha reported different amounts of depreciation in 1998 than they did in previous years, since 1998 depreciation was based on the new estimate. While Southeast's depreciation expenses for 1994–1998 are consistent, the amounts reported in Southeast's comparative statements for 1994–1997 *differ* from the amounts *originally* reported in those years.

The financial statements of these four hypothetical companies, then, may not permit users to make intelligent investment decisions, because four different approaches were used to account for and disclose the same accounting change. Which of those approaches yields the most useful financial statements if the characteristics of relevance, reliability, comparability, and consistency are considered? There is no definitive answer to this question because, as was discussed in Chapter 2, trade-offs must sometimes be made among qualitative characteristics.

APB Opinion No. 20, "Accounting Changes," was issued in 1971 to reduce the diversity in the reporting of accounting changes. The next several sections of this

C O N C E P T U A L

Accounting changes require trade-offs among the qualitative characteristics of financial reporting.

EXHIBIT 19–1 Information from Four Airlines' Comparative Financial Statements, 1994–1998

Transstate, Southeast, Northern, and Alpha Airlines
Income Statements for the Years Ended December 31

	1998	1997	1996	1995	1994
Transstate					
Depreciation expense	$ (1,200,000)	$ (2,000,000)	$ (2,000,000)	$ (2,000,000)	$ (2,000,000)
Accounting change	3,200,000				
Southeast					
Depreciation expense (restated)	(1,200,000)	(1,200,000)	(1,200,000)	(1,200,000)	(1,200,000)
Northern					
Depreciation expense	(1,200,000)	(2,000,000)	(2,000,000)	(2,000,000)	(2,000,000)
Alpha					
Depreciation expense	(666,667)	(2,000,000)	(2,000,000)	(2,000,000)	(2,000,000)

Balance Sheets, December 31

	1998	1997	1996	1995	1994
Transstate					
Airplanes	$12,000,000	$12,000,000	$12,000,000	$12,000,000	$12,000,000
Accumulated depreciation	(6,000,000)	(8,000,000)	(6,000,000)	(4,000,000)	(2,000,000)
	$ 6,000,000	$ 4,000,000	$ 6,000,000	$ 8,000,000	$10,000,000
Southeast					
Airplanes	$12,000,000	$12,000,000	$12,000,000	$12,000,000	$12,000,000
Accumulated depreciation (after restatement)	(6,000,000)	(4,800,000)	(3,600,000)	(2,400,000)	(1,200,000)
	$ 6,000,000	$ 7,200,000	$ 8,400,000	$ 9,600,000	$10,800,000
Northern					
Airplanes	$12,000,000	$12,000,000	$12,000,000	$12,000,000	$12,000,000
Accumulated depreciation	(6,000,000)	(8,000,000)	(6,000,000)	(4,000,000)	(2,000,000)
	$ 6,000,000	$ 4,000,000	$ 6,000,000	$ 8,000,000	$10,000,000
Alpha					
Airplanes	$12,000,000	$12,000,000	$12,000,000	$12,000,000	$12,000,000
Accumulated depreciation	(8,666,667)	(8,000,000)	(6,000,000)	(4,000,000)	(2,000,000)
	$ 3,333,333	$ 4,000,000	$ 6,000,000	$ 8,000,000	$10,000,000

chapter are based on this *Opinion.* First, we will describe three different types of accounting changes and give some examples of each. Next, we will discuss alternative approaches to recording and reporting accounting changes. Finally, we will discuss the accounting and reporting requirements of *Opinion No. 20.*

Types of Accounting Changes

Distinguish among a change in accounting principle, a change in accounting estimate, and a change in the reporting entity.

There are three types of accounting changes: (1) a change in accounting principle, (2) a change in accounting estimate, and (3) a change in the reporting entity. Each type is discussed in the following pages.

Change in Accounting Principle

A **change in accounting principle** occurs when a company adopts a generally accepted accounting principle that differs from the one it used previously. Some examples of such changes include:

1. A change in the method of inventory pricing (e.g., a change from FIFO to LIFO).
2. A change in depreciation methods for previously recorded assets (e.g., from straight-line to accelerated depreciation).
3. A change in the method of accounting for long-term construction contracts (e.g., from the completed-contract method to the percentage-of-completion method).

A change in accounting principle also includes a change in the *method of applying* the principle. For example, a change from the aggregate approach to the individual-item approach in applying the lower-of-cost-or-market method to inventories is a change in accounting principle. However, a change from an accounting principle that is *not* generally accepted to one that *is* generally accepted does not qualify as a change in accounting principle. Changes of this type are classified as error corrections. Error corrections are discussed later in the chapter.

Change in Accounting Estimate

Estimates are inherent in the accounting process. For example, estimates are made for uncollectible receivables, salvage values and useful lives of depreciable assets, and inventory obsolescence. Occasionally, accountants must revise their estimates as time passes, circumstances change, or additional information is obtained. The case of the four airlines discussed earlier is an example of a **change in accounting estimate.** To give another example, you probably continually revise your estimate of your grade in an accounting class as you move through the quarter or semester and are exposed to new material and obtain feedback on your examinations. Your original grade estimate was not *wrong,* since it was based on all the facts you knew at the time. As additional information becomes available, however, your revised estimates probably become more accurate.

Many companies include a discussion of the use of estimates in their financial statements. The following discussion appeared in the annual report of Entergy Corporation:

Use of Estimates in the Preparation of Financial Statements

The preparation of Entergy Corporation and its subsidiaries' financial statements, in conformity with generally accepted accounting principles, requires management to make estimates and assumptions that affect reported amounts of assets and liabilities and disclosure of contingent assets and liabilities as of December 31, 1995 and 1994, and the reported amounts of revenues and expenses during fiscal years 1995, 1994, and 1993. Adjustments to the reported amounts of assets and liabilities may be necessary in the future to the extent that future estimates or actual results are different from the estimates used in 1995 financial statements.

Under certain circumstances, distinguishing between a change in accounting principle and a change in accounting estimate may be difficult. For example, because of a change in estimated future benefits, a company may begin recording certain costs as assets and amortizing them over future periods instead of expensing them as they are incurred. Since the change in principle arises as a result of a change in estimated future benefits, separating the two types of changes is difficult. In these circumstances the change must be classified as a change in estimate.[4]

Change in Reporting Entity

An accounting change that involves the preparation of financial statements for a new accounting entity is called a **change in reporting entity.** Changes of this type include:

1. Presenting consolidated or combined statements in place of statements of individual companies.

2. Changing the specific subsidiaries that are included in the group of companies for which consolidated statements are presented.

3. Changing the specific companies included in combined financial statements.

Because this type of change is usually covered in courses that cover consolidated financial statements, they are not discussed further in this text.

Approaches to Recording and Reporting Accounting Changes

Three approaches have been suggested for reporting accounting changes. One is to report the total financial statement effects of the change in the *current period.* Another is to report them *retroactively.* A third approach is to report them *prospectively.* We shall discuss each in turn.

Current Period Approach

Under the **current period approach,** the *cumulative effect* of the accounting change on the financial statements is calculated—that is, the cumulative effect on assets or liabilities—at the beginning of the period in which the change is made. The cumulative effect is the difference between the present carrying value of the asset or liability and the amount the carrying value would have been if the accounting change had been in effect in all previous periods. The cumulative effect is recorded by adjusting the asset or liability. The offsetting debit or credit is made to the account *cumulative effect of change in accounting principle,* which is reported on the income statement. Revenues or expenses that are affected by the accounting change in the period in which the change is made are based on the new accounting method. However, the financial statements of prior periods reported currently for comparative purposes are *not* restated. In the airline example discussed earlier (pages 1023–1025), *Transtate used the current period approach.*

The rationale for the current period approach is that by recording and reporting the effect of the change in the current period, the credibility of prior period statements and of financial reporting in general is maintained. Again, many

2 **Calculate the cumulative effect of a change in accounting principle and prepare the journal entry to record the change under the current period approach.**

CONCEPTUAL

The current period approach maintains the credibility of prior period statements.

---

[4]"Accounting Changes," *Opinions of the Accounting Principles Board No. 20* (New York: AICPA, 1971), para. 10.

accountants believe that if prior period statements are *continually* restated, users may begin to question their reliability and credibility.

Retroactive Approach

Calculate the cumulative effect of a change in accounting principle and prepare the journal entry to record the change under the retroactive approach.

The **retroactive approach** is similar to the current period approach, since the cumulative effect of the accounting change is calculated at the beginning of the period in which the change is made. In recording and disclosure, however, this approach differs from the current period approach. The cumulative effect is *recorded* by adjusting the asset or liability, with an offsetting debit or credit to *retained earnings*. The change is *disclosed* by restating the financial statements of prior periods. In the earlier example, *Southeast used the retroactive approach.*

Support for the retroactive approach is based on *interperiod comparability or consistency.* When accounting changes are treated retroactively, prior period financial statements are consistent with present and future statements.

CONCEPTUAL

The retroactive approach increases interperiod comparability (consistency).

Prospective Approach

CONCEPTUAL

The prospective approach maintains financial statement credibility.

As its name implies, the **prospective approach** is "forward looking"; that is, prior period financial statements are not restated under this approach. If future periods are not affected, the accounting effect of the change is reported in the current period. If the change affects current and future periods, the financial effects of the change are reported in those periods. The argument for this approach is similar to that for the current period approach—it maintains financial statement credibility. Another argument is that since previously reported results have affected past decisions and behavior, mathematical reconstruction of what already has happened may not be meaningful. In the hypothetical example presented earlier, *Alpha used the prospective approach.*

Now that we have introduced the types of accounting changes and some approaches for recording and reporting them, we will discuss how each type is recorded and disclosed under generally accepted accounting principles.

CCOUNTING FOR CHANGES IN ACCOUNTING PRINCIPLE

A general accounting and reporting requirement governs accounting for and reporting changes in accounting principle. Two groups of exceptions may be made to the general requirement. Both the requirements and the exceptions are presented in the next several sections.

General Requirement: Current Period Approach

CONCEPTUAL

The cumulative effect of a change in accounting principle is reported in the income statement.

Generally, changes in accounting principle are accounted for under the current period approach. That is, the cumulative effect of the change, as of the beginning of the period in which the change is made, is reported in the current period income statement. As was stated earlier (page 1027), the cumulative effect of the change means that the asset or liability affected is adjusted to the amount it would have been if the new principle had been used in previous periods. This approach is sometimes referred to as a **catch-up approach.** The *new* accounting principle is applied to the asset or liability in current and future periods.

To illustrate, assume that in 1998, Bowie Corporation decides to change the depreciation method on its plant and equipment from sum-of-the-years'-digits to

EXHIBIT 19-2	Calculation of the Cumulative Effect of a Change in Accounting Principle

Bowie Corporation

Depreciation Under:

Year	(1) Sum-of-the-Years'- Digits Method	(2) Straight-Line Method	(3) Difference
1994	10/55 × $110,000 = $20,000	$110,000/10 = $11,000	$ 9,000
1995	9/55 × $110,000 = 18,000	11,000	7,000
1996	8/55 × $110,000 = 16,000	11,000	5,000
1997	7/55 × $110,000 = 14,000	11,000	3,000
	$68,000	$44,000	$24,000

straight-line. The assets were purchased at the beginning of 1994 for $110,000; they have a useful life of 10 years and no salvage value. Bowie will continue to use the sum-of-the-years'-digits method for tax purposes. The applicable tax rate is 30 percent.

The cumulative effect of this change in accounting principle is determined as shown in Exhibit 19–2. Notice that the cumulative effect is calculated as of the end of 1997 (or the beginning of 1998). This approach is logical because presumably the economic conditions that justify the new depreciation method apply to 1998 and the following years. Therefore, depreciation expense for 1998 will be based on the new accounting principle, and thus will be a better financial representation of the asset's currently expiring service potential.

Using the data in Exhibit 19–2, the entry to record the change in accounting principle is as follows:

```
Accumulated depreciation ....................... 24,000
    Deferred tax liability (.3 × $24,000) ..............          7,200
    Cumulative effect of change in accounting principle
      ($24,000 – $7,200)........................          16,800
```

Accumulated depreciation is reduced by $24,000, so that the new balance in the account is $44,000 ($68,000 – $24,000). This balance is the total depreciation that would have been recorded on the plant assets by the beginning of 1998 if the straight-line method had been used in previous periods. The deferred tax liability of $7,200 is the expected tax consequence of the difference between the tax basis and the "book" basis of plant assets at the end of 1997. As the plant and equipment balance is recovered, the deferred tax liability will decrease because the difference between the asset's tax basis and book basis will decrease. When the asset has been fully depreciated, the deferred tax liability account will be zero.

Depreciation expense for 1998, based on the new method, is recorded as follows:

```
Depreciation expense ........................... 11,000
    Accumulated depreciation ....................          11,000
```

At the end of 1998, the plant assets have been 50 percent depreciated, and the accumulated depreciation account balance is now $55,000:

Accumulated depreciation

Accounting change		Balance, 12/31/97	68,000
adjustment	24,000	Depreciation, 1998	11,000
		Balance, 12/31/98	55,000

EXHIBIT 19–3   **Disclosure of a Change in Accounting Principle, Current Period Approach**

Bowie Corporation
Comparative Income Statements

	1998	1997	1996
Revenues	$50,000	$50,000	$50,000
Depreciation (Note A)	(11,000)	(14,000)	(16,000)
Other expenses.	(10,000)	(10,000)	(10,000)
Income taxes	(8,700)	(7,800)	(7,200)
Income before change in accounting principle.	$20,300		
Cumulative effect of change in accounting principle (Note A)	16,800		
Net income	$37,100	$18,200	$16,800
Earnings per share.	$3.71	$1.82	$1.68

*Assumes 10,000 common shares outstanding.

Pro Forma (Note A)

	1998	1997	1996
Net income	$20,300[a]	$20,300[b]	$20,300[c]
Earnings per share.	$2.03	$2.03	$2.03

Note A

Prior to 1998, Bowie used sum-of-the-years'-digits depreciation on its plant assets. In 1998, Bowie changed to the straight-line method of depreciation, which management felt better represented the service expiration of its plant assets. The cumulative effect of the change in accounting principle of $16,800 (net of tax) has been included in 1998 net income. The pro forma data report what net income would have been had the straight-line method been used prior to 1998.

[a]$37,100 − $16,800, since the straight-line method was used in 1998.
[b]$18,200 + (.7 × $3,000) (from Exhibit 19–2).
[c]$16,800 + (.7 × $5,000) (from Exhibit 19–2).

4

Explain how to report the effects of a change in accounting principle under the current period approach.

The change in accounting principle is disclosed by reporting its cumulative effect in the 1998 income statement. Exhibit 19–3 shows this disclosure in Bowie's comparative income statement data (figures assumed). The cumulative effect is disclosed between extraordinary items and net income. Though it is not an extraordinary item, it should be reported in a similar manner.[5]

Opinion No. 20 requires that the cumulative effect of the change in accounting principle also must be applied *retroactively* on a *pro forma* ("as if") basis. Thus, net income and earnings per share for all prior periods must be presented as if the new method had been in effect during those periods. This pro forma information is shown in Note A in Exhibit 19–3. The *additional* disclosure requirement increases the interperiod comparability of the disclosures. The previously reported amounts for income and earnings per share for earlier periods are still presented in the body

---

[5]Ibid., para. 20.

of the statements. Finally, a footnote is included to describe the accounting change and its effects for financial statement users.[6]

Notice that in the primary statements, the cumulative effect of the change in depreciation method is shown in the 1998 income statement, and depreciation expense for 1998 is based on the new depreciation method. The additional pro forma disclosures show that if the straight-line method had been used in previous periods, net income and earnings per share would have been equal for all three years, since revenues and other expenses were the same in those years.

Exceptions to the General Requirement

There are two exceptions to the general requirement of reporting the cumulative effect of a change in accounting principle in the current period income statement. One deals with retroactive reporting of *some* changes in accounting principle. The other applies to changes in accounting principle whose cumulative effect is not determinable. Both are addressed in the following sections.

Retroactive Reporting of Some Changes in Accounting Principle

Even though many changes in accounting principle are not reported retroactively, except on the pro forma basis just discussed, the following changes in accounting principle *must* be reported retroactively:

1. A change *from* LIFO to another inventory valuation method.

2. A change in the method of accounting for long-term construction contracts (e.g., from the completed contract to the percentage of completion method).

3. A change to or from the full-cost method of accounting for exploration costs in the extractive industries.

4. A change in accounting principle that is made by a company issuing comparative financial statements for the first time, in order to effect a business combination, register securities, or obtain equity financing.

5. A retroactive change in accounting principle is required by an authoritative pronouncement. For example, in Chapter 13 we pointed out that a change from the cost method to the equity method must be treated retroactively (see page 697).

In the first three situations, and possibly the fifth, retroactive application of a change in accounting principle is thought to be more meaningful than the current period approach. For these items, the cumulative effect can be quite material; thus, retroactive application prevents a large catch-up amount from distorting the current period's income statement. In the fourth situation, retroactive application is more relevant to users, since the company is issuing comparative

---

[6]*APB Opinion No. 20* specifies that when the cumulative effect is calculated for inclusion in the primary financial statements, only *direct effects* of the change and the related income tax should be considered. The direct effect of the change in Bowie Corporation's depreciation methods, for example, was calculated in Exhibit 19–2. The direct effect involved only two items—depreciation and taxes. In the pro forma presentation, however, *indirect effects* also should be considered. For example, if Bowie Corporation had a bonus agreement with employees that was tied to net income, the indirect effect should also be considered in the pro forma disclosures. If the straight-line method had been used in previous periods, net income excluding the bonus would have been greater. When the hypothetical bonus is considered, the pro forma net income and earnings per share numbers would be less than those shown in Exhibit 19–3.

financial statements for the first time; interperiod comparisons are therefore enhanced.

Many *FASB Statements* require retroactive application when a company begins applying the provisions of a new *Statement*. These mandatory accounting changes and disclosure requirements, called **transition rules,** should be distinguished from *voluntary changes* in accounting principle. A voluntary change is one that results from a decision to substitute one generally accepted accounting principle for another.

To illustrate retroactive application of a change in accounting principle, assume that Crane Company uses the completed-contract method to account for long-term construction contracts. The company changes to the percentage-of-completion method in 1998 because management believes that reliable construction costs and completion estimates can be made, and the new method will provide more useful cash flow signals. The company will continue to use the completed-contract method for tax purposes; the applicable tax rate is 30 percent. Crane's comparative statements cover a three-year period. The comparative income statements for 1995, 1996, and 1997 issued under the completed-contract method contain the following information:

	1997	1996	1995
Construction revenue	$500,000	$450,000	$400,000
Cost of construction revenue	(400,000)	(355,000)	(330,000)
Income before taxes	$100,000	$ 95,000	$ 70,000
Income tax expense (30% rate)	(30,000)	(28,500)	(21,000)
Net income	$ 70,000	$ 66,500	$ 49,000

Crane's comparative statements of retained earnings for the same three years contain the following information:

	1997	1996	1995
Retained earnings, beginning	$867,000	$828,000	$800,000
Net income	70,000	66,500	49,000
Dividends	(30,000)	(27,500)	(21,000)
Retained earnings, ending	$907,000	$867,000	$828,000

Exhibit 19–4 shows how the cumulative effect of the change from the completed-contract method to the percentage-of-completion method is calculated. The entry to record the change, at the beginning of 1998, is:

```
Construction in progress . . . . . . . . . . . . . . . . . . . . . . 155,000
    Deferred tax liability (.3 × $155,000) . . . . . . . . . . . .        46,500
    Retained earnings ($155,000 – $46,500) . . . . . . . . . .        108,500
```

As we saw in Chapter 7, under the percentage-of-completion method, income from construction activity is recorded as an increase in construction in progress. The debit to construction in progress increases the balance in this account to what it would have been if the percentage-of-completion method had been used in prior years. The credit to the deferred tax liability is the cumulative tax effect of the temporary differences that would have existed at the end of 1997 (beginning of 1998) had the percentage-of-completion method been used in prior years for financial reporting purposes and the completed-contract method for tax purposes. The credit to retained earnings represents the cumulative increase in income, net of taxes, that would have resulted under the percentage-of-completion method.

EXHIBIT 19–4   Cumulative Effect of a Change in Accounting Method, Long-Term Construction Contract

Crane Company

Pretax Accounting Income

Year	(1) Percentage-of-Completion Method[a]	(2) Completed-Contract Method	(3) Difference
Before 1995	$300,000	$180,000[a]	$120,000
1995	100,000	70,000	30,000
1996	90,000	95,000	(5,000)
1997	110,000	100,000	10,000
Total (as of 1/1/98)	$600,000	$445,000	$155,000
1998 (current year)	$ 80,000	$ 72,000[a]	$ 8,000
Tax at 30%	(24,000)		
Net income for 1998	$ 56,000		

[a]Assumed.

Exhibit 19–5 shows the retroactive disclosure of the change in accounting method in Crane's comparative financial statements. The $108,500 credit to retained earnings in the formal journal entry on page 1032 is a credit to the retained earnings account as of the beginning of 1998. It also affects the restated comparative statements as follows:

5 Explain how to report the effects of a change in accounting principle under the retroactive approach.

$ 84,000	increase in beginning 1995 retained earnings, which is the cumulative effect (net of taxes) for years prior to 1995 (.7 × $120,000 = $84,000)
+ 21,000	increase in 1995 net income (.7 × $30,000)
= $105,000	increase in 1996 beginning retained earnings
− 3,500	decrease in 1996 net income (.7 × $5,000)
= $101,500	increase in beginning 1997 retained earnings
+ 7,000	increase in 1997 net income (.7 × $10,000)
$108,500	cumulative increase in retained earnings at the beginning of 1998.

Cumulative Effect of a Change Not Determinable

Occasionally, the cumulative effect of a change in accounting principle cannot be determined. In these cases, disclosure is limited to showing the effect of the change on the operating results of the period of change and explaining the reason for omitting the cumulative effect and disclosure of pro forma amounts.[7]

One type of change in accounting principle whose cumulative effect generally cannot be calculated is a change *to* the LIFO method of inventory. Companies often change to LIFO in periods of inflation to obtain a better matching of current cost and current revenue and reduce income taxes. Under LIFO, as was pointed out in Chapter 10, "layers" are added as the physical inventory increases over time. If a company is changing to LIFO, however, it is unlikely to have the information

---

[7]*APB Opinion No. 20*, para. 26.

EXHIBIT 19-5	**Retroactive Disclosure of a Change in Accounting Principle**

Crane Company
Comparative Income Statements, 1996–1998

	1998	1997	1996
Construction revenue	$500,000	$510,000	$445,000
Cost of construction revenue	(420,000)	(400,000)	(355,000)
Income before taxes	$ 80,000	$110,000	$ 90,000
Income tax expense	(24,000)	(33,000)	(27,000)
Net income	$ 56,000	$ 77,000	$ 63,000

Comparative Statements of Retained Earnings*

	1998	1997	1996
Retained earnings, beginning (as previously reported)	$ 907,000	$ 867,000	$828,000
Cumulative effect of change in accounting principle, applied retroactively (Note A)	108,500	101,500	105,000
Balance, as adjusted	$1,015,500	$ 968,500	$933,000
Net income	56,000	77,000	63,000
Dividends (assumed)	(22,000)	(30,000)	(27,500)
Retained earnings, ending	$1,049,500	$1,015,500	$968,500

Note A

In 1998, the company changed to the percentage-of-completion method to account for long-term construction contracts. The completed-contract method was used in previous years. The change was made because management determined that estimates of construction costs could be made with a high degree of reliability. The new method therefore provides more useful information to users. The completed-contract method is continued for tax purposes. The effect of the accounting change on 1998 net income was an increase of $5,600 after related taxes, and net income for 1995, 1996, and 1997 (as previously reported) increased (decreased) by $21,000, ($3,500), and $7,000, respectively, net of related taxes. The retained earnings balances (as previously reported) have been adjusted for retroactive application of the change in accounting principle.

*An alternative presentation is as follows:

	1998	1997	1996
Retained earnings, beginning	$1,015,500	$ 968,500	$828,000
Prior period adjustment to apply change in accounting principle retroactively (see analysis for years prior to 1996) (Note A)			105,000
Net income	56,000	77,000	63,000
Dividends (assumed).	(22,000)	(30,000)	(27,500)
Retained earnings, ending	$1,049,500	$1,015,500	$968,500

needed to calculate the LIFO layers that would have existed had LIFO been used in prior periods. Therefore, the beginning inventory for the period in which the change is made is designated as the initial LIFO layer, or base inventory. No cumulative effect is calculated, and no adjusting entry is required.[8]

---

[8]As we saw in Chapter 10, an entry may be required to adjust the beginning inventory to cost if it is carried at the lower of cost or market.

Accounting for Changes in Accounting Estimates

As we have seen, estimates are an inherent part of the accounting process. Even though estimates may be made in good faith and based on all known facts and circumstances at the time, subsequent experience may indicate a need to revise them. (Estimates that are not made in good faith represent errors, which are discussed later in this chapter.)

Changes in accounting estimates must be accounted for prospectively. If the change affects the current period only, the effect of a change in estimate is accounted for and reported in the current period. If a change in estimate affects both current and future periods, it is accounted for and reported in those periods.

To illustrate the prospective application of a change in estimate, assume that Zero Corporation uses the allowance method of accounting for uncollectible accounts. Zero calculates its periodic uncollectible accounts expense by aging its accounts receivable. In 1998, after a review of its collection experience, Zero revised the estimates used in its aging procedure, which resulted in the recording of $3,000 in uncollectible accounts expense for 1998. This amount was $1,500 lower than uncollectible accounts expense would have been had the estimate not been revised.

The entry to record the 1998 uncollectible accounts expense would be as follows:

> **6** Prepare the journal entry to record a change in accounting estimate and describe the disclosure requirements for the change.

Uncollectible accounts expense.	3,000	
Allowance for doubtful accounts		3,000

The effect of the change in estimate on 1998 income would be disclosed in a footnote, as follows:

NOTE X

In 1998 the company revised its estimate of uncollectible accounts. The revised estimates provide a better measure of the net realizable value of accounts receivable. The effect of the change in estimate was to increase 1998 net income by $1,500.

Or take another illustration. Assume that W. Nelson, Inc., acquired plant assets at the beginning of 1994 at a cost of $100,000. The assets were expected to have a useful life of 10 years with no salvage value, and straight-line depreciation was used. The book value of the assets at the beginning of 1998 was therefore $60,000:

Original cost	**$100,000**
Accumulated depreciation ($10,000 × 4)	**(40,000)**
Book value	**$ 60,000**

During 1998 the estimated remaining useful life of the assets was revised downward to 4 years. Since a change in estimate is applied prospectively, depreciation for 1998 would be based on the new estimate. Thus, the net book value at the beginning of 1998 would be depreciated over the revised remaining useful life of 4 years. The depreciation expense for 1998 and subsequent years therefore would be $15,000, calculated as follows:

$$\frac{\text{Book value at beginning of 1998 (\$60,000)}}{\text{Remaining life based on new estimate (4 years)}} = \$15,000$$

The entry to record 1998 depreciation expense would be as follows:

Depreciation expense	15,000	
Accumulated depreciation		15,000

Disclosure would be limited to showing the effect of the change on 1998 income. The change would decrease income by $5,000 ($15,000 – $10,000).

Notice that in this example, the change in estimate affected both current and future periods (1998 and subsequent years). In the uncollectible accounts example, the change in estimate affected only the current period.

Ⓢ UMMARY AND EVALUATION OF ACCOUNTING CHANGES

The intent of *APB Opinion No. 20* was to increase the usefulness of financial information by increasing comparability in the manner in which accounting changes are recorded and reported. A brief summary of the accounting requirements of *APB Opinion No. 20* appears in Exhibit 19–6.

As was stated at the beginning of the chapter, arguments can be made for each of the various methods of reporting an accounting change. For example, many accountants believe that retroactive application is preferable for all accounting changes because it increases the comparability of financial statements. Others agree with this argument but are concerned about the effect of retroactive application on the credibility and reliability of financial statements. As a result, they prefer prospective application. Notice the trade-offs that must be made among the qualitative characteristics discussed in Chapter 2.

Some accountants believe that almost *all* changes in accounting principle are necessitated by changes in estimates. According to this view, there is no such thing as a change in accounting principle that is not tied directly to a change in estimate. Presumably a company should not change from, say, the completed-contract to the percentage-of-completion method unless construction costs estimates have become more accurate. Is that not a change in principle necessitated by a change in estimate? Presumably a company should not change its depreciation method unless the *estimated* pattern of future benefits to be received from an asset has changed. Is that not a change in principle necessitated by a change in estimate?

EXHIBIT 19–6	Summary of Accounting and Reporting Requirements for Accounting Changes	
Type of Accounting Change	**Basic Accounting Requirement**	**Other Disclosure Requirements**
Change in accounting principle:		
Generally	Cumulative effect included in current period income statement; comparative statements not restated	Effects of change on current period income disclosed; also, on a pro forma basis, cumulative effect applied retroactively to income and per share data
Exceptions:		
Some changes in accounting principle	Cumulative effect applied retroactively by restating prior period statements presented for comparative purposes	Effects of change on current period income disclosed
Cumulative effect not determinable	No cumulative effect calculated	Effects of change on current period income disclosed
Change in accounting estimate	Applied prospectively in current period or in current and future periods	Effects of change on current period income disclosed

Finally, we saw that the transition rules for many of the *FASB Statements* require retroactive application of the *Statements'* provisions. As a result, critics claim that current accounting practice is inconsistent in the manner of accounting and reporting for changes in accounting principle. The current period approach is used for some changes, and the retroactive approach for many others.

As was pointed out in Chapters 1 and 2, accounting standard setting cannot be perfect and free of criticism. Individual preferences differ, choices are necessary, and compromises are made. Any pronouncement will invariably please some constituents and displease others. While certain aspects of *Opinion No. 20* are subject to criticism, on balance it appears to have improved financial reporting without undue economic consequences.

ERROR CORRECTION AND ANALYSIS

Occasionally, a company will make an **error** in recording a transaction. For example, a company may purchase a long-lived asset, such as a machine, and improperly record the acquisition as an expense. In such a situation, the accountant must be able to assess the error's impact on the financial statements, correct the error in the accounts, and disclose the correction in the final statements.

A listing of all the possible accounting errors that could be made is almost impossible. However, errors generally arise as a result of one or more of the following conditions:

1. Mathematical mistakes in the calculation of quantities and amounts of inventory, depreciation, salary expense, and other items.

2. Use of an incorrect accounting principle in a given economic circumstance (e.g., use of the installment method of revenue recognition when estimates of uncollectible receivables can be made).

3. Oversight or misuse of available facts (e.g., recording an expenditure as an asset when no future benefits exist).

4. Incorrect classification in the income statement or balance sheet, intentionally or through oversight.

Correction and Disclosure of Errors

As soon as an error is discovered, it should be corrected.[9] An error may be discovered in the same accounting period in which it was made. If so, the incorrect entry should be reversed and the correct entry made. When an error is discovered *after* the period in which it was made, it should be corrected *as of the beginning of the period* in which the discovery is made. Prior period statements presented for comparative purposes should then be restated to correct for the error.

1 Prepare correcting entries for errors and explain how error corrections are reported.

Four Basic Steps in Error Correction

Because of the many types of errors that can be made, it is difficult to formulate any specific rules or procedures that always can be relied on to correct errors. However, four steps are helpful:

1. Determine the entry that *was made* or *omitted* and that gave rise to the error.

2. Determine the entry that *should have been made*.

3. Determine the effect of the error on the current and previous (if applicable) financial statements.

---

[9]All errors discussed in this text are assumed to be material. In practice, auditors often do not insist on correction of immaterial errors.

4. Determine the entry, if any, that is necessary to correct the error and determine how the prior period statements should be restated, if necessary.

To illustrate the application of these steps, assume that on January 2, 1994, Edd Corporation purchased a machine at a cost of $100,000. The machine had an expected life of 10 years, with no salvage value, and was to be depreciated on a straight-line basis. When the bookkeeper recorded the purchase, however, he erred by expensing the entire cost of the machine. The error also occurred on Edd's tax return. Assume that the error was discovered during the audit for the year ending December 31, 1998. Edd Corporation issues three-year comparative financial statements. Its 1998 income statement and statement of retained earnings, along with the 1997 and 1996 statements, appear below (before correction for the error). Edd's tax rate is 40 percent.

Income Statements for the Years Ended 12/31

	1998	1997	1996
Revenues	$200,000	$180,000	$150,000
Expenses, including depreciation	(120,000)	(100,000)	(90,000)
Income tax expense.........................	(32,000)	(32,000)	(24,000)
Net income...............................	$ 48,000	$ 48,000	$ 36,000

Statements of Retained Earnings for the Years Ended 12/31

	1998	1997	1996
Retained earnings, 1/1	$300,000	$274,000	$250,000
Net income................................	48,000	48,000	36,000
Dividends	(24,000)	(22,000)	(12,000)
Retained earnings, 12/31	$324,000	$300,000	$274,000

Applying the first two steps on page 1038, the entry that *was made in error* to record the equipment purchase on January 2, 1994, was:

Other expenses	100,000	
Cash		100,000

The entry that *should have been made* is:

Machinery................................	100,000	
Cash		100,000

In addition, the entry for each year's depreciation expense *should have been:*

Depreciation expense........................	10,000	
Accumulated depreciation, machinery		10,000

The third step is to determine the effect of the error on the current year's and previous years' financial statements. Exhibit 19–7 shows the financial statement effects of the error for the years 1994–1998. In 1994, the company recorded other expenses of $100,000 instead of depreciation expense of $10,000. Therefore, both 1994 income before taxes and taxable income are understated by $90,000 ($100,000 – $10,000). Income tax expense is understated by $36,000 (.4 × $90,000), and net income is understated by $54,000 ($90,000 – $36,000). On the balance sheet at the end of 1994, machinery, net of accumulated depreciation, is understated by $90,000 ($100,000 original cost less $10,000 accumulated depreciation), and income taxes payable is understated by $36,000.[10] Retained earnings is understated

---

[10] In practice, an error made on a tax return may give rise to a tax deficiency penalty, plus interest, if the error increases the taxpayer's income tax liability (as in this example). For simplicity, this deficiency is ignored.

EXHIBIT 19-7 Effects of an Error on the Financial Statements

Edd Corporation
Income Statements for the Years Ended 12/31

	1998	1997	1996	1995	1994
Depreciation expense	$10,000 *U*	$10,000 *U*	$10,000 *U*	$10,000 *U*	$ 10,000 *U*
Other expenses.	—	—	—	—	100,000 *O*
Income tax expense	4,000 *O*	4,000 *O*	4,000 *O*	4,000 *O*	36,000 *U*
Net income	6,000 *O*	6,000 *O*	6,000 *O*	6,000 *O*	54,000 *U*

Balance Sheets, 12/31

	1998	1997	1996	1995	1994
Assets:					
Machinery (net of					
accumulated					
depreciation)	$50,000 *U*	$60,000 *U*	$70,000 *U*	$80,000 *U*	$90,000 *U*
Liabilities:					
Income taxes payable.	20,000 *U*	24,000 *U*	28,000 *U*	32,000 *U*	36,000 *U*
Owners' equity:					
Retained earnings	30,000 *U*	36,000 *U*	42,000 *U*	48,000 *U*	54,000 *U*

Note: U = understated; *O* = overstated.

by $54,000 because of the $54,000 understatement of 1994 net income which was closed to retained earnings.

On the income statement for 1995, depreciation expense is understated by $10,000. Tax expense is overstated by $4,000 ($10,000 × .4), and net income is overstated by $6,000 (the $10,000 understatement of depreciation expense less $4,000 overstatement of tax expense). On the balance sheet at the end of 1995, the machinery is now understated by $80,000 (its $100,000 cost minus *two* years' depreciation of $10,000 per year). Income taxes payable is understated by $32,000, since the previous year's understatement of $36,000 is reduced by the 1995 overstatement of taxes of $4,000. Retained earnings is understated by $48,000, the cumulative effect of the error as of the end of 1995. (The beginning 1995 retained earnings is *understated* by $54,000, and 1995 net income is *overstated* by $6,000.) The effects of the error on the 1996, 1997, and 1998 financial statements can be analyzed in a similar manner.

The last step is to correct the error. If the error was discovered before the books were closed for 1998, it would be corrected *as of the beginning of 1998:*

Machinery.	100,000	
Accumulated depreciation, machinery		40,000
Income taxes payable		24,000
Retained earnings		36,000
To correct the error as of 1/1/98.		
Depreciation expense	10,000	
Accumulated depreciation, machinery		10,000
To record depreciation for 1998.		
Income taxes payable.	4,000	
Income tax expense		4,000
To reduce income taxes payable and 1998 income tax		
expense as a result of the $10,000 additional		
1998 depreciation expense.		

In the first entry above, a temporary account, *prior period adjustment—error correction,* could be credited instead of retained earnings. This temporary account would then be closed to retained earnings at the end of the accounting period. And instead of three separate entries, one compound correcting entry could have been made. The corrections and adjustments, when posted to the appropriate accounts, will bring the accounts up to date at the end of 1998.

Exhibit 19–8 shows Edd Corporation's comparative income statements, statements of retained earnings, and partial balance sheet increases restated to show the effects of the error correction. On the restated income statements, net income is $6,000 lower each year as a result of the $10,000 depreciation expense, less the $4,000 reduction in tax expense. On the retained earnings statements, the $48,000

EXHIBIT 19–8	Comparative Financial Statements Restated for Error Correction

Edd Corporation
Income Statements for the Years Ended 12/31

	1998	1997	1996
Revenues.	$200,000	$180,000	$150,000
Expenses, including depreciation . . .	(130,000)	(110,000)	(100,000)
Income tax expense	(28,000)	(28,000)	(20,000)
Net income	$ 42,000	$ 42,000	$ 30,000

Statements of Retained Earnings for the Years Ended 12/31[a]

	1998	1997	1996
Retained earnings, 1/1, as previously reported	$300,000	$274,000	$250,000
Prior period adjustment— cumulative effect of error	36,000	42,000	48,000
Retained earnings, 1/1, as corrected	$336,000	$316,000	$298,000
Net income	42,000	42,000	30,000
Dividends	(24,000)	(22,000)	(12,000)
Retained earnings, 12/31	$354,000	$336,000	$316,000

Partial Balance Sheet Increases, 12/31

	1998	1997	1996
Assets:			
Machinery, net of accumulated depreciation	$50,000	$60,000	$70,000
Liabilities:			
Income taxes payable.	20,000	24,000	28,000
Owners' equity:			
Retained earnings	30,000	36,000	42,000

[a]Alternatively, the statements of retained earnings could be presented as follows:			
	1998	1997	1996
Retained earnings, 1/1.	$336,000	$316,000	$250,000
Prior period adjustment to beginning retained earnings for correction of error (net of tax)			48,000
Net income	42,000	42,000	30,000
Dividends	(24,000)	(22,000)	(12,000)
Retained earnings, 12/31.	$354,000	$336,000	$316,000

increase in retained earnings as of January 1, 1996, is the cumulative effect of the error as of that date:

Error (overstatement of expense) when machine was purchased	**$100,000**
Understatement of 1994 depreciation	**(10,000)**
Error at 12/31/94, before tax	**$ 90,000**
Error at 12/31/94, net of tax [$90,000 − .4($90,000)]	**$ 54,000**
Overstatement of 1995 net income	**(6,000)**
Cumulative error at 12/31/95 (1/1/96)	**$ 48,000**

Finally, the correcting entry to retained earnings on page 1039 can be reconciled to the comparative retained earnings statements as follows:

Cumulative error as of 12/31/95	**$48,000**
Overstatement of 1996 income	**(6,000)**
Overstatement of 1997 income	**(6,000)**
Correction of retained earnings required as of 1/1/98	**$36,000**

Tax Effects of Errors

One final point should be made about the tax effect of errors. We have assumed that Edd Corporation's error was made for both book and tax purposes and thus resulted in an additional tax liability. If an error results in an overstatement of taxable income, a tax refund can be claimed. Occasionally a company may make an error in its books but not on its tax return. In that case, there is no effect on its tax liability or claim. The difference between pretax financial income and taxable income that results from this type of error results from one of the following occurrences:

1. In error, the company considered the difference to be a temporary difference, which affected a deferred tax account. In that case, correction of the error involves correction of a deferred tax account.

2. In error, the company ignored the difference and reported as income tax expense the amount due on the tax return. In that case, correction of the error is limited to correction of the affected real and nominal accounts, excluding any current or deferred tax accounts.

Disclosure of Error Correction

Companies usually include a description of any error corrections in their financial statement notes. The following description appeared in the notes to financial statements in Marietta Corporation's annual report:

2. Prior Period Adjustments

During fiscal 1991 the Company discovered an embezzlement of approximately $400,000 by a former financial officer and other irregularities in its financial statements. As a result of these irregularities, the Company directed its auditors and Company counsel to conduct an investigation and a special committee of independent directors was appointed to oversee the inquiry. As a result of the investigation, the financial statements for the fiscal years 1987 through 1990 were restated to reflect adjustments identified during the investigation. The restatements of the financial statements principally involved adjustments to property, plant and equipment, sales, cost of sales, other expenses, income and retained earnings. The adjustments were treated as corrections of errors and the financial statements for the respective periods were restated.

As part of the Company's detailed review of its assets for fiscal 1992, it has been determined that property, plant, and equipment and net income, as restated, were overstated by $218,167 for the fiscal year ended September 30, 1989. The Company has further restated its financial statements for fiscal 1989 to correct for this overstatement. In addition, it has further restated its 1990 balance sheet and statement of shareholders' equity and has restated its 1991 balance sheet and statement of shareholders' equity to adjust property, plant, and equipment and retained earnings for this item.

Analysis of Errors

In the previous section, we discussed and illustrated how errors are corrected and disclosed in financial statements. Error analysis, the subject of this section, is an extension of the previous section. In this section, we will discuss classification errors that do not affect net income. We will also discuss how errors that affect both the income statement and balance sheet may or may not correct themselves over time. These errors are classified as counterbalancing and noncounterbalancing errors. The use of a worksheet to facilitate error analysis is covered in Appendix 19–1.

Classification Errors That Do Not Affect Income

8 Distinguish among a classification error that does not affect income, a counterbalancing error, and a noncounterbalancing error.

Occasionally, a company will make a **classification error** in its balance sheet or income statement, but the error will have no effect on net income. For example, a company may issue common stock at a price in excess of par and credit the excess to common stock instead of contributed capital in excess of par. This classification error affects only the balance sheet (stockholders' equity); it has no effect on income. When errors of this kind are discovered, they should be corrected. Prior period statements issued for comparative purposes should also be restated to show the proper classification. To give another example, if a company's accounting system is computerized, salary expense may be recorded as cost of goods sold as the result of an error in coding. Again, though a classification error exists in the income statement, net income is not affected. If the error is discovered in a subsequent period, no correcting entry can be made, since these nominal accounts already have been closed. If comparative statements are presented, however, the income statement data (here, cost of goods sold and salary expense) for the period in which the error was made should be corrected to show the proper classification.

Errors That Affect Both Income Statement and Balance Sheet

While classification errors can be misleading to users, far more serious are errors that affect net income. For net income to be misstated, an error must affect *both* the income statement and the balance sheet. Accountants sometimes categorize these errors as *counterbalancing* and *noncounterbalancing* errors.

Counterbalancing Errors

9 Analyze the effects of counterbalancing errors on the financial statements and prepare any necessary correcting entries.

Counterbalancing errors are those that are automatically corrected through the recording process over a two-year period. In one year, net income and a corresponding asset or liability may be overstated or understated; but in the following year, net income and the corresponding asset or liability are misstated in the opposite direction. Thus, for the two years together, there is no cumulative effect on net income, assets, or liabilities.

Counterbalancing errors usually involve the following types of current asset and current liability accounts:

1. Inventories. Inventory errors usually result from errors either in the physical count of inventories or the recording of purchases. Inventory errors were discussed in Chapter 9 on pages 483–485. You should review these pages at this point.

2. Prepayments—prepaid expenses and unearned revenues. Errors involving these items usually result from recording cash expenditures/cash receipts as expenses/revenues instead of assets/liabilities or from failure to make proper adjusting entries involving prepaid expenses and unearned revenues.

3. Accruals—accrued expenses and accrued revenues. Errors involving these items usually result from failure to make adjusting entries for accrued expenses and accrued revenues.

Whether a correcting entry is required when one of these types of errors is discovered depends on when the error is discovered, as the examples that follow demonstrate.

Errors Involving Prepayments Prepayments involve transactions in which the cash flows precede the earnings activities; that is, a cash inflow or outflow precedes the earning of revenue or the incurring of an expense. Since a company's internal control system normally is effective in controlling cash receipts and disbursements, errors involving prepayments usually do not affect the cash account. Rather, these types of errors result from failure to allocate the prepaid expense or unearned revenue to the correct period.

To illustrate an error involving a prepayment, assume that on January 1, 1997, Tandy Company purchased a two-year insurance policy on its building and paid the two $900 annual premiums in advance. The company expensed the entire $1,800 in 1997. This error caused the following amounts of overstatement and understatement on Tandy's financial statements for 1997 and 1998:

Income Statements for the Years Ended 12/31

	1998	1997
Insurance expense	$900 *U*	$900 *O*
Net income	900 *O*	900 *U*

Balance Sheets, 12/31

	1998	1997
Assets (prepaid insurance)	*N*	$900 *U*
– Liabilities	*N*	*N*
= Owners' equity	*N*	900 *U*

How should this error be corrected? If the books for 1998 have *not* been closed, the correcting entry is:

| Insurance expense | 900 | |
| Retained earnings (beginning) | | 900 |

If the books for 1998 have been closed, no correcting entry is made. Correction of the financial statements depends on whether single-year or comparative statements are presented. If only the 1998 statements are presented, beginning retained earnings must be increased by $900; insurance expense (after the correction) is then stated properly. If 1997 and 1998 comparative statements are presented, insurance expense and net income must be decreased and increased, respectively, by $900 on the 1997 income statement. On the ending 1997 balance sheet, prepaid insurance and retained earnings must be increased by $900. The 1998 financial data will be correct after the correcting entry is made.

Errors Involving Accruals   Accruals involve transactions in which the earnings activities precede the cash flows. Accrued revenues arise when revenues have been earned but cash has not yet been collected. Revenue accruals increase assets on the balance sheet and revenue on the income statement. Accrued expenses arise when an expense has been incurred but has not yet been paid. Expense accruals increase expenses on the income statement and liabilities on the balance sheet. Errors involving accruals probably constitute one of the most frequent types of errors, because the accrual transactions, which in error are not recorded, occur before the related cash inflow or outflow. The error counterbalances when the cash is received or paid.

To illustrate an error involving an accrual, assume that Trene Company failed to record accrued interest revenue of $1,800 on a note receivable at the end of 1997. The company recorded the interest as revenue in 1998, when the cash was received. Analysis of the effects of this error on Trene's financial statements would reveal the following:

Income Statements for the Years Ended 12/31

	1998	1997
Interest revenue..........................	$1,800 *O*	$1,800 *U*
Net income...............................	1,800 *O*	1,800 *U*

Balance Sheets, 12/31

	1998	1997
Assets (interest receivable)............	*N*	$1,800 *U*
− Liabilities...........................	*N*	*N*
= Owners' equity	*N*	1,800 *U*

If the books for 1998 have *not* been closed, the correcting entry should be:

Interest revenue	1,800	
Retained earnings (beginning)		1,800

If the books for 1998 have been closed, no correcting entry is required. If 1998 statements are issued, beginning retained earnings are increased by $1,800, and interest revenue is not included on the income statement for 1998. Other 1998 financial data will be correct after the correction.

If 1997 and 1998 comparative statements are issued, interest revenue and net income are increased $1,800 on the 1997 income statement. On the ending 1997 balance sheet, interest receivable and retained earnings are increased $1,800. The 1998 financial data will be correct after the correcting entry.

This illustration dealt with an error involving accrued revenues. A similar analysis would be made for an error involving accrued expenses.

Noncounterbalancing Errors

Though counterbalancing errors automatically correct themselves over a two-year period, **noncounterbalancing errors** do not. Noncounterbalancing errors usually require several periods to self-correct. Generally, errors involving long-lived assets and long-term liabilities are noncounterbalancing. The case of Edd Corporation on pages 1038–1041 provides a good example of a noncounterbalancing error. In that example, the cost of a new machine was mistakenly expensed when the machine was purchased. The net income understatement of $54,000 in 1994 (see Exhibit 19–7) was gradually offset (counterbalanced) by the net income overstatements of $6,000 in subsequent years as the machine was used over its useful life. By the end of 2003, when the machine's service potential had expired, the original error of $54,000 was completely counterbalanced.

Worksheet Analysis of Errors

Many companies find that a worksheet facilitates error analysis and correction. The preparation of a worksheet is presented and discussed in Appendix 19–1.

SUMMARY OF LEARNING OBJECTIVES

1. **Distinguish among a change in accounting principle, a change in accounting estimate, and a change in the reporting entity.**

   A change in accounting *principle* occurs when a company adopts a generally accepted accounting principle that is different from the generally accepted accounting principle previously used. A change in accounting *estimate* occurs when a company revises or changes a previously used estimate as a part of applying an accounting principle or procedure. A change in reporting *entity* occurs when financial statements are prepared for a new accounting entity.

2. **Calculate the cumulative effect of a change in accounting principle and prepare the journal entry to record the change under the current period approach.**

   The cumulative effect of a change in accounting principle is the difference between the present carrying value of an asset or liability and the amount the carrying value would have been if the new accounting principle had been in effect in all previous periods of the asset's or liability's existence. The cumulative effect is calculated net of applicable taxes and is reported in the current period income statement.

3. **Calculate the cumulative effect of a change in accounting principle and prepare the journal entry to record the change under the retroactive approach.**

   For those changes in accounting principle that are applied retroactively, the cumulative effect is calculated net of applicable taxes and is recorded as an adjustment to beginning-of-period retained earnings.

4. **Explain how to report the effects of a change in accounting principle under the current period approach.**

   Under the current period approach, the cumulative effect of a change in accounting principle is reported in the income statement for the period of change. Prior period financial statements presented for comparative purposes are not restated. Instead, the cumulative effect is applied retroactively on a pro forma (as if) basis. The new accounting principle is used in the financial statements for the current period.

5. **Explain how to report the effects of a change in accounting principle under the retroactive approach.**

   Under the retroactive approach, the cumulative effect is reported in retained earnings. Prior period financial statements are restated to reflect the effects of the change. The new accounting principle is used in the financial statements for the current period.

6. **Prepare the journal entry to record a change in accounting estimate and describe the disclosure requirements for the change.**

   Changes in accounting estimate are accounted for prospectively. That is, the effects are reported in the current period and future periods, if applicable. The effect of the change on current period income must be disclosed.

7. **Prepare correcting entries for errors and explain how error corrections are reported.**

   When an error is discovered in a given period, all current period accounts affected by the error must be corrected. If the error affects prior period statements, those statements must be restated to correct for the error.

8. **Distinguish among a classification error that does not affect income, a counterbalancing error, and a noncounterbalancing error.**

   Some errors, such as recording salary expense as supplies expense, are classification errors that do not affect net income. A counterbalancing error is one that is automatically corrected through the recording process over a two-year period. Noncounterbalancing errors require several periods to self-correct.

9. Analyze the effects of counterbalancing errors on the financial statements and prepare any necessary correcting entries.

A schedule usually assists in the analysis of counterbalancing errors. The schedule shows the accounts affected by the error with the error's effect—an overstatement, understatement, or no effect. If the books have been closed, the correcting entry may affect the end-of-period balance sheet accounts only; or no entry may be required because the error has been counterbalanced and the affected accounts closed. If the books have *not* been closed, the correcting entry will affect both an income statement account and a balance sheet account.

KEY TERMS

accounting changes 1022

catch-up approach 1028

change in accounting estimate 1026

change in accounting principle 1026

change in reporting entity 1027

classification error 1042

counterbalancing errors 1042

current period approach 1027

error 1037

noncounterbalancing errors 1044

prospective approach 1028

retroactive approach 1028

transition rules 1032

APPENDIX 19-1

Worksheet Analysis of Errors

Use of a worksheet facilitates the analysis of errors. While a company is unlikely to make as many errors as we assume in the following illustration, the worksheet we will prepare is helpful for both analytical and instructional purposes. The illustration also provides a good summary of error correction and analysis.

Identification of Errors

Assume that Dandy Don Corporation reported the following amounts of net income for the years ended December 31, 1996, 1997, and 1998:

1996	$127,000
1997	110,000
1998	98,500

You are performing the audit for the year ended December 31, 1998. During your examination you discover the following errors:

1. As a result of errors in the physical count, ending inventories were misstated as follows:

12/31/97	$14,000 overstated
12/31/98	22,000 understated

2. On December 29, 1998, Dandy Don recorded as a purchase, merchandise in transit that cost $10,000. The merchandise was shipped f.o.b. destination and had not arrived by December 31. It was not included in the ending inventory.

3. Dandy Don records sales on the accrual basis, but failed to record sales on account made near the end of year as follows:

1996	$3,500
1997	5,500
1998	2,000

Instead, the sales were recorded in each of the following years, when the cash was received.

4. On December 30, 1996, Dandy Don purchased the net assets of Jamey Company, paying $40,000 in excess of the fair value of Jamey's identifiable assets. The excess, which should have been recorded as goodwill and amortized over a 10-year period, was instead expensed on December 30, 1996. Assume that goodwill amortization is not tax deductible.

5. The company failed to record accrued office salaries, as follows:

12/31/96	$10,000
12/31/97	12,000

6. On March 1, 1997, a small stock dividend was declared and distributed. The par value of the shares distributed was $10,000; their fair value was $13,000. The stock dividend was recorded as follows:

Miscellaneous expense	13,000	
Common stock		10,000
Retained earnings		3,000

7. Dandy Don rented an office building to a CPA firm. The company recorded rent revenue when the cash was received, and failed to record unearned rent at the end of each year, as follows (for tax purposes, rent is taxable when cash is received):

12/31/96	$15,000
12/31/97	12,000

8. On July 1, 1997, Dandy Don acquired a three-year insurance policy. The three-year premium of $4,800 was paid on that date, and the entire premium recorded as insurance expense.

9. On December 30, 1997, Dandy Don sold a tract of land with a carrying value of $10,000 for $18,000. The sale was recorded as follows:

Cash	18,000	
Land		18,000

10. Unless otherwise indicated, all errors made for financial reporting purposes were also made on each year's tax return. The tax rate each year was 30 percent.

Worksheet Analysis of Errors

A worksheet to correct these errors appears in Exhibit 19–9. Each item in the worksheet is explained below. The tax effect of all errors is considered in item 10 of Exhibit 19–9.

1. *Errors in the physical count of inventories.* Since the ending 1997 inventory was overstated by $14,000, net income for 1997 was also overstated by $14,000 because of the $14,000 understatement in cost of goods sold. The overstatement of 1997 net income is counterbalanced, however, by an understatement of 1998 income. The

EXHIBIT 19–9 **Worksheet Analysis of Errors**

	Net Income			Correcting Entry, 12/31/98		
	1996	1997	1998			
1. Error in physical count of ending inventories:						
End of 1997, overstated		(14,000)	14,000	Retained earnings	14,000	
End of 1998, understated			22,000	Inventory . . . . Cost of goods sold	22,000	36,000
2. Error on in-transit merchandise shipment.			10,000	Accounts payable . . . . . . Cost of goods sold	10,000	10,000
3. Error on unrecorded sales:						
End of 1996	3,500	(3,500)		Sales ($5,500 – $2,000) . .	3,500	
End of 1997		5,500	(5,500)	Accounts receivable	2,000	
End of 1998			2,000	Retained earnings		5,500
4. Error in recording goodwill	40,000	(4,000)	(4,000)	Goodwill . . . . Goodwill amortization . . . Retained earnings	32,000 4,000	36,000
5. Error in recording accrued salaries:						
1996	(10,000)	10,000		Retained earnings	12,000	
1997		(12,000)	12,000	Salary expense		12,000
6. Error in recording stock dividend		13,000		Retained earnings . . . . . . Contributed capital in excess of par	3,000	3,000
7. Error in recording unearned rent:						
End of 1996	(15,000)	15,000		Retained earnings	12,000	
End of 1997		(12,000)	12,000	Rent revenue		12,000
8. Error in recording prepaid insurance:						
End of 1997		4,000		Insurance expense	1,600	
End of 1998			(1,600)	Prepaid insurance . . . . . . Retained earnings	2,400	4,000

counterbalancing error comes about because the beginning 1998 inventory overstatement of $14,000 caused 1998 cost of goods sold to be overstated by $14,000. The ending inventory for 1998 was understated by $22,000, which caused cost of goods sold for 1998 to be overstated and net income to be understated by $22,000.

The correcting entry for the two inventory errors appears to the right in Exhibit 19–9. Beginning retained earnings is debited for $14,000 to correct the overstatement of 1997 net income. Ending inventory for 1998 is debited for $22,000, since assets are understated. Together, the two errors cause 1998 cost of goods sold to be overstated by $36,000. Therefore, cost of goods sold is credited for $36,000, which reduces cost of goods sold and increases 1995 income by $36,000, as shown in the 1998 net income column.

2. *Error in the recording of a merchandise shipment.* Since the company recorded the purchase and liability in error, cost of goods sold was overstated and net income

	Net Income			**Correcting Entry, 12/31/98**	
	1996	**1997**	**1998**		
9. Error on sale of land					
1997		8,000		Land 8,000	
				Retained earnings	8,000
10. Tax effect (see				Retained earnings	
below)	(5,550)	(4,200)	(19,470)	($5,550 + $4,200) 9,750	
Adjustment				Income tax expense 19,470	
to net income				Income taxes payable	
(after taxes)	12,950	5,800	41,430	(see below)	29,220
Net income as					
previously					
reported	127,000	110,000	98,500		
Net income					
(corrected)	139,950	115,800	139,930		

Tax Effect of Errors

	1996	**1997**	**1998**
Effect of errors, before taxes (summation of errors 1 through 9)	$18,500	$10,000	$60,900
Goodwill amortization error (no future tax consequences)		4,000	4,000
Increase in pretax financial income	$18,500	$14,000	$64,900
Additional income tax expense:			
1996 $18,500 × .3 = $ 5,550			
1997 $14,000 × .3 = 4,200			
1998 $64,900 × .3 = 19,470			
Temporary differences on unearned rent	15,000	(15,000)	
		12,000	(12,000)
Increase in taxable income	$35,500	$11,000	$52,900
Additional taxes payable:			
1996 $33,500 × .3 = $10,050			
1997 $11,000 × .3 = 3,300			
1998 $52,900 × .3 = 15,870			
	$29,220		

understated by $10,000. Thus, the entry in the right-hand column of Exhibit 19–9 corrects the error, and 1998 net income is increased by $10,000. The ending inventory is not affected, since the company correctly excluded the shipment in transit from the ending inventory.

3. *Failure to record sales.* The sales that were made near the end of 1996, 1997, and 1998 but were not recorded until the year immediately following. As a result, failure to record the sales of $3,500 made in 1996 until 1997 caused 1996 net income to be understated by $3,500 and 1997 net income to be overstated by $3,500.

The entry to correct the accounts at the end of 1998 is shown in the right-hand column of Exhibit 19–9. The debit of $3,500 to sales is the difference between the $5,500 overstatement of sales made in 1997 but recorded in 1998 and the $2,000 understatement of sales for 1998. Accounts receivable is debited for $2,000, and beginning retained earnings is credited for

$5,500. The $5,500 credit to retained earnings corrects 1997 net income, which was understated because of failure to record 1997 sales.

4. *Error in recording goodwill.* When goodwill was purchased, it was expensed. To correct for that error, net income for 1996 is increased by $40,000, while net income for the years 1997 and 1998 is decreased by $4,000 each year—the amount of goodwill amortization for those years. The debit of $32,000 to good-will is the unamortized goodwill at the end of 1998 ($40,000 − $4,000 − $4,000). Goodwill amortization is debited for the current year's amortization, and the credit to beginning retained earnings corrects for the cumulative effect of the error as of the beginning of 1998.

5. *Error in recording accrued salaries.* This error may be analyzed in much the same way as the unrecorded sales in transaction 3. The only difference between the two is that since no error was made in salary accruals at the end of 1998, a real account, salaries payable, is not misstated at the end of 1998.

6. *Error in recording a stock dividend.* This error may be analyzed most efficiently by comparing the erroneous entry with the entry that should have been made:

Entry made in error:			*Correct entry:*		
Expense.	13,000		Retained earnings. .	13,000	
Common stock .		10,000	Common stock . .		10,000
Retained			Contributed		
earnings		3,000	capital in excess		
			of par		3,000

In the 1997 worksheet column, $13,000 is added to net income because 1997 expenses were overstated and net income understated by $13,000. Since net income is closed to retained earnings, however, the net debit to retained earnings in the error entry is $10,000 ($13,000 − $3,000). Since retained earnings should have been debited for $13,000, it was overstated by $3,000. The correcting entry reduces retained earnings by $3,000 and increases contributed capital in excess of par by $3,000.

7. *Error in recording unearned rent.* This error is similar to the sales and salaries errors in transactions 3 and 5, except that it involves a prepayment rather than an accrual. The company recorded rent revenue when cash was received and failed to make appropriate adjusting entries at the end of 1996 and 1997. The failure to adjust for unearned rent of $15,000 at the end of 1996 overstated 1996 net income by $15,000. This error, however, was counterbalanced by an understatement of rent revenue of $15,000, which was earned in 1997 instead of 1996. The $15,000 error was counterbalanced at the end of 1997, so no correcting entry is necessary in 1998.

8. *Error in recording prepaid insurance.* This error is not a counterbalancing one. It will not automatically correct itself over two consecutive years, because the premium covers a three-year period. The annual premium expense should have been $1,600 ($4,800 ÷ 3). The $4,000 addition to 1997 income on the left side of the worksheet is the amount of insurance expense that was over-stated at the end of 1997 [$4,800 − ($1,600 ÷ 2)]. Net income for 1998 must be reduced by $1,600 to compensate for the understatement of insurance expense in 1998.

The correcting entry at the end of 1998 appears in the right-hand column of Exhibit 19–9. Insurance expense is debited for $1,600. Prepaid insurance is debited for $2,400, which is the unexpired insurance at the end of 1998 (at the end of 1998, the policy had a remaining life of 1 1/2 years). The credit to beginning retained earnings corrects for the 1997 understatement of net income of $4,000.

9. *Error in recording a sale of land.* The gain should have been included in 1997 net income. The correcting entry increases land and retained earnings.

Tax Effects of Errors

The tax effects of these errors are calculated in item 10 in Exhibit 19–9. We have assumed that unless otherwise indicated, errors made for book purposes were also made for tax purposes. In calculating the tax effects of the errors, however, we must adjust the before-tax effect of errors for temporary differences between pretax financial income and taxable income. Furthermore, we have assumed that goodwill is not deductible for tax purposes. The $4,000 annual amortization that was included in transaction 4 must therefore be added back to the 1997 and 1998 income adjustments so that we can calculate the additional tax expense and tax payable applicable to the net income increases for those years. Finally, since rent is taxable when it is received, a temporary difference arises for the portion of the rent that is unearned at the end of 1996 and 1997. These temporary differences become deductible amounts in the following years, when the rent is earned.

The entry to record the tax effects of the errors is shown in the right-hand column of the worksheet. Beginning retained earnings is debited for $9,750, which is the additional tax expense arising from the increased income for 1996 and 1997. Tax expense is debited for the tax expense related to the 1998 income adjustments, and taxes payable is credited for the additional tax liability of $29,220. Finally, the net income adjustments are added to the previously reported net income amounts to arrive at the corrected net income amounts for the three years.

QUESTIONS

Q 19-1. Define a change in accounting principle, give an example of such a change, and describe the *general rule* of accounting for and disclosing changes in accounting principles.

Q 19-2. Identify the exceptions to the general rule of reporting the cumulative effect of a change in accounting principle.

Q 19-3. How do pro forma data relate to changes in accounting principle?

Q 19-4. Distinguish between a voluntary change in accounting principle and one arising from transition rules.

Q 19-5. Define a change in accounting estimate and give an example of such a change.

Q 19-6. Give some examples of a change in reporting entity.

Q 19-7. How are the following accounting changes recorded in the accounts and reported in the financial statements for the current year?

1. A change in the estimated salvage value of machinery.
2. A change in the estimated useful life of machinery.
3. A change from LIFO to FIFO for merchandise inventories.
4. A change from FIFO to LIFO for merchandise inventories.
5. A change from the cash basis to the accrual basis of accounting.
6. A change from the direct write-off method to the allowance method for uncollectible receivables.
7. A change in depreciation methods for plant and equipment.
8. A change in the estimated amount recoverable from investments.
9. A change from deferring and amortizing marketing costs to expensing these costs as incurred because of increased uncertainty regarding future benefits.
10. A change from the percentage-of-completion to the completed-contract method for long-term construction contracts.
11. A change from recognizing revenue at the point of sale to recognition prior to sale because of an improved ability to estimate the amount of revenue to be received prior to the point of sale. Assume the earnings process is deemed complete before the point of sale.

Q 19-8. Describe how an error discovered in the current period that affects previously issued financial statements should be corrected and disclosed.

Q 19-9. Why must an error that affects net income affect both the balance sheet and the income statement?

Q 19-10.   Give an example of each of the following types of errors:
  I.   An error that affects the balance sheet only.
  2.   An error that affects the income statement only.
  3.   An error that affects both the balance sheet and the income statement.

Q 19-11.   Distinguish between counterbalancing and noncounterbalancing errors and give an example of each.

Q 19-12.   "All errors sooner or later correct themselves." Discuss.

CASES

C 19-1.   **ACCOUNTING CHANGES; ERROR CORRECTIONS; ETHICAL ISSUES**   Don Wood recently completed the audit of the December 31, 1998, financial statements of Best Products, Inc. Wood disagreed with the accounting treatment of a change in depreciation methods during the year. He decided to review the facts prior to meeting with Jack Reese, the controller of Best Products.

Best Products purchased a group of machines for $360,000 on January 3, 1995. The estimated useful life of the machines was five years with no residual value. The sum-of-the-years'-digits depreciation method was used. A decision was made during 1998 to change to the straight-line method effective with the depreciation recorded for the year ended December 31, 1998.

During the audit, Don Wood discovered that a $90,000 error had been made in recording depreciation for 1995. Depreciation had been incorrectly recorded as $210,000 instead of $120,000. The effect of the error was to understate 1995 net income by $90,000. This amount was included in the accounting change entry that was recorded on December 31, 1998, as follows:

Accumulated depreciation—machinery 162,000
     Income effect of change in depreciation   162,000

Don Wood knew the entry was wrong because the error correction amount should have been recorded as an adjustment to retained earnings. He was prepared to recommend to Jack Reese an audit adjusting entry as follows:

Income effect of change in depreciation 90,000
     Retained earnings   90,000

Wood pointed out during the meeting that the $90,000 error correction qualified as a prior period item and should be accounted for as an adjustment to the January 1, 1998, retained earnings balance. Reese insisted that since the error was discovered at the same time that the accounting change entry was recorded, it was acceptable to credit the entire amount to income. Furthermore, according to Reese, revenue for the last quarter of 1998 was below budgeted levels. The $90,000 part of the income adjustment would help to offset most of the effects of the revenue decline on net income for the year. This was important in light of an anticipated stock sale by Best Products during 1999.

The meeting between Don Wood and Jack Reese ended without agreement on Wood's proposed audit adjustment. Reese pointed out that the December 31, 1998, retained earnings balance would be the same regardless of the approach followed. Under these circumstances and in view of the pending stock sale, the position of Best Products is that the accounting change entry is acceptable.

REQUIRED   What ethical and professional issues should be of concern to Don Wood in deciding on a course of action? What would you do?

C 19-2.   **ACCOUNTING CHANGES; ERROR CORRECTION**   On January 1, 1998, Jesse Garon hired you as the company's controller. During 1998, you made several accounting changes and corrections for several errors recorded during the current and previous years. Garon's financial statements for the year ending December 31, 1998, will include 1997 statements for comparative purposes. These changes and error corrections were as follows:
  a)   Because of technology changes, you determined that Garon's equipment, previously being depreciated over 20 years, should be depreciated over 14 years.
  b)   You changed Garon's inventory costing system from LIFO to FIFO.
  c)   During 1998, you discovered that an insurance premium paid and expensed in 1997 was for a three-year period ending December 31, 1999.
  d)   Garon instituted a health care plan in 1998 and adopted the provisions of *Statement No. 106*. Jessie Garon had not had a health care plan previously.

e) You changed Garon's method of recording depreciation from the straight-line method to an accelerated method.

f) Because Garon's equity ownership interest in G-land increased from 10 percent to 40 percent during 1998, you changed from the fair value method to the equity method.

g) Because of a computerized credit analysis system and increased attention paid to uncollectible accounts by the credit department, you increased Garon's allowance for doubtful accounts from 5 percent of ending accounts receivable in previous years to 2 percent of ending accounts receivable for 1998.

REQUIRED   For each item above, write a brief paragraph that describes how each item would be classified—for example, accounting change (and type of accounting change) or error correction—and then outline the general accounting and reporting requirements for each item.

C 19-3.   **ACCOUNTING CHANGES**   Pitt Manufacturing Company is preparing its year-end financial statements. The controller is confronted with several decisions about statement presentation with regard to the following items:

a) Management has decided to switch from the FIFO method to the LIFO method for all inventories.

b) Pitt's Custom Division manufactures large-scale, custom-designed machinery on a contract basis. Management decided to switch from the completed-contract method to the percentage-of-completion method of accounting for long-term contracts.

c) The vice-president of sales indicated that one product line has lost its customer appeal and will be phased out over the next three years. Therefore, a decision has been made to lower the estimated lives of related production equipment from the remaining five years to three years.

d) Estimating the lives of new products in the Leisure Products Division has become very difficult because of the highly competitive conditions in this market. Therefore, the practice of deferring and amortizing preproduction costs has been abandoned in favor of expensing such costs as they are incurred.

e) The REO Building was converted from a sales office to offices for the accounting department at the beginning of this year. Therefore, the expense related to this building will now appear as an administrative expense rather than as a selling expense on current and future years' income statements.

REQUIRED   For each of the five changes or errors Pitt Manufacturing Company has made in the current year, identify and explain whether the change is a change in accounting principle or a change in estimate. If any of the changes is not one of these, explain why.

(IMA, adapted)

C 19-4.   **METHODS OF DISCLOSING ACCOUNTING CHANGES**   You are discussing the audit and financial statements of Compare Corporation with the company's board of directors. During the course of the discussion, three board members begin to debate the merits of various approaches to accounting for and disclosure of accounting changes. (Compare Corporation changed an accounting principle during the current year.)

Board Member Mr. Lorne: "I don't understand why all accounting changes shouldn't be accounted for on a prospective basis. What's past is past!"

Board Member Mr. Green: "It seems to me that accounting changes should be made retroactively. Just because a previous year's statements have already been issued doesn't mean we shouldn't clean up spilled milk!"

Board Member Ms. Cartright: "You're both wrong. Why mess up previous and future years' statements because of an accounting change? Changes are made all the time. Report the effect of the change in the period in which it's made!"

REQUIRED   **1.** Write a short paper listing the positive and negative features of the following approaches to the reporting of accounting changes:

a) Prospective approach.

b) Retroactive approach.

c) Current period approach (catch-up shown in current period).

2. Which of the above approaches generally is required under *APB Opinion No. 20* for the following types of accounting changes?

a) A change in accounting principle.

b) A change in accounting estimate.

C 19-5.   **ERROR CORRECTION AND DISCLOSURE**   Magellan is a high-flying conglomerate and has shown tremendous growth over the past 10 years through acquisitions of smaller companies. These acquisitions have always been made for cash, since the company has generated tremendous inflows of cash.

Magellan is considering going public, and you have been engaged to audit the company's financial statements for 1998. During the course of your work you discover that on several occasions the company has paid a substantial premium above the fair value of the assets of smaller companies it has acquired. Magellan has paid the premium because ownership and control of these assets have given Magellan several intangible benefits related to transportation economies, locational advantages, assured sources of supply, and a broader market for its products and services. For example, Magellan recently purchased Humble, a company critical to its manufacturing units, for $10 million. The fair value of Humble's individual assets was $8 million.

Magellan's accounting policy has been to write off the premium paid against its stockholders' equity on the date of acquisition. Management is aware that this practice is in violation of GAAP and has agreed to change its policy to conform to GAAP. Under GAAP, the premium paid should be recorded as an intangible asset, called goodwill, and amortized over a period not to exceed 40 years.

REQUIRED

1. Discuss the nature of the decision to change the procedure to conform with GAAP and discuss the disclosures Magellan must make in its comparative statements so as to conform to GAAP.

2. Given that the amounts involved are material, discuss the effect that the company's write-off procedures have had on the following financial statement elements:
   a) Assets.
   b) Liabilities.
   c) Stockholders' equity.
   d) Expenses.
   e) Net income.

3. What entries must Magellan make in order to conform with GAAP?

C 19-6.   **ERROR CORRECTION**   In reviewing the working papers for the audit of Shogren Corporation for the year ended December 31, 1998, you find the following adjusting and correcting entries that were made, without explanation, by the controller:

a)	Machinery	100,000	
	Depreciation expense	10,000	
	Retained earnings		30,000
	Accumulated depreciation		80,000
b)	Retained earnings	14,000	
	Wages payable		14,000
c)	Rent revenue	10,000	
	Retained earnings		10,000
d)	Inventory	18,000	
	Cost of goods sold		18,000
e)	Prepaid insurance	4,000	
	Insurance expense	1,000	
	Retained earnings		5,000

REQUIRED   For each item above, describe the type of error that probably was made and state when the error probably occurred.

C 19-7.   **MCDONNELL DOUGLAS ACCOUNTING CHANGE; RECOVERABLE VALUE**   This case, some of which has been extracted from *The Financial Times Limited*, January 19, 1996, page 22, extends the McDonnell Douglas headline article at the beginning of this chapter.

Doubts were raised over the future of McDonnell Douglas's wide-bodied MD-11 airliner yesterday after the U.S. defense and aerospace company recognized a shortfall in demand for the aircraft by taking a $1.8 billion charge to fourth-quarter profits. The charge stems from the fact that the costs of developing and manufacturing the MD-11 may have to be spread over a smaller number of aircraft than the company had expected.

Until now, McDonnell Douglas had followed standard industry practice of basing the cost of sales for each MD-11 delivery on an average cost per aircraft for the expected life of the MD-11 program. Yesterday, however, it said disappointing demand had forced it to change to a new method of accounting. From the beginning of the fourth quarter, it said, it had started to base the cost of sales of each delivery on the actual cost of producing each aircraft. In accounting terms, this means that the company has switched from a "program basis" of accounting to a "specific unit basis." As a result, it had to take a $1.8 billion pre-tax charge for deferred production costs and for the reduction in the valuation of support and tooling costs. This change to the specific unit costing method for the MD-11 program was made in recognition of production rates, existing order base, and length of time required to achieve program deliveries, and thus, the resultant increased difficulty in making estimates relating to program accounting.

Assume that the following data are representative of the manufacturing cost (in 000s) for each aircraft over the MD-11 program:

| | NUMBER OF MD-11'S PRODUCED AND SOLD | | | |
	1–5	6–20	21–50	50–100
Direct materials.............................	$1,000	$ 800	$ 500	$ 400
Direct labor..............................	4,000	2,800	1,800	1,200
Overhead................................	3,500	3,400	3,400	3,200
Total................................	$8,500	$7,000	$5,700	$4,800

REQUIRED

1. Discuss the underlying theory and possible motivation for using the program method of accounting for the MD-11.
2. Discuss the type of accounting change made by McDonnell Douglas and prepare a journal entry to record the change.
3. For this requirement, ignore the accounting change and assume that McDonnell Douglas expects to sell each MD-11 for $7,000. Using the program method of accounting and the per plane cost data above, prepare summary journal entries to record sales, cost of sales, and deferred production costs for each "group" of planes manufactured and sold—e.g., planes 1–5, planes 6–20, etc.—over the MD-11 program.
4. Refer to requirement 3. Now assume that after McDonnell Douglas had manufactured and sold 30 MD-11s, the demand for MD-11s softened. As a result, the company estimated that perhaps only between 10 and 20 additional MD-11s might be sold at a reduced market price of $6,000 per plane. Explain why McDonnell Douglas would find it necessary to switch from the program basis to a specific unit basis. Support your discussion and analysis with any necessary calculations.
5. We pointed out in the text that many accountants believe that all changes in accounting principle are necessitated by changes in estimates. Discuss how this view applies in the MD-11 situation.
6. Some accountants have suggested that the two methods of accounting for aircraft production and sale—program basis versus specific unit basis—are similar to certain methods of accounting for exploration costs in the oil and gas industry. Do you see any similarities between the methods? Discuss.

EXERCISES

E 19-1. **ACCOUNTING CHANGES; DEPRECIABLE ASSETS** During 1998, the management of Bat Corporation decided to change from sum-of-the-years'-digits to straight-line depreciation for equipment that was acquired at the beginning of 1995 at a cost of $220,000. The equipment has a useful life of 10 years from the date of purchase and no salvage value. Accumulated depreciation through 1997 was $108,000. If Bat had used the straight-line method, it would have been $66,000. Net income for the years ending December 31, before consideration of the cumulative effect of the change, was as follows:

1995	$130,000
1996	138,000
1997	146,000
1998	166,000 (depreciation expense for this year is based on the new method)

REQUIRED

1. Describe the type of accounting change made by Bat Corporation.
2. Prepare the entry, if any, to record the accounting change, and record the depreciation entry for 1998.

3. Show how the change would be disclosed on the December 31, 1998, income statement, and on income statements for 1995–1997, which are presented for comparative purposes.

E 19-2. **ACCOUNTING CHANGES; DEPRECIABLE ASSETS**   At the beginning of 1996, Singleton acquired a building at a cost of $120,000. At that time the estimated life of the building was 10 years, with an estimated salvage value of $10,000. Singleton uses straight-line depreciation on all buildings.

Near the end of 1998, management revised the estimated remaining life of the building to 5 years and the salvage value to $5,000.

Net income numbers were as follows (Singleton's fiscal year ends on December 31):

1996	$40,000
1997	60,000
1998	70,000 (depreciation expense for this year is based on the new estimates)

REQUIRED
1. Describe the type of accounting change made by Singleton.
2. Prepare the entry, if any, to record the accounting change, and record the depreciation entry for 1998.
3. Discuss how the change would be disclosed.

E 19-3. **ACCOUNTING CHANGES; INVENTORIES**   During 1998, Travis, Inc., which began operations at the beginning of 1994, decided to change its inventory pricing methods from FIFO to average cost. Net income for the pertinent years under each method was as follows (Travis's fiscal year ends on December 31):

YEAR	FIFO	AVERAGE COST
1994	$64,000	$62,000
1995	58,000	59,000
1996	69,000	62,000
1997	72,000	72,000
1998	75,000	70,000

REQUIRED
1. Describe the type of accounting change made by Travis.
2. Prepare the entry, if any, to record the accounting change.
3. Show how the change would be disclosed on the December 31, 1998, income statement and in the income statements for 1994–1997, which are presented for comparative purposes.

E 19-4. **ACCOUNTING CHANGES; INVENTORY METHODS**   The numbers below represent what net income would be (excluding any cumulative effects of changes in inventory methods) under various inventory pricing methods.

YEAR	FIFO	AVERAGE COST	LIFO
1996	$150,000	$141,000	$124,000
1997	153,000	142,500	120,000
1998	159,000	146,000	128,000

REQUIRED
For each independent case below, determine the appropriate net income number that would appear on the 1998 income statements and show the net income for 1997 and 1996 for comparative purposes (ignore taxes and pro forma data).
1. Change from FIFO to average cost.
2. Change from LIFO to FIFO.

E 19-5. **ACCOUNTING CHANGES; INVENTORIES, RECEIVABLES**   Near the end of 1998, management of Ernstman Corporation decided to make the following accounting changes.
a) Management decided to change from LIFO to FIFO in accounting for inventories. The resulting effect on net income was as follows:

YEAR	INCREASE IN INCOME
Before 1997	$164,000
1997	38,000
1998	26,000

b) Ernstman uses the allowance method of accounting for uncollectible accounts and determines annual uncollectible accounts expense by aging accounts receivable. Aging of the receivables at the end of 1998 indicated that the allowance account should be increased by $5,000.

c) Net income for 1997 was $175,000; net income for 1998 before any accounting changes (i.e., under the previous accounting procedures) was $180,000.

d) Ignore all income tax effects.

e) The books have not been closed for 1998.

REQUIRED

1. Prepare all necessary journal entries related to the above accounting changes at the end of 1998.

2. Calculate net income for 1998 and for 1997 for comparative purposes.

3. Prepare comparative statements of retained earnings for 1997 and 1998. Ernstman declared no dividends in 1997 and 1998, and retained earnings at the end of 1996 were $600,000.

E 19-6. **ACCOUNTING CHANGES; ERRORS** Childers Company purchased a plant asset at a cost of $110,000. The asset had an estimated useful life of 10 years and no salvage value. Three independent situations related to the plant asset acquisition appear below.

Situation A: At the end of the fifth year, an audit revealed that no depreciation on the plant asset had ever been recorded. Straight-line depreciation is appropriate.

Situation B: At the end of the fifth year, the total estimated life was revised from 10 years to 15 years.

Situation C: At the end of the fifth year, Childers changed from straight-line to sum-of-the-years'-digits depreciation.

REQUIRED For each situation, perform the following (ignore taxes):

1. Indicate whether an error correction or an accounting change (specify the type of accounting change) is involved.

2. Prepare the journal entry to correct the error or to record the accounting change. For each situation, assume that Childers's books have not been closed.

3. Calculate the appropriate amount of depreciation expense for the fifth year.

E 19-7. **ACCOUNTING CHANGES** For several years, Chatham Corporation has used the installment method of accounting. At the end of 1998, the current year, management decides to change from the installment method to the accrual method for sales made on account. Prior to the current year, management was not able to make reliable estimates of uncollectible accounts.

At the end of 1998, Chatham's accounts receivable balances were as follows:

Accounts receivable arising from 1998 sales	**$100,000**
Accounts receivable arising from 1997 sales	**24,000**
Accounts receivable arising from 1996 sales	**4,000**

The gross profit ratio for each year's credit sales was 40 percent in 1998, 45 percent in 1997, and 48 percent in 1996. Based on an aging of the ending accounts receivable, the estimates of uncollectible receivables are as follows: 1996, 85 percent; 1997, 20 percent; 1998, 5 percent.

REQUIRED Prepare the journal entry at the end of 1998 to record the accounting change for Chatham Corporation. Ignore taxes.

E 19-8. **ACCOUNTING CHANGES** At the beginning of 1996, Kaminski Company issued $100,000 of zero-coupon notes with a maturity of 10 years. The notes were issued at an effective rate of 8 percent. During 1996 and 1997, Kaminski accounted for the notes using the straight-line method, which was not materially different from the effective interest method. Because of external environmental factors that were expected to cause a permanent reduction in Kaminski's operations and that would cause a material difference between the straight-line method and the effective interest method, management decided to change to the effective interest method of accounting for the notes, beginning with December 31, 1998, financial statements.

REQUIRED

1. Prepare the 1998 journal entry to record the accounting change. Ignore taxes.

2. Calculate Kaminski's interest expense for 1998.

E 19-9. **ERROR ANALYSIS** Certain errors listed on page 1058 were made by Atchley Window Corporation. Indicate the effects of the errors on the company's statements by inserting in the spaces *O* to indicate overstatement, *U* to indicate understatement, and *N* to indicate no effect.

	TOTAL REVENUE	TOTAL EXPENSE	TOTAL ASSETS	TOTAL LIABILITIES	OWNERS' EQUITY
a)					
b)					
c)					
d)					
e)					

a) Failed to accrue interest on notes payable.
b) Failed to adjust unearned revenue for portion earned during the year.
c) Failed to record supplies used during the year.
d) Recorded the receipt of cash on an account receivable by a debit to cash and a credit to accounts payable.
e) Failed to record a sale made on account.

E 19-10. **ERROR CORRECTION** You are conducting the audit of Hall Corporation for 1998. The books for 1998 have not been closed. For each of the errors that follow, indicate the effects on 1997 and 1998 income by placing the amount in the proper columns. If income is understated because of the error, write *U* and the amount of understatement. If income is overstated because of the error, write *O* and the amount of overstatement. If income is not affected by the error, write *N* (no effect). In the last column, give the entry or entries, if any are needed, to correct the books or to record the accounting change.

	1997 INCOME	1998 INCOME	ENTRY AT 12/31/98
a) Failed to record depreciation expense of $3,000 in 1997.			
b) Failed to record merchandise purchased on account totaling $1,000 near the end of 1997. The merchandise was properly included in the ending inventory at the end of 1997.			
c) A machine costing $2,000 (useful life of 10 years, no salvage) was expensed when purchased at the end of 1996. Straight-line depreciation is proper.			
d) Hall failed to record interest accrued on notes payable at the end of 1997. The interest totaled $1,400 and was paid early in 1998.			
e) In 1998, common stock with a par value of $300 was issued for $500. The difference of $200 was included in revenue.			
f) Inventory at the end of 1997 was understated by $1,200 because of an error in the physical count.			

E 19-11. **ERROR ANALYSIS; INVENTORIES AND PURCHASES** Listed below are three accounting errors. Using the format shown below, indicate the effect, if any, of each error on the items shown. The company uses a periodic inventory method. Use *O* to indicate that an item is too high as a result of the error (overstated), *U* to indicate that it is too low (understated), and *N* to indicate no effect.

	1997 STATEMENTS			1998 STATEMENTS		
	COST OF GOODS SOLD	TOTAL ASSETS	NET INCOME	COST OF GOODS SOLD	TOTAL ASSETS	NET INCOME
a)						
b)						
c)						

a) Goods bought in 1997 were included in 12/31/97 inventory. In error, the purchase and liability were recorded in early 1998.

b) Goods were bought in 1997 and the purchase was recorded in that year, but the goods were not included in 12/31/97 inventory.

c) Goods received in 1997 were incorrectly excluded from 12/31/97 inventory.

(CGAA, adapted)

E 19-12. **ERROR ANALYSIS** Your employer approaches you for help regarding the financial statements prepared for the years ending December 31, 1997 and 1998. The owner is not satisfied with the previous accountant's work and has asked you to check on the accuracy of the statements prepared. Your examination reveals the following:

a) A three-year insurance policy was purchased for $2,400 on June 30, 1997, and the full amount was expensed at that time.

b) Accrued salaries at the end of 1997 and 1998 amounted to $500 and $400, respectively. The accountant did not make the necessary year-end adjustments.

c) On October 1, 1997, the company purchased at par $10,000 of 8 percent corporate bonds. The bonds were dated October 1, 1997, and pay interest semiannually. The accountant recorded interest revenue when the cash was received.

d) Depreciation was not recorded in 1997 and 1998. The amounts were $1,600 for 1997 and $2,000 for 1998.

REQUIRED

1. Indicate the amount of the understatement (*U*) or overstatement (*O*) of each of the above errors. Indicate no effect by *N*. Treat each item independently. Ignore taxes.

2. Prepare any necessary correcting entries for items *a* through *d*. The books for 1998 have not been closed.

	NET INCOME		TOTAL ASSETS, 12/31		TOTAL LIABILITIES, 12/31	
	1997	1998	1997	1998	1997	1998
a)						
b)						
c)						
d)						

E 19-13.   **ERROR CORRECTION; ACCRUALS, PREPAYMENTS** Below are several errors made by Calk Corporation in 1998.

a) 12/1/98: Purchased a two-year fire insurance policy on equipment. The two-year premium of $4,800 was paid in advance and the company expensed the entire $4,800 premium.

b) 12/10/98: Purchased supplies at a cost of $800. Failed to record supplies used during 1998 costing $300. The remaining supplies were used in 1999.

c) 12/31/98: Failed to record accrued salaries payable of $750. The monthly salary payments of $1,600 were paid on January 15, 1999, and recorded as an expense at that time.

d) 12/31/98: Received $700 advance on a sales contract. The receipt was recorded as sales revenue, although performance of the contract began in March 1999 and was completed in May 1999.

REQUIRED   For each error outlined above, prepare the correcting entry required, if any (ignore taxes), assuming that the error was discovered before the 1998 books were closed and before any 1999 transactions related to the errors occurred.

E 19-14.   **ERROR ANALYSIS AND CORRECTION** Unaudited comparative income statements for DeLeo Corporation are as follows:

	1999		1998	
	UNCORRECTED	**CORRECTED**	**UNCORRECTED**	**CORRECTED**
Sales	$100,000	_____	$80,000	_____
Cost of sales	(60,000)	_____	(50,000)	_____
Depreciation	(2,000)	_____	(5,000)	_____
Net income	$ 38,000	_____	$25,000	_____

In your audit you discover the following errors:

a) DeLeo failed to record sales of $10,000 on account made near the end of 1998. The sales were recorded in 1999 when the cash was collected.

b) The ending inventory for 1998 was overstated by $6,000 as a result of an error in the physical count.

c) At the beginning of 1998, DeLeo purchased a fixed asset for $4,400. Although the estimated life of the asset was five years, the entire cost was expensed in 1998. DeLeo uses straight-line depreciation on all fixed assets.

REQUIRED   1. Prepare the entries to correct DeLeo's books at the end of 1999, assuming the books have not been closed. Ignore taxes.

2. Fill in the blanks above to show the correct income statement items for 1999 and 1998.

E 19-15.   **ERROR ANALYSIS** Following is a list of seven accounting errors. Using the format shown, indicate the effect, if any, on each of the six items indicated by the column headings. If the error would cause an item to be too high, write a +; if too low, write –; if it has no effect, write *0*. You may assume the business has been operating for a number of years and has adjusted and closed its books annually each December 31. Each case is independent. The first item serves as an example.

ERROR

	1998 INCOME STATEMENT			BALANCE SHEET, 12/31/98		
	NET INCOME	COST OF GOODS SOLD	OTHER EXPENSE	ASSETS	LIABILITIES	OWNERS' EQUITY
a) Inventory on 12/31/97 was overstated.	–	+	0	0	0	0
b) Recorded too much depreciation in 1998.						
c) Failed to adjust for unexpired insurance. Debits during 1998 were made to insurance expense.						
d) Inventory on 12/31/98 was overstated.						
e) Office supplies inventory at the end of 1998 was overstated. Purchases during the year were debited to supplies expense.						
f) Failed to accrue interest on notes receivable at the end of 1997.						
g) Failed to adjust for accrued wages at the end of 1997.						

PROBLEMS   The problems marked with an asterisk (*) refers to Appendix 19–1.

P 19-1.   **ACCOUNTING CHANGES AND ERROR CORRECTIONS; DEPRECIABLE ASSETS** Southern Railway Corporation owns three locomotives that it leases to grain companies to move grain cars to market. During December 1998, management made the following discoveries and decisions:

a) Locomotive C was purchased at the beginning of 1992 at a cost of $1,640,000. The firm has depreciated this locomotive on a straight-line basis for book and tax purposes, using an estimated useful life of 10 years and $40,000 salvage value. Based on company experience, it was decided that the remaining useful life as of January 1, 1998, should be 8 years and that the estimated salvage value should be $80,000. The changes apply for both book and tax purposes.

b) Locomotive X was acquired at the beginning of 1995 at a cost of $2 million. The estimated life of the locomotive was 10 years with no estimated salvage value. Double-declining-balance depreciation was used for book and tax purposes. During December 1998, management decided to change to the straight-line method for book purposes, although the double-declining-balance method would be continued for tax purposes.

c) Locomotive Y was acquired at the beginning of 1996 at a cost of $1,500,000. This locomotive has an estimated useful life of 8 years with an estimated salvage value of $60,000. Straight-line depreciation is appropriate for book purposes. Management discovered that no depreciation had been recorded on this locomotive for either book or tax purposes. For tax purposes, the following percentages apply for a 3-year recovery period: 1996, 50 percent; 1997, 30 percent; 1998, 20 percent.

Additional data:

d) The applicable income tax rate for all years is 30 percent.

e) Southern's only source of revenue is from the leasing of the locomotives, and revenues for 1998 totaled $1,600,000. Southern's only expenses are depreciation, income taxes, and administrative expenses. Administrative expenses for 1998 totaled $100,000. No depreciation has been recorded for 1998.

REQUIRED   **I.** Prepare all necessary entries related to items *a* through *c* at the end of 1998.

2. Prepare the income statement for 1998. Ignore pro forma data.

P 19-2.   **DISCLOSURE OF ACCOUNTING CHANGES AND ERRORS**   Refer to Problem 19-1. Assume that Southern wishes to issue a 1998 income statement with 1996 and 1997 income statements presented for comparative purposes. Net income previously reported for 1996 and 1997 is as follows:

1996	$500,000
1997	580,000

REQUIRED   Calculate the amounts of net income for 1996, 1997, and 1998 that would appear on the three-year comparative income statements. Include pro forma data where applicable.

P 19-3.   **ACCOUNTING CHANGES; LONG-TERM CONSTRUCTION CONTRACTS**   In 1998, Kovar Construction Company switched from the completed-contract to the percentage-of-completion method of accounting for long-term construction contracts. The company continued to use the completed-contract method for tax purposes, and the tax rate was 30 percent. Before-tax net income under the two methods was as follows:

YEAR	COMPLETED CONTRACT	PERCENTAGE OF COMPLETION
Before 1996	$160,000	$240,000
1996	40,000	20,000
1997	40,000	60,000
1998	50,000	55,000

REQUIRED   **I.** Prepare the entry to record the change in accounting principle.

2. Assuming that Kovar's retained earnings at the beginning of 1996 was $200,000 and that Kovar prepares three-year comparative statements, indicate how the net income numbers and statement of retained earnings would appear. Use the following format:

Income Statements for the Years Ended 12/31

	1998	1997	1996
Income before taxes..................................			
Income tax expense....................................	_____	_____	_____
Net income...			

Statements of Retained Earnings for the Years

	1998	1997	1996
Beginning retained earnings			$200,000
Cumulative effect of change in accounting principle, applied retroactively			
Beginning retained earnings, as adjusted			
Net income			
Dividends (assumed)............................	(25,000)	(22,000)	(16,000)
Ending retained earnings			

P 19-4. **ERROR CORRECTION** Capco is a privately held company that is being audited in connection with a bank loan. The following information pertains to the audit for the year ending December 31, 1998:

a) At the beginning of 1997, Capco entered into a four-year lease of equipment, which qualified as a capital lease for both financial reporting and tax purposes. The leased equipment had an estimated useful life of five years from January 1, 1997. The annual lease payments, payable at the beginning of each year, were $10,000. Capco's incremental borrowing rate is 8 percent. Capco has been accounting for this lease incorrectly as an operating lease for financial reporting purposes but correctly as a capital lease for tax purposes. Straight-line depreciation is appropriate for both book purposes and tax purposes.

b) During 1998, Capco sold available-for-sale securities for $50,000. The securities had a carrying value of $48,000 (cost of $35,000). Capco credited the proceeds of $50,000 to the investment account. Capco's tax basis gain is $15,000 ($50,000 – $35,000).

c) Merchandise inventory, based on a physical count on December 31, 1998, was reported at $125,000. A review of the inventory procedure revealed that some inventory was counted twice, resulting in an overstatement of $25,000.

d) On December 31, 1998, the funded status of Capco's defined benefit pension plan was as follows:

Projected benefit obligation	$(300,000)
Plan assets at fair value	160,000
Funded status	$(140,000)
Unrecognized prior service cost	200,000
Net pension asset (also reported on Capco's 12/31/98 balance sheet)	$ 60,000

Capco's accumulated benefit obligation is 60 percent of the projected benefit obligation.

e) Near the end of 1998, a lawsuit was filed against Capco. Although Capco has not recognized any amounts in its financial statements, Capco's attorneys believe that an unfavorable outcome in the amount of $40,000, payable in 1999, is probable.

f) At the beginning of 1998, Capco installed an e-mail system at a cost of $100,000. Capco expensed this cost, although the estimated life of the system, for both book and tax purposes, was four years with no estimated salvage value.

g) Capco's tax rate for 1997 and 1998 was 30 percent. The tax rate for 1999 and future years (enacted in 1998) is expected to be 25 percent.

REQUIRED Prepare journal entries to record the effects of the foregoing data on Capco's accounting records for the year ending December 31, 1998. For each item above, prepare a separate journal entry to record any effects on income tax expense.

P 19-5. **ERROR CORRECTION** Early in January 1999, you assume your new post as controller of Mexico Joe's. Your predecessor has prepared the following preliminary income statement for the company's fiscal year ending December 31, 1998:

Income Statement for the Year Ended December 31, 1998

Sales		$586,700
Cost of goods sold	$300,000	
Depreciation	77,700	
Wages and salaries	70,000	
Interest and insurance	19,600	
Advertising	35,000	(502,300)
Net income		$ 84,400

In the course of examining the records, you discover the following:

a) A $1,000 purchase invoice dated December 27 was received December 31 and incorrectly recorded as a purchase. The goods had not been shipped to Mexico Joe's by year-end and were correctly excluded from ending inventory.

b) A $700 purchase of merchandise was received on December 31 and included in the inventory. The invoice did not arrive until after the trial balance was prepared, and therefore the merchandise was not recorded among the December purchases.

c) A sale for $2,700, dated December 27, had been properly recorded as a sale. The goods, which cost $1,800, had not been shipped and were included incorrectly in inventory on December 30, the date of the physical inventory count. The goods were shipped to the customer on December 31.

d) A $1,200 item of office equipment, received on December 31, was erroneously recorded as a purchase of merchandise. The company depreciates office equipment on a straight-line basis over a five-year service life.

e) The $70,000 of wages and salaries represented debits to this account during the year. Your predecessor failed to recognize $800 of accrued wages and salaries expense at December 31, 1997, and $1,200 at December 31, 1998.

REQUIRED

1. Determine the correct cost of goods sold.

2. Determine the correct depreciation expense.

3. Determine the correct wages and salaries expense.

4. Prepare a corrected income statement.

P 19-6. **ERROR ANALYSIS AND CORRECTION** Bolivar has been in business since January 1, 1994, but has never had an audit. In the course of the first audit for the year ended December 31, 1998, the errors listed below were discovered.

a) Because of an error in the physical count, the December 31, 1994, inventory was overstated by $4,000.

b) In 1995, a purchase of $9,000 was not recorded as a purchase or included in the December 31, 1995, inventory. Title to the goods passed to Bolivar when they were shipped. The overstatement of the December 31, 1994, inventory was not discovered in 1995.

c) The goods in transit on December 31, 1995, were received and recorded as a purchase in 1996, and payment was made to the seller. In addition, a sale on account on December 30, 1996, totaling $1,000, was not recorded.

d) The $1,000 sale on December 30, 1996, was recorded as a sale in 1997, when the cash payment was received. In addition, inventory for December 31, 1997, was understated by $12,000, and accrued wages of $1,500 were not recorded on that date.

e) The accrued wages in item *d* were paid and expensed in early 1998. The December 31, 1998, inventory was overstated by $10,200, and the 1997 inventory error was not discovered. In the end-of-the-year adjustments for 1998, depreciation was overstated by $1,000 and accrued interest expense was overstated by $900.

REQUIRED

1. Indicate the effects that the above errors have on all items in the financial statements below. Indicate the effects as *O* = overstatement and *U* = understatement, and the amounts (e.g., $12,000 *U*). If there is no effect, leave blank. Assume that items not mentioned are correct unless a counterbalancing error is involved. Ignore taxes. The 12/31/94 column has been completed as a guide.

2. Assuming that the books are not closed, prepare the entry to correct Bolivar's books as of December 31, 1998. Ignore taxes.

	1994	1995	1996	1997	1998
INCOME STATEMENT FOR THE YEAR ENDED 12/31					
Sales......................					
Beginning inventory..........					
Purchases...................					
Goods available for sale					
Ending inventory.............	4,000 *O*				
Cost of goods sold	4,000 *U*				
Gross margin	4,000 *O*				
Operating expenses..........					
Net income.................	4,000 *O*				
BALANCE SHEET, 12/31					
Current assets	4,000 *O*				
Total assets	4,000 *O*				
Current liabilities............					
Total liabilities					
Stockholders' equity	4,000 *O*				

P 19-7.   **ERROR ANALYSIS AND CORRECTION**   On January 1, 1995, Harley paid $40,000 for 40 percent interest in Suzuki, which had net assets of $100,000 on that date.

    You are conducting Harley's audit for the year ended December 31, 1998, and discover that Harley has, in error, been using the cost method instead of the equity method to account for its investment in Suzuki. Suzuki's net income and dividends paid since 1/1/95 are as follows:

YEAR	NET INCOME (LOSS)	DIVIDENDS
1995	$10,000	$4,000
1996	3,000	1,000
1997	(2,000)	1,000
1998	5,000	2,000

Harley has recorded the dividends received each year in the investment revenue account.

REQUIRED

1. Calculate the error made by Harley with respect to the investment revenue account for 1998.
2. Prepare the entry to correct Harley's books as of December 31, 1998. The books have not been closed for 1998.
3. Assume that Harley plans to issue comparative income statements for 1996, 1997, and 1998. Using the format below, indicate the correct amounts to be reported.

Income Statement

	1998	1997	1996
Investment revenue	_____	_____	_____

Retained Earnings Statement

	1998	1997	1996
Beginning balance, as originally reported	*xx*	*xx*	*xx*
Prior period adjustment	_____	_____	_____
Net income	_____	_____	_____
Ending balance	*xx*	*xx*	*xx*

P 19-8.   **ERROR CORRECTION**   Bickle Corporation was incorporated on December 1, 1997, and began operations one week later. Bickle is a nonpublic enterprise. Before closing the books for the fiscal year ended November 30, 1998, Bickle's controller prepared the following financial statements:

Balance Sheet
As of November 30, 1998

Assets:

  Current assets:

Cash	$ 150,000
Trading securities, at cost	60,000
Accounts receivable	450,000
Less allowance for doubtful accounts	(59,000)
Inventories	430,000
Prepaid insurance	15,000
Total current assets	$ 1,046,000
Property, plant, and equipment	426,000
Less accumulated depreciation	(40,000)
Research and development costs	120,000
Total assets	$ 1,552,000

Liabilities and stockholders' equity:

  Current liabilities:

Accounts payable and accrued expenses	$ 592,000
Income taxes payable	224,000
Total current liabilities	$ 816,000
Stockholders' equity:	
Common stock, $10 par value	$ 400,000
Retained earnings	336,000
Total stockholders' equity	$ 736,000
Total liabilities and stockholders' equity	$ 1,552,000

Income Statement
For the Year Ended November 30, 1998

Net sales		$ 2,950,000
Operating expenses:		
Cost of sales	$(1,670,000)	
Selling and administrative	(650,000)	
Depreciation	(40,000)	
Research and development	(30,000)	(2,390,000)
Income before income taxes		$ 560,000
Income tax expense		(224,000)
Net income		$ 336,000

Bickle is in the process of negotiating a loan for expansion purposes, and the bank has requested audited financial statements. During the course of the audit, the following additional information was obtained:

a) The trading securities have a fair value of $45,000 as of November 30, 1998.

b) Based on an aging of the accounts receivable as of November 30, 1998, it was estimated that $40,000 of the receivables will be uncollectible.

c) Inventories at November 30, 1998, did not include work-in-process inventory costing $22,000 sent to an outside processor on November 29, 1998.

d) A $3,000 insurance premium paid on November 30, 1998, on a policy expiring one year later was debited to insurance expense.

e) Bickle adopted a pension plan on June 1, 1998, for eligible employees, to be administered by a trustee. Based on actuarial computations, the first 12 months' pension expense was estimated at $45,000. None of this amount was funded. Bickle has made no entry for pension expense. Bickle's minimum liability, calculated under *Statement No. 87*, was $10,000.

f) On June 1, 1998, a production machine purchased for $48,000 was charged to repairs and maintenance. Bickle depreciates machines of this type on the straight-line method over a five-year life, with no salvage value, for financial and tax purposes.

g) Research and development costs of $150,000 were incurred in the development of a patent that Bickle expects to be granted during the fiscal year ending November 30, 1999. Bickle initiated a five-year amortization of the $150,000 total cost during the fiscal year ended November 30, 1998.

h) During November 1998, a competitor company filed suit against Bickle for patent infringement, claiming $200,000 in damages. Bickle's legal counsel believes that an unfavorable outcome is probable. A reasonable estimate of the court's award to the plaintiff is $80,000.

i) A 40 percent effective tax rate was determined to be appropriate for calculating the provision for income taxes for the fiscal year ended November 30, 1998. Ignore computation of the deferred portion of income taxes.

REQUIRED Prepare a four-column schedule for Bickle to correct the November 30, 1998, balance sheet and the income statement for the year ended November 30, 1998. Use the same format for account titles as appears in the problem data. The schedule should have the following column headings:

	UNADJUSTED	ADJUSTMENTS		CORRECTED
ACCOUNT	BALANCE	DR	CR	BALANCE

(AICPA, adapted)

*P 19-9.   ERROR CORRECTION; USE OF A WORKSHEET   Bud's Toyland has prepared the following trial balance on December 31, 1998:

	DR	CR
Cash	$ 10,000	
Accounts receivable	18,000	
Allowance for doubtful accounts		$ 300
Inventory (12/31/98)	50,000	
Building and equipment	40,000	
Accumulated depreciation		18,000
Accounts payable		40,000
Bud Lucy, capital		61,000
Sales		200,000
Rent revenue		32,700
Cost of goods sold	117,500	
Salaries expense	100,000	
Insurance expense	9,600	
Bud's personal expenses	3,900	
Utilities expense	3,000	
	$352,000	$352,000

During your audit of Bud's Toyland for the year ending December 31, 1998, you discover the following errors that affect the above trial balance:

a) The company failed to record a credit sale of $2,000 made near the end of 1997. The sale was recorded in 1998, when the cash was collected. Additionally, credit sales totaling $8,000 were not recorded on December 30, 1998.

b) The balance in allowance for doubtful accounts at the beginning of the fiscal year was $600. During the year, customers' accounts totaling $300 were written off as uncollectible. The ending balance in the allowance account should be 2 percent of ending accounts receivable.

c) Due to an error in a software program used to track physical quantities of inventory, the ending inventory on 12/31/97 was overstated by $6,200; the ending inventory on 12/31/98 was understated by $9,500.

d) The amount in the insurance expense account represents the cost of a two-year liability insurance policy purchased on November 1, 1998.

e) The salaries expense account includes $3,000 per month paid to Bud Lucy. He also received $325 per month in personal expenses during 1998.

f) The company failed to record the following accrued expenses at December 31, 1997 and 1998:

	1997	1998
Utilities expense	$2,000	$3,000
Salaries expense	1,500	1,800

g) On October 1, 1998, the company rented a small portion of its adjacent office building to Ship-n-Boxes, a company that specializes in shipping toys around the world. The annual rental amount was $32,700 and was recorded as rent revenue.

h) On December 31, 1998, a shipment of merchandise costing $3,500, shipped FOB factory, was in the freight company's warehouse. This purchase was not recorded by the toy shop and was not included in the 12/31/98 ending inventory.

i) The company failed to record depreciation expense in the amount of $4,000.

REQUIRED   Prepare a six-column worksheet to correct Bud Toyland's trial balance on December 31, 1998. Your worksheet should be set up with the following headings:

ACCOUNT TITLE	UNCORRECTED TRIAL BALANCE		ADJUSTMENTS		CORRECTED TRIAL BALANCE	
	DR	CR	DR	CR	DR	CR

P 19-10. **ACCOUNTING CHANGES; ERROR CORRECTION** Ponca Corporation is in the process of negotiating a loan for expansion purposes. The books and records have never been audited, and the bank has requested that an audit be performed for the year ending December 31, 1998. During the course of the audit, the following items were brought to your attention:

a) An analysis of collections and losses on accounts receivable during 1997 and 1998 indicated a drop in anticipated losses due to bad debts. After consultation with management, it was agreed that the allowance account at December 31, 1998, should be reduced by $10,000.

b) The merchandise inventory as of December 31, 1997, was overstated by $4,000, and the merchandise inventory as of December 31, 1998, was overstated by $6,100.

c) On January 2, 1997, equipment costing $12,000 (estimated useful life of 10 years and residual value of $1,000) was incorrectly charged to operating expenses. Ponca records depreciation by the straight-line method. In 1998, fully depreciated equipment (with no residual value) that originally cost $17,500 was sold as scrap for $3,500. Ponca credited the proceeds of $3,500 to the equipment account.

d) An analysis of 1997 operating expenses revealed that Ponca recorded as an expense a three-year insurance premium of $5,400 on January 3, 1997.

e) During 1998, Ponca changed its inventory method from LIFO to FIFO, and FIFO has been used in 1998. The cumulative effect of the change, as of January 1, 1998, was a $34,000 increase in the inventory account. Of this amount, $27,000 applies to years prior to 1997, and $7,000 applies to 1997. Ponca currently shows the $34,000 cumulative effect in its 1998 income statement.

f) Ponca failed to apply "mark-to-market" accounting to certain debt and equity securities. With respect to the trading securities portfolio, fair value exceeded carrying value on December 31, 1998, by $12,000. With respect to the available-for-sale securities portfolio, carrying value exceeded fair value on December 31, 1998, by $8,000.

g) On January 1, 1996, Ponca entered into a 10-year noncancelable equipment lease. The present value of the minimum lease payments was $33,795 and was recorded properly on January 1, 1996 as a capital lease. The annual lease payments, payable at the beginning of each year, were $5,000. During 1996, 1997, and 1998, Ponca accounted for the lease as an operating lease by recording the annual lease payments as rent expense. Ponca's incremental borrowing rate (and the implicit rate in the lease) was 10 percent.

h) At the beginning of 1997, Ponca initiated a defined benefit pension plan for its employees. Prior service cost at the plan inception date was $100,000 and was to be amortized over 20 years. During 1997 and 1998, Ponca failed to include prior service cost in the calculation of pension expense. Ponca also failed to include the expected return on plan assets for 1997 and 1998, which equaled the actual return for both years, in the pension expense calculation. These amounts were as follows: 1997, $3,000; 1998, $6,000.

i) Ponca declares cash dividends on its common stock outstanding in December of each year. The dividends are paid the following January. Ponca has recorded the dividends as they are paid, rather than when they are declared. During 1997 and 1998, dividend declarations were $12,000 and $15,000, respectively.

j) Ponca uses the par value method of accounting for treasury stock. During 1998, Ponca sold 4,000 shares of $5 par treasury stock for $12 per share. Ponca recorded the difference between the total issue price and the total par value as a gain on the sale of treasury stock.

k) Ponca reported the following amounts of net income for the years ending December 31, 1997 and 1998: 1997, $200,000; 1998, $240,000.

REQUIRED **1.** Prepare the journal entries to correct the books as of December 31, 1998. The books for 1998 have *not* been closed. Ignore income taxes.

2. Prepare a schedule showing the calculation of corrected net income for the years ended December 31, 1998 and 1997, assuming that any adjustments are to be reported on comparative statements for the two years. The first item on your schedule should be the net income for each year. Ignore income taxes.

(AICPA, adapted)

P 19-11.   **ERROR ANALYSIS AND CORRECTION**   During your audit of Doyle Corporation for the year ending January 31, 1998, you discover five errors made by Doyle's chief accountant. Information about each error appears below:

a)   On January 22, 1997, Doyle failed to record a purchase of merchandise on account. The merchandise was received near the end of January and was properly included in the ending inventory at January 31, 1997. The following entry was made on February 20, 1997, when payment was made to the creditor:

Purchases 4,000
   Cash 4,000

b)   In the physical count of inventory on January 30, 1998, Doyle failed to include merchandise costing $5,750. This merchandise was on display in an adjacent showroom.

c)   In the adjusting entry process, Doyle failed to record accrued interest revenue of $1,800 for the year ending January 31, 1997. When the cash was received in February of 1997, Doyle made the following entry:

Cash 1,800
   Interest revenue 1,800

Doyle also failed to record accrued interest revenue of $1,800 for the year ending January 31, 1998. (By the audit date, no cash interest had been received from Doyle's debtor.)

d)   On February 1, 1995, Doyle purchased a computer system at a cost of $12,000. Although Doyle's depreciation policy was to depreciate the cost of the computer system on a straight-line basis over a five-year period (no salvage value), no depreciation has been recorded to date.

e)   On February 1, 1997, Doyle purchased a four-year liability insurance policy at a cost of $8,000. The following entry was made on this date:

Insurance expense 8,000
   Cash 8,000

For the three years ending January 31, 1996, 1997, and 1998, Doyle reported the following amounts of net income:

1996	$60,000
1997	80,000
1998	100,000

REQUIRED   **1.**   Prepare a columnar schedule to show the correct amount of net income for each of the three years ending January 31.

2.   Assuming that Doyle Corporation's books have not been closed for the year ending January 31, 1998, prepare any necessary correcting entries for each of the above errors.

P 19-12.   **ACCOUNTING CHANGES; ERRORS**   Comparative statements of income and retained earnings of Bakker Construction Corporation for the years ended December 31, 1997, and December 31, 1998, are as follows:

	1998	1997
Construction revenues	$350,000	$240,000
Construction expenses	(250,000)	(195,000)
Administrative and other expenses	(50,000)	(15,000)
Income before taxes and extraordinary items	$ 50,000	$ 30,000
Income tax expense	(15,000)	(9,000)
Net income	$ 35,000	$ 21,000
Retained earnings, January 1	200,000	179,000
Retained earnings, December 31	$235,000	$200,000

The following three *unrelated* situations incorporate accounting changes, error correction, and classification. Each situation is based on Bakker's comparative statements shown above and requires revisions in these statements. The income tax rate is 30 percent.

a)   On January 1, 1996, Bakker purchased an office building at a cost of $30,000. Bakker adopted straight-line depreciation and estimated the building's useful life to be 10 years with no salvage value. At the beginning of 1998, Bakker switched to the double-declining-balance method, with no change in the estimated useful life or salvage value. Due to a computer-programming error, however, the straight-line method was used in 1998. Depreciation expense is included in administrative and other expenses on the income statement. Bakker had been using the double-declining-balance method for tax purposes.

b) Prior to 1998, Bakker used the completed-contract method in accounting for construction activities. During 1998, Bakker switched to the percentage-of-completion method for book purposes, although the completed-contract method was continued for tax purposes. The 1998 financial statements are based on the new method. Construction revenues less construction expenses under the two methods for 1997 and prior years are as follows:

	1997	PRIOR YEARS
Completed-contract method:		
Revenues..	$240,000	$800,000
Expenses..	195,000	670,000
Percentage-of-completion method:		
Revenues..	320,000	900,000
Expenses..	260,000	740,000

c) Bakker failed to record the following prepayments and accruals at the end of:

	1996	1997	1998
Supplies..	$8,000	$5,000	$4,000
Salaries payable................................	3,000	5,000	6,000

Supplies expense and salaries expense are included in administrative and other expenses on the income statement. These errors also were made on Bakker's tax return.

REQUIRED For each of the three *unrelated* situations described above, prepare revised comparative statements of income and retained earnings for the years ended December 31, 1998, and December 31, 1997. The revised statements for each situation should recognize the appropriate accounting changes, errors, and other items outlined in the situation. Ignore any pro forma calculations and presentations.

P 19-13. **ACCOUNTING CHANGES; ERROR CORRECTION** Refer to the information in P 19-12 above and assume that Bakker's books for 1998 have *not* been closed.

REQUIRED Prepare any necessary correcting entries for items *a, b,* and *c.*

*P 19-14. **WORKSHEET ANALYSIS OF ERRORS** For three years Silman Wholesale failed to recognize accruals, prepayments, and other transactions in its accounts. Reported net income and a listing of the errors appear below.

		1996	1997	1998
	Reported net income (loss)	$12,000	$4,000	$(1,000)
a)	Failed to record accrued revenues...........	2,000	2,500	4,800
b)	Failed to record uncollectible accounts expense	600	800	200
c)	Failed to record accrued salaries	1,300	1,800	—
d)	Understated depreciation expense	1,200	1,500	1,500
e)	Overstated ending inventories	3,600	2,800	—
f)	Failed to record purchase on account; merchandise properly included in ending inventory................................	—	—	4,000
g)	Failed to recognize unused supplies as an asset (expensed them instead)	300	—	400
h)	Failed to recognize gain on sale of land; land credited for amount of proceeds........	600	—	—
i)	Failed to recognize unearned revenue at end of year...........................	—	500	900

REQUIRED Prepare a four-column worksheet to correct the reported net income for each year. In the fourth column prepare the entry, if necessary, to correct the books at the end of 1998, assuming that the books have not been closed. Ignore taxes.

P 19-15.   COMPREHENSIVE; ACCOUNTING CHANGES, ERRORS, DISCLOSURE   You are conducting the audit for Traugh Company for the year ended December 31, 1998. The company has never been audited, and the financial statements appearing below have been presented to you for review in connection with the audit.

Comparative Financial Statements
(Unaudited)

	INCOME STATEMENTS FOR THE YEARS		
	1998	**1997**	**1996**
Sales	$310,000	$280,000	$260,000
Cost of goods sold	(150,000)	(145,000)	(120,000)
Depreciation expense	(35,000)	(36,000)	(30,000)
Other expenses	(45,000)	(42,000)	(40,000)
Income tax expense	(24,000)	(17,100)	(21,000)
Net income	$ 56,000	$ 39,900	$ 49,000

	BALANCE SHEETS, DECEMBER 31		
	1998	**1997**	**1996**
Assets:			
Cash and receivables	$165,000	$148,000	$125,000
Inventories (average cost)	95,000	83,000	70,000
Property, plant, and equipment (net)	438,000	440,000	350,000
Other assets	32,000	40,000	44,000
Total	$730,000	$711,000	$589,000
Liabilities and owners' equity:			
Accounts payable	$170,150	$176,650	$109,000
Income taxes payable	52,000	58,000	40,000
Other liabilities	81,500	85,000	60,000
Common stock (no-par)	200,000	200,000	200,000
Retained earnings	226,350	191,350	180,000
Total	$730,000	$711,000	$589,000

	STATEMENTS OF RETAINED EARNINGS FOR THE YEARS		
	1998	**1997**	**1996**
Retained earnings, 1/1	$191,350	$180,000	$165,500
Net income	56,000	39,900	49,000
Dividends	(21,000)	(28,550)	(34,500)
Retained earnings, 12/31	$226,350	$191,350	$180,000

During the audit examination, five items come to your attention:

a)   During 1998 management decided to change from average cost to FIFO for inventory valuation purposes. Average cost will be continued for tax purposes. Cost of goods sold under each of the methods is as follows:

	COST OF GOODS SOLD	
YEAR	AVERAGE COST	FIFO
Before 1996	$760,000	$720,000
1996	120,000	110,000
1997	145,000	142,000
1998	150,000	140,000

b)   Traugh's products are warranted against defects for two years. The company accrues estimated warranty expenses. Before 1998 the annual warranty expenses were estimated at 5 percent of sales. In 1998 the company wishes to revise the estimate to 8 percent of sales because the previous years' estimates appeared to be lower than actual warranty claims. Warranty expenses are included in other expenses on the income statement. For tax purposes, warranty expenses are not deductible until costs are actually incurred. Warranty expenditures, deductible for tax purposes, totaled $24,800 in 1998.

c) The company owns several machines. On June 30, 1997, the company acquired a machine at a cost of $120,000. The asset had a 10-year life with no salvage value and was to be depreciated by the straight-line method. Your examination reveals that the machine acquired was debited to land. No depreciation has been recorded for book or tax purposes since the acquisition date.

d) The company failed to record accrued salaries of $20,000 at the end of 1997. The salaries were recorded as expenses in 1998, when the cash was paid. For tax purposes, the salaries were deducted in 1998.

e) The company has failed to record a cash dividend in the amount of $25,000 declared near the end of 1998.

None of the above accounting changes or errors has been reflected or corrected in the financial statements. Any deferred tax assets and deferred tax liabilities should be included in other assets and other liabilities. The income tax rate is 30 percent.

REQUIRED

1. Prepare all necessary entries for items *a* through *e*.
2. Prepare new financial statements giving effect to the adjusting entries in part 1. Prepare pro forma data as necessary.
3. Draft any footnotes that are appropriate for the above items.

P 19-16. **RESEARCH PROBLEM ON ACCOUNTING CHANGES** Accounting changes are reported frequently in company annual reports. Obtain access to a database of company annual reports through your library, *LEXIS, Disclosure,* or other sources.

REQUIRED Search the databases available to you and perform the following:

1. Find two companies that reported a change in accounting *principle*. For each company, write a short paragraph that summarizes the nature of the change in accounting principle, whether the change was a voluntary change or mandatory change, how the change was reported (current period versus retroactive approach), and what footnote disclosures were included in the annual report related to the change in accounting principle.

2. Find two companies that reported a change in accounting *estimate*. For each company, write a short paragraph that summarizes the nature of the change in accounting estimate, what effect the change had on the current period's net income, and what footnote disclosures were included in the annual report related to the change in accounting estimate.

Earnings per Share

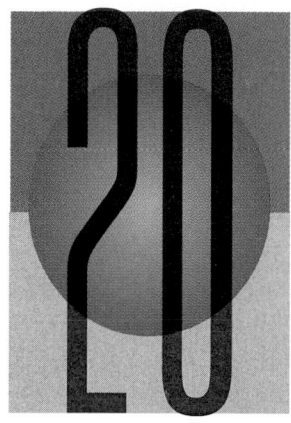

C H A P T E R

20

LEARNING OBJECTIVES

After studying this chapter, you should be able to:

1. State what is meant by basic earnings per share and diluted earnings per share.

2. Calculate the amount of income applicable to common stock for the basic earnings per share calculation.

3. Calculate the weighted average number of common shares for the basic earnings per share calculation.

4. Adjust the weighted average number of common shares for stock dividends, stock splits, and reverse splits.

5. Use the treasury stock method to include stock options, warrants, and their equivalents in diluted earnings per share calculations.

6. Use the if-converted method to include the dilutive effect of convertible securities in diluted earnings per share calculations.

7. Determine the order of entry of potentially dilutive securities into the diluted earnings per share calculations, based on the securities' relative income per incremental common share effects.

8. State the major reporting and disclosure requirements for earnings per share.

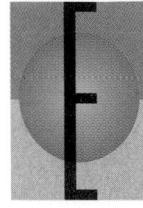

arnings per share (EPS) "is perhaps the most often cited and reported measure of an enterprise's performance. Investors, creditors, analysts and others use the statistic to evaluate how successful an enterprise has been in attaining its profit goal. Financial statement users also use EPS data to assess earnings potential and prospects for future dividends."[1] The popularity of EPS stems from the importance placed on income by investors, creditors, and others, and from the fact that as a measure *per share* of common stock, EPS is meaningful to individual stockholders. EPS figures appear in prospectuses, in proxy statements, in annual reports to stockholders, in reports filed with the SEC, and in the financial press, and are published by investment services. Investors, creditors, and other external decision makers use EPS to evaluate the past and present performance of a company and to predict its future performance.

The purpose of this chapter is to discuss and illustrate how EPS is calculated and reported in the financial statements. A brief historical background of EPS reporting and disclosure requirements is followed by an overview of current EPS reporting and disclosure requirements under the recently-issued *Statement No. 128.* The next section describes how EPS is calculated. The chapter concludes with a discussion of EPS reporting and disclosure issues.

ISTORICAL BACKGROUND OF EPS REPORTING

Before the late 1960s, companies were not required by GAAP to calculate and disclose EPS, although they often did so. EPS figures typically were presented only as supplementary data in annual reports to stockholders and other summaries of financial data. Moreover, both the procedure for calculating EPS and its disclosure varied widely among companies. In 1966, the APB issued *Opinion No. 9,* which provided guidance for calculating EPS as well as a format for its presentation in the income statement, and strongly recommended that EPS be disclosed in the income statement.[2]

In 1969, the APB changed its recommendation to a requirement by issuing *Opinion No. 15,* which required at a minimum that EPS for both income before extraordinary items and net income be disclosed on the face of the income statement.[3] *Opinion No. 15* also provided complex guidelines for calculating EPS. Because of the complexity of *Opinion No. 15,* the AICPA soon issued an unofficial interpretation that was more than 100 pages long.[4]

The complexities of *Opinion No. 15* and the FASB's objective of making EPS disclosures more comparable to the international EPS standards established by the IASC, resulted in the issuance of *Statement No. 128* in 1997.[5] The FASB worked closely with the IASC in developing its standards for EPS reporting and disclosure. Therefore, the requirements of *Statement No. 128* are substantially the same as *International Accounting Standard No. 33.* An overview of the *Statement No. 128* requirements is presented in the following section.

VERVIEW OF EPS REPORTING REQUIREMENTS

The EPS reporting and disclosure requirements depend on whether a company has a simple or a complex capital structure. A **simple capital structure** means that a company does not have any potentially dilutive securities, also called **potential**

[1]D. M. Blasch, J. Kelliher, and W. J. Reed, "The FASB and the IASC Redeliberate EPS," *Journal of Accountancy,* February 1996, pp. 43–47.
[2]"Reporting the Results of Operations," *Opinions of the Accounting Principles Board No. 9* (New York: AICPA, 1966).
[3]"Earnings per Share," *Opinions of the Accounting Principles Board No. 15* (New York: AICPA, 1969).
[4]*Computing Earnings per Share: Unofficial Accounting Interpretations of APB Opinion No. 15* (New York: AICPA, 1970).
[5]"Earnings per Share," *Statement of Financial Accounting Standards No. 128* (Norwalk, Conn.: FASB, 1997).

common shares, outstanding. **Potentially dilutive securities** include stock options, stock purchase warrants, contingently issuable common shares, convertible preferred stock, and convertible bonds. A **complex capital structure** means that the company does have some potentially dilutive securities outstanding.

For companies with simple capital structures, *Statement No. 128* requires that an EPS number called **basic earnings per share (BEPS)** be disclosed on the income statement. *Basic earnings per share is calculated by dividing net income available to common stockholders by the weighted-average number of common shares outstanding for the period.* Contingently issuable shares (shares that are issuable for little or no cash consideration when certain conditions have been satisfied) should be included in the BEPS denominator as of the date that all necessary conditions have been satisfied. Basic earnings per share must be reported for both income from continuing operations and net income.

For companies with complex capital structures, *Statement No. 128* requires that a dual presentation of EPS be disclosed on the income statement. The first presentation is basic earnings per share (BEPS). The second presentation is called **diluted earnings per share (DEPS).** Diluted earnings per share is an extension of BEPS in that it includes or reflects the *potential dilution* of (reduction in) EPS that could have occurred if certain potentially dilutive securities (potential common shares) had been exercised in exchange for common stock or had been converted into common stock. Contingently issuable shares should be included in the calculation of DEPS as of the beginning of the period, if the contingent conditions have been met by the end of the reporting period. If the conditions have not been met, the number of contingently issuable shares included in DEPS should be based on the number of shares that *would be issuable* if the end of the reporting period were the end of the contingency period. Like BEPS, DEPS must be calculated for both income from continuing operations and net income. Income from continuing operations is the control figure for determining whether potential common shares are dilutive.

Statement No. 128 also requires additional disclosures related to how BEPS and DEPS were calculated. These disclosures will be summarized at the end of the chapter. The following two sections will illustrate how to calculate BEPS and DEPS.

> **1** State what is meant by basic earnings per share and diluted earnings per share.

Basic Earnings per Share (BEPS)

If the concept of "earnings per share" is taken literally, the calculation of EPS is very simple:

$$\text{EPS} = \frac{\text{Income (or loss) for period}}{\text{Number of shares of common stock outstanding at end of period}}$$

However, the complexities of a corporation's capital structure and changes in that structure often require that the calculation of EPS be adjusted to better reflect economic reality and to improve the consistency and comparability of EPS figures. The next few sections explain how such adjustments are made.

Determining Income Applicable to Common Stock

If we examine the formulation of the EPS calculation shown above, we can see a potential deficiency in the numerator. How do we account for the claims of owners of outstanding securities that are senior to—that is, must be paid before—the claims of the common stockholders? To determine the income (or loss) applicable to shares of common stock, senior claims, such as dividends declared on nonconvertible preferred stock, must be deducted from income (or added to a loss) for the period. Hence, we must adjust the EPS formula presented earlier as shown below:

> **2** Calculate the amount of income applicable to common stock for the basic earnings per share calculation.

$$\text{EPS} = \frac{\text{Income (or loss) for period} - \text{Income applicable to senior securities}}{\text{Number of shares of common stock outstanding at end of period}}$$

To illustrate, assume that Benson Corporation earned $100,000 after taxes during fiscal year 1998 and that during the entire period 10,000 shares of common stock and 5,000 shares of nonconvertible preferred stock (with a dividend rate of $2 per share) were outstanding. In this case, net income must be adjusted for the income applicable to the nonconvertible preferred stock. Hence,

$$\text{EPS for 1998} = \frac{\$100,000 - \$2(5,000 \text{ shares})}{10,000 \text{ common shares}} = \frac{\$90,000}{10,000 \text{ shares}} = \$9$$

Income must be adjusted by the amount of dividends on *noncumulative* preferred stock outstanding any time those dividends for the current period have been paid or declared. Also, *cumulative* preferred dividends *for the current period,* even when not paid or declared, must be deducted from income in order to determine income applicable to common stock. However, preferred dividends that are cumulative *only if they are earned* are deducted from income only to the extent that they are earned. Dividends declared or accumulated *during a prior period* are not deducted in calculating EPS for the current period, even though they may have been paid during the current period. Those dividends would have been deducted from income when EPS was calculated for the particular prior period in which they were declared or accumulated.

Calculating the Weighted Average Number of Common Shares

Having adjusted the numerator of the EPS formulation to yield income applicable to common stock, we now turn our attention to the denominator. Notice that in the EPS formula just presented, income applicable to common stock is divided by the number of shares of common stock outstanding *at the end of the accounting period.* In effect, we are saying that the income that was earned *during* the accounting period was generated from the amount of capital corresponding to the common shares outstanding at the *end* of the period. This statement can be true only if there has been no change in the number of common shares outstanding during the period.

Since the earning process occurs continuously throughout the accounting period, we must recognize that the income for the period was generated from the capital available *during* the period, rather than from the amount of capital represented by the common stock at the end of the period. Therefore, we must adjust the denominator to reflect the lengths of time during the period that different amounts of capital (or net assets), represented by different numbers of common shares outstanding, were available to generate income. More specifically, we must "weight" the number of shares outstanding at any time during the accounting period by the length of time (e.g., the number of months) those shares were outstanding. In short, BEPS is calculated as follows:

$$\text{BEPS} = \frac{\text{Income (or loss) for period} - \text{Income applicable to senior securities}}{\substack{\text{Weighted average number of shares} \\ \text{of common stock outstanding during period}}}$$

The weighting procedure can be demonstrated by using a simple case in which 3,000 shares of common stock are outstanding for an entire year and 1,000 additional shares are issued and outstanding for the last three months of the year. In this case, at the end of the year the 3,000 shares would be multiplied by a weighting factor of 12/12, meaning that the 3,000 shares were outstanding for 12 of the 12 months in the year. The 1,000 shares would be multiplied by a weighting factor of 3/12, meaning that the 1,000 shares were outstanding for 3 of the 12 months. As a result of our calculations, the weighted average number of shares in this case

3 **Calculate the weighted average number of common shares for the basic earnings per share calculation.**

C O N C E P T U A L

The number of common stock shares outstanding at any time during the period must be weighted by the length of time those shares were outstanding.

is 3,250 [3,000(12/12) + 1,000(3/12)]. In cases in which the number of shares of common stock changes frequently during the year, the weighted average number of common shares may need to be calculated on the basis of days rather than months outstanding.

To further illustrate the weighted average procedure, assume that Adams, Inc., earned $100,000 after taxes during fiscal year 1998 and that Adams started 1998 with 6,000 common shares outstanding, issued 6,000 new common shares at the end of three months, and retired 2,000 common shares at the end of six months. Because the number of shares changed during the year, it is necessary to calculate the *weighted average* number of common shares outstanding during the year. The calculation of the weighted average number of common shares outstanding during 1998 is as follows:

$$6,000(12/12) + 6,000(9/12) - 2,000(6/12) = 6,000 + 4,500 - 1,000$$
$$= 9,500 \text{ weighted average}$$
$$\text{common shares}[6]$$

Using the adjusted equation for BEPS, we find:

$$\text{BEPS for 1998} = \frac{\$100,000}{9,500 \text{ shares}} = \$10.53$$

In determining the weighted average number of common shares to be used in calculating BEPS, acquisition of treasury stock is treated like a retirement of shares, since net assets are decreased when treasury stock is acquired. Correspondingly, reissue of treasury stock is treated like an issuance of new shares.

If convertible securities, such as convertible preferred stock or convertible bonds, are converted into common stock during the period, the weighted average number of common shares outstanding must be adjusted to reflect the shares of common stock issued upon conversion. In addition, income must be reduced by any dividend claims of convertible preferred stock that arose during the current period and *before* the conversion date. When a convertible bond is converted to common stock during the current period, the conversion must be considered in determining the weighted average number of common shares, but income need not be adjusted for bond interest expense incurred during the current period before the conversion date. The bond interest expense incurred before conversion of the bond would have been deducted when net income for the period was calculated.

To illustrate the inclusion of a preferred stock conversion in the BEPS calculation, assume that Acker, Inc., earned $50,000 after taxes for fiscal year 1998. Further assume that as of the beginning of the fiscal year, Acker had two classes of stock outstanding—2,500 shares of common stock and 5,000 shares of a convertible preferred stock that pays a $1 dividend per share at the end of the year. The conversion rate of the preferred stock is 2 preferred shares for 1 common share. Finally, assume that at the end of the ninth month of Acker's fiscal year, 3,200 of the preferred shares were converted to common shares.

There are two problems to be dealt with in this case. First, we must determine the income applicable to the common stock. Second, we must determine the weighted average number of common shares to be used in calculating the BEPS. Since only 1,800 preferred shares (5,000 shares – 3,200 shares converted) remain outstanding at the end of fiscal year 1998, the senior claim on income, preferred stock dividends, is $1,800 (1,800 shares × $1). Income applicable to the common stock, therefore, equals $48,200 ($50,000 – $1,800). With 2,500 common shares outstanding for the entire accounting period, and 1,600 (3,200 ÷ 2) new common

CONCEPTUAL

Shares issued when convertible securities are converted to common stock must be weighted to reflect the length of time the shares were outstanding.

---

[6]An alternative approach to calculating the weighted average number of common shares outstanding is to weight the number of shares outstanding by the proportion of the year that those shares were outstanding. Based on the data provided, this approach yields the following:

$$6,000(3/12) + 12,000(3/12) + 10,000(6/12) = 9,500 \text{ weighted average common shares}$$

shares outstanding for the final three months due to the conversion of preferred stock, the weighted average number of common shares is:

$$2,500(12/12) + 1,600(3/12) = 2,500 + 400 = 2,900 \text{ shares}$$

Therefore, in this case, the BEPS for fiscal year 1998 is:

$$\text{BEPS} = \frac{\$50,000 - \$1,800}{2,900 \text{ shares}} = \frac{\$48,200}{2,900 \text{ shares}} = \$16.62 \text{ per share}$$

CONCEPTUAL

Shares issued when options, rights, or warrants are exercised must be weighted to reflect the length of time the shares were outstanding.

The exercise of stock options, stock purchase rights, or stock warrants increases the number of common shares outstanding. When the exercise occurs *during* the accounting period for which BEPS is being calculated, the weighted average number of common shares outstanding must be adjusted to reflect the issuance of new common shares. For example, assume that on January 1, 1998, 3,300 shares of Partel Corporation common stock and 720 stock purchase warrants were outstanding. The warrants specified that the purchase of one share of Partel common stock required the exercise of a warrant and the payment of $50. Suppose that all the stock purchase warrants were exercised on March 1, 1998. To calculate BEPS, we must determine the weighted average number of common shares outstanding during the period, given the exercise of the warrants.

$$\begin{aligned}\text{Weighted average number of common shares} &= [3,300 \text{ shares} \times (12/12)] + [720 \text{ shares} \times (10/12)] \\ &= 3,300 \text{ shares} + 600 \text{ shares} = 3,900 \text{ shares}\end{aligned}$$

Adjusting the Weighted Average for Stock Dividends, Stock Splits, or Reverse Splits

4 Adjust the weighted average number of common shares for stock dividends, stock splits, and reverse splits.

Calculation of the weighted average number of common shares may also require an adjustment for stock dividends, stock splits, or reverse splits. When a stock dividend or stock split occurs, a stockholder has more shares (or fewer shares in the case of a reverse split) but no greater (no less) *proportionate* interest in the corporation. Therefore, when a stock dividend or stock split occurs during the year for which BEPS is being calculated, the resulting number of shares must be treated as if they were outstanding for the *entire* year (or since the issue date of the stock, if the stock was issued after the beginning of the year). This retroactive-to-the-beginning-of-the-fiscal-year treatment of a stock split or stock dividend is required because even though the number of shares changes as a result of the split or dividend, the invested capital represented by the new number of shares is exactly the same as the capital represented by the old number of shares. That is, there is no change in corporate assets as a result of a stock split or stock dividend. The effect of the retroactive treatment is to generate a BEPS figure that results in the same earnings *per investor* after the stock split or stock dividend as would have been calculated had there been no stock split or stock dividend.

To illustrate, assume that Taylor, Inc., earned $90,000 after income taxes during fiscal year 1998. Also assume that at the end of the fiscal year Taylor had 10,000 shares of common stock outstanding following a 2-for-1 stock split at the end of the fourth month. Recognizing that the 10,000 end-of-the-year shares represent no more invested capital than was represented by the 5,000 shares outstanding before the 2-for-1 split, we should treat the stock split as if the total ownership of the entity remained unchanged during 1998. That is, the BEPS calculation should be made as if the 10,000 shares were outstanding *throughout* the 1998 fiscal year. Therefore,

$$\text{BEPS for 1998} = \frac{\$90,000}{10,000 \text{ shares}} = \$9$$

When stock dividends, stock splits, or reverse splits occur, BEPS calculation rules require the retroactive-to-the-beginning-of-the-accounting-period adjustment just demonstrated. In addition, the weighted average number of common shares for all prior periods that are presented for comparative purposes also must be adjusted retroactively, and BEPS recalculated to reflect the stock dividend or stock split. The point to remember is that stock dividends, stock splits, and reverse splits *are not weighted* by the length of time the dividend or split is outstanding during the period, because there is no change in assets as a result of a stock dividend or stock split.

If a stock dividend or stock split occurs after the end of the accounting period but before the financial statements are issued, the weighted average number of common shares for the period for which BEPS is being calculated must be restated and BEPS recalculated to reflect the stock dividend or split. In addition, the weighted average number of common shares for any prior periods presented for comparative purposes also must be restated and BEPS adjusted accordingly. When EPS figures are adjusted for stock dividends or stock splits occurring after the balance sheet date, pertinent facts about the adjustment and its effect on EPS should be disclosed in a note to the financial statements.

To summarize this section, basic earnings per share (BEPS) is calculated by dividing the net income available to common stockholders (net income less any preferred dividend requirements) by the weighted-average number of common shares outstanding during the period. When stock dividends or stock splits occur during the period, the weighted-average number of shares must be adjusted accordingly. Any prior period BEPS numbers, presented for comparative purposes, must also be restated for any current period stock dividends or stock splits.

Now that we have covered how to calculate and report BEPS, we will consider the calculation of diluted earnings per share. As we shall see, several hypothetical assumptions underlie the calculation of DEPS. For example, if a company has stock options outstanding and their potential dilutive effects are to be included in DEPS, we must assume that they were exercised in exchange for common stock. Given this assumption, we must then make some assumption about how the proceeds from the exercise of the options would be used. To give another example, if a company has convertible bonds outstanding and their potential dilutive effects are to be included in DEPS, we must assume that they were converted into common shares. Given this assumption, we must then make some assumption about *when* the bonds might have been converted and what the corresponding effect *would have been* on net income. Given that the objective of DEPS is to show the maximum potential dilution of (reduction in) BEPS that is associated with potentially dilutive securities, the assumptions we make generally are based on the most advantageous results for the holders of those securities.

CONCEPTUAL

Stock dividends and stock splits require a retroactive-to-the-beginning-of-the-accounting-period treatment when BEPS is calculated.

DILUTED EARNINGS PER SHARE (DEPS)

This section explains how to calculate diluted earnings per share (DEPS). We will begin by discussing what is meant by the concept of dilution. We will then use the treasury stock method to include potentially dilutive stock options and warrants in the DEPS calculation. A discussion of the inclusion of contingently issuable common shares in the DEPS calculation follows. Next, we discuss and illustrate the "if-converted method" of including convertible securities, such as convertible preferred stock and convertible bonds, in the DEPS calculation. We then illustrate how potentially dilutive securities must be ranked by dilutive effect and included sequentially from most dilutive effect to least dilutive effect in the DEPS calculations. A comprehensive example of calculating and reporting BEPS and DEPS follows this section.

The Concept of Dilution

Convertible securities and stock purchase warrants are not actually common stock, but they do enable the holder to obtain common stock through conversion or exercise. Thus, in discussing DEPS calculations, they are called potentially dilutive securities or potential common shares. Potentially dilutive securities include convertible preferred stock, convertible bonds, stock purchase rights, stock warrants, and contingent shares.

CONCEPTUAL

Dilutive securities reduce the earnings per share of common stock.

The exercise or conversion of a potentially dilutive security increases the number of shares of common stock outstanding, reducing (or diluting) the earnings per share. Conservatism influences the rules for the calculation of DEPS, in that inclusion of the effect of dilutive securities in DEPS calculations is required only when a corporation has net income from continuing operations. (In the examples of this chapter, income from continuing operations usually is referred to simply as net income.) When a corporation has a net loss, such securities are antidilutive and therefore must be excluded from DEPS calculations. Thus, *only the weighted average number of common shares actually outstanding is considered when calculating net loss per share.*

The purpose of including dilutive securities in DEPS calculations is to place substance over form and to provide a reasonably conservative measure of corporate profitability per share of common stock outstanding. In addition, the inclusion of dilutive securities in DEPS calculations provides relevant and timely information about the effect that the exercise or conversion of the securities *could* have on DEPS.

To demonstrate the impact of a dilutive security on DEPS calculations, assume that Howard, Inc., earned $25,000 after taxes for fiscal year 1998. Ten thousand shares of Howard common stock were outstanding throughout 1998. Throughout 1998, Howard also had convertible bonds outstanding, which the bondholders could convert into 2,000 shares of common stock. Interest expense on the bonds was $500 per year. Ignoring Howard's convertible bonds for the moment, BEPS for 1998 would be:

$$\text{BEPS} = \frac{\$25,000}{10,000 \text{ shares}} = \$2.50 \text{ per share}$$

CONCEPTUAL

A dilutive security is included in DEPS calculations by assuming exercise or conversion of the security.

A dilutive security is included in DEPS calculations by *assuming* its exercise or conversion. That is, the assumed exercise or conversion allows us to determine what DEPS would have been if the dilutive security actually had been exercised or converted. In Howard's case, a hypothetical conversion of the convertible bonds into common stock at the beginning of 1998 requires two adjustments of the DEPS calculation. First, income applicable to common stock must be increased by $500, because the interest on the bonds would not have been paid if the bonds had been converted at the beginning of the period. Because tax-deductible expenses would have been reduced by $500, however, income applicable to common stock also must be decreased because of the increased tax. Assuming the 1998 tax rate was 34 percent, income must be decreased by $170 (.34 × $500). Hence, if the bonds had been converted at the beginning of 1998, income applicable to common stock would have been:

$$\$25,000 + \$500 - \$170 = \$25,330$$

Second, conversion of the bonds would require the issuance of 2,000 new shares of common stock, which would raise the number of common shares outstanding to 12,000. As a result, conversion of the bonds would make 1998 DEPS:

$$\text{DEPS} = \frac{\$25,330}{12,000 \text{ shares}} = \$2.11$$

As you can see, conversion of the convertible bonds would result in adjustments to both the numerator and the denominator of the DEPS fraction. The effect of conversion on DEPS would be:

$$\frac{\$330 \text{ additional after-tax income applicable to common stock}}{2,000 \text{ additional shares of common stock}} = \$.165$$

Since the effect of the conversion ($.165) is well below DEPS before inclusion of the dilutive security ($2.50), DEPS is lower ($2.11) after inclusion of the dilutive security. Later in the chapter we will discuss how the EPS effect of potentially dilutive securities is used to determine the order of entry of such securities into the DEPS calculations.

An **antidilutive security** is a security that increases DEPS or decreases the loss per share when included in DEPS calculations. For example, convertible debt is antidilutive if its assumed or actual conversion causes the income applicable to common stock to increase (because of the after-tax interest adjustment) by a greater amount per additional common share (because of the conversion) than DEPS was before conversion of the security.

Let us modify the facts given in the previous example for Howard, Inc. Assume now that the annual interest expense related to Howard's convertible bonds is $3,000, and that the bonds are convertible into only 700 common shares. We shall continue to assume $25,000 income after taxes for 1998, 10,000 shares of common stock outstanding if the bonds are not converted, and a 34 percent tax rate. In this case, the hypothetical conversion of the convertible bonds into common stock at the beginning of 1998 requires that income applicable to the common stock be adjusted as follows:

$$\$25,000 + [\$3,000 - .34(\$3,000)] = \$26,980$$

Given the incremental 700 common shares issuable upon conversion of the bonds, Howard's DEPS after inclusion of the convertible bonds would be:

$$DEPS = \frac{\$26,980}{10,700 \text{ shares}} = \$2.52$$

Because the conversion of the bonds has increased Howard's DEPS, the convertible bonds are antidilutive.

We could also have identified the convertible bonds as antidilutive by examining the incremental DEPS resulting from assumed conversion:

$$\frac{\$1,980 \text{ additional after-tax income applicable to common stock}}{700 \text{ additional shares of common stock}} = \$2.83$$

This amount is greater than DEPS before assumed conversion of the bonds ($2.50). *Antidilutive securities, like Howard's convertible bonds, should not be included in DEPS calculations.*

CONCEPTUAL

Antidilutive securities should not be included in DEPS calculations.

Including Potentially Dilutive Securities in DEPS Calculations

We have seen that including potentially dilutive securities in DEPS calculations allows us to determine what DEPS would have been if common stock actually had been issued to replace the potentially dilutive security. The following sections illustrate the procedures for including potentially dilutive securities in DEPS.

Stock Options and Warrants and Their Equivalents

Stock options and warrants and their equivalents are *always* classified as potentially dilutive securities. However, options and warrants are included in DEPS calculations *only if they are dilutive.* Stock purchase contracts, stock subscriptions not fully paid, and stock-based compensation arrangements are considered the equivalents of stock options and warrants for purposes of calculating DEPS.

The **treasury stock method** is the procedure used to include the dilutive effects of stock options, stock purchase rights, warrants, and their equivalents in DEPS calculations. Use of the treasury stock method increases the number of common

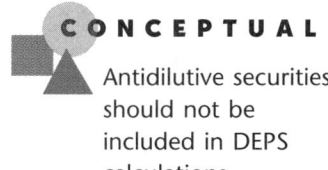

Use the treasury stock method to include stock options, warrants, and their equivalents in diluted earnings per share calculations.

shares *assumed* to be outstanding when the exercise price of a stock option or its equivalent is below the average market price of the common stock during the period. When the treasury stock method is used, we assume that the corporation would use the cash proceeds it would receive when the options or their equivalents are exercised to purchase ("buy back") shares of its own common stock at the *average market price* for the accounting period.

To illustrate the treasury stock method, assume that the current year's income for Arnold Company was $270,000. During the year Arnold had a weighted average of 45,000 shares of common stock outstanding; at year-end Arnold had 52,000 common shares outstanding. Throughout the year options to purchase 10,000 shares of Arnold's common stock at $10 per share were outstanding. The average price of Arnold's common stock during the year was $12. Arnold's BEPS would be $6 ($270,000 ÷ 45,000). Arnold's DEPS would be calculated as follows:

	DEPS
Shares that would have been issued under assumed exercise of options	10,000
Hypothetical proceeds from assumed exercise of options ($10 × 10,000 shares): $100,000	
Shares assumed purchased with proceeds: ($100,000 ÷ $12)	(8,333)
Incremental equivalent shares	1,667
Weighted average shares outstanding during year	45,000
Common shares plus incremental equivalent shares	46,667
DEPS ($270,000 ÷ 46,667 shares)	$5.79

Stock options, stock purchase rights, warrants, and their equivalents are included in DEPS calculations only when they are dilutive. In effect, this requirement means that *options, warrants, and their equivalents are included in DEPS calculations only when the average market price of the common stock for the period is above the exercise price of the option, warrant, or equivalent.*

At this point, the logic of the treasury stock method should be apparent. The treasury stock method is used *only* when the exercise (option) price of the stock option (or its equivalent) is *less* than the average market price of the common stock during the accounting period. Despite the fact that outstanding options means these options were not exercised, the treasury stock method *assumes that the options were exercised and that the proceeds were used to retire outstanding common shares.* Thus, even though no options were exercised, the relationship between the option price and market price—that is, an option price below the average market price—implies that exercise of the option is probable. The treasury stock method recognizes that fact. On the other hand, the treasury stock method is *not* used when the option price is *above* the average market price during the period. In those cases, exercise of the option probably would not occur and would not be a rational expectation. A holder of an option with an exercise price above the average market price could purchase shares of common stock directly in the market at a price that is lower than the option exercise price.

Contingently Issuable Shares of Common Stock

Contingently issuable shares of common stock are potentially dilutive securities that will be issued after some specified future event occurs—attainment of a specified level of income, perhaps, or simply the passage of time. Shares of common stock that are to be issued after the mere passage of time should be classified as outstanding shares when DEPS is calculated. Shares of common stock that are issuable for little or no consideration when specified conditions are met should also be considered outstanding stock in DEPS calculations when the specified conditions have been met. For example, if attainment or maintenance of a particular level of income is the specified condition, and that level of income is currently being attained, the contingently issuable shares of stock should be considered outstanding when DEPS is calculated.

To illustrate, assume that in 1998, Mead, Inc., purchased Atkinson Company and, as part of the purchase agreement, is to give Atkinson's stockholders 10,000 additional shares of Atkinson common stock if Atkinson's 1999 income after taxes is $100,000 or more. If Atkinson earns $100,000 in 1998, the 10,000 contingently issuable shares should be included in DEPS calculations for 1998, just as if they had been outstanding in 1998.

Convertible Securities

Convertible securities are another type of potentially dilutive security. The **if-converted method** is used to include the dilutive effect of convertible securities in DEPS calculations. The if-converted method *assumes that convertible securities were converted into common stock as of the beginning of the accounting period, or the issue date if the securities were issued during the period.* Income applicable to common stock must be adjusted for the effects of interest expense (after taxes) on convertible bonds and for dividends on convertible preferred stock that would not have to be paid if the securities were converted. For example, if convertible bonds actually were converted into common stock at the beginning of the period, there would be no interest expense on the bonds for the period. Since interest expense would have been deducted when income was determined, and tax expense would have been based on that income, assumed conversion of the bonds would mean that

> **6** Use the if-converted method to include the dilutive effect of convertible securities in diluted earnings per share calculations.

$$\left(\begin{array}{c} \text{Cash} \\ \text{interest} \end{array} - \begin{array}{c} \text{Premium} \\ \text{amortization} \end{array} \text{ or } + \begin{array}{c} \text{Discount} \\ \text{amortization} \end{array} \right) \times (1 - \text{Tax rate})$$

must be added back to after-tax income applicable to common stock.

In the case of convertible preferred stock, the assumed conversion would mean that any dividends that were deducted in the determination of income applicable to common stock must be added back. Such dividends would not exist if the preferred stock actually had been converted. Because dividends paid are not deductible for tax purposes, there is no tax effect for this adjustment.

The assumed conversion of convertible securities, whether bonds or preferred stocks, also requires an adjustment of the weighted average number of common shares to reflect the additional shares that would be issued upon conversion of the securities. For convertible securities issued during the accounting period, the assumed new shares must be weighted for the length of time from the issue date to the end of the period.

To illustrate the if-converted method, assume that Nantel Company had a net income of $320,000 for the year and an average of 20,000 shares of common stock outstanding during the year. Nantel also had two types of convertible securities outstanding. The first was 2,500 shares of convertible cumulative preferred stock that were issued in a prior year. These shares pay an annual dividend of $1.50, and are convertible into 5,000 shares of common stock. The second convertible security outstanding was a $50,000, 7 percent convertible bond issued at the beginning of the fifth month of the current fiscal year. This bond is convertible into 2,400 shares of common stock. Nantel is taxed at a 34 percent rate.

Nantel's *basic* earnings per share is calculated as follows:

Net income for the year *before* adjustment for preferred dividends	**$320,000**
Less: Preferred dividends	**(3,750)**
Income available to common stockholders	**$316,250**
Shares of common stock outstanding	**20,000**

$$\text{BEPS} = \frac{\$316,250}{20,000 \text{ shares}} = \$15.81$$

Nantel's *diluted* earnings per share is calculated as follows, given an order-of-entry analysis (discussed in next section) that shows the dilutive effect of both convertible securities should be included in DEPS:

Income available to common stockholders	**$316,250**
Add: Preferred dividends	**3,750**
Add: Adjustment for interest expense (net of tax)	
on the bond issue for the last eight months	
of the current year [$50,000 × .07 × 2/3 × (1 − .34 tax rate)]	**1,540**
Income available to common stockholders,	
plus assumed conversion	**$321,540**
Average number of shares outstanding during the year	**20,000**
Shares assumed to be issued upon conversion	
of the preferred stock	**5,000**
Weighted shares assumed to be issued upon conversion	
of the convertible bond issue (2,400 shares × 2/3 year)	**1,600**
Common shares plus assumed shares from conversion	**26,600**

$$\text{DEPS} = \frac{\$321,540}{26,600 \text{ shares}} = \$12.09$$

Notice that when BEPS was calculated, preferred stock dividends were subtracted from net income to determine income available to common stockholders. In calculating DEPS, we assumed that the preferred shares were converted at the beginning of the year and that the convertible bond issue was converted into 2,400 shares of common stock. Because the bonds were issued at the beginning of the fifth month of the year, the common shares related to the bonds were weighted by two-thirds. Similarly, only two-thirds of a year's interest expense, net of tax, was added back to net income for the year. This interest expense would not have been incurred had the bond issue been converted on the date of issuance.

Determining the Order of Entry of Potentially Dilutive Securities into DEPS Calculations

When several potentially dilutive securities are to be considered for inclusion in the DEPS calculations, the first step is to calculate the "income per incremental common share effect" embodied in each potentially dilutive security under consideration. Next, the securities should be ranked from the smallest income per incremental share effect (potentially the most dilutive) to the largest income per incremental share effect (potentially the least dilutive). The smallest income per incremental share effect should then be compared with the DEPS amount just before the inclusion of the security under consideration. If the previous DEPS is larger, the security should be included in the DEPS calculation, because it will be dilutive. A new DEPS amount should be calculated, including the security just tested, and the new DEPS amount should be compared with the next lowest income per incremental share effect. Once again, if the income per incremental share effect is smaller than the newly calculated DEPS, the security under consideration

7 **Determine the order of entry of potentially dilutive securities into the diluted earnings per share calculations, based on the securities' relative income per incremental common share effects.**

is dilutive and should therefore be included in the calculation of another DEPS amount. This process should continue, testing each increasing income per incremental share effect in turn and including the security under consideration in a new DEPS calculation, until an income per incremental share effect is reached that exceeds the previous DEPS amount.[7] At that point, antidilutive securities have been encountered, and the potentially dilutive securities remaining on the list should *not* be included in the DEPS calculations.

To illustrate this process of ordering potentially dilutive securities for entry into DEPS calculations, assume that Wixom Company has three potentially dilutive securities outstanding. These securities must be ordered for possible entry into Wixom's DEPS calculations. The three potentially dilutive securities are:

1. Stock options which, if exercised, would not change the numerator of DEPS, but would add 1,000 incremental common shares to the denominator. Hence, the income per incremental share effect would be $0 \div 1,000$ shares = $0.

2. Six percent convertible bonds which, if converted, would reduce Wixom's after-tax interest expense by $500, increasing the numerator of DEPS and adding 1,500 incremental common shares to the denominator of DEPS. Hence, the income per incremental share effect would be $500 \div 1,500$ shares = $.33.

3. Eight percent convertible bonds which, if converted, would reduce after-tax interest expense by $750, increasing the numerator of DEPS and adding 1,000 incremental common shares to the denominator of DEPS. Hence, the income per incremental share effect would be $750 \div 1,000$ shares = $.75.

These three securities would be considered for entry into Wixom's DEPS calculation on the basis of their income per incremental share effects, from the smallest income per incremental share effect (the stock options' effect of $0) to the largest income per incremental share effect (the 8 percent convertible bonds' effect of $.75). As each security is considered for inclusion in the DEPS calculation, its income per incremental share effect would be compared with the most recently calculated DEPS. The security would be included in the DEPS calculation only if its income per incremental share effect is lower than the previous DEPS amount—that is, if the security is dilutive.

EPORTING EPS AND RELATED DISCLOSURES

Corporations with simple capital structures (those with only common stock outstanding) are required to present BEPS amounts for income from continuing operations (or income before extraordinary items or accounting changes, if those items exist) and net income on the face of the income statement. An example of EPS presentation for a corporation with a simple capital structure appears in Exhibit 20–1. Corporations with complex capital structures are required to present BEPS and DEPS for income from continuing operations (or income before extraordinary items or accounting changes, if those items exist) and net income on the face of the income statement. An example of EPS presentation for a corporation with a complex capital structure appears in Exhibit 20–2. As shown in Exhibits 20–1 and 20–2 with regard to an extraordinary item, companies that report a discontinued operation, an extraordinary item, or the cumulative effect of an accounting change must report BEPS and DEPS amounts for those line items either on the face of the income statement or in the notes to the financial statements.[8]

8 State the major reporting and disclosure requirements for earnings per share.

[7]A graphical analysis of the order of entry procedure appears in L. Chasteen and M. Keener, "Ranking Convertible Securities for Earnings per Share: A Graphical Analysis," *Issues in Accounting Education,* Fall 1988.
[8]*Statement No. 128,* paras. 36–37.

EXHIBIT 20–1	Partial Income Statement and Presentation of BEPS for a Company with a Simple Capital Structure		
		1998	1997
Income before extraordinary item		$18,300,000	$15,300,000
Extraordinary item—gain on sale of property less applicable income taxes		1,800,000	
Net income		$20,100,000	$15,300,000
Earnings per common share:			
Income before extraordinary item		$5.54	$4.64
Extraordinary item		.56	
Net income		$6.10	$4.64

EXHIBIT 20–2	Partial Income Statement and Presentation of EPS for a Company with a Complex Capital Structure		
		1998	1997
Income before extraordinary item		$25,800,000	$20,600,000
Extraordinary item—gain on sale of property less applicable income taxes		1,800,000	
Net income		$27,600,000	$20,600,000
Earnings per common share (BEPS):			
Income before extraordinary item		$6.40	$5.50
Extraordinary item		.44	
Net income		$6.84	$5.50
Earnings per common share, assuming dilution (DEPS):			
Income before extraordinary item		$6.22	$5.32
Extraordinary item		.42	
Net income		$6.64	$5.32

Earnings per share amounts must be presented for all periods for which an income statement or a summary of earnings is presented. If DEPS amounts are reported for one period, they must be reported for all periods presented, even if DEPS and BEPS amounts are the same.[9] In addition, for each period for which an income statement is presented, the following items must be disclosed.[10]

1. A reconciliation of the numerators and denominators of the BEPS and DEPS calculations for income from continuing operations. The reconciliation must include the individual income and share amount effects of all securities that affect earnings per share. An example of the required reconciliation, based on the Nantel Company data and illustration presented earlier in the chapter on pages 1085–1086, appears in Exhibit 20–3.

2. The effect of preferred dividends on the income available to common stockholders used in calculating BEPS. This is illustrated in Exhibit 20–3.

---

[9]Ibid., para. 38.
[10]Ibid., para. 40.

EXHIBIT 20-3	Reconciliation of the Numerators and Denominators of BEPS and DEPS, Based on Data for Nantel Company		
	For the Year Ended 19XX		
	Income (Numerator)	**Shares (Denominator)**	**Per-Share Amount**
Income from continuing operations..............	$320,000		
Less: Preferred dividends	(3,750)		
Basic EPS			
Income applicable to common stockholders	$316,250	20,000	$15.81
Convertible preferred stock	3,750	5,000	
7% convertible bond........................	1,540	1,600	
Diluted EPS			
Income applicable to common stockholders, plus assumed conversions....................	$321,500	26,600	$12.09

3. Securities that could potentially dilute BEPS in the future but were not included in the calculation of DEPS because they were antidilutive for the periods presented.

For the latest period for which an income statement is presented, a company must provide a description of any transaction (such as the issuance or acquisition of common shares or the issuance of warrants, options, or convertible securities) that occurred after the end of the current period but before the financial statements were issued, and that would have changed materially the number of common shares or potential common shares outstanding at the end of the period if the transaction had occurred before the end of the period.[11]

The next section presents some comprehensive illustrations of the calculation and reporting of earnings per share.

COMPREHENSIVE ILLUSTRATION OF CALCULATING AND REPORTING EPS

Assume that Rex, Inc., began 1998 with 8,000 shares of common stock outstanding. Rex acquired 2,000 of those outstanding shares for treasury stock at the beginning of April, and reissued 1,200 of them at the beginning of November. In addition, assume that:

1. Rex had 1,000 shares of $20 par, 8 percent nonconvertible cumulative preferred stock outstanding during all of 1998.

2. At the end of 1998, Rex had stock options outstanding for 1,012 shares of common stock, with an exercise price of $20 per share. Options on 460 shares were outstanding during the entire year, and options on 552 shares were issued on May 1, 1998.

3. The average common stock price for the year was $23.

---

[11]Ibid., para. 41.

4. During 1998, Rex earned $75,000 after income taxes.

5. Rex had two different issues of convertible bonds outstanding throughout fiscal year 1998:

    a) $20,000 of 10-year, $1,000, 7 percent bonds, each convertible into 50 shares of common stock. These bonds were issued at 107.4, which provided an effective yield of 6 percent. For tax purposes, the bond premium is being amortized on a straight-line basis.

    b) $25,000 of 10-year, $1,000, 8 percent bonds, each convertible into 50 shares of common stock. These bonds were issued at 100.

6. The average income tax rate applicable to Rex, Inc., is 34 percent.

Since the average common stock price during the accounting period was above the $20 exercise price of the stock options, it is appropriate to assume that the options were exercised as prescribed by the treasury stock method.

Calculating Basic EPS

Basic EPS for Rex, Inc., would be calculated as follows:

$$\text{Income applicable to common stock} = \$75,000 - \$1.60(1,000 \text{ preferred shares})^a$$
$$= \$75,000 - \$1,600$$
$$= \$73,400$$

[a]Because the preferred stock is cumulative, the dividends would be deducted whether or not they had been declared for the current year. If the preferred stock had not been cumulative, the dividends would not be deducted unless they were paid or declared for the current year.

$$\text{Weighted average number of common shares} = 8,000(12/12) - 2,000(9/12) + 1,200(2/12)$$
$$= 8,000 - 1,500 + 200$$
$$= 6,700 \text{ shares}$$

$$\text{BEPS} = \frac{\$73,400}{6,700 \text{ shares}}$$
$$= \underline{\underline{\$10.96}}$$

Calculating Diluted EPS

The process of calculating DEPS for Rex, Inc., consists of the following steps:

1. Determination of income applicable to common stock. We did this when calculating BEPS.

Net income	**$75,000**
Less: Cumulative preferred dividends	**(1,600)**
Income applicable to common stock	**$73,400**

2. Detailed analysis of all outstanding securities:

    a) *Common stock.* When calculating BEPS, we determined the basic weighted average number of common shares to be 6,700.

    b) *$20 par, 8 percent nonconvertible cumulative preferred stock.* Being nonconvertible, this security is ignored because it cannot be dilutive. We know from the BEPS calculation that these preferred shares have a senior claim on income of $1,600, which was deducted in step 1 above to calculate income applicable to common stock.

    c) *Stock options.* The stock options must be considered when DEPS is calculated. Using the treasury stock method, we can determine the net weighted average number of common share equivalents of the stock options:

	NUMBER OF SHARES
Common share equivalents for options outstanding on 1/1/98	460
Weighted average common share equivalents	
for options issued 5/1/98: 552 shares × (8/12)	368
Weighted average treasury shares assumed purchased	
at *average* market price: [($20 × 460 shares)/$23] + [(8/12) ×	
($20 × 552 shares)/$23]	(720)
Net weighted average number of common share	
equivalents of stock options	108

d) *Convertible securities.* Rex, Inc., has two convertible securities, both of which are convertible bonds and must be considered in calculating DEPS.

Deciding whether each potentially dilutive security has a dilutive or an antidilutive effect on DEPS requires that, as each security is considered for entry into the DEPS calculations, we compare its "income per incremental common share effect" with the DEPS amount that applies just before the possible entry of the security in question. If the security's income per incremental share effect is less than the previous DEPS amount, the security is dilutive and should be included in the DEPS calculations. Otherwise, the security is antidilutive and should not be included in the DEPS calculations.

As discussed on page 1086, the "income per incremental common share effect" of each potentially dilutive security is also important because it is the basis for deciding the order in which dilutive securities will enter the DEPS calculations. Potentially dilutive securities enter the DEPS calculations beginning with the security that has the smallest income per incremental share effect and proceeding to securities with increasingly larger income per incremental share effects, until an antidilutive security is encountered. In preparation for calculating Rex's DEPS, the income per incremental share effect for each of Rex's potentially dilutive securities must be determined as follows:

1. *Stock options.* Exercise of these options would not change the numerator of EPS, but 108 incremental common shares must be added to the denominator. Income per incremental share is $0 ÷ 108 shares = $0.

2. *Seven percent convertible bonds.* If these bonds were converted as of the beginning of the year, they would increase the numerator of DEPS by the after-tax interest expense savings of $826: [($70 × 20 bonds) − $148 premium amortization] × (1 − .34). They would also add 1,000 incremental common shares to the denominator of DEPS. Income per incremental share is therefore $826 ÷ 1,000 shares = $.826.

3. *Eight percent convertible bonds.* If these bonds were converted as of the beginning of the year, they would increase the numerator of DEPS by the after-tax interest savings of $1,320 [($80 × 25 bonds) × (1 − .34)] and would add 1,250 incremental common shares to the denominator of DEPS. Income per incremental share is therefore $1,320 ÷ 1,250 shares = $1.06.

Given the income per incremental common share effect of each security, the securities should enter the DEPS calculations in the following order: stock options, 7 percent convertible bonds, and 8 percent convertible bonds.

We are now ready to begin calculating DEPS. *DEPS can be calculated by building on the BEPS calculations presented on page 1090.* In calculating DEPS for Rex, Inc., there are three potentially dilutive securities, which will be included in the DEPS calculations beginning with the security having the smallest income per incremental share effect (the stock options) and ending with the security having the largest income per incremental share effect (the 8 percent convertible bonds), provided that each security is dilutive. For purposes of calculating DEPS, assumed exercise of the stock options has no effect on the numerator of DEPS, but increases the denominator by a net 108 shares. Tentatively, DEPS is now:

$$\frac{\$73,400}{6,700 \text{ shares} + 108 \text{ shares}} = \$10.78$$

Next we consider the 7 percent convertible bonds. These bonds are dilutive because their \$.826 income per share effect is below the previous DEPS amount of \$10.78. Including the 7 percent convertibles in the DEPS calculations results in an increase in the numerator of \$826 (from the after-tax interest expense savings) and an increase in the denominator by 1,000 shares. Consequently, DEPS is now:

$$\frac{\$73,400 + \$826}{6,700 \text{ shares} + 108 \text{ shares} + 1,000 \text{ shares}} = \$9.51$$

When compared with the previous DEPS amount of \$9.51, the 8 percent convertible bonds, with an income per share effect of \$1.06, are dilutive. Including the 8 percent convertible bonds in the calculations increases the numerator of DEPS by \$1,320 (the after-tax interest expense savings) and the denominator by 1,250 shares. After the 8 percent convertible bonds have been included, the DEPS amount for Rex in the current year is:

$$\frac{\$73,400 + \$826 + \$1,320}{6,700 \text{ shares} + 108 \text{ shares} + 1,000 \text{ shares} + 1,250 \text{ shares}} = \$8.34$$

Reporting EPS

Now that the BEPS and DEPS amounts for Rex, Inc., have been calculated, the next step is to present both EPS amounts in Rex's income statement.

One possible presentation of the two amounts would be a dual presentation on the face of the income statement, with an accompanying footnote, as follows:

	1998
Net income..	$75,000
Earnings per common share (basic EPS) (Note A).........................	$10.96
Earnings per common share, assuming dilution (diluted EPS).................	$8.34

NOTE A
During 1998, 2,000 shares of common stock were acquired as treasury stock. Twelve hundred of those shares were subsequently reissued. At the end of 1998, 7,200 common shares were outstanding. One thousand shares of $20 par, 8 percent nonconvertible cumulative preferred stock were outstanding throughout 1998. Options are outstanding for 1,012 shares of common stock at an option price of $20. Options on 460 shares were outstanding during all of 1998, and options on 552 shares were granted on May 1, 1998. At the end of 1998 two issues of convertible bonds were outstanding: twenty $1,000, 7 percent convertible bonds, each convertible into 50 shares of common stock, and twenty-five $1,000, 8 percent convertible bonds, each convertible into 50 shares of common stock.

For purposes of calculating the basic earnings per share ($10.96), income applicable to common stockholders was $73,400, and the weighted average number of common shares was 6,700. For purposes of calculating diluted earnings per share ($8.34), several adjustments were made to the denominator of the basic earnings per share calculation. The number of common shares was increased by a net 108 shares, representing the difference between the number of shares issuable upon exercise of the stock options (828 shares) and the number of shares that could be purchased (720) with the exercise proceeds at the average market price of 1998. The number of common shares was further increased by the 1,000 shares issuable upon the hypothetical beginning-of-year conversion of the 7 percent convertible bonds, and the 1,250 shares issuable upon the hypothetical beginning-of-year conversion of the 8 percent convertible bonds. The numerator of the basic earnings per share was increased by $826, the after-tax interest expense saving that would result from conversion of the 7 percent convertible bonds; and $1,320, the after-tax interest expense saving that would result from conversion of the 8 percent convertible bonds.

The numerators and denominators of the basic and diluted earnings per share amounts for 1998 may be reconciled as follows:

| | FOR THE YEAR ENDED 12/31/98 | | |
	INCOME (NUMERATOR)	SHARES (DENOMINATOR)	PER-SHARE AMOUNT
Income from continuing operations	$75,000		
Less: Preferred dividends	(1,600)		
Basic EPS			
Income available to common stockholders	$73,400	6,700	$10.96
Stock options		108	
7% convertible bonds	826	1,000	
8% convertible bonds	1,320	1,250	
Diluted EPS			
Income available to common stockholders, plus assumed conversion	$75,546	9,058	$ 8.34

Exhibit 20–4 summarizes the process of calculating EPS. As we have seen, while the concept of EPS is simple, its calculation under GAAP can be complex. You should become very familiar with Exhibit 20–4 and use it as a format for organizing your solutions to the exercises and problems at the end of the chapter.

 NTERNATIONAL PERSPECTIVE

There are only a few countries other than the United States, such as Great Britain and Japan, where the disclosure of EPS is required. (For example, neither Germany nor Australia requires disclosure of EPS.) One reason for this situation is that in many countries, banks or the national government provide most of the capital needed by business. Because organized securities markets are not a major source of financing, there is less need to report shareholder-oriented information such as EPS.

Recently there has been a concerted effort by the International Accounting Standards Committee (IASC) to develop international standards regarding calculating and presenting EPS.[12] The FASB's *Statement No. 128* is the result of a desire to get the United States more in line with international harmonization of accounting standards. *Statement No. 128* not only simplifies the calculation of EPS, but is compatible with the EPS standards of other countries and with standards being developed by the IASC. As a result, comparisons of the EPS amounts of companies, both national and multinational, should be enhanced.

---

[12]In February 1997, the IASC issued *International Accounting Standard No. 33*, "Earning Per Share."

EXHIBIT 20–4   Summary of EPS Calculations

Collect the necessary data for EPS calculations.

Calculate income applicable to common stock, after adjusting
for senior claims, if any, on income.
Calculate weighted average number of common shares outstanding.

Calculate basic EPS:

$$BEPS = \frac{\text{Income applicable to common stock}}{\text{Weighted average number of common shares outstanding during the period}}$$

If simple capital structure   If complex capital structure

Present BEPS on the face
of the income statement.

1. Assume replacement of potentially
   dilutive securities with shares of
   common stock.[a]

2. *Stock options, warrants, and
   equivalents.* If dilutive, use the
   treasury stock method and the
   average market price for assumed
   conversion.

3. *Contingently issuable shares of
   common stock.* If dilutive,
   include in EPS calculation.

4. *Convertible securities.* If dilutive,
   include in EPS calculation
   using the *if-converted method.*

Calculate diluted EPS:

$$DEPS = \frac{\text{Income applicable to common stock adjusted for after-tax interest expense on dilutive convertible bonds and for dividends on dilutive convertible preferred stock}}{\text{Weighted average number of shares of common stock outstanding, assuming dilution from potentially dilutive securities}}$$

Present BEPS and DEPS on the face
of the income statement.

[a]Multiple potentially dilutive securities enter the EPS calculations beginning with the smallest income per incremental common share effect security and proceeding to the next largest income per incremental common share effect security, until an antidilutive security is encountered.

UMMARY OF LEARNING OBJECTIVES

1. **State what is meant by basic earnings per share and diluted earnings per share.**
   Basic earnings per share (BEPS) is calculated by dividing net income available to common stockholders by the weighted-average number of common shares outstanding for the period. Diluted earnings per share is similar to (or an extension of) BEPS, except that it includes or reflects the potential dilution of EPS that could occur if certain potentially dilutive securities (potential common shares) were exchanged for or converted into common stock.

2. **Calculate the amount of income applicable to common stock for the basic earnings per share calculation.**
   Senior claims on income, such as dividends declared on nonconvertible preferred stock, must be deducted from income (or added to a loss) for the period to determine the income (or loss) applicable to shares of common stock.

3. **Calculate the weighted average number of common shares for the basic earnings per share calculation.**
   The denominator of the EPS calculation must be adjusted to reflect the lengths of time during the period that different amounts of capital, from different numbers of common shares outstanding, were available to generate income. Therefore, the number of shares of common stock outstanding at any time during the period must be weighted by the length of time those shares were outstanding.

4. **Adjust the weighted average number of common shares for stock dividends, stock splits, and reverse splits.**
   When a stock dividend or stock split occurs during the year for which EPS is being calculated, the resulting number of shares must be treated as if the shares were outstanding for the entire year (or since the issue date, if the stock was issued after the beginning of the year). This retroactive-to-the-beginning-of-the-fiscal-year treatment of a stock split or stock dividend is required because even though the number of shares changes as a result of the split or dividend, the invested capital represented by the new number of shares is exactly the same as the capital represented by the old number of shares.

5. **Use the treasury stock method to include stock options, warrants, and their equivalents in diluted earnings per share calculations.**
   Use of the treasury stock method increases the number of common shares assumed to be outstanding when the exercise price of a stock option or its equivalent is below the average market price of the common stock during the period. Under these conditions, the option or its equivalent is assumed to be exercised at the exercise price. It is assumed also that the corporation would use the cash proceeds it would receive from the exercise of the option or its equivalents to purchase (buy back) shares of its own common stock at the average market price for the period.

6. **Use the if-converted method to include the dilutive effect of convertible securities in diluted earnings per share calculations.**
   Under the if-converted method, convertible securities are assumed to have been converted into common stock as of the beginning of the accounting period, or the issue date of the securities if they were issued during the period. Furthermore, the income applicable to common stock must be adjusted for the effects of interest expense (after taxes) on convertible bonds and for dividends on convertible preferred stock that would not have to be paid if the securities were converted. The assumed conversion of convertible securities also requires the adjustment of the weighted average number of common shares to reflect the additional shares that would be issued upon conversion of the securities. For convertible securities issued during the accounting period, the assumed new shares must be weighted by the length of time from the issue date to the end of the period.

7. **Determine the order of entry of potentially dilutive securities into the diluted earnings per share calculations, based on the securities' relative income per incremental common share effects.**

First, calculate the income per incremental common share effect that is embodied in each potentially dilutive security under consideration. Next, rank the securities from the smallest income per incremental share effect (potentially the most dilutive) to the largest income per incremental share effect (potentially the least dilutive). The smallest income per incremental share effect should be compared with the DEPS amount just before the inclusion of the security under consideration. If the previous DEPS is larger, the security should be included in the DEPS calculation because it will be dilutive. A new DEPS amount should be calculated, including the security just tested. The new DEPS amount should be compared with the next lowest income per incremental share effect. Once again, if the income per incremental share effect is smaller than the newly calculated DEPS, the security under consideration is dilutive and should be included in the calculation of another DEPS amount. This process should continue, testing each increasing income per incremental share effect in turn and including the security under consideration in a new DEPS calculation, until an income per incremental share effect is reached that exceeds the previous DEPS amount.

8. **State the major reporting and disclosure requirements for earnings per share.**

Corporations with simple capital structures (those with only common stock outstanding) are required to present BEPS amounts for income from continuing operations (or income before extraordinary items or accounting changes, if such items exist) and net income on the face of the income statement. Corporations with complex capital structures are required to present BEPS and DEPS for income from continuing operations (or income before extraordinary items or accounting changes, if such items exist) and net income on the face of the income statement. Earnings per share amounts must be presented for all periods for which an income statement or summary of earnings is presented. If DEPS amounts are reported for one period, they must be reported for all periods presented, even if DEPS and BEPS amounts are the same. In addition, for each period for which an income statement is presented, the following must be disclosed:

a) A reconciliation of the numerators and denominators of the basic and diluted EPS calculations for income from continuing operations (or income before extraordinary items or accounting changes, if such items exist). The reconciliation must include the individual income and share amount effects of all securities that affect earnings per share.

b) The effect of preferred dividends on income available to common stockholders used in calculating BEPS.

c) Securities that could potentially dilute BEPS in the future but were not included in the calculation of DEPS because they were antidilutive for the periods presented.

For the latest period for which an income statement is presented, a company must provide a description of any transaction (such as the issuance or acquisition of common shares or the issuance of warrants, options, or convertible securities) that occurred after the end of the most recent period but before the issuance of the financial statements and that would have changed materially the number of common shares or potential common shares outstanding at the end of the period if the transaction had occurred before the end of the period.

KEY TERMS

antidilutive security 1083

basic earnings per share (BEPS) 1077

complex capital structure 1077

contingently issuable shares 1084

diluted earnings per share (DEPS) 1077

if-converted method 1085

potential common shares 1077

potentially dilutive securities 1077

simple capital structure 1076

treasury stock method 1083

QUESTIONS

Q 20-1. Explain the term *senior securities* within the context of corporate capital structure.

Q 20-2. Why are senior claims on income important in EPS calculations?

Q 20-3. For purposes of calculating income applicable to common stock, how do dividends on cumulative preferred stock differ from dividends on noncumulative preferred stock?

Q 20-4. What is the reasoning behind calculation of a weighted average number of common shares for an accounting period?

Q 20-5. For purposes of EPS calculations, how should the acquisition and reissue of treasury stock be treated?

Q 20-6. How do annual interest expense and dividends on preferred stock affect income applicable to common stock?

Q 20-7. Describe the nature of a stock split or stock dividend with respect to the total ownership of a corporation.

Q 20-8. Explain how a stock split or stock dividend should be handled in calculating the weighted average number of common shares.

Q 20-9. Is a stock dividend or stock split that occurs after the end of the accounting period relevant to EPS calculations for the accounting period? If so, what treatment should they be given?

Q 20-10. What does the term *dilution* mean in the context of EPS calculations?

Q 20-11. What does the term *antidilution* mean in the context of EPS calculations?

Q 20-12. Explain what is meant by potentially dilutive securities.

Q 20-13. For purposes of calculating EPS, what does it mean to say that a corporation has a simple capital structure? A complex capital structure?

Q 20-14. Is it possible for a corporation to have a simple capital structure in one accounting period and a complex capital structure in the next? Explain.

Q 20-15. Distinguish between a single presentation and a dual presentation of EPS.

Q 20-16. Explain the treasury stock method used for stock options and their equivalents in calculating DEPS.

Q 20-17. Explain the if-converted method in DEPS calculations.

Q 20-18. Explain what is meant by the "income per additional common share effect" as it applies to convertible securities in DEPS calculations.

Q 20-19. Why must potentially dilutive securities be ranked for order of entry into DEPS calculations?

Q 20-20. What disclosures must accompany EPS figures reported in the income statement?

CASES

C 20-1. **COMMON STOCK EQUIVALENTS AND SENIOR SECURITIES** Laker Corporation has current year net income of $257,000 and has had 60,000 common shares outstanding for the entire year. Other securities outstanding include:

a) $200,000 of 9 percent convertible bonds that had been issued at par. Each $1,000 bond is convertible into 20 shares of common stock.

b) $60,000 par value of 10 percent, cumulative, convertible preferred stock. The preferred shares are convertible into 1,000 shares of common stock.

c) $300,000 of 8 percent convertible bonds. Each $1,000 bond is convertible into 24 shares of common stock.

Laker's president is under the impression that earnings per share is about $4.28 ($257,000 ÷ 60,000 shares).

REQUIRED

1. Discuss the reasons why securities other than common stock should be considered common stock when calculating DEPS.

2. Why is the 10 percent preferred stock called a *senior security,* and, if the preferred stock was not convertible, how would the preferred stock affect the determination of EPS?

C 20-2. **EPS CONCEPTS AND PROCEDURES** Financial analysts and others place great emphasis on the earnings per share figures of corporations. Daily stock price quotations often include a "times earnings" amount that is based on earnings per share. EPS is significant because of the importance of income to the success of a corporation and because, as a measure per share of common stock, EPS is meaningful to individual stockholders.

REQUIRED

1. Explain how EPS calculations are affected by dividends or dividend requirements on outstanding shares of preferred stock.

2. The treasury stock method is the procedure used to include the dilutive effect of stock options, stock purchase rights, warrants, and their equivalents in EPS calculations. When should the treasury stock method be used?

3. How are convertible debentures treated for purposes of EPS calculations?

C 20-3. **EARNINGS PER SHARE AND DILUTION** M. Latine is the president of Husky Manufacturing, a company engaged in personal computer development. Latine has called you to his office to discuss a proposed stock offering intended to provide capital for the rapidly expanding operations of the company.

The company's board of directors has decided to obtain additional capital by creating a new class of preferred stock rather than by issuing additional shares of common stock. This approach will allow the board to maintain operating control of the company. Latine has presented a proposal to the board that would result in issuance of 10,000 shares of Class A preferred stock. The stock would be convertible, noncumulative, nonparticipating, 7 percent preferred stock with a $100 par value per share. The conversion feature would allow investors to obtain two shares of common stock for each share of preferred stock. Through consultation with investment bankers, Latine has determined that issuance of the preferred shares should provide about $1,000,000 of additional capital.

One of the directors has expressed some concern about the proposed offering of preferred stock. The director is worried about the possibility of additional dilution of earnings per common share as a result of the issuance of the preferred stock and has requested that Latine have you prepare an analysis of the situation.

Husky had 100,000 shares of common stock outstanding for all of the current year and reported after-tax net income for the year of $1,500,000. Husky had no other securities outstanding during the current year.

REQUIRED Write a memorandum to M. Latine discussing:

1. The director's concern about additional dilution. If Husky had issued the preferred stock as of January 1 of the current year, how would reported earnings per share have been affected?

2. At least two alternative means for raising the needed capital and avoiding most or all of the dilutive potential of the preferred stock issuance. (One alternative that might be proposed would be to issue a nonconvertible preferred stock. However, this type of security would still require that declared or paid dividends on the preferred be deducted from income to determine income applicable to common [thus causing some minor dilution], and a nonconvertible preferred would be less attractive to investors and, therefore, probably would require a higher dividend yield.) Given the nature of the earnings per share calculation, explain how your suggested alternatives would avoid the dilution problem.

C 20-4. **EARNINGS PER SHARE AND THE CONCEPTUAL FRAMEWORK** Karen Wallace recently became the new controller for New York–based City Slickers, Inc. As part of her duties, Karen has been assigned to prepare the financial statements for the year ended December 31, 1998. In making the earnings per share calculations, Karen finds that the company has outstanding stock options allowing investors to purchase 20,000 shares of common stock at an exercise price of $25 per share. The options were issued on January 1, 1996, and expire on December 31, 2002. Karen determines that the options are dilutive and should be included in diluted earnings per share calculations for 1998 because the exercise price was below the average market price of the common stock for the period.

While preparing the comparative financial statements, Karen notes that the 20,000 stock options were not included in diluted earnings per share calculations for 1997.

REQUIRED
1. What has happened here? Describe a situation in which it is possible that both the 1997 and 1998 earnings per share calculations were made correctly.
2. The FASB's *Statement of Financial Accounting Concepts No. 2* describes the qualitative characteristics of useful accounting information. Consider your answer to part 1 and critique current earnings per share reporting requirements in light of *Statement of Concepts No. 2*. You need not address all of the qualitative characteristics in your critique.

C 20-5. **EARNINGS PER SHARE: ETHICAL AND PROFESSIONAL ISSUES** Kaplan Industries develops, designs, and sells computer hardware. During the current year Kaplan experienced a decline in net income and earnings per share as a result of competitive pressures. Recently, at a meeting with Tom Fisher, Kaplan's chief accounting officer, and Stuart Kaplan, Kaplan's president, Ron Lehman, the chief financial officer, expressed the view that "We have to get earnings per share higher in our year-end report than it has been during the first three quarters of the year. If we don't, our ability to raise needed capital next year may be seriously impaired."

Ron Lehman recommended that Kaplan Industries offer to buy back shares of its own common stock. He felt that the recent dramatic decline in stock prices for Kaplan and several other competitor companies, which Lehman felt was temporary, might provide the necessary incentive for stockholders to sell their shares to the company. Lehman believed that enough shares could be purchased from stockholders to boost earnings per share up to the desired level by year-end. He stated that increased earnings per share at year-end should benefit Kaplan Industries in two ways. First, the company could take advantage of the expected turnaround in stock prices in the computer hardware industry by reissuing shares above the buy-back price. Second, the increased level of earnings per share should help the company in its efforts to obtain new financing next year for potential expansion of the company into new markets.

Tom Fisher doubted whether Ron Lehman's recommendation was in the best interests of the existing stockholders. Fisher stated that those stockholders opting to sell their shares to the company might lose out if stock prices rebounded next year as anticipated. Fisher believed that if the potential expansion turned out to be as successful as expected, there would be a good chance that Kaplan Industries would have higher earnings and be able to increase dividend payments to stockholders. Fisher also noted that potential stockholders might be misled by the higher earnings per share at the end of the current year. The increase above current levels would be due to the stock acquisition rather than increased earnings. Fisher suggested that more attention should be paid to increasing sales and cutting costs as ways to boost net income and earnings per share.

Stuart Kaplan and Ron Lehman were sensitive to Tom Fisher's concerns. However, they both agreed that the quickest and most certain solution to the low earnings per share problem was Lehman's stock acquisition plan. Fisher reiterated his position, but he agreed to go along with the Lehman plan because he was a team player.

REQUIRED What ethical and professional issues are raised by the facts of this case? Do you think that the plan to buy back shares from existing stockholders is the "right" thing to do?

EXERCISES

E 20-1. **WEIGHTED AVERAGE NUMBER OF SHARES** Kelly Corporation had 800,000 common shares outstanding on January 1, issued 1,200,000 shares on April 1, and had income applicable to common stock of $3.4 million for the year ended December 31, 1998.

REQUIRED Calculate Kelly's BEPS for 1998.

E 20-2. **WEIGHTED AVERAGE NUMBER OF SHARES** Gill Corporation is a large conglomerate headquartered in the Midwest. On January 1, 1998, Gill had 120,000 shares of common stock outstanding. In order to provide funds for construction of a new glue factory, Gill issued an additional 30,000 shares on February 1 at a price of $125 per share. On May 1, Gill purchased 15,000 shares of its own common stock in the open market at a price of $120. These shares are held as treasury stock. Profits from operation of the glue factory were phenomenal. On October 1, Gill issued 5,000 shares of the treasury stock as a bonus to the vice-president who had created the concept. The vice-president made no payment to Gill for these shares.

REQUIRED Calculate the weighted average number of shares outstanding for each of the following periods:
1. The quarter ended March 31, 1998.
2. The six months ended June 30, 1998.
3. The year ended December 31, 1998.

E 20-3. **WEIGHTED AVERAGE NUMBER OF SHARES; INCOME APPLICABLE TO COMMON STOCK** Quickline, Inc., had 600,000 shares of common stock outstanding and 150,000 shares of noncumulative, nonconvertible, $100 par value preferred stock outstanding on January 1, 1998. An additional 240,000 shares of common stock were issued on August 1. On December 31, Quickline paid cash dividends of $5.00 per share on the preferred stock and $2.00 per share on the common stock. Earnings per share on common stock for 1998 was $3.25.

REQUIRED Determine Quickline's net income for 1998.

E 20-4. **WEIGHTED AVERAGE NUMBER OF SHARES; INCOME APPLICABLE TO COMMON STOCK** Staley Company's net income for the year ended December 31, 1998, was $10,000. During 1998, Staley declared and paid $1,750 cash dividends on preferred stock and $1,500 cash dividends on common stock.

On December 31, 1998, 12,000 shares of common stock were issued and outstanding, 8,000 of which had been issued and outstanding throughout the year and 4,000 of which were issued on July 1, 1998. There were *no* other common stock transactions during the year, and there is *no* potential dilution of earnings per share.

REQUIRED Calculate Staley Company's 1998 BEPS.

(AICPA, adapted)

E 20-5. **WEIGHTED AVERAGE NUMBER OF SHARES; INCOME APPLICABLE TO COMMON STOCK** On December 31, 1997, Newton Company had 35,000 shares of common stock issued and outstanding. On April 1, 1998, an additional 20,000 shares of common stock were issued. Newton's net income for the year ended December 31, 1998, was $172,500. During 1998, Newton declared and paid $80,000 cash dividends on its nonconvertible preferred stock.

REQUIRED What is Newton's BEPS for the year ended December 31, 1998?

(AICPA, adapted)

E 20-6. **WEIGHTED AVERAGE NUMBER OF SHARES; EXTRAORDINARY ITEM** Hill Company had 90,000 shares of common stock outstanding on December 31, 1997. During 1998, Hill issued 20,000 new shares on April 1 and retired 5,000 shares on October 1. Hill's after-tax income for 1998 was $280,000 before an extraordinary loss of $40,000 (net of tax).

REQUIRED Give the EPS figures that should appear at the bottom of Hill's income statement. Provide schedules showing the calculations leading to the EPS figures.

E 20-7. **WEIGHTED AVERAGE NUMBER OF SHARES; CONVERTIBLE BONDS** Teak, Inc., had 3 million shares of common stock outstanding on December 31, 1997. An additional 1 million shares of common stock were issued on April 1, 1998, and 400,000 more shares were issued on July 1, 1998. On October 1, 1998, Teak issued 10,000 $1,000 face value, 7 percent convertible bonds. Each bond is convertible into 30 shares of common stock. No bonds were converted into common stock in 1998. Assume that the convertible bonds are dilutive.

REQUIRED   What is the number of shares to be used in calculating BEPS and DEPS, respectively?

(AICPA, adapted)

E 20-8.   **WEIGHTED AVERAGE NUMBER OF SHARES; STOCK SPLIT**   Tiger, Inc., earned $620,000 after taxes in 1998. Tiger began 1998 with 200,000 shares of common stock outstanding. On May 1, 30,000 new shares were issued, and on October 31, 6,000 shares were acquired as treasury stock. On December 1, Tiger split its common stock 2 for 1.

In addition to common stock, Tiger had 40,000 shares of $100 par, 8 percent cumulative nonconvertible preferred stock outstanding during all of 1998.

REQUIRED   Calculate Tiger's BEPS for 1998. Provide a schedule showing determination of the weighted average number of common shares used in the BEPS calculation.

E 20-9.   **DILUTED EPS**   On December 31, 1997, Royston Company had 600,000 shares of common stock outstanding. On October 1, 1998, an additional 80,000 shares of common stock were issued. In addition, Royston had $10 million of 8 percent convertible bonds outstanding on December 31, 1997, which were issued at face value and are convertible into 225,000 shares of common stock. No bonds were converted into common stock in 1998. The net income for the year ended December 31, 1998, was $4 million and the tax rate was 34 percent.

REQUIRED   Calculate Royston Company's DEPS for the year ended December 31, 1998.

(AICPA, adapted)

E 20-10.   **DILUTED EPS**   On December 31, 1997, Catron Company had 350,000 shares of common stock outstanding. On September 1, 1998, an additional 225,000 shares of common stock were issued. In addition, Catron had $10 million of 8 percent convertible bonds outstanding on December 31, 1997, which are convertible into 200,000 shares of common stock. No bonds were converted into common stock in 1998. The net income for the year ended December 31, 1998, was $3.8 million, and the income tax rate was 34 percent.

REQUIRED   Calculate DEPS for Catron Company for the year ended December 31, 1998.

(AICPA, adapted)

E 20-11.   **STOCK OPTIONS AND EPS CALCULATIONS**   On January 1, 1998, Harkins Corporation granted options to purchase 10,000 of its common shares at $8 each. The market price of common averaged $8.80 per share during 1998. There was no change in the 50,000 shares of outstanding common stock during 1998. Net income for 1998 was $8,268.

REQUIRED   What number of shares should be used in calculating DEPS for 1998?

(AICPA, adapted)

E 20-12.   **STOCK OPTIONS AND WARRANTS AND EPS CALCULATIONS**   Reston Manufacturing has 200,000 shares of common stock, all of which have been outstanding for the entire current year. During 1998, Reston reported net income of $520,000, which includes interest expense on nonconvertible bonds in the amount of $20,000. The following information is available concerning outstanding warrants and stock options:

a)   The nonconvertible bonds were originally issued on July 1, 1991. Investors found the bonds particularly attractive because they were accompanied by 10-year, Series II warrants that allowed a total purchase of 5,000 shares of common stock at a price of $29 per share. No warrants have been exercised as of December 31, 1998. These warrants will expire on June 30, 2001.

b)   Reston sold Series III warrants to the public in 1994. These warrants permitted a possible total purchase of 3,000 common shares at a price of $26 each. The Series III warrants expired on May 31, 1998. No Series III warrants were ever exercised.

c)   The company offers a bonus plan for top executives that includes a stock option plan. Options are issued to executives in those years when net income exceeds a target amount of $600,000. The actual number of options issued varies with the excess of net income over the target amount.

The target net income was exceeded in 1994. Series A options were issued, allowing executives to purchase 1,000 shares of common stock at an exercise price of $24. The options could be exercised at any time after January 1, 1996. The options expire 10 years after the earliest exercise date. None was exercised during 1998.

The target net income was again exceeded in 1996. Series B options were issued, allowing executives to purchase 1,500 shares of common stock at an exercise price of $28. The options could be exercised at any time after January 1, 1998. The options expire 10 years after the earliest exercise date. None was exercised during 1998.

During 1998, Reston's shares traded at an average price of $30. The closing price was $31 per share on December 31, 1998.

REQUIRED   Calculate Reston's DEPS for 1998.

E 20-13.   **TREASURY STOCK METHOD** Dotson Company earned $450,000 and had 85,000 shares of common stock outstanding during the current year. In addition, throughout the entire year there were options outstanding to purchase 20,000 shares of Dotson's common stock at $15 per share. The average market price of Dotson's common stock for the year was $16. Dotson's outstanding debt during the year consisted of $100,000 of 10 percent short-term notes. Dotson is subject to a 34 percent tax rate.

REQUIRED   **1.** How many common and potential common shares should be used to calculate Dotson's BEPS and DEPS for the current year?
            2. Calculate Dotson's BEPS and DEPS for the current year. Show all calculations.

E 20-14.   **TREASURY STOCK METHOD** A partial balance sheet and other selected information for NewSound Recording Studios, Inc., for the year ended December 31, 1998, are presented below.

Bonds payable (10%, nonconvertible, due 12/31/04) $500,000
Preferred stock (6%, noncumulative, nonconvertible, $100 par;
  1,000 shares issued and outstanding)   100,000
Common stock ($10 par; 60,000 shares issued
  and outstanding)   600,000

NewSound reported net income of $360,000 for 1998 and has an effective tax rate of 34 percent. NewSound declared and paid preferred dividends of $6,000 during the year. NewSound common stock is considered a high-growth stock and currently pays no dividends. The $50,000 bond interest expense was paid on December 31, 1998.

NewSound's common stock traded at an average price of $20 during 1998 and closed at $25 on December 31. The preferred shares traded at an average price of $120 during 1998 and closed at $105 on December 31.

NewSound has stock options outstanding for 15,000 shares. The options have an exercise price of $18 and expire on June 30, 2002.

There were no transactions in bonds, preferred shares, common shares, or options during 1998 that directly involved NewSound. The common and preferred shares were actively traded on the Pacific Stock Exchange during the year.

REQUIRED   Calculate DEPS for 1998.

E 20-15.   **CONTINGENTLY ISSUABLE COMMON SHARES** In 1995, Easton Company's board of directors adopted a plan under which Easton's stockholders will receive 6,000 additional shares of Easton common stock if Easton's income after taxes is at least $100,000 in 2000. In 1998, Easton earned $120,000 and had 16,000 common shares outstanding. Easton also had $4,000 of 6 percent bonds outstanding throughout 1998. These bonds are convertible into 2,000 shares of common stock. Easton is subject to a 34 percent tax rate.

REQUIRED   Calculate BEPS and DEPS for Easton Company for 1998. Show your calculations.

E 20-16.   **CONTINGENTLY ISSUABLE COMMON SHARES** During the current year, Impel, Inc., earned $115,000. A weighted average of 12,000 shares of Impel's common stock was outstanding during the year, and 10,000 shares were outstanding at year-end. The average price of Impel's common stock for the year was $5 per share, and the year-end price was $6.50. Throughout the year, there were stock options outstanding to purchase 1,000 shares of Impel's common stock for $4.80 per share.

In an effort to stimulate management, Impel's board of directors established a contingent issuance agreement stating that management would receive 900 shares of common stock if Impel's annual after-tax income next year is 5 percent more than was earned in the current year.

REQUIRED   Calculate BEPS and DEPS for Impel, Inc., for the current year. Show your calculations.

E 20-17.   **CONVERTIBLE SECURITIES AND EPS CALCULATIONS**   Information concerning the capital structure of Swain Corporation is as follows:

	12/31/97	12/31/98
Common stock	95,000 shares	95,000 shares
Convertible preferred stock	10,000 shares	10,000 shares
8% convertible bonds	$1,000,000	$1,000,000

During 1998, Swain paid dividends of $1.00 per share on its common stock and $2.20 per share on its preferred stock. The preferred stock is convertible into 20,000 shares of common stock. The 8 percent convertible bonds are convertible into 25,000 shares of common stock. The net income after taxes for the year ended December 31, 1998, was $290,000. The income tax rate was 34 percent.

REQUIRED   Calculate the BEPS and DEPS for Swain for the year ended December 31, 1998.

(AICPA, adapted)

E 20-18.   **IF-CONVERTED METHOD**   Noonan Company is preparing EPS data for 1998. Net income for 1998 was $380,000, and there were 60,000 shares of common stock outstanding during the entire year. Noonan has the following two convertible securities outstanding:

10% convertible bonds (each $1,000 bond is convertible into 25 shares of common stock)	$100,000
4% convertible $100 par value preferred stock (each share is convertible into two shares of common stock)	50,000

Both convertible securities were issued at face value in 1995. There were no conversions during 1998, and Noonan's income tax rate is 34 percent. The preferred stock is cumulative, and the dividends are paid quarterly (1 percent per quarter).

REQUIRED   **1.**   Calculate Noonan Company's BEPS and DEPS for 1998.
2.   Recalculate Noonan Company's BEPS and DEPS for 1998, assuming instead that the preferred stock pays a 14 percent dividend (3.5 percent per quarter).

E 20-19.   **IF-CONVERTED METHOD WHEN ACTUAL CONVERSIONS OCCUR**   Assume the same facts as are given in Exercise 20-18 (exclusive of requirement 2).

REQUIRED   **1.**   Calculate BEPS and DEPS for Noonan Company, assuming that $20,000 par value of the preferred stock actually was converted into common stock on October 1, 1998.
2.   Ignoring the conversion assumption made in part 1, calculate BEPS and DEPS for Noonan Company, assuming instead that 40 percent of the convertible bonds were converted to common stock on April 1, 1998.
3.   What is the impact on EPS calculations of actual conversions during the year?

E 20-20.   **IF-CONVERTED METHOD WITH BOND DISCOUNT**   Cable Company has 10,000 shares of common stock and $30,000 of 20-year, $1,000, 8 percent convertible bonds outstanding. Each bond is convertible into 100 shares of common stock. The bonds were issued at 97 in 1991. The bond discount is being amortized by the straight-line method. After including the effect of bond interest expense, Cable earned $125,000 before taxes in 1998 and is subject to a 34 percent income tax rate.

REQUIRED   Calculate Cable's 1998 BEPS and DEPS.

E 20-21.   **ORDER OF ENTRY INTO EPS CALCULATION**   Kevin's Kards, Inc., operates a large chain of sports card retail stores in the Midwest. Kevin's operations have been financed by a wide variety of alternative debt and equity offerings. Initially, Kevin's authorized and issued 200,000 shares of $5 par value common stock in January 1993, of which 51 percent are owned by Mr. Kevin, who serves as president, chairman of the board, chief operating officer, and chief financial officer of the company.

Kevin's also issued 10,000 shares of 6 percent, $100 par value, noncumulative, nonparticipating, convertible preferred stock for $1,000,000 to Mr. James, a local venture capitalist, in February 1993. The preferred shares may be exchanged for common shares at a ratio of 1:2.

David's Bakeries, Inc., a long-standing client of Mr. James, expressed some interest in investing in Kevin's Kards. Kevin's seized the opportunity to obtain additional capital and sold $200,000 of 8 percent convertible bonds to David's at par value on January

30, 1995. David's may convert the bonds, exchanging them for 3,000 shares of common stock, at any time prior to their maturity on January 29, 2005.

In November 1997, Kevin's sold 5,000 stock options to Mr. James for $5 each. Each option entitles the investor to purchase one share of stock at an exercise price of $35. The options expire in 2000, and none has been exercised to date.

During 1998, Kevin's reported net income of $1,260,000. Kevin's Kards' earnings are taxed at an effective rate of 34 percent. Total cash dividends of $260,000 were declared and paid during the year. Net income also reflects the payment of 1998 interest expense on the bonds. Kevin's common stock performed well during 1998, selling at an average price of $40 per share and closing at an all-time high of $50 on December 31. Kevin's engaged in no additional securities transactions in 1998.

REQUIRED
1. Show the correct order of entry into 1998 earnings per share calculations for any potentially dilutive securities issued by Kevin's Kards, Inc.
2. Calculate Kevin's BEPS and DEPS for 1998.

PROBLEMS

P 20-1. **WEIGHTED AVERAGE NUMBER OF COMMON SHARES** Milton Company had the following account titles on its December 31, 1998, trial balance:
  6 percent cumulative convertible preferred stock, $100 par value
  Contributed capital in excess of par, preferred stock
  Common stock, $1 stated value
  Contributed capital in excess of stated value, common stock
  Retained earnings

The following additional information about the Milton Company is available for the year ended December 31, 1998:

a) There were 2 million shares of preferred stock authorized, of which 900,000 were outstanding. All 900,000 shares outstanding were issued on January 2, 1995, for $120 a share. The preferred stock is convertible into common stock on a 1:1 basis until December 31, 2004; then the preferred stock ceases to be convertible and is callable at par value by the company. No preferred stock has been converted into common stock, and there were no dividends in arrears on December 31, 1998.

b) The common stock has been issued at amounts above stated value per share since incorporation in 1980. Of the 5 million shares authorized, 3.5 million shares were outstanding on January 1, 1998. The market price of the outstanding common stock has increased slowly but consistently since 1993.

c) The company has an employee stock option plan whereby certain key employees and officers may purchase shares of common stock at 100 percent of the market price at the date of the option grant. All options are exercisable in installments of one-third each year, commencing one year after the date of the grant, and expire four years after the grant date if they have not been exercised by that date. On January 1, 1998, options for 70,000 shares were outstanding at prices ranging from $47 to $83 a share. Options for 20,000 shares were exercised at $47 to $79 a share during 1998. No options expired during 1998, and additional options for 15,000 shares were granted at $86 a share during the year. The 65,000 options outstanding on December 31, 1998, were exercisable at $54 to $86 a share. Of these options, 30,000 were exercisable at that date at prices ranging from $54 to $79 a share.

d) The company also has an employee stock purchase plan whereby the company pays one-half and the employee pays one-half of the market price of the stock at the date of the subscription. During 1998, employees subscribed to 60,000 shares at an average price of $87 a share. All 60,000 shares were paid for and issued late in September 1998.

e) On December 31, 1998, 355,000 shares of common stock were set aside for the granting of future stock options and for future purchases under the employee stock purchase plan.

The only other changes in stockholders' equity for 1998 were for 1998 net income and cash dividends paid.

REQUIRED
1. Prepare the stockholders' equity section of the balance sheet of Milton Company as of December 31, 1998. Where appropriate, substitute x's for unknown dollar amounts. Use good form and provide full disclosure. Write appropriate footnotes as they should appear in the published financial statements.

2. Write a memorandum explaining how the amount of the denominator should be determined to calculate DEPS for presentation in the financial statements. Be specific as to the handling of each item. If additional information is needed to determine whether an item should be included or excluded or the extent to which an item should be included, identify the information needed and how the item would be handled if the information were known. Assume Milton Company had substantial net income for the year ended December 31, 1998.

(AICPA, adapted)

P 20-2. **WEIGHTED AVERAGE NUMBER OF SHARES; CALCULATING EPS** The following schedule sets forth the long-term debt and stockholders' equity of Torre Company as of December 31, 1998. The president of Torre has requested that you assist the controller in preparing figures for earnings per share calculations.

Long-term debt:

4% convertible debentures due 4/15/2011	$15,000,000
Other long-term debt less current portions	10,000,000
Total long-term debt	$25,000,000

Stockholders' equity:

$4 cumulative convertible preferred stock, par value $20 per share: authorized, 1,000,000 shares; issued and outstanding, 600,000 shares; liquidation preference, $30 per share, aggregating $18,000,000	$12,000,000
Common stock, par value $1 per share: authorized, 10,000,000 shares; issued, 3,250,000 shares, including 250,000 shares held in treasury	3,250,000
Contributed capital in excess of par	2,100,000
Retained earnings	38,250,000
Total	$55,600,000
Less: Cost of 250,000 shares of common stock held in treasury (acquired prior to 1998)	(450,000)
Total stockholders' equity	$55,150,000
Total long-term debt and stockholders' equity	$80,150,000

Additional information that may be useful is as follows:

a) The other long-term debt and the related amounts due within one year are amounts due on unsecured promissory notes that require payments each year to maturity. The effective interest rates on these borrowings range from 6 percent to 7 percent.

b) The 4 percent convertible debentures were issued at their face value of $15 million in 1996. The debentures are convertible into the common stock of Torre at the rate of 25 shares for each $1,000 debenture.

c) The $4 cumulative convertible preferred stock was issued in 1997. On July 1, 1998, and October 1, 1998, holders of the preferred stock converted 40,000 and 10,000 preferred shares, respectively, into common stock. Each share of preferred stock is convertible into 1.2 shares of common stock.

d) On April 1, 1998, Torre acquired the assets and business of Harsen Industries by the issuance of 300,000 shares of Torre common stock.

e) On October 1, 1997, the company granted options to its officers and selected employees to purchase 50,000 shares of Torre's common stock at a price of $33 per share.

f) Both the average and ending market prices of Torre common stock during 1998 were $34.

g) Dividends on the preferred stock are paid quarterly and have been paid through December 31, 1998. Dividends paid on the common stock were $.50 per share for each quarter.

h) The net income of Torre Company for the year ended December 31, 1998, was $4.4 million. There were *no* extraordinary items. The provision for income taxes was calculated at a rate of 34 percent.

REQUIRED Calculate:

1. BEPS.

2. DEPS.

P 20-3. **WEIGHTED AVERAGE NUMBER OF SHARES; CALCULATING EPS** The stockholders' equity section of Miller Company's balance sheet as of December 31, 1998, contains the following:

$1 cumulative convertible preferred stock, par value $25 a share:	
authorized, 1,600,000 shares; issued, 1,400,000 shares; converted	
to common, 600,000 shares; outstanding, 800,000 shares;	
involuntary liquidation value, $30 a share, aggregating $24,000,000	$20,000,000
Common stock, par value $.25 a share:	
authorized, 15,000,000 share; issued and outstanding,	
6,600,000 shares	1,650,000
Contributed capital in excess of par	32,750,000
Retained earnings	40,595,000
Total stockholders' equity	$94,995,000

Other relevant information is as follows:

a) On January 1, 1998, Miller Company acquired the business and assets and assumed the liabilities of Bates Corporation. For each of Bates Corporation's 2.4 million shares of $.25 par value common stock outstanding, the owner received one share of common stock of Miller Company.

b) Included in the liabilities of Miller Company are 5 percent convertible subordinated debentures issued at their face value of $20 million in 1997. The debentures are due in 2017 and until then are convertible into the common stock of Miller Company at the rate of five shares of common stock for each $100 debenture. To date, none of these debentures has been converted.

c) On January 1, 1998, Miller Company issued 1.4 million shares of convertible preferred stock at $40 per share. Quarterly dividends to December 31, 1998, have been paid on these shares. The preferred stock is convertible into common stock at the rate of two shares of common for each share of preferred. On July 1 and October 1, 1998, 150,000 and 450,000 shares, respectively, were converted into common stock.

d) During July 1997, Miller Company granted options to its officers and key employees to purchase 500,000 shares of the company's common stock at a price of $20 a share.

e) During 1998, dividend payments were $.50 per share and the average market price of the Miller common stock was $25. On December 31, 1998, the closing price of the common stock was $25 a share.

f) Miller Company's consolidated net income for the year ended December 31, 1998, was $9 million.

g) The provision for income taxes was calculated at a rate of 34 percent.

REQUIRED For 1998, calculate:

1. BEPS.
2. DEPS.

(AICPA, adapted)

P 20-4. **CALCULATING WEIGHTED AVERAGE NUMBER OF SHARES AND EPS** Pavlik Corporation's capital structure is as follows:

	12/31/98	12/31/97
Outstanding shares:		
Common stock...	360,000	320,000
Nonconvertible preferred stock	10,000	10,000
8% convertible bonds	$1,000,000	$1,000,000

The following additional information is available:

a) On September 1, 1998, Pavlik sold 40,000 additional shares of common stock.

b) Net income for the year ended December 31, 1998, was $800,000.

c) During 1998, Pavlik paid dividends of $3 per share on its nonconvertible preferred stock.

d) The 8 percent convertible bonds are convertible into 40 shares of common stock for each $1,000 bond.

e) Unexercised stock options to purchase 30,000 shares of common stock at $22.50 per share were outstanding at the beginning and end of 1998. The average market price of Pavlik's common stock was $34 per share during 1998. The market price was $33 per share on December 31, 1998.

f) Warrants to purchase 20,000 shares of common stock at $38 per share were attached to the preferred stock at the time of issuance. The warrants, which expire on December 31, 2003, were outstanding on December 31, 1998.

g) Pavlik's effective income tax rate was 34 percent for 1997 and 1998.

REQUIRED   Calculate BEPS and DEPS for the year ended December 31, 1998.

(AICPA, adapted)

P 20-5. **WEIGHTED AVERAGE NUMBER OF SHARES; INCOME APPLICABLE TO EPS CALCULATIONS**   Daley Company had 20,000 shares of common stock outstanding on December 31, 1998. No dividends were paid on the common stock in 1998. On October 1, 1998, Daley acquired 1,000 shares of its common for use as treasury stock.

The company issued 5,000 shares of 8 percent convertible preferred stock in 1997 at the $100 par value. Each share of preferred stock is convertible into two shares of common stock. Holders of the preferred stock converted 2,000 shares into common stock on July 1, 1998. Dividends have been paid on the preferred stock at the end of each quarter.

Daley issued 20, 20-year bonds ($1,000 face) on April 1, 1998, at $1,100 per bond. Each bond is convertible into 50 shares of common stock. Interest is payable at 7 percent of face value.

Daley issued options in 1997 to its executives to purchase 2,500 shares of common stock. Each option entitles the holder to buy one share of common at $20. None of the options has been exercised. The average market price per share of common stock during 1998 was $24.

Daley's fiscal year ends December 31, and its effective income tax rate for 1998 is 34 percent. On January 1, 1998, the amount of retained earnings was $102,000, and on December 31, 1998, retained earnings is $148,000.

REQUIRED   Calculate the 1998:

1. BEPS.

2. DEPS.

P 20-6. **WEIGHTED AVERAGE NUMBER OF SHARES; INCOME APPLICABLE TO EPS CALCULATIONS**   Tyler Company had 49,000 shares of common stock outstanding on December 31, 1998, after acquiring 2,000 shares of common as treasury stock on April 1, 1998. No dividends were declared on the common stock in 1998.

Tyler issued 3,000 shares of 7 percent cumulative convertible preferred stock in 1996. The shares were issued at their par value of $50 per share. Each share of preferred is convertible into 2 shares of common stock. Holders of the preferred stock converted 2,500 shares on July 1, 1998. Dividends were paid on the preferred stock at the end of each of the first three quarters of 1998. In order to conserve cash, the company's board of directors did not declare a dividend for the fourth quarter of 1998.

On July 1, 1996, Tyler Company issued 100 convertible debentures. The bonds were dated July 1, 1996, and were sold for their face value of $1,000 per bond. The bonds have a stated interest rate of 10 percent, with interest payable each January 1 and July 1. Each bond is convertible into 15 shares of common stock. The bonds mature on July 1, 2016. None of the bonds was converted as of December 31, 1998.

On July 1, 1998, Tyler Company issued 200 convertible debentures. The bonds were dated July 1, 1998, and were sold at 110. Each bond has a face value of $1,000 and a nominal interest rate of 6.5 percent. Interest is payable each January 1 and July 1. Each bond is convertible into 25 shares of common stock. The bonds mature on July 1, 2018. None of the bonds has been converted.

In 1997, the company issued options for the purchase of 9,000 shares of common stock to its key executives. Each option entitles the holder to buy one share of common stock at $20. None of the options has been exercised as of December 31, 1998. The average market price per share of common stock for 1998 was $23.

Tyler's fiscal year ends on December 31, and its effective income tax rate for 1998 was 34 percent. Retained earnings was $211,575 and $302,750 on January 1, 1998, and December 31, 1998, respectively.

REQUIRED   Calculate the 1998:

1. BEPS.

2. DEPS.

P 20-7. **EPS PROCEDURES AND TREND ANALYSIS** Space Products Corporation was formed on January 1, 1994, to manufacture and supply the National Aeronautics and Space Administration (NASA) with high-quality precision instruments to be used on the space shuttle. Because of the nature of the agreement with NASA, Space Products was assured of earning a 10 percent annual rate of return on stockholders' equity. Stockholders' equity was $200,000 on January 1, 1994, which represented 10,000 shares of common stock issued at $20 per share. Since its formation, Space Products has declared and paid a cash dividend each year equal to that year's net income (10 percent return on beginning stockholders' equity).

No common stock transactions occurred during 1994 and 1995. On July 1, 1996, Space Products issued 800 shares of common stock for $16,000, and at the end of 1997, the company effected a 2-for-1 stock split. On April 1, 1998, Space Products issued 1,000 shares of common stock for $10 per share (the market price of the stock declined after the stock split). Space Products also declared and distributed a 20 percent stock dividend on October 1, 1998.

Space Products' net income each year, based on the assured 10 percent rate of return, was as follows:

1994: $.10 \times \$200,000$ = $20,000
1995: $.10 \times \$200,000$ = $20,000
1996: $.10 \times \$200,000 + 1/2\,(.10 \times 16,000) = \$20,800$
1997: $.10 \times \$216,000$ = $21,600
1998: $.10 \times \$216,000 + 3/4\,(.10 \times 10,000) = \$22,350$

Space Products reported the following EPS numbers for the years ending December 31, 1994 through 1998:

1994: $\dfrac{\$20,000}{10,000} = \$2.00$

1995: $\dfrac{\$20,000}{10,000} = \$2.00$

1996: $\dfrac{\$20,800}{10,800} = \$1.926$
(10,800 shares outstanding, end of 1996)

1997: $\dfrac{\$21,600}{21,600} = \$1.00$
$(10,800 \times 2 = 21,600)$

1998: $\dfrac{\$22,350}{27,120} = \$.8242$
$[21,600 + 1,000 + .20(21,600 + 1,000) = 27,120]$

The EPS numbers above were also reported in Space Products' five-year comparative statements for the year ending December 31, 1998.

Space Products' president was very disturbed when she was provided with the five-year EPS data. She was concerned about the effect the declining EPS numbers would have on investors' evaluations and assessments of the company's earnings trend. She could not understand how EPS could show a downward trend, especially since the company's profitability had not declined (a 10 percent return on stockholders' equity has been realized since the company was formed). In addition, she pointed out that the stock split and stock dividend had not caused a reduction in the company's net assets.

REQUIRED
1. Recalculate the EPS numbers that should have been reported for each year.
2. Prepare the EPS data as they should have appeared on the five-year comparative statements for the year ending December 31, 1998.
3. Prepare a brief written response to the president's concern about the declining earnings trend and explain how the presentation in part 2 will alleviate her concern.

P 20-8. **EARNINGS PER SHARE; DILUTION AND ANTIDILUTION** Allen Corporation has gathered the following information for purposes of presenting EPS data for the year ending December 31, 1998:
a) Net income for 1998 was $265,000.
b) Common shares outstanding at December 31, 1998, 60,000 shares. There were no common stock transactions during 1998.

c) Several years ago, Allen issued at par $200,000 in 10 percent convertible bonds. Each $1,000 bond is convertible into 20 shares of common stock.

d) At the beginning of 1998, Allen Corporation issued, for $58,000, 10 percent preferred stock with a par value of $50,000. These shares are convertible into 1,000 shares of common stock.

e) During 1996, Allen issued options to purchase 4,000 common shares. The option price was $6 per share. The average market price of Allen's shares was $8 per share during 1998. No options have been exercised since they were issued.

f) The income tax rate is 34 percent.

REQUIRED   Calculate the 1998:

1. BEPS.

2. DEPS.

P 20-9.   **ORDER OF ENTRY INTO EPS CALCULATIONS**   Harrison Development Corporation had a weighted average of 160,000 shares of common stock outstanding during the current year and 170,000 shares outstanding at year-end. Harrison's current net income, after taxes, is $177,000. Harrison's tax rate is 30 percent. The common stock is selling for $15 per share at year-end and had an average price of $13.50 per share during the year. Harrison has no outstanding warrants or stock options, but does have several issues of convertible securities (all of which were outstanding throughout the current year).

The following summary information on convertible securities is taken from Harrison's current year-end balance sheet:

Bonds payable:

Series I (7%, convertible, due in 10 years)	$350,000
Series II (9%, convertible, due in 15 years)	250,000
Series III (8%, convertible, due in 20 years)	400,000

Preferred stock:

Class A (6%, $100 par, cumulative, convertible, 1,000 shares issued and outstanding)	100,000
Class B (8%, $200 par, cumulative, convertible, 1,000 shares issued and outstanding)	200,000

Additional information concerning the convertible securities follows:

a) The Series I bonds were issued in 1993. Each $1,000 par value bond is convertible into 75 common shares.

b) The Series II bonds were issued in 1995. Each $1,000 par value bond is convertible into 70 common shares.

c) The Series III bonds were issued in 1997. Each $1,000 par value bond is convertible into 80 common shares.

d) The Class A preferred shares were issued in 1991. Each preferred share is convertible into 8 common shares.

e) The Class B preferred shares were issued in 1996. Each preferred share is convertible into 15 common shares.

f) All convertible issues were originally issued at par value and may be converted at any time prior to maturity.

REQUIRED   **1.** Show the correct order of entry into earnings per share calculations for any potentially dilutive securities issued by Harrison Development Corporation. Show all supporting calculations.

2. Calculate Harrison's basic and diluted EPS for the current year.

P 20-10.   **ORDER OF ENTRY INTO EPS CALCULATIONS**   Ilgen, Inc., had income after taxes of $500,000 for the current year. An average of 125,000 shares of Ilgen's common stock was outstanding for the entire year. In addition, options were outstanding throughout the year to buy 12,000 shares of Ilgen common stock at $7.50 per share. During the year, Ilgen's common stock had an average market price of $9 per share. Ilgen is subject to a 34 percent tax rate.

Ilgen had the following convertible securities outstanding throughout the current year:

a) 6 percent, cumulative, convertible preferred stock. Each $10 par value share is convertible into 1.5 common shares. A total of $100,000 par value is outstanding.

b) 10-year, $1,000 par, 8 percent convertible bonds that were issued at 105. Total par value outstanding is $100,000. Each bond converts into 90 shares of common stock.

c) 5-year, $1,000 par, 13 percent convertible bonds that were issued at 97. Total par value outstanding is $30,000. Each bond converts into 30 shares of common stock.

d) 8-year, $1,000 par, 7 percent convertible bonds that were issued at 95. Total par value outstanding is $60,000. Each bond converts into 20 shares of common stock.

Any bond premium or discount is amortized on a straight-line basis.

REQUIRED

1. Determine the income per incremental common share effect for each of Ilgen's convertible securities. Order the securities from lowest per share effect to the highest per share effect. Show your calculations.

2. Calculate Ilgen's BEPS and DEPS for the current year. Show your calculations.

CHAPTER

Revisiting the Statement of Cash Flows; Additional Disclosure Topics

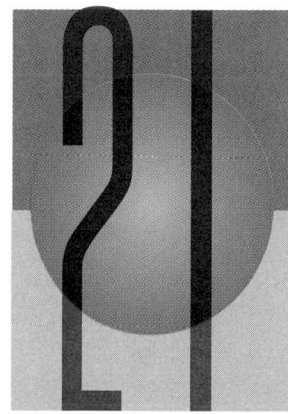

L EARNING OBJECTIVES

PART A • Revisiting the Statement of Cash Flows
After studying Part A of this chapter, you should be able to:

1. State the information that is provided by a statement of cash flows.

2. Describe the general format of a statement of cash flows and the general types of transactions that affect cash flows from operating, investing, and financing activities.

3. Use both the direct approach and the indirect approach to report cash flows from operating activities.

4. Determine cash flows from investing activities.

5. Determine cash flows from financing activities.

6. Use a worksheet to prepare a statement of cash flows.

PART B • Additional Disclosure Topics
After studying Part B of this chapter, you should be able to:

7. Describe the general guidelines for interim financial reporting under GAAP.

8. State the information that companies must disclose, at a minimum, in interim financial reports.

9. State the basis for reporting segment information, including the definition of an operating segment.

10. List the several categories of segment information that must be provided for reportable operating segments under GAAP.

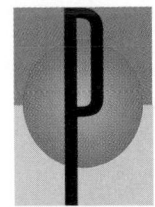art A of this chapter, like Chapter 6, discusses preparation of the statement of cash flows. However, in this chapter we assume that the reader has at least an intermediate–level knowledge of financial accounting. The discussion is best suited for students who already have an introductory-level understanding of the cash flow statement, such as is provided in introductory accounting texts or in Chapter 6 of this text. The illustration in Part A of this chapter includes transactions related to available-for-sale securities, pensions, deferred taxes, leases, and treasury stock. In addition, use of a worksheet to prepare the statement of cash flows is discussed and illustrated.

Part B of this chapter is concerned with two additional disclosure topics: interim reporting and segment reporting. The material in Part B adds to the disclosure coverage found in Chapters 4, 5, and 6.

Part A • Revisiting the Statement of Cash Flows

If you are studying Part A of this chapter without previously studying Chapter 6, it would be worthwhile to turn to Chapter 6 and read the first part, including the overview of the statement of cash flows and the section on the usefulness of the statement of cash flows (pages 277–283). These sections provide some perspective for the material presented in this chapter.

A statement of cash flows must be included in a set of financial statements purporting to report both financial position and results of operations.[1] The primary purpose of the statement of cash flows is to provide information regarding a company's cash inflows and outflows during an accounting period. In addition, the statement of cash flows provides information about a company's operating, investing, and financing activities. In recognition of the fact that companies often invest idle cash in highly liquid assets, cash and cash equivalents are combined when preparing the statement of cash flows. That is, the statement of cash flows provides information explaining the net increase or decrease in cash and cash equivalents during an accounting period. **Cash equivalents** are defined as short-term, highly liquid investments that are readily convertible to known amounts of cash.[2] Some examples of cash equivalents include Treasury bills, commercial paper, and money-market funds.

The statement of cash flows is organized using an **activity format,** which classifies cash flows in terms of operating, investing, and financing activities, as shown in Exhibit 21–1. As can be seen from Exhibit 21–1, investing and financing activities that do not affect cash (e.g., the purchase of equipment by issuing a note payable) are reported in a supplementary schedule. Alternatively, they may be reported in a narrative footnote. In either case, any cash flows also related to such transactions should be clearly indicated.

Operating activities relate to a company's primary revenue-generating activities. Cash flows from operating activities are generally the cash effects of transactions and economic events included in the determination of income. In addition, cash flows from buying, selling, and the maturing of trading securities are classified as cash flows from operating activities.[3]

Investing activities include lending money and collecting on those loans, buying and selling productive assets that are expected to generate revenues over long periods, and buying, selling, and the maturing of available-for-sale and held-to-maturity securities.

Financing activities include borrowing money from creditors and repaying the amounts borrowed, as well as obtaining resources from owners and providing

Margin notes

1 State the information that is provided by a statement of cash flows.

CONCEPTUAL

The statement of cash flows provides information explaining the net increase or decrease in cash and cash equivalents for a period.

2 Describe the general format of a statement of cash flows and the general types of transactions that affect cash flows from operating, investing, and financing activities.

---

[1]"Statement of Cash Flows," *Statement of Financial Accounting Standards No. 95* (Stamford, Conn.: FASB, 1987).

[2]Generally, only investments with original maturities of three months or less qualify as cash equivalents.

[3]Trading securities, available-for-sale securities, and held-to-maturity securities are described in Chapters 13 and 14.

EXHIBIT 21–1   **Format for the Statement of Cash Flows**

Company Name
Statement of Cash Flows
Period Covered

Cash flows from operating activities:

    ⋮

  Net cash provided (or used) by operating activities . . . . $xx
Cash flows from investing activities:

    ⋮

  Net cash provided (or used) by investing activities xx
Cash flows from financing activities:

    ⋮

  Net cash provided (or used) by financing activities xx
Net increase (or decrease) in cash . . . . $xx
Cash at beginning of period xx
Cash at end of period . . . . $xx

Investing and financing activities not affecting cash:
  (List of individual transactions clearly stating
    cash and noncash portions) . . . . $xx

---

them with both a return on their investment (through dividends) and a return of their investment. Exhibit 21–2 summarizes the types of transactions that appear on the statement of cash flows by the activities involved.

TWO APPROACHES TO REPORTING CASH FLOWS FROM OPERATING ACTIVITIES

3   Use both the direct approach and the indirect approach to report cash flows from operating activities.

Two approaches may be used to report cash flows from operating activities—the direct approach and the indirect approach. *Statement No. 95* encourages the use of the direct approach but permits the indirect approach.

Under the **direct approach,** at a minimum the following major sources of operating cash inflows and outflows are reported:

1. Cash collected from customers and cash collected from lessees, licensees, and similar parties.
2. Interest and dividends received.
3. Cash received from sale or maturity of trading securities.
4. Any other operating cash receipts.
5. Cash paid to employees and other suppliers of goods or services, including suppliers of insurance, advertising, and similar services.
6. Interest paid.
7. Income taxes paid.
8. Cash paid to purchase trading securities.
9. Any other operating cash payments.

CONCEPTUAL

The direct approach directly converts individual accrual-basis income statement accounts to a cash basis, while the indirect approach arrives at net cash from operating activities by adjusting accrual-basis net income to a cash basis.

EXHIBIT 21-2   **Cash Flows by Major Activities**

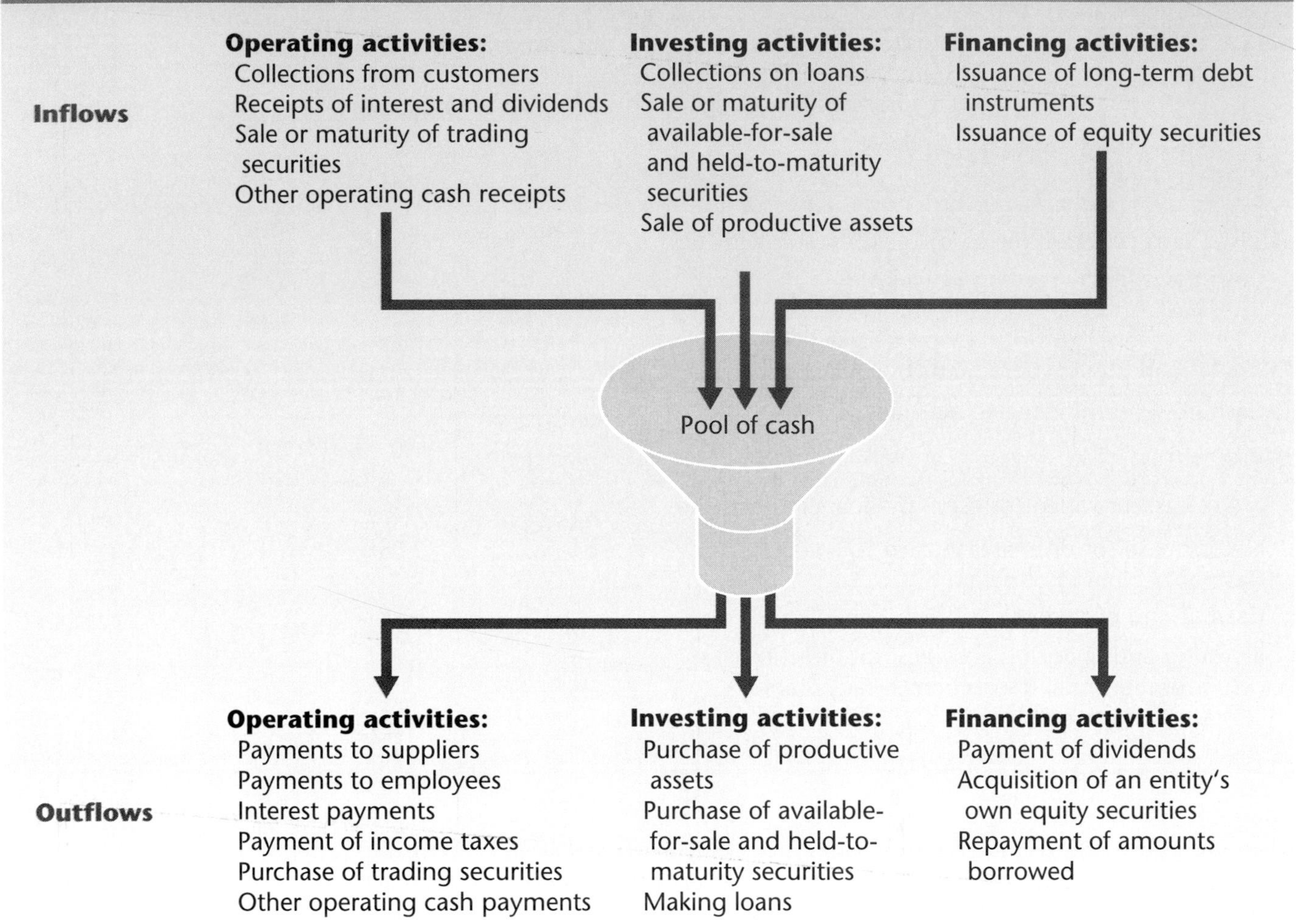

Inflows

Operating activities:
Collections from customers
Receipts of interest and dividends
Sale or maturity of trading
 securities
Other operating cash receipts

Investing activities:
Collections on loans
Sale or maturity of
 available-for-sale
 and held-to-maturity
 securities
Sale of productive assets

Financing activities:
Issuance of long-term debt
 instruments
Issuance of equity securities

Pool of cash

Outflows

Operating activities:
Payments to suppliers
Payments to employees
Interest payments
Payment of income taxes
Purchase of trading securities
Other operating cash payments

Investing activities:
Purchase of productive
 assets
Purchase of available-
 for-sale and held-to-
 maturity securities
Making loans

Financing activities:
Payment of dividends
Acquisition of an entity's
 own equity securities
Repayment of amounts
 borrowed

CONCEPTUAL

The direct approach
to determining cash
flows from operating
activities is more
understandable, more
relevant, and more
representationally
faithful than the
indirect approach.

The Box Energy Corporation's statements of cash flow, shown in Exhibit 6–3 (page 280), illustrate use of the direct approach.

Under the **indirect approach,** cash flows from operating activities are reported by adjusting net income for revenues, expenses, gains, and losses that appear on the income statement but do not have an effect on cash. In addition, net income is adjusted for operating cash flows that do *not* appear on the income statement. Companies that use the indirect approach also must disclose in footnotes the amounts of interest and income taxes paid. While the direct approach directly converts the accrual-basis income statement (and other accruals and deferrals) to a cash basis, the indirect approach arrives at net cash provided or used by operating activities by adjusting the final net income number to a cash basis. The U.S. Air consolidated statements of cash flows shown in Exhibit 6–4 (page 282) were prepared using the indirect approach.

The indirect approach is used by most companies, probably because of its historical popularity and because many companies feel that their accounting systems cannot capture the data required by the direct approach. However, the FASB prefers the direct approach. The direct approach is more straightforward and less confusing than the indirect approach. It clearly shows that cash inflows are from customers and other sources and that cash outflows are for merchandise, salaries, interest, taxes, and other operating activities. The direct approach is thus more *understandable,* more *relevant,* and more *representationally faithful* than the indirect approach. Users of financial statements should find that a statement of cash flows prepared using the direct approach is the most logical and the simplest form of statement because the cash flows shown are not affected by *recognition, measurement,* or *estimation* issues. Given the FASB's preference for the direct approach, this chapter will emphasize it, although the indirect approach will also be presented. (Both approaches are illustrated in Chapter 6, with an emphasis on the more widely used indirect approach.)

PREPARATION OF THE STATEMENT OF CASH FLOWS

This section will explain how to prepare the statement of cash flows. For instructional purposes, the completed statement is presented first, followed by an analysis of how each inflow and outflow of cash was determined.

The balance sheet and income statement for NewMart, Inc., appear in Exhibit 21–3. The following information further describes events and transactions affecting NewMart, Inc., during 1998:

1. The allowance for uncollectible accounts was increased by $5,000. No accounts receivable were written off.

2. NewMart sold its investment in Miller common stock, which had been classified as an available-for-sale security, for $4,500.

3. Equipment with an original cost of $50,000 and accumulated depreciation of $30,000 was sold for $30,000.

4. A $25,000 lease payment was made, resulting in a $20,000 reduction of the lease liability. In addition, depreciation of $10,000 was recorded on the leased property.

5. The decrease in bonds payable was due to premium amortization.

6. NewMart's 1998 pension expense exceeded funding by $2,000.

7. Outstanding common stock with a book value of $30,000 was purchased for $35,000 and retired; the $5,000 difference was debited to retained earnings.

8. Treasury stock, accounted for at a cost of $10,000, was reissued for $18,000.

9. Income tax payments were $15,950, of which $5,000 related to taxes deferred in prior years.

10. Dividends declared and paid during 1998 totaled $15,000.

The statement of cash flows is prepared as follows:

1. Determine the net increase or decrease in cash and cash equivalents for the period. Referring to Exhibit 21–3, we see that NewMart's cash balance increased by $35,550 during 1998. (NewMart had no cash equivalents.) This amount serves as a control figure. Once we have completed the statement of cash flows, the net cash inflow or outflow must agree with the $35,550 net change in the cash account on the comparative balance sheets.

2. Analyze any available income statement data, changes in the noncash balance sheet accounts, and any additional information provided in order to determine the transactions that caused inflows and outflows of cash during the period.

3. Prepare the statement of cash flows on the basis of the two previous steps.[4]

Exhibit 21–4 presents a statement of cash flows for NewMart, Inc. Notice that the statement follows the activity format shown in Exhibit 21–1. Under each activity, the sources and uses (inflows and outflows) of cash are summarized. Furthermore,

---

[4]In Chapter 3, we prepared the statement of cash flows directly from the cash ledger account. Although that approach appears to be a logical one, in practice the volume of cash transactions could make that approach inefficient.

EXHIBIT 21-3	Financial Statements Used as Basis for Statement of Cash Flows

NewMart, Inc.
Comparative Balance Sheets

			Net Change	
	12/31/97	12/31/98	Dr	Cr
Assets:				
Cash.	$ 35,000	$ 70,550	$35,550	
Accounts receivable	80,000	70,000		$10,000
Allowance for uncollectible accounts.	(10,000)	(15,000)		5,000
Inventories	100,000	75,000		25,000
Investment in Miller common stock	5,500	–0–		5,500
Plant and equipment	200,000	190,000		10,000
Accumulated depreciation on plant and equipment . . .	(40,000)	(35,000)	5,000	
Leased property	100,000	100,000		
Accumulated depreciation on leased property	–0–	(10,000)		10,000
Land.	30,000	38,000	8,000	
Total	$500,500	$483,550		
Liabilities and stockholders' equity:				
Accounts payable.	$ 70,000	$ 80,000		10,000
Salaries payable	10,000	15,000		5,000
Deferred tax liability	18,000	13,000	5,000	
Lease liability.	100,000	80,000	20,000	
Bonds payable ($100,000 face; 12% stated rate) . . .	110,000	108,000	2,000	
Pension liability	20,000	22,000		2,000
Common stock	80,000	60,000	20,000	
Contributed capital in excess of par	40,000	38,000	2,000	
Unrealized holding gain on investment in				
Miller common.	500	–0–	500	
Retained earnings.	62,000	67,550		5,550
Treasury stock	(10,000)	–0–		10,000
Total	$500,500	$483,550	$98,050	$98,050

Income Statement
For the Year Ended December 31, 1998

Revenues	$250,000
Cost of goods sold	(120,000)
Uncollectible accounts expense	(5,000)
Salaries expense.	(40,000)
Pension expense	(8,000)
Interest expense	(15,000)
Depreciation expense	(35,000)
Realized loss on sale of Miller common stock	(500)
Gain on sale of equipment	10,000
Net income before income taxes	$ 36,500
Income tax expense	(10,950)
Net income.	$ 25,550

EXHIBIT 21–4   **Statement of Cash Flows, Direct Approach**

NewMart, Inc.
Statement of Cash Flows
For the Year Ended December 31, 1998

Cash flows from operating activities:

Cash collections from customers.	$260,000	
Cash payments to merchandise suppliers.	(85,000)	
Cash payments for salaries.	(35,000)	
Cash payments for pension plan	(6,000)	
Cash payments for interest	(17,000)	
Cash payments for income taxes	(15,950)	
Net cash provided by operating activities		$101,050

Cash flows from investing activities:

Sale of investment in Miller common	$ 4,500	
Sale of equipment	30,000	
Purchase of equipment	(40,000)	
Purchase of land	(8,000)	
Net cash used by investing activities		(13,500)

Cash flows from financing activities:

Payment of lease obligation	$ (20,000)	
Retirement of common stock	(35,000)	
Reissue of treasury stock	18,000	
Payment of dividends	(15,000)	
Net cash used by financing activities		(52,000)
Net increase in cash		$ 35,550
Cash at beginning of year.		35,000
Cash at end of year		$ 70,550

the cash flows from NewMart's operating activities are reported using the direct approach. As we proceed through the following analysis, refer to Exhibit 21–4 to see how each transaction that affected cash is reported.

Cash Flows from Operating Activities

The first section of the statement of cash flows summarizes the cash flows associated with a company's operating activities. As discussed earlier, the major recurring cash inflow for most companies comes from sales of primary products or services— or stated another way, *cash inflows from customer collections. Operating cash outflows* include payments to suppliers of merchandise, payments to employees for wages and salaries, payments to creditors for interest, and payments to governmental agencies for taxes.

Because the income statement is based on accrual accounting, the equality between net income and net cash flows from operating activities rarely holds for short periods of time. For example, depreciation expense is an item that appears on the income statement under accrual accounting. However, depreciation expense is a noncash expense, and therefore would not be part of net cash flows. To give another example, interest accrued on notes receivable would appear on the income statement under accrual accounting. However, this revenue accrual would not represent a cash inflow.

In general, two distinct classes of items cause differences between "income flows" and cash flows, and must therefore be kept in mind when an income statement is used to determine cash flows from operating activities:

1. Items that appear on the income statement that do not represent inflows and outflows of cash, such as depreciation expense and amortization expense, or items whose cash effects do not relate to operating activities, such as gains on sales of depreciable assets.

2. Operating cash inflows and outflows that do not appear on the income statement but that must be reported on the statement of cash flows.

As an example of the second class of items, a company may collect, in the current period, cash arising from credit sales made in a previous period. Or, current period cash payments to employees may be made for settlement of salary expenses accrued in the previous accounting period. Because most current asset and current liability accounts arise from, and are affected by, transactions related to a company's operating activities, an analysis of changes in these accounts is necessary in order to adjust the accrual-basis income statement to a cash basis. The following sections explain how each operating cash inflow and outflow is determined.

Cash Collections from Customers

As Exhibit 21–4 shows, NewMart's cash collections from customers were $260,000, although the company's revenues for 1998 were only $250,000. The $10,000 difference is attributable to a $10,000 *decrease in accounts receivable* during the year:

Revenues reported on income statement.................................	**$250,000**
Add: Decrease in accounts receivable	**10,000**
Cash collections from customers.......................................	**$260,000**

The $10,000 decrease in accounts receivable represents cash collections from customers in excess of revenues reported on the income statement. We can see why this decrease in accounts receivable must be added to revenues to determine cash collections by examining the source of differences in revenues under the accrual basis and the cash basis, illustrated by Exhibit 21–5.

Cash Payments to Merchandise Suppliers

NewMart paid merchandise suppliers $85,000 in cash during 1998, although the company's cost of goods sold was $120,000. The difference of $35,000 is attributable to, and can be reconciled by, changes in two balance sheet accounts—inventories and accounts payable:

Cost of goods sold reported on the income statement	**$120,000**
Deduct: Decrease in inventories..	**(25,000)**
Increase in accounts payable	**(10,000)**
Cash payments to merchandise suppliers	**$ 85,000**

First let us look at the decrease in inventories. If there had been no change in inventories during the year, the cost of goods sold would have equaled purchases for the year. However, the decrease in inventories increased cost of goods sold, decreasing net income; yet this decrease in inventory had no corresponding effect on cash. Because the inventory decrease of $25,000 is included in the calculation of cost of goods sold and net income, yet does not represent a cash outflow, it must be subtracted from cost of goods sold when determining cash payments to suppliers.

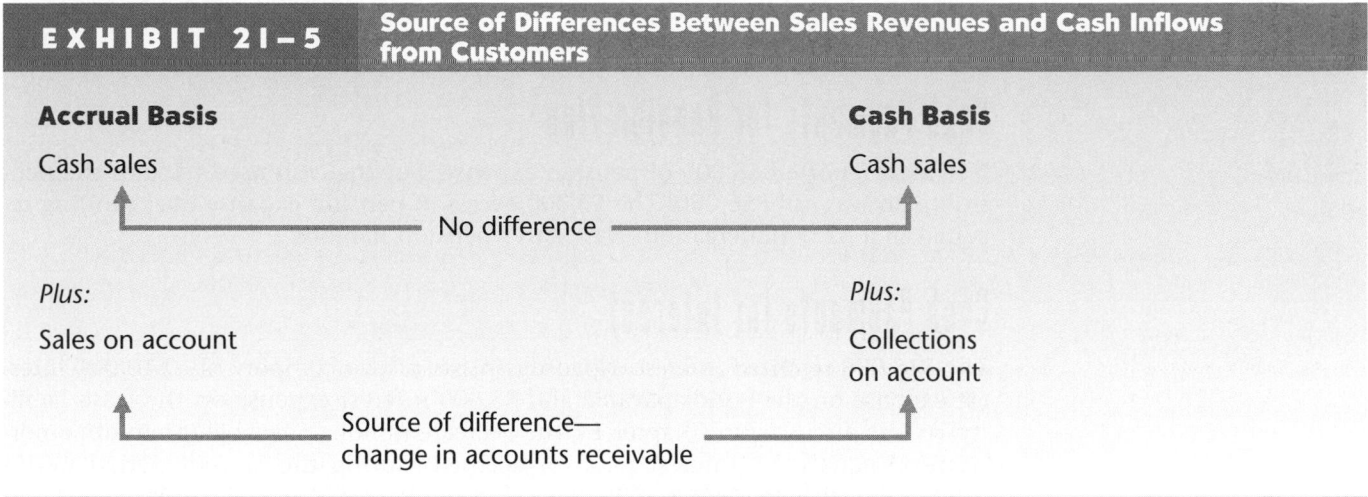

EXHIBIT 21–5 Source of Differences Between Sales Revenues and Cash Inflows from Customers

Accrual Basis   **Cash Basis**

Cash sales   Cash sales

⬆ ──────────── No difference ──────────── ⬆

Plus: *Plus:*

Sales on account   Collections on account

⬆ ──────── Source of difference— ──────── ⬆
            change in accounts receivable

The $10,000 increase in accounts payable represents additional purchases on credit over and above the cash payments made to suppliers during the year. Because these additional credit purchases increased goods available for sale but did not cause an outflow of cash, the $10,000 increase must be subtracted from cost of goods sold when determining cash payments to suppliers.

Notice that both the inventory and accounts payable adjustments are necessary to convert cost of goods sold from an accrual basis to a cash basis. The sources of differences between the accrual-basis cost of goods sold and the cash outflows to merchandise suppliers are shown in Exhibit 21–6.

Cash Payments for Salaries

Although NewMart's salary expense was $40,000, cash payments for salaries were only $35,000. This difference is attributable to the increase in salaries payable during 1998.

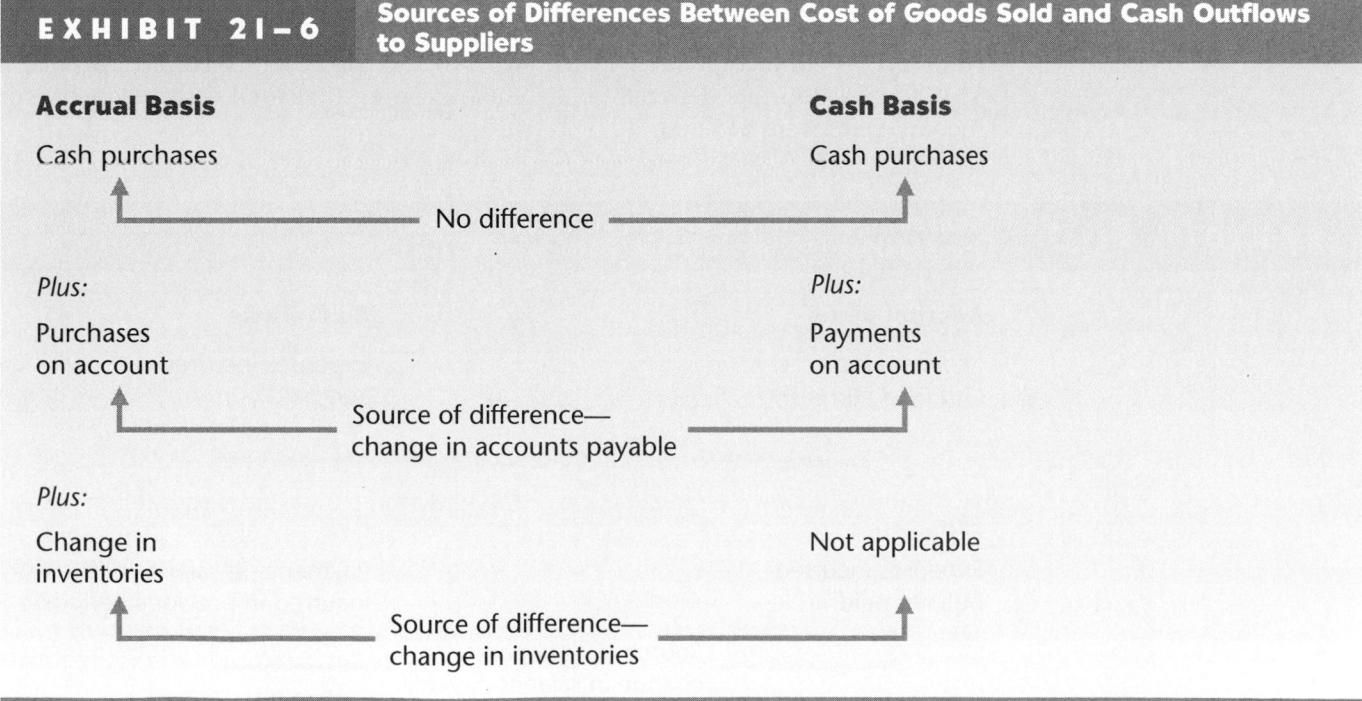

EXHIBIT 21–6 Sources of Differences Between Cost of Goods Sold and Cash Outflows to Suppliers

Accrual Basis   **Cash Basis**

Cash purchases   Cash purchases

⬆ ──────────── No difference ──────────── ⬆

Plus: *Plus:*

Purchases on account   Payments on account

⬆ ──────── Source of difference— ──────── ⬆
            change in accounts payable

Plus:

Change in inventories   Not applicable

⬆ ──────── Source of difference— ──────── ⬆
            change in inventories

Exhibit 21–7 further clarifies why salaries expense must be reduced by $5,000 to arrive at cash payments for salaries.

Cash Payments for Pension Plan

NewMart reported $8,000 of pension expense, but the cash used to fund the pension plan was only $6,000. The $2,000 excess of pension expense over funding resulted in a $2,000 increase in NewMart's pension liability.

Cash Payments for Interest

The $15,000 reported interest expense consists of two components: $10,000 interest expense on the bonds payable and $5,000 interest expense on the lease liability. As was discussed in Chapter 14, the decrease in bonds payable (premium amortization) equals the interest paid (or accrued) during the current period minus interest expense. In 1998, the decrease in bonds payable (amortization of the bond premium) reduced interest expense by $2,000, compared to the amount of cash paid to bondholders. This effect may be seen more clearly if we reconstruct New-Mart's entry to record 1998 interest expense on the bonds:

Interest expense ($12,000 – $2,000)	10,000	
Bonds payable	2,000	
Cash (.12 × $100,000)		12,000

NewMart also paid $25,000 on its lease contract, which resulted in a $20,000 reduction of its lease liability. In other words, $5,000 of the lease payment was a payment of interest incurred on the lease liability during 1998. The entry that New-Mart made to record its lease payment was as follows:

Interest expense	5,000	
Lease liability	20,000	
Cash		25,000

By examining both the entries to record interest expense for 1998, we can see that NewMart used $17,000 ($12,000 + $5,000) of cash to pay interest.

Cash Payments for Income Taxes

NewMart's 1998 income tax expense was $10,950. However, NewMart also had a $5,000 decrease in its deferred tax liability, meaning that total cash payments for income taxes were $15,950.

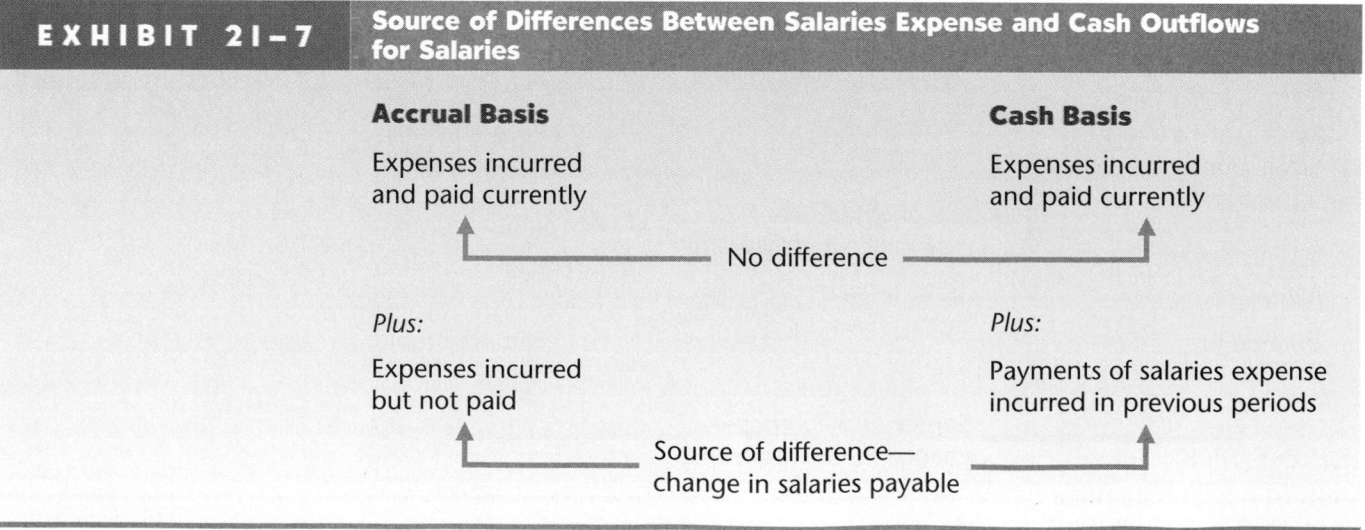

EXHIBIT 21–7	**Source of Differences Between Salaries Expense and Cash Outflows for Salaries**

Accrual Basis   **Cash Basis**

Expenses incurred and paid currently   Expenses incurred and paid currently

—————— No difference ——————

Plus: *Plus:*

Expenses incurred but not paid   Payments of salaries expense incurred in previous periods

————— Source of difference— change in salaries payable

Other Noncash Income Statement Items

Several items on NewMart's income statement—uncollectible accounts expense, depreciation expense, loss on the sale of Miller common stock, and gain on the sale of equipment—are not part of net cash flows. Uncollectible accounts expense and depreciation expense are noncash expenses that do not affect cash flows. The $500 realized loss on the sale of Miller common stock—the difference between the proceeds of $4,500 and the cost of $5,000 ($5,500 fair value at the end of 1997 minus the unrealized holding gain of $500 at the end of 1997)—and the $10,000 gain on the sale of equipment are not part of operating cash flows, for *two* reasons. First, the dollar amounts of the loss and gain are not measures of the cash flows that occurred in the transactions. The Miller common stock was sold for $4,500, and the equipment was sold for $30,000. Second, neither the loss nor the gain relates to operating activities. Revenues and expenses arise from a company's *primary* operating activities; losses and gains relate to *peripheral* activities—in this case, investment activities.

Remember, *Statement No. 115* specifies that sales and purchases of investments in available-for-sale securities are to be classified as *investment* activities for statement of cash flows purposes. More accurate information about operating cash flows results when losses and gains relating to investing and financing activities are excluded. The cash provided by the sale of the Miller common stock and the equipment sale are therefore reported under cash flows from investing activities, which we will discuss later.

Reconciliation of Income Flows and Cash Flows

If a company uses the direct approach to report cash flows from operating activities, it must provide a supplementary schedule that reconciles net income with net cash provided or used by operating activities. Because NewMart used the direct approach (see Exhibit 21–4), the required supplementary schedule must also be reported by New-Mart:

Net income	$ 25,550
Adjustments to reconcile net income to net cash provided	
by operating activities:	
Uncollectible accounts expense	5,000
Depreciation expense	35,000
Amortization of bond premium	(2,000)
Realized loss on sale of Miller common stock	500
Gain on sale of equipment	(10,000)
Decrease in accounts receivable	10,000
Decrease in inventories	25,000
Increase in accounts payable	10,000
Increase in salaries payable	5,000
Decrease in deferred tax liability	(5,000)
Increase in pension liability	2,000
Net cash provided by operating activities	$101,050

Note that the first five adjustments to reported income consist of income statement items that have no effect on cash flows. The last six adjustments consist of accruals and deferrals that affect operating cash inflows and outflows, but do not appear on the income statement. The decrease in accounts receivable is added to net income to determine net cash provided by operating activities, because cash was collected in excess of the current period's revenues. The decrease in inventories is added because cash was not used to pay for goods sold. The increase in accounts payable is added because cash was not used to purchase goods. The increase in salaries payable is added because cash was not used when salaries expense was incurred. The decrease in deferred tax liability is subtracted because the liability was reduced by using cash. The increase in pension liability is added because cash was not used when pension expense was incurred.

This form of reconciliation is called the indirect approach to reporting cash flows from operating activities. *If a company uses the indirect approach in the operating activities section of the statement of cash flows, the reconciliation on page 1121 would replace the data in the first section of Exhibit 21–4, and a supplementary schedule would not be required.* Exhibit 6–8 on page 287 provides a summary of the more common additions to and deductions from net income when the indirect approach is used.

Cash Flows from Investing Activities

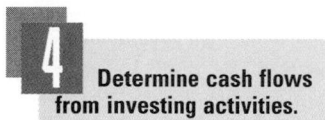

4 Determine cash flows from investing activities.

C O N C E P T U A L

Investing activities include purchases and sales of productive assets, purchases and sales of available-for-sale and held-to-maturity securities, and lending money and collecting on those loans.

As shown in Exhibits 21–1 and 21–4, in addition to operating activities, two other major activities may produce cash inflows and outflows: investing activities and financing activities. NewMart's investing activities are discussed in this section, and its financing activities are discussed in the next section. These discussions are organized in the order in which accounts other than current assets and current liabilities appear in NewMart's balance sheet. (Current assets other than cash and current liabilities were discussed in connection with the operating activities section of the statement of cash flows.)

Investing activities include purchases and sales of productive assets that are expected to generate revenues over long periods, purchases and sales of available-for-sale and held-to-maturity securities, and lending money and collecting on those loans. As we analyze each of NewMart's investing activities, refer to Exhibit 21–4 to see how each transaction is reported on the statement of cash flows.

Sale of Investment in Common Stock

At the beginning of 1998, NewMart had a $5,500 investment in Miller common stock, on which a $500 unrealized holding gain had been recorded in a prior period. (See the stockholders' equity section in NewMart's 1997 balance sheet in Exhibit 21–3.) This stock, with a $5,000 cost (the $5,500 fair value minus the $500 unrealized holding gain), was sold for $4,500, resulting in the realized loss of $500, reported in NewMart's 1998 income statement. The cash proceeds from the sale would be reported as follows:

Sale of investment in Miller common stock. $4,500

Sale of Equipment

Equipment with a book value of $20,000 (original cost of $50,000 less accumulated depreciation of $30,000) was sold for $30,000 cash. This investment transaction would appear in the statement of cash flows as:

Sale of equipment $30,000

Purchase of Equipment

From the comparative balance sheets in Exhibit 21–3, we can see that the plant and equipment account decreased by $10,000. Since the equipment that was sold had an original cost of $50,000, which was removed from the account at the time of sale, additional equipment costing $40,000 must have been purchased for cash:

Beginning balance + Purchases − Sales = Ending balance
$200,000 + $40,000 − $50,000 = $190,000

Thus, the purchase of equipment decreased cash by $40,000, which would appear in the investment activity section of the statement of cash flows:

Purchase of equipment. **$40,000**

Accumulated Depreciation

The accumulated depreciation on plant and equipment decreased by $5,000. Earlier we noted that $30,000 of accumulated depreciation was removed from the books at the time of the equipment sale. Therefore, we can conclude that depreciation expense and accumulated depreciation on plant and equipment recorded for 1998 was $25,000 (resulting in the net decrease in accumulated depreciation on plant and equipment of only $5,000). Accumulated depreciation on leased property increased by $10,000, which is explained by the 1998 entry to record depreciation expense related to the leased property. The $25,000 depreciation expense on plant and equipment plus the $10,000 depreciation expense on leased property equals the $35,000 depreciation expense reported in NewMart's income statement (see Exhibit 21–3). This depreciation expense was included in our earlier discussion of noncash income statement items (see page 1121).

Purchase of Land

No information was provided about this transaction. However, by inspecting the comparative balance sheets in Exhibit 21–3, we can see that the land account increased by $8,000 during 1998. From this fact we can infer that land was purchased for $8,000. Thus, an investing activity cash outflow of $8,000 would be reported on the statement of cash flows:

Purchase of land. **$8,000**

Cash Flows from Financing Activities

5 Determine cash flows from financing activities.

Financing activities include borrowing money from creditors and repaying the amounts borrowed, as well as obtaining resources from owners and providing them with both a return on their investment (through dividends) and a return of their investment.

Payment of Lease Obligation

In 1998, NewMart made a $25,000 lease payment. Earlier we observed that $5,000 of this payment was for interest expense and would be reported in the operating activities section of the statement of cash flows. The remaining $20,000 of the payment reduced the principal of the lease obligation and would therefore be reported as a cash outflow in the financing activities section of the statement of cash flows:

Payment of lease obligation **$20,000**

Bonds Payable and Premium on Bonds

There was no change in the bonds payable account other than the $2,000 decrease in the premium. That decrease was considered when we calculated cash payments for interest in preparing the cash flows from operating activities section.

Increase in Pension Obligation

As discussed earlier, the increase in the pension liability is related entirely to the fact that operating cash outflows to fund the pension plan were $2,000 less than

CONCEPTUAL

Financing activities include borrowing money, repaying amounts borrowed, issuing equity securities, acquiring the entity's own equity securities, and paying dividends.

the pension expense that was analyzed in determining cash flows from operating activities.

Retirement of Common Stock

Common stock with a book value of $30,000 was purchased for $35,000 and retired; the $5,000 difference was debited to retained earnings. We also know that treasury stock, accounted for at a cost of $10,000, was reissued for $18,000. This reissue of treasury stock would have resulted in an $8,000 credit to contributed capital in excess of par; yet contributed capital in excess of par had a net decline (debit) of $2,000 in 1998. Therefore, we can conclude that when the common stock was purchased, a $10,000 debit to contributed capital in excess of par was recorded, and common stock was debited for $20,000, as in the following entry:

Common stock	20,000	
Contributed capital in excess of par	10,000	
Retained earnings	5,000	
Cash		35,000

On the statement of cash flows, this financing activity would be reported as:

Retirement of common stock **$35,000**

Reissue of Treasury Stock

As has just been mentioned, the reissue of treasury stock generated a cash inflow of $18,000, along with a reduction of (credit to) treasury stock of $10,000 and an increase in (credit to) contributed capital in excess of par of $8,000. The cash inflow related to the treasury stock transaction would be reported in the financing activities section of the statement of cash flows as follows:

Reissue of treasury stock **$18,000**

Payment of Dividends

We are told that cash dividends declared and paid in 1998 were $15,000, which would be reported as a financing activity cash outflow. We could have *calculated* the $15,000 dividends declared by adding the $25,550 1998 net income to the 1997 retained earnings of $62,000, deducting the $5,000 decrease in retained earnings related to the purchase of outstanding common stock and then comparing the balance ($82,550) with 1998 retained earnings ($67,550). Since there are no dividends payable, all declared dividends were paid. (See the discussion of retained earnings below.)

Payments of dividends **$15,000**

Contributed Capital Accounts

The $20,000 decrease in the common stock account resulted from the purchase and retirement of common stock, as was discussed in the section on the retirement of shares of NewMart's stock. Also, as was discussed earlier, the $2,000 decrease in contributed capital in excess of par is the difference between the $10,000 reduction at the time NewMart purchased its own common stock and the $8,000 increase that occurred when the shares of treasury stock were reissued.

Unrealized Holding Gain on Common Stock

The unrealized holding gain was eliminated when the investment in Miller common stock was sold. The sale of the Miller common for $4,500, when the investment was on the books at $5,500, including a $500 unrealized holding gain, was a financing activity. As a result of the sale, a $500 realized loss was reported in the income statement (see Exhibit 21–3).

Retained Earnings

As shown in Exhibit 21–3, the retained earnings account increased by $5,550 during the year. This increase can be reconciled by summarizing the transactions that affected retained earnings, all of which were discussed in earlier analyses.

Net income	**$25,550 Cr**
Amount paid in excess of book value of common stock retired	**5,000 Dr**
Dividends	**15,000 Dr**
Net change in retained earnings	**$ 5,550 Cr**

The statement of cash flows for NewMart, Inc., is now complete (see Exhibit 21–4). The net cash provided by operating activities was $101,050, net cash used by investing activities totaled $13,500, and net cash used by financing activities was $52,000. These three activities and the inflows and outflows of cash within each activity summarize how NewMart's cash balance increased by $35,550 during 1998.

Investing and Financing Activities That Do Not Affect Cash

As was mentioned earlier, significant investing and financing activities that do not affect cash must be disclosed in the statement of cash flows, either in a *supplementary schedule* or in a *narrative*. Examples of noncash investing and financing activities are converting debt to equity; acquiring assets by assuming directly related liabilities, as in the purchase of a building by incurring a mortgage to the seller; obtaining an asset by entering into a capital lease; and exchanging noncash assets or liabilities for other noncash assets or liabilities.

Some transactions are part cash and part noncash; only the cash portions of those transactions should be reported in the body of the statement of cash flows. However, disclosure of any noncash activity should clearly indicate both the cash and noncash portions of the transaction. To illustrate, assume that a company acquired plant and equipment with a fair value of $100,000 by paying $30,000 cash and issuing common stock for the $70,000 balance. Exhibit 21–8 shows how this transaction should be reported in a supplementary schedule to the statement of cash flows.

S UMMARY OF CASH FLOW REPORTING OBJECTIVES

The examples and discussion presented to this point have illustrated most of the basic concepts and procedures related to preparation of the statement of cash flows. As was stated earlier, information that is reported in the statement of cash flows, when used with other financial statement information, helps users to assess a company's future cash flow potential. Such information also helps users to assess a company's ability to pay its debts, to pay dividends, and to meet its external financing needs. Finally, the statement of cash flows helps users to understand differences between a company's income flows and cash flows and to assess both cash and noncash aspects of the company's investing and financing activities during the period.

EXHIBIT 21-8	Reporting Noncash Transactions in a Supplementary Schedule to the Statement of Cash Flows

Operating activities:

   .
   .
   .

Investing activities:

  Purchased plant and equipment . . . . $ (30,000)

Financing activities:

   .
   .
   .

Net increase (decrease) in cash . . . . $ *xx*

Cash at beginning of year. . . . .   *xx*

Cash at end of year . . . . $ *xx*

Noncash investing and financing activities:

  Acquisition of plant and equipment $100,000

  Less: Common stock issued in acquisition . . . . (70,000)

  Cash paid for plant and equipment. . . . . $ 30,000

OTHER ISSUES IN STATEMENT OF CASH FLOWS PREPARATION AND DISCLOSURE

This section reinforces the discussion to this point and addresses some additional concepts associated with the statement of cash flows. Some of those concepts relate to statement preparation, while others relate to disclosure issues.

Income Flows versus Cash Flows

In the NewMart illustration on the preceding pages, cash flows from operating activities were determined by converting the accrual-basis income statement to a cash basis. In making this conversion, we considered two distinct classes of items: (1) income statement items that have no effect on cash (e.g., depreciation expense) and (2) current period operating cash inflows and outflows that have no effect on net income for the current period (e.g., collections on accounts receivable arising from sales made in the previous period).

Exhibit 21–9 presents a model that describes the relationship between income flows (income statement items) and cash flows from operating activities. Exhibit 21–9 is a *general model* that captures all the procedures discussed so far for determining NewMart's cash flows from operating activities. The left-hand column of Exhibit 21–9 shows the types of transactions that affect revenues, expenses, and net income in the current period. Notice that under accrual accounting, *three* types of items—cash, accruals, and prepayments (deferrals or unearned items)—make up these transactions. These types of items apply to both revenues and expenses. The middle column of Exhibit 21–9 shows those operating cash inflows and outflows that have no effect on current period income. The right-hand column shows the adjustments required to calculate cash flows from operating activities. In other words, the right-hand column shows the adjustments required to convert from an accrual basis to a cash basis. The transactions listed in the left-hand and middle columns are the types of items that necessitate the adjustments in the right-hand column.

EXHIBIT 21–9   **Reconciliation of Income Flows with Cash Flows**

Accrual-Basis Income Statement	Other Operating Cash Inflows and Outflows	Cash Flows from Operating Activities
(Items affecting current period income)	*(Items not affecting current period income)*	

Revenues:

1. Earned and collected in current period

→ Accrual-basis revenues

2. Accrued but not collected in current period (increase in an *asset* account)

7. Revenues accrued in previous periods; collected in current period (decrease in an *asset* account)

Add: Net decrease (**2** < **7**)
Deduct: Net increase (**2** > **7**)

3. Collected in previous periods; earned in current period (decrease in a *liability* account)

8. Collected but unearned in current period (increase in a *liability* account)

Add: Net increase (**3** < **8**)
Deduct: Net decrease (**3** > **8**)

Accrual-basis revenues (**1** + **2** + **3**)

Equals: Cash inflows

Expenses:

4. Incurred and paid in current period

→ Accrual-basis expenses

5. Accrued but not paid in current period (increase in a *liability* account)

9. Accrued in previous periods; paid in current period (decrease in a *liability* account)

Add: Net decrease (**5** < **9**)
Deduct: Net increase (**5** > **9**)

6. Incurred in current period; cash payments in previous periods (decrease in an *asset* account)

10. Current period payments for asset that will be an expense in future period(s) (increase in an *asset* account)

Add: Net increase (**6** < **10**)
Deduct: Net decrease (**6** > **10**)

Accrual-basis expenses (**4** + **5** + **6**)

Equals: Cash outflows

Summary:
    Accrual-basis revenues
  − Accrual-basis expenses
  = Net income

Summary:
    Cash inflows
  − Cash outflows
  = Net cash provided by operating activities

Current Assets and Current Liabilities Not Related to Operations

In calculating NewMart's cash flows from operating activities, we analyzed the company's current asset and current liability accounts (other than cash), because they were directly related to its operating activities. We eliminated (or omitted) revenues, expenses, gains, and losses that did not affect cash in order to complete the conversion of the accrual-basis income statement to a cash basis.

In some cases, a current asset or current liability may be affected by a financing or investing transaction rather than by a transaction related to operations. For example, a company might borrow money on a short-term basis (a financing transaction); or it might acquire plant and equipment on account or by issuing a short-term note (an investing and financing transaction). On the statement of cash flows, the first transaction would be reported as a financing activity. The second transaction would be reported as a noncash investing and financing activity. To give another example, a company might declare dividends but defer payment until the following accounting period. Dividends paid would be reported as a financing activity. Dividends declared but not paid (evidenced by dividends payable) would be reported as a noncash financing activity.

Extraordinary Items

Statement No. 95 does not address directly the disclosure of extraordinary items on the statement of cash flows. However, it does require that cash flows from transactions and other events whose effects are included in income, but which are unrelated to operations, be reported as investing or financing activities, as appropriate. For example, assume that a company extinguished debt by paying debt holders $50,000 and as a result recognized an extraordinary gain on the extinguishment of $8,000. In the statement of cash flows, the $8,000 gain would be excluded from operating cash flows, and the $50,000 cash outflow would be reported as a financing activity (and perhaps labeled extraordinary).

Classification Issues

Some transactions are difficult to classify clearly as operating, investing, or financing activities. For example, payments to retire bonds and payments on notes are classified as financing transactions. But should payments of interest on those bonds and notes payable be classified as financing activities or operating activities? To give another example, under GAAP a distinction is made between extraordinary gains and losses and those gains and losses that are not extraordinary. Should gains and losses on sales of assets, which do not meet extraordinary criteria, be classified as operating activities or investing activities? No clear-cut answers can be given to these questions; arguments can be made in support of each view. *Statement No. 95*, however, requires that interest or dividends received and interest paid be classified as operating activities and that cash flows associated with gains and losses on sales of assets be classified as investing activities rather than operating activities.

Cash Flow per Share

For many years the accounting profession and other groups have debated the issue of whether net cash flows from operating activities should be expressed on a per share basis. Some users have expressed a desire for such data. Income theorists, on the other hand, have feared that presenting cash flow per share might imply that such data are an alternative to earnings per share as an indicator of performance. Because of potential misinterpretation and confusion, *Statement No. 95* prohibits the reporting of cash flow data on a per share basis.

Transactions and Events Not Disclosed on the Statement of Cash Flows

Many transactions and events, such as stock dividends, stock splits, retained earnings appropriations, and reversals of appropriations, affect only stockholders' equity accounts. Since these economic events are *reclassifications within stockholders' equity,* they are not shown on the statement of cash flows. They have no effect on cash and are not significant investing and financing activities. However, a conversion of preferred stock to common stock would be disclosed as a noncash financing activity in a supplementary schedule to the statement of cash flows, in a manner similar to the illustration in Exhibit 21–8.

USE OF A WORKSHEET TO PREPARE THE STATEMENT OF CASH FLOWS

A worksheet is a useful tool for preparing a statement of cash flows. The primary advantage of a worksheet is that all the data to be analyzed appear in one place, so that the analysis can be performed in a well-organized and efficient manner. The worksheet does not take the place of the formal statement of cash flows. However, the statement can be prepared very easily by copying data from the completed worksheet.

> **6** Use a worksheet to prepare a statement of cash flows.

In this section we will use an extended example to prepare a worksheet. Comparative balance sheets for the Harrison Company appear in Exhibit 21–10. Assume further that additional information about the company's transactions in 1998 is as follows:

1. Cash dividends declared and paid were $10,000.

2. Plant and equipment, with an original cost of $35,000 and accumulated depreciation of $10,000 was sold at a loss of $10,000. The loss, not extraordinary

EXHIBIT 21–10	Comparative Balance Sheets for Harrison Company			
	December 31		**Net Change**	
	1997	**1998**	**Dr**	**Cr**
Assets:				
Cash	$ 60,000	$117,000	$ 57,000	
Accounts receivable	50,000	64,000	14,000	
Allowance for doubtful accounts	(10,000)	(16,000)		$ 6,000
Inventory	126,000	100,000		26,000
Plant and equipment	120,000	105,000		15,000
Accumulated depreciation	(40,000)	(50,000)		10,000
Land	60,000	30,000		30,000
Investment in Adkins common stock	250,000	330,000	80,000	
Goodwill	30,000	28,000		2,000
Total	$646,000	$708,000		
Liabilities and stockholders' equity:				
Accounts payable	$ 75,000	$ 50,000	25,000	
Salaries payable	20,000	12,000	8,000	
Other current liabilities	6,000	8,000		2,000
Deferred tax liability (noncurrent)	30,000	18,000	12,000	
Bonds payable (10% stated rate)	45,000	–0–	45,000	
Preferred stock (no par)	70,000	35,000	35,000	
Common stock ($2 par)	100,000	205,000		105,000
Contributed capital in excess of par	100,000	180,000		80,000
Retained earnings	200,000	200,000		
Total	$646,000	$708,000	$276,000	$276,000

EXHIBIT 21–11 Worksheet for the Statement of Cash Flows

Harrison Company
Balance Sheet

		Transactions and Analysis		
	12/31/97	Dr	Cr	12/31/98
Assets:				
Cash	60,000	(24) 57,000	(13) 10,000	117,000
Accounts receivable	50,000	(14) 24,000	(12) 16,000	64,000
Allowance for doubtful accounts	(10,000)	(13) 10,000		(16,000)
Inventory	126,000		(15) 26,000	100,000
Plant and equipment	120,000	(3) 20,000	(2) 35,000	105,000
Accumulated depreciation	(40,000)	(2) 10,000	(16) 20,000	(50,000)
Land	60,000	(5) 30,000	(4) 60,000	30,000
Investment in Adkins common stock	250,000	(7) 80,000		330,000
Goodwill	30,000		(18) 2,000	28,000
Total	646,000			708,000
Liabilities and stockholders' equity:				
Accounts payable	75,000	(15) 25,000		50,000
Salaries payable	20,000	(17) 8,000		12,000
Other current liabilities	6,000		(20) 2,000	8,000
Deferred tax liability	30,000	(21) 12,000		18,000
Bonds payable	45,000	(8) 46,000	(19) 1,000	–0–
Preferred stock	70,000	(9) 35,000		35,000
Common stock	100,000		(6) 15,000 (10) 30,000 (11) 10,000 (22) 50,000	205,000
Contributed capital in excess of par	100,000		(6) 15,000 (10) 5,000 (11) 10,000 (22) 50,000	180,000
Retained earnings	200,000	(1) 10,000 (11) 20,000	(23) 30,000	200,000
	646,000			708,000

Income Statement
For the Year Ended 12/31/98

Account	Amount	Dr ref	Dr	Cr ref	Cr
Sales revenue	300,000			(14)	300,000
Investment revenue	80,000			(7)	80,000
Cost of goods sold	(250,000)	(15)	250,000		
Depreciation expense	(20,000)	(16)	20,000		
Salaries expense	(37,000)	(17)	37,000		
Other expenses	(42,000)	(2)	10,000		
		(12)	16,000		
		(18)	2,000		
		(19)	6,000		
		(20)	8,000		
Income tax expense	(10,000)	(21)	10,000		
Gain on bond retirement (extraordinary)	9,000			(8)	9,000
Net income	30,000	(23)	30,000		

Statement of Cash Flows

Item	Dr ref	Dr	Cr ref	Cr
Cash flows from operating activities:				
Collections from customers	(14)	276,000		
Payments to merchandise suppliers			(15)	249,000
Payments to employees for salaries			(17)	45,000
Payments to creditors for interest			(19)	5,000
Payments for miscellaneous expenses			(20)	6,000
Payments for income taxes			(8)	6,000
			(21)	22,000
Cash flows from investing activities:				
Sale of equipment	(2)	15,000		
Purchase of equipment			(3)	20,000
Sale of land	(4)	60,000		
Cash flows from financing activities:				
Payment of dividends			(1)	10,000
Retirement of debt (extraordinary item)			(8)	31,000
Issuance of common stock	(22)	100,000		
Investing and financing activities not affecting cash:				
Land acquired by issuing common stock	(6)	30,000	(5)	30,000
Conversion of preferred stock to common stock	(10)	35,000	(9)	35,000
Net increase in cash			(24)	57,000
		1,296,000		1,296,000

was included in other expenses. Additional equipment was purchased at a cost of $20,000.

3. Land costing $60,000 was sold at book value. In addition, land with a fair value of $30,000 was acquired by issuing common stock with a par value of $15,000.

4. Harrison uses the equity method in accounting for its long-term investment in Adkins common stock. No dividends were declared by the investee.

5. Bonds payable with a carrying value of $46,000 were retired at the end of 1998. The extraordinary gain was $9,000 net of taxes of $6,000.

6. Preferred stock was converted to common stock. The book value method was used. The common stock issued had a par value of $30,000.

7. A stock dividend of 5,000 shares was declared and distributed. The shares distributed had a fair value of $4 per share.

8. Uncollectible accounts expense for 1998 was $16,000 (included in other expenses); receivables of $10,000 were written off against the allowance account.

9. Harrison's condensed income statement was as follows:

Sales revenue	$300,000
Investment revenue	80,000
Cost of goods sold	(250,000)
Depreciation expense	(20,000)
Salaries expense	(37,000)
Other expenses	(42,000)
Income tax expense	(10,000)
Income before extraordinary gain	$ 21,000
Extraordinary gain (debt extinguishment, net of tax)	9,000
Net income	$ 30,000

A worksheet for Harrison Company's statement of cash flows appears in Exhibit 21–11. The worksheet is divided into three parts. The upper part contains the beginning and ending balances for each balance sheet item. The middle part contains Harrison's income statement for 1998. The bottom part, which follows an activity format, contains the cash inflows and outflows that will appear on the formal statement of cash flows. The two middle columns in the worksheet are used to record, in summary form, the transactions that caused changes in cash during the year. *The bottom part and the two middle columns have been completed for instructional purposes. Normally they are completed as part of the analysis of changes in the balance sheet accounts, the income statement, and any additional data available.*

The worksheet in Exhibit 21–11 is completed by making summary journal entries in the two middle columns. Entries made to balance sheet accounts are designed to reconcile or explain changes in account balances during the period. Entries made to income statement accounts are designed to re-create the revenue, expense, gain, and loss amounts appearing in the first column. As a general rule, debits made to noncash balance sheet and income statement accounts in the upper and middle parts are associated with credits made in the lower part of the worksheet. Similarly, credits made to noncash balance sheet and income statement accounts in the upper and middle parts are associated with debits made in the lower part of the worksheet. The debits and credits in the lower portion correspond to cash inflows and outflows, respectively. Once the analysis has been completed, the formal statement of cash flows can be prepared from the lower part of the worksheet.

The following discussion explains each worksheet entry and, as appropriate, how each transaction was recorded originally by Harrison Company. You should study each worksheet entry carefully and trace it into the worksheet.

Explanation of the Worksheet Entries

Entry 1: Additional information item 1, dividends declared and paid (financing activity):

ORIGINAL ENTRY		WORKSHEET ENTRY (1)	
Retained earnings . . . 10,000		Retained earnings . . . 10,000	
Cash	10,000	Payment	
		of dividends	10,000

Retained earnings is debited for $10,000 in the balance sheet part of the worksheet. The $10,000 credit is entered as a payment of dividends under financing activities, in the bottom part of the worksheet.

Entry 2: Additional information item 2, sale of equipment (investing activity):

ORIGINAL ENTRY		WORKSHEET ENTRY (2)	
Cash 15,000		Sale of equipment . . . 15,000	
Accumulated		Accumulated	
depreciation 10,000		depreciation 10,000	
Loss on sale		Other expenses 10,000	
of equipment 10,000		Equipment	35,000
Equipment	35,000		

Since the sale of the equipment generated cash of $15,000, it is entered on the worksheet as a $15,000 debit under investing activities. Accumulated depreciation is debited for $10,000 because that account was debited when the sale was recorded. The $10,000 loss is included among other expenses and is entered as an income statement item. Because the loss has no effect on cash and does not relate to operations, it does not appear in the statement of cash flows section of the worksheet. Finally, the equipment account is credited for $35,000.

Entry 3: Additional information item 2, equipment purchase (investing activity):

ORIGINAL ENTRY		WORKSHEET ENTRY (3)	
Equipment 20,000		Equipment 20,000	
Cash	20,000	Purchase of	
		equipment	20,000

The equipment account is debited for $20,000 in the upper portion of the worksheet. In the lower portion of the worksheet, cash used to purchase the equipment is credited for $20,000.

Entry 4: Additional information item 3, sale of land at book value (investing activity):

ORIGINAL ENTRY		WORKSHEET ENTRY (4)	
Cash 60,000		Sale of land 60,000	
Land	60,000	Land	60,000

Entries 5 and 6: Additional information item 3; issued stock for land with a fair value of $30,000 (noncash investing and financing activity):

ORIGINAL ENTRY			**WORKSHEET ENTRIES (5) AND (6)**		
Land 30,000			Land. 30,000		
Common stock . . .	15,000		Land acquired		
Contributed capital			by issuing		
in excess of par . .	15,000		common stock . . .		30,000
			Land acquired		
			by issuing		
			common stock. 30,000		
			Common stock. . . .		15,000
			Contributed capital		
			in excess of par . . .		15,000

This entry records a transaction that is a noncash investing and financing activity. On the worksheet, two entries are made. In entry 5, land is debited for $30,000, while the credit is entered under "investing and financing activities not affecting cash." In entry 6, the debit is entered under "investing and financing activities not affecting cash." The credits are made to common stock for the par value of the shares issued, and to contributed capital in excess of par for the difference between the fair value of the land and the par value of the shares issued. From the standpoint of the accounts in the upper portion of the worksheet, entry 5 is similar to the one that would have been made if the land had been acquired with cash. Entry 6 is similar to one that would have been made if the stock had been issued for cash.

Entry 7: Additional information item 4; investment revenue from use of equity method, $80,000 (operating activity):

ORIGINAL ENTRY		**WORKSHEET ENTRY (7)**
Investment in		(Same as original entry)
Adkins common . . . 80,000		
Investment		
revenue	80,000	

Since the investment revenue reported on Harrison's income statement has no effect on cash, this amount does not appear in the cash flows part of the worksheet.

Entry 8: Additional information item 5; early extinguishment of debt at a gain (net of tax) of $9,000 (financing activity):

ORIGINAL ENTRIES		
Bonds payable. 46,000		
Cash		31,000
Gain on bond retirement (extraordinary).		15,000
To record before-tax gain.		
Gain on bond retirement (extraordinary) 6,000		
Cash		6,000
To record payment of taxes on gain and		
to show gain net of tax.		

WORKSHEET ENTRY (8)

Bonds payable...............................	46,000	
Retirement of debt—extraordinary item.............		31,000
Payments for income taxes.....................		6,000
Gain on bond retirement (extraordinary)...........		9,000

For instructional purposes, two original entries are shown above. The first entry is to record the bond retirement before taxes are considered; the second is to record the income taxes on the gain. Since the gain must be shown net of tax, the tax of $6,000 is shown as a reduction of the gain. In the worksheet entry, bonds payable is debited for $46,000. (See Entry 19 on page 1137 for a discussion of the discount amortization.) Cash used for retirement of the debt is credited for $31,000, which is the amount of cash associated with the early extinguishment. Payments for income taxes is credited for $6,000.

Entries 9 and 10: Additional information item 6; conversion of preferred stock to common stock, $35,000 (noncash financing activity):

ORIGINAL ENTRY			WORKSHEET ENTRIES (9) AND (10)		
Preferred stock 35,000			Preferred stock...... 35,000		
Common stock ...	30,000		Conversion of		
Contributed capital			preferred stock to		
in excess of par ..	5,000		common stock ...		35,000
			Conversion of		
			preferred stock		
			to common stock... 35,000		
			Common stock....		30,000
			Contributed capital		
			in excess of par...		5,000

This transaction is a financing activity that has no effect on cash. It is recorded on the worksheet in a manner similar to worksheet entries 5 and 6.

Entry 11: Additional item 7; stock dividend of $20,000:

ORIGINAL ENTRY		WORKSHEET ENTRY (11)
Retained earnings ... 20,000		(Same as original entry)
Common stock ...	10,000	
Contributed capital		
in excess of par ..	10,000	

A stock dividend has no effect on cash, and constitutes neither an investing activity nor a financing activity. As was discussed earlier, the stock dividend is *merely a reclassification within stockholders' equity.* Therefore, it does not appear in the bottom portion of the worksheet.

Entries 12 and 13: Additional information item 8; uncollectible accounts expense and write-off of customers' accounts (operating activity):

ORIGINAL ENTRIES		**WORKSHEET ENTRIES (12) AND (13)**	
Uncollectible		Other expenses 16,000	
accounts expense. . . 16,000		Allowance for	
Allowance for		doubtful accounts .	16,000
doubtful accounts .	16,000		
Allowance for		(Same as original entry)	
doubtful accounts . . 10,000			
Accounts			
receivable	10,000		

Uncollectible accounts expense is a noncash expense (among other expenses) on the income statement. Therefore, the worksheet entry is a debit to other expenses and a credit to the allowance account. The write-off of customers' accounts has no effect on either the income statement or the statement of cash flows.

Now that each item of additional information has been analyzed, we must inspect the income statement. Analysis of items on the income statement, together with an analysis of net changes in related balance sheet accounts, will allow us to determine operating cash inflows and outflows.

Entry 14: Cash collections from customers (operating activity):

ORIGINAL ENTRIES		**WORKSHEET ENTRY (14)**	
(Various entries to record		Collections from	
sales and collections)		customers 276,000	
		Accounts	
		receivable 24,000	
		Sales revenue . . .	300,000

During the year, accounts receivable had a *net* increase of $14,000 ($64,000 − $50,000). Because we already have determined that $10,000 in customers' accounts was written off as uncollectible (entry 13), we can conclude that the accounts receivable account increased by $24,000. This $24,000 increase may be interpreted as credit sales that must be subtracted from sales revenue in order to arrive at cash collections from customers. Another logical way to arrive at this same conclusion is to assume that the $276,000 cash inflow consists of collection of the beginning accounts receivable balance less write-offs ($50,000 − $10,000 = $40,000) plus $236,000 of current period revenues ($300,000 − $64,000): $40,000 + $236,000 = $276,000.

Entry 15: Payments to merchandise suppliers (operating activity):

ORIGINAL ENTRIES		**WORKSHEET ENTRY (15)**	
(Various entries to record		Accounts payable. . 25,000	
purchases on account,		Cost of goods sold . 250,000	
payments on account,		Inventory	26,000
and cost of goods sold)		Payments to	
		merchandise	
		suppliers	249,000

The decrease in accounts payable represents additional cash payments in excess of current period purchases (purchases are a component of cost of goods sold). The decrease in inventories increased cost of goods sold, but had no effect on cash.

Entry 16: Depreciation expense (operating activity):

ORIGINAL ENTRY	WORKSHEET ENTRY (16)
Depreciation expense. 20,000	(Same as original entry)
Accumulated depreciation 20,000	

Depreciation expense appears on the income statement, but has no effect on cash. Therefore, the worksheet entry appears in the upper and middle portions of the worksheet.

Entry 17: Payments to employees for salaries (operating activity):

ORIGINAL ENTRIES	WORKSHEET ENTRY (17)

(Various entries to record salaries expense and payments to employees)	Salaries payable . . . 8,000
	Salaries expense . . . 37,000
	  Payments to
	  employees for
	  salaries 45,000

The $8,000 decrease in salaries payable represents cash payments to employees in excess of salaries expense reported on the income statement.

The next item on Harrison's income statement is other expenses of $42,000. We have analyzed $26,000 of this expense in entries 2 and 12. We must return to the balance sheet accounts at the top of the worksheet in order to analyze the remainder of this expense.

Entry 18: Goodwill account; amortization of goodwill for 1998 (operating activity):

ORIGINAL ENTRY	WORKSHEET ENTRY (18)
Other expenses (amortization of goodwill). 2,000	(Same as original entry)
Goodwill 2,000	

This worksheet entry is made in the balance sheet and income statement sections of the worksheet. Because goodwill amortization is a noncash expense, it does not appear in the bottom portion of the worksheet.

Entry 19: Cash payments to creditors for interest (operating activity):

ORIGINAL ENTRY	WORKSHEET ENTRY (19)
Interest expense 6,000	Interest expense 6,000
Bonds payable 1,000	Bonds payable 1,000
Cash	Payments to
(.10 $\times$ \$50,000) . . . 5,000	creditors for
	interest 5,000

Interest expense for the year was $6,000, which consisted of the $5,000 cash paid plus amortization of the discount on bonds payable. Notice that this worksheet entry and entry 8 to record the bond retirement fully explain the change in the bonds payable account for the year. (Amortization of the discount in the amount of $1,000 is the reason the bonds had a book value of $46,000 at the retirement date.)

Entry 20: Cash payments for miscellaneous expenses (operating activity):

ORIGINAL ENTRIES	WORKSHEET ENTRY (20)
(Various entries to record miscellaneous expenses accrued and paid in cash)	Other expenses . . . 8,000 Other current liabilities. . . . . . 2,000 Payments for miscellaneous expenses. 6,000

The increase in current liabilities during the year means that expenses reported on Harrison's income statement exceeded cash payments by $6,000.

Entry 21: Cash payments for income taxes (operating activity):

ORIGINAL ENTRY	WORKSHEET ENTRY (21)

Income tax expense . . 10,000
Deferred tax liability . . 12,000
   Cash 22,000
	Income tax expense . . 10,000
	Deferred tax liability . . 12,000
	   Payments for income taxes 22,000

The decrease in the deferred tax liability account during the year means that cash payments for taxes exceeded income tax expense by $12,000. Thus, payments for income taxes in the amount of $22,000 are entered in the worksheet under cash flows from operating activities.

At this point, we have analyzed the additional information and income statement items for Harrison Company. We must now inspect and analyze each non-cash balance sheet account to determine whether all cash transactions have been included in the statement of cash flows. Scanning the balance sheet to see whether each balance sheet account has been fully reconciled, we find only three accounts that have not been reconciled—common stock, contributed capital in excess of par, and retained earnings.

Entry 22: Common stock and contributed capital in excess of par accounts; issuance of stock for $100,000 (financing activity):

The contributed capital accounts that have not been reconciled are common stock and contributed capital in excess of par:

	BEGINNING BALANCE	+ PREVIOUS CREDITS	– ENDING BALANCE =	UNRECONCILED DEBIT (CREDIT)
Common stock	$100,000	+ $15,000 + 30,000 + 10,000	– $205,000 =	$(50,000)
Contributed capital in excess of par	$100,000	+ $15,000 + 5,000 + 10,000	– $180,000 =	$(50,000)

These unreconciled credits (increases) represent an issuance of common stock. The entries appear below:

ORIGINAL ENTRY	WORKSHEET ENTRY (22)

Cash 100,000
   Common stock . . . 50,000
   Contributed capital in excess of par . . 50,000
	Issuance of common stock 100,000
	   Common stock . . 50,000
	   Contributed capital in excess of par . . 50,000

Entry 23: Net income for 1998, $30,000:

ORIGINAL ENTRY		WORKSHEET ENTRY (23)	
Income summary . . . 30,000		Net income 30,000	
Retained earnings. .	30,000	Retained earnings . .	30,000

This worksheet entry transfers the net income of $30,000, shown at the bottom of the income statement section, to retained earnings.

Entry 24: Net increase in cash during the period, $57,000:

By inspecting the worksheet, you can see that all changes in the noncash account balances have been reconciled. In addition, summary entries for items on Harrison's income statement have been entered in the middle columns of the worksheet. Each income statement entry has been offset either with a balance sheet entry or with an entry in the statement of cash flows section of the worksheet. Therefore, the final worksheet entry records the increase in cash of $57,000 by debiting cash in the upper portion of the worksheet and crediting net increase in cash in the lower portion of the worksheet.

Preparation of the Statement of Cash Flows from the Worksheet

The statement of cash flows for Harrison Company, which is based on the data in the bottom portion of the worksheet, appears in Exhibit 21–12. Notice that Harrison's operations for 1998 resulted in a net use of cash. In addition, the noncash investing and financing activities and the reconciliation of net income to net cash used by operating activities are disclosed in supplementary schedules.

Part B • Additional Disclosure Topics

In this section we will discuss two additional disclosure topics, interim reporting and segment (or disaggregated information) reporting.

INTERIM REPORTING

As we saw in Chapter 2, to be useful, information must be disclosed on a timely basis. Because investment, credit, and other types of decisions that affect entities are made frequently, a significant demand exists for **interim reporting**—that is, reporting of information that covers periods of less than one year. As a result, *quarterly* reporting of selected financial information has become quite common in the United States. Internationally, semiannual reporting is more typical.

Companies whose stock is traded on an organized exchange, such as the New York Stock Exchange, must issue quarterly financial information. Quarterly reports must be filed with the Securities and Exchange Commission on Form 10-Q. *APB Opinion No. 28* governs the preparation of quarterly reports to stockholders.[5] Quarterly reports are much less detailed than annual reports, often containing only con-

---

[5]"Interim Financial Reporting," *Opinions of the Accounting Principles Board No. 28* (New York: AICPA, 1973).

EXHIBIT 21–12   **Statement of Cash Flows, Direct Approach**

Harrison Company
Statement of Cash Flows
For the Year Ended December 31, 1998

Cash flows from operating activities:

Collections from customers	$276,000	
Payments to merchandise suppliers	(249,000)	
Payments to employees for salaries	(45,000)	
Payments to creditors for interest	(5,000)	
Payments for miscellaneous expenses	(6,000)	
Payments for income taxes	(28,000)	
Net cash used by operating activities		$ (57,000)

Cash flows from investing activities:

Sale of equipment	$ 15,000	
Sale of land	60,000	
Purchase of equipment	(20,000)	
Net cash provided by investing activities		55,000

Cash flows from financing activities:

Issuance of common stock	$100,000	
Retirement of debt (extraordinary item)	(31,000)	
Payment of dividends	(10,000)	
Net cash provided by financing activities		59,000
Net increase in cash		$ 57,000
Cash at beginning of year		60,000
Cash at end of year		$117,000

densed earnings information; they need not be audited. To prevent misleading inferences, each page of an unaudited interim report should be clearly labeled "Unaudited."

Several inherent difficulties complicate interim reporting. Because of seasonal factors, the revenues of some companies fluctuate widely from one interim period to the next. In other companies, heavy fixed costs incurred in one interim period may benefit other interim periods. In still other situations, costs and expenses related to the full year's activities are incurred at irregular intervals, and must be allocated to products in process or to other interim periods to avoid distorting interim financial results. In addition, because of the limited time available to prepare interim reports, many costs and expenses must be estimated. For example, reviewing each type of inventory item may not be practical, nor may precise income tax calculations for each interim period be possible. Moreover, subsequent refinement of interim estimates may distort the operating results of later interim periods.

CONCEPTUAL

There are two fundamentally different views of the relationship between interim periods and the annual period.

Interim reporting is further complicated by the existence of two fundamentally different views of the relationship between interim periods and the annual period. One view holds that each interim period is a basic accounting period that stands on its own, and therefore the results of operations for each interim period should be determined in essentially the same manner as for an annual accounting period. In this view, the same principles used to prepare annual reports should be used to report deferrals, accruals, and estimations at the end of each interim period. The second view is that each interim period is an integral part of the annual period. In this view, deferrals, accruals, and estimations made at the end of each interim period necessarily depend on judgments made on each interim date about the results of operations for the entire annual period. Also, an expense occurring within the fiscal year could be allocated among interim periods on the basis of the passage of time, sales volume, production volume, or some other activity factor.

The guidelines set forth in *Opinion No. 28* reflect the APB's view that each interim period should be considered an integral part of the annual period. In general, the Board believed that the results for each interim period should be based on the accounting principles and practices used to prepare the company's most recent annual financial statements. The Board concluded, however, that certain accounting principles and practices followed in preparing the annual report might require modification at interim report dates, so that interim financial information would better relate to information in the annual report, and thus be more useful.

The next few sections summarize GAAP for interim reporting.

Revenue

Revenue from products sold or services rendered should be recognized for interim periods on the same basis that is used for the annual period. Companies engaged in seasonal business activities must disclose that fact. Supplemental information should be provided for the current and preceding 12-month periods ending at the interim date so users will not be misled by seasonally influenced interim results.

Expenses Associated with Revenue

Expenses that can be associated directly with, or allocated to, products sold or services rendered should be matched against interim revenue on the same basis or bases as those used for annual reporting purposes. Such expenses may include costs of materials used, wages and salaries and related fringe benefits, manufacturing overhead, and warranty expense.

In determining inventory costs and cost of goods sold, companies generally should use the same cost flow assumptions (e.g., FIFO, LIFO, average cost) for interim reporting as for annual reporting. Some exceptions, however, are appropriate for interim reporting purposes:

1. Companies may use an estimation method for interim inventory valuation. However, disclosure of the method used at the interim date as well as any significant adjustments needed to reconcile interim figures with the annual inventory are required.

2. An apparently *permanent* inventory loss due to market price declines should be recognized in the interim period in which the decline occurs. If the loss is later recovered as a result of market price increases within the same fiscal year, a gain should be recognized in the interim period in which the loss is recovered. However, the gain from price recovery cannot exceed the previously recognized loss. *Temporary* market price declines need not be recognized in interim periods because no loss is expected for the annual period.

3. Companies that use standard cost accounting systems to determine inventory and product costs should defer recognition of *planned* price, volume, or cost variances expected to be absorbed by the end of the annual period. *Unplanned* or unanticipated variances, however, should be recognized in interim periods in accordance with the same procedures used at the end of the annual period.

Other Expenses

Expenses other than those associated directly with, or allocated to, products sold or services rendered should be accounted for in interim periods, as follows:

1. In calculating interim period income, expenses should be deducted as they are incurred or allocated among interim periods on the basis of an estimate of time

CONCEPTUAL

For reporting purposes, each interim period should be considered an integral part of the annual period.

1 Describe the general guidelines for interim financial reporting under GAAP.

expired, benefit received, or activity associated with a period. The allocation procedures used should be consistent with those used for annual reporting purposes. For example, utility expense, rent expense, and interest expense should be recognized in the interim periods in which they are incurred. On the other hand, expenses such as insurance premiums and property taxes should be allocated among the interim periods.

2. Interim expenses that cannot be readily identified with the activities or benefits of other interim periods should be recognized in the interim period in which they are incurred, rather than arbitrarily assigned to other interim periods.

3. Interim gains and losses that are similar to those that would not be deferred at year-end—such as a gain or loss on the sale of property, plant, or equipment—should be recognized in the interim period in which they occur.

Income Tax Expense

To determine income tax expense at the end of each interim period, a company must estimate its effective tax rate for the full fiscal year. The estimated effective annual tax rate is equal to the expected annual income tax expense divided by expected annual pretax income. This rate should *not* include significant unusual, infrequent, or extraordinary items that will be reported separately or net of income tax effects for the interim or annual period. At the end of each interim period, the estimated effective annual tax rate should be used to calculate estimated year-to-date taxes on income from continuing operations. The income tax expense for the current interim period is equal to the estimated year-to-date tax on income from continuing operations minus the income tax expense for all previous interim periods in the fiscal year.

To illustrate, assume that Nelson Company reported taxable income from continuing operations of $40,000 in the first quarter of the current year, and $35,000 in the second quarter. The estimated income tax expenses on each of these amounts, as calculated at the end of each quarter, were reported as $12,000 and $10,000, respectively. Nelson is now in the process of determining its income tax expense for the third-quarter interim report. The company has calculated its third-quarter taxable income from continuing operations as $25,000, and anticipates earnings of $30,000 in the fourth quarter. Assume that the company has a tax rate of 22 percent on the first $25,000 of taxable income, and 34 percent on taxable income over $25,000. At the end of the third quarter, Nelson would estimate its effective annual tax rate as follows:

ESTIMATE OF ANNUAL TAXABLE INCOME

Actual 1st-quarter income	$ 40,000
Actual 2nd-quarter income	35,000
Actual 3rd-quarter income	25,000
Estimated 4th-quarter income	30,000
Estimated annual income	$130,000

ESTIMATE OF EFFECTIVE ANNUAL TAX RATE

22% of first $25,000	$ 5,500
34% of remaining $105,000	35,700
Estimated total annual tax expense	$41,200

$$\text{Estimated effective annual tax rate} = \frac{\$41,200 \text{ estimated total annual taxes}}{\$130,000 \text{ estimated total annual income}}$$

$$= 32\%$$

This estimated effective annual tax rate can now be used to calculate Nelson's estimated year-to-date income tax expense as well as its income tax expense for the current quarter:

$$32\% \times (\$40,000 + \$35,000 + \$25,000) = \genfrac{}{}{0pt}{}{\$32,000 \text{ estimated year-to-date}}{\text{income tax expense}}$$

ESTIMATED THIRD-QUARTER INCOME TAX EXPENSE

Estimated taxes on income of first three quarters		$32,000
Actual tax expense for 1st quarter	$12,000	
Actual tax expense for 2nd quarter	10,000	(22,000)
Estimated 3rd-quarter income tax expense		$10,000

Earnings per Share

Following the guidelines of *Statement No. 128,* companies must include in their interim reports basic and diluted earnings per share (EPS) related to net income, income from continuing operations, extraordinary items, and discontinued operations.

Disclosure in Interim Financial Reports

In addition to the interim financial data described in the preceding sections, companies must disclose the following information, at a minimum, in their interim financial reports:

1. Sales or gross revenues, income tax expense, extraordinary items, cumulative effect of a change in accounting principles, and net income.

2. Earnings per share data for each period presented, determined in accordance with *Statement No. 128.*

3. Seasonal revenues, costs, or expenses.

4. Significant changes in estimated or actual income tax expense.

5. Disposal of a segment of the company, and extraordinary, unusual, or infrequent items.

6. Contingent items.

7. Changes in accounting principles or accounting estimates.

8. Significant cash flows.

8 State the information that companies must disclose, at a minimum, in interim financial reports.

When disclosing the above information for an interim period, data should be presented for the current fiscal year to date or the last 12 months to date, along with comparable data for the preceding year. In addition, the following information about reportable operating segments (defined on page 1145) must be disclosed in interim financial statements:[6]

1. Revenues from external customers.

2. Intersegment revenues.

3. Segment profit or loss.

4. A description of differences from the last annual report in the basis of segmentation or in the basis of measurement of segment profit or loss.

5. A reconciliation of the total of the reportable segments' profits or losses to the enterprises consolidated income before income taxes, extraordinary items, discontinued operations, and the cumulative effect of changes in accounting principles.

---

[6]"Disclosures about Segments of an Enterprise and Related Information," *Statement of Financial Accounting Standards No. 131* (Norwalk, Conn.: FASB, 1997), para. 33.

6. Total assets for which there has been a material change from the amount reported in the last annual report.

Companies also are encouraged, but not required, to publish a balance sheet and a statement of cash flows on interim dates. If a balance sheet and statement of cash flows are not presented, the company must disclose any material changes in liquid assets, net working capital, long-term liabilities, and stockholders' equity since the last reporting period.

Disclosure of Special Items

How should special items, such as the disposal of a segment of a business or changes in accounting principles or accounting estimates, be presented in interim reports? Extraordinary items that are material in relation to annual net income should be disclosed separately and included in the determination of net income for the interim period in which they occur. Likewise, companies must disclose separately the effects of the disposal of a business segment as well as unusual or infrequent transactions and events that are material with respect to net income for the interim period.

Interim financial reports should indicate any change in accounting principles or accounting estimates from those used in (1) the comparable interim period of the prior year, (2) the preceding interim periods in the current year, or (3) the prior annual report. If a change in accounting principle requiring the cumulative effect treatment is made in the first interim period of a company's fiscal year, the cumulative effect of the change on retained earnings at the beginning of that fiscal year should be included in the net income of the first interim period. If a cumulative effect change in accounting principle is made in other than the first interim period, no cumulative effect should be included in the net income of the period of change. Instead, financial data of *prechange* interim periods within the current fiscal year should be restated by applying the new accounting principle. In addition, the cumulative effect of the change on the retained earnings at the beginning of the fiscal year should be included in the restated net income of the first interim period.[7] The effect of a change in accounting estimate should be accounted for in the interim period in which the change in estimate is made.

S EGMENT REPORTING

Businesses with multiple operating units (subsidiaries) typically prepare consolidated financial statements. For example, the consolidated financial statements of General Electric Company, presented in Appendix B, represent the company's manufacturing and nonfinancial services businesses as well as the accounts of General Electric Capital Services, Inc. In consolidated financial statements, the revenues, expenses, assets, liabilities, and other financial statement elements of the controlling (parent) company and its subsidiaries are combined for reporting purposes. A consolidated dollar amount is reported for each account.

Although consolidated financial statements provide useful information, there also is a demand for information about segments of an enterprise among external users of financial statements. Beginning in 1976, *FASB Statement No. 14* provided guidelines for reporting segment information.[8] *Statement No. 14* required business

---

[7]"Reporting Accounting Changes in Interim Financial Statements," *Statement of Financial Accounting Standards No. 3* (Stamford, Conn.: FASB, 1974), paras. 9 and 10.

[8]"Financial Reporting for Segments of a Business Enterprise," *Statement of Financial Accounting Standards No. 14* (Stamford, Conn.: FASB, 1976).

enterprises to report segment information on two bases: by industry and by geographic area. It also required disclosure of information about export sales and major customers. Yet users of financial statements continued to press for financial information that was disaggregated to a much greater extent than that required by *Statement No. 14.*

As a result, in 1997, the FASB issued *Statement No. 131,* which changed the way public business enterprises report segment information in their annual financial statements and required that selected segment information be reported in interim financial reports to shareholders. The FASB and the Accounting Standards Board of the Canadian Institute of Chartered Accountants cooperated in developing these revised standards for reporting segment information. At about the same time, the International Accounting Standards Committee undertook a similar project to reconsider *International Accounting Standard No. 14,* "Reporting Financial Information by Segment." *Statement No. 131* supersedes *Statement No. 14* for financial statements issued for periods beginning after December 15, 1997. The provisions of the *Statement* are not applicable to interim financial statements in the initial year of its application, however. The *Statement* applies only to public (not to not-for-profit or nonpublic) enterprises.

Statement No. 131 requires that public business enterprises report segment information *based on management's organization of the enterprise*—that is, on reportable operating segments.[9] Information about the enterprises's products and services, the geographic areas in which it operates, and its major customers must be included. The objective of providing this information is to help users of financial statements to better understand the enterprise's performance, to better assess its prospects for future cash flows, and to make more informed judgments about the enterprise. If a company changes the composition of its operating segments, the corresponding segment information for earlier periods should be restated unless doing so is impracticable.

9 State the basis for reporting segment information, including the definition of an operating segment.

Operating Segments

An **operating segment** is a business component (1) that engages in business activities from which revenues are earned and expenses incurred; (2) whose operating results are reviewed regularly by the company's chief operating decision maker (whether an individual or a group of senior officers) for purposes of performance evaluation and future resource allocation; and (3) for which discrete financial information generated by, or based on, the company's internal financial reporting system is available. Not every part of a business is necessarily an operating segment. For example, administrative headquarters and some functional departments may not be directly involved in earning revenues.

Identification of operating segments based on an enterprise's internal organizational structure has several potential benefits. First, information that is segmented along operating lines highlights the risks and opportunities perceived by management. Thus, operating segment information improves a user's ability to predict management's actions or reactions. Furthermore, the incremental cost of providing operating segment information is relatively low, because information about operating segments is already available for managerial use. Finally, segment information that is based on the enterprise's internal operating structure should produce less subjective reporting than was the case under *Statement No. 14,* which required information based on "industry" segments.

---

[9]Ibid., paras. 4–5 and 16–18.

| 10 | **List the several categories of segment information that must be provided for reportable operating segments under GAAP.** |

General Information

Management is required to disclose general information about those factors considered most significant in determining operating segments as well as the revenue-generating products and services of each segment.[10] Based on illustrations provided by the FASB, appropriate general information disclosures for Harrell Company would be:

> Harrell Company's operating segments are strategic business units that were acquired as separate entities, and that provide different products and services. At the time of acquisition, the management of each business unit was retained. Each segment continues to be managed separately because each requires different technology and marketing strategies.
>
> Harrell Company has three operating segments: Recreational Vehicles, Appliances, and Finance. The Recreational Vehicles segment produces pleasure boats and snowmobiles for sale to retailers such as marinas and boat shops. The Appliances segment produces refrigerators, ovens, stove-tops, microwaves, and dishwashers for sale to retailers. The Finance segment includes all the company's financial operations, including the financing of customer purchases from the other two segments.

Information about Segment Profits (Losses) and Assets

Management is required to provide explanations of the measurements of segment profit or loss, as well as total assets for each reportable segment.[11] At a minimum, the company must provide information about:

1. The basis of accounting for any transactions between reportable segments.

2. Differences (including policies for allocation of centrally incurred costs) between the measurements of the reportable segments' profits or losses and the measurement of the company's consolidated income before income taxes, extraordinary items, discontinued operations, and the cumulative effect of changes in accounting principle.

3. Differences (including policies of allocating jointly used assets or centrally incurred liabilities) between the measurements of reportable segments' assets and the company's consolidated assets.

4. The nature of any changes from prior periods in the measurement methods used to determine reported segment profit or loss and the effect, if any, of those changes on the measure of segment profit or loss.

5. The nature and effect of any assymetrical allocations to segments (such as the allocation of depreciation expense to a segment without a corresponding allocation of the related depreciable assets).

Based on FASB illustrations, appropriate explanations of Harrell Company's measurement of segment profit or loss and segment assets might read as follows:

> The accounting policies of the segments are the same as those described in the Company's Summary of Significant Accounting Policies, except that pension expense for each segment is recognized and measured on the basis of cash payments to the pension plan. Harrell Company evaluates performance based on profit or loss from operations before income taxes, not including nonrecurring gains and losses and foreign exchange gains and losses.

---

[10]Ibid., para. 26.
[11]Ibid., para. 31.

Segment profit or loss, derived using the company's internal financial reporting system, must be disclosed for each reportable segment. If these amounts are included in the determination of segment profit or loss, the information disclosed for each segment must include:[12]

1. Revenues from external customers.

2. Revenues from transactions with other operating segments of the company.

3. Interest revenue and interest expense.

4. Depreciation, depletion, and amortization expense.

5. Unusual items (per *APB Opinion No. 30*, para 26).

6. Equity in the net income of investees accounted for by the equity method.

7. Income tax expense or benefit.

8. Extraordinary items.

9. Significant noncash items other than depreciation, depletion, and amortization expense.

Each operating segment's total assets and total liabilities, measured using the company's internal financial reporting system, must also be reported. Information about each segment must include:[13]

1. The amount of investment in equity method investees included in segment assets.

2. Total expenditures for additions to long-lived segment assets other than financial instruments, long-term customer relationships of a financial institution, mortgage and other servicing rights, deferred policy acquisition costs, or deferred tax assets.

Based on FASB illustrations, and using amounts assumed to have been taken from internal financial information about each operating segment that is used by the chief operating decision maker, a presentation of the profit or loss and assets information related to the operating segments of Harrell Company follows:

	RECREATIONAL VEHICLES	APPLIANCES	FINANCE	TOTALS
Revenues from external customers . .	$13,000	$12,000	$7,000	$32,000
Intersegment revenues	3,000	2,500	—	5,500
Segment profit	1,200	1,800	1,000	4,000
Interest revenue	—	—	5,000	5,000
Interest expense	—	—	3,500	3,500
Depreciation and amortization	400	1,500	1,000	2,900
Other significant noncash item:				
Cost in excess of billings				
on long-term contracts	250	—	—	250
Segment assets.	10,000	13,000	59,000	82,000
Expenditures for segment assets	1,500	1,600	700	3,800

Reconciliation of Segment Amounts with Consolidated Amounts

Statement No. 131 requires a reconciliation of the total of the reportable segments' profits or losses with the company's consolidated income before income taxes, extraordinary items, discontinued operations, and the cumulative effect of changes in accounting principles. A reconciliation of the total of the segments' revenues

[12]Ibid., para. 27.
[13]Ibid., para. 28.

with the company's consolidated revenues must also be provided. It also is necessary to provide reconciliations of the total reportable segments' assets with the company's consolidated assets. Finally, the total of the reportable segments' amounts for every other significant item of information disclosed should be reconciled to the corresponding consolidated amount.[14]

Using the FASB's illustrations as a basis, and assuming that Harrell Company has no discontinued operations or cumulative effects of changes in accounting principles, but does have a few small operating segments that are not reportable segments, the following are examples of reconciliations of segment revenues, segment profit or loss, and segment assets with the consolidated amounts:

REVENUES

Total revenues for reportable segments	$37,500
Other revenues	1,000
Elimination of intersegment revenues	(5,500)
Total consolidated revenues	$33,000

PROFIT OR LOSS

Total profit or loss for reportable segments	$ 4,000
Other profit or loss	100
Elimination of intersegment profits	(600)
Unallocated amounts:	
Litigation settlement received	400
Other corporate expenses	(800)
Adjustment to pension expense in consolidation	(300)
Income before income taxes and extraordinary items	$ 2,800

ASSETS

Total assets for reportable segments	$82,000
Other assets	1,800
Elimination of receivables from corporate headquarters	(1,000)
Goodwill not allocated to segments	3,000
Other unallocated amounts	1,500
Consolidated totals	$87,300

Enterprise-Wide Disclosures

The enterprise-wide disclosures discussed in this section are required only if the information is not provided as part of the reportable segment information required by *Statement No. 131*. Enterprise-wide disclosures may be needed with regard to: information about products and services, information about geographic areas, and information about major customers.

Unless it is impracticable to do so, an enterprise must report the revenues from external customers for each product and service or each group of similar products and services,[15] as well as certain geographic information.[16] Since Harrell Company reported revenues from external customers on a segment basis (see page 1147), no further enterprise-wide report of this information is needed.

---

[14]Ibid., para. 32.
[15]Ibid., para. 37.
[16]Ibid., para. 38.

The required geographic information is: (1) revenues from external customers (a) attributed to the enterprise's home country and (b) attributed to all foreign countries in total from which the enterprise derives revenues; and (2) long-lived assets (other than financial instruments, long-term customer relationships of a financial institution, mortgage and other servicing rights, deferred policy acquisition costs and deferred tax assets) (a) located in the enterprise's home country and (b) located in all foreign countries in which the enterprise holds assets. Based on FASB illustrations, the following example shows how Harrell Company might report the required geographic information:

GEOGRAPHIC INFORMATION

	REVENUES	LONG-LIVED ASSETS
United States	$19,000	$11,300
Canada	5,700	6,500
Japan	3,000	3,500
Other foreign countries	4,300	1,700
Total	$32,000	$23,000

An enterprise also must provide information about the extent of its reliance on its major customers. If revenues from transactions with a single external customer equal 10 percent or more of total enterprise revenues, the enterprise must disclose that fact, the total amount of revenues from each such customer, and the identity of the segment or segments reporting the revenues. It is not necessary to disclose the identity of a major customer or the amount of revenues reported by each segment from that customer.[17] If Harrell had a qualifying major customer, it might have reported the required information as follows:

> One customer of the Recreational Vehicle segment accounts for approximately $6,500 of the Company's consolidated revenues.

International Reporting Practices

Currently, the segment reporting requirements for U.S. companies are the most comprehensive in the world. To the extent that segment reporting requirements exist in countries other than the United States, the most common requirement is for disclosures of sales by line of business and geographic area.

Many non-U.S. multinational companies present no segment data. However, the amount of disclosure of segment data seems to be influenced by the extent to which a company operates in global capital markets. Companies that are relatively active participants in global capital markets may present quite extensive product-line and geographic segment information. In fact, a number of those companies provide more extensive disclosures than do U.S. companies, despite less comprehensive international requirements. Japanese multinational corporations are a notable exception; few provide segment data, even if they do operate in international capital markets.

As indicated earlier, the International Accounting Standards Committee is reconsidering *International Accounting Standard No. 14,* which relates to segment reporting. Depending on the outcome of that activity, there may be some change in international practices related to segment reporting.

---

[17]Ibid., para. 39.

SUMMARY OF LEARNING OBJECTIVES

PART A • Revisiting the Statement of Cash Flows

1. State the information that is provided by a statement of cash flows.

The statement of cash flows provides information regarding a company's cash inflows and outflows during an accounting period as well as information about its operating, investing, and financing activities.

2. Describe the general format of a statement of cash flows and the general types of transactions that affect cash flows from operating, investing, and financing activities.

The statement of cash flows is organized using an activity format, in which cash flows are classified in terms of operating, investing, and financing activities. Operating activities relate to a company's primary revenue-generating activities. Cash flows from buying, selling, and the maturing of trading securities are also classified as cash flows from operating activities. Investing activities include lending money and collecting on those loans; buying and selling productive assets; and buying, selling, and the maturing of available-for-sale and held-to-maturity securities. Financing activities include borrowing money and repaying the amounts borrowed as well as obtaining resources from owners and providing them with both a return on their investment and a return of their investment.

3. Use both the direct approach and the indirect approach to report cash flows from operating activities.

Under the direct approach, the following major sources of operating cash inflows and outflows are reported, at a minimum: cash collected from customers, lessees, licensees, and similar parties; interest and dividends received; cash received from the sale or maturity of trading securities; any other operating cash receipts; cash paid to employees and other suppliers of goods and services; interest paid; income taxes paid; cash paid to purchase trading securities; and any other operating cash payments. Under the indirect approach, cash flows from operating activities are reported by adjusting net income for revenues, expenses, gains, and losses that appear on the income statement but do not have an effect on cash. In addition, net income is adjusted for operating cash flows that do not appear on the income statement.

4. Determine cash flows from investing activities.

Investing activities include purchases and sales of productive assets that are expected to generate revenues over long periods; purchases and sales of available-for-sale and held-to-maturity securities; and lending money and collecting on those loans.

5. Determine cash flows from financing activities.

Financing activities include borrowing money and repaying the amounts borrowed, as well as obtaining resources from owners and providing them with both a return on their investment (through dividends) and a return of their investment.

6. Use a worksheet to prepare a statement of cash flows.

The use of a worksheet to prepare a statement of cash flows is illustrated on pages 1129–1139.

PART B • Additional Disclosure Topics

7. Describe the general guidelines for interim financial reporting under GAAP.

Each interim period should be considered an integral part of the annual period. The results for each interim period should be based on the accounting principles and practices used to prepare the company's most recent annual financial statements, unless modification of those principles and practices at interim report dates would yield interim information that better relates to the information in the annual report.

8. State the information that companies must disclose, at a minimum, in interim financial reports.

At a minimum, the following items must be disclosed in interim financial reports: sales or gross revenues, income tax expense, extraordinary items, the cumulative effect of a change in accounting principle, and net income; earnings per share data for each period presented; seasonal revenues, costs, or expenses; significant changes in estimated or actual income tax expense; disposal of a segment of the company and extraordinary, unusual, or infrequent items; contingent items; changes in accounting principles or accounting estimates; and significant cash flows. In addition, the following information about reportable operating segments must be disclosed: revenues from external customers of each operating segment; intersegment revenues for each segment; segment profit or loss for each segment; a description of differences from the last annual report in the basis of measurement of segment profit or loss; a reconciliation of the total of the segments' profits or losses to the company's consolidated income before income taxes, extraordinary items, discontinued operations, and the cumulative effect of changes in accounting principles; and total assets of each segment for which there has been a material change from the amount reported in the last annual report.

9. **State the basis for reporting segment information, including the definition of an operating segment.**
   Segment information must be reported based on management's organization of the company (that is, on its operating segments), including information about the company's products and services, the geographic areas in which it operates, and its major customers. An operating segment is a business component (1) that engages in business activities from which revenues are earned and expenses incurred, (2) whose operating results are reviewed regularly by the company's chief operating decision maker, whether an individual or a group of senior officers, for purposes of performance evaluation and future resource allocations, and (3) for which discrete financial information, generated by or based on the company's internal financial reporting system, is available. Not every part of a business is necessarily part of an operating segment.

10. **List the several categories of segment information that must be provided for reportable operating segments under GAAP.**
    The categories of segment information that must be provided for material operating segments are: general information about factors significant in determining operating segments and the revenue-generating products and services of each segment; information about segment profits (losses) and assets; reconciliations of segment revenues, profits (losses), and assets with consolidated amounts; geographic information; and information about major customers.

KEY TERMS

PART A
activity format 1112
cash equivalents 1112
direct approach 1113
financing activities 1112
indirect approach 1114

investing activities 1112
operating activities 1112

PART B
interim reporting 1139
operating segment 1145

EXHIBIT 21–13　　**Preparation of the Statement of Cash Flows Using the T-Account Approach**

NewMart, Inc.

Cash

Net change	35,550		

Investment in Miller common

		Net change	5,500
		(9)	5,500

Bonds payable

		Net change	2,000
		(6)	2,000

Operating activities

(1)	260,000	(2)	85,000
		(4)	35,000
		(5)	6,000
		(6)	17,000
		(7)	15,950

Plant and equipment

(11)	40,000	Net change	10,000
		(10)	50,000

Pension liability

		Net change	2,000
		(5)	2,000

Investing activities

(9)	4,500	(11)	40,000
(10)	30,000	(12)	8,000

Acc. depr.—plant & equip.

Net change	5,000	(8)	25,000
(10)	30,000		

Common stock

Net change	20,000		
(13)	20,000		

Financing activities

(14)	18,000	(6)	20,000
		(13)	35,000
		(15)	15,000

Acc. depr.—leased property

		Net change	10,000
		(8)	10,000

Contrib. cap. in excess of par

		Net change	2,000
		(14)	8,000
		(13)	10,000

Accounts receivable

		Net change	10,000
		(1)	10,000

Land

Net change	8,000		
(12)	8,000		

Unrealized holding gain

		Net change	500
		(9)	500

Allowance for uncoll. accounts

		Net change	5,000
		(3)	5,000

Accounts payable

		Net change	10,000
		(2)	10,000

Retained earnings

(13)	5,000	Net change	5,500
(15)	15,000	(16)	25,500

Inventories

		Net change	25,000
		(2)	25,000

Salaries payable

		Net change	5,000
		(4)	5,000

Treasury stock

		Net change	10,000
		(14)	10,000

Deferred taxes payable

Net change	5,000		
(7)	5,000		

Lease liability

Net change	20,000		
(6)	20,000		

Income summary

(2)	120,000	(1)	250,000
(3)	5,000	(9)	500
(4)	40,000	(10)	10,000
(5)	8,000		
(6)	15,000		
(7)	10,950		
(8)	35,000		
(9)	1,000		
(16)	25,550		

Explanation of T-account entries:
(1) Collections from customers.
(2) Payments to suppliers.
(3) Uncollectible accounts expense.
(4) Payments for salaries.
(5) Payments for pension plan.
(6) Payments for interest.
(7) Payments for income taxes.
(8) Depreciation.
(9) Sale of investment in Miller common.
(10) Sale of equipment.
(11) Purchase of equipment.
(12) Purchase of land.
(13) Retirement of common stock.
(14) Reissue of treasury stock.
(15) Payment of dividends.
(16) Close income summary.

PPENDIX 21-1

Using T-Accounts to Prepare the Statement of Cash Flows

An alternative to the worksheet approach for analyzing data to prepare the statement of cash flows is the T-account approach. Instead of making summary entries on a worksheet to develop data for preparing the formal statement, we could make them in T-accounts.

Exhibit 21–13 illustrates the T-account approach based on the data for New-Mart, Inc., on page 1115 and in Exhibit 21–3. First, the net change in cash and the net change in each of the noncash accounts are entered in the appropriate T-accounts. An income summary T-account is used to accumulate income statement transactions. Cash inflows are entered on the debit side of the cash T-account, and cash outflows on the credit side. For each debit or credit entry made in the cash T-account, an offsetting debit or credit is made in the appropriate noncash or income summary T-account. Entries are made until all the net changes in the noncash accounts have been reconciled.

The idea behind the T-account approach is the same as that for the worksheet approach. The only difference is that the debits and credits made in the "transactions and analysis" columns of the worksheet are entered on the debit and credit sides of the T-accounts.

QUESTIONS

PART A • Revisiting the Statement of Cash Flows

Q 21-1. What is the purpose of the statement of cash flows?

Q 21-2. How is *cash equivalent* defined?

Q 21-3. Distinguish among a company's operating activities, investing activities, and financing activities.

Q 21-4. List three examples of investing activities and three examples of financing activities.

Q 21-5. Give an example of each of the following transactions:
 1. A transaction that appears on the income statement and is an inflow of cash.
 2. An expense transaction that appears on the income statement but is not an outflow of cash.
 3. A transaction that appears as an inflow on the statement of cash flows but is not on the income statement.

Q 21-6. List three types of transactions that have no effect on cash but that must be disclosed either in a narrative or in a supplementary schedule to the statement of cash flows.

Q 21-7. Give two examples of a cash equivalent.

Q 21-8. Two approaches that can be used to determine the amount of cash flows from operating activities are the direct approach and the indirect approach. How do the two approaches differ?

Q 21-9. When cash collections from customers are calculated, why must sales revenue be adjusted for a change in accounts receivable during the period?

Q 21-10. Indicate how each item listed below should be considered in determining cash flows from operating activities under the direct approach:
 1. Depreciation expense.
 2. Amortization of goodwill.

3. Gain on sale of equipment.
4. Increase in accounts payable.
5. Loss on sale of an investment classified as a cash equivalent.
6. Decrease in noncurrent deferred tax liability.
7. Stock dividends distributed.
8. Amortization of discount on long-term capital lease.
9. Uncollectible accounts expense.
10. Loss on held-to-maturity securities.
11. Write-off of uncollectible accounts (allowance method used).
12. Decrease in deferred investment credit classified as noncurrent.

Q 21-11. How would interest revenue accrued on a cash equivalent be reported on the statement of cash flows?

Q 21-12. A company made an annual lease payment of $18,000, which covered $4,000 of interest expense and reduced the lease liability by $14,000. How should this transaction be reported on a statement of cash flows?

Q 21-13. During 1998, Snow Corporation, which uses the allowance method of accounting for doubtful accounts, recorded $15,000 of uncollectible accounts expense and wrote off $8,000 of uncollectible accounts. What effect did these combined transactions have on Snow's balance sheet reporting of accounts receivable, net of allowance for doubtful accounts?

Q 21-14. Explain how a company could report a net loss for the year and still have cash flows generated from operations.

Q 21-15. If the indirect approach is used, indicate how the following numbered transactions would appear on a statement of cash flows. Use the lettered key for your answers:
a) Income statement adjustment for determining operating cash flows.
b) Investing activity.
c) Financing activity.
d) Supplementary schedule (noncash investing and/or financing activity).
e) None of the above.
1. Declaration (but not payment) of a cash dividend.
2. Proceeds from sale of a trading security.
3. Interest accrued on short-term notes receivable.
4. Interest accrued on long-term notes receivable.
5. Issuance of long-term notes for cash.
6. Issuance of short-term notes for cash.
7. Amortization of patents.
8. Proceeds from sale of a held-to-maturity security.
9. Proceeds from sale of an available-for-sale security.
10. Loss on sale of land.
11. Appropriation of retained earnings for cost of treasury stock purchased.
12. Issue of treasury stock in excess of cost.
13. Issue of treasury stock at less than cost.
14. Interest expense on bonds issued at par.

Q 21-16. Give an example of a transaction that affects current assets or current liabilities and that does not relate to operations.

PART B • Additional Disclosure Topics

Q 21-17. Discuss some of the circumstances that may complicate interim reporting.

Q 21-18. What general guideline should be followed when GAAP is applied to interim financial reporting?

Q 21-19. Describe the proper treatment of (a) permanent and (b) temporary inventory losses from market price declines during an interim reporting period.

Q 21-20. What information must companies disclose, as a minimum, in interim financial reports?

Q 21-21. Why might an analyst wish to have segment information when attempting to evaluate the financial condition and profitability of a company that has different operating segments or operations in different geographic areas?

Q 21-22. Define an operating segment.

Q 21-23. Under GAAP, what information must a company provide for each reportable operating segment?

Q 21-24. Under what conditions must information about major customers be disclosed?

CASES

PART A • Revisiting the Statement of Cash Flows

C 21-1.   **ANALYSIS OF CASH FLOWS**   Harold Associates, a high-tech research and development company, has decided to expand its operations and is preparing a registration statement for the SEC in connection with a new stock offering. The company has never prepared a statement of cash flows and must include one in the registration statement. The controller is puzzled about how several items should be reported. You have agreed to assist the controller in determining how the following events that occurred during the current year should be reported on the statement of cash flows:

a) Used research equipment, which was secured by a mortgage of $80,000, was sold for $300,000 cash. The mortgage was assumed by the buyer, and a gain of $45,000 was recorded on the transaction. Depreciation of $120,000 had been recorded on the equipment since acquisition.

b) During the year, the company borrowed $410,000 in cash to be used for plant expansion. The funds are being held by a bank under a trust arrangement, and $36,000 had not been spent at the end of the year. The debt matures in five years.

c) The company holds, as an investment, common stock of Garrison Corporation. During the current year, Harold acquired additional shares of Garrison stock at a cost of $65,000 and received cash dividends of $10,000 from Garrison. The purchase of Garrison's stock was financed by a $15,000 note and a cash payment of $50,000.

d) Cash proceeds from the sale of assets of discontinued operations amounted to $11,000. The loss on sale was $89,000; $82,000 of this amount had been accrued in the previous year, when management made the decision to dispose of the segment.

e) The company wrote off $12,000 in uncollectible receivables during the year and recorded uncollectible accounts expense of $20,000 at the end of the year.

f) Harold's cost of goods sold during the year was $84,000, and accounts payable for these goods decreased by $6,000. Because of demand for the goods, Harold's inventory also decreased by $4,000 during the year.

g) Near the end of the current year, the company acquired all of the assets of Walsh Services by issuing common stock. The fair value of the assets acquired was $60,000:

Inventories	$25,000
Land	10,000
Plant and equipment	20,000
Supplies	5,000

h) During the current year, the company's long-term bonds payable account increased by $10,000. A gain of $20,000 was recorded on an open market purchase and retirement of bonds with a book value of $75,000. Near the end of the year, Harold issued bonds for cash.

i) During the year, Harold declared and paid a cash dividend of $45,000.

j) To encourage Harold to expand, the county donated land with a fair value of $80,000 to Harold.

REQUIRED   Discuss how each of the 10 items above should be reported in Harold's statement of cash flows. The company has not decided on whether the direct approach or the indirect approach will be used in reporting cash flows from operating activities.

C 21-2.   **NET CASH FLOWS FROM OPERATING ACTIVITIES**   At lunch recently, your aunt commented that she had just received annual reports from two companies in which she had invested. She pointed out that the two companies used different methods of arriving at net cash flows from operating activities on their statement of cash flows. She stated, "One company started the calculation with net income and added and deducted strange things that seem to have nothing to do with cash flows; the other company listed certain cash inflows and outflows that seem to have nothing to do with income." She further stated, "These companies are in similar businesses; however, their cash flow statements are bewildering!"

REQUIRED   Prepare a memorandum that:

1. Discusses the two approaches that the companies are using to determine and report net cash flows from operating activities.

2. Summarizes the primary arguments supporting each of the approaches used by the two companies.

3. Discusses how each item below would affect the calculations in preparing the statement of cash flows under "net cash flows from operating activities" using the direct approach. For the purposes of this case, consider each item independently and ignore how the items would appear on a supporting reconciliation schedule.

    a)   Decrease in an accounts receivable account.

    b)   Uncollectible accounts expense.

    c)   Increase in an inventory account.

    d)   Depreciation expense.

    e)   Increase in a salaries payable account.

    f)   Loss on sale of land.

    g)   Write-off of uncollectible accounts (allowance method used).

    h)   Amortization of premium on bonds payable.

    i)   Dividends declared and paid during the year.

    j)   Increase in an interest receivable account.

C 21-3.   **STATEMENT OF CASH FLOWS PREPARATION**   Yale Engineering Company is a young and growing producer of electronic measuring instruments and technical equipment. You have been retained by the company to advise it in the preparation of a statement of cash flows. You have obtained the following information concerning certain events and transactions for the company during the fiscal year ended October 31, 1998:

    a)   The amount of net income for the fiscal year was $800,000, which included a deduction for an extraordinary loss of $93,000 (see item *e* below).

    b)   Depreciation expense of $240,000 was included in the income statement.

    c)   Uncollectible accounts receivable of $30,000 were written off against the allowance for uncollectible accounts. Also, $37,000 of bad debts expense was included in the determination of income for the fiscal year, and the same amount was added to the allowance for uncollectible accounts.

    d)   A gain of $4,700 was realized on the sale of a machine. The machine originally cost $75,000, of which $25,000 was undepreciated on the date of sale.

    e)   On April 1, 1998, a freak storm caused an uninsured inventory loss of $93,000 ($180,000 loss, less reduction in income taxes of $87,000). This extraordinary loss was included in the determination of income, as indicated in item *a* above.

    f)   On July 3, 1998, a building and some land were purchased for $600,000. Yale gave in payment $100,000 cash, $200,000 market value of its unissued common stock, and a $300,000 mortgage note.

    g)   On August 3, 1998, Yale purchased $100,000 of its common stock on the open market.

    h)   The board of directors declared a $320,000 cash dividend on October 20, 1998, payable on November 15, 1998, to stockholders of record on November 5, 1998.

REQUIRED   Write a brief explanation of how each of the items above should be disclosed in Yale's statement of cash flows for the fiscal year ended October 31, 1998. If any item is neither an inflow nor an outflow of cash, explain why it is not and indicate how the item should be disclosed, if at all, in Yale's statement of cash flows. Yale uses the direct approach in reporting cash flows from operating activities.

(AICPA, adapted)

PART B • Additional Disclosure Topics

C 21-4.   **INTERIM REPORTING**   Nation's Best Pool Fence Company manufactures, sells, and installs pool fences. The company is publicly held and is issuing its interim financial statements for the third quarter. The following information must be evaluated in preparing the third-quarter financial statements.

    a)   The company earns two-thirds of its revenues during the second quarter. The accounting manager believes that fact need not be disclosed.

    b)   A major contract is being accounted for appropriately by the completed-contract method, under which the entire income effect is reported in the period in which the contract is completed. The contract is scheduled to be completed in the fourth quarter. However, it is estimated that 40 percent of the contract was completed during the third quarter. The chief executive officer wants to include income related to 40 percent of the contract in the third-quarter results.

    c)   The first semiannual interest payment on newly issued debt was made during the third quarter. Monthly accruals for interest expense have not been made during the year. The entire payment was recorded as an expense in the third quarter. The accounting manager believes no adjustment is necessary for the quarterly report.

d) Comparative income data are presented for the same quarter last year. The printers have said there is room for only one set of EPS figures on the page and suggest omitting last year's from the report.

e) Third-quarter revenues were below projections. As a result, the estimated effective tax rate for the year is less than previously projected. A company tax department employee has suggested calculating the income tax expense for the quarter by multiplying the new effective rate for the year by the quarterly income.

REQUIRED   Discuss whether the suggestions would be in accordance with GAAP. If the suggestions are not in accordance with GAAP, indicate why and how the item should be presented or treated.

C 21-5.   **SEGMENT REPORTING**   An organization composed of financial officers and senior accounting officials of companies that recently have become multiproduct, multidivision, or multigeographic area firms has asked you to present a seminar on GAAP for segment reporting. The members of this organization either know that segment reporting soon will be required for their companies or are trying to determine whether it will be required. Although the organization's representatives have indicated that you should emphasize those aspects of GAAP for segment reporting that you consider the most important, they have asked that, as a minimum, you address the following questions:

a) In general, what segment information must be reported under GAAP, and what is the objective of providing this information?

b) What is an operating segment, and what characteristics does it have?

c) At a minimum, what information must be reported for each segment related to profit or loss, assets, and liabilities?

d) In addition to reporting operating segment profit or loss, assets, and liabilities, what other information must be disclosed that is related to profit or loss, assets, and liabilities?

REQUIRED   Prepare a brief draft of the comments you think should be made at the seminar. Be sure to include responses to each of the specific questions presented to you.

EXERCISES

PART A • Revisiting the Statement of Cash Flows

E 21-1.   **CASH COLLECTIONS FROM CUSTOMERS**   During 1998, Jackson Corporation wrote off customer accounts totaling $35,000 and made sales, all on account, of $610,000. Other information about the company's sales activities is as follows:

	BEGINNING OF 1998	END OF 1998
Accounts receivable	$180,000	$150,000
Allowance for uncollectible accounts	16,000	40,000

In addition, in 1998, Jackson accepted a $4,000 note from a customer whose account was overdue. Jackson collected $1,600 on this note during 1998.

REQUIRED   Prepare a schedule showing the amount of cash collected from customers during 1998.

E 21-2.   **CASH FLOWS FROM OPERATING ACTIVITIES; ACCRUAL-BASIS INCOME**   The following appeared in the statement of cash flows for James Company for the year ended January 31, 1998:

Cash collections from customers	$130,000
Cash paid to suppliers for merchandise	(26,000)
Cash paid to employees for salaries	(40,000)
Cash interest paid	(10,000)
Cash paid for income taxes	(15,000)
Net cash flows from operating activities	$ 39,000

Other pertinent information is as follows:

	FEBRUARY 1, 1997	JANUARY 31, 1998
Accounts receivable	$22,000	$33,000
Allowance for doubtful accounts	5,000	8,000
Inventories	16,000	10,000
Salaries payable...................................	8,000	–0–
Income taxes payable	2,000	9,000

REQUIRED Assuming that uncollectible accounts of $3,000 were written off against the allowance account and that depreciation expense for the year was $4,000, prepare James Company's income statement for the year ended January 31, 1998.

E 21-3. **CASH FLOWS; FINANCIAL STATEMENT RELATIONSHIPS** Refer to Exercise 21-2. Use the balance sheet accounts to calculate James' net income for the year ended January 31, 1998. Assume that the beginning balances for cash and plant and equipment were $0 and $4,000, respectively.

E 21-4. **CALCULATING CASH FLOWS FROM OPERATING ACTIVITIES** An income statement for Stein Corporation is as follows:

Revenues from sales of product		$300,000
Cost of goods sold:		
Beginning inventory.......................................	$ 40,000	
Purchases...	190,000	
Ending inventory	(140,000)	(90,000)
Depreciation expense		(40,000)
Uncollectible accounts expense		(5,000)
Salary expense		(35,000)
Insurance expense		(5,000)
Income tax expense		(20,000)
Income before extraordinary item and cumulative effect		$105,000
Extraordinary gain on retirement of bonds		
(net of taxes of $10,000)		40,000
Cumulative effect of change from straight-line depreciation		
to accelerated depreciation (net of taxes of $8,000)		(20,000)
Net income		$125,000

Additional information related to Stein Corporation's operations:
a) Decrease in accounts receivable (net of allowance for doubtful accounts), $30,000.
b) The change in accounting principle was made for financial reporting purposes but not for tax purposes.
c) The prepaid insurance account increased by $4,000 during the year.
d) Included in salary expenses are salaries of $8,000 accrued at the end of the year; there were no unpaid salaries at the beginning of the year.
e) At the date of retirement, the bonds payable had a book value of $200,000.

REQUIRED Prepare a schedule showing the net cash flows generated by the operating activities of Stein Corporation. Use the direct approach.

E 21-5. **CASH COLLECTIONS FROM CUSTOMERS** Branson Company reported revenues of $27,000 for the fiscal year just ended. Changes (Dr or Cr) in selected current accounts for the year were as follows:

Accounts receivable	$5,000 Dr
Allowance for doubtful accounts	400 Cr

Customers' accounts totaling $600 were written off as uncollectible.

REQUIRED Calculate the amount of cash collected from customers.

E 21-6. **RELATIONSHIP BETWEEN BALANCE SHEET AND STATEMENT OF CASH FLOWS** Selected financial statements for Quaker Company, a sole proprietorship, are as follows:

Balance Sheet
December 31, 1997

Assets:

Cash	$20,000
Equipment	24,000
Accumulated depreciation on equipment	(7,500)
Leased property	12,000
Total	$48,500

Liabilities and owner's equity:

Lease liability	$12,000
Quaker, capital	36,500
Total	$48,500

Statement of Cash Flows
For the Year Ended December 31, 1998

Cash flows from operating activities:		
Collections from customers	$25,000	
Payments for salaries	(5,500)	
Payments for other expenses	(4,500)	
Net cash provided by operating activities		$15,000
Cash flows from investing activities:		
Sale of equipment	$ 3,500	
Purchase of land	(9,000)	
Purchase of investments	(15,000)	
Net cash used by investing activities		(20,500)
Cash flows from financing activities:		
Payment on lease liability	$ (2,000)	
Issue of long-term notes	10,000	
Owner withdrawals	(8,000)	
Net cash from financing activities		–0–
Net decrease in cash		$ (5,500)

Additional information:

a) Net income for 1998, $9,500.

b) Depreciation expense for 1998: on equipment, $5,500; on leased property, $2,000.

c) A $2,500 lease payment was made in 1998, reducing the lease liability by $2,000.

d) 1998 gain on sale of equipment, $2,000; accumulated depreciation on equipment sold, $3,000.

REQUIRED Based on the above data, prepare the December 31, 1998, balance sheet for Quaker Company.

E 21-7. **TRANSACTION ANALYSIS FOR THE STATEMENT OF CASH FLOWS** The following information relates to 1998 financial data for Isley Corporation:

a) During 1998, Isley sold its only holding in the common stock of Lisa, Inc. The stock, which had a cost of $150,000 and a carrying amount of $320,000, was sold for $360,000. Taxes of $50,000 were paid on the realized gain.

b) In early 1998, bonds with a par (face) value of $100,000 were issued for $90,000. The discount amortization for 1998 was $1,000.

c) Near the end of 1998, Isley issued common stock with a par value of $50,000 for land with a fair value of $200,000.

d) On December 30, 1998, Isley declared a cash dividend of $30,000. The dividend is payable on January 21, 1999.

e) Inventory purchases on account during 1998 totaled $200,000. Accounts payable decreased by $25,000.

f) For the past two years, Isley has been engaged in self-construction of an energy-saving device designed to recirculate heat exhaust through its manufacturing facilities. Construction expenditures for 1998 were $45,000. Of this amount, $4,000 had not been paid by the end of 1998.

REQUIRED   Indicate how each transaction above would appear on Isley's statement of cash flows for the year ended December 31, 1998.

E 21-8.   **INCOME FLOWS VS. CASH FLOWS**   At the beginning of the year, the balance sheet for Dave's Body Shop was as follows:

ASSETS		LIABILITIES AND EQUITY	
Cash........................	$30,000	Accounts payable..............	$10,000
Accounts receivable...........	10,000	Unearned revenue	4,000
Supplies.....................	5,000	Notes payable to bank..........	25,000
Equipment	50,000	Dave Smith, capital	46,000
Accumulated depreciation—equipment	(10,000)		
Total.....................	$85,000	Total	$85,000

Below are several transactions and other events that occurred during the year:
a) Supplies purchased on account, $2,000.
b) Cash sales during the year, $22,000.
c) Sales on account during the year, $48,000.
d) Made interest payment on note payable to bank, $1,000.
e) Made principal payment on note payable to bank, $10,000.
f) Depreciation expense for the year, $5,000.
g) Collections on accounts receivable, $55,000.
h) Beginning-of-year unearned revenue earned during the year, $4,000.
i) Supplies used during the year, $4,000.
j) Payments made on accounts payable during the year $9,900.
k) Paid salaries of employees, $8,000.
l) Cash received in advance for body work to be performed next year, $3,000.
m) Cash withdrawals by Dave for personal use during the year, $1,000.
n) Salaries expense accrued but not paid at the end of the year, $800.
o) Dave invested $6,000 of additional equipment at the end of the year.

REQUIRED   Prepare a table to show the income effect and the cash effect of transactions *a* through *o*. Indicate the effects as + for increase, – for decrease, and *NE* for no effect. Also indicate whether each transaction is an operating activity, an investing activity, or a financing activity. Use the following format (an example transaction is provided):

	INCOME EFFECT	CASH EFFECT	ACTIVITY
Purchased supplies with cash, $600	*NE*	—	Operating

E 21-9.   **INCOME FLOWS VS. CASH FLOWS**   A model for reconciling income flows and cash flows appears in Exhibit 21–9 on page 1127. In this exhibit are 10 general classes of transactions that may be used to reconcile income flows and cash flows.

REQUIRED   Refer to transactions *a* through *o* in Exercise 21-8. Indicate where each one belongs in Exhibit 21–9. For example, the purchase of supplies example in Exercise 21-8 would be classified under item 10 in Exhibit 21–9. If the transaction would not appear, indicate why.

PART B • Additional Disclosure Topics

E 21-10.   **REPORTING IN INTERIM FINANCIAL STATEMENTS**   The following information is available for Rossel Corporation for 1998:
a) On January 1, 1998, Rossel paid property taxes amounting to $40,000 on its plant for the calendar year 1998. In late March 1998, Rossel made annual major repairs to its machinery amounting to $99,000. These repairs will benefit the remainder of the calendar year's operations.

b) An inventory loss of $380,000 from market decline occurred in April 1998. Rossel recorded this loss in April 1998 after its March 31 quarterly report was issued. None of this loss had been recovered by the end of 1998.

REQUIRED   State the dollar amounts that should appear in Rossel Corporation's March 31, June 30, September 30, and December 31, 1998, quarterly financial statements to report:
1. Property taxes.
2. Major repairs to machinery.
3. Inventory loss from market decline.

(AICPA, adapted)

E 21-11. **DETERMINING INTERIM TAX PROVISION** Davidson Publications, Inc., has the following income before income tax provision and estimated effective annual income tax rates for the first three quarters of 1998:

QUARTER	INCOME BEFORE INCOME TAX PROVISION	ESTIMATED EFFECTIVE ANNUAL TAX RATE AT END OF QUARTER
1st	$60,000	30%
2nd	70,000	34
3rd	40,000	36

REQUIRED   What should be Davidson Publications' income tax provision in the third-quarter interim income statement?

(AICPA, adapted)

E 21-12. **PREPARING SEGMENT INFORMATION** The 1998 income statement for Dawson, Inc., which has two operating segments—Industrial Parts and Small Engines—is as follows:

Sales revenue (Note A)		$475,000
Less operating expenses:		
Cost of goods sold (Note A)	$250,000	
Selling and administrative (Note B)	110,000	
Research and development	50,000	
Depreciation	55,000	(465,000)
Operating profit before taxes		$ 10,000
Other revenues and expenses:		
Interest revenue	$ 17,500	
Interest expense	(4,000)	13,500
Income before taxes		$ 23,500
Income taxes (40 percent tax rate)		(9,400)
Net income		$ 14,100

Note A: The Industrial Parts segment had sales revenue of $5,000 and cost of goods sold of $3,000 related to intersegment sales. These amounts are not included in the consolidated sales revenue ($475,000) and cost of goods sold ($250,000).

Note B: Selling and administrative expense includes $25,000 of general corporate expenses.

All consolidated revenues and expenses other than those mentioned in Notes A and B are directly allocable to the operating segments as follows:

	INDUSTRIAL PARTS	SMALL ENGINES
Sales revenues	60%	40%
Segment profit	65%	35%
Interest revenue	55%	45%
Interest expense	70%	30%
Depreciation	50%	50%

REQUIRED
1. Prepare a schedule to report information about segment profit and related matters for each operating segment.
2. Prepare schedules to (*a*) reconcile total segment revenues to total consolidated revenues and (*b*) reconcile total segment profit or loss before taxes to consolidated net income before taxes.

PROBLEMS

PART A • Revisiting the Statement of Cash Flows

P 21-1.   **CASH FLOWS; FINANCIAL STATEMENT RELATIONSHIPS**   Lilley Corporation's beginning balance sheet and its statement of cash flows appear below:

Lilley Corporation
Balance Sheet
December 31, 1997

Assets:

Cash	$ 21,300
Trading securities	17,000
Accounts receivable	49,500
Inventories	78,000
Land	25,000
Plant and equipment	72,000
Accumulated depreciation	(17,000)
Investment in Geo	18,000
Total assets	**$263,800**

Liabilities and equity:

Accounts payable and accrued expenses	$ 82,300
Bonds payable (maturity value, $50,000)	51,800
Common stock ($20 par)	60,000
Contributed capital in excess of par	24,400
Retained earnings	45,300
Total liabilities and equity	**$263,800**

Lilley Corporation
Statement of Cash Flows
For the Year Ended December 31, 1998

Cash flows from operating activities:		
Net cash provided by operating activities (see Schedule 1)		$10,700
Cash flows from investing activities:		
Sale of equipment	$ 3,300	
Purchases of equipment	(39,200)	
Net cash used by investing activities		(35,900)
Cash flows from financing activities:		
Issuance of long-term notes	$45,000	
Dividends	(4,000)	
Net cash provided by financing activities		41,000
Net increase in cash and cash equivalents		$15,800
Noncash investing and financing activities:		
Acquired land by issuing common stock		$12,000

Lilley Corporation
Schedule 1
Reconciliation of Income Flows and Cash Flows

	INCOME FLOWS	CASH FLOWS
Revenues from sales, interest, and dividends	$100,000	$91,000
Gain on sale of equipment	500	–0–
Cost of goods sold (increase in inventories, $11,500)	(40,000)	(57,800)
Depreciation expense	(14,900)	–0–
Interest expense	(8,350)	(8,550)
Miscellaneous expenses	(1,950)	(1,950)
Income tax expense	(10,000)	(12,000)
Net income	$ 25,300	
Net cash provided by operating activities		$10,700

Additional information:

a) During 1998, Lilley sold all of its trading securities for $19,000 cash, which included accrued interest revenue of $2,000.

b) In April 1998, Lilley issued 200 shares of its common stock for land with a fair value of $12,000.

c) On May 31, 1998, Lilley borrowed $45,000 cash. The note is payable in three equal annual installments of $15,000 and bears interest at 12 percent, payable monthly. The first installment payment is due on May 31, 1999.

d) During 1998, Lilley purchased equipment for $39,200 cash. The company also sold equipment with an original cost of $5,200 and accumulated depreciation of $2,400 for $3,300 cash.

e) In September 1998, Lilley paid a $2,000 additional income tax assessment because of an error on its 1993 tax return. The payment was recorded correctly as an error correction (prior period adjustment).

f) The only entries in retained earnings were for net income, dividends declared and paid, and the error correction.

REQUIRED On the basis of the information provided above, prepare the balance sheet for Lilley Corporation on December 31, 1998.

P 21-2. STATEMENT OF CASH FLOWS Presented below are comparative statements of financial position of Horizon Corporation as of December 31, 1998, and December 31, 1997.

Statements of Financial Position

	12/31/98	12/31/97	INCREASE (DECREASE)
Assets:			
Cash	$ 175,000	$ 123,000	$ 52,000
Accounts receivable (net of allowance for uncollectible accounts)	210,000	140,000	70,000
Inventories	260,000	220,000	40,000
Land	325,000	200,000	125,000
Plant and equipment	580,000	633,000	(53,000)
Less: Accumulated depreciation	(90,000)	(100,000)	10,000
Total assets	$1,460,000	$1,216,000	$244,000
Liabilities and stockholders' equity:			
Liabilities:			
Accounts payable	$ 330,000	$ 250,000	$ 80,000
Accrued wages	270,000	260,000	10,000
Long-term bonds (due 12/15/04)	130,000	180,000	(50,000)
Total liabilities	$ 730,000	$ 690,000	$ 40,000
Stockholders' equity:			
Common stock, par value $5, authorized, 100,000 shares; issued and outstanding, 50,000 and 42,000 shares, respectively	$ 250,000	$ 210,000	$ 40,000
Additional paid-in capital	233,000	170,000	63,000
Retained earnings	247,000	146,000	101,000
Total stockholders' equity	$ 730,000	$ 526,000	$204,000
Total liabilities and stockholders' equity	$1,460,000	$1,216,000	$244,000

The income statement of Horizon Corporation for the year ended December 31, 1998, is as follows:

Income Statement
For the Year Ended December 31, 1998

Sales	$ 800,000
Expenses:	
Cost of sales	$ 360,000
Salaries and wages	193,000
Depreciation	20,000
Loss on sale of equipment	4,000
Interest	16,000
Miscellaneous (includes uncollectible accounts expense of $5,000)	8,000
Total expenses	$(601,000)
Income before income taxes and extraordinary item	$ 199,000
Income tax expense	(90,000)
Income before extraordinary item	$109,000
Extraordinary item—gain on extinguishment of debt (net of $10,000 income tax)	12,000
Net income	$ 121,000

Additional information:

a) On February 2, 1998, Horizon issued 4,200 shares of common stock to stockholders of record for cash. The issue price per share was $15.

b) On March 1, 1998, Horizon issued 3,800 shares of common stock for land. The common stock and land had current market values of approximately $40,000 on March 1, 1998.

c) On April 15, 1998, Horizon extinguished long-term bonds with a face value of $50,000. The gain was reported as an extraordinary item on the income statement.

d) On June 30, 1998, Horizon sold equipment costing $53,000, with a book value of $23,000, for $19,000 cash.

e) On September 30, 1998, Horizon declared and paid a $.40 per share cash dividend to stockholders.

f) On October 10, 1998, Horizon purchased land for $85,000 cash.

REQUIRED

1. Prepare a schedule that reconciles each of Horizon Corporation's income statement items for 1998 with Horizon's major operating cash receipts and payments for 1998.

2. Prepare Horizon's statement of cash flows for the year ended December 31, 1998, under the direct approach. A schedule reconciling net income to net cash provided by operating activities also should be prepared.

P 21-3. **STATEMENT OF CASH FLOWS** Harley Manufacturing Company is in the process of preparing its statement of cash flows for the year ending December 31, 1998. The beginning and ending balances of Harley's ledger accounts and other information appear below:

	12/31/98 (ENDING)	12/31/97 (BEGINNING)	INCREASE (DECREASE)
Debits:			
Buildings	$ 810,000	$ 560,000	$250,000
Land	140,000	150,000	(10,000)
Equipment	330,000	200,000	130,000
Bond investment (long-term)	18,000	15,000	3,000
Inventories	210,000	218,000	(8,000)
Accounts receivable	180,000	92,000	88,000
Notes receivable—trade	21,000	27,000	(6,000)
Cash and cash equivalents	290,700	279,000	11,700
Prepaid insurance—equipment	1,200	1,400	(200)
	$2,000,900	$1,542,400	$458,500
Credits:			
Capital stock	$ 700,000	$ 400,000	$300,000
Bonds payable (1998 par, $150,000)	147,900	97,500	50,400
Accounts payable	58,000	52,000	6,000
Notes payable—trade	14,500	16,800	(2,300)
Interest payable	10,000	6,000	4,000
Income taxes payable	5,000	3,000	2,000
Allowance for doubtful accounts	4,500	2,300	2,200
Accumulated depreciation	271,200	181,000	90,200
Retained earnings	789,800	783,800	6,000
	$2,000,900	$1,542,400	$458,500

The following transactions were among those taking place during 1998:

a) A $20,000 cash dividend was declared and paid during the year.

b) Common stock was issued during the year for $300,000.

c) Equipment that cost $4,500 was sold for $1,200. Accumulated depreciation on the equipment was $3,300.

d) Land costing $10,000 was sold at book value to the Rotary Club.

e) Bonds were issued at par.

f) The discount amortization for the year on bonds payable was $400.

g) The income statement for the year ended December 31, 1998, was as follows:

Sales (net)		$1,250,000
Operating expenses:		
Material and supplies	$250,000	
Direct labor	440,000	
Manufacturing overhead	181,500	
Depreciation	93,500	
Selling expenses	245,000	
Interest expense	7,500	
Income tax expense	6,500	
Total operating expenses		(1,224,000)
Net income		$ 26,000

REQUIRED Use the direct approach to prepare a statement of cash flows for Harley for 1998. A reconciliation of net income to net cash provided by operating activities should be provided.

P 21-4. **INCOME FLOWS AND CASH FLOWS** In the process of reviewing the drafts of financial statements for the year ending December 31, 1998, the officers of Rather Brothers are puzzled and confused. Net income of $583,000 is reported on the income statement; however, the statement of cash flows reports only $50,000 for net cash flows from operating activities. The president, Don Rather, cannot understand how or why these two numbers can be so far apart. He asks Sharon Rather, the company's controller, to assemble the information necessary to reconcile these two numbers. Sharon brings you a copy of the income statement, a schedule showing the changes in Rather Brothers' current asset and current liability accounts, and additional facts about Rather Brothers' operating activities for the year ending December 31, 1998. This information appears below:

Income Statement for the Year Ended December 31, 1998

Sales		$8,520,000
Operating expenses:		
Cost of goods sold	$4,575,000	
Salaries and wages	1,459,000	
Selling and administrative	467,700	
Interest	110,500	
Depreciation	189,300	
Utilities and insurance	655,500	
Income taxes	390,000	(7,847,000)
Income from continuing operations		$ 673,000
Discontinued operations:		
Loss on sale of subsidiary (net of $60,000 tax benefit)		(90,000)
Net income		$ 583,000

Schedule of Changes in Current Asset and Current Liability Accounts
(*in thousands of dollars*)

ACCOUNT	INCREASE (DECREASE)
Cash	$100.5
Accounts receivable, net of allowance	348.0
Inventory	300.5
Prepaid expenses	(25.0)
Accounts payable (trade)	(270.8)
Accrued wages	7.5
Accrued liabilities	(39.7)
Cash dividends payable	25.0
Income taxes payable	54.2

Additional information:

a) Rather Brothers sold a subsidiary during the year for $590,000. The carrying value of the investment was $740,000. The loss on the sale of the subsidiary ($90,000 net of taxes) was reflected as discontinued operations on the income statement.

b) During the year, write-offs of uncollectible accounts were $95,000; uncollectible accounts expense for the year was $100,000.

REQUIRED

I. Using Rather Brothers' income statement and the additional facts, verify the company's cash flows from operating activities for the year ended May 31, 1998.

2. Explain how the cash flow data reveal important factors regarding Rather Brothers' operations for the current fiscal year.

P 21-5. **PREPARATION OF A WORKSHEET FOR THE STATEMENT OF CASH FLOWS** Comparative balance sheets and an income statement for Thelan Corporation are as follows:

	12/31/97	12/31/98
Assets:		
Cash	$ 9,000	$ 7,000
Accounts receivable	3,000	5,000
Inventories	12,000	12,000
Prepaid expenses	500	200
Plant and equipment, net of accumulated depreciation	38,000	33,000
Long-term investments	12,000	15,000
Total assets	$74,500	$72,200
Liabilities and stockholders' equity:		
Accounts payable	$ 3,000	$10,100
Interest payable	400	500
Notes payable	29,000	20,000
Common stock	30,000	25,000
Contributed capital in excess of par	3,000	2,500
Retained earnings	9,100	14,100
Total liabilities and stockholders' equity	$74,500	$72,200

Income Statement for the Year Ended December 31, 1998

Revenues	$30,200
Investment revenue	1,200
Cost of goods sold	(14,000)
Depreciation expense	(5,000)
Interest expense	(1,800)
Other expenses	(600)
Net income	$10,000

Additional data:
a) Dividends declared and paid, $4,500.
b) Investments purchased during the year, $3,000.
c) During the year common stock was retired; the excess of the amount paid over the original issue price was $500 and was debited to retained earnings.

REQUIRED Prepare a worksheet for the statement of cash flows.

P 21-6. **PREPARATION OF A WORKSHEET FOR THE STATEMENT OF CASH FLOWS** The records of Hillard Company showed the following data:

	BALANCE SHEET		CHANGE
	12/31/97	12/31/98	DR (CR)
Cash..	$173,300	$185,200	$ 11,900
Plant and equipment..........................	96,000	100,500	4,500
Accumulated depreciation....................	(30,000)	(34,000)	(4,000)
Investments................................	35,000	32,000	(3,000)
Total..................................	$274,300	$283,700	$ 9,400
Accounts payable...........................	$ 43,300	$ 58,800	$(15,500)
Bonds payable (8%).........................	48,750	–0–	48,750
Common stock..............................	155,000	165,000	(10,000)
Contributed capital in excess of par...........	–0–	40,000	(40,000)
Retained earnings...........................	27,250	19,900	7,350
Total..................................	$274,300	$283,700	$ (9,400)

Additional data for 1998:

a) Dividends declared and paid, $18,500.

b) Fully depreciated equipment (original cost, $10,500) was sold for $1,500. The remaining changes in the plant and equipment and accumulated depreciation accounts represent equipment purchases and depreciation expense.

c) Investments purchased with cash totaled $17,000. Other investments, with a cost and carrying amount of $20,000, were sold at a realized loss of $6,000.

d) On December 31, 1998, the bonds outstanding matured and were retired at book value.

e) The equipment purchased was acquired by issuing common stock (par value of shares issued, $2,000). The remaining common stock was issued for cash.

f) Hillard's condensed income statement for the year ended December 31, 1998, was as follows:

Revenues...	$75,400	
Gain on sale of equipment................................	1,500	$76,900
Depreciation expense....................................	$14,500	
Interest expense.......................................	3,900	
Other expenses..	41,350	
Loss on sale of investments..............................	6,000	(65,750)
Net income..		$11,150

REQUIRED Prepare a worksheet for the statement of cash flows for Hillard Company.

P 21-7. **STATEMENT OF CASH FLOWS** Klawson Corporation is preparing to go public, and you are assisting the firm with its statement of cash flows for the year ending December 31, 1998. You have been provided the following income statement for the year ending December 31, 1998, and comparative balance sheets at December 31, 1997 and 1998.

Klawson Corporation
Income Satement
For the Year Ended December 31, 1998

Sales	$ 2,650,000
Cost of goods sold	(1,800,000)
Gross margin on sales	$ 850,000
Selling, general, and administrative expenses	(281,500)
Operating income	$ 568,500
Other:	
Interest expense	(56,000)
Equity in earnings of investee	37,500
Gain on sale of equipment	192,500
Income from continuing operations	$ 742,500
Discontinued operations:	
Loss on disposal of segment, net of applicable	
deferred tax liability of $36,000	(39,000)
Income before taxes	$ 703,500
Income tax expense:	
Current	$344,400
Deferred	12,000 (356,400)
Net income	$ 347,100

Klawson Corporation
Balance Sheets

	12/31/98	12/31/97
Assets:		
Cash	$ 155,250	$ 40,500
Accounts receivable, net of allowance	310,500	307,000
Inventories	686,500	666,500
Prepaid expenses	80,000	87,500
Investment in and advances to Flywheel Corporation	470,000	312,500
Land	27,100	77,100
Buildings	379,000	429,000
Machinery and equipment	792,000	687,000
Accumulated depreciation	(248,500)	(413,000)
Total assets	$2,651,850	$2,194,100
Liabilities and stockholders' equity:		
Accounts payable	$ 350,900	$ 374,000
Accrued liabilities	93,750	135,500
Current portion of long-term debt	35,000	25,000
Income taxes payable	5,000	13,000
Serial bonds payable	450,000	475,000
Secured notes payable	190,000	–0–
Deferred tax liability	59,500	83,500
Preferred stock	250,000	–0–
Common stock	810,500	810,500
Retained earnings	474,700	277,600
Treasury stock (common, at cost)	(67,500)	–0–
Total liabilities and stockholders' equity	$2,651,850	$2,194,100

The following information has been provided to you at your request:

a) At the beginning of March 1998, Klawson acquired machinery and equipment at a cost of $500,000. Klawson paid $50,000 cash, issued 2,500 shares of preferred stock with a fair value of $250,000, and issued a $200,000, 8 percent note. The note is secured by the machinery and equipment and is payable in 20 equal annual installments plus interest in March of each year until fully paid.

b) During 1998, machinery and equipment with a cost of $360,000 and accumulated depreciation of $260,000 was sold for cash.

c) Uncollectible accounts expense for the year was $6,000 and is included in selling, general, and administrative expenses.

d) Depreciation expense for the year was $100,500.

e) During 1998, Klawson advanced $120,000 to Flywheel Corporation as a loan. Klawson owns a 40 percent equity interest in Flywheel.

f) In early 1998, Klawson disposed of a business segment. The carrying values of the segment assets sold were as follows:

Inventories	$ 20,000
Land	50,000
Buildings	50,000
Machinery and equipment	35,000
Accumulated depreciation	(5,000)
	$150,000

g) The only entries in retained earnings during 1998 were for net income and cash dividends.

REQUIRED Use the direct approach to prepare Klawson Corporation's statement of cash flows for the year ending December 31, 1998. A reconciliation of net income to net cash provided by operating activities should be provided.

P 21-8. **STATEMENT OF CASH FLOWS** Presented below and on the next page are Smith Corporation's condensed income statement for the year ending December 31, 1998 and comparative balance sheets as of December 31, 1998 and 1997.

Smith Corporation
Income Statement
For the Year Ended December 31, 1998

Revenues:	
Sales	$ 2,038,000
Dividend revenues	6,000
Gain on sale of equipment	7,000
Realized gain on sale of trading securities	20,000
Total revenues	$ 2,071,000
Expenses:	
Cost of goods sold	$(1,385,000)
Depreciation expense	(149,000)
Interest expense	(65,000)
Uncollectible accounts expense	(10,000)
Other	(100,000)
Income tax expense	(107,000)
Total expenses	$(1,816,000)
Net income	$ 255,000

Smith Corporation
Balance Sheets

	12/31/98	12/31/97	INCREASE (DECREASE)
Assets:			
Cash	$ 518,000	$ 308,000	$210,000
Accounts receivable, net	585,000	495,000	90,000
Trading securities, at fair value	–0–	75,000	(75,000)
Inventories	895,000	780,000	115,000
Investment in Mack (at fair value)	200,000	180,000	20,000
Land	350,000	250,000	100,000
Leased property	158,000	–0–	158,000
Plant and equipment	1,052,000	720,000	332,000
Accumulated depreciation	(284,000)	(170,000)	(114,000)
Total assets	$3,474,000	$2,638,000	$836,000
Liabilities and stockholders' equity:			
Current portion of notes payable	$ 150,000	$ –0–	$150,000
Accounts payable	700,000	800,000	(100,000)
Accrued liabilities	60,000	23,000	37,000
Lease liability	133,000	–0–	133,000
Notes payable, long-term	300,000	–0–	300,000
Bonds payable (par value $500,000)	514,000	518,000	(4,000)
Deferred tax liability	30,000	35,000	(5,000)
Common stock, $20 par value	640,000	600,000	40,000
Contributed capital in excess of par	304,000	244,000	60,000
Retained earnings	613,000	408,000	205,000
Unrealized holding gain/(loss)	30,000	10,000	20,000
Total liabilities and stockholders' equity	$3,474,000	$2,638,000	$836,000

Additional information:

a) Smith declared and paid a cash dividend on common stock.

b) Smith issued 2,000 shares of common stock for land with a fair value of $100,000.

c) Smith borrowed $450,000 from a savings and loan. Interest is payable monthly, and the principal is payable in three annual installments of $150,000. The first installment is due in February 1999.

d) Smith sold for cash equipment costing $60,000 with a book value of $25,000. Smith also purchased equipment during the year.

e) Smith paid, and recorded as a prior period adjustment, a $20,000 penalty to the IRS in connection with an error in a previous year's tax return.

f) On December 31, 1998, Smith entered into a capital lease for equipment. The present value of the minimum lease payments was $158,000. The annual lease payments are $25,000 and are due on December 31 each year, beginning December 31, 1998. The $25,000 lease payment due on December 31, 1999, will consist of $9,000 principal and $16,000 interest.

g) Smith owns 10 percent of the common stock of Mack Corporation and reports the investment at fair value. Smith classifies the investment as an available-for-sale security.

REQUIRED Use the direct approach to prepare Smith Corporation's statement of cash flows for the year ended December 31, 1998. A reconciliation of net income to net cash provided by operating activities should be provided.

P 21-9. COMPREHENSIVE REVIEW OF FINANCIAL STATEMENT RELATIONSHIPS The following information applies to the Barron Company for the year ended December 31, 1998. The omitted balances, numbered from 1 through 13, can be calculated from the other information provided.

Statement of Cash Flows

Cash flows from operating activities		
(see reconciliation schedule below)		$ 2,615
Cash flows from investing activities:		
Sale of equipment	$12,000	
Purchase of land	(14,715)	
Net cash used by investing activities		(2,715)
Cash flows from financing activities:		
Issue of common stock	$11,400	
Retirement of debt at maturity	(7,200)	
Net cash provided by financing activities		4,200
Net increase in cash		$ 4,100
Cash at beginning of year		22,000
Cash at end of year		$26,100

Reconciliation of Income Flows and Cash Flows From Operating Activities

	INCOME STATEMENT	ADJUSTMENT	CASH FLOWS
Revenues	$15,380	$ –0–	$15,380
Gain on sale of equipment	2,000	(2,000)	–0–
Depreciation expense	(3,000)	3,000	–0–
Interest expense	(3,500)	(500)	(4,000)
Other expenses	(12,780)	3,200	(9,580)
Tax credit:			
Refund	$815		
Reduction of taxes payable	200 1,015	(200)	815
Net loss	$ (885)		
Net cash provided by operating activities			$ 2,615

Balance Sheets

	1/1/98	12/31/98
Assets:		
Cash	$22,000	$ (5)
Building and equipment	92,000	(6)
Accumulated depreciation	(25,000)	(7)
Land	(1)	(8)
Total assets	$ (?)	$ (?)
Liabilities and stockholders' equity:		
Current liabilities (operating)	$ (2)	$ (9)
Bonds payable (8%; premium at 1/1/98, $2,600)	(3)	(10)
Income taxes payable	(4)	1,700
Common stock	73,000	(11)
Paid-in capital	13,000	(12)
Retained earnings (deficit)	(6,000)	(13)
Total liabilities and stockholders' equity	$ (?)	$ (?)

Additional information:

a) The book value of the equipment sold was two-thirds of the cost of that equipment.

b) Selected ratios of accounts in the January 1 and December 31 balance sheets are as follows:

	1/1/98	12/31/98
Current ratio	?	3:1
Total stockholders' equity divided by total liabilities	4:3	?

c) The common stock issued had a par value of $9,000.

REQUIRED Calculate the correct balance for each balance sheet account or group of accounts. (The totals are shown as question marks. Calculation of these amounts may be necessary to calculate the numbered balances.)

(AICPA, adapted)

PART B • Additional Disclosure Topics

P 21-10. **INTERIM REPORTING** Riley Manufacturing Company budgeted activities for 1998 as follows:

Net sales (1,000,000 units)	$6,000,000
Cost of goods sold	(3,600,000)
Gross margin	$2,400,000
Selling, general, and administrative expenses	(1,400,000)
Operating income	$1,000,000
Nonoperating revenues and expenses	–0–
Income before income taxes	$1,000,000
Estimated income taxes (current and deferred)	(550,000)
Net income	$ 450,000
Earnings per share of common stock	$4.50

Riley has operated profitably for many years and has experienced a seasonal pattern of sales volume and production similar to the following patterns forecast for 1998.

Sales volume is expected to follow a pattern of 10, 20, 35, and 35 percent for the four quarters, because of the seasonality of the industry. Also, because of production and storage capacity limitations, it is expected that production will follow a pattern of 20, 25, 30, and 25 percent per quarter.

At the conclusion of the first quarter of 1998, Riley's controller has prepared and issued the following interim report for public release:

Net sales (100,000 units)	$ 600,000
Cost of goods sold	(360,000)
Gross margin	$ 240,000
Selling, general, and administrative expenses	(275,000)
Operating loss	$ (35,000)
Loss from warehouse fire	(175,000)
Loss before income taxes	$(210,000)
Estimated income taxes	–0–
Net loss	$(210,000)
Loss per share of common stock	$(2.10)

The following additional information is available for the just-completed first quarter but was not included in the public information released:

a) The company uses a standard cost system in which standards are set at currently attainable levels on an annual basis. At the end of the first quarter, underapplied fixed factory overhead (volume variance) of $50,000 was treated as an asset. Production during the quarter was 200,000 units, of which 100,000 were sold.

b) The selling, general, and administrative expenses were budgeted on a basis of $900,000 fixed expenses for the year plus $.50 variable expenses per unit of sales.

c) The warehouse fire loss met the conditions of an extraordinary loss. The warehouse had an undepreciated cost of $320,000; $145,000 was recovered from insurance on the warehouse. No other gains or losses are anticipated this year from similar events or transactions, nor has Riley had any similar losses in preceding years. Thus, the full loss will be deductible as an ordinary loss for income tax purposes.

d) The effective income tax rate, for federal and state taxes combined, is expected to average 40 percent of income before income taxes during 1998.

e) Earnings per share were calculated on the basis of 100,000 shares of capital stock outstanding. Riley has only one class of stock issued, no long-term debt outstanding, and no stock option plan.

REQUIRED

1. Without reference to the specific situation described above, what are the standards of disclosure for interim financial data (published interim financial reports) for publicly traded companies? Explain.

2. Identify the weaknesses in form and content of Riley's interim report without reference to the additional information.

3. Indicate the preferable treatment for each of the five items of additional information for interim reporting purposes and explain why that treatment is preferable.

(AICPA, adapted)

P 21-11.   **INTERIM REPORTING**   Eller Company issues quarterly reports to its shareholders. The income statement for the first quarter of 1998 is shown below.

Eller Company
Income Statement
For the Quarter Ended March 31, 1998
(*in thousands*)

Sales..		$475,000
Cost of goods sold		(325,000)
Gross profit..		$150,000
Operating expenses:		
Depreciation expense	$25,000	
Salary expense	47,000	
General and administrative expenses	30,000	(102,000)
Operating profit		$ 48,000
Other revenues and expenses:		
Unrealized holding loss on trading securities	$ (5,000)	
Interest revenue	8,500	
Interest expense..	(11,500)	(8,000)
Income from continuing operations before taxes................		$ 40,000
Provision for income taxes		(20,000)
Net income...		$ 20,000
Earnings per common share (100,000 shares)...................		$ .20

Additional information:

a) Cost of goods sold is estimated for the quarterly reports. Eller estimates that the average gross profit for the first six months of 1998 is 35 percent. Sales for the second quarter are $400,000.

b) An error occurred in recording depreciation expense for the first quarter of 1998. Depreciation expense was underrecorded by $2,000 in the first quarter and was recorded during the second quarter. Depreciation expense for the first six months of 1998 per the trial balance is $55,000.

c) No interest expense has been recorded during the second quarter of 1998. The next semiannual interest payment of $23,000 is due September 30.

d) The market value of Eller's trading securities recovered during the second quarter. At the end of the first quarter, the market value was $45,000. At the end of the second quarter, the market value was $52,000. The securities were purchased for $50,000 on December 31, 1997.

e) Eller holds a note receivable from a longtime customer who is having financial difficulties. The note was recorded at $10,000. The customer paid $4,000 during the second quarter and has promised to pay an additional $4,000 in the third quarter. It is probable that the remaining $2,000 will not be collected.

f) Eller's June 30, 1998, trial balance included the following additional items: salaries expense, $90,000; general and administrative expense, $44,000; interest revenue, $15,000.

g) Eller hired a new tax consultant, who has estimated that the company's effective rate for 1998 is 20 percent.

REQUIRED   Draft Eller Company's income statement for the quarter ended June 30, 1998.

Concepts of Present and Future Value

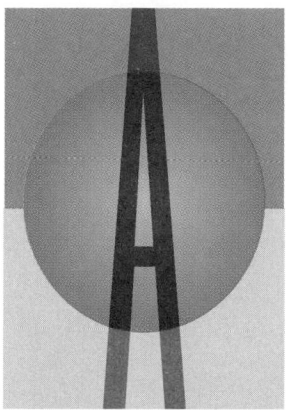

APPENDIX

A

LEARNING OBJECTIVES

After studying this Appendix, you should be able to:

1. Explain the concept of interest.

2. Explain the variables that affect the dollar amount of interest.

3. Differentiate between simple interest and compound interest.

4. Explain the concept and calculate the future value of a single amount.

5. Explain the concept and calculate the present value of a single amount.

6. Define an annuity and distinguish between an ordinary annuity and an annuity due.

7. Explain the concept and calculate the future value of an ordinary annuity.

8. Explain the concept and calculate the present value of an ordinary annuity.

9. Explain the concept and calculate the future value of an annuity due.

10. Explain the concept and calculate the present value of an annuity due.

11. Explain the concept and calculate the future value of a deferred annuity.

12. Explain the concept and calculate the present value of a deferred annuity.

13. Apply the concepts of future value and present value to the measurement of and accounting for long-term debt, pension obligations, and lease obligations.

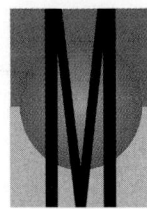

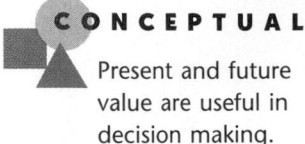

oney has a time value. **Time value** means that a dollar is worth more now than one year from now, because one dollar held today can be invested to earn interest or some other form of return—and thus will be worth more than one dollar one year from now.[1] In this appendix we will examine the concepts of **present value**—the present worth of an amount to be paid or received at some future date—and **future value**—the future worth of an amount invested today. You may be familiar with the concepts of present and future value, and you probably are aware of the impact of these concepts on accounting theory and practice, as well as on your personal financial activities. Accountants use the concepts of present and future value to measure and record economic events, to interpret accounting data, and to provide managers and external users of accounting information with relevant data for decision making.

Present value and future value concepts are used in business and accounting as well as in personal activities. For example, present values are used to value assets and liabilities in the financial statements. In Chapter 2, we pointed out that under the historical cost (exchange price) principle, transactions are recorded at exchange prices established at the exchange date. We also pointed out that historical cost is at least a *minimum* estimate of the present value of the future cash flows associated with an asset or liability at the date of exchange. Frequently, present value techniques are used to determine the historical exchange price at the transaction date. Subsequent to the transaction date, present value techniques are used to value and to account for monetary assets and liabilities, such as long-term notes and bonds, lease obligations, and pension obligations.

One of the most *significant* applications of present value in our society relates to the provision of information about companies' postretirement benefit obligations, such as an obligation under a pension plan. Many employees earn pension retirement benefits each year as they provide services to their employers. Because these benefits will not be paid until the employees retire (which may be several years in the distant future), present value concepts are used to measure the employer's obligation to its employees at the end of each year during the employees' service (working) period. A comparison of the present value of this obligation with the fair value of pension fund assets provides important information to users of financial statements. Many pension funds in the United States currently are "in the red"; that is, the present value of the employer's pension obligation exceeds the fair value of the pension fund assets. A recent search of the LEXIS/NEXIS computerized database found over 300 articles relating to the unfunded pension obligations of many companies and not-for-profit organizations, such as cities and other governmental units.

Present and future value concepts are also used in a wide variety of personal investing and financing decisions. For example, if you purchase a $30,000 automobile and make equal monthly payments of $600 over a 60-month period, what is the effective annual interest rate in your loan agreement? Or, if you purchase a $250,000 home and finance the purchase price over a 25-year period at an annual interest rate of 7 percent, what are your monthly mortgage payments? Or, say you can invest your savings at 8 percent. How much should you save each year to be able to retire at 55 and receive a $5,000 monthly retirement benefit?

Finally, present value concepts apply to lottery winnings and other prizes. For example, the following article appeared in a local newspaper column:

Dear Mister Economy:

    Like every red-blooded patriotic citizen, I buy my share of lottery tickets. Sooner or later I'm going to win. That's not really a problem. However, I understand that a lottery payoff is not quite what I, and most other people, think it is. How is that possible? What's going on?

—A Sure Winner

---

[1]"A bird in the hand is worth two in the bush," the old saying goes; but it may be worth three or more in inflationary periods. In periods of inflation, investors demand higher rates of return on their investments. We assume in this appendix either that inflation is minimal or that interest rates include an adjustment for its effects.

Dear Shirley:

The reason for this pseudo-scientific gambit is that big-money lotteries, whether government sanctioned or commercially sponsored, pay out prize money over several years. A $20 million dollar lottery windfall, for example, might pay $1 million a year for 20 years. Is the first million-dollar payment really the same as the twentieth? And if not, is the prize pot really $20 million? Mister Economy thinks not! Suppose, for example, that you have $370,000 tucked away in your sock drawer—a nice little stash for emergency spending. This little stash, however, would become a bigger stash in an interest-paying bank account. A modest 5 percent interest rate, compounded annually, creates a balance of $1 million after two decades. Working in reverse, a million-dollar lottery payment in 20 years has a present value of only $370,000. Adjusting all of the annual payments in a like manner means that the present value of your $20 million prize is in the $12.5 million range. A higher interest rate would reduce the present value of your jackpot even further.[2]

One final example shows how present value concepts apply in practice. Several years ago a fire killed 84 people at the MGM Grand Hotel (now Bally's) in Las Vegas. Shortly *after* the fire, MGM purchased a liability insurance policy, which the insurance company *backdated* to 20 days before the fire.[3] Evidently, the insurer had calculated that the premium charged MGM would allow a profit sufficient to cover the present value of liability judgments, which sometimes are litigated over a lengthy period.

The examples presented in the following pages cover only a few of the many applications of present and future value. Other applications that appear throughout the text employ the fundamentals presented in this appendix.

① NTEREST AND THE TIME VALUE OF MONEY

Interest is the *cost* of borrowing money or the *return* from lending money. If you lend someone $5 today and you receive $6 one year from today, the difference of $1 represents interest that you earned on the amount lent. From the borrower's standpoint, the $1 difference also represents interest paid on the amount borrowed. Interest rates usually are stated as, or understood to be, annual rates. If you borrow $100 from a bank at 6 percent per annum (year), you must pay the bank $100 plus $6 (.06 × $100), or $106 at the end of the year.

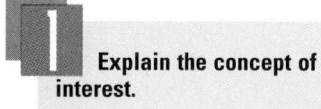

The interest rate applicable in an economic transaction is affected by the perceived risk or probability of nonpayment in the transaction. To illustrate, a bank may lend money to Customer *A*, a low-risk customer, at a 5 percent rate of interest while charging Customer *B*, a high-risk customer, 8 percent interest. Investors attempt to balance risk and return in their investment decisions and will undertake more risky investments only if the prospective rates of return are higher. For example, a money-market certificate of deposit that pays 5 percent interest is less risky than an investment in an oil-drilling venture that may pay a 100 percent rate of return *if* the well is successful.

CONCEPTUAL

More risky investments require higher expected rates of return.

In theory, as well as in practice, an interest rate has three components:

I. A *risk-free* component based on an economic concept called the *marginal productivity of capital.* Many economists believe that this rate is about 3 or 4 percent in a risk-free and inflation-free environment.

---

[2]Orley Amos, "Ask Mr. Economy," *Stillwater News Press/News Plus,* February 28, 1996, p. 4. Mr. Economy can be found napping on the World Wide Web at: http://amos.bus.okstate.edu/ame/
[3]M. Smith and R. Witt, "Retroactive Liability Insurance—The Economics of Insuring a Known Loss," *CPCU Journal,* September 1983, pp. 147–153.

2. A *risk* component to compensate for uncertainty. The higher the perceived risk, the higher the rate of interest.

3. An *inflation* component applicable in periods of inflation. In periods of inflation, lenders demand higher rates of return to compensate for the expected decline in purchasing power between the time money is loaned and the time it is repaid.

The *dollar* amount of interest in a given situation is a function of three variables:

1. The *amount* borrowed or invested. This amount sometimes is called the **principal.** The larger the principal, the larger the dollar amount of interest.

2. The *rate of interest.* The higher the rate of interest on a given principal, the larger will be the dollar amount of interest.

3. The *time period* covered by the loan. The longer the period of time for which money is borrowed, the larger the dollar amount of interest.[4]

Explain the variables that affect the dollar amount of interest.

Simple Interest

Simple interest is interest that is earned only on the original principal. The formula for calculating simple interest is as follows:

$$I = (p)(i)(n)$$

where I = simple interest
   p = principal (amount borrowed or lent)
   i = interest rate per year
   n = number of years (or fractional portion of a year)

If you borrow $100 for one year at 10 percent, the interest for the year is $10:

$$I = (p)(i)(n)$$
$$= (\$100)(.10)(1)$$
$$= \$10$$

If you borrow $100 for 3 months at 10 percent, the interest is $2.50:

$$I = (\$100)(.10)(.25) \quad \left(\frac{3 \text{ months}}{12 \text{ months}} = .25 \text{ of a year} \right)$$
$$= \$2.50$$

Differentiate between simple interest and compound interest.

Compound Interest

Compound interest is interest that is earned on both principal *and* interest. Under simple interest, interest is earned only on the original principal. When interest is compounded, however, interest is earned each period on the original principal *and* on the interest accumulated for the preceding periods. Stated another way, the principal increases each period as interest earned for that period is added to it. For example, assume that you deposited $1,000 today in a bank savings account that paid 10 percent interest compounded annually (i.e., interest is calculated and added to your account once a year). The amount of interest earned over a four-year period under compound interest as compared with simple interest is shown in Exhibit A–1.

We have seen that interest rates normally are stated as annual rates. When interest is compounded for periods of less than a year, the following steps are necessary before compound interest can be calculated:

1. Divide the annual rate by the number of compounding periods per year to determine the interest rate per compounding period.

---

[4]In this text we have considered time periods as years, months, or days. A month is considered to be 1/12 of a year, and a day to be 1/360 of a year. When banks calculate interest, however, they consider a day to be 1/365 of a year.

EXHIBIT A-1	Amount Earned over Four Years at Simple and Compound Interest of 10 Percent		
End of Year	**Interest Earned**	**Cumulative Interest Earned**	**Investment Balance**
	Simple Interest		
1	$1,000(.10) = $100	$100	$1,100
2	$1,000(.10) = 100	200	1,200
3	$1,000(.10) = 100	300	1,300
4	$1,000(.10) = 100	400	1,400
	Compound Interest		
1	$1,000(.10) = $100.00	$100.00	$1,100.00
2	$1,100(.10) = 110.00	210.00	1,210.00
3	$1,210(.10) = 121.00	331.00	1,331.00
4	$1,331(.10) = 133.10	464.10	1,464.10

2. Multiply the number of years involved by the number of compounding periods per year to obtain the total number of interest compounding periods.

Notice that these steps refer to interest compounding periods rather than to years. The four examples in Exhibit A–2 illustrate these two steps, which will be used later in this appendix.

When interest is compounded more frequently than once a year, the *effective annual* interest rate can be calculated as follows:

$$\text{Effective annual rate} = \left(1 + \frac{i}{c}\right)^c - 1$$

where i = annual interest rate
c = number of compoundings per year

In terms of the four examples in Exhibit A–2:

CONCEPTUAL

Effective annual interest rates.

EXAMPLE		EFFECTIVE ANNUAL RATE
1	$\left(1 + \frac{.12}{1}\right) - 1 = 1.12 - 1 \quad =$	12.00%
2	$\left(1 + \frac{.06}{2}\right)^2 - 1 = 1.0609 - 1 =$	6.09%
3	$\left(1 + \frac{.06}{4}\right)^4 - 1 = 1.0614 - 1 =$	6.14%
4	$\left(1 + \frac{.18}{12}\right)^{12} - 1 = 1.1956 - 1 =$	19.56%

These calculations are made easily with spreadsheet software or a hand calculator.[5]

Some banks offer daily or even *continuous* compounding on money deposited in savings accounts. Continuous compounding requires the use of natural logarithms. The underlying concepts are mathematically complex and therefore are not discussed in this text.

---

[5]The effective annual rate for many combinations of annual interest rates and compoundings per year also can be found by using Table A at the end of this appendix. Table A is discussed in the next section.

| | | EXHIBIT A-2 | Calculation of Compound Interest at Four Interest Rates and Compounding Periods | | |

Example	Annual Interest Rate	Interest Compounded	Interest Rate per Compounding Period	Number of Compounding Periods
1	12%	Annually for 3 years	$.12 \div 1 = .12$	3 years × 1 compounding period = 3 periods
2	6%	Semiannually for 4 years	$.06 \div 2 = .03$	4 years × 2 compounding periods = 8 periods
3	6%	Quarterly for 5 years	$.06 \div 4 = .015$	5 years × 4 compounding periods = 20 periods
4	18%	Monthly for 9 years	$.18 \div 12 = .015$	9 years × 12 compounding periods = 108 periods

(P) RESENT AND FUTURE VALUES OF SINGLE AMOUNTS

We are now ready to discuss present and future values based on the principle of compound interest. Time diagrams are used to help you visualize the cash flows associated with present and future value concepts.

Time Diagrams

CONCEPTUAL

A time diagram is helpful in understanding the pattern of cash flows.

Since cash flows have a time value, a **time diagram** is a convenient way to visualize these cash flows over time. A typical time diagram appears as follows:

Present ... Future
0   1   2   3   4   5

Point 0 on the diagram represents the present date in a problem situation. The horizontal line is divided into equal time periods, which represent the interest or compounding periods. This time diagram contains five interest periods. Time diagrams are presented often in this appendix, since they are useful in visualizing cash flows. You will also find them a valuable aid in solving any problems that deal with the time value of money.

Future Value of a Single Amount

4 Explain the concept and calculate the future value of a single amount.

When an amount is invested for several interest periods at a specified rate of interest, it will accumulate to a larger amount because of compounding. This larger amount, which exists at the end of the last interest period, is called the **future value of a single amount** and is represented by the symbol a.

To illustrate, if $354.60 is invested today, what is the *future value* of this amount in four years at an interest rate of 5 percent compounded annually? We may view this problem on a time diagram as follows:

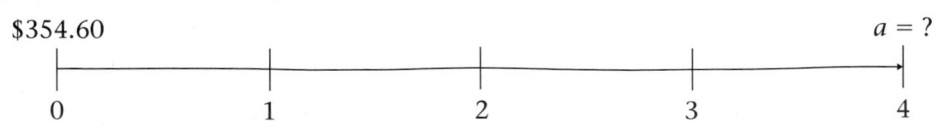

$354.60 $a = ?$
0   1   2   3   4

One way to solve this problem is to calculate how much has been accumulated at the end of each period:

	AMOUNT	CALCULATION
Beginning principal (year 0)	$354.60	
Interest (year 1)	17.73	($354.60)(.05)
Amount (end of year 1)	$372.33	($354.60)(1.05)
Interest (year 2)	18.62	($372.33)(.05)
Amount (end of year 2)	$390.95	($372.33)(1.05)
Interest (year 3)	19.55	($390.95)(.05)
Amount (end of year 3)	$410.50	($390.95)(1.05)
Interest (year 4)	20.52	($410.50)(.05)
Amount (end of year 4)	$431.02	($410.50)(1.05)

Based on the calculations in the right-hand column above, a general formula for the future value of a single amount may be expressed as follows:

$$a = p\,(a_{\overline{n}|i})$$

where a = future value of a single amount

p = beginning principal

$a_{\overline{n}|i}$ (read "small a angle n at i") = $(1 + i)^n$

i = interest rate per period

n = number of interest periods

The symbols a and $a_{\overline{n}|i}$ should not be confused. The symbol $a_{\overline{n}|i}$ is simply a shorthand notation for the formula $(1 + i)^n$. The symbol a represents the future value of a single amount and is determined by multiplying *any* principal (p) times the appropriate interest factor, $(1 + i)^n$, when i and n are given. In this example:

$$a = \$354.60(a_{\overline{4}|5\%})$$
$$= \$354.60(1.05)^4$$
$$= \$354.60(1.2155)$$
$$= \$431.02$$

Although we can calculate $(1.05)^4$ by hand or with a calculator, tables have been constructed that provide future value factors ($a_{\overline{n}|i}$) for various interest rates and time periods. Table A at the end of this appendix provides these future value factors. To use Table A, simply multiply the principal amount by the appropriate interest factor in the table to obtain the future value.

To illustrate how a future value table is used, assume you borrow $10,000 today from a bank. How much will you owe the bank at the end of five years if the rate of interest is 12 percent compounded semiannually? The solution is:

$$a = \$10,000(a_{\overline{10}|6\%})$$
$$= \$10,000(1.7908)$$
$$= \$17,908$$

Note that because we are compounding semiannually, the number of periods is 10, and the interest rate per period is 6 percent. Reading from Table A, we find that the factor corresponding to 10 periods at 6 percent is 1.7908. Thus, if we borrow $10,000 today from a bank, we will owe the bank $17,908 at the end of the fifth year if the bank charges interest at 12 percent compounded semiannually.[6]

Some of the examples that follow include an illustration showing how the answer was derived. In most of the examples, however, the proof is not provided. In these cases, you are encouraged to verify how the answer "proves out." You may wish to perform this task using a handheld calculator or a personal computer

[6]The effective annual rate in this example is 12.36% $[(1 + .12/2)^2 - 1]$. This amount is found in Table A under the 6% column (12% ÷ 2) and the $n = 2$ row (two compoundings per year).

using spreadsheet software such as Excel. For example, you may wish to verify the $17,908 debt at the end of year 5 in the preceding example.

Present Value of a Single Amount

Determining future values of single amounts is important in many investing and lending situations. The concept of the **present value of a single amount,** however, has more applications in financial accounting. The present value concept provides an answer to the following general question: What is the value today (the present value) of an amount to be received or paid at some future date?

To illustrate, assume that in five years you desire to have a "nest egg" of $4,000 in the bank. If the interest rate you can earn is 10 percent compounded annually, how much must you invest today so that your original investment and interest will accumulate to $4,000 at the end of the fifth year?

A time diagram for this problem follows:

Future value (a)
$4,000

$p = ?$

| 0 | 1 | 2 | 3 | 4 | 5 |

Notice that we wish to find the *present value* of a future amount when the future amount is known. (Earlier we wished to find the *future value* when the present value was known.)

Since $a = p(a_{\overline{n}|i}) = p(1 + i)^n$,

$$p = \frac{a}{a_{\overline{n}|i}} = \frac{a}{(1 + i)^n}$$

This relationship means that to find the present value of a future amount, we can divide the known future amount by the appropriate factor in Table A. Therefore, our problem can be solved as follows:

$$p = \frac{a}{a_{\overline{n}|i}}$$

$$= \frac{\$4,000}{a_{\overline{5}|10\%}}$$

$$= \frac{\$4,000}{1.6105}$$

$$= \$2,483.70$$

The $2,483.70 amount represents the present value of $4,000, *discounted* for five years at 10 percent per year. In other words, if you invest $2,483.70 at 10 percent interest compounded annually, the investment will grow to $4,000 at the end of year 5.

This result is shown in Exhibit A–3. Notice the pattern in which the interest of $1,516.30 ($4,000.00 – $2,483.70) is earned over the five-year period. This pattern is characteristic of the **effective interest method** of calculating interest. Under the effective interest method, *periodic interest expense is calculated by multiplying the effective interest rate by the beginning-of-period balance.* Under this method, the dollar amount of periodic interest increases (decreases) as the investment increases (decreases). The changing dollar amount of periodic interest represents a *constant* rate of return (10 percent, in this case) on the beginning-of-period investment. *The effective interest method is one of the most pervasive and important concepts in accounting and finance.* Be sure you understand it before you proceed further.

CONCEPTUAL

The effective interest method is a very important concept.

EXHIBIT A–3	Growth of Initial Investment (Present Value) of $2,483.70 to $4,000 in Five Years at 10 Percent Interest Compounded Annually		

Year	(a) Beginning Investment	(b) Interest for Year (a × .10)	(c) Ending Investment (a + b)
1	$2,483.70	$ 248.37	$2,732.07
2	2,732.07	273.21	3,005.28
3	3,005.28	300.53	3,305.81
4	3,305.81	330.58	3,636.39
5	3,636.39	363.61[a]	4,000.00
		$1,516.30	

[a]Rounded down by $.03.

Although we can use Table A to solve present value problems, tables have been constructed to provide present value factors directly. Table B at the end of this appendix contains factors for the present value of 1 at various interest rates and over various time periods. Inspect Table B at this point. The present value factors in Table B are reciprocals of the future value factors in Table A, as Exhibit A–4 shows. Thus, the present value of a single amount is:

$$p = a(p\overline{n}|i)$$

where p = present value of a single future amount

a = the future value

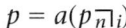 $p\overline{n}|i$ (read "small p angle n at i") = $\dfrac{1}{(1 + i)^n}$

i = interest rate per period

n = number of periods

To illustrate, assume you have the opportunity to purchase a zero-coupon bond that will pay $13,000 at its maturity date at the end of six years. (A zero-coupon bond pays no periodic cash interest.) What is the present value of this investment at a rate of return of 8 percent? That is, if the required rate of return is 8 percent, how much would we be willing to invest now to receive $13,000 at the end of six years?

$$p = a(p\overline{n}|i)$$
$$= \$13,000(p\overline{6}|8\%)$$
$$= \$13,000(.6302)$$
$$= \$8,192.60$$

EXHIBIT A–4	Relationship Between Table A and Table B (10% Interest Column)			

n	1 ÷	TABLE A FACTOR	=	TABLE B FACTOR
1	1 ÷	1.1000	=	.9091
2	1 ÷	1.2100	=	.8264
3	1 ÷	1.3310	=	.7513
⋮	⋮	⋮		⋮
12	1 ÷	3.1384	=	.3186
⋮		⋮		⋮
20	1 ÷	6.7275	=	.1486

The present value factor is determined by finding the amount in Table B that corresponds to six periods at 8 percent interest per year. Multiplying this factor, .6302, by the future amount yields the present value of $8,192.60.

If the investment is purchased for $8,192.60, the difference between our cost of $8,192.60 and the maturity value of $13,000 represents interest revenue over the six-year period. The effective interest method would be used to calculate the amount of interest revenue recognized each year:

Year 1: $.08 \times \$8{,}192.60 = \$655.41$
Year 2: $.08 \times (\$8{,}192.60 + \$655.41) = \$707.84$

Notice that this pattern is the same as the pattern illustrated in Exhibit A–3.

Other Values Related to Single Amounts

So far this appendix has illustrated future and present values of single amounts when the number of periods and the rate of interest are given. In this section we shall look at some different but related problems. Our purpose here is to demonstrate that if we know the values of any three of the four variables (p, a, i, and n), we can determine the value of the fourth variable.

Finding n When p, a, and i Are Known

Assume that your client needs $25,000 for major construction expenditures. At the present time the firm has only $11,580 in funds. How many years will it take to accumulate $25,000, if the $11,580 is invested at 8 percent?

In this example, both the present and future values are known ($11,580 and $25,000, respectively), as is the interest rate. We are trying to determine the number of periods (n) required for $11,580 invested at 8 percent per period to accumulate to $25,000. A time diagram follows:

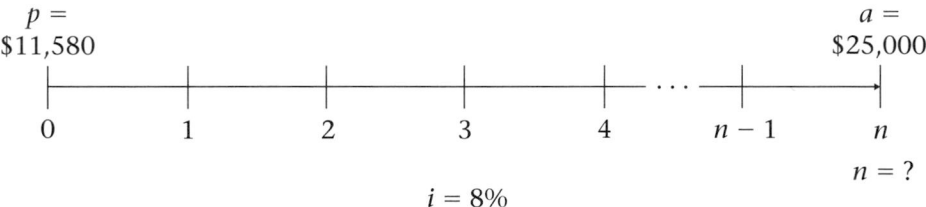

Since both the present and future values are known, we will approach the problem from the present value perspective (although we could also use a future value perspective):

$$p = a(p\,\overline{_n|}\,8\%)$$
$$\$11{,}580 = \$25{,}000(p\,\overline{_n|}\,8\%)$$
$$p\,\overline{_n|}\,8\% = \frac{\$11{,}580}{\$25{,}000} = .4632$$

Thus, we need to find how many interest periods correspond to the present value factor of .4632 when $i = 8$ percent. Using Table B and reading down the 8 percent column, we find that the number of periods (n) corresponding to .4632 is 10. Thus, it will take 10 years for $11,580 to accumulate to $25,000 at an earnings rate of 8 percent per year.

Finding i When p, a, and n Are Known

What interest rate is necessary for a single amount of $5,645 invested today to accumulate to $10,000 in six years?

A time diagram and the solution follow. While the problem can be approached as either a present value or future value problem, we present the solution in terms of present value:

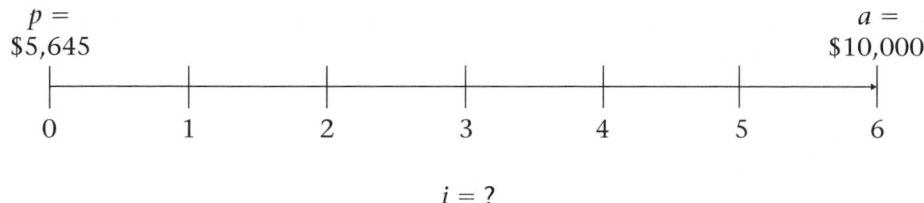

$$p = a(p\overline{6}|_i)$$
$$\$5,645 = \$10,000(p\overline{6}|_i)$$
$$p\overline{6}|_i = \frac{\$5,645}{\$10,000}$$
$$p\overline{6}|_i = .5645$$

Using Table B and reading across the $n = 6$ row, we find that .5645 corresponds to an interest rate of 10 percent. Thus, if \$5,645 is invested at 10 percent, it will accumulate to \$10,000 at the end of the sixth year.

Changing Interest Rates

In our economy, interest rates change because of monetary policy, inflation, fluctuations in the supply of and demand for money, investors' perceptions of risk, and other factors. To illustrate a situation with changing interest rates, assume that Polly Frank deposited \$15,000 in a savings account on January 1, year 1. What is the amount in her savings account at the end of 16 years, if the rate of interest is 6 percent for the first 10 years and 10 percent for the remaining 6 years?

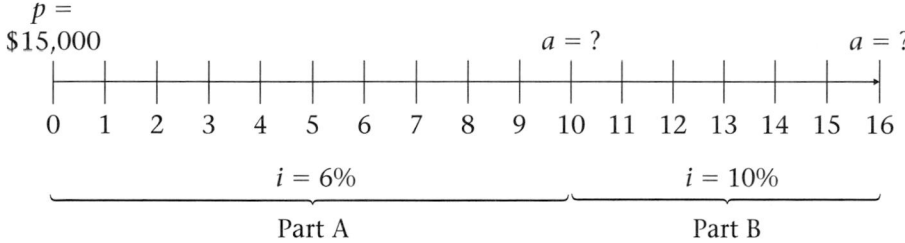

The solution is fairly straightforward if we visualize the problem in two parts, as illustrated in the following time diagram:

Part A: Future value at the end of year 10:

$$a = \$15,000(a\overline{10}|_{6\%})$$
$$= \$15,000(1.7908)$$
$$= \$26,862$$

Part B: Future value at the end of year 16:

$$a = \$26,862(a\overline{6}|_{10\%})$$
$$= \$26,862(1.7716)$$
$$= \$47,588.72$$

Thus, the \$15,000 will earn interest at 6 percent for 10 years and will accumulate to \$26,862 at the end of the tenth year. Beginning in the eleventh year, the \$26,862 will earn interest at 10 percent and will accumulate to \$47,588.72 at the end of the sixteenth year.

PRESENT AND FUTURE VALUES OF ANNUITIES

6 Define an annuity and distinguish between an ordinary annuity and an annuity due.

In the previous section, we discussed the concepts of the present and future values of *single* amounts. In this section we shall discuss present and future value concepts related to a *series* of equal cash flows, called an annuity. An **annuity** is a series of equal cash flows occurring at equal intervals over a period of time.[7] If the first cash flow occurs at the *end* of the first interest period, the annuity is an **ordinary annuity** (or an annuity in arrears). If the first cash flow occurs at the *beginning* of the first interest period, the annuity is called an **annuity due** (or an annuity in advance). The difference between an ordinary annuity and an annuity due is illustrated in Exhibit A–5.

Annuities have many applications in accounting. Many of the cash flows related to bonds, notes, leases, and pensions, for example, are annuities. As with single amounts, the basic annuity problems are (1) determining to what amount the periodic cash flows (i.e., an annuity) will accumulate at some future point and (2) determining the present value of a series of equal, periodic future cash flows. The first part of this section deals with ordinary annuities; annuities due will be discussed later.

Future Value of an Ordinary Annuity

7 Explain the concept and calculate the future value of an ordinary annuity.

To illustrate how the **future value of an ordinary annuity** is determined, assume that you deposit $100 in a savings account at the end of each year for four years. What will be the amount in your savings account at the end of the fourth year if the interest rate is 5 percent compounded annually?[8] A time diagram follows:

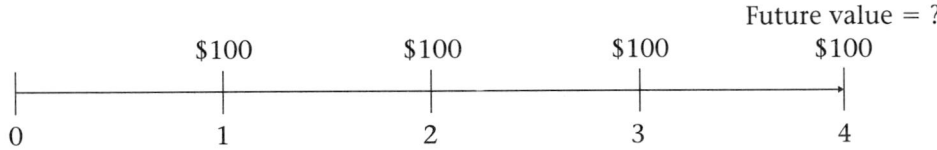

EXHIBIT A–5   Time Diagrams of an Ordinary Annuity and an Annuity Due

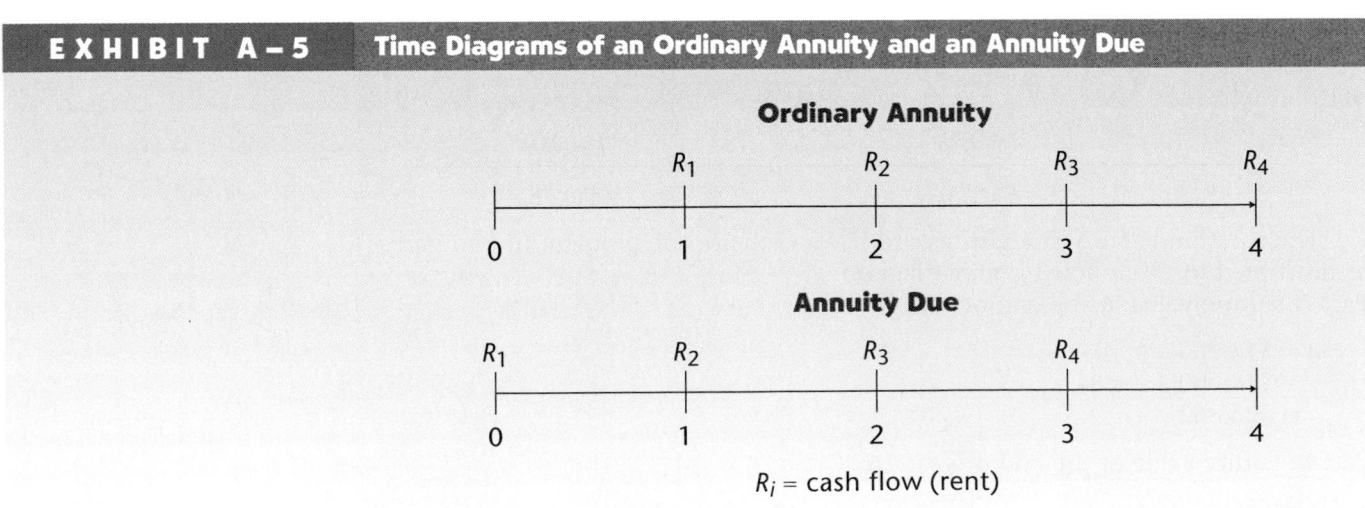

R_i = cash flow (rent)

---

[7]These cash flows are often called *rents*.

[8]In all of the examples in this book, we have assumed that the periodic rents (e.g., $100 each year in this example) coincide with the compounding period (e.g., annually in this example). Cases in which the compounding period differs from the timing of the cash flows are beyond the scope of this textbook.

To find the future value, we can treat each cash flow as a single amount and calculate the future value of each:

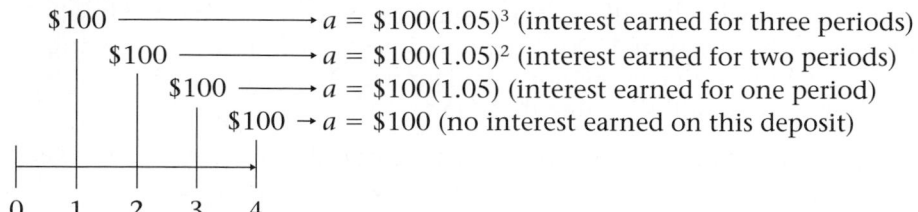

$$\text{Future value of an ordinary annuity} = \$100(1.05)^3 + \$100(1.05)^2 + \$100(1.05) + \$100$$

$$= \$100[(1.05)^3 + (1.05)^2 + (1.05) + 1]$$
$$= \$100(1.1576 + 1.1025 + 1.05 + 1)$$
$$= \$100(4.3101)$$
$$= \$431.01$$

Thus, if you deposit $100 in a savings account at the end of each year for four years, your balance at the end of the fourth year will be $431.01. Exhibit A–6 illustrates how your savings will grow over the four-year period.

As you might imagine, this approach can become tedious and time-consuming as the number of rents increases. Fortunately, the calculation is based on a geometric progression (not derived here) that can be used to obtain $\$100\left[\dfrac{(1 + .05)^4 - 1}{.05}\right]$. Thus, the formula for the future value of an ordinary annuity is as follows:

$$A = R(A_{\overline{n}|i})$$

where A = future value of an ordinary annuity
R = periodic cash flows (rents)

$$A_{\overline{n}|i} \text{ (read "capital A angle } n \text{ at } i\text{")} = \frac{(1 + i)^n - 1}{i}$$

n = number of rents
i = interest rate per period

Table C at the end of this appendix gives the future value of ordinary annuity factors for various values of i and n. To use the Table C factors in the formula, simply multiply the periodic rent by the annuity factor that corresponds to the appropriate i and n to obtain the future value of the ordinary annuity.

EXHIBIT A–6	Growth in Investment from an Ordinary Annuity of $100 Each Year for Four Years at 5 Percent			
Year	(a) Beginning Investment Balance	(b) Interest Earned (a × .05)	(c) Annual Deposit at Year-End	(d) Ending Investment Balance (a + b + c)
1	—	—	$100	$100.00
2	$100.00	$ 5.00	100	205.00
3	205.00	10.25	100	315.25
4	315.25	15.76	100	431.01

To illustrate the use of the formula for the future value of an annuity together with Table C, assume that Goody Corporation must accumulate a pension fund for retiring employees. If today is the beginning of year 1, how much will be accumulated in five years, if $200 is deposited each six months in a savings account that earns 12 percent compounded semiannually? Assume that the first deposit will be made in six months. A time diagram and the solution follow:

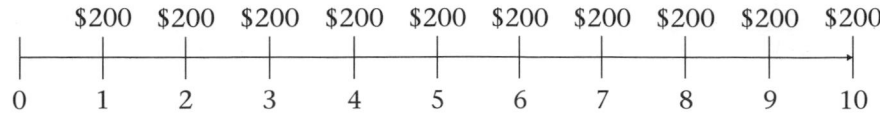

$$A = R(A_{\overline{n}|i})$$
$$= \$200\ (A_{\overline{10}|6\%})$$
$$= \$200\ (13.1808)$$
$$= \$2,636.16$$

Thus, if Goody makes the 10 semiannual deposits on the indicated dates, funds totaling $2,636.16 will be available in five years.

It should be apparent that Table C (the future value of an ordinary annuity of 1) and Table A (the future value of 1) are related, since as was stated earlier, we can treat each cash flow of an annuity as a single amount, find the future value of each cash flow, and then add the individual future values of all of the cash flows to obtain the future value of an ordinary annuity. This relationship is shown in Exhibit A–7. As the exhibit demonstrates, Table C's factors may be derived from Table A's factors by subtracting 1 from Table A's factors and dividing the result by the interest rate (i).

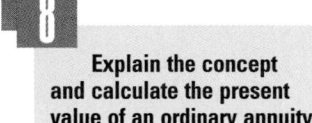

Explain the concept and calculate the present value of an ordinary annuity.

Present Value of an Ordinary Annuity

Accountants use the concept of the **present value of an ordinary annuity** in solving many accounting problems. For example, assume that your client Tim Dubois is considering investing in a solar energy unit that will provide annual cash savings of $1,200 each year for five years. The first cash saving will occur at the end of the current year. What is the present value of this investment at an interest rate, or rate of return, of 10 percent? That is, how much should your client be willing to invest to save $1,200 per year for five years, if he expects to earn a 10 percent rate of return?

EXHIBIT A–7	Relationship Between Table A and Table C				
n	**Table A:** Future Value of 1 at 5% $a_{\overline{n}|i} = (1 + i)^n$	$(1 + i)^n - 1$	÷	i	=	**Table C:** Future Value of an Ordinary Annuity of 1 at 5% $A_{\overline{n}|i} = \dfrac{(1 + i)^n - 1}{i}$
1	1.0500	.0500	.05		1.0000
2	1.1025	.1025	.05		2.0500
3	1.1576	.1576	.05		3.1520
5	1.2763	.2763	.05		5.5260
10	1.6289	.6289	.05		12.5780
20	2.6533	1.6533	.05		33.0660

A time diagram for this problem would look like this:

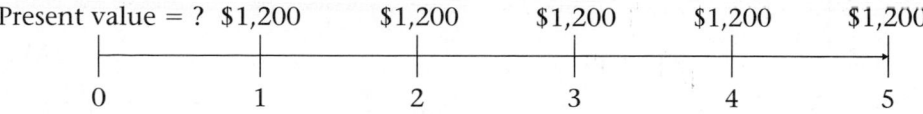

Present value = ? $1,200 $1,200 $1,200 $1,200 $1,200

| | | | | |
0   1   2   3   4   5

To determine the present value of this ordinary annuity, we may treat each $1,200 cash flow as a single amount, find the present value of each single amount, and then add the individual present values to obtain the total present value:

$$\text{Present value of ordinary annuity} = \frac{\$1,200}{(1.10)} + \frac{\$1,200}{(1.10)^2} + \frac{\$1,200}{(1.10)^3} + \frac{\$1,200}{(1.10)^4} + \frac{\$1,200}{(1.10)^5}$$

or

$$\text{Present value of ordinary annuity} = \$1,200\left[\frac{1}{(1.10)} + \frac{1}{(1.10)^2} + \frac{1}{(1.10)^3} + \frac{1}{(1.10)^4} + \frac{1}{(1.10)^5}\right]$$

$$= \$1,200(.9091 + .8264 + .7513 + .6830 + .6209)$$
$$= \$1,200(3.7908)$$
$$= \$4,548.95$$

This solution may be interpreted as follows: If your client invests $4,548.95 in a solar unit that provides cash savings of $1,200 each year for five years, the rate of return earned on the investment is 10 percent per year.

Needless to say, such a calculation can become cumbersome when an annuity covers several periods. Therefore, the use of a formula is more efficient. The formula for the present value of an ordinary annuity is as follows:

$$P = R(P_{\overline{n}|i})$$

where P = present value of an ordinary annuity
R = periodic cash flows (rents)

$$P_{\overline{n}|i} \text{ (read "capital } P \text{ angle } n \text{ at } i\text{") } = \frac{1 - \dfrac{1}{(1 + i)^n}}{i}$$

n = number of rents
i = interest (discount) rate per period

Table D at the end of this appendix gives the factors for the present value of an ordinary annuity for various values of i and n. To use the Table D factors in the formula, multiply the periodic rents by the annuity factor that corresponds to the appropriate i and n. Applying the formula and Table D to the previous example, we obtain:

$$P = R(P_{\overline{n}|i})$$
$$= \$1,200(P_{\overline{5}|10\%})$$
$$= \$1,200(3.7908)$$
$$= \$4,548.95$$

To further illustrate the calculations for the present value of an ordinary annuity, assume that Roderick wishes to deposit in a financial institution an amount that will enable him to withdraw cash of $1,250 per year for 10 years, with the first withdrawal to be made at the end of year 1. How much should be deposited at the beginning of year 1, if the deposit earns 10 percent compounded annually? The problem can be solved as follows:

$$P = R(P_{\overline{n}|i})$$
$$= \$1,250(P_{\overline{10}|10\%})$$
$$= \$1,250(6.1446)$$
$$= \$7,680.75$$

Thus, if Roderick deposits $7,680.75, he will be able to withdraw $1,250 at the end of each year for 10 years. The schedule in Exhibit A–8 shows how the amount on

EXHIBIT A-8	Schedule of Decline in Deposit from Annual Withdrawals						
Year	(1) Beginning Balance	+	(2) Interest at 10%[a]	−	(3) Withdrawal	=	(4) Ending Balance
1	$7,680.75		$768.08		$1,250.00		$7,198.83
2	7,198.83		719.88		1,250.00		6,668.71
3	6,668.71		666.87		1,250.00		6,085.58
4	6,085.58		608.56		1,250.00		5,444.14
5	5,444.14		544.41		1,250.00		4,738.55
6	4,738.55		473.86		1,250.00		3,962.41
7	3,962.41		396.24		1,250.00		3,108.65
8	3,108.65		310.86		1,250.00		2,169.51
9	2,169.51		216.95		1,250.00		1,136.46
10	1,136.46		113.64		1,250.00		0.00[b]

[a]10% of the beginning balance on deposit.
[b]Rounding error of $.10.

deposit gradually decreases to zero over the 10-year period. Notice that the annual interest earnings in column 2 *increase* the amount on deposit, while the annual withdrawals in column 3 *decrease* the amount on deposit. Another way to interpret Exhibit A–8 is to view each periodic withdrawal as consisting of two distinct elements: (1) withdrawal of the interest earned during the period; and (2) withdrawal of a portion of the principal. For example, in year 5, the $1,250 withdrawal consists of interest in the amount of $544.41 and principal in the amount of $705.59 ($1,250.00 – $544.41). The principal withdrawal causes the amount on deposit to decrease from $5,444.14 to $4,738.55—a reduction of $705.59.

Exhibit A–9 presents the deposit data from Exhibit A–8 in the form of a graph. The upward-sloping lines in the exhibit represent the annual growth in the investment as a result of the interest earned at a 10 percent rate. The dotted lines represent the cash withdrawals of $1,250 at the end of each year. Notice that the pattern of the graph resembles the teeth on a saw. *This "saw-toothed curve" is a pattern that applies to a large number of present value applications in accounting, in terms of the carrying-value of an asset (a deposit, in this case) or a liability over time.*

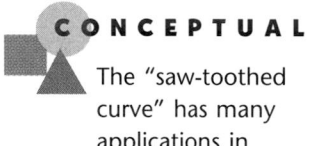

CONCEPTUAL

The "saw-toothed curve" has many applications in accounting.

Two observations may be made about this exhibit. First, notice that because the periodic cash flows (withdrawals) are greater than the periodic interest earned, the asset (deposit) decreases over time, finally reaching a terminal point (zero in this case). Second, if the periodic cash flows were less than the periodic interest earned, the asset would grow continuously. (An example of such a case appears in Exhibit A–3.) Study Exhibit A–9 carefully and thoroughly. It has numerous applications in the study of notes, bonds, leases, pensions, and other topics in this text.

As with the two future value tables, there is a relationship between the two present value tables, Table B and Table D. That relationship is shown in Exhibit A–10. Notice that the present value factors in Table D are the cumulative summations of the present value factors in Table B.

CONCEPTUAL

The factors in Table D are cumulative summations of the factors in Table B.

Other Values Related to Ordinary Annuities

Earlier in this appendix we discussed how other variables related to single amounts (e.g., the interest rate or the number of periods) can be determined when both the present and future values of those amounts are known. These same concepts also apply to annuities.

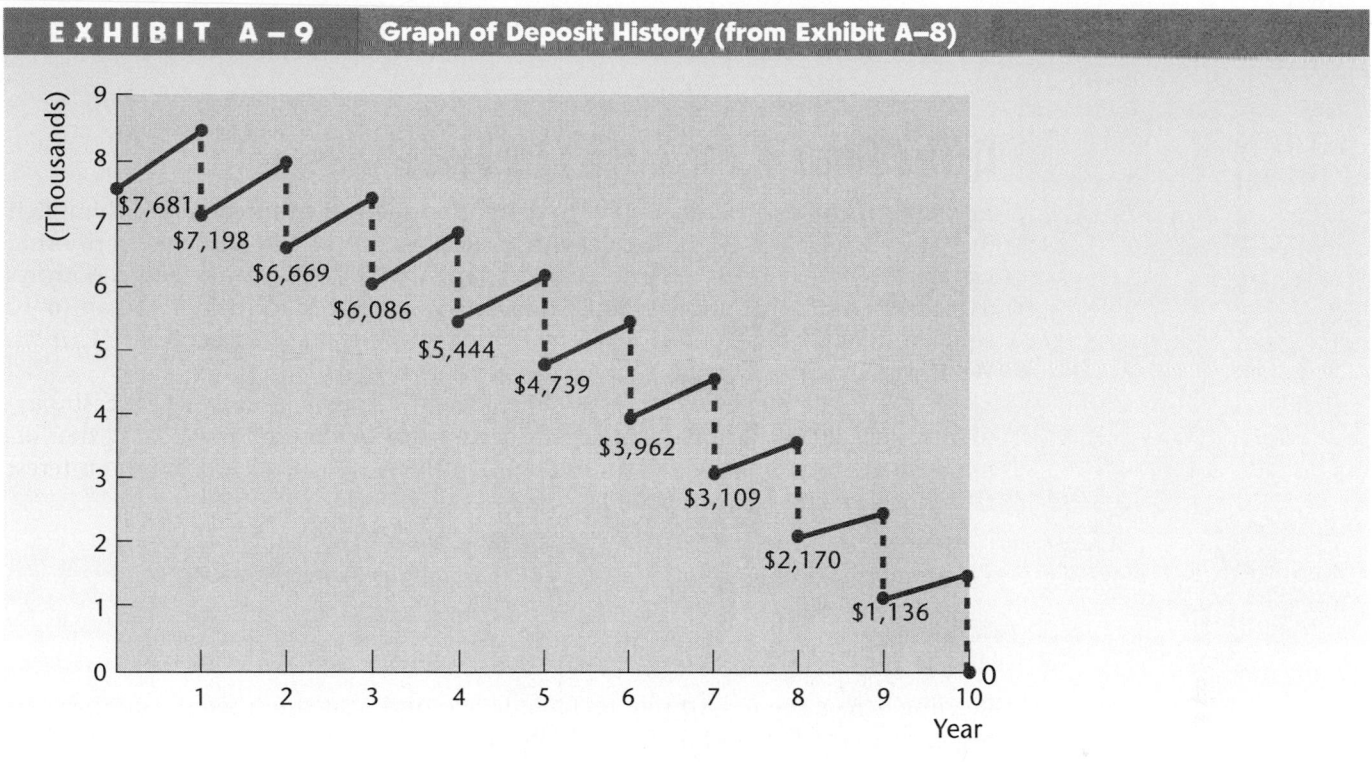

EXHIBIT A-9   Graph of Deposit History (from Exhibit A-8)

$7,681
$7,198
$6,669
$6,086
$5,444
$4,739
$3,962
$3,109
$2,170
$1,136

EXHIBIT A-10   Relationship Between Table B and Table D

n	Table B: Present Value of 1 at 5%	Table D: Present Value of Ordinary Annuity of 1 at 5%
1	.9524	.9524
2	.9070	.9524 + .9070 = 1.8594
3	.8638	.9524 + .9070 + .8638 = 2.7232
4	.8227	.9524 + .9070 + .8638 + .8227 = 3.5460
5	.7835	.9524 + .9070 + .8638 + .8227 + .7835 = 4.3295

Finding n When R, P or A, and i Are Known

Accountants frequently need to determine the annuity payments necessary to accumulate a certain dollar amount. For example, a company may need to accumulate funds to retire a debt at some point in the future. If today is January 1, 1998, how many year-end deposits of $10,000, the first to be made at the end of 1998, are necessary to accumulate a total of $61,051, if the interest rate is 10 percent compounded annually?

Notice that $61,051 represents the *future value* of n (to be determined) $10,000 year-end cash flows, at an interest rate of 10 percent. Thus,

$$A = R(A_{\overline{n}|i})$$
$$\$61,051 = \$10,000(A_{\overline{n}|10\%})$$

$$A_{\overline{n}|10\%} = \frac{\$61,051}{\$10,000} = 6.1051$$

Consulting Table C (the future value of an ordinary annuity) and reading down the 10 percent column, we find that the number of periods (n) corresponding to

6.1051 is five. Thus, it will take five $10,000 year-end deposits (or five years) to accumulate $61,051 at an interest rate (rate of return) of 10 percent.

Finding *i* When *R*, *P* or *A*, and *n* Are Known

Accountants often are called upon to determine the rate of interest that is implicit in a loan agreement. In these cases the interest rate must be calculated from other variables. For example, assume that on January 1, 1998, Pam Tedder borrows $10,170 from Sixth National Bank. The bank requires her to repay the loan in 10 equal annual payments of $1,800. The first payment is due on December 31, 1998. What rate of interest is the bank charging on the loan?

The $10,170 borrowed represents the present value of 10 end-of-year cash payments of $1,800 at an interest rate of i percent (to be determined). Using the formula for the present value of an ordinary annuity, we can determine the interest rate as follows:

$$P = R(P_{\overline{n}|i})$$
$$\$10,170 = \$1,800(P_{\overline{10}|i})$$
$$P_{\overline{10}|i} = \frac{\$10,170}{\$1,800} = 5.6500$$

Reading across the $n = 10$ row in Table D, we find that the interest rate that corresponds to the factor of 5.6500 is 12 percent. Thus, the bank is charging Pam Tedder an interest rate of 12 percent on the unpaid balance of the loan.

Finding *R* When *P* or *A*, *i*, and *n* Are Known

Many present value problems require calculation of either the periodic cash payments necessary to liquidate a current debt or the periodic cash investment necessary to accumulate a given future amount. A good example of the use of periodic payments to liquidate a debt is the typical home mortgage. To illustrate, assume that a couple borrows $40,000 for a home improvement, agreeing to mortgage their home as collateral. The bank loan must be repaid over a 50-month period, with interest at 1 percent per month. The monthly mortgage payments, due at the end of each month, would be calculated as follows:

$$\text{Present value of an ordinary annuity } (P) = \text{Monthly payments } (R)(P_{\overline{n}|i})$$
$$\$40,000 = R(P_{\overline{50}|1\%})$$
$$\$40,000 = R(39.1961)$$
$$R = \$1,020.51$$

A schedule showing the monthly interest, monthly payments, and loan balance at the end of each month appears in Exhibit A–11. This exhibit provides another example of the effective interest method. Notice that each month's interest is calculated by multiplying the effective interest rate of 1 percent by the loan balance at the beginning of the month. Also notice that as the loan balance declines over time, the periodic interest also declines.

Annuities Due

Up to this point we have discussed ordinary annuities, in which the periodic cash flows occur at the *end* of each interest period. In many business transactions, such as lease payments, the annuity payment occurs at the *beginning* of each interest period and is called an *annuity due*.

EXHIBIT A–11   Schedule of Interest and Book Value for a Home Mortgage

Month	(1) Interest[a]	(2) Payment[b]	(3) Balance[c]	Month	(1) Interest[a]	(2) Payment[b]	(3) Balance[c]
			$40,000.00	26	$224.75	$1,020.51	$21,679.05
1	$400.00	$1,020.51	39,379.49	27	216.79	1,020.51	20,875.33
2	393.79	1,020.51	38,752.77	28	208.75	1,020.51	20,063.57
3	387.53	1,020.51	38,119.79	29	200.64	1,020.51	19,243.70
4	381.20	1,020.51	37,480.48	30	192.44	1,020.51	18,415.63
5	374.80	1,020.51	36,834.78	31	184.16	1,020.51	17,579.27
6	368.35	1,020.51	36,182.61	32	175.79	1,020.51	16,734.56
7	361.83	1,020.51	35,523.93	33	167.35	1,020.51	15,881.39
8	355.24	1,020.51	34,858.66	34	158.81	1,020.51	15,019.70
9	348.59	1,020.51	34,186.74	35	150.20	1,020.51	14,149.38
10	341.87	1,020.51	33,508.09	36	141.49	1,020.51	13,270.37
11	335.08	1,020.51	32,822.66	37	132.70	1,020.51	12,382.56
12	328.23	1,020.51	32,130.38	38	123.83	1,020.51	11,485.88
13	321.30	1,020.51	31,431.17	39	114.86	1,020.51	10,580.22
14	314.31	1,020.51	30,724.98	40	105.80	1,020.51	9,665.52
15	307.25	1,020.51	30,011.72	41	96.66	1,020.51	8,741.66
16	300.12	1,020.51	29,291.32	42	87.42	1,020.51	7,808.57
17	292.91	1,020.51	28,563.73	43	78.09	1,020.51	6,866.14
18	285.64	1,020.51	27,828.85	44	68.66	1,020.51	5,914.30
19	278.29	1,020.51	27,086.63	45	59.14	1,020.51	4,952.93
20	270.87	1,020.51	26,336.99	46	49.53	1,020.51	3,981.95
21	263.37	1,020.51	25,579.85	47	39.82	1,020.51	3,001.26
22	255.80	1,020.51	24,815.14	48	30.01	1,020.51	2,010.76
23	248.15	1,020.51	24,042.78	49	20.11	1,020.51	1,010.36
24	240.43	1,020.51	23,262.70	50	10.10	1,020.51	0.00[d]
25	232.63	1,020.51	22,474.81				

[a].01 × previous balance in col. 3.
[b]Monthly payments (given).
[c]Previous balance + col. 3 − col. 2.
[d]Rounding error of $.05.

Table C and Table D provide the future value and present value factors corresponding to ordinary annuities. For annuity due problems, a formula modification must be made before Tables C and D can be used.

Future Values of an Annuity Due

We will begin by illustrating how the **future value of an annuity due** is calculated. Assume that at the beginning of year 1, Drew Cody makes four annual deposits of $100 to a savings account. How much does she have in the account at the end of year 4, if the savings account pays 12 percent interest compounded annually?

As the following time diagram illustrates, these deposits represent an annuity due, since they are made at the *beginning* of each interest period instead of at the end, as in an ordinary annuity.

9 Explain the concept and calculate the future value of an annuity due.

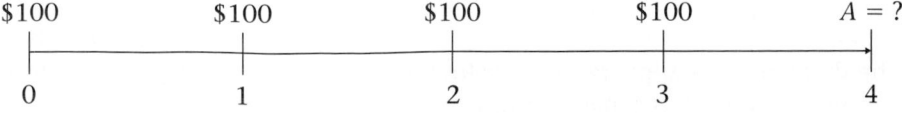

$100	$100	$100	$100	A = ?
0	1	2	3	4

To make the situation represented by this time diagram appear as an ordinary annuity, we can extend the time line back one period (one year in this example). Also, if we temporarily ignore the last interest period, the time diagram represents an ordinary annuity of four rents for four periods ending at the end of year 3:

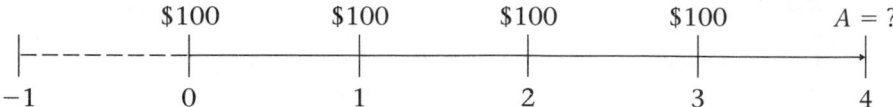

Once we have calculated the future value of the ordinary annuity as of the end of year 3, *we can treat this future value as a single amount and compound the amount for one period.* This final calculation will give us the future value at the end of year 4.

Better still, we can combine these two steps by modifying the formula for the future value of an ordinary annuity, to obtain the formula for the future value of an annuity due, as follows:

FUTURE VALUE OF	FORMULA
Ordinary annuity (A)	$A = R(A_{\overline{n}|\,i})$
Annuity due (A_D)	$A_D = R(A_{\overline{n}|\,i})(1 + i)$

The future value of the annuity due in the example on page 1195 is calculated as follows:

$$A_D = \$100(A_{\overline{4}|\,12\%})(1.12)$$
$$= \$100(4.7793)(1.12)$$
$$= \$100(5.3528)$$
$$= \$535.28$$

Present Value of an Annuity Due

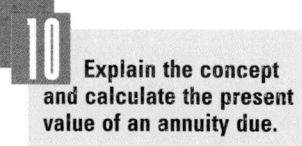

Explain the concept and calculate the present value of an annuity due.

To demonstrate the modifications for the **present value of an annuity due,** assume that at the beginning of year 1, Parker Thomas leases a building for six years, agreeing to make six annual lease payments of $600 each, the first of which is due at the beginning of year 1. What is the *present value* of this obligation if the interest rate is 8 percent? In other words, what equivalent lump-sum amount should the building owner agree to take if Parker agrees to pay the entire lease obligation at the beginning of year 1?

Here is the corresponding time diagram:

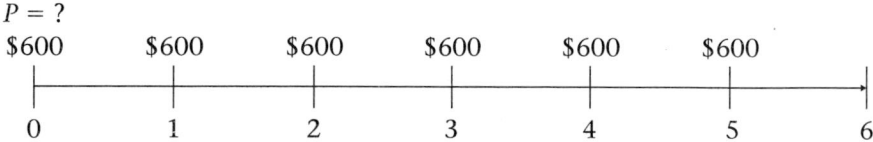

Because we are calculating the present value, there is no interest for the sixth period. After making the last lease payment, Parker has no further obligations, although he will use the building through year 6. If we extend the time diagram back one period, it will appear as follows:

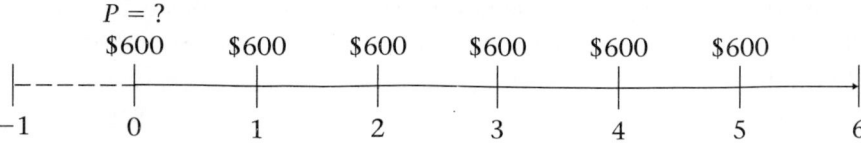

The diagram now appears as an ordinary annuity. We can find the present value of this annuity at the beginning of year 0, and *then compound that amount for*

one period. These adjustments will modify the formula for the present value of an ordinary annuity to the formula for the present value of an annuity due, as follows:

PRESENT VALUE OF	FORMULA
Ordinary annuity (P)	$P = R(P_{\overline{n}|i})$
Annuity due (P_D)	$P_D = R(P_{D_{\overline{n}|i}})$ where $P_{D_{\overline{n}|i}} = (P_{\overline{n}|i})(1 + i)$

Thus, the present value of Parker Thomas's lease obligation is calculated as follows:

$$P_D = \$600(P_{\overline{6}|8\%})(1.08)$$
$$= \$600(4.6229)(1.08)$$
$$= \$600(4.9927)$$
$$= \$2,995.62$$

Table E at the end of this appendix gives the factors for the present value of an annuity due. It is related to Table D as shown in Exhibit A–12. Though Table D can be used to solve problems that deal with the present value of an annuity due (using the modifications discussed above), using the factors in Table E is easier. Table E will be useful to you in solving many of the problems that appear in Chapter 15 on leases.

Deferred Annuities

The final type of annuity we will discuss is called a deferred annuity. A **deferred annuity** is an annuity in which the first rent occurs after at least two interest periods have expired. The time diagram for a five-year ordinary annuity deferred for three periods would appear as follows:

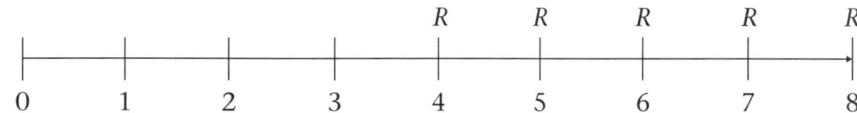

Present date

Notice that in this case, four interest periods elapse before the cash flows begin. Notice also that from an end-of-period-3 vantage point, the annuity appears to be an ordinary annuity.

To illustrate how to determine the **future value of a deferred annuity,** assume that at the beginning of year 1 you decide to make five $1,000 annual deposits in a savings account, the first deposit to be made at the end of year 4. How

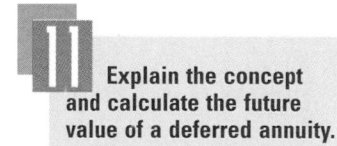

11 Explain the concept and calculate the future value of a deferred annuity.

EXHIBIT A–12	Relationship Between Table D (Present Value of an Ordinary Annuity) and Table E (Present Value of an Annuity Due)			
	Interest Rate (i) = 10%			
	Table D Factors			**Table E Factors**
n	$P_{\overline{n}|10\%}$	$\times$	$(1 + i)$	$=$	$(P_{\overline{n}|10\%})(1.10)$
1	.9091		1.10		1.0000
2	1.7355		1.10		1.9091
3	2.4869		1.10		2.7355
4	3.1699		1.10		3.4869
5	3.7908		1.10		4.1699
6	4.3553		1.10		4.7908

much will be in the account at the end of year 8 if the savings account earns interest at 10 percent? The time diagram for this example is as follows:

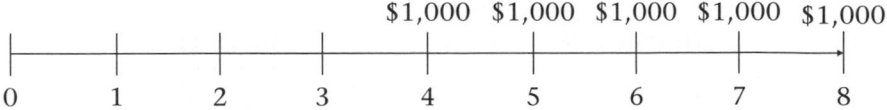

Since no deposits are made before the end of year 4, we can view the deferred annuity as the future value of a $1,000 ordinary annuity for five rents at 10 percent:

$$A = \$1,000(A_{\overline{5}|10\%})$$
$$= \$1,000(6.1051)$$
$$= \$6,105.10$$

Notice that the future value of a deferred annuity is exactly the same as the future value of an ordinary annuity. The three-year deferral has no effect on the future value, because the first cash flow does not occur until the end of year 4.

12 Explain the concept and calculate the present value of a deferred annuity.

Many problems in accounting practice deal with the **present value of a deferred annuity.** Accountants often are required to find the present value of a stream of cash flows that will begin several years in the future. Determining the present value of future retirement benefits from a pension plan is one example. Or, assume that you want to make five annual withdrawals of $1,000 from a savings account, the first withdrawal to be made at the end of year 4. How much must you deposit at the beginning of year 1 if the savings account will earn interest at 10 percent?

To find the present value of this deferred annuity, we can split the problem into two parts, as demonstrated by the following time diagram and calculations:

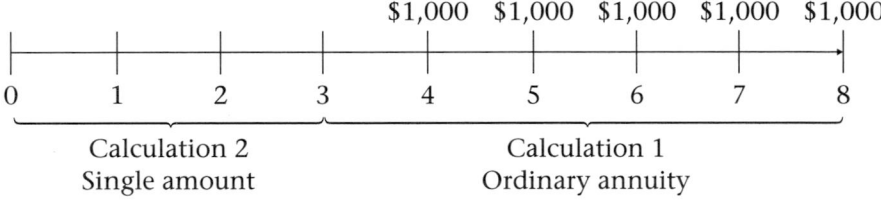

Calculations:

1. Find the present value of the ordinary annuity at the end of year 3.

1. $P = \$1,000(P_{\overline{5}|10\%})$
   $= \$1,000(3.7908)$
   $= \$3,790.80$

2. Consider the answer in part 1 as a single amount at the end of year 3. Find the present value of this amount at the beginning of year 1.

2. $p = \$3,790.80(p_{\overline{3}|10\%})$
   $= \$3,790.80(.7513)$
   $= \$2,848.00$

These two calculations can be combined into one calculation, as follows:

$$P = \$1,000(P_{\overline{5}|10\%})(p_{\overline{3}|10\%})$$
$$= \$1,000(3.7908)(.7513)$$
$$= \$2,848.00$$

In summary, if, at the beginning of year 1, $2,848.00 is deposited in a savings account that earns 10 percent interest, the account will total $3,790.80 at the end of year 3. That amount will allow annual withdrawals of $1,000, beginning at the end of year 4. After the fifth withdrawal at the end of year 8, the savings account balance will be zero, Exhibit A–13 is based on this problem, and shows that the savings account will be exhausted at the end of year 8. Notice that the amount on deposit at the end of year 3 corresponds, except for rounding, to the first calculation in the first approach for determining the present value of the deferred annuity.

Exhibit A–14 summarizes the present and future value concepts discussed in this appendix. As you study the exhibit, use the time diagram to visualize the cash flows.

EXHIBIT A-13		Schedule of Interest and Withdrawals for a Deferred Annuity				
Year	Beginning Balance	+	Interest at 10%[a]	− Withdrawals	=	Ending Balance
0						$2,848.00
1	$2,848.00		$284.80	—		3,132.80
2	3,132.80		313.28	—		3,446.08
3	3,446.08		344.61	—		3,790.69
4	3,790.69		379.07	$1,000		3,169.76
5	3,169.76		316.98	1,000		2,486.74
6	2,486.74		248.68	1,000		1,735.42
7	1,735.42		173.54	1,000		908.96
8	908.96		90.90	1,000		0.00[b]

[a]10% times the beginning balance.
[b]Rounding error of $.14.

ACCOUNTING APPLICATIONS OF PRESENT AND FUTURE VALUE

We are now ready to consider some specific accounting applications of present and future value concepts. These illustrations are by no means exhaustive. Other applications of present and future values appear throughout this text.

Valuing Long-Term Bonds

A company that issues a long-term bond usually incurs *two* obligations: (1) the obligation to pay interest periodically over the life of the bond; and (2) the obligation to pay the maturity value, or face value, of the bond at maturity. Present value concepts are used to calculate the issue price of the bond given the face amount, the market interest rate, the stated interest rate on the bond, and the bond's maturity date.

Assume, for example, that Pilloff Corporation plans to issue bonds that have a maturity value of $100,000, pay annual interest at 6 percent, and mature in 10 years. What is the issue price of the bonds if, at the date of sale, the current market rate of interest for bonds of similar risk is (1) 6 percent, (2) 10 percent, and (3) 4 percent?

Intuitively, you probably suspect that if the stated interest rate on the bonds equals the market rate of 6 percent, the bonds will sell at par value (the face amount of $100,000). You also may suspect that if the current market rate of interest is 10 percent but the stated rate on the bonds is only 6 percent, no one will pay par value, because doing so will provide a rate of return each year of only 6 percent (rate of return = interest ÷ principal = $6,000 ÷ $100,000). Economic theory tells us that under these circumstances, the demand for these bonds will not support an issue price of $100,000. A buyer will pay no more than a price that provides an *effective yield* equal to the current market rate of interest. A similar statement can be made where the market rate of interest—say 4 percent—is less than the stated rate. In this instance, the price will be bid up over the par value until the effective yield equals the current market rate of interest.

Notice that the cash flows for a bond's interest payments are an annuity and the principal payment is a single amount. The issue price of the bond can therefore be calculated by finding the present values of the interest annuity and of the

13 Apply the concepts of future and present value to the measurement of and accounting for long-term debt, pension obligations, and lease obligations.

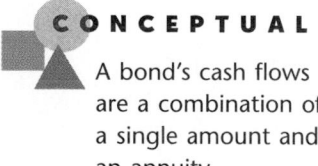

CONCEPTUAL

A bond's cash flows are a combination of a single amount and an annuity.

EXHIBIT A–14   Representative Problems Based on Concepts of Present and Future Value

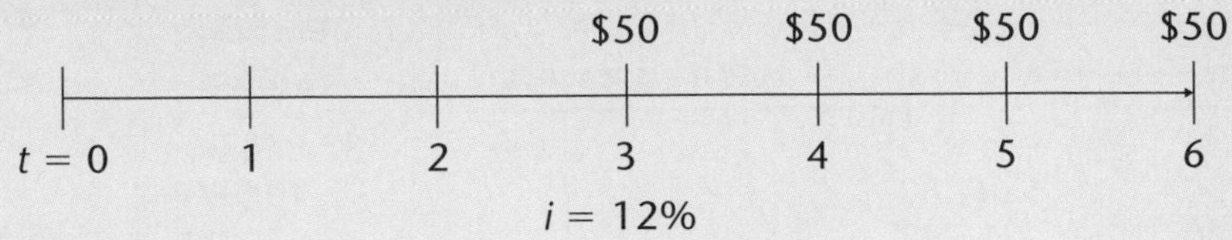

$$\$50 \quad \$50 \quad \$50 \quad \$50$$

$$t = 0 \quad 1 \quad 2 \quad 3 \quad 4 \quad 5 \quad 6$$

$$i = 12\%$$

Problem	Concept	Solution
1. What is the future value at $t = 6$ of the $\$50$ cash flow occurring at $t = 3$?	Future value of a single amount	$a = p(a_{\overline{3}\rceil 12\%})$ $= \$50(1.4049)$ $= \$70.25$
2. What is the present value at $t = 2$ of the $\$50$ cash flow occurring at $t = 6$?	Present value of a single amount	$p = a(p_{\overline{4}\rceil 12\%})$ $= \$50(.6355)$ $= \$31.78$
3. At $t = 2$, what is the future value at the end of period 6 of the $\$50$ cash flows occurring at $t = 3$ through 6?	Future value of an ordinary annuity	$A = R(A_{\overline{4}\rceil 12\%})$ $= \$50(4.7793)$ $= \$238.97$
4. At $t = 3$, what is the future value at the end of period 6 of the $\$50$ cash flows occurring at $t = 3$ through 5?	Future value of an annuity due	$A_D = R(A_{\overline{3}\rceil 12\%})(1.12)$ $= \$50(3.7793)$ $= \$188.97$
5. What is the present value at $t = 2$ of the $\$50$ cash flows occurring at $t = 3$ through 6?	Present value of an ordinary annuity	$P = R(P_{\overline{4}\rceil 12\%})$ $= \$50(3.0373)$ $= \$151.87$
6. What is the present value at $t = 3$ of the $\$50$ cash flows occurring at $t = 3$ through 5?	Present value of an annuity due	$P_D = R(P_{D\overline{3}\rceil 12\%})$ $= \$50(2.6901)$ $= \$134.51$
7. At $t = 0$, what is the future value at the end of period 6 of the $\$50$ cash flows occurring at $t = 3$ through 6?	Future value of a deferred annuity	$A = R(A_{\overline{4}\rceil 12\%})$ $= \$50(4.7793)$ $= \$238.97$
8. What is the present value at $t = 0$ of the $\$50$ cash flows occurring at $t = 3$ through 6?	Present value of a deferred annuity	$P = R(P_{\overline{4}\rceil 12\%})$ $= \$50(3.0373)$ $= \$151.87$ and $p = \$151.87\,(p_{\overline{2}\rceil 12\%})$ $= \$151.87(.7972)$ $= \$121.07$

principal amount due on the maturity date. The issue price calculations appear in Exhibit A–15. The time diagram for the cash flows appears as follows:

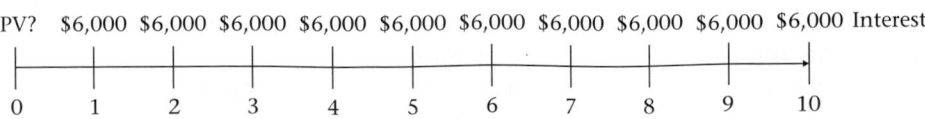

$100,000 Principal

PV? $6,000 $6,000 $6,000 $6,000 $6,000 $6,000 $6,000 $6,000 $6,000 $6,000 Interest

0   1   2   3   4   5   6   7   8   9   10

The calculations show that to yield 4 percent, the bonds must sell for $116,225. That is, they will sell at a *premium* of $16,225 over their par value. On the other

EXHIBIT A–15	Using Present Value Concepts in Bond Valuation		
	Selling Price of Bonds to Provide an Effective Yield of		
	4%	**6%**	**10%**
Present value of principal:			
$100,000(.6756)[a]	$ 67,560		
100,000(.5584)[b]		$ 55,840	
100,000(.3855)[c]			$38,550
plus			
Present value of interest:			
$6,000(8.1109)[d]	48,665		
6,000(7.3601)[e]		44,160	
6,000(6.1446)[f]			36,868
Issue price	$116,225	$100,000	$75,418

[a] $p\,\overline{_{10}}\,_{4\%} = .6756$ [c] $p\,\overline{_{10}}\,_{10\%} = .3855$ [e] $P\,\overline{_{10}}\,_{6\%} = 7.3601$
[b] $p\,\overline{_{10}}\,_{6\%} = .5584$ [d] $P\,\overline{_{10}}\,_{4\%} = 8.1109$ [f] $P\,\overline{_{10}}\,_{10\%} = 6.1446$

hand, to yield an effective rate of 10 percent, the bonds must sell for $75,418—a *discount* of $24,582 (the $100,000 par value minus $75,418). Accounting for bonds and other types of debt is discussed in depth in Chapter 14.

Obligations Arising Under Employer Pension Plans

Accountants often are required to determine the present value of a company's pension obligations for financial reporting purposes. To illustrate, assume that at the beginning of year 1, Sullivan Corporation initiated a pension plan under which each of its employees would receive a pension annuity of $1,000 per year, beginning one year after retirement and continuing until death. Employee A will retire at the end of year 7 and, according to mortality tables, is expected to live long enough to receive eight pension payments. What is the present value of Sullivan Corporation's pension obligation to Employee A at the beginning of year 1, if the interest rate is 10 percent?

As Exhibit A–16 indicates, the pension payments represent a *deferred annuity*. The present value of the deferred annuity is calculated in the exhibit. We find that Sullivan Corporation's pension obligation at the beginning of year 1 is $2,737.87. In practice, pension plans are much more complicated than this example. Our purpose here is merely to show how present value concepts apply to the determination of pension obligations. Accounting for pensions is discussed in more detail in Chapter 16.

EXHIBIT A–16	Using Present Value Concepts to Determine Pension Obligations

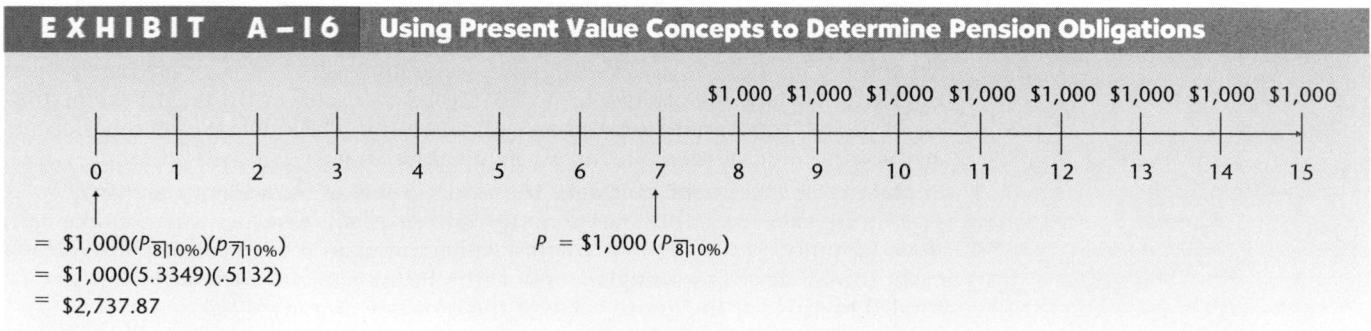

Notice that we can treat the present value of the ordinary annuity at the end of year 7 as a single amount ($5,334.90) and then find its present value at the beginning of year 1.

Lease Obligations

Many companies lease, rather than purchase, property for use in their business. For example, on July 1, 1998, Key signed a 25-year noncancelable lease agreement with Chace Real Estate for a building. The lease term covered the remaining life of the building. The annual lease payments were $12,000 payable each July 1; the first lease payment was due July 1, 1998. What is the present value of this lease obligation at a discount rate of 10 percent?

Because the first lease payment is due on the date of the lease agreement, we are calculating the present value of an annuity due:

$$P_D = R(P_{\overline{n}|i})(1 + i)$$
$$= \$12,000(P_{\overline{25}|10\%})(1.10)$$
$$= \$12,000(9.0770)(1.10)$$
$$= \$12,000(9.9847)$$
$$= \$119,816$$

The present value of this lease obligation, $119,816, may also be thought of as the cash equivalent exchange price of the building. Many accountants and users of financial statements believe that present values of lease obligations should be disclosed in the financial statements in order to satisfy the financial reporting objectives discussed in Chapter 2. This leasing issue and others are discussed in Chapter 15.

SUMMARY OF LEARNING OBJECTIVES

1. Explain the concept of interest.
Interest is the cost of borrowing money or the return from lending money.

2. Explain the variables that affect the dollar amount of interest.
Other things being equal, the larger the amount of principal, the larger the amount of interest; the higher the rate of interest, the larger the amount of interest; and the longer the time period, the larger the amount of interest.

3. Differentiate between simple interest and compound interest.
Simple interest is interest earned only on the original amount borrowed or lent (principal). Compound interest is interest earned on both principal and interest. The principal increases each period as interest for that period is added to it.

4. Explain the concept and calculate the future value of a single amount.
The future value of a single amount is an amount that is borrowed/invested for several interest periods at a specified rate of interest and that accumulates to a larger amount because of compounding.

5. Explain the concept and calculate the present value of a single amount.
The present value of a single amount is the value today (the present value) of a single amount to be received/paid at some future date. The interest (discount) factor for the present value of a single amount is the reciprocal of the interest factor for the future value of a single amount.

6. Define an annuity and distinguish between an ordinary annuity and an annuity due.
An annuity is a series of equal cash flows, sometimes called rents, occurring at equal intervals over a period of time. If the first cash flow occurs at the end of the first interest period, the annuity is called an ordinary annuity. If the first cash flows occurs at the beginning of the first interest period, the annuity is called an annuity due.

7. Explain the concept and calculate the future value of an ordinary annuity.
The future value of an ordinary annuity is the amount to which the periodic cash flows (annuity) plus compound interest will accumulate at some future point. If each cash flow is viewed as a single amount, the future value of each cash flow can be totaled to arrive at the future value of the ordinary annuity.

8. Explain the concept and calculate the present value of an ordinary annuity.
The present value of an ordinary annuity is the value today of the periodic cash flows (annuity) discounted at a given rate of interest. If each cash flow is viewed as

a single amount, the present value of each cash flow can be totaled to arrive at the present value of the ordinary annuity.

9. **Explain the concept and calculate the future value of an annuity due.**
   The future value of an annuity due is the amount to which the periodic cash flows (annuity) plus compound interest will accumulate at some future point. If each cash flow is viewed as a single amount, the future value of each cash flow can be totaled to arrive at the future value of the annuity due.

10. **Explain the concept and calculate the present value of an annuity due.**
    The present value of an annuity due is the value today of the periodic cash flows (annuity) discounted at a given rate of interest. If each cash flow is viewed as a single amount, the present value of each cash flow can be totaled to arrive at the present value of the annuity due.

11. **Explain the concept and calculate the future value of a deferred annuity.**
    A deferred annuity is an annuity in which the first cash flow occurs after at least two interest periods have passed. The future value of a deferred annuity is calculated in exactly the same manner as the future value of an ordinary annuity and the results are the same.

12. **Explain the concept and calculate the present value of a deferred annuity.**
    A deferred annuity is an annuity in which the first cash flow occurs after at least two interest periods have passed. The present value of a deferred annuity is calculated in two parts: first, find the present value of the ordinary annuity one interest period before the first cash flow; second, treat this present value as a single amount and find its present value at the present date.

13. **Apply the concepts of future value and present value to the measurement of and accounting for long-term debt, pension obligations, and lease obligations.**
    Present values (single amounts and ordinary annuities) are used to determine the issue price of long-term debt. Present value concepts (deferred annuities) are used to calculate current obligations associated with pension benefits paid during an employee's retirement period. Present value concepts (annuities) are used to determine present obligations associated with long-term leases.

KEY TERMS

annuity 1188

annuity due 1188

compound interest 1180

deferred annuity 1197

effective interest method 1184

future value 1178

future value of a deferred annuity 1197

future value of an annuity due 1195

future value of an ordinary annuity 1188

future value of a single amount 1182

interest 1179

ordinary annuity 1188

present value 1178

present value of a deferred annuity 1198

present value of an annuity due 1196

present value of an ordinary annuity 1190

present value of a single amount 1184

principal 1180

simple interest 1180

time diagram 1182

time value 1178

PRESENT AND FUTURE VALUE TABLES

The tables used to determine the future and present values of 1, the future and present values of an ordinary annuity of 1, and the present value of an annuity due of 1 are presented on pages 1204–1213.

TABLE A	Future Value of I (*a*)

This table shows the compound amount of $1 at various interest rates and for various time periods. The table may be used to find the future value of *any* dollar amount by multiplying the dollar amount by the factor below corresponding to the appropriate interest rate (*i*) and number of periods (*n*).

i

n	1%	1.5%	2%	2.5%	3%	4%	5%
1	1.0100	1.0150	1.0200	1.0250	1.0300	1.0400	1.0500
2	1.0201	1.0302	1.0404	1.0506	1.0609	1.0816	1.1025
3	1.0303	1.0457	1.0612	1.0769	1.0927	1.1249	1.1576
4	1.0406	1.0614	1.0824	1.1038	1.1255	1.1699	1.2155
5	1.0510	1.0773	1.1041	1.1314	1.1593	1.2167	1.2763
6	1.0615	1.0934	1.1262	1.1597	1.1941	1.2653	1.3401
7	1.0721	1.1098	1.1487	1.1887	1.2299	1.3159	1.4071
8	1.0829	1.1265	1.1717	1.2184	1.2668	1.3686	1.4775
9	1.0937	1.1434	1.1951	1.2489	1.3048	1.4233	1.5513
10	1.1046	1.1605	1.2190	1.2801	1.3439	1.4802	1.6289
11	1.1157	1.1779	1.2434	1.3121	1.3842	1.5395	1.7103
12	1.1268	1.1956	1.2682	1.3449	1.4258	1.6010	1.7959
13	1.1381	1.2136	1.2936	1.3785	1.4685	1.6651	1.8856
14	1.1495	1.2318	1.3195	1.4130	1.5126	1.7317	1.9799
15	1.1610	1.2502	1.3459	1.4483	1.5580	1.8009	2.0789
16	1.1726	1.2690	1.3728	1.4845	1.6047	1.8730	2.1829
17	1.1843	1.2880	1.4002	1.5216	1.6528	1.9479	2.2920
18	1.1961	1.3073	1.4282	1.5597	1.7024	2.0258	2.4066
19	1.2081	1.3270	1.4568	1.5987	1.7535	2.1068	2.5270
20	1.2202	1.3469	1.4859	1.6386	1.8061	2.1911	2.6533
21	1.2324	1.3671	1.5157	1.6796	1.8603	2.2788	2.7860
22	1.2447	1.3876	1.5460	1.7216	1.9161	2.3699	2.9253
23	1.2572	1.4084	1.5769	1.7646	1.9736	2.4647	3.0715
24	1.2697	1.4295	1.6084	1.8087	2.0328	2.5633	3.2251
25	1.2824	1.4509	1.6406	1.8539	2.0938	2.6658	3.3864
30	1.3478	1.5631	1.8114	2.0976	2.4273	3.2434	4.3219
50	1.6446	2.1052	2.6916	3.4371	4.3839	7.1067	11.4674

$$a = a_{\overline{n}|i} = (1 + i)^n$$

			i			
6%	8%	10%	12%	16%	20%	*n*
1.0600	1.0800	1.1000	1.1200	1.1600	1.2000	1
1.1236	1.1664	1.2100	1.2544	1.3456	1.4400	2
1.1910	1.2597	1.3310	1.4049	1.5609	1.7280	3
1.2625	1.3605	1.4641	1.5735	1.8106	2.0736	4
1.3382	1.4693	1.6105	1.7623	2.1003	2.4883	5
1.4185	1.5869	1.7716	1.9738	2.4364	2.9860	6
1.5036	1.7138	1.9487	2.2107	2.8262	3.5832	7
1.5938	1.8509	2.1436	2.4760	3.2784	4.2998	8
1.6895	1.9990	2.3579	2.7731	3.8030	5.1598	9
1.7908	2.1589	2.5937	3.1058	4.4114	6.1917	10
1.8983	2.3316	2.8531	3.4786	5.1173	7.4301	11
2.0122	2.5182	3.1384	3.8960	5.9360	8.9161	12
2.1329	2.7196	3.4523	4.3635	6.8858	10.6993	13
2.2609	2.9372	3.7975	4.8871	7.9875	12.8392	14
2.3966	3.1722	4.1772	5.4736	9.2655	15.4070	15
2.5404	3.4259	4.5950	6.1304	10.7480	18.4884	16
2.6928	3.7000	5.0545	6.8660	12.4677	22.1861	17
2.8543	3.9960	5.5599	7.6900	14.4625	26.6233	18
3.0256	4.3157	6.1159	8.6128	16.7765	31.9480	19
3.2071	4.6610	6.7275	9.6463	19.4608	38.3376	20
3.3996	5.0338	7.4002	10.8039	22.5745	46.0051	21
3.6035	5.4365	8.1403	12.1003	26.1864	55.2061	22
3.8198	5.8715	8.9543	13.5523	30.3762	66.2474	23
4.0489	6.3412	9.8497	15.1786	35.2364	79.4969	24
4.2919	6.8485	10.8347	17.0001	40.8742	95.3962	25
5.7435	10.0627	17.4494	29.9599	85.8499	237.3763	30
18.4202	46.9016	117.3909	289.0022	1670.7038	9100.4382	50

TABLE B — Present Value of I (p)

This table shows the present value of $1 discounted at various rates of interest and for various time periods. The table may be used to find the present value of *any* future dollar amount by multiplying the future dollar amount by the table factor corresponding to the appropriate interest rate (*i*) and number of periods (*n*).

i

n	1%	1.5%	2%	2.5%	3%	4%	5%
1	0.9901	0.9852	0.9804	0.9756	0.9709	0.9615	0.9524
2	0.9803	0.9707	0.9612	0.9518	0.9426	0.9246	0.9070
3	0.9706	0.9563	0.9423	0.9286	0.9151	0.8890	0.8638
4	0.9610	0.9422	0.9238	0.9060	0.8885	0.8548	0.8227
5	0.9515	0.9283	0.9057	0.8839	0.8626	0.8219	0.7835
6	0.9420	0.9145	0.8880	0.8623	0.8375	0.7903	0.7462
7	0.9327	0.9010	0.8706	0.8413	0.8131	0.7599	0.7107
8	0.9235	0.8877	0.8535	0.8207	0.7894	0.7307	0.6768
9	0.9143	0.8746	0.8368	0.8007	0.7664	0.7026	0.6446
10	0.9053	0.8617	0.8203	0.7812	0.7441	0.6756	0.6139
11	0.8963	0.8489	0.8043	0.7621	0.7224	0.6496	0.5847
12	0.8874	0.8364	0.7885	0.7436	0.7014	0.6246	0.5568
13	0.8787	0.8240	0.7730	0.7254	0.6810	0.6006	0.5303
14	0.8700	0.8118	0.7579	0.7077	0.6611	0.5775	0.5051
15	0.8613	0.7999	0.7430	0.6905	0.6419	0.5553	0.4810
16	0.8528	0.7880	0.7284	0.6736	0.6232	0.5339	0.4581
17	0.8444	0.7764	0.7142	0.6572	0.6050	0.5134	0.4363
18	0.8360	0.7649	0.7002	0.6412	0.5874	0.4936	0.4155
19	0.8277	0.7536	0.6864	0.6255	0.5703	0.4746	0.3957
20	0.8195	0.7425	0.6730	0.6103	0.5537	0.4564	0.3769
21	0.8114	0.7315	0.6598	0.5954	0.5375	0.4388	0.3589
22	0.8034	0.7207	0.6468	0.5809	0.5219	0.4220	0.3418
23	0.7954	0.7100	0.6342	0.5667	0.5067	0.4057	0.3256
24	0.7876	0.6995	0.6217	0.5529	0.4919	0.3901	0.3101
25	0.7798	0.6892	0.6095	0.5394	0.4776	0.3751	0.2953
30	0.7419	0.6398	0.5521	0.4767	0.4120	0.3083	0.2314
50	0.6080	0.4750	0.3715	0.2909	0.2281	0.1407	0.0872

$$p = p_{\overline{n}|i} = \frac{1}{(1 + i)^n}$$

i

6%	8%	10%	12%	16%	20%	n
0.9434	0.9259	0.9091	0.8929	0.8621	0.8333	1
0.8900	0.8573	0.8264	0.7972	0.7432	0.6944	2
0.8396	0.7938	0.7513	0.7118	0.6407	0.5787	3
0.7921	0.7350	0.6830	0.6355	0.5523	0.4823	4
0.7473	0.6806	0.6209	0.5674	0.4761	0.4019	5
0.7050	0.6302	0.5645	0.5066	0.4104	0.3349	6
0.6651	0.5835	0.5132	0.4523	0.3538	0.2791	7
0.6274	0.5403	0.4665	0.4039	0.3050	0.2326	8
0.5919	0.5002	0.4241	0.3606	0.2630	0.1938	9
0.5584	0.4632	0.3855	0.3220	0.2267	0.1615	10
0.5268	0.4289	0.3505	0.2875	0.1954	0.1346	11
0.4970	0.3971	0.3186	0.2567	0.1685	0.1122	12
0.4688	0.3677	0.2897	0.2292	0.1452	0.0935	13
0.4423	0.3405	0.2633	0.2046	0.1252	0.0779	14
0.4173	0.3152	0.2394	0.1827	0.1079	0.0649	15
0.3936	0.2919	0.2176	0.1631	0.0930	0.0541	16
0.3714	0.2703	0.1978	0.1456	0.0802	0.0451	17
0.3503	0.2502	0.1799	0.1300	0.0691	0.0376	18
0.3305	0.2317	0.1635	0.1161	0.0596	0.0313	19
0.3118	0.2145	0.1486	0.1037	0.0514	0.0261	20
0.2942	0.1987	0.1351	0.0926	0.0443	0.0217	21
0.2775	0.1839	0.1228	0.0826	0.0382	0.0181	22
0.2618	0.1703	0.1117	0.0738	0.0329	0.0151	23
0.2470	0.1577	0.1015	0.0659	0.0284	0.0126	24
0.2330	0.1460	0.0923	0.0588	0.0245	0.0105	25
0.1741	0.0994	0.0573	0.0334	0.0116	0.0042	30
0.0543	0.0213	0.0085	0.0035	0.0006	0.0001	50

| TABLE C | Future Value of an Ordinary Annuity of I (*A*) |

This table shows the future value of an ordinary annuity of $1 at various rates of interest and for various rents. The table may be used to find the future value of an ordinary annuity of *any* dollar amount by multiplying the dollar amount of the rents by the factor corresponding to the appropriate interest rate (*i*) and number of rents (*n*).

i

n	1%	1.5%	2%	2.5%	3%	4%	5%
1	1.0000	1.0000	1.0000	1.0000	1.0000	1.0000	1.0000
2	2.0100	2.0150	2.0200	2.0250	2.0300	2.0400	2.0500
3	3.0301	3.0452	3.0604	3.0756	3.0909	3.1216	3.1525
4	4.0604	4.0909	4.1216	4.1525	4.1836	4.2465	4.3101
5	5.1010	5.1523	5.2040	5.2563	5.3091	5.4163	5.5256
6	6.1520	6.2296	6.3081	6.3877	6.4684	6.6330	6.8019
7	7.2135	7.3230	7.4343	7.5474	7.6625	7.8983	8.1420
8	8.2857	8.4328	8.5830	8.7361	8.8923	9.2142	9.5491
9	9.3685	9.5593	9.7546	9.9545	10.1591	10.5828	11.0266
10	10.4622	10.7027	10.9497	11.2034	11.4639	12.0061	12.5779
11	11.5668	11.8633	12.1687	12.4835	12.8078	13.4864	14.2068
12	12.6825	13.0412	13.4121	13.7956	14.1920	15.0258	15.9171
13	13.8093	14.2368	14.6803	15.1404	15.6178	16.6268	17.7130
14	14.9474	15.4504	15.9739	16.5190	17.0863	18.2919	19.5986
15	16.0969	16.6821	17.2934	17.9319	18.5989	20.0236	21.5786
16	17.2579	17.9324	18.6393	19.3802	20.1569	21.8245	23.6575
17	18.4304	19.2014	20.0121	20.8647	21.7616	23.6975	25.8404
18	19.6148	20.4894	21.4123	22.3864	23.4144	25.6454	28.1324
19	20.8109	21.7967	22.8406	23.9460	25.1169	27.6712	30.5390
20	22.0190	23.1237	24.2974	25.5447	26.8704	29.7781	33.0660
21	23.2392	24.4705	25.7833	27.1833	28.6765	31.9692	35.7193
22	24.4716	25.8376	27.2990	28.8629	30.5368	34.2480	38.5052
23	25.7163	27.2251	28.8450	30.5844	32.4529	36.6179	41.4305
24	26.9735	28.6335	30.4219	32.3490	34.4265	39.0826	44.5020
25	28.2432	30.0630	32.0303	34.1578	36.4593	41.6459	47.7271
30	34.7849	37.5387	40.5681	43.9027	47.5754	56.0849	66.4389
50	64.4632	73.6828	84.5794	97.4844	112.7969	152.6671	209.3480

$$A = A_{\overline{n}|i} = \frac{(1 + i)^n - 1}{i}$$

			i			
6%	8%	10%	12%	16%	20%	n
1.0000	1.0000	1.0000	1.0000	1.0000	1.0000	1
2.0600	2.0800	2.1000	2.1200	2.1600	2.2000	2
3.1836	3.2464	3.3100	3.3744	3.5056	3.6400	3
4.3746	4.5061	4.6410	4.7793	5.0665	5.3680	4
5.6371	5.8666	6.1051	6.3528	6.8771	7.4416	5
6.9753	7.3359	7.7156	8.1152	8.9775	9.9299	6
8.3938	8.9228	9.4872	10.0890	11.4139	12.9159	7
9.8975	10.6366	11.4359	12.2997	14.2401	16.4991	8
11.4913	12.4876	13.5795	14.7757	17.5185	20.7989	9
13.1808	14.4866	15.9374	17.5487	21.3215	25.9587	10
14.9716	16.6455	18.5312	20.6546	25.7329	32.1504	11
16.8699	18.9771	21.3843	24.1331	30.8502	39.5805	12
18.8821	21.4953	24.5227	28.0291	36.7862	48.4966	13
21.0151	24.2149	27.9750	32.3926	43.6720	59.1959	14
23.2760	27.1521	31.7725	37.2797	51.6595	72.0351	15
25.6725	30.3243	35.9497	42.7533	60.9250	87.4421	16
28.2129	33.7502	40.5447	48.8837	71.6730	105.9306	17
30.9057	37.4502	45.5992	55.7497	84.1407	128.1167	18
33.7600	41.4463	51.1591	63.4397	98.6032	154.7400	19
36.7856	45.7620	57.2750	72.0524	115.3797	186.6880	20
39.9927	50.4229	64.0025	81.6987	134.8405	225.0256	21
43.3923	55.4568	71.4027	92.5026	157.4150	271.0307	22
46.9958	60.8933	79.5430	104.6029	183.6014	326.2369	23
50.8156	66.7648	88.4973	118.1552	213.9776	392.4842	24
54.8645	73.1059	98.3471	133.3339	249.2140	471.9811	25
79.0582	113.2832	164.4940	241.3327	530.3117	1181.8816	30
290.3359	573.7702	1163.9085	2400.0183	10435.6488	45497.1910	50

TABLE D | Present Value of an Ordinary Annuity of I (P)

This table shows the present value of an ordinary annuity of $1 at various interest rates and for various rents. The table may be used to find the present value of an ordinary annuity of *any* dollar amount by multiplying the dollar amounts of the rents by the factor corresponding to the appropriate interest rate (*i*) and number of rents (*n*).

i

n	1%	1.5%	2%	2.5%	3%	4%	5%
1	0.9901	0.9852	0.9804	0.9756	0.9709	0.9615	0.9524
2	1.9704	1.9559	1.9416	1.9274	1.9135	1.8861	1.8594
3	2.9410	2.9122	2.8839	2.8560	2.8286	2.7751	2.7232
4	3.9020	3.8544	3.8077	3.7620	3.7171	3.6299	3.5460
5	4.8534	4.7826	4.7135	4.6458	4.5797	4.4518	4.3295
6	5.7955	5.6972	5.6014	5.5081	5.4172	5.2421	5.0757
7	6.7282	6.5982	6.4720	6.3494	6.2303	6.0021	5.7864
8	7.6517	7.4859	7.3255	7.1701	7.0197	6.7327	6.4632
9	8.5660	8.3605	8.1622	7.9709	7.7861	7.4353	7.1078
10	9.4713	9.2222	8.9826	8.7521	8.5302	8.1109	7.7217
11	10.3676	10.0711	9.7868	9.5142	9.2526	8.7605	8.3064
12	11.2551	10.9075	10.5753	10.2578	9.9540	9.3851	8.8633
13	12.1337	11.7315	11.3484	10.9832	10.6350	9.9856	9.3936
14	13.0037	12.5434	12.1063	11.6909	11.2961	10.5631	9.8986
15	13.8651	13.3432	12.8493	12.3814	11.9379	11.1184	10.3797
16	14.7179	14.1313	13.5777	13.0550	12.5611	11.6523	10.8378
17	15.5623	14.9077	14.2919	13.7122	13.1661	12.1657	11.2741
18	16.3983	15.6726	14.9920	14.3534	13.7535	12.6593	11.6896
19	17.2260	16.4262	15.6785	14.9789	14.3238	13.1339	12.0853
20	18.0456	17.1686	16.3514	15.5892	14.8775	13.5903	12.4622
21	18.8570	17.9001	17.0112	16.1846	15.4150	14.0292	12.8212
22	19.6604	18.6208	17.6581	16.7654	15.9369	14.4511	13.1630
23	20.4558	19.3309	18.2922	17.3321	16.4436	14.8568	13.4886
24	21.2434	20.0304	18.9139	17.8850	16.9355	15.2470	13.7986
25	22.0232	20.7196	19.5235	18.4244	17.4132	15.6221	14.0939
30	25.8077	24.0158	22.3965	20.9303	19.6004	17.2920	15.3725
50	39.1961	34.9997	31.4236	28.3623	25.7298	21.4822	18.2559

$$P = P_{\overline{n}|i} = \frac{1 - \dfrac{1}{(1 + i)^n}}{i}$$

6%	8%	10%	12%	16%	20%	n
0.9434	0.9259	0.9091	0.8929	0.8621	0.8333	1
1.8334	1.7833	1.7355	1.6901	1.6052	1.5278	2
2.6730	2.5771	2.4869	2.4018	2.2459	2.1065	3
3.4651	3.3121	3.1699	3.0373	2.7982	2.5887	4
4.2124	3.9927	3.7908	3.6048	3.2743	2.9906	5
4.9173	4.6229	4.3553	4.1114	3.6847	3.3255	6
5.5824	5.2064	4.8684	4.5638	4.0386	3.6046	7
6.2098	5.7466	5.3349	4.9676	4.3436	3.8372	8
6.8017	6.2469	5.7590	5.3283	4.6065	4.0310	9
7.3601	6.7101	6.1446	5.6502	4.8332	4.1925	10
7.8869	7.1390	6.4951	5.9377	5.0286	4.3271	11
8.3838	7.5361	6.8137	6.1944	5.1971	4.4392	12
8.8527	7.9038	7.1034	6.4235	5.3423	4.5327	13
9.2950	8.2442	7.3667	6.6282	3.4675	4.6106	14
9.7122	8.5595	7.6061	6.8109	5.5755	4.6755	15
10.1059	8.8514	7.8237	6.9740	5.6685	4.7296	16
10.4773	9.1216	8.0216	7.1196	5.7487	4.7746	17
10.8276	9.3719	8.2014	7.2497	5.8178	4.8122	18
11.1581	9.6036	8.3649	7.3658	5.8775	4.8435	19
11.4699	9.8181	8.5136	7.4694	5.9288	4.8696	20
11.7641	10.0168	8.6487	7.5620	5.9731	4.8913	21
12.0416	10.2007	8.7715	7.6446	6.0113	4.9094	22
12.3034	10.3711	8.8832	7.7184	6.0442	4.9245	23
12.5504	10.5288	8.9847	7.7843	6.0726	4.9371	24
12.7834	10.6748	9.0770	7.8431	6.0971	4.9476	25
13.7648	11.2578	9.4269	8.0552	6.1772	4.9789	30
15.7619	12.2335	9.9148	8.3045	6.2463	4.9995	50

| **TABLE E** | | **Present Value of an Annuity Due of $1 ($P_D$)** | | | | | |

This table shows the present value of an annuity due of $1 at various rates of interest and for various numbers of rents. The table may be used to find the present value of an annuity due of *any* dollar amount by multiplying the dollar amount of the rents by the appropriate factors corresponding to the interest rate (*i*) and number of rents (*n*).

i

n	1%	1.5%	2%	2.5%	3%	4%	5%
1	1.0000	1.0000	1.0000	1.0000	1.0000	1.0000	1.0000
2	1.9901	1.9852	1.9804	1.9756	1.9709	1.9615	1.9524
3	2.9704	2.9559	2.9416	2.9274	2.9135	2.8861	2.8594
4	3.9410	3.9122	3.8839	3.8560	3.8286	3.7751	3.7232
5	4.9020	4.8544	4.8077	4.7620	4.7171	4.6299	4.5460
6	5.8534	5.7826	5.7135	5.6458	5.5797	5.4518	5.3295
7	6.7955	6.6972	6.6014	6.5081	6.4172	6.2421	6.0757
8	7.7282	7.5982	7.4720	7.3494	7.2303	7.0021	6.7864
9	8.6517	8.4859	8.3255	8.1701	8.0197	7.7327	7.4632
10	9.5660	9.3605	9.1622	8.9709	8.7861	8.4353	8.1078
11	10.4713	10.2222	9.9826	9.7521	9.5302	9.1109	8.7217
12	11.3676	11.0711	10.7869	10.5142	10.2526	9.7605	9.3064
13	12.2551	11.9075	11.5753	11.2578	10.9540	10.3851	9.8633
14	13.1337	12.7315	12.3484	11.9832	11.6350	10.9857	10.3936
15	14.0037	13.5434	13.1063	12.6909	12.2961	11.5631	10.8986
16	14.8651	14.3432	13.8493	13.3814	12.9379	12.1184	11.3797
17	15.7179	15.1313	14.5777	14.0550	13.5611	12.6523	11.8378
18	16.5623	15.9077	15.2919	14.7122	14.1661	13.1657	12.2741
19	17.3983	16.6726	15.9920	15.3534	14.7535	13.6593	12.6896
20	18.2260	17.4262	16.6785	15.9789	15.3238	14.1339	13.0853
21	19.0456	18.1686	17.3514	16.5892	15.8775	14.5903	13.4622
22	19.8570	18.9001	18.0112	17.1846	16.4150	15.0292	13.8212
23	20.6604	19.6208	18.6581	17.7654	16.9369	15.4511	14.1630
24	21.4558	20.3309	19.2922	18.3321	17.4436	15.8568	14.4886
25	22.2434	21.0304	19.9139	18.8850	17.9355	16.2470	14.7986
30	26.0658	24.3761	22.8444	21.4536	20.1885	17.9837	16.1411
50	39.5881	35.5247	32.0521	29.0714	26.5017	22.3415	19.1687

$$P_D = P_{D\overline{n}|i} = (P_{\overline{n}|i})(1 + i) = \left[\frac{1 - \dfrac{1}{(1 + i)^n}}{i}\right][1 + i]$$

i

6%	8%	10%	12%	16%	20%	n
1.0000	1.0000	1.0000	1.0000	1.0000	1.0000	1
1.9434	1.9259	1.9091	1.8929	1.8621	1.8333	2
2.8334	2.7833	2.7355	2.6901	2.6052	2.5278	3
3.6730	3.5771	3.4869	3.4018	3.2459	3.1065	4
4.4651	4.3121	4.1699	4.0373	3.7982	3.5887	5
5.2124	4.9927	4.7908	4.6048	4.2743	3.9906	6
5.9173	5.6229	5.3553	5.1114	4.6847	4.3255	7
6.5824	6.2064	5.8684	5.5638	5.0386	4.6046	8
7.2098	6.7466	6.3349	5.9676	5.3436	4.8372	9
7.8017	7.2469	6.7590	6.3283	5.6065	5.0310	10
8.3601	7.7101	7.1446	6.6502	5.8332	5.1925	11
8.8869	8.1390	7.4951	6.9377	6.0286	5.3271	12
9.3838	8.5361	7.8137	7.1944	6.1971	5.4392	13
9.8527	8.9038	8.1034	7.4235	6.3423	5.5327	14
10.2950	9.2442	8.3667	7.6282	6.4675	5.6106	15
10.7123	9.5595	8.6061	7.8109	6.5755	5.6755	16
11.1059	9.8514	8.8237	7.9740	6.6685	5.7296	17
11.4773	10.1216	9.0216	8.1196	6.7487	5.7746	18
11.8276	10.3719	9.2014	8.2497	6.8178	5.8122	19
12.1581	10.6036	9.3649	8.3658	6.8775	5.8435	20
12.4699	10.8182	9.5136	8.4694	6.9288	5.8696	21
12.7641	11.0168	9.6487	8.5620	6.9731	5.8913	22
13.0416	11.2007	9.7715	8.6446	7.0113	5.9094	23
13.3034	11.3711	9.8832	8.7184	7.0442	5.9245	24
13.5504	11.5288	9.9847	8.7843	7.0726	5.9371	25
14.5907	12.1584	10.3696	9.0218	7.1656	5.9747	30
16.7076	13.2122	10.9063	9.3010	7.2457	5.9993	50

QUESTIONS

Q A-1. How are present and future value concepts used by the professional accountant?

Q A-2. Define interest.

Q A-3. Distinguish between simple interest and compound interest, and between interest and discount.

Q A-4. Since interest rates usually are stated as annual rates, what adjustments must be made when compounding or discounting occurs more often than once each year?

Q A-5. Given an interest rate of 12 percent, calculate the interest rate per period and the number of compounding periods for each of the following situations:
1. Semiannual compounding for 4 years.
2. Annual compounding for 10 years.
3. Quarterly compounding for 6 years.
4. Monthly compounding for 12 years.

Q A-6. Define an annuity.

Q A-7. Distinguish between an ordinary annuity and an annuity due.

Q A-8. Construct a time diagram for the present value of an ordinary annuity of cash flows of $R for three years, if the interest rate is 10 percent compounded semiannually.

Q A-9. How is the future value of an ordinary annuity related to the future value of a single amount?

Q A-10. How is the present value of an ordinary annuity related to the present value of a single amount?

Q A-11. How is the future value of a single amount related to the present value of a single amount?

Q A-12. What is a deferred annuity?

Q A-13. What formula modification must be made to use Table C to find future values of annuities due?

Q A-14. What formula modification must be made to use Table D to find present values of annuities due?

Q A-15. Explain how the future value-of-1 formula, $(1 + i)^n$, and the related future value factors pertain to the following:
1. Present value of 1.
2. Future value of an ordinary annuity.
3. Future value of an annuity due.
4. Present value of an ordinary annuity.
5. Present value of an annuity due.

CASES

C A-1 **PRESENT AND FUTURE VALUE RELATIONSHIPS** A hard-nosed professor teaching accounting at a prestigious university once remarked to a colleague: "On *my* examinations that cover present and future value, the only table that I provide to students is a table that gives the future value factors for a single amount. With that, they can solve any present or future value problem. Otherwise, I have failed as their teacher."

REQUIRED Recognizing that the table the professor was referring to is represented by Table A in this appendix, discuss the validity of the assertion that with it students "can solve any present or future value problem." Give examples to support your position.

C A-2 **ANNUITY APPLICATION** A bank in Oklahoma City advertised the following proposal in order to attract deposits: "If you will deposit $1,000 per year (at the end of each year) for 10 years in our bank, at the end of 10 years you may begin withdrawing $1,594 annually for the rest of *your* life, for the rest of your *children's* lives, for the rest of your *grandchildren's* lives. These annual withdrawals may continue forever and ever!"

REQUIRED Assume that the bank pays 10 percent interest on deposits. Explain and demonstrate how the bank could make such an attractive proposal.

C A-3 **AN ETHICAL ISSUE INVOLVING PRESENT VALUE** Sammy Joe's Oil Company is an oil and gas exploration company. The company leases land, performs geological surveys,

and drills for oil and gas deposits. Sammy Joe's top executives participate in a profit-sharing plan, whereby they receive stock options and cash bonuses based on net income each year.

Federal authorities specify quite extensive reclamation guidelines for restoring leased land to its original and natural condition, and failure to follow these guidelines can result in significant fines. During the current year, Sammy Joe was fined $10 million for failing to follow federal reclamation guidelines. The company's chief accountant proposed recording this fine by debiting expenses and crediting a liability for $10 million. Management, on the other hand, was reluctant to record this fine as it would result in a huge net loss for the current year, reduce Sammy Joe's equity, and increase its liabilities to the point where the company would be in violation of all of its debt covenants.

Given the bureaucratic nature of the federal agency that levied the fine and the possible length of a potential appeals process, it was not certain when Sammy Joe would be required to pay the fine. Therefore, management decided to record the fine at its present value of $1.08 million, under the assumption that an appropriate discount rate was 16 percent and that the fine might not be paid for at least 15 years.

REQUIRED
1. What are the ethical issues in this case?
2. What stakeholders could be harmed by management's accounting policy decision?
3. What are your recommendations about how the fine should be recorded?

EXERCISES

E A-1. **CONCEPT APPLICATIONS** For each of the lettered amounts, select the numbered concept that applies to the problem and name the table (Table A, Table B, etc.) that should be used to solve the problem.

1. Future value of a single amount.
2. Present value of a single amount.
3. Future value of an ordinary annuity.
4. Present value of an ordinary annuity.
5. Future value of an annuity due.
6. Present value of an annuity due.
7. Future value of a deferred annuity.
8. Present value of a deferred annuity.

a) The amount owed today if a debt of $xx is due in 10 years.
b) The amount that will accumulate if $xx is deposited at the beginning of each year for 10 years.
c) The annual periodic payment required to liquidate a debt due today. The payments will be made at the end of each year and will be made for 10 years.
d) The amount to which $xx deposited today will accumulate in 15 years.
e) The present value of 10 semiannual payments of $xx, the first of which is to be received in 2 1/2 years.
f) The annual periodic deposit required to accumulate $xx at the end of 15 years. The deposits are made at the beginning of each year, beginning today.
g) Same as item f, except that the first payment is made at the beginning of the fourth year.
h) The amount of proceeds if an interest-bearing bond maturing in 10 years is sold today.
i) The amount of proceeds if a non-interest-bearing note maturing in 5 years is issued today.
j) The amount required to liquidate a debt 10 years before maturity. The debt is due 15 years from today.

E A-2. **USE OF PRESENT AND FUTURE VALUE TABLES** Using the tables in this appendix, find the appropriate table factors for the following present value and future value concepts, where i = annual interest rate and n = number of years.

1. Present value of 1 when i = 10 percent compounded annually, n = 10.
2. Future value of 1 when i = 12 percent compounded quarterly, n = 4.
3. Future value of an ordinary annuity when i = 10 percent compounded semiannually, n = 10.
4. Present value of annuity due when i = 6 percent compounded annually, n = 10.
5. Present value of an ordinary annuity when i = 12 percent compounded monthly, n = 2.
6. Future value of annuity due when i = 8 percent compounded annually, n = 15.
7. Present value of a deferred annuity when i = 6 percent compounded annually, n = 10. The first cash flow occurs at the end of Year 3.

E A-3.   **FUTURE VALUES AND PRESENT VALUES OF SINGLE AMOUNTS**

1. Calculate the future value of the following amounts for the indicated interest rates and years:

	AMOUNT INVESTED	*i*	COMPOUNDED	YEARS
a)	$4,800	10%	Semiannually	5
b)	3,600	8	Annually	4
c)	3,600	12	Quarterly	4

2. Calculate the present value of the following future amounts for the indicated interest rates and years:

	FUTURE VALUE	*i*	COMPOUNDED	YEARS
a)	$60,000	6%	Annually	8
b)	21,000	8	Semiannually	5
c)	24,000	12	Monthly	2

E A-4.   **FUTURE VALUES AND PRESENT VALUES OF ANNUITIES**

1. Calculate the future value of the following ordinary annuities at the indicated interest rates and interest periods:

	PERIODIC CASH FLOW	*i*	COMPOUNDED	YEARS
a)	$1,000	10%	Annually	4
b)	1,600	12	Quarterly	4
c)	2,000	10	Semiannually	5

2. Use the same instructions as in part 1, but now assume that the annuities are annuities due.

3. Calculate the present value of the following ordinary annuities at the indicated interest rates and interest periods:

	PERIODIC CASH FLOW	*i*	COMPOUNDED	YEARS
a)	$10,000	4%	Annually	10
b)	10,000	8	Semiannually	6
c)	10,000	8	Quarterly	4

4. Use the same instructions as in part 3, but now assume that the annuities are annuities due.

E A-5.   **FINDING UNKNOWN VARIABLES**   For each situation below, all of which deal with single amounts, find the unknown variable (*x*). Assume that interest is compounded annually.

	FUTURE VALUE	PRESENT VALUE	*i*	*n* (YEARS)
1.	$48,000	$ *x*	10%	10
2.	16,000	4,988.80	*x*	20
3.	31,722	10,000.00	8	*x*
4.	16,098	8,000.00	*x*	12
5.	25,000	17,624.00	6	*x*

E A-6. **FINDING UNKNOWN VARIABLES** For each situation below, all of which deal with annuities, find the unknown variable (x). Assume that each cash flow occurs at the end of each year and that interest is compounded annually.

	FUTURE VALUE (A) OR PRESENT VALUE (P)	R	i	n
1.	$12,000 ($A$)	$ x	8%	6
2.	10,000 (P)	x	10	15
3.	8,000 (A)	1,500	4	x
4.	18,000 (A)	1,000	x	13
5.	16,500 (P)	2,000	10	x
6.	20,000 (P)	2,000	x	24

E A-7. **SINGLE AMOUNTS** On December 25, 1998, Ms. Kris Kringle received for her twenty-first birthday the sum of $25,000, the result of an investment her father made on the date of her birth.

REQUIRED Calculate the amount of the original investment at an earnings rate of 8 percent compounded annually.

E A-8. **SINGLE AMOUNTS** On January 1, 1998, Mr. James Raye deposited $6,000 in a savings account that earns interest at the rate of 8 percent compounded semiannually.

REQUIRED Calculate the balance in the account at the end of 2004.

E A-9. **ANNUITIES** Ms. Lau wishes to accumulate $50,000 by investing $5,000 at the beginning of each year in a sinking fund that yields 10 percent compounded annually.

REQUIRED
1. Find the year in which the sinking fund will reach $50,000.
2. Ignoring your answer in part 1, calculate the annuity payments that Ms. Lau could make under this plan to ensure that she had $50,000 at the end of the fifteenth year.
(CGAA, adapted)

E A-10. **VALUATION OF BONDS** Sorter LLP is planning to issue $500,000 (par value) of bonds that mature in 12 years and pay interest at the rate of 8 percent at the end of each year.

REQUIRED Find the selling price of the bonds at the following market (effective) rates of interest:
1. 4%
2. 10%

E A-11. **ANNUITIES—PRESENT AND FUTURE VALUES** On March 1, 1995, Ike Guest made the first of 10 equal annual deposits in a sinking fund. Beginning on March 1, 2011, he will make the first of 10 annual withdrawals of $2,000 from the fund, after which the fund will be exhausted. The interest rate is 8 percent compounded annually.

REQUIRED Calculate the amount of the annual deposits.

E A-12. **CONCEPTS OF PRESENT AND FUTURE VALUE** For each amount below, state which present or future value concept applies and then solve the problem.
1. The amount to which $5,000 will accumulate in 5 years at 6 percent compounded annually.
2. The present value of $3,000 due in 8 years at 6 percent, compounded semiannually.
3. The present value of an ordinary annuity of $2,000 every six months for 10 years at 8 percent, compounded semiannually.
4. The amount of an annuity due of $2,000 every three months for 4 years at 12 percent, compounded quarterly.
5. The present value of an ordinary annuity of $3,000 per year for 15 years at 3 percent, compounded annually.
6. The present value of $4,000 due in 6 years at 8 percent, compounded quarterly.

E A-13. **INTEREST SCHEDULES FOR ANNUITIES**
1. If $50,000 is invested today to earn an annual return of 10 percent, what equal amounts can be withdrawn at the end of the second, third, and fourth years? Construct a schedule showing that the fund balance will be zero at the end of the fourth year.
2. Calculate the semiannual, end-of-period deposit necessary to accumulate a $20,000 fund at the end of three years, if the fund earns interest at the annual rate of 8

percent compounded semiannually. Prepare a schedule showing the accumulation for the three-year period.

3. If $10,000 is invested at the beginning of year 1 at 6 percent, what amount can be withdrawn at the end of each year for three years? Construct a schedule showing that the fund balance will be zero at the end of the third year.

E A-14. **DETERMINING RENTS AND OTHER VARIABLES** Crystal Pour is allowed $3,000 for her old half-ton truck on the purchase of a $20,000 camper. She makes a down payment and retires the debt with 24 monthly payments of $600 each. Money is worth 12 percent per annum compounded monthly.

REQUIRED Calculate the amount of the down payment.

(CGAA, adapted)

E A-15. **DETERMINING RENTS AND OTHER VARIABLES** Ken Murray borrows $45,000 today and wishes to repay it in 20 equal annual installments, the first being payable one year from today. The debt bears interest at 8 percent per year.

REQUIRED Calculate the annual installment payment.

E A-16. **ORDINARY ANNUITY** Mike Jackson will retire five years from today. He wishes to accumulate $60,000 in a trust fund over this period by making 10 equal successive semiannual payments. The first payment will be made six months from today and the last one five years from today's date. The trust fund will earn 3 percent each six months.

REQUIRED Calculate the amount of each semiannual payment that will be necessary to meet his objective.

E A-17. **ANNUITIES DUE** On May 1, 1998, Mr. Thompson opens a new savings account with an initial deposit of $200. He continues to deposit $200 on the first of each month, provided that the accumulated value just before the deposit is less than $5,200; otherwise, he makes no further deposits. The account earns interest at 12 percent compounded monthly.

REQUIRED Find the amount in the account on July 1, 2001.

(CGAA, adapted)

E A-18. **ANNUITIES** Mr. Douglas's mortgage of $300 per month on the first of each month will finally be paid in full on November 1, 1998. The interest rate is 12 percent compounded monthly. After his payment on June 1, 1998, Mr. Douglas wishes to know the present value of the remaining payments.

REQUIRED Find the present value of the remaining payments on June 1, 1998.

(CGAA, adapted)

E A-19. **IMPLICIT INTEREST RATES** A motorcycle can be purchased for either $10,000 cash or $1,274 cash plus 12 successive monthly payments of $800 each.

REQUIRED **1.** Calculate the effective rate of interest per month implicit in the deferred payments.
2. Based on your answer in part 1, calculate the effective *annual* rate.

E A-20. **ANNUITY AND AMOUNT APPLICATIONS** Your client has agreed to sell land for $60,000. He is to receive $5,000 cash at the date of sale, 20 notes of equal amount which will not bear interest, and a lump-sum amount of $5,000 on the date that the last note is paid. The notes are due serially, one each six months, starting six months from the date of sale. It is agreed that the notes will include on their face an amount that will equal 6 percent interest compounded semiannually.

REQUIRED Calculate the amount of each note.

E A-21. **ANNUITIES** Bert Jacobson, an employee of Colvin Centre, asks your advice on the following matter: He is eligible to participate in a company insurance and retirement plan. His payment into the company plan would amount to $1,200 each six months for the next 10 years; and starting with the eleventh year, he would receive an annual payment of $4,000 for life. He does not need insurance protection and states that he can save and invest each six months the amounts otherwise paid into the company plan. His investment will earn 10 percent compounded semiannually. Also, he can continue to earn the same rate on his investment after retirement. He would like to receive an equal amount of funds each six months for 15 years after retirement.

REQUIRED Assuming that he can carry out his personal saving and investing plan, how much can Jacobson expect to have available *each six months* for the 15 years following his retirement?

(AICPA, adapted)

E A-22. **PRESENT AND FUTURE VALUES**

1. Tim DcLco will owe $50,000 at the end of 2002. The interest rate is 8 percent compounded annually. Calculate the four equal annual payments necessary to retire his debt, the first payment to be made at the end of 1999.

2. On May 1, 1998, Evelyn Wertz purchased a new car on a one-year installment contract that required payments of $400 on May 1, 1998, and $400 on the first day of each month thereafter, with the last payment due on April 1, 1999. The annual interest rate is 12 percent compounded monthly. Calculate the apparent cash price for the car at May 1, 1998.

3. Joe Ward has an investment that will be worth $12,000 at the end of year 10. If the interest rate is 8 percent compounded annually, what is the present value of the investment at the beginning of year 1?

E A-23. **ANNUITIES—CHANGING RENTS** Jerry and Gerri Nelson would like to double their annual home mortgage payments. They have a 10 percent mortgage, which at the current rate of payment will be fully paid off in 20 years. If they decide to double their annual payments, how many years will it take them to pay it off? For simplicity, assume that mortgage payments are made once a year, at the end of the year.

E A-24. **CALCULATING RENTS** Ms. Monroe has obligations of $8,000 due August 1, 2000, and $9,000 due August 1, 2001. She and her creditor agree to settle the debt with two equal payments on August 1, 1998, and August 1, 1999. The interest rate is 12 percent compounded annually.

REQUIRED Find the size of the two equal payments.

E A-25. **ANNUITIES; SEVERAL RENTS** In calculating the present value of an ordinary annuity, we use the table factor from Table D, which is based on the formula

$$P_{\overline{n}|i} = \frac{1 - \dfrac{1}{(1+i)^n}}{i}$$

REQUIRED

1. Assuming that $i = 10$ percent, calculate the present value of an ordinary annuity of $30 each period for (a) 25 periods and (b) 50 periods.

2. Are your answers to part 1 fairly close to $300? If so, what might you conclude about present values of annuities that extend over *very* long periods of time? (*Hint:* Notice that the table factors under the 10 percent column get closer and closer to the factor of 10.000 and that the $30 cash flow $\div$ .10 = $300.)

E A-26. **ORDINARY ANNUITIES AND PRESENT VALUES** The city of Sugarland wishes to accumulate $400,000 by making equal successive payments into a fund at the end of each six months for five years. The fund bears interest at 5 percent, compounded semiannually.

REQUIRED Calculate the amount of each of the payments.

E A-27. **ORDINARY ANNUITIES AND PRESENT VALUES** Refer to Exercise A-26, but assume instead that the city desires to make one lump-sum payment immediately that would accumulate to $400,000 by the end of the fifth year.

REQUIRED Calculate the amount of the payment.

E A-28. **CHANGING INTEREST RATES** Franz deposited $2,000 at the end of each year in a savings account. Six deposits were made over a six-year period.

REQUIRED

1. How much had accumulated at the end of the sixth year if the account earned 8 percent each of the first three years and 10 percent each of the last three years?

2. Prepare a schedule showing the growth in the savings account during the six-year period.

E A-29. **ANNUITIES** On January 1, 1998, an inventor sold the rights to a patent to a university and received a cash payment of $12,000. The university also agreed to pay an additional $1,200 five years from January 1, 1998, and at the end of each succeeding year forever.

REQUIRED Find the present value of these payments on January 1, 1998, at a 10 percent annual rate of return.

E A-30. **PRESENT AND FUTURE VALUES; TABLE SELECTION** Reproduced below are the first three lines from the 2 percent columns of each of several present and future value tables. For each of the following items, you are to select from among these fragmentary tables the one from which the amount required can be obtained *most directly* (assuming that the complete table is available in each instance):

1. The amount to which a single sum would accumulate at compound interest by the end of a specified period (interest compounded annually).

2. The amount that must be appropriated at the end of each of a specific number of years to provide for the accumulation, at annually compounded interest, of a certain sum.

3. The amount that must be deposited in a fund that will earn interest at a specified rate, compounded annually, in order to make possible the withdrawal of certain equal sums annually over a specified period starting one year from date of deposit.

4. The amount of interest that will accumulate on a single deposit by the end of a specified period (interest compounded semiannually).

5. The amount, net of compound discount, that if paid now would settle a debt of larger amount due at a specified future date.

PERIODS	TABLE A	TABLE B	TABLE C	TABLE D	TABLE E	TABLE F
0	1.0000		1.0000			
1	0.9804	1.0200	1.0200	1.0000	0.9804	1.0200
2	0.9612	2.0604	1.0404	0.4950	1.9416	0.5150
3		3.1216		0.3268	2.8839	0.3468

(AICPA, adapted)

PROBLEMS

P A-I. **PRESENT VALUE ANALYSIS** Okoma State University is planning on building a modern all-sports facility. The project will be financed as follows: Okoma will receive $9,000,000 in cash by issuing "revenue" debt with a stated interest rate of 6 percent. The cash will be used to construct the facility. Once the facility has been in operation for three years, the debt will be retired by making a series of equal payments at the end of each year to the debtholders. Each equal payment will include interest at the 6 percent rate. The net cash inflows from sports events (cash operating revenues less cash operating expenses) will provide the funds for retiring the debt.

Okoma estimates that the annual net cash inflows available to service the debt (principal and interest payments) will be $1,500,000. Okoma's Board of Regents would like to be able to retire the debt in ten years, once the facility is in operation.

REQUIRED   Determine if Okoma State University will be able to retire the debt in ten years, once its sports facility is in operation.

P A-2. **PRESENT VALUE ANALYSIS** Mel-Lacy Investment Corporation is considering buying a piece of property and renting it to off-road vehicle enthusiasts. Mel-Lacy estimates that the property can be rented each year for $4,000, payable at the beginning of each year, and that $500 per year will be required in property taxes and other costs, payable at the end of each year. At the end of fifteen years, the property can be sold to the county for $12,500. Mel-Lacy Corporation requires an 8 percent return on investments of similar risks.

REQUIRED   Calculate the maximum amount that Mel-Lacy should pay for the property.

P A-3. **SOLVING FOR UNKNOWN VARIABLES—SINGLE AMOUNTS** Mary Melody made a deposit of $75,000 in a savings account. After she had left the amount on deposit for 12 years at 8 percent interest, the resultant accumulation was $188,865.

REQUIRED   1. Show how the accumulated amount could be determined.
2. Assume that the number of interest periods is unknown but the other three values are known. Show how the number of periods could be determined.
3. Assume that the interest rate is unknown but the other three values are known. Show how the interest rate could be determined.

P A-4. **SOLVING FOR UNKNOWN VARIABLES—ANNUITIES** Rocky Duckworth received $2,000 per year for nine years, beginning at the end of year 1. At an interest rate of 10 percent, the value of this annuity at the beginning of year 1 was $11,518.

REQUIRED   1. Show how the amount received could be determined.
2. Assume that the number of interest periods is unknown but the other three values are known. Show how the number of periods could be determined.
3. Assume that the interest rate is unknown but the other three values are known. Show how the interest rate could be determined.

P A-5. **PRESENT VALUE ANALYSIS** One of your clients is considering leasing a new dump truck for twelve years from Farmer Brown Construction Company. The dump truck has a fair value of $60,000 at the beginning of the lease term. The lease agreement requires your client to make annual lease payments of $6,416 at the beginning of each year for twelve years. At the end of the lease term, the dump truck is returned to Farmer Brown. You are aware that the lease payments provide a 6 percent rate of return to Farmer Brown. The 6 percent rate of return considers the residual value of the dump truck that accrues to Farmer Brown at the end of the lease term.

REQUIRED Calculate the residual value of the dump truck at the end of the lease term (the end of the twelfth year).

P A-6. **ANNUITIES** Exactly eight years ago the Trennepohls bought an interest in a condominium for $20,000. They paid $2,000 down and $2,000 on each subsequent anniversary date. Rather than paying the usual $2,000, which is due today, they have decided to pay off the entire debt. The agreement permits them to pay off any part of the debt without penalty.

REQUIRED Calculate the amount of cash the Trennepohls will need to pay off the entire debt if the interest rate on the debt is 8 percent.

P A-7. **DEFERRED ANNUITIES** A company wishes to know how much must be invested today ($t = 0$) in a trust fund earning interest at 8 percent compounded annually in order to make the following withdrawals:

t	AMOUNT WITHDRAWN AT END OF PERIOD
7	$4,500
8	4,500
9	8,000
10	8,000

REQUIRED Calculate the amount that must be deposited.

P A-8. **DEFERRED ANNUITIES** Jesse Garon will begin attending college 10 years from today. His father estimates his son's expenses to be $15,000 per year for each of the first 2 years and $20,000 for each of the last 3 years that Jesse will attend school. His father plans to invest an equal amount each year, beginning a year from today, for 9 years and estimates that the investment will earn 10 percent compounded annually. Assume that each year's investment will be made at the end of the year and that Jesse's expenses occur at the beginning of each school year.

REQUIRED Calculate how much Jesse's father must invest each year.

P A-9. **RATE OF RETURN; EFFECTIVE INTEREST METHOD** Blackstone, Inc., acquires an asset with a fair value of $100,000 by issuing a $100,000, 8 percent note payable. The asset will generate end-of-year cash flows of $41,635 each year for three years and will have zero salvage value at the end of the third year. The note will be paid in three equal end-of-year payments. Each payment will include interest.

The company's president disagrees with the controller on how to account for the asset, liability, and net income over the three-year period. The president feels that, in order to smooth income and with the increased emphasis on cash flows, net income each year should be the difference between the cash inflow from the asset and the cash payment on the note. The controller believes that net income should be the difference between the earnings on the asset (based on the asset's effective rate of return) and the interest expense on the note, calculated using the effective interest method.

REQUIRED 1. Calculate (a) the effective rate of return on the asset and (b) the annual end-of-year payments on the note.
2. Using the president's approach, calculate each year's net income and the total net income over the three-year period.
3. Using the controller's approach, calculate each year's net income and the total net income over the three-year period.
4. Do you prefer the president's approach or the controller's approach? Give reasons for your answer.

P A-10. **PRESENT VALUE APPLICATIONS** Several years ago, Creative Finance Company (CFC) issued, at face value, $100,000 of 10 percent notes. The notes pay interest annually and mature in six years. Since the market rate of interest for similar bonds currently is above 10 percent, CFC would like to retire these notes and report a retirement gain on its income statement. However, state regulatory authorities will not permit the retirement.

On the advice of counsel, CFC has decided to invest cash in a certificate of deposit issued by Financenet. The CD currently is paying 12 percent on six-year certificates. The amount to be deposited will be the present value of CFC's note obligation, discounted at 12 percent. This amount will be sufficient to service the interest on the notes and to retire the notes at maturity. If CFC signs a written agreement to leave the certificate of deposit at Financenet during the six-year period, regulatory authorities will permit CFC to report a gain equal to the difference between the $100,000 carrying value of the notes and the amount of the certificate of deposit.

REQUIRED
1. Calculate the amount of the Financenet certificate of deposit and the amount of the gain.
2. Prepare a schedule that demonstrates that the cash flows from the certificate of deposit will be sufficient to service the notes. Assume that interest on the certificate of deposit is paid annually and that CFC can adjust the principal amount of the certificate at the end of each year; that is, interest may be added to the principal at the end of each year.

P A-11. **PRESENT VALUE; LOTTERIES** On the morning of January 3, 1998, Alaina Harrington purchased a "pick six" lottery ticket in her state and won the $5,000,000 jackpot that afternoon. The jackpot was payable over a 25-year period. On January 3, 1998, the state paid Alaina $200,000 cash and issued her a note for $4,800,000, payable in 25 installments of $192,000 each December 31, beginning on December 31, 1998. In order to provide assured funding for payment of the lottery jackpot over the 25-year period, the state purchased an annuity from an insurance company on January 3, 1998, at a cost of $2,049,562. This annuity would provide the annual lottery prize payments for Alaina Harrington.

REQUIRED
1. Calculate the effective interest rate associated with the annuity contract.
2. Calculate the state's 1998 expense associated with the lottery prize award.
3. Prepare the state's journal entry associated with the lottery award and annuity purchase.

P A-12. **CHANGING INTEREST RATES** Churchhill deposited $20,000 in a savings account on January 1, 1998, and left it on deposit for eight years.

REQUIRED
1. How much had accumulated on December 31, 2005, if the savings account earned 8 percent for each of the first two years, 10 percent for each of the next three years, and 12 percent for each of the last three years?
2. Prepare a schedule showing the growth in the savings account from January 1, 1998, through December 31, 2005.

P A-13. **DEFERRED ANNUITIES** Pickens is contemplating making a tender offer for the common stock of McGee Corporation. Although McGee presently is not generating any net cash inflows, Pickens estimates that McGee's average annual net cash flows will be $400,000 beginning 6 years from now and continuing for 30 years. Pickens desires a 12 percent rate of return on its investments.

REQUIRED
Calculate the amount that Pickens should offer for McGee's stock using the following approaches:
1. Find the present value of McGee's cash flows at the end of year 5; then find the present value at the beginning of the first year.
2. Find the future value of McGee's cash flows at the end of year 35; then find the present value at the beginning of the first year.

P A-14. **PRESENT AND FUTURE VALUE; MISCELLANEOUS**
1. A company has a $100,000 bond issue due and payable on January 1, 2005. What amount must be deposited on January 1, 1998, in order to accumulate $100,000? The deposit earns 10 percent compounded annually.
2. A company wishes to invest an amount on January 1, 1998, that will allow the company to pay each of its 20 employees an annual retirement benefit of $8,000. These payments will begin on December 31, 2003, and will extend through December 31, 2009. The investment will earn 8 percent compounded annually. How much should the company invest on January 1, 1998?
3. A couple purchased a car for $30,000. They made a down payment of $2,500 and financed the balance, to be repaid over 50 months, from their credit union. The

credit union's interest rate is 12 percent compounded monthly, and payments are due at the end of each month. Calculate the couple's monthly payments to the credit union.

4. Refer to part 3. Assume that immediately after making the 30th payment, the couple decides to pay off the loan to the credit union. Calculate the amount to be paid to the credit union.

5. On January 1, 1998, you purchase a bond that will mature in 15 years and will have a maturity value of $25,000 at that time. The bond is a non-interest-bearing bond (sometimes called a zero-coupon bond). At the time of your purchase, the effective annual yield on this bond is 10 percent. Calculate your purchase price.

6. On January 1, 1998, you invest $5,000 in a mutual stock fund that has been earning a rate of return of 8 percent compounded annually. You also plan to invest an additional $2,000 each year for 10 years, beginning on December 31, 1998. Calculate the value of your mutual fund investment one year after having made your tenth $2,000 investment.

P A-15. **EFFECTIVE INTEREST RATES AND RENTS** You recently have inherited $100,000 from a rich aunt and are comparing savings accounts at four banks. You plan to deposit the $100,000 inheritance in one of the banks for a two-year period, after which you will use the proceeds to buy either a catamaran or a small beach house. The following savings plans apply at the four banks:

BANK	INTEREST PAID ON DEPOSITS
ONEOK	12% compounded annually
Mercantile Trust	12% compounded semiannually
Farmer's National	12% compounded quarterly
J. James State	12% compounded monthly

REQUIRED

1. Calculate the effective annual interest rate (yield) for each bank.

2. Assume that you deposited $25,000 (1/4 × $100,000) in each bank at the beginning of year 1. Calculate the total amount of your investment at the end of the second year.

3. Assume instead that you decided to make your $100,000 deposit in J. James State (this bank gave free travel miles). After making the deposit at the beginning of year 1, you decided to make 12 equal monthly withdrawals, beginning at the end of the first month of year 2. Calculate the amount of each withdrawal.

4. Refer to part 3. Assume instead that you decided to withdraw $5,000 at the end of each month for 12 months, beginning at the end of the first month of year 2. Calculate your deposit balance at the end of the second year.

P A-16. **ANNUITY APPLICATIONS**

1. Barry Bickle deposits $8,000 in a savings account at the beginning of 1998. What is the approximate number of quarterly $1,000 withdrawals that he can make if the interest rate is 8 percent compounded quarterly? The first withdrawal will be made at the end of the first quarter of 1999.

2. Wayne Thomas is considering an investment that promises annual cash flows of $900 at the end of each year for six years starting at the end of year 4. If the interest rate is 6 percent, what is the present value of the investment at the beginning of year 1?

3. Prepare a schedule for part 2 which demonstrates that the present value is sufficient to allow six cash flows of $900 beginning at the end of year 4.

P A-17. **ANNUITY AND SINGLE AMOUNT APPLICATIONS**

1. Your client wishes to provide for the payment of an obligation of $300,000 due on July 1, 2006. She plans to deposit $24,000 in a special fund each July 1 for eight years, starting July 1, 1999. She also wishes to make an initial deposit on July 1, 1998, of an amount which, with its accumulated interest, will bring the fund up to $300,000 at the maturity of the obligation. She expects that the fund will earn interest at the rate of 4 percent compounded annually. Calculate the amount to be deposited on July 1, 1998.

2. Your client has made annual payments of $5,000 into a fund at the close of each year for the past nine years. The fund balance immediately after the ninth payment totaled $52,914. She has asked you how many more $5,000 annual payments will be required to bring the fund to $75,000, assuming that the fund continues to earn interest at 4 percent compounded annually. Calculate the number of full payments required and the amount of the final payment if the entire $5,000 is not required.

(AICPA, adapted)

P A-18. **VALUATION OF NOTES** On January 1, 1998, Culpepper Corporation issued $1 million in five-year, 8 percent installment notes to be repaid in the amount of $200,000 on January 1, 1999, 2000, 2001, 2002, and 2003. Interest is payable at the end of each year. The notes were sold to yield a rate of 6 percent.

REQUIRED **1.** Construct a time diagram showing the cash flow obligations for Culpepper Corporation in connection with the notes issued.

2. Prepare a schedule showing the calculation of the total amount received from the issuance of the installment notes.

(AICPA, adapted)

P A-19. **INTEREST-BEARING AND ZERO-COUPON BONDS** HiRollers, an investment club, is considering investing in one of two security issues. The two investment alternatives are as follows:

Alternative 1: Invest $12,418 in zero-coupon (non-interest-bearing) notes of Sports Company. The notes, which have a maturity value of $20,000, mature in five years.

Alternative 2: Invest $12,418 in interest-bearing bonds of Unlimited Company. The bonds pay 10 percent interest at the end of each year. The bonds have a maturity value of $12,418 and mature in five years.

The securities of both companies are of equal risk. The investment club desires a 10 percent rate of return on its investments.

REQUIRED **1.** Demonstrate that the effective rate of return on the Sports Company notes is 10 percent.

2. Assuming that the investment club can invest funds at a 10 percent rate of return over the next five years, prepare a schedule showing that both alternatives allow the accumulation of $20,000 at the end of the fifth year.

P A-20. **NOTE VALUATION** James Jackson purchases a tract of land with a fair value of $120,000 by paying $30,000 cash and issuing a five-year, non-interest-bearing note for the balance. The seller of the land desires an 8 percent rate of return on financing activities. Thus, the note's maturity value should reflect an 8 percent interest cost.

REQUIRED **1.** Calculate the necessary maturity value of the note at the end of the five-year period.

2. Prepare a schedule that shows James Jackson's interest expense for each year and the carrying value of the note payable at the end of each year.

P A-21. **FINANCING ALTERNATIVES** Herrmann has decided to purchase a new automobile for $15,000 and to finance the purchase either through the automobile dealer, a local bank, or her credit union. The financing arrangement for each alternative is as follows:

Automobile dealer: Ten percent down, with the balance payable in eight equal monthly installments, beginning one month from the purchase date. The interest rate charged on the loan is 1 percent per month on the outstanding balance.

Local bank: Twenty percent down, eight monthly payments of $1,500, beginning one month from the purchase date, with a lump-sum balloon payment at the end of eight months. The interest rate charged is 1½ percent per month on the outstanding balance.

Credit union: No down payment and eight equal monthly payments, beginning on the purchase date. The interest rate charged is 1 percent per month on the outstanding balance.

REQUIRED For each alternative, prepare a schedule showing the beginning-of-month loan balance, interest expense for the month, the monthly cash payment, and the end-of-month loan balance.

P A-22. **ASSET VALUATION AT PRESENT VALUE** On January 1, 1998, Jean Canning founded Canning Racing Company by investing $30,000 cash. The company immediately acquired a De Soto GT for use in stock car racing. The car was to be used in three races—one race at the end of each year, beginning December 31, 1998. Canning estimated that the net cash inflow from racing at the end of each year would be $11,000, $12,100, and $13,310 for 1998, 1999, and 2000, respectively. These net cash inflows would provide Canning Racing Company a 10 percent rate of return on its $30,000 investment. At the end of the three-year period, the De Soto GT's estimated resale value (salvage value) will be zero.

Canning Racing Company is considering investing in other similar racing cars. Jean Canning will have to finance these investments by raising funds from the general public

and is considering how to present financial information about the De Soto GT's operating income and cash flows.

REQUIRED
1. Verify that the above cash flows provide a 10 percent rate of return.
2. Assume that Canning Racing Company applies generally accepted accounting principles. Canning will use straight-line depreciation over the three-year period for the De Soto GT. Prepare income statements for each year.
3. Refer to part 2 and your solution. Calculate Canning's rate of return on racing activities each year by dividing each year's net income by the beginning-of-year book value (cost less accumulated depreciation). Comment briefly on your results.
4. Canning has heard of a new method of depreciation called "direct valuation." Under this method, assets are valued in terms of the present value of future cash flows. Depreciation expense each year is the decline in the present value of the net cash flows associated with the asset. Calculate depreciation expense each year using this method.
5. Refer to part 4 and your solution. Prepare income statements for each year using "value depreciation."
6. Refer to part 5 and your solution. Calculate Canning's rate of return on racing activities each year by dividing each year's net income by the beginning-of-year book value (cost less accumulated depreciation). Comment briefly on your results.
7. Discuss some difficulties in applying "direct valuation" as a general method of accounting for depreciable assets.

P A-23. **FINANCIAL REPORTING PROBLEM: GENERAL ELECTRIC** The annual report for General Electric Corporation appears in Appendix B of this text. Refer to the following sections of the annual report that are covered by the auditors' report: earnings, financial position, cash flows, and notes to consolidated financial statements.

REQUIRED
Write a short report that lists and describes General Electric's 1995 business transactions, financial statement accounts, or other events that mention the concept of interest.

General Electric Annual Report 1995

Contents

Financial Section

Revenues

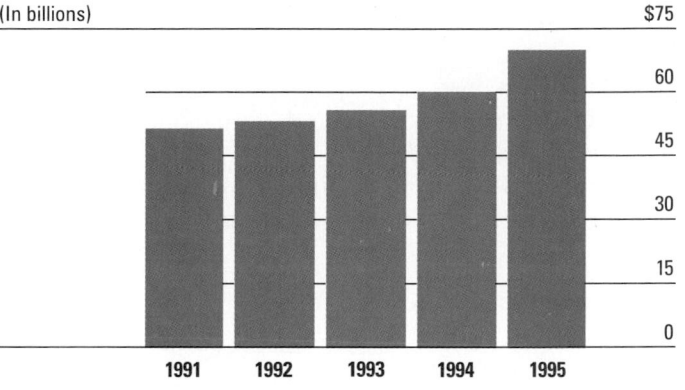

Earnings per share from continuing operations before accounting changes

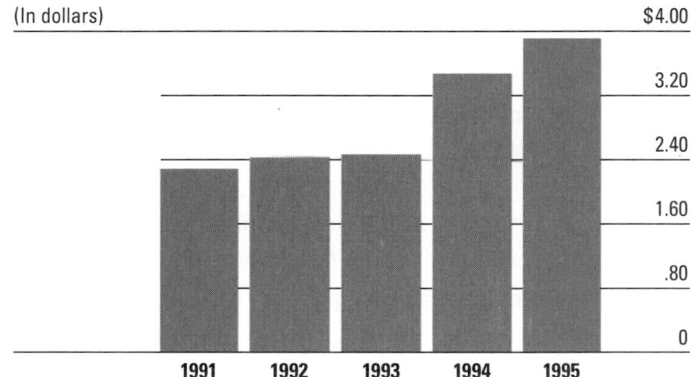

Dividends per share

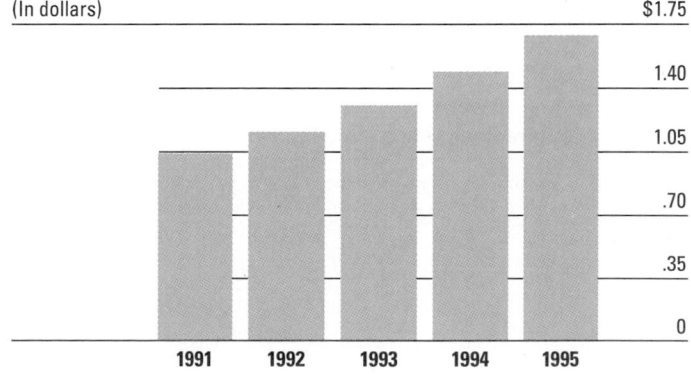

Statement of Earnings

For the years ended December 31 (In millions)	General Electric Company and consolidated affiliates		
	1995	1994	1993
Revenues			
Sales of goods	$33,157	$30,740	$29,509
Sales of services	9,733	8,803	8,268
Other income (note 3)	752	793	735
Earnings of GECS from continuing operations	—	—	—
GECS revenues from operations (note 4)	26,386	19,773	17,189
Total revenues	70,028	60,109	55,701
Costs and expenses (note 5)			
Cost of goods sold	24,288	22,748	22,606
Cost of services sold	6,682	6,214	6,308
Interest and other financial charges	7,286	4,949	4,054
Insurance losses and policyholder and annuity benefits	5,285	3,507	3,172
Provision for losses on financing receivables (note 8)	1,117	873	987
Other costs and expenses	15,429	12,987	12,287
Minority interest in net earnings of consolidated affiliates	204	170	151
Total costs and expenses	60,291	51,448	49,565
Earnings from continuing operations before income taxes and accounting change	9,737	8,661	6,136
Provision for income taxes (note 9)	(3,164)	(2,746)	(1,952)
Earnings from continuing operations before accounting change	6,573	5,915	4,184
Earnings (loss) from discontinued operations (note 2)	—	(1,189)	993
Earnings before accounting change	6,573	4,726	5,177
Cumulative effect of accounting change (note 20)	—	—	(862)
Net earnings	$ 6,573	$ 4,726	$ 4,315
Net earnings per share (in dollars)			
Continuing operations before accounting change	$ 3.90	$ 3.46	$ 2.45
Discontinued operations before accounting change	—	(0.69)	0.58
Earnings before accounting change	3.90	2.77	3.03
Cumulative effect of accounting change	—	—	(0.51)
Net earnings per share	$ 3.90	$ 2.77	$ 2.52
Dividends declared per share (in dollars)	$ 1.69	$ 1.49	$ 1.305

The notes to consolidated financial statements on pages 45-64 are an integral part of this statement.

	GE			GECS		
	1995	1994	1993	**1995**	1994	1993
	$33,177	$30,767	$29,533	$ —	$ —	$ —
	9,836	8,863	8,289	—	—	—
	753	783	730	—	—	—
	2,415	2,085	1,567	—	—	—
	—	—	—	26,492	19,875	17,276
	46,181	42,498	40,119	26,492	19,875	17,276
	24,308	22,775	22,630	—	—	—
	6,785	6,274	6,329	—	—	—
	649	410	525	6,661	4,545	3,538
	—	—	—	5,285	3,507	3,172
	—	—	—	1,117	873	987
	5,743	5,211	5,124	9,769	7,862	7,236
	64	31	17	140	139	134
	37,549	34,701	34,625	22,972	16,926	15,067
	8,632	7,797	5,494	3,520	2,949	2,209
	(2,059)	(1,882)	(1,310)	(1,105)	(864)	(642)
	6,573	5,915	4,184	2,415	2,085	1,567
	—	(1,189)	993	—	(1,189)	240
	6,573	4,726	5,177	2,415	896	1,807
	—	—	(862)	—	—	—
	$ 6,573	$ 4,726	$ 4,315	$ 2,415	$ 896	$ 1,807

In the consolidating data on this page, "GE" means the basis of consolidation as described in note 1 to the consolidated financial statements; "GECS" means General Electric Capital Services, Inc. and all of its affiliates and associated companies. Transactions between GE and GECS have been eliminated from the "General Electric Company and consolidated affiliates" columns on page 26.

Statement of Financial Position

At December 31 (In millions)	General Electric Company and consolidated affiliates	
	1995	1994
Assets		
Cash and equivalents	**$ 2,823**	$ 2,591
Investment securities (note 10)	**41,067**	30,965
Current receivables (note 11)	**8,735**	7,527
Inventories (note 12)	**4,395**	3,880
GECS financing receivables (investment in time sales, loans and financing leases) — net (notes 8 and 13)	**93,272**	76,357
Other GECS receivables	**12,417**	5,763
Property, plant and equipment (including equipment leased to others) — net (note 14)	**25,679**	23,465
Investment in GECS	**—**	—
Intangible assets (note 15)	**13,342**	11,373
All other assets (note 16)	**26,305**	23,950
Total assets	**$228,035**	$185,871
Liabilities and equity		
Short-term borrowings (note 18)	**$ 64,463**	$ 57,781
Accounts payable, principally trade accounts	**9,061**	6,766
Progress collections and price adjustments accrued	**1,812**	2,065
Dividends payable	**767**	699
All other GE current costs and expenses accrued (note 17)	**5,898**	5,543
Long-term borrowings (note 18)	**51,027**	36,979
Insurance liabilities, reserves and annuity benefits (note 19)	**39,699**	29,438
All other liabilities (note 20)	**15,363**	13,161
Deferred income taxes (note 22)	**7,380**	5,205
Total liabilities	**195,470**	157,637
Minority interest in equity of consolidated affiliates (note 23)	**2,956**	1,847
Common stock (1,857,013,000 shares issued)	**594**	594
Unrealized gains (losses) on investment securities	**1,000**	(810)
Other capital	**1,663**	1,122
Retained earnings	**34,528**	30,793
Less common stock held in treasury	**(8,176)**	(5,312)
Total share owners' equity (notes 24 and 25)	**29,609**	26,387
Total liabilities and equity	**$228,035**	$185,871

The notes to consolidated financial statements on pages 45-64 are an integral part of this statement. Year-end 1994 assets and liabilities of Kidder, Peabody Group Inc., the discontinued securities broker-dealer of GECS, have been reclassified to "All other liabilities."

	GE			GECS	
	1995	1994		**1995**	1994
	$ 874	$ 1,373		$ 1,949	$ 1,218
	4	93		41,063	30,872
	8,891	7,807		—	—
	4,395	3,880		—	—
	—	—		93,272	76,357
	—	—		12,897	6,012
	10,234	9,525		15,445	13,940
	12,774	9,380		—	—
	6,643	6,336		6,699	5,037
	11,901	12,419		14,404	11,531
	$55,716	$50,813		**$185,729**	$144,967
	$ 1,666	$ 906		$ 62,808	$ 57,087
	3,968	3,141		5,952	3,777
	1,812	2,065		—	—
	767	699		—	—
	5,747	5,798		—	—
	2,277	2,699		48,790	34,312
	—	—		39,699	29,438
	8,928	8,468		6,312	4,571
	508	268		6,872	4,937
	25,673	24,044		170,433	134,122
	434	382		2,522	1,465
	594	594		1	1
	1,000	(810)		989	(821)
	1,663	1,122		2,266	2,006
	34,528	30,793		9,518	8,194
	(8,176)	(5,312)		—	—
	29,609	26,387		12,774	9,380
	$55,716	$50,813		**$185,729**	$144,967

In the consolidating data on this page, "GE" means the basis of consolidation as described in note 1 to the consolidated financial statements; "GECS" means General Electric Capital Services, Inc. and all of its affiliates and associated companies. Transactions between GE and GECS have been eliminated from the "General Electric Company and consolidated affiliates" columns on page 28.

Statement of Cash Flows

For the years ended December 31 (In millions)	1995	1994	1993
Cash flows from operating activities			
Net earnings	$ 6,573	$ 4,726	$ 4,315
Adjustments for discontinued operations	—	1,189	(993)
Adjustments to reconcile net earnings to cash provided from operating activities			
Cumulative effect of accounting change	—	—	862
Depreciation, depletion and amortization	3,594	3,207	3,223
Earnings retained by GECS — continuing operations	—	—	—
Deferred income taxes	1,047	1,228	548
Decrease (increase) in GE current receivables	(632)	668	(571)
Decrease (increase) in GE inventories	55	(56)	750
Increase (decrease) in accounts payable	244	697	639
Increase in insurance liabilities, reserves and annuity benefits	2,490	1,624	1,479
Provision for losses on financing receivables	1,117	873	987
All other operating activities	458	(2,399)	782
Cash from operating activities	14,946	11,757	12,021
Cash flows from investing activities			
Additions to property, plant and equipment	(6,447)	(7,492)	(4,727)
Dispositions of property, plant and equipment	1,542	2,506	1,139
Net increase in GECS financing receivables	(11,309)	(9,525)	(4,164)
Payments for principal businesses purchased	(5,641)	(2,606)	(2,090)
All other investing activities	(3,362)	372	(6,518)
Cash used for investing activities	(25,217)	(16,745)	(16,360)
Cash flows from financing activities			
Net change in borrowings (maturities of 90 days or less)	(3,487)	(2,784)	2,406
Newly issued debt (maturities longer than 90 days)	37,604	23,239	15,468
Repayments and other reductions (maturities longer than 90 days)	(18,580)	(13,098)	(11,851)
Net purchase of GE shares for treasury	(2,523)	(353)	(364)
Dividends paid to share owners	(2,770)	(2,462)	(2,153)
All other financing activities	259	181	(69)
Cash from (used for) financing activities	10,503	4,723	3,437
Cash from (used for) discontinued operations	—	(200)	962
Increase (decrease) in cash and equivalents during year	232	(465)	60
Cash and equivalents at beginning of year	2,591	3,056	2,996
Cash and equivalents at end of year	$ 2,823	$ 2,591	$ 3,056
Supplemental disclosure of cash flows information			
Cash paid during the year for interest	$ (6,645)	$ (4,524)	$ (3,754)
Cash recovered (paid) during the year for income taxes	(1,483)	(1,777)	(1,644)

The notes to consolidated financial statements on pages 45-64 are an integral part of this statement. Data for 1994 and 1993 have been reclassified to combine cash flows of discontinued operations.

	GE			GECS		
	1995	1994	1993	**1995**	1994	1993
	$ 6,573	$ 4,726	$ 4,315	$ 2,415	$ 896	$ 1,807
	—	1,189	(993)	—	1,189	(240)
	—	—	862	—	—	—
	1,581	1,545	1,631	2,013	1,662	1,592
	(1,324)	(1,181)	(957)	—	—	—
	369	575	120	678	653	428
	(739)	754	(625)	—	—	—
	55	(56)	750	—	—	—
	462	810	114	418	(222)	540
	—	—	—	2,490	1,624	1,479
	—	—	—	1,117	873	987
	(912)	(2,291)	(16)	946	140	770
	6,065	6,071	5,201	10,077	6,815	7,363
	(1,831)	(1,743)	(1,588)	(4,616)	(5,749)	(3,139)
	38	86	55	1,504	2,420	1,084
	—	—	—	(11,309)	(9,525)	(4,164)
	(238)	(575)	—	(5,403)	(2,031)	(2,090)
	408	14	298	(3,913)	176	(6,793)
	(1,623)	(2,218)	(1,235)	(23,737)	(14,709)	(15,102)
	1,061	(566)	46	(4,510)	(2,261)	2,404
	826	766	215	36,778	22,473	15,253
	(1,535)	(1,399)	(2,325)	(17,045)	(11,699)	(9,526)
	(2,523)	(353)	(364)	—	—	—
	(2,770)	(2,462)	(2,153)	(1,091)	(904)	(610)
	—	(2)	—	259	183	(69)
	(4,941)	(4,016)	(4,581)	14,391	7,792	7,452
	—	—	962	—	(200)	—
	(499)	(163)	347	731	(302)	(287)
	1,373	1,536	1,189	1,218	1,520	1,807
	$ 874	$ 1,373	$ 1,536	$ 1,949	$ 1,218	$ 1,520
	$ (468)	$ (374)	$ (473)	$ (6,177)	$ (4,150)	$ (3,281)
	(1,651)	(1,456)	(1,455)	168	(321)	(189)

In the consolidating data on this page, "GE" means the basis of consolidation as described in note 1 to the consolidated financial statements; "GECS" means General Electric Capital Services, Inc. and all of its affiliates and associated companies. Transactions between GE and GECS have been eliminated from the "General Electric Company and consolidated affiliates" columns on page 30.

Management's Discussion of Operations

Overview

General Electric Company's consolidated financial statements represent the combination of the Company's manufacturing and nonfinancial services businesses ("GE") and the accounts of General Electric Capital Services, Inc. ("GECS"). See note 1 to the consolidated financial statements, which explains how the various financial data are presented.

Management's Discussion of Operations is presented in four parts: Consolidated Operations, GE Continuing Operations, GECS Continuing Operations and International Operations.

Consolidated Operations

GE achieved record revenues and earnings in 1995, as broad strength across its businesses, coupled with continued emphasis on globalization, productivity and effective asset management, produced top-line growth, higher margins and strong cash generation. Consolidated revenues, including acquisitions, rose to a record $70.0 billion, a 17% increase that was attributable primarily to the Company's increasing international activities. Eleven of twelve businesses increased revenues, with six businesses — led by GE Capital Services, Plastics and NBC — achieving double-digit increases.

Consolidated earnings per share from continuing operations increased to $3.90, up 13% from last year's $3.46 from continuing operations, and earnings increased 11% to $6.573 billion. Earnings per share grew faster than earnings, reflecting the cumulative impact of $3.2 billion of shares purchased under a three-year, $9 billion share repurchase program initiated in December 1994.

Net earnings in 1995 were 39% higher than 1994's $4.726 billion ($2.77 per share), which were 10% higher than 1993's $4.315 billion ($2.52 per share). Three factors affecting 1994 and 1993 are important to these comparisons: discontinued operations of the GECS securities broker-dealer and the GE Aerospace businesses; 1993 restructuring provisions; and the effect of an accounting change in 1993. Each is discussed separately below. Excluding the effects of these items, 1994 earnings would have been $5.915 billion, up 22% from $4.862 billion in 1993.

- *Discontinued operations* reflected the results of the GECS securities broker-dealer, Kidder, Peabody Group Inc. (Kidder, Peabody) in 1994 and 1993, and the results of the discontinued GE Aerospace businesses in 1993. Note 2 provides additional information about these discontinued operations. The 1994 loss from discontinued operations included a provision of $868 million after taxes for exit costs related to the liquidation of Kidder, Peabody. This liquidation was substantially complete as of December 31, 1995.

- *Restructuring provisions* in 1993, amounting to $678 million after taxes, covered costs of actions that have reduced GE's cost structure. Essentially all restructuring expenditures were completed by the end of 1994. Savings arising from these restructuring programs can best be observed in the growth in operating margin seen in the chart at the bottom of the page and in the productivity measurements discussed on page 33.

- *The 1993 accounting change* represented effects of adopting Statement of Financial Accounting Standards (SFAS) No. 112, *Employers' Accounting for Postemployment Benefits* (see note 20). The transition effect of the accounting change decreased net earnings by $862 million ($0.51 per share), with a corresponding decrease in share owners' equity.

Two newly issued accounting standards will be adopted in the first quarter of 1996 and are not expected to have a material effect on financial position or results of operations of GE or GECS. A summary of these standards follows.

- SFAS No. 121, *Accounting for the Impairment of Long-Lived Assets and for Long-Lived Assets to be Disposed Of,* requires that certain long-lived assets be reviewed for impairment when events or circumstances indicate that the carrying amounts of the assets may not be recoverable. If such review indicates that the carrying amount of an asset exceeds the sum of its expected future cash flows, the asset's carrying value must be written down to fair value.

- SFAS No. 122, *Accounting for Mortgage Servicing Rights,* requires that capitalized rights to service mortgage loans be assessed for impairment by individual risk stratum by comparing each stratum's carrying amount with its fair value. Impairment, if any, would be recognized in earnings.

GE operating margin as a percentage of sales

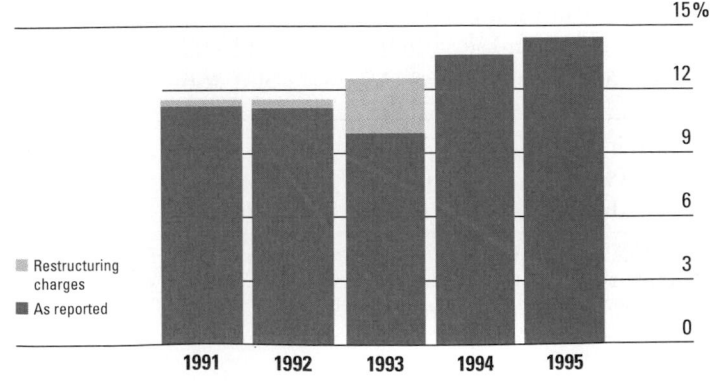

Dividends declared totaled $2.838 billion in 1995. Per-share dividends of $1.69 were up 13% from the previous year, following a 14% increase from the year before. The 1995 increase marks the 20th consecutive year of dividend growth. The chart at right compares GE's dividend growth for the last five years with dividend growth of companies in the Standard and Poor's 500 stock index.

GE Continuing Operations

GE total revenues were $46.2 billion in 1995, compared with $42.5 billion in 1994 and $40.1 billion in 1993.

• GE's sales of goods and services were $43.0 billion in 1995, an increase of 9% from 1994, which in turn was 5% higher than in 1993. The improvement was led by Plastics and NBC. Volume was about 8% higher in 1995, reflecting growth in most businesses and the effect of consolidating Nuovo Pignone, a European energy equipment manufacturer. The effects of selling prices on sales differed markedly among businesses during the year. Overall, selling prices were essentially flat in 1995, while the effect of currency exchange rates on the translation of sales denominated in other than U.S. dollars contributed modestly to the sales increase. Volume in 1994 was about 6% higher than in 1993, but was partially offset by the effects of lower selling prices. Currency exchange rates had a minor negative effect on 1994 sales.

• GE's other income, earned from a wide variety of sources, was $753 million in 1995, $783 million in 1994 and $730 million in 1993. Details of GE's other income are provided in note 3.

• Earnings of GECS from continuing operations were up 16% in 1995, following a 33% increase the year before. See page 36 for an analysis of these earnings.

Principal costs and expenses for GE are those classified as costs of goods and services sold, and selling, general and administrative expenses.

Operating margin is sales of goods and services less the costs of goods and services sold, and selling, general and administrative expenses. In 1995, GE's operating margin rose to a record 14.4% of sales, an improvement of 0.8 percentage points from 1994. The operating margin increase was led by strong improvements in Plastics, Aircraft Engines and NBC. Operating margin was 13.6% of sales in 1994, compared with 12.5% (before restructuring provisions) in 1993. Including restructuring provisions, 1993 operating margin

GE/S&P dividend growth since 1990

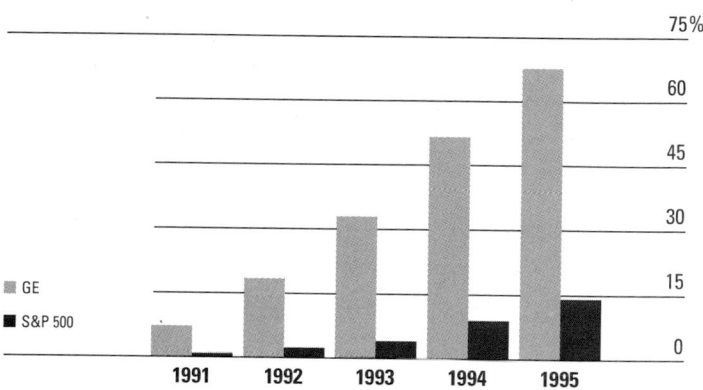

was 9.9% of sales. The improved performance in 1994 was attributable to Appliances, NBC, Power Systems and Transportation Systems, which increased their margin rates by one percentage point or more.

Total cost productivity (sales in relation to costs, both on a constant dollar basis) has been a major source of improvements in operating margin, accounting for more than $1 billion of the increases in margin in each of the last three years. The productivity rate was 3.7% in 1995, reflecting the sharp improvement at Aircraft Engines and improvements at Plastics and Medical Systems, largely offset by adverse productivity performance by Power Systems, the result of its lower 1995 capacity utilization. While the productivity rate in 1994 was reasonably strong throughout most businesses, at 3.2% overall, it reflected adverse results of Aircraft Engines' lower volume. Cost savings provided by productivity improvements more than offset the impact of inflation in each of the last three years.

GE interest expense in 1995 was $649 million, up from $410 million in 1994, which was down from $525 million in 1993. The increase in interest expense was attributable to a number of factors, including higher interest rates and average borrowing levels. The decrease in interest expense in 1994 was primarily the result of lower borrowings partially offset by the effects of higher interest rates.

Entering 1996 with excellent cash flows and a strong balance sheet, the Company continues to be well positioned to deliver strong performance in the current global economic environment.

GE industry segment revenues and operating profit for the past five years are shown in the table on page 35. For additional information, including a description of the products and services included in each segment, see note 27.

• *Aircraft Engines* revenues increased 7% from 1994, which was down 13% from 1993. The revenue increase was primarily attributable to higher volume in commercial and military spares and related services, partially offset by effects of lower selling prices. Operating profit increased 26% from 1994, as significant productivity gains and, to a lesser degree, higher volume more than offset the effects of lower prices. Operating profit increased 17% during 1994, principally because there was no counterpart to 1993 restructuring provisions ($267 million). Excluding 1993 restructuring provisions, operating profit decreased 12% in 1994, largely as a result of lower volume.

In 1995, $1.7 billion of revenues were from sales to the U.S. government, down $0.1 billion from 1994, which was $0.6 billion lower than in 1993. The lower 1994 revenues were primarily attributable to declines in sales for the F110 and T700 engine programs.

Firm orders received during 1995 totaled $5.9 billion, up 7% from $5.5 billion in 1994. The firm orders backlog at year-end 1995 was $7.7 billion ($7.6 billion at the end of 1994), about 38% of which was scheduled for delivery in 1996.

• *Appliances* revenues were about the same as in 1994, as softening North American sales offset strong growth in Europe and Asia. Operating profit increased 2% despite higher material costs, primarily as a result of productivity. Operating profit rose 84% in 1994 on a 7% increase in revenues, in part because there was no counterpart to restructuring provisions of $136 million in 1993. Excluding 1993 restructuring provisions, operating profit increased 34% in 1994, primarily as a result of strong productivity and higher volume.

• *Broadcasting* revenues increased 17% in 1995, following an 8% increase in 1994. The revenue increase in both years was principally attributable to sharply stronger prime-time ratings and improved cable and owned-and-operated station performance, resulting in improved advertising prices throughout the period. Operating profit was up 48% in 1995, as a result of the stronger advertising revenues. Operating profit also increased sharply in 1994, in part because of restructuring provisions of $81 million in 1993. Excluding the effect of those provisions, operating profit improved 45% from 1993, reflecting the impact of stronger advertising, improved ratings performance and substantially improved cable operations.

• *Industrial Products and Systems* revenues rose 8% in 1995, following a 10% increase in 1994. The improvements in revenues in both years were largely attributable to increased volume in Transportation Systems, Lighting, and Motors and Industrial Systems (Motors). Operating profit increased 14% in 1995, after a 47% increase in 1994. The improvement in 1995 resulted from the combination of productivity across the segment and the volume increases, which more than offset higher material costs. The 1994 increase in operating profit reflected primarily the effect of $253 million of restructuring provisions in 1993. Absent restructuring provisions, operating profit increased 15% in 1994, principally because of improved European operations in Lighting and the combination of higher volume and productivity in Motors and Transportation Systems.

Transportation Systems received orders of $1.6 billion in 1995, down $1.2 billion from 1994's record level. The backlog at year-end 1995 was $3.4 billion ($3.5 billion at the end of 1994), about 29% of which was scheduled for shipment in 1996.

• *Materials* revenues increased 17% in 1995, reflecting principally the effects of higher selling prices and the consolidation of Toshiba Silicones. Operating profit increased 51%, primarily because of higher prices, productivity and volume growth, the combination of which more than offset increases in material costs. Revenues were up 13% in 1994, primarily because of increased volume across all major product groups. Operating profit rose 16% in 1994, in part because there was no counterpart to $52 million of restructuring provisions in 1993. Excluding 1993 restructuring provisions, operating profit increased 9%, as ongoing productivity and improved volume more than offset the impact of lower selling prices and much higher material costs.

• *Power Generation* revenues were 10% higher in 1995, following a 7% increase in 1994. The current-year revenue increase was more than accounted for by the 1995 consolidation of Nuovo Pignone ($1.5 billion in revenues). Excluding Nuovo Pignone, the revenue decrease in 1995 resulted from lower volume in both gas and steam turbines. Operating profit decreased 38% in 1995, as the profit contribution of Nuovo Pignone was more than offset by the effects of difficult market conditions on volume and prices, cost inflation, and modification costs related to series "F" gas turbines. Operating profit in 1994 increased 21%, reflecting the effect of 1993 restructuring provisions of $82 million. Adjusting for 1993 restructuring provisions, operating profit increased 12%, primarily as a result of lower material costs and volume improvements that more than offset lower selling prices.

Summary of Industry Segments

For the years ended December 31 (In millions)	General Electric Company and consolidated affiliates				
	1995	1994	1993	1992	1991
Revenues					
GE					
Aircraft Engines	**$ 6,098**	$ 5,714	$ 6,580	$ 7,368	$ 7,777
Appliances	**5,933**	5,965	5,555	5,330	5,225
Broadcasting	**3,919**	3,361	3,102	3,363	3,121
Industrial Products and Systems	**10,194**	9,406	8,575	8,210	8,248
Materials	**6,647**	5,681	5,042	4,853	4,736
Power Generation	**6,545**	5,933	5,530	5,106	4,813
Technical Products and Services	**4,424**	4,285	4,174	4,674	4,686
All Other	**2,707**	2,348	1,803	1,581	1,485
Corporate items and eliminations	**(286)**	(195)	(242)	(399)	(538)
Total GE	**46,181**	42,498	40,119	40,086	39,553
GECS					
Financing	**19,042**	14,932	12,399	10,544	10,069
Specialty Insurance	**7,444**	4,926	4,862	3,863	2,989
All Other	**6**	17	15	11	(5)
Total GECS	**26,492**	19,875	17,276	14,418	13,053
Eliminations	**(2,645)**	(2,264)	(1,694)	(1,453)	(1,323)
Consolidated revenues	**$70,028**	$60,109	$55,701	$53,051	$51,283
Operating profit					
GE					
Aircraft Engines	**$ 1,176**	$ 935	$ 798	$ 1,274	$ 1,390
Appliances	**697**	683	372	386	400
Broadcasting	**738**	500	264	204	209
Industrial Products and Systems	**1,519**	1,328	901	1,071	1,088
Materials	**1,465**	967	834	740	800
Power Generation	**769**	1,238	1,024	854	679
Technical Products and Services	**801**	787	706	912	693
All Other	**2,683**	2,309	1,725	1,495	1,405
Total GE	**9,848**	8,747	6,624	6,936	6,664
GECS					
Financing	**3,045**	2,662	1,727	1,366	1,327
Specialty Insurance	**1,020**	589	770	641	501
All Other	**(545)**	(302)	(288)	(272)	(290)
Total GECS	**3,520**	2,949	2,209	1,735	1,538
Eliminations	**(2,396)**	(2,072)	(1,554)	(1,317)	(1,199)
Consolidated operating profit	**10,972**	9,624	7,279	7,354	7,003
GE interest and financial charges, net of eliminations	**(644)**	(417)	(529)	(752)	(881)
GE items not traceable to segments	**(591)**	(546)	(614)	(629)	(515)
Earnings from continuing operations before income taxes and accounting changes	**$ 9,737**	$ 8,661	$ 6,136	$ 5,973	$ 5,607

The notes to consolidated financial statements on pages 45-64 are an integral part of this statement. "GE" means the basis of consolidation as described in note 1 to the consolidated financial statements; "GECS" means General Electric Capital Services, Inc. and all of its affiliates and associated companies. Operating profit of GE segments excludes interest and other financial charges; operating profit of GECS includes interest and discount expense, which is the largest element of GECS' operating costs.

Power Generation orders were $6.7 billion for 1995, compared with $5.7 billion in 1994. The backlog of unfilled orders at year-end 1995 was $10.2 billion ($9.4 billion at the end of 1994), about 43% of which was scheduled to be shipped in 1996. The increases in orders and backlog were more than accounted for by the consolidation of Nuovo Pignone in 1995.

- *Technical Products and Services* revenues were up 3% in 1995, following a similar increase in 1994, as higher volume was partially offset by lower selling prices in both Medical Systems and Information Services. Medical Systems achieved strong volume growth in Asia and Europe, but the U.S. market was weak throughout both years. Information Services revenues increased in 1995 and 1994, reflecting continued worldwide growth in services associated with electronic commerce. Segment operating profit increased 2% in 1995, primarily a result of productivity gains. The 1994 increase in operating profit of 11% was partially attributable to 1993 restructuring provisions of $60 million. Excluding such provisions, 1994 operating profit was 3% ahead of 1993, reflecting productivity and volume improvements that were partially offset by weaker pricing at both Medical Systems and Information Services.

Orders received by Medical Systems in 1995 were $3.7 billion, up 12% from 1994. The backlog of unfilled orders at year-end 1995 was $1.6 billion ($1.5 billion at the end of 1994), about 94% of which was scheduled to be shipped in 1996.

- *All Other* consists primarily of GECS' earnings, which are discussed in the next section. Also included are revenues derived from licensing the use of GE technology to others.

GECS Continuing Operations

GECS conducts its operations in two segments: Financing and Specialty Insurance. The Financing segment includes financing operations of General Electric Capital Corporation (GE Capital). The Specialty Insurance segment includes operations of GE Global Insurance Holding Corporation (GE Global Insurance), the principal subsidiary of which is Employers Reinsurance Corporation (ERC), and the other insurance businesses described on page 61.

Improved operating results for 1995 and 1994 reflect the effects of asset growth with approximately equal contributions from origination volume and from acquisitions of businesses and portfolios.

- GECS revenues from operations were $26.5 billion in 1995, up 33% from 1994, which was up 15% from 1993.

- GECS earnings from continuing operations were $2.4 billion in 1995, up 16% from 1994, which was up 33% from 1993. The 1995 increase reflected asset growth

partially offset by a decrease in financing spreads (the excess of yields over interest rates on borrowings). The 1994 increase resulted primarily from asset growth, increased financing spreads and improved asset quality, which were partially offset by higher insurance losses.

- GECS interest on borrowings in 1995 was $6.7 billion, 47% higher than in 1994, which was 28% higher than in 1993. Increases in 1995 and 1994 reflected the effects of higher average borrowings used to finance asset growth as well as the effects of higher interest rates. Part of the 1995 increase resulted from a shift during the year to longer-term funding. The composite interest rate on GECS' borrowings was 6.76% in 1995, compared with 5.47% in 1994 and 4.96% in 1993.

- GECS insurance losses and policyholder and annuity benefits increased to $5.3 billion during 1995, compared with $3.5 billion in 1994 and $3.2 billion in 1993, primarily because of business acquisitions and growth in originations throughout the period.

- GECS other costs and expenses increased to $9.8 billion in 1995 from $7.9 billion in 1994 and $7.2 billion in 1993, reflecting costs associated with acquired businesses and portfolios, and higher investment levels.

GECS industry segment revenues and operating profit for the past five years are shown in the table on page 35. Revenues from operations (earned income) are detailed in note 4.

- *Financing segment* revenues from operations were $19.0 billion in 1995, up 28% from 1994, which was up 20% from 1993. Asset growth and increased yields were significant factors in both years.

Operating profit was $3.0 billion in 1995, up 14% from 1994, as the effects of the asset growth were partially offset by declining financing spreads and losses from adverse market conditions in the Mortgage Services business. Financing spreads declined during 1995, as the increase in borrowing rates outpaced the improvements in yields. Operating profit increased 54% in 1994 over 1993, the result of asset growth of 14%, increased financing spreads and improved asset quality. The provision for losses on financing receivables increased in 1995, principally reflecting portfolio growth, following a decline in 1994 that was attributable to improved quality of the portfolio. Other costs and expenses increased in both years, primarily as a result of asset growth.

The portfolio of financing receivables, before allowance for losses, increased to $95.8 billion at the end of 1995 from $78.4 billion at the end of 1994. Financing receivables are the Financing segment's largest asset and its primary source of revenues. The related allowance for losses at the end of

1995 amounted to $2.5 billion (2.63% of receivables — the same as for 1994 and 1993) and, in management's judgment, is appropriate given the risk profile of the portfolio. Amounts written off in 1995 were approximately 1.01% of the year's average financing receivables, compared with 1.04% and 1.59% during 1994 and 1993, respectively. A discussion of the quality of certain elements of the Financing segment portfolio follows. Nonearning receivables are those that are 90 days or more delinquent and reduced-earning receivables are receivables whose terms have been restructured to a below-market yield.

Consumer receivables at year-end 1995 and 1994 are shown in the following table:

(In millions)	1995	1994
Credit card and personal loans	$23,937	$19,124
Auto loans	5,555	3,991
Auto finance leases	12,461	7,473
Total consumer	$41,953	$30,588
Noncarning and reduced-earning	$ 671	$ 422
— As percentage of total	1.6%	1.4%
Receivable write-offs for the year	$ 644	$ 482

Most of the nonearning consumer receivables were U.S. private-label credit card loans, the majority of which were subject to various loss-sharing agreements that provide full or partial recourse to the originating retailer. Delinquencies in the consumer portfolio were slightly higher at the end of 1995 than for 1994, consistent with overall industry experience.

Commercial real estate portfolio at year-end 1995 and 1994 amounted to $17.4 billion and $16.9 billion, respectively, as shown in the following table:

(In millions)	1995	1994
Commercial real estate loans	$13,405	$13,282
Nonearning and reduced-earning loans	179	179
Receivable write-offs for the year	147	209
Assets acquired for resale	2,335	2,103
Other (primarily ventures)	1,651	1,508

Commercial real estate loans are generally secured by first mortgages. Assets are acquired for resale from various financial institutions. Values realized during 1995 and 1994 on disposition of assets acquired for resale have met or exceeded expectations at the time of purchase.

The commercial real estate portfolio includes investments in a variety of property types and continues to be well dispersed geographically, principally in the continental United States. Write-offs in the commercial real estate portfolio declined during 1995, as markets continued to stabilize.

GECS earnings from continuing operations

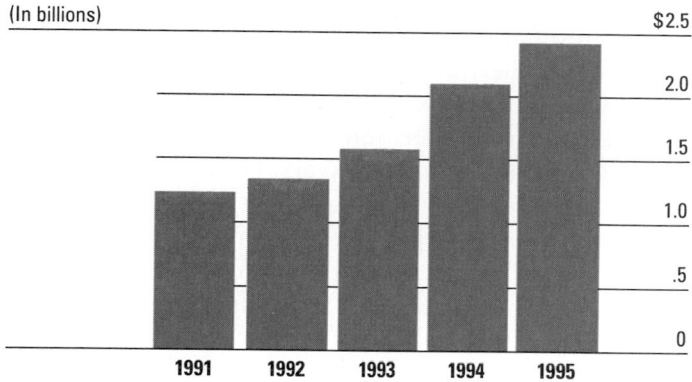

(In billions)

Other financing receivables, totaling $40.4 billion at December 31, 1995, consisted of a diverse commercial, industrial and equipment loan and lease portfolio. This portfolio increased $5.9 billion during 1995, primarily because of acquisitions. The related nonearning and reduced-earning receivables increased to $285 million at year-end 1995 from $165 million at year-end 1994.

GECS held loans and leases to commercial airlines, as discussed in note 16, amounting to $8.3 billion at the end of 1995, up from $7.6 billion at the end of 1994, reflecting purchases of aircraft. At year-end 1995, GECS' commercial aircraft positions included financial guaranties and funding commitments amounting to $409 million ($506 million at year-end 1994) and conditional commitments to purchase aircraft at a cost of $141 million ($81 million at year-end 1994). On January 22, 1996, GECS announced that it had placed a multi-year order for various Boeing aircraft with list prices approximating $4 billion.

• *Specialty Insurance segment* revenues from operations were $7.4 billion in 1995, an increase of 51% from 1994, which was essentially the same as 1993. The increase in 1995 reflected growth, primarily associated with business acquisitions, in the property and casualty reinsurance business. Operating profit increased to $1,020 million in 1995 from $589 million in 1994, principally because there was no current-year counterpart to the 1994 adverse loss development in the private mortgage pool insurance, the result of poor economic conditions and housing value declines in southern California. Operating profit in 1995 also was enhanced by improved returns on investment securities and effects of acquisitions. For 1994, private mortgage pool insurance losses more than offset operating profit increases in other parts of the segment, including primary mortgage insurance.

International Operations

Estimated results of international operations include all exports from the United States plus the results of GE's and GECS' operations located outside the United States. International revenues in 1995 were $26.9 billion (38% of consolidated revenues), compared with $20.0 billion in 1994 and $18.2 billion in 1993. In 1995, about 46% of GE's sales of goods and services were international, compared with about 40% in the previous two years. The chart below left depicts the growth in international revenues in relation to total revenues over the past five years. International operating profit was $3.0 billion (27% of consolidated operating profit) in 1995, compared with $2.6 billion in 1994 and $2.3 billion in 1993.

GE's international revenues were $20.2 billion in 1995, an increase of 24% from 1994, reflecting strong growth in Europe and the Pacific Basin. European revenues increased by $2.5 billion, largely because of the 1995 consolidation of Nuovo Pignone's $1.5 billion of sales. Additionally, many GE businesses, especially Aircraft Engines and Plastics, achieved strong revenue performance in Europe during the year. GE's Pacific Basin revenues were up $0.9 billion in 1995, the result of consolidating Toshiba Silicones in the Plastics business, as well as growth across many other businesses, particularly Medical Systems and Lighting.

GECS' international revenues were $6.7 billion in 1995 and year-end assets were about $43.3 billion. These revenues, which were derived primarily from operations in Europe, Canada and the Pacific Basin, were up sharply from

$3.7 billion in 1994; year-end assets more than doubled during the year from approximately $21.5 billion at the end of 1994. The increase is attributable to expansion of GECS' operations into the international marketplace — expansion that management expects to continue.

The accompanying financial results reported in U.S. dollars are unavoidably affected by currency exchange. A number of techniques are used to manage the effects of currency exchange, including selective borrowings in local currencies and selective hedging of significant cross-currency transactions. International activity is diverse, as shown for revenues in the chart at the bottom right of this page. Principal currencies include those of countries in the European Monetary Union, as well as the Japanese yen and the Canadian dollar.

GE's export sales by major world areas follow.

GE's total exports from the United States

(In millions)	1995	1994	1993
Pacific Basin	$3,397	$3,260	$2,645
Europe	1,701	1,319	2,320
Americas	1,023	1,027	981
Other	964	821	1,039
Exports to external customers	7,085	6,427	6,985
Exports to affiliates	2,123	1,683	1,513
Total exports	$9,208	$8,110	$8,498

GE made a positive 1995 contribution of approximately $5.2 billion to the U.S. balance of trade. Total exports in 1995 were $9.2 billion; direct imports from external suppliers were $2.8 billion; and imports from GE affiliates were $1.2 billion.

Consolidated revenues

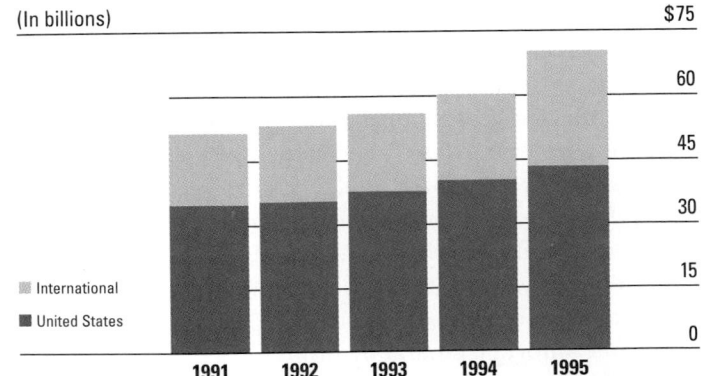

Consolidated international revenues

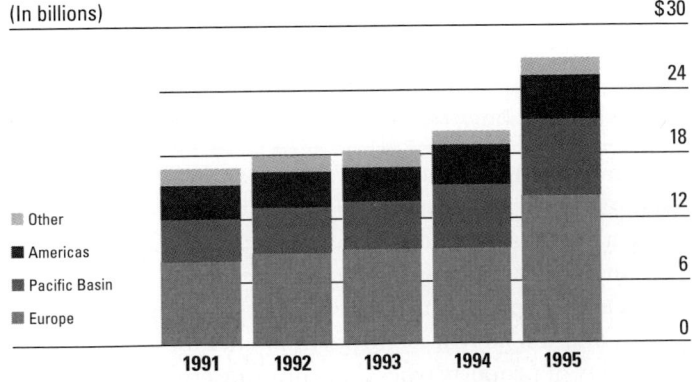

Management's Discussion of Financial Resources and Liquidity

Overview

This discussion of financial resources and liquidity focuses on the Statement of Financial Position (page 28) and the Statement of Cash Flows (page 30).

Throughout the discussion, it is important to understand the differences between the businesses of GE and GECS. Although GE's manufacturing and nonfinancial services activities involve a variety of different businesses, their underlying characteristics are development, preparation for market and delivery of tangible goods and services. Risks and rewards are directly related to the ability to manage and finance those activities.

GECS' principal businesses provide financing, asset management, insurance and other financial services to third parties. The underlying characteristics of these businesses involve the management of financial risk. GECS' risks and rewards stem from the abilities of its businesses to continue to design and provide a wide range of financial services in a competitive marketplace and to receive adequate compensation for such services. GECS is not a "captive finance company" nor a vehicle for "off-balance-sheet financing" for GE; very little of GECS' business is directly related to other GE operations.

Despite the different business profiles of GE and GECS, the global commercial airline industry is one significant example of an important source of business for both. GE assumes financing positions primarily in support of engine sales, whereas GECS is a significant source of lease and loan financing for the industry (see details in note 16). Management believes that, particularly as the industry regains financial strength, these financing positions are reasonably protected by collateral values and by its ability to control assets, either by ownership or security interests.

The fundamental differences between GE and GECS are reflected in the measurements commonly used by investors, rating agencies and financial analysts. These differences will become clearer in the discussion that follows with respect to the more significant items in the financial statements.

Statement of Financial Position

• *Investment securities* for each of the past two years comprised mainly investment-grade debt securities held by GECS' specialty insurance and annuity businesses in support of obligations to policyholders and annuitants. The increase of $10.2 billion at GECS during 1995 was principally related to acquisitions, increases in fair value resulting from lower year-end interest rates and investment of premiums.

• *GE's current receivables* were $8.9 billion and $7.8 billion at the end of 1995 and 1994, respectively, and included $6.6 billion and $5.7 billion due from customers at the end

GE annual inventory turnover

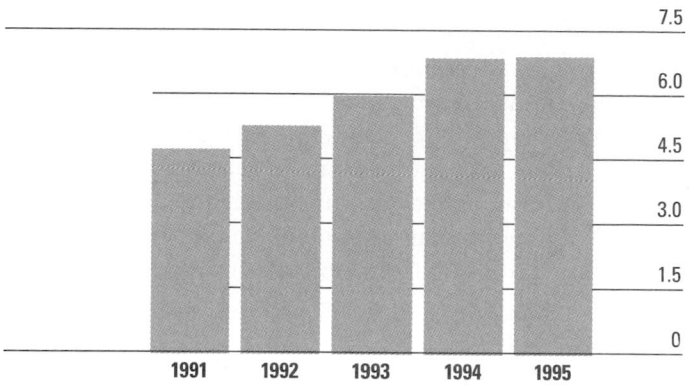

of 1995 and 1994, respectively. As a measure of asset utilization, customer receivables turnover was 6.7 in 1995, compared with 6.9 in 1994, a decline solely attributable to consolidation of Nuovo Pignone. Current receivables other than amounts owed by customers are primarily amounts that did not originate from sales of GE goods or services, such as advances to suppliers in connection with large contracts.

• *Inventories* were $4.4 billion at December 31, 1995, up $0.5 billion from the end of 1994. As a measure of inventory utilization, turnover was 6.9 in 1995, about the same as in 1994. Absent the consolidation of Nuovo Pignone, inventory turnover would have been 7.2 in 1995, continuing the improvements achieved over the past five years. Last-in, first-out (LIFO) revaluations decreased $87 million in 1995, compared with decreases of $197 million in 1994 and $179 million in 1993. Included in these changes were decreases of $88 million, $72 million and $101 million (1995, 1994 and 1993, respectively) that resulted from lower LIFO inventory levels. There was no cost change in 1995 and net cost decreases in 1994 and 1993.

• *GECS financing receivables* were $93.3 billion at year-end 1995, net of allowance for doubtful accounts, up $16.9 billion over 1994. These receivables are discussed on page 36 and in notes 8 and 13.

• *GECS other receivables* were $12.9 billion and $6.0 billion at December 31, 1995 and 1994, respectively. The 1995 increase was almost entirely attributable to premiums receivable and reinsurance recoverables, reflecting acquired businesses and a general increase in underwriting activity.

• *Property, plant and equipment* (including equipment leased to others) was $25.7 billion at December 31, 1995, up $2.2 billion from 1994. GE's property, plant and equipment consists of investments for its own productive use, whereas the largest element of GECS' investment is in equipment provided to third parties on operating leases. Details by category of investment can be found in note 14.

GE's total expenditures for new plant and equipment during 1995 totaled $1.8 billion, up slightly from $1.7 billion in 1994. Total expenditures for the past five years were $8.8 billion, of which 36% was investment in productivity, through new equipment and process improvements; 35% was investment for growth, through new capacity and product development; and 29% was investment for such other purposes as improvement of research and development facilities and safety and environmental protection.

GECS' additions to its equipment leased to others were $4.5 billion during 1995 ($5.6 billion during 1994).

• *Intangible assets* were $13.3 billion at year-end 1995, up from $11.4 billion at year-end 1994. GE's intangibles increased to $6.6 billion from $6.3 billion at the end of 1994. The $1.7 billion increase in GECS' intangibles was primarily goodwill attributable to various acquisitions, none of which was individually material.

• *All other assets* totaled $26.3 billion at year-end 1995, an increase of $2.4 billion from the end of 1994. GE's other assets decreased $0.5 billion, reflecting the 1995 consolidation of Nuovo Pignone, which was classified in other assets in 1994, and an increase in the prepaid pension asset. GECS' increase of $2.9 billion related principally to acquisitions.

• *Insurance liabilities, reserves and annuity benefits* were $39.7 billion, $10.3 billion higher than in 1994. The increase was primarily attributable to acquisitions.

• *Consolidated borrowings* aggregated $115.5 billion at December 31, 1995, compared with $94.8 billion at the end of 1994. The major debt-rating agencies evaluate the financial condition of GE and of GE Capital (GECS' major public borrowing entity) differently because of their distinct business characteristics. Using criteria appropriate to each and considering their combined strength, those major rating agencies continue to give the highest ratings to debt of both GE and GE Capital.

GE has committed to contribute capital to GE Capital in the event of either a significant, specified decrease in the ratio of GE Capital's earnings to fixed charges or a failure to maintain a specified debt-to-equity ratio in the event certain GE Capital preferred stock is redeemed. GE also has guaranteed subordinated debt of GECS with a face amount of $1,000 million and $700 million at December 31, 1995 and 1994, respectively. Management believes the likelihood that GE will be required to contribute capital under either the commitments or the guaranties is remote.

GE's total borrowings were $3.9 billion at year-end 1995 ($1.6 billion short-term, $2.3 billion long-term), an increase of about $0.3 billion from year-end 1994. GE's total debt at the end of 1995 equaled 11.6% of total capital, down from 11.9% at the end of 1994.

GECS' total borrowings were $111.6 billion at December 31, 1995, of which $62.8 billion is due in 1996 and $48.8 billion is due in subsequent years. Comparable amounts at the end of 1994 were $91.4 billion total, $57.1 billion due within one year and $34.3 billion due thereafter. GECS' composite interest rates are discussed on page 36. A large portion of GECS' borrowings ($41.2 billion and $43.7 billion at the end of 1995 and 1994, respectively) was issued in active commercial paper markets that management believes will continue to be a reliable source of short-term financing. Most of this commercial paper is issued by GE Capital. The average remaining terms and interest rates of GE Capital's commercial paper were 41 days and 5.88%, respectively, at the end of 1995, compared with 45 days and 5.90% at the end of 1994. GE Capital's leverage (ratio of debt to equity, excluding from equity all net unrealized gains and losses on investment securities) was 7.89 to 1 at the end of 1995, compared with 7.94 to 1 at the end of 1994. By comparison, including in equity all net unrealized gains and losses on investment securities, GE Capital's ratio of debt to equity was 7.59 to 1 at the end of 1995, compared with 8.43 to 1 at the end of 1994.

Interest rate and currency risk management

Both GE and GECS are exposed to various types of risk, although the nature of their activities means that the respective risks are different. The multinational nature of GE's operations and the relatively low level of GE's borrowings means that currency management is more important than managing exposure to changes in interest rates.

On the other hand, changes in interest rates are the more significant exposure for GECS because of the potential effects of such changes on financing spreads.

The correlation between interest rate changes and financing spreads is subject to many factors and cannot be forecast with reliability. Although not necessarily rele-

GE borrowings as a percentage of total capital invested

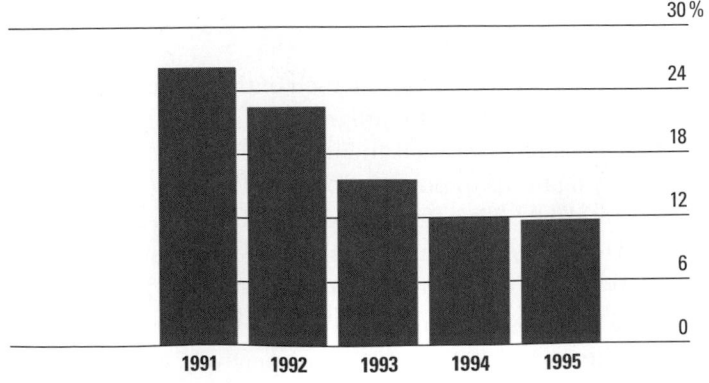

vant to future effects, management estimates that, all else constant, an increase of 100 basis points in interest rates for all of 1995 would have reduced GECS net earnings by approximately $65 million.

GE and GECS use various financial instruments, particularly interest rate, currency and basis swaps, but also options and currency forwards, to manage their respective risks. GE and GECS are exclusively end users of these instruments, which are commonly referred to as derivatives; neither GE nor GECS engages in trading, market-making or other speculative activities in the derivatives markets. Established practices require that derivative financial instruments relate to specific asset, liability or equity transactions or to currency exposures. The total exposure of GE and GECS to credit risk associated with in-the-money derivatives at December 31, 1995, was $50 million and $680 million, respectively. Management does not anticipate any loss from this exposure.

More detailed information regarding these financial instruments, as well as the strategies and policies for their use, is contained in notes 1, 18 and 29.

Statement of Cash Flows

Because cash management activities of GE and GECS are separate and distinct, it is more useful to review their cash flows statements separately.

GE

GE's cash and equivalents aggregated $0.9 billion at the end of 1995, about $0.5 billion lower than at the end of 1994. During 1995, GE generated $6.1 billion in cash from operating activities, about the same as in 1994. The 1995 cash generation provided most of the resources to repurchase $3.1 billion of GE common stock under share repurchase programs, to pay $2.8 billion in dividends to share owners, and to invest $1.8 billion in new plant and equipment.

Operating activities are the principal source of GE's cash flows from continuing operations. Over the past three years, operating activities have provided more than $17.3 billion of cash. Principal applications were payment of dividends to share owners ($7.4 billion), investment in new plant and equipment ($5.2 billion) and reduction of debt ($2.9 billion). In addition, the Company repurchased and placed into treasury $3.4 billion of its common stock during the past three years under share repurchase programs.

In December 1994, GE's Board of Directors authorized the repurchase of up to $5 billion of the Company's common stock over the following two years. In December 1995, the Board increased the authorized amount of the repurchase to $9 billion and extended the program through 1997. This program is a direct result of GE's solid financial condi-

GE cumulative cash flows

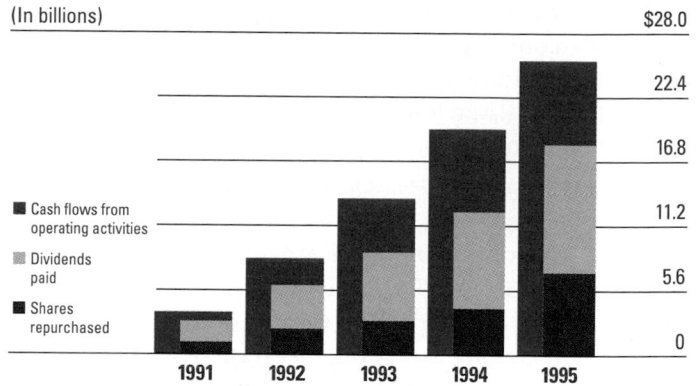

tion and cash-generating capability, and it was authorized after evaluating various alternatives to enhance long-term share owner value.

Based on past performance and current expectations, in combination with the financial flexibility that comes with a strong balance sheet and the highest credit ratings, management believes that GE is in a sound position to complete the share repurchase program, to grow dividends in line with earnings, and to continue making long-term investments for future growth, including selective acquisitions and investments in joint ventures. Expenditures for new plant and equipment in 1996 are expected to be about 20% higher than in 1995, principally for productivity and growth.

GECS

GECS' primary source of cash is financing activities involving the continued rollover of short-term borrowings and appropriate addition of borrowings with a reasonable balance of maturities. Over the past three years, GECS' borrowings with maturities of 90 days or less have decreased by $4.4 billion. New borrowings of $74.5 billion having maturities longer than 90 days were added during those years, while $38.3 billion of such longer-term borrowings were retired. GECS also generated $24.3 billion from continuing operating activities.

GECS' principal use of cash has been investing in assets to grow its businesses. Of the $53.5 billion that GECS invested over the past three years, $25.0 billion was used for additions to financing receivables, $13.5 billion was used to invest in new equipment, principally for lease to others, and $9.5 billion was used for acquisitions of new businesses.

With the financial flexibility that comes with excellent credit ratings, management believes that GECS should be well positioned to meet the global needs of its customers for capital and to continue providing GE share owners with good returns.

Management's Discussion of Selected Financial Data

Selected financial data summarizes on the opposite page some data frequently requested about General Electric Company. The data are divided into three sections: upper portion — consolidated data; middle portion — GE data that reflect various conventional measurements for industrial enterprises; and lower portion — GECS data that reflect key information pertinent to financial services.

GE's total research and development expenditures were $1,892 million in 1995, up $151 million (or 9%) from 1994. In 1995, expenditures of $1,299 million were from GE's own funds, up 10% from 1994. Expenditures reflected continuing research and development work related to new product programs, including the next generation of gas turbines, a more powerful version of the recently introduced AC locomotive and, in Aircraft Engines, introduction of the new GE90 and development of more fuel-efficient versions of the best-selling CFM56. Expenditures from funds provided by customers (mainly the U.S. government) were $593 million in 1995, up $28 million from 1994, primarily reflecting additional research efforts in advanced propulsion technologies at Aircraft Engines.

GE's total backlog of firm unfilled orders at the end of 1995 was $25.5 billion, up $1.2 billion from the 1994 level. The increase was more than accounted for by the 1995 consolidation of Nuovo Pignone. Orders constituting this backlog may be canceled or deferred by customers, subject in certain cases to cancellation penalties. See Industry Segments beginning on page 34 for further discussion on unfilled orders of relatively long-cycle manufacturing businesses. About 46% of total unfilled orders at the end of 1995 was scheduled to be shipped in 1996, with most of the remainder to be shipped in the two years after that. For comparison, about 50% of the 1994 backlog was expected to be shipped in 1995.

Regarding environmental matters, the Company's operations, like operations of other companies engaged in similar businesses, involve the use, disposal and cleanup of substances regulated under environmental protection laws.

In 1995, GE had capital expenditures of about $75 million for projects related to the environment. The comparable amount in 1994 was $63 million. These amounts exclude expenditures for remediation actions, which are principally expensed and are discussed below. Capital expenditures for environmental purposes have included pollution control devices — such as wastewater treatment plants, groundwater monitoring devices, air strippers or separators, and incinerators — at new and existing facilities constructed or upgraded in the normal course of business. Consistent with policies stressing environmental responsibility, average annual capital expenditures other than for remediation

projects are presently expected to be about $85 million over the next two years. This level is in line with existing levels for new or expanded programs to build facilities or modify manufacturing processes to minimize waste and reduce emissions.

GE also is involved in a sizable number of remediation actions to clean up hazardous wastes as required by federal and state laws. Such statutes require that responsible parties fund remediation actions regardless of fault, legality of original disposal or ownership of a disposal site. Expenditures for site remediation actions amounted to approximately $76 million in 1995, compared with $98 million in 1994. It is presently expected that remediation actions will require average annual expenditures in the range of $80 million to $110 million over the next two years. Liabilities for remediation costs are based on management's best estimate of future costs; when there appears to be a range of possible costs with equal likelihood, liabilities are based on the lower end of such range. Possible insurance recoveries are not considered in estimating liabilities.

It is difficult to estimate with any meaning the annual level of future remediation expenditures because of the many uncertainties, including uncertainties about the status of laws, regulations, technology and information related to individual sites. Subject to the foregoing, management believes that capital expenditures and remediation actions to comply with the present laws governing environmental protection will not have a material effect on consolidated earnings, liquidity or competitive position. In making this determination, management considered the fact that, if remediation expenditures were to continue at the 1995 level, liabilities recorded at the end of 1995 would be sufficient to cover expenditures through the end of 2001, and that the probability of incurring more than nominal expenditures beyond 2015 is remote. Of course, lower annual expenditures could be incurred over a longer period without increasing the total expenditures.

GE share price activity

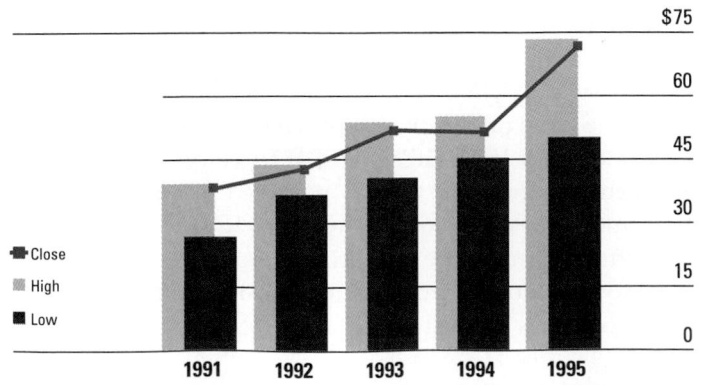

Selected Financial Data

(Dollar amounts in millions; per-share amounts in dollars)	1995	1994	1993	1992	1991
General Electric Company and consolidated affiliates					
Revenues	$ 70,028	$ 60,109	$ 55,701	$ 53,051	$ 51,283
Earnings from continuing operations	6,573	5,915	4,184	4,137	3,943
Earnings (loss) from discontinued operations	—	(1,189)	993	588	492
Earnings before accounting changes	6,573	4,726	5,177	4,725	4,435
Net earnings	6,573	4,726	4,315	4,725	2,636
Dividends declared	2,838	2,546	2,229	1,985	1,808
Earned on average share owners' equity	23.5%	18.1%	17.5%	20.9%	12.2%
Per share					
Earnings from continuing operations	$ 3.90	$ 3.46	$ 2.45	$ 2.41	$ 2.27
Earnings (loss) from discontinued operations	—	(0.69)	0.58	0.34	0.28
Earnings before accounting changes	3.90	2.77	3.03	2.75	2.55
Net earnings	3.90	2.77	2.52	2.75	1.51
Dividends declared	1.69	1.49	1.305	1.16	1.04
Stock price range	$73\frac{1}{8}$-$49\frac{7}{8}$	$54\frac{7}{8}$-45	$53\frac{1}{2}$-$40\frac{3}{8}$	$43\frac{3}{4}$-$36\frac{3}{8}$	39-$26\frac{1}{2}$
Total assets of continuing operations	228,035	185,871	166,413	135,472	123,115
Long-term borrowings	51,027	36,979	28,194	25,298	22,602
Shares outstanding — average (in thousands)	1,683,812	1,708,738	1,707,979	1,714,396	1,737,863
Share owner accounts — average	460,000	458,000	464,000	481,000	495,000
Employees at year end					
United States	150,000	156,000	157,000	168,000	173,000
Other countries	72,000	60,000	59,000	58,000	62,000
Discontinued operations (primarily U.S.)	—	5,000	6,000	42,000	49,000
Total employees	222,000	221,000	222,000	268,000	284,000
GE data					
Short-term borrowings	$ 1,666	$ 906	$ 2,391	$ 3,448	$ 3,482
Long-term borrowings	2,277	2,699	2,413	3,420	4,332
Minority interest	434	382	355	350	353
Share owners' equity	29,609	26,387	25,824	23,459	21,683
Total capital invested	$ 33,986	$ 30,374	$ 30,983	$ 30,677	$ 29,850
Return on average total capital invested	21.3%	15.9%	15.2%	16.9%	11.1%
Borrowings as a percentage of total capital invested	11.6%	11.9%	15.5%	22.4%	26.2%
Working capital	$ 204	$ 544	$ (419)	$ (822)	$ (231)
Property, plant and equipment additions	1,831	1,743	1,588	1,445	2,164
Year-end orders backlog	25,507	24,324	22,861	25,434	26,049
GECS data					
Revenues	$ 26,492	$ 19,875	$ 17,276	$ 14,418	$ 13,053
Earnings from continuing operations	2,415	2,085	1,567	1,331	1,221
Earnings (losses) from discontinued operations	—	(1,189)	240	168	54
Net earnings	2,415	896	1,807	1,499	1,256
Share owner's equity	12,774	9,380	10,809	8,884	7,758
Minority interest	2,522	1,465	1,301	994	865
Borrowings from others	111,598	91,399	81,052	72,360	63,313
Ratio of debt to equity at GE Capital (a)	7.89:1	7.94:1	7.96:1	7.91:1	7.80:1
Total assets of GE Capital	$160,825	$130,904	$117,939	$ 92,632	$ 80,528
Reserve coverage on financing receivables	2.63%	2.63%	2.63%	2.63%	2.63%
Insurance premiums written	$ 6,158	$ 3,962	$ 3,956	$ 2,900	$ 2,155

(a) Equity excludes unrealized gains and losses on investment securities.

See note 20 to the consolidated financial statements for information about the 1993 accounting change. The 1991 accounting change represented the adoption of SFAS No. 106, *Employers' Accounting for Postretirement Benefits Other Than Pensions.* "GE" means the basis of consolidation as described in note 1 to the consolidated financial statements; "GECS" means General Electric Capital Services, Inc. and all of its affiliates and associated companies. Transactions between GE and GECS have been eliminated from the "consolidated information."

Management's Discussion of Financial Responsibility

The financial data in this report, including the audited financial statements, have been prepared by management using the best available information and applying judgment. Accounting principles used in preparing the financial statements are those that are generally accepted in the United States.

Management believes that a sound, dynamic system of internal financial controls that balances benefits and costs provides the best safeguard for Company assets. Professional financial managers are responsible for implementing and overseeing the financial control system, reporting on management's stewardship of the assets entrusted to it by share owners and maintaining accurate records.

GE is dedicated to the highest standards of integrity, ethics and social responsibility. This dedication is reflected in written policy statements covering, among other subjects, environmental protection, potentially conflicting outside interests of employees, compliance with antitrust laws, proper business practices and adherence to the highest standards of conduct and practices in transactions with the U.S. government. Management continually emphasizes to all employees that even the appearance of impropriety can erode public confidence in the Company. Ongoing educa-

tion and communication programs and review activities, such as those conducted by the Company's Policy Compliance Review Board, are designed to create a strong compliance culture — one that encourages employees to raise their policy questions and concerns and that prohibits retribution for doing so.

KPMG Peat Marwick LLP provides an objective, independent review of management's discharge of its obligations relating to the fairness of reporting operating results and financial condition. Their report for 1995 appears below.

The Audit Committee of the Board (consisting solely of Directors from outside GE) maintains an ongoing appraisal — on behalf of share owners — of the activities and independence of the Company's independent auditors, the activities of its internal audit staff, financial reporting process, internal financial controls and compliance with key Company policies.

John F. Welch, Jr.
Chairman of the Board and
Chief Executive Officer

February 9, 1996

Dennis D. Dammerman
Senior Vice President
Finance

Independent Auditors' Report

To Share Owners and Board of Directors of
General Electric Company

We have audited the accompanying statement of financial position of General Electric Company and consolidated affiliates as of December 31, 1995 and 1994, and the related statements of earnings and cash flows for each of the years in the three-year period ended December 31, 1995. These consolidated financial statements are the responsibility of the Company's management. Our responsibility is to express an opinion on these consolidated financial statements based on our audits.

We conducted our audits in accordance with generally accepted auditing standards. Those standards require that we plan and perform the audit to obtain reasonable assurance about whether the financial statements are free of material misstatement. An audit includes examining, on a test basis, evidence supporting the amounts and disclosures in the financial statements. An audit also includes assessing the accounting principles used and significant estimates made by management, as well as evaluating the overall financial

statement presentation. We believe that our audits provide a reasonable basis for our opinion.

In our opinion, the aforementioned financial statements appearing on pages 26-31, 35, and 45-64 present fairly, in all material respects, the financial position of General Electric Company and consolidated affiliates at December 31, 1995 and 1994, and the results of their operations and their cash flows for each of the years in the three-year period ended December 31, 1995, in conformity with generally accepted accounting principles.

As discussed in note 20 to the consolidated financial statements, the Company in 1993 adopted a required change in its method of accounting for postemployment benefits.

KPMG Peat Marwick LLP
Stamford, Connecticut

February 9, 1996

Notes to Consolidated Financial Statements

1 Summary of Significant Accounting Policies

Consolidation. The consolidated financial statements represent the adding together of all affiliates — companies that General Electric directly or indirectly controls, either through majority ownership or otherwise. Results of associated companies — generally companies that are 20% to 50% owned and over which GE, directly or indirectly, has significant influence — are included in the financial statements on a "one-line" basis.

Financial statement presentation. Financial data and related measurements are presented in the following categories.

- **GE.** This represents the adding together of all affiliates other than General Electric Capital Services, Inc. ("GECS"), whose continuing operations are presented on a one-line basis.

- **GECS.** This affiliate owns all of the common stock of General Electric Capital Corporation (GE Capital) and GE Global Insurance Holding Corporation (GE Global Insurance). GE Capital, GE Global Insurance and their respective affiliates are consolidated in the GECS columns and constitute its business.

- **Consolidated.** These data represent the adding together of GE and GECS.

The effects of transactions among related companies within and between each of the above-mentioned groups are eliminated. Transactions between GE and GECS are not material.

Certain prior-year amounts have been reclassified to conform to the 1995 presentation.

The preparation of financial statements in conformity with generally accepted accounting principles requires management to make estimates and assumptions that affect reported amounts and related disclosures. Actual results could differ from those estimates.

Sales of goods and services. A sale is recorded when title passes to the customer or when services are performed in accordance with contracts.

GECS revenues from operations ("earned income"). Income on all loans is recognized on the interest method. Accrual of interest income is suspended at the earlier of the time at which collection of an account becomes doubtful or the account becomes 90 days delinquent. Interest income on impaired loans is recognized either as cash is collected or on a cost-recovery basis as conditions warrant.

Financing lease income is recorded on the interest method so as to produce a level yield on funds not yet recovered. Estimated unguarantied residual values of leased assets are based primarily on periodic independent appraisals of the values of leased assets remaining at expiration of the lease terms.

Operating lease income is recognized on a straight-line basis over the terms of underlying leases.

Origination, commitment and other nonrefundable fees related to fundings are deferred and recorded in earned income on the interest method. Commitment fees related to loans not expected to be funded and line-of-credit fees are deferred and recorded in earned income on a straight-line basis over the period to which the fees relate. Syndication fees are recorded in earned income at the time related services are performed unless significant contingencies exist.

Premiums on insurance contracts are reported as earned income over the terms of the related reinsurance treaties or insurance policies. In general, earned premiums are calculated on a pro rata basis or are determined based on reports received from reinsureds. Premium adjustments under retrospectively rated reinsurance contracts are recorded based on estimated losses and loss expenses, including both case and incurred-but-not-reported reserves. Premiums received under annuity contracts that do not have significant mortality or morbidity risk are not reported as revenues but as annuity benefits — a liability — and are adjusted according to terms of the respective policies.

Depreciation and amortization. The cost of most of GE's manufacturing plant and equipment is depreciated using an accelerated method based primarily on a sum-of-the-years digits formula. If manufacturing plant and equipment is subject to abnormal economic conditions or obsolescence, additional depreciation is provided.

The cost of GECS' equipment leased to others on operating leases is amortized, principally on a straight-line basis, to estimated net salvage value over the lease term or over the estimated economic life of the equipment. Depreciation of property and equipment for GECS' own use is recorded on either a sum-of-the-years digits formula or a straight-line basis over the lives of the assets.

Recognition of losses on financing receivables and investments. GECS maintains an allowance for losses on financing receivables at an amount that it believes is sufficient to provide adequate protection against future losses in the portfolio. When collateral is repossessed in satisfaction of a loan, the receivable is written down against the allowance for losses to estimated fair value less costs to sell, transferred to other assets and subsequently carried at the lower of cost or estimated fair value less costs to sell. This accounting method has been employed principally for specialized financing transactions.

See note 8 for further information on GECS' allowance for losses on financing receivables.

Cash equivalents. Marketable securities with original maturities of three months or less are included in cash equivalents.

Investment securities. The Company has designated its investments in debt securities and marketable equity securities as available-for-sale. Those securities are reported at fair value, with net unrealized gains and losses included in equity, net of applicable taxes. Unrealized losses that are other than temporary are recognized in earnings.

Inventories. All inventories are stated at the lower of cost or realizable values. Cost for virtually all of GE's U.S. inventories is stated on a last-in, first-out (LIFO) basis; cost of other inventories is primarily determined on a first-in, first-out (FIFO) basis.

Intangible assets. Goodwill is amortized over its estimated period of benefit on a straight-line basis; other intangible assets are amortized on appropriate bases over their estimated lives. No amortization period exceeds 40 years. Goodwill in excess of associated expected operating cash flows is considered to be impaired and is written down to fair value.

Deferred insurance acquisition costs. For the property and casualty business, deferred insurance acquisition costs are amortized pro rata over the contract periods in which the related premiums are earned. For the life insurance business, these costs are amortized over the premium-paying periods of the contracts in proportion either to anticipated premium income or to gross profit, as appropriate. For certain annuity contracts, such costs are amortized on the basis of anticipated gross profits. For other lines of business, acquisition costs are amortized over the life of the related insurance contracts. Deferred insurance acquisition costs are reviewed for recoverability; anticipated investment income is considered in making recoverability evaluations.

Interest rate and currency risk management. As a matter of policy, neither GE nor GECS engages in derivatives trading, market-making or other speculative activities. Any instrument designated but ineffective as a hedge is marked to market and recognized in operations immediately.

GE and GECS use swaps primarily to optimize funding costs. To a lesser degree, and in combination with options and limit contracts, GECS uses swaps to stabilize cash flows from mortgage-related assets.

Interest rate and currency swaps that modify borrowings or designated assets, including swaps associated with forecasted commercial paper renewals, are accounted for on an accrual basis. Both GE and GECS require all other swaps, as well as options and forwards, to be designated and accounted for as hedges of specific assets, liabilities or committed transactions; resulting payments and receipts are recognized contemporaneously with effects of hedged transactions. A payment or receipt arising from early termination of an effective hedge is accounted for as an adjustment to the basis of the hedged transaction.

2 Discontinued Operations

A summary of discontinued operations follows.

(In millions)	1994	1993
Earnings (loss) from GECS securities broker-dealer	$(1,189)	$ 240
Earnings from GE Aerospace	—	753
Earnings (loss) from discontinued operations	$(1,189)	$ 993

GECS securities broker-dealer. In November 1994, GE elected to terminate the operations of Kidder, Peabody Group Inc. (Kidder, Peabody), the GECS securities broker-dealer, by initiating an orderly liquidation of its assets and liabilities. As part of the liquidation plan, GE received securities of Paine Webber Group Inc. valued at $657 million in exchange for certain broker-dealer assets and operations. Summary operating results of the discontinued broker-dealer operations follow.

(In millions)	1994	1993
Revenues	$ 4,578	$4,861
Earnings (loss) before income taxes	$ (551)	$ 439
Income tax benefit (provision)	230	(199)
Earnings (loss) from discontinued operations	(321)	240
Provision for loss, net of income tax benefit of $266	(868)	—
Earnings (loss) from GECS securities broker-dealer	$(1,189)	$ 240

The 1994 provision of $868 million after taxes, shown in the summary above, related to exit costs associated with liquidation of Kidder, Peabody. This liquidation was substantially complete as of December 31, 1995.

GE Aerospace. In April 1993, General Electric Company transferred GE's Aerospace business segment, GE Government Services, Inc., and a component of GE that operated Knolls Atomic Power Laboratory under a contract with the U.S. Department of Energy to a new company controlled by the shareholders of Martin Marietta Corporation in a transaction valued at $3.3 billion. Summary operating results of discontinued aerospace operations follow.

(In millions)	1993
Revenues	$ 996
Earnings before income taxes	$ 119
Provision for income taxes	(44)
Earnings from discontinued operations	75
Gain on transfer, net of income taxes of $752	678
Earnings from GE Aerospace	$ 753

3 GE Other Income

(In millions)	1995	1994	1993
Royalty and technical agreements	**$453**	$395	$371
Associated companies	**111**	115	65
Marketable securities and bank deposits	**70**	77	75
Customer financing	**26**	28	29
Other investments			
Dividends	**62**	62	50
Interest	**18**	21	21
Other items	**13**	85	119
	$753	$783	$730

4 GECS Revenues from Operations

(In millions)	1995	1994	1993
Time sales, loan, investment and other income	**$13,004**	$ 9,709	$ 7,997
Financing leases	**3,176**	2,539	2,315
Operating lease rentals	**4,080**	3,802	3,267
Premium and commission income of insurance affiliates	**6,232**	3,825	3,697
	$26,492	$19,875	$17,276

Included in earned income from financing leases were pretax gains on the sale of equipment at lease completion of $191 million in 1995, $180 million in 1994 and $145 million in 1993.

5 Supplemental Cost Details

Total expenditures for research and development were $1,892 million, $1,741 million and $1,955 million in 1995, 1994 and 1993, respectively. The Company-funded portion aggregated $1,299 million in 1995, $1,176 million in 1994 and $1,297 million in 1993.

Rental expense under operating leases is shown below.

(In millions)	1995	1994	1993
GE	**$523**	$514	$635
GECS	**524**	468	413

At December 31, 1995, minimum rental commitments under noncancelable operating leases aggregated $2,705 million and $3,119 million for GE and GECS, respectively. Amounts payable over the next five years are shown below.

(In millions)	1996	1997	1998	1999	2000
GE	$358	$324	$275	$216	$164
GECS	434	384	345	320	288

GE's selling, general and administrative expense totaled $5,743 million in 1995, $5,211 million in 1994 and $5,124 million in 1993. Insignificant amounts of interest were capitalized by GE and GECS in 1995, 1994 and 1993.

6 Pension Benefits

GE and its affiliates sponsor a number of pension plans. Principal pension plans are discussed below; other pension plans are not significant individually or in the aggregate.

Principal pension plans are the GE Pension Plan and the GE Supplementary Pension Plan.

The GE Pension Plan covers substantially all GE employees and 65% of GECS employees in the United States. Generally, benefits are based on the greater of a formula recognizing career earnings or a formula recognizing length of service and final average earnings. Benefit provisions are subject to collective bargaining. At the end of 1995, the GE Pension Plan covered approximately 462,000 participants, including 134,000 employees, 147,000 former employees with vested rights to future benefits, and 181,000 retirees and beneficiaries receiving benefits.

The GE Supplementary Pension Plan is an unfunded plan providing supplementary retirement benefits primarily to higher-level, longer-service U.S. employees.

Details of income for principal pension plans follow.

Pension plan income

(In millions)	1995	1994	1993
Actual return on plan assets	**$ 5,439**	$ 316	$ 3,221
Unrecognized portion of return	**(3,087)**	1,951	(1,066)
Service cost for benefits earned (a)	**(469)**	(496)	(452)
Interest cost on benefit obligation	**(1,580)**	(1,491)	(1,486)
Amortization	**394**	294	352
Total pension plan income	**$ 697**	$ 574	$ 569

(a) Net of employee contributions.

Actual return on trust assets in 1995 was 21.2%, compared with the 9.5% assumed return on such assets. The effect of this higher return will be recognized in future years.

The 1993 gain on transfer of discontinued Aerospace operations included a pretax pension plan curtailment/settlement loss of $125 million.

Funding policy for the GE Pension Plan is to contribute amounts sufficient to meet minimum funding requirements as set forth in employee benefit and tax laws plus such additional amounts as GE may determine to be appropriate. GE has not made contributions since 1987 because the fully funded status of the GE Pension Plan precludes current tax deduction and because any Company contribution would require payment of annual excise taxes.

Funded status of pension plans

December 31 (In millions)	1995	1994
Market-related value of assets	$27,795	$25,441
Projected benefit obligation	23,119	19,334

The market-related value of pension assets recognizes market appreciation or depreciation in the portfolio over five years, a method that reduces the short-term impact of market fluctuations.

Plan assets are held in trust and consist mainly of common stock and fixed-income investments. GE common stock represents about 3% of trust assets.

An analysis of amounts shown in the Statement of Financial Position is shown below.

Prepaid pension asset

December 31 (In millions)	1995	1994
Fair value of trust assets	$ 30,200	$ 26,166
Projected benefit obligation	(23,119)	(19,334)
Assets in excess of obligation	7,081	6,832
Add (deduct) unamortized balances		
SFAS No. 87 transition gain	(769)	(923)
Experience gains	(2,127)	(2,548)
Plan amendments	523	602
Pension liability	564	526
Prepaid pension asset	$ 5,272	$ 4,489

The accumulated benefit obligation was $22,052 million and $18,430 million at year-end 1995 and 1994, respectively; the vested benefit obligation was approximately equal to the accumulated benefit obligation at the end of both years.

Actuarial assumptions and techniques used to determine costs and benefit obligations for principal pension plans follow.

Actuarial assumptions

December 31	1995	1994
Discount rate	7.0%	8.5%
Compensation increases	4.0	5.5
Return on assets for the year	9.5	9.5

Experience gains and losses, as well as the effects of changes in actuarial assumptions and plan provisions, are amortized over employees' average future service period.

7 Retiree Health and Life Benefits

GE and its affiliates sponsor a number of retiree health and life insurance benefit plans. Principal retiree benefit plans are discussed below; other such plans are not significant individually or in the aggregate.

Principal retiree benefit plans generally provide health and life insurance benefits to employees who retire under the GE Pension Plan with 10 or more years of service. Retirees share in the cost of their health care benefits. Benefit provisions are subject to collective bargaining. At the end of 1995, these plans covered approximately 252,000 retirees and dependents.

Details of cost for principal retiree benefit plans follow.

Cost of retiree benefit plans

(In millions)	1995	1994	1993
Retiree health plans			
Service cost for benefits earned	$ 73	$ 78	$ 49
Interest cost on benefit obligation	189	191	192
Actual return on plan assets	—	—	(3)
Unrecognized portion of return	—	(1)	1
Amortization	(12)	(3)	(26)
Retiree health plan cost	250	265	213
Retiree life plans			
Service cost for benefits earned	13	24	21
Interest cost on benefit obligation	108	105	111
Actual return on plan assets	(329)	(2)	(152)
Unrecognized portion of return	206	(120)	42
Amortization	1	8	7
Retiree life plan cost (income)	(1)	15	29
Total cost	$ 249	$ 280	$ 242

The 1993 gain on transfer of discontinued Aerospace operations included a pretax retiree health and life plan curtailment/settlement gain of $245 million.

Funding policy for retiree health benefits is generally to pay covered expenses as they are incurred. GE funds retiree life insurance benefits at its discretion and within limits imposed by tax laws.

Funded status of retiree benefit plans

December 31 (In millions)	1995	1994
Market-related value of assets	$1,430	$1,346
Accumulated postretirement benefit obligation	4,089	3,701

The market-related value of assets of retiree life plans recognizes market appreciation or depreciation in the portfolio over five years, a method that reduces the short-term impact of market fluctuations.

Plan assets are held in trust and consist mainly of common stock and fixed-income investments. GE common stock represents about 2% of trust assets.

An analysis of amounts shown in the Statement of Financial Position is shown below.

Retiree benefit liability/asset

December 31 (In millions)	Retiree health plans		Retiree life plans	
	1995	1994	**1995**	1994
Accumulated postretirement benefit obligation				
Retirees and dependents	**$1,984**	$1,858	**$ 1,314**	$ 1,099
Employees eligible to retire	**95**	101	**53**	55
Other employees	**451**	427	**192**	161
	2,530	2,386	**1,559**	1,315
Less fair value of trust assets	**—**	—	**(1,556)**	(1,323)
Obligation over (under) assets	**2,530**	2,386	**3**	(8)
Add (deduct) unamortized balances				
Experience losses	**(292)**	(112)	**(199)**	(198)
Plan amendments	**177**	188	**119**	130
Retiree benefit liability (prepaid asset)	**$2,415**	$2,462	**$ (77)**	$ (76)

Actuarial assumptions and techniques used to determine costs and benefit obligations for principal retiree benefit plans are shown below.

Actuarial assumptions

December 31	1995	1994
Discount rate	**7.0%**	8.5%
Compensation increases	**4.0**	5.5
Health care cost trend	**8.5**(a)	9.0(b)
Return on assets for the year	**9.5**	9.5

(a) Gradually declining to 5.0% after 2002.
(b) Gradually declining to 5.0% after 2022.

Increasing the health care cost trend rates by one percentage point would not have had a material effect on the December 31, 1995, accumulated postretirement benefit obligation or the annual cost of retiree health plans.

Experience gains and losses, as well as the effects of changes in actuarial assumptions and plan provisions, are amortized over employees' average future service period.

8 GECS Allowance for Losses on Financing Receivables

GECS allowance for losses on financing receivables represented 2.63% of total financing receivables at year-end 1995 and 1994. The allowance for small-balance receivables is determined principally on the basis of actual experience during the preceding three years. Further allowances are provided to reflect management's judgment of additional loss potential. For other receivables, principally the larger loans and leases, the allowance for losses is determined primarily on the basis of management's judgment of net loss potential, including specific allowances for known troubled accounts. The table below shows the activity in the allowance for losses on financing receivables during each of the past three years.

(In millions)	1995	1994	1993
Balance at January 1	**$2,062**	$1,730	$1,607
Provisions charged to operations	**1,117**	873	987
Net transfers related to companies acquired or sold	**217**	199	126
Amounts written off — net	**(877)**	(740)	(990)
Balance at December 31	**$2,519**	$2,062	$1,730

All accounts or portions thereof deemed to be uncollectible or to require an excessive collection cost are written off to the allowance for losses. Generally, small-balance accounts are progressively written down (from 10% when more than three months delinquent to 100% when 9 to 12 months delinquent) to record the balances at estimated realizable value. If at any time during that period an account is judged to be uncollectible, such as in the case of a bankruptcy, the uncollectible balance is written off. Large-balance accounts are reviewed at least quarterly, and those accounts with amounts that are judged to be uncollectible are written down to estimated realizable value.

9 Provision for Income Taxes

(In millions)	1995	1994	1993
GE			
Estimated amounts payable	**$1,696**	$1,305	$1,207
Deferred tax expense from temporary differences	**373**	592	120
Investment credit amortized — net	**(10)**	(15)	(17)
	2,059	1,882	1,310
GECS			
Estimated amounts payable	**434**	447	221
Deferred tax expense from temporary differences	**678**	431	428
Investment credit amortized — net	**(7)**	(14)	(7)
	1,105	864	642
Consolidated			
Estimated amounts payable	**2,130**	1,752	1,428
Deferred tax expense from temporary differences	**1,051**	1,023	548
Investment credit amortized — net	**(17)**	(29)	(24)
	$3,164	$2,746	$1,952

GE includes GECS in filing a consolidated U.S. federal income tax return. GECS' provision for estimated taxes payable includes its effect on the consolidated return.

Estimated consolidated amounts payable includes amounts applicable to non-U.S. jurisdictions of $721 million, $453 million and $302 million in 1995, 1994 and 1993, respectively.

Deferred income tax balances reflect the impact of temporary differences between the carrying amounts of assets and liabilities and their tax bases and are stated at enacted tax rates expected to be in effect when taxes are actually paid or recovered. See note 22 for details.

Except for certain earnings that GE intends to reinvest indefinitely, provision has been made for the estimated U.S. federal income tax liabilities applicable to undistributed earnings of affiliates and associated companies.

Based on location (not tax jurisdiction) of the business providing goods and services, consolidated U.S. income before taxes was $8.1 billion in 1995, $7.5 billion in 1994 and $5.6 billion in 1993. The corresponding amounts for non-U.S. based operations were $1.6 billion in 1995, $1.2 billion in 1994 and $0.5 billion in 1993.

Reconciliation of U.S. federal statutory tax rate to actual rate	Consolidated			GE			GECS		
	1995	1994	1993	**1995**	1994	1993	**1995**	1994	1993
Statutory U.S. federal income tax rate	**35.0%**	35.0%	35.0%	**35.0%**	35.0%	35.0%	**35.0%**	35.0%	35.0%
Increase (reduction) in rate resulting from:									
Inclusion of after-tax earnings of GECS in before-tax earnings of GE	—	—	—	**(9.8)**	(9.4)	(10.0)	—	—	—
Rate increase — deferred taxes	—	—	1.6	—	—	(0.2)	—	—	5.2
Amortization of goodwill	**1.1**	1.1	1.5	**0.8**	0.8	1.2	**1.1**	1.0	1.2
Tax-exempt income	**(2.1)**	(2.4)	(2.9)	—	—	—	**(5.8)**	(6.9)	(8.3)
Foreign Sales Corporation tax benefits	**(0.9)**	(1.1)	(1.3)	**(1.1)**	(1.2)	(1.5)	—	—	—
Dividends received, not fully taxable	**(0.5)**	(0.5)	(0.7)	**(0.2)**	(0.3)	(0.3)	**(0.8)**	(0.8)	(1.2)
All other — net	**(0.1)**	(0.4)	(1.4)	**(0.8)**	(0.8)	(0.4)	**1.9**	1.0	(2.8)
	(2.5)	(3.3)	(3.2)	**(11.1)**	(10.9)	(11.2)	**(3.6)**	(5.7)	(5.9)
Actual income tax rate	**32.5%**	31.7%	31.8%	**23.9%**	24.1%	23.8%	**31.4%**	29.3%	29.1%

10 GECS Investment Securities

(In millions)	Amortized cost	Gross unrealized gains	Gross unrealized losses	Estimated fair value
December 31, 1995				
Corporate and other	$12,313	$ 463	$ (63)	$12,713
State and municipal	9,460	570	(11)	10,019
Mortgage-backed	5,991	255	(65)	6,181
Non-U.S.	6,887	213	(37)	7,063
Equity	2,843	412	(59)	3,196
U.S. government and federal agency	1,817	77	(3)	1,891
	$39,311	$1,990	$ (238)	$41,063
December 31, 1994				
Corporate and other	$10,883	$ 4	$ (763)	$10,124
State and municipal	9,193	146	(392)	8,947
Mortgage-backed	4,927	82	(220)	4,789
Non-U.S.	3,892	20	(76)	3,836
Equity	2,147	201	(180)	2,168
U.S. government and federal agency	1,185	—	(177)	1,008
	$32,227	$ 453	$(1,808)	$30,872

At December 31, 1995, contractual maturities of debt securities, other than mortgage-backed securities, were as follows:

**GECS contractual maturities
(excluding mortgage-backed securities)**

(In millions)	Amortized cost	Estimated fair value
Due in		
1996	$ 2,359	$ 2,386
1997-2000	9,753	9,982
2001-2005	6,821	7,129
2006 and later	11,544	12,189

It is expected that actual maturities will differ from contractual maturities because borrowers have the right to call or prepay certain obligations, sometimes without call or prepayment penalties. Proceeds from sales of investment securities in 1995 were $11,017 million ($5,821 million in 1994 and $6,112 million in 1993). Gross realized gains were $503 million in 1995 ($281 million in 1994 and $173 million in 1993). Gross realized losses were $157 million in 1995 ($112 million in 1994 and $34 million in 1993).

11 GE Current Receivables

December 31 (In millions)	1995	1994
Aircraft Engines	$1,373	$1,183
Appliances	595	499
Broadcasting	556	493
Industrial Products and Systems	1,525	1,503
Materials	1,322	1,256
Power Generation	2,334	1,925
Technical Products and Services	692	603
All Other	94	282
Corporate	631	268
	9,122	8,012
Less allowance for losses	(231)	(205)
	$8,891	$7,807

Of receivables balances at December 31, 1995 and 1994 before allowance for losses, $6,582 million and $5,668 million, respectively, were from sales of goods and services to customers, and $293 million and $196 million, respectively, were from transactions with associated companies.

Current receivables of $322 million at year-end 1995 and $387 million at year-end 1994 arose from sales, principally of aircraft engine goods and services, on open account to various agencies of the U.S. government, which is GE's largest single customer. About 5%, 6% and 8% of GE's sales of goods and services were to the U.S. government in 1995, 1994 and 1993, respectively.

12 GE Inventories

December 31 (In millions)	1995	1994
Raw materials and work in process	$3,205	$ 2,933
Finished goods	2,277	2,165
Unbilled shipments	258	214
	5,740	5,312
Less revaluation to LIFO	(1,345)	(1,432)
	$4,395	$ 3,880

LIFO revaluations decreased $87 million in 1995, compared with decreases of $197 million in 1994 and $179 million in 1993. Included in these changes were decreases of $88 million, $72 million and $101 million in 1995, 1994 and 1993, respectively, that resulted from lower LIFO inventory levels. There was no cost change in 1995 and net cost decreases in 1994 and 1993. As of December 31, 1995, GE is obligated to acquire raw materials at market prices through the year 2000 under various take-or-pay or similar arrangements. Annual minimum commitments under these arrangements are insignificant.

13   GECS Financing Receivables (investment in time sales, loans and financing leases)

December 31 (In millions)	1995	1994
Time sales and loans		
Consumer services	$33,430	$25,906
Specialized financing	18,230	17,988
Mid-market financing	8,795	5,916
Equipment management	1,371	1,516
Specialty insurance	189	—
	62,015	51,326
Deferred income	(2,424)	(1,305)
Time sales and loans — net	59,591	50,021
Investment in financing leases		
Direct financing leases	33,291	25,916
Leveraged leases	2,909	2,482
Investment in financing leases	36,200	28,398
	95,791	78,419
Less allowance for losses	(2,519)	(2,062)
	$93,272	$76,357

Time sales and loans represents transactions in a variety of forms, including time sales, revolving charge and credit, mortgages, installment loans, intermediate-term loans and revolving loans secured by business assets. The portfolio includes time sales and loans carried at the principal amount on which finance charges are billed periodically, and time sales and loans carried at gross book value, which includes finance charges. At year-end 1995 and 1994, specialized financing and consumer services loans included $13,405 million and $13,282 million, respectively, for commercial real estate loans. Note 16 contains information on airline loans and leases.

At December 31, 1995, contractual maturities for time sales and loans were $24,543 million in 1996; $11,933 million in 1997; $6,635 million in 1998; $5,052 million in 1999; $4,424 million in 2000; and $9,428 million thereafter — aggregating $62,015 million. Experience has shown that a substantial portion of receivables will be paid prior to contractual maturity. Accordingly, the maturities of time sales and loans are not to be regarded as forecasts of future cash collections.

Investment in financing leases consists of direct financing and leveraged leases of aircraft, railroad rolling stock, autos, other transportation equipment, data processing equipment and medical equipment, as well as other manufacturing, power generation, mining and commercial equipment and facilities.

As the sole owner of assets under direct financing leases and as the equity participant in leveraged leases, GECS is taxed on total lease payments received and is entitled to tax deductions based on the cost of leased assets and tax deductions for interest paid to third-party participants. GECS generally is entitled to any residual value of leased assets.

Investment in direct financing and leveraged leases represents unpaid rentals and estimated unguarantied residual values of leased equipment, less related deferred income. GECS has no general obligation for principal and interest on notes and other instruments representing third-party participation related to leveraged leases; such notes and other instruments have not been included in liabilities but have been offset against the related rentals receivable. GECS' share of rentals receivable on leveraged leases is subordinate to the share of other participants who also have security interests in the leased equipment.

Net investment in financing leases	Total financing leases		Direct financing leases		Leveraged leases	
December 31 (In millions)	1995	1994	1995	1994	1995	1994
Total minimum lease payments receivable	$50,059	$39,968	$37,434	$30,338	$12,625	$ 9,630
Less principal and interest on third-party nonrecourse debt	(9,329)	(7,103)	—	—	(9,329)	(7,103)
Net rentals receivable	40,730	32,865	37,434	30,338	3,296	2,527
Estimated unguarantied residual value of leased assets	5,768	4,889	4,630	3,767	1,138	1,122
Less deferred income	(10,298)	(9,356)	(8,773)	(8,189)	(1,525)	(1,167)
Investment in financing leases (as shown above)	36,200	28,398	33,291	25,916	2,909	2,482
Less amounts to arrive at net investment						
Allowance for losses	(745)	(570)	(669)	(471)	(76)	(99)
Deferred taxes arising from financing leases	(5,746)	(5,075)	(2,959)	(2,470)	(2,787)	(2,605)
Net investment in financing leases	$29,709	$22,753	$29,663	$22,975	$ 46	$ (222)

At December 31, 1995, contractual maturities for rentals receivable under financing leases were $8,780 million in 1996; $10,418 million in 1997; $6,837 million in 1998; $3,631 million in 1999; $2,126 million in 2000; and $8,938 million thereafter — aggregating $40,730 million. As with time sales and loans, experience has shown that a portion of receivables will be paid prior to contractual maturity, and these amounts should not be regarded as forecasts of future cash flows.

Nonearning consumer receivables, primarily private-label credit card receivables, amounted to $671 million and $422 million at December 31, 1995 and 1994, respectively. A majority of these receivables were subject to various loss-sharing arrangements that provide full or partial recourse to the originating private-label entity. Nonearning and re-duced-earning receivables other than consumer receivables were $464 million and $346 million at year-end 1995 and 1994, respectively.

On January 1, 1995, GE adopted Statement of Financial Accounting Standards (SFAS) No. 114, *Accounting by Creditors for Impairment of a Loan,* and the related SFAS No. 118, *Accounting by Creditors for Impairment of a Loan — Income Recognition and Disclosures.* These Statements do not apply to, among other things, leases or large groups of smaller-balance, homogeneous loans, and therefore are principally relevant to GECS' commercial loans. There was no effect of adopting the Statements on 1995 results of operations or financial position because the allowance for losses established under the previous accounting policy continued to be appropriate following the accounting change. The Statements require disclosures of impaired loans — loans for which it is probable that the lender will be unable to col-lect all amounts due according to original contractual terms of the loan agreement, based on current information and events. At December 31, 1995, loans that required dis-closure as impaired amounted to $867 million, principally commercial real estate loans. For $647 million of such loans, the required allowance for losses was $285 million. The remaining $220 million of loans represents the re-corded investment in loans that are fully recoverable, but only because the recorded investment had been reduced through charge-offs or deferral of income recognition. These loans must be disclosed under the Statements' tech-nical definition of "impaired" because GECS will be unable to collect all amounts due according to original contractual terms of the loan agreement. Under the Statements, such loans do not require an allowance for losses. GECS' average investment in impaired loans requiring disclosure under the Statements was $1,037 million during 1995, with revenue of $49 million recognized, principally on the cash basis.

14 Property, Plant and Equipment (including equipment leased to others)

December 31 (In millions)	1995	1994
Original cost		
GE		
Land and improvements	$ 496	$ 416
Buildings, structures and related equipment	6,063	5,547
Machinery and equipment	17,184	15,847
Leasehold costs and manufacturing plant under construction	1,100	1,073
Other	24	24
	24,867	22,907
GECS		
Buildings and equipment	2,616	1,875
Equipment leased to others		
Aircraft (a)	5,682	4,601
Vehicles	4,948	4,542
Marine shipping containers	3,253	3,333
Railroad rolling stock	1,811	1,605
Other	2,769	2,807
	21,079	18,763
	$45,946	$41,670
Accumulated depreciation, depletion and amortization		
GE	$14,633	$13,382
GECS		
Buildings and equipment	964	794
Equipment leased to others	4,670	4,029
	$20,267	$18,205

(a) Includes $101 million and $226 million of commercial aircraft off-lease in 1995 and 1994, respectively.

Amortization of GECS' equipment leased to others was $1,702 million, $1,435 million and $1,395 million in 1995, 1994 and 1993, respectively. Noncancelable future rentals due from customers for equipment on operating leases at year-end 1995 totaled $8,412 million and are due as follows: $2,501 million in 1996; $1,657 million in 1997; $1,119 mil-lion in 1998; $732 million in 1999; $450 million in 2000; and $1,953 million thereafter.

15 Intangible Assets

December 31 (In millions)	1995	1994
GE		
Goodwill	$ 5,901	$ 5,605
Other intangibles	742	731
	6,643	6,336
GECS		
Goodwill	3,984	2,513
Mortgage servicing rights	1,688	1,351
Other intangibles	1,027	1,173
	6,699	5,037
	$13,342	$11,373

GE's intangible assets are shown net of accumulated amortization of $2,347 million in 1995 and $2,049 million in 1994. GECS' intangible assets are net of accumulated amortization of $1,494 million in 1995 and $988 million in 1994.

16 All Other Assets

December 31 (In millions)	1995	1994
GE		
Investments		
Associated companies (a)	$ 1,201	$ 1,945
Government and government-guarantied securities	100	273
Other	1,572	1,713
	2,873	3,931
Prepaid pension asset	5,272	4,489
Other	3,756	3,999
	11,901	12,419
GECS		
Investments		
Assets acquired for resale	3,998	3,867
Associated companies (a)	3,566	2,098
Real estate ventures	1,564	1,400
Other	2,072	1,652
	11,200	9,017
Deferred insurance acquisition costs	1,336	1,290
Other	1,868	1,224
	14,404	11,531
	$26,305	$23,950

(a) Includes advances.

In line with industry practice, sales of commercial jet aircraft engines often involve long-term customer financing commitments. In making such commitments, it is GE's general practice to require that it have or be able to establish a secured position in the aircraft being financed. Under such airline financing programs, GE had issued loans and guaranties (principally guaranties) amounting to $1,433 million at year-end 1995 and $1,260 million at year-end 1994; and it had entered into commitments totaling $1,505 million and $1,136 million at year-end 1995 and 1994, respectively, to provide financial assistance on future aircraft engine sales. Estimated fair values of the aircraft securing these receivables and associated guaranties exceeded the related account balances and guarantied amounts at December 31, 1995. GE sells certain long-term receivables from the airline industry with recourse. Proceeds from such sales amounted to $297 million in 1995 and $137 million in 1993. No receivables were sold in 1994. Balances outstanding were $487 million and $269 million at December 31, 1995 and 1994, respectively. GECS acts as a lender and lessor to the commercial airline industry. At December 31, 1995 and 1994, the balance of such GECS loans, leases and equipment leased to others was $8,337 million and $7,571 million, respectively. In addition, GECS had issued financial guaranties and funding commitments of $409 million at December 31, 1995 ($506 million at year-end 1994) and had conditional commitments to purchase aircraft at a cost of $141 million ($81 million at year-end 1994).

At year-end 1995, the National Broadcasting Company had $7,953 million of commitments to acquire broadcast material or the rights to broadcast television programs, including U.S. television rights to future Olympic games, and commitments under long-term television station affiliation agreements that require payments through the year 2008.

In connection with numerous projects, primarily power generation bids and contracts, GE had issued various bid and performance bonds and guaranties totaling $2,462 million at year-end 1995 and $2,229 million at year-end 1994.

17 GE All Other Current Costs and Expenses Accrued

At year-end 1995 and 1994, this account included taxes accrued of $1,598 million and $1,238 million, respectively, and compensation and benefit accruals of $1,233 million and $1,191 million, respectively. Also included are amounts for product warranties, estimated costs on shipments billed to customers and a variety of sundry items.

18 Borrowings

Short-term borrowings

December 31 (In millions)	1995 Amount	1995 Average rate	1994 Amount	1994 Average rate
GE				
Payable to banks	$ 266	8.18%	$ 353	8.21%
Commercial paper (U.S.)	403	5.72	—	
Current portion of long-term debt	697		243	
Other	300		310	
	1,666		906	
GECS				
Commercial paper				
U.S.	37,432	5.82	41,759	5.88
Non-U.S.	3,796	6.33	1,938	6.27
Current portion of long-term debt	15,719		9,695	
Other	5,861		3,695	
	62,808		57,087	
Eliminations	(11)		(212)	
	$64,463		$57,781	

Long-term borrowings

December 31 (In millions)	Weighted average interest rate (a)	Maturities	1995	1994
GE				
Senior notes	7.16%	1997-2000	$ 988	$ 1,480
Payable to banks	6.11	1997-2003	482	283
Industrial development/ pollution control bonds	3.90	1997-2019	260	261
Other (b)			547	675
			2,277	2,699
GECS				
Senior notes	6.56	1997-2055	47,794	33,615
Subordinated notes (c)	7.88	2006-2035	996	697
			48,790	34,312
Eliminations			(40)	(32)
			$51,027	$36,979

(a) Includes the effects of associated interest rate and currency swaps.
(b) Includes a variety of obligations having various interest rates and maturities, including certain borrowings by parent operating components and affiliates.
(c) Guarantied by GE.

Interest rate and currency swaps are employed by GE and GECS to achieve the lowest cost of funds for a particular funding strategy. GECS enters into interest rate swaps and currency swaps (including non-U.S. currency and cross-currency interest rate swaps) to modify interest rates and/or currencies of specific debt instruments. For example, to fund U.S. operations, GE Capital may issue fixed-rate debt denominated in a currency other than the U.S. dollar and simultaneously enter into a currency swap to create synthetic fixed-rate U.S. dollar debt with a lower yield than could be achieved directly. Such interest rate and currency swaps have been designated as modifying interest rates, currencies, or both. Neither GE nor GECS engages in derivatives trading, market-making or other speculative activities.

GECS used a portion of this interest rate swap portfolio to convert interest rate exposure on short-term and floating rate long-term borrowings to interest rates that are fixed over the terms of the related swaps; interest rate basis swaps also are employed to manage short-term financing factors — for example, to convert commercial paper-based interest costs to prime rate-based costs. At December 31, 1995 and 1994, such swaps were outstanding for principal amounts equivalent to $11,451 million and $9,301 million with maturities from 1996 to 2029 and weighted average interest rates of 6.86% and 6.80%, respectively.

Aggregate amounts of long-term borrowings that mature during the next five years are as follows.

(In millions)	1996	1997	1998	1999	2000
GE	$ 697	$ 527	$ 1,011	$ 28	$ 276
GECS	15,719	14,012	11,517	5,480	4,494

Additional information about GE and GECS borrowings, as well as associated swaps, is provided in note 29.

Confirmed credit lines of approximately $3.1 billion had been extended to GE by 32 banks at year-end 1995. Substantially all of GE's credit lines are available to GECS and its affiliates in addition to their own credit lines.

At year-end 1995, GECS and its affiliates had committed lines of credit aggregating $20.4 billion with 128 banks, including $9.5 billion of revolving credit agreements pursuant to which it has the right to borrow funds for periods exceeding one year. A total of $1.5 billion of GE Capital's credit lines is available for use by GE.

During 1995, neither GE nor GECS borrowed under any of these credit lines. Both GE and GECS compensate banks for credit facilities in the form of fees, which were insignificant in each of the past three years.

19 Insurance Liabilities, Reserves and Annuity Benefits

Insurance liabilities, reserves and annuity benefits comprises policyholders' benefits, unearned premiums and reserves for policy losses in GECS' insurance and annuity businesses. The estimated liability for insurance losses and loss expenses consists of both case and incurred-but-not-reported reserves. Where GECS' experience is not sufficient to determine reserves, industry averages are used. Estimated amounts of salvage and subrogation recoverable on paid and unpaid losses are deducted from outstanding losses. The insurance subsidiaries of GECS have no significant permitted statutory accounting practices that differ from either statutorily prescribed or generally accepted accounting principles.

Activity in the liability for unpaid claims and claims adjustment expenses is summarized below.

(In millions)	1995	1994	1993
Balance at January 1 — gross	$ 7,032	$ 6,405	$ 5,484
Less reinsurance recoverables	(1,084)	(1,142)	(1,191)
Balance at January 1 — net	5,948	5,263	4,293
Claims and expenses incurred			
Current year	3,268	2,016	2,051
Prior years	492	558	359
Claims and expenses paid			
Current year	(706)	(543)	(378)
Prior years	(1,908)	(1,432)	(1,048)
Claim reserves related to acquired companies	3,696	49	—
Other	19	37	(14)
Balance at December 31 — net	10,809	5,948	5,263
Add reinsurance recoverables	1,853	1,084	1,142
Balance at December 31 — gross	$12,662	$ 7,032	$ 6,405

The liability for future policy benefits of the life insurance affiliates has been computed mainly by a net-level-premium method based on assumptions for investment yields, mortality and terminations that were appropriate at date of purchase or at the time the policies were developed, including provisions for adverse deviations. Average yields used in these computations ranged from 2.0% to 9.0% in 1995 and 4.0% to 9.1% in 1994.

Financial guaranties and credit life risk of insurance affiliates are summarized below.

December 31 (In millions)	1995	1994
Guaranties, principally on municipal bonds and structured finance issues	$119,406	$106,726
Mortgage insurance risk in force	32,599	31,463
Credit life insurance risk in force	13,670	13,713
Other	110	147
Less reinsurance	(21,749)	(19,426)
	$144,036	$132,623

20 GE All Other Liabilities

This account includes noncurrent compensation and benefit accruals at year-end 1995 and 1994 of $4,858 million and $4,632 million, respectively. Also included are amounts for deferred incentive compensation, deferred income, product warranties and a variety of sundry items.

SFAS No. 112, *Employers' Accounting for Postemployment Benefits*, was adopted as of January 1, 1993. This Statement requires that employers recognize over the service lives of employees the costs of postemployment benefits if certain conditions are met. The principal effect for GE was to change the method of accounting for severance benefits. Under the previous accounting policy, the total cost of severance benefits was expensed when the severance event occurred. The cumulative effect of the accounting change as of January 1, 1993, amounted to $1,306 million before taxes ($862 million, or $0.51 per share, after taxes).

21 Restricted Net Assets of Affiliates

Certain GECS consolidated affiliates are restricted from remitting funds to GECS in the form of dividends or loans by a variety of regulations, the purpose of which is to protect affected insurance policyholders, depositors or investors. At year-end 1995, net assets of GECS' regulated affiliates amounted to $14.7 billion, of which $12.5 billion was restricted.

Aggregate deferred tax amounts are summarized below.

December 31 (In millions)	1995	1994
Assets		
GE	$ 3,851	$ 3,720
GECS	2,183	2,642
	6,034	6,362
Liabilities		
GE	4,359	3,988
GECS	9,055	7,579
	13,414	11,567
Net deferred tax liability	$ 7,380	$ 5,205

Principal components of the net deferred tax liability balances for GE and GECS are as follows:

December 31 (In millions)	1995	1994
GE		
Provisions for expenses	$ (2,539)	$ (2,422)
Retiree insurance plans	(818)	(835)
Prepaid pension asset	1,845	1,571
Depreciation	928	860
Other — net	1,092	1,094
	508	268
GECS		
Financing leases	5,746	5,075
Operating leases	1,367	1,234
Net unrealized gains (losses) on securities	608	(468)
Allowance for losses	(852)	(876)
Insurance reserves	(497)	(460)
Other — net	500	432
	6,872	4,937
Net deferred tax liability	$ 7,380	$ 5,205

23   Minority Interest in Equity of Consolidated Affiliates

Minority interest in equity of consolidated GECS affiliates includes preferred stock issued by GE Capital and by a subsidiary of GE Capital. The preferred stock pays cumulative dividends at variable rates. The liquidation preference of the preferred shares is summarized below.

December 31 (In millions)	1995	1994
GE Capital	$1,800	$875
GE Capital subsidiary	360	240

Dividend rates on the preferred stock ranged from 4.2% to 5.2% during 1995, from 2.3% to 4.9% during 1994 and from 2.3% to 2.8% during 1993.

24   Share Owners' Equity

(In millions)	1995	1994	1993
Common stock issued			
Balance at January 1	$ 594	$ 584	$ 584
Adjustment for stock split	—	9	—
Newly issued stock	—	1	—
Balance at December 31	$ 594	$ 594	$ 584
Unrealized gains (losses) on investment securities	$ 1,000	$ (810)	$ 848
Other capital			
Balance at January 1	$ 1,122	$ 550	$ 719
Currency translation adjustments	127	180	(279)
Gains on treasury stock dispositions	414	215	110
Newly issued stock	—	186	—
Adjustment for stock split	—	(9)	—
Balance at December 31	$ 1,663	$ 1,122	$ 550
Retained earnings			
Balance at January 1	$30,793	$28,613	$26,527
Net earnings	6,573	4,726	4,315
Dividends declared	(2,838)	(2,546)	(2,229)
Balance at December 31	$34,528	$30,793	$28,613
Common stock held in treasury			
Balance at January 1	$ 5,312	$ 4,771	$ 4,407
Purchases	4,016	1,124	770
Dispositions	(1,152)	(583)	(406)
Balance at December 31	$ 8,176	$ 5,312	$ 4,771

In December 1994, GE's Board of Directors authorized the repurchase of up to $5 billion of Company common stock over a two-year period with funds generated largely from free cash flow. In December 1995, the Board increased the authorized amount of the repurchase to $9 billion, which will allow the program to continue through 1997. A total of 54.7 million shares having an aggregate cost of $3.2 billion had been repurchased under this program and placed into treasury as of December 31, 1995.

Common shares issued and outstanding are summarized in the table below.

Shares of GE common stock December 31 (In thousands)	1995	1994	1993
Issued	1,857,013	1,857,013	1,853,128
In treasury	(190,501)	(151,046)	(145,826)
Outstanding	1,666,512	1,705,967	1,707,302

GE has 50 million authorized shares of preferred stock ($1.00 par value), but no such shares have been issued.

The effects of translating to U.S. dollars the financial statements of non-U.S. affiliates whose functional currency is the local currency are included in other capital. Asset and liability accounts are translated at year-end exchange rates, while revenues and expenses are translated at average rates for the period. The cumulative currency translation adjustment was an addition to other capital of $61 million at year-end 1995 and a reduction of other capital of $66 million and $246 million at December 31, 1994 and 1993, respectively.

25 Other Stock-Related Information

Stock option plans, stock appreciation rights (SARs), restricted stock and restricted stock units are described in GE's current Proxy Statement. More than 20,000 individuals, nearly one third of all exempt professionals at GE and GECS, hold stock options. With certain restrictions, requirements for stock option shares can be met from either unissued or treasury shares.

Stock option activity

(Shares in thousands)	Shares subject to option	Average per share Exercise price	Average per share Market price
Balance at January 1, 1993	48,164	$32.19	$42.75
Options granted	17,580	45.90	45.90
Replacement options	882	28.60	28.60
Options exercised	(6,072)	28.33	47.57
Options terminated	(1,200)	36.84	—
Balance at December 31, 1993	59,354	36.50	52.44
Options granted	15,134	50.66	50.66
Replacement options	340	36.44	36.44
Options exercised	(4,163)	30.35	50.58
Options terminated	(1,167)	44.04	—
Balance at December 31, 1994	69,498	39.82	51.00
Options granted	12,089	55.88	55.88
Replacement options	753	41.82	41.82
Options exercised	(7,784)	31.44	59.21
Options terminated	(2,119)	47.33	—
Balance at December 31, 1995	72,437	43.20	72.00

Options granted have been adjusted for the April 1994 2-for-1 stock split. Without giving effect to that adjustment, options granted (in thousands) were 12,089 in 1995; 10,117 in 1994; and 8,790 in 1993.

The replacement options replaced canceled SARs and have identical terms thereto. At year-end 1995, there were 8.3 million SARs outstanding at an average exercise price of $45.55. There were 4.4 million restricted stock shares and restricted stock units outstanding at year-end 1995.

There were 20.8 million and 16.1 million shares available for grants of options, SARs, restricted stock and restricted stock units at December 31, 1995 and 1994, respectively. Under the 1990 Long-Term Incentive Plan, 0.95% of the Company's issued common stock (including treasury shares) as of the first day of each calendar year during which the Plan is in effect becomes available for granting awards in such year. Any unused portion, in addition to shares allocated to awards that are canceled or forfeited, is available for later years.

Outstanding options and SARs expire on various dates through December 14, 2005. Restricted stock grants vest on various dates up to normal retirement of grantees.

GE adopted the disclosure-only option under SFAS No. 123, *Accounting for Stock-Based Compensation*, as of December 31, 1995. If the accounting provisions of the new Statement had been adopted as of the beginning of 1995, the effect on 1995 net earnings would have been immaterial. Further, based on current and anticipated use of stock options, it is not envisioned that the impact of the Statement's accounting provisions would be material in any future period.

The following table summarizes information about stock options outstanding at December 31, 1995.

Stock options outstanding
(Shares in thousands)

Exercise price range	Outstanding Shares	Outstanding Average life (a)	Outstanding Average exercise price	Exercisable Shares	Exercisable Average exercise price
$19¾ – $33¹⁵⁄₁₆	14,705	4.2	$29.25	14,705	$29.25
$34⁵⁄₁₆–$43¹⁄₁₆	16,539	6.1	37.39	15,644	37.23
$43¼ –$51	20,087	7.8	47.02	6,383	43.94
$51¹⁄₁₆–$72⅜	21,106	8.8	53.84	55	51.69
Total	72,437	7.0	43.20	36,787	35.23

(a) Average contractual life remaining in years.

At December 31, 1994, there were approximately 38 million options exercisable at an average exercise price of $33.43.

Stock options expire in 10 years from the date they are granted; options vest over service periods that range from one to five years.

26

Supplemental Cash Flows Information

Changes in operating assets and liabilities are net of acquisitions and dispositions of businesses.

"Payments for principal businesses purchased" in the Statement of Cash Flows is net of cash acquired and includes debt assumed and immediately repaid in acquisitions.

"All other operating activities" in the Statement of Cash Flows consists principally of adjustments to current and noncurrent accruals of costs and expenses, amortization of premium and discount on debt, and adjustments to assets such as amortization of goodwill and intangibles.

The Statement of Cash Flows excludes certain noncash transactions that had no significant effects on the investing or financing activities of GE or GECS.

Certain supplemental information related to GE and GECS cash flows is shown below.

For the years ended December 31 (In millions)	1995	1994	1993
GE			
Net purchase of GE shares for treasury			
Open market purchases under share repurchase programs	$ (3,101)	$ (69)	$ (217)
Other purchases	(915)	(1,055)	(553)
Dispositions (mainly to employee and dividend reinvestment plans)	1,493	771	406
	$ (2,523)	$ (353)	$ (364)
GECS			
Financing receivables			
Increase in loans to customers	$ (46,154)	$ (37,059)	$ (30,002)
Principal collections from customers	44,840	31,264	27,571
Investment in equipment for financing leases	(17,182)	(10,528)	(7,204)
Principal collections on financing leases	8,821	8,461	6,011
Net change in credit card receivables	(3,773)	(2,902)	(1,645)
Sales of financing receivables with recourse	2,139	1,239	1,105
	$ (11,309)	$ (9,525)	$ (4,164)
All other investing activities			
Purchases of securities by insurance and annuity businesses	$ (14,452)	$ (8,663)	$ (10,488)
Dispositions and maturities of securities by insurance and annuity businesses	12,460	6,338	7,698
Proceeds from principal business dispositions	575	—	—
Other	(2,496)	2,501	(4,003)
	$ (3,913)	$ 176	$ (6,793)
Newly issued debt having maturities longer than 90 days			
Short-term (91 to 365 days)	$ 2,545	$ 3,214	$ 4,315
Long-term (longer than one year)	32,507	19,228	10,885
Long-term subordinated	298	—	—
Proceeds — nonrecourse, leveraged lease debt	1,428	31	53
	$ 36,778	$ 22,473	$ 15,253
Repayments and other reductions of debt having maturities longer than 90 days			
Short-term (91 to 365 days)	$ (16,075)	$ (10,460)	$ (9,008)
Long-term (longer than one year)	(678)	(930)	(206)
Principal payments — nonrecourse, leveraged lease debt	(292)	(309)	(312)
	$ (17,045)	$ (11,699)	$ (9,526)
All other financing activities			
Proceeds from sales of investment and annuity contracts	$ 1,754	$ 1,207	$ 509
Preferred stock issued by GE Capital	1,045	240	—
Redemption of investment and annuity contracts	(2,540)	(1,264)	(578)
	$ 259	$ 183	$ (69)
Other			
Cash from (used for) discontinued operations			
Cash from GE Aerospace operating activities	$ —	$ —	$ 76
Cash from GE Aerospace investing activities	—	—	886
Cash from (used for) GECS securities broker-dealer operating activities	1,414	1,635	(1,910)
Cash from (used for) GECS securities broker-dealer investing activities	92	334	(107)
Cash from (used for) GECS securities broker-dealer financing activities	(1,506)	(2,169)	2,017
	$ —	$ (200)	$ 962

27 Industry Segments

(In millions)	Revenues For the years ended December 31								
	Total revenues			Intersegment revenues			External revenues		
	1995	1994	1993	1995	1994	1993	1995	1994	1993
GE									
Aircraft Engines	$ 6,098	$ 5,714	$ 6,580	$ 115	$ 43	$ 59	$ 5,983	$ 5,671	$ 6,521
Appliances	5,933	5,965	5,555	4	3	3	5,929	5,962	5,552
Broadcasting	3,919	3,361	3,102	—	—	—	3,919	3,361	3,102
Industrial Products and Systems	10,194	9,406	8,575	436	368	409	9,758	9,038	8,166
Materials	6,647	5,681	5,042	19	43	50	6,628	5,638	4,992
Power Generation	6,545	5,933	5,530	57	44	135	6,488	5,889	5,395
Technical Products and Services	4,424	4,285	4,174	19	18	18	4,405	4,267	4,156
All Other	2,707	2,348	1,803	—	—	—	2,707	2,348	1,803
Corporate items and eliminations	(286)	(195)	(242)	(650)	(519)	(674)	364	324	432
Total GE	46,181	42,498	40,119	—	—	—	46,181	42,498	40,119
GECS									
Financing	19,042	14,932	12,399	—	—	—	19,042	14,932	12,399
Specialty Insurance	7,444	4,926	4,862	—	—	—	7,444	4,926	4,862
All Other	6	17	15	—	—	—	6	17	15
Total GECS	26,492	19,875	17,276	—	—	—	26,492	19,875	17,276
Eliminations	(2,645)	(2,264)	(1,694)	—	—	—	(2,645)	(2,264)	(1,694)
Consolidated revenues	$70,028	$60,109	$55,701	$ —	$ —	$ —	$70,028	$60,109	$55,701

GE revenues include income from sales of goods and services to customers and other income. Sales from one Company component to another generally are priced at equivalent commercial selling prices. "All Other" GE revenues consists primarily of GECS' earnings.

(In millions)	Assets At December 31			Property, plant and equipment (including equipment leased to others) For the years ended December 31					
				Additions			Depreciation, depletion and amortization		
	1995	1994	1993	1995	1994	1993	1995	1994	1993
GE									
Aircraft Engines	$ 4,890	$ 4,751	$ 5,329	$ 266	$ 254	$ 207	$ 273	$ 261	$ 333
Appliances	2,304	2,309	2,193	143	159	129	93	84	125
Broadcasting	3,915	3,881	3,742	97	86	56	64	67	98
Industrial Products and Systems	6,117	5,862	5,442	425	400	397	308	363	332
Materials	9,095	8,628	8,181	521	417	374	478	443	413
Power Generation	5,679	4,887	3,875	155	176	212	166	143	143
Technical Products and Services	2,200	2,362	2,179	110	154	124	109	95	88
All Other	13,113	9,768	11,604	1	—	1	1	2	3
Corporate items and eliminations	8,403	8,365	8,589	113	97	88	89	87	96
Total GE	55,716	50,813	51,134	1,831	1,743	1,588	1,581	1,545	1,631
GECS									
Financing	150,062	121,966	106,854	5,144	5,889	3,352	1,962	1,607	1,545
Specialty Insurance	34,795	22,058	18,915	132	62	15	24	16	9
All Other	872	943	868	36	44	59	27	39	38
Total GECS	185,729	144,967	126,637	5,312	5,995	3,426	2,013	1,662	1,592
Eliminations	(13,410)	(9,909)	(11,358)	—	—	—	—	—	—
Consolidated totals	$228,035	$185,871	$166,413	$7,143	$7,738	$5,014	$3,594	$3,207	$3,223

"All Other" GE assets consists primarily of investment in GECS.

Details of operating profit by industry segment can be found on page 35 of this report. A description of industry segments for General Electric Company and consolidated affiliates follows.

- **Aircraft Engines.** Jet engines and replacement parts and repair services for all categories of commercial aircraft (short/medium, intermediate and long-range); for a wide variety of military aircraft, including fighters, bombers, tankers and helicopters; and for executive and commuter aircraft. Sold worldwide to airframe manufacturers, airlines and government agencies. Also, aircraft engine derivatives used as marine propulsion and industrial power sources.

- **Appliances.** Major appliances and related services for products such as refrigerators, freezers, electric and gas ranges, dishwashers, clothes washers and dryers, microwave ovens and room air conditioning equipment. Sold in North America and in global markets under various GE and private-label brands. Distributed to retail outlets, mainly for the replacement market, and to building contractors and distributors for new installations.

- **Broadcasting.** Primarily the National Broadcasting Company (NBC). Principal businesses are the furnishing of U.S. network television services to more than 200 affiliated stations, production of television programs, operation of six VHF television broadcasting stations, operation of five cable/satellite networks around the world, and investment and programming activities in multimedia and cable television.

- **Industrial Products and Systems.** Lighting products (including a wide variety of lamps, lighting fixtures, wiring devices and quartz products); electrical distribution and control equipment (including power delivery and control products such as transformers, meters, relays, capacitors and arresters); transportation systems products (including diesel-electric locomotives, transit propulsion equipment and motorized wheels for off-highway vehicles); electric motors and related products; a broad range of electrical and electronic industrial automation products, including drive systems; installation, engineering and repair services, which includes management and technical expertise for large projects such as process control systems; and GE Supply, a network of electrical supply houses. Markets are extremely diverse. Products are sold to commercial and industrial end users, including utilities, to original equipment manufacturers, to electrical distributors, to retail outlets, to railways and to transit authorities. Increasingly, products are developed for and sold in global markets.

- **Materials.** High-performance engineered plastics used in applications such as automobiles and housings for computers and other business equipment; ABS resins; silicones; superabrasives such as man-made diamonds; and laminates. Sold worldwide to a diverse customer base consisting mainly of manufacturers.

- **Power Generation.** Products and related maintenance services, mainly for the generation of electricity. Markets and competition are global. Gas turbines are sold principally as packaged power plants for electric utilities and for industrial cogeneration and mechanical drive applications. Steam turbine-generators are sold to electric utilities, to the U.S. Navy and, for cogeneration, to industrial and other power customers. Marine steam turbines are sold to the U.S. Navy. Power Generation also includes nuclear reactors and fuel and support services for GE's installed boiling water reactors.

- **Technical Products and Services.** Medical systems such as magnetic resonance (MR) and computed tomography (CT) scanners, x-ray, nuclear imaging, ultrasound, other diagnostic equipment and related services sold worldwide to hospitals and medical facilities. This segment also includes a full range of computer-based information and data interchange services for internal use and external commercial and industrial customers.

- **GECS Financing.** Operations of GE Capital, as follows:

Consumer services — private-label and bank credit card loans, time sales and revolving credit and inventory financing for retail merchants, auto leasing and inventory financing, mortgage servicing, and annuity and mutual fund sales.

Specialized financing — loans and financing leases for major capital assets, including industrial facilities and equipment, and energy-related facilities; commercial and residential real estate loans and investments; and loans to and investments in management buyouts, including those with high leverage, and corporate recapitalizations.

Equipment management — leases, loans and asset management services for portfolios of commercial and transportation equipment, including aircraft, trailers, auto fleets, modular space units, railroad rolling stock, data processing equipment, oceangoing containers and satellites.

Mid-market financing — loans and financing and operating leases for middle-market customers, including manufacturers, distributors and end users, for a variety of equipment that includes data processing equipment, medical and diagnostic equipment, and equipment used in construction, manufacturing, office applications and telecommunications activities.

Very few of the products financed by GE Capital are manufactured by other GE segments.

- **GECS Specialty Insurance.** U.S. and international multiple-line property and casualty reinsurance, certain directly written specialty insurance and life reinsurance; financial guaranty insurance, principally on municipal bonds and structured finance issues; private mortgage insurance; and creditor insurance covering international customer loan repayments.

28 Geographic Segment Information (consolidated)

Revenues and operating profit shown below are classified according to their country of origin (including exports from such areas). Revenues and operating profit classified under the caption "United States" include royalty and licensing income from non-U.S. sources. U.S. exports to international customers by major areas of the world are shown on page 38.

At year-end 1995, net assets of operations classified under the captions "Europe" and "Other areas of the world" were $20,793 million and $6,942 million, respectively.

(In millions)	**Revenues** For the years ended December 31								
	Total revenues			Intersegment revenues			External revenues		
	1995	1994	1993	**1995**	1994	1993	**1995**	1994	1993
United States	**$54,319**	$49,920	$47,495	**$2,123**	$1,683	$1,513	**$52,196**	$48,237	$45,982
Europe	**12,417**	7,797	6,722	**656**	579	525	**11,761**	7,218	6,197
Other areas of the world	**6,967**	5,493	4,171	**896**	839	649	**6,071**	4,654	3,522
Intercompany eliminations	**(3,675)**	(3,101)	(2,687)	**(3,675)**	(3,101)	(2,687)	**—**	—	—
Total	**$70,028**	$60,109	$55,701	**$ —**	$ —	$ —	**$70,028**	$60,109	$55,701

(In millions)	**Operating profit** For the years ended December 31			**Assets** At December 31		
	1995	1994	1993	**1995**	1994	1993
United States	**$ 9,175**	$8,351	$6,635	**$168,878**	$152,151	$145,390
Europe	**1,063**	673	360	**45,167**	22,464	14,257
Other areas of the world	**725**	595	307	**14,164**	11,439	6,954
Intercompany eliminations	**9**	5	(23)	**(174)**	(183)	(188)
Total	**$10,972**	$9,624	$7,279	**$228,035**	$185,871	$166,413

29 Additional Information about Financial Instruments

This note contains estimated fair values of certain financial instruments to which GE and GECS are parties. Apart from GE's and GECS' own borrowings and certain marketable securities, relatively few of these instruments are actively traded. Thus, fair values must often be determined by using one or more models that indicate value based on estimates of quantifiable characteristics as of a particular date. Because this undertaking is, by its nature, difficult and highly judgmental, for a limited number of instruments, alternative valuation techniques may have produced disclosed values different from those that could have been realized at December 31, 1995 or 1994. Moreover, the disclosed values are representative of fair values only as of the dates indicated. Assets that, as a matter of accounting policy, are reflected in the accompanying financial statements at fair value are not included in the following disclosures; such assets include cash and equivalents and investment securities.

Values are estimated as follows:

Borrowings. Based on quoted market prices or market comparables. Fair values of interest rate and currency swaps on borrowings are based on quoted market prices and include the effects of counterparty creditworthiness.

Time sales and loans. Based on quoted market prices, recent transactions and/or discounted future cash flows, using rates at which similar loans would have been made to similar borrowers.

Annuity benefits. Based on expected future cash flows, discounted at currently offered discount rates for immediate annuity contracts or cash surrender values for single premium deferred annuities.

Financial guaranties. Based on future cash flows, considering expected renewal premiums, claims, refunds and servicing costs, discounted at a market rate.

All other instruments. Based on comparable transactions, market comparables, discounted future cash flows, quoted market prices, and/or estimates of the cost to terminate or otherwise settle obligations to counterparties.

Financial instruments

At December 31 (In millions)	1995 Notional amount	1995 Assets (liabilities) Carrying amount (net)	1995 Assets (liabilities) Estimated fair value High	1995 Assets (liabilities) Estimated fair value Low	1994 Notional amount	1994 Assets (liabilities) Carrying amount (net)	1994 Assets (liabilities) Estimated fair value High	1994 Assets (liabilities) Estimated fair value Low
GE								
Investments	$ (a)	$ 1,796	$ 2,886	$ 2,886	$ (a)	$ 2,128	$ 2,289	$ 2,269
Borrowings and related instruments								
Borrowings (b)(c)	(a)	(3,943)	(3,981)	(3,981)	(a)	(3,605)	(3,530)	(3,530)
Interest rate swaps	89	—	(16)	(16)	89	—	2	2
Currency swaps	180	—	50	50	393	—	26	26
Financial guaranties	1,722	—	—	—	1,520	—	—	—
Other firm commitments								
Currency forwards and options	3,774	—	131	131	3,195	—	—	—
Financing commitments	1,505	—	—	—	1,153	—	—	—
GECS								
Assets								
Time sales and loans	(a)	57,817	59,188	58,299	(a)	48,529	49,496	48,840
Integrated interest rate swaps	1,703	—	(93)	(93)	1,183	—	64	64
Purchased options	1,213	24	11	11	103	2	2	2
Mortgage-related positions								
Mortgage purchase commitments	1,360	—	17	17	205	—	(2)	(2)
Mortgage sale commitments	1,334	—	(11)	(11)	1,792	—	2	2
Memo: mortgages held for sale (d)	(a)	1,663	1,663	1,663	(a)	1,764	1,764	1,764
Options, including "floors"	18,522	67	144	144	—	—	—	—
Interest rate swaps	1,990	—	31	31	950	—	(127)	(127)
Other cash financial instruments	(a)	1,514	1,967	1,705	(a)	1,897	2,026	1,924
Liabilities								
Borrowings and related instruments								
Borrowings (b)(c)	(a)	(111,598)	(113,105)	(113,105)	(a)	(91,399)	(89,797)	(89,797)
Interest rate swaps	43,681	—	(630)	(630)	21,996	—	198	195
Currency swaps	22,342	—	937	937	11,695	—	86	86
Purchased options	2,751	26	12	11	130	12	11	12
Other	515	—	(65)	(65)	—	—	—	—
Annuity benefits	(a)	(11,994)	(11,728)	(11,728)	(a)	(13,186)	(12,788)	(12,788)
Insurance — financial guaranties and credit life	144,036	(1,570)	(832)	(922)	132,623	(1,562)	(663)	(806)
Credit and liquidity support — securitizations	7,035	(58)	(65)	(65)	5,808	(22)	(22)	(22)
Performance guaranties — principally letters of credit	2,920	(48)	(78)	(78)	2,227	(18)	(98)	(101)
Other — principally liquidity commitments	3,556	1	(36)	(45)	3,166	—	42	38
Other firm commitments								
Currency forwards and options	7,657	—	69	69	3,372	—	12	12
Currency swaps	280	—	(22)	(22)	488	—	(3)	(3)
Ordinary course of business lending commitments	6,929	—	(60)	(60)	6,687	—	(50)	(50)
Unused revolving credit lines								
Commercial	3,223	—	—	—	2,580	—	—	—
Consumer — principally credit cards	118,710	—	—	—	101,582	—	—	—

(a) Not applicable.
(b) Includes interest rate and currency swaps.
(c) See note 18.
(d) Included in other cash financial instruments.

Additional information about certain financial instruments in the above table follows.

Currency forwards and options are employed by GE and GECS to manage exposures to changes in currency exchange rates associated with commercial purchase and sale transactions. These financial instruments generally are used to fix the local currency cost of purchased goods or services or selling prices denominated in currencies other than the functional currency. Currency exposures that result from net investments in affiliates are managed principally by funding assets denominated in local currency with debt denominated in those same currencies. In certain circumstances, net investment exposures are managed using currency forwards and currency swaps.

Options other than currency options. GECS is exposed to prepayment risk in certain of its business activities, such as in its mortgage servicing and annuities activities. In order to hedge those exposures, GECS uses one-sided financial instruments containing option features. These instruments generally behave based on limits ("caps," "floors" or "collars") on interest rate movement.

Interest rate and currency swaps are used by both GE and GECS to optimize borrowing costs for a particular funding strategy (see note 18) and by GECS to establish specific hedges of mortgage-related assets and to manage net investment exposures. Such swaps are evaluated by management under the credit criteria set forth below. In addition, as part of its ongoing customer activities, GECS may enter into swaps that are integrated with investments in or loans to particular customers and do not involve assumption of third-party credit risk. Such integrated swaps are evaluated and monitored like their associated investments or loans, and are not therefore subject to the same credit criteria that would apply to a stand-alone swap.

Counterparty credit risk. Given the ways in which GE and GECS each use swaps, purchased options and forwards, the principal risk is credit risk — risk that counterparties will be financially unable to make payments in accordance with the agreements. Associated market risk is meaningful only as it relates to how changes in market value affect credit exposure to individual counterparties. Except as noted above for positions that are integrated into financings, all swaps, purchased options and forwards are carried out within the following credit policy constraints:

• Once a counterparty exceeds credit exposure limits (see table below), no additional transactions are permitted until the exposure with that counterparty is reduced to an amount that is within the established limit. Open contracts remain in force.

Counterparty credit criteria	Credit rating	
	Moody's	Standard & Poor's
Term of transaction		
Between one and five years	Aa3	AA–
Greater than five years	Aaa	AAA
Credit exposure limits		
Up to $50 million	Aa3	AA–
Up to $75 million	Aaa	AAA

• All swaps are executed under master swap agreements containing mutual credit downgrade provisions that provide the ability to require assignment or termination in the event either party is downgraded below A3 or A–.

More credit latitude is permitted for transactions having original maturities shorter than one year because of their lower risk.

30 Quarterly Information (unaudited)

(Dollar amounts in millions; per-share amounts in dollars)	First quarter		Second quarter		Third quarter		Fourth quarter	
	1995	1994	**1995**	1994	**1995**	1994	**1995**	1994
Consolidated operations								
Earnings from continuing operations	**$1,372**	$1,219	**$ 1,726**	$ 1,554	**$ 1,610**	$1,457	**$ 1,865**	$ 1,685
Losses from discontinued operations	—	(151)	—	(32)	—	(89)	—	(49)
Provision for loss on discontinued securities broker-dealer operations	—	—	—	—	—	—	—	(868)
Net earnings	**$1,372**	$1,068	**$ 1,726**	$ 1,522	**$ 1,610**	$1,368	**$ 1,865**	$ 768
Per share								
Earnings from continuing operations	**$ 0.81**	$ 0.71	**$ 1.02**	$ 0.91	**$ 0.96**	$ 0.85	**$ 1.12**	$ 0.99
Losses from discontinued operations	—	(0.09)	—	(0.02)	—	(0.05)	—	(0.54)
Net earnings	**$ 0.81**	$ 0.62	**$ 1.02**	$ 0.89	**$ 0.96**	$ 0.80	**$ 1.12**	$ 0.45
Selected data								
GE								
Sales of goods and services	**$9,278**	$8,264	**$11,237**	$10,038	**$10,106**	$9,384	**$12,392**	$ 11,944
Gross profit from sales	**2,567**	2,282	**3,219**	2,743	**2,794**	2,441	**3,340**	3,115
GECS								
Revenues from operations	**5,754**	4,393	**6,415**	4,730	**7,099**	5,097	**7,224**	5,655
Operating profit	**826**	668	**818**	684	**1,048**	857	**828**	740

For GE, gross profit from sales is sales of goods and services less costs of goods and services sold. For GECS, operating profit is income before taxes.

First-quarter 1994 discontinued operations included a $210 million ($350 million before tax) charge resulting from the discovery of false trading profits created by the then head U.S. government securities trader in the discontinued securities broker-dealer. Approximately $143 million ($238 million before tax) of the charge related to periods prior to 1994.

Earnings-per-share amounts for each quarter are required to be computed independently and, as a result, their sums do not equal the total year earnings-per-share amounts.

Photographs *Page 1* Rivera Collection/SuperStock; *31* Courtesy of Albert D. Phelps, Inc.; *101* P.R. Productions/SuperStock; *167* © Gene Fitzer; *207* © Gene Fitzer; *275* © Gene Fitzer; *329* © Jeff Greenberg/Rainbow; *389* Dwight Ellefsen/SuperStock; *475* © R. Lord/The Image Works; *531* © Jeff Greenberg/Rainbow; *573* © Dan McCoy/Rainbow; *621* Scott Barrow/SuperStock; *669* Charles Orricco/SuperStock; *715* © Eric Schnakenberg/FPG International; *787* © Fritz Hoffmann/The Image Works; *843* SuperStock; *907* © Bob Daemmrich/Stock Boston; *953* © Catherine Ursillo/Photo Researchers, Inc.; *1021* Florian Franke/SuperStock; *1075* © Gene Fitzer; *1111* © Gene Fitzer.

Acknowledgments

Material from: Uniform CPA Examination Questions and Unofficial Answers, copyright © 1951, 1952, 1953, 1954, 1957, 1959, 1961, 1962, 1963, 1964, 1965, 1966, 1967, 1968, 1969, 1970, 1971, 1972, 1973, 1974, 1975, 1976, 1977, 1978, 1979, 1980, 1981, 1982, 1983, 1984 by the American Institute of Certified Public Accountants, Inc., is adapted with permission.

Material is reprinted, with permission, from the 1975 Chartered Accountants Examination, published by the Canadian Institute of Chartered Accountants, Toronto, Canada.

Materials issued by the FASB are copyright © by Financial Accounting Standards Board, 401 Merritt 7, P.O.B. 5116, Norwalk, CT 06856-5116, and reprinted with permission. Copies of the complete documents are available from the FASB.

Material from the Certificate in Management Accounting Examination, copyright © 1977, 1978, 1981 by the National Association of Accountants, is reprinted and/or adapted with permission.

Page 32: Excerpt from "Proposed Cut-Rate Financial Statements for Small Business Meet Opposition," by Lee Berton, *The Wall Street Journal*, August 18, 1995. Reprinted by permission of The Wall Street Journal, © 1995 Dow Jones & Company, Inc. All Rights Reserved Worldwide.
Page 36: Excerpt from "Bean Counters, Unite," *The Economist*, June 10, 1995, pp. 67–68. © 1995 The Economist Newspaper Group, Inc. Reprinted with permission; further reproduction prohibited.
Page 80: Excerpt from a speech by Lawrence Weinbach to the Institute of Management Accountants, September 1995, used by permission of Lawrence A. Weinbach.
Page 83: Excerpt from "Now You See It, Now You Don't," *Forbes*, June 5, 1995, pp. 42–43. Reprinted by permission of Forbes Magazine, © Forbes Inc., 1995.
Pages 98–99: "How a Corporate Watchdog Nearly Lost Its Bite," by Robert Kutner, *Business Week*, May 20, 1996, p. 24. Reprinted from Business Week by special permission, © 1996 by The McGraw-Hill Companies, Inc.
Page 99: "Keeping Options Under Wraps," by Gene Koretz, *Business Week*, June 3, 1996, p. 26. Reprinted from Business Week by special permission, © 1996 by The McGraw-Hill Companies, Inc.

Page 168: Excerpt from "Ben & Jerry's Writes Down Investment, Reports $4.9 Million Loss for 4th Period," by David Stipp, *The Wall Street Journal*, March 6, 1995, p. B-7E. Reprinted by permission of The Wall Street Journal, © 1995 Dow Jones & Company, Inc. All Rights Reserved Worldwide.
Page 203: "How to Get DEC Back on Track," by Paul C. Judge and Ira Sager, *Business Week*, November 4, 1996, p. 46. Reprinted from Business Week by special permission, © 1996 by The McGraw-Hill Companies, Inc.
Pages 204–205: Excerpts from the Digital Equipment Corporation 1996 Annual Report used by permission of Digital Equipment Corporation.
Pages 325–328: Excerpts from the 1996 Walt Disney Company Annual Report used by permission of the Walt Disney Company.
Page 330: Excerpt from "Piping Up: Natural Gas Industry Is Reinventing Itself by Going International," *The Wall Street Journal*, April 19, 1994, pp. A-1 and A-12. Reprinted by permission of The Wall Street Journal, © 1994 Dow Jones & Company, Inc. All Rights Reserved Worldwide.
Page 497: Excerpts from "Price Rises Make Look at Valuing Timely," *Crain's Cleveland Business*, March 13, 1995, p. S-3. Reprinted by permission of Crain Communication, Inc. All Rights Reserved.
Pages 660–661: "A Real-Life Hollywood Horror Story," by Ronald Grover, *Business Week*, July 1, 1996, p. 14. Reprinted from Business Week by special permission, © 1996 by The McGraw-Hill Companies, Inc.
Pages 666–668: Excerpts from The Philip Morris Companies, Inc., 1996 Annual Report used by permission of The Philip Morris Companies.
Page 716: Excerpt from "Junk Buy-Backs Take Off; Issuers Spring at Discounts," *The Wall Street Journal*, June 1, 1990, pp. C-1 and C-13. Reprinted by permission of The Wall Street Journal, © 1990 Dow Jones & Company, Inc. All Rights Reserved Worldwide.
Page 788: Excerpt from "As IBM's Woes Grew, Its Accounting Tactics Got Less Conservative," *The Wall Street Journal*, April 7, 1993, p. A-6. Reprinted by permission of The Wall Street Journal, © 1990 Dow Jones & Company, Inc. All Rights Reserved Worldwide.
Pages 949–951: Excerpts from Reynolds Metals Companies 1995 Annual Report used by permission of Reynolds Metals Company.
Page 960: Excerpts from McDonald's 1995 Annual Report reprinted with permission of McDonald's Corporation.
Pages 1018–1020: Excerpts from the 1995 Bristol-Myers Squibb Annual Report used by permission of Bristol-Myers Squibb.
Page 1022: Excerpt from "Suit Leasing Firm Can Help You Fit the Company Image," by Gale Tollin, as appeared in *Tulsa World*, March 22, 1981. Copyright © 1981 Associated Press. Reprinted by permission.
Pages 1178–1179: Excerpt from "Ask Mr. Economy," by Orley Amos, from *Stillwater* [Oklahoma] *News Press*, February 28, 1996, p. 4. Copyright © 1996 Orley Amos. Used by permission of Orley Amos.
Pages 1227–1266: Excerpts from the 1995 GE Annual Report used by permission of General Electric Company.